The Sporting News

BASEBALL GUIDE

1999 EDITION

Editors / Baseball Guide

CRAIG CARTER
DAVE SLOAN

The Sporting News

Efrem Zimbalist III, President and Chief Executive Officer, Times Mirror Magazines; **James H. Nuckols,** President, The Sporting News; **Francis X. Farrell,** Senior Vice President, Publisher; **John D. Rawlings,** Senior Vice President, Editorial Director; **John Kastberg,** Vice President, General Manager; **Kathy Kinkeade,** Vice President, Operations; **Steve Meyerhoff,** Executive Editor; **Joe Hoppel,** Senior Editor; **Sean Stewart,** Associate Editor; **Mark Bonavita and Brendan Roberts,** Assistant Editors; **Marilyn Kasal,** Production Director; **Terry Shea,** Database Analyst; **Michael Bruner,** Prepress Director; **Michael Behrens,** Art Director, Special Projects; **Christen Webster,** Production Artist; **David Polmer,** Editorial Assistant.

**A Times Mirror
Company**

EXPLANATION OF STATISTICAL ABBREVIATIONS

A: assists. **AB:** at-bats. **Avg.:** batting average (hits divided by at-bats). **BB:** bases on balls. **Bk.:** balks. **CG:** complete games. **CS:** caught stealing. **E:** errors. **ER:** earned runs. **ERA:** earned-run average (earned runs times nine divided by innings pitched). **G:** games. **GB:** games behind. **GF:** games finished. **GDP:** grounding into double plays. **GS:** games started. **H:** hits. **HB:** hit batsmen. **HP:** hit by pitches. **HR:** home runs. **IBB:** intentional bases on balls. **IP:** innings pitched. **L:** losses. **OBP:** on-base percentage (hits plus bases on balls plus hit by pitches divided by at-bats plus bases on balls plus hit by pitches plus sacrifice flies). **Pct.:** winning percentage. **PO:** putouts. **Pos.:** position. **R:** runs. **RBI:** runs batted in. **SB:** stolen bases. **SF:** sacrifice flies (run-scoring flyouts). **SH:** sacrifice hits (bunts that advance one or more runners but result in the batter being retired at first base or reaching first on an error). **ShO:** shutouts. **Slg.:** slugging percentage (total bases divided by at-bats). **SO:** strikeouts. **Sv.:** saves. **TB:** total bases (hits plus doubles plus two times the number of triples plus three times the number of home runs). **TBF:** total batters faced. **TC:** total chances (putouts plus assists plus errors). **TPA:** total plate appearances (at-bats plus bases on balls plus sacrifice hits plus sacrifice flies plus hit by pitches plus times reaching base on catcher's interference). **W:** wins. **WP:** wild pitches. **2B:** doubles. **3B:** triples.

World Series, A.L. Championship Series, N.L. Championship Series, A.L. Division Series, N.L. Division Series and All-Star Game highlights written by Joe Hoppel, Brendan Roberts and Ron Smith of THE SPORTING NEWS.

Major league statistics compiled by STATS, Inc., Lincolnwood, Ill.

Minor league statistics compiled by Howe Sportsdata International Inc., Boston.

ISBN: 0-89204-604-X

10 9 8 7 6 5 4 3 2 1

CONTENTS

1999 SEASON...5
  Major league baseball 6
    Commissioner's office 6
    American League 6
    National League 6
    Other organizations..............................6
  Individual teams section (schedules, directories,
    rosters, 1998 results and more)........................8
    Anaheim Angels...................................8
    Baltimore Orioles 13
    Boston Red Sox...................................18
    Chicago White Sox 23
    Cleveland Indians..............................28
    Detroit Tigers.....................................33
    Kansas City Royals 38
    Minnesota Twins................................43
    New York Yankees 48
    Oakland Athletics 53
    Seattle Mariners.................................58
    Tampa Bay Devil Rays 63
    Texas Rangers 68
    Toronto Blue Jays 73
    Arizona Diamondbacks 78
    Atlanta Braves...................................83
    Chicago Cubs.....................................88
    Cincinnati Reds..................................93
    Colorado Rockies...............................98
    Florida Marlins.................................103
    Houston Astros.................................108
    Los Angeles Dodgers........................113
    Milwaukee Brewers..........................118
    Montreal Expos.................................123
    New York Mets 128
    Philadelphia Phillies.........................133
    Pittsburgh Pirates 138
    St. Louis Cardinals............................143
    San Diego Padres.............................148
    San Francisco Giants 153

1998 REVIEW 159
  Year in review 160
    Final standings..................................167
  A.L. Division Series................................168
  N.L. Division Series 176
  A.L. Championship Series.......................184
  N.L. Championship Series 190
  World Series 196
  All-Star Game..204
  Notable performances............................207
    Box scores of no-hit games................207
    Low-hit games...................................207
    15-strikeout games............................208
    10-strikeout games............................209
    1-0 games..209
    Four or more hits in one game 210
    Five- and six-hit games.......................211

Hitting streaks of 15 or more games........211
Multi-homer games 211
Three-homer games 212
Grand slams 212
Transactions..215
Award winners 222
  The Sporting News 222
  Baseball Writers' Assoc. of America.........222
Miscellaneous 224
  Attendance...224
  Debuts 224
  Salary arbitration results.......................227
  Free-agent filings 227
  Major league Rule 5 draft 227
Necrology...229

1998 AMERICAN LEAGUE STATISTICS....233
  Batting 234
  Designated hitting.................................241
  Pinch-hitting 244
  Pitching...248
  Fielding 253
  Miscellaneous 259
    Shutout games 259
    Home record......................................259
    Road record.......................................259
    Pitching against each club 260
    Home runs by parks 264

1998 NATIONAL LEAGUE STATISTICS.....267
  Batting 268
  Designated hitting.................................278
  Pinch-hitting 280
  Pitching...285
  Fielding 291
  Miscellaneous 298
    Shutout games 298
    Home record......................................298
    Road record.......................................298
    Pitching against each club 299
    Home runs by parks 304

HISTORY..307
  All-time results......................................308
    American League Champions 308
    National League Champions 308
    World Series 309
    Division Series....................................310
    Championship Series...........................310
    All-Star Game 311
  Award winners 313
    The Sporting News 313
    Baseball Writers' Assoc. of America.........331
    Early Most Valuable Player awards 334
  Hall of Fame..335
  Team by team 339

American League 339
National League 355

MINOR LEAGUES **373**
  Farm systems 374
  Class AAA 375
    International League 375
    Mexican League 397
    Pacific Coast League.............................. 414
  Class AA.. 438
    Eastern League 438
    Southern League...................................... 452
    Texas League 467
  Class A.. 480

California League 480
Carolina League 493
Florida State League 504
Midwest League.. 521
New York-Pennsylvania League............... 536
Northwest League..................................... 550
South Atlantic League.............................. 559
Summer Class A 574
  Appalachian League................................. 574
  Arizona League 584
  Gulf Coast League.................................... 592
  Pioneer League 606
Minor league index 615

ON THE COVER: The 1998 World Series champion New York Yankees. (Cover designed by Michael Behrens/THE SPORTING NEWS. Foreground photo by Robert Seale/THE SPORTING NEWS; background photo by John Cordes for THE SPORTING NEWS.)

Spine photo of Roger Clemens by Robert Seale/THE SPORTING NEWS.

1999 SEASON

Major League Baseball directories

Team by team

MAJOR LEAGUE BASEBALL

Address
245 Park Avenue
New York, NY 10167
Telephone
212-931-7800
FAX
212-355-0007
Commissioner of baseball
Allan H. "Bud" Selig
COO, Major League Baseball
Paul Beeston

Vice president, marketing
Kathleen Francis
Director, special events
Carolyn Taylor
Exec. dir., security/facility management
Kevin Hallinan
Executive director, public relations
Richard Levin
Executive director, baseball operations
William Murray

General counsel
Thomas J. Ostertag
Exec. director, minor league relations
Jimmie Lee Solomon
Chief financial officer
Jeffrey White
V.p., broadcasting and new media dev.
Leslie Sullivan
Sr. v.p., domestic and int'l properties
Timothy Brosnan

AMERICAN LEAGUE

Address
350 Park Avenue
New York, NY 10022
Telephone
212-339-7600
President
Gene A. Budig
Vice president
Carl R. Pohlad
Executive director of umpiring
Martin J. Springstead
Senior vice president
Phyllis Merhige
Vice president of finance
Derek Irwin
Director, waivers and player records
Brian Small
Media relations assistant
Bill Melchior

Administrator of umpires/travel
Tess Basta-Marino
Administrative assistant
Carolyn Coen
Umpires
Larry Barnett
Joseph Brinkman
Gary Cederstrom
Alan Clark
Drew Coble
Derryl Cousins
Terry Craft
James Evans
Dale Ford
Richard Garcia
Ted Hendry
Ed Hickox
John Hirschbeck
Mark Johnson
Jim Joyce

Kenneth Kaiser
Greg Kosc
Tim McClelland
Larry McCoy
James McKean
Chuck Meriwether
Durwood Merrill
Dan Morrison
David Phillips
Rick Reed
Michael Reilly
John (Rocky) Roe
Dale Scott
John Shulock
Tim Tschida
Tim Welke
Larry Young

NATIONAL LEAGUE

Address
350 Park Avenue
New York, NY 10022
Telephone
212-339-7700
President and treasurer
Leonard S. Coleman Jr.
Senior vice president and secretary
Katy Feeney
Executive director, public relations
Ricky Clemons
Director of umpire supervision
Paul Runge
Executive director, player records
Nancy Crofts
Executive secretary
Rita Aughavin

Administrative assistant, umpires
Cathy Davis
Public relations assistant
Moises Rodriguez
Umpires
Wally Bell
Greg Bonin
Jerry Crawford
Gary Darling
Bob Davidson
Gerry Davis
Dana DeMuth
Bruce Froemming
Brian Gorman
Eric Gregg
Tom Hallion
Angel Hernandez
Mark Hirschbeck

Bill Hohn
Jeff Kellogg
Jerry Layne
Randy Marsh
Ed Montague
Larry Poncino
Frank Pulli
Ed Rapuano Jr.
Charlie Reliford
Rich Rieker
Steve Rippley
Terry Tata
Larry Vanover
Joe West
Charlie Williams
Mike Winters

OTHER ORGANIZATIONS

PLAYER RELATIONS COMMITTEE

Address
245 Park Avenue
New York, NY 10167
Telephone
212-931-7401
212-949-5690 (FAX)

Executive vice president of labor and
human resources and labor counsel
Robert D. Manfred Jr.
General labor counsel
Francis X. Coonelly

Associate counsels
Louis Melendez
John Westhoff
Contract administrator
John Ricco

NATIONAL ASSOCIATION OF PROFESSIONAL BASEBALL LEAGUES

Address
P.O. Box A
St. Petersburg, FL 33731
Telephone
727-822-6937
727-821-5819 (FAX)
President
Mike Moore
Vice president/administration
Pat O'Conner
Chief operating officer
Rob Dlugozima
General counsel
Ben Hayes
Director/licensing
Brian Earle
Director/media relations
Jim Ferguson
Director of operations
Tim Brunswick
Director of marketing
Rod Meadows
Director of business/finance
Eric Krupa
General supervisor or Professional Baseball Umpire Corporation
Mike Fitzpatrick
Director of Professional Baseball Employment Opportunities
Ann Perkins

ASSOCIATION OF PROFESSIONAL BASEBALL PLAYERS OF AMERICA

Address
12062 Valley View, Suite 211
Garden Grove, CA 92645
Telephone
714-892-9900
714-897-0233 (FAX)
President
John J. McHale
Vice presidents
Joe DiMaggio
Arthur Richman
Robert Kennedy
Secretary/treasurer
Dick Beverage

BASEBALL ASSISTANCE TEAM INC.

Address
245 Park Avenue
New York, NY 10167
Telephone
212-931-7821
Chairman
Ralph Branca
President
Joe Garagiola
Vice presidents
Joe Black
Earl Wilson
Executive director
James J. Martin
Secretary/treasurer
Tom Ostertag

NATIONAL BASEBALL HALL OF FAME AND MUSEUM

Address
P.O. Box 590
Cooperstown, NY 13326
Telephone
607-547-7200
607-547-2044 (FAX)
Chairman of Hall of Fame
Edward W. Stack
Vice president
Frank Simio
Curator
William T. Spencer Jr.
Curator of exhibits
Peter P. Clark
Executive director of retail marketing
Barbara Shinn
Controller
Frances L. Althiser
Librarian
James L. Gates
Executive director of communications and education
Jeff Idelson

MAJOR LEAGUE BASEBALL MAJOR LEAGUE SCOUTING BUREAU

Address
23712 Birtcher Dr., Suite A
Lake Forest, CA 92630
Telephone
949-458-7600
949-458-9454 (FAX)
Director
Frank Marcos

MAJOR LEAGUE BASEBALL PLAYERS ASSOCIATION

Address
12 E. 49th St., 24th Floor
New York, NY 10017
Telephone
212-826-0808
212-752-3649 (FAX)
Executive director and general counsel
Donald M. Fehr
Special assistant
Tony Bernazard
Associate general counsel
Eugene D. Orza
Assistant general counsel
Doyle R. Pryor
Michael Weiner
Counsel
Robert Leneghan
Director of licensing
Judy Heeter
Director of communications
To be announced

MAJOR LEAGUE BASEBALL PLAYERS ALUMNI ASSOC.

Address
1631 Mesa Ave., Suite C
Colorado Springs, CO 80906
Telephone
719-477-1870
719-477-1875 (FAX)
President
Brooks Robinson
Vice presidents
Bobby Bonds
Bob Boone
George Brett
Mike Hegan
Chuck Hinton
Al Kaline
Carl Erskine
Rusty Staub
Robin Yount
Secretary/treasurer
Fred Valentine

ELIAS SPORTS BUREAU

Address
500 Fifth Ave.
New York, NY 10110
Telephone
212-869-1530
212-354-0980 (FAX)
General manager
Seymour Siwoff

MAJOR LEAGUE UMPIRES ASSOCIATION

Address
1735 Market St., Suite 3420
Philadelphia, PA 19103
Telephone
215-979-3220
215-979-3201 (FAX)
General counsel
Richard G. Phillips

BASEBALL WRITERS' ASSOCIATION OF AMERICA

President
Bob Elliott, Toronto Sun
Vice president
Charles Scoggins, Lowell (Mass.) Sun
Secretary/treasurer
Jack O'Connell, Hartford Courant

HOWE SPORTSDATA INTERNATIONAL INC.

Address
Boston Fish Pier
West Building No. 1, Suite 302
Boston, MA 02210
Telephone
617-951-0070
617-951-1379 (stats request)
617-737-9960 (FAX)
President
Jay Virshbo
Historical consultant
William Weiss

ANAHEIM ANGELS
AMERICAN LEAGUE WEST DIVISION

1999 Angels Schedule
Home games shaded. *—All-Star Game at Fenway Park (Boston).
D—Day game (any game starting before 5 p.m.).

April

SUN	MON	TUE	WED	THU	FRI	SAT
				1	2	3
4	5	6 CLE	7 CLE	8 CLE	9 TEX	10 TEX
11 D TEX	12 D TEX	13 OAK	14 OAK	15 D OAK	16 SEA	17 SEA
18 D SEA	19	20 TOR	21 TOR	22 TOR	23 KC	24 D KC
25 KC	26 TOR	27 TOR	28 TOR	29 TOR	30 CWS	

May

SUN	MON	TUE	WED	THU	FRI	SAT
						1 D CWS
2 CWS	3 CWS	4 DET	5 DET	6 DET	7 BOS	8 D BOS
9 D BOS	10	11 NYY	12 NYY	13 NYY	14 TB	15 TB
16 TB	17	18 BAL	19 BAL	20 BAL	21 TB	22 TB
23 D TB	24	25 BAL	26 BAL	27 BAL	28 KC	29 KC
30 KC	31 MIN					

June

SUN	MON	TUE	WED	THU	FRI	SAT
		1 MIN	2 MIN	3	4 LA	5 D LA
6 D LA	7 SF	8 SF	9 D SF	10	11 ARI	12 ARI
13 ARI	14	15 TOR	16 TOR	17 TOR	18 NYY	19 D NYY
20 NYY	21 D	22 SEA	23 SEA	24 SEA	25 OAK	26 OAK
27 OAK	28 TEX	29 TEX	30 TEX			

July

SUN	MON	TUE	WED	THU	FRI	SAT
				1	2 D OAK	3 OAK
4 D OAK	5 SEA	6 SEA	7 SEA	8	9 COL	10 COL
11 D COL	12	13 *	14	15 LA	16 LA	17 D LA
18 SD	19 SD	20 D SD	21 TEX	22 TEX	23 BAL	24 D BAL
25 BAL	26 TB	27 TB	28 TB	29	30 MIN	31 MIN

August

SUN	MON	TUE	WED	THU	FRI	SAT
1 MIN	2 KC	3 KC	4 KC	5 BOS	6 D BOS	7 BOS
8 BOS	9 CLE	10 CLE	11 CLE	12	13 DET	14 D DET
15 DET	16 CWS	17 CWS	18 CWS	19 D CWS	20 DET	21 DET
22 DET	23 D DET	24 TOR	25 TOR	26	27 BOS	28 D BOS
29 D BOS	30 CLE	31 CLE				

September

SUN	MON	TUE	WED	THU	FRI	SAT
			1 CLE	2 CLE	3 NYY	4 D NYY
5 NYY	6 NYY	7 CWS	8 CWS	9	10 MIN	11 D MIN
12 MIN	13 MIN	14 KC	15 KC	16 D KC	17 BAL	18 BAL
19 BAL	20 TB	21 TB	22 TB	23	24 SEA	25 SEA
26 SEA	27	28 OAK	29 OAK	30 OAK		

October

SUN	MON	TUE	WED	THU	FRI	SAT
					1 TEX	2 TEX
3 D TEX	4	5	6	7	8	9

1999 SEASON
CLUB DIRECTORY

Owner
The Walt Disney Company
Chairman and CEO, The Walt Disney Co.
Michael Eisner
President
Tony Tavares
Vice president and general manager
Bill Bavasi
Vice president, business operations
Spencer Neumann
Vice president of finance/administration
Andy Roundtree
V.p., advertising sales and broadcasting
Bob Wagner
Vice president, sales and marketing
Ron Minegar
Vice president, communications
Tim Mead
Vice president, ballpark operations
Kevin Uhlich
V.p., business and legal affairs
Rick Schlesinger
Assistant general manager
Ken Forsch
Special assistants to general manager
Preston Gomez, Bob Harrison
Legal counsel/contract negotiations
Mark Rosenthal
Director, player personnel and scouting
Bob Fontaine Jr.
Director, player development
Jeff Parker
Manager, baseball operations
Tony Reagins
Equipment manager
Ken Higdon
Visiting clubhouse manager
Brian Harkins
Senior video coordinator
Diego Lopez
Manager, baseball information
Larry Babcock
Manager, media services
Nancy Mazmanian

Manager, publications
Doug Ward
Manager, community relations
Dennis Bickmeier
Manager, civic affairs
Marie Moreno
Media services/travel coordinator
Tom Taylor
Dir., ticket sales and customer service
Lawrence Cohen
Manager, marketing
Lisa Manning
Manager, ticket operations
Sheila Brazelton
Medical director
Dr. Lewis Yocum
Team physician
Dr. Craig Milhouse
Head athletic trainer
Ned Bergert
Athletic trainer
Rick Smith
Strength and conditioning coach
Brian Grapes
Sports psychologist
Ken Ravizza
Scouts
Don Archer, John Burden, Tom Burns, Todd Claus, Pete Coachman, Tom Davis, Red Gaskill, Jose Gomez, Steve Gruwell, Felipe Gutierrez, Ta Honda, Rick Ingalls, Hal Keller, Tim Kelly, Kris Kline, Tom Kotchman, Tony LaCava, George Lauzerique, Jose Leiva, Ron Marigny, Jim McLaughlin, Mario Mendoza, Darrell Miller, Jon Neiderer, Steve Oleschuk, Tom Osowski, Eusebio Perez, Paul Robinson, Rick Schlenker, Rick Schroeder, Jerry Streeter, Rip Tutor, Jack Uhey, Victor Villa, Dick Wilson
Major league scouts
Dave Garcia, Jay Hankins, Bob Harrison, Nick Kamzic, Matt Keough, Joe McDonald, Moose Stubing, Dale Sutherland, Gary Sutherland

MINOR LEAGUE AFFILIATES

Class	Team	League	Manager
AAA	Edmonton	Pacific Coast	Carney Lansford
AA	Erie	Eastern	Garry Templeton
A	Boise	Northwest	Tom Kotchman
A	Cedar Rapids	Midwest	Mitch Seoane
A	Lake Elsinore	California	Mario Mendoza
Rookie	Butte	Pioneer	Joe Urso

BROADCAST INFORMATION

Radio: KRLA-AM (1110).
TV: KCAL-TV (Channel 9).
Cable TV: Fox Sports West.

SPRING TRAINING

Ballpark (city): Tempe Diablo Stadium (Tempe, Ariz.).
Ticket information: 602-254-3300, 800-326-0331.

SPRING TRAINING ROSTER

Manager—Terry Collins (1).
Coaches—Larry Bowa (2), Rod Carew (29), Joe Coleman (47), George Hendrick (24), Joe Maddon (70), Dick Pole.

No.	PITCHERS	B/T	Ht./Wt.	Born	1998 clubs
	Belcher, Tim	R/R	6-3/225	10-19-61	Kansas City
41	DeLucia, Rich	R/R	6-0/190	10-7-64	Anaheim
19	Dickson, Jason	L/R	6-0/202	3-30-73	Anaheim, Vancouver
55	Edsell, Geoff	R/R	6-2/194	12-10-71	Vancouver
31	Finley, Chuck	L/L	6-6/226	11-26-62	Anaheim
68	Harriger, Mark	R/R	6-2/196	4-29-75	Lake Elsinore, Cedar Rapids
48	Harris, Pep	R/R	6-2/253	9-23-72	Lake Elsinore, Vancouver, Anaheim
21	Hasegawa, Shigetoshi	R/R	5-11/171	8-1-68	Anaheim
44	Hill, Ken	R/R	6-2/214	12-14-65	Anaheim, Cedar Rapids, Lake Elsinore
65	Holtz, Mike	L/L	5-9/180	10-10-72	Anaheim, Vancouver
46	James, Mike	R/R	6-3/205	8-15-67	Anaheim
72	McDowell, Jack	R/R	6-5/190	1-16-66	Anaheim, Vancouver, Lake Elsinore, Midland
39	Olivares, Omar	R/R	6-0/205	7-6-67	Anaheim
62	Ortiz, Ramon	R/R	6-0/165	3-23-76	Midland
40	Percival, Troy	R/R	6-3/230	8-9-69	Anaheim
34	Petkovsek, Mark	R/R	6-0/185	11-18-65	St. Louis
60	Schoeneweis, Scott	L/L	6-0/186	10-2-73	Vancouver
23	Sparks, Steve	R/R	6-0/180	7-2-65	Vancouver, Anaheim, Midland
56	Washburn, Jarrod	L/L	6-1/200	8-13-74	Anaheim, Vancouver, Midland

No.	CATCHERS	B/T	Ht./Wt.	Born	1998 clubs
8	Greene, Todd	R/R	5-10/208	5-8-71	Lake Elsinore, Vancouver, Anaheim
4	Hemphill, Bret	B/R	6-3/200	12-17-71	Vancouver
20	Nevin, Phil	R/R	6-2/231	1-19-71	Anaheim
22	O'Brien, Charlie	R/R	6-2/205	5-1-61	Chicago A.L., Midland, Anaheim
6	Walbeck, Matt	B/R	5-11/206	10-2-69	Anaheim

No.	INFIELDERS	B/T	Ht./Wt.	Born	1998 clubs
13	Baughman, Justin	R/R	5-11/180	8-1-74	Anaheim, Vancouver
	Castro, Nelson	R/B	5-10/190	6-4-76	Lake Elsinore
9	DiSarcina, Gary	R/R	6-2/205	11-19-67	Anaheim
14	Glaus, Troy	R/R	6-5/225	8-3-76	Anaheim, Vancouver, Midland
10	Hollins, Dave	B/R	6-1/232	5-25-66	Anaheim
28	Pritchett, Chris	L/R	6-4/212	1-31-70	Vancouver, Anaheim
42	Vaughn, Mo	L/R	6-1/240	12-15-67	Boston
18	Velarde, Randy	R/R	6-0/200	11-24-62	Lake Elsinore, Anaheim, Vancouver

No.	OUTFIELDERS	B/T	Ht./Wt.	Born	1998 clubs
16	Anderson, Garret	L/L	6-3/215	6-30-72	Anaheim
25	Edmonds, Jim	L/L	6-1/218	6-27-70	Anaheim
17	Erstad, Darin	L/L	6-2/210	6-4-74	Anaheim
35	Hutchins, Norm	R/L	5-11/200	11-20-75	Midland, Vancouver
	Luke, Matt	L/L	6-5/220	2-26-71	Los Angeles, Cleveland
3	Palmeiro, Orlando	L/R	5-11/175	1-19-69	Vancouver, Anaheim
15	Salmon, Tim	R/R	6-3/241	8-24-68	Anaheim
12	Williams, Reggie	B/R	6-1/180	5-5-66	Anaheim, Vancouver

BALLPARK INFORMATION

Ballpark (capacity, surface)
Edison International Field of Anaheim (45,050, grass)
Address
2000 Gene Autry Way
Anaheim, CA 92806
Business phone
714-940-2000
Ticket information
714-663-9000
Ticket prices
$19 (field box)
$17.50 (terrace box, terrace disabled MVP)
$13 (lower view MVP)
$11 (lower view box)
$10 (upper value box, terrace disabled box)
$8 (terrace/club pavilion-adult)
$6 (left field pavilion-adult)
$5.50 (terrace/club pavilion-child)
$3 (left field pavilion-child)
Field dimensions (from home plate)
To left field at foul line, 333 feet
To center field, 404 feet
To right field at foul line, 333 feet
First game played
April 19, 1966 (White Sox 3, Angels 1)

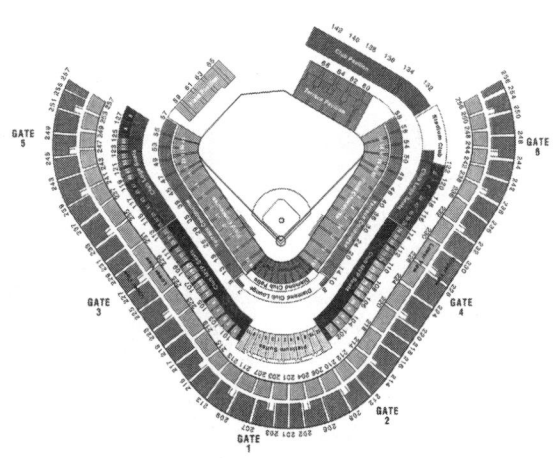

1998 REVIEW
DAY BY DAY

Date	Opp.	Res.	Score	(inn.*)	Hits	Opp. hits	Winning pitcher	Losing pitcher	Save	Record	Pos.	GB
4-1	N.Y.	W	4-1		11	5	Finley	Pettitte	Percival	1-0	1st	+1.0
4-2	N.Y.	W	10-2		14	7	Hill	Wells		2-0	1st	+1.0
4-3	Cle.	L	2-6		8	10	Burba	McDowell		2-1	T1st	...
4-4	Cle.	L	0-11		4	13	Colon	Watson		2-2	T1st	...
4-5	Cle.	L	4-6		7	9	Nagy	Dickson	Jackson	2-3	T2nd	1.0
4-6	Bos.	W	2-1	(11)	9	5	Holtz	Gordon		3-3	T1st	...
4-7	Bos.	W	6-1		9	6	Hill	Wakefield		4-3	1st	+0.5
4-8	Bos.	W	2-1		5	8	McDowell	Lowe	Percival	5-3	1st	+1.0
4-10	At Cle.	L	5-8	(10)	10	15	Plunk	Percival		5-4	2nd	0.5
4-11	At Cle.	L	5-8		9	9	Nagy	Dickson	Jackson	5-5	2nd	0.5
4-12	At Cle.	W	12-1		14	9	Finley	Wright		6-5	2nd	0.5
4-15	At N.Y.∞	L	3-6		4	13	Wells	Hill	Nelson	6-6	2nd	2.5
4-16	T.B.	L	5-6		7	11	Saunders	Holtz	Hernandez	6-7	2nd	3.0
4-17	T.B.	W	5-0		11	6	Finley	Gorecki		7-7	2nd	3.0
4-18	T.B.	L	1-8		6	14	Alvarez	Dickson		7-8	2nd	3.0
4-19	T.B.	L	0-6		6	9	Arrojo	Watson		7-9	3rd	3.0
4-20	Bal.	W	4-3		6	8	Hill	Drabek	Percival	8-9	3rd	3.5
4-21	Bal.	L	3-8		11	14	Rhodes	McDowell		8-10	3rd	4.5
4-22	Bal.	W	7-6		12	12	Holtz	Mathews	Percival	9-10	3rd	4.5
4-24	At T.B.	W	10-3		13	8	Watson	Alvarez		10-10	T2nd	3.0
4-25	At T.B.	W	7-1		11	7	Hill	Arrojo		11-10	2nd	3.0
4-26	At T.B.	W	2-1		6	7	Olivares	Springer	Percival	12-10	2nd	3.0
4-27	At Bal.	W	3-1		9	4	Finley	Erickson	Percival	13-10	2nd	3.0
4-28	At Bal.	W	6-5		9	12	Dickson	Rodriguez	Percival	14-10	2nd	3.0
4-29	At Bos.	L	4-8		9	15	Wakefield	Watson	Gordon	14-11	2nd	4.0
4-30	At Bos.	W	7-2		10	9	Hill	Checo		15-11	2nd	3.0
5-1	Chi.	W	7-1		10	5	Hasegawa	Baldwin		16-11	2nd	2.0
5-2	Chi.	W	5-3		10	7	DeLucia	Sirotka	Percival	17-11	2nd	2.0
5-3	Chi.	L	1-12		5	15	Bere	Dickson		17-12	2nd	2.0
5-4	Chi.	L	5-6		11	9	T. Castillo	DeLucia	Karchner	17-13	2nd	2.5
5-5	Tor.	L	11-13		14	17	Plesac	Percival	Myers	17-14	2nd	2.5
5-6	Tor.	L	5-6		12	10	Escobar	Hasegawa	Myers	17-15	2nd	2.5
5-8	Det.	W	5-3		7	7	Watson	Moehler	Percival	18-15	2nd	2.0
5-9	Det.	L	3-7		11	10	Castillo	Finley		18-16	2nd	3.0
5-10	Det.	W	4-2		7	10	Hill	Worrell	Percival	19-16	2nd	3.0
5-12	At Chi.	L	2-5		4	8	C. Castillo	Olivares		19-17	2nd	4.5
5-13	At Chi.	W	8-3		12	12	Watson	Sirotka		20-17	2nd	3.5
5-14	At Tor.	L	4-5		9	13	Myers	DeLucia		20-18	2nd	4.5
5-15	At Tor.	L	1-9		3	11	Hentgen	Hill		20-19	2nd	4.5
5-16	At Det.	W	8-6		14	9	Dickson	Worrell	Percival	21-19	2nd	3.5
5-17	At Det.	L	3-4		14	4	Florie	DeLucia	Jones	21-20	2nd	4.5
5-18	At Det.	L	2-11		8	19	Moehler	Watson		21-21	2nd	5.0
5-19	Oak.	W	4-3	(10)	8	7	Hasegawa	Taylor		22-21	2nd	5.0
5-20	Oak.	W	5-4		7	10	Hill	Oquist	Percival	23-21	2nd	5.0
5-21	Oak.	W	12-2		14	8	Dickson	Stein		24-21	2nd	5.0
5-22	Min.	W	10-3		13	8	Olivares	Tewksbury		25-21	2nd	5.0
5-23	Min.	L	5-9		8	14	Hawkins	Watson	Swindell	25-22	2nd	6.0
5-24	Min.	L	1-9		3	11	Radke	Finley		25-23	2nd	6.0
5-25	K.C.	L	4-6		7	8	Belcher	Hill	Montgomery	25-24	2nd	6.0
5-27	K.C.	L	0-4		5	5	Rosado	Olivares		25-25	2nd	6.0
5-29	At Min.	W	3-1		11	5	Finley	Hawkins	Percival	26-25	2nd	4.5
5-30	At Min.	L	1-8		8	12	Radke	Hill		26-26	2nd	5.5
5-31	At Min.	W	6-5		10	12	Dickson	Swindell	Percival	27-26	2nd	5.5
6-1	At K.C.	W	6-3		13	8	Hasegawa	Pichardo	Percival	28-26	2nd	4.5
6-2	At K.C.	W	7-5		11	5	Washburn	Haney	Percival	29-26	2nd	4.5
6-3	At Sea.	W	8-1		14	6	Finley	Johnson		30-26	2nd	4.5
6-4	At Sea.	W	6-2		13	6	Hill	Cloude	Hasegawa	31-26	2nd	3.5
6-5	Col.	W	5-0		11	6	Dickson	Jones		32-26	2nd	3.5
6-6	Col.	W	2-1		9	7	Olivares	Kile	Percival	33-26	2nd	3.5
6-7	Col.	W	6-5		10	14	Cadaret	DiPoto		34-26	2nd	2.5
6-9	At Ari.	W	10-8		16	8	Finley	Sodowsky	Percival	35-26	2nd	3.0
6-10	At Ari.	L	2-10		5	15	Daal	Hill		35-27	2nd	3.0
6-11	At Ari.	W	10-5		11	10	Dickson	Wolcott	Percival	36-27	2nd	2.5
6-12	At Tex.	W	5-1		10	6	Olivares	Burkett	Cadaret	37-27	2nd	1.5
6-13	At Tex.	W	18-6		21	8	Washburn	Sele		38-27	2nd	0.5
6-14	At Tex.	L	2-4		4	13	Helling	Finley	Wetteland	38-28	2nd	1.5
6-15	At Tex.	W	8-5		12	10	Sparks	Witt	Percival	39-28	2nd	0.5
6-16	Sea.	W	3-2		7	7	Dickson	Swift	Percival	40-28	1st	+1.5
6-17	Sea.	W	4-2		9	4	Olivares	Fassero	Percival	41-28	1st	+1.5
6-18	Sea.	W	11-5		15	8	Washburn	Spoljaric	DeLucia	42-28	1st	+1.5
6-19	Tex.	L	3-7		11	8	Helling	Finley		42-29	1st	+0.5
6-20	Tex.	W	8-3		10	6	Sparks	Van Poppel		43-29	1st	+1.5

– 10 –

Date	Opp.	Res.	Score	(inn.*)	Hits	Opp. hits	Winning pitcher	Losing pitcher	Save	Record	Pos.	GB
6-21	Tex.	W	10-7		14	11	Dickson	Perisho	Percival	44-29	1st	+2.5
6-22	L.A.	W	6-5		9	9	Percival	McMichael		45-29	1st	+3.5
6-23	L.A.	W	6-4		11	13	Harris	Brunson	DeLucia	46-29	1st	+3.5
6-24	At L.A.	L	5-6	(11)	11	12	Osuna	Cadaret		46-30	1st	+2.5
6-25	At L.A.	W	3-2		3	5	Sparks	Reyes	Percival	47-30	1st	+2.5
6-26	At S.D.	L	3-6		5	12	Brown	Dickson	Hoffman	47-31	1st	+1.5
6-27	At S.D.	L	1-5		2	10	Hitchcock	Olivares		47-32	1st	+1.5
6-28	At S.D.	W	11-3		14	12	Washburn	Hamilton		48-32	1st	+2.5
6-30	S.F.	W	4-3		9	8	Finley	Estes	Percival	49-32	1st	+3.5
7-1	S.F.	L	3-6	(10)	8	12	Nen	Cadaret		49-33	1st	+3.5
7-2	S.F.	L	4-7		15	10	Rueter	Dickson		49-34	1st	+3.5
7-3	Oak.	L	6-10		13	14	Candiotti	Olivares		49-35	1st	+3.5
7-4	Oak.	L	3-8		6	9	Oquist	Washburn	Taylor	49-36	1st	+2.5
7-5	Oak.	L	4-5		6	9	Fetters	Percival	Taylor	49-37	1st	+1.5
7-9	At Sea.	L	6-8		10	12	Fassero	Olivares	Timlin	49-38	1st	+0.5
7-10	At Sea.	W	5-3	(11)	11	8	Percival	Ayala		50-38	1st	+0.5
7-11	At Sea.	L	0-2		5	4	Johnson	Sparks		50-39	2nd	0.5
7-12	At Sea.	W	8-5		10	9	Dickson	Swift	Percival	51-39	1st	+0.5
7-13	At Oak.	L	2-5		8	10	Oquist	Washburn	Taylor	51-40	1st	+0.5
7-14	At Oak.	L	2-6		8	9	Rogers	Olivares		51-41	1st	+0.5
7-15	T.B.	W	4-2		7	8	Hasegawa	Alvarez	Percival	52-41	1st	+1.5
7-16	T.B.	L	1-8		3	12	Arrojo	Sparks		52-42	1st	+1.5
7-17	Bal.	L	1-4		6	9	Drabek	Dickson	Benitez	52-43	1st	+0.5
7-18	Bal.	W	8-3		13	5	Washburn	Rodriguez		53-43	1st	+0.5
7-19	Bal.	L	4-7		7	9	Orosco	Percival		53-44	2nd	0.5
7-21	At Min.	L	2-4		7	10	Hawkins	Watson	Aguilera	53-45	2nd	1.5
7-22	At Min.	W	5-3		12	7	Hasegawa	Swindell	Percival	54-45	2nd	0.5
7-23	At Min.	W	6-5	(10)	13	10	Harris	Carrasco	Percival	55-45	2nd	0.5
7-24	At K.C.	L	3-4		8	6	Pichardo	Finley	Montgomery	55-46	2nd	0.5
7-25	At K.C.	W	6-5		11	8	Harris	Belcher	Holtz	56-46	1st	+0.5
7-26	At K.C.	L	4-9		13	13	Rosado	Olivares		56-47	1st	+0.5
7-27	At K.C.	W	6-1		9	4	Watson	Rapp	Hasegawa	57-47	1st	+1.0
7-28	N.Y.	L	3-9		8	14	Cone	Dickson		57-48	1st	+1.0
7-29	N.Y.	W	10-5		19	7	Sparks	Hernandez		58-48	1st	+1.0
7-30	N.Y.	L	0-3	(10)	11	5	Mendoza	DeLucia	Rivera	58-49	1st	+1.0
7-31	Bos.	L	2-7		7	6	Saberhagen	Olivares	Gordon	58-50	1st	+1.0
8-1	Bos.	L	3-11		6	10	Martinez	Watson	Lowe	58-51	T1st	...
8-2	Bos.	L	7-8		9	10	Wakefield	Dickson	Gordon	58-52	2nd	1.0
8-3	Cle.	W	11-4		10	9	Sparks	Wright		59-52	2nd	0.5
8-4	Cle.	W	5-4		12	8	Hasegawa	Jones	Percival	60-52	2nd	0.5
8-5	Cle.	L	5-6		11	10	Shuey	Percival	Assenmacher	60-53	2nd	1.5
8-8†	At Chi.	L	5-7		9	8	Sirotka	Dickson	Simas	60-54		
8-8‡	At Chi.	L	3-4		8	9	Bradford	Hasegawa		60-55	2nd	3.0
8-9	At Chi.	W	9-0		13	4	Finley	Baldwin		61-55	2nd	2.0
8-10	At Det.	W	6-2		12	6	Olivares	Castillo		62-55	2nd	1.5
8-11	At Det.	W	5-4	(11)	8	7	Fetters	Runyan	Percival	63-55	2nd	1.5
8-12	At Det.	W	3-2		7	9	Sparks	Greisinger	Percival	64-55	2nd	0.5
8-13	At Tor.	L	3-4		9	8	Risley	Hasegawa	Plesac	64-56	2nd	0.5
8-14	At Tor.	W	7-5		15	10	Watson	Hentgen	Percival	65-56	1st	+0.5
8-15	At Tor.	W	6-3	(11)	10	8	DeLucia	Sinclair		66-56	1st	+0.5
8-16	At Tor.	L	4-6		10	9	Carpenter	Juden	Quantrill	66-57	1st	+0.5
8-17	Chi.	W	7-2		10	10	Sparks	Parque		67-57	1st	+1.0
8-18	Chi.	L	3-4		7	9	Snyder	Finley	Simas	67-58	1st	+1.5
8-19	Det.	W	2-0		9	6	McDowell	Thompson	Percival	68-58	1st	+1.5
8-20	Det.	W	13-2		16	8	Olivares	Powell		69-58	1st	+1.5
8-21	Tor.	L	4-9		8	11	Carpenter	Juden		69-59	1st	+1.5
8-22	Tor.	W	5-1		8	8	Sparks	Escobar	Hasegawa	70-59	1st	+2.5
8-23	Tor.	W	3-2		5	6	Finley	Almanzar	Percival	71-59	1st	+2.5
8-24	At N.Y.	W	7-3		12	7	McDowell	Pettitte		72-59	1st	+2.5
8-25	At N.Y.	W	7-6		12	17	Watson	Stanton	Percival	73-59	1st	+3.5
8-26§	At N.Y.	W	6-4		9	5	Juden	Bradley	Percival	74-59		
8-26§	At N.Y.	L	6-7		13	8	Rivera	Fetters		74-60	1st	+3.0
8-27	At N.Y.	L	5-6	(11)	11	11	Tessmer	Fetters		74-61	1st	+2.5
8-28	At Bos.	W	7-6		13	12	Hill	Avery		75-61	1st	+3.0
8-29	At Bos.	L	1-6		7	8	Martinez	McDowell		75-62	1st	+2.0
8-30	At Bos.	W	8-6		11	8	Hasegawa	Wakefield	Percival	76-62	1st	+3.0
9-1	At Cle.	L	6-7		8	16	Reed	DeLucia		76-63	1st	+2.5
9-2	At Cle.	W	13-5		21	8	Sparks	Colon		77-63	1st	+2.5
9-4	K.C.	L	3-5		8	11	Bones	Holtz	Montgomery	77-64	1st	+1.5
9-5	K.C.	W	2-1		9	6	McDowell	Barber	DeLucia	78-64	1st	+2.5
9-6	K.C.	W	3-0		7	3	Finley	Belcher	Hasegawa	79-64	1st	+3.5
9-8	Min.	L	0-5		8	10	Radke	Sparks		79-65	1st	+2.0
9-9	Min.	W	10-8		13	12	Olivares	Rodriguez	Percival	80-65	1st	+2.0
9-11	At Bal.	L	3-8		9	12	Erickson	Finley		80-66	1st	+2.0
9-12	At Bal.	L	2-3		8	9	Mills	Percival		80-67	1st	+1.0
9-13	At Bal.	L	7-12		8	13	Key	Washburn		80-68	1st	+1.0
9-14	At T.B.	W	4-2		9	7	Hasegawa	Lopez	Percival	81-68	1st	+2.0

Date	Opp.	Res.	Score	(inn.*)	Hits	Opp. hits	Winning pitcher	Losing pitcher	Save	Record	Pos.	GB
9-15	At T.B.	L	1-8		5	10	Arrojo	Juden		81-69	1st	+1.0
9-16	At Tex.	L	3-5		8	10	Stottlemyre	Finley		81-70	T1st	...
9-17	At Tex.	L	6-7		11	12	Crabtree	Harris	Wetteland	81-71	2nd	1.0
9-18	Sea.	L	3-5	(12)	10	9	Timlin	DeLucia		81-72	2nd	2.0
9-19	Sea.	W	5-3		9	8	McDowell	Spoljaric	Percival	82-72	2nd	1.0
9-20	Sea.	W	3-1		5	8	Olivares	Abbott	Percival	83-72	T1st	...
9-21	Tex.	L	1-9		7	14	Stottlemyre	Sparks		83-73	2nd	1.0
9-22	Tex.	L	1-9		4	8	Helling	Finley		83-74	2nd	2.0
9-23	Tex.	L	1-7		4	7	Burkett	Hill		83-75	2nd	3.0
9-24	At Oak.	W	10-6		13	11	Dickson	Haynes		84-75	2nd	3.0
9-25	At Oak.	L	2-7		7	10	Rogers	Olivares		84-76	2nd	3.0
9-26	At Oak.	L	3-4		9	7	Mathews	Percival		84-77	2nd	3.0
9-27	At Oak.	W	4-2		11	4	Washburn	Witasick	Hasegawa	85-77	2nd	3.0

Monthly records: April (15-11), May (12-15), June (22-6), July (9-18), August (18-12), September (9-15).
*Innings, if other than nine. †First game of doubleheader. ‡Second game of doubleheader. §Two games in one day (separate admissions). ∞Game played at Shea Stadium due to repairs being made at Yankee Stadium.

HIGHLIGHTS

High point: In an August 24-27 series at New York, the Angels came from behind to win the first three games against the Yankees and increase their division lead over Texas to four. The Angels were thinking sweep before the Yankees scored in the bottom of the ninth to win the fourth game and the bottom of the 11th to win the fifth.
Low point: The Angels and Rangers were tied atop the A.L. West entering a September 21 series at Anaheim. Three nights later, after being outscored by a combined 25-3, the Angels were three games back with four to play.
Turning point: Baltimore shortstop Mike Bordick's stunning game-tying, two-run homer off closer Troy Percival in the bottom of the ninth at Camden Yards September 12. The shellshocked Angels never recovered from that 3-2 loss, losing 12 of their last 17 games.
Most valuable player: Center fielder Jim Edmonds hit .307 with 25 homers, led the team in RBIs (91), doubles (42) and runs (115), and won his second straight Gold Glove.
Most valuable pitcher: Japanese reliever Shigetoshi Hasegawa was phenomenal in a variety of roles, going 8-3 with a 3.14 ERA and five saves and allowing only 16-of-55 inherited runners to score.
Most improved player: After a combined 6-10, 4.97-ERA season for Detroit and Seattle in 1997, Omar Olivares was a consistent and reliable starter, going 9-9 with a 4.03 ERA and 112 strikeouts in 183 innings.
Most pleasant surprise: Knuckleballer Steve Sparks was a combined 0-8 in Class AA and AAA when the Angels called him up June 15. The righthander, who missed all of 1997 because of elbow surgery, won his first three starts and finished 9-4 with a 4.34 ERA.
Biggest disappointment: The third base spot. Dave Hollins hit a dismal .242 before suffering a season-ending shoulder injury in early August; then highly touted rookie Troy Glaus, who had hit 35 homers in four months in the minors, fizzled amid a blur of big-league breaking balls.
Key injuries: Right fielder Tim Salmon was limited to DH because of a torn ligament in his foot; first baseman Darin Erstad sat out two weeks in August and most of September because of a strained hamstring; pitchers Ken Hill and Jack McDowell missed two months each because of elbow injuries, and reliever Mike James had season-ending elbow surgery in July.
Notable: The Angels gave up only 164 home runs, the second-lowest total in the major leagues, and their bullpen combined for an A.L.-low 3.91 ERA. . . . After going 4-12 in interleague play in 1997, the Angels went 10-6 against N.L. West opponents in 1998. . . . The Angels used the disabled list a club-record 23 times.
—MIKE DiGIOVANNA

RECORDS

1998 regular-season record: 85-77 (2nd in A.L. West); 42-39 at home; 43-38 on road; 27-28 vs. East; 29-26 vs. Central; 19-17 vs. A.L. West; 10-6 vs. N.L.; 23-18 vs. lefthanded starters; 62-59 vs. righthanded starters; 71-68 on grass; 14-9 on turf; 13-19 in daytime; 72-58 at night; 24-19 in one-run games; 6-6 in extra-inning games; 0-1-0 in doubleheaders. **Team record past five years:** 364-381 (.489, ranks 8th in league in that span).

TEAM LEADERS

Batting average: Jim Edmonds (.307).
At-bats: Garret Anderson (622).
Runs: Jim Edmonds (115).
Hits: Jim Edmonds (184).
Total bases: Jim Edmonds (303).
Doubles: Jim Edmonds (42).
Triples: Garret Anderson (7).
Home runs: Tim Salmon (26).
Runs batted in: Jim Edmonds (91).
Stolen bases: Darin Erstad (20).
Slugging percentage: Tim Salmon (.533).
On-base percentage: Tim Salmon (.410).
Wins: Chuck Finley (11).
Earned-run average: Chuck Finley (3.39).
Complete games: Chuck Finley, Omar Olivares, Allen Watson (1).
Shutouts: Chuck Finley (1).

Saves: Troy Percival (42).
Innings pitched: Chuck Finley (223.1).
Strikeouts: Chuck Finley (212).

GAMES BY POSITION

Catcher: Matt Walbeck 104, Phil Nevin 69, Charlie O'Brien 5, Chad Kreuter 3, Ben Molina 2.
First base: Cecil Fielder 72, Darin Erstad 70, Chris Pritchett 29, Craig Shipley 8, Dave Hollins 7, Mark Johnson 5, Todd Greene 3, Gregg Jefferies 3, Phil Nevin 2, Frank Bolick 1.
Second base: Justin Baughman 59, Norberto Martin 54, Randy Velarde 51, Carlos Garcia 11, Craig Shipley 11.
Third base: Dave Hollins 91, Troy Glaus 48, Craig Shipley 48, Frank Bolick 7, Norberto Martin 5.
Shortstop: Gary DiSarcina 157, Carlos Garcia 5, Craig Shipley 5, Justin Baughman 3, Norberto Martin 2.
Outfield: Garret Anderson 155, Jim Edmonds 153, Darin Erstad 72, Orlando Palmeiro 54, Damon Mashore 35, Reggie Williams 24, Tim Salmon 19, Gregg Jefferies 15, Todd Greene 12, Norberto Martin 5, Craig Shipley 2, Frank Bolick 1.
Designated hitter: Tim Salmon 111, Cecil Fielder 31, Norberto Martin 10, Frank Bolick 9, Damon Mashore 7, Todd Greene 4, Carlos Garcia 3, Phil Nevin 3, Orlando Palmeiro 3, Darin Erstad 2, Dave Hollins 2, Mark Johnson 2, Matt Walbeck 2, Reggie Williams 2, Justin Baughman 1, Craig Shipley 1.

TOP DRAFT CHOICES

1. **Seth Etherton,** RHP, U. of Southern California
2. **Brandon Emanuel,** RHP, Northwestern State U.
3. **Paul French,** RHP, Northgate H.S., Concord, Calif.
4. **Brian Oliver,** SS, U. of California
5. **Darren Blakely,** OF, U. of Hawaii
6. **Jay Hood,** SS, Georgia Tech
7. **Jeff Hundley,** LHP, Bowling Green State U.
8. **Jason Hill,** C, U. of California
9. **Kevin McClain,** RHP, Central Fla. C.C.
10. **Justin Lehr,** RHP-C, U.C. Santa Barbara

BALTIMORE ORIOLES
AMERICAN LEAGUE EAST DIVISION

1999 Orioles Schedule
Home games shaded. *—All-Star Game at Fenway Park (Boston). D—Day game (any game starting before 5 p.m.).

April
SUN	MON	TUE	WED	THU	FRI	SAT
				1	2	3
4	5 TB	D 6	7 TB	8 TB	9 TOR	10 D TOR
11 TOR	D 12	13 NYY	14 NYY	15 NYY	16 TOR	17 D TOR
18 TOR	D 19	20 TB	21 TB	22 TB	23 OAK	24 D OAK
25 OAK	D 26	27 KC	28 KC	29 KC	30 MIN	

May
SUN	MON	TUE	WED	THU	FRI	SAT
						1 MIN
2 MIN	D 3	4 CWS	5 CWS	6 CWS	D 7 DET	8 D DET
9 DET	D 10	11 CLE	12 CLE	13 TEX	14 TEX	15 TEX
16 TEX	D 17	18 ANA	19 ANA	20 ANA	21 TEX	22 D TEX
23 TEX	D 24	25 ANA	26 ANA	27 ANA	28 OAK	29 OAK
30 OAK	D 31 SEA					

June
SUN	MON	TUE	WED	THU	FRI	SAT
		1 SEA	2 SEA	3	4 PHI	5 PHI
6 PHI	D 7 FLA	8 FLA	9 FLA	10	11 ATL	12 D ATL
13 ATL	14 KC	15 KC	16 KC	D 17 CWS	18 D CWS	19 CWS
20 CWS	D 21	22 BOS	23 BOS	24 BOS	25 NYY	26 D NYY
27 NYY	D 28	29 TOR	30 TOR			

July
SUN	MON	TUE	WED	THU	FRI	SAT
				D 1 TOR	2 NYM	3 D NYM
4 NYM	D 5 NYM	6 TOR	7 TOR	8 TOR	9 PHI	10 PHI
11 PHI	D 12	13	* 14	15 MON	16 MON	17 MON
18 NYM	D 19 NYM	20 NYM	21 BOS	22 BOS	23 ANA	24 D ANA
25 ANA	D 26	27 TEX	28 TEX	29 D TEX	30 SEA	31 D SEA

August
SUN	MON	TUE	WED	THU	FRI	SAT
1 SEA	D 2 OAK	3 OAK	4 OAK	D 5 DET	6 DET	DET
8 DET	D 9 TB	10 TB	11 TB	12	13 CLE	14 D CLE
15 CLE	D 16	17 MIN	18 MIN	19 MIN	D 20 CWS	21 CWS
22 CWS	D 23 KC	24 KC	25 KC	26 KC	27 DET	28 DET
29 DET	D 30	31				

September
SUN	MON	TUE	WED	THU	FRI	SAT
			TB	TB	CLE	CLE
5 CLE	D 6 CLE	D 7 MIN	8 MIN	9 MIN	10 SEA	11 D SEA
12 SEA	D 13 SEA	14 OAK	15 OAK	16 OAK	17 ANA	18 ANA
19 ANA	20	21 TEX	22 TEX	23	24 BOS	25 D BOS
26 BOS	D 27 BOS	28 NYY	29 NYY	30 NYY		

October
SUN	MON	TUE	WED	THU	FRI	SAT
					BOS	2 BOS
3 BOS	D 4	5	6	7	8	9

1999 SEASON
CLUB DIRECTORY

Chairman of the board/CEO
Peter Angelos
Executive vice president
John Angelos
Vice chairman, chief operating officer
Joe Foss
General manager
Frank Wren
Assistant general manager
Bruce Manno
V.p., marketing & broadcasting
Mike Lehr
Director of player development
Tom Trebelhorn
Asst. director of player development
Don Buford
Scouting director
Tony DeMacio
Special assistants to the g.m.
Syd Thrift
Fred Uhlman Sr.
Assistant, player development
Tripp Norton
Vice president/chief financial officer
Robert Ames
Traveling secretary
Phil Itzoe
Director of public relations
John Maroon
Asst. director of public relations
Bill Stetka
Director of marketing and advertising
Scott Nickle
Director of ballpark operations
Roger Hayden
Director of community relations
Julie Wagner

Dir. of ballpark ent. & on-line services
Spiro Alafassos
Director of computer services
James Kline
Director of ticket operations
Audrey Brown
Trainers
Richard Bancells
Brian Ebel
Strength and conditioning
Tim Bishop
Scouts
Carlos Bernhardt
Dean Decillis
Lane Decker
John Gillette
Jesus Halabi
Ubaldo Heredia
Jim Howard
Deacon Jones
Ray Krawczik
Gil Kubski
Mike Ledna
Jeff Morris
Curt Motton
Lamar North
Shawn Pender
Salvador Ramirez
Arturo Sanchez
Harry Shelton
Ed Sprague
Marc Tramuta
Mike Tullier
Brett Ward
Don Welke
Logan White
Earl Winn
Jeff Wren
Marc Ziegler

MINOR LEAGUE AFFILIATES

Class	Team	League	Manager
AAA	Rochester	International	Dave Machemer
AA	Bowie	Eastern	Joe Ferguson
A	Frederick	Carolina	Andy Etchebarren
A	Delmarva	South Atlantic	Butch Davis
Rookie	Bluefield	Appalachian	Duffy Dyer
Rookie	Gulf Coast Orioles	Gulf Coast	Jesus Alfaro

BROADCAST INFORMATION

Radio: WBAL-AM (1090).
TV: WJZ (Channel 13), WNUV (Channel 54), WFTY (Channel 50).
Cable TV: Home Team Sports.

SPRING TRAINING

Ballpark (city): Ft. Lauderdale Stadium (Ft. Lauderdale, Fla.).
Ticket information: 954-523-3309, 305-358-5885, 561-776-9116.

SPRING TRAINING ROSTER

Manager—Ray Miller (31).
Coaches—Terry Crowley, Marv Foley, Elrod Hendricks (44), Bruce Kison, Eddie Murray (33), Sam Perlozzo (2).

No.	PITCHERS	B/T	Ht./Wt.	Born	1998 clubs
	Blood, Darin	R/R	6-2/200	8-13-74	Fresno, Rochester
25	Bones, Ricky	R/R	6-0/202	4-7-69	Salt Lake, Omaha, Kansas City
	Coppinger, Rocky	R/R	6-5/245	3-19-74	Bowie, Rochester, Baltimore
	Dykhoff, Radhames	L/L	6-0/160	9-27-74	Baltimore, Bowie
19	Erickson, Scott	R/R	6-4/230	2-2-68	Baltimore
	Fussell, Chris	R/R	6-2/200	5-19-76	Baltimore, Rochester, Bowie
57	Guzman, Juan	R/R	5-11/195	10-28-66	Toronto, Baltimore
	Hernandez, Xavier	L/R	6-2/195	8-16-65	Texas, Tulsa, Oklahoma
55	Johns, Doug	R/L	6-2/195	12-19-67	Rochester, Baltimore
30	Kamieniecki, Scott	R/R	6-0/200	4-19-64	Baltimore, Bowie
	Medina, Carlos	L/L	6-2/160	5-16-77	Delmarva, Bowie
	Molina, Gabe	R/R	5-11/190	5-3-75	Bowie
35	Mussina, Mike	R/R	6-2/185	12-8-68	Baltimore
47	Orosco, Jesse	R/L	6-2/205	4-21-57	Baltimore
43	Ponson, Sidney	R/R	6-1/220	11-2-76	Baltimore, Rochester
53	Rhodes, Arthur	L/L	6-2/205	10-24-69	Baltimore, Rochester
40	Timlin, Mike	R/R	6-4/210	3-10-66	Seattle

No.	CATCHERS	B/T	Ht./Wt.	Born	1998 clubs
	Alley, Chip	B/R	6-3/190	12-20-76	Frederick
23	Hoiles, Chris	R/R	6-0/220	3-20-65	Baltimore
26	Johnson, Charles	R/R	6-2/220	7-20-71	Florida, Los Angeles
42	Webster, Lenny	R/R	5-9/200	2-10-65	Baltimore

No.	INFIELDERS	B/T	Ht./Wt.	Born	1998 clubs
14	Bordick, Mike	R/R	5-11/175	7-21-65	Baltimore
80	Casimiro, Carlos	R/R	5-11/175	11-8-76	Frederick
	Clark, Will	L/L	6-1/200	3-13-64	Texas
	Coffie, Ivanon	L/R	6-1/170	5-16-77	Frederick
7	DeShields, Delino	L/R	6-1/175	1-15-69	St. Louis, Arkansas
	Garcia, Jesse	R/R	5-10/155	9-24-73	Bowie, Rochester
	Hairston, Jerry	R/R	5-10/170	5-29-76	Baltimore, Frederick, Bowie
10	Minor, Ryan	R/R	6-7/225	1-5-74	Bowie, Baltimore
52	Otanez, Willis	R/R	6-1/200	4-19-73	Rochester, Baltimore
6	Pickering, Calvin	L/L	6-3/286	9-29-76	Bowie, Baltimore
36	Reboulet, Jeff	R/R	6-0/175	4-30-64	Baltimore
8	Ripken, Cal	R/R	6-4/220	8-24-60	Baltimore

No.	OUTFIELDERS	B/T	Ht./Wt.	Born	1998 clubs
	Amaral, Rich	R/R	6-0/175	4-1-62	Seattle
9	Anderson, Brady	L/L	6-1/202	1-18-64	Baltimore
3	Baines, Harold	L/L	6-2/195	3-15-59	Baltimore
88	Belle, Albert	R/R	6-2/225	8-25-66	Chicago A.L.
41	Clyburn, Danny	R/R	6-0/220	4-6-74	Baltimore, Rochester
40	Kingsale, Gene	B/R	6-3/190	8-20-76	Bowie, Rochester, Baltimore
28	Mouton, Lyle	R/R	6-4/240	5-13-69	Rochester, Baltimore
17	Surhoff, B.J.	L/R	6-1/200	8-4-64	Baltimore

BALLPARK INFORMATION

Ballpark (capacity, surface)
Oriole Park at Camden Yards (48,876, grass)
Address
333 W. Camden St.
Baltimore, MD 21201
Business phone
410-685-9800
Ticket information
410-481-7328, 888-848-2473
Ticket prices
$35 (club box)
$30 & $27 (field box)
$23 & $20 (terrace box)
$22 (left field club, lower box)
$18 (left field lower box, upper box)
$16 (left field upper box, lower reserve)
$13 (upper reserve, lower reserve)
$11 (left field upper reserve)
$9 (bleacher)
$7 (standing room)
Field dimensions (from home plate)
To left field at foul line, 333 feet
To center field, 400 feet
To right field at foul line, 318
First game played
April 6, 1992 (Orioles 2, Indians 0)

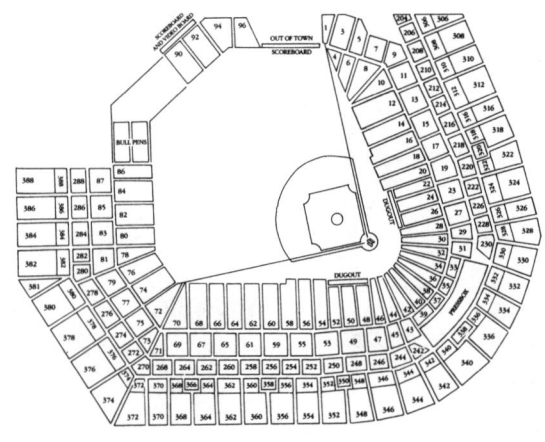

1998 REVIEW
DAY BY DAY

Date	Opp.	Res.	Score	(inn.*)	Hits	Opp. hits	Winning pitcher	Losing pitcher	Save	Record	Pos.	GB
3-31	K.C.	L	1-4		5	8	Belcher	Mussina	Montgomery	0-1	T1st	...
4-1	K.C.	W	10-1		11	4	Erickson	Rusch		1-1	T3rd	0.5
4-2	K.C.	W	4-3		5	9	Benitez	Montgomery		2-1	T2nd	0.5
4-3	Det.	W	10-2		8	7	Drabek	Sanders		3-1	1st	+0.5
4-4	Det.	W	2-1		4	5	Kamieniecki	Keagle	Benitez	4-1	1st	+1.0
4-5	Det.	W	6-3		10	10	Mussina	Thompson	Orosco	5-1	1st	+1.0
4-7	At K.C.	W	11-7		16	12	Erickson	Rusch		6-1	1st	+2.0
4-9	At K.C.	W	2-1		7	9	Key	Rosado	Benitez	7-1	1st	+2.5
4-10	At Det.	L	1-7		6	12	Worrell	Drabek		7-2	1st	+2.5
4-11	At Det.	W	2-0		4	2	Mussina	Thompson	Benitez	8-2	1st	+2.5
4-12	At Det.	W	6-3		8	11	Erickson	Keagle	Benitez	9-2	1st	+2.5
4-14	Chi.	W	4-3		8	5	Key	Eyre	Orosco	10-2	1st	+2.5
4-15	Chi.	L	6-7		7	11	Baldwin	Drabek	Karchner	10-3	1st	+1.5
4-16	Chi.	L	2-8		7	12	Sirotka	Mussina		10-4	1st	+1.0
4-17	At Tex.	L	4-6		10	14	Pavlik	Erickson	Wetteland	10-5	T1st	...
4-18	At Tex.	W	10-8		15	11	Kamieniecki	Burkett		11-5	2nd	+0.5
4-19	At Tex.	L	7-11		12	16	Witt	Key	Wetteland	11-6	T1st	...
4-20	At Ana.	L	3-4		8	6	Hill	Drabek	Percival	11-7	4th	1.0
4-21	At Ana.	W	8-3		14	11	Rhodes	McDowell		12-7	3rd	0.5
4-22	At Ana.	L	6-7		12	12	Holtz	Mathews	Percival	12-8	3rd	1.5
4-24	Oak.	L	1-10		8	13	Rogers	Kamieniecki		12-9	3rd	2.5
4-25	Oak.	W	8-2		15	4	Key	Haynes		13-9	3rd	2.5
4-26	Oak.	L	4-12		6	15	Candiotti	Drabek		13-10	3rd	3.0
4-27	Ana.	L	1-3		4	9	Finley	Erickson	Percival	13-11	3rd	4.0
4-28	Ana.	L	5-6		12	9	Dickson	Rodriguez	Percival	13-12	3rd	4.0
4-29	At Chi.	L	7-16		6	15	Navarro	Ponson		13-13	3rd	5.0
4-30	At Chi.	W	4-1		5	5	Key	Eyre	Benitez	14-13	3rd	5.0
5-1	Min.	W	6-3		11	9	Drabek	Radke	Benitez	15-13	3rd	5.0
5-2	Min.	L	7-8	(11)	14	13	Aguilera	Johns		15-14	3rd	6.0
5-3	Min.	W	2-0		4	3	Mussina	Milton	Rhodes	16-14	3rd	6.0
5-5	At Cle.	L	5-6		11	9	Assenmacher	Benitez		16-15	3rd	7.0
5-6	At Cle.	L	5-14		8	17	Burba	Erickson		16-16	3rd	8.0
5-8	At T.B.	W	8-2		14	4	Rhodes	Lopez		17-16	3rd	8.0
5-9	At T.B.	W	7-0		11	5	Mussina	Springer		18-16	3rd	7.0
5-10	At T.B.	L	3-4		7	7	Yan	Mills	Hernandez	18-17	3rd	8.0
5-11	At Min.	W	4-0		7	5	Erickson	Tewksbury		19-17	3rd	7.5
5-12	At Min.	L	4-7		12	13	Hawkins	Rhodes	Aguilera	19-18	3rd	8.5
5-13	Cle.	W	8-1		10	6	Drabek	Ogea		20-18	3rd	8.5
5-14	Cle.	L	4-5		12	10	Nagy	Rhodes	Jackson	20-19	3rd	8.5
5-15	T.B.	L	1-4		6	9	Alvarez	Key	Hernandez	20-20	3rd	8.5
5-16	T.B.	L	2-5		6	11	Arrojo	Erickson	Hernandez	20-21	3rd	9.5
5-17	T.B.	L	3-7		6	9	Mecir	Mills		20-22	3rd	10.5
5-18	T.B.	L	3-6		6	10	Lopez	Drabek	Hernandez	20-23	T4th	11.0
5-19	At N.Y.	L	5-9		7	14	Stanton	Charlton		20-24	5th	12.0
5-20	At N.Y.	L	6-9		12	15	Irabu	Key		20-25	5th	13.0
5-21	At N.Y.	L	1-3		8	5	Pettitte	Erickson	Rivera	20-26	5th	14.0
5-22	At Oak.	L	5-9		12	10	Candiotti	Kamieniecki		20-27	5th	14.0
5-23	At Oak.	W	9-1		11	4	Drabek	Haynes		21-27	5th	14.0
5-24	At Oak.	W	2-1		6	8	Orosco	Taylor	Ponson	22-27	5th	14.0
5-25	At Sea.	L	4-12		8	15	Swift	Rodriguez		22-28	5th	15.0
5-26	At Sea.	W	8-3		11	6	Erickson	Fassero		23-28	5th	15.0
5-28	Tex.	W	5-2		11	7	Drabek	Witt	Orosco	24-28	4th	14.5
5-29	Tex.	W	6-3		12	8	Johns	Sele	Benitez	25-28	4th	14.5
5-30	Tex.	L	8-10		11	12	Hernandez	Ponson	Wetteland	25-29	4th	14.5
5-31	Tex.	L	5-9		12	15	Oliver	Erickson	Patterson	25-30	4th	14.5
6-1	Sea.	W	10-9		14	11	Mills	Fossas	Benitez	26-30	4th	14.5
6-2	Sea.	W	9-8	(10)	11	12	Charlton	Ayala		27-30	4th	14.5
6-3	At Bos.	W	3-0		7	5	Johns	Lowe	Rhodes	28-30	4th	14.5
6-4	At Bos.	L	1-9		8	14	Saberhagen	Ponson		28-31	4th	15.5
6-5	Atl.	W	3-2		6	7	Erickson	Neagle		29-31	4th	15.5
6-6	Atl.	L	5-10		8	14	Millwood	Mussina		29-32	4th	16.5
6-7	Atl.	L	0-9		4	14	Maddux	Drabek		29-33	4th	17.5
6-8	At Phi.	W	14-8		18	14	Rhodes	Winston	Orosco	30-33	4th	17.0
6-9	At Phi.	L	0-2		3	8	Beech	Ponson	Leiter	30-34	4th	18.0
6-10	At Phi.	W	5-2	(10)	8	10	Benitez	Leiter		31-34	4th	18.0
6-12	At Tor.	W	9-5		13	14	Mussina	Guzman		32-34	T3rd	17.0
6-13	At Tor.	L	8-9		13	12	Person	Drabek	Myers	32-35	4th	17.5
6-14	At Tor.	L	4-7		7	12	Clemens	Smith	Myers	32-36	4th	18.5
6-15	N.Y.	W	7-4		14	7	Erickson	Wells	Orosco	33-36	4th	17.5
6-16	N.Y.	W	2-0		8	2	Ponson	Irabu	Rhodes	34-36	T3rd	16.5
6-17	N.Y.	L	3-5		7	9	Pettitte	Mussina	Rivera	34-37	T3rd	17.5

Date	Opp.	Res.	Score	(inn.*)	Hits	Opp. hits	Winning pitcher	Losing pitcher	Save	Record	Pos.	GB
6-18	Tor.	L	6-13		13	18	Carpenter	Johns		34-38	4th	18.5
6-19	Tor.	W	7-4	(15)	15	10	Charlton	Risley		35-38	T3rd	17.5
6-20	Tor.	W	11-3		16	12	Erickson	Williams		36-38	3rd	17.5
6-21	Tor.	L	3-7		10	11	Hentgen	Ponson	Myers	36-39	T3rd	17.5
6-22	N.Y. (NL)	W	7-2		14	2	Mussina	Jones		37-39	T3rd	17.5
6-23	N.Y. (NL)	L	3-6		8	15	Hudek	Rhodes	J. Franco	37-40	4th	17.5
6-24	At N.Y. (NL)	L	3-6		14	9	Reed	Smith	J. Franco	37-41	4th	18.5
6-25	At N.Y.	L	2-3		6	9	Cook	Benitez		37-42	4th	19.5
6-26	At Mon.	L	4-9		10	12	Hermanson	Ponson		37-43	4th	20.5
6-27	At Mon.	L	1-3		6	10	Pavano	Mussina	Urbina	37-44	4th	21.5
6-28	At Mon.	L	4-8		7	11	Vazquez	Drabek	Urbina	37-45	4th	21.5
6-30	Fla.	L	5-7		8	11	Edmondson	Mills	Mantei	37-46	4th	22.5
7-1	Fla.	L	3-5		11	8	Hernandez	Smith	Powell	37-47	4th	23.5
7-2	Fla.	W	5-3		10	9	Ponson	Fontenot	Benitez	38-47	4th	23.5
7-3	At N.Y.	L	2-3		4	9	Pettitte	Orosco		38-48	4th	24.5
7-4	At N.Y.	L	3-4		8	10	Hernandez	Drabek	Rivera	38-49	4th	25.5
7-5	At N.Y.	L	0-1		7	7	Cone	Erickson	Rivera	38-50	4th	26.5
7-9	Bos.	W	3-2		9	6	Orosco	Corsi	Benitez	39-50	4th	26.5
7-10	Bos.	W	3-2		5	7	Orosco	Martinez	Benitez	40-50	4th	26.5
7-11	Bos.	W	2-1		11	4	Erickson	Wakefield	Orosco	41-50	4th	26.5
7-12	Bos.	W	11-7		12	9	Johns	Cho	Mills	42-50	4th	26.5
7-13	Tor.	W	5-0		8	3	Rodriguez	Guzman		43-50	4th	25.5
7-14	Tor.	W	11-5		14	7	Mussina	Williams		44-50	4th	25.5
7-15	At Tex.	W	14-3		19	11	Ponson	Helling		45-50	4th	25.5
7-16	At Tex.	W	9-3		18	8	Erickson	Sele		46-50	4th	24.5
7-17	At Ana.	W	4-1		9	6	Drabek	Dickson	Benitez	47-50	4th	23.5
7-18	At Ana.	L	3-8		5	13	Washburn	Rodriguez		47-51	4th	24.5
7-19	At Ana.	W	7-4		9	7	Orosco	Percival		48-51	4th	23.5
7-21	Oak.	W	7-1		10	6	Erickson	Candiotti		49-51	4th	23.5
7-22	Oak.	W	5-4		10	6	Benitez	Fetters		50-51	4th	23.5
7-23	Oak.	W	9-7		12	9	Benitez	Fetters		51-51	3rd	23.0
7-24	Sea.	W	7-4		14	7	Mussina	Swift	Benitez	52-51	3rd	23.0
7-25	Sea.	L	2-4		11	10	Fassero	Kamieniecki	Timlin	52-52	3rd	23.0
7-26	Sea.	L	4-10		6	13	Moyer	Erickson		52-53	3rd	24.0
7-28	At Det.	W	6-5		10	8	Ponson	Florie	Benitez	53-53	3rd	24.0
7-29	At Det.	W	14-2		18	8	Mussina	Castillo	Johns	54-53	3rd	23.0
7-30	At Det.	W	6-4		7	8	Smith	Anderson	Benitez	55-53	3rd	23.0
7-31	At K.C.	L	6-9		7	15	Rosado	Erickson		55-54	3rd	24.0
8-1	At K.C.	L	5-9		5	9	Haney	Kamieniecki		55-55	3rd	25.0
8-2	At K.C.	W	9-2		16	8	Ponson	Rusch		56-55	3rd	24.0
8-4	Det.	W	4-0		11	2	Mussina	Florie		57-55	3rd	25.0
8-5	Det.	W	6-1		9	5	Guzman	Thompson		58-55	3rd	24.0
8-7	At Min.	W	16-9		19	11	Key	Miller		59-55	3rd	24.5
8-8	At Min.	W	6-3		11	12	Ponson	Radke	Orosco	60-55	3rd	24.5
8-9	At Min.	L	4-5		9	14	Serafini	Mussina	Aguilera	60-56	3rd	25.5
8-10	At T.B.	W	2-1		7	3	Guzman	Saunders	Benitez	61-56	3rd	25.5
8-11	At T.B.	L	1-2		3	11	Mecir	Benitez		61-57	3rd	26.5
8-12	At T.B.	W	7-0		10	5	Erickson	Alvarez		62-57	3rd	26.5
8-13	At Cle.	W	7-4	(12)	15	6	Smith	Reed	Benitez	63-57	3rd	26.5
8-14	At Cle.	W	15-3		16	9	Mussina	Nagy		64-57	3rd	26.5
8-15	At Cle.	W	9-8	(10)	16	7	Benitez	Jones		65-57	3rd	25.5
8-16	At Cle.	L	3-5		9	6	Wright	Kamieniecki	Jackson	65-58	3rd	26.5
8-17	Min.	W	3-2		9	7	Erickson	Hawkins	Benitez	66-58	3rd	26.5
8-18	Min.	W	7-1		10	7	Ponson	Radke		67-58	3rd	26.5
8-19	T.B.	W	6-4		12	12	Mussina	Arrojo	Benitez	68-58	3rd	25.5
8-20	T.B.	L	2-4		4	7	Saunders	Rhodes	Hernandez	68-59	3rd	25.5
8-21	Cle.	L	3-6		5	12	Wright	Kamieniecki		68-60	3rd	26.5
8-22	Cle.	W	6-3		9	7	Erickson	Colon		69-60	3rd	26.5
8-23	Cle.	L	1-4		5	11	Gooden	Ponson	Jackson	69-61	3rd	26.5
8-25	At Chi.	L	4-6		7	11	Bradford	Mussina		69-62	3rd	26.0
8-26	At Chi.	L	5-12		6	15	Baldwin	Guzman		69-63	3rd	26.5
8-27	At Chi.	L	4-7		11	8	Parque	Erickson	Simas	69-64	3rd	27.5
8-28	K.C.	L	5-6		9	10	Rapp	Ponson	Montgomery	69-65	3rd	28.5
8-29	K.C.	L	1-2		3	8	Barber	Mussina	Montgomery	69-66	4th	29.5
8-30	K.C.	L	2-3		6	6	Haney	Guzman	Montgomery	69-67	4th	29.5
8-31	Chi.	L	1-4		7	8	Baldwin	Erickson	Howry	69-68	4th	30.0
9-1	Chi.	L	5-9		10	10	Parque	Drabek	Navarro	69-69	4th	31.0
9-2	Chi.	L	2-3		3	6	Snyder	Mills	Howry	69-70	4th	31.0
9-4	At Sea.	W	10-1		10	5	Guzman	Spoljaric		70-70	4th	31.0
9-5	At Sea.	L	5-6		8	13	McCarthy	Benitez	Timlin	70-71	4th	31.0
9-6	At Sea.	W	5-2		8	4	Mussina	Fassero	Rhodes	71-71	4th	30.0
9-7	At Sea.	L	1-11		3	15	Moyer	Drabek		71-72	4th	30.0
9-8	At Oak.	W	5-2		11	7	Rhodes	Heredia	Benitez	72-72	4th	30.0
9-9	At Oak.	W	6-2		10	7	Guzman	Haynes		73-72	4th	30.0
9-11	Ana.	W	8-3		12	9	Erickson	Finley		74-72	4th	29.5
9-12	Ana.	W	3-2		9	8	Mills	Percival		75-72	4th	28.5

Date	Opp.	Res.	Score	(inn.*)	Hits	Opp. hits	Winning pitcher	Losing pitcher	Save	Record	Pos.	GB
9-13	Ana.	W	12-7		13	8	Key	Washburn		76-72	4th	27.5
9-14	Tex.	W	1-0		8	5	Mills	Hernandez	Benitez	77-72	4th	27.5
9-15	Tex.	L	5-6		10	8	Crabtree	Benitez	Wetteland	77-73	4th	27.5
9-16	Bos.	L	3-4		10	14	Saberhagen	Erickson	Gordon	77-74	4th	27.5
9-17	Bos.	L	2-3	(10)	6	8	Eckersley	Benitez	Gordon	77-75	4th	28.5
9-18	N.Y.	L	5-15		12	15	Wells	Guzman		77-76	4th	29.5
9-19	N.Y.	W	5-3		13	10	Ponson	Cone	Mills	78-76	4th	28.5
9-20	N.Y.	L	4-5		8	16	Hernandez	Johns	Rivera	78-77	4th	29.5
9-21	At Tor.	L	1-3		8	9	Clemens	Erickson	Plesac	78-78	4th	29.5
9-22	At Tor.	L	3-7		6	8	Carpenter	Mussina		78-79	4th	31.0
9-23	At Tor.	L	3-6		10	8	Escobar	Guzman	Person	78-80	4th	32.0
9-24	At Bos.	L	6-9		8	18	Martinez	Ponson	Gordon	78-81	4th	33.0
9-25	At Bos.	L	3-8		7	11	Wakefield	Fussell		78-82	4th	34.0
9-26	At Bos.	W	5-2		6	7	Erickson	Saberhagen	Benitez	79-82	4th	34.0
9-27	At Bos.	L	4-6		13	9	Valdez	Mussina	Gordon	79-83	4th	35.0

Monthly records: March (0-1), April (14-12), May (11-17), June (12-16), July (18-8), August (14-14), September (10-15).
*Innings, if other than nine. †First game of doubleheader. ‡Second game of doubleheader.

HIGHLIGHTS

High point: The Orioles defeated the White Sox 4-3 on April 14 to improve their record to 10-2 and take a 2.5-game lead in the A.L. East. Lefthander Jimmy Key improved to 2-0 as the defending division champions appeared ready to assume control.

Low point: Mike Mussina was struck in the face by a line drive off the bat of Indians catcher Sandy Alomar. He suffered a laceration over his right eye and a badly broken nose and was placed on the disabled list for the second time in a month.

Turning point: The club followed its 10-2 start with a 3-11 slump and an eight-game turnabout in the standings. The O's slipped steadily out of contention after that, though they did rebound enough to make the Red Sox sweat out the wild-card race in September.

Most valuable player: First baseman Rafael Palmeiro had another outstanding season, batting .296 with 43 home runs and 121 RBIs.

Most valuable pitcher: Scott Erickson was the only Orioles starter who didn't miss a scheduled start. He led the league with 36 starts en route to a 16-13 record and 4.01 ERA.

Most improved player: Spot starter/middle reliever Doug Johns came out of nowhere to appear in 31 games (10 starts) and he played an unexpected role on the Orioles' injury-depleted staff.

Most pleasant surprise: Veteran outfielder Eric Davis came back less than a year after cancer surgery to bat .327 with 28 home runs and 89 RBIs.

Biggest disappointment: Center fielder Brady Anderson tried to play through injuries in the early weeks and got off to an abysmal start. He finished with a .236 average, 18 homers and 51 RBIs, well below expectations.

Key injuries: Mussina went on the D.L. twice, first with a wart on his pitching hand and then when he was struck in the face by a line drive. Key missed much of the season with an inflamed shoulder. Anderson was on the D.L. from April 21-May 8 with a shoulder problem and played through assorted other injuries. Pitcher Scott Kamieniecki was limited to 11 starts by a variety of injuries.

Notable: Cal Ripken's record string of 2,632 straight games ended when he took himself out of the lineup September 20. . . . Chris Hoiles became the first catcher in big-league history to hit two grand slams in one game on August 14. . . . Davis hit in a club-record 30 straight games from July 12-August 15. . . . The Orioles set a record by committing only 81 errors and set a club record with a .987 fielding percentage.

—PETER SCHMUCK

RECORDS

1998 regular-season record: 79-83 (4th in A.L. East); 42-39 at home; 37-44 on road; 19-29 vs. A.L. East; 29-25 vs. Central; 26-18 vs. West; 5-11 vs. N.L.; 22-27 vs. lefthanded starters; 57-56 vs. righthanded starters; 66-67 on grass; 13-16 on turf; 25-22 in daytime; 54-61 at night; 18-24 in one-run games; 5-2 in extra-inning games; 0-0 in doubleheaders.

Team record past five years: 399-343 (.538, ranks 3rd in league in that span).

TEAM LEADERS

Batting average: Eric Davis (.327).
At-bats: Rafael Palmeiro (619).
Runs: Rafael Palmeiro (98).
Hits: Rafael Palmeiro (183).
Total bases: Rafael Palmeiro (350).
Doubles: Roberto Alomar, Rafael Palmeiro (36).
Triples: Brady Anderson (3).
Home runs: Rafael Palmeiro (43).
Runs batted in: Rafael Palmeiro (121).
Stolen bases: Brady Anderson (21).
Slugging percentage: Eric Davis (.582).
On-base percentage: Eric Davis (.388).
Wins: Scott Erickson (16).
Earned-run average: Mike Mussina (3.49).
Complete games: Scott Erickson (11).
Shutouts: Scott Erickson, Mike Mussina (2).
Saves: Armando Benitez (22).
Innings pitched: Scott Erickson (251.1).
Strikeouts: Scott Erickson (186).

GAMES BY POSITION

Catcher: Lenny Webster 102, Chris Hoiles 83, Charlie Greene 13.

First base: Rafael Palmeiro 159, Chris Hoiles 6, Calvin Pickering 5, Ryan Minor 3, Joe Carter 1, B.J. Surhoff 1.

Second base: Roberto Alomar 144, Jeff Reboulet 28, P.J. Forbes 7, Jerry Hairston Jr. 4.

Third base: Cal Ripken Jr. 161, Jeff Reboulet 23, Ryan Minor 6, P.J. Forbes 1, Ozzie Guillen 1.

Shortstop: Mike Bordick 150, Jeff Reboulet 28, Ozzie Guillen 6, P.J. Forbes 1.

Outfield: B.J. Surhoff 157, Brady Anderson 130, Eric Davis 72, Rich Becker 60, Jeffrey Hammonds 53, Joe Carter 50, Lyle Mouton 16, Willie Greene 14, Danny Clyburn 8, Jesus Tavarez 8, Gene Kingsale 4, Willis Otanez 2.

Designated hitter: Harold Baines 80, Eric Davis 54, Joe Carter 32, Jeffrey Hammonds 7, Chris Hoiles 6, Lenny Webster 4, Roberto Alomar 3, Rafael Palmeiro 3, Calvin Pickering 3, Rich Becker 2, Lyle Mouton 2, Brady Anderson 1, Danny Clyburn 1, Willie Greene 1, Gene Kingsale 1, Ryan Minor 1.

TOP DRAFT CHOICES

1a. **Rick Elder**, OF, Sprayberry H.S., Marietta, Ga.

1b. **Mamon Tucker**, OF, Stephen F. Austin H.S., Austin, Tex.

2a. **Ben Knapp**, RHP, Oviedo (Fla.) H.S.

2b. **Alex Hart**, RHP, Chambersburg (Pa.) Area H.S.

3. **Stephen Bechler**, RHP, S. Medford H.S., Medford (Ore.)

4. **Chris Davidson**, RHP, W. Carolina U.

5. **Josh Yarno**, RHP, Moscow (Ida.) H.S.

6. **Tim Raines Jr.**, OF, Seminole H.S., Sanford, Fla.

7. **Tim Nelson**, 3B, Allen Hancock (Calif.) J.C.

8. **Randy Perez**, LHP, El Capitan H.S., Lakeside, Calif.

9. **Francisco Monzon**, C, Lorenzo Vizcarrondo H.S., Carolina, P.R.

10. **Dustin Emberley**, RHP, Composite H.S., Weyburn, Sask.

BOSTON RED SOX
AMERICAN LEAGUE EAST DIVISION

1999 Red Sox Schedule
Home games shaded. *—All-Star Game at Fenway Park (Boston).
D—Day game (any game starting before 5 p.m.).

April
SUN	MON	TUE	WED	THU	FRI	SAT
				1	2	3
4	5 D KC	6	7 KC	8 KC	9 TB	10 TB
11 D TB	12	13 D CWS	14	15 CWS	16 TB	17 D TB
18 TB	19 D TB	20 DET	21 DET	22 D DET	23 CLE	24 D CLE
25 CLE	26 MIN	27 MIN	28 D MIN	29	30 OAK	

May
SUN	MON	TUE	WED	THU	FRI	SAT
						1 D OAK
2 OAK	3 D OAK	4	5 TEX	6 TEX	7 ANA	8 D ANA
9 ANA	10 D SEA	11 SEA	12 SEA	13	14 TOR	15 D TOR
16 TOR	17 TOR	18 NYY	19 NYY	20 NYY	21 TOR	22 D TOR
23 TOR	24 NYY	25 NYY	26 NYY	27	28 CLE	29 D CLE
30 CLE	31 D DET					

June
SUN	MON	TUE	WED	THU	FRI	SAT
		1 DET	2 DET	3	4 ATL	5 D ATL
6 ATL	7 MON	8 MON	9 MON	10	11 NYM	12 D NYM
13 NYM	14 MIN	15 MIN	16 MIN	17	18 TEX	19 TEX
20 TEX	21 TEX	22 BAL	23 BAL	24 BAL	25 CWS	26 D CWS
27 CWS	28 CWS	29	30 TB			

July
SUN	MON	TUE	WED	THU	FRI	SAT
				1 TB	2 CWS	3 D CWS
4 D CWS	5 D TB	6 TB	7 TB	8 TB	9 ATL	10 D ATL
11 D ATL	12	13	* 14	15 PHI	16 PHI	17 D PHI
18 FLA	19 FLA	20 FLA	21 BAL	22 DET	23 DET	24 DET
25 DET	26	27 TOR	28 TOR	29	30 NYY	31 NYY

August
SUN	MON	TUE	WED	THU	FRI	SAT
1 NYY	2 CLE	3 CLE	4 CLE	5 ANA	6 ANA	7 ANA
8 ANA	9 KC	10 KC	11 KC	12	13 SEA	14 D SEA
15 SEA	16 OAK	17 OAK	18 OAK	19 OAK	20 TEX	21 TEX
22 TEX	23 MIN	24 MIN	25 MIN	26	27 ANA	28 D ANA
29 ANA	30 D KC	31 KC				

September
SUN	MON	TUE	WED	THU	FRI	SAT
			1 KC	2 KC	3 SEA	4 D SEA
5 SEA	6 D SEA	7 D OAK	8 OAK	9 D	10 NYY	11 D NYY
12 NYY	13 CLE	14 CLE	15 CLE	16	17 DET	18 D DET
19 DET	20	21 TOR	22 TOR	23 TOR	24 BAL	25 D BAL
26 BAL	27 BAL	28 CWS	29 CWS	30 CWS		

October
SUN	MON	TUE	WED	THU	FRI	SAT
					1 BAL	2 BAL
3 BAL	4	5	6	7	8	9

1999 SEASON
CLUB DIRECTORY

Chief executive officer
John L. Harrington
Exec. v.p. and general manager
Daniel F. Duquette
Exec. vice president, administration
John S. Buckley
V.p. and chief financial officer
Robert C. Furbush
Vice president, baseball operations
Michael D. Port
V.p., broadcasting and technology
James P. Healey
Vice president, public affairs
Richard L. Bresciani
Vice president, sales and marketing
Lawrence C. Cancro
Vice president, stadium operations
Joseph F. McDermott
Vice president, assistant g.m. and legal counsel
Elaine W. Steward
Assistant general manager
Edward P. Kenney
Dir. of com. and baseball information
Kevin J. Shea
Dir. of human resources and office mgmt.
Michele Julian
Vice president, scouting
W. Wayne Britton
Exec. dir. of int'l baseball operations
R. Ray Poitevint
Director of minor league operations
Kent A. Qualls
Coordinator of Florida operations
Marci S. Blacker
Traveling secretary
John F. McCormick
Special asst. for player development
John M. Pesky
Major league scout
Frank J. Malzone
Major league special assignment scout
G. Edwin Haas
Medical director
Arthur M. Pappas, M.D.
Trainer
James W. Rowe Jr.
Physical therapist
Richard M. Zawacki
Strength and conditioning coordinator
Merle V. "B.J." Baker III
Baseball information coordinator
Glenn Wilburn
Baseball operations assistant
Thomas L. Moore

Communications coordinator
Kathleen J. Gordon
Instructors
Theodore S. Williams, Carl M. Yastrzemski
Executive administrative assistant
Lorraine Leong
Equip. manager and clubhouse operations
J. Joseph Cochran
Controller
Stanley H. Tran
Director of advertising and sponsorships
Jeffrey E. Goldenberg
Director of facilities management
Thomas L. Queenan Jr.
Director of food services
Patricia T. Flanagan
Director of ticket operations
Joseph P. Helyar
Executive consultant, public affairs
James "Lou" Gorman
Superintendent of grounds and maint.
Joseph P. Mooney
Box office manager
Richard J. Beaton Jr.
Broadcasting manager
James E. Shannahan
Community relations manager
Ronald E. Burton Jr.
Customer relations manager
Ann Marie C. Starzyk
Ground crew manager
Casey Erven
Promotions manager
Marcita Thompson
Publications manager
Debra A. Matson
Scouts
Ray Blanco, Raymond Boone, Buzz Bowers, Kevin Burrell, Julian Camilo, Ben Cherington, Ray Crone Jr., George Digby, Danny Doyle, William Enos, Ray Fagnant, Mark Garcia, Robinson Garcia, Eddie Haas, Matt Haas, Ernie Jacobs, Wally Komatsubara, Chuck Koney, Kenneth Lee, Don Lenhardt, Frank Malzone, Luis Marin, Sebastian Martinez, Joe Mason, Jose Maza, Steve McAllister, Levy Ochoa, Ray Poitevint, Gary Rajsich, Carlos Ramirez, Rafael Rios, Eddie Robinson, Jim Robinson, Reuben Rodriguez, Ed Roebuck, Edward Scott, Mathew Sczesny, Lee Sigman, Harry Smith, Dick Sorkin, Jerry Stephenson, Joseph Stephenson, Lee Thomas, Fay Thompson, Michael Victoria, Charles Wagner, Luke Wrenn, Jeffrey Zona

MINOR LEAGUE AFFILIATES

Class	Team	League	Manager
AAA	Pawtucket	International	Gary Jones
AA	Trenton	Eastern	DeMarlo Hale
A	Sarasota	Florida State	Butch Hobson
A	Augusta	South Atlantic	Billy Gardner Jr.
A	Lowell	New York-Pennsylvania	Luis Aguayo
Rookie	Gulf Coast Red Sox	Gulf Coast	John Sanders

BROADCAST INFORMATION

Radio: WEEI-AM (680).
TV: WABU-TV (Channel 68).
Cable TV: New England Sports Network.

SPRING TRAINING

Ballpark (city): City of Palms Park (Fort Myers, Fla.).
Ticket information: 941-334-4700.

SPRING TRAINING ROSTER

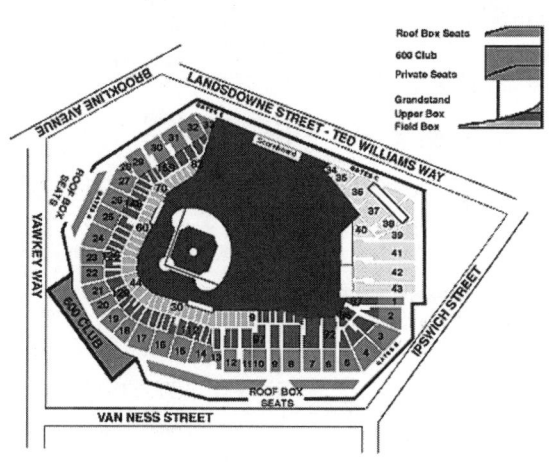

Manager—Jimy Williams (22).
Coaches—John Cumberland, Dave Jauss (41), Joe Kerrigan (16), Wendell Kim (31), Grady Little (35), Jim Rice (14).

No.	PITCHERS	B/T	Ht./Wt.	Born	1998 clubs
	Adamson, Joel	L/L	6-4/185	7-2-71	Arizona
59	Barkley, Brian	L/L	6-2/180	12-8-75	Pawtucket, Boston
	Cho, Jin Ho	R/R	6-3/210	8-16-75	Trenton, Boston, Sarasota
41	Corsi, Jim	R/R	6-1/220	9-9-61	Boston, Pawtucket
	Cressend, Jack	R/R	6-1/185	5-13-75	Trenton
36	Gordon, Tom	R/R	5-9/180	11-18-67	Boston
	Gross, Kip	R/R	6-2/194	8-24-64	Nippon (Japan)
	Guthrie, Mark	R/L	6-4/207	9-22-65	Los Angeles
32	Lowe, Derek	R/R	6-6/170	6-1-73	Boston
57	Mahay, Ron	L/L	6-2/190	6-28-71	Pawtucket, Boston
45	Martinez, Pedro J.	R/R	5-11/170	7-25-71	Boston
	Pena, Juan	R/R	6-5/211	6-27-77	Pawtucket
	Portugal, Mark	R/R	6-0/208	10-30-62	Philadelphia
	Ramsay, Robert	L/L	6-5/230	12-3-73	Trenton
	Rapp, Pat	R/R	6-3/215	7-13-67	Kansas City
19	Rose, Brian	R/R	6-3/212	2-13-76	Boston, Pawtucket
17	Saberhagen, Bret	R/R	6-1/200	4-11-64	Boston
	Santana, Marino	R/R	6-1/190	5-10-72	Toledo, Detroit
49	Wakefield, Tim	R/R	6-2/206	8-2-66	Boston
46	Wasdin, John	R/R	6-2/193	8-5-72	Boston, Pawtucket

No.	CATCHERS	B/T	Ht./Wt.	Born	1998 clubs
10	Hatteberg, Scott	L/R	6-1/195	12-14-69	Boston
	Hillenbrand, Shea	R/R	6-1/190	8-27-75	Michigan
	Lomasney, Steve	R/R	6-0/185	8-29-77	Sarasota
47	Varitek, Jason	B/R	6-2/210	4-11-72	Boston

No.	INFIELDERS	B/T	Ht./Wt.	Born	1998 clubs
3	Frye, Jeff	R/R	5-9/165	8-31-66	Boston
5	Garciaparra, Nomar	R/R	6-0/167	7-23-73	Boston
18	Jefferson, Reggie	L/L	6-4/215	9-25-68	Boston, Gulf Coast Red Sox, Sarasota
	Liniak, Cole	R/R	6-1/182	8-23-76	Pawtucket, Gulf Coast Red Sox
	Merloni, Lou	R/R	5-10/195	4-6-71	Pawtucket, Boston, Gulf Coast Red Sox
30	Offerman, Jose	B/R	6-0/190	11-8-68	Kansas City
52	Sadler, Donnie	R/R	5-6/165	6-17-75	Pawtucket, Boston
24	Stanley, Mike	R/R	6-0/190	6-25-63	Toronto, Boston
13	Valentin, John	R/R	6-0/180	2-18-67	Boston
	Veras, Wilton	R/R	6-2/186	1-19-78	Trenton

No.	OUTFIELDERS	B/T	Ht./Wt.	Born	1998 clubs
2	Buford, Damon	R/R	5-10/170	6-12-70	Boston
44	Coleman, Michael	R/R	5-11/180	8-16-75	Pawtucket
29	Cummings, Midre	L/R	6-0/190	10-14-71	Boston
20	Lewis, Darren	R/R	6-0/189	8-28-67	Boston
7	Nixon, Trot	L/L	6-2/196	4-11-74	Pawtucket, Boston
25	O'Leary, Troy	L/L	6-0/198	8-4-69	Boston

BALLPARK INFORMATION

Ballpark (capacity, surface)
Fenway Park (33,455; grass)
Address
4 Yawkey Way
Boston, MA 02215-3496
Business phone
617-267-9440
Ticket information
617-267-1700, 617-482-4769
Ticket prices
$35 (field box)
$32 (loge box and infield roof)
$26 (right-field boxes and right-field roof)
$24 (reserved grandstand)
$18 (outfield grandstand)
$14 (lower bleachers)
$12 (upper bleachers)
Field dimensions (from home plate)
To left field at foul line, 310 feet
To center field, 420 feet
To right field at foul line, 302 feet
First game played
April 20, 1912
(Red Sox 7, New York Highlanders 6)

1998 REVIEW
DAY BY DAY

Date	Opp.	Res.	Score	(inn.*)	Hits	Opp. hits	Winning pitcher	Losing pitcher	Save	Record	Pos.	GB
4-1	At Oak.	W	2-0		7	4	Martinez	Candiotti	Gordon	1-0	T1st	...
4-2	At Oak.	W	6-3		11	7	Wasdin	Taylor	Gordon	2-0	1st	+0.5
4-3	At Sea.	L	6-11		9	13	Cloude	Lowe		2-1	2nd	0.5
4-4	At Sea.	L	6-12		9	12	Swift	Rose		2-2	T3rd	1.5
4-5	At Sea.	W	10-5		9	8	Saberhagen	Johnson		3-2	3rd	1.5
4-6	At Ana.	L	1-2	(11)	5	9	Holtz	Gordon		3-3	3rd	2.0
4-7	At Ana.	L	1-6		6	9	Hill	Wakefield		3-4	3rd	3.0
4-8	At Ana.	L	1-2		8	5	McDowell	Lowe	Percival	3-5	5th	3.5
4-10	Sea.	W	9-7		6	12	Garces	Timlin		4-5	4th	3.0
4-11	Sea.	W	5-0		13	2	Martinez	Moyer		5-5	4th	3.0
4-12	Sea.	W	8-7		13	14	Wasdin	Slocumb		6-5	4th	3.0
4-13	Oak.	W	6-3		11	4	Saberhagen	Rogers	Gordon	7-5	4th	2.5
4-14	Oak.	W	8-6		9	11	Gordon	Taylor		8-5	2nd	2.5
4-15	Oak.	W	4-3		11	7	Eckersley	Mathews		9-5	2nd	1.5
4-17	Cle.	W	3-2	(10)	14	6	Gordon	Assenmacher		10-5	T1st	...
4-18	Cle.	L	4-7		9	10	Martin	Eckersley	Jackson	10-6	2nd	0.5
4-19	Cle.	W	2-0		10	7	Saberhagen	Burba	Gordon	11-6	T1st	...
4-20	Cle.	W	6-5	(11)	16	9	Gordon	Plunk		12-6	T1st	...
4-21	At Det.	W	11-4		12	7	Rose	Worrell		13-6	2nd	+0.5
4-22	At Det.	W	8-5		12	9	Corsi	Jones	Gordon	14-6	2nd	+0.5
4-24	At Cle.	W	7-5		7	8	Wakefield	Burba	Gordon	15-6	2nd	+0.5
4-25	At Cle.	W	3-2		9	7	Saberhagen	Colon	Gordon	16-6	2nd	+0.5
4-27	Det.	W	6-5		8	10	Eckersley	Runyan	Gordon	17-6	2nd	+0.5
4-28	Det.	L	5-7		13	13	Florie	Shouse	Jones	17-7	2nd	+0.5
4-29	Ana.	W	8-4		15	9	Wakefield	Watson	Gordon	18-7	2nd	+0.5
4-30	Ana.	L	2-7		9	10	Hill	Checo		18-8	2nd	0.5
5-1	Tex.	W	5-3		9	7	Wasdin	Sele	Gordon	19-8	2nd	0.5
5-2	Tex.	L	6-7		12	11	Helling	Rose	Wetteland	19-9	2nd	1.5
5-3	Tex.	W	2-1		9	5	Martinez	Oliver	Gordon	20-9	2nd	1.5
5-5	Min.	W	4-2		7	5	Wakefield	Tewksbury	Gordon	21-9	2nd	1.5
5-6	Min.	L	7-8		9	13	Hawkins	Checo		21-10	2nd	2.5
5-7	At K.C.	L	3-5		10	5	Rapp	Rose	Montgomery	21-11	2nd	3.0
5-8	At K.C.	W	14-3		20	8	Saberhagen	Haney	Garces	22-11	2nd	3.0
5-9	At K.C.	W	3-1		10	5	Martinez	Belcher	Gordon	23-11	2nd	2.0
5-10	At K.C.	W	3-1		5	2	Wakefield	Rosado	Gordon	24-11	2nd	2.0
5-11	At Tex.	L	2-8		5	11	Witt	Wasdin		24-12	2nd	2.5
5-12	At Tex.	L	3-6		7	7	Sele	Rose	Wetteland	24-13	2nd	3.5
5-13	At Min.	L	4-7		9	9	Radke	Saberhagen	Aguilera	24-14	2nd	4.5
5-14	At Min.	L	1-2	(12)	9	9	Trombley	Wasdin		24-15	2nd	4.5
5-15	K.C.	W	5-2		8	9	Wakefield	Rosado	Eckersley	25-15	2nd	3.5
5-16	K.C.	W	5-0		10	4	Avery	Walker	Gordon	26-15	2nd	3.5
5-17	K.C.	W	5-3		9	10	Mahay	Rusch	Gordon	27-15	2nd	3.5
5-19	Chi.	L	5-9		11	12	Bere	Saberhagen		27-16	2nd	4.5
5-20	Chi.	W	6-2		11	8	Martinez	Navarro	Gordon	28-16	2nd	4.5
5-22	N.Y.	W	5-4		11	7	Wakefield	Nelson	Gordon	29-16	2nd	4.0
5-23	N.Y.	L	3-12		6	15	Wells	Lowe		29-17	2nd	5.0
5-24	N.Y.	L	4-14		12	17	Cone	Saberhagen		29-18	2nd	6.0
5-25	Tor.	L	5-7		8	12	Hentgen	Martinez	Myers	29-19	2nd	7.0
5-26	Tor.	L	2-5		7	8	Guzman	Avery	Myers	29-20	2nd	8.0
5-28	At N.Y.	L	3-8		13	11	Wells	Wakefield	Stanton	29-21	2nd	8.5
5-29	At N.Y.	L	2-6		5	11	Cone	Lowe		29-22	2nd	9.5
5-30	At N.Y.	W	3-2		3	7	Saberhagen	Irabu	Gordon	30-22	2nd	8.5
5-31	At N.Y.	W	13-7		17	14	Martinez	Pettitte		31-22	2nd	7.5
6-1	At Tor.	W	9-5		13	7	Corsi	Myers		32-22	2nd	7.5
6-2	At Tor.	W	11-3		11	8	Avery	Carpenter		33-22	2nd	7.5
6-3	Bal.	L	0-3		5	7	Johns	Lowe	Rhodes	33-23	2nd	8.5
6-4	Bal.	W	9-1		14	8	Saberhagen	Ponson		34-23	2nd	8.5
6-5	N.Y. (NL)	L	2-9		5	11	Leiter	Martinez		34-24	2nd	9.5
6-6	N.Y. (NL)	L	0-1		4	2	Jones	Wakefield	J. Franco	34-25	2nd	10.5
6-7	N.Y. (NL)	W	5-0		8	4	Avery	Yoshii		35-25	2nd	10.5
6-8	At Atl.	L	6-7		12	11	Embree	Wasdin		35-26	2nd	11.0
6-9	At Atl.	W	9-3		13	8	Saberhagen	Martinez		36-26	2nd	11.0
6-10	At Atl.	W	10-6		13	10	Martinez	Neagle		37-26	2nd	11.0
6-12	T.B.	W	5-1		9	10	Wakefield	Arrojo		38-26	2nd	10.0
6-14	T.B.	W	3-2	(10)	10	13	Gordon	Lopez		39-26	2nd	10.0
6-15	At Chi.	L	2-3		6	6	Parque	Saberhagen	Karchner	39-27	2nd	10.0
6-16	At Chi.	W	6-1		12	7	Martinez	Bere		40-27	2nd	9.0
6-17	At Chi.	W	12-5		13	4	Wakefield	Eyre	Gordon	41-27	2nd	9.0
6-18	At T.B.	W	7-5	(10)	14	8	Wasdin	Yan	Gordon	42-27	2nd	9.0
6-19	At T.B.	W	4-1		4	6	Avery	Saunders	Gordon	43-27	2nd	8.0
6-20	At T.B.	L	5-8		10	9	Santana	Saberhagen	Hernandez	43-28	2nd	9.0
6-21	At T.B.	W	3-1		11	2	Martinez	Johnson	Gordon	44-28	2nd	8.0
6-22	Phi.	L	8-9	(10)	13	13	Gomes	Gordon	Leiter	44-29	2nd	9.0

Date	Opp.	Res.	Score	(inn.*)	Hits	Opp. hits	Winning pitcher	Losing pitcher	Save	Record	Pos.	GB
6-23	Phi.	L	2-3		7	11	Portugal	Lowe		44-30	2nd	9.0
6-24	At Phi.	L	8-11		10	13	Loewer	Avery	Leiter	44-31	2nd	10.0
6-25	At Phi.	W	7-5		10	9	Saberhagen	Beech	Mahay	45-31	2nd	10.0
6-26	At Fla.	W	6-1		11	5	Martinez	Fontenot		46-31	2nd	10.0
6-27	At Fla.	W	9-4		14	8	Wakefield	Sanchez		47-31	2nd	10.0
6-28	At Fla.	L	1-5		6	8	Dempster	Lowe	Alfonseca	47-32	2nd	10.0
6-30	Mon.	W	7-4		12	6	Avery	C. Perez	Gordon	48-32	2nd	10.0
7-1	Mon.	W	6-1		12	6	Saberhagen	Hermanson		49-32	2nd	10.0
7-2	Mon.	W	15-0		20	3	Martinez	Pavano		50-32	2nd	10.0
7-3	Chi.	W	15-2		17	7	Wakefield	Sirotka		51-32	2nd	10.0
7-4	Chi.	L	0-3		5	7	Snyder	Cho	Simas	51-33	2nd	11.0
7-5	Chi.	W	15-14		20	12	Reyes	Howry	Gordon	52-33	2nd	11.0
7-9	At Bal.	L	2-3		6	9	Orosco	Corsi	Benitez	52-34	2nd	12.0
7-10	At Bal.	L	2-3		7	5	Orosco	Martinez	Benitez	52-35	2nd	13.0
7-11	At Bal.	L	1-2		4	11	Erickson	Wakefield	Orosco	52-36	2nd	14.0
7-12	At Bal.	L	7-11		9	12	Johns	Cho	Mills	52-37	2nd	15.0
7-13	At T.B.	W	2-0		10	7	Avery	Santana	Gordon	53-37	2nd	14.0
7-14	At T.B.	L	4-5		8	11	Lopez	Mahay		53-38	2nd	15.0
7-15	Cle.	W	1-0		7	4	Martinez	Colon		54-38	2nd	15.0
7-16	Cle.	W	15-5		17	8	Wakefield	Gooden	Lowe	55-38	2nd	14.0
7-17	At Det.	L	4-6		9	11	Powell	Cho	Jones	55-39	2nd	14.0
7-18	At Det.	W	9-4		10	7	Avery	Castillo	Lowe	56-39	2nd	14.0
7-19	At Det.	L	1-3		7	9	Thompson	Gordon		56-40	2nd	14.0
7-21§	At Cle.	W	10-7		12	12	Martinez	Gooden		57-40		
7-21§	At Cle.	L	2-4	(8)	8	8	Ogea	Wakefield	Jackson	57-41	2nd	14.5
7-22	At Cle.	L	3-4		8	9	Nagy	Garces	Jackson	57-42	2nd	15.5
7-23	Tor.	W	8-7	(10)	13	15	Gordon	Myers		58-42	2nd	15.0
7-24	Tor.	L	6-10		7	13	Guzman	Avery	Quantrill	58-43	2nd	16.0
7-25	Tor.	W	5-3		9	7	Lowe	Williams	Gordon	59-43	2nd	15.0
7-26	Tor.	W	6-3		12	10	Martinez	Hentgen		60-43	2nd	15.0
7-28	At Oak.	W	8-4		13	7	Wakefield	Haynes	Gordon	61-43	2nd	15.0
7-29	At Oak.	W	10-2		15	8	Wasdin	Oquist	Lowe	62-43	2nd	14.0
7-30	At Oak.	L	5-6		8	6	Rogers	Avery	Taylor	62-44	2nd	15.0
7-31	At Ana.	W	7-2		6	7	Saberhagen	Olivares	Gordon	63-44	2nd	15.0
8-1	At Ana.	W	11-3		10	6	Martinez	Watson	Lowe	64-44	2nd	15.0
8-2	At Ana.	W	8-7		10	9	Wakefield	Dickson	Gordon	65-44	2nd	14.0
8-3	At Sea.	L	1-3		7	9	Cloude	Wasdin	Timlin	65-45	2nd	15.0
8-4	At Sea.	W	2-1		7	2	Avery	McCarthy	Gordon	66-45	2nd	15.5
8-6	At Tex.	L	4-7		10	11	Burkett	Saberhagen	Wetteland	66-46	2nd	15.5
8-7	At Tex.	L	3-4		8	8	Helling	Martinez	Wetteland	66-47	2nd	17.0
8-8	At Tex.	W	11-1		18	7	Wakefield	Sele		67-47	2nd	17.0
8-9	At Tex.	W	14-8		12	9	Corsi	Stottlemyre		68-47	2nd	17.0
8-11	K.C.	W	7-4	(10)	13	9	Gordon	Montgomery		69-47	2nd	17.5
8-12	K.C.	L	4-8		5	16	Service	Swindell		69-48	2nd	18.5
8-13	Min.	W	8-7		16	12	Eckersley	Miller	Gordon	70-48	2nd	18.5
8-14	Min.	W	13-12		15	17	Lowe	Baptist	Gordon	71-48	2nd	18.5
8-15	Min.	L	2-3		8	14	Rodriguez	Schourek	Aguilera	71-49	2nd	18.5
8-16§	Min.	L	3-6		6	13	Milton	Avery	Aguilera	71-50	2nd	19.5
8-18§	Tex.	W	4-1		7	5	Martinez	Burkett	Gordon	72-50		
8-18§	Tex.	W	5-4		9	10	Lowe	Patterson	Gordon	73-50	2nd	19.5
8-19	At K.C.	W	11-1		14	5	Wakefield	Barber		74-50	2nd	18.5
8-20	At K.C.	L	2-8		5	12	Pichardo	Schourek		74-51	2nd	18.5
8-21	At Min.	W	9-2		12	6	Avery	Milton		75-51	2nd	18.5
8-22	At Min.	L	3-4		6	10	Trombley	Swindell		75-52	2nd	19.5
8-23	At Min.	W	5-1		15	9	Martinez	Radke		76-52	2nd	18.5
8-25	Oak.	W	3-2		10	7	Swindell	Rogers	Gordon	77-52	2nd	17.0
8-26	Oak.	W	7-4		10	6	Wasdin	Worrell	Gordon	78-52	2nd	16.5
8-27	Oak.	L	3-6		8	13	Candiotti	Schourek	Taylor	78-53	2nd	17.5
8-28	Ana.	L	6-7		12	13	Hill	Avery		78-54	2nd	18.5
8-29	Ana.	W	6-1		8	7	Martinez	McDowell		79-54	2nd	18.5
8-30	Ana.	L	6-8		8	11	Hasegawa	Wakefield	Percival	79-55	2nd	18.5
8-31	Sea.	W	5-1		8	4	Saberhagen	Fassero		80-55	2nd	18.0
9-1	Sea.	L	3-7		11	9	Moyer	Lowe		80-56	2nd	19.0
9-2	Sea.	W	7-3		7	15	Gordon	Ayala		81-56	2nd	18.0
9-3	At Tor.	L	3-4	(11)	12	9	Person	Veras		81-57	2nd	18.5
9-4	At Tor.	L	1-12		6	12	Hentgen	Wakefield	Stieb	81-58	2nd	19.5
9-5	At Tor.	L	3-4		4	10	Clemens	Saberhagen	Quantrill	81-59	2nd	19.5
9-6	At Tor.	L	7-8		8	8	Quantrill	Lowe	Person	81-60	2nd	19.5
9-7	N.Y.	W	4-3		6	6	Swindell	Wells	Gordon	82-60	2nd	18.5
9-8	N.Y.	L	2-3		6	5	Cone	Martinez	Rivera	82-61	2nd	19.5
9-9	N.Y.	L	5-7		8	7	Mendoza	Wakefield	Rivera	82-62	2nd	20.5
9-11	Det.	W	6-2		9	10	Saberhagen	Powell	Gordon	83-62	2nd	20.0
9-12	Det.	L	2-3		4	7	Anderson	Gordon	Jones	83-63	2nd	20.0
9-13	Det.	L	1-4		5	6	Moehler	Swindell	Jones	83-64	2nd	20.0
9-14	At N.Y.	L	0-3		3	7	Hernandez	Martinez		83-65	2nd	21.0
9-15	At N.Y.	W	9-4		9	8	Wakefield	Jerzembeck		84-65	2nd	20.0

Date	Opp.	Res.	Score	(inn.*)	Hits	Opp. hits	Winning pitcher	Losing pitcher	Save	Record	Pos.	GB
9-16	At Bal.	W	4-3		14	10	Saberhagen	Erickson	Gordon	85-65	2nd	19.0
9-17	At Bal.	W	3-2	(10)	8	6	Eckersley	Benitez	Gordon	86-65	2nd	19.0
9-18	At Chi.	L	9-11		14	18	Parque	Avery	Simas	86-66	2nd	20.0
9-19	At Chi.	L	2-5		10	5	Snyder	Martinez		86-67	2nd	20.0
9-20	At Chi.	L	4-6		8	8	Sirotka	Corsi	Ward	86-68	2nd	21.0
9-21†	T.B.	W	4-3		9	9	Saberhagen	Saunders	Gordon	87-68		
9-21‡	T.B.	L	4-8		6	13	Wade	Reyes		87-69	2nd	20.5
9-22	T.B.	W	11-2		11	6	Schourek	Santana		88-69	2nd	21.0
9-23	T.B.	W	5-4		6	9	Avery	Rekar	Gordon	89-69	2nd	21.0
9-24	Bal.	W	9-6		18	8	Martinez	Ponson	Gordon	90-69	2nd	21.0
9-25	Bal.	W	8-3		11	7	Wakefield	Fussell		91-69	2nd	21.0
9-26	Bal.	L	2-5		7	6	Erickson	Saberhagen	Benitez	91-70	2nd	22.0
9-27	Bal.	W	6-4		9	13	Valdez	Mussina	Gordon	92-70	2nd	22.0

Monthly records: April (18-8), May (13-14), June (17-10), July (15-12), August (17-11), September (12-15).
*Innings, if other than nine. †First game of doubleheader. ‡Second game of doubleheader. §Two games in one day (separate admissions).

HIGHLIGHTS

High point: The tone of the season was set with a dramatic victory in the home opener. On April 10 at Fenway Park, the Red Sox scored seven runs in the ninth inning to earn a 9-7 victory over the Mariners. The game ended when Mo Vaughn hit a grand slam.

Low point: On October 3, the season ended when closer Tom Gordon blew his first save since April 14—a span of 43 opportunities. Leading 1-0 in Game 4 of an A.L. Division Series, the Red Sox turned the game over to Gordon to start the eighth. The Indians took the lead on a two-run double by David Justice and held on for a 2-1 victory.

Turning point: The Red Sox started the season with a 3-5 West Coast trip and were coming off a three-game losing streak when they made their Fenway Park debut April 10. Vaughn's homer turned the season around.

Most valuable player: Shortstop Nomar Garciaparra did the unthinkable by topping his historic rookie season. Garciaparra hit .323 with 35 homers and 122 RBIs.

Most valuable pitcher: In his first full season as closer, Gordon set a franchise record with 46 saves and reeled off a major league-record 43 in a row, including a run of 28 perfect appearances.

Most improved player: A career reserve, infielder Mike Benjamin was a career .204 hitter before the second base job fell into his lap. He hit a career-high .274 with 23 doubles, four homers and 39 RBIs.

Most pleasant surprise: After missing almost two full seasons with a severe shoulder injury, Bret Saberhagen did not miss a beat. He was 15-8 with a 3.96 ERA.

Biggest disappointment: After consecutive seasons with 15 homers and 80 RBIs as a semi-regular, Troy O'Leary earned a four-year contract and the starting left field job. O'Leary was making the team look smart in the first half, when he hit .296 with 14 homers and 47 RBIs. But his production slipped after the break and he hit just .238 over the last 73 games.

Key injuries: Second baseman Jeff Frye was penciled in as the leadoff hitter, but a knee injury in spring training ended his season. His replacement, Mark Lemke, suffered a concussion and his season was over after 37 games. The rotation missed lefthander Butch Henry, whose knee injury ended his season after two starts. Rookie pitcher Brian Rose suffered a season-ending elbow injury that limited his season to eight starts.

Notable: Vaughn's .337 average was the highest by a Red Sox player since Wade Boggs hit .366 in 1988. . . . Garciaparra became the fifth player in major league history to hit 30 or more homers in each of his first two seasons.

—PAUL DOYLE

RECORDS

1998 regular-season record: 92-70 (2nd in A.L. East); 51-30 at home; 41-40 on road; 25-23 vs. A.L. East; 31-23 vs. Central; 27-17 vs. West; 9-7 vs. N.L.; 31-15 vs. lefthanded starters; 61-55 vs. righthanded starters; 81-57 on grass; 11-13 on turf; 23-25 in daytime; 69-45 at night; 24-25 in one-run games; 7-4 in extra-inning games; 0-0-1 in doubleheaders.

Team record past five years: 395-350 (.530, ranks 4th in league in that span).

TEAM LEADERS

Batting average: Mo Vaughn (.337).
At-bats: Troy O'Leary (611).
Runs: John Valentin (113).
Hits: Mo Vaughn (205).
Total bases: Mo Vaughn (360).
Doubles: John Valentin (44).
Triples: Nomar Garciaparra, Troy O'Leary (8).
Home runs: Mo Vaughn (40).
Runs batted in: Nomar Garciaparra (122).
Stolen bases: Darren Lewis (29).
Slugging percentage: Mo Vaughn (.591).
On-base percentage: Mo Vaughn (.402).
Wins: Pedro Martinez (19).
Earned-run average: Pedro Martinez (2.89).
Complete games: Pedro Martinez (3).

Shutouts: Pedro Martinez (2).
Saves: Tom Gordon (46).
Innings pitched: Pedro Martinez (233.2).
Strikeouts: Pedro Martinez (251).

GAMES BY POSITION

Catcher: Scott Hatteberg 108, Jason Varitek 75, Mandy Romero 4, Jim Leyritz 1.
First base: Mo Vaughn 142, Mike Stanley 13, Mike Benjamin 10, Reggie Jefferson 7, Billy Ashley 2, Jim Leyritz 1.
Second base: Mike Benjamin 87, Donnie Sadler 50, Lou Merloni 32, Mark Lemke 31, Chris Snopek 3, Damon Buford 1, Keith Johns 1, John Valentin 1.
Third base: John Valentin 153, Mike Benjamin 11, Lou Merloni 5, Chris Snopek 3, Damon Buford 1.
Shortstop: Nomar Garciaparra 143, Mike Benjamin 20, Donnie Sadler 4, Lou Merloni 1.
Outfield: Troy O'Leary 155, Darren Lewis 152, Darren Bragg 124, Damon Buford 67, Midre Cummings 17, Keith Mitchell 10, Trot Nixon 7, Billy Ashley 2, Orlando Merced 1.
Designated hitter: Reggie Jefferson 48, Jim Leyritz 39, Mike Stanley 34, Midre Cummings 31, Damon Buford 15, Keith Mitchell 12, Mo Vaughn 12, Billy Ashley 5, Darren Bragg 4, Trot Nixon 4, Donnie Sadler 4, Mandy Romero 3, Jason Varitek 3, Mike Benjamin 2, Chris Snopek 2, Keith Johns 1, Darren Lewis 1, Orlando Merced 1.

TOP DRAFT CHOICES

1. **Adam Everett,** SS, U. of S. Carolina
2. None
3. **Mike Maroth,** LHP, U. of Central Fla.
4. **Jerome Gamble,** RHP, Benjamin Russell H.S., Alexander City, Ala.
5. **Josh Hancock,** RHP, Tupelo, Miss.
6. **Rick Riccobono,** RHP, Commack (N.Y.) H.S.
7. **Syketo Anderson,** 2B, Prattville (Ala.) H.S.
8. **Frederick Silverthorn,** LHP, Pearce H.S., Richardson, Tex.
9. **Mark Teixeira,** 3B, Mt. St. Joseph H.S., Severna Park, Md.
10. **Lenny Dinardo,** LHP, Santa Fe H.S., High Spring, Fla.

CHICAGO WHITE SOX
AMERICAN LEAGUE CENTRAL DIVISION

1999 White Sox Schedule
Home games shaded. *—All-Star Game at Fenway Park (Boston). D—Day game (any game starting before 5 p.m.).

April
SUN	MON	TUE	WED	THU	FRI	SAT
				1	2	3
4	5 SEA	6 SEA	7 SEA	8	9 D KC	10 D KC
11 KC	D 12	13 D BOS	14	15 BOS	16 KC	17 D KC
18 D KC	19	20 SEA	21 SEA	22 D SEA	23 DET	24 D DET
25 D DET	26	27 TB	28 TB	29 D TB	30 ANA	

May
SUN	MON	TUE	WED	THU	FRI	SAT
						1 ANA
2 ANA	3 D ANA	4 BAL	5 BAL	6 D BAL	7 OAK	8 OAK
9 D OAK	10 TEX	11 TEX	12 TEX	13	14 NYY	15 D NYY
16 D NYY	17 CLE	18 CLE	19 CLE	20	21 NYY	22 NYY
23 D NYY	24 CLE	25 CLE	26 CLE	27 DET	28 DET	29 D DET
30 D DET	31					

June
SUN	MON	TUE	WED	THU	FRI	SAT
		1 TOR	2 TOR	3 D TOR	4 PIT	5 PIT
6 D PIT	7 HOU	8 HOU	9 HOU	10	11 D CUB	12 D CUB
13 CUB	14 TB	15 TB	16 TB	17 D BAL	18 D BAL	19 BAL
20 BAL	21	22 MIN	23 MIN	24 D MIN	25 BOS	26 D BOS
27 D BOS	28 BOS	29 KC	30 KC			

July
SUN	MON	TUE	WED	THU	FRI	SAT
				1 KC	2 BOS	3 D BOS
4 D BOS	5	6 D KC	7 KC	8 KC	9 CUB	10 D CUB
11 D CUB	12	13 *	14	15 STL	16 STL	17 STL
18 D MIL	19 MIL	20 MIL	21 MIN	22 MIN	23 D TOR	24 TOR
25 TOR	26 D NYY	27 NYY	28 NYY	29 D CLE	30 CLE	31 D CLE

August
SUN	MON	TUE	WED	THU	FRI	SAT
1 CLE	D 2 DET	3 DET	4	5 D OAK	6 OAK	7 OAK
8 D OAK	9 SEA	10 SEA	11 SEA	12	13 TEX	14 TEX
15 D TEX	16 ANA	17 ANA	18 ANA	19 D ANA	20 BAL	21 BAL
22 BAL	23 TB	24 TB	25 TB	26 D OAK	27 OAK	28 OAK
29 D SEA	30 SEA	31 SEA				

September
SUN	MON	TUE	WED	THU	FRI	SAT
			1 SEA	2	3 TEX	4 D TEX
5 TEX	6 TEX	7 ANA	8 ANA	9	10 CLE	11 CLE
12 D CLE	13 DET	14 DET	15 DET	16	17 TOR	18 D TOR
19 D TOR	20	21 NYY	22 NYY	23 NYY	24 MIN	25 MIN
26 D MIN	27	28 BOS	29 BOS	30 BOS		

October
SUN	MON	TUE	WED	THU	FRI	SAT
					1 MIN	2 MIN
3 D MIN	4	5	6	7	8	9

1999 SEASON
CLUB DIRECTORY

Chairman
Jerry Reinsdorf
Vice chairman
Eddie Einhorn
Executive vice president
Howard Pizer
Senior v.p., major league operations
Ron Schueler
Sr. v.p., marketing and broadcasting
Rob Gallas
Senior vice president, baseball
Jack Gould
V.p., administration and finance
Tim Buzard
Vice president, stadium operations
Terry Savarise
V.p., free agent and major league scouting
Larry Monroe
Vice president, player development
Ken Williams
Dir. of baseball operations/asst. g.m.
Dan Evans
Special assistants to Ron Schueler
Ed Brinkman
Dave Yoakum
Special assignment
Mike Pazik
Director of scouting
Duane Shaffer
Director of minor league instruction
Jim Snyder
Traveling secretary
Ed Cassin
Asst. dir. of min. league & scouting admin.
Grace Guerrero Zwit
Asst. dir. of scouting & min. league op.
Daniel Fabian
Director of marketing and broadcasting
Bob Grim
Director of community relations
Christine Makowski
Director of sales
Jim Muno

Director of ticket operations
Bob Devoy
Dir. of management information services
Don Brown
Director of human resources
Moira Foy
Controller
Bill Waters
Director of public relations
Scott Reifert
Trainers
Herm Schneider
Mark Anderson
Director of conditioning
Steve Odgers
Team physicians
Dr. James Boscardin
Dr. Hugo Cuadros
Dr. Bernard Feldman
Dr. David Orth
Dr. Scott Price
Dr. Lowell Scott Weil
Scouting national cross-checker
Doug Laumann
Scouting supervisors
George Bradley
Ed Pebley
Ken Stauffer
Full-time scouts
Juan Ramon Bernhardt, Joseph Butler, Scott Cerny, Hernan Cortes, Alex Cosmidis, Nathan Durst, Denny Gonzalez, Larry Grefer, Warren Hughes, Miguel Ibarra, George Kachigian, Joe Karp, John Kazanas, Reginald Lewis, Jose Ortega, Gary Pellant, Paul Provas, Hector Rincones, Michael Sgobba, Ken Stauffer, John Tumminia
Part-time scouts
Tom Butler, Javier Ceteno, Mike Davenport, John Doldeorian, Roberto Espinoza, Joe Ingalls, Jack Jolly, Dario Lodigiani, Donald Metzger, Paul Murphy, Al Otto, Michael Paris, Oswaldo Salazar

MINOR LEAGUE AFFILIATES

Class	Team	League	Manager
AAA	Charlotte	International	Tom Spencer
AA	Birmingham	Southern	Chris Cron
A	Burlington	Midwest	Nick Capra
A	Winston-Salem	Carolina	Jerry Terrell
Rookie	Bristol	Appalachian	Mark Haley
Rookie	Gulf Coast White Sox	Gulf Coast	Jerry Hairston

BROADCAST INFORMATION

Radio: ESPN-AM (1000).
TV: WGN-TV (Channel 9).
Cable TV: Fox Sports Chicago.

SPRING TRAINING

Ballpark (city): Tucson Electric Park (Tucson, Ariz.).
Ticket information: 888-683-3900.

SPRING TRAINING ROSTER

Manager—Jerry Manuel (7).
Coaches—Nardi Contreras, Wallace Johnson (18), Von Joshua, Art Kusyner (53), Bryan Little (20), Joe Nossek (21).

No.	PITCHERS	B/T	Ht./Wt.	Born	1998 clubs
	Ambrose, John	R/R	6-5/180	11-1-74	Birmingham
37	Baldwin, James	R/R	6-3/210	7-15-71	Chicago A.L.
	Barcelo, Lorenzo	R/R	6-4/226	9-10-77	Arizona White Sox
	Beirne, Kevin	L/R	6-4/210	1-1-74	Birmingham, Calgary
44	Bradford, Chad	R/R	6-5/205	9-14-74	Chicago A.L., Birmingham, Calgary
43	Castillo, Carlos	R/R	6-2/250	4-21-75	Chicago A.L., Calgary
	Chapman, Walker	R/R	6-3/201	2-25-76	Fort Myers, New Britain
36	Eyre, Scott	L/L	6-1/190	5-30-72	Chicago A.L.
31	Fordham, Tom	L/L	6-2/205	2-20-74	Chicago A.L., Calgary
29	Foulke, Keith	R/R	6-0/195	10-19-72	Chicago A.L.
	Hall, Darren	R/R	6-3/207	7-14-64	Los Angeles, San Bernardino, San Antonio
62	Howry, Bobby	L/R	6-5/215	8-4-73	Calgary, Chicago A.L.
	Jacobs, Dwayne	R/R	6-10/225	7-17-76	Danville
	Lundquist, David	R/R	6-2/200	6-4-73	Winston-Salem, Birmingham, Calgary
38	Navarro, Jaime	R/R	6-4/230	3-27-68	Chicago A.L.
	Olsen, Jason	R/R	6-4/210	3-16-75	Birmingham
40	Parque, Jim	L/L	5-11/165	2-8-75	Chicago A.L., Calgary
41	Simas, Bill	L/R	6-3/220	11-28-71	Calgary, Chicago A.L.
33	Sirotka, Mike	L/L	6-1/200	5-13-71	Chicago A.L.
59	Snyder, John	R/R	6-3/185	8-16-74	Chicago A.L., Calgary
56	Ward, Bryan	L/L	6-2/210	1-25-72	Birmingham, Chicago A.L.

No.	CATCHERS	B/T	Ht./Wt.	Born	1998 clubs
57	Johnson, Mark	L/R	6-0/185	9-12-75	Chicago A.L., Birmingham
55	Machado, Robert	R/R	6-1/205	6-3-73	Calgary, Chicago A.L.
	Paul, Josh	R/R	6-1/185	5-19-75	Winston-Salem

No.	INFIELDERS	B/T	Ht./Wt.	Born	1998 clubs
17	Caruso, Mike	L/R	6-0/172	5-27-77	Chicago A.L.
5	Durham, Ray	B/R	5-8/170	11-30-71	Chicago A.L.
	Konerko, Paul	R/R	6-3/211	3-5-76	Los Angeles, Albuquerque, Cincinnati, Indianapolis
	Lee, Carlos	R/R	6-2/202	6-20-76	Birmingham
31	Norton, Greg	B/R	6-1/190	7-6-72	Chicago A.L.
35	Thomas, Frank	R/R	6-5/257	5-27-68	Chicago A.L.
34	Valdez, Mario	L/R	6-2/190	11-19-74	Calgary
28	Wilson, Craig	R/R	6-0/185	9-3-70	Chicago A.L., Calgary

No.	OUTFIELDERS	B/T	Ht./Wt.	Born	1998 clubs
45	Abbott, Jeff	R/L	6-2/190	8-17-72	Chicago A.L.
	Christensen, McKay	L/L	5-11/180	8-14-75	Winston-Salem
	Liefer, Jeff	L/R	6-3/195	8-17-74	Birmingham, Calgary
30	Ordonez, Magglio	R/R	5-11/170	1-28-74	Chicago A.L.
	Pendergrass, Tyrone	B/R	6-1/174	7-31-76	Danville, Greenville
27	Simmons, Brian	B/R	6-2/190	9-4-73	Calgary, Arizona White Sox, Chicago A.L.
	Singleton, Chris	L/L	6-2/195	8-15-72	Columbus

BALLPARK INFORMATION

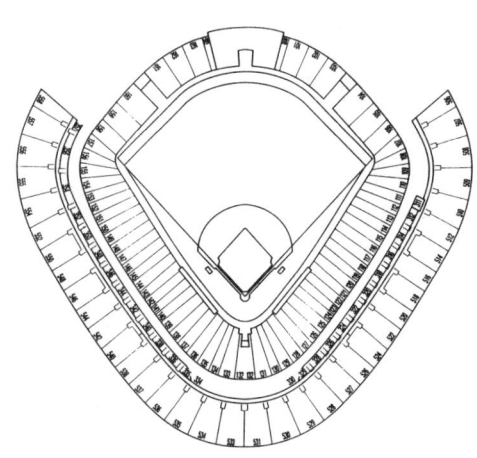

Ballpark (capacity, surface)
Comiskey Park (44,321, grass)

Address
333 W. 35th St.
Chicago, IL 60616

Business phone
312-674-1000

Ticket information
312-674-1000

Ticket prices
$22 (lower deck box, club level)
$17 (lower deck reserved)
$15 (upper deck box)
$14 (bleacher reserved)
$10 (upper deck reserved)

Field dimensions (from home plate)
To left field at foul line, 347 feet
To center field, 400 feet
To right field at foul line, 347 feet

First game played
April 18, 1991 (Tigers 16, White Sox 0)

Date	Opp.	Res.	Score	(inn.*)	Hits	Opp. hits	Winning pitcher	Losing pitcher	Save	Record	Pos.	GB
3-31	At Tex.	W	9-2		13	8	Navarro	Burkett		1-0	T1st	...
4-2	At Tex.	L	4-20		8	23	Sele	Sirotka	Pavlik	1-1	T2nd	1.0
4-3	At T.B.	W	10-4		15	11	Baldwin	Gorecki		2-1	2nd	1.0
4-4	At T.B.	L	2-8		7	15	Springer	Eyre		2-2	3rd	2.0
4-5	At T.B.	L	0-5		4	8	Alvarez	Bere		2-3	T3rd	3.0
4-6	Tex.	W	5-4		11	7	Foulke	Pavlik	Karchner	3-3	T2nd	2.5
4-9	Tex.	L	0-11		3	11	Sele	Baldwin		3-4	3rd	3.0
4-10	T.B.	W	3-0		10	5	Sirotka	Saunders	Karchner	4-4	2nd	3.0
4-11	T.B.	L	1-5		4	12	Gorecki	Bere		4-5	3rd	4.0
4-12	T.B.	L	1-4		4	12	Alvarez	Navarro	Hernandez	4-6	3rd	4.0
4-14	At Bal.	L	3-4		5	8	Key	Eyre	Orosco	4-7	4th	5.5
4-15	At Bal.	W	7-6		11	7	Baldwin	Drabek	Karchner	5-7	4th	4.5
4-16	At Bal.	W	8-2		12	7	Sirotka	Mussina		6-7	3rd	4.0
4-17	At Tor.	L	1-6		6	10	Clemens	Bere		6-8	4th	4.0
4-18	At Tor.	L	4-9		9	12	Hentgen	Navarro		6-9	4th	5.0
4-19	At Tor.	L	4-5	(12)	7	7	Carpenter	C. Castillo		6-10	4th	5.0
4-21	At Cle.	L	6-14		10	14	Mesa	Baldwin		6-11	4th	5.5
4-22	At Cle.	W	14-7		16	11	Sirotka	Nagy		7-11	4th	4.5
4-23	At Cle.	L	4-5		8	8	Plunk	T. Castillo	Jackson	7-12	4th	5.5
4-24	Tor.	L	1-3		6	6	Hentgen	Navarro	Myers	7-13	4th	5.5
4-25	Tor.	W	8-1		7	4	Eyre	Guzman		8-13	4th	4.5
4-26	Tor.	T	5-5	(6)	7	8	......	......		8-13	4th	4.5
4-27	Cle.	W	10-3		13	8	Sirotka	Ogea		9-13	4th	3.5
4-28	Cle.	L	1-4		4	9	Nagy	Karchner	Jackson	9-14	4th	4.5
4-29	Bal.	W	16-7		15	6	Navarro	Ponson		10-14	4th	3.5
4-30	Bal.	L	1-4		5	5	Key	Eyre	Benitez	10-15	4th	3.5
5-1	At Ana.	L	1-7		5	10	Hasegawa	Baldwin		10-16	4th	4.5
5-2	At Ana.	L	3-5		7	10	DeLucia	Sirotka	Percival	10-17	4th	5.5
5-3	At Ana.	W	12-1		15	5	Bere	Dickson		11-17	4th	5.5
5-4	At Ana.	W	6-5		9	11	T. Castillo	DeLucia	Karchner	12-17	2nd	5.0
5-5	At Sea.	L	1-8		3	9	Fassero	Eyre		12-18	3rd	6.0
5-6	At Sea.	L	9-10		13	13	Slocumb	C. Castillo	Ayala	12-19	4th	7.0
5-8	At Oak.	W	5-3		5	5	Sirotka	Fetters		13-19	3rd	6.5
5-9	At Oak.	L	7-15		15	17	Rogers	Bere	Fetters	13-20	4th	6.5
5-10	At Oak.	W	4-3		3	12	Navarro	Stein	Simas	14-20	2nd	5.5
5-12	Ana.	W	5-2		8	4	C. Castillo	Olivares		15-20	2nd	5.0
5-13	Ana.	L	3-8		12	12	Watson	Sirotka		15-21	3rd	4.0
5-14	Sea.	W	5-3		8	8	Fordham	Johnson	Simas	16-21	3rd	4.0
5-15	Sea.	W	6-3		11	7	Navarro	Swift	Foulke	17-21	3rd	4.0
5-16	Oak.	L	3-11		10	17	Stein	C. Castillo		17-22	3rd	5.0
5-17	Oak.	L	7-9		13	10	Groom	Simas	Taylor	17-23	3rd	5.0
5-18	Oak.	L	0-14		6	17	Haynes	Sirotka		17-24	3rd	5.5
5-19	At Bos.	W	9-5		12	11	Bere	Saberhagen		18-24	3rd	5.5
5-20	At Bos.	L	2-6		8	11	Martinez	Navarro	Gordon	18-25	3rd	6.5
5-22	Det.	L	5-9		9	18	Thompson	Eyre		18-26	4th	8.0
5-23	Det.	W	7-1		12	4	Sirotka	Moehler		19-26	3rd	7.0
5-24	Det.	L	4-8		6	15	Sager	Bere		19-27	4th	7.0
5-25	N.Y.	L	0-12		6	14	Irabu	Navarro		19-28	4th	8.0
5-26	N.Y.	L	5-7		7	10	Nelson	Foulke	Rivera	19-29	4th	9.0
5-27	N.Y.	W	12-9		17	6	Simas	Nelson	Karchner	20-29	3rd	8.5
5-28	At Det.	W	11-7	(10)	11	9	Karchner	Duran		21-29	3rd	8.5
5-29	At Det.	L	7-8		14	6	Crow	C. Castillo	Jones	21-30	3rd	9.5
5-30	At Det.	L	0-6		7	12	Moehler	Navarro		21-31	4th	9.5
5-31	At Det.	W	8-2		14	6	Parque	Castillo		22-31	3rd	9.5
6-1	At N.Y.	L	4-5	(10)	7	8	Nelson	Karchner		22-32	3rd	10.5
6-2	At N.Y.	L	3-6		7	11	Wells	Sirotka	Rivera	22-33	3rd	11.5
6-3	At K.C.	W	10-5		15	8	C. Castillo	Rapp		23-33	3rd	10.5
6-4	At K.C.	W	7-1		12	8	Navarro	Rusch		24-33	3rd	10.5
6-5	At Chi. (NL)	L	5-6	(12)	10	12	Mulholland	T. Castillo		24-34	3rd	10.5
6-6	At Chi. (NL)	L	6-7		12	7	Tapani	Eyre	Beck	24-35	3rd	11.5
6-7	At Chi. (NL)	L	7-13		11	14	Gonzalez	Sirotka		24-36	3rd	12.5
6-8	St.L.	W	8-6		8	8	Bere	Petkovsek	Karchner	25-36	3rd	12.5
6-9	St.L.	L	4-5		8	10	Painter	Navarro	Brantley	25-37	3rd	12.5
6-10	St.L.	W	10-8	(11)	13	12	Karchner	Lowe		26-37	3rd	11.5
6-12	At Min.	L	7-8		9	16	Aguilera	Simas		26-38	3rd	12.0
6-13	At Min.	W	3-2		11	4	Sirotka	Tewksbury	Karchner	27-38	3rd	11.5
6-14	At Min.	L	1-2		4	9	Hawkins	Navarro	Aguilera	27-39	3rd	11.5
6-15	Bos.	W	3-2		6	6	Parque	Saberhagen	Karchner	28-39	3rd	10.5
6-16	Bos.	L	1-6		7	12	Martinez	Bere		28-40	3rd	11.5
6-17	Bos.	L	5-12		4	13	Wakefield	Eyre	Gordon	28-41	3rd	11.5
6-18	Min.	L	1-4	(5)	5	9	Tewksbury	Sirotka		28-42	T3rd	11.5

Date	Opp.	Res.	Score	(inn.*)	Hits	Opp. hits	Winning pitcher	Losing pitcher	Save	Record	Pos.	GB
6-19	Min.	L	6-10		13	10	Trombley	Navarro	Swindell	28-43	4th	12.5
6-20	Min.	W	8-7	(11)	20	11	Simas	Aguilera		29-43	T3rd	11.5
6-21	Min.	L	1-6		5	6	Morgan	Bere	Carrasco	29-44	4th	12.5
6-22	At Pit.	W	5-4		10	10	C. Castillo	Dessens	Karchner	30-44	4th	12.5
6-23	At Pit.	W	5-4		10	7	Sirotka	Schmidt	Karchner	31-44	4th	12.5
6-24	Cin.	W	4-2		9	5	Navarro	Winchester	Simas	32-44	T3rd	12.5
6-25	Cin.	L	5-7		15	9	Tomko	Parque	Shaw	32-45	4th	13.5
6-26	Mil.	L	1-2		4	9	Juden	Simas	Wickman	32-46	4th	14.5
6-27	Mil.	L	5-10		7	10	Woodall	Fordham		32-47	4th	14.5
6-28	Mil.	W	10-8		17	15	Simas	Myers		33-47	4th	13.5
6-30	At Hou.	L	2-17		7	18	Bergman	Navarro		33-48	4th	13.5
7-1	At Hou.	L	4-10		9	12	Schourek	Parque		33-49	4th	14.5
7-2	At Hou.	W	4-3		7	5	Baldwin	Lima	Simas	34-49	4th	14.5
7-3	At Bos.	L	2-15		7	17	Wakefield	Sirotka		34-50	4th	15.5
7-4	At Bos.	W	3-0		7	5	Snyder	Cho	Simas	35-50	4th	14.5
7-5	At Bos.	L	14-15		12	20	Reyes	Howry	Gordon	35-51	4th	15.5
7-9	K.C.	L	4-6		7	12	Belcher	Sirotka	Montgomery	35-52	5th	15.5
7-10	K.C.	W	10-3		15	8	Navarro	Rosado		36-52	5th	15.5
7-11	K.C.	W	4-3		7	9	Baldwin	Rapp	Karchner	37-52	5th	15.5
7-12	K.C.	L	3-4		6	13	Service	Karchner	Montgomery	37-53	5th	15.5
7-13	Min.	W	5-2		7	10	Snyder	Serafini	Simas	38-53	4th	15.5
7-14	Min.	W	8-5		11	12	Foulke	Aguilera		39-53	4th	14.5
7-15†	Tor.	W	9-3		14	7	Navarro	Hentgen		40-53		
7-15‡	Tor.	W	5-2		9	8	C. Castillo	Stieb	Simas	41-53	4th	13.0
7-16	Tor.	L	2-5		4	11	Carpenter	Baldwin	Myers	41-54	4th	13.0
7-17	Cle.	W	4-3		7	10	Simas	Shuey		42-54	4th	12.0
7-18	Cle.	L	9-15		11	15	Shuey	Karchner	Jackson	42-55	4th	13.0
7-19	Cle.	W	8-1		9	4	Sirotka	Burba		43-55	4th	12.0
7-20	Cle.	L	4-5		7	6	Colon	Navarro	Jackson	43-56	4th	13.0
7-21	At Tor.	W	6-3		11	9	Baldwin	Hentgen	Simas	44-56	3rd	12.5
7-22	At Tor.	L	0-4		4	5	Clemens	Parque		44-57	4th	13.5
7-24	At N.Y.	L	4-5		9	6	Pettitte	Ward	Rivera	44-58	4th	14.0
7-25	At N.Y.	W	6-2		9	10	Sirotka	Irabu	Simas	45-58	4th	14.0
7-26	At N.Y.	L	3-6		7	7	Wells	Navarro	Rivera	45-59	4th	14.0
7-28	T.B.	W	4-1		8	4	Baldwin	Arrojo	Simas	46-59	T3rd	14.0
7-29	T.B.	L	2-7		4	12	Saunders	Parque		46-60	T3rd	15.0
7-31	At Tex.	W	10-2		11	8	Snyder	Burkett		47-60	4th	14.5
8-1	At Tex.	L	1-8		9	12	Helling	Sirotka		47-61	4th	14.5
8-2	At Tex.	L	3-12		10	17	Sele	Navarro		47-62	4th	14.5
8-3	At T.B.	W	6-1		10	8	Baldwin	Arrojo		48-62	4th	13.5
8-4	At T.B.	W	8-6		17	8	C. Castillo	Saunders	Simas	49-62	4th	12.5
8-5	At T.B.	L	3-7		9	12	Hernandez	Howry		49-63	4th	13.5
8-8†	Ana.	W	7-5		8	9	Sirotka	Dickson	Simas	50-63		
8-8‡	Ana.	W	4-3		9	8	Bradford	Hasegawa		51-63	T3rd	13.5
8-9	Ana.	L	0-9		4	13	Finley	Baldwin		51-64	4th	13.5
8-10	Oak.	W	5-3		8	4	Parque	Rogers	Simas	52-64	T2nd	13.0
8-11	Oak.	L	4-6		6	8	Candiotti	Snyder	Taylor	52-65	T2nd	13.0
8-12	Oak.	W	2-0		9	2	Eyre	Haynes	Simas	53-65	2nd	13.0
8-14	Sea.	W	14-2		16	9	Sirotka	Cloude		54-65	3rd	11.5
8-15	Sea.	L	7-13		17	17	Swift	Navarro		54-66	3rd	11.5
8-16	Sea.	W	5-3		13	5	Foulke	Fassero	Simas	55-66	2nd	11.5
8-17	At Ana.	L	2-7		10	10	Sparks	Parque		55-67	2nd	12.5
8-18	At Ana.	W	4-3		9	7	Snyder	Finley	Simas	56-67	2nd	12.5
8-19	At Oak.	L	0-6		2	8	Stein	Sirotka		56-68	2nd	12.5
8-20	At Oak.	L	1-3		7	8	Rogers	Fordham	Taylor	56-69	2nd	12.5
8-21	At Sea.	L	4-5		9	8	Paniagua	Foulke	Timlin	56-70	3rd	13.5
8-22	At Sea.	L	4-5	(11)	8	15	Timlin	Navarro		56-71	4th	13.5
8-23	At Sea.	L	2-3		3	3	Spoljaric	Snyder	Paniagua	56-72	4th	14.5
8-24	At Sea.	L	10-11		12	13	Cloude	Sirotka	Timlin	56-73	4th	15.0
8-25	Bal.	W	6-4		11	7	Bradford	Mussina		57-73	4th	15.0
8-26	Bal.	W	12-5		15	6	Baldwin	Guzman		58-73	4th	15.0
8-27	Bal.	W	7-4		8	11	Parque	Erickson	Simas	59-73	T3rd	14.0
8-28†	Tex.	L	5-6	(10)	6	12	Hernandez	Howry	Wetteland	59-74		
8-28‡	Tex.	W	8-7		13	9	Ward	Gunderson	Howry	60-74	3rd	13.5
8-29	Tex.	L	3-5		6	10	Sele	Sirotka	Wetteland	60-75	3rd	13.5
8-30	Tex.	W	5-3		8	8	C. Castillo	Stottlemyre	Howry	61-75	3rd	13.5
8-31	At Bal.	W	4-1		8	7	Baldwin	Erickson	Howry	62-75	3rd	13.5
9-1	At Bal.	W	9-5		10	10	Parque	Drabek	Navarro	63-75	3rd	13.5
9-2	At Bal.	W	3-2		6	3	Snyder	Mills	Howry	64-75	T2nd	12.5
9-4	N.Y.	L	6-11		10	15	Lloyd	Bradford		64-76	3rd	14.0
9-5	N.Y.	W	9-5		12	10	J. Abbott	Pettitte		65-76	T2nd	14.0
9-6	N.Y.	W	6-5		12	8	Baldwin	Irabu	Howry	66-76	2nd	13.0
9-7	Det.	W	7-5		8	10	Parque	Moehler	Bradford	67-76	2nd	12.0
9-8	Det.	W	12-6		17	10	Snyder	Thompson		68-76	2nd	11.5
9-9	Det.	L	6-8		12	14	Greisinger	Sirotka		68-77	2nd	12.5

– 26 –

Date	Opp.	Res.	Score	(inn.*)	Hits	Opp. hits	Winning pitcher	Losing pitcher	Save	Record	Pos.	GB
9-11	At Cle.	W	3-2		7	6	J. Abbott	Nagy	Howry	69-77	2nd	11.5
9-12	At Cle.	W	6-4		10	8	Baldwin	Shuey	Howry	70-77	2nd	10.5
9-13	At Cle.	L	3-6		6	7	Shuey	Ward	Jackson	70-78	2nd	11.5
9-14	At Det.	W	17-16	(12)	19	22	Eyre	Bochtler		71-78	2nd	11.5
9-15	At Det.	L	0-2		5	8	Greisinger	Sirotka	Jones	71-79	2nd	12.5
9-16	K.C.	W	9-4		12	6	J. Abbott	Bevil		72-79	2nd	12.5
9-17	K.C.	L	4-13		11	16	Belcher	Baldwin		72-80	2nd	13.5
9-18	Bos.	W	11-9		18	14	Parque	Avery	Simas	73-80	2nd	13.5
9-19	Bos.	W	5-2		5	10	Snyder	Martinez		74-80	2nd	12.5
9-20	Bos.	W	6-4		8	8	Sirotka	Corsi	Ward	75-80	2nd	12.5
9-21	At Min.	W	7-1		11	8	J. Abbott	Tewksbury		76-80	2nd	12.5
9-22	At Min.	W	4-1		9	6	Baldwin	Milton		77-80	2nd	11.0
9-23	At Min.	L	6-7	(12)	17	11	Trombley	Eyre		77-81	2nd	11.0
9-24	At K.C.	L	4-6		7	11	Rosado	Navarro	Montgomery	77-82	2nd	11.0
9-25	At K.C.	W	3-0		9	4	Sirotka	Bones	Howry	78-82	2nd	10.0
9-26	At K.C.	W	13-5		15	11	J. Abbott	Barber		79-82	2nd	10.0
9-27	At K.C.	W	7-6		9	6	Baldwin	Belcher	Howry	80-82	2nd	9.0

Monthly records: March (1-0), April (9-15), May (12-16), June (11-17), July (14-12), August (15-15), September (18-7).
*Innings, if other than nine. †First game of doubleheader. ‡Second game of doubleheader.

HIGHLIGHTS

High point: After falling 17 games below .500 at the end of August, the White Sox won the final three games of the season in Kansas City to finish just two games below the break-even mark.

Low point: Beginning with a 13-7 loss to Seattle August 15, the club lost eight of 10 games, including six straight, to lower its record to 56-73.

Turning point: After limping into the All-Star break with a 35-51 record, manager Jerry Manuel challenged his young team to close the season with a purpose and that's exactly what happened. The team went 45-31 in the second half and wound up finishing second in the A.L. Central.

Most valuable player: Popular or not, Albert Belle had a monster year at the plate and ranked among league leaders in 11 of the 14 major offensive categories.

Most valuable pitcher: In early May, James Baldwin and his 2-3 record (7.57 ERA) were shipped to the bullpen and the once-promising starting pitcher's career was in jeopardy. Over the next six weeks, Baldwin labored in relief but something finally clicked and he dominated hitters over the second half of the season. The righthander was 10-3 with a 3.68 ERA after the break and he'll get the ball when the team opens the 1999 season at Seattle.

Most improved player: Mike Sirotka wound up winning 14 games after previously posting just five victories in parts of three seasons. A tired arm and some porous defensive backing did help stick Sirotka with 15 losses, but he had a solid season.

Biggest disappointment: Just about any player would be happy with 29 home runs and 109 RBIs in a season, but Frank Thomas isn't any player. That's why the team's prolific designated hitter couldn't wait for the year to end so he could start getting ready for 1999. Thomas' power numbers were actually pretty good, but his batting average (.265) was 65 points below the career mark he brought into the season.

Key injuries: On a team that stayed pretty healthy all season, only reliever Keith Foulke missed a considerable amount of time. The righthander was placed on the disabled list in late August and missed the rest of the season after having surgery to remove bone chips in his throwing shoulder.

Notable: The team used 18 rookies over the course of the season and their average age (26.1) was the youngest in the league. . . . The team had the fourth-best record (45-31) in the majors after the All-Star break. . . . The team hit 198 home runs, the most in franchise history.

—SCOT GREGOR

RECORDS

1998 regular-season record: 80-82 (2nd in A.L. Central); 44-37 at home; 36-45 on road; 28-26 vs. East; 26-22 vs. A.L. Central; 19-25 vs. West; 7-9 vs. N.L.; 17-25 vs. lefthanded starters; 63-57 vs. righthanded starters; 70-64 on grass; 10-18 on turf; 20-29 in daytime; 60-53 at night; 20-22 in one-run games; 4-6 in extra-inning games; 2-0-1 in doubleheaders.

Team record past five years: 380-362 (.512, ranks 5th in league in that span).

TEAM LEADERS

Batting average: Albert Belle (.328).
At-bats: Ray Durham (635).
Runs: Ray Durham (126).
Hits: Albert Belle (200).
Total bases: Albert Belle (399).
Doubles: Albert Belle (48).
Triples: Ray Durham (8).
Home runs: Albert Belle (49).
Runs batted in: Albert Belle (152).
Stolen bases: Ray Durham (36).
Slugging percentage: Albert Belle (.655).
On-base percentage: Albert Belle (.399).
Wins: Mike Sirotka (14).
Earned-run average: Mike Sirotka (5.06).

Complete games: Mike Sirotka (5).
Shutouts: None.
Saves: Bill Simas (18).
Innings pitched: Mike Sirotka (211.2).
Strikeouts: Mike Sirotka (128).

GAMES BY POSITION

Catcher: Chad Kreuter 91, Charlie O'Brien 57, Robert Machado 34, Mark L. Johnson 7.
First base: Wil Cordero 83, Greg Norton 79, Frank Thomas 14, Chris Snopek 1.
Second base: Ray Durham 158, Chris Snopek 12, Craig Wilson 4, Greg Norton 1.
Third base: Robin Ventura 161, Greg Norton 11, Chris Snopek 3, Craig Wilson 2.
Shortstop: Mike Caruso 131, Chris Snopek 33, Craig Wilson 8.
Outfield: Albert Belle 159, Magglio Ordonez 145, Mike Cameron 138, Jeff Abbott 76, Ruben Sierra 14, Wil Cordero 11, Brian Simmons 5, Lou Frazier 3, Chris Snopek 1.
Designated hitter: Frank Thomas 146, Ruben Sierra 5, Albert Belle 4, Jeff Abbott 2, Greg Norton 2, Lou Frazier 1, Chris Snopek 1.

TOP DRAFT CHOICES

1a. **Kip Wells,** RHP, Baylor University
1b. **Aaron Roward,** OF, Cal St. Fullerton
2. **Gary Majewski,** RHP, St. Pius X H.S., Houston
3a. **Josh Fogg,** RHP, U. of Florida
3b. **Daniel Mozingo,** LHP, Ashtabula Harbor H.S. Ashtabula, O.
4. **Juan Santamarina,** 3B, Gulliver Prep, Miami
5. **Steve Kelly,** RHP, Fairfield H.S., Hamilton, O.
6. **Matt Borne,** RHP, U. of Kentucky
7. **Eric Fischer,** LHP, Moeller H.S., Cincinnati
8. **Mitch Wylie,** RHP, St. Ambrose (Ia.) University
9. **Gus Mosley,** OF, Wakulla H.S., Crawfordville, Fla.
10. **Stephen Bess,** RHP, Rice University

CLEVELAND INDIANS
AMERICAN LEAGUE CENTRAL DIVISION

1999 Indians Schedule
Home games shaded. *—All-Star Game at Fenway Park (Boston). D—Day game (any game starting before 5 p.m.).

April
SUN	MON	TUE	WED	THU	FRI	SAT
				1	2	3
4	5	6 ANA	7 ANA	8 ANA	9 MIN	10 MIN
11 MIN	12 D KC	13	14 KC	15 KC	16 MIN	17 D MIN
18 MIN	19	20 OAK	21 OAK	22 OAK	23 BOS	24 D BOS
25 BOS	26 OAK	27 OAK	28 OAK	29 D OAK	30 TEX	

May
SUN	MON	TUE	WED	THU	FRI	SAT
						1 TEX
2 D TEX	3 D TEX	4	5 SEA	6 SEA	7 TB	8 TB
9 TB	10 BAL	11 BAL	12 BAL	13	14 DET	15 D DET
16 DET	17 CWS	18 CWS	19 CWS	20	21 DET	22 DET
23 DET	24 CWS	25 CWS	26 CWS	27	28 BOS	29 D BOS
30 BOS	31 D NYY					

June
SUN	MON	TUE	WED	THU	FRI	SAT
		1 NYY	2 NYY	3	4 CUB	5 D CUB
6 CUB	7	8 MIL	9 MIL	10 MIL	11 CIN	12 CIN
13 D CIN	14	15 OAK	16 OAK	17 OAK	18 SEA	19 D SEA
20 SEA	21 D SEA	22 TOR	23 TOR	24 TOR	25 KC	26 KC
27 KC	28 KC	29 MIN	30 MIN			

July
SUN	MON	TUE	WED	THU	FRI	SAT
				1 MIN	2 KC	3 D KC
4 KC	5	6 MIN	7 MIN	8 MIN	9 CIN	10 D CIN
11 CIN	12	13 *	14	15 PIT	16 PIT	17 D PIT
18 HOU	19 HOU	20 HOU	21 TOR	22 TOR	23 NYY	24 D NYY
25 NYY	26 DET	27 DET	28 DET	29	30 CWS	31 D CWS

August
SUN	MON	TUE	WED	THU	FRI	SAT
1 CWS	2 D BOS	3 BOS	4 BOS	5 D	6 TB	7 TB
8 TB	9 ANA	10 ANA	11 ANA	12	13 BAL	14 D BAL
15 BAL	16 TEX	17 TEX	18 TEX	19 TEX	20 SEA	21 D SEA
22 SEA	23 D OAK	24 OAK	25 D OAK	26	27 TB	28 D TB
29 TB	30 D ANA	31 ANA				

September
SUN	MON	TUE	WED	THU	FRI	SAT
			1 ANA	2 ANA	3 BAL	4 D BAL
5 BAL	6 D BAL	7 TEX	8 TEX	9	10 CWS	11 CWS
12 CWS	13 D BOS	14 BOS	15 BOS	16 NYY	17 NYY	18 NYY
19 NYY	20 DET	21 DET	22 DET	23 DET	24 TOR	25 D TOR
26 D TOR	27 KC	28 KC	29 TOR	30 TOR		

October
SUN	MON	TUE	WED	THU	FRI	SAT
					1 TOR	2 TOR
3 D TOR	4	5	6	7	8	9

1999 SEASON
CLUB DIRECTORY

Board of directors
Richard E. Jacobs, Martin J. Cleary, Edward G. Ptaszek Jr., William B. Summers Jr., Dr. Robert W. Brown, M.D., Raymond P. Park

Executive vice president, general manager
John Hart

Executive vice president, business
Dennis Lehman

V.p., marketing and communications
Jeff Overton

Vice president
Martin J. Cleary

Vice president, public relations
Bob DiBiasio

Vice president, finance
Ken Stefanov

Vice president of baseball operations/asst. general manager
Mark Shapiro

Dir. of baseball operations/asst. g.m.
Dan O'Dowd

Assistant, baseball operations
Chris Antonetti

Director, scouting
Josh Byrnes

Director, team travel
Mike Seghi

Director, player development
Neal Huntington

Administrator, player personnel
Wendy Hoppel

Assistant director, scouting
Brad Grant

Director, media relations
Bart Swain

Manager, media relations, administrations & credentials
Susie Giuliano

Director, community relations
Allen Davis

Manager, community relations
Melissa Zapanta

Manager, promotions
Chris Previte

Sr. dir., corp. marketing & broadcasting
Jon Starrett

Manager, advertising/publications
Bernadette Repko

Director, corp. planning & development
Ron McQuate

Director, advertising/publications
Valerie Arcuri

Director, ticket services
John Schulze

Director, ticket sales
Scott Sterneckert

Coordinator, season/group sales
Diane Stack

Senior director, ballpark operations
Jim Folk

Sr. director, merchandising/licensing
Jayne Churchmack

Controller
Lisa Ostry

Home clubhouse mgr./equipment mgr.
Ted Walsh

Equipment manager
Jeff Sipos

Visiting clubhouse manager
Cy Buynak

Medical director
William T. Wilder, M.D.

Head trainer
Paul Spicuzza

Assistant trainer
Jim Warfield

Strength and conditioning coach
Fernando Montes

Team physicians
Ronald Golovan M.D., Godofredo Domingo, M.D., K.V. Gopal, M.D., Zenos Vangelos, M.D.

Major league/spec. assignment scouts
Dan Carnevale, Dom Chiti, Tom Giordano, Ted Simmons, Bill Werle

National crosschecker
Bill Schmidt

West Coast supervisor
Jesse Flores

East Coast supervisor
Jerry Jordan

Midwest supervisor
Bob Mayer

Full-time scouts
Steve Abney, Steve Avila, Doug Baker, Keith Boeck, Ted Brzenk, Paul Cogan, Henry Cruz, Jim Gabella, Rene Gayo, Mark Germann, Chris Jefts, Chad MacDonald, Guy Mader, Chuck Ricci, Bill Schudlich, Max Semler

MINOR LEAGUE AFFILIATES

Class	Team	League	Manager
AAA	Buffalo	International	Jeff Datz
AA	Akron	Eastern	Joel Skinner
A	Kinston	Carolina	To be announced
A	Columbus	South Atlantic	Brad Komminsk
A	Mahoning Valley	New York-Pennsylvania	To be announced
Rookie	Burlington	Appalachian	To be announced

BROADCAST INFORMATION
Radio: WTAM (1100 AM).
TV: WUAB-TV (Channel 43).
Cable TV: Fox Sports Ohio.

SPRING TRAINING
Ballpark (city): Chain O'Lakes (Winter Haven, Fla.).
Ticket information: 941-293-3900.

SPRING TRAINING ROSTER

Manager—Mike Hargrove (21).
Coaches—Brian Graham, Luis Isaac (4), Clarence Jones, Charlie Manuel (32), Jeff Newman (55), Phil Regan.

No.	PITCHERS	B/T	Ht./Wt.	Born	1998 clubs
45	Assenmacher, Paul	L/L	6-3/210	12-10-60	Cleveland
64	Brammer, J.D.	R/R	6-4/235	1-30-75	Akron, Kinston
34	Burba, Dave	R/R	6-4/240	7-7-66	Cleveland
40	Colon, Bartolo	R/R	6-0/185	5-24-75	Cleveland
16	Gooden, Dwight	R/R	6-3/210	11-16-64	Buffalo, Cleveland
63	Hamilton, Jimmy	L/L	6-3/190	8-1-75	Kinston
42	Jackson, Mike	R/R	6-2/225	12-22-64	Cleveland
20	Karsay, Steve	R/R	6-3/209	3-24-72	Buffalo, Cleveland
36	Martin, Tom	L/L	6-1/200	5-21-70	Cleveland, Buffalo
71	Martinez, Willie	R/R	6-2/185	1-4-78	Akron
69	Matthews, Mike	L/L	6-2/175	10-24-73	Buffalo
41	Nagy, Charles	L/R	6-3/200	5-5-67	Cleveland
67	Negrette, Richard	R/R	6-2/175	3-6-76	Columbus, Kinston
59	Rakers, Jason	R/R	6-2/200	6-29-73	Akron, Cleveland, Buffalo
39	Reed, Steve	R/R	6-2/212	3-11-66	San Francisco, Cleveland
73	Rincon, Ricardo	L/L	5-10/187	4-13-70	Carolina, Nashville, Pittsburgh
53	Shuey, Paul	R/R	6-3/215	9-16-70	Cleveland, Akron, Buffalo
57	Smiley, John	L/L	6-4/210	3-17-65	Cleveland
48	Spradlin, Jerry	B/R	6-7/246	6-14-67	Philadelphia
47	Villone, Ron	L/L	6-3/235	1-16-70	Buffalo, Cleveland
27	Wright, Jaret	R/R	6-2/230	12-29-75	Cleveland

No.	CATCHERS	B/T	Ht./Wt.	Born	1998 clubs
15	Alomar, Sandy	R/R	6-5/215	6-18-66	Cleveland
2	Diaz, Einar	R/R	5-10/165	12-28-72	Cleveland, Buffalo

No.	INFIELDERS	B/T	Ht./Wt.	Born	1998 clubs
12	Alomar, Roberto	B/R	6-0/185	2-5-68	Baltimore
66	Branyan, Russell	L/R	6-3/195	12-19-75	Akron, Cleveland
72	Cabrera, Jolbert	R/R	6-0/177	12-8-72	Cleveland, Buffalo
17	Fryman, Travis	R/R	6-1/195	3-25-69	Cleveland
72	McDonald, John	R/R	5-11/175	9-24-74	Akron
68	Peoples, Danny	R/R	6-1/207	1-20-75	Akron
44	Sexson, Richie	R/R	6-6/206	12-29-74	Buffalo, Cleveland
25	Thome, Jim	L/R	6-4/230	8-27-70	Cleveland
13	Vizquel, Omar	B/R	5-9/170	4-24-67	Cleveland
35	Wilson, Enrique	B/R	5-11/160	7-27-75	Cleveland, Buffalo

No.	OUTFIELDERS	B/T	Ht./Wt.	Born	1998 clubs
51	Cruz, Jacob	L/L	6-0/179	1-28-73	Fresno, San Francisco, Buffalo, Cleveland
23	Justice, David	L/L	6-3/200	4-14-66	Cleveland
7	Lofton, Kenny	L/L	6-0/180	5-31-67	Cleveland
62	Morgan, Scott	R/R	6-7/230	7-19-73	Akron
61	Ramirez, Alex	R/R	5-11/176	10-3-74	Buffalo, Cleveland
24	Ramirez, Manny	R/R	6-0/190	5-30-72	Cleveland
12	Whiten, Mark	B/R	6-3/235	11-25-66	Cleveland

BALLPARK INFORMATION

Ballpark (capacity, surface)
Jacobs Field (43,863, grass)
Address
2401 Ontario St.
Cleveland, OH 44115
Business phone
216-420-4200
Ticket information
216-241-8888
Ticket prices
$30 (field box)
$22 (lower box & view box)
$18 (lower reserved, upper box
& mezzanine seating)
$14 (bleachers)
$10 (upper reserved)
$6 (reserved g.a., standing room only)
Field dimensions (from home plate)
To left field at foul line, 325 feet
To center field, 405 feet
To right field at foul line, 325 feet
First game played
April 4, 1994
(Indians 4, Mariners 3, 11 innings)

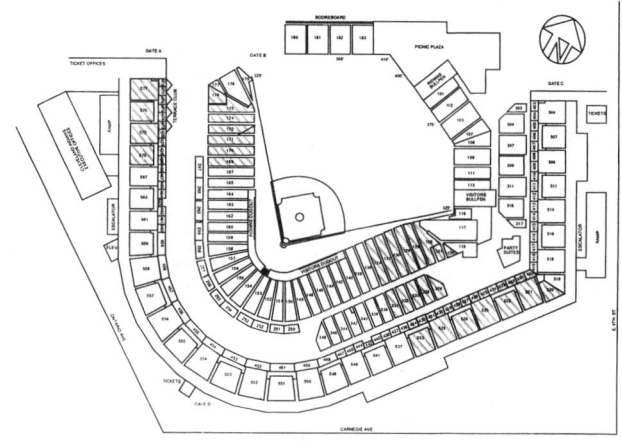

1998 REVIEW
DAY BY DAY

Date	Opp.	Res.	Score	(inn.*)	Hits	Opp. hits	Winning pitcher	Losing pitcher	Save	Record	Pos.	GB
3-31	At Sea.	W	10-9		14	12	Mesa	Fossas	Jackson	1-0	T1st	...
4-1	At Sea.	W	9-7		14	7	Wright	Moyer	Jackson	2-0	T1st	...
4-3	At Ana.	W	6-2		10	8	Burba	McDowell		3-0	1st	+1.0
4-4	At Ana.	W	11-0		13	4	Colon	Watson		4-0	1st	+1.5
4-5	At Ana.	W	6-4		9	7	Nagy	Dickson	Jackson	5-0	1st	+2.5
4-6	At Oak.	W	6-5		7	14	Krivda	Candiotti	Jackson	6-0		
4-8	At Oak.	L	1-3		4	8	Rogers	Burba	Taylor	6-1	1st	+2.5
4-10	Ana.	W	8-5	(10)	15	10	Plunk	Percival		7-1	1st	+3.0
4-11	Ana.	W	8-5		9	9	Nagy	Dickson	Jackson	8-1	1st	+3.5
4-12	Ana.	L	1-12		9	14	Finley	Wright		8-2	1st	+2.5
4-13	Sea.	W	6-5		8	8	Burba	Cloude	Jackson	9-2	1st	+3.5
4-14	Sea.	W	8-3		7	7	Assenmacher	Slocumb		10-2	1st	+3.5
4-15	Sea.	L	3-5		5	7	Spoljaric	Assenmacher	Ayala	10-3	1st	+3.0
4-17	At Bos.	L	2-3	(10)	6	14	Gordon	Assenmacher		10-4	1st	+3.5
4-18	At Bos.	W	7-4		10	9	Martin	Eckersley	Jackson	11-4	1st	+4.5
4-19	At Bos.	L	0-2		7	10	Saberhagen	Burba	Gordon	11-5	1st	+4.0
4-20	At Bos.	L	5-6	(11)	9	16	Gordon	Plunk		11-6	1st	+4.0
4-21	Chi.	W	14-6		14	10	Mesa	Baldwin		12-6	1st	+4.0
4-22	Chi.	L	7-14		11	16	Sirotka	Nagy		12-7	1st	+4.0
4-23	Chi.	W	5-4		8	8	Plunk	T. Castillo	Jackson	13-7	1st	+4.5
4-24	Bos.	L	5-7		8	7	Wakefield	Burba	Gordon	13-8	1st	+3.5
4-25	Bos.	L	2-3		7	9	Saberhagen	Colon	Gordon	13-9	1st	+3.5
4-27	At Chi.	L	3-10		8	13	Sirotka	Ogea		13-10	1st	+3.5
4-28	At Chi.	W	4-1		9	4	Nagy	Karchner	Jackson	14-10	1st	+4.5
4-29	Oak.	L	4-11		6	16	Rogers	Wright		14-11	1st	+3.5
4-30	Oak.	L	2-5		8	11	Mathews	Assenmacher	Taylor	14-12	1st	+2.5
5-1	T.B.	W	7-5		11	10	Colon	Springer	Jackson	15-12	1st	+3.5
5-2	T.B.	W	5-1		9	4	Ogea	Saunders		16-12	1st	+4.5
5-3	T.B.	W	10-8		16	14	Mesa	Hernandez		17-12	1st	+5.5
5-5	Bal.	W	6-5		9	11	Assenmacher	Benitez		18-12	1st	+5.5
5-6	Bal.	W	14-5		17	8	Burba	Erickson		19-12	1st	+6.5
5-7	At Tex.	W	7-2		12	4	Colon	Sele		20-12	1st	+6.5
5-8	At Tex.	L	3-6		9	7	Hernandez	Mesa	Wetteland	20-13	1st	+6.5
5-9	At Tex.	L	3-7		7	13	Oliver	Nagy		20-14	1st	+6.0
5-10	At Tex.	L	3-5		6	10	Burkett	Wright	Wetteland	20-15	1st	+5.5
5-11	At T.B.	L	2-4		5	7	Arrojo	Burba	Hernandez	20-16	1st	+5.0
5-12	At T.B.	L	5-6	(14)	10	10	Santana	Jackson		20-17	1st	+4.0
5-13	At Bal.	L	1-8		6	10	Drabek	Ogea		20-18	1st	+4.0
5-14	At Bal.	W	5-4		10	12	Nagy	Rhodes	Jackson	21-18	1st	+4.0
5-15	Tex.	W	3-2	(14)	10	10	Krivda	Levine		22-18	1st	+4.0
5-16	Tex.	W	10-3		12	7	Burba	Witt		23-18	1st	+5.0
5-17	Tex.	L	0-1		5	5	Sele	Colon	Wetteland	23-19	1st	+5.0
5-19	At K.C.	W	16-3		20	7	Ogea	Rapp		24-19	1st	+5.0
5-20	At K.C.	W	14-5		16	13	Nagy	Belcher		25-19	1st	+6.0
5-21	At K.C.	W	6-2		11	6	Wright	Rosado		26-19	1st	+7.0
5-22	Tor.	W	9-7		11	14	Burba	Hanson	Jackson	27-19	1st	+7.5
5-23	Tor.	L	2-7		3	11	Clemens	Colon		27-20	1st	+7.0
5-24	Tor.	L	0-5		5	10	Williams	Gooden		27-21	1st	+6.0
5-25	Det.	W	7-4		9	10	Nagy	Castillo		28-21	1st	+6.0
5-26	Det.	W	9-2		14	12	Wright	Worrell		29-21	1st	+6.5
5-28	At Tor.	W	6-2		11	5	Burba	Carpenter		30-21	1st	+6.5
5-29	At Tor.	W	7-3		10	5	Colon	Clemens		31-21	1st	+7.5
5-30	At Tor.	L	2-4		6	6	Williams	Gooden	Myers	31-22	1st	+6.5
5-31	At Tor.	W	8-3		12	8	Nagy	Hentgen	Mesa	32-22	1st	+7.5
6-1	At Det.	W	2-0		7	3	Wright	Florie		33-22	1st	+8.5
6-2	At Det.	W	8-3		15	6	Burba	Thompson		34-22	1st	+8.5
6-3	At Min.	L	2-3		7	7	Swindell	Colon	Aguilera	34-23	1st	+7.5
6-4	At Min.	W	3-2		7	10	Gooden	Radke	Jackson	35-23	1st	+8.5
6-5	At Cin.	L	1-2		5	10	Harnisch	Nagy	Shaw	35-24	1st	+8.5
6-6	At Cin.	W	10-1		15	3	Wright	Remlinger		36-24	1st	+9.5
6-7	At Cin.	W	6-1		10	9	Burba	Klingenbeck		37-24	1st	+9.5
6-8	Pit.	W	8-0		15	4	Colon	Peters		38-24	1st	+10.5
6-9	Pit.	L	4-7		9	12	Lieber	Morman	Rincon	38-25	1st	+9.5
6-10	Pit.	L	3-4	(11)	10	15	Loaiza	Mesa	Loiselle	38-26	1st	+8.5
6-14	At N.Y.	L	2-4		6	10	Cone	Wright	Rivera	38-27	1st	+7.5
6-15	K.C.	L	6-7	(10)	16	13	Montgomery	Mesa	Whisenant	38-28	1st	+7.5
6-16	K.C.	W	9-1		10	6	Colon	Pichardo		39-28	1st	+7.5
6-17	K.C.	L	3-4		9	10	Rosado	Gooden	Montgomery	39-29	1st	+7.5
6-18	N.Y.	L	2-5		8	8	Nelson	Assenmacher	Rivera	39-30	1st	+6.5
6-19	N.Y.	W	7-4		12	8	Wright	Cone	Jackson	40-30	1st	+6.5
6-20	N.Y.	L	3-5		11	7	Wells	Burba	Rivera	40-31	1st	+6.5

- 30 -

Date	Opp.	Res.	Score	(inn.*)	Hits	Opp. hits	Winning pitcher	Losing pitcher	Save	Record	Pos.	GB
6-21	N.Y.	W	11-0		13	4	Colon	Irabu		41-31	1st	+6.5
6-22	At Chi. (NL)	W	3-1		10	7	Gooden	Tapani	Jackson	42-31	1st	+6.5
6-23	At Chi. (NL)	W	5-4		11	6	Plunk	Adams	Jackson	43-31	1st	+7.5
6-24	St.L.	W	14-3		18	9	Wright	Petkovsek		44-31	1st	+8.5
6-25	St.L.	W	8-2		10	6	Burba	Aybar		45-31	1st	+9.5
6-26	Hou.	W	4-2		11	5	Colon	Magnante	Jackson	46-31	1st	+9.5
6-27	Hou.	L	5-9	(11)	12	15	Wagner	Mesa		46-32	1st	+9.5
6-28	Hou.	L	3-12		9	16	Reynolds	Nagy	Nitkowski	46-33	1st	+8.5
6-30	At Mil.	L	4-5		10	11	Eldred	Wright	Wickman	46-34	1st	+8.5
7-1	At Mil.	W	5-2		8	5	Burba	Juden	Jackson	47-34	1st	+8.5
7-2	At Mil.	W	7-2		10	13	Colon	Woodall		48-34	1st	+9.5
7-3	At K.C.	W	2-1		2	6	Shuey	Rosado	Jackson	49-34	1st	+10.5
7-4	At K.C.	L	3-5		9	12	Rapp	Nagy	Montgomery	49-35	1st	+10.5
7-5	At K.C.	W	12-3		14	6	Wright	Rusch		50-35	1st	+10.5
7-9	Min.	L	0-3		4	6	Tewksbury	Burba	Aguilera	50-36	1st	+9.5
7-10	Min.	W	6-5		10	11	Jackson	Trombley		51-36	1st	+10.5
7-11	Min.	W	12-2		19	5	Gooden	Radke		52-36	1st	+11.5
7-12	Min.	L	6-11		8	17	Milton	Nagy		52-37	1st	+10.5
7-13	N.Y.	W	4-1		10	8	Wright	Hernandez	Jackson	53-37	1st	+11.5
7-14	N.Y.	L	1-7		6	12	Pettitte	Burba		53-38	1st	+11.5
7-15	At Bos.	L	0-1		4	7	Martinez	Colon		53-39	1st	+11.5
7-16	At Bos.	L	5-15		8	17	Wakefield	Gooden	Lowe	53-40	1st	+11.5
7-17	At Chi.	L	3-4		10	7	Simas	Shuey		53-41	1st	+10.5
7-18	At Chi.	W	15-9		15	11	Shuey	Karchner	Jackson	54-41	1st	+10.5
7-19	At Chi.	L	1-8		4	9	Sirotka	Burba		54-42	1st	+10.5
7-20	At Chi.	W	5-4		6	7	Colon	Navarro	Jackson	55-42	1st	+11.0
7-21†	Bos.	L	7-10		12	12	Martinez	Gooden	Gordon	55-43		
7-21†	Bos.	W	4-2	(8)	8	8	Ogea	Wakefield	Jackson	56-43	1st	+10.5
7-22	Bos.	W	4-3		9	8	Nagy	Garces	Jackson	57-43	1st	+11.5
7-23	Det.	L	2-3		10	10	Castillo	Wright	Jones	57-44	1st	+11.5
7-24	Det.	W	2-1	(11)	9	8	Reed	Bochtler		58-44	1st	+11.5
7-25	Det.	W	6-5		7	13	Colon	Greisinger	Jackson	59-44	1st	+11.5
7-26	Det.	L	1-8		8	16	Moehler	Gooden		59-45	1st	+10.5
7-28	At Sea.	W	4-3		4	9	Nagy	Johnson	Jackson	60-45	1st	+10.5
7-29	At Sea.	W	8-7		13	11	Ogea	McCarthy	Jackson	61-45	1st	+10.5
7-30	At Sea.	W	9-8	(17)	16	19	Shuey	Wells		62-45	1st	+11.5
7-31	At Oak.	L	2-12		7	12	Candiotti	Colon		62-46	1st	+10.5
8-1	At Oak.	L	5-6	(10)	12	9	Mathews	Karsay		62-47	1st	+10.5
8-2	At Oak.	L	5-7		9	8	Mohler	Nagy	Taylor	62-48	1st	+10.5
8-3	At Ana.	L	4-11		9	10	Sparks	Wright		62-49	1st	+10.0
8-4	At Ana.	L	4-5		8	12	Hasegawa	Jones	Percival	62-50	1st	+10.0
8-5	At Ana.	W	6-5		10	11	Shuey	Percival	Assenmacher	63-50	1st	+11.0
8-7	At T.B.	W	5-1		6	6	Gooden	Alvarez		64-50	1st	+12.5
8-8	At T.B.	W	6-2		12	3	Nagy	Rekar		65-50	1st	+13.5
8-9	At T.B.	L	1-2		4	10	Mecir	Assenmacher		65-51	1st	+12.5
8-11	Tex.	L	1-2		7	8	Loaiza	Karsay	Wetteland	65-52	1st	+13.0
8-12	Tex.	W	6-3		13	11	Colon	Burkett	Jackson	66-52	1st	+13.0
8-13	Bal.	L	4-7	(12)	6	15	Smith	Reed	Benitez	66-53	1st	+12.5
8-14	Bal.	L	3-15		9	16	Mussina	Nagy		66-54	1st	+11.5
8-15	Bal.	L	8-9	(10)	7	16	Benitez	Jones		66-55	1st	+11.5
8-16	Bal.	W	5-3		6	9	Wright	Kamieniecki	Jackson	67-55	1st	+11.5
8-17	T.B.	W	4-3		7	8	Colon	Alvarez	Jackson	68-55	1st	+12.5
8-18	T.B.	W	4-2		8	11	Gooden	Rekar	Jackson	69-55	1st	+12.5
8-19	At Tex.	L	1-3		5	6	Sele	Nagy	Wetteland	69-56	1st	+12.5
8-20	At Tex.	L	2-8		12	9	Stottlemyre	Burba	Patterson	69-57	1st	+12.5
8-21	At Bal.	W	6-3		12	5	Wright	Kamieniecki		70-57	1st	+13.5
8-22	At Bal.	L	3-6		7	9	Erickson	Colon		70-58	1st	+12.5
8-23	At Bal.	W	4-1		11	5	Gooden	Ponson	Jackson	71-58	1st	+12.5
8-25	Sea.	W	10-4		11	12	Nagy	Swift		72-58	1st	+13.0
8-26	Sea.	W	5-3		9	8	Burba	Fassero	Jackson	73-58	1st	+13.0
8-27	Sea.	L	4-10		10	13	Moyer	Wright		73-59	1st	+13.0
8-28	Oak.	L	6-14	(10)	13	24	Heredia	Reed		73-60	1st	+12.0
8-29	Oak.	L	6-11		11	16	Haynes	Martin	Taylor	73-61	1st	+11.0
8-30	Oak.	W	9-4		15	10	Nagy	Rogers	Jackson	74-61	1st	+11.0
8-31	Oak.	W	15-6		14	13	Burba	Stein	Jones	75-61	1st	+11.5
9-1	Ana.	W	7-6		16	8	Reed	DeLucia		76-61	1st	+12.5
9-2	Ana.	L	5-13		8	21	Sparks	Colon		76-62	1st	+12.5
9-3	At Det.	W	2-1		7	7	Gooden	Thompson	Jackson	77-62	1st	+13.0
9-4	At Det.	W	10-2		13	5	Nagy	Greisinger		78-62	1st	+13.0
9-5	At Det.	W	5-4		9	8	Burba	Powell	Jackson	79-62	1st	+14.0
9-6	At Det.	L	2-3		7	6	Florie	Wright	Jones	79-63	1st	+13.0
9-7	At Tor.	L	1-15		4	18	Escobar	Ogea		79-64	1st	+12.0
9-9	At Tor.	W	6-3	(13)	7	9	Jones	Almanzar	Jackson	80-64	1st	+12.5
9-11	Chi.	L	2-3		6	7	J. Abbott	Nagy	Howry	80-65	1st	+11.5
9-12	Chi.	L	4-6		8	10	Baldwin	Shuey	Howry	80-66	1st	+10.5
9-13	Chi.	W	6-3		7	6	Shuey	Ward	Jackson	81-66	1st	+11.5

– 31 –

Date	Opp.	Res.	Score	(inn.*)	Hits	Opp. hits	Winning pitcher	Losing pitcher	Save	Record	Pos.	GB
9-14	Tor.	W	6-3		12	7	Gooden	Sinclair	Jackson	82-66	1st	+11.5
9-15	Tor.	W	7-5		13	10	Ogea	Stieb	Assenmacher	83-66	1st	+12.5
9-16	Min.	W	8-6		13	13	Nagy	Tewksbury	Assenmacher	84-66	1st	+12.5
9-17	Min.	W	9-1		15	4	Burba	Milton		85-66	1st	+13.5
9-18	K.C.	W	4-1		6	6	Wright	Appier	Shuey	86-66	1st	+13.5
9-19	K.C.	L	6-7		6	15	Service	Shuey	Montgomery	86-67	1st	+12.5
9-20	K.C.	W	5-3		8	12	Colon	Rapp	Jackson	87-67	1st	+12.5
9-21	At N.Y.	W	4-1		9	5	Nagy	Pettitte	Shuey	88-67	1st	+12.5
9-22†	At N.Y.	L	4-10		9	15	Mendoza	Burba		88-68		
9-22†	At N.Y.	L	1-5		5	7	Irabu	Ogea		88-69	1st	+11.0
9-23	At N.Y.	L	4-8		8	10	Bradley	Jacome		88-70	1st	+11.0
9-24	At Min.	L	0-2		4	6	Radke	Wright	Aguilera	88-71	1st	+11.0
9-25	At Min.	L	4-5		6	11	Aguilera	Shuey		88-72	1st	+10.0
9-26	At Min.	W	9-5		11	12	Burba	Tewksbury		89-72	1st	+10.0
9-27	At Min.	L	2-6		7	9	Milton	Colon	Trombley	89-73	1st	+9.0

Monthly records: March (1-0), April (13-12), May (18-10), June (14-12), July (16-12), August (13-15), September (14-12).
*Innings, if other than nine. †Two games in one day (separate admissions).

HIGHLIGHTS

High point: A Division Series victory over the Red Sox, who had won eight of 11 meetings in the regular season. The underachieving Indians looked like good candidates for an early playoff ouster.

Low point: An ALCS loss to the powerful Yankees, after the Indians had taken a shocking 2-1 lead in the series.

Turning point: It came early. The Indians rallied from a 9-3 deficit against Randy Johnson to beat the Mariners 10-9 on opening day. That triggered a six-game winning streak to open the season and the Indians never fell out of first place en route to their fourth straight Central Division title.

Most valuable player: Manny Ramirez had the best offensive season of his career, batting .294 with career highs of 45 home runs and 145 RBIs. Ramirez also eliminated many of the defensive and baserunning mistakes that plagued him the first four years of his career.

Most valuable pitcher: Hargrove moved Mike Jackson into the closer's role two days before the season. It turned out to be a master stroke. Jackson converted 40 of his 45 save chances and had a 1.55 ERA.

Most improved player: Bartolo Colon went from a prospect to an All-Star. The righthander finished 14-9 with a 3.71 ERA and was the team's best starter for most of the season.

Most pleasant surprise: The team's starters, questionable entering the season, finished with the fourth best ERA in the league. Dave Burba and Charles Nagy both won 15 games. Colon emerged to win 14, Dwight Gooden came back to be the team's best starter in the second half and even though Jaret Wright struggled at times, he still won 12 games.

Biggest disappointment: The once-proud offense fell to sixth in the league in runs scored and batting average and tied for seventh in home runs.

Key injuries: Gooden didn't pitch until late May because of a sore shoulder. Ogea was on the disabled list three times with knee, chest and shoulder injuries. A broken hand sidelined Jim Thome from August 7 to September 16. David Justice was bothered all season with knee and elbow problems. Sandy Alomar Jr. played with back and knee injuries.

Notable: The Indians became the seventh team to lead their division/league from start to finish. . . . Since opening the 1995 season, the Indians have been in first place or tied for first for 639 of the 700 days. . . . The Indians have won the last four division titles by a combined 59.5 games. . . . Hargrove goes into the 1999 season with a career record of 624-526, good for second place on the team's all-time list for wins by a manager. Lou Boudreau leads with 728.

—STEVE HERRICK

RECORDS

1998 regular-season record: 89-73 (1st in A.L. Central); 46-35 at home; 43-38 on road; 27-27 vs. East; 29-19 vs. A.L. Central; 23-21 vs. West; 10-6 vs. N.L.; 25-20 vs. lefthanded starters; 64-53 vs. righthanded starters; 74-63 on grass; 15-10 on turf; 21-29 in daytime; 68-44 at night; 23-23 in one-run games; 5-10 in extra-inning games; 0-0 in doubleheaders.

Team record past five years: 440-301 (.594, ranks 2nd in league in that span).

TEAM LEADERS

Batting average: Manny Ramirez (.294).
At-bats: Kenny Lofton (600).
Runs: Manny Ramirez (108).
Hits: Kenny Lofton (169).
Total bases: Manny Ramirez (342).
Doubles: David Justice (39).
Triples: Kenny Lofton, Omar Vizquel (6).
Home runs: Manny Ramirez (45).
Runs batted in: Manny Ramirez (145).
Stolen bases: Kenny Lofton (54).
Slugging percentage: Manny Ramirez (.599).
On-base percentage: Jim Thome (.413).
Wins: Dave Burba, Charles Nagy (15).
Earned-run average: Bartolo Colon (3.71).

Complete games: Bartolo Colon (6).
Shutouts: Bartolo Colon (2).
Saves: Mike Jackson (40).
Innings pitched: Charles Nagy (210.1).
Strikeouts: Bartolo Colon (158).

GAMES BY POSITION

Catcher: Sandy Alomar Jr. 111, Pat Borders 53, Einar Diaz 17.
First base: Jim Thome 117, Richie Sexson 45, Jeff Manto 7, Jeff Branson 3, Cecil Fielder 3, David Bell 1.
Second base: David Bell 101, Jeff Branson 31, Shawon Dunston 24, Enrique Wilson 22, Joey Cora 21, Torey Lovullo 5, Jeff Manto 1.
Third base: Travis Fryman 144, Jeff Branson 20, Jeff Manto 8, David Bell 6, Enrique Wilson 2, Pat Borders 1, Russ Branyan 1, Torey Lovullo 1.
Shortstop: Omar Vizquel 151, Shawon Dunston 14, Enrique Wilson 10, Travis Fryman 3, Jeff Branson 2, David Bell 1, Jolbert Cabrera 1.
Outfield: Kenny Lofton 154, Manny Ramirez 148, Brian S. Giles 101, Mark Whiten 72, David Justice 21, Geronimo Berroa 14, Shawon Dunston 12, Alex Ramirez 3, Richie Sexson 3.
Designated hitter: David Justice 123, Cecil Fielder 10, Shawon Dunston 7, Brian S. Giles 6, Jim Thome 6, Geronimo Berroa 3, Mark Whiten 5, Sandy Alomar Jr. 3, Travis Fryman 2, Manny Ramirez 2, Richie Sexson 2.

TOP DRAFT CHOICES

1. **C.C. Sabathia,** LHP, Vallejo (Calif.) H.S.
2. **Zach Sorensen,** SS, Wichita State U.
3. **Scott Pratt,** SS, Auburn University
4. **Ron Marietta,** LHP, St. John's Univ.
5. **Ryan Drese,** RHP, U. of California
6. **Tyler Minges,** OF, Ross H.S., Hamilton, O.
7. **Brody Percell,** LHP, Oregon State U.
8. **Chris Reinike,** RHP, Miss. State U.
9. **Paul Day,** 3B, Long Beach State U.
10. **Michael McPadden,** RHP, Port St. Lucie (Fla.) H.S.

DETROIT TIGERS
AMERICAN LEAGUE CENTRAL DIVISION

1999 Tigers Schedule

Home games shaded. ●—All-Star Game at Fenway Park (Boston). D—Day game (any game starting before 5 p.m.).

April

SUN	MON	TUE	WED	THU	FRI	SAT
				1	2	3
4	5 TEX	D 6 TEX	7 TEX	8	9 D NYY	10 D NYY
11 D NYY	12 D MIN	D 13	14 MIN	15 MIN	16 NYY	17 D NYY
18 D NYY	19	20 BOS	21 BOS	22 D BOS	23 CWS	24 D CWS
25 D CWS	26 SEA	27 SEA	28 SEA	29 D SEA	30 TB	

May

SUN	MON	TUE	WED	THU	FRI	SAT
						1 TB
2 TB	D 3 TB	ANA	ANA	6 ANA	7 BAL	8 D BAL
9 BAL	D 10	11 OAK	12 OAK	13	14 CLE	15 D CLE
16 D CLE	17 TOR	18 TOR	19 TOR	20 TOR	21 CLE	22 D CLE
23 CLE	24 TOR	25 TOR	26 TOR	27 CWS	28 CWS	29 D CWS
30 D CWS	31 D BOS					

June

SUN	MON	TUE	WED	THU	FRI	SAT
		1 BOS	2 BOS	3	4 STL	5 STL
6 D STL	7 PIT	8 PIT	9 PIT	10	11 STL	12 STL
13 D STL	14 SEA	15 SEA	16 SEA	17 SEA	18 OAK	19 OAK
20 OAK	21 OAK	22 KC	23 KC	24 D KC	25 MIN	26 MIN
27 D MIN	28	29 NYY	30 D NYY			

July

SUN	MON	TUE	WED	THU	FRI	SAT
				1 NYY	2 MIN	3 MIN
4 MIN	D 5	6 NYY	7 NYY	8 NYY	9 MIL	10 MIL
11 D MIL	12	13	* 14	15 HOU	16 HOU	17 D HOU
18 D CIN	19 CIN	20 CIN	21 KC	22 KC	23 BOS	24 BOS
25 D BOS	26 CLE	27 CLE	28 CLE	29	30 TOR	31 D TOR

August

SUN	MON	TUE	WED	THU	FRI	SAT
1 TOR	2 CWS	CWS	4	5 BAL	6 BAL	7 BAL
8 D BAL	9 TEX	10 TEX	11 TEX	12 TEX	13 ANA	14 D ANA
15 D ANA	16 TB	17 TB	18 TB	19	20 ANA	21 ANA
22 ANA	23 SEA	24 SEA	25 SEA	26	27 BAL	28 BAL
29 BAL	30 TEX	31 TEX				

September

SUN	MON	TUE	WED	THU	FRI	SAT
			1 TEX	2 TEX	D 3 OAK	4 D OAK
5 OAK	D 6 OAK	7	8 TB	9 TB	10 TOR	11 TOR
12 D TOR	13 CWS	14 CWS	15 CWS	16	17 BOS	18 D BOS
19 D BOS	20 CLE	21 CLE	22 CLE	23 CLE	24 KC	25 KC
26 D KC	27 KC	28 MIN	29 MIN	30 MIN		

October

SUN	MON	TUE	WED	THU	FRI	SAT
					1 KC	2 KC
3 D KC	D 4	5	6	7	8	9

1999 SEASON
CLUB DIRECTORY

Owners
Michael Ilitch

President, chief executive officer
John McHale Jr.

Vice president, baseball operations/g.m.
Randy Smith

Vice president, business operations
David H. Glazier

Assistant general manager
Steve Lubratich

Assistant to baseball operations
Ricky Bennett

Special assistants to the g.m.
Al Hargesheimer
Randy Johnson

Director of scouting
Greg Smith

Director minor league operations
Dave Miller

Advance scout
Tom Runnells

Special assignment scout
Larry Bearnarth

Traveling secretary
Bill Brown

Director of public relations
Tyler Barnes

Assistant director of public relations
David Matheson

Manager, community relations
Celia Bobrowsky

Coordinator, community relations
Herman Jenkins

Coordinator, public relations
Giovanni Loria

Asst., public relations-publications
Melanie Waters

Asst., public relations-administrative
To be announced

Coordinator, community relations
Christina Branham

Marketing manager
Howard Krugel

Director of stadium operations
Tom Folk

Head groundskeeper
Frank Feneck

Senior director, corporate sales
Gary Vitto

Director of corporate sales
Martin Pawlusiak

Controller
Jennifer Marosso

Director of ticket services
Ken Marchetti

Director of ticket sales
Mike Stanfield

Season ticket manager
Kevin Marcy

Director of merchandise
Kayla French

Head trainer
Russ Miller

Assistant trainer
Steve Carter

Strength and conditioning coach
Brad Andress

Manager, home clubhouse
Jim Schmakel

Assistant manager, visiting clubhouse
John Nelson

Team physicians
Michael Workings, M.D.
David Collon, M.D.
Terry Lock, M.D.
Louis Saco, M.D. (Florida)

Scouts
Larry Bearnarth, Ricky Bennett, Bill Buck, Tom Chandler, Nathan Durst, Louis Eljaua, Tim Grieve, Rob Guzik, Jack Hays, Ray Hayward, Mike Humphreys, Steve Lemke, Dennis Lieberthal, Jeff Malinoff, John Mirabelli, Mark Monahan, Glenn Murdock, Pat Murtaugh, Jim Olander, David Owen, Ramon Pena, Rusty Pendergrass, Buddy Poine, Dave Roberts, Derrick Ross, Tom Runnells, Mike Stafford, Chuck Stone, Dan Warthen, Clyde Weir, Jeff Wetherby, Rob Wilfong, Ellis Williams, Gary York

MINOR LEAGUE AFFILIATES

Class	Team	League	Manager
AAA	Toledo	International	Gene Roof
AA	Jacksonville	Southern	Dave Anderson
A	Lakeland	Florida State	To be announced
A	West Michigan	Midwest	To be announced
A	Oneonta	To be announced	To be announced
Rookie	Gulf Coast Tigers	Gulf Coast	To be announced

BROADCAST INFORMATION

Radio: WJR-AM (760).
TV: WKBD (Channel 50).
Cable TV: FOX Sports Detroit.

SPRING TRAINING

Ballpark (city): Marchant Stadium (Lakeland, Fla.).
Ticket information: 941-603-6278 or 941-603-6279.

SPRING TRAINING ROSTER

Manager—Larry Parrish.
Coaches—Rick Adair (35), Perry Hill (13), Jeff Jones, Lance Parrish, Juan Samuel, Alan Trammell.

No.	PITCHERS	B/T	Ht./Wt.	Born	1998 clubs
14	Anderson, Matt	R/R	6-4/200	8-17-76	Lakeland, Detroit, Jacksonville
	Blair, Willie	R/R	6-1/185	12-18-65	Arizona, New York N.L.
	Blanco, Alberto	L/L	6-1/200	6-27-76	Kissimmee, Jackson
	Borkowski, David	R/R	6-1/200	2-7-77	Jacksonville
26	Brocail, Doug	L/R	6-5/235	5-16-67	Detroit
58	Brunson, Will	L/L	6-6/185	3-20-70	Los Angeles, Detroit, Albuquerque
	Cordero, Francisco	R/R	6-2/200	8-11-77	Jacksonville, Lakeland
	Corey, Bryan	R/R	6-0/170	10-21-73	Tucson, Arizona
	Drews, Matt	R/R	6-8/230	8-29-74	Toledo
	Drumright, Mike	L/R	6-4/210	4-19-74	Toledo
39	Florie, Bryce	R/R	5-11/192	5-21-70	Detroit, Toledo
	Garcia, Apostol	R/R	6-0/155	8-3-76	Lakeland
50	Greisinger, Seth	R/R	6-3/200	7-29-75	Toledo, Detroit
59	Jones, Todd	R/R	6-3/230	4-24-68	Detroit
	Kida, Masao	R/R	6-2/210	9-12-68	Orix
38	Moehler, Brian	R/R	6-3/235	12-31-71	Detroit
	Nitkowski, C.J.	L/L	6-3/205	3-9-73	Houston, New Orleans
	Roberts, Willis	R/R	6-3/175	6-19-75	Jacksonville, Toledo
44	Runyan, Sean	L/L	6-3/200	6-21-74	Detroit
22	Thompson, Justin	L/L	6-4/215	3-8-73	Detroit

No.	CATCHERS	B/T	Ht./Wt.	Born	1998 clubs
	Ausmus, Brad	R/R	5-11/195	4-14-69	Houston
33	Casanova, Raul	B/R	6-0/195	8-23-72	Detroit, Toledo
41	Fick, Rob	L/R	6-1/189	3-15-74	Detroit, Jacksonville
	Haselman, Bill	R/R	6-3/223	5-25-66	Texas

No.	INFIELDERS	B/T	Ht./Wt.	Born	1998 clubs
20	Alvarez, Gabe	R/R	6-1/205	3-6-74	Toledo, Detroit
27	Catalanotto, Frank	L/R	6-0/195	4-27-74	Detroit, Toledo
17	Clark, Tony	B/R	6-7/245	6-15-72	Detroit
8	Cruz, Deivi	R/R	6-0/184	11-6-75	Lakeland, Toledo, Detroit
9	Easley, Damion	R/R	5-11/185	11-11-69	Detroit
	Garcia, Luis	R/R	6-0/175	5-20-75	Toledo
	Jefferies, Gregg	B/R	5-10/184	8-1-67	Philadelphia, Anaheim
	Palmer, Dean	R/R	6-1/210	12-27-68	Kansas City
43	Wood, Jason	R/R	6-1/170	12-16-69	Oakland, Edmonton, Toledo, Detroit

No.	OUTFIELDERS	B/T	Ht./Wt.	Born	1998 clubs
12	Bartee, Kimera	B/R	6-0/190	7-21-72	Detroit, Toledo
34	Encarnacion, Juan	R/R	6-3/187	3-8-76	Lakeland, Toledo, Detroit
24	Garcia, Karim	L/L	6-0/172	10-29-75	Arizona, Tucson
4	Higginson, Bobby	L/R	5-11/195	8-18-70	Detroit
21	Hunter, Brian	R/R	6-3/180	3-25-71	Detroit
51	Kapler, Gabe	R/R	6-2/190	8-31-75	Detroit, Jacksonville

BALLPARK INFORMATION

Ballpark (capacity, surface)
Tiger Stadium (46,945, grass)

Address
Tiger Stadium
Detroit, MI 48216

Business phone
313-962-4000

Ticket information
313-963-2050

Ticket prices
$20 and $15 (box seats)
$12 and $8 (reserved seats)
$10 (Coca Cola fan stands)
$5 (bleacher seats)

Field dimensions (from home plate)
To left field at foul line, 340 feet
To center field, 440 feet
To right field at foul line, 325 feet

First game played
April 20, 1912
(Tigers 6, Cleveland Naps 5, 11 innings)

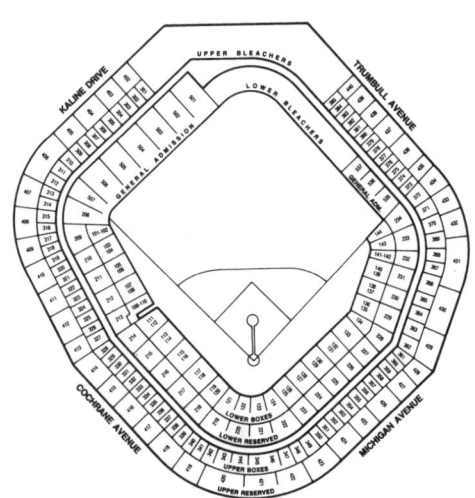

1999 SEASON   *Detroit Tigers*

Date	Opp.	Res.	Score	(inn.*)	Hits	Opp. hits	Winning pitcher	Losing pitcher	Save	Record	Pos.	GB
3-31	At T.B.	W	11-6		18	12	Thompson	Alvarez		1-0	T1st	...
4-1	At T.B.	L	8-11		13	18	Arrojo	Moehler		1-1	T3rd	1.0
4-2	At T.B.	L	1-7		5	12	Yan	Worrell		1-2	T4th	1.5
4-3	At Bal.	L	2-10		7	8	Drabek	Sanders		1-3	5th	2.5
4-4	At Bal.	L	1-2		5	4	Kamieniecki	Keagle	Benitez	1-4	5th	3.5
4-5	At Bal.	L	3-6		10	10	Mussina	Thompson	Orosco	1-5	5th	4.5
4-7	T.B.	W	3-1		8	10	Florie	Arrojo	Jones	2-5	5th	4.0
4-10	Bal.	W	7-1		12	6	Worrell	Drabek		3-5	5th	4.0
4-11	Bal.	L	0-2		2	4	Mussina	Thompson	Benitez	3-6	5th	5.0
4-12	Bal.	L	3-6		11	8	Erickson	Keagle	Benitez	3-7	5th	5.0
4-13	At Tex.	L	1-10		8	14	Witt	Moehler		3-8	5th	6.0
4-14	At Tex.	L	2-11		7	19	Sele	Sanders		3-9	5th	7.0
4-15	At Tex.	L	3-7		7	9	Helling	Worrell		3-10	5th	7.0
4-17	N.Y.	L	2-11		7	12	Pettitte	Thompson		3-11	5th	7.0
4-18	N.Y.	L	3-8		13	13	Cone	Keagle		3-12	5th	8.0
4-19	N.Y.	W	2-1		4	3	Moehler	Holmes	Jones	4-12	5th	7.0
4-21	Bos.	L	4-11		7	12	Rose	Worrell		4-13	5th	7.5
4-22	Bos.	L	5-8		9	12	Corsi	Jones	Gordon	4-14	5th	7.5
4-24	At N.Y.	L	4-8		6	13	Cone	Keagle		4-15	5th	8.0
4-25	At N.Y.	L	4-5		5	6	Wells	Runyan	Rivera	4-16	5th	8.0
4-27	At Bos.	L	5-6		10	8	Eckersley	Runyan	Gordon	4-17	5th	8.0
4-28	At Bos.	W	7-5		13	13	Florie	Shouse	Jones	5-17	5th	8.0
4-29	Tex.	L	1-4		4	7	Burkett	Keagle	Wetteland	5-18	5th	8.0
4-30	Tex.	W	7-2		14	6	Moehler	Witt		6-18	5th	7.0
5-1	At Sea.	W	17-3		20	9	Worrell	Swift		7-18	5th	7.0
5-2	At Sea.	L	0-4		3	6	Moyer	Thompson		7-19	5th	8.0
5-3	At Sea.	L	6-10		8	13	Johnson	Castillo		7-20	5th	9.0
5-6	At Oak.	W	10-5		9	10	Brocail	Groom		8-20	5th	9.5
5-7	At Oak.	W	6-3		12	3	Thompson	Candiotti	Jones	9-20	5th	9.5
5-8	At Ana.	L	3-5		7	7	Watson	Moehler	Percival	9-21	5th	9.5
5-9	At Ana.	W	7-3		10	11	Castillo	Finley		10-21	5th	8.5
5-10	At Ana.	L	2-4		10	7	Hill	Worrell	Percival	10-22	5th	8.5
5-12	Sea.	L	2-4		6	5	Spoljaric	Thompson	Ayala	10-23	5th	8.0
5-13	Sea.	W	8-5		10	5	Moehler	Cloude	Jones	11-23	5th	7.0
5-14	Oak.	W	8-3		10	7	Sager	Rogers		12-23	5th	7.0
5-15	Oak.	W	8-3		10	6	Castillo	Oquist		13-23	5th	7.0
5-16	Ana.	L	6-8		9	14	Dickson	Worrell	Percival	13-24	5th	8.0
5-17	Ana.	W	4-3		4	14	Florie	DeLucia	Jones	14-24	5th	7.0
5-18	Ana.	W	11-2		19	8	Moehler	Watson		15-24	4th	6.5
5-19	At Min.	L	3-8		5	15	Radke	Sager		15-25	4th	7.5
5-20	At Min.	W	12-11		20	15	Runyan	Naulty	Jones	16-25	4th	7.5
5-21	At Min.	W	6-3	(11)	17	7	Brocail	Trombley	Jones	17-25	4th	7.5
5-22	At Chi.	W	9-5		18	9	Thompson	Eyre		18-25	2nd	7.5
5-23	At Chi.	L	1-7		4	12	Sirotka	Moehler		18-26	4th	7.5
5-24	At Chi.	W	8-4		15	6	Sager	Bere		19-26	3rd	6.5
5-25	At Cle.	L	4-7		10	9	Nagy	Castillo		19-27	3rd	7.5
5-26	At Cle.	L	2-9		12	14	Wright	Worrell		19-28	3rd	8.5
5-28	Chi.	L	7-11	(10)	9	11	Karchner	Duran		19-29	4th	9.5
5-29	Chi.	W	8-7		6	14	Crow	C. Castillo	Jones	20-29	4th	9.5
5-30	Chi.	W	6-0		12	7	Moehler	Navarro		21-29	3rd	8.5
5-31	Chi.	L	2-8		6	14	Parque	Castillo		21-30	4th	9.5
6-1	Cle.	L	0-2		3	7	Wright	Florie		21-31	4th	10.5
6-2	Cle.	L	3-8		6	15	Burba	Thompson		21-32	4th	11.5
6-3	At Tor.	L	1-5		4	8	Clemens	Greisinger		21-33	4th	11.5
6-4	At Tor.	L	6-9		8	12	Williams	Moehler	Myers	21-34	4th	12.5
6-5	At Mil.	L	3-7		9	9	Eldred	Castillo	Wickman	21-35	5th	12.5
6-6	At Mil.	W	9-3		16	10	Florie	Karl		22-35	4th	12.5
6-7	At Mil.	W	4-1		7	3	Thompson	Woodard		23-35	4th	12.5
6-8	Hou.	L	5-9		9	14	Henry	Jones		23-36	4th	13.5
6-9	Hou.	L	3-5		9	10	Hampton	Jones	Wagner	23-37	4th	13.5
6-10	Hou.	L	3-10		6	9	Schourek	Castillo		23-38	4th	13.5
6-12	At K.C.	L	3-7		10	10	Rosado	Florie		23-39	5th	14.0
6-13	At K.C.	W	7-1		14	5	Thompson	Rapp		24-39	4th	13.5
6-14	At K.C.	L	0-2		7	5	Rusch	Greisinger		24-40	5th	13.5
6-15	Min.	W	3-2		8	7	Moehler	Radke	Jones	25-40	5th	12.5
6-16	Min.	L	5-8		11	12	Serafini	Harriger	Aguilera	25-41	5th	13.5
6-17	Min.	W	6-2		10	7	Florie	Milton		26-41	5th	12.5
6-18	K.C.	L	3-5		12	12	Rapp	Thompson	Montgomery	26-42	5th	12.5
6-19	K.C.	L	4-8		11	11	Rusch	Greisinger	Bones	26-43	5th	13.5
6-20	K.C.	W	4-3		10	10	Moehler	Belcher	Jones	27-43	5th	12.5
6-21	K.C.	L	5-6		8	7	Pichardo	Harriger	Montgomery	27-44	5th	13.5

Date	Opp.	Res.	Score	(inn.*)	Hits	Opp. hits	Winning pitcher	Losing pitcher	Save	Record	Pos.	GB
6-22	At St.L.	L	1-4		7	8	Stottlemyre	Florie	Croushore	27-45	5th	14.5
6-23	At St.L.	W	8-1		11	4	Thompson	Bottenfield		28-45	5th	14.5
6-24	Chi. (NL)	W	7-6	(11)	13	13	Brocail	Pisciotta		29-45	5th	14.5
6-25	Chi. (NL)	W	6-4		6	7	Anderson	Adams	Jones	30-45	5th	14.5
6-26	Cin.	L	3-4		4	11	Harnisch	Brocail	Shaw	30-46	5th	15.5
6-27	Cin.	L	5-6	(13)	15	13	White	Harriger		30-47	5th	15.5
6-28	Cin.	L	2-5		11	10	Parris	Thompson	Shaw	30-48	5th	15.5
6-30	At Pit.	W	3-0		7	5	Moehler	Lieber		31-48	5th	14.5
7-1	At Pit.	W	9-1		10	7	Greisinger	Peters		32-48	5th	14.5
7-2	At Pit.	L	2-5		8	9	Loaiza	Powell	Loiselle	32-49	5th	15.5
7-3	At Min.	W	5-4	(10)	12	9	Brocail	Naulty	Jones	33-49	5th	15.5
7-4	At Min.	W	4-2		9	9	Thompson	Serafini	Jones	34-49	5th	14.5
7-5	At Min.	L	4-5		9	11	Hawkins	Moehler	Aguilera	34-50	5th	15.5
7-9	Tor.	W	4-3		8	8	Anderson	Plesac	Jones	35-50	4th	14.5
7-10	Tor.	W	3-2	(10)	12	8	Jones	Quantrill		36-50	4th	14.5
7-11	Tor.	W	5-2		8	4	Moehler	Carpenter	Runyan	37-50	4th	14.5
7-12	Tor.	L	2-7		5	7	Clemens	Brocail		37-51	4th	14.5
7-13	K.C.	L	4-6	(10)	6	9	Whisenant	Jones	Montgomery	37-52	5th	15.5
7-14	K.C.	W	8-3		12	10	Thompson	Belcher		38-52	5th	14.5
7-15	N.Y.	L	0-11		5	13	Irabu	Greisinger		38-53	5th	14.5
7-16	N.Y.	W	3-1		7	7	Moehler	Cone	Jones	39-53	5th	13.5
7-17	Bos.	W	6-4		11	9	Powell	Cho	Jones	40-53	5th	12.5
7-18	Bos.	L	4-9		7	10	Avery	Castillo	Lowe	40-54	5th	13.5
7-19	Bos.	W	3-1		9	7	Thompson	Gordon		41-54	5th	12.5
7-20†	At N.Y.	W	4-3	(17)	14	13	Sager	Holmes		42-54		
7-20‡	At N.Y.	L	3-4		5	10	Irabu	Florie	Rivera	42-55	5th	13.0
7-21	At N.Y.	L	1-5		9	7	Cone	Moehler		42-56	5th	13.5
7-22	At N.Y.	L	2-13		12	12	Hernandez	Powell	Holmes	42-57	5th	14.5
7-23	At Cle.	W	3-2		10	10	Castillo	Wright	Jones	43-57	5th	13.5
7-24	At Cle.	L	1-2	(11)	8	9	Reed	Bochtler		43-58	5th	14.5
7-25	At Cle.	L	5-6		13	7	Colon	Greisinger	Jackson	43-59	5th	15.5
7-26	At Cle.	W	8-1		16	8	Moehler	Gooden		44-59	5th	14.5
7-28	Bal.	L	5-6		8	10	Ponson	Florie	Benitez	44-60	5th	15.5
7-29	Bal.	L	2-14		8	18	Mussina	Castillo	Johns	44-61	5th	16.5
7-30	Bal.	L	4-6		8	7	Smith	Anderson	Benitez	44-62	5th	17.5
7-31	At T.B.	L	1-5		5	12	Santana	Greisinger	Hernandez	44-63	5th	17.5
8-1	At T.B.	W	8-0		12	5	Moehler	Alvarez		45-63	5th	16.5
8-2	At T.B.	W	3-2		10	6	Powell	Rekar	Jones	46-63	5th	15.5
8-4	At Bal.	L	0-4		2	11	Mussina	Florie		46-64	5th	15.0
8-5	At Bal.	L	1-6		5	9	Guzman	Thompson		46-65	5th	16.0
8-7†	Sea.	L	3-6		7	11	Slocumb	Crow	Timlin	46-66		
8-7‡	Sea.	L	1-7		8	13	Moyer	Moehler		46-67	5th	17.5
8-8	Sea.	L	3-9		9	13	Cloude	Powell		46-68	5th	18.5
8-9	Sea.	L	3-6		9	11	Wells	Runyan	Timlin	46-69	5th	18.5
8-10	Ana.	L	2-6		6	12	Olivares	Castillo		46-70	5th	19.0
8-11	Ana.	L	4-5	(11)	7	8	Fetters	Runyan	Percival	46-71	5th	19.0
8-12	Ana.	L	2-3		9	7	Sparks	Greisinger	Percival	46-72	5th	20.0
8-14	Oak.	W	13-4		15	8	Thompson	Stein	Sager	47-72	5th	18.5
8-15	Oak.	L	8-10	(11)	15	21	Taylor	Crow		47-73	5th	18.5
8-16	Oak.	W	6-4		8	6	Florie	Oquist	Jones	48-73	5th	18.5
8-17	At Sea.	L	1-3		8	8	Moyer	Moehler	Timlin	48-74	5th	19.5
8-18	At Sea.	W	7-6		10	13	Greisinger	Ayala	Jones	49-74	5th	19.5
8-19	At Ana.	L	0-2		6	9	McDowell	Thompson	Percival	49-75	5th	19.5
8-20	At Ana.	L	2-13		8	16	Olivares	Powell		49-76	5th	19.5
8-21	At Oak.	L	2-4		7	9	Oquist	Florie	Taylor	49-77	5th	20.5
8-22†	At Oak.	L	2-7		9	9	Heredia	Moehler	Mathews	49-78		
8-22‡	At Oak.	L	1-7		6	12	Candiotti	Castillo		49-79	5th	21.0
8-23	At Oak.	W	5-4		7	8	Greisinger	Haynes	Jones	50-79	5th	21.0
8-24	At Tex.	L	5-6		12	9	Sele	Thompson	Wetteland	50-80	5th	21.5
8-25	At Tex.	W	8-7		16	12	Powell	Stottlemyre		51-80	5th	21.5
8-26	At Tex.	L	6-8		8	12	Loaiza	Florie	Wetteland	51-81	5th	22.5
8-28	T.B.	L	3-4		7	8	Mecir	Moehler	Hernandez	51-82	5th	22.0
8-29†	T.B.	L	6-10		5	17	Springer	Thompson		51-83		
8-29‡	T.B.	W	8-2		11	4	Greisinger	Rekar		52-83	5th	21.5
8-30	T.B.	L	5-10		8	13	Arrojo	Powell	Hernandez	52-84	5th	22.5
8-31	Tex.	L	2-13		6	14	Loaiza	Florie		52-85	5th	23.5
9-1	Tex.	W	12-8		17	11	Anderson	Crabtree	Sager	53-85	5th	23.5
9-2	Tex.	L	3-5		8	11	Helling	Moehler	Wetteland	53-86	5th	23.5
9-3	Cle.	L	1-2		7	7	Gooden	Thompson	Jackson	53-87	5th	24.5
9-4	Cle.	L	2-10		5	13	Nagy	Greisinger		53-88	5th	25.5
9-5	Cle.	L	4-5		8	9	Burba	Powell	Jackson	53-89	5th	26.5
9-6	Cle.	W	3-2		6	7	Florie	Wright	Jones	54-89	5th	25.5
9-7	At Chi.	L	5-7		10	8	Parque	Moehler	Bradford	54-90	5th	25.5
9-8	At Chi.	L	6-12		10	17	Snyder	Thompson		54-91	5th	26.0
9-9	At Chi.	W	8-6		14	12	Greisinger	Sirotka		55-91	5th	26.0
9-11	At Bos.	L	2-6		10	9	Saberhagen	Powell	Gordon	55-92	5th	26.0

Date	Opp.	Res.	Score	(inn.*)	Hits	Opp. hits	Winning pitcher	Losing pitcher	Save	Record	Pos.	GB
9-12	At Bos.	W	3-2		7	4	Anderson	Gordon	Jones	56-92	5th	25.0
9-13	At Bos.	W	4-1		6	5	Moehler	Swindell	Jones	57-92	5th	25.0
9-14	Chi.	L	16-17	(12)	22	19	Eyre	Bochtler		57-93	5th	26.0
9-15	Chi.	W	2-0		8	5	Greisinger	Sirotka	Jones	58-93	5th	26.0
9-16	Tor.	L	1-2		4	4	Clemens	Powell	Person	58-94	5th	27.0
9-17	Tor.	W	7-4		15	10	Brocail	Person		59-94	5th	27.0
9-18	Min.	W	5-4	(11)	10	5	Anderson	Trombley		60-94	5th	27.0
9-19	Min.	W	8-7	(10)	12	14	Sager	Aguilera		61-94	5th	26.0
9-20	Min.	L	0-3		4	6	Sampson	Greisinger	Aguilera	61-95	5th	27.0
9-21	At K.C.	W	7-5		11	10	Crow	Service	Jones	62-95	5th	27.0
9-22	At K.C.	W	14-4		18	6	Thompson	Belcher	Castillo	63-95	5th	25.5
9-23	At K.C.	W	5-1		11	4	Florie	Appier		64-95	5th	24.5
9-25	At Tor.	W	7-5		10	12	Moehler	Williams	Jones	65-95	5th	23.0
9-26	At Tor.	L	4-5	(13)	12	13	Risley	Sager		65-96	5th	24.0
9-27	At Tor.	L	1-2		1	5	Halladay	Thompson		65-97	5th	24.0

Monthly records: March (1-0), April (5-18), May (15-12), June (10-18), July (13-15), August (8-22), September (13-12).
*Innings, if other than nine. †First game of doubleheader. ‡Second game of doubleheader.

1999 SEASON   Detroit Tigers

HIGHLIGHTS

High point: The team went into New York on July 20 and beat the Yankees 4-3 in 17 innings in the first game of a twinight doubleheader, surviving one threat after another that would have won the game for the Yankees. After that, however, it was back to normal. The Tigers lost 18 of their next 20.

Low point: The team fell apart in August, going 8-22. After allowing 33 runs in three losses at the end of the month, the team fired manager Buddy Bell.

Turning point: At 3-5, the start had been rocky but not disastrous. But then the team lost seven straight to fall eight games back—just a little more than two weeks into the season. After a victory over New York, the team lost another five in a row.

Most valuable player: Damion Easley had a breakout season. Easley set career highs with 100 RBIs, 27 home runs, 38 doubles and 153 games played. Defensively, he led A.L. second basemen with a .985 fielding percentage.

Most valuable pitcher: Brian Moehler led the club in wins with 14 and his 3.90 ERA was the lowest of the starting rotation. Moehler allowed fewer than four runs in 22 of his 33 starts and his three shutouts were the most by a Detroit pitcher since Jack Morris tossed six in 1986.

Most improved player: When Paul Bako was acquired from the Reds for Melvin Nieves following the 1997 season, the thought was that he'd be a good addition for Class AAA Toledo. Instead, he proved to be a good addition at the major league level. He hit .272 in 96 big-league games last season.

Most pleasant surprise: Lefthanded reliever Sean Runyan was consistent his entire rookie season. He had a 3.45 ERA before the All-Star break and a 3.74 ERA after the break. His 88 appearances were a major league record for a rookie and his 3.58 ERA was third-best among American League lefthanded relievers with more than 50 innings.

Biggest disappointment: There weren't what you'd call high hopes at the start of the year for righthander Frank Castillo, but there were moderate hopes that he

would reach double figures in victories. Castillo went 3-9 with an 8.32 ERA in 19 starts. He was much more effective (1.13 ERA) in eight relief appearances, but he was used in relief only because he'd flopped as a starter.

Key injuries: Shortstop Deivi Cruz broke his ankle while playing winter ball and wasn't able to play at the major league level until April 27.

Notable: Center fielder Brian Hunter's walks dropped from 66 to 36. His stolen bases fell from 74 to 42 and his runs from 112 to 67.

—TOM GAGE

RECORDS

1998 regular-season record: 65-97 (5th in A.L. Central); 32-49 at home; 33-48 on road; 19-35 vs. East; 23-25 vs. A.L. Central; 16-28 vs. West; 7-9 vs. N.L.; 17-25 vs. lefthanded starters; 48-72 vs. righthanded starters; 53-84 on grass; 12-13 on turf; 19-28 in day-time; 46-69 at night; 20-21 in one-run games; 7-8 in extra-inning games; 0-2-2 in doubleheaders.
Team record past five years: 310-435 (.416, ranks 13th in league in that span).

TEAM LEADERS

Batting average: Tony Clark (.291).
At-bats: Bob Higginson (612).
Runs: Bob Higginson (92).
Hits: Tony Clark (175).
Total bases: Tony Clark (314).
Doubles: Damion Easley (38).
Triples: Luis Gonzalez (5).
Home runs: Tony Clark (34).
Runs batted in: Tony Clark (103).
Stolen bases: Brian L. Hunter (42).
Slugging percentage: Tony Clark (.522).
On-base percentage: Tony Clark (.358).
Wins: Brian Moehler (14).
Earned-run average: Brian Moehler (3.90).
Complete games: Justin Thompson (5).
Shutouts: Brian Moehler (3).
Saves: Todd Jones (28).
Innings pitched: Justin Thompson (222.0).
Strikeouts: Justin Thompson (149).

GAMES BY POSITION

Catcher: Paul Bako 94, Joe Oliver 48, Joe Siddall 27, Raul Casanova 14, Robert Fick 3.
First base: Tony Clark 142, Frank Catalanotto 18, Jeff Manto 10, Jason Wood 6, Joe Oliver 2, Billy Ripken 2, Robert Fick 1, Joe Randa 1.
Second base: Damion Easley 140, Frank Catalanotto 31, Joe Randa 20, Billy Ripken 2, Bip Roberts 1.
Third base: Joe Randa 118, Gabe Alvarez 55, Frank Catalanotto 3, Billy Ripken 2.
Shortstop: Deivi Cruz 135, Damion Easley 30, Billy Ripken 21, Jason Wood 1.
Outfield: Bob Higginson 153, Brian L. Hunter 139, Luis Gonzalez 132, Juan Encarnacion 39, Kimera Bartee 29, Gabe Kapler 6, Andy Tomberlin 5, Trey Beamon 4, Geronimo Berroa 4, Bip Roberts 2, Pete Incaviglia 1, Jeff Manto 1, Joe Siddall 1.
Designated hitter: Geronimo Berroa 37, Bip Roberts 29, Frank Catalanotto 22, Andy Tomberlin 21, Luis Gonzalez 19, Tony Clark 15, Trey Beamon 11, Kimera Bartee 10, Jeff Manto 6, Pete Incaviglia 4, Jason Wood 3, Gabe Alvarez 2, Damion Easley 2, Robert Fick 2, Bob Higginson 2, Juan Encarnacion 1, Gabe Kapler 1, Joe Oliver 1, Joe Randa 1, Billy Ripken 1.

TOP DRAFT CHOICES

1a. **Jeff Weaver**, RHP, Fresno State Univ.
1b. **Nate Cornejo**, RHP, Wellington (Kan.) H.S.
2a. **Brandon Inge**, SS-RHP, Virginia Commonwealth Univ.
2b. **Adam Pettyjohn**, LHP, Fresno St. U.
3. **Tommy Marx**, LHP, Brother Rice H.S., W. Bloomfield, Mich.
4. **Andres Torres**, OF, Miami-Dade C.C. North
5. **Greg Peterson**, RHP-OF, St. John's U.
6. **Bobby Sismondo**, LHP, Ohio Univ.
7. **Clint Smith**, RHP, U. of Oklahoma
8. **Barry Tolli**, OF, Newbury Park H.S., Thousand Oaks, Calif.
9. **Donny Sevieri**, OF, El Dorado H.S., Albuquerque, N.M.
10. **Billy Rich**, OF, U. of Connecticut

KANSAS CITY ROYALS
AMERICAN LEAGUE CENTRAL DIVISION

1999 Royals Schedule
Home games shaded. *—All-Star Game at Fenway Park (Boston).
D—Day game (any game starting before 5 p.m.).

April
SUN	MON	TUE	WED	THU	FRI	SAT
				1	2	3
4	5 D BOS	6	7 BOS	8 BOS	9 D CWS	10 D CWS
11 CWS	12 D CLE	13	14 CLE	15 CLE	16 D CWS	17 D CWS
18 CWS	19 D MIN	20 MIN	21 MIN	22	23 ANA	24 D ANA
25 D ANA	26	27 BAL	28 BAL	29 BAL	30 NYY	

May
SUN	MON	TUE	WED	THU	FRI	SAT
						1 NYY
2 NYY	3 D NYY	4 TB	5 TB	6 TB	7 D MIN	8 MIN
9 MIN	10 D MIN	11 TOR	12 TOR	13 D TOR	14 SEA	15 SEA
16 D SEA	17	18 OAK	19 OAK	20 OAK	21 SEA	22 SEA
23 SEA	24 OAK	25 OAK	26 D OAK	27 D ANA	28 ANA	29 ANA
30 ANA	31 TEX					

June
SUN	MON	TUE	WED	THU	FRI	SAT
		1 TEX	2 D TEX	3	4 CIN	5 CIN
6 CIN	7 D STL	8 STL	9 STL	10	11 PIT	12 PIT
13 D PIT	14 BAL	15 BAL	16 D BAL	17	18 TOR	19 D TOR
20 D TOR	21 TOR	22 DET	23 DET	24 D DET	25 D CLE	26 CLE
27 D CLE	28 CLE	29 CWS	30 CWS			

July
SUN	MON	TUE	WED	THU	FRI	SAT
				1 CWS	2 CLE	3 D CLE
4 D CLE	5	6 CWS	7 D CWS	8 D HOU	9 HOU	10 HOU
11 HOU	12	13	14 *	15 MIL	16 MIL	17 MIL
18 CUB	19 D CUB	20 CUB	21 DET	22 DET	23 D OAK	24 OAK
25 D OAK	26	27 SEA	28 SEA	29 D SEA	30 TEX	31 TEX

August
SUN	MON	TUE	WED	THU	FRI	SAT
1 TEX	2 ANA	3 ANA	4 ANA	5	6 D MIN	7 MIN
8 MIN	9 BOS	10 BOS	11 D TB	12 TB	13 TB	14 TB
15 D TB	16	17 NYY	18 NYY	19 D NYY	20 TB	21 TB
22 D TB	23 BAL	24 BAL	25 BAL	26 BAL	27 MIN	28 MIN
29 D MIN	30 BOS	31 BOS				

September
SUN	MON	TUE	WED	THU	FRI	SAT
			1 BOS	2 BOS	3 D TOR	4 TOR
5 D TOR	6	7 NYY	8 NYY	9	10 TEX	11 TEX
12 TEX	13 TEX	14 ANA	15 ANA	16 ANA	17 OAK	18 D OAK
19 OAK	20 SEA	21 SEA	22	23 DET	24 DET	25 DET
26 DET	27 D DET	28 D CLE	29 CLE	30		

October
SUN	MON	TUE	WED	THU	FRI	SAT
					1 DET	2 DET
3 D DET	4	5	6	7	8	9

1999 SEASON
CLUB DIRECTORY

Board of directors
David Glass
Richard Green
Mike Herman
Julia I. Kauffman
Janice Kreamer
Louis Smith
Joseph McGuff
Chairman of the board & CEO
David Glass
President
Mike Herman
Exec. v.p. and general manager
Spencer (Herk) Robinson
Sr. v.p., business operations & admin.
Art Chaudry
Vice president, baseball operations
George Brett
V.p., development and administration
Lloyd Arnsmeyer
Vice president and asst. general manager
Allard Baird
V.p., marketing and communications
Mike Levy
Vice president, finance
Dale Rohr
Sr. special assistant to g.m.
Art Stewart
Assistant g.m., baseball administration
Jay Hinrichs
Senior director, communications
Jim Lachimia
Senior director, scouting
Terry Wetzel
Senior director, minor league operations
Bob Hegman
Senior director, stadium administration
John Johnson
Director, media relations
Steve Fink
Director, team travel
David Witty
Director, marketing
Tonya Mangels
Director, corporate sponsorships
Vernice Givens
Director, stadium operations
Rodney Lewallen
Director, event operations
John Walker

Director, season ticket services
Joe Grigoli
Senior director/controller
John Luther
Director, payroll and benefit accounting
Tom Pfannenstiel
Director, group sales
Michelle Kammerer
Director, Lancer program
Larry Sherrard
Director, information systems
Jim Edwards
Dir., groundskeeping and landscaping
Trevor Vance
Assistant director, player personnel
Dan Glass
Equipment manager
Mike Burkhalter
Team physician
Dr. Steve Joyce
Trainer
Nick Swartz
Assistant trainer
Lee Kuntz
Major league scouts
Gary Blaylock
Gail Henley
Dick Wiencek
Advance scout
Ron Clark
National crosschecker
Steve Flores
Regional crosscheckers
Carl Blando, Pat Jones, Jeff McKay
Territorial scouts
Frank Baez, Paul Baretta, Bob Bishop,
Monte Bothwell, Jason Bryans, Balos
Davis, Paul Faulk, Albert Gonzalez, Dave
Herrera, Keith Hughes, Gary Johnson,
Mike Lee, Cliff Pastornicky, Bill Price,
Johnny Ramos, Wil Rutenschroer, Chet
Sergo, Greg Smith, Gerald Turner,
Dennis Woody
International special assignment scout
Carlos Pascual
Latin American scouting supervisor
Luis Silverio
Canadian scouting supervisor
Jason Bryans

MINOR LEAGUE AFFILIATES

Class	Team	League	Manager
AAA	Omaha	Pacific Coast	Ron Johnson
AA	Wichita	Texas	John Mizerock
A	Wilmington	Carolina	To be announced
A	Charleston (WV)	Midwest	Tom Paquette
A	Spokane	Northwest	Jeff Garber
Rookie	Gulf Coast Royals	Gulf Coast	Andre David

BROADCAST INFORMATION

Radio: KMBZ-AM (980).
TV: KMBC (Channel 9), KCWB
(Channel 29).
Cable TV: Fox Sports Midwest.

SPRING TRAINING

Ballpark (city): Baseball City Stadium
(Davenport, Fla.).
Ticket information: 941-424-2500,
407-839-3900.

SPRING TRAINING ROSTER

Manager—Tony Muser (40).
Coaches—Tom Burgmeier (39), Rich Dauer, Lamar Johnson, Jamie Quirk (9), Frank White (20), Mark Wiley.

No.	PITCHERS	B/T	Ht./Wt.	Born	1998 clubs
17	Appier, Kevin	R/R	6-2/200	12-6-67	Gulf Coast Royals, Lansing, Wichita, Omaha, Kansas City
44	Barber, Brian	R/R	6-1/190	3-4-73	Omaha, Kansas City
58	Byrdak, Tim	L/L	5-11/160	10-31-73	Omaha, Wichita, Kansas City
45	Evans, Bart	R/R	6-2/210	12-30-70	Omaha, Kansas City
21	Montgomery, Jeff	R/R	5-11/175	1-7-62	Kansas City
	Moreno, Orber	R/R	6-2/190	4-27-77	Wichita, Wilmington
52	Morman, Alvin	L/L	6-3/210	1-6-69	Cleveland, Buffalo, San Francisco, Fresno
	Mullen, Scott	R/L	6-2/190	1-17-75	Wichita, Wilmington
35	Pichardo, Hipolito	R/R	6-1/195	8-22-69	Kansas City, Lansing
34	Pittsley, Jim	R/R	6-7/220	4-3-74	Kansas City
61	Ray, Ken	R/R	6-2/200	1-27-74	Wichita
50	Rosado, Jose	L/L	6-0/185	11-9-74	Kansas City
53	Rusch, Glendon	L/L	6-1/195	11-7-74	Kansas City, Omaha
49	Santiago, Jose	R/R	6-3/215	11-5-74	Wichita, Kansas City, Omaha
48	Service, Scott	R/R	6-6/230	2-26-67	Kansas City
37	Suppan, Jeff	R/R	6-2/210	1-2-75	Arizona, Tucson, Kansas City
31	Veras, Dario	R/R	6-1/155	3-13-73	Las Vegas, Pawtucket, Boston
56	Whisenant, Matt	R/L	6-3/215	6-8-71	Kansas City

No.	CATCHERS	B/T	Ht./Wt.	Born	1998 clubs
26	Fasano, Sal	R/R	6-2/220	8-10-71	Kansas City, Omaha
	Kreuter, Chad	B/R	6-2/200	8-26-64	Chicago A.L., Anaheim
	Sweeney, Mike	R/R	6-2/215	7-22-73	Kansas City

No.	INFIELDERS	B/T	Ht./Wt.	Born	1998 clubs
43	Febles, Carlos	R/R	5-11/170	5-24-76	Wichita, Kansas City
4	Halter, Shane	R/R	6-0/180	11-8-69	Kansas City, Omaha
2	Hansen, Jed	R/R	6-1/195	8-19-72	Kansas City, Omaha
7	King, Jeff	R/R	6-1/188	12-26-64	Kansas City
32	Lopez, Mendy	R/R	6-2/190	10-15-74	Omaha, Kansas City
19	Randa, Joe	R/R	5-11/190	12-18-69	Detroit
	Sanchez, Rey	R/R	5-9/170	10-5-67	San Francisco
22	Sutton, Larry	L/L	6-0/185	5-14-70	Kansas City

No.	OUTFIELDERS	B/T	Ht./Wt.	Born	1998 clubs
36	Beltran, Carlos	B/R	6-0/175	4-24-77	Wichita, Kansas City, Wilmington
27	Brown, Dermal	L/R	5-11/210	3-27-78	Kansas City, Wilmington
19	Conine, Jeff	R/R	6-1/220	6-27-66	Kansas City, Omaha
18	Damon, Johnny	L/L	6-2/190	11-5-73	Kansas City
24	Dye, Jermaine	R/R	6-4/210	1-28-74	Omaha, Kansas City
15	Giambi, Jeremy	L/L	6-0/185	9-30-74	Kansas City
62	Quinn, Mark	R/R	6-1/175	5-21-74	Wichita

BALLPARK INFORMATION

Ballpark (capacity, surface)
Kauffman Stadium (40,625, grass)

Address
P.O. Box 419969
Kansas City, MO 64141-6969

Business phone
816-921-8000

Ticket information
816-921-8000

Ticket prices
$17 (club box)
$15 (field box)
$13 (plaza reserved)
$12 (view upper box)
$11 (view upper reserved)
$7 (general admission)
$5.50 (Royal nights)

Field dimensions (from home plate)
To left field at foul line, 330 feet
To center field, 400 feet
To right field at foul line, 330 feet

First game played
April 10, 1973 (Royals 12, Rangers 1)

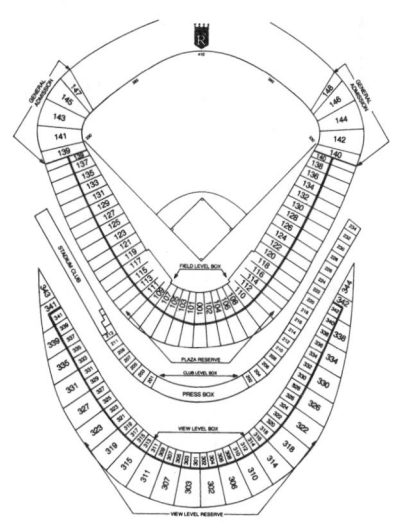

1998 REVIEW
DAY BY DAY

Date	Opp.	Res.	Score	(inn.*)	Hits	Opp. hits	Winning pitcher	Losing pitcher	Save	Record	Pos.	GB
3-31	At Bal.	W	4-1		8	5	Belcher	Mussina	Montgomery	1-0	T1st	...
4-1	At Bal.	L	1-10		4	11	Erickson	Rusch		1-1	T3rd	1.0
4-2	At Bal.	L	3-4		9	5	Benitez	Montgomery		1-2	T4th	1.5
4-3	At Min.	W	9-5		15	10	Haney	Radke		2-2	3rd	1.5
4-4	At Min.	W	3-2	(10)	13	4	Bevil	Guardado	Montgomery	3-2	2nd	1.5
4-5	At Min.	L	1-10		7	14	Milton	Belcher		3-3	2nd	2.5
4-7	Bal.	L	7-11		12	16	Erickson	Rusch		3-4	4th	3.0
4-9	Bal.	L	1-2		9	7	Key	Rosado	Benitez	3-5	4th	3.5
4-10	Min.	W	5-4		13	7	Bevil	Aguilera		4-5	T3rd	3.5
4-11	Min.	L	3-8		8	10	Milton	Belcher		4-6	4th	4.5
4-12	Min.	L	2-7		8	12	Tewksbury	Pichardo	Aguilera	4-7	4th	4.5
4-13	Tor.	W	11-1		14	8	Rusch	Hentgen		5-7	3rd	4.5
4-14	Tor.	L	1-5		5	7	Guzman	Rapp	Quantrill	5-8	3rd	5.5
4-15	Tor.	W	7-3		14	7	Haney	Williams		6-8	3rd	4.5
4-16	At Oak.	L	7-12		9	14	Candiotti	Belcher		6-9	4th	5.0
4-17	At Oak.	W	4-1	(12)	13	7	Service	Dougherty	Montgomery	7-9	3rd	4.0
4-18	At Oak.	L	2-3		7	6	Rogers	Rusch	Taylor	7-10	3rd	5.0
4-19	At Oak.	W	7-3		15	10	Rapp	Prieto	Rosado	8-10	2nd	4.0
4-20	At Sea.	L	7-8		12	12	Lira	Rios	Ayala	8-11	2nd	4.0
4-21	At Sea.	W	5-3		10	9	Bevil	Fossas	Montgomery	9-11	2nd	4.0
4-22	At Sea.	L	5-11		8	17	Fassero	Pichardo		9-12	2nd	4.0
4-24	Tex.	W	11-4		12	12	Rusch	Burkett		10-12	2nd	3.5
4-25	Tex.	L	8-11		12	14	Witt	Rapp	Wetteland	10-13	2nd	3.5
4-26	Tex.	L	4-11		9	15	Sele	Haney		10-14	3rd	4.0
4-28	Sea.	L	1-5		6	7	Johnson	Service		10-15	T2nd	4.5
4-29	At Tor.	W	7-2		12	7	Pichardo	Hentgen		11-15	T2nd	3.5
4-30	At Tor.	W	7-4		11	9	Rusch	Guzman	Montgomery	12-15	2nd	2.5
5-1	N.Y.	L	1-2		2	6	Irabu	Rapp	Rivera	12-16	2nd	3.5
5-2	N.Y.	L	6-12		12	14	Pettitte	Haney		12-17	T2nd	4.5
5-3	N.Y.	L	1-10		4	13	Mendoza	Belcher		12-18	T2nd	5.5
5-5	T.B.	W	4-2		11	8	Pichardo	Alvarez	Montgomery	13-18	2nd	5.5
5-6	T.B.	L	0-5		3	12	Arrojo	Rusch		13-19	T2nd	6.5
5-7	Bos.	W	5-3		5	10	Rapp	Rose	Montgomery	14-19	2nd	6.5
5-8	Bos.	L	3-14		8	20	Saberhagen	Haney	Garces	14-20	2nd	6.5
5-9	Bos.	L	1-3		5	10	Martinez	Belcher	Gordon	14-21	3rd	6.5
5-10	Bos.	L	1-3		2	5	Wakefield	Rosado	Gordon	14-22	4th	6.5
5-12	At N.Y.	L	2-3		5	4	Wells	Rusch	Rivera	14-23	4th	6.0
5-13	At T.B.	W	4-0		9	4	Rapp	Saunders		15-23	4th	5.0
5-14	At T.B.	W	10-2		12	10	Belcher	Springer		16-23	4th	5.0
5-15	At Bos.	L	2-5		9	8	Wakefield	Rosado	Eckersley	16-24	4th	6.0
5-16	At Bos.	L	0-5		4	10	Avery	Walker	Gordon	16-25	4th	7.0
5-17	At Bos.	L	3-5		10	9	Mahay	Rusch	Gordon	16-26	4th	7.0
5-19	Cle.	L	3-16		7	20	Ogea	Rapp		16-27	5th	8.0
5-20	Cle.	L	5-14		13	16	Nagy	Belcher		16-28	5th	9.0
5-21	Cle.	L	2-6		6	11	Wright	Rosado		16-29	5th	10.0
5-22	At Tex.	L	10-13		15	13	Wetteland	Montgomery		16-30	5th	11.0
5-23	At Tex.	L	3-7		8	10	Sele	Rusch		16-31	5th	11.0
5-24	At Tex.	W	8-3		11	11	Rapp	Helling	Pichardo	17-31	5th	10.0
5-25	At Ana.	W	6-4		8	7	Belcher	Hill	Montgomery	18-31	5th	10.0
5-27	At Ana.	W	4-0		5	5	Rosado	Olivares		19-31	5th	10.0
5-29	Oak.	W	5-3		9	6	Haney	Mohler	Montgomery	20-31	5th	10.5
5-30	Oak.	L	4-10		10	14	Taylor	Pichardo		20-32	5th	10.5
5-31	Oak.	W	10-4		16	9	Belcher	Mathews		21-32	5th	10.5
6-1	Ana.	L	3-6		8	13	Hasegawa	Pichardo	Percival	21-33	5th	11.5
6-2	Ana.	L	5-7		5	11	Washburn	Haney	Percival	21-34	5th	12.5
6-3	Chi.	L	5-10		8	15	C. Castillo	Rapp		21-35	5th	12.5
6-4	Chi.	L	1-7		8	12	Navarro	Rusch		21-36	5th	13.5
6-5	At Hou.	W	3-0		6	8	Belcher	Schourek	Montgomery	22-36	4th	12.5
6-6	At Hou.	L	0-6		5	9	Lima	Rosado		22-37	5th	13.5
6-7	At Hou.	L	1-7		8	11	Reynolds	Pittsley		22-38	5th	14.5
6-8	Mil.	W	8-7		10	17	Rapp	Juden	Montgomery	23-38	5th	14.5
6-9	Mil.	L	3-6	(10)	13	8	Wickman	Montgomery	Jones	23-39	5th	14.5
6-10	Mil.	L	6-9	(15)	16	11	Patrick	Pichardo		23-40	5th	14.5
6-12	Det.	W	7-3		10	10	Rosado	Florie		24-40	4th	14.0
6-13	Det.	L	1-7		5	14	Thompson	Rapp		24-41	5th	14.5
6-14	Det.	W	2-0		5	7	Rusch	Greisinger		25-41	4th	13.5
6-15	At Cle.	W	7-6	(10)	13	16	Montgomery	Mesa	Whisenant	26-41	4th	12.5
6-16	At Cle.	L	1-9		6	10	Colon	Pichardo		26-42	4th	13.5
6-17	At Cle.	W	4-3		10	9	Rosado	Gooden	Montgomery	27-42	4th	12.5
6-18	At Det.	W	5-3		12	12	Rapp	Thompson	Montgomery	28-42	T3rd	11.5
6-19	At Det.	W	8-4		11	11	Rusch	Greisinger	Bones	29-42	3rd	11.5

Date	Opp.	Res.	Score	(inn.*)	Hits	Opp. hits	Winning pitcher	Losing pitcher	Save	Record	Pos.	GB
6-20	At Det.	L	3-4		10	10	Moehler	Belcher	Jones	29-43	T3rd	11.5
6-21	At Det.	W	6-5		7	8	Pichardo	Harriger	Montgomery	30-43	3rd	11.5
6-22	At Cin.	W	3-0		7	8	Pittsley	Remlinger	Montgomery	31-43	3rd	11.5
6-23	At Cin.	W	6-4		11	10	Rapp	Klingenbeck	Service	32-43	3rd	11.5
6-24	Pit.	L	3-10		10	19	Peters	Rusch		32-44	T3rd	12.5
6-25	Pit.	W	6-1		10	4	Belcher	Lieber		33-44	3rd	12.5
6-26	Chi. (NL)	W	6-3		10	8	Pichardo	Trachsel	Montgomery	34-44	3rd	12.5
6-27	Chi. (NL)	W	4-3	(10)	13	8	Service	Beck		35-44	3rd	11.5
6-28	Chi. (NL)	L	3-6		11	8	Gonzalez	Rapp	Beck	35-45	3rd	11.5
6-30	At St.L.	W	6-1		9	7	Rusch	Aybar	Service	36-45	3rd	10.5
7-1	At St.L.	W	6-4		12	7	Belcher	Mercker	Montgomery	37-45	3rd	10.5
7-2	At St.L.	L	0-3		7	5	Acevedo	Pichardo	Brantley	37-46	3rd	11.5
7-3	Cle.	L	1-2		6	2	Shuey	Rosado	Jackson	37-47	3rd	12.5
7-4	Cle.	W	5-3		12	9	Rapp	Nagy	Montgomery	38-47	3rd	11.5
7-5	Cle.	L	3-12		6	14	Wright	Rusch		38-48	3rd	12.5
7-9	At Chi.	W	6-4		12	7	Belcher	Sirotka	Montgomery	39-48	3rd	11.5
7-10	At Chi.	L	3-10		8	15	Navarro	Rosado		39-49	3rd	12.5
7-11	At Chi.	L	3-4		9	7	Baldwin	Rapp	Karchner	39-50	3rd	13.5
7-12	At Chi.	W	4-3		13	6	Service	Karchner	Montgomery	40-50	3rd	12.5
7-13	At Det.	W	6-4	(10)	9	6	Whisenant	Jones	Montgomery	41-50	3rd	12.5
7-14	At Det.	L	3-8		10	12	Thompson	Belcher		41-51	3rd	12.5
7-15	At Oak.	W	5-1		9	3	Rosado	Candiotti		42-51	T2nd	11.5
7-16	At Oak.	L	3-5		6	7	Stein	Rapp	Taylor	42-52	T2nd	11.5
7-17	At Sea.	L	5-18		8	22	Swift	Rusch		42-53	3rd	11.5
7-18	At Sea.	L	5-8		5	14	Ayala	Service		42-54	3rd	12.5
7-19	At Sea.	W	4-1		8	5	Belcher	Fassero	Montgomery	43-54	3rd	11.5
7-21	Tex.	L	5-15		7	16	Helling	Rosado		43-55	4th	12.5
7-22	Tex.	W	7-4		12	8	Rapp	Sele	Montgomery	44-55	3rd	12.5
7-23	Tex.	L	4-8		12	18	Hernandez	Rusch		44-56	3rd	12.5
7-24	Ana.	W	4-3		6	8	Pichardo	Finley	Montgomery	45-56	3rd	12.5
7-25	Ana.	L	5-6		8	11	Harris	Belcher	Holtz	45-57	3rd	13.5
7-26	Ana.	W	9-4		13	13	Rosado	Olivares		46-57	3rd	12.5
7-27	Ana.	L	1-6		4	9	Watson	Rapp	Hasegawa	46-58	3rd	13.0
7-28	Min.	L	0-3		4	6	Radke	Rusch	Aguilera	46-59	T3rd	14.0
7-29	Min.	L	3-5		4	8	Milton	Pichardo	Aguilera	46-60	T3rd	15.0
7-30	Min.	W	7-3		14	6	Belcher	Serafini		47-60	3rd	15.0
7-31	Bal.	W	9-6		15	7	Rosado	Erickson		48-60	3rd	14.0
8-1	Bal.	W	9-5		9	5	Haney	Kamieniecki		49-60	3rd	13.0
8-2	Bal.	L	2-9		8	16	Ponson	Rusch		49-61	3rd	13.0
8-4	At Min.	W	12-4		16	10	Pichardo	Milton		50-61	3rd	11.5
8-5	At Min.	W	4-3		7	6	Belcher	Rodriguez	Montgomery	51-61	3rd	11.5
8-6	At Min.	W	8-7		11	12	Service	Aguilera	Montgomery	52-61	2nd	11.0
8-7§	At N.Y.	L	2-8		8	12	Cone	Rapp		52-62		
8-7§	At N.Y.	L	2-14		6	18	Wells	Haney		52-63	2nd	12.5
8-8	At N.Y.	L	1-14		4	15	Hernandez	Rusch		52-64	3rd	13.5
8-9	At N.Y.	L	4-5		8	8	Mendoza	Service	Rivera	52-65	3rd	13.5
8-11	At Bos.	L	4-7	(10)	9	13	Gordon	Montgomery		52-66	4th	13.5
8-12	At Bos.	W	8-4		16	5	Service	Swindell		53-66	3rd	13.5
8-13	T.B.	W	6-4	(10)	11	12	Montgomery	Hernandez		54-66	2nd	12.5
8-14	T.B.	W	11-9		13	12	Haney	Arrojo	Service	55-66	2nd	11.5
8-15	T.B.	L	6-8	(11)	13	13	Mecir	Bones	Hernandez	55-67	2nd	11.5
8-16	T.B.	L	3-8		7	13	Santana	Belcher		55-68	3rd	12.5
8-17	N.Y.	L	1-7		6	10	Cone	Rosado		55-69	3rd	13.5
8-18	N.Y.	L	2-3	(13)	8	11	Borowski	Whisenant		55-70	3rd	14.5
8-19	Bos.	L	1-11		5	14	Wakefield	Barber		55-71	4th	14.5
8-20	Bos.	W	8-2		12	5	Pichardo	Schourek		56-71	4th	13.5
8-21	At T.B.	W	6-5	(11)	9	14	Whisenant	Yan	Montgomery	57-71	2nd	13.5
8-22	At T.B.	W	3-2		7	4	Rosado	Alvarez	Montgomery	58-71	2nd	12.5
8-23	At T.B.	W	11-5		13	11	Rapp	Rekar		59-71	2nd	12.5
8-24	At Tor.	W	7-3		13	7	Barber	Hentgen	Whisenant	60-71	2nd	12.0
8-25	At Tor.	L	0-3		3	6	Clemens	Haney		60-72	2nd	13.0
8-26	At Tor.	W	7-2		15	3	Belcher	Carpenter		61-72	2nd	13.0
8-27	At Tor.	L	1-11		7	15	Escobar	Rosado		61-73	2nd	13.0
8-28	At Bal.	W	6-5		10	9	Rapp	Ponson	Montgomery	62-73	2nd	12.0
8-29	At Bal.	W	2-1		8	3	Barber	Mussina	Montgomery	63-73	2nd	11.0
8-30	At Bal.	W	3-2		6	6	Haney	Guzman	Montgomery	64-73	2nd	11.0
9-1	Tor.	L	1-2		5	10	Carpenter	Belcher	Quantrill	64-74	2nd	12.5
9-2	Tor.	L	0-5		4	5	Escobar	Rosado	Quantrill	64-75	T2nd	12.5
9-4	At Ana.	W	5-3		11	8	Bones	Holtz	Montgomery	65-75	2nd	13.0
9-5	At Ana.	L	1-2		6	9	McDowell	Barber	DeLucia	65-76	T2nd	14.0
9-6	At Ana.	L	0-3		3	7	Finley	Belcher	Hasegawa	65-77	3rd	14.0
9-8	At Tex.	L	6-7		15	14	Patterson	Montgomery		65-78	3rd	14.0
9-9	At Tex.	L	0-8		6	15	Sele	Rapp		65-79	3rd	15.0
9-11†	Sea.	L	3-6		5	10	Fassero	Barber	Timlin	65-80		
9-11‡	Sea.	W	8-5		13	8	Appier	Swift	Rusch	66-80	3rd	14.5
9-12	Sea.	W	5-2		8	5	Belcher	Moyer	Montgomery	67-80	3rd	13.5

Date	Opp.	Res.	Score	(inn.*) Hits	Opp. hits	Winning pitcher	Losing pitcher	Save	Record	Pos.	GB
9-14	Oak.	W	16-6	19	10	Bones	Stein	Service	68-80	3rd	14.0
9-15	Oak.	W	6-3	9	6	Rapp	Rogers	Montgomery	69-80	3rd	14.0
9-16	At Chi.	L	4-9	6	12	J. Abbott	Bevil		69-81	3rd	15.0
9-17	At Chi.	W	13-4	16	11	Belcher	Baldwin		70-81	3rd	15.0
9-18	At Cle.	L	1-4	6	6	Wright	Appier	Shuey	70-82	3rd	16.0
9-19	At Cle.	W	7-6	15	6	Service	Shuey	Montgomery	71-82	3rd	15.0
9-20	At Cle.	L	3-5	12	8	Colon	Rapp	Jackson	71-83	3rd	16.0
9-21	Det.	L	5-7	10	11	Crow	Service	Jones	71-84	3rd	17.0
9-22	Det.	L	4-14	6	18	Thompson	Belcher	Castillo	71-85	3rd	16.5
9-23	Det.	L	1-5	4	11	Florie	Appier		71-86	3rd	16.5
9-24	Chi.	W	6-4	11	7	Rosado	Navarro	Montgomery	72-86	3rd	15.5
9-25	Chi.	L	0-3	4	9	Sirotka	Bones	Howry	72-87	3rd	15.5
9-26	Chi.	L	5-13	11	15	J. Abbott	Barber		72-88	3rd	16.5
9-27	Chi.	L	6-7	6	9	Baldwin	Belcher	Howry	72-89	3rd	16.5

Monthly records: March (1-0), April (11-15), May (9-17), June (15-13), July (12-15), August (16-13), September (8-16).
*Innings, if other than nine. †First game of doubleheader. ‡Second game of doubleheader. §Two games in one day (separate admissions).

HIGHLIGHTS

High point: On August 30, the Royals completed a sweep of Baltimore at Camden Yards to finish a 9-of-11 stretch that pulled them within nine games of .500.

Low point: After a June 2 brawl during a game against Anaheim, shortstop Felix Martinez was sent packing to Class AAA for sucker-punching an Angels player and manager Tony Muser was relegated to watching his team from a TV van in the parking lot while serving an eight-game suspension.

Turning point: The brawl was the closest thing to a turning point. Two days into Muser's suspension, the Royals woke up and strung together 15 victories in their final 23 games before the All-Star break.

Most valuable player: Dean Palmer provided a consistent buzz with his power, hitting 34 home runs and finishing with a career-high 119 RBIs. He even swiped eight bases in 10 attempts and earned his first trip to the All-Star Game.

Most valuable pitcher: Closer Jeff Montgomery got back to pre-arm surgery form with 36 saves. It was the fifth time in his 11-year career that he recorded 30 or more in a season.

Most improved player: At age 31, Scott Service enjoyed his first full big-league season and he didn't just occupy space. Service was reliable as a setup man from the right side, recording 19 holds with a 6-4 record and four saves in 73 appearances.

Most pleasant surprise: Second baseman Jose Offerman had the best offensive season of his career while hitting in four different spots and was a close second to Palmer in the team MVP sweepstakes. Offerman led the A.L. in triples (13) and ranked high in numerous offensive categories while batting .315.

Biggest disappointments: Although solid and versatile in the outfield when he did play, veteran Jeff Conine wasn't around enough to be a factor on offense, where he was really needed.

Key injuries: The biggest setback was Kevin Appier's March shoulder injury that held him out of the rotation until September. Conine had two stints on the D.L. that limited him to 93 games. Jermaine Dye struggled with various injuries, including a strained quadriceps that forced him to start his season at Class AAA.

Notable: Offerman had a 27-game hitting streak. . . . Johnny Damon hit 18 homers in 1998, more than his three previous seasons combined. He was also one of six A.L. players to appear in all of his team's games. . . . Tim Belcher's 14 wins led the team for the third straight season. . . . Kansas City went 0-10 against the Yankees. . . . The Royals' 43-38 road record was one of the best in the majors. Their 29-51 home record was the worst.

—LUCIANA CHAVEZ

RECORDS

1998 regular-season record: 72-89 (3rd in A.L. Central); 29-51 at home; 43-38 on road; 23-31 vs. East; 21-27 vs. A.L. Central; 19-24 vs. West; 9-7 vs. N.L.; 19-30 vs. lefthanded starters; 53-59 vs. righthanded starters; 53-80 on grass; 19-9 on turf; 18-23 in daytime; 54-66 at night; 17-16 in one-run games; 7-5 in extra-inning games; 0-0-1 in doubleheaders.

Team record past five years: 348-394 (.469, ranks 9th in league in that span).

TEAM LEADERS

Batting average: Jose Offerman (.315).
At-bats: Johnny Damon (642).
Runs: Johnny Damon (104).
Hits: Jose Offerman (191).
Total bases: Dean Palmer (292).
Doubles: Johnny Damon (30).
Triples: Jose Offerman (13).
Home runs: Dean Palmer (34).
Runs batted in: Dean Palmer (119).
Stolen bases: Jose Offerman (45).
Slugging percentage: Dean Palmer (.510).
On-base percentage: Jose Offerman (.403).
Wins: Tim Belcher (14).
Earned-run average: Tim Belcher (4.27).
Complete games: Tim Belcher, Jose Rosado (2).
Shutouts: Pat Rapp, Jose Rosado, Glendon Rusch (1).
Saves: Jeff Montgomery (36).
Innings pitched: Tim Belcher (234.0).
Strikeouts: Jose Rosado (135).

GAMES BY POSITION

Catcher: Mike Sweeney 91, Sal Fasano 70, Tim Spehr 11, Chris Turner 4, Mike Macfarlane 3, Hector Ortiz 3.
First base: Jeff King 112, Hal Morris 46, Jeff Conine 12, Larry Sutton 6, Sal Fasano 5, Shane Halter 1, Hector Ortiz 1.
Second base: Jose Offerman 152, Carlos Febles 11, Shane Halter 7, Luis Rivera 6, Jed Hansen 2, Felix Martinez 2.
Third base: Dean Palmer 129, Terry Pendleton 23, Scott Leius 15, Shane Halter 8, Luis Rivera 6, Jeff King 4, Mendy Lopez 2, Sal Fasano 1.
Shortstop: Mendy Lopez 72, Shane Halter 66, Felix Martinez 32, Luis Rivera 30, Scott Leius 2.
Outfield: Johnny Damon 158, Jeff Conine 80, Larry Sutton 79, Jermaine Dye 59, Hal Morris 39, Shane Mack 32, Jermaine Allensworth 27, Ernie Young 24, Carlos Beltran 14, Jeremy Giambi 9, Shane Halter 9, Chris Hatcher 5, Dermal Brown 2.
Designated hitter: Terry Pendleton 40, Hal Morris 39, Dean Palmer 22, Shane Mack 21, Jeff King 16, Jeremy Giambi 7, Jose Offerman 6, Dermal Brown 3, Jeff Conine 3, Larry Sutton 3, Joe Vitiello 2, Scott Leius 1.

TOP DRAFT CHOICES

1a. **Jeff Austin**, RHP, Stanford University
1b. **Matt Burch**, RHP, Va. Commonwealth
1c. **Chris George**, LHP, Klein (Tex.) H.S.
2. **Robbie Morrison**, RHP, U. of Maine
3. **Ben Cordova**, OF, Marian Catholic H.S., Chula Vista, Calif.
4. **Monty Ward**, RHP, Texas Tech
5. **Scott Chiasson**, RHP, Eastern Connecticut State U.
6. **Mike Curry**, OF, U. of South Carolina
7. **Jeremy Dodson**, OF, Baylor University
8. **Norris Hopper**, SS, Shelby (N.C.) H.S.
9. **Paul Phillips**, OF, U. of Alabama
10. **Jeremy Jackson**, LHP, Miss. St. U.

MINNESOTA TWINS
AMERICAN LEAGUE CENTRAL DIVISION

1999 Twins Schedule

Home games shaded. *—All-Star Game at Fenway Park (Boston).
D—Day game (any game starting before 5 p.m.).

April

SUN	MON	TUE	WED	THU	FRI	SAT
				1	2	3
4	5	6 TOR	7 TOR	8 TOR	9 CLE	10 CLE
11 D CLE	12 D DET	13	14 DET	15 DET	16 CLE	17 D CLE
18 CLE	19 KC	20 KC	21 KC	22 TEX	23 TEX	24 TEX
25 TEX	26 BOS	27 BOS	28 D BOS	29	30 BAL	

May

SUN	MON	TUE	WED	THU	FRI	SAT
						1 BAL
2 D BAL	3	4 NYY	5 NYY	6 D NYY	7 KC	8 KC
9 D KC	10 KC	11 TB	12 D TB	13	14 OAK	15 D OAK
16 D OAK	17	18 SEA	19 SEA	20	21 OAK	22 OAK
23 D OAK	24 SEA	25 SEA	26 D SEA	27	28 TEX	29 TEX
30 D TEX	31 ANA					

June

SUN	MON	TUE	WED	THU	FRI	SAT
		1 ANA	2 ANA	3	4 HOU	5 HOU
6 D HOU	7 CIN	8 CIN	9 CIN	10	11 MIL	12 MIL
13 D MIL	14 BOS	15 BOS	16 BOS	17 BOS	18 TB	19 TB
20 D TB	21 D TB	22 CWS	23 CWS	24 D CWS	25 DET	26 DET
27 D DET	28 D CLE	29 CLE	30 CLE			

July

SUN	MON	TUE	WED	THU	FRI	SAT
				1 CLE	2 DET	3 DET
4 D DET	5	6 CLE	7 CLE	8 CLE	9 PIT	10 PIT
11 D PIT	12	13	14	15 CUB	16 D CUB	17 D CUB
18 D STL	19 STL	20	21 CWS	22 CWS	23 SEA	24 SEA
25 D SEA	26 OAK	27 OAK	28 D OAK	29	30 ANA	31 ANA

August

SUN	MON	TUE	WED	THU	FRI	SAT
1 ANA	2 TEX	3 TEX	4 TEX	5	6 KC	7 KC
8 D KC	9	10 TOR	11 TOR	12 D TOR	13 NYY	14 D NYY
15 D NYY	16	17 BAL	18 BAL	19 D BAL	20 NYY	21 NYY
22 NYY	23 BOS	24 BOS	25 BOS	26	27 KC	28 KC
29 D KC	30 TOR	31 TOR				

September

SUN	MON	TUE	WED	THU	FRI	SAT
			1 TOR	2 TOR	3 TB	4 TB
5 D TB	6 D TB	7 BAL	8 BAL	9 BAL	10 ANA	11 D ANA
12 D ANA	13 ANA	14 TEX	15 TEX	16	17 SEA	18 SEA
19 D SEA	20 OAK	21 OAK	22 D OAK	23	24 CWS	25 CWS
26 D CWS	27 CWS	28 DET	29 DET	30 DET		

October

SUN	MON	TUE	WED	THU	FRI	SAT
					1 CWS	2 CWS
3 D CWS	4	5	6	7	8	9

1999 SEASON
CLUB DIRECTORY

Owner
Carl R. Pohlad

President
Jerry Bell

Chairman of executive committee
Howard Fox

Directors
Carl R. Pohlad
Eloise Pohlad
James O. Pohlad
Robert C. Pohlad
William M. Pohlad
T. Geron (Jerry) Bell
Kirby Puckett
Chris Clouser

Vice president, general manager
Terry Ryan

Vice president, asst. general manager
Bill Smith

Assistant general manager
Wayne Krivsky

Executive vice president, baseball
Kirby Puckett

Vice president, operations
Matt Hoy

Director of minor leagues
Jim Rantz

Director of scouting
Mike Radcliff

Director of baseball operations
Rob Antony

Traveling secretary
Remzi Kiratli

Manager, media relations
Sean Harlin

Club physicians
Dr. Leonard J. Michienzi
Dr. John Steubs

Scouts
Ellsworth Brown
Ray Coley
Gene DeBoer
Cal Ermer
Marty Esposito
Vern Followell (west supervisor)
Earl Frishman (east supervisor)
Scott Groot
Bill Harford
Deron Johnson
John Leavitt
Joel Lepel
Bill Lohr
Greg Miller
Bill Milos
Kevin Murphy
Tim O'Neil
Mark Quimuyog
Clair Rierson
Eddie Robinson
Mike Ruth (midwest supervisor)
Ricky Taylor
Brad Weitzel
John Wilson

International scouts
Enrique Brito
Howard Norsetter
Johnny Sierra

MINOR LEAGUE AFFILIATES

Class	Team	League	Manager
AAA	Salt Lake	Pacific Coast	Phil Roof
AA	New Britain	Eastern	John Russell
A	Fort Myers	Florida State	Mike Boulanger
A	Quad City	Midwest	To be announced
Rookie	Elizabethton	Appalachian	To be announced
Rookie	Gulf Coast Twins	Gulf Coast	To be announced

BROADCAST INFORMATION

Radio: WCCO-AM (830).
TV: WCCO-TV (Channel 4).
Cable TV: Midwest SportsChannel.

SPRING TRAINING

Ballpark (city): Lee County Sports Complex (Fort Myers, Fla.).
Ticket information: 800-338-9467.

SPRING TRAINING ROSTER

Manager—Tom Kelly (10).
Coaches—Ron Gardenhire (35), Rick Stelmaszek (43), Dick Such (44), Scott Ullger (45), Jerry White (13).

No.	PITCHERS	B/T	Ht./Wt.	Born	1998 clubs
38	Aguilera, Rick	R/R	6-5/203	12-31-61	Minnesota
24	Baptist, Travis	L/L	6-0/196	12-30-71	, Minnesota, Salt Lake
58	Carrasco, Hector	R/R	6-2/225	10-22-69	Minnesota
	Espinal, Jose	R/R	6-1/185	8-31-76	Daytona
18	Guardado, Eddie	R/L	6-0/195	10-2-70	Minnesota
32	Hawkins, LaTroy	R/R	6-5/202	12-21-72	Minnesota
46	Kinney, Matt	R/R	6-4/200	12-16-76	Fort Myers, Sarasota
19	Lincoln, Mike	R/R	6-2/211	4-10-75	New Britain
53	Mays, Joe	B/R	6-1/160	10-10-75	New Britain, Fort Myers
20	Miller, Travis	R/L	6-3/211	11-2-72	Salt Lake, Minnesota
41	Milton, Eric	L/L	6-3/200	8-4-75	Minnesota
54	Mota, Danny	R/R	6-0/180	10-9-75	Fort Myers, Fort Wayne
49	Perkins, Dan	R/R	6-2/193	3-15-75	New Britain, Salt Lake
22	Radke, Brad	R/R	6-2/184	10-27-72	Minnesota
55	Redman, Mark	L/L	6-5/220	1-5-74	Salt Lake, New Britain
33	Rodriguez, Frank	R/R	6-0/202	12-11-72	Minnesota, Salt Lake
53	Sampson, Benj	L/L	6-2/210	4-27-75	Minnesota, Salt Lake
16	Serafini, Daniel	B/L	6-1/195	1-25-74	Salt Lake, Minnesota
37	Stentz, Brent	R/R	6-5/224	7-24-75	New Britain
21	Trombley, Mike	R/R	6-2/204	4-14-67	Minnesota

No.	CATCHERS	B/T	Ht./Wt.	Born	1998 clubs
39	Moeller, Chad	R/R	6-3/207	2-18-75	New Britain, Fort Myers
9	Pierzynski, A.J.	L/R	6-3/220	12-30-76	New Britain, Salt Lake, Minnesota
	Steinbach, Terry	R/R	6-1/195	3-2-62	Minnesota
26	Valentin, Javier	B/R	5-10/192	9-19-75	Minnesota

No.	INFIELDERS	B/T	Ht./Wt.	Born	1998 clubs
8	Coomer, Ron	R/R	5-11/210	11-18-66	Minnesota
56	Davidson, Cleatus	B/R	5-10/170	11-1-76	Fort Myers
51	Espada, Josue	R/R	5-10/175	8-30-75	Huntsville
15	Guzman, Cristian	B/R	6-0/150	3-21-78	New Britain
7	Hocking, Denny	B/R	5-10/189	4-2-70	Minnesota
47	Koskie, Corey	L/R	6-3/217	6-28-73	Salt Lake, Minnesota
51	Mientkiewicz, Doug	L/R	6-2/193	6-19-74	Minnesota, New Britain
27	Ortiz, David	L/L	6-4/237	11-18-75	Minnesota, Salt Lake
12	Walker, Todd	L/R	6-0/181	5-25-73	Minnesota

No.	OUTFIELDERS	B/T	Ht./Wt.	Born	1998 clubs
31	Allen, Chad	R/R	6-1/195	2-6-75	New Britain
30	Buchanan, Brian	R/R	6-4/220	7-21-73	Salt Lake
40	Cordova, Marty	R/R	6-0/206	7-10-69	Minnesota
1	Felston, Anthony	L/L	5-9/175	11-26-74	New Britain, Fort Myers
48	Hunter, Torii	R/R	6-2/201	7-18-75	New Britain, Minnesota, Salt Lake
11	Jones, Jacque	L/L	5-10/176	4-25-75	New Britain
28	Latham, Chris	B/R	6-0/195	5-26-73	Salt Lake, Minnesota
50	Lawton, Matt	L/R	5-10/192	11-3-71	Minnesota

BALLPARK INFORMATION

Ballpark (capacity, surface)
Hubert H. Humphrey Metrodome (48,678, artificial)
Address
34 Kirby Puckett Place
Minneapolis, MN 55415
Business phone
612-375-1366
Ticket information
1-800-338-9467
Ticket prices
$19 (VIP level, lower deck club level)
$16 (lower deck club)
$13 (lower deck reserved)
$11 (upper deck club level)
$7 (g.a., lower left field)
$4 (g.a., upper deck)
Field dimensions (from home plate)
To left field at foul line, 343 feet
To center field, 408 feet
To right field at foul line, 327 feet
First game played
April 6, 1982 (Mariners 11, Twins 7)

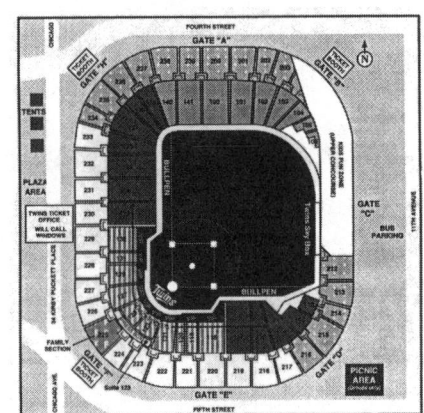

1998 REVIEW
DAY BY DAY

Date	Opp.	Res.	Score	(inn.*)	Hits	Opp. hits	Winning pitcher	Losing pitcher	Save	Record	Pos.	GB
4-1	At Tor.	L	2-3		4	6	Clemens	Tewksbury	Myers	0-1	5th	1.5
4-2	At Tor.	W	3-2		8	3	Guardado	Escobar	Aguilera	1-1	T2nd	1.0
4-3	K.C.	L	5-9		10	15	Haney	Radke		1-2	4th	2.0
4-4	K.C.	L	2-3	(10)	4	13	Bevil	Guardado	Montgomery	1-3	4th	3.0
4-5	K.C.	W	10-1		14	7	Milton	Belcher		2-3	T3rd	3.0
4-7	Tor.	W	12-2		11	3	Tewksbury	Clemens		3-3	T2nd	2.5
4-8	Tor.	L	6-9		10	11	Hentgen	Hawkins	Myers	3-4	T3rd	3.0
4-9	Tor.	W	13-2		13	7	Radke	Guzman		4-4	2nd	2.5
4-10	At K.C.	L	4-5		7	13	Bevil	Aguilera		4-5	T3rd	3.5
4-11	At K.C.	W	8-3		10	8	Milton	Belcher		5-5	2nd	3.5
4-12	At K.C.	W	7-2		12	8	Tewksbury	Pichardo	Aguilera	6-5	2nd	2.5
4-13	At T.B.	L	12-13	(14)	22	19	Yan	Trombley		6-6	2nd	3.5
4-14	At T.B.	W	8-2		12	9	Radke	Springer		7-6	2nd	3.5
4-16	Sea.	L	2-3	(10)	11	10	Timlin	Aguilera	Ayala	7-7	2nd	3.5
4-17	Sea.	L	6-11		10	15	Fassero	Milton		7-8	2nd	3.5
4-18	Sea.	L	3-5		9	12	Cloude	Tewksbury	Ayala	7-9	2nd	4.5
4-19	Sea.	L	4-7		6	13	Swift	Hawkins	Timlin	7-10	3rd	4.5
4-20	At Oak.	L	2-3		10	8	Groom	Swindell	Taylor	7-11	3rd	4.5
4-21	At Oak.	L	4-5	(12)	10	15	Mathews	Carrasco		7-12	3rd	5.5
4-22	At Oak.	W	4-2		7	11	Guardado	Mathews	Aguilera	8-12	3rd	4.5
4-24	At Sea.	L	2-4		9	6	Cloude	Tewksbury	Ayala	8-13	3rd	5.0
4-25	At Sea.	W	8-2		12	5	Aguilera	Timlin		9-13	3rd	4.0
4-26	At Sea.	W	2-0		5	6	Radke	Moyer	Aguilera	10-13	2nd	3.5
4-27	Tex.	L	4-9		9	13	Helling	Morgan		10-14	T2nd	3.5
4-28	Tex.	L	2-7		5	14	Oliver	Milton		10-15	T2nd	4.5
4-29	T.B.	W	2-0		6	5	Tewksbury	Alvarez	Aguilera	11-15	T2nd	3.5
4-30	T.B.	L	0-2		3	8	Arrojo	Hawkins		11-16	3rd	3.5
5-1	At Bal.	L	3-6		9	11	Drabek	Radke	Benitez	11-17	3rd	4.5
5-2	At Bal.	W	8-7	(11)	13	14	Aguilera	Johns		12-17	T2nd	4.5
5-3	At Bal.	L	0-2		3	4	Mussina	Milton	Rhodes	12-18	T2nd	5.5
5-5	At Bos.	L	2-4		5	7	Wakefield	Tewksbury	Gordon	12-19	4th	6.5
5-6	At Bos.	W	8-7		13	9	Hawkins	Checo		13-19	T2nd	6.5
5-8	N.Y.	L	1-5		5	11	Irabu	Radke	Nelson	13-20	4th	7.0
5-9	N.Y.	W	8-1		12	7	Morgan	Pettitte		14-20	3rd	6.0
5-10	N.Y.	L	0-7		5	16	Mendoza	Milton		14-21	3rd	6.0
5-11	Bal.	L	0-4		5	7	Erickson	Tewksbury		14-22	T3rd	6.0
5-12	Bal.	W	7-4		13	12	Hawkins	Rhodes	Aguilera	15-22	3rd	5.0
5-13	Bos.	W	7-4		9	9	Radke	Saberhagen	Aguilera	16-22	2nd	4.0
5-14	Bos.	W	2-1	(12)	9	9	Trombley	Wasdin		17-22	2nd	4.0
5-15	At N.Y.	W	7-6		12	10	Milton	Pettitte	Aguilera	18-22	2nd	4.0
5-16	At N.Y.	L	2-5		4	12	Mendoza	Tewksbury	Rivera	18-23	2nd	5.0
5-17	At N.Y.	L	0-4		0	6	Wells	Hawkins		18-24	2nd	5.0
5-19	Det.	W	8-3		15	5	Radke	Sager		19-24	2nd	5.0
5-20	Det.	L	11-12		15	20	Runyan	Naulty	Jones	19-25	2nd	6.0
5-21	Det.	L	3-6	(11)	7	17	Brocail	Trombley	Jones	19-26	2nd	7.0
5-22	At Ana.	L	3-10		8	13	Olivares	Tewksbury		19-27	3rd	8.0
5-23	At Ana.	W	9-5		14	8	Hawkins	Watson	Swindell	20-27	2nd	7.0
5-24	At Ana.	W	9-1		11	3	Radke	Finley		21-27	2nd	6.0
5-25	At Tex.	W	9-3		12	6	Morgan	Oliver		22-27	2nd	6.0
5-27	At Tex.	W	6-5		11	11	Trombley	Hernandez	Aguilera	23-27	2nd	6.0
5-29	Ana.	L	1-3		5	11	Finley	Hawkins	Percival	23-28	2nd	7.5
5-30	Ana.	W	8-1		12	8	Radke	Hill		24-28	2nd	6.5
5-31	Ana.	L	5-6		12	10	Dickson	Swindell	Percival	24-29	2nd	7.5
6-1	Oak.	L	5-8		12	12	Oquist	Milton	Taylor	24-30	2nd	8.5
6-2	Oak.	W	10-3		15	6	Serafini	Candiotti		25-30	2nd	8.5
6-3	Cle.	W	3-2		7	7	Swindell	Colon	Aguilera	26-30	2nd	7.5
6-4	Cle.	L	2-3		10	7	Gooden	Radke	Jackson	26-31	2nd	8.5
6-5	At Pit.	L	1-6		5	12	Silva	Morgan		26-32	2nd	8.5
6-6	At Pit.	L	3-4	(12)	11	12	Loaiza	Aguilera		26-33	2nd	9.5
6-7	At Pit.	W	3-2		8	6	Serafini	Schmidt	Aguilera	27-33	2nd	9.5
6-8	Chi. (NL)	L	1-8		10	13	Clark	Hawkins		27-34	2nd	10.5
6-9	Chi. (NL)	W	8-0		10	4	Radke	Wood		28-34	2nd	9.5
6-10	Chi. (NL)	W	5-1		10	4	Morgan	Trachsel	Aguilera	29-34	2nd	8.5
6-12	Chi.	W	8-7		16	9	Aguilera	Simas		30-34	2nd	8.0
6-13	Chi.	L	2-3		4	11	Sirotka	Tewksbury	Karchner	30-35	2nd	8.5
6-14	Chi.	W	2-1		9	4	Hawkins	Navarro	Aguilera	31-35	2nd	7.5
6-15	At Det.	L	2-3		7	8	Moehler	Radke	Jones	31-36	2nd	7.5
6-16	At Det.	W	8-5		12	11	Serafini	Harriger	Aguilera	32-36	2nd	7.5
6-17	At Det.	L	2-6		7	10	Florie	Milton		32-37	2nd	7.5
6-18	At Chi.	W	4-1	(5)	9	5	Tewksbury	Sirotka		33-37	2nd	6.5
6-19	At Chi.	W	10-6		10	13	Trombley	Navarro	Swindell	34-37	2nd	6.5
6-20	At Chi.	L	7-8	(11)	11	20	Simas	Aguilera		34-38	2nd	6.5

– 45 –

Date	Opp.	Res.	Score	(inn.*)	Hits	Opp. hits	Winning pitcher	Losing pitcher	Save	Record	Pos.	GB
6-21	At Chi.	W	6-1		6	5	Morgan	Bere	Carrasco	35-38	2nd	6.5
6-22	At Hou.	W	5-3		10	4	Milton	Lima	Aguilera	36-38	2nd	6.5
6-23	At Hou.	L	0-9		5	13	Reynolds	Tewksbury		36-39	2nd	7.5
6-24	Mil.	L	1-3		9	8	Woodard	Hawkins	Wickman	36-40	2nd	8.5
6-25	Mil.	L	2-9		6	11	Eldred	Radke		36-41	2nd	9.5
6-26	St.L.	W	5-1		12	5	Swindell	Acevedo		37-41	2nd	9.5
6-27	St.L.	L	2-7		5	10	Stottlemyre	Milton		37-42	2nd	9.5
6-28	St.L.	W	3-2		11	10	Carrasco	Bottenfield	Aguilera	38-42	2nd	8.5
6-30	At Cin.	L	3-6		9	13	Tomko	Hawkins	Shaw	38-43	2nd	8.5
7-1	At Cin.	W	2-1		7	10	Radke	Sullivan	Aguilera	39-43	2nd	8.5
7-2	At Cin.	L	7-8		14	11	Shaw	Aguilera		39-44	2nd	9.5
7-3	Det.	L	4-5	(10)	9	12	Brocail	Naulty	Jones	39-45	2nd	10.5
7-4	Det.	L	2-4		9	9	Thompson	Serafini	Jones	39-46	2nd	10.5
7-5	Det.	W	5-4		11	9	Hawkins	Moehler	Aguilera	40-46	2nd	10.5
7-9	At Cle.	W	3-0		6	4	Tewksbury	Burba	Aguilera	41-46	2nd	9.5
7-10	At Cle.	L	5-6		11	10	Jackson	Trombley		41-47	2nd	10.5
7-11	At Cle.	L	2-12		5	19	Gooden	Radke		41-48	2nd	11.5
7-12	At Cle.	W	11-6		17	8	Milton	Nagy		42-48	2nd	10.5
7-13	At Chi.	L	2-5		10	7	Snyder	Serafini	Simas	42-49	2nd	11.5
7-14	At Chi.	L	5-8		12	11	Foulke	Aguilera		42-50	2nd	11.5
7-15	At Sea.	L	1-4		6	7	Moyer	Hawkins	Timlin	42-51	T2nd	11.5
7-16	At Sea.	L	0-3		1	7	Johnson	Radke		42-52	T2nd	11.5
7-17	At Oak.	W	8-7		16	10	Carrasco	Taylor	Aguilera	43-52	2nd	10.5
7-18	At Oak.	W	4-3		7	9	Carrasco	Oquist	Aguilera	44-52	2nd	10.5
7-19	At Oak.	L	2-5		7	7	Rogers	Serafini		44-53	2nd	10.5
7-21	Ana.	W	4-2		10	7	Hawkins	Watson	Aguilera	45-53	2nd	11.5
7-22	Ana.	L	3-5		7	12	Hasegawa	Swindell	Percival	45-54	2nd	11.5
7-23	Ana.	L	5-6	(10)	10	13	Harris	Carrasco	Percival	45-55	2nd	11.5
7-24	Tex.	W	5-3		13	11	Serafini	Loaiza	Aguilera	46-55	2nd	11.5
7-25	Tex.	W	7-6		11	8	Swindell	Patterson	Aguilera	47-55	2nd	11.5
7-26	Tex.	W	11-3		14	8	Hawkins	Helling		48-55	2nd	10.5
7-28	At K.C.	W	3-0		6	4	Radke	Rusch	Aguilera	49-55	2nd	10.5
7-29	At K.C.	W	5-3		8	4	Milton	Pichardo	Aguilera	50-55	2nd	10.5
7-30	At K.C.	L	3-7		6	14	Belcher	Serafini		50-56	2nd	11.5
7-31	Tor.	W	6-4		10	7	Rodriguez	Williams	Aguilera	51-56	2nd	10.5
8-1	Tor.	L	9-10		13	16	Hentgen	Hawkins	Myers	51-57	2nd	10.5
8-2	Tor.	L	4-6		9	12	Clemens	Radke	Myers	51-58	2nd	10.5
8-4	K.C.	L	4-12		10	16	Pichardo	Milton		51-59	2nd	10.0
8-5	K.C.	L	3-4		6	7	Belcher	Rodriguez	Montgomery	51-60	2nd	11.0
8-6	K.C.	L	7-8		12	11	Service	Aguilera	Montgomery	51-61	3rd	11.5
8-7	Bal.	L	9-16		11	19	Key	Miller		51-62	2nd	12.5
8-8	Bal.	L	3-6		12	11	Ponson	Radke	Orosco	51-63	T3rd	13.5
8-9	Bal.	W	5-4		14	9	Serafini	Mussina	Aguilera	52-63	2nd	12.5
8-10	At N.Y.	L	3-7		5	10	Irabu	Rodriguez		52-64	T2nd	13.0
8-11	At N.Y.	L	0-7		4	13	Wells	Milton		52-65	T2nd	13.0
8-12	At N.Y.	L	2-11		8	18	Cone	Hawkins		52-66	4th	14.0
8-13	At Bos.	L	7-8		12	16	Eckersley	Miller	Gordon	52-67	4th	14.0
8-14	At Bos.	L	12-13		17	15	Lowe	Baptist	Gordon	52-68	4th	14.0
8-15	At Bos.	W	3-2		14	8	Rodriguez	Schourek	Aguilera	53-68	4th	13.0
8-16	At Bos.	W	6-3		13	6	Milton	Avery	Aguilera	54-68	4th	13.0
8-17	At Bal.	L	2-3		7	9	Erickson	Hawkins	Benitez	54-69	4th	14.0
8-18	At Bal.	L	1-7		7	10	Ponson	Radke		54-70	4th	15.0
8-19	N.Y.	W	5-3		9	7	Serafini	Pettitte	Aguilera	55-70	3rd	14.0
8-20	N.Y.	W	9-4		14	11	Rodriguez	Buddie		56-70	3rd	13.0
8-21	Bos.	L	2-9		6	12	Avery	Milton		56-71	4th	14.0
8-22	Bos.	W	4-3		10	6	Trombley	Swindell		57-71	3rd	13.0
8-23	Bos.	L	1-5		9	15	Martinez	Radke		57-72	3rd	14.0
8-25	At T.B.	W	4-1		10	7	Rodriguez	Arrojo	Aguilera	58-72	3rd	14.0
8-26	At T.B.	W	7-3		12	10	Tewksbury	Saunders	Aguilera	59-72	3rd	14.0
8-27	At T.B.	L	3-10		5	16	Santana	Milton		59-73	T3rd	14.0
8-28	At Tor.	L	6-7		8	10	Williams	Trombley	Plesac	59-74	4th	14.0
8-29	At Tor.	L	7-14		10	18	Stieb	Radke		59-75	4th	14.0
8-30	At Tor.	L	0-6		2	9	Clemens	Rodriguez		59-76	4th	15.0
8-31	T.B.	W	2-1		8	7	Tewksbury	Saunders	Aguilera	60-76	4th	15.0
9-1	T.B.	W	6-5	(10)	10	10	Serafini	Hernandez		61-76	4th	15.0
9-2	T.B.	L	1-4		5	11	Yan	Hawkins	Lopez	61-77	4th	15.0
9-3	T.B.	W	5-4	(12)	10	9	Guardado	White		62-77	4th	15.0
9-4	At Tex.	L	3-9		9	12	Sele	Rodriguez		62-78	4th	16.0
9-5	At Tex.	W	7-4		14	13	Trombley	Hernandez	Aguilera	63-78	4th	16.0
9-6	At Tex.	W	6-5		13	11	Carrasco	Hernandez	Aguilera	64-78	4th	15.0
9-7	At Tex.	L	0-6		3	10	Helling	Hawkins		64-79	4th	15.0
9-8	At Ana.	W	5-0		10	8	Radke	Sparks		65-79	4th	14.5
9-9	At Ana.	L	8-10		12	13	Olivares	Rodriguez	Percival	65-80	4th	15.5
9-11	Oak.	L	2-3		4	11	Rogers	Tewksbury		65-81	4th	15.5
9-12	Oak.	L	5-6		10	8	Witasick	Milton	Taylor	65-82	4th	15.5
9-13	Oak.	L	6-9	(12)	12	12	Holzemer	Aguilera	Taylor	65-83	4th	16.5

– 46 –

Date	Opp.	Res.	Score	(inn.*)	Hits	Opp. hits	Winning pitcher	Losing pitcher	Save	Record	Pos.	GB
9-14	Sea.	L	3-10		6	15	Suzuki	Radke		65-84	4th	17.5
9-15	Sea.	L	7-12		12	16	Abbott	Rodriguez		65-85	4th	18.5
9-16	At Cle.	L	6-8		13	13	Nagy	Tewksbury	Assenmacher	65-86	4th	19.5
9-17	At Cle.	L	1-9		4	15	Burba	Milton		65-87	4th	20.5
9-18	At Det.	L	4-5	(11)	5	10	Anderson	Trombley		65-88	4th	21.5
9-19	At Det.	L	7-8	(10)	14	12	Sager	Aguilera		65-89	4th	21.5
9-20	At Det.	W	3-0		6	4	Sampson	Greisinger	Aguilera	66-89	4th	21.5
9-21	Chi.	L	1-7		8	11	J. Abbott	Tewksbury		66-90	4th	22.5
9-22	Chi.	L	1-4		6	9	Baldwin	Milton		66-91	4th	22.0
9-23	Chi.	W	7-6	(12)	11	17	Trombley	Eyre		67-91	4th	21.0
9-24	Cle.	W	2-0		6	4	Radke	Wright	Aguilera	68-91	4th	20.0
9-25	Cle.	W	5-4		11	6	Aguilera	Shuey		69-91	4th	19.0
9-26	Cle.	L	5-9		12	11	Burba	Tewksbury		69-92	4th	20.0
9-27	Cle.	W	6-2		9	7	Milton	Colon	Trombley	70-92	4th	19.0

Monthly records: April (11-16), May (13-13), June (14-14), July (13-13), August (9-20), September (10-16).
*Innings, if other than nine. †First game of doubleheader. ‡Second game of doubleheader.

HIGHLIGHTS

High point: Although there never were title hopes, the team was anchored solidly in second place in the A.L. Central after opening the post-All-Star schedule with a win at Cleveland.

Low point: The May 17 perfect game by Yankees lefty David Wells was a crystal-clear example of where the Twins stood in 1998. That day's lineup featured No. 9 hitter Pat Meares with a .290 average and other hitters with (No. 1 through 8) .239, .123, .250, .247, .264, .244, .143 and .220 marks.

Turning point: When veteran starters Mike Morgan and Bob Tewksbury went on the disabled list two days apart in July, any hopes for a strong finish disappeared.

Most valuable player: Second baseman Todd Walker was among the league's hitting leaders most of the year before a late slump left him with a .316 average. He stepped in after Chuck Knoblauch was traded to the Yankees and finally displayed in the big leagues what he had shown all year in the minors.

Most valuable pitcher: Righthanded reliever Mike Trombley set career highs in games and strikeouts and tied his career high with six wins. After Greg Swindell was traded to Boston on July 31, Trombley took over as the No. 1 middle reliever and excelled.

Most improved player: Right fielder Matt Lawton turned his season around after a lousy start, lifting his batting average from .218 on June 1 to .278 by season's end. He began to show solid power late in the year, along with the ability to become a .300 hitter.

Most pleasant surprise: A tie between Walker and Lawton. Walker's batting average rose from .237 in 52 games in 1997 to .316 in 143 games. Lawton hit .248 in 1997 and .278 in 1998. Walker was deep in doubt after his abysmal 1997, and Lawton had not shown much in the big leagues. But 1998 appeared to be a breakthrough year for both.

Biggest disappointment: Left fielder Marty Cordova's home run total fell for the third season in a row, going from 24

in 1995 to 16, 15 and 10. Injuries dogged him during a poor 1997 season, but the reasons weren't so clear in 1998. **Key injuries:** Rookie first baseman David Ortiz spent 60 days on the disabled list with a broken wrist, and it ruined what had the looks of a solid campaign by the lefthanded slugger. Tewksbury was on the D.L. twice, as was Morgan. Otis Nixon was out from April 29 to May 30 with a fractured jaw, Cordova was on the D.L. from April 29 to May 12 with a strained neck and Paul Molitor was out from June 21 to July 15 with a broken rib.

Notable: Brad Radke went from a 20-10 record in 1997 to 12-14 in '98. Still, he led the team in wins for the third time in four years. . . . The Twins' longest winning streak was five games, their longest losing streak six games. . . . Ron Coomer tied the Yankees' Paul O'Neill for the A.L. lead in grounding into double plays (22). . . . Molitor announced his retirement after 21 big-league seasons and 3,319 hits, eighth on the all-time list.

— JOHN MILLEA

RECORDS

1998 regular-season record: 70-92 (4th in A.L. Central); 35-46 at home; 35-46 on road; 24-30 vs. East; 21-27 vs. A.L. Central; 18-26 vs. West; 7-9 vs. N.L.; 16-19 vs. lefthanded starters; 54-73 vs. righthanded starters; 26-32 on grass; 44-60 on turf; 22-25 in day-time; 48-67 at night; 25-29 in one-run games; 5-12 in extra-inning games; 0-0 in doubleheaders.

Team record past five years: 325-418 (.437, ranks 12th in league in that span).

TEAM LEADERS

Batting average: Todd Walker (.316).
At-bats: Matt Lawton (557).
Runs: Matt Lawton (91).
Hits: Todd Walker (167).
Total bases: Matt Lawton (266).
Doubles: Todd Walker (41).
Triples: Matt Lawton, Otis Nixon (6).
Home runs: Matt Lawton (21).

Runs batted in: Matt Lawton (77).
Stolen bases: Otis Nixon (37).
Slugging percentage: Matt Lawton (.478).
On-base percentage: Matt Lawton (.387).
Wins: Brad Radke (12).
Earned-run average: Brad Radke (4.30).
Complete games: Brad Radke (5).
Shutouts: Brad Radke (1).
Saves: Rick Aguilera (38).
Innings pitched: Brad Radke (213.2).
Strikeouts: Brad Radke (146).

GAMES BY POSITION

Catcher: Terry Steinbach 119, Javier Valentin 53, A.J. Pierzynski 6.
First base: David Ortiz 71, Ron Coomer 54, Orlando Merced 38, Paul Molitor 9, Doug Mientkiewicz 8, Scott Stahoviak 4, Denny Hocking 2, Brent Gates 1, Jon Shave 1.
Second base: Todd Walker 140, Denny Hocking 48, Brent Gates 21.
Third base: Brent Gates 77, Ron Coomer 76, Jon Shave 15, Denny Hocking 11, Corey Koskie 10.
Shortstop: Pat Meares 149, Denny Hocking 28, Brent Gates 1, Jon Shave 1.
Outfield: Matt Lawton 151, Marty Cordova 115, Otis Nixon 108, Alex Ochoa 74, Chris Latham 32, Denny Hocking 24, Orlando Merced 13, Torii Hunter 6, Ron Coomer 3, Scott Stahoviak 1.
Designated hitter: Paul Molitor 115, Ron Coomer 13, David Ortiz 10, Orlando Merced 8, Marty Cordova 4, Alex Ochoa 3, Terry Steinbach 3, Brent Gates 2, Denny Hocking 2, Jon Shave 1, Javier Valentin 1, Todd Walker 1.

TOP DRAFT CHOICES

1. **Ryan Mills,** LHP, Arizona State Univ.
2. **Marcus Sents,** RHP, Cookeville (Tenn.) H.S.
3. **Brent Hoard,** LHP, Stanford University
4. **Pete Fisher,** RHP, Univ. of Alabama
5. **Mickey Blount,** RHP, Kansas State U.
6. **Brad Pautz,** RHP, U. of Minnesota
7. **Sam Taulli,** LHP, Lafayette (La.) H.S.
8. **John Edwards,** C, Triton (Ill.) J.C.
9. **Saul Rivera,** RHP, U. of Mobile (Ala.)
10. **Ryan Lundquist,** OF, U. of Arkansas

NEW YORK YANKEES
AMERICAN LEAGUE EAST DIVISION

1999 Yankees Schedule
Home games shaded. *—All-Star Game at Fenway Park (Boston).
D—Day game (any game starting before 5 p.m.).

April
SUN	MON	TUE	WED	THU	FRI	SAT
				1	2	3
4	5 OAK	6 OAK	7 OAK	8 D	9 D DET	10 D DET
11 DET	12	13 BAL	14 BAL	15 BAL	16 DET	17 D DET
18 D DET	19	20 TEX	21 TEX	22	23 TOR	24 D TOR
25 TOR	26	27 TEX	28 TEX	29 TEX	30 KC	

May
SUN	MON	TUE	WED	THU	FRI	SAT
						1 KC
2 D KC	3 KC	4 MIN	5 MIN	6 D MIN	7 SEA	8 D SEA
9 SEA	10	11 ANA	12 ANA	13 ANA	14 CWS	15 D CWS
16 CWS	17	18 BOS	19 BOS	20 BOS	21 CWS	22 CWS
23 CWS	24 BOS	25 BOS	26 BOS	27	28 TOR	29 D TOR
30 D TOR	31 CLE					

June
SUN	MON	TUE	WED	THU	FRI	SAT
		1 CLE	2 CLE	3	4 NYM	5 D NYM
6 NYM	7 PHI	8 PHI	9 PHI	10	11 FLA	12 FLA
13 FLA	14 TEX	15 TEX	16 TEX	17	18 ANA	19 D ANA
20 D ANA	21	22 TB	23 TB	24 TB	25 BAL	26 D BAL
27 D BAL	28	29 DET	30 DET			

July
SUN	MON	TUE	WED	THU	FRI	SAT
				1 DET	2 BAL	3 D BAL
4 BAL	5 BAL	6 DET	7 DET	8 DET	9 NYM	10 D NYM
11 NYM	12	13 *	14	15 ATL	16 ATL	17 D ATL
18 MON	19 MON	20 MON	21 TB	22 TB	23 CLE	24 CLE
25 CLE	26	27 CWS	28 CWS	29 CWS	30 BOS	31 D BOS

August
SUN	MON	TUE	WED	THU	FRI	SAT
1 D BOS	2 TOR	3 TOR	4 TOR	5 SEA	6 D SEA	7 SEA
8 SEA	9 OAK	10 OAK	11 OAK	12	13 MIN	14 D MIN
15 MIN	16 MIN	17 KC	18 KC	19 D KC	20 MIN	21 MIN
22 MIN	23 TEX	24 TEX	25 TEX	26	27 SEA	28 SEA
29 SEA	30 OAK	31 OAK				

September
SUN	MON	TUE	WED	THU	FRI	SAT
			1 OAK	2 OAK	3 D ANA	4 D ANA
5 ANA	6 ANA	7 KC	8 KC	9 D BOS	10 BOS	11 D BOS
12 BOS	13 TOR	14 TOR	15 CLE	16 CLE	17 CLE	18 D CLE
19 D CLE	20	21 CWS	22 CWS	23 CWS	24 TB	25 TB
26 D TB	27 TB	28 BAL	29 BAL	30 BAL		

October
SUN	MON	TUE	WED	THU	FRI	SAT
					1 TB	2 TB
3 D TB	4	5	6	7	8	9

1999 SEASON
CLUB DIRECTORY

Principal owner
George M. Steinbrenner III
General partners
Harold Z. Steinbrenner, Steven W. Swindal
Executive v.p., general counsel
Lonn Trost
Vice president, ticket operations
Frank Swaine
Vice president, business development
Joseph M. Perello
Vice president, chief financial officer
Marty Greenspun
Controller
Robert Brown
Special advisory group
Clyde King, Dick Williams
Vice president, general manager
Brian Cashman
Vice president, player development
Mark Newman
Director of major league scouting
Gene Michael
Assistant general manager
Kim Ng
Major league administrator
Tom May
Traveling secretary
David Szen
Director of stadium operations
Sonny Hight
Director of customer service
Joel White
Dir. of office administration and services
Harvey C. Winston
Manager, stadium operations
Kirk Randazzo
Assistant, stadium operations
Bob Pelegrino
Stadium superintendent
Bob Wilkinson
Head groundskeeper
Dan Cunningham
Director, video and broadcast operations
Doyal Martin
Asst. dir., video and broadcast operations
Joe Pullia
Public address announcer
Bob Sheppard
Stadium organist
Eddie Layton
Executive director of ticket operations
Jeff Kline
Ticket director
Ken Skrypek
Director of media relations and publicity
Rick Cerrone

Director, publications and multimedia
Dan Cahalane
Asst. dir. of media relations and publicity
Jason Zillo
Senior advisor
Arthur Richman
Director of marketing
Deborah A. Tymon
Dir. of community relations/special assistant to George M. Steinbrenner
Brian Smith
Director of Yankee Alumni Association
Jim Ogle
Director of entertainment
Stanley Kay
Special assistant
Joe Pepitone
Dir. of television and video production
Joe Violone
Manager of publications and multimedia
Kara McGovern
Team photographer
Steve Crandall
Assistant director of scouting
Joe Caro
Coord. of Latin American player dev.
Ken Dominguez
Team physician
Dr. Stuart Hershon
Head trainer
Gene Monahan
Assistant trainer
Steve Donohue
Strength & conditioning coach
Jeff Mangold
Cross-checkers
John Cox, Damon Oppenheimer, Donnie Rowland
Special assignment scouts
Ket Barber, Bill Emslie
Scouts
Rich Arena, Joe Arnold, Mike Baker, Mark Batchko, Bobby Dejardin, Lee Elder, Tim Kelly, Greg Orr, Scott Pleis, Cesar Presbott, Joe Robison, Phil Rossi, Steve Webber, J. Leon Wurth, Bill Young
Coordinator of international scouting
Gordon Blakeley
Coordinator of Canadian scouting
Dick Groch
Foreign scouts
Karl Heron, Ricardo Heron, Ruddy Jabalera, Francisco Lugo, Victor Mata, Manuel Medina, Roberto Morillo, Jorge Oquendo, Raul Ortega, Jim Patterson, Marc Picard, Jose Quintero, Luis Ramos, Arquimedes Rojas, Dale Tilleman, Modesto Ulloa

MINOR LEAGUE AFFILIATES

Class	Team	League	Manager
AAA	Columbus	International	Trey Hillman
AA	Norwich	Eastern	Lee Mazzilli
A	Tampa	Florida State	Tom Nieto
A	Greensboro	South Atlantic	Stan Hough
A	Watertown	New York-Pennsylvania	To be announced
Rookie	Gulf Coast Yankees	Gulf Coast	To be announced

BROADCAST INFORMATION
Radio: WABC-AM (770).
TV: WNYW-TV (Channel 5).
Cable TV: Madison Square Garden Network.

SPRING TRAINING
Ballpark (city): Legends Field (Tampa, Fla.).
Ticket information: 813-879-2244, 813-287-8844.

SPRING TRAINING ROSTER

Manager—Joe Torre (6).
Coaches—Jose Cardenal (53), Chris Chambliss (48), Tony Cloninger (40), Willie Randolph (30), Mel Stottlemyre (34), Don Zimmer (50).

No.	PITCHERS	B/T	Ht./Wt.	Born	1998 clubs
58	Bradley, Ryan	R/R	6-4/226	10-26-75	Norwich, Columbus, Tampa, New York A.L.
61	Bruske, Jim	R/R	6-1/185	10-7-64	Los Angeles, San Diego, Las Vegas, Columbus, New York A.L.
52	Buddie, Mike	R/R	6-3/210	12-12-70	Columbus, New York A.L.
36	Cone, David	L/R	6-1/190	1-2-63	New York A.L.
	De Los Santos, Luis	R/R	6-2/187	11-1-77	Norwich, Tampa
79	Einertson, Chief	R/R	6-2/190	9-4-72	Columbus
54	Erdos, Todd	R/R	6-1/190	11-21-73	Columbus, New York A.L.
26	Hernandez, Orlando	R/R	6-2/210	10-11-69	Tampa, Columbus, New York A.L.
40	Holmes, Darren	R/R	6-0/202	4-25-66	New York A.L., Tampa
14	Irabu, Hideki	R/R	6-4/240	5-5-69	New York A.L.
78	Jerzembeck, Mike	R/R	6-1/185	5-18-72	Columbus, New York A.L.
27	Lloyd, Graeme	L/L	6-7/234	4-9-67	New York A.L.
55	Mendoza, Ramiro	R/R	6-2/154	6-15-72	New York A.L.
	Naulty, Dan	R/R	6-6/224	1-6-70	Salt Lake, Minnesota
43	Nelson, Jeff	R/R	6-8/235	11-17-66	New York A.L., Tampa
46	Pettitte, Andy	L/L	6-5/235	6-15-72	New York A.L.
42	Rivera, Mariano	R/R	6-2/170	11-29-69	New York A.L.
29	Stanton, Mike	L/L	6-1/215	6-2-67	New York A.L.
62	Tessmer, Jay	R/R	6-3/190	12-26-71	Norwich, Columbus, New York A.L.
33	Wells, David	L/L	6-4/225	5-20-63	New York A.L.

No.	CATCHERS	B/T	Ht./Wt.	Born	1998 clubs
	Figga, Mike	R/R	6-0/200	7-31-70	Columbus, New York A.L.
25	Girardi, Joe	R/R	5-11/200	10-14-64	New York A.L.
20	Posada, Jorge	B/R	6-2/205	8-17-71	New York A.L.

No.	INFIELDERS	B/T	Ht./Wt.	Born	1998 clubs
18	Brosius, Scott	R/R	6-1/202	8-15-66	New York A.L.
22	Bush, Homer	R/R	5-10/180	11-12-72	New York A.L.
2	Jeter, Derek	R/R	6-3/195	6-26-74	New York A.L., Columbus
	Jimenez, D'Angelo	R/R	6-0/160	12-21-77	Norwich, Columbus
11	Knoblauch, Chuck	R/R	5-9/170	7-7-68	New York A.L.
60	Lowell, Mike	R/R	6-4/193	2-24-74	Columbus, New York A.L.
24	Martinez, Tino	L/R	6-2/210	12-7-67	New York A.L.
19	Sojo, Luis	R/R	5-11/175	1-3-66	Tampa, Columbus, New York A.L.
	Soriano, Alfonso	/R	6-1/160	1-7-78	DID NOT PLAY

No.	OUTFIELDERS	B/T	Ht./Wt.	Born	1998 clubs
28	Curtis, Chad	R/R	5-10/185	11-6-68	New York A.L.
20	Davis, Chili	B/R	6-3/240	1-17-60	New York A.L., Norwich, Columbus
17	Ledee, Ricky	L/L	6-1/160	11-22-73	Columbus, New York A.L.
84	McDonald, Donzell	B/R	5-11/165	2-20-75	Norwich, Tampa
21	O'Neill, Paul	L/L	6-4/215	2-25-63	New York A.L.
47	Spencer, Shane	R/R	5-11/210	2-20-72	Columbus, New York A.L.
51	Williams, Bernie	B/R	6-2/205	9-13-68	New York A.L., Tampa, Norwich

BALLPARK INFORMATION

Ballpark (capacity, surface)
Yankee Stadium (57,546, grass)

Address
Yankee Stadium
E. 161 St. and River Ave.
Bronx, NY 10451

Business phone
718-293-4300

Ticket information
212-307-1212, 718-293-6013

Ticket prices
$25 (field, main and loge boxes)
$23 (main and loge boxes)
$23 (main reserved-infield)
$20 (tier boxes, main reserved-outfield)
$12 (tier reserved)
$7 (bleachers)
$2 (senior citizens)

Field dimensions (from home plate)
To left field at foul line, 318 feet
To center field, 408 feet
To right field at foul line, 314 feet

First game played
April 18, 1923 (Yankees 4, Red Sox 1)

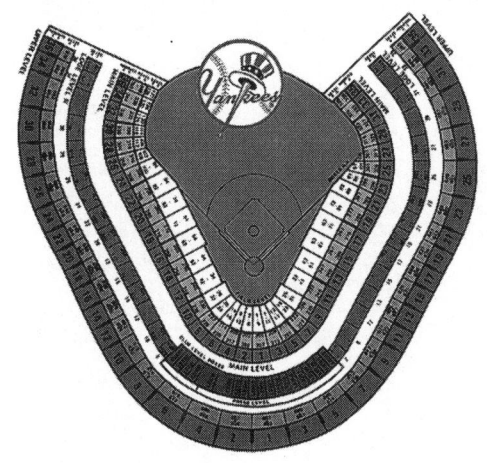

1998 REVIEW
DAY BY DAY

Date	Opp.	Res.	Score	(inn.*)	Hits	Opp. hits	Winning pitcher	Losing pitcher	Save	Record	Pos.	GB
4-1	At Ana.	L	1-4		5	11	Finley	Pettitte	Percival	0-1	5th	1.0
4-2	At Ana.	L	2-10		7	14	Hill	Wells		0-2	5th	2.0
4-4	At Oak.	L	3-7		8	11	Haynes	Cone		0-3	5th	3.0
4-5	At Oak.	W	9-7	(10)	11	12	Nelson	Mohler		1-3	5th	3.0
4-6	At Sea.	L	0-8		3	12	Moyer	Pettitte		1-4	5th	3.5
4-7	At Sea.	W	13-7		18	14	Wells	Bullinger		2-4	T4th	3.5
4-8	At Sea.	W	4-3		10	10	Lloyd	Ayala	Stanton	3-4	T3rd	3.0
4-10	Oak.	W	17-13		16	16	Buddie	Dougherty		4-4	T2nd	2.5
4-11	Oak.	W	3-1		8	6	Pettitte	Candiotti	Stanton	5-4	T2nd	2.5
4-12	Oak.	W	7-5		11	8	Buddie	Mathews	Stanton	6-4	T2nd	2.5
4-15	Ana.∞	W	6-3		13	4	Wells	Hill	Nelson	7-4	3rd	2.0
4-17	At Det.	W	11-2		12	7	Pettitte	Thompson		8-4	T1st	...
4-18	At Det.	W	8-3		13	13	Cone	Keagle		9-4	1st	+0.5
4-19	At Det.	L	1-2		3	4	Moehler	Holmes	Jones	9-5	3rd	0.5
4-20	At Tor.	W	3-2	(11)	9	7	Banks	Risley	Stanton	10-5	T1st	...
4-21	At Tor.	W	5-3	(10)	13	9	Stanton	Plesac		11-5	1st	+0.5
4-22	At Tor.	W	9-1		10	6	Pettitte	Clemens		12-5	1st	+0.5
4-24	Det.	W	8-4		13	6	Cone	Keagle		13-5	1st	+0.5
4-25	Det.	W	5-4		6	5	Wells	Runyan	Rivera	14-5	1st	+0.5
4-27	Tor.	W	1-0		3	9	Pettitte	Clemens	Rivera	15-5	1st	+0.5
4-28	Tor.	L	2-5		9	8	Williams	Mendoza	Myers	15-6	1st	+0.5
4-29	Sea.	W	8-5		12	10	Cone	Fassero	Rivera	16-6	1st	+0.5
4-30	Sea.	W	9-8	(10)	15	11	Rivera	Ayala		17-6	1st	+0.5
5-1	At K.C.	W	2-1		6	2	Irabu	Rapp	Rivera	18-6	1st	+0.5
5-2	At K.C.	W	12-6		14	12	Pettitte	Haney		19-6	1st	+1.5
5-3	At K.C.	W	10-1		13	4	Mendoza	Belcher		20-6	1st	+1.5
5-5	At Tex.	W	7-2		13	4	Cone	Burkett		21-6	1st	+1.5
5-6	At Tex.	W	15-13		18	15	Stanton	Patterson	Rivera	22-6	1st	+2.5
5-8	At Min.	W	5-1		11	5	Irabu	Radke	Nelson	23-6	1st	+3.0
5-9	At Min.	L	1-8		7	12	Morgan	Pettitte		23-7	1st	+2.0
5-10	At Min.	W	7-0		16	5	Mendoza	Milton		24-7	1st	+2.0
5-12	K.C.	W	3-2		4	5	Wells	Rusch	Rivera	25-7	1st	+3.5
5-13	Tex.	W	8-6		13	12	Cone	Helling	Rivera	26-7	1st	+4.5
5-14	Tex.	L	5-7	(13)	13	12	Patterson	Banks	Wetteland	26-8	1st	+4.5
5-15	Min.	L	6-7		10	12	Milton	Pettitte	Aguilera	26-9	1st	+3.5
5-16	Min.	W	5-2		12	4	Mendoza	Tewksbury	Rivera	27-9	1st	+3.5
5-17	Min.	W	4-0		6	0	Wells	Hawkins		28-9	1st	+4.5
5-19	Bal.	W	9-5		14	7	Stanton	Charlton		29-9	1st	+4.5
5-20	Bal.	W	9-6		15	12	Irabu	Key		30-9	1st	+4.5
5-21	Bal.	W	3-1		5	8	Pettitte	Erickson	Rivera	31-9	1st	+4.5
5-22	At Bos.	L	4-5		7	11	Wakefield	Nelson	Gordon	31-10	1st	+4.0
5-23	At Bos.	W	12-3		15	6	Wells	Lowe		32-10	1st	+5.0
5-24	At Bos.	W	14-4		17	12	Cone	Saberhagen		33-10	1st	+6.0
5-25	At Chi.	W	12-0		14	6	Irabu	Navarro		34-10	1st	+7.0
5-26	At Chi.	W	7-5		10	7	Nelson	Foulke	Rivera	35-10	1st	+8.0
5-27	At Chi.	L	9-12		6	17	Simas	Nelson	Karchner	35-11	1st	+7.5
5-28	Bos.	W	8-3		11	13	Wells	Wakefield	Stanton	36-11	1st	+8.5
5-29	Bos.	W	6-2		11	5	Cone	Lowe		37-11	1st	+9.5
5-30	Bos.	L	2-3		7	3	Saberhagen	Irabu	Gordon	37-12	1st	+8.5
5-31	Bos.	W	7-13		14	17	Martinez	Pettitte		37-13	1st	+7.5
6-1	Chi.	W	5-4	(10)	8	7	Nelson	Karchner		38-13	1st	+7.5
6-2	Chi.	W	6-3		11	7	Wells	Sirotka	Rivera	39-13	1st	+7.5
6-3	T.B.	W	7-1		8	5	Hernandez	Saunders		40-13	1st	+8.5
6-4	T.B.	W	6-1		11	6	Irabu	Springer		41-13	1st	+8.5
6-5	Fla.	W	5-1		7	5	Pettitte	Fontenot		42-13	1st	+9.5
6-6	Fla.	W	4-2		10	4	Mendoza	Sanchez	Rivera	43-13	1st	+10.5
6-7	Fla.	W	4-1		8	2	Cone	Dempster		44-13	1st	+10.5
6-9	At Mon.	W	11-1		17	4	Hernandez	C. Perez		45-13	1st	+11.0
6-10	At Mon.	W	6-2		11	6	Irabu	Hermanson		46-13	1st	+11.0
6-11	At Mon.	L	5-7		6	8	Valdes	Nelson	Urbina	46-14	1st	+10.5
6-14	Cle.	W	4-2		10	6	Cone	Wright	Rivera	47-14	1st	+10.0
6-15	At Bal.	L	4-7		7	14	Erickson	Wells	Orosco	47-15	1st	+10.0
6-16	At Bal.	L	0-2		2	8	Ponson	Irabu	Rhodes	47-16	1st	+9.0
6-17	At Bal.	W	5-3		9	7	Pettitte	Mussina		48-16	1st	+9.0
6-18	At Cle.	W	5-2		8	8	Nelson	Assenmacher	Rivera	49-16	1st	+9.0
6-19	At Cle.	L	4-7		8	12	Wright	Cone	Jackson	49-17	1st	+8.0
6-20	At Cle.	W	5-3		7	11	Wells	Burba	Rivera	50-17	1st	+9.0
6-21	At Cle.	L	0-11		4	13	Colon	Irabu		50-18	1st	+8.0
6-22	Atl.	W	6-4		11	9	Nelson	Martinez	Rivera	51-18	1st	+9.0
6-23	Atl.	L	2-7		7	11	Glavine	Hernandez		51-19	1st	+9.0
6-24	At Atl.	W	10-6		13	7	Cone	Millwood	Rivera	52-19	1st	+10.0
6-25	At Atl.	W	6-0		4	6	Wells	Neagle		53-19	1st	+10.0

Date	Opp.	Res.	Score	(inn.*)	Hits	Opp. hits	Winning pitcher	Losing pitcher	Save	Record	Pos.	GB
6-26	At N.Y. (NL)	W	8-4		13	7	Mendoza	Leiter	Rivera	54-19	1st	+10.0
6-27	At N.Y. (NL)	W	7-2		8	5	Pettitte	Jones		55-19	1st	+10.0
6-28	At N.Y. (NL)	L	1-2		2	3	Cook	Mendoza		55-20	1st	+10.0
6-30	Phi.	W	9-2		9	5	Cone	Loewer		56-20	1st	+10.0
7-1	Phi.	W	5-2		7	8	Wells	Beech	Rivera	57-20	1st	+10.0
7-2	Phi.	W	9-8	(11)	14	13	Buddie	Spradlin		58-20	1st	+10.0
7-3	Bal.	W	3-2		9	4	Pettitte	Orosco		59-20	1st	+10.0
7-4	Bal.	W	4-3		10	8	Hernandez	Drabek	Rivera	60-20	1st	+11.0
7-5	Bal.	W	1-0		7	7	Cone	Erickson	Rivera	61-20	1st	+11.0
7-9	At T.B.	W	2-0		4	5	Pettitte	Rekar	Rivera	62-20	1st	+12.0
7-10	At T.B.	W	8-4		9	12	Irabu	Alvarez	Mendoza	63-20	1st	+13.0
7-11	At T.B.	W	2-0		8	5	Cone	Arrojo	Rivera	64-20	1st	+14.0
7-12	At T.B.	W	9-2		11	6	Stanton	Hernandez		65-20	1st	+15.0
7-13	At Cle.	L	1-4		8	10	Wright	Hernandez	Jackson	65-21	1st	+14.0
7-14	At Cle.	W	7-1		12	6	Pettitte	Burba		66-21	1st	+15.0
7-15	At Det.	W	11-0		13	5	Irabu	Greisinger		67-21	1st	+15.0
7-16	At Det.	L	1-3		7	7	Moehler	Cone	Jones	67-22	1st	+14.0
7-17	At Tor.	L	6-9		12	10	Clemens	Holmes	Myers	67-23	1st	+14.0
7-18	At Tor.	W	10-3		13	8	Hernandez	Guzman		68-23	1st	+14.0
7-19	At Tor.	L	3-9		7	8	Williams	Pettitte		68-24	1st	+14.0
7-20†	Det.	L	3-4	(17)	13	14	Sager	Holmes		68-25		
7-20‡	Det.	W	4-3		10	5	Irabu	Florie	Rivera	69-25	1st	+14.0
7-21	Det.	W	5-1		7	9	Cone	Moehler		70-25	1st	+14.5
7-22	Det.	W	13-2		12	12	Hernandez	Powell	Holmes	71-25	1st	+15.5
7-24	Chi.	W	5-4		6	9	Pettitte	Ward	Rivera	72-25	1st	+16.0
7-25	Chi.	L	2-6		10	9	Sirotka	Irabu	Simas	72-26	1st	+15.0
7-26	Chi.	W	6-3		7	7	Wells	Navarro	Rivera	73-26	1st	+15.0
7-28	At Ana.	W	9-3		14	8	Cone	Dickson		74-26	1st	+15.0
7-29	At Ana.	L	5-10		7	19	Sparks	Hernandez		74-27	1st	+14.0
7-30	At Ana.	W	3-0	(10)	5	11	Mendoza	DeLucia	Rivera	75-27	1st	+15.0
7-31	At Sea.	W	5-3		12	6	Irabu	Fassero	Rivera	76-27	1st	+15.0
8-1	At Sea.	W	5-2		11	8	Wells	Moyer		77-27	1st	+15.0
8-2	At Sea.	L	3-6		9	9	Wells	Cone	Timlin	77-28	1st	+14.0
8-3	At Oak.	W	14-1		17	3	Hernandez	Oquist		78-28	1st	+15.0
8-4†	At Oak.	W	10-4		10	7	Mendoza	Witasick	Stanton	79-28		
8-4‡	At Oak.	W	10-5		16	9	Lloyd	Taylor		80-28	1st	+15.5
8-5	At Oak.	L	1-3		4	2	Candiotti	Irabu		80-29	1st	+15.0
8-7§	K.C.	W	8-2		12	8	Cone	Rapp		81-29		
8-7§	K.C.	W	14-2		18	6	Wells	Haney		82-29	1st	+17.0
8-8	K.C.	W	14-1		15	4	Hernandez	Rusch		83-29	1st	+17.0
8-9	K.C.	W	5-4		8	8	Mendoza	Service	Rivera	84-29	1st	+17.0
8-10	Min.	W	7-3		10	5	Irabu	Rodriguez		85-29	1st	+17.5
8-11	Min.	W	7-0		13	4	Wells	Milton		86-29	1st	+17.5
8-12	Min.	W	11-2		18	8	Cone	Hawkins		87-29	1st	+18.5
8-13	Tex.	W	2-0		3	2	Hernandez	Helling	Rivera	88-29	1st	+18.5
8-14	Tex.	W	6-4		9	11	Pettitte	Sele	Rivera	89-29	1st	+18.5
8-15	Tex.	L	5-16		12	19	Stottlemyre	Irabu		89-30	1st	+18.5
8-16	Tex.	W	6-5		17	12	Rivera	Hernandez		90-30	1st	+19.5
8-17	At K.C.	W	7-1		10	6	Cone	Rosado		91-30	1st	+20.0
8-18	At K.C.	W	3-2	(13)	11	8	Borowski	Whisenant		92-30	1st	+19.5
8-19	At Min.	L	3-5		7	9	Serafini	Pettitte	Aguilera	92-31	1st	+18.5
8-20	At Min.	L	4-9		11	14	Rodriguez	Buddie		92-32	1st	+18.5
8-21	At Tex.	W	5-0		10	6	Wells	Loaiza		93-32	1st	+18.5
8-22	At Tex.	W	12-9		17	13	Bradley	Hernandez	Rivera	94-32	1st	+19.5
8-23	At Tex.	L	10-12		13	14	Helling	Hernandez	Wetteland	94-33	1st	+18.5
8-24	Ana.	L	3-7		7	12	McDowell	Pettitte		94-34	1st	+18.0
8-25	Ana.	L	6-7		17	12	Watson	Stanton	Percival	94-35	1st	+17.0
8-26§	Ana.	L	4-6		5	9	Juden	Bradley	Percival	94-36		
8-26§	Ana.	W	7-6		8	13	Rivera	Fetters		95-36	1st	+16.5
8-27	Ana.	W	6-5	(11)	11	11	Tessmer	Fetters		96-36	1st	+17.5
8-28	Sea.	W	10-3		12	4	Hernandez	Spoljaric		97-36	1st	+18.5
8-29	Sea.	W	11-6		19	11	Pettitte	Cloude		98-36	1st	+18.5
8-30	Sea.	L	3-13		7	15	Swift	Irabu		98-37	1st	+18.5
9-1	Oak.	W	7-0		12	2	Wells	Candiotti		99-37	1st	+19.0
9-2	Oak.	L	0-2		6	6	Heredia	Cone	Taylor	99-38	1st	+18.0
9-4	At Chi.	W	11-6		15	10	Lloyd	Bradford		100-38	1st	+19.5
9-5	At Chi.	L	5-9		10	12	J. Abbott	Pettitte		100-39	1st	+19.5
9-6	At Chi.	L	5-6		8	12	Baldwin	Irabu	Howry	100-40	1st	+19.5
9-7	At Bos.	L	3-4		6	6	Swindell	Wells	Gordon	100-41	1st	+18.5
9-8	At Bos.	W	3-2		5	6	Cone	Martinez	Rivera	101-41	1st	+19.5
9-9	At Bos.	W	7-5		7	8	Mendoza	Wakefield	Rivera	102-41	1st	+20.5
9-10	Tor.	W	8-5		13	8	Pettitte	Hentgen	Holmes	103-41	1st	+21.0
9-11	Tor.	L	4-5		9	7	Almanzar	Irabu	Person	103-42	1st	+20.0
9-12	Tor.	L	3-5		4	8	Carpenter	Wells	Person	103-43	1st	+20.0
9-13	Tor.	L	3-5		8	15	Escobar	Cone	Person	103-44	1st	+20.0
9-14	Bos.	W	3-0		7	3	Hernandez	Martinez		104-44	1st	+21.0
9-15	Bos.	L	4-9		8	9	Wakefield	Jerzembeck		104-45	1st	+20.0

Date	Opp.	Res.	Score	(inn.*)	Hits	Opp. hits	Winning pitcher	Losing pitcher	Save	Record	Pos.	GB
9-16	At T.B.	L	0-7		7	8	Saunders	Pettitte		104-46	1st	+19.0
9-17	At T.B.	W	4-0	16	2		Irabu	Santana		105-46	1st	+19.0
9-18	At Bal.	W	15-5		15	12	Wells	Guzman		106-46	1st	+20.0
9-19	At Bal.	L	3-5	10		13	Ponson	Cone	Mills	106-47	1st	+20.0
9-20	At Bal.	W	5-4	16	8		Hernandez	Johns	Rivera	107-47	1st	+21.0
9-21	Cle.	L	1-4		5	9	Nagy	Pettitte	Shuey	107-48	1st	+20.5
9-22§	Cle.	W	10-4	15	9		Mendoza	Burba		108-48		
9-22§	Cle.	W	5-1	7	5		Irabu	Ogea		109-48	1st	+21.0
9-23	Cle.	W	8-4	10	8		Bradley	Jacome		110-48	1st	+21.0
9-24	T.B.	W	5-2	5	6		Buddie	Alvarez	Nelson	111-48	1st	+21.0
9-25	T.B.	W	6-1	9	7		Hernandez	Eiland		112-48	1st	+21.0
9-26	T.B.	W	3-1	12	7		Cone	Wade		113-48	1st	+22.0
9-27	T.B.	W	8-3	10	11		Bruske	White		114-48	1st	+22.0

Monthly records: April (17-6), May (20-7), June (19-7), July (20-7), August (22-10), September (16-11). *Innings, if other than nine. †First game of doubleheader. ‡Second game of doubleheader. §Two games in one day (separate admissions). ∞Game played at Shea Stadium due to repairs being made at Yankee Stadium.

HIGHLIGHTS

High point: The Yankees won their 24th World Series title by sweeping the Padres, completing an incredible season in which they won 125 games, including playoffs. The Yankees' 3-0 Game 4 victory gave them status with some of the greatest teams in baseball history.

Low point: It came April 4, when little-known A's pitcher Jimmy Haynes beat the Yankees, 7-3, and dropped their record to 0-3. After a stellar spring training, the Yankees opened the season with three bad losses—they were outscored 21-6—on the West Coast.

Turning point: The Yankees swept the Indians in a September 22 doubleheader, ending a 4-7 stretch and igniting a 7-0 finish that would set up a successful playoff run. The 5-1 nightcap victory over the Indians allowed them to equal the major league record for wins in a 162-game schedule, with 109.

Most valuable player: Derek Jeter was the best player on baseball's best team. He finished third in A.L. MVP voting and was among league leaders in average (fifth at .324), runs (first at 127), hits (third with 203), triples (tied for fourth with eight) and at-bats (sixth with 626).

Most valuable pitcher: David Wells, dogged previously by the belief that he could not concentrate for a full game, put that talk to rest in a remarkable season that was highlighted by his May 17 perfect game against Minnesota.

Most improved player: Hideki Irabu failed to meet the overreaching hype during the 1997 season and was one of the more generous starting pitchers in baseball. In his second season, Irabu finished 13-9 with a 4.06 ERA, which is good enough to be a No. 2 or 3 starter on most teams.

Most pleasant surprise: Scott Brosius came to spring training uncertain whether he would be the club's starting third baseman but wound up as World Series MVP.

Biggest disappointment: Chuck Knoblauch hit .265, 40 points below his career mark in Minnesota, and raised

questions about whether he was made for New York.

Key injuries: Luis Sojo missed four weeks with a broken hand suffered in spring training. Mariano Rivera missed 18 days in April with a strained groin muscle. Chili Davis missed four months with a torn tendon in his ankle. Bernie Williams missed five weeks in June and July with a strained knee. Jeff Nelson missed two months with a back ailment. Jeter missed two weeks in June with a strained abdominal muscle.

Notable: By going 114-48, the Yankees set the A.L. record for most victories, breaking the 1954 Indians' mark of 111. . . . The team held a lead in 48 consecutive games, a major league record. . . . David Cone broke the big-league record for longest stretch between 20-victory seasons. He won 20 for the first time in 10 years.

—JON HEYMAN

RECORDS

1998 regular-season record: 114-48 (1st in A.L. East); 62-19 at home; 52-29 on road; 33-15 vs. A.L. East; 39-15 vs. Central; 29-15 vs. West; 13-3 vs. N.L.; 33-11 vs. lefthanded starters; 81-37 vs. righthanded starters; 97-39 on grass; 17-9 on turf; 37-13 in daytime; 77-35 at night; 21-10 in one-run games; 9-2 in extra-inning games; 1-0-1 in doubleheaders.

Team record past five years: 451-292 (.607, ranks 1st in league in that span).

TEAM LEADERS

Batting average: Bernie Williams (.339).
At-bats: Derek Jeter (626).
Runs: Derek Jeter (127).
Hits: Derek Jeter (203).
Total bases: Paul O'Neill (307).
Doubles: Paul O'Neill (40).
Triples: Derek Jeter (8).
Home runs: Tino Martinez (28).
Runs batted in: Tino Martinez (123).
Stolen bases: Chuck Knoblauch (31).
Slugging percentage: Bernie Williams (.575).

On-base percentage: Bernie Williams (.422).
Wins: David Cone (20).
Earned-run average: David Wells (3.49).
Complete games: David Wells (8).
Shutouts: David Wells (5).
Saves: Mariano Rivera (36).
Innings pitched: Andy Pettitte (216.1).
Strikeouts: David Cone (209).

GAMES BY POSITION

Catcher: Jorge Posada 99, Joe Girardi 78, Mike Figga 1.
First base: Tino Martinez 142, Dale Sveum 21, Luis Sojo 19, Scott Brosius 3, Jorge Posada 1, Shane Spencer 1.
Second base: Chuck Knoblauch 149, Homer Bush 24, Luis Sojo 8.
Third base: Scott Brosius 150, Mike Lowell 7, Luis Sojo 6, Dale Sveum 6, Homer Bush 3.
Shortstop: Derek Jeter 148, Luis Sojo 20, Homer Bush 2.
Outfield: Paul O'Neill 150, Chad Curtis 148, Bernie Williams 123, Tim Raines 47, Ricky Ledee 42, Shane Spencer 22, Darryl Strawberry 16, Scott Brosius 1.
Designated hitter: Darryl Strawberry 81, Tim Raines 56, Chili Davis 34, Homer Bush 13, Jorge Posada 6, Bernie Williams 5, Shane Spencer 4, Dale Sveum 3, Chad Curtis 2, Luis Sojo 2, Chuck Knoblauch 1, Mike Lowell 1, Paul O'Neill 1.

TOP DRAFT CHOICES

1a. **Andy Brown,** OF, Richmond (Ind.) H.S.
1b. **Mark Prior,** RHP, University H.S., San Diego
2. **Randy Keisler,** LHP, Louisiana State U.
3. **Drew Henson,** 3B-RHP, Brighton (Mich.) H.S.
4. **Ivan Reyes,** SS, Liceo Hispano Americano H.S., Bayamon, P.R.
5. **Brian Rogers,** RHP, The Citadel
6. **Brett Jodie,** RHP, U. of South Carolina
7. **Ryan Ridenour,** LHP, Tex. Christian U.
8. **David Fowler,** OF, McCluer North H.S., Florissant, Mo.
9. **Allen Greene,** OF, U. of Notre Dame
10. **Damon Thames,** SS, Rice University

OAKLAND ATHLETICS
AMERICAN LEAGUE WEST DIVISION

1999 A's Schedule
Home games shaded. (*—All-Star Game at Fenway Park (Boston).
D—Day game (any game starting before 5 p.m.).

April
SUN	MON	TUE	WED	THU	FRI	SAT
				1	2	3
4	5 NYY	6 NYY	7 D NYY	8	9 SEA	10 SEA
11 D SEA	12 SEA	13 ANA	14 ANA	15 D ANA	16 TEX	17 D TEX
18 D TEX	19	20 CLE	21 CLE	22 CLE	23 BAL	24 D BAL
25 D BAL	26 CLE	27 CLE	28 CLE	29 D CLE	30 BOS	

May
SUN	MON	TUE	WED	THU	FRI	SAT
						1 D BOS
2 D BOS	3 D BOS	4 D TOR	5 TOR	6 TOR	7 CWS	8 CWS
9 D CWS	10	11 DET	12 DET	13	14 MIN	15 D MIN
16 D MIN	17	18 KC	19 KC	20 KC	21 MIN	22 MIN
23 D MIN	24	25 KC	26 D KC	27 D KC	28 BAL	29 BAL
30 D BAL	31 TB					

June
SUN	MON	TUE	WED	THU	FRI	SAT
		1 TB	2 TB	3 D	4 SF	5 D SF
6 D SF	7	8 SD	9 SD	10 D LA	11 D LA	12 D LA
13 D LA	14	15 CLE	16 CLE	17 CLE	18 DET	19 DET
20 DET	21	22 TEX	23 TEX	24 TEX	25 ANA	26 ANA
27 ANA	28	29 SEA	30 SEA			

July
SUN	MON	TUE	WED	THU	FRI	SAT
				1 D SEA	2 ANA	3 ANA
4 D ANA	5 TEX	6 TEX	7 TEX	8	9 ARI	10 ARI
11 D ARI	12	13 *	14	15 SF	16 D SF	17 D SF
18 D COL	19 COL	20 COL	21 SEA	22 D SEA	23 KC	24 KC
25 D KC	26 MIN	27 MIN	28 D MIN	29	30 TB	31 TB

August
SUN	MON	TUE	WED	THU	FRI	SAT
1 D TB	2 BAL	3 BAL	4 BAL	5 D CWS	6 CWS	7 D CWS
8 D CWS	9	10 NYY	11 NYY	12	13 TOR	14 D TOR
15 D TOR	16 BOS	17 BOS	18 BOS	19 BOS	20 TOR	21 TOR
22 D TOR	23 D TOR	24 CLE	25 CLE	26	27 CWS	28 CWS
29 D CWS	30 NYY	31 NYY				

September
SUN	MON	TUE	WED	THU	FRI	SAT
			1 NYY	2 NYY	3 D DET	4 D DET
5 D DET	6 D DET	7 BOS	8 D BOS	9	10 TB	11 TB
12 D TB	13 TB	14 BAL	15 BAL	16 BAL	17 KC	18 D KC
19 D KC	20 MIN	21 MIN	22 D MIN	23	24 TEX	25 TEX
26 D TEX	27	28 ANA	29 ANA	30 ANA		

October
SUN	MON	TUE	WED	THU	FRI	SAT
					1 SEA	2 D SEA
3 D SEA	4	5	6	7	8	9

1999 SEASON
CLUB DIRECTORY

Owners
Stephen C. Schott
Ken Hofmann
President
Mike Crowley
Chief financial officer
To be announced
Special assistants to the g.m.
Bill Rigney, J.P. Ricciardi
General manager
Billy Beane
Assistant general manager
Paul DePodesta
Director of player development
Keith Lieppman
Director of scouting
Grady Fuson
Assistant to the general manager
Dave Seifert
Director of baseball administration
Pam Pitts
Traveling secretary
Mickey Morabito
Baseball information manager
Mike Selleck
Scouting and player development asst.
Danny McCormack
Sr. dir. of broadcasting communications
Ken Pries
Broadcasting manager
Robert Buan
Public relations manager
Eric Carrington
Sr. director of stadium operations
David Rinetti

Director of corporate sales
Franklin Lowe
Director of sales and marketing
David Alioto
Director of events and promotions
Susan Bress
Director of ticket sales
Dennis Murphy
Admin. assistant, executive office
Erin Buckert
Director of information resources
David Lozow
Team physician
Dr. Allan Pont
Team orthopedist
Dr. Jerrald Goldman
Trainers
Steven Sayles
Larry Davis
Equipment manager
Steve Vucinich
Visiting clubhouse manager
Mike Thalblum
Special assignment scout
Dick Bogard
National crosschecker
Ron Hopkins
Pacific Rim coordinator
Eric Kubota
Scouts
Steve Bowden, Tom Clark, Ruben Escalera, Tim Holt, John Kuehl, Rick Magnante, Gary McGraw, Billy Owens, Chris Pittaro, John Poloni, Jim Pransky, Will Schock, Mike Soper, Rich Sparks, Ron Vaughn

MINOR LEAGUE AFFILIATES

Class	Team	League	Manager
AAA	Vancouver	Pacific Coast	Mike Quade
AA	Midland	Texas	Tony DeFrancesco
A	Modesto	California	Bob Geren
A	Visalia	California	Juan Navarette
A	Southern Oregon	Northwest	Greg Sparks
Rookie	Phoenix A's	Arizona	John Kuehl

BROADCAST INFORMATION
Radio: KNEW-AM (910).
TV: KICU-TV (Channel 36).
Cable TV: Fox Sports Bay Area.

SPRING TRAINING
Ballpark (city): Phoenix Stadium (Phoenix, Ariz.).
Ticket information: 602-392-0074.

SPRING TRAINING ROSTER

Manager—Art Howe (18).
Coaches—Thad Bosley, Brad Fischer (35), Dave Hudgens, Ken Macha, Rick Peterson, Ron Washington (38).

No.	PITCHERS	B/T	Ht./Wt.	Born	1998 clubs
49	Candiotti, Tom	R/R	6-2/221	8-31-57	Oakland
63	D'Amico, Jeff	R/R	6-3/195	11-9-74	Huntsville, Arizona Athletics
53	Dale, Carl	R/R	6-2/215	12-7-72	Huntsville, Modesto, Edmonton
29	Groom, Buddy	L/L	6-2/208	7-10-65	Oakland
51	Haynes, Jimmy	R/R	6-3/180	9-5-72	Oakland
31	Heredia, Gil	R/R	6-1/195	10-26-65	Edmonton, Oakland
30	Holzemer, Mark	L/L	6-0/165	8-20-69	Edmonton, Oakland
	Jones, Doug	R/R	6-2/224	6-24-57	Milwaukee, Cleveland
58	Laxton, Brett	L/R	6-2/205	10-5-73	Huntsville, Edmonton
33	Mathews, T.J.	R/R	6-2/200	1-19-70	Oakland, Edmonton
50	Perez, Juan	L/L	6-0/155	3-28-73	Huntsville, Edmonton
48	Prieto, Ariel	R/R	6-3/245	10-22-69	Edmonton, Oakland
57	Rigby, Brad	R/R	6-6/213	5-14-73	Edmonton
37	Rogers, Kenny	L/L	6-1/205	11-10-64	Oakland
59	Stein, Blake	R/R	6-7/210	8-3-73	Edmonton, Oakland
22	Taylor, Bill	R/R	6-8/230	10-16-61	Oakland
61	Vizcaino, Luis	R/R	6-1/170	6-1-77	Huntsville, Modesto
52	Witasick, Jay	R/R	6-4/210	8-28-72	Oakland, Edmonton
36	Worrell, Tim	R/R	6-4/215	7-5-67	Oakland, Cleveland, Detroit

No.	CATCHERS	B/T	Ht./Wt.	Born	1998 clubs
17	Ardoin, Danny	R/R	6-0/205	7-8-74	Huntsville
55	Hernandez, Ramon	R/R	6-0/203	5-20-76	Huntsville
23	Hinch, A.J.	R/R	6-1/205	5-15-74	Oakland
15	Macfarlane, Mike	R/R	6-1/210	4-12-64	Kansas City, Oakland

No.	INFIELDERS	B/T	Ht./Wt.	Born	1998 clubs
10	Bellhorn, Mark	B/R	6-1/190	8-23-74	Edmonton, Oakland
3	Chavez, Eric	L/R	6-1/195	12-7-77	Huntsville, Edmonton, Oakland
16	Giambi, Jason	L/R	6-3/235	1-8-71	Oakland
60	Ortiz, Jose	R/R	5-9/160	6-13-77	Huntsville
9	Saenz, Olmedo	R/R	6-0/185	10-8-70	Calgary
21	Spiezio, Scott	B/R	6-2/222	9-21-72	Oakland, Edmonton
4	Tejada, Miguel	R/R	5-9/192	5-25-76	Edmonton, Huntsville, Oakland
13	Velandia, Jorge	R/R	5-9/160	1-12-75	Oakland, Edmonton

No.	OUTFIELDERS	B/T	Ht./Wt.	Born	1998 clubs
28	Christenson, Ryan	R/R	5-11/175	3-28-74	Oakland, Edmonton
11	Encarnacion, Mario	R/R	6-2/187	9-24-77	Huntsville
14	Grieve, Ben	L/R	6-4/226	5-4-76	Oakland
20	Lesher, Brian	R/L	6-5/216	3-5-71	Edmonton, Oakland
2	McDonald, Jason	B/R	5-7/182	3-20-72	Oakland, Edmonton, Huntsville
6	Phillips, Tony	B/R	5-10/175	4-25-59	Syracuse, Toronto, New York N.L.
12	Stairs, Matt	L/R	5-9/206	2-27-68	Oakland
26	Stuckenschneider, Eric	R/R	6-0/200	8-24-71	Albuquerque, San Antonio

BALLPARK INFORMATION

Ballpark (capacity, surface)
Network Associates Coliseum (43,662, grass)

Address
Oakland Athletics
7677 Oakport St., Suite 200
Oakland, CA 94621

Business phone
510-638-4900

Ticket information
510-638-4627

Ticket prices
$22 (plaza club)
$20 (MVP infield)
$17.50 (MVP)
$14 (field level-infield)
$13 (field level, plaza-infield)
$9 (plaza)
$5 (upper reserved)
$4 (bleachers)

Field dimensions (from home plate)
To left field at foul line, 330 feet
To center field, 400 feet
To right field at foul line, 330 feet

First game played
April 17, 1968 (Orioles 4, Athletics 1)

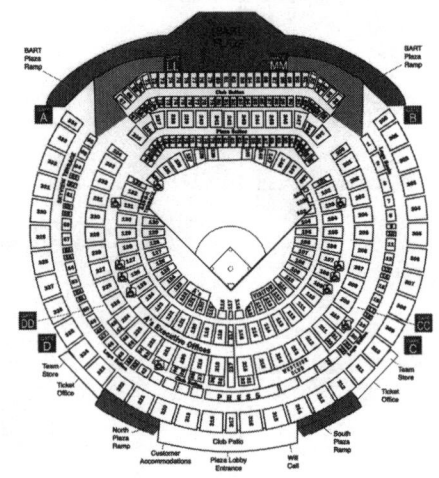

Date	Opp.	Res.	Score	(inn.*)	Hits	Opp. hits	Winning pitcher	Losing pitcher	Save	Record	Pos.	GB
4-1	Bos.	L	0-2		4	7	Martinez	Candiotti	Gordon	0-1	T2nd	1.0
4-2	Bos.	L	3-6		7	11	Wasdin	Taylor	Gordon	0-2	T3rd	2.0
4-4	N.Y.	W	7-3		11	8	Haynes	Cone		1-2	4th	0.5
4-5	N.Y.	L	7-9	(10)	12	11	Nelson	Mohler		1-3	4th	1.5
4-6	Cle.	L	5-6		14	7	Krivda	Candiotti	Jackson	1-4		
4-8	Cle.	W	3-1		8	4	Rogers	Burba	Taylor	2-4	4th	2.0
4-10	At N.Y.	L	13-17		16	16	Buddie	Dougherty		2-5	4th	2.5
4-11	At N.Y.	L	1-3		6	8	Pettitte	Candiotti	Stanton	2-6	4th	2.5
4-12	At N.Y.	L	5-7		8	11	Buddie	Mathews	Stanton	2-7	4th	3.5
4-13	At Bos.	L	3-6		4	11	Saberhagen	Rogers	Gordon	2-8	4th	4.5
4-14	At Bos.	L	6-8		11	9	Gordon	Taylor		2-9	4th	5.5
4-15	At Bos.	L	3-4		7	11	Eckersley	Mathews		2-10	4th	6.5
4-16	K.C.	W	12-7		14	9	Candiotti	Belcher		3-10	4th	6.0
4-17	K.C.	L	1-4	(12)	7	13	Service	Dougherty	Montgomery	3-11	4th	7.0
4-18	K.C.	W	3-2		6	7	Rogers	Rusch	Taylor	4-11	4th	6.0
4-19	K.C.	L	3-7		10	15	Rapp	Prieto	Rosado	4-12	4th	7.0
4-20	Min.	W	3-2		8	10	Groom	Swindell	Taylor	5-12	4th	6.5
4-21	Min.	W	5-4	(12)	15	10	Mathews	Carrasco		6-12	4th	6.5
4-22	Min.	L	2-4		11	7	Guardado	Mathews	Aguilera	6-13	4th	7.5
4-24	At Bal.	W	10-1		13	8	Rogers	Kamieniecki		7-13	4th	6.0
4-25	At Bal.	L	2-8		9	15	Key	Haynes		7-14	4th	7.0
4-26	At Bal.	W	12-4		15	6	Candiotti	Drabek		8-14	4th	7.0
4-27	At T.B.	W	7-6		8	6	Mathews	Hernandez	Taylor	9-14	4th	7.0
4-28	At T.B.	W	4-3		9	6	Small	Johnson	Taylor	10-14	4th	7.0
4-29	At Cle.	W	11-4		16	6	Rogers	Wright		11-14	4th	7.0
4-30	At Cle.	W	5-2		11	8	Mathews	Assenmacher	Taylor	12-14	3rd	6.0
5-1	Tor.	W	5-2		10	6	Candiotti	Hanson	Taylor	13-14	3rd	5.0
5-2	Tor.	L	0-7		1	11	Clemens	Oquist		13-15	3rd	6.0
5-3	Tor.	L	3-6		5	10	Williams	Telgheder	Myers	13-16	4th	6.0
5-4	Tor.	W	7-4		12	8	Rogers	Hentgen		14-16	T3rd	5.5
5-6	Det.	L	5-10		10	9	Brocail	Groom		14-17	4th	5.0
5-7	Det.	L	3-6		3	12	Thompson	Candiotti	Jones	14-18	4th	5.0
5-8	Chi.	L	3-5		5	5	Sirotka	Fetters		14-19	4th	6.0
5-9	Chi.	W	15-7		17	15	Rogers	Bere	Fetters	15-19	4th	5.0
5-10	Chi.	L	3-4		12	3	Navarro	Stein	Simas	15-20	4th	7.0
5-12	At Tor.	L	3-4	(10)	8	8	Myers	Taylor		15-21	4th	8.5
5-13	At Tor.	W	4-2		5	6	Haynes	Clemens	Fetters	16-21	4th	7.5
5-14	At Det.	L	3-8		7	10	Sager	Rogers		16-22	4th	8.5
5-15	At Det.	L	3-8		6	10	Castillo	Oquist		16-23	4th	8.5
5-16	At Chi.	W	11-3		17	10	Stein	C. Castillo		17-23	4th	7.5
5-17	At Chi.	W	9-7		10	13	Groom	Simas	Taylor	18-23	4th	7.5
5-18	At Chi.	W	14-0		17	6	Haynes	Sirotka		19-23	4th	7.0
5-19	At Ana.	L	3-4	(10)	7	8	Hasegawa	Taylor		19-24	4th	8.0
5-20	At Ana.	L	4-5		10	7	Hill	Oquist	Percival	19-25	4th	9.0
5-21	At Ana.	L	2-12		8	14	Dickson	Stein		19-26	4th	10.0
5-22	Bal.	W	9-5		10	12	Candiotti	Kamieniecki		20-26	4th	10.0
5-23	Bal.	L	1-9		4	11	Drabek	Haynes		20-27	4th	11.0
5-24	Bal.	L	1-2		8	6	Orosco	Taylor	Ponson	20-28	4th	11.0
5-25	T.B.	W	8-2		12	5	Oquist	Ruebel		21-28	4th	10.0
5-26	T.B.	L	2-7		6	14	Arrojo	Candiotti		21-29	4th	10.5
5-29	At K.C.	L	3-5		6	9	Haney	Mohler	Montgomery	21-30	4th	9.5
5-30	At K.C.	W	10-4		14	10	Taylor	Pichardo		22-30	4th	9.5
5-31	At K.C.	L	4-10		9	16	Belcher	Mathews		22-31	4th	10.5
6-1	At Min.	W	8-5		12	12	Oquist	Milton	Taylor	23-31	4th	9.5
6-2	At Min.	L	3-10		6	15	Serafini	Candiotti		23-32	4th	10.5
6-3	Tex.	L	10-16		13	19	Crabtree	Stein		23-33	4th	11.5
6-4	Tex.	W	6-1		9	5	Haynes	Helling	Taylor	24-33	4th	10.5
6-5	Ari.	W	2-1	(11)	7	7	Mohler	Springer		25-33	4th	10.5
6-6	Ari.	W	10-5		14	9	Oquist	Benes		26-33	4th	10.5
6-7	Ari.	L	4-12		6	15	Anderson	Candiotti		26-34	4th	10.5
6-8	At L.A.	W	7-3		8	5	Stein	Martinez		27-34	3rd	10.5
6-9	At L.A.	L	1-5		7	9	Park	Haynes		27-35	4th	11.5
6-10	At L.A.	L	0-1		2	3	Valdes	Rogers		27-36	4th	11.5
6-11	Sea.	W	5-2		7	11	Oquist	Fassero	Taylor	28-36	3rd	11.0
6-12	Sea.	L	0-5		3	10	Moyer	Candiotti		28-37	4th	11.0
6-13	Sea.	W	7-3		9	3	Stein	Johnson	Fetters	29-37	3rd	10.0
6-14	Sea.	W	4-3	(10)	9	9	Taylor	Slocumb		30-37	3rd	10.0
6-16	At Tex.	W	9-7		7	9	Groom	Perisho	Taylor	31-37	3rd	9.0
6-17	At Tex.	W	3-2		11	6	Rogers	Burkett	Taylor	32-37	3rd	9.0
6-18	At Tex.	L	2-3		9	6	Sele	Candiotti	Wetteland	32-38	3rd	10.0
6-19	At Sea.	L	1-9		8	7	Johnson	Stein		32-39	3rd	10.0
6-20	At Sea.	W	6-2		10	8	Haynes	Cloude		33-39	3rd	10.0

Date	Opp.	Res.	Score	(inn.*)	Hits	Opp. hits	Winning pitcher	Losing pitcher	Save	Record	Pos.	GB
6-21	At Sea.	L	5-10		8	11	Swift	Oquist		33-40	3rd	11.0
6-22	S.F.	L	8-12		13	13	Rueter	Small		33-41	3rd	12.0
6-23	S.F.	L	2-4		7	6	Gardner	Candiotti	Nen	33-42	3rd	13.0
6-24	At S.F.	W	7-6		10	8	Mohler	Poole	Taylor	34-42	3rd	12.0
6-25	At S.F.	W	5-2		7	8	Haynes	Estes	Taylor	35-42	3rd	12.0
6-26	At Col.	L	6-12		10	19	Munoz	Oquist		35-43	3rd	12.0
6-27	At Col.	W	8-6		9	10	Mathews	DiPoto	Taylor	36-43	3rd	11.0
6-28	At Col.	L	10-11		13	11	DeJean	Fetters	Veres	36-44	3rd	12.0
6-30	S.D.	W	12-10		12	14	Taylor	Miceli	Fetters	37-44	3rd	12.0
7-1	S.D.	L	4-8		8	12	Brown	Stein		37-45	3rd	12.0
7-2	S.D.	W	7-2		10	6	Rogers	Hitchcock		38-45	3rd	11.0
7-3	At Ana.	W	10-6		14	13	Candiotti	Olivares		39-45	3rd	10.0
7-4	At Ana.	W	8-3		9	6	Oquist	Washburn	Taylor	40-45	3rd	9.0
7-5	At Ana.	W	5-4		9	6	Fetters	Percival	Taylor	41-45	3rd	8.0
7-9	Tex.	L	1-4		5	6	Burkett	Taylor	Wetteland	41-46	3rd	8.0
7-10	Tex.	L	0-1		4	9	Helling	Taylor	Wetteland	41-47	3rd	9.0
7-11	Tex.	L	2-4		7	6	Hernandez	Fetters	Wetteland	41-48	3rd	9.5
7-12	Tex.	W	7-5		11	13	Haynes	Oliver	Taylor	42-48	3rd	9.0
7-13	Ana.	W	5-2		10	8	Oquist	Washburn	Taylor	43-48	3rd	8.0
7-14	Ana.	W	6-2		9	8	Rogers	Olivares		44-48	3rd	7.0
7-15	K.C.	L	1-5		3	9	Rosado	Candiotti		44-49	3rd	8.0
7-16	K.C.	W	5-3		7	6	Stein	Rapp	Taylor	45-49	3rd	7.0
7-17	Min.	L	7-8		10	16	Carrasco	Taylor	Aguilera	45-50	3rd	7.0
7-18	Min.	L	3-4		9	7	Carrasco	Oquist	Aguilera	45-51	3rd	8.0
7-19	Min.	W	5-2		7	7	Rogers	Serafini		46-51	3rd	7.5
7-21	At Bal.	L	1-7		6	10	Erickson	Candiotti		46-52	3rd	8.5
7-22	At Bal.	L	4-5		6	10	Benitez	Fetters		46-53	3rd	8.5
7-23	At Bal.	L	7-9		9	12	Benitez	Fetters		46-54	3rd	9.5
7-24	At T.B.	L	0-6		5	14	Saunders	Oquist		46-55	3rd	9.5
7-25	At T.B.	L	5-7		11	8	Hernandez	Rogers		46-56	4th	10.0
7-26	At T.B.	L	1-3		3	10	Alvarez	Candiotti	Yan	46-57	4th	10.0
7-27	At T.B.	L	5-11		9	11	Rekar	Stein		46-58	4th	11.0
7-28	Bos.	L	4-8		7	13	Wakefield	Haynes	Gordon	46-59	4th	11.0
7-29	Bos.	L	2-10		8	15	Wasdin	Oquist	Lowe	46-60	4th	12.0
7-30	Bos.	W	6-5		6	8	Rogers	Avery	Taylor	47-60	4th	11.0
7-31	Cle.	W	12-2		12	7	Candiotti	Colon		48-60	T3rd	10.0
8-1	Cle.	W	6-5	(10)	9	12	Mathews	Karsay		49-60	3rd	9.0
8-2	Cle.	W	7-5		8	9	Mohler	Nagy	Taylor	50-60	3rd	9.0
8-3	N.Y.	L	1-14		3	17	Hernandez	Oquist		50-61	T3rd	9.5
8-4†	N.Y.	L	4-10		7	10	Mendoza	Witasick	Stanton†	50-62		
8-4‡	N.Y.	L	5-10		9	16	Lloyd	Taylor		50-63	4th	11.0
8-5	N.Y.	W	3-1		2	4	Candiotti	Irabu		51-63	3rd	11.0
8-7	At Tor.	W	7-6		8	9	Haynes	Williams	Fetters	52-63	4th	11.5
8-8	At Tor.	L	5-6	(10)	7	10	Plesac	Fetters		52-64	4th	11.5
8-9	At Tor.	L	3-4		5	9	Quantrill	Mohler		52-65	4th	11.5
8-10	At Chi.	L	3-5		4	8	Parque	Rogers	Simas	52-66	4th	12.0
8-11	At Chi.	W	6-4		8	6	Candiotti	Snyder	Taylor	53-66	4th	12.0
8-12	At Chi.	L	0-2		2	9	Eyre	Haynes	Simas	53-67	4th	12.0
8-14	At Det.	L	4-13		8	15	Thompson	Stein	Sager	53-68	4th	12.0
8-15	At Det.	W	10-8	(11)	21	15	Taylor	Crow		54-68	4th	12.0
8-16	At Det.	L	4-6		6	8	Florie	Oquist	Jones	54-69	4th	12.0
8-17	Tor.	L	2-4		6	8	Escobar	Candiotti	Plesac	54-70	4th	13.0
8-18	Tor.	W	10-5		9	13	Haynes	Williams		55-70	4th	12.0
8-19	Chi.	W	6-0		8	2	Stein	Sirotka		56-70	4th	12.0
8-20	Chi.	W	3-1		8	7	Rogers	Fordham	Taylor	57-70	3rd	12.0
8-21	Det.	W	4-2		9	7	Oquist	Florie	Taylor	58-70	3rd	11.0
8-22†	Det.	W	7-2		9	9	Heredia	Moehler	Mathews	59-70		
8-22‡	Det.	W	7-1		12	6	Candiotti	Castillo		60-70	3rd	10.5
8-23	Det.	L	4-5		8	7	Greisinger	Haynes	Jones	60-71	4th	11.5
8-25	At Bos.	L	2-3		7	10	Swindell	Rogers	Gordon	60-72	4th	13.0
8-26	At Bos.	L	4-7		6	10	Wasdin	Worrell	Gordon	60-73	4th	13.5
8-27	At Bos.	W	6-3		13	8	Candiotti	Schourek	Taylor	61-73	4th	12.5
8-28	At Cle.	W	14-6	(10)	24	13	Heredia	Reed		62-73	3rd	12.5
8-29	At Cle.	W	11-6		16	11	Haynes	Martin	Taylor	63-73	3rd	11.5
8-30	At Cle.	L	4-9		10	15	Nagy	Rogers	Jackson	63-74	3rd	12.5
8-31	At Cle.	L	6-15		13	14	Burba	Stein	Jones	63-75	3rd	13.0
9-1	At N.Y.	L	0-7		2	12	Wells	Candiotti		63-76	4th	13.0
9-2	At N.Y.	W	2-0		6	6	Heredia	Cone	Taylor	64-76	3rd	13.0
9-4	T.B.	L	2-5		5	12	Arrojo	Haynes	Hernandez	64-77	3rd	13.0
9-5	T.B.	W	3-0		8	9	Rogers	Saunders		65-77	3rd	13.0
9-6	T.B.	W	9-2		7	7	Candiotti	Santana		66-77	3rd	13.0
9-8	Bal.	L	2-5		7	11	Rhodes	Heredia	Benitez	66-78	3rd	13.0
9-9	Bal.	L	2-6		7	10	Guzman	Haynes		66-79	4th	14.0
9-11	At Min.	W	3-2		11	4	Rogers	Tewksbury		67-79	T3rd	13.0
9-12	At Min.	W	6-5		8	10	Witasick	Milton	Taylor	68-79	3rd	12.0

Date	Opp.	Res.	Score	(inn.*)	Hits	Opp. hits	Winning pitcher	Losing pitcher	Save	Record	Pos.	GB
9-13	At Min.	W	9-6	(12)	12	12	Holzemer	Aguilera	Taylor	69-79	3rd	11.0
9-14	At K.C.	L	6-16		10	19	Bones	Stein	Service	69-80	3rd	12.0
9-15	At K.C.	L	3-6		6	9	Rapp	Rogers	Montgomery	69-81	4th	12.0
9-16	Sea.	L	1-4		6	7	Fassero	Heredia	Timlin	69-82	4th	12.0
9-17	Sea.	L	0-8		4	16	Moyer	Candiotti		69-83	4th	13.0
9-18	At Tex.	L	1-3		6	6	Burkett	Oquist	Wetteland	69-84	4th	14.0
9-19	At Tex.	W	8-4		17	8	Haynes	Sele		70-84	4th	13.0
9-20	At Tex.	W	6-3		8	10	Rogers	Loaiza	Taylor	71-84	4th	12.0
9-21	At Sea.	L	2-5		6	10	Paniagua	Heredia	Timlin	71-85	4th	13.0
9-22	At Sea.	L	6-7		12	13	Moyer	Witasick	Timlin	71-86	4th	14.0
9-23	At Sea.	W	8-3		9	9	Mathews	Slocumb	Taylor	72-86	4th	14.0
9-24	Ana.	L	6-10		11	13	Dickson	Haynes		72-87	4th	15.0
9-25	Ana.	W	7-2		10	7	Rogers	Olivares		73-87	4th	14.0
9-26	Ana.	W	4-3		7	9	Mathews	Percival		74-87	4th	13.0
9-27	Ana.	L	2-4		4	11	Washburn	Witasick	Hasegawa	74-88	4th	14.0

Monthly records: April (12-14), May (10-17), June (15-13), July (11-16), August (15-15), September (11-13).
*Innings, if other than nine. †First game of doubleheader. ‡Second game of doubleheader.

HIGHLIGHTS

High point: One day late in the season, Ben Grieve admitted he was having trouble with his confidence at the plate, a human admission that shows the young man not only has a velvet swing, he also has the ability to scrutinize what he does—and always get better.

Low point: At the end of July, the A's suffered a four-game sweep in Tampa to round out a winless trip. It does not get much worse than losing four in a row to an expansion team.

Turning point: When Rafael Palmeiro batted with two out in the ninth inning of a July game at Baltimore and won it with an all-wrist homer off Mike Fetters, the A's were dead in the water.

Most valuable player: Rickey Henderson led baseball in steals and the A.L. in walks, but his leadership was just as important. Hall of Fame tutelage for young players makes all the difference.

Most valuable pitcher: Kenny Rogers not only piled up an impressive 16-8 record with a 3.18 ERA, third-best in the A.L., he also went out there every night with the kind of winner's arrogance a team needs to right itself. Rogers also fielded his position like a rookie shortstop trying to impress the manager.

Most improved player: He faded, but rookie center fielder Ryan Christenson showed he's going to be the team's center fielder for years to come. People around the league will know his name soon enough.

Most pleasant surprise: Journeyman pitcher Gil Heredia gave the A's a real boost, especially when he shut out the Yankees through 7.2 innings at Yankee Stadium on September 2, carrying the A's to a 2-0 win that kept the Yankees from celebrating win No. 100 that day.

Biggest disappointment: Ed Sprague, acquired late in the season from Toronto even though he offered an almost eerie approximation of what Mike Blowers had been giving the A's, hit .149 in 27 games, and his defense was bad, too.

Key injuries: Dave Magadan was hitting .321 after 35 games, but he hurt his hand, expecting to be out a couple of weeks at the most, and never returned.

Notable: Grieve, who led all major league rookies in runs, hits, walks and on-base percentage, was named A.L. Rookie of the Year, and the A's saw just enough from 20-year-old Eric Chavez to know he will head into the 1999 season on many lists of Rookie of the Year candidates. . . . At 39, Henderson became the oldest player to lead his league in stolen bases. . . . The A's have finished under .500 six consecutive years, the longest such streak since moving to Oakland.

—STEVE KETTMANN

RECORDS

1998 regular-season record: 74-88 (4th in A.L. West); 39-42 at home; 35-46 on road; 18-37 vs. East; 30-25 vs. Central; 18-18 vs. A.L. West; 8-8 vs. N.L.; 23-29 vs. lefthanded starters; 51-59 vs. righthanded starters; 64-76 on grass; 10-12 on turf; 33-38 in daytime; 41-50 at night; 16-19 in one-run games; 7-5 in extra-inning games; 1-1-0 in doubleheaders.

Team record past five years: 335-409 (.450, ranks 11th in league in that span).

TEAM LEADERS

Batting average: Jason Giambi (.295).
At-bats: Ben Grieve (583).
Runs: Rickey Henderson (101).
Hits: Ben Grieve (168).
Total bases: Jason Giambi (275).
Doubles: Ben Grieve (41).
Triples: Mike Blowers, Ryan Christenson, Ben Grieve (2).
Home runs: Jason Giambi (27).
Runs batted in: Jason Giambi (110).
Stolen bases: Rickey Henderson (66).
Slugging percentage: Matt Stairs (.511).
On-base percentage: Ben Grieve (.386).
Wins: Kenny Rogers (16).
Earned-run average: Kenny Rogers (3.17).

Complete games: Kenny Rogers (7).
Shutouts: Jimmy Haynes, Kenny Rogers, Blake Stein (1).
Saves: Billy Taylor (33).
Innings pitched: Kenny Rogers (238.2).
Strikeouts: Kenny Rogers (138).

GAMES BY POSITION

Catcher: A.J. Hinch 118, Mike Macfarlane 70, Izzy Molina 5.
First base: Jason Giambi 146, Jack Voigt 27, Mike Blowers 8, Dave Magadan 7, Matt Stairs 6, Kevin Mitchell 2, Brian Lesher 1, Ed Sprague 1.
Second base: Scott Spiezio 112, Rafael Bournigal 48, Bip Roberts 30, Mark Bellhorn 1, Jorge Velandia 1.
Third base: Mike Blowers 120, Dave Magadan 30, Ed Sprague 23, Eric Chavez 13, Mark Bellhorn 5, Bip Roberts 3, Jack Voigt 2, Kurt Abbott 1, Jason Wood 1.
Shortstop: Miguel Tejada 104, Rafael Bournigal 38, Kurt Abbott 28, Jorge Velandia 7, Mark Bellhorn 2, Jason Wood 2.
Outfield: Ben Grieve 151, Rickey Henderson 151, Ryan Christenson 116, Jason McDonald 60, Bip Roberts 22, Jack Voigt 20, Matt Stairs 12, Kevin Mitchell 10, Mike Neill 6, Kurt Abbott 5, Brian Lesher 4.
Designated hitter: Matt Stairs 120, Kevin Mitchell 23, Jason Giambi 7, Kurt Abbott 3, Ben Grieve 3, Jack Voigt 3, Mark Bellhorn 2, Mike Blowers 2, Rafael Bournigal 1, Jason McDonald 1, Izzy Molina 1, Scott Spiezio 1.

TOP DRAFT CHOICES

1. **Mark Mulder,** LHP, Michigan State U.
2. **Gerald Laird,** C, La Quinta H.S., Westminster, Calif.
3. **Kevin Miller,** SS, Univ. of Washington
4. **Jeff Schultz,** RHP, Cypress (Calif.) J.C.
5. **Jason Hart,** 1B, SW Missouri State U.
6. **Gary Schneidmiller,** SS, Don Lugo H.S., Chino, Calif.
7. **Donato Calandriello,** LHP, College of Charleston
8. **Eric Byrnes,** OF, UCLA
9. **Jon Adkins,** RHP, Oklahoma State U.
10. **Bert Snow,** RHP, Vanderbilt Univ.

SEATTLE MARINERS
AMERICAN LEAGUE WEST DIVISION

1999 Mariners Schedule
Home games shaded. *—All-Star Game at Fenway Park (Boston).
D—Day game (any game starting before 5 p.m.).

April
SUN	MON	TUE	WED	THU	FRI	SAT
				1	2	3
4	5 CWS	6 CWS	7 CWS	8	9 D OAK	10 OAK
11 D OAK	12 OAK	13 TEX	14 TEX	15 D TEX	16 D ANA	17 ANA
18 D ANA	19	20 CWS	21 CWS	22 D CWS	23 TB	24 TB
25 D TB	26 DET	27 DET	28 DET	29 D DET	30 TOR	

May
SUN	MON	TUE	WED	THU	FRI	SAT
						1 TOR
2 D TOR	3 D TOR	4	5 CLE	6 CLE	7 NYY	8 NYY
9 NYY	10 BOS	11 BOS	12 BOS	13	14 KC	15 KC
16 KC	17 D MIN	18 MIN	19 MIN	20	21 KC	22 KC
23 KC	24 D MIN	25 MIN	26 D MIN	27	28 D TB	29 TB
30 TB	31 BAL					

June
SUN	MON	TUE	WED	THU	FRI	SAT
		1 BAL	2 BAL	3	4 D SD	5 SD
6 D SD	7 COL	8 COL	9 COL	10	11 D SF	12 SF
13 SF	14 DET	15 DET	16 DET	17 DET	18 CLE	19 D CLE
20 D CLE	21 D ANA	22 ANA	23 ANA	24 TEX	25 D TEX	26 D TEX
27 D TEX	28	29 OAK	30 OAK			

July
SUN	MON	TUE	WED	THU	FRI	SAT
				1 D OAK	2 TEX	3 TEX
4 TEX	5 ANA	6 ANA	7 ANA	8 LA	9 LA	10 LA
11 D LA	12	13	* 14	15 D SD	16 D SD	17 D SD
18 D ARI	19 ARI	20 ARI	21 OAK	22 D OAK	23 MIN	24 MIN
25 D MIN	26	27 KC	28 KC	29 D KC	30 D BAL	31 BAL

August
SUN	MON	TUE	WED	THU	FRI	SAT
1 BAL	2 TB	3 TB	4 TB	5 NYY	6 NYY	7 NYY
8 NYY	9 D CWS	10 CWS	11 CWS	12 BOS	13 BOS	14 D BOS
15 BOS	16 TOR	17 TOR	18 D TOR	19	20 CLE	21 D CLE
22 CLE	23 D DET	24 DET	25 DET	26	27 NYY	28 D NYY
29 NYY	30 CWS	31 CWS				

September
SUN	MON	TUE	WED	THU	FRI	SAT
			1 CWS	2	3 BOS	4 BOS
5 D BOS	6 D BOS	7 D TOR	8 TOR	9	10 BAL	11 D BAL
12 D BAL	13 TB	14 TB	15 TB	16	17 MIN	18 MIN
19 D MIN	20 KC	21 KC	22 KC	23	24 ANA	25 ANA
26 D ANA	27 TEX	28 TEX	29 TEX	30 TEX		

October
SUN	MON	TUE	WED	THU	FRI	SAT
					1 OAK	2 D OAK
3 D OAK	4	5	6	7	8	9

1999 SEASON
CLUB DIRECTORY

Board of directors
John Ellis, chairman; Minoru Arakawe; Chris Larson; Howard Lincoln; John McCaw; Frank Shrontz; Craig Watjen

Chairman and chief executive officer
John Ellis

President and chief operating officer
Chuck Armstrong

Vice president, baseball operations
Woody Woodward

Vice president, communications
Randy Adamack

V.p., finance and administration
Kevin Mather

Vice president, business development
Paul Isaki

V.p., scouting and player development
Roger Jongewaard

V.p., ballpark planning and development
John Palmer

Controller
Tim Kornegay

Vice president, baseball administration
Lee Pelekoudas

Assistants to v.p., baseball operations
George Zuraw
Larry Beinfest

Director of player development
Benny Looper

Coordinator of minor league instruction
Mike Goff

Director, team travel
Ron Spellacy

Director, community relations
David Venneri

Vice president, sales
Bob Aylward

Director, sales
Joe Chard

Director, merchandising
Todd Vecchio

Director, public relations
Tim Hevly

Director, stadium operations
Tony Pereira

Assistant director, public relations
To be announced

Exec. asst., ownership/business dev.
Janet O'Brien

Manager, payroll and benefits admin.
Shirley Shreve

Trainers
Rick Griffin, Tom Newberg

Video coordinator
Carl Hamilton

Home clubhouse manager
Scott Gilbert

Visiting clubhouse manager
Henry Genzale

Strength and conditioning coach
Allen Wirtala

Club physicians
Dr. Larry Pedegana
Dr. Mitchel Storey

Club dentist
Dr. Richard Leshgold

Public address announcer
Tom Hutyler

Director of professional scouting
Ken Compton

Director of scouting
Frank Mattox

Major league scouts
Brandy Davis, Bill Kearns, Steve Pope

Advance scout
John Moses

Scouting supervisors
Fernando Arguelles, Ken Madeja, John McMichen, Carroll Sembera

Scouts
Dave Alexander, Maximo Alvarez, Brian Ballentine, Jeff Brisson, Mark Brown, Rodney Davis, Ramon de los Santos, Murray Gage-Cole, Phil Geisler, Ron Hafner, Des Hamilton, Larry Harper, Ted Heid, Jae Lee, Jay Lee, Stan Lewis, Wilmer Madera, Luis Martinez, Tom McNamara, John Martin, Mauro Mazzotti, Billy Merkel, Julio Molina, Omer Munoz Sr., Myron Pines, Don Poplin, Phil Pote, Steve Rath, Jesus Salazar, Raul Santana, Alex Smith, Jim Stewart, Harry Stricklett, Derek Valenzuela, Kyle Van Hook, Ray Vince, Curtis Wallace, Selwyn Young

MINOR LEAGUE AFFILIATES

Class	Team	League	Manager
AAA	Tacoma	Pacific Coast	Dave Myers
AA	New Haven	Eastern	Dan Rohn
A	Lancaster	California	Darrin Garner
A	Wisconsin	Midwest	Steve Roadcap
A	Everett	Northwest	Terry Pohreisz
Rookie	Peoria Mariners	Arizona	Gary Thurman

BROADCAST INFORMATION
Radio: KIRO-AM (710).
TV: KIRO-TV (Channel 7).
Cable TV: Fox Sports Northwest.

SPRING TRAINING
Ballpark: Peoria Sports Complex (Peoria, Ariz.).
Ticket information: 602-784-4444.

SPRING TRAINING ROSTER

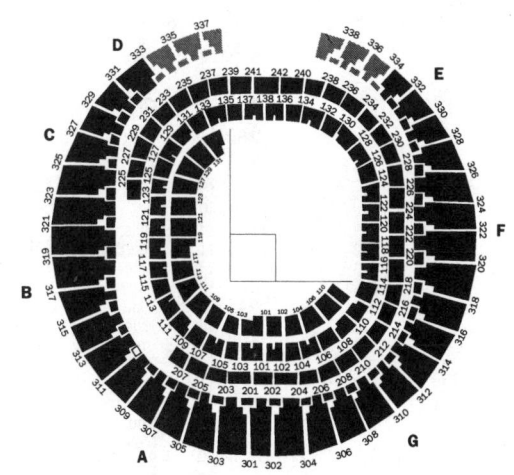

Manager—Lou Piniella (14).
Coaches—Jesse Barfield (29), John McLaren (7), Sam Mejias (49), Matt Sinatro (15), Steve Smith (10), Stan Williams.

No.	PITCHERS	B/T	Ht./Wt.	Born	1998 clubs
31	Ayala, Bobby	R/R	6-3/210	7-8-69	Seattle
22	Carmona, Rafael	L/R	6-2/185	10-2-72	Lancaster, Orlando
27	Cloude, Ken	R/R	6-1/180	1-9-75	Seattle, Tacoma
	De La Rosa, Maximo	R/R	5-11/170	7-12-71	Tacoma, Orlando
13	Fassero, Jeff	L/L	6-1/195	1-5-63	Seattle
	Fuentes, Brian	L/L	6-4/220	8-9-75	Lancaster
	Garcia, Freddy	R/R	6-4/235	10-6-76	New Orleans, Jackson, Tacoma
	Halama, John	L/L	6-5/200	2-22-72	Houston, New Orleans
	Henry, Butch	L/L	6-1/205	10-7-68	Sarasota, Boston
68	Hinchliffe, Brett	R/R	6-5/190	7-21-74	Lancaster, Tacoma
	Leiter, Mark	R/R	6-3/220	4-13-63	Philadelphia
37	Marte, Damaso	L/L	6-0/170	2-14-75	Orlando
39	McCarthy, Greg	L/L	6-2/215	10-30-68	Tacoma, Seattle
	Mesa, Jose	R/R	6-3/225	5-22-66	Cleveland, San Francisco
50	Moyer, Jamie	L/L	6-0/170	11-18-62	Seattle
30	Paniagua, Jose	R/R	6-2/185	8-20-73	Tacoma, Seattle
	Scheffer, Aaron	L/R	6-2/185	10-15-75	Lancaster, Orlando
33	Smith, Cam	R/R	6-3/190	9-20-73	Orlando, Lancaster
	Stark, Dennis	R/R	6-2/210	10-27-74	Lancaster, Arizona Mariners
35	Suzuki, Mac	R/R	6-3/195	5-31-75	Tacoma, Seattle
	Swift, Bill	R/R	6-0/197	10-27-61	Seattle
	Weaver, Eric	R/R	6-5/230	8-4-73	Albuquerque, Los Angeles
26	Zimmerman, Jordan	R/L	6-0/200	4-28-75	Lancaster, Arizona Mariners

No.	CATCHERS	B/T	Ht./Wt.	Born	1998 clubs
	Lampkin, Tom	L/R	5-11/185	3-4-64	St. Louis
6	Wilson, Dan	R/R	6-3/202	3-25-69	Seattle

No.	INFIELDERS	B/T	Ht./Wt.	Born	1998 clubs
2	Bell, David	R/R	5-10/175	9-14-72	St. Louis, Cleveland, Seattle
19	Buhner, Jay	R/R	6-3/215	8-13-64	Seattle, Tacoma
18	Davis, Russ	R/R	6-0/195	9-13-69	Seattle
34	Guevara, Giomar	B/R	5-8/150	10-23-72	Lancaster, Orlando, Seattle
5	Guillen, Carlos	R/R	6-1/180	9-30-75	New Orleans, Tacoma, Seattle
	Mabry, John	L/R	6-4/195	10-17-70	St. Louis
11	Martinez, Edgar	R/R	5-11/200	1-2-63	Seattle
3	Rodriguez, Alex	R/R	6-3/195	7-27-75	Seattle

No.	OUTFIELDERS	B/T	Ht./Wt.	Born	1998 clubs
16	Gipson, Charles	R/R	6-2/180	12-16-72	Tacoma, Seattle
24	Griffey Jr., Ken	L/L	6-3/205	11-21-69	Seattle
42	Huskey, Butch	R/R	6-3/244	11-10-71	New York N.L., Norfolk
38	Ibanez, Raul	L/R	6-2/200	6-2-72	Tacoma, Seattle
	Mieske, Matt	R/R	6-0/195	2-13-68	Chicago N.L., Iowa
12	Monahan, Shane	L/R	6-0/195	8-12-74	Tacoma, Seattle
15	Robinson, Kerry	L/L	6-0/175	10-3-73	Tampa Bay, Orlando, Durham
21	Segui, David	B/L	6-1/202	7-19-66	Seattle

BALLPARK INFORMATION

Ballpark (capacity, surface)
The Kingdome (59,856, artificial) The Mariners are scheduled to play in SAFECO Field (45,600, grass) beginning July 15, 1999.

Address
P.O. Box 4100
83 King St.
Seattle, WA 98104

Business phone
206-346-4000

Ticket information
206-622-4487

Ticket prices
$28 (box)
$25 (field)
$22 (club)
$16 (view box)
$13 (view)
$11 (view, children 14 and under)
$10 (outfield reserved, family)
$8 (family, children 14 and under)
$8 (of reserved, children 14 and under)
$6 (Southwest Airlines Cloud Crowd)

Field dimensions (from home plate)
To left field at foul line, 331 feet
To center field, 405 feet
To right field at foul line, 312 feet

First game played
April 6, 1977 (Angels 7, Mariners 0)

1998 REVIEW
DAY BY DAY

Date	Opp.	Res.	Score	(inn.*)	Hits	Opp. hits	Winning pitcher	Losing pitcher	Save	Record	Pos.	GB
3-31	Cle.	L	9-10		12	14	Mesa	Fossas	Jackson	0-1	T1st	...
4-1	Cle.	L	7-9		7	14	Wright	Moyer	Jackson	0-2	T2nd	1.5
4-3	Bos.	W	11-6		13	9	Cloude	Lowe		1-2	3rd	1.0
4-4	Bos.	W	12-6		12	9	Swift	Rose		2-2	T1st	...
4-5	Bos.	L	5-10		8	9	Saberhagen	Johnson		2-3	T2nd	1.0
4-6	N.Y.	W	8-0		12	3	Moyer	Pettitte		3-3	T1st	...
4-7	N.Y.	L	7-13		14	18	Wells	Bullinger		3-4	3rd	1.0
4-8	N.Y.	L	3-4		10	10	Lloyd	Ayala	Stanton	3-5	3rd	2.0
4-10	At Bos.	L	7-9		12	6	Garces	Timlin		3-6	3rd	2.5
4-11	At Bos.	L	0-5		2	13	Martinez	Moyer		3-7	3rd	2.5
4-12	At Bos.	L	7-8		14	13	Wasdin	Slocumb		3-8	3rd	3.5
4-13	At Cle.	L	5-6		8	8	Burba	Cloude	Jackson	3-9	3rd	4.5
4-14	At Cle.	L	3-8		7	7	Assenmacher	Slocumb		3-10	3rd	5.5
4-15	At Cle.	W	5-3		7	5	Spoljaric	Assenmacher	Ayala	4-10	3rd	5.5
4-16	At Min.	W	3-2	(10)	10	11	Timlin	Aguilera	Ayala	5-10	3rd	5.0
4-17	At Min.	W	11-6		15	10	Fassero	Milton		6-10	3rd	5.0
4-18	At Min.	W	5-3		12	9	Cloude	Tewksbury	Ayala	7-10	3rd	4.0
4-19	At Min.	W	7-4		13	5	Swift	Hawkins	Timlin	8-10	2nd	4.0
4-20	K.C.	W	8-7		12	12	Lira	Rios	Ayala	9-10	2nd	3.5
4-21	K.C.	L	3-5		9	10	Bevil	Fossas	Montgomery	9-11	2nd	4.5
4-22	K.C.	W	11-5		17	8	Fassero	Pichardo		10-11	2nd	4.5
4-24	Min.	W	4-2		6	9	Cloude	Tewksbury	Ayala	11-11	T2nd	3.0
4-25	Min.	L	2-8		5	12	Aguilera	Timlin		11-12	3rd	4.0
4-26	Min.	L	0-2		6	5	Radke	Moyer	Aguilera	11-13	3rd	5.0
4-28	At K.C.	W	5-1		7	6	Johnson	Service		12-13	3rd	5.5
4-29	At N.Y.	L	5-8		10	12	Cone	Fassero	Rivera	12-14	3rd	6.5
4-30	At N.Y.	L	8-9	(10)	11	15	Rivera	Ayala		12-15	4th	6.5
5-1	Det.	L	3-17		9	20	Worrell	Swift		12-16	4th	6.5
5-2	Det.	W	4-0		6	3	Moyer	Thompson		13-16	4th	6.5
5-3	Det.	W	10-6		13	8	Johnson	Castillo		14-16	3rd	5.5
5-5	Chi.	W	8-1		9	3	Fassero	Eyre		15-16	3rd	4.5
5-6	Chi.	W	10-9		13	13	Slocumb	C. Castillo	Ayala	16-16	3rd	3.5
5-7	Tor.	L	0-6		11	13	Clemens	Moyer		16-17	3rd	3.5
5-8	Tor.	W	8-3		9	9	Johnson	Williams		17-17	3rd	3.5
5-9	Tor.	L	1-4		8	9	Hentgen	Swift	Myers	17-18	3rd	4.5
5-10	Tor.	W	3-1		5	5	Fassero	Guzman	Ayala	18-18	3rd	4.5
5-12	At Det.	W	4-2		5	6	Spoljaric	Thompson	Ayala	19-18	3rd	5.0
5-13	At Det.	L	5-8		5	10	Moehler	Cloude	Jones	19-19	3rd	5.0
5-14	At Chi.	L	3-5		8	8	Fordham	Johnson	Simas	19-20	3rd	6.0
5-15	At Chi.	L	3-6		7	11	Navarro	Swift	Foulke	19-21	3rd	6.0
5-16	At Tor.	W	8-1		7	5	Fassero	Guzman		20-21	3rd	5.0
5-17	At Tor.	L	3-4		11	8	Plesac	Slocumb		20-22	3rd	6.0
5-18	At Tor.	W	9-4		12	7	Spoljaric	Clemens		21-22	3rd	5.5
5-19	At Tex.	L	4-10		9	11	Helling	Johnson	Hernandez	21-23	3rd	6.5
5-20	At Tex.	L	7-8		8	13	Crabtree	Timlin	Wetteland	21-24	3rd	7.5
5-21	At Tex.	L	8-9		14	16	Bailes	Ayala		21-25	3rd	8.5
5-22	T.B.	L	2-5		8	14	Johnson	Moyer	Hernandez	21-26	3rd	9.5
5-23	T.B.	L	3-6		9	8	Yan	Ayala	Hernandez	21-27	3rd	10.5
5-24	T.B.	W	3-1		11	7	Johnson	Springer		22-27	3rd	9.5
5-25	Bal.	W	12-4		15	8	Swift	Rodriguez		23-27	3rd	8.5
5-26	Bal.	L	3-8		6	11	Erickson	Fassero		23-28	3rd	9.0
5-28	At T.B.	W	5-2		9	11	Moyer	Johnson		24-28	3rd	7.5
5-29	At T.B.	W	6-2		13	3	Johnson	Saunders		25-28	3rd	6.5
5-30	At T.B.	L	2-5		4	8	Springer	Cloude	Hernandez	25-29	3rd	7.5
5-31	At T.B.	W	11-6		17	12	Swift	White		26-29	3rd	7.5
6-1	At Bal.	L	9-10		11	14	Mills	Fossas	Benitez	26-30	3rd	7.5
6-2	At Bal.	L	8-9	(10)	12	11	Charlton	Ayala		26-31	3rd	8.5
6-3	Ana.	L	1-8		6	14	Finley	Johnson		26-32	3rd	9.5
6-4	Ana.	L	2-6		6	13	Hill	Cloude	Hasegawa	26-33	3rd	9.5
6-5	L.A.	W	4-0		9	9	Swift	Valdes		27-33	3rd	9.5
6-6	L.A.	L	6-10		10	10	Bruske	Wells	Osuna	27-34	3rd	10.5
6-7	L.A.	L	4-7		13	12	Dreifort	Moyer	Osuna	27-35	3rd	10.5
6-8	At S.F.	L	3-4		11	8	Darwin	Johnson	Rodriguez	27-36	4th	11.5
6-9	At S.F.	L	6-7		13	11	Johnstone	Cloude	Nen	27-37	4th	12.5
6-10	At S.F.	W	4-1		10	7	Swift	Hershiser	Slocumb	28-37	3rd	11.5
6-11	At Oak.	L	2-5		11	7	Oquist	Fassero	Taylor	28-38	4th	12.0
6-12	At Oak.	W	5-0		10	3	Moyer	Candiotti		29-38	3rd	11.0
6-13	At Oak.	L	3-7		3	9	Stein	Johnson	Fetters	29-39	4th	11.0
6-14	At Oak.	L	3-4	(10)	9	9	Taylor	Slocumb		29-40	4th	12.0
6-16	At Ana.	L	2-3		7	7	Dickson	Swift	Percival	29-41	4th	12.0
6-17	At Ana.	L	2-4		4	9	Olivares	Fassero	Percival	29-42	4th	13.0

Date	Opp.	Res.	Score	(inn.*)	Hits	Opp. hits	Winning pitcher	Losing pitcher	Save	Record	Pos.	GB
6-18	At Ana.	L	5-11		8	15	Washburn	Spoljaric	DeLucia	29-43	4th	14.0
6-19	Oak.	W	9-1		7	8	Johnson	Stein		30-43	4th	13.0
6-20	Oak.	L	2-6		8	10	Haynes	Cloude		30-44	4th	14.0
6-21	Oak.	W	10-5		11	8	Swift	Oquist		31-44	4th	14.0
6-22	S.D.	L	3-5		5	7	Miceli	Fassero	Hoffman	31-45	4th	15.0
6-23	S.D.	W	5-3		10	10	Moyer	Hamilton	Slocumb	32-45	4th	15.0
6-24	At S.D.	W	2-1		8	6	Johnson	Ashby		33-45	4th	14.0
6-25	At S.D.	L	0-6		6	10	Langston	Cloude	Wall	33-46	4th	15.0
6-26	At Ari.	L	8-13		11	14	Sodowsky	Spoljaric		33-47	4th	15.0
6-27	At Ari.	W	6-4		10	11	Fassero	Benes	Slocumb	34-47	4th	14.0
6-28	At Ari.	L	2-3		6	8	Embree	Ayala		34-48	4th	15.0
6-30	Col.	L	4-6		8	10	Astacio	Johnson	Munoz	34-49	4th	16.0
7-1	Col.	W	9-5		16	8	Cloude	Saipe		35-49	4th	15.0
7-2	Col.	W	10-3		12	10	Swift	Kile		36-49	4th	14.0
7-3	At Tex.	W	8-2		12	8	Fassero	Burkett		37-49	4th	13.0
7-4	At Tex.	L	2-9		8	12	Sele	Moyer		37-50	4th	13.0
7-5	At Tex.	L	4-8		7	9	Hernandez	Johnson		37-51	4th	13.0
7-9	Ana.	W	8-6		12	10	Fassero	Olivares	Timlin	38-51	4th	12.0
7-10	Ana.	L	3-5	(11)	8	11	Percival	Ayala		38-52	4th	13.0
7-11	Ana.	W	2-0		4	5	Johnson	Sparks		39-52	4th	12.5
7-12	Ana.	L	5-8		9	10	Dickson	Swift	Percival	39-53	4th	13.0
7-13	Tex.	W	10-3		15	9	Cloude	Van Poppel		40-53	4th	12.0
7-14	Tex.	W	6-3		11	6	Fassero	Burkett	Timlin	41-53	4th	11.0
7-15	Min.	W	4-1		7	6	Moyer	Hawkins	Timlin	42-53	4th	11.0
7-16	Min.	W	3-0		7	1	Johnson	Radke		43-53	4th	10.0
7-17	K.C.	W	18-5		22	8	Swift	Rusch		44-53	4th	9.0
7-18	K.C.	W	8-5		14	5	Ayala	Service		45-53	4th	9.0
7-19	K.C.	L	1-4		5	8	Belcher	Fassero	Montgomery	45-54	4th	9.5
7-21	At T.B.	W	8-3		12	7	Moyer	Alvarez		46-54	4th	9.5
7-22	At T.B.	L	5-7		10	11	Lopez	Johnson	Hernandez	46-55	4th	9.5
7-24	At Bal.	L	4-7		7	14	Mussina	Swift	Benitez	46-56	4th	10.0
7-25	At Bal.	W	4-2		10	11	Fassero	Kamieniecki	Timlin	47-56	3rd	9.5
7-26	At Bal.	W	10-4		13	6	Moyer	Erickson		48-56	3rd	8.5
7-28	Cle.	L	3-4		9	4	Nagy	Johnson	Jackson	48-57	3rd	9.0
7-29	Cle.	L	7-8		11	13	Ogea	McCarthy	Jackson	48-58	3rd	10.0
7-30	Cle.	L	8-9	(17)	19	16	Shuey	Wells		48-59	3rd	10.0
7-31	N.Y.	L	3-5		6	12	Irabu	Fassero	Rivera	48-60	T3rd	10.0
8-1	N.Y.	L	2-5		8	11	Wells	Moyer		48-61	4th	10.0
8-2	N.Y.	W	6-3		9	9	Wells	Cone	Timlin	49-61	4th	10.0
8-3	Bos.	W	3-1		9	7	Cloude	Wasdin	Timlin	50-61	T3rd	9.5
8-4	Bos.	L	1-2		2	7	Avery	McCarthy	Gordon	50-62	3rd	10.5
8-7†	At Det.	W	6-3		11	7	Slocumb	Crow	Timlin	51-62		
8-7‡	At Det.	W	7-1		13	8	Moyer	Moehler		52-62	3rd	11.0
8-8	At Det.	W	9-3		13	9	Cloude	Powell		53-62	3rd	10.0
8-9	At Det.	W	6-3		11	9	Wells	Runyan	Timlin	54-62	3rd	9.0
8-11	At Tor.	L	4-7		9	11	Carpenter	Fassero	Quantrill	54-63	3rd	10.0
8-12	At Tor.	L	5-11		7	13	Rodriguez	Ayala		54-64	3rd	10.0
8-14	At Chi.	L	2-14		9	16	Sirotka	Cloude		54-65	3rd	10.0
8-15	At Chi.	W	13-7		17	17	Swift	Navarro		55-65	3rd	10.0
8-16	At Chi.	L	3-5		5	13	Foulke	Fassero	Simas	55-66	3rd	10.0
8-17	Det.	W	3-1		8	8	Moyer	Moehler	Timlin	56-66	3rd	10.0
8-18	Det.	L	6-7		13	10	Greisinger	Ayala	Jones	56-67	3rd	10.0
8-19	Tor.	L	2-16		6	21	Hentgen	Cloude	Stieb	56-68	3rd	11.0
8-20	Tor.	L	0-7		3	14	Clemens	Swift		56-69	4th	12.0
8-21	Chi.	W	5-4		8	9	Paniagua	Foulke	Timlin	57-69	4th	11.0
8-22	Chi.	W	5-4	(11)	15	8	Timlin	Navarro		58-69	4th	11.0
8-23	Chi.	W	3-2		3	3	Spoljaric	Snyder	Paniagua	59-69	3rd	11.0
8-24	Chi.	W	11-10		13	12	Cloude	Sirotka	Timlin	60-69	3rd	11.0
8-25	At Cle.	L	4-10		12	11	Nagy	Swift		60-70	3rd	12.0
8-26	At Cle.	L	3-5		8	9	Burba	Fassero	Jackson	60-71	3rd	12.5
8-27	At Cle.	W	10-4		13	10	Moyer	Wright		61-71	3rd	11.5
8-28	At N.Y.	L	3-10		4	12	Hernandez	Spoljaric		61-72	4th	12.5
8-29	At N.Y.	L	6-11		11	19	Pettitte	Cloude		61-73	4th	12.5
8-30	At N.Y.	W	13-3		15	7	Swift	Irabu		62-73	4th	12.5
8-31	At Bos.	L	1-5		4	8	Saberhagen	Fassero		62-74	4th	13.0
9-1	At Bos.	W	7-3		9	11	Moyer	Lowe		63-74	3rd	12.0
9-2	At Bos.	L	3-7		15	7	Gordon	Ayala		63-75	4th	13.0
9-4	Bal.	L	1-10		5	10	Guzman	Spoljaric		63-76	4th	13.0
9-5	Bal.	W	6-5		13	8	McCarthy	Benitez	Timlin	64-76	4th	13.0
9-6	Bal.	L	2-5		4	8	Mussina	Fassero	Rhodes	64-77	4th	14.0
9-7	Bal.	W	11-1		15	3	Moyer	Drabek		65-77	4th	13.5
9-8	T.B.	L	0-10		2	15	Alvarez	Suzuki		65-78	4th	13.5
9-9	T.B.	W	5-2		11	7	Abbott	Arrojo	Timlin	66-78	3rd	13.5
9-11†	At K.C.	W	6-3		10	5	Fassero	Barber	Timlin	67-78		
9-11‡	At K.C.	L	5-8		8	13	Appier	Swift	Rusch	67-79	T3rd	13.0

– 61 –

Date	Opp.	Res.	Score	(inn.*)	Hits	Opp. hits	Winning pitcher	Losing pitcher	Save	Record	Pos.	GB
9-12	At K.C.	L	2-5		5	8	Belcher	Moyer	Montgomery	67-80	4th	13.0
9-14	At Min.	W	10-3		15	6	Suzuki	Radke		68-80	4th	12.5
9-15	At Min.	W	12-7		16	12	Abbott	Rodriguez		69-80	3rd	11.5
9-16	At Oak.	W	4-1		7	6	Fassero	Heredia	Timlin	70-80	3rd	10.5
9-17	At Oak.	W	8-0		16	4	Moyer	Candiotti		71-80	3rd	10.5
9-18	At Ana.	W	5-3	(12)	9	10	Timlin	DeLucia		72-80	3rd	10.5
9-19	At Ana.	L	3-5		8	9	McDowell	Spoljaric	Percival	72-81	3rd	10.5
9-20	At Ana.	L	1-3		8	5	Olivares	Abbott	Percival	72-82	3rd	10.5
9-21	Oak.	W	5-2		10	6	Paniagua	Heredia	Timlin	73-82	3rd	10.5
9-22	Oak.	W	7-6		13	12	Moyer	Witasick	Timlin	74-82	3rd	10.5
9-23	Oak.	L	3-8		9	9	Mathews	Slocumb	Taylor	74-83	3rd	11.5
9-24	Tex.	L	3-9		8	15	Sele	Suzuki		74-84	3rd	12.5
9-25	Tex.	W	15-4		17	8	Abbott	Loaiza		75-84	3rd	11.5
9-26	Tex.	W	5-2		10	8	Fassero	Gunderson	Timlin	76-84	3rd	10.5
9-27	Tex.	L	6-12		10	14	Fossas	Spoljaric		76-85	3rd	11.5

Monthly records: March (0-1), April (12-14), May (14-14), June (8-20), July (14-11), August (14-14), September (14-11).
*Innings, if other than nine. †First game of doubleheader. ‡Second game of doubleheader.

HIGHLIGHTS

High point: During a three-game stretch from April 18-20, shortstop Alex Rodriguez, who would become the third player in major league history to post 40 home runs and 40 stolen bases in the same season, hit four doubles, two triples and two homers, a hot streak that coincided with the Mariners' season-best five-game winning streak.

Low point: Deflated and distracted by the constant Randy Johnson trade rumors, the Mariners lost 20 games in June to destroy any hopes of repeating as A.L. West champions.

Turning point: On opening night against the Indians, Johnson took a 9-3 lead into the sixth inning, but neither he nor the bullpen could hold it and the Mariners lost 10-9. It was the first of many signs that Johnson wasn't his usual dominant force and the bullpen was going to be ineffective.

Most valuable player: Rodriguez and center fielder Ken Griffey Jr. had MVP-type seasons. Rodriguez set an A.L. record for shortstops with 46 homers while Griffey led the league with his second straight 56-homer season.

Most valuable pitcher: With Johnson down and eventually out, lefthander Jamie Moyer emerged as the most dependable starter, posting a 15-win season that would have been better if the bullpen had not squandered four leads.

Most improved player: Jose Paniagua, claimed on waivers during spring training, was called up in August and flourished as the late-inning setup reliever with a 2.05 ERA in 18 appearances. The Mariners were 11-1 in games Paniagua pitched.

Most pleasant surprise: After two injury-plagued seasons with the Rockies, Bill Swift returned to Seattle and finished with 11 wins, the most since he won 21 games for the Giants in 1993. He allowed three or fewer runs in 18 of 26 starts.

Biggest disappointment: After management decided not to offer Johnson a contract extension beyond the '98 season and didn't trade him before spring training, the franchise's best-ever pitcher went into a mental funk that created a dark cloud. Johnson sulked his way to a 9-10 record, taking the team down with him.

Key injuries: Right fielder Jay Buhner's string of 40-plus home runs ended at three because of injuries that limited him to 72 games. Catcher Dan Wilson went on the D.L. for the first time in his career on July 20 after tearing the ligaments in his ankle. He didn't return until September 1.

Notable: For the fourth straight season, the Mariners had at least three players—Griffey, Rodriguez and Edgar Martinez—drive in at least 100 runs. . . . During the 1990s, the team is 351-407 record in even-numbered years and 334-297 in odd-numbered years. . . . The Mariners posted the best post-All Star Game record (39-34) in the AL West.

—JIM STREET

RECORDS

1998 regular-season record: 76-85 (3rd in A.L. West); 42-39 at home; 34-46 on road; 22-33 vs. East; 32-22 vs. Central; 15-21 vs. A.L. West; 7-9 vs. N.L.; 14-18 vs. lefthanded starters; 62-67 vs. righthanded starters; 22-41 on grass; 54-44 on turf; 24-23 in daytime; 52-62 at night; 10-20 in one-run games; 3-5 in extra-inning games; 1-0-1 in doubleheaders.

Team record past five years: 379-362 (.511, ranks 7th in league in that span).

TEAM LEADERS

Batting average: Edgar Martinez (.322).
At-bats: Alex Rodriguez (686).
Runs: Alex Rodriguez (123).
Hits: Alex Rodriguez (213).
Total bases: Ken Griffey Jr. (387).
Doubles: Edgar Martinez (47).
Triples: Joey Cora (6).
Home runs: Ken Griffey Jr. (56).
Runs batted in: Ken Griffey Jr. (146).
Stolen bases: Alex Rodriguez (46).
Slugging percentage: Ken Griffey Jr. (.611).
On-base percentage: Edgar Martinez (.429).
Wins: Jamie Moyer (15).
Earned-run average: Jamie Moyer (3.53).
Complete games: Jeff Fassero (7).

Shutouts: Jamie Moyer (3).
Saves: Mike Timlin (19).
Innings pitched: Jamie Moyer (234.1).
Strikeouts: Randy Johnson (213).

GAMES BY POSITION

Catcher: Dan Wilson 94, John Marzano 48, Joe Oliver 29, Rick Wilkins 6, Raul Chavez 1.
First base: David Segui 134, Raul Ibanez 16, Rich Amaral 7, Jeff Huson 7, Rick Wilkins 6, David Bell 5, Edgar Martinez 4, Dave McCarty 2, Ken Griffey Jr. 1, Ryan Radmanovich 1.
Second base: Joey Cora 130, David Bell 14, Rich Amaral 11, Carlos Guillen 10, Jeff Huson 8, Rico Rossy 6, Giomar Guevara 5.
Third base: Russ Davis 137, Rico Rossy 25, Jeff Huson 8, David Bell 5, Charles Gipson 4, Rich Amaral 1.
Shortstop: Alex Rodriguez 160, Giomar Guevara 5, Rico Rossy 4, Jeff Huson 1.
Outfield: Ken Griffey Jr. 158, Rob Ducey 83, Glenallen Hill 71, Jay Buhner 70, Shane Monahan 62, Rich Amaral 52, Charles Gipson 36, Ryan Radmanovich 24, Raul Ibanez 17, Robert Perez 17, Dave McCarty 5, Rickey Cradle 4, Russ Davis 3, David Bell 1, Jeff Huson 1, David Segui 1.
Designated hitter: Edgar Martinez 147, Rich Amaral 5, Ken Griffey Jr. 3, Jay Buhner 1, Charles Gipson 1, Giomar Guevara 1, Jeff Huson 1, Raul Ibanez 1, John Marzano 1, Alex Rodriguez 1, Rico Rossy 1, Rick Wilkins 1.

TOP DRAFT CHOICES

1. **Matt Thornton,** LHP, Grand Valley State (Mich.) U.
2. **Jeff Verplancke,** RHP, Cal State L.A.
3. **Andy Van Hekken,** LHP, Holland (Mich.) H.S.
4. **Juan Amador,** OF, Luis Felipe Crespo H.S., Camuy, P.R.
5. **Corey Freeman,** SS, King H.S., Tamp
6. **Jake Weber,** OF, North Carolina St. U.
7. **Shawn McCorkle,** 1B, Montclair State (N.J.) University
8. **Craig Kuzmic,** C-3B, Texas A&M U.
9. **Neil Longo,** RHP, Manhattan College
10. **Jason Pomar,** RHP, U. of S. Carolina

TAMPA BAY DEVIL RAYS
AMERICAN LEAGUE EAST DIVISION

1999 Devil Rays Schedule

Home games shaded. *—All-Star Game at Fenway Park (Boston). D—Day game (any game starting before 5 p.m.).

April
SUN	MON	TUE	WED	THU	FRI	SAT
				1	2	3
4	5 D	6	7 BAL	8 BAL	9 BOS	10 BOS
11 BOS	12 TOR	13 TOR	14 TOR	15 TOR	16 BOS	17 D BOS
18 BOS	19 BOS	20 BAL	21 BAL	22 BAL	23 SEA	24 SEA
25 SEA	26	27 CWS	28 CWS	29 CWS	30 D DET	

May
SUN	MON	TUE	WED	THU	FRI	SAT
						1 DET
2 DET	3 DET	4 KC	5 KC	6 D KC	7 CLE	8 D CLE
9 CLE	10	11 MIN	12 D MIN	13	14 ANA	15 ANA
16 ANA	17 TEX	18 TEX	19 D TEX	20	21 ANA	22 ANA
23 ANA	24 TEX	25 TEX	26 TEX	27	28 SEA	29 SEA
30 SEA	31 OAK					

June
SUN	MON	TUE	WED	THU	FRI	SAT
		1 OAK	2 OAK	D 3	4 FLA	5 FLA
6 FLA	7 ATL	8 ATL	9 ATL	10	11 MON	12 MON
13 MON	14 CWS	15 CWS	16 CWS	17	18 MIN	19 MIN
20 MIN	21 D MIN	22 NYY	23 NYY	24 NYY	25 TOR	26 TOR
27 TOR	28 TOR	29	30 BOS			

July
SUN	MON	TUE	WED	THU	FRI	SAT
				1 BOS	2 D TOR	3 D TOR
4 D TOR	5 BOS	6 BOS	7 BOS	8 FLA	9 FLA	10 FLA
11 D FLA	12	13	* 14	15 NYM	16 NYM	17 D NYM
18 D PHI	19 PHI	20 D NYY	21 D NYY	22 NYY	23 TEX	24 TEX
25 TEX	26 D ANA	27 ANA	28 ANA	29	30 OAK	31 D OAK

August
SUN	MON	TUE	WED	THU	FRI	SAT
1 OAK	2 SEA	3 SEA	4 SEA	5	6 D CLE	7 CLE
8 CLE	9 BAL	10 BAL	11 BAL	12 KC	13 KC	14 KC
15 KC	16 DET	17 DET	18 DET	19	20 KC	21 KC
22 KC	23 D CWS	24 CWS	25 CWS	26 D CWS	27 CLE	28 D CLE
29 CLE	30	31 BAL				

September
SUN	MON	TUE	WED	THU	FRI	SAT
			1 BAL	2 BAL	3 MIN	4 MIN
5 D MIN	6 D MIN	7	8 DET	9 DET	10 OAK	11 OAK
12 OAK	13 D SEA	14 SEA	15 SEA	16 TEX	17 TEX	18 TEX
19 D TEX	20 D ANA	21 ANA	22 ANA	23	24 NYY	25 D NYY
26 D NYY	27 TOR	28 TOR	29 TOR	30		

October
SUN	MON	TUE	WED	THU	FRI	SAT
					1 NYY	2 NYY
3 D NYY	4	5	6	7	8	9

1999 SEASON
CLUB DIRECTORY

Managing general partner/CEO
Vincent J. Naimoli
Senior vice president, baseball operations/general manager
Chuck LaMar
Senior vice president/chief financial officer
Raymond Naimoli
Senior vice president/general counsel
John P. Higgins
Vice president/stadia operations & facilities
Rick Nafe
Senior vice president/sales and marketing
Mike Veeck
Vice president/public relations
Rick Vaughn
Manager of media relations
Chris Costello
Public relations assistant
Steve Matesich
Assistant to V.P., public relations
Carmen Molina
Admin. asst., managing general partner/CEO
Diane Villanova
Special assistant to general manager
Eddie Bane
Asst. general manager/baseball operations
Bart Braun
Assistant general manager/administration
Scott Proefrock
Director of player personnel
Bill Livesey
Special assistant to the general manager
Bart Johnson
Director of scouting
Dan Jennings
Assistant/scouting & player development
Michael Hill
Director of minor league operations
Tom Foley
Manager of suites and liason
Cass Halpin
Director of ticket operations
Robert Bennett
Director of corporate sales
Larry McCabe
Director of corporate sales
John Brown
Director of merchandising
Rob Katz

Director, business administration
Bill Wiener, Jr.
Senior account executive
Noel Beaulieu
Ticket sales coordinator
Drew Cloud
Director of community relations
Julie Williamson
Community relations assistant
Liz Lauck
Publications director
Mike Flanagan
Assistant publications director
Matt Lorenz
Dir. of event productions & entertainment
John Franzone
Traveling secretary
To be announced
Medical director
Dr. James Andrews
Trainers
Jamie Reed, Ken Crenshaw
Strength and conditioning coach
Kevin Harmon
Head groundskeeper
Mike Williams
Home clubhouse manager
Carlos Ledesma
Visiting clubhouse manager
Guy Gallagher
Major League scouts
Jerry Gardner, Bart Johnson, Al LaMacchia, Don Lindeberg, Don Williams
Crosscheckers
Jack Gillis, R.J. Harrison, Stan Meek
Area scouts
Fernando Arango, Todd Brown, Skip Bundy, Tim Corcoran, Matt Dodd, Kevin Elfering, Steve Foster, Doug Gassaway, Matt Kinzer, Paul Kirsch, Mark McKnight, Edwin Rodriguez, Rudy Santin, Charles Scott, Craig F. Weissmann
Part-time scouts
Jorge Calvo Sr., Jorge Calvo Jr., Philip Elhage, Mark Lummus, Daniel McConnon, Adrian T. Meagher, Juan Pringle, Gustavo Rodriguez, Freddy Torres, Jesus Valdivia, Mel Zitter

MINOR LEAGUE AFFILIATES

Class	Team	League	Manager
AAA	Durham	International	Bill Evers
AA	Orlando	Southern	Bill Russell
A	St. Petersburg	Florida State	Roy Silver
A	Charleston (S.C.)	South Atlantic	Charlie Montoyo
A	Hudson Valley	New York-Pennsylvania	To be announced
Rookie	Princeton	Appalachian	Bobby Ramos

BROADCAST INFORMATION

Radio: WFLA-AM (970).
TV: WWWB (Channel 32).
Cable TV: SportsChannel Florida.

SPRING TRAINING

Ballpark (city): Al Lang Stadium (St. Petersburg, Fla.).
Ticket information: 813-825-3250.

1999 SEASON *Tampa Bay Devil Rays*

Manager—Larry Rothschild (11).
Coaches—Billy Hatcher (22), Frank Howard (33), Greg Riddoch (7), Leon Roberts, Rick Williams (38).

No.	PITCHERS	B/T	Ht./Wt.	Born	1998 clubs
37	Aldred, Scott	L/L	6-4/228	6-12-68	Durham, Tampa Bay
40	Alvarez, Wilson	L/L	6-1/235	3-24-70	Tampa Bay, Gulf Coast Devil Rays, St. Petersburg, Durham
30	Arrojo, Rolando	R/R	6-4/215	7-18-68	Tampa Bay
	Duvall, Mike	R/L	6-0/185	10-11-74	Tampa Bay, Durham, St. Petersburg
	Gaillard, Eddie	R/R	6-1/200	8-13-70	Tampa Bay, Gulf Coast Devil Rays, Durham, St. Petersburg
55	Gorecki, Rick	R/R	6-3/167	8-27-73	Tampa Bay, Gulf Coast Devil Rays, St. Petersburg
39	Hernandez, Roberto	R/R	6-4/235	11-11-64	Tampa Bay
41	Johnson, Jason	R/R	6-6/235	10-27-73	Durham, Tampa Bay
	LeRoy, John	R/R	6-3/175	4-19-75	Durham, Orlando, St. Petersburg
	Lidle, Cory	R/R	5-11/180	3-22-72	High Desert, Tucson
32	Lopez, Albie	R/R	6-2/185	8-18-71	Tampa Bay, Durham, St. Petersburg
45	Mecir, Jim	B/R	6-1/195	5-16-70	Tampa Bay
	Newman, Al	L/L	6-6/240	10-2-69	Las Vegas
56	Rekar, Bryan	R/R	6-3/210	6-3-72	St. Petersburg, Durham, Tampa Bay
60	Santana, Julio	R/R	6-0/185	1-20-74	Texas, Tampa Bay
31	Saunders, Tony	L/L	6-2/205	4-29-74	Tampa Bay
52	Tatis, Ramon	L/L	6-3/185	1-5-73	Durham, Tampa Bay
36	Wade, Terrell	L/L	6-3/205	1-25-73	St. Petersburg, Durham, Tampa Bay
51	White, Rick	R/R	6-4/215	12-23-68	Durham, Tampa Bay
43	Yan, Esteban	R/R	6-4/230	6-22-74	Tampa Bay

No.	CATCHERS	B/T	Ht./Wt.	Born	1998 clubs
8	Difelice, Mike	R/R	6-2/205	5-28-69	Tampa Bay
23	Flaherty, John	R/R	6-1/200	10-21-67	Tampa Bay, Durham
	Mosquera, Julio	R/R	6-0/190	1-29-72	Syracuse, Knoxville

No.	INFIELDERS	B/T	Ht./Wt.	Born	1998 clubs
12	Boggs, Wade	L/R	6-2/197	6-15-58	Tampa Bay
13	Cairo, Miguel	R/R	6-1/180	5-4-74	Tampa Bay
	Lamb, David	B/R	6-2/165	6-6-75	Bowie, Rochester
4	Ledesma, Aaron	R/R	6-2/200	6-3-71	Tampa Bay
20	McClain, Scott	R/R	6-4/210	5-19-72	Durham, Tampa Bay
29	McGriff, Fred	L/L	6-3/215	10-31-63	Tampa Bay
9	Smith, Bobby	R/R	6-3/190	5-10-74	Tampa Bay
44	Sorrento, Paul	L/R	6-2/220	11-17-65	Tampa Bay
19	Stocker, Kevin	B/R	6-1/175	2-13-70	Tampa Bay

No.	OUTFIELDERS	B/T	Ht./Wt.	Born	1998 clubs
10	Butler, Rich	L/R	6-1/205	5-1-73	Tampa Bay, Durham
33	Canseco, Jose	R/R	6-4/240	7-2-64	Toronto
24	Kelly, Mike	R/R	6-4/195	6-2-70	Tampa Bay, Durham
14	Martinez, Dave	L/L	5-10/175	9-26-64	Tampa Bay
3	McCracken, Quinton	B/R	5-7/173	3-16-70	Tampa Bay
18	Mendoza, Carlos	L/L	5-11/165	11-14-74	St. Petersburg, Durham, Gulf Coast Devil Rays, Orlando
	Sanchez, Alex	L/L	5-10/180	8-26-76	St. Petersburg
21	Trammell, Bubba	R/R	6-2/220	11-6-71	Tampa Bay, Durham
2	Winn, Randy	B/R	6-2/175	6-9-74	Tampa Bay, Durham

Ballpark (capacity, surface)
Tropicana Field (43,819, artificial)
Address
One Tropicana Drive
St. Petersburg, FL 33607
Business phone
727-825-3137
Ticket information
727-825-3250
Ticket prices
$27 (club field, club loge)
$19 (main box, loge box)
$16.50 (tier box)
$16 (main reserved)
$11.50 (tier reserved)
$6 (bleachers)
Field dimensions (from home plate)
To left field at foul line, 315 feet
To center field, 404 feet
To right field at foul line, 320 feet
First game played
March 31, 1998 (Tigers 11, Devil Rays 6)

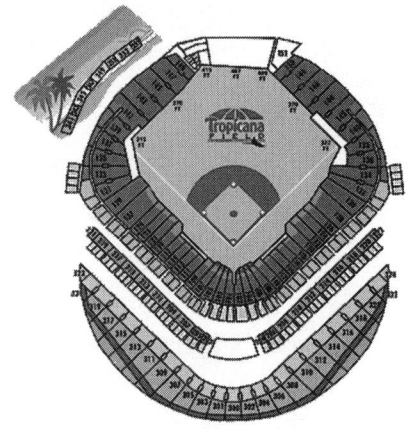

Date	Opp.	Res.	Score	(inn.*)	Hits	Opp. hits	Winning pitcher	Losing pitcher	Save	Record	Pos.	GB
3-31	Det.	L	6-11		12	18	Thompson	Alvarez		0-1	T1st	...
4-1	Det.	W	11-8		18	13	Arrojo	Moehler		1-1	T3rd	0.5
4-2	Det.	W	7-1		12	5	Yan	Worrell		2-1	T2nd	0.5
4-3	Chi.	L	4-10		11	15	Baldwin	Gorecki		2-2	3rd	1.0
4-4	Chi.	W	8-2		15	7	Springer	Eyre		3-2	2nd	1.0
4-5	Chi.	W	5-0		8	4	Alvarez	Bere		4-2	2nd	1.0
4-7	At Det.	L	1-3		10	8	Florie	Arrojo		4-3	2nd	2.0
4-10	At Chi.	L	0-3		5	10	Sirotka	Saunders	Karchner	4-4	T2nd	2.5
4-11	At Chi.	W	5-1		12	4	Gorecki	Bere		5-4	T2nd	2.5
4-12	At Chi.	W	4-1		12	4	Alvarez	Navarro	Hernandez	6-4	T2nd	2.5
4-13	Min.	W	13-12	(14)	19	22	Yan	Trombley		7-4	2nd	2.0
4-14	Min.	L	2-8		9	12	Radke	Springer		7-5	4th	3.0
4-16	At Ana.	W	6-5		11	7	Saunders	Holtz	Hernandez	8-5	4th	1.5
4-17	At Ana.	L	0-5		6	11	Finley	Gorecki		8-6	4th	1.5
4-18	At Ana.	W	8-1		14	6	Alvarez	Dickson		9-6	4th	1.0
4-19	At Ana.	W	6-0		9	6	Arrojo	Watson		10-6	4th	0.5
4-21	At Tex.	L	0-4		4	6	Sele	Springer		10-7	4th	1.5
4-22	At Tex.	L	2-7		10	12	Helling	Saunders		10-8	4th	2.5
4-23	At Tex.	W	12-5		16	8	Johnson	Oliver		11-8	4th	2.0
4-24	Ana.	L	3-10		8	13	Watson	Alvarez		11-9	4th	3.0
4-25	Ana.	L	1-7		7	11	Hill	Arrojo		11-10	4th	4.0
4-26	Ana.	L	1-2		7	6	Olivares	Springer	Percival	11-11	4th	4.5
4-27	Oak.	L	6-7		6	8	Mathews	Hernandez	Taylor	11-12	4th	5.5
4-28	Oak.	L	3-4		6	9	Small	Johnson	Taylor	11-13	4th	5.5
4-29	At Min.	L	0-2		5	6	Tewksbury	Alvarez	Aguilera	11-14	4th	6.5
4-30	At Min.	W	2-0		8	3	Arrojo	Hawkins		12-14	4th	6.5
5-1	At Cle.	L	5-7		10	11	Colon	Springer	Jackson	12-15	4th	7.5
5-2	At Cle.	L	1-5		4	9	Ogea	Saunders		12-16	4th	8.5
5-3	At Cle.	L	8-10		14	16	Mesa	Hernandez		12-17	T4th	9.5
5-5	At K.C.	L	2-4		8	11	Pichardo	Alvarez	Montgomery	12-18	5th	10.5
5-6	At K.C.	W	5-0		12	3	Arrojo	Rusch		13-18	5th	10.5
5-8	Bal.	L	2-8		4	14	Rhodes	Lopez		13-19	5th	11.5
5-9	Bal.	L	0-7		5	11	Mussina	Springer		13-20	5th	11.5
5-10	Bal.	W	4-3		7	7	Yan	Mills	Hernandez	14-20	5th	11.5
5-11	Cle.	W	4-2		7	5	Arrojo	Burba	Hernandez	15-20	5th	11.0
5-12	Cle.	W	6-5	(14)	10	10	Santana	Jackson		16-20	5th	11.0
5-13	K.C.	L	0-4		4	9	Rapp	Saunders		16-21	5th	12.0
5-14	K.C.	L	2-10		10	12	Belcher	Springer		16-22	5th	12.0
5-15	At Bal.	W	4-1		9	6	Alvarez	Key	Hernandez	17-22	5th	11.0
5-16	At Bal.	W	5-2		11	6	Arrojo	Erickson	Hernandez	18-22	5th	11.0
5-17	At Bal.	W	7-3		9	6	Mecir	Mills		19-22	5th	11.0
5-18	At Bal.	W	6-3		10	6	Lopez	Drabek	Hernandez	20-22	3rd	10.5
5-19	At Tor.	L	1-3		2	4	Williams	Springer	Myers	20-23	4th	11.5
5-20	At Tor.	L	1-9		9	7	Hentgen	Alvarez		20-24	4th	12.5
5-21	At Tor.	L	1-6		4	10	Guzman	Arrojo		20-25	4th	13.5
5-22	At Sea.	W	5-2		14	8	Johnson	Moyer	Hernandez	21-25	4th	12.5
5-23	At Sea.	W	6-3		8	9	Yan	Ayala	Hernandez	22-25	4th	12.5
5-24	At Sea.	L	1-3		7	11	Johnson	Springer		22-26	4th	13.5
5-25	At Oak.	L	2-8		5	12	Oquist	Ruebel		22-27	4th	14.5
5-26	At Oak.	W	7-2		14	6	Arrojo	Candiotti		23-27	4th	14.5
5-28	Sea.	L	2-5		11	9	Moyer	Johnson		23-28	5th	15.0
5-29	Sea.	L	2-6		3	13	Johnson	Saunders		23-29	5th	16.0
5-30	Sea.	W	5-2		8	4	Springer	Cloude	Hernandez	24-29	5th	15.0
5-31	Sea.	L	6-11		12	17	Swift	White		24-30	5th	15.0
6-1	Tex.	W	4-1		8	5	Arrojo	Burkett	Hernandez	25-30	5th	15.0
6-2	Tex.	L	3-7		9	11	Witt	Johnson		25-31	5th	16.0
6-3	At N.Y.	L	1-7		5	8	Hernandez	Saunders		25-32	5th	17.0
6-4	At N.Y.	L	1-6		6	11	Irabu	Springer		25-33	5th	18.0
6-5	Mon.	L	2-5		5	12	Hermanson	White		25-34	5th	19.0
6-6	Mon.	L	5-7		13	10	Telford	Ruebel	Urbina	25-35	5th	20.0
6-7	Mon.	W	4-3	(11)	12	5	Lopez	Kline		26-35	5th	20.0
6-8	At N.Y. (NL)	L	0-3		3	7	Reed	Springer		26-36	5th	20.5
6-9	At N.Y. (NL)	W	5-4	(11)	10	11	Mecir	Hudek	Hernandez	27-36	5th	20.5
6-10	At N.Y. (NL)	L	2-3		6	4	Leiter	White	Rojas	27-37	5th	21.5
6-12	At Bos.	L	1-5		10	9	Wakefield	Arrojo		27-38	5th	21.5
6-14	At Bos.	L	2-3	(10)	13	10	Gordon	Lopez		27-39	5th	22.5
6-15	Tor.	W	8-7		9	9	White	Quantrill	Hernandez	28-39	5th	21.5
6-16	Tor.	W	4-3		8	10	Mecir	Myers		29-39	5th	20.5
6-17	Tor.	W	2-1		6	7	Arrojo	Guzman	Hernandez	30-39	5th	20.5
6-18	Bos.	L	5-7	(10)	8	14	Wasdin	Yan	Gordon	30-40	5th	21.5
6-19	Bos.	L	1-4		6	4	Avery	Saunders	Gordon	30-41	5th	21.5

Date	Opp.	Res.	Score	(inn.*)	Hits	Opp. hits	Winning pitcher	Losing pitcher	Save	Record	Pos.	GB
6-20	Bos.	W	8-5		9	10	Santana	Saberhagen	Hernandez	31-41	5th	21.5
6-21	Bos.	L	1-3		2	11	Martinez	Johnson	Gordon	31-42	5th	21.5
6-22	Fla.	L	2-3	(12)	12	9	Alfonseca	Mecir		31-43	5th	22.5
6-23	Fla.	W	6-4		10	7	Lopez	Dempster	Hernandez	32-43	5th	21.5
6-24	At Fla.	L	4-8		13	10	Meadows	Saunders		32-44	5th	22.5
6-25	At Fla.	L	1-5		8	10	Hernandez	Santana		32-45	5th	23.5
6-26	At Phi.	L	0-7		3	12	Green	Johnson		32-46	5th	24.5
6-27	At Phi.	W	5-1		13	6	Arrojo	Schilling		33-46	5th	24.5
6-28	At Phi.	W	5-4		13	11	Lopez	Gomes	Hernandez	34-46	5th	23.5
6-30	Atl.	L	2-7		6	8	Neagle	Saunders		34-47	5th	24.5
7-1	Atl.	L	5-6		10	8	Springer	Hernandez	Ligtenberg	34-48	5th	25.5
7-2	Atl.	L	0-6		5	11	Maddux	Arrojo		34-49	5th	26.5
7-3	At Tor.	L	2-3	(10)	7	12	Myers	Yan		34-50	5th	27.5
7-4	At Tor.	L	0-8		4	11	Carpenter	Springer		34-51	5th	28.5
7-5	At Tor.	L	1-2		6	8	Quantrill	White	Myers	34-52	5th	29.5
7-9	N.Y.	L	0-2		5	4	Pettitte	Rekar	Rivera	34-53	5th	30.5
7-10	N.Y.	L	4-8		12	9	Irabu	Alvarez	Mendoza	34-54	5th	31.5
7-11	N.Y.	L	0-2		5	8	Cone	Arrojo	Rivera	34-55	5th	32.5
7-12	N.Y.	L	2-9		6	11	Stanton	Hernandez		34-56	5th	33.5
7-13	Bos.	L	0-2		7	10	Avery	Santana	Gordon	34-57	5th	33.5
7-14	Bos.	W	5-4		11	8	Lopez	Mahay		35-57	5th	33.5
7-15	At Ana.	L	2-4		8	7	Hasegawa	Alvarez	Percival	35-58	5th	34.5
7-16	At Ana.	W	8-1		12	3	Arrojo	Sparks		36-58	5th	33.5
7-17	At Tex.	L	4-7		11	8	Oliver	Mecir	Wetteland	36-59	5th	33.5
7-18	At Tex.	L	8-9	(10)	12	18	Crabtree	Yan		36-60	5th	34.5
7-19	At Tex.	L	4-7		11	10	Burkett	Rekar	Wetteland	36-61	5th	34.5
7-21	Sea.	L	3-8		7	12	Moyer	Alvarez		36-62	5th	35.5
7-22	Sea.	W	7-5		11	10	Lopez	Johnson	Hernandez	37-62	5th	35.5
7-24	Oak.	W	6-0		14	5	Saunders	Oquist		38-62	5th	35.5
7-25	Oak.	W	7-5		8	11	Hernandez	Rogers		39-62	5th	34.5
7-26	Oak.	W	3-1		10	3	Alvarez	Candiotti	Yan	40-62	5th	34.5
7-27	Oak.	W	11-5		11	9	Rekar	Stein		41-62	5th	34.0
7-28	At Chi.	L	1-4		4	8	Baldwin	Arrojo	Simas	41-63	5th	35.0
7-29	At Chi.	W	7-2		12	4	Saunders	Parque		42-63	5th	34.0
7-31	Det.	W	5-1		12	5	Santana	Greisinger	Hernandez	43-63	5th	34.5
8-1	Det.	L	0-8		5	12	Moehler	Alvarez		43-64	5th	35.5
8-2	Det.	L	2-3		6	10	Powell	Rekar	Jones	43-65	5th	35.5
8-3	Chi.	L	1-6		8	10	Baldwin	Arrojo		43-66	5th	36.5
8-4	Chi.	L	6-8		8	17	C. Castillo	Saunders	Simas	43-67	5th	38.0
8-5	Chi.	W	7-3		12	9	Hernandez	Howry		44-67	5th	37.0
8-7	Cle.	L	1-5		6	6	Gooden	Alvarez		44-68	5th	38.5
8-8	Cle.	L	2-6		3	12	Nagy	Rekar		44-69	5th	39.5
8-9	Cle.	W	2-1		10	4	Mecir	Assenmacher		45-69	5th	39.5
8-10	Bal.	L	1-2		3	7	Guzman	Saunders	Benitez	45-70	5th	40.5
8-11	Bal.	W	2-1		11	3	Mecir	Benitez		46-70	5th	40.5
8-12	Bal.	L	0-7		5	10	Erickson	Alvarez		46-71	5th	41.5
8-13	At K.C.	L	4-6	(10)	12	11	Montgomery	Hernandez		46-72	5th	42.5
8-14	At K.C.	L	9-11		12	13	Haney	Arrojo	Service	46-73	5th	43.5
8-15	At K.C.	W	8-6	(11)	13	13	Mecir	Bones	Hernandez	47-73	5th	42.5
8-16	At K.C.	W	8-3		13	7	Santana	Belcher		48-73	5th	42.5
8-17	At Cle.	L	3-4		8	7	Colon	Alvarez	Jackson	48-74	5th	43.5
8-18	At Cle.	L	2-4		11	8	Gooden	Rekar	Jackson	48-75	5th	44.5
8-19	At Bal.	L	4-6		12	12	Mussina	Arrojo	Benitez	48-76	5th	44.5
8-20	At Bal.	W	4-2		7	4	Saunders	Rhodes	Hernandez	49-76	5th	43.5
8-21	K.C.	L	5-6	(11)	14	9	Whisenant	Yan	Montgomery	49-77	5th	44.5
8-22	K.C.	L	2-3		4	7	Rosado	Alvarez	Montgomery	49-78	5th	45.5
8-23	K.C.	L	5-11		11	13	Rapp	Rekar		49-79	5th	45.5
8-25	Min.	L	1-4		7	10	Rodriguez	Arrojo	Aguilera	49-80	5th	45.0
8-26	Min.	L	3-7		10	12	Tewksbury	Saunders	Aguilera	49-81	5th	45.5
8-27	Min.	W	10-3		16	5	Santana	Milton		50-81	5th	45.5
8-28	At Det.	W	4-3		8	7	Mecir	Moehler	Hernandez	51-81	5th	45.5
8-29†	At Det.	W	10-6		17	5	Springer	Thompson		52-81		
8-29‡	At Det.	L	2-8		4	11	Greisinger	Rekar		52-82	5th	46.0
8-30	At Det.	W	10-5		13	8	Arrojo	Powell	Hernandez	53-82	5th	45.0
8-31	At Min.	L	1-2		7	8	Tewksbury	Saunders	Aguilera	53-83	5th	45.5
9-1	At Min.	L	5-6	(10)	10	10	Serafini	Hernandez		53-84	5th	46.5
9-2	At Min.	W	4-1		11	5	Yan	Hawkins	Lopez	54-84	5th	45.5
9-3	At Min.	L	4-5	(12)	9	10	Guardado	White		54-85	5th	46.0
9-4	At Oak.	W	5-2		12	5	Arrojo	Haynes	Hernandez	55-85	5th	46.0
9-5	At Oak.	L	0-3		9	8	Rogers	Saunders		55-86	5th	46.0
9-6	At Oak.	L	2-9		7	7	Candiotti	Santana		55-87	5th	46.0
9-8	At Sea.	W	10-0		15	2	Alvarez	Suzuki		56-87	5th	45.5
9-9	At Sea.	L	2-5		7	11	Abbott	Arrojo	Timlin	56-88	5th	46.5
9-11	Tex.	W	3-2		5	4	Saunders	Stottlemyre	Hernandez	57-88	5th	46.0
9-12	Tex.	L	2-8		9	15	Helling	Santana		57-89	5th	46.0

Date	Opp.	Res.	Score	(inn.*)	Hits	Opp. hits	Winning pitcher	Losing pitcher	Save	Record	Pos.	GB
9-13	Tex.	W	10-5		17	9	White	Loaiza		58-89	5th	45.0
9-14	Ana.	L	2-4		7	9	Hasegawa	Lopez	Percival	58-90	5th	46.0
9-15	Ana.	W	8-1		10	5	Arrojo	Juden		59-90	5th	45.0
9-16	N.Y.	W	7-0		8	7	Saunders	Pettitte		60-90	5th	44.0
9-17	N.Y.	L	0-4		2	16	Irabu	Santana		60-91	5th	45.0
9-18	Tor.	W	6-1		9	3	Rekar	Escobar		61-91	5th	45.0
9-19	Tor.	W	7-5		8	10	Lopez	VanRyn	Hernandez	62-91	5th	44.0
9-20	Tor.	L	5-7	(12)	13	11	Risley	Lopez		62-92	5th	45.0
9-21†	At Bos.	L	3-4		9	9	Saberhagen	Saunders	Gordon	62-93		
9-21‡	At Bos.	W	8-4		13	6	Wade	Reyes		63-93	5th	44.5
9-22	At Bos.	L	2-11		6	11	Schourek	Santana		63-94	5th	46.0
9-23	At Bos.	L	4-5		9	6	Avery	Rekar	Gordon	63-95	5th	47.0
9-24	At N.Y.	L	2-5		6	5	Buddie	Alvarez	Nelson	63-96	5th	48.0
9-25	At N.Y.	L	1-6		7	9	Hernandez	Eiland		63-97	5th	49.0
9-26	At N.Y.	L	1-3		7	12	Cone	Wade		63-98	5th	50.0
9-27	At N.Y.	L	3-8		11	10	Bruske	White		63-99	5th	51.0

Monthly records: March (0-1), April (12-13), May (12-16), June (10-17), July (9-16), August (10-20), September (10-16).
*Innings, if other than nine. †First game of doubleheader. ‡Second game of doubleheader.

HIGHLIGHTS

High point: The Devil Rays, after a 16-22 start, rolled into Camden Yards May 15 and beat the Orioles four straight, becoming the first expansion team to sweep a four-game series from a defending league or division champion in its home park.

Low point: The Rays dropped their final six games and finished 51 games behind the Yankees, the largest gap between first and last place since divisional play began in 1969.

Turning point: The Rays had sprinted to a 10-6 start, but reality caught up with them, and it was particularly painful during a May 3 loss at Cleveland. One strike away from an 8-6 victory over the A.L.-champion Indians, closer Roberto Hernandez gave up a grand slam to Sandy Alomar, turning the game into a 10-8 loss.

Most valuable player: Quinton McCracken set an expansion record with 18 assists, and was an offensive force. McCracken led the team in hits, runs, total bases, doubles, multi-hit games, extra-base hits, games played and at-bats.

Most valuable pitcher: Rolando Arrojo turned into the ace of the staff. He won 14 games, breaking the single-season expansion record, while the rest of the starters combined to win 25.

Most improved player: Bubba Trammell made the team out of spring training, but a 3-for-17 start led to him being sent to Class AAA. When the Rays recalled him at the All-Star break, he responded with a .297 average, 11 homers and 34 RBIs in 52 games.

Most pleasant surprise: Randy Winn seemed to come out of nowhere to be the Rays' starting center fielder during the second half. All Winn did was hit .285 at Class AAA Durham to earn a May 11 promotion, then start 78 games in the big leagues, hitting .278 with 26 steals, tops among major league rookies.

Biggest disappointment: Lefthander Wilson Alvarez, in the first year of a $35 million, five-season contract, was inconsistent, injured and exasperating. Alvarez lost a career-high 14 games, posted his highest ERA (4.73) in six seasons and did not look like a staff ace.

Key injuries: Outfielder Dave Martinez was out for the rest of the season after a severe hamstring strain on July 21. Shortstop Kevin Stocker saw his season end August 29 with a broken hand. Alvarez missed six weeks with shoulder tendinitis. Pitchers Rick Gorecki (shoulder pain) and Jason Johnson (stress fracture in his back) had their seasons cut short.

Notable: The Devil Rays ranked fourth in the A.L. in team ERA (4.35) and second in fielding percentage (.985). The Rays hit the fewest homers in the league and were the lowest-scoring team in the majors.
—MARC TOPKIN

RECORDS

1998 regular-season record: 63-99 (5th in A.L. East); 33-48 at home; 30-51 on road; 16-32 vs. A.L. East; 22-33 vs. Central; 20-24 vs. West; 5-11 vs. N.L.; 13-27 vs. lefthanded starters; 50-72 vs. righthanded starters; 23-38 on grass; 40-61 on turf; 18-22 in daytime; 45-77 at night; 15-20 in one-run games; 5-10 in extra-inning games; 0-2 in doubleheaders.
Team record past five years: 63-99 in one year (.389).

TEAM LEADERS

Batting average: Quinton McCracken (.292).
At-bats: Quinton McCracken (614).
Runs: Quinton McCracken (77).
Hits: Quinton McCracken (179).
Total bases: Quinton McCracken (252).
Doubles: Quinton McCracken (38).
Triples: Quinton McCracken (7).
Home runs: Fred McGriff (19).
Runs batted in: Fred McGriff (81).
Stolen bases: Randy Winn (26).
Slugging percentage: Fred McGriff (.443).
On-base percentage: Fred McGriff (.371).
Wins: Rolando Arrojo (14).

Earned-run average: Rolando Arrojo (3.56).
Complete games: Rolando Arrojo, Tony Saunders (2).
Shutouts: Rolando Arrojo (2).
Saves: Roberto Hernandez (26).
Innings pitched: Rolando Arrojo (202.0).
Strikeouts: Tony Saunders (172).

GAMES BY POSITION

Catcher: John Flaherty 91, Mike DiFelice 84, Tim Laker 2.
First base: Fred McGriff 135, Paul Sorrento 27, Scott McClain 5, Aaron Ledesma 3, Dave Martinez 1.
Second base: Miguel Cairo 148, Aaron Ledesma 19, Bobby Smith 6, Dave Silvestri 2.
Third base: Bobby Smith 97, Wade Boggs 78, Aaron Ledesma 7, Scott McClain 3, Dave Silvestri 3.
Shortstop: Kevin Stocker 110, Aaron Ledesma 57, Bobby Smith 7, Dave Silvestri 1.
Outfield: Quinton McCracken 153, Randy Winn 96, Mike Kelly 93, Dave Martinez 86, Rich Butler 61, Bubba Trammell 37, Paul Sorrento 18, Jerome Walton 8, Kerry Robinson 2.
Designated hitter: Paul Sorrento 86, Wade Boggs 33, Bubba Trammell 19, Fred McGriff 14, Bobby Smith 7, Mike Kelly 6, Aaron Ledesma 6, Randy Winn 4, Jerome Walton 3, Dave Silvestri 2, Miguel Cairo 1, Tim Laker 1, Dave Martinez 1.

TOP DRAFT CHOICES

1. None
2. None
3. None
4. **Josh Pressley,** 1B-RHP, Westminster Acad., Ft. Lauderdale, Fla.
5. **Aubrey Huff,** 3B, Univ. of Miami
6. **Ryan Rupe,** RHP, Texas A&M Univ.
7. **John Jacobs,** 3B, Marin Catholic H.S., Kentfield, Calif.
8. **Joseph Kennedy,** LHP, Grossmont (Calif.) J.C.
9. **Brian Martin,** C, Central Union H.S., El Centro, Calif.
10. **Ben Keiter,** RHP, Arvada (Colo.) West H.S.

TEXAS RANGERS
AMERICAN LEAGUE WEST DIVISION

1999 Rangers Schedule
Home games shaded. *—All-Star Game at Fenway Park (Boston).
D—Day game (any game starting before 5 p.m.).

April

SUN	MON	TUE	WED	THU	FRI	SAT
				1	2	3
4	5 DET	6 DET	7 DET	8	9 ANA	10 ANA
11 ANA	12 ANA	13 SEA	14 SEA	15 D SEA	16 OAK	17 D OAK
18 D OAK	19	20 NYY	21 NYY	22 MIN	23 MIN	24 MIN
25 MIN	26	27 NYY	28 NYY	29 NYY	30 CLE	

May

SUN	MON	TUE	WED	THU	FRI	SAT
						1 CLE D
2 CLE	3 D CLE	4	5 BOS	6 BOS	7 TOR	8 D TOR
9 TOR	10 CWS	11 CWS	12 CWS	13 BAL	14 BAL	15 BAL
16 BAL	17 D TB	18 TB	19 D TB	20	21 BAL	22 D BAL
23 BAL	24 TB	25 TB	26 TB	27	28 MIN	29 MIN
30 D MIN	31 KC					

June

SUN	MON	TUE	WED	THU	FRI	SAT
		1 KC	2 D KC	3	4 ARI	5 ARI
6 ARI	7 LA	8 LA	9 LA	10	11 COL	12 COL
13 COL	14 NYY	15 NYY	16 NYY	17 NYY	18 BOS	19 D BOS
20 BOS	21 BOS	22 OAK	23 OAK	24 OAK	25 SEA	26 D SEA
27 SEA	28 ANA	29 ANA	30 ANA			

July

SUN	MON	TUE	WED	THU	FRI	SAT
				1	2 SEA	3 SEA
4 SEA	5 OAK	6 OAK	7 OAK	8	9 SD	10 D SD
11 SD	12	13 *	14	15 ARI	16 ARI	17 ARI
18 SF	19 SF	20 SF	21 ANA	22 ANA	23 TB	24 TB
25 TB	26	27 BAL	28 BAL	29 D BAL	30 KC	31 KC

August

SUN	MON	TUE	WED	THU	FRI	SAT
1 KC	2 MIN	3 MIN	4 MIN	5	6 TOR	7 TOR
8 TOR	9 TOR	10 DET	11 DET	12 D DET	13 CWS	14 CWS
15 CWS	16 CLE	17 CLE	18 CLE	19 CLE	20 BOS	21 BOS
22 BOS	23 NYY	24 NYY	25 NYY	26	27 TOR	28 D TOR
29 TOR	30 DET	31 DET				

September

SUN	MON	TUE	WED	THU	FRI	SAT
			1 DET	2 DET	3 D CWS	4 CWS
5 CWS	6 CWS	7 CLE	8 CLE	9	10 KC	11 KC
12 KC	13 KC	14 MIN	15 MIN	16	17 TB	18 TB
19 D TB	20	21 BAL	22 BAL	23	24 OAK	25 OAK
26 OAK	27 D SEA	28 SEA	29 SEA	30 SEA		

October

SUN	MON	TUE	WED	THU	FRI	SAT
					1 ANA	2 ANA
3 ANA	D 4	5	6	7	8	9

1999 SEASON
CLUB DIRECTORY

Chairman of the board and owner
Thomas O. Hicks
President
J. Thomas Schieffer
Assistant to the president
Nolan Ryan
Exec. v.p., general manager
R. Douglas Melvin
Exec. v.p., bus. operations/treasurer
John F. McMichael
Vice president, human resources
Kimberly A. Smith
Vice president, information technology
Steve McNeill
Vice president, marketing
Charles R. Seraphin
Vice president, public relations
John Blake
Vice president, community development
Norman Lyons
Director, Legends of the Game Museum
Tom Smith
Assistant vice president, controller
Chip Sawicki
Assistant vice president, facilities
Billy Ray Johnson
Assistant v.p., customer service
Tim Murphy
Director, grounds
Tom Burns
Assistant general manager
Dan O'Brien
Director of scouting
Chuck McMichael
Director, player development
Reid Nichols
Director of travel
Chris Lyngos
Director, major league administration
Judy Johns
Asst. dir., professional and int'l scouting
Monty Clegg
Medical director
Dr. John Conway
Visiting clubhouse manager
Joe Macko
Equipment and home clubhouse manager
Zack Minasian

Assistant controller
Susan Capps
Director, purchasing
Millicent Van Wie
Director, corporate sales
Mike Phillips
Director, camps and clinics
Jack Lazorko
Director, in-park entertainment
Chuck Morgan
Director, merchandising
Nancy Hill
Director, ticket operations
To be announced
Director, sales
Ross Scott
Director, special events
Jennifer Lumley
Director, player relations
Taunee Taylor
Dir., Spanish broadcasting and Latin American liason
Luis R. Mayoral
Director, publications
Michelle Lancaster
Assistant director, public relations
Brad Horn
Asst. dir., public relations, community & ballpark activities
Lydia Traina
Coordinator, public relations
Amy Gunter
National crosscheckers
Tim Hallgren
David Klipstein
Jeff Taylor
Scouts
Manny Batista (Latin coordinator), Dave Birecki, Mike Cadahia, Carl Cassell, Jim Cuthbert, Mike Daughtry, Jay Eddings, Kip Fagg, Jim Fairey, Tim Fortugno, Mark Giegler, Les Gonzalez, Joel Grampiero, Mike Grouse, Todd Guggiana, Doug Harris, Bobby Heck, Zackary Hoyrst, Jim Lentine, Dennis Meeks, Sammy Melendez, Gary Neibauer, Mike Paustian, Demerius Pittman, Randy Taylor, Ron Toenjes, Greg Whitworth

MINOR LEAGUE AFFILIATES

Class	Team	League	Manager
AAA	Oklahoma	Pacific Coast	Greg Biagini
AA	Tulsa	Texas	Bobby Jones
A	Charlotte	Florida State	Jim Byrd
A	Savannah	South Atlantic	Paul Carey
Rookie	Pulaski	Appalachian	Bruce Crabbe
Rookie	Gulf Coast Rangers	Gulf Coast	Darryl Kennedy

BROADCAST INFORMATION

Radio: KRLD-AM (1080).
TV: KXAS-TV (Channel 5); KXTX-TV (Channel 39).
Cable TV: Fox Sports Southwest.

SPRING TRAINING

Ballpark (city): Charlotte County Stadium (Port Charlotte, Fla.).
Ticket information: 941-625-9500.

SPRING TRAINING ROSTER

Manager—Johnny Oates (26).
Coaches—Dick Bosman (17), Bucky Dent (20), Larry Hardy (25), Rudy Jaramillo (8), Ed Napoleon (12), Jerry Narron (5).

No.	PITCHERS	B/T	Ht./Wt.	Born	1998 clubs
33	Burkett, John	R/R	6-3/215	11-28-64	Texas
54	Clark, Mark	R/R	6-5/235	5-12-68	Chicago N.L.
47	Cook, Derrick	R/R	6-2/195	8-6-75	Charlotte
23	Crabtree, Tim	R/R	6-4/200	10-13-69	Texas
46	Davis, Doug	R/L	6-3/185	9-21-75	Charlotte
49	Glynn, Ryan	R/R	6-3/195	11-1-74	Tulsa
53	Gunderson, Eric	R/L	6-0/190	3-29-66	Texas
32	Helling, Rick	R/R	6-3/220	12-15-70	Texas
50	Johnson, Jonathon	R/R	6-0/180	7-16-74	Oklahoma, Texas, Charlotte
57	Knight, Brandon	L/R	6-0/170	10-1-75	Tulsa, Oklahoma City
36	Kolb, Danny	R/R	6-4/185	3-29-75	Tulsa, Oklahoma
55	Lee, Corey	B/L	6-2/180	12-26-74	Tulsa
43	Levine, Al	L/R	6-3/180	5-22-68	Oklahoma, Texas
22	Loaiza, Esteban	R/R	6-3/205	12-31-71	Pittsburgh, Texas
56	Patterson, Danny	R/R	6-0/225	2-17-71	Tulsa, Oklahoma, Texas
40	Perisho, Matt	L/L	6-0/190	6-8-75	Tulsa, Oklahoma, Texas
30	Sele, Aaron	R/R	6-5/215	6-25-70	Texas
51	Venafro, Mike	L/L	5-10/170	8-2-73	Tulsa, Oklahoma City
35	Wetteland, John	R/R	6-2/215	8-21-66	Texas

No.	CATCHERS	B/T	Ht./Wt.	Born	1998 clubs
41	King, Cesar	R/R	6-0/175	2-28-78	Tulsa
7	Rodriguez, Ivan	R/R	5-9/205	11-30-71	Texas
8	Zaun, Gregg	B/R	5-10/180	4-14-71	Florida

No.	INFIELDERS	B/T	Ht./Wt.	Born	1998 clubs
10	Alicea, Luis	B/R	5-9/176	7-29-65	Texas
11	Clayton, Royce	R/R	6-0/183	1-2-70	St. Louis, Texas
44	Dransfeldt, Kelly	R/R	6-2/195	4-16-75	Charlotte, Tulsa
45	Gallagher, Shawn	R/R	6-0/187	11-8-76	Charlotte
3	McLemore, Mark	B/R	5-11/207	10-4-64	Texas
25	Palmeiro, Rafael	L/L	6-0/190	9-24-64	Baltimore
28	Sasser, Rob	R/R	6-3/205	3-9-75	Texas, Charlotte, Tulsa
15	Shave, Jon	R/R	6-0/185	11-4-67	Salt Lake, Minnesota
9	Stevens, Lee	L/L	6-4/235	7-10-67	Texas, Oklahoma
27	Zeile, Todd	R/R	6-1/205	9-9-65	Los Angeles, Texas, Florida

No.	OUTFIELDERS	B/T	Ht./Wt.	Born	1998 clubs
19	Gonzalez, Juan	R/R	6-3/220	10-16-69	Texas
24	Goodwin, Tom	L/R	6-1/175	7-27-68	Texas
29	Greer, Rusty	L/L	6-0/195	1-21-69	Texas
39	Kelly, Roberto	R/R	6-2/198	10-1-64	Texas
38	Mateo, Ruben	R/R	6-0/170	2-10-78	Tulsa, Charlotte
16	Simms, Mike	R/R	6-4/230	1-12-67	Texas
37	Williams, Ricky	R/R	6-0/225	5-21-77	Batavia
31	Zywica, Michael	R/R	6-4/190	9-14-74	Charlotte, Tulsa

BALLPARK INFORMATION

Ballpark (capacity, surface)
The Ballpark in Arlington (49,166, grass)
Address
1000 Ballpark Way
Arlington, TX 76011
Business phone
817-273-5222
Ticket information
817-273-5100
Ticket prices
$30 (lower box, club box)
$25 (corner box, club box)
$20 (terrace club box)
$15 (left field reserved, lower HR porch)
$14 (upper box)
$12 (upper reserved, upper HR porch)
$10 (upper box-adult, bleachers-adult)
$7 (grandstand reserved-adult)
$5 (upper box-children, grandstand-adult)
$4 (bleachers-children)
$3 (grandstand reserved-children)
$2 (grandstand-children)
Field dimensions (from home plate)
To left field at foul line, 334 feet
To center field, 400 feet
To right field at foul line, 325 feet
First game played
April 11, 1994 (Brewers 4, Rangers 3)

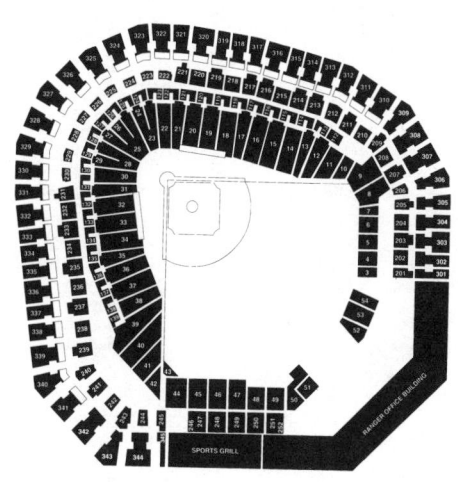

1998 REVIEW
DAY BY DAY

Date	Opp.	Res.	Score	(inn.*)	Hits	Opp. hits	Winning pitcher	Losing pitcher	Save	Record	Pos.	GB
3-31	Chi.	L	2-9		8	13	Navarro	Burkett		0-1	T1st	...
4-2	Chi.	W	20-4		23	8	Sele	Sirotka	Pavlik	1-1	2nd	1.0
4-3	At Tor.	W	5-0		9	4	Helling	Guzman		2-1	T1st	...
4-4	At Tor.	L	2-9		4	13	Williams	Oliver		2-2	T1st	...
4-5	At Tor.	W	6-5		10	6	Burkett	Risley	Wetteland	3-2	1st	+1.0
4-6	At Chi.	L	4-5		7	11	Foulke	Pavlik	Karchner	3-3	T1st	...
4-9	At Chi.	W	11-0		11	3	Sele	Baldwin		4-3	2nd	0.5
4-10	Tor.	W	4-3		11	7	Helling	Plesac	Wetteland	5-3	1st	+0.5
4-11	Tor.	L	8-9		17	13	Almanzar	Oliver	Myers	5-4	1st	+0.5
4-12	Tor.	W	3-1		8	7	Wetteland	Quantrill		6-4	1st	+0.5
4-13	Det.	W	10-1		14	8	Witt	Moehler		7-4	1st	+1.0
4-14	Det.	W	11-2		19	7	Sele	Sanders		8-4	1st	+1.5
4-15	Det.	W	7-3		9	7	Helling	Worrell		9-4	1st	+2.5
4-17	Bal.	W	6-4		14	10	Pavlik	Erickson	Wetteland	10-4	1st	+3.0
4-18	Bal.	L	8-10		11	15	Kamieniecki	Burkett		10-5	1st	+3.0
4-19	Bal.	W	11-7		16	12	Witt	Key	Wetteland	11-5	1st	+4.0
4-21	T.B.	W	4-0		6	4	Sele	Springer		12-5	1st	+4.5
4-22	T.B.	W	7-2		12	10	Helling	Saunders		13-5	1st	+4.5
4-23	T.B.	L	5-12		8	16	Johnson	Oliver		13-6	1st	+4.0
4-24	At K.C.	L	4-11		12	12	Rusch	Burkett		13-7	1st	+3.0
4-25	At K.C.	W	11-8		14	12	Witt	Rapp	Wetteland	14-7	1st	+3.0
4-26	At K.C.	W	11-4		15	9	Sele	Haney		15-7	1st	+3.0
4-27	At Min.	W	9-4		13	9	Helling	Morgan		16-7	1st	+3.0
4-28	At Min.	W	7-2		14	5	Oliver	Milton		17-7	1st	+3.0
4-29	At Det.	W	4-1		7	4	Burkett	Keagle	Wetteland	18-7	1st	+4.0
4-30	At Det.	L	2-7		6	14	Moehler	Witt		18-8	1st	+3.0
5-1	At Bos.	L	3-5		7	9	Wasdin	Sele	Gordon	18-9	1st	+2.0
5-2	At Bos.	W	7-6		11	12	Helling	Rose	Wetteland	19-9	1st	+2.0
5-3	At Bos.	L	1-2		5	9	Martinez	Oliver	Gordon	19-10	1st	+2.0
5-5	N.Y.	L	2-7		4	13	Cone	Burkett		19-11	1st	+2.5
5-6	N.Y.	L	13-15		15	18	Stanton	Patterson	Rivera	19-12	1st	+2.5
5-7	Cle.	L	2-7		4	12	Colon	Sele		19-13	1st	+2.0
5-8	Cle.	W	6-3		7	9	Hernandez	Mesa	Wetteland	20-13	1st	+2.0
5-9	Cle.	W	7-3		13	7	Oliver	Nagy		21-13	1st	+3.0
5-10	Cle.	W	5-3		10	6	Burkett	Wright	Wetteland	22-13	1st	+3.0
5-11	Bos.	W	8-2		11	5	Witt	Wasdin		23-13	1st	+3.5
5-12	Bos.	W	6-3		7	7	Sele	Rose	Wetteland	24-13	1st	+4.5
5-13	At N.Y.	L	6-8		12	13	Cone	Helling	Rivera	24-14	1st	+3.5
5-14	At N.Y.	W	7-5	(13)	12	13	Patterson	Banks	Wetteland	25-14	1st	+4.5
5-15	At Cle.	L	2-3	(14)	10	10	Krivda	Levine		25-15	1st	+4.5
5-16	At Cle.	L	3-10		7	12	Burba	Witt		25-16	1st	+3.5
5-17	At Cle.	W	1-0		5	5	Sele	Colon	Wetteland	26-16	1st	+4.5
5-19	Sea.	W	10-4		11	9	Helling	Johnson	Hernandez	27-16	1st	+5.0
5-20	Sea.	W	8-7		13	8	Crabtree	Timlin	Wetteland	28-16	1st	+5.0
5-21	Sea.	W	9-8		16	14	Bailes	Ayala		29-16	1st	+5.0
5-22	K.C.	W	13-10		13	15	Wetteland	Montgomery		30-16	1st	+5.0
5-23	K.C.	W	7-3		10	8	Sele	Rusch		31-16	1st	+6.0
5-24	K.C.	L	3-8		11	11	Rapp	Helling	Pichardo	31-17	1st	+6.0
5-25	Min.	L	3-9		6	12	Morgan	Oliver		31-18	1st	+6.0
5-27	Min.	L	5-6		11	11	Trombley	Hernandez	Aguilera	31-19	1st	+6.0
5-28	At Bal.	L	2-5		7	11	Drabek	Witt	Orosco	31-20	1st	+5.5
5-29	At Bal.	L	3-6		8	12	Johns	Sele	Benitez	31-21	1st	+4.5
5-30	At Bal.	W	10-8		12	11	Hernandez	Ponson	Wetteland	32-21	1st	+5.5
5-31	At Bal.	W	9-5		15	12	Oliver	Erickson	Patterson	33-21	1st	+5.5
6-1	At T.B.	L	1-4		5	8	Arrojo	Burkett	Hernandez	33-22	1st	+4.5
6-2	At T.B.	W	7-3		11	9	Witt	Johnson		34-22	1st	+4.5
6-3	At Oak.	W	16-10		19	13	Crabtree	Stein		35-22	1st	+4.5
6-4	At Oak.	L	1-6		5	9	Haynes	Helling	Taylor	35-23	1st	+3.5
6-5	S.D.	W	8-7		15	13	Crabtree	Wall	Wetteland	36-23	1st	+3.5
6-6	S.D.	W	3-0		9	6	Burkett	Hitchcock	Wetteland	37-23	1st	+3.5
6-7	S.D.	L	8-17		9	15	Miceli	Patterson		37-24	1st	+2.5
6-8	At Col.	W	3-1		8	6	Sele	Astacio	Wetteland	38-24	1st	+3.0
6-9	At Col.	W	5-2		12	5	Helling	Thomson	Wetteland	39-24	1st	+3.0
6-10	At Col.	L	8-9	(10)	14	14	DiPoto	Gunderson		39-25	1st	+3.0
6-12	Ana.	L	1-5		6	10	Olivares	Burkett	Cadaret	39-26	1st	+1.5
6-13	Ana.	L	6-18		8	21	Washburn	Sele		39-27	1st	+0.5
6-14	Ana.	W	4-2		13	4	Helling	Finley	Wetteland	40-27	1st	+1.5
6-15	Ana.	L	5-8		10	12	Sparks	Witt	Percival	40-28	1st	+0.5
6-16	Oak.	L	7-9		9	7	Groom	Perisho	Taylor	40-29	2nd	0.5
6-17	Oak.	L	2-3		6	11	Rogers	Burkett	Taylor	40-30	2nd	1.5
6-18	Oak.	W	3-2		6	9	Sele	Candiotti	Wetteland	41-30	2nd	1.5

Date	Opp.	Res.	Score	(inn.*)	Hits	Opp. hits	Winning pitcher	Losing pitcher	Save	Record	Pos.	GB
6-19	At Ana.	W	7-3		8	11	Helling	Finley		42-30	2nd	0.5
6-20	At Ana.	L	3-8		6	10	Sparks	Van Poppel		42-31	2nd	1.5
6-21	At Ana.	L	7-10		11	14	Dickson	Perisho	Percival	42-32	2nd	2.5
6-22	Ari.	L	0-6		7	11	Benes	Burkett		42-33	2nd	3.5
6-23	Ari.	W	16-5		19	13	Sele	Anderson		43-33	2nd	3.5
6-24	At Ari.	W	3-2		9	5	Helling	Blair	Wetteland	44-33	2nd	2.5
6-25	At Ari.	W	9-4		13	6	Van Poppel	Telemaco		45-33	2nd	2.5
6-26	At S.F.	W	7-3		12	10	Oliver	Hershiser	Wetteland	46-33	2nd	1.5
6-27	At S.F.	L	5-6	(10)	10	9	Nen	Patterson		46-34	2nd	1.5
6-28	At S.F.	L	0-7		3	7	Gardner	Sele		46-35	2nd	2.5
6-30	L.A.	L	1-4		3	8	Dreifort	Helling	Osuna	46-36	2nd	3.5
7-1	L.A.	L	5-7		9	11	Radinsky	Wetteland	Osuna	46-37	2nd	3.5
7-2	L.A.	L	1-4		7	11	Park	Oliver	Radinsky	46-38	2nd	3.5
7-3	Sea.	L	2-8		8	12	Fassero	Burkett		46-39	2nd	3.5
7-4	Sea.	W	9-2		12	8	Sele	Moyer		47-39	2nd	2.5
7-5	Sea.	W	8-4		9	7	Hernandez	Johnson		48-39	2nd	1.5
7-9	At Oak.	W	4-1		6	5	Burkett	Taylor	Wetteland	49-39	2nd	0.5
7-10	At Oak.	W	1-0		9	4	Helling	Taylor	Wetteland	50-39	2nd	0.5
7-11	At Oak.	W	4-2		6	7	Hernandez	Fetters	Wetteland	51-39	1st	+0.5
7-12	At Oak.	L	5-7		13	11	Haynes	Oliver	Taylor	51-40	2nd	0.5
7-13	At Sea.	L	3-10		9	15	Cloude	Van Poppel		51-41	2nd	0.5
7-14	At Sea.	L	3-6		6	11	Fassero	Burkett	Timlin	51-42	2nd	0.5
7-15	Bal.	L	3-14		11	19	Ponson	Helling		51-43	2nd	1.5
7-16	Bal.	L	3-9		8	18	Erickson	Sele		51-44	2nd	1.5
7-17	T.B.	W	7-4		8	11	Oliver	Mecir	Wetteland	52-44	2nd	0.5
7-18	T.B.	W	9-8	(10)	18	12	Crabtree	Yan		53-44	2nd	0.5
7-19	T.B.	W	7-4		10	11	Burkett	Rekar	Wetteland	54-44	1st	+1.5
7-21	At K.C.	W	15-5		16	7	Helling	Rosado		55-44	1st	+1.5
7-22	At K.C.	L	4-7		8	12	Rapp	Sele	Montgomery	55-45	1st	+0.5
7-23	At K.C.	W	8-4		18	12	Hernandez	Rusch	Wetteland	56-45	1st	+0.5
7-24	At Min.	L	3-5		11	13	Serafini	Loaiza	Aguilera	56-46	1st	+0.5
7-25	At Min.	L	6-7		8	11	Swindell	Patterson	Aguilera	56-47	2nd	0.5
7-26	At Min.	L	3-11		8	14	Hawkins	Helling		56-48	2nd	0.5
7-28	At Tor.	L	3-8		7	11	Clemens	Sele		56-49	2nd	1.0
7-29	At Tor.	W	9-6		11	8	Oliver	Carpenter	Wetteland	57-49	2nd	1.0
7-30	At Tor.	L	0-1		5	4	Guzman	Loaiza	Myers	57-50	2nd	1.0
7-31	Chi.	L	2-10		8	11	Snyder	Burkett		57-51	2nd	1.0
8-1	Chi.	W	8-1		12	9	Helling	Sirotka		58-51	T1st	...
8-2	Chi.	W	12-3		17	10	Sele	Navarro		59-51	1st	+1.0
8-4	Tor.	W	11-9		11	12	Stottlemyre	Carpenter	Wetteland	60-51	1st	+0.5
8-5	Tor.	W	4-3		6	7	Wetteland	Myers		61-51	1st	+1.5
8-6	Bos.	W	7-4		11	10	Burkett	Saberhagen	Wetteland	62-51	1st	+2.0
8-7	Bos.	W	4-3		8	8	Helling	Martinez	Wetteland	63-51	1st	+2.5
8-8	Bos.	L	1-11		7	18	Wakefield	Sele		63-52	1st	+3.0
8-9	Bos.	L	8-14		9	12	Corsi	Stottlemyre		63-53	1st	+2.0
8-11	At Cle.	W	2-1		8	7	Loaiza	Karsay	Wetteland	64-53	1st	+1.5
8-12	At Cle.	L	3-6		11	13	Colon	Burkett	Jackson	64-54	1st	+0.5
8-13	At N.Y.	L	0-2		2	3	Hernandez	Helling	Rivera	64-55	1st	+0.5
8-14	At N.Y.	L	4-6		11	9	Pettitte	Sele	Rivera	64-56	2nd	0.5
8-15	At N.Y.	W	16-5		19	12	Stottlemyre	Irabu		65-56	2nd	0.5
8-16	At N.Y.	L	5-6		12	17	Rivera	Hernandez		65-57	2nd	0.5
8-18§	At Bos.	L	1-4		5	7	Martinez	Burkett	Gordon	65-58		
8-18§	At Bos.	L	4-5		10	9	Lowe	Patterson	Gordon	65-59	2nd	1.5
8-19	Cle.	W	3-1		6	5	Sele	Nagy	Wetteland	66-59	2nd	1.5
8-20	Cle.	W	8-2		9	12	Stottlemyre	Burba	Patterson	67-59	2nd	1.5
8-21	N.Y.	L	0-5		6	10	Wells	Loaiza		67-60	2nd	1.5
8-22	N.Y.	L	9-12		13	17	Bradley	Hernandez	Rivera	67-61	2nd	2.5
8-23	N.Y.	W	12-10		14	13	Helling	Hernandez	Wetteland	68-61	2nd	2.5
8-24	Det.	W	6-5		9	12	Sele	Thompson	Wetteland	69-61	2nd	2.5
8-25	Det.	L	7-8		12	16	Powell	Stottlemyre		69-62	2nd	3.5
8-26	Det.	W	8-6		12	8	Loaiza	Florie	Wetteland	70-62	2nd	3.0
8-28†	At Chi.	W	6-5	(10)	12	6	Hernandez	Howry	Wetteland	71-62		
8-28‡	At Chi.	L	7-8		9	13	Ward	Gunderson	Howry	71-63	2nd	3.0
8-29	At Chi.	W	5-3		10	6	Sele	Sirotka	Wetteland	72-63	2nd	2.0
8-30	At Chi.	L	3-5		8	8	C. Castillo	Stottlemyre	Howry	72-64	2nd	3.0
8-31	At Det.	W	13-2		14	6	Loaiza	Florie		73-64	2nd	2.5
9-1	At Det.	L	8-12		11	17	Anderson	Crabtree	Sager	73-65	2nd	2.5
9-2	At Det.	W	5-3		11	8	Helling	Moehler	Wetteland	74-65	2nd	2.5
9-4	Min.	W	9-3		12	9	Sele	Rodriguez		75-65	2nd	1.5
9-5	Min.	L	4-7		13	14	Trombley	Hernandez	Aguilera	75-66	2nd	2.5
9-6	Min.	L	5-6		11	13	Carrasco	Hernandez	Aguilera	75-67	2nd	3.5
9-7	Min.	W	6-0		10	3	Helling	Hawkins		76-67	2nd	3.0
9-8	K.C.	W	7-6		14	15	Patterson	Montgomery		77-67	2nd	2.0
9-9	K.C.	W	8-0		15	6	Sele	Rapp		78-67	2nd	2.0
9-11	At T.B.	L	2-3		4	5	Saunders	Stottlemyre	Hernandez	78-68	2nd	2.0

Date	Opp.	Res.	Score	(inn.*)	Hits	Opp. hits	Winning pitcher	Losing pitcher	Save	Record	Pos.	GB
9-12	At T.B.	W	8-2		15	9	Helling	Santana		79-68	2nd	1.0
9-13	At T.B.	L	5-10		9	17	White	Loaiza		79-69	2nd	1.0
9-14	At Bal.	L	0-1		5	8	Mills	Hernandez	Benitez	79-70	2nd	2.0
9-15	At Bal.	W	6-5		8	10	Crabtree	Benitez	Wetteland	80-70	2nd	1.0
9-16	Ana.	W	5-3		10	8	Stottlemyre	Finley		81-70	T1st	...
9-17	Ana.	W	7-6		12	11	Crabtree	Harris	Wetteland	82-70	1st	+1.0
9-18	Oak.	W	3-1		6	6	Burkett	Oquist	Wetteland	83-70	1st	+2.0
9-19	Oak.	L	4-8		8	17	Haynes	Sele		83-71	1st	+1.0
9-20	Oak.	L	3-6		10	8	Rogers	Loaiza	Taylor	83-72	T1st	...
9-21	At Ana.	W	9-1		14	7	Stottlemyre	Sparks		84-72	1st	+1.0
9-22	At Ana.	W	9-1		8	4	Helling	Finley		85-72	1st	+2.0
9-23	At Ana.	W	7-1		7	4	Burkett	Hill		86-72	1st	+3.0
9-24	At Sea.	W	9-3		15	8	Sele	Suzuki		87-72	1st	+3.0
9-25	At Sea.	L	4-15		8	17	Abbott	Loaiza		87-73	1st	+3.0
9-26	At Sea.	L	2-5		8	10	Fassero	Gunderson	Timlin	87-74	1st	+3.0
9-27	At Sea.	W	12-6		14	10	Fossas	Spoljaric		88-74	1st	+3.0

Monthly records: March (0-1), April (18-7), May (15-13), June (13-15), July (11-15), August (16-13), September (15-10).
*Innings, if other than nine. †First game of doubleheader. ‡Second game of doubleheader. §Two games in one day (separate admissions).

HIGHLIGHTS

High point: Over the final two weeks, the Rangers played Anaheim five times (two in Texas and three in Anaheim) and won all of them en route to sealing their second A.L. West Division title in three seasons.

Low point: The reliable bullpen had incalculable collapses on September 5 and 6 against Minnesota at The Ballpark in Arlington. Following their 6-5 loss to the Twins on September 6, Texas trailed Anaheim by 3.5 games with 20 remaining.

Turning point: The September 21 meeting in Anaheim turned the tide of the division race. The Rangers scored a run in the first inning off Anaheim knuckleballer Steve Sparks and survived a bases-loaded scare in the bottom of the inning before pulling away for a 9-1 victory.

Most valuable player: Right fielder Juan Gonzalez won his second league MVP award in three seasons with a phenomenal offensive outburst (.318, 45 HR, 157 RBIs). Gonzalez also became only the second player in history to collect more than 100 RBIs (101) before the All-Star break.

Most valuable pitcher: Rick Helling became just the third pitcher in club history to win 20 games (he went 20-7). He led the club in wins, innings (216.1) and complete games (4).

Most improved player: The scrutiny on center fielder Tom Goodwin became intense when the Rangers placed their trust in him to be the leadoff hitter. He responded with career highs in batting average (.290), runs (102) and walks (73) and had a respectable .378 on-base percentage.

Most pleasant surprise: Aaron Sele posted career highs in wins (19), innings (212.2) and strikeouts (167). Ridiculed for being a weak pitcher in the second half, Sele responded to critics by pitching at least six innings in eight of his final nine starts.

Biggest disappointment: The Rangers traded second baseman-of-the-future Warren Morris for righthander Esteban Loaiza, who had been described by scouts as not keeping his head in a game and lacking a breaking ball. In his final

four starts of the season, Loaiza worked past the fourth inning once and could not deliver when the Rangers had a chance to clinch the division September 25.

Key injuries: Righthanders Xavier Hernandez and Danny Patterson (rotator cuff); righthander Roger Pavlik (broken finger, torn rotator cuff); outfielder Roberto Kelly (hamstring); second baseman Mark McLemore (hamstring); shortstop Kevin Elster (shoulder); lefthander Darren Oliver (shoulder muscle strain); and DH Lee Stevens (strained oblique muscle) all missed time.

Notable: The Rangers finished the season with a 20-16 record against their American League brethren. It was their first winning record within their division since baseball realigned divisions in 1994 and only their second in the 1990s.

—KEVIN LONNQUIST

RECORDS

1998 regular-season record: 88-74 (1st in A.L. West); 48-33 at home; 40-41 on road; 27-28 vs. East; 33-22 vs. Central; 20-16 vs. A.L. West; 8-8 vs. N.L.; 26-22 vs. lefthanded starters; 62-52 vs. righthanded starters; 79-61 on grass; 9-13 on turf; 16-22 in daytime; 72-52 at night; 19-17 in one-run games; 3-3 in extra-inning games; 0-0-1 in doubleheaders.

Team record past five years: 381-363 (.512, ranks 6th in league in that span).

TEAM LEADERS

Batting average: Ivan Rodriguez (.321).
At-bats: Juan Gonzalez (606).
Runs: Juan Gonzalez (110).
Hits: Juan Gonzalez (193).
Total bases: Juan Gonzalez (382).
Doubles: Juan Gonzalez (50).
Triples: Rusty Greer (5).
Home runs: Juan Gonzalez (45).
Runs batted in: Juan Gonzalez (157).
Stolen bases: Tom Goodwin (38).
Slugging percentage: Juan Gonzalez (.630).

On-base percentage: Rusty Greer (.386).
Wins: Rick Helling (20).
Earned-run average: Aaron Sele (4.23).
Complete games: Rick Helling (4).
Shutouts: Rick Helling, Aaron Sele (2).
Saves: John Wetteland (42).
Innings pitched: Rick Helling (216.1).
Strikeouts: Aaron Sele (167).

GAMES BY POSITION

Catcher: Ivan Rodriguez 139, Bill Haselman 36.
First base: Will Clark 134, Lee Stevens 37, Mike Simms 16, Scott Sheldon 1.
Second base: Mark McLemore 122, Luis Alicea 45, Domingo Cedeno 7.
Third base: Fernando Tatis 94, Todd Zeile 52, Luis Alicea 26, Scott Sheldon 3.
Shortstop: Kevin Elster 84, Royce Clayton 52, Domingo Cedeno 35, Scott Sheldon 2.
Outfield: Rusty Greer 154, Tom Goodwin 150, Juan Gonzalez 116, Roberto Kelly 71, Mike Simms 43, Lee Stevens 7, Warren Newson 6, Milt Cuyler 3, Luis Alicea 2.
Designated hitter: Lee Stevens 72, Juan Gonzalez 38, Mike Simms 24, Luis Alicea 18, Domingo Cedeno 15, Will Clark 15, Ivan Rodriguez 6, Milt Cuyler 3, Bill Haselman 3, Warren Newson 3, Roberto Kelly 2, Mark McLemore 2, Chris Tremie 2, Tom Goodwin 1, Scott Sheldon 1.

TOP DRAFT CHOICES

1. **Carlos Pena**, 1B, Northeastern Univ.
2. **Cody Nowlin**, OF, Clovis (Calif.) H.S.
3. **Barry Zito**, LHP, L.A. Pierce J.C.
4. **Antwon Rollins**, OF, Encinal H.S., Alameda, Calif.
5. **Ryan Dittfurth**, RHP, Union H.S., Tulsa, Okla.
6. **Frankie McGill**, RHP, Tate H.S., Gonzalez, Fla.
7. **John Stewart**, LHP, W. Michigan U.
8. **Brad Ticehurst**, OF, U. of Southern California
9. **Andrew Pratt**, LHP, Chino Valley (Ariz.) H.S.
10. **Justin Backsmeyer**, RHP, DeSmet H.S., St. Louis

TORONTO BLUE JAYS
AMERICAN LEAGUE EAST DIVISION

1999 Blue Jays Schedule

Home games shaded. ●—All-Star Game at Fenway Park (Boston).
D—Day game (any game starting before 5 p.m.)

April

SUN	MON	TUE	WED	THU	FRI	SAT
				1	2	3
4	5	6 MIN	7 MIN	8 MIN	9 BAL	10 D BAL
11 D BAL	12 TB	13 TB	14 TB	15 TB	16 BAL	17 D BAL
18 D BAL	19	20 ANA	21 ANA	22 ANA	23 NYY	24 D NYY
25 D NYY	26 ANA	27 ANA	28 ANA	29 ANA	30 SEA	

May

SUN	MON	TUE	WED	THU	FRI	SAT
						1 SEA
2 D SEA	3 D SEA	4 D OAK	5 OAK	6 OAK	7 TEX	8 D TEX
9 D TEX	10	11 KC	12 KC	13 D KC	14 BOS	15 D BOS
16 D BOS	17 DET	18 DET	19 DET	20 DET	21 BOS	22 D BOS
23 D BOS	24 DET	25 DET	26 DET	27	28 NYY	29 D NYY
30 D NYY	31					

June

SUN	MON	TUE	WED	THU	FRI	SAT
		1 CWS	2 CWS	3 D CWS	4 D MON	5 D MON
6 D MON	7	8 NYM	9 NYM	10	11 PHI	12 PHI
13 D PHI	14	15 ANA	16 ANA	17 ANA	18 KC	19 D KC
20 D KC	21 KC	22 CLE	23 CLE	24 D CLE	25 TB	26 TB
27 D TB	28 TB	29 BAL	30 BAL			

July

SUN	MON	TUE	WED	THU	FRI	SAT
				1 D BAL	2 D TB	3 D TB
4 D TB	5	6 BAL	7 BAL	8 BAL	9 MON	10 MON
11 D MON	12	13	* 14	15 FLA	16 FLA	17 D FLA
18 D ATL	19 ATL	20 ATL	21 CLE	22 CLE	23 CWS	24 CWS
25 D CWS	26 CWS	27 BOS	28 BOS	29	30 DET	31 D DET

August

SUN	MON	TUE	WED	THU	FRI	SAT
1 D DET	2 NYY	3 NYY	4 NYY	5 D	6 TEX	7 TEX
8 TEX	9 TEX	10 MIN	11 MIN	12 D MIN	13 OAK	14 D OAK
15 D OAK	16 SEA	17 SEA	18 D	19	20 OAK	21 OAK
22 D OAK	23 D OAK	24 D ANA	25 ANA	26	27 TEX	28 D TEX
29 D TEX	30 MIN	31 MIN				

September

SUN	MON	TUE	WED	THU	FRI	SAT
			1 MIN	2 MIN	3 D KC	4 KC
5 D KC	6	7 SEA	8 SEA	9	10 DET	11 DET
12 D DET	13 D NYY	14 NYY	15 NYY	16	17 CWS	18 D CWS
19 D CWS	20	21 BOS	22 BOS	23 BOS	24 CLE	25 D CLE
26 D CLE	27	28 TB	29 TB	30 CLE		

October

SUN	MON	TUE	WED	THU	FRI	SAT
				1	2 CLE	D
3 D CLE	4	5	6	7	8	9

1999 SEASON
CLUB DIRECTORY

Chairman and chief executive officer
Sam Pollock
Vice president and general manager
Gord Ash
Executive vice president, business
Bob Nicholson
Vice president, baseball
Bob Mattick
Senior advisor, baseball operations
Bob Engle
Assistant general managers
Tim McCleary
Dave Stewart
Special asst. to v.p., baseball, g.m.
Al Widmar
Wayne Morgan
Vice president, media relations
Howard Starkman
V.p., stadium and ticket operations
George Holm
Director, finance
Susan Quigley
Director, scouting
Tim Wilken
Assistant director, scouting
Chris Buckley
Director, player development
Jim Hoff
Director, Canadian scouting
Bill Byckowski
Director, baseball administration
Bob Nelson
Director, Florida operations
Ken Carson

Director, communications
Peter Cosentino
Director, corporate partnerships
Mark Lemmon
Asst. dir., tickets and box office mgr.
Randy Low
General manager, TBJ merchandising
Michael Andrejek
Manager, team travel
John Brioux
Manager, game operations
Mario Coutinho
Trainers
Tommy Craig
Scott Shannon
Strength and conditioning coordinator
Brian McNamee
Team physicians
Dr. Ron Taylor
Dr. Anthony Miniaci
Dr. Allan Gross
Dr. Steve Mirabello
Advance scout
Pat Kelly
Scouts
Charles Aliano, Tony Arias, Andy Beene, David Blume, Bus Campbell, Rick Cerrone, John Cole, Jeff Cornell, Ellis Dungan, Joe Ford, Tom Hinkle, Tim Huff, Jim Hughes, Ted Lekas, Ben McLure, Marty Miller, Bill Moore, Ty Nichols, Andy Pienovi, Jorge Rivera, Marteese Robinson, Joe Siers, Mark Snipp, Ron Tostenson, Steve Williams

MINOR LEAGUE AFFILIATES

Class	Team	League	Manager
AAA	Syracuse	International	Terry Bevington
AA	Knoxville	Southern	Omar Malave
A	Dunedin	Florida State	Rocket Wheeler
A	Hagerstown	South Atlantic	Rolando Pino
A	St. Catharines	New York-Penn.	Eddie Rodriguez
Rookie	Medicine Hat	Pioneer	Paul Elliott

BROADCAST INFORMATION

Radio: CHUM (1050).
TV: CBC-TV.
Cable TV: The Sports Network, CTV SportsNet.

SPRING TRAINING

Ballpark (city): Dunedin Stadium at Grant Field (Dunedin, Fla.).
Ticket information: 800-707-8269; 727-733-0429.

SPRING TRAINING ROSTER

Manager—Tim Johnson (17).
Coaches—Sal Butera (22), Jim Lett (10), Gary Matthews (36), Lloyd Moseby (16), Marty Pevey (30), Mel Queen (34).

No.	PITCHERS	B/T	Ht./Wt.	Born	1998 clubs
49	Bale, John	L/L	6-4/195	5-22-74	Knoxville, Dunedin
26	Carpenter, Chris	R/R	6-6/215	4-27-75	Toronto
21	Clemens, Roger	R/R	6-4/230	8-4-62	Toronto
43	Davey, Tom	R/R	6-7/215	9-11-73	Knoxville
45	Escobar, Kelvim	R/R	6-1/195	4-11-76	Toronto, Syracuse
66	Estrella, Leo	R/R	6-1/175	2-20-75	Columbia, Hagerstown
53	Giron, Isabel	R/R	6-2/170	11-17-77	Knoxville, Hagerstown
51	Glover, Gary	R/R	6-5/205	12-3-76	Knoxville, Dunedin
32	Halladay, Roy	R/R	6-6/205	5-14-77	Syracuse, Toronto
50	Hamilton, Joey	R/R	6-4/230	9-9-70	San Diego
41	Hentgen, Pat	R/R	6-2/195	11-13-68	Toronto
40	Ludwick, Eric	R/R	6-5/220	12-14-71	Florida, Charlotte
50	Munro, Peter	R/R	6-2/204	6-14-75	Pawtucket, Syracuse
31	Person, Robert	R/R	6-0/195	10-6-69	Toronto, Syracuse
19	Plesac, Dan	L/L	6-5/217	2-4-62	Toronto
48	Quantrill, Paul	L/R	6-1/185	11-3-68	Toronto
55	Risley, Bill	R/R	6-2/210	5-29-67	Toronto
39	Rodriguez, Nerio	R/R	6-1/195	3-22-73	Rochester, Baltimore, Bowie, Toronto
46	Sinclair, Steve	L/L	6-2/190	8-2-71	Toronto, Syracuse

No.	CATCHERS	B/T	Ht./Wt.	Born	1998 clubs
14	Brown, Kevin	R/R	6-2/215	4-21-73	Toronto, Syracuse
5	Dalesandro, Mark	R/R	6-0/195	5-14-68	Toronto, Syracuse
9	Fletcher, Darrin	L/R	6-2/200	10-3-66	Toronto
54	Lawrence, Joe	R/R	6-2/190	2-13-77	Dunedin
11	Matheny, Mike	R/R	6-3/205	9-22-70	Milwaukee, Beloit

No.	INFIELDERS	B/T	Ht./Wt.	Born	1998 clubs
28	Blake, Casey	R/R	6-2/195	8-23-73	Knoxville, Dunedin
3	Crespo, Felipe	B/R	5-11/200	3-5-73	Toronto
25	Delgado, Carlos	L/R	6-3/225	6-25-72	Dunedin, Syracuse, Toronto
2	Evans, Tom	R/R	6-1/200	7-9-74	Syracuse, Toronto
1	Fernandez, Tony	B/R	6-2/195	6-30-62	Toronto
8	Gonzalez, Alex	R/R	6-0/200	4-8-73	Toronto
4	Grebeck, Craig	R/R	5-7/155	12-29-64	Toronto
13	Perez, Tomas	B/R	5-11/177	12-29-73	Syracuse, Toronto
6	Witt, Kevin	L/R	6-4/200	1-5-76	Toronto, Syracuse

No.	OUTFIELDERS	B/T	Ht./Wt.	Born	1998 clubs
35	Berroa, Geronimo	R/R	6-0/210	3-18-65	Cleveland, Detroit
23	Cruz, Jose	B/R	6-0/195	4-19-74	Toronto, Syracuse
38	Freel, Ryan	R/R	5-10/175	3-8-76	Syracuse
15	Green, Shawn	L/L	6-4/200	11-10-72	Toronto
20	Lennon, Patrick	R/R	6-2/230	4-27-68	Syracuse, Toronto
27	Sanders, Anthony	R/R	6-2/200	3-2-74	Syracuse, Knoxville
24	Stewart, Shannon	R/R	6-1/194	2-25-74	Toronto

BALLPARK INFORMATION

Ballpark (capacity, surface)
SkyDome (50,516, artificial)

Address
One Blue Jays Way
Suite 3200
Toronto, Ontario M5V 1J1

Business phone
416-341-1000

Ticket information
416-341-1000

Ticket prices
$27.50 (esplanade IF, club level OF)
$20 (skydeck IF, esplanade OF)
$13 (skydeck)
$4 (skydeck outfield)

Field dimensions (from home plate)
To left field at foul line, 330 feet
To center field, 400 feet
To right field at foul line, 330 feet

First game played
June 5, 1989 (Brewers 5, Blue Jays 3)

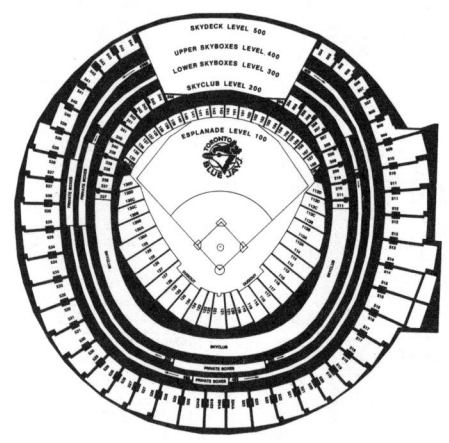

Date	Opp.	Res.	Score	(inn.*)	Hits	Opp. hits	Winning pitcher	Losing pitcher	Save	Record	Pos.	GB
4-1	Min.	W	3-2		6	4	Clemens	Tewksbury	Myers	1-0	T1st	...
4-2	Min.	L	2-3		3	8	Guardado	Escobar	Aguilera	1-1	4th	1.0
4-3	Tex.	L	0-5		4	9	Helling	Guzman		1-2	4th	1.5
4-4	Tex.	W	9-2		13	4	Williams	Oliver		2-2	T3rd	1.5
4-5	Tex.	L	5-6		6	10	Burkett	Risley	Wetteland	2-3	4th	2.5
4-7	At Min.	L	2-12		3	11	Tewksbury	Clemens		2-4	T4th	3.5
4-8	At Min.	W	9-6		11	10	Hentgen	Hawkins	Myers	3-4	T3rd	3.0
4-9	At Min.	L	2-13		7	13	Radke	Guzman		3-5	T4th	4.0
4-10	At Tex.	L	3-4		7	11	Helling	Plesac	Wetteland	3-6	5th	4.0
4-11	At Tex.	W	9-8		13	17	Almanzar	Oliver	Myers	4-6	5th	4.0
4-12	At Tex.	L	1-3		7	8	Wetteland	Quantrill		4-7	5th	5.0
4-13	At K.C.	L	1-11		8	14	Rusch	Hentgen		4-8	5th	5.5
4-14	At K.C.	W	5-1		7	5	Guzman	Rapp	Quantrill	5-8	5th	5.5
4-15	At K.C.	L	3-7		7	14	Haney	Williams		5-9	5th	5.5
4-17	Chi.	W	6-1		10	6	Clemens	Bere		6-9	5th	4.0
4-18	Chi.	W	9-4		12	9	Hentgen	Navarro		7-9	5th	3.5
4-19	Chi.	W	5-4	(12)	7	7	Carpenter	C. Castillo		8-9	5th	3.0
4-20	N.Y.	L	2-3	(11)	7	9	Banks	Risley	Stanton	8-10	5th	4.0
4-21	N.Y.	L	3-5	(10)	9	13	Stanton	Plesac		8-11	5th	4.5
4-22	N.Y.	L	1-9		6	10	Pettitte	Clemens		8-12	5th	5.5
4-24	At Chi.	W	3-1		6	6	Hentgen	Navarro	Myers	9-12	5th	5.5
4-25	At Chi.	L	1-8		4	7	Eyre	Guzman		9-13	5th	6.5
4-26	At Chi.	T	5-5	(6)	8	7	......	......		9-13	5th	6.5
4-27	At N.Y.	L	0-1		9	3	Pettitte	Clemens	Rivera	9-14	5th	7.5
4-28	At N.Y.	L	5-2		8	9	Williams	Mendoza	Myers	10-14	5th	6.5
4-29	K.C.	L	2-7		7	12	Pichardo	Hentgen		10-15	5th	7.5
4-30	K.C.	L	4-7		9	11	Rusch	Guzman	Montgomery	10-16	5th	8.5
5-1	At Oak.	L	2-5		6	10	Candiotti	Hanson	Taylor	10-17	5th	9.5
5-2	At Oak.	W	7-0		11	1	Clemens	Oquist		11-17	5th	9.5
5-3	At Oak.	W	6-3		10	5	Williams	Telgheder	Myers	12-17	T4th	9.5
5-4	At Oak.	L	4-7		8	12	Rogers	Hentgen		12-18	5th	10.0
5-5	At Ana.	W	13-11		17	14	Plesac	Percival	Myers	13-18	4th	10.0
5-6	At Ana.	W	6-5		10	12	Escobar	Hasegawa	Myers	14-18	4th	10.0
5-7	At Sea.	W	6-0		13	11	Clemens	Moyer		15-18	4th	9.5
5-8	At Sea.	L	3-8		9	9	Johnson	Williams		15-19	4th	10.5
5-9	At Sea.	W	4-1		9	8	Hentgen	Swift	Myers	16-19	4th	9.5
5-10	At Sea.	L	1-3		5	5	Fassero	Guzman	Ayala	16-20	4th	10.5
5-12	Oak.	W	4-3	(10)	8	8	Myers	Taylor		17-20	4th	10.5
5-13	Oak.	L	2-4		6	5	Haynes	Clemens	Fetters	17-21	4th	11.5
5-14	Ana.	W	5-4		13	9	Myers	DeLucia		18-21	4th	10.5
5-15	Ana.	W	9-1		11	3	Hentgen	Hill		19-21	4th	9.5
5-16	Sea.	L	1-8		5	7	Fassero	Guzman		19-22	4th	10.5
5-17	Sea.	W	4-3		8	11	Plesac	Slocumb		20-22	T3rd	10.5
5-18	Sea.	L	4-9		7	12	Spoljaric	Clemens		20-23	T4th	11.0
5-19	T.B.	W	3-1		4	2	Williams	Springer	Myers	21-23	3rd	11.0
5-20	T.B.	W	9-1		7	9	Hentgen	Alvarez		22-23	3rd	11.0
5-21	T.B.	W	6-1		10	4	Guzman	Arrojo		23-23	3rd	11.0
5-22	At Cle.	L	7-9		14	11	Burba	Hanson	Jackson	23-24	3rd	11.0
5-23	At Cle.	W	7-2		11	3	Clemens	Colon		24-24	3rd	11.0
5-24	At Cle.	W	5-0		10	5	Williams	Gooden		25-24	3rd	11.0
5-25	At Bos.	W	7-5		12	8	Hentgen	Martinez	Myers	26-24	3rd	11.0
5-26	At Bos.	W	5-2		8	7	Guzman	Avery	Myers	27-24	3rd	11.0
5-28	Cle.	L	2-6		5	11	Burba	Carpenter		27-25	3rd	11.5
5-29	Cle.	L	3-7		5	10	Colon	Clemens		27-26	3rd	12.5
5-30	Cle.	W	4-2		6	6	Williams	Gooden	Myers	28-26	3rd	11.5
5-31	Cle.	W	3-8		8	12	Nagy	Hentgen	Mesa	28-27	3rd	11.5
6-1	Bos.	L	5-9		7	13	Corsi	Myers		28-28	3rd	12.5
6-2	Bos.	L	3-11		8	11	Avery	Carpenter		28-29	3rd	13.5
6-3	Det.	W	5-1		8	4	Clemens	Greisinger		29-29	3rd	13.5
6-4	Det.	W	9-6		12	8	Williams	Moehler	Myers	30-29	3rd	13.5
6-5	Phi.	L	7-8		6	15	Green	Risley	Leiter	30-30	3rd	14.5
6-6	Phi.	L	6-10		10	16	Gomes	Guzman		30-31	3rd	15.5
6-7	Phi.	W	3-1		9	10	Carpenter	Schilling	Myers	31-31	3rd	15.5
6-8	At Fla.	L	3-4	(17)	13	14	Edmondson	Hanson		31-32	3rd	16.0
6-9	At Fla.	L	4-5		9	12	Hernandez	Quantrill		31-33	3rd	17.0
6-10	At Fla.	W	4-3	(10)	9	11	Person	Powell	Myers	32-33	3rd	17.0
6-12	Bal.	L	5-9		14	13	Mussina	Guzman		32-34	T3rd	17.0
6-13	Bal.	W	9-8		12	13	Person	Drabek	Myers	33-34	3rd	16.5
6-14	Bal.	W	7-4		12	7	Clemens	Smith	Myers	34-34	3rd	16.5
6-15	At T.B.	L	7-8		9	9	White	Quantrill	Hernandez	34-35	3rd	16.5
6-16	At T.B.	L	3-4		10	8	Mecir	Myers		34-36	T3rd	16.5
6-17	At T.B.	L	1-2		7	6	Arrojo	Guzman	Hernandez	34-37	T3rd	17.5

Date	Opp.	Res.	Score	(inn.*)	Hits	Opp. hits	Winning pitcher	Losing pitcher	Save	Record	Pos.	GB
6-18	At Bal.	W	13-6		18	13	Carpenter	Johns		35-37	3rd	17.5
6-19	At Bal.	L	4-7	(15)	10	15	Charlton	Risley		35-38	T3rd	17.5
6-20	At Bal.	L	3-11		12	16	Erickson	Williams		35-39	4th	18.5
6-21	At Bal.	W	7-3		11	10	Hentgen	Ponson	Myers	36-39	T3rd	17.5
6-22	Mon.	W	14-2		18	7	Guzman	Pavano		37-39	T3rd	17.5
6-23	Mon.	W	3-2		7	10	Carpenter	Batista	Myers	38-39	3rd	16.5
6-24	At Mon.	W	7-6		10	13	Clemens	Boskie	Myers	39-39	3rd	16.5
6-25	At Mon.	W	1-0		5	5	Williams	C. Perez		40-39	3rd	16.5
6-26	At Atl.	W	6-4		10	11	Hentgen	Smoltz	Myers	41-39	3rd	16.5
6-27	At Atl.	L	0-2		8	4	Maddux	Guzman		41-40	3rd	17.5
6-28	At Atl.	L	3-10		6	14	Glavine	Carpenter		41-41	3rd	17.5
6-30	N.Y. (NL)	W	6-3		11	6	Clemens	Reed		42-41	3rd	17.5
7-1	N.Y. (NL)	W	15-10		15	14	Plesac	Rojas		43-41	3rd	17.5
7-2	N.Y. (NL)	L	1-9		5	11	Jones	Hentgen		43-42	3rd	18.5
7-3	T.B.	W	3-2	(10)	12	7	Myers	Yan		44-42	3rd	18.5
7-4	T.B.	W	8-0		11	4	Carpenter	Springer		45-42	3rd	18.5
7-5	T.B.	W	2-1		8	6	Quantrill	White	Myers	46-42	3rd	18.5
7-9	At Det.	L	3-4		8	8	Anderson	Plesac	Jones	46-43	3rd	19.5
7-10	At Det.	L	2-3	(10)	8	12	Jones	Quantrill		46-44	3rd	20.5
7-11	At Det.	L	2-5		4	8	Moehler	Carpenter	Runyan	46-45	3rd	21.5
7-12	At Det.	W	7-2		7	5	Clemens	Brocail		47-45	3rd	21.5
7-13	At Bal.	L	0-5		3	8	Rodriguez	Guzman		47-46	3rd	21.5
7-14	At Bal.	L	5-11		7	14	Mussina	Williams		47-47	3rd	22.5
7-15†	At Chi.	L	3-9		7	14	Navarro	Hentgen		47-48		
7-15‡	At Chi.	L	2-5		8	9	C. Castillo	Stieb	Simas	47-49	3rd	24.0
7-16	At Chi.	W	5-2		11	4	Carpenter	Baldwin	Myers	48-49	3rd	23.0
7-17	N.Y.	W	9-6		10	12	Clemens	Holmes	Myers	49-49	3rd	22.0
7-18	N.Y.	L	3-10		8	13	Hernandez	Guzman		49-50	3rd	23.0
7-19	N.Y.	W	9-3		8	7	Williams	Pettitte		50-50	3rd	22.0
7-21	Chi.	L	3-6		9	11	Baldwin	Hentgen	Simas	50-51	3rd	23.0
7-22	Chi.	W	4-0		5	4	Clemens	Parque		51-51	3rd	23.0
7-23	At Bos.	L	7-8	(10)	15	13	Gordon	Myers		51-52	4th	23.5
7-24	At Bos.	W	10-6		13	7	Guzman	Avery	Quantrill	52-52	4th	23.5
7-25	At Bos.	L	3-5		7	9	Lowe	Williams	Gordon	52-53	4th	23.5
7-26	At Bos.	L	3-6		10	12	Martinez	Hentgen		52-54	4th	24.5
7-28	Tex.	W	8-3		11	7	Clemens	Sele		53-54	4th	24.5
7-29	Tex.	L	6-9		8	11	Oliver	Carpenter	Wetteland	53-55	4th	24.5
7-30	Tex.	W	1-0		4	5	Guzman	Loaiza	Myers	54-55	4th	24.5
7-31	At Min.	L	4-6		7	10	Rodriguez	Williams	Aguilera	54-56	4th	25.5
8-1	At Min.	W	10-9		16	13	Hentgen	Hawkins	Myers	55-56	4th	25.5
8-2	At Min.	W	6-4		12	9	Clemens	Radke	Myers	56-56	4th	24.5
8-4	At Tex.	L	9-11		12	11	Stottlemyre	Carpenter	Wetteland	56-57	4th	26.5
8-5	At Tex.	L	3-4		7	6	Wetteland	Myers		56-58	4th	26.5
8-7	Oak.	L	6-7		9	8	Haynes	Williams	Fetters	56-59	4th	28.0
8-8	Oak.	W	6-5	(10)	10	7	Plesac	Fetters		57-59	4th	28.0
8-9	Oak.	W	4-3		9	5	Quantrill	Mohler		58-59	4th	28.0
8-11	Sea.	W	7-4		11	9	Carpenter	Fassero	Quantrill	59-59	4th	28.5
8-12	Sea.	W	11-5		13	7	Rodriguez	Ayala		60-59	4th	28.5
8-13	Ana.	W	4-3		8	9	Risley	Hasegawa	Plesac	61-59	4th	28.5
8-14	Ana.	L	5-7		10	15	Watson	Hentgen	Percival	61-60	4th	29.5
8-15	Ana.	L	3-6	(11)	8	10	DeLucia	Sinclair		61-61	4th	29.5
8-16	Ana.	W	6-4		9	10	Carpenter	Juden	Quantrill	62-61	4th	29.5
8-17	At Oak.	W	4-2		8	6	Escobar	Candiotti	Plesac	63-61	4th	29.5
8-18	At Oak.	L	5-10		13	9	Haynes	Williams		63-62	4th	30.5
8-19	At Sea.	W	16-2		21	6	Hentgen	Cloude	Stieb	64-62	4th	29.5
8-20	At Sea.	W	7-0		14	3	Clemens	Swift		65-62	4th	28.5
8-21	At Ana.	W	9-4		11	8	Carpenter	Juden		66-62	4th	28.5
8-22	At Ana.	L	1-5		8	8	Sparks	Escobar	Hasegawa	66-63	4th	29.5
8-23	At Ana.	L	2-3		6	5	Finley	Almanzar	Percival	66-64	4th	29.5
8-24	K.C.	L	3-7		7	13	Barber	Hentgen	Whisenant	66-65	4th	29.5
8-25	K.C.	W	3-0		6	3	Clemens	Haney		67-65	4th	28.5
8-26	K.C.	L	2-7		3	15	Belcher	Carpenter		67-66	4th	29.0
8-27	K.C.	W	11-1		15	7	Escobar	Rosado		68-66	4th	29.0
8-28	Min.	W	7-6		10	8	Williams	Trombley	Plesac	69-66	4th	29.0
8-29	Min.	W	14-7		18	10	Stieb	Radke		70-66	3rd	29.0
8-30	Min.	W	6-0		9	2	Clemens	Rodriguez		71-66	3rd	28.0
9-1	At K.C.	W	2-1		10	5	Carpenter	Belcher	Quantrill	72-66	3rd	28.0
9-2	At K.C.	W	5-0		5	4	Escobar	Rosado	Quantrill	73-66	3rd	27.0
9-3	Bos.	W	4-3	(11)	9	12	Person	Veras		74-66	3rd	26.5
9-4	Bos.	W	12-1		12	6	Hentgen	Wakefield	Stieb	75-66	3rd	26.5
9-5	Bos.	W	4-3		10	4	Clemens	Saberhagen	Quantrill	76-66	3rd	25.5
9-6	Bos.	W	8-7		8	8	Quantrill	Lowe	Person	77-66	3rd	24.5
9-7	Cle.	W	15-1		18	4	Escobar	Ogea		78-66	3rd	23.5
9-9	Cle.	L	3-6	(13)	9	7	Jones	Almanzar	Jackson	78-67	3rd	25.0
9-10	At N.Y.	L	5-8		8	13	Pettitte	Hentgen	Holmes	78-68	3rd	26.0

Date	Opp.	Res.	Score	(inn.*)	Hits	Opp. hits	Winning pitcher	Losing pitcher	Save	Record	Pos.	GB
9-11	At N.Y.	W	5-4		7	9	Almanzar	Irabu	Person	79-68	3rd	25.0
9-12	At N.Y.	W	5-3		8	4	Carpenter	Wells	Person	80-68	3rd	24.0
9-13	At N.Y.	W	5-3		15	8	Escobar	Cone	Person	81-68	3rd	23.0
9-14	At Cle.	L	3-6		7	12	Gooden	Sinclair	Jackson	81-69	3rd	24.0
9-15	At Cle.	L	5-7		10	13	Ogea	Stieb	Assenmacher	81-70	3rd	24.0
9-16	At Det.	W	2-1		4	4	Clemens	Powell	Person	82-70	3rd	23.0
9-17	At Det.	L	4-7		10	15	Brocail	Person		82-71	3rd	24.0
9-18	At T.B.	L	1-6		3	9	Rekar	Escobar		82-72	3rd	25.0
9-19	At T.B.	L	5-7		10	8	Lopez	VanRyn	Hernandez	82-73	3rd	25.0
9-20	At T.B.	W	7-5	(12)	11	13	Risley	Lopez		83-73	3rd	25.0
9-21	Bal.	W	3-1		9	8	Clemens	Erickson	Plesac	84-73	3rd	24.0
9-22	Bal.	W	7-3		8	6	Carpenter	Mussina		85-73	3rd	24.5
9-23	Bal.	W	6-3		8	10	Escobar	Guzman	Person	86-73	3rd	24.5
9-25	Det.	L	5-7		12	10	Moehler	Williams	Jones	86-74	3rd	26.0
9-26	Det.	W	5-4	(13)	13	12	Risley	Sager		87-74	3rd	26.0
9-27	Det.	W	2-1		5	1	Halladay	Thompson		88-74	3rd	26.0

Monthly records: April (10-16), May (18-11), June (14-14), July (12-15), August (17-10), September (17-8).
*Innings, if other than nine. †First game of doubleheader. ‡Second game of doubleheader.

HIGHLIGHTS

High point: An 11-game winning streak from August 26 to September 7 pulled the Blue Jays close to Boston in the hunt for a wild-card playoff spot. They hit .320 with 21 homers during the 11-game span as the pitchers combined for a 2.58 ERA.
Low point: After Kansas City defeated Pat Hentgen and Juan Guzman on consecutive nights at SkyDome, the Jays fell to 10-16 for April—the lowest win total of any month. A team optimistic about a fast start couldn't reach .500 until May 23. By then, the Yankees had opened an 11-game spread in the A.L. East.
Turning point: Trading Mike Stanley and Ed Sprague at the end of July allowed Jose Canseco to move from the outfield to DH, Tony Fernandez to transfer from second to third base, and Craig Grebeck to come off the bench and play second. The tightened defense helped the Jays go 34-18 over their final 52 games.
Most valuable player: First baseman Carlos Delgado led in homers (38) and RBIs (115) despite missing the first three weeks while recovering from shoulder surgery.
Most valuable pitcher: Roger Clemens (20-6, 2.65 ERA, 271 strikeouts) earned both the triple crown of pitching and a Cy Young Award for the second consecutive year. It was his fifth career Cy Young.
Most improved player: Shawn Green, given steady playing time and the No. 2 slot in the batting order, became the first 30-30 man in club history and reached 100 RBIs, nearly double his previous best (54).
Most pleasant surprise: The Blue Jays pulled Canseco off the free-agent scrap heap and he responded with a career-high 46 homers, reached the 100-RBI mark for the first time since 1990 and fell one steal shy of becoming the first hitter to assemble 30-30 seasons 10 years apart.
Biggest disappointment: After hitting 26 homers in 104 games as a rookie, Jose Cruz Jr. was plugged into center field and the 5-hole in the batting order. He averaged .253 with 11 homers in 105 games—and was demoted to Class AAA Syracuse for six weeks.

Key injuries: Catcher Benito Santiago, projected as the starter, suffered multiple injuries in a January car accident and couldn't play until September. Pat Hentgen tweaked an elbow ligament in spring training, pitched through the pain and wound up affecting his shoulder. The Jays shut him down in mid-September with a 5.17 ERA. Pitcher Kelvim Escobar missed three starts with an elbow strain.
Notable: The 88 wins improved on the previous season total by 12. . . . After May 1, Toronto went 78-58, better than any A.L. team except the Yankees. . . . The 221 homers established a franchise record. . . . Four players hit at least 20 homers for the second time in franchise history: Canseco (46), Delgado (38), Green (35) and Stanley (22). . . . The Jays led the majors with 184 stolen bases and 81 times caught stealing.

—TOM MALONEY

RECORDS

1998 regular-season record: 88-74 (3rd in A.L. East); 51-30 at home; 37-44 on road; 27-21 vs. A.L. East; 28-26 vs. Central; 24-20 vs. West; 9-7 vs. N.L.; 23-19 vs. lefthanded starters; 65-55 vs. righthanded starters; 27-34 on grass; 61-40 on turf; 35-14 in daytime; 53-60 at night; 28-17 in one-run games; 8-8 in extra-inning games; 0-1-0 in doubleheaders.
Team record past five years: 349-396 (.468, ranks 10th in league in that span).

TEAM LEADERS

Batting average: Tony Fernandez (.321).
At-bats: Shawn Green (630).
Runs: Shawn Green (106).
Hits: Shawn Green (175).
Total bases: Shawn Green (321).
Doubles: Carlos Delgado (43).
Triples: Shawn Green (4).
Home runs: Jose Canseco (46).
Runs batted in: Carlos Delgado (115).
Stolen bases: Shannon Stewart (51).
Slugging percentage: Carlos Delgado (.592).

On-base percentage: Tony Fernandez (.387).
Wins: Roger Clemens (20).
Earned-run average: Roger Clemens (2.65).
Complete games: Roger Clemens (5).
Shutouts: Roger Clemens (3).
Saves: Randy Myers (28).
Innings pitched: Roger Clemens (234.2).
Strikeouts: Roger Clemens (271).

GAMES BY POSITION

Catcher: Darrin Fletcher 121, Kevin L. Brown 52, Mark Dalesandro 18, Benito Santiago 15.
First base: Carlos Delgado 141, Mike Stanley 22, Juan Samuel 3, Mark Dalesandro 2, Felipe Crespo 1, Kevin Witt 1.
Second base: Craig Grebeck 91, Tony Fernandez 82, Felipe Crespo 8, Juan Samuel 2, Tomas Perez 1.
Third base: Ed Sprague 105, Tony Fernandez 54, Mark Dalesandro 8, Tom Evans 7, Craig Grebeck 4, Felipe Crespo 2.
Shortstop: Alex Gonzalez 158, Craig Grebeck 6, Tomas Perez 4.
Outfield: Shawn Green 157, Shannon Stewart 144, Jose Cruz Jr. 105, Jose Canseco 73, Felipe Crespo 42, Tony Phillips 13, Juan Samuel 10, Patrick Lennon 2, Mark Dalesandro 1, Mike Stanley 1.
Designated hitter: Jose Canseco 78, Mike Stanley 73, Juan Samuel 11, Felipe Crespo 2, Carlos Delgado 1, Tony Fernandez 1, Darrin Fletcher 1.

TOP DRAFT CHOICES

1. **Felipe Lopez,** SS, Lake Brantley H.S., Altamonte Springs, Fla.
2. None
3. None
4. **Ryan Bundy,** C, U. of Washington
5. **Lee Delfino,** SS, Pickering (Ontario) H.S.
6. **Joe Orloski,** RHP, Green Valley H.S. Henderson, Nev.
7. **Tyler Thompson,** OF, Indiana State U.
8. **Mike Kremblas,** C, Ohio State Univ.
9. **Steve Murray,** LHP, St. Peter H.S., Peterborough, Ont.
10. **Jarrod Kingrey,** RHP, U. of Alabama

ARIZONA DIAMONDBACKS
NATIONAL LEAGUE WEST DIVISION

1999 Diamondbacks Schedule

Home games shaded. *—All-Star Game at Fenway Park (Boston). D—Day game (any game starting before 5 p.m.).

April

SUN	MON	TUE	WED	THU	FRI	SAT
				1	2	3
4	5 D LA	6 D LA	7 LA	8	9 ATL	10 ATL
11 D ATL	12 D LA	13 LA	14 LA	15 D LA	16 SF	17 D SF
18 SF	19 PHI	20 PHI	21 PHI	22	23 SD	24 SD
25 SD	26 D HOU	27 HOU	28 HOU	29 D HOU	30 MIL	

May

SUN	MON	TUE	WED	THU	FRI	SAT
						1 D MIL
2 D MIL	3 CIN	4 CIN	5 CIN	6	7 NYM	8 D NYM
9 NYM	10 D MON	11 MON	12 MON	13	14 COL	15 D COL
16 COL	17 SF	18 SF	19 D SF	20 COL	21 COL	22 D COL
23 COL	24 SD	25 SD	26 SD	27	28 NYM	29 D NYM
30 D NYM	31 MON					

June

SUN	MON	TUE	WED	THU	FRI	SAT
		1 MON	2 MON	3	4 TEX	5 TEX
6 TEX	7 CUB	8 CUB	9 CUB	10	11 ANA	12 ANA
13 ANA	14 FLA	15 FLA	16 FLA	17	18 ATL	19 ATL
20 ATL	21 CIN	22 CIN	23 CIN	24 STL	25 STL	26 STL
27 STL	28	29 CIN	30 CIN			

July

SUN	MON	TUE	WED	THU	FRI	SAT
				1 CIN	2 STL	3 D STL
4 STL	5 D STL	6 D HOU	7 HOU	8 HOU	9 OAK	10 OAK
11 D OAK	12	13	* 14	15 TEX	16 TEX	17 TEX
18 D SEA	19 SEA	20 SEA	21 HOU	22 HOU	23 LA	24 LA
25 LA	26	27 SD	28 SD	29 D SD	30 LA	31 LA

August

SUN	MON	TUE	WED	THU	FRI	SAT
1 LA	2 SF	3 SF	4 SF	5	6 PHI	7 PHI
8 PHI	9 CUB	10 CUB	11 CUB	12	13 MIL	14 MIL
15 MIL	16 CUB	17 CUB	18 CUB	19	20 PIT	21 PIT
22 PIT	23 PIT	24 FLA	25 FLA	26 D FLA	27 NYM	28 NYM
29 NYM	30 MON	31 MON				

September

SUN	MON	TUE	WED	THU	FRI	SAT
			1 MON	2	3 ATL	4 ATL
5 ATL	6 D MIL	7 MIL	8 MIL	9 D PHI	10 PHI	11 PHI
12 PHI	13 PIT	14 PIT	15 PIT	16	17 FLA	18 D FLA
19 FLA	20 COL	21 COL	22 D COL	23	24 SF	25 D SF
26 SF	27 COL	28 COL	29 COL	30		

October

SUN	MON	TUE	WED	THU	FRI	SAT
					1 SD	2 SD
3 SD	4	5	6	7	8	9

1999 SEASON
CLUB DIRECTORY

Managing general partner
Jerry Colangelo
President
Richard Dozer
Vice president and general manager
Joe Garagiola Jr.
Senior executive vice president, baseball operations
Roland Hemond
Senior vice president, sales and marketing
Scott Brubaker
Vice president, finance
Thomas Harris
V.p., tickets and special services
Dianne Aquilar
Vice president, sales
Blake Edwards
Senior assistant to the general manager
Mel Didier
Director of baseball administration
Ralph Nelson
Director of Hispanic marketing
Richard Saenz
Director of Tucson operations
Mark Fernandez
Director of public relations
Mike Swanson
Director of community affairs
Craig Pletenik
Director of ballpark services
Russ Amaral
Director of suite services
Diney Mahoney
Director of team travel
Roger Riley
Director of minor league operations
Tommy Jones
Director of Pacific Rim operations
Jim Marshall
Trainer
Paul Lessard

Assistant trainer
Dave Edwards
Club physician
Dr. David Zeman
Director of scouting
Don Mitchell
Assistant director of scouting
Bob Miller
Scouting coordinators
Kendall Carter, Clay Daniel, Junior Noboa
Professional scouts
Brannon Bonifay, Ed Durkin, Bill Earnhart, Julian Mock
Major league advanced scouts
Mack (Shooty) Babitt, Ron Massbay, Dick Scott
National scouting supervisors
Howard McCullough, Mike Rizzo, Steve Springer
Area scouting supervisors
David Cassidy, Arnold Cochran, Ray Corbett, Jason Goligoski, Brian Guinn, Scott Jaster, James Keller, Chris Knabenshue, Greg Lonigro, David May Jr., Louie Medina, Matt Merullo, Mike Piatnik, Mac Siebert, Steve Swail, Mike Valarezo, Brad Vaughn, Harold Zonder
Scouts
Monte Aldrich, Rogel Andrade, Ossie Alvarez, Pete Carmona, Gary Davenport, Leo Figueroa, Doug Gonring, David Hall, Scott Jamieson, Min Su Kim, Hal Kurtzman, Rafael Mena, Hiiroyuki Oya, Arturo Pena, Jose Diaz Perez, Carlos Porte, Juan Carlos Salabarria, Tomas Santana, Williams Jose Sarmiento, Mark Smelko, Modesto Ulloa, Jorge Urribari, Cesar Valasquez, Roberto Perez Vilchis, John Wadsworth, Doyle Wilson, John Wright

MINOR LEAGUE AFFILIATES

Class	Team	League	Manager
AAA	Tucson	Pacific Coast	Chris Speier
AA	El Paso	Texas	Don Wakamatsu
A	High Desert	California	Derek Bryant
A	South Bend	Midwest	Mike Brumley
Rookie	Missoula	Pioneer	Joe Almaraz
Rookie	Tucson	Arizona	Roly de Armas

BROADCAST INFORMATION

Radio: KTAR-AM (620).
TV: KTVK (Channel 3)
Cable TV: Fox Sports Arizona.

SPRING TRAINING

Ballpark (city): Tucson Electric Park (Tucson, Ariz.).
Ticket information: 800-638-4253, 520-434-1111.

Manager—Buck Showalter (11).
Coaches—Brian Butterfield (55), Mark Connor (52), Dwayne Murphy (21), Jim Presley (17), Glenn Sherlock (53), Carlos Tosca (14).

No.	PITCHERS	B/T	Ht./Wt.	Born	1998 clubs
34	Anderson, Brian	B/L	6-1/190	4-26-72	Arizona
40	Benes, Andy	R/R	6-6/245	8-20-67	Arizona
62	Boyd, Jason	R/R	6-3/170	2-23-73	Tucson
	Brohawn, Troy	L/L	6-1/190	1-14-73	Fresno
41	Chouinard, Bobby	R/R	6-1/185	5-1-72	Louisville, Milwaukee, Tucson, Arizona
37	Daal, Omar	L/L	6-3/185	3-1-72	Arizona, Tucson
66	Figueroa, Nelson	B/R	6-1/155	5-18-74	Binghamton, Tucson
50	Ford, Ben	R/R	6-7/200	8-15-75	Arizona, Tucson
57	Jacob, Russell	R/R	6-6/225	1-2-75	High Desert
51	Johnson, Randy	R/L	6-10/230	9-10-63	Seattle, Houston
	Nunez, Vladimir	R/R	6-4/235	3-15-75	Tucson, Arizona
30	Olson, Gregg	R/R	6-4/210	10-11-66	Arizona
	Randolph, Steve	L/L	6-3/185	5-1-74	Tucson, High Desert
27	Reynoso, Armando	R/R	6-0/204	5-1-66	St. Lucie, Norfolk, New York N.L.
39	Shouse, Brian	L/L	5-11/180	9-26-68	Pawtucket, Boston
31	Small, Aaron	R/R	6-5/214	11-23-71	Oakland, Arizona
36	Sodowsky, Clint	L/R	6-4/200	7-13-72	Arizona, Tucson
32	Stottlemyre, Todd	L/R	6-3/200	5-20-65	St. Louis, Texas
22	Swindell, Greg	R/L	6-3/230	1-2-65	Minnesota, Boston
44	Telemaco, Amaury	R/R	6-3/214	1-19-74	Chicago N.L., Arizona

No.	CATCHERS	B/T	Ht./Wt.	Born	1998 clubs
26	Miller, Damian	R/R	6-2/190	10-13-69	Tucson, Arizona
35	Stinnett, Kelly	R/R	5-11/195	2-14-70	Arizona

No.	INFIELDERS	B/T	Ht./Wt.	Born	1998 clubs
10	Batista, Tony	R/R	6-0/195	12-9-73	Arizona
33	Bell, Jay	R/R	6-0/182	12-11-65	Arizona
28	Colbrunn, Greg	R/R	6-0/205	7-26-69	Colorado, Atlanta
59	Diaz, Edwin	R/R	5-11/170	1-15-75	Arizona, Tucson
2	Frias, Hanley	B/R	6-0/165	12-5-73	Tucson, Arizona
7	Klassen, Danny	R/R	6-0/175	9-22-75	Arizona, Tucson
16	Lee, Travis	L/L	6-3/210	5-26-75	Arizona
64	Spivey, Junior	R/R	6-0/185	1-28-75	Tulsa, High Desert
9	Williams, Matt	R/R	6-2/210	11-28-65	Arizona, Tucson

No.	OUTFIELDERS	B/T	Ht./Wt.	Born	1998 clubs
43	Benitez, Yamil	R/R	6-2/195	5-10-72	Arizona
63	Conti, Jason	L/R	5-11/180	1-27-75	Tulsa
25	Dellucci, David	L/L	5-10/180	10-31-73	Tucson, Arizona
12	Finley, Steve	L/L	6-2/180	3-12-65	San Diego
6	Fox, Andy	L/R	6-4/205	1-12-71	Arizona
23	Gilkey, Bernard	R/R	6-0/200	9-24-66	New York N.L., Arizona
28	Gonzalez, Luis	L/R	6-2/190	9-3-67	Detroit
	Powell, Dante	R/R	6-2/185	8-25-73	Fresno, San Francisco
65	Ryan, Rob	L/L	5-11/190	6-24-73	Tucson

1999 SEASON Arizona Diamondbacks

BALLPARK INFORMATION

Ballpark (capacity, surface)
Bank One Ballpark (49,075)

Address
401 East Jefferson
Phoenix, AZ 85003

Business phone
602-462-6500

Ticket information
602-514-8400

Ticket prices
$10 to $22.50 (lower level)
$1 to $15.50 (upper level)
$35 to 55 (lower level premium seats)
$27 and $33 (Infiniti Diamond level)

Field dimensions (from home plate)
To left field at foul line, 330 feet
To center field, 407 feet
To right field at foul line, 334 feet

First game played
March 31, 1998 (Rockies 9, Diamondbacks 2)

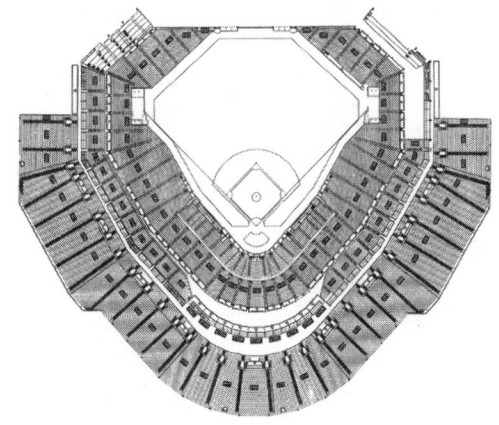

1998 REVIEW
DAY BY DAY

Date	Opp.	Res.	Score	(inn.*)	Hits	Opp. hits	Winning pitcher	Losing pitcher	Save	Record	Pos.	GB
3-31	Col.	L	2-9		6	13	Kile	Benes		0-1	T4th	1.0
4-1	Col.	L	0-6		3	16	Thomson	Blair		0-2	T4th	2.0
4-2	Col.	L	4-6	11	9	Astacio	Anderson	DiPoto	0-3	T4th	3.0
4-3	S.F.	L	3-8		6	12	Gardner	Suppan		0-4	T4th	3.0
4-4	S.F.	L	3-5		8	7	Darwin	Olson	Nen	0-5	T4th	4.0
4-5	S.F.	W	3-2		8	7	Benes	Estes	Rodriguez	1-5	5th	3.0
4-7	At L.A.	L	1-9		8	13	Park	Blair		1-6	5th	4.0
4-8	At L.A.	W	3-0		5	8	Anderson	Nomo	Rodriguez	2-6	5th	4.0
4-9	At L.A.	L	2-7		10	10	Valdes	Suppan		2-7	5th	5.0
4-10	At S.D.	L	4-6		5	9	Miceli	Rodriguez		2-8	5th	6.0
4-11	At S.D.	L	0-7		6	9	Smith	Adamson		2-9	5th	7.0
4-12	At S.D.	L	2-4		4	5	Hamilton	Blair	Hoffman	2-10	5th	8.0
4-13	At S.D.	L	0-1		4	3	Ashby	Anderson		2-11	5th	9.0
4-14	At St.L.	L	5-15		4	13	Busby	Sodowsky		2-12	5th	9.0
4-16†	At St.L.	L	4-5		11	5	Stottlemyre	Adamson	Brantley	2-13		
4-16‡	At St.L.	W	8-2		10	7	Benes	Osborne		3-13	5th	9.5
4-17	Fla.	W	7-5		12	4	Springer	Darensbourg	Rodriguez	4-13	5th	9.5
4-18	Fla.	W	7-5		12	5	Manuel	Alfonseca	Rodriguez	5-13	5th	9.5
4-19	Fla.	L	3-4		10	8	Meadows	Suppan	Stanifer	5-14	5th	10.0
4-20	Fla.	W	15-4		16	10	Sodowsky	Hernandez		6-14	5th	9.5
4-22	At Atl.	L	2-5		7	9	Smoltz	Benes		6-15	5th	10.0
4-23	At Atl.	L	1-3		7	5	Glavine	Blair	Wohlers	6-16	5th	11.0
4-24	At Atl.	L	5-6		13	14	Ligtenberg	Springer		6-17	5th	11.0
4-25	At Fla.	W	4-3	(11)	10	8	Brow	Darensbourg	Rodriguez	7-17	5th	11.0
4-26	At Fla.	L	6-12		8	11	Ludwick	Adamson		7-18	5th	11.0
4-27	Atl.	L	5-6		11	9	Cather	Daal	Wohlers	7-19	5th	11.0
4-28	Atl.	L	2-12		6	18	Glavine	Blair		7-20	5th	12.0
5-1	At Mon.	L	4-7		7	10	Vazquez	Anderson	Urbina	7-21	5th	12.5
5-2	At Mon.	L	4-5	(12)	10	13	Bennett	Springer		7-22	5th	13.5
5-3	At Mon.	L	1-4		2	8	Hermanson	Blair		7-23	5th	13.5
5-4	At N.Y.	W	4-2	(11)	9	7	Olson	Bohanon		8-23	5th	13.5
5-5	At N.Y.	L	1-9		6	13	Mlicki	Daal		8-24	5th	14.5
5-6	At N.Y.	L	2-8		8	9	Rojas	Sodowsky		8-25	5th	14.5
5-7	At Phi.	L	1-4		3	8	Schilling	Benes	Leiter	8-26	5th	14.5
5-8	At Phi.	L	4-6		6	8	Green	Olson	Leiter	8-27	5th	15.5
5-10	At Phi.	L	4-7		7	8	Winston	Suppan	Leiter	8-28	5th	15.0
5-11	Chi.	L	2-4		7	10	Wood	Anderson	Beck	8-29	5th	16.0
5-12	Chi.	L	6-7		8	7	Adams	Rodriguez	Beck	8-30	5th	16.5
5-13	Mil.	L	3-8		7	14	Juden	Blair	Wickman	8-31	5th	16.5
5-14	Mil.	W	4-1		6	4	Springer	Eldred	Olson	9-31	5th	17.0
5-15	Pit.	W	6-1		15	3	Suppan	Cordova		10-31	5th	17.0
5-16	Pit.	L	3-6		11	11	Schmidt	Anderson	Loiselle	10-32	5th	18.0
5-17	Pit.	W	8-2		11	9	Benes	Loaiza		11-32	5th	18.0
5-18	Pit.	W	9-2		15	8	Blair	Lieber		12-32	5th	17.5
5-20	At Fla.	W	7-3		9	8	Daal	Larkin	Olson	13-32	5th	16.5
5-21	At Fla.	W	6-4		8	7	Telemaco	Darensbourg	Olson	14-32	5th	15.5
5-22	L.A.	L	0-5		6	10	Dreifort	Benes		14-33	5th	16.5
5-23	L.A.	L	1-7		2	14	Martinez	Anderson		14-34	5th	16.5
5-24	L.A.	W	8-5		9	9	Blair	Park	Olson	15-34	5th	15.5
5-25	S.D.	W	3-2		6	4	Springer	Ashby	Olson	16-34	5th	14.5
5-26	S.D.	L	1-12		10	16	Brown	Suppan		16-35	5th	15.5
5-27	S.D.	L	4-6		14	12	Wall	Benes	Hoffman	16-36	5th	16.5
5-28	At S.F.	W	8-7		12	9	Anderson	Darwin	Olson	17-36	5th	16.0
5-29	At S.F.	L	1-3		4	6	Estes	Blair	Nen	17-37	5th	16.0
5-30	At S.F.	L	1-4		2	10	Hershiser	Daal	Nen	17-38	5th	17.0
5-31	At S.F.	L	4-7		10	10	Rueter	Suppan		17-39	5th	18.0
6-1	At Col.	W	6-4		9	7	Benes	Kile	Olson	18-39	5th	18.0
6-2	At Col.	W	9-3		14	5	Anderson	Wright		19-39	5th	17.0
6-3	At Col.	L	2-3		8	8	McElroy	Olson		19-40	5th	17.0
6-4	At Col.	L	2-5		4	12	Thomson	Daal		19-41	5th	18.0
6-5	At Oak.	L	1-2	(11)	7	7	Mohler	Springer		19-42	5th	18.0
6-6	At Oak.	L	5-10		9	14	Oquist	Benes		19-43	5th	19.0
6-7	At Oak.	W	12-4		15	6	Anderson	Candiotti		20-43	5th	19.0
6-9	Ana.	L	8-10		8	16	Finley	Sodowsky	Percival	20-44	5th	20.5
6-10	Ana.	W	10-2		15	5	Daal	Hill		21-44	5th	19.5
6-11	Ana.	L	5-10		10	11	Dickson	Wolcott	Percival	21-45	5th	20.0
6-12	St.L.	L	4-9		8	10	Stottlemyre	Benes		21-46	5th	21.0
6-13	St.L.	W	7-4		11	9	Springer	Brantley	Olson	22-46	5th	21.0
6-14	St.L.	L	0-2		4	10	Petkovsek	Blair	Bottenfield	22-47	5th	22.0
6-16	At Cin.	W	5-1		10	9	Daal	Harnisch		23-47	5th	22.0
6-17	At Cin.	W	4-1		8	7	Benes	Remlinger	Olson	24-47	5th	22.0

Date	Opp.	Res.	Score	(inn.*)	Hits	Opp. hits	Winning pitcher	Losing pitcher	Save	Record	Pos.	GB
6-18	At Cin.	W	4-2		9	5	Anderson	Klingenbeck	Olson	25-47	5th	22.0
6-19	At St.L.	L	0-5		6	10	Petkovsek	Blair		25-48	5th	23.0
6-20	At St.L.	L	2-4		7	7	Aybar	Banks	Croushore	25-49	5th	23.0
6-21	At St.L.	L	4-5		8	9	Raggio	Sodowsky	Brantley	25-50	5th	24.0
6-22	At Tex.	W	6-0		11	7	Benes	Burkett		26-50	5th	24.0
6-23	At Tex.	L	5-16		13	19	Sele	Anderson		26-51	5th	24.0
6-24	Tex.	L	2-3		5	9	Helling	Blair	Wetteland	26-52	5th	24.0
6-25	Tex.	L	4-9		6	13	Van Poppel	Telemaco		26-53	5th	25.0
6-26	Sea.	W	13-8		14	11	Sodowsky	Spoljaric		27-53	5th	25.0
6-27	Sea.	L	4-6		11	10	Fassero	Benes	Slocumb	27-54	5th	26.0
6-28	Sea.	W	3-2		8	6	Embree	Ayala		28-54	5th	25.0
6-30	At Chi.	W	5-4		9	9	Blair	Clark	Olson	29-54	5th	24.0
7-1	At Chi.	L	4-6		4	11	Wood	Telemaco	Beck	29-55	5th	25.0
7-2	At Chi.	L	2-3		8	6	Trachsel	Suppan	Beck	29-56	5th	25.0
7-3	At Hou.	L	5-6		15	9	Reynolds	Benes	Wagner	29-57	5th	26.0
7-4	At Hou.	W	7-4		11	12	Anderson	Hampton		30-57	5th	26.0
7-5	At Hou.	L	2-5		8	10	Bergman	Blair	Wagner	30-58	5th	27.0
7-10	Cin.	L	4-5		11	12	Tomko	Benes		30-59	5th	26.5
7-11	Cin.	L	0-8		3	12	Remlinger	Blair		30-60	5th	27.5
7-12	Cin.	L	3-5		9	13	Hudek	Anderson		30-61	5th	28.5
7-13	Hou.	W	5-3		7	5	Telemaco	Schourek	Olson	31-61	5th	27.5
7-14	Hou.	L	2-4		5	12	Reynolds	Daal	Wagner	31-62	5th	28.5
7-15	Hou.	W	9-8	(11)	15	12	Embree	Magnante		32-62	5th	28.5
7-17	Col.	W	9-6		12	11	Blair	Astacio	Olson	33-62	5th	28.5
7-18	Col.	W	4-2		11	7	Anderson	Jones	Olson	34-62	5th	28.5
7-19	Col.	W	6-4		9	11	Small	Munoz	Embree	35-62	5th	28.5
7-20	At S.F.	L	3-5		3	9	Rodriguez	Chouinard	Nen	35-63	5th	28.5
7-21	At S.F.	W	5-3		10	10	Benes	Hershiser	Olson	36-63	5th	28.5
7-22	At S.D.	L	3-9		9	9	Ashby	Blair		36-64	5th	29.5
7-23	At S.D.	L	0-3		4	6	Hamilton	Anderson	Hoffman	36-65	5th	30.5
7-24	At L.A.	L	1-3		3	9	Park	Telemaco	Shaw	36-66	5th	30.5
7-25	At L.A.	W	5-3		7	8	Daal	Dreifort	Olson	37-66	5th	30.5
7-26	At L.A.	L	3-5		9	9	Valdes	Benes	Shaw	37-67	5th	31.5
7-27	Chi.	L	2-6		3	7	Trachsel	Blair		37-68	5th	32.0
7-28	Chi.	W	7-5		13	10	Wolcott	Clark	Olson	38-68	5th	31.0
7-29	Chi.	L	3-7		7	10	Wengert	Telemaco	Adams	38-69	5th	31.0
7-30	Chi.	W	4-0		10	4	Daal	Tapani		39-69	5th	31.0
7-31	At Mil.	W	8-2		11	7	Benes	Juden		40-69	5th	31.0
8-1	At Mil.	W	5-4		7	9	Banks	Fox	Olson	41-69	5th	30.0
8-2	At Mil.	L	2-7		7	10	Woodall	Anderson		41-70	5th	31.0
8-3	At Chi.	W	6-5		10	15	Telemaco	Wengert	Olson	42-70	5th	30.0
8-4	At Chi.	L	0-2		5	5	Tapani	Daal	Beck	42-71	5th	31.0
8-5	At Chi.	W	10-7		14	7	Benes	Wood	Olson	43-71	5th	31.0
8-7	At Mon.	W	6-4		10	9	Anderson	Vazquez	Olson	44-71	5th	30.5
8-8	At Mon.	L	3-5		9	10	Hermanson	Telemaco	Urbina	44-72	5th	31.0
8-9	At Mon.	L	2-8		6	9	Bennett	Wolcott	Kline	44-73	5th	32.0
8-10	Phi.	L	0-3		3	6	Schilling	Daal		44-74	5th	32.0
8-11	Phi.	W	7-3		13	8	Benes	Portugal		45-74	5th	32.0
8-12	Phi.	L	4-7		8	8	Grace	Anderson		45-75	5th	33.0
8-14	N.Y.	L	2-3		9	6	Reed	Telemaco	Wendell	45-76	5th	33.5
8-15	N.Y.	L	4-5		7	11	Reynoso	Chouinard	J. Franco	45-77	5th	34.0
8-16	N.Y.	W	6-1		7	2	Daal	Nomo		46-77	5th	33.5
8-17	Mon.	W	6-1		7	3	Benes	Powell		47-77	5th	33.0
8-18	Mon.	L	1-7		4	12	Vazquez	Anderson		47-78	5th	34.0
8-19	Mon.	L	2-8		4	10	Hermanson	Telemaco		47-79	5th	34.0
8-20†	At Phi.	L	1-11		4	13	Schilling	Wolcott		47-80		
8-20‡	At Phi.	W	12-9	(11)	15	14	Embree	Bottalico		48-80	5th	34.5
8-21	At Phi.	L	0-1		5	9	Portugal	Daal	Gomes	48-81	5th	34.5
8-22	At N.Y.	L	4-9		8	6	Jones	Benes		48-82	5th	34.5
8-23	At N.Y.	W	4-3		8	7	Anderson	Leiter	Olson	49-82	5th	34.5
8-24	At N.Y.	W	9-5		12	9	Telemaco	Yoshii	Banks	50-82	5th	34.5
8-25	Pit.	L	6-9		10	11	Lawrence	Sodowsky	Loiselle	50-83	5th	35.5
8-26	Pit.	L	3-4		9	13	Tabaka	Daal	Loiselle	50-84	5th	36.5
8-27	Mil.	L	0-4		2	13	Roque	Benes	Plunk	50-85	5th	37.5
8-28	Mil.	W	6-3		9	7	Anderson	Woodall	Olson	51-85	5th	37.5
8-29	Mil.	W	4-3		7	7	Small	Wickman		52-85	5th	36.5
8-30	Mil.	W	7-3		11	8	Sodowsky	Karl		53-85	5th	35.5
9-1	At Pit.	W	4-3		9	8	Daal	Peters	Olson	54-85	5th	36.0
9-2	At Pit.	W	2-1	(11)	8	5	Small	Tabaka	Olson	55-85	5th	35.0
9-3	At Pit.	W	1-0		4	3	Anderson	Cordova		56-85	5th	34.5
9-4	Hou.	W	3-1		8	7	Telemaco	Lima	Olson	57-85	5th	33.5
9-5	Hou.	L	5-6	(12)	13	10	Wagner	Embree		57-86	5th	34.5
9-6	Hou.	L	1-10		9	17	Hampton	Daal		57-87	5th	34.5
9-7	L.A.	W	4-2		7	6	Benes	Mlicki	Olson	58-87	5th	33.5
9-8	L.A.	L	5-6	(11)	11	17	Kubenka	Embree	Shaw	58-88	5th	33.5

Date	Opp.	Res.	Score	(inn.*)	Hits	Opp. hits	Winning pitcher	Losing pitcher	Save	Record	Pos.	GB
9-9	L.A.	L	2-6		9	8	Perez	Telemaco		58-89	5th	34.5
9-11	At Cin.	L	1-13		5	11	Tomko	Sodowsky		58-90	5th	35.0
9-12	At Cin.	L	0-3		3	6	Parris	Daal	White	58-91	5th	36.0
9-13	At Cin.	W	5-0		9	1	Benes	Bere	Olson	59-91	5th	35.0
9-14	S.F.	W	14-2		17	7	Anderson	Estes		60-91	5th	35.0
9-15	S.F.	W	7-6	(11)	15	6	Olson	Mesa		61-91	5th	34.0
9-16	S.F.	L	5-6	(10)	9	10	Johnstone	Olson	Nen	61-92	5th	34.0
9-17	Atl.	L	0-1		4	4	Neagle	Daal	Ligtenberg	61-93	5th	34.0
9-18	Atl.	W	5-0		10	5	Benes	Maddux		62-93	5th	33.0
9-19	Atl.	L	0-5		6	12	Glavine	Anderson		62-94	5th	34.0
9-20	Atl.	L	0-10		4	13	Chen	Telemaco		62-95	5th	34.0
9-22	At Col.	W	8-6		12	7	Daal	Wright	Olson	63-95	5th	33.0
9-23	At Col.	L	11-14		16	15	Wainhouse	Banks	Veres	63-96	5th	34.0
9-25	S.D.	W	6-3		8	9	Olson	R. Myers		64-96	5th	33.0
9-26	S.D.	W	3-2		7	6	Telemaco	Hitchcock	Olson	65-96	5th	32.0
9-27	S.D.	L	2-3		5	9	Clement	Small	Hoffman	65-97	5th	33.0

Monthly records: March (0-1), April (7-19), May (10-19), June (12-15), July (11-15), August (13-16), September (12-12).
*Innings, if other than nine. †First game of doubleheader. ‡Second game of doubleheader.

HIGHLIGHTS

High point: Andy Benes put together a gem of a start September 13 in Cincinnati. Needing just two outs for his first career no-hitter, Reds first baseman Sean Casey lined a single to right to end the quest. It represented an incredible turnaround from the beginning of the season.

Low point: Losing 31 of their first 39 games, the Diamondbacks drew nationwide comparisons to the laughable 1962 New York Mets.

Turning point: A 4-1 victory over Milwaukee on May 14 began the club's slow climb toward respectability. Arizona posted a 57-66 record from that point on and began to be taken seriously by opponents in the second half of the season.

Most valuable player: Andy Fox, acquired in a trade with the Yankees, managed to play in 139 games while starting at six different positions. Fox's .277 average and 67 runs scored ranked second and fifth, respectively, for the club.

Most valuable pitcher: Gregg Olson latched onto a spring training invitation and wound up turning his baseball life around. He was successful in 30 of 34 save situations.

Most improved player: After rarely seeing game action during the first three months, Tony Batista began playing regularly and wound up with 18 home runs in just 293 at-bats.

Most pleasant surprise: A second-round pick in the expansion draft from Toronto, Omar Daal, who began the season in the bullpen, had the fifth-lowest ERA in the league at 2.88. His record was an unimpressive 8-12, but the club averaged only 3.2 runs in his starts.

Biggest disappointment: Veteran third baseman Matt Williams rarely looked like his old self at the plate. His 71 RBIs were the second-lowest total of his career in a full season. Throw in just 20 home runs, tying his career worst.

Key injuries: Rookie Travis Lee was placed on the 15-day disabled list because of a groin strain. His numbers slipped dramatically after his return. Daal spent 15 days on the disabled list after suffering hamstring pulls in both legs on June 21. Catcher Jorge Fabregas tore tendons in his ankle in mid-May, missing the next six weeks. He was traded to the Mets. Joel Adamson began the season in the rotation but managed only five starts before being diagnosed with a rotator cuff injury. He never returned.

Notable: Benes' 14 victories tied Tampa Bay's Rolando Arrojo for the most ever by an expansion pitcher. . . . David Dellucci led the league with 12 triples. . . . Arizona's 100 errors were the second-fewest in the National League to Atlanta's 91. Devon White became the first expansion player to hit at least 20 home runs and steal 20 bases. . . . The Diamondbacks finished the year with a total home attendance of 3,600,412, the third highest mark in the majors. Only Colorado and Baltimore drew more fans.

—PEDRO GOMEZ

RECORDS

1998 regular-season record: 65-97 (5th in N.L. West); 34-47 at home; 31-50 on road; 15-29 vs. East; 27-30 vs. Central; 18-30 vs. N.L. West; 5-8 vs. A.L.; 18-22 vs. lefthanded starters; 47-75 vs. righthanded starters; 55-83 on grass; 10-14 on turf; 16-25 in daytime; 49-72 at night; 16-23 in one-run games; 6-5 in extra-inning games; 0-0-2 in doubleheaders.

Team record past five years: 65-97 in one year (.401).

TEAM LEADERS

Batting average: Devon White (.286).
At-bats: Devon White (563).
Runs: Devon White (84).
Hits: Devon White (157).
Total bases: Devon White (257).
Doubles: Devon White (32).
Triples: David Dellucci (12).
Home runs: Devon White, Travis Lee (22).
Runs batted in: Devon White (85).
Stolen bases: Devon White (22).

Slugging percentage: Devon White (.456).
On-base percentage: Andy Fox (.355).
Wins: Andy Benes (14).
Earned-run average: Omar Daal (2.88).
Complete games: Omar Daal (3).
Shutouts: Omar Daal, Brian Anderson (1).
Saves: Gregg Olson (30).
Innings pitched: Andy Benes (231.1).
Strikeouts: Andy Benes (164).

GAMES BY POSITION

Catcher: Kelly Stinnett 86, Damian Miller 46, Jorge Fabregas 41.
First base: Travis Lee 146, Brent Brede 12, Andy Fox 12, Damian Miller 1.
Second base: Andy Stankiewicz 61, Andy Fox 60, Tony Batista 41, Danny Klassen 29, Jay Bell 15, Edwin Diaz 3, Hanley Frias 3.
Third base: Matt Williams 134, Andy Fox 26, Tony Batista 15, Hanley Frias 2.
Shortstop: Jay Bell 138, Tony Batista 34, Hanley Frias 2.
Outfield: Devon White 144, David Dellucci 117, Karim Garcia 103, Yamil Benitez 62, Brent Brede 58, Andy Fox 48, Bernard Gilkey 27, Chris Jones 8, Hensley Meulens 4, Damian Miller 2.
Designated hitter: Yamil Benitez 2, Damian Miller 2, Mike Robertson 2, Brent Brede 1, Kelly Stinnett 1.

TOP DRAFT CHOICES

1. None
2. None
3. **Darryl Conyer,** OF, Mission Bay H.S., San Diego
4. **Javier Lopez,** LHP, U. of Virginia
5. **J.D. Closser,** C, Monroe H.S., Alexandria, Ind.
6. **Brock McCarty,** OF, Ouachita Parish H.S., Monroe, La.
7. **Jeff Pass,** LHP, Chrysler H.S., New Castle, Ind.
8. **Andrew Good,** RHP, Rochester H.S., Rochester Hills, Mich.
9. **Brendan Fuller,** RHP, Clearwater (Fla.) H.S.
10. **Tom Kail,** OF, Baldwin H.S., Pittsburgh

ATLANTA BRAVES
NATIONAL LEAGUE EAST DIVISION

1999 Braves Schedule

Home games shaded. *—All-Star Game at Fenway Park (Boston). D—Day game (any game starting before 5 p.m.).

April

SUN	MON	TUE	WED	THU	FRI	SAT
				1	2	3
4	5 D PHI	6 PHI	7 PHI	8 PHI	9 ARI	10 ARI
11 D ARI	12 D PHI	13	14 PHI	15 PHI	16 COL	17 D COL
18 COL	19 LA	20 LA	21 LA	22	23 FLA	24 FLA
25 FLA	26 FLA	27 PIT	28 PIT	29 PIT	30 CIN	

May

SUN	MON	TUE	WED	THU	FRI	SAT
						1 CIN
2 D CIN	3 STL	4 STL	5 STL	6 D	7 SD	8 SD
9 SD	10 SF	11 SF	12 D SF	13	14 D CUB	15 D CUB
16 D CUB	17 PIT	18 PIT	19 PIT	20 CUB	21 CUB	22 CUB
23 CUB	24 MIL	25 MIL	26 MIL	27 D MIL	28 LA	29 LA
30 D LA	31 COL					

June

SUN	MON	TUE	WED	THU	FRI	SAT
		1 COL	2 COL	3	4 BOS	5 D BOS
6 D BOS	7 TB	8 TB	9 TB	10	11 BAL	12 D BAL
13 BAL	14 HOU	15 HOU	16 HOU	17 HOU	18 ARI	19 ARI
20 ARI	21 MON	22 MON	23 MON	24 D NYM	25 NYM	26 NYM
27 NYM	28 MON	29 MON	30 MON			

July

SUN	MON	TUE	WED	THU	FRI	SAT
				1 D MON	2 D NYM	3 D NYM
4 NYM	5 FLA	6 FLA	7 FLA	8 FLA	9 BOS	10 D BOS
11 D BOS	12	13	14 *	15 NYY	16 NYY	17 D NYY
18 TOR	19 TOR	20 TOR	21 FLA	22 FLA	23 PHI	24 PHI
25 D PHI	26 MIL	27 MIL	28 MIL	29	30 PHI	31 PHI

August

SUN	MON	TUE	WED	THU	FRI	SAT
1 PHI	2	3 PIT	4 PIT	5 PIT	6 D SF	7 D SF
8 SF	9 HOU	10 HOU	11 HOU	12	13 LA	14 LA
15 LA	16 COL	17 COL	18 D COL	19	20 SD	21 D SD
22 SD	23 CIN	24 CIN	25 CIN	26	27 STL	28 D STL
29 STL	30 CIN	31 CIN				

September

SUN	MON	TUE	WED	THU	FRI	SAT
			1 CIN	2	3 ARI	4 ARI
5 ARI	6 D STL	7 STL	8 STL	9	10 SF	11 D SF
12 SF	13 SD	14 SD	15 SD	16	17 D MON	18 MON
19 MON	20 D NYM	21 NYM	22 NYM	23 D NYM	24 MON	25 MON
26 MON	27 NYM	28 NYM	29 NYM	30 NYM		

October

SUN	MON	TUE	WED	THU	FRI	SAT
					1 FLA	2 FLA
3 FLA	4	5	6	7	8	9

1999 SEASON
CLUB DIRECTORY

Owner
R.E. Turner III
Chairman of the board of directors
William C. Bartholomay
President
Stanley H. Kasten
Executive vice president and general manager
John Schuerholz
Senior v.p. and assistant to the president
Henry L. Aaron
Senior vice president, administration
Bob Wolfe
V.p., director of marketing and broadcasting
Wayne Long
Vice president
Lee Douglas
Vice president of development
Janet Marie Smith
Assistant general manager
Dean Taylor
Director of scouting and player development
Paul Snyder
Director of minor league operations
Deric Ladnier
Assistant director of scouting
Dayton Moore
Baseball operations assistant
Tyrone Brooks
Special assistants to general manager
Bill Lajoie, Brian Murphy
Special assistant to g.m./player development
Jose Martinez
Special asst., scouting and player development
Guy Hansen
Director of team travel, equipment manager
Bill Acree
Executive assistant
June Cornillaud
Senior director of promotions and civic affairs
Miles McRea
Vice president/Controller
Chip Moore
Director of ticket sales
Paul Adams
Director of minor league business operations
Bruce Baldwin
Director of stadium operations and security
Larry Bowman
Director of Braves foundation
Danny Goodwin
Field director
Ed Mangan
Director of ticket operations
Ed Newman
Team counsel
David Payne

Director of stadium operations and security
Larry Bowman
Director of community relations
Cara Maglione
Director of special events
David Lee
Director of audio video operations
Jennifer Berger
Director of corporate sales
Jim Allen
Director of advertising
Amy Richter
Dir. of community relations, fan development
Dexter Santos
Director of sports human resources
Lisa Stricklin
Director of public relations
Jim Schultz
Media relations manager
Glen Serra
Public relations assistants
Steve Copses, Robert Gahagan, Joan Hicks, Kim Zieglar
Trainer
Dave Pursley
Club physician
Dr. David T. Watson
Associate physicians
Dr. William Barber, Dr. John Cantwell, Dr. Norman Elliott
Major league scouts
Dick Balderson, Scott Nethery, Fred Shaffer, Bobby Wine
National supervisors
Roy Clark, Bob Wadsworth
Regional supervisors
Butch Baccala, Harold Cronin, John Flannery
Area supervisors
Stu Cann, Bill Clark, Sherard Clinkscales, Bob Dunning, Rob English, Rene Francisco, Ralph Garr, Rod Gilbreath, John Hagemann, J. Harrison, Dexter Harris, J. Harrison, Ray Jackson, Kurt Kemp, Brian Kohlscheen, Jim Martz, Marco Paddy, John Ramey, Doug Smith, John Stewart
Scouts
Mike Baker, Jim Buchert, Joe Caputo, Todd Cook, Edgar Fernandez, Jose Figueroa, Pedro Flores, Felix Francisco, Bill Froberg, Ruben Garcia, Gil Garrido, Luis Herrera, Bob Isabelle, Rafael Josela, James Kane, Seong Yeol Kwak, Al Kubski, Duk Jung Lee, Jose Leon, Robert Lucas, William Marcot, Giorgio Moretti, Jose Mota, Dario Paulino, Ernie Pedersen, Rolando Petit, Elvis Pineda, Eric Robinson, Mark Ross, Ubaldo Salinas, Olivio Sanasota, Charlie Smith, Miguel Teren, Ted Thornton, Marv Throneberry, Carlos Torres, Fernando Villaescusa, Murray Zuk

MINOR LEAGUE AFFILIATES

Class	Team	League	Manager
AAA	Richmond	International	Randy Ingle
AA	Greenville	Southern	Paul Runge
A	Myrtle Beach	Carolina	Brian Snitker
A	Macon	South Atlantic	Jeff Treadway
A	Jamestown	New York-Pennsylvania	Jim Saul
Rookie	Danville	Appalachian	J.J. Cannon
Rookie	Gulf Coast Braves	Gulf Coast	Rick Albert

BROADCAST INFORMATION

Radio: WSB-AM (750).
TV: TBS-TV (Channel 17).
Cable TV: Fox SportsSouth.

SPRING TRAINING

Ballpark (city): Disney's Wide World of Sports Baseball Stadium (Kissimmee, Fla.).
Ticket information: 407-839-3900, 407-939-1418.

SPRING TRAINING ROSTER

Manager—Bobby Cox (6).
Coaches—Don Baylor, Pat Corrales (39), Bobby Dews (22), Glenn Hubbard, Leo Mazzone (54), Ned Yost (42).

No.	PITCHERS	B/T	Ht./Wt.	Born	1998 clubs
63	Bowie, Micah	L/L	6-4/185	11-10-74	Greenville
38	Cather, Mike	R/R	6-2/195	12-17-70	Richmond, Atlanta
48	Chen, Bruce	B/L	6-1/180	6-19-77	Greenville, Richmond, Atlanta
62	Ebert, Derrin	R/L	6-3/200	8-21-76	Richmond
47	Glavine, Tom	L/L	6-1/185	3-25-66	Atlanta
46	Ligtenberg, Kerry	R/R	6-2/205	5-11-71	Atlanta
31	Maddux, Greg	R/R	6-0/175	4-14-66	Atlanta
34	Millwood, Kevin	R/R	6-4/205	12-24-74	Atlanta
61	Moss, Damian	L/R	6-0/187	11-24-76	DID NOT PLAY
45	Perez, Odalis	L/L	6-0/150	6-7-78	Richmond, Atlanta, Greenville
37	Remlinger, Mike	L/L	6-1/210	3-26-66	Cincinnati
72	Rivera, Luis	R/R	6-3/163	6-21-78	Macon
49	Rocker, John	R/L	6-4/210	10-17-74	Richmond, Atlanta
40	Seanez, Rudy	R/R	5-10/190	10-20-68	Richmond, Atlanta
29	Smoltz, John	R/R	6-3/205	5-15-67	Greenville, Macon, Atlanta
36	Springer, Russ	R/R	6-4/205	11-7-68	Arizona, Atlanta
70	Villegas, Ismael	R/R	6-1/188	8-12-76	Greenville
43	Wohlers, Mark	R/R	6-4/207	1-23-70	Richmond, Atlanta, Greenville

No.	CATCHERS	B/T	Ht./Wt.	Born	1998 clubs
8	Lopez, Javy	R/R	6-3/200	11-5-70	Atlanta
65	Lunar, Fernando	R/R	6-1/190	5-25-77	Danville
12	Perez, Eddie	R/R	6-1/185	5-4-68	Atlanta

No.	INFIELDERS	B/T	Ht./Wt.	Born	1998 clubs
24	Boone, Bret	R/R	5-10/180	4-6-69	Cincinnati
2	DeRosa, Mark	R/R	6-1/190	2-2-75	Atlanta, Greenville
14	Galarraga, Andres	R/R	6-3/235	6-18-61	Atlanta
11	Graffanino, Tony	R/R	6-1/195	6-6-72	Atlanta
13	Guillen, Ozzie	L/R	5-11/165	1-20-64	Baltimore, Atlanta
9	Helms, Wes	R/R	6-4/230	5-12-76	Richmond, Atlanta
10	Jones, Chipper	B/R	6-4/210	4-24-72	Atlanta
7	Lockhart, Keith	L/R	5-10/170	11-10-64	Atlanta
20	Malloy, Marty	L/R	5-10/160	7-6-72	Richmond, Atlanta
15	Simon, Randall	L/L	6-0/180	5-26-75	Richmond, Atlanta
22	Weiss, Walt	B/R	6-0/175	11-28-63	Atlanta
	Williams, Glenn	R/R	6-2/170	7-18-77	Danville

No.	OUTFIELDERS	B/T	Ht./Wt.	Born	1998 clubs
17	Bautista, Danny	R/R	5-11/170	5-24-72	Atlanta, Greenville
25	Jones, Andruw	R/R	6-1/185	4-23-77	Atlanta
33	Jordan, Brian	R/R	6-1/205	3-29-67	St. Louis
18	Klesko, Ryan	L/L	6-3/220	6-12-71	Atlanta
26	Lombard, George	L/R	6-0/208	9-14-75	Greenville, Atlanta
1	Nixon, Otis	B/R	6-2/180	1-9-59	Minnesota
19	Pride, Curtis	L/R	6-0/200	12-17-68	Atlanta, Richmond
27	Williams, Gerald	R/R	6-2/187	8-10-66	Atlanta

BALLPARK INFORMATION

Ballpark (capacity, surface)
Turner Field (50,062, grass)

Address
P.O. Box 4064
Atlanta, GA 30302

Business phone
404-522-7630

Ticket information
404-249-6400 or 800-326-4000

Ticket prices
$33 (dugout level)
$27 (club level)
$22 (field level, terrace level)
$16 (field pavilion, terrace pavilion)
$11 (upper level)
$5 (upper pavilion)
$1 (skyline)

Field dimensions (from home plate)
To left field at foul line, 335 feet
To center field, 401 feet
To right field at foul line, 330 feet

First game played
April 4, 1997 (Braves 5, Cubs 4)

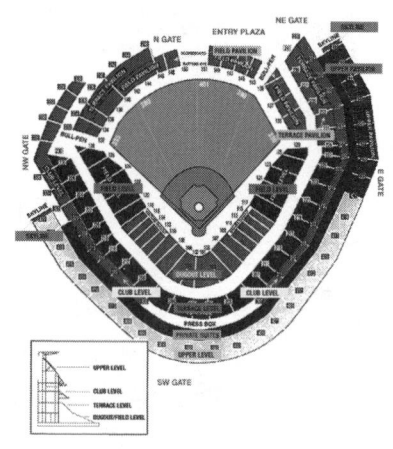

Date	Opp.	Res.	Score	(inn.*)	Hits	Opp. hits	Winning pitcher	Losing pitcher	Save	Record	Pos.	GB
3-31	Mil.	W	2-1		8	7	Ligtenberg	Wickman		1-0	T1st	...
4-2	Mil.	L	6-8	(11)	11	14	Myers	Butler		1-1	T1st	...
4-3	Phi.	W	5-1		10	5	Neagle	Grace		2-1	T1st	...
4-4	Phi.	W	5-4		9	13	Martinez	Brewer	Wohlers	3-1	T1st	...
4-5	Phi.	L	1-2		5	5	Schilling	Maddux		3-2	2nd	1.0
4-7	At Pit.	W	11-3		14	10	Glavine	Schmidt		4-2	2nd	0.5
4-8	At Pit.	L	3-5		7	8	Loaiza	Neagle	Loiselle	4-3	T2nd	1.0
4-9	At Pit.	W	4-3		6	9	Millwood	Lieber	Wohlers	5-3	T1st	...
4-10	At Phi.	L	0-1		2	6	Schilling	Cather		5-4	T2nd	0.5
4-11	At Phi.	L	5-6		9	10	Green	Martinez		5-5	3rd	1.5
4-12	At Phi.	W	3-2		7	8	Glavine	Stephenson	Wohlers	6-5	3rd	1.0
4-13	At Phi.	L	8-11		13	12	Spradlin	Ligtenberg	Bottalico	6-6	3rd	1.5
4-14	Pit.	W	6-0		6	1	Millwood	Lieber		7-6	3rd	1.5
4-15	Pit.	W	7-0		13	6	Maddux	Silva		8-6	3rd	1.5
4-16	Pit.	W	3-1		9	5	Smoltz	Cordova	Wohlers	9-6	2nd	0.5
4-18	At Col.	W	11-4		12	7	Neagle	Astacio		10-6	T1st	...
4-19†	At Col.	W	5-3		8	7	Millwood	Thompson	Wohlers	11-6		
4-19†	At Col.	L	7-10		13	14	Wright	Martinez	DiPoto	11-7	2nd	0.5
4-20	At Col.	W	7-5		13	8	Maddux	Kile	Ligtenberg	12-7	2nd	0
4-22	Ari.	W	5-2		9	7	Smoltz	Benes		13-7	1st	+0.5
4-23	Ari.	W	3-1		5	7	Glavine	Blair	Wohlers	14-7	1st	+1.0
4-24	Ari.	W	6-5		14	13	Ligtenberg	Springer		15-7	1st	+1.0
4-25	Col.	L	7-11		11	14	Kile	Millwood		15-8	1st	+1.0
4-26	Col.	L	6-7		10	13	Wright	Maddux	DiPoto	15-9	1st	+0.5
4-27	At Ari.	W	6-5		9	11	Cather	Daal	Wohlers	16-9	1st	+1.5
4-28	At Ari.	W	12-2		18	6	Glavine	Blair		17-9	1st	+2.5
4-30	S.F.	W	6-0		8	5	Neagle	Hershiser		18-9	1st	+4.0
5-1	S.F.	W	6-2		11	6	Maddux	Rueter		19-9	1st	+4.5
5-2	S.F.	W	4-3		10	7	Ligtenberg	Nen		20-9	1st	+5.5
5-3	S.F.	L	8-12		10	13	Darwin	Glavine		20-10	1st	+4.5
5-4	L.A.	W	4-2		8	5	Millwood	Guthrie	Ligtenberg	21-10	1st	+5.5
5-5	L.A.	W	8-3		11	7	Neagle	Valdes		22-10	1st	+5.5
5-6	L.A.	W	7-0		10	7	Maddux	Dreifort		23-10	1st	+5.5
5-7	S.D.	W	6-3		10	5	Smoltz	Hamilton	Ligtenberg	24-10	1st	+5.5
5-8	S.D.	L	2-3		9	6	Ashby	Glavine	Hoffman	24-11	1st	+4.5
5-9	S.D.	W	6-4		10	7	Millwood	VanRyn	Ligtenberg	25-11	1st	+5.0
5-10	S.D.	W	8-5		9	12	Cather	Wall	Ligtenberg	26-11	1st	+5.5
5-11	At Cin.	W	8-1		9	4	Maddux	Remlinger		27-11	1st	+6.5
5-12	At Cin.	W	5-1		11	4	Smoltz	Weathers		28-11	1st	+7.0
5-13	At St.L.	W	10-2		12	4	Glavine	Politte		29-11	1st	+7.0
5-14	At St.L.	W	7-3		12	5	Rocker	Acevedo		30-11	1st	+8.5
5-15	At Hou.	W	3-2		4	7	Neagle	Lima	Martinez	31-11	1st	+9.5
5-16	At Hou.	L	2-3		6	7	Henry	Ligtenberg		31-12	1st	+8.5
5-17	At Hou.	L	1-8		4	10	Bergman	Smoltz		31-13	1st	+8.5
5-18	At Hou.	W	4-0		12	7	Glavine	Hampton		32-13	1st	+9.0
5-20	Col.	W	5-1		11	4	Millwood	Thomson		33-13	1st	+9.0
5-21	Col.	W	2-0		9	8	Neagle	Kile	Ligtenberg	34-13	1st	+9.0
5-22	Chi.	W	8-2		10	6	Maddux	Clark		35-13	1st	+9.0
5-23	Chi.	L	6-10	(11)	14	14	Beck	Edmondson		35-14	1st	+8.0
5-24	Chi.	W	2-1		7	3	Glavine	Adams		36-14	1st	+8.0
5-25	Chi.	W	9-5		18	7	Millwood	Tapani		37-14	1st	+8.5
5-26	Mon.	W	9-3		11	11	Neagle	Batista		38-14	1st	+8.5
5-27	Mon.	W	2-0		3	7	Maddux	Vazquez	Ligtenberg	39-14	1st	+8.5
5-28	Mon.	L	5-9		10	12	Maddux	Wohlers		39-15	1st	+8.0
5-29	At Chi.	L	3-5	(11)	7	12	Adams	Rocker		39-16	1st	+7.0
5-30	At Chi.	L	8-9		11	15	Trachsel	Millwood	Patterson	39-17	1st	+6.0
5-31	At Chi.	L	2-4		7	11	Tapani	Neagle	Beck	39-18	1st	+5.0
6-1	At Mil.	W	5-2		11	5	Maddux	Woodard		40-18	1st	+6.0
6-2	At Mil.	W	9-0		12	12	Martinez	Wagner		41-18	1st	+7.0
6-3	At Mil.	W	5-2		4	8	Glavine	Juden	Wohlers	42-18	1st	+8.0
6-5	At Bal.	L	2-3		7	6	Erickson	Neagle		42-19	1st	+7.0
6-6	At Bal.	W	10-5		14	8	Millwood	Mussina		43-19	1st	+7.0
6-7	At Bal.	W	9-0		14	4	Maddux	Drabek		44-19	1st	+8.0
6-8	Bos.	W	7-6		11	12	Embree	Wasdin		45-19	1st	+8.0
6-9	Bos.	L	3-9		8	13	Saberhagen	Martinez		45-20	1st	+8.0
6-10	Bos.	L	6-10		10	13	Martinez	Neagle		45-21	1st	+7.0
6-12	Mon.	L	5-7		11	9	Batista	Cather	Urbina	45-22	1st	+6.5
6-13	Mon.	W	9-7		11	14	Glavine	Johnson	Martinez	46-22	1st	+6.5
6-14	Mon.	W	5-1		9	4	Millwood	C. Perez		47-22	1st	+7.5
6-16	Fla.	W	7-0		9	4	Neagle	Fontenot		48-22	1st	+7.5
6-17	Fla.	W	6-2		7	4	Maddux	Sanchez		49-22	1st	+8.5

Date	Opp.	Res.	Score	(inn.*)	Hits	Opp. hits	Winning pitcher	Losing pitcher	Save	Record	Pos.	GB
6-18	Fla.	L	2-3		7	10	Ojala	Glavine	Alfonseca	49-23	1st	+8.5
6-19	At Mon.	L	1-14		7	15	Boskie	Millwood		49-24	1st	+8.5
6-20	At Mon.	W	5-1		12	4	Smoltz	C. Perez		50-24	1st	+9.5
6-21	At Mon.	L	1-4		6	6	Hermanson	Neagle	Urbina	50-25	1st	+8.5
6-22	At N.Y. (AL)	L	4-6		9	11	Nelson	Martinez	Rivera	50-26	1st	+8.5
6-23	At N.Y. (AL)	W	7-2		11	7	Glavine	Hernandez		51-26	1st	+8.5
6-24	N.Y.	L	6-10		7	13	Cone	Millwood	Rivera	51-27	1st	+7.5
6-25	N.Y.	L	0-6		6	4	Wells	Neagle		51-28	1st	+6.5
6-26	Tor.	L	4-6		11	10	Hentgen	Smoltz	Myers	51-29	1st	+6.5
6-27	Tor.	W	2-0		4	8	Maddux	Guzman		52-29	1st	+7.5
6-28	Tor.	W	10-3		14	6	Glavine	Carpenter		53-29	1st	+7.5
6-30	At T.B.	W	7-2		8	6	Neagle	Saunders		54-29	1st	+8.5
7-1	At T.B.	W	6-5		8	10	Springer	Hernandez	Ligtenberg	55-29	1st	+9.5
7-2	At T.B.	W	6-0		11	5	Maddux	Arrojo		56-29	1st	+9.5
7-3	N.Y.	W	3-2		9	12	Glavine	Bohanon	Ligtenberg	57-29	1st	+10.5
7-4	N.Y.	W	4-1		8	6	Millwood	Yoshii		58-29	1st	+11.5
7-5	N.Y.	W	3-2	(11)	8	7	Seanez	J. Franco		59-29	1st	+12.5
7-9	At Fla.	W	6-4		7	11	Smoltz	Hernandez	Ligtenberg	60-29	1st	+13.5
7-10	At Fla.	L	1-3		6	6	Sanchez	Neagle	Heredia	60-30	1st	+13.5
7-11	At Fla.	L	3-4		6	7	Mantei	Maddux		60-31	1st	+12.5
7-12	At Fla.	L	3-5		7	11	Meadows	Glavine	Alfonseca	60-32	1st	+11.5
7-14	At N.Y.	W	4-2		8	6	Smoltz	Jones	Ligtenberg	61-32	1st	+12.5
7-15	At N.Y.	W	12-1		16	6	Neagle	Yoshii		62-32	1st	+13.5
7-16	Mil.	W	4-3		7	5	Maddux	Eldred	Seanez	63-32	1st	+13.5
7-17	Mil.	W	4-1		10	7	Glavine	Woodall	Rocker	64-32	1st	+14.5
7-18	Mil.	L	1-7		4	13	Woodard	Millwood		64-33	1st	+13.5
7-19	Mil.	W	11-6		13	12	Smoltz	Juden		65-33	1st	+13.5
7-20	Chi.	L	4-11		10	11	Tapani	Neagle		65-34	1st	+13.5
7-21	Chi.	L	0-3		6	7	Wood	Maddux	Beck	65-35	1st	+12.5
7-22	At Phi.	W	14-2		16	4	Glavine	Loewer		66-35	1st	+13.0
7-23	At Phi.	W	3-2		9	9	Millwood	Green	Ligtenberg	67-35	1st	+13.0
7-24	At Pit.	W	3-0		8	3	Smoltz	Peters		68-35	1st	+12.5
7-25	At Pit.	L	1-4		6	10	Cordova	Neagle	Christiansen	68-36	1st	+12.5
7-26	At Pit.	W	2-1		9	4	Maddux	Schmidt	Ligtenberg	69-36	1st	+13.5
7-27	At Cin.	W	3-2	(10)	10	6	Seanez	Belinda	Ligtenberg	70-36	1st	+14.0
7-28	At Cin.	L	1-13		5	12	Sullivan	Millwood		70-37	1st	+13.0
7-29	At Cin.	W	11-5		13	11	Seanez	Parris		71-37	1st	+13.0
7-30	At Cin.	W	13-3		16	9	Neagle	Krivda		72-37	1st	+14.0
7-31	St.L.	L	2-3		7	8	Mercker	Maddux	Painter	72-38	1st	+14.0
8-1	St.L.	W	3-1		10	7	Seanez	Croushore	Ligtenberg	73-38	1st	+14.0
8-2	St.L.	W	4-3		9	6	Millwood	Witt	Ligtenberg	74-38	1st	+14.0
8-4	Cin.	W	4-2		11	8	Smoltz	Sullivan	Ligtenberg	75-38	1st	+14.5
8-5	Cin.	L	9-13		10	16	Hudek	Springer		75-39	1st	+14.5
8-6	Cin.	W	5-0		8	3	Maddux	Remlinger		76-39	1st	+14.5
8-7	At S.F.	W	5-0		10	3	Glavine	Rueter		77-39	1st	+14.5
8-8	At S.F.	W	14-6		20	8	Millwood	Darwin		78-39	1st	+14.5
8-9	At S.F.	W	7-5		8	6	Martinez	Mesa	Ligtenberg	79-39	1st	+15.5
8-11	At S.D.	L	1-3		6	6	Hamilton	Neagle	Hoffman	79-40	1st	+14.0
8-12	At S.D.	L	1-5		5	4	Ashby	Maddux		79-41	1st	+14.0
8-13	At S.D.	W	5-0		10	2	Glavine	Langston		80-41	1st	+14.5
8-14	At L.A.	W	5-2		10	8	Millwood	Mlicki	Ligtenberg	81-41	1st	+14.5
8-15	At L.A.	W	5-3		12	8	Smoltz	Park	Ligtenberg	82-41	1st	+14.5
8-16	At L.A.	L	0-1		2	7	Radinsky	Neagle	Shaw	82-42	1st	+14.5
8-18	S.F.	W	8-4		9	7	Maddux	Rueter		83-42	1st	+14.0
8-19	S.F.	L	2-6		7	11	Gardner	Glavine		83-43	1st	+13.0
8-20	S.D.	L	0-2		11	6	Brown	Millwood	Hoffman	83-44	1st	+12.5
8-21	S.D.	W	5-4		7	8	Smoltz	Hamilton	Ligtenberg	84-44	1st	+13.0
8-22	L.A.	W	7-5		8	10	Neagle	Dreifort	Ligtenberg	85-44	1st	+13.0
8-23	L.A.	W	12-7		15	11	Maddux	Perez		86-44	1st	+14.0
8-24	L.A.	W	4-3		9	10	Glavine	Shaw	Ligtenberg	87-44	1st	+15.0
8-25	At Hou.	L	2-3		7	9	Hampton	Millwood	Wagner	87-45	1st	+15.0
8-26	At Hou.	W	6-2		10	8	Smoltz	Bergman		88-45	1st	+15.0
8-27	At St.L.	W	6-4		10	7	Neagle	Morris	Ligtenberg	89-45	1st	+16.0
8-28	At St.L.	L	4-5	(10)	12	9	Acevedo	Martinez		89-46	1st	+15.0
8-29	At St.L.	W	4-3		6	3	Glavine	Bottenfield	Seanez	90-46	1st	+15.0
8-30	At St.L.	L	7-8		11	11	Petkovsek	Martinez	Acevedo	90-47	1st	+15.0
8-31	Hou.	L	3-4		8	8	Powell	Smoltz	Wagner	90-48	1st	+14.0
9-1	Hou.	W	6-4		11	12	Neagle	Elarton	Ligtenberg	91-48	1st	+15.0
9-2	Hou.	L	2-4		5	12	R. Johnson	Maddux	Wagner	91-49	1st	+14.0
9-4	At N.Y.	L	1-2		5	6	Leiter	Glavine		91-50	1st	+13.0
9-5	At N.Y.	L	4-5		6	10	Wendell	Seanez	J. Franco	91-51	1st	+12.0
9-6	At N.Y.	W	4-0		8	3	Smoltz	Reed		92-51	1st	+13.0
9-7	At N.Y.	L	7-8		10	11	McMichael	Rocker	J. Franco	92-52	1st	+12.0
9-8	At Mon.	L	3-6		6	6	Batista	Maddux	Urbina	92-53	1st	+12.0
9-9	At Mon.	L	2-3		7	6	Urbina	Rocker		92-54	1st	+11.0

Date	Opp.	Res.	Score	(inn.*)	Hits	Opp. hits	Winning pitcher	Losing pitcher	Save	Record	Pos.	GB
9-10	At Mon.	W	7-4		7	10	Millwood	Thurman	Ligtenberg	93-54	1st	+11.0
9-11	Fla.	W	8-2		9	10	Smoltz	Ojala		94-54	1st	+12.0
9-12	Fla.	W	4-2		7	6	Chen	Hernandez	Ligtenberg	95-54	1st	+13.0
9-13	Fla.	L	5-6		6	6	Sanchez	O. Perez	Mantei	95-55	1st	+12.0
9-14	Phi.	W	4-2		7	10	Glavine	Schilling	Ligtenberg	96-55	1st	+12.0
9-15	Phi.	W	3-0		8	8	Millwood	Green	Charlton	97-55	1st	+12.5
9-16	Phi.	W	5-1		7	6	Smoltz	Loewer		98-55	1st	+12.5
9-17	At Ari.	W	1-0		4	4	Neagle	Daal	Ligtenberg	99-55	1st	+13.0
9-18	At Ari.	L	0-5		5	10	Benes	Maddux		99-56	1st	+13.0
9-19	At Ari.	W	5-0		12	6	Glavine	Anderson		100-56	1st	+13.0
9-20	At Ari.	W	10-0		13	4	Chen	Telemaco		101-56	1st	+13.0
9-22	At Fla.	W	4-1		8	7	Millwood	Medina	Ligtenberg	102-56	1st	+14.0
9-23	At Fla.	W	11-0		19	3	Smoltz	Ojala		103-56	1st	+15.0
9-25	N.Y.	W	6-5		10	11	Martinez	Reed	Rocker	104-56	1st	+16.0
9-26	N.Y.	W	4-0		6	7	Neagle	Leiter		105-56	1st	+17.0
9-27	N.Y.	W	7-2		14	8	Maddux	Reynoso		106-56	1st	+18.0

Monthly records: March (1-0), April (17-9), May (21-9), June (15-11), July (18-9), August (18-10), September (16-8).
*Innings, if other than nine. †Two games in one day (separate admissions).

HIGHLIGHTS

High point: With a win over the Phillies on September 14, the Braves became the first team in major league history to win seven straight division championships.

Low point: The club's National League-record home run streak was snapped at 25 consecutive games by the Cardinals on May 14.

Turning point: John Smoltz proved his surgically repaired elbow was healthy with five shutout innings against the Pirates in his first start on April 16 and wound up winning 17 games.

Most valuable player: Javy Lopez. He joined the ranks of the game's elite catchers with his best season, hitting 34 homers and driving in 106 runs. In addition, he led all major league catchers with a .995 fielding percentage and led all N.L. catchers by throwing out runners at a 33.8 percent rate.

Most valuable pitcher: Tom Glavine. He won 20 games for the fourth time and posted a career-low 2.47 ERA. The left-hander has quietly emerged as one of the game's most consistent pitchers, second only to Greg Maddux in wins among active pitchers over the last 10 years.

Most improved player: Ozzie Guillen. The veteran shortstop was supposedly washed up after being released by the Orioles, but he showed the Braves he was still capable of playing every day when Walt Weiss was hurt. Guillen hit .277 in 83 games and played solid defense.

Most pleasant surprise: Kevin Millwood. In his first full season in the majors, he won 17 games and finished among the league's top 10 in winning percentage and strikeouts (8.4) per nine innings.

Biggest disappointment: Ryan Klesko. Since hitting 34 homers and driving in 93 runs in 1996, his power and production has fallen each season. His numbers tumbled to 18 homers and 70 RBIs and he struggled against lefthanders, hitting only .213.

Key injuries: Weiss was limited to 96 games by quadriceps and groin injuries. Klesko missed nine games following an appendectomy on June 29. Rafael Belliard missed virtually the entire season after suffering a torn quadriceps muscle April 10. Mark Wohlers was never the same after straining an oblique muscle in May. He returned in two weeks, but eventually landed on the disabled list again because of his inability to pitch.

Notable: Kerry Ligtenberg became the first rookie since Todd Worrell (36 in 1986) to record 30 saves. . . . With 106 victories, the Braves set a franchise record for most wins in a season. . . . Bobby Cox became the franchise's all-time winningest manager when he surpassed Frank Selee's mark of 1,004 wins. . . . Led by Andres Galarraga's 44 homers, the most-ever by a first baseman in franchise history, the Braves eclipsed the club record with 215 home runs.

—BILL ZACK

RECORDS

1998 regular-season record: 106-56 (1st in N.L. East); 56-25 at home; 50-31 on road; 30-18 vs. N.L. East; 34-20 vs. Central; 33-11 vs. West; 9-7 vs. A.L.; 25-13 vs. lefthanded starters; 81-43 vs. righthanded starters; 86-43 on grass; 20-13 on turf; 33-12 in daytime; 73-44 at night; 23-21 in one-run games; 2-4 in extra-inning games; 0-0-0 in doubleheaders.

Team record past five years: 461-283 (.620, ranks 1st in league in that span).

TEAM LEADERS

Batting average: Chipper Jones (.313).
At-bats: Chipper Jones (601).
Runs: Chipper Jones (123).
Hits: Chipper Jones (188).
Total bases: Andres Galarraga (330).
Doubles: Andruw Jones (33).
Triples: Andruw Jones (8).
Home runs: Andres Galarraga (44).
Runs batted in: Andres Galarraga (121).
Stolen bases: Andruw Jones (27).
Slugging percentage: Andres Galarraga (.595).

On-base percentage: Chipper Jones (.404).
Wins: Tom Glavine (20).
Earned-run average: Greg Maddux (2.22).
Complete games: Greg Maddux (9).
Shutouts: Greg Maddux (5).
Saves: Kerry Ligtenberg (30).
Innings pitched: Greg Maddux (251.0).
Strikeouts: Greg Maddux (204).

GAMES BY POSITION

Catcher: Javy Lopez 128, Eddie Perez 45.
First base: Andres Galarraga 149, Greg Colbrunn 9, Eddie Perez 8, Ryan Klesko 7, Randall Simon 4, Ozzie Guillen 1.
Second base: Keith Lockhart 98, Tony Graffanino 93, Marty Malloy 10, Ozzie Guillen 2.
Third base: Chipper Jones 158, Wes Helms 4, Tony Graffanino 1, Ozzie Guillen 1, Keith Lockhart 1.
Shortstop: Walt Weiss 96, Ozzie Guillen 71, Rafael Belliard 7, Ray Holbert 7, Mark DeRosa 4, Tony Graffanino 2.
Outfield: Andruw Jones 159, Ryan Klesko 120, Gerald Williams 120, Michael Tucker 118, Danny Bautista 58, Curtis Pride 22, Damon Hollins 3, George Lombard 2, Greg Colbrunn 1.
Designated hitter: Andres Galarraga 2, Keith Lockhart 2, Curtis Pride 2, Danny Bautista 1, Javy Lopez 1, Eddie Perez 1.

TOP DRAFT CHOICES

1. None
2. **Matt Belisle,** RHP, McCallum H.S., Austin, Tex.
3. **Ryan Langerhans,** OF, Round Rock (Tex.) H.S.
4. **Johnny McGinnis,** RHP, Dacula (Ga.) H.S.
5. **Damien Jones,** OF, Vigor H.S., Whistler, Ala.
6. **Victor Menocal,** SS, Gainesville (Ga.) H.S.
7. **Scott Sobkowiak,** RHP, U. of N. Iowa
8. **Josh Karp,** RHP, Bothell (Wash.) H.S.
9. **Matt Targac,** LHP, Sacred Heart H.S., Hallettsville, Tex.
10. **Charlie Bilezikjian,** OF, Port Richmond H.S., Staten Island, N.Y.

CHICAGO CUBS
NATIONAL LEAGUE CENTRAL DIVISION

1999 Cubs Schedule
Home games shaded. *—All-Star Game at Fenway Park (Boston). D—Day game (any game starting before 5 p.m.)

April
SUN	MON	TUE	WED	THU	FRI	SAT
				1	2	3
4	5	6 HOU	7 HOU	8 HOU	9 D PIT	10 D PIT
11 D PIT	12 D CIN	13	14 D CIN	15 D CIN	16 D MIL	17 D MIL
18 D MIL	19	20 HOU	21 HOU	22 D HOU	23 D NYM	24 D NYM
25 D NYM	26	27 FLA	28 FLA	29 D FLA	30 D SD	

May
SUN	MON	TUE	WED	THU	FRI	SAT
						1 SD
2 D SD	3 COL	4 D COL	5 D COL	6	7 CIN	8 D CIN
9 CIN	10 D LA	11 LA	12 LA	13	14 ATL	15 D ATL
16 ATL	17 D FLA	18 FLA	19 FLA	20 ATL	21 ATL	22 ATL
23 D ATL	24 FLA	25 FLA	26 FLA	27	28 STL	29 D STL
30 D STL	31					

June
SUN	MON	TUE	WED	THU	FRI	SAT
		1 SD	2 SD	3 D SD	4 CLE	5 D CLE
6 D CLE	7 ARI	8 ARI	9 ARI	10	11 D CWS	12 D CWS
13 CWS	14 MIL	15 MIL	16 D MIL	17 SF	18 SF	19 D SF
20 SF	21	22 COL	23 COL	24 D COL	25 D PHI	26 D PHI
27 D PHI	28	29 MIL	30 D MIL			

July
SUN	MON	TUE	WED	THU	FRI	SAT
				1 MIL	2 PHI	3 PHI
4 D PHI	5 D PIT	6 D PIT	7 PIT	8 PIT	9 CWS	10 D CWS
11 D CWS	12	13 *	14 MIN	15 MIN	16 D MIN	17 D MIN
18 KC	19 KC	20 KC	21 PIT	22 PIT	23 NYM	24 D NYM
25 NYM	26 MON	27 MON	28 MON	29	30 NYM	31 D NYM

August
SUN	MON	TUE	WED	THU	FRI	SAT
1 NYM	2 MON	3 MON	4 MON	5 MON	6 D HOU	7 HOU
8 HOU	9 ARI	10 ARI	11 ARI	12	13 STL	14 D STL
15 STL	16 ARI	17 ARI	18 ARI	19	20 D COL	21 COL
22 D COL	23 SF	24 D SF	25 SF	26 SF	27 LA	28 D LA
29 LA	30 SD	31 SD				

September
SUN	MON	TUE	WED	THU	FRI	SAT
		1 SD	2	3 D LA	4 D LA
5 D LA	6 CIN	7 CIN	8 CIN	9 CIN	10 D HOU	11 D HOU
12 HOU	13	14 CIN	15 CIN	16 CIN	17 D MIL	18 D MIL
19 MIL	20 STL	21 STL	22 D PIT	23 PIT	24 PIT	25 D PIT
26 D PIT	27	28 PHI	29 PHI	30 PHI		

October
SUN	MON	TUE	WED	THU	FRI	SAT
				1 STL	2 D STL
3 D STL	4	5	6	7	8	9

1999 SEASON
CLUB DIRECTORY

Board of directors
James Dowdle
Andrew B. MacPhail
Andrew McKenna

President and chief executive officer
Andrew B. MacPhail

Vice president, general manager
Ed Lynch

Director, baseball operations
Scott Nelson

Special assistants to the g.m.
Larry Himes
Ken Kravec

Major league advance scout
Keith Champion

Traveling secretary
Jimmy Bank

Assistant general manager
David Wilder

Field coordinator
Alan Regier

Hitting coordinator
Randy Bush

Pitching coordinator
Lester Strode

Roving infield instructor
Sandy Alomar

Roving outfield instructor
Jimmy Piersall

Equipment manager
Michael Burkhart

Director, player development & scouting
Jim Hendry

Coordinator of scouting
John Stockstill

Regional scouting supervisors
Joe Housey
Brad Kelley
Larry Maxie

Latin American coordinator
Oneri Fleita

Director, media relations
Sharon Pannozzo

Media information coordinator
Chuck Wasserstrom

Team physicians
John Marquardt, M.D.
Michael Schafer, M.D.

Head athletic trainer
David Tumbas

Assistant athletic trainer
Steve Melendez

Strength coordinator
Bruce Hammel

Equipment manager
Yosh Kawano

Assistant equipment manager
Dana Noeltner

Visiting clubhouse manager
Tom Hellmann

Exec. v.p., business operations
Mark McGuire

V.p., marketing and broadcasting
John McDonough

Director, promotions and advertising
Jay Blunk

Mgr., Cubs Care/community relations
Rebecca Polihronis

Director, publications/special projects
Ernie Roth

Photographer
Stephen Green

Director, stadium operations
Paul Rathje

Director, ticket operations
Frank Maloney

Scouts
Mark Adair, Billy Blitzer, Jim Crawford, Steve Fuller, Al Geddes, John Gracio, Gene Handley, Bill Harford, Steve Hinton, Sam Hughes, Spider Jorgensen, Buzzy Keller, Leon Lee, Scott May, Brian Milner, Fred Peterson, Alberto Rondon, Marc Russo, Jose Serra, Mark Servais, Tom Shafer, Billy Swoope, Jose Trujillo, Harry Von Suskil

MINOR LEAGUE AFFILIATES

Class	Team	League	Manager
AAA	Iowa	Pacific Coast	Terry Kennedy
AA	West Tenn	Southern	Dave Trembley
A	Daytona	Florida State	Nate Oliver
A	Lansing	Midwest	Oscar Acosta
A	Eugene	Northwest	Bob Ralston
Rookie	Mesa Cubs	Arizona	Carmelo Martinez

BROADCAST INFORMATION
Radio: WGN-AM (720).
TV: WGN-TV (Channel 9).
Cable TV: CLTV.

SPRING TRAINING
Ballpark (city): HoHoKam Park (Mesa, Ariz.).
Ticket information: 800-638-4253.

SPRING TRAINING ROSTER

Manager—Jim Riggleman (5).
Coaches—Dave Bialas, Marty DeMerritt, Tom Gamboa (39), Jeff Pentland (2), Dan Radison (42) Billy Williams (26).

No.	PITCHERS	B/T	Ht./Wt.	Born	1998 clubs
51	Adams, Terry	R/R	6-3/205	3-6-73	Chicago N.L., Iowa
	Barker, Richie	R/R	6-2/220	10-29-72	West Tenn
47	Beck, Rod	R/R	6-1/235	8-3-68	Chicago N.L.
	Farnsworth, Kyle	B/R	6-4/205	4-14-76	Iowa, West Tenn
30	Gonzalez, Jeremi	R/R	6-2/210	1-8-75	Chicago N.L.
49	Heredia, Felix	L/L	6-0/180	6-18-76	Florida, Chicago N.L.
	Hernandez, Elvin	R/R	6-1/195	8-20-77	Carolina
52	Karchner, Matt	R/R	6-4/215	6-28-67	Chicago A.L., Chicago N.L.
	King, Ray	L/L	6-1/225	1-15-74	Iowa, West Tenn
32	Lieber, Jon	L/R	6-3/225	4-2-70	Pittsburgh
	McNichol, Brian	L/L	6-5/225	5-20-74	Iowa, West Tenn
53	Miller, Kurt	R/R	6-5/225	8-24-72	Iowa, Chicago N.L.
45	Mulholland, Terry	R/L	6-3/220	3-9-63	Chicago N.L.
59	Myers, Rod	R/R	6-1/205	6-26-69	Iowa, Chicago N.L.
	Norton, Phillip	R/L	6-1/185	2-1-76	West Tenn, Daytona
41	Pisciotta, Marc	R/R	6-5/225	8-7-70	Chicago N.L., Iowa
57	Ryan, Jason	B/R	6-3/185	1-23-76	West Tenn
27	Sanders, Scott	R/R	6-4/220	3-25-69	Detroit, Las Vegas, San Diego
36	Tapani, Kevin	R/R	6-1/195	2-18-64	Chicago N.L.
46	Trachsel, Steve	R/R	6-4/205	10-31-70	Chicago N.L.
34	Wood, Kerry	R/R	6-5/225	6-16-77	Iowa, Chicago N.L.

No.	CATCHERS	B/T	Ht./Wt.	Born	1998 clubs
22	Cline, Pat	R/R	6-3/225	10-9-74	Iowa
7	Houston, Tyler	L/R	6-1/210	1-17-71	Chicago N.L.
15	Martinez, Sandy	L/R	6-2/215	10-3-72	Chicago N.L.
9	Santiago, Benito	R/R	6-1/195	3-9-65	Dunedin, Syracuse, Toronto

No.	INFIELDERS	B/T	Ht./Wt.	Born	1998 clubs
24	Alexander, Manny	R/R	5-10/180	3-20-71	Chicago N.L.
4	Blauser, Jeff	R/R	6-1/190	11-8-65	Chicago N.L.
8	Gaetti, Gary	R/R	6-0/205	8-19-58	St. Louis, Chicago N.L.
17	Grace, Mark	L/L	6-2/200	6-28-64	Chicago N.L.
18	Hernandez, Jose	R/R	6-1/180	7-14-69	Chicago N.L.
50	Maxwell, Jason	R/R	6-1/180	3-26-72	Iowa, Chicago N.L.
	Meyers, Chad	R/R	6-0/190	8-8-75	West Tenn, Daytona
12	Morandini, Mickey	L/R	5-11/180	4-22-66	Chicago N.L.
11	Nieves, Jose	R/R	6-1/185	6-16-75	Iowa, West Tenn

No.	OUTFIELDERS	B/T	Ht./Wt.	Born	1998 clubs
	Brown, Roosevelt	L/R	5-11/195	8-3-75	Iowa, West Tenn, Daytona
6	Hill, Glenallen	R/R	6-3/230	3-22-65	Seattle, Chicago N.L.
29	Jennings, Robin	L/L	6-2/210	4-11-72	West Tenn, Iowa
1	Johnson, Lance	L/L	5-11/165	7-6-63	Chicago N.L.
40	Rodriguez, Henry	L/L	6-2/220	11-8-67	Chicago N.L.
21	Sosa, Sammy	R/R	6-0/210	11-12-68	Chicago N.L.

BALLPARK INFORMATION

Ballpark (capacity, surface)
Wrigley Field (38,902, grass)

Address
1060 W. Addison St.
Chicago, IL 60613-4397

Business phone
773-404-2827

Ticket information
773-404-2827

Ticket prices
$25 (club box, field box)
$20 (terrace box, upper deck box, family section)
$16 (terrace reserved)
$15 (bleachers)
$10 (adult upper deck reserved)
$6 (under 14 upper deck reserved)

Field dimensions (from home plate)
To left field at foul line, 355 feet
To center field, 400 feet
To right field at foul line, 353 feet

First game played
April 20, 1916 (Cubs 7, Reds 6)

1998 REVIEW
DAY BY DAY

Date	Opp.	Res.	Score	(inn.*)	Hits	Opp. hits	Winning pitcher	Losing pitcher	Save	Record	Pos.	GB
3-31	At Fla.	L	6-11		10	14	Hernandez	Tapani		0-1	T2nd	1.0
4-1	At Fla.	W	10-3		10	8	Clark	Heredia		1-1	T3rd	0.5
4-2	At Fla.	W	8-7		12	8	Patterson	Powell	Beck	2-1	3rd	0.5
4-3	Mon.	W	6-2		9	6	Trachsel	Vazquez	Beck	3-1	1st	+0.5
4-4	Mon.	W	3-1		8	5	Mulholland	Valdes	Beck	4-1	1st	+0.5
4-5	Mon.	W	7-2		8	6	Tapani	Moore		5-1	1st	+0.5
4-6	Mon.	W	3-2		9	7	Clark	C. Perez	Beck	6-1	1st	+0.5
4-7	N.Y.	L	2-3		8	8	Leiter	Gonzalez	J. Franco	6-2	2nd	0.5
4-9	N.Y.	W	8-7		14	10	Trachsel	Reed	Beck	7-2	1st	+0.5
4-10	At Mon.	W	13-0		16	3	Tapani	Valdes		8-2	1st	+0.5
4-11	At Mon.	L	4-5	(10)	12	11	Kline	Adams		8-3	1st	+0.5
4-12	At Mon.	L	1-4		5	9	Hermanson	Wood	Urbina	8-4	1st	+0.5
4-14	At N.Y.	L	0-6		6	12	Leiter	Gonzalez		8-5	T2nd	0.5
4-15	At N.Y.	L	1-2		5	5	Reed	Trachsel	J. Franco	8-6	3rd	0.5
4-16	At N.Y.	W	8-4		13	12	Tapani	Mlicki		9-6	T2nd	0.5
4-17	L.A.	L	3-11		4	14	Park	Clark	Lankford	9-7	3rd	1.5
4-18	L.A.	W	8-1		6	5	Wood	Nomo		10-7	3rd	1.5
4-19	L.A.	W	2-1		9	6	Gonzalez	Valdes	Beck	11-7	3rd	1.5
4-21	S.D.	W	5-3		7	7	Trachsel	Brown	Beck	12-7	3rd	1.5
4-22	S.D.	L	2-3	(14)	9	9	Boehringer	Telemaco	Reyes	12-8	3rd	1.5
4-23	S.D.	L	1-4		9	11	Ashby	Clark	Hoffman	12-9	3rd	2.5
4-24	At L.A.	L	4-12		5	10	Valdes	Wood		12-10	T3rd	3.5
4-25	At L.A.	L	2-3		5	3	Guthrie	Gonzalez	Radinsky	12-11	4th	3.5
4-26	At L.A.	L	3-4	(12)	6	13	Clontz	Pisciotta		12-12	4th	3.5
4-27	At S.D.	W	3-1		8	5	Tapani	Hamilton	Beck	13-12	4th	3.5
4-28	At S.D.	L	3-7		8	13	Ashby	Clark	Hitchcock	13-13	4th	3.5
4-30	St.L.	W	8-3		15	8	Wood	Petkovsek		14-13	4th	3.0
5-1	St.L.	W	6-5		6	10	Gonzalez	Stottlemyre	Beck	15-13	4th	3.0
5-2	St.L.	W	4-3	(11)	13	9	Adams	Bottenfield		16-13	T3rd	3.0
5-3	St.L.	L	5-8		8	12	Petkovsek	Mulholland	Brantley	16-14	4th	3.0
5-5	Hou.	L	5-10		6	11	Lima	Clark	Nitkowski	16-15	4th	4.0
5-6	Hou.	W	2-0		8	1	Wood	Reynolds		17-15	T3rd	3.0
5-8	S.F.	W	5-4	(14)	8	15	Telemaco	Tavarez		18-15	3rd	2.0
5-9†	S.F.	L	1-5		9	9	Darwin	Tapani		18-16		
5-9‡	S.F.	W	6-0		11	6	Gonzalez	Estes		19-16	3rd	2.5
5-10	S.F.	L	0-3		3	5	Hershiser	Clark	Nen	19-17	3rd	3.5
5-11	At Ari.	W	4-2		10	7	Wood	Anderson	Beck	20-17	3rd	3.5
5-12	At Ari.	W	7-6		7	8	Adams	Rodriguez	Beck	21-17	2nd	3.5
5-13	At Col.	W	9-3		19	8	Trachsel	Astacio		22-17	2nd	3.5
5-14	At Col.	W	9-7		15	21	Tapani	Thomson	Beck	23-17	2nd	2.5
5-15	At Cin.	L	3-11		8	14	Harnisch	Gonzalez		23-18	2nd	2.5
5-16	At Cin.	W	5-4		11	8	Clark	Remlinger	Beck	24-18	2nd	2.5
5-17	At Cin.	W	10-1		11	3	Wood	Weathers	Mulholland	25-18	2nd	2.5
5-19	L.A.	W	6-3		11	9	Trachsel	Park	Beck	26-18	2nd	1.0
5-20	L.A.	W	5-0		10	3	Tapani	Nomo		27-18	2nd	1.0
5-21	L.A.	L	3-7		8	12	Valdes	Adams	Osuna	27-19	2nd	2.0
5-22	At Atl.	L	2-8		6	10	Maddux	Clark		27-20	2nd	2.0
5-23	At Atl.	W	10-6	(11)	14	14	Beck	Edmondson		28-20	2nd	2.0
5-24	At Atl.	L	1-2		3	7	Glavine	Adams		28-21	2nd	3.0
5-25	At Atl.	L	5-9		7	18	Millwood	Tapani		28-22	2nd	3.0
5-27	Phi.	L	5-10		8	14	Grace	Gonzalez		28-23	2nd	3.5
5-28	Phi.	L	7-8		11	12	Winston	Beck	Leiter	28-24	2nd	4.0
5-29	Atl.	W	5-3	(11)	12	7	Adams	Rocker		29-24	2nd	4.0
5-30	Atl.	W	9-8		15	11	Trachsel	Millwood	Patterson	30-24	2nd	3.0
5-31	Atl.	W	4-2		11	7	Tapani	Neagle	Beck	31-24	2nd	2.0
6-1	Fla.	W	10-2		14	5	Gonzalez	Dempster		32-24	2nd	1.5
6-2	Fla.	W	2-1		5	8	Adams	Heredia		33-24	2nd	1.5
6-3	Fla.	W	5-1		10	6	Wood	Hernandez		34-24	2nd	1.5
6-5	Chi. (AL)	W	6-5	(12)	12	10	Mulholland	T. Castillo		35-24	T1st	...
6-6	Chi. (AL)	W	7-6		7	12	Tapani	Eyre	Beck	36-24	T1st	...
6-7	Chi. (AL)	W	13-7		14	11	Gonzalez	Sirotka		37-24	T1st	...
6-8	At Min.	W	8-1		13	10	Clark	Hawkins		38-24	T1st	...
6-9	At Min.	L	0-8		4	10	Radke	Wood		38-25	2nd	1.0
6-10	At Min.	L	1-5		4	10	Morgan	Trachsel	Aguilera	38-26	2nd	2.0
6-12	At Phi.	L	0-4		5	10	Schilling	Tapani		38-27	2nd	2.0
6-13	At Phi.	W	10-8	(10)	12	18	Adams	Spradlin		39-27	2nd	1.0
6-14	At Phi.	L	2-4		5	10	Loewer	Clark		39-28	2nd	2.0
6-15	Mil.	W	6-5		12	3	Adams	Jones	Beck	40-28	2nd	2.0
6-16	Mil.	L	2-11		5	16	Woodall	Trachsel		40-29	2nd	2.0
6-17	Mil.	L	5-6		8	11	Patrick	Tapani	Wickman	40-30	2nd	3.0
6-18	Phi.	W	12-5		16	9	Gonzalez	Portugal	Mulholland	41-30	2nd	2.0

Date	Opp.	Res.	Score	(inn.*)	Hits	Opp. hits	Winning pitcher	Losing pitcher	Save	Record	Pos.	GB
6-19	Phi.	L	8-9	(12)	12	19	Spradlin	Mulholland		41-31	2nd	3.0
6-20	Phi.	W	9-4		15	10	Wood	Beech		42-31	2nd	3.0
6-21	Phi.	L	2-7		8	9	Green	Trachsel		42-32	2nd	4.0
6-22	Cle.	L	1-3		7	10	Gooden	Tapani	Jackson	42-33	2nd	4.0
6-23	Cle.	L	4-5		6	11	Plunk	Adams	Jackson	42-34	2nd	5.0
6-24	At Det.	L	6-7	(11)	13	13	Brocail	Pisciotta		42-35	2nd	5.0
6-25	At Det.	L	4-6		7	6	Anderson	Adams	Jones	42-36	2nd	5.0
6-26	At K.C.	L	3-6		8	10	Pichardo	Trachsel	Montgomery	42-37	3rd	5.0
6-27	At K.C.	L	3-4	(10)	8	13	Service	Beck		42-38	3rd	6.0
6-28	At K.C.	W	6-3		8	11	Gonzalez	Rapp	Beck	43-38	T2nd	6.0
6-30	Ari.	L	4-5		9	9	Blair	Clark	Olson	43-39	3rd	7.0
7-1	Ari.	W	6-4		11	4	Wood	Telemaco	Beck	44-39	3rd	7.0
7-2	Ari.	W	3-2		6	8	Trachsel	Suppan	Beck	45-39	2nd	6.0
7-3	Pit.	W	12-9		12	14	Tapani	Cordova	Beck	46-39	2nd	6.0
7-4	Pit.	W	5-4		12	7	Pisciotta	Schmidt	Beck	47-39	2nd	5.0
7-5	Pit.	W	7-6		11	14	Stevens	Loiselle	Beck	48-39	2nd	5.0
7-9	At Mil.	L	9-12		12	12	Reyes	Patterson	Wickman	48-40	2nd	6.0
7-10	At Mil.	L	5-6		8	7	Patrick	Wood		48-41	2nd	6.0
7-11	At Mil.	W	11-8		12	7	Trachsel	Eldred	Beck	49-41	2nd	5.0
7-12	At Mil.	W	3-0		6	3	Clark	Woodall		50-41	2nd	4.0
7-13	At Pit.	L	2-6		6	10	Lieber	Gonzalez		50-42	2nd	4.0
7-14	At Pit.	W	7-4		11	10	Tapani	Peters	Beck	51-42	2nd	4.0
7-15	At Pit.	L	0-3		4	5	Cordova	Wood	Rincon	51-43	2nd	4.0
7-17	At Fla.	W	6-1		11	5	Trachsel	Dempster		52-43	2nd	4.0
7-18	At Fla.	L	1-2		7	5	Meadows	Clark	Mantei	52-44	2nd	5.0
7-19	At Fla.	W	7-6	(12)	10	12	Mulholland	Stanifer	Beck	53-44	2nd	5.0
7-20	At Atl.	W	11-4		11	10	Tapani	Neagle		54-44	2nd	5.0
7-21	At Atl.	W	3-0		7	6	Wood	Maddux	Beck	55-44	2nd	4.0
7-22	Mon.	W	9-5		11	9	Adams	Batista	Beck	56-44	2nd	3.0
7-23	Mon.	W	2-1		4	6	Clark	Powell	Beck	57-44	2nd	3.0
7-24†	N.Y.	L	0-5		5	13	Reynoso	Gonzalez		57-45		
7-24‡	N.Y.	L	3-7		7	11	Cook	Adams		57-46	2nd	4.5
7-25	N.Y.	W	3-2		4	7	Tapani	J. Franco	Beck	58-46	2nd	3.5
7-26	N.Y.	W	3-1		7	6	Wood	Reed	Beck	59-46	2nd	2.5
7-27	At Ari.	W	6-2		7	3	Trachsel	Blair		60-46	2nd	2.5
7-28	At Ari.	L	5-7		10	13	Wolcott	Clark	Olson	60-47	2nd	3.5
7-29	At Ari.	W	7-3		10	7	Wengert	Telemaco	Adams	61-47	2nd	3.5
7-30	At Ari.	L	0-4		4	10	Daal	Tapani		61-48	2nd	3.5
7-31	Col.	W	9-1		8	6	Wood	Wright	Mulholland	62-48	2nd	3.5
8-1	Col.	W	3-2		7	12	Trachsel	Thomson	Beck	63-48	2nd	3.5
8-2	Col.	L	3-6		6	11	Astacio	Clark	McElroy	63-49	2nd	4.5
8-3	Ari.	L	5-6		15	10	Telemaco	Wengert	Olson	63-50	2nd	4.5
8-4	Ari.	W	2-0		5	5	Tapani	Daal	Beck	64-50	2nd	4.5
8-5	Ari.	L	7-10		7	14	Benes	Wood	Olson	64-51	2nd	4.5
8-7	At St.L.	L	3-16		5	17	Bottenfield	Trachsel		64-52	2nd	5.5
8-8	At St.L.	L	8-9	(13)	13	16	Witt	Stevens		64-53	2nd	6.5
8-9	At St.L.	L	1-2		5	5	Oliver	Wengert	Brantley	64-54	2nd	7.5
8-10	At S.F.	W	8-5		9	11	Tapani	Ortiz	Beck	65-54	2nd	7.5
8-11	At S.F.	L	7-8		11	10	Mesa	Adams	Nen	65-55	2nd	8.5
8-12	At S.F.	W	10-2		12	7	Trachsel	Rueter		66-55	2nd	8.5
8-14	At Hou.	W	6-4		11	8	Clark	Reynolds	Beck	67-55	2nd	8.0
8-15	At Hou.	L	4-5	(11)	8	9	Wagner	Mulholland		67-56	2nd	9.0
8-16	At Hou.	W	2-1	(11)	7	3	Karchner	Powell	Beck	68-56	2nd	8.0
8-18	St.L.	W	4-1		13	6	Trachsel	Mercker	Beck	69-56	2nd	7.5
8-19	St.L.	L	6-8	(10)	9	18	Acevedo	Mulholland		69-57	2nd	8.5
8-20	S.F.	W	7-3		12	7	Tapani	Ortiz		70-57	2nd	7.5
8-21	S.F.	W	6-5		12	9	Heredia	Nen		71-57	2nd	7.5
8-22	Hou.	L	3-8		5	15	R. Johnson	Wengert		71-58	2nd	8.5
8-23	Hou.	L	3-13		11	15	Lima	Trachsel		71-59	2nd	9.5
8-24	Hou.	L	3-12		9	11	Reynolds	Clark		71-60	2nd	10.5
8-25	At Cin.	L	9-10		11	12	Hudek	Mulholland	White	71-61	2nd	11.5
8-26	At Cin.	W	9-2		11	4	Wood	Tomko		72-61	2nd	10.5
8-27	At Col.	W	11-10	(10)	19	15	Mulholland	Munoz	Beck	73-61	2nd	10.0
8-28	At Col.	W	10-5		15	15	Trachsel	Thomson		74-61	2nd	10.0
8-29	At Col.	L	3-7		5	13	Jones	Clark		74-62	2nd	11.0
8-30	At Col.	W	4-3		10	9	Tapani	Kile	Beck	75-62	2nd	11.0
8-31	Cin.	W	5-4		6	6	Wood	Tomko	Beck	76-62	2nd	11.0
9-1	Cin.	W	6-5		11	10	Karchner	White	Beck	77-62	2nd	10.0
9-2	Cin.	W	4-2		9	7	Heredia	White	Beck	78-62	2nd	10.0
9-4	At Pit.	W	5-2		11	4	Karchner	Williams	Beck	79-62	2nd	9.0
9-5	At Pit.	W	8-4		8	8	Tapani	Lawrence	Beck	80-62	2nd	9.0
9-6	At Pit.	L	3-4	(10)	11	9	Loiselle	Stevens		80-63	2nd	10.0
9-7	At St.L.	L	2-3		9	5	Oliver	Morgan	Acevedo	80-64	2nd	11.0
9-8	At St.L.	L	3-6		12	5	Mercker	Trachsel	Acevedo	80-65	2nd	12.0
9-9	Pit.	W	4-2		6	5	Clark	Schmidt	Beck	81-65	2nd	12.0

Date	Opp.	Res.	Score	(inn.*)	Hits	Opp. hits	Winning pitcher	Losing pitcher	Save	Record	Pos.	GB
9-10	Pit.	W	5-2		6	8	Tapani	Silva	Beck	82-65	2nd	12.0
9-11	Mil.	L	11-13		15	15	Plunk	Wengert	Wickman	82-66	2nd	13.0
9-12	Mil.	W	15-12		18	16	Beck	Wickman		83-66	2nd	13.0
9-13	Mil.	W	11-10	(10)	17	13	Beck	Reyes		84-66	2nd	12.0
9-14	At S.D.	L	3-4		5	9	Miceli	Karchner	Hoffman	84-67	2nd	12.0
9-15	At S.D.	W	4-2		10	6	Tapani	Brown	Beck	85-67	2nd	11.5
9-16	At S.D.	W	6-3		11	8	Mulholland	Miceli	Beck	86-67	2nd	10.5
9-17	At S.D.	W	4-3	(10)	9	7	Heredia	Hoffman	Beck	87-67	2nd	10.0
9-18	Cin.	L	4-6		6	12	Parris	Wengert	White	87-68	2nd	11.0
9-19	Cin.	L	2-7		3	11	Bere	Clark		87-69	2nd	11.0
9-20	Cin.	L	3-7		10	13	Harnisch	Tapani	White	87-70	2nd	12.0
9-22	At Mil.	W	5-2		9	9	Mulholland	Pulsipher		88-70	2nd	11.0
9-23	At Mil.	L	7-8		10	10	Fox	Beck		88-71	2nd	12.0
9-25	At Hou.	L	2-6		5	11	Lima	Tapani		88-72	2nd	13.0
9-26	At Hou.	W	3-2		11	7	Clark	Powell	Beck	89-72	2nd	12.0
9-27	At Hou.	L	3-4	(11)	7	12	Elarton	Beck		89-73	2nd	13.0
9-28	S.F.	W	5-3		10	6	Trachsel	Gardner	Beck	90-73	2nd	12.5

Monthly records: March (0-1), April (14-12), May (17-11), June (12-15), July (19-9), August (14-14), September (14-11).
*Innings, if other than nine. †First game of doubleheader. ‡Second game of doubleheader.

HIGHLIGHTS

High point: In a season full of highs, the Cubs enjoyed the best of all when they beat the Giants September 28 in baseball's first wild-card playoff tie-breaker.
Low point: It didn't occur until October 3, when the Braves completed a three-game sweep of the Cubs in the Division Series. The Cubs were outscored, 15-4, and outhomered, 4-1.
Turning point: The Cubs were 16-15, had lost 8-of-13 and looked sluggish and tentative until rookie Kerry Wood took the mound May 6 in his fifth big-league start. All he did was tie Roger Clemens' major league record with 20 strikeouts. Beginning with that game, the Cubs went on a 21-9 run and began to believe they could compete for a playoff spot.
Most valuable player: Sammy Sosa. Who can argue with 66 home runs, 158 RBIs and an N.L. MVP?
Most valuable pitcher: Terry Mulholland. Without his versatility, Jim Riggleman would have had no chance to manage this team to a wild-card berth.
Most improved player: Brant Brown, who contributed 14 homers and 48 RBIs in just 347 at-bats while learning a new position (center field) at midseason.
Most pleasant surprise: Unhappily thrust into a relief role, Mulholland was spectacular as a setup man. He saved the Cubs by taking the ball 70 times (2.89 ERA) and pitching 112 innings.
Biggest disappointment: Shortstop Jeff Blauser, who signed for two years and $8 million prior to the season. When he wasn't injured, Blauser was just plain bad. He hit .219 with four homers, 26 RBIs, 93 strikeouts and 14 errors while batting just 361 times.
Key injuries: Wood won only two games the final two months because of a sore elbow. Henry Rodriguez never homered after injuring his ankle August 24. Blauser was hampered by elbow chips all season. Lance Johnson was bothered by a hand injury most of the season. Jeremi Gonzalez was lost for at least a year when he had elbow surgery in late July.
Notable: The Cubs won 22 more games

(90) than they did in 1997, and piled up 49 come-from-behind victories. They won 24 games in their final at-bat. After August 8, the Cubs were never more than one game up or one game out in the wild-card race. They hit a club-record 212 homers, surpassing the previous record of 209 (1987). . . . Pitchers struck out a team-record 1,207 batters. . . . Kevin Tapani's 19 wins were the most by a Cubs pitcher since Greg Maddux won 20 in 1992. . . . Rod Beck became the fifth reliever in history to record 50 saves, but his 51 weren't enough to match the club record of 53 set by Randy Myers (1993).

—BARRY ROZNER

RECORDS

1998 regular-season record: 90-73 (2nd in N.L. Central); 51-31 at home; 39-42 on road; 27-18 vs. East; 28-28 vs. N.L. Central; 30-19 vs. West; 5-8 vs. A.L.; 23-22 vs. lefthanded starters; 67-51 vs. righthanded starters; 78-59 on grass; 12-14 on turf; 52-41 in daytime; 38-32 at night; 30-27 in one-run games; 11-11 in extra-inning games; 0-1-1 in doubleheaders.
Team record past five years: 356-388 (.478, ranks 11th in league in that span).

TEAM LEADERS

Batting average: Mark Grace (.309).
At-bats: Sammy Sosa (643).
Runs: Sammy Sosa (134).
Hits: Sammy Sosa (198).
Total bases: Sammy Sosa (416).
Doubles: Mark Grace (39).
Triples: Brant Brown, Jose Hernandez (7).
Home runs: Sammy Sosa (66).
Runs batted in: Sammy Sosa (158).
Stolen bases: Sammy Sosa (18).
Slugging percentage: Sammy Sosa (.647).
On-base percentage: Mark Grace (.401).
Wins: Kevin Tapani (19).
Earned-run average: Kerry Wood (3.40).

Complete games: Mark Clark, Kevin Tapani (2).
Shutouts: Kevin Tapani (2).
Saves: Rod Beck (51).
Innings pitched: Kevin Tapani (219.0).
Strikeouts: Kerry Wood (233).

GAMES BY POSITION

Catcher: Scott Servais 110, Tyler Houston 63, Sandy Martinez 33.
First base: Mark Grace 156, Brant Brown 7, Tyler Houston 7, Jose Hernandez 3, Scott Servais 1.
Second base: Mickey Morandini 152, Manny Alexander 27, Jose Hernandez 2, Jason Maxwell 1.
Third base: Jose Hernandez 72, Kevin Orie 57, Gary Gaetti 36, Manny Alexander 19, Tyler Houston 12, Jason Hardtke 7.
Shortstop: Jeff Blauser 106, Manny Alexander 50, Jose Hernandez 45, Jose Nieves 1.
Outfield: Sammy Sosa 159, Henry Rodriguez 114, Brant Brown 102, Lance Johnson 78, Matt Mieske 62, Jose Hernandez 54, Glenallen Hill 34, Terrell Lowery 22, Pedro Valdes 17, Orlando Merced 4, Manny Alexander 1, Jason Hardtke 1, Derrick White 1.
Designated hitter: Henry Rodriguez 5, Manny Alexander 2, Jason Hardtke 1, Derrick White 1.

TOP DRAFT CHOICES

1. **Corey Patterson,** OF, Harrison H.S., Kennesaw, Ga.
2a. **David Kelton,** SS, Troup County H.S., La Grange, Ga.
2b. **Jeff Goldbach,** C, Princeton (Ind.) Community H.S.
3. **Kevin Bass,** 3B, Fayette County H.S., Fayette, Ala.
4. **Jeramy Gomer,** LHP, Durant H.S., Plant City, Fla.
5. **Aaron Sams,** LHP, James Madison U.
6. **Tony Schrager,** 2B, Stanford University
7. **Keola De la Tori,** RHP, Triton (Ill.) J.C.
8. **Will Ohman,** LHP, Pepperdine Univ.
9. **Steven Reba,** RHP, Concordia Lutheran H.S., Fort Wayne, Ind.
10. **Nate Frese,** SS, University of Iowa

CINCINNATI REDS
NATIONAL LEAGUE CENTRAL DIVISION

1999 Reds Schedule
Home games shaded. *—All-Star Game at Fenway Park (Boston). D—Day game (any game starting before 5 p.m.).

April

SUN	MON	TUE	WED	THU	FRI	SAT
				1	2	3
4	5 SF	6 D SF	7 D SF	8	9 STL	10 D STL
11 D STL	12 D CUB	13	14 D CUB	15 D CUB	16 PIT	17 D PIT
18 D PIT	19	20 NYM	21 NYM	22 NYM	23 HOU	24 D HOU
25 D HOU	26	27 PHI	28 PHI	29 PHI	30 ATL	

May

SUN	MON	TUE	WED	THU	FRI	SAT
						1 ATL
2 D ATL	3 ARI	4 ARI	5 ARI	6	7 CUB	8 D CUB
9 D CUB	10	11 MIL	12 MIL	13	14 SD	15 SD
16 D SD	17 COL	18 COL	19 D COL	20	21 SD	22 SD
23 D SD	24	25 LA	26 LA	27 D LA	28 FLA	29 FLA
30 D FLA	31 D NYM					

June

SUN	MON	TUE	WED	THU	FRI	SAT
		1 NYM	2 NYM	3	4 KC	5 KC
6 KC	7 MIN	8 MIN	9 MIN	10	11 CLE	12 CLE
13 CLE	14 NYM	15 NYM	16 D NYM	17 MIL	18 MIL	19 MIL
20 D MIL	21 ARI	22 ARI	23 ARI	24 HOU	25 HOU	26 D HOU
27 HOU	28	29 ARI	30 ARI			

July

SUN	MON	TUE	WED	THU	FRI	SAT
				1 ARI	2 HOU	3 HOU
4 D HOU	5 D HOU	6 STL	7 STL	8 STL	9 CLE	10 D CLE
11 D CLE	12	13 *	14	15 COL	16 COL	17 D COL
18 D DET	19 DET	20 STL	21 STL	22 D STL	23 SF	24 D SF
25 SF	26 LA	27 LA	28 LA	29 D SF	30 SF	31 SF

August

SUN	MON	TUE	WED	THU	FRI	SAT
1 D SF	2	3 COL	4 COL	5 D COL	6 MIL	7 MIL
8 D MIL	9 PIT	10 PIT	11 PIT	12	13 MIL	14 MIL
15 D MIL	16 PIT	17 PIT	18 PIT	19 MON	20 MON	21 MON
22 MON	23 ATL	24 ATL	25 D ATL	26 MON	27 MON	28 MON
29 D MON	30 ATL	31 ATL				

September

SUN	MON	TUE	WED	THU	FRI	SAT
			1 ATL	2	3 PHI	4 PHI
5 PHI	6 D CUB	7 D CUB	8 CUB	9 D CUB	10 FLA	11 FLA
12 D FLA	13 D CUB	14 CUB	15 CUB	16 D CUB	17 PIT	18 PIT
19 D PIT	20 SD	21 SD	22 SD	23	24 STL	25 D STL
26 D STL	27 D HOU	28 HOU	29 HOU	30		

October

SUN	MON	TUE	WED	THU	FRI	SAT
				1 MIL	2 D MIL	
3 D MIL	4	5	6	7	8	9

1999 SEASON
CLUB DIRECTORY

General partner
Marge Schott
President and chief executive officer
Marge Schott
Managing executive
John Allen
General manager
Jim Bowden
Assistant general manager
Darrell "Doc" Rodgers
Assistant/baseball operations
Brad Kullman
Special assistant to the general manager
Gene Bennett
Senior advisor, major leagues and player development
Chief Bender
Special assistant to the g.m.
Al Goldis
Director, player development
Muzzy Jackson
Director, scouting
De Jon Watson
Director, baseball operations
Larry Barton Jr.
Special consultant to g.m.
Johnny Bench
Senior advisor, player personnel
Bob Boone
Assistant, baseball operations
Brad Kullman
Senior advisor, baseball operations
Bob Zuk
Controller
Anthony Ward
Director, stadium operations
Jody Pettyjohn
Director, ticket department
John O'Brien
Director, season ticket sales
Pat McCaffrey
Director, group sales
Barb McManus
Marketing consultant
Cal Levy
Director of communications
Mike Ringering
Director, media relations
Rob Butcher

Assistant director, media relations
Mark Walpole
Assistant/publicity
Larry Herms
Traveling secretary
Gary Wahoff
Assistant ticket director
Ken Ayer
Chief administrative assistant
Joyce Pfarr
Administrative assistant, business
Ginny Kamp
Head trainer
Greg Lynn
Assistant trainer
Mark Mann
Field superintendent
Dennis McMullen
Sr. clubhouse & equipment manager
Bernie Stowe
Reds clubhouse & equipment manager
Rick Stowe
Visiting clubhouse & equip. manager
Mark Stowe
Executive asst. to the general manager
Lois Schneider
Director of scouting administration
Wilma Mann
Admin. asst., player development
Lois Hudson
Cross-checkers
Johnny Almaraz, Jeff Barton, Hank Sargent, Thomas Wilson
Scouting supervisors
Johnny Almaraz, Ray Bellino, John Brinckley, George Brill, Bobby Filotei, Jerry Flowers, Chris Gill, Jimmy Gonzales, Dick Hager, David Jennings, Robert Koontz, Steve Kring, Mike Mangan, Tom Severtson, Bob Szymkowski, Marion "Bo" Trumbo, Mike Wallace, Brian Wilson
Scouts
John Bellino, Fred Blair, Ismael Cruz, Felix Delgado, Jim Grief, Don Gust, Fred Hayes, Thomas Herrera, Don Hill, Les Houser, Fred Leone, Anthony Lowe, Armando Morales, Jose Moreno, Denny Nagel, Jerry Raddatz, Glenn Serviente, Douglas Stuart, Marlon Styles Jr., Lee Toole, John Walsh, Nathan Ware, Roger Weberg

MINOR LEAGUE AFFILIATES

Class	Team	League	Manager
AAA	Indianapolis	International	Dave Miley
AA	Chattanooga	Southern	Phillip Wellman
A	Clinton	Midwest	To be announced
A	Rockford	Midwest	To be announced
Rookie	Billings	Pioneer	Russ Nixon

BROADCAST INFORMATION

Radio: WLW-AM (700).
TV: WKRC-TV (Channel 12).
Cable TV: Fox Sports Ohio.

SPRING TRAINING

Ballpark (city): Ed Smith Stadium (Sarasota, Fla.).
Ticket information: 941-954-4101.

SPRING TRAINING ROSTER

Manager—Jack McKeon (15).
Coaches—Harry Dunlop (2), Ken Griffey Sr. (30), Don Gullett (35), Tom Hume (47)Denis Menke (19), Ron Oester (7).

No.	PITCHERS	B/T	Ht./Wt.	Born	1998 clubs
33	Avery, Steve	L/L	6-4/205	4-14-70	Boston, Pawtucket
48	Barrios, Manuel	R/R	6-0/185	9-21-74	Charlotte, Florida, Albuquerque, Los Angeles
37	Belinda, Stan	R/R	6-3/215	8-6-66	Cincinnati
50	Bell, Rob	R/R	6-5/225	1-17-77	Danville
51	Bere, Jason	R/R	6-3/215	5-26-71	Chicago A.L., Cincinnati
	Crowell, Jim	R/L	6-3/230	5-14-74	Chattanooga, Charleston, W.Va., Indianapolis
32	Graves, Danny	R/R	5-11/185	8-7-73	Indianapolis, Cincinnati
38	Harnisch, Pete	R/R	6-0/228	9-23-66	Cincinnati
	Hudek, John	B/R	6-1/205	8-8-66	New York N.L., Cincinnati
15	Neagle, Denny	L/L	6-2/225	9-13-68	Atlanta
58	Parris, Steve	R/R	6-0/195	12-17-67	Indianapolis, Cincinnati
49	Reyes, Dennis	L/L	6-3/246	4-19-77	Albuquerque, Los Angeles, Indianapolis, Cincinnati
	Rose, Teddy	L/R	6-2/185	8-23-73	Chattanooga
56	Sullivan, Scott	R/R	6-3/210	3-13-71	Cincinnati
40	Tomko, Brett	R/R	6-4/215	4-7-73	Cincinnati
36	White, Gabe	L/L	6-2/200	11-20-71	Cincinnati
53	Williams, Todd	R/R	6-3/210	2-13-71	Indianapolis, Cincinnati
	Winchester, Scott	R/R	6-2/210	4-20-73	Indianapolis, Cincinnati

No.	CATCHERS	B/T	Ht./Wt.	Born	1998 clubs
6	Fordyce, Brook	R/R	6-0/190	5-7-70	Cincinnati, Indianapolis
	Johnson, Brian	R/R	6-2/210	1-8-68	San Francisco, Fresno
60	LaRue, Jason	R/R	5-11/200	3-19-74	Indianapolis, Chattanooga
10	Taubensee, Eddie	L/R	6-3/200	10-31-68	Cincinnati

No.	INFIELDERS	B/T	Ht./Wt.	Born	1998 clubs
17	Boone, Aaron	R/R	6-2/200	3-9-73	Cincinnati, Indianapolis
	Branson, Jeff	L/R	6-0/180	1-26-67	Cleveland, Buffalo
21	Casey, Sean	L/R	6-4/225	7-2-74	Cincinnati, Indianapolis
12	Jackson, Damian	R/R	5-11/185	8-16-73	Indianapolis, Cincinnati
11	Larkin, Barry	R/R	6-0/185	4-28-64	Cincinnati
26	Lewis, Mark	R/R	6-1/185	11-30-69	Philadelphia
3	Reese, Pokey	R/R	5-11/180	6-10-73	Cincinnati

No.	OUTFIELDERS	B/T	Ht./Wt.	Born	1998 clubs
	Cameron, Mike	R/R	6-2/190	1-8-73	Chicago A.L.
55	Frank, Mike	L/L	6-2/185	1-14-75	Indianapolis, Cincinnati, Chattanooga
4	Hammonds, Jeffrey	R/R	6-0/195	3-5-71	Baltimore, Bowie, Cincinnati
70	Ingram, Darron	R/R	6-3/218	6-7-76	Chattanooga
	Myers, Rod	L/L	6-1/190	1-14-73	Wichita, Omaha
22	Nunnally, Jon	L/R	5-10/190	11-9-71	Cincinnati, Indianapolis
16	Sanders, Reggie	R/R	6-1/185	12-1-67	Cincinnati
23	Stynes, Chris	R/R	5-10/185	1-19-73	Cincinnati
34	Tucker, Michael	L/R	6-2/185	6-25-71	Atlanta
25	Young, Dmitri	B/R	6-2/235	10-11-73	Cincinnati

BALLPARK INFORMATION

Ballpark (capacity, surface)
Cinergy Field (52,953, artificial)

Address
100 Cinergy Field
Cincinnati, OH 45202

Business phone
513-421-4510

Ticket information
513-421-7337, 1-800-829-5353

Ticket prices
$17, $15 (blue level box seats)
$13, $12 (green level box seats)
$12 (yellow level box seats)
$10 (red level box seats)
$9 (green level reserved seats)
$7 (red level reserved seats)
$4 ("top six" reserved seats)

Field dimensions (from home plate)
To left field at foul line, 330 feet
To center field, 404 feet
To right field at foul line, 330 feet

First game played
June 30, 1970 (Braves 8, Reds 2)

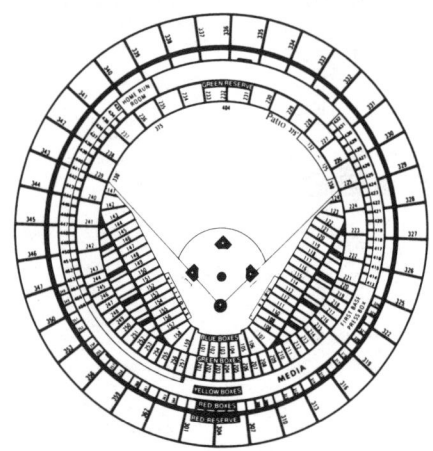

DAY BY DAY

Date	Opp.	Res.	Score	(inn.*)	Hits	Opp. hits	Winning pitcher	Losing pitcher	Save	Record	Pos.	GB
3-31	S.D.	L	2-10		6	10	Brown	Remlinger		0-1	T2nd	1.0
4-1	S.D.	L	9-10		13	10	Hamilton	Sullivan	Hoffman	0-2	T5th	1.5
4-2	S.D.	W	5-1		9	6	Cooke	Ashby	Shaw	1-2	T5th	1.5
4-3	L.A.	W	6-3		6	7	Weathers	Hall	Shaw	2-2	T5th	1.0
4-4	L.A.	W	3-1		8	3	Tomko	Valdes	Shaw	3-2	4th	1.0
4-5	L.A.	L	0-1		2	6	Martinez	Remlinger	Radinsky	3-3	T4th	2.0
4-7	At S.D.	L	2-3	(10)	6	9	Hoffman	Shaw		3-4	T5th	3.0
4-8	At S.D.	L	3-6		6	13	Ashby	White	Hoffman	3-5	6th	3.5
4-9	At S.D.	L	2-6		8	9	Boehringer	Tomko		3-6	6th	4.0
4-10	At Col.	W	18-7		17	18	Jordan	Kile	Sullivan	4-6	6th	4.0
4-11	At Col.	W	12-5		21	14	Remlinger	Thomson	Belinda	5-6	6th	3.0
4-12	At Col.	W	10-4		11	11	Harnisch	Astacio		6-6	6th	2.0
4-13	At Col.	L	4-8		7	12	Leskanic	Belinda		6-7	6th	2.5
4-15	Hou.	W	4-1		8	3	Tomko	Reynolds	Shaw	7-7	4th	1.5
4-16	Hou.	L	4-7		11	12	Hampton	Weathers	Wagner	7-8	5th	2.5
4-17	N.Y.	W	4-3		8	4	Remlinger	Jones	Shaw	8-8	5th	2.5
4-18	N.Y.	L	4-5	(10)	10	6	Rojas	Belinda	J. Franco	8-9	5th	3.5
4-19	N.Y.	L	0-14		4	16	Leiter	White		8-10	5th	4.5
4-21	At Phi.	W	6-3		9	8	Tomko	Schilling	Shaw	9-10	5th	4.5
4-22	At Phi.	L	4-5		11	9	Green	White	Bottalico	9-11	5th	4.5
4-23	At Phi.	L	3-6		7	8	Spradlin	Sullivan	Leiter	9-12	T5th	5.5
4-24	At N.Y.	L	2-3		5	5	Jones	Shaw	J. Franco	9-13	6th	6.5
4-25	At N.Y.	W	2-0		6	6	Weathers	Yoshii	Shaw	10-13	T5th	5.5
4-27	Phi.	W	3-1		5	3	Belinda	Green		11-13	5th	5.0
4-28	Phi.	L	8-11	(10)	12	15	Leiter	Belinda	Winston	11-14	5th	5.0
4-29	Phi.	W	1-0		5	2	Harnisch	Grace		12-14	5th	4.5
5-1	At Mil.	L	2-5		8	10	Karl	Remlinger	Jones	12-15	5th	5.5
5-2	At Mil.	W	8-5		13	10	White	Fox	Shaw	13-15	5th	5.5
5-3	At Mil.	W	5-3		10	8	Tomko	Eldred	Shaw	14-15	5th	4.5
5-4	At Mon.	W	4-1		7	4	Winchester	Moore	Shaw	15-15	5th	4.0
5-5	At Mon.	L	2-3		11	9	Urbina	Belinda		15-16	5th	5.0
5-6	At Mon.	W	4-2		9	9	Remlinger	Vazquez	Shaw	16-16	5th	4.0
5-7	At Pit.	L	7-8		13	9	Dessens	Belinda	Loiselle	16-17	5th	4.5
5-8	At Pit.	W	5-3	(10)	7	9	Belinda	Rincon	Shaw	17-17	T4th	3.5
5-9	At Pit.	L	1-6		6	12	Silva	Winchester	Peters	17-18	5th	4.5
5-10	At Pit.	W	4-3	(12)	7	6	Belinda	Loiselle		18-18	T4th	4.5
5-11	Atl.	L	1-8		4	9	Maddux	Remlinger		18-19	5th	5.5
5-12	Atl.	L	1-5		4	11	Smoltz	Weathers		18-20	T5th	6.5
5-13	Fla.	W	10-4		14	8	Tomko	Pall		19-20	5th	6.5
5-14	Fla.	W	11-8		17	12	Winchester	Larkin	Shaw	20-20	T4th	5.5
5-15	Chi.	W	11-3		14	8	Harnisch	Gonzalez		21-20	4th	4.5
5-16	Chi.	L	4-5		8	11	Clark	Remlinger	Beck	21-21	T4th	5.5
5-17	Chi.	L	1-10		3	11	Wood	Weathers	Mulholland	21-22	5th	6.5
5-19†	At N.Y.	L	3-7		4	8	Jones	Tomko		21-23		
5-19‡	At N.Y.	L	3-5		8	10	Bohanon	Winchester	J. Franco	21-24	T5th	6.5
5-20	At N.Y.	W	8-6		15	8	Harnisch	Hudek	Shaw	22-24	5th	6.5
5-21	At N.Y.	L	1-6		9	6	Yoshii	Hutton		22-25	6th	7.5
5-22	Col.	L	2-3		8	10	Wright	Weathers	DiPoto	22-26	6th	7.5
5-23	Col.	W	4-1	(7)	9	4	Winchester	Astacio		23-26	6th	7.5
5-24	Col.	L	1-3		2	8	Jones	Tomko	DiPoto	23-27	6th	8.5
5-25	S.F.	L	1-3		4	5	Hershiser	Harnisch	Nen	23-28	6th	8.5
5-26	S.F.	L	2-5		9	6	Rueter	Remlinger	Nen	23-29	6th	9.5
5-27	S.F.	W	7-5		11	9	Sullivan	Poole	Shaw	24-29	T5th	8.5
5-28	At L.A.	L	3-4		11	11	Bruske	Belinda		24-30	6th	9.0
5-29	At L.A.	W	8-4	(12)	15	9	Shaw	Reyes		25-30	5th	9.0
5-30	At L.A.	W	7-3		12	9	Harnisch	Nomo		26-30	5th	8.0
5-31	At L.A.	W	6-5		11	6	Graves	Radinsky	Shaw	27-30	5th	7.0
6-1	At S.F.	L	3-16		6	16	Gardner	Priest		27-31	6th	7.5
6-2	At S.F.	L	2-4		7	8	Darwin	Winchester	Nen	27-32	6th	8.5
6-3	At S.F.	L	5-8		10	13	Estes	Tomko	Nen	27-33	6th	9.5
6-5	Cle.	W	2-1		10	5	Harnisch	Nagy	Shaw	28-33	6th	8.0
6-6	Cle.	L	1-10		3	15	Wright	Remlinger		28-34	6th	9.0
6-7	Cle.	L	1-6		9	10	Burba	Klingenbeck		28-35	6th	10.0
6-8	At S.D.	L	2-4		8	6	Hamilton	Sullivan	Hoffman	28-36	6th	11.0
6-9	At S.D.	L	1-5		8	6	Ashby	Tomko	Hoffman	28-37	6th	12.0
6-10	At S.D.	L	1-2		9	5	Brown	Shaw		28-38	6th	13.0
6-12	Hou.	W	8-1		12	4	Remlinger	Lima		29-38	6th	12.0
6-13	Hou.	W	7-4		10	7	Klingenbeck	Reynolds	Shaw	30-38	6th	11.0
6-14	Hou.	L	3-6	(10)	11	11	Wagner	Shaw		30-39	6th	12.0
6-15	Hou.	L	2-13		6	17	Magnante	Tomko		30-40	6th	13.0
6-16	Ari.	L	1-5		9	10	Daal	Harnisch		30-41	6th	13.0

Date	Opp.	Res.	Score	(inn.*)	Hits	Opp. hits	Winning pitcher	Losing pitcher	Save	Record	Pos.	GB
6-17	Ari.	L	1-4		7	8	Benes	Remlinger	Olson	30-42	6th	14.0
6-18	Ari.	L	2-4		5	9	Anderson	Klingenbeck	Olson	30-43	6th	14.0
6-19	At Hou.	L	2-4		9	10	Bergman	Winchester	Wagner	30-44	6th	15.0
6-20	At Hou.	L	8-9		10	12	Nitkowski	Krivda	Wagner	30-45	6th	16.0
6-21	At Hou.	L	1-3		7	8	Schourek	Harnisch	Magnante	30-46	6th	17.0
6-22	K.C.	L	0-3		8	7	Pittsley	Remlinger	Montgomery	30-47	6th	17.0
6-23	K.C.	L	4-6		10	11	Rapp	Klingenbeck	Service	30-48	6th	18.0
6-24	At Chi. (AL)	L	2-4		5	9	Navarro	Winchester	Simas	30-49	6th	18.0
6-25	At Chi. (AL)	W	7-5		9	15	Tomko	Parque	Shaw	31-49	6th	17.0
6-26	At Det.	W	4-3		11	4	Harnisch	Brocail	Shaw	32-49	6th	16.0
6-27	At Det.	W	6-5	(13)	13	15	White	Harriger		33-49	6th	16.0
6-28	At Det.	W	5-2		10	11	Parris	Thompson	Shaw	34-49	6th	16.0
6-30	Min.	W	6-3		13	9	Tomko	Hawkins	Shaw	35-49	6th	16.0
7-1	Min.	L	1-2		10	7	Radke	Sullivan	Aguilera	35-50	6th	17.0
7-2	Min.	W	8-7		11	14	Shaw	Aguilera		36-50	6th	16.0
7-3	St.L.	W	6-3		9	7	Remlinger	Stottlemyre	Shaw	37-50	6th	16.0
7-4	St.L.	W	5-4		7	5	Graves	Croushore		38-50	6th	15.0
7-5	St.L.	W	6-1		9	7	Tomko	Mercker		39-50	6th	15.0
7-10	At Ari.	W	5-4		12	11	Tomko	Benes		40-50	6th	14.5
7-11	At Ari.	W	8-0		12	3	Remlinger	Blair		41-50	5th	13.5
7-12	At Ari.	W	5-3		13	9	Hudek	Anderson		42-50	5th	12.5
7-13	At St.L.	W	6-5	(13)	16	9	White	Witt		43-50	5th	11.5
7-14	At St.L.	W	7-4		12	8	Sullivan	Stottlemyre	Graves	44-50	4th	11.5
7-15	At St.L.	W	4-2	(11)	11	8	White	Frascatore		45-50	4th	10.5
7-17	S.D.	L	3-13		8	15	Ashby	Remlinger		45-51	4th	11.5
7-18	S.D.	L	1-2		5	7	Hamilton	Harnisch	Hoffman	45-52	4th	12.5
7-19	S.D.	L	6-7		9	7	Wall	Hudek	Hoffman	45-53	T5th	13.5
7-20	At L.A.	L	0-2		1	6	Dreifort	Parris	Shaw	45-54	6th	14.5
7-21	At L.A.	L	2-4		6	7	Valdes	Tomko	Shaw	45-55	6th	14.5
7-23§	At Col.	L	4-6		10	13	Astacio	Remlinger	Veres	45-56		
7-23§	At Col.	L	4-6		9	12	Jones	Harnisch	Leskanic	45-57	6th	15.5
7-24	At S.F.	L	2-12		5	15	Gardner	Winchester		45-58	6th	16.5
7-25	At S.F.	W	9-8		14	11	Belinda	Ortiz	Graves	46-58	6th	15.5
7-26	At S.F.	L	1-2	(10)	5	3	Mesa	Belinda		46-59	6th	15.5
7-27	Atl.	L	2-3	(10)	6	10	Seanez	Belinda	Ligtenberg	46-60	6th	16.5
7-28	Atl.	W	13-1		12	5	Sullivan	Millwood		47-60	6th	16.5
7-29	Atl.	L	5-11		11	13	Seanez	Parris		47-61	6th	17.5
7-30	Atl.	L	3-13		6	16	Neagle	Krivda		47-62	6th	17.5
7-31	At Fla.	W	3-2		8	5	Tomko	Mantei	White	48-62	6th	17.5
8-1	At Fla.	W	9-7	(10)	12	11	Hudek	Mantei		49-62	6th	17.5
8-2	At Fla.	W	5-1		9	6	Reyes	Ojala	Graves	50-62	6th	17.5
8-4	At Atl.	L	2-4		8	11	Smoltz	Sullivan	Ligtenberg	50-63	6th	18.0
8-5	At Atl.	W	13-9		16	10	Hudek	Springer		51-63	T5th	17.0
8-6	At Atl.	L	0-5		3	8	Maddux	Remlinger		51-64	T5th	17.5
8-7	Mil.	W	17-0		14	6	Harnisch	Woodall		52-64	5th	17.5
8-8	Mil.	W	4-0		5	5	Reyes	Woodard		53-64	5th	17.5
8-9	Mil.	L	3-4		8	8	Karl	Parris	Wickman	53-65	5th	18.5
8-11	Pit.	L	0-7		6	8	Cordova	Tomko		53-66	T5th	20.0
8-12	Pit.	L	4-5		8	7	Schmidt	Remlinger	Rincon	53-67	6th	21.0
8-13	Pit.	L	6-9		7	11	McCurry	Harnisch	Rincon	53-68	6th	22.0
8-14	Mon.	W	3-2		7	3	White	Kline		54-68	6th	21.0
8-15	Mon.	W	6-4		12	10	Parris	Thurman	White	55-68	T5th	21.0
8-16	Mon.	W	8-1		13	5	Tomko	Pavano		56-68	T5th	20.0
8-18	At Mil.	L	4-8		8	14	Woodall	Remlinger		56-69	6th	20.5
8-19	At Mil.	W	8-2		12	7	Harnisch	Woodard		57-69	6th	20.5
8-20	At Pit.	L	5-6		9	13	Christiansen	Graves		57-70	6th	20.5
8-21	At Pit.	L	2-14		7	17	Peters	Tomko		57-71	6th	21.5
8-22	At Mon.	W	4-0		6	3	Parris	Powell		58-71	6th	21.5
8-23	At Mon.	W	10-0		13	4	Bere	Vazquez		59-71	6th	21.5
8-24	At Mon.	W	8-1		11	3	Harnisch	Hermanson		60-71	6th	21.5
8-25	Chi.	W	10-9		12	11	Hudek	Mulholland	White	61-71	6th	21.5
8-26	Chi.	L	2-9		4	11	Wood	Tomko		61-72	6th	21.5
8-27	Fla.	W	12-3		15	5	Parris	Hernandez		62-72	6th	21.0
8-28	Fla.	W	10-8		10	15	Sullivan	Stanifer	White	63-72	6th	21.0
8-29	Fla.	W	7-5		13	10	Remlinger	Meadows	Graves	64-72	T4th	21.0
8-30	Fla.	W	14-7		13	10	Reyes	Medina		65-72	3rd	21.0
8-31	At Chi.	L	4-5		6	6	Wood	Tomko	Beck	65-73	5th	22.0
9-1	At Chi.	L	5-6		10	11	Karchner	White	Beck	65-74	5th	22.0
9-2	At Chi.	L	2-4		7	9	Heredia	White	Beck	65-75	6th	23.0
9-4	At St.L.	W	3-2		9	7	Harnisch	Frascatore	White	66-75	T4th	22.0
9-5	At St.L.	L	0-7		3	9	Osborne	Reyes		66-76	5th	23.0
9-6	At St.L.	L	2-5		7	7	Acevedo	Hudek		66-77	5th	24.0
9-7	At Hou.	L	0-1		6	4	R. Johnson	Parris		66-78	5th	25.0
9-8	At Hou.	L	7-13		9	16	Bergman	Bere		66-79	6th	26.0
9-9	St.L.	W	6-3		8	5	Harnisch	Witt	Graves	67-79	5th	26.0

Date	Opp.	Res.	Score	(inn.*)	Hits	Opp. hits	Winning pitcher	Losing pitcher	Save	Record	Pos.	GB
9-10	St.L.	L	7-8		13	6	Aybar	Remlinger	Acevedo	67-80	5th	27.0
9-11	Ari.	W	13-1		11	5	Tomko	Sodowsky		68-80	5th	27.0
9-12	Ari.	W	3-0		6	3	Parris	Daal	White	69-80	5th	27.0
9-13	Ari.	L	0-5		1	9	Benes	Bere	Olson	69-81	5th	27.0
9-14	Mil.	L	1-2		7	6	Woodard	Harnisch	Wickman	69-82	5th	27.0
9-15	Mil.	W	5-1		14	7	Remlinger	Karl	Graves	70-82	5th	26.5
9-16	Mil.	L	0-2		5	10	Pulsipher	Tomko	Wickman	70-83	5th	26.5
9-18	At Chi.	W	6-4		12	6	Parris	Wengert	White	71-83	5th	26.5
9-19	At Chi.	W	7-2		11	3	Bere	Clark		72-83	T4th	25.5
9-20	At Chi.	W	7-3		13	10	Harnisch	Tapani	White	73-83	4th	25.5
9-21	Phi.	W	8-5		9	6	Sullivan	Leiter	Graves	74-83	4th	25.0
9-22	Phi.	L	8-10	(11)	11	14	Spradlin	Williams	Bottalico	74-84	4th	25.0
9-23	Phi.	L	2-4		5	8	Portugal	Parris	Bottalico	74-85	4th	26.0
9-25	Pit.	W	4-1		8	6	Bere	Cordova	Graves	75-85	4th	26.0
9-26	Pit.	W	6-2		8	6	Harnisch	Schmidt	White	76-85	4th	25.0
9-27	Pit.	W	4-1		5	5	Tomko	Silva		77-85	4th	25.0

Monthly records: March (0-1), April (12-13), May (15-16), June (8-19), July (13-13), August (17-11), September (12-12).
*Innings, if other than nine. †First game of doubleheader. ‡Second game of doubleheader. §Two games in one day (separate admissions).

HIGHLIGHTS

High point: The team won 10 in a row, capped by a 4-2, 11-inning victory over St. Louis on July 15. During the streak, the team hit .309 with 12 home runs and 60 runs scored, and posted an ERA of 3.00.

Low point: The Reds bottomed out with an 11-game losing streak in June. The streak tied Florida for the longest in the league in 1998 and left the team 30-49, 18 games out of first place.

Turning point: On June 1, with a respectable 27-30 record, the team sent Eddie Priest out for his second major league start. Priest lasted only one-third of an inning, allowing four hits and three runs, and the Giants won 16-3. Infielder Lenny Harris pitched an inning of relief in that game, which started a run of 19 losses in 22 games.

Most valuable player: Second baseman Bret Boone won the Gold Glove and turned around his offensive slide of seasons past. Boone led the team in home runs (24) and RBIs (95) and received his first All-Star berth.

Most valuable pitcher: After overcoming problems with insomnia and anxiety in 1997, Pete Harnisch went 14-7 with a 3.14 ERA and struck out 157 while walking only 64 in 209 innings.

Most improved player: In his first year with Cincinnati, Dmitri Young hit .310 with 14 home runs and 83 RBIs in 144 games. He became the everyday left fielder, and his 48 doubles tied for second in the major leagues.

Most pleasant surprise: Gabe White blossomed in the second half, going 3-2 with a 2.86 ERA after the All-Star break. He ascended to the co-closer role with Danny Graves and recorded all nine of his saves after the All-Star break.

Biggest disappointment: Reggie Sanders struggled through periods of injuries and inconsistency. The only place in the line-up he enjoyed success was the leadoff spot, but the team really couldn't afford to have him hit there.

Key injuries: Barry Larkin started the season on the D.L. after having back surgery and returned April 7. Sean Casey went on the D.L. April 2 with a broken facial bone and was activated May 5. Stan Belinda went on the D.L. June 3 with inflammation in his spinal cord. He returned July 9 then went back on the D.L. August 10 for the rest of the season. Pokey Reese injured his thumb in July and missed the rest of the season.

Notable: On September 27, Bret (second base) and Aaron Boone (third base), and Barry (shortstop) and Stephen Larkin (first base) became the first sets of brothers to play for the same major league team in the same regular-season game.

—MIKE BASS

RECORDS

1998 regular-season record: 77-85 (4th in N.L. Central); 39-42 at home; 38-43 on road; 26-19 vs. East; 27-29 vs. N.L. Central; 17-31 vs. West; 7-6 vs. A.L.; 14-23 vs. lefthanded starters; 63-62 vs. righthanded starters; 30-31 on grass; 47-54 on turf; 28-28 in daytime; 49-57 at night; 16-26 in one-run games; 7-7 in extra-inning games; 0-1-0 in doubleheaders.

Team record past five years: 385-359 (.517, ranks 4th in league in that span).

TEAM LEADERS

Batting average: Dmitri Young (.310).
At-bats: Bret Boone (583).
Runs: Barry Larkin (93).
Hits: Barry Larkin, Dmitri Young (166).
Total bases: Barry Larkin (271).
Doubles: Dmitri Young (48).
Triples: Barry Larkin (10).
Home runs: Bret Boone (24).
Runs batted in: Bret Boone (95).
Stolen bases: Barry Larkin (26).
Slugging percentage: Barry Larkin (.504).
On-base percentage: Barry Larkin (.397).
Wins: Pete Harnisch (14).

Earned-run average: Pete Harnisch (3.14).
Complete games: Pete Harnisch (2).
Shutouts: Pete Harnisch, Steve Parris, Mike Remlinger (1).
Saves: Jeff Shaw (23).
Innings pitched: Brett Tomko (210.2).
Strikeouts: Brett Tomko (162).

GAMES BY POSITION

Catcher: Eddie Taubensee 126, Brook Fordyce 54, Guillermo Garcia 11.
First base: Sean Casey 86, Eduardo Perez 51, Dmitri Young 44, Roberto Petagine 15, Paul Konerko 7, Stephen Larkin 1.
Second base: Bret Boone 156, Chris Stynes 11, Pokey Reese 3, Aaron Boone 1.
Third base: Willie Greene 76, Aaron Boone 52, Pokey Reese 32, Chris Stynes 22, Paul Konerko 9, Eduardo Perez 1.
Shortstop: Barry Larkin 145, Pokey Reese 18, Damian Jackson 10, Willie Greene 2, Chris Stynes 2, Aaron Boone 1.
Outfield: Reggie Sanders 131, Dmitri Young 105, Chris Stynes 80, Pat Watkins 77, Jon Nunnally 70, Lenny Harris 32, Mike Frank 28, Willie Greene 28, Jeffrey Hammonds 25, Melvin Nieves 25, Roberto Petagine 15, Paul Konerko 7, Tony Tarasco 7, Damian Jackson 3, Eduardo Perez 1.
Designated hitter: Melvin Nieves 3, Willie Greene 1, Lenny Harris 1.

TOP DRAFT CHOICES

1. **Austin Kearns,** OF, Lafayette H.S., Lexington, Ky.
2. **Adam Dunn,** OF, New Caney (Tex.) H.S.
3. **Greg Porter,** SS, Keller (Tex.) H.S.
4. **Darrell Hussman,** RHP, U. of Arizona
5. **Jayson Larman,** RHP, Wayne (Okla.) H.S.
6. **Robert Madritsch,** LHP, Point Park (Pa.) College
7. **Josh Hall,** RHP, Lynchburg, Va.
8. **Clint Vaughn,** 1B, Okla. Christian U.
9. **David Themeau,** RHP, Bellevue (Neb.) U.
10. **Jacob Wallis,** C, Paschal H.S., Joshua, Tex.

COLORADO ROCKIES
NATIONAL LEAGUE WEST DIVISION

1999 Rockies Schedule

Home games shaded. *—All-Star Game at Fenway Park (Boston).
D—Day game (any game starting before 5 p.m.).

April

SUN	MON	TUE	WED	THU	FRI	SAT
				1	2	3
4 SD	5	6 SD	7 D SD	8 LA	9 LA	10 D LA
11 D LA	12 D SD	13	14 SD	15 D SD	16 ATL	17 D ATL
18 D ATL	19 MON	20 MON	21 D SF	22 SF	23 SF	24 D SF
25 SF	26	27 STL	28 STL	29 D STL	30 PIT	

May

SUN	MON	TUE	WED	THU	FRI	SAT
						1 D PIT
2 D PIT	3 D CUB	4 CUB	5 D CUB	6	7 PHI	8 D PHI
9 D PHI	10 NYM	11 NYM	12 D NYM	13	14 ARI	15 D ARI
16 ARI	17 CIN	18 CIN	19 D CIN	20 D ARI	21 ARI	22 D ARI
23 ARI	24 HOU	25 HOU	26 D HOU	27 HOU	28 PHI	29 PHI
30 PHI	31 ATL					

June

SUN	MON	TUE	WED	THU	FRI	SAT
		1 ATL	2 ATL	3	4 D MIL	5 MIL
6 MIL	7 D SEA	8 SEA	9 SEA	10	11 TEX	12 TEX
13 D TEX	14 D SF	15 SF	16 D SF	17 D	18 FLA	19 FLA
20 D FLA	21	22 CUB	23 CUB	24 D CUB	25 SD	26 SD
27 D SD	28 SD	29 SF	30 D SF			

July

SUN	MON	TUE	WED	THU	FRI	SAT
				1 SF	2 D SD	3 SD
4 D SD	5 D LA	6 LA	7 LA	8 LA	9 ANA	10 ANA
11 D ANA	12	13 *	14	15 CIN	16 CIN	17 D CIN
18 D OAK	19 OAK	20 D OAK	21 LA	22 D LA	23 STL	24 D STL
25 STL	26 D HOU	27 HOU	28 HOU	29 D HOU	30 STL	31 STL

August

SUN	MON	TUE	WED	THU	FRI	SAT
1 STL	2 D	3 CIN	4 CIN	5 CIN	6 D FLA	7 FLA
8 FLA	9 MIL	10 MIL	11 MIL	12	13 D MON	14 MON
15 D MON	16 ATL	17 ATL	18 D ATL	19	20 D CUB	21 D CUB
22 D CUB	23	24 PIT	25 PIT	26 PIT	27 D PHI	28 PHI
29 D PHI	30 PIT	31 PIT				

September

SUN	MON	TUE	WED	THU	FRI	SAT
			1 D PIT	2	3 NYM	4 NYM
5 NYM	6 D MON	7 D MON	8 D MON	9	10 D MIL	11 D MIL
12 MIL	13 NYM	14 NYM	15 D NYM	16	17 D LA	18 D LA
19 LA	20 ARI	21 ARI	22 D ARI	23	24 FLA	25 FLA
26 FLA	27 D ARI	28 ARI	29 ARI	30		

October

SUN	MON	TUE	WED	THU	FRI	SAT
					1 SF	2 SF
3 D SF	4 SF	5	6	7	8	9

1999 SEASON
CLUB DIRECTORY

Chairman, president and CEO
Jerry McMorris

Exec. vice president/general manager
Bob Gebhard

Exec. vice president/business operations
Keli McGregor

Sr. v.p./secretary and corporate counsel
Clark Weaver

Sr. vice president/chief financial officer
Hal Roth

Director, baseball administration
Tony Siegle

Vice president/finance
Michael Kent

Director/player development
Paul Egins

Vice president/player personnel
Gary Hughes

Vice president/sales and marketing
Greg Feasel

Vice president/scouting
Pat Daugherty

Vice president/ticket operations
Sue Ann McClaren

Senior director, Coors Field operations
Kevin Kahn

Director, broadcasting
Eric Brummond

Director, information systems
Mary Burns

Dir., promotions and special events
Alan Bossart

Director, public relations
Jay Alves

Director, publications
Jimmy Oldham

Director, team travel
To be announced

Director, ticket operations
Chuck Javernick

Dir., charitable and community affairs
Roger Kinney

Director, int'l & professional scouting
Jeff Schugel

Assistant director, player development
Marc Gustafson

Assistant director, scouting
Coley Brannon

Head groundskeeper
Mark Razum

Coordinator of instruction
Rick Mathews

National cross-checkers
Dave Holliday
Bill Gayton

Regional cross-checkers
Jay Darnell
Robyn Lynch
Danny Montgomery

Major league scouts
Jim Fanning, Bill Harford, Larry High, John Van Ornum, Bill Wood

Scouts
John Cedarburg, Ty Coslow, Dar Cox, Mike Ericson, Abe Flores, Mike Garlatti, Bert Holt, Greg Hopkins, Bill Hughes, Damon Iannelli, Eric Johnson, Bill Mackenzie, Jay Matthews, Lance Nichols, Steve Payne, Art Pontarelli, Ed Santa, Nick Venuto, Tom Wheeler

International scouts
Phil Allen, Dario Arias, Francisco Cartava, Roland de Lima Gamez, Cristobal A. Giron, Jim Hovorka, Oscar Martinez, Brian McRobie, Atanacio Mendez, Jimmy Moreno, Jorge Posada, Jesus Rizales, Reed Spencer, Ron Steele

MINOR LEAGUE AFFILIATES

Class	Team	League	Manager
AAA	Colorado Springs	Pacific Coast	Bill Hayes
AA	Carolina	Southern	Jay Loviglio
A	Salem	Carolina	Ron Gideon
A	Asheville	South Atlantic	Jim Eppard
A	Portland	Northwest	Alan Cockrell
Rookie	Rockies	Arizona	P.J. Carey

BROADCAST INFORMATION

Radio: KOA-AM (850), KCUV-AM (1150).
TV: KWGN-TV (Channel 2).
Cable TV: Fox Sports Rocky Mountain.

SPRING TRAINING

Ballpark (city): Hi Corbett Field (Tucson, Ariz.).
Ticket information: 1-800-388-ROCK.

SPRING TRAINING ROSTER

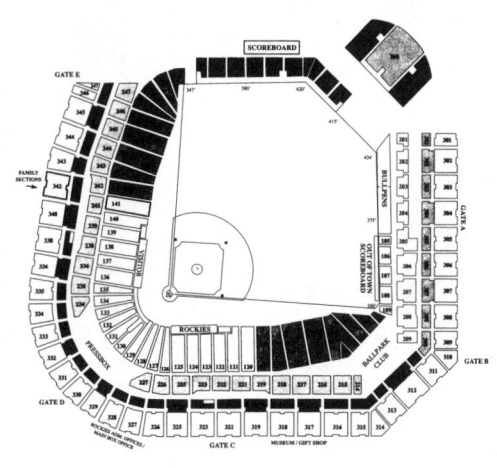

Manager—Jim Leyland.
Coaches—Lorenzo Bundy, Rich Donnelly, Clint Hurdle, Bruce Kimm, Milt May, Tommy Sandt.

No.	PITCHERS	B/T	Ht./Wt.	Born	1998 clubs
34	Astacio, Pedro	R/R	6-2/208	11-28-69	Colorado
41	Bohanon, Brian	L/L	6-2/240	8-1-68	New York N.L., Los Angeles
	Brester, Jason	L/L	6-3/190	12-7-76	New Haven, Shreveport
46	Brownson, Mark	L/R	6-2/185	6-17-75	Colorado Springs, Colorado
44	DeJean, Mike	R/R	6-2/212	9-28-70	Colorado
45	DiPoto, Jerry	R/R	6-2/205	5-24-68	Colorado
38	Gonzalez, Lariel	R/R	6-4/228	5-25-76	New Haven, Colorado
36	Jones, Bobby	R/L	6-0/178	4-11-72	Colorado
57	Kile, Darryl	R/R	6-5/212	12-2-68	Colorado
	Kusiewicz, Mike	R/L	6-2/190	11-1-76	New Haven
	Lee, David	R/R	6-1/202	3-12-73	Salem
16	Leskanic, Curtis	R/R	6-0/186	4-2-68	Colorado
	Martin, Chandler	R/R	6-1/192	10-23-73	Salem
23	McElroy, Chuck	L/L	6-0/205	10-1-67	Colorado
49	Ramirez, Roberto	L/L	5-11/170	8-17-72	Las Vegas, San Diego
48	Randall, Scott	R/R	6-3/190	10-29-75	New Haven
30	Ritz, Kevin	R/R	6-4/229	6-8-65	Colorado Springs, Colorado, New Haven
51	Shoemaker, Steve	L/R	6-1/214	2-3-73	New Haven, Colorado Springs
39	Stoops, Jim	R/R	6-2/180	6-30-72	Colorado Springs, Salem, San Jose, Colorado
52	Thomson, John	R/R	6-3/187	10-1-73	Colorado, Asheville
47	Veres, Dave	R/R	6-2/220	10-19-66	Colorado
41	Wainhouse, Dave	L/R	6-2/196	11-7-67	Colorado Springs, Colorado
21	Wright, Jamey	R/R	6-5/221	12-24-74	Colorado

No.	CATCHERS	B/T	Ht./Wt.	Born	1998 clubs
8	Manwaring, Kirt	R/R	5-11/198	7-15-65	Colorado
15	Reed, Jeff	L/R	6-2/202	11-12-62	Colorado

No.	INFIELDERS	B/T	Ht./Wt.	Born	1998 clubs
7	Abbott, Kurt	R/R	6-0/198	6-2-69	Edmonton, Oakland, Colorado
9	Castilla, Vinny	R/R	6-1/205	7-4-67	Colorado
17	Helton, Todd	L/L	6-2/206	8-20-73	Colorado
3	Lansing, Mike	R/R	6-0/195	4-3-68	Colorado
5	Perez, Neifi	B/R	6-0/175	2-2-75	Colorado
4	Sexton, Chris	R/R	5-11/178	8-3-71	Colorado Springs
	Sosa, Juan	R/R	6-1/175	8-19-75	Salem

No.	OUTFIELDERS	B/T	Ht./Wt.	Born	1998 clubs
10	Bichette, Dante	R/R	6-3/238	11-18-63	Colorado
19	Clemente, Edgard	R/R	5-11/188	12-15-75	Colorado Springs, Colorado
11	Echevarria, Angel	R/R	6-3/226	5-25-71	Colorado Springs, Colorado
24	Gibson, Derrick	R/R	6-2/244	2-5-75	Colorado Springs, Colorado
1	Goodwin, Curtis	L/L	5-11/180	9-30-72	Colorado
12	Hamilton, Darryl	L/R	6-1/192	12-3-64	San Francisco, Colorado
28	Harris, Lenny	L/R	5-10/220	10-28-64	Cincinnati, New York N.L.
33	Walker, Larry	L/R	6-3/237	12-1-66	Colorado
	White, Derrick	R/R	6-1/225	10-12-69	Iowa, Chicago N.L., Colorado, Colorado Springs

BALLPARK INFORMATION

Ballpark (capacity, surface)
Coors Field (50,249, grass)

Address
2001 Blake St.
Denver, CO 80205-2000

Business phone
303-292-0200

Ticket information
800-388-7625

Ticket prices
$30 (club level)
$25 (infield box)
$20 (outfield box)
$13/14 (lower reserved)
$12 (upper reserved, RF box)
$10 (RF mezzanine)
$8 (lower pavilion)
$6 (lower RF reserved)
$5 (upper RF reserved)
$4 (rockpile)
$1 (rockpile)

Field dimensions (from home plate)
To left field at foul line, 347 feet
To center field, 415 feet
To right field at foul line, 350

First game played
April 26, 1995 (Rockies 11, Mets 9, 14 innings)

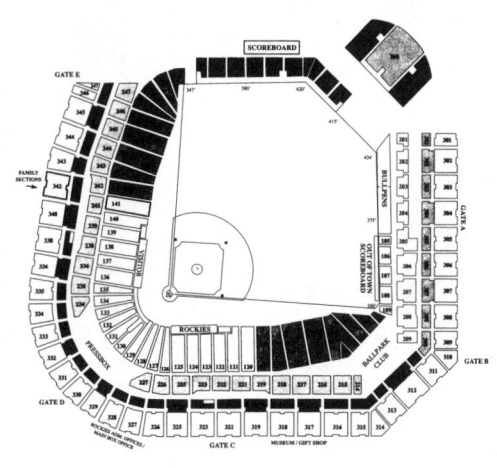

1999 SEASON *Colorado Rockies*

Date	Opp.	Res.	Score	(inn.*)	Hits	Opp. hits	Winning pitcher	Losing pitcher	Save	Record	Pos.	GB
3-31	At Ari.	W	9-2		13	6	Kile	Benes		1-0	T1st	...
4-1	At Ari.	W	6-0		16	3	Thomson	Blair		2-0	T1st	...
4-2	At Ari.	W	6-4		9	11	Astacio	Anderson	DiPoto	3-0	1st	+1.0
4-3	At Hou.	L	2-15		6	18	Lima	Wright		3-1	T1st	...
4-4	At Hou.	W	5-3		9	12	Thompson	Bergman	DiPoto	4-1	T1st	...
4-5	At Hou.	L	2-6		10	6	Reynolds	Kile		4-2	T1st	...
4-6	At Hou.	L	4-13		13	15	Hampton	Thomson		4-3	3rd	0.5
4-7	St.L.	L	11-12		14	14	Politte	Astacio	Bottenfield	4-4	3rd	1.5
4-8	St.L.	L	9-13		13	14	Aybar	Wright		4-5	3rd	2.5
4-9	St.L.	L	5-7		13	9	Busby	Leskanic	Brantley	4-6	3rd	3.5
4-10	Cin.	L	7-18		18	17	Jordan	Kile	Sullivan	4-7	4th	4.5
4-11	Cin.	L	5-12		14	21	Remlinger	Thomson	Belinda	4-8	4th	5.5
4-12	Cin.	L	4-10		11	11	Harnisch	Astacio		4-9	4th	6.5
4-13	Cin.	W	8-4		12	7	Leskanic	Belinda		5-9	4th	6.5
4-14	L.A.	W	6-3		12	10	DeJean	Valdes	DiPoto	6-9	4th	5.5
4-16	L.A.	L	3-4	(10)	7	7	Radinsky	DiPoto	Bruske	6-10	4th	6.5
4-18	Atl.	L	4-11		7	12	Neagle	Astacio		6-11	4th	8.0
4-19§	Atl.	L	3-5		7	8	Millwood	Thompson	Wohlers	6-12		
4-19§	Atl.	W	10-7		14	13	Wright	Martinez	DiPoto	7-12	4th	8.0
4-20	Atl.	L	5-7		8	13	Maddux	Kile	Ligtenberg	7-13	4th	8.5
4-22	At Fla.	L	2-3		5	7	Powell	Leskanic		7-14	4th	9.0
4-23	At Fla.	W	4-3		5	7	DiPoto	Stanifer		8-14	4th	9.0
4-24	At Fla.	L	1-5		9	10	Meadows	Thompson		8-15	4th	9.0
4-25	At Atl.	W	11-7		14	11	Kile	Millwood		9-15	4th	9.0
4-26	At Atl.	W	7-6		13	10	Wright	Maddux	DiPoto	10-15	4th	8.0
4-27	Fla.	L	4-5	(10)	6	9	Powell	Leskanic	Alfonseca	10-16	4th	8.0
4-28	Fla.	W	8-7		14	14	Astacio	Larkin	Leskanic	11-16	4th	8.0
4-30	At N.Y.	W	4-0		7	4	Kile	Jones		12-16	4th	8.0
5-2	At N.Y.	W	7-3		7	8	Leskanic	Cook		13-16	4th	7.5
5-3	At N.Y.	L	2-5		7	5	Reed	Astacio		13-17	4th	7.5
5-4	At Phi.	W	11-2		14	6	Thomson	Stephenson		14-17	4th	7.5
5-5	At Phi.	W	6-1		13	7	Kile	Grace		15-17	4th	7.5
5-6	At Phi.	L	6-7	(10)	10	13	Leiter	McElroy		15-18	4th	7.5
5-7	At Mon.	L	1-2		7	5	C. Perez	Wright	Urbina	15-19	4th	7.5
5-8	At Mon.	W	7-5		9	10	Astacio	Hermanson	DiPoto	16-19	4th	7.5
5-9	At Mon.	L	0-4		7	8	Moore	Thomson	Urbina	16-20	4th	7.5
5-10	At Mon.	W	5-3		8	5	Kile	Kline	DiPoto	17-20	4th	6.5
5-11	At Pit.	L	2-5		9	11	Schmidt	Ritz		17-21	4th	7.5
5-12	At Pit.	L	0-6		5	8	Loaiza	Wright		17-22	4th	8.0
5-13	Chi.	L	3-9		8	19	Trachsel	Astacio		17-23	4th	8.0
5-14	Chi.	L	7-9		21	15	Tapani	Thomson	Beck	17-24	4th	9.5
5-15	Mil.	L	5-8		9	16	Woodard	Kile	Myers	17-25	4th	10.5
5-16	Mil.	L	5-7		10	10	Karl	Ritz	Jones	17-26	4th	11.5
5-17	Mil.	W	2-1		7	7	Wright	Woodall	DiPoto	18-26	4th	11.5
5-18	Mil.	W	8-5		11	7	Astacio	Juden	DiPoto	19-26	4th	11.0
5-20	At Atl.	L	1-5		4	11	Millwood	Thomson		19-27	4th	11.0
5-21	At Atl.	L	0-2		8	9	Neagle	Kile	Ligtenberg	19-28	4th	11.0
5-22	At Cin.	W	3-2		10	8	Wright	Weathers	DiPoto	20-28	4th	11.0
5-23	At Cin.	L	1-4	(7)	4	9	Winchester	Astacio		20-29	4th	11.0
5-24	At Cin.	W	3-1		8	2	Jones	Tomko	DiPoto	21-29	4th	10.0
5-25	At St.L.	W	6-1		11	5	Thomson	Busby		22-29	4th	9.0
5-27	At St.L.	L	1-2		5	4	Stottlemyre	Kile	Brantley	22-30	4th	10.5
5-28	At St.L.	L	1-4		7	8	Mercker	Wright	King	22-31	4th	11.0
5-29	Hou.	L	6-7		8	14	Hampton	Astacio	Wagner	22-32	4th	11.0
5-30	Hou.	W	6-3		10	8	Thomson	Schourek	DiPoto	23-32	4th	11.0
5-31	Hou.	W	7-5		12	10	McElroy	Henry		24-32	4th	11.0
6-1	Ari.	L	4-6		7	9	Benes	Kile	Olson	24-33	4th	12.0
6-2	Ari.	L	3-9		5	14	Anderson	Wright		24-34	4th	12.0
6-3	Ari.	W	3-2		8	8	McElroy	Olson		25-34	4th	11.0
6-4	Ari.	W	5-2		12	4	Thomson	Daal		26-34	4th	11.0
6-5	At Ana.	L	0-5		6	11	Dickson	Jones		26-35	4th	11.0
6-6	At Ana.	L	1-2		7	9	Olivares	Kile	Percival	26-36	4th	12.0
6-7	At Ana.	L	5-6		14	10	Cadaret	DiPoto		26-37	4th	13.0
6-8	Tex.	L	1-3		6	8	Sele	Astacio	Wetteland	26-38	4th	14.0
6-9	Tex.	L	2-5		5	12	Helling	Thomson	Wetteland	26-39	4th	15.0
6-10	Tex.	W	9-8	(10)	14	14	DiPoto	Gunderson		27-39	4th	14.0
6-12	At L.A.	L	1-2		6	5	Mlicki	Kile	McMichael	27-40	4th	15.0
6-13	At L.A.	W	4-2		8	5	Wright	Dreifort	DiPoto	28-40	4th	15.0
6-14	At L.A.	W	3-2	(12)	9	6	DeJean	Radinsky	McElroy	29-40	4th	15.0
6-15	At S.F.	W	4-3	(12)	6	5	Leskanic	Johnstone	DiPoto	30-40	4th	14.5
6-16	At S.F.	L	3-5		8	13	Tavarez	Jones	Nen	30-41	4th	15.5

Date	Opp.	Res.	Score	(inn.*)	Hits	Opp. hits	Winning pitcher	Losing pitcher	Save	Record	Pos.	GB
6-17	At S.F.	L	3-6		7	12	Rueter	Kile	Nen	30-42	4th	16.5
6-18	L.A.	L	0-5		7	7	Mlicki	Wright		30-43	4th	17.5
6-19	L.A.	L	3-4	(10)	8	12	Osuna	DiPoto		30-44	4th	18.5
6-20	L.A.	W	7-6		11	10	Munoz	Reyes	Veres	31-44	4th	17.5
6-21	L.A.	W	11-6		12	10	Jones	Park		32-44	4th	17.5
6-22	At Mil.	L	2-3		6	7	Reyes	McElroy	Wickman	32-45	4th	18.5
6-23	At Mil.	L	5-7		8	9	Patrick	Wright	Wickman	32-46	4th	18.5
6-24	Hou.	W	8-6		14	6	Astacio	Bergman	Veres	33-46	4th	17.5
6-25	Hou.	W	6-5	(12)	14	13	Leskanic	Magnante		34-46	4th	17.5
6-26	Oak.	W	12-6		19	10	Munoz	Oquist		35-46	4th	17.5
6-27	Oak.	L	6-8		10	9	Mathews	DiPoto	Taylor	35-47	4th	18.5
6-28	Oak.	W	11-10		11	13	DeJean	Fetters	Veres	36-47	4th	17.5
6-30	At Sea.	W	6-4		10	8	Astacio	Johnson	Munoz	37-47	4th	16.5
7-1	At Sea.	L	5-9		8	16	Cloude	Saipe		37-48	4th	17.5
7-2	At Sea.	L	3-10		10	12	Swift	Kile		37-49	4th	17.5
7-3	At S.D.	L	2-4		8	8	Hamilton	DeJean	Hoffman	37-50	4th	18.5
7-4	At S.D.	L	1-9		8	12	Langston	Jones		37-51	4th	19.5
7-5	At S.D.	L	2-7		5	9	Ashby	Astacio		37-52	4th	20.5
7-10	S.F.	W	11-2		19	8	Kile	Estes		38-52	4th	19.0
7-11	S.F.	W	5-4		9	11	McElroy	Hershiser	Munoz	39-52	4th	19.0
7-12	S.F.	W	5-3		9	9	Astacio	Rueter	Munoz	40-52	4th	19.0
7-13	S.D.	W	9-5		11	8	Jones	Hitchcock		41-52	4th	18.0
7-14	S.D.	L	7-8		14	10	Sanders	Kile	Hoffman	41-53	4th	19.0
7-15	S.D.	L	2-6		12	10	Brown	Wright		41-54	4th	20.0
7-17	At Ari.	L	6-9		11	12	Blair	Astacio	Olson	41-55	4th	21.0
7-18	At Ari.	L	2-4		7	11	Anderson	Jones	Olson	41-56	4th	22.0
7-19	At Ari.	L	4-6		11	9	Small	Munoz	Embree	41-57	4th	23.0
7-20	At Hou.	L	9-10		13	18	Henry	Veres		41-58	4th	23.0
7-21	At Hou.	W	5-0		8	4	Brownson	Hampton		42-58	4th	23.0
7-23§	Cin.	W	6-4		13	10	Astacio	Remlinger	Veres	43-58		
7-23§	Cin.	W	6-4		12	9	Jones	Harnisch	Leskanic	44-58	4th	23.0
7-24	St.L.	W	12-3		18	7	Kile	Stottlemyre		45-58	4th	22.0
7-25	St.L.	W	5-2		11	7	McElroy	Morris	DeJean	46-58	4th	22.0
7-26	St.L.	L	1-3		7	8	Mercker	Thomson	Croushore	46-59	4th	23.0
7-27	Pit.	W	8-7	(13)	16	18	Leskanic	McCurry		47-59	4th	22.5
7-28	Pit.	W	12-6		15	6	Astacio	Lieber		48-59	4th	21.5
7-29	Pit.	L	1-12		5	19	Peters	Kile		48-60	4th	21.5
7-31	At Chi.	L	1-9		6	8	Wood	Wright	Mulholland	48-61	4th	23.0
8-1	At Chi.	L	2-3		12	7	Trachsel	Thomson	Beck	48-62	4th	23.0
8-2	At Chi.	W	6-3		11	6	Astacio	Clark	McElroy	49-62	4th	23.0
8-3	At Pit.	W	7-2		13	5	Jones	Lieber		50-62	4th	22.0
8-4	At Pit.	L	5-13		11	21	Christiansen	Kile		50-63	4th	23.0
8-5	At Pit.	W	6-2		8	5	Wright	Cordova		51-63	4th	23.0
8-6	At Pit.	W	5-1		9	4	Thomson	Schmidt		52-63	4th	22.0
8-7	N.Y.	L	7-8		14	13	Reed	Astacio	J. Franco	52-64	4th	23.0
8-8	N.Y.	L	3-4		12	9	Reynoso	Jones	J. Franco	52-65	4th	23.5
8-9	N.Y.	W	11-4		17	10	Kile	Nomo		53-65	4th	23.5
8-10	Mon.	W	6-2		8	7	Wright	Telford		54-65	4th	22.5
8-11	Mon.	W	15-6		18	16	Thomson	Powell		55-65	4th	22.5
8-12	Mon.	W	3-2		6	9	Astacio	Vazquez	DiPoto	56-65	4th	22.5
8-14	Phi.	L	2-6		9	6	Loewer	Jones		56-66	4th	23.0
8-15	Phi.	W	7-3		16	8	Kile	Gomes		57-66	4th	22.5
8-16	Phi.	L	7-8		10	12	Portugal	Wright	Leiter	57-67	4th	23.0
8-18†	At N.Y.	L	2-6		10	8	Leiter	Astacio		57-68		
8-18‡	At N.Y.	L	3-6		8	12	Rojas	McElroy	J. Franco	57-69	4th	24.5
8-19	At N.Y.	L	1-2		9	6	Yoshii	Jones	J. Franco	57-70	4th	24.5
8-20	At Mon.	W	6-3		10	11	Kile	Thurman	DeJean	58-70	4th	24.5
8-21	At Mon.	W	3-2		11	6	Veres	Urbina		59-70	4th	23.5
8-22	At Phi.	L	1-6		5	10	Byrd	Astacio		59-71	4th	23.5
8-23	At Phi.	W	5-2		9	9	Thomson	Grace	DiPoto	60-71	4th	23.5
8-24	At Phi.	W	3-1		7	6	Jones	Loewer	Veres	61-71	4th	23.5
8-25	Mil.	W	11-6		11	13	Veres	Weathers		62-71	4th	23.5
8-26	Mil.	L	5-6		6	14	Pulsipher	Wright		62-72	4th	24.5
8-27	Chi.	L	10-11	(10)	15	19	Mulholland	Munoz	Beck	62-73	4th	25.5
8-28	Chi.	L	5-10		15	15	Trachsel	Thomson		62-74	4th	26.5
8-29	Chi.	W	7-3		13	5	Jones	Clark		63-74	4th	25.5
8-30	Chi.	L	3-4		9	10	Tapani	Kile	Beck	63-75	4th	25.5
9-1	At Mil.	W	12-3		14	8	Wright	Pulsipher		64-75	4th	26.0
9-2	At Mil.	L	4-8		9	10	Roque	Astacio		64-76	4th	26.0
9-3	At Mil.	L	3-7		11	10	Woodall	Thomson		64-77	4th	26.5
9-4	S.D.	W	11-5		14	9	Veres	Sanders		65-77	4th	25.5
9-5	S.D.	L	2-4		6	10	Brown	Kile	Hoffman	65-78	4th	26.5
9-6	S.D.	W	12-2		14	6	Wright	Hamilton		66-78	4th	25.5
9-7	Fla.	W	15-10		21	16	Leskanic	Ludwick		67-78	4th	24.5
9-8	Fla.	W	11-10		18	13	McElroy	Mantei		68-78	4th	23.5

– 101 –

Date	Opp.	Res.	Score	(inn.*)	Hits	Opp. hits	Winning pitcher	Losing pitcher	Save	Record	Pos.	GB
9-9	Fla.	W	9-8		15	9	McElroy	Speier		69-78	4th	23.5
9-10	Fla.	W	3-1		10	2	Kile	Medina		70-78	4th	22.5
9-11	At S.F.	W	7-6		11	15	Stoops	Morman	DiPoto	71-78	4th	22.5
9-12	At S.F.	W	1-0		8	6	Astacio	Nen	DiPoto	72-78	4th	22.5
9-13	At S.F.	L	3-4		7	6	Johnstone	McElroy	Nen	72-79	4th	22.5
9-14	At L.A.	L	1-4		7	9	Perez	Jones		72-80	4th	23.5
9-15	At L.A.	W	5-4		7	12	Kile	Park	DiPoto	73-80	4th	22.5
9-16	At L.A.	L	0-2		8	6	Bohanon	Wright	Shaw	73-81	4th	22.5
9-18	At S.D.	W	4-1		10	7	Astacio	Ashby	Veres	74-81	4th	21.0
9-19	At S.D.	L	1-4		7	8	Clement	Thomson	Hoffman	74-82	4th	22.0
9-20	At S.D.	W	1-0	(11)	7	4	Kile	R. Myers	Veres	75-82	4th	21.0
9-22	Ari.	L	6-8		7	12	Daal	Wright	Olson	75-83	4th	21.0
9-23	Ari.	W	14-11		15	16	Wainhouse	Banks	Veres	76-83	4th	21.0
9-25	S.F.	L	6-8		7	15	Johnstone	Leskanic	Nen	76-84	4th	21.0
9-26	S.F.	L	4-8		8	15	Hershiser	Kile		76-85	4th	21.0
9-27	S.F.	W	9-8		15	12	DiPoto	Nen		77-85	4th	21.0

Monthly records: March (1-0), April (11-16), May (12-16), June (13-15), July (11-14), August (15-14), September (14-10).
*Innings, if other than nine. †First game of doubleheader. ‡Second game of doubleheader. §Two games in one day (separate admissions).

HIGHLIGHTS

High point: Things looked rosy when the Rockies opened the season with a three-game sweep of the Diamondbacks. Included was a 9-1 season-opening victory by Darryl Kile and a shutout started by John Thomson.

Low point: The Rockies limped into the All-Star break with a 37-52 mark, bottoming out at 20.5 games behind the Padres when former teammate Andy Ashby needed only 77 pitches in a complete game to beat them 7-2.

Turning point: It was all downhill after the season's first homestand turned into a 3-10 disaster. The Rockies began the stand at 4-3 and finished at 7-13, eight games out of first place.

Most valuable player: Vinny Castilla improved upon his consistently outstanding numbers by hitting .319 with 46 homers and 144 RBIs—all career bests.

Most valuable pitcher: A hard category to fill on this team, but nobody did his job better than Chuck McElroy. The veteran lefthander kept his ERA under 2.00 for much of the season and he did it while setting a club record with 78 appearances. He also recorded two saves and struck out 61 in 68 innings.

Most improved player: Bobby Jones went to spring training as a longshot to make the staff and finished with a 7-8 record as the No. 5 starter. He set a club record for a lefthander by making 20 starts, during which the Rockies compiled a 12-8 record.

Most pleasant surprise: After being acquired in an overlooked expansion draft-day deal for Harvey Pulliam, McElroy led the club in appearances and allowed only three homers in 68.2 innings.

Biggest disappointment: Not only did the Rockies give up three prospects for Mike Lansing, they gave him a four-year, $23.75 million contract one year before he was eligible for free agency. Lansing struggled in all phases of the game and needed a strong finish to end up with mediocre numbers.

Key injuries: Larry Walker was stripped of much of his power and run-production capabilities because of lingering pain in his elbow, which was operated on in January 1998. Walker spent two weeks on the disabled list and missed 33 games. He also suffered a sprained finger and back spasms.

Notable: Walker joined Andres Galarraga as the club's second batting champion in its six-year history. . . . The offense set a club record with a .291 team average, highest in the National League since 1939. . . . Dante Bichette led the majors and set a club record with 219 hits. Castilla had 206 hits, giving the Rockies the first pair of 200-hit men in the N.L. since St. Louis in 1979.

—TONY DeMARCO

RECORDS

1998 regular-season record: 77-85 (4th in N.L. West); 42-39 at home; 35-46 on road; 24-20 vs. East; 25-33 vs. Central; 24-24 vs. N.L. West; 4-8 vs. A.L.; 18-32 vs. lefthanded starters; 59-53 vs. righthanded starters; 61-71 on grass; 16-14 on turf; 25-27 in daytime; 52-58 at night; 23-24 in one-run games; 6-5 in extra-inning games; 0-1-0 in doubleheaders.

Team record past five years: 373-374 (.499, ranks 6th in league in that span).

TEAM LEADERS

Batting average: Larry Walker (.363).
At-bats: Dante Bichette (662).
Runs: Larry Walker (113).
Hits: Dante Bichette (219).
Total bases: Vinny Castilla (380).
Doubles: Dante Bichette (48).
Triples: Neifi Perez (9).
Home runs: Vinny Castilla (46).
Runs batted in: Vinny Castilla (144).
Stolen bases: Dante Bichette, Larry Walker (14).
Slugging percentage: Larry Walker (.630).
On-base percentage: Larry Walker (.445).
Wins: Pedro Astacio, Darryl Kile (13).
Earned-run average: Darryl Kile (5.20).
Complete games: Darryl Kile (4).
Shutouts: Mark Brownson, Darryl Kile (1).
Saves: Jerry DiPoto (19).

Innings pitched: Darryl Kile (230.1).
Strikeouts: Pedro Astacio (170).

GAMES BY POSITION

Catcher: Kirt Manwaring 108, Jeff Reed 99, Mark Strittmatter 3, Greg Colbrunn 1, Neifi Perez 1.
First base: Todd Helton 146, Greg Colbrunn 27, Angel Echevarria 4, John Vander Wal 2.
Second base: Mike Lansing 153, Jason Bates 17, Kurt Abbott 7, Terry Shumpert 6, Nelson Liriano 3, Larry Walker 1.
Third base: Vinny Castilla 162, Kurt Abbott 3, Jason Bates 3, Mike Lansing 1, Larry Walker 1.
Shortstop: Neifi Perez 162, Kurt Abbott 7, Jason Bates 3, Vinny Castilla 1, Nelson Liriano 1.
Outfield: Dante Bichette 156, Larry Walker 123, Ellis Burks 98, Curtis Goodwin 91, Darryl Hamilton 48, John Vander Wal 25, Jeff Barry 10, Kurt Abbott 9, Edgard Clemente 7, Derrick Gibson 7, Greg Colbrunn 5, Angel Echevarria 4, Derrick White 2.
Designated hitter: Greg Colbrunn 3, John Vander Wal 3, Kurt Abbott 1, Dante Bichette 1, Larry Walker 1.

TOP DRAFT CHOICES

1a. None
1b. **Matt Roney,** RHP, Edmond North H.S., Edmond, Okla.
1c. **Choo Freeman,** OF, Dallas Christian H.S., Mesquite, Tex.
1d. **Jeff Winchester,** C, Archbishop Rummel H.S., Metairie, La.
2a. **Jermaine Van Buren,** RHP, Hattiesburg (Miss.) H.S.
2b. **Jody Gerut,** OF, Stanford University
3. **Kevin Gordon,** RHP, U. of Central Fla.
4. **Luke Hudson,** RHP, U. of Tennessee
5. **Ryan Shealy,** 1B, Cardinal Gibbons H.S., Fort Lauderdale, Fla.
6. **Javier Guzman,** OF, Univ. Garden H.S., Rio Piedras, P.R.
7. **Matt Holliday,** 3B, Stillwater (Okla.) H.S.
8. **Justin Lincoln,** 3B-RHP, Manatee (Fla.) J.C.
9. **Justin Carter,** LHP, U. of S. Alabama
10. **Andrew Beinbrink,** 3B, Arizona St.

FLORIDA MARLINS
NATIONAL LEAGUE EAST DIVISION

1999 Marlins Schedule
Home games shaded. *—All-Star Game at Fenway Park (Boston). D—Day game (any game starting before 5 p.m.).

April
SUN	MON	TUE	WED	THU	FRI	SAT
				1	2	3
4	5 NYM	D 6 NYM	7 NYM	8	9 PHI	10 PHI
11 PHI	12 D NYM	D 13	14 NYM	15 NYM	16 PHI	17 PHI
18 PHI	19 SF	20 SF	21 SF	D 22	23 ATL	24 ATL
25 ATL	26 ATL	27 CUB	28 CUB	29 CUB	D 30 HOU	

May
SUN	MON	TUE	WED	THU	FRI	SAT
						1 HOU
2 HOU	D 3 MIL	4 MIL	5 MIL	D 6	7 LA	8 LA
9 LA	D 10 SD	11 SD	12 SD	13	14 MIL	15 MIL
16 MIL	D 17 CUB	18 CUB	19 CUB	20 PIT	21 PIT	22 PIT
23 PIT	24 CUB	25 CUB	26 CUB	D 27	28 CIN	29 CIN
30 CIN	D 31 STL					

June
SUN	MON	TUE	WED	THU	FRI	SAT
		1 STL	2 STL	3 STL	4 TB	5 TB
6 TB	D 7 BAL	8 BAL	9 BAL	10	11 NYY	12 NYY
13 NYY	D 14 ARI	15 ARI	16 ARI	17	18 COL	19 COL
20 COL	D 21	22 NYM	23 NYM	24 NYM	D 25 MON	26 MON
27 MON	D 28 NYM	29 NYM	30 NYM			

July
SUN	MON	TUE	WED	THU	FRI	SAT
				1 NYM	2 MON	3 MON
4 MON	D 5 ATL	6 ATL	7 ATL	8 ATL	9 TB	10 TB
11 TB	D 12	13	* 14	15 TOR	16 TOR	17 D TOR
18 BOS	D 19 BOS	20 BOS	21 ATL	22 ATL	23 MIL	24 MIL
25 MIL	26 PHI	27 PHI	28 PHI	29 PHI	30 PIT	31 PIT

August
SUN	MON	TUE	WED	THU	FRI	SAT
1 PIT	D 2	3 PHI	4 PHI	5 PHI	6 COL	7 COL
8 COL	D 9 SF	10 SF	11 SF	D 12	13 SD	14 SD
15 SD	D 16 LA	17 LA	18 LA	19	20 HOU	21 HOU
22 HOU	D 23	24 ARI	25 ARI	26 ARI	D 27 HOU	28 HOU
29 HOU	D 30 STL	31 STL				

September
SUN	MON	TUE	WED	THU	FRI	SAT
		1 STL	2	3 SD	4 SD
5 SD	D 6 LA	7 LA	8 LA	9	10 CIN	11 CIN
12 CIN	D 13 CIN	14 SF	15 SF	16 SF	17 ARI	18 D ARI
19 ARI	20	21 MON	22 MON	23 MON	D 24 COL	25 COL
26 COL	D 27 MON	28 MON	29 MON	30		

October
SUN	MON	TUE	WED	THU	FRI	SAT
					1 ATL	2 ATL
3 ATL	D 4	5	6	7	8	9

1999 SEASON
CLUB DIRECTORY

Chairman
H. Wayne Huizenga
President
To be announced
Exec. vice president and general manager
David Dombrowski
Vice president of finance & administration
Jonathan Mariner
Vice president of sales and marketing
Jim Ross
Assistant general manager
Dave Littlefield
Director of major league administration
Dan Lunetta
Senior advisor, special asst. to the g.m.
Whitey Lockman
Dir. of scouting including Latin American operations
Al Avila
Director of team travel
Bill Beck
Special asst. to the general manager
Tony Perez
Dir. of baseball information and publicity
Ron Colangelo
Director of community affairs
Nancy Olson
Director of communications
Mark Geddis
Director of scouting
Orrin Freeman
Director of marketing
John Pierce
Director of marketing partnerships
Ben Creed
Director of season & group sales
Lou De Paoli
Asst. dir. of baseball info. and publicity
Julio C. Sarmiento

Director of Brevard County operations
Andy Dunn
Equipment manager
Mike Wallace
Team physician
Dr. Dan Kanell
Head trainer
Larry Starr
Major league scouts and special asst. to the general manager
Orrin Freeman, Scott Reid
Manager of scouting administration
Cheryl Evans
Scouting assistant
James Orr
National crosscheckers
Jax Robertson, Bill Singer, Murray Cook, David Chedd, Tim Schmidt
Scouts
Dick Egan, Manny Estrada, Will George, Kelvin Bowles, Lou Fitzgerald, Charlie Silvers, Ty Brown, John Castleberry, John Deeble, Whitey Dehart, Brad Del Barba, Louis Eljaua, David Finley, Bob Laurie, Steve Minor, Steve Mondile, Cucho Rodriguez, Jimmy Rough, Mike Russell, Dennis Sheehan, Keith Snider, Wally Walker, Stan Zielinski
Director Dominican Republic operations
Jesus Alou
Dominican Republic scouts
Pablo Lantigua, Cesar Santiago
Puerto Rico scouts
Cucho Rodriguez, Pedro Cintron
Venezuela scout
Miguel Angel Garcia
Colombia scout
Holbert Cabrera
Panama scout
Ramon Webster

MINOR LEAGUE AFFILIATES

Class	Team	League	Manager
AAA	Calgary	Pacific Coast	Lynn Jones
AA	Portland	Eastern	Frank Cacciatore
A	Brevard County	Florida State	Dave Huppert
A	Kane County	Midwest	Rick Renteria
A	Utica	New York-Pennsylvania	Ken Joyce
Rookie	Gulf Coast Marlins	Gulf Coast	Jon Deeble

BROADCAST INFORMATION

Radio: WQAM-AM (560); WQBA-AM (1140, Spanish language).
TV: WAMI (Channel 69).
Cable TV: Sports Channel Florida.

SPRING TRAINING

Ballpark (city): Space Coast Stadium (Melbourne, Fla.).
Ticket information: To be announced.

SPRING TRAINING ROSTER

Manager—John Boles
Coaches—Joe Breeden, Rich Dubee, Fredi Gonzalez, Rusty Kuntz, Jack Maloof, Tony Taylor.

No.	PITCHERS	B/T	Ht./Wt.	Born	1998 clubs
57	Alfonseca, Antonio	R/R	6-5/235	4-16-72	Florida
56	Almanza, Armando	L/L	6-3/205	10-26-72	Memphis, Arkansas
48	Billingsley, Brent	L/L	6-2/200	4-19-75	Portland
49	Burnett, A.J.	R/R	6-5/204	1-3-77	Kane County
40	Darensbourg, Vic	L/L	5-10/165	11-13-70	Florida
50	Dempster, Ryan	R/R	6-1/201	5-3-77	Portland, Florida, Charlotte
20	Edmondson, Brian	R/R	6-2/175	1-29-73	Atlanta, Florida
32	Fernandez, Alex	R/R	6-1/225	8-13-69	Florida
54	Fontenot, Joe	R/R	6-2/185	3-20-77	Portland, Florida, Charlotte
61	Hernandez, Livan	R/R	6-2/225	2-20-75	Florida
53	Lara, Nelson	R/R	6-4/185	7-15-78	Brevard County, Kane County
23	Looper, Braden	R/R	6-5/225	10-28-74	St. Louis, Memphis
33	Mantei, Matt	R/R	6-1/190	7-7-73	Charlotte, Florida
34	Meadows, Brian	R/R	6-4/210	11-21-75	Florida
47	Medina, Rafael	R/R	6-3/195	2-15-75	Florida, Charlotte
24	Ojala, Kirt	L/L	6-2/215	12-24-68	Florida
21	Sanchez, Jesus	L/L	5-10/155	10-11-74	Florida
35	Speier, Justin	R/R	6-4/205	11-6-73	Iowa, Chicago N.L., Florida
58	Tejera, Michael	L/L	5-9/175	10-18-76	Portland, Kane County

No.	CATCHERS	B/T	Ht./Wt.	Born	1998 clubs
29	Castro, Ramon	R/R	6-3/225	3-1-76	Portland, Jackson
14	Fabregas, Jorge	L/R	6-3/215	3-13-70	Arizona, Tucson, New York N.L.
9	Garcia, Guillermo	R/R	6-3/215	4-4-72	Indianapolis, Cincinnati
52	Redmond, Mike	R/R	6-1/185	5-5-71	Portland, Florida, Charlotte

No.	INFIELDERS	B/T	Ht./Wt.	Born	1998 clubs
10	Berg, Dave	R/R	5-11/185	9-3-70	Florida
1	Castillo, Luis	B/R	5-11/175	9-12-75	Charlotte, Florida
30	Counsell, Craig	L/R	6-0/175	8-21-70	Florida
45	Garcia, Amaury	R/R	5-10/160	5-20-75	Portland
6	Gonzalez, Alex	R/R	6-0/170	2-15-77	Charlotte, Florida
3	Jackson, Ryan	L/L	6-3/185	11-11-71	Florida, Charlotte
25	Lee, Derrek	R/R	6-5/225	9-6-75	Florida
27	Orie, Kevin	R/R	6-4/215	9-1-72	Iowa, Chicago N.L., Florida
26	Rolison, Nate	L/R	6-5/225	3-27-77	Portland

No.	OUTFIELDERS	B/T	Ht./Wt.	Born	1998 clubs
	Bates, Fletcher	B/R	6-1/193	3-24-74	Portland
17	Dunwoody, Todd	L/L	6-1/195	4-11-75	Charlotte, Florida
15	Floyd, Cliff	L/R	6-4/235	12-5-72	Florida
41	Jones, Jaime	L/L	6-3/190	8-2-76	Portland
7	Kotsay, Mark	L/L	6-0/190	12-2-75	Florida
28	Ramirez, Julio	R/R	5-11/170	8-10-77	Brevard County
36	Watkins, Pat	R/R	6-2/195	9-2-72	Cincinnati, Indianapolis
44	Wilson, Preston	R/R	6-2/193	7-19-74	New York N.L., Florida, Charlotte, Norfolk

BALLPARK INFORMATION

Ballpark (capacity, surface)
Pro Player Stadium (42,530, grass)
Address
2267 N.W. 199th St.
Miami, Fla. 33056
Business phone
305-626-7400
Ticket information
305-350-5050
Ticket prices
$28 (club level section A)
$21 (infield box)
$20 (club level section B)
$15 (club level section C)
$12.50 (terrace box, mezzanine box)
$9 (outfield reserved, adult)
$7 (mezzanine reserved, adult)
$4 (outfield reserved, children)
$2 (mezzanine reserved, children)
Field dimensions (from home plate)
To left field at foul line, 330 feet
To center field, 434 feet
To right field at foul line, 345 feet
First game played
April 5, 1993 (Marlins 6, Dodgers 3)

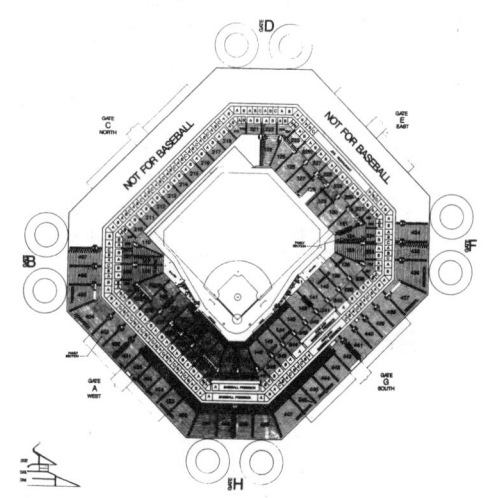

1999 SEASON *Florida Marlins*

Date	Opp.	Res.	Score	(inn.*)	Hits	Opp. hits	Winning pitcher	Losing pitcher	Save	Record	Pos.	GB
3-31	Chi.	W	11-6		14	10	Hernandez	Tapani		1-0	T1st	...
4-1	Chi.	L	3-10		8	10	Clark	Heredia		1-1	3rd	0.5
4-2	Chi.	L	7-8		8	12	Patterson	Powell	Beck	1-2	4th	0.5
4-3	Mil.	L	1-7		7	8	Woodard	Ludwick		1-3	4th	1.5
4-4	Mil.	L	2-6		9	15	Juden	Meadows		1-4	4th	2.5
4-5	Mil.	L	2-5		10	8	Reyes	Hernandez	Jones	1-5	4th	3.5
4-6	Mil.	L	5-8		8	11	Woodard	Heredia	Jones	1-6	4th	3.5
4-7	At Phi.	L	8-9	(10)	9	15	Bottalico	Sanchez		1-7	4th	4.5
4-8	At Phi.	L	5-9		7	14	Grace	Ludwick		1-8	4th	5.0
4-10	At Pit.	L	1-4		7	8	Silva	Meadows	Loiselle	1-9	5th	5.0
4-11	At Pit.	L	6-7	(10)	8	11	Loiselle	Powell		1-10	5th	6.0
4-12	At Pit.	L	3-7		6	9	Schmidt	Medina		1-11	5th	6.5
4-13	At Pit.	W	7-2		8	9	Larkin	Loaiza		2-11	5th	6.0
4-15	Phi.	W	3-2		4	3	Meadows	Schilling	Heredia	3-11	5th	6.5
4-16	Phi.	W	12-4		12	9	Hernandez	Green		4-11	5th	5.5
4-17	At Ari.	L	5-7		4	12	Springer	Darensbourg	Rodriguez	4-12	5th	5.5
4-18	At Ari.	L	5-7		5	12	Manuel	Alfonseca	Rodriguez	4-13	5th	6.5
4-19	At Ari.	W	4-3		8	10	Meadows	Suppan	Stanifer	5-13	5th	6.5
4-20	At Ari.	L	4-15		10	16	Sodowsky	Hernandez		5-14	5th	7.0
4-22	Col.	W	3-2		7	5	Powell	Leskanic		6-14	5th	7.0
4-23	Col.	L	3-4		7	5	DiPoto	Stanifer		6-15	5th	8.0
4-24	Col.	W	5-1		10	9	Meadows	Thompson		7-15	5th	8.0
4-25	Ari.	L	3-4	(11)	8	10	Brow	Darensbourg	Rodriguez	7-16	5th	8.0
4-26	Ari.	W	12-6		11	8	Ludwick	Adamson		8-16	4th	7.0
4-27	At Col.	W	5-4	(10)	9	6	Powell	Leskanic	Alfonseca	9-16	4th	7.0
4-28	At Col.	L	7-8		14	14	Astacio	Larkin	Leskanic	9-17	4th	8.0
4-30	S.D.	L	1-4		4	9	Smith	Meadows	Hoffman	9-18	4th	9.0
5-1	S.D.	W	6-5	(11)	9	12	Powell	Miceli		10-18	4th	9.0
5-2	S.D.	L	7-8		11	13	Hamilton	Ludwick	Hoffman	10-19	4th	10.0
5-3	S.D.	W	1-0		9	5	Sanchez	Ashby	Powell	11-19	4th	9.0
5-4	S.F.	L	0-8		4	12	Estes	Larkin		11-20	4th	10.0
5-5	S.F.	L	2-8	(10)	3	9	Nen	Darensbourg		11-21	4th	11.0
5-6	S.F.	L	9-10		13	11	Reed	Darensbourg	Nen	11-22	5th	12.0
5-7	L.A.	L	3-4		6	8	Martinez	Stanifer	Radinsky	11-23	5th	13.0
5-8	L.A.	W	12-6		15	7	Sanchez	Park		12-23	4th	12.0
5-9	L.A.	W	7-4		14	6	Larkin	Nomo		13-23	5th	12.0
5-10	L.A.	L	2-4		5	9	Valdes	Meadows	Radinsky	13-24	5th	13.0
5-11	At Hou.	L	2-5		8	11	Reynolds	Hernandez	Wagner	13-25	5th	14.0
5-12	At Hou.	L	2-4		5	10	Bergman	Hammond	Wagner	13-26	5th	15.0
5-13	At Cin.	L	4-10		8	14	Tomko	Pall		13-27	5th	16.0
5-14	At Cin.	L	8-11		12	17	Winchester	Larkin	Shaw	13-28	5th	17.0
5-15	At St.L.	W	8-7		15	13	Meadows	Raggio	Powell	14-28	5th	17.0
5-16	At St.L.	L	4-5		7	9	Stottlemyre	Darensbourg		14-29	5th	17.0
5-17	At St.L.	L	4-13		12	15	Mercker	Hammond		14-30	5th	17.0
5-18	At St.L.	W	7-3		9	6	Sanchez	Aybar		15-30	5th	17.0
5-20	Ari.	L	3-7		8	9	Daal	Larkin	Olson	15-31	5th	18.0
5-21	Ari.	L	4-6		7	8	Telemaco	Darensbourg	Olson	15-32	5th	19.0
5-22	Pit.	W	3-1		9	9	Hernandez	Loaiza		16-32	5th	19.0
5-23	Pit.	L	4-10		6	11	Lieber	Fontenot	Rincon	16-33	5th	19.0
5-24	Pit.	W	4-3		7	9	Powell	Christiansen		17-33	5th	19.0
5-26	N.Y.	L	6-10		9	15	Bohanon	Larkin		17-34	5th	20.5
5-27	N.Y.	L	2-8		9	15	Yoshii	Meadows		17-35	5th	21.5
5-29	At Mil.	L	3-4	(11)	10	10	Wickman	Powell		17-36	5th	21.0
5-30	At Mil.	L	4-12		6	16	Eldred	Fontenot		17-37	5th	21.0
5-31	At Mil.	L	6-7		11	7	Woodall	Alfonseca	Wickman	17-38	5th	21.0
6-1	At Chi.	L	2-10		5	14	Gonzalez	Dempster		17-39	5th	22.0
6-2	At Chi.	L	1-2		8	5	Adams	Heredia		17-40	5th	23.0
6-3	At Chi.	L	1-5		6	10	Wood	Hernandez		17-41	5th	24.0
6-5	At N.Y. (AL)	L	1-5		5	7	Pettitte	Fontenot		17-42	5th	24.0
6-6	At N.Y. (AL)	L	2-4		4	10	Mendoza	Sanchez	Rivera	17-43	5th	25.0
6-7	At N.Y. (AL)	L	1-4		2	8	Cone	Dempster		17-44	5th	26.0
6-8	Tor.	W	4-3	(17)	14	13	Edmondson	Hanson		18-44	5th	26.0
6-9	Tor.	W	5-4		12	9	Hernandez	Quantrill		19-44	5th	25.0
6-10	Tor.	L	3-4	(10)	11	9	Person	Powell	Myers	19-45	5th	25.0
6-11	N.Y.	L	3-5		9	9	Jones	Sanchez	J. Franco	19-46	5th	25.5
6-12	N.Y.	W	4-3		9	8	Mantei	Bohanon		20-46	5th	24.5
6-13	N.Y.	L	4-7		7	7	Reed	Meadows	J. Franco	20-47	5th	25.5
6-14	N.Y.	W	5-4		12	12	Mantei	Hudek		21-47	5th	25.5
6-16	At Atl.	L	0-7		4	9	Neagle	Fontenot		21-48	5th	26.5
6-17	At Atl.	L	2-6		4	7	Maddux	Sanchez		21-49	5th	27.5
6-18	At Atl.	W	3-2		10	7	Ojala	Glavine	Alfonseca	22-49	5th	26.5

Date	Opp.	Res.	Score	(inn.*)	Hits	Opp. hits	Winning pitcher	Losing pitcher	Save	Record	Pos.	GB
6-19	At N.Y.	W	3-2		6	9	Meadows	Reed	Mantei	23-49	5th	25.5
6-20	At N.Y.	W	8-3		13	8	Hernandez	Nomo		24-49	5th	25.5
6-21	At N.Y.	L	2-3		8	6	Leiter	Fontenot	J. Franco	24-50	5th	25.5
6-22	At T.B.	W	3-2	(12)	9	12	Alfonseca	Mecir		25-50	5th	24.5
6-23	At T.B.	L	4-6		7	10	Lopez	Dempster	Hernandez	25-51	5th	25.5
6-24	T.B.	W	8-4		10	13	Meadows	Saunders		26-51	5th	24.5
6-25	T.B.	W	5-1		10	8	Hernandez	Santana		27-51	5th	23.5
6-26	Bos.	L	1-6		5	11	Martinez	Fontenot		27-52	5th	23.5
6-27	Bos.	L	4-9		8	14	Wakefield	Sanchez		27-53	5th	24.5
6-28	Bos.	W	5-1		8	6	Dempster	Lowe	Alfonseca	28-53	5th	24.5
6-30	At Bal.	W	7-5		11	8	Edmondson	Mills	Mantei	29-53	5th	24.5
7-1	At Bal.	W	5-3		8	11	Hernandez	Smith	Powell	30-53	5th	24.5
7-2	At Bal.	L	3-5		9	10	Ponson	Fontenot	Benitez	30-54	5th	25.5
7-3	At Mon.	L	4-8		8	13	Vazquez	Sanchez		30-55	5th	26.5
7-4	At Mon.	W	3-2		9	7	Edmondson	Boskie	Alfonseca	31-55	5th	26.5
7-5	At Mon.	W	2-1		10	9	Meadows	C. Perez	Alfonseca	32-55	5th	26.5
7-9	Atl.	L	4-6		11	7	Smoltz	Hernandez	Ligtenberg	32-56	5th	27.5
7-10	Atl.	W	3-1		6	6	Sanchez	Neagle	Heredia	33-56	5th	26.5
7-11	Atl.	W	4-3		7	6	Mantei	Maddux		34-56	5th	25.5
7-12	Atl.	W	5-3		11	7	Meadows	Glavine	Alfonseca	35-56	5th	24.5
7-13	Mon.	W	8-7		11	13	Alfonseca	Telford		36-56	5th	24.0
7-14	Mon.	L	1-2		5	6	Hermanson	Hernandez	Urbina	36-57	5th	25.0
7-15	Mon.	L	5-9		11	16	C. Perez	Edmondson		36-58	5th	26.0
7-17	Chi.	L	1-6		5	11	Trachsel	Dempster		36-59	5th	27.5
7-18	Chi.	W	2-1		5	7	Meadows	Clark	Mantei	37-59	5th	26.5
7-19	Chi.	L	6-7	(12)	12	10	Mulholland	Stanifer	Beck	37-60	5th	27.5
7-20	Mil.	L	3-5		6	9	Karl	Hernandez	Wickman	37-61	5th	27.5
7-21	Mil.	L	4-6		8	10	Reyes	Alfonseca		37-62	5th	27.5
7-22	At Pit.	L	4-6		9	9	Van Poppel	Dempster	Christiansen	37-63	5th	28.5
7-23	At Pit.	L	1-9		12	14	Lieber	Meadows		37-64	5th	29.5
7-24†	At Phi.	L	4-6	(12)	9	8	Gomes	Alfonseca		37-65		
7-24‡	At Phi.	L	6-7	(12)	17	9	Leiter	Darensbourg		37-66	5th	31.0
7-25	At Phi.	W	5-4		9	8	Hernandez	Schilling	Mantei	38-66	5th	30.0
7-26	At Phi.	L	9-10		11	18	Leiter	Alfonseca		38-67	5th	31.0
7-27	At Hou.	L	1-9		6	14	Lima	Meadows		38-68	5th	32.0
7-28	At Hou.	L	3-7		10	8	Bergman	Ojala		38-69	5th	32.0
7-29	At Hou.	L	6-10		10	14	Schourek	Larkin	Elarton	38-70	5th	33.0
7-30	At Hou.	W	4-3		6	5	Hernandez	Reynolds		39-70	5th	33.0
7-31	Cin.	L	2-3		5	8	Tomko	Mantei	White	39-71	5th	33.0
8-1	Cin.	L	7-9	(10)	11	12	Hudek	Mantei		39-72	5th	34.0
8-2	Cin.	L	1-5		6	9	Reyes	Ojala	Graves	39-73	5th	35.0
8-3	Hou.	W	11-3		13	6	Larkin	Bergman	Mantei	40-73	5th	34.5
8-4	Hou.	L	5-9		13	13	Reynolds	Hernandez		40-74	5th	35.5
8-5	Hou.	W	5-3		9	6	Sanchez	Hampton	Mantei	41-74	5th	34.5
8-7	At S.D.	L	3-6	(13)	11	12	Sanders	Speier		41-75	5th	36.0
8-9	At S.D.	L	5-6		7	8	Hitchcock	Larkin	Hoffman	41-76	5th	37.5
8-10	At S.D.	W	3-2		7	5	Hernandez	Brown		42-76	5th	37.0
8-11	At L.A.	W	8-6		17	9	Sanchez	Dreifort		43-76	5th	36.0
8-12	At L.A.	W	3-2		9	7	Stanifer	Osuna	Mantei	44-76	5th	35.0
8-13	At L.A.	L	2-5		6	9	Bohanon	Meadows	Shaw	44-77	5th	36.0
8-14	At S.F.	L	0-10		6	10	Gardner	Larkin		44-78	5th	37.0
8-15	At S.F.	L	3-4	(10)	10	12	Mesa	Mantei		44-79	5th	38.0
8-16	At S.F.	L	2-3		11	9	Hershiser	Sanchez	Nen	44-80	5th	38.0
8-18	S.D.	L	5-7		13	11	Miceli	Alfonseca	Hoffman	44-81	5th	39.0
8-19	S.D.	W	6-0		10	11	Meadows	Hitchcock		45-81	5th	38.0
8-20	L.A.	L	1-2	(10)	7	4	Radinsky	Speier	Shaw	45-82	5th	38.0
8-21	L.A.	L	1-5		4	10	Park	Hernandez		45-83	5th	39.0
8-22	S.F.	L	4-5	(10)	6	8	Rodriguez	Edmondson	Nen	45-84	5th	40.0
8-23	S.F.	L	5-10		9	12	Rueter	Ojala		45-85	5th	41.0
8-24	S.F.	L	4-7		10	14	Rodriguez	Edmondson	Nen	45-86	5th	42.0
8-25	At St.L.	W	4-3		6	6	Medina	Osborne	Alfonseca	46-86	5th	41.0
8-26	At St.L.	W	7-6	(10)	10	14	Alfonseca	Acevedo		47-86	5th	41.0
8-27	At Cin.	L	3-12		5	15	Parris	Hernandez		47-87	5th	42.0
8-28	At Cin.	L	8-10		15	10	Sullivan	Stanifer	White	47-88	5th	42.0
8-29	At Cin.	L	5-7		10	13	Remlinger	Meadows	Graves	47-89	5th	43.0
8-30	At Cin.	L	7-14		10	13	Reyes	Medina		47-90	5th	43.0
8-31	St.L.	L	3-5		10	9	Oliver	Ojala	Acevedo	47-91	5th	43.0
9-1	St.L.	L	1-7		6	13	Morris	Hernandez		47-92	5th	44.0
9-2	St.L.	L	4-14		8	13	Mercker	Sanchez		47-93	5th	44.0
9-4	Mon.	L	0-8		3	11	Hermanson	Meadows		47-94	5th	44.0
9-5	Mon.	L	1-7		5	5	Thurman	Medina		47-95	5th	44.0
9-6	Mon.	W	6-2		7	9	Ojala	Pavano	Darensbourg	48-95	5th	44.0
9-7	At Col.	L	10-15		16	21	Leskanic	Ludwick		48-96	5th	44.0
9-8	At Col.	L	10-11		13	18	McElroy	Mantei		48-97	5th	44.0
9-9	At Col.	L	8-9		9	15	McElroy	Speier		48-98	5th	44.0

Date	Opp.	Res.	Score	(inn.*)	Hits	Opp. hits	Winning pitcher	Losing pitcher	Save	Record	Pos.	GB
9-10	At Col.	L	1-3		2	10	Kile	Medina		48-99	5th	45.0
9-11	At Atl.	L	2-8	10	9		Smoltz	Ojala		48-100	5th	46.0
9-12	At Atl.	L	2-4	6	7		Chen	Hernandez	Ligtenberg	48-101	5th	47.0
9-13	At Atl.	W	6-5	6	6		Sanchez	O. Perez	Mantei	49-101	5th	46.0
9-14	At Mon.	L	2-4	5	6		Hermanson	Meadows	Urbina	49-102	5th	47.0
9-15	At Mon.	W	7-4	11	11		Medina	Thurman		50-102	5th	47.0
9-16	At Mon.	L	2-3	9	5		Kline	Ojala		50-103	5th	48.0
9-18	At N.Y.	W	7-6	14	11		Edmondson	J. Franco	Mantei	51-103	5th	47.5
9-19	At N.Y.	L	3-4	9	7		Yoshii	Sanchez	J. Franco	51-104	5th	48.5
9-20	At N.Y.	L	0-5	5	10		Leiter	Meadows		51-105	5th	49.5
9-22	Atl.	L	1-4	7	8		Millwood	Medina	Ligtenberg	51-106	5th	50.5
9-23	Atl.	L	0-11	3	19		Smoltz	Ojala		51-107	5th	51.5
9-26†	Phi.	W	4-3	(10)	9	7	Alfonseca	Perez		52-107		
9-26‡	Phi.	W	1-0	(13)	6	6	Stanifer	Bottalico		53-107	5th	51.5
9-27†	Phi.	W	6-5		9	15	Meadows	Green	Alfonseca	54-107		
9-27‡	Phi.	L	3-7		10	12	Loewer	Medina		54-108	5th	52

Monthly records: March (1-0), April (8-18), May (8-20), June (12-15), July (10-18), August (8-20), September (7-17).
*Innings, if other than nine. †First game of doubleheader. ‡Second game of doubleheader.

1999 SEASON *Florida Marlins*

HIGHLIGHTS

High point: On August 26 in St. Louis, the Marlins trailed the Cardinals 6-0 heading into the top of the ninth, and manager Jim Leyland had been ejected. But Florida rallied to tie the game with four home runs in the ninth and Randy Knorr won the game with an RBI double in the top of the 10th.

Low point: It was midnight, May 15, when the official word came that Gary Sheffield, Bobby Bonilla, Charles Johnson and Jim Eisenreich had all been traded to the Dodgers for Mike Piazza and Todd Zeile (both of whom were soon to be shipped out themselves).

Turning point: On September 9, Dave Dombrowski, who was all but assured of the Dodgers' G.M. job, accepted an offer to stay with the Marlins. Prospective new owner John Henry had convinced Dombrowski that he would be buying the team and getting it pointed in the right direction again.

Most valuable player: Left fielder Cliff Floyd hit .282 with 22 home runs and 90 RBIs. More important for the injury-prone Floyd, however, was that he played in 153 games.

Most valuable pitcher: Livan Hernandez was 10-12 with a 4.72 ERA, but he made 33 starts, pitched 234.1 innings, and completed nine games.

Most improved player: Righthander Matt Mantei didn't make the team out of spring training. But once he got called up in May, he posted nine saves in 12 chances with a 2.96 ERA, 63 strikeouts and just 23 walks in 54.2 innings.

Most pleasant surprise: Lefthander Jesus Sanchez began the season in the bullpen, but when Leyland slid him into the rotation in April, he never left. The rookie dazzled opponents with his surprisingly quick fastball, his slider and his knee-buckling curve.

Biggest disappointment: Catcher Gregg Zaun finally got the chance to be a starting catcher in the majors. Well, Zaun finished the season with a .188 batting

average, and he didn't make up for it with good defense.

Key injuries: Second baseman Craig Counsell missed the final two months after having his jaw broken by a pitch on August 3. Shortstop Edgar Renteria finished his season with a nagging knee injury that kept him out of most of the team's September games. Third baseman Bobby Bonilla began the season on the disabled list, recovering from offseason wrist and ankle surgeries. Righthander Alex Fernandez missed the entire season while recovering from rotator cuff surgery.

Notable: The Marlins' 54-108 mark shattered the record for the worst defending World Series champion ever. The previous record was held by the 1991 Cincinnati Reds, who finished 74-88.

—DAN GRAZIANO

RECORDS

1998 regular-season record: 54-108 (5th in N.L. East); 31-50 at home; 23-58 on road; 21-27 vs. N.L. East; 12-42 vs. Central; 13-31 vs. West; 8-8 vs. A.L.; 11-25 vs. lefthanded starters; 43-83 vs. righthanded starters; 47-83 on grass; 7-25 on turf; 19-30 in daytime; 35-78 at night; 31-29 in one-run games; 7-14 in extra-inning games; 1-1 in doubleheaders.

Team record past five years: 344-400 (.462, ranks 12th in league in that span).

TEAM LEADERS

Batting average: Edgar Renteria (.282).
At-bats: Cliff Floyd (588).
Runs: Cliff Floyd (85).
Hits: Cliff Floyd (166).
Total bases: Cliff Floyd (283).
Doubles: Cliff Floyd (45).
Triples: Todd Dunwoody, Mark Kotsay (7).
Home runs: Cliff Floyd (22).
Runs batted in: Cliff Floyd (90).
Stolen bases: Edgar Renteria (41).

Slugging percentage: Cliff Floyd (.481).
On-base percentage: Edgar Renteria (.347).
Wins: Brian Meadows (11).
Earned-run average: Jesus Sanchez (4.47).
Complete games: Livan Hernandez (9).
Shutouts: None.
Saves: Matt Mantei (9).
Innings pitched: Livan Hernandez (234.1).
Strikeouts: Livan Hernandez (162).

GAMES BY POSITION

Catcher: Gregg Zaun 88, Mike Redmond 37, Charles Johnson 31, Randy Knorr 15, Mike Piazza 4.
First base: Derrek Lee 132, Ryan Jackson 44, Jim Eisenreich 10, Brian Daubach 4, Mark Kotsay 3, John Roskos 1.
Second base: Craig Counsell 104, Luis Castillo 44, Dave Berg 27, Gregg Zaun 1.
Third base: Todd Zeile 65, Kevin Orie 48, Bobby Bonilla 26, Dave Berg 25, John Wehner 8, Josh Booty 7, Kevin Millar 2.
Shortstop: Edgar Renteria 130, Alex Gonzalez 25, Dave Berg 17.
Outfield: Cliff Floyd 146, Mark Kotsay 145, Todd Dunwoody 111, John Cangelosi 45, Gary Sheffield 37, Ryan Jackson 32, John Wehner 23, Preston Wilson 11, Jim Eisenreich 8.
Designated hitter: Ryan Jackson 5, Cliff Floyd 3, John Cangelosi 1.

TOP DRAFT CHOICES

1. **Chip Ambres,** OF, West Brook H.S., Beaumont, Tex.
2. **Derek Wathan,** SS, U. of Oklahoma
3. **David Callahan,** 1B, Palm Bay (Fla.) H.S.
4. **Heath Honeycutt,** 3B, Georgia Tech
5. **Matt Padgett,** OF, Clemson University
6. **Phill Lowery,** LHP, Arizona State Univ.
7. **Ryan Harber,** LHP, Butler University
8. **Marc Sauer,** RHP, Bishop Eustace H.S., Gloucester, N.J.
9. **Mike Trussell,** RHP, Menchville H.S., Newport News, Va.
10. **Chris Heck,** LHP, St. Joseph's (Pa.) U.

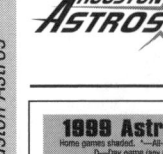

HOUSTON ASTROS
NATIONAL LEAGUE CENTRAL DIVISION

1999 Astros Schedule
Home games shaded. *—All-Star Game at Fenway Park (Boston).
D—Day game (any game starting before 5 p.m.).

April

SUN	MON	TUE	WED	THU	FRI	SAT
				1	2	3
4	5	6 CUB	7 CUB	8 CUB	9 MIL	10 MIL
11 D MIL	D 12	13 SF	14 SF	15 D SF	16 STL	17 STL
18 D STL	D 19	20 CUB	21 D CUB	22 D CUB	23 CIN	24 D CIN
25 D CIN	ARI	27 ARI	28 ARI	29 D ARI	30 FLA	

May

SUN	MON	TUE	WED	THU	FRI	SAT
						1 FLA
2 D FLA	D 3 NYM	4 NYM	5 NYM	6	7 D MON	8 MON
9 MON	D 10 PIT	11 PIT	12 PIT	13	14 SF	15 SF
16 SF	17	18 LA	19 LA	20 LA	21 SF	22 D SF
23 SF	24 COL	25 COL	26 COL	27 D COL	28 PIT	29 PIT
30 D PIT	31					

June

SUN	MON	TUE	WED	THU	FRI	SAT
		1 MIL	2 MIL	3 D MIL	4 MIN	5 MIN
6 MIN	D 7 CWS	8 CWS	9 CWS	10	11 SD	12 SD
13 D SD	D 14 ATL	15 ATL	16 ATL	17 ATL	18 MON	19 MON
20 D MON	D 21 STL	22 STL	23 STL	24 CIN	25 CIN	26 D CIN
27 D CIN	28	29 STL	30 STL			

July

SUN	MON	TUE	WED	THU	FRI	SAT
				1 STL	2 CIN	3 CIN
4 CIN	D 5 CIN	D 6 ARI	7 ARI	8 ARI	9 KC	10 KC
11 KC	D 12	13 *	14	15 DET	16 DET	17 D DET
18 D CLE	19 CLE	20 CLE	21 ARI	22 ARI	23 SD	24 D SD
25 D SD	26 COL	27 COL	28 COL	29 D COL	30 SD	31 D SD

August

SUN	MON	TUE	WED	THU	FRI	SAT
1 D SD	D 2	3 LA	4 LA	5 LA	6 D 7 CUB	D CUB
8 CUB	9 ATL	10 ATL	11 ATL	12	13 PIT	14 PIT
15 D PIT	D 16 MIL	17 MIL	18 MIL	19 D MIL	20 FLA	21 FLA
22 D FLA	D 23 NYM	24 NYM	25 NYM	26	27 FLA	28 FLA
29 D FLA	D 30 NYM	31 NYM				

September

SUN	MON	TUE	WED	THU	FRI	SAT
			1 NYM	2	3 D MON	4 MON
5 MON	D 6 PHI	7 PHI	8 PHI	9	10 D CUB	11 D CUB
12 CUB	D 13 PHI	14 PHI	15 D PHI	16	17 STL	18 D STL
19 D STL	D 20 PIT	21 PIT	22	23	24 MIL	25 MIL
26 D MIL	D 27	28 CIN	29 CIN	30		

October

SUN	MON	TUE	WED	THU	FRI	SAT
					1 LA	2 LA
3 D LA	D 4	5	6	7	8	9

1999 SEASON
CLUB DIRECTORY

Chairman and chief executive officer
Drayton McLane Jr.

President
Tal Smith

Senior vice president, business operations
Bob McClaren

General manager
Gerry Hunsicker

Assistant general manager/player development
Tim Purpura

Special assistant to the general manager for international scouting
Andros Reiner

Director of scouting
David Lakey

Director of baseball administration
Barry Waters

Vice president of marketing
Pam Gardner

Director of media relations
Rob Matwick

Assistant director of media relations
Alyson Footer

Assistant director of media relations
Warren Miller

Director of broadcasting and promotions
Jamie Hildreth

Director of community development
Marian Harper

Director of ticket sales and services
John Sorrentino

Controller
Robert McBurnett

Professional scouts
Leo Labossiere, Kimball Crossley, Fred Nelson, Joe Pittman, Tom Romenesko, Scipio Spinks, Lynwood Stallings.

Major league scouts
Stan Benjamin, Walt Matthews, Tom Mooney, Bob Skinner, Paul Weaver, Tom Wiedenbauer.

Full-time scouts
Bob Blair, Ralph Bratton, Chuck Carlson, Gerry Craft, Doug Deutsch, David Henderson, Dan Huston, Brian Keegan, Bill Kelso, Bob King, Mike Maggart, Jerry Marik, Mel Nelson, Joe Robinson, Tad Slowik, Steve Smith, Tim Tolman, Gene Wellman

Foreign scouts
Ricardo Aponte, Jesus Aristimuno, Sergio A. Beltre, Rafael Cariel, Alexis Corro, Mario Gonzalez, Julio Linares, Omar Lopez, Ramon Morales, Oscar Padron, Guillermo Ramirez, Rafael Ramirez, Wolfgang Ramos, Anibal Reluz, Adriano Rodriguez, Dr. Lester Storey, Pablo Torrealba, Calixto Vargas, Mark Van Zanten

MINOR LEAGUE AFFILIATES

Class	Team	League	Manager
AAA	New Orleans	Pacific Coast	Tony Pena
AA	Jackson	Texas	Jim Pankovits
A	Kissimmee	Florida State	Manny Acta
A	Michigan	Midwest	Al Pedrique
A	Auburn	New York-Pennsylvania	Lyle Yates
Rookie	Gulf Coast Astros	Gulf Coast	Brad Wellman

BROADCAST INFORMATION

Radio: KILT-AM (610); KXYZ-AM (1320, Spanish language).
TV: KTXH-TV (Channel 20).
Cable TV: Fox Sports Southwest.

SPRING TRAINING

Ballpark (city): Osceola County Stadium (Kissimmee, Fla.).
Ticket information: 407-839-3900.

SPRING TRAINING ROSTER

Manager—Larry Dierker (49).
Coaches—Jose Cruz (25), Mike Cubbage (24), Matt Galante (8), Tom McCraw (16), Vern Ruhle (48), John Tamargo.

No.	PITCHERS	B/T	Ht./Wt.	Born	1998 clubs
38	Bergman, Sean	R/R	6-4/225	4-11-70	Houston
51	Cabrera, Jose	R/R	6-0/160	3-24-72	New Orleans, Houston
	Crow, Dean	L/R	6-4/215	8-21-72	Toledo, Detroit
50	Elarton, Scott	R/R	6-7/240	2-23-76	New Orleans, Houston
23	Grzanich, Mike	R/R	6-1/180	8-24-72	New Orleans, Houston, Kissimmee
10	Hampton, Mike	R/L	5-10/180	9-9-72	Houston
19	Henry, Doug	R/R	6-4/205	12-10-63	Houston
45	Holt, Chris	R/R	6-4/205	9-18-71	Kissimmee
42	Lima, Jose	R/R	6-2/205	9-30-72	Houston
	McKnight, Tony	R/R	6-5/205	6-29-77	Kissimmee
46	Miller, Trever	R/L	6-4/195	5-29-73	Houston
	Miller, Wade	R/R	6-2/185	9-13-76	Jackson
	Powell, Brian	R/R	6-2/205	10-10-73	Toledo, Detroit, Jacksonville
39	Powell, Jay	R/R	6-4/225	1-19-72	Florida, Houston
37	Reynolds, Shane	R/R	6-3/210	3-26-68	Houston
	Root, Derek	L/L	6-5/215	5-26-75	Kissimmee, New Orleans, Jackson
55	Sikorski, Brian	R/R	6-1/190	7-27-73	New Orleans, Jackson
13	Wagner, Billy	L/L	5-11/180	7-25-71	Houston, Jackson

No.	CATCHERS	B/T	Ht./Wt.	Born	1998 clubs
	Bako, Paul	L/R	6-2/205	6-20-72	Toledo, Detroit
20	Eusebio, Tony	R/R	6-2/210	4-27-67	Houston
4	Meluskey, Mitch	B/R	6-0/185	9-18-73	New Orleans, Houston

No.	INFIELDERS	B/T	Ht./Wt.	Born	1998 clubs
5	Bagwell, Jeff	R/R	6-0/195	5-27-68	Houston
7	Biggio, Craig	R/R	5-11/180	12-14-65	Houston
27	Bogar, Timothy	R/R	6-2/198	10-28-66	Houston
29	Caminiti, Ken	B/R	6-0/200	4-21-63	San Diego
12	Gutierrez, Ricky	R/R	6-1/175	5-23-70	Houston
63	Hernandez, Carlos	R/R	5-9/175	12-12-75	New Orleans
36	Howell, Jack	L/R	6-0/190	8-18-61	Houston
19	Johnson, Russ	R/R	5-10/180	2-22-73	New Orleans, Houston
	Lugo, Julio	R/R	6-1/165	11-16-75	Kissimmee
28	Spiers, Bill	L/R	6-2/190	6-5-66	Houston
	Truby, Chris	R/R	6-2/190	12-9-73	Kissimmee, New Orleans, Jackson
	Villalobos, Carlos	R/R	6-0/170	4-5-74	Jacksonville
	Ward, Daryle	L/L	6-2/230	6-27-75	New Orleans, Houston

No.	OUTFIELDERS	B/T	Ht./Wt.	Born	1998 clubs
18	Alou, Moises	R/R	6-3/195	7-3-66	Houston
	Barker, Glen	R/R	5-10/180	5-10-71	Jacksonville
14	Bell, Derek	R/R	6-2/215	12-11-68	Houston
35	Clark, Dave	L/R	6-2/210	9-3-62	Houston
3	Everett, Carl	B/R	6-0/190	6-3-71	Houston
15	Hidalgo, Richard	R/R	6-3/190	7-2-75	Houston, New Orleans

BALLPARK INFORMATION

Ballpark (capacity, surface)
The Astrodome (54,313, artificial)

Address
P.O. Box 288
Houston, TX 77001-0288

Business phone
713-799-9500

Ticket information
713-799-9567

Ticket prices
$26 (star deck)
$21 (field level)
$18 (club level)
$17 (mezzanine)
$12 (loge level, mezzanine OF, sky box)
$8 (upper box)
$6 (upper reserved)
$4 (adult pavilion)
$1 (youth pavilion)

Field dimensions (from home plate)
To left field at foul line, 325 feet
To center field, 400 feet
To right field at foul line, 325 feet

First game played
April 12, 1965 (Phillies 2, Astros 0)

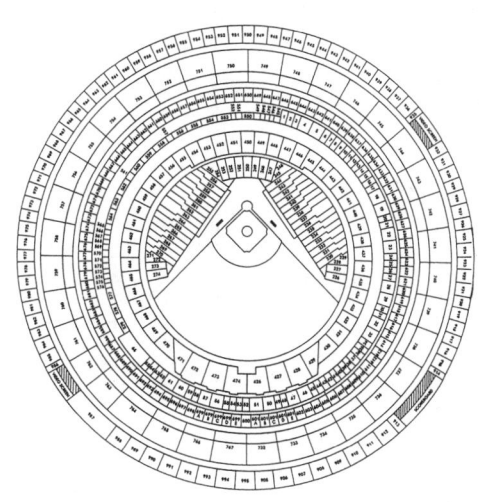

1998 REVIEW
DAY BY DAY

Date	Opp.	Res.	Score	(inn.*)	Hits	Opp. hits	Winning pitcher	Losing pitcher	Save	Record	Pos.	GB
3-31	S.F.	L	4-9	(13)	9	16	Johnstone	Nitkowski		0-1	T2nd	1.0
4-1	S.F.	W	7-6		8	11	Miller	Tavarez	Wagner	1-1	T3rd	0.5
4-2	S.F.	L	2-9		3	16	Rueter	Halama		1-2	T5th	1.5
4-3	Col.	W	15-2		18	6	Lima	Wright		2-2	T5th	1.0
4-4	Col.	L	3-5		12	9	Thompson	Bergman	DiPoto	2-3	6th	2.0
4-5	Col.	W	6-2		6	10	Reynolds	Kile		3-3	T4th	2.0
4-6	Col.	W	13-4		15	13	Hampton	Thomson		4-3	4th	2.0
4-7	At S.F.	L	4-5	(10)	5	10	Nen	Wagner		4-4	4th	2.5
4-8	At S.F.	W	6-3		12	10	Lima	Rueter	Wagner	5-4	4th	2.0
4-9	At S.F.	W	3-1		6	8	Bergman	Gardner	Nitkowski	6-4	4th	1.5
4-10	At L.A.	L	2-7		4	13	Martinez	Reynolds		6-5	4th	2.5
4-11	At L.A.	W	6-2		10	7	Hampton	Dreifort	Henry	7-5	4th	1.5
4-12	At L.A.	L	6-7	(10)	11	11	Osuna	Wagner		7-6	5th	1.5
4-13	At L.A.	L	1-3		6	5	Nomo	Lima	Radinsky	7-7	5th	2.0
4-15	At Cin.	L	1-4		3	8	Tomko	Reynolds	Shaw	7-8	T5th	2.0
4-16	At Cin.	W	7-4		12	11	Hampton	Weathers	Wagner	8-8	4th	2.0
4-17	Mon.	W	5-3		6	7	Halama	Hermanson	Wagner	9-8	4th	2.0
4-18	Mon.	W	4-3		8	9	Henry	Batista		10-8	4th	2.0
4-19	Mon.	L	4-5		10	11	Telford	Magnante	Urbina	10-9	4th	3.0
4-21	At N.Y.	W	6-0		13	7	Hampton	Reed		11-9	4th	3.0
4-22	At N.Y.	L	7-10		10	10	Cook	Henry		11-10	4th	3.0
4-24	At Mon.	W	8-4		10	11	Lima	Valdes		12-10	T3rd	3.5
4-25	At Mon.	W	4-3		9	10	Magnante	Urbina	Wagner	13-10	3rd	2.5
4-26	At Mon.	W	15-0		18	5	Bergman	Moore	Miller	14-10	T2nd	1.5
4-27	At N.Y.	W	4-3		7	10	Nitkowski	J. Franco	Wagner	15-10	T2nd	1.5
4-28	N.Y.	W	4-3	(10)	13	9	Magnante	Hudek		16-10	2nd	0.5
4-29	N.Y.	W	6-1		12	8	Lima	Mlicki		17-10	2nd	0.0
5-1	At Phi.	W	12-5		14	11	Reynolds	Beech		18-10	2nd	0.0
5-2	At Phi.	W	4-1		7	8	Hampton	Schilling	Wagner	19-10	1st	+1.0
5-3	At Phi.	L	3-5		7	10	Gomes	Bergman	Leiter	19-11	1st	+1.0
5-5	At Chi.	W	10-5		11	6	Lima	Clark	Nitkowski	20-11	1st	+2.5
5-6	At Chi.	L	0-2		1	8	Wood	Reynolds		20-12	1st	+1.5
5-8	At Mil.	L	1-4		6	8	Juden	Hampton	Jones	20-13	1st	+0.5
5-9	At Mil.	W	11-6		13	9	Schourek	Eldred		21-13	1st	+1.5
5-10	At Mil.	W	7-1		12	11	Lima	Woodard		22-13	1st	+2.5
5-11	Fla.	W	5-2		11	8	Reynolds	Hernandez	Wagner	23-13	1st	+3.5
5-12	Fla.	W	4-2		10	5	Bergman	Hammond	Wagner	24-13	1st	+3.5
5-13	Pit.	W	1-0		7	6	Hampton	Lieber	Wagner	25-13	1st	+3.5
5-14	Pit.	L	2-7		6	13	Silva	Schourek		25-14	1st	+2.5
5-15	Atl.	L	2-3		7	4	Neagle	Lima	Martinez	25-15	1st	+2.5
5-16	Atl.	W	3-2		7	6	Henry	Ligtenberg		26-15	1st	+2.5
5-17	Atl.	W	8-1		10	4	Bergman	Smoltz		27-15	1st	+2.5
5-18	Atl.	L	0-4		7	12	Glavine	Hampton		27-16	1st	+2.0
5-19	At Mon.	L	2-4		6	10	C. Perez	Schourek	Urbina	27-17	1st	+1.0
5-20	At Mon.	W	4-3		10	10	Henry	Telford	Wagner	28-17	1st	+1.0
5-21	At Mon.	W	6-0		13	5	Reynolds	Bennett		29-17	1st	+2.0
5-22	S.D.	L	6-9		10	16	Miceli	Nitkowski	Hoffman	29-18	1st	+2.0
5-23	S.D.	W	4-3		8	4	Miller	Miceli	Wagner	30-18	1st	+2.0
5-24	S.D.	W	5-2		8	9	Schourek	Hamilton	Wagner	31-18	1st	+3.0
5-25	L.A.	L	3-4	(10)	10	12	Bruske	Scanlan	Radinsky	31-19	1st	+3.0
5-26	L.A.	W	13-2		11	9	Reynolds	Valdes		32-19	1st	+3.5
5-27	L.A.	L	1-3		5	8	Dreifort	Bergman	Radinsky	32-20	1st	+3.5
5-29	At Col.	W	7-6		14	8	Hampton	Astacio	Wagner	33-20	1st	+4.0
5-30	At Col.	L	3-6		8	10	Thomson	Schourek	DiPoto	33-21	1st	+3.0
5-31	At Col.	L	5-7		10	12	McElroy	Henry		33-22	1st	+2.0
6-2	At S.D.	W	4-3		10	8	Reynolds	Reyes	Wagner	34-22	1st	+1.5
6-3	At S.D.	W	8-2		8	10	Bergman	Hamilton		35-22	1st	+1.5
6-4	At S.D.	L	1-5		8	6	Ashby	Hampton		35-23	1st	+1.0
6-5	K.C.	L	0-3		8	6	Belcher	Schourek	Montgomery	35-24	T1st	...
6-6	K.C.	W	6-0		9	5	Lima	Rosado		36-24	T1st	...
6-7	K.C.	W	7-1		11	8	Reynolds	Pittsley		37-24	T1st	...
6-8	At Det.	W	9-5		14	9	Henry	Jones		38-24	T1st	...
6-9	At Det.	W	5-3		10	9	Hampton	Jones	Wagner	39-24	1st	+1.0
6-10	At Det.	W	10-3		9	6	Schourek	Castillo		40-24	1st	+2.0
6-12	At Cin.	L	1-8		4	12	Remlinger	Lima		40-25	1st	+2.0
6-13	At Cin.	L	4-7		7	10	Klingenbeck	Reynolds	Shaw	40-26	1st	+1.0
6-14	At Cin.	W	6-3	(10)	11	11	Wagner	Shaw		41-26	1st	+2.0
6-15	At Cin.	W	13-2		17	6	Magnante	Tomko		42-26	1st	+2.0
6-16	St.L.	L	4-9		8	12	Acevedo	Schourek		42-27	1st	+2.0
6-17	St.L.	W	6-5		12	11	Nitkowski	Brantley		43-27	1st	+3.0
6-18	St.L.	L	6-7		13	9	Bottenfield	Reynolds	Croushore	43-28	1st	+2.0

Date	Opp.	Res.	Score	(inn.*)	Hits	Opp. hits	Winning pitcher	Losing pitcher	Save	Record	Pos.	GB
6-19	Cin.	W	4-2		10	9	Bergman	Winchester	Wagner	44-28	1st	+3.0
6-20	Cin.	W	9-8		12	10	Nitkowski	Krivda	Wagner	45-28	1st	+3.0
6-21	Cin.	W	3-1		8	7	Schourek	Harnisch	Magnante	46-28	1st	+4.0
6-22	Min.	L	3-5		4	10	Milton	Lima	Aguilera	46-29	1st	+4.0
6-23	Min.	W	9-0		13	5	Reynolds	Tewksbury		47-29	1st	+5.0
6-24	At Col.	L	6-8		6	14	Astacio	Bergman	Veres	47-30	1st	+5.0
6-25	At Col.	L	5-6	(12)	13	14	Leskanic	Magnante		47-31	1st	+5.0
6-26	At Cle.	L	2-4		5	11	Colon	Magnante	Jackson	47-32	1st	+5.0
6-27	At Cle.	W	9-5	(11)	15	12	Wagner	Mesa		48-32	1st	+5.0
6-28	At Cle.	W	12-3		16	9	Reynolds	Nagy	Nitkowski	49-32	1st	+6.0
6-30	Chi. (AL)	W	17-2		18	7	Bergman	Navarro		50-32	1st	+6.0
7-1	Chi. (AL)	W	10-4		12	9	Schourek	Parque		51-32	1st	+7.0
7-2	Chi. (AL)	L	3-4		5	7	Baldwin	Lima	Simas	51-33	1st	+6.0
7-3	Ari.	W	6-5		9	15	Reynolds	Benes	Wagner	52-33	1st	+6.0
7-4	Ari.	L	4-7		12	11	Anderson	Hampton		52-34	1st	+5.0
7-5	Ari.	W	5-2		10	8	Bergman	Blair	Wagner	53-34	1st	+5.0
7-9	At St.L.	W	5-4		10	7	Reynolds	Stottlemyre	Wagner	54-34	1st	+6.0
7-10	At St.L.	L	3-6		6	9	King	Nitkowski	Brantley	54-35	1st	+6.0
7-11	At St.L.	L	3-4	(11)	9	6	Painter	Wagner		54-36	1st	+5.0
7-12	At St.L.	L	4-6		9	10	Acevedo	Bergman	Croushore	54-37	1st	+4.0
7-13	At Ari.	L	3-5		5	7	Telemaco	Schourek	Olson	54-38	1st	+4.0
7-14	At Ari.	W	4-2		12	5	Reynolds	Daal	Wagner	55-38	1st	+4.0
7-15	At Ari.	L	8-9	(11)	12	15	Embree	Magnante		55-39	1st	+4.0
7-17	S.F.	W	10-7		17	10	Lima	Rueter		56-39	1st	+4.0
7-18	S.F.	W	7-2		10	7	Bergman	Darwin		57-39	1st	+5.0
7-19	S.F.	W	4-3	(12)	9	7	Henry	Nen		58-39	1st	+5.0
7-20	Col.	W	10-9		18	13	Henry	Veres		59-39	1st	+5.0
7-21	Col.	L	0-5		4	8	Brownson	Hampton		59-40	1st	+4.0
7-22	At L.A.	L	4-6		6	11	Bohanon	Lima	Shaw	59-41	1st	+3.0
7-23	At L.A.	W	8-6	(10)	11	10	Henry	Hall	Powell	60-41	1st	+3.0
7-24	At S.D.	W	2-1		7	5	Schourek	Hitchcock	Magnante	61-41	1st	+4.5
7-25	At S.D.	L	5-6		11	9	Langston	Reynolds	Hoffman	61-42	1st	+3.5
7-26	At S.D.	L	4-5	(10)	9	11	Wall	Magnante		61-43	1st	+2.5
7-27	Fla.	W	9-1		14	6	Lima	Meadows		62-43	1st	+2.5
7-28	Fla.	W	7-3		8	10	Bergman	Ojala		63-43	1st	+3.5
7-29	Fla.	W	10-6		14	10	Schourek	Larkin	Elarton	64-43	1st	+3.5
7-30	Fla.	L	3-4		5	6	Hernandez	Reynolds		64-44	1st	+3.5
7-31	At Pit.	W	7-4		10	12	Hampton	Cordova	Henry	65-44	1st	+3.5
8-1	At Pit.	W	2-1		10	5	Lima	Williams		66-44	1st	+3.5
8-2	At Pit.	W	6-2		10	6	R. Johnson	Christiansen	Elarton	67-44	1st	+4.5
8-3	At Fla.	L	3-11		6	13	Larkin	Bergman	Mantei	67-45	1st	+4.5
8-4	At Fla.	W	9-5		13	13	Reynolds	Hernandez		68-45	1st	+4.5
8-5	At Fla.	L	3-5		6	9	Sanchez	Hampton	Mantei	68-46	1st	+4.5
8-7	Phi.	W	9-0		9	5	R. Johnson	Welch		69-46	1st	+5.5
8-8	Phi.	W	7-6		15	10	Henry	Leiter		70-46	1st	+6.5
8-9	Phi.	W	11-2		12	8	Reynolds	Beech		71-46	1st	+7.5
8-10	Mil.	W	5-2		10	9	Elarton	Fox	Wagner	72-46	1st	+7.5
8-11	Mil.	W	6-5	(10)	14	11	Magnante	Plunk		73-46	1st	+8.5
8-12	Mil.	W	3-0		9	5	R. Johnson	Woodall		74-46	1st	+8.5
8-13	Mil.	W	6-2		7	5	Lima	Woodard		75-46	1st	+9.0
8-14	Chi.	L	4-6		8	11	Clark	Reynolds	Beck	75-47	1st	+8.0
8-15	Chi.	W	5-4	(11)	9	8	Wagner	Mulholland		76-47	1st	+9.0
8-16	Chi.	L	1-2	(11)	3	7	Karchner	Powell	Beck	76-48	1st	+8.0
8-17	At Phi.	L	0-4		4	9	Byrd	R. Johnson		76-49	1st	+7.5
8-18	At Phi.	W	8-2		10	4	Lima	Grace		77-49	1st	+7.5
8-19	At Phi.	W	4-3		11	7	Reynolds	Leiter	Wagner	78-49	1st	+8.5
8-20	At Mil.	L	5-6	(10)	17	13	Wickman	Magnante		78-50	1st	+7.5
8-21	At Mil.	W	5-2		9	8	Bergman	Pulsipher	Powell	79-50	1st	+7.5
8-22	At Chi.	W	8-3		15	5	R. Johnson	Wengert		80-50	1st	+8.5
8-23	At Chi.	W	13-3		15	11	Lima	Trachsel		81-50	1st	+9.5
8-24	At Chi.	W	12-3		11	9	Reynolds	Clark		82-50	1st	+10.5
8-25	Atl.	W	3-2		9	7	Hampton	Millwood	Wagner	83-50	1st	+11.5
8-26	Atl.	L	2-6		8	10	Smoltz	Bergman		83-51	1st	+10.5
8-28	Pit.	W	2-0		4	7	R. Johnson	Cordova		84-51	1st	+10.0
8-29	Pit.	W	6-3		12	9	Lima	Schmidt	Powell	85-51	1st	+11.0
8-30	Pit.	W	11-4		14	7	Reynolds	McCurry		86-51	1st	+11.0
8-31	At Atl.	W	4-3		8	8	Powell	Smoltz	Wagner	87-51	1st	+11.0
9-1	At Atl.	L	4-6		12	11	Neagle	Elarton	Ligtenberg	87-52	1st	+10.0
9-2	At Atl.	W	4-2		12	5	R. Johnson	Maddux	Wagner	88-52	1st	+10.0
9-4	At Ari.	L	1-3		7	8	Telemaco	Lima	Olson	88-53	1st	+9.0
9-5	At Ari.	W	6-5	(12)	10	13	Wagner	Embree		89-53	1st	+9.0
9-6	At Ari.	W	10-1		17	9	Hampton	Daal		90-53	1st	+10.0
9-7	Cin.	W	1-0		4	6	R. Johnson	Parris		91-53	1st	+11.0
9-8	Cin.	W	13-7		16	9	Bergman	Bere		92-53	1st	+12.0
9-9	Mil.	W	6-2		14	8	Lima	Woodard	Wagner	93-53	1st	+12.0

Date	Opp.	Res.	Score	(inn.*)	Hits	Opp. hits	Winning pitcher	Losing pitcher	Save	Record	Pos.	GB
9-10	Mil.	W	7-1		7	7	Reynolds	Karl		94-53	1st	+12.0
9-11	St.L.	W	8-2		14	8	Powell	Morris		95-53	1st	+13.0
9-12	St.L.	W	3-2		6	5	R. Johnson	Oliver	Wagner	96-53	1st	+13.0
9-13	St.L.	L	2-3		9	6	Mercker	Bergman	Acevedo	96-54	1st	+12.0
9-14	N.Y.	L	4-7	(13)	9	13	McMichael	Magnante	J. Franco	96-55	1st	+12.0
9-15†	N.Y.	W	6-5	(12)	13	11	Powell	Tam		97-55		
9-15‡	N.Y.	L	4-8		8	10	Leiter	Powell	Wendell	97-56	1st	+11.5
9-16	N.Y.	L	3-4	(11)	5	13	McMichael	Bergman	Wendell	97-57	1st	+10.5
9-18	At Pit.	W	5-2		14	5	R. Johnson	Dessens	Powell	98-57	1st	+11.0
9-19	At Pit.	L	1-7		8	10	Cordova	Lima		98-58	1st	+11.0
9-20	At Pit.	W	2-0		7	10	Reynolds	Schmidt	Wagner	99-58	1st	+11.0
9-22	At St.L.	L	0-4		5	4	Morris	Hampton		99-59	1st	+11.0
9-23	At St.L.	W	7-1		15	9	R. Johnson	Oliver		100-59	1st	+12.0
9-25	Chi.	W	6-2		11	5	Lima	Tapani		101-59	1st	+13.0
9-26	Chi.	L	2-3		7	11	Clark	Powell	Beck	101-60	1st	+12.0
9-27	Chi.	W	4-3	(11)	12	7	Elarton	Beck		102-60	1st	+13.0

Monthly records: March (0-1), April (17-9), May (16-12), June (17-10), July (15-12), August (22-7), September (15-9).
*Innings, if other than nine. †First game of doubleheader. ‡Second game of doubleheader.

HIGHLIGHTS

High point: The Astros began to have realistic expectations of reaching the World Series for the first time in franchise history on July 31, the day they traded three prospects to Seattle for dominant lefthanded pitcher Randy Johnson. Johnson compiled a 10-1 record with 116 strikeouts in 84.1 innings for the Astros.

Low point: Despite the best regular-season record in franchise history and a charged-up Big Unit for the playoffs, the Astros were bounced in the first round for the second year in a row.

Turning point: By outscoring the Cubs 33-9 during a three-game sweep at Wrigley Field, the Astros increased their N.L. Central lead to 10.5 games and all but locked up their second straight division title.

Most valuable player: It's a close call between Moises Alou and Craig Biggio, but Biggio gets the nod. He was the spark that ignited the explosive offense, hitting .325 with 20 homers, 88 RBIs, 51 doubles and 50 stolen bases.

Most valuable pitcher: Righthander Shane Reynolds was the horse from beginning to end, posting a 19-8 record with a 3.51 ERA in 233.1 innings. Reynolds may be one of the best-kept secrets in baseball.

Most improved player: Getting out of the pressure-packed environment of New York did wonders for center fielder Carl Everett, who enjoyed the finest year of his career. The switch-hitting outfielder hit .296, raising his average by 52 points.

Most pleasant surprise: The Astros had no intention of putting Jose Lima into the rotation when the club reported to spring training. But injuries to Chris Holt, Ramon Garcia and Pete Schourek left the team desperately in need of a starter. Lima took advantage of the opportunity, winning 16 games while walking just 32 batters in 233.1 innings.

Biggest disappointment: Lefthanded reliever Mike Magnante arguably was the most consistent performer in the Astros'

bullpen in 1997, but he was haunted by walks during the first half of 1998 and wasn't quite the same pitcher as the year before. Magnante was left off the post-season roster and won't be with the club in 1999.

Key injuries: Righthanded pitchers Holt and Garcia combined for 17 wins and 368 innings in 1997, but neither threw a pitch during the regular season in 1998. Righthanded reliever Jose Cabrera suffered an arm injury in April and never returned to action. First/third baseman Jack Howell missed most of the season because of a broken bone in his wrist.

Notable: The Astros won a club-record 102 games and claimed their third division title. . . . Larry Dierker was named N.L. Manager of the Year, and G.M. Gerry Hunsicker earned recognition as TSN's Executive of the Year.

—CARLTON THOMPSON

RECORDS

1998 regular-season record: 102-60 (1st in N.L. Central); 55-26 at home; 47-34 on road; 30-15 vs. East; 38-18 vs. N.L. Central; 24-23 vs. West; 10-4 vs. A.L.; 24-17 vs. lefthanded starters; 78-43 vs. righthanded starters; 30-27 on grass; 72-33 on turf; 31-20 in daytime; 71-40 at night; 30-18 in one-run games; 10-12 in extra-inning games; 0-0-1 in doubleheaders.

Team record past five years: 410-335 (.550, ranks 2nd in league in that span).

TEAM LEADERS

Batting average: Craig Biggio (.325).
At-bats: Craig Biggio (646).
Runs: Jeff Bagwell (124).
Hits: Craig Biggio (210).
Total bases: Moises Alou (340).
Doubles: Craig Biggio (51).
Triples: Moises Alou (5).
Home runs: Moises Alou (38).
Runs batted in: Moises Alou (124).
Stolen bases: Craig Biggio (50).
Slugging percentage: Moises Alou (.582).

On-base percentage: Jeff Bagwell (.424).
Wins: Shane Reynolds (19).
Earned-run average: Mike Hampton (3.36).
Complete games: Randy Johnson (4).
Shutouts: Randy Johnson (4).
Saves: Billy Wagner (30).
Innings pitched: Jose Lima, Shane Reynolds (233.1).
Strikeouts: Shane Reynolds (209).

GAMES BY POSITION

Catcher: Brad Ausmus 124, Tony Eusebio 54, Mitch Meluskey 3.
First base: Jeff Bagwell 147, J.R. Phillips 12, Jack Howell 10, Bill Spiers 7.
Second base: Craig Biggio 159, Tim Bogar 11, Bill Spiers 9, Russ Johnson 1.
Third base: Bill Spiers 99, Sean Berry 87, Tim Bogar 11, Russ Johnson 5, Jack Howell 2.
Shortstop: Ricky Gutierrez 141, Tim Bogar 55, Bill Spiers 2.
Outfield: Moises Alou 154, Derek Bell 154, Carl Everett 123, Richard Hidalgo 72, Dave Clark 22, J.R. Phillips 6, Pete Incaviglia 3, Ray Montgomery 2.
Designated hitter: Dave Clark 4, Moises Alou 1, Sean Berry 1, Craig Biggio 1, Tim Bogar 1.

TOP DRAFT CHOICES

1a. **Brad Lidge**, RHP, U. of Notre Dame
1b. None
1c. **Mike Nannini**, RHP, Green Valley H.S., Henderson, Nev.
2. None
3. **Brad Busbin**, RHP, Dr. Phillips H.S., Orlando, Fla.
4. **Jason Van Meetren**, OF, Bishop Gorman H.S., Las Vegas, Nev.
5. **Scott Barrett**, LHP, San Jacinto (Tex.) J.C.
6. **David Matranga**, SS, Pepperdine U.
7. **John Buck**, C, Taylorsville H.S., Salt Lake City, Utah
8. **Jesse Joyce**, 3B, Cal State L.A.
9. **Morgan Ensberg**, 3B, U. of Southern California
10. **Keith Ginter**, 2B, Texas Tech

LOS ANGELES DODGERS
NATIONAL LEAGUE WEST DIVISION

1999 Dodgers Schedule
Home games shaded. *—All-Star Game at Fenway Park (Boston).
D—Day game (any game starting before 5 p.m.).

April

SUN	MON	TUE	WED	THU	FRI	SAT
				1	2	3
4	5 D ARI	6 ARI	7 ARI	8 ARI	9 COL	10 D COL
11 D COL	12 ARI	13 ARI	14 ARI	15 ARI	16 SD	17 SD
18 SD	19 ATL	20 ATL	21 ATL	22	23 STL	24 STL
25 STL	26	27 MIL	28 MIL	29 D MIL	30 PHI	

May

SUN	MON	TUE	WED	THU	FRI	SAT
						1 PHI
2 PHI	3 D MON	4 MON	5 MON	6	7 FLA	8 FLA
9 FLA	10 D CUB	11 CUB	12 CUB	13	14 STL	15 STL
16 D STL	17	18 HOU	19 HOU	20 HOU	21 STL	22 STL
23 STL	24	25 CIN	26 CIN	27 CIN	28 D ATL	29 ATL
30 ATL	31 D PIT					

June

SUN	MON	TUE	WED	THU	FRI	SAT
		1 PIT	2 PIT	3	4 D ANA	5 D ANA
6 D OAK	7	8 TEX	9 TEX	10	11 OAK	12 D OAK
13 D OAK	14	15 PIT	16 PIT	17 PIT	18 PHI	19 D PHI
20 PHI	21	22 SD	23 SD	24 SD	25 SF	26 D SF
27 SF	28	29 SD	30 SD			

July

SUN	MON	TUE	WED	THU	FRI	SAT
				1 D SD	2 SF	3 D SF
4 SF	5 COL	6 COL	7 COL	8 COL	9 SEA	10 SEA
11 SEA	12	13	* 14	15 ANA	16 ANA	17 D ANA
18 PIT	19 PIT	20 D PIT	21 COL	22 D COL	23 ARI	24 ARI
25 ARI	26 CIN	27 CIN	28 CIN	29 CIN	30 ARI	31 ARI

August

SUN	MON	TUE	WED	THU	FRI	SAT
1 ARI	2	3 HOU	4 HOU	5	6 D NYM	7 NYM
8 NYM	9 NYM	10 MON	11 MON	12 D MON	13 D ATL	14 ATL
15 ATL	16 FLA	17 FLA	18 FLA	19	20 PHI	21 PHI
22 PHI	23 MIL	24 MIL	25 D MIL	26	27 CUB	28 D CUB
29 CUB	30 MIL	31 MIL				

September

SUN	MON	TUE	WED	THU	FRI	SAT
			1 D MIL	2	3 CUB	4 D CUB
5 CUB	6 D FLA	7 FLA	8 FLA	9	10 NYM	11 NYM
12 NYM	13 MON	14 MON	15 MON	16	17 COL	18 D COL
19 COL	20 SF	21 SF	22 SF	23 SF	24 SD	25 D SD
26 SD	27	28 SF	29 SF	30 D SF		

October

SUN	MON	TUE	WED	THU	FRI	SAT
					1 HOU	2 HOU
3 D HOU	4	5	6	7	8	9

1999 SEASON
CLUB DIRECTORY

Board of directors
Chase Carey, Peter Chernin, Bob Graziano, Sam Fernandez

President and CEO
Bob Graziano

Executive vice president and g.m.
Kevin Malone

Vice president
Tommy Lasorda

Vice president, communications
Tommy Hawkins

Vice president, marketing
Barry Stockhamer

Vice president, Campo Las Palmas
Ralph Avila

Director, stadium operations
Doug Duennes

Director, broadcasting and publications
Brent Shyer

Director, accounting and finance
Cristine Hurley

Director, community relations
Don Newcombe

Director, public affairs
Monique Brandon

Dir., management information services
Mike Mularky

Assistants to the general manager
Bill Geivett, Ed Creech

Asst. director, publicity/media relations
John Olguin

Asst. dir., publicity/baseball information
Shaun Rachau

Traveling secretary
Bill DeLury

Director, ticket operations
Debra Kay Duncan

Asst. secretary and general counsel
Santiago Fernandez

Club physicians
Dr. Frank W. Jobe, Dr. Michael F. Mellman, Dr. Herndon Harding

Assistant director of scouting
Matt Slater

Coordinator of minor league pro scouting
Terry Reynolds

Scouts
Julio Alcala, Eleodoro Arias, John Barr, Rick Birmingham, Gib Bodet, Florez Bolivar, Mike Brito, Ray Brown, Brian Cakebread, Jim Chapman, Dominick Christy, Bob Darwin, Juan Davalillo, Felix Feliz, Joe Ferrone, Juan Garcia, Jim Garland, George Genovese, Rafael Gonzalez, Carl Greene, Gene Grimaldi, Scott Groot, Mazimo Gross, Bob Hale, Mike Hankins, Art Harris, Julio Imbert, Henny Jenken, Hank Jones, Lon Joyce, John Kosciak, Jimmy Lester, Mike Leuzinger, Carl Loewenstine, Alexander Mata, Theodore Mata, Ed Mathes, Ken McGee, Dale McReynolds, Bump Merriweather, Camilo Pascual, Pablo Peguero, Luis Penalver, Ramon Perez, Tony Petek, Bill Pleis, Willie Powell, Silvano Quesada, Eddie Rodriguez, Jose Salado, Mark Sheehy, Chris Smith, Alan Tanner, Leon Taylor, Tom Thomas, Glen VanProyen, Peter Worboys, Jack Zduriencik

MINOR LEAGUE AFFILIATES

Class	Team	League	Manager
AAA	Albuquerque	Pacific Coast	Mike Scioscia
AA	San Antonio	Texas	Jim Johnson
A	San Bernardino	California	Rick Burleson
A	Vero Beach	Florida State	Alvaro Espinosa
A	Yakima	Northwest	Dino Ebel
Rookie	Great Falls	Pioneer	To be announced

BROADCAST INFORMATION

Radio: KXTA-AM (1150); KWKW-AM (1330, Spanish language).
TV: KTLA-TV (Channel 5); Fox Sports West.

SPRING TRAINING

Ballpark (city): Holman Stadium (Vero Beach, Fla.).
Ticket information: 561-569-6858.

SPRING TRAINING ROSTER

Manager—Davey Johnson.
Coaches—Rick Dempsey, Rick Down, Glenn Hoffman, Charlie Hough, Manny Mota, John Shelby, Jim Tracy.

No.	PITCHERS	B/T	Ht./Wt.	Born	1998 clubs
	Borbon, Pedro	L/L	6-1/205	11-15-67	Macon, Greenville
27	Brown, Kevin	R/R	6-4/200	3-14-65	San Diego
	Cadaret, Greg	L/L	6-3/215	2-27-62	Anaheim, Vancouver, Texas
37	Dreifort, Darren	R/R	6-2/211	5-3-72	Los Angeles
	Gagne, Eric	R/R	6-2/195	1-7-76	Vero Beach
	Galvez, Randy	R/R	6-2/165	7-26-78	Mexico City Red Devils
	Gooch, Arnold	R/R	6-2/210	11-12-76	Binghamton
60	Judd, Mike	R/R	6-1/217	6-30-75	Los Angeles, Albuquerque
67	Kubenka, Jeff	R/L	6-1/191	8-24-74	Los Angeles, San Antonio, Albuquerque
	Masaoka, Onan	R/L	6-0/188	10-27-77	San Antonio
75	Mills, Alan	B/R	6-1/195	10-18-66	Baltimore
38	Mlicki, Dave	R/R	6-4/205	6-8-68	New York N.L., Los Angeles
13	Osuna, Antonio	R/R	5-11/206	4-12-73	Los Angeles
61	Park, Chan Ho	R/R	6-2/204	6-30-73	Los Angeles
33	Perez, Carlos	L/L	6-3/210	1-14-71	Montreal, Gulf Coast Expos, Los Angeles
51	Rojas, Mel	R/R	5-11/212	12-10-66	New York N.L.
41	Shaw, Jeff	R/R	6-2/200	7-7-66	Cincinnati, Los Angeles
59	Valdes, Ismael	R/R	6-3/215	8-21-73	Los Angeles, Vero Beach, San Bernardino

No.	CATCHERS	B/T	Ht./Wt.	Born	1998 clubs
9	Hundley, Todd	B/R	5-11/199	5-27-69	St. Lucie, Gulf Coast Mets, Norfolk, New York N.L.
64	LoDuca, Paul	R/R	5-10/185	4-12-72	Los Angeles, Albuquerque
63	Pena, Angel	R/R	5-10/228	2-16-75	Los Angeles, San Antonio

No.	INFIELDERS	B/T	Ht./Wt.	Born	1998 clubs
29	Beltre, Adrian	R/R	5-11/170	4-7-78	San Antonio, Los Angeles
17	Castro, Juan	R/R	5-10/187	6-20-72	Los Angeles
3	Cora, Alex	L/R	6-0/180	10-18-75	Los Angeles, Albuquerque
8	Grudzielanek, Mark	R/R	6-1/185	6-30-70	Montreal, Los Angeles
	Hansen, Dave	L/R	6-0/195	11-24-68	Japan
23	Karros, Eric	R/R	6-4/226	11-4-67	San Bernardino, Los Angeles
14	Riggs, Adam	R/R	6-0/190	10-4-72	Albuquerque
10	Vizcaino, Jose	B/R	6-1/180	3-26-68	Los Angeles
26	Young, Eric	R/R	5-9/170	5-18-67	Los Angeles

No.	OUTFIELDERS	B/T	Ht./Wt.	Born	1998 clubs
66	Bocachica, Hiram	R/R	5-11/165	3-4-76	Harrisburg, Ottawa, Albuquerque
28	Hollandsworth, Todd	L/L	6-2/215	4-20-73	Los Angeles
47	Hubbard, Trenidad	R/R	5-9/185	5-11-66	Los Angeles, Albuquerque
43	Mondesi, Raul	R/R	5-11/215	3-12-71	Los Angeles
10	Sheffield, Gary	R/R	5-11/205	11-18-68	Florida, Los Angeles
22	White, Devon	B/R	6-2/190	12-29-62	Arizona

BALLPARK INFORMATION

Ballpark (capacity, surface)
Dodger Stadium (56,000, grass)
Address
1000 Elysian Park Ave.
Los Angeles, CA 90012
Business phone
323-224-1500
Ticket information
323-224-1448
Ticket prices
$16 (field box)
$13 (preferred reserve)
$12 (loge box)
$8 (reserve)
$6 (top deck, pavilion-adult)
$3 (top deck, pavilion, children)
Field dimensions (from home plate)
To left field at foul line, 330 feet
To center field, 395 feet
To right field at foul line, 330 feet
First game played
April 10, 1962 (Reds 6, Dodgers 3)

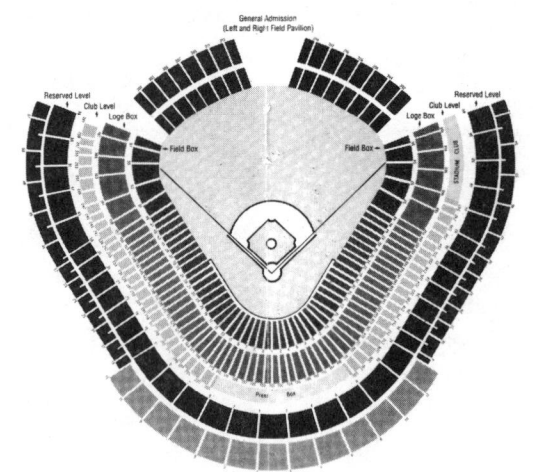

Date	Opp.	Res.	Score	(inn.*)	Hits	Opp. hits	Winning pitcher	Losing pitcher	Save	Record	Pos.	GB
3-31	At St.L.	L	0-6		3	13	Stottlemyre	Martinez		0-1	T4th	1.0
4-2	At St.L.	L	5-8	(12)	9	16	Acevedo	Lankford		0-2	T4th	2.5
4-3	At Cin.	L	3-6		7	6	Weathers	Hall	Shaw	0-3	T4th	2.5
4-4	At Cin.	L	1-3		3	8	Tomko	Valdes	Shaw	0-4	T4th	3.5
4-5	At Cin.	W	1-0		6	2	Martinez	Remlinger	Radinsky	1-4	4th	2.5
4-7	Ari.	W	9-1		13	8	Park	Blair		2-4	4th	2.5
4-8	Ari.	L	0-3		8	5	Anderson	Nomo	Rodriguez	2-5	4th	3.5
4-9	Ari.	W	7-2		10	10	Valdes	Suppan		3-5	4th	3.5
4-10	Hou.	W	7-2		13	4	Martinez	Reynolds		4-5	3rd	3.5
4-11	Hou.	L	2-6		7	10	Hampton	Dreifort	Henry	4-6	3rd	4.5
4-12	Hou.	W	7-6	(10)	11	11	Osuna	Wagner		5-6	3rd	4.5
4-13	Hou.	W	3-1		5	6	Nomo	Lima	Radinsky	6-6	3rd	4.5
4-14	At Col.	L	3-6		10	12	DeJean	Valdes	DiPoto	6-7	3rd	4.5
4-16	At Col.	W	4-3	(10)	7	7	Radinsky	DiPoto	Bruske	7-7	3rd	4.5
4-17	At Chi.	W	11-3		14	4	Park	Clark	Lankford	8-7	3rd	4.5
4-18	At Chi.	L	1-8		5	6	Wood	Nomo		8-8	3rd	5.5
4-19	At Chi.	L	1-2		6	9	Gonzalez	Valdes	Beck	8-9	3rd	6.0
4-21	At Mil.	L	2-5		9	5	Juden	Martinez		8-10	3rd	6.0
4-22	At Mil.	W	9-6		11	8	Osuna	Wickman	Radinsky	9-10	3rd	6.0
4-23	At Mil.	L	1-2		7	3	Mercedes	Nomo	Jones	9-11	3rd	7.0
4-24	Chi.	W	12-4		10	5	Valdes	Wood		10-11	2nd	6.0
4-25	Chi.	W	3-2		3	5	Guthrie	Gonzalez	Radinsky	11-11	2nd	5.0
4-26	Chi.	W	4-3	(12)	13	6	Clontz	Pisciotta		12-11	2nd	5.0
4-27	Mil.	L	2-3	(13)	10	10	Reyes	Lankford		12-12	3rd	5.0
4-28	Mil.	W	6-3		8	3	Nomo	Mercedes		13-12	3rd	5.0
4-30	At Pit.	W	14-6		19	14	Clontz	Dessens		14-12	2nd	5.0
5-1	At Pit.	L	4-5		9	9	Tabaka	Dreifort	Loiselle	14-13	2nd	5.0
5-2	At Pit.	W	5-4		12	8	Martinez	Lieber	Radinsky	15-13	2nd	5.0
5-3	At Pit.	W	10-5		13	8	Park	Silva		16-13	2nd	4.0
5-4	At Atl.	L	2-4		5	8	Millwood	Guthrie	Ligtenberg	16-14	2nd	5.0
5-5	At Atl.	L	3-8		7	11	Neagle	Valdes		16-15	3rd	6.0
5-6	At Atl.	L	0-7		7	10	Maddux	Dreifort		16-16	3rd	6.0
5-7	At Fla.	W	4-3		8	6	Martinez	Stanifer	Radinsky	17-16	3rd	5.0
5-8	At Fla.	L	6-12		7	15	Sanchez	Park		17-17	3rd	6.0
5-9	At Fla.	L	4-7		6	14	Larkin	Nomo		17-18	3rd	6.0
5-10	At Fla.	W	4-2		9	5	Valdes	Meadows	Radinsky	18-18	3rd	6.0
5-11	Phi.	L	2-5		5	15	Beech	Dreifort	Leiter	18-19	3rd	6.0
5-12	Phi.	L	3-5		11	12	Schilling	Radinsky	Leiter	18-20	3rd	6.5
5-13	Phi.	W	9-4		11	7	Park	Green		19-20	3rd	5.5
5-14	Phi.	L	0-4		2	9	Portugal	Nomo		19-21	3rd	7.0
5-15	Mon.	L	2-4		7	10	Batista	Valdes	Urbina	19-22	3rd	8.0
5-16	Mon.	W	9-4		11	6	Dreifort	Vazquez		20-22	3rd	8.0
5-17	Mon.	W	6-3		10	4	Martinez	Johnson	Radinsky	21-22	3rd	8.0
5-19	At Chi.	L	3-6		9	11	Trachsel	Park	Beck	21-23	3rd	8.0
5-20	At Chi.	L	0-5		3	10	Tapani	Nomo		21-24	3rd	8.5
5-21	At Chi.	W	7-3		12	8	Valdes	Adams	Osuna	22-24	3rd	7.5
5-22	At Ari.	W	5-0		10	6	Dreifort	Benes		23-24	3rd	7.5
5-23	At Ari.	W	7-1		14	2	Martinez	Anderson		24-24	3rd	6.5
5-24	At Ari.	L	5-8		9	9	Blair	Park	Olson	24-25	3rd	6.5
5-25	At Hou.	W	4-3	(10)	12	10	Bruske	Scanlan	Radinsky	25-25	3rd	5.5
5-26	At Hou.	L	2-13		9	11	Reynolds	Valdes		25-26	3rd	6.5
5-27	At Hou.	W	3-1		8	5	Dreifort	Bergman	Radinsky	26-26	3rd	6.5
5-28	Cin.	W	4-3		11	11	Bruske	Belinda		27-26	3rd	6.0
5-29	Cin.	L	4-8	(12)	9	15	Shaw	Reyes		27-27	3rd	6.0
5-30	Cin.	L	3-7		9	12	Harnisch	Nomo		27-28	3rd	7.0
5-31	Cin.	L	5-6		6	11	Graves	Radinsky	Shaw	27-29	3rd	8.0
6-2	St.L.	L	4-7		8	11	Mercker	Dreifort	Brantley	27-30	3rd	8.5
6-3	St.L.	W	7-4		11	8	Martinez	Petkovsek	Radinsky	28-30	3rd	7.5
6-4	St.L.	W	3-2		9	7	Radinsky	Brantley		29-30	3rd	7.5
6-5	At Sea.	L	0-4		9	9	Swift	Valdes		29-31	3rd	7.5
6-6	At Sea.	W	10-6		10	10	Bruske	Wells	Osuna	30-31	3rd	7.5
6-7	At Sea.	W	7-4		12	13	Dreifort	Moyer	Osuna	31-31	3rd	7.5
6-8	Oak.	L	3-7		5	8	Stein	Martinez		31-32	3rd	8.5
6-9	Oak.	W	5-1		9	7	Park	Haynes		32-32	3rd	8.5
6-10	Oak.	W	1-0		3	2	Valdes	Rogers		33-32	3rd	7.5
6-12	Col.	W	2-1		5	6	Mlicki	Kile	McMichael	34-32	3rd	7.5
6-13	Col.	L	2-4		5	8	Wright	Dreifort	DiPoto	34-33	3rd	8.5
6-14	Col.	L	2-3	(12)	6	9	DeJean	Radinsky	McElroy	34-34	3rd	9.5
6-16	At S.D.	L	6-10		11	10	Brown	Park	Hoffman	34-35	3rd	10.5
6-17	At S.D.	L	2-3	(12)	6	8	Hoffman	Reyes		34-36	3rd	11.5
6-18	At Col.	W	5-0		7	7	Mlicki	Wright		35-36	3rd	11.5

Date	Opp.	Res.	Score	(inn.*)	Hits	Opp. hits	Winning pitcher	Losing pitcher	Save	Record	Pos.	GB
6-19	At Col.	W	4-3	(10)	12	8	Osuna	DiPoto		36-36	3rd	11.5
6-20	At Col.	L	6-7		10	11	Munoz	Reyes	Veres	36-37	3rd	11.5
6-21	At Col.	L	6-11		10	12	Jones	Park		36-38	3rd	12.5
6-22	At Ana.	L	5-6		9	9	Percival	McMichael		36-39	3rd	13.5
6-23	At Ana.	L	4-6		13	11	Harris	Brunson	DeLucia	36-40	3rd	13.5
6-24	Ana.	W	6-5	(11)	12	11	Osuna	Cadaret		37-40	3rd	12.5
6-25	Ana.	L	2-3		5	3	Sparks	Reyes	Percival	37-41	3rd	13.5
6-26	Pit.	W	5-2		11	11	Park	Loaiza	Osuna	38-41	3rd	13.5
6-27	Pit.	W	2-0		5	1	Valdes	Cordova		39-41	3rd	13.5
6-28	Pit.	L	4-6		6	8	Williams	Radinsky	Loiselle	39-42	3rd	13.5
6-30	At Tex.	W	4-1		8	3	Dreifort	Helling	Osuna	40-42	3rd	12.5
7-1	At Tex.	W	7-5		11	9	Radinsky	Wetteland	Osuna	41-42	3rd	12.5
7-2	At Tex.	W	4-1		11	7	Park	Oliver	Radinsky	42-42	3rd	11.5
7-3	At S.F.	L	3-6		5	12	Hershiser	Valdes	Nen	42-43	3rd	12.5
7-4	At S.F.	W	9-5		12	10	Mlicki	Gardner		43-43	3rd	12.5
7-5	At S.F.	L	0-3		8	8	Estes	Dreifort	Nen	43-44	3rd	13.5
7-9	S.D.	W	12-3		14	8	Park	Langston		44-44	3rd	12.5
7-10	S.D.	W	6-2		11	6	Osuna	Miceli		45-44	3rd	11.5
7-11	S.D.	L	1-4		4	7	Ashby	Valdes	Hoffman	45-45	3rd	12.5
7-12	S.D.	L	3-6		9	7	Hamilton	Bohanon	Hoffman	45-46	3rd	13.5
7-13	S.F.	W	7-5		12	9	Mlicki	Darwin	Shaw	46-46	3rd	12.5
7-14	S.F.	W	2-1		5	6	Radinsky	Johnstone		47-46	3rd	12.5
7-15	S.F.	L	3-5		7	8	Hershiser	Dreifort	Nen	47-47	3rd	13.5
7-16	At St.L.	W	8-2		15	6	Valdes	Mercker		48-47	3rd	13.0
7-17	At St.L.	L	1-4		5	5	Acevedo	Bohanon	Croushore	48-48	3rd	14.0
7-18	At St.L.	W	10-8		11	11	Guthrie	Brantley	Shaw	49-48	3rd	14.0
7-19	At St.L.	L	4-5		9	11	Petkovsek	Radinsky		49-49	3rd	15.0
7-20	Cin.	W	2-0		6	1	Dreifort	Parris	Shaw	50-49	3rd	14.0
7-21	Cin.	W	4-2		7	6	Valdes	Tomko	Shaw	51-49	3rd	14.0
7-22	Hou.	W	6-4		11	6	Bohanon	Lima	Shaw	52-49	3rd	14.0
7-23	Hou.	L	6-8	(10)	10	11	Henry	Hall	Powell	52-50	3rd	15.0
7-24	Ari.	W	3-1		9	3	Park	Telemaco	Shaw	53-50	3rd	14.0
7-25	Ari.	L	3-5		8	7	Daal	Dreifort	Olson	53-51	3rd	15.0
7-26	Ari.	W	5-3		9	9	Valdes	Benes	Shaw	54-51	3rd	14.0
7-28	At Phi.	W	7-3		9	11	Bohanon	Green		55-51	3rd	14.0
7-29	At Phi.	L	3-8		11	13	Loewer	Mlicki		55-52	3rd	14.0
7-30	At Phi.	W	3-1		7	2	Park	Beech	Shaw	56-52	3rd	14.0
7-31	At N.Y.	W	4-3		11	10	Osuna	J. Franco	Shaw	57-52	3rd	14.0
8-1	At N.Y.	L	1-2		6	5	Reed	Shaw		57-53	3rd	14.0
8-2	At N.Y.	L	3-9		5	10	Reynoso	Bohanon		57-54	3rd	15.0
8-3	At N.Y.	W	8-5		11	10	Mlicki	McMichael	Shaw	58-54	3rd	14.0
8-4	At Mon.	L	4-5	(10)	10	10	Kline	Hall		58-55	3rd	15.0
8-5	At Mon.	L	1-5		8	6	Pavano	Dreifort	Urbina	58-56	3rd	16.0
8-6	At Mon.	L	0-9		2	10	Powell	Perez		58-57	3rd	16.0
8-7	Pit.	W	3-1		8	2	Bohanon	Van Poppel	Shaw	59-57	3rd	16.0
8-8	Pit.	W	2-1		11	4	Osuna	Christiansen		60-57	3rd	15.5
8-9	Pit.	L	1-2		5	6	Peters	Park	Rincon	60-58	3rd	16.5
8-11	Fla.	L	6-8		9	17	Sanchez	Dreifort		60-59	3rd	17.0
8-12	Fla.	L	2-3		7	9	Stanifer	Osuna	Mantei	60-60	3rd	17.0
8-13	Fla.	W	5-2		9	6	Bohanon	Meadows	Shaw	61-60	3rd	17.0
8-14	Atl.	L	2-5		8	10	Millwood	Mlicki	Ligtenberg	61-61	3rd	18.0
8-15	Atl.	L	3-5		8	12	Smoltz	Park	Ligtenberg	61-62	3rd	18.5
8-16	Atl.	W	1-0		7	2	Radinsky	Neagle	Shaw	62-62	3rd	18.0
8-18	At Pit.	L	4-6		12	10	Schmidt	Perez	Loiselle	62-63	3rd	19.0
8-19	At Pit.	L	5-6		6	7	Williams	Bohanon	Christiansen	62-64	3rd	19.0
8-20	At Fla.	W	2-1	(10)	4	7	Radinsky	Speier	Shaw	63-64	3rd	19.0
8-21	At Fla.	W	5-1		10	4	Park	Hernandez		64-64	3rd	18.0
8-22	At Atl.	L	5-7		10	8	Neagle	Dreifort	Ligtenberg	64-65	3rd	18.0
8-23	At Atl.	L	7-12		11	15	Maddux	Perez		64-66	3rd	19.0
8-24	At Atl.	L	3-4		10	9	Glavine	Shaw	Ligtenberg	64-67	3rd	20.0
8-25	Mon.	W	4-3		6	10	Mlicki	Thurman	Shaw	65-67	3rd	20.0
8-26	Mon.	W	4-3		9	6	Shaw	Kline		66-67	3rd	20.0
8-27	Mon.	W	10-9		11	12	Dreifort	Powell	Radinsky	67-67	3rd	20.0
8-28	N.Y.	L	4-5	(10)	13	8	Cook	Shaw	J. Franco	67-68	3rd	21.0
8-29	N.Y.	L	3-4		6	12	Leiter	Shaw	J. Franco	67-69	3rd	21.0
8-30	N.Y.	W	4-2		9	8	Mlicki	Yoshii		68-69	3rd	20.0
8-31	N.Y.	L	3-8		9	14	Reed	Park		68-70	3rd	21.0
9-1	Phi.	W	3-2		4	9	Valdes	Byrd	Shaw	69-70	3rd	21.0
9-2	Phi.	W	6-0		11	2	Perez	Green		70-70	3rd	20.0
9-4	S.F.	W	8-5		10	10	Dreifort	Estes	Shaw	71-70	3rd	19.0
9-5	S.F.	W	6-3		11	4	Park	Hershiser		72-70	3rd	19.0
9-6	S.F.	L	2-6		5	7	Gardner	Bohanon		72-71	3rd	19.0
9-7	At Ari.	L	2-4		6	7	Benes	Mlicki	Olson	72-72	3rd	19.0
9-8	At Ari.	W	6-5	(11)	17	11	Kubenka	Embree	Shaw	73-72	3rd	18.0
9-9	At Ari.	W	6-2		8	9	Perez	Telemaco		74-72	3rd	18.0

Date	Opp.	Res.	Score	(inn.*)	Hits	Opp. hits	Winning pitcher	Losing pitcher	Save	Record	Pos.	GB
-10	At S.D.	W	4-3		3	5	Park	Brown	Shaw	75-72	3rd	17.0
-11	At S.D.	L	0-1		7	7	Hamilton	Bohanon	Hoffman	75-73	3rd	18.0
-12	At S.D.	L	7-8		10	7	Sanders	Maloney	Hoffman	75-74	3rd	19.0
-13	At S.D.	W	5-4	(10)	6	8	Weaver	Wall	Shaw	76-74	3rd	18.0
-14	Col.	W	4-1		9	7	Perez	Jones		77-74	3rd	18.0
-15	Col.	L	4-5		12	7	Kile	Park	DiPoto	77-75	3rd	18.0
-16	Col.	W	2-0		6	8	Bohanon	Wright	Shaw	78-75	3rd	17.0
-18	At S.F.	L	3-4		7	9	Tavarez	Radinsky	Nen	78-76	3rd	16.5
-19	At S.F.	L	4-18		12	19	Ortiz	Valdes		78-77	3rd	17.5
-20	At S.F.	W	1-0		2	4	Perez	Estes		79-77	3rd	16.5
-22	S.D.	W	3-2		6	8	Park	Hamilton	Shaw	80-77	3rd	15.5
-23	S.D.	L	2-3		8	8	Ashby	Bohanon	Hoffman	80-78	3rd	16.5
-24	Mil.	W	4-1		3	5	Weaver	Fox	Shaw	81-78	3rd	16.0
-25	Mil.	W	3-2		5	9	Valdes	Woodall	Shaw	82-78	3rd	15.0
-26	Mil.	L	1-6		7	9	Karl	Perez		82-79	3rd	15.0
-27	Mil.	W	2-1		7	10	Park	Pulsipher	Shaw	83-79	3rd	15.0

Monthly records: March (0-1), April (14-11), May (13-17), June (13-13), July (17-10), August (11-18), September (15-9). *Innings, if other than nine. †First game of doubleheader. ‡Second game of doubleheader.

HIGHLIGHTS

High point: When the Dodgers acquired Gary Sheffield, Bobby Bonilla, Charles Johnson, Jim Eisenreich and Manuel Barrios for Mike Piazza and Todd Zeile on May 15, they trailed the N.L. West-leading Padres by eight games. The move seemingly put the Dodgers in contention for the wild-card berth.

Low point: On August 6, the Expos routed the Dodgers, 9-0, completing a three-game sweep. The Dodgers were defeated by rookie pitchers in two games and fell 16 games behind the Padres after going 4-6 on a 10-game, three-city East Coast trip. They never recovered.

Turning point: The Dodgers squandered a 3-0 lead in the eighth inning August 24 in Atlanta and lost, 4-3, when closer Jeff Shaw gave up back-to-back home runs in the bottom of the inning. That completed the Braves' three-game sweep and effectively ended the Dodgers' hopes of a wild-card berth.

Most valuable player: First baseman Eric Karros, who sat out the first 21 games, batted .296 with 23 home runs and 87 RBIs. Karros was the only everyday player to bat at least .300 with runners in scoring position.

Most valuable pitcher: Chan Ho Park went 15-9 with a 3.71 ERA, striking out 191 in 220.2 innings. In only his second season as a starter, Park led the club in wins, strikeouts and innings.

Most improved player: Juan Castro batted only .195, but he made significant strides at the plate, improving on his 1997 average of .147 and hitting his first two big-league home runs. The middle infielder was dazzling defensively.

Most pleasant surprise: Hard-working rookie outfielder Matt Luke provided a spark off the bench, batting .236 with 12 homers and 34 RBIs. He provided left-handed power, something the Dodgers sorely needed.

Biggest disappointment: Outfielder Roger Cedeno entered spring training as the starting center fielder but lost the job because of repeated mental lapses and poor baserunning. He batted .242 with two home runs and 17 RBIs as his role diminished throughout the season. The Dodgers finally gave up on Cedeno during the offseason, including him in a trade with the Mets.

Key injuries: Ramon Martinez, who declined surgery after suffering a rotator cuff tear in 1997, suffered an increased rotator cuff tear and a cartilage tear last season. Martinez missed the remainder of the season after undergoing surgery June 30. He is not expected to pitch again until the second half of the 1999 season—at the earliest. Second baseman Eric Young was sidelined 45 games because of leg and foot injuries. Outfielder Gary Sheffield missed the final 25 games because of a severely sprained ankle.

Notable: Outfielder Trenidad Hubbard was the only member of the club's opening day lineup who was not traded or lost for the season because of an injury.

—JASON REID

RECORDS

1998 regular-season record: 83-79 (3rd in N.L. West); 48-33 at home; 35-46 on road; 19-25 vs. East; 31-26 vs. Central; 25-23 vs. N.L. West; 8-5 vs. A.L.; 19-19 vs. lefthanded starters; 64-60 vs. righthanded starters; 73-68 on grass; 10-11 on turf; 21-23 in daytime; 62-56 at night; 30-24 in one-run games; 9-8 in extra-inning games; 0-0 in doubleheaders.

Team record past five years: 397-347 (.534, ranks 3rd in league in that span).

TEAM LEADERS

Batting average: Eric Karros (.296).
At-bats: Raul Mondesi (580).
Runs: Raul Mondesi (85).
Hits: Raul Mondesi (162).
Total bases: Raul Mondesi (288).
Doubles: Raul Mondesi (26).
Triples: Raul Mondesi (5).
Home runs: Raul Mondesi (30).
Runs batted in: Raul Mondesi (90).
Stolen bases: Eric Young (42).
Slugging percentage: Raul Mondesi (.497).

On-base percentage: Eric Young (.355).
Wins: Chan Ho Park (15).
Earned-run average: Chan Ho Park (3.71).
Complete games: Carlos Perez (4).
Shutouts: Carlos Perez, Ismael Valdes (2).
Saves: Jeff Shaw (25).
Innings pitched: Chan Ho Park (220.2).
Strikeouts: Chan Ho Park (191).

GAMES BY POSITION

Catcher: Charles Johnson 100, Mike Piazza 37, Tom Prince 32, Paul LoDuca 4, Angel Pena 4.
First base: Eric Karros 136, Paul Konerko 23, Matt Luke 18, Jim Eisenreich 9, Todd Zeile 1.
Second base: Eric Young 114, Juan Castro 38, Wilton Guerrero 32, Alex Cora 4, Mike Metcalfe 1.
Third base: Adrian Beltre 74, Bobby Bonilla 59, Todd Zeile 40, Juan Castro 12, Paul Konerko 11, Trenidad Hubbard 1.
Shortstop: Jose Vizcaino 66, Mark Grudzielanek 51, Juan Castro 47, Alex Cora 21, Wilton Guerrero 14, Adrian Beltre 2.
Outfield: Raul Mondesi 148, Gary Sheffield 89, Trenidad Hubbard 81, Roger Cedeno 77, Matt Luke 63, Todd Hollandsworth 51, Thomas Howard 29, Jim Eisenreich 24, Bobby Bonilla 12, Paul Konerko 11, Wilton Guerrero 7, Mike Devereaux 5, Damon Hollins 4.
Designated hitter: Paul Konerko 3, Jim Eisenreich 2, Eric Karros 2, Thomas Howard 1, Eric Young 1.

TOP DRAFT CHOICES

1. **Bubba Crosby,** OF, Rice University
2. **Mike Fischer,** RHP, U. of S. Alabama
3. **Alex Santos,** RHP, University of Miami
4. **Eric Riggs,** SS, U. of Central Florida
5. **Scott Proctor,** RHP, Florida State U.
6. **Ryan Moskau,** RHP-1B, U. of Arizona
7. **David Ross,** C, University of Florida
8. **Thomari Story-Hardin,** 1B, El Cerrito H.S., Richmond, Calif.
9. **Joel Williams,** RHP, Yoncalla (Ore.) H.S.
10. **Lance Caraccioli,** LHP, Northeast Louisiana University

MILWAUKEE BREWERS
NATIONAL LEAGUE CENTRAL DIVISION

1999 Brewers Schedule
Home games shaded. *—All-Star Game at Fenway Park (Boston).
D—Day game (any game starting before 5 p.m.).

April

SUN	MON	TUE	WED	THU	FRI	SAT
				1	2	3
4	5 D	6	7 STL	8 D STL	9 HOU	10 HOU
11 D HOU	12	13 STL	14 MON	15 D MON	16 D CUB	17 D CUB
18 D CUB	19 STL	20	21 D STL	22	23 PIT	24 D PIT
25 D PIT	26	27 LA	28 LA	29 D LA	30 ARI	

May

SUN	MON	TUE	WED	THU	FRI	SAT
						1 ARI
2 D ARI	3 FLA	4 FLA	5 FLA	6 D	7 SF	8 D SF
9 D SF	10	11 CIN	12 CIN	13	14 FLA	15 FLA
16 D FLA	17 NYM	18 NYM	19 NYM	20 NYM	21 MON	22 MON
23 MON	24 ATL	25 ATL	26 ATL	27 ATL	28 SD	29 SD
30 D SD	31 D SD					

June

SUN	MON	TUE	WED	THU	FRI	SAT
		1 HOU	2 HOU	3 D HOU	4 COL	5 COL
6 COL	7 D	8 CLE	9 CLE	10 CLE	11 MIN	12 MIN
13 D MIN	14 CUB	15 CUB	16 D CUB	17 CIN	18 CIN	19 CIN
20 D CIN	21 SF	22 SF	23 D SF	24	25 PIT	26 PIT
27 D PIT	28	29 CUB	30 D CUB			

July

SUN	MON	TUE	WED	THU	FRI	SAT
				1 D CUB	2 D PIT	3 PIT
4 PIT	5 D PHI	6 PHI	7 PHI	8	9 DET	10 DET
11 D DET	12	13 *	14	15 KC	16 KC	17 KC
18 D CWS	19 CWS	20 CWS	21 PHI	22 PHI	23 FLA	24 FLA
25 FLA	26 ATL	27 ATL	28 ATL	29	30 MON	31 MON

August

SUN	MON	TUE	WED	THU	FRI	SAT
1 MON	2 NYM	3 NYM	4	5	6 CIN	7 CIN
8 D CIN	9 COL	10 COL	11 D COL	12	13 ARI	14 ARI
15 ARI	16 HOU	17 HOU	18 HOU	19 D HOU	20 D SF	21 D SF
22 D SF	23 LA	24 LA	25 D LA	26 D SD	27 SD	28 SD
29 D SD	30 LA	31 LA				

September

SUN	MON	TUE	WED	THU	FRI	SAT
		1 D LA	2	3 STL	4 STL	5 D
5 D STL	6	7 ARI	8 ARI	9 ARI	10 COL	11 D COL
12 COL	13 STL	14 STL	15 STL	16	17 CUB	18 D CUB
19 CUB	20 PHI	21 PHI	22 PHI	23 PHI	24 HOU	25 HOU
26 D HOU	27	28 PIT	29 PIT	30 PIT		

October

SUN	MON	TUE	WED	THU	FRI	SAT
					1 CIN	2 CIN
3 D CIN	4	5	6	7	8	9

1999 SEASON
CLUB DIRECTORY

President, chief executive officer
Wendy Selig-Prieb

Sr. vice president, baseball operations
Sal Bando

Vice president & general counsel
Tom Gausden

Assistant general counsel
Eugene (Pepi) Randolph

V.p., new ballpark development
Michael Bucek

Vice president, stadium operations
Scott Jenkins

Vice president, corporate affairs
Laurel Prieb

Vice president, finance
Paul Baniel

Vice president, ticket sales
Bob Voight

Director, community relations
Michael Downs

Director, event services
Steve Ethier

Director, grounds
Gary Vandenberg

Director, media relations
Jon Greenberg

Director, player development
Cecil Cooper

Director of Brewers Gold Club
Mike Harlan

Director of publications
Mario Ziino

Director of ticket operations
John Barnes

Traveling secretary
Dan Larrea

Trainers
John Adam
Al Price

Strength and conditioning coach
John Rewolinski

Team physicians
Dr. Dennis Sullivan
Dr. Drew Palin

Scouting director
Ken Califano

Pro. scouting and special assignments
Larry Haney
Al Monchak
Chuck Tanner

Special assignments
Felix Delgado
Walter Youse

Midwest supervisor/crosschecker
Fred Beene

Southeast supervisor/crosschecker
Russ Bove

West coast supervisor/crosschecker
Kevin Christman

Northeast supervisor/crosschecker
Ron Rizzi

Southwest supervisor/crosschecker
Ric Wilson

International supervisor
Epy Guerrero

Scouts
Walter Boggen, Jeff Brookens, Domingo Carrasquel, Rich Chiles, Steve Connelly, Dick Fanning, Mike Farrell, Dick Foster, Danny Garcia, Mike Gibbons, Manolo Hernandez, Elvio Jimenez, Brian Johnson, Harvey Kuenn Jr., John Logan, Demie Mainieri, Alex Morales, Douglas Reynolds, Corey Rodriguez, Bruce Seid, Bob Sloan, Jonathan Story, Tom Tanous, John Viney, Red Whitsett, David Young

MINOR LEAGUE AFFILIATES

Class	Team	League	Manager
AAA	Louisville	International	Gary Allenson
AA	Huntsville	Southern	Darrell Evans
A	Stockton	California	Bernie Moncallo
A	Beloit	Midwest	Don Money
Rookie	Helena	Pioneer	Carlos Lezcano
Rookie	Ogden	Pioneer	Jon Pont

BROADCAST INFORMATION

Radio: WTMJ-AM (620).
TV: WCGV-TV (Channel 24).
Cable TV: Midwest Sports Channel.

SPRING TRAINING

Ballpark (city): Maryvale Baseball Park (Maryvale, Ariz.).
Ticket information: 602-784-4444.

SPRING TRAINING ROSTER

Manager—Phil Garner (3).
Coaches—Bill Campbell, Bill Castro (35), Jim Lefebvre, Doug Mansolino (38), Bob Melvin.

No.	PITCHERS	B/T	Ht./Wt.	Born	1998 clubs
52	Borowski, Joe	R/R	6-2/225	5-4-71	Columbus, New York A.L.
13	D'Amico, Jeff	R/R	6-7/250	12-27-75	Milwaukee
	De Los Santos, Valerio	L/L	6-2/180	9-6-75	El Paso, Milwaukee, Louisville
21	Eldred, Cal	R/R	6-4/237	11-24-67	Milwaukee
	Estrada, Horacio	L/L	6-0/160	10-19-75	El Paso, Louisville
40	Fox, Chad	R/R	6-3/190	9-3-70	Milwaukee, Beloit
42	Karl, Scott	L/L	6-2/206	8-9-71	Milwaukee
57	Mullins, Greg	L/L	5-10/160	12-13-71	Louisville, Milwaukee
28	Myers, Mike	L/L	6-4/205	6-26-69	Milwaukee
	Passini, Brian	L/L	6-3/195	1-24-75	Stockton, El Paso
29	Plunk, Eric	R/R	6-6/220	9-3-63	Cleveland, Milwaukee
46	Pulsipher, Bill	L/L	6-3/200	10-9-73	Norfolk, New York N.L., Milwaukee
47	Reyes, Al	R/R	6-1/206	4-10-71	Milwaukee, Louisville
	Roque, Rafael	L/L	6-4/185	1-1-72	El Paso, Louisville, Milwaukee
49	Weathers, Dave	R/R	6-3/220	9-25-69	Cincinnati, Milwaukee
27	Wickman, Bob	R/R	6-1/212	2-6-69	Milwaukee
48	Woodall, Brad	B/L	6-0/175	6-25-69	Louisville, Milwaukee
37	Woodard, Steve	L/R	6-4/236	5-15-75	Milwaukee

No.	CATCHERS	B/T	Ht./Wt.	Born	1998 clubs
34	Greene, Charlie	R/R	6-2/190	1-23-71	Rochester, Baltimore
33	Hughes, Bobby	R/R	6-4/237	3-10-71	Milwaukee
7	Nilsson, David	L/R	6-3/229	12-14-69	Beloit, El Paso, Milwaukee

No.	INFIELDERS	B/T	Ht./Wt.	Born	1998 clubs
	Barker, Kevin	R/R	6-3/205	7-26-75	El Paso, Louisville
11	Belliard, Ron	R/R	5-8/180	7-4-76	Louisville, Milwaukee
	Berry, Sean	R/R	5-11/200	3-22-66	Houston
26	Cirillo, Jeff	R/R	6-1/193	9-23-69	Milwaukee
6	Collier, Lou	R/R	5-10/183	8-21-73	Pittsburgh, Lynchburg
8	Loretta, Mark	R/R	6-0/180	8-14-71	Milwaukee
	Perez, Santiago	B/R	6-2/150	12-30-75	El Paso, Louisville
2	Valentin, Jose	L/R	5-10/173	10-12-69	Milwaukee
1	Vina, Fernando	L/R	5-9/170	4-16-69	Milwaukee

No.	OUTFIELDERS	B/T	Ht./Wt.	Born	1998 clubs
25	Banks, Brian	B/R	6-3/200	9-28-70	Louisville, Milwaukee
	Becker, Rich	L/L	5-10/193	2-1-72	New York N.L., Baltimore
20	Burnitz, Jeromy	L/R	6-0/205	4-15-69	Milwaukee
	Green, Chad	R/R	5-10/180	6-28-75	Stockton, El Paso
9	Grissom, Marquis	R/R	5-11/190	4-17-67	Milwaukee
	Iapoce, Anthony	B/L	5-10/175	8-23-73	El Paso
	Jenkins, Geoffrey	L/R	6-1/200	7-21-74	Louisville, Milwaukee
	Krause, Scott	R/R	6-1/187	8-16-73	Louisville
	Martinez, Greg	B/R	5-10/170	1-27-72	Milwaukee, Louisville
25	Ochoa, Alex	R/R	6-0/195	3-29-72	Minnesota

BALLPARK INFORMATION

Ballpark (capacity, surface)
County Stadium (53,192, grass)

Address
County Stadium
P.O. Box 3099
Milwaukee, WI 53201-3099

Business phone
414-933-4114

Ticket information
414-933-9000, 800-933-7890

Ticket prices
$25 (mezzanine diamond box)
$20 (lower box)
$14 (upper box, lower grandstand)
$8 (upper grandstand)
$7 (general admission)
$5 (bleachers)

Field dimensions (from home plate)
To left field at foul line, 315 feet
To center field, 402 feet
To right field at foul line, 315 feet

First game played
April 7, 1970 (Angels 12, Brewers 0)

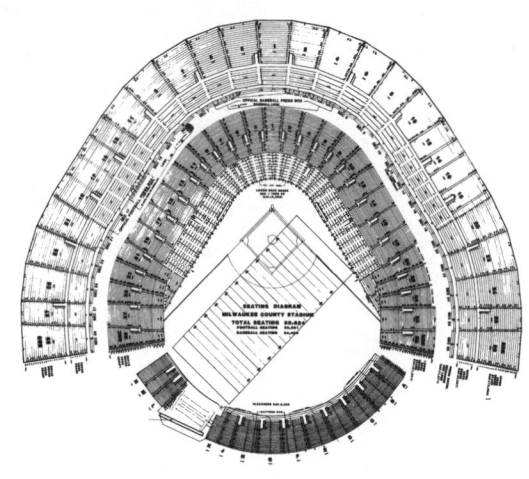

1999 SEASON *Milwaukee Brewers*

Date	Opp.	Res.	Score	(inn.*)	Hits	Opp. hits	Winning pitcher	Losing pitcher	Save	Record	Pos.	GB
3-31	At Atl.	L	1-2		7	8	Ligtenberg	Wickman		0-1	T2nd	1.0
4-2	At Atl.	W	8-6	(11)	14	11	Myers	Butler		1-1	4th	1.0
4-3	At Fla.	W	7-1		8	7	Woodard	Ludwick		2-1	T2nd	0.5
4-4	At Fla.	W	6-2		15	9	Juden	Meadows		3-1	T2nd	0.5
4-5	At Fla.	W	5-2		8	10	Reyes	Hernandez	Jones	4-1	2nd	0.5
4-6	At Fla.	W	8-5		11	8	Woodard	Heredia	Jones	5-1	2nd	0.5
4-7	Mon.	W	6-4		12	8	Karl	Hermanson	Jones	6-1	1st	+0.5
4-9	Mon.	L	5-6		6	14	Telford	Wickman	Urbina	6-2	T2nd	0.5
4-10	N.Y.	W	5-3		7	8	Juden	Mlicki	Jones	7-2	2nd	0.5
4-11	N.Y.	L	1-2		6	5	Cook	Wickman	J. Franco	7-3	T2nd	0.5
4-12	N.Y.	L	4-6		8	8	Wendell	Wagner	Rojas	7-4	T2nd	0.5
4-14	At Mon.	W	7-4		10	9	Karl	Vazquez		8-4	1st	+0.5
4-15	At Mon.	L	3-4		6	8	Moore	Juden	Urbina	8-5	T1st	...
4-16	At Mon.	W	5-3	(14)	17	9	Jones	Bennett		9-5	1st	+0.5
4-17	S.F.	W	5-2		7	5	Mercedes	Estes	Jones	10-5	1st	+0.5
4-18	S.F.	W	3-1		6	7	Wagner	Hershiser	Jones	11-5	1st	+0.5
4-19	S.F.	W	3-2	(12)	11	11	Wickman	Johnstone		12-5	1st	+0.5
4-21	L.A.	W	5-2		5	9	Juden	Martinez		13-5	1st	+0.5
4-22	L.A.	L	6-9		8	11	Osuna	Wickman	Radinsky	13-6	1st	+0.5
4-23	L.A.	W	2-1		3	7	Mercedes	Nomo	Jones	14-6	1st	+1.5
4-24	At S.F.	W	7-5		9	9	Karl	Hershiser	Jones	15-6	1st	+2.5
4-25	At S.F.	L	1-2		3	4	Rueter	Wagner	Nen	15-7	1st	+1.5
4-26	At S.F.	L	7-8		15	12	Reed	Jones		15-8	1st	+1.5
4-27	At L.A.	W	3-2	(13)	10	10	Reyes	Lankford		16-8	1st	+1.5
4-28	At L.A.	L	3-6		3	8	Nomo	Mercedes		16-9	1st	+0.5
5-1	Cin.	W	5-2		10	8	Karl	Remlinger	Jones	17-9	1st	+0.0
5-2	Cin.	L	5-8		10	13	White	Fox	Shaw	17-10	2nd	1.0
5-3	Cin.	L	3-5		8	10	Tomko	Eldred	Shaw	17-11	2nd	1.0
5-4	S.D.	L	5-13		14	18	Hitchcock	Mercedes	Wengert	17-12	2nd	1.5
5-5	S.D.	L	4-13		12	11	Smith	Wagner		17-13	2nd	2.5
5-6	S.D.	W	3-2		12	8	Jones	Reyes		18-13	2nd	1.5
5-8	Hou.	W	4-1		8	6	Juden	Hampton	Jones	19-13	2nd	0.5
5-9	Hou.	L	6-11		9	13	Schourek	Eldred		19-14	2nd	1.5
5-10	Hou.	L	1-7		11	12	Lima	Woodard		19-15	2nd	2.5
5-11	At St.L.	L	0-7		2	10	Stottlemyre	Karl		19-16	2nd	3.5
5-12	At St.L.	L	5-6	(10)	11	12	Busby	Jones		19-17	T3rd	4.5
5-13	At Ari.	W	8-3		14	7	Juden	Blair	Wickman	20-17	3rd	4.5
5-14	At Ari.	L	1-4		4	6	Springer	Eldred	Olson	20-18	3rd	4.5
5-15	At Col.	W	8-5		16	9	Woodard	Kile	Myers	21-18	3rd	3.5
5-16	At Col.	W	7-5		10	10	Karl	Ritz	Jones	22-18	3rd	3.5
5-17	At Col.	L	1-2		7	7	Wright	Woodall	DiPoto	22-19	3rd	4.5
5-18	At Col.	L	5-8		7	11	Astacio	Juden	DiPoto	22-20	3rd	4.5
5-19	S.F.	W	9-6		11	13	Jones	Poole		23-20	3rd	3.5
5-20	S.F.	L	2-4		7	14	Hershiser	Woodard	Nen	23-21	T3rd	4.5
5-21	S.F.	L	1-8		2	17	Rueter	Karl		23-22	T3rd	5.5
5-22	At N.Y.	L	2-3		6	4	Reed	Woodall	J. Franco	23-23	4th	5.5
5-23	At N.Y.	L	0-3		4	11	Leiter	Juden		23-24	4th	6.5
5-24	At N.Y.	L	3-8		10	15	Jones	Eldred		23-25	4th	7.5
5-26	Pit.	W	3-2		10	6	Myers	Loiselle		24-25	4th	7.0
5-27	Pit.	W	3-2	(10)	11	6	Woodall	Rincon		25-25	4th	6.0
5-29	Fla.	W	4-3	(11)	10	10	Wickman	Powell		26-25	4th	6.0
5-30	Fla.	W	12-4		16	6	Eldred	Fontenot		27-25	4th	5.0
5-31	Fla.	W	7-6		7	11	Woodall	Alfonseca	Wickman	28-25	3rd	4.0
6-1	Atl.	L	2-5		5	11	Maddux	Woodard		28-26	3rd	4.5
6-2	Atl.	L	0-9		12	12	Martinez	Wagner		28-27	4th	5.5
6-3	Atl.	L	2-5		8	4	Glavine	Juden	Wohlers	28-28	4th	6.5
6-5	Det.	W	7-3		9	9	Eldred	Castillo	Wickman	29-28	3rd	5.0
6-6	Det.	L	3-9		10	16	Florie	Karl		29-29	4th	6.0
6-7	Det.	L	1-4		3	7	Thompson	Woodard		29-30	4th	7.0
6-8	At K.C.	L	7-8		17	10	Rapp	Juden	Montgomery	29-31	4th	8.0
6-9	At K.C.	W	6-3	(10)	8	13	Wickman	Montgomery	Jones	30-31	4th	8.0
6-10	At K.C.	W	9-6	(15)	11	16	Patrick	Pichardo		31-31	4th	8.0
6-12	At Pit.	W	4-2		9	7	Karl	Cordova	Wickman	32-31	3rd	7.0
6-13	At Pit.	W	8-1		9	5	Juden	Schmidt		33-31	3rd	6.0
6-14	At Pit.	L	2-7		5	13	Peters	Woodard		33-32	3rd	7.0
6-15	At Chi.	L	5-6		3	12	Adams	Jones	Beck	33-33	3rd	8.0
6-16	At Chi.	W	11-2		16	8	Woodall	Trachsel		34-33	3rd	7.0
6-17	At Chi.	W	6-5		11	8	Patrick	Tapani	Wickman	35-33	3rd	7.0
6-18	Pit.	L	0-1		4	8	Dessens	Jones	Rincon	35-34	3rd	7.0
6-19	Pit.	W	2-1		8	5	Woodard	Peters	Wickman	36-34	3rd	7.0
6-20	Pit.	L	2-4		4	10	Lieber	Eldred	Rincon	36-35	3rd	8.0

Date	Opp.	Res.	Score	(inn.*)	Hits	Opp. hits	Winning pitcher	Losing pitcher	Save	Record	Pos.	GB
6-21	Pit.	L	7-8		11	11	Loaiza	Juden	Rincon	36-36	4th	9.0
6-22	Col.	W	3-2		7	6	Reyes	McElroy	Wickman	37-36	4th	8.0
6-23	Col.	W	7-5		9	8	Patrick	Wright	Wickman	38-36	3rd	8.0
6-24	At Min.	W	3-1		8	9	Woodard	Hawkins	Wickman	39-36	3rd	7.0
6-25	At Min.	W	9-2		11	6	Eldred	Radke		40-36	3rd	6.0
6-26	At Chi. (AL)	W	2-1		9	4	Juden	Simas	Wickman	41-36	2nd	5.0
6-27	At Chi. (AL)	W	10-5		10	7	Woodall	Fordham		42-36	2nd	5.0
6-28	At Chi. (AL)	L	8-10		15	17	Simas	Myers		42-37	T2nd	6.0
6-30	Cle.	W	5-4		11	10	Eldred	Wright	Wickman	43-37	2nd	6.0
7-1	Cle.	L	2-5		5	8	Burba	Juden	Jackson	43-38	2nd	7.0
7-2	Cle.	L	2-7		13	10	Colon	Woodall		43-39	3rd	7.0
7-3	At Phi.	L	0-2		6	7	Schilling	Karl	Leiter	43-40	3rd	8.0
7-4	At Phi.	L	5-6		9	8	Gomes	Wickman		43-41	3rd	8.0
7-5	At Phi.	L	3-4		9	7	Loewer	Eldred	Leiter	43-42	3rd	9.0
7-9	Chi.	W	12-9		12	12	Reyes	Patterson	Wickman	44-42	3rd	9.0
7-10	Chi.	W	6-5		7	8	Patrick	Wood		45-42	3rd	8.0
7-11	Chi.	L	8-11		7	12	Trachsel	Eldred	Beck	45-43	3rd	8.0
7-12	Chi.	L	0-3		3	6	Clark	Woodall		45-44	3rd	8.0
7-13	Phi.	W	4-2		5	8	Woodard	Green	Wickman	46-44	3rd	7.0
7-14	Phi.	L	2-4		8	11	Gomes	Juden	Leiter	46-45	3rd	8.0
7-15	Phi.	W	3-2		8	8	Karl	Schilling	Wickman	47-45	3rd	7.0
7-16	At Atl.	L	3-4		5	7	Maddux	Eldred	Seanez	47-46	3rd	7.5
7-17	At Atl.	L	1-4		7	10	Glavine	Woodall	Rocker	47-47	3rd	8.5
7-18	At Atl.	W	7-1		13	4	Woodard	Millwood		48-47	3rd	8.5
7-19	At Atl.	L	6-11		12	13	Smoltz	Juden		48-48	3rd	9.5
7-20	At Fla.	W	5-3		9	6	Karl	Hernandez	Wickman	49-48	3rd	9.5
7-21	At Fla.	W	6-4		10	8	Reyes	Alfonseca		50-48	3rd	8.5
7-22†	N.Y.	L	5-7		12	11	Cook	Wickman	J. Franco	50-49		
7-22‡	N.Y.	L	1-6		6	15	Nomo	Patrick		50-50	3rd	9.0
7-23	N.Y.	L	5-6		9	16	McMichael	Myers	J. Franco	50-51	3rd	10.0
7-24†	Mon.	W	10-7		11	15	Weathers	Hermanson		51-51		
7-24‡	Mon.	L	2-11		9	13	Thurman	Wagner		51-52	3rd	10.5
7-25	Mon.	W	4-3		8	7	Wickman	Telford		52-52	3rd	9.5
7-26	Mon.	W	6-5		5	14	Wickman	Bennett		53-52	3rd	8.5
7-28	At St.L.	W	13-10		16	15	Weathers	Croushore	Wickman	54-52	3rd	9.0
7-29	At St.L.	W	2-1		6	6	Woodard	Witt	Wickman	55-52	3rd	9.0
7-30	At St.L.	L	2-3		6	7	Morris	Karl	Croushore	55-53	3rd	9.0
7-31	Ari.	L	2-8		7	11	Benes	Juden		55-54	3rd	10.0
8-1	Ari.	L	4-5		9	7	Banks	Fox	Olson	55-55	3rd	11.0
8-2	Ari.	W	7-2		10	7	Woodall	Anderson		56-55	3rd	11.0
8-3	St.L.	W	6-5		12	8	Woodard	Oliver	Wickman	57-55	3rd	10.0
8-4	St.L.	L	1-2		4	6	Morris	Karl		57-56	3rd	11.0
8-5	St.L.	L	1-5		4	8	Mercker	Juden		57-57	3rd	11.0
8-7	At Cin.	L	0-17		6	14	Harnisch	Woodall		57-58	3rd	12.0
8-8	At Cin.	L	0-4		5	5	Reyes	Woodard		57-59	3rd	13.0
8-9	At Cin.	W	4-3		8	8	Karl	Parris	Wickman	58-59	3rd	13.0
8-10	At Hou.	L	2-5		9	10	Elarton	Fox	Wagner	58-60	3rd	14.0
8-11	At Hou.	L	5-6	(10)	11	14	Magnante	Plunk		58-61	3rd	15.0
8-12	At Hou.	L	0-3		5	9	R. Johnson	Woodall		58-62	3rd	16.0
8-13	At Hou.	L	2-6		5	7	Lima	Woodard		58-63	3rd	17.0
8-14	At S.D.	L	0-7		5	10	Hitchcock	Karl		58-64	4th	17.0
8-16†	At S.D.	L	0-4		1	7	Brown	Roque		58-65		
8-16‡	At S.D.	W	4-2		7	9	Pulsipher	Hamilton	Wickman	59-65	4th	17.0
8-18	Cin.	W	8-4		14	8	Woodall	Remlinger		60-65	3rd	16.5
8-19	Cin.	L	2-8		7	12	Harnisch	Woodard		60-66	4th	17.5
8-20	Hou.	W	6-5	(10)	13	17	Wickman	Magnante		61-66	4th	16.5
8-21	Hou.	L	2-5		8	9	Bergman	Pulsipher	Powell	61-67	4th	17.5
8-22	S.D.	W	8-4		14	12	Roque	Langston	Wickman	62-67	T3rd	17.5
8-23	S.D.	L	11-13	(10)	15	18	Hoffman	Wickman		62-68	T3rd	18.5
8-24	S.D.	L	2-7		8	13	Hitchcock	Woodard		62-69	5th	19.5
8-25	At Col.	L	6-11		13	11	Veres	Weathers		62-70	5th	20.5
8-26	At Col.	W	6-5		14	6	Pulsipher	Wright		63-70	4th	19.5
8-27	At Ari.	W	4-0		13	2	Roque	Benes	Plunk	64-70	4th	19.0
8-28	At Ari.	L	3-6		7	9	Anderson	Woodall	Olson	64-71	4th	20.0
8-29	At Ari.	L	3-4		7	7	Small	Wickman		64-72	T4th	21.0
8-30	At Ari.	L	3-7		8	11	Sodowsky	Karl		64-73	6th	22.0
9-1	Col.	L	3-12		8	14	Wright	Pulsipher		64-74	6th	22.5
9-2	Col.	W	8-4		10	9	Roque	Astacio		65-74	4th	22.5
9-3	Col.	W	7-3		10	11	Woodall	Thomson		66-74	4th	22.0
9-4	Phi.	L	2-6		8	7	Schilling	Woodard		66-75	T4th	22.0
9-5	Phi.	W	3-2	(14)	13	6	Weathers	Bottalico		67-75	4th	22.0
9-6	Phi.	W	5-4		9	11	Weathers	Gomes		68-75	4th	22.0
9-7	At Pit.	W	6-3		8	6	Roque	Dessens	Wickman	69-75	4th	22.0
9-8	At Pit.	L	7-8		8	12	Williams	Plunk	Loiselle	69-76	4th	23.0
9-9	At Hou.	L	2-6		8	14	Lima	Woodard	Wagner	69-77	4th	24.0

Date	Opp.	Res.	Score	(inn.*)	Hits	Opp. hits	Winning pitcher	Losing pitcher	Save	Record	Pos.	GB
9-10	At Hou.	L	1-7		7	7	Reynolds	Karl		69-78	4th	25.0
9-11	At Chi.	W	13-11		15	15	Plunk	Wengert	Wickman	70-78	4th	25.0
9-12	At Chi.	L	12-15		16	18	Beck	Wickman		70-79	4th	26.0
9-13	At Chi.	L	10-11	(10)	13	17	Beck	Reyes		70-80	4th	26.0
9-14	At Cin.	W	2-1		6	7	Woodard	Harnisch	Wickman	71-80	4th	25.0
9-15	At Cin.	L	1-5		7	14	Remlinger	Karl	Graves	71-81	4th	25.5
9-16	At Cin.	W	2-0		10	5	Pulsipher	Tomko	Wickman	72-81	4th	24.5
9-18	St.L.	L	2-5		8	9	Oliver	Roque	Acevedo	72-82	4th	25.5
9-19	St.L.	L	4-7		8	10	Jimenez	Woodard	Acevedo	72-83	T4th	25.5
9-20	St.L.	L	6-11		13	10	Aybar	Karl		72-84	5th	26.5
9-22	Chi.	L	2-5		9	9	Mulholland	Pulsipher		72-85	5th	26.5
9-23	Chi.	W	8-7		10	10	Fox	Beck		73-85	5th	26.5
9-24	At L.A.	L	1-4		5	3	Weaver	Fox	Shaw	73-86	5th	27.0
9-25	At L.A.	L	2-3		9	5	Valdes	Woodall	Shaw	73-87	5th	28.0
9-26	At L.A.	W	6-1		9	7	Karl	Perez		74-87	5th	27.0
9-27	At L.A.	L	1-2		10	7	Park	Pulsipher	Shaw	74-88	5th	28.0

Monthly records: March (0-1), April (16-8), May (12-16), June (15-12), July (12-17), August (9-19), September (10-15).
*Innings, if other than nine. †First game of doubleheader. ‡Second game of doubleheader.

HIGHLIGHTS

High point: In its first month of National League play, the club sprinted to a 17-9 record. Right fielder Jeromy Burnitz led the way with eight homers and 24 RBIs in April and lefty Scott Karl won his first four decisions.

Low point: With a 57-57 record on August 6, the club embarked on a pivotal 10-game trip with stops at Cincinnati, Houston and San Diego. A 17-0 loss in the opener set the tone and the club went on to lose nine of 10 games.

Turning point: First baseman John Jaha, the most indispensable player in the line-up, broke his foot and ripped his hamstring April 22. He was sidelined for a month and never returned with a solid contribution.

Most valuable player: With virtually no support in the middle of the lineup, Burnitz put together one of the best offensive seasons in franchise history.

Most valuable pitcher: Bob Wickman had some hiccups in the second half of the season, but he held the bullpen together by taking over the closer's role after Doug Jones pitched his way out of town.

Most improved player: After six frustrating seasons in the minors, Bobby Hughes got his chance and made the most of it. He made the team as the third catcher. By season's end, he was No. 1.

Most pleasant surprise: Righthander Chad Fox, acquired in the offseason from Atlanta, spent his first full season in the majors and was practically unhittable until a shoulder injury put him on the disabled list in mid-May.

Biggest disappointment: There were plenty of candidates, but the award goes to David Nilsson. He opened the season on the D.L. and sputtered at the plate until the final month, when the club was already out of contention.

Key injuries: Cal Eldred (broken arm) and Jose Mercedes (shoulder) were out of the rotation at midseason. Jaha was ineffective for most of the year because of foot and hamstring injuries. Jesse Levis, the club's top pinch hitter, was shelved with a shoulder injury. Marquis Grissom was bothered by back and leg injuries for most of the year.

Notable: The pitching staff tied the big-league record and set the National League record for fewest complete games in a season (2). Both of those were thrown by Jeff Juden, who was traded at midseason. . . . Manager Phil Garner, who picked up his 500th victory, has won and lost more games than any skipper in franchise history. He ended the season with a 511-557 record in seven seasons. . . . Jeff Cirillo tied for eighth in the league in hitting, but also grounded into an N.L.-high 26 double plays. . . . The defense led the majors with 192 double plays. . . . The Brewers had a 9-0 record against Florida, the first season sweep in club history.

—DREW OLSON

RECORDS

1998 regular-season record: 74-88 (5th in N.L. Central); 38-43 at home; 36-45 on road; 22-23 vs. East; 22-34 vs. N.L. Central; 22-25 vs. West; 8-6 vs. A.L.; 20-27 vs. lefthanded starters; 54-61 vs. righthanded starters; 64-73 on grass; 10-15 on turf; 24-29 in daytime; 50-59 at night; 26-26 in one-run games; 10-4 in extra-inning games; 0-1-2 in doubleheaders.

Team record past five years: 350-394 (.470).

TEAM LEADERS

Batting average: Jeff Cirillo (.321).
At-bats: Fernando Vina (637).
Runs: Fernando Vina (101).
Hits: Fernando Vina (198).
Total bases: Jeromy Burnitz (304).
Doubles: Fernando Vina (39).
Triples: Fernando Vina (7).
Home runs: Jeromy Burnitz (38).
Runs batted in: Jeromy Burnitz (125).
Stolen bases: Fernando Vina (22).
Slugging percentage: Jeromy Burnitz (.499).

On-base percentage: Jeff Cirillo (.402).
Wins: Steve Woodard, Scott Karl (10).
Earned-run average: Steve Woodard (4.18).
Complete games: Jeff Juden (2).
Shutouts: None.
Saves: Bob Wickman (25).
Innings pitched: Scott Karl (192.1).
Strikeouts: Steve Woodard (135).

GAMES BY POSITION

Catcher: Mike Matheny 107, Bobby Hughes 72, Jesse Levis 14, Dave Nilsson 7, Brian Banks 5, Marcus Jensen 1.

First base: Mark Loretta 70, John Jaha 57, Bob Hamelin 51, Dave Nilsson 49, Jeff Cirillo 6, Brian Banks 2.

Second base: Fernando Vina 158, Mark Loretta 13, Eric Owens 4, Ron Belliard 1.

Third base: Jeff Cirillo 149, Mark Loretta 22, Brian Banks 1.

Shortstop: Jose Valentin 139, Mark Loretta 56.

Outfield: Jeromy Burnitz 161, Marquis Grissom 137, Darrin Jackson 94, Geoff Jenkins 81, Marc Newfield 55, Dave Nilsson 37, Eric Owens 16, Greg Martinez 6, Bobby Hughes 3, Brian Banks 1, Mark Loretta 1.

Designated hitter: John Jaha 8, Darrin Jackson 2, Marc Newfield 2, Bob Hamelin 1, Jose Valentin 1, Brad Woodall 1.

TOP DRAFT CHOICES

1. **J.M. Gold,** RHP, Toms River North H.S., Toms River, N.J.
2. **Nick Neugebauer,** RHP, Arlington H.S., Riverside, Calif.
3. **Derry Hammond,** OF, West Point (Miss.) H.S.
4. **Rhett Parrott,** RHP, Northwest Whitfield H.S., Dalton, Ga.
5. **Chris Pine,** RHP, Oregon State U.
6. **William Hall,** SS, Nettleton (Miss.) H.S.
7. **Jason Fox,** OF, Florida Southern College
8. **Mike Penney,** RHP, U. of Southern California
9. **Ryan Bordenick,** C, U. of S. Carolina
10. **James Johnson,** LHP, U. of Arizona

MONTREAL EXPOS
NATIONAL LEAGUE EAST DIVISION

1999 Expos Schedule
Home games shaded. *—All-Star Game at Fenway Park (Boston). D—Day game (any game starting before 5 p.m.).

April

SUN	MON	TUE	WED	THU	FRI	SAT
				1	2	3
4	5 PIT	6 PIT	7 PIT	8 NYM	9 NYM	10 D NYM
11 NYM	12	13 MIL	14 MIL	15 D MIL	16 NYM	17 D NYM
18 D NYM	19 COL	20 COL	21 D COL	22	23 PHI	24 PHI
25 PHI	26	27 SF	28 SF	29 SF	30 STL	

May

SUN	MON	TUE	WED	THU	FRI	SAT
						1 STL
2	3 D LA	4 LA	5 LA	6	7 HOU	8 HOU
9 HOU	10 ARI	11 ARI	12 ARI	13	14 PIT	15 D PIT
16 PIT	17 PHI	18 PHI	19 PHI	20	21 MIL	22 MIL
23 MIL	24 D PHI	25 PHI	26 PHI	27	28 SF	29 SF
30 SF	31 ARI					

June

SUN	MON	TUE	WED	THU	FRI	SAT
		1 ARI	2 ARI	3	4 TOR	5 D TOR
6 D TOR	7 BOS	8 BOS	9 BOS	10	11 TB	12 TB
13 TB	14 STL	15 STL	16 STL	17	18 HOU	19 HOU
20 HOU	21	22 ATL	23 ATL	24 D ATL	25 FLA	26 FLA
27 D FLA	28 ATL	29 ATL	30 ATL			

July

SUN	MON	TUE	WED	THU	FRI	SAT
				1 D ATL	2 FLA	3 FLA
4 D FLA	5 NYM	6 NYM	7 NYM	8 D NYM	9 TOR	10 TOR
11 D TOR	12	13	14 *	15 BAL	16 BAL	17 BAL
18 D NYY	19 NYY	20 NYY	21 NYM	22 NYM	23 PIT	24 PIT
25 D PIT	26 CUB	27 CUB	28 CUB	29	30 MIL	31 MIL

August

SUN	MON	TUE	WED	THU	FRI	SAT
1 D MIL	2 CUB	3 CUB	4 CUB	5 D SD	6 D SD	7 SD
8 D SD	9 SD	10 LA	11 LA	12 D LA	13 COL	14 COL
15 D COL	16 SF	17 SF	18 D SF	19	20 CIN	21 CIN
22 D CIN	23 STL	24 STL	25 STL	26 CIN	27 CIN	28 CIN
29 D CIN	30 ARI	31 ARI				

September

SUN	MON	TUE	WED	THU	FRI	SAT
			1 ARI	2	3 D HOU	4 HOU
5 HOU	6 D COL	7 COL	8 COL	9 D SD	10 SD	11 SD
12 SD	13 LA	14 LA	15 LA	16	17 ATL	18 ATL
19 ATL	20	21 FLA	22 FLA	23 D FLA	24 ATL	25 ATL
26 ATL	27 FLA	28 FLA	29 FLA	30		

October

SUN	MON	TUE	WED	THU	FRI	SAT
					1 PHI	2 PHI
3 D PHI	4	5	6	7	8	9

1999 SEASON
CLUB DIRECTORY

President and general partner
Claude R. Brochu

Chairman of the partnership committee
L. Jacques Menard

Vice chairmen of the partnership comm.
Raymond Bachand
Jocelyn Proteau
Andre Aubin

Vice president, baseball operations
Bill Stoneman

Vice president and general manager
Jim Beattie

V.p. and dir. of international operations
Fred Ferreira

Director, scouting
Jim Fleming

Director, player development
Don Reynolds

Assistant director, scouting
Gregg Leonard

Executive vice president, development
Laurier M. Carpentier

Vice president, finance and treasurer
Michel Bussiere

Vice president, sales and marketing
Richard Morency

Vice president, communications
Johanne Heroux

Vice president, stadium operations
Claude Delorme

Director, media relations
P.J. Loyello

Director, media services
Monique Giroux

Director, Olympic Stadium ticket office
Hubert Richard

Director, stadium operations
Denis Pare

Directors, advertising sales
Luigi Carola
John Di Terlizzi
Danielle La Roche

Director, season ticket sales
Gilles Beauregard

Director, business development
Real Sureau

Club physician
Dr. Mike Thomassin

Club orthopedist
Dr. Larry Coughlin

Scouts
Alex Agostino, Matt Anderson, Mark Baca, Mike Berger, Bob Cluck, Dennis Cardoza, Robby Corsaro, Dave Dangler, Marc Del Piano, Dan Freed, Scott Goldby, John Hughes, Joe Jordan, Mark Leavit, Dave Malpass, Darryl Monroe, Bob Oldis, Scott Stanley, Len Strelitz, Tommy Thompson

MINOR LEAGUE AFFILIATES

Class	Team	League	Manager
AAA	Ottawa	International	Jeff Cox
AA	Harrisburg	Eastern	Doug Sisson
A	Jupiter	Florida State	To be announced
A	Cape Fear	South Atlantic	To be announced
A	Vermont	New York-Pennsylvania	To be announced
Rookie	Gulf Coast Expos	Gulf Coast	To be announced

BROADCAST INFORMATION

Radio: CIQC-AM (600); CKAC-AM (73, French language).
TV: SRC (Channel 4).
Cable TV: The Sports Network; RDS (French language).

SPRING TRAINING

Ballpark (city): Roger Dean Stadium (Jupiter, Fla.).
Ticket information: 561-775-1818.

SPRING TRAINING ROSTER

Manager—Felipe Alou (17).
Coaches—Pierre Arsenault (67), Bobby Cuellar (23), Gene Glynn, Tommy Harper (1), Pete Mackanin (25), Luis Pujols (55).

No.	PITCHERS	B/T	Ht./Wt.	Born	1998 clubs
	Armas, Tony	R/R	6-4/175	4-29-78	Jupiter
48	Batista, Miguel	R/R	6-2/190	2-19-71	Montreal
21	Bennett, Shayne	R/R	6-5/215	4-10-72	Montreal
34	DeHart, Rick	L/L	6-1/190	3-21-70	Montreal, Ottawa
	Duran, Roberto	L/L	6-0/205	3-6-73	Detroit, Toledo, Lakeland
30	Hermanson, Dustin	R/R	6-2/200	12-21-72	Montreal
	Johnson, Mike	L/R	6-2/175	10-3-75	Harrisburg, Ottawa, Montreal
44	Kline, Steve	B/L	6-2/210	8-22-72	Ottawa, Montreal
	Lilly, Ted	L/L	6-1/177	1-4-76	San Antonio, Albuquerque, Ottawa
29	Moore, Trey	L/L	6-1/200	10-2-72	Montreal, Ottawa
	Mota, Guillermo	R/R	6-6/200	7-25-73	Jupiter, Harrisburg
45	Pavano, Carl	R/R	6-5/228	1-8-76	Jupiter, Ottawa, Montreal
	Powell, Jeremy	R/R	6-6/225	6-18-76	Montreal, Harrisburg
	Smart, J.D.	R/R	6-2/180	11-12-73	Cape Fear, Harrisburg, Ottawa
	Smith, Dan	R/R	6-3/210	9-15-75	Tulsa, Oklahoma City
32	Telford, Anthony	R/R	6-0/195	3-6-66	Montreal
35	Thurman, Mike	R/R	6-4/210	7-22-73	Ottawa, Montreal
41	Urbina, Ugueth	R/R	6-2/205	2-15-74	Montreal
28	Vazquez, Javier	R/R	6-2/180	7-25-76	Montreal

No.	CATCHERS	B/T	Ht./Wt.	Born	1998 clubs
13	Henley, Bob	R/R	6-2/205	1-30-73	Jupiter, Ottawa, Montreal
16	Widger, Chris	R/R	6-3/210	5-21-71	Montreal

No.	INFIELDERS	B/T	Ht./Wt.	Born	1998 clubs
11	Andrews, Shane	R/R	6-1/215	8-28-71	Montreal
5	Barrett, Michael	R/R	6-3/185	10-22-76	Harrisburg, Montreal
2	Cabrera, Orlando	R/R	5-9/165	11-2-74	Ottawa, Montreal
	Coquillette, Trace	R/R	5-11/175	6-4-74	Harrisburg, Ottawa
	Fernandez, Jose	L/R	6-2/190	11-2-74	Harrisburg
20	Fullmer, Brad	L/R	6-1/205	1-17-75	Montreal
4	Guerrero, Wilton	R/R	5-11/175	10-24-74	Los Angeles, Albuquerque, Montreal
6	McGuire, Ryan	L/L	6-2/200	11-23-71	Montreal
15	Mordecai, Mike	R/R	5-11/175	12-13-67	Montreal, Jupiter, Ottawa
37	Vidro, Jose	B/R	6-0/185	8-27-74	Montreal, Ottawa

No.	OUTFIELDERS	B/T	Ht./Wt.	Born	1998 clubs
27	Guerrero, Vladimir	R/R	6-2/200	2-9-76	Montreal
9	Jones, Terry	B/R	5-10/165	2-15-71	Ottawa, Montreal
30	Martinez, Manny	R/R	6-2/169	10-3-70	Nashville, Pittsburgh
33	Seguignol, Fernando	B/R	6-5/190	1-17-75	Montreal, Harrisburg, Ottawa
	Staton, T.J.	L/L	6-3/210	2-17-75	Carolina, Nashville
	Stowers, Christopher	L/L	6-3/195	8-18-74	Harrisburg
22	White, Rondell	R/R	6-1/210	2-23-72	Montreal

BALLPARK INFORMATION

Ballpark (capacity, surface)
Olympic Stadium (46,500, artificial)

Address
4549 Pierre-de-Coubertin Ave.
Montreal, QC H1V 3N7

Business phone
514-790-1245, 800-678-5440 (in U.S.), 800-361-4595 (in Canada)

Ticket information
800-GO-EXPOS

Ticket prices
$33 (VIP box seats)
$23 (box seats)
$13 (terrace)
$7 (general admission)

Field dimensions (from home plate)
To left field at foul line, 325 feet
To center field, 404 feet
To right field at foul line, 325 feet

First game played
April 15, 1977 (Phillies 7, Expos 2)

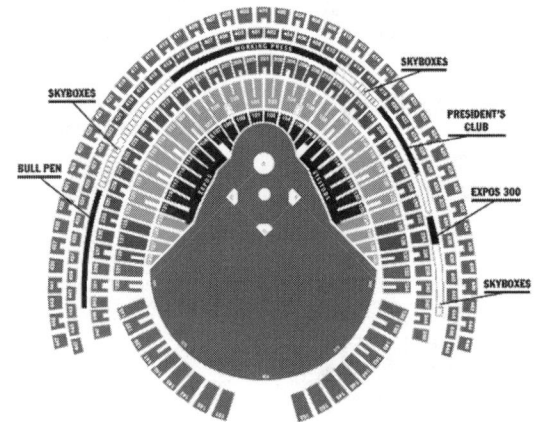

1999 SEASON *Montreal Expos*

Date	Opp.	Res.	Score	(inn.*)	Hits	Opp. hits	Winning pitcher	Losing pitcher	Save	Record	Pos.	GB
4-1	Pit.	L	0-4		5	7	Cordova	C. Perez		0-1	T4th	1.0
4-2	Pit.	L	3-4		8	10	Schmidt	Maddux	Loiselle	0-2	5th	1.0
4-3	At Chi.	L	2-6		6	9	Trachsel	Vazquez	Beck	0-3	5th	2.0
4-4	At Chi.	L	1-3		5	8	Mulholland	Valdes	Beck	0-4	5th	3.0
4-5	At Chi.	L	2-7		6	8	Tapani	Moore		0-5	5th	4.0
4-6	At Chi.	L	2-3		7	9	Clark	C. Perez	Beck	0-6	5th	4.0
4-7	At Mil.	L	4-6		8	12	Karl	Hermanson	Jones	0-7	5th	5.0
4-9	At Mil.	W	6-5		14	6	Telford	Wickman	Urbina	1-7	4th	4.0
4-10	Chi.	L	0-13		3	16	Tapani	Valdes		1-8	4th	4.5
4-11	Chi.	W	5-4	(10)	11	12	Kline	Adams		2-8	4th	4.5
4-12	Chi.	W	4-1		9	5	Hermanson	Wood	Urbina	3-8	4th	4.0
4-14	Mil.	L	4-7		9	10	Karl	Vazquez		3-9	4th	5.0
4-15	Mil.	W	4-3		8	6	Moore	Juden	Urbina	4-9	4th	5.0
4-16	Mil.	L	3-5	(14)	9	17	Jones	Bennett		4-10	4th	5.0
4-17	At Hou.	L	3-5		7	6	Halama	Hermanson	Wagner	4-11	4th	6.0
4-18	At Hou.	L	3-4		9	8	Henry	Batista		4-12	4th	6.0
4-19	At Hou.	W	5-4		11	10	Telford	Magnante	Urbina	5-12	4th	6.0
4-21	St.L.	L	3-5		5	11	Stottlemyre	Moore	Brantley	5-13	4th	6.5
4-22	St.L.	W	3-2		12	9	Urbina	Bottenfield		6-13	4th	6.5
4-23	St.L.	W	5-2		10	5	Hermanson	Politte	Urbina	7-13	4th	6.5
4-24	Hou.	L	4-8		11	10	Lima	Valdes		7-14	4th	7.5
4-25	Hou.	L	3-4		10	9	Magnante	Urbina	Wagner	7-15	4th	7.5
4-26	Hou.	L	0-15		5	18	Bergman	Moore	Miller	7-16	5th	7.5
4-27	At St.L.	L	0-7		4	10	Osborne	C. Perez		7-17	5th	8.5
4-29	At St.L.	L	7-13		7	12	Busby	Kline		7-18	5th	9.5
5-1	Ari.	W	7-4		10	7	Vazquez	Anderson	Urbina	8-18	5th	10.0
5-2	Ari.	W	5-4	(12)	13	10	Bennett	Springer		9-18	5th	10.0
5-3	Ari.	W	4-1		8	2	Hermanson	Blair		10-18	5th	9.0
5-4	Cin.	L	1-4		4	7	Winchester	Moore	Shaw	10-19	5th	10.0
5-5	Cin.	W	3-2		9	11	Urbina	Belinda		11-19	5th	10.0
5-6	Cin.	L	2-4		9	9	Remlinger	Vazquez	Shaw	11-20	4th	11.0
5-7	Col.	W	2-1		5	7	C. Perez	Wright	Urbina	12-20	4th	11.0
5-8	Col.	L	5-7		10	9	Astacio	Hermanson	DiPoto	12-21	4th	11.0
5-9	Col.	W	4-0		8	7	Moore	Thomson	Urbina	13-21	4th	11.0
5-10	Col.	L	3-5		5	8	Kile	Kline	DiPoto	13-22	4th	12.0
5-11	At S.F.	L	2-7		11	9	Rueter	Vazquez		13-23	4th	13.0
5-13	At S.F.	W	9-5		15	7	C. Perez	Gardner		14-23	4th	13.5
5-14†	At S.F.	L	1-6		6	11	Estes	Hermanson	Tavarez	14-24		
5-14‡	At S.F.	L	0-2		4	7	Darwin	Moore	Nen	14-25	4th	15.0
5-15	At L.A.	W	4-2		10	7	Batista	Valdes	Urbina	15-25	4th	15.0
5-16	At L.A.	L	4-9		6	11	Dreifort	Vazquez		15-26	4th	15.0
5-17	At L.A.	L	3-6		4	10	Martinez	Johnson	Radinsky	15-27	4th	15.0
5-19	Hou.	W	4-2		10	6	C. Perez	Schourek	Urbina	16-27	4th	15.0
5-20	Hou.	L	3-4		10	10	Henry	Telford	Wagner	16-28	4th	16.0
5-21	Hou.	L	0-6		5	13	Reynolds	Bennett		16-29	4th	17.0
5-22	Phi.	L	5-7	(10)	8	15	Gomes	Telford	Leiter	16-30	4th	18.0
5-23	Phi.	W	3-2		5	3	Urbina	Schilling		17-30	4th	17.0
5-24	Phi.	W	5-4		4	7	C. Perez	Spradlin	Urbina	18-30	4th	17.0
5-25	Phi.	L	3-5	(14)	13	13	Gomes	Bennett	Spradlin	18-31	4th	18.0
5-26	At Atl.	L	3-9		11	11	Neagle	Batista		18-32	4th	19.0
5-27	At Atl.	L	0-2		7	3	Maddux	Vazquez	Ligtenberg	18-33	4th	20.0
5-28	At Atl.	W	9-5		12	10	Maddux	Wohlers		19-33	4th	19.0
5-29	At Pit.	W	4-1		10	9	C. Perez	Lieber	Urbina	20-33	4th	18.0
5-30	At Pit.	L	7-8		11	12	Christiansen	Urbina		20-34	4th	18.0
5-31	At Pit.	L	4-9		7	8	Cordova	Batista		20-35	4th	18.0
6-1	At Phi.	L	2-6		7	8	Gomes	Maddux		20-36	4th	19.0
6-2	At Phi.	W	4-3		10	6	Pavano	Schilling	Urbina	21-36	4th	19.0
6-3	At Phi.	W	3-2		8	7	C. Perez	Gomes		22-36	4th	19.0
6-5	At T.B.	W	5-2		12	5	Hermanson	White		23-36	4th	18.0
6-6	At T.B.	W	7-5		10	13	Telford	Ruebel	Urbina	24-36	4th	18.0
6-7	At T.B.	L	3-4	(11)	5	12	Lopez	Kline		24-37	4th	19.0
6-9	N.Y. (AL)	L	1-11		4	17	Hernandez	C. Perez		24-38	4th	19.5
6-10	N.Y. (AL)	L	2-6		6	11	Irabu	Hermanson		24-39	4th	19.5
6-11	N.Y. (AL)	W	7-5		8	6	Valdes	Nelson	Urbina	25-39	4th	19.0
6-12	At Atl.	W	7-5		9	11	Batista	Cather	Urbina	26-39	4th	18.0
6-13	At Atl.	L	7-9		14	11	Glavine	Johnson	Martinez	26-40	4th	19.0
6-14	At Atl.	L	1-5		4	9	Millwood	C. Perez		26-41	4th	20.0
6-16	N.Y.	L	0-2		5	6	Leiter	Hermanson		26-42	4th	21.0
6-17	N.Y.	W	5-4		12	8	Urbina	Rojas		27-42	4th	21.0
6-18	N.Y.	W	7-6		7	14	Bennett	Yoshii	Urbina	28-42	4th	20.0
6-19	Atl.	W	14-1		15	7	Boskie	Millwood		29-42	4th	19.0
6-20	Atl.	L	1-5		4	12	Smoltz	C. Perez		29-43	4th	20.0

Date	Opp.	Res.	Score	(inn.*)	Hits	Opp. hits	Winning pitcher	Losing pitcher	Save	Record	Pos.	GB
6-21	Atl.	W	4-1		6	6	Hermanson	Neagle	Urbina	30-43	4th	19.0
6-22	At Tor.	L	2-14		7	18	Guzman	Pavano		30-44	4th	19.0
6-23	At Tor.	L	2-3	10	7		Carpenter	Batista	Myers	30-45	4th	20.0
6-24	Tor.	L	6-7	13	10		Clemens	Boskie	Myers	30-46	4th	20.0
6-25	Tor.	L	0-1		5	5	Williams	C. Perez		30-47	4th	20.0
6-26	Bal.	W	9-4		12	10	Hermanson	Ponson		31-47	4th	19.0
6-27	Bal.	W	3-1		10	6	Pavano	Mussina	Urbina	32-47	4th	19.0
6-28	Bal.	W	8-4		11	7	Vazquez	Drabek	Urbina	33-47	4th	19.0
6-30	At Bos.	L	4-7		6	12	Avery	C. Perez	Gordon	33-48	4th	20.0
7-1	At Bos.	L	1-6		6	12	Saberhagen	Hermanson		33-49	4th	21.0
7-2	At Bos.	L	0-15		3	20	Martinez	Pavano		33-50	4th	22.0
7-3	Fla.	W	8-4		13	8	Vazquez	Sanchez		34-50	4th	22.0
7-4	Fla.	L	2-3		7	9	Edmondson	Boskie	Alfonseca	34-51	4th	23.0
7-5	Fla.	L	1-2		9	10	Meadows	C. Perez	Alfonseca	34-52	4th	24.0
7-9	At N.Y.	W	9-8	(11)	18	15	Maddux	J. Franco	Urbina	35-52	4th	24.0
7-10	At N.Y.	W	8-6		11	12	Bennett	J. Franco	Urbina	36-52	4th	23.0
7-11	At N.Y.	L	4-8		12	11	Reed	Pavano		36-53	4th	23.0
7-12	At N.Y.	L	2-5		2	11	Tam	Vazquez	Cook	36-54	4th	23.0
7-13	At Fla.	L	7-8		13	11	Alfonseca	Telford		36-55	4th	23.5
7-14	At Fla.	W	2-1		6	5	Hermanson	Hernandez	Urbina	37-55	4th	23.5
7-15	At Fla.	W	9-5		16	11	C. Perez	Edmondson		38-55	4th	23.5
7-16	Pit.	W	10-5		12	11	Pavano	Schmidt	Maddux	39-55	4th	23.5
7-17	Pit.	L	1-5		8	11	Williams	Vazquez	Christiansen	39-56	4th	24.5
7-18	Pit.	L	2-5		5	11	Lieber	Boskie		39-57	4th	24.5
7-19	Pit.	L	1-6		6	13	Peters	Hermanson		39-58	4th	25.5
7-20	Phi.	L	1-3		5	6	Schilling	C. Perez		39-59	4th	25.5
7-21	Phi.	L	2-3		4	9	Portugal	Pavano		39-60	4th	25.5
7-22	At Chi.	L	5-9		9	11	Adams	Batista	Beck	39-61	4th	26.5
7-23	At Chi.	L	1-2		6	4	Clark	Powell	Beck	39-62	4th	27.5
7-24†	At Mil.	L	7-10		15	11	Weathers	Hermanson		39-63		
7-24‡	At Mil.	W	11-2		13	9	Thurman	Wagner		40-63	4th	28.0
7-25	At Mil.	L	3-4		7	8	Wickman	Telford		40-64	4th	28.0
7-26	At Mil.	L	5-6		14	5	Wickman	Bennett		40-65	4th	29.0
7-28	S.F.	L	1-7		2	11	Rueter	Vazquez		40-66	4th	29.5
7-29	S.F.	W	6-0		9	5	Hermanson	Darwin		41-66	4th	29.5
7-30	S.F.	W	12-6		14	9	Thurman	Gardner	Bennett	42-66	4th	29.5
7-31	S.D.	L	4-5		9	8	Brown	Pavano	Hoffman	42-67	4th	29.5
8-1	S.D.	W	4-2		7	5	Bennett	Langston	Urbina	43-67	4th	29.5
8-2	S.D.	L	1-4		6	9	Ashby	Vazquez	Hoffman	43-68	4th	30.5
8-3	S.D.	W	6-1		9	4	Hermanson	Boehringer		44-68	4th	30.0
8-4	L.A.	W	5-4	(10)	10	10	Kline	Hall		45-68	4th	30.0
8-5	L.A.	W	5-1		6	8	Pavano	Dreifort	Urbina	46-68	4th	29.0
8-6	L.A.	W	9-0		10	2	Powell	Perez		47-68	4th	29.0
8-7	Ari.	L	4-6		9	10	Anderson	Vazquez	Olson	47-69	4th	30.0
8-8	Ari.	W	5-3		10	9	Hermanson	Telemaco	Urbina	48-69	4th	30.0
8-9	Ari.	W	8-2		9	6	Bennett	Wolcott	Kline	49-69	4th	30.0
8-10	At Col.	L	2-6		7	8	Wright	Telford		49-70	4th	30.5
8-11	At Col.	L	6-15		16	18	Thomson	Powell		49-71	4th	30.5
8-12	At Col.	L	2-3		9	6	Astacio	Vazquez	DiPoto	49-72	4th	30.5
8-14	At Cin.	L	2-3		3	7	White	Kline		49-73	4th	32.0
8-15	At Cin.	L	4-6		10	12	Parris	Thurman	White	49-74	4th	33.0
8-16	At Cin.	L	1-8		5	13	Tomko	Pavano		49-75	4th	33.0
8-17	At Ari.	L	1-6		3	7	Benes	Powell		49-76	4th	33.5
8-18	At Ari.	W	7-1		12	4	Vazquez	Anderson		50-76	4th	33.5
8-19	At Ari.	W	8-2		10	4	Hermanson	Telemaco		51-76	4th	32.5
8-20	Col.	L	3-6		11	10	Kile	Thurman	DeJean	51-77	4th	32.5
8-21	Col.	L	2-3		6	11	Veres	Urbina		51-78	4th	33.5
8-22	Cin.	L	0-4		3	6	Parris	Powell		51-79	4th	34.5
8-23	Cin.	L	0-10		4	13	Bere	Vazquez		51-80	4th	35.5
8-24	Cin.	L	1-8		3	11	Harnisch	Hermanson		51-81	4th	36.5
8-25	At L.A.	L	3-4		10	6	Mlicki	Thurman	Shaw	51-82	4th	36.5
8-26	At L.A.	L	3-4		6	9	Shaw	Kline		51-83	4th	37.5
8-27	At L.A.	L	9-10		12	11	Dreifort	Powell	Radinsky	51-84	4th	38.5
8-28	At S.D.	L	8-12		12	10	Wall	Maddux		51-85	4th	38.5
8-29	At S.D.	W	3-1		6	3	Hermanson	Hitchcock	Urbina	52-85	4th	38.5
8-30	At S.D.	W	2-1		8	3	Bullinger	Brown	Urbina	53-85	4th	37.5
8-31	At S.D.	L	2-5		6	9	Hamilton	Pavano	Hoffman	53-86	4th	37.5
9-1	At S.F.	L	7-9		12	14	Johnstone	Kline	Nen	53-87	4th	38.5
9-2	At S.F.	L	3-12		8	14	Rueter	Vazquez		53-88	4th	38.5
9-4	At Fla.	W	8-0		11	3	Hermanson	Meadows		54-88	4th	37.5
9-5	At Fla.	W	7-1		5	5	Thurman	Medina		55-88	4th	36.5
9-6	At Fla.	L	2-6		9	7	Ojala	Pavano	Darensbourg	55-89	4th	37.5
9-8	Atl.	W	6-3		6	6	Batista	Maddux	Urbina	56-89	4th	36.0
9-9	Atl.	W	3-2		6	7	Urbina	Rocker		57-89	4th	35.0
9-10	Atl.	L	4-7		10	7	Millwood	Thurman	Ligtenberg	57-90	4th	36.0

ate	Opp.	Res.	Score	(inn.*)	Hits	Opp. hits	Winning pitcher	Losing pitcher	Save	Record	Pos.	GB
-11	N.Y.	W	5-1		7	4	Pavano	Jones	Urbina	58-90	4th	36.0
-12	N.Y.	W	5-3		7	7	Maddux	Reed	Urbina	59-90	4th	36.0
-13	N.Y.	L	0-1		4	4	Blair	Telford	J. Franco	59-91	4th	36.0
-14	Fla.	W	4-2		6	5	Hermanson	Meadows	Urbina	60-91	4th	36.0
-15	Fla.	L	4-7		11	11	Medina	Thurman		60-92	4th	37.0
-16	Fla.	W	3-2		5	9	Kline	Ojala		61-92	4th	37.0
-18	At Phi.	W	11-4		18	10	Vazquez	Portugal	Telford	62-92	4th	36.5
-19	At Phi.	L	3-4		5	10	Schilling	Maddux		62-93	4th	37.5
-20	At Phi.	L	3-6		6	10	Byrd	Hermanson	Bottalico	62-94	4th	38.5
-22	At N.Y.	W	5-3		10	5	Thurman	Reynoso	Urbina	63-94	4th	38.5
-23	At N.Y.	W	3-0		7	3	Pavano	Jones	Urbina	64-94	4th	38.5
-24	At St.L.	L	3-6		6	11	Osborne	Vazquez	Acevedo	64-95	4th	39.0
-25	At St.L.	L	5-6		10	12	Jimenez	Bennett	Acevedo	64-96	4th	40.0
-26	At St.L.	W	7-6		9	8	Urbina	Busby	DeHart	65-96	4th	40.0
-27	At St.L.	L	3-6		9	9	Frascatore	Pavano	Acevedo	65-97	4th	41.0

Monthly records: April (7-18), May (13-17), June (13-13), July (9-19), August (11-19), September (12-11).

Innings, if other than nine. †First game of doubleheader. ‡Second game of doubleheader.

HIGHLIGHTS

High point: June 11, against the Yankees. In this matchup of the most vs. the least, the Expos were losing 5-0 in the seventh inning when they stormed back against the Yankees' bullpen. Led by Vladimir Guerrero, the Expos scored seven unanswered runs and salvaged a 7-5 victory.

Low point: At Olympic Stadium, April 26, in a 15-0 loss that capped off a series sweep—and back-to-back shutouts—by the Astros. The game also featured five Expos errors.

Turning point: On a frigid April evening at Milwaukee, after seven consecutive losses to open the season and a rainout the previous day, the Expos eked out a 6-4 victory over the Brewers that broke the ice—literally—on the 1998 season.

Most valuable player: At age 22, Vladimir Guerrero was called upon to carry the club offensively July 20 when center fielder Rondell White went down with a season-ending injury. Guerrero delivered, moving into the cleanup spot and continually driving in whatever baserunners managed to get on ahead of him.

Most valuable pitcher: Dustin Hermanson. In only his second full year as a starter, the righthander grabbed the No. 1 spot with his tremendous competitive fire and became the stopper. A 14-11 record and a 3.13 ERA on a team that lost 97 games is no small feat.

Most improved player: Guerrero. In his first full big-league season, Guerrero hit 38 homers and drove in 119 runs for a team that wasn't blessed with an abundance of baserunners. He finished the season with a .324 average, setting six franchise records and coming close to matching two more.

Most pleasant surprise: Even at Class AAA Ottawa, Orlando Cabrera batted only .232, did not walk enough and flew out far too often. But after being called up following the trade of shortstop Mark Grudzielanek, Cabrera showed he belonged. He hit a solid .280 and made only three errors in 52 games.

Biggest disappointment: White was well on his way to a big offensive output when he was lost for the season. His loss carved a major hole in the team's offense.

Key injuries: White (torn thumb ligament); reliever Marc Valdes (Tommy John surgery).

Notable: Wilton Guerrero appeared to turn his career around after coming over in trade from the Dodgers. Not only did it reunite him with brother Vladimir, but the elder Guerrero was a solid hitter, speedy on the basepaths, and his teamwork with Cabrera in the middle infield bodes well for spectacular things to come.

—STEPHANIE MYLES

RECORDS

1998 regular-season record: 65-97 (4th in N.L. East); 39-42 at home; 26-55 on road; 26-22 vs. N.L. East; 13-41 vs. Central; 20-24 vs. West; 6-10 vs. A.L.; 14-22 vs. lefthanded starters; 51-75 vs. righthanded starters; 19-42 on grass; 46-55 on turf; 14-31 in daytime; 51-66 at night; 21-27 in one-run games; 4-4 in extra-inning games; 0-1-1 in doubleheaders.

Team record past five years: 371-373 (.499, ranks 8th in league in that span).

TEAM LEADERS

Batting average: Vladimir Guerrero (.324).
At-bats: Vladimir Guerrero (623).
Runs: Vladimir Guerrero (108).
Hits: Vladimir Guerrero (202).
Total bases: Vladimir Guerrero (367).
Doubles: Brad Fullmer (44).
Triples: Vladimir Guerrero (7).
Home runs: Vladimir Guerrero (38).
Runs batted in: Vladimir Guerrero (109).
Stolen bases: Terry Jones, Rondell White (16).
Slugging percentage: Vladimir Guerrero (.589).
On-base percentage: Vladimir Guerrero (.371).
Wins: Dustin Hermanson (14).

Earned-run average: Dustin Hermanson (3.13).
Complete games: Carlos Perez (3).
Shutouts: None.
Saves: Ugueth Urbina (34).
Innings pitched: Dustin Hermanson (187.0).
Strikeouts: Dustin Hermanson (154).

GAMES BY POSITION

Catcher: Chris Widger 123, Bob Henley 35, Mike Hubbard 24, Michael Barrett 3.
First base: Brad Fullmer 137, Ryan McGuire 78, Fernando Seguignol 7, Scott Livingstone 3, Mike Mordecai 1.
Second base: Jose Vidro 56, Wilton Guerrero 52, F.P. Santangelo 35, Orlando Cabrera 28, Mike Mordecai 21, Ray Holbert 1, Mike Hubbard 1.
Third base: Shane Andrews 147, Scott Livingstone 17, Mike Mordecai 11, Jose Vidro 7, Michael Barrett 3, F.P. Santangelo 1.
Shortstop: Mark Grudzielanek 105, Orlando Cabrera 52, Mike Mordecai 30.
Outfield: Vladimir Guerrero 157, Rondell White 96, F.P. Santangelo 92, Terry Jones 60, Derrick May 49, DaRond Stovall 47, Ryan McGuire 46, Robert Perez 29, Fernando Seguignol 9.
Designated hitter: Scott Livingstone 5, Derrick May 2, Rondell White 1.

TOP DRAFT CHOICES

1a. **Josh McKinley**, SS, Malvern Prep, Downington, Pa.
1b. **Brad Wilkerson**, OF-LHP, U. of Fla.
2. **Eric Good**, LHP, Mishawaka (Ind.) H.S.
3a. **Clyde Williams**, 1B, Seminole H.S., Sanford, Fla.
3b. **Kevin Kelly**, 3B, Gloucester Catholic H.S., Brooklawn, N.J.
4. **Rob Castelli**, RHP, Eastern Illinois U.
5. **Ryan Lentz**, 3B, U. of Washington
6. **Wes Chisnall**, RHP, Etiwanda H.S., Alta Loma, Calif.
7. **Brad Piercy**, C, North Carolina State U.
8. **Scott Sandusky**, C, Texas A&M U.
9. **Juan Ortiz**, OF, Eastern District H.S., Brooklyn, N.Y.
10. **Ryan Grantham**, RHP, Burlington, Ontario

NEW YORK METS
NATIONAL LEAGUE EAST DIVISION

1999 Mets Schedule
Home games shaded. *—All-Star Game at Fenway Park (Boston).
D—Day game (any game starting before 5 p.m.).

April
SUN	MON	TUE	WED	THU	FRI	SAT
				1	2	3
4	5 D FLA	6 FLA	7 FLA	8 MON	9 MON	10 D MON
11 D MON	12 D FLA	13	14 FLA	15 FLA	16 MON	17 D MON
18 D MON	19	20 CIN	21 CIN	22 CIN	23 D CUB	24 D CUB
25 D CUB	26	27 SD	28 SD	29 D SD	30 SF	

May
SUN	MON	TUE	WED	THU	FRI	SAT
						1 D SF
2 D SF	3 HOU	4 HOU	5 HOU	6	7 ARI	8 D ARI
9 ARI	10 D COL	11 COL	12 D COL	13	14 PHI	15 PHI
16 D PHI	17 MIL	18 MIL	19 MIL	20 MIL	21 PHI	22 PHI
23 PHI	24 PIT	25 PIT	26 PIT	27	28 ARI	29 D ARI
30 ARI	31 D CIN					

June
SUN	MON	TUE	WED	THU	FRI	SAT
		1 CIN	2 CIN	3	4 NYY	5 D NYY
6 D NYY	7 TOR	8 TOR	9 TOR	10	11 BOS	12 D BOS
13 D BOS	14 CIN	15 CIN	16 D STL	17 STL	18 STL	19 D STL
20 STL	21	22 FLA	23 FLA	24 D FLA	25 ATL	26 ATL
27 D ATL	28 FLA	29 FLA	30 FLA			

July
SUN	MON	TUE	WED	THU	FRI	SAT
				1 FLA	2 ATL	3 D ATL
4 ATL	5 MON	6 MON	7 MON	8 MON	9 NYY	10 D NYY
11 B NYY	12	13 *	14	15 TB	16 TB	17 D TB
18 D BAL	19 BAL	20 BAL	21 MON	22 MON	23 CUB	24 D CUB
25 D CUB	26 PIT	27 PIT	28 D PIT	29	30 D CUB	31 CUB

August
SUN	MON	TUE	WED	THU	FRI	SAT
1 D CUB	2 MIL	3 MIL	4 MIL	5	6 LA	7 LA
8 D LA	9 SD	10 SD	11 SD	12 D SF	13 SF	14 D SF
15 D SF	16 SD	17 SD	18 SD	19	20 STL	21 D STL
22 STL	23 HOU	24 HOU	25 HOU	26	27 ARI	28 ARI
29 ARI	30 HOU	31 HOU				

September
SUN	MON	TUE	WED	THU	FRI	SAT
			1 HOU	2	3 COL	4 COL
5 COL	6 D SF	7 SF	8 D LA	9 LA	10 LA	11 LA
12 LA	13 COL	14 COL	15 D COL	16	17 PHI	18 PHI
19 B PHI	20	21 ATL	22 ATL	23 ATL	24 D PHI	25 PHI
26 D PHI	27	28 ATL	29 ATL	30 ATL		

October
SUN	MON	TUE	WED	THU	FRI	SAT
					1 PIT	2 PIT
3 D PIT	4	5	6	7	8	9

1999 SEASON
CLUB DIRECTORY

Chairman of the board
Nelson Doubleday
President and chief executive officer
Fred Wilpon
Directors
Nelson Doubleday, Fred Wilpon, Saul B. Katz, Steve Phillips, Marvin B. Tepper
Special advisor to the board of directors
Richard Cummins
Senior v.p., general manager
Steve Phillips
Sr. asst. g.m./international scouting dir.
Omar Minaya
Assistant g.m./player personnel
Jim Duquette
Assistant g.m./amateur scouting
Gary Larocque
Assistant g.m./professional scouting
Carmen Fusco
Senior exec. advisor for player personnel
Dave Wallace
Special assistants to the g.m.
Harry Minor, Darrell Johnson, Larry Doughty
Assistant director of amateur scouting
Fred Wright
Assistant director of player personnel
Kevin Morgan
Senior v.p. and treasurer
Harold W. O'Shaughnessy
Senior v.p. of business & legal affairs
David Howard
Vice president, marketing
Mark Bingham
Vice president, stadium operations
Bob Mandt
Vice president, ticket sales and services
Bill Ianniciello
Senior v.p. and consultant
J. Frank Cashen
Director of marketing
Kit Geis
Director of marketing production
Tim Gunkel
Director of human resources
Ray Scott

General counsel
David Cohen
Dir., admin. and data processing
Russ Richardson
Director, community outreach
Jill Knee
Director of promotions
James Plummer
Director of media relations
Jay Horwitz
Director, ticket operations
Dan DeMato
Manager, customer relations
Joann Galardy
Club physicians
Dr. David Altchek
Club psychologist/E.A.P.
Dr. Allan Lans
Team trainers
Fred Hina, Scott Lawrenson
Professional scouts
Edwin Bryant, Howard Johnson, Roland Johnson, Bill Latham, Mike Toomey, John Stearns
International scouts
Isao O'Jimi, George Santiago, Eddy Toledo, Boris Villa, Julio Molina Jr., Gregorio Machado, Cornelio Pena, Roberto Alfonzo, Guadalupe Salinas, Guadalupe Canol, Donald Canedo, James Waddell
National cross-checker
Jack Bowen
Regional scouting supervisors
Paul Fryer, Gene Kerns, Terry Tripp
Area supervisors
Tom Allison, Kevin Blankenship, Quincy Boyd, Larry Chase, Joe DelliCarri, Chuck Hensley Jr., Bob Lavallee, Dave Lottsfeldt, Fred Mazuca, Marlin McPhail, Randy Milligan, Bob Minor, Joe Morlan, Joe Nigro, Jim Reeves, Junior Roman, Bob Rossi, Joe Salermo, Greg Tubbs
Part-time scouts
Chet Atkins, Steve Free, Rich Hinell, Joe Hoagland, Buddy Kerr, Doug Sisk, George Walden, Joe Willingham

MINOR LEAGUE AFFILIATES

Class	Team	League	Manager
AAA	Norfolk	International	John Gibbons
AA	Binghamton	Eastern	Doug Davis
A	St. Lucie	Florida State	Howie Freiling
A	Capital City	South Atlantic	Dave Engle
A	Pittsfield	New York-Pennsylvania	Tony Tijerina
Rookie	Kingsport	Appalachian	To be announced
Rookie	Gulf Coast Mets	Gulf Coast	To be announced

BROADCAST INFORMATION

Radio: WFAN-AM (660).
TV: WWOR-TV (Channel 9).
Cable TV: Fox Sports New York.

SPRING TRAINING

Ballpark (city): Thomas J. White Stadium (Port St. Lucie, Fla.).
Ticket information: 561-871-2115.

SPRING TRAINING ROSTER

Manager—Bobby Valentine (2).
Coaches—Bob Apodaca (34), Bruce Benedict (20), Randy Niemann, Tom Robson (53), Cookie Rojas (4), Mookie Wilson (51).

No.	PITCHERS	B/T	Ht./Wt.	Born	1998 clubs
43	Beltran, Rigo	L/L	5-11/185	11-13-69	Norfolk, New York N.L.
49	Benitez, Armando	R/R	6-4/225	11-3-72	Baltimore
27	Cook, Dennis	L/L	6-3/190	10-4-62	New York N.L.
29	Dotel, Octavio	R/R	6-0/175	11-25-75	Binghamton, Norfolk
31	Franco, John	L/L	5-10/185	9-17-60	New York N.L.
40	Henriquez, Oscar	R/R	6-6/220	1-28-74	Charlotte, Florida
44	Isringhausen, Jason	R/R	6-3/196	9-7-72	New York N.L.
28	Jones, Bobby	R/R	6-4/225	2-10-70	New York N.L.
22	Leiter, Al	L/L	6-3/220	10-23-65	New York N.L.
36	McMichael, Greg	R/R	6-3/215	12-1-66	New York N.L., Los Angeles
64	Murray, Dan	R/R	6-1/193	11-21-73	Binghamton
16	Nomo, Hideo	R/R	6-2/230	8-31-68	Los Angeles, New York N.L.
35	Reed, Rick	R/R	6-1/195	8-16-65	New York N.L.
67	Roberts, Grant	R/R	6-3/205	9-13-77	St. Lucie
38	Tam, Jeff	R/R	6-1/202	8-19-70	New York N.L., Norfolk
47	Wallace, Derek	R/R	6-3/215	9-1-71	Norfolk
99	Wendell, Turk	L/R	6-2/205	5-19-67	New York N.L.
32	Wilson, Paul	R/R	6-5/235	3-28-73	St. Lucie, Norfolk
21	Yoshii, Masato	R/R	6-2/210	4-20-65	New York N.L.

No.	CATCHERS	B/T	Ht./Wt.	Born	1998 clubs
31	Piazza, Mike	R/R	6-3/215	9-4-68	Los Angeles, Florida, New York N.L.
7	Pratt, Todd	R/R	6-3/230	2-9-67	Norfolk, New York N.L., St. Lucie, Gulf Coast Mets
3	Wilson, Vance	R/R	5-11/190	3-17-73	St. Lucie, Norfolk

No.	INFIELDERS	B/T	Ht./Wt.	Born	1998 clubs
13	Alfonzo, Edgardo	R/R	5-11/187	11-8-73	New York N.L.
62	Bruce, Mo	R/R	5-10/190	5-1-75	Columbia
15	Franco, Matt	L/R	6-1/210	8-19-69	New York N.L., Norfolk
33	Kinkade, Mike	R/R	6-1/210	5-6-73	Louisville, Norfolk, New York N.L.
17	Lopez, Luis	B/R	5-11/166	9-4-70	New York N.L.
26	Milliard, Ralph	R/R	5-11/175	12-30-73	Norfolk, New York N.L.
5	Olerud, John	L/L	6-5/220	8-5-68	New York N.L.
10	Ordonez, Rey	R/R	5-9/159	11-11-72	New York N.L.
4	Ventura, Robin	L/R	6-1/198	7-14-67	Chicago A.L.

No.	OUTFIELDERS	B/T	Ht./Wt.	Born	1998 clubs
23	Allensworth, Jermaine	R/R	6-0/190	1-11-72	Pittsburgh, Kansas City, New York N.L.
25	Bonilla, Bobby	B/R	6-4/240	2-23-63	Florida, Los Angeles
	Cedeno, Roger	B/R	6-1/205	8-16-74	Los Angeles, Vero Beach
24	Henderson, Rickey	R/L	5-10/190	12-25-58	Oakland
66	Hunter, Scott	R/R	6-1/210	12-17-75	Binghamton, Norfolk
65	Long, Terrence	L/L	6-1/190	2-29-76	Binghamton
56	McRae, Brian	B/R	6-0/195	8-27-67	New York N.L.
12	Payton, Jay	R/R	5-10/185	11-22-72	Norfolk, New York N.L., St. Lucie

BALLPARK INFORMATION

Ballpark (capacity, surface)
Shea Stadium (55,601, grass)

Address
123-10 Roosevelt Ave.
Flushing, NY 11368

Business phone
718-507-6387

Ticket information
718-507-8499

Ticket prices
$45 (Metropolitan Club seating)
$30 (inner field box, inner loge box)
$25 (outer field box, outer loge box,
        mezzanine box)
$22 (loge reserved)
$25 (mezzanine box, upper box)
$10 (upper reserved, back rows loge and mezzanine)

Field dimensions (from home plate)
To left field at foul line, 338 feet
To center field, 410 feet
To right field at foul line, 338 feet

First game played
April 17, 1964 (Pirates 4, Mets 3)

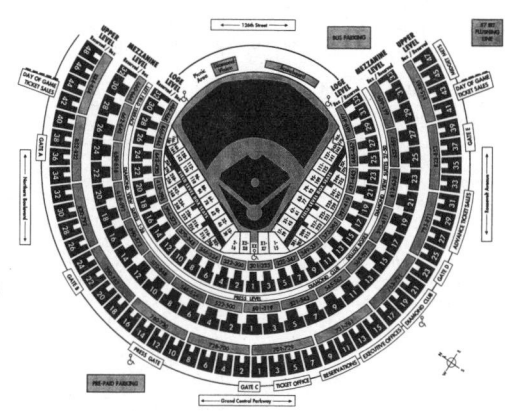

1999 SEASON New York Mets

Date	Opp.	Res.	Score	(inn.*)	Hits	Opp. hits	Winning pitcher	Losing pitcher	Save	Record	Pos.	GB
3-31	Phi.	W	1-0	(14)	7	9	Wendell	Bottalico		1-0	T1st	...
4-2	Phi.	L	5-6		6	11	Portugal	Leiter	Bottalico	1-1	T1st	...
4-3	Pit.	W	2-1		5	8	McMichael	Peters		2-1	T1st	...
4-4	Pit.	W	7-6	(13)	14	14	Wendell	Peters		3-1	T1st	...
4-5	Pit.	W	7-0		13	5	Yoshii	Silva		4-1	1st	+1.0
4-6	Pit.	L	2-4		8	8	Cordova	Jones	Loiselle	4-2	1st	+0.5
4-7	At Chi.	W	3-2		8	8	Leiter	Gonzalez	J. Franco	5-2	1st	+0.5
4-9	At Chi.	L	7-8		10	14	Trachsel	Reed	Beck	5-3	T1st	...
4-10	At Mil.	L	3-5		8	7	Juden	Mlicki	Jones	5-4	T2nd	0.5
4-11	At Mil.	W	2-1		5	6	Cook	Wickman	J. Franco	6-4	2nd	0.5
4-12	At Mil.	W	6-4		8	8	Wendell	Wagner	Rojas	7-4	1st	+0.5
4-14	Chi.	W	6-0		12	6	Leiter	Gonzalez		8-4	1st	+0.5
4-15	Chi.	W	2-1		5	5	Reed	Trachsel	J. Franco	9-4	1st	+1.5
4-16	Chi.	L	4-8		12	13	Tapani	Mlicki		9-5	1st	+0.5
4-17	At Cin.	L	3-4		4	8	Remlinger	Jones	Shaw	9-6	T1st	...
4-18	At Cin.	W	5-4	(10)	6	10	Rojas	Belinda	J. Franco	10-6	T1st	...
4-19	At Cin.	W	14-0		16	4	Leiter	White		11-6	1st	+0.5
4-21	Hou.	L	0-6		7	13	Hampton	Reed		11-7	2nd	0.5
4-22	Hou.	W	10-7		10	10	Cook	Henry		12-7	2nd	0.5
4-24	Cin.	W	3-2		5	5	Jones	Shaw	J. Franco	13-7	2nd	1.0
4-25	Cin.	L	0-2		6	6	Weathers	Yoshii	Shaw	13-8	2nd	1.0
4-27	Hou.	L	3-4		10	7	Nitkowski	J. Franco	Wagner	13-9	2nd	1.5
4-28	At Hou.	L	3-4	(10)	9	13	Magnante	Hudek		13-10	2nd	2.5
4-29	At Hou.	L	1-6		8	12	Lima	Mlicki		13-11	2nd	3.0
4-30	Col.	L	0-4		4	7	Kile	Jones		13-12	2nd	4.0
5-2	Col.	L	3-7		8	7	Leskanic	Cook		13-13	2nd	5.5
5-3	Col.	W	5-2		5	7	Reed	Astacio		14-13	2nd	4.5
5-4	Ari.	L	2-4	(11)	7	9	Olson	Bohanon		14-14	2nd	5.5
5-5	Ari.	W	9-1		13	6	Mlicki	Daal		15-14	2nd	5.5
5-6	Ari.	W	8-2		9	8	Rojas	Sodowsky		16-14	2nd	5.5
5-7	St.L.	W	4-1		7	2	Yoshii	Osborne	J. Franco	17-14	2nd	5.5
5-8	St.L.	W	9-2		12	5	Reed	Politte		18-14	2nd	4.5
5-11	At S.D.	L	1-2		4	5	Brown	Leiter	Hoffman	18-15	2nd	6.5
5-13	At S.D.	W	4-3		10	6	Jones	Hamilton	J. Franco	19-15	2nd	7.0
5-14†	At S.D.	L	1-3		8	9	Boehringer	Cook	Hoffman	19-16		
5-14‡	At S.D.	L	2-6		4	7	Miceli	McMichael		19-17	2nd	8.5
5-15	At S.F.	L	2-3		5	9	Hershiser	McMichael	Nen	19-18	T2nd	9.5
5-16	At S.F.	W	4-1		8	7	Reed	Rueter	J. Franco	20-18	2nd	8.5
5-17	At S.F.	L	2-4		7	9	Gardner	Leiter	Nen	20-19	2nd	8.5
5-19†	Cin.	W	7-3		8	4	Jones	Tomko		21-19		
5-19‡	Cin.	W	5-3		10	8	Bohanon	Winchester	J. Franco	22-19	2nd	8.0
5-20	Cin.	L	6-8		8	15	Harnisch	Hudek	Shaw	22-20	2nd	9.0
5-21	Cin.	W	6-1		6	9	Yoshii	Hutton		23-20	2nd	9.0
5-22	Mil.	W	3-2		4	6	Reed	Woodall	J. Franco	24-20	2nd	9.0
5-23	Mil.	W	3-0		11	4	Leiter	Juden		25-20	2nd	8.0
5-24	Mil.	W	8-3		15	10	Jones	Eldred		26-20	2nd	8.0
5-26	At Fla.	W	10-6		15	9	Bohanon	Larkin		27-20	2nd	8.5
5-27	At Fla.	W	8-2		15	9	Yoshii	Meadows		28-20	2nd	8.5
5-29	At Phi.	W	11-0		16	5	Reed	Beech		29-20	2nd	7.0
5-30	At Phi.	W	6-4		9	7	Leiter	Green	J. Franco	30-20	2nd	6.0
5-31	At Phi.	W	8-6		19	12	Rojas	Winston	J. Franco	31-20	2nd	5.0
6-1	At Pit.	L	3-4		6	7	Schmidt	Mlicki	Rincon	31-21	2nd	6.0
6-2	At Pit.	L	2-5		7	7	Peters	Bohanon	Rincon	31-22	2nd	7.0
6-3	At Pit.	L	0-3		4	4	Lieber	Reed	Christiansen	31-23	2nd	8.0
6-5	At Bos.	W	9-2		11	5	Leiter	Martinez		32-23	2nd	7.0
6-6	At Bos.	W	1-0		2	4	Jones	Wakefield	J. Franco	33-23	2nd	7.0
6-7	At Bos.	L	0-5		4	8	Avery	Yoshii		33-24	2nd	8.0
6-8	T.B.	W	3-0		7	3	Reed	Springer		34-24	2nd	8.0
6-9	T.B.	L	4-5	(11)	11	10	Mecir	Hudek	Hernandez	34-25	2nd	8.0
6-10	T.B.	W	3-2		4	6	Leiter	White	Rojas	35-25	2nd	7.0
6-11	At Fla.	W	5-3		9	9	Jones	Sanchez	J. Franco	36-25	2nd	6.5
6-12	At Fla.	L	3-4		8	9	Mantei	Bohanon		36-26	2nd	6.5
6-13	At Fla.	W	7-4		7	7	Reed	Meadows	J. Franco	37-26	2nd	6.5
6-14	At Fla.	L	4-5		12	12	Mantei	Hudek		37-27	2nd	7.5
6-16	At Mon.	W	2-0		6	5	Leiter	Hermanson		38-27	2nd	7.5
6-17	At Mon.	L	4-5		8	12	Urbina	Rojas		38-28	2nd	8.5
6-18	At Mon.	L	6-7		14	7	Bennett	Yoshii	Urbina	38-29	2nd	8.5
6-19	Fla.	L	2-3		9	6	Meadows	Reed	Mantei	38-30	2nd	8.5
6-20	Fla.	L	3-8		8	13	Hernandez	Nomo		38-31	2nd	9.5
6-21	Fla.	W	3-2		6	8	Leiter	Fontenot	J. Franco	39-31	2nd	8.5
6-22	At Bal.	L	2-7		2	14	Mussina	Jones		39-32	2nd	8.5

Date	Opp.	Res.	Score	(inn.*)	Hits	Opp. hits	Winning pitcher	Losing pitcher	Save	Record	Pos.	GB
6-23	At Bal.	W	6-3		15	8	Hudek	Rhodes	J. Franco	40-32	2nd	8.5
6-24	Bal.	W	6-3		9	14	Reed	Smith	J. Franco	41-32	2nd	7.5
6-25	Bal.	W	3-2		9	6	Cook	Benitez		42-32	2nd	6.5
6-26	N.Y. (AL)	L	4-8		7	13	Mendoza	Leiter	Rivera	42-33	2nd	6.5
6-27	N.Y. (AL)	L	2-7		5	8	Pettitte	Jones		42-34	2nd	7.5
6-28	N.Y. (AL)	W	2-1		3	2	Cook	Mendoza		43-34	2nd	7.5
6-30	At Tor.	L	3-6		6	11	Clemens	Reed		43-35	2nd	8.5
7-1	At Tor.	L	10-15		14	15	Plesac	Rojas		43-36	2nd	9.5
7-2	At Tor.	W	9-1		11	5	Jones	Hentgen		44-36	2nd	9.5
7-3	At Atl.	L	2-3		12	9	Glavine	Bohanon	Ligtenberg	44-37	2nd	10.5
7-4	At Atl.	L	1-4		6	8	Millwood	Yoshii		44-38	2nd	11.5
7-5	At Atl.	L	2-3	(11)	7	8	Seanez	J. Franco		44-39	2nd	12.5
7-9	Mon.	L	8-9	(11)	15	18	Maddux	J. Franco	Urbina	44-40	2nd	13.5
7-10	Mon.	L	6-8		12	11	Bennett	J. Franco	Urbina	44-41	2nd	13.5
7-11	Mon.	W	8-4		11	12	Reed	Pavano		45-41	2nd	12.5
7-12	Mon.	W	5-2		11	2	Tam	Vazquez	Cook	46-41	2nd	11.5
7-14	Atl.	L	2-4		6	8	Smoltz	Jones	Ligtenberg	46-42	2nd	12.5
7-15	Atl.	L	1-12		6	16	Neagle	Yoshii		46-43	2nd	13.5
7-16	Phi.	L	2-4		9	11	Portugal	Reed	Leiter	46-44	3rd	14.5
7-17	Phi.	W	6-0		9	4	Nomo	Loewer		47-44	T2nd	14.5
7-18	Phi.	W	7-0		10	3	Leiter	Green		48-44	2nd	13.5
7-19	Phi.	L	6-7	(10)	10	13	Leiter	Cook		48-45	T2nd	14.5
7-20	Pit.	L	1-3		5	8	Cordova	Yoshii	Rincon	48-46	3rd	14.5
7-21	Pit.	W	4-0		6	8	Reed	Schmidt		49-46	3rd	13.5
7-22†	At Mil.	W	7-5		11	12	Cook	Wickman	J. Franco	50-46		
7-22‡	At Mil.	W	6-1		15	6	Nomo	Patrick		51-46	2nd	13.0
7-23	At Mil.	W	6-5		16	9	McMichael	Myers	J. Franco	52-46	2nd	13.0
7-24†	At Chi.	W	5-0		13	5	Reynoso	Gonzalez		53-46		
7-24‡	At Chi.	W	7-3		11	7	Cook	Adams		54-46	2nd	12.5
7-25	At Chi.	L	2-3		7	4	Tapani	J. Franco	Beck	54-47	2nd	12.5
7-26	At Chi.	L	1-3		6	7	Wood	Reed	Beck	54-48	2nd	13.5
7-28	S.D.	W	7-3		11	10	Nomo	Ashby	McMichael	55-48	2nd	13.0
7-29	S.D.	W	7-6		14	12	Rojas	Wall	J. Franco	56-48	2nd	13.0
7-30	S.D.	L	1-3	(10)	5	8	Miceli	Cook	Hoffman	56-49	2nd	14.0
7-31	L.A.	L	3-4		10	11	Osuna	J. Franco	Shaw	56-50	2nd	14.0
8-1	L.A.	W	2-1		5	6	Reed	Shaw		57-50	2nd	14.0
8-2	L.A.	W	9-3		10	5	Reynoso	Bohanon		58-50	2nd	14.0
8-3	L.A.	L	5-8		10	11	Mlicki	McMichael	Shaw	58-51	2nd	14.5
8-4	S.F.	W	7-6	(10)	15	10	Cook	Mesa		59-51	2nd	14.5
8-5	S.F.	L	4-6		8	14	Ortiz	Jones	Nen	59-52	2nd	14.5
8-6	S.F.	W	9-8		16	13	Wendell	Nen		60-52	2nd	14.5
8-7	At Col.	W	8-7		13	14	Reed	Astacio	J. Franco	61-52	2nd	14.5
8-8	At Col.	W	4-3		9	12	Reynoso	Jones	J. Franco	62-52	2nd	14.5
8-9	At Col.	L	4-11		10	17	Kile	Nomo		62-53	2nd	15.5
8-10	At St.L.	W	4-2		8	6	Leiter	Morris	J. Franco	63-53	2nd	15.0
8-11	At St.L.	W	8-3		17	10	Jones	Mercker		64-53	2nd	14.0
8-12	At St.L.	L	4-5	(14)	11	12	Frascatore	J. Franco		64-54	2nd	14.0
8-14	At Ari.	W	3-2		6	9	Reed	Telemaco	Wendell	65-54	2nd	14.5
8-15	At Ari.	W	5-4		11	7	Reynoso	Chouinard	J. Franco	66-54	2nd	14.5
8-16	At Ari.	L	1-6		2	7	Daal	Nomo		66-55	2nd	14.5
8-18†	Col.	W	6-2		8	10	Leiter	Astacio		67-55		
8-18‡	Col.	W	6-3		12	8	Rojas	McElroy	J. Franco	68-55	2nd	14.0
8-19	Col.	W	2-1		6	9	Yoshii	Jones	J. Franco	69-55	2nd	13.0
8-20†	St.L.	L	0-2		4	3	Osborne	Blair	Acevedo	69-56		
8-20‡	St.L.	W	5-4		9	6	Reed	Oliver	Wendell	70-56	2nd	12.5
8-21†	St.L.	L	5-10		9	11	Morris	Nomo		70-57		
8-21‡	St.L.	W	1-0		7	3	Reynoso	Aybar	J. Franco	71-57	2nd	13.0
8-22	Ari.	W	9-4		6	8	Jones	Benes		72-57	2nd	13.0
8-23	Ari.	L	3-4		7	8	Anderson	Leiter	Olson	72-58	2nd	14.0
8-24	Ari.	L	5-9		9	12	Telemaco	Yoshii	Banks	72-59	2nd	15.0
8-25	At S.F.	L	3-7		7	12	Ortiz	Reed		72-60	2nd	15.0
8-26	At S.F.	W	4-1		9	3	Nomo	Hershiser		73-60	2nd	15.0
8-27	At S.F.	L	3-11		10	16	Darwin	Reynoso		73-61	2nd	16.0
8-28	At L.A.	W	5-4	(10)	8	13	Cook	Shaw	J. Franco	74-61	2nd	15.0
8-29	At L.A.	W	4-3		12	6	Leiter	Shaw	J. Franco	75-61	2nd	15.0
8-30	At L.A.	L	2-4		8	9	Mlicki	Yoshii		75-62	2nd	15.0
8-31	At L.A.	W	8-3		14	9	Reed	Park		76-62	2nd	14.0
9-1	At S.D.	L	8-9		10	10	R. Myers	Wendell	Hoffman	76-63	2nd	15.0
9-2	At S.D.	W	4-1		6	5	Reynoso	Ashby	J. Franco	77-63	2nd	14.0
9-4	Atl.	W	2-1		6	5	Leiter	Glavine		78-63	2nd	13.0
9-5	Atl.	W	5-4		10	6	Wendell	Seanez	J. Franco	79-63	2nd	12.0
9-6	Atl.	L	0-4		3	8	Smoltz	Reed		79-64	2nd	13.0
9-7	Atl.	W	8-7		11	10	McMichael	Rocker	J. Franco	80-64	2nd	12.0
9-8	At Phi.	L	4-16		11	17	Byrd	Nomo		80-65	2nd	12.0
9-9	At Phi.	W	6-2		13	8	Reynoso	Schilling	J. Franco	81-65	2nd	11.0

Date	Opp.	Res.	Score	(inn.*)	Hits	Opp. hits	Winning pitcher	Losing pitcher	Save	Record	Pos.	GB
9-10	At Phi.	W	7-5		8	6	Leiter	Green	J. Franco	82-65	2nd	11.0
9-11	At Mon.	L	1-5		4	7	Pavano	Jones	Urbina	82-66	2nd	12.0
9-12	At Mon.	L	3-5		7	7	Maddux	Reed	Urbina	82-67	2nd	13.0
9-13	At Mon.	W	1-0		4	4	Blair	Telford	J. Franco	83-67	2nd	12.0
9-14	At Hou.	W	7-4	(13)	13	9	McMichael	Magnante	J. Franco	84-67	2nd	12.0
9-15†	At Hou.	L	5-6	(12)	11	13	Powell	Tam		84-68		
9-15‡	At Hou.	W	8-4		10	8	Leiter	Powell	Wendell	85-68	2nd	12.5
9-16	At Hou.	W	4-3	(11)	13	5	McMichael	Bergman	Wendell	86-68	2nd	12.5
9-18	Fla.	L	6-7		11	14	Edmondson	J. Franco	Mantei	86-69	2nd	13.0
9-19	Fla.	W	4-3		7	9	Yoshii	Sanchez	J. Franco	87-69	2nd	13.0
9-20	Fla.	W	5-0		10	5	Leiter	Meadows		88-69	2nd	13.0
9-22	Mon.	L	3-5		5	10	Thurman	Reynoso	Urbina	88-70	2nd	14.0
9-23	Mon.	L	0-3		3	7	Pavano	Jones	Urbina	88-71	2nd	15.0
9-25	At Atl.	L	5-6		11	10	Martinez	Reed	Rocker	88-72	2nd	16.0
9-26	At Atl.	L	0-4		7	6	Neagle	Leiter		88-73	2nd	17.0
9-27	At Atl.	L	2-7		8	14	Maddux	Reynoso		88-74	2nd	18.0

Monthly records: March (1-0), April (12-12), May (18-8), June (12-15), July (13-15), August (20-12), September (12-12).
*Innings, if other than nine. †First game of doubleheader. ‡Second game of doubleheader.

HIGHLIGHTS

High point: The team won a season-high nine consecutive games from May 21-31. It averaged six runs over that span and was only five games behind the division-leading Braves by the end of the streak.

Low point: Playing Todd Hundley in left field in July and August was a disaster. He made five errors and had trouble catching fly balls. By September, Hundley was the backup catcher.

Turning point: On September 20, the Mets had a one-game lead in the N.L. wild-card race. But they lost their final five games and were eliminated September 27.

Most valuable player: With Hundley sidelined by an elbow injury, the Mets acquired Mike Piazza from the Marlins on May 22. Piazza provided leadership and hit .348 with 23 home runs and 76 RBIs. The Mets went 66-53 after his arrival and were in the wild-card race until the final week of the season.

Most valuable pitcher: Despite missing four weeks because of a knee injury, Al Leiter won 17 games and had a 2.47 ERA, which ranked third in the N.L.

Most improved player: Journeyman Dennis Cook had his best season, pitching a career-high 73 games and posting a 2.38 ERA.

Most pleasant surprise: Brian McRae had a career-high 21 home runs and hit .293 over the second half of the season.

Biggest disappointment: The Mets had heard that Hideo Nomo had lost velocity off his fastball. That might explain why he had a 5.05 ERA when the Dodgers designated him for assignment on June 1. But the Mets ignored the scouting reports and acquired Nomo three days later. Unfortunately, he didn't pitch any better for them, winning four games and posting a 4.82 ERA. Nomo was so ineffective, manager Bobby Valentine took him out of the rotation during September and replaced him with Willie Blair.

Key injuries: Leiter missed four weeks because of a partially torn patella tendon in his knee. Hundley spent the first three months recuperating from elbow surgery. Butch Huskey had hamstring problems,

which limited him to 35 games over the second half of the season. Arm and shoulder problems limited Armando Reynoso to 11 games.

Notables: Carlos Baerga should be exclusively a lefthanded hitter. Over the last three seasons, he batted .200 while averaging a homer and 11 RBIs from the right side. As a lefty hitter during that same period, Baerga batted .285 and averaged eight home runs and 46 RBIs. . . . . John Olerud's .353 batting average established a team record for a single season.

—WILLIAM LADSON

RECORDS

1998 regular-season record: 88-74 (2nd in N.L. East); 47-34 at home; 41-40 on road; 22-26 vs. N.L. East; 33-21 vs. Central; 24-20 vs. West; 9-7 vs. A.L.; 25-19 vs. lefthanded starters; 63-55 vs. righthanded starters; 75-60 on grass; 13-14 on turf; 33-26 in daytime; 55-48 at night; 35-26 in one-run games; 7-9 in extra-inning games; 4-1-3 in doubleheaders.

Team record past five years: 371-372 (.499, ranks 7th in league in that span).

TEAM LEADERS

Batting average: John Olerud (.354).
At-bats: Edgardo Alfonzo, John Olerud (557).
Runs: Edgardo Alfonzo (94).
Hits: John Olerud (197).
Total bases: John Olerud (307).
Doubles: Brian McRae, John Olerud (36).
Triples: Brian McRae (5).
Home runs: Mike Piazza (23).
Runs batted in: John Olerud (93).
Stolen bases: Brian McRae (20).
Slugging percentage: John Olerud (.551).
On-base percentage: John Olerud (.447).
Wins: Al Leiter (17).
Earned-run average: Al Leiter (2.47).
Complete games: Al Leiter (4).
Shutouts: Al Leiter (2).

Saves: John Franco (38).
Innings pitched: Rick Reed (212.1).
Strikeouts: Al Leiter (174).

GAMES BY POSITION

Catcher: Mike Piazza 99, Alberto Castillo 35, Tim Spehr 21, Todd Pratt 16, Jorge Fabregas 12, Jimmy Tatum 4, Rick Wilkins 4, Todd Hundley 2.
First base: John Olerud 157, Matt Franco 11, Jimmy Tatum 9, Todd Pratt 3, Craig Paquette 2, Lenny Harris 1, Tim Spehr 1.
Second base: Carlos Baerga 144, Luis Lopez 50, Ralph Milliard 5, Lenny Harris 2, Todd Haney 1.
Third base: Edgardo Alfonzo 144, Matt Franco 13, Luis Lopez 11, Lenny Harris 10, Craig Paquette 4, Jimmy Tatum 3, Shawn Gilbert 1, Mike Kinkade 1.
Shortstop: Rey Ordonez 151, Luis Lopez 39, Edgardo Alfonzo 1, Ralph Milliard 1.
Outfield: Brian McRae 154, Butch Huskey 103, Bernard Gilkey 77, Lenny Harris 65, Tony Phillips 51, Rich Becker 41, Todd Hundley 34, Jermaine Allensworth 31, Wayne Kirby 19, Matt Franco 13, Jay Payton 10, Benny Agbayani 9, Luis Lopez 9, Preston Wilson 7, Jimmy Tatum 4, Todd Haney 1, Craig Paquette 1.
Designated hitter: Mike Piazza 4, Matt Franco 2, Alberto Castillo 1, Butch Huskey 1, Jimmy Tatum 1.

TOP DRAFT CHOICES

1. **Jason Tyner,** OF, Texas A&M Univ.
2. **Pat Strange,** RHP, Central H.S., Springfield, Mass.
3. **Jason Saenz,** LHP, U. of Southern California
4. **Jason Moates,** RHP, Meridian (Miss.) C.C.
5. **Craig Brazell,** C, Jeff Davis H.S., Montgomery, Ala.
6. **Marvin Seale,** OF, Durango (Colo.) H.S.
7. **Ryan Smith,** C, Mifflinburg (Pa.) Area H.S.
8. **Vince Vazquez,** RHP, Chaminade H.S., Hollywood, Fla.
9. **Todd Bellhorn,** LHP, U. of Central Fla.
10. **Larnell Hamn,** OF, Potomac H.S., Triangle, Va.

PHILADELPHIA PHILLIES
NATIONAL LEAGUE EAST DIVISION

1999 Phillies Schedule
Home games shaded. *—All-Star Game at Fenway Park (Boston). D—Day game (any game starting before 5 p.m.).

April
SUN	MON	TUE	WED	THU	FRI	SAT
				1	2	3
4	5 D ATL	6 D ATL	7 ATL	8 ATL	9 FLA	10 FLA
11 D FLA	12 D ATL	13 ATL	14 ATL	15 ATL	16 FLA	17 FLA
18 D FLA	19 ARI	20 ARI	21 ARI	22	23 MON	24 MON
25 D MON	26	27 CIN	28 CIN	29 CIN	30 LA	

May
SUN	MON	TUE	WED	THU	FRI	SAT
						1 LA
2 D LA	3 D SD	4 D SD	5 D SD	6	7 COL	8 D COL
9 COL	10 D STL	11 STL	12 D STL	13	14 NYM	15 NYM
16 D NYM	17 MON	18 MON	19 MON	20	21 NYM	22 D NYM
23 NYM	24 MON	25 MON	26 MON	27	28 COL	29 COL
30 D COL	31 SF					

June
SUN	MON	TUE	WED	THU	FRI	SAT
		1 SF	2 SF	3 D BAL	4 D BAL	5 BAL
6 D BAL	7 NYY	8 NYY	9 NYY	10	11 TOR	12 TOR
13 D TOR	14	15 SD	16 SD	17 D SD	18 D LA	19 D LA
20 D LA	21	22 PIT	23 PIT	24 PIT	25 D CUB	26 D CUB
27 D CUB	28 PIT	29 PIT	30 PIT			

July
SUN	MON	TUE	WED	THU	FRI	SAT
				1 PIT	2 CUB	3 CUB
4 CUB	5 MIL	6 MIL	7 MIL	8	9 BAL	10 BAL
11 D BAL	12	13	14 *	15 BOS	16 BOS	17 D BOS
18 TB	19 TB	20 D TB	21 MIL	22 MIL	23 ATL	24 ATL
25 D ATL	26 FLA	27 FLA	28 FLA	29 FLA	30 ATL	31 ATL

August
SUN	MON	TUE	WED	THU	FRI	SAT
1 D ATL	2	3 FLA	4 FLA	5 FLA	6 ARI	7 D ARI
8 D ARI	9 STL	10 STL	11 STL	12	13 CIN	14 CIN
15 D CIN	16 D STL	17 STL	18 STL	19	20 LA	21 LA
22 D LA	23 SD	24 SD	25 SD	26	27 COL	28 COL
29 D COL	30 SF	31 SF				

September
SUN	MON	TUE	WED	THU	FRI	SAT
			1 D SF	2 SF	3 D CIN	4 CIN
5 CIN	6 HOU	7 HOU	8 HOU	9	10 ARI	11 ARI
12 ARI	13 HOU	14 HOU	15 HOU	16	17 NYM	18 NYM
19 NYM	20 MIL	21 MIL	22 MIL	23 D NYM	24 NYM	25 NYM
26 D NYM	27	28 CUB	29 CUB	30 CUB		

October
SUN	MON	TUE	WED	THU	FRI	SAT
					1 MON	2 MON
3 D MON	4	5	6	7	8	9

1999 SEASON
CLUB DIRECTORY

Managing general partner, president, CEO
David Montgomery
Chairman, general partner
Bill Giles
Partners
Claire S. Betz, Tri-Play Associates (Alexander K. Buck, J. Mahlon Buck Jr., William C. Buck), Double Play, Inc. (Herbert H. Middleton Jr.), Fitz Eugene Dixon Jr.
Secretary and general counsel
Bill Webb
Senior v.p., finance and planning
Jerry Clothier
Special assistant to the president
Sharon Swainson
Director, business development
Joe Giles
Vice president and general manager
Ed Wade
Assistant general manager
Ruben Amaro Jr.
Controller
John Fusco
Director, scouting
Mike Arbuckle
Senior advisors to general manager
Dallas Green, Paul Owens
Director, minor league personnel
Lee Elia
Director, minor league operations
Steve Noworyta
Executive asst. to the general manager
Susan Ingersoll
Traveling secretary
Eddie Ferenz
Vice president, public relations
Larry Shenk
Manager, publicity
Leigh Tobin
Manager, media relations
Gene Dias
Vice president, advertising sales
Dave Buck

Director, information systems
Brian Lamoreaux
Vice president, ticket operations
Richard Deats
Director, ticket department
Dan Goroff
Director, sales
John Weber
Director, broadcasting and video services
Rory McNeil
Director, stadium operations
Mike DiMuzio
Club physician
Dr. Phillip Marone
Club trainers
Jeff Cooper, Mark Andersen
Mgr., equipment and home clubhouse
Frank Coppenbarger
Manager, visiting clubhouse
Levin Steinhour
National supervisor
Marti Wolever
Director, Florida Operations
John Timberlake
Director, Latin American Operations
Sal Artiaga
Director, Major League scouts
Gordon Lakey
Major League scout
Jimmy Stewart
Advance scout, Major Leagues
Hank King
Special assignment scouts
Jim Fregosi Jr., Dean Jongewaard
Coordinator, professional coverage
Dick Lawlor
Regular scouts
Sal Agostinelli, Emil Belich, Jim Fregosi Jr., Steve Gillispie, Bill Harper, Ken Hultzapple, Jerry Lafferty, Terry Logan, Miguel Machado, Lloyd Merritt, Venice Murray, Arthur Parrack, Mark Ralston, Scott Ramsay, Mitch Sokol, Doug Takaragawa, Roy Tanner

MINOR LEAGUE AFFILIATES

Class	Team	League	Manager
AAA	Scranton/Wilkes-Barre	International	Marc Bombard
AA	Reading	Eastern	Gary Varsho
A	Clearwater	Florida State	Bill Dancy
A	Piedmont	South Atlantic	Ken Oberkfell
A	Batavia	New York-Pennsylvania	Greg Legg
Rookie	Gulf Coast Phillies	Gulf Coast	Ramon Aviles

BROADCAST INFORMATION
Radio: Talk Radio 1210.
TV: UPN 57.
Cable TV: Comcast Sportsnet.

SPRING TRAINING
Ballpark (city): Jack Russell Stadium (Clearwater, Fla.).
Ticket information: 215-463-1000 or 727-442-8496.

SPRING TRAINING ROSTER

Manager—Terry Francona (7).
Coaches—Galen Cisco (43), Chuck Cottier (3), Ramon Henderson, Hal McRae (56), Brad Mills (9), John Vukovich (18).

No.	PITCHERS	B/T	Ht./Wt.	Born	1998 clubs
55	Beech, Matt	L/L	6-2/194	1-20-72	Philadelphia
45	Brantley, Jeff	R/R	5-10/190	9-5-63	Arkansas, St. Louis
34	Byrd, Paul	R/R	6-1/185	12-3-70	Richmond, Atlanta, Philadelphia
72	Coggin, Dave	R/R	6-4/205	10-30-76	Reading
61	Gomes, Wayne	R/R	6-2/226	1-15-73	Philadelphia
44	Grace, Mike	R/R	6-4/219	6-20-70	Philadelphia, Scranton/Wilkes-Barre
28	Green, Tyler	R/R	6-5/208	2-18-70	Philadelphia
46	Loewer, Carlton	B/R	6-6/220	9-24-73	Philadelphia, Scranton/Wilkes-Barre
39	Nye, Ryan	R/R	6-2/214	6-24-73	Scranton/Wilkes-Barre, Philadelphia
33	Ogea, Chad	L/R	6-2/220	11-9-70	Buffalo, Cleveland
48	Perez, Yorkis	B/L	6-0/180	9-30-67	Scranton/Wilkes-Barre, Philadelphia, Reading
35	Politte, Cliff	R/R	5-11/185	2-27-74	Memphis, Arkansas, St. Louis
	Poole, Jim	L/L	6-2/195	4-28-66	San Francisco, Buffalo, Cleveland
51	Ryan, Ken	R/R	6-3/230	10-24-68	Clearwater, Scranton/Wilkes-Barre, Philadelphia
38	Schilling, Curt	R/R	6-4/228	11-14-66	Philadelphia
65	Shumaker, Anthony	L/L	6-5/223	5-14-73	Reading
50	Spoljaric, Paul	R/L	6-3/210	9-24-70	Seattle
47	Welch, Mike	L/R	6-2/210	8-25-72	Scranton/Wilkes-Barre, Philadelphia

No.	CATCHERS	B/T	Ht./Wt.	Born	1998 clubs
14	Bennett, Gary	R/R	6-0/190	4-17-72	Scranton/Wilkes-Barre, Philadelphia
27	Estalella, Robert	R/R	6-1/210	8-23-74	Scranton/Wilkes-Barre, Philadelphia
24	Lieberthal, Mike	R/R	6-0/186	1-18-72	Philadelphia
12	Prince, Tom	R/R	5-11/206	8-13-64	Los Angeles

No.	INFIELDERS	B/T	Ht./Wt.	Born	1998 clubs
16	Anderson, Marlon	L/R	5-11/200	1-6-74	Scranton/Wilkes-Barre
26	Arias, Alex	R/R	6-3/197	11-20-67	Philadelphia
2	Brogna, Rico	L/L	6-2/205	4-18-70	Philadelphia
76	Burrell, Pat	R/R	6-4/225	10-10-76	Clearwater
15	Doster, Dave	R/R	5-10/181	10-8-70	Scranton/Wilkes-Barre
67	Duncan, Carlos	R/R	6-1/185	6-30-77	Piedmont, Batavia
23	Jordan, Kevin	R/R	6-1/206	10-9-69	Philadelphia
30	Relaford, Desi	B/R	5-9/175	9-16-73	Philadelphia
17	Rolen, Scott	R/R	6-4/225	4-4-75	Philadelphia
11	Sefcik, Kevin	R/R	5-10/180	2-10-71	Philadelphia

No.	OUTFIELDERS	B/T	Ht./Wt.	Born	1998 clubs
53	Abreu, Bob	L/R	6-0/186	3-11-74	Philadelphia
60	Carver, Steve	L/R	6-3/215	9-27-72	Reading, Scranton/Wilkes-Barre
	Ducey, Rob	L/R	6-2/180	5-24-65	Seattle
5	Gant, Ron	R/R	6-0/200	3-2-65	St. Louis
6	Glanville, Doug	R/R	6-2/180	8-25-70	Philadelphia
29	Magee, Wendell	R/R	6-0/220	8-3-72	Scranton/Wilkes-Barre, Philadelphia
	Miller, David	L/L	6-4/200	12-9-73	Buffalo
63	Taylor, Reggie	L/R	6-1/178	1-12-77	Reading

BALLPARK INFORMATION

Ballpark (capacity, surface)
Veterans Stadium (62,409, artificial)

Address
P.O. Box 7575
Philadelphia, PA 19101

Business phone
215-463-6000

Ticket information
215-463-1000

Ticket prices
$20 (field box)
$17 (sections 258-274)
$17 (terrace box)
$16 (loge box)
$12 (reserved, 600 level)
$6 (reserved, 700 level)

Field dimensions (from home plate)
To left field at foul line, 330 feet
To center field, 408 feet
To right field at foul line, 330 feet

First game played
April 10, 1971 (Phillies 4, Expos 1)

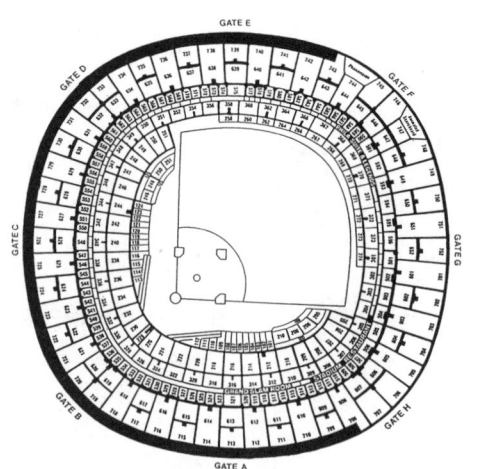

1998 REVIEW
DAY BY DAY

Date	Opp.	Res.	Score	(inn.*)	Hits	Opp. hits	Winning pitcher	Losing pitcher	Save	Record	Pos.	GB
3-31	At N.Y.	L	0-1	(14)	9	7	Wendell	Bottalico		0-1	T4th	1.0
4-2	At N.Y.	W	6-5		11	6	Portugal	Leiter	Bottalico	1-1	T1st	...
4-3	At Atl.	L	1-5		5	10	Neagle	Grace		1-2	3rd	1.0
4-4	At Atl.	L	4-5		13	9	Martinez	Brewer	Wohlers	1-3	3rd	2.0
4-5	At Atl.	W	2-1		5	5	Schilling	Maddux		2-3	3rd	2.0
4-7	Fla.	W	9-8	(10)	15	9	Bottalico	Sanchez		3-3	3rd	1.5
4-8	Fla.	W	9-5		14	7	Grace	Ludwick		4-3	T2nd	1.0
4-10	Atl.	W	1-0		6	2	Schilling	Cather		5-3	1st	+0.5
4-11	Atl.	W	6-5		10	9	Green	Martinez		6-3	1st	+0.5
4-12	Atl.	L	2-3		8	7	Glavine	Stephenson	Wohlers	6-4	2nd	0.5
4-13	Atl.	W	11-8		12	13	Spradlin	Ligtenberg	Bottalico	7-4	T1st	...
4-15	At Fla.	L	2-3		3	4	Meadows	Schilling	Heredia	7-5	2nd	1.5
4-16	At Fla.	L	4-12		9	12	Hernandez	Green		7-6	3rd	1.5
4-17	At St.L.	L	5-8		11	10	Politte	Whiteside	Bottenfield	7-7	3rd	1.5
4-18	At St.L.	L	5-6		9	10	Aybar	Grace	Brantley	7-8	3rd	2.5
4-19	At St.L.	L	2-3		11	8	Mercker	Beech	Acevedo	7-9	3rd	3.5
4-21	Cin.	L	3-6		8	9	Tomko	Schilling	Shaw	7-10	3rd	4.0
4-22	Cin.	W	5-4		9	11	Green	White	Bottalico	8-10	3rd	4.0
4-23	Cin.	W	6-3		8	7	Spradlin	Sullivan	Leiter	9-10	3rd	4.0
4-24	St.L.	W	8-4		10	10	Whiteside	Mercker		10-10	3rd	4.0
4-25	St.L.	L	5-8		9	11	Petkovsek	Spradlin	Brantley	10-11	3rd	4.0
4-26	St.L.	W	9-3		11	8	Schilling	Stottlemyre		11-11	3rd	3.0
4-27	At Cin.	L	1-3		3	5	Belinda	Green		11-12	3rd	4.0
4-28	At Cin.	W	11-8	(10)	15	12	Leiter	Belinda	Winston	12-12	3rd	4.0
4-29	At Cin.	L	0-1		2	5	Harnisch	Grace		12-13	3rd	4.5
5-1	Hou.	L	5-12		11	14	Reynolds	Beech		12-14	3rd	6.0
5-2	Hou.	L	1-4		8	7	Hampton	Schilling	Wagner	12-15	3rd	7.0
5-3	Hou.	W	5-3		10	7	Gomes	Bergman	Leiter	13-15	3rd	6.0
5-4	Col.	L	2-11		6	14	Thomson	Stephenson		13-16	3rd	7.0
5-5	Col.	L	1-6		7	13	Kile	Grace		13-17	3rd	8.0
5-6	Col.	W	7-6	(10)	13	10	Leiter	McElroy		14-17	3rd	8.0
5-7	Ari.	W	4-1		8	3	Schilling	Benes	Leiter	15-17	3rd	8.0
5-8	Ari.	W	6-4		8	6	Green	Olson	Leiter	16-17	3rd	7.0
5-10	Ari.	W	7-4		8	7	Winston	Suppan	Leiter	17-17	3rd	7.5
5-11	At L.A.	W	5-2		15	5	Beech	Dreifort	Leiter	18-17	3rd	7.5
5-12	At L.A.	W	5-3		12	11	Schilling	Radinsky	Leiter	19-17	3rd	7.5
5-13	At L.A.	L	4-9		7	11	Park	Green		19-18	3rd	8.5
5-14	At L.A.	W	4-0		9	2	Portugal	Nomo		20-18	3rd	8.5
5-15	At S.D.	L	6-7		12	10	Boehringer	Grace	Hoffman	20-19	T2nd	9.5
5-16	At S.D.	L	2-3		9	7	Reyes	Leiter		20-20	3rd	9.5
5-17	At S.D.	L	1-3		7	7	Wall	Schilling	Hoffman	20-21	3rd	9.5
5-19	St.L.	L	8-10		10	15	Frascatore	Gomes	Acevedo	20-22	3rd	10.5
5-20	St.L.	L	5-8		11	15	Busby	Portugal	Brantley	20-23	3rd	11.5
5-21	St.L.	W	4-3		9	6	Grace	Stottlemyre	Leiter	21-23	3rd	11.5
5-22	At Mon.	W	7-5	(10)	15	8	Gomes	Telford	Leiter	22-23	3rd	11.5
5-23	At Mon.	L	2-3		3	5	Urbina	Schilling		22-24	3rd	11.5
5-24	At Mon.	L	4-5		7	4	C. Perez	Spradlin	Urbina	22-25	3rd	12.5
5-25	At Mon.	W	5-3	(14)	13	13	Gomes	Bennett	Spradlin	23-25	3rd	12.5
5-27	At Chi.	W	10-5		14	8	Grace	Gonzalez		24-25	3rd	13.0
5-28	At Chi.	W	8-7		12	11	Winston	Beck	Leiter	25-25	3rd	12.0
5-29	N.Y.	L	0-11		5	16	Reed	Beech		25-26	3rd	12.0
5-30	N.Y.	L	4-6		7	9	Leiter	Green	J. Franco	25-27	3rd	12.0
5-31	N.Y.	L	6-8		12	19	Rojas	Winston	J. Franco	25-28	3rd	12.0
6-1	Mon.	W	6-2		8	7	Gomes	Maddux		26-28	3rd	12.0
6-2	Mon.	L	3-4		6	10	Pavano	Schilling	Urbina	26-29	3rd	13.0
6-3	Mon.	L	2-3		7	8	C. Perez	Gomes		26-30	3rd	14.0
6-5	At Tor.	W	8-7		15	6	Green	Risley	Leiter	27-30	4th	13.0
6-6	At Tor.	W	10-6		16	10	Gomes	Guzman		28-30	3rd	13.0
6-7	At Tor.	L	1-3		10	9	Carpenter	Schilling	Myers	28-31	3rd	14.0
6-8	Bal.	L	8-14		14	18	Rhodes	Winston	Orosco	28-32	3rd	15.0
6-9	Bal.	W	2-0		8	3	Beech	Ponson	Leiter	29-32	3rd	14.0
6-10	Bal.	L	2-5	(10)	10	8	Benitez	Leiter		29-33	3rd	14.0
6-12	Chi.	W	4-0		10	5	Schilling	Tapani		30-33	3rd	13.0
6-13	Chi.	L	8-10	(10)	18	12	Adams	Spradlin		30-34	3rd	14.0
6-14	Chi.	W	4-2		10	5	Loewer	Clark		31-34	3rd	14.0
6-15	Pit.	W	2-1		8	4	Beech	Lieber	Leiter	32-34	3rd	13.5
6-16	Pit.	W	8-7		8	13	Dodd	Loiselle		33-34	3rd	13.5
6-17	Pit.	W	3-1		8	2	Schilling	Cordova		34-34	3rd	13.5
6-18	At Chi.	L	5-12		9	16	Gonzalez	Portugal	Mulholland	34-35	3rd	13.5
6-19	At Chi.	W	9-8	(12)	19	12	Spradlin	Mulholland		35-35	3rd	12.5
6-20	At Chi.	L	4-9		10	15	Wood	Beech		35-36	3rd	13.5

Date	Opp.	Res.	Score	(inn.*)	Hits	Opp. hits	Winning pitcher	Losing pitcher	Save	Record	Pos.	GB
6-21	At Chi.	W	7-2		9	8	Green	Trachsel		36-36	3rd	12.5
6-22	At Bos.	W	9-8	(10)	13	13	Gomes	Gordon	Leiter	37-36	3rd	11.5
6-23	At Bos.	W	3-2		11	7	Portugal	Lowe		38-36	3rd	11.5
6-24	Bos.	W	11-8		13	10	Loewer	Avery	Leiter	39-36	3rd	10.5
6-25	Bos.	L	5-7		9	10	Saberhagen	Beech	Mahay	39-37	3rd	10.5
6-26	T.B.	W	7-0		12	3	Green	Johnson		40-37	3rd	9.5
6-27	T.B.	L	1-5		6	13	Arrojo	Schilling		40-38	3rd	10.5
6-28	T.B.	L	4-5		11	13	Lopez	Gomes	Hernandez	40-39	3rd	11.5
6-30	At N.Y. (AL)	L	2-9		5	9	Cone	Loewer		40-40	3rd	12.5
7-1	At N.Y. (AL)	L	2-5		8	7	Wells	Beech	Rivera	40-41	3rd	13.5
7-2	At N.Y. (AL)	L	8-9	(11)	13	14	Buddie	Spradlin		40-42	3rd	14.5
7-3	Mil.	W	2-0		7	6	Schilling	Karl	Leiter	41-42	3rd	14.5
7-4	Mil.	W	6-5		8	9	Gomes	Wickman		42-42	3rd	14.5
7-5	Mil.	W	4-3		7	9	Loewer	Eldred	Leiter	43-42	3rd	14.5
7-10	At Pit.	W	7-6		14	9	Schilling	Cordova		44-42	3rd	14.0
7-11	At Pit.	W	1-0		8	7	Portugal	Loiselle	Leiter	45-42	3rd	13.0
7-12	At Pit.	W	10-4		8	10	Loewer	Loaiza		46-42	3rd	12.0
7-13	At Mil.	L	2-4		8	5	Woodard	Green	Wickman	46-43	3rd	12.5
7-14	At Mil.	W	4-2		11	8	Gomes	Juden	Leiter	47-43	3rd	12.5
7-15	At Mil.	L	2-3		8	8	Karl	Schilling	Wickman	47-44	3rd	13.5
7-16	At N.Y.	W	4-2		11	9	Portugal	Reed	Leiter	48-44	3rd	13.5
7-17	At N.Y.	L	0-6		4	9	Nomo	Loewer		48-45	T2nd	14.5
7-18	At N.Y.	L	0-7		3	10	Leiter	Green		48-46	3rd	14.5
7-19	At N.Y.	W	7-6	(10)	13	10	Leiter	Cook		49-46	T2nd	14.5
7-20	At Mon.	W	3-1		6	5	Schilling	C. Perez		50-46	2nd	13.5
7-21	At Mon.	W	3-2		9	4	Portugal	Pavano		51-46	2nd	12.5
7-22	Atl.	L	2-14		4	16	Glavine	Loewer		51-47	3rd	13.5
7-23	Atl.	L	2-3		9	9	Millwood	Green	Ligtenberg	51-48	3rd	14.5
7-24†	Fla.	W	6-4	(12)	8	9	Gomes	Alfonseca		52-48		
7-24‡	Fla.	W	7-6	(12)	9	17	Leiter	Darensbourg		53-48	3rd	14.0
7-25	Fla.	L	4-5		8	9	Hernandez	Schilling	Mantei	53-49	3rd	14.0
7-26	Fla.	W	10-9		18	11	Leiter	Alfonseca		54-49	3rd	14.0
7-28	L.A.	L	3-7		11	9	Bohanon	Green		54-50	3rd	14.5
7-29	L.A.	W	8-3		13	11	Loewer	Mlicki		55-50	3rd	14.5
7-30	L.A.	L	1-3		2	7	Park	Beech	Shaw	55-51	3rd	15.5
7-31	S.F.	L	6-7		10	13	Mesa	Perez	Nen	55-52	3rd	15.5
8-1	S.F.	L	7-8	(10)	12	14	Nen	Bottalico	Rodriguez	55-53	3rd	16.5
8-2	S.F.	L	3-15		7	19	Rueter	Welch		55-54	3rd	17.5
8-3	S.F.	L	1-6		8	12	Darwin	Loewer		55-55	3rd	18.0
8-4	At S.D.	L	1-3		8	9	Hitchcock	Beech	Hoffman	55-56	3rd	19.0
8-5	At S.D.	L	0-4		5	9	Brown	Schilling		55-57	3rd	19.0
8-6	At S.D.	W	3-2	(11)	9	8	Leiter	Hoffman		56-57	3rd	19.0
8-7	At Hou.	L	0-9		5	9	R. Johnson	Welch		56-58	3rd	20.0
8-8	At Hou.	L	6-7		10	15	Henry	Leiter		56-59	3rd	21.0
8-9	At Hou.	L	2-11		8	12	Reynolds	Beech		56-60	3rd	22.0
8-10	At Ari.	W	3-0		6	3	Schilling	Daal		57-60	3rd	21.5
8-11	At Ari.	L	3-7		8	13	Benes	Portugal		57-61	3rd	21.5
8-12	At Ari.	W	7-4		8	8	Grace	Anderson	Leiter	58-61	3rd	20.5
8-14	At Col.	W	6-2		6	9	Loewer	Jones		59-61	3rd	21.0
8-15	At Col.	L	3-7		8	16	Kile	Gomes		59-62	3rd	22.0
8-16	At Col.	W	8-7		12	10	Portugal	Wright	Leiter	60-62	3rd	21.0
8-17	Hou.	W	4-0		9	4	Byrd	R. Johnson		61-62	3rd	20.5
8-18	Hou.	L	2-8		4	10	Lima	Grace		61-63	3rd	21.5
8-19	Hou.	L	3-4		7	11	Reynolds	Leiter	Wagner	61-64	3rd	21.5
8-20†	Ari.	W	11-1		13	4	Schilling	Wolcott		62-64		
8-20‡	Ari.	L	9-12	(11)	14	15	Embree	Bottalico		62-65	3rd	21.0
8-21	Ari.	W	1-0		9	5	Portugal	Daal	Gomes	63-65	3rd	21.0
8-22	Col.	W	6-1		10	5	Byrd	Astacio		64-65	3rd	21.0.
8-23	Col.	L	2-5		9	9	Thomson	Grace	DiPoto	64-66	3rd	22.0
8-24	Col.	L	1-3		6	7	Jones	Loewer	Veres	64-67	3rd	23.0
8-25	S.D.	L	3-5		5	9	Brown	Schilling	Hoffman	64-68	3rd	23.0
8-26	S.D.	L	0-2		5	8	Hamilton	Portugal	Hoffman	64-69	3rd	24.0
8-27	S.D.	L	1-8		8	11	Spencer	Byrd		64-70	3rd	25.0
8-28	At S.F.	W	4-3	(10)	7	6	Leiter	Nen		65-70	3rd	24.0
8-29	At S.F.	L	3-10		8	13	Gardner	Loewer		65-71	3rd	25.0
8-30	At S.F.	W	5-4		10	7	Schilling	Ortiz		66-71	3rd	24.0
8-31	At S.F.	L	2-6		7	7	Mesa	Gomes		66-72	3rd	24.0
9-1	At L.A.	L	2-3		9	4	Valdes	Byrd	Shaw	66-73	3rd	25.0
9-2	At L.A.	L	0-6		2	11	Perez	Green		66-74	3rd	25.0
9-4	At Mil.	W	6-2		7	8	Schilling	Woodard		67-74	3rd	24.0
9-5	At Mil.	L	2-3	(14)	6	13	Weathers	Bottalico*		67-75	3rd	24.0
9-6	At Mil.	L	4-5		11	9	Weathers	Gomes		67-76	3rd	25.0
9-8	N.Y.	W	16-4		17	11	Byrd	Nomo		68-76	3rd	23.5
9-9	N.Y.	L	2-6		8	13	Reynoso	Schilling	J. Franco	68-77	3rd	23.5
9-10	N.Y.	L	5-7		6	8	Leiter	Green	J. Franco	68-78	3rd	24.5

Date	Opp.	Res.	Score	(inn.*)	Hits	Opp. hits	Winning pitcher	Losing pitcher	Save	Record	Pos.	GB
9-11	Pit.	L	1-6		7	12	Peters	Loewer		68-79	3rd	25.5
9-12	Pit.	W	13-4		16	9	Portugal	Dessens		69-79	3rd	25.5
9-13	Pit.	W	4-1		5	3	Byrd	Cordova	Leiter	70-79	3rd	24.5
9-14	At Atl.	L	2-4		10	7	Glavine	Schilling	Ligtenberg	70-80	3rd	25.5
9-15	At Atl.	L	0-3		8	8	Millwood	Green	Charlton	70-81	3rd	26.5
9-16	At Atl.	L	1-5		6	7	Smoltz	Loewer		70-82	3rd	27.5
9-18	Mon.	L	4-11		10	18	Vazquez	Portugal	Telford	70-83	3rd	28.0
9-19	Mon.	W	4-3		10	5	Schilling	Maddux		71-83	3rd	28.0
9-20	Mon.	W	6-3		10	6	Byrd	Hermanson	Bottalico	72-83	3rd	28.0
9-21	At Cin.	L	5-8		6	9	Sullivan	Leiter	Graves	72-84	3rd	28.5
9-22	At Cin.	W	10-8	(11)	14	11	Spradlin	Williams	Bottalico	73-84	3rd	28.5
9-23	At Cin.	W	4-2		8	5	Portugal	Parris	Bottalico	74-84	3rd	28.5
9-26†	At Fla.	L	3-4	(10)	7	9	Alfonseca	Perez		74-85		
9-26‡	At Fla.	L	0-1	(13)	6	6	Stanifer	Bottalico		74-86	3rd	30.5
9-27†	At Fla.	L	5-6		15	9	Meadows	Green	Alfonseca	74-87		
9-27‡	At Fla.	W	7-3		12	10	Loewer	Medina		75-87	3rd	31.0

Monthly records: March (0-1), April (12-12), May (13-15), June (15-12), July (15-12), August (11-20), September (9-15).
*Innings, if other than nine. †First game of doubleheader. ‡Second game of doubleheader.

HIGHLIGHTS

High point: After a 4-2 mid-July victory at New York, the Phillies were 48-44 and held sole possession of second place in the N.L. East. The club's surprisingly strong performance through 100 games fueled short-lived talk of competing for the wild card.

Low point: While suffering a three-game sweep at Houston August 7-9, the Phillies were outscored, 27-8. The lopsided series pounded home the reality that the Phillies were not ready to compete with the N.L.'s elite clubs.

Turning point: On August 2, during the seventh inning of a 15-3 loss to San Francisco at Veterans Stadium, reliever Ricky Bottalico hit Giants left fielder Barry Bonds with a pitch and Bonds rushed the mound, tomahawking Bottalico to the ground. Both players were ejected and the Phillies went on to lose 33 of their final 53 games.

Most valuable player: Third baseman Scott Rolen captured his first Gold Glove and improved upon his 1997 production in almost every offensive category. Rolen (.290 batting average, 120 runs scored, 31 home runs, 110 RBIs, 45 doubles) became the youngest player (23) in team history to reach 100 RBIs.

Most valuable pitcher: Curt Schilling was 15-14 with a major league-leading 15 complete games and a 3.25 ERA, even though he received three or fewer runs in 22 of 35 starts. He became only the fifth pitcher in history to record back-to-back 300-strikeout seasons.

Most improved player: First baseman Rico Brogna played a brilliant first base and joined Rolen to give the Phillies two players with 100 or more RBIs for the first time since 1993. His .265 average was a 13-point improvement over 1997.

Most pleasant surprise: Right fielder Bobby Abreu, obtained in a November 1997 trade, led Phillies regulars with a .312 average. In 151 games, he clubbed 29 doubles and 17 homers and drove in 74 runs.

Biggest disappointment: The starting trio of Tyler Green (6-12, 5.03 ERA), Mike Grace (4-7, 5.48) and Garrett Stephenson (0-2, 9.00) was counted upon to bolster the rotation. Instead, Stephenson allowed 24 runs in 23 innings and earned a minor league demotion while Green and Grace were erratic.

Key injuries: Bottalico underwent arthroscopic surgery on his elbow in late April, spent nine weeks on the disabled list and wound up saving just six games. Center fielder Lenny Dykstra (recurring back problems) missed the entire season and retired. Catcher Mike Lieberthal missed the final two months after being diagnosed with a pelvic stress reaction. Lefty Matt Beech missed the final 46 games while having elbow surgery.

Notable: Relievers Wayne Gomes (71 appearances), Mark Leiter (69) and Jerry Spradlin (65) gave the club three pitchers with 65 or more appearances for the first time in history. . . . On September 8 at the Vet, second baseman Marlon Anderson became the first-ever Phillie to record a pinch-hit homer in his first big-league plate appearance.

—CHRIS EDWARDS

RECORDS

1998 regular-season record: 75-87 (3rd in N.L. East); 40-41 at home; 35-46 on road; 21-27 vs. N.L. East; 29-25 vs. Central; 18-26 vs. West; 7-9 vs. A.L.; 15-25 vs. lefthanded starters; 60-62 vs. righthanded starters; 23-37 on grass; 52-50 on turf; 22-25 in daytime; 53-62 at night; 29-28 in one-run games; 13-9 in extra-inning games; 1-1-2 in doubleheaders.

Team record past five years: 333-412 (.447, ranks 13th in league in that span).

TEAM LEADERS

Batting average: Bob Abreu (.312).
At-bats: Doug Glanville (678).
Runs: Scott Rolen (120).
Hits: Doug Glanville (189).
Total bases: Scott Rolen (320).
Doubles: Scott Rolen (45).
Triples: Doug Glanville (7).
Home runs: Scott Rolen (31).

Runs batted in: Scott Rolen (110).
Stolen bases: Doug Glanville (23).
Slugging percentage: Scott Rolen (.532).
On-base percentage: Bob Abreu (.409).
Wins: Curt Schilling (15).
Earned-run average: Curt Schilling (3.25).
Complete games: Curt Schilling (15).
Shutouts: Curt Schilling (2).
Saves: Mark Leiter (23).
Innings pitched: Curt Schilling (268.2).
Strikeouts: Curt Schilling (300).

GAMES BY POSITION

Catcher: Mike Lieberthal 83, Bobby Estalella 47, Mark Parent 34, Gary Bennett 9.
First base: Rico Brogna 151, Kevin Jordan 24, Jon Zuber 4, Rex Hudler 1.
Second base: Mark Lewis 140, Kevin Jordan 22, Marlon Anderson 9, Alex Arias 1, Kevin Sefcik 1.
Third base: Scott Rolen 159, Kevin Jordan 6, Alex Arias 5, Kevin Sefcik 2.
Shortstop: Desi Relaford 137, Alex Arias 38.
Outfield: Doug Glanville 158, Bob Abreu 146, Gregg Jefferies 121, Kevin Sefcik 60, Ruben Amaro 51, Wendell Magee 19, Rex Hudler 9, Jon Zuber 5.
Designated hitter: Kevin Jordan 8, Kevin Sefcik 1.

TOP DRAFT CHOICES

1a. **Pat Burrell,** 3B-1B, Univ. of Miami
1b. **Eric Valent,** OF, UCLA
2. **Brad Baisley,** RHP, Land O'Lakes (Fla.) H.S.
3. **Jorge Padilla,** OF, Florida Air Acad., Melbourne, Fla.
4. **Jason Michaels,** OF, Univ. of Miami
5. **Kinnon McArthur,** C, Sylacauga (Ala.) H.S.
6. **Tommy Whiteman,** SS, Midwest City (Okla.) H.S.
7. **Jarrod Lawson,** RHP, Potosi (Mo.) H.S.
8. **Mike Wilson,** RHP, Granite Hills H.S., El Cajon, Calif.
9. **Ryan Madson,** RHP, Valley View H.S., Moreno Valley, Calif.
10. **Ken Westmoreland,** RHP, U. of Alabama-Huntsville

PITTSBURGH PIRATES
NATIONAL LEAGUE CENTRAL DIVISION

1999 Pirates Schedule
Home games shaded. *—All-Star Game at Fenway Park (Boston).
D—Day game (any game starting before 5 p.m.).

April
SUN	MON	TUE	WED	THU	FRI	SAT
				1	2	3
4	5 MON	6 MON	7 MON	8	9 CUB	10 D CUB
11 D CUB	12	13 STL	14 STL	15 STL	16 CIN	17 D CIN
18 D CIN	19 SD	20 SD	21 SD	22	23 MIL	24 D MIL
25 D MIL	26	27 ATL	28 ATL	29 ATL	30 COL	

May
SUN	MON	TUE	WED	THU	FRI	SAT
						1 D COL
2 D COL	3 SF	4 SF	5 SF	6 STL	7 STL	8 STL
9 D STL	10 HOU	11 HOU	12 HOU	13	14 MON	15 D MON
16 D MON	17 ATL	18 ATL	19 D ATL	20 FLA	21 FLA	22 FLA
23 FLA	24 NYM	25 NYM	26 NYM	27	28 HOU	29 HOU
30 D HOU	31 D LA					

June
SUN	MON	TUE	WED	THU	FRI	SAT
		1 LA	2 LA	3	4 CWS	5 CWS
6 CWS	7 DET	8 DET	9 DET	10	11 KC	12 KC
13 D KC	14	15 LA	16 LA	17 LA	18 SD	19 SD
20 SD	21	22 PHI	23 PHI	24 D PHI	25 MIL	26 MIL
27 MIL	28 PHI	29 PHI	30 PHI			

July
SUN	MON	TUE	WED	THU	FRI	SAT
				1 PHI	2 MIL	3 MIL
4 MIL	5 D CUB	6 D CUB	7 D CUB	8 CUB	9 MIN	10 MIN
11 MIN	12	13 *	14	15 CLE	16 CLE	17 D CLE
18 LA	19 LA	20 D CUB	21 D CUB	22 CUB	23 MON	24 MON
25 D MON	26 NYM	27 NYM	28 D NYM	29	30 FLA	31 FLA

August
SUN	MON	TUE	WED	THU	FRI	SAT
1 D FLA	2	3 ATL	4 ATL	5 ATL	6 STL	7 STL
8 STL	9 CIN	10 CIN	11 CIN	12	13 HOU	14 HOU
15 HOU	16 CIN	17 CIN	18 CIN	19 CIN	20 ARI	21 ARI
22 ARI	23 COL	24 COL	25 COL	26 D COL	27 SF	28 D SF
29 SF	30 COL	31 COL				

September
SUN	MON	TUE	WED	THU	FRI	SAT
			1 COL	2 D	3 SF	4 SF
5 SF	6 D SD	7 SD	8 SD	9 D	10 STL	11 STL
12 STL	13 ARI	14 ARI	15 ARI	16	17 CIN	18 CIN
19 CIN	20 HOU	21 HOU	22 HOU	23 CUB	24 D CUB	25 CUB
26 CUB	27	28 MIL	29 MIL	30 MIL		

October
SUN	MON	TUE	WED	THU	FRI	SAT
					1 NYM	2 NYM
3 D NYM	4	5	6	7	8	9

1999 SEASON
CLUB DIRECTORY

General partner
Kevin S. McClatchy
Board of directors
William B. Allen
Donald Beaver
Frank Brenner
Chip Ganassi
Kevin S. McClatchy
Mayor Tom Murphy
G. Ogden Nutting
William E. Springer
Chief operating officer
Dick Freeman
Sr. v.p. and general manager
Cam Bonifay
Assistant g.m./baseball operations
John Sirignano
Assistant g.m./player personnel
Roy Smith
Sr. advisor/player personnel
Lenny Yochim
Special assistants to the g.m.
Chet Montgomery
Ken Parker
Willie Stargell
V.p., finance and administration
Jim Plake
V.p., broadcasting and marketing
Vic Gregovits
V.p., communications and new ballpark dev.
Steven N. Greenberg
Vice president, operations
Dennis DaPra
Controller
David Bowman
Director of finance
Patti Mistick
Traveling secretary
Greg Johnson
Dir. of corporate sales & broadcasting
Mark Ferraco
Director of Bradenton baseball operations
Jeff Podobnik
Director of community services & sales
Al Gordon
Director of corporate relations
Nellie Briles

Director of human resources
Sarah Torosky
Director of information systems
Terry Zeigler
Director of in-game entertainment
Eric Wolff
Director of marketing communications
Mike Gordon
Director of media relations
Jim Trdinich
Director of merchandising
Joe Billetdeaux
Director of player development
Paul Tinnell
Dir. of community & player relations
Kathy Guy
Dir. of promotions and advertising
Rick Orienza
Asst. director of player development
Bill Bryk
Director of sales
Mike Harmon
Director of scouting
Mickey White
Club physician
Dr. Joseph Coroso
Team orthopedist
Dr. Jack Failla
Head trainer
Kent Biggerstaff
Equipment manager
Roger Wilson
Scouting coordinators
Tom Barnard, Steve Fleming, Scott Littlefield
Special assignment scouts
John Green, Jim Guinn
Latin America coordinators
Pablo Cruz, Jose Luna
Scouting supervisors
Jason Angel, Russell Bowen, Grant Brittain, Dana Brown, Dan Durst, Duane Gustavson, James House, Mike Kendall, Craig Kornfeld, Jose Luna, Greg McClain, Jack Powell, Steve Riha, Delvy Santiago, Rob Sidwell, George Swain, Michael Williams

MINOR LEAGUE AFFILIATES

Class	Team	League	Manager
AAA	Nashville	Pacific Coast	Trent Jewett
AA	Altoona	Eastern	Marty Brown
A	Lynchburg	Carolina	Scott Little
A	Hickory	South Atlantic	Tracy Woodson
A	Williamsport	New York-Pennsylvania	Curtis Wilkerson
Rookie	Gulf Coast Pirates	Gulf Coast	Woody Huyke

BROADCAST INFORMATION

Radio: KDKA-AM (1020).
Cable TV: Fox Sports Pittsburgh.

SPRING TRAINING

Ballpark (city): McKechnie Field (Bradenton, Fla.).
Ticket information: 941-748-4610.

SPRING TRAINING ROSTER

Manager—Gene Lamont (32).
Coaches—Joe Jones (37), Jack Lind (45), Lloyd McClendon (23), Rick Renick, Pete Vuckovich (50), Spin Williams (54).

No.	PITCHERS	B/T	Ht./Wt.	Born	1998 clubs
55	Anderson, Jimmy	L/L	6-1/190	1-22-76	Nashville
41	Christiansen, Jason	R/L	6-5/242	9-21-69	Pittsburgh
67	Cordova, Francisco	R/R	6-1/191	4-26-72	Pittsburgh
71	Dessens, Elmer	R/R	6-0/187	1-13-72	Pittsburgh, Nashville
51	Loiselle, Rich	R/R	6-5/250	1-12-72	Pittsburgh, Nashville
36	Martinez, Javier	R/R	6-2/235	2-5-77	Pittsburgh
58	O'Connor, Brian	L/L	6-2/190	1-4-77	Lynchburg, Carolina
	Pena, Alex	R/R	6-2/205	9-9-77	Lynchburg, Augusta
38	Peters, Chris	L/L	6-1/165	1-28-72	Pittsburgh
26	Phillips, Jason	R/R	6-6/225	3-22-74	Nashville, Carolina
59	Pickford, Kevin	L/L	6-4/205	3-12-75	Nashville, Carolina
	Sauerbeck, Scott	R/L	6-3/190	11-9-71	Norfolk
22	Schmidt, Jason	R/R	6-5/211	1-29-73	Pittsburgh
	Schourek, Pete	L/L	6-5/205	5-10-69	Kissimmee, Houston, Boston
56	Silva, Jose	R/R	6-5/227	12-19-73	Pittsburgh, Nashville
49	Tabaka, Jeff	R/L	6-2/201	1-17-64	Pittsburgh, Nashville
39	Wallace, Jeff	L/L	6-2/228	4-12-76	Pittsburgh
35	Wilkins, Marc	R/R	5-11/221	10-21-70	Pittsburgh, Carolina, Nashville
43	Williams, Mike	R/R	6-3/209	7-29-68	Pittsburgh, Nashville

No.	CATCHERS	B/T	Ht./Wt.	Born	1998 clubs
31	Haad, Yamid	R/R	6-2/204	9-2-77	Lynchburg
18	Kendall, Jason	R/R	6-0/193	6-26-74	Pittsburgh
15	Osik, Keith	R/R	6-0/198	10-22-68	Pittsburgh

No.	INFIELDERS	B/T	Ht./Wt.	Born	1998 clubs
2	Benjamin, Mike	R/R	6-0/169	11-22-65	Boston
14	Garcia, Freddy	R/R	6-2/224	8-1-72	Pittsburgh, Nashville
10	Nunez, Abraham	B/R	5-11/175	3-16-76	Nashville, Lynchburg, Pittsburgh
16	Ramirez, Aramis	R/R	6-1/215	6-25-78	Pittsburgh, Nashville
	Sprague, Ed	R/R	6-2/205	7-25-67	Toronto, Oakland
17	Strange, Doug	B/R	6-1/188	4-13-64	Pittsburgh, Carolina
5	Womack, Tony	L/R	5-9/159	9-25-69	Pittsburgh
7	Wright, Ron	R/R	6-1/230	1-21-76	Nashville, Gulf Coast Pirates
29	Young, Kevin	R/R	6-3/225	6-16-69	Pittsburgh

No.	OUTFIELDERS	B/T	Ht./Wt.	Born	1998 clubs
13	Brown, Adrian	B/R	6-0/185	2-7-74	Nashville, Pittsburgh
	Brown, Brant	L/L	6-3/205	6-22-71	Chicago N.L., Iowa
19	Brown, Emil	R/R	6-2/192	12-29-74	Carolina, Pittsburgh
24	Giles, Brian	L/L	5-11/200	1-20-71	Cleveland, Buffalo
11	Guillen, Jose	R/R	5-11/195	5-17-76	Pittsburgh
3	Hermansen, Chad	R/R	6-2/185	9-10-77	Nashville
52	Hernandez, Alex	L/L	6-4/186	5-28-77	Carolina
28	Martin, Al	L/L	6-2/214	11-24-67	Pittsburgh
12	Ward, Turner	B/R	6-2/204	4-11-65	Pittsburgh

BALLPARK INFORMATION

Ballpark (capacity, surface)
Three Rivers Stadium (47,972, artificial)

Address
600 Stadium Circle
Pittsburgh, PA 15212

Business phone
412-323-5000

Ticket information
800-BUY-BUCS

Ticket prices
$18 (field boxes)
$16 (club boxes)
$12 (terrace boxes)
$12 (family boxes)
$9 (reserved seats)
$6 (general admission)
$3 (g.a., children 14 and under)

Field dimensions (from home plate)
To left field at foul line, 335 feet
To center field, 400 feet
To right field at foul line, 335 feet

First game played
July 16, 1970 (Reds 3, Pirates 2)

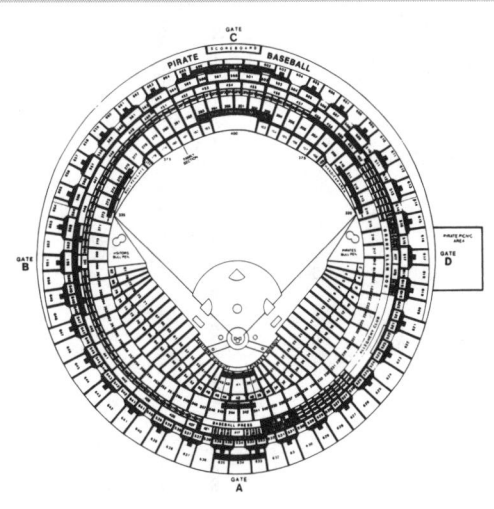

1999 SEASON *Pittsburgh Pirates*

Date	Opp.	Res.	Score	(inn.*)	Hits	Opp. hits	Winning pitcher	Losing pitcher	Save	Record	Pos.	GB
4-1	At Mon.	W	4-0		7	5	Cordova	C. Perez		1-0	T1st	...
4-2	At Mon.	W	4-3		10	8	Schmidt	Maddux	Loiselle	2-0	T1st	...
4-3	At N.Y.	L	1-2		8	5	McMichael	Peters		2-1	T2nd	0.5
4-4	At N.Y.	L	6-7	(13)	14	14	Wendell	Peters		2-2	5th	1.5
4-5	At N.Y.	L	0-7		5	13	Yoshii	Silva		2-3	6th	2.5
4-6	At N.Y.	W	4-2		8	8	Cordova	Jones	Loiselle	3-3	T5th	2.5
4-7	Atl.	L	3-11		10	14	Glavine	Schmidt		3-4	T5th	3.0
4-8	Atl.	W	5-3		8	7	Loaiza	Neagle	Loiselle	4-4	5th	2.5
4-9	Atl.	L	3-4		9	6	Millwood	Lieber	Wohlers	4-5	5th	3.0
4-10	Fla.	W	4-1		8	7	Silva	Meadows	Loiselle	5-5	5th	3.0
4-11	Fla.	W	7-6	(10)	11	8	Loiselle	Powell		6-5	5th	2.0
4-12	Fla.	W	7-3		9	6	Schmidt	Medina		7-5	4th	1.0
4-13	Fla.	L	2-7		9	8	Larkin	Loaiza		7-6	4th	1.5
4-14	At Atl.	L	0-6		1	6	Millwood	Lieber		7-7	T4th	2.0
4-15	At Atl.	L	0-7		6	13	Maddux	Silva		7-8	T5th	2.0
4-16	At Atl.	L	1-3		5	9	Smoltz	Cordova	Wohlers	7-9	6th	3.0
4-17	S.D.	L	5-7		11	8	Boehringer	Tabaka	Hoffman	7-10	6th	4.0
4-18	S.D.	L	5-7	(10)	14	15	Miceli	Loiselle	Hoffman	7-11	6th	5.0
4-21	S.F.	L	3-6		6	11	Gardner	Lieber		7-12	6th	6.5
4-22	S.F.	W	5-2		8	7	Silva	Darwin	Loiselle	8-12	6th	5.5
4-23	S.F.	W	7-0		10	5	Cordova	Estes		9-12	T5th	5.5
4-24	At S.D.	W	4-2		6	5	Schmidt	Smith	Rincon	10-12	5th	5.5
4-25	At S.D.	L	3-4	(16)	7	17	Reyes	J. Martinez		10-13	T5th	5.5
4-26	At S.D.	W	6-0		13	3	Lieber	Brown		11-13	5th	4.5
4-27	At S.F.	L	5-6		9	8	Nen	Loiselle		11-14	6th	5.5
4-28	At S.F.	L	1-2		3	6	Estes	Cordova	Nen	11-15	6th	5.5
4-30	L.A.	L	6-14		14	19	Clontz	Dessens		11-16	6th	6.0
5-1	L.A.	W	5-4		9	9	Tabaka	Dreifort	Loiselle	12-16	6th	6.0
5-2	L.A.	L	4-5		8	12	Martinez	Lieber	Radinsky	12-17	6th	7.0
5-3	L.A.	L	5-10		8	13	Park	Silva		12-18	6th	7.0
5-5	St.L.	W	5-2		10	6	Cordova	Mercker	Loiselle	13-18	6th	7.0
5-6	St.L.	W	5-0		6	4	Schmidt	Stottlemyre		14-18	6th	6.0
5-7	Cin.	W	8-7		9	13	Dessens	Belinda	Loiselle	15-18	6th	5.5
5-8	Cin.	L	3-5	(10)	9	7	Belinda	Rincon	Shaw	15-19	6th	5.5
5-9	Cin.	W	6-1		12	6	Silva	Winchester	Peters	16-19	6th	5.5
5-10	Cin.	L	3-4	(12)	6	7	Belinda	Loiselle		16-20	6th	6.5
5-11	Col.	W	5-2		11	9	Schmidt	Ritz		17-20	6th	6.5
5-12	Col.	W	6-0		8	5	Loaiza	Wright		18-20	T5th	6.5
5-13	At Hou.	L	0-1		6	7	Hampton	Lieber	Wagner	18-21	6th	7.5
5-14	At Hou.	W	7-2		13	6	Silva	Schourek		19-21	6th	6.5
5-15	At Ari.	L	1-6		3	15	Suppan	Cordova		19-22	6th	6.5
5-16	At Ari.	W	6-3		11	11	Schmidt	Anderson	Loiselle	20-22	6th	6.5
5-17	At Ari.	L	2-8		9	11	Benes	Loaiza		20-23	6th	7.5
5-18	At Ari.	L	2-9		8	15	Blair	Lieber		20-24	6th	7.5
5-19	S.D.	W	3-0		10	5	Silva	Hamilton	Loiselle	21-24	T5th	6.5
5-20†	S.D.	W	5-2		9	6	Cordova	Ashby	Loiselle	22-24		
5-20‡	S.D.	L	3-8		11	9	Hitchcock	Peters		22-25	6th	7.0
5-21	S.D.	W	3-2		8	6	Schmidt	Brown	Rincon	23-25	5th	7.0
5-22	At Fla.	L	1-3		9	9	Hernandez	Loaiza		23-26	5th	7.0
5-23	At Fla.	W	10-4		11	6	Lieber	Fontenot	Rincon	24-26	5th	7.0
5-24	At Fla.	L	3-4		9	7	Powell	Christiansen		24-27	5th	8.0
5-26	At Mil.	L	2-3		6	10	Myers	Loiselle		24-28	5th	8.5
5-27	At Mil.	L	2-3	(10)	6	11	Woodall	Rincon		24-29	T5th	8.5
5-29	Mon.	L	1-4		9	10	C. Perez	Lieber	Urbina	24-30	6th	9.5
5-30	Mon.	W	8-7		12	11	Christiansen	Urbina		25-30	6th	8.5
5-31	Mon.	W	9-4		8	7	Cordova	Batista		26-30	6th	7.5
6-1	N.Y.	W	4-3		7	6	Schmidt	Mlicki	Rincon	27-30	5th	7.0
6-2	N.Y.	W	5-2		7	7	Peters	Bohanon	Rincon	28-30	5th	7.0
6-3	N.Y.	W	3-0		4	4	Lieber	Reed	Christiansen	29-30	5th	7.0
6-5	Min.	W	6-1		12	5	Silva	Morgan		30-30	4th	5.5
6-6	Min.	W	4-3	(12)	12	11	Loaiza	Aguilera		31-30	3rd	5.5
6-7	Min.	L	2-3		6	8	Serafini	Schmidt	Aguilera	31-31	3rd	6.5
6-8	At Cle.	L	0-8		4	15	Colon	Peters		31-32	3rd	7.5
6-9	At Cle.	W	7-4		12	9	Lieber	Morman	Rincon	32-32	3rd	7.5
6-10	At Cle.	W	4-3	(11)	15	10	Loaiza	Mesa	Loiselle	33-32	3rd	7.5
6-12	Mil.	L	2-4		7	9	Karl	Cordova	Wickman	33-33	4th	7.5
6-13	Mil.	L	1-8		5	9	Juden	Schmidt		33-34	4th	7.5
6-14	Mil.	W	7-2		13	5	Peters	Woodard		34-34	4th	7.5
6-15	At Phi.	L	1-2		4	8	Beech	Lieber	Leiter	34-35	4th	8.5
6-16	At Phi.	L	7-8		13	8	Dodd	Loiselle		34-36	4th	8.5
6-17	At Phi.	L	1-3		2	8	Schilling	Cordova		34-37	4th	9.5
6-18	At Mil.	W	1-0		8	4	Dessens	Jones	Rincon	35-37	T4th	8.5

Date	Opp.	Res.	Score	(inn.*)	Hits	Opp. hits	Winning pitcher	Losing pitcher	Save	Record	Pos.	GB
6-19	At Mil.	L	1-2		5	8	Woodard	Peters	Wickman	35-38	5th	9.5
6-20	At Mil.	W	4-2		10	4	Lieber	Eldred	Rincon	36-38	5th	9.5
6-21	At Mil.	W	8-7		11	11	Loaiza	Juden	Rincon	37-38	5th	9.5
6-22	Chi. (AL)	L	4-5		10	10	C. Castillo	Dessens	Karchner	37-39	5th	9.5
6-23	Chi. (AL)	L	4-5		7	10	Sirotka	Schmidt	Karchner	37-40	5th	10.5
6-24	At K.C.	W	10-3		19	10	Peters	Rusch		38-40	5th	9.5
6-25	At K.C.	L	1-6		4	10	Belcher	Lieber		38-41	5th	9.5
6-26	At L.A.	L	2-5		11	11	Park	Loaiza	Osuna	38-42	5th	9.5
6-27	At L.A.	L	0-2		1	5	Valdes	Cordova		38-43	5th	10.5
6-28	At L.A.	W	6-4		8	6	Williams	Radinsky	Loiselle	39-43	5th	10.5
6-30	Det.	L	0-3		5	7	Moehler	Lieber		39-44	5th	11.5
7-1	Det.	L	1-9		7	10	Greisinger	Peters		39-45	5th	12.5
7-2	Det.	W	5-2		9	8	Loaiza	Powell	Loiselle	40-45	5th	11.5
7-3	At Chi.	L	9-12		14	12	Tapani	Cordova	Beck	40-46	5th	12.5
7-4	At Chi.	L	4-5		7	12	Pisciotta	Schmidt	Beck	40-47	5th	12.5
7-5	At Chi.	L	6-7		14	11	Stevens	Loiselle	Beck	40-48	5th	13.5
7-10	Phi.	L	6-7		9	14	Schilling	Cordova		40-49	5th	14.0
7-11	Phi.	L	0-1		7	8	Portugal	Loiselle	Leiter	40-50	6th	14.0
7-12	Phi.	L	4-10		10	8	Loewer	Loaiza		40-51	6th	14.0
7-13	Chi.	W	6-2		10	6	Lieber	Gonzalez		41-51	6th	13.0
7-14	Chi.	L	4-7		10	11	Tapani	Peters	Beck	41-52	6th	14.0
7-15	Chi.	W	3-0		5	4	Cordova	Wood	Rincon	42-52	6th	13.0
7-16	At Mon.	L	5-10		11	12	Pavano	Schmidt	Maddux	42-53	6th	13.5
7-17	At Mon.	W	5-1		11	8	Williams	Vazquez	Christiansen	43-53	6th	13.5
7-18	At Mon.	W	5-2		11	5	Lieber	Boskie		44-53	6th	13.5
7-19	At Mon.	W	6-1		13	6	Peters	Hermanson		45-53	T5th	13.5
7-20	At N.Y.	W	3-1		8	5	Cordova	Yoshii	Rincon	46-53	5th	13.5
7-21	At N.Y.	L	0-4		8	6	Reed	Schmidt		46-54	5th	13.5
7-22	Fla.	W	6-4		9	9	Van Poppel	Dempster	Christiansen	47-54	5th	12.5
7-23	Fla.	W	9-1		14	12	Lieber	Meadows		48-54	5th	12.5
7-24	Atl.	L	0-3		3	8	Smoltz	Peters		48-55	5th	13.5
7-25	Atl.	W	4-1		10	6	Cordova	Neagle	Christiansen	49-55	4th	12.5
7-26	Atl.	L	1-2		4	9	Maddux	Schmidt	Ligtenberg	49-56	5th	12.5
7-27	At Col.	L	7-8	(13)	18	16	Leskanic	McCurry		49-57	5th	13.5
7-28	At Col.	L	6-12		6	15	Astacio	Lieber		49-58	5th	14.5
7-29	At Col.	W	12-1		19	5	Peters	Kile		50-58	4th	14.5
7-31	Hou.	L	4-7		12	10	Hampton	Cordova	Henry	50-59	5th	15.0
8-1	Hou.	L	1-2		5	10	Lima	Williams		50-60	5th	16.0
8-2	Hou.	L	2-6		6	10	R. Johnson	Christiansen	Elarton	50-61	5th	17.0
8-3	Col.	L	2-7		5	13	Jones	Lieber		50-62	5th	17.0
8-4	Col.	W	13-5		21	11	Christiansen	Kile		51-62	5th	17.0
8-5	Col.	L	2-6		5	8	Wright	Cordova		51-63	T5th	17.0
8-6	Col.	L	1-5		4	9	Thomson	Schmidt		51-64	T5th	17.5
8-7	At L.A.	L	1-3		2	8	Bohanon	Van Poppel	Shaw	51-65	6th	18.5
8-8	At L.A.	L	1-2		4	11	Osuna	Christiansen		51-66	6th	19.5
8-9	At L.A.	W	2-1		6	5	Peters	Park	Rincon	52-66	6th	19.5
8-11	At Cin.	W	7-0		8	6	Cordova	Tomko		53-66	T5th	20.0
8-12	At Cin.	W	5-4		7	8	Schmidt	Remlinger	Rincon	54-66	5th	20.0
8-13	At Cin.	W	9-6		11	7	McCurry	Harnisch	Rincon	55-66	5th	20.0
8-14	At St.L.	L	5-10		12	8	Osborne	Lieber		55-67	5th	20.0
8-15	At St.L.	L	7-8	(12)	10	12	Painter	McCurry		55-68	5th	21.0
8-16	At St.L.	W	4-1		10	7	Cordova	Morris	Lieber	56-68	T5th	20.0
8-18	L.A.	W	6-4		10	12	Schmidt	Perez	Loiselle	57-68	5th	19.5
8-19	L.A.	W	6-5		7	6	Williams	Bohanon	Christiansen	58-68	5th	19.5
8-20	Cin.	W	6-5		13	9	Christiansen	Graves		59-68	5th	18.5
8-21	Cin.	W	14-2		17	7	Peters	Tomko		60-68	5th	18.5
8-22	St.L.	W	14-4		16	9	Cordova	Witt		61-68	5th	18.5
8-23	St.L.	W	4-3		9	11	Schmidt	Mercker	Christiansen	62-68	T3rd	18.5
8-24	St.L.	T	5-5	(7)	6	7	......	......		62-68	T3rd	19.0
8-25	At Ari.	W	9-6		11	10	Lawrence	Sodowsky	Loiselle	63-68	3rd	19.0
8-26	At Ari.	W	4-3		13	9	Tabaka	Daal	Loiselle	64-68	3rd	18.0
8-28	At Hou.	L	0-2		7	4	R. Johnson	Cordova		64-69	3rd	19.0
8-29	At Hou.	L	3-6		9	12	Lima	Schmidt	Powell	64-70	3rd	20.0
8-30	At Hou.	L	4-11		7	14	Reynolds	McCurry		64-71	4th	21.0
9-1	Ari.	L	3-4		8	9	Daal	Peters	Olson	64-72	4th	21.5
9-2	Ari.	L	1-2	(11)	5	8	Small	Tabaka	Olson	64-73	4th	22.5
9-3	Ari.	L	0-1		3	4	Anderson	Cordova		64-74	6th	23.0
9-4	Chi.	L	2-5		4	11	Karchner	Williams	Beck	64-75	6th	23.0
9-5	Chi.	L	4-8		8	8	Tapani	Lawrence	Beck	64-76	6th	24.0
9-6	Chi.	W	4-3	(10)	9	11	Loiselle	Stevens		65-76	6th	24.0
9-7	Mil.	L	3-6		6	8	Roque	Dessens	Wickman	65-77	6th	25.0
9-8	Mil.	W	8-7		12	8	Williams	Plunk	Loiselle	66-77	5th	25.0
9-9	At Chi.	L	2-4		5	6	Clark	Schmidt	Beck	66-78	6th	26.0
9-10	At Chi.	L	2-5		8	6	Tapani	Silva	Beck	66-79	6th	27.0
9-11	At Phi.	W	6-1		12	7	Peters	Loewer		67-79	6th	27.0

Date	Opp.	Res.	Score	(inn.*)	Hits	Opp. hits	Winning pitcher	Losing pitcher	Save	Record	Pos.	GB
9-12	At Phi.	L	4-13		9	16	Portugal	Dessens		67-80	6th	28.0
9-13	At Phi.	L	1-4		3	5	Byrd	Cordova	Leiter	67-81	6th	28.0
9-14	At St.L.	L	3-7		7	11	Jimenez	Schmidt		67-82	6th	28.0
9-15†	At St.L.	W	8-6		9	9	Lawrence	Osborne	Loiselle	68-82		
9-15‡	At St.L.	L	3-9		7	14	Aybar	Silva	Acevedo	68-83	6th	28.0
9-16	At St.L.	L	0-4		4	6	Morris	Van Poppel		68-84	6th	28.0
9-18	Hou.	L	2-5		5	14	R. Johnson	Dessens	Powell	68-85	6th	29.0
9-19	Hou.	W	7-1		10	8	Cordova	Lima		69-85	6th	28.0
9-20	Hou.	L	0-2		10	7	Reynolds	Schmidt	Wagner	69-86	6th	29.0
9-21	At S.F.	L	1-8		7	8	Hershiser	Silva		69-87	6th	29.5
9-22	At S.F.	L	2-14		7	17	Rueter	Lieber		69-88	6th	29.5
9-23	At S.F.	L	1-4		6	10	Gardner	Peters	Nen	69-89	6th	30.5
9-24	At S.F.	L	2-6		9	10	Ortiz	Dessens		69-90	6th	31.0
9-25	At Cin.	L	1-4		6	8	Bere	Cordova	Graves	69-91	6th	32.0
9-26	At Cin.	L	2-6		6	8	Harnisch	Schmidt	White	69-92	6th	32.0
9-27	At Cin.	L	1-4		5	5	Tomko	Silva		69-93	6th	33.0

Monthly records: April (11-16), May (15-14), June (13-14), July (11-15), August (14-12), September (5-22).
*Innings, if other than nine. †First game of doubleheader. ‡Second game of doubleheader.

HIGHLIGHTS

High point: The Pirates won nine of 11 games from May 30 to June 10, the last time they were over .500. The stretch started with a three-run, ninth-inning rally against Montreal and ended with an 11th-inning win that sealed an improbable series victory over Cleveland.

Low point: A 5-22 September embarrassed an organization that promised maximum effort. The Pirates were apathetic as they played out the string.

Turning point: The season took a bad turn on June 16 in Philadelphia, a game that saw the Pirates lose pitcher Jose Silva to a broken arm and then blow a 7-1 lead in the ninth inning and lose, 8-7. The Pirates went 35-57 (.380) the rest of the way.

Most valuable player: Catcher Jason Kendall noses out Kevin Young, the result of the latter's September fade. Kendall set career highs in nearly every offensive category. His .327 average was the best by a Pirates player in a non-strike season since Dave Parker led the league with a .334 average in 1978.

Most valuable pitcher: Righthander Francisco Cordova. His best moments weren't as good as they were in 1997, but he didn't wear down the way he did in '97, either. Cordova was dependable, throwing a career-high 220 innings and answering questions about his durability.

Most improved player: Lefthander Chris Peters. Given a chance in the rotation, Peters showed he belonged, learning how to change speeds and pitch out of trouble. He showed consistent improvement.

Most pleasant surprise: Lefthander Jeff Tabaka and righthander Mike Williams. Both veterans were signed as minor league free agents in December 1997, moves that got little notice. Both, however, turned out to be contributors out of the bullpen. Lefthanders hit only .175 against Tabaka. Williams even contributed an emergency start the night Esteban Loaiza was traded.

Biggest disappointment: Al Martin. There's plenty of competition for this cat-

egory but Martin stands above the rest. Martin's .239 average was his lowest in six major league seasons. Runnerup is Rich Loiselle, who had eight blown saves in 27 opportunities and lost the closer's job for a time.

Key injuries: Silva spent nearly three months on the disabled list with a broken forearm, delaying his development. Marc Wilkins, a useful righthanded reliever, didn't pitch after May 23 because of a rotator cuff strain that required surgery. Tabaka missed nearly six weeks with a broken jaw.

Notable: The Pirates led the National League with 159 stolen bases but hit a major league-low 107 home runs. . . . Kendall's 95 runs were a club record for a catcher.

—JOHN MEHNO

RECORDS

1998 regular-season record: 69-93 (6th in N.L. Central); 40-40 at home; 29-53 on road; 21-24 vs. East; 23-33 vs. N.L. Central; 19-29 vs. West; 6-7 vs. A.L.; 19-24 vs. lefthanded starters; 50-69 vs. righthanded starters; 19-40 on grass; 50-53 on turf; 15-30 in daytime; 54-63 at night; 19-30 in one-run games; 4-9 in extra-inning games; 0-0-2 in doubleheaders.

Team record past five years: 332-412 (.446, ranks 14th in league in that span).

TEAM LEADERS

Batting average: Jason Kendall (.327).
At-bats: Tony Womack (655).
Runs: Jason Kendall (95).
Hits: Tony Womack (185).
Total bases: Kevin Young (285).
Doubles: Kevin Young (40).
Triples: Tony Womack (7).
Home runs: Kevin Young (27).
Runs batted in: Kevin Young (108).
Stolen bases: Tony Womack (58).
Slugging percentage: Kevin Young (.481).
On-base percentage: Jason Kendall (.411).

Wins: Francisco Cordova (13).
Earned-run average: Francisco Cordova (3.31).
Complete games: Francisco Cordova (3).
Shutouts: Francisco Cordova (2).
Saves: Rich Loiselle (19).
Innings pitched: Francisco Cordova (220.1).
Strikeouts: Jason Schmidt (158).

GAMES BY POSITION

Catcher: Jason Kendall 144, Keith Osik 26, Tim Laker 1.
First base: Kevin Young 157, Mark Smith 6, Freddy Garcia 4, Tim Laker 4, Doug Strange 3.
Second base: Tony Womack 152, Kevin Polcovich 15, Doug Strange 9, Chance Sanford 1.
Third base: Aramis Ramirez 71, Freddy Garcia 47, Doug Strange 42, Kevin Polcovich 8, Keith Osik 7, Chance Sanford 5.
Shortstop: Lou Collier 107, Kevin Polcovich 54, Abraham Nunez 23, Tony Womack 2, Chance Sanford 1.
Outfield: Jose Guillen 151, Al Martin 114, Turner Ward 97, Jermaine Allensworth 66, Manny Martinez 62, Adrian Brown 38, Mark Smith 24, Emil Brown 10, Tony Womack 5, Steve Bieser 1.
Designated hitter: Mark Smith 3, Al Martin 2, Manny Martinez 2, Turner Ward 1.

TOP DRAFT CHOICES

1. **Clint Johnston,** LHP-OF, Vanderbilt U.
2. **Jeremy Cotten,** 3B-RHP, Fuquay-Varina (N.C.) H.S.
3. **Jeremy Harts,** OF-LHP, Columbia H.S., Decatur, Ga.
4. **Eddy Furniss,** 1B, Louisiana State U.
5. **Rayner Cardona,** C, Patria la Torres Ramirez H.S., San Sebastian, P.R.
6. **Brice Pelfrey,** SS, Tate H.S., Gonzalez, Fla.
7. **James Whte,** RHP, Chico (Calif.) H.S.
8. **Chuck Crowder,** LHP, Georgia Tech
9. **Giovanni Gonzalez,** RHP, Northwest Christian Acad., Miami
10. **David Diaz,** C, Hialeah-Miami Lakes H.S., Hialeah, Fla.

ST. LOUIS CARDINALS
NATIONAL LEAGUE CENTRAL DIVISION

1999 Cardinals Schedule
Home games shaded. *—All-Star Game at Fenway Park (Boston).
D—Day game (any game starting before 5 p.m.).

April

SUN	MON	TUE	WED	THU	FRI	SAT
				1	2	3
4	5 D MIL	6	7 MIL	8 MIL	9 D CIN	10 D CIN
11 CIN	12 D	13 PIT	14 PIT	15 PIT	16 HOU	17 HOU
18 HOU	19 D MIL	20 MIL	21 MIL	22 D	23 LA	24 LA
25 LA	26	27 COL	28 D COL	29 D COL	30 MON	

May

SUN	MON	TUE	WED	THU	FRI	SAT
						1 MON
2 D MON	3 ATL	4 ATL	5 ATL	6 D PIT	7 PIT	8 PIT
9 D PIT	10 PHI	11 PHI	12 PHI	13 D	14 LA	15 LA
16 LA	17 SD	18 SD	19 SD	20 D SD	21 LA	22 LA
23 D LA	24	25 SF	26 SF	27 D SF	28 D CUB	29 D CUB
30 D CUB	31 D FLA					

June

SUN	MON	TUE	WED	THU	FRI	SAT
		1 FLA	2 FLA	3 FLA	4 DET	5 DET
6 DET	7 D KC	8 KC	9 KC	10	11 DET	12 DET
13 D DET	14 D MON	15 MON	16 MON	17 NYM	18 NYM	19 NYM
20 D NYM	21 HOU	22 HOU	23 HOU	24 ARI	25 ARI	26 ARI
27 ARI	28	29 HOU	30 HOU			

July

SUN	MON	TUE	WED	THU	FRI	SAT
				1 D HOU	2 D ARI	3 D ARI
4 ARI	5 D ARI	6 D CIN	7 CIN	8 CIN	9 SF	10 D SF
11 SF	12 D	13 *	14	15 CWS	16 CWS	17 CWS
18 MIN	19 MIN	20 MIN	21 CIN	22 CIN	23 D COL	24 D COL
25 COL	26 D SF	27 SF	28 D SF	29	30 COL	31 COL

August

SUN	MON	TUE	WED	THU	FRI	SAT
1 COL	2 D SD	3 SD	4 SD	5 SD	6 PIT	7 PIT
8 D PIT	9 D PHI	10 PHI	11 PHI	12	13 D CUB	14 D CUB
15 CUB	16 D PHI	17 PHI	18 PHI	19	20 NYM	21 D NYM
22 D NYM	23 D MON	24 MON	25 MON	26	27 ATL	28 ATL
29 ATL	30 FLA	31 FLA				

September

SUN	MON	TUE	WED	THU	FRI	SAT
			1 FLA	2 MIL	3 MIL	4 D MIL
5 MIL	6 D ATL	7 ATL	8 ATL	9	10 PIT	11 PIT
12 PIT	13 D MIL	14 MIL	15 MIL	16	17 HOU	18 D HOU
19 HOU	20 CUB	21 CUB	22 CUB	23	24 CIN	25 D CIN
26 CIN	27 D CIN	28 SD	29 SD	30		

October

SUN	MON	TUE	WED	THU	FRI	SAT
					1 CUB	2 D CUB
3 D CUB	4	5	6	7	8	9

1999 SEASON
CLUB DIRECTORY

Chairman of the board/general partner
William O. DeWitt Jr.
Chairman
Frederick O. Hanser
Secretary-treasurer
Andrew N. Baur
President
Mark C. Lamping
Admin. assistant to the president
Julie Laningham
Vice president, general manager
Walt Jocketty
Sr. exec. asst. to v.p., general manager
Judy Carpenter-Barada
Vice president/player personnel
Jerry Walker
Vice president, corporate sales
Dan Farrell
Vice president, controller
Brad Wood
Vice president, community relations
Marty Hendin
Vice president, business development
Bill DeWitt III
Vice president, stadium operations
Joe Abernathy
Director, ticket operations
Josie Arnold
Group director, sales
Kevin Wade
Director, group sales
Joe Strohm
Manager, ticket sales
Mark Murray
Director, corporate sales/marketing
Thane van Breusegen
Director, target marketing
Ted Savage
Director, media relations
Brian Bartow
Mgr., media relations & publications
Steve Zesch

Assistant to director, media relations
Brad Hainje
Traveling secretary
C.J. Cherre
Director, player development
Mike Jorgensen
Director, player procurement
Jeff Scott
Director, scouting operations
John Mozeliak
Dir., baseball admin., int'l operations
Tim Hanser
Director, minor league operations
Scott Smulczenski
Mgr., baseball info./player development
John Vuch
National cross-checker
Mike Roberts
East coast cross-checker
Tim Conroy
West coast cross-checker
Clark Crist
Special assignment scouts
Marty Keough, Fred McAlister, Joe Sparks, Mike Squires
Scouts
Randy Benson, Doug Carpenter, Roberto Diaz, Ben Galante, Steve Grilli, Manny Guerra, Dave Karaff, Scott Melvin, Scott Nichols, Jay North, Miguel Nova, , Dan Ontiveros, Tommy Shields, Roger Smith, Dane Walker
Major league trainer
Barry Weinberg
Assistant major league trainer
Brad Henderson
Medical/rehabilitation coordinator
Mark O'Neal
Equipment manager
Buddy Bates
Assistant equipment manager
Rip Rowan

MINOR LEAGUE AFFILIATES

Class	Team	League	Manager
AAA	Memphis	Pacific Coast	Gaylen Pitts
AA	Arkansas	Texas	Chris Maloney
A	Potomac	Carolina	Joe Cunningham
A	Peoria	Midwest	Jose Oquendo
A	New Jersey	New York-Pennsylvania	Jeff Shireman
Rookie	Johnson City	Appalachian	Steve Turco

BROADCAST INFORMATION

Radio: KMOX-AM (1120).
TV: KPLR-TV (Channel 11).
Cable TV: Fox Sports Midwest.

SPRING TRAINING

Ballpark (city): Roger Dean Stadium (Jupiter, Fla.).
Ticket information: 561-966-3309.

SPRING TRAINING ROSTER

Manager—Tony La Russa (10).
Coaches—Mark DeJohn (34), Dave Duncan (18), Mike Easler, Rene Lachemann (15), Dave McKay (39).

No.	PITCHERS	B/T	Ht./Wt.	Born	1998 clubs
53	Acevedo, Juan	R/R	6-2/228	5-5-70	St. Louis, Memphis
38	Aybar, Manny	R/R	6-1/165	10-5-74	St. Louis, Memphis
41	Benes, Alan	R/R	6-5/215	1-21-72	St. Louis
52	Bottalico, Ricky	L/R	6-1/217	8-26-69	Philadelphia, Scranton/Wilkes-Barre
37	Bottenfield, Kent	R/R	6-3/240	11-14-68	St. Louis
54	Busby, Mike	R/R	6-4/210	12-27-72	St. Louis
44	Croushore, Rick	R/R	6-4/210	8-7-70	Memphis, St. Louis
66	DeWitt, Matthew	R/R	6-4/220	9-4-77	Prince William
50	Frascatore, John	R/R	6-1/210	2-4-70	St. Louis
	Heiserman, Rick	R/R	6-7/225	2-22-73	Memphis, Arkansas
32	Hutchinson, Chad	R/R	6-5/230	2-21-77	New Jersey, Prince William
63	Jimenez, Jose	R/R	6-3/195	7-7-73	Arkansas, St. Louis
57	King, Curtis	R/R	6-5/205	10-25-70	Memphis, St. Louis
	Lowe, Sean	R/R	6-2/205	3-29-71	Memphis, St. Louis
43	Mercker, Kent	L/L	6-2/195	2-1-68	St. Louis
35	Morris, Matt	R/R	6-5/210	8-9-74	Arkansas, Memphis, St. Louis
33	Oliver, Darren	R/L	6-2/210	10-6-70	Texas, Oklahoma, St. Louis
31	Osborne, Donovan	L/L	6-2/195	6-21-69	Memphis, Arkansas, St. Louis
28	Painter, Lance	L/L	6-1/197	7-21-67	St. Louis
36	Radinsky, Scott	L/L	6-3/204	3-3-68	Los Angeles
	Raggio, Brady	R/R	6-4/210	9-17-72	Memphis, St. Louis
59	Stephenson, Garrett	R/R	6-5/208	1-2-72	Philadelphia, Scranton/Wilkes-Barre

No.	CATCHERS	B/T	Ht./Wt.	Born	1998 clubs
	Castillo, Alberto	R/R	6-0/185	2-10-70	New York N.L., Norfolk
26	Marrero, Eli	R/R	6-1/180	11-17-73	St. Louis, Memphis

No.	INFIELDERS	B/T	Ht./Wt.	Born	1998 clubs
61	Haas, Chris	L/R	6-1/205	10-15-76	Arkansas
29	Howard, David	B/R	6-0/175	2-26-67	St. Louis
48	McEwing, Joe	R/R	5-11/170	10-19-72	Memphis, Arkansas, St. Louis
25	McGwire, Mark	R/R	6-5/250	10-1-63	St. Louis
11	Ordaz, Luis	R/R	5-11/170	8-12-75	Memphis, St. Louis
27	Polanco, Placido	R/R	5-10/168	10-10-75	Memphis, St. Louis
5	Renteria, Edgar	R/R	6-1/160	8-7-75	Florida
23	Tatis, Fernando	R/R	6-1/175	1-1-75	Texas, St. Louis
64	Woolf, Jason	B/R	6-1/170	6-6-77	Arkansas

No.	OUTFIELDERS	B/T	Ht./Wt.	Born	1998 clubs
	Bragg, Darren	L/R	5-9/180	9-7-69	Boston
24	Davis, Eric	R/R	6-3/185	5-29-62	Baltimore
8	Drew, J.D.	L/R	6-1/195	11-20-75	St. Paul, Arkansas, St. Louis
16	Lankford, Ray	L/L	5-11/198	6-5-67	St. Louis
58	Little, Mark	R/R	6-0/195	7-11-72	Oklahoma, Memphis, St. Louis
51	McGee, Willie	B/R	6-1/185	11-2-58	St. Louis
65	Saturria, Luis	R/R	6-2/165	7-21-76	Prince William

BALLPARK INFORMATION

Ballpark (capacity, surface)
Busch Stadium (50,297, grass)

Address
250 Stadium Plaza
St. Louis, MO 63102

Business phone
314-421-3060

Ticket information
314-421-2400

Ticket prices
$28 (field boxes-infield)
$26 (loge boxes-infield)
$23 (field boxes-outfield, loge boxes-outfield)
$18 (terrace boxes-infield, loge reserved-infield)
$16 (terrace boxes-outfield, loge reserved-outfield)
$13 (terrace reserved-adults)
$8 (bleachers)
$7 (ter. reserved-children, upper ter. reserved-adults)
$3 (upper terrace reserved-children)

Field dimensions (from home plate)
To left field at foul line, 330 feet
To center field, 402 feet
To right field at foul line, 330 feet

First game played
May 12, 1966 (Cardinals 4, Braves 3)

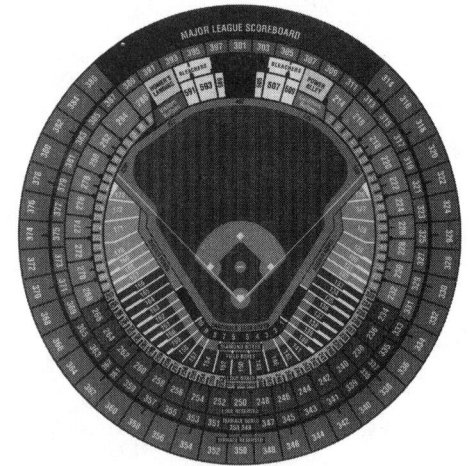

Date	Opp.	Res.	Score	(inn.*)	Hits	Opp. hits	Winning pitcher	Losing pitcher	Save	Record	Pos.	GB
3-31	L.A.	W	6-0		13	3	Stottlemyre	Martinez		1-0	1st	+0.5
4-2	L.A.	W	8-5	(12)	16	9	Acevedo	Lankford		2-0	T1st	...
4-3	S.D.	L	5-13		6	13	Langston	Aybar		2-1	T2nd	0.5
4-4	S.D.	W	8-6		14	8	Mercker	Smith	Bottenfield	3-1	T2nd	0.5
4-5	S.D.	L	7-8		13	8	Hoffman	Looper	Miceli	3-2	3rd	1.5
4-7	At Col.	W	12-11		14	14	Politte	Astacio	Bottenfield	4-2	3rd	1.5
4-8	At Col.	W	13-9		14	13	Aybar	Wright		5-2	3rd	1.0
4-9	At Col.	W	7-5		9	13	Busby	Leskanic	Brantley	6-2	T2nd	0.5
4-10	At S.F.	L	3-5		11	10	Tavarez	Frascatore	Nen	6-3	3rd	1.5
4-11	At S.F.	W	7-2		8	10	Bottenfield	Estes		7-3	T2nd	0.5
4-12	At S.F.	L	1-2		7	7	Nen	Frascatore		7-4	T2nd	0.5
4-13	At S.F.	L	2-8		8	11	Rueter	Aybar		7-5	3rd	1.0
4-14	Ari.	W	15-5		13	4	Busby	Sodowsky		8-5	T2nd	0.5
4-16†	Ari.	W	5-4		5	11	Stottlemyre	Adamson	Brantley	9-5		
4-16‡	Ari.	L	2-8		7	10	Benes	Osborne		9-6	T2nd	0.5
4-17	Phi.	W	8-5		10	11	Politte	Whiteside	Bottenfield	10-6	2nd	0.5
4-18	Phi.	W	6-5		10	9	Aybar	Grace	Brantley	11-6	2nd	0.5
4-19	Phi.	W	3-2		8	11	Mercker	Beech	Acevedo	12-6	2nd	0.5
4-21	At Mon.	W	5-3		11	5	Stottlemyre	Moore	Brantley	13-6	2nd	0.5
4-22	At Mon.	L	2-3		9	12	Urbina	Bottenfield		13-7	2nd	0.5
4-23	At Mon.	L	2-5		5	10	Hermanson	Politte	Urbina	13-8	2nd	1.5
4-24	At Phi.	L	4-8		10	10	Whiteside	Mercker		13-9	2nd	2.5
4-25	At Phi.	W	8-5		11	9	Petkovsek	Spradlin	Brantley	14-9	2nd	1.5
4-26	At Phi.	L	3-9		8	11	Schilling	Stottlemyre		14-10	T2nd	1.5
4-27	Mon.	W	7-0		10	4	Osborne	C. Perez		15-10	T2nd	1.5
4-29	Mon.	W	13-7		12	7	Busby	Kline		16-10	2nd	0.5
4-30	At Chi.	L	3-8		8	15	Wood	Petkovsek		16-11	3rd	1.0
5-1	At Chi.	L	5-6		10	6	Gonzalez	Stottlemyre	Beck	16-12	3rd	2.0
5-2	At Chi.	L	3-4	(11)	9	13	Adams	Bottenfield		16-13	T3rd	3.0
5-3	At Chi.	W	8-5		12	8	Petkovsek	Mulholland	Brantley	17-13	3rd	2.0
5-5	At Pit.	L	2-5		6	10	Cordova	Mercker	Loiselle	17-14	3rd	3.0
5-6	At Pit.	L	0-5		4	6	Schmidt	Stottlemyre		17-15	T3rd	3.0
5-7	At N.Y.	L	1-4		2	7	Yoshii	Osborne	J. Franco	17-16	4th	3.5
5-8	At N.Y.	L	2-9		5	12	Reed	Politte		17-17	T4th	3.5
5-11	Mil.	W	7-0		10	2	Stottlemyre	Karl		18-17	4th	4.5
5-12	Mil.	W	6-5	(10)	12	11	Busby	Jones		19-17	T3rd	4.5
5-13	Atl.	L	2-10		4	12	Glavine	Politte		19-18	4th	5.5
5-14	Atl.	L	3-7		5	12	Rocker	Acevedo		19-19	T4th	5.5
5-15	Fla.	L	7-8		13	15	Meadows	Raggio	Powell	19-20	5th	5.5
5-16	Fla.	W	5-4		9	7	Stottlemyre	Darensbourg		20-20	T4th	5.5
5-17	Fla.	W	13-4		15	12	Mercker	Hammond		21-20	4th	5.5
5-18	Fla.	L	3-7		6	9	Sanchez	Aybar		21-21	4th	5.5
5-19	At Phi.	W	10-8		15	10	Frascatore	Gomes	Acevedo	22-21	4th	4.5
5-20	At Phi.	W	8-5		15	11	Busby	Portugal	Brantley	23-21	T3rd	4.5
5-21	At Phi.	L	3-4		6	9	Grace	Stottlemyre	Leiter	23-22	T3rd	4.5
5-22	S.F.	W	4-3	(12)	10	9	King	Tavarez		24-22	3rd	4.5
5-23	S.F.	W	11-10		15	9	Painter	Johnstone	King	25-22	3rd	4.5
5-24	S.F.	L	6-9	(17)	14	19	Poole	Mercker	Reed	25-23	3rd	5.5
5-25	Col.	L	1-6		5	11	Thomson	Busby		25-24	3rd	5.5
5-27	Col.	W	2-1		4	5	Stottlemyre	Kile	Brantley	26-24	3rd	5.0
5-28	Col.	W	4-1		8	7	Mercker	Wright	King	27-24	3rd	4.5
5-29	At S.D.	W	8-3		8	6	Petkovsek	Hamilton		28-24	3rd	4.5
5-30	At S.D.	L	2-3		9	9	Ashby	Brantley		28-25	3rd	4.5
5-31	At S.D.	L	3-7		7	10	Brown	Lowe		28-26	4th	4.5
6-1	At S.D.	L	2-3		8	8	Hitchcock	Stottlemyre	Hoffman	28-27	4th	5.0
6-2	At L.A.	W	7-4		11	8	Mercker	Dreifort	Brantley	29-27	3rd	5.0
6-3	At L.A.	L	4-7		8	11	Martinez	Petkovsek	Radinsky	29-28	3rd	6.0
6-4	At L.A.	L	2-3		7	9	Radinsky	Brantley		29-29	T3rd	6.0
6-5	S.F.	L	2-3		8	7	Hershiser	Bottenfield	Nen	29-30	5th	6.0
6-6	S.F.	L	4-5	(14)	14	10	Rodriguez	Lowe		29-31	5th	7.0
6-7	S.F.	L	5-6		10	13	Gardner	Mercker	Nen	29-32	5th	8.0
6-8	At Chi. (AL)	L	6-8		8	8	Bere	Petkovsek	Karchner	29-33	5th	9.0
6-9	At Chi. (AL)	W	5-4		10	8	Painter	Navarro	Brantley	30-33	5th	9.0
6-10	At Chi. (AL)	L	8-10	(11)	12	13	Karchner	Lowe		30-34	5th	10.0
6-12	At Ari.	W	9-4		10	8	Stottlemyre	Benes		31-34	5th	9.0
6-13	At Ari.	L	4-7		9	11	Springer	Brantley	Olson	31-35	5th	9.0
6-14	At Ari.	W	2-0		10	4	Petkovsek	Blair	Bottenfield	32-35	5th	9.0
6-16	At Hou.	W	9-4		12	8	Acevedo	Schourek		33-35	5th	8.5
6-17	At Hou.	L	5-6		11	12	Nitkowski	Brantley		33-36	5th	9.5
6-18	At Hou.	W	7-6		9	13	Bottenfield	Reynolds	Croushore	34-36	T4th	8.5
6-19	Ari.	W	5-0		10	6	Petkovsek	Blair		35-36	4th	8.5

Date	Opp.	Res.	Score	(inn.*)	Hits	Opp. hits	Winning pitcher	Losing pitcher	Save	Record	Pos.	GB
6-20	Ari.	W	4-2		7	7	Aybar	Banks	Croushore	36-36	4th	8.5
6-21	Ari.	W	5-4		9	8	Raggio	Sodowsky	Brantley	37-36	3rd	8.5
6-22	Det.	W	4-1		8	7	Stottlemyre	Florie	Croushore	38-36	3rd	7.5
6-23	Det.	L	1-8		4	11	Thompson	Bottenfield		38-37	4th	8.5
6-24	At Cle.	L	3-14		9	18	Wright	Petkovsek		38-38	4th	8.5
6-25	At Cle.	L	2-8		6	10	Burba	Aybar		38-39	4th	8.5
6-26	At Min.	L	1-5		5	12	Swindell	Acevedo		38-40	4th	8.5
6-27	At Min.	W	7-2		10	5	Stottlemyre	Milton		39-40	4th	8.5
6-28	At Min.	L	2-3		10	11	Carrasco	Bottenfield	Aguilera	39-41	4th	9.5
6-30	K.C.	L	1-6		7	9	Rusch	Aybar	Service	39-42	4th	10.5
7-1	K.C.	L	4-6		7	12	Belcher	Mercker	Montgomery	39-43	4th	11.5
7-2	K.C.	W	3-0		5	7	Acevedo	Pichardo	Brantley	40-43	4th	10.5
7-3	At Cin.	L	3-6		7	9	Remlinger	Stottlemyre	Shaw	40-44	4th	11.5
7-4	At Cin.	L	4-5		5	7	Graves	Croushore		40-45	4th	11.5
7-5	At Cin.	L	1-6		7	9	Tomko	Mercker		40-46	4th	12.5
7-9	Hou.	L	4-5		7	10	Reynolds	Stottlemyre	Wagner	40-47	4th	13.5
7-10	Hou.	W	6-3		9	6	King	Nitkowski	Brantley	41-47	4th	12.5
7-11	Hou.	W	4-3	(11)	6	9	Painter	Wagner		42-47	4th	11.5
7-12	Hou.	W	6-4		10	9	Acevedo	Bergman	Croushore	43-47	4th	10.5
7-13	Cin.	L	5-6	(13)	9	16	White	Witt		43-48	4th	10.5
7-14	Cin.	L	4-7		8	12	Sullivan	Stottlemyre	Graves	43-49	5th	11.5
7-15	Cin.	L	2-4	(11)	8	11	White	Frascatore		43-50	5th	11.5
7-16	L.A.	L	2-8		6	15	Valdes	Mercker		43-51	5th	12.0
7-17	L.A.	W	4-1		5	5	Acevedo	Bohanon	Croushore	44-51	5th	12.0
7-18	L.A.	L	8-10		11	11	Guthrie	Brantley	Shaw	44-52	5th	13.0
7-19	L.A.	W	5-4		11	9	Petkovsek	Radinsky		45-52	4th	13.0
7-20	At S.D.	W	13-1		16	3	Morris	Langston		46-52	4th	13.0
7-21	At S.D.	L	3-6		10	12	Brown	Mercker	Hoffman	46-53	4th	13.0
7-22	At S.F.	W	3-2		6	5	Witt	Rueter	Croushore	47-53	4th	12.0
7-23	At S.F.	W	8-1		11	4	Bottenfield	Darwin		48-53	4th	12.0
7-24	At Col.	L	3-12		7	18	Kile	Stottlemyre		48-54	4th	13.0
7-25	At Col.	L	2-5		7	11	McElroy	Morris	DeJean	48-55	5th	13.0
7-26	At Col.	W	3-1		8	7	Mercker	Thomson	Croushore	49-55	4th	12.0
7-28	Mil.	L	10-13		15	16	Weathers	Croushore	Wickman	49-56	4th	13.5
7-29	Mil.	L	1-2		6	6	Woodard	Witt	Wickman	49-57	5th	14.5
7-30	Mil.	W	3-2		7	6	Morris	Karl	Croushore	50-57	4th	13.5
7-31	At Atl.	W	3-2		8	7	Mercker	Maddux	Painter	51-57	4th	13.5
8-1	At Atl.	L	1-3		7	10	Seanez	Croushore	Ligtenberg	51-58	4th	14.5
8-2	At Atl.	L	3-4		6	9	Millwood	Witt	Ligtenberg	51-59	4th	15.5
8-3	At Mil.	L	5-6		8	12	Woodard	Oliver	Wickman	51-60	4th	15.5
8-4	At Mil.	W	2-1		6	4	Morris	Karl		52-60	4th	15.5
8-5	At Mil.	W	5-1		8	4	Mercker	Juden		53-60	4th	14.5
8-7	Chi.	W	16-3		17	5	Bottenfield	Trachsel		54-60	4th	14.5
8-8	Chi.	W	9-8	(13)	16	13	Witt	Stevens		55-60	4th	14.5
8-9	Chi.	W	2-1		5	5	Oliver	Wengert	Brantley	56-60	4th	14.5
8-10	N.Y.	L	2-4		6	8	Leiter	Morris	J. Franco	56-61	4th	15.5
8-11	N.Y.	L	3-8		10	17	Jones	Mercker		56-62	4th	16.5
8-12	N.Y.	W	5-4	(14)	12	11	Frascatore	J. Franco		57-62	4th	16.5
8-14	Pit.	W	10-5		8	12	Osborne	Lieber		58-62	3rd	16.0
8-15	Pit.	W	8-7	(12)	12	10	Painter	McCurry		59-62	3rd	16.0
8-16	Pit.	L	1-4		7	10	Cordova	Morris	Lieber	59-63	3rd	16.0
8-18	At Chi.	L	1-4		6	13	Trachsel	Mercker	Beck	59-64	4th	16.5
8-19	At Chi.	W	8-6	(10)	18	9	Acevedo	Mulholland		60-64	3rd	16.5
8-20†	At N.Y.	W	2-0		3	4	Osborne	Blair	Acevedo	61-64		
8-20‡	At N.Y.	L	4-5		6	9	Reed	Oliver	Wendell	61-65	3rd	16.0
8-21†	At N.Y.	W	10-5		11	9	Morris	Nomo		62-65		
8-21‡	At N.Y.	L	0-1		3	7	Reynoso	Aybar	J. Franco	62-66	3rd	16.5
8-22	At Pit.	L	4-14		9	16	Cordova	Witt		62-67	T3rd	17.5
8-23	At Pit.	L	3-4		11	9	Schmidt	Mercker	Christiansen	62-68	T3rd	18.5
8-24	At Pit.	T	5-5	(7)	7	6	......	......		62-68	T3rd	19.0
8-25	Fla.	L	3-4		6	6	Medina	Osborne	Alfonseca	62-69	4th	20.0
8-26	Fla.	W	6-7	(10)	14	10	Alfonseca	Acevedo		62-70	5th	20.0
8-27	Atl.	L	4-6		7	10	Neagle	Morris	Ligtenberg	62-71	5th	20.5
8-28	Atl.	W	5-4	(10)	9	12	Acevedo	Martinez		63-71	5th	20.5
8-29	Atl.	L	3-4		3	6	Glavine	Bottenfield	Seanez	63-72	6th	21.5
8-30	Atl.	W	8-7		11	11	Petkovsek	Martinez	Acevedo	64-72	5th	21.5
8-31	At Fla.	W	5-3		9	10	Oliver	Ojala	Acevedo	65-72	3rd	21.5
9-1	At Fla.	W	7-1		13	6	Morris	Hernandez		66-72	3rd	20.5
9-2	At Fla.	W	14-4		13	8	Mercker	Sanchez		67-72	3rd	20.5
9-4	Cin.	L	2-3		7	9	Harnisch	Frascatore	White	67-73	3rd	20.5
9-5	Cin.	W	7-0		9	3	Osborne	Reyes		68-73	3rd	20.5
9-6	Cin.	W	5-2		7	7	Acevedo	Hudek		69-73	3rd	20.5
9-7	Chi.	W	3-2		5	9	Oliver	Morgan	Acevedo	70-73	3rd	20.5
9-8	Chi.	W	6-3		5	12	Mercker	Trachsel	Acevedo	71-73	3rd	20.5
9-9	At Cin.	L	3-6		5	8	Harnisch	Witt	Graves	71-74	3rd	21.5

Date	Opp.	Res.	Score	(inn.*)	Hits	Opp. hits	Winning pitcher	Losing pitcher	Save	Record	Pos.	GB
9-10	At Cin.	W	8-7		6	13	Aybar	Remlinger	Acevedo	72-74	3rd	21.5
9-11	At Hou.	L	2-8		8	14	Powell	Morris		72-75	3rd	22.5
9-12	At Hou.	L	2-3		5	6	R. Johnson	Oliver	Wagner	72-76	3rd	23.5
9-13	At Hou.	W	3-2		6	9	Mercker	Bergman	Acevedo	73-76	3rd	22.5
9-14	Pit.	W	7-3		11	7	Jimenez	Schmidt		74-76	3rd	21.5
9-15†	Pit.	L	6-8		9	9	Lawrence	Osborne	Loiselle	74-77		
9-15‡	Pit.	W	9-3		14	7	Aybar	Silva	Acevedo	75-77	3rd	21.5
9-16	Pit.	W	4-0		6	4	Morris	Van Poppel		76-77	3rd	20.5
9-18	At Mil.	W	5-2		9	8	Oliver	Roque	Acevedo	77-77	3rd	20.5
9-19	At Mil.	W	7-4		10	8	Jimenez	Woodard	Acevedo	78-77	3rd	19.5
9-20	At Mil.	W	11-6		10	13	Aybar	Karl		79-77	3rd	19.5
9-22	Hou.	W	4-0		4	5	Morris	Hampton		80-77	3rd	18.5
9-23	Hou.	L	1-7		9	15	R. Johnson	Oliver		80-78	3rd	19.5
9-24	Mon.	W	6-3		11	6	Osborne	Vazquez	Acevedo	81-78	3rd	19.0
9-25	Mon.	W	6-5		12	10	Jimenez	Bennett	Acevedo	82-78	3rd	19.0
9-26	Mon.	L	6-7		8	9	Urbina	Busby	DeHart	82-79	3rd	19.0
9-27	Mon.	W	6-3		9	9	Frascatore	Pavano	Acevedo	83-79	3rd	19.0

Monthly records: March (1-0), April (15-11), May (12-15), June (11-16), July (12-15), August (14-15), September (18-7).
*Innings, if other than nine. †First game of doubleheader. ‡Second game of doubleheader.

HIGHLIGHTS

High point: Any number of Mark McGwire's home runs, but No. 62 on September 8 and No. 70 on September 27 were the showstoppers. Next came No. 61 on September 7 and the 400th of his career on May 8 in New York. The team high point came in late September when the Cardinals finally climbed over .500.

Low point: A two-game series in Cleveland on June 24-25 in which the Cardinals were outscored, 22-7. This series personified the Cardinals' poor 4-9 record against the A.L. Central Division. The Cardinals did not win any of the five series against that division.

Turning point: The Cardinals began dropping out of sight after going 1-6 on a three-city trip to Chicago, Pittsburgh and New York the first week of May.

Most valuable player: Mark McGwire. Without him, the Cardinals would have won about 40 games and drawn about 1 million fewer customers at Busch Stadium. McGwire also was the MVP before games as he rained batting-practice pitches into the left field seats, both in the lower deck and upper deck.

Most valuable pitcher: Juan Acevedo became the club's closer almost by accident, but when he took over, he ran off 13 straight saves at the end of the season. This for a team that had blown a major league-high 31 save opportunities.

Most improved player: Acevedo not only pitched well in the rotation before suffering an elbow-related injury, but he was almost unhittable in relief.

Most pleasant surprise: Pitcher Rick Croushore. Although Croushore struggled late, he reeled off eight saves as the Cardinals' interim closer between Jeff Brantley and Acevedo.

Biggest disappointment: Brantley converted only 14-of-22 save opportunities. Plagued by periodic arm problems, he allowed a whopping 12 home runs in 40 innings, most of them coming in game-deciding situations.

Key Injuries: Donovan Osborne was limited to 14 starts because of groin and arm injuries. Matt Morris missed half a season with a shoulder problem. Brantley's arm, one year removed from serious shoulder surgery, was almost never right.

Notable: Ray Lankford had his best year with 31 homers and 105 runs batted in. . . . Brian Jordan went from no homers and 10 RBIs in 1997 to 25 and 91 last season. . . . Lefthanded reliever Lance Painter fielded 1.000, batted 1.000 (one at-bat) and had a perfect 4-0 pitching record. . . . The Cardinals were 10 games over .500 with the pitcher batting eighth over the last 76 games.

—RICK HUMMEL

RECORDS

1998 regular-season record: 83-79 (3rd in N.L. Central); 48-34 at home; 35-45 on road; 23-22 vs. East; 30-26 vs. N.L. Central; 26-22 vs. West; 4-9 vs. A.L.; 26-22 vs. lefthanded starters; 57-57 vs. righthanded starters; 74-61 on grass; 9-18 on turf; 25-26 in day-time; 58-53 at night; 28-30 in one-run games; 9-7 in extra-inning games; 0-0-4 in doubleheaders.

Team record past five years: 359-384 (.483, ranks 10th in league in that span).

TEAM LEADERS

Batting average: Brian Jordan (.316).
At-bats: Brian Jordan (564).
Runs: Mark McGwire (130).
Hits: Brian Jordan (178).
Total bases: Mark McGwire (383).
Doubles: Ray Lankford (37).
Triples: Delino DeShields (8).
Home runs: Mark McGwire (70).
Runs batted in: Mark McGwire (147).
Stolen bases: Delino DeShields, Ray Lankford (26).
Slugging percentage: Mark McGwire (.752).
On-base percentage: Mark McGwire (.470).
Wins: Kent Mercker (11).
Earned-run average: None.
Complete games: Todd Stottlemyre (3).

Shutouts: Matt Morris, Donovan Osborne (1).
Saves: Juan Acevedo (15).
Innings pitched: Kent Mercker (161.2).
Strikeouts: Todd Stottlemyre (147).

GAMES BY POSITION

Catcher: Eli Marrero 73, Tom Lampkin 62, Tom Pagnozzi 44.
First base: Mark McGwire 151, John Mabry 16, Brian Hunter 10, Gary Gaetti 3, Tom Lampkin 2, Eli Marrero 2, Delino DeShields 1, Willie McGee 1.
Second base: Delino DeShields 111, Pat Kelly 41, David Howard 19, Placido Polanco 14, Joe McEwing 6, Shawn Gilbert 2, David Bell 1, Gary Gaetti 1, Luis Ordaz 1.
Third base: Gary Gaetti 83, Fernando Tatis 55, John Mabry 38, David Howard 14, David Bell 4, Luis Ordaz 2, Brian Jordan 1.
Shortstop: Royce Clayton 90, Luis Ordaz 54, Placido Polanco 28, David Howard 16, Fernando Tatis 3, Pat Kelly 2.
Outfield: Ray Lankford 145, Brian Jordan 141, Ron Gant 104, Willie McGee 88, John Mabry 80, Brian Hunter 25, J.D. Drew 11, Mark Little 7, Tom Lampkin 5, Pat Kelly 3, Joe McEwing 3, David Howard 2, Gary Gaetti 1.
Designated hitter: Brian Jordan 3, Willie McGee 3, Brian Hunter 1, Ray Lankford 1.

TOP DRAFT CHOICES

1a. **J.D. Drew**, OF, St. Paul (Northern League)
1b. **Ben Diggins**, 1B-RHP, Bradshaw Mountain H.S., Dewey, Ariz.
2a. **Chad Hutchinson**, RHP, Stanford U.
2b. **Tim Lemon**, OF, La Mirada (Calif.) H.S.
3. **Gabriel Johnson**, C, Atlantic H.S., Delray Beach, Fla.
4. **Bud Smith**, LHP, L.A. Harbor J.C.
5. **Steve Stemle**, RHP, W. Kentucky U.
6. **Kristopher Rayborn**, LHP, Purvis (Miss.) H.S.
7. **Brad Freeman**, SS-OF, Miss. State U.
8. **Greg Clark**, C, Univ. of Arizona
9. **Jack Wilson**, SS, Oxnard (Calif.) J.C.
10. **Pedro Zazueta**, RHP, Amphitheater H.S., Tucson

SAN DIEGO PADRES
NATIONAL LEAGUE WEST DIVISION

1999 Padres Schedule

Home games shaded. *—All-Star Game at Fenway Park (Boston). D—Day game (any game starting before 5 p.m.).

April

SUN	MON	TUE	WED	THU	FRI	SAT
				1	2	3
4 COL	5	6 COL	7 COL	8 D SF	9 D SF	10 D SF
11 D SF	12 COL	13	14 COL	15 D COL	16 LA	17 LA
18 D LA	19 PIT	20 PIT	21 PIT	22	23 ARI	24 ARI
25 ARI	26	27 NYM	28 NYM	29 D NYM	30 D CUB	

May

SUN	MON	TUE	WED	THU	FRI	SAT
						1 D CUB
2 D CUB	3 PHI	4 FLA	5 D FLA	6		8 ATL
9 D ATL	10 FLA	11 FLA	12 FLA	13	14 CIN	15 CIN
16 D CIN	17	18 STL	19 STL	20 D STL	21 CIN	22 CIN
23 D CIN	24 ARI	25 ARI	26 ARI	27	28 MIL	29 MIL
30 MIL	31 D MIL					

June

SUN	MON	TUE	WED	THU	FRI	SAT
		1 CUB	2 CUB	3 D CUB	4 D SEA	5 SEA
6 D SEA	7	8 OAK	9 OAK	10 D OAK	11 HOU	12 HOU
13 D HOU	14	15 PHI	16 PHI	17 D PHI	18 PIT	19 PIT
20 D PIT	21	22 LA	23 LA	24 LA	25 D COL	26 COL
27 COL	28 COL	29 LA	30 LA			

July

SUN	MON	TUE	WED	THU	FRI	SAT
				1 D LA	2 COL	3 COL
4 D COL	5 SF	6 SF	7	8	9 TEX	10 D TEX
11 D TEX	12	13	* 14	15 D SEA	16 SEA	17 D SEA
18 ANA	19 ANA	20 D ANA	21 SF	22 D SF	23 HOU	24 D HOU
25 D HOU	26	27 ARI	28 ARI	29 D ARI	30 HOU	31 D HOU

August

SUN	MON	TUE	WED	THU	FRI	SAT
1 HOU	2 D STL	3 STL	4 STL	5 D MON	6 MON	7 MON
8 MON	9 MON	10 NYM	11 NYM	12 D NYM	13 FLA	14 FLA
15 D FLA	16 NYM	17 NYM	18 NYM	19	20 ATL	21 D ATL
22 D ATL	23 PHI	24 PHI	25 D PHI	26 D MIL	27 MIL	28 MIL
29 MIL	30 CUB	31 CUB				

September

SUN	MON	TUE	WED	THU	FRI	SAT
			1 CUB	2	3 D FLA	4 FLA
5 FLA	6 D PIT	7 D PIT	8 PIT	9 D MON	10 MON	11 MON
12 D MON	13 ATL	14 ATL	15 ATL	16	17 SF	18 D SF
19 D SF	20 CIN	21 CIN	22 CIN	23	24 LA	25 D LA
26 LA	27	28 STL	29 STL	30 ARI		

October

SUN	MON	TUE	WED	THU	FRI	SAT
				1 ARI	2 ARI	
3 D ARI	4	5	6	7	8	9

1999 SEASON
CLUB DIRECTORY

Chairman
John Moores
President & chief executive officer
Larry Lucchino
Executive vice president
Bill Adams
Sr. v.p./baseball operations and g.m.
Kevin Towers
Sr. vice president/public affairs
Charles Steinberg
Vice president/corporate development
Michael Dee
Vice president/marketing
Don Johnson
Vice president/general counsel
Alan Ostfield
Vice president/finance
Bob Wells
Assistant general manager
Fred Uhlman Jr.
Director/community relations
Michele Anderson
Director/merchandising
Michael Babida
Controller
Steve Fitch
Director/administrative services
Lucy Freeman
Director/ticket operations & services
Dave Gilmore
Director/stadium operations
Mark Guglielmo
Dir./Hispanic & multicultural marketing
Enrique Morones
Director/player development
Jim Skaalen
Director/minor league operations
Priscilla Oppenheimer
Director/team travel
Brian Prilaman
Director/public relations
Glenn Geffner

Director/fan services
Tim Katzman
Director/sales
Louie Ruvane
Director/scouting
Brad Sloan
Trainer
Todd Hutcheson
Assistant trainer
Jim Daniel
Strength and conditioning coach
Sam Gannelli
Club physicians
Cliff Colwell
Jan Fronek
Paul Hirshman
Blaine Phillips
Major league scouts
Ken Bracey, Ray Crone, Moose Johnson
Advance scout
Jeff Gardner
Supervisors
Bob Cummings, Andy Hancock, Jim Woodward
Professional scouts
Chas Bolton, Gary Roenicke, Gene Watson
Full-time scouts
Freddy Barbosa, Cesar Berroteran, Miguel Blanco, Joe Bochy, Rich Bordi, Bob Buob, Julio Coronado, Jimmy Dreyer, Celestino Espinal, Ronquito Garcia, Robert Gutierrez, Chris Gwynn, Rich Hacker, Tim Harkness, Mike Keenan, Gary Kendall, William Killian, Steve Leavitt, Ramon Silva Lopez, Don Lyle, Tim McWilliam, Bill Mele, Juan Melo, Darryl Milne, Rene Mons, Steve Nichols, Chuck Pierce, Jack Pierce, Van Smith, Gene Thompson, Mark Wasinger

MINOR LEAGUE AFFILIATES

Class	Team	League	Manager
AAA	Las Vegas	Pacific Coast	Mike Ramsey
AA	Mobile	Southern	Mike Basso
A	Rancho Cucamonga	California	Tom Le Vasseur
A	Fort Wayne	Midwest	Dan Simonds
Rookie	Idaho Falls	Pioneer	Don Werner
Rookie	Peoria Padres	Arizona	Randy Whisler

BROADCAST INFORMATION

Radio: KFMB-AM (760), KURS-AM (1040, Spanish)
TV: KUSI (Channel 9).
Cable TV: Channel 4 Padres.

SPRING TRAINING

Ballpark (city): Peoria Stadium (Peoria, Ariz.).
Ticket information: 602-878-4337, 800-409-1511.

SPRING TRAINING ROSTER

Manager—Bruce Bochy (15).
Coaches—Greg Booker, Tim Flannery (11), Davey Lopes (30), Rob Picciolo (5), Merv Rettenmund (16), Dave Smith.

No.	PITCHERS	B/T	Ht./Wt.	Born	1998 clubs
40	Almanzar, Carlos	R/R	6-2/200	11-6-73	Toronto, Syracuse
43	Ashby, Andy	R/R	6-5/190	7-11-67	San Diego
37	Boehringer, Brian	B/R	6-2/190	1-8-70	San Diego
31	Clement, Matt	R/R	6-3/190	8-12-74	Las Vegas, San Diego
	Cunnane, Will	R/R	6-2/175	4-24-74	Las Vegas, San Diego
	Guzman, Domingo	R/R	6-0/180	4-5-75	Mobile, Rancho Cucamonga
41	Hitchcock, Sterling	L/L	6-1/192	4-29-71	San Diego
51	Hoffman, Trevor	R/R	6-0/205	10-13-67	San Diego
33	Miceli, Dan	R/R	6-0/216	9-9-70	San Diego
	Murray, Heath	L/L	6-4/205	4-19-73	Las Vegas
18	Myers, Randy	L/L	6-1/210	9-19-62	Toronto, San Diego
	Sak, Jim	R/R	6-1/195	8-18-73	Mobile
	Serrano, Wascar	R/R	6-2/178	6-2-78	Clinton
58	Spencer, Stan	R/R	6-4/205	8-7-69	Las Vegas, San Diego
	Vosberg, Ed	L/L	6-1/190	9-28-61	DID NOT PLAY
36	Wall, Donne	R/R	6-1/180	7-11-67	Las Vegas, San Diego
30	Williams, Woody	R/R	6-0/190	8-19-66	Toronto
	Wolff, Bryan	R/R	6-1/195	3-16-72	Las Vegas, Mobile

No.	CATCHERS	B/T	Ht./Wt.	Born	1998 clubs
25	Davis, Ben	B/R	6-4/205	3-10-77	Mobile, San Diego
9	Hernandez, Carlos	R/R	5-11/215	5-24-67	San Diego
13	Leyritz, Jim	R/R	6-0/195	12-27-63	Boston, San Diego
20	Myers, Greg	L/R	6-2/208	4-14-66	San Diego, Rancho Cucamonga, Las Vegas

No.	INFIELDERS	B/T	Ht./Wt.	Born	1998 clubs
14	Arias, George	R/R	5-11/190	3-12-72	Las Vegas, San Diego
	Carmona, Cesarin	B/R	5-10/155	12-20-76	Rancho Cucamonga
17	Giovanola, Ed	L/R	5-10/170	3-4-69	San Diego, Las Vegas
10	Gomez, Chris	R/R	6-1/195	6-16-71	San Diego
22	Joyner, Wally	L/L	6-2/200	6-16-62	San Diego
17	Magadan, Dave	L/R	6-4/215	9-30-62	Oakland
	Melo, Juan	B/R	6-1/180	5-11-76	Las Vegas
3	Sheets, Andy	R/R	6-2/180	11-19-71	San Diego
4	Veras, Quilvio	B/R	5-9/166	4-3-71	San Diego

No.	OUTFIELDERS	B/T	Ht./Wt.	Born	1998 clubs
	Darr, Mike	L/R	6-3/205	3-21-76	Mobile
19	Gwynn, Tony	L/L	5-11/220	5-9-60	San Diego
5	Mack, Shane	R/R	6-0/190	12-7-63	Oakland, Kansas City
	Matthews, Gary	B/R	6-0/200	8-25-74	Mobile
28	Rivera, Ruben	R/R	6-3/200	11-14-73	Las Vegas, San Diego
8	Sweeney, Mark	L/L	6-1/195	10-26-69	San Diego
44	Vander Wal, John	L/L	6-2/197	4-29-66	Colorado, San Diego
23	Vaughn, Greg	R/R	6-0/202	7-3-65	San Diego

BALLPARK INFORMATION

Ballpark (capacity, surface)
Qualcomm Stadium (56,133, grass)

Address
P.O. Box 2000
San Diego, CA 92112-2000

Business phone
619-881-6500

Ticket information
888-723-7379

Ticket prices
$18 (club level, field level, IF)
$16 (plaza level/IF)
$14 (plaza level, loge level)
$11 (press level)
$8 (grandstand)
$7 (view level/IF)
$6 (view level)
$5 (RF & LF bleachers, view level)

Field dimensions (from home plate)
To left field at foul line, 327 feet
To center field, 405 feet
To right field at foul line, 330 feet

First game played
April 8, 1969 (Padres 2, Astros 1)

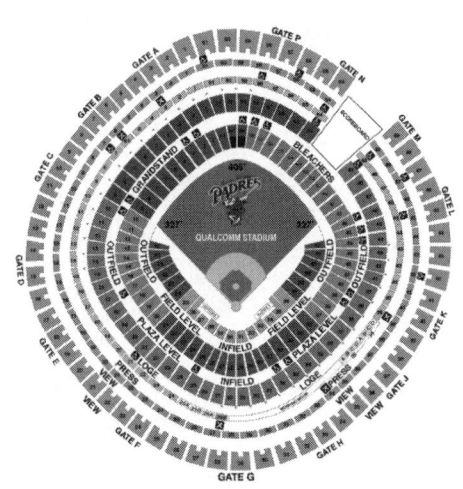

1999 SEASON *San Diego Padres*

Date	Opp.	Res.	Score	(inn.*)	Hits	Opp. hits	Winning pitcher	Losing pitcher	Save	Record	Pos.	GB
3-31	At Cin.	W	10-2		10	6	Brown	Remlinger		1-0	T1st	...
4-1	At Cin.	W	10-9		10	13	Hamilton	Sullivan	Hoffman	2-0	T1st	...
4-2	At Cin.	L	1-5		6	9	Cooke	Ashby	Shaw	2-1	T2nd	1.0
4-3	At St.L.	W	13-5		13	6	Langston	Aybar		3-1	1st	...
4-4	At St.L.	L	6-8		8	14	Mercker	Smith	Bottenfield	3-2	3rd	1.0
4-5	At St.L.	W	8-7		8	13	Hoffman	Looper	Miceli	4-2	T1st	...
4-7	Cin.	W	3-2	(10)	9	6	Hoffman	Shaw		5-2	T1st	...
4-8	Cin.	W	6-3		13	6	Ashby	White	Hoffman	6-2	1st	+1.0
4-9	Cin.	W	6-2		9	8	Boehringer	Tomko		7-2	1st	+2.0
4-10	Ari.	W	6-4		9	5	Miceli	Rodriguez		8-2	1st	+2.0
4-11	Ari.	W	7-0		9	6	Smith	Adamson		9-2	1st	+3.0
4-12	Ari.	W	4-2		5	4	Hamilton	Blair	Hoffman	10-2	1st	+3.0
4-13	Ari.	W	1-0		3	4	Ashby	Anderson		11-2	1st	+3.0
4-14	At S.F.	L	7-13		15	12	Tavarez	Boehringer		11-3	1st	+2.0
4-15	At S.F.	W	1-0		9	4	Brown	Darwin		12-3	1st	+3.0
4-17	At Pit.	W	7-5		8	11	Boehringer	Tabaka	Hoffman	13-3	1st	+4.0
4-18	At Pit.	W	7-5	(10)	15	14	Miceli	Loiselle	Hoffman	14-3	1st	+5.0
4-21	At Chi.	L	3-5		7	7	Trachsel	Brown	Beck	14-4	1st	+4.5
4-22	At Chi.	W	3-2	(14)	9	9	Boehringer	Telemaco	Reyes	15-4	1st	+5.5
4-23	At Chi.	W	4-1		11	9	Ashby	Clark	Hoffman	16-4	1st	+6.5
4-24	Pit.	L	2-4		5	6	Schmidt	Smith	Rincon	16-5	1st	+6.0
4-25	Pit.	W	4-3	(16)	17	7	Reyes	J. Martinez		17-5	1st	+6.0
4-26	Pit.	L	0-6		3	13	Lieber	Brown		17-6	1st	+5.0
4-27	Chi.	L	1-3		5	8	Tapani	Hamilton	Beck	17-7	1st	+4.5
4-28	Chi.	W	7-3		13	8	Ashby	Clark	Hitchcock	18-7	1st	+4.5
4-30	At Fla.	W	4-1		9	4	Smith	Meadows	Hoffman	19-7	1st	+5.0
5-1	At Fla.	L	5-6	(11)	12	9	Powell	Miceli		19-8	1st	+5.0
5-2	At Fla.	W	8-7		13	11	Hamilton	Ludwick	Hoffman	20-8	1st	+5.0
5-3	At Fla.	L	0-1		5	9	Sanchez	Ashby	Powell	20-9	1st	+4.0
5-4	At Mil.	W	13-5		18	14	Hitchcock	Mercedes	Wengert	21-9	1st	+5.0
5-5	At Mil.	W	13-4		11	12	Smith	Wagner		22-9	1st	+5.5
5-6	At Mil.	L	2-3		8	12	Jones	Reyes		22-10	1st	+4.5
5-7	At Atl.	L	3-6		5	10	Smoltz	Hamilton	Ligtenberg	22-11	1st	+4.0
5-8	At Atl.	W	3-2		6	9	Ashby	Glavine	Hoffman	23-11	1st	+5.0
5-9	At Atl.	L	4-6		7	10	Millwood	VanRyn	Ligtenberg	23-12	1st	+4.0
5-10	At Atl.	L	5-8		12	9	Cather	Wall	Ligtenberg	23-13	1st	+3.5
5-11	N.Y.	W	2-1		5	4	Brown	Leiter	Hoffman	24-13	1st	+3.5
5-13	N.Y.	L	3-4		6	10	Jones	Hamilton	J. Franco	24-14	1st	+3.5
5-14†	N.Y.	W	3-1		9	8	Boehringer	Cook	Hoffman	25-14		
5-14‡	N.Y.	W	6-2		7	4	Miceli	McMichael		26-14	1st	+3.5
5-15	Phi.	W	7-6		10	12	Boehringer	Grace	Hoffman	27-14	1st	+3.5
5-16	Phi.	W	3-2		7	9	Reyes	Leiter		28-14	1st	+4.5
5-17	Phi.	W	3-1		7	7	Wall	Schilling	Hoffman	29-14	1st	+4.5
5-19	At Pit.	L	0-3		5	10	Silva	Hamilton	Loiselle	29-15	1st	+4.5
5-20†	At Pit.	L	2-5		6	9	Cordova	Ashby	Loiselle	29-16		
5-20‡	At Pit.	W	8-3		9	11	Hitchcock	Peters		30-16	1st	+4.0
5-21	At Pit.	L	2-3		6	8	Schmidt	Brown	Rincon	30-17	1st	+3.0
5-22	At Hou.	W	9-6		16	10	Miceli	Nitkowski	Hoffman	31-17	1st	+4.0
5-23	At Hou.	L	3-4		4	8	Miller	Miceli	Wagner	31-18	1st	+4.0
5-24	At Hou.	L	2-5		9	8	Schourek	Hamilton	Wagner	31-19	1st	+3.0
5-25	At Ari.	L	2-3		4	6	Springer	Ashby	Olson	31-20	1st	+2.0
5-26	At Ari.	W	12-1		16	10	Brown	Suppan		32-20	1st	+2.0
5-27	At Ari.	W	6-4		12	14	Wall	Benes	Hoffman	33-20	1st	+3.0
5-29	St.L.	L	3-8		6	8	Petkovsek	Hamilton		33-21	1st	+2.5
5-30	St.L.	W	3-2		9	9	Ashby	Brantley		34-21	1st	+2.5
5-31	St.L.	W	7-3		10	7	Brown	Lowe		35-21	1st	+2.5
6-1	St.L.	W	3-2		8	8	Hitchcock	Stottlemyre	Hoffman	36-21	1st	+2.5
6-2	Hou.	L	3-4		8	10	Reynolds	Reyes	Wagner	36-22	1st	+1.5
6-3	Hou.	L	2-8		10	8	Bergman	Hamilton		36-23	1st	+0.5
6-4	Hou.	W	5-1		6	8	Ashby	Hampton		37-23	1st	+1.0
6-5	At Tex.	L	7-8		13	15	Crabtree	Wall	Wetteland	37-24	T1st	...
6-6	At Tex.	L	0-3		6	9	Burkett	Hitchcock	Wetteland	37-25	2nd	1.0
6-7	At Tex.	W	17-8		15	9	Miceli	Patterson		38-25	2nd	1.0
6-8	Cin.	W	4-2		6	8	Hamilton	Sullivan	Hoffman	39-25	2nd	1.0
6-9	Cin.	W	5-1		6	8	Ashby	Tomko	Hoffman	40-25	2nd	1.0
6-10	Cin.	W	2-1		5	9	Brown	Shaw		41-25	T1st	...
6-12	S.F.	W	10-3		15	9	Miceli	Reed		42-25	1st	+1.0
6-13	S.F.	W	4-2		8	4	Hamilton	Gardner	Hoffman	43-25	1st	+2.0
6-14	S.F.	W	3-2		6	9	Ashby	Darwin	Hoffman	44-25	1st	+3.0
6-16	L.A.	W	10-6		10	11	Brown	Park	Hoffman	45-25	1st	+3.5
6-17	L.A.	W	3-2	(12)	8	6	Hoffman	Reyes		46-25	1st	+3.5

Date	Opp.	Res.	Score	(inn.*)	Hits	Opp. hits	Winning pitcher	Losing pitcher	Save	Record	Pos.	GB
6-18	At S.F.	W	7-6		9	10	Ramirez	Johnstone	Miceli	47-25	1st	+4.5
6-19	At S.F.	W	9-5	12		7	Ashby	Darwin		48-25	1st	+5.5
6-20	At S.F.	L	2-5		6	11	Estes	Langston	Nen	48-26	1st	+4.5
6-21	At S.F.	W	5-1		9	8	Brown	Hershiser	Hoffman	49-26	1st	+5.5
6-22	At Sea.	W	5-3		7	5	Miceli	Fassero	Hoffman	50-26	1st	+5.5
6-23	At Sea.	L	3-5		10	10	Moyer	Hamilton	Slocumb	50-27	1st	+4.5
6-24	Sea.	L	1-2		6	8	Johnson	Ashby		50-28	1st	+4.5
6-25	Sea.	W	6-0		10	6	Langston	Cloude	Wall	51-28	1st	+5.5
6-26	Ana.	W	6-3		12	5	Brown	Dickson	Hoffman	52-28	1st	+6.5
6-27	Ana.	W	5-1		10	2	Hitchcock	Olivares		53-28	1st	+6.5
6-28	Ana.	L	3-11		12	14	Washburn	Hamilton		53-29	1st	+5.5
6-30	At Oak.	L	10-12		14	12	Taylor	Miceli	Fetters	53-30	1st	+5.5
7-1	At Oak.	W	8-4		12	8	Brown	Stein		54-30	1st	+5.5
7-2	At Oak.	L	2-7		6	10	Rogers	Hitchcock		54-31	1st	+4.5
7-3	Col.	W	4-2		8	8	Hamilton	DeJean	Hoffman	55-31	1st	+4.5
7-4	Col.	W	9-1		12	8	Langston	Jones		56-31	1st	+5.5
7-5	Col.	W	7-2		9	5	Ashby	Astacio		57-31	1st	+5.5
7-9	At L.A.	L	3-12		8	14	Park	Langston		57-32	1st	+5.0
7-10	At L.A.	L	2-6		6	11	Osuna	Miceli		57-33	1st	+5.0
7-11	At L.A.	W	4-1		7	4	Ashby	Valdes	Hoffman	58-33	1st	+6.0
7-12	At L.A.	W	6-3		7	9	Hamilton	Bohanon	Hoffman	59-33	1st	+7.0
7-13	At Col.	L	5-9		8	11	Jones	Hitchcock		59-34	1st	+7.0
7-14	At Col.	W	8-7		10	14	Sanders	Kile	Hoffman	60-34	1st	+8.0
7-15	At Col.	W	6-2		10	12	Brown	Wright		61-34	1st	+8.0
7-17	At Cin.	W	13-3		15	8	Ashby	Remlinger		62-34	1st	+9.0
7-18	At Cin.	W	2-1		7	5	Hamilton	Harnisch	Hoffman	63-34	1st	+10.0
7-19	At Cin.	W	7-6		7	9	Wall	Hudek	Hoffman	64-34	1st	+11.0
7-20	St.L.	L	1-13		3	16	Morris	Langston		64-35	1st	+10.0
7-21	St.L.	W	6-3		12	10	Brown	Mercker	Hoffman	65-35	1st	+11.0
7-22	Ari.	W	9-3		9	9	Ashby	Blair		66-35	1st	+12.0
7-23	Ari.	W	3-0		6	4	Hamilton	Anderson	Hoffman	67-35	1st	+13.0
7-24	Hou.	L	1-2		5	7	Schourek	Hitchcock	Magnante	67-36	1st	+12.0
7-25	Hou.	W	6-5		9	11	Langston	Reynolds	Hoffman	68-36	1st	+13.0
7-26	Hou.	W	5-4	(10)	11	9	Wall	Magnante		69-36	1st	+13.0
7-28	At N.Y.	L	3-7		10	11	Nomo	Ashby	McMichael	69-37	1st	+12.0
7-29	At N.Y.	L	6-7		12	14	Rojas	Wall	J. Franco	69-38	1st	+12.0
7-30	At N.Y.	W	3-1	(10)	8	5	Miceli	Cook	Hoffman	70-38	1st	+13.0
7-31	At Mon.	W	5-4		8	9	Brown	Pavano	Hoffman	71-38	1st	+13.0
8-1	At Mon.	L	2-4		5	7	Bennett	Langston	Urbina	71-39	1st	+12.0
8-2	At Mon.	W	4-1		9	6	Ashby	Vazquez	Hoffman	72-39	1st	+12.0
8-3	At Mon.	L	1-6		4	9	Hermanson	Boehringer		72-40	1st	+11.0
8-4	Phi.	W	3-1		9	8	Hitchcock	Beech	Hoffman	73-40	1st	+12.0
8-5	Phi.	W	4-0		9	5	Brown	Schilling		74-40	1st	+12.0
8-6	Phi.	L	2-3	(11)	8	9	Leiter	Hoffman		74-41	1st	+12.0
8-7	Fla.	W	6-3	(13)	12	11	Sanders	Speier		75-41	1st	+13.0
8-9	Fla.	W	6-5		8	7	Hitchcock	Larkin	Hoffman	76-41	1st	.14.5
8-10	Fla.	L	2-3		5	7	Hernandez	Brown		76-42	1st	+14.5
8-11	Atl.	W	3-1		6	6	Hamilton	Neagle	Hoffman	77-42	1st	+14.5
8-12	Atl.	W	5-1		8	5	Ashby	Maddux		78-42	1st	+15.5
8-13	Atl.	L	0-5		2	10	Glavine	Langston		78-43	1st	+15.0
8-14	Mil.	W	7-0		10	5	Hitchcock	Karl		79-43	1st	+15.0
8-16†	Mil.	W	4-0		7	1	Brown	Roque		80-43		
8-16‡	Mil.	L	2-4		9	7	Pulsipher	Hamilton	Wickman	80-44	1st	+14.0
8-18	At Fla.	W	7-5		11	13	Miceli	Alfonseca	Hoffman	81-44	1st	+15.0
8-19	At Fla.	L	0-6		11	10	Meadows	Hitchcock		81-45	1st	+14.0
8-20	At Atl.	W	2-0		6	11	Brown	Millwood	Hoffman	82-45	1st	+15.0
8-21	At Atl.	L	4-5		8	7	Smoltz	Hamilton	Ligtenberg	82-46	1st	+15.0
8-22	At Mil.	L	4-8		12	14	Roque	Langston	Wickman	82-47	1st	+14.0
8-23	At Mil.	W	13-11	(10)	18	15	Hoffman	Wickman		83-47	1st	+14.0
8-24	At Mil.	W	7-2		13	8	Hitchcock	Woodard		84-47	1st	+14.0
8-25	At Phi.	W	5-3		9	5	Brown	Schilling	Hoffman	85-47	1st	+14.0
8-26	At Phi.	W	2-0		8	5	Hamilton	Portugal	Hoffman	86-47	1st	+15.0
8-27	At Phi.	W	8-1		11	8	Spencer	Byrd		87-47	1st	+15.0
8-28	Mon.	W	12-8		10	12	Wall	Maddux		88-47	1st	+16.0
8-29	Mon.	L	1-3		3	6	Hermanson	Hitchcock	Urbina	88-48	1st	+15.0
8-30	Mon.	L	1-2		3	8	Bullinger	Brown	Urbina	88-49	1st	+15.0
8-31	Mon.	W	5-2		9	6	Hamilton	Pavano	Hoffman	89-49	1st	+15.0
9-1	N.Y.	W	9-8		10	10	R. Myers	Wendell	Hoffman	90-49	1st	+15.0
9-2	N.Y.	L	1-4		5	6	Reynoso	Ashby	J. Franco	90-50	1st	+14.0
9-4	At Col.	L	5-11		9	14	Veres	Sanders		90-51	1st	+14.0
9-5	At Col.	W	4-2		10	6	Brown	Kile	Hoffman	91-51	1st	+15.0
9-6	At Col.	L	2-12		6	14	Wright	Hamilton		91-52	1st	+14.0
9-7	S.F.	L	4-5		10	9	Tavarez	R. Myers	Nen	91-53	1st	+13.0
9-8	S.F.	L	1-5		4	10	Rueter	Ashby		91-54	1st	+12.0
9-9	S.F.	W	8-3		7	6	Hitchcock	Estes	Hoffman	92-54	1st	+13.0

Date	Opp.	Res.	Score	(inn.*)	Hits	Opp. hits	Winning pitcher	Losing pitcher	Save	Record	Pos.	GB
9-10	L.A.	L	3-4		5	3	Park	Brown	Shaw	92-55	1st	+12.5
9-11	L.A.	W	1-0		7	7	Hamilton	Bohanon	Hoffman	93-55	1st	+13.5
9-12	L.A.	W	8-7		7	10	Sanders	Maloney	Hoffman	94-55	1st	+14.5
9-13	L.A.	L	4-5	(10)	8	6	Weaver	Wall	Shaw	94-56	1st	+13.5
9-14	Chi.	W	4-3		9	5	Miceli	Karchner	Hoffman	95-56	1st	+14.5
9-15	Chi.	L	2-4		6	10	Tapani	Brown	Beck	95-57	1st	+14.5
9-16	Chi.	L	3-6		8	11	Mulholland	Miceli	Beck	95-58	1st	+13.5
9-17	Chi.	L	3-4	(10)	7	9	Heredia	Hoffman	Beck	95-59	1st	+13.0
9-18	Col.	L	1-4		7	10	Astacio	Ashby	Veres	95-60	1st	+12.0
9-19	Col.	W	4-1		8	7	Clement	Thomson	Hoffman	96-60	1st	+12.0
9-20	Col.	L	0-1	(11)	4	7	Kile	R. Myers	Veres	96-61	1st	+12.0
9-22	At L.A.	L	2-3		8	6	Park	Hamilton	Shaw	96-62	1st	+10.5
9-23	At L.A.	W	3-2		8	8	Ashby	Bohanon	Hoffman	97-62	1st	+10.5
9-25	At Ari.	L	3-6		9	8	Olson	R. Myers		97-63	1st	+9.0
9-26	At Ari.	L	2-3		6	7	Telemaco	Hitchcock	Olson	97-64	1st	+8.0
9-27	At Ari.	W	3-2		9	5	Clement	Small	Hoffman	98-64	1st	+9.0

Monthly records: March (1-0), April (18-7), May (16-14), June (18-9), July (18-8), August (18-11), September (9-15).
*Innings, if other than nine. †First game of doubleheader. ‡Second game of doubleheader.

HIGHLIGHTS

High point: The Padres clinched their second N.L. West title in three years when they rallied to beat the Dodgers, 8-7, on September 12. Greg Vaughn's two-run single provided the winning run and capped a rally from a 7-0 deficit. It was only San Diego's third division title in 30 seasons.

Low point: A 3-0 June 6 loss at Texas dropped the club out of first place for the first time since April 4. But four days later, the Padres regained the lead for good when Kevin Brown pitched a 2-1 victory over the Reds.

Turning point: A June 12-14 sweep of the Giants (in the midst of an 11-game winning streak) triggered a runaway division title and set a franchise record for home attendance in a three-game series. The teams were tied for first place entering the series, but San Francisco left town three games back.

Most valuable player: Teammates said Greg Vaughn carried the offense for the first three months, after which the club cruised toward the playoffs. Vaughn hit a franchise-record 50 home runs and led the team in RBIs (119) and slugging percentage (.597).

Most valuable pitcher: Reliever Trevor Hoffman and No. 1 starter Kevin Brown shared the honors. Hoffman converted 53-of-54 save chances, a major league-record success rate of .981. Brown ranked among league leaders in every major pitching category. He had an 18-7 record, 2.38 ERA and franchise-record 257 strikeouts.

Most improved player: Vaughn went from question mark to exclamation point. He seldom resembled the slugger who batted .216 in 1997 with 110 strikeouts in 120 games, and he also provided solid defense and good baserunning.

Most pleasant surprise: Donne Wall excelled in his first season as a reliever. He didn't allow an earned run in 35-of-45 appearances. The righthander held lefty batters to a .204 average.

Biggest disappointment: Steve Finley. For the second straight season, the speedster posted the lowest on-base percentage (.301) of any Padres regular. The club didn't strongly pursue Finley after the season, and he signed a four-year contract with the Diamondbacks.

Key injuries: Third baseman Ken Caminiti suffered from leg and back ailments throughout the season. Pained by acute tendinitis in his left biceps, first baseman Wally Joyner batted .239 in September and was 0-for-4 in the World Series. A shoulder injury limited second baseman Quilvio Veras and required postseason surgery. Tendinitis derailed pitcher Andy Ashby, who plummeted in mid-August after becoming the National League's first 16-game winner.

Notable: The 54 home wins set a club record, as did the attendance total of 2,555,901.

—TOM KRASOVIC

RECORDS

1998 regular-season record: 98-64 (1st in N.L. West); 54-27 at home; 44-37 on road; 26-18 vs. East; 35-22 vs. Central; 31-17 vs. N.L. West; 6-7 vs. A.L.; 28-24 vs. lefthanded starters; 70-40 vs. righthanded starters; 83-55 on grass; 15-9 on turf; 31-21 in daytime; 67-43 at night; 31-23 in one-run games; 9-5 in extra-inning games; 1-0-2 in doubleheaders.

Team record past five years: 382-365 (.511, ranks 5th in league in that span).

TEAM LEADERS

Batting average: Tony Gwynn (.321).
At-bats: Steve Finley (619).
Runs: Greg Vaughn (112).
Hits: Greg Vaughn (156).
Total bases: Greg Vaughn (342).
Doubles: Steve Finley (40).
Triples: Steve Finley (6).
Home runs: Greg Vaughn (50).
Runs batted in: Greg Vaughn (119).
Stolen bases: Quilvio Veras (24).
Slugging percentage: Greg Vaughn (.597).

On-base percentage: Quilvio Veras (.373).
Wins: Kevin Brown (18).
Earned-run average: Kevin Brown (2.38).
Complete games: Kevin Brown (7).
Shutouts: Kevin Brown (3).
Saves: Trevor Hoffman (53).
Innings pitched: Kevin Brown (257.0).
Strikeouts: Kevin Brown (257).

GAMES BY POSITION

Catcher: Carlos Hernandez 122, Greg Myers 52, Jim Leyritz 24, Mandy Romer 6, Ben Davis 1.
First base: Wally Joyner 127, Mark Sweeney 21, Jim Leyritz 20, Archi Cianfrocco 19, Eddie Williams 7, John Vander Wal 3, Andy Sheets 2, George Arias 1, Carlos Hernandez 1.
Second base: Quilvio Veras 131, Ed Giovanola 36, Andy Sheets 22, Archi Cianfrocco 3.
Third base: Ken Caminiti 126, Ed Giovanola 37, Andy Sheets 23, George Arias 14, Archi Cianfrocco 13, Jim Leyritz 1.
Shortstop: Chris Gomez 143, Andy Sheets 39, Ed Giovanola 2.
Outfield: Steve Finley 157, Greg Vaughn 151, Tony Gwynn 116, Ruben Rivera 91, Mark Sweeney 34, James Mouton 33, John Vander Wal 5, Archi Cianfrocco 3, Jim Leyritz 1.
Designated hitter: Greg Vaughn 4, Tony Gwynn 3, James Mouton 1, Mark Sweeney 1.

TOP DRAFT CHOICES

1. **Sean Burroughs**, 3B, Wilson H.S., Long Beach, Calif.
2. None
3. **Beau Craig**, C, Grossmont H.S., La Mesa, Calif.
4. **Travis Devine**, RHP, Dacula (Ga.) H.S.
5. **Kevin Eberwein**, 3B-OF, UNLV
6. **Dale Deveraux**, RHP, American Fork (Utah) H.S.
7. **Brian Berryman**, RHP, U. of Michigan
8. **Jeremy Owens**, OF, Middle Tennessee State U.
9. **Sean Campbell**, C, UNLV
10. **John Meyers**, RHP, Grayson County (Tex.) J.C.

SAN FRANCISCO GIANTS
NATIONAL LEAGUE WEST DIVISION

1999 Giants Schedule
Home games shaded. *—All-Star Game at Fenway Park (Boston).
D—Day game (any game starting before 5 p.m.)

April
SUN	MON	TUE	WED	THU	FRI	SAT
				1	2	3
4	5 D CIN	6 CIN	7 D CIN	8 D SD	9 SD	10 D SD
11 D	12	13 HOU	14 HOU	15 HOU	16 D ARI	17 D ARI
18 D ARI	19 FLA	20 FLA	21 D FLA	22 D COL	23 COL	24 D COL
25 D COL	26	27 MON	28 MON	29 MON	30 NYM	

May
SUN	MON	TUE	WED	THU	FRI	SAT
						1 D NYM
2 NYM	3 D PIT	4 PIT	5 D PIT	6	7 MIL	8 D MIL
9 MIL	10 D ATL	11 ATL	12 D ATL	13	14 HOU	15 HOU
16 HOU	17 D ARI	18 ARI	19 D ARI	20	21 D HOU	22 D HOU
23 D HOU	24	25 STL	26 D STL	27 D STL	28 MON	29 MON
30 MON	31 PHI					

June
SUN	MON	TUE	WED	THU	FRI	SAT
		1 PHI	2 PHI	3 D PHI	4 D OAK	5 OAK
6 OAK	7 D	8 D ANA	9 D ANA	10	11 SEA	12 SEA
13 SEA	14 COL	15 COL	16 D COL	17 D CUB	18 CUB	19 D CUB
20 CUB	21 D MIL	22 D MIL	23 D MIL	24	25 LA	26 D LA
27 LA	28	29 D COL	30 D COL			

July
SUN	MON	TUE	WED	THU	FRI	SAT
				1 COL	2 D LA	3 D LA
4 LA	5 SD	6 SD	7 SD	8	9 D STL	10 D STL
11 D STL	12	13 *	14	15 OAK	16 D OAK	17 D OAK
18 TEX	19 TEX	20 TEX	21 SD	22 D SD	23 CIN	24 D CIN
25 CIN	26 STL	27 D STL	28 D STL	29	30 CIN	31 CIN

August
SUN	MON	TUE	WED	THU	FRI	SAT
1 CIN	2 D ARI	3 ARI	4 ARI	5	6 ATL	7 D ATL
8 ATL	9 D FLA	10 FLA	11 D FLA	12	13 NYM	14 D NYM
15 NYM	16 D MON	17 D MON	18 D MON	19	20 MIL	21 D MIL
22 MIL	23 CUB	24 D CUB	25 D CUB	26 D CUB	27 PIT	28 D PIT
29 PIT	30 D PHI	31 PHI				

September
SUN	MON	TUE	WED	THU	FRI	SAT
			1 PHI	2 D PHI	3 D PIT	4 PIT
5 PIT	6 D NYM	7 D NYM	8 D NYM	9	10 ATL	11 D ATL
12 ATL	13	14 FLA	15 FLA	16 D FLA	17 D SD	18 D SD
19 D SD	20 LA	21 LA	22 LA	23 LA	24 ARI	25 D ARI
26 D ARI	27	28 LA	29 LA	30 LA		

October
SUN	MON	TUE	WED	THU	FRI	SAT
					1 COL	2 D COL
3 D COL	4	5	6	7	8	9

1999 SEASON
CLUB DIRECTORY

President and managing general partner
Peter A. Magowan
Executive vice president/COO
Larry Baer
Senior v.p. and general manager
Brian Sabean
Sr. vice president, business operations
Pat Gallagher
Special assistant to the general manager
Jim Fregosi
Vice president and assistant g.m.
Ned Colletti
Vice president of player personnel
Dick Tidrow
Special assistant, player personnel
Ted Uhloender
Director of player development
Jack Hiatt
Coordinator of international operations
Rick Ragazzo
Sr. v.p. and chief financial officer
John Yee
V.p., stadium operations/security
Jorge Costa
Vice president, communications
Bob Rose
Vice president, marketing/sales
Mario Alioto
General manager, retail/Internet
Connie Kullberg
Director of stadium operations
Gene Telucci

Vice president, ticket sales
Mark Norrelli
Vice president, ticket services
Russ Stanley
Director of travel
Reggie Younger Jr.
Vice president and general counsel
Jack Bair
Media relations manager
Jim Moorehead
National cross-checker
Randy Waddill
Eastern cross-checker
Paul Turco
Western cross-checker
Doug Mapson
Major league advance scout
Pat Dobson
Major league scout
Cal Emery
Special assignment scouts
Joe DiCarlo, Stan Saleski, Bob Hartsfield
Scouts
Jorge Aranzamendi, Steve Arnjeri, Jose Cassino, Richard Cole, Joe DiCarlo, John Dipuglia, Tom Korenek, Alan Marr, Doug McMillan, Bob Myrick, Cesar Navarro, Matt Nerland, Bo Osborne, Carlos Ramirez, John Shafer, Joe Strain, Todd Thomas, Glenn Tufts, Ciro Villalobos, Darren Wittake, Tom Zimmer

MINOR LEAGUE AFFILIATES
Class	Team	League	Manager
AAA	Fresno	Pacific Coast	Ron Roenicke
AA	Shreveport	Texas	Shane Turner
A	San Jose	California	Lenn Sakata
A	Bakersfield	California	Keith Comstock
Rookie	Salem-Keizer	Northwest	Frank Reberger

BROADCAST INFORMATION
Radio: KNBR-AM (680); KIQI-AM (1010, Spanish language).
TV: KTVU-TV (Channel 2).
Cable TV: FOX Sports Bay Area.

SPRING TRAINING
Ballpark (city): Scottsdale Stadium (Scottsdale, Ariz.).
Ticket information: 602-990-7972 or 602-784-4444.

SPRING TRAINING ROSTER

Manager— Dusty Baker (12).
Coaches—Carlos Alfonso (17), Gene Clines (20), Sonny Jackson (15), Ron Perranoski (16), Ron Wotus (10).

No.	PITCHERS	B/T	Ht./Wt.	Born	1998 clubs
41	Bailey, Cory	R/R	6-1/200	1-24-71	Fresno, San Francisco
51	Brock, Chris	R/R	6-0/185	2-5-70	Fresno, San Francisco
	Connelly, Steve	R/R	6-4/210	4-27-74	Oakland, Edmonton
	Crabtree, Robbie	R/R	6-0/175	11-25-72	San Jose, Shreveport, Fresno
56	Embree, Alan	L/L	6-2/190	1-23-70	Atlanta, Arizona
55	Estes, Shawn	R/L	6-2/192	2-18-73	San Francisco, Bakersfield, Fresno
26	Gardner, Mark	R/R	6-1/220	3-1-62	San Francisco
	Hansell, Greg	R/R	6-5/224	3-12-71	Edmonton, Omaha
49	Johnstone, John	R/R	6-3/210	11-25-68	San Francisco
36	Nathan, Joe	R/R	6-4/195	11-22-74	Shreveport, San Jose
31	Nen, Robb	R/R	6-5/215	11-28-69	San Francisco
48	Ortiz, Russ	R/R	6-1/210	6-5-74	San Francisco, Fresno
	Patrick, Bronswell	R/R	6-1/220	9-16-70	Milwaukee, Louisville
	Rodriguez, Felix	R/R	6-1/190	12-5-72	Arizona, Arizona Diamondbacks, Tucson
33	Rodriguez, Rich	L/L	6-0/205	3-1-63	San Francisco
46	Rueter, Kirk	L/L	6-3/205	12-1-70	San Francisco
39	Soderstrom, Steve	R/R	6-2/190	4-3-72	Fresno
50	Tavarez, Julian	R/R	6-2/190	5-22-73	San Francisco, Fresno
	Wilson, Trevor	L/L	6-1/185	6-7-66	Anaheim, Vancouver

No.	CATCHERS	B/T	Ht./Wt.	Born	1998 clubs
9	Mayne, Brent	L/R	6-1/192	4-19-68	San Francisco
19	Mirabelli, Doug	R/R	6-1/218	10-18-70	Fresno, San Francisco
5	Torrealba, Yorvit	R/R	5-11/180	7-19-78	Fresno, Shreveport, San Jose

No.	INFIELDERS	B/T	Ht./Wt.	Born	1998 clubs
35	Aurilia, Rich	R/R	6-1/185	9-2-71	San Francisco
29	Canizaro, Jay	R/R	5-9/178	7-4-73	Shreveport, Fresno
62	Delgado, Wilson	B/R	5-11/160	7-15-75	Fresno, San Francisco
2	Feliz, Pedro	R/R	6-1/195	4-27-77	Fresno, Shreveport
13	Hayes, Charlie	R/R	6-0/220	5-29-65	San Francisco
21	Kent, Jeff	R/R	6-1/205	3-7-68	San Francisco
34	Martinez, Ramon	R/R	6-1/187	10-10-72	Fresno, San Francisco
30	Minor, Damon	L/L	6-7/230	1-5-74	Shreveport, San Jose
32	Mueller, Bill	B/R	5-10/180	3-17-71	San Francisco
6	Snow, J.T.	B/L	6-2/205	2-26-68	San Francisco

No.	OUTFIELDERS	B/T	Ht./Wt.	Born	1998 clubs
7	Benard, Marvin	L/L	5-9/185	1-20-70	San Francisco
25	Bonds, Barry	L/L	6-2/210	7-24-64	San Francisco
23	Burks, Ellis	R/R	6-2/205	9-11-64	Colorado, San Francisco
28	Javier, Stan	B/R	6-0/202	1-9-64	San Francisco
8	Murray, Calvin	R/R	5-11/190	7-30-71	Fresno, Shreveport
1	Rios, Armando	L/L	5-9/185	9-13-71	Fresno, San Francisco
	Santangelo, F.P.	B/R	5-10/170	10-24-67	Montreal, Ottawa

BALLPARK INFORMATION

Ballpark (capacity, surface)
3Com Park at Candlestick Point (63,000, grass)

Address
3Com Park
San Francisco, CA 94124

Business phone
415-468-3700

Ticket information
415-468-3700

Ticket prices
$21 (lower box)
$14 (upper box)
$18 (lower reserved)
$9 (upper reserved)
$6 (pavilion)
$6 (reserved bleachers)

Field dimensions (from home plate)
To left field at foul line, 335 feet
To center field, 400 feet
To right field at foul line, 328 feet

First game played
April 12, 1960 (Giants 3, Cardinals 1)

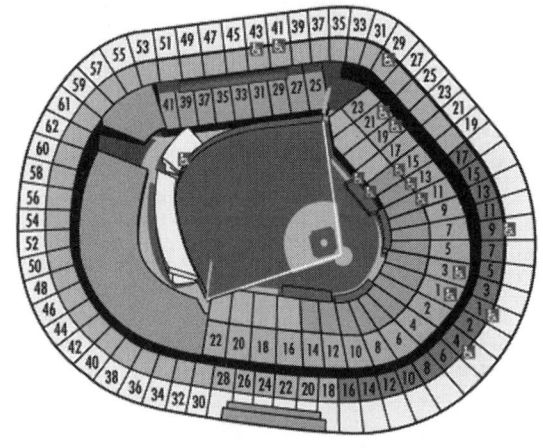

Date	Opp.	Res.	Score	(inn.*)	Hits	Opp. hits	Winning pitcher	Losing pitcher	Save	Record	Pos.	GB
3-31	At Hou.	W	9-4	(13)	16	9	Johnstone	Nitkowski		1-0	T1st	...
4-1	At Hou.	L	6-7		11	8	Miller	Tavarez	Wagner	1-1	3rd	1.0
4-2	At Hou.	W	9-2		16	3	Rueter	Halama		2-1	T2nd	1.0
4-3	At Ari.	W	8-3		12	6	Gardner	Suppan		3-1	T1st	...
4-4	At Ari.	W	5-3		7	8	Darwin	Olson	Nen	4-1	T1st	...
4-5	At Ari.	L	2-3		7	8	Benes	Estes	Rodriguez	4-2	T1st	...
4-7	Hou.	W	5-4	(10)	10	5	Nen	Wagner		5-2	T1st	...
4-8	Hou.	L	3-6		10	12	Lima	Rueter	Wagner	5-3	2nd	1.0
4-9	Hou.	L	1-3		8	6	Bergman	Gardner	Nitkowski	5-4	2nd	2.0
4-10	St.L.	W	5-3		10	11	Tavarez	Frascatore	Nen	6-4	2nd	2.0
4-11	St.L.	L	2-7		10	8	Bottenfield	Estes		6-5	2nd	3.0
4-12	St.L.	W	2-1		7	7	Nen	Frascatore		7-5	2nd	3.0
4-13	St.L.	W	8-2		11	8	Rueter	Aybar		8-5	2nd	3.0
4-14	S.D.	W	13-7		12	15	Tavarez	Boehringer		9-5	2nd	2.0
4-15	S.D.	L	0-1		4	9	Brown	Darwin		9-6	2nd	3.0
4-17	At Mil.	L	2-5		5	7	Mercedes	Estes	Jones	9-7	2nd	4.0
4-18	At Mil.	L	1-3		7	6	Wagner	Hershiser	Jones	9-8	2nd	5.0
4-19	At Mil.	L	2-3	(12)	11	11	Wickman	Johnstone		9-9	2nd	5.5
4-21	At Pit.	W	6-3		11	6	Gardner	Lieber		10-9	2nd	4.5
4-22	At Pit.	L	2-5		7	8	Silva	Darwin	Loiselle	10-10	2nd	5.5
4-23	At Pit.	L	0-7		5	10	Cordova	Estes		10-11	2nd	6.5
4-24	Mil.	L	5-7		9	9	Karl	Hershiser	Jones	10-12	3rd	6.5
4-25	Mil.	W	2-1		4	3	Rueter	Wagner	Nen	11-12	3rd	6.5
4-26	Mil.	W	8-7		12	15	Reed	Jones		12-12	3rd	5.5
4-27	Pit.	W	6-5		8	9	Nen	Loiselle		13-12	2nd	4.5
4-28	Pit.	W	2-1		6	3	Estes	Cordova	Nen	14-12	2nd	4.5
4-30	At Atl.	L	0-6		5	8	Neagle	Hershiser		14-13	3rd	5.5
5-1	At Atl.	L	2-6		6	11	Maddux	Rueter		14-14	3rd	5.5
5-2	At Atl.	L	3-4		7	10	Ligtenberg	Nen		14-15	3rd	6.5
5-3	At Atl.	W	12-8		13	10	Darwin	Glavine		15-15	3rd	5.5
5-4	At Fla.	W	8-0		12	4	Estes	Larkin		16-15	3rd	5.5
5-5	At Fla.	W	8-2	(10)	9	3	Nen	Darensbourg		17-15	2nd	5.5
5-6	At Fla.	W	10-9		11	13	Reed	Darensbourg	Nen	18-15	2nd	4.5
5-8	At Chi.	L	4-5	(14)	15	8	Telemaco	Tavarez		18-16	2nd	5.0
5-9†	At Chi.	W	5-1		9	9	Darwin	Tapani		19-16		
5-9‡	At Chi.	L	0-6		6	11	Gonzalez	Estes		19-17	2nd	4.5
5-10	At Chi.	W	3-0		5	3	Hershiser	Clark	Nen	20-17	2nd	3.5
5-11	Mon.	W	7-2		9	11	Rueter	Vazquez		21-17	2nd	3.5
5-13	Mon.	L	5-9		7	15	C. Perez	Gardner		21-18	2nd	3.5
5-14†	Mon.	W	6-1		11	6	Estes	Hermanson	Tavarez	22-18		
5-14‡	Mon.	W	2-0		7	4	Darwin	Moore	Nen	23-18	2nd	3.5
5-15	N.Y.	W	3-2		9	5	Hershiser	McMichael	Nen	24-18	2nd	3.5
5-16	N.Y.	L	1-4		7	8	Reed	Rueter	J. Franco	24-19	2nd	4.5
5-17	N.Y.	W	4-2		9	7	Gardner	Leiter	Nen	25-19	2nd	4.5
5-19	At Mil.	L	6-9		13	11	Jones	Poole		25-20	2nd	4.5
5-20	At Mil.	W	4-2		14	7	Hershiser	Woodard	Nen	26-20	2nd	4.0
5-21	At Mil.	W	8-1		17	2	Rueter	Karl		27-20	2nd	3.0
5-22	At St.L.	L	3-4	(12)	9	10	King	Tavarez		27-21	2nd	4.0
5-23	At St.L.	L	10-11		9	15	Painter	Johnstone	King	27-22	2nd	4.0
5-24	At St.L.	W	9-6	(17)	19	14	Poole	Mercker	Reed	28-22	2nd	3.0
5-25	At Cin.	W	3-1		5	4	Hershiser	Harnisch	Nen	29-22	2nd	2.0
5-26	At Cin.	W	5-2		6	9	Rueter	Remlinger	Nen	30-22	2nd	2.0
5-27	At Cin.	L	5-7		9	11	Sullivan	Poole	Shaw	30-23	2nd	3.0
5-28	Ari.	L	7-8		9	12	Anderson	Darwin	Olson	30-24	2nd	3.5
5-29	Ari.	W	3-1		6	4	Estes	Blair	Nen	31-24	2nd	2.5
5-30	Ari.	W	4-1		10	2	Hershiser	Daal	Nen	32-24	2nd	2.5
5-31	Ari.	W	7-4		10	10	Rueter	Suppan		33-24	2nd	2.5
6-1	Cin.	W	16-3		16	6	Gardner	Priest		34-24	2nd	2.5
6-2	Cin.	W	4-2		8	7	Darwin	Winchester	Nen	35-24	2nd	1.5
6-3	Cin.	W	8-5		13	10	Estes	Tomko	Nen	36-24	2nd	0.5
6-5	At St.L.	W	3-2		7	8	Hershiser	Bottenfield	Nen	37-24	T1st	...
6-6	At St.L.	W	5-4	(14)	10	14	Rodriguez	Lowe		38-24	1st	+1.0
6-7	At St.L.	W	6-5		13	10	Gardner	Mercker	Nen	39-24	1st	+1.0
6-8	Sea.	W	4-3		8	11	Darwin	Johnson	Rodriguez	40-24	1st	+1.0
6-9	Sea.	W	7-6		11	13	Johnstone	Cloude	Nen	41-24	1st	+1.0
6-10	Sea.	L	1-4		7	10	Swift	Hershiser	Slocumb	41-25	T1st	...
6-12	At S.D.	L	3-10		9	15	Miceli	Reed		41-26	2nd	1.0
6-13	At S.D.	L	2-4		4	8	Hamilton	Gardner	Hoffman	41-27	2nd	2.0
6-14	At S.D.	L	2-3		9	6	Ashby	Darwin	Hoffman	41-28	2nd	3.0
6-15	Col.	L	3-4	(12)	5	6	Leskanic	Johnstone	DiPoto	41-29	2nd	3.5
6-16	Col.	W	5-3		13	8	Tavarez	Jones	Nen	42-29	2nd	3.5

Date	Opp.	Res.	Score	(inn.*)	Hits	Opp. hits	Winning pitcher	Losing pitcher	Save	Record	Pos.	GB
6-17	Col.	W	6-3		12	7	Rueter	Kile	Nen	43-29	2nd	3.5
6-18	S.D.	L	6-7		10	9	Ramirez	Johnstone	Miceli	43-30	2nd	4.5
6-19	S.D.	L	5-9		7	12	Ashby	Darwin		43-31	2nd	5.5
6-20	S.D.	W	5-2		11	6	Estes	Langston	Nen	44-31	2nd	4.5
6-21	S.D.	L	1-5		8	9	Brown	Hershiser	Hoffman	44-32	2nd	5.5
6-22	At Oak.	W	12-8		13	13	Rueter	Small		45-32	2nd	5.5
6-23	At Oak.	W	4-2		6	7	Gardner	Candiotti	Nen	46-32	2nd	4.5
6-24	Oak.	L	6-7		8	10	Mohler	Poole	Taylor	46-33	2nd	4.5
6-25	Oak.	L	2-5		8	7	Haynes	Estes	Taylor	46-34	2nd	5.5
6-26	Tex.	L	3-7		10	12	Oliver	Hershiser	Wetteland	46-35	2nd	6.5
6-27	Tex.	W	6-5	(10)	9	10	Nen	Patterson		47-35	2nd	6.5
6-28	Tex.	W	7-0		7	3	Gardner	Sele		48-35	2nd	5.5
6-30	At Ana.	L	3-4		8	9	Finley	Estes	Percival	48-36	2nd	5.5
7-1	At Ana.	W	6-3	(10)	12	8	Nen	Cadaret		49-36	2nd	5.5
7-2	At Ana.	W	7-4		10	15	Rueter	Dickson		50-36	2nd	4.5
7-3	L.A.	W	6-3		12	5	Hershiser	Valdes	Nen	51-36	2nd	4.5
7-4	L.A.	L	5-9		10	12	Mlicki	Gardner		51-37	2nd	5.5
7-5	L.A.	W	3-0		8	8	Estes	Dreifort	Nen	52-37	2nd	5.5
7-10	At Col.	L	2-11		8	19	Kile	Estes		52-38	2nd	5.0
7-11	At Col.	L	4-5		11	9	McElroy	Hershiser	Munoz	52-39	2nd	6.0
7-12	At Col.	L	3-5		9	9	Astacio	Rueter	Munoz	52-40	2nd	7.0
7-13	At L.A.	L	5-7		9	12	Mlicki	Darwin	Shaw	52-41	2nd	7.0
7-14	At L.A.	L	1-2		6	5	Radinsky	Johnstone		52-42	2nd	8.0
7-15	At L.A.	W	5-3		8	7	Hershiser	Dreifort	Nen	53-42	2nd	8.0
7-17	At Hou.	L	7-10		10	17	Lima	Rueter		53-43	2nd	9.0
7-18	At Hou.	L	2-7		7	10	Bergman	Darwin		53-44	2nd	10.0
7-19	At Hou.	L	3-4	(12)	7	9	Henry	Nen		53-45	2nd	11.0
7-20	Ari.	W	5-3		9	3	Rodriguez	Chouinard	Nen	54-45	2nd	10.0
7-21	Ari.	L	3-5		10	10	Benes	Hershiser	Olson	54-46	2nd	11.0
7-22	St.L.	L	2-3		5	6	Witt	Rueter	Croushore	54-47	2nd	12.0
7-23	St.L.	L	1-8		4	11	Bottenfield	Darwin		54-48	2nd	13.0
7-24	Cin.	W	12-2		15	5	Gardner	Winchester		55-48	2nd	12.0
7-25	Cin.	L	8-9		11	14	Belinda	Ortiz	Graves	55-49	2nd	13.0
7-26	Cin.	W	2-1	(10)	3	5	Mesa	Belinda		56-49	2nd	13.0
7-28	At Mon.	W	7-1		11	2	Rueter	Vazquez		57-49	2nd	12.0
7-29	At Mon.	L	0-6		5	9	Hermanson	Darwin		57-50	2nd	12.0
7-30	At Mon.	L	6-12		9	14	Thurman	Gardner	Bennett	57-51	2nd	13.0
7-31	At Phi.	W	7-6		13	10	Mesa	Perez	Nen	58-51	2nd	13.0
8-1	At Phi.	W	8-7	(10)	14	12	Nen	Bottalico	Rodriguez	59-51	2nd	12.0
8-2	At Phi.	W	15-3		19	7	Rueter	Welch		60-51	2nd	12.0
8-3	At Phi.	W	6-1		12	8	Darwin	Loewer		61-51	2nd	11.0
8-4	At N.Y.	L	6-7	(10)	10	15	Cook	Mesa		61-52	2nd	12.0
8-5	At N.Y.	W	6-4		14	8	Ortiz	Jones	Nen	62-52	2nd	12.0
8-6	At N.Y.	L	8-9		13	16	Wendell	Nen		62-53	2nd	12.0
8-7	Atl.	L	0-5		3	10	Glavine	Rueter		62-54	2nd	13.0
8-8	Atl.	L	6-14		8	20	Millwood	Darwin		62-55	2nd	13.5
8-9	Atl.	L	5-7		6	8	Martinez	Mesa	Ligtenberg	62-56	2nd	14.5
8-10	Chi.	L	5-8		11	9	Tapani	Ortiz	Beck	62-57	2nd	14.5
8-11	Chi.	W	8-7		10	11	Mesa	Adams	Nen	63-57	2nd	14.5
8-12	Chi.	L	2-10		7	12	Trachsel	Rueter		63-58	2nd	15.5
8-14	Fla.	W	10-0		10	6	Gardner	Larkin		64-58	2nd	15.0
8-15	Fla.	W	4-3	(10)	12	10	Mesa	Mantei		65-58	2nd	14.5
8-16	Fla.	W	3-2		9	11	Hershiser	Sanchez	Nen	66-58	2nd	14.0
8-18	At Atl.	L	4-8		7	9	Maddux	Rueter		66-59	2nd	15.0
8-19	At Atl.	W	6-2		11	7	Gardner	Glavine		67-59	2nd	14.0
8-20	At Chi.	L	3-7		7	12	Tapani	Ortiz		67-60	2nd	15.0
8-21	At Chi.	L	5-6		9	12	Heredia	Nen		67-61	2nd	15.0
8-22	At Fla.	W	5-4	(10)	8	6	Rodriguez	Edmondson	Nen	68-61	2nd	14.0
8-23	At Fla.	W	10-5		12	9	Rueter	Ojala		69-61	2nd	14.0
8-24	At Fla.	W	7-4		14	10	Rodriguez	Edmondson	Nen	70-61	2nd	14.0
8-25	N.Y.	W	7-3		12	7	Ortiz	Reed		71-61	2nd	14.0
8-26	N.Y.	L	1-4		3	9	Nomo	Hershiser		71-62	2nd	15.0
8-27	N.Y.	W	11-3		16	10	Darwin	Reynoso		72-62	2nd	15.0
8-28	Phi.	L	3-4	(10)	6	7	Leiter	Nen		72-63	2nd	16.0
8-29	Phi.	W	10-3		13	8	Gardner	Loewer		73-63	2nd	15.0
8-30	Phi.	L	4-5		7	10	Schilling	Ortiz		73-64	2nd	15.0
8-31	Phi.	W	6-2		7	7	Mesa	Gomes		74-64	2nd	15.0
9-1	Mon.	W	9-7		14	12	Johnstone	Kline	Nen	75-64	2nd	15.0
9-2	Mon.	W	12-3		14	8	Rueter	Vazquez		76-64	2nd	14.0
9-4	At L.A.	L	5-8		10	10	Dreifort	Estes	Shaw	76-65	2nd	14.0
9-5	At L.A.	L	3-6		4	11	Park	Hershiser		76-66	2nd	15.0
9-6	At L.A.	W	6-2		7	5	Gardner	Bohanon		77-66	2nd	14.0
9-7	At S.D.	W	5-4		9	10	Tavarez	R. Myers	Nen	78-66	2nd	13.0
9-8	At S.D.	W	5-1		10	4	Rueter	Ashby		79-66	2nd	12.0
9-9	At S.D.	L	3-8		6	7	Hitchcock	Estes	Hoffman	79-67	2nd	13.0

Date	Opp.	Res.	Score	(inn.*)	Hits	Opp. hits	Winning pitcher	Losing pitcher	Save	Record	Pos.	GB
9-11	Col.	L	6-7		15	11	Stoops	Morman	DiPoto	79-68	2nd	13.5
9-12	Col.	L	0-1		6	8	Astacio	Nen	DiPoto	79-69	2nd	14.5
9-13	Col.	W	4-3		6	7	Johnstone	McElroy	Nen	80-69	2nd	13.5
9-14	At Ari.	L	2-14		7	17	Anderson	Estes		80-70	2nd	14.5
9-15	At Ari.	L	6-7	(11)	6	15	Olson	Mesa		80-71	2nd	14.5
9-16	At Ari.	W	6-5	(10)	10	9	Johnstone	Olson	Nen	81-71	2nd	13.5
9-18	L.A.	W	4-3		9	7	Tavarez	Radinsky	Nen	82-71	2nd	12.0
9-19	L.A.	W	18-4		19	12	Ortiz	Valdes		83-71	2nd	12.0
9-20	L.A.	L	0-1		4	2	Perez	Estes		83-72	2nd	12.0
9-21	Pit.	W	8-1		8	7	Hershiser	Silva		84-72	2nd	11.5
9-22	Pit.	W	14-2		17	7	Rueter	Lieber		85-72	2nd	10.5
9-23	Pit.	W	4-1		10	6	Gardner	Peters	Nen	86-72	2nd	10.5
9-24	Pit.	W	6-2		10	9	Ortiz	Dessens		87-72	2nd	10.0
9-25	At Col.	W	8-6		15	7	Johnstone	Leskanic	Nen	88-72	2nd	9.0
9-26	At Col.	W	8-4		15	8	Hershiser	Kile		89-72	2nd	8.0
9-27	At Col.	L	8-9		12	15	DiPoto	Nen		89-73	2nd	9.0
9-28	At Chi.	L	3-5		6	10	Trachsel	Gardner	Beck	89-74	2nd	9.5

Monthly records: March (1-0), April (13-13), May (19-11), June (15-12), July (10-15), August (16-13), September (15-10).
*Innings, if other than nine. †First game of doubleheader. ‡Second game of doubleheader.

HIGHLIGHTS

High point: June 9. After a 7-6 victory over the Mariners, their 11th straight win, the surprising Giants were 41-24 and leading the N.L. West by one game.
Low point: On the final day of the season, the Giants blew a 7-0 lead at Colorado and lost 9-8 on a Neifi Perez homer off Robb Nen in the 10th inning. A victory would have given the Giants the N.L. wild-card. Instead, they lost a one-game playoff at Chicago the next night.
Turning point: Jeff Kent, pivoting on a double-play attempt in a June 10 game, took a hit from Mariners shortstop Alex Rodriguez and injured his knee. The Giants' most productive hitter missed a month, during which the club fell out of first place, never to return.
Most valuable player: Despite missing that month, Kent still set career highs with 31 homers and 128 RBIs while batting .297 and becoming a clubhouse leader.
Most valuable pitcher: Mark Gardner. Although he opened the season as the No. 4 starter, Gardner was the most consistent man in the rotation, especially down the stretch when he went 5-0 and kept the Giants in the playoff hunt.
Most improved player: After a disappointing 1997 season, Darryl Hamilton became a force at the top of the order. The Giants traded him to Colorado July 31 because they needed Ellis Burks' power, a deal that might not have been possible had Hamilton not improved so much.
Most pleasant surprise: Marvin Benard had been tagged as a pinch hitter and defensive replacement, but he stunned everybody by hitting .371 over his last 65 games, mostly as the leadoff hitter and Hamilton's replacement in center.
Biggest disappointment: Shawn Estes. The lefthander who won 19 games in 1997 went 7-12. Estes was often wild and seemed lost on the mound, not understanding what he needed to do to get hitters out. In one season, his ERA soared from 3.18 to 5.06.
Key injuries: Kent's sprained knee cost him a month, during which the team went 11-24. Estes had a strained shoul-

der that forced him to miss 44 games. Catcher Brian Johnson was twice forced onto the disabled list with a fracture in his hand. First baseman J.T. Snow strained his shoulder in June, requiring periodic rest and affecting his hitting.
Notable: Kent became just the second second baseman in major league history to drive in more than 120 runs in multiple seasons. . . . The 842 runs scored was the second-highest total in San Francisco history. . . . Barry Bonds became the first player in history to reach 400 homers and 400 steals when he went deep off Florida's Kirt Ojala August 23.

—HENRY SCHULMAN

RECORDS

1998 regular-season record: 89-74 (2nd in N.L. West); 49-32 at home; 40-42 on road; 28-16 vs. East; 31-27 vs. Central; 22-26 vs. N.L. West; 8-5 vs. A.L.; 23-17 vs. lefthanded starters; 66-57 vs. righthanded starters; 79-65 on grass; 10-9 on turf; 42-29 in daytime; 47-45 at night; 25-29 in one-run games; 12-8 in extra-inning games; 1-0-1 in doubleheaders.
Team record past five years: 369-377 (.495, ranks 9th in league in that span).

TEAM LEADERS

Batting average: Barry Bonds (.303).
At-bats: Barry Bonds (552).
Runs: Barry Bonds (120).
Hits: Barry Bonds (167).
Total bases: Barry Bonds (336).
Doubles: Barry Bonds (44).
Triples: Barry Bonds (7).
Home runs: Barry Bonds (37).
Runs batted in: Jeff Kent (128).
Stolen bases: Barry Bonds (28).
Slugging percentage: Barry Bonds (.609).
On-base percentage: Barry Bonds (.438).
Wins: Kirk Rueter (16).

Earned-run average: Mark Gardner (4.33).
Complete games: Mark Gardner (4).
Shutouts: Mark Gardner (2).
Saves: Robb Nen (40).
Innings pitched: Mark Gardner (212.0).
Strikeouts: Mark Gardner (151).

GAMES BY POSITION

Catcher: Brian Johnson 95, Brent Mayne 88, Doug Mirabelli 10.
First base: J.T. Snow 136, Charlie Hayes 45, Joe Carter 16, Jeff Ball 1, Jeff Kent 1.
Second base: Jeff Kent 134, Rey Sanchez 36, Ramon E. Martinez 14, Bill Mueller 10, Shawon Dunston 1.
Third base: Bill Mueller 137, Charlie Hayes 46.
Shortstop: Rich Aurilia 120, Rey Sanchez 76, Shawon Dunston 9, Wilson Delgado 6.
Outfield: Barry Bonds 155, Stan Javier 121, Darryl Hamilton 96, Marvin Benard 79, Ellis Burks 41, Chris Jones 29, Alex Diaz 21, Joe Carter 17, Dante Powell 8, Shawon Dunston 6, Armando Rios 5, Brian Johnson 1.
Designated hitter: Marvin Benard 2, Charlie Hayes 2, Chris Jones 2.

TOP DRAFT CHOICES

1a. **Tony Torcato**, 3B, Woodland (Calif.) H.S.
1b. **Nate Bump**, RHP, Penn State Univ.
1c. **Arturo McDowell**, OF, Forest Hill H.S., Jackson, Miss.
1d. **Chris Jones**, LHP, S. Mecklenburg H.S., Charlotte, N.C.
1e. **Jeff Urban**, LHP, Ball State Univ.
2a. **Sammy Serrano**, C, Stetson Univ.
2b. **Chris Magruder**, OF, U. of Washington
3. **Mike Dean**, C, Oral Roberts Univ.
4. **Josh Santos**, LHP, U. of Connecticut
5. **Ryan Vogelsong**, RHP, Kutztown (Pa.) Univ.
6. **Jake Esteves**, RHP, Louisiana State U.
7. **Doug Clark**, OF, U. of Massachusetts
8. **Todd Ozias**, RHP, Univ. of Miami
9. **Bryan Ransom**, SS, Grand Canyon U.
10. **Chris Jackson**, RHP, Wasson H.S., Colorado Springs, Colo.

1998 REVIEW

Year in review

American League Division Series

National League Division Series

American League Championship Series

National League Championship Series

World Series

All-Star Game

Notable Performances

Transactions

Award Winners

Miscellaneous

Necrology

YEAR IN REVIEW

THE TOP STORIES OF THE PAST YEAR

By STEVE GIETSCHIER
TSN Archivist

No sooner had New York Yankees third baseman Scott Brosius thrown out San Diego Padres pinch-hitter Mark Sweeney to wrap up the World Series in four games than baseball fans everywhere began to debate whether this edition of the Yankees, 125-50 during regular and postseason play, was the best team ever.

Regardless of how one chose to answer this question, opinion was more nearly universal that the 1998 season, taken as a whole, ranked with the greatest of all time. For sheer excitement, the events of the year, headlined by the hoopla surrounding Mark McGwire's new single-season home run record, seemed hard to top. Add to this a handful of other special achievements plus the fact that the home-run chase was a dual assault, energized by Sammy Sosa's matching McGwire's pace nearly every step of the way, and 1998 stood out as one of the game's finest campaigns.

Not entirely lost in the radiance of this quest for baseball immortality were other events that in less breath-taking years would have garnered more headlines. Baseball owners named a fulltime commissioner for the first time since 1992. A veteran pitcher threw a perfect game, and a rookie set strikeout records. Two expansion teams began play in new ballparks. Congress passed and President Bill Clinton signed the Curt Flood Act, repealing that part of baseball's antitrust exemption dealing with labor relations. Five teams with the largest payrolls made luxury-tax payments in the first year of the plan implemented after the 1994-95 work stoppage. On the field, players engaged in a series of early-season brawls that alarmed league officials, who threatened to clamp down on transgressors. Umpires continued to be widely criticized for both their behavior and their judgment: Perceived arrogance, liberal and inconsistent interpretation of the strike zone and, in too many key situations, bad decisions.

NEW HOME RUN RECORD

Talk of a fresh challenge to Roger Maris's still-controversial record (61 home runs in 1961) had risen sporadically whenever one of the game's acknowledged sluggers had gotten off to a hot start. During the 1990s, such chatter became an annual occurrence. True or not, many baseball fans believed that hitters were stronger and pitchers decidedly less skilled than in days gone by and that the modern-day baseball was wound too tightly—"juiced" to provide an artificial offensive jolt. From 1920, when Babe Ruth did it first, through 1989, batters hit 50 or more home runs in a season only 17 times. In the six succeeding seasons, the feat was accomplished six times.

Even after McGwire hit 52 home runs in 1996 and 58 in 1997 (34 for the Oakland A's and 24 after being traded to the St. Louis Cardinals), many fans would have picked Ken Griffey Jr. as the player most likely to break Maris' record. The Seattle slugger had hit 49 homers in 1996 and 56 in 1997 and, at 28, was generally considered to be in the prime of his career. McGwire refocused attention on himself in 1998 by hitting a grand slam on opening day and three more homers in the Cardinals' next three games. He finished April with 11 (on a pace to hit 66), May with 27 (pace: 83) and June with 37 (pace: 74).

The Chicago Cubs' Sosa had never hit more than 40 home runs in a season (in 1996), and he hit only six in April and seven in May. In June, though, he joined the race by hitting 20, five more than the major-league record for that month, for a season total of 33. Both Sosa and McGwire broke the record for most home runs by the end of June and, despite tapering off in July (eight homers for McGwire and nine for Sosa), both stood in good shape for a run at the record as the season entered its final two months.

Among the curiosities of this two-man entertainment was how often both hit homers on the same day (21 times) and how difficult it was for Sosa despite applying constant and encouraging pressure to McGwire and tying him several times, to surpass him. No day ended with Sosa ahead of McGwire in the home-run race. Both hitters finished August with 55 home runs, one short of Hack Wilson's N.L. mark set in 1930. McGwire hit two homers on September 1 to break Wilson's record, and hit his 60th home run on September 5, tying Babe Ruth's 1927 standard in the Cardinals' 142nd game. He hit No. 61 on September 7 and No. 62 the next night against Sosa's teammate, righthander Steve Trachsel of the Cubs. Sosa hit his 56th on September 2, his 57th on September 4 and his 60th on September 12. Nos. 61 and 62 came in the same game on September 13 against Bronswell Patrick and Eric Plunk of the Milwaukee Brewers.

Lost in all these numbers was the tremendous adulation heaped upon both players. Fans in every ballpark greeted each McGwire plate appearance with a sustained standing ovation, and Sosa won people's hearts with his infectious enthusiasm and public insistence that McGwire, and not he, was the man of the moment. McGwire weathered a small tempest when a New York Post story reported that he used androstenedione, a controversial muscle building dietary supplement, legal in baseball but banned by several other major sports organizations.

As both players approached and then passed Maris' mark, baseball enjoyed much greater attention than it had in the recent past. These were no simply Cubs and Cardinals fans expressing their usual intense partisanship nor even just baseball fans generally enjoying a stunning occasion. Rather the McGwire-Sosa competition appealed to a much wider audience that, for the moment at least, chose to place baseball closer to the center of America's cultural life than it had been in a long time.

Still, with McGwire having been first to the new record, the question became who the ultimate home run champion would be. McGwire hit No. 65 on September 20, but Sosa answered with Nos. 64 and 65 three days later. On the Friday of the season's final weekend, Sosa reached 66 first, but the lead lasted only 45 minutes as McGwire responded yet again. Sosa hit no more homers, even in the Cubs' one-game playoff against the Giants for the N.L. wild-card spot. McGwire, defying all odds, hit two more homers on September 26 and two more again on September 27 for a very grand total of 70.

SELIG NAMED COMMISSIONER

After serving as chairman of the Executive Committee and interim commissioner for nearly six years, Allan H. (Bud) Selig, president and chief executive officer of the Brewers, accepted a five-year term as commissioner on July 9. Selig was elected baseball's ninth commissioner by unanimous vote of the owners and given an annual salary estimated at between $2.25 and $3 million. He had expressed his desire not to take the position many times over the preceding years, during which a search committee had labored in vain to identify a candidate it considered better qualified.

Principal owner of the Brewers since that franchise moved from Seattle in 1970, Selig, 63, had assumed a position of public prominence within baseball's governance in the months before the forced resignation of the eighth commissioner, Francis T. (Fay) Vincent, on September 7, 1992. During his 2,131 days of service as acting commissioner, a term longer than that of four of his predecessors, Selig presided over the rearrangement of each league into three divisions with a wild card becoming eligible for the postseason, the introduction of a plan to share revenue between large-revenue and small-revenue clubs, the start of interleague play, and the modified realignment that took effect in 1998. He also was in charge during the 230-day strike that saw the 1994 season end prematurely and the World Series cancelled.

Upon his election, Selig made plans to resign as an officer of the trust that owned the Brewers. Day-to-day operation of the club passed to his daughter, Wendy Selig-Prieb.

INTERLEAGUE PLAY CONTINUES

Regular season games between A.L. clubs and N.L. clubs continued for the second year. The '98 schedule called for two periods of interleague play: June 5-11 and June 22-July 2. Each team played between 12 and 16 games, three or four against each team in the corresponding division of the other league.

Overall, A.L. teams won 114 interleague games and lost 110. The Yankees compiled the best interleague record among A.L. teams (13-3), and the Baltimore Orioles and the Tampa Bay Devil Rays had the worst (5-11). In the N.L., the Houston Astros finished best (10-4) while the Cardinals were worst (4-9).

Attendance at interleague games averaged 31,447, down six percent from 1997's 33,407, but 16 percent higher than the average for intraleague games played prior to the interleague periods.

1999 SCHEDULE

By mutual agreement between owners and the Players Association, interleague play will continue in 1999 with much the same format. However, four pairs of rivals (New York Mets-Yankees, Los Angeles Dodgers-Anaheim Angels, Montreal Expos-Toronto Blue Jays and San Francisco Giants-A's) will play six games between them instead of three. The A.L. will experiment with an unbalanced schedule for the first time since 1976, returning to a nearly balanced schedule in 2000 unless three-fourths of its teams vote to stay unbalanced. The N.L. will retain its unbalanced schedule in 1999 and beyond unless league owners vote otherwise.

YANKEES BREAK WINS RECORD

The Yankees' four-game World Series triumph over the Padres put an exclamation point behind one of the most successful seasons a team has ever enjoyed. New York celebrated the 75th anniversary of Yankee Stadium by reaching postseason play for the fourth year in a row, winning the team's 35th A.L. pennant and its 24th world championship, the second in three years.

The Yankees capped the year winning nine of 11 postseason games, but it was their regular season performance that suggested they deserve a place among the greatest teams ever. They were 61-20 in the first half of the season, breaking the previous major league record for most wins in the first half of a 162-game schedule (58-23, by the 1970 Cincinnati Reds). They reached 90 wins in only 120 games, tying the record of the 1944 Cardinals. They set a major league record by holding a lead in 48 consecutive games and tied another by going 24 straight series without losing one. They won their 100th game on September 4 against only 38 losses, thereby breaking the major league mark for earliest date to reach 100 wins by five days and breaking the A.L. mark for fewest amount of games to reach 100 wins by two games. New York finished the regular season with a 114-48 record, setting an A.L. record for most wins in a season and a major league record for most wins in a 162-game schedule.

A significant number of fans had relished the prospect of a Series matchup between the Yankees and the Atlanta Braves, arguably the best team in the N.L., but these fans were disappointed. Despite high television ratings in the New York area, interest in the postseason declined markedly from the excitement fostered by the McGwire-Sosa home run chase. Viewership for the Series hit an all-time low, worse than 1989's earthquake-interrupted Series, casting doubt upon the opinion that baseball had somehow regained the prominence it had enjoyed before the strike of 1994-95.

In 1996, human interest in the Yankees' quest was heightened by imminent heart transplant surgery for manager Joe Torre's brother, former major leaguer Frank Torre. In 1998, similar emotions were stirred when doctors diagnosed outfielder Darryl Strawberry with colon cancer on October 1 with the Yankees in the midst of their division series against the Texas Rangers. Strawberry, whose once-shining career had been besmirched by a series of off-the-field troubles, underwent successful surgery on October 3. His teammates added his number, 39, to their caps.

ATLANTA WINS DIVISION AGAIN

The Braves won 106 games, a franchise record, en route to capturing the N.L. East for the fourth year in a row. Leaving aside the incomplete 1994 season, Atlanta has now won an unprecedented seven straight division titles. The Braves started slowly (6-6) but ended April at 18-9, four games ahead of the Mets, and were never headed after that. They led the division by 8.5 games at the end of June, 12.5 games at the All-Star break and 14 games at the end of August. They clinched the division on September 14 by beating the Philadelphia Phillies, 4-2.

Atlanta's powerful offense set franchise records for runs scored (826, tied for third in the N.L.) and home runs (215, second in the league). The Braves tied a major league record by hitting at least one home run in 25 consecutive games and became the third franchise in major league history (after the Dodgers and the Colorado Rockies) to have four players hit 30 or more home runs. Free-agent signee Andres Galarraga led the team with 44, Chipper Jones and Javy Lopez each hit 34 and Andruw Jones added 31. Galarraga batted .305 with 121 RBIs, Chipper Jones hit .313 with 107 RBIs and Lopez had 106 RBIs.

Atlanta's pitching was, once again, superior. The staff finished first in the league in ERA, complete games, shutouts, fewest hits allowed, fewest home runs allowed and strikeouts. The Braves became the second team in major league history (after the 1902 Pittsburgh Pirates) to have five pitchers win 16 or more games. Tom Glavine led the league with 20 wins and was tied for third in ERA (2.47). Greg Maddux won 18 (including five shutouts), John Smoltz and Kevin Millwood 17 each and Denny Neagle 16. Maddux won 10 games in a row. He led the N.L. in ERA (2.22) and finished fifth in strikeouts (204). Smoltz finished first in winning percentage (.850) and Glavine was second (.769). Rookie Kerry Ligtenberg saved 30 games.

HOUSTON WINS 2ND N.L. CENTRAL TITLE

The Astros won the N.L. Central title for the second consecutive year, finishing 12.5 games ahead of the Cubs. Houston held the division lead most of the season and took over first place for good on June 9. They led Chicago by five games at the All-Star break, by 11 games at the end of August and clinched the division when the Cubs lost on September 17.

The Astros led the N.L. in runs (874) and were second in batting average (.280). Moises Alou, acquired from the Florida Marlins in November 1997, hit .312 with 38 home runs and 124 RBIs. Craig Biggio hit .325, led the league in doubles (51), finished second in hits (210) and stolen bases (50) and tied for fourth in runs scored (123). Jeff Bagwell hit 34 homers, and Derek Bell drove in 108 runs.

Shane Reynolds led Houston's pitchers with 19 wins, second best in the league, and struck out 209 (fourth in the league). Righthander Jose Lima spent his first full year in the majors and earned 16 wins, and Sean Bergman added 12. The Houston staff was bolstered considerably by the acquisition of Randy Johnson from Seattle on July 31. Johnson started 11 games for the Astros and compiled 10 wins. His combined strikeout total, 329, was the most in the majors since Nolan Ryan's 341 in 1977. Billy Wagner tallied 30 saves.

CUBS WIN PLAYOFF FOR WILD CARD

The Cubs defeated the Giants, 5-3, in the first playoff for the N.L. wild card. From August 8 on, the Cubs and the Mets waged a nip-and-tuck battle for the wild-card spot, never more than a game apart. The Mets, though, lost their last five games to finish one game behind the Cubs and the resurgent Giants, who rebounded from five games back on September 17 to tie Chicago with two games to play. Each team then split its last two games to set up the playoff.

Besides Sosa, who hit .308 and drove in a major league-leading 158 runs to complement his 66 homers, the Cubs were led by Mark Grace, who hit .309, Henry Rodriguez, who hit 31 home runs, and Jose Hernandez, who added 23. Kevin Tapani led Chicago with 19 wins and Steve Trachsel 15, but the Cubs' pitching sensation was rookie Kerry Wood, who won 13 games and struck out 233 batters in 166.2 innings. Wood set an N.L. record and tied the major league mark on May 6 by striking out 20 Astros while pitching a one-hitter in just his fifth major league start. The Sporting News named him its N.L. Rookie Pitcher of the Year.

The Marlins, last year's N.L. wild card, finished at 54-108, the worst record ever for a defending World Series champion and the poorest record for any major league team since the 1979 Blue Jays finished at 53-109.

PADRES TAKE N.L. WEST

San Diego won its second division title in three years with a franchise-record 98 wins. Thus, for the second consecutive season, the N.L. West crown went to a team that had finished last the year before (the Giants did it in '97). The Padres led their division for nearly the entire season. They enjoyed at least a share of first place for 175 of the season's 181 days and were in the division lead alone from June 12 on. For this achievement, The Sporting News named Bruce Bochy N.L. Manager of the Year. San Diego led the West by 5.5 games at the All-Star break and 15 games on September 1. The Padres clinched the title with an 8-7 win over Los Angeles on September 12.

San Diego's offense was led by Greg Vaughn, who batted .272, hit 50 home runs (third behind McGwire and Sosa) and drove in 119 runs. The Sporting News named him N.L. Comeback Player of the Year. Ken Caminiti hit 29 homers and had 82 RBIs, and Wally Joyner added 80 RBIs.

Kevin Brown, TSN's N.L. Pitcher of the Year, led the Padres with 18 wins. Andy Ashby added 17 and Joey Hamilton had 13. Trevor Hoffman recorded 53 saves to tie the N.L. record and had an ERA of 1.48. He was named TSN's N.L. Fireman of the Year.

YANKEES TAKE A.L. EAST

The Yankees won their division handily. After a 10-5 start, they took over first place on April 21 and were never headed. They led by 7.5 games at the end of May, 10 games at the end of June and 15 games at the end of July. New York clinched the division on September 9, with a 7-5 win over the Boston Red Sox, who finished in second place, 22 games behind.

The Yankees hit 207 home runs, second-highest in franchise history, but no player reached 30. Tino Martinez led New York with 28 homers. Bernie Williams had 26, and Darryl Strawberry and Paul O'Neill added 24 each. Williams led the A.L. in batting (.339), Derek Jeter hit .324 and O'Neill hit .317. Martinez led the team in RBIs with 123. O'Neill had 116, Scott Brosius 98 and Williams 97.

David Cone tied for the league lead in wins with 20. David Wells added 18, Andy Pettitte had 16 and Hideki Irabu 13. Wells led the league in winning percentage (.818) and put together winning streaks of eight and nine games. On May 17, he pitched a perfect game against the Minnesota Twins, winning 4-0. On September 1, he took a second attempt at a perfect game into the seventh inning against Oakland before Jason Giambi singled with two out.

BOSTON SETTLES FOR WILD CARD

Despite winning 92 games, the Red Sox had to settle for the A.L. wild-card spot. Led by Mo Vaughn, Nomar Garciaparra and pitchers Pedro Martinez, Tim Wakefield and Tom Gordon (TSN's A.L. Fireman of the Year), the Red Sox held off successive challenges from the Orioles, Rangers, Angels and the fast-closing Blue Jays. Boston clinched the wild card on September 24, defeating Baltimore, 9-6.

INDIANS WIN FOURTH A.L. CENTRAL TITLE

The Cleveland Indians became the seventh team in major league history to go wire-to-wire, winning their fourth straight A.L. Central division title by nine games over the White Sox. Cleveland led the division by 10.5 games at the All-Star break and clinched the division crown on September 16 with an 8-6 win over Minnesota.

Compared to their previous three seasons, Cleveland struggled offensively, finishing sixth in the league in batting, sixth in runs and tied for seventh in home runs. No Indians regular batted .300, but Manny Ramirez hit .294 with 45 home runs and 145 RBIs. Ramirez's home runs came in bunches. He had eight multi-homer games and hit six in three games in mid-September. Jim Thome hit 30 homers despite missing 35 games with a broken hand, and Travis Fryman added 28 with 96 RBIs. Kenny Lofton stole 54 bases, second in the league.

Dave Burba, acquired from Cincinnati on March 30, won 15 games, as did Charles Nagy. Bartolo Colon added 14 wins, and Mike Jackson had 40 saves, fourth best in the A.L.

TEXAS WINS A.L. WEST

The Rangers won the A.L. West for the second time in three seasons. Texas held at least a share of first place for 103 days, but they battled the Angels throughout the season. After spending the first part of August in first, the Rangers fell behind the Angels for 34 days. Texas bounced back to tie Anaheim on September 16 and seize first place for good on September 21. They clinched the pennant on September 25, despite losing to Seattle, as Anaheim lost to the A's.

Texas led the A.L. in batting (.289) and was second in runs scored (940). The Rangers hit .304 at home and scored 10 or more runs 20 times. Juan Gonzalez hit .318 with 45 home runs and led the A.L. with 157 RBIs. Ivan Rodriguez (.321, 21 HRs, 91 RBIs) and Will Clark (.305, 23 HRs, 102 RBIs) also starred offensively.

The Rangers pitching staff ranked 12th in ERA, 14th in hits allowed and 10th in strikeouts. Righthander Rick Helling won 20 games (tied for the A.L. lead), and Aaron Sele added 19, but no other Ranger won more than nine games. John Wetteland recorded 42 saves to tie for second in the league.

CHANGES IN POSTSEASON FORMAT

On January 14, the Executive Council approved a new format for postseason play, replacing the rotation system for determining home-field advantage in the division series and the league championship series with a merit system. The proposal, later ratified by the owners, the Players Association and the television networks, called for division series matchups to be based on won-loss records with the division champion having the best record meeting the playoff qualifier with the worst record, unless they are in the same division. The plan also gave the teams with home-field advantage in the division series Games 1, 2 and 5 at home. Similarly, of the two teams advancing to each league championship series, the one with the better record would play Games 1, 2, 6 and 7 at home.

None of the division series went to a fifth game. In the N.L., the Braves swept the wild-card Cubs, and the Padres ousted Houston in four games. Kevin Brown struck out 16 Astros in Game 1 to defeat Randy Johnson, who also lost Game 4. In the A.L., the Yankees swept Texas, giving up only one run, and Cleveland came back from a Game 1 loss to beat the wild-card Red Sox in four games.

PADRES SHOCK BRAVES IN SIX

In the N.L. Championship Series, the Braves and their vaunted starting pitching staff quickly found themselves on the verge of being swept by the Padres. John Smoltz started Game 1, but San Diego third baseman Ken Caminiti won it with a 10th-inning home run off Kerry Ligtenberg. Kevin Brown pitched a three-hitter to best Tom Glavine, 3-0, in Game 2, and Sterling Hitchcock and four relievers stymied Atlanta, 4-1, in Game 3, beating Greg Maddux.

Prior to this series, 21 teams had fallen behind three games to none in postseason play, and only three had managed to extend their series to a fifth game. The Braves not only won Game 4 but Game 5 as well, an unprecedented feat. Atlanta won Game 4, 8-3, with Denny Neagle starting, and Game 5, 7-6, with both Maddux and Brown pitching in relief.

Back in Atlanta for Game 6, the Braves' hope to push the Padres to the limit was squashed by Hitchcock and the bullpen again. Five pitchers held Atlanta to two hits as San Diego won, 5-0. Thus, after consecutive World Series appearances in 1995 and 1996, Atlanta failed to survive the championship series for the second year in a row.

YANKEES OUST INDIANS IN SIX

The Yankees and the Indians split the first two games of the A.L. Championship Series in New York. The Yankees won Game 1, 7-2, blasting Jaret Wright, Cleveland's 1997 postseason hero, for five runs in the first inning. Cleveland bounced back to win Game 2, 4-1, in 12 innings, aided by a controversial play in the last inning. Indians third baseman Travis Fryman laid down a sacrifice bunt to move pinch-runner Enrique Wilson to second. First baseman Tino Martinez fielded the bunt and threw to second baseman Chuck Knoblauch, covering first. The throw hit Fryman in the back, and Knoblauch, aware that Fryman had run nearly all the way to first inside the baseline, looked in vain toward home plate umpire Ted Hendry, who declined to call Fryman out for interference. Knoblauch stood dumbstruck instead of retrieving the ball, and Wilson came all the way around to score the go-ahead run.

Cleveland took a 2-1 lead in games when the Series shifted to Jacobs Field. Bartolo Colon pitched a complete game to win Game 3, 6-1, with two home runs by Jim Thome and one each from Mark Whiten and Manny Ramirez. The Yankees won Game 4, 4-0, behind the pitching of Cuban refugee Orlando (El Duque) Hernandez, half-brother of 1997 World Series MVP Livan Hernandez. New York also won Game 5, 5-3, with David Wells pitching well after a shaky first inning.

Returning to Yankee Stadium, New York wrapped up the pennant with a wild 9-5 victory. The Yankees nearly squandered a 6-0 lead when Thome hit a grand slam in the fifth inning, but relievers Ramiro Mendoza and Mariano Rivera shut Cleveland out on one hit over the last four innings.

YANKEES SWEEP PADRES

The World Series opened in New York with the Yankees winning Game 1, 9-6. Neither Brown nor Wells pitched particularly well. San Diego took a 5-2 lead into the seventh inning only to have Knoblauch tie the game with a three-run homer and Martinez follow with a grand slam.

The Yankees won Game 2, 9-3, piling up 16 hits and driving starter Andy Ashby from the game in the third inning.

New York continued its winning ways in San Diego. Third baseman Scott Brosius hit two home runs in Game 3, including a three-run drive in the eighth inning off Trevor Hoffman that propelled the Yankees to a 5-4 victory. The following night, Brown worked on three days' rest for San Diego but could not best Andy Pettitte, who hadn't pitched in 12 days. Pettitte allowed just five hits in 7.1 innings as the Yankees won, 3-0. New York scored one run in the seventh on an infield out and two more in the eighth on a bases-loaded single by Brosius and a sacrifice fly by Ricky Ledee.

Each member of the Yankees voted a full World Series share received $312,042.41. San Diego's full shares came to $204,143.82. Both figures were records, attributable to a doubling of World Series ticket prices.

OTHER FEATS AND EVENTS

Cal Ripken of the Orioles ended his record streak of consecutive games played at 2,632 when he decided not to play on September 20 against New York, the Orioles' last home game of the season. Ryan Minor played third base for Baltimore in a 5-4 loss. Ripken's streak, begun on May 30, 1982, surpassed Lou Gehrig by 502 games and left Albert Belle as the new leader in consecutive games played, with 327.

Dennis Martinez, who had announced his retirement during the 1997 season, signed a minor-league contract with the Braves on January 29 and became the winningest Latin pitcher in major league history. He tied Juan Marichal at 243 wins by shutting out Milwaukee on June 2 and got his 244th win in relief against the Giants on August 9. He added one more win on September 25.

Dennis Eckersley of the Red Sox surpassed Hoyt Wilhelm as the all-time leader in pitching appearances when he pitched in his 1,071st game on September 26 against Baltimore. Roger Clemens of the Blue Jays joined Grover Alexander, Lefty Grove and Sandy Koufax by winning the triple crown for pitching for the second year in a row. He tied for the league lead in wins (20) and led in ERA (2.65) and strikeouts (271). He became the 11th pitcher to reach 3,000 strikeouts on July 5, fanning Randy Winn of Tampa Bay in a 2-1 victory. TSN named Clemens its A.L. Pitcher of the Year.

Larry Walker of Colorado led the N.L. in batting with a .363 average, and the Yankees' Bernie Williams hit .339 to win the A.L. batting title. Ken Griffey led the A.L. in homers with 56.

Randy Johnson led the majors in strikeouts with 329 (213 in the A.L. and 116 in the N.L.). Curt Schilling of the Phillies led the N.L. with 300.

On July 9, Cardinals manager Tony La Russa batted his starting pitcher, Todd Stottlemyre, eighth and had second baseman Placido Polanco hit ninth. La Russa retained this departure from tradition for the rest of the season. Not since 1979 had a starting pitcher hit anywhere else but ninth.

TWO TEAMS MAKE DEBUT

The 1998 season marked the debut of the two teams granted major league franchises in 1995. Assigned to the N.L. West, the Arizona Diamondbacks played their first game on March 31, losing at their home, Ball One Ballpark, 9-2, to the Rockies. Andy Benes was the starting and losing pitcher. Rookie first baseman Travis Lee got the Diamondbacks' first hit, a single in the first inning, and hit the team's first home run in the sixth inning. Arizona finished the season 65-97, in fifth place.

On the same date, Tampa Bay, playing in the A.L. East, lost its first game at its home, Tropicana Field, to the Detroit Tigers, 11-6. Wilson Alvarez was the starting pitcher for the Devil Rays and took the loss. Dave Martinez got Tampa Bay's first hit, a single in the third inning, and Wade Boggs hit the team's first home run in the sxith inning. The Devil Rays won more games before the end of April than any previous expansion team, 12, but finished in fifth place with a record of 63-99.

The arrival of the two teams caused some limited realignment. Milwaukee, an A.L. team since 1970, moved from the A.L. Central to the N.L. Central, and the Tigers shifted from the A.L. East to the A.L. Central. The Brewers thus became the first team this century to change leagues, returning N.L. baseball to Milwaukee for the first time since 1965.

Despite the McGwire-Sosa home run onslaught and the impact of expansion, the total number of home runs rose only 1.5 percent from 1997. A total of 5,064 homers were hit in 2,431 games in 1998, an average of 2.08 per game. The 1997 average was 2.05 per game. Thirty-three players hit 30 or more homers in 1998 compared to 31 in 1997.

ATTENDANCE HIGHEST EVER

Major league attendance for 1998, abetted by the two expansion clubs, totalled 70,615,217, surpassing the previous record of 70,256,459 set in 1993. The 16 N.L. teams outdrew the 14 A.L. teams, 38,424,321 to 31,915,479. Average attendance was 29,386, 3.9 percent better than 1997 but less than 1994's record average of 31,612.

Seven teams drew more than three million fans: Colorado (which led both leagues with 3,789,347, exceeding the three-million mark for a record sixth consecutive year), Arizona, Atlanta, St. Louis and Los Angeles in the N.L. and Baltimore and Cleveland in the A.L. Eleven others clubs exceeded the two-million mark, and all other clubs except Montreal drew at least one million.

The Diamondbacks drew 3,600,412 in their first year. Tampa Bay attracted 2,261,158. The Angels showed the greatest increase, up 751,777 to 2,519,107, while the Marlins declined the most, down 613,992 to 1,750,395.

FOUR MANAGERIAL CHANGES

Two teams changed managers during the season, and two others made changes after the season. The Dodgers fired both general manager Fred Claire and manager Bill Russell on June 21 as the team sat in third place in the N.L. West with a record of 36-38. Russell thus became the first Dodgers manager to be fired since Charlie Dressen after the 1953 season. Tommy Lasorda, Russell's predecessor as manager, replaced Claire as interim G.M. and minor league manager Glenn Hoffman became interim manager. Hoffman guided the Dodgers to a 47-41 record, still good for third place in the division. Los Angeles named Kevin Malone general manager on September 11. Malone relieved Hoffman at the end of the season and hired Davey Johnson, previous manager of the Mets, Reds and Orioles, on October 24.

The Tigers fired Buddy Bell on September 1 with the team at 52-85, last in the A.L. Central. Bench coach Larry Parrish was named interim manager on that date. He led Detroit to a 13-12 mark in September and signed a two-year contract on October 14.

The Rockies, having finished in fourth place in the N.L. West (77-85), fired Don Baylor on September 28, the day after the season's end. Colorado replaced him with Jim Leyland, former Florida manager, on October 5. Leyland had resigned from the Marlins on October 1, receiving a $500,000 buyout because the team was in the process of being sold. The Marlins replaced Leyland with John Boles, their vice president for player development, on October 2. Boles had served as interim manager in 1996 after the team had fired Rene Lachemann.

OWNERS AND BALLPARKS

Fourteen months after Peter O'Malley announced his intention to sell the Dodgers—the team his family had owned for nearly half a century—and six months after O'Malley had reached an agreement in principle to sell the club to the Fox Group, an affiliate of Rupert Murdoch's News Corporation, for a reported $311 million (a record), major league owners approved the sale on March 19. Despite a move to oppose the sale led by Atlanta owner Ted Turner, only the Braves and White Sox voted no (with the Mets abstaining). The sale included the franchise, Dodger Stadium and its 300 surrounding acres, a spring training facility in Vero Beach, Fla., and other facilities in the Dominican Republic. Bob Graziano became president and chief operating officer, replacing O'Malley, who remained chairman of the board through the end of the year.

A 500-pound concrete and steel beam fell from beneath the upper deck of Yankee Stadium into empty seats below on April 13, necessitating the ballpark's temporary abandonment and a full-scale inspection. The team was forced to postpone April 13 and 14 games against the Angels and to play its April 15 game at Shea Stadium. The Yankees won, 6-3, and that night the Mets beat the Cubs, 2-1. Thus, for the first time this century two regular-season games involving four teams were played in one stadium on the same day. The Yankees' weekend series against the Tigers was moved to Detroit, and their series the following weekend, scheduled for Detroit, was moved to the reopened stadium. The incident gave a certain force to owner George Steinbrenner's contention, encouraged by New York Mayor Rudolph Giuliani, that the Yankees need a new ballpark located somewhere other than the Bronx.

Voters in Forsyth and Guilford counties, North Carolina, defeated a proposed referendum on May 5 that would have raised taxes to fund construction of a ballpark in the Triad region (Greensboro, High Point and Winston-Salem). The proposal would have raised $13 million per year for 20 years through a 1 percent sales tax on restaurant food and a 50-cent surcharge on tickets sold at the stadium. The defeat rebuffed the plan of Hickory, N.C., businessman Don Beaver to buy and relocate the Twins.

On June 10, owners unanimously approved the sale of the Rangers from a group headed by George W. Bush to Tom Hicks, owner of more than 400 radio stations and the NHL Dallas Stars. The deal for a reported $250 million, the highest selling price in A.L. history, included the franchise, the lease for The Ballpark in Arlington, the office building and restaurant in the ballpark, 43 acres of land and an option to buy 227 additional acres.

MLB officials confirmed on October 22 that Marge Schott, Cincinnati's general partner, had signed a letter-of-intent to sell her controlling interest in the club rather than face an indefinite suspension over falsifying records at her car dealerships. Schott, whose previous suspension expired at the end of the World Series, planned to retain only one of the 6.5 shares she owned in a 15-share partnership.

On November 3, San Diego voters approved a proposition to build a downtown ballpark for the Padres. The plan called for the city to contribute $275 million ($50 million from a redevelopment agency and $225 million from a hotel tax) and for the Padres to pay $115 million and to pledge to recruit at least $400 million in additional development surrounding the park.

H. Wayne Huizenga reached agreement on November 6 to sell the Marlins to south Florida businessman John Henry for an estimated $150 million. Huizenga had a tentative agreement with club president Don Smiley to sell the club, but Smiley was not able to complete the financial arrangements to close the deal.

Late in the year, a group headed by New York attorney Miles Prentice, but with substantial local financial support, announced an agreement to purchase the Kansas City Royals for $75 million from the foundation set up by the Royals' late owner, Ewing Kauffman.

EIGHT SALARY ARBITRATION CASES

Eighty-one players filed for salary arbitration, but only eight cases proceeded all the way through the hearing and decision stage. A total of 60 players and their teams exchanged figures. Bernie Williams of the Yankees filed for a record $9 million, and New York countered with an offer of $7.5 million, also a record. They settled at $8.25 million. Jeromy Burnitz, who earned $225,000 in 1997, signed a four-year, $14.5 million contract with the Brewers. His average of $3,625,000 per season is the largest percentage increase ever: 1,511 percent.

Three players (Joey Hamilton, Charles Johnson and Jose Mercedes) won their cases while five (Damon Buford, Jorge Fabregas, Todd Hollandsworth, Frank Rodriguez and Tony Tarasco) lost theirs. These eight decisions gave the owners a three-year winning streak and a record of 227 cases won and 179 lost since 1974, arbitration's first year. Johnson, winner of the final case to be decided, won a 1,040 percent raise, up from $290,000 to $3,300,000. For the first time, some of the hearings were held before three-person panels instead of a single arbitrator.

The 81 players who filed saw their average salary rise 150 percent, according to the Associated Press, from $774,323 to $1,936,400, just short of the 1997 record. The 60 players who exchanged salary figures with their clubs earned raises averaging $677,730, with 23 of the 60 getting raises of more than $1 million. Part of the reason for the large increases was the owners' recent success holding down salaries for players in their first three seasons before they are eligible for arbitration. These salaries tend to escalate dramatically when players reach their first arbitration year.

SALARIES RISE

Figures compiled by USA Today at the end of the season showed an average major league salary of $1,377,196, up 4.8 percent over 1997. Of the players listed on opening-day rosters, a record 317 were scheduled to earn a million dollars or more while 64 received the minimum salary of $170,000. The Expos had the lowest total payroll, $8,317,500, and the Orioles the highest, a record $73,995,921.

Criticism of high salaries, rampant for years from fans and owners, continued unabated. The eight teams advancing to the postseason were among the top 12 teams in total payroll, adding fuel to the argument that clubs were being divided into two economic groups: the 'haves' and the 'have nots.'

BROWN SIGNS RECORD CONTRACT

Despite predictions of an economic Armageddon, some teams seemed quite willing to sign players to lucrative contract extensions during the season and to attract free agents with astounding new contracts after the season.

Even before the season began, the Red Sox signed Nomar Garciaparra to a five-year contract worth $23.25 million with two team options that could raise his total compensation to $44.25 million. Later, the Phillies signed Scott Rolen (four years, $10 million), the Cardinals extended Ray Lankford's contract (five years, $34 million) and the Orioles signed an extension with Scott Erickson (five years, $32 million).

Two premier players left teams with whom they had become stars following salary disputes. Mike Piazza turned down a six-year, $80 million contract offer from the Dodgers on April 6 and broke off negotiations two days later. On May 15, the Dodgers traded him and Todd Zeile to the Marlins for Gary Sheffield, Charles Johnson, Bobby Bonilla, Jim Eisenreich and Manuel Barrios. A week later, the Marlins sent Piazza to the Mets for Preston Wilson, Ed Yarnall and Geoff Goetz. On October 24, Piazza signed a seven-year contract with the Mets for $91 million, at that time the largest total contract in history.

The Mariners had announced in 1997 that they would not offer a contract extension to Randy Johnson after the 1998 season. Johnson opened the year in Seattle but looked to be traded before the season was finished. He labored to a 9-10 record with an ERA of 4.33 before being traded to Houston. After the season, Johnson signed a contract with Arizona (four years, $53 million).

In other postseason deals, the Red Sox signed Jose Offerman (four years, $26 million); Dean Palmer left Kansas City for Detroit (five years, $36 million); the Braves added Brian Jordan (five years, $40 million); Cleveland signed Roberto Alomar (four years, $32 million); the Yankees kept Bernie Williams (seven years, $87.5 million); Mo Vaughn signed with Anaheim (six years, $80 million); Albert Belle joined the Orioles (five years, $65 million); and Rafael Palmeiro returned to Texas from Baltimore (five years, $45 million).

The Dodgers made Kevin Brown the game's first $100-million player on December 12, signing the pitcher to a seven-year contract worth $105 million. Brown received a $5 million signing bonus, $10 million in 1999 and $15 million in each of the next six years. Brown also got a hotel suite on Dodgers road trips and 12 charter round trips for his family each year from Macon, Georgia, to wherever he is pitching.

RETIREMENTS

Three outstanding players retired at the end of the season. Paul Molitor concluded a 21-year career with Milwaukee, Toronto and Minnesota, having accumulated 3,319 hits (eighth on the all-time list), 1,307 RBIs and 504 stolen bases with a .306 batting average. Joe Carter retired after a 15-year career with five clubs. He hit .259 and recorded 2,184 hits, 396 home runs and 1,445 RBIs. Dennis Eckersley ended his 24-year career with the Red Sox. His won-lost record stood at 197-171 with 390 saves.

CONCLUSION

In the Yankees' clubhouse following the World Series, Joe Torre was asked to assess the place of his team in baseball's annals. "I only have about 40 years of history," he said, "but it's the best club I've ever been around. The '27 Yankees, they may be a better club—but we had the best record."

However baseball historians will come to judge this edition of the Yankees and the overall significance of the season—one in which the Yankees emerged as world champions and Mark McGwire and Sammy Sosa were glorified as heroes—here is how the game on the field ended up in 1998:

FINAL STANDINGS

AMERICAN LEAGUE

EAST DIVISION

Team	N.Y.	Bos.	Tor.	Bal.	T.B.	Cle.	Chi.	K.C.	Min.	Det.	Tex.	Ana.	Sea.	Oak.	Atl.	Fla.	Mon.	N.Y.	Phi.	W	L	Pct.	GB
New York	....	7	6	9	11	7	7	10	7	8	8	5	8	8	3-1	3-0	2-1	2-1	3-0	114	48	.704	....
Boston	5	....	5	6	9	8	5	8	5	5	6	5	7	9	2-1	2-1	3-0	1-2	1-3	92	70	.568	22.0
Toronto	6	7	....	7	7	4	6	5	7	6	4	7	7	6	1-2	1-2	4-0	2-1	1-2	88	74	.543	26.0
Baltimore	3	6	5	....	5	5	2	5	7	10	6	6	6	8	1-2	1-2	0-3	1-3	2-1	79	83	.488	35.0
Tampa Bay	1	3	5	7	....	3	6	3	4	6	4	5	5	6	0-3	1-3	1-2	1-2	2-1	63	99	.389	51.0

CENTRAL DIVISION

Team	Cle.	Chi.	K.C.	Min.	Det.	N.Y.	Bos.	Tor.	Bal.	T.B.	Tex.	Ana.	Sea.	Oak.	Chi.	Cin.	Hou.	Mil.	Pit.	St.L.	W	L	Pct.	GB
Cleveland	....	6	8	6	9	4	3	7	6	7	4	7	9	3	2-0	2-1	1-2	2-1	1-2	2-0	89	73	.549	....
Chicago	6	....	8	6	6	4	6	4	9	5	5	6	4	4	0-3	1-1	1-2	1-2	2-0	2-1	80	82	.494	9.0
Kansas City	4	4	....	7	6	0	3	6	6	8	3	5	4	7	2-1	2-0	1-2	1-2	1-1	2-1	72	89	.447	16.5
Minnesota	6	6	5	....	4	4	6	4	3	7	7	5	2	4	2-1	1-2	1-1	0-2	1-2	2-1	70	92	.432	19.0
Detroit	3	6	6	8	....	3	5	5	1	5	3	3	3	7	2-0	0-3	0-3	2-1	2-1	1-1	65	97	.401	24.0

WEST DIVISION

Team	Tex.	Ana.	Sea.	Oak.	N.Y.	Bos.	Tor.	Bal.	T.B.	Cle.	Chi.	K.C.	Min.	Det.	Ari.	Col.	L.A.	S.D.	S.F.	W	L	Pct.	GB
Texas	....	7	7	6	3	5	7	5	7	7	6	8	4	8	3-1	2-1	0-3	2-1	1-2	88	74	.543	....
Anaheim	5	....	9	5	6	6	4	5	6	4	5	6	6	8	2-1	3-0	3-1	1-2	1-2	85	77	.525	3.0
Seattle	5	3	....	7	3	4	5	6	2	7	6	9	8	7	1-2	2-1	1-2	2-2	1-2	76	85	.472	11.5
Oakland	6	7	5	....	3	2	5	3	5	8	7	4	7	4	2-1	1-2	1-2	2-1	2-2	74	88	.457	14.0

NOTE: Read across for wins, down for losses.

Clinching dates: New York (East)—September 9; Cleveland (Central)—September 16; Texas (West)—September 25; Boston (wild card)—September 24.

NATIONAL LEAGUE

EAST DIVISION

Team	Atl.	N.Y.	Phi.	Mon.	Fla.	Hou.	Chi.	St.L.	Cin.	Mil.	Pit.	S.D.	S.F.	L.A.	Col.	Ari.	Bal.	Bos.	N.Y.	T.B.	Tor.	W	L	Pct.	GB
Atlanta	....	9	8	6	7	4	3	6	7	7	7	5	7	8	5	8	2-1	1-2	1-3	3-0	2-1	106	56	.654	....
New York	3	....	8	4	7	4	5	6	6	8	4	4	5	6	5	6	3-1	2-1	1-2	2-1	1-2	88	74	.543	18.0
Phila.	4	4	....	7	6	2	6	3	5	5	8	1	2	4	4	7	1-2	3-1	0-3	1-2	2-1	75	87	.463	31.0
Montreal	6	8	5	....	7	2	2	3	1	3	2	4	3	4	2	7	3-0	0-3	1-2	2-1	0-4	65	97	.401	41.0
Florida	5	5	6	5	....	3	2	4	0	3	4	0	4	3	2	2	2-1	1-2	0-3	3-1	2-1	54	108	.333	52.0

CENTRAL DIVISION

Team	Hou.	Chi.	St.L.	Cin.	Mil.	Pit.	Atl.	N.Y.	Phi.	Mon.	Fla.	S.D.	S.F.	L.A.	Col.	Ari.	Chi.	Cle.	Det.	K.C.	Min.	W	L	Pct.	GB
Houston	....	7	5	8	9	9	5	5	7	7	6	5	6	3	5	5	2-1	2-1	3-0	2-1	1-1	102	60	.630	....
Chicago	4	....	4	6	6	8	6	4	3	7	7	5	7	4	7	7	3-0	0-2	0-2	1-2	1-2	90	73	.552	12.5
St. Louis	7	7	....	3	8	5	3	3	6	6	5	3	5	5	6	7	1-2	0-2	1-1	1-2	1-2	83	79	.512	19.0
Cincinnati	3	5	8	....	6	5	2	3	4	8	9	1	2	5	4	5	1-1	1-2	3-0	0-2	2-1	77	85	.475	25.0
Milwaukee	2	6	3	5	....	6	2	1	4	6	9	3	5	4	7	3	2-1	1-2	1-2	2-1	2-0	74	88	.457	28.0
Pittsburgh	2	3	6	7	5	....	2	5	1	7	6	5	2	5	4	3	0-2	2-1	1-2	1-1	2-1	69	93	.426	33.0

WEST DIVISION

Team	S.D.	S.F.	L.A.	Col.	Ari.	Atl.	N.Y.	Phi.	Mon.	Fla.	Hou.	Chi.	St.L.	Cin.	Mil.	Pit.	Ana.	Oak.	Sea.	Tex.	W	L	Pct.	GB
San Diego	....	8	7	7	9	4	5	8	4	5	4	4	6	11	6	4	2-1	1-2	2-2	1-2	98	64	.605	....
San Fran.	4	....	6	5	7	2	5	6	6	9	3	3	7	4	7	2	2-1	2-2	2-1	1-2	89	74	.546	9.5
Los Angeles	5	6	....	6	8	1	3	5	5	6	5	4	4	5	7	1-3	2-1	2-1	3-0	83	79	.512	15.0
Colorado	5	7	6	....	6	3	3	5	7	6	6	2	3	5	4	5	0-3	2-1	1-2	1-2	77	85	.475	21.0
Arizona	3	5	4	6	....	1	4	2	2	6	4	5	2	4	6	6	1-2	1-2	2-1	1-3	65	97	.401	33.0

NOTE: Read across for wins, down for losses.

Clinching dates: Atlanta (East)—September 14; Houston (Central)—September 14; San Diego (West)—September 12; Chicago (wild card)—September 28.

A.L. DIVISION SERIES
CLEVELAND VS. BOSTON

The bottom line: The Cleveland Indians claimed their third A.L. Championship Series berth in four years with an action-packed four-game Division Series victory over the post-season-plagued Boston Red Sox. The A.L. Central Division-champion Indians finished with an 89-73 regular-season record, the worst among A.L. playoff qualifiers, but they responded from a Game 1 rout in Cleveland with clutch hitting that produced two wins in Boston. The Red Sox, who earned an A.L. wild-card berth with a 92-70 record, entered the series with 13 straight post-season losses and had not won a World Series in 80 years.

Why the Indians won: Game 1 starting pitcher Jaret Wright was shelled and Game 2 starter Dwight Gooden was ejected in the first inning, but veteran Charles Nagy and 23-year-old Bartolo Colon pitched masterfully in Boston to keep the series from going five games. That was a blessing for the Indians—Boston ace and Game 1 winner Pedro Martinez was slated for Game 5. The Indians, who had little success against Martinez all season, welcomed Pete Schourek as the Game 4 starter. Schourek pitched well, but the Indians got to closer Tom Gordon, the A.L. leader with 46 saves, in the eighth inning for the clinching win.

The turning points:

Game 1: It took only 15 pitches for Boston to draw first blood at Jacobs Field en route to an 11-3 win. Singles by Darren Lewis and John Valentin and a Mo Vaughn three-run homer off Wright gave the Red Sox a lead they would not relinquish. Nomar Garciaparra added a three-run homer in the fifth inning and Vaughn, who finished with seven RBIs, homered again in the sixth to give Boston ace Martinez an 8-0 lead. Martinez, who was 2-0 with a 1.44 ERA in three starts against the Indians in the regular season, allowed just two singles in his first five innings, striking out six.

Game 2: The first-inning ejections of manager Mike Hargrove and starting pitcher Dwight Gooden appeared to energize the silent Indians bats and the Tribe went on to hammer Boston starter Tim Wakefield and earn a 9-5 victory. Down 2-0 and without Hargrove and Gooden, the Indians scored six runs, three on a David Justice home run, in the first two innings and Dave Burba, called upon to replace Gooden, pitched five-plus innings to earn the win with relief help from Paul Shuey, Paul Assenmacher and Mike Jackson. Although the Indians were able to quiet Vaughn, they were hurt by Garciaparra, who collected three more RBIs (giving him seven in two games), two on a first-inning double.

Game 3: Fifth-, sixth-, seventh- and ninth-inning solo home runs gave Cleveland a 4-3 victory at Boston's Fenway Park. Thanks to two homers by Manny Ramirez and one each by Jim Thome and Kenny Lofton, the Indians took a 4-1 lead into the bottom of the ninth—and survived a two-run Garciaparra homer. Nagy was masterful, allowing only one run over eight innings. Nagy, who induced 15 groundball outs while surrendering four singles without issuing a walk, improved his career record to 8-1 against the Red Sox and 5-0 at Fenway, where he has fashioned a 1.27 ERA. Boston starter Bret Saberhagen matched Nagy pitch for pitch through four innings before Thome connected in the fifth, Lofton in the sixth and Ramirez in the seventh. Ramirez's booming shot to left off reliever Dennis Eckersley in the ninth produced the decisive run.

Game 4: Justice prevailed, and so did the Indians in a 2-1 victory that dashed Boston's playoff hopes at Fenway Park. With the Indians already trailing 1-0 in the sixth inning and John Valentin stationed on second with one out, Mike Stanley lined a single to left and Justice, who had started only 20 of his 136 regular-season games in the outfield, cut down Valentin trying to score with a perfect one-hop throw to catcher Sandy Alomar Jr. Two innings later, Justice made his defensive play seem even bigger when he lined a two-run double to center field off Boston closer Gordon, who had converted a major league-record 43 straight save opportunities. The Justice double followed one-out, broken-bat singles by Lofton and Omar Vizquel, who snapped an 0-for-14 slump. Colon, making his first post-season start, allowed only a fourth-inning homer by Garciaparra in his 5.2 innings and five relievers combined to blank the Red Sox the rest of the way, with Jackson picking up the save.

Notable:

Red Sox: Before Game 1, the Red Sox had not won a post-season game since Game 5 of the 1986 World Series. . . . Valentin took exception to a Jackson inside pitch in the ninth inning of Game 2, gesturing at Jackson and causing both benches and bullpens to empty. However, no brawl developed. . . . Game 3 was played on the 20th anniversary of Boston's 5-4 loss to the New York Yankees in a one-game playoff for the A.L. East Division title at Fenway Park. . . . Vaughn and Garciaparra combined for 18 of Boston's 19 RBIs in the series. . . . Boston's 1 through 4 hitters were 24-for-61 (.393) and its 5 through 9 hitters were 10-for-73 (.137) with one RBI and one run scored.

Indians: The 11-3 loss in Game 1 was the worst for Cleveland in 55 post-season contests. . . . Entering the series, Game 2 starter Gooden was the loser in the last post-season game won by the Red Sox—Game 5 of the 1986 World Series. . . . The Indians lost their seventh straight playoff-series opener. The last time they had won an opener was 1995, a 13-inning 5-4 victory over the Red Sox in the Division Series. . . . Hargrove was ejected by home-plate umpire Joe Brinkman just three pitches into Game 2 after Gooden had questioned two calls on leadoff batter Darren Lewis. Gooden was ejected three batters later, when he exploded over a questionable safe call by Brinkman at home plate.

Quotable:

Red Sox: Manager Jimy Williams, on the temptation to start Martinez on three days' rest in Game 4: "Temptation? Yeah. Come to my senses? No. I'll live with it, regardless of what other people believe." . . . Martinez, on not getting the Game 4 start: "I asked for it. Jimy Williams said no . . . It's his decision. He's the one on the spot. I'm only a worker here." . . . Saberhagen, on allowing three Game 3 homers: "I needed to be a groundball pitcher today, and I ended up being a fly-ball pitcher." . . . Gordon, after losing Game 4: "I just stuck with my game, which is high fastballs. And I broke two bats, but they fought them off for hits. I wouldn't take those pitches back."

Indians: Thome, on losing Game 1: "It's discouraging, but then again it isn't. We lost the first game three times last year and came back to win." . . . Hargrove, on the performances of Vaughn and Garciaparra in Game 1: "We had to pitch to them today. Every time they came up, they had runners on base and we had no place else to put them. The best way we can change is to get the people out in front of them." . . . Hargrove, after Game 4: "I don't think you get to the post-season by being lucky. I don't think you continue in post-season by being lucky." . . . Justice, explaining why he celebrated wildly after his eighth-inning double in Game 4: "I didn't care if people thought I was crazy or acted like a child . . . I'm going to retire in four years and the only thing I'm going to have left is my memories."

GAME 1 BOX SCORE

BOSTON 11, CLEVELAND 3

TUESDAY, SEPTEMBER 29, AT CLEVELAND

Boston	AB	R	H	RBI	PO	A
Lewis, cf	2	1	2	0	0	0
Buford, pr-cf	1	2	0	1	1	0
Valentin, 3b	4	4	3	0	1	2
Vaughn, 1b	5	2	3	7	9	0
Garciaparra, ss	4	1	1	4	1	1
Stanley, dh	4	0	1	0	0	0
O'Leary, lf	5	0	0	0	2	0
Bragg, rf	5	0	1	0	2	0
Hatteberg, c	4	0	1	0	9	0
Benjamin, 2b	4	1	0	0	2	3
Martinez, p	0	0	0	0	0	0
Corsi, p	0	0	0	0	0	0
Totals	38	11	12	11	27	6

Cleveland	AB	R	H	RBI	PO	A
Lofton, cf	4	1	2	2	3	0
Cora, 2b	4	0	0	0	0	1
Justice, dh	4	0	1	0	0	0
M. Ramirez, rf	4	0	1	0	2	0
Thome, 1b	4	1	1	1	7	0
Fryman, 3b	4	0	0	0	1	3
Giles, lf	4	0	1	0	3	0

Cleveland	AB	R	H	RBI	PO	A
Alomar, c	3	1	1	0	10	0
Vizquel, ss	3	0	0	0	0	2
Wright, p	0	0	0	0	0	0
Jones, p	0	0	0	0	0	0
Reed, p	0	0	0	0	0	0
Poole, p	0	0	0	0	0	0
Shuey, p	0	0	0	0	1	0
Assenmacher, p	0	0	0	0	0	0
Totals	34	3	7	3	27	7

Boston	3	0 0	0 3 2	0 3 0—11
Cleveland	0	0 0	0 0 2	1 0 0— 3

Boston	IP	H	R	ER	BB	SO
Martinez (W)	7.0	6	3	3	0	8
Corsi	2.0	1	0	0	0	2

Cleveland	IP	H	R	ER	BB	SO
Wright (L)	4.1	7	6	6	2	6
Jones	2.2	3	2	2	1	1
Reed	*0.0	1	3	3	1	0
Poole	†0.0	1	0	0	0	0
Shuey	1.0	0	0	0	0	1
Assenmacher	1.0	0	0	0	0	2

*Pitched to three batters in eighth.
†Pitched to one batter in eighth.
DP—Boston 1. LOB—Boston 7, Cleveland 4. 2B—Vaughn, Alomar, Justice, Giles. HR—Vaughn 2, Garciaparra, Lofton, Thome. SF—Garciaparra. HBP—By Wright (Lewis), by Reed (Buford). WP—Martinez. T—3:16. A—45,185. U—Scott, plate; Brinkman, first; Hirschbeck, second; McCoy, third; Phillips, left field; Meriwether, right field.

GAME 2 BOX SCORE

CLEVELAND 9, BOSTON 5

WEDNESDAY, SEPTEMBER 30, AT CLEVELAND

Boston	AB	R	H	RBI	PO	A
Lewis, cf	4	2	1	0	2	0
Valentin, 3b	4	1	1	0	2	0
Vaughn, 1b	4	0	1	0	10	1
Garciaparra, ss	4	1	2	3	2	3
Stanley, dh	4	1	2	0	0	0
O'Leary, lf	3	0	1	0	2	0
Bragg, rf	3	0	0	0	0	0
Buford, ph	0	0	0	0	0	0
Cummings, ph	1	0	0	0	0	0
Sadler, 2b	0	0	0	0	0	0
Varitek, c	4	0	1	1	5	0
Benjamin, 2b	3	0	1	0	3	6
Nixon, ph-rf	0	0	0	0	0	0
Wakefield, p	0	0	0	0	0	0
Wasdin, p	0	0	0	0	0	0
Lowe, p	0	0	0	0	0	0
Swindell, p	0	0	0	0	0	0
Gordon, p	0	0	0	0	0	1
Totals	34	5	10	4	24	13

Cleveland	AB	R	H	RBI	PO	A
Lofton, cf	4	2	2	1	1	0
Vizquel, ss	4	0	0	0	3	5
Justice, dh	4	2	2	4	0	0
M. Ramirez, rf	3	0	2	1	1	0
Thome, 1b	4	0	0	0	5	0
Sexson, 1b	0	0	0	0	2	0
Fryman, 3b	3	1	1	0	1	1
Giles, lf	2	1	0	0	1	0
Alomar, c	4	1	2	2	8	0
Cora, 2b	2	2	0	0	5	4
Gooden, p	0	0	0	0	0	0
Burba, p	0	0	0	0	0	0
Shuey, p	0	0	0	0	0	0
Assenmacher, p	0	0	0	0	0	0
Jackson, p	0	0	0	0	0	1
Totals	30	9	9	8	27	11

Boston	2	0 1	0 0 2	0 0 0—5
Cleveland	1	5 1	0 0 1	0 1 x—9

Boston	IP	H	R	ER	BB	SO
Wakefield (L)	1.1	3	5	5	2	1
Wasdin	1.2	2	2	2	1	2

Boston	IP	H	R	ER	BB	SO
Lowe	2.2	3	1	1	1	0
Swindell	1.1	0	0	0	1	1
Gordon	1.0	1	1	1	2	1

Cleveland	IP	H	R	ER	BB	SO
Gooden	0.1	1	2	2	2	1
Burba (W)	5.1	4	3	3	2	4
Shuey	*1.1	3	0	0	0	3
Assenmacher	*0.0	1	0	0	0	0
Jackson (S)	2.0	1	0	0	1	0

*Pitched to one batter in eighth.

E—Alomar. DP—Boston 2, Cleveland 2. LOB—Boston 8, Cleveland 8. 2B—Garciaparra, Lewis, Alomar 2, Lofton, M. Ramirez 2, Justice. HR—Justice. SF—Garciaparra, Justice. SB—Lewis, Lofton. HBP—By Wakefield (Ramirez), by Wasdin (M. Ramirez), by Lowe (Giles). WP—Gordon. PB—Varitek 2. T—3:25. A—45,229. U—Brinkman, plate; Hirschbeck, first; McCoy, second; Phillips, third; Meriwether, left field; Scott, right field.

GAME 3 BOX SCORE

CLEVELAND 4, BOSTON 3

FRIDAY, OCTOBER 2, AT BOSTON

Cleveland	AB	R	H	RBI	PO	A
Lofton, cf	4	1	1	1	2	0
Vizquel, ss	4	0	0	0	0	4
Justice, lf	4	0	0	0	4	0
M. Ramirez, rf	3	2	2	2	0	0
Thome, 1b	4	1	1	1	14	0
Sexson, 1b	0	0	0	0	2	0
Fryman, 3b	4	0	0	0	1	3
Giles, dh	4	0	1	0	0	0
Alomar, c	3	0	0	0	3	0
Cora, 2b	2	0	0	0	1	6
Nagy, p	0	0	0	0	0	1
Jackson, p	0	0	0	0	0	0
Totals	32	4	5	4	27	14

Boston	AB	R	H	RBI	PO	A
Lewis, cf	4	1	1	0	3	0
Valentin, 3b	4	0	1	0	2	3
Vaughn, 1b	4	1	2	0	6	0
Garciaparra, ss	4	1	1	3	0	1
Stanley, dh	4	0	0	0	0	0
O'Leary, lf	4	0	0	0	1	0
Nixon, rf	3	0	1	0	3	0
Hatteberg, c	3	0	0	0	8	0
Benjamin, 2b	2	0	0	0	4	0
Cummings, ph	1	0	0	0	0	0
Sadler, 2b	0	0	0	0	0	0
Saberhagen, p	0	0	0	0	0	0
Corsi, p	0	0	0	0	0	0
Eckersley, p	0	0	0	0	0	0
Totals	33	3	6	3	27	4

Cleveland		0	0	0		0	1	1		1	0	1—4
Boston		0	0	0		1	0	0		0	0	2—3

Cleveland	IP	H	R	ER	BB	SO
Nagy (W)	8.0	4	1	1	0	3
Jackson (S)	1.0	2	2	2	0	0

Boston	IP	H	R	ER	BB	SO
Saberhagen (L)	7.0	4	3	3	1	7
Corsi	1.0	0	0	0	1	0
Eckersley	1.0	1	1	1	0	1

LOB—Cleveland 3, Boston 3. HR—Thome, Lofton, M. Ramirez 2, Garciaparra. T—2:27. A—33,114. U—Garcia, plate; Tschida, first; Coble, second; Craft, third; Joyce, left field; Merrill, right field.

GAME 4 BOX SCORE

CLEVELAND 2, BOSTON 1

SATURDAY, OCTOBER 3, AT BOSTON

Cleveland	AB	R	H	RBI	PO	A
Lofton, cf	4	1	1	0	4	0
Vizquel, ss	4	1	1	0	1	5
Justice, lf	4	0	2	2	1	1
M. Ramirez, rf	4	0	0	0	1	0
Fryman, 3b	2	0	1	0	2	1
Thome, dh	3	0	0	0	0	0
Sexson, 1b	2	0	0	0	8	1
Alomar, c	3	0	0	0	8	0
Wilson, 2b	2	0	0	0	2	2
Cora, ph-2b	2	0	0	0	0	1
Colon, p	0	0	0	0	0	0
Poole, p	0	0	0	0	0	0
Reed, p	0	0	0	0	0	0
Assenmacher, p	0	0	0	0	0	0
Shuey, p	0	0	0	0	0	0
Jackson, p	0	0	0	0	0	0
Totals	30	2	5	2	27	11

Boston	AB	R	H	RBI	PO	A
Lewis, cf	4	0	1	0	5	0
Valentin, 3b	3	0	2	0	2	3
Vaughn, 1b	4	0	1	0	5	3
Sadler, pr-2b	0	0	0	0	1	1
Garciaparra, ss	3	1	1	1	0	2
Stanley, dh	3	0	1	0	0	0
Buford, pr-dh	0	0	0	0	0	0
O'Leary, lf	4	0	0	0	3	0
Hatteberg, c	2	0	0	0	3	0
Benjamin, 2b-1b	2	0	0	0	4	0
Cummings, ph	1	0	0	0	0	0
Bragg, rf	4	0	0	0	2	0
Schourek, p	0	0	0	0	2	1
Lowe, p	0	0	0	0	0	0
Gordon, p	0	0	0	0	0	0
Totals	30	1	6	1	27	10

Cleveland		0	0	0		0	0	0		0	2	0—2
Boston		0	0	0		1	0	0		0	0	0—1

Cleveland	IP	H	R	ER	BB	SO
Colon	5.2	5	1	1	3	3
Poole	1.0	0	0	0	1	2
Reed (W)	0.2	0	0	0	0	1
Assenmacher	*0.0	1	0	0	0	0
Shuey	0.2	0	0	0	1	0
Jackson (S)	1.0	0	0	0	0	1

Boston	IP	H	R	ER	BB	SO
Schourek	5.1	2	0	0	4	1
Lowe	1.2	0	0	0	0	2
Gordon (L)	2.0	3	2	2	2	0

*Pitched to one batter in eighth.

DP—Cleveland 1, Boston 1. LOB—Cleveland 7, Boston 8. 2B—Fryman, Justice 2, Lewis, Valentin, Vaughn. HR—Garciaparra. SH—Benjamin. SB—Fryman, Lofton. CS—Fryman. T—3:00. A—33,537. U—Tschida, plate; Coble, first; Craft, second; Joyce, third; Merrill, left field; Garcia, right field.

STATISTICS

CLEVELAND INDIANS' BATTING AND FIELDING AVERAGES

Player, position	G	AB	R	H	TB	2B	3B	HR	RBI	BB	IBB	SO	Avg.	PO	A	E	Avg.
Lofton, cf	4	16	5	6	13	1	0	2	4	1	0	1	.375	10	0	0	1.000
M. Ramirez, rf	4	14	2	5	13	2	0	2	3	1	0	4	.357	4	0	0	1.000
Justice, dh-lf	4	16	2	5	12	4	0	1	6	0	0	1	.313	5	1	0	1.000
Alomar, c	4	13	2	3	6	3	0	0	2	1	0	4	.231	29	0	1	.967
Giles, lf-dh	3	10	1	2	3	1	0	0	0	1	0	4	.200	0	0	0	1.000
Fryman, 3b	4	13	1	2	3	1	0	0	0	3	0	4	.154	5	8	0	1.000
Thome, 1b-dh	4	15	2	2	8	0	0	2	2	2	1	5	.133	26	1	0	1.000

Player, position	G	AB	R	H	TB	2B	3B	HR	RBI	BB	IBB	SO	Avg.	PO	A	E	Avg.
Vizquel, ss	4	15	1	1	1	0	0	0	0	1	0	0	.067	4	16	0	1.000
Cora, 2b-ph	4	10	2	0	0	0	0	0	0	3	0	2	.000	6	12	0	1.000
Sexson, 1b	3	2	0	0	0	0	0	0	0	2	0	1	.000	12	1	0	1.000
Wilson, 2b	1	2	0	0	0	0	0	0	0	0	0	0	.000	2	2	0	1.000
Assenmacher, p	3	0	0	0	0	0	0	0	0	0	0	0	.000	0	0	0	.000
Jackson, p	3	0	0	0	0	0	0	0	0	0	0	0	.000	0	1	0	1.000
Shuey, p	3	0	0	0	0	0	0	0	0	0	0	0	.000	1	0	0	1.000
Poole, p	2	0	0	0	0	0	0	0	0	0	0	0	.000	0	0	0	.000
Reed, p	2	0	0	0	0	0	0	0	0	0	0	0	.000	0	0	0	.000
Burba, p	1	0	0	0	0	0	0	0	0	0	0	0	.000	0	0	0	.000
Colon, p	1	0	0	0	0	0	0	0	0	0	0	0	.000	0	0	0	.000
Gooden, p	1	0	0	0	0	0	0	0	0	0	0	0	.000	0	0	0	.000
Jones, p	1	0	0	0	0	0	0	0	0	0	0	0	.000	0	0	0	.000
Nagy, p	1	0	0	0	0	0	0	0	0	0	0	0	.000	0	1	0	1.000
Wright, p	1	0	0	0	0	0	0	0	0	0	0	0	.000	0	0	0	.000
Totals	4	126	18	26	59	12	0	7	17	15	1	26	.206	108	43	1	.993

CLEVELAND INDIANS' PITCHING RECORDS

Pitcher	G	GS	CG	IP	H	R	ER	HR	BB	IBB	SO	HB	WP	W	L	Pct.	ERA
Shuey	3	0	0	3.0	3	0	0	0	1	0	4	0	0	0	0	.000	0.00
Assenmacher	3	0	0	1.0	2	0	0	0	0	0	2	0	0	0	0	.000	0.00
Poole	2	0	0	1.0	1	0	0	0	1	0	2	0	0	0	0	.000	0.00
Nagy	1	1	0	8.0	4	1	1	0	0	0	3	0	0	1	0	1.000	1.13
Colon	1	1	0	5.2	5	1	1	1	3	1	3	0	0	0	0	.000	1.59
Jackson	3	0	0	4.0	3	2	2	1	1	0	1	0	0	0	0	.000	4.50
Burba	1	0	0	5.1	4	3	3	0	2	0	4	0	0	1	0	1.000	5.06
Jones	1	0	0	2.2	3	2	2	1	1	0	1	0	0	0	0	.000	6.75
Wright	1	1	0	4.1	7	6	6	2	2	0	6	1	0	0	1	.000	12.46
Reed	2	0	0	0.2	1	3	3	0	1	0	1	1	0	1	0	1.000	40.50
Gooden	1	1	0	0.1	1	2	2	0	2	0	1	0	0	0	0	.000	54.00
Totals	4	4	0	36.0	34	20	20	5	14	1	28	2	0	3	1	.750	5.00

No shutouts. Saves—Jackson 3.

BOSTON RED SOX'S BATTING AND FIELDING AVERAGES

Player, position	G	AB	R	H	TB	2B	3B	HR	RBI	BB	IBB	SO	Avg.	PO	A	E	Avg.
Valentin, 3b	4	15	5	7	8	1	0	0	0	3	0	1	.467	5	10	0	1.000
Vaughn, 1b	4	17	3	7	15	2	0	2	7	1	0	5	.412	30	4	0	1.000
Lewis, cf	4	14	4	5	7	2	0	0	0	1	0	3	.357	10	0	0	1.000
Garciaparra, ss	4	15	4	5	15	1	0	3	11	1	1	0	.333	3	7	0	1.000
Nixon, ph-rf	2	3	0	1	1	0	0	0	0	1	0	0	.333	3	0	0	1.000
Stanley, dh	4	15	1	4	4	0	0	0	0	2	0	5	.267	0	0	0	.000
Varitek, c	1	4	0	1	1	0	0	0	1	0	0	1	.250	5	0	0	1.000
Hatteberg, c	3	9	0	1	1	0	0	0	0	3	0	1	.111	20	0	0	1.000
Benjamin, 2b-1b	4	11	1	1	1	0	0	0	0	1	0	3	.091	13	9	0	1.000
Bragg, rf	3	12	0	1	1	0	0	0	0	0	0	5	.083	4	0	0	1.000
O'Leary, lf	4	16	0	1	1	0	0	0	0	1	0	4	.063	8	0	0	1.000
Buford, pr-cf-ph-dh	3	1	2	0	0	0	0	0	0	0	0	0	.000	1	0	0	1.000
Cummings, ph	3	3	0	0	0	0	0	0	0	0	0	0	.000	0	0	0	.000
Sadler, 2b-pr	3	0	0	0	0	0	0	0	0	0	0	0	.000	1	1	0	1.000
Corsi, p	2	0	0	0	0	0	0	0	0	0	0	0	.000	0	0	0	.000
Gordon, p	2	0	0	0	0	0	0	0	0	0	0	0	.000	0	1	0	1.000
Lowe, p	2	0	0	0	0	0	0	0	0	0	0	0	.000	0	0	0	.000
Eckersley, p	1	0	0	0	0	0	0	0	0	0	0	0	.000	0	0	0	.000
Martinez, p	1	0	0	0	0	0	0	0	0	0	0	0	.000	0	0	0	.000
Saberhagen, p	1	0	0	0	0	0	0	0	0	0	0	0	.000	0	0	0	.000
Schourek, p	1	0	0	0	0	0	0	0	0	0	0	0	.000	2	1	0	1.000
Swindell, p	1	0	0	0	0	0	0	0	0	0	0	0	.000	0	0	0	.000
Wakefield, p	1	0	0	0	0	0	0	0	0	0	0	0	.000	0	0	0	.000
Wasdin, p	1	0	0	0	0	0	0	0	0	0	0	0	.000	0	0	0	.000
Totals	4	135	20	34	55	6	0	5	19	14	1	28	.252	105	33	0	1.000

BOSTON RED SOX'S PITCHING RECORDS

Pitcher	G	GS	CG	IP	H	R	ER	HR	BB	IBB	SO	HB	WP	W	L	Pct.	ERA
Schourek	1	1	0	5.1	2	0	0	0	4	0	1	0	0	0	0	.000	0.00
Corsi	2	0	0	3.0	1	0	0	0	1	0	2	0	0	0	0	.000	0.00
Swindell	1	0	0	1.1	0	0	0	0	1	0	1	0	0	0	0	.000	0.00
Lowe	2	0	0	4.1	3	1	1	0	1	1	2	1	0	0	0	.000	2.08
Martinez	1	1	0	7.0	6	3	3	2	0	0	8	0	1	1	0	1.000	3.86
Saberhagen	1	1	0	7.0	4	3	3	3	1	0	7	0	0	0	1	.000	3.86

Pitcher	G	GS	CG	IP	H	R	ER	HR	BB	IBB	SO	HB	WP	W	L	Pct.	ERA
Gordon	2	0	0	3.0	4	3	3	0	4	0	1	0	1	0	1	.000	9.00
Eckersley	1	0	0	1.0	1	1	1	1	0	0	1	0	0	0	0	.000	9.00
Wasdin	1	0	0	1.2	2	2	2	1	1	0	2	1	0	0	0	.000	10.80
Wakefield	1	1	0	1.1	3	5	5	0	2	0	1	1	0	0	1	.000	33.75
Totals	4	4	0	35.0	26	18	18	7	15	1	26	3	2	1	3	.250	4.63

No shutouts or saves.

SCORE BY INNINGS

Cleveland..1 5 1   0 1 4   2 3   1—18
Boston ....5 0 1   2 3 4   0 3   2—20

MISCELLANEOUS STATISTICS

Sacrifice hits—Benjamin.
Sacrifice flies—Garciaparra 2, Justice.
Stolen bases—Lofton 2, Fryman, Lewis.
Caught stealing—Fryman.
Double plays—Garciaparra, Benjamin and Vaughn; Jackson, Cora and Sexson; Valentin, Benjamin and Vaughn; Valentin, Sadler and Benjamin; Valentin and Vaughn; Vizquel, Cora and Thome; Vizquel, Wilson and Sexson.
Left on bases—Cleveland 4, 8, 3, 7—22; Boston 7, 8, 3, 8—26.
Hit by pitcher—M. Ramirez 2, Buford, Giles, Lewis.
Passed balls—Varitek 2.
Balks—None.
Time of games—First game, 3:16; second game, 3:25; third game, 2:27; fourth game, 3:00.
Attendance—First game, 45,185; second game, 45,229; third game, 33,114; fourth game, 33,537.
Umpires—Scott, Brinkman, Hirschbeck, McCoy, Phillips, Meriwether, Garcia, Tschida, Coble, Craft, Joyce and Merrill.
Official scorers—Hank Kozloski, Charlie Scoggins.

NEW YORK VS. TEXAS

HIGHLIGHTS

The bottom line: The New York Yankees, after breaking the American League regular-season record with 114 wins, used superior pitching to sweep the West Division-champion Texas Rangers and advance to the Championship Series. Although the Yankees finished 114-48, critics had questioned their ability to shut down a Rangers lineup that led the A.L. in hitting and put up big numbers against them in the regular season. The Yankees met that challenge in impressive fashion, winning three low-scoring games and moving a step closer to their major league-record 35th pennant and 24th World Series victory. The victory also added fuel to their claim as the best team in baseball history.

Why the Yankees won: The old baseball adage is that great pitching stops good hitting. It certainly applied in this case. The Rangers' regular-season team averages of .289 and 5.80 runs per game meant little to David Wells, Andy Pettitte, David Cone and a handful of relievers, who held Texas hitters to one run and a .141 (13-for-92) mark in the Division Series. Although the Yankees didn't make the offensive statement they had hoped, they were able to put up enough runs to back their excellent starting pitchers. While the big bats in the Yankees lineup slumbered, rookie Shane Spencer and Scott Brosius collected seven of the team's eight RBIs in the series.

The turning points:

Game 1: With David Wells combining with closer Mariano Rivera to silence the Rangers in a 2-0 victory at Yankee Stadium, the Yankees manufactured all the runs they would need in the second inning—and the bottom of the lineup did all the damage. After Jorge Posada walked, left fielder Chad Curtis, start-ing more for defensive purposes, doubled to right and Brosius, the team's No. 9 hitter, followed with an RBI single. The Yankees executed the double steal to perfection for the second run. Brosius took off on the pitch but stopped between first and second when the throw from catcher Ivan Rodriguez beat him easily. Curtis scored before the Rangers could chase down Brosius. Wells, who had been hammered in two of three regular-season starts against the Rangers, allowed only three runners to reach second base in eight innings. Stottlemyre allowed only three more hits after the second in his complete-game loss.

Game 2: It was Pettitte's turn to silence the Rangers at Yankee Stadium, and he did so nearly as successfully as Wells in a 3-1 victory. He pinpointed the outside corner with his fastball and changeup, taking advantage of home-plate umpire Durwood Merrill's generous strike zone. He struck out eight in seven innings, allowing just a fifth-inning RBI single to Rodriguez. Again some unlikely candidates were the offensive heroes. Although the first five spots in the Yankees lineup were a combined 1-for-19, Spencer hit a solo homer in his first post-season at-bat and Brosius added a two-run homer to back Pettitte. Rick Helling, a 20-game winner during the regular season, was the tough-luck loser for Texas, striking out nine in his six innings.

Game 3: Just minutes before a torrential downpour forced a 3-hour, 16-minute rain delay and knocked out Yankees starter Cone in the sixth inning, veteran Paul O'Neill hit a solo homer and Spencer added a three-run shot to give the Yankees the 4-0 lead they would carry to victory. Cone was masterful in his 5.2 innings, allowing just two hits and striking out six before the game was halted. When play resumed at 12:24 a.m., relievers Graeme Lloyd, Jeff Nelson and Mariano Rivera put the finishing touches on the second shutout of the series and the Yankees' impressive sweep. Spencer hit his second homer in as many games off Texas starter Aaron Sele—the second-toughest starter in the A.L. to homer against. Spencer hit a slow curve through a strong wind 371 feet into the left field stands.

Notable:

Yankees: Wells' 135-pitch outing in Game 1 was his longest of the year and he appeared to run out of gas in the eighth inning. . . . Pettitte, making his ninth playoff start, recorded a career post-season-high eight strikeouts in Game 2. . . . Pettitte's performance was encouraging, considering he was 3-5 with a 6.14 ERA in his last nine starts of the regular season. . . . Spencer's Game 3 homer was his ninth in his last 33 at-bats. He also hit three grand slams during a nine-day stretch in September. . . . The first six hitters in the Yankees lineup were a combined 11-for-63 (.175); the bottom three hitters were a surprising 12-for-28 (.429).

Rangers: Stottlemyre, traded to the Rangers on July 31, was pitching under the watchful eye of his father Mel, the Yankees pitching coach and a former Yankee pitcher. The two have combined for 287 regular-season wins, the most by a father-son combo. . . . Before Well's outing in Game 1, lefthanded starting pitching was 12-23 with a 6.49 ERA in 48 starts against the Rangers. . . . Game 2 loser Helling attended the same high school as Yankees great Roger Maris. . . . Sele allowed 0.59 home runs per inning (14 in 212.2) this season, second only to Toronto's Roger Clemens, who allowed just 0.37. . . . The big bats in the Texas lineup—Rusty Greer, Juan Gonzalez, Will Clark and Rodriguez—were a combined 4-for-44 (.091) in the series and 0-for-13 in Game 3.

Quotable:

Yankees: Wells, on getting the Game 1 start: "This is crunch time; I love this stuff. I want to be the hero or the goat, the guy they blame if we get our butts kicked and the guy who gets the pat on the back if we do well. I want that ball, and if I don't get my way I get ticked off." . . . Manager Joe Torre, on Wells tiring in the eighth inning of Game 1: "He was running on fumes." . . . Mel Stottlemyre, on his son's performance: "Tonight's game probably ended the best way. My son pitched well and we won. That's my job." . . . Spencer, on his opportunity to be a Yankees hero: "I've thought about the fact that maybe if I had been with another team, I would have gotten a shot earlier. But I made it with the best organization ever, and that's a great accomplishment." . . . Pettitte, after winning Game 2: "What really feels good is that the critics were there, but my manager stuck with me." . . . Cone, on continuing the tradition of great Yankee pitching: "Boomer (Wells) set the pace in the opener and Andy (Pettitte) kept it going. I didn't want to drop the baton."

Rangers: Manager Johnny Oates, after being shut out by Wells: "I've accused David of throwing everything but the kitchen sink out there, and that's what he did tonight." . . . Oates on Spencer: "He doesn't get cheated. He uses that piece of wood—and not to clean off his shoes." . . . Gonzalez, recapping the series: "It was very frustrating. Their pitching dominated the best team in the A.L. . . . it was good pitching stopping good hitting over three games." . . . Greer, disappointed after the Game 3 loss: "We played for seven months and hit the ball well, but couldn't hit when we needed to."

GAME 1 BOX SCORE

NEW YORK 2, TEXAS 0

TUESDAY, SEPTEMBER 29, AT NEW YORK

Texas	AB	R	H	RBI	PO	A
McLemore, 2b	3	0	1	0	1	4
Kelly, cf	4	0	0	0	2	0
Greer, lf	4	0	1	0	2	1
Gonzalez, rf	4	0	0	0	2	0
Clark, 1b	4	0	1	0	6	0
Rodriguez, c	4	0	0	0	9	2
Zeile, dh	3	0	1	0	0	2
Simms, dh	3	0	1	0	0	0
Clayton, ss	3	0	0	0	2	2
Stottlemyre, p	0	0	0	0	0	1
Totals	**32**	**0**	**5**	**0**	**24**	**12**

New York	AB	R	H	RBI	PO	A
Knoblauch, 2b	3	0	1	0	2	2
Jeter, ss	2	0	0	0	0	2
O'Neill, rf	3	0	1	0	1	0
B. Williams, cf	3	0	0	0	2	0
Martinez, 1b	3	0	1	0	8	0
Davis, dh	3	0	0	0	0	0
Posada, c	2	1	0	0	11	1
Curtis, lf	3	1	2	0	3	0
Brosius, 3b	3	0	1	1	0	1
Wells, p	0	0	0	0	0	2
Rivera, p	0	0	0	0	0	0
Totals	**25**	**2**	**6**	**1**	**27**	**8**

Texas	0	0	0		0	0	0		0	0	0—0
New York	0	2	0		0	0	0		0	x—2

Texas	IP	H	R	ER	BB	SO
Stottlemyre (L)	8.0	6	2	2	4	8

New York	IP	H	R	ER	BB	SO
Wells (W)	8.0	5	0	0	1	9
Rivera (S)	1.0	0	0	0	0	1

DP—Texas 2. LOB—Texas 6, New York 5. 2B—McLemore, O'Neill, Curtis, Martinez. SH—Jeter. CS—Brosius, Curtis. HBP—By Stottlemyre (Knoblauch). PB—Rodriguez. T—3:02. A—57,362. U—Joyce, plate; Merrill, first; Garcia, second; Tschida, third; Coble, left field; Craft, right field.

GAME 2 BOX SCORE

NEW YORK 3, TEXAS 1

WEDNESDAY, SEPTEMBER 30, AT NEW YORK

Texas	AB	R	H	RBI	PO	A
McLemore, 2b	4	0	0	0	2	3
Kelly, cf	3	0	1	0	1	0
Goodwin, cf	1	0	1	0	0	0
Greer, lf	4	0	0	0	2	0
Gonzalez, rf	4	1	1	0	2	0
Clark, 1b	4	0	0	0	5	1
Rodriguez, c	3	0	1	1	11	0
Zeile, 3b	3	0	0	0	0	0
Simms, dh	2	0	0	0	0	0
Alicea, ph-dh	1	0	0	0	0	0
Clayton, ss	3	0	1	0	0	2
Helling, p	0	0	0	0	1	0
Crabtree, p	0	0	0	0	0	0
Totals	**32**	**1**	**5**	**1**	**24**	**6**

New York	AB	R	H	RBI	PO	A
Knoblauch, 2b	4	0	0	0	2	3
Jeter, ss	3	0	0	0	1	0
O'Neill, rf	4	0	1	0	0	0
B. Williams, cf	4	0	0	0	4	0
Martinez, 1b	4	0	0	0	8	0
Davis, dh	3	0	1	0	0	0
Bush, pr-dh	0	0	0	0	0	0
Raines, ph-dh	1	0	0	0	0	0
Spencer, lf	3	2	2	1	1	0
Curtis, lf	0	0	0	0	0	0
Brosius, 3b	3	1	2	2	2	4
Girardi, c	3	0	2	0	9	0
Pettitte, p	0	0	0	0	0	1
Nelson, p	0	0	0	0	0	0
Rivera, p	0	0	0	0	0	0
Totals	32	3	8	3	27	8

Texas	0	0	0		0	1	0		0 0 0—1
New York	0	1	0		2	0	0		0 0 x—3

Texas	IP	H	R	ER	BB	SO
Helling (L)	6.0	8	3	3	1	9
Crabtree	2.0	0	0	0	0	1

New York	IP	H	R	ER	BB	SO
Pettitte (W)	7.0	3	1	1	0	8
Nelson	0.2	1	0	0	0	0
Rivera (S)	1.1	1	0	0	0	1

LOB—Texas 4, New York 6. 2B—Gonzalez, Kelly, O'Neill. HR—Spencer, Brosius. SB—Bush. T—2:58. A—57,360. U—Merrill, plate; Garcia, first; Tschida, second; Coble, third; Craft, left field; Joyce, right field.

GAME 3 BOX SCORE

NEW YORK 4, TEXAS 0

FRIDAY, OCTOBER 2, AT TEXAS

New York	AB	R	H	RBI	PO	A
Knoblauch, 2b	4	0	0	0	0	5
Jeter, ss	4	0	1	0	3	3
O'Neill, rf	4	1	2	1	1	0
B. Williams, cf	4	0	0	0	2	0

New York	AB	R	H	RBI	PO	A
Martinez, 1b	4	1	2	0	11	1
Raines, dh	3	1	1	0	0	0
Spencer, lf	3	1	1	3	0	0
Curtis, lf	0	0	0	0	0	0
Brosius, 3b	4	0	1	0	0	1
Girardi, c	4	0	1	0	10	0
Cone, p	0	0	0	0	0	1
Lloyd, p	0	0	0	0	0	0
Nelson, p	0	0	0	0	0	0
Rivera, p	0	0	0	0	0	0
Totals	34	4	9	4	27	12

Texas	AB	R	H	RBI	PO	A
Goodwin, cf	3	0	0	0	1	0
McLemore, 2b	3	0	0	0	1	5
Greer, lf	3	0	0	0	0	0
Gonzalez, rf	4	0	0	0	4	0
Clark, 1b	3	0	0	0	10	1
Rodriguez, c	3	0	0	0	7	1
Stevens, dh	3	0	0	0	0	0
Zeile, 3b	3	0	2	0	0	2
Clayton, ss	3	0	1	0	3	4
Sele, p	0	0	0	0	1	0
Crabtree, p	0	0	0	0	0	0
Wetteland, p	0	0	0	0	0	0
Totals	28	0	3	0	27	13

New York	0	0	0		0	0	4		0 0 0—4
Texas	0	0	0		0	0	0		0 0 0—0

New York	IP	H	R	ER	BB	SO
Cone (W)	5.2	2	0	0	1	6
Lloyd	0.1	0	0	0	0	0
Nelson	2.0	1	0	0	1	2
Rivera	1.0	0	0	0	1	0

Texas	IP	H	R	ER	BB	SO
Sele (L)	6.0	8	4	4	1	4
Crabtree	2.0	1	0	0	0	1
Wetteland	1.0	0	0	0	1	1

E—Knoblauch, Clayton. DP—New York 2, Texas 2. LOB—New York 5, Texas 5. 2B—Martinez, Raines. HR—O'Neill, Spencer. SH—Goodwin. SB—Curtis. CS—Zeile. T—2:58. A—49,950. U—Hirschbeck, plate; McCoy, first; Phillips, second; Scott, third; Brinkman, left.

STATISTICS

NEW YORK YANKEES' BATTING AND FIELDING AVERAGES

Player, position	G	AB	R	H	TB	2B	3B	HR	RBI	BB	IBB	SO	Avg.	PO	A	E	Avg.
Curtis, lf	3	3	1	2	3	1	0	0	0	1	0	1	.667	3	0	0	1.000
Spencer, lf	2	6	3	3	9	0	0	2	4	0	0	1	.500	1	0	0	1.000
Girardi, c	2	7	0	3	3	0	0	0	0	0	0	0	.429	19	1	0	1.000
Brosius, 3b	3	10	1	4	7	0	0	1	3	0	0	3	.400	2	6	0	1.000
O'Neill, rf	3	11	1	4	9	2	0	1	1	1	0	1	.364	2	0	0	1.000
Martinez, 1b	3	11	1	3	5	2	0	0	0	0	0	2	.273	27	1	0	1.000
Raines, ph-dh	2	4	1	1	2	1	0	0	0	1	0	1	.250	0	0	0	.000
Davis, dh	2	6	0	1	1	0	0	0	0	0	0	0	.167	0	0	0	.000
Jeter, ss	3	9	0	1	1	0	0	0	0	2	0	2	.111	4	5	0	1.000
Knoblauch, 2b	3	11	0	1	1	0	0	0	0	0	0	4	.091	4	10	1	.933
Bush, pr-dh	1	0	0	0	0	0	0	0	0	0	0	0	.000	0	0	0	.000
Posada, c	1	2	1	0	0	0	0	0	0	1	0	0	.000	11	1	0	1.000
Williams, cf	3	11	0	0	0	0	0	0	0	1	0	4	.000	8	0	0	1.000
Rivera, p	3	0	0	0	0	0	0	0	0	0	0	0	.000	0	0	0	.000
Nelson, p	2	0	0	0	0	0	0	0	0	0	0	0	.000	0	0	0	.000
Cone, p	1	0	0	0	0	0	0	0	0	0	0	0	.000	0	1	0	1.000
Lloyd, p	1	0	0	0	0	0	0	0	0	0	0	0	.000	0	0	0	.000
Pettitte, p	1	0	0	0	0	0	0	0	0	0	0	0	.000	0	1	0	1.000
Wells, p	1	0	0	0	0	0	0	0	0	0	0	0	.000	0	2	0	1.000
Totals	3	91	9	23	41	6	0	4	8	7	0	24	.253	81	28	1	.991

NEW YORK YANKEES' PITCHING RECORDS

Pitcher	G	GS	CG	IP	H	R	ER	HR	BB	IBB	SO	HB	WP	W	L	Pct.	ERA
Wells	1	1	0	8.0	5	0	0	0	1	0	9	0	0	1	0	1.000	0.00
Cone	1	1	0	5.2	2	0	0	0	1	0	6	0	0	1	0	1.000	0.00
Rivera	3	0	0	3.1	1	0	0	0	1	0	2	0	0	0	0	.000	0.00
Nelson	2	0	0	2.2	2	0	0	0	1	0	2	0	0	0	0	.000	0.00

Pitcher	G	GS	CG	IP	H	R	ER	HR	BB	IBB	SO	HB	WP	W	L	Pct.	ERA
Lloyd	1	0	0	0.1	0	0	0	0	0	0	0	0	0	0	0	.000	0.00
Pettitte	1	1	0	7.0	3	1	1	0	0	0	8	0	0	1	0	1.000	1.29
Totals	3	3	0	27.0	13	1	1	0	4	0	27	0	0	3	0	1.000	0.33

Shutouts—Wells and Rivera (combined); Cone, Lloyd, Nelson and Rivera (combined). Saves—Rivera 2.

TEXAS RANGERS' BATTING AND FIELDING AVERAGES

					BATTING										FIELDING		
Player, position	G	AB	R	H	TB	2B	3B	HR	RBI	BB	IBB	SO	Avg.	PO	A	E	Avg.
Zeile, 3b	3	9	0	3	3	0	0	0	0	0	0	2	.333	0	4	0	1.000
Goodwin, cf	2	4	0	1	1	0	0	0	0	0	0	1	.250	1	0	0	1.000
Clayton, ss	3	9	0	2	2	0	0	0	0	0	0	4	.222	5	8	1	.929
Simms, dh	2	5	0	1	1	0	0	0	0	0	0	2	.200	0	0	0	.000
Kelly, cf	2	7	0	1	2	1	0	0	0	0	0	2	.143	3	0	0	1.000
McLemore, 2b	3	10	0	1	2	1	0	0	0	2	0	3	.100	4	12	0	1.000
Rodriguez, c	3	10	0	1	1	0	0	0	1	0	0	5	.100	27	3	0	1.000
Clark, 1b	3	11	0	1	1	0	0	0	0	1	0	2	.091	21	2	0	1.000
Greer, lf	3	11	0	1	1	0	0	0	0	1	0	2	.091	4	1	0	1.000
Gonzalez, rf	3	12	1	1	2	1	0	0	0	0	0	3	.083	8	0	0	1.000
Alicea, ph-dh	1	1	0	0	0	0	0	0	0	0	0	0	.000	0	0	0	.000
Stevens, dh	1	3	0	0	0	0	0	0	0	0	0	1	.000	0	0	0	.000
Crabtree, p	2	0	0	0	0	0	0	0	0	0	0	0	.000	0	0	0	.000
Helling, p	1	0	0	0	0	0	0	0	0	0	0	0	.000	1	0	0	1.000
Sele, p	1	0	0	0	0	0	0	0	0	0	0	0	.000	1	0	0	1.000
Stottlemyre, p	1	0	0	0	0	0	0	0	0	0	0	0	.000	0	1	0	1.000
Wetteland, p	1	0	0	0	0	0	0	0	0	0	0	0	.000	0	0	0	.000
Totals	3	92	1	13	16	3	0	0	1	4	0	27	.141	75	31	1	.991

TEXAS RANGERS' PITCHING RECORDS

Pitcher	G	GS	CG	IP	H	R	ER	HR	BB	IBB	SO	HB	WP	W	L	Pct.	ERA
Crabtree	2	0	0	4.0	1	0	0	0	0	0	2	0	0	0	0	.000	0.00
Wetteland	1	0	0	1.0	0	0	0	0	1	0	1	0	0	0	0	.000	0.00
Stottlemyre	1	1	1	8.0	6	2	2	0	4	0	8	1	0	0	1	.000	2.25
Helling	1	1	0	6.0	8	3	3	2	1	0	9	0	0	0	1	.000	4.50
Sele	1	1	0	6.0	8	4	4	2	1	0	4	0	0	0	1	.000	6.00
Totals	3	3	1	25.0	23	9	9	4	7	0	24	1	0	0	3	.000	3.24

No shutouts or saves.

SCORE BY INNINGS

New York...0 3 0 2 0 4 0 0 0 —9
Texas...0 0 0 0 1 0 0 0 0 —1

MISCELLANEOUS STATISTICS

Sacrifice hits—Goodwin, Jeter.
Sacrifice flies—None.
Stolen bases—Bush, Curtis.
Caught stealing—Brosius, Curtis, Zeile.
Double plays—McLemore, Clayton and Clark 2; Clayton, McLemore and Clark; Girardi, Jeter and Martinez; Jeter and Martinez; Rodriguez, McLemore and Clark..
Left on bases—New York 5, 6, 5—16; Texas 6, 4, 5—15.
Hit by pitcher—Knoblauch.
Passed ball—Rodriguez.
Balks—None.
Time of games—First game, 3:02; second game, 2:58; third game, 2:58.
Attendance—First game, 57,362; second game, 57,360; third game, 49,950.
Umpires—Joyce, Merrill, Garcia, Tschida, Coble, Craft, Hirschbeck, McCoy, Phillips, Scott and Brinkman.
Official scorers—Red Foley, Kurt Iverson.

N.L. DIVISION SERIES
SAN DIEGO VS. HOUSTON

The bottom line: The San Diego Padres, gunning for the second pennant in their 30th National League season, defied the odds with a four-game Division Series victory over Houston and claimed a berth in the N.L. Championship Series for the first time since 1984. The West Division-champion Padres shut down the National League's highest-scoring offense in three games and took the Astros into the bottom of the ninth before losing the other. The Central Division-champion Astros, 102-game regular-season winners and favored by many to reach their first World Series, batted a paltry .182 against Padres pitchers. The loss was Houston's fifth in as many post-season appearances.

Why the Padres won: Because they outpitched the Astros and got a welcome offensive pickup from backup catcher and first baseman Jim Leyritz. Kevin Brown won twice, including a 16-strikeout, two-hit series-opening victory over Randy Johnson, and Sterling Hitchcock came back to beat the dominating Johnson in the Game 4 clincher. "They said we couldn't beat Johnson twice in a five-game series," Hitchcock said. "Well, we beat him twice in a four-game series." Padres pitchers, who limited the Astros to one run in three of the four games, also held Houston's Killer B's—Craig Biggio, Jeff Bagwell and Derek Bell—to 6 hits in 41 at-bats and 124-RBI man Moises Alou to 3-for-16.

The turning points:

Game 1: There was not a specific turning point in San Diego's 2-1 victory because Brown was so dominant. He worked eight scoreless innings, fell one short of Bob Gibson's post-season strikeout record and allowed only two harmless singles to No. 8 hitter Brad Ausmus. Brown struck out every Houston batter at least once, allowed only four balls out of the infield and held the Biggio-Bagwell-Bell-Alou quartet hitless in 11 at-bats with eight strikeouts. Johnson surrendered only a sixth-inning sacrifice fly to Leyritz and Greg Vaughn's eighth-inning home run, but the performance was not good enough to keep him from losing for the first time at the Astrodome after five regular-season victories there. The only Houston run was scored in the ninth inning off closer Trevor Hoffman on third baseman Ken Caminiti's throwing error.

Game 2: Ricky Gutierrez and Bill Spiers provided the save in the bottom of the ninth after closer Billy Wagner couldn't provide it in the top of the inning. After Wagner had surrendered a two-out, game-tying, two-run homer to pinch hitter Leyritz, Gutierrez led off the bottom of the ninth with an infield single. Ausmus sacrificed and Gutierrez shocked everybody on the field, a near-capacity Astrodome crowd and a national television audience by stealing third base on the first pitch from reliever Trevor Hoffman. With Gutierrez now stationed at third with less than two out, Hoffman walked Biggio intentionally and Spiers stroked his third hit of the night—a single to right that gave Houston a 5-4 victory and knotted the series at a game apiece.

Game 3: Leyritz struck again, delivering a seventh-inning, game-deciding homer off reliever Scott Elarton in the first contest at San Diego's Qualcomm Stadium. Leyritz broke a 1-1 tie with his 402-foot shot into the left field seats after Brown, working on three days' rest, had walked in the tying run in the top of the inning. The homer was the fifth in 14 play-off games for the opportunistic Leyritz, who had delivered a Game 4 winner for the New York Yankees that turned around the 1996 World Series against Atlanta. The home run was one of three hits surrendered by Mike Hampton and Elarton, but Brown, Dan Miceli and Hoffman limited the Astros to four.

Game 4: Miceli provided the lift in the clincher when he preserved a 2-1 Padres lead by striking out Ausmus with one out and the bases loaded in the seventh inning and forcing pinch hitter Carl Everett to pop out. Not only did Miceli preserve the lead, his strikeout of Ausmus forced Astros manager Larry Dierker to pinch hit for Johnson and the Padres put the game out of reach with four eighth-inning runs—two on John Vander Wal's triple and two more on Wally Joyner's home run. Miceli also had entered the seventh inning of Game 3 with the bases loaded and struck out Spiers. The Padres' first run off Johnson came on a second-inning homer by Leyritz—his third in as many games.

Notable:

Astros: When the Astros scored in the ninth inning of Game 2, they secured their 28th last-at-bat victory of the season. . . . The Game 2 win also snapped Houston's six-game playoff losing streak dating back to the 1986 NLCS against the New York Mets. . . . Bell's Game 2 home run ended an 0-for-20 post-season hitless streak dating back to the 1997 playoffs. . . . Johnson suffered two Division Series losses despite working 14 innings and allowing only three earned runs. The losses were his fourth and fifth straight in post-season play after winning his first two decisions.

Padres: The Game 3 crowd of 65,235 at Qualcomm Stadium was a Division Series record and the largest ever to see a baseball game in San Diego. . . . The only player remaining from the 1984 Padres team that lost to Detroit in the World Series was Tony Gwynn. But manager Bruce Bochy and coaches Tim Flannery and Greg Booker also played on that team. . . . When the Padres scored six runs in Game 4, it marked the first time in 17 games they had scored more than four.

Quotable:

Astros: Bagwell, after Brown had outdueled Johnson in Game 1: "I know we had our best guy out there, but they had their best guy, too. He can dominate as well as Randy.". . . Bagwell, on losing a series the Astros were expected to win: "It's just kind of hard for me to think about. It's just too devastating to even think about.". . . Johnson, on his series performance: "I didn't have my best stuff, but you give up three earned runs in 14 innings, you don't feel like you're going to lose too many ballgames."

Padres: Brown, after his 16-strikeout masterpiece: "I didn't think I had great stuff, but it must have been moving pretty good.". . . Gwynn, after his team's surprising victory: "Coming into this series, a lot of people wrote us off. And I'll be honest with you. I think the only people who thought we could win this thing were the players.". . . Leyritz, on his series performance: "I'm numb right now. I can't believe all that's gone on. I don't even want to think about it. Let it just keep rolling, man!"

GAME 1 BOX SCORE

SAN DIEGO 2, HOUSTON 1

TUESDAY, SEPTEMBER 29, AT HOUSTON

San Diego	AB	R	H	RBI	PO	A
Veras, 2b	4	0	0	0	0	2
Sheets, pr-2b	0	0	0	0	0	0
Gwynn, rf	3	1	1	0	0	0
Rivera, rf	2	0	0	0	2	0
Vaughn, lf	4	1	3	1	0	0
Caminiti, 3b	4	0	1	0	0	1
Leyritz, 1b	3	0	1	1	6	0
Joyner, 1b	0	0	0	0	1	0
Finley, cf	3	0	0	0	2	0
Hernandez, c	4	0	2	0	15	2
Gomez, ss	3	0	1	0	1	2
Brown, p	3	0	0	0	0	0
Vander Wal, ph	1	0	0	0	0	0
Hoffman, p	0	0	0	0	0	0
Totals	34	2	9	2	27	7

Houston	AB	R	H	RBI	PO	A
Biggio, 2b	2	0	0	0	0	4
Spiers, 3b	4	1	1	0	1	4
Bell, rf	4	0	0	0	4	0
Bagwell, 1b	4	0	0	0	6	1
Alou, lf	4	0	1	0	0	0
Everett, cf	4	0	0	0	3	0
Gutierrez, ss	3	0	0	0	1	1
Ausmus, c	3	0	2	0	12	0
Johnson, p	2	0	0	0	0	1
Clark, ph	0	0	0	0	0	0
Powell, p	0	0	0	0	0	0
Henry, p	0	0	0	0	0	0
Totals	30	1	4	0	27	8

San Diego	0	0	0	0	0	1	0	1	0—2
Houston	0	0	0	0	0	0	0	0	1—1

San Diego	IP	H	R	ER	BB	SO
Brown (W)	8.0	2	0	0	2	16
Hoffman (S)	1.0	2	1	0	0	1

Houston	IP	H	R	ER	BB	SO
Johnson (L)	8.0	9	2	2	1	9
Powell	0.2	0	0	0	1	1
Henry	0.1	0	0	0	0	1

E—Caminiti. DP—San Diego 1. LOB—San Diego 9, Houston 5. 2B—Gwynn, Spiers. HR—Vaughn. SF—Leyritz. CS—Vaughn. HBP—By Brown (Biggio), by Powell (Veras). WP—Powell. PB—Hernandez 2. T—2:38. A—50,080. U—Rapuano, plate; Kellogg, first; Darling, second; Davidson, third; Froemming, left field; Hernandez, right field.

GAME 2 BOX SCORE

HOUSTON 5, SAN DIEGO 4

THURSDAY, OCTOBER 1, AT HOUSTON

San Diego	AB	R	H	RBI	PO	A
Veras, 2b	3	1	1	0	2	4
Finley, cf	4	1	1	1	0	0
Gwynn, rf	4	0	1	1	2	0
Caminiti, 3b	4	1	1	0	0	0
Vaughn, lf	4	0	0	0	1	0
Joyner, 1b	3	0	0	0	12	0
Leyritz, ph-1b	1	1	1	2	1	0
Hernandez, c	4	0	2	0	6	3
Sheets, pr	0	0	0	0	0	0
Myers, c	0	0	0	0	0	0
Gomez, ss	4	0	1	0	1	4
Ashby, p	1	0	0	0	0	0
Vander Wal, ph	1	0	0	0	0	0
Hamilton, p	0	0	0	0	0	1
Sweeney, ph	1	0	0	0	0	0
Wall, p	0	0	0	0	0	1
Arias, ph	1	0	0	0	0	0
Miceli, p	0	0	0	0	0	1
Hoffman, p	0	0	0	0	0	0
Totals	35	4	8	4	25	14

Houston	AB	R	H	RBI	PO	A
Biggio, 2b	3	2	1	0	1	2
Spiers, 3b	5	1	3	1	0	3
Bell, rf	4	1	1	1	0	0
Bagwell, 1b	4	0	1	3	9	2
Alou, lf	4	0	0	0	1	0
Everett, cf	4	0	1	0	4	0
Eusebio, c	3	0	1	0	6	0
Wagner, p	0	0	0	0	0	0
Gutierrez, ss	4	1	3	0	3	3
Reynolds, p	2	0	0	0	0	2
Powell, p	0	0	0	0	2	0
Ausmus, c	0	0	0	1	1	0
Totals	33	5	11	5	27	12

San Diego	0	0	0	0	0	2	0	0	2—4
Houston	1	0	2	0	0	0	0	1	1—5

One out when winning run scored.

San Diego	IP	H	R	ER	BB	SO
Ashby	4.0	6	3	3	1	4
Hamilton	3.0	1	0	0	0	3
Wall	1.0	2	1	1	0	2
Miceli (L)	0.1	1	1	1	0	0
Hoffman	*0.0	1	0	0	1	0

Houston	IP	H	R	ER	BB	SO
Reynolds	7.0	4	2	2	1	5
Powell	1.0	0	0	0	0	1
Wagner (W)	1.0	4	2	2	0	1

*Pitched to three batters in ninth.

E—Joyner, Biggio. DP—San Diego 1, Houston 1. LOB—San Diego 5, Houston 8. 2B—Finley, Spiers 2, Eusebio. HR—Leyritz, Bell. SH—Reynolds, Ausmus. SB—Gutierrez. HBP—By Ashby (Eusebio). T—2:53. A—45,550. U—Kellogg, plate; Darling, first; Davidson, second; Froemming, third; Hernandez, left field; Rapuano, right field.

GAME 3 BOX SCORE

SAN DIEGO 2, HOUSTON 1

SATURDAY, OCTOBER 3, AT SAN DIEGO

Houston	AB	R	H	RBI	PO	A
Biggio, 2b	3	0	0	1	6	3
Spiers, 3b	3	0	0	0	0	1
Bell, rf	4	0	1	0	0	0
Bagwell, 1b	3	0	0	0	9	1
Alou, lf	4	0	2	0	1	0
Everett, cf	4	1	1	0	1	0
Gutierrez, ss	1	0	0	0	2	7
Ausmus, c	3	0	0	0	5	1
Incaviglia, ph	1	0	0	0	0	0
Hampton, p	2	0	0	0	0	1
Clark, ph	0	0	0	0	0	0
Elarton, p	0	0	0	0	0	0
Totals	28	1	4	1	24	14

San Diego	AB	R	H	RBI	PO	A
Veras, 2b	4	0	1	0	3	2
Gwynn, rf	4	0	0	1	2	1
Hoffman, p	0	0	0	0	0	0
Vaughn, lf	3	0	0	0	0	0
Caminiti, 3b	3	0	0	0	1	3
Leyritz, 1b	3	1	1	1	4	0
Joyner, 1b	0	0	0	0	1	0
Finley, cf	3	0	0	0	3	0
Hernandez, c	2	0	0	0	11	0
Gomez, ss	2	1	1	0	2	2
Brown, p	0	0	0	0	0	0
Miceli, p	0	0	0	0	0	0
Sweeney, ph	0	0	0	0	0	0
Rivera, rf	0	0	0	0	0	0
Totals	24	2	3	2	27	8

Houston									
Houston	0	0	0	0	0	0	1	0	0—1
San Diego	0	0	0	0	0	1	1	0	x—2

Houston	IP	H	R	ER	BB	SO
Hampton	6.0	2	1	1	1	2
Elarton (L)	2.0	1	1	1	1	3

San Diego	IP	H	R	ER	BB	SO
Brown	6.2	3	1	1	5	5
Miceli (W)	1.1	1	0	0	0	2
Hoffman (S)	1.0	0	0	0	0	3

DP—San Diego 2. LOB—Houston 7, San Diego 3. HR—Leyritz. SH—Brown 2. CS—Sweeney. HBP—By Brown 2 (Bagwell, Gutierrez), by Elarton (Hernandez). WP—Hampton. T—2:32. A—65,235. U—Layne, plate; Marsh, first; Pulli, second; Bell, third; Winters, left field; Hohn, right field.

GAME 4 BOX SCORE

SAN DIEGO 6, HOUSTON 1

SUNDAY, OCTOBER 4, AT SAN DIEGO

Houston	AB	R	H	RBI	PO	A
Biggio, 2b	3	1	1	0	2	1
Hidalgo, cf	4	0	1	0	1	0
Bell, rf	4	0	0	0	1	0
Bagwell, 1b	3	0	1	1	7	0
Alou, lf	4	0	0	0	2	0
Berry, 3b	2	0	0	0	0	2
Spiers, ph-3b	2	0	0	0	0	0

Houston	AB	R	H	RBI	PO	A
Gutierrez, ss	2	0	0	0	1	2
Ausmus, c	3	0	0	0	10	0
Johnson, p	2	0	0	0	0	1
Everett, ph	1	0	0	0	0	0
Miller, p	0	0	0	0	0	0
Henry, p	0	0	0	0	0	1
Powell, p	0	0	0	0	0	0
Totals	30	1	3	1	24	7

San Diego	AB	R	H	RBI	PO	A
Veras, 2b	4	0	0	0	3	4
Gwynn, rf	4	0	1	0	0	0
Finley, pr-cf	0	1	0	0	1	0
Vaughn, lf	4	1	2	0	1	0
Caminiti, 3b	3	1	0	0	1	1
Leyritz, c	3	1	1	1	11	0
Hamilton, p	0	0	0	0	0	0
Miceli, p	0	0	0	0	0	0
Vander Wal, ph	1	1	1	2	0	0
Hoffman, p	0	0	0	0	0	0
Joyner, 1b	3	1	1	2	5	1
Rivera, cf-rf	4	0	0	0	1	0
Gomez, ss	2	0	0	0	2	1
Hitchcock, p	2	0	0	0	0	0
Hernandez, c	2	0	1	0	2	1
Totals	32	6	7	5	27	8

Houston									
Houston	0	0	0	1	0	0	0	0	0—1
San Diego	0	1	0	0	0	1	0	4	x—6

Houston	IP	H	R	ER	BB	SO
Johnson (L)	6.0	3	2	1	1	8
Miller	*0.0	0	0	0	1	0
Henry	1.1	2	1	1	0	0
Powell	0.2	2	3	3	2	1

San Diego	IP	H	R	ER	BB	SO
Hitchcock (W)	6.0	3	1	1	0	11
Hamilton	0.1	0	0	0	2	0
Miceli	1.2	0	0	0	0	2
Hoffman	1.0	0	0	0	0	0

*Pitched to one batter in seventh.

E—Berry, Gomez. DP—San Diego 1. LOB—Houston 5, San Diego 6. 2B—Biggio, Vaughn, Gwynn. 3B—Vander Wal. HR—Leyritz, Joyner. HBP—By Hitchcock (Biggio). T—2:39. A—64,898. U—Marsh, plate; Pulli, first; Winters, second; Hohn, third; Layne, left field; Bell, right field.

STATISTICS

SAN DIEGO PADRES' BATTING AND FIELDING AVERAGES

Player, position	G	AB	R	H	TB	2B	3B	HR	RBI	BB	IBB	SO	Avg.	PO	A	E	Avg.
Hernandez, c	4	12	0	5	5	0	0	0	0	0	0	0	.417	34	6	0	1.000
Leyritz, 1b-ph-c	4	10	3	4	13	0	0	3	5	0	0	2	.400	22	0	0	1.000
Vander Wal, ph	3	3	1	1	3	0	1	0	2	0	0	1	.333	0	0	0	.000
Vaughn, lf	4	15	2	5	9	1	0	1	1	0	0	4	.333	2	0	0	1.000
Gomez, ss	4	11	1	3	3	0	0	0	0	4	0	1	.273	6	9	1	.938
Gwynn, rf	4	15	1	3	5	2	0	0	2	0	0	2	.200	4	1	0	1.000
Joyner, 1b	4	6	1	1	4	0	0	1	2	1	0	0	.167	19	1	1	.952
Caminiti, 3b	4	14	2	2	2	0	0	0	0	1	1	3	.143	2	5	1	.875
Veras, 2b	4	15	1	2	2	0	0	0	0	1	0	6	.133	8	12	0	1.000
Finley, cf-pr	4	10	2	1	2	1	0	0	1	1	0	4	.100	6	0	0	1.000
Arias, ph	1	1	0	0	0	0	0	0	0	0	0	1	.000	0	0	0	.000
Ashby, p	1	1	0	0	0	0	0	0	0	0	0	0	.000	0	0	0	.000
Brown, p	2	3	0	0	0	0	0	0	0	0	0	2	.000	0	0	0	.000
Myers, c	1	0	0	0	0	0	0	0	0	0	0	0	.000	0	0	0	.000
Hamilton, p	2	0	0	0	0	0	0	0	0	0	0	0	.000	0	1	0	1.000
Hitchcock, p	1	2	0	0	0	0	0	0	0	0	0	1	.000	0	0	0	.000
Hoffman, p	4	0	0	0	0	0	0	0	0	0	0	0	.000	0	0	0	.000
Miceli, p	3	0	0	0	0	0	0	0	0	0	0	0	.000	0	1	0	1.000
Rivera, rf-cf	3	6	0	0	0	0	0	0	0	0	0	3	.000	3	0	0	1.000
Sheets, pr-2b	2	0	0	0	0	0	0	0	0	0	0	0	.000	0	0	0	.000
Sweeney, ph	2	1	0	0	0	0	0	0	0	1	0	0	.000	0	0	0	.000
Wall, p	1	0	0	0	0	0	0	0	0	0	0	0	.000	0	1	0	1.000
Totals	4	125	14	27	48	4	1	5	13	9	1	32	.216	106	37	3	.979

SAN DIEGO PADRES' PITCHING RECORDS

Pitcher	G	GS	CG	IP	H	R	ER	HR	BB	IBB	SO	HB	WP	W	L	Pct.	ERA
Hamilton	2	0	0	3.1	1	0	0	0	2	1	3	0	0	0	0	.000	0.00
Hoffman	4	0	0	3.0	3	1	0	0	1	1	4	0	0	0	0	.000	0.00
Brown	2	2	0	14.2	5	1	1	0	7	0	21	3	0	1	0	1.000	0.61
Hitchcock	1	1	0	6.0	3	1	1	0	0	0	11	1	0	1	0	1.000	1.50
Miceli	3	0	0	3.1	2	1	1	0	0	0	4	0	0	1	1	.500	2.70
Ashby	1	1	0	4.0	6	3	3	0	1	0	4	1	0	0	0	.000	6.75
Wall	1	0	0	1.0	2	1	1	1	0	0	2	0	0	0	0	.000	9.00
Totals	4	4	0	35.1	22	8	7	1	11	2	49	5	0	3	1	.750	1.78

No shutouts. Saves—Hoffman 2.

HOUSTON ASTROS' BATTING AND FIELDING AVERAGES

Player, position	G	AB	R	H	TB	2B	3B	HR	RBI	BB	IBB	SO	Avg.	PO	A	E	Avg.
Eusebio, c	1	3	0	1	2	1	0	0	0	0	0	2	.333	6	0	0	1.000
Gutierrez, ss	4	10	1	3	3	0	0	0	0	3	1	7	.300	7	13	0	1.000
Spiers, 3b-ph	4	14	2	4	7	3	0	0	1	1	0	3	.286	1	5	0	1.000
Hidalgo, cf	1	4	0	1	1	0	0	0	0	0	0	1	.250	1	0	0	1.000
Ausmus, c	4	9	0	2	2	0	0	0	0	0	0	4	.222	28	1	0	1.000
Alou, lf	4	16	0	3	3	0	0	0	0	0	0	2	.188	4	0	0	1.000
Biggio, 2b	4	11	3	2	3	1	0	0	1	4	1	4	.182	9	10	1	.950
Everett, cf-ph	4	13	1	2	2	0	0	0	0	0	0	4	.154	8	0	0	1.000
Bagwell, 1b	4	14	0	2	2	0	0	0	4	1	0	6	.143	31	4	0	1.000
Bell, rf	4	16	1	2	5	0	0	1	1	0	0	7	.125	5	0	0	1.000
Berry, 3b	1	2	0	0	0	0	0	0	0	0	0	1	.000	0	2	1	.667
Clark, ph	2	0	0	0	0	0	0	0	0	2	0	0	.000	0	0	0	.000
Elarton, p	1	0	0	0	0	0	0	0	0	0	0	0	.000	0	0	0	.000
Hampton, p	1	2	0	0	0	0	0	0	0	0	0	2	.000	0	1	0	1.000
Henry, p	2	0	0	0	0	0	0	0	0	0	0	0	.000	0	1	0	1.000
Incaviglia, ph	1	1	0	0	0	0	0	0	0	0	0	1	.000	0	0	0	.000
Johnson, p	2	4	0	0	0	0	0	0	0	0	0	4	.000	0	2	0	1.000
Powell, p	3	0	0	0	0	0	0	0	0	0	0	0	.000	2	0	0	1.000
Reynolds, p	1	2	0	0	0	0	0	0	0	0	0	1	.000	0	2	0	1.000
Miller, p	1	0	0	0	0	0	0	0	0	0	0	0	.000	0	0	0	.000
Wagner, p	1	0	0	0	0	0	0	0	0	0	0	0	.000	0	0	0	.000
Totals	4	121	8	22	30	5	0	1	7	11	2	49	.182	102	41	2	.986

HOUSTON ASTROS' PITCHING RECORDS

Pitcher	G	GS	CG	IP	H	R	ER	HR	BB	IBB	SO	HB	WP	W	L	Pct.	ERA
Miller	1	0	0	0.0	0	0	0	0	1	0	0	0	0	0	0	.000	0.00
Hampton	1	1	0	6.0	2	1	1	0	1	0	2	0	1	0	0	.000	1.50
Johnson	2	2	0	14.0	12	4	3	2	2	0	17	0	0	0	2	.000	1.93
Reynolds	1	1	0	7.0	4	2	2	0	1	0	5	0	0	0	0	.000	2.57
Elarton	1	0	0	2.0	1	1	1	1	1	0	3	1	0	0	1	.000	4.50
Henry	2	0	0	1.2	2	1	1	0	0	0	1	0	0	0	0	.000	5.40
Powell	3	0	0	2.1	2	3	3	1	3	1	3	1	1	0	0	.000	11.57
Wagner	1	0	0	1.0	4	2	2	1	0	0	1	0	0	1	0	1.000	18.00
Totals	4	4	0	34.0	27	14	13	5	9	1	32	2	2	1	3	.250	3.44

No shutouts or saves.

SCORE BY INNINGS

San Diego	0	1	0	0	0	5	1	5	2	—14
Houston	1	0	2	1	0	0	1	1	2	— 8

MISCELLANEOUS STATISTICS

Sacrifice hits—Brown 2, Ausmus, Reynolds.
Sacrifice fly—Leyritz.
Stolen base—Gutierrez.
Caught stealing—Sweeney, Vaughn.
Double plays—Veras, Gomez and Joyner 2; Gomez, Veras and Joyner; Reynolds, Gutierrez and Bagwell; Veras, Gomez and Leyritz; Veras and Leyritz.
Left on bases—San Diego 9, 5, 3, 6—23; Houston 5, 8, 7, 5—25.
Hit by pitcher—Biggio 2, Bagwell, Eusebio, Gutierrez, Hernandez, Veras.
Passed balls—Hernandez 2.
Balks—None.
Time of games—First game, 2:38; second game, 2:53; third game, 2:32; fourth game, 2:39.
Attendance—First game, 50,080; second game, 45,550; third game, 65,235; fourth game, 64,898.
Umpires—Rapuano, Kellogg, Darling, Davidson, Froemming, Hernandez, Layne, Marsh, Pulli, Bell, Winters and Hohn.
Official scorers—Rick Blount, Bill Zavestoski.

ATLANTA VS. CHICAGO

The bottom line: Atlanta swept past the outmanned Chicago Cubs and into its seventh straight N.L. Championship Series, thanks to the 1-2-3 pitching punch of John Smoltz, Tom Glavine and Greg M addux, the clutch work of an oft-maligned bullpen and a timely Game 2 offensive lift from catcher Javy Lopez. The Cubs manufactured only four runs in their first post-season venture since 1989 after earning the N.L. wild-card berth with a victory over San Francisco in a special one-game playoff. The N.L. East Division-champion Braves continued their first-round playoff domination by lifting their Division Series record to 12-1 with their third consecutive sweep.

Why the Braves won: "It all starts with pitching. That's how you do it," said Braves manager Bobby Cox after watching his Big Three starters limit the Cubs to 15 hits over 21.2 innings and his bullpen hold them to two hits over 6.1 scoreless innings. Chicago right fielder Sammy Sosa, who had hit 66 home runs and driven in a major league-high 158 runs in the regular season, was held to a double and single in 11 non-productive at-bats. The series turned in Game 2 when the Cubs and righthander Kevin Tapani carried a 1-0 lead into the bottom of the ninth inning at Atlanta's Turner Field, only to see the Braves rally for an extra-inning victory.

The turning points:

Game 1: An errant second-inning forkball that Cubs starter Mark Clark tried to bounce ended up in the right field stands, courtesy of Braves right fielder Michael Tucker. With a runner on second base, two out and pitcher Smoltz in the on-deck circle, Clark wanted to see if Tucker would chase a 3-2 pitch out of the strike zone. But he got the pitch too close and Tucker gave Smoltz all the runs he needed for an opening 7-1 victory. Smoltz, who allowed only an eighth-inning home run to Chicago catcher Tyler Houston, was in complete command over the weary Cubs, who had defeated the Giants a day earlier in their one-game regular season-extending wild-card playoff. Smoltz also benefited from superb defense and a victory-securing seventh-inning grand slam by Ryan Klesko off Chicago reliever Matt Karchner. Smoltz held Mark Grace, Henry Rodriguez and Gary Gaetti—the Cubs' fourth, fifth and sixth hitters—hitless in 11 at-bats.

Game 2: One out, bottom of the ninth. The Braves trail Tapani and the Cubs, 1-0. No problem. Lopez brought the largest crowd in Turner Field history to life by drilling a Tapani pitch into the left-center field seats, and the Cubs self-destructed in an ugly 10th inning that allowed the Braves to gain a two-games-to-none series advantage before heading for Chicago's Wrigley Field. The Cubs missed a golden opportunity to regain the lead in the top of the 10th when former Braves shortstop Jeff Blauser, pinch-hitting with one out and runners on first and third,

swung through a 3-2 pitch from Odaliz Perez and watched Mickey Morandini get thrown out trying to steal second base. In the bottom of the 10th, the Cubs botched a sacrifice bunt by Tony Graffanino, and Chipper Jones followed with a game-winning single down the left field line. It was a rocky ending to what had been an outstanding pitching duel between Tapani and Glavine.

Game 3: Maddux held Chicago scoreless through seven innings, but he also made a major contribution with his bat. He doubled in the third inning off Cubs rookie Kerry Wood, moved to third on a groundout and scored on a passed ball. He made that run stand up until the eighth when the Braves broke through for five more, four coming on catcher Eddie Perez's grand slam off Chicago ace reliever Rod Beck. Maddux's 6-2 victory, which was secured by two scoreless innings of relief by Kerry Ligtenberg, came at the expense of the team and the city he had abandoned as a free agent after his 1992 Cy Young season.

Notable:

Cubs: The Cubs finished the regular season with six wins in nine games against Atlanta—the best record of any N.L. team against the Braves. . . . The Cubs tacked on another year to their dubious distinction of not having won a post-season series since capturing the 1908 World Series. Entering the series, the Braves had played 72 post-season games since the Cubs had made their last playoff appearance. . . . Chicago's six-game playoff losing streak dates back to Game 2 of the 1989 NLCS against the Giants. . . . Wood, who had been battling a tender elbow, made his first appearance since August 31 in Game 3 and pitched five solid innings in a losing cause. . . . First baseman Grace, the only holdover from the Cubs' 1989 playoff team, was a disappointing 1-for-12 against the Braves.

Braves: Game 1 victor Smoltz became the winningest post-season pitcher in baseball history. He lifted his record to 11-3 in 21 starts, breaking the record he shared with Whitey Ford and Dave Stewart. . . . Game 2 drew a Turner Field record crowd of 51,713—6,000 more than attended Game 1. . . . When the Cubs scored in the sixth inning of Game 2, it marked the first time the Braves had trailed in a Division Series game since 1996—a span of 44.1 innings. . . . Game 2 starter Glavine did not allow a hit through six innings, and only one ball was hit out of the infield.

Quotable:

Cubs: Manager Jim Riggleman on his decision to stay with Kevin Tapani in the ninth inning of Game 2 instead of going to his bullpen: "It was a tough decision. When you've got a guy like Beck, it's a great temptation to turn it over to him. I just felt Tap . . . was at the top of his game.". . . Reliever Terry Mulholland, the loser in tough-luck Game 2: "They didn't beat us. We beat us."

Braves: Maddux, on how he likes pitching at Wrigley Field, his former home park: "Time flies. This is a great park. I love pitching here with the atmosphere and the history I had in this park, but it's pretty hard for me sometimes." . . . Manager Cox, on the Braves' playoff success in the 1990s: "It's really something. Maybe someday this will sink in, but it hasn't yet. It's something that's going to be hard for just about any other club to do with the current format."

GAME 1 BOX SCORE

ATLANTA 7, CHICAGO 1
WEDNESDAY, SEPTEMBER 30, AT ATLANTA

Chicago	AB	R	H	RBI	PO	A
Johnson, cf	4	0	1	0	2	0
Morandini, 2b	3	0	0	0	0	2
Sosa, rf	4	0	2	0	2	0
Grace, 1b	4	0	0	0	7	1
Rodriguez, lf	3	0	0	0	1	0
Gaetti, 3b	4	0	0	0	0	1
Houston, c	3	1	1	1	6	0
Hernandez, ss	3	0	0	0	5	0
Clark, p	2	0	1	0	1	0
Heredia, p	0	0	0	0	0	1
Karchner, p	0	0	0	0	0	0
Blauser, ph	1	0	0	0	0	0
Morgan, p	0	0	0	0	0	0
Totals	31	1	5	1	24	5
Atlanta	AB	R	H	RBI	PO	A
Weiss, ss	4	1	1	0	0	1
Lockhart, 2b	3	1	1	0	2	3
C. Jones, 3b	3	1	0	0	1	2
Galarraga, 1b	4	1	1	0	6	0
Klesko, lf	4	1	2	4	2	0
Bautista, lf	0	0	0	0	2	0
Lopez, c	4	0	1	0	8	1
A. Jones, cf	3	1	0	1	3	0
Tucker, rf	4	1	1	2	3	0
Ligtenberg, p	0	0	0	0	0	0
Smoltz, p	2	0	1	0	0	0
Rocker, p	0	0	0	0	0	0
Colbrunn, ph	1	0	0	0	0	0
Williams, rf	0	0	0	0	0	0
Totals	32	7	8	7	27	7

Chicago	0	0 0	0 0 0	0 1	0—1
Atlanta	0	2 0	0 0 1	4 0	x—7

Chicago	IP	H	R	ER	BB	SO
Clark (L)	*6.0	7	4	2	1	4
Heredia	0.1	0	2	2	2	0
Karchner	0.2	1	1	1	0	1
Morgan	1.0	0	0	0	0	1
Atlanta	IP	H	R	ER	BB	SO
Smoltz (W)	7.2	5	1	1	0	6
Rocker	0.1	0	0	0	0	0
Ligtenberg	1.0	0	0	0	2	2

*Pitched to one batter in seventh.
E—Hernandez. LOB—Chicago 5, Atlanta 5. 2B—Sosa. HR—Houston, Tucker, Klesko. SF—A. Jones. SB—A. Jones. CS—Sosa. T—2:34. A—45,598. U—Winters, plate; Hohn, first; Layne, second; Marsh, third; Pulli, left field; Bell, right field.

GAME 2 BOX SCORE

ATLANTA 2, CHICAGO 1
THURSDAY, OCTOBER 1, AT ATLANTA

Chicago	AB	R	H	RBI	PO	A
Johnson, cf	4	0	0	1	4	0
Alexander, ss	4	0	0	0	2	2
Grace, 1b	4	0	0	0	6	1
Sosa, rf	3	0	0	0	3	0
Hill, lf	3	0	1	0	3	0

Chicago	AB	R	H	RBI	PO	A
Gaetti, 3b	3	0	0	0	1	3
Morandini, 2b	3	1	1	0	3	1
Servais, c	3	0	2	0	6	1
Rodriguez, ph	0	0	0	0	0	0
Blauser, ph	1	0	0	0	0	0
Mulholland, p	0	0	0	0	0	0
Tapani, p	1	0	0	0	0	1
Houston, c	0	0	0	0	0	0
Totals	29	1	4	1	28	9
Atlanta	AB	R	H	RBI	PO	A
Weiss, ss	4	1	0	0	5	0
Lockhart, 2b	4	0	1	0	5	3
Graffanino, ph	0	0	0	0	0	0
C. Jones, 3b	4	0	1	0	1	0
Galarraga, 1b	4	0	1	0	3	2
Klesko, lf	4	0	1	0	2	0
Lopez, c	3	1	1	1	12	2
A. Jones, cf	4	0	0	0	1	0
Tucker, rf	3	0	1	0	1	0
Glavine, p	1	0	0	0	0	1
Guillen, ph	1	0	0	0	0	0
Rocker, p	0	0	0	0	0	0
Seanez, p	0	0	0	0	0	0
Ligtenberg, p	0	0	0	0	0	0
O. Perez, p	0	0	0	0	0	0
Colbrunn, ph	1	0	0	0	0	0
Totals	33	2	6	2	30	8

Chicago	0 0 0	0 0 1	0 0 0	0—1
Atlanta	0 0 0	0 0 0	0 0 1	1—2

One out when winning run scored.

Chicago	IP	H	R	ER	BB	SO
Tapani	9.0	5	1	1	3	6
Mulholland (L)	0.1	1	1	1	1	0
Atlanta	IP	H	R	ER	BB	SO
Glavine	7.0	3	1	1	1	8
Rocker	1.0	1	0	0	0	2
Seanez	1.0	0	0	0	0	0
Ligtenberg	0.1	0	0	0	2	0
O. Perez (W)	0.2	0	0	0	0	1

E—Mulholland. DP—Atlanta 2. LOB—Chicago 4, Atlanta 9. HR—Lopez. SH—Tapani 2, Gaetti, Glavine, Graffanino. SB—Hill, Tucker. CS—Sosa, Morandini. Balk—Tapani. T—2:47. A—51,713. U—Hohn, plate; Layne, first; Marsh, second; Pulli, third; Bell, left field; Winters, right field.

GAME 3 BOX SCORE

ATLANTA 2, CHICAGO 1
SATURDAY, OCTOBER 3, AT CHICAGO

Atlanta	AB	R	H	RBI	PO	A
Weiss, ss	5	0	1	0	1	2
Lockhart, 2b	5	1	2	0	2	3
C. Jones, 3b	3	1	1	0	0	0
Galarraga, 1b	4	0	1	0	8	3
Klesko, lf	3	0	0	0	1	0
Williams, rf	2	1	1	1	2	0
A. Jones, cf	2	1	0	0	4	0
E. Perez, c	5	1	1	4	6	0
Tucker, rf	1	0	0	0	2	0
Bautista, lf	2	0	1	0	0	0
Maddux, p	4	1	1	0	1	2
Ligtenberg, p	0	0	0	0	0	0
Totals	36	6	9	5	27	10
Chicago	AB	R	H	RBI	PO	A
Johnson, cf	4	0	1	0	4	0
Morandini, 2b	3	0	1	1	2	0
Sosa, rf	4	0	0	0	0	0
Grace, 1b	4	0	1	1	7	0
Rodriguez, lf	4	0	1	0	4	1
Gaetti, 3b	4	0	1	0	1	2
Houston, c	3	0	0	0	7	0
Beck, p	0	0	0	0	0	1
Morgan, p	0	0	0	0	0	0
Alexander, ph	1	0	0	0	0	0
Hernandez, ss	4	1	2	0	0	1
Wood, p	1	0	0	0	1	0
Brown, ph	1	0	0	0	0	0

Chicago	AB	R	H	RBI	PO	A
Mulholland, p	0	0	0	0	0	1
Martinez, c	1	1	1	0	1	0
Totals	34	2	8	2	27	6

Atlanta	0 0 1	0 0 0	0 5 0—6
Chicago	0 0 0	0 0 0	0 2 0—2

Atlanta	IP	H	R	ER	BB	SO
Maddux (W)	*7.0	7	2	2	0	4
Ligtenberg	2.0	1	0	0	0	1

Chicago	IP	H	R	ER	BB	SO
Wood (L)	5.0	3	1	1	4	5
Mulholland	†2.0	1	2	2	1	2
Beck	1.2	5	3	3	2	1
Morgan	0.1	0	0	0	0	0

*Pitched to three batters in eighth.
†Pitched to two batters in eighth.

E—Gaetti, Hernandez. DP—Chicago 1. LOB—Atlanta 10, Chicago 6. 2B—Maddux, Bautista, Rodriguez. HR—E. Perez. SF—Morandini. SB—A. Jones. PB—Houston. T—2:57. A—39,597. U—Darling, plate; Davidson, first; Froemming, second; Hernandez, third; Rapuano, left field; Kellogg, right field.

STATISTICS

ATLANTA BRAVES' BATTING AND FIELDING AVERAGES

Player, position	G	AB	R	H	TB	2B	3B	HR	RBI	BB	IBB	SO	Avg.	PO	A	E	Avg.
Bautista, lf	2	2	0	1	2	1	0	0	0	0	0	0	.500	2	0	0	1.000
Smoltz, p	1	2	0	1	1	0	0	0	0	1	0	1	.500	0	0	0	.000
Williams, rf	2	2	1	1	1	0	0	0	1	0	0	1	.500	2	0	0	1.000
Lockhart, 2b	3	12	2	4	4	0	0	0	0	1	0	0	.333	9	9	0	1.000
Lopez, c	2	7	1	2	5	0	0	1	1	1	0	1	.286	20	3	0	1.000
Klesko, lf	3	11	1	3	6	0	0	1	4	0	0	3	.273	5	0	0	1.000
Galarraga, 1b	3	12	1	3	3	0	0	0	0	1	0	3	.250	17	5	0	1.000
Maddux, p	1	4	1	1	2	1	0	0	0	0	0	1	.250	1	2	0	1.000
Tucker, rf	3	8	1	2	5	0	0	1	2	2	1	0	.250	6	0	0	1.000
C. Jones, 3b	3	10	2	2	2	0	0	0	1	4	0	3	.200	2	2	0	1.000
E. Perez, c	1	5	1	1	4	0	0	1	4	0	0	2	.200	6	0	0	1.000
Weiss, ss	3	13	2	2	2	0	0	0	0	1	0	3	.154	6	3	0	1.000
A. Jones, cf	3	9	2	0	0	0	0	0	1	3	1	2	.000	8	0	0	1.000
Colbrunn, ph	2	2	0	0	0	0	0	0	0	0	0	0	.000	0	0	0	.000
Glavine, p	1	1	0	0	0	0	0	0	0	0	0	0	.000	0	1	0	1.000
Graffanino, ph	1	0	0	0	0	0	0	0	0	0	0	0	.000	0	0	0	.000
Guillen, ph	1	1	0	0	0	0	0	0	0	0	0	0	.000	0	0	0	.000
Ligtenberg, p	3	0	0	0	0	0	0	0	0	0	0	0	.000	0	0	0	.000
O. Perez, p	1	0	0	0	0	0	0	0	0	0	0	0	.000	0	0	0	.000
Rocker, p	2	0	0	0	0	0	0	0	0	0	0	0	.000	0	0	0	.000
Seanez, p	1	0	0	0	0	0	0	0	0	0	0	0	.000	0	0	0	.000
Totals	3	101	15	23	37	2	0	4	14	14	2	20	.228	84	25	0	1.000

ATLANTA BRAVES' PITCHING RECORDS

Pitcher	G	GS	CG	IP	H	R	ER	HR	BB	IBB	SO	HB	WP	W	L	Pct.	ERA
Ligtenberg	3	0	0	3.1	1	0	0	0	4	1	3	0	0	0	0	.000	0.00
Rocker	2	0	0	1.1	1	0	0	0	2	0	0	0	0	0	0	.000	0.00
Seanez	1	0	0	1.0	0	0	0	0	0	0	0	0	0	0	0	.000	0.00
O. Perez	1	0	0	0.2	0	0	0	0	0	1	0	0	1	0	0	.000	0.00
Smoltz	1	1	0	7.2	5	1	1	1	0	0	6	0	0	1	0	1.000	1.17
Glavine	1	1	0	7.0	3	1	1	0	1	0	8	0	0	0	0	.000	1.29
Maddux	1	1	0	7.0	7	2	2	0	0	0	4	0	0	1	0	1.000	2.57
Totals	3	3	0	28.0	17	4	4	1	5	1	24	0	0	3	0	1.000	1.29

No shutouts or saves.

CHICAGO CUBS' BATTING AND FIELDING AVERAGES

Player, position	G	AB	R	H	TB	2B	3B	HR	RBI	BB	IBB	SO	Avg.	PO	A	E	Avg.
Martinez, c	1	1	1	1	1	0	0	0	0	0	0	0	1.000	1	0	0	1.000
Servais, c	1	3	0	2	2	0	0	0	0	0	0	0	.667	6	1	0	1.000
Clark, p	1	2	0	1	1	0	0	0	0	0	0	0	.500	1	0	0	1.000
Hill, lf	1	3	0	1	1	0	0	0	0	1	0	2	.333	3	0	0	1.000
Hernandez, ss	2	7	1	2	2	0	0	0	0	0	0	2	.286	5	1	2	.875
Morandini, 2b	3	9	1	2	2	0	0	0	1	2	1	2	.222	5	3	0	1.000
Sosa, rf	3	11	0	2	3	1	0	0	1	0	0	4	.182	5	0	0	1.000
Houston, c	3	6	1	1	4	0	0	1	1	0	0	3	.167	13	0	0	1.000
Johnson, cf	3	12	0	2	2	0	0	0	1	0	0	1	.167	10	0	0	1.000
Rodriguez, lf-ph	3	7	0	1	2	1	0	0	0	1	0	2	.143	5	1	0	1.000
Gaetti, 3b	3	11	0	1	1	0	0	0	0	0	0	4	.091	2	6	1	.889
Grace, 1b	3	12	0	1	1	0	0	0	1	0	0	2	.083	20	2	0	1.000
Alexander, ss-ph	2	5	0	0	0	0	0	0	0	0	0	1	.000	2	2	0	1.000
Beck, p	1	0	0	0	0	0	0	0	0	0	0	0	.000	0	1	0	1.000
Blauser, ph	2	2	0	0	0	0	0	0	0	0	0	1	.000	0	0	0	.000
Brown, p	1	1	0	0	0	0	0	0	0	0	0	0	.000	0	0	0	.000
Heredia, p	1	0	0	0	0	0	0	0	0	0	0	0	.000	0	1	0	1.000
Karchner, p	1	0	0	0	0	0	0	0	0	0	0	0	.000	0	0	0	.000

Player, position	G	AB	R	H	TB	2B	3B	HR	RBI	BB	IBB	SO	Avg.	PO	A	E	Avg.
Morgan, p	2	0	0	0	0	0	0	0	0	0	0	0	.000	0	0	0	.000
Mulholland, p	2	0	0	0	0	0	0	0	0	0	0	0	.000	0	1	1	.500
Tapani, p	1	1	0	0	0	0	0	0	0	0	0	0	.000	0	1	0	1.000
Wood, p	1	1	0	0	0	0	0	0	0	0	0	0	.000	1	0	0	1.000
Totals	3	94	4	17	22	2	0	1	4	5	1	24	.181	79	20	4	.961

CHICAGO CUBS' PITCHING RECORDS

Pitcher	G	GS	CG	IP	H	R	ER	HR	BB	IBB	SO	HB	WP	W	L	Pct.	ERA
Morgan	2	0	0	1.1	0	0	0	0	0	0	1	0	0	0	0	.000	0.00
Tapani	1	1	0	9.0	5	1	1	1	3	0	6	0	0	0	0	.000	1.00
Wood	1	1	0	5.0	3	1	1	0	4	1	5	0	0	0	1	.000	1.80
Clark	1	1	0	6.0	7	4	2	1	1	0	4	0	0	0	1	.000	3.00
Mulholland	2	0	0	2.1	2	3	3	0	2	0	2	0	0	0	1	.000	11.57
Karchner	1	0	0	0.2	1	1	1	1	0	0	1	0	0	0	0	.000	13.50
Beck	1	0	0	1.2	5	3	3	1	2	1	1	0	0	0	0	.000	16.20
Heredia	1	0	0	0.1	0	2	2	0	2	0	0	0	0	0	0	.000	54.00
Totals	3	3	0	26.1	23	15	13	4	14	2	20	0	0	0	3	.000	4.44

No shutouts or saves.

SCORE BY INNINGS

```
Atlanta .................................................................................................0  2  1    0  0  1    4  5  1    1 —15
Chicago .................................................................................................0  0  0    0  0  1    0  3  0    0 — 4
```

MISCELLANEOUS STATISTICS

Sacrifice hits—Tapani 2, Gaetti, Glavine, Graffanino.
Sacrifice flies—A. Jones, Morandini.
Stolen bases—A. Jones 2, Hill, Tucker.
Caught stealing—Sosa 2, Morandini.
Double plays—Lopez and Weiss 2; Rodriguez, Hernandez and Morandini.
Left on bases—Atlanta 5, 9, 10—24; Chicago 5, 4, 6—15.
Hit by pitcher—None.
Passed ball—Houston.
Balk—Tapani.
Time of games—First game, 2:34; second game, 2:47; third game, 2:57.
Attendance—First game, 45,598; second game, 51,713; third game, 39,597.
Umpires—Winters, Hohn, Layne, Marsh, Pulli, Bell, Darling, Davidson, Froemming, Hernandez, Rapuano and Kellogg.
Official scorers—Mark Frederickson, Don Friske.

1998 REVIEW N.L. Division Series

A.L. CHAMPIONSHIP SERIES

The bottom line: The Yankees added another chapter to their storybook season by capturing the American League championship in a six-game battle against the Cleveland Indians. The Yankees, 1996 World Series champions, improved their 1998 record to 121-50 (.708), even though they got plenty of resistance from the Tribe, the defending A.L. champions. Outstanding pitching performances by Charles Nagy in Game 2 and Bartolo Colon in Game 3 put Cleveland up two games to one and gave Cleveland fans hope for a shocking upset of the Yankees. But New York responded by winning three straight games, two of them in Cleveland, and advanced to World Series play for a record 35th time.

Why the Yankees won: Despite a valiant effort, Cleveland simply didn't have the starting pitching to hang with the Yankees. The Yankees have five pitchers who could be No. 1 or No. 2 starters on most Major League teams and two were solid Cy Young candidates in 1998. The Indians were overmatched by the Yankees hitters and three starters failed to make it past the third inning. The underrated Indians hitters might have matched up well on paper against the Yankees, but they rarely were able to string together hits against the tough New York staff.

The turning points:

Game 1: Revenge from the start. The Yankees scored an ALCS-record five runs in the first inning off Cleveland starter Jaret Wright, who was masterful against the Yankees in the 1997 Division Series. This was more than enough support for David Wells, who did not allow a run until the ninth inning of a 7-2 Yankees victory in New York. Chuck Knoblauch, Derek Jeter, Paul O'Neill and Bernie Williams, all of whom had struggled in a Division Series victory over Texas, led off the first with singles and the Yankees went on to bat around, collecting six singles and a walk while chasing Wright. The Cleveland right-hander lasted two-thirds of an inning—the worst ALCS start since 1976. There was no such problem for Wells, who retired 11 straight Indians at one stretch and 15 of 16. He had worked 23 consecutive shutout post-season innings before allowing a two-run, ninth-inning home run to Manny Ramirez.

Game 2: A seemingly harmless bunt down the first-base line turned out to be the difference in the Indians' 4-1, 12-inning victory in New York. With pinch runner Enrique Wilson stationed on first with no one out in the top of the 12th, Travis Fryman laid down a bunt that first baseman Tino Martinez fielded inside the line. Martinez fired the ball to second baseman Knoblauch covering the bag, but it hit Fryman in the back and caromed 20 feet away. Fryman appeared to be running illegally inside the baseline, but umpire Ted Hendry did not call interference. Knoblauch, instead of chasing the ball, argued the non-call with Hendry, allowing Wilson to score all the way from first. Kenny Lofton added a two-run single moments later for the final margin. It was an ugly ending for what had otherwise been a well-played game that featured Nagy and David Cone in a good, old-fashioned pitching duel.

Game 3: With the Indians leading 2-1 in the fifth inning, Yankees starter Andy Pettitte unraveled, allowing three homers and four runs in a 13-pitch sequence that sent him to the bench in disbelief and the Yankees into a 2-1 hole with two games remaining at Jacobs Field. However, the star of the Indians' 6-1 victory was not a hitter, but 23-year-old Colon, who fired a complete-game four-hitter. Colon, who can throw the ball in the upper 90s, held the Yankee 2-through-8 hitters to 1-for-21 while earning his first post-season win. With two out in the Indians' fifth, Ramirez hit a solo homer to right. Jim Thome added a two-run homer, his second homer of the day, two batters later and former Yankee Mark Whiten hit a 416-foot shot to left to end the barrage against Pettitte.

Game 4: The game's big moment came in the Indians' half of the sixth inning. After retiring nine consecutive batters and resting comfortably on a 3-0 lead with one out, Yankees starter Orlando Hernandez allowed a single to Omar Vizquel and hit David Justice with a pitch, setting the table for Cleveland's power men—Ramirez and Thome. But Hernandez went right at the sluggers, striking out both and preserving the lead. Reliever Mike Stanton faced the same odds in the eighth, but got out of trouble with a double-play ball. Hernandez, a 29-year-old Cuban defector and the older brother of 1997 World Series MVP Livan Hernandez, combined with Stanton and Mariano Rivera for the 4-0 shutout at Jacobs Field and pulled the Yankees out of their 2-1 hole.

Game 5: A wild three-run first inning highlighted the Yankees' 5-3 victory in Cleveland. Indians starter Chad Ogea struggled early, loading the bases with one out. New York DH Chili Davis hit a high bouncer up the middle, a sure double-play ball for Gold Glove shortstop Vizquel. But Ogea, seeing Knoblauch break from third, lunged for the ball and deflected it into left field, allowing two runs to score. A Tim Raines groundout added another first-inning run, turning a potential double-play ball into a three-run lead. Wells also allowed two runs in the first, but he settled down and pitched the Yankees to victory, improving his post-season record to 7-1—4-0 against Cleveland.

Game 6: After a five-run fifth inning off starter David Cone brought the Indians back to within a run, the Yankees responded with three sixth-inning insurance runs and clinched the series with a 9-5 victory at Yankee Stadium. The key play in the winning rally came when Ramirez misjudged a Jeter fly ball and allowed it to hit the base of the wall. Jeter was credited with a two-run triple and eventually scored to give the Yankees a four-run lead—plenty of insurance for a bullpen that allowed just three earned runs in 33.2 innings over nine post-season games. Thome's towering third-deck grand slam off Cone was the big Cleveland highlight.

Notable:

Indians: Wright had hit Luis Sojo with a pitch during spring training, breaking a bone in his hand. He also had beaned O'Neill during the season. The Yankees would use these infractions as added incentive for their Game 1 barrage against Wright. . . . Dwight Gooden holds the distinction of having made the most career post-season starts (nine) without a victory. . . . Hargrove was forced to start three rookies in Game 5 because of injuries. Richie Sexson, Einar Diaz and Wilson went a combined 1-for-10. . . . Vizquel's Game 6 throwing error snapped a 46-game playoff errorless streak, spanning 237 chances.

Yankees: Before Ramirez's ninth-inning homer in Game 1, the Yankees had set a team record with 21 consecutive shutout innings in post-season play, surpassing their 20 scoreless innings against the New York Giants in the 1921 World Series. . . . The Yankees batted around for the 37th time in 1998 in the first inning of Game 1. . . . With the Game 4 victory, the Yankees broke the all-time record for wins in a year (119). . . . After Game 4, the Yankees were batting just .194 in the Postseason after .288 in the regular season. . . . Wells was named ALCS MVP, thanks to his 2-0 record and 2.87 ERA. . . . The pennant brought a World Series to New York for the 49th time in the 94 years a fall classic has been played.

Quotable:

Indians: Ogea, on the balanced Yankees lineup: "I looked and saw Scott Brosius batting ninth and I thought, 'This is a guy who would be hitting third or fourth for most teams!' " . . . David Justice, on Wilson stumbling between third and home before scoring the go-ahead run in Game 2: "Man, he had a monkey on his back and a sniper started shooting at him." . . . Manager Mike Hargrove after Game 5: "You don't win 114 games by being lucky. These guys are good."

Yankees: Wells, after his Game 1 victory: "The message this sent to the fans was unbelievable. They hold a grudge more than we hold a grudge." . . . Manager Joe Torre, on the lack of an interference call on Fryman in Game 2: "He was on the grass, it was so blatant. It was a terrible call. I'm not sure we would have won the game, but you don't want to lose it that way." . . . Knoblauch, recalling his Game 2 mistake: "I don't feel like I didn't play the ball out. It's not that I was trying to be an umpire. I thought it was a no-doubter." . . . Torre, on Hernandez handling the pressure in Game 4: "I saw El Duque at a buffet luncheon at the hotel passing out plates of food to people as if he was one of the waiters. He seemed pretty relaxed to me." . . . Wells, on the vulgar chants he endured from Cleveland fans while warming up in the bullpen before Game 5: "I don't appreciate stuff like that. I appreciate the fans who appreciate a good game of baseball. To all those idiots out there, this (win's) for you."

GAME 1 BOX SCORE

NEW YORK 7, CLEVELAND 2

TUESDAY, OCTOBER 6, AT NEW YORK

Cleveland	AB	R	H	RBI	PO	A
Lofton, cf	4	0	0	0	1	0
Cora, 2b	3	1	1	0	1	3
Justice, lf	4	0	1	0	3	0
Ramirez, rf	4	1	2	2	2	0
Fryman, 3b	4	0	0	0	1	1
Thome, dh	3	0	0	0	0	0
Sexson, 1b	3	0	0	0	8	1
Alomar, c	3	0	0	0	5	0
Diaz, c	0	0	0	0	1	1
Vizquel, ss	3	0	1	0	1	3
Wright, p	0	0	0	0	0	0
Ogea, p	0	0	0	0	1	1
Poole, p	0	0	0	0	0	0
Reed, p	0	0	0	0	0	0
Shuey, p	0	0	0	0	0	0
Totals	31	2	5	2	24	10

New York	AB	R	H	RBI	PO	A
Knoblauch, 2b	5	1	1	0	1	4
Jeter, ss	4	1	2	0	1	3
O'Neill, rf	5	2	2	1	1	0
Williams, cf	4	0	2	2	4	0
Martinez, 1b	5	1	0	0	9	0
Raines, dh	2	0	0	0	0	0
Spencer, lf	2	1	0	0	1	0
Ledee, ph-lf	1	0	0	0	0	0
Posada, c	3	1	2	2	10	0
Brosius, 3b	4	0	2	1	0	1
Wells, p	0	0	0	0	0	0
Nelson, p	0	0	0	0	0	0
Totals	35	7	11	6	27	8

Cleveland	0 0 0	0 0 0	0 0 2—2
New York	5 0 0	0 0 1	1 0 x—7

Cleveland	IP	H	R	ER	BB	SO
Wright (L)	0.2	5	5	5	1	1
Ogea	*5.1	5	2	2	2	2
Poole	0.1	0	0	0	1	1
Reed	0.2	0	0	0	0	0
Shuey	1.0	1	0	0	2	2

New York	IP	H	R	ER	BB	SO
Wells (W)	8.1	5	2	2	1	7
Nelson	0.2	0	0	0	0	1

*Pitched to two batters in seventh.
DP—New York 1. LOB—Cleveland 4, New York 10. 2B—O'Neill, Williams. HR—Ramirez, Posada. SB—Vizquel, Martinez, Jeter. HBP—By Wells (Thome). WP—Wright, Shuey. U—Evans, plate; Hendry, first; Shulock, second; Young, third; Welke, left field; McKean, right field. T—3:31. A—57,138.

GAME 2 BOX SCORE

CLEVELAND 4, NEW YORK 1 (12 INNINGS)

WEDNESDAY, OCTOBER 7, AT NEW YORK

Cleveland	AB	R	H	RBI	PO	A
Lofton, cf	6	0	1	2	3	0
Vizquel, ss	6	0	1	0	1	4
Justice, dh	4	1	2	1	0	0
Ramirez, rf	4	0	0	0	4	0
Thome, 1b	5	0	1	0	9	3
Wilson, pr-2b	0	1	0	0	0	0
Fryman, 3b	4	1	1	0	0	1
Giles, lf	4	0	0	0	3	0
Alomar, c	4	1	1	0	11	0
Cora, 2b	4	0	0	0	1	3
Sexson, 1b	0	0	0	0	1	0
Nagy, p	0	0	0	0	3	1
Reed, p	0	0	0	0	0	1
Poole, p	0	0	0	0	0	0
Shuey, p	0	0	0	0	0	0

Cleveland	AB	R	H	RBI	PO	A
Assenmacher, p	0	0	0	0	0	0
Burba, p	0	0	0	0	0	0
Jackson, p	0	0	0	0	0	0
Totals	41	4	7	3	36	13

New York	AB	R	H	RBI	PO	A
Knoblauch, 2b	6	0	0	0	3	3
Jeter, ss	5	0	1	0	3	1
O'Neill, rf	5	0	1	0	2	0
Williams, cf	4	1	1	0	3	0
Martinez, 1b	4	0	0	0	9	2
Raines, dh	4	0	1	0	0	0
Bush, pr-dh	0	0	0	0	0	0
Davis, ph	1	0	1	0	0	0
Ledee, pr-dh	0	0	0	0	0	0
Spencer, lf	5	0	1	0	3	1
Brosius, 3b	4	0	1	1	0	1
Girardi, c	3	0	0	0	8	1
Posada, ph-c	2	0	0	0	2	0
Cone, p	0	0	0	0	1	2
Rivera, p	0	0	0	0	2	0
Stanton, p	0	0	0	0	0	0
Nelson, p	0	0	0	0	0	0
Lloyd, p	0	0	0	0	0	1
Totals	43	1	7	1	36	12

Cleveland....	0	0	0		1	0	0		0	0	0		0	0	3—4
New York....	0	0	0		0	0	0		1	0	0		0	0	0—1

Cleveland	IP	H	R	ER	BB	SO
Nagy	6.2	5	1	1	1	5
Reed	0.2	0	0	0	1	0
Poole	0.1	0	0	0	0	0
Shuey	2.0	1	0	0	2	2
Assenmacher	1.0	0	0	0	0	2
Burba (W)	0.1	1	0	0	0	0
Jackson (S)	1.0	0	0	0	0	2

New York	IP	H	R	ER	BB	SO
Cone	8.0	5	1	1	3	5
Rivera	2.0	0	0	0	0	2
Stanton	0.2	0	0	0	0	0
Nelson (L)	0.2	2	3	3	1	2
Lloyd	0.2	1	0	0	0	0

E—Fryman, Martinez. DP—Cleveland 1, New York 1. LOB—Cleveland 7, New York 10. 2B—Jeter, O'Neill, Brosius. 3B—Vizquel. HR—Justice. SB—Jeter, Bush. SH—Fryman. HBP—By Nelson (Alomar). U—Hendry, plate; Shulock, first; Young, second; Welke, third; McKean, left field; Evans, right field. T—4:28. A—57,128.

GAME 3 BOX SCORE

CLEVELAND 6, NEW YORK 1

FRIDAY, OCTOBER 9, AT CLEVELAND

New York	AB	R	H	RBI	PO	A
Knoblauch, 2b	3	1	2	0	2	5
Jeter, ss	3	0	0	0	0	1
O'Neill, rf	3	0	0	0	1	0
Williams, cf	4	0	1	1	3	0
Martinez, 1b	4	0	0	0	9	0
Davis, dh	1	0	0	0	0	0
Spencer, lf	3	0	0	0	3	0
Brosius, 3b	3	0	0	0	1	2
Girardi, c	2	0	1	0	3	0
Posada, ph-c	1	0	0	0	2	0
Pettitte, p	0	0	0	0	0	0
Mendoza, p	0	0	0	0	0	0
Stanton, p	0	0	0	0	0	0
Totals	27	1	4	1	24	8

Cleveland	AB	R	H	RBI	PO	A
Lofton, cf	5	0	0	0	1	0
Vizquel, ss	4	0	3	0	4	7
Justice, dh	5	0	0	0	0	0
Ramirez, rf	4	1	3	1	1	0
Fryman, 3b	3	1	1	0	0	1
Thome, 1b	4	2	2	3	14	0
Whiten, lf	3	2	2	1	2	0
Alomar, c	4	0	0	0	4	0
Wilson, 2b	4	0	1	1	1	3
Colon, p	0	0	0	0	0	3
Totals	36	6	12	6	27	14

New York	1	0	0		0	0	0		0	0	0—1
Cleveland	0	2	0		0	4	0		0	0	x—6

New York	IP	H	R	ER	BB	SO
Pettitte (L)	4.2	8	6	6	3	1
Mendoza	*1.1	3	0	0	0	0
Stanton	2.0	1	0	0	1	3

Cleveland	IP	H	R	ER	BB	SO
Colon (W)	9.0	4	1	1	4	3

*Pitched to two batters in seventh.

DP—Cleveland 3. LOB—New York 4, Cleveland 10. 2B—Ramirez, Whiten. HR—Thome 2, Ramirez, Whiten. SH—Jeter. U—Shulock, plate; Young, first; Welke, second; McKean, third; Evans, left field; Hendry, right field. T—2:53. A—44,904.

GAME 4 BOX SCORE

NEW YORK 4, CLEVELAND 0

SATURDAY, OCTOBER 10, AT CLEVELAND

New York	AB	R	H	RBI	PO	A
Knoblauch, 2b	5	0	0	0	2	1
Jeter, ss	4	0	0	0	3	2
O'Neill, rf	3	2	1	1	2	0
Williams, cf	1	1	0	0	1	0
Davis, dh	4	0	1	0	0	0
Martinez, 1b	2	0	1	1	5	0
Bush, pr	0	1	0	0	0	0
Sojo, 1b	0	0	0	0	1	1
Posada, c	4	0	0	0	10	0
Curtis, lf	3	0	0	0	1	0
Brosius, 3b	3	0	1	1	1	2
Hernandez, p	0	0	0	0	0	1
Stanton, p	0	0	0	0	0	0
Rivera, p	0	0	0	0	1	0
Totals	29	4	4	4	27	7

Cleveland	AB	R	H	RBI	PO	A
Lofton, cf	4	0	1	0	1	0
Vizquel, ss	4	0	3	0	0	7
Justice, dh	3	0	0	0	0	0
Ramirez, rf	3	0	0	0	2	0
Thome, 1b	4	0	0	0	13	1
Fryman, 3b	4	0	0	0	0	1
Giles, lf	3	0	0	0	1	0
Alomar, c	2	0	0	0	4	0
Diaz, c	1	0	0	0	3	1
Wilson, 2b	2	0	0	0	2	4
Gooden, p	0	0	0	0	1	0
Poole, p	0	0	0	0	0	0
Burba, p	0	0	0	0	0	0
Shuey, p	0	0	0	0	0	0
Totals	30	0	4	0	27	14

New York	1	0	0		2	0	0		0	0	1—4
Cleveland	0	0	0		0	0	0		0	0	0—0

New York	IP	H	R	ER	BB	SO
Hernandez (W)	*7.0	3	0	0	2	6
Stanton	1.0	1	0	0	0	1
Rivera	1.0	0	0	0	0	1

Cleveland	IP	H	R	ER	BB	SO
Gooden (L)	4.2	3	3	3	3	3
Poole	0.1	0	0	0	0	1
Burba	3.1	1	1	1	3	4
Shuey	0.2	0	0	0	0	0

*Pitched to one batter in eighth.

E—Alomar 2, Lofton. DP—New York 1, Cleveland 1. LOB—New York 6, Cleveland 6. 2B—Davis, Martinez, Lofton. HR—O'Neill. SB—Vizquel 2, Martinez, O'Neill, Jeter, Williams. SF—Martinez, Brosius. HBP—By Hernandez (Justice). WP—Burba. U—Young, plate; Welke, first; McKean, second; Evans, third; Hendry, left field; Shulock, right field. T—3:31. A—44,981.

GAME 5 BOX SCORE

NEW YORK 5, CLEVELAND 3

SUNDAY, OCTOBER 11, AT CLEVELAND

New York	AB	R	H	RBI	PO	A
Knoblauch, 2b	1	2	0	0	1	3
Jeter, ss	4	0	0	0	2	4

New York	AB	R	H	RBI	PO	A
O'Neill, rf	4	1	2	1	3	0
Williams, cf	4	1	1	0	1	0
Davis, dh	5	1	2	3	0	0
Martinez, 1b	1	0	0	0	7	1
Raines, lf	4	0	0	1	1	0
Curtis, lf	1	0	0	0	0	0
Posada, c	1	0	0	0	11	1
Brosius, 3b	3	0	1	0	1	1
Wells, p	0	0	0	0	0	1
Nelson, p	0	0	0	0	0	0
Rivera, p	0	0	0	0	0	0
Totals	28	5	6	5	27	11

Cleveland	AB	R	H	RBI	PO	A
Lofton, cf	4	1	1	1	1	0
Vizquel, ss	3	1	2	0	4	3
Fryman, 3b	3	0	1	0	0	2
Ramirez, rf	3	0	1	1	0	0
Whiten, lf	4	0	0	0	1	0
Thome, dh	3	1	2	1	0	0
Sexson, 1b	3	0	0	0	11	2
Giles, ph	1	0	0	0	0	0
Diaz, c	3	0	0	0	7	1
Justice, ph	0	0	0	0	0	0
Wilson, 2b	4	0	1	0	2	7
Ogea, p	0	0	0	0	0	1
Wright, p	0	0	0	0	1	0
Reed, p	0	0	0	0	0	0
Assenmacher, p	0	0	0	0	0	0
Shuey, p	0	0	0	0	0	0
Totals	31	3	8	3	27	17

New York	3	1	0	1	0	0	0	0	0—5
Cleveland	2	0	0	0	0	1	0	0	0—3

New York	IP	H	R	ER	BB	SO
Wells (W)	7.1	7	3	3	1	11
Nelson	*0.0	1	0	0	0	0
Rivera (S)	1.2	0	0	0	1	1

Cleveland	IP	H	R	ER	BB	SO
Ogea (L)	1.1	4	4	4	3	2
Wright	6.0	2	1	1	7	3
Reed	0.1	0	0	0	0	0
Assenmacher	0.1	0	0	0	0	0
Shuey	1.0	0	0	0	1	2

*Pitched to two batters in eighth.
DP—New York 2, Cleveland 2. LOB—New York 11, Cleveland 6. HR—Lofton, Davis, Thome. SB—O'Neill, Vizquel, Fryman. CS—Posada, Vizquel. SH—Jeter, Brosius. SF—Ramirez. HBP—By Wells (Vizquel), by Nelson (Fryman), by Ogea 2 (Knoblauch, Martinez). WP—Wells. U—Welke, plate; McKean, first; Evans, second; Hendry, third; Shulock, left field; Young, right field. T—3:33. A—44,966.

NEW YORK 9, CLEVELAND 5
TUESDAY, OCTOBER 13, AT NEW YORK

Cleveland	AB	R	H	RBI	PO	A
Lofton, cf	4	1	2	0	1	0
Vizquel, ss	5	1	1	0	1	2
Justice, dh	3	1	0	1	0	0
Ramirez, rf	3	0	1	0	3	0
Thome, 1b	4	1	2	4	9	0
Fryman, 3b	4	0	0	0	0	1
Giles, lf	4	0	1	0	3	0
Alomar, c	3	0	0	0	5	1
Branson, ph	1	0	0	0	0	0
Diaz, c	0	0	0	0	2	0
Wilson, 2b	4	1	1	0	0	5
Nagy, p	0	0	0	0	0	0
Burba, p	0	0	0	0	0	0
Poole, p	0	0	0	0	0	0
Shuey, p	0	0	0	0	0	0
Assenmacher, p	0	0	0	0	0	0
Totals	35	5	8	5	24	9

New York	AB	R	H	RBI	PO	A
Knoblauch, 2b	5	0	2	0	0	1
Jeter, ss	5	2	2	2	0	2
O'Neill, rf	5	1	1	0	1	0
Williams, cf	4	1	3	2	2	0
Davis, dh	3	1	0	1	0	0
Martinez, 1b	3	0	1	0	8	1
Ledee, lf	4	0	0	0	3	0
Brosius, 3b	3	2	1	3	1	3
Girardi, c	3	2	1	0	11	0
Cone, p	0	0	0	0	1	0
Mendoza, p	0	0	0	0	0	0
Rivera, p	0	0	0	0	0	1
Totals	35	9	11	8	27	8

Cleveland	0	0	0	0	5	0	0	0	0—5
New York	2	1	3	0	0	3	0	0	x—9

Cleveland	IP	H	R	ER	BB	SO
Nagy (L)	3.0	8	6	3	0	0
Burba	2.1	1	3	1	2	4
Poole	0.1	0	0	0	0	0
Shuey	1.2	2	0	0	2	1
Assenmacher	0.2	0	0	0	0	1

New York	IP	H	R	ER	BB	SO
Cone (W)	5.0	7	5	5	3	8
Mendoza	3.0	1	0	0	0	0
Rivera	1.0	0	0	0	0	1

E—Giles, Wilson, Vizquel, Brosius. LOB—Cleveland 6, New York 7. 2B—Knoblauch. 3B—Jeter. HR—Brosius, Thome. SB—Lofton. CS—Williams. SF—Davis. WP—Burba. U—McKean, plate; Evans, first; Hendry, second; Shulock, third; Young, left field; Welke, right field. T—3:31. A—57,142.

STATISTICS

NEW YORK YANKEES' BATTING AND FIELDING AVERAGES

Player, position	BATTING													FIELDING			
	G	AB	R	H	TB	2B	3B	HR	RBI	BB	IBB	SO	Avg.	PO	A	E	Avg.
Williams, cf	6	21	4	8	9	1	0	0	5	7	0	4	.381	14	0	0	1.000
Brosius, 3b	6	20	2	6	10	1	0	1	6	2	2	4	.300	4	10	1	.933
Davis, ph-dh	5	14	2	4	8	1	0	1	5	2	0	3	.286	0	0	0	.000
O'Neill, rf	6	25	6	7	12	2	0	1	3	3	0	4	.280	10	0	0	1.000
Girardi, c	3	8	2	2	2	0	0	0	0	1	0	0	.250	22	1	0	1.000
Jeter, ss	6	25	3	5	8	1	1	0	2	2	0	5	.200	9	13	0	1.000
Knoblauch, 2b	6	25	4	5	6	1	0	0	0	4	0	2	.200	9	17	0	1.000
Posada, c-ph	5	11	1	2	5	0	0	1	2	4	0	2	.182	35	1	0	1.000
Martinez, 1b	6	19	1	2	3	1	0	0	1	6	0	8	.105	47	4	1	.981
Raines, dh-lf	3	10	0	1	1	0	0	0	1	2	0	5	.100	1	0	0	1.000
Spencer, lf	3	10	1	1	1	0	0	0	0	1	0	3	.100	7	1	0	1.000
Bush, pr-dh	2	0	1	0	0	0	0	0	0	0	0	0	.000	0	0	0	.000
Cone, p	2	0	0	0	0	0	0	0	0	0	0	0	.000	2	2	0	1.000
Hernandez, p	1	0	0	0	0	0	0	0	0	0	0	0	.000	0	1	0	1.000
Lloyd, p	1	0	0	0	0	0	0	0	0	0	0	0	.000	0	1	0	1.000
Mendoza, p	2	0	0	0	0	0	0	0	0	0	0	0	.000	0	0	0	.000

Player, position	G	AB	R	H	TB	2B	3B	HR	RBI	BB	IBB	SO	Avg.	PO	A	E	Avg.
						BATTING									**FIELDING**		
Nelson, p	3	0	0	0	0	0	0	0	0	0	0	0	.000	0	0	0	.000
Pettitte, p	1	0	0	0	0	0	0	0	0	0	0	0	.000	0	0	0	.000
Rivera, p	4	0	0	0	0	0	0	0	0	0	0	0	.000	3	1	0	1.000
Sojo, 1b	1	0	0	0	0	0	0	0	0	0	0	0	.000	1	1	0	1.000
Stanton, p	3	0	0	0	0	0	0	0	0	0	0	0	.000	0	0	0	.000
Wells, p	2	0	0	0	0	0	0	0	0	0	0	0	.000	0	1	0	1.000
Curtis, lf	2	4	0	0	0	0	0	0	0	1	0	2	.000	1	0	0	1.000
Ledee, ph-lf-pr-dh	3	5	0	0	0	0	0	0	0	0	0	0	.000	3	0	0	1.000
Totals	6	197	27	43	65	8	1	4	25	35	2	42	.218	168	54	2	.991

CLEVELAND INDIANS' BATTING AND FIELDING AVERAGES

Player, position	G	AB	R	H	TB	2B	3B	HR	RBI	BB	IBB	SO	Avg.	PO	A	E	Avg.
						BATTING									**FIELDING**		
Vizquel, ss	6	25	2	11	13	0	1	0	0	1	0	3	.440	11	26	1	.974
Ramirez, rf	6	21	2	7	14	1	0	2	4	4	0	9	.333	12	0	0	1.000
Thome, dh-1b	6	23	4	7	19	1	0	4	8	1	0	8	.304	45	4	0	1.000
Whiten, lf	2	7	2	2	6	1	0	1	1	1	1	3	.286	3	0	0	1.000
Wilson, pr-2b	5	14	2	3	3	0	0	0	1	1	0	3	.214	5	19	1	.960
Lofton, cf	6	27	2	5	9	1	0	1	3	1	0	7	.185	8	0	1	.889
Fryman, 3b	6	23	2	4	4	0	0	0	0	1	0	5	.174	1	7	1	.889
Justice, lf-dh-ph	6	19	2	3	6	0	0	1	2	3	0	3	.158	3	0	0	1.000
Cora, 2b	2	7	1	1	1	0	0	0	0	2	0	1	.143	2	6	0	1.000
Giles, lf-ph	4	12	0	1	1	0	0	0	0	1	0	3	.083	7	0	1	.875
Alomar, c	5	16	1	1	1	0	0	0	0	0	0	2	.063	29	1	2	.938
Assenmacher, p	3	0	0	0	0	0	0	0	0	0	0	0	.000	0	0	0	.000
Burba, p	3	0	0	0	0	0	0	0	0	0	0	0	.000	0	0	0	.000
Colon, p	1	0	0	0	0	0	0	0	0	0	0	0	.000	0	3	0	1.000
Gooden, p	1	0	0	0	0	0	0	0	0	0	0	0	.000	1	0	0	1.000
Jackson, p	1	0	0	0	0	0	0	0	0	0	0	0	.000	0	0	0	.000
Nagy, p	2	0	0	0	0	0	0	0	0	0	0	0	.000	3	1	0	1.000
Ogea, p	2	0	0	0	0	0	0	0	0	0	0	0	.000	1	2	0	1.000
Poole, p	4	0	0	0	0	0	0	0	0	0	0	0	.000	0	0	0	.000
Reed, p	3	0	0	0	0	0	0	0	0	0	0	0	.000	0	1	0	1.000
Shuey, p	5	0	0	0	0	0	0	0	0	0	0	0	.000	0	0	0	.000
Wright, p	2	0	0	0	0	0	0	0	0	0	0	0	.000	1	1	0	1.000
Branson, ph	1	1	0	0	0	0	0	0	0	0	0	0	.000	0	0	0	.000
Diaz, c	4	4	0	0	0	0	0	0	0	0	0	1	.000	13	3	0	1.000
Sexson, 1b	3	6	0	0	0	0	0	0	0	0	0	3	.000	20	3	0	1.000
Totals	6	205	20	45	77	3	1	9	19	16	1	51	.220	165	77	7	.972

NEW YORK YANKEES' PITCHING RECORDS

Pitcher	G	GS	CG	IP	H	R	ER	HR	BB	IBB	SO	HB	WP	W	L	Pct.	ERA
Hernandez	1	1	0	7.0	3	0	0	0	2	0	6	1	0	1	0	1.000	0.00
Rivera	4	0	0	5.2	0	0	0	0	1	0	5	0	0	0	0	.000	0.00
Mendoza	2	0	0	4.1	4	0	0	0	0	0	1	0	0	0	0	.000	0.00
Stanton	3	0	0	3.2	2	0	0	0	1	1	4	0	0	0	0	.000	0.00
Lloyd	1	0	0	0.2	1	0	0	0	0	0	0	0	0	0	0	.000	0.00
Wells	2	2	0	15.2	12	5	5	3	2	0	18	2	1	2	0	1.000	2.87
Cone	2	2	0	13.0	12	6	6	2	6	0	13	0	0	1	0	1.000	4.15
Pettitte	1	1	0	4.2	8	6	6	4	3	0	1	0	0	0	1	.000	11.57
Nelson	3	0	0	1.1	3	3	3	0	1	0	3	2	0	0	1	.000	20.25
Totals	6	6	0	56.0	45	20	20	9	16	1	51	5	1	4	2	.667	3.21

Shutout—Hernandez, Stanton and Rivera (combined). Save—Rivera.

CLEVELAND INDIANS' PITCHING RECORDS

Pitcher	G	GS	CG	IP	H	R	ER	HR	BB	IBB	SO	HB	WP	W	L	Pct.	ERA
Shuey	5	0	0	6.1	4	0	0	0	7	2	7	0	1	0	0	.000	0.00
Assenmacher	3	0	0	2.0	0	0	0	0	0	0	3	0	0	0	0	.000	0.00
Reed	3	0	0	1.2	0	0	0	0	1	0	0	0	0	0	0	.000	0.00
Poole	4	0	0	1.1	0	0	0	0	1	0	2	0	0	0	0	.000	0.00
Jackson	1	0	0	1.0	0	0	0	0	0	0	2	0	0	0	0	.000	0.00
Colon	1	1	1	9.0	4	1	1	0	4	0	3	0	0	1	0	1.000	1.00
Burba	3	0	0	6.0	3	4	2	0	5	0	8	0	2	1	0	1.000	3.00
Nagy	2	2	0	9.2	13	7	4	1	1	0	6	0	0	0	1	.000	3.72
Gooden	1	1	0	4.2	3	3	3	1	3	0	3	0	0	0	1	.000	5.79
Ogea	2	1	0	6.2	9	6	6	1	5	0	4	2	0	0	1	.000	8.10
Wright	2	1	0	6.2	7	6	6	1	8	0	4	0	1	0	1	.000	8.10
Totals	6	6	1	55.0	43	27	22	4	35	2	42	2	4	2	4	.333	3.60

No shutouts. Save—Jackson.

SCORE BY INNINGS

New York	12	2	3	3	0	4	2	0	1	0	0	0—27
Cleveland	2	2	0	1	9	1	0	0	2	0	0	3—20

MISCELLANEOUS STATISTICS

Sacrifice hits—Jeter 2, Brosius, Fryman.

Sacrifice flies—Brosius, Davis, Martinez, Ramirez.

Stolen bases—Vizquel 4, Jeter 3, Martinez 2, O'Neill 2, Bush, Fryman, Lofton, Williams.

Caught stealing—Posada, Vizquel, Williams.

Double plays—Knoblauch, Jeter and Martinez 3; Jeter, Knoblauch and Martinez 2; Vizquel, Wilson and Thome 2; Cora, Vizquel and Thome; Sexson and Vizquel; Vizquel and Thome; Vizquel, Wilson and Sexson; Wilson, Vizquel and Thome.

Left on bases—New York 10, 10, 4, 6, 11, 7—48; Cleveland 4, 7, 10, 6, 6, 6—39.

Hit by pitcher—By Wells 2 (Thome, Vizquel), by Nelson 2 (Alomar, Fryman), by Hernandez (Justice), by Ogea 2 (Knoblauch, Martinez).

Passed balls—None.

Balks—None.

Time of games—First game, 3:31; second game, 4:28; third game, 2:53; fourth game, 3:31; fifth game, 3:33; sixth game, 3:31.

Attendance—First game, 57,138; second game, 57,128; third game, 44,904; fourth game, 44,981; fifth game, 44,966; sixth game, 57,142.

Umpires—Evans, Hendry, Shulock, Young, Welke and McKean.

Official scorers—Hank Kozloski, Bill Shannon.

N.L. CHAMPIONSHIP SERIES

The bottom line: The San Diego Padres, a dark horse in the National League playoffs that featured high-powered teams from Houston and Atlanta, claimed the second pennant of their 30-year existence and first since 1984 with a six-game NLCS victory over the Eastern Division champion Braves. The Padres, who won 98 regular-season games en route to the Western Division title, qualified for a World Series date with the New York Yankees by pounding out postseason victories over the N.L.'s two most successful 1998 teams. The loss was very disappointing for the Braves, who had won a club-record 106 regular-season games and qualified for their record seventh straight NLCS. They became the winningest team that failed to reach the World Series.

Why the Padres won: Because they were able to beat the Braves at their own game—pitching and defense—and were able to win three times at Atlanta's Turner Field. San Diego pitchers, led by righthanders Kevin Brown and Andy Ashby and lefty Sterling Hitchcock, finished the series with a 2.78 ERA and held Atlanta hitters to a .235 average. Especially significant was the job the Padres did on power men Chipper Jones (.208) and Andres Galarraga (.095), who combined for five RBIs. San Diego fans survived a scare when the Braves became the first team in baseball history to force a Game 6 after losing the first three games of a series, but the Padres rebounded behind Hitchcock for a pennant-clinching shutout.

The turning points:

Game 1: The Braves won their first battle against premier closer Trevor Hoffman, but they couldn't win the war. Trailing 2-1 entering the bottom of the ninth inning at Turner Field, the Braves accomplished something few teams could do during the season against Hoffman: They scored a run on Andruw Jones' sacrifice fly and forced extra innings. Then, after the Padres regained the lead in the 10th on Ken Caminiti's opposite-field home run, the Braves put two runners on base in the bottom of the inning, but Donne Wall relieved Hoffman and ended the game on Galarraga's long fly ball. The first seven innings of the rain-delayed NLCS opener featured a pitching duel between Ashby and John Smoltz, but the Padres broke a 1-1 tie in the eighth when Ruben Rivera, a fifth-inning replacement for injured left fielder Greg Vaughn, made a daring dash home from third base on an infield dribbler that resulted in an unusual double error for first baseman Andres Galarraga.

Game 2: The turning point came in the first inning when Brown made it perfectly clear the Braves were in for a long night. Eight innings later, he was enjoying the glow of a three-hit, 11-strikeout, 3-0 victory that lowered his 1998 postseason ERA to 0.38. "Against us, this is the best I've seen (from Brown)," Braves manager Bobby Cox said after watching his team sink into a two-game hole. Brown not only limited the Braves to three singles, he also singled twice himself to key rallies. Brown outdueled 20-game winner Tom Glavine, who issued six walks and six hits in six innings.

Game 3: There were three distinct turning points in a game the Padres won 4-1 behind Hitchcock and four relievers. The Braves loaded the bases in the fourth, sixth and eighth innings—twice with less than two outs—but failed to score in any of those situations. Hitchcock pitched out of the first jam, Dan Miceli came out of the bullpen in the sixth to strike out consecutive pinch hitters and Hoffman came on in the eighth to strike out Javy Lopez representing the potential winning run. The Padres couldn't break through against Greg Maddux until the fifth, when Steve Finley doubled home one run and Caminiti delivered an RBI single. Then they scored twice in the eighth on an error by left fielder Ryan Klesko and a passed ball.

Game 4: A grand slam by Galarraga was the big blow in a six-run Atlanta seventh, but an RBI single by backup shortstop Ozzie Guillen set the table for Galarraga and an 8-3 series-extending Braves victory. The score was tied 3-3, thanks to a leadoff homer by Lopez in the seventh, when Guillen battled reliever Randy Myers with two out and Andruw Jones stationed at second. Guillen fought off several tough pitches, singled home the go-ahead run and advanced to third on an infield hit by Keith Lockhart and a walk to Chipper Jones. Galarraga greeted reliever Miceli with a 459-foot drive over the left-center field wall—only his second hit of the series and his first RBIs.

Game 5: A 3-2, eighth-inning pitch to Michael Tucker rescued the Braves from the brink of elimination and sent the suddenly competitive series back to Atlanta with the Braves hoping to make history. The 7-6 victory before 58,988 frustrated Padres fans at Qaulcomm Stadium allowed the Braves to become the first team in baseball history to come back from a 3-0 postseason deficit and force a sixth game. Not only did Tucker turn a 4-2 Padres' advantage into a 5-4 Atlanta lead with a three-run homer, he did it off San Diego ace Brown, who had made a surprising seventh-inning bullpen appearance as manager Bruce Bochy went for the kill. Brown escaped a jam in the seventh, but he walked Klesko leading off the eighth and Lopez reached on an infield single to set up Tucker's dramatic home run. Ironically, Braves ace Maddux made a ninth-inning relief appearance and picked up his first career save.

Game 6: A five-run sixth inning turned a scoreless duel between Hitchcock and Glavine into a 5-0 victory that short-circuited Atlanta's attempt to stage the greatest single-series comeback in baseball history. The five-run outburst featured six singles, a walk and a key bases-loaded error by left fielder Danny

Bautista, who lost Hitchcock's low line drive in the lights and dropped the ball after a dive. Hitchcock, pitching on three days' rest, combined with four relievers to on a two-hitter that set up the Padres' World Series date with the Yankees.

Notable:

Braves: The Braves drew 42,117 fans to the rain-delayed opener and 43,083 to Game 2—both crowds well below the 50,062 capacity of Turner Field. . . . Galarraga's Game 4 grand slam was the sixth in NLCS history and the first since 1996, when St. Louis' Gary Gaetti hit one against the Braves. . . . When Atlanta scored six runs in the seventh inning of Game 4, it marked the first multi-run inning for the Braves in the NLCS. . . . Glavine, a two-time loser in the series, saw his postseason record drop to 9-11. He has lost eight times in NLCS play. . . . In Glavine's three 1998 playoff starts covering 18.2 innings, the Braves did not score a run while he was in the game.

Padres: The Padres became the sixth consecutive team to win the opener of the NLCS and go on to win the series. . . . Jim Leyritz's Game 4 homer was his fourth of this postseason and seventh overall in 43 career playoff at-bats. . . . Mark Langston, a 15-year veteran, made his playoff debut with a Game 4 relief appearance. . . . Hitchcock entered the World Series following playoff victories over Houston's Randy Johnson and Atlanta's Greg Maddux and Tom Glavine. . . . Through NLCS play, the Padres had won 181 consecutive games when leading after eight innings—a streak that dated back to July 1996. . . . The Padres became only the second team to win three road games in a League Championship Series.

Quotable:

Braves: Tucker, after hitting his dramatic Game 5 home run off Brown: "The feeling in the dugout was that we were going to get him. He really didn't have the extra giddy-up you really want to have." . . . Cox, after watching his team fail to reach the World Series for the fifth time in the decade: "If you don't get hot in these things, you're not going to win them. We don't have anything to be ashamed about."

Padres: Bochy, after Brown's Game 2 masterpiece: "When Kevin Brown is on, he's as tough as any pitcher in the game. He's as tough a competitor as I've ever seen, and he's locked in right now." . . . Leyritz, after getting hit by a Maddux pitch in Game 3: "What really bothered me was him throwing at my head. The only reason I didn't charge the mound was this is the postseason and you have to stay in the game." . . . Gwynn, after San Diego's Game 6 win: "Not many people gave us a chance against Houston. Not many people gave us a chance against Atlanta. But here we are."

GAME 1 BOX SCORE

SAN DIEGO 3, ATLANTA 2 (10 INNINGS)
WEDNESDAY, OCTOBER 7, AT ATLANTA

San Diego	AB	R	H	RBI	PO	A
Veras, 2b	3	0	0	0	2	3
Gwynn, rf	5	0	2	1	0	0

San Diego	AB	R	H	RBI	PO	A
Vaughn, lf	3	0	0	0	1	0
Rivera, lf	2	1	1	0	0	0
Caminiti, 3b	5	1	1	1	2	2
Joyner, 1b	3	0	0	0	11	1
Leyritz, ph-1b	2	0	0	1	1	0
Finley, cf	2	0	1	0	4	0
Hernandez, c	4	1	2	0	7	2
Gomez, ss	4	0	0	0	1	2
Hoffman, p	0	0	0	0	0	0
Wall, p	0	0	0	0	0	0
Ashby, p	2	0	0	0	1	4
R. Myers, p	0	0	0	0	0	0
Miceli, p	0	0	0	0	0	0
Sheets, ss	1	0	0	0	0	1
Totals	36	3	7	3	30	15

Atlanta	AB	R	H	RBI	PO	A
Weiss, ss	5	0	0	0	2	3
Lockhart, 2b	3	0	2	0	1	3
Graffanino, ph	0	0	0	0	0	0
Guillen, ph	1	0	1	0	0	0
Ligtenberg, p	0	0	0	0	0	0
Glavine, ph	0	0	0	0	0	0
C. Jones, 3b	4	0	0	0	0	1
Galarraga, 1b	5	0	0	0	11	2
Klesko, lf	3	1	0	0	0	0
Lopez, c	4	0	2	0	6	0
Bautista, pr	0	0	0	0	0	0
E. Perez, c	0	0	0	0	1	0
A. Jones, cf	3	1	1	2	5	0
Tucker, rf	1	0	1	0	2	0
Williams, ph-rf	2	0	0	0	0	0
Smoltz, p	2	0	0	0	2	2
Rocker, p	0	0	0	0	0	0
Martinez, p	0	0	0	0	0	1
Colbrunn, p	1	0	1	0	0	0
Malloy, pr-2b	1	0	0	0	0	0
Totals	35	2	8	2	30	13

San Diego	0	0	0	0	1	0	0	1	0	1—3
Atlanta	0	0	1	0	0	0	0	0	1	0—2

San Diego	IP	H	R	ER	BB	SO
Ashby	7.0	5	1	1	1	3
R. Myers	0.2	1	0	0	0	2
Miceli	*0.0	1	0	0	0	0
Hoffman (W)	2.0	0	1	1	2	3
Wall (S)	0.1	0	0	0	1	0

Atlanta	IP	H	R	ER	BB	SO
Smoltz	*7.0	4	2	2	5	5
Rocker	0.1	0	0	0	0	0
Martinez	0.2	1	0	0	1	0
Ligtenberg (L)	2.0	2	1	1	0	2

*Pitched to one batter in eighth.

E—Galarraga 2, Smoltz. DP—San Diego 2, Atlanta 2. LOB—San Diego 10, Atlanta 8. 2B—Rivera, Lockhart, Tucker. HR—A. Jones, Caminiti. SB—Finley. SH—Ashby. SF—A. Jones. U—Tata, plate; Poncino, first; Hallion, second; Bonin, third; Davis, left field; Rippley, right field. T—3:27. A—42,117.

GAME 2 BOX SCORE

SAN DIEGO 3, ATLANTA 0
THURSDAY, OCTOBER 8, AT ATLANTA

San Diego	AB	R	H	RBI	PO	A
Veras, 2b	5	1	3	1	0	4
Finley, cf	5	0	2	1	2	0
Gwynn, rf	4	0	1	0	0	0
Caminiti, 3b	1	0	0	0	0	0
Joyner, 1b	3	0	1	1	9	2
Hernandez, c	5	0	0	0	11	0
Rivera, lf	5	0	0	0	2	0
Gomez, ss	3	1	2	0	1	2
Brown, p	4	1	2	0	2	1
Totals	35	3	11	3	27	9

Atlanta	AB	R	H	RBI	PO	A
Weiss, ss	3	0	0	0	0	3
Colbrunn, ph	1	0	1	0	0	0
O. Perez, p	0	0	0	0	0	0
Ligtenberg, p	0	0	0	0	0	0

Atlanta	AB	R	H	RBI	PO	A
Lockhart, 2b	4	0	0	0	1	1
C. Jones, 3b	4	0	1	0	1	2
Galarraga, 1b	3	0	0	0	9	1
Klesko, lf	2	0	0	0	0	0
Lopez, c	3	0	0	0	11	0
A. Jones, cf	3	0	0	0	2	0
Tucker, rf	3	0	0	0	2	0
Glavine, p	2	0	1	0	0	1
Rocker, p	0	0	0	0	1	0
Seanez, p	0	0	0	0	0	0
Guillen, ph-ss	1	0	0	0	0	0
Malloy, pr	0	0	0	0	0	0
Totals	29	0	3	0	27	8

San Diego	0 0 0	0 0 1	0 0 2—3			
Atlanta	0 0 0	0 0 0	0 0 0—0			

San Diego	IP	H	R	ER	BB	SO
Brown (W)	9.0	3	0	0	3	11

Atlanta	IP	H	R	ER	BB	SO
Glavine (L)	6.0	6	1	1	6	6
Rocker	1.0	1	0	0	0	1
Seanez	1.0	0	0	0	0	0
O. Perez	0.1	4	2	2	1	0
Ligtenberg	0.2	0	0	0	0	1

E—Lopez. DP—San Diego 1, Atlanta 1. LOB—San Diego 13, Atlanta 5. 2B—Veras, Gomez. SH—Gwynn. WP—Brown. U—Poncino, plate; Hallion, first; Bonin, second; Davis, third; Rippley, left field; Tata, right field. T—2:54. A—43,093.

GAME 3 BOX SCORE

SAN DIEGO 4, ATLANTA 1

SATURDAY, OCTOBER 10, AT SAN DIEGO

Atlanta	AB	R	H	RBI	PO	A
Weiss, ss	5	0	3	1	2	2
Williams, rf	5	0	0	0	2	0
C. Jones, 3b	4	0	1	0	0	1
Galarraga, 1b	3	0	1	0	6	4
A. Jones, cf	4	0	1	0	2	0
E. Perez, c	3	0	2	0	4	0
Malloy, pr	0	0	0	0	0	0
Seanez, p	0	0	0	0	0	0
Bautista, lf	2	0	0	0	2	0
Klesko, ph-lf	0	0	0	0	1	0
Graffanino, 2b	0	1	0	0	1	2
Tucker, ph	1	0	0	0	0	0
Lockhart, 2b	1	0	0	0	1	1
Maddux, p	1	0	0	0	1	0
Colbrunn, ph	1	0	0	0	0	0
Martinez, p	0	0	0	0	0	0
Rocker, p	0	0	0	0	1	1
Lopez, ph-c	1	0	0	0	2	0
Totals	31	1	8	1	24	12

San Diego	AB	R	H	RBI	PO	A
Veras, 2b	3	0	0	0	2	0
Finley, cf	4	1	2	1	1	0
Gwynn, rf	3	0	0	0	2	0
Caminiti, 3b	4	0	1	1	0	2
Joyner, 1b	2	1	0	0	4	0
Leyritz, c	2	0	0	0	9	0
Hernandez, c	1	1	1	0	4	0
Vander Wal, lf	3	0	1	0	2	1
Rivera, lf	1	0	0	0	1	0
Gomez, ss	4	0	0	0	1	3
Hitchcock, p	2	1	1	0	1	1
Wall, p	0	0	0	0	0	0
Sweeney, ph	1	0	0	0	0	0
Miceli, p	0	0	0	0	0	0
R. Myers, p	0	0	0	0	0	0
Hoffman, p	0	0	0	0	0	0
Totals	30	4	7	2	27	7

Atlanta	0 0 1	0 0 0	0 0 0—1			
San Diego	0 0 0	0 2 0	0 2 x—4			

Atlanta	IP	H	R	ER	BB	SO
Maddux (L)	5.0	5	2	2	2	3
Martinez	1.0	0	0	0	0	0
Rocker	1.0	0	0	0	1	1
Seanez	1.0	2	2	2	1	2

San Diego	IP	H	R	ER	BB	SO
Hitchcock (W)	*5.0	3	1	1	5	6
Wall	2.0	2	0	0	1	3
Miceli	0.1	2	0	0	0	0
R. Myers	0.1	0	0	0	1	0
Hoffman (S)	1.1	1	0	0	0	3

*Pitched to one batter in sixth.
E—Galarraga, Klesko. DP—Atlanta 1, San Diego 1. LOB—Atlanta 12, San Diego 7. 2B—Finley, Hernandez. SB—Weiss, Rivera. CS—Veras. SH—Maddux, E. Perez. HBP—By Maddux (Leyritz). PB—Lopez. U—Hallion, plate; Bonin, first; Davis, second; Rippley, third; Tata, left field; Poncino, right field. T—3:00. A—62,779.

GAME 4 BOX SCORE

ATLANTA 8, SAN DIEGO 3

SUNDAY, OCTOBER 11, AT SAN DIEGO

Atlanta	AB	R	H	RBI	PO	A
Guillen, ss	5	1	1	1	0	2
Lockhart, 2b	5	2	2	0	2	4
C. Jones, 3b	4	2	1	1	0	2
Galarraga, 1b	2	1	1	4	7	1
Klesko, lf	4	0	1	1	1	0
Rocker, p	0	0	0	0	0	0
O. Perez, p	0	0	0	0	0	0
Seanez, p	0	0	0	0	0	0
Ligtenberg, p	0	0	0	0	0	0
Lopez, c	4	1	1	1	12	0
A. Jones, cf	4	1	2	0	1	0
Tucker, rf	2	0	1	0	3	0
Williams, ph-rf	2	0	1	0	0	0
Neagle, p	2	0	0	0	1	1
Martinez, p	0	0	0	0	0	0
Colbrunn, ph	1	0	0	0	0	0
Bautista, lf	1	0	0	0	0	0
Totals	36	8	12	8	27	10

San Diego	AB	R	H	RBI	PO	A
Veras, 2b	4	1	0	0	2	5
Finley, cf	4	0	1	0	3	0
Gwynn, rf	4	1	1	1	1	0
Caminiti, 3b	3	0	1	0	1	2
Leyritz, 1b	3	1	2	2	4	0
Joyner, 1b	1	0	1	0	4	0
Hernandez, c	4	0	1	0	7	0
Rivera, lf	3	0	1	0	4	1
Sweeney, ph	1	0	0	0	0	0
Gomez, ss	3	0	0	0	1	2
Miceli, p	0	0	0	0	0	0
Boehringer, p	0	0	0	0	0	0
Langston, p	0	0	0	0	0	0
G. Myers, ph	1	0	0	0	0	0
Hamilton, p	2	0	0	0	0	1
R. Myers, p	0	0	0	0	0	0
Sheets, ss	1	0	0	0	0	1
Vander Wal, ph	1	0	0	0	0	0
Totals	34	3	8	3	27	12

Atlanta	0 0 0	1 0 1	6 0 0—8			
San Diego	0 0 2	0 0 1	0 0 0—3			

Atlanta	IP	H	R	ER	BB	SO
Neagle	5.2	7	3	3	1	7
Martinez (W)	0.1	0	0	0	0	0
Rocker	1.1	0	0	0	0	3
O. Perez	†0.0	1	0	0	1	0
Seanez	0.2	0	0	0	0	0
Ligtenberg	1.0	0	0	0	1	2

San Diego	IP	H	R	ER	BB	SO
Hamilton (L)	*6.0	7	4	4	2	5
R. Myers	0.2	2	3	3	1	0
Miceli	0.1	1	1	1	0	1
Boehringer	1.0	2	0	0	0	0
Langston	1.0	0	0	0	0	0

*Pitched to two batters in seventh. †Pitched to two batters in eighth.
DP—Atlanta 1, San Diego 2. LOB—Atlanta 4, San Diego 7. 2B—C. Jones, Gwynn, Rivera. 3B—Lockhart. HR—Leyritz, Lopez, Galarraga. WP—R. Myers. Bk—Ligtenberg. U—Bonin, plate; Davis, first; Rippley, second; Tata, third; Poncino, left field; Hallion, right field. T—2:58. A—65,042.

GAME 5 BOX SCORE

ATLANTA 7, SAN DIEGO 6
MONDAY, OCTOBER 12, AT SAN DIEGO

Atlanta	AB	R	H	RBI	PO	A
Guillen, ss	5	0	3	0	1	4
Lockhart, 2b	3	0	0	0	0	2
Colbrunn, ph	1	0	0	0	0	0
Graffanino, 2b	1	1	1	1	0	0
C. Jones, 3b	4	0	1	0	0	0
Galarraga, 1b	5	0	0	0	13	3
Klesko, lf	3	1	0	0	1	0
Williams, lf-rf	1	0	0	0	0	0
Lopez, c	4	1	2	0	8	2
Malloy, pr	0	1	0	0	0	0
E. Perez, c	1	0	1	0	1	0
A. Jones, cf	4	1	2	0	2	0
Tucker, rf	5	1	3	5	0	0
Ligtenberg, p	0	0	0	0	0	0
Maddux, p	0	0	0	0	0	0
Smoltz, p	3	0	1	0	1	3
Rocker, p	0	0	0	0	0	0
Seanez, p	0	0	0	0	0	1
Bautista, lf	0	0	0	0	0	0
Totals	40	7	14	6	27	15

Atlanta	AB	R	H	RBI	PO	A
Veras, 2b	5	0	2	0	1	1
Finley, cf	3	1	0	0	3	0
Gwynn, rf	5	0	0	0	1	0
Caminiti, 3b	4	1	1	2	1	2
Joyner, 1b	3	1	2	0	9	2
Sheets, ph	1	0	0	0	0	0
Boehringer, p	0	0	0	0	0	0
R. Myers, p	0	0	0	0	0	0
Vander Wal, lf	3	1	2	2	3	0
Langston, p	0	0	0	0	0	0
Brown, p	0	0	0	0	0	0
Wall, p	0	0	0	0	0	0
Leyritz, ph-1b	1	0	0	0	0	0
Hernandez, c	3	0	1	0	5	2
Sweeney, ph	0	1	0	0	0	0
Gomez, ss	3	0	1	0	4	3
G. Myers, ph	1	1	1	2	0	0
Ashby, p	2	0	0	0	3	0
Rivera, lf	1	0	0	0	1	0
Vaughn, ph	1	0	0	0	0	0
Totals	36	6	10	6	27	10

Atlanta	0	0	0	1	0	1	0	5	0—7
San Diego	2	0	0	0	0	2	0	0	2—6

Atlanta	IP	H	R	ER	BB	SO
Smoltz	6.2	9	4	4	1	8
Rocker (W)	1.0	0	0	0	0	0
Seanez	0.1	0	0	0	0	0
Ligtenberg	†0.0	1	2	2	1	0
Maddux (S)	1.0	0	0	0	1	1

San Diego	IP	H	R	ER	BB	SO
Ashby	6.0	9	2	2	1	2
Langston	*0.0	1	0	0	0	0
Brown (L)	1.1	2	3	3	1	1
Wall	0.2	1	2	1	2	1
Boehringer	0.2	1	0	0	0	0
R. Myers	0.1	0	0	0	0	1

*Pitched to one batter in seventh. †Pitched to two batters in ninth.
E—Galarraga, Gomez. LOB—Atlanta 10, San Diego 6. 2B—Graffanino. HR—Caminiti, Vander Wal, Tucker, G. Myers. SB—A. Jones. CS—A. Jones. U—Davis, plate; Rippley, first; Tata, second; Poncino, third; Hallion, left field; Bonin, right field. T—3:17. A—58,988.

GAME 6 BOX SCORE

SAN DIEGO 5, ATLANTA 0
WEDNESDAY, OCTOBER 14, AT ATLANTA

San Diego	AB	R	H	RBI	PO	A
Veras, 2b	4	0	1	1	0	0
Gwynn, rf	5	0	2	0	1	0
Hoffman, p	0	0	0	0	0	0
Vaughn, lf	4	1	2	0	1	0
Caminiti, 3b	5	1	2	0	1	2
Leyritz, c	4	0	0	1	10	1
Hamilton, p	0	0	0	0	1	1
Rivera, ph-rf	1	0	0	0	1	0
Joyner, 1b	4	1	1	1	8	1
Finley, cf	3	1	1	0	2	0
Gomez, ss	3	1	0	0	1	2
Hitchcock, p	3	0	0	0	0	0
Boehringer, p	0	0	0	0	0	0
Langston, p	0	0	0	0	0	0
Hernandez, c	1	0	1	0	2	0
Totals	37	5	10	3	27	7

Atlanta	AB	R	H	RBI	PO	A
Weiss, ss	2	0	0	0	0	3
Williams, rf-lf	3	0	1	0	1	0
C. Jones, 3b	4	0	0	0	0	6
Galarraga, 1b	3	0	0	0	17	0
Lopez, c	4	0	1	0	4	0
A. Jones, cf	4	0	0	0	3	0
Bautista, lf	2	0	0	0	0	0
Tucker, ph-rf	1	0	0	0	0	0
Graffanino, 2b	2	0	0	0	1	3
Lockhart, ph-2b	1	0	0	0	1	1
Glavine, p	2	0	0	0	0	1
Rocker, p	0	0	0	0	0	0
Martinez, p	0	0	0	0	0	2
Colbrunn, ph	1	0	0	0	0	0
Neagle, p	0	0	0	0	0	0
Totals	29	0	2	0	27	16

San Diego	0	0	0	0	0	5	0	0	0—5
Atlanta	0	0	0	0	0	0	0	0	0—0

San Diego	IP	H	R	ER	BB	SO
Hitchcock (W)	*5.0	2	0	0	3	8
Boehringer	1.1	0	0	0	1	1
Langston	0.1	0	0	0	0	0
Hamilton	1.1	0	0	0	1	1
Hoffman	1.0	0	0	0	0	1

Atlanta	IP	H	R	ER	BB	SO
Glavine (L)	5.2	7	5	2	3	2
Rocker	*0.0	2	0	0	0	0
Martinez	1.1	0	0	0	0	0
Neagle	2.0	1	0	0	1	2

*Pitched to two batters in sixth.
E—Bautista. DP—Atlanta 1. LOB—San Diego 9, Atlanta 7. SB—Williams. WP—Hitchcock 2. U—Rippley, plate; Tata, first; Poncino, second; Hallion, third; Bonin, left field; Davis, right field. T—3:10. A—50,988.

STATISTICS

SAN DIEGO PADRES' BATTING AND FIELDING AVERAGES

Player, position	G	AB	R	H	TB	2B	3B	HR	RBI	BB	IBB	SO	Avg.	PO	A	E	Avg.
G. Myers, ph	2	1	1	1	4	0	0	1	2	1	0	0	1.000	0	0	0	.000
Brown, p	2	4	1	2	2	0	0	0	0	0	0	1	.500	2	1	0	1.000
Vander Wal, lf-ph	3	7	1	3	6	0	0	1	2	0	0	2	.429	5	1	0	1.000
Finley, cf	6	21	3	7	8	1	0	0	2	6	1	2	.333	15	0	0	1.000
Hernandez, c	6	18	2	6	7	1	0	0	0	1	0	5	.333	36	4	0	1.000
Joyner, 1b	6	16	3	5	5	0	0	0	2	4	0	3	.313	45	6	0	1.000
Caminiti, 3b	6	22	3	6	12	0	0	2	4	5	1	4	.273	5	10	0	1.000

Player, position	G	AB	R	H	TB	2B	3B	HR	RBI	BB	IBB	SO	Avg.	PO	A	E	Avg.
Veras, 2b	6	24	2	6	7	1	0	0	2	5	0	7	.250	7	13	0	1.000
Vaughn, lf-ph	3	8	1	2	2	0	0	0	0	1	0	1	.250	2	0	0	1.000
Gwynn, rf	6	26	1	6	7	1	0	0	2	1	1	2	.231	5	0	0	1.000
Rivera, lf-ph-rf	6	13	1	3	5	2	0	0	0	0	0	7	.231	8	1	0	1.000
Hitchcock, p	2	5	1	1	1	0	0	0	0	0	0	0	.200	1	1	0	1.000
Leyritz, ph-1b-c	5	12	1	2	5	0	0	1	4	0	0	2	.167	24	1	0	1.000
Gomez, ss	6	20	2	3	4	1	0	0	0	2	0	5	.150	5	14	1	.950
Boehringer, p	3	0	0	0	0	0	0	0	0	0	0	0	.000	0	0	0	.000
Hoffman, p	3	0	0	0	0	0	0	0	0	0	0	0	.000	0	0	0	.000
Langston, p	3	0	0	0	0	0	0	0	0	0	0	0	.000	0	0	0	.000
Miceli, p	3	0	0	0	0	0	0	0	0	0	0	0	.000	0	0	0	.000
R. Myers, p	4	0	0	0	0	0	0	0	0	0	0	0	.000	0	0	0	.000
Wall, p	3	0	0	0	0	0	0	0	0	0	0	0	.000	0	0	0	.000
Hamilton, p	2	2	0	0	0	0	0	0	0	0	0	1	.000	1	2	0	1.000
Sweeney, ph	3	2	1	0	0	0	0	0	0	1	0	1	.000	0	0	0	.000
Sheets, ss-ph	3	3	0	0	0	0	0	0	0	0	0	1	.000	0	2	0	1.000
Ashby, p	2	4	0	0	0	0	0	0	0	0	0	4	.000	4	4	0	1.000
Totals	6	208	24	53	75	7	0	5	20	27	3	48	.255	165	60	1	.996

ATLANTA BRAVES' BATTING AND FIELDING AVERAGES

Player, position	G	AB	R	H	TB	2B	3B	HR	RBI	BB	IBB	SO	Avg.	PO	A	E	Avg.
E. Perez, c	3	4	0	3	3	0	0	0	0	0	0	0	.750	6	0	0	1.000
Guillen, ph-ss	4	12	1	5	5	0	0	0	1	0	0	1	.417	1	6	0	1.000
Tucker, rf-ph	6	13	1	5	9	1	0	1	5	2	0	5	.385	7	0	0	1.000
Colbrunn, ph	6	6	0	2	2	0	0	0	0	0	0	2	.333	0	0	0	.000
Graffanino, ph-2b	4	3	2	1	2	1	0	0	1	2	1	1	.333	2	5	0	1.000
Lopez, c-ph	6	20	2	6	9	0	0	1	1	0	0	7	.300	43	2	1	.978
A. Jones, cf	6	22	3	6	9	0	0	1	2	1	0	4	.273	15	0	0	1.000
Glavine, ph-p	3	4	0	1	1	0	0	0	0	1	0	2	.250	0	2	0	1.000
Lockhart, 2b-ph	6	17	2	4	7	1	0	0	0	0	0	4	.235	5	12	0	1.000
C. Jones, 3b	6	24	2	5	6	1	0	0	1	4	0	5	.208	1	12	0	1.000
Weiss, ss	4	15	0	3	3	0	0	0	1	2	0	5	.200	4	11	0	1.000
Smoltz, p	2	5	0	1	1	0	0	0	0	0	0	1	.200	3	5	1	.889
Williams, ph-rf-lf	5	13	0	2	2	0	0	0	1	0	0	6	.154	3	0	0	1.000
Galarraga, 1b	6	21	1	2	5	0	0	1	4	6	0	6	.095	63	11	4	.949
Klesko, lf-ph	5	12	2	1	1	0	0	0	1	6	1	3	.083	3	0	1	.750
Ligtenberg, p	4	0	0	0	0	0	0	0	0	0	0	0	.000	0	0	0	.000
Martinez, p	4	0	0	0	0	0	0	0	0	0	0	0	.000	0	3	0	1.000
O. Perez, p	2	0	0	0	0	0	0	0	0	0	0	0	.000	0	0	0	.000
Rocker, p	6	0	1	0	0	0	0	0	0	1	0	0	.000	2	1	0	1.000
Seanez, p	4	0	0	0	0	0	0	0	0	0	0	0	.000	0	1	0	1.000
Maddux, p	2	1	0	0	0	0	0	0	0	0	0	0	.000	1	1	0	1.000
Malloy, pr-2b	4	1	1	0	0	0	0	0	0	0	0	1	.000	0	1	0	1.000
Neagle, p	2	2	0	0	0	0	0	0	0	0	0	0	.000	1	1	0	1.000
Bautista, pr-lf	5	5	0	0	0	0	0	0	0	0	0	1	.000	2	0	1	.667
Totals	6	200	18	47	65	4	1	4	17	26	2	54	.235	162	74	8	.967

SAN DIEGO PADRES' PITCHING RECORDS

Pitcher	G	GS	CG	IP	H	R	ER	HR	BB	IBB	SO	HB	WP	W	L	Pct.	ERA
Boehringer	3	0	0	3.0	3	0	0	0	1	0	1	0	0	0	0	.000	0.00
Langston	3	0	0	1.1	1	0	0	0	0	0	1	0	0	0	0	.000	0.00
Hitchcock	2	2	0	10.0	5	1	1	0	8	1	14	0	2	2	0	1.000	0.90
Ashby	2	2	0	13.0	14	3	3	1	2	0	5	0	0	1	0	.000	2.08
Hoffman	3	0	0	4.1	2	1	1	0	2	0	7	0	0	1	0	1.000	2.08
Brown	2	1	1	10.1	5	3	3	1	4	0	12	0	1	1	1	.500	2.61
Wall	3	0	0	3.0	3	2	1	0	4	1	4	0	0	0	0	.000	3.00
Hamilton	2	1	0	7.1	7	4	4	1	3	0	6	0	0	0	1	.000	4.91
R. Myers	4	0	0	2.0	3	3	3	0	2	0	3	0	1	0	0	.000	13.50
Miceli	3	0	0	0.2	4	1	1	1	0	0	1	0	0	0	0	.000	13.50
Totals	6	6	1	55.0	47	18	17	4	26	2	54	0	4	4	2	.667	2.78

Shutouts—Brown; Hitchcock, Boehringer, Langston, Hamilton and Hoffman (combined). Saves—Hoffman, Wall.

ATLANTA BRAVES' PITCHING RECORDS

Pitcher	G	GS	CG	IP	H	R	ER	HR	BB	IBB	SO	HB	WP	W	L	Pct.	ERA
Rocker	6	0	0	4.2	3	0	0	0	1	0	5	0	0	1	0	1.000	0.00
Martinez	4	0	0	3.1	1	0	0	0	1	1	0	0	0	1	0	1.000	0.00
Glavine	2	2	0	11.2	13	6	3	0	9	0	8	0	0	0	2	.000	2.31
Maddux	2	1	0	6.0	5	2	2	0	3	1	4	1	0	0	1	.000	3.00

Pitcher	G	GS	CG	IP	H	R	ER	HR	BB	IBB	SO	HB	WP	W	L	Pct.	ERA
Neagle...........................	2	1	0	7.2	8	3	3	1	2	0	9	0	0	0	0	.000	3.52
Smoltz..........................	2	2	0	13.2	13	6	6	2	6	0	13	0	0	0	0	.000	3.95
Seanez	4	0	0	3.0	2	2	2	0	1	0	4	0	0	0	0	.000	6.00
Ligtenberg.....................	4	0	0	3.2	3	3	3	2	2	0	5	0	0	0	1	.000	7.36
O. Perez	2	0	0	0.1	5	2	2	0	2	1	0	0	0	0	0	.000	54.00
Totals	6	6	0	54.0	53	24	21	5	27	3	48	1	0	2	4	.333	3.50

No shutouts. Save—Maddux.

SCORE BY INNINGS

San Diego 2	0	2		0	3	9		0	3	4		1—24
Atlanta 0	0	2		2	0	2		6	5	1		0—18

MISCELLANEOUS STATISTICS

Sacrifice hits—Ashby, Gwynn, Maddux, E. Perez.
Sacrifice flies—A. Jones.
Stolen bases—Finley, A. Jones, Rivera, Weiss, Williams.
Caught stealing—A. Jones, Veras.
Double plays—Weiss, Lockhart and Galarraga 2; Ashby and Caminiti; Galarraga and Weiss; Gomez and Joyner; Gomez, Veras and Joyner; Gomez, Veras and Leyritz; Guillen, Lockhart and Galarraga; C. Jones, Graffanino and Galarraga; Joyner, Gomez and Brown; Veras, Hernandez and Caminiti; Weiss, Graffanino and Galarraga.
Left on bases—San Diego 10, 13, 7, 7, 6, 9—52; Atlanta 8, 5, 12, 4, 10, 7—46.
Hit by pitcher—By Maddux (Leyritz).
Passed ball—Lopez.
Balk—Ligtenberg.
Time of games—First game, 3:27; second game, 2:54; third game, 3:00; fourth game, 2:58; fifth game, 3:17; sixth game, 3:10.
Attendance—First game, 42,117; second game, 43,093; third game, 62,779; fourth game, 65,042; fifth game, 58,988; sixth game, 50,988.
Umpires—Tata, Poncino, Hallion, Bonin, Davis, Rippley.
Official scorers—Phil Collier, Mark Frederickson, Bill Zavestoski.

1998 REVIEW N.L. Championship Series

WORLD SERIES

GAME 1
HIGHLIGHTS
NEW YORK 9, SAN DIEGO 6

Why the Yankees won: Tino Martinez, having added to his history of postseason futility with a .105 batting average in the 1998 A.L. Championship Series, picked a most opportune time to shake out of his funk.

Why the Padres lost: San Diego's questionable middle relief came up small just when it needed to come up big.

The turning points:

1. When Padres ace Kevin Brown was struck on the left shin by Chili Davis' second-inning smash that went for a single. The play ignited a two-run Yankees rally—rookie Ricky Ledee accounted for the runs with a bases-loaded double into Yankee Stadium's right field corner—and it led to Brown's premature departure from the game (in the seventh) when the righthander struggled with his control, apparently because he was favoring the leg.

2. After Donne Wall relieved Brown in the seventh inning and yielded a game-tying three-run homer to the Yankees' Chuck Knoblauch, Mark Langston seemingly escaped a bases-loaded jam later in the inning when he whistled a 2-2 fastball past Martinez. But umpire Richie Garcia said the pitch just missed low, and the New York first baseman followed with a grand slam. Trailing 5-2 entering the inning, the Yankees had seized a 9-5 lead.

Notable: Padres outfielder Greg Vaughn, coming off a remarkable turnaround season in which he hit 50 home runs after producing only 18 the year before, continued his extraordinary slugging with a two-run homer in the third inning and a bases-empty shot in the fifth. . . . Tony Gwynn, the eight-time N.L. batting champion playing in his first World Series game in 14 years, hit a two-run homer in the fifth that gave San Diego a 4-2 lead. He had a 3-for-4 night. . . . David Wells was hardly his dominant self, but the Yankees' lefthander pitched well enough to win—and he did just that despite allowing five runs in seven innings. . . . The Yankees' seventh-inning outburst was helped along by a two-out intentional walk to Bernie Williams, who already had a strike on him. Williams was put aboard in a 5-5 game after Langston's wild pitch advanced Derek Jeter (who had singled) from first to second base. Sometimes a pitcher struggles with his control after an intentional pass and, sure enough, Langston proceeded to walk Davis, filling the bases. Then came the fateful Langston-Martinez matchup.

Quotable: Padres manager Bruce Bochy said "we would have liked to have had it (the critical 2-2 pitch to Martinez). Langston thought it was there, and Carlos (Hernandez, San Diego's catcher) thought it was there. Mark was frustrated. He was upset. Mark

had to come at him, and he (Martinez) got all of it." Martinez's take: "I thought it was down. (Garcia) did a great job behind the plate all night." . . . Why was Wall summoned to face Knoblauch in such a key situation earlier in the seventh inning? "Because you've got to stay with what got you here," Bochy said. "All year we've used him in the seventh inning, and he's done a good job there." True, the reliever had a 2.43 regular-season ERA, but he had experienced some off moments in the N.L. playoffs. . . . Bochy, watching Brown closely after his ace was hit by Davis' drive, said the Padres "were going to get him" if he showed signs of weakening. When two Yankees reached base in the seventh ahead of Knoblauch, it was time. . . . Knoblauch, who got considerable grief in the ALCS for letting a ball roll away while he argued a call, wasn't buying into a redemption theory after contributing his key homer. "I don't think so," he said. The second baseman said he was probably more excited when Martinez hit his home run. "We've been trying to help each other out," he explained. . . . New York manager Joe Torre said Martinez's home run "relieved everybody's pressure in the dugout." And Martinez, acknowledging his poor postseason resume, said it "was definitely a big relief to get a hit in that situation."

BOX SCORE

SATURDAY, OCTOBER 17, AT NEW YORK

San Diego	AB	R	H	RBI	PO	A
Veras, 2b	4	1	1	0	1	4
Gwynn, rf	4	1	3	2	2	0
Vaughn, lf	4	3	2	3	2	0
Caminiti, 3b	3	0	0	0	0	1
Leyritz, dh	4	0	0	0	0	0
Joyner, 1b	3	0	0	0	7	0
Finley, cf	4	0	1	0	3	1
C. Hernandez, c	3	0	0	0	8	0
*G. Myers, ph	1	0	0	0	0	0
Gomez, ss	3	1	1	0	1	2
†Vander Wal, ph	1	0	0	0	0	0
Brown, p	0	0	0	0	0	0
Wall, p	0	0	0	0	0	0
Langston, p	0	0	0	0	0	0
Boehringer, p	0	0	0	0	0	0
Myers, p	0	0	0	0	0	0
Totals	34	6	8	5	24	8

New York	AB	R	H	RBI	PO	A
Knoblauch, 2b	4	1	2	3	2	1
Jeter, ss	4	1	1	0	1	0
O'Neill, rf	5	0	0	0	4	0
Williams, cf	4	1	0	0	1	0
Davis, dh	3	2	1	0	0	0
Martinez, 1b	3	2	1	4	8	0
Brosius, 3b	4	0	1	0	1	1
Posada, c	3	1	1	0	7	0
Ledee, lf	3	1	2	2	3	0
Wells, p	0	0	0	0	0	0
Nelson, p	0	0	0	0	0	1
M. Rivera, p	0	0	0	0	0	0
Totals	33	9	9	9	27	3

San Diego	0	0	2	0	3	0	0	1	0—6
New York	0	2	0	0	0	0	7	0	x—9

San Diego	IP	H	R	ER	BB	SO
Brown	6.1	6	4	4	3	5
Wall (L)	*0.0	2	2	2	0	0

San Diego	IP	H	R	ER	BB	SO
Langston	0.2	1	3	3	2	0
Boehringer	0.1	0	0	0	1	1
R. Myers	0.2	0	0	0	0	2

New York	IP	H	R	ER	BB	SO
Wells (W)	7.0	7	5	5	2	4
Nelson	0.2	1	1	0	1	1
Rivera (S)	1.1	0	0	0	0	2

*Pitched to two batters in seventh.

Bases on balls—Off Brown 3 (Martinez, Posada, Ledee), off Langston 2 (Williams, Davis), off Boehringer 1 (Jeter), off Wells 2 (Veras, Joyner), off Nelson 1 (Caminiti).

Strikeouts—By Brown 5 (Williams 2, Brosius, Knoblauch, Martinez), by Boehringer 1 (Posada), by R. Myers 2 (O'Neill, Williams), by Wells 4 (Caminiti 2, Joyner, Leyritz), by Nelson 1 (Leyritz), by M. Rivera 2 (G. Myers, Vander Wal).

*Struck out for C. Hernandez in ninth. †Struck out for Gomez in ninth. E—Vaughn, Knoblauch. DP—New York 2. LOB—San Diego 4, New York 7. 2B—Finley, Ledee. HR—Vaughn 2, Gwynn, Williams, Martinez. HBP—By Boehringer (Knoblauch). WP—Langston. U—Garcia (A.L.), plate; Hirschbeck (N.L.), first; Scott (A.L.), second; DeMuth (N.L.), third; Tschida (A.L.), left field; Crawford (N.L.), right field. T—3:29. A—56,712.

PLAY BY PLAY

FIRST INNING

San Diego—Veras walked. Gwynn singled to left as Veras went to second. Vaughn grounded into a double play, Knoblauch to Martinez, as Veras went to third. Caminiti struck out.

New York—Knoblauch popped to Gomez. Jeter grounded out, Veras to Joyner. O'Neill grounded out, Gomez to Joyner.

SECOND INNING

San Diego—Leyritz grounded out to Martinez. Joyner struck out. Finley doubled to right-center. C. Hernandez flied to O'Neill.

New York—Williams grounded out, Caminiti to Joyner. Davis singled to the pitcher. Martinez walked. Brosius struck out. Posada walked. Ledee doubled down the right-field line, scoring Davis and Martinez, as Posada went to third. Knoblauch struck out. **N.Y. 2, S.D. 0.**

THIRD INNING

San Diego—Gomez singled to left. Veras flied to O'Neill. Gwynn grounded out to Martinez as Gomez went to second. Vaughn homered to right-center, scoring Gomez. Caminiti struck out. **N.Y. 2, S.D. 2.**

New York—Jeter flied to Gwynn. O'Neill flied to Vaughn. Williams struck out.

FOURTH INNING

San Diego—Leyritz struck out. Joyner lined to Ledee. Finley grounded to Martinez.

New York—Davis and Martinez flied to Finley. Brosius singled to left-center, but was out trying to stretch the hit to a double, Finley to Veras.

FIFTH INNING

San Diego—C. Hernandez flied to Ledee. Gomez popped to Jeter. Veras singled to center. Gwynn homered to right, scoring Veras. Vaughn homered to left. Caminiti flied to Ledee. **S.D. 5, N.Y. 2.**

New York—Posada grounded out, Veras to Joyner. Ledee singled to right. Knoblauch singled to right as Ledee went to second. Jeter grounded out, Gomez to Joyner, as Ledee went to third and Knoblauch to second. O'Neill grounded out, Veras to Joyner.

SIXTH INNING

San Diego—Leyritz flied to O'Neill. Joyner walked. Finley lined to Martinez, who doubled Joyner off of first, unassisted.

New York—Williams struck out. Davis flied to Vaughn. Martinez struck out.

SEVENTH INNING

San Diego—C. Hernandez flied to Williams. Gomez grounded out, Brosius to Martinez. Veras flied to O'Neill.

New York—Brosius grounded out, Veras to Joyner. Posada singled to right. Ledee walked. Wall now pitching. Knoblauch homered to left, scoring Posada and Ledee. Jeter singled to center. Langston now pitching. O'Neill flied to Gwynn. Jeter went to second on a wild pitch. Williams was walked intentionally. Davis

walked. Martinez hit a home run to right, scoring Jeter, Williams and Davis. Brosius flied to Finley. **N.Y. 9, S.D. 5.**

EIGHTH INNING

San Diego—Nelson now pitching. Gwynn singled to right. Vaughn forced Gwynn at second, Nelson to Knoblauch. Caminiti walked. Leyritz struck out. M. Rivera now pitching. Joyner reached first on an error by Knoblauch, scoring Vaughn as Caminiti went to second. Finley grounded to Martinez. **N.Y. 9, S.D. 6.**

New York—Boehringer now pitching. Posada struck out. Ledee reached first on an error by Vaughn. Knoblauch hit by pitch. Jeter walked. R. Myers now pitching. O'Neill and Williams struck out.

NINTH INNING

San Diego—G. Myers, pinch-hitting for C. Hernandez, struck out. Vander Wal, pinch-hitting for Gomez, struck out. Veras popped to Brosius in foul territory. **Final score: N.Y. 9, S.D. 6.**

GAME 2
HIGHLIGHTS

NEW YORK 9, SAN DIEGO 3

Why the Yankees won: They got the all-around contributions that marked their run to an A.L.-record 114 regular-season victories. Every player in the starting lineup managed at least one hit (and only one starter failed to score a run), the defense was flawless and the pitching was effective.

Why the Padres lost: Andy Ashby had a fine season (17-9 record, 3.34 ERA) as the No. 2 man in San Diego's rotation, but the righthander nevertheless was viewed as a considerable dropoff from the club's lead man, Kevin Brown, and he proved to be just that. Furthermore, Ashby was not 100 percent physically fit for Game 2. Battling flu symptoms (as well as the knowledge that even Brown looked mortal against the Yankees the night before), Ashby was hammered for 10 hits in 2⅔ innings. Also, shaky defense put the Padres in a hole early.

The turning points:

1. When the Padres muffed a chance to seize a first-inning lead, an edge that might have done wonders for the N.L. champions' collective psyche. After leadoff hitter Quilvio Veras struck out against Orlando "El Duque" Hernandez, Tony Gwynn stroked a single and Greg Vaughn drew a walk. But Ken Caminiti struck out and the Yankees' Paul O'Neill made a leaping catch against the right field wall on Wally Joyner's line drive.

2. When the Yankees did exactly what San Diego feared—they gained a psychological edge by jumping on top immediately after the Padres fumbled their opportunity. Chuck Knoblauch, getting a second chance when catcher Greg Myers failed to make a sliding catch of his pop foul, led off the first with a walk, stole second and scored when third baseman Caminiti made an errant throw to first on O'Neill's grounder. By inning's end, Chili Davis and Scott Brosius had added RBI singles and New York had built a 3-0 advantage.

Notable: Yankees center fielder Bernie Williams, playing amid reports that the free agent-to-be might wind up elsewhere in 1999, highlighted another three-run New York salvo in the second inning with a two-run homer. . . . Ninth-place hitter Ricky Ledee, enjoying his second consecutive two-hit game, boosted the Yanks to a 7-0 lead in the third with a double that scored Tino Martinez, and eighth-place hitter Jorge Posada capped the victors' scoring with a two-run homer in the fifth. . . . Martinez, coming out of his postseason doldrums in grand style, collected three hits. . . . The bottom four hitters in the Yankees' lineup were 9-for-17 with four RBIs and three runs scored. . . . Hernandez, whose brother Livan of the Florida Marlins was the 1997 World Series MVP, left after seven innings with the game safely in hand.

Quotable: "On a play like that, you just go for it," New York's O'Neill said of his momentum-snuffing catch of Joyner's drive in the first inning. ... "The first inning was really the difference in the ballgame," San Diego manager Bruce Bochy said. "We're close to getting three runs there and we don't score. They come back and get three unearned runs. That's a six-run difference." . . . Joe Torre's decision to use Ledee in the Series seemed to be another masterstroke for the Yankees' manager, who had shown a knack for making the right moves all season. But, Torre acknowledged, he had stationed Ledee in left field because of his defense. "Shows you how smart I am," said Torre, alluding to Ledee's offensive contributions (4-for-6 with three RBIs) in the first two games. . . . Asked if he might be distracted by the speculation about his future, the Yankees' Williams responded: "This is my future right now. This is what you play for. This is what every major leaguer wants—an opportunity to play in the World Series."

BOX SCORE

SUNDAY, OCTOBER 18, AT NEW YORK

San Diego	AB	R	H	RBI	PO	A
Veras, 2b	5	0	1	1	1	4
Gwynn, rf	4	0	1	0	2	0
Vaughn, lf	4	0	0	0	0	0
Caminiti, 3b	5	1	1	0	2	0
Joyner, 1b	2	0	0	0	8	0
*Leyritz, ph-1b	1	0	0	0	0	0
Finley, cf	4	0	0	0	2	0
Vander Wal, lf	3	0	2	0	1	0
†R. Rivera, ph-lf	1	1	1	1	0	0
G. Myers, c	3	0	0	0	4	1
‡C. Hernandez, ph-c	1	0	1	0	2	0
Gomez, ss	3	1	2	0	2	3
§Sweeney, ph	1	0	1	1	0	0
Sheets, ss	0	0	0	0	0	0
Ashby, p	0	0	0	0	0	2
Boehringer, p	0	0	0	0	0	0
Wall, p	0	0	0	0	0	1
Miceli, p	0	0	0	0	0	1
Totals	37	3	10	3	24	12

New York	AB	R	H	RBI	PO	A
Knoblauch, 2b	3	2	2	0	1	2
Jeter, ss	5	1	2	1	3	0
O'Neill, rf	5	1	1	0	1	0
Williams, cf	4	1	1	2	1	0
Davis, dh	3	1	1	1	0	0
∞Bush, pr-dh	0	0	0	0	0	0
Martinez, 1b	5	1	3	0	6	1
Brosius, 3b	5	1	3	1	0	2
Posada, c	4	1	1	2	10	0
Ledee, lf	3	0	2	1	4	0

New York	AB	R	H	RBI	PO	A
O. Hernandez, p	0	0	0	0	1	1
Stanton, p	0	0	0	0	0	0
Nelson, p	0	0	0	0	0	0
Totals	37	9	16	8	27	6

San Diego	0	0	0	0	1	0	0	2	0—3
New York	3	3	1	0	2	0	0	0	x—9

San Diego	IP	H	R	ER	BB	SO
Ashby (L)	2.2	10	7	4	1	1
Boehringer	1.2	4	2	2	1	2
Wall	2.2	1	0	0	3	1
Miceli	1.0	1	0	0	2	1

New York	IP	H	R	ER	BB	SO
O. Hernandez (W)	7.0	6	1	1	3	7
Stanton	0.2	3	2	2	0	1
Nelson	1.1	1	0	0	0	2

Bases on balls—Off Ashby 1 (Knoblauch), off Boehringer 1 (Ledee), off Wall 3 (Davis, Posada, Knoblauch), off Miceli 2 (Williams, Davis), off O. Hernandez 3 (Vaughn, Joyner, Gwynn).

Strikeouts—By Ashby 1 (Davis), by Boehringer 2 (Knoblauch, Davis), by Wall 1 (Jeter), by Miceli 1 (Brosius), by O. Hernandez 7 (Veras 2, Caminiti, Finley, Vander Wal, G. Myers, Vaughn), by Stanton 1 (Leyritz), by Nelson 2 (Veras, Caminiti).

*Struck out for Joyner in eighth. †Doubled for Vander Wal in eighth. ‡Singled for G. Myers in eighth. §Singled for Gomez in eighth. ∞Ran for Davis in eighth. E—Caminiti. DP—San Diego 3. LOB—San Diego 10, New York 11. 2B—Veras, Caminiti, Vander Wal, R. Rivera, Ledee. 3B—Gomez. HR—Williams, Posada. SB—Knoblauch. CS—Ledee. U—Hirschbeck (N.L.), plate; Scott (A.L.), first; DeMuth (N.L.), second; Tschida (A.L.), third; Crawford (N.L.), left field; Garcia (A.L.), right field. T—3:13. A—56,692.

PLAY BY PLAY

FIRST INNING

San Diego—Veras struck out. Gwynn singled to left. Vaughn walked. Caminiti struck out. Joyner flied to O'Neill.

New York—Knoblauch walked. Knoblauch stole second. Jeter grounded out, Ashby to Joyner. O'Neill reached first on a throwing error by Caminiti as Knoblauch scored. Williams grounded out, Ashby to Joyner, as O'Neill went to second. Davis singled to center, scoring O'Neill. Martinez singled down the right-field line, as Davis went to third. Brosius singled to left, scoring Davis as Martinez went to second. Posada grounded out, Veras to Joyner. **N.Y. 3, S.D. 0.**

SECOND INNING

San Diego—Finley struck out. Vander Wal singled to left-center. G. Myers flied to Williams. Gomez grounded out, Brosius to Martinez.

New York—Ledee singled to right. Knoblauch singled to third as Ledee went to second. Ledee was caught trying to steal third, G. Myers to Caminiti, as Knoblauch went to second. Jeter singled to center, scoring Knoblauch. O'Neill flied to Vander Wal. Williams homered to right-center, scoring Jeter. Davis struck out. **N.Y. 6, S.D. 0.**

THIRD INNING

San Diego—Veras struck out. Gwynn flied to Ledee. Vaughn popped to Jeter.

New York—Martinez singled to center. Brosius singled to left as Martinez went to second. Posada grounded into a double play, Veras to Gomez to Joyner, as Martinez went to third. Ledee doubled to left, scoring Martinez. Boehringer now pitching. Knoblauch struck out. **N.Y. 7, S.D. 0.**

FOURTH INNING

San Diego—Caminiti lined to Martinez. Joyner grounded out, Knoblauch to Martinez. Finley grounded out, Martinez to O. Hernandez.

New York—Jeter singled to center. O'Neill grounded out, Gomez to Joyner, as Jeter went to second. Williams flied to Finley. Davis struck out.

FIFTH INNING

San Diego—Vander Wal struck out. G. Myers struck out. Gomez tripled to right-center. Veras doubled down the right-field line, scoring Gomez. Gwynn grounded out, O. Hernandez to Martinez. **N.Y. 7, S.D. 1.**

New York—Martinez popped to Caminiti. Brosius singled to left. Posada homered to right-center, scoring Brosius. Ledee

- 198 -

walked. Knoblauch singled to right as Ledee went to second. Wall now pitching. Jeter struck out. O'Neill grounded out, Veras to Joyner. **N.Y. 9, S.D. 1.**

SIXTH INNING

San Diego—Vaughn struck out. Caminiti flied to Ledee. Joyner walked. Finley popped to Knoblauch.

New York—Williams lined to Gwynn. Davis walked. Martinez singled to left as Davis went to second. Brosius grounded into a double play, Veras to Joyner.

SEVENTH INNING

San Diego—Vander Wal doubled down the left-field line. G. Myers flied to Ledee. Gomez singled to center as Vander Wal went to third. Veras flied to Ledee. Gwynn walked. Vaughn popped to Jeter.

New York—Posada walked. Ledee flied to Gwynn. Knoblauch walked. Jeter grounded into a double play, Wall to Gomez to Joyner.

EIGHTH INNING

San Diego—Stanton now pitching. Caminiti hit a ground-rule double down the left-field line. Leyritz, pinch-hitting for Joyner, struck out. Finley grounded out, Knoblauch to Martinez, as Caminiti went to third. R. Rivera, pinch-hitting for Vander Wal, doubled to left-center, scoring Caminiti. C. Hernandez, pinch-hitting for G. Myers, singled to second as R. Rivera went to third. Nelson now pitching. Sweeney, pinch-hitting for Gomez, singled to right, scoring R. Rivera as C. Hernandez went to second. Veras struck out. **N.Y. 9, S.D. 3.**

New York—Sheets now at short, Leyritz at first, R. Rivera in left, C. Hernandez catching and Miceli pitching. O'Neill singled to center. Williams and Davis walked. Bush now pinch-running for Davis. Martinez forced O'Neill at home, Miceli to C. Hernandez, as Williams went to third and Bush to second. Brosius struck out. Posada flied to Finley.

NINTH INNING

San Diego—Gwynn lined to Jeter. Vaughn grounded out, Brosius to Martinez. Caminiti struck out. **Final score: N.Y. 9, S.D. 3.**

GAME 3
HIGHLIGHTS
NEW YORK 5, SAN DIEGO 4

Why the Yankees won: Scott Brosius, a .300 hitter in the regular season with 98 RBIs after batting .203 for Oakland in 1997, continued his storybook year with two home runs—including the game-winner, a three-run smash to center field at Qualcomm Stadium.

Why the Padres lost: San Diego was forced to call on closer Trevor Hoffman an inning earlier than usual—and the move didn't work.

The turning points:

1. When Padres manager Bruce Bochy summoned Hoffman with no one out in the eighth inning to protect a 3-2 lead. Hoffman, coming off a phenomenal season (53 saves and a 1.48 ERA), was being called on to do what he had done only four times in 66 regular-season games—pitch two full innings. Whether it was a mind-set problem or plain ineffectiveness, Hoffman couldn't get the job done. With one runner already on base, the reliever retired Bernie Williams on a long drive to right field before walking Tino Martinez and then being tagged for a home run by Brosius.

2. When Bochy, his team trailing 5-4 in the ninth inning, used pinch hitter extraordinaire John Vander Wal as a pinch runner. Carlos Hernandez and pinch hitter Mark Sweeney collected two-out singles

against Yankees closer Mariano Rivera, but the left-handed-hitting Vander Wal—having been sent in to run for Hernandez—wasn't available when reserve shortstop Andy Sheets came to the plate. Righthander Rivera struck out the righthanded-hitting Sheets to end the game.

Notable: Brosius, who batted .400 in the Division Series and .300 in the ALCS and collected nine RBIs in those nine playoff games, was now 7-for-13 in the World Series with five RBIs. . . . Padres third baseman Ken Caminiti, whose mobility was severely limited by a groin injury, made his second error of the Series and saw his batting average plummet to .100. . . . Yankees righthander David Cone didn't allow a hit until the sixth inning, when Padres pitcher Sterling Hitchcock ignited a three-run inning with a leadoff single. . . . Hitchcock immediately gave back one of those runs when Brosius began the Yankees' seventh with his first home run of the night. After Shane Spencer followed with a double, Hitchcock gave way to Joey Hamilton. Spencer eventually scored on a ground ball. . . . San Diego center fielder Steve Finley got the game off to a rousing start with a sliding, juggling catch of Chuck Knoblauch's fly ball. Lying on the ground, Finley batted at the ball after it popped out of his glove and then pulled it safely to his chest.

Quotable: "This is the type of thing that, as a kid, you dream about," Brosius said of his big night. . . . Bochy didn't second-guess himself about using Hoffman, saying, "This was a big game for us. We had to win today. And it just got away from us." . . . New York manager Joe Torre, defending Bochy's move, said "it would really be hell if you don't win a game and you don't get a chance to get your best guy out there. There would be no way to ever question that." . . . Hoffman said he needed to be more aggressive with his fastball, considering he couldn't get his prized changeup over the plate. "I won't say it was a bad pitch," Hoffman said of the fastball that Brosius hit over the wall in center. "I'd rather say he put a good swing on it." . . . As for using Vander Wal as a pinch runner and letting Sheets bat in the ninth, Bochy said the Padres "felt like the righthanded hitters are getting as good at-bats (against righthander Rivera) as our lefthanders."

BOX SCORE

TUESDAY, OCTOBER 20, AT SAN DIEGO

New York	AB	R	H	RBI	PO	A
Knoblauch, 2b	4	0	1	0	2	2
Jeter, ss	4	0	1	0	2	3
O'Neill, rf	4	1	1	0	2	0
Williams, cf	4	0	0	0	2	0
Martinez, 1b	3	1	0	0	8	2
Brosius, 3b	4	2	3	4	1	1
Spencer, lf	3	1	1	0	2	1
‡Ledee, ph-lf	1	0	0	0	0	0
Girardi, c	2	0	0	0	4	0
*Posada, ph-c	2	0	1	0	3	0
Cone, p	2	0	1	0	1	0
†Davis, ph	1	0	0	1	0	0
∞Bush, pr	0	0	0	0	0	0
Lloyd, p	0	0	0	0	0	0

New York	AB	R	H	RBI	PO	A
Mendoza, p	1	0	0	0	0	0
M. Rivera, p	0	0	0	0	0	0
Totals	35	5	9	5	27	9

San Diego	AB	R	H	RBI	PO	A
Veras, 2b	3	2	1	0	4	3
Gwynn, rf	4	1	2	1	1	0
▲R. Rivera, pr-rf	0	0	0	0	1	0
Vaughn, lf	3	0	0	1	1	0
Caminiti, 3b	2	0	0	1	0	0
Joyner, 1b	3	0	0	0	7	0
Finley, cf	4	0	0	0	4	0
Leyritz, c	2	0	0	0	8	0
C. Hernandez, c	2	0	1	0	0	0
◆Vander Wal, pr	0	0	0	0	0	0
Gomez, ss	3	0	1	0	1	3
Hoffman, p	0	0	0	0	0	0
§Sweeney, ph	1	0	1	0	0	0
Hitchcock, p	2	1	1	0	0	1
Hamilton, p	0	0	0	0	0	0
R. Myers, p	0	0	0	0	0	0
Sheets, ss	2	0	0	0	0	2
Totals	31	4	7	3	27	9

New York	0	0	0	0	0	0	2	3	0—5
San Diego	0	0	0	0	0	3	0	1	0—4

New York	IP	H	R	ER	BB	SO
Cone	6.0	2	3	2	3	4
Lloyd	0.1	0	0	0	0	0
Mendoza (W)	1.0	2	1	1	0	1
M. Rivera (S)	1.2	3	0	0	0	2

San Diego	IP	H	R	ER	BB	SO
Hitchcock	6.0	7	2	1	1	7
Hamilton	*1.0	0	0	0	1	1
R. Myers	†0.0	0	1	1	1	0
Hoffman (L)	2.0	2	2	2	1	0

*Pitched to two batters in seventh. †Pitched to one batter in eighth.

Bases on balls—Off Cone 3 (Joyner, Caminiti, Veras), off Hitchcock 1 (Jeter), off Hamilton 1 (Knoblauch), off R. Myers 1 (O'Neill), off Hoffman 1 (Martinez).

Strikeouts—By Cone 4 (Caminiti, Leyritz, Gomez, Finley), by Mendoza 1 (C. Hernandez), by M. Rivera 2 (Caminiti, Sheets), by Hitchcock 7 (Williams 2, Spencer 2, O'Neill, Girardi, Jeter), by Hamilton 1 (Posada).

*Struck out for Girardi in seventh. †Reached on error for Cone in seventh. ‡Grounded out for Spencer in eighth. §Singled for Hoffman in ninth. ∞Ran for Davis in seventh. ▲Ran for Gwynn in eighth. ◆Ran for C. Hernandez in ninth. E—O'Neill, Caminiti. DP—San Diego 2. LOB—New York 7, San Diego 5. 2B—Spencer, Veras. HR—Brosius 2. SB—Finley. SF—Caminiti, Vaughn. PB—Leyritz. U—Scott (A.L.), plate; DeMuth (N.L.), first; Tschida (A.L.), second; Crawford (N.L.), third; Garcia (A.L.), left field; Hirschbeck (N.L.), right field. T—3:14. A—64,667.

PLAY BY PLAY

FIRST INNING

New York—Knoblauch flied to Finley. Jeter walked. O'Neill grounded into a double play, Gomez to Veras to Joyner.

San Diego—Veras grounded out, Jeter to Martinez. Gwynn flied to Spencer. Vaughn lined to Martinez.

SECOND INNING

New York—Williams struck out. Martinez and Brosius flied to Finley.

San Diego—Caminiti struck out. Joyner walked. Finley forced Joyner at second, Martinez to Jeter. Finley stole second. Leyritz struck out.

THIRD INNING

New York—Spencer struck out. Girardi grounded out, Veras to Joyner. Cone flied to Vaughn.

San Diego—Gomez struck out. Hitchcock grounded out, Jeter to Martinez. Veras grounded out, Knoblauch to Martinez.

FOURTH INNING

New York—Knoblauch flied to Finley. Jeter singled to left. O'Neill struck out. Williams forced Jeter at second, Gomez to Veras.

San Diego—Gwynn flied to Williams. Vaughn lined to Spencer. Caminiti walked. Joyner popped to Brosius in foul territory.

FIFTH INNING

New York—Martinez grounded out, Hitchcock to Joyner. Brosius singled to left-center. Spencer and Girardi struck out.

San Diego—Finley struck out. Leyritz popped to Knoblauch. Gomez lined to O'Neill.

SIXTH INNING

New York—Cone singled to left. Knoblauch singled to third as Cone went to second. Jeter struck out. O'Neill singled to center as Cone went to third and Knoblauch to second. Williams struck out. Martinez popped to Veras.

San Diego—Hitchcock singled to right. Veras walked. Gwynn singled to right. On the play, O'Neill made a throwing error which scored Hitchcock and Veras, and advanced Gwynn to third. Vaughn grounded out, Jeter to Martinez. Caminiti hit a sacrifice fly to Williams, scoring Gwynn. Joyner grounded out, Martinez to Cone. **S.D. 3, N.Y. 0.**

SEVENTH INNING

New York—Brosius homered to left-center. Spencer doubled to left-center. Hamilton now pitching. With Posada pinch-hitting for Girardi, Leyritz committed a passed ball, advancing Spencer to third. Posada struck out. Davis, pinch-hitting for Cone, reached first on a fielding error by Caminiti as Spencer scored. Bush now pinch-running for Davis. C. Hernandez now catching. Knoblauch walked. Jeter lined into a double play to Gomez, who threw to Veras. **S.D. 3, N.Y. 2.**

San Diego—Posada now catching and Lloyd pitching. Finley grounded out, Knoblauch to Martinez. Mendoza now pitching. C. Hernandez struck out. Gomez singled to left, but was out trying to stretch the hit into a double, Spencer to Knoblauch.

EIGHTH INNING

New York—R. Myers now pitching. O'Neill walked. Hoffman now pitching and Sheets at shortstop. Williams flied to Gwynn. Martinez walked. Brosius homered to center, scoring O'Neill and Martinez. Ledee, pinch-hitting for Spencer, grounded out, Veras to Joyner. Posada singled to center. Mendoza grounded out, Sheets to Joyner. **N.Y. 5, S.D. 3.**

San Diego—Ledee now in left field. Sheets grounded out, Brosius to Martinez. Veras doubled to left-center. M. Rivera now pitching. Gwynn singled to left as Veras went to third. R. Rivera now pinch-running for Gwynn. Vaughn hit a sacrifice fly to O'Neill, scoring Veras. Caminiti struck out. **N.Y. 5, S.D. 4.**

NINTH INNING

New York—R. Rivera now in right field. Knoblauch flied to R. Rivera. Jeter grounded out, Sheets to Joyner. O'Neill grounded to Joyner.

San Diego—Joyner lined to Jeter. Finley grounded to Martinez. C. Hernandez singled to left-center. Vander Wal now pinch-running for C. Hernandez. Sweeney, pinch-hitting for Hoffman, singled to right as Vander Wal went to third. Sheets struck out. **Final score: N.Y. 5, S.D. 4.**

GAME 4

HIGHLIGHTS

NEW YORK 3, SAN DIEGO 0

Why the Yankees won: The bounces went New York's way—literally. The Yankees broke a scoreless deadlock in the sixth inning when Derek Jeter beat out a bouncer to shortstop Chris Gomez, advanced to third on Paul O'Neill's double and scored on Bernie Williams' bouncer back to Padres pitcher Kevin Brown. In the eighth, Jeter walked and O'Neill followed with a chopper to first baseman Jim Leyritz, who slid to the bag in an attempt to beat O'Neill. Umpire Tim Tschida ruled O'Neill safe. Yet another bouncing ball—this one off Williams' bat to third baseman Ken Caminiti—moved the runners to second and third. After Tino Martinez drew an intentional walk, Scott Brosius netted one run with a pop-fly single and Ricky Ledee brought home another with a sacrifice fly.

Why the Padres lost: They couldn't solve left-hander Andy Pettitte, who had not pitched in 12 days (since he was pounded by Cleveland in Game 3 of the ALCS) and seemed to have fallen into disfavor after seeing his ERA balloon from 2.88 in the 1997 season to 4.24 in 1998. Pettitte was his old self on this night, outdueling Padres ace Brown and allowing only five hits in 7.1 scoreless innings.

The turning points:

1. Trying desperately to jump ahead early and thereby enable Brown to work aggressively with a lead, the Padres filled the bases in the second inning on two walks and a single. But a breakthrough was not to be, the inning ending when Brown himself was thrown out by catcher Joe Girardi on a bunt attempt.

2. With two out and the bases loaded in the San Diego eighth and New York guarding a 3-0 lead, Jim Leyritz—a hero in the Yankees' 1996 World Series championship—had a chance to get the Padres back into the game. But closer Mariano Rivera got him to line out to center.

Notable: Padres center fielder Ruben Rivera lifted his club's hopes with a one-out double in the seventh—San Diego trailed 1-0 at the time—but he was caught off base on Carlos Hernandez's ensuing grounder and thrown out at third. . . . In the spotlight because of his prominent role with the Yankees two years earlier, Leyritz wound up up having a dreadful World Series. He went hitless in 10 at-bats, striking out four times. . . . The World Series clincher was New York's 125th victory of the year (114 in the regular season, three in the Division Series and four each in the ALCS and World Series) against only 50 losses. . . . In winning their 24th World Series crown, the Yankees scored the first sweep in the fall classic since 1990. . . . Brosius was named the Series MVP after going 8-for-17 (.471) with two home runs and six RBIs. . . . Tony Gwynn, who batted .263 in his first World Series in 1984, hit .500 this time around. . . . The Yanks' Rivera recorded saves in three of the four games.

Quotable: As soon as the last out was made, the debate started over where this Yankees club ranked among the great teams in history. "I'll let people smarter than me argue about it," said New York pitcher David Cone. "It's tough to compare yourself with ghosts of the past . . . but we made our mark. We've heard about it since the All-Star break, and it created pressure. We just kept our tunnel vision and let them argue about it." Martinez's view: "I love it. When you play as well as we have for six months and win the World Series, you deserve to be compared with the best." And Bochy's reaction: "There's no weakness on that Yankees team." . . . San Diego's Brown didn't take much solace in losing to such a juggernaut. "I can't tell you one break we had in the entire Series," he said. "Balls bounced differently or whatever. That's what makes it hard to accept. . . . No matter how well you pitch, somewhere down the line you've got to have some luck. You give up that many infield hits, that many broken-bat hits, and

you're not going to win." . . . The jubilant Yankees gathered in a circle in the clubhouse after the game and chanted "Strawman," a tribute to teammate Darryl Strawberry, who was recovering from recent cancer surgery.

BOX SCORE

WEDNESDAY, OCTOBER 21, AT SAN DIEGO

New York	AB	R	H	RBI	PO	A
Knoblauch, 2b	5	0	1	0	2	5
Jeter, ss	4	2	2	0	1	5
O'Neill, rf	5	1	2	0	1	0
Williams, cf	4	0	0	1	2	0
Martinez, 1b	2	0	1	0	14	0
Brosius, 3b	4	0	1	1	1	2
Ledee, lf	3	0	2	1	1	0
Girardi, c	4	0	0	0	5	2
Pettitte, p	2	0	0	0	0	4
Nelson, p	0	0	0	0	0	0
M. Rivera, p	1	0	0	0	0	0
Totals	34	3	9	3	27	18
San Diego	**AB**	**R**	**H**	**RBI**	**PO**	**A**
Veras, 2b	3	0	0	0	3	5
Gwynn, rf	4	0	2	0	1	0
Vaughn, lf	4	0	0	0	1	0
Caminiti, 3b	4	0	1	0	0	1
Leyritz, 1b	3	0	0	0	11	0
R. Rivera, cf	4	0	3	0	2	0
C. Hernandez, c	4	0	0	0	8	1
Gomez, ss	2	0	0	0	1	1
†Sweeney, ph	1	0	0	0	0	0
Brown, p	2	0	1	0	0	4
*Vander Wal, ph	1	0	0	0	0	0
Miceli, p	0	0	0	0	0	0
R. Myers, p	0	0	0	0	0	0
Totals	32	0	7	0	27	12

New York	0	0	0		0	0	1		0	2	0—3
San Diego	0	0	0		0	0	0		0	0	0—0

New York	IP	H	R	ER	BB	SO
Pettitte (W)	7.1	5	0	0	3	4
Nelson	0.1	0	0	0	0	1
M. Rivera (S)	1.1	2	0	0	0	0
San Diego	**IP**	**H**	**R**	**ER**	**BB**	**SO**
Brown (L)	8.0	8	3	3	3	8
Miceli	0.2	1	0	0	0	0
R. Myers	0.1	0	0	0	0	0

Bases on balls—Off Pettitte 3 (Leyritz, Gomez, Veras), off Brown 3 (Martinez 2, Jeter). Strikeouts—By Pettitte 4 (C. Hernandez 2, Veras, Caminiti), by Nelson 1 (Vaughn), by Brown 8 (Pettitte 2, Brosius 2, Jeter, Martinez, Ledee, Girardi). *Flied out for Brown in eighth. †Grounded out for Gomez in ninth. DP—New York 2. LOB—New York 9, San Diego 8. 2B—O'Neill, Ledee, R. Rivera. SH—Pettitte. SF—Ledee. U—DeMuth (N.L.), plate; Tschida (A.L.), first; Crawford (N.L.), second; Garcia (A.L.), third; Hirschbeck (N.L.), left field; Scott (A.L.), right field. T—2:58. A—65,427.

PLAY BY PLAY

FIRST INNING

New York—Knoblauch grounded out, Gomez to Leyritz. Jeter struck out. O'Neill grounded out, Brown to Leyritz.

San Diego—Veras struck out. Gwynn grounded out, Knoblauch to Martinez. Vaughn flied to Ledee.

SECOND INNING

New York—Williams grounded out, Brown to Leyritz. Martinez struck out. Brosius flied to R. Rivera.

San Diego—Caminiti grounded out, Brosius to Martinez. Leyritz walked. R. Rivera singled to the mound as Leyritz went to second. C. Hernandez struck out. Gomez walked. Brown grounded out, Girardi to Martinez.

THIRD INNING

New York—Ledee struck out. Girardi flied to Gwynn. Pettitte struck out.

San Diego—Veras grounded to Martinez. Gwynn grounded out, Knoblauch to Martinez. Vaughn grounded out, Jeter to Martinez.

FOURTH INNING

New York—Knoblauch grounded out, Veras to Leyritz. Jeter singled to right. O'Neill grounded out, Veras to Leyritz, as Jeter went to second. Williams popped to Gomez.

San Diego—Caminiti struck out. Leyritz grounded out, Girardi to Martinez. R. Rivera grounded out, Jeter to Martinez.

FIFTH INNING

New York—Martinez singled to left. Brosius struck out. Ledee doubled to right as Martinez went to third. Girardi grounded out, Brown to Leyritz. Pettitte struck out.

San Diego—C. Hernandez struck out. Gomez grounded out, Pettitte to Martinez. Brown singled to right-center. Veras grounded out, Pettitte to Martinez.

SIXTH INNING

New York—Knoblauch grounded out, Veras to Leyritz. Jeter singled to short. O'Neill doubled to right as Jeter went to third. Williams grounded out, Brown to Leyritz, as Jeter scored and O'Neill went to third. Martinez was walked intentionally. Brosius struck out. **N.Y. 1, S.D. 0.**

San Diego—Gwynn singled to first. Vaughn forced Gwynn at second, Jeter to Knoblauch. Caminiti grounded into a double play, Knoblauch to Jeter to Martinez.

SEVENTH INNING

New York—Ledee singled to right-center. Girardi struck out. Pettitte hit a sacrifice bunt, C. Hernandez to Veras, as Ledee went to second. Knoblauch grounded out, Veras to Leyritz.

San Diego—Leyritz grounded out, Pettitte to Martinez. R. Rivera doubled to right. C. Hernandez reached first on a fielder's choice as R. Rivera was thrown out, Pettitte to Knoblauch to Brosius. Gomez flied out to O'Neill.

EIGHTH INNING

New York—Jeter walked. O'Neill singled to first as Jeter went to second. Williams grounded out, Caminiti to Leyritz, as Jeter went to third and O'Neill to second. Martinez was walked intentionally. Brosius singled to left, scoring Jeter, as ONeill went to third and Martinez to second. Ledee hit a sacrifice fly to Vaughn, scoring O'Neill. Girardi grounded out, Veras to Leyritz. **N.Y. 3, S.D. 0.**

San Diego—Vander Wal, pinch-hitting for Brown, flied to Williams. Veras walked. Gwynn singled to center as Veras went to second. Nelson now pitching. Vaughn struck out. M. Rivera now pitching with a 2-0 count on Caminiti. Caminiti singled to right as Veras went to third and Gwynn to second. Leyritz lined to Williams.

NINTH INNING

New York—Miceli now pitching. M. Rivera popped to Veras. Knoblauch singled to center. Jeter flied to R. Rivera. R. Myers now pitching. O'Neill lined to Veras.

San Diego—R. Rivera singled to center. C. Hernandez grounded into a double play, Jeter to Knoblauch to Martinez. Sweeney, pinch-hitting for Gomez, grounded out, Brosius to Martinez. **Final score: N.Y. 3, S.D. 0.**

STATISTICS

NEW YORK YANKEES' BATTING AND FIELDING AVERAGES

Player, position	G	AB	R	H	TB	2B	3B	HR	RBI	BB	IBB	SO	Avg.	PO	A	E	Avg.
Ledee, lf-ph	4	10	1	6	9	3	0	0	4	2	0	1	.600	8	0	0	1.000
Cone, p	1	2	0	1	1	0	0	0	0	0	0	0	.500	1	0	0	1.000
Brosius, 3b	4	17	3	8	14	0	0	2	6	0	0	4	.471	3	6	0	1.000
Martinez, 1b	4	13	4	5	8	0	0	1	4	4	2	2	.385	36	3	0	1.000
Knoblauch, 2b	4	16	3	6	9	0	0	1	3	3	0	2	.375	7	10	1	.944
Jeter, ss	4	17	4	6	6	0	0	0	1	3	0	3	.353	7	8	0	1.000
Posada, c-ph	3	9	2	3	6	0	0	1	2	2	0	2	.333	20	0	0	1.000
Spencer, lf	1	3	1	1	2	1	0	0	0	0	0	2	.333	2	1	0	1.000
Davis, dh-ph	3	7	3	2	2	0	0	0	2	3	0	2	.286	0	0	0	.000
O'Neill, rf	4	19	3	4	5	1	0	0	0	1	0	2	.211	8	0	1	.889
Williams, cf	4	16	2	1	4	0	0	1	3	2	1	5	.063	6	0	0	1.000
Bush, pr-dh	2	0	0	0	0	0	0	0	0	0	0	0	.000	0	0	0	.000
Lloyd, p	1	0	0	0	0	0	0	0	0	0	0	0	.000	0	0	0	.000
Nelson, p	3	0	0	0	0	0	0	0	0	0	0	0	.000	0	1	0	1.000
O. Hernandez, p	1	0	0	0	0	0	0	0	0	0	0	0	.000	1	1	0	1.000
Stanton, p	1	0	0	0	0	0	0	0	0	0	0	0	.000	0	0	0	.000
Wells, p	1	0	0	0	0	0	0	0	0	0	0	0	.000	0	0	0	.000
M. Rivera, p	3	1	0	0	0	0	0	0	0	0	0	0	.000	0	0	0	.000
Mendoza, p	1	1	0	0	0	0	0	0	0	0	0	0	.000	0	0	0	.000
Pettitte, p	1	2	0	0	0	0	0	0	0	0	0	2	.000	0	4	0	1.000
Girardi, c	2	6	0	0	0	0	0	0	0	0	0	2	.000	9	2	0	1.000
Totals	4	139	26	43	66	5	0	6	25	20	3	29	.309	108	36	2	.986

SAN DIEGO PADRES' BATTING AND FIELDING AVERAGES

Player, position	G	AB	R	H	TB	2B	3B	HR	RBI	BB	IBB	SO	Avg.	PO	A	E	Avg.
R. Rivera, ph-lf-pr-rf-cf	3	5	1	4	6	2	0	0	1	0	0	0	.800	3	0	0	1.000
Sweeney, ph	3	3	0	2	2	0	0	0	1	0	0	0	.667	0	0	0	.000
Gwynn, rf	4	16	2	8	11	0	0	1	3	1	0	0	.500	6	0	0	1.000
Brown, p	2	2	0	1	1	0	0	0	0	0	0	0	.500	0	4	0	1.000
Hitchcock, p	1	2	1	1	1	0	0	0	0	0	0	0	.500	0	1	0	1.000
Vander Wal, ph-lf-pr	4	5	0	2	3	1	0	0	0	0	0	2	.400	1	0	0	1.000
Gomez, ss	4	11	2	4	6	0	1	0	1	0	0	1	.364	5	9	0	1.000
Veras, 2b	4	15	3	3	5	2	0	0	1	3	0	4	.200	9	16	0	1.000
C. Hernandez, c-ph	4	10	0	2	2	0	0	0	0	0	0	3	.200	18	1	0	1.000
Caminiti, 3b	4	14	1	2	3	1	0	0	1	2	0	7	.143	2	2	2	.667
Vaughn, lf-dh	4	15	3	2	8	0	0	2	4	1	0	2	.133	4	0	1	.800

Player, position	G	AB	R	H	TB	2B	3B	HR	RBI	BB	IBB	SO	Avg.	PO	A	E	Avg.
Finley, cf	3	12	0	1	2	1	0	0	0	0	0	2	.083	9	1	0	1.000
Ashby, p	1	0	0	0	0	0	0	0	0	0	0	0	.000	0	2	0	1.000
Boehringer, p	2	0	0	0	0	0	0	0	0	0	0	0	.000	0	0	0	.000
Hamilton, p	1	0	0	0	0	0	0	0	0	0	0	0	.000	0	0	0	.000
Hoffman, p	1	0	0	0	0	0	0	0	0	0	0	0	.000	0	0	0	.000
Langston, p	1	0	0	0	0	0	0	0	0	0	0	0	.000	0	0	0	.000
Miceli, p	2	0	0	0	0	0	0	0	0	0	0	0	.000	0	1	0	1.000
R. Myers, p	3	0	0	0	0	0	0	0	0	0	0	0	.000	0	0	0	.000
Wall, p	2	0	0	0	0	0	0	0	0	0	0	0	.000	0	1	0	1.000
Sheets, ss	2	2	0	0	0	0	0	0	0	0	0	1	.000	0	2	0	1.000
G. Myers, ph-c	2	4	0	0	0	0	0	0	0	0	0	2	.000	4	1	0	1.000
Joyner, 1b	3	8	0	0	0	0	0	0	3	0	0	1	.000	22	0	0	1.000
Leyritz, dh-ph-1b-c	4	10	0	0	0	0	0	0	0	1	0	4	.000	19	0	0	1.000
Totals	4	134	13	32	50	7	1	3	11	12	0	29	.239	102	41	3	.979

NEW YORK YANKEES' PITCHING RECORDS

Pitcher	G	GS	CG	IP	H	R	ER	HR	BB	IBB	SO	HB	WP	W	L	Pct.	ERA
Pettitte	1	1	0	7.1	5	0	0	0	3	0	4	0	0	1	0	1.000	0.00
M. Rivera	3	0	0	4.1	5	0	0	0	0	0	4	0	0	0	0	.000	0.00
Nelson	3	0	0	2.1	2	1	0	0	1	0	4	0	0	0	0	.000	0.00
Lloyd	1	0	0	0.1	0	0	0	0	0	0	0	0	0	0	0	.000	0.00
O. Hernandez	1	1	0	7.0	6	1	1	0	3	0	7	0	0	1	0	1.000	1.29
Cone	1	1	0	6.0	2	3	2	0	3	0	4	0	0	0	0	.000	3.00
Wells	1	1	0	7.0	7	5	5	3	2	0	4	0	0	1	0	1.000	6.43
Mendoza	1	0	0	1.0	2	1	1	0	0	0	1	0	0	1	0	1.000	9.00
Stanton	1	0	0	0.2	3	2	2	0	0	0	1	0	0	0	0	.000	27.00
Totals	4	4	0	36.0	32	13	11	3	12	0	29	0	0	4	0	1.000	2.75

Shutout—Pettitte, Nelson and Rivera (combined). Saves—M. Rivera 3.

SAN DIEGO PADRES' PITCHING RECORDS

Pitcher	G	GS	CG	IP	H	R	ER	HR	BB	IBB	SO	HB	WP	W	L	Pct.	ERA
Miceli	2	0	0	1.2	2	0	0	0	2	0	1	0	0	0	0	.000	0.00
Hamilton	1	0	0	1.0	0	0	0	0	1	0	1	0	0	0	0	.000	0.00
Hitchcock	1	1	0	6.0	7	2	1	1	1	0	7	0	0	0	0	.000	1.50
Brown	2	2	0	14.1	14	7	7	0	6	2	13	0	0	0	1	.000	4.40
Wall	2	0	0	2.2	3	2	2	1	3	0	1	0	0	0	1	.000	6.75
Boehringer	2	0	0	2.0	4	2	2	1	2	0	3	1	0	0	0	.000	9.00
Hoffman	1	0	0	2.0	2	2	2	1	1	0	0	0	0	0	1	.000	9.00
R. Myers	3	0	0	1.0	0	1	1	0	1	0	2	0	0	0	0	.000	9.00
Ashby	1	1	0	2.2	10	7	4	1	1	0	1	0	0	0	1	.000	13.50
Langston	1	0	0	0.2	1	3	3	1	2	1	0	0	1	0	0	.000	40.50
Totals	4	4	0	34.0	43	26	22	6	20	3	29	1	1	0	4	.000	5.82

No shutouts or saves.

SCORE BY INNINGS

New York	3	5	1	0	2	1	9	5	0—26
San Diego	0	0	2	0	4	3	0	4	0—13

MISCELLANEOUS STATISTICS

Sacrifice hit—Pettitte.
Sacrifice flies—Caminiti, Ledee, Vaughn.
Stolen bases—Finley, Knoblauch.
Caught stealing—Ledee.
Double plays—Gomez and Veras; Gomez, Veras and Joyner; Jeter, Knoblauch and Martinez; Knoblauch, Jeter and Martinez; Knoblauch and Martinez; Martinez (unassisted); Veras, Gomez and Joyner; Veras and Joyner; Wall, Gomez and Joyner.
Left on bases—New York 7, 11, 7, 9—34; San Diego 4, 10, 5, 8—27.
Hit by pitcher—By Boehringer (Knoblauch).
Passed balls—None.
Balks—None.
Time of games—First game, 3:29; second game, 3:13; third game, 3:14; fourth game, 2:58.
Attendance—First game, 56,712; second game, 56,692; third game, 64,667; fourth game, 65,427.
Umpires—Garcia, Hirschbeck, Scott, DeMuth, Tschida and Crawford.
Official scorers—Phil Collier, Red Foley, Tom Krasovic, Jim Street.

1998 REVIEW *World Series*

ALL-STAR GAME

AT COORS FIELD, COLORADO, JULY 7, 1998

HIGHLIGHTS

AMERICAN LEAGUE 13, NATIONAL LEAGUE 8

Why the American League won: Because manager Mike Hargrove sent his players into attack mode and they responded with a 19-hit, five-stolen base barrage that seemed to catch their N.L. rivals by surprise. The chief protagonist was Baltimore second baseman Roberto Alomar, who collected three hits, stroked a solo home run, stole a base and earned MVP honors—one year after his brother, Sandy Alomar Jr., had captured the family's first All-Star MVP trophy.

Why the National League lost: Because its pitchers couldn't hold two early leads or the daring A.L. runners, who flitted around the bases almost at will and disrupted their rhythm and concentration. "They came out very aggressive," N.L. manager Jim Leyland said, "and we let them run at will a little bit."

The turning points:

1. The American League trailed 2-0 when it finally got the offense rolling against Braves lefthander Tom Glavine in the fourth inning. The A.L.'s Rodriguez boys, Texas catcher Ivan and Seattle shortstop Alex, hit consecutive singles and Baltimore's Cal Ripken drove both home with his 11th All-Star hit—a towering double off the right field wall. Two more A.L. runs scored on a bases-loaded walk to Ken Griffey Jr. and a sacrifice fly.

2. After San Francisco's Barry Bonds had propelled the N.L. back into the lead with his first All-Star homer—a three-run fifth-inning shot off Cleveland's Bartolo Colon—the A.L. got its "ugly game" in full gear. The three-run, sixth-inning rally off Montreal righthander Ugueth Urbina featured four stolen bases and runners crossing the plate on a wild pitch and passed ball. Ahead 8-6, the A.L. methodically added to a lead it would never relinquish.

Notable:

The A.L.'s 13 runs tied the All-Star Game record and the 21 combined runs broke the All-Star record. The 3-hour, 38-minute marathon was 28 minutes longer than any previous midsummer classic. . . . The A.L.'s five stolen bases also were an All-Star record. . . . Bonds joined his father, Bobby Bonds, as the second father-son combination to hit All-Star homers. The only other father-son duo to accomplish the feat is Ken Griffey Jr. and Ken Griffey Sr. . . . The Alomars, Sandy and Roberto, became the first brother combination to win All-Star MVP honors. . . . Ivan Rodriguez set an All-Star record for catchers with his three-hit performance. . . . None of the three players showing early signs of challenging the single-season home run record came close to finding the range at homer-friendly Coors Field. St. Louis' Mark McGwire, the All-Star break leader with 37,

was 0-for-2 with a walk. Griffey collected two singles and Cubs right fielder Sammy Sosa dressed for the game but didn't play because of a sore shoulder.

Quotable:

Leyland on the surprising strategy employed by the A.L.: "Maybe it was my fault that we kind of let them run at will, but I'll take that responsibility. We didn't have a game plan for a lot of running. If we had our own staff, we could have done that. But not this way.". . . Hargrove, on the unusual offensive tone of the All-Star Game: "I'd forgotten how deep the outfielders have to play here to make up for the way the ball carries. A lot of balls that are hit softly fall in that normally wouldn't.". . .Leyland on the same subject: "You saw some balls bloop in, freak hits, passed balls and wild pitches. These kind of things seem to happen here.". . . Alex Rodriguez, on his solo home run in the fifth inning: "I had no idea it was a home run when I hit it. I was hoping and trying to blow it out."

BOX SCORE

American League	AB	R	H	RBI	PO	A
Lofton, lf (Indians)	3	0	1	0	2	0
Erstad, lf-cf (Angels)	2	1	0	0	3	0
R. Alomar, 2b (Orioles)	4	2	3	1	3	2
▼Durham, ph-2b (White Sox) .	1	1	1	1	0	0
Griffey, cf (Mariners)	3	1	2	1	0	0
O'Neill, lf (Yankees)	2	0	0	0	0	1
Gonzalez, rf (Rangers)	3	0	0	1	0	0
Ramirez, rf (Indians)	1	0	0	1	0	0
Thome, 1b (Indians)	2	1	0	0	4	0
Palmeiro, 1b (Orioles)	2	1	2	1	2	0
A. Rodriguez, ss (Mariners)	3	2	2	1	1	2
Jeter, ss (Yankees)	1	0	0	0	0	2
▲Vizquel, ph-ss (Indians)	2	0	1	0	1	1
I. Rodriguez, c (Rangers)	4	1	3	1	5	0
S. Alomar, c (Indians)	1	0	1	1	5	0
Ripken, 3b (Orioles)	4	1	1	2	1	1
Arrojo, p (Devil Rays)	0	0	0	0	0	0
Wetteland, p (Rangers)	0	0	0	0	0	0
◆Palmer, ph (Royals)	1	0	0	0	0	0
Gordon, p (Red Sox)	0	0	0	0	0	0
Percival, p (Angels)	0	0	0	0	0	0
Wells, p (Yankees)	1	0	0	0	0	0
Clemens, p (Blue Jays)	0	0	0	0	0	0
*Easley, ph (Tigers)	1	1	1	0	0	0
Radke, p (Twins)	0	0	0	0	0	0
‡Grieve, ph (Athletics)	0	0	0	0	0	0
Colon, p (Indians)	0	0	0	0	0	0
Brosius, 3b (Yankees)	2	1	1	0	0	0
Totals	43	13	19	11	27	9
National League	**AB**	**R**	**H**	**RBI**	**PO**	**A**
Biggio, 2b (Astros)	3	0	0	0	2	4
Hoffman, p (Padres)	0	0	0	0	0	0
Shaw, p (Dodgers)	0	0	0	0	0	0
■Vaughn, ph-lf (Padres)	1	0	1	2	0	0
Gwynn, rf (Padres)	2	0	1	2	0	0
White, cf (Diamondbacks)	3	1	3	0	0	0
Nen, p (Giants)	0	0	0	0	0	0
McGwire, 1b (Cardinals)	2	1	0	0	6	0
Galarraga, 1b (Braves)	2	0	0	0	7	0
Bonds, lf (Giants)	2	1	1	3	1	0
Bichette, lf-rf (Rockies)	2	0	0	0	1	0
C. Jones, 3b (Braves)	2	1	0	0	0	0
Castilla, 3b (Rockies)	2	0	0	0	0	2
Piazza, c (Mets)	3	0	1	0	2	0
Lopez, c (Braves)	1	0	0	0	3	0
•Kendall, ph (Pirates)	1	0	1	0	0	0

National League	AB	R	H	RBI	PO	A
Walker, cf-rf (Rockies)	1	1	0	0	2	0
§Alou, ph-rf-cf (Astros)	3	1	1	0	0	0
Weiss, ss (Braves)	3	1	2	1	2	2
Renteria, ss (Marlins)	1	1	0	0	0	3
Maddux, p (Braves)	0	0	0	0	0	1
Glavine, p (Braves)	0	0	0	0	0	1
Brown, p (Padres)	0	0	0	0	0	0
†Sheffield, ph (Dodgers)	1	0	0	0	0	0
Ashby, p (Padres)	0	0	0	0	0	0
Urbina, p (Expos)	0	0	0	0	0	0
∞Vina, ph-2b (Brewers)	1	0	1	0	1	1
Totals	**36**	**8**	**12**	**8**	**27**	**14**

American League	0	0	0	4	1	3	1 1	3—13
National League..............	0	0	2	1	3	0	0 2	0— 8

American League	IP	H	R	ER	BB	SO
Wells (Yankees)	2.0	0	0	0	1	1
Clemens (Blue Jays)	1.0	2	2	2	1	1
Radke (Twins)	1.0	2	1	1	1	1
Colon (Indians)	1.0	2	3	3	1	1
Arrojo (Devil Rays)	1.0	2	0	0	0	1
Wetteland (Rangers)	1.0	0	0	0	1	0
Gordon (Red Sox)	1.0	3	2	2	1	0
Percival (Angels)	1.0	1	0	0	0	2

National League	IP	H	R	ER	BB	SO
Maddux (Braves)	2.0	3	0	0	1	1
Glavine (Braves)	1.1	5	4	4	3	0
Brown (Padres)	0.2	0	0	0	1	1
Ashby (Padres)	1.0	1	1	1	1	0
Urbina (Expos)	1.0	3	3	3	1	2
Hoffman (Padres)	1.0	1	1	1	0	1
Shaw (Dodgers)	1.0	3	1	1	0	0
Nen (Giants)	1.0	3	3	1	0	0

Winning pitcher—Colon. Losing pitcher—Urbina.

*Singled for Clemens in fourth. †Flied out for Brown in fourth. ‡Walked for Radke in fifth. §Struck out for Walker in fifth. ∞Singled for Urbina in sixth. ▲Singled for Jeter in eighth. ◆Grounded into double play for Wetteland in eighth. ■Singled for Shaw in eighth. ▼Singled for R. Alomar in ninth. •Singled for Lopez in ninth. E—Griffey, Brosius, Vina. DP—A.L. 2, N.L. 2. LOB—A.L. 11, N.L. 8. 2B—Ripken. 3B—White. HR—A. Rodriguez, Bonds, R. Alomar. SB—Lofton, R. Alomar, Griffey, I. Rodriguez, Brosius. SH—Glavine. SF—Gonzalez, Ramirez. HBP—By Clemens (Biggio). WP—Urbina. PB—Lopez. BB—Off Wells 1 (Bonds), off Clemens 1 (Walker), off Radke 1 (C. Jones), off Colon 1 (McGwire), off Gordon 1 (Vina), off Maddux 1 (Thome), off Glavine 3 (Lofton, R. Alomar, Griffey), off Ashby 1 (Grieve), off Urbina 1 (Thome). SO—By Wells 1 (Biggio), by Clemens 1 (McGwire), by Radke 1 (Biggio), by Colon 1 (Alou), by Arrojo 1 (Biggio), by Wetteland 1 (Lopez), by Percival 2 (Bichette, Alou), by Maddux 1 (A. Rodriguez), by Brown 1 (Thome), by Urbina 2 (Gonzalez, Jeter), by Hoffman 1 (Brosius). T—3:38. A—51,267. U—Montague (N.L.), plate; Cousins (A.L.), first; Gorman (N.L.), second; Reed (A.L.), third; Rieker (N.L.), left field; McClelland (A.L.), right field. Official scorers—Tony DeMarco, Frank Haraway and Jim Street.

Players listed on rosters but not used: A.L.—Martinez (Red Sox), Sele (Rangers); N.L.—Boone (Reds), Reed (Mets), Schilling (Phillies).

PLAY BY PLAY

FIRST INNING
A.L.—Lofton singled to left. Lofton stole second. R. Alomar singled to first, Lofton went to third. Griffey fouled to McGwire. Gonzalez grounded out, Maddux to McGwire, as R. Alomar went to second. Thome walked. A. Rodriguez struck out.

N.L.—Biggio struck out. Gwynn flied to Lofton. McGwire grounded out, A. Rodriguez to Thome.

SECOND INNING
A.L.—I. Rodriguez singled to right. Ripken grounded into a double play, Biggio to Weiss to McGwire. Wells grounded out, Biggio to McGwire.

N.L.—Bonds walked. C. Jones grounded into a double play, A. Rodriguez to R. Alomar to Thome. Piazza flied to R. Alomar.

THIRD INNING
A.L.—Glavine now pitching. Lofton walked. R. Alomar flied to Biggio. Griffey singled to right-center as Lofton went to third. Gonzalez flied to Biggio. Thome fouled to Bonds.

N.L.—Clemens now pitching. Walker walked. Weiss singled to left as Walker went to second. Glavine sacrificed Walker to third

and Weiss to second, Ripken to R. Alomar. Biggio was hit by a pitch. Gwynn singled to center, scoring Walker and Weiss, as Biggio went to third. McGwire struck out. Bonds flied to Lofton. **N.L. 2, A.L. 0.**

FOURTH INNING
A.L.—A. Rodriguez singled to right. I. Rodriguez singled to left-center as A. Rodriguez went to second. Ripken doubled to right, scoring. A. Rodriguez and I. Rodriguez. Easley, pinch-hitting for Clemens, singled to second as Ripken went to third. Lofton grounded out, Glavine to McGwire. R. Alomar walked. Griffey walked, scoring Ripken. Brown now pitching. Gonzalez hit a sacrifice fly to Walker, scoring Easley. Thome struck out. **A.L. 4, N.L. 2.**

N.L.—Radke now pitching. C. Jones walked. Piazza singled to center and C. Jones reached third on an error by Griffey. Walker fouled to Ripken. Weiss singled to right, scoring C. Jones as Piazza went to second. Sheffield, pinch-hitting for Brown, flied to A. Rodriguez. Biggio struck out. **A.L. 4, N.L. 3.**

FIFTH INNING
A.L.—Ashby now pitching, White in center field and Walker moves from center to right field. A. Rodriguez homered to right-center. I. Rodriguez flied to Walker. Ripken grounded out, Weiss to McGwire. Grieve, pinch-hitting for Radke, walked. Lofton forced Grieve at second, Biggio to Weiss. **A.L. 5, N.L. 3.**

N.L.—Colon now pitching, Jeter at short and Erstad in left field. White tripled to center. McGwire walked. Bonds homered to right-center, scoring White and McGwire. C. Jones grounded out, R. Alomar to Thome. Piazza grounded out, Jeter to Thome. Alou, pinch-hitting for Walker, struck out. **N.L. 6, A.L. 5.**

SIXTH INNING
A.L.—Urbina now pitching, Galarraga at first, Castilla at third, Alou in right field and Lopez catching. R. Alomar singled to second. Griffey singled to the pitcher as R. Alomar went to second. Gonzalez struck out. With Thome batting, R. Alomar stole third and Griffey stole second. Thome walked. A passed ball scored R. Alomar and advanced Griffey to third and Thome to second. Jeter struck out. A wild pitch scored Griffey and advanced Thome to third. I. Rodriguez singled to left, scoring Thome. I. Rodriguez stole second. Ripken grounded out, Biggio to Galarraga. **A.L. 8, N.L. 6.**

N.L.—Arrojo now pitching, Palmeiro at first, Brosius at third, O'Neill in left field, Ramirez in right field and Erstad moved from left to center field. Weiss flied to Erstad. Vina, pinch-hitting for Urbina, singled to left-center. Biggio struck out. White singled to center as Vina went to second. Galarraga flied to Erstad.

SEVENTH INNING
A.L.—Hoffman now pitching, Vina at second, Renteria at short and Bichette in left field. Brosius struck out. Erstad grounded out, Renteria to Galarraga. R. Alomar homered to right. O'Neill grounded out, Castilla to Galarraga. **A.L. 9, N.L. 6.**

N.L.—Wetteland now pitching and S. Alomar catching. Bichette grounded out, Jeter to Palmeiro. Castilla fouled to S. Alomar. Lopez struck out.

EIGHTH INNING
A.L.—Shaw now pitching. Ramirez grounded out, Castilla to Galarraga. Palmeiro singled to left. Vizquel, pinch-hitting for Jeter, singled to left-center as Palmeiro went to third. S. Alomar singled to right-center, scoring Palmeiro as Vizquel went to third. Palmer, pinch-hitting for Wetteland, grounded into a double play, Renteria to Vina to Galarraga. **A.L. 10, N.L. 6.**

N.L.—Gordon now pitching and Vizquel at short. Alou singled to right-center. Renteria reached first on an error by Brosius as Alou went to second. Vina walked. Vaughn, pinch-hitting for Shaw, singled to left, scoring Alou and Renteria, as Vina went to second. White singled to left, but Vina was thrown out at home, O'Neill to S. Alomar, while Vaughn went to second. Galarraga grounded into a double play, Vizquel to Palmeiro. **A.L. 10, N.L. 8.**

NINTH INNING
A.L.—Nen now pitching, Vaughn in left field, Bichette in right

field and Alou moved from right to center field. Brosius singled to center. Brosius stole second. Erstad reached first on an error by Vina as Brosius went to third. Durham, pinch-hitting for R. Alomar, singled to right, scoring Brosius, as Erstad went to third and Durham to second on the fielder's choice. O'Neill grounded to Galarraga. Ramirez hit a sacrifice fly to Bichette, scoring Erstad. Palmeiro singled to right-center, scoring Durham. Vizquel grounded out, Renteria to Galarraga. **A.L. 13, N.L. 8.**

N.L.—Percival now pitching and Durham at second. Bichette struck out. Castilla flied to Erstad. Kendall, pinch-hitting for Lopez, singled to center. Alou struck out. **Final score: A.L. 13, N.L. 8.**

NOTABLE PERFORMANCES

BOX SCORES OF NO-HIT GAMES

DAVID WELLS (PERFECT GAME)

MAY 17

New York 4, Minnesota 0 (D)

MINNESOTA	AB	R	H	RBI	NEW YORK	AB	R	H	RBI
Lawton, cf	3	0	0	0	Knoblauch, 2b	4	0	0	0
Gates, 2b	3	0	0	0	Jeter, ss	3	0	1	0
Molitor, dh	3	0	0	0	O'Neill, rf	4	0	0	0
Cordova, lf	3	0	0	0	Martinez, 1b	4	0	0	0
Coomer, 1b	3	0	0	0	Williams, cf	3	3	3	1
Ochoa, rf	3	0	0	0	Strawberry, dh	3	1	1	1
Shave, 3b	3	0	0	0	Curtis, lf	3	0	1	1
Valentin, c	3	0	0	0	Posada, c	3	0	0	0
Meares, ss	3	0	0	0	Brosius, 3b	3	0	0	0
TOTALS	27	0	0	0	**TOTALS**	30	4	6	3

```
Minnesota . . . . . . . . . .   0 0 0      0 0 0      0 0 0—0
New York . . . . . . . . . .   0 1 0      1 0 0      2 0 0—4
```

LOB—Minnesota 0, New York 3. 2B—Williams 2. 3B—Strawberry. HR—Williams. SB—Jeter, Curtis.

MINNESOTA	IP	H	R	ER	BB	SO
Hawkins (L, 2-4)	7.0	6	4	4	0	5
Naulty	0.1	0	0	0	1	0
Swindell	0.2	0	0	0	0	1
NEW YORK	**IP**	**H**	**R**	**ER**	**BB**	**SO**
Wells (W, 5-1)	9.0	0	0	0	0	11

WP—Hawkins. PB—Valentin. T—2:40. A—49,820. Umpires—HP, McClelland; 1B, Hirschbeck; 2B, Garcia; 3B, Reilly.

LOW-HIT GAMES
AMERICAN LEAGUE

ONE-HIT GAMES

Date   Pitcher(s), Team, Opponent, Result—Player with hit
5-2   Roger Clemens (7 innings) and Paul Quantrill (2 innings), Toronto at Oakland, W 7-0—Ben Grieve (single in seventh)
7-16   Randy Johnson, Seattle vs. Minnesota, W 3-0—Brent Gates (single in eighth)
9-27   Roy Halladay, Toronto vs. Detroit, W 2-1—Bob Higginson (home run in ninth)

TWO-HIT GAMES

Date   Pitcher(s), Team, Opponent, Result—Player(s) with hit(s)
4-11   Mike Mussina (8 innings) and Armando Benitez (1 inning), Baltimore at Detroit, W 2-0—Damion Easley (single in second), Bob Higginson (single in fourth)
4-11   Pedro Martinez, Boston vs. Seattle, W 5-0—Joey Cora (single in fourth), Alex Rodriguez (single in sixth)
5-1   Hideki Irabu (7.1 innings), Mike Stanton (0.2 inning) and Mariano Rivera (1 inning), New York at Kansas City, W 2-1—Hal Morris (single in first), Johnny Damon (home run in third)
5-10   Tim Wakefield (8.2 innings) and Tom Gordon (0.1 inning), Boston at Kansas City, W 3-1—Shane Mack (single in seventh), Johnny Damon (single in ninth)
5-19   Woody Williams (8 innings) and Randy Myers (1 inning), Toronto vs. Tampa Bay, W 3-1—Kevin Stocker (single in eighth), Wade Boggs (single in ninth)
6-6   Tim Wakefield (8 innings) and Tom Gordon (1 inning), Boston vs. New York N.L., L 0-1—Edgardo Alfonzo (single in second), John Olerud (single in ninth)
6-7   David Cone, New York vs. Florida N.L., W 4-1—Gregg Zaun (single in third), Todd Dunwoody (double in eighth)
6-16   Sidney Ponson (6.2 innings) and Arthur Rhodes (2.1 innings), Baltimore vs. New York, W 2-0—Luis Sojo (single in third), Jorge Posada (single in seventh)
6-21   Pedro Martinez (8 innings) and Tom Gordon (1 inning), Boston at Tampa Bay, W 3-1—Miguel Cairo (triple in fifth), Dave Martinez (single in ninth)
6-22   Mike Mussina vs. New York N.L., W 7-2—Brian McRae (home run in second), Butch Huskey (home run in second)
7-3   Jose Rosado, Kansas City vs. Cleveland, L 1-2—Manny Ramirez (home runs in sixth and ninth)
8-4   Steve Avery (6 innings), Derek Lowe (2 innings) and Tom Gordon (1 inning), Boston at Seattle, W 2-1—Ken Griffey Jr. (single in fourth), Jay Buhner (home run in fifth)
8-4   Mike Mussina, Baltimore vs. Detroit, W 4-0—Frank Catalanotto (double in eighth), Deivi Cruz (single in ninth)
8-5   Hideki Irabu, New York at Oakland, L 1-3—Rafael Bournigal (single in fifth), Rickey Henderson (home run in eighth)
8-12   Scott Eyre (5 innings), Keith Foulke (2 innings), Bob Howry (1 inning) and Bill Simas (1 inning), Chicago vs. Oakland, W 2-0—Jason Giambi (single in eighth), Bip Roberts (single in ninth)
8-13   Orlando Hernandez (8.1 innings) and Mariano Rivera (0.2 innings), New York vs. Texas, W 2-0—Mark McLemore (double in fourth), Todd Zeile (double in seventh)
8-19   Blake Stein, Oakland vs. Chicago, W 6-0—Mike Caruso (single in first), Magglio Ordonez (triple in second)
8-30   Roger Clemens, Toronto vs. Minnesota, W 6-0—Alex Ochoa (single in first), Todd Walker (single in seventh)

1998 REVIEW *Notable performances*

Date	Pitcher(s), Team, Opponent, Result—Player(s) with hit(s)
9-1	David Wells, New York vs. Oakland, W 7-0—Jason Giambi (single in seventh), Mike Blowers (single in eighth)
9-8	Wilson Alvarez (7 innings), Jim Mecir (1 inning) and Bryan Rekar (1 inning), Tampa Bay at Seattle, W 10-0—Charles Gipson (single in third), David Bell (double in sixth)
9-17	Hideki Irabu (8 innings) and Mike Stanton (1 inning), New York at Tampa Bay, W 4-0—Aaron Ledesma (single in second), Randy Winn (single in third)

NATIONAL LEAGUE

ONE-HIT GAMES

Date	Pitcher(s), Team, Opponent, Result—Player with hit
4-14	Kevin Millwood, Atlanta vs. Pittsburgh, W 6-0—Jermaine Allensworth (double in fifth)
5-6	Kerry Wood, Chicago vs. Houston, W 2-0—Ricky Gutierrez (single in third)
6-27	Ismael Valdes, Los Angeles vs. Pittsburgh, W 2-0—Kevin Young (single in eighth)
7-20	Darren Dreifort (8 innings) and Jeff Shaw (1 inning), Los Angeles vs. Cincinnati, W 2-0—Willie Greene (double in second)
8-16	Kevin Brown, San Diego vs. Milwaukee, W 4-0—Jeromy Burnitz (single in seventh)
9-13	Andy Benes (8.1 innings) and Gregg Olson (0.2 innings), Arizona at Cincinnati, W 5-0—Sean Casey (single in ninth)

TWO-HIT GAMES

Date	Pitcher(s), Team, Opponent, Result—Player(s) with hit(s)
4-5	Ramon Martinez (8 innings) and Scott Radinsky (1 inning), Los Angeles at Cincinnati, W 1-0—Eddie Taubensee (single in eighth), Chris Stynes (single in ninth)
4-10	Curt Schilling, Philadelphia vs. Atlanta, W 1-0—Tony Graffanino (single in second), Chipper Jones (single in fourth)
4-29	Pete Harnisch, Cincinnati vs. Philadelphia, W 1-0—Kevin Sefcik (double in first), Alex Arias (single in fifth)
5-3	Dustin Hermanson, Montreal vs. Arizona, W 4-1—Brent Brede (double in second), Jay Bell (single in fourth)
5-7	Masato Yoshii (7 innings), Greg McMichael (1 inning) and John Franco (1 inning), New York vs. St. Louis, W 4-1—Mark McGwire (single in first), Brian Jordan (home run in fourth)
5-11	Todd Stottlemyre (8 innings) and Jeff Brantley (1 inning), St. Louis vs. Milwaukee, W 7-0—Jeromy Burnitz (double in first), Bob Hamelin (single in third)
5-14	Mark Portugal (8 innings) and Mark Leiter (1 inning), Philadelphia at Los Angeles, W 4-0—Thomas Howard (double in sixth), Todd Hollandsworth (single in eighth)
5-21	Kirk Rueter (8 innings) and John Johnstone (1 inning), San Francisco at Milwaukee, W 8-1—Jeromy Burnitz (home run in second), Jeff Cirillo (single in ninth)
5-23	Ramon Martinez, Los Angeles at Arizona, W 7-1—Andy Fox (single in first), Brent Brede (home run in ninth)
5-24	Bobby M. Jones (7 innings), Chuck McElroy (1 inning) and Jerry DiPoto (1 inning), Colorado at Cincinnati, W 3-1—Jon Nunnally (double in fourth), Dmitri Young (single in fourth)
5-30	Orel Hershiser (6 innings), Rich Rodriguez (1 inning), Steve Reed (1 inning) and Robb Nen (1 inning), San Francisco vs. Arizona, W 4-1—Jorge Fabregas (single in fourth), Tony Batista (double in fifth)
6-10	Ismael Valdes, Los Angeles vs. Oakland A.L., W 1-0—Matt Stairs (single in seventh), Mike Macfarlane (single in eighth)
6-17	Curt Schilling, Philadelphia vs. Pittsburgh, W 3-1—Jason Kendall (single in first and home run in fourth)
6-27	Sterling Hitchcock, San Diego vs. Anaheim A.L., W 5-1—Phil Nevin (home run in eighth), Damon Mashore (single in eighth)
6-28	Masato Yoshii (7 innings) and Dennis Cook (2 innings), New York vs. New York A.L., W 2-1—Derek Jeter (single in fifth), Scott Brosius (home run in seventh)
7-12	Hideo Nomo (5.1 innings), Jeff Tam (1.2 innings), Greg McMichael (1 inning) and Dennis Cook (1 inning), New York vs. Montreal, W 5-2—Rondell White (single in second), Javier Vazquez (single in third)
7-28	Kirk Rueter, San Francisco at Montreal, W 7-1—Terry Jones (single in first), Orlando Cabrera (single in ninth)
7-30	Chan Ho Park (8 innings) and Jeff Shaw (1 inning), Los Angeles at Philadelphia, W 3-1—Doug Glanville (single in fourth), Gregg Jefferies (single in fourth)
8-6	Jeremy Powell (6 innings), Mike Maddux (2 innings) and Anthony Telford (1 inning), Montreal vs. Los Angeles, W 9-0—Trenidad Hubbard (single in first), Eric Young (single in sixth)
8-7	Brian Bohanon (7.1 innings), Antonio Osuna (0.2 inning) and Jeff Shaw (1 inning), Los Angeles vs. Pittsburgh, W 3-1—Manny Martinez (double in fourth), Kevin Young (double in fourth)
8-13	Tom Glavine, Atlanta at San Diego, W 5-0—Carlos Hernandez (single in sixth), Andy Sheets (single in sixth)
8-16	Darren Dreifort (7 innings), Scott Radinsky (1 inning) and Jeff Shaw (1 inning), Los Angeles vs. Atlanta, W 1-0—Javy Lopez (single in second), Andres Galarraga (double in eighth)
8-16	Omar Daal (8 innings) and Willie Banks (1 inning), Arizona vs. New York, W 6-1—Jermaine Allensworth (home run in fourth), Mike Piazza (double in fourth)
8-27	Rafael Roque (7 innings) and Eric Plunk (2 innings), Milwaukee at Arizona, W 4-0—Travis Lee (single in second), Jay Bell (single in seventh)
9-2	Carlos Perez, Los Angeles vs. Philadelphia, W 6-0—Mark Lewis (single in second), Kevin Sefcik (single in sixth)
9-10	Darryl Kile, Colorado vs. Florida, W 3-1—Luis Castillo (single in third), Todd Dunwoody (triple in ninth)
9-20	Shawn Estes (8 innings) and Julian Tavarez (1 inning), San Francisco vs. Los Angeles, L 0-1—Trenidad Hubbard (home run in first), Eric Karros (single in seventh)

15-STRIKEOUT GAMES

Date	Pitcher, Team, Opponent	IP	H	R	ER	BB	SO	Result
4-5	Curt Schilling, Philadelphia N.L. at Atlanta	9	5	1	1	1	15	W 2-1
4-10	Randy Johnson, Seattle A.L. at Boston	8	2	2	2	3	15	L 7-9
5-6	Kerry Wood, Chicago N.L. vs. Houston	9	1	0	0	0	20	W 2-0
5-24	Randy Johnson, Seattle A.L. vs. Tampa Bay	9	7	1	1	2	15	W 3-1
7-11	Randy Johnson, Seattle A.L. vs. Anaheim	9	5	0	0	2	15	W 2-0
8-15	Roger Clemens, Toronto A.L. vs. Anaheim	8	6	2	2	1	15	L 3-6
8-25	Roger Clemens, Toronto A.L. vs. Kansas City	9	3	0	0	0	18	W 3-0

Date	Pitcher, Team, Opponent	IP	H	R	ER	BB	SO	Result
8-26	Kerry Wood, Chicago N.L. at Cincinnati	8	3	2	1	3	16	W 9-2
8-28	Randy Johnson, Houston N.L. vs. Pittsburgh	9	7	0	0	0	16	W 2-0
8-29	Sterling Hitchcock, San Diego N.L. vs. Montreal ...	8	6	3	3	0	15	L 1-3
9-21	Roger Clemens, Toronto A.L. vs. Baltimore	8	7	1	1	3	15	W 3-1

10-STRIKEOUT GAMES

AMERICAN LEAGUE

Team	No.	Pitchers
Seattle	17	Randy Johnson 13, Ken Cloude 2, Jamie Moyer 1, Jeff Fassero 1.
Toronto	15	Roger Clemens 11, Kelvim Escobar 2, Juan Guzman 1, Chris Carpenter 1.
New York	14	David Cone 9, David Wells 4, Orlando Hernandez 1.
Baltimore	9	Mike Mussina 7, Scott Erickson 2.
Boston	8	Pedro Martinez 8.
Cleveland	5	Bartolo Colon 3, Charles Nagy 1, Jaret Wright 1.
Anaheim	3	Chuck Finley 3.
Texas	3	Aaron Sele 1, Darren Oliver 1, Rick Helling 1.
Detroit	2	Bryce Florie 1, Justin Thompson 1.
Minnesota	2	Brad Radke 2.
Oakland	2	Jimmy Haynes 1, Blake Stein 1.
Kansas City	1	Pat Rapp 1.
Tampa Bay	1	Tony Saunders 1.
Chicago	0	None.

NATIONAL LEAGUE

Team	No.	Pitchers
Philadelphia	19	Curt Schilling 15, Tyler Green 2, Matt Beech 2.
Houston	15	Randy Johnson 7, Shane Reynolds 5, Jose Lima 2, Mike Hampton 1.
San Diego	14	Kevin Brown 9, Andy Ashby 2, Joey Hamilton 2, Sterling Hitchcock 1.
Chicago	13	Kerry Wood 9, Mark Clark 3, Jeremi Gonzalez 1.
Atlanta	9	John Smoltz 3, Greg Maddux 2, Tom Glavine 2, Denny Neagle 1, Kevin Millwood 1.
Los Angeles	6	Chan Ho Park 2, Ramon Martinez 1, Brian Bohanon 1, Darren Dreifort 1, Hideo Nomo 1.
New York	6	Al Leiter 2, Rick Reed 1, Bobby Jones 1, Hideo Nomo 1, Masato Yoshii 1.
St. Louis	5	Todd Stottlemyre 3, Matt Morris 2.
San Francisco	4	Shawn Estes 3, Mark Gardner 1.
Cincinnati	3	Pete Harnisch 1, Mike Remlinger 1, Dennis Reyes 1.
Colorado	3	Darryl Kile 2, John Thomson 1.
Florida	3	Jesus Sanchez 3.
Arizona	2	Andy Benes 1, Omar Daal 1.
Milwaukee	2	Bill Pulsipher 1, Steve Woodard 1.
Pittsburgh	1	Francisco Cordova 1.
Montreal	0	None.

1-0 GAMES

AMERICAN LEAGUE

Date	Winner	Loser	Inn.*	Site
4-27	†Andy Pettitte, New York	†Roger Clemens, Toronto	3	New York
5-17	†Aaron Sele, Texas	†Bartolo Colon, Cleveland	4	Cleveland
6-25	Woody Williams, Toronto	Carlos Perez, Montreal N.L.	4	Montreal
7-5	†David Cone, New York	Scott Erickson, Baltimore	3	New York
7-10	†Rick Helling, Texas	†Billy Taylor, Oakland	9	Oakland
7-15	Pedro Martinez, Boston	Bartolo Colon, Cleveland	5	Boston
7-30	†Juan Guzman, Toronto	Esteban Loaiza, Texas	5	Toronto
9-14	†Alan Mills, Baltimore	†Xavier Hernandez, Texas	8	Baltimore

PLAYERS HITTING HOME RUNS IN 1-0 GAMES: 6-25—Mike Stanley, Toronto; 7-15—Midre Cummings, Boston.

*Inning in which run scored. †Did not pitch complete game. Note: Interleague 1-0 games are listed in the winning club's league.

NATIONAL LEAGUE

Date	Winner	Loser	Inn.*	Site
3-31	†Turk Wendell, New York	†Ricky Bottalico, Philadelphia	14	New York
4-5	†Ramon Martinez, Los Angeles	†Mike Remlinger, Cincinnati	7	Cincinnati
4-10	Curt Schilling, Philadelphia	†Mike Cather, Atlanta	9	Philadelphia
4-13	Andy Ashby, San Diego	Brian Anderson, Arizona	5	San Diego
4-15	Kevin Brown, San Diego	†Danny Darwin, San Francisco	2	San Francisco
4-29	Pete Harnisch, Cincinnati	†Mike Grace, Philadelphia	1	Cincinnati
5-3	†Jesus Sanchez, Florida	†Andy Ashby, San Diego	2	Florida
5-13	†Mike Hampton, Houston	Jon Lieber, Pittsburgh	4	Houston
6-6	†Bobby Jones, New York	†Tim Wakefield, Boston A.L.	6	Boston
6-10	Ismael Valdes, Los Angeles	†Kenny Rogers, Oakland A.L.	3	Los Angeles
6-18	†Elmer Dessens, Pittsburgh	†Doug Jones, Milwaukee	7	Milwaukee
7-11	†Mark Portugal, Philadelphia	†Rich Loiselle, Pittsburgh	8	Pittsburgh
8-16	†Scott Radinsky, Los Angeles	Denny Neagle, Atlanta	8	Los Angeles
8-21	†Mark Portugal, Philadelphia	†Omar Daal, Arizona	4	Philadelphia
8-21‡	†Armando Reynoso, New York	†Manny Aybar, St. Louis	1	New York
9-3	Brian Anderson, Arizona	Francisco Cordova, Pittsburgh	3	Pittsburgh
9-7	Randy Johnson, Houston	†Steve Parris, Cincinnati	6	Houston
9-11	†Joey Hamilton, San Diego	Brian Bohanon, Los Angeles	1	San Diego
9-12	†Pedro Astacio, Colorado	†Robb Nen, San Francisco	9	San Francisco
9-13	†Willie Blair, New York	†Anthony Telford, Montreal	8	Montreal
9-17	†Denny Neagle, Atlanta	†Omar Daal, Arizona	3	Arizona

Date	Winner	Loser	Inn.*	Site
9-20	†Darryl Kile, Colorado	†Randy Myers, San Diego	11	San Diego
9-20	Carlos Perez, Los Angeles	†Shawn Estes, San Francisco	1	San Francisco
9-26‡	†Robby Stanifer, Florida	†Ricky Bottalico, Philadelphia	13	Florida

PLAYERS HITTING HOME RUNS IN 1-0 GAMES: 4-5—Raul Mondesi, Los Angeles; 4-13—Archi Cianfrocco, San Diego; 4-15—Greg Vaughn, San Diego; 8-16—Eric Young, Los Angeles; 8-21—Edgardo Alfonzo, New York; 9-7—Derek Bell, Houston; 9-20—Trenidad Hubbard, Los Angeles; 9-26—Alex Gonzalez, Florida.

*Inning in which run scored. †Did not pitch complete game. ‡Second game of doubleheader. Note: Interleague 1-0 games are listed in the winning club's league.

FOUR OR MORE HITS IN ONE GAME
AMERICAN LEAGUE

Team	No.	Hitters
New York	21	Derek Jeter 5, Paul O'Neill 4, Chuck Knoblauch 4, Bernie Williams 3, Tim Raines 1, Joe Girardi 1, Luis Sojo 1, Tino Martinez 1, Shane Spencer 1.
Seattle	21	Alex Rodriguez 6, Joey Cora 3, Edgar Martinez 3, Ken Griffey Jr. 3, David Segui 3, Glenallen Hill 1, Rob Ducey 1, Rico Rossy 1.
Chicago	20	Albert Belle 4, Ray Durham 4, Mike Caruso 4, Robin Ventura 3, Magglio Ordonez 2, Wil Cordero 1, Jeff Abbott 1, Craig Wilson 1.
Baltimore	16	Roberto Alomar 4, Rafael Palmeiro 3, Harold Baines 2, Cal Ripken Jr. 2, Brady Anderson 2, Eric Davis 1, B.J. Surhoff 1, Lenny Webster 1.
Toronto	16	Shannon Stewart 5, Tony Fernandez 3, Shawn Green 2, Alex Gonzalez 2, Jose Canseco 1, Darrin Fletcher 1, Craig Grebeck 1, Carlos Delgado 1.
Anaheim	15	Gary DiSarcina 4, Darin Erstad 3, Jim Edmonds 2, Garret Anderson 2, Randy Velarde 1, Gregg Jefferies 1, Tim Salmon 1, Orlando Palmeiro 1, Justin Baughman 1.
Kansas City	13	Hal Morris 4, Jose Offerman 2, Johnny Damon 2, Dean Palmer 1, Jeff Conine 1, Mike Sweeney 1, Sal Fasano 1, Larry Sutton 1.
Minnesota	13	Otis Nixon 4, Matt Lawton 2, Todd Walker 2, Paul Molitor 1, Terry Steinbach 1, Brent Gates 1, Ron Coomer 1, Marty Cordova 1.
Cleveland	12	Travis Fryman 2, Kenny Lofton 2, Brian S. Giles 2, Omar Vizquel 1, David Justice 1, Jim Thome 1, Manny Ramirez 1, David Bell 1, Richie Sexson 1.
Detroit	11	Brian L. Hunter 2, Bob Higginson 2, Tony Clark 2, Juan Encarnacion 2, Andy Tomberlin 1, Deivi Cruz 1, Paul Bako 1.
Boston	10	Darren Bragg 3, Nomar Garciaparra 3, Mike Benjamin 1, Darren Lewis 1, Troy O'Leary 1, Scott Hatteberg 1.
Oakland	10	Ben Grieve 4, Rickey Henderson 2, Mike Blowers 1, Matt Stairs 1, Jason Giambi 1, Ryan Christenson 1.
Texas	10	Ivan Rodriguez 3, Will Clark 1, Roberto Kelly 1, Juan Gonzalez 1, Lee Stevens 1, Domingo Cedeno 1, Rusty Greer 1, Fernando Tatis 1.
Tampa Bay	10	Fred McGriff 3, Paul Sorrento 2, Bobby Smith 2, Wade Boggs 1, Quinton McCracken 1, Randy Winn 1.

NATIONAL LEAGUE

Team	No.	Hitters
Colorado	28	Dante Bichette 9, Todd Helton 4, Vinny Castilla 3, Mike Lansing 3, Neifi Perez 3, Ellis Burks 2, Jeff Reed 1, Larry Walker 1, Darryl Hamilton 1, Derrick Gibson 1.
Houston	17	Craig Biggio 3, Derek Bell 3, Carl Everett 3, Moises Alou 2, Sean Berry 2, Bill Spiers 1, Jeff Bagwell 1, Brad Ausmus 1, Richard Hidalgo 1.
New York	15	John Olerud 3, Carlos Baerga 2, Brian McRae 2, Mike Piazza 2, Edgardo Alfonzo 2, Rey Ordonez 2, Tony Phillips 1, Butch Huskey 1.
Atlanta	12	Chipper Jones 4, Keith Lockhart 2, Andruw Jones 2, Andres Galarraga 1, Javy Lopez 1, Michael Tucker 1, Tony Graffanino 1.
San Francisco	12	Barry Bonds 2, Rich Aurilia 2, Marvin Benard 2, Bill Mueller 2, Stan Javier 1, Darryl Hamilton 1, Charlie Hayes 1, Jeff Kent 1.
Milwaukee	11	Fernando Vina 4, Jeff Cirillo 4, Jose Valentin 1, Mike Matheny 1, Geoff Jenkins 1.
Chicago	10	Mickey Morandini 3, Lance Johnson 2, Glenallen Hill 1, Mark Grace 1, Jose Hernandez 1, Henry Rodriguez 1, Brant Brown 1.
Montreal	10	Rondell White 3, Mark Grudzielanek 3, Wilton Guerrero 1, Orlando Cabrera 1, Brad Fullmer 1, Bob Henley 1.
Philadelphia	10	Alex Arias 2, Rico Brogna 2, Mike Lieberthal 2, Bob Abreu 2, Gregg Jefferies 1, Desi Relaford 1.
St. Louis	10	Delino DeShields 3, Brian Jordan 2, Willie McGee 1, Mark McGwire 1, Ray Lankford 1, John Mabry 1, Fernando Tatis 1.
Cincinnati	9	Bret Boone 4, Dmitri Young 2, Barry Larkin 1, Eddie Taubensee 1, Chris Stynes 1.
Florida	8	Mark Kotsay 3, Cliff Floyd 2, Gary Sheffield 1, Gregg Zaun 1, Derrek Lee 1.
Arizona	7	Devon White 4, Matt Williams 1, Andy Fox 1, David Dellucci 1.
Los Angeles	7	Raul Mondesi 3, Eric Karros 2, Eric Young 1, Wilton Guerrero 1.
Pittsburgh	6	Kevin Young 2, Jason Kendall 2, Tony Womack 1, Jose Guillen 1.
San Diego	5	Tony Gwynn 2, Steve Finley 2, Mark Sweeney 1.

FIVE- AND SIX-HIT GAMES

Date	Player, Team, Opponent	AB	R	H	2B	3B	HR	RBI	Result
3-31	Jeff Kent, San Francisco N.L. at Houston	7	2	5	1	0	1	4	W 9-4
4-6	Dante Bichette, Colorado N.L. at Houston	5	1	5	1	0	0	2	L 4-13
4-10	Henry Rodriguez, Chicago N.L. at Montreal	5	2	5	0	0	1	3	W 13-0

Date	Player, Team, Opponent	AB	R	H	2B	3B	HR	RBI	Result
4-16	Fernando Vina, Milwaukee N.L. at Montreal	5	0	5	0	1	0	1	W 5-3
4-27	Raul Mondesi, Los Angeles N.L. vs. Milwaukee	6	1	5	1	0	1	1	L 2-3
4-28	Tony Gwynn, San Diego N.L. vs. Chicago N.L.	5	3	5	0	0	1	2	W 7-3
4-29	Ben Grieve, Oakland A.L. at Cleveland	5	4	5	2	0	0	2	W 11-4
5-7	Carlos Delgado, Toronto A.L. at Seattle	5	1	5	0	0	1	4	W 6-0
5-8	Mark Grudzielanek, Montreal N.L. vs. Colorado	5	1	5	0	0	0	0	L 5-7
5-14	Vinny Castilla, Colorado N.L. vs. Chicago N.L.	6	3	5	1	0	1	3	L 7-9
5-17	Brian Jordan, St. Louis N.L. vs. Florida	5	2	5	1	0	1	4	W 13-4
6-9	Darin Erstad, Anaheim A.L. at Arizona N.L.	5	3	5	1	0	0	1	W 10-8
6-13	Gary DiSarcina, Anaheim A.L. at Texas	5	1	5	2	1	0	4	W 18-6
6-22	Mark Kotsay, Florida N.L. at Tampa Bay A.L.	6	0	5	1	0	0	1	W 3-2
6-28	Jeff Cirillo, Milwaukee N.L. at Chicago A.L.	5	1	5	1	0	0	2	L 8-10
8-7	Brady Anderson, Baltimore A.L. at Minnesota	6	3	5	2	0	2	4	W 16-9
8-7†	Shane Spencer, New York A.L. vs. Kansas City	5	4	5	2	0	2	3	W 14-2
8-8	Paul Molitor, Minnesota A.L. vs. Baltimore	5	2	5	1	0	0	0	L 3-6
8-12	Hal Morris, Kansas City A.L. at Boston	6	0	5	2	0	0	2	W 8-4
8-18	Alex Rodriguez, Seattle A.L. vs. Detroit	5	2	5	2	0	0	2	L 6-7
8-23	Fernando Tatis, St. Louis N.L. at Pittsburgh	5	1	5	0	0	1	1	L 3-4
9-12	Alex Arias, Philadelphia N.L. vs. Pittsburgh	5	2	5	3	0	0	2	W 13-4
9-14	Albert Belle, Chicago A.L. at Detroit	8	1	5	3	0	0	5	W17-16
9-14	Juan Encarnacion, Detroit A.L. vs. Chicago A.L.	6	5	5	0	1	1	4	L16-17
9-24	Gary DiSarcina, Anaheim A.L. at Oakland	5	3	5	2	0	0	2	W 10-6

†Second game of doubleheader

HITTING STREAKS OF 15 OR MORE GAMES

AMERICAN LEAGUE

G	Player, Team	Span of streak
30	Eric Davis, Baltimore	July 12-Aug. 15
28	Garret Anderson, Anaheim	June 28-July 31
27	Jose Offerman, Kansas City	July 11-Aug. 7
24	Nomar Garciaparra, Boston	June 7-July 3
20	Joey Cora, Seattle-Cleveland	Aug. 15-Sept. 4
	Juan Gonzalez, Texas	Aug. 20-Sept. 9
19	Damion Easley, Detroit	May 10-May 30
	Carlos Delgado, Toronto	May 21-June 9
	Damion Easley, Detroit	July 3-July 23
18	Scott Spiezio, Oakland	May 21-June 9
	Jose Cruz Jr., Toronto	Aug. 5-Aug. 24
	Quinton McCracken, Tampa Bay	Aug. 18-Sept. 9
17	Paul O'Neill, New York	May 24-June 10
	Jason Giambi, Oakland	July 16-Aug. 2
	Paul Molitor, Minnesota	Aug. 31-Sept. 19
16	Joey Cora, Seattle	Mar. 31-Apr. 17
	Nomar Garciaparra, Boston	Apr. 2-Apr. 19
	Jim Thome, Cleveland	May 25-June 10
	Bernie Williams, New York	July 31-Aug. 14
	Will Clark, Texas	Aug. 22-Sept. 7

G	Player, Team	Span of streak
16	Jason Giambi, Oakland	Sept. 5-Sept. 24
	Mo Vaughn, Boston	Sept. 13-Sept. 27
15	Darin Erstad, Anaheim	Apr. 1-Apr. 18
	Shane Mack, Kansas City	Apr. 10-Apr. 26
	Derek Jeter, New York	May 2-May 20

Note: Gregg Jefferies compiled a 15-game hitting streak from August 20 through September 5 for Philadelphia N.L. (nine games) and Anaheim A.L. (six games).

NATIONAL LEAGUE

G	Player, Team	Span of streak
23	John Olerud, New York	July 19-Aug. 9
20	Larry Walker, Colorado	May 4-May 25
18	Doug Glanville, Philadelphia	May 1-May 20
	Delino DeShields, St. Louis	May 30-June 20
17	Bill Mueller, San Francisco	Apr. 24-May 14
	Doug Glanville, Philadelphia	May 30-June 17
16	Tony Womack, Pittsburgh	July 3-July 22
15	Andres Galarraga, Atlanta	Apr. 23-May 8
	Neifi Perez, Colorado	July 27-Aug. 11

MULTI-HOMER GAMES

AMERICAN LEAGUE

Team	No.	Hitters
Seattle	21	Ken Griffey Jr. 7, Edgar Martinez 3, David Segui 3, Russ Davis 3, Alex Rodriguez 3, Glenallen Hill 1, Jay Buhner 1.
Toronto	19	Carlos Delgado 6, Jose Canseco 5, Shawn Green 4, Mike Stanley 2, Ed Sprague 2.
Boston	18	Mo Vaughn 4, Nomar Garciaparra 4, John Valentin 3, Troy O'Leary 2, Mike Stanley 1, Jim Leyritz 1, Reggie Jefferson 1, Darren Bragg 1, Jason Varitek 1.
Texas	15	Juan Gonzalez 6, Lee Stevens 3, Roberto Kelly 2, Mark McLemore 1, Kevin Elster 1, Will Clark 1, Rusty Greer 1.
Chicago	14	Albert Belle 5, Jeff Abbott 2, Ruben Sierra 1, Robin Ventura 1, Frank Thomas 1, Wil Cordero 1, Greg Norton 1, Craig Wilson 1, Brian Simmons 1.
Cleveland	14	Manny Ramirez 8, Jim Thome 2, David Justice 1, Travis Fryman 1, Brian S. Giles 1, Richie Sexson 1.
New York	14	Darryl Strawberry 2, Paul O'Neill 2, Tino Martinez 2, Jorge Posada 2, Shane Spencer 2, Chuck Knoblauch 1, Bernie Williams 1, Scott Brosius 1, Derek Jeter 1.
Baltimore	12	Eric Davis 4, B.J. Surhoff 2, Brady Anderson 2, Chris Hoiles 2, Rafael Palmeiro 1, Lenny Webster 1.
Detroit	11	Damion Easley 4, Tony Clark 3, Bob Higginson 2, Luis Gonzalez 1, Gabe Alvarez 1.
Oakland	8	Matt Stairs 2, Jason Giambi 2, Mike Macfarlane 1, Mike Blowers 1, Scott Spiezio 1, Ben Grieve 1.
Anaheim	6	Jim Edmonds 2, Cecil Fielder 1, Dave Hollins 1, Tim Salmon 1, Darin Erstad 1.
Tampa Bay	5	Mike Kelly 3, Fred McGriff 1, Quinton McCracken 1.
Kansas City	3	Jeff King 1, Dean Palmer 1, Johnny Damon 1.
Minnesota	2	Terry Steinbach 1, Pat Meares 1.

NATIONAL LEAGUE

Team	No.	Hitters
Atlanta	21	Andres Galarraga 8, Andruw Jones 4, Javy Lopez 2, Chipper Jones 2, Ryan Klesko 1, Gerald Williams 1, Keith Lockhart 1, Michael Tucker 1, Eddie Perez 1.
Chicago	18	Sammy Sosa 11, Henry Rodriguez 3, Mark Grace 1, Jose Hernandez 1, Tyler Houston 1, Brant Brown 1.
St. Louis	15	Mark McGwire 10, J.D. Drew 2, Gary Gaetti 1, Ron Gant 1, Ray Lankford 1.
Colorado	12	Vinny Castilla 6, Larry Walker 2, Todd Helton 2, Ellis Burks 1, Mike Lansing 1.
Houston	11	Moises Alou 3, Jeff Bagwell 3, Craig Biggio 2, Richard Hidalgo 2, Carl Everett 1.
Philadelphia	11	Rico Brogna 4, Scott Rolen 2, Bobby Estalella 2, Kevin Sefcik 1, Doug Glanville 1, Bob Abreu 1.
San Diego	11	Greg Vaughn 7, Ken Caminiti 2, Tony Gwynn 1, Chris Gomez 1.
San Francisco	11	Barry Bonds 2, Jeff Kent 2, J.T. Snow 2, Brian Johnson 2, Stan Javier 1, Rich Aurilia 1, Bill Mueller 1.
Milwaukee	8	Jeromy Burnitz 3, Jose Valentin 2, Marquis Grissom 1, Dave Nilsson 1, Jeff Cirillo 1.
Los Angeles	7	Eric Karros 2, Mike Piazza 2, Raul Mondesi 2, Matt Luke 1.
Montreal	7	Chris Widger 2, Rondell White 1, Shane Andrews 1, Mark Grudzielanek 1, Vladimir Guerrero 1, Brad Fullmer 1.
Arizona	6	Travis Lee 2, Devon White 1, Matt Williams 1, Karim Garcia 1, Tony Batista 1.
Cincinnati	6	Bret Boone 3, Barry Larkin 2, Jon Nunnally 1.
Florida	3	Bobby Bonilla 1, Cliff Floyd 1, Charles Johnson 1.
New York	3	John Olerud 1, Mike Piazza 1, Edgardo Alfonzo 1.
Pittsburgh	1	Freddy Garcia 1.

THREE-HOMER GAMES

Date	Player, Team, Opponent	AB	R	H	2B	3B	HR	RBI	Result
4-3	Jose Valentin, Milwaukee N.L. at Florida	3	3	3	0	0	3	5	W 7-1
4-13	Lee Stevens, Texas A.L. vs. Detroit	4	3	3	0	0	3	4	W 10-1
4-14	Mark McGwire, St. Louis N.L. vs. Arizona	3	4	3	0	0	3	5	W 15-5
5-19	Mark McGwire, St. Louis N.L. at Philadelphia	5	3	3	0	0	3	6	W 10-8
6-15	Sammy Sosa, Chicago N.L. vs. Milwaukee	4	3	3	0	0	3	3	W 6-5
6-18	Brant Brown, Chicago N.L. vs. Philadelphia	5	3	4	0	0	3	5	W 12-5
7-12	Ken Caminiti, San Diego N.L. at Los Angeles	4	3	3	0	0	3	5	W 6-3
8-4	Carlos Delgado, Toronto A.L. at Texas	5	3	3	0	0	3	4	L 9-11
9-15	Manny Ramirez, Cleveland A.L. vs. Toronto	4	3	3	0	0	3	5	W 7-5
9-20	Bret Boone, Cincinnati N.L. at Chicago N.L.	4	3	3	0	0	3	6	W 7-3
9-22	Mike Lansing, Colorado N.L. vs. Arizona	4	3	3	0	0	3	4	L 6-8

GRAND SLAMS
AMERICAN LEAGUE

Date	Batter, Team	Pitcher, Team	Inn.*	Site
4-1	Cal Ripken Jr., Baltimore	Glendon Rusch, Kansas City	1	Baltimore
4-2	Juan Gonzalez, Texas	Tom Fordham, Chicago	7	Texas
4-4	Scott Spiezio, Oakland	David Cone, New York	6	Oakland
4-10	Mo Vaughn, Boston	Paul Spoljaric, Seattle	9	Boston
4-16	Matt Stairs, Oakland	Tim Belcher, Kansas City	4	Oakland
4-17	Tino Martinez, New York	Justin Thompson, Detroit	1	Detroit
4-25	Ron Coomer, Minnesota	Heathcliff Slocumb, Seattle	9	Seattle
4-26	Rickey Henderson, Oakland	Alan Mills, Baltimore	7	Baltimore
4-29	Wil Cordero, Chicago	Terry Mathews, Baltimore	5	Chicago
5-1	Darin Erstad, Anaheim	Tony Castillo, Chicago	6	Anaheim
5-2	Darryl Strawberry, New York	Scott Service, Kansas City	9	Kansas City
5-3	Paul Sorrento, Tampa Bay	Charles Nagy, Cleveland	3	Cleveland
5-3	Sandy Alomar Jr., Cleveland	Roberto Hernandez, Tampa Bay	9	Cleveland
5-3	Dan Wilson, Seattle	Frank Castillo, Detroit	1	Seattle
5-7	Carlos Delgado, Toronto	Jamie Moyer, Seattle	3	Seattle
5-9	Matt Lawton, Minnesota	Andy Pettitte, New York	6	Minnesota
5-13	Bernie Williams, New York	Rick Helling, Texas	5	New York
5-14	Johnny Damon, Kansas City	Dennis Springer, Tampa Bay	2	Tampa Bay
5-17	Mike Blowers, Oakland	Bill Simas, Chicago	8	Chicago
5-18	Scott Spiezio, Oakland	James Baldwin, Chicago	7	Chicago
5-22	Shane Mack, Kansas City	Xavier Hernandez, Texas	7	Texas
5-23	Chuck Knoblauch, New York	Derek Lowe, Boston	2	Boston
5-23	Jeffrey Hammonds, Baltimore	Jimmy Haynes, Oakland	4	Oakland
5-25	Garret Anderson, Anaheim	Tim Belcher, Kansas City	1	Anaheim
5-31	Juan Gonzalez, Texas	Scott Erickson, Baltimore	3	Baltimore
6-3	Rickey Henderson, Oakland	Aaron Sele, Texas	5	Oakland
6-9	Cecil Fielder, Anaheim	Willie Blair, Arizona N.L.	3	Arizona
6-19	David Segui, Seattle	Blake Stein, Oakland	2	Seattle
6-21	Brent Gates, Minnesota	Jason Bere, Chicago	4	Chicago
6-24	Manny Ramirez, Cleveland	Mark Petkovsek, St. Louis N.L.	1	Cleveland
6-24	Matt Stairs, Oakland	Steve Reed, San Francisco N.L.	8	San Francisco
6-27	Paul Sorrento, Tampa Bay	Curt Schilling, Philadelphia N.L.	8	Philadelphia

Date	Batter, Team	Pitcher, Team	Inn.*	Site
7-3	Billy Ashley, Boston	Jason Bere, Chicago	5	Boston
7-5	Manny Ramirez, Cleveland	Glendon Rusch, Kansas City	6	Kansas City
7-12	Eric Davis, Baltimore	Jin Ho Cho, Boston	3	Baltimore
7-14	Chris Hoiles, Baltimore	Woody Williams, Toronto	1	Baltimore
7-16	Troy O'Leary, Boston	Dwight Gooden, Cleveland	5	Boston
7-17	Shawn Green, Toronto	Mike Stanton, New York	7	Toronto
7-18	Brian S. Giles, Cleveland	John Snyder, Chicago	1	Chicago
7-18	Tim Raines, New York	Robert Person, Toronto	8	Toronto
7-19	Jose Canseco, Toronto	Andy Pettitte, New York	3	Toronto
7-23	Damon Buford, Boston	Dan Plesac, Toronto	8	Boston
7-28	Gabe Alvarez, Detroit	Sidney Ponson, Baltimore	1	Detroit
7-31	Frank Thomas, Chicago	John Burkett, Texas	5	Texas
8-4†	Darryl Strawberry, New York	Billy Taylor, Oakland	9	Oakland
8-5	Rafael Palmeiro, Baltimore	Sean Runyan, Detroit	8	Baltimore
8-12	Carlos Delgado, Toronto	Greg McCarthy, Seattle	7	Toronto
8-14	Chris Hoiles, Baltimore	Charles Nagy, Cleveland	3	Cleveland
8-14	Chris Hoiles, Baltimore	Ron Villone, Cleveland	8	Cleveland
8-14	Damion Easley, Detroit	Blake Stein, Oakland	2	Detroit
8-15	Rusty Greer, Texas	Hideki Irabu, New York	2	New York
8-18	Bob Higginson, Detroit	Greg McCarthy, Seattle	6	Seattle
8-24	Robin Ventura, Chicago	Mike Timlin, Seattle	9	Seattle
8-30	Richie Sexson, Cleveland	Tim Worrell, Oakland	7	Cleveland
9-1	Deivi Cruz, Detroit	Danny Patterson, Texas	7	Detroit
9-2	Nomar Garciaparra, Boston	Bobby Ayala, Seattle	9	Boston
9-7	Ken Griffey Jr., Seattle	Jimmy Key, Baltimore	6	Seattle
9-9	Scott Hatteberg, Boston	Orlando Hernandez, New York	4	Boston
9-13	Wade Boggs, Tampa Bay	Esteban Loaiza, Texas	2	Tampa Bay
9-18	Shane Spencer, New York	Jesse Orosco, Baltimore	9	Baltimore
9-21	Enrique Wilson, Cleveland	Andy Pettitte, New York	5	New York
9-24	Shane Spencer, New York	Wilson Alvarez, Tampa Bay	6	New York
9-27	Shane Spencer, New York	Albie Lopez, Tampa Bay	5	New York

*Inning in which grand slam was hit. †Second game of doubleheader.

NATIONAL LEAGUE

Date	Batter, Team	Pitcher, Team	Inn.*	Site
3-31	Mark McGwire, St. Louis	Ramon Martinez, Los Angeles	5	St. Louis
4-2	Jeromy Burnitz, Milwaukee	Brian Edmondson, Atlanta	11	Atlanta
4-7	Derrek Lee, Florida	Garrett Stephenson, Philadelphia	5	Philadelphia
4-9	Mike Piazza, Los Angeles	Jeff Suppan, Arizona	3	Los Angeles
4-10	Mike Piazza, Los Angeles	Mike Magnante, Houston	8	Los Angeles
4-10	Steve Finley, San Diego	Felix Rodriguez, Arizona	9	San Diego
4-12	Bret Boone, Cincinnati	Pedro Astacio, Colorado	3	Colorado
4-13	Derrek Lee, Florida	Esteban Loaiza, Pittsburgh	3	Pittsburgh
4-14	Matt Williams, Arizona	Kent Mercker, St. Louis	4	St. Louis
4-16	Craig Counsell, Florida	Tyler Green, Philadelphia	1	Florida
4-21	John Jaha, Milwaukee	Ramon Martinez, Los Angeles	5	Milwaukee
4-24	Mike Piazza, Los Angeles	Kerry Wood, Chicago	2	Los Angeles
4-26	Barry Bonds, San Francisco	Jeff Juden, Milwaukee	3	San Francisco
5-2	Ellis Burks, Colorado	Greg McMichael, New York	9	New York
5-5	Wally Joyner, San Diego	Paul Wagner, Milwaukee	2	Milwaukee
5-6	Larry Walker, Colorado	Jerry Spradlin, Philadelphia	6	Philadelphia
5-6	Brent Mayne, San Francisco	Antonio Alfonseca, Florida	7	Florida
5-8	Todd Zeile, Los Angeles	Jesus Sanchez, Florida	1	Florida
5-9	Chipper Jones, Atlanta	Dan Miceli, San Diego	7	Atlanta
5-14	Henry Rodriguez, Chicago	John Thomson, Colorado	3	Colorado
5-20	Matt Williams, Arizona	Andy Larkin, Florida	5	Florida
5-26	Javy Lopez, Atlanta	Marc Valdes, Montreal	7	Atlanta
5-26	Ryan Jackson, Florida	Dave Mlicki, New York	1	Florida
5-29	Larry Walker, Colorado	Doug Henry, Houston	8	Colorado
5-30	Brad Fullmer, Montreal	Jose Silva, Pittsburgh	5	Pittsburgh
5-31	Raul Mondesi, Los Angeles	Mike Remlinger, Cincinnati	1	Los Angeles
6-9	Greg Vaughn, San Diego	Brett Tomko, Cincinnati	7	San Diego
6-9	Yamil Benitez, Arizona	Chuck Finley, Anaheim A.L.	3	Arizona
6-12	DaRond Stovall, Montreal	Mike Cather, Atlanta	9	Atlanta
6-12	Mark McGwire, St. Louis	Andy Benes, Arizona	3	Arizona
6-16	Ryan Klesko, Atlanta	Joe Fontenot, Florida	1	Atlanta
6-21	Jose Guillen, Pittsburgh	Jeff Juden, Milwaukee	3	Milwaukee
6-26	Devon White, Arizona	Bob Wells, Seattle A.L.	6	Arizona
6-28	J.T. Snow, San Francisco	Aaron Sele, Texas A.L.	2	San Francisco
7-17	Ruben Rivera, San Diego	Rick Krivda, Cincinnati	4	Cincinnati
7-20	Kevin Tapani, Chicago	Denny Neagle, Atlanta	3	Atlanta

Date	Batter, Team	Pitcher, Team	Inn.*	Site
7-20	Ray Lankford, St. Louis	Roberto Ramirez, San Diego	9	San Diego
7-24	Jeff Kent, San Francisco	Scott Winchester, Cincinnati	4	San Francisco
7-25	J.T. Snow, San Francisco	Steve Parris, Cincinnati	1	San Francisco
7-27	Sammy Sosa, Chicago	Alan Embree, Arizona	8	Arizona
7-28	Ray Lankford, St. Louis	Mike Myers, Milwaukee	8	St. Louis
7-28	Darrin Jackson, Milwaukee	Rich Croushore, St. Louis	9	St. Louis
7-28	Sammy Sosa, Chicago	Bob Wolcott, Arizona	5	Arizona
8-10	Dante Bichette, Colorado	Anthony Telford, Montreal	7	Colorado
8-16	Bobby Estalella, Philadelphia	Jamey Wright, Colorado	3	Colorado
8-16	Jeff Reed, Colorado	Ricky Bottalico, Philadelphia	8	Colorado
8-20	Glenallen Hill, Chicago	Julian Tavarez, San Francisco	5	Chicago
8-22	Mike Piazza, New York	Andy Benes, Arizona	2	New York
8-27	Chris Widger, Montreal	Darren Dreifort, Los Angeles	8	Los Angeles
9-2	Kent Mercker, St. Louis	Jesus Sanchez, Florida	4	Florida
9-8	Jeff Bagwell, Houston	Rick Krivda, Cincinnati	3	Houston
9-11	Gerald Williams, Atlanta	Kirt Ojala, Florida	3	Atlanta
9-16	Sammy Sosa, Chicago	Brian Boehringer, San Diego	8	San Diego
9-19	Bill Mueller, San Francisco	Ismael Valdes, Los Angeles	3	San Francisco
9-19	Jeff Kent, San Francisco	Mike Judd, Los Angeles	4	San Francisco
9-21	Tony Tarasco, Cincinnati	Mark Leiter, Philadelphia	7	Cincinnati
9-23	Karim Garcia, Arizona	Pedro Astacio, Colorado	3	Colorado

*Inning in which grand slam was hit.

TRANSACTIONS

JANUARY 5
Royals organization signed P Brian Barber.
Mets released P Joe Crawford.

JANUARY 6
Indians organization signed 2B Carlos Garcia.
Twins organization signed P Ricky Bones.
Expos organization signed OF Derrick May.
Cardinals signed P Kent Bottenfield.

JANUARY 7
Twins organization signed P Dan Smith.
Mariners organization signed OF Glenallen Hill.
Diamondbacks signed P Omar Daal.
Reds organization signed P Junichi Iwasaki.
Dodgers organization signed OF Thomas Howard.
Padres organization signed P Mark Langston.

JANUARY 8
Indians organization signed P John Cummings, P John Ericks, P Jason Grimsley and P Jamie McAndrew.
Tigers signed P Tim Worrell.
Diamondbacks signed IF Andy Stankiewicz.
Reds signed P Jose Rijo.
Mets organization signed C Tim Spehr.

JANUARY 9
White Sox organization signed OF Ruben Sierra and P Jim Bullinger.
Diamondbacks organization signed P Mark Davis.
Astros organization signed P Pete Schourek and P Reggie Harris.

JANUARY 10
Angels signed P William VanLandingham and IF Norberto Martin.

JANUARY 12
Royals organization signed P Chris Hammond.
Twins organization signed OF Orlando Merced.

JANUARY 13
White Sox organization signed P Larry Casian and OF Lou Frazier.
Indians organization signed C Ron Karkovice, P Jimmy Williams, P Andy Croghan, P Anthony Young, C Sean Mulligan and IF Brandon Wilson.
Mets signed P Masato Yoshii.
Padres organization signed 1B Eddie Williams.

JANUARY 14
Astros traded OF James Mouton to Padres for P Sean Bergman.
Brewers organization signed IF Bob Hamelin.

JANUARY 15
Devil Rays signed SS Kevin Stocker.
Diamondbacks signed C Kelly Stinnett.
Cubs signed P Rod Beck.

JANUARY 16
Red Sox signed P Curtis Shaw.
Rockies signed P David Veres.
Expos organization signed IF Mike Mordecai.
Padres signed OF James Mouton and P Dan Miceli.

JANUARY 19
Angels organization signed P Rich Robertson.
Indians organization signed IF Jolbert Cabera.

JANUARY 20
Royals organization signed P Lee Smith and IF Terry Pendleton.
Yankees claimed P Hector Ramirez on waivers from Orioles.

Blue Jays organization signed OF Phil Plantier.
Diamondbacks signed P Russ Springer.

JANUARY 21
Mets signed OF Rick Parker.

JANUARY 22
Angels signed OF Gary Thurman.
Royals signed P Pat Rapp.
Athletics signed OF Rickey Henderson.
Reds signed P Pete Harnisch.
Padres traded P Jim Baron to Yankees for P Salvador Rodriguez.
Giants signed SS Rey Sanchez.

JANUARY 23
Red Sox signed IF Julio Cesar Guerrero.
Braves signed P Tommy Greene.

JANUARY 25
Mets organization signed P Efrain Valdez.

JANUARY 26
Reds signed P Curt Lyons.
Rockies released P Robbie Beckett.

JANUARY 27
Cardinals signed IF Craig Shipley.

JANUARY 28
Diamondbacks signed P Chris Clemons, P Marty Janzen, P Jeff Suppan, IF Edwin Diaz and OF Brent Brede.
Reds signed P Mark Hutton.

JANUARY 29
Orioles organization signed SS Ozzie Guillen.
Indians signed OF Geronimo Berroa.
Tigers organization signed OF Pete Incaviglia.
Braves organization signed P Dennis Martinez.
Giants signed P John Johnstone.
Giants traded IF-OF David McCarty to Mariners for OF Jalal Leach and OF Scott Smith.

JANUARY 30
Angels organization signed OF Patrick Lennon.
Devil Rays signed IF Herbert Perry, P Esteban Yan and P Rick Gorecki.

JANUARY 31
Diamondbacks organization signed P Gregg Olson.

FEBRUARY 2
White Sox signed C Johnny Cardenas.
Devil Rays signed OF Randy Winn.
Rangers signed P Larry Thomas.
Cubs organization signed P Terry Mulholland.

FEBRUARY 3
Diamondbacks signed P Andy Benes.
Expos organization signed P Shawn Boskie, P Mike Campbell and OF Chuck Carr.

FEBRUARY 4
Blue Jays signed OF Jose Canseco.

FEBRUARY 5
Devil Rays signed P Chuck Bauer and P Juan Williams.
Mets traded 1B-OF Roberto Petagine to Reds for SS Yuri Sanchez.

FEBRUARY 6
Yankees traded P Eric Milton, P Danny Mota, OF Brian Buchanan, SS Cristain Guzman and cash to Twins for 2B Chuck Knoblauch.
Rangers signed P Aaron Sele and P Matt Perisho.

Diamondbacks signed P Hector Carrasco.
Braves signed OF Curtis Pride.
Rockies signed OF Curtis Goodwin.
Mets traded P Jesus Sanchez, P A.J. Burnett and OF Robert Stratton to Marlins for P Al Leiter and IF Ralph Milliard.
Padres signed IF Andy Sheets and P Donne Wall.

FEBRUARY 10
Diamondbacks traded IF Mike Bell to Mets for P Joe Lisio.

FEBRUARY 12
Devil Rays signed P Albie Lopez.

FEBRUARY 13
Dodgers announced the retirement of P Mark Gubicza.

FEBRUARY 14
Padres organization signed P Rob Dibble.

FEBRUARY 16
Indians signed IF Shawon Dunston.

FEBRUARY 17
Blue Jays sold P Ken Robinson to Diamondbacks.

FEBRUARY 20
Marlins claimed P Kirt Ojala on waivers from Diamondbacks.

FEBRUARY 21
Mets organization signed OF Joe Orsulak.

FEBRUARY 23
Tigers signed 3B Joe Randa and OF Trey Beamon.

FEBRUARY 24
Twins signed OF Brian Buchanan.
Phillies released OF Midre Cummings.

FEBRUARY 25
Angels signed P Jack McDowell.

FEBRUARY 26
Yankees organization signed P Ricardo Aramboles.
Mariners claimed P Maximo de la Rosa on waivers from Indians.
Diamondbacks released OF David Hulse.

FEBRUARY 27
Reds organization signed OF Midre Cummings.
Padres organization signed P Ryan Bowen.

MARCH 3
Tigers released pitcher Robert Ellis.

MARCH 5
Twins signed OF Alex Ochoa.

MARCH 6
Yankees signed P Orlando Hernandez.
Rangers released P Tanyon Sturtze.
Phillies organization signed P Toby Borland.

MARCH 7
Yankees traded IF Andy Fox to Arizona for P Marty Janzen and P Todd Erdos.
Diamondbacks announced the retirement of P Mark Davis.

MARCH 9
White Sox signed C Mark Johnson, IF Benji Gil and IF Sergio Nunez.
Indians released IF Chad Fonville.
Tigers signed P Rikki Johnston.
Athletics organization signed OF Kevin Mitchell.

MARCH 11
Angels released OF Patrick Lennon.
Indians traded P Ben McDonald to Brewers for P Mark Watson.
Indians organization signed OF Osmani Santana.
Yankees released P Jim Converse and P Joey Eischen.
Mariners signed C Francisco Santiestevan.

MARCH 12
Rangers organization released P Scott Klingenbeck.
Dodgers claimed P Steve Montgomery on waivers from Orioles.

MARCH 13
Astros released P Bob McDonald.

MARCH 14
Yankees released P Dave Fleming and P Pat Linton.
Blue Jays traded P Tim Crabtree to Rangers for C Kevin Brown.
Mets organization signed IF Chad Fonville.

MARCH 16
White Sox announced the retirement of P Roger McDowell.

MARCH 17
Athletics sold OF Ernie Young to Royals.

MARCH 19
Red Sox claimed OF Midre Cummings on waivers from Reds.
Blue Jays released OF Phil Plantier.
Reds signed P Joey Eischen.

MARCH 20
Reds traded 1B Tim Belk to Tigers for SS Kevin Baez.
Dodgers organization signed P Sean Maloney.
Mets traded P Brandon Villafuerte and a player to be named to Marlins for OF Robert Stratton; Mets sent 2B Cesar Crespo to complete deal (September 14).
Cardinals claimed OF Luis Saturria on waivers from Blue Jays.

MARCH 21
Reds traded IF Eric Owens to Marlins for a player to be named; Marlins sent P Jesus Martinez to Reds organization to complete deal (March 26).

MARCH 23
White Sox signed OF Wil Cordero.
Rangers released P Matt Whiteside.

MARCH 24
Orioles released OF Tony Tarasco and P Rick Krivda.
Indians claimed P Rick Krivda on waivers from Orioles.
Tigers signed IF Bill Ripken and C Joe Oliver.
Royals released P Chris Hammond.
Rangers organization released IF Scott Cooper.
Blue Jays released OF Jacob Brumfield.
Reds claimed OF Tony Tarasco on waivers from Orioles.

MARCH 25
Indians released 2B Carlos Garcia.
Tigers signed P Doug Bochtler.
Tigers released C Marcus Jensen.
Mariners released SS Pat Listach and IF Aaron Holbert.
Devil Rays released OF Dwight Smith.
Blue Jays organization signed SS Juan Bell and OF Patrick Lennon.
Diamondbacks released P Hector Carrasco.
Braves released P Brad Clontz.
Marlins sold IF-OF Eric Owens to Brewers.
Dodgers signed OF Thomas Howard.
Cardinals released C Danny Sheaffer.

MARCH 26
Red Sox organization signed 2B Mark Lemke.
Red Sox released IF Mike Gallego.
White Sox traded P Jim Bullinger to Mariners for P Marty Weymouth.
Royals claimed P Danny Rios on waivers from Yankees.
Mariners claimed P Jose Paniagua on waivers from Devil Rays.
Blue Jays released P Carey Paige, P Alan Meinershagen and OF Scott Bullett.
Mets released IF Chad Fonville.

MARCH 27
Mariners claimed OF Ryan Radmanovich on waivers from Twins, and claimed P Jose Paniagua on waivers from Devil Rays.
Diamondbacks released IF Darnell Coles.
Expos signed IF Mike Mordecai.
Phillies released P Rich Hunter.

MARCH 28
Phillies traded C Chris Tremie to Rangers for future considerations.

Rangers announced retirement of P Jose Guzman.
Mets traded P Juan Acevedo to Cardinals for P Rigo Beltran.
Mets released OF Joe Orsulak.

MARCH 30
Angels traded IF Chip Hale to Cardinals for IF Craig Shipley.
Angels signed 2B Carlos Garcia.
Red Sox signed P Jin Ho Cho.
Red Sox organization signed OF Billy Ashley.
Indians traded 1B Sean Casey to Reds for P Dave Burba.
Mariners claimed OF Robert Perez on waivers from Blue Jays.
Rangers organization signed P Jeff Granger.
Brewers released P Ben McDonald.
Expos claimed C Mike Hubbard on waivers from Cubs.
Expos released OF Chuck Carr.

APRIL 1
Twins signed P Hector Carrasco.

APRIL 2
Devil Rays claimed P Eddie Gaillard on waivers from Tigers.

APRIL 6
Astros organization signed P David West.

APRIL 7
Mets traded P Chris Roberts to Athletics for a player to be named.
Mets organization signed P Dan Pontes.

APRIL 8
Indians organization signed IF Pat Listach.
Royals traded C Mike Macfarlane to Athletics for OF Shane Mack and a player to be named; Athletics sent P Greg Hansell to complete deal (May 9).
Padres traded P Marc Kroon to Reds for P Buddy Carlyle.

APRIL 9
Dodgers signed P Brad Clontz.

APRIL 10
Expos organization signed P Ulmer Urbina.

APRIL 11
Cubs organization released OF Stoney Briggs.

APRIL 13
Indians organization signed P Huck Flener and P Jim Brower.
Mets organization signed IF Robert Eenhoorn.

APRIL 14
Indians claimed IF David Bell on waivers from Cardinals.

APRIL 18
Reds traded OF Chad Mottola to Rangers for a player to be named.

APRIL 20
Diamondbacks organization signed P John Rosengren.

APRIL 22
Tigers released OF Pete Incaviglia.

APRIL 23
Padres organization signed P Roberto Ramirez.

APRIL 24
Tigers claimed IF Jeff Manto on waivers from Indians.

APRIL 27
Devil Rays claimed P Julio Santana on waivers from Rangers.
Giants traded P Ricky Pickett to Diamondbacks for OF Chris Jones.

APRIL 28
Indians organization signed IF Phil Hiatt.

MAY 1
Orioles organization signed P Steve Ontiveros and P Jim Converse, and released IF Ozzie Guillen.

MAY 5
White Sox traded P Brian Woods to Rockies for P Mike Zolecki.
Cubs traded P Ben VanRyn to Padres for P Don Wengert.

MAY 6
Indians signed OF Mark Whiten.
Braves signed SS Ozzie Guillen.
Tigers traded P Scott Sanders to Padres for a player to be named; Padres sent OF Rod Lindsey to complete deal (June 1).

MAY 7
Blue Jays traded P Dane Johnson to Brewers for future considerations.

MAY 8
Expos traded C Raul Chavez to Mariners for OF Robert Perez.

MAY 9
Mets signed 1B-OF Phil Plantier and C Steve Decker.

MAY 12
Twins claimed OF Ken Ramos on waivers from Astros.
Astros organization signed OF Pete Incaviglia.
Mariners traded C Rick Wilkins to Mets for P Lindsay Gulin.

MAY 14
Diamondbacks claimed P Amaury Telemaco on waivers from Cubs.
Marlins traded OF Gary Sheffield, 3B Bobby Bonilla, C Charles Johnson, OF Jim Eisenreich and P Manuel Barrios to Dodgers for C Mike Piazza and 3B Todd Zeile.
Dodgers sold P Frank Lankford to Yankees.

MAY 20
Mets organization signed IF Kenji Sonofuku.

MAY 22
Marlins traded C Mike Piazza to Mets for OF Preston Wilson, P Ed Yarnall and P Geoff Goetz.

MAY 23
Diamondbacks signed SS John Brock.

MAY 26
Devil Rays released OF Jerome Walton.
Blue Jays signed P Mark Hendrickson.
Astros signed P-3B Derek Stanford.

MAY 27
White Sox organization signed P Jim Abbott.
Indians organization signed OF Aaron Gordnier and P Jason Farmer.

MAY 29
Orioles signed P Matt Riley.
Yankees signed OF Mike Vento.

Rockies acquired P Tom Doyle from Duluth-Superior of the Northern League for a player to be named.

JUNE 2
Orioles organization signed P Scott Taylor.
Diamondbacks claimed P Bobby Chouinard on waivers from Brewers.
Phillies signed P Hut Smith.

JUNE 3
Astros sold IF Luis Rivera to Royals.

JUNE 4
Diamondbacks traded P Scott Brow and P Joe Lisio to Yankees for P Willie Banks.
Marlins claimed P Brian Edmonson on waivers from Braves.
Dodgers traded P Hideo Nomo and P Brad Clontz to Mets for P Dave Mlicki and P Greg McMichael.

JUNE 6
Astros organization signed P Lee Smith.

JUNE 8
Indians claimed OF Matt Luke on waivers from Dodgers.

JUNE 9
Orioles traded P Eric Estes to Padres for P Pete Smith.

Athletics traded IF Kurt Abbott to Rockies for a player to be named and cash; Rockies sent P Ara Petrosian to complete deal (June 18).
Padres organization signed OF Mike Devereaux.

JUNE 10
Braves signed P Rodney Dickinson.
Cardinals traded OF Wayne Kirby to Mets for IF Shawn Gilbert and a player to be named.

JUNE 16
Orioles claimed OF Rich Becker on waivers from Mets.
Indians organization signed IF Jeff Manto.
Mariners released P Tony Fossas.
Blue Jays released P Erik Hanson and signed C Ryan Bundy.
Reds traded P Eddie Priest and OF Christian Rojas to Indians for P Rick Krivda.
Phillies signed IF Takahito Ishida and P Masahiro Tanaka.

JUNE 18
Red Sox traded P Mike Blais to Astros for P David West.
Reds released IF Pete Rose Jr.

JUNE 19
Cubs organization signed P Tony Fossas.

JUNE 20
Red Sox traded C Jim Leyritz and OF Ethan Faggett to Padres for P Carlos Reyes, P Dario Veras and C Mandy Romero.
White Sox released P Tony Castillo.
Cleveland Indians sold OF Matt Luke to Dodgers.
Mets signed OF Ruben Sierra.

JUNE 22
Rangers traded P Bobby Witt to Cardinals for a player to be named.
Cubs released 1B Rod McCall.
Phillies signed SS Pat Listach.

JUNE 23
Tigers traded IF Bip Roberts to Athletics for a player to be named; Athletics sent IF Jason Wood to complete deal (July 18).
Diamondbacks traded P Russ Springer to Braves for P Alan Embree.

JUNE 24
Indians traded OF Geronimo Berroa to Tigers for OF Dave Roberts, and claimed P Tim Worrell on waivers from Tigers.
Blue Jays signed P Tyler Renwick.
Brewers claimed P David Weathers on waivers from Reds.
Phillies released OF Rex Hudler.

JUNE 25
Angels organization signed P Erik Hanson.
Royals signed P Robbie Morrison.
Rockies claimed P Fred Rath on waivers from Twins.

JUNE 26
Diamondbacks claimed P Aaron Small on waivers from Athletics.
Pirates signed IF Pete Rose Jr.

JUNE 27
Royals traded P Manuel Bernal to Pirates for OF Jermaine Allensworth.

JUNE 30
Astros organization released P Lee Smith.
Mets sold P Mark Mimbs to Orix Bluerays (Japan).

JULY 1
Blue Jays organization signed OF Tony Phillips.

JULY 2
Indians organization signed IF-OF Rex Hudler.
Rockies released P Brian Richardson.

JULY 3
Reds traded OF-IF Lenny Harris to Mets for P John Hudek.

JULY 4
Astros traded C Ramon Castro to Marlins for P Jay Powell and C Scott Makarewicz.

Dodgers traded IF Paul Konerko and P Dennis Reyes to Reds for P Jeff Shaw.

JULY 6
Indians released C Ron Karkovice.
Cubs claimed Glenallen Hill on waivers from Mariners.

JULY 10
Blue Jays released P Luis Andujar.
Mets traded P Brian Bohanon to Dodgers for P Greg McMichael and cash.

JULY 12
Indians traded P Tim Worrell to Athletics for a player to be named; Athletics sent SS Adam Robinson to complete deal (July 28).
Cubs released P Bob Patterson.

JULY 15
Tigers released C Joe Oliver.

JULY 16
White Sox released P Jason Bere.
Blue Jays sold contract of 2B Pat Kelly to Cardinals.

JULY 17
Rockies claimed OF Derrick White on waivers from Cubs.
Pirates traded P Esteban Loaiza to Rangers for P Todd Van Poppel and 2B Warren Morris.

JULY 18
Tigers released IF Billy Ripken.

JULY 21
Reds organization signed pitcher Jason Bere.

JULY 22
Indians organization signed P Jim Poole.
Mariners signed C Joe Oliver.

JULY 23
Orioles traded OF-DH Joe Carter to Giants for P Darin Blood.
Indians traded P Jose Mesa, IF Shawon Dunston and P Al Morman to Giants for P Steve Reed and OF Jacob Cruz.
Brewers traded P Doug Jones to Indians for P Eric Plunk.
Padres traded P Widd Workman to Dodgers for P Jim Bruske.

JULY 28
Orioles released P Norm Charlton.

JULY 29
White Sox traded P Matt Karchner to Cubs for P Jon Garland.

JULY 30
White Sox traded C Charlie O'Brien to Angels for P Jason Stockstill and P Brian Tokarse.
Blue Jays traded 1B-DH Mike Stanley to Red Sox for P Peter Munro and P Jay Yennaco.
Braves traded P David Cortes, P Mike Porzio, and a player to be named to Rockies for 1B Greg Colbrunn; Braves sent P Antony Briggs to complete deal (September 9).

JULY 31
Red Sox traded P Joe Hudson to Brewers for IF Eddy Diaz.
Twins traded 1B Orlando Merced and P Greg Swindell to Red Sox for P Matt Kinney, P Joe Thomas and P John Barnes.
Mariners traded P Randy Johnson to Astros for IF Carlos Guillen, P Freddy Garcia and a player to be named; Astros sent P John Halama to complete deal (October 1).
Marlins traded 3B Todd Zeile to Rangers for 3B Jose Santos and P Daniel DeYoung.
Rangers traded P Darren Oliver, 3B Fernando Tatis and a player to be named to Cardinals for P Todd Stottlemyre and SS Royce Clayton; Rangers sent OF Mark Little to complete deal (August 9).
Rangers released SS Kevin Elster.
Blue Jays traded P Juan Guzman to Orioles for P Nerio Rodriguez and OF Shannon Carter.
Blue Jays traded OF Tony Phillips to Mets for P Leoncio Ramirez Estrella.
Blue Jays traded 3B Ed Sprague to Athletics for P Scott Rivette.
Marlins traded P Felix Heredia and P Steve Hoff to Cubs for 3B Kevin Orie, P Todd Noel and P Justin Speier.

Rockies traded OF Ellis Burks to Giants for OF Darryl Hamilton, P James Stoops and a player to be named; Giants sent P Jason Brester to complete deal (August 18).

Mets traded P Bill Pulsipher to Brewers for IF Mike Kinkade.

Expos traded P Carlos Perez, SS Mark Grudzielanek and OF Hiram Bocachica to Dodgers for 2B Wilton Guerrero, P Ted Lilly, OF Peter Bergeron and 1B Jonathan Tucker.

Mets traded OF Bernard Gilkey, P Nelson Figueroa and cash to Diamondbacks for P Willie Blair, C Jorge Fabregas and a player to be named; Diamondbacks sent cash to complete deal (September 3).

AUGUST 1

Diamondbacks traded OF Hensley Meulens to White Sox for a player to be named.

Cardinals released OF Brian Hunter.

AUGUST 3

Athletics released OF-DH Kevin Mitchell.

AUGUST 4

Cubs released P Tony Fossas.

AUGUST 5

Braves organization signed P Norm Charlton and P Paul Wagner.

AUGUST 6

Blue Jays traded P Randy Myers to Padres for C Brian Loyd and a player to be named.

Astros sold P Pete Schourek to White Sox.

AUGUST 7

Brewers traded P Jeff Juden to Angels for a player to be named and cash.

AUGUST 8

Rangers signed OF Wes Chamberlain

Athletics traded OF Jack Voight to Rangers for a player to be named.

AUGUST 10

Athletics traded P Mike Fetters to Angels for a player to be named and cash.

Orioles traded OF Jeffrey Hammonds to Reds for OF-3B Willie Greene.

Royals traded OF Jermaine Allensworth to Mets for a player to be named; Mets sent cash to complete deal (September 3).

AUGUST 13

Indians signed 1B-DH Cecil Fielder.

AUGUST 14

Cardinals released 3B Gary Gaetti.

AUGUST 16

Cardinals released C Tom Pagnozzi.

Phillies claimed pitcher Paul Byrd on waivers from Braves.

AUGUST 19

Cubs signed 3B Gary Gaetti.

Rockies traded P David Cortes to Braves for a player to be named.

AUGUST 25

Rangers claimed P Greg Cadaret on waivers from Angels.

Twins traded P Mike Morgan to Cubs for cash and a player to be named; Cubs sent P Scott Downs to complete deal (November 3).

AUGUST 28

Phillies traded OF Gregg Jefferies to Angels for a player to be named; Angels sent P Doug Nickle to complete deal (September 9).

AUGUST 31

Red Sox released OF Orlando Merced.

White Sox traded IF Chris Snopek to Red Sox for OF Corey Jenkins.

Indians traded IF David Bell to Mariners for 2B Joey Cora.

Mets sold C Tim Spehr to Royals.

Cubs released OF Gerald Connell.

Rockies traded IF John Vander Wal to Padres for a player to be named; Padres sent OF Kevin Burford to complete deal (October 29).

SEPTEMBER 5

Tigers claimed P Will Brunson on waivers from Dodgers.

Cubs signed OF Orlando Merced.

SEPTEMBER 7

Rangers signed OF Milt Cuyler.

Mets signed 1B-OF Jorge Luis Toca.

SEPTEMBER 8

Rangers claimed outfielder Scarborough Green on waivers from Cardinals.

SEPTEMBER 9

Braves traded OF Damon Hollins to Dodgers for 2B Jose Pimentel.

SEPTEMBER 11

Angels claimed 1B Mark Johnson on waivers from Reds.

SEPTEMBER 12

Royals sold P Chris Haney to Cubs.

SEPTEMBER 14

Giants released OF Alex Diaz.

SEPTEMBER 18

White Sox sold C Chad Kreuter to Angels.

Indians released 1B-DH Cecil Fielder.

SEPTEMBER 23

Devil Rays claimed C Julio Mosquera on waivers from Blue Jays.

Blue Jays signed C Guillermo Quiroz.

SEPTEMBER 25

Mariners signed P Cha Sueng Baek.

SEPTEMBER 28

Twins claimed P Fred Rath on waivers from Rockies.

OCTOBER 1

Reds claimed P Eddie Priest on waivers from Indians.

OCTOBER 6

Dodgers claimed P Doug Bochtler on waivers from Tigers.

Brewers released C Jesse Levis, C Marcus Jensen and P Joe Hudson.

OCTOBER 7

Devil Rays claimed P Cory Lidle on waivers from Diamondbacks.

OCTOBER 8

Diamondbacks released P Ken Robinson and P Efrain Valdez.

OCTOBER 12

Dodgers traded P Eric Weaver to Mariners for P Scott Prouty.

OCTOBER 15

Twins claimed P Elvin Hernandez on waivers from Pirates.

OCTOBER 20

Marlins claimed OF Bruce Aven on waivers from Indians.

OCTOBER 29

Mariners organization signed IF Davide Dallospedale, P Jose Klepaski and IF Brendan Kingman.

OCTOBER 30

Royals organization IF Rico Rossy.

NOVEMBER 5

Orioles organization signed OF Mike Murphy and C Julio Vinas.

Phillies organization signed P Joel Bennett, P Steve Schrenk, P Steve Montgomery, P Shad Williams, P Billy Brewer, C Alberto Castillo, IF Lou Lucca, IF Torey Lovullo and OF Lou Frazier.

NOVEMBER 6

Devil Rays released P Dennis Springer.

Diamondbacks released OF Brent Brede.

Rockies signed OF Lenny Harris.

Dodgers signed CF Devon White.

NOVEMBER 7

Rockies signed P Brian Bohanon.
Giants signed P Mark Gardner.

NOVEMBER 9

Mariners traded P Paul Spoljaric to Phillies for P Mark Leiter.

NOVEMBER 10

Braves traded P Denny Neagle, OF Michael Tucker and P Rob Bell to Reds for 2B Bret Boone and P Mike Remlinger.
Reds released OF Tony Tarasco and P Rick Krivda.
Diamondbacks traded P Alan Embree to Giants for OF Dante Powell.

NOVEMBER 11

Diamondbacks traded P Bob Wolcott to Red Sox for a player to be named.
White Sox traded OF Mike Cameron to Reds for 1B Paul Konerko.
Tigers signed 3B Dean Palmer.
Diamondbacks signed P Greg Swindell and 1B Greg Colbrunn.
Dodgers traded OF-IF Bobby Bonilla to Mets for P Mel Rojas.

NOVEMBER 12

Orioles signed P Mike Timlin.
Mariners signed P Jose Mesa.
Marlins organization signed OF DaRond Stovall.

NOVEMBER 13

Red Sox signed 2B Jose Offerman.
Indians traded P Chad Ogea to Phillies for P Jerry Spradlin.
Cubs organization signed 1B Scott Stahoviak, P Steve Gajkowski, P Andrew Lorraine, P Scott Watkins, OF Allen Battle and C Alan Zinter.
Dodgers signed P Alan Mills.

NOVEMBER 14

Astros signed 3B Ken Caminiti.

NOVEMBER 16

Angels released P Jeff Juden and P Rich Robertson.
Twins traded P Dan Naulty to Yankees for 3B Allen Butler.

NOVEMBER 17

Reds organization signed IF Jeff Branson, P Kevin Foster, P Marty Janzen and P Todd Etler.
Marlins organization signed IF Russ Morman and P Archie Corbin.
Pirates signed IF Mike Benjamin.
Padres released IF Archi Cianfrocco and P Scott Sanders.

NOVEMBER 18

Angels organization signed P Brett Grebe, P Michael Hartung, P Luis Pote, P Norman Montoya, P Kevin Loman, P Jeff Ware, P DeSean Warren, P Darren Winston, P Mike Fyhrie, P Keith Troutman, P Travis Thurmond, P Mike Bovee, P Joe Jacobsen, C Steve Decker, 3B Tim Unroe, IF Jeff Huson, SS Loyce Coveli, OF Benji Simonton, OF Eddie Christian, OF Chris White and OF Jason Herrick.
Indians traded OF Brian Giles to Pirates for P Ricardo Rincon.
Blue Jays released P Shannon Withem.

NOVEMBER 19

White Sox claimed P Dwayne Jacobs on waivers from Braves.
Indians released P Jason Jacome.
Mariners released P Bob Wells and P Tim Davis, and claimed OF Kerry Robinson on waivers from Devil Rays.
Devil Rays organization signed P Larry Casian, C Cesar Devarez, P Vaughn Eshelman, OF Terrell Lowery, P Bobby Munoz, P Alan Newman, P Erik Plantenberg, P Mark Sievert and C Tom Wilson.
Rangers claimed IF Jon Shave on waivers from Twins, and signed P Eric Moody.
Rangers organization signed SS Juan Bautista.
Diamondbacks signed P Todd Stottlemyre, P Brian Shouse, P Chris Clemons and P Neil Weber.
Braves organization signed P Chris Seelbach.
Cubs claimed P Elvin Hernandez on waivers from Twins.
Phillies traded P Ricky Bottalico and P Garrett Stephenson to Cardinals for OF Ron Gant, P Jeff Brantley and P Cliff Politte.
Phillies released P Calvin Maduro.
Cardinals signed OF Eric Davis and P Scott Radinsky.

NOVEMBER 20

Rockies released IF Jason Bates, P Luther Hackman and P Mike Vrarek.
Mets traded C Jorge Fabregas to Marlins for P Oscar Henriquez and cash.

NOVEMBER 23

Tigers signed P Masao Kida.
Marlins traded C Gregg Zaun to Rangers for a player to be named or cash.
Braves signed OF Brian Jordan.

NOVEMBER 24

Indians signed 2B Roberto Alomar.
Diamondbacks signed P Armando Reynoso.
Marlins released IF-OF Brian Daubach.

NOVEMBER 25

Angels signed 1B Mo Vaughn.

NOVEMBER 30

Diamondbacks signed P Randy Johnson.

DECEMBER 1

Orioles signed OF Albert Belle.
Orioles claimed C Charlie Greene on waivers from Brewers.
Rangers signed 1B Rafael Palmeiro.
Braves signed OF Otis Nixon.
Expos organization signed P Luis Torres.
Mets traded C Todd Hundley and P Arnold Gooch to Dodgers for C Charles Johnson and OF Roger Cedeno.
Mets traded C Charles Johnson to Orioles for P Armando Benitez.

DECEMBER 2

Cubs signed P Scott Sanders.
Marlins traded P Manuel Barrios to Reds for C Guillermo Garcia.
Reds sold 1B-OF Roberto Petagine to Yakult Swallows (Japan).
Mets signed 3B Robin Ventura.

DECEMBER 4

Orioles signed 2B Delino DeShields.
Indians signed P John Burke.
Braves signed P Mike Remlinger.
Brewers claimed P Joe Borowski on waivers from Yankees, and claimed C Charlie Greene on waivers from Orioles.
Mets traded P Willie Blair to Tigers for IF Joe Randa.
Giants signed P Greg Hansell.
Giants organization signed P Bronswell Patrick.

DECEMBER 5

Orioles signed 1B Will Clark.

DECEMBER 7

Angels organization signed IF Craig Shipley.
Tigers claimed P Bryan Corey on waivers from Diamondbacks.
Royals claimed P Dario Veras on waivers from Red Sox.
Diamondbacks signed OF Steve Finley.

DECEMBER 8

Yankees traded OF Chris Singleton to White Sox for a player to be named.
Rangers signed P Mark Clark.
Diamondbacks traded P Felix Rodriguez to Giants for future considerations; Giants sent P Troy Brohawn and OF Chris Van Rossum to complete deal (December 21).
Brewers signed 3B Sean Berry.

DECEMBER 9

Red Sox signed P Mark Portugal.
Devil Rays signed OF Jose Canseco.
Cubs signed C Benito Santiago.
Rangers organization signed P Rich Robertson.
Rockies released OF Derrick White.

DECEMBER 10

Tigers sold P Marino Santana to Red Sox.
Royals released SS Rey Sanchez.
Mets traded IF Joe Randa to Royals for OF Juan LeBron.
Mariners signed C Tom Lampkin.

DECEMBER 11

Athletics signed OF Tony Phillips.
Devil Rays signed C John Flaherty.
Texas released IF Domingo Cedeno.
Reds signed P Steve Avery.

DECEMBER 12

Padres traded P Joey Hamilton to Blue Jays for P Woody Williams, P Carlos Almanzar and OF Peter Tucci.
Reds signed IF Mark Lewis and released 1B Eduardo Perez.
Dodgers signed P Kevin Brown.
Mets signed OF Rickey Henderson.

DECEMBER 14

Red Sox released P Carlos Reyes.
Tigers signed C Bill Haselman and released OF Trey Beamon.
Royals signed C Chad Kreuter and released OF Roderick Myers.
Twins traded OF Alex Ochoa to Brewers for a player to be named; Brewers sent OF Darrell Nicholas to complete deal (December 15).
Athletics released IF Rafael Bournigal.
Tigers traded P Eric Ludwick to Toronto for P Beiker Graterol.
Marlins traded SS Edgar Renteria to Cardinals for P Braden Looper, P Armando Almanza and SS Pablo Ozuna.
Marlins sold P Alberto Blanco to Tigers.
Brewers released P Frankie Rodriguez.
Pirates traded P Jon Lieber to Cubs for OF Brant Brown.
Pirates released OF Manny Martinez.
Expos claimed P Dan Smith on waivers from Rangers.
Mets traded OF Butch Huskey to Mariners for P Lesli Brea.
Cardinals traded P Mark Petkovsek to Angels for a player to be named or cash; Angels sent C Mark Garrick to complete deal (December 18).

DECEMBER 15

Mariners signed P Butch Henry.
Expos sold OF Ricky Williams to Rangers.
Twins organization signed IF Brent Gates, OF Melvin Nieves, 1B Eddie Williams and P Ryan Hancock.
Reds organization signed SS Pat Listach, 1B D.T. Cromer, IF Jason Hardtke, IF Phil Hiatt, OF Damon Hollins, 1B Rod McCall, C Jayhawk Owens, OF Darrell Whitmore and P Mark Thompson.
Phillies signed P Jim Poole and C Tom Prince.
Pirates signed IF Ed Sprague.

DECEMBER 16

Red Sox claimed pitcher Steve Connelly on waivers from Athletics.
Indians signed P Jerry Spradlin.
Mariners signed P Butch Henry and claimed OF Matt Mieske on waivers from Cubs.

DECEMBER 17

Orioles signed P Xavier Hernandez.
Orioles organization signed P Doug Linton.
Royals organization signed P John Cummings, P Chris George, P Erik Hanson, P Rick Krivda, P Ricky Pickett, P Joe Roa, P Kennie Steenstra, P David Swartzbaugh, C Henry Mercedes, IF Ray Holbert, IF Scott Leius, IF Rico Rossy, OF Steve Gibralter, OF Les Norman, OF Scott Pose and OF Joe Vitiello.
Diamondbacks organization signed OF Pete Incaviglia, IF Scott Coolbaugh, P Dan Carlson, P George Glinatsis, C Marcus Hanel, P Al Kermode, C Izzy Molina, P Matt Ruebel, 1B Desi Wilson and OF Ernie Young.
Expos claimed OF Manny Martinez on waivers from Pirates.
Pirates signed P Pete Schourek.

DECEMBER 18

Angels signed P Tim Belcher.
Red Sox organization signed 1B-OF Brian Daubach.
Tigers organization signed OF Luis Polonia, IF David McCarty, IF Alejandro Freire and P Beiker Graterol.
Twins claimed P Jose Espinal on waivers from Cubs.
Twins organization signed C George Williams and P Gary Rath.
Devil Rays organization signed SS Aaron Holbert, P Mark Hutton, C Jesse Levis, IF Chris Martin, P Roger Bailey, P John LeRoy and P Tim Davis.
Reds organization signed P John Riedling, and claimed OF Roderick Myers on waivers from Royals.
Rockies organization signed C Henry Blanco, IF Chris Hajek, IF J.R. Phillips, IF Terry Shumpert, IF Chris Peterson, OF Jim Tatum, OF Jeff Barry, OF Miguel Correa, OF Chris Hatcher, OF Dwight Maness, P Ryan Jacobs and P Mike Rossiter.
Brewers released OF Marc Newfield, and claimed IF Lou Collier on waivers from Pirates.
Padres organization signed OF Shane Mack.

DECEMBER 19

Red Sox signed P Mark Guthrie.

DECEMBER 21

Orioles signed IF-OF Rich Amaral and P Ricky Bones.
Orioles organization signed IF Jesse Garcia and P Carlos Medina.
Royals signed P Alvin Morman.

DECEMBER 22

Angels released IF Mark Johnson, allowing him to sign with the Hanshin Tigers (Japan).
Red Sox signed P Tomokazu Oka.
White Sox signed P Kip Wells.
Phillies signed OF Rob Ducey.
Pirates organization signed SS Rafael Bournigal, P Jim Dougherty, P Todd Ritchie, C Chris Tremie, IF Matt Howard, OF Ray Montgomery and 1B Ivan Cruz.

DECEMBER 23

Twins signed IF Denny Hocking.
Athletics organization signed IF Domingo Cedeno.
Pirates organization signed P Jim Baron, P Johann Lopez, P Bob Milacki, C Mel Rosario and C-IF Reed Secrist.
Blue Jays signed C Mike Matheny.

DECEMBER 28

Tigers signed OF Gregg Jefferies.
Diamondbacks traded OF Karim Garcia to Detroit for OF Luis Gonzalez and cash.

DECEMBER 29

Dodgers signed P Pedro Borbon.

DECEMBER 30

Mariners signed IF-OF John Mabry.

AWARD WINNERS

THE SPORTING NEWS

AMERICAN LEAGUE

Pitcher of the Year: Roger Clemens, Toronto
Rookie Player of the Year: Ben Grieve, Oakland, OF
Rookie Pitcher of the Year: Rolando Arrojo, Tampa Bay
Fireman of the Year: Tom Gordon, Boston
Comeback Player of the Year: Bret Saberhagen, Boston
Manager of the Year: Joe Torre, New York

NATIONAL LEAGUE

Pitcher of the Year: Kevin Brown, San Diego
Rookie Player of the Year: Todd Helton, Colorado, 1B
Rookie Pitcher of the Year: Kerry Wood, Chicago
Fireman of the Year: Trevor Hoffman, San Diego
Comeback Player of the Year: Greg Vaughn, San Diego
Manager of the Year: Bruce Bochy, San Diego

MAJOR LEAGUE

Player of the Year: Sammy Sosa, Chicago
Executive of the Year: Gerry Hunsicker, Houston

MINOR LEAGUE

Player of the Year: Gabe Kapler, Jacksonville, Southern
Manager of the Year: Doug Davis, Columbia, South Atlantic
Executive of the Year: Chuck Domino, Reading, Eastern

BASEBALL WRITERS' ASSOCIATION OF AMERICA

AMERICAN LEAGUE

MOST VALUABLE PLAYER

Player, Team	1	2	3	4	5	6	7	8	9	10	Pts.
Juan Gonzalez, Texas	21	7	-	-	-	-	-	-	-	-	357
Nomar Garciaparra, Boston	5	7	7	2	1	3	1	1	-	1	232
Derek Jeter, New York	2	6	3	3	2	5	2	2	1	-	180
Mo Vaughn, Boston	-	3	1	3	9	1	1	3	3	1	135
Ken Griffey Jr., Seattle	-	-	4	4	5	5	1	4	1	2	135
Manny Ramirez, Cleveland	-	1	3	4	3	4	5	1	2	1	127
Bernie Williams, New York	-	1	3	3	1	3	3	2	4	2	103
Albert Belle, Chicago	-	-	4	4	2	-	2	2	3	6	98
Alex Rodriguez, Seattle	-	2	1	2	-	3	6	1	4	2	92
Ivan Rodriguez, Texas	-	-	-	1	1	2	1	6	2	1	50
Roger Clemens, Toronto	-	1	1	-	2	-	4	-	1	2	49
Paul O'Neill, New York	-	-	-	2	-	2	1	2	1	-	36
Tom Gordon, Boston	-	-	1	-	1	-	-	2	3	1	27
Darin Erstad, Anaheim	-	-	-	-	1	-	-	-	-	-	7
Tim Salmon, Anaheim	-	-	-	-	-	-	1	-	-	3	7
David Wells, New York	-	-	-	-	-	-	-	1	-	-	3
John Wetteland, Texas	-	-	-	-	-	-	-	1	-	-	3
Eric Davis, Baltimore	-	-	-	-	-	-	-	-	1	-	2
Travis Fryman, Cleveland	-	-	-	-	-	-	-	-	1	-	2
Rafael Palmeiro, Baltimore	-	-	-	-	-	-	-	-	1	-	2
Carlos Delgado, Toronto	-	-	-	-	-	-	-	-	-	1	1
Rick Helling, Texas	-	-	-	-	-	-	-	-	-	1	1
Mike Jackson, Cleveland	-	-	-	-	-	-	-	-	-	1	1
Pedro Martinez, Boston	-	-	-	-	-	-	-	-	-	1	1
Jim Thome, Cleveland	-	-	-	-	-	-	-	-	-	1	1

Fourteen points awarded for a first-place vote, nine for second and down to one for 10th.

CY YOUNG AWARD

Pitcher, Team	1	2	3	Pts.
Roger Clemens, Toronto	28	-	-	140
Pedro Martinez, Boston	-	20	5	65
David Wells, New York	-	4	19	31
David Cone, New York	-	4	4	16

Five points awarded for a first-place vote, three for second and one for third.

ROOKIE OF THE YEAR

Player, Team	1	2	3	Pts.
Ben Grieve, Oakland	23	5	-	130
Rolando Arrojo, Tampa Bay	4	10	11	61
Mike Caruso, Chicago	-	9	7	34
Orlando Hernandez, New York	1	4	8	25
Magglio Ordonez, Chicago	-	-	1	1
Sidney Ponson, Baltimore	-	-	1	1

Five points awarded for a first-place vote, three for second and one for third.

MANAGER OF THE YEAR

Manager, Team	1	2	3	Pts.
Joe Torre, New York	23	4	1	128
Jimy Williams, Boston	3	12	8	59
Terry Collins, Anaheim	2	7	7	38
Johnny Oates, Texas	-	2	5	11
Mike Hargrove, Cleveland	-	1	5	8
Tim Johnson, Toronto	-	1	1	4
Jerry Manuel, Chicago	-	1	1	4

Five points awarded for a first-place vote, three for second and one for third.

MOST VALUABLE PLAYER

Player, Team	1	2	3	4	5	6	7	8	9	10	Pts.
Sammy Sosa, Chicago	30	2	-	-	-	-	-	-	-	-	438
Mark McGwire, St. Louis	2	20	3	1	4	1	1	-	-	-	272
Moises Alou, Houston	-	6	8	9	3	1	1	1	1	2	215
Greg Vaughn, San Diego	-	-	7	8	6	4	2	2	1	1	185
Craig Biggio, Houston	-	3	5	7	2	2	5	-	2	1	163
Andres Galarraga, Atlanta	-	-	1	1	6	9	10	3	1	-	147
Trevor Hoffman, San Diego	-	-	5	5	3	4	-	-	2	-	117
Barry Bonds, San Francisco	-	1	-	-	1	2	3	5	6	2	66
Chipper Jones, Atlanta	-	-	2	-	1	2	2	4	1	2	56
Jeff Kent, San Francisco	-	-	1	-	2	2	2	4	2	2	56
Vinny Castilla, Colorado	-	-	-	-	2	2	-	5	3	6	49
John Olerud, New York	-	-	-	-	1	1	2	2	5	3	38
Vladimir Guerrero, Montreal	-	-	-	-	-	-	2	2	2	7	25
Mike Piazza, Fla.-L.A.-N.Y.	-	-	-	-	-	1	-	2	2	-	15
Tony Gwynn, San Diego	-	-	-	-	1	1	-	-	-	-	11
Kevin Brown, San Diego	-	-	-	-	-	-	1	1	-	1	8
Larry Walker, Colorado	-	-	-	1	-	-	-	-	-	-	7
Rod Beck, Chicago	-	-	-	-	-	-	-	1	1	-	5
Jeromy Burnitz, Milwaukee	-	-	-	-	-	-	1	-	-	-	4
Scott Rolen, Philadelphia	-	-	-	-	-	-	-	-	1	1	3
Tom Glavine, Atlanta	-	-	-	-	-	-	-	-	1	-	2
Randy Johnson, Houston	-	-	-	-	-	-	-	-	1	-	2
Dante Bichette, Colorado	-	-	-	-	-	-	-	-	-	2	2
Javier Lopez, Atlanta	-	-	-	-	-	-	-	-	-	1	1
Mickey Morandini, Chicago	-	-	-	-	-	-	-	-	-	1	1

Fourteen points awarded for a first-place vote, nine for second and down to one for 10th.

MANAGER OF THE YEAR

Manager, Team	1	2	3	Pts.
Larry Dierker, Houston	16	6	4	102
Bruce Bochy, San Diego	5	13	6	70
Jim Riggleman, Chicago	5	7	9	55
Dusty Baker, San Francisco	6	2	3	39
Bobby Cox, Atlanta	-	3	8	17
Bobby Valentine, New York	-	1	2	5

Five points awarded for a first-place vote, three for second and one for third.

ROOKIE OF THE YEAR

Player, Team	1	2	3	Pts.
Kerry Wood, Chicago	16	16	-	128
Todd Helton, Colorado	15	14	2	119
Travis Lee, Arizona	-	2	15	21
Kerry Ligtenberg, Atlanta	1	-	13	18
Brad Fullmer, Montreal	-	-	2	2

Five points awarded for a first-place vote, three for second and one for third.

CY YOUNG AWARD

Pitcher, Team	1	2	3	Pts.
Tom Glavine, Atlanta	11	13	5	99
Trevor Hoffman, San Diego	13	5	8	88
Kevin Brown, San Diego	8	8	12	76
John Smoltz, Atlanta	-	3	1	10
Greg Maddux, Atlanta	-	2	4	10
Al Leiter, New York	-	1	-	3
Randy Johnson, Houston	-	-	2	2

Five points awarded for a first-place vote, three for second and one for third.

1998 REVIEW *Award winners*

MISCELLANEOUS

ATTENDANCE

AMERICAN LEAGUE

	Home	Road
Baltimore	3,685,194	2,064,020
Cleveland	3,467,299	2,054,625
Texas	2,927,409	1,945,773
New York	2,919,046	2,314,089
Seattle	2,644,305	2,102,205
Anaheim	2,519,107	1,892,207
Toronto	2,454,283	1,949,880
Boston	2,343,947	2,159,639
Tampa Bay	2,261,158	1,943,996
Kansas City	1,494,875	2,027,669
Detroit	1,409,391	1,937,582
Chicago	1,391,146	2,004,024
Oakland	1,232,339	2,045,648
Minnesota	1,165,980	1,967,993
Totals	**31,915,479**	**28,409,350**

Note: American League road attendance figures exclude inter-league games played in National League parks.

NATIONAL LEAGUE

	Home	Road
Colorado	3,789,347	2,154,522
Arizona	3,600,412	2,158,785
Atlanta	3,361,350	2,699,094
St. Louis	3,194,092	2,766,615
Los Angeles	3,089,201	2,641,382
Chicago	2,623,000	2,900,959
San Diego	2,555,901	2,322,937
Houston	2,450,451	2,235,431
New York	2,287,942	2,168,956
San Francisco	1,925,634	2,601,854
Milwaukee	1,811,548	2,331,670
Cincinnati	1,793,679	2,192,004
Florida	1,750,395	2,409,594
Philadelphia	1,715,702	2,208,257
Pittsburgh	1,560,950	2,316,100
Montreal	914,717	2,313,762
Totals	**38,424,321**	**38,421,922**

DEBUTS

Player	Pos.	Team	Birth date	Birthplace	Debut
Agbayani, Benny Peter	RF	New York N.L.	12-28-71	Honolulu, Hawaii	6-17
Alvarez, Gabe	3B	Detroit	3- 6-74	Navojoa, Mexico	6-22
Anderson, Marlon Ordell	PH	Philadelphia	1- 6-74	Montgomery, Alabama	9-8
Anderson, Matt	P	Detroit	8-17-76	Louisville, Kentucky	6-25
Arrojo, Luis Rolando	P	Tampa Bay	7-18-68	Havana, Cuba	4-1
Bako, Paul	C	Detroit	6-20-72	Lafayette, Louisiana	4-30
Ball, Jeff D.	PH	San Francisco	4-17-69	Merced, California	6-10
Baptist, Travis Steven	P	Minnesota	12-30-71	Forest Grove, Oregon	8-1
Barkley, Brian Edward	P	Boston	12- 8-75	Conroe, Texas	5-28
Barrett, Michael	3B	Montreal	10-22-76	Atlanta, Georgia	9-19
Baughman, Justin Reis	2B	Anaheim	8- 1-74	Mountain View, California	5-17
Belliard, Ronald	PR	Milwaukee	4- 7-75	Bronx, New York	9-12
Beltran, Carlos Ivan	CF	Kansas City	4-24-77	Manati, Puerto Rico	9-14
Beltre, Adrian	3B	Los Angeles	4- 7-78	Santo Domingo, Dominican Republic	6-24
Bennett, Joel Todd	P	Baltimore	1-31-70	Binghamton, New York	7-15
Berg, David Scott	PR	Florida	9- 3-70	Roseville, California	4-2
Bradford, Chad	P	Chicago A.L.	9-14-74	Jackson, Mississippi	8-1
Bradley, Ryan J.	P	New York A.L.	10-26-75	Covina, California	8-22
Branyan, Russell	3B	Cleveland	12-19-75	Warner Robins, Georgia	9-26
Brown, Dermal	PR	Kansas City	3-27-78	Bronx, New York	9-14
Brownson, Mark Phillip	P	Colorado	6-17-75	Lake Worth, Florida	7-21
Brunson, William	P	Los Angeles	3-20-70	Irving, Texas	6-21
Buddie, Michael J.	P	New York A.L.	12-12-70	Cleveland, Ohio	4-6
Bullinger, Kirk Matthew	P	Montreal	10-28-69	New Orleans, Louisiana	8-30
Butler, Adam Christpher	P	Atlanta	8-17-73	Fairfax, Virginia	3-31
Byrdak, Timothy	P	Kansas City	10-31-73	Oak Forest, Illinois	8-7
Cabrera, Jolbert Alexis	SS	Cleveland	12- 8-72	Cartagena, Colombia	4-12
Caruso, Michael J.	SS	Chicago A.L.	5-27-77	Queens, New York	3-31
Chavez, Eric Cesar	PH	Oakland	12- 7-77	Los Angeles, California	9-8
Chen, Bruce Kastulo	P	Atlanta	6-19-77	Panama City, Panama	9-7
Cho, Jin Ho	P	Boston	8-16-75	Jun Ju City, South Korea	7-4
Christenson, Ryan Alan	CF	Oakland	3-28-74	Redlands, California	4-20
Clement, Matthew Paul	P	San Diego	8-12-74	McCandless Township, Pennsylvania	9-6
Clemente, Edgard Velazque	RF	Colorado	12-15-75	Santurce, Puerto Rico	9-10
Connelly, Steven Lee	P	Oakland	4-27-74	Long Beach, California	6-28
Cora, Alex	2B	Los Angeles	10-18-75	Caquas, Puerto Rico	6-7
Corey, Bryan Scott	P	Arizona	10-21-73	Thousand Oaks, California	5-13
Cradle, Rickey Nelson	LF	Seattle	6-20-73	Norfolk, Virginia	7-1
Croushore, Richard Steven	P	St. Louis	8- 7-70	Lakehurst, New Jersey	5-18
Crow, Dean	P	Detroit	8-21-72	Garland, Texas	5-29
Darensbourg, Victor Anthony	P	Florida	11-13-70	Los Angeles, California	4-1
Daubach, Brian Michael	1B	Florida	2-11-72	Belleville, Illinois	9-10
Davis, Matthew Benjami	C	San Diego	3-10-77	Chester, Pennsylvania	9-25
De Los Santos, Valerio Lorenzo	P	Milwaukee	9- 6-75	Las Matas, Dominican Republic	7-31

Player	Pos.	Team	Birth date	Birthplace	Debut
Dempster, Ryan Scott	P	Florida	5- 3-77	Sachelt, British Columbia	5-23
DeRosa, Mark Thomas	PH	Atlanta	2- 2-75	Passaic, New Jersey	9-2
Diaz, Edwin Roasario	2B	Arizona	1-15-75	Bayamon, Puerto Rico	3-31
Dodd, Robert Wayne	P	Philadelphia	3-14-73	Kansas City, Kansas	5-28
Drew, J.D.	PH	St. Louis	11-20-75	Valdosta, Georgia	9-8
Duvall, Mike	P	Tampa Bay	10-11-74	Warrenton, Virginia	9-22
Dykhoff, Radhames Alviro	P	Baltimore	9-27-74	Paradera, Aruba	6-7
Edmondson, Brian	P	Atlanta	1-29-73	Fontana, California	4-2
Elarton, Vincent Scott	P	Houston	2-23-76	Lamar, Colorado	6-20
Evans, Bart Steven	P	Kansas City	12-30-70	Springfield, Missouri	6-16
Febles, Carlos Manuel	PH	Kansas City	5-24-76	El Seybo, Dominican Republic	9-14
Fick, Robert Charles	DH	Detroit	3-15-74	Torrance, California	9-19
Fontenot, Joseph D.	P	Florida	3-20-77	Lafayette, Louisiana	5-23
Forbes, Patrick J.	2B	Baltimore	9-22-67	Pittsburg, Kansas	7-21
Ford, Benjamin	P	Arizona	8-15-75	Cedar Rapids, Iowa	8-20
Frank, Stephen Michael	CF	Cincinnati	1-14-75	Pomona, California	6-19
Fussell, Christopher Wre	P	Baltimore	5-19-76	Oregon, Ohio	9-15
Gajkowski, Stephen Robert	P	Seattle	12-30-69	Seattle, Washington	5-25
Garcia, Guillermo Antio	C	Cincinnati	4- 4-72	Santo Domingo, Dominican Republic	7-19
Giambi, Jeremy Dean	DH	Kansas City	9-30-74	San Jose, California	9-1
Gibson, Derrick Lamont	LF	Colorado	2- 5-75	Winter Haven, Florida	9-8
Gipson, Charles Wells	LF	Seattle	12-16-72	Orange, California	3-31
Glauber, Keith H.	P	Cincinnati	1-18-72	Brooklyn, New York	9-8
Glaus, Troy	3B	Anaheim	8- 3-76	Tarzana, California	7-31
Gonzalez, Alexander	SS	Florida	2-15-77	Cagua, Venezuela	8-25
Gonzalez, Gabriel	P	Florida	5-24-72	Long Beach, California	4-1
Gonzalez, Lariel	P	Colorado	5-25-76	San Cristobal, Dominican Republic	9-22
Greisinger, Seth	P	Detroit	7-29-75	Kansas City, Kansas	6-3
Grzanich, Michael Edward	P	Houston	8-24-72	Canton, Illinois	5-14
Guillen, Carlos	2B	Seattle	9-30-75	Maracay, Venezuela	9-6
Hairston Jr., Jerry W	2B	Baltimore	5-29-76	Naperville, Illinois	9-11
Halama, John	P	Houston	2-22-72	Brooklyn, New York	4-2
Halladay, Roy	P	Toronto	5-14-77	Denver, Colorado	9-20
Harriger, Dennis Scott	P	Detroit	7-21-69	Kittanning, Pennsylvania	6-16
Hatcher, Chris	LF	Kansas City	1- 7-69	Anaheim, California	9-6
Heathcott, Michael Joseph	P	Chicago A.L.	5-16-69	Chicago, Illinois	8-28
Helms, Wesley Ray	PH	Atlanta	5-12-76	Gastonia, North Carolina	9-5
Henley, Robert Clifton	C	Montreal	1-30-73	Mobile, Alabama	7-19
Hernandez, Orlando	P	New York A.L.	10-11-69	Villa Clara, Cuba	6-3
Hinch, Andrew Jay	C	Oakland	5-15-74	Waverly, Iowa	4-1
Holdridge, David Allen	P	Seattle	2- 5-69	Wayne, Michigan	8-8
Hollins, Damon Jamall	LF	Atlanta	6-12-74	Fairfield, California	4-24
Howry, Bobby Dean	P	Chicago A.L.	8- 4-73	Phoenix, Arizona	6-21
Hughes, Robert E.	PH	Milwaukee	4-10-71	Burbank, California	4-2
Jackson, Ryan De Witte	1B	Florida	11-11-71	Sarasota, Florida	3-31
Jenkins, Geoff	LF	Milwaukee	7-21-74	Olympia, Washington	4-24
Jerzembeck, Michael Joseph	P	New York A.L.	5-18-72	Queens, New York	8-8
Jimenez, Jose	P	St. Louis	7- 7-73	San Pedro de Macoris, Dominican Rep.	9-9
Johns, Keith Robert	PH	Boston	7-19-71	Jacksonville, Florida	5-23
Johnson, Jonathan	P	Texas	7-16-74	LaGrange, Georgia	9-27
Johnson, Mark Landon	C	Chicago A.L.	9-12-75	Wheat Ridge, Colorado	9-14
Kapler, Gabe	RF	Detroit	8-31-75	Hollywood, California	9-20
Kinkade, Mike	3B	New York N.L.	5- 6-73	Livonia, Michigan	9-8
Klassen, Daniel Victor	2B	Arizona	9-22-75	Leamington, Ontario	7-4
Koskie, Cordel Leonard	3B	Minnesota	6-28-73	Anola, Manitoba	9-9
Kubenka, Jeffrey	P	Los Angeles	8-24-74	Weimer, Texas	9-6
Lankford, Frank	P	Los Angeles	3-26-71	Atlanta, Georgia	3-31
Larkin, Stephen Karari	1B	Cincinnati	7-24-73	Cincinnati, Ohio	9-27
Lawrence, Sean Christophe	P	Pittsburgh	9- 2-70	Oak Park, Illinois	8-25
Ledee, Ricardo Alberto	LF	New York A.L.	11-22-73	Ponce, Puerto Rico	6-14
Lee, Travis R.	1B	Arizona	5-26-75	San Diego, California	3-31
Little, Mark	RF	St. Louis	7-11-72	Edwardsville, Illinois	9-12
LoDuca, Paul	PH	Los Angeles	4-12-72	Brooklyn, New York	6-21
Loewer, Carlton	P	Philadelphia	9-24-73	Lafayette, Louisiana	6-14
Lombard, George Paul	PR	Atlanta	9-14-75	Atlanta, Georgia	9-4
Looper, Braden LaVern	P	St. Louis	10-28-74	Weatherford, Oklahoma	3-31
Lopez, Mendy Aude	SS	Kansas City	10-15-74	Santo Domingo, Dominican Republic	6-3
Lowell, Michael A.	3B	New York A.L.	2-24-74	San Juan, Puerto Rico	9-13
Malloy, Marty Thomas	2B	Atlanta	7- 6-72	Gainesville, Florida	9-6
Martinez, Gregory A.	PR	Milwaukee	1-27-72	Las Vegas, Nevada	3-31
Martinez, Javier Antonio	P	Pittsburgh	2- 5-77	Bayamon, Puerto Rico	4-2
Martinez, Ramon E.	2B	San Francisco	10-10-72	Philadelphia, Pennsylvania	6-20
Maxwell, Jason Ramond	PH	Chicago N.L.	3-26-72	Lewisburg, Tennessee	9-1

Player	Pos.	Team	Birth date	Birthplace	Debut
McClain, Scott Michael	PH	Tampa Bay	5-19-72	Simi Valley, California	5-14
McEwing, Joseph E.	PH	St. Louis	10-19-72	Bristol, Pennsylvania	9-2
Meadows, Brian	P	Florida	11-21-75	Montgomery, Alabama	4-4
Medina, Rafael	P	Florida	2-15-75	Panama City, Panama	4-2
Meluskey, Mitch	PH	Houston	9-18-73	Yakima, Washington	8-30
Merloni, Louis William	2B	Boston	4- 6-71	Framingham, Massachusetts	5-10
Metcalfe, Mike	PH	Los Angeles	1- 2-73	Quantico, Virginia	9-18
Michalak, Christian	P	Arizona	1- 4-71	Joliet, Illinois	8-22
Mientkiewicz, Douglas Andrew	1B	Minnesota	6-19-74	Toledo, Ohio	9-18
Millar, Kevin	PH	Florida	9-24-71	Los Angeles, California	4-11
Milton, Eric Robert	P	Minnesota	8- 4-75	State College, Pennsylvania	4-5
Minor, Ryan Dale	PH	Baltimore	1- 5-74	Canton, Ohio	9-13
Molina, Ben	C	Anaheim	7-20-74	Rio Piedras, Puerto Rico	9-21
Monahan, Shane Hartland	LF	Seattle	8-12-74	Syosset, New York	7-9
Moore, Warren Neal	P	Montreal	10- 2-72	Houston, Texas	4-5
Mullins, Greg	P	Milwaukee	12-13-71	Palatka, Florida	9-18
Neill, Michael Robert	LF	Oakland	4-27-70	Martinsville, Virginia	7-27
Nieves, Jose Miguel	SS	Chicago N.L.	6-16-75	Guacara, Venezuela	8-7
Nunez, Vladimir Zaraba	P	Arizona	3-15-75	Havana, Cuba	9-11
Ortiz, Hector	C	Kansas City	10-14-69	Rio Piedras, Puerto Rico	9-14
Ortiz, Russ	P	San Francisco	6- 5-74	Encino, California	4-2
Otanez, Willis	RF	Baltimore	4-19-73	Vega Baja, Puerto Rico	8-25
Parque, Jim Vo	P	Chicago A.L.	2- 8-76	Norwalk, California	5-26
Patrick, Bronswell Dante	P	Milwaukee	9-16-70	Greenville, North Carolina	5-18
Pavano, Carl Anthony	P	Montreal	1- 8-76	New Britain, Connecticut	5-23
Payton, Jason Lee	LF	New York N.L.	11-22-72	Zanesville, Ohio	9-1
Pena, Angel	PH	Los Angeles	2-16-75	San Pedro de Macoris, Dominican Rep.	9-8
Perez, Odalis Amadol	P	Atlanta	6- 7-78	La Matas de Farfan, Dominican Rep.	9-1
Pickering, Calvin E.	DH	Baltimore	9-29-76	St. Thomas, Virgin Islands	9-12
Pickett, Ricky	P	Arizona	1-19-70	Fort Worth, Texas	4-28
Pierzynski, Anthony John	C	Minnesota	12-30-76	Bridgehampton, New York	9-9
Polanco, Placido Enrique	2B	St. Louis	10-10-75	Santo Domingo, Dominican Republic	7-3
Politte, Cliff A.	P	St. Louis	2-27-74	St. Louis, Missouri	4-2
Ponson, Sidney Alton	P	Baltimore	11- 2-76	Noord, Aruba	4-19
Powell, Jeremy Robert	P	Montreal	6-18-76	La Miranda, California	7-23
Powell, William Brian	P	Detroit	10-10-73	Bainbridge, Georgia	6-27
Priest, Eddie Lee	P	Cincinnati	4- 8-74	Boaz, Alabama	5-27
Radmanovich, Ryan Ashley	RF	Seattle	8- 9-71	Calgary, Alberta	4-13
Rakers, Jason Paul	P	Cleveland	6-29-73	Pittsburgh, Pennsylvania	5-6
Ramirez, Alex	LF	Cleveland	10- 3-74	Caracas, Venezuela	9-19
Ramirez, Aramis Nin	3B	Pittsburgh	6-25-78	Santo Domingo, Dominican Republic	5-26
Ramirez, Roberto	P	San Diego	8-17-72	El Laurel, Veracruz, Mexico	6-12
Rath, Frederick Helsh	P	Colorado	1- 5-73	Dallas, Texas	7-29
Rath, Gary	P	Los Angeles	1-10-73	Gulfport, Mississippi	6-2
Redmond, Michael Patrick	C	Florida	5- 5-71	Seattle, Washington	5-31
Rios, Armando	PH	San Francisco	9-13-71	Santurce, Puerto Rico	9-1
Rizzo, Todd Michael	P	Chicago A.L.	5-24-71	Clifton Heights, Pennsylvania	4-2
Robinson, Kerry	LF	Tampa Bay	10- 3-73	St. Louis, Missouri	9-22
Rocker, John Loy	P	Atlanta	10-17-74	Statesboro, Georgia	5-5
Roque, Rafael	P	Milwaukee	10- 27-72	Cotui, Dominican Republic	8-1
Roskos, John Edwards	1B	Florida	11-19-74	Victorville, California	4-20
Runyan, Sean David	P	Detroit	6-21-74	Fort Smith, Arkansas	3-31
Sadler, Donnie	2B	Boston	6-17-75	Gohlson, Texas	4-1
Saipe, Michael Eric	P	Colorado	9-10-73	San Diego, California	6-25
Sampson, Benjamin Damon	P	Minnesota	4-27-75	Des Moines, Iowa	9-9
Sanchez, Jesus Paulino	P	Florida	10-11-74	Nizao Bani, Dominican Republic	3-31
Sanford, Chance Steven	3B	Pittsburgh	6- 2-72	Houston, Texas	4-30
Santana, Marino	P	Detroit	5-10-72	San Jose de Los Llanos, Dom. Rep.	9-4
Sasser, Robert Doffell	PH	Texas	3- 9-75	Philadelphia, Pennsylvania	7-31
Seguignol, Fernando	LF	Montreal	1-17-75	Bocas Del Toro, Panama	9-5
Simmons, Brian Lee	LF	Chicago A.L.	9- 4-73	Lebanon, Pennsylvania	9-21
Sinclair, Steven Scott	P	Toronto	8- 2-71	Victoria, British Columbia	4-25
Smith, Robert	PH	Tampa Bay	5-10-74	Oakland, California	3-31
Smith, Travis William	P	Milwaukee	11- 7-72	Springfield, Oregon	6-21
Snyder, John Michael	P	Chicago A.L.	8-16-74	Southfield, Michigan	6-30
Speier, Justin James	P	Chicago N.L.	11- 6-73	Walnut Creek, California	5-27
Spencer, Michael Shane	PH	New York A.L.	2-20-72	Key West, Florida	4-10
Spencer, Stanley R.	P	San Diego	8- 7-69	Vancouver, British Columbia	8-27
Steenstra, Kenneth Gregory	P	Chicago N.L.	10-13-70	Springfield, Missouri	5-21
Stein, William Blake	P	Oakland	8- 3-73	McComb, Mississippi	5-10
Stoops, Jim	P	Colorado	6-30-72	Edison, New Jersey	9-9
Stovall, DaRond Tyrone	CF	Montreal	1- 3-73	St. Louis, Missouri	4-1
Strittmatter, Mark Arthur	C	Colorado	4- 4-69	Huntington, New York	9-3

Player	Pos.	Team	Birth date	Birthplace	Debut
Tam, Jeffrey Eugene	P	New York N.L.	8-19-70	Fullerton, California	6-30
Tessmer, Jay W.	P	New York A.L.	12-26-71	Meadville, Pennsylvania	8-27
Vazquez, Javier	P	Montreal	7-25-76	Ponce, Puerto Rico	4-3
Ward, Bryan Matthew	P	Chicago A.L.	1-25-72	Bristol, Pennsylvania	7-3
Ward, Daryle Lamar	PH	Houston	6-27-75	Lynwood, California	5-14
Washburn, Jarrod Michael	P	Anaheim	8-13-74	La Crosse, Wisconsin	6-2
Weaver, Eric	P	Los Angeles	8- 4-73	Springfield, Illinois	5-30
Weber, Neil Aaron	P	Arizona	12- 6-72	Newport Beach, California	9-11
Welch, Michael Paul	P	Philadelphia	8-25-72	Haverhill, Massachusetts	7-17
Wilson, Craig Franklin	SS	Chicago A.L.	9- 3-70	Chicago, Illinois	9-5
Wilson, Preston	LF	New York N.L.	7-19-74	Bamberg, South Carolina	5-7
Winn, Dwight Randolph	PR	Tampa Bay	6- 9-74	Los Angeles, California	5-11
Withem, Shannon	P	Toronto	9-21-72	Ann Arbor, Michigan	9-18
Witt, Kevin	PH	Toronto	1- 5-76	High Point, North Carolina	9-15
Wood, Jason William	SS	Oakland	12-16-69	San Bernadino, California	4-1
Wood, Kerry Lee	P	Chicago N.L.	6-16-77	Irving, Texas	4-12
Yoshii, Masato	P	New York N.L.	4-20-65	Osaka, Japan	4-5
Young, Timothy R.	P	Montreal	10-15-73	Gulfport, Mississippi	9-5

SALARY ARBITRATION RESULTS

WINNERS

Player, Team	Salary awarded	Team's offer
Joey Hamilton, San Diego	$3,250,000	$2,375,000
Charles Johnson, Florida	$3,300,000	$2,250,000
Jose Mercedes, Milwaukee	$1,050,000	$615,000

LOSERS

Player, Team	Salary awarded	Player's request
Jorge Fabregas, Arizona	$875,000	$1,500,000
Todd Hollandsworth, Los Angeles	$700,000	1,150,000
Damon Buford, Boston	$460,000	$750,000
Frank Rodriguez, Minnesota	$425,000	$880,000
Tony Tarasco, Baltimore	$340,000	$485,000

1998 FREE-AGENT FILINGS

AMERICAN LEAGUE

Anaheim: Mike Fetters, Gregg Jefferies, Chad Krueter, Jack McDowell, Craig Shipley, Randy Velarde, Trevor Wilson.
Baltimore: Roberto Alomar, Eric Davis, Doug Drabek, Jimmy Key, Alan Mills, Rafael Palmeiro, Pete Smith, B.J. Surhoff.
Boston: Steve Avery, Mike Benjamin, Dennis Eckersley, Butch Henry, Mark Lemke, Darren Lewis, Tim Naehring, Pete Schourek, Greg Swindell, Mo Vaughn.
Chicago: Jim Abbott, Albert Belle, Wil Cordero, Robin Ventura.
Cleveland: Pat Borders, Jeff Branson, Joey Cora, Doug Jones, Jim Poole, Mark Whiten.
Detroit: Geronimo Berroa, Frank Castillo.
Kansas City: Tim Belcher, Ricky Bones, Scott Leius, Shane Mack, Jeff Montgomery, Hal Morris, Jose Offerman, Dean Palmer, Terry Pendleton.
Minnesota: Paul Molitor, Otis Nixon, Terry Steinbach, Bob Tewksbury.
New York: Scott Brosius, David Cone, Tim Raines, Darryl Strawberry, Bernie Williams.
Oakland: Mike Blowers, Rickey Henderson, Mike Macfarlane, Dave Magadan, Bip Roberts, Ed Sprague.
Seattle: Rich Amaral, John Marzano, Joe Oliver, Heathcliff Slocumb, Bill Swift, Mike Timlin.
Tampa Bay: None.
Texas: Scott Bailes, Greg Cadaret, Will Clark, Royce Clayton, Bill Haselman, Xavier Hernandez, Roger Pavlik, Todd Stottlemyre.
Toronto: Jose Canseco, Craig Grebeck, Juan Samuel, Benito Santiago, Dave Stieb.

NATIONAL LEAGUE

Arizona: Andy Stankiewicz, Devon White.
Atlanta: Rafael Belliard, Norm Charlton, Greg Colbrunn, Ozzie Guillen, Dennis Martinez.
Chicago: Mark Clark, Gary Gaetti, Chris Haney, Glenallen Hill, Orlando Merced, Mike Morgan, Terry Mulholland, Henry Rodriguez, Scott Servais.
Cincinnati: None.
Colorado: Darryl Hamilton, Kirt Manwaring, Mike Munoz.
Florida: None.
Houston: Sean Berry, Tim Bogar, Randy Johnson, Mike Magnante.
Los Angeles: Brian Bohanon, Jim Eisenreich, Mark Guthrie, Tom Prince, Scott Radinsky.
Milwaukee: Darrin Jackson, John Jaha.
Montreal: None.
New York: Carlos Baerga, Dennis Cook, Lenny Harris, Tony Phillips, Armando Reynoso.
Philadelphia: Mark Lewis, Mark Parent, Mark Portugal.
Pittsburgh: None.
St. Louis: Delino DeShields, Brian Jordan, Pat Kelly, Tom Lampkin, Willie McGee, Bobby Whitt.
San Diego: Kevin Brown, Ken Caminiti, Steve Finley, Carlos Hernandez, Mark Langston, John Vander Wal.
San Francisco: Ellis Burks, Joe Carter, Danny Darwin, Shawon Dunston, Mark Gardner, Orel Hershiser, Jose Mesa, Rey Sanchez.

MAJOR LEAGUE RULE 5 DRAFT

(Listed in order of selection)

Player	Pos.	Drafted by	Drafted from (major league organization)
Alberto Blanco	P	Florida	Jackson, Texas (Astros)
David Lamb	SS	Tampa Bay	Rochester, International League (Orioles)
Eric Ludwick	P	Detroit	Charlotte, S.C., International League (Marlins)
Ricky Williams	OF	Montreal	Scranton/Wilkes-Barre, International League (Phillies)

Player	Pos.	Drafted by	Drafted from (major league organization)
Josue Espada	SS	Minnesota	Edmonton, Pacific Coast League (Athletics)
Scott Sauerbeck	P	Pittsburgh	Norfolk, International League (Mets)
Eric Stuckenschneider	OF	Oakland	Albuquerque, Pacific Coast League (Dodgers)
David Miller	OF	Philadelphia	Buffalo, International League (Indians)
Jay Walker Chapman	P	Chicago A.L.	Salt Lake City, Pacific Coast League (Twins)
Alberto Castillo	C	St. Louis	Scranton/Wilkes-Barre, International League (Phillies)
Joel Adamson	P	Boston	Edmonton, Pacific Coast League (Athletics)
Glen Barker	OF	Houston	Toledo, International League (Tigers)
Tyrone Pendergrass	OF	Chicago A.L.	Richmond, International League (Braves)

NECROLOGY

Wayne Ambler, 82, at Ponte Vedra, Fla., on January 3. Infielder Ambler played 271 games for the Athletics from 1937 through 1939 and batted .224.

Harry Anderson, 66, at Greenville, Del., on June 11. Anderson, an outfielder, had a standout sophomore season for the Phillies in 1958, batting .301 with 23 home runs and 97 RBIs. But Anderson's average dropped 61 points the next year and he was out of the majors by 1961.

Gene Autry, 91, at Los Angeles on October 2. Owner of the Angels franchise since the A.L. club was founded in December 1960, the recording and motion picture star and businessman extraordinaire ran the team for 3½ decades before yielding operating control to the Walt Disney Co. in 1996.

Red Badgro, 95, at Kent, Wash., on July 13. A Pro Football Hall of Famer, Badgro was a reserve outfielder for the Browns in 1929 and 1930 and batted .257 in 143 games.

Frank (Red) Barrett, 84, at Leesburg, Fla., on March 8. Barrett, who pitched in 104 big-league games, made a total of 73 relief appearances for the Red Sox in 1944 and 1945 and was 12-10 overall in those seasons.

Frankie Baumholtz, 79, at Winter Springs, Fla., on December 14, 1997. Baumholtz, an outfielder for the Reds, Cubs and Phillies, batted .290 over 10 big-league seasons. In 1952, his career-high .325 average ranked second to Stan Musial's .336 figure in the N.L. batting race.

Joe Becker, 89, at Sunset Hills, Mo., on January 11. Becker, who saw brief duty as an Indians catcher in 1936 and 1937, was a coach for three World Series championship teams—the 1955, 1959 and 1963 Dodgers.

Mark Belanger, 54, at New York on October 6. Winner of eight Gold Gloves, Belanger was considered one of top defensive shortstops of all time. He spent 17 seasons with the Orioles and played in four World Series. His best offensive season was 1969, when he batted .287.

Ron Blackburn, 63, at Morganton, N.C., on April 29. Blackburn, primarily a reliever, pitched in a total of 64 games for the Pirates in 1958 and 1959, compiling a 3-2 record.

Jack Bolling, 81, at Panama City, Fla., on April 13. First baseman Bolling was a key reserve for the 1944 Dodgers, batting .351 in 56 games.

Larry Bradford, 48, at Atlanta on September 11. Bradford, who spent four seasons in the Braves' bullpen, posted an ERA of 0.95 in 21 appearances in 1979 and a career figure of 2.51 in 104 games.

Jack Brickhouse, 82, at Chicago on August 6. Brickhouse was a Cubs radio and television broadcaster from 1941 to 1981 and also broadcast White Sox games for more than a quarter century. Brickhouse is a member of the broadcasters' wing of the Hall of Fame.

Leon Brinkopf, 71, at Cape Girardeau. Mo., on July 2. Infielder Brinkopf appeared in nine games for the 1952 Cubs.

George Brophy, 72, at Edina, Minn., on November 20. Brophy, longtime head of Minnesota's minor league and scouting department, was a Twins official from 1961 through 1985. He later worked as a major league scout for the Astros.

Al Campanis, 81, at Fullerton, Calif., on June 21. As Los Angeles general manager from 1968 to 1987, he helped put together Dodgers teams that won four pennants and one World Series. Campanis, an infielder and minor league teammate of Jackie Robinson, played briefly with Brooklyn in 1943 before embarking on a long career as a Dodgers executive. Fired as G.M. for making racially insensitive remarks in an '87 television interview, he was supported by past and present Dodgers players and

officials who said unwavering fairness and shrewdness in judging talent were hallmarks of his career.

Milo Candini, 80, at Manteca, Calif., on March 17. Candini's first year in the majors was his best. Breaking in with the Senators in 1943, Candini went 11-7 with a 2.49 ERA.

Harry Caray, 83, at Rancho Mirage, Calif., on February 18. Caray broadcast major league baseball for 53 seasons—25 of them for the Cardinals (1945-1969) and 16 for the Cubs (1982-1997). Having already attracted a wide and devoted following, the folksy-yet-opinionated Caray achieved icon status with the Cubs when viewers nationwide tuned in cable-TV broadcasts of that team's games. He is a Hall of Fame inductee.

Slick Castleman, 84, at Nashville on March 2. Giants righthander Castleman went 15-6 in 1935 and 11-6 in 1937. In the 1936 World Series, he worked in relief against the Yankees in Game 6 and pitched 4⅓ innings of one-run ball.

Ed Connolly, 58, at New Canaan, Conn., on July 1. Connolly, a lefthander, compiled a 4-11 record for the 1964 Red Sox and a 2-1 mark for the 1967 Indians.

Jess Dobernic, 80, at St. Louis on July 16. Dobernic pitched in 76 big-league games, all in relief. In 1948, he made 54 appearances for the Cubs and went 7-2 with a 3.15 ERA.

Slim Emmerich, 78, at Allentown, Pa., on September 17. Emmerich pitched in 33 big-league games—31 of them for the 1945 Giants, for whom he went 4-4.

Mike Fornieles, 66, at St. Petersburg, Fla., on February 11. A 12-season major leaguer, he pitched for the Senators, White Sox, Orioles, Red Sox and Twins. Fornieles, who threw a one-hitter for Washington in his big-league debut in 1952, had his best season in 1960 when he made 70 relief appearances for the Red Sox and went 10-5 with a 2.64 ERA.

Bill Froats, 67, at Minneapolis on February 9. Pitching for the Tigers in 1955, Froats hurled two scoreless innings in his only major league game.

Denny Galehouse, 86, at Doylestown, Ohio, on October 12. Righthander Galehouse won 109 games in the majors in a 15-year career. He pitched two complete games for the Browns in the 1944 World Series, beating the Cardinals, 2-1, in Game 1 and losing Game 5 by a 2-0 score.

Joe Gallagher, 83, at Houston on February 25. Outfielder Gallagher split the 1939 season between the Yankees and Browns and the 1940 season between the Browns and Dodgers. Overall, he hit .273 in 165 games.

Sam Gentile, 81, at Everett, Mass., on May 4. Gentile was an outfielder whose major league career consisted of eight games with the 1943 Braves.

M. Donald Grant, 94, at Hobe Sound, Fla., on November 28. Grant was chairman of the board of the Mets from the team's inception in 1962 through 1978. In June 1977, he became embroiled in a contract dispute with pitcher Tom Seaver and drew heavy criticism when the club dealt the future Hall of Famer to Cincinnati.

Lee Grissom, 90, at Corning, Calif., on October 4. Lefthander Grissom, pitching for the last-place Reds, tied for the N.L. lead in shutouts with five in 1937, a year in which he went 12-17 and appeared in the All-Star Game. Two years later, he was 9-7 for Cincinnati and pitched in relief in the World Series.

Earl Harrist, 79, at Simsboro, La., on September 1. Primarily a relief pitcher, Harrist went 12-28 in five big-league seasons. He was in and out of the majors from 1945 to 1953 and pitched for the Reds, White Sox (two stints), Senators, Browns and Tigers.

Fred Hatfield, 73, at Tallahassee, Fla., on May 22. A versatile infielder, Hatfield played in 722 big-league games in the 1950s and batted .242. He was with the Red Sox, Tigers, White Sox, Indians and Reds.

Phil Haugstad, 74, at Black River Falls, Wis., on October 21. Pitcher Haugstad saw major league service in four seasons, his most extensive duty coming in 1951 when he appeared in 21 games for the Dodgers. His career record: 1-1.

Jim Hearn, 77, at Boca Grande, Fla., on June 10. Hearn, obtained on waivers by the Giants from the Cardinals in July 1950, topped the N.L. in ERA that season with a figure of 2.49. He then went 17-9 for the pennant-winning Giants in 1951 and won Game 3 of the '51 World Series against the Yankees. Overall, he was 109-89 in 13 big-league seasons.

Chet Hoff, 107, at Daytona Beach, Fla., on September 17. Lefthander Hoff broke into the majors in 1911 with the A.L.'s New York franchise—when the Yankees-to-be were known as the Highlanders and Yankee Stadium was more than a decade away from being opened. He compiled a 2-4 record in four big-league seasons.

Gene Host, 65, at Nashville on August 20. After starting one game (no decision) for the Tigers in 1956, lefthander Host pitched in 11 games (nine in relief) for the Athletics in 1957 and went 0-2.

John Kennedy, 71, at Jacksonville on April 27. Infielder Kennedy became the first black player in Phillies history when he appeared in an April 22, 1957, game. He played in only four other big-league games.

Rufino Linares, 47, in a car accident in the Dominican Republic on May 16. Outfielder Linares spent four years in the majors. In 1982, he batted .298 in 77 games for a Braves team that won the N.L. West.

Johnny Lipon, 75, at Houston on August 17. The Tigers' No. 1 shortstop from 1948 through 1951, he hit .290 in '48 and .293 in '50. The nine-season major leaguer went on to longtime service as a minor league manager.

Ad Liska, 92, at Portland, Ore., on November 30. Liska, who pitched in the big leagues for five seasons, enjoyed his best year in 1930 when he went 9-7 for the Senators with a 3.29 ERA.

Verdell Mathis, 83, at Memphis on October 30. Mathis was an outstanding Negro leagues pitcher for the Memphis Red Sox throughout the 1940s. The lefthander was the winning pitcher in the 1944 and 1945 East-West all-star games and contributed three hits in three at-bats in those games.

Ronnie Miller, 79, at Ferguson, Mo., on January 6. Miller pitched in one game for the 1941 Senators.

Al "Hiker" Moran, 86, at Saratoga Springs, N.Y., on January 7. Moran pitched in a total of seven N.L. games for Boston in 1938 and 1939.

Ray Moss, 96, at Chattanooga, Tenn., on August 9. Moss, a righthander, pitched in the majors for six seasons and had his best year in 1929 when he went 11-6 for the Dodgers.

Hal Newhouser, 77, at Detroit on November 10. Hall of Famer Newhouser, who pitched for his hometown Tigers in 15 of his 17 big-league seasons, compiled a 207-150 career record. He is the only pitcher to collect consecutive MVP awards, winning A.L. honors in 1944 (29-9 record, 2.22 ERA) and 1945 (25-9, 1.81, eight shutouts). The lefthander capped the '45 season with a complete-game victory in Detroit's World Series-clinching triumph against the Cubs. He was dazzling again in 1946, finishing 26-9 with a 1.94 ERA, and won 21 games in 1948.

Ray Noble, 79, at Brooklyn, N.Y., on May 9. Noble was a back-up catcher for the 1951 pennant-winning Giants and made two pinch-hitting appearances in the '51 World Series.

Marv Olson, 90, at Tyndall, S.D., on February 5. Second baseman Olson had 403 of his 457 career at-bats in 1932 and hit .248 for the Red Sox that season.

Gabe Paul, 88, at Rochester, N.Y., on April 26. Paul was an executive who spent a quarter century with the Reds in a tenure that ran through 1960 and later was part owner of the Yankees. He also spent a decade with the Indians and was briefly with Houston when that N.L. expansion franchise was being formed.

Dick Phillips, 66, at Burnaby, B.C., on March 29. Phillips, a first baseman, played briefly for the Giants in 1962 and then appeared in 258 games for the Senators over three seasons.

Nick Picciuto, 76, at Winchester, Va., on January 10. Infielder Picciuto played 36 games for the 1945 Phillies.

Elmo Plaskett, 60, in the Virgin Islands on November 2. Plaskett, primarily a catcher, played in a total of 17 games for the 1962 and 1963 Pirates.

Dan Quisenberry, 45, at Leawood, Kan., on September 30. Pitching for the Royals from 1979 to 1988, Quisenberry led the A.L. in saves five times and established a major league record (since broken) with 45 saves in 1983. His emergence helped Kansas City win its first pennant in 1980 and its first World Series title in 1985. He also pitched for the Cardinals and Giants.

Hal Rice, 73, at St. Augustine, Fla., on December 22, 1997. Rice was an effective part-time player for the Cardinals in 1952, batting .288 in 295 at-bats. In June 1953, the outfielder was traded to Pittsburgh, where he batted .311 in 286 at-bats.

Rafael Robles, 50, at New York on August 13. He was the Padres' shortstop in the first game in franchise history—April 8, 1969, against Houston—but played only 47 games in the majors over three seasons.

Packy Rogers, 85, at Elmira, N.Y., on May 15. Rogers appeared in only 23 big-league games—all in 1938 for the Dodgers—but managed to see duty at shortstop, third base, second base and in the outfield.

Ed Sanicki, 73, at Old Bridge, N.J., on July 6. Playing for the Phillies, outfielder Sanicki homered in his first major league at-bat in September 1949. In 13 at-bats during his call-up stint, he collected three hits—all of them home runs. He also played briefly for the Phils in 1951.

George Schmees, 74, at San Jose, Calif., on October 30. Outfielder Schmees divided his lone season in the majors, 1952, between the Browns and Red Sox and batted only .168 in 125 at-bats. He made two pitching appearances with Boston.

Walter Sessi, 79, at Mobile, Ala., on April 18. Outfielder Sessi played briefly for the Cardinals before and after World War II, appearing in five games in 1941 and 15 games in 1946.

Strick Shofner, 79, at Crawford, Texas, on October 10. Third baseman Shofner appeared in five games for the 1947 Red Sox.

Dick Sisler, 78, at Nashville on November 20. His three-run home run against Brooklyn in the 10th inning of the final game of the 1950 season clinched the pennant for the Phillies, who entered the day with a one-game lead over the Dodgers. The '50 season was the most productive (.296 average, 83 RBIs) of an eight-year career for Sisler, an outfielder/first baseman and a son of Hall of Famer George Sisler.

Dave Smith, 83, at Whiteville, N.C., on April 11. Smith pitched for the Athletics in 1938 and 1939, going 2-1 in 22 games.

Bill Sodd, 83, at Fort Worth, Texas, on May 14. Sodd, an outfielder, had one at-bat in the big leagues—for the Indians in 1937. He struck out as a pinch hitter.

Dewey Soriano, 78, at Seattle on April 6. Soriano, former president of the Pacific Coast League, was president of the Seattle Pilots, a 1969 A.L. expansion team that moved to Milwaukee in 1970 and became the Brewers.

Ray Stoviak, 82, in Costa Rica on February 23. In 10 at-bats for the 1938 Phillies, outfielder Stoviak went hitless.

Elvin Tappe, 71, at Quincy, Ill., on October 10. Tappe was part of the Cubs' College of Coaches, whose members rotated in 1961 and 1962 and assumed duties previously held by a manager. Earlier, Tappe was a reserve catcher for the Cubs.

Bob Thurman, 81, at Wichita, Kan., on October 31. After military service, stints in the Negro leagues and minor leagues and two years out of U.S. professional baseball, Thurman reached the majors in April 1955, one month before he turned 38. The outfielder wound up playing 334 games in the big leagues, all for the Reds. He had a three-homer game against the Braves in '56 and hit 16 homers in 190 at-bats in '57. Thurman bowed out of the majors in '59, having hit 35 homers in 663 career at-bats.

Jim Turner, 95, at Nashville on November 29. Turner had two tenures as Yankees pitching coach, the most notable from 1949 through 1959 when he helped mold a staff that led the Yanks to nine pennants and seven World Series titles. He also was pitching coach for the 1961 pennant-winning Reds. As a player, he spent 12 years in the minor leagues before reaching the majors at age 33 in 1937—a year in which he won 20 games for the Boston Bees (nee Braves) and led the N.L. with a 2.38 ERA.

Bill Tuttle, 69, at Anoka, Minn., on July 27. Tuttle, who in his fight against cancer became a leading spokesman against tobacco use, was a fixture in center field for the Tigers and Athletics from 1954 through 1960 and later played for the Twins. He scored 102 runs for the '55 Tigers and batted .300 for the '59 A's.

Elmer Valo, 77, at Palmerton, Pa., on July 19. Outfielder Valo played in the majors for 20 seasons and batted .282. He spent 13 of his years with the Philadelphia A's, hitting .300 or higher for that club from 1946 through 1948. In 1955, Valo batted .452 as a pinch hitter for the A's in their first season in Kansas City.

Ed Walczak, 79, at Norwich, Conn., on March 10. Infielder Walczak appeared in 20 games for the 1945 Phillies.

Charlie White, 69, at Seattle on May 26. White, a catcher, played in 50 games for the Braves in 1954 and in 12 games for the Milwaukee club in 1955. On April 23, 1954, Braves rookies White and Hank Aaron hit their first major league home runs. White never hit another homer; Aaron hit 754 more.

John Wyatt, 62, at Omaha, Neb., on April 6. Wyatt was the No. 1 reliever for the pennant-winning Red Sox of 1967, making 60 appearances and going 10-7 with a 2.60 ERA. The righthander, who pitched in an A.L.-leading 81 games in 1964 for the Athletics, worked in 435 games in his nine years in the majors.

Jerry Zimmerman, 63, at Neskowin, Ore., on September 9. Catcher Zimmerman played 76 games for the N.L. champion Reds in 1961 and 83 games for the A.L. champion Twins in 1965 and saw brief World Series duty both years. He spent eight seasons in the majors.

1998 A.L. STATISTICS

Batting

Designated hitting

Pinch-hitting

Pitching

Fielding

Miscellaneous

BATTING

TEAM

Team	Avg.	G	TPA	AB	R	H	TB	2B	3B	HR	RBI	SH	SF	HP	BB	IBB	SO	SB	CS	GDP	LOB	ShO	Slg.	OBP
Texas	.289	162	6401	5672	940	1637	2618	314	32	201	894	41	54	39	595	27	1045	82	47	137	1184	6	.462	.357
New York	.288	162	6444	5643	965	1625	2598	290	31	207	907	32	59	57	653	34	1025	153	63	145	1203	5	.460	.364
Boston	.280	162	6299	5601	876	1568	2591	338	35	205	827	35	52	70	541	32	1049	72	39	144	1150	4	.463	.348
Seattle	.276	161	6327	5628	859	1553	2632	321	28	234	822	36	48	57	558	26	1081	115	39	107	1189	6	.468	.345
Baltimore	.273	162	6304	5565	817	1520	2487	303	11	214	783	44	44	58	593	30	903	86	48	136	1187	3	.447	.347
Cleveland	.272	162	6376	5616	850	1530	2518	334	30	198	811	30	59	41	630	35	1061	143	60	123	1169	6	.448	.347
Anaheim	.272	162	6278	5630	787	1530	2339	314	27	147	739	49	41	48	510	31	1028	93	45	122	1180	6	.415	.335
Chicago	.271	163	6280	5585	861	1516	2477	291	38	198	806	38	59	47	551	34	916	127	46	119	1104	9	.444	.339
Minnesota	.266	162	6262	5641	734	1499	2193	285	32	115	691	18	52	45	506	33	915	112	54	155	1151	10	.389	.328
Toronto	.266	163	6323	5580	816	1482	2499	316	19	221	776	43	49	87	564	43	1132	184	81	108	1133	4	.448	.340
Detroit	.264	162	6242	5664	722	1494	2353	306	29	165	691	16	45	62	455	25	1070	122	62	111	1131	8	.415	.323
Kansas City	.263	161	6191	5546	714	1459	2215	274	40	134	686	45	65	60	475	24	984	135	50	118	1140	10	.399	.324
Tampa Bay	.261	162	6156	5555	620	1450	2136	267	43	111	579	53	37	37	473	24	1101	120	73	127	1155	17	.385	.321
Oakland	.257	162	6282	5490	804	1413	2181	295	13	149	755	58	46	55	633	22	1122	131	47	120	1159	9	.397	.338
Totals	.271	1134	88165	78416	11365	21276	33837	4248	408	2499	10767	538	711	763	7737	420	14438	1675	754	1772	16325	103	.432	.340

INDIVIDUAL

TOP QUALIFIERS FOR BATTING CHAMPIONSHIP

Minimum 502 plate appearances. *Lefthanded batter. †Switch-hitter.

Player, Team	Avg.	G	TPA	AB	R	H	TB	2B	3B	HR	RBI	SH	SF	HP	BB	IBB	SO	SB	CS	GDP	Slg.	OBP
Belle, Albert, Chi.	.328	163	706	609	113	200	399	48	2	49	152	0	15	1	81	10	84	6	4	17	.655	.399
Gonzalez, Juan, Tex.	.318	154	669	606	110	193	382	50	2	45	157	0	11	6	46	9	126	2	1	20	.630	.366
Griffey, Ken Jr., Sea.*	.284	161	720	633	120	180	387	33	3	56	146	0	4	7	76	11	121	20	5	14	.611	.365
Ramirez, Manny, Cle.	.294	150	663	571	108	168	342	35	2	45	145	0	10	6	76	6	121	5	3	18	.599	.377
Delgado, Carlos, Tor.*	.292	142	620	530	94	155	314	43	1	38	115	0	6	11	73	13	139	3	0	8	.592	.385
Vaughn, Mo, Bos.*	.337	154	681	609	107	205	360	31	2	40	115	0	3	8	61	13	144	0	0	13	.591	.402
Garciaparra, Nomar, Bos.	.323	143	652	604	111	195	353	37	8	35	122	0	7	8	33	1	62	12	6	20	.584	.362
Thome, Jim, Cle.*	.293	123	537	440	89	129	257	34	2	30	85	0	4	4	89	8	141	1	0	7	.584	.413
Davis, Eric, Bal.	.327	131	508	452	81	148	263	29	1	28	89	0	7	5	44	0	108	7	6	13	.582	.388
Williams, Bernie, N.Y.†	.339	128	578	499	101	169	287	30	5	26	97	0	4	1	74	9	81	15	9	19	.575	.422
Martinez, Edgar, Sea.	.322	154	672	556	86	179	314	46	1	29	102	0	7	3	106	4	96	1	1	13	.565	.429
Palmeiro, Rafael, Bal.*	.296	162	709	619	98	183	350	36	1	43	121	0	4	7	79	8	91	11	7	14	.565	.379
Rodriguez, Alex, Sea.	.310	161	748	686	123	213	384	35	5	42	124	3	4	10	45	0	121	46	13	12	.560	.360
Salmon, Tim, Ana.	.300	136	566	463	84	139	247	28	1	26	88	0	10	3	90	5	100	0	1	4	.533	.410
Clark, Tony, Det.†	.291	157	673	602	84	175	314	37	0	34	103	0	5	3	63	5	128	3	3	16	.522	.358

DEPARTMENTAL LEADERS: G—Belle, Chi., 163; AB—Rodriguez, Sea., 686; R—Jeter, N.Y., 127; H—Rodriguez, Sea., 213; TB—Belle, Chi., 399; 2B—Gonzalez, Tex., 50; 3B—Offerman, K.C., 13; HR—Griffey, Sea., 56; RBI—Gonzalez, Tex., 157; SH—Bordick, Bal., 15; SF—Belle, Chi., 15; HP—Knoblauch, N.Y., 18; BB—Henderson, Oak., 118; IBB—Ventura, Chi., 15; SO—Canseco, Tor., 159; SB—Henderson, Oak., 66; CS—Goodwin, Tex., 20; GIDP—Coomer, Min., O'Neill, N.Y., 22; Slg. Pct.—Belle, Chi., .655; OB. Pct.—Martinez, Sea., .429.

ALL PLAYERS

*Lefthanded batter. †Switch-hitter.

Player, Team	Avg.	G	TPA	AB	R	H	TB	2B	3B	HR	RBI	SH	SF	HP	BB	IBB	SO	SB	CS	GDP	Slg.	OBP
Abbott, Jeff, Chi.	.279	89	260	244	33	68	120	14	1	12	41	2	5	0	9	1	28	3	3	2	.492	.298
Abbott, Kurt, Oak.	.268	35	136	123	17	33	48	7	1	2	9	1	1	1	10	0	34	2	1	3	.390	.326
Alicea, Luis, Tex.†	.274	101	308	259	51	71	110	15	3	6	33	4	3	5	37	0	40	4	3	1	.425	.372
Allensworth, Jermaine, K.C.	.205	30	91	73	15	15	20	5	0	0	3	5	0	4	9	0	17	7	0	0	.274	.326
Alomar, Roberto, Bal.†	.282	147	657	588	86	166	246	36	1	14	56	3	5	2	59	3	70	18	5	11	.418	.347
Alomar, Sandy Jr., Cle.	.235	117	438	409	45	96	144	26	2	6	44	5	3	3	18	0	45	0	3	15	.352	.270
Alvarez, Gabe, Det.	.231	58	221	199	16	46	72	11	0	5	29	0	2	2	18	1	65	1	3	2	.362	.299
Amaral, Rich, Sea.	.276	73	149	134	25	37	46	6	0	1	4	0	1	1	13	0	24	11	1	1	.343	.342
Anderson, Brady, Bal.*	.236	133	574	479	84	113	201	28	3	18	51	4	1	15	75	1	78	21	7	7	.420	.356
Anderson, Garret, Ana.*	.294	156	658	622	62	183	283	41	7	15	79	3	3	1	29	8	80	8	3	13	.455	.325
Arrojo, Rolando, T.B.	.000	32	3	3	0	0	0	0	0	0	0	0	0	0	0	0	2	0	0	0	.000	.000
Ashley, Billy, Bos.	.292	13	26	24	3	7	19	3	0	3	7	0	0	0	2	0	11	0	0	0	.792	.346
Avery, Steve, Bos.*	.000	39	1	1	2	0	0	0	0	0	0	0	0	0	0	0	0	0	0	0	.000	.000
Baines, Harold, Bal.*	.300	104	328	293	40	88	132	17	0	9	57	0	2	1	32	4	40	0	0	17	.451	.369
Bako, Paul, Det.*	.272	96	333	305	23	83	106	12	1	3	30	1	4	0	23	4	82	1	1	3	.348	.319
Baldwin, James, Chi.	.000	37	2	2	0	0	0	0	0	0	0	0	0	0	0	0	1	0	0	0	.000	.000
Bartee, Kimera, Det.†	.194	57	105	98	20	19	35	5	1	3	15	0	1	0	6	0	35	9	5	1	.357	.238
Baughman, Justin, Ana.	.255	63	211	196	24	50	64	9	1	1	20	5	3	1	6	0	36	10	4	4	.327	.277
Beamon, Trey, Det.*	.262	28	48	42	4	11	15	4	0	0	2	1	0	0	5	0	13	1	0	3	.357	.340
Becker, Rich, Bal.*	.204	79	139	113	22	23	33	1	0	3	11	2	0	2	22	0	34	2	0	6	.292	.343
Belcher, Tim, K.C.	.200	34	6	5	1	1	1	0	0	0	0	1	0	0	0	0	2	0	0	0	.200	.200
Bell, David, Cle.-Sea.	.274	128	455	420	48	115	178	29	2	10	49	1	5	2	27	4	62	0	4	11	.424	.317
Belle, Albert, Chi.	.328	163	706	609	113	200	399	48	2	49	152	0	15	1	81	10	84	6	4	17	.655	.399
Bellhorn, Mark, Oak.†	.083	11	16	12	1	1	1	0	0	0	1	0	0	1	3	0	4	2	0	0	.167	.313
Beltran, Carlos, K.C.†	.276	14	63	58	12	16	27	5	3	0	7	0	1	1	3	0	12	3	0	2	.466	.317
Benjamin, Mike, Bos.	.272	124	385	349	46	95	130	23	0	4	39	13	2	6	15	1	73	3	0	11	.372	.312
Berroa, Geronimo, Cle.-Det.	.225	72	217	191	23	43	57	7	2	1	13	0	2	2	24	1	44	1	1	5	.298	.318
Blowers, Mike, Oak.	.237	129	455	409	56	97	158	24	2	11	71	2	4	1	39	1	116	1	0	13	.386	.302
Boggs, Wade, T.B.*	.280	123	483	435	51	122	174	23	4	7	52	0	2	0	45	6	54	3	2	13	.400	.348
Bolick, Frank, Ana.†	.156	21	56	45	3	7	12	2	0	1	2	0	0	0	11	0	8	0	0	1	.267	.321

Player, Team	Avg.	G	TPA	AB	R	H	TB	2B	3B	HR	RBI	SH	SF	HP	BB	IBB	SO	SB	CS	GDP	Slg.	OBP
Bones, Ricky, K.C.	.000	32	1	1	0	0	0	0	0	0	0	0	0	0	0	0	0	0	0	0	.000	.000
Borders, Pat, Cle.	.238	54	175	160	12	38	44	6	0	0	6	2	1	2	10	0	40	0	2	3	.275	.289
Bordick, Mike, Bal.	.260	151	533	465	59	121	191	29	1	13	51	15	4	10	39	0	65	6	7	13	.411	.328
Bournigal, Rafael, Oak.	.225	85	229	209	23	47	61	11	0	1	19	6	2	2	10	1	11	6	1	6	.292	.265
Bragg, Darren, Bos.*	.279	129	465	409	51	114	173	29	3	8	57	4	4	6	42	0	99	5	3	16	.423	.351
Branson, Jeff, Cle.*	.200	63	105	100	6	20	29	4	1	1	9	1	1	0	3	0	21	0	0	1	.290	.221
Branyan, Russ, Cle.*	.000	1	4	4	0	0	0	0	0	0	0	0	0	0	0	0	2	0	0	0	.000	.000
Brosius, Scott, N.Y.	.300	152	603	530	86	159	250	34	0	19	98	8	3	10	52	1	97	11	8	4	.472	.371
Brown, Dermal, K.C.*	.000	5	3	3	2	0	0	0	0	0	0	0	0	0	0	0	1	0	0	0	.000	.000
Brown, Kevin, Tor.	.264	52	128	110	17	29	44	7	1	2	15	3	4	2	9	0	31	0	0	1	.400	.320
Buford, Damon, Bos.	.282	86	241	216	37	61	113	14	4	10	42	0	2	1	22	1	43	5	5	5	.523	.349
Buhner, Jay, Sea.	.242	72	286	244	33	59	113	7	1	15	45	1	2	1	38	0	71	0	0	2	.463	.344
Burba, Dave, Cle.	.167	32	6	6	1	1	4	0	0	1	2	0	0	0	0	0	1	0	0	0	.667	.167
Burkett, John, Tex.	.000	32	3	3	1	0	0	0	0	0	0	0	0	0	0	0	1	0	0	0	.000	.000
Bush, Homer, N.Y.	.380	45	78	71	17	27	33	3	0	1	5	2	0	0	5	0	19	6	3	1	.465	.421
Butler, Rich, T.B.*	.226	72	237	217	25	49	79	3	3	7	20	0	3	2	15	0	37	4	2	4	.364	.278
Cabrera, Jolbert, Cle.	.000	1	2	2	0	0	0	0	0	0	0	0	0	0	0	0	1	0	0	0	.000	.000
Cairo, Miguel, T.B.	.268	150	558	515	49	138	189	26	5	5	46	11	2	6	24	0	44	19	8	9	.367	.307
Cameron, Mike, Chi.	.210	141	443	396	53	83	133	16	5	8	43	1	3	6	37	0	101	27	11	6	.336	.285
Candiotti, Tom, Oak.	1.000	33	2	1	0	1	2	1	0	0	1	0	0	0	0	0	0	0	0	0	2.000	1.000
Canseco, Jose, Tor.	.237	151	658	583	98	138	302	26	0	46	107	0	4	6	65	5	159	29	17	7	.518	.318
Carpenter, Chris, Tor.	.000	33	1	1	0	0	0	0	0	0	0	0	0	0	0	0	0	0	0	0	.000	.000
Carter, Joe, Bal.	.247	85	303	283	36	70	120	15	1	11	34	0	2	2	18	4	48	3	1	7	.424	.297
Caruso, Mike, Chi.*	.306	133	555	523	81	160	204	17	6	5	55	8	3	7	14	0	38	22	6	8	.390	.331
Casanova, Raul, Det.†	.143	16	48	42	4	6	11	2	0	1	3	0	0	1	5	0	10	0	0	3	.262	.250
Castillo, Carlos, Chi.	.000	54	1	1	0	0	0	0	0	0	0	0	0	0	0	0	0	0	0	0	.000	.000
Castillo, Frank, Det.	.000	27	1	1	0	0	0	0	0	0	0	0	0	0	0	0	0	0	0	0	.000	.000
Catalanotto, Frank, Det.*	.282	89	234	213	23	60	95	13	2	6	25	0	5	4	12	1	39	3	2	4	.446	.325
Cedeno, Domingo, Tex.†	.262	61	153	141	19	37	54	9	1	2	21	1	1	0	10	0	32	2	1	4	.383	.309
Chavez, Eric, Oak.*	.311	16	48	45	6	14	20	4	1	0	6	0	0	0	3	1	5	1	1	1	.444	.354
Chavez, Raul, Sea.	.000	1	1	1	0	0	0	0	0	0	0	0	0	0	0	0	0	0	0	0	.000	.000
Christenson, Ryan, Oak.	.257	117	421	370	56	95	136	22	2	5	40	10	4	1	36	0	106	5	6	1	.368	.321
Clark, Tony, Det.†	.291	157	673	602	84	175	314	37	0	34	103	0	5	3	63	5	128	3	3	16	.522	.358
Clark, Will, Tex.*	.305	149	636	554	98	169	281	41	1	23	102	0	7	3	72	5	97	1	0	15	.507	.384
Clayton, Royce, Tex.	.285	52	206	186	30	53	82	12	1	5	24	3	3	1	13	0	32	5	5	6	.441	.330
Clemens, Roger, Tor.	.000	33	6	4	0	0	0	0	0	0	0	1	0	0	1	0	0	0	0	0	.000	.200
Cloude, Ken, Sea.	.000	30	3	3	0	0	0	0	0	0	0	0	0	0	0	0	0	0	0	1	.000	.000
Clyburn, Danny, Bal.	.280	11	26	25	6	7	10	0	0	1	3	0	0	0	1	0	10	0	0	0	.400	.308
Colon, Bartolo, Cle.	.500	31	2	2	0	1	1	0	0	0	0	1	0	0	0	0	1	0	0	0	.500	.500
Cone, David, N.Y.*	.000	31	4	3	1	0	0	0	0	0	0	1	1	0	0	0	0	0	0	0	.000	.000
Conine, Jeff, K.C.	.256	93	343	309	30	79	129	26	0	8	43	0	6	2	26	1	68	3	0	8	.417	.312
Coomer, Ron, Min.	.276	137	555	529	54	146	215	22	1	15	72	0	8	0	18	1	72	2	2	22	.406	.295
Cora, Joey, Sea.-Cle.†	.276	155	695	602	111	166	223	27	6	6	32	12	3	5	73	0	59	15	6	5	.370	.357
Cordero, Wil, Chi.	.267	96	371	341	58	91	152	18	2	13	49	1	4	3	22	0	66	2	1	7	.446	.314
Cordova, Marty, Min.	.253	119	499	438	52	111	165	20	2	10	69	0	6	5	50	3	103	3	6	14	.377	.333
Corsi, Jim, Bos.	.000	59	1	1	0	0	0	0	0	0	0	0	0	0	0	0	0	0	0	0	.000	.000
Crabtree, Tim, Tex.	.000	64	1	1	0	0	0	0	0	0	0	0	0	0	0	0	0	0	0	0	.000	.000
Cradle, Rickey, Sea.	.143	5	8	7	0	1	1	0	0	0	2	0	0	0	1	0	5	1	0	0	.143	.250
Crespo, Felipe, Tor.†	.262	66	153	130	11	34	47	8	1	1	15	4	2	2	15	1	27	4	3	1	.362	.342
Cruz, Deivi, Det.	.260	135	477	454	52	118	161	22	3	5	45	5	2	3	13	0	55	3	4	11	.355	.284
Cruz, Jacob, Cle.*	.000	1	1	1	0	0	0	0	0	0	0	0	0	0	0	0	1	0	0	0	.000	.000
Cruz, Jose Jr., Tor.†	.253	105	413	352	55	89	142	14	3	11	42	0	4	0	57	3	99	11	4	0	.403	.354
Cummings, Midre, Bos.*	.283	67	140	120	20	34	57	8	0	5	15	1	0	2	17	0	19	3	3	2	.475	.381
Curtis, Chad, N.Y.	.243	151	545	456	79	111	164	21	1	10	56	1	6	7	75	3	80	21	5	11	.360	.355
Cuyler, Milt, Tex.†	.500	7	7	6	3	3	8	2	0	1	3	0	0	0	1	0	0	0	0	0	1.333	.571
Dalesandro, Mark, Tor.	.299	32	69	67	8	20	31	5	0	2	14	0	1	0	1	0	6	0	0	3	.463	.304
Damon, Johnny, K.C.*	.277	161	710	642	104	178	282	30	10	18	66	3	3	4	58	4	84	26	12	4	.439	.339
Davis, Chili, N.Y.†	.291	35	118	103	11	30	46	7	0	3	9	0	1	0	14	1	18	0	1	6	.447	.373
Davis, Eric, Bal.	.327	131	508	452	81	148	263	29	1	28	89	0	7	5	44	0	108	7	6	13	.582	.388
Davis, Russ, Sea.	.259	141	550	502	68	130	222	30	1	20	82	2	9	3	34	1	134	4	3	10	.442	.305
Delgado, Carlos, Tor.*	.292	142	620	530	94	155	314	43	1	38	115	0	6	11	73	13	139	3	0	8	.592	.385
Diaz, Einar, Cle.	.229	17	56	48	8	11	18	1	0	2	9	0	3	2	3	0	2	0	0	2	.375	.286
Dickson, Jason, Ana.*	.000	27	5	4	1	0	0	0	0	0	0	0	0	0	0	0	1	0	0	0	.000	.200
DiFelice, Mike, T.B.	.230	84	269	248	17	57	84	12	3	3	23	3	2	1	15	0	56	0	0	12	.339	.274
DiSarcina, Gary, Ana.	.287	157	595	551	73	158	212	39	3	3	56	12	3	8	21	0	51	11	7	11	.385	.321
Drabek, Doug, Bal.	.000	23	1	1	0	0	0	0	0	0	0	0	0	0	0	0	1	0	0	0	.000	.000
Ducey, Rob, Sea.*	.240	97	250	217	30	52	89	18	2	5	23	0	1	9	23	2	61	4	3	4	.410	.336
Dunston, Shawon, Cle.	.237	62	166	156	26	37	63	11	3	3	12	0	3	1	6	0	18	9	2	2	.404	.265
Durham, Ray, Chi.†	.285	158	723	635	126	181	289	35	8	19	67	6	3	6	73	3	105	36	9	5	.455	.363
Dye, Jermaine, K.C.	.234	60	230	214	24	50	72	5	1	5	23	0	4	1	11	2	46	2	2	8	.336	.270
Easley, Damion, Det.	.271	153	651	594	84	161	284	38	2	27	100	0	2	16	39	2	112	15	5	8	.478	.332
Edmonds, Jim, Ana.*	.307	154	659	599	115	184	303	42	1	25	91	1	1	1	57	7	114	7	5	16	.506	.368
Elster, Kevin, Tex.	.232	84	336	297	33	69	105	10	1	8	37	2	2	2	33	0	66	1	2	7	.354	.311
Encarnacion, Juan, Det.	.329	40	175	164	30	54	92	9	4	7	21	0	3	1	7	0	31	7	4	2	.561	.354
Erickson, Scott, Bal.	.000	36	6	2	2	0	0	0	0	0	0	0	1	0	3	0	2	0	0	0	.000	.600
Erstad, Darin, Ana.*	.296	133	590	537	84	159	261	39	3	19	82	1	3	6	43	7	77	20	6	2	.486	.353
Evans, Tom, Tor.	.000	7	11	10	0	0	0	0	0	0	0	0	0	0	1	0	2	0	0	1	.000	.091
Eyre, Scott, Chi.*	.000	33	3	3	0	0	0	0	0	0	0	0	0	0	0	0	3	0	0	0	.000	.000
Fasano, Sal, K.C.	.227	74	247	216	21	49	83	10	0	8	31	3	2	16	10	1	56	1	0	4	.384	.307
Fassero, Jeff, Sea.*	.000	32	3	3	0	0	0	0	0	0	0	0	0	0	0	0	2	0	0	0	.000	.000
Febles, Carlos, K.C.	.400	11	29	25	5	10	15	1	2	0	2	0	0	0	4	0	7	2	1	0	.600	.483

Player, Team	Avg.	G	TPA	AB	R	H	TB	2B	3B	HR	RBI	SH	SF	HP	BB	IBB	SO	SB	CS	GDP	Slg.	OBP
Fernandez, Tony, Tor.†	.321	138	551	486	71	156	223	36	2	9	72	3	6	11	45	5	53	13	8	11	.459	.387
Fick, Rob, Det.*	.364	7	24	22	6	8	18	1	0	3	7	0	0	0	2	0	7	1	0	1	.818	.417
Fielder, Cecil, Ana.-Cle.	.233	117	476	416	49	97	167	17	1	17	68	0	3	4	53	1	111	0	1	18	.401	.324
Figga, Mike, N.Y.	.250	1	4	4	1	1	1	0	0	0	0	0	0	0	0	0	1	0	0	0	.250	.250
Finley, Chuck, Ana.*	.000	34	4	4	0	0	0	0	0	0	0	0	0	0	0	0	3	0	0	0	.000	.000
Flaherty, John, T.B.	.207	91	334	304	21	63	83	11	0	3	24	4	3	1	22	0	46	0	5	9	.273	.261
Fletcher, Darrin, Tor.*	.283	124	446	407	37	115	167	23	1	9	52	1	7	6	25	7	39	0	0	19	.410	.328
Florie, Bryce, Det.	.333	42	6	3	0	1	1	0	0	0	0	1	0	0	2	0	1	0	0	0	.333	.600
Forbes, P.J., Bal.	.100	9	10	10	0	1	1	0	0	0	2	0	0	0	0	0	0	0	0	0	.100	.100
Fordham, Tom, Chi.*	.000	29	1	1	0	0	0	0	0	0	0	0	0	0	0	0	1	0	0	0	.000	.000
Frazier, Lou, Chi.†	.000	7	10	7	0	0	0	0	0	0	0	1	0	0	2	0	6	4	0	0	.000	.222
Fryman, Travis, Cle.	.287	146	608	557	74	160	281	33	2	28	96	0	4	3	44	0	125	10	8	12	.504	.340
Garcia, Carlos, Ana.	.143	19	40	35	4	5	6	1	0	0	0	1	0	1	3	0	11	2	0	0	.171	.231
Garciaparra, Nomar, Bos.	.323	143	652	604	111	195	353	37	8	35	122	0	7	8	33	1	62	12	6	20	.584	.362
Gates, Brent, Min.†	.249	107	377	333	31	83	107	15	0	3	42	3	3	2	36	0	46	3	3	6	.321	.324
Giambi, Jason, Oak.*	.295	153	657	562	92	166	275	28	0	27	110	0	9	5	81	7	102	2	2	16	.489	.384
Giambi, Jeremy, K.C.*	.224	18	70	58	6	13	23	4	0	2	8	0	1	0	11	0	9	0	1	3	.397	.343
Giles, Brian, Cle.*	.269	112	430	350	56	94	161	19	0	16	66	1	3	3	73	8	75	10	5	7	.460	.396
Gipson, Charles, Sea.	.235	44	57	51	11	12	13	1	0	0	2	0	0	1	5	1	9	2	1	1	.255	.316
Girardi, Joe, N.Y.	.276	78	279	254	31	70	98	11	4	3	31	8	1	2	14	1	38	2	4	10	.386	.317
Glaus, Troy, Ana.	.218	48	182	165	19	36	48	9	0	1	23	0	2	0	15	0	51	1	0	3	.291	.280
Gonzalez, Alex, Tor.	.239	158	618	568	70	136	205	28	1	13	51	13	3	6	28	1	121	21	6	13	.361	.281
Gonzalez, Juan, Tex.	.318	154	669	606	110	193	382	50	2	45	157	0	11	6	46	9	126	2	1	20	.630	.366
Gonzalez, Luis, Det.*	.267	154	620	547	84	146	260	35	5	23	71	0	8	8	57	7	62	12	7	9	.475	.340
Gooden, Dwight, Cle.	.000	23	2	2	0	0	0	0	0	0	0	0	0	0	0	0	1	0	0	0	.000	.000
Goodwin, Tom, Tex.*	.290	154	608	520	102	151	176	13	3	2	33	10	3	2	73	0	90	38	20	2	.338	.378
Grebeck, Craig, Tor.	.256	102	344	301	33	77	104	17	2	2	27	8	2	4	29	0	42	2	2	8	.346	.327
Green, Shawn, Tor.*	.278	158	689	630	106	175	321	33	4	35	100	1	3	5	50	2	142	35	12	6	.510	.334
Greene, Charlie, Bal.	.190	13	22	21	1	4	5	1	0	0	0	0	1	0	0	0	8	0	0	1	.238	.190
Greene, Todd, Ana.	.254	29	73	71	3	18	25	4	0	1	7	0	0	0	2	0	20	0	0	0	.352	.274
Greene, Willie, Bal.*	.150	24	53	40	8	6	10	1	0	1	5	0	0	0	13	0	10	1	0	2	.250	.358
Greer, Rusty, Tex.*	.306	155	691	598	107	183	272	31	5	16	108	0	9	4	80	1	93	2	4	18	.455	.386
Greisinger, Seth, Det.	.250	21	4	4	0	1	1	0	0	0	1	0	0	0	0	0	0	0	0	0	.250	.250
Grieve, Ben, Oak.*	.288	155	678	583	94	168	267	41	2	18	89	0	1	9	85	3	123	2	2	18	.458	.386
Griffey, Ken Jr., Sea.*	.284	161	720	633	120	180	387	33	3	56	146	0	4	7	76	11	121	20	5	14	.611	.365
Guevara, Giomar, Sea.	.231	11	18	13	4	3	5	2	0	0	0	0	0	1	4	0	4	0	0	1	.385	.444
Guillen, Carlos, Sea.†	.333	10	42	39	9	13	16	1	1	0	5	0	0	0	3	0	9	2	0	0	.410	.381
Guillen, Ozzie, Bal.*	.063	12	18	16	2	1	1	0	0	0	0	0	1	0	1	0	2	0	1	1	.063	.118
Guzman, Juan, Tor.-Bal.	.000	33	2	2	0	0	0	0	0	0	0	0	0	0	0	0	0	0	0	0	.000	.000
Hairston, Jerry Jr., Bal.	.000	5	7	7	2	0	0	0	0	0	0	0	0	0	0	0	1	0	0	0	.000	.000
Halter, Shane, K.C.	.221	86	226	204	17	45	63	12	0	2	13	7	2	1	12	0	38	2	5	3	.309	.265
Hammonds, Jeffrey, Bal.	.269	63	203	171	36	46	78	12	1	6	28	0	3	3	26	1	38	7	2	2	.456	.369
Hansen, Jed, K.C.	.000	4	3	3	0	0	0	0	0	0	0	0	0	0	0	0	3	0	0	0	.000	.000
Haselman, Bill, Tex.	.314	40	110	105	11	33	57	6	0	6	17	0	2	0	3	0	17	0	0	2	.543	.327
Hatcher, Chris, K.C.	.067	8	16	15	0	1	1	0	0	0	1	0	0	0	1	0	7	0	0	0	.067	.125
Hatteberg, Scott, Bos.*	.276	112	410	359	46	99	160	23	1	12	43	0	3	5	43	3	58	0	0	11	.446	.359
Hawkins, LaTroy, Min.	.000	33	1	1	0	0	0	0	0	0	0	0	0	0	0	0	1	0	0	0	.000	.000
Haynes, Jimmy, Oak.	.000	33	4	3	1	0	0	0	0	0	0	0	0	0	1	0	3	0	0	0	.000	.250
Helling, Rick, Tex.	.200	33	6	5	0	1	1	0	0	0	0	1	0	0	0	0	2	0	0	0	.200	.200
Henderson, Rickey, Oak.	.236	152	670	542	101	128	188	16	1	14	57	2	3	5	118	0	114	66	13	5	.347	.376
Hentgen, Pat, Tor.	.000	29	6	5	0	0	0	0	0	0	0	0	0	0	0	0	2	0	0	0	.000	.000
Hernandez, Orlando, N.Y.	.000	21	8	7	0	0	0	0	0	0	0	1	0	0	0	0	5	0	0	0	.000	.000
Higginson, Bobby, Det.*	.284	157	685	612	92	174	294	37	4	25	85	0	4	6	63	2	101	3	5	16	.480	.355
Hill, Glenallen, Sea.	.290	74	277	259	37	75	135	20	2	12	33	0	1	3	14	1	45	1	1	13	.521	.332
Hill, Ken, Ana.	.000	19	1	1	0	0	0	0	0	0	0	0	0	0	0	0	0	0	0	0	.000	.000
Hinch, A.J., Oak.	.231	120	391	337	34	78	115	10	0	9	35	13	7	4	30	0	89	3	0	6	.341	.296
Hocking, Denny, Min.†	.202	110	219	198	32	40	57	6	1	3	15	3	2	0	16	1	44	2	1	2	.288	.259
Hoiles, Chris, Bal.	.262	97	318	267	36	70	127	12	0	15	56	5	4	4	38	0	50	0	1	5	.476	.358
Hollins, Dave, Ana.†	.242	101	418	363	60	88	141	16	2	11	39	2	2	7	44	2	69	11	3	5	.388	.334
Hunter, Brian L., Det.	.254	142	636	595	67	151	198	29	3	4	36	2	1	2	36	0	94	42	12	8	.333	.298
Hunter, Torii, Min.	.235	6	19	17	0	4	5	1	0	0	2	0	0	0	2	0	6	0	1	1	.294	.316
Huson, Jeff, Sea.*	.163	31	54	49	8	8	12	1	0	1	4	0	0	0	5	0	6	1	1	0	.245	.241
Ibanez, Raul, Sea.*	.255	37	103	98	12	25	40	7	1	2	12	0	0	0	5	0	22	0	0	4	.408	.291
Incaviglia, Pete, Det.	.071	7	15	14	0	1	1	0	0	0	0	0	0	0	1	0	6	0	0	0	.071	.133
Irabu, Hideki, N.Y.	.250	29	5	4	0	1	1	0	0	0	0	0	0	1	0	0	3	0	0	0	.250	.250
Jefferies, Gregg, Ana.†	.347	19	72	72	7	25	34	6	0	1	10	0	0	0	0	0	5	1	0	2	.472	.347
Jefferson, Reggie, Bos.*	.306	62	219	196	24	60	102	16	1	8	31	0	1	1	21	2	40	0	0	7	.520	.374
Jeter, Derek, N.Y.	.324	149	694	626	127	203	301	25	8	19	84	3	3	5	57	1	119	30	6	13	.481	.384
Johns, Doug, Bal.	1.000	31	2	2	1	2	2	0	0	0	0	0	0	0	0	0	0	0	0	0	1.000	1.000
Johns, Keith, Bos.	.000	2	1	0	0	0	0	0	0	0	0	0	0	0	1	0	0	0	0	0	.000	1.000
Johnson, Jason, T.B.	.000	13	2	2	0	0	0	0	0	0	0	0	0	0	0	0	0	0	0	0	.000	.000
Johnson, Mark L., Chi.*	.087	7	24	23	2	2	6	0	2	0	1	0	0	0	1	0	8	0	0	0	.261	.125
Johnson, Mark P., Ana.*	.071	10	14	14	1	1	1	0	0	0	1	0	0	0	0	0	6	0	0	1	.071	.071
Johnson, Randy, Sea.	.143	23	7	7	1	1	1	0	0	0	0	0	0	0	0	0	2	0	0	0	.143	.143
Justice, David, Cle.*	.280	146	625	540	94	151	257	39	2	21	88	0	9	0	76	7	98	9	3	9	.476	.363
Kapler, Gabe, Det.	.200	7	26	25	3	5	7	0	1	0	0	0	0	0	1	0	4	2	0	0	.280	.231
Kelly, Mike, T.B.	.240	106	303	279	39	67	112	11	2	10	33	1	1	0	22	1	80	13	6	8	.401	.295
Kelly, Roberto, Tex.	.323	75	270	257	48	83	144	7	3	16	46	1	1	3	8	0	46	0	2	4	.560	.349
King, Jeff, K.C.	.263	131	540	486	83	128	219	17	1	24	93	0	10	2	42	1	73	10	2	10	.451	.319
Kingsale, Eugene, Bal.†	.000	11	2	2	1	0	0	0	0	0	0	0	0	0	0	0	1	0	0	0	.000	.000
Knoblauch, Chuck, N.Y.	.265	150	706	603	117	160	244	25	4	17	64	2	7	18	76	1	70	31	12	13	.405	.361
Koskie, Corey, Min.*	.138	11	31	29	2	4	7	0	0	1	2	0	0	0	2	0	10	0	0	0	.241	.194

Player, Team	Avg.	G	TPA	AB	R	H	TB	2B	3B	HR	RBI	SH	SF	HP	BB	IBB	SO	SB	CS	GDP	Slg.	OBP
Kreuter, Chad, Chi.-Ana.†	.250	96	294	252	27	63	81	10	1	2	33	5	1	3	33	1	49	1	0	8	.321	.343
Laker, Tim, T.B.	.200	3	6	5	1	1	1	0	0	0	0	0	0	0	1	0	1	0	1	0	.200	.333
Latham, Chris, Min.†	.160	34	108	94	14	15	19	1	0	1	5	1	0	0	13	0	36	4	2	0	.202	.262
Lawton, Matt, Min.*	.278	152	662	557	91	155	266	36	6	21	77	0	4	15	86	6	64	16	8	10	.478	.387
Ledee, Ricky, N.Y.*	.241	42	87	79	13	19	31	5	2	1	12	0	1	0	7	0	29	3	1	1	.392	.299
Ledesma, Aaron, T.B.	.324	95	315	299	30	97	119	16	3	0	29	4	2	1	9	1	51	9	7	8	.398	.344
Leius, Scott, K.C.	.174	17	47	46	2	8	8	0	0	0	4	0	0	1	0	6	0	0	2	.174	.191
Lemke, Mark, Bos.†	.187	31	100	91	10	17	21	4	0	0	7	1	2	0	6	0	15	0	1	0	.231	.232
Lennon, Patrick, Tor.	.500	2	4	4	1	2	4	2	0	0	0	0	0	0	0	0	1	0	0	0	1.000	.500
Lesher, Brian, Oak.	.143	7	7	7	0	1	2	1	0	0	1	0	0	0	0	0	3	0	0	0	.286	.143
Lewis, Darren, Bos.	.268	155	670	585	95	157	212	25	3	8	63	2	5	8	70	0	94	29	12	12	.362	.352
Leyritz, Jim, Bos.	.287	52	156	129	17	37	67	6	0	8	24	0	4	2	21	1	34	0	0	4	.519	.385
Lofton, Kenny, Cle.*	.282	154	698	600	101	169	248	31	6	12	64	3	6	2	87	1	80	54	10	7	.413	.371
Lopez, Albie, T.B.	.000	54	1	1	0	0	0	0	0	0	0	0	0	0	0	0	0	0	0	0	.000	.000
Lopez, Mendy, K.C.	.243	74	225	206	18	50	67	10	2	1	15	5	1	1	12	0	40	5	2	6	.325	.286
Lovullo, Torey, Cle.†	.211	6	21	19	1	4	5	1	0	0	1	1	0	0	1	0	2	0	0	1	.263	.250
Lowe, Derek, Bos.	.000	63	5	4	0	0	0	0	0	0	0	0	0	0	1	0	3	0	0	0	.000	.200
Lowell, Mike, N.Y.	.267	8	15	15	1	4	4	0	0	0	0	0	0	0	0	0	1	0	0	0	.267	.267
Luke, Matt, Cle.*	.000	2	2	2	0	0	0	0	0	0	0	0	0	0	0	0	0	0	0	0	.000	.000
Macfarlane, Mike, K.C.-Oak. ..	.243	81	238	218	29	53	86	12	0	7	34	1	3	4	12	0	36	1	0	3	.394	.291
Machado, Robert, Chi.	.207	34	121	111	14	23	38	6	0	3	15	3	0	0	7	0	22	0	0	3	.342	.254
Mack, Shane, Oak.-K.C.	.278	69	231	209	31	58	93	15	1	6	29	0	1	6	15	0	36	8	2	6	.445	.342
Magadan, Dave, Oak.*	.321	35	123	109	12	35	46	8	0	1	13	0	1	0	13	1	12	0	1	5	.422	.390
Manto, Jeff, Cle.-Det.-Cle.	.239	31	73	67	14	16	28	3	0	3	9	0	0	1	5	0	21	1	1	5	.418	.301
Martin, Norberto, Ana.	.215	79	206	195	20	42	47	2	0	1	13	3	2	0	6	0	29	3	1	9	.241	.236
Martinez, Tino, N.Y.*	.281	142	608	531	92	149	268	33	1	28	123	0	10	6	61	3	83	2	1	18	.505	.355
Martinez, Dave, T.B.*	.256	90	347	309	31	79	99	11	0	3	20	0	1	2	35	4	52	8	7	5	.320	.334
Martinez, Edgar, Sea.	.322	154	672	556	86	179	314	46	1	29	102	0	7	3	106	4	96	1	1	13	.565	.429
Martinez, Felix, K.C.†	.129	34	95	85	7	11	14	1	1	0	5	4	0	1	5	0	21	3	1	1	.165	.187
Martinez, Pedro, Bos.	.000	33	7	7	0	0	0	0	0	0	0	0	0	0	0	0	5	0	0	0	.000	.000
Marzano, John, Sea.	.233	50	153	133	13	31	52	7	1	4	12	2	0	9	9	1	24	0	0	3	.391	.325
Mashore, Damon, Ana.	.235	43	111	98	13	23	35	6	0	2	11	1	0	3	9	0	22	1	0	3	.357	.318
McCarty, David, Sea.	.278	8	23	18	1	5	8	0	0	1	2	0	0	0	5	0	4	1	0	0	.444	.435
McClain, Scott, T.B.	.100	9	23	20	2	2	2	0	0	0	0	0	0	1	2	0	6	0	0	0	.100	.217
McCracken, Quinton, T.B.†	.292	155	675	614	77	179	252	38	7	7	59	9	8	3	41	1	107	19	10	12	.410	.335
McDonald, Jason, Oak.†	.251	70	212	175	25	44	56	9	0	1	16	6	1	3	27	0	33	10	4	2	.320	.359
McGriff, Fred, T.B.*	.284	151	649	564	73	160	250	33	0	19	81	0	4	2	79	9	118	7	2	14	.443	.371
McLemore, Mark, Tex.†	.247	126	567	461	79	114	146	15	1	5	53	12	3	2	89	1	64	12	4	15	.317	.369
Meares, Pat, Min.	.260	149	581	543	56	141	200	26	3	9	70	3	5	6	24	1	86	7	4	12	.368	.296
Mecir, Jim, T.B.†	.000	68	1	1	0	0	0	0	0	0	0	0	0	0	0	0	0	0	0	0	.000	.000
Mendoza, Ramiro, N.Y.	.000	41	1	0	0	0	0	0	0	0	0	1	0	0	0	0	0	0	0	0	.000	.000
Merced, Orlando, Min.-Bos.* ..	.277	72	235	213	22	59	86	12	0	5	35	0	2	1	19	3	32	1	4	4	.404	.336
Merloni, Lou, Bos.	.281	100	96	10	27	36	6	0	1	15	1	0	2	7	1	20	1	0	1	.375	.343
Mientkiewicz, Doug, Min.*	.200	8	29	25	1	5	6	1	0	0	2	0	0	0	4	0	3	1	1	0	.240	.310
Milton, Eric, Min.*	.444	32	9	9	0	4	4	0	0	0	1	0	0	0	0	0	4	0	0	0	.444	.444
Minor, Ryan, Bal.	.429	9	14	14	3	6	7	1	0	0	1	0	0	0	0	0	3	0	0	0	.500	.429
Mitchell, Keith, Bos.	.273	23	40	33	4	9	11	2	0	0	6	0	0	0	7	1	5	1	0	0	.333	.400
Mitchell, Kevin, Oak.	.228	51	136	127	14	29	44	7	1	2	21	0	0	0	9	0	26	0	0	4	.346	.279
Moehler, Brian, Det.	.000	33	4	4	1	0	0	0	0	0	0	0	0	0	0	0	2	0	0	0	.000	.000
Molina, Ben, Ana.	.000	2	1	1	0	0	0	0	0	0	0	0	0	0	0	0	0	0	0	0	.000	.000
Molina, Izzy, Oak.	.500	6	2	2	1	1	1	0	0	0	0	0	0	0	0	0	0	0	0	0	.500	.500
Molitor, Paul, Min.	.281	126	559	502	75	141	192	29	5	4	69	1	10	1	45	5	41	9	2	19	.382	.335
Monahan, Shane, Sea.*	.242	62	223	211	17	51	73	8	1	4	28	4	0	0	8	0	53	1	2	0	.346	.269
Morgan, Mike, Min.	.500	18	2	2	1	1	1	0	0	0	0	0	0	0	0	0	1	0	0	0	.500	.500
Morris, Hal, K.C.*	.309	128	516	472	50	146	180	27	2	1	40	4	7	1	32	6	52	1	0	15	.381	.350
Mouton, Lyle, Bal.	.308	18	43	39	5	12	20	2	0	2	7	0	0	0	4	0	8	0	0	2	.513	.372
Moyer, Jamie, Sea.*	.000	34	2	2	0	0	0	0	0	0	0	0	0	0	0	0	0	0	0	0	.000	.000
Mussina, Mike, Bal.*	.000	29	2	2	0	0	0	0	0	0	0	0	0	0	0	0	0	0	0	0	.000	.000
Myers, Randy, Tor.*	.000	41	1	1	0	0	0	0	0	0	0	0	0	0	0	0	1	0	0	0	.000	.000
Nagy, Charles, Cle.*	.000	33	5	5	0	0	0	0	0	0	0	0	0	0	0	0	4	0	0	0	.000	.000
Navarro, Jaime, Chi.	.000	37	1	1	0	0	0	0	0	0	0	0	0	0	0	0	1	0	0	0	.000	.000
Neill, Mike, Oak.*	.267	6	17	15	2	4	5	1	0	0	0	0	0	0	2	0	4	0	0	0	.333	.353
Nelson, Jeff, N.Y.	.000	45	2	1	0	0	0	0	0	0	0	1	0	0	0	0	0	0	0	0	.000	.000
Nevin, Phil, Ana.	.228	75	261	237	27	54	88	8	1	8	27	0	2	5	17	0	67	0	0	6	.371	.291
Newson, Warren, Tex.*	.190	10	22	21	1	4	5	1	0	0	2	0	0	0	1	1	5	0	0	1	.238	.227
Nixon, Trot, Bos.*	.259	13	28	27	3	7	8	1	0	0	1	0	0	0	1	0	3	0	0	0	.296	.286
Nixon, Otis, Min.†	.297	110	500	448	71	133	154	6	6	1	20	4	2	2	44	0	56	37	7	14	.344	.361
Norton, Greg, Chi.†	.237	105	330	299	38	71	119	17	2	9	36	1	2	2	26	1	77	3	3	11	.398	.301
O'Brien, Charlie, Chi.-Ana. ...	.257	62	193	175	13	45	66	9	0	4	18	3	3	2	10	0	33	0	0	3	.377	.300
Ochoa, Alex, Min.	.257	94	260	249	35	64	88	14	2	2	25	0	0	1	10	0	35	6	3	7	.353	.288
Offerman, Jose, K.C.†	.315	158	709	607	102	191	266	28	13	7	66	2	6	5	89	1	96	45	12	7	.438	.403
O'Leary, Troy, Bos.*	.270	156	657	611	95	165	286	36	3	23	83	0	5	5	36	2	108	2	2	17	.468	.314
Olivares, Omar, Ana.	.000	40	3	2	1	0	0	0	0	0	0	0	0	0	1	0	1	0	0	0	.000	.333
Oliver, Darren, Tex.	.167	19	6	6	1	1	2	1	0	0	1	0	0	0	0	0	2	0	0	0	.333	.167
Oliver, Joe, Det.-Sea.	.225	79	263	240	20	54	83	11	0	6	32	2	4	0	17	0	48	1	1	8	.346	.272
O'Neill, Paul, N.Y.*	.317	152	672	602	95	191	307	40	2	24	116	0	11	2	57	2	103	15	1	22	.510	.372
Oquist, Mike, Oak.	.000	31	2	1	0	0	0	0	0	0	0	1	0	0	0	0	0	0	0	0	.000	.000
Ordonez, Magglio, Chi.	.282	145	578	535	70	151	222	25	2	14	65	2	4	9	28	1	53	9	7	19	.415	.326
Ortiz, David, Min.*	.277	86	326	278	47	77	124	20	0	9	46	0	4	5	39	3	72	1	0	8	.446	.371
Ortiz, Hector, K.C.	.000	4	4	4	1	0	0	0	0	0	0	0	0	0	0	0	1	0	0	0	.000	.000
Otanez, Willis, Bal.	.200	3	5	5	0	1	1	0	0	0	0	0	0	0	0	0	2	0	0	0	.200	.200
Palmeiro, Orlando, Ana.*	.321	75	192	165	28	53	64	7	2	0	21	7	0	0	20	1	11	5	4	2	.388	.395

Player, Team	Avg.	G	TPA	AB	R	H	TB	2B	3B	HR	RBI	SH	SF	HP	BB	IBB	SO	SB	CS	GDP	Slg.	OBP
Palmeiro, Rafael, Bal.*	.296	162	709	619	98	183	350	36	1	43	121	0	4	7	79	8	91	11	7	14	.565	.379
Palmer, Dean, K.C.	.278	152	639	572	84	159	292	27	2	34	119	0	13	6	48	3	134	8	2	18	.510	.333
Parque, Jim, Chi.*	.000	21	3	1	0	0	0	0	0	0	0	2	0	0	0	0	0	0	0	0	.000	.000
Pendleton, Terry, K.C.†	.257	79	254	237	17	61	80	10	0	3	29	0	2	0	15	1	49	1	0	2	.338	.299
Perez, Robert, Sea.	.171	17	35	35	3	6	13	1	0	2	6	0	0	0	0	0	5	0	0	1	.371	.171
Perez, Tomas, Tor.†	.111	6	11	9	1	1	1	0	0	0	0	1	0	0	1	0	3	0	0	1	.111	.200
Pettitte, Andy, N.Y.*	.000	33	6	4	0	0	0	0	0	0	0	2	0	0	0	0	3	0	0	0	.000	.000
Phillips, Tony, Tor.†	.354	13	60	48	9	17	25	5	0	1	7	0	1	2	9	1	6	0	0	2	.521	.467
Pichardo, Hipolito, K.C.	.000	27	2	2	0	0	0	0	0	0	0	0	0	0	0	0	2	0	0	0	.000	.000
Pickering, Calvin, Bal.*	.238	9	24	21	4	5	11	0	0	2	3	0	0	0	3	0	4	1	0	2	.524	.333
Pierzynski, A.J., Min.*	.300	7	13	10	1	3	3	0	0	0	1	0	1	1	1	0	2	0	0	0	.300	.385
Pittsley, Jim, K.C.	.000	39	3	2	0	0	0	0	0	0	0	1	0	0	0	0	2	0	0	0	.000	.000
Ponson, Sidney, Bal.	.500	31	4	4	1	2	2	0	0	0	0	0	0	0	0	0	2	0	0	0	.500	.500
Posada, Jorge, N.Y.†	.268	111	409	358	56	96	170	23	0	17	63	0	4	0	47	7	92	0	1	14	.475	.350
Powell, Brian, Det.	.000	18	1	1	0	0	0	0	0	0	0	0	0	0	0	0	1	0	0	0	.000	.000
Pritchett, Chris, Ana.*	.288	31	84	80	12	23	33	2	1	2	8	0	0	0	4	0	16	2	0	3	.413	.321
Radke, Brad, Min.	.000	32	2	2	0	0	0	0	0	0	0	0	0	0	0	0	1	0	0	0	.000	.000
Radmanovich, Ryan, Sea.*	.217	25	75	69	5	15	25	4	0	2	10	2	0	0	4	1	25	1	1	0	.362	.260
Raines, Tim, N.Y.†	.290	109	382	321	53	93	123	13	1	5	47	0	3	3	55	1	49	8	3	5	.383	.395
Ramirez, Alex, Cle.	.125	3	8	8	1	1	1	0	0	0	0	0	0	0	0	0	3	0	0	0	.125	.125
Ramirez, Manny, Cle.	.294	150	663	571	108	168	342	35	2	45	145	0	10	6	76	6	121	5	3	18	.599	.377
Randa, Joe, Det.	.254	138	514	460	56	117	169	21	2	9	50	3	3	7	41	1	70	8	7	9	.367	.323
Rapp, Pat, K.C.	.000	32	3	2	0	0	0	0	0	0	0	0	1	0	0	0	1	0	0	0	.000	.000
Reboulet, Jeff, Bal.	.246	79	155	126	20	31	40	6	0	1	8	7	1	2	19	0	34	0	1	3	.317	.351
Rhodes, Arthur, Bal.*	.500	45	2	2	0	1	1	0	0	0	0	0	0	0	0	0	1	0	0	0	.500	.500
Ripken, Cal, Bal.	.271	161	659	601	65	163	234	27	1	14	61	1	2	4	51	0	68	0	2	9	.389	.331
Ripken, Billy, Det.	.270	27	81	74	8	20	23	3	0	0	5	0	1	1	5	0	10	3	2	2	.311	.321
Rivera, Luis, K.C.	.247	42	98	89	14	22	26	4	0	0	7	2	0	0	7	0	17	1	1	1	.292	.302
Roberts, Bip, Det.-Oak.†	.268	95	333	295	45	79	99	17	0	1	24	2	1	4	31	0	38	16	4	7	.336	.344
Robinson, Kerry, T.B.*	.000	2	3	3	0	0	0	0	0	0	0	0	0	0	0	0	1	0	0	0	.000	.000
Rodriguez, Alex, Sea.	.310	161	748	686	123	213	384	35	5	42	124	3	4	10	45	0	121	46	13	12	.560	.360
Rodriguez, Ivan, Tex.	.321	145	617	579	88	186	297	40	4	21	91	0	3	3	32	4	88	9	0	18	.513	.358
Rogers, Kenny, Oak.*	.000	34	4	4	1	0	0	0	0	0	0	0	0	0	0	0	2	0	0	0	.000	.000
Romero, Mandy, Bos.†	.231	12	16	13	2	3	4	1	0	0	1	0	0	0	3	0	3	0	0	1	.308	.375
Rosado, Jose, K.C.*	.500	38	2	2	0	1	1	0	0	0	0	0	0	0	0	0	1	0	0	0	.500	.500
Rossy, Rico, Sea.	.198	37	89	81	12	16	25	6	0	1	4	2	0	0	6	0	13	0	0	0	.309	.253
Rusch, Glendon, K.C.*	.000	29	3	3	0	0	0	0	0	0	0	0	0	0	0	0	1	0	0	0	.000	.000
Saberhagen, Bret, Bos.	.000	31	5	5	0	0	0	0	0	0	0	0	0	0	0	0	2	0	0	0	.000	.000
Sadler, Donnie, Bos.	.226	58	139	124	21	28	49	4	4	3	15	5	1	3	6	0	28	4	0	1	.395	.276
Sager, A.J., Det.	.000	31	1	1	0	0	0	0	0	0	0	0	0	0	0	0	0	0	0	0	.000	.000
Salmon, Tim, Ana.	.300	136	566	463	84	139	247	28	1	26	88	0	10	3	90	5	100	0	1	4	.533	.410
Samuel, Juan, Tor.	.180	43	59	50	14	9	14	2	0	1	2	1	0	1	7	0	13	13	6	0	.280	.293
Santana, Julio, Tex.-T.B.	.000	35	4	4	0	0	0	0	0	0	0	0	0	0	0	0	3	0	0	0	.000	.000
Santiago, Benito, Tor.	.310	15	30	29	3	9	14	5	0	0	4	0	0	0	1	0	6	0	0	1	.483	.333
Sasser, Rob, Tex.	.000	1	1	1	0	0	0	0	0	0	0	0	0	0	0	0	0	0	0	0	.000	.000
Saunders, Tony, T.B.*	1.000	31	2	2	0	2	2	2	0	0	0	0	0	0	0	0	0	0	0	0	1.000	1.000
Segui, David, Sea.†	.305	143	580	522	79	159	254	36	1	19	84	0	9	0	49	4	80	3	1	12	.487	.359
Sele, Aaron, Tex.	.250	33	4	4	0	1	2	1	0	0	0	0	0	0	0	0	0	0	0	0	.500	.250
Serafini, Dan, Min.†	.000	28	1	1	0	0	0	0	0	0	0	0	0	0	0	0	0	0	0	0	.000	.000
Service, Scott, K.C.	.000	73	1	1	0	0	0	0	0	0	0	0	0	0	0	0	1	0	0	0	.000	.000
Sexson, Richie, Cle.	.310	49	183	174	28	54	103	14	1	11	35	0	0	3	6	0	42	1	1	3	.592	.344
Shave, Jon, Min.	.250	19	43	40	7	10	16	3	0	1	5	0	0	3	0	0	10	1	2	0	.400	.302
Sheldon, Scott, Tex.	.125	7	17	16	0	2	2	0	0	0	1	0	0	0	1	0	6	0	0	1	.125	.176
Shipley, Craig, Ana.	.259	77	162	147	18	38	53	7	1	2	17	4	1	5	5	0	22	0	4	3	.361	.304
Shuey, Paul, Cle.	.000	43	1	1	0	0	0	0	0	0	0	0	0	0	0	0	0	0	0	0	.000	.000
Siddall, Joe, Det.*	.185	29	74	65	3	12	18	3	0	1	6	2	0	0	7	0	25	0	0	1	.277	.264
Sierra, Ruben, Chi.†	.216	27	77	74	7	16	34	4	1	4	11	0	0	0	3	0	11	2	0	2	.459	.247
Silvestri, Dave, T.B.	.071	8	14	14	0	1	1	0	0	0	0	0	0	0	0	0	2	0	0	1	.071	.071
Simmons, Brian, Chi.†	.368	5	19	19	4	7	13	0	0	2	6	0	0	0	0	0	2	0	1	0	.684	.368
Simms, Mike, Tex.	.296	86	215	186	36	55	114	11	0	16	46	0	2	3	24	0	47	0	1	4	.613	.381
Sirotka, Mike, Chi.*	.000	33	5	4	0	0	0	0	0	0	0	1	0	0	0	0	1	0	0	0	.000	.200
Smith, Pete, Bal.	.000	27	2	2	0	0	0	0	0	0	0	0	0	0	0	0	1	0	0	0	.000	.000
Smith, Bobby, T.B.	.276	117	416	370	44	102	156	15	3	11	55	2	4	6	34	0	110	5	5	9	.422	.343
Snopek, Chris, Chi.-Bos.	.204	61	155	137	19	28	33	2	0	1	6	0	1	1	16	0	29	3	0	4	.241	.290
Sojo, Luis, N.Y.	.231	54	153	147	16	34	39	3	1	0	14	1	1	0	4	0	15	1	0	5	.265	.250
Sorrento, Paul, T.B.*	.225	137	495	435	40	98	176	27	0	17	57	0	3	3	54	1	133	2	3	8	.405	.313
Sparks, Steve, Ana.	.000	22	3	1	1	0	0	0	0	0	0	1	0	0	1	0	1	0	0	0	.000	.500
Spehr, Tim, K.C.	.240	11	36	25	5	6	11	2	0	1	2	1	0	2	8	0	3	0	0	1	.440	.457
Spencer, Shane, N.Y.	.373	27	73	67	18	25	61	6	0	10	27	0	1	0	5	0	12	0	1	0	.910	.411
Spiezio, Scott, Oak.†	.259	114	461	406	54	105	153	19	1	9	50	7	2	2	44	3	56	1	3	10	.377	.333
Sprague, Ed Jr., Tor.-Oak.	.222	132	510	469	57	104	189	25	0	20	58	0	2	13	26	2	90	1	2	16	.403	.280
Springer, Dennis, T.B.	.000	29	1	1	0	0	0	0	0	0	0	0	0	0	0	0	1	0	0	0	.000	.000
Stahoviak, Scott, Min.*	.105	9	19	19	1	2	5	0	0	1	1	0	0	0	0	0	7	0	0	0	.263	.105
Stairs, Matt, Oak.*	.294	149	593	523	88	154	267	33	1	26	106	1	4	6	59	4	93	8	3	13	.511	.370
Stanley, Mike, Tor.-Bos.	.256	145	593	497	74	127	239	25	0	29	79	0	7	7	82	5	129	3	1	12	.481	.364
Stanton, Mike, N.Y.*	.000	67	1	1	0	0	0	0	0	0	0	0	0	0	0	0	1	0	0	0	.000	.000
Stein, Blake, Oak.	.000	24	6	5	0	0	0	0	0	0	0	1	0	0	0	0	4	0	0	0	.000	.000
Steinbach, Terry, Min.	.242	124	465	422	45	102	173	25	2	14	54	0	1	4	38	0	89	0	1	16	.410	.310
Stevens, Lee, Tex.*	.265	120	376	344	52	91	176	17	4	20	59	0	1	0	31	4	93	0	2	6	.512	.324
Stewart, Shannon, Tor.	.279	144	605	516	90	144	215	29	3	12	55	6	1	15	67	1	77	51	18	5	.417	.371
Stieb, Dave, Tor.	.000	19	1	1	0	0	0	0	0	0	0	0	0	0	0	0	0	0	0	0	.000	.000
Stocker, Kevin, T.B.†	.208	112	381	336	37	70	105	11	3	6	25	8	2	8	27	1	80	5	3	7	.313	.282

Player, Team	Avg.	G	TPA	AB	R	H	TB	2B	3B	HR	RBI	SH	SF	HP	BB	IBB	SO	SB	CS	GDP	Slg.	OBP
Strawberry, Darryl, N.Y.*	.247	101	345	295	44	73	160	11	2	24	57	0	1	3	46	4	90	8	7	1	.542	.354
Surhoff, B.J., Bal.*	.279	162	634	573	79	160	262	34	1	22	92	1	10	1	49	9	81	9	7	13	.457	.332
Sutton, Larry, K.C.*	.245	111	351	310	29	76	109	14	2	5	42	4	5	3	29	3	46	3	3	5	.352	.311
Sveum, Dale, N.Y.†	.155	30	64	58	6	9	9	0	0	0	3	0	2	0	4	0	16	0	0	2	.155	.203
Sweeney, Mike, K.C.	.259	92	311	282	32	73	115	18	0	8	35	2	1	2	24	1	38	2	3	7	.408	.320
Swift, Bill, Sea.	.000	29	5	5	0	0	0	0	0	0	0	0	0	0	0	0	2	0	0	0	.000	.000
Tatis, Fernando, Tex.	.270	95	350	330	41	89	119	17	2	3	32	4	0	4	12	2	66	6	2	10	.361	.303
Tavarez, Jesus, Bal.†	.182	8	13	11	2	2	5	0	0	1	1	0	0	0	2	0	3	0	1	0	.455	.308
Tejada, Miguel, Oak.	.233	105	407	365	53	85	140	20	1	11	45	4	3	7	28	0	86	5	6	8	.384	.298
Tewksbury, Bob, Min.	.000	26	1	1	0	0	0	0	0	0	0	0	0	0	0	0	1	0	0	0	.000	.000
Thomas, Frank, Chi.	.265	160	712	585	109	155	281	35	2	29	109	0	11	6	110	2	93	7	0	14	.480	.381
Thome, Jim, Cle.*	.293	123	537	440	89	129	257	34	2	30	85	0	4	4	89	8	141	1	0	7	.584	.413
Thompson, Justin, Det.*	.143	34	7	7	1	1	1	0	0	0	0	0	0	0	0	0	3	0	0	0	.143	.143
Tomberlin, Andy, Det.*	.217	32	75	69	8	15	23	2	0	2	12	0	0	3	3	1	25	1	0	3	.333	.280
Trammell, Bubba, T.B.	.286	59	216	199	28	57	113	18	1	12	35	0	1	0	16	0	45	0	2	4	.568	.338
Tremie, Chris, Tex.	.333	2	4	3	2	1	2	1	0	0	0	0	0	0	1	0	1	0	0	0	.667	.500
Turner, Chris, K.C.	.000	4	10	9	0	0	0	0	0	0	0	0	0	0	1	0	4	0	0	1	.000	.100
Valentin, John, Bos.	.247	153	681	588	113	145	260	44	1	23	73	2	5	9	77	3	82	4	5	9	.442	.340
Valentin, Javier, Min.†	.198	55	177	162	11	32	50	7	1	3	18	3	1	0	11	1	30	0	0	7	.309	.247
Van Poppel, Todd, Cle.	.000	4	4	2	1	0	0	0	0	0	0	0	0	0	0	0	0	0	0	0	.000	.000
Varitek, Jason, Bos.†	.253	86	247	221	31	56	90	13	0	7	33	4	3	2	17	1	45	2	2	8	.407	.309
Vaughn, Mo, Bos.*	.337	154	681	609	107	205	360	31	2	40	115	0	3	8	61	13	144	0	0	13	.591	.402
Velandia, Jorge, Oak.	.250	8	4	4	0	1	1	0	0	0	0	0	0	0	0	0	1	0	0	0	.250	.250
Velarde, Randy, Ana.	.261	51	224	188	29	49	76	13	1	4	26	0	1	1	34	0	42	7	2	8	.404	.375
Ventura, Robin, Chi.*	.263	161	674	590	84	155	257	31	4	21	91	1	3	1	79	15	111	1	1	10	.436	.349
Vitiello, Joe, K.C.	.143	3	8	7	0	1	1	0	0	0	0	0	0	0	1	0	2	0	0	0	.143	.250
Vizquel, Omar, Cle.†	.288	151	660	576	86	166	214	30	6	2	50	12	6	4	62	1	64	37	12	10	.372	.358
Voigt, Jack, Oak.	.139	57	79	72	7	10	17	4	0	1	10	1	0	0	6	0	19	5	1	1	.236	.205
Wakefield, Tim, Bos.	.000	37	5	2	0	0	0	0	0	0	0	2	0	0	1	0	2	0	0	0	.000	.333
Walbeck, Matt, Ana.†	.257	108	380	338	41	87	124	15	2	6	46	5	5	2	30	0	68	1	1	9	.367	.317
Walker, Todd, Min.*	.316	143	581	528	85	167	250	41	3	12	62	0	4	2	47	9	65	19	7	13	.473	.372
Walton, Jerome, T.B.	.324	12	36	34	4	11	14	3	0	0	3	0	0	2	0	6	0	0	1	.412	.361
Wasdin, John, Bos.	.000	47	1	0	1	0	0	0	0	0	0	0	0	0	1	0	0	0	0	0	.000	1.000
Washburn, Jarrod, Ana.*	.000	15	3	1	0	0	0	0	0	0	0	2	0	0	0	0	1	0	0	0	.000	.000
Webster, Lenny, Bal.	.285	108	328	309	37	88	134	16	0	10	46	3	1	0	15	0	38	0	0	10	.434	.317
Wells, David, N.Y.*	.250	30	4	4	0	1	1	0	0	0	0	0	0	0	0	0	1	0	0	0	.250	.250
White, Rick, T.B.	.333	38	3	3	0	1	1	0	0	0	0	0	0	0	0	0	1	0	0	1	.333	.333
Whiten, Mark, Cle.†	.283	88	259	226	31	64	96	14	0	6	29	1	0	3	29	0	60	2	1	7	.425	.372
Wilkins, Rick, Sea.*	.195	19	46	41	5	8	14	1	1	1	4	0	1	0	4	0	14	0	0	1	.341	.261
Williams, Bernie, N.Y.†	.339	128	578	499	101	169	287	30	5	26	97	0	4	1	74	9	81	15	9	19	.575	.422
Williams, Woody, Tor.	.333	32	6	6	0	2	2	0	0	0	0	0	0	0	0	0	1	0	0	0	.333	.333
Williams, Reggie, Ana.†	.361	29	45	36	7	13	17	1	0	1	5	1	0	1	7	0	11	3	3	0	.472	.477
Wilson, Craig, Chi.	.468	13	53	47	14	22	36	5	0	3	10	2	1	0	3	0	6	1	0	0	.766	.490
Wilson, Dan, Sea.	.252	96	368	325	39	82	128	17	1	9	44	8	6	5	24	0	56	2	1	6	.394	.308
Wilson, Enrique, Cle.†	.322	32	97	90	13	29	41	6	0	2	12	1	1	1	4	0	8	2	4	1	.456	.354
Winn, Randy, T.B.†	.278	109	379	338	51	94	124	9	9	1	17	11	0	1	29	0	69	26	12	2	.367	.337
Witt, Kevin, Tor.*	.143	5	7	7	0	1	1	0	0	0	0	0	0	0	0	0	3	0	0	0	.143	.143
Witt, Bobby, Tex.	.000	15	1	1	0	0	0	0	0	0	0	0	0	0	0	0	0	0	0	0	.000	.000
Wood, Jason, Oak.-Det.	.333	13	27	24	6	8	13	2	0	1	1	0	0	0	3	0	5	0	1	0	.542	.407
Wright, Jaret, Cle.	.429	32	7	7	2	3	3	0	0	0	1	0	0	0	0	0	2	0	0	0	.429	.429
Young, Ernie, K.C.	.189	25	56	53	2	10	16	3	0	1	3	0	0	1	2	0	9	2	1	3	.302	.232
Zeile, Todd, Tex.	.261	52	213	180	26	47	81	14	1	6	28	1	3	1	28	0	32	0	0	3	.450	.358

AWARDED FIRST BASE ON OBSTRUCTION OR CATCHER'S INTERFERENCE—Erstad, Anaheim 2 (Hoiles, Fletcher); Lewis, Boston 2 (Widger, Bako); J. Abbott, Chicago (Fletcher); Cordova, Minnesota (Girardi); Cummings, Boston (Borders); DiFelice, Tampa Bay (Marzano); Higginson, Detroit (Valentin); Macfarlane, K.C.-Oak. (Diaz).

PLAYERS WITH TWO OR MORE TEAMS

Player, Team	Avg.	G	TPA	AB	R	H	TB	2B	3B	HR	RBI	SH	SF	HP	BB	IBB	SO	SB	CS	GDP	Slg.	OBP
Bell, David, Cle.	.262	107	370	340	37	89	144	21	2	10	41	1	5	2	22	4	54	0	4	8	.424	.306
Bell, David, Sea.	.325	21	85	80	11	26	34	8	0	0	8	0	0	0	5	0	8	0	0	3	.425	.365
Berroa, Geronimo, Cle.	.200	20	72	65	6	13	18	3	1	0	3	0	0	0	7	0	17	1	0	2	.277	.278
Berroa, Geronimo, Det.	.238	52	145	126	17	30	39	4	1	1	10	0	0	2	17	1	27	0	1	3	.310	.338
Cora, Joey, Sea.†	.283	131	598	519	95	147	200	23	6	6	26	10	3	4	62	0	50	13	5	2	.385	.362
Cora, Joey, Cle.†	.229	24	97	83	16	19	23	4	0	0	6	2	0	1	11	0	9	2	1	3	.277	.326
Fielder, Cecil, Ana.	.241	103	439	381	48	92	161	16	1	17	68	0	3	3	52	1	98	0	1	17	.423	.335
Fielder, Cecil, Cle.	.143	14	37	35	1	5	6	1	0	0	0	0	0	1	1	0	13	0	0	1	.171	.189
Guzman, Juan, Bal.	.000	11	0	0	0	0	0	0	0	0	0	0	0	0	0	0	0	0	0	0	.000	.000
Guzman, Juan, Tor.	.000	22	2	2	0	0	0	0	0	0	0	2	0	0	0	0	0	0	0	0	.000	.000
Kreuter, Chad, Chi.†	.253	93	286	245	26	62	79	9	1	2	33	5	1	3	32	1	45	1	0	8	.322	.345
Kreuter, Chad, Ana.†	.143	3	8	7	1	1	2	1	0	0	0	0	0	0	1	0	4	0	0	0	.286	.250
Macfarlane, Mike, K.C.	.091	3	11	11	1	1	1	0	0	0	0	0	0	0	0	0	2	0	0	0	.091	.091
Macfarlane, Mike, Oak.	.251	78	227	207	28	52	85	12	0	7	34	1	3	4	12	0	34	1	0	3	.411	.301
Mack, Shane, Oak.	.000	3	2	2	1	0	0	0	0	0	0	0	0	0	0	0	0	0	0	0	.000	.000
Mack, Shane, K.C.	.280	66	229	207	30	58	93	15	1	6	29	0	1	6	15	0	36	8	2	6	.449	.345
Manto, Jeff, Cle.	.216	15	39	37	8	8	15	1	0	2	6	0	0	2	0	10	0	1	4	.405	.256
Manto, Jeff, Det.	.267	16	34	30	6	8	13	2	0	1	3	0	1	0	3	0	11	1	0	1	.433	.353
Merced, Orlando, Min.*	.289	63	223	204	22	59	86	12	0	5	33	0	1	1	17	3	29	1	4	4	.422	.345
Merced, Orlando, Bos.*	.000	9	12	9	0	0	0	0	0	0	2	0	1	0	2	0	3	0	0	0	.000	.167
O'Brien, Charlie, Chi.	.262	57	181	164	12	43	64	9	0	4	18	3	2	9	0	31	0	0	3	.390	.303
O'Brien, Charlie, Ana.	.182	5	12	11	1	2	2	0	0	0	0	0	0	1	0	2	0	0	0	.182	.250
Oliver, Joe, Det.	.226	50	166	155	8	35	55	8	0	4	22	0	4	0	7	0	33	0	1	5	.355	.253
Oliver, Joe, Sea.	.224	29	97	85	12	19	28	3	0	2	10	2	0	0	10	0	15	1	0	3	.329	.305

Player, Team	Avg.	G	TPA	AB	R	H	TB	2B	3B	HR	RBI	SH	SF	HP	BB	IBB	SO	SB	CS	GDP	Slg.	OBP
Roberts, Bip, Det.†	.248	34	132	113	17	28	34	6	0	0	9	1	0	2	16	0	14	6	1	3	.301	.351
Roberts, Bip, Oak.†	.280	61	201	182	28	51	65	11	0	1	15	1	1	2	15	0	24	10	3	4	.357	.340
Santana, Julio, Tex.	.000	3	0	0	0	0	0	0	0	0	0	0	0	0	0	0	0	0	0	0	.000	.000
Santana, Julio, T.B.	.000	32	4	4	0	0	0	0	0	0	0	0	0	0	0	0	3	0	0	0	.000	.000
Snopek, Chris, Chi.	.208	53	141	125	17	26	31	2	0	1	4	0	1	1	14	0	24	3	0	4	.248	.291
Snopek, Chris, Bos.	.167	8	14	12	2	2	2	0	0	0	2	0	0	0	2	0	5	0	0	0	.167	.286
Sprague, Ed, Tor.	.238	105	419	382	49	91	162	20	0	17	51	0	2	11	24	1	73	0	2	15	.424	.301
Sprague, Ed, Oak.	.149	27	91	87	8	13	27	5	0	3	7	0	0	2	2	1	17	1	0	1	.310	.187
Stanley, Mike, Tor.	.240	98	405	341	49	82	161	13	0	22	47	0	3	5	56	3	86	2	1	6	.472	.353
Stanley, Mike, Bos.	.288	47	188	156	25	45	78	12	0	7	32	0	4	2	26	2	43	1	0	6	.500	.388
Wood, Jason, Oak.	.000	3	1	1	1	0	0	0	0	0	0	0	0	0	0	0	1	0	0	0	.000	.000
Wood, Jason, Det.	.348	10	26	23	5	8	13	2	0	1	1	0	0	0	3	0	4	0	1	0	.565	.423

DESIGNATED HITTING

TEAM

Team	Avg.	G	TPA	AB	R	H	TB	2B	3B	HR	RBI	SH	SF	HP	BB	IBB	SO	SB	CS	GDP	Slg.	OBP
Seattle	.312	153	683	568	91	177	308	45	1	28	102	0	7	3	105	3	100	2	1	13	.542	.417
Baltimore	.307	154	686	618	93	190	291	29	4	24	109	0	4	5	59	4	107	4	3	24	.471	.370
Texas	.295	154	663	587	100	173	309	37	6	29	112	1	6	4	65	7	129	1	3	15	.526	.366
Anaheim	.288	154	682	565	95	163	278	36	2	25	100	1	10	5	101	5	128	2	2	9	.492	.395
Boston	.282	154	672	577	91	163	288	33	1	30	97	1	6	4	84	6	140	8	2	19	.499	.374
Minnesota	.279	154	688	620	85	173	235	35	6	5	83	1	11	2	54	7	62	11	2	21	.379	.333
Oakland	.278	154	676	597	103	166	288	36	1	28	110	0	4	4	71	4	109	8	4	17	.482	.357
New York	.276	154	672	568	89	157	280	24	3	31	93	0	7	4	93	5	130	13	12	9	.493	.378
Detroit	.270	154	659	585	83	158	243	32	1	17	71	2	5	7	60	5	119	15	7	15	.415	.342
Kansas City	.269	154	672	606	81	163	245	29	1	17	91	2	6	1	57	4	117	6	3	15	.404	.330
Cleveland	.268	154	688	601	100	161	266	46	1	19	87	0	7	3	77	6	121	9	3	12	.443	.350
Tampa Bay	.265	154	656	586	70	155	254	47	2	16	73	0	3	3	64	3	145	10	6	9	.433	.338
Chicago	.259	155	690	571	102	148	268	34	4	26	99	0	10	6	103	2	91	5	1	12	.469	.372
Toronto	.228	155	680	597	94	136	287	22	0	43	101	1	6	8	68	1	170	14	13	6	.481	.312
Totals	.277	1078	9467	8246	1277	2283	3840	485	29	338	1328	9	92	59	1061	68	1668	108	62	196	.466	.360

TOP DESIGNATED HITTERS

Minimum 100 at-bats. *Lefthanded batter. †Switch-hitter.

Player, Team	Avg.	G	TPA	AB	R	H	TB	2B	3B	HR	RBI	SH	SF	HP	BB	IBB	SO	SB	CS	GDP	Slg.	OBP
Davis, Eric, Bal.	.335	54	208	194	32	65	102	10	0	9	37	0	3	3	8	0	49	2	2	5	.526	.365
Boggs, Wade, T.B.*	.333	33	145	132	17	44	65	8	2	3	19	0	1	0	12	2	17	2	0	1	.492	.386
Gonzalez, Juan, Tex.	.329	38	163	143	28	47	85	12	1	8	39	0	3	3	14	2	35	0	1	5	.594	.393
Martinez, Edgar, Sea.	.320	147	652	540	83	173	303	44	1	28	100	0	7	3	102	3	93	1	1	13	.561	.426
Baines, Harold, Bal.*	.308	80	305	273	38	84	125	14	0	9	52	0	1	1	30	3	33	0	0	17	.458	.377
Stevens, Lee, Tex.*	.305	72	260	236	38	72	139	14	4	15	48	0	0	0	24	4	57	0	2	4	.589	.369
Salmon, Tim, Ana.	.304	111	483	398	69	121	207	27	1	19	75	0	10	2	73	5	82	0	1	4	.520	.406
Stairs, Matt, Oak.*	.298	120	510	450	79	134	235	30	1	23	89	0	3	4	53	4	76	7	3	12	.522	.375
Morris, Hal, K.C.*	.298	39	175	161	19	48	59	8	0	1	16	2	1	0	11	2	17	0	0	7	.366	.341
Jefferson, Reggie, Bos.*	.298	48	189	171	20	51	86	12	1	7	23	0	1	0	17	1	35	0	0	7	.503	.360
Davis, Chili, N.Y.†	.294	34	117	102	11	30	46	7	0	3	9	0	1	0	14	1	18	0	1	6	.451	.376
Raines, Tim, N.Y.†	.289	56	191	159	25	46	63	6	1	3	25	0	2	2	28	0	22	2	1	1	.396	.398
Justice, David, Cle.*	.287	123	532	460	83	132	223	38	1	17	75	0	7	0	65	6	81	8	3	8	.485	.370
Leyritz, Jim, Bos.	.284	39	138	116	16	33	62	5	0	8	23	0	4	1	17	1	32	0	0	4	.534	.370
Molitor, Paul, Min.	.279	115	521	466	70	130	179	27	5	4	67	1	10	0	44	5	36	9	2	17	.384	.335

ALL DESIGNATED HITTERS

*Lefthanded batter. †Switch-hitter.

Player, Team	Avg.	G	TPA	AB	R	H	TB	2B	3B	HR	RBI	SH	SF	HP	BB	IBB	SO	SB	CS	GDP	Slg.	OBP
Abbott, Jeff, Chi.	.000	2	2	2	0	0	0	0	0	0	0	0	0	0	0	0	0	1	0	0	.000	.000
Abbott, Kurt, Oak.	.286	3	15	14	2	4	5	1	0	0	0	0	0	0	0	0	3	0	0	1	.357	.333
Alicea, Luis, Tex.†	.206	18	41	34	4	7	10	1	1	0	3	0	1	0	6	0	6	0	0	0	.294	.317
Alomar, Roberto, Bal.†	.222	3	10	9	1	2	3	1	0	0	1	0	0	0	1	0	1	0	0	0	.333	.300
Alomar, Sandy Jr., Cle.	.300	3	11	10	1	3	6	0	0	1	6	0	0	0	1	0	2	0	0	0	.600	.364
Alvarez, Gabe, Det.	.364	2	12	11	1	4	8	1	0	1	2	0	0	0	1	0	3	1	0	0	.727	.417
Amaral, Rich, Sea.	.000	5	1	1	3	0	0	0	0	0	0	0	0	0	0	0	0	0	0	0	.000	.000
Anderson, Brady, Bal.*	.000	1	0	0	0	0	0	0	0	0	0	0	0	0	0	0	0	0	0	0	.000	.000
Ashley, Billy, Bos.	.375	5	17	16	3	6	17	2	0	3	6	0	0	0	1	0	8	0	0	0	1.063	.412
Baines, Harold, Bal.*	.308	80	305	273	38	84	125	14	0	9	52	0	1	1	30	3	33	0	0	17	.458	.377
Bartee, Kimera, Det.†	.222	10	20	18	2	4	7	0	0	1	6	0	1	0	1	0	5	1	4	0	.389	.250
Baughman, Justin, Ana.	.000	1	1	0	1	0	0	0	0	0	0	1	0	0	0	0	0	0	1	0	.000	.000
Beamon, Trey, Det.*	.348	11	28	23	2	8	11	3	0	0	2	1	0	0	4	0	9	0	0	1	.478	.444
Becker, Rich, Bal.*	.333	2	3	3	1	1	1	0	0	0	0	0	0	0	0	0	0	0	0	0	.333	.333
Belle, Albert, Chi.	.267	4	17	15	3	4	5	1	0	0	0	0	0	0	2	0	1	0	1	0	.333	.353
Bellhorn, Mark, Oak.†	.000	2	2	2	0	0	0	0	0	0	0	0	0	0	0	0	1	1	0	0	.000	.000
Benjamin, Mike, Bos.	.000	2	1	1	1	0	0	0	0	0	0	0	0	0	0	0	0	0	0	0	.000	.000
Berroa, Geronimo, Cle.-Det.	.246	42	147	130	17	32	41	4	1	1	11	0	0	2	15	1	32	0	0	1	.315	.333
Blowers, Mike, Oak.	.286	2	8	7	1	2	3	1	0	0	0	0	0	0	1	0	0	0	0	0	.429	.375
Boggs, Wade, T.B.*	.333	33	145	132	17	44	65	8	2	3	19	0	1	0	12	2	17	2	0	1	.492	.386
Bolick, Frank, Ana.†	.167	9	23	18	2	3	5	2	0	0	1	0	0	0	5	0	3	0	0	0	.278	.348
Bournigal, Rafael, Oak.	.000	1	1	0	1	0	0	0	0	0	0	0	0	0	1	0	0	0	0	0	.000	1.000
Bragg, Darren, Bos.*	.000	4	4	4	0	0	0	0	0	0	0	0	0	0	0	0	3	0	0	0	.000	.000
Brown, Dermal, K.C.*	.000	3	2	2	1	0	0	0	0	0	0	0	0	0	0	0	1	0	0	0	.000	.000
Buford, Damon, Bos.	.111	15	10	9	3	1	1	0	0	0	0	0	0	0	1	0	2	1	0	0	.111	.200
Buhner, Jay, Sea.	.000	1	5	5	0	0	0	0	0	0	0	0	0	0	0	0	2	0	0	0	.000	.000
Bush, Homer, N.Y.	.000	13	4	3	5	0	0	0	0	0	0	0	0	0	0	0	2	2	3	0	.000	.250
Cairo, Miguel, T.B.	.000	2	1	1	0	0	0	0	0	0	0	0	0	0	0	0	0	0	0	0	.000	.000
Canseco, Jose, Tor.	.219	78	348	319	51	70	158	13	0	25	57	0	3	3	23	4	94	9	10	2	.495	.276
Carter, Joe, Bal.	.286	32	104	98	11	28	47	4	0	5	14	0	0	1	5	1	13	1	1	1	.480	.327
Catalanotto, Frank, Det.*	.343	23	78	70	10	24	36	9	0	1	8	0	2	1	5	1	9	1	0	1	.514	.385
Cedeno, Domingo, Tex.†	.200	15	17	15	4	3	4	1	0	0	0	1	0	0	1	0	3	1	0	0	.267	.250
Clark, Tony, Det.†	.269	15	60	52	10	14	30	1	0	5	11	0	1	0	7	1	10	0	0	3	.577	.350
Clark, Will, Tex.*	.294	15	60	51	6	15	22	4	0	1	6	0	1	0	8	0	12	0	0	1	.431	.383
Clyburn, Danny, Bal.	.250	1	5	4	2	1	1	0	0	0	0	0	0	0	1	0	1	0	0	0	.250	.400
Conine, Jeff, K.C.	.250	3	12	12	0	3	4	1	0	0	1	0	0	0	0	0	4	0	0	1	.333	.250

Player, Team	Avg.	G	TPA	AB	R	H	TB	2B	3B	HR	RBI	SH	SF	HP	BB	IBB	SO	SB	CS	GDP	Slg.	OBP
Coomer, Ron, Min.	.306	13	50	49	3	15	20	2	0	1	6	0	1	0	0	0	4	0	0	2	.408	.300
Cordova, Marty, Min.	.235	4	18	17	2	4	5	1	0	0	1	0	0	0	1	1	4	0	0	1	.294	.278
Crespo, Felipe, Tor.†	.000	2	2	2	0	0	0	0	0	0	0	0	0	0	0	0	2	0	0	0	.000	.000
Cummings, Midre, Bos.*	.294	31	82	68	13	20	32	3	0	3	6	1	0	1	12	0	9	3	2	1	.471	.407
Curtis, Chad, N.Y.	.500	2	4	2	1	1	4	0	0	1	3	0	0	0	2	0	1	0	0	0	2.000	.750
Cuyler, Milt, Tex.†	.000	3	0	0	1	0	0	0	0	0	0	0	0	0	0	0	0	0	0	0	.000	.000
Davis, Chili, N.Y.†	.294	34	117	102	11	30	46	7	0	3	9	0	1	0	14	1	18	0	1	6	.451	.376
Davis, Eric, Bal.	.335	54	208	194	32	65	102	10	0	9	37	0	3	3	8	0	49	2	2	5	.526	.365
Delgado, Carlos, Tor.*	.500	1	5	4	0	2	2	0	0	0	2	0	0	0	1	0	1	0	0	0	.500	.600
Dunston, Shawon, Cle.	.133	7	16	15	2	2	4	2	0	0	0	0	0	0	1	0	2	1	0	0	.267	.188
Easley, Damion, Det.	.286	2	7	7	0	2	2	0	0	0	0	0	0	0	0	0	1	0	0	2	.286	.286
Encarnacion, Juan, Det.	.000	1	1	1	0	0	0	0	0	0	0	0	0	0	0	0	0	0	0	0	.000	.000
Erstad, Darin, Ana.*	.556	2	9	9	2	5	11	0	0	2	2	0	0	0	0	0	1	0	0	0	1.222	.556
Fernandez, Tony, Tor.†	.000	1	5	4	0	0	0	0	0	0	0	0	0	1	0	0	1	0	0	0	.000	.200
Fick, Rob, Det.*	.375	2	8	8	3	3	7	1	0	1	2	0	0	0	0	0	3	1	0	1	.875	.375
Fielder, Cecil, Ana.-Cle.	.230	41	158	135	16	31	52	7	1	4	20	0	0	2	21	0	44	0	0	5	.385	.342
Fletcher, Darrin, Tor.*	.000	1	4	4	0	0	0	0	0	0	0	0	0	0	0	0	0	0	0	0	.000	.000
Frazier, Lou, Chi.†	.000	1	0	0	0	0	0	0	0	0	0	0	0	0	0	0	0	0	0	0	.000	.000
Fryman, Travis, Cle.	.250	2	8	8	1	2	3	1	0	0	0	0	0	0	0	0	4	0	0	0	.375	.250
Garcia, Carlos, Ana.	.000	3	0	0	1	0	0	0	0	0	0	0	0	0	0	0	0	0	0	0	.000	.000
Gates, Brent, Min.†	1.000	2	2	2	0	2	2	0	0	0	0	0	0	0	0	0	0	1	0	0	1.000	1.000
Giambi, Jason, Oak.*	.250	7	32	28	7	7	13	0	0	2	4	0	0	0	4	0	8	0	0	1	.464	.344
Giambi, Jeremy, K.C.*	.261	7	29	23	4	6	11	2	0	1	2	0	1	0	5	0	2	0	1	0	.478	.379
Giles, Brian, Cle.*	.100	6	22	20	1	2	3	1	0	0	0	0	0	0	2	0	3	0	0	1	.150	.182
Gipson, Charles, Sea.	.000	1	0	0	0	0	0	0	0	0	0	0	0	0	0	0	0	0	0	0	.000	.000
Gonzalez, Juan, Tex.	.329	38	163	143	28	47	85	12	1	8	39	0	3	3	14	2	35	0	1	5	.594	.393
Gonzalez, Luis, Det.*	.250	19	73	68	10	17	30	4	0	3	8	0	1	0	4	1	8	3	1	2	.441	.288
Goodwin, Tom, Tex.*	.000	1	1	1	0	0	0	0	0	0	0	0	0	0	0	0	1	0	0	0	.000	.000
Greene, Todd, Ana.	.000	4	11	9	0	0	0	0	0	0	0	0	0	0	2	0	4	0	0	0	.000	.182
Greene, Willie, Bal.*	.000	1	0	0	1	0	0	0	0	0	0	0	0	0	0	0	0	0	0	0	.000	.000
Grieve, Ben, Oak.*	.200	3	12	10	2	2	5	0	0	1	3	0	1	0	1	0	3	0	0	0	.500	.250
Griffey, Ken Jr., Sea.*	.167	3	13	12	1	2	2	0	0	0	1	0	0	0	1	0	3	0	0	0	.167	.231
Guevara, Giomar, Sea.	.000	1	0	0	0	0	0	0	0	0	0	0	0	0	0	0	0	0	0	0	.000	.000
Hammonds, Jeffrey, Bal.	.500	7	5	4	2	2	2	0	0	0	1	0	0	0	1	0	1	0	0	0	.500	.600
Haselman, Bill, Tex.	.000	3	5	4	0	0	0	0	0	0	0	1	0	0	0	0	1	0	0	1	.000	.000
Higginson, Bobby, Det.*	.429	2	9	7	1	3	6	0	0	1	1	0	0	0	2	0	2	1	0	0	.857	.556
Hocking, Denny, Min.†	.500	2	2	2	0	1	1	0	0	0	0	0	0	0	0	0	0	0	0	0	.500	.500
Hoiles, Chris, Bal.	.125	6	15	8	1	1	1	0	0	0	0	0	0	0	7	0	2	0	0	0	.125	.533
Hollins, Dave, Ana.†	.333	2	6	6	1	2	2	0	0	0	0	0	0	0	0	0	1	0	1	1	.333	.333
Huson, Jeff, Sea.*	.000	1	1	1	1	0	0	0	0	0	0	0	0	0	0	0	0	0	0	0	.000	.000
Ibanez, Raul, Sea.*	.000	1	1	1	0	0	0	0	0	0	0	0	0	0	0	0	1	0	0	0	.000	.000
Incaviglia, Pete, Det.	.083	4	12	12	0	1	1	0	0	0	0	0	0	0	0	0	5	0	0	0	.083	.083
Jefferson, Reggie, Bos.*	.298	48	189	171	20	51	86	12	1	7	23	0	1	0	17	1	35	0	0	7	.503	.360
Johns, Keith, Bos.	.000	1	1	0	0	0	0	0	0	0	0	0	0	0	1	0	0	0	0	0	.000	1.000
Johnson, Mark P., Ana.*	.000	2	4	4	0	0	0	0	0	0	0	0	0	0	0	0	1	0	0	0	.000	.000
Justice, David, Cle.*	.287	123	532	460	83	132	223	38	1	17	75	0	7	0	65	6	81	8	3	8	.485	.370
Kapler, Gabe, Det.	.000	1	2	2	0	0	0	0	0	0	0	0	0	0	0	0	0	0	0	0	.000	.000
Kelly, Mike, T.B.	.000	6	7	6	2	0	0	0	0	0	0	0	0	0	1	0	3	1	0	0	.000	.143
Kelly, Roberto, Tex.	.333	2	3	3	1	1	1	0	0	0	0	0	0	0	0	0	0	0	0	0	.333	.333
King, Jeff, K.C.	.254	16	65	59	9	15	26	2	0	3	12	0	1	0	5	0	15	1	0	1	.441	.308
Kingsale, Eugene, Bal.†	.000	1	0	0	0	0	0	0	0	0	0	0	0	0	0	0	0	0	0	0	.000	.000
Knoblauch, Chuck, N.Y.	.000	1	5	3	0	0	0	0	0	0	0	0	0	0	2	0	1	0	1	0	.000	.400
Laker, Tim, T.B.	.500	1	3	2	1	1	1	0	0	0	0	0	0	0	1	0	1	0	0	0	.500	.667
Ledesma, Aaron, T.B.	.235	6	17	17	3	4	5	1	0	0	1	0	0	0	0	0	2	0	0	0	.294	.235
Leius, Scott, K.C.	.000	1	2	2	0	0	0	0	0	0	0	0	0	0	0	0	1	0	0	0	.000	.000
Lewis, Darren, Bos.	.000	1	0	0	0	0	0	0	0	0	0	0	0	0	0	0	0	1	0	0	.000	.000
Leyritz, Jim, Bos.	.284	39	138	116	16	33	62	5	0	8	23	0	4	1	17	1	32	0	0	4	.534	.370
Lowell, Mike, N.Y.	.000	1	0	0	0	0	0	0	0	0	0	0	0	0	0	0	0	0	0	0	.000	.000
Mack, Shane, K.C.	.266	21	86	79	11	21	31	5	1	1	10	0	0	1	6	0	13	3	0	1	.392	.326
Manto, Jeff, Det.	.333	6	14	12	4	4	7	0	0	1	2	0	0	0	2	0	4	1	0	1	.583	.429
Martin, Norberto, Ana.	.333	10	3	3	2	1	1	0	0	0	1	0	0	0	0	0	0	0	0	0	.333	.333
Martinez, Dave, T.B.*	.333	1	5	3	1	1	1	0	0	0	0	0	0	0	2	1	0	0	0	0	.333	.600
Martinez, Edgar, Sea.	.320	147	652	540	83	173	303	44	1	28	100	0	7	3	102	3	93	1	1	13	.561	.426
Marzano, John, Sea.	.000	1	1	0	1	0	0	0	0	0	0	0	0	0	1	0	0	0	0	0	.000	1.000
Mashore, Damon, Ana.	.000	7	0	0	2	0	0	0	0	0	0	0	0	0	0	0	0	0	0	0	.000	.000
McDonald, Jason, Oak.†	.000	1	1	0	0	0	0	0	0	0	0	0	0	0	1	0	0	0	0	0	.000	1.000
McGriff, Fred, T.B.*	.340	14	61	53	7	18	31	7	0	2	8	0	0	0	8	0	11	1	0	0	.585	.426
McLemore, Mark, Tex.†	.000	2	5	4	0	0	0	0	0	0	0	0	0	0	1	0	1	0	0	0	.000	.200
Merced, Orlando, Min.-Bos.*	.300	9	35	30	5	9	10	1	0	0	3	0	0	0	5	1	5	0	0	0	.333	.400
Minor, Ryan, Bal.	1.000	1	1	1	1	1	1	0	0	0	0	0	0	0	0	0	0	0	0	0	1.000	1.000
Mitchell, Keith, Bos.	.333	12	17	12	2	4	5	1	0	0	3	0	0	0	5	1	1	1	0	0	.417	.529
Mitchell, Kevin, Oak.	.200	23	89	80	11	16	26	4	0	2	14	0	0	0	9	0	16	0	0	3	.325	.281
Molina, Izzy, Oak.	.000	1	0	0	0	0	0	0	0	0	0	0	0	0	0	0	0	0	0	0	.000	.000
Molitor, Paul, Min.	.279	115	521	466	70	130	179	27	5	4	67	1	10	0	44	5	36	9	2	17	.384	.335
Morris, Hal, K.C.*	.298	39	175	161	19	48	59	8	0	1	16	2	1	0	11	2	17	0	0	7	.366	.341
Mouton, Lyle, Bal.	.000	2	1	0	1	0	0	0	0	0	0	0	0	0	1	0	0	0	0	0	.000	1.000
Nevin, Phil, Ana.	.333	3	5	3	0	1	1	0	0	0	0	0	0	0	2	0	0	0	0	0	.333	.600
Newson, Warren, Tex.*	.231	3	14	13	1	3	3	0	0	0	1	0	0	0	1	1	3	0	0	1	.231	.286
Nixon, Trot, Bos.*	.000	4	5	5	0	0	0	0	0	0	0	0	0	0	0	0	2	0	0	0	.000	.000
Norton, Greg, Chi.†	.500	2	2	2	0	1	3	0	1	0	0	0	0	0	0	0	0	0	0	0	1.500	.500
Ochoa, Alex, Min.	.167	3	7	6	1	1	3	0	1	0	1	0	0	0	1	0	1	0	0	0	.500	.286
Offerman, Jose, K.C.†	.350	6	24	20	1	7	10	0	0	1	7	0	1	0	3	0	3	1	2	2	.500	.417

– 242 –

Player, Team	Avg.	G	TPA	AB	R	H	TB	2B	3B	HR	RBI	SH	SF	HP	BB	IBB	SO	SB	CS	GDP	Slg.	OBP
Oliver, Joe, Det.	.000	1	1	1	0	0	0	0	0	0	0	0	0	0	0	0	0	0	0	0	.000	.000
O'Neill, Paul, N.Y.*	.000	1	2	1	0	0	0	0	0	0	0	1	0	1	0	0	1	0	0	0	.000	.500
Ortiz, David, Min.*	.286	10	41	35	3	10	14	4	0	0	5	0	0	2	4	0	9	1	0	0	.400	.390
Palmeiro, Orlando, Ana.* ...	.500	3	2	2	1	1	2	1	0	0	1	0	0	0	0	0	0	0	0	0	1.000	.500
Palmeiro, Rafael, Bal.*	.200	3	12	10	0	2	2	0	0	0	2	0	0	0	2	0	3	0	0	0	.200	.333
Palmer, Dean, K.C.	.256	22	96	82	21	21	48	3	0	8	22	0	1	0	13	1	25	1	0	3	.585	.354
Pendleton, Terry, K.C.†	.253	40	162	150	13	38	51	7	0	2	20	0	1	0	11	1	32	0	0	2	.340	.302
Pickering, Calvin, Bal.*	.222	3	10	9	2	2	5	0	0	1	1	0	0	0	1	0	3	1	0	0	.556	.300
Posada, Jorge, N.Y.†	.353	6	21	17	3	6	10	1	0	1	3	0	1	0	3	0	2	0	0	0	.588	.429
Raines, Tim, N.Y.†	.289	56	191	159	25	46	63	6	1	3	25	0	2	2	28	0	22	2	1	1	.396	.398
Ramirez, Manny, Cle.	.250	2	9	8	0	2	2	0	0	0	2	0	0	0	1	0	1	0	0	1	.250	.333
Randa, Joe, Det.	.000	1	1	1	0	0	0	0	0	0	0	0	0	0	0	0	0	0	0	0	.000	.000
Ripken, Billy, Det.	.333	1	4	3	0	1	1	0	0	0	0	0	0	0	1	0	0	0	0	0	.333	.500
Roberts, Bip, Det.†	.252	29	120	103	16	26	32	6	0	0	9	1	0	1	15	0	13	5	0	2	.311	.353
Rodriguez, Alex, Sea.	.500	1	4	4	1	2	3	1	0	0	1	0	0	0	0	0	1	0	0	0	.750	.500
Rodriguez, Ivan, Tex.	.423	6	27	26	7	11	20	3	0	2	6	0	0	0	1	0	1	0	0	1	.769	.444
Romero, Mandy, Bos.†	.167	3	8	6	1	1	1	0	0	0	0	0	0	0	2	0	0	0	0	1	.167	.375
Rossy, Rico, Sea.	.000	1	0	0	1	0	0	0	0	0	0	0	0	0	0	0	0	0	0	0	.000	.000
Sadler, Donnie, Bos.	.000	4	0	0	0	0	0	0	0	0	0	0	0	0	0	0	0	1	0	0	.000	.000
Salmon, Tim, Ana.	.304	111	483	398	69	121	207	27	1	19	75	0	10	2	73	5	82	0	1	4	.520	.406
Samuel, Juan, Tor.	.333	11	10	6	7	2	5	0	0	1	1	1	0	1	2	0	1	4	2	0	.833	.556
Sexson, Richie, Cle.	.000	2	5	5	0	0	0	0	0	0	0	0	0	0	0	0	2	0	0	1	.000	.000
Shave, Jon, Min.	.000	1	0	0	1	0	0	0	0	0	0	0	0	0	0	0	0	0	0	0	.000	.000
Sheldon, Scott, Tex.	.000	1	1	1	0	0	0	0	0	0	0	0	0	0	0	0	1	0	0	0	.000	.000
Shipley, Craig, Ana.	.000	1	0	0	0	0	0	0	0	0	0	0	0	0	0	0	0	0	0	0	.000	.000
Sierra, Ruben, Chi.†	.200	5	21	20	0	4	8	2	1	0	2	0	0	0	1	0	5	0	0	0	.400	.238
Silvestri, Dave, T.B.	.000	2	2	2	0	0	0	0	0	0	0	0	0	0	0	0	1	0	0	1	.000	.000
Simms, Mike, Tex.	.245	26	62	53	8	13	23	1	0	3	8	0	0	1	8	0	7	0	0	2	.434	.355
Smith, Bobby, T.B.	.250	7	9	8	2	2	3	1	0	0	2	0	0	0	1	0	2	0	0	0	.375	.333
Snopek, Chris, Chi.-Bos.	.000	3	5	4	1	0	0	0	0	0	0	0	0	0	1	0	0	0	0	0	.000	.200
Sojo, Luis, N.Y.	.500	2	2	2	1	1	1	0	0	0	0	0	0	0	0	0	0	0	0	0	.500	.500
Sorrento, Paul, T.B.*	.225	86	323	285	23	64	110	19	0	9	34	0	2	3	33	0	92	2	2	5	.386	.310
Spencer, Shane, N.Y.	.167	4	7	6	0	1	1	0	0	0	1	0	1	0	0	0	1	0	0	0	.167	.143
Spiezio, Scott, Oak.†	.250	1	4	4	0	1	1	0	0	0	0	0	0	0	0	0	2	0	0	0	.250	.250
Stairs, Matt, Oak.*	.298	120	510	450	79	134	235	30	1	23	89	0	3	4	53	4	76	7	3	12	.522	.375
Stanley, Mike, Tor.-Bos.	.258	107	441	372	56	96	179	17	0	22	64	0	4	5	60	5	104	2	1	9	.481	.365
Steinbach, Terry, Min.	.111	3	10	9	0	1	1	0	0	0	1	0	0	0	1	0	4	0	0	0	.111	.200
Stevens, Lee, Tex.*	.305	72	260	236	38	72	139	14	4	15	48	0	0	0	24	4	57	0	2	4	.589	.369
Strawberry, Darryl, N.Y.*	.254	81	291	248	35	63	137	10	2	20	44	0	1	2	40	4	76	8	6	1	.552	.361
Sutton, Larry, K.C.*	.300	3	12	10	2	3	4	1	0	0	1	0	0	0	2	0	2	0	0	0	.400	.417
Sveum, Dale, N.Y.†	.000	3	4	3	0	0	0	0	0	0	0	0	0	0	1	0	3	0	0	0	.000	.250
Thomas, Frank, Chi.	.261	146	648	532	98	139	252	31	2	26	97	0	10	6	100	2	85	4	0	12	.474	.378
Thome, Jim, Cle.*	.273	6	26	22	4	6	9	0	0	1	1	0	0	2	2	0	8	0	0	0	.409	.385
Tomberlin, Andy, Det.*	.226	22	68	62	5	14	19	2	0	1	9	0	0	3	3	1	22	1	0	2	.306	.294
Trammell, Bubba, T.B.	.284	19	72	67	10	19	36	11	0	2	9	0	0	0	5	0	14	0	2	1	.537	.333
Tremie, Chris, Tex.	.333	2	4	3	2	1	2	1	0	0	0	0	0	0	1	0	1	0	0	0	.667	.500
Valentin, Javier, Min.†	.000	1	3	3	0	0	0	0	0	0	0	0	0	0	0	0	0	0	0	1	.000	.000
Varitek, Jason, Bos.†	.333	3	3	3	0	1	1	0	0	0	0	0	0	0	0	0	1	0	0	0	.333	.333
Vaughn, Mo, Bos.*	.267	12	52	45	12	12	26	2	0	4	12	0	0	0	7	1	12	0	0	1	.578	.365
Vitiello, Joe, K.C.	.167	2	7	6	0	1	1	0	0	0	0	0	0	0	1	0	2	0	0	0	.167	.286
Voigt, Jack, Oak.	.000	3	2	2	0	0	0	0	0	0	0	0	0	0	0	0	0	0	1	0	.000	.000
Walbeck, Matt, Ana.†	.500	2	2	2	0	1	1	0	0	0	0	0	0	0	0	0	1	0	0	0	.500	.500
Walker, Todd, Min.*	.000	1	4	4	0	0	0	0	0	0	0	0	0	0	0	0	1	0	0	0	.000	.000
Walton, Jerome, T.B.	.200	3	11	10	2	2	2	0	0	0	0	0	0	0	1	0	2	0	0	1	.200	.273
Webster, Lenny, Bal.	.200	4	7	5	0	1	1	0	0	0	1	0	0	0	2	0	1	0	0	1	.200	.429
Whiten, Mark, Cle.†	.417	5	15	12	5	5	8	3	0	0	2	0	0	0	3	0	1	0	0	0	.667	.533
Wilkins, Rick, Sea.*	.000	2	5	4	0	0	0	0	0	0	0	0	0	0	1	0	1	0	0	0	.000	.200
Williams, Bernie, N.Y.†	.409	5	24	22	8	9	18	0	0	3	7	0	0	0	2	0	3	1	0	1	.818	.458
Williams, Reggie, Ana.†	.500	2	3	2	0	1	1	0	0	0	0	0	0	0	1	0	0	1	0	0	.500	.667
Winn, Randy, T.B.†	.000	4	0	0	2	0	0	0	0	0	0	0	0	0	0	0	0	3	1	0	.000	.000
Wood, Jason, Det.	.444	3	10	9	4	4	8	1	0	1	1	0	0	0	1	0	0	0	0	1	.889	.500

DESIGNATED HITTERS WITH TWO OR MORE TEAMS

Player, Team	Avg.	G	TPA	AB	R	H	TB	2B	3B	HR	RBI	SH	SF	HP	BB	IBB	SO	SB	CS	GDP	Slg.	OBP
Berroa, Geronimo, Cle.	.200	5	16	15	2	3	3	0	0	0	1	0	0	0	1	0	8	0	0	0	.200	.250
Berroa, Geronimo, Det.	.252	37	131	115	15	29	38	4	1	1	10	0	0	2	14	1	24	0	1	0	.330	.344
Fielder, Cecil, Ana.	.248	31	130	109	15	27	47	6	1	4	20	0	0	1	20	0	35	0	0	4	.431	.369
Fielder, Cecil, Cle.	.154	10	28	26	1	4	5	1	0	0	0	0	0	1	1	0	9	0	0	1	.192	.214
Merced, Orlando, Min.*	.333	8	30	27	5	9	10	1	0	0	2	0	0	0	3	1	3	0	0	0	.370	.400
Merced, Orlando, Bos.*	.000	1	5	3	0	0	0	0	0	0	1	0	0	0	2	0	2	0	0	0	.000	.400
Snopek, Chris, Chi.	.000	1	0	0	1	0	0	0	0	0	0	0	0	0	0	0	0	0	0	0	---	---
Snopek, Chris, Bos.	.000	2	5	4	0	0	0	0	0	0	0	0	0	0	1	0	0	0	0	0	.000	.200
Stanley, Mike, Tor.	.240	73	306	258	36	62	122	9	0	17	41	0	3	3	42	3	71	1	1	4	.473	.350
Stanley, Mike, Bos.	.298	34	135	114	20	34	57	8	0	5	23	0	1	2	18	2	33	1	0	5	.500	.394

The following designated hitters, each of whom appeared in at least one game, had no plate appearances, runs scored or stolen base attempts: Anderson, Brady, Baltimore; Frazier, Lou, Chicago; Gipson, Charles, Seattle; Guevara, Giomar, Seattle; Kingsale, Gene, Baltimore; Lowell, Mike, New York; Molina, Izzy, Oakland; Shipley, Craig, Anaheim.

PINCH-HITTING

TEAM

Team	Avg.	G	TPA	AB	R	H	TB	2B	3B	HR	RBI	SH	SF	HP	BB	IBB	SO	SB	CS	GDP	Slg.	OBP
Minnesota	.301	64	99	83	6	25	30	5	0	0	12	0	2	0	14	1	20	2	0	4	.361	.394
Oakland	.299	85	136	117	13	35	44	6	0	1	24	1	2	0	16	1	24	3	0	3	.376	.378
Tampa Bay	.272	78	126	114	18	31	46	6	0	3	25	1	0	0	11	0	33	2	0	2	.404	.336
Cleveland	.250	61	87	76	8	19	30	4	2	1	17	0	2	1	8	1	23	0	1	1	.395	.322
Texas	.235	82	128	115	19	27	38	5	0	2	22	0	3	0	10	1	29	1	0	2	.330	.289
Boston	.220	90	156	132	11	29	46	9	1	2	18	1	2	3	18	1	35	0	0	1	.348	.323
Baltimore	.209	104	157	129	13	27	35	5	0	1	23	0	5	2	21	1	34	0	1	3	.271	.318
Toronto	.204	45	60	54	4	11	17	3	0	1	5	0	2	1	3	1	21	1	0	2	.315	.250
New York	.203	70	91	69	8	14	23	3	0	2	23	1	4	1	16	0	19	0	0	2	.333	.344
Anaheim	.195	73	99	87	4	17	22	5	0	0	8	1	0	1	10	1	20	1	1	3	.253	.289
Detroit	.190	84	126	116	9	22	36	2	0	4	16	0	1	1	8	0	31	1	0	6	.310	.246
Seattle	.187	70	93	75	8	14	21	5	1	0	9	1	3	2	12	0	19	0	0	1	.280	.304
Chicago	.186	47	65	59	4	11	19	3	1	1	9	0	0	0	6	0	14	1	0	0	.322	.262
Kansas City	.186	83	127	118	6	22	29	4	0	1	12	0	0	3	6	0	26	1	0	4	.246	.244
Totals	.226	1036	1550	1344	131	304	436	65	5	19	223	6	26	15	159	8	348	13	3	34	.324	.310

TOP PINCH-HITTERS

Minimum 20 at-bats. *Lefthanded batter. †Switch-hitter.

Player, Team	Avg.	G	TPA	AB	R	H	TB	2B	3B	HR	RBI	SH	SF	HP	BB	IBB	SO	SB	CS	GDP	Slg.	OBP
Cummings, Midre, Bos.*	.346	31	31	26	4	9	19	4	0	2	7	0	0	1	4	0	5	0	0	0	.731	.452
Mitchell, Kevin, Oak.	.304	23	23	23	2	7	8	1	0	0	4	0	0	0	0	0	6	0	0	1	.348	.304
Branson, Jeff, Cle.*	.300	21	21	20	1	6	8	0	1	0	6	0	1	0	0	0	6	0	0	0	.400	.286
Pendleton, Terry, K.C.†	.286	22	22	21	1	6	7	1	0	0	3	0	0	0	1	0	5	0	0	0	.333	.318
Varitek, Jason, Bos.†	.286	24	23	21	1	6	7	1	0	0	2	0	0	0	2	1	3	0	0	0	.333	.348
Cedeno, Domingo, Tex.†	.286	22	22	21	4	6	8	2	0	0	5	0	0	0	1	0	3	0	0	0	.381	.318
Catalanotto, Frank, Det.*	.250	38	37	32	3	8	11	0	0	1	3	0	1	0	4	0	5	0	0	1	.344	.324
Palmeiro, Orlando, Ana.*	.238	21	21	21	1	5	7	2	0	0	2	0	0	0	0	0	1	0	0	0	.333	.238
Alicea, Luis, Tex.†	.192	28	28	26	5	5	6	1	0	0	1	0	0	0	2	0	7	0	0	0	.231	.250
Baines, Harold, Bal.*	.167	28	27	24	2	4	7	3	0	0	5	0	1	0	2	1	8	0	0	0	.292	.222
Sutton, Larry, K.C.*	.115	29	29	26	1	3	3	0	0	0	2	0	0	0	3	0	5	0	0	0	.115	.207

ALL PINCH-HITTERS

*Lefthanded batter. †Switch-hitter.

Player, Team	Avg.	G	TPA	AB	R	H	TB	2B	3B	HR	RBI	SH	SF	HP	BB	IBB	SO	SB	CS	GDP	Slg.	OBP
Abbott, Jeff, Chi.	.143	14	14	14	2	2	6	1	0	1	1	0	0	0	0	0	3	1	0	0	.429	.143
Abbott, Kurt, Oak.	.000	1	1	1	0	0	0	0	0	0	0	0	0	0	0	0	0	0	0	0	.000	.000
Alicea, Luis, Tex.†	.192	28	28	26	5	5	6	1	0	0	1	0	0	0	2	0	7	0	0	0	.231	.250
Allensworth, Jermaine, K.C.	.000	4	4	4	0	0	0	0	0	0	1	0	0	0	0	0	1	0	0	0	.000	.000
Alomar, Roberto, Bal.†	.000	4	4	4	0	0	0	0	0	0	0	0	0	0	0	0	1	0	0	0	.000	.000
Alomar, Sandy Jr., Cle.	.250	4	4	4	0	1	1	0	0	0	2	0	0	0	0	0	0	0	0	0	.250	.250
Alvarez, Gabe, Det.	.000	1	1	1	0	0	0	0	0	0	0	0	0	0	0	0	0	0	0	0	.000	.000
Amaral, Rich, Sea.	.250	5	5	4	1	1	2	1	0	0	0	0	0	0	1	0	0	0	0	0	.500	.400
Anderson, Brady, Bal.*	.000	5	5	3	0	0	0	0	0	0	0	0	0	0	2	0	1	0	0	0	.000	.400
Anderson, Garret, Ana.*	1.000	3	3	2	0	2	2	0	0	0	1	0	0	0	1	1	0	0	0	0	1.000	1.000
Ashley, Billy, Bos.	.000	6	5	5	0	0	0	0	0	0	0	0	0	0	0	0	4	0	0	0	.000	.000
Baines, Harold, Bal.*	.167	28	27	24	2	4	7	3	0	0	5	0	1	0	2	1	8	0	0	0	.292	.222
Bako, Paul, Det.*	.200	5	5	5	0	1	1	0	0	0	0	0	0	0	0	0	1	0	0	0	.200	.200
Bartee, Kimera, Det.†	.571	8	7	7	1	4	8	1	0	0	3	0	0	0	0	0	3	0	0	0	1.143	.571
Beamon, Trey, Det.*	.176	17	17	17	1	3	4	1	0	0	1	0	0	0	0	0	4	0	0	2	.235	.176
Becker, Rich, Bal.*	.176	24	24	17	4	3	3	0	0	0	0	0	0	1	6	0	6	0	0	0	.176	.417
Bell, David, Cle.-Sea.	.000	3	3	3	0	0	0	0	0	0	0	0	0	0	0	0	2	0	0	0	.000	.000
Bellhorn, Mark, Oak.†	.333	3	3	3	0	1	2	1	0	0	1	0	0	0	0	0	2	0	0	0	.667	.333
Benjamin, Mike, Bos.	.000	4	4	3	1	0	0	0	0	0	0	0	0	0	1	0	0	0	0	0	.000	.250
Berroa, Geronimo, Cle.-Det.	.083	18	14	12	1	1	1	0	0	0	0	0	0	0	2	0	5	0	0	1	.083	.214
Blowers, Mike, Oak.	.333	11	11	9	2	3	3	0	0	0	3	0	0	0	2	0	3	0	0	0	.333	.455
Boggs, Wade, T.B.*	.200	15	15	15	0	3	4	1	0	0	2	0	0	0	0	0	2	0	0	0	.267	.200
Bolick, Frank, Ana.†	.000	6	6	5	0	0	0	0	0	0	0	0	0	0	1	0	2	0	0	0	.000	.167
Borders, Pat, Cle.	.667	3	3	3	1	2	4	2	0	0	0	0	0	0	0	0	0	0	0	1	1.333	.667
Bournigal, Rafael, Oak.	.500	4	4	2	1	1	1	0	0	0	0	0	1	0	0	0	1	0	0	0	.500	.667
Bragg, Darren, Bos.*	.250	8	8	8	1	2	2	0	0	0	0	0	0	0	0	0	2	0	0	0	.250	.250
Branson, Jeff, Cle.*	.300	21	21	20	1	6	8	0	1	0	6	0	1	0	0	0	6	0	0	0	.400	.286
Brosius, Scott, N.Y.	.000	2	2	1	0	0	0	0	0	0	0	0	1	0	0	0	1	0	0	0	.000	.000
Brown, Dermal, K.C.*	.000	3	3	3	0	0	0	0	0	0	0	0	0	0	0	0	1	0	0	0	.000	.000
Brown, Kevin, Tor.	.000	1	1	1	0	0	0	0	0	0	0	0	0	0	1	0	0	0	0	0	.000	1.000
Buford, Damon, Bos.	.214	18	16	14	1	3	6	1	1	0	3	0	1	0	1	0	2	0	0	0	.429	.250
Buhner, Jay, Sea.	.000	1	1	1	0	0	0	0	0	0	0	0	0	0	0	0	0	0	0	0	.000	.000
Bush, Homer, N.Y.	.500	2	2	2	0	1	1	0	0	0	0	0	0	0	0	0	1	0	0	0	.500	.500
Butler, Rich, T.B.*	.167	13	13	12	0	2	2	0	0	0	1	0	0	0	1	0	6	1	0	0	.167	.231
Cairo, Miguel, T.B.	.000	3	3	2	0	0	0	0	0	0	0	0	0	0	0	0	0	0	0	0	.000	.000
Cameron, Mike, Chi.	.000	3	3	3	0	0	0	0	0	0	0	0	0	0	0	0	1	0	0	0	.000	.000
Carter, Joe, Bal.	.214	16	16	14	1	3	4	1	0	0	3	0	0	1	1	0	4	0	0	1	.286	.313
Caruso, Mike, Chi.*	.000	1	1	1	0	0	0	0	0	0	0	0	0	0	0	0	0	0	0	0	.000	.000
Casanova, Raul, Det.†	.000	2	2	2	0	0	0	0	0	0	0	0	0	0	0	0	1	0	0	0	.000	.000
Catalanotto, Frank, Det.*	.250	38	37	32	3	8	11	0	0	1	3	0	1	0	4	0	5	0	0	1	.344	.324
Cedeno, Domingo, Tex.†	.286	22	22	21	4	6	8	2	0	0	5	0	0	0	1	0	3	0	0	0	.381	.318

Player, Team	Avg.	G	TPA	AB	R	H	TB	2B	3B	HR	RBI	SH	SF	HP	BB	IBB	SO	SB	CS	GDP	Slg.	OBP
Chavez, Eric, Oak.*	.000	5	5	5	0	0	0	0	0	0	0	0	0	0	0	0	1	0	0	0	.000	.000
Christenson, Ryan, Oak.	.000	1	1	1	0	0	0	0	0	0	0	0	0	0	0	0	1	0	0	0	.000	.000
Clark, Will, Tex.*	1.000	1	1	1	0	1	1	0	0	0	1	0	0	0	0	0	0	0	0	0	1.000	1.000
Clyburn, Danny, Bal.	.000	1	1	1	0	0	0	0	0	0	0	0	0	0	0	0	1	0	0	0	.000	.000
Conine, Jeff, K.C.	.250	4	4	4	0	1	1	0	0	0	1	0	0	0	0	0	1	0	0	0	.250	.250
Coomer, Ron, Min.	.400	10	10	10	1	4	7	3	0	0	3	0	0	0	0	0	1	0	0	0	.700	.400
Cora, Joey, Sea.-Cle.†	.000	7	7	6	0	0	0	0	0	0	0	0	0	0	1	0	1	0	0	0	.000	.143
Cordero, Wil, Chi.	.500	4	4	4	0	2	2	0	0	0	1	0	0	0	0	0	0	0	0	0	.500	.500
Cordova, Marty, Min.	.000	1	1	1	0	0	0	0	0	0	0	0	0	0	0	0	0	0	0	0	.000	.000
Cradle, Rickey, Sea.	.000	2	2	2	0	0	0	0	0	0	0	0	0	0	0	0	2	0	0	0	.000	.000
Crespo, Felipe, Tor.†	.182	15	15	11	0	2	2	0	0	0	1	0	1	1	2	1	6	0	0	0	.182	.333
Cruz, Jacob, Cle.*	.000	1	1	1	0	0	0	0	0	0	0	0	0	0	0	0	0	0	0	0	.000	.000
Cruz, Jose Jr., Tor.†	.000	1	1	1	0	0	0	0	0	0	0	0	0	0	0	0	1	0	0	0	.000	.000
Cummings, Midre, Bos.*	.346	31	31	26	4	9	19	4	0	2	7	0	0	1	4	0	5	0	0	0	.731	.452
Curtis, Chad, N.Y.	.333	7	6	3	1	1	2	1	0	0	3	0	0	0	3	0	1	0	0	0	.667	.667
Dalesandro, Mark, Tor.	.200	6	5	5	0	1	1	0	0	0	2	0	0	0	0	0	1	0	0	2	.200	.200
Damon, Johnny, K.C.*	.200	5	5	5	1	1	1	0	0	0	0	0	0	0	0	0	1	0	0	1	.200	.200
Davis, Chili, N.Y.†	.500	9	9	8	1	4	5	1	0	0	1	0	0	0	1	0	1	0	0	1	.625	.556
Davis, Eric, Bal.	.385	16	16	13	1	5	6	1	0	0	4	0	1	0	2	0	5	0	1	0	.462	.438
Davis, Russ, Sea.	.250	5	5	4	0	1	1	0	0	0	1	0	1	0	0	0	1	0	0	0	.250	.250
Diaz, Einar, Cle.	1.000	1	1	1	0	1	1	0	0	0	0	0	0	0	0	0	0	0	0	0	1.000	1.000
Ducey, Rob, Sea.*	.133	20	19	15	1	2	3	1	0	0	1	0	0	2	2	0	8	0	0	0	.200	.316
Dunston, Shawon, Cle.	.143	7	7	7	1	1	4	0	0	1	1	0	0	0	0	0	1	0	1	0	.571	.143
Durham, Ray, Chi.†	.000	1	1	0	0	0	0	0	0	0	0	0	0	0	1	0	0	0	0	0	.000	1.000
Dye, Jermaine, K.C.	.000	2	2	2	1	0	0	0	0	0	0	0	0	0	0	0	0	0	0	1	.000	.000
Edmonds, Jim, Ana.*	.000	1	1	1	0	0	0	0	0	0	0	0	0	0	0	0	0	0	0	0	.000	.000
Encarnacion, Juan, Det.	.000	1	1	1	0	0	0	0	0	0	0	0	0	0	0	0	1	0	0	0	.000	.000
Erstad, Darin, Ana.*	.000	4	4	3	0	0	0	0	0	0	0	0	0	0	1	0	1	0	0	0	.000	.250
Fasano, Sal, K.C.	.000	1	1	1	0	0	0	0	0	0	0	0	0	0	0	0	0	0	0	0	.000	.000
Febles, Carlos, K.C.	1.000	1	1	1	0	1	1	0	0	0	0	0	0	0	0	0	0	0	0	0	1.000	1.000
Fernandez, Tony, Tor.†	.500	3	3	2	1	1	1	0	0	0	1	0	1	0	0	0	1	0	0	0	.500	.333
Fick, Rob, Det.*	.000	1	1	1	0	0	0	0	0	0	0	0	0	0	0	0	1	0	0	0	.000	.000
Fielder, Cecil, Cle.	.000	4	3	2	0	0	0	0	0	0	0	0	0	0	1	0	0	0	0	1	.000	.333
Fletcher, Darrin, Tor.*	.250	8	8	8	0	2	3	1	0	0	0	0	0	0	0	0	2	0	0	0	.375	.250
Forbes, P.J., Bal.	.000	1	1	1	0	0	0	0	0	0	0	0	0	0	0	0	0	0	0	0	.000	.000
Frazier, Lou, Chi.†	.000	3	3	3	0	0	0	0	0	0	0	0	0	0	0	0	3	0	0	0	.000	.000
Garcia, Carlos, Ana.	.500	2	2	2	1	1	1	0	0	0	0	0	0	0	0	0	0	0	0	0	.500	.500
Gates, Brent, Min.†	.286	17	17	14	1	4	4	0	0	0	0	0	0	0	3	0	2	1	0	0	.286	.412
Giambi, Jeremy, K.C.*	.000	2	2	2	0	0	0	0	0	0	0	0	0	0	0	0	1	0	0	0	.000	.000
Giles, Brian, Cle.*	.500	7	7	2	0	1	1	0	0	0	3	0	1	1	3	1	1	0	0	0	.500	.714
Gipson, Charles, Sea.	.333	6	6	6	2	2	2	0	0	0	1	0	0	0	0	0	0	0	0	0	.333	.333
Gonzalez, Juan, Tex.	.000	1	1	1	0	0	0	0	0	0	0	0	0	0	0	0	0	0	0	0	.000	.000
Gonzalez, Luis, Det.*	.000	6	6	6	0	0	0	0	0	0	0	0	0	0	0	0	3	0	0	0	.000	.000
Goodwin, Tom, Tex.*	.143	9	9	7	1	1	1	0	0	0	1	0	1	0	1	0	3	1	0	0	.143	.222
Grebeck, Craig, Tor.	.200	5	5	5	0	1	1	0	0	0	0	0	0	0	0	0	2	0	0	0	.200	.200
Green, Shawn, Tor.*	.000	2	2	2	0	0	0	0	0	0	0	0	0	0	0	0	0	0	0	0	.000	.000
Greene, Todd, Ana.	.167	13	13	12	0	2	3	1	0	0	2	0	0	0	1	0	5	0	0	0	.250	.231
Greene, Willie, Bal.*	.125	10	10	8	1	1	1	0	0	0	2	0	0	0	2	0	4	0	0	0	.125	.300
Greer, Rusty, Tex.*	.000	2	2	2	0	0	0	0	0	0	0	0	0	0	0	0	1	0	0	0	.000	.000
Grieve, Ben, Oak.*	.000	2	2	2	0	0	0	0	0	0	0	0	0	0	0	0	1	0	0	0	.000	.000
Guevara, Giomar, Sea.	.000	1	1	1	0	0	0	0	0	0	0	0	0	0	0	0	0	0	0	0	.000	.000
Guillen, Ozzie, Bal.*	.000	7	6	6	0	0	0	0	0	0	0	0	0	0	0	0	1	0	0	1	.000	.000
Halter, Shane, K.C.	.200	5	5	5	0	1	1	0	0	0	0	0	0	0	0	0	2	0	0	0	.200	.200
Hammonds, Jeffrey, Bal.	.200	7	6	5	0	1	1	0	0	0	1	0	0	0	1	0	1	0	0	0	.200	.333
Hansen, Jed, K.C.	.000	1	1	1	0	0	0	0	0	0	0	0	0	0	0	0	0	0	0	0	.000	.000
Haselman, Bill, Tex.	.333	4	4	3	0	1	1	0	0	0	1	0	1	0	0	0	1	0	0	0	.333	.250
Hatcher, Chris, K.C.	.000	3	3	3	0	0	0	0	0	0	0	0	0	0	0	0	1	0	0	0	.000	.000
Hatteberg, Scott, Bos.*	.000	5	4	3	0	0	0	0	0	0	0	0	1	0	0	0	2	0	0	0	.000	.250
Henderson, Rickey, Oak.	.250	4	4	4	0	1	1	0	0	0	0	0	0	0	0	0	0	0	0	0	.250	.250
Higginson, Bobby, Det.*	.500	2	2	2	1	1	4	0	0	1	1	0	0	0	0	0	1	0	0	0	2.000	.500
Hill, Glenallen, Sea.	.500	4	4	4	2	2	4	0	1	0	0	0	0	0	0	0	1	0	0	0	1.000	.500
Hinch, A.J., Oak.	.000	3	3	3	0	0	0	0	0	0	0	0	0	0	0	0	1	0	0	0	.000	.000
Hocking, Denny, Min.†	.250	6	6	4	1	1	1	0	0	0	0	0	0	0	2	0	0	0	0	0	.250	.500
Hoiles, Chris, Bal.	.333	10	10	6	1	2	5	0	0	1	6	0	2	0	2	0	2	0	0	0	.833	.400
Hollins, Dave, Ana.†	.000	2	2	2	0	0	0	0	0	0	0	0	0	0	0	0	1	0	0	0	.000	.000
Hunter, Brian L., Det.	.000	1	1	1	0	0	0	0	0	0	0	0	0	0	0	0	0	0	0	0	.000	.000
Hunter, Torii, Min.	1.000	1	1	1	0	1	1	0	0	0	0	0	0	0	0	0	0	0	0	0	1.000	1.000
Huson, Jeff, Sea.*	.000	7	7	6	0	0	0	0	0	0	0	0	0	0	1	0	0	0	0	0	.000	.143
Ibanez, Raul, Sea.*	.167	8	6	6	0	1	2	1	0	0	2	0	0	0	0	0	0	0	0	1	.333	.167
Incaviglia, Pete, Det.	.000	4	4	3	0	0	0	0	0	0	0	0	0	0	1	0	1	0	0	0	.000	.250
Jefferies, Gregg, Ana.†	.000	1	1	1	0	0	0	0	0	0	0	0	0	0	0	0	0	0	0	0	.000	.000
Jefferson, Reggie, Bos.*	.143	8	8	7	0	1	1	0	0	0	2	0	0	0	1	0	4	0	0	0	.143	.250
Jeter, Derek, N.Y.	.000	1	1	1	0	0	0	0	0	0	0	0	0	0	0	0	0	0	0	0	.000	.000
Johns, Keith, Bos.	.000	1	1	0	0	0	0	0	0	0	0	0	0	0	1	0	0	0	0	0	.000	1.000
Johnson, Mark P., Ana.*	.000	4	4	4	0	0	0	0	0	0	0	0	0	0	0	0	0	0	0	1	.000	.000
Justice, David, Cle.*	.375	9	9	8	3	3	6	1	1	0	3	0	0	0	1	0	2	0	0	0	.750	.444
Kapler, Gabe, Det.	.000	1	1	1	0	0	0	0	0	0	0	0	0	0	0	0	0	0	0	0	.000	.000
Kelly, Mike, T.B.	.333	16	16	15	3	5	5	0	0	0	2	0	0	0	1	0	5	0	0	1	.333	.375
Kelly, Roberto, Tex.	.333	12	12	12	4	4	8	1	0	1	4	0	0	0	0	0	1	0	0	2	.667	.333
King, Jeff, K.C.	.000	3	3	3	0	0	0	0	0	0	0	0	0	0	0	0	1	0	0	1	.000	.000
Koskie, Corey, Min.*	1.000	2	2	1	0	1	1	0	0	0	0	0	0	0	1	0	0	0	0	0	1.000	1.000
Kreuter, Chad, Chi.†	.250	5	5	4	0	1	1	0	0	0	2	0	0	0	1	0	1	0	0	0	.250	.400

Player, Team	Avg.	G	TPA	AB	R	H	TB	2B	3B	HR	RBI	SH	SF	HP	BB	IBB	SO	SB	CS	GDP	Slg.	OBP
Latham, Chris, Min.†	.000	3	3	2	1	0	0	0	0	0	0	0	0	0	1	0	1	0	0	0	.000	.333
Lawton, Matt, Min.*	1.000	3	3	2	0	2	2	0	0	0	1	0	0	0	1	1	0	0	0	0	1.000	1.000
Ledee, Ricky, N.Y.*	.000	1	0	0	0	0	0	0	0	0	0	0	0	0	0	0	0	0	0	0	.000	.000
Ledesma, Aaron, T.B.	.333	12	12	12	3	4	6	2	0	0	3	0	0	0	0	0	1	0	0	0	.500	.333
Leius, Scott, K.C.	.250	4	4	4	0	1	1	0	0	0	1	0	0	0	0	0	0	0	0	0	.250	.250
Lesher, Brian, Oak.	.000	1	1	1	0	0	0	0	0	0	0	0	0	0	0	0	1	0	0	0	.000	.000
Lewis, Darren, Bos.	.000	1	1	1	0	0	0	0	0	0	0	0	0	0	0	0	0	0	0	0	.000	.000
Leyritz, Jim, Bos.	.286	21	21	14	1	4	5	1	0	0	1	0	0	1	6	0	5	0	0	1	.357	.524
Lowell, Mike, N.Y.	.000	1	1	1	0	0	0	0	0	0	0	0	0	0	0	0	0	0	0	0	.000	.000
Luke, Matt, Cle.*	.000	2	2	2	0	0	0	0	0	0	0	0	0	0	0	0	0	0	0	0	.000	.000
Macfarlane, Mike, Oak.	.636	13	13	11	2	7	8	1	0	0	3	0	0	0	2	0	1	0	0	0	.727	.692
Mack, Shane, Oak.-K.C.	.385	16	16	13	2	5	9	1	0	1	4	0	0	3	0	0	2	1	0	0	.692	.500
Magadan, Dave, Oak.*	.333	6	6	3	0	1	1	0	0	0	2	0	1	0	2	1	0	0	0	1	.333	.500
Manto, Jeff, Cle.-Det.-Cle.	.200	6	6	5	1	1	1	0	0	0	0	0	0	0	1	0	1	0	0	0	.200	.333
Martin, Norberto, Ana.	.000	4	3	3	0	0	0	0	0	0	0	0	0	0	0	0	0	0	0	0	.000	.000
Martinez, Dave, T.B.*	.200	6	6	5	0	1	1	0	0	0	0	0	0	0	1	0	0	0	0	0	.200	.333
Martinez, Edgar, Sea.	.000	3	3	2	0	0	0	0	0	0	0	0	0	0	1	0	0	0	0	0	.000	.333
Martinez, Felix, K.C.†	.000	2	2	2	0	0	0	0	0	0	0	0	0	0	0	0	0	0	0	0	.000	.000
Martinez, Tino, N.Y.*	.000	1	1	1	0	0	0	0	0	0	0	0	0	0	0	0	1	0	0	0	.000	.000
Marzano, John, Sea.	.000	3	3	1	1	0	0	0	0	0	0	0	0	0	2	0	1	0	0	0	.000	.667
Mashore, Damon, Ana.	.000	2	2	2	0	0	0	0	0	0	0	0	0	0	0	0	1	0	0	0	.000	.000
McCarty, David, Sea.	.000	1	1	1	0	0	0	0	0	0	0	0	0	0	0	0	0	0	0	0	.000	.000
McClain, Scott, T.B.	.000	1	1	1	0	0	0	0	0	0	0	0	0	0	0	0	0	0	0	0	.000	.000
McCracken, Quinton, T.B.†	.200	6	6	5	1	1	2	1	0	0	1	0	0	0	1	0	1	0	0	1	.400	.333
McDonald, Jason, Oak.†	.286	11	11	7	1	2	2	0	0	0	0	0	0	0	4	0	1	0	0	0	.286	.545
McGriff, Fred, T.B.*	.333	3	3	3	0	1	1	0	0	0	0	0	0	0	0	0	2	0	0	0	.333	.333
McLemore, Mark, Tex.†	.333	3	3	3	1	1	1	0	0	0	1	0	0	0	0	0	1	0	0	0	.333	.333
Meares, Pat, Min.	.000	2	2	2	0	0	0	0	0	0	0	0	0	0	0	0	0	0	0	2	.000	.000
Merced, Orlando, Min.-Bos.*	.200	13	12	10	1	2	3	1	0	0	3	0	2	0	0	0	2	0	0	0	.300	.167
Merloni, Lou, Bos.	.500	2	2	2	0	1	2	1	0	0	0	0	0	0	0	0	0	0	0	1	1.000	.500
Mientkiewicz, Doug, Min.*	1.000	1	1	1	0	1	1	0	0	0	1	0	0	0	0	0	0	0	0	0	1.000	1.000
Minor, Ryan, Bal.	1.000	1	1	1	1	1	1	0	0	0	0	0	0	0	0	0	0	0	0	0	1.000	1.000
Mitchell, Keith, Bos.	.000	9	7	5	0	0	0	0	0	0	1	0	0	0	2	0	2	0	0	0	.000	.286
Mitchell, Kevin, Oak.	.304	23	23	23	2	7	8	1	0	0	4	0	0	0	0	0	6	0	0	1	.348	.304
Molina, Ben, Ana.	.000	1	1	1	0	0	0	0	0	0	0	0	0	0	0	0	0	0	0	0	.000	.000
Molina, Izzy, Oak.	1.000	1	1	1	1	1	1	0	0	0	0	0	0	0	0	0	0	0	0	0	1.000	1.000
Molitor, Paul, Min.	.000	2	2	2	0	0	0	0	0	0	0	0	0	0	0	0	1	0	0	0	.000	.000
Morris, Hal, K.C.*	.200	10	10	10	0	2	3	1	0	0	0	0	0	0	0	0	0	0	0	0	.300	.200
Mouton, Lyle, Bal.	.000	3	2	1	1	0	0	0	0	0	0	0	0	0	1	0	1	0	0	0	.000	.500
Neill, Mike, Oak.*	.000	1	1	1	0	0	0	0	0	0	0	0	0	0	0	0	0	0	0	0	.000	.000
Nevin, Phil, Ana.	.000	2	2	2	0	0	0	0	0	0	0	0	0	0	0	0	1	0	0	0	.000	.000
Nixon, Otis, Min.†	.500	2	2	2	0	1	1	0	0	0	0	0	0	0	0	0	0	0	0	0	.500	.500
Nixon, Trot, Bos.*	.000	7	6	6	0	0	0	0	0	0	0	0	0	0	0	0	2	0	0	0	.000	.000
Norton, Greg, Chi.†	.167	20	20	18	2	3	5	0	1	0	2	0	0	0	2	0	4	0	0	0	.278	.250
Ochoa, Alex, Min.	.263	23	21	19	1	5	5	0	0	0	3	0	0	0	2	0	4	1	0	2	.263	.333
Offerman, Jose, K.C.†	.000	1	1	1	0	0	0	0	0	0	0	0	0	0	0	0	0	0	0	0	.000	.000
O'Leary, Troy, Bos.*	.500	2	2	2	1	1	1	0	0	0	0	0	0	0	0	0	1	0	0	0	.500	.500
Olivares, Omar, Ana.	.000	1	1	1	0	0	0	0	0	0	0	0	0	0	0	0	1	0	0	0	.000	.000
Oliver, Joe, Det.-Sea.	.000	4	4	2	1	0	0	0	0	0	1	0	0	0	2	0	0	0	0	0	.000	.500
O'Neill, Paul, N.Y.*	.000	2	2	1	0	0	0	0	0	0	1	0	1	0	0	0	1	0	0	0	.000	.000
Ortiz, David, Min.*	.000	6	6	3	0	0	0	0	0	0	0	0	0	0	3	0	2	0	0	0	.000	.500
Otanez, Willis, Bal.	.000	1	1	1	0	0	0	0	0	0	0	0	0	0	0	0	1	0	0	0	.000	.000
Palmeiro, Orlando, Ana.*	.238	21	21	21	1	5	7	2	0	0	2	0	0	0	0	0	1	0	0	0	.333	.238
Palmeiro, Rafael, Bal.*	.000	1	1	0	0	0	0	0	0	0	1	0	1	0	0	0	0	0	0	0	.000	.000
Palmer, Dean, K.C.	.000	1	1	1	0	0	0	0	0	0	0	0	0	0	0	0	1	0	0	0	.000	.000
Pendleton, Terry, K.C.†	.286	22	22	21	1	6	7	1	0	0	3	0	0	0	1	0	5	0	0	0	.333	.318
Perez, Robert, Sea.	.500	2	2	2	0	1	1	0	0	0	0	0	0	0	0	0	0	0	0	0	.500	.500
Pickering, Calvin, Bal.*	.000	1	1	1	0	0	0	0	0	0	0	0	0	0	0	0	1	0	0	0	.000	.000
Pierzynski, A.J., Min.*	1.000	1	1	1	0	1	1	0	0	0	0	0	0	0	0	0	0	0	0	0	1.000	1.000
Posada, Jorge, N.Y.†	.000	19	19	14	2	0	0	0	0	0	2	0	1	0	4	0	3	0	0	1	.000	.211
Pritchett, Chris, Ana.*	.333	3	3	3	0	1	1	0	0	0	0	0	0	0	0	0	1	0	0	0	.333	.333
Raines, Tim, N.Y.†	.133	24	24	15	0	2	2	0	0	0	6	0	2	1	6	0	2	0	0	0	.133	.375
Randa, Joe, Det.	.111	10	9	9	0	1	1	0	0	0	2	0	0	0	0	0	2	0	0	0	.111	.111
Reboulet, Jeff, Bal.	.500	6	6	6	1	3	3	0	0	0	0	0	0	0	0	0	1	0	0	0	.500	.500
Roberts, Bip, Det.-Oak.†	.294	19	19	17	1	5	6	1	0	0	2	0	1	1	1	0	2	2	0	2	.353	.368
Rodriguez, Ivan, Tex.	.000	1	1	1	0	0	0	0	0	0	0	0	0	0	0	0	0	0	0	0	.000	.000
Romero, Mandy, Bos.†	.286	7	7	7	1	2	3	1	0	0	1	0	0	0	0	0	2	0	0	0	.429	.286
Rossy, Rico, Sea.	1.000	1	1	1	0	1	1	0	0	0	0	0	0	0	0	0	0	0	0	0	1.000	1.000
Sadler, Donnie, Bos.	.000	1	1	1	0	0	0	0	0	0	0	0	0	0	0	0	0	0	0	0	.000	.000
Salmon, Tim, Ana.	.250	6	6	4	0	1	1	0	0	0	0	0	0	0	2	0	1	0	0	0	.250	.500
Samuel, Juan, Tor.	.250	8	8	8	1	2	5	0	0	1	1	0	0	0	0	0	1	0	0	0	.625	.250
Santiago, Benito, Tor.	.250	4	4	4	0	1	2	1	0	0	0	0	0	0	0	0	2	0	0	0	.500	.250
Sasser, Rob, Tex.	.000	1	1	1	0	0	0	0	0	0	0	0	0	0	0	0	0	0	0	0	.000	.000
Segui, David, Sea.†	.250	9	9	8	0	2	4	2	0	0	1	0	0	0	1	0	3	0	0	0	.500	.333
Sexson, Richie, Cle.	.000	2	2	2	0	0	0	0	0	0	1	0	0	0	0	0	0	0	0	0	.000	.000
Shave, Jon, Min.	.333	4	4	3	0	1	1	0	0	0	0	0	0	0	1	0	2	0	0	0	.333	.500
Sheldon, Scott, Tex.	.333	3	3	3	0	1	1	0	0	0	1	0	0	0	0	0	2	0	0	0	.333	.333
Shipley, Craig, Ana.	.222	12	12	9	1	2	4	2	0	0	2	1	0	1	1	0	0	0	0	2	.444	.364
Siddall, Joe, Det.*	.000	1	1	1	0	0	0	0	0	0	0	0	0	0	0	0	0	0	0	0	.000	.000
Sierra, Ruben, Chi.†	.250	10	10	8	0	2	4	2	0	0	3	0	0	0	2	0	1	0	0	0	.500	.400
Silvestri, Dave, T.B.	.000	2	2	2	0	0	0	0	0	0	0	0	0	0	0	0	1	0	0	0	.000	.000
Simms, Mike, Tex.	.333	20	18	15	1	5	8	0	0	1	6	0	1	0	2	0	2	0	0	0	.533	.389

Player, Team	Avg.	G	TPA	AB	R	H	TB	2B	3B	HR	RBI	SH	SF	HP	BB	IBB	SO	SB	CS	GDP	Slg.	OBP
Smith, Bobby, T.B.	.364	13	13	11	4	4	5	1	0	0	2	0	0	0	2	0	4	0	0	0	.455	.462
Snopek, Chris, Chi.-Bos.	.200	5	5	5	0	1	1	0	0	0	0	0	0	0	0	0	1	0	0	0	.200	.200
Sojo, Luis, N.Y.	.333	6	6	6	2	2	2	0	0	0	1	0	0	0	0	0	1	0	0	0	.333	.333
Sorrento, Paul, T.B.*	.222	12	12	9	2	2	8	0	0	2	6	0	0	0	3	0	5	0	0	0	.889	.417
Spencer, Shane, N.Y.	.400	6	5	5	0	2	3	1	0	0	1	0	0	0	0	0	1	0	0	0	.600	.400
Spiezio, Scott, Oak.†	.500	3	3	2	1	1	2	1	0	0	1	0	0	0	1	0	0	0	0	0	1.000	.667
Sprague, Ed Jr., Oak.	.333	3	3	3	0	1	2	1	0	0	1	0	0	0	0	0	1	0	0	0	.667	.333
Stahoviak, Scott, Min.*	.000	4	4	4	0	0	0	0	0	0	0	0	0	0	0	0	2	0	0	0	.000	.000
Stairs, Matt, Oak.*	.455	14	14	11	2	5	8	0	0	1	8	0	1	0	2	0	3	0	0	0	.727	.500
Stanley, Mike, Tor.-Bos.	.000	3	3	3	0	0	0	0	0	0	0	0	0	0	0	0	2	0	0	0	.000	.000
Steinbach, Terry, Min.	.000	4	4	4	0	0	0	0	0	0	0	0	0	0	0	0	3	0	0	0	.000	.000
Stevens, Lee, Tex.*	.059	22	20	17	1	1	1	0	0	0	1	0	0	0	3	1	7	0	0	0	.059	.200
Stewart, Shannon, Tor.	.500	2	2	2	1	1	2	1	0	0	0	0	0	0	0	0	1	1	0	0	1.000	.500
Strawberry, Darryl, N.Y.*	.333	7	7	6	2	2	8	0	0	2	8	0	0	0	1	0	2	0	0	0	1.333	.429
Surhoff, B.J., Bal.*	.000	8	8	7	0	0	0	0	0	0	0	0	0	0	1	0	0	0	0	1	.000	.125
Sutton, Larry, K.C.*	.115	29	29	26	1	3	3	0	0	0	2	0	0	0	3	0	5	0	0	0	.115	.207
Sveum, Dale, N.Y.†	.000	6	6	5	0	0	0	0	0	0	0	0	0	0	1	0	3	0	0	0	.000	.167
Sweeney, Mike, K.C.	.000	4	4	3	0	0	0	0	0	0	0	0	0	0	0	0	1	0	0	1	.000	.250
Thome, Jim, Cle.*	.000	3	3	1	1	0	0	0	0	0	0	0	0	0	2	0	1	0	0	0	.000	.667
Tomberlin, Andy, Det.*	.111	10	9	9	1	1	4	0	0	1	3	0	0	0	0	0	5	0	0	1	.444	.111
Trammell, Bubba, T.B.	.400	6	6	5	2	2	5	0	0	1	5	0	0	0	1	0	1	0	0	0	1.000	.500
Tremie, Chris, Tex.	1.000	2	2	1	2	1	2	1	0	0	0	0	0	0	1	0	0	0	0	0	2.000	1.000
Valentin, Javier, Min.†	.000	1	1	1	0	0	0	0	0	0	0	0	0	0	0	0	0	0	0	0	.000	.000
Varitek, Jason, Bos.†	.286	24	23	21	1	6	7	1	0	0	2	0	0	0	2	1	3	0	0	0	.333	.348
Velarde, Randy, Ana.	1.000	1	1	1	0	1	1	0	0	0	1	0	0	0	0	0	0	0	0	0	1.000	1.000
Vitiello, Joe, K.C.	.000	1	1	1	0	0	0	0	0	0	0	0	0	0	0	0	0	0	0	0	.000	.000
Voigt, Jack, Oak.	.000	10	10	9	0	0	0	0	0	0	0	0	0	0	1	0	1	0	0	0	.000	.100
Wakefield, Tim, Bos.	.000	1	1	0	0	0	0	0	0	0	0	1	0	0	0	0	0	0	0	0	.000	.000
Walbeck, Matt, Ana.†	.200	7	7	5	1	1	1	0	0	0	0	0	0	0	2	0	3	0	0	0	.200	.429
Walker, Todd, Min.*	1.000	2	2	1	0	1	2	1	0	0	2	0	1	0	0	0	0	0	0	0	2.000	.500
Walton, Jerome, T.B.	.200	5	5	5	0	1	2	1	0	0	1	0	0	0	0	0	1	0	0	0	.400	.200
Webster, Lenny, Bal.	.400	12	11	10	0	4	4	0	0	0	1	0	0	0	1	0	1	0	0	0	.400	.455
Whiten, Mark, Cle.†	.286	14	14	14	1	4	5	1	0	0	1	0	0	0	0	0	7	0	0	0	.357	.286
Wilkins, Rick, Sea.*	.000	8	5	3	0	0	0	0	0	0	1	0	1	0	1	0	2	0	0	0	.000	.200
Williams, Reggie, Ana.†	.333	4	4	3	0	1	1	0	0	0	0	0	0	0	1	0	2	1	1	0	.333	.500
Wilson, Dan, Sea.	.500	4	4	2	0	1	1	0	0	0	1	1	1	0	0	0	0	0	0	0	.500	.333
Wilson, Enrique, Cle.†	.000	2	2	1	0	0	0	0	0	0	0	0	0	0	1	0	0	0	0	0	.000	.500
Winn, Randy, T.B.†	.417	13	13	12	3	5	5	0	0	0	2	0	0	0	1	0	1	1	0	0	.417	.462
Witt, Bobby, Tex.	.000	1	1	1	0	0	0	0	0	0	0	0	0	0	0	0	0	0	0	0	.000	.000
Witt, Kevin, Tor.*	.000	4	4	4	0	0	0	0	0	0	0	0	0	0	0	0	2	0	0	0	.000	.000
Young, Ernie, K.C.	.250	5	5	4	0	1	2	1	0	0	0	0	0	0	1	0	0	0	0	0	.500	.400

PINCH-HITTERS WITH TWO OR MORE TEAMS

Player, Team	Avg.	G	TPA	AB	R	H	TB	2B	3B	HR	RBI	SH	SF	HP	BB	IBB	SO	SB	CS	GDP	Slg.	OBP
Bell, David, Cle.	.000	2	2	2	0	0	0	0	0	0	0	0	0	0	0	0	1	0	0	0	.000	.000
Bell, David, Sea.	.000	1	1	1	0	0	0	0	0	0	0	0	0	0	0	0	0	0	0	0	.000	.000
Berroa, Geronimo, Cle.	.000	2	2	2	0	0	0	0	0	0	0	0	0	0	0	0	1	0	0	0	.000	.000
Berroa, Geronimo, Det.	.100	16	12	10	1	1	1	0	0	0	2	0	0	0	2	0	4	0	0	1	.100	.250
Cora, Joey, Sea.†	.000	5	5	4	0	0	0	0	0	0	0	0	0	0	1	0	0	0	0	0	.000	.200
Cora, Joey, Cle.†	.000	2	2	2	0	0	0	0	0	0	0	0	0	0	0	0	1	0	0	0	.000	.000
Mack, Shane, Oak.	.000	2	2	2	0	0	0	0	0	0	0	0	0	0	0	0	0	0	0	0	.000	.000
Mack, Shane, K.C.	.455	14	14	11	2	5	9	1	0	1	4	0	0	3	0	0	2	1	0	0	.818	.571
Manto, Jeff, Cle.	.000	2	2	2	0	0	0	0	0	0	0	0	0	0	0	0	1	0	0	0	.000	.000
Manto, Jeff, Det.	.333	4	4	3	1	1	1	0	0	0	0	0	0	0	1	0	0	0	0	0	.333	.500
Merced, Orlando, Min.*	.400	6	6	5	1	2	3	1	0	0	2	0	1	0	0	0	1	0	0	0	.600	.333
Merced, Orlando, Bos.*	.000	7	6	5	0	0	0	0	0	0	1	0	1	0	0	0	1	0	0	0	.000	.000
Oliver, Joe, Det.	.000	1	1	1	0	0	0	0	0	0	0	0	0	0	0	0	0	0	0	0	.000	.000
Oliver, Joe, Sea.	.000	3	3	1	1	0	0	0	0	0	0	0	0	0	2	0	0	0	0	0	.000	.667
Roberts, Bip, Det.†	.250	5	5	4	0	1	1	0	0	0	1	0	0	1	0	0	0	1	0	1	.250	.400
Roberts, Bip, Oak.†	.308	14	14	13	1	4	5	1	0	0	1	0	0	1	0	0	2	1	0	1	.385	.357
Snopek, Chris, Chi.	.250	4	4	4	0	1	1	0	0	0	0	0	0	0	0	0	1	0	0	0	.250	.250
Snopek, Chris, Bos.	.000	1	1	1	0	0	0	0	0	0	0	0	0	0	0	0	0	0	0	0	.000	.000
Stanley, Mike, Tor.	.000	2	2	2	0	0	0	0	0	0	0	0	0	0	0	0	2	0	0	0	.000	.000
Stanley, Mike, Bos.	.000	1	1	1	0	0	0	0	0	0	0	0	0	0	0	0	0	0	0	0	.000	.000

PITCHING

TEAM

Team	W	L	Pct.	ERA	G	ShO	Rel.	Sv.	IP	H	TBF	R	ER	HR	SH	SF	HB	BB	IBB	SO	WP	Bk.
New York........	114	48	.704	3.82	162	16	334	48	1456.2	1357	6100	656	619	156	34	47	68	466	25	1080	37	5
Boston..............	92	70	.568	4.18	162	8	432	53	1436.0	1406	6141	729	667	168	26	47	53	504	33	1025	62	2
Toronto.............	88	74	.543	4.28	163	11	384	47	1465.0	1443	6352	768	697	169	42	44	45	587	26	1154	34	4
Tampa Bay	63	99	.389	4.35	162	7	410	28	1443.0	1425	6269	751	698	173	34	45	81	643	27	1008	43	3
Cleveland.........	89	73	.549	4.44	162	4	423	47	1460.0	1552	6393	779	721	171	43	49	67	563	48	1037	35	5
Anaheim..........	85	77	.525	4.49	162	5	415	54	1444.0	1481	6326	783	720	164	44	57	47	630	23	1091	70	4
Baltimore..........	79	83	.488	4.74	162	10	402	37	1431.1	1505	6213	785	754	169	46	50	46	535	33	1065	51	6
Minnesota	70	92	.432	4.75	162	8	432	42	1447.2	1622	6322	818	764	180	37	68	44	457	21	952	55	5
Oakland............	74	88	.457	4.81	162	4	408	39	1434.0	1555	6310	866	766	179	44	53	56	529	29	922	68	5
Detroit..............	65	97	.401	4.93	162	4	446	32	1446.1	1551	6327	863	792	185	46	49	40	595	53	947	60	0
Seattle..............	76	85	.472	4.93	161	7	368	31	1424.1	1530	6271	855	781	196	46	37	60	528	23	1156	61	6
Texas...............	88	74	.543	4.99	162	8	402	46	1431.1	1624	6357	871	794	164	35	63	45	519	32	994	62	2
Kansas City	72	89	.447	5.15	161	5	388	46	1436.1	1590	6369	899	822	196	30	58	60	568	28	999	72	5
Chicago............	80	82	.494	5.22	163	4	405	42	1438.2	1569	6368	931	835	211	32	51	54	580	20	911	58	10
Totals...........	1135	1131	.501	4.65	1134	101	5649	590	20194.2	21210	88118	11354	10430	2479	542	718	766	7704	421	14341	768	62

NOTE—Totals for earned runs for several clubs do not agree with composite total for all pitchers of each respective club due to instances in which provisions of Section 10.18(i) of the Scoring Rules were applied. The following differences are to be noted: Boston pitchers add to 668; Toronto pitchers add to 698; Cleveland pitchers add to 722; Minnesota pitchers add to 765; Oakland pitchers add to 769; Detroit pitchers add to 793; Seattle pitchers add to 784; Texas pitchers add to 795; Kansas City pitchers add to 824; Chicago pitchers add to 837.

INDIVIDUAL

TOP QUALIFIERS FOR EARNED-RUN AVERAGE TITLE

Minimum 162 innings. *Throws lefthanded.

Pitcher, Team	W	L	Pct.	ERA	G	GS	CG	ShO	GF	Sv.	IP	H	TBF	R	ER	HR	SH	SF	HB	BB	IBB	SO	WP	Bk.
Clemens, Roger, Tor.	20	6	.769	2.65	33	33	5	3	0	0	234.2	169	961	78	69	11	8	2	7	88	0	271	6	0
Martinez, Pedro, Bos.	19	7	.731	2.89	33	33	3	2	0	0	233.2	188	951	82	75	26	4	7	8	67	3	251	9	0
Rogers, Kenny, Oak.*	16	8	.667	3.17	34	34	7	1	0	0	238.2	215	970	96	84	19	4	5	7	67	0	138	5	2
Finley, Chuck, Ana.*	11	9	.550	3.39	34	34	1	1	0	0	223.1	210	976	97	84	20	3	5	6	109	1	212	8	0
Wells, David, N.Y.*	18	4	.818	3.49	30	30	8	5	0	0	214.1	195	851	86	83	29	2	2	1	29	0	163	2	0
Mussina, Mike, Bal.	13	10	.565	3.49	29	29	4	2	0	0	206.1	189	835	85	80	22	6	3	4	41	3	175	10	0
Moyer, Jamie, Sea.*	15	9	.625	3.53	34	34	4	3	0	0	234.1	234	974	99	92	23	4	3	10	42	2	158	3	1
Cone, David, N.Y.	20	7	.741	3.55	31	31	3	0	0	0	207.2	186	866	89	82	20	4	4	15	59	1	209	6	0
Arrojo, Rolando, T.B.	14	12	.538	3.56	32	32	2	2	0	0	202.0	195	853	84	80	21	5	3	19	65	2	152	3	1
Colon, Bartolo, Cle.	14	9	.609	3.71	31	31	6	2	0	0	204.0	205	883	91	84	15	10	2	3	79	5	158	4	0
Moehler, Brian, Det.	14	13	.519	3.90	33	33	4	3	0	0	221.1	220	912	103	96	30	3	3	2	56	1	123	4	0
Saberhagen, Bret, Bos.	15	8	.652	3.96	31	31	0	0	0	0	175.0	181	725	82	77	22	2	3	6	29	1	100	4	0
Fassero, Jeff, Sea.*	13	12	.520	3.97	32	32	7	0	0	0	224.2	223	954	115	99	33	8	8	10	66	2	176	12	0
Erickson, Scott, Bal.	16	13	.552	4.01	36	36	11	2	0	0	251.1	284	1102	125	112	23	7	2	13	69	4	186	4	0
Olivares, Omar, Ana.	9	9	.500	4.03	37	26	1	0	6	0	183.0	189	805	92	82	19	6	4	5	91	1	112	5	0

DEPARTMENTAL LEADERS: W—Clemens, Tor.; Cone, N.Y., Helling, Tex., 20; L—Candiotti, Oak.; Guzman, Bal.-Tor., Navarro, Chi., 16; G—Runyan, Det., 88; GS—Erickson, Bal., 36; CG—Erickson, Bal., 11; ShO—Wells, N.Y., 5; GF—Gordon, Bos., 69; Sv.—Gordon, Bos., 46; IP—Erickson, Bal., 251; H—Erickson, Bal., 284; TBF—Erickson, Bal., 1102; R—Nagy, Cle., 139; ER—Burkett, Tex., 123; HR—Belcher, K.C., 37; SH—Colon, Cle., Thompson, Det., 10; SF—Haney, K.C., 11; HB—Arrojo, T.B., 19; BB—Saunders, T.B., 111; IBB—Nagy, Cle., 12; SO—Clemens, Tor., 271; WP—Navarro, Chi., 18; BK—C. Castillo, Chi., Jackson, Cle., Parque, Chi., 3.

ALL PITCHERS

*Throws lefthanded.

Pitcher, Team	W	L	Pct.	ERA	G	GS	CG	ShO	GF	Sv.	IP	H	TBF	R	ER	HR	SH	SF	HB	BB	IBB	SO	WP	Bk.
Abbott, Jim, Chi.*	5	0	1.000	4.55	5	5	0	0	0	0	31.2	35	134	16	16	2	0	1	1	12	0	14	0	0
Abbott, Paul, Sea.	3	1	.750	4.01	4	4	0	0	0	0	24.2	24	105	11	11	2	0	1	0	10	0	22	3	0
Aguilera, Rick, Min.	4	9	.308	4.24	68	0	0	0	64	38	74.1	75	307	35	35	8	3	2	1	15	1	57	1	0
Aldred, Scott, T.B.*	0	0	.000	3.73	48	0	0	0	9	0	31.1	33	135	13	13	1	3	0	2	13	3	21	2	0
Almanzar, Carlos, Tor.	2	2	.500	5.34	25	0	0	0	8	0	28.2	34	129	18	17	4	1	0	1	8	2	20	0	0
Alvarez, Wilson, T.B.*	6	14	.300	4.73	25	25	0	0	0	0	142.2	130	624	78	75	18	1	2	9	68	0	107	4	0
Anderson, Matt, Det.	5	1	.833	3.27	42	0	0	0	10	0	44.0	38	194	16	16	3	6	3	2	31	4	44	2	0
Andujar, Luis, Tor.	0	0	.000	9.53	5	0	0	0	3	0	5.2	12	30	6	6	0	0	0	0	2	0	1	1	0
Appier, Kevin, K.C.	1	2	.333	7.80	3	3	0	0	0	0	15.0	21	69	13	13	3	0	1	1	5	1	9	1	0
Arrojo, Rolando, T.B.	14	12	.538	3.56	32	32	2	2	0	0	202.0	195	853	84	80	21	5	3	19	65	2	152	3	1
Assenmacher, Paul, Cle.*	2	5	.286	3.26	69	0	0	0	17	3	47.0	54	213	22	17	5	2	2	1	19	6	43	0	0
Avery, Steve, Bos.*	10	7	.588	5.02	34	23	0	0	4	0	123.2	128	546	74	69	14	3	0	4	64	0	57	7	0
Ayala, Bobby, Sea.	1	10	.091	7.29	62	0	0	0	36	8	75.1	100	351	66	61	9	8	6	1	26	4	68	4	0
Bailes, Scott, Tex.*	0	1	1.000	6.47	46	0	0	0	13	0	40.1	61	187	33	29	5	0	2	0	11	0	30	3	0
Baldwin, James, Chi.	13	6	.684	5.32	37	24	1	0	3	0	159.0	176	712	103	94	18	5	3	10	60	2	108	5	1
Banks, Willie, N.Y.	1	1	.500	10.05	9	0	0	0	5	0	14.1	20	77	16	16	4	2	0	1	12	2	8	1	0
Baptist, Travis, Min.*	0	1	1.000	5.67	13	0	0	0	4	0	27.0	34	123	18	17	5	0	0	0	11	1	11	0	0
Barber, Brian, K.C.	2	4	.333	6.00	8	8	0	0	0	0	42.0	45	180	28	28	5	0	1	1	13	1	24	4	0
Barkley, Brian, Bos.*	0	0	.000	9.82	6	0	0	0	1	0	11.0	16	59	13	12	2	0	2	1	9	1	2	1	0
Belcher, Tim, K.C.	14	14	.500	4.27	34	34	2	0	0	0	234.0	247	1003	127	111	37	5	9	7	73	0	130	6	1
Benitez, Armando, Bal.	5	6	.455	3.82	71	0	0	0	54	22	68.1	48	289	29	29	10	3	2	4	39	2	87	0	0
Bennett, Joel, Bal.	0	0	.000	4.50	2	0	0	0	2	0	2.0	2	11	1	1	0	0	0	0	3	0	0	0	0
Bere, Jason, Chi.	3	7	.300	6.45	18	15	0	0	0	0	83.2	98	404	71	60	14	4	5	2	58	0	53	7	0
Bevil, Brian, K.C.	3	1	.750	6.30	39	0	0	0	10	0	40.0	47	194	29	28	4	1	2	3	22	1	47	6	0
Bochtler, Doug, Det.	0	2	.000	6.15	51	0	0	0	11	0	67.1	73	312	48	46	17	2	3	3	42	6	45	6	0
Bones, Ricky, K.C.	2	2	.500	3.04	32	0	0	0	12	1	53.1	49	231	18	18	4	5	0	1	24	5	38	2	0

Pitcher, Team	W	L	Pct.	ERA	G	GS	CG	ShO	GF	Sv.	IP	H	TBF	R	ER	HR	SH	SF	HB	BB	IBB	SO	WP	Bk.
Borowski, Joe, N.Y.	1	0	1.000	6.52	8	0	0	0	6	0	9.2	11	42	7	7	0	0	0	0	4	0	7	0	0
Bradford, Chad, Chi.	2	1	.667	3.23	29	0	0	0	8	1	30.2	27	125	16	11	0	0	0	0	7	0	11	1	1
Bradley, Ryan, N.Y.	2	1	.667	5.68	5	1	0	0	1	0	12.2	12	59	9	8	2	0	1	1	9	0	13	0	0
Brocail, Doug, Det.	5	2	.714	2.73	60	0	0	0	24	0	62.2	47	247	23	19	2	2	3	1	18	3	55	6	0
Brunson, Will, Det.*	0	0	.000	0.00	8	0	0	0	1	0	3.0	2	11	0	0	0	0	0	0	1	0	1	1	0
Bruske, Jim, N.Y.	1	0	1.000	3.00	3	1	0	0	0	0	9.0	9	36	3	3	2	0	0	0	1	0	3	0	0
Buddie, Mike, N.Y.	4	1	.800	5.62	24	2	0	0	8	0	41.2	46	180	29	26	5	1	1	3	13	1	20	2	1
Bullinger, Jim, Sea.	0	1	.000	15.88	2	1	0	0	0	0	5.2	13	33	10	10	3	0	1	0	2	0	4	0	0
Burba, Dave, Cle.	15	10	.600	4.11	32	31	0	0	0	0	203.2	210	870	100	93	30	3	10	7	69	4	132	6	0
Burkett, John, Tex.	9	13	.409	5.68	32	32	0	0	0	0	195.0	230	854	131	123	19	7	5	8	46	1	131	3	0
Byrdak, Tim, K.C.*	0	0	.000	5.40	3	0	0	0	0	0	1.2	5	9	1	1	1	0	0	0	0	0	1	0	0
Cadaret, Greg, Ana.-Tex.*	1	2	.333	4.23	50	0	0	0	14	1	44.2	49	203	21	21	7	2	1	3	18	0	42	8	0
Candiotti, Tom, Oak.	11	16	.407	4.84	33	33	3	0	0	0	201.0	222	878	124	108	30	7	8	9	63	2	98	14	0
Carlson, Dan, T.B.	0	0	.000	7.64	10	0	0	0	1	0	17.2	25	86	15	15	3	2	1	3	8	0	16	0	0
Carpenter, Chris, Tor.	12	7	.632	4.37	33	24	1	1	4	0	175.0	177	742	97	85	18	4	5	5	61	1	136	5	0
Carrasco, Hector, Min.	4	2	.667	4.38	63	0	0	0	20	1	61.2	75	287	30	30	4	0	8	1	31	1	46	8	0
Casian, Larry, Chi.*	0	0	.000	11.25	4	0	0	0	3	0	4.0	8	23	5	5	0	0	0	2	1	0	6	0	0
Castillo, Tony, Chi.*	1	2	.333	8.00	25	0	0	0	4	0	27.0	38	129	25	24	7	0	0	2	11	0	14	0	0
Castillo, Carlos, Chi.	6	4	.600	5.11	54	2	0	0	11	0	100.1	94	431	61	57	17	2	7	5	35	1	64	4	3
Castillo, Frank, Det.	3	9	.250	6.83	27	19	0	0	4	1	116.0	150	531	91	88	17	2	6	5	44	0	81	0	0
Charlton, Norm, Bal.*	2	1	.667	6.94	36	0	0	0	11	0	35.0	46	178	27	27	5	1	1	0	25	0	41	5	0
Checo, Robinson, Bos.	0	2	.000	9.39	2	2	0	0	0	0	7.2	11	34	8	8	3	0	0	0	5	0	5	1	0
Cho, Jin Ho, Bos.	0	3	.000	8.20	4	4	0	0	0	0	18.2	28	87	17	17	4	0	1	1	3	0	15	1	0
Clemens, Roger, Tor.	20	6	.769	2.65	33	33	5	3	0	0	234.2	169	961	78	69	11	8	2	7	88	0	271	6	0
Cloude, Ken, Sea.	8	10	.444	6.37	30	30	0	0	0	0	155.1	187	722	116	110	29	4	4	3	80	4	114	2	1
Colon, Bartolo, Cle.	14	9	.609	3.71	31	31	6	2	0	0	204.0	205	883	91	84	15	10	2	3	79	5	158	4	0
Cone, David, N.Y.	20	7	.741	3.55	31	31	3	0	0	0	207.2	186	866	89	82	20	4	4	15	59	1	209	6	0
Connelly, Steve, Oak.	0	0	.000	1.93	3	0	0	0	1	0	4.2	10	28	1	1	0	0	0	1	4	0	1	0	0
Coppinger, Rocky, Bal.	0	0	.000	5.17	6	1	0	0	3	0	15.2	16	72	9	9	3	0	0	0	7	1	13	0	0
Corsi, Jim, Bos.	3	2	.600	2.59	59	0	0	0	9	0	66.0	58	274	23	19	6	2	1	1	23	2	49	3	0
Crabtree, Tim, Tex.	6	1	.857	3.59	64	0	0	0	14	0	85.1	86	371	40	34	3	1	6	3	35	2	60	6	0
Crow, Dean, Det.	2	2	.500	3.94	32	0	0	0	15	0	45.2	55	197	22	20	6	2	1	2	16	6	18	0	0
DeLucia, Rich, Ana.	2	6	.250	4.27	61	0	0	0	18	3	71.2	56	314	36	34	10	5	7	3	46	5	73	8	1
Dickson, Jason, Ana.	10	10	.500	6.05	27	18	0	0	5	0	122.0	147	545	89	82	17	4	9	6	41	1	61	6	0
Dougherty, Jim, Oak.	0	2	.000	8.25	9	0	0	0	4	0	12.0	17	59	11	11	2	1	0	1	7	0	3	0	0
Drabek, Doug, Bal.	6	11	.353	7.29	23	21	1	0	1	0	108.2	138	484	90	88	20	0	7	5	29	2	55	1	0
Duran, Roberto, Det.*	0	1	.000	5.87	18	0	0	0	5	0	15.1	9	74	10	10	0	2	0	2	17	0	12	2	0
Duvall, Mike, T.B.*	0	0	.000	6.75	3	0	0	0	0	0	4.0	4	17	3	3	0	0	0	0	2	0	1	0	0
Dykhoff, Radhames, Bal.*	0	0	.000	18.00	1	0	0	0	1	0	1.0	2	6	2	2	0	0	0	0	1	0	1	0	0
Eckersley, Dennis, Bos.	4	1	.800	4.76	50	0	0	0	13	1	39.2	46	171	21	21	6	2	1	2	8	3	22	0	0
Eiland, Dave, T.B.	0	1	.000	20.25	1	1	0	0	0	0	2.2	6	17	6	6	0	0	0	0	3	0	1	0	0
Erdos, Todd, N.Y.	0	0	.000	9.00	2	0	0	0	1	0	2.0	5	11	2	2	0	0	0	0	1	1	0	0	0
Erickson, Scott, Bal.	16	13	.552	4.01	36	36	11	2	0	0	251.1	284	1102	125	112	23	7	2	13	69	4	186	4	0
Escobar, Kelvim, Tor.	7	3	.700	3.73	22	10	0	0	2	0	79.2	72	342	37	33	5	0	3	0	35	0	72	0	0
Evans, Bart, K.C.	0	0	.000	2.00	8	0	0	0	3	0	9.0	7	34	3	2	1	0	0	0	0	0	7	0	0
Eyre, Scott, Chi.*	3	8	.273	5.38	33	17	0	0	10	0	107.0	114	491	78	64	24	2	3	2	64	0	73	7	0
Fassero, Jeff, Sea.*	13	12	.520	3.97	32	32	7	0	0	0	224.2	223	954	115	99	33	8	8	10	66	2	176	12	0
Fetters, Mike, Oak.-Ana.	2	8	.200	4.30	60	0	0	0	28	5	58.2	62	264	34	28	5	4	2	1	25	2	43	6	0
Finley, Chuck, Ana.*	11	9	.550	3.39	34	34	1	1	0	0	223.1	210	976	97	84	20	3	5	6	109	1	212	8	0
Florie, Bryce, Det.	8	9	.471	4.80	42	16	0	0	6	0	133.0	141	580	80	71	16	3	2	4	59	6	97	9	0
Fordham, Tom, Chi.*	1	2	.333	6.75	29	5	0	0	5	0	48.0	51	228	36	36	7	1	1	1	42	0	23	1	0
Fossas, Tony, Sea.-Tex.*	1	3	.250	5.30	33	0	0	0	9	0	18.2	22	84	11	11	1	1	1	0	10	0	17	1	0
Foulke, Keith, Chi.	3	2	.600	4.13	54	0	0	0	18	1	65.1	51	267	31	30	9	2	2	4	20	3	57	3	1
Fussell, Chris, Bal.	0	1	.000	8.38	3	2	0	0	0	0	9.2	11	47	9	9	1	1	1	0	9	1	8	0	0
Gaillard, Eddie, T.B.	0	0	.000	5.87	6	0	0	0	1	0	7.2	4	30	5	5	3	0	0	0	3	0	5	0	0
Gajkowski, Steve, Sea.	0	0	.000	7.27	9	0	0	0	3	0	8.2	14	42	8	7	3	0	0	2	4	0	3	0	0
Garces, Rich, Bos.	1	1	.500	3.33	30	0	0	0	11	1	46.0	36	201	19	17	6	2	1	2	27	3	34	1	1
Gooden, Dwight, Cle.	8	6	.571	3.76	23	23	0	0	0	0	134.0	135	580	59	56	13	1	4	9	51	0	83	3	0
Gordon, Tom, Bos.	7	4	.636	2.72	73	0	0	0	69	46	79.1	55	317	24	24	2	2	2	0	25	1	78	9	0
Gorecki, Rick, T.B.	1	2	.333	4.86	3	3	0	0	0	0	16.2	15	70	9	9	1	0	2	0	10	0	7	1	0
Greisinger, Seth, Det.	6	9	.400	5.12	21	21	0	0	0	0	130.0	142	562	79	74	17	2	5	4	48	2	66	3	0
Groom, Buddy, Oak.*	3	1	.750	4.24	75	0	0	0	13	0	57.1	62	251	30	27	4	1	3	1	20	1	36	1	0
Guardado, Eddie, Min.*	3	1	.750	4.52	79	0	0	0	12	0	65.2	66	286	34	33	10	3	6	0	28	6	53	2	0
Gunderson, Eric, Tex.*	0	3	.000	5.19	68	1	0	0	13	0	67.2	88	303	43	39	13	1	3	1	19	4	41	4	0
Guzman, Juan, Tor.-Bal.	10	16	.385	4.35	33	33	2	0	0	0	211.0	193	918	117	102	23	2	5	8	98	2	168	11	0
Halladay, Roy, Tor.	1	0	1.000	1.93	2	2	1	0	0	0	14.0	9	53	4	3	2	0	0	0	2	0	13	0	0
Halter, Shane, K.C.	0	0	.000	0.00	1	0	0	0	1	0	1.0	1	3	0	0	0	0	0	0	0	0	0	0	0
Haney, Chris, K.C.*	6	6	.500	7.03	33	12	0	0	2	0	97.1	125	450	78	76	18	2	11	5	36	0	51	4	1
Hanson, Erik, Tor.	0	3	.000	6.24	11	8	0	0	3	0	49.0	73	243	34	34	10	3	0	1	29	1	21	1	1
Harriger, Denny, Det.	0	3	.000	6.75	4	2	0	0	2	0	12.0	17	61	12	9	1	1	0	0	8	2	3	0	0
Harris, Pep, Ana.	3	1	.750	4.35	49	0	0	0	13	0	60.0	55	257	32	29	7	3	1	0	23	4	34	2	0
Hasegawa, Shigetoshi, Ana.	8	3	.727	3.14	61	0	0	0	20	5	97.1	86	401	37	34	14	4	6	2	32	2	73	5	2
Hawkins, LaTroy, Min.	7	14	.333	5.25	33	33	0	0	0	0	190.1	227	840	126	111	27	4	10	5	61	1	105	10	2
Haynes, Jimmy, Oak.	11	9	.550	5.09	33	33	1	1	0	0	194.1	229	875	124	110	25	5	9	5	88	4	134	11	0
Heathcott, Mike, Chi.	0	0	.000	3.00	1	0	0	0	0	0	3.0	2	12	1	1	0	0	0	0	1	0	3	2	0
Helling, Rick, Tex.	20	7	.741	4.41	33	33	4	2	0	0	216.1	209	922	109	106	27	6	10	1	78	6	164	10	0
Henry, Butch, Bos.*	0	0	.000	4.00	2	2	0	0	0	0	9.0	8	38	4	4	2	0	0	1	3	0	6	0	0
Hentgen, Pat, Tor.	12	11	.522	5.17	29	29	0	0	0	0	177.2	208	795	109	102	28	5	7	5	69	1	94	7	1
Heredia, Gil, Oak.	3	3	.500	2.74	8	6	0	0	2	0	42.2	43	175	14	13	4	1	0	3	3	0	27	0	0
Hernandez, Xavier, Tex.	6	6	.500	3.57	46	0	0	0	15	1	58.0	43	243	27	23	5	2	2	1	30	1	41	4	0
Hernandez, Orlando, N.Y.	12	4	.750	3.13	21	21	3	1	0	0	141.0	113	574	53	49	11	3	5	6	52	1	131	5	2
Hernandez, Roberto, T.B.	2	6	.250	4.04	67	0	0	0	58	26	71.1	55	310	33	32	5	4	0	5	41	4	55	1	0

Pitcher, Team	W	L	Pct.	ERA	G	GS	CG	ShO	GF	Sv.	IP	H	TBF	R	ER	HR	SH	SF	HB	BB	IBB	SO	WP	Bk.
Hill, Ken, Ana.	9	6	.600	4.98	19	19	0	0	0	0	103.0	123	458	60	57	6	7	5	3	47	0	57	3	0
Holdridge, David, Sea.	0	0	.000	4.05	7	0	0	0	3	0	6.2	6	31	3	3	0	0	1	0	4	0	6	3	0
Holmes, Darren, N.Y.	0	3	.000	3.33	34	0	0	0	13	2	51.1	53	215	19	19	4	0	3	2	14	3	31	1	0
Holtz, Mike, Ana.*	2	2	.500	4.75	53	0	0	0	9	1	30.1	38	137	16	16	0	1	2	1	15	1	29	4	0
Holzemer, Mark, Oak.*	1	0	1.000	5.59	13	0	0	0	4	0	9.2	13	44	6	6	1	0	1	1	3	0	3	1	0
Howry, Bobby, Chi.	0	3	.000	3.15	44	0	0	0	15	9	54.1	37	217	20	19	7	2	3	2	19	2	51	2	0
Irabu, Hideki, N.Y.	13	9	.591	4.06	29	28	2	1	0	0	173.0	148	732	79	78	27	6	6	9	76	1	126	6	1
Jackson, Mike, Cle.	1	1	.500	1.55	69	0	0	0	57	40	64.0	43	239	11	11	4	1	0	4	13	0	55	1	3
Jacome, Jason, Cle.*	0	0	.000	14.40	1	1	0	0	0	0	5.0	10	26	8	8	2	0	0	0	3	0	2	0	0
James, Mike, Ana.	0	0	.000	1.93	11	0	0	0	3	0	14.0	10	55	3	3	0	0	0	0	7	0	12	0	0
Jerzembeck, Mike, N.Y.	0	1	.000	12.79	3	2	0	0	1	0	6.1	9	31	9	9	2	0	1	0	4	0	1	1	1
Johns, Doug, Bal.*	3	3	.500	4.57	31	10	0	0	5	1	86.2	108	382	46	44	9	4	6	4	32	2	34	3	0
Johnson, Jason, T.B.	2	5	.286	5.70	13	13	0	0	0	0	60.0	74	274	38	38	9	1	1	3	27	0	36	2	0
Johnson, Jonathan, Tex.	0	0	.000	8.31	1	1	0	0	0	0	4.1	5	22	4	4	0	0	1	0	5	0	3	0	0
Johnson, Randy, Sea.*	9	10	.474	4.33	23	23	6	2	0	0	160.0	146	685	90	77	19	5	1	11	60	0	213	7	2
Jones, Doug, Cle.	1	2	.333	3.45	23	0	0	0	8	1	31.1	34	133	12	12	2	2	3	0	6	3	28	0	1
Jones, Todd, Det.	1	4	.200	4.97	65	0	0	0	53	28	63.1	58	279	38	35	7	2	6	2	36	4	57	5	0
Juden, Jeff, Ana.	1	3	.250	6.75	8	6	0	0	1	0	40.0	33	172	32	30	7	0	0	2	18	0	39	4	0
Kamieniecki, Scott, Bal.	2	6	.250	6.75	12	11	0	0	1	0	54.2	67	249	41	41	7	3	2	4	26	0	25	2	0
Karchner, Matt, Chi.	2	4	.333	5.15	32	0	0	0	23	11	36.2	33	167	21	21	2	3	4	5	19	6	30	0	0
Karsay, Steve, Cle.	0	2	.000	5.92	11	1	0	0	4	0	24.1	31	111	16	16	3	1	2	2	6	1	13	2	0
Keagle, Greg, Det.	0	5	.000	5.59	9	7	0	0	0	0	38.2	46	180	26	24	5	0	0	4	20	0	25	2	0
Key, Jimmy, Bal.*	6	3	.667	4.20	25	11	0	0	4	0	79.1	77	327	39	37	5	1	1	3	23	0	53	1	1
Krivda, Rick, Cle.*	0	0	.000	3.24	11	1	0	0	5	0	25.0	24	112	10	9	2	0	0	0	16	1	10	1	1
Levine, Al, Tex.	0	1	.000	4.50	30	0	0	0	11	0	58.0	68	251	30	29	6	1	3	0	16	1	19	5	0
Lewis, Richie, Bal.	0	0	.000	15.43	2	1	0	0	0	0	4.2	8	25	8	8	2	0	1	0	5	0	4	1	0
Lira, Felipe, Sea.	1	0	1.000	4.60	7	0	0	0	3	0	15.2	22	75	10	8	5	0	1	0	5	0	16	1	0
Lloyd, Graeme, N.Y.*	3	0	1.000	1.67	50	0	0	0	8	0	37.2	26	145	10	7	3	0	1	2	6	2	20	2	0
Loaiza, Esteban, Tex.	3	6	.333	5.90	14	14	1	0	0	0	79.1	103	357	57	52	15	2	5	2	22	3	55	3	0
Lopez, Albie, T.B.	7	4	.636	2.60	54	0	0	0	12	1	79.2	73	335	31	23	7	4	3	3	32	4	62	5	0
Lorraine, Andrew, Sea.*	0	0	.000	2.45	4	0	0	0	1	0	3.2	3	16	1	1	0	0	0	0	4	0	0	1	0
Lowe, Derek, Bos.	3	9	.250	4.02	63	10	0	0	8	4	123.0	126	527	60	55	5	4	5	4	42	5	77	8	0
Mahay, Ron, Bos.*	1	1	.500	3.46	29	0	0	0	6	1	26.0	26	120	16	10	2	0	4	2	15	1	14	3	0
Martin, Tom, Cle.*	1	1	.500	12.89	14	0	0	0	1	0	14.2	29	85	21	21	3	1	1	0	12	0	9	2	0
Martinez, Pedro, Bos.	19	7	.731	2.89	33	33	3	2	0	0	233.2	188	951	82	75	26	4	7	8	67	3	251	9	0
Mathews, Terry, Bal.	0	1	.000	6.20	17	0	0	0	2	0	20.1	26	90	15	14	6	5	1	0	8	3	10	0	0
Mathews, T.J., Oak.	7	4	.636	4.58	66	0	0	0	15	1	72.2	71	319	44	37	6	2	9	4	29	3	53	1	0
McCarthy, Greg, Sea.*	1	2	.333	5.01	29	0	0	0	5	0	23.1	18	106	13	13	6	2	0	3	17	2	25	1	0
McDill, Allen, K.C.*	0	0	.000	10.50	7	0	0	0	1	0	6.0	9	29	7	7	3	0	0	0	5	0	3	0	0
McDowell, Jack, Ana.	5	3	.625	5.09	14	14	0	0	0	0	76.0	96	334	45	43	11	3	2	1	19	1	45	2	0
Mecir, Jim, T.B.	7	2	.778	3.11	68	0	0	0	23	0	84.0	68	343	30	29	6	3	2	3	33	5	77	2	0
Mendoza, Ramiro, N.Y.	10	2	.833	3.25	41	14	1	1	6	1	130.1	131	548	50	47	9	6	7	9	30	6	56	3	0
Mesa, Jose, Cle.	3	4	.429	5.17	44	0	0	0	18	1	54.0	61	244	36	31	7	2	2	4	20	3	35	2	0
Miller, Travis, Min.*	0	2	.000	3.86	14	0	0	0	2	0	23.1	25	104	10	10	0	0	1	0	11	1	23	2	0
Mills, Alan, Bal.	3	4	.429	3.74	72	0	0	0	13	2	77.0	55	327	32	32	8	2	3	1	50	8	57	4	0
Milton, Eric, Min.*	8	14	.364	5.64	32	32	1	0	0	0	172.1	195	772	113	108	25	2	6	2	70	0	107	1	0
Moehler, Brian, Det.	14	13	.519	3.90	33	33	4	3	0	0	221.1	220	912	96	96	30	3	3	2	56	1	123	4	0
Mohler, Mike, Oak.*	3	3	.500	5.16	57	0	0	0	16	0	61.0	70	277	38	35	6	3	2	4	26	3	42	3	1
Montgomery, Jeff, K.C.	2	5	.286	4.98	56	0	0	0	54	36	56.0	58	247	35	31	8	2	1	2	22	2	54	0	1
Morgan, Mike, Min.	4	2	.667	3.49	18	17	0	0	0	0	98.0	108	412	41	38	13	0	3	7	24	1	50	1	0
Morman, Alvin, Cle.*	0	1	.000	5.32	31	0	0	0	5	0	22.0	25	96	13	13	1	0	1	0	11	1	16	2	0
Moyer, Jamie, Sea.*	15	9	.625	3.53	34	34	4	3	0	0	234.1	234	974	99	92	23	4	3	10	42	2	158	3	1
Munoz, Bobby, Bal.	0	0	.000	5.75	9	1	0	0	5	0	12.0	18	58	13	13	4	1	3	1	6	0	6	0	1
Mussina, Mike, Bal.	13	10	.565	3.49	29	29	4	2	0	0	206.1	189	835	85	80	22	6	3	4	41	3	175	10	0
Myers, Randy, Tor.*	3	4	.429	4.46	41	0	0	0	37	28	42.1	44	190	21	21	4	2	1	2	19	4	32	2	0
Nagy, Charles, Cle.	15	10	.600	5.22	33	33	2	0	0	0	210.1	250	930	139	122	34	8	6	9	66	12	120	3	0
Naulty, Dan, Min.	0	0	.000	4.94	19	0	0	0	9	0	23.2	25	104	16	13	3	0	1	0	10	1	15	0	0
Navarro, Jaime, Chi.	8	16	.333	6.36	37	27	1	0	4	1	172.2	223	802	135	122	30	3	7	7	77	1	71	18	0
Nelson, Jeff, N.Y.	5	3	.625	3.79	45	0	0	0	13	3	40.1	44	192	18	17	1	1	3	8	22	4	35	2	0
Ogea, Chad, Cle.	5	4	.556	5.61	19	9	0	0	1	0	69.0	74	307	44	43	9	1	3	7	25	1	43	0	0
Olivares, Omar, Ana.	9	9	.500	4.03	37	26	1	0	6	0	183.0	189	805	92	82	19	6	4	5	91	1	112	5	0
Oliver, Darren, Tex.*	6	7	.462	6.53	19	19	2	0	0	0	103.1	140	493	84	75	11	3	6	10	43	1	58	6	1
Oquist, Mike, Oak.	7	11	.389	6.22	31	29	0	0	2	0	175.0	210	777	125	121	27	5	6	5	57	1	112	4	0
Orosco, Jesse, Bal.*	4	1	.800	3.18	69	0	0	0	26	7	56.2	46	243	20	20	6	4	2	1	28	1	50	3	1
Paniagua, Jose, Sea.	2	0	1.000	2.05	18	0	0	0	2	1	22.0	15	83	5	5	3	0	5	0	6	2	16	2	0
Parque, Jim, Chi.*	7	5	.583	5.10	21	21	0	0	0	0	113.0	135	507	72	64	14	1	0	6	49	0	77	0	3
Patterson, Danny, Tex.	2	5	.286	4.45	56	0	0	0	21	2	60.2	64	257	31	30	11	1	1	2	19	2	33	3	0
Pavlik, Roger, Tex.	1	1	.500	3.86	5	0	0	0	2	1	14.0	16	63	8	6	2	0	1	1	5	1	8	1	0
Pennington, Brad, T.B.*	0	0	.000	---	1	0	0	0	0	0	0.0	1	4	1	1	0	0	0	0	3	0	0	0	0
Percival, Troy, Ana.	2	7	.222	3.65	67	0	0	0	60	42	66.2	45	287	31	27	5	3	2	3	37	4	87	3	0
Perisho, Matt, Tex.*	0	2	.000	27.00	2	2	0	0	0	0	1.2	5	15	40	17	15	2	0	0	2	8	0	2	0	0
Person, Robert, Tor.	3	1	.750	7.04	27	0	0	0	14	6	38.1	45	184	31	30	9	2	5	2	22	1	31	0	0
Pettitte, Andy, N.Y.*	16	11	.593	4.24	33	32	5	0	0	0	216.1	226	932	110	102	20	6	7	6	87	1	146	5	0
Pichardo, Hipolito, K.C.	7	8	.467	5.13	27	18	0	0	2	1	112.1	126	503	73	64	11	3	3	4	43	2	55	2	0
Pittsley, Jim, K.C.	1	1	.500	6.59	39	2	0	0	11	0	68.1	88	320	56	50	13	3	5	2	37	1	44	6	0
Plesac, Dan, Tor.*	4	3	.571	3.78	78	0	0	0	16	4	50.0	41	203	23	21	4	0	3	1	16	1	55	0	0
Plunk, Eric, Cle.	3	1	.750	4.83	37	0	0	0	6	0	41.0	44	178	23	22	6	3	2	2	15	1	38	0	0
Ponson, Sidney, Bal.	8	9	.471	5.27	31	20	0	0	5	1	135.0	157	588	82	79	19	3	4	3	42	2	85	4	1
Poole, Jim, Cle.*	0	0	.000	5.14	12	0	0	0	1	0	7.0	9	34	4	4	0	0	0	1	3	1	11	0	0
Powell, Brian, Det.	3	8	.273	6.35	18	16	0	0	0	0	83.2	101	383	67	59	17	1	1	2	36	2	46	3	0
Prieto, Ariel, Oak.	0	1	.000	11.88	2	2	0	0	0	0	8.1	17	47	11	11	2	0	0	1	5	1	8	0	0
Quantrill, Paul, Tor.	3	4	.429	2.59	82	0	0	0	32	7	80.0	88	345	26	23	5	7	4	3	22	6	59	1	0

Pitcher, Team	W	L	Pct.	ERA	G	GS	CG	ShO	GF	Sv.	IP	H	TBF	R	ER	HR	SH	SF	HB	BB	IBB	SO	WP	Bk.
Radke, Brad, Min.	12	14	.462	4.30	32	32	5	1	0	0	213.2	238	904	109	102	23	9	3	9	43	1	146	3	1
Rakers, Jason, Cle.	0	0	.000	9.00	1	0	0	0	1	0	1.0	0	6	1	1	0	0	1	0	3	0	0	0	0
Rapp, Pat, K.C.	12	13	.480	5.30	32	32	1	1	0	0	188.1	208	855	117	111	24	3	6	10	107	7	132	14	0
Reed, Steve, Cle.	2	2	.500	6.66	20	0	0	0	5	0	25.2	26	109	19	19	4	0	0	1	8	0	23	0	0
Rekar, Bryan, T.B.	2	8	.200	4.98	16	15	1	0	1	0	86.2	95	369	56	48	16	1	8	2	21	0	55	1	0
Reyes, Carlos, Bos.	1	1	.500	3.52	24	0	0	0	10	0	38.1	35	158	15	15	2	0	1	1	14	2	23	3	0
Rhodes, Arthur, Bal.*	4	4	.500	3.51	45	0	0	0	10	4	77.0	65	321	30	30	8	2	5	1	34	2	83	1	1
Rios, Danny, K.C.	0	1	.000	6.14	5	0	0	0	1	0	7.1	9	38	9	5	1	0	1	1	6	0	6	1	0
Risley, Bill, Tor.	3	4	.429	5.27	44	0	0	0	18	0	54.2	52	245	37	32	7	3	3	4	34	4	42	3	1
Ritchie, Todd, Min.	0	0	.000	5.63	15	0	0	0	7	0	24.0	30	113	17	15	1	0	0	0	9	0	21	3	0
Rivera, Mariano, N.Y.	3	0	1.000	1.91	54	0	0	0	49	36	61.1	48	246	13	13	3	2	3	1	17	1	36	0	0
Rizzo, Todd, Chi.*	0	0	.000	13.50	9	0	0	0	1	0	6.2	12	38	12	10	0	0	1	0	6	0	3	2	0
Robertson, Rich, Ana.*	0	0	.000	15.88	5	0	0	0	0	0	5.2	11	31	11	10	3	0	1	0	2	0	3	0	0
Rodriguez, Frankie, Min.	4	6	.400	6.56	20	11	0	0	4	0	70.0	88	329	58	51	6	1	5	3	30	0	62	6	1
Rodriguez, Nerio, Bal.-Tor.	2	3	.400	8.56	13	4	0	0	3	0	27.1	35	133	26	26	1	0	2	1	17	0	11	1	0
Rogers, Kenny, Oak.*	16	8	.667	3.17	34	34	7	1	0	0	238.2	215	970	96	84	19	4	5	7	67	0	138	5	2
Rosado, Jose, K.C.*	8	11	.421	4.69	38	25	2	1	1	1	174.2	180	757	106	91	25	1	3	5	57	2	135	6	1
Rose, Brian, Bos.	1	4	.200	6.93	8	8	0	0	0	0	37.2	43	168	32	29	9	0	1	2	14	0	18	0	0
Ruebel, Matt, T.B.*	0	2	.000	6.23	7	1	0	0	1	0	8.2	11	39	7	6	3	0	0	0	4	0	6	0	0
Runyan, Sean, Det.*	1	4	.200	3.58	88	0	0	0	11	1	50.1	47	223	23	20	7	2	7	2	28	3	39	5	0
Rusch, Glendon, K.C.*	6	15	.286	5.88	29	24	1	1	2	1	154.2	191	686	104	101	22	1	2	4	50	0	94	1	0
Saberhagen, Bret, Bos.	15	8	.652	3.96	31	31	0	0	0	0	175.0	181	725	82	77	22	2	3	6	29	1	100	4	0
Sager, A.J., Det.	4	2	.667	6.52	31	3	0	0	7	2	59.1	79	274	47	43	7	5	2	1	23	4	23	4	0
Sampson, Ben, Min.*	1	0	1.000	1.56	5	2	0	0	1	0	17.1	10	67	3	3	0	0	2	1	6	0	16	2	0
Sanders, Scott, Det.	0	2	.000	17.69	3	2	0	0	1	0	9.2	24	57	19	19	1	0	0	0	6	2	6	1	0
Santana, Julio, Tex.-T.B.	5	6	.455	4.39	35	19	1	0	5	0	145.2	151	630	77	71	18	2	5	5	62	3	61	3	0
Santana, Marino, Det.	0	0	.000	3.68	7	0	0	0	2	0	7.1	9	39	3	3	1	1	0	1	8	2	10	3	0
Santiago, Jose, K.C.	0	0	.000	9.00	2	0	0	0	2	0	2.0	4	9	2	2	0	0	0	0	0	0	2	0	0
Saunders, Tony, T.B.*	6	15	.286	4.12	31	31	2	0	0	0	192.1	191	855	95	88	15	6	10	7	111	1	172	2	1
Schourek, Pete, Bos.*	1	3	.250	4.30	10	8	0	0	0	0	44.0	45	183	21	21	7	0	3	1	14	1	36	2	0
Sele, Aaron, Tex.	19	11	.633	4.23	33	33	3	2	0	0	212.2	239	954	116	100	14	5	7	13	84	6	167	4	0
Serafini, Dan, Min.*	7	4	.636	6.48	28	9	0	0	3	0	75.0	95	345	58	54	10	3	6	1	29	1	46	2	0
Service, Scott, K.C.	6	4	.600	3.48	73	0	0	0	26	4	82.2	70	353	35	32	7	2	5	9	34	4	95	10	1
Shouse, Brian, Bos.*	0	1	.000	5.63	7	0	0	0	4	0	8.0	9	36	5	5	2	0	0	0	4	0	5	0	0
Shuey, Paul, Cle.	5	4	.556	3.00	43	0	0	0	16	2	51.0	44	222	19	17	6	2	0	3	25	5	58	3	0
Simas, Bill, Chi.	4	3	.571	3.57	60	0	0	0	41	18	70.2	54	287	29	28	12	2	0	1	22	4	56	1	0
Sinclair, Steve, Tor.*	0	2	.000	3.60	24	0	0	0	3	0	15.0	13	61	7	6	0	0	0	0	5	0	8	0	0
Sirotka, Mike, Chi.*	14	15	.483	5.06	33	33	5	0	0	0	211.2	255	911	137	119	30	5	7	2	47	0	128	3	1
Slocumb, Heathcliff, Sea.	2	5	.286	5.32	57	0	0	0	29	3	67.2	72	313	40	40	5	4	2	1	44	1	51	10	0
Small, Aaron, Oak.	1	1	.500	7.25	24	0	0	0	4	0	36.0	51	174	34	29	3	3	1	3	14	3	19	4	0
Smith, Pete, Bal.	2	3	.400	6.20	27	4	0	0	3	0	45.0	57	204	31	31	7	3	2	0	16	1	29	6	1
Snyder, John, Chi.	7	2	.778	4.80	15	14	1	0	0	0	86.1	96	367	49	46	14	2	4	2	23	1	52	2	0
Sparks, Steve, Ana.	9	4	.692	4.34	22	20	0	0	1	0	128.2	130	562	66	62	14	2	3	5	58	0	90	6	0
Spoljaric, Paul, Sea.*	4	6	.400	6.48	53	6	0	0	10	0	83.1	85	387	67	60	14	5	3	1	55	3	89	10	0
Springer, Dennis, T.B.	3	11	.214	5.45	29	17	1	0	8	0	115.2	120	517	77	70	21	1	2	12	60	1	46	6	0
Stanton, Mike, N.Y.*	4	1	.800	5.47	67	0	0	0	26	6	79.0	71	330	51	48	13	1	2	4	26	1	69	0	0
Stein, Blake, Oak.	5	9	.357	6.37	24	20	1	1	0	0	117.1	117	538	92	83	22	1	2	5	71	3	89	15	0
Stieb, Dave, Tor.	1	2	.333	4.83	19	3	0	0	7	2	50.1	58	228	31	27	6	0	2	5	17	1	27	0	0
Stottlemyre, Todd, Tex.	5	4	.556	4.33	10	10	0	0	0	0	60.1	68	275	33	29	5	1	3	0	30	1	57	1	0
Suppan, Jeff, K.C.	0	0	.000	0.71	4	1	0	0	2	0	12.2	9	46	1	1	1	0	0	0	1	0	12	0	0
Suzuki, Mac, Sea.	1	2	.333	7.18	6	5	0	0	0	0	26.1	34	127	23	21	3	0	0	0	15	0	19	0	0
Swift, Bill C., Sea.	11	9	.550	5.85	29	26	0	0	0	0	144.2	183	663	103	94	21	2	2	10	51	2	77	1	2
Swindell, Greg, Min.-Bos.*	5	6	.455	3.59	81	0	0	0	15	2	90.1	92	385	40	36	13	4	2	3	31	3	63	3	0
Tatis, Ramon, T.B.*	0	0	.000	13.89	22	0	0	0	7	0	11.2	23	72	19	18	2	0	0	1	16	1	5	1	1
Taylor, Bill, Oak.	4	9	.308	3.58	70	0	0	0	58	33	73.0	71	311	37	29	7	3	5	3	22	4	58	0	1
Telgheder, Dave, Oak.	0	1	.000	3.60	8	2	0	0	4	0	20.0	19	91	12	8	4	2	0	2	6	0	5	2	1
Tessmer, Jay, N.Y.	1	0	1.000	3.12	7	0	0	0	3	0	8.2	4	33	3	3	1	0	1	0	4	0	6	1	0
Tewksbury, Bob, Min.	7	13	.350	4.79	26	25	1	0	0	0	148.1	174	635	82	79	19	7	6	6	20	1	60	5	0
Thompson, Justin, Det.*	11	15	.423	4.05	34	34	5	0	0	0	222.0	227	946	114	100	20	10	6	2	79	4	149	4	0
Timlin, Mike, Sea.	3	3	.500	2.95	70	0	0	0	40	19	79.1	78	321	26	26	5	4	2	3	16	2	60	0	0
Trombley, Mike, Min.	6	5	.545	3.63	77	1	0	0	17	1	96.2	90	413	41	39	16	2	1	5	41	3	89	6	1
Valdez, Carlos, Bos.	1	0	1.000	0.00	4	0	0	0	1	0	3.1	1	16	0	0	0	0	1	0	5	0	4	0	0
Van Poppel, Todd, Tex.	1	2	.333	8.84	4	4	0	0	0	0	19.1	26	95	20	19	5	0	1	1	10	0	10	2	0
VanRyn, Ben, Tor.*	0	1	.000	9.00	10	0	0	0	3	0	4.0	6	17	4	4	0	0	0	0	2	0	3	0	0
Veras, Dario, Bos.	0	1	.000	10.13	7	0	0	0	4	0	8.0	12	43	9	9	0	0	0	1	7	0	2	2	0
Villone, Ron, Cle.*	0	0	.000	6.00	25	0	0	0	6	0	27.0	30	129	18	18	3	2	2	2	22	0	15	0	0
Wade, Terrell, T.B.*	1	1	.500	5.06	2	2	0	0	0	0	10.2	14	46	6	6	3	0	0	0	2	0	8	1	0
Wakefield, Tim, Bos.	17	8	.680	4.58	36	33	2	0	1	0	216.0	211	939	123	110	30	1	8	14	79	1	146	6	1
Walker, Jamie, K.C.*	0	1	.000	9.87	6	2	0	0	2	0	17.1	30	86	20	19	5	1	1	2	3	0	15	0	0
Ward, Bryan, Chi.*	1	2	.333	3.33	28	0	0	0	9	1	27.0	30	116	13	10	4	0	1	0	7	0	17	0	0
Wasdin, John, Bos.	6	4	.600	5.25	47	8	0	0	13	0	96.0	111	424	57	56	14	3	6	2	27	8	59	1	0
Washburn, Jarrod, Ana.*	6	3	.667	4.62	15	11	0	0	0	0	74.0	70	317	40	38	11	2	3	3	27	1	48	0	0
Watson, Allen, Ana.*	6	7	.462	6.04	28	14	1	0	4	0	92.1	122	421	67	62	12	0	6	3	34	0	64	6	1
Wells, David, N.Y.*	18	4	.818	3.49	30	30	8	5	0	0	214.1	195	851	86	83	29	2	2	1	29	0	163	2	0
Wells, Bob, Sea.	2	2	.500	6.10	30	0	0	0	4	0	51.2	54	228	38	35	12	2	1	2	16	1	29	1	0
West, David, Bos.*	0	0	.000	27.00	6	0	0	0	0	0	2.0	7	20	6	6	1	0	0	0	7	0	4	1	0
Wetteland, John, Tex.	3	1	.750	2.03	63	0	0	0	59	42	62.0	47	249	17	14	6	2	2	0	14	1	72	1	0
Whisenant, Matt, K.C.*	2	1	.667	4.90	70	0	0	0	23	2	60.2	61	267	37	33	3	1	5	3	33	2	45	9	0
White, Rick, T.B.	2	6	.250	3.80	38	3	0	0	12	2	68.2	66	289	32	29	8	0	3	2	23	2	39	3	0
Whiten, Mark, Cle.	0	0	.000	9.00	1	0	0	0	1	0	1.0	1	7	1	1	0	0	0	1	2	0	3	0	0
Williams, Woody, Tor.	10	9	.526	4.46	32	32	1	1	0	0	209.2	196	894	112	104	36	5	6	2	81	3	151	2	1
Wilson, Trevor, Ana.*	0	0	.000	3.52	15	0	0	0	2	0	7.2	8	37	4	3	0	0	1	1	5	2	6	0	0

Pitcher, Team	W	L	Pct.	ERA	G	GS	CG	ShO	GF	Sv.	IP	H	TBF	R	ER	HR	SH	SF	HB	BB	IBB	SO	WP	Bk.
Witasick, Jay, Oak.	1	3	.250	6.33	7	3	0	0	1	0	27.0	36	131	24	19	9	0	0	0	15	1	29	2	0
Withem, Shannon, Tor.	0	0	.000	3.00	1	0	0	0	0	0	3.0	3	14	1	1	0	0	0	0	2	0	2	0	0
Witt, Bobby, Tex.	5	4	.556	7.66	14	13	0	0	0	0	69.1	95	329	62	59	14	2	4	0	33	1	30	2	1
Worrell, Tim, Det.-Cle.-Oak. ...	2	7	.222	5.24	43	9	0	0	5	0	103.0	106	440	62	60	16	2	3	1	29	3	82	2	0
Wright, Jaret, Cle. ....:	12	10	.545	4.72	32	32	1	1	0	0	192.2	207	855	109	101	22	4	6	11	87	4	140	6	0
Yan, Esteban, T.B.	5	4	.556	3.86	64	0	0	0	18	1	88.2	78	381	41	38	11	1	3	5	41	2	77	6	0

COMBINATION SHUTOUTS: **Anaheim (4)**—Dickson, Cadaret, DeLucia and Percival; Finley and Harris; McDowell, Hasegawa and Percival; Finley and Hasegawa. **Baltimore (6)**—Mussina and Benitez; Mussina and Rhodes; Johns and Rhodes; Ponson and Rhodes; Rodriguez, Smith, Benitez and Orosco; Guzman, Mills and Benitez. **Boston (6)**—Martinez, Eckersley and Gordon; Saberhagen, Corsi and Gordon; Avery, Garces and Gordon; Avery and Garces; Martinez, Wasdin and Reyes; Avery, Lowe, Mahay and Gordon. **Chicago (4)**—Sirotka and Karchner; Snyder, Howry and Simas; Eyre, Foulke, Howry and Simas; Sirotka and Howry. **Cleveland (1)**—Colon and Villone. **Detroit (1)**—Greisinger and Jones. **Kansas City (2)**—Belcher and Montgomery; Pittsley, Bones, Whisenant and Montgomery. **Minnesota (7)**—Radke, Trombley, Swindell and Aguilera; Tewksbury and Aguilera; Tewksbury, Swindell and Aguilera; Radke, Swindell and Aguilera; Radke, Guardado, Trombley and Aguilera; Radke and Guardado; Sampson, Baptist, Guardado and Aguilera. **New York (8)**—Pettitte, Nelson, Stanton and Rivera; Cone and Rivera; Pettitte and Rivera; Cone and Rivera; Irabu and Buddie; Pettitte, Mendoza and Rivera; Hernandez and Rivera; Irabu and Stanton. **Oakland (1)**—Heredia, Mathews and Taylor. **Seattle (2)**—Moyer and Spoljaric; Swift, Timlin and Slocumb. **Tampa Bay (5)**—Alvarez, Yan and Mecir; Arrojo, Carlson and Hernandez; Saunders and Mecir; Alvarez, Mecir and Rekar; Saunders, Lopez and Hernandez. **Texas (4)**—Sele and Wetteland; Burkett and Wetteland; Helling and Wetteland; Sele, Fossas, Hernandez and Levine. **Toronto (6)**—Clemens and Quantrill; Clemens and Quantrill; Williams, Risley and Quantrill; Guzman and Myers; Clemens and Quantrill; Escobar and Quantrill.

PITCHERS WITH TWO OR MORE TEAMS

Pitcher, Team	W	L	Pct.	ERA	G	GS	CG	ShO	GF	Sv.	IP	H	TBF	R	ER	HR	SH	SF	HB	BB	IBB	SO	WP	Bk.
Cadaret, Greg, Ana.*	1	2	.333	4.14	39	0	0	0	11	1	37.0	38	167	17	17	6	1	0	3	15	0	37	5	0
Cadaret, Greg, Tex.*	0	0	.000	4.70	11	0	0	0	3	0	7.2	11	36	4	4	1	1	0	0	3	0	5	3	0
Fetters, Mike, Oak.	1	6	.143	3.99	48	0	0	0	22	5	47.1	48	214	26	21	3	4	2	1	21	2	34	3	0
Fetters, Mike, Ana.	1	2	.333	5.56	12	0	0	0	6	0	11.1	14	50	8	7	2	0	0	0	4	0	9	3	0
Fossas, Tony, Sea.*	0	3	.000	8.74	23	0	0	0	8	0	11.1	19	55	11	11	1	1	1	0	6	0	10	0	0
Fossas, Tony, Tex.*	1	0	1.000	0.00	10	0	0	0	1	0	7.1	3	29	0	0	0	0	0	4	0	7	1	0
Guzman, Juan, Tor.	6	12	.333	4.41	22	22	2	0	0	0	145.0	133	632	83	71	19	2	3	6	65	1	113	6	0
Guzman, Juan, Bal.	4	4	.500	4.23	11	11	0	0	0	0	66.0	60	286	34	31	4	0	2	2	33	1	55	5	0
Rodriguez, Nerio, Bal.	1	3	.250	8.05	6	4	0	0	0	0	19.0	25	89	17	17	0	0	2	0	9	0	8	1	0
Rodriguez, Nerio, Tor.	1	0	1.000	9.72	7	0	0	0	3	0	8.1	10	44	9	9	1	0	0	1	8	0	3	0	0
Santana, Julio, Tex.	0	0	.000	8.44	3	0	0	0	0	0	5.1	7	27	5	5	0	0	0	0	4	1	1	0	0
Santana, Julio, T.B.	5	6	.455	4.23	32	19	1	0	5	0	140.1	144	603	72	66	18	2	5	5	58	2	60	3	0
Swindell, Greg, Min.*	3	3	.500	3.66	52	0	0	0	12	2	66.1	67	281	27	27	10	3	2	3	18	2	45	3	0
Swindell, Greg, Bos.*	2	3	.400	3.38	29	0	0	0	3	0	24.0	25	104	13	9	3	1	0	0	13	1	18	0	0
Worrell, Tim, Det.	2	6	.250	5.98	15	9	0	0	0	0	61.2	66	265	42	41	11	0	1	1	19	2	47	0	0
Worrell, Tim, Cle.	0	0	.000	5.06	3	0	0	0	1	0	5.1	6	24	3	3	0	0	2	0	2	0	2	0	0
Worrell, Tim, Oak.	0	1	.000	4.00	25	0	0	0	4	0	36.0	34	151	17	16	5	2	0	0	8	1	33	2	0

FIELDING

TEAM

Team	Pct.	G	PO	A	E	TC	DP	PB	Team	Pct.	G	PO	A	E	TC	DP	PB
Baltimore	.987	162	4294	1760	81	6135	144	12	Texas	.980	162	4294	1580	121	5995	140	10
Tampa Bay	.985	162	4329	1765	94	6188	178	19	Kansas City	.980	161	4309	1689	125	6123	172	11
New York	.984	162	4370	1642	98	6110	146	12	Toronto	.979	163	4395	1532	125	6052	131	9
Boston	.983	162	4308	1625	105	6038	128	35	Seattle	.979	161	4273	1572	125	5970	139	11
Anaheim	.983	162	4332	1646	106	6084	146	28	Chicago	.977	163	4316	1706	140	6162	161	9
Cleveland	.982	162	4380	1727	110	6217	146	8	Oakland	.977	162	4302	1654	141	6097	155	13
Minnesota	.982	162	4343	1585	108	6036	135	11	**Totals**	.981	1134	60584	23295	1594	5473	2085	202
Detroit	.982	162	4339	1812	115	6266	164	14	TRIPLE PLAYS: None.								

INDIVIDUAL

FIRST BASEMEN

NOTE: All caps denotes fielding-percentage leader based on 81 games for catchers, 108 for all other non-pitchers and 162 innings for pitchers. *Throws lefthanded.

Player, Team	Pct.	G	PO	A	E	TC	DP
Amaral, Rich, Sea.	1.000	7	16	2	0	18	1
Ashley, Billy, Bos.	.857	2	6	0	1	7	2
Bell, David, Cle.-Sea.	1.000	6	39	2	0	41	3
Benjamin, Mike, Bos.	1.000	10	41	9	0	50	3
Blowers, Mike, Oak.	1.000	8	47	0	0	47	3
Bolick, Frank, Ana.	1.000	1	2	0	0	2	1
Branson, Jeff, Cle.	1.000	3	9	2	0	11	0
Brosius, Scott, N.Y.	1.000	3	7	2	0	9	1
Carter, Joe, Bal.	1.000	1	3	1	0	4	0
Catalanotto, Frank, Det.	1.000	18	124	10	0	134	9
Clark, Tony, Det.	.991	142	1265	102	13	1380	134
Clark, Will, Tex.*	.989	134	1079	73	13	1165	112
Conine, Jeff, K.C.	1.000	12	101	3	0	104	15
Coomer, Ron, Min.	.998	54	371	34	1	406	32
Cordero, Wil, Chi.	.992	83	698	66	6	770	78
Crespo, Felipe, Tor.	.800	1	4	0	1	5	0
Dalesandro, Mark, Tor.	1.000	2	5	0	0	5	0
Delgado, Carlos, Tor.	.992	141	1165	87	10	1262	110
Erstad, Darin, Ana.*	.996	70	464	39	2	505	46
Fasano, Sal, K.C.	1.000	5	16	0	0	16	2
Fick, Rob, Det.	1.000	1	9	0	0	9	0
Fielder, Cecil, Ana.-Cle.	.995	75	562	41	3	606	61
Gates, Brent, Min.	1.000	1	2	0	0	2	1
Giambi, Jason, Oak.	.990	146	1255	73	14	1342	120
Greene, Todd, Ana.	1.000	3	16	1	0	17	2
Griffey, Ken, Sea.*	.000	1	0	0	0	0	0
Halter, Shane, K.C.	1.000	1	2	0	0	2	0
Hocking, Denny, Min.	1.000	2	3	0	0	3	0
Hoiles, Chris, Bal.	1.000	6	13	0	0	13	3
Hollins, Dave, Ana.	.980	7	44	5	1	50	4
Huson, Jeff, Sea.	1.000	7	22	1	0	23	1
Ibanez, Raul, Sea.	.990	16	93	6	1	100	12
Jefferies, Gregg, Ana.	1.000	3	23	2	0	25	2
Jefferson, Reggie, Bos.*	.953	7	37	4	2	43	2
Johnson, Mark P., Ana.*	1.000	5	13	1	0	14	2
King, Jeff, K.C.	.995	112	932	85	5	1022	103
Ledesma, Aaron, T.B.	1.000	2	4	0	0	4	1
Lesher, Brian, Oak.*	.000	1	0	0	1	1	0
Leyritz, Jim, Bos.	1.000	1	3	0	0	3	1
Magadan, Dave, Oak.	1.000	7	33	3	0	36	3
Manto, Jeff, Cle.-Det.-Cle.	.979	17	92	2	2	96	7
Martinez, Tino, N.Y.	.992	142	1180	93	10	1283	111
Martinez, Dave, T.B.*	1.000	1	1	0	0	1	0
Martinez, Edgar, Sea.	1.000	4	22	6	0	28	3
McCarty, David, Sea.*	1.000	2	14	0	0	14	0
McClain, Scott, T.B.	.966	5	24	4	1	29	1
McGriff, Fred, T.B.*	.995	135	1150	81	6	1237	140
Merced, Orlando, Min.	.982	38	299	21	6	326	32
Mientkiewicz, Doug, Min.	1.000	8	61	3	0	64	3
Minor, Ryan, Bal.	1.000	3	5	1	0	6	2
Mitchell, Kevin, Oak.	1.000	2	5	0	0	5	1
Molitor, Paul, Min.	1.000	9	79	7	0	86	4
Morris, Hal, K.C.*	.990	46	349	34	4	387	35
Nevin, Phil, Ana.	1.000	2	3	0	0	3	2
Norton, Greg, Chi.	.994	79	642	30	4	676	57
Oliver, Joe, Det.	1.000	2	2	1	0	3	0
Ortiz, David, Min.*	.989	70	503	46	6	555	51
Ortiz, Hector, K.C.	.000	1	0	0	0	0	0
Palmeiro, Rafael, Bal.*	.994	159	1435	124	9	1568	127
Pickering, Calvin, Bal.*	.969	5	31	0	1	32	3
Posada, Jorge, N.Y.	1.000	1	7	1	0	8	2
Pritchett, Chris, Ana.	.995	29	190	20	1	211	12
Radmanovich, Ryan, Sea.	1.000	1	1	0	0	1	0
Randa, Joe, Det.	1.000	1	4	0	0	4	1
Ripken, Billy, Det.	1.000	2	5	0	0	5	0
Samuel, Juan, Tor.	1.000	3	2	0	0	2	0
Segui, David, Sea.*	.999	134	1045	116	1	1162	107
Sexson, Richie, Cle.	.984	45	321	38	6	365	36
Shave, Jon, Min.	1.000	1	1	0	0	1	0
Sheldon, Scott, Tex.	.000	1	0	0	0	0	0
Shipley, Craig, Ana.	.968	8	27	3	1	31	3
Simms, Mike, Tex.	.976	16	73	7	2	82	8
Snopek, Chris, Chi.	1.000	1	9	0	0	9	1
Sojo, Luis, N.Y.	.991	19	106	8	1	115	8
Sorrento, Paul, T.B.	1.000	27	219	24	0	243	22
Spencer, Shane, N.Y.	1.000	1	3	1	0	4	0
Sprague, Ed, Oak.*	1.000	1	1	0	0	1	0
Stahoviak, Scott, Min.	.975	4	35	4	1	40	4
Stairs, Matt, Oak.	1.000	6	45	8	0	53	6
Stanley, Mike, Tor.-Bos.	.997	35	279	18	1	298	28
Stevens, Lee, Tex.*	.996	37	208	15	1	224	11
Surhoff, B.J., Bal.	1.000	1	2	0	0	2	0
Sutton, Larry, K.C.*	1.000	6	32	3	0	35	5
Sveum, Dale, N.Y.	.975	21	108	9	3	120	9
Thomas, Frank, Chi.	.984	14	116	6	2	124	12
Thome, Jim, Cle.	.991	117	998	85	10	1093	97
Vaughn, Mo, Bos.	.991	142	1176	90	12	1278	91
Voigt, Jack, Oak.	.987	27	73	2	1	76	8
Wilkins, Rick, Sea.	1.000	6	42	2	0	44	2
Witt, Kevin, Tor.	1.000	1	5	1	0	6	0
Wood, Jason, Det.	1.000	6	36	2	0	38	4

FIRST BASEMEN WITH TWO OR MORE TEAMS

Player, Team	Pct.	G	PO	A	E	TC	DP
Bell, David, Cle.	1.000	1	4	0	0	4	0
Bell, David, Sea.	1.000	5	35	2	0	37	3
Fielder, Cecil, Ana.	.997	72	550	39	2	591	60
Fielder, Cecil, Cle.	.933	3	12	2	1	15	1
Manto, Jeff, Det.	.977	10	43	0	1	44	3
Manto, Jeff, Cle.	.981	7	49	2	1	52	4
Stanley, Mike, Tor.	.995	22	171	12	1	184	14
Stanley, Mike, Bos.	1.000	13	108	6	0	114	14

SECOND BASEMEN

Player, Team	Pct.	G	PO	A	E	TC	DP
Alicea, Luis, Tex.	.970	45	81	111	6	198	26
Alomar, Roberto, Bal.	.985	144	251	449	11	711	86
Amaral, Rich, Sea.	1.000	11	17	10	0	27	1
Baughman, Justin, Ana.	.977	59	104	153	6	263	22
Bell, David, Cle.-Sea.	.982	115	216	333	10	559	69
Bellhorn, Mark, Oak.	.000	1	0	0	0	0	0
Benjamin, Mike, Bos.	.994	87	160	189	2	351	40
Bournigal, Rafael, Oak.	1.000	48	56	81	0	137	20
Branson, Jeff, Cle.	.960	31	35	37	3	75	14
Buford, Damon, Bos.	.000	1	0	0	0	0	0
Bush, Homer, N.Y.	.971	24	37	29	2	68	4
Cairo, Miguel, T.B.	.978	148	278	429	16	723	109
Catalanotto, Frank, Det.	.974	31	38	36	2	76	10
Cedeno, Domingo, Tex.	.889	7	4	12	2	18	1
Cora, Joey, Sea.-Cle.	.965	151	243	310	20	573	76

Player, Team	Pct.	G	PO	A	E	TC	DP
Crespo, Felipe, Tor.	.870	8	6	14	3	23	2
Dunston, Shawon, Cle.	.978	24	32	55	2	89	9
Durham, Ray, Chi.	.976	158	282	438	18	738	128
Easley, Damion, Det.	.985	140	285	439	11	735	102
Febles, Carlos, K.C.	1.000	11	16	18	0	34	2
Fernandez, Tony, Tor.	.975	82	128	222	9	359	43
Forbes, P.J., Bal.	1.000	7	6	9	0	15	2
Garcia, Carlos, Ana.	.978	11	19	25	1	45	7
Gates, Brent, Min.	.971	21	23	43	2	68	8
Grebeck, Craig, Tor.	.975	91	145	250	10	405	38
Guevara, Giomar, Sea.	1.000	5	6	9	0	15	2
Guillen, Carlos, Sea.	1.000	10	15	29	0	44	5
Hairston, Jerry, Bal.	.750	4	4	2	2	8	1
Halter, Shane, K.C.	.909	6	2	8	1	11	0
Hansen, Jed, K.C.	1.000	2	1	0	0	1	0
Hocking, Denny, Min.	1.000	47	38	46	0	84	9
Huson, Jeff, Sea.	1.000	8	7	6	0	13	2
Johns, Keith, Bos.	1.000	1	1	1	0	2	1
Knoblauch, Chuck, N.Y.	.981	149	275	408	13	696	86
Ledesma, Aaron, T.B.	.979	19	39	54	2	95	10
Lemke, Mark, Bos.	1.000	31	38	71	0	109	15
Lovullo, Torey, Cle.	.947	5	4	14	1	19	3
Manto, Jeff, Cle.	1.000	1	0	1	0	1	1
Martin, Norberto, Ana.	.982	54	86	138	4	228	31
Martinez, Felix, K.C.	.000	2	0	0	0	0	0
McLemore, Mark, Tex.	.975	122	249	332	15	596	71
Merloni, Lou, Bos.	.974	32	47	66	3	116	10
Norton, Greg, Chi.	1.000	1	0	2	0	2	0
Offerman, Jose, K.C.	.974	152	277	440	19	736	113
Perez, Tomas, Tor.	1.000	1	0	1	0	1	0
Randa, Joe, Det.	1.000	20	25	40	0	65	9
Reboulet, Jeff, Bal.	.974	28	26	49	2	77	13
Ripken, Billy, Det.	1.000	2	2	2	0	4	1
Rivera, Luis, K.C.	1.000	6	5	6	0	11	0
Roberts, Bip, Det.-Oak.	.971	31	40	61	3	104	21
Rossy, Rico, Sea.	1.000	6	1	12	0	13	1
Sadler, Donnie, Bos.	.972	50	76	95	5	176	16
Samuel, Juan, Tor.	1.000	2	2	4	0	6	0
Shipley, Craig, Ana.	1.000	11	20	31	0	51	11
Silvestri, Dave, T.B.	1.000	2	4	5	0	9	1
Smith, Bobby, T.B.	.968	6	11	19	1	31	3
Snopek, Chris, Chi.-Bos.	.933	15	7	21	2	30	3
Sojo, Luis, N.Y.	1.000	8	7	14	0	21	4
Spiezio, Scott, Oak.	.975	112	198	316	13	527	72
Valentin, John, Bos.	.000	1	0	0	0	0	0
Velandia, Jorge, Oak.	1.000	1	1	3	0	4	0
Velarde, Randy, Ana.	.982	51	88	132	4	224	25
Walker, Todd, Min.	.978	140	219	363	13	595	72
Wilson, Craig, Chi.	1.000	4	7	9	0	16	4
Wilson, Enrique, Cle.	.989	22	34	52	1	87	6

SECOND BASEMEN WITH TWO OR MORE TEAMS

Player, Team	Pct.	G	PO	A	E	TC	DP
Bell, David, Cle.	.982	101	192	294	9	495	58
Bell, David, Sea.	.984	14	24	39	1	64	11
Cora, Joey, Sea.	.962	130	212	270	19	501	68
Cora, Joey, Cle.	.986	21	31	40	1	72	8
Roberts, Bip, Det.	1.000	1	2	3	0	5	3
Roberts, Bip, Oak.	.970	30	38	58	3	99	18
Snopek, Chris, Chi.	.962	12	6	19	1	26	3
Snopek, Chris, Bos.	.750	3	1	2	1	4	0

THIRD BASEMEN

Player, Team	Pct.	G	PO	A	E	TC	DP
Abbott, Kurt, Oak.	.000	1	0	0	0	0	0
Alicea, Luis, Tex.	.940	26	15	32	3	50	1
Alvarez, Gabe, Det.	.873	55	38	93	19	150	6
Amaral, Rich, Sea.	.000	1	0	0	0	0	0
Bell, David, Cle.-Sea.	1.000	11	6	17	0	23	1
Bellhorn, Mark, Oak.	1.000	5	3	7	0	10	0
Benjamin, Mike, Bos.	1.000	11	6	19	0	25	0
Blowers, Mike, Oak.	.927	120	66	174	19	259	15
Boggs, Wade, T.B.	.973	78	52	131	5	188	12
Bolick, Frank, Ana.	1.000	7	5	7	0	12	0
Borders, Pat, Cle.	1.000	1	0	1	0	1	0
Branson, Jeff, Cle.	.913	20	5	16	2	23	1
Branyan, Russ, Cle.	1.000	1	0	1	0	1	0
Brosius, Scott, N.Y.	.948	150	107	292	22	421	29
Buford, Damon, Bos.	.000	1	0	0	0	0	0
Bush, Homer, N.Y.	1.000	3	1	6	0	7	0
Catalanotto, Frank, Det.	.833	3	0	5	1	6	1
Chavez, Eric, Oak.	1.000	13	11	21	0	32	2

Player, Team	Pct.	G	PO	A	E	TC	DP
Coomer, Ron, Min.	.972	75	56	116	5	177	9
Crespo, Felipe, Tor.	1.000	2	1	2	0	3	0
Dalesandro, Mark, Tor.	.889	8	3	5	1	9	0
Davis, Russ, Sea.	.906	137	55	254	32	341	26
Evans, Tom, Tor.	.889	7	5	3	1	9	0
Fasano, Sal, K.C.	.000	1	0	0	0	0	0
Fernandez, Tony, Tor.	.963	54	32	73	4	109	3
Forbes, P.J., Bal.	1.000	1	0	0	0	0	0
Fryman, Travis, Cle.	.963	144	100	237	13	350	21
Gates, Brent, Min.	.961	77	59	113	7	179	5
Gipson, Charles, Sea.	.900	4	6	3	1	10	0
Glaus, Troy, Ana.	.941	48	27	85	7	119	7
Grebeck, Craig, Tor.	.857	4	2	4	1	7	0
Guillen, Ozzie, Bal.	.000	1	0	0	0	0	0
Halter, Shane, K.C.	1.000	8	1	3	0	4	0
Hocking, Denny, Min.	1.000	11	1	11	0	12	1
Hollins, Dave, Ana.	.929	91	63	145	16	224	13
Huson, Jeff, Sea.	.800	8	1	7	2	10	0
King, Jeff, K.C.	1.000	4	3	6	0	9	2
Koskie, Corey, Min.	.941	10	6	10	1	17	1
Ledesma, Aaron, T.B.	.846	7	5	6	2	13	0
Leius, Scott, K.C.	.867	15	8	18	4	30	2
Lopez, Mendy, K.C.	1.000	2	1	4	0	5	0
Lovullo, Torey, Cle.	1.000	1	0	1	0	1	0
Lowell, Mike, N.Y.	1.000	7	2	5	0	7	1
Magadan, Dave, Oak.	.918	30	15	52	6	73	7
Manto, Jeff, Cle.	1.000	8	0	5	0	5	2
Martin, Norberto, Ana.	1.000	5	2	4	0	6	0
McClain, Scott, T.B.	1.000	3	2	2	0	4	0
Merloni, Lou, Bos.	.857	5	5	7	2	14	0
Minor, Ryan, Bal.	.833	6	1	4	1	6	0
Norton, Greg, Chi.	.917	11	12	10	2	24	0
Palmer, Dean, K.C.	.921	129	69	187	22	278	16
Pendleton, Terry, K.C.	.957	23	12	33	2	47	2
Randa, Joe, Det.	.976	118	73	212	7	292	18
Reboulet, Jeff, Bal.	.900	23	1	8	1	10	2
Ripken, Cal, Bal.	.979	161	101	265	8	374	22
Ripken, Billy, Det.	1.000	2	2	5	0	7	1
Rivera, Luis, K.C.	1.000	6	1	3	0	4	0
Roberts, Bip, Oak.	1.000	3	3	3	0	6	0
Rossy, Rico, Sea.	1.000	25	11	44	0	55	5
Shave, Jon, Min.	1.000	15	6	20	0	26	2
Sheldon, Scott, Tex.	1.000	3	1	4	0	5	2
Shipley, Craig, Ana.	.963	48	15	37	2	54	1
Silvestri, Dave, T.B.	1.000	3	1	1	0	2	0
Smith, Bobby, T.B.	.963	97	71	164	9	244	11
Snopek, Chris, Chi.-Bos.	1.000	6	0	2	0	2	0
Sojo, Luis, N.Y.	1.000	6	4	8	0	12	1
Sprague, Ed, Tor.-Oak.	.921	128	110	194	26	330	10
Sveum, Dale, N.Y.	.909	6	4	6	1	11	0
Tatis, Fernando, Tex.	.945	94	74	184	15	273	15
Valentin, John, Bos.	.965	153	121	292	15	428	28
Ventura, Robin, Chi.	.966	161	102	330	15	447	38
Voigt, Jack, Oak.	1.000	2	0	1	0	1	0
Wilson, Craig, Chi.	1.000	2	0	1	0	1	0
Wilson, Enrique, Cle.	1.000	2	1	0	0	1	0
Wood, Jason, Oak.	1.000	1	0	1	0	1	0
Zeile, Todd, Tex.	.915	52	38	91	12	141	7

THIRD BASEMEN WITH TWO OR MORE TEAMS

Player, Team	Pct.	G	PO	A	E	TC	DP
Bell, David, Cle.	1.000	6	4	12	0	16	1
Bell, David, Sea.	1.000	5	2	5	0	7	0
Snopek, Chris, Chi.	1.000	3	0	0	0	0	0
Snopek, Chris, Bos.	1.000	3	0	2	0	2	0
Sprague, Ed, Tor.	.924	105	87	157	20	264	8
Sprague, Ed, Oak.	.909	23	23	37	6	66	2

SHORTSTOPS

Player, Team	Pct.	G	PO	A	E	TC	DP
Abbott, Kurt, Oak.	.909	28	40	70	11	121	16
Baughman, Justin, Ana.	.667	3	2	2	2	6	0
Bell, David, Sea.	1.000	1	1	0	0	1	0
Bellhorn, Mark, Oak.	.000	2	0	0	0	0	0
Benjamin, Mike, Bos.	.988	20	26	58	1	85	11
Bordick, Mike, Bal.	.990	150	236	446	7	689	91
Bournigal, Rafael, Oak.	1.000	38	53	89	0	142	18
Branson, Jeff, Cle.	.000	2	0	0	0	0	0
Bush, Homer, N.Y.	1.000	2	0	3	0	3	0
Cabrera, Jolbert, Cle.	1.000	1	2	2	0	4	0
Caruso, Mike, Chi.	.944	131	216	378	35	629	91
Cedeno, Domingo, Tex.	.963	35	37	67	4	108	14

Player, Team	Pct.	G	PO	A	E	TC	DP
Clayton, Royce, Tex.	.972	52	88	152	7	247	26
Cruz, Deivi, Det.	.983	135	196	445	11	652	100
DiSarcina, Gary, Ana.	.980	157	253	437	14	704	103
Dunston, Shawon, Cle.	.944	14	13	21	2	36	3
Easley, Damion, Det.	.986	30	27	41	1	69	10
Elster, Kevin, Tex.	.976	84	107	257	9	373	49
Forbes, P.J., Bal.	.000	1	0	0	0	0	0
Fryman, Travis, Cle.	1.000	3	1	5	0	6	2
Garcia, Carlos, Ana.	1.000	5	5	8	0	13	2
Garciaparra, Nomar, Bos.	.962	143	228	402	25	655	68
Gates, Brent, Min.	1.000	1	1	1	0	2	0
Gonzalez, Alex, Tor.	.976	158	259	427	17	703	98
Grebeck, Craig, Tor.	1.000	6	4	15	0	19	3
Guevara, Giomar, Sea.	1.000	5	2	4	0	6	1
Guillen, Ozzie, Bal.	.933	6	3	11	1	15	1
Halter, Shane, K.C.	.964	66	73	166	9	248	29
Hocking, Denny, Min.	.960	28	29	43	3	75	7
Huson, Jeff, Sea.	.000	1	0	0	0	0	0
Jeter, Derek, N.Y.	.986	148	223	393	9	625	82
Ledesma, Aaron, T.B.	.971	58	103	167	8	278	51
Leius, Scott, K.C.	1.000	2	0	1	0	1	0
Lopez, Mendy, K.C.	.955	72	101	221	15	337	53
Martin, Norberto, Ana.	1.000	2	1	2	0	3	0
Martinez, Felix, K.C.	.956	32	49	80	6	135	23
Meares, Pat, Min.	.966	149	263	412	24	699	92
Merloni, Lou, Bos.	.000	1	0	0	0	0	0
Perez, Tomas, Tor.	1.000	4	6	5	0	11	1
Reboulet, Jeff, Bal.	.967	28	24	63	3	90	8
Ripken, Billy, Det.	.926	21	23	52	6	81	11
Rivera, Luis, K.C.	.961	30	42	81	5	128	20
Rodriguez, Alex, Sea.	.975	160	268	445	18	731	90
Rossy, Rico, Sea.	1.000	4	3	4	0	7	0
Sadler, Donnie, Bos.	1.000	4	5	6	0	11	2
Shave, Jon, Min.	.000	1	0	0	0	0	0
Sheldon, Scott, Tex.	.933	2	7	7	1	15	3
Shipley, Craig, Ana.	1.000	5	6	5	0	11	4
Silvestri, Dave, T.B.	.750	1	0	3	1	4	0
Smith, Bobby, T.B.	.900	7	7	20	3	30	4
Snopek, Chris, Chi.	.972	33	47	93	4	144	16
Sojo, Luis, N.Y.	.973	20	29	44	2	75	12
Stocker, Kevin, T.B.	.979	110	186	335	11	532	81
Tejada, Miguel, Oak.	.951	104	173	327	26	526	75
Velandia, Jorge, Oak.	.909	7	3	7	1	11	1
Vizquel, Omar, Cle.	.993	151	273	442	5	720	94
Wilson, Craig, Chi.	1.000	8	13	17	0	30	4
Wilson, Enrique, Cle.	.970	10	8	24	1	33	4
Wood, Jason, Oak.-Det.	1.000	3	3	2	0	5	1

SHORTSTOPS WITH TWO OR MORE TEAMS

Player, Team	Pct.	G	PO	A	E	TC	DP
Wood, Jason, Oak.	1.000	2	1	2	0	3	1
Wood, Jason, Det.	1.000	1	2	0	0	2	0

OUTFIELDERS

Player, Team	Pct.	G	PO	A	E	TC	DP
Abbott, Jeff, Chi.*	.971	76	132	0	4	136	0
Abbott, Kurt, Oak.	1.000	5	6	0	0	6	0
Alicea, Luis, Tex.	1.000	2	1	0	0	1	0
Allensworth, Jermaine, K.C.	.982	27	54	0	1	55	0
Amaral, Rich, Sea.	1.000	52	57	2	0	59	0
Anderson, Brady, Bal.*	.985	130	269	1	4	274	0
Anderson, Garret, Ana.*	.983	155	326	11	6	343	3
Ashley, Billy, Bos.	1.000	2	0	1	0	1	0
Bartee, Kimera, Det.	.964	29	51	3	2	56	0
Beamon, Trey, Det.	1.000	4	7	0	0	7	0
Becker, Rich, Bal.*	.984	60	59	1	1	61	0
Bell, David, Sea.	.000	1	0	0	0	0	0
Belle, Albert, Chi.	.976	159	316	11	8	335	3
Beltran, Carlos, K.C.	.978	14	44	0	1	45	0
Berroa, Geronimo, Cle.-Det.	1.000	18	31	1	0	32	0
Bolick, Frank, Ana.	1.000	1	2	0	0	2	0
Bragg, Darren, Bos.	.996	124	218	6	1	225	3
Brosius, Scott, N.Y.	.000	1	0	0	0	0	0
Brown, Dermal, K.C.	1.000	2	1	0	0	1	0
Buford, Damon, Bos.	1.000	67	134	4	0	138	1
Buhner, Jay, Sea.	.985	70	127	5	2	134	2
Butler, Rich, T.B.	1.000	61	113	4	0	117	1
Cameron, Mike, Chi.	.988	138	313	6	4	323	0
Canseco, Jose, Tor.	.960	73	117	4	5	126	2
Carter, Joe, Bal.	.962	50	96	4	4	104	1
Christenson, Ryan, Oak.	.983	116	284	7	5	296	2
Clyburn, Danny, Bal.	1.000	8	11	0	0	11	0
Conine, Jeff, K.C.	.993	80	134	4	1	139	0
Coomer, Ron, Min.	1.000	3	1	0	0	1	0
Cordero, Wil, Chi.	.938	11	15	0	1	16	0
Cordova, Marty, Min.	.978	115	257	5	6	268	1
Cradle, Rickey, Sea.	1.000	4	2	0	0	2	0
Crespo, Felipe, Tor.	1.000	42	56	1	0	57	1
Cruz, Jose, Tor.	.984	105	247	7	4	258	1
Cummings, Midre, Bos.	.941	17	16	0	1	17	0
Curtis, Chad, N.Y.	.984	148	306	8	5	319	3
Cuyler, Milt, Tex.	1.000	3	5	0	0	5	0
Dalesandro, Mark, Tor.	.000	1	0	0	0	0	0
Damon, Johnny, K.C.*	.990	158	372	10	4	386	1
Davis, Eric, Bal.	.992	72	119	4	1	124	0
Davis, Russ, Sea.	.333	3	1	0	2	3	0
Ducey, Rob, Sea.	.970	83	127	4	4	135	1
Dunston, Shawon, Cle.	1.000	12	18	0	0	18	0
Dye, Jermaine, K.C.	.987	59	152	4	2	158	3
Edmonds, Jim, Ana.*	.988	153	392	10	5	407	1
Encarnacion, Juan, Det.	.985	39	60	4	1	65	1
Erstad, Darin, Ana.*	.992	72	116	4	1	121	2
Frazier, Lou, Chi.	1.000	3	5	0	0	5	0
Giambi, Jeremy, K.C.*	1.000	9	14	1	0	15	0
Giles, Brian, Cle.*	.978	101	213	7	5	225	1
Gipson, Charles, Sea.	.973	36	34	2	1	37	1
Gonzalez, Juan, Tex.	.982	116	213	8	4	225	2
Gonzalez, Luis, Det.	.988	132	232	8	3	243	0
Goodwin, Tom, Tex.	.992	150	370	5	3	378	2
Green, Shawn, Tor.*	.979	157	311	14	7	332	4
Greene, Todd, Ana.	1.000	12	12	0	0	12	0
Greene, Willie, Bal.	.941	14	15	1	1	17	0
Greer, Rusty, Tex.*	.990	154	304	6	3	313	0
Grieve, Ben, Oak.	.993	151	262	7	2	271	0
Griffey, Ken, Sea.*	.988	158	409	11	5	425	3
Halter, Shane, K.C.	1.000	9	13	0	0	13	0
Hammonds, Jeffrey, Bal.	.980	53	94	2	2	98	1
Hatcher, Chris, K.C.	1.000	5	7	0	0	7	0
Henderson, Rickey, Oak.*	.988	151	327	3	4	334	1
Higginson, Bobby, Det.	.982	153	303	18	6	327	3
Hill, Glenallen, Sea.	.965	71	107	2	4	113	1
Hocking, Denny, Min.	.980	24	47	2	1	50	1
Hunter, Brian L., Det.	.988	139	386	11	5	402	0
Hunter, Torii, Min.	1.000	6	8	0	0	8	0
Huson, Jeff, Sea.	1.000	1	1	0	0	1	0
Ibanez, Raul, Sea.	1.000	17	12	1	0	13	0
Incaviglia, Pete, Det.	.000	1	0	0	0	0	0
Jefferies, Gregg, Ana.	1.000	15	25	0	0	25	0
Justice, David, Cle.*	1.000	21	37	0	0	37	0
Kapler, Gabe, Det.	1.000	6	9	0	0	9	0
Kelly, Mike, T.B.	1.000	93	137	4	0	141	1
Kelly, Roberto, Tex.	.976	71	155	5	4	164	1
Kingsale, Eugene, Bal.	1.000	4	2	0	0	2	0
Latham, Chris, Min.	.972	32	69	1	2	72	0
Lawton, Matt, Min.	.990	151	398	12	4	414	5
Ledee, Ricky, N.Y.*	.981	42	47	4	1	52	0
Lennon, Patrick, Tor.	1.000	2	3	0	0	3	0
Lesher, Brian, Oak.*	1.000	4	4	2	0	6	1
Lewis, Darren, Bos.	.992	152	382	6	3	391	0
Lofton, Kenny, Cle.*	.978	154	339	19	8	366	4
Mack, Shane, K.C.	.982	32	54	1	1	56	1
Manto, Jeff, Det.	.000	1	0	0	0	0	0
Martin, Norberto, Ana.	1.000	5	2	0	0	2	0
Martinez, Dave, T.B.*	.994	86	162	9	1	172	1
Mashore, Damon, Ana.	1.000	35	53	1	0	54	0
McCarty, David, Sea.*	1.000	5	7	0	0	7	0
McCracken, Quinton, T.B.	.992	153	343	18	3	364	3
McDonald, Jason, Oak.	.956	60	122	7	6	135	1
Merced, Orlando, Min.-Bos.	1.000	14	27	2	0	29	1
Mitchell, Keith, Bos.	1.000	10	6	0	0	6	0
Mitchell, Kevin, Oak.	1.000	10	10	0	0	10	0
Monahan, Shane, Sea.	.992	62	117	3	1	121	1
Morris, Hal, K.C.*	1.000	39	47	1	0	48	0
Mouton, Lyle, Bal.	1.000	16	19	1	0	20	0
Neill, Mike, Oak.*	1.000	6	14	0	0	14	0
Newson, Warren, Tex.*	1.000	7	16	0	0	16	0
Nixon, Trot, Bos.*	1.000	4	2	0	0	2	0
Nixon, Otis, Min.	.989	108	278	4	3	285	0
Ochoa, Alex, Min.	.969	74	117	8	4	129	0
O'Leary, Troy, Bos.*	.990	155	303	9	3	315	1
O'Neill, Paul, N.Y.*	.987	150	293	11	4	308	6
Ordonez, Magglio, Chi.	.985	145	323	10	5	338	2
Otanez, Willis, Bal.	1.000	2	1	0	0	1	0
Palmeiro, Orlando, Ana.*	1.000	54	92	0	0	92	0

Player, Team	Pct.	G	PO	A	E	TC	DP
Perez, Robert, Sea.	1.000	17	20	1	0	21	0
Phillips, Tony, Tor.	.960	13	24	0	1	25	0
Radmanovich, Ryan, Sea.	1.000	24	33	2	0	35	0
Raines, Tim, N.Y.	.985	47	61	3	1	65	2
Ramirez, Alex, Cle.	.833	3	5	0	1	6	0
Ramirez, Manny, Cle.	.977	148	291	10	7	308	1
Roberts, Bip, Det.-Oak.	.953	24	41	0	2	43	0
Robinson, Kerry, T.B.*	1.000	2	4	0	0	4	0
Salmon, Tim, Ana.	.959	19	46	1	2	49	0
Samuel, Juan, Tor.	.882	10	15	0	2	17	0
Segui, David, Sea.*	.000	1	0	0	0	0	0
Sexson, Richie, Cle.	1.000	3	4	0	0	4	0
Shipley, Craig, Ana.	1.000	2	4	0	0	4	0
Siddall, Joe, Det.	.000	1	0	0	0	0	0
Sierra, Ruben, Chi.	1.000	14	19	1	0	20	0
Simmons, Brian, Chi.	1.000	5	13	0	0	13	0
Simms, Mike, Tex.	1.000	43	45	1	0	46	0
Snopek, Chris, Chi.	.000	1	0	0	0	0	0
Sorrento, Paul, T.B.	1.000	18	30	0	0	30	0
Spencer, Shane, N.Y.	1.000	22	26	1	0	27	0
Stahoviak, Scott, Min.	.000	1	0	0	0	0	0
Stairs, Matt, Oak.	1.000	12	22	3	0	25	0
Stanley, Mike, Tor.	1.000	1	1	0	0	1	0
Stevens, Lee, Tex.*	1.000	7	12	0	0	12	0
Stewart, Shannon, Tor.	.980	144	295	4	6	305	1
Strawberry, Darryl, N.Y.*	.905	16	19	0	2	21	0
Surhoff, B.J., Bal.	.989	157	254	12	3	269	2
Sutton, Larry, K.C.*	.987	79	147	4	2	153	2
Tavarez, Jesus, Bal.	1.000	8	7	0	0	7	0
Tomberlin, Andy, Det.*	1.000	5	5	0	0	5	0
Trammell, Bubba, T.B.	1.000	37	50	3	0	53	0
Voigt, Jack, Oak.	1.000	20	29	2	0	31	0
Walton, Jerome, T.B.	1.000	8	13	2	0	15	0
Whiten, Mark, Cle.	.970	72	124	7	4	135	1
Williams, Bernie, N.Y.	.990	123	298	4	3	305	1
Williams, Reggie, Ana.	1.000	24	25	0	0	25	0
Winn, Randy, T.B.	.980	96	192	7	4	203	1
Young, Ernie, K.C.	1.000	24	43	2	0	45	0

OUTFIELDERS WITH TWO OR MORE TEAMS

Player, Team	Pct.	G	PO	A	E	TC	DP
Berroa, Geronimo, Cle.	1.000	14	27	1	0	28	0
Berroa, Geronimo, Det.	1.000	4	4	0	0	4	0
Merced, Orlando, Min.	1.000	13	25	2	0	27	1
Merced, Orlando, Bos.	1.000	1	2	0	0	2	0
Roberts, Bip, Det.	1.000	2	1	0	0	1	0
Roberts, Bip, Oak.	.952	22	40	0	2	42	0

CATCHERS

Player, Team	Pct.	G	PO	A	E	TC	DP	PB
Alomar, Sandy, Cle.	.992	111	712	42	6	760	7	4
Bako, Paul, Det.	.989	94	493	45	6	544	5	9
Borders, Pat, Cle.	.974	53	283	19	8	310	1	4
Brown, Kevin, Tor.	.993	52	261	19	2	282	2	5
Casanova, Raul, Det.	.967	14	81	6	3	90	0	0
Chavez, Raul, Sea.	1.000	1	3	0	0	3	0	0
Dalesandro, Mark, Tor.	.986	18	68	4	1	73	0	0
Diaz, Eomar, Cle.	.973	17	101	9	3	113	0	0
DiFelice, Mike, T.B.	.993	84	483	52	4	539	8	13
Fasano, Sal, K.C.	.996	70	421	25	2	448	5	2
Fick, Rob, Det.	.950	3	18	1	1	20	0	0
Figga, Mike, N.Y.	1.000	1	3	1	0	4	0	0
Flaherty, John, T.B.	.993	91	542	45	4	591	2	5
Fletcher, Darrin, Tor.	.991	121	832	51	8	891	1	3
Girardi, Joe, N.Y.	.995	78	541	38	3	582	5	5
Greene, Charlie, Bal.	1.000	13	58	4	0	62	0	1
Haselman, Bill, Tex.	.995	36	176	8	1	185	0	0
Hatteberg, Scott, Bos.	.993	108	664	61	5	730	7	17
Hinch, A.J., Oak.	.986	118	602	47	9	658	8	8
Hoiles, Chris, Bal.	.995	83	516	39	3	558	6	2
Johnson, Mark L., Chi.	1.000	7	36	2	0	38	1	0
Kreuter, Chad, Chi.-Ana.	.981	94	438	36	9	483	4	5
Laker, Tim, T.B.	1.000	2	5	0	0	5	0	1
Leyritz, Jim, Bos.	1.000	1	10	0	0	10	0	0
Macfarlane, Mike, K.C.-Oak.	.990	73	368	23	4	395	7	5
Machado, Robert, Chi.	.981	34	189	17	4	210	0	3
Marzano, John, Sea.	.997	48	317	24	1	342	2	5
Molina, Ben, Ana.	1.000	2	1	0	0	1	0	0
Molina, Izzy, Oak.	1.000	5	8	1	0	9	0	0
Nevin, Phil, Ana.	.989	69	399	32	5	436	3	20
O'Brien, Charlie, Chi.-Ana.	.989	62	325	24	4	353	3	1
Oliver, Joe, Det.-Sea.	.983	77	433	25	8	466	2	3

Player, Team	Pct.	G	PO	A	E	TC	DP	PB
Ortiz, Hector, K.C.	1.000	3	4	0	0	4	0	0
Pierzynski, A.J., Min.	1.000	6	33	2	0	35	1	0
Posada, Jorge, N.Y.	.994	99	587	46	4	637	3	7
Rodriguez, Ivan, Tex.	.994	139	864	72	6	942	7	10
Romero, Mandy, Bos.	1.000	4	11	0	0	11	0	0
Santiago, Benito, Tor.	1.000	15	45	2	0	47	0	1
Siddall, Joe, Det.	.994	27	142	16	1	159	3	3
Spehr, Tim, K.C.	1.000	11	62	2	0	64	0	0
Steinbach, Terry, Min.	.990	119	665	52	7	724	3	4
Sweeney, Mike, K.C.	.984	91	517	33	9	559	6	9
Turner, Chris, K.C.	1.000	4	16	0	0	16	0	0
Valentin, Javier, Min.	.983	53	281	17	5	303	0	7
Varitek, Jason, Bos.	.988	75	367	32	5	404	3	18
Walbeck, Matt, Ana.	.990	104	682	46	7	735	3	8
Webster, Lenny, Bal.	.993	102	528	39	4	571	5	9
Wilkins, Rick, Sea.	1.000	6	28	2	0	30	0	1
Wilson, Dan, Sea.	.994	94	677	35	4	716	6	5

CATCHERS WITH TWO OR MORE TEAMS

Player, Team	Pct.	G	PO	A	E	TC	DP	PB
Kreuter, Chad, Chi.	.985	91	424	35	7	466	4	5
Kreuter, Chad, Ana.	.882	3	14	1	2	17	0	0
Macfarlane, Mike, K.C.	1.000	3	13	3	0	16	1	0
Macfarlane, Mike, Oak.	.989	70	355	20	4	379	6	5
O'Brien, Charlie, Chi.	.988	57	305	22	4	331	3	1
O'Brien, Charlie, Ana.	1.000	5	20	2	0	22	0	0
Oliver, Joe, Det.	.982	48	259	16	5	280	2	2
Oliver, Joe, Sea.	.984	29	174	9	3	186	0	1

PITCHERS

Player, Team	Pct.	G	PO	A	E	TC	DP
Abbott, Jim, Chi.*	1.000	5	2	10	0	12	1
Abbott, Jeff, Sea.	1.000	4	1	3	0	4	0
Aguilera, Rick, Min.	1.000	68	3	9	0	12	2
Aldred, Scott, T.B.*	1.000	48	3	7	0	10	2
Almanzar, Carlos, Tor.	.833	25	2	3	1	6	0
Alvarez, Wilson, T.B.*	1.000	25	5	6	0	11	1
Anderson, Matt, Det.	.889	42	0	8	1	9	0
Andujar, Luis, Tor.	1.000	5	0	1	0	1	0
Appier, Kevin, K.C.	1.000	3	0	1	0	1	0
Arrojo, Rolando, T.B.	.934	32	17	40	4	61	5
Assenmacher, Paul, Cle.*	1.000	69	2	4	0	6	0
Avery, Steve, Bos.*	.979	34	7	39	1	47	5
Ayala, Bobby, Sea.	.762	62	8	8	5	21	1
Bailes, Scott, Tex.*	.833	46	2	3	1	6	0
Baldwin, James, Chi.	.815	37	7	15	5	27	0
Banks, Willie, N.Y.	.875	9	3	4	1	8	1
Baptist, Travis, Min.*	1.000	13	6	2	0	8	0
Barber, Brian, K.C.	1.000	8	0	3	0	3	0
Barkley, Brian, Bos.*	1.000	6	1	0	0	1	0
Belcher, Tim, K.C.	.946	34	18	17	2	37	3
Benitez, Armando, Bal.	1.000	71	3	5	0	8	0
Bennett, Joel, Bal.	.000	2	0	0	0	0	0
Bere, Jason, Chi.	.929	18	7	6	1	14	0
Bevil, Brian, K.C.	1.000	39	1	1	0	2	0
Bochtler, Doug, Det.	.833	51	6	4	2	12	0
Bones, Ricky, K.C.	.958	32	8	15	1	24	1
Borowski, Joe, N.Y.	1.000	8	0	2	0	2	0
Bradford, Chad, Chi.	.900	29	1	8	1	10	0
Bradley, Ryan, N.Y.	1.000	5	2	0	0	2	0
Brocail, Doug, Det.	1.000	60	8	7	0	15	1
Brunson, Will, Det.*	1.000	8	0	1	0	1	0
Bruske, Jim, N.Y.	1.000	3	2	1	0	3	0
Buddie, Mike, N.Y.	1.000	24	4	3	0	7	0
Bullinger, Jim, Sea.	1.000	2	1	0	0	1	0
Burba, Dave, Cle.	.953	32	15	26	2	43	4
Burkett, John, Tex.	.967	32	11	18	1	30	0
Byrdak, Tim, K.C.*	.000	3	0	0	0	0	0
Cadaret, Greg, Ana.-Tex.*	1.000	50	1	4	0	5	1
Candiotti, Tom, Oak.	.982	33	16	39	1	56	2
Carlson, Dan, T.B.	1.000	10	1	1	0	2	0
Carpenter, Chris, Tor.	.971	33	20	13	1	34	2
Carrasco, Hector, Min.	1.000	63	9	6	0	15	0
Casian, Larry, Chi.*	1.000	4	1	1	0	2	0
Castillo, Tony, Chi.*	1.000	25	1	9	0	10	2
Castillo, Carlos, Chi.	.955	54	5	16	1	22	1
Castillo, Tony, Det.	1.000	27	8	14	0	22	1
Charlton, Norm, Bal.*	.917	36	4	7	1	12	0
Checo, Robinson, Bos.	.000	2	0	0	0	0	0
Cho, Jin Ho, Bos.	1.000	4	3	0	0	3	0
Clemens, Roger, Tor.	.971	33	7	27	1	35	1
Cloude, Ken, Sea.	.929	30	11	15	2	28	2

Player, Team	Pct.	G	PO	A	E	TC	DP
Colon, Bartolo, Cle.	.979	31	13	34	1	48	1
Cone, David, N.Y.	.974	31	12	25	1	38	3
Connelly, Steve, Oak.	1.000	3	1	1	0	2	0
Coppinger, Rocky, Bal.	1.000	6	1	0	0	1	0
Corsi, Jim, Bos.	.905	59	3	16	2	21	2
Crabtree, Tim, Tex.	.923	64	4	8	1	13	2
Crow, Dean, Det.	1.000	32	2	7	0	9	0
DeLucia, Rich, Ana.	1.000	61	0	6	0	6	0
Dickson, Jason, Ana.	.950	27	9	10	1	20	0
Dougherty, Jim, Oak.	1.000	9	1	5	0	6	2
Drabek, Doug, Bal.	.958	23	8	15	1	24	1
Duran, Roberto, Det.*	1.000	18	1	2	0	3	0
Duvall, Mike, T.B.*	1.000	3	2	1	0	3	0
Dykhoff, Radhames, Bal.*	.000	1	0	0	0	0	0
Eckersley, Dennis, Bos.	.857	50	2	4	1	7	0
Eiland, Dave, T.B.	.000	1	0	0	0	0	0
Erdos, Todd, N.Y.	.000	2	0	0	0	0	0
Erickson, Scott, Bal.	.961	36	23	51	3	77	5
Escobar, Kelvin, Tor.	1.000	22	2	4	0	6	0
Evans, Bart, K.C.	1.000	8	1	1	0	2	0
Eyre, Scott, Chi.*	.947	33	1	17	1	19	3
Fassero, Jeff, Sea.*	.955	32	11	31	2	44	0
Fetters, Mike, Oak.-Ana.	.895	60	2	15	2	19	1
Finley, Chuck, Ana.*	.925	34	13	24	3	40	4
Florie, Bryce, Det.	.923	42	14	22	3	39	5
Fordham, Tom, Chi.*	1.000	29	3	11	0	14	0
Fossas, Tony, Sea.-Tex.*	1.000	33	3	2	0	5	0
Foulke, Keith, Chi.	.818	54	1	8	2	11	0
Fussell, Chris, Bal.	1.000	3	1	2	0	3	1
Gaillard, Eddie, T.B.	1.000	6	0	1	0	1	0
Gajkowski, Steve, Sea.	.000	9	0	0	0	0	0
Garces, Rich, Bos.	1.000	30	2	5	0	7	0
Gooden, Dwight, Cle.	1.000	23	6	18	0	24	1
Gordon, Tom, Bos.	1.000	73	7	1	0	8	0
Gorecki, Rick, T.B.	1.000	3	0	2	0	2	0
Greisinger, Seth, Det.	.900	21	3	15	2	20	0
Groom, Buddy, Oak.*	1.000	75	1	6	0	7	0
Guardado, Eddie, Min.*	1.000	79	6	5	0	11	0
Gunderson, Eric, Tex.*	1.000	68	6	10	0	16	0
Guzman, Juan, Tor.-Bal.	.886	33	11	20	4	35	2
Halladay, Roy, Tor.	1.000	2	1	2	0	3	0
Halter, Shane, K.C.	1.000	1	1	0	0	1	0
Haney, Chris, K.C.*	1.000	33	3	21	0	24	3
Hanson, Erik, Tor.	1.000	11	8	7	0	15	1
Harriger, Denny, Det.	1.000	4	1	1	0	2	0
Harris, Pep, Ana.	.895	49	4	13	2	19	1
Hasegawa, Shigetoshi, Ana.	1.000	61	3	16	0	19	2
Hawkins, LaTroy, Min.	1.000	33	17	29	0	46	5
Haynes, Jimmy, Oak.	.968	33	11	19	1	31	1
Heathcott, Mike, Chi.	.000	1	0	0	0	0	0
Helling, Rick, Tex.	.952	33	8	12	1	21	0
Henry, Buth, Bos.*	1.000	2	1	3	0	4	0
Hentgen, Pat, Tor.	.949	29	15	22	2	39	1
Heredia, Gil, Oak.	1.000	8	1	9	0	10	0
Hernandez, Xavier, Tex.	1.000	46	3	3	0	6	0
Hernandez, Orlando, N.Y.	1.000	21	10	23	0	33	0
Hernandez, Roberto, T.B.	.929	67	4	9	1	14	0
Hill, Ken, Ana.	1.000	19	14	20	0	34	3
Holdridge, David, Sea.	.000	7	0	0	0	0	0
Holmes, Darren, N.Y.	.900	34	4	5	1	10	2
Holtz, Mike, Ana.*	1.000	53	0	2	0	2	0
Holzemer, Mark, Oak.*	1.000	13	2	0	0	2	0
Howry, Bobby, Chi.	.900	44	2	7	1	10	0
Irabu, Hideki, N.Y.	.920	29	6	17	2	25	1
Jackson, Mike, Cle.	.944	69	6	11	1	18	2
Jacome, Jason, Cle.*	.000	1	0	0	0	0	0
James, Mike, Ana.	1.000	11	0	1	0	1	0
Jerzembeck, Mike, N.Y.	1.000	3	0	1	0	1	0
Johns, Doug, Bal.*	.968	31	5	25	1	31	2
Johnson, Jason, T.B.	1.000	13	2	4	0	6	0
Johnson, Jonathan, Tex.	1.000	1	1	1	0	2	0
Johnson, Randy, Sea.*	.778	23	5	23	8	36	2
Jones, Doug, Cle.	1.000	23	0	7	0	7	1
Jones, Todd, Det.	1.000	65	7	7	0	14	2
Juden, Jeff, Ana.	.714	8	1	4	2	7	1
Kamieniecki, Scott, Bal.	1.000	12	12	10	0	22	0
Karchner, Matt, Chi.	1.000	32	2	6	0	8	0
Karsay, Steve, Oak.	1.000	11	3	2	0	5	0
Keagle, Greg, Det.	1.000	9	3	5	0	8	0
Key, Jimmy, Bal.*	1.000	25	4	11	0	15	3
Krivda, Rick, Cle.*	1.000	11	2	3	0	5	0
Levine, Al, Tex.	1.000	30	4	7	0	11	1

Player, Team	Pct.	G	PO	A	E	TC	DP
Lewis, Richie, Bal.	1.000	2	1	0	0	1	0
Lira, Felipe, Sea.	1.000	7	2	2	0	4	0
Lloyd, Graeme, N.Y.*	.889	50	3	5	1	9	1
Loaiza, Esteban, Tex.	1.000	14	11	6	0	17	0
Lopez, Albie, T.B.	1.000	54	3	16	0	19	0
Lorraine, Andrew, Sea.*	.000	4	0	0	0	0	0
Lowe, Derek, Bos.	.900	63	12	24	4	40	4
Mahay, Ron, Bos.*	.750	29	1	2	1	4	0
Martin, Tom, Cle.*	1.000	14	1	2	0	3	0
Martinez, Pedro, Bos.	.879	33	11	18	4	33	3
Mathews, Terry, Bal.	1.000	17	3	6	0	9	0
Mathews, T.J., Oak.	.917	66	4	7	1	12	1
McCarthy, Greg, Sea.*	1.000	29	1	6	0	7	0
McDill, Allen, K.C.*	1.000	7	0	1	0	1	0
McDowell, Jack, Ana.	1.000	14	3	12	0	15	1
Mecir, Jim, T.B.	1.000	68	9	16	0	25	2
Mendoza, Ramiro, N.Y.	.973	41	11	25	1	37	3
Mesa, Jose, Cle.	.933	44	4	10	1	15	1
Miller, Travis, Min.*	.750	14	1	2	1	4	0
Mills, Alan, Bal.	1.000	72	8	9	0	17	2
Milton, Eric, Min.*	1.000	32	8	20	0	28	1
Moehler, Brian, Det.	.979	33	11	35	1	47	1
Mohler, Mike, Oak.*	.889	57	1	7	1	9	1
Montgomery, Jeff, K.C.	1.000	56	5	4	0	9	1
Morgan, Mike, Min.	.967	18	13	16	1	30	1
Morman, Alvin, Cle.*	1.000	31	2	4	0	6	0
Moyer, Jamie, Sea.*	.979	34	16	31	1	48	1
Munoz, Bobby, Bal.	1.000	9	1	2	0	3	0
Mussina, Mike, Bal.	1.000	29	12	38	0	50	1
Myers, Randy, Tor.*	1.000	41	0	2	0	2	0
Nagy, Charles, Cle.	.969	33	17	46	2	65	4
Naulty, Dan, Min.	1.000	19	1	0	0	1	0
Navarro, Jaime, Chi.	.966	37	8	20	1	29	1
Nelson, Jeff, N.Y.	1.000	45	3	9	0	12	0
Ogea, Chad, Cle.	1.000	19	2	9	0	11	1
Olivares, Omar, Ana.	.923	37	21	39	5	65	3
Oliver, Darren, Tex.*	.952	19	5	15	1	21	0
Oquist, Mike, Oak.	1.000	31	7	15	0	22	3
Orosco, Jesse, Bal.*	1.000	69	1	5	0	6	1
Paniagua, Jose, Sea.	1.000	18	2	5	0	7	1
Parque, Jim, Chi.*	1.000	21	7	16	0	23	0
Patterson, Danny, Tex.	1.000	56	3	8	0	11	0
Pavlik, Roger, Tex.	1.000	5	0	2	0	2	0
Pennington, Brad, T.B.*	.000	1	0	0	0	0	0
Percival, Troy, Ana.	.857	67	2	4	1	7	1
Perisho, Matt, Tex.*	.000	2	0	0	0	0	0
Person, Robert, Tor.	.800	27	2	2	1	5	0
Pettitte, Andy, N.Y.*	.980	33	11	37	1	49	5
Pichardo, Hipolito, K.C.	1.000	27	11	18	0	29	5
Pittsley, Jim, K.C.	.889	39	5	11	2	18	1
Plesac, Dan, Tor.*	1.000	78	0	1	0	1	0
Plunk, Eric, Cle.	.833	37	0	5	1	6	0
Ponson, Sidney, Bal.	.955	31	10	11	1	22	1
Poole, Jim, Cle.*	1.000	12	0	2	0	2	0
Powell, Brian, Det.	.933	18	6	8	1	15	0
Prieto, Ariel, Oak.	1.000	2	0	1	0	1	0
Quantrill, Paul, Tor.	1.000	82	4	14	0	18	2
Radke, Brad, Min.	.979	32	12	34	1	47	1
Rakers, Jason, Cle.	.000	1	0	0	0	0	0
Rapp, Pat, K.C.	.977	32	20	23	1	44	0
Reed, Steve, Cle.	1.000	20	2	3	0	5	1
Rekar, Brian, T.B.	.905	16	12	7	2	21	0
Reyes, Carlos, Bos.	1.000	24	3	5	0	8	0
Rhodes, Arthur, Bal.*	.778	45	2	5	2	9	0
Rios, Danny, K.C.	1.000	5	1	0	0	1	0
Risley, Bill, Tor.	1.000	44	2	3	0	5	1
Ritchie, Todd, Min.	.000	15	0	0	0	0	0
Rivera, Mariano, N.Y.	1.000	54	3	14	0	17	1
Rizzo, Todd, Chi.*	.000	9	0	1	0	1	0
Robertson, Rich, Ana.*	1.000	5	1	3	0	4	0
Rodriguez, Frankie, Min.	.895	20	8	9	2	19	0
Rodriguez, Nerio, Bal.-Tor.	1.000	13	0	1	0	1	0
Rogers, Kenny, Oak.*	.977	34	20	66	2	88	4
Rosado, Jose, K.C.*	.947	38	8	28	2	38	1
Rose, Brian, Bos.	1.000	8	4	4	0	8	1
Ruebel, Matt, T.B.*	1.000	7	1	0	0	1	0
Runyan, Sean, Det.*	1.000	88	2	1	0	3	0
Rusch, Glendon, K.C.*	.969	29	9	22	1	32	4
Saberhagen, Bret, Bos.	.971	31	13	20	1	34	1
Sager, A.J., Det.	1.000	31	2	14	0	16	2
Sampson, Ben, Min.*	1.000	5	0	1	0	1	0
Sanders, Scott, Det.	1.000	3	0	2	0	2	0

Player, Team	Pct.	G	PO	A	E	TC	DP
Santana, Julio, Tex.-T.B.	.895	35	5	12	2	19	0
Santana, Marino, Det.	1.000	7	0	1	0	1	0
Santiago, Jose, K.C.	1.000	2	0	1	0	1	0
Saunders, Tony, T.B.*	.968	31	12	18	1	31	4
Schourek, Pete, Bos.*	1.000	10	0	2	0	2	0
Sele, Aaron, Tex.	.949	33	17	20	2	39	3
Serafini, Dan, Min.*	1.000	28	1	8	0	9	1
Service, Scott, K.C.	.950	73	4	15	1	20	0
Shouse, Brian, Bos.*	1.000	7	0	2	0	2	0
Shuey, Paul, Cle.	.889	43	3	5	1	9	0
Simas, Bill, Chi.	1.000	60	9	5	0	14	1
Sinclair, Steve, Tor.*	1.000	24	0	4	0	4	1
Sirotka, Mike, Chi.*	.977	33	9	34	1	44	1
Slocumb, Heathcliff, Sea.	.938	57	6	9	1	16	0
Small, Aaron, Oak.	1.000	24	2	3	0	5	0
Smith, Pete, Bal.	.933	27	2	12	1	15	1
Snyder, John, Chi.	.957	15	8	14	1	23	0
Sparks, Steve, Ana.	1.000	22	12	31	0	43	2
Spoljaric, Paul, Sea.*	1.000	53	3	9	0	12	0
Springer, Dennis, T.B.	1.000	29	7	11	0	18	2
Stanton, Mike, N.Y.*	.929	67	7	6	1	14	0
Stein, Blake, Oak.	.938	24	0	15	1	16	1
Stieb, Dave, Tor.	1.000	19	5	5	0	10	0
Stottlemyre, Todd, Tex.	1.000	10	2	5	0	7	0
Suppan, Jeff, K.C.	1.000	4	1	3	0	4	1
Suzuki, Mac, Sea.	1.000	6	0	2	0	2	0
Swift, Bill, Sea.	.920	29	17	29	4	50	3
Swindell, Greg, Min.-Bos.*	1.000	81	10	10	0	20	1
Tatis, Ramon, T.B.*	1.000	22	1	4	0	5	1
Taylor, Bill, Oak.	1.000	70	4	8	0	12	2
Telgheder, Dave, Oak.	1.000	8	0	2	0	2	0
Tessmer, Jay, N.Y.	.000	7	0	0	0	0	0
Tewksbury, Bob, Min.	.956	26	12	31	2	45	3
Thompson, Justin, Det.*	1.000	34	6	35	0	41	2
Timlin, Mike, Sea.	1.000	70	10	13	0	23	1
Trombley, Mike, Min.	1.000	77	4	9	0	13	0
Valdez, Carlos, Bos.	.000	4	0	0	0	0	0
Van Poppel, Todd, Tex.	1.000	4	0	1	0	1	0
VanRyn, Ben, Tor.*	.000	10	0	0	0	0	0
Veras, Dario, Bos.	1.000	7	1	0	0	1	0
Villone, Ron, Cle.*	1.000	25	2	4	0	6	0
Wade, Terrell, T.B.*	.000	2	0	0	0	0	0
Wakefield, Tim, Bos.	.929	36	16	23	3	42	1
Walker, Jamie, K.C.*	1.000	6	2	4	0	6	1
Ward, Bryan, Chi.*	1.000	28	2	0	0	2	0
Wasdin, John, Bos.	.952	47	5	15	1	21	1
Washburn, Jarrod, Ana.*	1.000	15	4	8	0	12	0
Watson, Allen, Ana.*	1.000	28	4	15	0	19	0
Wells, David, N.Y.*	.921	30	8	27	3	38	1
Wells, Bob, Sea.	1.000	30	4	5	0	9	0
West, David, Bos.*	.000	6	0	0	0	0	0
Wetteland, John, Tex.	.900	63	2	7	1	10	0
Whisenant, Matt, K.C.*	1.000	70	3	10	0	13	1
White, Rick, T.B.	.889	38	5	11	2	18	1
Whiten, Marki, Cle.	.000	1	0	0	0	0	0
Williams, Woody, Tor.	.909	32	12	18	3	33	4
Wilson, Trevor, Ana.*	1.000	15	1	1	0	2	1
Witasick, Jay, Oak.	1.000	7	1	2	0	3	1
Withem, Shannon, Tor.	1.000	1	0	1	0	1	0
Witt, Bobby, Tex.	.714	14	2	3	2	7	0
Worrell, Tim, Det.-Cle.-Oak.	1.000	43	8	15	0	23	1
Wright, Jaret, Cle.	.977	32	16	26	1	43	0
Yan, Esteban, T.B.	.952	64	9	11	1	21	1

PITCHERS WITH TWO OR MORE TEAMS

Player, Team	Pct.	G	PO	A	E	TC	DP
Cadaret, Greg, Ana.*	1.000	39	1	3	0	4	1
Cadaret, Greg, Tex.*	1.000	11	0	1	0	1	0
Fetters, Mike, Oak.	.923	48	2	10	1	13	1
Fetters, Mike, Ana.	.833	12	0	5	1	6	0
Fossas, Tony, Sea.*	1.000	23	2	2	0	4	0
Fossas, Tony, Tex.*	1.000	10	1	0	0	1	0
Guzman, Juan, Tor.	.917	22	8	14	2	24	2
Guzman, Juan, Bal.	.818	11	3	6	2	11	0
Rodriguez, Nerio, Bal.	.000	6	0	0	0	0	0
Rodriguez, Nerio, Tor.	1.000	7	0	1	0	1	0
Santana, Julio, Tex.	1.000	3	0	1	0	1	0
Santana, Julio, T.B.	.889	32	5	11	2	18	0
Swindell, Greg, Min.*	1.000	52	8	6	0	14	0
Swindell, Greg, Bos.*	1.000	29	2	4	0	6	1
Worrell, Tim, Det.	1.000	15	7	7	0	14	1
Worrell, Tim, Cle.	1.000	3	1	3	0	4	0
Worrell, Tim, Oak.	1.000	25	0	5	0	5	0

1998 A.L. STATISTICS Fielding

MISCELLANEOUS

SHUTOUT GAMES

Read across for wins, down for losses.

Team	Bal.	N.Y.	Tor.	Bos.	Tex.	Sea.	Ana.	Min.	Cle.	K.C.	Det.	Chi.	Oak.	TB.	N.L.	W	L	Pct.
Baltimore	..	1	1	1	1	0	0	0	2	0	0	2	0	0	2	0	10	3	.769
New York	1	..	1	1	2	0	1	3	0	0	1	1	1	3	1	16	5	.762
Toronto	0	0	..	0	1	2	0	1	1	2	0	1	1	1	1	11	4	.733
Boston	0	0	0	..	0	1	0	0	2	1	0	0	1	1	2	8	4	.667
Texas	0	0	1	0	..	0	0	1	1	1	0	1	1	1	1	8	6	.571
Seattle	0	1	0	0	0	..	1	1	0	0	1	0	2	0	1	7	6	.538
Anaheim	0	0	0	0	0	0	..	0	0	1	1	1	0	1	1	5	6	.455
Minnesota	0	0	0	0	0	1	1	..	2	1	1	0	0	1	1	8	10	.444
Cleveland	0	1	0	0	0	0	1	0	..	0	1	0	0	0	1	4	6	.400
Kansas City	0	0	0	0	0	0	1	0	0	..	1	0	0	1	2	5	10	.333
Detroit	0	0	0	0	0	0	0	0	0	0	..	2	0	1	1	4	8	.333
Chicago	0	0	0	1	0	0	0	0	0	1	0	..	1	1	0	4	9	.308
Oakland	0	1	0	0	0	0	0	0	0	0	0	2	..	1	0	4	9	.308
Tampa Bay	0	1	0	0	0	1	1	1	0	1	0	1	1	..	0	7	17	.292
N.L. clubs	2	0	1	1	2	1	0	1	0	2	0	0	1	3	..			
Lost	3	5	4	4	6	6	6	10	6	10	8	9	9	17	..	101	103	.495

A.L. shutouts vs. N.L. clubs (12): Anaheim vs. Colorado; Boston vs. Montreal and New York N.L.; Cleveland vs. Pittsburgh; Detroit vs. Pittsburgh; Kansas City vs. Cincinnati and Houston; Minnesota vs. Chicago N.L.; New York A.L. vs. Atlanta; Seattle vs. Los Angeles; Texas vs. San Diego; Toronto vs. Montreal.

HOME RECORD

Read across for home wins, down for road losses.

Team	N.Y.	Bos.	Tor.	Tex.	Cle.	Chi.	Bal.	Ana.	Sea.	Oak.	Min.	TB.	Det.	K.C.	N.L.	W	L	Pct.
New York	..	3	2	4	4	4	6	3	4	4	5	6	5	5	7	62	19	.765
Boston	2	..	3	4	5	3	4	2	5	5	3	5	2	4	4	51	30	.630
Toronto	2	4	..	3	2	4	5	4	3	3	4	6	4	2	5	51	30	.630
Texas	1	4	4	..	5	3	2	3	5	2	2	5	5	4	3	48	33	.593
Cleveland	3	2	3	3	..	3	3	3	4	2	4	5	4	3	4	46	35	.568
Chicago	3	4	3	3	3	..	4	3	4	2	3	2	3	3	3	44	37	.543
Baltimore	3	4	4	3	2	1	..	3	3	4	4	1	5	2	3	42	39	.519
Anaheim	3	3	2	2	3	3	3	..	5	3	2	4	2		6	42	39	.519
Seattle	2	3	2	4	0	6	3	2	..	4	3	2	3	4	4	42	39	.519
Oakland	2	1	3	2	4	3	1	4	3	..	3	3	3	4	4	39	42	.481
Minnesota	3	3	3	3	4	3	2	2	0	1	..	4	2	1	4	35	46	.432
Tampa Bay	1	2	5	3	3	3	2	1	2	4	2	..	3	0	2	33	48	.407
Detroit	2	2	4	2	1	3	1	2	1	4	4	2	..	2	2	32	49	.395
Kansas City	0	2	2	2	1	1	2	2	2	4	2	3	2	..	4	29	51	.363
N.L. clubs	2	3	4	3	2	5	6	4	5	4	5	5	3	3	..			
Lost on road	29	40	44	41	38	45	44	38	46	46	46	51	48	38	..	596	537	.526

HOME RECORDS IN INTERLEAGUE GAMES

Team	Atl.	Fla.	Mon.	N.Y.	Phi.
Baltimore	1-2	1-2	..	1-1	..
Boston	..	..	3-0	1-2	0-2
New York	1-1	3-0	..	..	3-0
Tampa Bay	0-3	1-1	1-2	..	..
Toronto	..	..	2-0	2-1	1-2

Team	Chi.	Cin.	Hou.	Mil.	Pit.	St.L.
Chicago	..	1-1	..	1-2	..	2-1
Cleveland	..	..	1-2	..	1-2	2-0
Detroit	2-0	0-3	0-3	..	..	..
Kansas City	2-1	..	..	1-2	1-1	..
Minnesota	2-1	..	..	0-2	..	2-1

Team	Ariz.	Col.	L.A.	S.D.	S.F.
Anaheim	..	3-0	2-0	..	1-2
Oakland	2-1	..	..	2-1	0-2
Seattle	..	2-1	1-2	1-1	..
Texas	1-1	..	0-3	2-1	..

ROAD RECORD

Read across for road wins, down for home losses.

Team	N.Y.	Ana.	Cle.	K.C.	Bos.	Tex.	Bal.	Tor.	Chi.	Min.	Oak.	Sea.	Det.	TB.	N.L.	W	L	Pct.
New York	..	2	3	5	4	4	3	4	3	2	4	4	3	5	6	52	29	.642
Anaheim	3	..	2	4	3	3	2	2	2	4	2	4	4	4	4	43	38	.531
Cleveland	1	4	..	5	1	1	3	4	3	2	1	5	5	2	6	43	38	.531
Kansas City	0	3	3	..	1	1	4	4	3	5	3	2	4	5	4	43	38	.531
Boston	3	3	3	4	..	2	2	2	2	4	2	3	4	5		41	40	.506
Texas	2	4	2	4	1	..	3	3	2	4	2	3	2	5	4	40	41	.494
Baltimore	0	3	3	3	2	3	..	1	1	3	4	3	5	4	3	37	44	.457
Toronto	4	3	2	3	3	1	2	..	2	3	3	4	2	1	4	37	44	.457
Chicago	1	3	3	5	2	2	5	1	..	3	2	0	3	3	3	36	45	.444
Minnesota	1	3	2	4	3	4	1	1	3	..	3	2	2	3	3	35	46	.432
Oakland	1	3	4	1	1	4	2	2	4	4	..	2	1	2	4	35	46	.432
Seattle	1	1	2	2	1	1	2	2	1	6	3	..	5	4	3	34	46	.425
Detroit	1	1	2	4	3	1	0	1	3	4	3	2	..	3		33	48	.407
Tampa Bay	0	4	0	3	1	1	5	0	3	2	2	3	3	..	3	30	51	.370
N.L. clubs	1	2	4	4	4	5	5	3	4	4	4	4	6	6	..			
Lost at home	19	39	35	51	30	33	39	30	37	46	42	39	49	48	..	539	594	.476

ANAHEIM—85-77

Pitcher	Bal. W-L	Bos. W-L	Chi. W-L	Cle. W-L	Det. W-L	K.C. W-L	Min. W-L	N.Y. W-L	Oak. W-L	Sea. W-L	T.B. W-L	Tex. W-L	Tor. W-L	N.L. W-L	Total W-L
Cadaret, Greg	0-0	0-0	0-0	0-0	0-0	0-0	0-0	0-0	0-0	0-0	0-0	0-0	0-0	1-2	1-2
DeLucia, Rich	0-0	0-0	1-1	0-1	0-1	0-0	0-0	0-1	0-0	0-1	0-0	0-0	1-1	0-0	2-6
Dickson, Jason	1-1	0-1	0-2	0-2	1-0	0-0	1-0	0-1	2-0	2-0	0-1	1-0	0-0	2-2	10-10
Fetters, Mike	0-0	0-0	0-0	0-0	1-0	0-0	0-0	0-2	0-0	0-0	0-0	0-0	0-0	0-0	1-2
Finley, Chuck	1-1	0-0	1-1	1-0	0-1	1-1	1-1	1-0	1-0	1-0	0-4	1-0	2-0	1-0	11-9
Harris, Pep	0-0	0-0	0-0	0-0	0-0	1-0	1-0	0-0	0-0	0-0	0-1	0-0	1-0	1-0	3-1
Hasegawa, Shigetoshi	0-0	1-0	1-1	1-0	0-0	1-0	1-0	0-0	1-0	0-0	2-0	0-0	0-2	0-0	8-3
Hill, Ken	1-0	3-0	0-0	0-0	1-0	0-1	0-1	1-1	1-0	1-0	0-1	0-1	0-1	0-1	9-6
Holtz, Mike	1-0	1-0	0-0	0-0	0-0	0-1	0-0	0-0	0-0	0-0	0-0	0-0	0-0	0-0	2-2
James, Mike	0-0	0-0	0-0	0-0	0-0	0-0	0-0	0-0	0-0	0-0	0-0	0-0	0-0	0-0	0-0
Juden, Jeff	0-0	0-0	0-0	0-0	0-0	0-0	0-0	1-0	0-0	0-0	0-1	0-0	0-2	0-0	1-3
McDowell, Jack	0-1	1-1	0-0	0-1	1-0	1-0	0-0	1-0	0-0	1-0	0-0	0-0	0-0	0-0	5-3
Olivares, Omar	0-0	0-1	0-1	0-0	2-0	0-2	2-0	0-0	0-3	2-1	1-0	1-0	0-0	1-1	9-9
Percival, Troy	0-2	0-0	0-0	0-2	0-0	0-0	0-0	0-0	0-2	1-0	0-0	0-0	0-1	1-0	2-7
Robertson, Rich	0-0	0-0	0-0	0-0	0-0	0-0	0-0	0-0	0-0	0-0	0-0	0-0	0-0	0-0	0-0
Sparks, Steve	0-0	0-0	1-0	2-0	1-0	0-0	0-1	1-0	0-0	0-1	0-1	2-1	1-0	1-0	9-4
Washburn, Jarrod	1-1	0-0	0-0	0-0	0-0	0-0	0-0	0-0	1-2	1-0	0-0	1-0	0-0	1-0	6-3
Watson, Allen	0-0	0-2	1-0	0-1	1-1	0-0	1-0	0-2	1-0	0-0	0-0	1-1	0-0	1-0	6-7
Wilson, Trevor	0-0	0-0	0-0	0-0	0-0	0-0	0-0	0-0	0-0	0-0	0-0	0-0	0-0	0-0	0-0
Totals	5-6	6-5	5-6	4-7	8-3	6-5	6-5	6-5	5-7	9-3	6-5	5-7	4-7	10-6	85-77

INTERLEAGUE BREAKDOWN: Cadaret 0-1, Harris 1-0, Percival 1-0, Sparks 1-0 vs. Dodgers; Dickson 0-1, Olivares 0-1, Washburn 1-0 vs. Padres; Cadaret 0-1, Dickson 0-1, Finley 1-0 vs. Giants; Cadaret 1-0, Dickson 1-0, Olivares 1-0 vs. Rockies; Dickson 1-0, Finley 1-0, Hill 0-1 vs. Diamondbacks.

BALTIMORE—79-83

Pitcher	Ana. W-L	Bos. W-L	Chi. W-L	Cle. W-L	Det. W-L	K.C. W-L	Min. W-L	N.Y. W-L	Oak. W-L	Sea. W-L	T.B. W-L	Tex. W-L	Tor. W-L	N.L. W-L	Total W-L
Benitez, Armando	0-0	0-1	0-0	1-1	0-0	1-0	0-0	0-0	2-0	0-1	0-1	0-1	0-0	1-1	5-6
Bennett, Joel	0-0	0-0	0-0	0-0	0-0	0-0	0-0	0-0	0-0	0-0	0-0	0-0	0-0	0-0	0-0
Charlton, Norm	0-0	0-0	0-0	0-0	0-0	0-0	0-0	0-1	0-0	1-0	0-0	0-0	1-0	0-0	2-1
Coppinger, Rocky	0-0	0-0	0-0	0-0	0-0	0-0	0-0	0-0	0-0	0-0	0-0	0-0	0-0	0-0	0-0
Drabek, Doug	1-1	0-0	0-2	1-0	1-1	0-0	1-0	0-1	1-1	0-0	0-0	1-0	0-1	0-2	6-11
Dykhoff, Radhames	0-0	0-0	0-0	0-0	0-0	0-0	0-0	0-0	0-0	0-0	0-0	0-0	0-0	0-0	0-0
Erickson, Scott	1-1	2-1	0-2	1-1	1-0	2-1	2-0	1-2	1-0	1-1	1-1	1-2	1-1	1-0	16-13
Fussell, Chris	0-0	0-1	0-0	0-0	0-0	0-0	0-0	0-0	0-0	0-0	0-0	0-0	0-0	0-0	0-1
Guzman, Juan	0-0	0-0	0-1	0-0	1-0	0-1	0-0	1-0	1-0	1-0	0-0	0-1	0-0	0-0	4-4
Johns, Doug	0-0	2-0	0-0	0-0	0-0	0-0	0-1	0-1	0-0	0-0	1-0	0-0	0-0	0-0	3-3
Kamieniecki, Scott	0-0	0-0	0-0	0-2	1-0	0-1	0-0	0-0	0-2	0-1	0-0	1-0	0-0	0-0	2-6
Key, Jimmy	1-0	0-0	2-0	0-0	1-0	1-0	1-0	0-1	1-0	0-0	0-1	0-1	0-0	0-0	6-3
Lewis, Richie	0-0	0-0	0-0	0-0	0-0	0-0	0-0	0-0	0-0	0-0	0-0	0-0	0-0	0-0	0-0
Mathews, Terry	0-1	0-0	0-0	0-0	0-0	0-0	0-0	0-0	0-0	0-0	0-0	0-0	0-0	0-0	0-1
Mills, Alan	1-0	0-0	0-1	0-0	0-0	0-0	0-0	0-0	0-0	1-0	0-2	1-0	0-0	0-1	3-4
Munoz, Bobby	0-0	0-0	0-0	0-0	0-0	0-0	0-0	0-0	0-0	0-0	0-0	0-0	0-0	0-0	0-0
Mussina, Mike	0-0	0-1	0-2	1-0	4-0	0-2	1-1	0-0	2-0	2-0	0-0	2-1	1-2	0-0	13-10
Orosco, Jesse	1-0	2-0	0-0	0-0	0-0	1-1	0-0	0-0	0-0	0-0	0-0	0-0	0-0	0-0	4-1
Ponson, Sidney	0-0	0-2	0-1	0-1	1-0	1-1	2-0	2-0	1-0	0-0	0-0	1-1	0-1	1-2	8-9
Rhodes, Arthur	1-0	0-0	0-0	0-0	0-0	0-0	0-0	0-0	0-0	0-0	1-1	0-0	0-0	1-1	4-4
Rodriguez, Nerio	0-2	0-0	0-0	0-0	0-0	0-0	0-0	0-0	0-0	0-1	0-0	1-0	0-0	0-0	1-3
Smith, Pete	0-0	0-0	0-0	0-0	0-0	0-0	0-0	0-0	0-0	0-1	0-0	0-0	1-0	0-2	2-3
Totals	6-5	6-6	2-9	5-6	10-1	5-6	7-3	3-9	8-3	6-5	5-7	6-5	5-7	5-11	79-83

INTERLEAGUE BREAKDOWN: Drabek 0-1, Erickson 1-0, Mussina 0-1 vs. Braves; Drabek 0-1, Mussina 0-1, Ponson 0-1 vs. Expos; Benitez 0-1, Mussina 1-0, Rhodes 0-1, Smith 0-1 vs. Mets; Benitez 1-0, Ponson 0-1, Rhodes 1-0 vs. Phillies; Mills 0-1, Ponson 1-0, Smith 0-1 vs. Marlins.

BOSTON—92-70

Pitcher	Ana. W-L	Bal. W-L	Chi. W-L	Cle. W-L	Det. W-L	K.C. W-L	Min. W-L	N.Y. W-L	Oak. W-L	Sea. W-L	T.B. W-L	Tex. W-L	Tor. W-L	N.L. W-L	Total W-L
Avery, Steve	0-1	0-0	0-1	0-0	1-0	1-0	1-1	0-0	0-1	1-0	3-0	0-0	1-2	2-1	10-7
Barkley, Brian	0-0	0-0	0-0	0-0	0-0	0-0	0-0	0-0	0-0	0-0	0-0	0-0	0-0	0-0	0-0
Checo, Robinson	0-1	0-0	0-0	0-0	0-0	0-0	0-1	0-0	0-0	0-0	0-0	0-0	0-0	0-0	0-2
Cho, Jin Ho	0-0	0-1	0-1	0-0	0-1	0-0	0-0	0-0	0-0	0-0	0-0	0-0	0-0	0-0	0-3
Corsi, Jim	0-0	0-1	0-1	0-0	1-0	0-0	0-0	0-0	0-0	0-0	1-0	1-0	0-0	0-0	3-2
Eckersley, Dennis	0-0	1-0	0-0	0-1	1-0	0-0	1-0	0-0	1-0	0-0	0-0	0-0	0-0	0-0	4-1
Garces, Rich	0-0	0-0	0-0	0-1	0-0	0-0	0-0	0-0	1-0	0-0	0-0	0-0	0-0	0-0	1-1
Gordon, Tom	0-1	0-0	0-0	2-0	0-2	1-0	0-0	0-0	1-0	1-0	1-0	0-0	0-1	0-0	7-4
Henry, Butch	0-0	0-0	0-0	0-0	0-0	0-0	0-0	0-0	0-0	0-0	0-0	0-0	0-0	0-0	0-0
Lowe, Derek	0-1	0-1	0-0	0-0	0-0	0-0	1-0	0-2	0-0	0-2	0-0	1-0	1-1	0-2	3-9
Mahay, Ron	0-0	0-0	0-0	0-0	0-0	1-0	0-0	0-0	0-0	0-0	0-0	0-0	0-0	0-0	1-1
Martinez, Pedro	2-0	1-1	2-1	2-0	0-0	1-0	1-0	1-2	1-0	1-0	1-0	2-1	1-1	3-1	19-7
Reyes, Carlos	0-0	0-0	1-0	0-0	0-0	0-0	0-0	0-0	0-0	0-1	0-0	0-0	0-0	0-0	1-1
Rose, Brian	0-0	0-0	0-0	0-0	1-0	0-1	0-0	0-0	0-1	0-0	0-2	0-0	0-0	0-0	1-4
Saberhagen, Bret	1-0	2-1	0-2	2-0	1-0	1-0	0-1	1-1	0-0	2-0	1-1	0-1	0-1	3-0	15-8
Schourek, Pete	0-0	0-0	0-0	0-0	0-0	0-1	0-1	0-0	0-1	0-0	1-0	0-0	0-0	0-0	1-3
Shouse, Brian	0-0	0-0	0-0	0-0	0-1	0-0	0-0	0-0	0-0	0-0	0-0	0-0	0-0	0-0	0-1
Swindell, Greg	0-0	0-0	0-0	0-0	0-1	0-1	0-1	1-0	1-0	0-0	0-0	0-0	0-0	0-0	2-3
Valdez, Carlos	0-0	1-0	0-0	0-0	0-0	0-0	0-0	0-0	0-0	0-0	0-0	0-0	0-0	0-0	1-0
Veras, Dario	0-0	0-0	0-0	0-0	0-0	0-0	0-0	0-0	0-0	0-0	0-0	0-0	0-1	0-0	0-1
Wakefield, Tim	2-2	1-1	2-0	2-1	0-0	3-0	1-0	2-2	1-0	0-0	1-0	1-0	0-1	1-1	17-8
Wasdin, John	2-0	0-0	0-0	0-0	0-0	0-0	0-1	0-0	3-0	1-1	0-0	1-1	0-0	0-1	6-4
West, David	0-0	0-0	0-0	0-0	0-0	0-0	0-0	0-0	0-0	0-0	0-0	0-0	0-0	0-0	0-0
Totals	5-6	6-6	5-6	8-3	5-5	8-3	5-6	5-7	9-2	7-4	9-3	6-5	5-7	9-7	92-70

INTERLEAGUE BREAKDOWN: Martinez 1-0, Saberhagen 1-0, Wasdin 0-1 vs. Braves; Avery 1-0, Martinez 1-0, Saberhagen 1-0 vs. Expos; Avery 1-0, Martinez 0-1, Wakefield 0-1 vs. Mets; Avery 0-1, Gordon 0-1, Lowe 0-1, Saberhagen 1-0 vs. Phillies; Lowe 0-1, Martinez 1-0, Wakefield 1-0 vs. Marlins.

1998 A.L. STATISTICS Miscellaneous

CHICAGO—80-82

Pitcher	Ana. W-L	Bal. W-L	Bos. W-L	Cle. W-L	Det. W-L	K.C. W-L	Min. W-L	N.Y. W-L	Oak. W-L	Sea. W-L	T.B. W-L	Tex. W-L	Tor. W-L	N.L. W-L	Total W-L
Abbott, Jim	0-0	0-0	0-0	1-0	0-0	2-0	1-0	1-0	0-0	0-0	0-0	0-0	0-0	0-0	5-0
Baldwin, James	0-2	3-0	0-0	1-1	0-0	2-1	1-0	1-0	0-0	0-0	3-0	0-1	1-1	1-0	13-6
Bere, Jason	1-0	0-0	1-1	0-0	0-1	0-0	0-1	0-0	0-1	0-0	0-2	0-0	0-1	1-0	3-7
Bradford, Chad	1-0	1-0	0-0	0-0	0-0	0-0	0-0	0-1	0-0	0-0	0-0	0-0	0-0	0-0	2-1
Casian, Larry	0-0	0-0	0-0	0-0	0-0	0-0	0-0	0-0	0-0	0-0	0-0	0-0	0-0	0-0	0-0
Castillo, Carlos	1-0	0-0	0-0	0-0	0-1	1-0	0-0	0-0	0-1	0-1	1-0	1-0	1-1	1-0	6-4
Castillo, Tony	1-0	0-0	0-0	0-1	0-0	0-0	0-0	0-0	0-0	0-0	0-0	0-0	0-0	0-1	1-2
Eyre, Scott	0-0	0-2	0-1	0-0	1-1	0-0	0-1	0-0	1-0	0-1	0-1	0-0	1-0	0-1	3-8
Fordham, Tom	0-0	0-0	0-0	0-0	0-0	0-0	0-0	0-0	0-1	1-0	0-0	0-0	0-0	0-1	1-2
Foulke, Keith	0-0	0-0	0-0	0-0	0-0	0-0	1-0	0-1	0-0	1-1	0-0	1-0	0-0	0-0	3-2
Heathcott, Mike	0-0	0-0	0-0	0-0	0-0	0-0	0-0	0-0	0-0	0-0	0-0	0-0	0-0	0-0	0-0
Howry, Bob	0-0	0-0	0-1	0-0	0-0	0-0	0-0	0-0	0-0	0-0	0-1	0-1	0-0	0-0	0-3
Karchner, Matt	0-0	0-0	0-0	0-2	1-0	0-1	0-0	0-1	0-0	0-0	0-0	0-0	0-0	1-0	2-4
Navarro, Jaime	0-0	1-0	0-1	0-1	0-1	2-1	0-2	0-2	1-0	1-2	0-1	1-1	1-2	1-2	8-16
Parque, Jim	0-1	2-0	2-0	0-0	2-0	0-0	0-0	0-0	0-0	0-1	0-0	0-0	0-1	0-2	7-5
Rizzo, Todd	0-0	0-0	0-0	0-0	0-0	0-0	0-0	0-0	0-0	0-0	0-0	0-0	0-0	0-0	0-0
Simas, Bill	0-0	0-0	0-0	1-0	0-0	0-0	1-1	1-0	0-1	0-0	0-0	0-0	0-0	1-1	4-3
Sirotka, Mike	1-2	1-0	1-1	3-0	1-2	1-1	1-1	1-1	1-2	1-1	1-0	0-3	0-1	0-1	14-15
Snyder, John	1-0	1-0	2-0	0-0	1-0	0-0	1-0	0-0	0-1	0-1	0-0	1-0	0-0	0-0	7-2
Ward, Bryan	0-0	0-0	0-0	0-1	0-0	0-0	0-0	0-1	0-0	0-0	0-0	1-0	0-0	0-0	1-2
Totals	6-5	9-2	6-5	6-6	6-6	8-4	6-6	4-7	4-7	4-7	5-6	5-6	4-6	7-9	80-82

INTERLEAGUE BREAKDOWN: Fordham, 0-1, Simas 1-1 vs. Brewers; T. Castillo 0-1, Eyre 0-1, Sirotka, 0-1 vs. Cubs; Navarro 1-0, Parque 0-1 vs. Reds; Baldwin 1-0, Navarro 0-1, Parque 0-1 vs. Astros; C. Castillo 1-0, Sirotka 1-0 vs. Pirates; Bere 1-0, Karchner 1-0, Navarro 0-1 vs. Cardinals.

CLEVELAND—89-73

Pitcher	Ana. W-L	Bal. W-L	Bos. W-L	Chi. W-L	Det. W-L	K.C. W-L	Min. W-L	N.Y. W-L	Oak. W-L	Sea. W-L	T.B. W-L	Tex. W-L	Tor. W-L	N.L. W-L	Total W-L
Assenmacher, Paul	0-0	1-0	0-1	0-0	0-0	0-0	0-0	0-1	0-1	1-1	0-1	0-0	0-0	0-0	2-5
Burba, Dave	1-0	1-0	0-2	0-1	2-0	0-0	2-1	0-3	1-1	2-0	0-1	1-1	2-0	3-0	15-10
Colon, Bartolo	1-1	0-1	0-2	1-0	1-0	2-0	0-2	1-0	0-1	0-0	2-0	2-1	1-1	3-0	14-9
Gooden, Dwight	0-0	1-0	0-2	0-0	1-1	0-1	2-0	0-0	0-0	0-0	2-0	0-0	1-2	1-0	8-6
Jackson, Mike	0-0	0-0	0-0	0-0	0-0	0-0	1-0	0-0	0-0	0-0	0-1	0-0	0-0	0-0	1-1
Jacome, Jason	0-0	0-0	0-0	0-0	0-0	0-0	0-0	0-1	0-0	0-0	0-0	0-0	0-0	0-0	0-1
Jones, Doug	0-1	0-1	0-0	0-0	0-0	0-0	0-0	0-0	0-1	0-0	0-0	0-0	1-0	0-0	1-2
Karsay, Steve	0-0	0-0	0-0	0-0	0-0	0-0	0-0	0-0	0-1	0-0	0-1	0-0	0-0	0-0	0-2
Krivda, Rick	0-0	0-0	0-0	0-0	0-0	0-0	0-0	0-0	1-0	0-0	1-0	0-0	0-0	0-0	2-0
Martin, Tom	0-0	0-0	1-0	0-0	0-0	0-0	0-0	0-0	0-1	0-0	0-0	0-0	0-0	0-0	1-1
Mesa, Jose	0-0	0-0	0-0	1-0	0-0	0-0	0-0	0-0	0-0	1-0	1-0	0-1	0-0	0-2	3-4
Morman, Alvin	0-0	0-0	0-0	0-0	0-0	0-0	0-0	0-0	0-0	0-0	0-0	0-0	0-0	0-1	0-1
Nagy, Charles	2-0	1-1	1-0	1-2	2-0	1-1	1-1	1-0	1-1	2-0	1-0	0-2	1-0	0-2	15-10
Ogea, Chad	0-0	0-1	1-0	0-1	0-0	1-0	1-0	0-0	0-1	0-0	1-0	0-0	1-1	0-0	5-4
Plunk, Eric	1-0	0-0	0-1	1-0	0-0	0-0	0-0	0-0	0-0	0-0	0-0	0-0	1-0	0-0	3-1
Poole, Jim	0-0	0-0	0-0	0-0	0-0	0-0	0-0	0-0	0-0	0-0	0-0	0-0	0-0	0-0	0-0
Rakers, Jason	0-0	0-0	0-0	0-0	0-0	0-0	0-0	0-0	0-0	0-0	0-0	0-0	0-0	0-0	0-0
Reed, Steve	1-0	0-1	0-0	0-0	1-0	0-0	0-0	0-0	0-1	0-0	0-0	0-0	0-0	0-0	2-2
Shuey, Paul	1-0	0-0	0-0	2-2	0-0	1-1	0-1	0-0	1-0	0-0	0-0	0-0	0-0	0-0	5-4
Villone, Ron	0-0	0-0	0-0	0-0	0-0	0-0	0-0	0-0	0-0	0-0	0-0	0-0	0-0	0-0	0-0
Whiten, Mark	0-0	0-0	0-0	0-0	0-0	0-0	0-0	0-0	0-0	0-0	0-0	0-0	0-0	0-0	0-0
Worrell, Tim	0-0	0-0	0-0	0-0	0-0	0-0	0-0	0-0	0-0	0-0	0-0	0-0	0-0	0-0	0-0
Wright, Jaret	0-2	2-0	0-0	0-0	2-2	3-0	0-0	2-1	0-1	1-1	0-0	0-1	0-0	2-0	12-10
Totals	7-4	6-5	3-8	6-6	9-3	8-4	6-6	4-7	3-8	9-2	7-3	4-7	7-4	10-6	89-73

INTERLEAGUE BREAKDOWN: Burba 1-0, Colon 1-0, Wright 0-1 vs. Brewers; Gooden 1-0, Plunk 1-0 vs. Cubs; Burba 1-0, Nagy 0-1, Wright 1-0 vs. Reds; Colon 1-0, Mesa 0-1, Nagy 0-1 vs. Astros; Colon 1-0, Mesa 0-1, Morman 0-1 vs. Pirates; Burba 1-0, Wright 1-0 vs. Cardinals.

DETROIT—65-97

Pitcher	Ana. W-L	Bal. W-L	Bos. W-L	Chi. W-L	Cle. W-L	K.C. W-L	Min. W-L	N.Y. W-L	Oak. W-L	Sea. W-L	T.B. W-L	Tex. W-L	Tor. W-L	N.L. W-L	Total W-L
Anderson, Matt	0-0	0-1	1-0	0-0	0-0	0-0	0-0	1-0	0-0	0-0	0-0	0-0	1-0	1-0	5-1
Bochtler, Doug	0-0	0-0	0-0	0-1	0-1	0-0	0-0	0-0	0-0	0-0	0-0	0-0	0-0	0-0	0-2
Brocail, Doug	0-0	0-0	0-0	0-0	0-0	0-0	2-0	0-0	1-0	0-0	0-0	0-0	1-1	1-1	5-2
Brunson, Will	0-0	0-0	0-0	0-0	0-0	0-0	0-0	0-0	0-0	0-0	0-0	0-0	0-0	0-0	0-0
Castillo, Frank	1-1	0-1	0-1	0-1	1-1	0-0	0-0	0-0	1-1	0-1	0-0	0-0	0-0	0-2	3-9
Crow, Dean	0-0	0-0	0-0	1-0	0-0	1-0	0-0	0-0	0-1	0-1	0-0	0-0	0-0	0-0	2-2
Duran, Roberto	0-0	0-0	0-0	0-1	0-1	0-0	0-0	0-0	0-0	0-0	0-0	0-0	0-0	0-0	0-1
Florie, Bryce	1-0	0-2	1-0	0-0	1-1	1-1	1-0	0-1	1-1	0-0	1-0	0-2	0-0	1-1	8-9
Greisinger, Seth	0-1	0-0	0-0	2-0	0-2	0-2	0-1	0-1	1-0	1-0	1-1	0-0	0-1	1-0	6-9
Harriger, Denny	0-0	0-0	0-1	0-0	0-1	0-0	0-1	0-0	0-0	0-0	0-0	0-0	0-0	0-1	0-3
Jones, Todd	0-0	0-0	0-1	0-0	0-0	0-0	0-0	0-0	0-0	0-0	0-0	0-0	1-0	0-2	1-4
Keagle, Greg	0-0	0-2	0-0	0-0	0-0	0-0	0-2	0-0	0-0	0-0	0-1	0-0	0-0	0-0	0-5
Moehler, Brian	1-1	0-0	1-0	1-2	1-0	1-0	1-1	2-1	0-1	1-2	1-2	1-2	2-1	1-0	14-13
Powell, Brian	0-1	0-0	1-1	0-1	0-1	0-0	0-0	0-0	0-1	1-1	1-0	0-1	0-1	0-1	3-8
Runyan, Sean	0-1	0-0	0-1	0-0	0-0	0-0	1-0	0-1	0-0	0-0	0-0	0-0	0-0	0-0	1-4
Sager, A.J.	0-0	0-0	0-0	0-0	0-0	0-0	1-1	1-0	1-0	0-0	0-0	0-0	0-1	0-0	4-2
Sanders, Scott	0-0	0-1	0-0	0-0	0-0	0-0	0-0	0-0	0-0	0-0	0-0	0-1	0-0	0-0	0-2
Santana, Marino	0-0	0-0	0-0	0-0	0-0	0-0	0-0	0-0	0-0	0-0	0-0	0-0	0-0	0-0	0-0
Thompson, Justin	0-1	0-3	1-0	1-1	0-2	3-1	1-0	0-1	2-0	0-2	1-1	0-1	0-1	2-1	11-15
Worrell, Tim	0-2	0-0	0-0	0-0	0-0	0-0	0-0	0-0	0-0	0-0	1-0	0-0	0-0	0-0	2-6
Totals	3-8	1-10	5-5	6-6	3-9	6-6	8-4	3-8	7-4	3-8	5-6	3-8	5-6	7-9	65-97

INTERLEAGUE BREAKDOWN: Castillo 0-1, Florie 1-0, Thompson 1-0 vs. Brewers; Anderson 1-0, Brocail 0-1 vs. Cubs; Brocail 0-1, Harriger 0-1, Thompson 0-1 vs. Reds; Castillo 0-1, Jones 0-2 vs. Astros; Greisinger 1-0, Moehler 1-0, Powell 0-1 vs. Pirates; Florie 0-1, Thompson 1-0 vs. Cardinals.

1998 A.L. STATISTICS — Miscellaneous

KANSAS CITY—72-89

Pitcher	Ana. W-L	Bal. W-L	Bos. W-L	Chi. W-L	Cle. W-L	Det. W-L	Min. W-L	N.Y. W-L	Oak. W-L	Sea. W-L	T.B. W-L	Tex. W-L	Tor. W-L	N.L. W-L	Total W-L
Appier, Kevin	0-0	0-0	0-0	0-0	0-1	0-1	0-0	0-0	0-0	1-0	0-0	0-0	0-0	0-0	1-2
Barber, Brian	0-1	1-0	0-1	0-1	0-0	0-0	0-0	0-0	0-0	0-1	0-0	0-0	1-0	0-0	2-4
Belcher, Tim	1-2	1-0	0-1	2-1	0-1	0-3	2-2	0-1	1-1	2-0	1-1	0-0	1-1	3-0	14-14
Bevil, Brian	0-0	0-0	0-0	0-1	0-0	0-0	2-0	0-0	0-0	1-0	0-0	0-0	0-0	0-0	3-1
Bones, Ricky	1-0	0-0	0-0	0-1	0-0	0-0	0-0	0-0	1-0	0-0	0-1	0-0	0-0	0-0	2-2
Byrdak, Tim	0-0	0-0	0-0	0-0	0-0	0-0	0-0	0-0	0-0	0-0	0-0	0-0	0-0	0-0	0-0
Evans, Bart	0-0	0-0	0-0	0-0	0-0	0-0	0-0	0-0	0-0	0-0	0-0	0-0	0-0	0-0	0-0
Halter, Shane	0-0	0-0	0-0	0-0	0-0	0-0	0-0	0-0	0-0	0-0	0-0	0-0	0-0	0-0	0-0
Haney, Chris	0-1	2-0	0-1	0-0	0-0	0-0	1-0	0-2	1-0	0-0	1-0	0-1	1-1	0-0	6-6
McDill, Allen	0-0	0-0	0-0	0-0	0-0	0-0	0-0	0-0	0-0	0-0	0-0	0-0	0-0	0-0	0-0
Montgomery, Jeff	0-0	0-1	0-1	0-0	1-0	0-0	0-0	0-0	0-0	0-0	1-0	0-2	0-0	0-1	2-5
Pichardo, Hipolito	1-1	0-0	1-0	0-0	0-1	1-0	1-2	0-0	0-1	0-1	1-0	0-0	0-0	1-2	7-8
Pittsley, Jim	0-0	0-0	0-0	0-0	0-0	0-0	0-0	0-0	0-0	0-0	0-0	0-0	0-0	1-1	1-1
Rapp, Pat	0-1	1-0	1-0	0-2	1-2	1-1	0-0	0-2	2-1	0-0	2-0	2-2	0-1	2-1	12-13
Rios, Danny	0-0	0-0	0-0	0-0	0-0	0-0	0-0	0-0	0-0	0-1	0-0	0-0	0-0	0-0	0-1
Rosado, Jose	2-0	1-1	0-2	1-1	1-2	1-0	0-0	0-1	1-0	0-0	1-0	0-1	0-2	0-1	8-11
Rusch, Glendon	0-0	0-3	0-1	0-1	0-1	2-0	0-1	0-2	0-1	0-1	0-1	1-2	2-0	1-1	6-15
Santiago, Jose	0-0	0-0	0-0	0-0	0-0	0-0	0-0	0-0	0-0	0-0	0-0	0-0	0-0	0-0	0-0
Service, Scott	0-0	0-0	1-0	1-0	1-0	0-1	1-0	0-1	1-0	0-2	0-0	0-0	0-0	1-0	6-4
Suppan, Jeff	0-0	0-0	0-0	0-0	0-0	0-0	0-0	0-0	0-0	0-0	0-0	0-0	0-0	0-0	0-0
Walker, Jamie	0-0	0-0	0-1	0-0	0-0	0-0	0-0	0-0	0-0	0-0	0-0	0-0	0-0	0-0	0-1
Whisenant, Matt	0-0	0-0	0-0	0-0	0-0	1-0	0-0	0-1	0-0	0-0	1-0	0-0	0-0	0-0	2-1
Totals	5-6	6-5	3-8	4-8	4-8	6-6	7-5	0-10	7-4	4-6	8-3	3-8	6-5	9-7	72-89

INTERLEAGUE BREAKDOWN: Montgomery 0-1, Pichardo 0-1, Rapp 1-0 vs. Brewers; Pichardo 1-0, Rapp 0-1, Service 1-0 vs. Cubs; Pittsley 1-0, Rapp 1-0 vs. Reds; Belcher 1-0, Pittsley 0-1, Rosado 0-1 vs. Astros; Belcher 1-0, Rusch 0-1 vs. Pirates; Belcher 1-0, Pichardo 0-1, Rusch 1-0 vs. Cardinals.

MINNESOTA—70-92

Pitcher	Ana. W-L	Bal. W-L	Bos. W-L	Chi. W-L	Cle. W-L	Det. W-L	K.C. W-L	N.Y. W-L	Oak. W-L	Sea. W-L	T.B. W-L	Tex. W-L	Tor. W-L	N.L. W-L	Total W-L
Aguilera, Rick	0-0	1-0	0-0	1-2	1-0	0-1	0-2	0-0	0-1	1-1	0-0	0-0	0-0	0-2	4-9
Baptist, Travis	0-0	0-0	0-1	0-0	0-0	0-0	0-0	0-0	0-0	0-0	0-0	0-0	0-0	0-0	0-1
Carrasco, Hector	0-1	0-0	0-0	0-0	0-0	0-0	0-0	0-0	2-1	0-0	1-0	1-0	1-0	1-0	4-2
Guardado, Eddie	0-0	0-0	0-0	0-0	0-0	0-0	0-1	0-0	1-0	0-0	1-0	0-0	1-0	0-0	3-1
Hawkins, LaTroy	2-1	1-1	1-0	1-0	0-0	1-0	0-0	0-2	0-0	0-2	0-2	1-1	0-2	0-3	7-14
Miller, Travis	0-0	0-1	0-1	0-0	0-0	0-0	0-0	0-0	0-0	0-0	0-0	0-0	0-0	0-0	0-2
Milton, Eric	0-0	0-0	1-1	0-1	2-1	0-1	3-1	1-2	0-2	0-1	0-1	0-1	0-0	1-1	8-14
Morgan, Mike	0-0	0-0	0-0	1-0	0-0	0-0	0-0	1-0	0-0	0-0	0-0	1-1	0-0	1-1	4-2
Naulty, Dan	0-0	0-0	0-0	0-0	0-0	0-2	0-0	0-0	0-0	0-0	0-0	0-0	0-0	0-0	0-2
Radke, Brad	3-0	0-3	1-1	0-0	1-2	1-1	1-1	0-1	0-0	1-2	1-0	0-0	1-2	2-1	12-14
Ritchie, Todd	0-0	0-0	0-0	0-0	0-0	0-0	0-0	0-0	0-0	0-0	0-0	0-0	0-0	0-0	0-0
Rodriguez, Frank	0-1	0-0	1-0	0-0	0-0	0-0	0-1	1-1	0-0	0-1	1-0	0-1	1-1	0-0	4-6
Sampson, Benj	0-0	0-0	0-0	0-0	0-0	1-0	0-0	0-0	0-0	0-0	0-0	0-0	0-0	0-0	1-0
Serafini, Dan	0-0	1-0	0-0	0-1	0-0	1-1	0-1	1-0	1-1	0-0	1-0	1-0	0-0	1-0	7-4
Swindell, Greg	0-2	0-0	0-0	0-0	1-0	0-0	0-0	0-0	0-1	1-0	1-0	0-0	1-0	1-0	3-3
Tewksbury, Bob	0-1	0-1	0-1	1-2	1-2	0-0	1-0	0-1	0-1	0-2	3-0	0-0	1-1	0-1	7-13
Trombley, Mike	0-0	0-0	2-0	2-0	0-1	0-2	0-0	0-0	0-0	0-0	0-1	2-0	0-1	0-0	6-5
Totals	5-6	3-7	6-5	6-6	6-6	4-8	5-7	4-7	4-7	2-9	7-4	7-4	4-7	7-9	70-92

INTERLEAGUE BREAKDOWN: Hawkins 0-1, Radke 0-1 vs. Brewers; Hawkins 0-1, Morgan 1-0, Radke 1-0 vs. Cubs; Aguilera 0-1, Hawkins 0-1, Radke 1-0 vs. Reds; Milton 1-0, Tewksbury 0-1 vs. Astros; Aguilera 0-1, Morgan 0-1, Serafini 1-0 vs. Pirates; Carrasco 1-0, Milton 0-1, Swindell 1-0 vs. Cardinals.

NEW YORK—114-48

Pitcher	Ana. W-L	Bal. W-L	Bos. W-L	Chi. W-L	Cle. W-L	Det. W-L	K.C. W-L	Min. W-L	Oak. W-L	Sea. W-L	T.B. W-L	Tex. W-L	Tor. W-L	N.L. W-L	Total W-L
Banks, Willie	0-0	0-0	0-0	0-0	0-0	0-0	0-0	0-0	0-0	0-0	0-0	0-1	1-0	0-0	1-1
Borowski, Joe	0-0	0-0	0-0	0-0	0-0	0-0	1-0	0-0	0-0	0-0	0-0	0-0	0-0	0-0	1-0
Bradley, Ryan	0-1	0-0	0-0	0-0	1-0	0-0	0-0	0-0	0-0	0-0	0-0	1-0	0-0	0-0	2-1
Brow, Scott	0-0	0-0	0-0	0-0	0-0	0-0	0-0	0-0	0-0	0-0	0-0	0-0	0-0	0-0	0-0
Bruske, Jim	0-0	0-0	0-0	0-0	0-0	0-0	0-0	0-0	0-0	0-0	1-0	0-0	0-0	0-0	1-0
Buddie, Mike	0-0	0-0	0-0	0-0	0-0	0-0	0-0	0-1	2-0	0-0	1-0	0-0	0-0	1-0	4-1
Cone, David	1-0	1-1	3-0	0-0	1-1	3-1	2-0	1-0	0-2	1-1	2-0	2-0	0-1	3-0	20-7
Erdos, Todd	0-0	0-0	0-0	0-0	0-0	0-0	0-0	0-0	0-0	0-0	0-0	0-0	0-0	0-0	0-0
Hernandez, Orlando	0-1	2-0	1-0	0-0	0-1	1-0	1-0	0-0	1-0	0-0	2-0	1-1	1-0	1-1	12-4
Holmes, Darren	0-0	0-0	0-0	0-0	0-0	0-2	0-0	0-0	0-0	0-0	0-0	0-0	0-1	0-0	0-3
Irabu, Hideki	0-0	1-1	0-1	1-2	1-1	2-0	1-0	2-0	0-1	1-1	3-0	0-1	0-1	1-0	13-9
Jerzembeck, Mike	0-0	0-0	0-1	0-0	0-0	0-0	0-0	0-0	0-0	0-0	0-0	0-0	0-0	0-0	0-1
Lankford, Frank	0-0	0-0	0-0	0-0	0-0	0-0	0-0	0-0	0-0	0-0	0-0	0-0	0-0	0-0	0-0
Lloyd, Graeme	0-0	0-0	0-0	1-0	0-0	0-0	0-0	1-0	0-0	0-0	0-0	0-0	0-0	1-0	3-0
Mendoza, Ramiro	1-0	0-0	1-0	0-0	1-0	0-0	2-0	2-0	1-0	0-0	0-0	0-0	0-1	2-1	10-2
Nelson, Jeff	0-0	0-0	0-1	2-1	1-0	0-0	0-0	0-0	0-0	0-0	0-0	0-0	1-0	1-1	5-3
Pettitte, Andy	0-2	3-0	0-1	1-1	1-1	1-0	1-0	0-3	1-0	1-1	1-1	1-0	3-1	2-0	16-11
Rivera, Mariano	1-0	0-0	0-1	0-0	1-0	0-0	0-0	0-0	0-0	1-0	0-0	1-0	0-0	0-0	3-0
Stanton, Mike	0-1	1-0	0-0	0-0	0-0	0-0	0-0	0-0	0-0	0-0	1-0	1-0	1-0	0-0	4-1
Tessmer, Jay	1-0	0-0	0-0	0-0	0-0	0-0	0-0	0-0	0-0	0-0	0-0	0-0	0-0	0-0	1-0
Wells, David	1-1	1-1	2-1	2-0	1-0	1-0	2-0	2-0	1-0	2-0	0-0	1-0	0-1	2-0	18-4
Totals	5-6	9-3	7-5	7-4	7-4	8-3	10-0	7-4	8-3	8-3	11-1	8-3	6-6	13-3	114-48

INTERLEAGUE BREAKDOWN: Cone 1-0, Hernandez 0-1, Nelson 1-0, Wells 1-0 vs. Braves; Hernandez 1-0, Irabu 1-0, Nelson 0-1 vs. Expos; Mendoza 1-1, Pettitte 1-0 vs. Mets; Buddie 1-0, Cone 1-0, Wells 1-0 vs. Phillies; Cone 1-0, Mendoza 1-0, Pettitte 1-0 vs. Marlins.

OAKLAND—74-88

Pitcher	Ana. W-L	Bal. W-L	Bos. W-L	Chi. W-L	Cle. W-L	Det. W-L	K.C. W-L	Min. W-L	N.Y. W-L	Sea. W-L	T.B. W-L	Tex. W-L	Tor. W-L	N.L. W-L	Total W-L
Candiotti, Tom	1-0	2-1	1-1	1-0	1-1	1-1	1-1	0-1	1-2	0-2	1-2	0-1	1-1	0-2	11-16
Connelly, Steve	0-0	0-0	0-0	0-0	0-0	0-0	0-0	0-0	0-0	0-0	0-0	0-0	0-0	0-0	0-0
Dougherty, Jim	0-0	0-0	0-0	0-0	0-0	0-0	0-1	0-0	0-1	0-0	0-0	0-0	0-0	0-0	0-2
Fetters, Mike	1-0	0-2	0-0	0-1	0-0	0-0	0-0	0-0	0-0	0-0	0-0	0-1	0-1	0-1	1-6
Groom, Buddy	0-0	0-0	0-0	1-0	0-0	0-1	0-0	1-0	0-0	0-0	0-0	1-0	0-0	0-0	3-1
Haynes, Jimmy	0-1	0-3	0-1	1-1	1-0	0-1	0-0	0-0	1-0	1-0	0-1	3-0	3-0	1-1	11-9
Heredia, Gil	0-0	0-1	0-0	0-0	1-0	1-0	0-0	0-0	1-0	0-2	0-0	0-0	0-0	0-0	3-3
Holzemer, Mark	0-0	0-0	0-0	0-0	0-0	0-0	0-0	1-0	0-0	0-0	0-0	0-0	0-0	0-0	1-0
Mathews, T.J.	1-0	0-0	0-1	0-0	2-0	0-0	0-1	1-1	0-1	1-0	1-0	0-0	0-0	1-0	7-4
Mohler, Mike	0-0	0-0	0-0	0-0	1-0	0-0	0-1	0-0	0-1	0-0	0-0	0-0	0-1	2-0	3-3
Oquist, Mike	2-1	0-0	0-1	0-0	0-0	1-2	0-0	1-1	0-1	1-1	1-1	0-1	0-1	1-1	7-11
Prieto, Ariel	0-0	0-0	0-0	0-0	0-0	0-0	0-1	0-0	0-0	0-0	0-0	0-0	0-0	0-0	0-1
Rogers, Kenny	2-0	1-0	1-2	2-1	2-1	0-1	1-1	2-0	0-0	0-0	1-1	2-0	1-0	1-1	16-8
Small, Aaron	0-0	0-0	0-0	0-0	0-0	0-0	0-0	0-0	0-0	0-0	1-0	0-0	0-0	0-1	1-1
Stein, Blake	0-1	0-0	0-0	2-1	0-1	0-1	1-1	0-0	0-0	1-1	0-1	0-1	0-0	1-1	5-9
Taylor, Billy	0-1	0-1	0-2	0-0	0-0	1-0	1-0	0-1	0-1	1-0	0-0	0-2	0-1	1-0	4-9
Telgheder, Dave	0-0	0-0	0-0	0-0	0-0	0-0	0-0	0-0	0-0	0-0	0-0	0-0	0-1	0-0	0-1
Witasick, Jay	0-1	0-0	0-0	0-0	0-0	0-0	0-0	1-0	0-1	0-1	0-0	0-0	0-0	0-0	1-3
Worrell, Tim	0-0	0-0	0-0	0-1	0-0	0-0	0-0	0-0	0-0	0-0	0-0	0-0	0-0	0-0	0-1
Totals	7-5	3-8	2-9	7-4	8-3	4-7	4-7	7-4	3-8	5-7	5-6	6-6	5-6	8-8	74-88

INTERLEAGUE BREAKDOWN:Haynes 0-1, Rogers 0-1, Stein 1-0 vs. Dodgers; Rogers 1-0, Stein 0-1, Taylor 1-0 vs. Padres; Candiotti 0-1, Haynes 1-0, Mohler 1-0, Small 0-1 vs. Giants; Fetters 0-1, Mathews 1-0, Oquist 0-1 vs. Rockies; Candiotti 0-1, Mohler 1-0, Oquist 1-0 vs. Diamondbacks.

SEATTLE—76-85

Pitcher	Ana. W-L	Bal. W-L	Bos. W-L	Chi. W-L	Cle. W-L	Det. W-L	K.C. W-L	Min. W-L	N.Y. W-L	Oak. W-L	T.B. W-L	Tex. W-L	Tor. W-L	N.L. W-L	Total W-L
Abbott, Paul	0-1	0-0	0-0	0-0	0-0	0-0	0-0	1-0	0-0	0-0	1-0	1-0	0-0	0-0	3-1
Ayala, Bobby	0-1	0-1	0-1	0-0	0-0	0-1	1-0	0-0	0-2	0-0	0-1	0-1	0-1	0-1	1-10
Bullinger, Jim	0-0	0-0	0-0	0-0	0-0	0-0	0-0	0-0	0-1	0-0	0-0	0-0	0-0	0-0	0-1
Cloude, Ken	0-1	0-0	2-0	1-1	0-1	1-1	0-0	2-0	0-1	0-1	0-1	1-0	0-1	1-2	8-10
Fassero, Jeff	1-1	1-2	0-1	1-1	0-1	0-0	2-1	1-0	0-2	1-1	0-0	3-0	2-1	1-1	13-12
Fossas, Tony	0-0	0-1	0-0	0-0	0-1	0-0	0-1	0-0	0-0	0-0	0-0	0-0	0-0	0-0	0-3
Gajkowski, Steve	0-0	0-0	0-0	0-0	0-0	0-0	0-0	0-0	0-0	0-0	0-0	0-0	0-0	0-0	0-0
Holdridge, David	0-0	0-0	0-0	0-0	0-0	0-0	0-0	0-0	0-0	0-0	0-0	0-0	0-0	0-0	0-0
Johnson, Randy	1-1	0-0	0-1	0-1	0-1	1-0	1-0	1-0	0-0	1-1	2-1	0-2	1-0	1-2	9-10
Lira, Felipe	0-0	0-0	0-0	0-0	0-0	0-0	1-0	0-0	0-0	0-0	0-0	0-0	0-0	0-0	1-0
Lorraine, Andrew	0-0	0-0	0-0	0-0	0-0	0-0	0-0	0-0	0-0	0-0	0-0	0-0	0-0	0-0	0-0
McCarthy, Greg	0-0	1-0	0-1	0-0	0-1	0-0	0-0	0-0	0-0	0-0	0-0	0-0	0-0	0-0	1-2
Moyer, Jamie	0-0	2-0	1-1	0-0	1-1	3-0	0-1	1-1	1-1	3-0	2-1	0-1	0-1	1-1	15-9
Paniagua, Jose	0-0	0-0	0-0	1-0	0-0	0-0	0-0	0-0	0-0	1-0	0-0	0-0	0-0	0-0	2-0
Slocumb, Heathcliff	0-0	0-0	0-0	1-0	0-1	1-0	0-0	0-0	0-0	0-2	0-0	0-0	0-0	0-0	2-5
Spoljaric, Paul	0-2	0-1	0-0	1-0	1-0	1-0	0-0	0-0	0-1	0-0	0-0	0-1	1-0	0-1	4-6
Suzuki, Makoto	0-0	0-0	0-0	0-0	0-0	0-0	1-0	0-0	0-0	0-0	0-1	0-1	0-0	0-0	1-2
Swift, Bill	0-2	1-1	1-0	1-1	0-1	0-1	1-1	1-0	1-0	1-0	1-0	0-0	0-2	3-0	11-9
Timlin, Mike	1-0	0-0	0-1	1-0	0-0	0-0	0-0	0-0	1-1	0-0	0-0	0-0	0-0	0-1	3-3
Wells, Bob	0-0	0-0	0-0	0-0	0-0	1-0	0-0	0-0	1-0	0-0	0-0	0-0	0-0	0-1	2-2
Totals	3-9	5-6	4-7	7-4	2-9	8-3	6-4	9-2	3-8	7-5	6-5	5-7	4-7	7-9	76-85

INTERLEAGUE BREAKDOWN: Moyer 0-1, Swift 1-0, Wells 0-1 vs. Dodgers; Cloude 0-1, Fassero 0-1, Johnson 1-0, Moyer 1-0 vs. Padres; Cloude 0-1, Fassero 1-0, Johnson 0-1, Swift 1-0 vs. Giants; Cloude 1-0, Johnson 0-1, Swift 1-0 vs. Rockies; Ayala 0-1, Fassero 1-0, Spoljaric 0-1 vs. Diamondbacks.

TAMPA BAY—63-99

Pitcher	Ana. W-L	Bal. W-L	Bos. W-L	Chi. W-L	Cle. W-L	Det. W-L	K.C. W-L	Min. W-L	N.Y. W-L	Oak. W-L	Sea. W-L	Tex. W-L	Tor. W-L	N.L. W-L	Total W-L
Aldred, Scott	0-0	0-0	0-0	0-0	0-0	0-0	0-0	0-0	0-0	0-0	0-0	0-0	0-0	0-0	0-0
Alvarez, Wilson	1-2	1-1	0-0	2-0	0-2	0-2	0-2	0-1	0-2	1-0	0-0	1-1	0-0	0-1	6-14
Arrojo, Rolando	3-1	1-1	0-1	0-2	1-0	2-1	1-1	1-1	0-1	2-0	0-1	1-0	1-1	1-1	14-12
Carlson, Dan	0-0	0-0	0-0	0-0	0-0	0-0	0-0	0-0	0-0	0-0	0-0	0-0	0-0	0-0	0-0
Duvall, Mike	0-0	0-0	0-0	0-0	0-0	0-0	0-0	0-0	0-0	0-0	0-0	0-0	0-0	0-0	0-0
Eiland, Dave	0-0	0-0	0-0	0-0	0-0	0-0	0-0	0-0	0-1	0-0	0-0	0-0	0-0	0-0	0-1
Gaillard, Eddie	0-0	0-0	0-0	0-0	0-0	0-0	0-0	0-0	0-0	0-0	0-0	0-0	0-0	0-0	0-0
Gorecki, Rick	0-1	0-0	0-0	1-1	0-0	0-0	0-0	0-0	0-0	0-0	0-0	0-0	0-0	0-0	1-2
Hernandez, Roberto	0-0	0-0	0-0	1-0	0-1	0-0	0-1	0-1	0-1	0-0	1-1	0-0	0-0	0-1	2-6
Johnson, Jason	0-0	0-0	0-1	0-0	0-0	0-0	0-0	0-0	0-1	0-0	0-1	1-1	1-1	0-1	2-5
Lopez, Albie	0-1	1-1	1-1	0-0	0-0	0-0	0-0	0-0	0-0	0-0	1-0	0-0	0-1	3-0	7-4
Mecir, Jim	0-0	2-0	0-0	0-0	1-0	0-0	1-0	0-0	0-0	0-0	0-0	0-1	1-0	1-1	7-2
Pennington, Brad	0-0	0-0	0-0	0-0	0-0	0-0	0-0	0-0	0-0	0-0	0-0	0-0	0-0	0-0	0-0
Rekar, Bryan	0-0	0-0	0-1	0-0	0-2	0-2	0-1	0-0	0-1	1-0	0-0	0-1	0-0	0-1	2-8
Ruebel, Matt	0-0	0-0	0-0	0-0	0-0	0-0	0-0	0-0	0-1	0-0	0-0	0-0	0-0	0-1	0-2
Santana, Julio	0-0	0-0	1-2	0-0	1-0	1-0	1-0	1-0	0-1	0-1	0-0	0-1	0-0	0-0	5-6
Saunders, Tony	1-0	1-1	0-2	1-2	0-1	0-0	0-1	0-2	1-1	1-1	0-1	1-1	0-0	0-2	6-15
Springer, Dennis	0-1	0-1	0-0	1-0	0-1	0-1	0-0	0-1	0-0	1-1	0-1	0-2	0-1	0-1	3-11
Tatis, Ramon	0-0	0-0	0-0	0-0	0-0	0-0	0-0	0-0	0-0	0-0	0-0	0-0	0-0	0-0	0-0
Wade, Terrell	0-0	0-0	1-0	0-0	0-0	0-0	0-0	0-0	0-1	0-0	0-0	0-0	0-0	0-0	1-1
White, Rick	0-0	0-0	0-0	0-0	0-0	1-0	0-1	0-0	0-1	0-0	0-1	1-0	1-1	0-2	2-6
Yan, Esteban	0-0	1-0	0-1	0-0	0-0	1-0	0-1	2-0	0-0	0-0	1-0	0-1	0-0	0-1	5-4
Totals	5-6	7-5	3-9	6-5	3-7	6-5	3-8	4-7	1-11	6-5	5-6	4-7	5-7	5-11	63-99

INTERLEAGUE BREAKDOWN: Arrojo 0-1, Hernandez 0-1, Saunders 0-1 vs. Braves; Lopez 1-0, Ruebel 0-1, White 0-1 vs. Expos; Mecir 1-0, Springer 0-1, White 0-1 vs. Mets; Arrojo 1-0, Johnson 0-1, Lopez 1-0 vs. Phillies; Lopez 1-0, Mecir 0-1, Santana 0-1, Saunders 0-1 vs. Marlins.

1998 A.L. STATISTICS Miscellaneous

TEXAS—88-74

Pitcher	Ana. W-L	Bal. W-L	Bos. W-L	Chi. W-L	Cle. W-L	Det. W-L	K.C. W-L	Min. W-L	N.Y. W-L	Oak. W-L	Sea. W-L	T.B. W-L	Tor. W-L	N.L. W-L	Total W-L
Bailes, Scott	0-0	0-0	0-0	0-0	0-0	0-0	0-0	0-0	0-0	0-0	0-0	1-0	0-0	0-0	1-0
Burkett, John	1-1	0-1	1-1	0-2	1-1	0-0	0-1	0-0	0-1	2-1	0-2	1-1	1-0	1-1	9-13
Cadaret, Greg	0-0	0-0	0-0	0-0	0-0	0-0	0-0	0-0	0-0	0-0	0-0	0-0	0-0	0-0	0-0
Crabtree, Tim	1-0	1-0	0-0	0-0	0-0	0-1	0-0	0-0	0-0	1-0	1-0	1-0	0-0	1-0	6-1
Fossas, Tony	0-0	0-0	0-0	0-0	0-0	0-0	0-0	0-0	0-0	0-0	1-0	0-0	0-0	0-0	1-0
Gunderson, Eric	0-0	0-0	0-0	0-1	0-0	0-0	0-0	0-0	0-0	0-0	0-1	0-0	0-0	0-1	0-3
Helling, Rick	3-0	0-0	2-0	1-0	0-0	2-0	1-1	2-1	1-2	1-1	1-0	2-0	2-0	2-1	20-7
Hernandez, Xavier	0-0	0-1	0-0	1-0	1-0	0-0	1-0	0-3	0-2	1-0	1-0	0-0	0-0	0-0	6-6
Johnson, Jonathan	0-0	0-0	0-0	0-0	0-0	0-0	0-0	0-0	0-0	0-0	0-0	0-0	0-0	0-0	0-0
Levine, Al	0-0	0-0	0-0	0-0	0-1	0-0	0-0	0-0	0-0	0-0	0-0	0-0	0-0	0-0	0-1
Loaiza, Esteban	0-0	0-0	0-0	0-0	0-0	0-0	2-0	0-0	0-1	0-1	0-1	0-1	0-1	0-1	3-6
Oliver, Darren	0-0	1-0	0-1	0-0	1-0	0-0	0-0	1-1	0-0	0-1	0-0	1-1	1-2	1-1	6-7
Pavlik, Roger	0-0	1-0	0-0	0-1	0-0	0-0	0-0	0-0	0-0	0-0	0-0	0-0	0-0	0-0	1-1
Perisho, Matt	0-1	0-0	0-0	0-0	0-0	0-0	0-0	0-0	0-0	0-1	0-0	0-0	0-0	0-0	0-2
Santana, Julio	0-0	0-0	0-0	0-0	0-0	0-0	0-0	0-0	0-0	0-0	0-0	0-0	0-0	0-0	0-0
Sele, Aaron	0-1	0-2	1-2	4-0	2-1	2-0	3-1	1-0	0-1	1-1	1-0	2-0	0-1	2-1	19-11
Stottlemyre, Todd	2-0	0-0	0-1	0-1	1-0	0-1	0-0	0-0	1-0	0-0	0-0	0-1	1-0	0-0	5-4
Van Poppel, Todd	0-1	0-0	0-0	0-0	0-0	0-0	0-0	0-0	0-0	0-1	0-0	0-0	0-0	1-0	1-2
Wetteland, John	0-0	0-0	0-0	0-0	0-0	0-0	1-0	0-0	0-0	0-0	0-0	0-0	2-0	0-1	3-1
Witt, Bobby	0-1	1-1	1-0	0-0	0-1	1-1	1-0	0-0	0-0	0-0	0-0	1-0	0-0	0-0	5-4
Totals	7-5	5-6	5-6	6-5	7-4	8-3	8-3	4-7	3-8	6-6	7-5	7-4	7-4	8-8	88-74

INTERLEAGUE BREAKDOWN: Helling 0-1, Oliver 0-1, Wetteland 0-1 vs. Dodgers; Burkett 1-0, Crabtree 1-0, Patterson 0-1 vs. Padres; Oliver 1-0, Patterson 0-1, Sele 0-1 vs. Giants; Gunderson 0-1, Helling 1-0, Sele 1-0 vs. Rockies; Burkett 0-1, Helling 1-0, Sele 1-0, Van Poppel 1-0 vs. Diamondbacks.

TORONTO—88-74

Pitcher	Ana. W-L	Bal. W-L	Bos. W-L	Chi. W-L	Cle. W-L	Det. W-L	K.C. W-L	Min. W-L	N.Y. W-L	Oak. W-L	Sea. W-L	Tex. W-L	T.B. W-L	N.L. W-L	Total W-L
Almanzar, Carlos	0-1	0-0	0-0	0-0	0-1	0-0	0-0	0-0	1-0	0-0	0-0	1-0	0-0	0-0	2-2
Andujar, Luis	0-0	0-0	0-0	0-0	0-0	0-0	0-0	0-0	0-0	0-0	0-0	0-0	0-0	0-0	0-0
Carpenter, Chris	2-0	2-0	0-1	2-0	0-1	0-1	1-1	0-0	1-0	0-0	1-0	0-2	1-0	2-1	12-7
Clemens, Roger	0-0	2-0	1-0	2-0	1-1	3-0	1-0	3-1	1-2	1-1	2-1	1-0	0-0	2-0	20-6
Escobar, Kelvim	1-1	0-0	1-0	0-0	1-0	0-0	2-0	0-1	1-0	1-0	0-0	0-1	0-0	0-0	7-3
Guzman, Juan	0-0	0-2	2-0	0-1	0-0	0-0	1-1	0-1	0-1	0-0	0-2	1-1	1-1	1-2	6-12
Halladay, Roy	0-0	0-0	0-0	0-0	0-0	0-0	0-0	0-0	0-0	0-0	0-0	0-0	0-0	0-0	1-0
Hanson, Erik	0-0	0-0	0-0	0-0	0-0	0-0	0-0	0-0	0-0	0-1	0-0	0-0	0-0	0-1	0-2
Hentgen, Pat	1-1	1-0	2-1	2-2	0-1	0-0	0-3	2-0	0-1	0-0	2-0	0-0	1-0	1-1	12-11
Myers, Randy	1-0	0-0	0-2	0-0	0-0	0-0	0-0	0-0	1-0	0-0	0-1	1-1	0-0	0-1	3-4
Person, Robert	0-0	1-0	1-0	0-0	0-0	0-0	0-0	0-0	0-0	0-0	0-0	0-0	0-1	1-0	3-1
Plesac, Dan	1-0	0-0	0-0	0-0	0-1	0-0	0-0	0-1	0-1	1-0	0-0	1-0	0-0	0-1	4-3
Quantrill, Paul	0-0	0-0	1-0	0-0	0-1	0-0	0-0	0-0	1-0	0-0	0-1	1-1	0-1	0-1	3-4
Risley, Bill	1-0	0-1	0-0	0-0	0-0	1-0	0-0	0-1	0-0	0-0	0-1	1-0	0-1	0-1	3-4
Rodriguez, Nerio	0-0	0-0	0-0	0-0	0-0	0-0	0-0	0-0	0-0	0-0	1-0	0-0	0-0	0-0	1-0
Sinclair, Steve	0-1	0-0	0-0	0-0	0-1	0-0	0-0	0-0	0-0	0-0	0-0	0-0	0-0	0-0	0-2
Stieb, Dave	0-0	0-0	0-0	0-1	0-0	0-0	1-0	0-0	0-0	0-0	0-0	0-0	0-0	0-0	1-2
VanRyn, Ben	0-0	0-0	0-0	0-0	0-0	0-0	0-0	0-0	0-0	0-0	0-0	0-0	0-1	0-0	0-1
Williams, Woody	0-0	0-2	0-1	0-0	2-0	1-1	0-1	1-1	2-0	1-2	0-1	1-0	1-0	1-0	10-9
Withem, Shannon	0-0	0-0	0-0	0-0	0-0	0-0	0-0	0-0	0-0	0-0	0-0	0-0	0-0	0-0	0-0
Totals	7-4	7-5	7-5	6-4	4-7	6-5	5-6	7-4	6-6	6-5	7-4	4-7	7-5	9-7	88-74

INTERLEAGUE BREAKDOWN: Carpenter 0-1, Guzman 0-1, Hentgen 1-0 vs. Braves; Carpenter 1-0, Clemens 1-0, Guzman 1-0, Williams 1-0 vs. Expos; Clemens 1-0, Hentgen 0-1, Plesac 1-0 vs. Mets; Carpenter 1-0, Guzman 0-1, Risley 0-1 vs. Phillies; Hanson 0-1, Person 1-0, Quantrill 0-1 vs. Marlins.

HOME RUNS BY PARKS

	At Ana.	At Bal.	At Bos.	At Chi.	At Cle.	At Det.	At K.C.	At Min.	At N.Y.	At Oak.	At Sea.	At T.B.	At Tex.	At Tor.	At N.L. Parks	Totals 1998	Totals 1997	HR Allow.
Anaheim	53	3	5	6	11	6	7	7	*7	4	6	4	12	3	13	147	161	164
Baltimore	6	109	12	11	10	9	7	11	4	6	10	6	1	4	8	214	196	169
Boston	8	6	93	9	7	13	8	7	7	7	6	7	10	9	8	205	185	168
Chicago	8	12	7	106	9	7	9	7	4	6	1	8	4	6	5	198	158	211
Cleveland	10	4	6	8	104	7	13	4	5	4	9	2	3	10	9	198	220	171
Detroit	6	1	5	6	5	92	10	7	1	5	3	6	1	8	9	165	176	185
Kansas City	1	2	0	4	2	5	76	7	1	5	8	6	6	6	5	134	158	196
Minnesota	7	1	4	6	5	7	6	51	2	4	3	9	4	2	4	115	132	180
New York	6	8	8	9	4	6	9	3	*97	12	12	5	14	4	10	207	161	156
Oakland	7	6	3	6	7	6	7	9	1	71	6	6	5	3	6	149	197	179
Seattle	3	9	5	6	7	11	6	9	12	10	117	13	6	10	10	234	264	196
Tampa Bay	4	4	3	4	4	4	5	3	1	3	2	67	4	0	3	111	....	171
Texas	7	8	6	10	1	6	11	8	12	3	9	7	101	1	11	201	187	164
Toronto	9	9	11	1	4	11	5	7	8	8	12	4	8	112	12	221	147	169
N.L. clubs	6	9	8	8	9	13	9	7	7	11	7	13	5	11	....	123	99	....
1998 Totals	141	191	176	200	187	205	186	144	*171	154	218	163	184	189	113	2499	....	2479
1997 Totals	210	196	152	151	185	189	182	151	146	203	233	....	186	140	....	....	†2477	

*There were actually 167 home runs hit in Yankee Stadium in 1998. The totals include one home run by the Yankees and three by the Angels at Shea Stadium on April 15. †The 1997 A.L. total includes Milwaukee.

AT ANAHEIM (141):

Anaheim (53)—Salmon 13, Edmonds 9, Erstad 9, Fielder 7, Hollins 4, Anderson 4, Walbeck 3, Nevin 3, Velarde 1. **Baltimore (6)**—Davis 2, Palmeiro 1, Hoiles 1, Webster 1, Bordick 1. **Boston (8)**—Benjamin 1, Vaughn 1, Valentin 1, Buford 1, O'Leary 1, Hatteberg 1, Garciaparra 1, Varitek 1. **Chicago (8)**—Belle 3, Ordonez 2, O'Brien 1, Thomas 1, Cordero 1. **Cleveland (10)**—M. Ramirez 4, Justice 2, Fryman 2, Giles 2. **Detroit (6)**—Clark 2, Oliver 1, Manto 1, Gonzalez 1, Catalanotto 1. **Kansas City (1)**—Palmer 1. **Minnesota (7)**—Steinbach 2, Molitor 1, Meares 1, Cordova 1, Lawton 1, Ortiz 1. **New York (6)**—Strawberry 2, Jeter 2, Martinez 1, Williams 1. **Oakland (7)**—Giambi 2, Henderson 1, Mitchell 1, Blowers 1, Tejada 1, Grieve 1. **Seattle (3)**—Griffey 1, Wilson 1, Rodriguez 1. **Tampa Bay (4)**—Sorrento 1, Flaherty 1, DiFelice 1, Smith 1. **Texas (7)**—Gonzalez 3, Alicea 2, Zeile 1, Greer 1. **Toronto (9)**—Canseco 2, Delgado 2, Fernandez 1, Stanley 1, Fletcher 1, Green 1, Stewart 1. **Los Angeles (2)**—Luke 1, Konerko 1. **San Francisco (4)**—Snow 2, Bonds 1, Mueller 1.

AT BALTIMORE (191):

Anaheim (3)—Fielder 1, Salmon 1, Edmonds 1. **Baltimore (109)**—Palmeiro 25, Davis 16, Bordick 10, Surhoff 9, Ripken 8, Anderson 7, Alomar 7, Carter 6, Webster 6, Baines 5, Hoiles 5, Reboulet 1, W. Greene 1, Hammonds 1, Becker 1, Pickering 1. **Boston (6)**—Vaughn 2, Valentin 2, Bragg 1, Sadler 1. **Chicago (12)**—Belle 3, J. Abbott 3, O'Brien 1, Ventura 1, Durham 1, Norton 1, Ordonez 1, Caruso 1. **Cleveland (4)**—Fryman 2, Thome 1, M. Ramirez 1. **Detroit (1)**—Easley 1. **Kansas City (2)**—Palmer 1, Sutton 1. **Minnesota (1)**—Coomer 1. **New York (8)**—Davis 1, Strawberry 1, O'Neill 1, Girardi 1, Martinez 1, Posada 1, Ledee 1, Spencer 1. **Oakland (6)**—Henderson 1, Stairs 1, Spiezio 1, Grieve 1, Hinch 1, Christenson 1. **Seattle (9)**—Martinez 2, Griffey 2, Cora 1, Marzano 1, Segui 1, Davis 1, Rodriguez 1. **Tampa Bay (4)**—Flaherty 1, Kelly 1, McCracken 1, Trammell 1. **Texas (8)**—Gonzalez 4, Elster 1, Stevens 1, Rodriguez 1, Tatis 1. **Toronto (9)**—Stanley 2, Sprague 2, Canseco 1, Delgado 1, Green 1, Gonzalez 1, Dalesandro 1. **Atlanta (6)**—Galarraga 2, Klesko 1, Lopez 1, Graffanino 1, A. Jones 1. **Florida (1)**—Lee 1. **New York N.L. (2)**—McRae 1, Huskey 1.

AT BOSTON (176):

Anaheim (5)—Anderson 2, Fielder 1, Hollins 1, Erstad 1. **Baltimore (12)**—Surhoff 5, Davis 1, Anderson 1, Alomar 1, Hoiles 1, Mouton 1, Clyburn 1, Pickering 1. **Boston (93)**—Vaughn 19, Garciaparra 17, O'Leary 12, Valentin 11, Leyritz 6, Lewis 5, Buford 4, Cummings 4, Hatteberg 4, Bragg 3, Benjamin 2, Jefferson 2, Stanley 1, Ashley 1, Varitek 1, Merloni 1. **Chicago (7)**—Sierra 1, Thomas 1, Cordero 1, Durham 1, Snopek 1, Cameron 1, Norton 1. **Cleveland (6)**—Justice 2, Fryman 1, M. Ramirez 1, Bell 1, Giles 1. **Detroit (5)**—Hunter 1, Randa 1, Higginson 1, Clark 1, Wood 1. **Minnesota (4)**—Coomer 2, Steinbach 1, Walker 1. **New York (8)**—O'Neill 2, Knoblauch 2, Jeter 2, Williams 1, Brosius 1. **Oakland (3)**—Blowers 1, Stairs 1, Hinch 1. **Seattle (5)**—Buhner 2, Rodriguez 2, Griffey 1. **Tampa Bay (3)**—Kelly 1, Trammell 1, Smith 1. **Texas (6)**—Elster 2, Kelly 1, Alicea 1, Gonzalez 1, Rodriguez 1. **Toronto (11)**—Canseco 3, Stanley 2, Sprague 2, Phillips 1, Fletcher 1, Green 1, Cruz 1. **Montreal (2)**—White 1, Andrews 1. **New York N.L. (4)**—Olerud 1, Gilkey 1, Lopez 1, Castillo 1. **Philadelphia (2)**—Lewis 1, Rolen 1.

AT CHICAGO (200):

Anaheim (6)—Fielder 1, Shipley 1, Velarde 1, Salmon 1, Edmonds 1, Erstad 1. **Baltimore (11)**—Palmeiro 3, Hammonds 2, Becker 2, Ripken 1, Carter 1, Webster 1, Bordick 1. **Boston (9)**—Vaughn 3, Buford 2, Lewis 1, Jefferson 1, Valentin 1, Garciaparra 1. **Chicago (106)**—Belle 29, Ventura 15, Thomas 15, Durham 10, Ordonez 8, Norton 6, Cordero 5, Cameron 5, J. Abbott 5, Caruso 3, Kreuter 2, Machado 2, Wilson 1. **Cleveland (8)**—Thome 2, Lofton 2, Justice 1, Fryman 1, M. Ramirez 1, Giles 1. **Detroit (6)**—Clark 2, Oliver 1, Gonzalez 1, Easley 1, Randa 1. **Kansas City (4)**—Damon 2, Conine 1, Fasano 1. **Minnesota (6)**—Cordova 2, Lawton 2, Meares 1, Gates 1. **New York (9)**—Williams 5, Davis 1, O'Neill 1, Martinez 1, Spencer 1. **Oakland (6)**—Blowers 2, Macfarlane 1, Stairs 1, Spiezio 1, Grieve 1. **Seattle (6)**—Buhner 2, Cora 1, Huson 1, Griffey 1, Davis 1. **Tampa Bay (4)**—Martinez 1, Stocker 1, Trammell 1, Winn 1. **Texas (10)**—Clark 2, Rodriguez 2, Clayton 2, Kelly 1, Gonzalez 1, Stevens 1, Greer 1. **Toronto (1)**—Canseco 1. **Cincinnati (2)**—Taubensee 1, Reese 1. **Milwaukee (2)**—Grissom 1, Hamelin 1. **St. Louis (4)**—McGwire 2, Jordan 1, Mabry 1.

AT CLEVELAND (187):

Anaheim (11)—Salmon 4, Edmonds 2, Erstad 2, Velarde 1, Hollins 1, Bolick 1. **Baltimore (10)**—Davis 2, Anderson 2, Hoiles 2, Baines 1, Palmeiro 1, Surhoff 1, Hammonds 1. **Boston (7)**—Jefferson 1, Valentin 1, O'Leary 1, Bragg 1, Hatteberg 1, Garciaparra 1, Varitek 1. **Chicago (7)**—Thomas 2, Cordero 2, Sierra 1, Ventura 1, Durham 1. **Cleveland (104)**—M. Ramirez 25, Thome 18, Fryman 16, Giles 10, Sexson 9, Justice 7, Lofton 6, Alomar 3, Whiten 3, Bell 2, Dunston 1, Manto 1, Branson 1, Diaz 1, Wilson 1. **Detroit (5)**—Easley 2, Clark 2, Gonzalez 1. **Kansas City (2)**—King 1, Giambi 1. **Minnesota (5)**—Ortiz 2, Steinbach 1, Coomer 1, Lawton 1. **New York (4)**—Brosius 2, Strawberry 1, Knoblauch 1. **Oakland (7)**—Stairs 2, Giambi 2, Henderson 1, Abbott 1, Grieve 1. **Seattle (7)**—Griffey 2, Segui 2, Cora 1, Martinez 1, Rodriguez 1. **Tampa Bay (4)**—Sorrento 2, Buford 1, Everett 1, Ausmus 1. **Pittsburgh (1)**—Young 1. **St. Louis (3)**—McGwire 2, Mabry 1.

AT DETROIT (205):

Anaheim (6)—Edmonds 3, Hollins 1, Salmon 1, Martin 1. **Baltimore (9)**—Davis 3, Anderson 2, Hoiles 2, Palmeiro 1, Webster 1. **Boston (13)**—Garciaparra 4, Vaughn 2, Benjamin 1, Lewis 1, Valentin 1, Ashley 1, O'Leary 1, Cummings 1, Sadler 1. **Chicago (9)**—Cordero 2, Durham 2, Wilson 2, Thomas 1, J. Abbott 1, Caruso 1. **Cleveland (7)**—M. Ramirez 2, Sexson 2, Vizquel 1, Fryman 1, Giles 1. **Detroit (92)**—Easley 19, Clark 18, Gonzalez 15, Higginson 10, Cruz 5, Encarnacion 4, Randa 3, Bartee 3, Catalanotto 3, Alvarez 3, Oliver 2, Bako 2, Berroa 1, Siddall 1, Tomberlin 1, Hunter 1, Casanova 1. **Kansas City (5)**—King 2, Palmer 1, Sweeney 1, Sutton 1. **Minnesota (7)**—Lawton 2, Molitor 1, Meares 1, Hocking 1, Coomer 1, Walker 1. **New York (6)**—Knoblauch 2, O'Neill 1, Martinez 1, Jeter 1, Posada 1. **Oakland (6)**—Magadan 1, Stairs 1, Giambi 1, Tejada 1, Grieve 1, Hinch 1. **Seattle (11)**—Martinez 3, Rodriguez 3, Davis 2, Hill 1, Ducey 1, Ibanez 1. **Tampa Bay (4)**—Kelly 2, Trammell 1, Smith 1. **Texas (6)**—Clark 2, Rodriguez 2, Kelly 1, Gonzalez 1. **Toronto (11)**—Sprague 4, Delgado 2, Stewart 2, Stanley 1, Green 1, Cruz 1. **Chicago N.L. (6)**—Sosa 2, Morandini 2, Rodriguez 2. **Cincinnati (3)**—Sanders 1, Greene 1, Young 1. **Houston (4)**—Alou 2, Biggio 1, Everett 1.

AT KANSAS CITY (186):

Anaheim (7)—Salmon 3, Fielder 2, Nevin 1, Baughman 1. **Baltimore (7)**—Davis 2, Hoiles 2, Ripken 1, Webster 1, Hammonds 1. **Boston (8)**—Stanley 3, O'Leary 3, Leyritz 1, Varitek 1. **Chicago (7)**—Belle 2, Simmons 2, Ventura 1, Thomas 1, J. Abbott 1. **Cleveland (13)**—M. Ramirez 5, Fryman 2, Thome 2, Dunston 1, Whiten 1, Lofton 1, Bell 1. **Detroit (10)**—Randa 2, Higginson 2, Fick 2, Gonzalez 1, Easley 1, Clark 1, Encarnacion 1. **Kansas City (76)**—Palmer 21, King 13, Damon 11, Sweeney 6, Offerman 4, Conine 4, Fasano 4, Mack 3, Dye 3, Sutton 3, Pendleton 2, Spehr 1, Lopez 1. **Minnesota (6)**—Meares 2, Molitor 1, Merced 1, Coomer 1, Valentin 1. **New York (9)**—Martinez 2, Williams 2, Raines 1, Strawberry 1, O'Neill 1, Jeter 1, Posada 1. **Oakland (7)**—Blowers 2, Henderson 1, Stairs 1, Giambi 1, Tejada 1, Hinch 1. **Seattle (6)**—Segui 2, Marzano 1, Griffey 1, Oliver 1, Wilson 1. **Tampa Bay (5)**—Smith 2, McGriff 1, Sorrento 1, Trammell 1. **Texas (11)**—Gonzalez 5, Kelly 2, Elster 1, Haselman 1, Simms 1, Greer 1. **Toronto (5)**—Gonzalez 3, Green 1, Stewart 1. **Chicago N.L. (2)**—Alexander 1, Houston 1. **Milwaukee (4)**—Grissom 1, Vina 1, Burnitz 1, Cirillo 1. **Pittsburgh (3)**—Smith 1, Guillen 1, Ramirez 1.

AT MINNESOTA (144):

Anaheim (7)—Edmonds 2, Anderson 2, Walbeck 1, Nevin 1, Erstad 1. **Baltimore (11)**—Anderson 3, Palmeiro 2, Surhoff 2, Alomar 2, Baines 1, Ripken 1. **Boston (7)**—Valentin 2, Vaughn 1, Buford 1, O'Leary 1, Hatteberg 1, Garciaparra 1. **Chicago (4)**—Ventura 1, Thomas 1, Cameron 1, J. Abbott 1. **Cleveland (4)**—Justice 2, Alomar 1, Thome 1. **Detroit (7)**—Gonzalez 2, Easley 2, Higginson 2, Randa 1. **Kansas City (7)**—King 2, Offerman 2, Palmer 1, Fasano 1, Halter 1. **Minnesota (51)**—Lawton 11, Walker 7, Steinbach 6, Coomer 6, Cordova 4, Merced 3, Meares 2, Ortiz 2, Nixon 1, Gates 1, Stahoviak 1, Hocking 1, Ochoa 1, Latham 1, Valentin 1, Koskie 1. **New York (3)**—Martinez 1, Brosius 1, Posada 1. **Oakland (9)**—Henderson 2, Grieve 2, Macfarlane 1, Stairs 1, Giambi 1, Spiezio 1, Tejada 1. **Seattle (9)**—Davis 3, Griffey 2, Rodriguez 2, Martinez 1, Segui 1. **Tampa Bay (3)**—McGriff 1, DiFelice 1, Butler 1. **Texas (8)**—Clark 3, Gonzalez 2, Stevens 2, Simms 1. **Toronto (7)**—Green 4, Canseco 2, Cruz 1. **Chicago N.L. (2)**—Sosa 1, Hernandez 1. **Milwaukee (2)**—Burnitz 1. **St. Louis (3)**—McGwire 1, Lankford 1, Hunter 1.

AT NEW YORK (171):

Anaheim (7)—Edmonds 2, *DiSarcina 1, Williams 1, Anderson 1, *Nevin 1, *Erstad 1. **Baltimore (4)**—Palmeiro 2, Surhoff 1, Alomar 1. **Boston (7)**—Jefferson 2, Vaughn 2, Varitek 2, Leyritz 1. **Chicago (2)**—Belle 1, Cordero 1, Durham 1. **Cleveland (5)**—Justice 2, Whiten 1, Lofton 1, Wilson 1. **Detroit (1)**—Higginson 1. **Kansas City (1)**—Damon 1. **Minnesota (2)**—Coomer 1, Lawton 1. **New York (97)**—*Strawberry 14, Williams 14, Martinez 12, O'Neill 10, Jeter 9, Brosius 8, Spencer 8, Curtis 6, Posada 6, Knoblauch 5, Raines 2, Davis 1, Girardi 1, Bush 1. **Oakland (1)**—Christenson 1. **Seattle (12)**—Griffey 6,

Rodriguez 2, Monahan 2, Ducey 1, Davis 1. **Tampa Bay (1)**—McGriff 1. **Texas (12)**—Greer 3, Kelly 2, Simms 2, Clark 1, Zeile 1, Gonzalez 1, Rodriguez 1, Clayton 1. **Toronto (8)**—Stewart 2, Cruz 2, Fernandez 1, Canseco 1, Sprague 1, Delgado 1. **Florida (1)**—Dunwoody 1. **Philadelphia (6)**—Brogna 2, Lewis 1, Lieberthal 1, Zuber 1, Rolen 1.

*Note: DiSarcina, Erstad, and Nevin of the Angels hit their home runs at Shea Stadium and Strawberry hit one of his at Shea Stadium.

AT OAKLAND (154):

Anaheim (4)—Edmonds 1, Anderson 1, Greene 1, Pritchett 1. **Baltimore (6)**—Palmeiro 2, Baines 1, Anderson 1, Alomar 1, Hammonds 1. **Boston (7)**—Garciaparra 2, Lewis 1, Vaughn 1, Ashley 1, O'Leary 1, Hatteberg 1. **Chicago (1)**—Thomas 1. **Cleveland (4)**—Alomar 1, Justice 1, Lofton 1, Bell 1. **Detroit (5)**—Higginson 2, Tomberlin 1, Clark 1, Encarnacion 1. **Kansas City (5)**—King 3, Palmer 1, Young 1. **Minnesota (4)**—Steinbach 1, Meares 1, Hocking 1, Ortiz 1. **New York (12)**—Strawberry 3, Knoblauch 3, O'Neill 2, Martinez 2, Curtis 1, Posada 1. **Oakland (71)**—Stairs 16, Giambi 12, Henderson 6, Spiezio 6, Macfarlane 5, Tejada 5, Grieve 5, Hinch 4, Sprague 3, Blowers 2, Christenson 2, Mitchell 1, Voigt 1, Bournigal 1, Abbott 1, McDonald 1. **Seattle (10)**—Hill 2, Buhner 2, Griffey 2, Rodriguez 2, Martinez 1, Segui 1. **Tampa Bay (3)**—Sorrento 1, McCracken 1, Cairo 1. **Texas (3)**—Alicea 1, Gonzalez 1, Simms 1. **Toronto (8)**—Canseco 2, Fernandez 1, Fletcher 1, Sprague 1, Delgado 1, Green 1, Brown 1. **Arizona (3)**—White 1, Benitez 1, Dellucci 1. **San Diego (5)**—Vaughn 2, Joyner 1, Hernandez 1, Leyritz 1. **San Francisco (3)**—Bonds 1, Sanchez 1, Snow 1.

AT SEATTLE (218):

Anaheim (6)—Erstad 2, Fielder 1, DiSarcina 1, Hollins 1, Mashore 1. **Baltimore (10)**—Ripken 2, Baines 1, Carter 1, Davis 1, Anderson 1, Alomar 1, Hoiles 1, Bordick 1, Mouton 1. **Boston (6)**—Vaughn 2, Garciaparra 2, O'Leary 1, Hatteberg 1. **Chicago (8)**—Sierra 2, Belle 2, Ventura 1, Thomas 1, Cordero 1, Ordonez 1. **Cleveland (9)**—M. Ramirez 4, Justice 2, Alomar 1, Thome 1, Bell 1. **Colorado (4)**—Castilla 2, Perez 1, Helton 1. **Detroit (3)**—Higginson 3. **Kansas City (8)**—Palmer 4, Mack 1, King 1, Sweeney 1, Halter 1. **Minnesota (3)**—Coomer 1, Ortiz 1, Valentin 1. **New York (12)**—Posada 3, Strawberry 2, Curtis 2, O'Neill 1, Martinez 1, Knoblauch 1, Brosius 1, Jeter 1. **Oakland (6)**—Giambi 3, Stairs 1, Grieve 1, Hinch 1. **Seattle (117)**—Griffey 30, Rodriguez 18, Martinez 17, Segui 10, Buhner 8, Davis 7, Wilson 6, Hill 5, Cora 2, Ducey 2, Perez 2, Radmanovich 2, Monahan 2, Oliver 1, Amaral 1, Wilkins 1, Rossy 1, McCarty 1, Ibanez 1. **Tampa Bay (2)**—McGriff 1, Cairo 1. **Texas (9)**—Stevens 3, Kelly 2, Elster 1, Cuyler 1, Rodriguez 1, Greer 1. **Toronto (12)**—Delgado 4, Fletcher 2, Green 2, Cruz 2, Canseco 1, Crespo 1. **Los Angeles (3)**—Sheffield 1, Karros 1, Konerko 1.

AT TAMPA BAY (163):

Anaheim (4)—Hollins 1, Edmonds 1, Anderson 1, Mashore 1. **Baltimore (6)**—Palmeiro 2, Ripken 1, Carter 1, Davis 1, Surhoff 1. **Boston (7)**—Garciaparra 3, Hatteberg 2, Vaughn 1, Varitek 1. **Chicago (8)**—Belle 2, Thomas 2, Durham 1, Machado 1, Norton 1, J. Abbott 1. **Cleveland (2)**—Manto 1, Giles 1. **Detroit (6)**—Hunter 2, Clark 2, Gonzalez 1, Higginson 1. **Kansas City (6)**—Palmer 2, Conine 1, Damon 1, Fasano 1, Dye 1. **Minnesota (9)**—Ortiz 2, Steinbach 1, Meares 1, Coomer 1, Cordova 1, Lawton 1, Ochoa 1, Walker 1. **New York (5)**—Girardi 1, Knoblauch 1, Williams 1, Brosius 1, Posada 1. **Oakland (6)**—Blowers 2, Henderson 1, Giambi 1, Tejada 1, Christenson 1. **Seattle (13)**—Martinez 2, Griffey 2, Davis 2, Rodriguez 2, Hill 1, Cora 1, Marzano 1, Ducey 1, Segui 1. **Tampa Bay (67)**—McGriff 14, Sorrento 10, Boggs 7, Trammell 6, Butler 6, McCracken 5, Stocker 4, Kelly 4, Smith 4, Cairo 3, Martinez 2, Flaherty 1, DiFelice 1. **Texas (7)**—Clark 1, Alicea 1, Gonzalez 1, Simms 1, Rodriguez 1, Clayton 1, Greer 1. **Toronto (4)**—Canseco 2, Fernandez 1, Gonzalez 1. **Atlanta (7)**—C. Jones 3, Galarraga 2, Lockhart 2. **Florida (2)**—Floyd 1, Kotsay 1. **Montreal (4)**—V. Guerrero 2, Widger 1, Fullmer 1.

AT TEXAS (184):

Anaheim (12)—Salmon 3, Edmonds 3, Anderson 2, Shipley 1, Jefferies 1, Walbeck 1, Nevin 1. **Baltimore (1)**—Palmeiro 1. **Boston (10)**—Vaughn 4, Bragg 2, Stanley 1, Valentin 1, Hatteberg 1, Sadler 1. **Chicago (4)**—Belle 1, Ventura 1, Thomas 1, Cameron 1. **Cleveland (3)**—Justice 1, Lofton 1, Bell 1. **Detroit (1)**—Catalanotto 1. **Kansas City (6)**—Mack 1, Offerman 1, Conine 1, Damon 1, Dye 1, Giambi 1. **Minnesota (4)**—Walker 2, Molitor 1, Shave 1. **New York (14)**—Martinez 3, O'Neill 2, Knoblauch 2, Brosius 2, Jeter 2, Posada 2, Raines 1. **Oakland (5)**—Grieve 3, Giambi 1, Tejada 1. **Seattle (6)**—Martinez 2, Rodriguez 2, Griffey 1, Segui 1. **Tampa Bay (4)**—Kelly 2, Trammell 1, Smith 1. **Texas (101)**—Gonzalez 21, Stevens 13, Rodriguez 12, Clark 11, Simms 9, Greer 8, Kelly 6, McLemore 4, Zeile 4, Haselman 4, Elster 3, Goodwin 2, Alicea 1, Clayton 1, Cedeno 1, Tatis 1. **Toronto (8)**—Canseco 3, Delgado 3, Stanley 2. **Arizona (1)**—Dellucci 1. **Los Angeles (3)**—Mondesi 1, Johnson 1, Beltre 1. **San Diego (1)**—Vaughn 1.

AT TORONTO (189):

Anaheim (3)—Velarde 1, Pritchett 1, Glaus 1. **Baltimore (4)**—Carter 1, Palmeiro 1, Surhoff 1, Tavarez 1. **Boston (9)**—Stanley 2, O'Leary 2, Garciaparra 2, Vaughn 1, Valentin 1, Bragg 1. **Chicago (6)**—Belle 2, Thomas 2, Durham 1, Ordonez 1. **Cleveland (10)**—Thome 3, Vizquel 1, Justice 1, Fryman 1, Whiten 1, M. Ramirez 1, Bell 1, Diaz 1. **Detroit (8)**—Clark 2, Easley 1, Randa 1, Higginson 1, Encarnacion 1, Catalanotto 1, Fick 1. **Kansas City (6)**—Palmer 2, Pendleton 1, Morris 1, King 1, Fasano 1. **Minnesota (2)**—Gates 1, Lawton 1. **New York (4)**—Raines 1, O'Neill 1, Williams 1, Jeter 1. **Oakland (3)**—Henderson 1, Giambi 1, Grieve 1. **Seattle (10)**—Rodriguez 4, Hill 2, Marzano 1, Buhner 1, Griffey 1, Davis 1. **Texas (1)**—Gonzalez 1. **Toronto (112)**—Canseco 25, Green 21, Delgado 20, Stanley 11, Gonzalez 7, Sprague 6, Stewart 6, Fernandez 4, Cruz 4, Fletcher 3, Grebeck 2, Samuel 1, Dalesandro 1, Brown 1. **Montreal (1)**—Fullmer 1. **New York N.L. (6)**—Alfonzo 2, Olerud 1, McRae 1, Pratt 1, Piazza 1. **Philadelphia (4)**—Glanville 2, Brogna 1, Abreu 1.

1998 N.L. STATISTICS

Batting

Designated hitting

Pinch-hitting

Pitching

Fielding

Miscellaneous

BATTING

TEAM

Team	Avg.	G	TPA	AB	R	H	TB	2B	3B	HR	RBI	SH	SF	HP	BB	IBB	SO	SB	CS	GDP	LOB	ShO	Slg.	OBP
Colorado	.291	162	6277	5632	826	1640	2594	333	36	183	791	98	41	37	469	29	949	67	47	148	1138	6	.461	.347
Houston	.280	162	6441	5641	874	1578	2458	326	28	166	818	58	49	72	621	52	1122	155	51	146	1217	6	.436	.356
San Francisco	.274	163	6484	5628	845	1540	2367	292	26	161	800	81	53	44	678	53	1040	102	51	123	1235	8	.421	.353
Atlanta	.272	162	6215	5484	826	1489	2483	297	26	215	794	76	46	61	548	37	1062	98	43	104	1148	6	.453	.342
Chicago	.264	163	6393	5494	831	1494	2448	250	34	212	788	67	37	39	601	51	1223	65	44	123	1162	7	.433	.337
Philadelphia	.264	162	6300	5617	713	1482	2218	286	36	126	672	65	65	45	508	44	1080	97	45	110	1179	11	.395	.326
Cincinnati	.262	162	6268	5496	750	1441	2209	298	28	138	723	78	49	37	608	39	1107	95	42	133	1183	10	.402	.337
Milwaukee	.260	162	6232	5541	707	1439	2195	266	17	152	673	61	32	66	532	36	1039	81	59	135	1148	11	.396	.330
New York	.259	162	6255	5510	706	1425	2170	289	24	136	671	88	48	37	572	55	1049	62	46	126	1193	9	.394	.330
St. Louis	.258	163	6413	5593	810	1444	2465	292	30	223	781	68	34	42	676	65	1179	133	41	117	1200	2	.441	.341
Pittsburgh	.254	163	6111	5493	650	1395	2057	271	35	107	613	78	56	91	393	22	1060	159	51	102	1089	14	.374	.311
San Diego	.253	162	6243	5490	749	1390	2243	292	30	167	715	56	45	48	604	40	1072	79	37	112	1179	7	.409	.330
Los Angeles	.252	162	6076	5459	669	1374	2114	209	27	159	630	91	43	36	447	31	1056	137	53	98	1069	9	.387	.310
Montreal	.249	162	6041	5418	644	1348	2133	280	32	147	602	87	37	60	439	31	1086	91	46	109	1068	13	.394	.310
Florida	.248	162	6227	5558	667	1381	2072	277	36	114	621	70	29	45	525	30	1120	115	57	121	1132	6	.373	.317
Arizona	.246	162	6116	5491	665	1353	2157	235	46	159	621	45	27	64	489	32	1239	73	38	125	1104	16	.393	.314
Totals	.262	1298	100092	88700	11932	23213	36383	4493	491	2565	11313	1167	691	824	8710	647	17455	1609	751	1932	18444	141	.410	.331

INDIVIDUAL

TOP QUALIFIERS FOR BATTING CHAMPIONSHIP

Minimum 502 plate appearances. *Lefthanded batter. †Switch-hitter.

Player, Team	Avg.	G	TPA	AB	R	H	TB	2B	3B	HR	RBI	SH	SF	HP	BB	IBB	SO	SB	CS	GDP	Slg.	OBP
McGwire, Mark, St.L	.299	155	681	509	130	152	383	21	0	70	147	0	4	6	162	28	155	1	0	8	.752	.470
Sosa, Sammy, Chi.	.308	159	722	643	134	198	416	20	0	66	158	0	5	1	73	14	171	18	9	20	.647	.377
Walker, Larry, Col.*	.363	130	524	454	113	165	286	46	3	23	67	0	2	4	64	2	61	14	4	11	.630	.445
Bonds, Barry, S.F.*	.303	156	697	552	120	167	336	44	7	37	122	1	6	8	130	29	92	28	12	15	.609	.438
Vaughn, Greg, S.D.	.272	158	661	573	112	156	342	28	4	50	119	0	4	5	79	6	121	11	4	7	.597	.363
Galarraga, Andres, Atl.	.305	153	648	555	103	169	330	27	1	44	121	0	5	25	63	11	146	7	6	8	.595	.397
Castilla, Vinny, Col.	.319	162	697	645	108	206	380	28	4	46	144	0	6	6	40	7	89	5	9	24	.589	.362
Guerrero, Vladimir, Mon.	.324	159	677	623	108	202	367	37	7	38	109	0	5	7	42	13	95	11	9	15	.589	.371
Alou, Moises, Hou.	.312	159	679	584	104	182	340	34	5	38	124	0	6	5	84	11	87	11	3	14	.582	.399
Piazza, Mike, L.A.-Fla.-N.Y.	.328	151	626	561	88	184	320	38	1	32	111	0	5	2	58	14	80	1	0	15	.570	.390
Bagwell, Jeff, Hou.	.304	147	661	540	124	164	301	33	1	34	111	0	5	7	109	8	90	19	7	14	.557	.424
Kent, Jeff, S.F.	.297	137	594	526	94	156	292	37	3	31	128	1	10	9	48	4	110	9	4	16	.555	.359
Olerud, John, N.Y.*	.354	160	665	557	91	197	307	36	4	22	93	1	7	4	96	11	73	2	2	15	.551	.447
Jones, Chipper, Atl.†	.313	160	707	601	123	188	329	29	5	34	107	1	8	1	96	1	93	16	6	17	.547	.404
Lankford, Ray, St.L*	.293	154	626	533	94	156	288	37	1	31	105	0	4	3	86	5	151	26	5	3	.540	.391
Lopez, Javy, Atl.	.284	133	534	489	73	139	264	21	1	34	106	1	8	6	30	1	85	5	3	22	.540	.328

DEPARTMENTAL LEADERS: G—Castilla, Col., Perez, Col., 162; AB—Glanville, Phi., 678; R—Sosa, Chi., 134; H—Bichette, Col., 219; TB—Sosa, Chi., 416; 1B—Womack, Pit., 149; 2B—Biggio, Hou., 51; 3B—Dellucci, Ari., 12; HR—McGwire, St.L., 70; RBI—Sosa, Chi., 158; SH—Perez, Col., 22; SF—Bell, Hou., Brogna, Phi., Kent, S.F., 10; HP—Kendall, Pit., 31; BB—McGwire, St.L., 162; IBB—Bonds, S.F., 29; SO—Sosa, Chi., 171; SB—Womack, Pit., 58; CS—Renteria, Fla., 22; GIDP—Cirillo, Mil., 26; Slg. Pct.—McGwire, St.L., .752; OB. Pct.—McGwire, St.L., .470.

ALL PLAYERS

*Lefthanded batter. †Switch-hitter.

Player, Team	Avg.	G	TPA	AB	R	H	TB	2B	3B	HR	RBI	SH	SF	HP	BB	IBB	SO	SB	CS	GDP	Slg.	OBP
Abbott, Kurt, Col.	.254	42	76	71	9	18	33	6	0	3	15	0	2	1	2	0	19	0	0	2	.465	.276
Abreu, Bobby, Phi.*	.312	151	589	497	68	155	247	29	6	17	74	4	4	0	84	14	133	19	10	6	.497	.409
Acevedo, Juan, St.L	.176	50	20	17	2	3	4	1	0	0	0	2	0	0	1	0	5	0	0	0	.235	.222
Adams, Terry, Chi.	.000	63	1	1	0	0	0	0	0	0	0	0	0	0	0	0	1	0	0	0	.000	.000
Adamson, Joel, Ari.*	.429	5	8	7	0	3	4	1	0	0	1	1	0	0	0	0	0	0	0	1	.571	.429
Agbayani, Benny, N.Y.	.133	11	16	15	1	2	2	0	0	0	0	0	0	0	1	0	5	0	2	1	.133	.188
Alexander, Manny, Chi.	.227	108	289	264	34	60	87	10	1	5	25	5	1	1	18	1	66	4	1	6	.330	.278
Alfonseca, Antonio, Fla.	.000	58	4	4	0	0	0	0	0	0	0	0	0	0	0	0	2	0	0	0	.000	.000
Alfonzo, Edgardo, N.Y.	.278	144	630	557	94	155	238	28	2	17	78	2	3	3	65	1	77	8	3	11	.427	.355
Allensworth, Jermaine, Pit.-NY	.289	103	318	287	39	83	119	15	3	5	28	3	1	8	19	0	59	8	6	1	.415	.349
Alou, Moises, Hou.	.312	159	679	584	104	182	340	34	5	38	124	0	6	5	84	11	87	11	3	14	.582	.399
Amaro, Ruben Jr., Phi.†	.187	92	117	107	7	20	28	5	0	1	10	1	3	0	6	0	15	0	0	1	.262	.224
Anderson, Brian, Ari.†	.106	35	75	66	6	7	7	0	0	0	0	6	0	0	3	0	19	1	0	1	.106	.145
Anderson, Marlon, Phi.*	.326	17	45	43	4	14	20	3	0	1	4	0	1	0	1	0	6	2	0	0	.465	.333
Andrews, Shane, Mon.	.238	150	559	492	48	117	224	30	1	25	69	2	7	0	58	3	137	1	6	10	.455	.314
Arias, Alex, Phi.	.293	56	149	133	17	39	50	8	0	1	16	1	1	1	13	3	18	2	0	1	.376	.358
Arias, George, S.D.	.194	20	41	36	4	7	13	1	1	1	4	0	0	2	3	0	16	0	0	0	.361	.293
Ashby, Andy, S.D.	.111	33	83	72	1	8	10	2	0	0	2	9	0	0	2	0	35	0	0	1	.139	.135
Astacio, Pedro, Col.	.129	35	75	62	4	8	10	2	0	0	3	11	0	0	2	0	21	0	0	1	.161	.156
Aurilia, Rich, S.F.	.266	122	453	413	54	110	168	27	2	9	49	5	2	2	31	3	62	3	3	3	.407	.319
Ausmus, Brad, Hou.	.269	128	472	412	62	111	147	10	4	6	45	3	1	3	53	1	60	10	3	18	.357	.356
Aybar, Manny, St.L	.222	20	28	27	4	6	9	0	0	1	3	1	0	0	0	0	9	0	0	0	.333	.222
Baerga, Carlos, N.Y.†	.266	147	551	511	46	136	186	27	1	7	53	3	7	6	24	6	55	0	1	21	.364	.303
Bagwell, Jeff, Hou.	.304	147	661	540	124	164	301	33	1	34	111	0	5	7	109	8	90	19	7	14	.557	.424
Ball, Jeff, S.F.	.250	2	4	4	0	1	1	0	0	0	0	0	0	0	0	0	0	0	0	0	.250	.250
Banks, Brian, Mil.†	.292	24	28	24	3	7	12	2	0	1	5	0	0	0	4	0	7	0	0	0	.500	.393
Banks, Willie, Ari.	.000	33	1	1	0	0	0	0	0	0	0	0	0	0	0	0	1	0	0	0	.000	.000

Player, Team	Avg.	G	TPA	AB	R	H	TB	2B	3B	HR	RBI	SH	SF	HP	BB	IBB	SO	SB	CS	GDP	Slg.	OBP
Barrett, Michael, Mon.	.304	8	27	23	3	7	12	2	0	1	2	0	0	1	3	0	6	0	0	0	.522	.407
Barry, Jeff, Col.†	.176	15	37	34	4	6	7	1	0	0	2	0	1	0	2	0	11	0	0	0	.206	.216
Bates, Jason, Col.†	.189	53	82	74	10	14	17	3	0	0	3	0	0	0	8	1	21	0	0	4	.230	.268
Batista, Miguel, Mon.	.000	56	34	32	0	0	0	0	0	0	0	2	0	0	0	0	21	0	0	0	.000	.000
Batista, Tony, Ari.	.273	106	318	293	46	80	152	16	1	18	41	0	4	3	18	0	52	1	1	7	.519	.318
Bautista, Danny, Atl.	.250	82	156	144	17	36	56	11	0	3	17	3	2	0	7	0	21	1	0	4	.389	.281
Beck, Rod, Chi.	.000	81	1	1	0	0	0	0	0	0	0	0	0	0	0	0	0	0	0	0	.000	.000
Becker, Rich, N.Y.*	.190	49	121	100	15	19	36	4	2	3	10	0	0	0	21	2	42	3	1	1	.360	.331
Beech, Matt, Phi.*	.152	21	39	33	2	5	5	0	0	0	2	6	0	0	0	0	10	0	0	1	.152	.152
Belinda, Stan, Cin.	.000	40	1	1	0	0	0	0	0	0	0	0	0	0	0	0	1	0	0	0	.000	.000
Bell, David, St.L	.222	4	9	9	0	2	3	1	0	0	0	0	0	0	0	0	3	0	0	0	.333	.222
Bell, Derek, Hou.	.314	156	695	630	111	198	309	41	2	22	108	0	10	4	51	0	126	13	3	14	.490	.364
Bell, Jay, Ari.	.251	155	645	549	79	138	237	29	5	20	67	5	3	7	81	3	129	3	5	14	.432	.353
Belliard, Rafael, Atl.	.250	7	20	20	1	5	5	0	0	0	1	0	0	0	0	0	1	0	0	2	.250	.250
Belliard, Ronnie, Mil.	.200	8	5	5	1	1	1	0	0	0	0	0	0	0	0	0	0	0	0	0	.200	.200
Beltran, Rigo, N.Y.*	.000	7	1	1	0	0	0	0	0	0	0	0	0	0	0	0	0	0	0	0	.000	.000
Beltre, Adrian, L.A.	.215	77	214	195	18	42	72	9	0	7	22	2	0	3	14	0	37	3	1	4	.369	.278
Benard, Marvin, S.F.*	.322	121	327	286	41	92	124	21	1	3	36	4	1	2	34	1	39	11	4	3	.434	.396
Benes, Andy, Ari.	.169	35	82	65	8	11	17	3	0	1	3	10	0	1	6	0	28	0	0	0	.262	.250
Benitez, Yamil, Ari.	.199	91	225	206	17	41	77	7	1	9	30	0	1	4	14	1	46	2	2	6	.374	.262
Bennett, Gary, Phi.	.290	9	37	31	4	9	9	0	0	0	3	0	1	0	5	0	5	0	0	1	.290	.378
Bennett, Shayne, Mon.	.000	62	8	6	0	0	0	0	0	0	0	1	0	0	1	0	1	0	0	0	.000	.143
Bere, Jason, Cin.	.000	9	15	14	0	0	0	0	0	0	0	0	0	0	1	0	5	0	0	1	.000	.067
Berg, Dave, Fla.	.313	81	215	182	18	57	74	11	0	2	21	4	3	0	26	1	46	3	0	1	.407	.393
Bergman, Sean, Hou.	.083	31	68	60	3	5	7	2	0	0	4	8	0	0	0	0	30	0	0	0	.117	.083
Berry, Sean, Hou.	.314	102	342	299	48	94	152	17	1	13	52	1	4	7	31	3	50	3	1	8	.508	.387
Bichette, Dante, Col.	.331	161	695	662	97	219	337	48	2	22	122	0	4	1	28	2	76	14	4	22	.509	.357
Bieser, Steve, Pit.*	.273	13	13	11	2	3	4	1	0	0	1	0	0	0	2	0	2	0	0	1	.364	.385
Biggio, Craig, Hou.	.325	160	738	646	123	210	325	51	2	20	88	1	4	23	64	6	113	50	8	10	.503	.403
Blair, Willie, Ari.-N.Y.	.096	34	59	52	3	5	5	0	0	0	4	0	0	3	0	0	27	0	0	0	.096	.145
Blauser, Jeff, Chi.	.219	119	435	361	49	79	108	11	3	4	26	3	3	8	60	1	93	2	2	5	.299	.340
Boehringer, Brian, S.D.†	.000	56	8	7	0	0	0	0	0	0	0	0	0	0	1	0	4	0	0	0	.000	.125
Bogar, Tim, Hou.	.154	79	169	156	12	24	33	4	1	1	8	1	1	2	9	2	36	2	1	5	.212	.208
Bohanon, Brian, N.Y.-L.A.*	.279	39	49	43	1	12	16	2	1	0	5	4	0	0	2	0	13	0	0	2	.372	.311
Bonds, Barry, S.F.*	.303	156	697	552	120	167	336	44	7	37	122	1	6	8	130	29	92	28	12	15	.609	.438
Bonilla, Bobby, Fla.-L.A.†	.249	100	380	333	39	83	129	11	1	11	45	0	6	0	41	4	59	1	2	16	.387	.326
Boone, Aaron, Cin.	.282	58	206	181	24	51	74	13	2	2	28	3	2	5	15	1	36	6	1	3	.409	.350
Boone, Bret, Cin.	.266	157	648	583	76	155	267	38	1	24	95	9	4	4	48	3	104	6	4	23	.458	.324
Booty, Josh, Fla.	.158	7	22	19	0	3	4	1	0	0	3	0	0	0	3	0	8	0	0	0	.211	.273
Boskie, Shawn, Mon.	.000	5	5	4	1	0	0	0	0	0	0	0	0	0	1	0	3	0	0	0	.000	.200
Bottenfield, Kent, St.L	.088	44	39	34	3	3	3	0	0	0	2	5	0	0	0	0	9	0	0	0	.088	.088
Brantley, Jeff, St.L	.000	48	1	0	0	0	0	0	0	0	0	1	0	0	0	0	0	0	0	0	.000	.000
Brede, Brent, Ari.*	.226	98	238	212	23	48	69	9	3	2	17	0	0	2	24	2	43	1	0	6	.325	.311
Brock, Chris, S.F.	.250	13	4	4	0	1	1	0	0	0	0	0	0	0	0	0	0	0	0	0	.250	.250
Brogna, Rico, Phi.*	.265	153	624	565	77	150	252	36	3	20	104	0	10	0	49	8	125	7	7	12	.446	.319
Brow, Scott, Ari.	.000	17	1	1	0	0	0	0	0	0	0	0	0	0	0	0	1	0	0	0	.000	.000
Brown, Adrian, Pit.†	.283	41	165	152	20	43	49	4	1	0	5	4	0	0	9	0	18	4	0	3	.322	.323
Brown, Brant, Chi.*	.291	124	380	347	56	101	174	17	7	14	48	1	1	1	30	2	95	4	5	1	.501	.348
Brown, Emil, Pit.	.256	13	41	39	2	10	11	1	0	0	3	0	0	1	1	0	11	0	0	2	.282	.293
Brown, Kevin, S.D.	.207	36	93	82	4	17	20	3	0	0	10	7	0	0	4	0	29	0	0	1	.244	.244
Brownson, Mark, Col.*	.000	2	5	5	0	0	0	0	0	0	0	0	0	0	0	0	0	0	0	0	.000	.000
Bruske, Jim, L.A.-S.D.	.000	39	3	3	0	0	0	0	0	0	0	0	0	0	0	0	1	0	0	0	.000	.000
Bullinger, Kirk, Mon.	.000	8	1	1	0	0	0	0	0	0	0	0	0	0	0	0	0	0	0	0	.000	.000
Burks, Ellis, Col.-S.F.	.292	142	582	504	76	147	250	28	6	21	76	6	9	5	58	1	111	11	8	12	.496	.365
Burnitz, Jeromy, Mil.*	.263	161	691	609	92	160	304	28	1	38	125	1	7	4	70	7	158	7	4	9	.499	.339
Busby, Mike, St.L	.000	26	4	3	0	0	0	0	0	0	0	1	0	0	1	0	1	0	0	0	.000	.250
Byrd, Paul, Atl.-Phi.	.167	9	20	18	1	3	3	0	0	0	1	0	0	1	1	0	7	0	0	0	.167	.250
Cabrera, Orlando, Mon.	.280	79	285	261	44	73	108	16	5	3	22	5	1	0	18	1	27	6	2	6	.414	.325
Caminiti, Ken, S.D.†	.252	131	535	452	87	114	230	29	0	29	82	0	8	4	71	4	108	6	2	6	.509	.353
Cangelosi, John, Fla.†	.251	104	208	171	19	43	54	8	0	1	10	5	1	1	30	0	23	2	3	5	.316	.363
Carter, Joe, S.F.	.295	41	115	105	15	31	59	7	0	7	29	0	4	0	6	0	13	1	0	2	.562	.322
Casey, Sean, Cin.*	.272	96	351	302	44	82	126	21	1	7	52	0	3	3	43	3	45	1	1	11	.417	.365
Castilla, Vinny, Col.	.319	162	697	645	108	206	380	28	4	46	144	0	6	6	40	7	89	5	9	24	.589	.362
Castillo, Alberto, N.Y.	.205	38	99	83	13	17	27	4	0	2	7	6	0	1	9	0	17	0	2	1	.325	.290
Castillo, Luis, Fla.	.203	44	177	153	21	31	41	3	2	1	10	1	0	1	22	0	33	3	0	1	.268	.307
Castro, Juan, L.A.	.195	89	246	220	25	43	56	7	0	2	14	9	2	0	15	0	37	0	0	5	.255	.245
Cedeno, Roger, L.A.†	.242	105	271	240	33	58	77	11	1	2	17	3	1	0	27	2	57	8	2	1	.321	.317
Charlton, Norm, Atl.†	.000	13	1	1	0	0	0	0	0	0	0	0	0	0	0	0	0	0	0	0	.000	.000
Chen, Bruce, Atl.*	.143	4	9	7	0	1	1	0	0	0	1	2	0	0	0	0	4	0	0	0	.143	.143
Chouinard, Bobby, Mil.-Ari.	.000	27	2	2	0	0	0	0	0	0	0	0	0	0	0	0	1	0	0	0	.000	.000
Christiansen, Jason, Pit.	.250	60	4	4	0	1	1	0	0	0	0	0	0	0	0	0	1	0	0	0	.250	.250
Cianfrocco, Archi, S.D.	.125	40	80	72	4	9	15	3	0	1	5	2	0	1	5	0	22	1	0	3	.208	.192
Cirillo, Jeff, Mil.	.321	156	694	604	97	194	269	31	1	14	68	5	2	4	79	3	88	10	4	26	.445	.402
Clark, Dave, Hou.*	.206	93	146	131	12	27	34	7	0	0	4	0	0	1	14	1	45	1	1	2	.260	.288
Clark, Mark, Chi.	.065	33	73	62	1	4	6	2	0	0	3	8	0	0	3	0	27	0	0	1	.097	.108
Clayton, Royce, St.L	.234	90	402	355	59	83	116	19	1	4	29	3	2	2	40	1	51	19	6	10	.327	.313
Clement, Matt, S.D.	.000	4	2	2	0	0	0	0	0	0	0	0	0	0	0	0	2	0	0	0	.000	.000
Clemente, Edgard, Col.	.353	11	19	17	2	6	8	0	1	0	2	0	0	0	2	0	8	0	0	0	.471	.421
Clontz, Brad, L.A.-N.Y.	.000	20	2	2	0	0	0	0	0	0	0	0	0	0	0	0	2	0	0	0	.000	.000
Colbrunn, Greg, Col.-Atl.	.307	90	180	166	18	51	75	11	2	3	23	0	0	4	10	0	34	4	3	1	.452	.361
Collier, Lou, Pit.	.246	110	379	334	30	82	113	13	6	2	34	3	5	6	31	6	70	2	2	8	.338	.316
Cook, Dennis, N.Y.*	.000	73	3	3	0	0	0	0	0	0	0	0	0	0	0	0	0	0	0	0	.000	.000

Player, Team	Avg.	G	TPA	AB	R	H	TB	2B	3B	HR	RBI	SH	SF	HP	BB	IBB	SO	SB	CS	GDP	Slg.	OBP
Cooke, Steve, Cin.	.500	1	2	2	0	1	1	0	0	0	0	0	0	0	0	0	0	0	0	0	.500	.500
Cora, Alex, L.A.*	.121	29	38	33	1	4	6	0	1	0	0	2	0	1	2	0	8	0	0	0	.182	.194
Cordova, Francisco, Pit.	.120	33	79	75	3	9	12	1	1	0	1	2	0	0	2	0	29	0	0	2	.160	.143
Counsell, Craig, Fla.*	.251	107	399	335	43	84	125	19	5	4	40	8	1	4	51	7	47	3	0	5	.373	.355
Cromer, Tripp, L.A.	.167	6	6	6	1	1	4	0	0	1	1	0	0	0	0	0	2	0	0	0	.667	.167
Croushore, Rick, St.L.	.000	41	2	0	0	0	0	0	0	0	0	2	0	0	0	0	0	0	0	0	.000	.000
Cruz, Jacob, S.F.*	.000	3	3	3	0	0	0	0	0	0	0	0	0	0	0	0	2	0	0	0	.000	.000
Daal, Omar, Ari.*	.109	33	56	46	3	5	5	0	0	0	1	5	0	0	5	0	17	0	0	1	.109	.196
Darensbourg, Vic, Fla.*	.000	60	9	8	0	0	0	0	0	0	0	0	0	0	1	0	3	0	0	1	.000	.111
Darwin, Danny, S.F.	.089	33	51	45	2	4	5	1	0	0	1	4	0	1	1	0	30	0	0	1	.111	.128
Daubach, Brian, Fla.*	.200	10	17	15	0	3	4	1	0	0	3	0	1	1	1	0	5	0	0	0	.267	.294
Davis, Ben, S.D.†	.000	1	1	1	0	0	0	0	0	0	0	0	0	0	0	0	0	0	0	0	.000	.000
DeJean, Mike, Col.	.000	59	5	5	0	0	0	0	0	0	0	0	0	0	0	0	4	0	0	1	.000	.000
Delgado, Wilson, S.F.†	.167	10	13	12	1	2	3	1	0	0	1	0	0	0	1	0	3	0	0	0	.250	.231
Dellucci, David, Ari.*	.260	124	453	416	43	108	166	19	12	5	51	0	1	3	33	2	103	3	5	6	.399	.318
Dempster, Ryan, Fla.	.000	14	14	13	0	0	0	0	0	0	0	1	0	0	0	0	8	0	0	1	.000	.000
DeRosa, Mark, Atl.	.333	5	3	3	2	1	1	0	0	0	0	0	0	0	0	0	1	0	0	0	.333	.333
DeShields, Delino, St.L.*	.290	117	484	420	74	122	180	21	8	7	44	4	4	0	56	2	61	26	10	6	.429	.371
Dessens, Elmer, Pit.	.000	43	12	8	0	0	0	0	0	0	1	3	0	0	1	0	4	0	0	0	.000	.111
Devereaux, Mike, L.A.	.308	9	16	13	0	4	5	1	0	0	1	0	0	0	3	0	2	0	1	2	.385	.438
Diaz, Alex, S.F.†	.129	34	62	62	5	8	10	2	0	0	5	0	0	0	0	0	15	1	1	0	.161	.129
Diaz, Edwin, Ari.	.000	3	7	7	0	0	0	0	0	0	0	0	0	0	0	0	0	0	0	0	.000	.000
Dipoto, Jerry, Col.	.000	68	2	1	0	0	0	0	0	0	0	0	0	0	1	0	0	0	0	1	.000	.500
Dreifort, Darren, L.A.	.224	33	56	49	10	11	14	0	0	1	2	5	0	0	2	0	22	0	0	0	.286	.255
Drew, J.D., St.L*	.417	14	41	36	9	15	35	3	1	5	13	0	1	0	4	0	10	0	0	4	.972	.463
Dunston, Shawon, S.F.	.176	36	55	51	10	9	20	2	0	3	8	1	0	3	0	0	10	0	2	1	.392	.222
Dunwoody, Todd, Fla.*	.251	116	462	434	53	109	165	27	7	5	28	3	0	4	21	0	113	5	1	6	.380	.292
Echevarria, Angel, Col.	.379	19	33	29	7	11	17	3	0	1	9	0	0	2	2	0	3	0	0	4	.586	.455
Edmondson, Brian, Atl.-Fla.	.000	53	13	12	0	0	0	0	0	0	0	1	0	0	0	0	5	0	0	0	.000	.000
Eisenreich, Jim, Fla.-L.A.*	.215	105	208	191	21	41	51	3	2	1	13	1	0	0	16	2	36	6	0	3	.267	.275
Elarton, Scott, Hou.	.000	28	10	7	0	0	0	0	0	0	0	3	0	0	0	0	4	0	0	0	.000	.000
Eldred, Cal, Mil.	.125	24	39	32	1	4	5	1	0	0	2	5	0	0	2	0	19	0	1	1	.156	.176
Embree, Alan, Atl.-Ari.*	.000	55	2	1	0	0	0	0	0	0	0	0	0	0	1	0	1	0	0	0	.000	.500
Estalella, Bobby, Phi.	.188	47	182	165	16	31	63	6	1	8	20	0	3	1	13	0	49	0	0	4	.382	.247
Estes, Shawn, S.F.	.190	27	51	42	4	8	9	1	0	0	0	8	0	0	1	0	17	0	0	0	.214	.209
Eusebio, Tony, Hou.	.253	66	203	182	13	46	57	6	1	1	36	0	2	1	18	2	31	1	0	8	.313	.320
Everett, Carl, Hou.†	.296	133	519	467	72	138	225	34	4	15	76	3	2	3	44	2	102	14	12	11	.482	.359
Fabregas, Jorge, Ari.-N.Y.*	.197	70	201	183	11	36	46	4	0	2	20	1	2	1	14	1	32	0	0	4	.251	.255
Finley, Steve, S.D.*	.249	159	674	619	92	154	248	40	6	14	67	3	4	3	45	0	103	12	3	9	.401	.301
Floyd, Cliff, Fla.*	.282	153	641	588	85	166	283	45	3	22	90	0	3	3	47	7	112	27	14	10	.481	.337
Fontenot, Joe, Fla.	.000	8	11	10	1	0	0	0	0	0	0	1	0	0	0	0	6	0	0	0	.000	.000
Fordyce, Brook, Cin.	.253	57	158	146	8	37	55	9	0	3	14	1	0	0	11	3	28	0	1	2	.377	.306
Fox, Andy, Ari.*	.277	139	564	502	67	139	199	21	6	9	44	0	1	18	43	0	97	14	7	2	.396	.355
Fox, Chad, Mil.	.000	49	4	3	0	0	0	0	0	0	0	1	0	0	0	0	2	0	0	0	.000	.000
Franco, John, N.Y.*	.000	61	2	2	0	0	0	0	0	0	0	0	0	0	0	0	1	0	0	0	.000	.000
Franco, Matt, N.Y.*	.273	103	187	161	20	44	58	7	2	1	13	1	1	1	23	6	26	0	1	8	.360	.366
Frank, Mike, Cin.*	.225	28	98	89	14	20	26	6	0	0	7	1	1	0	7	0	12	0	0	3	.292	.278
Frascatore, John, St.L	.167	69	6	6	0	1	1	0	0	0	0	0	0	0	0	0	3	0	0	1	.167	.167
Frias, Hanley, Ari.†	.130	15	23	23	4	3	8	0	1	1	2	0	0	0	0	0	5	0	0	1	.348	.130
Fullmer, Brad, Mon.*	.273	140	547	505	58	138	225	44	2	13	73	0	1	2	39	4	70	6	6	12	.446	.327
Gaetti, Gary, St.L-Chi.	.281	128	492	434	60	122	215	34	1	19	70	1	4	10	43	2	62	1	1	12	.495	.356
Galarraga, Andres, Atl.	.305	153	648	555	103	169	330	27	1	44	121	0	5	25	63	11	146	7	6	8	.595	.397
Gant, Ron, St.L	.240	121	438	383	60	92	189	17	1	26	67	0	2	2	51	2	92	8	0	6	.493	.331
Garcia, Freddy, Pit.	.256	56	193	172	27	44	84	11	1	9	26	0	1	2	18	3	45	0	2	3	.488	.332
Garcia, Guillermo, Cin.	.194	12	38	36	3	7	15	2	0	2	4	0	0	0	2	0	13	0	0	2	.417	.237
Garcia, Karim, Ari.*	.222	113	354	333	39	74	127	10	8	9	43	0	3	0	18	1	78	5	4	6	.381	.260
Gardner, Mark, S.F.	.164	33	83	73	4	12	13	1	0	0	4	4	0	1	5	0	26	0	0	3	.178	.228
Gibson, Derrick, Col.	.429	7	23	21	4	9	10	1	0	0	2	0	0	1	1	0	4	0	0	0	.476	.478
Gilbert, Shawn, N.Y.-St.L	.200	7	5	5	1	1	1	0	0	0	0	0	0	0	0	0	2	1	0	0	.200	.200
Gilkey, Bernard, N.Y.-Ari.	.233	111	419	365	41	85	115	15	0	5	33	3	3	5	43	1	80	9	3	11	.315	.320
Giovanola, Ed, S.D.*	.230	92	166	139	19	32	44	3	3	1	9	5	0	0	22	0	22	1	2	2	.317	.335
Glanville, Doug, Phi.	.279	158	735	678	106	189	255	28	7	8	49	5	4	6	42	1	89	23	6	7	.376	.325
Glauber, Keith, Cin.	.000	3	2	2	0	0	0	0	0	0	0	0	0	0	0	0	0	0	0	0	.000	.000
Glavine, Tom, Atl.*	.239	33	86	71	3	17	20	3	0	0	7	14	0	0	1	0	15	0	0	0	.282	.250
Gomes, Wayne, Phi.	.000	71	2	2	0	0	0	0	0	0	0	0	0	0	0	0	2	0	0	0	.000	.000
Gomez, Chris, S.D.	.267	145	515	449	55	120	170	32	3	4	39	7	3	5	51	7	87	1	3	11	.379	.346
Gonzalez, Alex, Fla.	.151	25	98	86	11	13	24	2	0	3	7	2	0	1	9	0	30	0	0	2	.279	.240
Gonzalez, Jeremi, Chi.	.188	21	40	32	0	6	7	1	0	0	2	8	0	0	0	0	11	0	0	3	.219	.188
Goodwin, Curtis, Col.*	.245	19	186	159	27	39	49	7	0	1	6	10	1	0	16	0	40	5	1	3	.308	.313
Grace, Mark, Chi.*	.309	158	698	595	92	184	280	39	3	17	89	0	7	3	93	8	56	4	7	17	.471	.401
Grace, Mike, Phi.	.087	21	28	23	1	2	2	0	0	0	1	3	0	0	2	0	11	0	0	1	.087	.160
Graffanino, Tony, Atl.	.211	111	317	289	32	61	92	14	1	5	22	1	1	2	24	0	68	1	4	7	.318	.275
Graves, Danny, Cin.	.000	62	4	4	0	0	0	0	0	0	0	0	0	0	0	0	3	0	0	0	.000	.000
Green, Tyler, Phi.	.146	27	51	41	2	6	7	1	0	0	3	6	2	0	2	0	21	0	0	0	.171	.178
Greene, Willie, Cin.*	.270	111	417	356	57	96	158	18	1	14	49	0	2	3	56	2	80	6	3	7	.444	.372
Grissom, Marquis, Mil.	.271	142	572	542	57	147	207	28	4	10	60	2	2	4	24	2	78	13	8	12	.382	.304
Grudzielanek, Mark, Mon.-L.A.	.272	156	641	589	62	160	213	21	1	10	62	8	7	11	26	2	73	18	5	18	.362	.311
Guerrero, Vladimir, Mon.	.324	159	677	623	108	202	367	37	7	38	109	0	5	7	42	13	95	11	9	15	.589	.371
Guerrero, Wilton, L.A.-Mon.†	.284	116	426	402	50	114	152	14	9	2	27	6	3	1	14	0	63	8	2	4	.378	.307
Guillen, Jose, Pit.	.267	153	605	573	60	153	237	38	2	14	84	1	4	6	21	0	100	3	5	7	.414	.298
Guillen, Ozzie, Atl.*	.277	83	295	264	35	73	93	15	1	1	22	4	2	1	24	0	25	1	4	2	.352	.337
Guthrie, Mark, L.A.†	.000	53	1	1	0	0	0	0	0	0	0	0	0	0	0	0	0	0	0	0	.000	.000

Player, Team	Avg.	G	TPA	AB	R	H	TB	2B	3B	HR	RBI	SH	SF	HP	BB	IBB	SO	SB	CS	GDP	Slg.	OBP
Gutierrez, Ricky, Hou.	.261	141	561	491	55	128	164	24	3	2	46	3	7	6	54	5	84	13	7	20	.334	.337
Gwynn, Tony, S.D.*	.321	127	505	461	65	148	231	35	0	16	69	0	8	1	35	6	18	3	1	14	.501	.364
Halama, John, Hou.*	.000	6	13	10	1	0	0	0	0	0	0	1	0	0	2	0	7	0	0	0	.000	.167
Hamelin, Bob, Mil.*	.219	109	167	146	15	32	59	6	0	7	22	1	3	1	16	1	30	0	1	7	.404	.295
Hamilton, Darryl, S.F.-Col.*	.308	148	661	561	95	173	225	28	3	6	51	12	3	3	82	1	73	13	9	6	.401	.398
Hamilton, Joey, S.D.	.141	35	74	71	1	10	15	0	1	1	6	2	0	0	1	0	31	0	0	0	.211	.153
Hammond, Chris, Fla.*	.200	3	5	5	0	1	1	0	0	0	0	0	0	0	0	0	2	0	0	0	.200	.200
Hammonds, Jeffrey, Cin.	.302	26	103	86	14	26	32	4	1	0	11	3	1	0	13	0	18	1	1	0	.372	.390
Hampton, Mike, Hou.	.262	32	76	61	3	16	20	4	0	0	2	7	0	1	7	0	12	2	0	2	.328	.348
Haney, Todd, N.Y.	.000	3	4	3	0	0	0	0	0	0	0	0	0	0	1	0	0	0	0	0	.000	.250
Hardtke, Jason, Chi.†	.238	18	23	21	2	5	5	0	0	0	2	0	0	0	2	0	6	0	0	0	.238	.304
Harnisch, Pete, Cin.	.106	32	76	66	3	7	7	0	0	0	1	9	0	0	1	0	22	0	0	1	.106	.119
Harris, Lenny, Cin.-N.Y.*	.259	132	317	290	30	75	108	15	0	6	27	4	4	2	17	3	21	6	5	13	.372	.300
Hayes, Charlie, S.F.	.286	111	366	329	39	94	138	8	0	12	62	1	2	0	34	0	61	2	1	4	.419	.351
Helms, Wes, Atl.	.308	7	13	13	2	4	8	1	0	1	2	0	0	0	0	0	4	0	0	0	.615	.308
Helton, Todd, Col.*	.315	152	595	530	78	167	281	37	1	25	97	1	5	6	53	5	54	3	3	15	.530	.380
Henley, Bob, Mon.	.304	41	132	115	16	35	54	8	1	3	18	2	1	3	11	0	26	3	0	4	.470	.377
Henriquez, Oscar, Fla.	.000	15	1	1	0	0	0	0	0	0	0	0	0	0	0	0	0	0	0	0	.000	.000
Henry, Doug, Hou.	.000	59	5	4	0	0	0	0	0	0	0	1	0	0	0	0	2	0	0	0	.000	.000
Heredia, Felix, Fla.-Chi.*	.000	71	3	3	0	0	0	0	0	0	0	0	0	0	0	0	1	0	0	0	.000	.000
Hermanson, Dustin, Mon.	.115	32	68	52	7	6	10	1	0	1	2	5	0	1	10	0	29	0	0	1	.192	.270
Hernandez, Carlos, S.D.	.262	129	417	390	34	102	144	15	0	9	52	0	2	9	16	2	54	2	2	19	.369	.305
Hernandez, Livan, Fla.	.195	35	84	82	3	16	19	3	0	0	6	1	0	1	0	0	20	0	0	4	.232	.205
Hernandez, Jose, Chi.	.254	149	533	488	76	124	230	23	7	23	75	2	2	1	40	3	140	4	6	12	.471	.311
Hershiser, Orel, S.F.	.152	34	78	66	7	10	12	2	0	0	1	8	0	1	3	0	16	1	0	0	.182	.200
Hidalgo, Richard, Hou.	.303	74	234	211	31	64	100	15	0	7	35	0	4	2	17	0	37	3	3	5	.474	.355
Hill, Glenallen, Chi.	.351	48	145	131	26	46	75	5	0	8	23	0	0	0	14	1	34	0	0	3	.573	.414
Hitchcock, Sterling, S.D.*	.140	39	56	50	5	7	7	0	0	0	2	5	0	0	1	0	21	0	0	0	.140	.157
Hoffman, Trevor, S.D.	.000	66	3	3	0	0	0	0	0	0	0	0	0	0	0	0	2	0	0	0	.000	.000
Holbert, Ray, Atl.-Mon.	.100	10	23	20	2	2	2	0	0	0	1	0	1	0	2	0	5	0	0	0	.100	.174
Hollandsworth, Todd, L.A.*	.269	55	187	175	23	47	70	6	4	3	20	2	0	1	9	0	42	4	3	2	.400	.308
Hollins, Damon, Atl.-L.A.	.200	8	15	15	1	3	3	0	0	0	2	0	0	0	0	0	3	0	1	0	.200	.200
Houston, Tyler, Chi.*	.255	95	270	255	26	65	101	7	1	9	33	1	1	0	13	1	53	2	2	6	.396	.290
Howard, David, St.L†	.245	46	117	102	15	25	34	1	1	2	12	2	1	0	12	2	22	0	0	2	.333	.322
Howard, Thomas, L.A.*	.184	47	79	76	9	14	24	4	0	2	4	0	0	0	3	0	15	1	0	2	.316	.215
Howell, Jack, Hou.*	.289	24	42	38	4	11	19	5	0	1	7	0	0	0	4	0	12	0	0	1	.500	.357
Hubbard, Mike, Mon.	.145	32	56	55	3	8	12	1	0	1	3	0	0	1	0	0	17	0	0	1	.218	.161
Hubbard, Trenidad, L.A.	.298	94	235	208	29	62	94	9	1	7	18	3	3	3	18	0	46	9	5	5	.452	.358
Hudek, John, N.Y.-Cin.†	.000	58	4	3	0	0	0	0	0	0	0	0	1	0	0	0	3	0	0	0	.000	.000
Hudler, Rex, Phi.	.122	25	45	41	2	5	6	1	0	0	2	0	0	4	0	0	12	0	0	1	.146	.200
Hughes, Bobby, Mil.	.229	85	237	218	28	50	88	7	2	9	29	1	1	1	16	1	54	1	2	3	.404	.284
Hundley, Todd, N.Y.†	.161	53	142	124	8	20	33	4	0	3	12	0	1	1	16	0	55	1	1	0	.266	.261
Hunter, Brian, St.L	.205	62	123	112	11	23	46	9	1	4	13	3	0	1	7	0	23	1	1	4	.411	.258
Huskey, Butch, N.Y.	.252	113	402	369	43	93	150	18	0	13	59	2	4	1	26	3	66	7	6	13	.407	.300
Hutton, Mark, Cin.	1.000	10	1	1	0	1	1	0	0	0	1	0	0	0	0	0	0	0	0	0	1.000	1.000
Incaviglia, Pete, Hou.	.125	13	17	16	0	2	3	1	0	0	2	0	0	0	1	0	4	0	0	1	.188	.176
Jackson, Damian, Cin.	.316	13	45	38	4	12	17	5	0	0	7	0	1	0	6	0	4	2	0	1	.447	.400
Jackson, Darrin, Mil.	.240	114	214	204	20	49	76	13	1	4	20	0	0	1	9	0	37	1	1	5	.373	.276
Jackson, Ryan, Fla.*	.250	11	284	260	26	65	97	15	1	5	31	2	1	1	20	0	73	1	1	3	.373	.305
Jaha, John, Mil.	.208	73	273	216	29	45	74	6	1	7	38	0	2	6	49	3	66	1	3	5	.343	.366
Javier, Stan, S.F.†	.290	135	490	417	63	121	156	13	5	4	49	4	3	1	65	4	63	21	5	13	.374	.385
Jefferies, Gregg, Phi.†	.294	125	520	483	65	142	194	22	3	8	48	1	6	1	29	4	27	11	3	17	.402	.331
Jenkins, Geoff, Mil.*	.229	84	285	262	33	60	101	12	1	9	28	0	1	2	20	4	61	1	3	7	.385	.288
Jensen, Marcus, Mil.†	.000	2	2	2	0	0	0	0	0	0	0	0	0	0	0	0	2	0	0	0	.000	.000
Jimenez, Jose, St.L	.000	4	8	6	0	0	0	0	0	0	0	1	2	0	0	0	4	0	0	0	.000	.000
Johnson, Brian, S.F.	.237	99	346	308	34	73	122	8	1	13	34	4	1	5	28	4	67	0	2	11	.396	.310
Johnson, Charles, Fla.-L.A.	.218	133	506	459	44	100	175	18	0	19	58	0	1	1	45	1	129	0	2	12	.381	.289
Johnson, Lance, Chi.*	.280	85	332	304	51	85	107	8	4	2	21	1	1	0	26	1	22	10	6	5	.352	.335
Johnson, Mike, Mon.*	.333	2	3	3	0	1	1	0	0	0	0	0	0	0	0	0	1	0	0	0	.333	.333
Johnson, Randy, Hou.	.063	11	35	32	1	2	3	1	0	0	2	3	0	0	0	0	17	0	0	1	.094	.063
Johnson, Russ, Hou.	.231	8	15	13	2	3	4	1	0	0	0	0	0	1	1	0	5	1	0	1	.308	.333
Johnstone, John, S.F.	.000	70	3	2	0	0	0	0	0	0	0	0	1	0	0	0	0	0	0	0	.000	.000
Jones, Andruw, Atl.	.271	159	631	582	89	158	300	33	8	31	90	1	4	4	40	8	129	27	4	10	.515	.321
Jones, Chris, Ari.-S.F.	.190	63	134	121	17	23	34	3	1	2	13	0	2	0	11	0	37	2	1	2	.281	.254
Jones, Doug, Mil.	.000	46	2	2	0	0	0	0	0	0	0	0	0	0	0	0	2	0	0	0	.000	.000
Jones, Chipper, Atl.†	.313	160	707	601	123	188	329	29	5	34	107	1	8	1	96	1	93	16	6	17	.547	.404
Jones, Bobby J., N.Y.	.188	30	62	48	1	9	10	1	0	0	4	12	0	0	2	0	21	0	0	1	.208	.220
Jones, Bobby M., Col.	.178	35	50	45	3	8	9	1	0	0	4	5	0	0	0	0	14	0	0	1	.200	.178
Jones, Terry, Mon.†	.217	60	248	212	30	46	60	7	2	1	15	15	0	0	21	1	46	16	4	2	.283	.288
Jordan, Brian, St.L	.316	150	617	564	100	178	301	34	7	25	91	0	4	9	40	1	66	17	5	18	.534	.368
Jordan, Kevin, Phi.	.276	112	261	250	23	69	88	13	0	2	27	0	1	2	8	1	30	0	0	5	.352	.303
Joyner, Wally, S.D.*	.298	131	494	439	58	131	199	30	1	12	80	0	3	1	51	8	44	1	2	11	.453	.370
Judd, Mike, L.A.	.000	7	1	1	0	0	0	0	0	0	0	0	0	0	0	0	0	0	0	0	.000	.000
Juden, Jeff, Mil.	.122	24	44	41	3	5	6	1	0	0	4	3	0	0	0	0	12	0	0	3	.146	.122
Karl, Scott, Mil.*	.071	34	69	56	3	4	6	0	1	0	9	9	0	0	4	0	17	0	0	1	.107	.133
Karros, Eric, L.A.	.296	139	564	507	59	150	241	20	1	23	87	0	7	3	47	1	93	7	2	7	.475	.355
Kelly, Pat, St.L	.216	53	170	153	18	33	50	5	0	4	14	1	1	2	13	0	48	5	1	3	.327	.284
Kendall, Jason, Pit.	.327	149	627	535	95	175	253	36	3	12	75	2	8	31	51	3	51	26	5	6	.473	.411
Kent, Jeff, S.F.	.297	137	594	526	94	156	292	37	3	31	128	1	10	9	48	4	110	9	4	16	.555	.359
Kile, Darryl, Col.	.254	39	84	71	5	18	23	5	0	0	5	9	0	0	4	0	22	0	0	1	.324	.293
King, Curtis, St.L	.000	36	5	5	0	0	0	0	0	0	0	0	0	0	0	0	1	0	0	1	.000	.000
Kinkade, Mike, N.Y.	.000	3	2	2	2	0	0	0	0	0	0	0	0	0	0	0	0	0	0	0	.000	.000

Player, Team	Avg.	G	TPA	AB	R	H	TB	2B	3B	HR	RBI	SH	SF	HP	BB	IBB	SO	SB	CS	GDP	Slg.	OBP
Kirby, Wayne, N.Y.*	.194	26	33	31	5	6	8	0	1	0	0	1	0	0	1	0	9	1	1	0	.258	.219
Klassen, Danny, Ari.	.194	29	118	108	12	21	34	2	1	3	8	0	1	0	9	0	33	1	1	5	.315	.263
Klesko, Ryan, Atl.*	.274	129	490	427	69	117	202	29	1	18	70	0	4	3	56	5	66	5	3	9	.473	.359
Kline, Steve, Mon.†	.000	78	5	4	0	0	0	0	0	0	0	1	0	0	0	0	1	0	0	0	.000	.000
Klingenbeck, Scott, Cin.	.000	4	6	6	0	0	0	0	0	0	0	0	0	0	0	0	4	0	0	0	.000	.000
Knorr, Randy, Fla.	.204	15	51	49	4	10	22	4	1	2	11	0	1	0	1	0	10	0	0	0	.449	.216
Konerko, Paul, L.A.-Cin.	.217	75	239	217	21	47	72	4	0	7	29	0	3	3	16	0	40	0	1	10	.332	.276
Kotsay, Mark, Fla.*	.279	154	623	578	72	161	233	25	7	11	68	7	3	1	34	2	61	10	5	17	.403	.318
Krivda, Rick, Cin.	.000	16	4	4	0	0	0	0	0	0	0	0	0	0	0	0	3	0	0	0	.000	.000
Laker, Tim, Pit.	.375	14	26	24	2	9	13	1	0	1	2	0	1	0	1	0	3	0	0	1	.542	.385
Lampkin, Tom, St.L*	.231	93	248	216	25	50	82	12	1	6	28	1	0	7	24	5	32	3	2	5	.380	.328
Langston, Mark, S.D.	.083	23	30	24	0	2	3	1	0	0	2	4	0	0	2	0	9	0	0	1	.125	.154
Lankford, Frank, L.A.	.000	12	2	2	0	0	0	0	0	0	0	0	0	0	0	0	1	0	0	0	.000	.000
Lankford, Ray, St.L*	.293	154	626	533	94	156	288	37	1	31	105	0	4	3	86	5	151	26	5	4	.540	.391
Lansing, Mike, Col.	.276	153	638	584	73	161	240	39	2	12	66	7	3	5	39	4	88	10	3	18	.411	.325
Larkin, Andy, Fla.	.138	17	32	29	1	4	4	0	0	0	2	0	0	1	0	0	19	0	0	1	.138	.167
Larkin, Barry, Cin.	.309	145	626	538	93	166	271	34	10	17	72	4	3	2	79	5	69	26	3	12	.504	.397
Larkin, Stephen, Cin.*	.333	1	3	3	0	1	1	0	0	0	0	0	0	0	0	0	1	0	0	0	.333	.333
Lawrence, Sean, Pit.*	.000	7	6	6	0	0	0	0	0	0	0	0	0	0	0	0	4	0	0	0	.000	.000
Lee, Derrek, Fla.	.233	141	513	454	62	106	188	29	1	17	74	0	2	10	47	1	120	5	2	12	.414	.318
Lee, Travis, Ari.*	.269	146	630	562	71	151	241	20	2	22	72	0	1	0	67	5	123	8	1	13	.429	.346
Leiter, Al, N.Y.*	.105	28	69	57	1	6	9	3	0	0	4	5	0	0	7	0	32	0	0	1	.158	.203
Leiter, Mark, Phi.	.000	69	2	2	0	0	0	0	0	0	0	0	0	0	0	0	2	0	0	0	.000	.000
Leskanic, Curtis, Col.	.000	66	3	2	1	0	0	0	0	0	0	1	0	0	0	0	1	0	0	0	.000	.000
Levis, Jesse, Mil.*	.351	22	48	37	4	13	13	0	0	0	4	1	1	2	7	2	6	1	0	3	.351	.468
Lewis, Mark, Phi.	.249	142	580	518	52	129	181	21	2	9	54	3	8	3	48	2	111	3	3	17	.349	.312
Leyritz, Jim, S.D.	.266	62	172	143	17	38	60	10	0	4	18	0	1	7	21	0	40	0	0	2	.420	.384
Lieber, Jon, Pit.*	.167	29	58	48	3	8	9	1	0	0	1	7	0	0	3	0	20	0	0	0	.188	.216
Lieberthal, Mike, Phi.	.256	86	342	313	39	80	125	15	3	8	45	0	5	7	17	1	44	2	1	4	.399	.304
Lima, Jose, Hou.	.139	33	91	79	6	11	13	2	0	0	4	9	1	0	2	0	27	0	0	0	.165	.159
Liriano, Nelson, Col.†	.000	12	17	17	0	0	0	0	0	0	0	0	0	0	0	0	7	0	0	1	.000	.000
Little, Mark, St.L	.083	7	15	12	0	1	1	0	0	0	0	0	1	0	2	0	5	1	0	0	.083	.214
Livingstone, Scott, Mon.*	.209	76	118	110	1	23	29	6	0	0	12	0	3	0	5	2	15	1	1	2	.264	.237
Loaiza, Esteban, Pit.	.241	21	33	29	2	7	7	0	0	0	3	3	0	0	1	0	5	0	0	1	.241	.267
Lockhart, Keith, Atl.*	.257	109	401	366	50	94	142	21	0	9	37	2	3	1	29	0	37	2	2	2	.388	.311
LoDuca, Paul, L.A.	.286	6	14	14	2	4	5	1	0	0	1	0	0	0	0	0	1	0	0	0	.357	.286
Loewer, Carlton, Phi.	.086	21	43	35	4	3	3	0	0	0	1	5	0	0	3	0	10	0	0	1	.086	.158
Loiselle, Rich, Pit.	.000	54	1	0	0	0	0	0	0	0	0	1	0	0	0	0	0	0	0	0	.000	.000
Lombard, George, Atl.*	.333	6	6	6	2	2	5	0	0	1	1	0	0	0	0	0	1	1	0	0	.833	.333
Lopez, Javy, Atl.	.284	133	534	489	73	139	264	21	1	34	106	1	8	6	30	1	85	5	3	22	.540	.328
Lopez, Luis M., N.Y.†	.252	117	295	266	37	67	90	13	2	2	22	3	2	4	20	3	60	2	2	10	.338	.312
Loretta, Mark, Mil.	.316	140	491	434	55	137	184	29	0	6	54	4	4	7	42	1	47	9	6	14	.424	.382
Lowe, Sean, St.L	.000	4	2	2	0	0	0	0	0	0	0	0	0	0	0	0	0	0	0	0	.000	.000
Lowery, Terrell, Chi.	.200	24	18	15	2	3	4	1	0	0	1	0	0	3	0	0	7	0	0	0	.267	.333
Ludwick, Eric, Fla.	.000	13	7	7	0	0	0	0	0	0	0	0	0	0	0	0	3	0	0	0	.000	.000
Luke, Matt, L.A.*	.236	102	257	237	34	56	106	12	1	12	34	1	1	1	17	2	60	2	1	4	.447	.289
Mabry, John, St.L*	.249	142	413	377	41	94	143	22	0	9	46	3	2	1	30	6	76	0	2	6	.379	.305
Maddux, Greg, Atl.	.240	34	85	75	4	18	21	3	0	0	4	6	0	0	4	0	18	0	1	0	.280	.278
Maddux, Mike, Mon.*	.000	51	2	2	0	0	0	0	0	0	0	0	0	0	0	0	1	0	0	0	.000	.000
Magee, Wendell Jr., Phi.	.293	20	82	75	9	22	33	6	1	1	11	0	0	0	7	0	11	0	0	4	.440	.354
Magnante, Mike, Hou.*	1.000	48	2	2	0	2	2	0	0	0	1	0	0	0	0	0	0	0	0	0	1.000	1.000
Malloy, Marty, Atl.*	.179	11	30	28	3	5	9	1	0	1	1	0	0	0	2	0	2	0	0	1	.321	.233
Maloney, Sean, L.A.	.000	11	1	1	0	0	0	0	0	0	0	0	0	0	0	0	1	0	0	0	.000	.000
Mantei, Matt, Fla.	.333	42	3	3	0	1	1	0	0	0	0	0	0	0	0	0	0	0	0	0	.333	.333
Manwaring, Kirt, Col.	.247	110	335	291	30	72	96	12	3	2	26	2	1	3	38	3	49	1	5	11	.330	.339
Marrero, Eli, St.L	.244	83	284	254	28	62	94	18	1	4	20	1	1	0	28	5	42	6	2	5	.370	.318
Martin, Al, Pit.*	.239	125	479	440	57	105	160	15	2	12	47	0	2	5	32	2	91	20	3	13	.364	.296
Martinez, Sandy, Chi.*	.264	45	102	87	7	23	34	9	1	0	7	0	1	1	13	0	21	1	0	3	.391	.363
Martinez, Greg, Mil.†	.000	13	4	3	2	0	0	0	0	0	0	0	0	0	1	0	2	2	0	0	.000	.250
Martinez, Javier, Pit.	.000	37	1	1	0	0	0	0	0	0	0	0	0	0	0	0	0	0	0	0	.000	.000
Martinez, Dennis, Atl.	.091	53	13	11	0	1	2	1	0	0	3	1	0	0	1	0	7	0	0	1	.182	.167
Martinez, Manny, Pit.	.250	73	196	180	21	45	78	11	2	6	24	3	2	2	9	0	44	0	3	3	.433	.290
Martinez, Ramon E., S.F.	.316	19	24	19	4	6	7	1	0	0	0	1	0	0	4	0	2	0	0	0	.368	.435
Martinez, Ramon J., L.A.*	.176	19	39	34	3	6	9	1	1	0	1	5	0	0	0	0	16	0	0	0	.265	.176
Matheny, Mike, Mil.	.238	108	341	320	24	76	107	13	0	6	27	3	0	7	11	0	63	1	0	6	.334	.278
Maxwell, Jason, Chi.	.333	7	4	3	2	1	4	0	0	1	2	1	0	0	0	0	0	0	0	0	1.333	.333
May, Derrick, Mon.*	.239	85	192	180	13	43	66	8	0	5	15	0	1	0	11	1	24	0	0	5	.367	.281
Mayne, Brent, S.F.*	.273	94	317	275	26	75	99	15	0	3	32	2	2	1	37	3	47	2	1	8	.360	.359
McElroy, Chuck, Col.*	.200	78	6	5	0	1	1	0	0	0	0	1	0	0	0	0	3	0	0	0	.200	.200
McEwing, Joe, St.L	.200	10	23	20	5	4	5	1	0	0	1	1	0	1	1	0	3	0	1	0	.250	.273
McGee, Willie, St.L†	.253	120	286	269	27	68	89	10	1	3	34	0	3	0	14	5	49	7	2	6	.331	.287
McGuire, Ryan, Mon.*	.186	130	244	210	17	39	51	9	0	1	10	1	1	0	32	0	55	0	0	9	.243	.292
McGwire, Mark, St.L	.299	155	681	509	130	152	383	21	0	70	147	0	4	6	162	28	155	1	0	8	.752	.470
McMichael, Greg, NY-LA-NY	.000	64	1	1	0	0	0	0	0	0	0	0	0	0	0	0	0	0	0	0	.000	.000
McRae, Brian, N.Y.†	.264	159	645	552	79	146	255	36	5	21	79	3	5	5	80	3	90	20	11	5	.462	.360
Meadows, Brian, Fla.	.130	31	61	54	4	7	7	0	0	0	3	2	1	0	4	0	19	0	0	2	.130	.161
Medina, Rafael, Fla.	.053	12	25	19	1	1	1	0	0	0	0	6	0	0	0	0	6	0	0	0	.053	.053
Meluskey, Mitch, Hou.†	.250	8	9	8	1	2	3	1	0	0	0	0	0	0	1	0	4	0	0	1	.375	.333
Merced, Orlando, Chi.*	.300	12	12	10	2	3	6	0	0	1	5	0	1	0	1	0	2	0	0	2	.600	.333
Mercedes, Jose, Mil.	.091	7	12	11	0	1	1	0	0	0	0	1	0	0	0	0	6	0	0	0	.091	.167
Mercker, Kent, St.L*	.148	32	61	54	3	8	13	0	1	1	6	5	0	0	2	0	25	0	0	1	.241	.179
Mesa, Jose, S.F.	.000	32	1	0	1	0	0	0	0	0	0	1	0	0	0	0	0	0	0	0	.000	1.000

Player, Team	Avg.	G	TPA	AB	R	H	TB	2B	3B	HR	RBI	SH	SF	HP	BB	IBB	SO	SB	CS	GDP	Slg.	OBP
Metcalfe, Mike, L.A.	.000	4	1	1	0	0	0	0	0	0	0	0	0	0	0	0	1	2	0	0	.000	.000
Meulens, Hensley, Ari.	.067	7	15	15	1	1	4	0	0	1	1	0	0	0	0	0	6	0	0	0	.267	.067
Miceli, Dan, S.D.	1.000	67	1	1	0	1	1	0	0	0	0	0	0	0	0	0	0	0	0	0	1.000	1.000
Mieske, Matt, Chi.	.299	77	111	97	16	29	39	7	0	1	12	1	1	1	11	1	17	0	0	0	.402	.373
Millar, Kevin, Fla.	.500	2	3	2	1	1	1	0	0	0	0	0	0	0	0	0	0	0	0	0	.500	.667
Miller, Damian, Ari.	.286	57	183	168	17	48	75	14	2	3	14	2	0	2	11	2	43	1	0	2	.446	.337
Miller, Trever, Hou.	.333	37	3	3	1	1	2	1	0	0	0	0	0	0	0	0	0	0	0	0	.667	.333
Milliard, Ralph, N.Y.	.000	10	1	1	3	0	0	0	0	0	0	0	0	0	0	0	1	0	0	0	.000	.000
Millwood, Kevin, Atl.	.080	31	62	50	1	4	5	1	0	0	1	6	0	0	6	0	22	0	0	0	.100	.179
Mirabelli, Doug, S.F.	.235	10	19	17	2	4	9	2	0	1	4	0	0	0	2	0	6	0	0	0	.529	.316
Mlicki, Dave, N.Y.-L.A.	.100	30	64	50	4	5	6	1	0	0	0	10	0	0	4	0	15	0	0	0	.120	.167
Mondesi, Raul, L.A.	.279	148	617	580	85	162	288	26	5	30	90	0	4	3	30	4	112	16	10	8	.497	.316
Montgomery, Ray, Hou.	.400	6	5	5	2	2	2	0	0	0	0	0	0	0	0	0	0	0	0	0	.400	.400
Moore, Trey, Mon.*	.235	14	19	17	1	4	5	1	0	0	0	1	0	0	1	0	3	0	0	0	.294	.278
Morandini, Mickey, Chi.*	.296	154	669	582	93	172	224	20	4	8	53	4	2	9	72	4	84	13	1	14	.385	.380
Mordecai, Mike, Mon.	.202	73	130	119	12	24	41	4	2	3	10	2	0	0	9	0	20	1	0	2	.345	.258
Morgan, Mike, Chi.	.667	5	7	6	0	4	5	1	0	0	0	1	0	0	0	0	2	0	0	0	.833	.667
Morris, Matt, St.L.	.069	17	41	29	1	2	3	1	0	0	3	7	0	0	5	0	16	0	0	0	.103	.206
Mouton, James, S.D.	.190	55	71	63	8	12	16	2	1	0	7	0	1	0	7	1	11	4	3	3	.254	.268
Mueller, Bill, S.F.†	.294	145	622	534	93	157	211	27	0	9	59	3	5	1	79	1	83	3	3	12	.395	.383
Mulholland, Terry, Chi.	.294	70	20	17	3	5	7	2	0	0	3	1	0	0	2	0	10	0	0	0	.412	.368
Munoz, Mike, Col.*	.000	40	3	2	1	0	0	0	0	0	0	1	0	0	0	0	2	0	0	0	.000	.000
Myers, Greg, S.D.*	.246	69	189	171	19	42	64	10	0	4	20	0	1	0	17	1	36	0	1	6	.374	.312
Myers, Rodney L., Chi.	.000	12	1	1	0	0	0	0	0	0	0	0	0	0	0	0	1	0	0	0	.000	.000
Neagle, Denny, Atl.*	.175	32	76	63	2	11	12	1	0	0	3	9	0	0	4	0	12	0	0	1	.190	.224
Nen, Robb, S.F.	.000	78	3	3	0	0	0	0	0	0	0	0	0	0	0	0	2	0	0	0	.000	.000
Newfield, Marc, Mil.	.237	93	209	186	15	44	60	7	0	3	25	0	3	1	19	1	29	0	1	7	.323	.306
Nieves, Jose, Chi.	.000	2	2	1	0	0	0	0	0	0	0	0	0	1	0	0	0	0	0	0	.000	.000
Nieves, Melvin, Cin.†	.252	83	147	119	8	30	40	4	0	2	17	0	2	0	26	1	42	0	0	3	.336	.381
Nilsson, David, Mil.*	.269	102	347	309	39	83	135	14	1	12	56	2	2	1	33	1	48	2	2	12	.437	.339
Nitkowski, C.J., Hou.*	.000	43	5	4	0	0	0	0	0	0	0	1	0	0	0	0	3	0	0	0	.000	.000
Nomo, Hideo, L.A.-N.Y.	.180	29	55	50	4	9	12	0	0	1	5	4	0	0	1	0	17	0	0	0	.240	.196
Nunez, Abraham, Pit.†	.192	24	67	52	6	10	15	2	0	1	2	3	0	0	12	0	14	4	2	1	.288	.344
Nunnally, Jon, Cin.*	.207	74	213	174	29	36	66	9	0	7	20	1	3	1	34	3	38	3	4	4	.379	.335
Ojala, Kirt, Fla.*	.154	41	31	26	2	4	5	1	0	0	3	2	0	0	3	0	10	0	0	1	.192	.241
Olerud, John, N.Y.*	.354	160	665	557	91	197	307	36	4	22	93	1	7	4	96	I1	73	2	2	15	.551	.447
Oliver, Darren, St.L	.087	11	24	23	0	2	3	1	0	0	0	0	0	0	1	0	12	0	0	1	.130	.125
Olson, Gregg, Ari.	.500	64	2	2	1	1	4	0	0	1	2	0	0	0	0	1	0	0	0	0	2.000	.500
Ordaz, Luis, St.L	.203	57	169	153	9	31	36	5	0	0	8	4	0	0	12	1	18	2	0	3	.235	.261
Ordonez, Rey, N.Y.	.246	153	548	505	46	124	151	20	2	1	42	15	4	1	23	7	60	3	6	11	.299	.278
Orie, Kevin, Chi.-Fla.	.219	112	425	379	47	83	131	22	1	8	38	2	4	8	32	2	59	2	1	8	.346	.291
Ortiz, Russ, S.F.	.280	22	32	25	3	7	10	0	0	1	2	5	0	0	2	0	4	0	0	0	.400	.333
Osborne, Donovan, St.L*	.040	14	32	25	0	1	1	0	0	0	0	4	0	0	3	0	5	0	0	1	.040	.143
Osik, Keith, Pit.	.214	39	116	98	8	21	25	4	0	0	7	2	1	2	13	2	16	1	2	4	.255	.316
Osuna, Antonio, L.A.	.000	54	2	2	0	0	0	0	0	0	0	0	0	0	0	0	0	0	0	0	.000	.000
Owens, Eric, Mil.	.125	34	43	40	5	5	10	2	0	1	4	1	0	0	2	0	6	0	0	3	.250	.167
Pagnozzi, Tom, St.L	.219	51	178	160	7	35	47	9	0	1	10	3	1	0	14	0	37	0	0	4	.294	.280
Painter, Lance, St.L*	1.000	65	2	1	0	1	1	0	0	0	0	1	0	0	0	0	0	0	0	0	1.000	1.000
Pall, Donn, Fla.	.000	23	2	2	0	0	0	0	0	0	0	0	0	0	0	0	1	0	0	0	.000	.000
Paquette, Craig, N.Y.	.263	7	19	19	3	5	7	2	0	0	0	0	0	0	0	0	6	1	0	3	.368	.263
Parent, Mark, Phi.	.221	34	126	113	7	25	32	4	0	1	13	0	3	0	10	0	30	1	1	1	.283	.278
Park, Chan Ho, L.A.	.194	34	80	72	2	14	18	2	1	0	3	6	0	0	2	0	30	0	0	0	.250	.216
Parris, Steve, Cin.	.138	18	32	29	0	4	4	0	0	0	3	3	0	0	0	0	9	0	0	0	.138	.138
Patrick, Bronswell, Mil.	.200	32	18	15	1	3	6	0	0	1	1	1	0	0	2	0	3	0	0	0	.400	.294
Patterson, Bob, Chi.	.000	33	1	0	0	0	0	0	0	0	0	1	0	0	0	0	0	0	0	0	.000	.000
Pavano, Carl, Mon.	.158	24	44	38	1	6	7	1	0	0	3	6	0	0	0	0	14	0	0	0	.184	.158
Payton, Jay, N.Y.	.318	15	23	22	2	7	8	1	0	0	0	0	0	0	1	0	4	0	0	0	.364	.348
Pena, Angel, L.A.	.231	6	13	13	1	3	3	0	0	0	0	0	0	0	0	0	6	0	0	0	.231	.231
Perez, Carlos, Mon.-L.A.*	.155	34	89	71	5	11	16	2	0	1	3	14	0	0	4	0	32	0	0	0	.225	.200
Perez, Eddie, Atl.	.336	61	167	149	18	50	80	12	0	6	32	1	0	2	15	0	28	1	1	3	.537	.404
Perez, Eduardo, Cin.	.238	84	198	172	20	41	57	4	0	4	30	1	2	2	21	2	45	0	1	2	.331	.325
Perez, Neifi, Col.†	.274	162	712	647	80	177	247	25	9	9	59	22	4	1	38	0	70	5	6	8	.382	.313
Perez, Robert, Mon.	.236	52	110	106	9	25	29	1	0	1	8	0	1	1	2	0	23	0	0	4	.274	.255
Perez, Yorkis, Phi.†	.000	57	2	2	0	0	0	0	0	0	0	0	0	0	0	0	1	0	0	0	.000	.000
Petagine, Roberto, Cin.*	.258	34	79	62	14	16	29	2	1	3	7	0	1	0	16	0	11	1	0	1	.468	.405
Peters, Chris, Pit.*	.231	39	44	39	2	9	9	0	0	0	2	4	0	0	1	0	9	1	0	0	.231	.250
Petkovsek, Mark, St.L	.318	48	25	22	5	7	8	1	0	0	1	2	0	0	1	0	2	0	0	0	.364	.348
Phillips, J.R., Hou.*	.190	36	65	58	4	11	17	0	0	2	9	0	0	0	7	1	22	0	0	1	.293	.277
Phillips, Tony, N.Y.†	.223	52	229	188	25	42	62	11	0	3	14	1	2	0	38	0	44	1	1	1	.330	.351
Piazza, Mike, L.A.-Fla.-N.Y.	.328	151	626	561	88	184	320	38	1	32	111	0	5	2	58	14	80	1	0	15	.570	.390
Pisciotta, Marc, Chi.	.333	43	3	3	0	1	1	0	0	0	0	0	0	0	0	0	0	0	0	0	.333	.333
Plunk, Eric, Mil.	.000	26	2	1	0	0	0	0	0	0	0	0	0	0	1	0	1	0	0	0	.000	.500
Polanco, Placido, St.L	.254	45	122	114	10	29	39	3	2	1	11	2	0	1	5	0	9	2	0	1	.342	.292
Polcovich, Kevin, Pit.	.189	81	238	212	18	40	52	12	0	0	14	3	3	5	15	2	33	4	3	7	.245	.255
Politte, Cliff, St.L	.071	8	16	14	0	1	1	0	0	0	0	0	0	1	0	0	8	0	0	1	.071	.133
Poole, Jim, S.F.*	.250	26	6	4	1	1	2	1	0	0	0	2	0	0	0	0	0	0	0	0	.500	.250
Portugal, Mark, Phi.	.260	26	58	50	6	13	18	5	0	0	4	4	0	0	4	0	10	0	0	2	.360	.315
Powell, Jay, Fla.-Hou.	.000	62	1	1	0	0	0	0	0	0	0	0	0	0	0	0	0	0	0	0	.000	.000
Powell, Jeremy, Mon.	.000	7	6	6	0	0	0	0	0	0	0	0	0	0	0	0	3	0	0	0	.000	.000
Powell, Dante, S.F.	.500	8	7	4	2	2	5	0	0	1	1	0	0	0	3	0	0	0	0	0	1.250	.714
Pratt, Todd, N.Y.	.275	41	71	69	9	19	36	9	1	2	18	0	0	0	2	0	20	0	0	0	.522	.296
Pride, Curtis, Atl.*	.252	70	121	107	19	27	44	6	1	3	9	1	1	3	9	0	29	4	0	2	.411	.325

Player, Team	Avg.	G	TPA	AB	R	H	TB	2B	3B	HR	RBI	SH	SF	HP	BB	IBB	SO	SB	CS	GDP	Slg.	OBP
Priest, Eddie, Cin.	.000	2	2	2	0	0	0	0	0	0	0	0	0	0	0	0	2	0	0	0	.000	.000
Prince, Tom, L.A.	.185	37	92	81	7	15	22	5	1	0	5	2	0	2	7	1	24	0	0	0	.272	.267
Pulsipher, Bill, N.Y.-Mil.*	.150	27	21	20	2	3	3	0	0	0	0	1	0	0	0	0	6	0	0	0	.150	.150
Raggio, Brady, St.L.	.000	4	1	1	0	0	0	0	0	0	0	0	0	0	0	0	0	0	0	0	.000	.000
Ramirez, Aramis, Pit.	.235	72	275	251	23	59	88	9	1	6	24	1	1	4	18	0	72	0	1	3	.351	.296
Rath, Fred, Col.	.000	2	2	2	0	0	0	0	0	0	0	0	0	0	0	0	1	0	0	0	.000	.000
Redmond, Mike, Fla.	.331	37	129	118	10	39	54	9	0	2	12	4	0	2	5	2	16	0	0	6	.458	.368
Reed, Jeff, Col.*	.290	113	303	259	43	75	121	17	1	9	39	3	3	1	37	4	57	0	0	6	.467	.377
Reed, Rick, N.Y.	.125	31	79	64	6	8	11	0	0	1	5	12	0	0	3	0	21	0	0	0	.172	.164
Reed, Steve, S.F.	.333	50	3	3	0	1	1	0	0	0	0	0	0	0	0	0	0	0	0	0	.333	.333
Reese, Pokey, Cin.	.256	59	151	133	20	34	43	2	2	1	16	2	2	0	14	1	28	3	2	3	.323	.322
Relaford, Desi, Phi.†	.245	142	546	494	45	121	167	25	3	5	41	10	6	3	33	4	87	9	5	9	.338	.293
Remlinger, Mike, Cin.*	.106	35	56	47	1	5	6	1	0	0	1	7	0	0	2	0	7	0	1	2	.128	.143
Renteria, Edgar, Fla.	.282	133	580	517	79	146	177	18	2	3	31	9	2	4	48	1	78	41	22	13	.342	.347
Reyes, Carlos, S.D.†	.000	22	1	0	0	0	0	0	0	0	0	1	0	0	0	0	0	0	0	0	.000	.000
Reyes, Dennis, L.A.-Cin.	.059	19	18	17	1	1	2	1	0	0	0	1	0	0	0	0	5	0	0	0	.118	.059
Reyes, Al, Mil.	.200	50	5	5	1	1	1	0	0	0	0	0	0	0	0	0	4	0	0	0	.200	.200
Reynolds, Shane, Hou.	.159	35	92	82	10	13	17	4	0	0	9	7	0	1	2	0	39	0	0	0	.207	.188
Reynoso, Armando, N.Y.	.167	11	31	30	2	5	7	2	0	0	0	1	0	0	0	0	15	0	0	0	.233	.167
Rincon, Ricardo, Pit.*	.000	60	2	2	0	0	0	0	0	0	0	0	0	0	0	0	1	0	0	1	.000	.000
Rios, Armando, S.F.*	.571	12	10	7	3	4	10	0	0	2	3	0	0	0	3	0	2	0	0	0	1.429	.700
Ritz, Kevin, Col.	.333	2	3	3	0	1	1	0	0	0	0	0	0	0	0	0	1	0	0	0	.333	.333
Rivera, Ruben, S.D.	.209	95	204	172	31	36	65	7	2	6	29	1	1	2	28	0	52	5	1	1	.378	.325
Robertson, Mike, Ari.*	.154	11	13	13	0	2	2	0	0	0	0	0	0	0	0	0	2	0	0	0	.154	.154
Rodriguez, Henry, Chi.*	.251	128	473	415	56	104	220	21	1	31	85	0	4	0	54	7	113	1	3	6	.530	.334
Rodriguez, Rich, S.F.*	.167	68	7	6	0	1	1	0	0	0	0	1	0	0	0	0	4	0	0	0	.167	.167
Rolen, Scott, Phi.	.290	160	711	601	120	174	320	45	4	31	110	0	6	11	93	6	141	14	7	10	.532	.391
Romero, Mandy, S.D.†	.000	6	10	9	1	0	0	0	0	0	0	0	0	1	0	0	3	0	0	0	.000	.100
Roque, Rafael, Mil.*	.077	9	17	13	0	1	1	0	0	0	1	4	0	0	0	0	6	0	0	0	.077	.077
Roskos, John, Fla.	.100	10	10	10	1	1	1	0	0	0	0	0	0	0	0	0	5	0	0	0	.100	.100
Rueter, Kirk, S.F.*	.209	34	76	67	7	14	15	1	0	0	3	9	0	0	0	0	12	0	1	1	.224	.209
Ryan, Ken, Phi.	.000	17	1	1	0	0	0	0	0	0	0	0	0	0	0	0	0	0	0	0	.000	.000
Saipe, Mike, Col.	.000	2	2	1	0	0	0	0	0	0	0	0	0	0	1	0	0	0	0	0	.000	.500
Sanchez, Jesus, Fla.*	.135	37	57	52	2	7	9	0	1	0	1	4	0	0	1	0	15	0	0	0	.173	.151
Sanchez, Rey, S.F.	.285	109	339	316	44	90	114	14	2	2	30	1	2	4	16	0	47	0	0	11	.361	.325
Sanders, Reggie, Cin.	.268	135	545	481	83	129	201	18	6	14	59	4	2	7	51	2	137	20	9	10	.418	.346
Sanders, Scott, S.D.	.000	23	1	0	0	0	0	0	0	0	0	1	0	0	0	0	0	0	0	0	.000	.000
Sanford, Chance, Pit.*	.143	14	29	28	3	4	7	1	1	0	3	0	0	0	1	0	6	0	0	1	.250	.172
Santangelo, F.P., Mon.†	.214	122	462	383	53	82	112	18	0	4	23	11	1	23	44	1	72	7	3	5	.292	.330
Schilling, Curt, Phi.	.132	35	91	76	3	10	12	2	0	0	3	12	0	0	3	0	26	0	0	0	.158	.165
Schmidt, Jason, Pit.	.097	33	77	62	1	6	8	2	0	0	2	12	1	0	2	0	25	0	0	1	.129	.123
Schourek, Pete, Hou.*	.211	15	24	19	2	4	5	1	0	0	2	5	0	0	0	0	6	1	0	0	.263	.211
Seanez, Rudy, Atl.	.000	34	1	1	0	0	0	0	0	0	0	0	0	0	0	0	1	0	0	0	.000	.000
Sefcik, Kevin, Phi.	.314	109	205	169	27	53	73	7	2	3	20	3	1	7	25	0	32	4	2	3	.432	.421
Seguignol, Fernando, Mon.†	.262	16	46	42	6	11	21	4	0	2	3	0	1	0	3	0	15	0	0	1	.500	.304
Servais, Scott, Chi.	.222	113	360	325	35	72	110	15	1	7	36	3	1	5	26	6	51	1	0	12	.338	.289
Shaw, Jeff, Cin.-L.A.	.000	73	3	2	0	0	0	0	0	0	0	1	0	0	0	0	2	0	0	0	.000	.000
Sheets, Andy, S.D.	.242	88	219	194	31	47	79	5	3	7	29	2	1	1	21	3	62	7	2	4	.407	.318
Sheffield, Gary, Fla.-L.A.	.302	130	549	437	73	132	229	27	2	22	85	0	9	8	95	12	46	22	7	7	.524	.428
Shumpert, Terry, Col.	.231	23	28	26	3	6	10	1	0	1	2	0	0	2	0	0	8	0	0	0	.385	.286
Silva, Jose, Pit.	.037	18	35	27	0	1	2	1	0	0	0	5	0	1	2	0	10	0	0	1	.074	.133
Simon, Randall, Atl.*	.188	7	17	16	2	3	3	0	0	0	4	0	1	0	0	0	1	0	0	0	.188	.176
Smith, Mark, Pit.	.195	59	144	128	18	25	37	6	0	2	13	0	3	3	10	0	26	7	0	1	.289	.264
Smith, Pete, S.D.	.071	11	17	14	1	1	1	0	0	0	1	1	0	0	2	0	6	0	0	0	.071	.188
Smith, Travis, Mil.	.000	1	1	1	0	0	0	0	0	0	0	0	0	0	0	0	0	0	0	0	.000	.000
Smoltz, John, Atl.	.196	26	68	51	4	10	11	1	0	0	5	8	0	1	8	0	16	0	0	1	.216	.317
Snow, J.T., S.F.†	.248	138	500	435	65	108	184	29	1	15	79	0	7	0	58	3	84	1	2	12	.423	.332
Sodowsky, Clint, Ari.†	.300	46	11	10	2	3	4	1	0	0	1	0	0	1	0	0	2	0	0	1	.400	.300
Sosa, Sammy, Chi.	.308	159	722	643	134	198	416	20	0	66	158	0	5	1	73	14	171	18	9	20	.647	.377
Spehr, Tim, N.Y.	.137	21	60	51	3	7	8	1	0	0	3	0	0	2	7	1	16	1	0	0	.157	.267
Spencer, Stan, S.D.	.111	6	12	9	0	1	2	1	0	0	0	3	0	0	0	0	4	0	0	1	.222	.111
Spiers, Bill, Hou.*	.273	123	437	384	66	105	152	27	4	4	43	1	2	5	45	0	62	11	2	9	.396	.356
Spradlin, Jerry, Phi.†	1.000	69	1	1	0	1	2	1	0	0	0	0	0	0	0	0	0	0	0	0	2.000	1.000
Springer, Russ, Ari.-Atl.	.000	48	1	1	0	0	0	0	0	0	0	0	0	0	0	0	0	0	0	0	.000	.000
Stanifer, Rob, Fla.	.000	38	5	5	0	0	0	0	0	0	0	0	0	0	0	0	3	0	0	0	.000	.000
Stankiewicz, Andy, Ari.	.207	77	155	145	9	30	35	5	0	0	8	0	1	2	7	0	33	1	0	3	.241	.252
Stephenson, Garrett, Phi.	.167	6	8	6	0	1	1	0	0	0	0	1	0	0	1	0	0	0	0	1	.167	.286
Stevens, Dave, Chi.	.250	31	4	4	0	1	1	0	0	0	0	0	0	0	0	0	2	0	0	0	.250	.250
Stinnett, Kelly, Ari.	.259	92	318	274	35	71	120	14	1	11	34	1	2	6	35	3	74	0	1	9	.438	.353
Stottlemyre, Todd, St.L.*	.226	23	62	53	3	12	12	0	0	0	1	5	0	0	4	0	24	0	0	1	.226	.281
Stovall, DaRond, Mon.†	.205	62	84	78	11	16	26	2	1	2	6	0	0	0	6	0	29	1	0	1	.333	.262
Strange, Doug, Pit.†	.173	90	201	185	9	32	40	8	0	0	14	3	2	1	10	1	39	1	0	5	.216	.217
Strittmatter, Mark, Col.	.000	4	4	4	0	0	0	0	0	0	0	0	0	0	0	0	3	0	0	0	.000	.000
Stynes, Chris, Cin.	.254	123	388	347	52	88	118	10	1	6	27	4	1	4	32	1	36	15	1	5	.340	.323
Sullivan, Scott, Cin.	.091	67	12	11	0	1	1	0	0	0	0	0	0	0	0	0	6	0	0	0	.091	.091
Suppan, Jeff, Ari.	.273	13	24	22	1	6	6	0	0	0	1	1	0	1	0	0	6	0	0	0	.273	.304
Sweeney, Mark, S.D.*	.234	122	222	192	17	45	65	8	3	2	15	0	3	1	26	0	37	1	2	5	.339	.324
Tabaka, Jeff, Pit.	.000	37	1	0	0	0	0	0	0	0	0	0	0	0	0	0	1	0	0	0	.000	.000
Tam, Jeff, N.Y.	.000	15	1	1	0	0	0	0	0	0	0	0	0	0	0	0	0	0	0	0	.000	.000
Tapani, Kevin, Chi.	.133	35	88	75	7	10	15	2	0	1	11	5	1	0	7	0	30	0	0	2	.200	.205
Tarasco, Tony, Cin.*	.208	15	28	24	5	5	10	2	0	1	4	1	0	0	3	0	5	0	0	0	.417	.296
Tatis, Fernando, St.L.	.287	55	229	202	28	58	102	16	2	8	26	0	1	2	24	1	57	7	3	6	.505	.296

Player, Team	Avg.	G	TPA	AB	R	H	TB	2B	3B	HR	RBI	SH	SF	HP	BB	IBB	SO	SB	CS	GDP	Slg.	OBP
Tatum, Jim, N.Y.	.180	35	57	50	4	9	20	1	2	2	13	0	4	0	3	0	19	0	0	0	.400	.211
Taubensee, Eddie, Cin.*	.278	130	491	431	61	120	180	27	0	11	72	2	6	0	52	6	93	1	0	4	.418	.352
Tavarez, Julian, S.F.*	.111	60	10	9	0	1	1	0	0	0	0	1	0	0	0	0	4	0	0	0	.111	.111
Telemaco, Amaury, Chi.-Ari.	.086	41	38	35	2	3	6	1	1	0	2	1	1	0	1	0	16	0	0	2	.171	.108
Telford, Anthony, Mon.	.250	77	4	4	0	1	1	0	0	0	1	0	0	0	0	0	0	0	0	0	.250	.250
Thompson, Mark, Col.	.143	6	7	7	1	1	1	0	0	0	0	0	0	0	0	0	3	0	0	0	.143	.143
Thomson, John, Col.	.120	26	63	50	4	6	6	0	0	0	2	9	2	0	2	0	23	0	1	1	.120	.148
Thurman, Mike, Mon.	.000	14	27	23	1	0	0	0	0	0	0	2	0	0	2	0	17	0	0	0	.000	.080
Tomko, Brett, Cin.	.108	36	79	65	4	7	8	1	0	0	3	9	1	0	4	0	29	0	0	0	.123	.157
Trachsel, Steve, Chi.	.266	33	80	64	11	17	23	3	0	1	8	9	0	0	7	0	18	0	0	1	.359	.338
Tucker, Michael, Atl.*	.244	130	469	414	54	101	173	27	3	13	46	1	2	3	49	10	112	8	3	4	.418	.327
Urbina, Ugueth, Mon.	.000	64	6	6	0	0	0	0	0	0	0	0	0	0	0	0	3	0	0	0	.000	.000
Valdes, Ismael, L.A.	.167	27	59	48	3	8	9	1	0	0	2	8	0	0	3	0	6	0	0	0	.188	.216
Valdes, Marc, Mon.	.400	20	6	5	1	2	2	0	0	0	0	0	0	1	0	0	2	0	0	0	.400	.500
Valdes, Pedro, Chi.*	.217	14	24	23	1	5	8	1	1	0	2	0	0	0	1	0	3	0	1	1	.348	.250
Valentin, Jose, Mil.†	.224	151	497	428	65	96	168	24	0	16	49	2	3	1	63	8	105	10	7	2	.393	.323
Vander Wal, John, Col.-S.D.* .	.279	109	152	129	21	36	66	13	1	5	20	0	1	0	22	0	34	0	0	2	.512	.382
Van Poppel, Todd, Pit.	.250	18	14	12	2	3	4	1	0	0	1	1	0	0	1	0	4	0	0	0	.333	.308
VanRyn, Ben, Chi.-S.D.*	.000	15	1	1	0	0	0	0	0	0	0	0	0	0	0	0	0	0	0	0	.000	.000
Vaughn, Greg, S.D.	.272	158	661	573	112	156	342	28	4	50	119	0	4	5	79	6	121	11	4	7	.597	.363
Vazquez, Javier, Mon.	.173	33	61	52	3	9	13	2	1	0	5	6	1	0	2	0	7	0	0	1	.250	.200
Veras, Quilvio, S.D.†	.267	138	612	517	79	138	184	24	2	6	45	1	4	6	84	2	78	24	9	6	.356	.373
Veres, Dave, Col.	.333	63	3	3	0	1	1	0	0	0	0	0	0	0	0	0	1	0	0	0	.333	.333
Vidro, Jose, Mon.	.220	83	245	205	24	45	57	12	0	0	18	6	3	4	27	0	33	2	2	5	.278	.318
Vina, Fernando, Mil.*	.311	159	722	637	101	198	272	39	7	7	45	5	1	25	54	2	46	22	16	7	.427	.386
Vizcaino, Jose, L.A.†	.262	67	267	237	30	62	80	9	0	3	29	10	2	1	17	0	35	7	3	4	.338	.311
Wagner, Paul, Mil.	.158	13	20	19	1	3	3	0	0	0	0	1	0	0	0	0	2	0	0	1	.158	.158
Wagner, Billy, Hou.*	.333	58	3	3	0	1	1	0	0	0	0	0	0	0	0	0	2	0	0	0	.333	.333
Wainhouse, David, Col.*	.000	10	1	1	0	0	0	0	0	0	0	0	0	0	0	0	0	0	0	0	.000	.000
Walker, Larry, Col.*	.363	130	524	454	113	165	286	46	3	23	67	0	2	4	64	2	61	14	4	11	.630	.445
Wall, Donne, S.D.	.286	46	7	7	0	2	2	0	0	0	0	0	0	0	0	0	3	0	0	0	.286	.286
Ward, Daryle, Hou.*	.333	4	4	3	1	1	1	0	0	0	0	0	0	1	0	0	2	0	0	0	.333	.500
Ward, Turner, Pit.†	.262	123	324	282	33	74	120	13	3	9	46	4	7	4	27	1	40	5	4	4	.426	.328
Watkins, Pat, Cin.	.265	83	162	147	11	39	55	8	1	2	15	2	4	1	8	0	26	1	3	3	.374	.300
Weathers, David, Cin.-Mil.	.087	44	29	23	2	2	5	0	0	1	1	4	0	0	2	0	14	0	0	0	.217	.160
Weaver, Eric, L.A.	.000	7	1	1	0	0	0	0	0	0	0	0	0	0	0	0	1	0	0	0	.000	.000
Wehner, John, Fla.	.227	53	96	88	10	20	22	2	0	0	5	0	1	0	7	0	12	1	0	3	.250	.281
Weiss, Walt, Atl.†	.280	96	424	347	64	97	119	18	2	0	27	12	3	3	59	0	53	7	1	4	.343	.386
Welch, Mike, Phi.*	.000	10	3	3	0	0	0	0	0	0	0	0	0	0	0	0	2	0	0	0	.000	.000
Wendell, Turk, N.Y.*	.000	66	4	4	0	0	0	0	0	0	0	0	0	0	0	0	2	0	0	0	.000	.000
Wengert, Don, S.D.-Chi.	.000	33	18	16	0	0	0	0	0	0	0	1	0	0	1	0	3	0	0	0	.000	.059
White, Derrick, Chi.-Col.	.053	20	19	19	1	1	4	0	0	1	2	0	0	0	0	0	9	0	0	1	.211	.053
White, Devon, Ari.†	.279	146	627	563	84	157	257	32	1	22	85	7	6	9	42	4	102	22	8	9	.456	.335
White, Gabe, Cin.*	.167	69	10	6	0	1	1	0	0	0	0	4	0	0	0	0	3	0	0	0	.167	.167
White, Rondell, Mon.	.300	97	397	357	54	107	183	21	2	17	58	0	3	7	30	2	57	16	7	7	.513	.363
Whiteside, Matt, Phi.	.000	10	2	2	0	0	0	0	0	0	0	0	0	0	0	0	2	0	0	0	.000	.000
Wickman, Bob, Mil.	.000	72	1	1	0	0	0	0	0	0	0	0	0	0	0	0	0	0	0	0	.000	.000
Widger, Chris, Mon.	.233	125	448	417	36	97	162	18	1	15	53	0	2	0	29	2	85	6	1	5	.388	.281
Wilkins, Rick, N.Y.*	.133	5	17	15	3	2	2	0	0	0	1	0	0	0	2	0	2	0	0	0	.133	.235
Williams, Eddie, S.D.	.143	17	31	28	1	4	4	0	0	0	3	0	1	0	2	0	6	0	0	1	.143	.194
Williams, Gerald, Atl.	.305	129	289	266	46	81	134	19	2	10	44	2	1	3	17	1	48	11	5	5	.504	.352
Williams, Matt, Ari.	.267	135	557	510	72	136	224	26	1	20	71	0	1	3	43	8	102	5	1	19	.439	.327
Williams, Mike, Pit.	.000	37	5	3	0	0	0	0	0	0	0	2	0	0	0	0	2	0	0	0	.000	.000
Williams, Todd, Cin.	.000	6	2	2	0	0	0	0	0	0	0	0	0	0	0	0	2	0	0	0	.000	.000
Wilson, Preston, N.Y.-Fla.	.157	22	60	51	7	8	13	2	0	1	3	2	0	1	6	0	21	1	1	0	.255	.259
Winchester, Scott, Cin.	.130	16	26	23	0	3	3	0	0	0	1	2	0	1	0	0	9	0	0	1	.130	.167
Winston, Darrin, Phi.	.000	27	1	1	0	0	0	0	0	0	0	0	0	0	0	0	0	0	0	0	.000	.000
Witt, Bobby, St.L	.200	17	12	10	0	2	3	1	0	0	1	1	0	0	1	0	5	0	0	0	.300	.273
Wolcott, Bob, Ari.	.222	6	9	9	1	2	2	0	0	0	0	0	0	0	0	0	1	0	0	0	.222	.222
Womack, Tony, Pit.*	.282	159	704	655	85	185	234	26	7	3	45	6	5	0	38	1	94	58	6	4	.357	.319
Wood, Kerry, Chi.	.130	26	63	54	3	7	13	0	0	2	8	8	0	0	1	0	16	0	0	0	.241	.145
Woodall, Brad, Mil.†	.237	37	47	38	7	9	13	1	0	1	2	5	0	0	4	0	10	0	0	1	.342	.310
Woodard, Steve, Mil.*	.140	34	52	50	1	7	9	2	0	0	4	2	0	0	0	0	12	0	0	1	.180	.140
Wright, Jamey, Col.	.175	34	68	57	5	10	17	2	1	1	4	8	0	0	3	0	29	0	0	1	.298	.217
Yoshii, Masato, N.Y.	.063	29	59	48	3	3	4	1	0	0	3	8	0	0	3	0	27	0	0	0	.083	.118
Young, Dmitri, Cin.†	.310	144	590	536	81	166	258	48	1	14	83	0	5	2	47	4	94	2	4	16	.481	.364
Young, Eric, L.A.	.285	117	513	452	78	129	179	24	1	8	43	9	2	5	45	0	32	42	13	4	.396	.355
Young, Kevin, Pit.	.270	159	656	592	88	160	285	40	2	27	108	0	9	11	44	1	127	15	7	20	.481	.328
Zaun, Gregg, Fla.†	.188	106	338	298	19	56	87	12	2	5	29	2	2	1	35	2	52	5	2	7	.292	.274
Zeile, Todd, L.A.-Fla.	.276	106	440	392	59	108	169	18	2	13	66	0	4	3	41	2	58	3	4	9	.431	.345
Zuber, Jon, Phi.*	.244	38	52	45	6	11	22	3	1	2	6	0	0	1	6	0	9	0	0	1	.489	.346

AWARDED FIRST BASE ON OBSTRUCTION OR CATCHER'S INTERFERENCE—Becker, New York 2 (Reed, Lampkin); Bonilla, L.A.-Fla. (Parent); Caminiti, San Diego (Houston); Counsell, Florida (Estalella); Gomez, San Diego (Manwaring); Houston, Chicago (Lampkin); Klesko, Atlanta (Marrero); M. Martinez, Pittsburgh (Taubensee); Millwood, Atlanta (Pratt); Santangelo, Montreal (Lampkin); Stynes, Cincinnati (Matheny); Young, Pittsburgh (Castillo).

PLAYERS WITH TWO OR MORE TEAMS

Player, Team	Avg.	G	TPA	AB	R	H	TB	2B	3B	HR	RBI	SH	SF	HP	BB	IBB	SO	SB	CS	GDP	Slg.	OBP
Allensworth, Jermaine, Pit.	.309	69	261	233	30	72	100	13	3	3	24	3	1	7	17	0	43	8	4	1	.429	.372
Allensworth, Jermaine, N.Y. .	.204	34	57	54	9	11	19	2	0	2	4	0	0	1	2	0	16	0	2	0	.352	.246

Player, Team	Avg.	G	TPA	AB	R	H	TB	2B	3B	HR	RBI	SH	SF	HP	BB	IBB	SO	SB	CS	GDP	Slg.	OBP
Blair, Willie, Ari.	.083	23	53	48	3	4	4	0	0	0	0	4	0	0	1	0	26	0	0	0	.083	.102
Blair, Willie, N.Y.	.250	11	6	4	0	1	1	0	0	0	0	0	0	0	2	0	1	0	0	0	.250	.500
Bohanon, Brian, N.Y.*	.429	25	14	14	1	6	7	1	0	0	3	0	0	0	0	0	4	0	0	0	.500	.429
Bohanon, Brian, L.A.*	.207	14	35	29	0	6	9	1	1	0	2	4	0	0	2	0	9	0	0	2	.310	.258
Bonilla, Bobby, Fla.†	.278	28	110	97	11	27	44	5	0	4	15	0	1	0	12	1	22	0	1	6	.454	.355
Bonilla, Bobby, L.A.†	.237	72	270	236	28	56	85	6	1	7	30	0	5	0	29	3	37	1	1	10	.360	.315
Bruske, Jim, L.A.	.000	35	3	3	0	0	0	0	0	0	0	0	0	0	0	0	1	0	0	0	.000	.000
Bruske, Jim, S.D.	.000	4	0	0	0	0	0	0	0	0	0	0	0	0	0	0	0	0	0	0	.000	.000
Burks, Ellis, Col.	.286	100	405	357	54	102	182	22	5	16	54	2	5	2	39	0	80	3	7	10	.510	.355
Burks, Ellis, S.F.	.306	42	177	147	22	45	68	6	1	5	22	4	4	3	19	1	31	8	1	2	.463	.387
Byrd, Paul, Atl.	.000	1	0	0	0	0	0	0	0	0	0	0	0	0	0	0	0	0	0	0	.000	.000
Byrd, Paul, Phi.	.167	8	20	18	1	3	3	0	0	0	1	0	0	1	1	0	7	0	0	0	.167	.250
Chouinard, Bobby, Mil.	.000	1	0	0	0	0	0	0	0	0	0	0	0	0	0	0	0	0	0	0	.000	.000
Chouinard, Bobby, Ari.	.000	26	2	2	0	0	0	0	0	0	0	0	0	0	0	0	1	0	0	1	.000	.000
Clontz, Brad, L.A.	.000	18	2	2	0	0	0	0	0	0	0	0	0	0	0	0	1	0	0	0	.000	.000
Clontz, Brad, N.Y.	.000	2	0	0	0	0	0	0	0	0	0	0	0	0	0	0	0	0	0	0	.000	.000
Colbrunn, Greg, Col.	.311	62	131	122	12	38	56	8	2	2	13	0	0	1	8	0	23	3	3	1	.459	.359
Colbrunn, Greg, Ari.	.295	28	49	44	6	13	19	3	0	1	10	0	0	3	2	0	11	1	0	0	.432	.367
Edmondson, Brian, Atl.	.000	10	2	2	0	0	0	0	0	0	0	0	0	0	0	0	0	0	0	0	.000	.000
Edmondson, Brian, Fla.	.000	43	11	10	0	0	0	0	0	0	0	1	0	0	0	0	5	0	0	0	.000	.000
Eisenreich, Jim, Fla.*	.250	30	68	64	9	16	20	1	0	1	7	0	0	0	4	1	14	2	0	1	.313	.294
Eisenreich, Jim, L.A.*	.197	75	140	127	12	25	31	2	2	0	6	1	0	0	12	1	22	4	0	2	.244	.266
Embree, Alan, Atl.*	.000	20	1	1	0	0	0	0	0	0	0	0	0	0	0	0	1	0	0	0	.000	.000
Embree, Alan, Ari.*	.000	35	1	0	0	0	0	0	0	0	0	0	0	0	1	0	0	0	0	0	.000	1.000
Fabregas, Jorge, Ari.*	.199	50	167	151	8	30	37	4	0	1	15	0	2	1	13	1	26	0	0	3	.245	.263
Fabregas, Jorge, N.Y.*	.188	20	34	32	3	6	9	0	0	1	5	1	0	0	1	0	6	0	0	1	.281	.212
Gaetti, Gary, St.L.	.265	91	345	306	39	81	139	23	1	11	43	0	3	5	31	1	39	1	1	10	.454	.339
Gaetti, Gary, Chi.	.320	37	147	128	21	41	76	11	0	8	27	1	1	5	12	1	23	0	0	2	.594	.397
Gilbert, Shawn, N.Y.	.000	3	3	3	1	0	0	0	0	0	0	0	0	0	0	0	1	0	0	0	.000	.000
Gilbert, Shawn, St.L	.500	4	2	2	0	1	1	0	0	0	0	0	0	0	0	0	1	0	0	0	.500	.500
Gilkey, Bernard, N.Y.	.227	82	305	264	33	60	87	15	0	4	28	2	3	4	32	1	66	5	1	6	.330	.317
Gilkey, Bernard, Ari.	.248	29	114	101	8	25	28	0	0	1	5	1	0	1	11	0	14	4	2	5	.277	.327
Grudzielanek, Mark, Mon.	.275	105	435	396	51	109	150	15	1	8	41	5	4	9	21	1	50	11	5	11	.379	.323
Grudzielanek, Mark, L.A.	.264	51	206	193	11	51	63	6	0	2	21	3	3	2	5	1	23	7	0	7	.326	.286
Guerrero, Wilton, L.A.†	.283	64	190	180	21	51	61	4	3	0	7	3	2	1	4	0	33	5	2	3	.339	.299
Guerrero, Wilton, Mon.†	.284	52	236	222	29	63	91	10	6	2	20	3	1	0	10	0	30	3	0	1	.410	.313
Hamilton, Darryl, S.F.*	.294	97	436	367	65	108	134	19	2	1	26	6	2	2	59	0	53	9	8	6	.365	.393
Hamilton, Darryl, Col.*	.335	51	225	194	30	65	91	9	1	5	25	6	1	1	23	1	20	4	1	0	.469	.406
Harris, Lenny, Cin.*	.295	57	133	122	12	36	44	8	0	0	10	0	2	1	8	2	9	1	3	8	.361	.338
Harris, Lenny, N.Y.*	.232	75	184	168	18	39	64	7	0	6	17	4	2	1	9	1	12	5	2	5	.381	.272
Heredia, Felix, Fla.*	.000	41	3	3	0	0	0	0	0	0	0	0	0	0	0	0	1	0	0	0	.000	.000
Heredia, Felix, Chi.*	.000	30	0	0	0	0	0	0	0	0	0	0	0	0	0	0	0	0	0	0	.000	.000
Holbert, Ray, Atl.	.133	8	18	15	2	2	2	0	0	0	1	0	1	0	2	0	4	0	0	0	.133	.222
Holbert, Ray, Mon.	.000	2	5	5	0	0	0	0	0	0	0	0	0	0	0	0	1	0	0	0	.000	.000
Hollins, Damon, Atl.	.167	3	6	6	0	1	1	0	0	0	0	0	0	0	0	0	1	0	0	0	.167	.167
Hollins, Damon, L.A.	.222	5	9	9	1	2	2	0	0	0	2	0	0	0	0	0	2	0	1	0	.222	.222
Hudek, John, N.Y.†	.000	28	0	0	0	0	0	0	0	0	0	0	0	0	0	0	0	0	0	0	.000	.000
Hudek, John, Cin.†	.000	30	4	3	0	0	0	0	0	0	0	1	0	0	0	0	0	0	0	0	.000	.000
Johnson, Charles, Fla.	.221	31	130	113	13	25	51	5	0	7	23	0	1	0	16	0	30	0	1	3	.451	.315
Johnson, Charles, L.A.	.217	102	376	346	31	75	124	13	0	12	35	0	0	1	29	1	99	0	1	9	.358	.279
Jones, Chris, Ari.	.194	20	34	31	3	6	7	1	0	0	3	0	0	0	3	0	9	0	0	2	.226	.265
Jones, Chris, S.F.	.189	43	100	90	14	17	27	2	1	2	10	0	2	0	8	0	28	2	1	0	.300	.250
Konerko, Paul, L.A.	.215	49	158	144	14	31	44	1	0	4	16	0	2	2	10	0	30	0	1	5	.306	.272
Konerko, Paul, Cin.	.219	26	81	73	7	16	28	3	0	3	13	0	1	1	6	0	10	0	0	5	.384	.284
McMichael, Greg, N.Y.	.000	52	1	1	0	0	0	0	0	0	0	0	0	0	0	0	0	0	0	0	.000	.000
McMichael, Greg, L.A.	.000	12	0	0	0	0	0	0	0	0	0	0	0	0	0	0	0	0	0	0	.000	.000
Mlicki, Dave, N.Y.	.188	10	21	16	3	3	3	0	0	0	0	3	0	0	2	0	5	0	0	0	.188	.278
Mlicki, Dave, L.A.	.059	20	43	34	1	2	3	1	0	0	0	7	0	0	2	0	10	0	0	0	.088	.111
Nomo, Hideo, L.A.	.050	12	22	20	1	1	4	0	0	1	2	2	0	0	0	0	6	0	0	0	.200	.050
Nomo, Hideo, N.Y.	.267	17	33	30	3	8	8	0	0	0	3	2	0	0	1	0	11	0	0	0	.267	.290
Orie, Kevin, Chi.	.181	64	230	204	24	37	57	14	0	2	21	1	4	3	18	0	35	1	1	4	.279	.253
Orie, Kevin, Fla.	.263	48	195	175	23	46	74	8	1	6	17	1	0	5	14	2	24	1	0	4	.423	.335
Perez, Carlos, Mon.*	.191	23	59	47	3	9	14	2	0	1	2	11	0	0	1	0	19	0	0	0	.298	.208
Perez, Carlos, L.A.*	.083	11	30	24	2	2	2	0	0	0	1	3	0	0	3	0	13	0	0	0	.083	.185
Piazza, Mike, L.A.	.282	37	161	149	20	42	74	5	0	9	30	0	1	0	11	4	27	0	0	3	.497	.329
Piazza, Mike, Fla.	.278	5	19	18	1	5	7	0	1	0	5	0	1	0	0	0	0	0	0	0	.389	.263
Piazza, Mike, N.Y.	.348	109	446	394	67	137	239	33	0	23	76	0	3	2	47	10	53	1	0	12	.607	.417
Powell, Jay, Fla.	.000	33	0	0	0	0	0	0	0	0	0	0	0	0	0	0	0	0	0	0	.000	.000
Powell, Jay, Hou.	.000	29	1	1	0	0	0	0	0	0	0	0	0	0	0	0	1	0	0	0	.000	.000
Pulsipher, Bill, N.Y.*	.000	16	1	1	0	0	0	0	0	0	0	0	0	0	0	0	0	0	0	0	.000	.000
Pulsipher, Bill, Mil.*	.158	11	20	19	2	3	3	0	0	0	0	1	0	0	0	0	6	0	0	0	.158	.158
Reyes, Dennis, L.A.	.000	11	6	5	0	0	0	0	0	0	0	1	0	0	0	0	2	0	0	0	.000	.000
Reyes, Dennis, Cin.	.083	8	12	12	1	1	2	1	0	0	0	0	0	0	0	0	3	0	0	0	.167	.083
Shaw, Jeff, Cin.	.000	39	3	2	0	0	0	0	0	0	0	1	0	0	0	0	2	0	0	0	.000	.000
Shaw, Jeff, L.A.	.000	34	0	0	0	0	0	0	0	0	0	0	0	0	0	0	0	0	0	0	.000	.000
Sheffield, Gary, Fla.	.272	40	166	136	21	37	68	11	1	6	28	0	2	2	26	1	16	4	2	3	.500	.392
Sheffield, Gary, L.A.	.316	90	383	301	52	95	161	16	1	16	57	0	7	6	69	11	30	18	5	4	.535	.444
Springer, Russ, Ari.	.000	26	1	1	0	0	0	0	0	0	0	0	0	0	0	0	1	0	0	0	.000	.000
Springer, Russ, Atl.	.000	22	0	0	0	0	0	0	0	0	0	0	0	0	0	0	0	0	0	0	.000	.000
Telemaco, Amaury, Chi.	.167	14	6	6	0	1	1	0	0	0	0	0	0	0	0	0	3	0	0	0	.167	.167
Telemaco, Amaury, Ari.	.069	27	32	29	2	2	5	1	1	0	2	1	0	1	0	0	13	0	0	2	.172	.097
Vander Wal, John, Col.*	.288	89	121	104	18	30	57	10	1	5	20	0	1	0	16	0	29	0	0	1	.548	.380

Player, Team	Avg.	G	TPA	AB	R	H	TB	2B	3B	HR	RBI	SH	SF	HP	BB	IBB	SO	SB	CS	GDP	Slg.	OBP
Vander Wal, John, S.D.*	.240	20	31	25	3	6	9	3	0	0	0	0	0	0	6	0	5	0	0	1	.360	.387
VanRyn, Ben, Chi.*	.000	9	1	1	0	0	0	0	0	0	0	0	0	0	0	0	0	0	0	0	.000	.000
VanRyn, Ben, S.D.*	.000	6	0	0	0	0	0	0	0	0	0	0	0	0	0	0	0	0	0	0	.000	.000
Weathers, David, Cin.	.067	16	20	15	1	1	4	0	0	1	1	3	0	0	2	0	10	0	0	0	.267	.176
Weathers, David, Mil.	.125	28	9	8	1	1	1	0	0	0	0	1	0	0	0	0	4	0	0	0	.125	.125
Wengert, Don, S.D.	.000	10	3	3	0	0	0	0	0	0	0	0	0	0	0	0	1	0	0	0	.000	.000
Wengert, Don, Chi.	.000	23	15	13	0	0	0	0	0	0	0	1	0	0	1	0	2	0	0	0	.000	.071
White, Derrick, Chi.	.100	11	10	10	1	1	4	0	0	1	2	0	0	0	0	0	5	0	0	0	.400	.100
White, Derrick, Col.	.000	9	9	9	0	0	0	0	0	0	0	0	0	0	0	0	4	0	0	0	.000	.000
Wilson, Preston, N.Y.	.300	8	22	20	3	6	8	2	0	0	2	0	0	0	2	0	8	1	1	0	.400	.364
Wilson, Preston, Fla.	.065	14	38	31	4	2	5	0	0	1	1	2	0	1	4	0	13	0	0	0	.161	.194
Zeile, Todd, L.A.	.253	40	170	158	22	40	69	6	1	7	27	0	1	1	10	0	24	1	1	5	.437	.300
Zeile, Todd, Fla.	.291	66	270	234	37	68	100	12	1	6	39	0	3	2	31	2	34	2	3	4	.427	.374

1998 N.L. STATISTICS *Batting*

DESIGNATED HITTING

TEAM

Team	Avg.	G	TPA	AB	R	H	TB	2B	3B	HR	RBI	SH	SF	HP	BB	IBB	SO	SB	CS	GDP	Slg.	OBP
Arizona	.316	5	21	19	2	6	9	0	0	1	3	0	0	1	1	0	2	0	0	0	.474	.381
Philadelphia	.303	8	36	33	5	10	12	2	0	0	3	0	0	1	2	0	3	0	0	0	.364	.361
St. Louis	.294	8	37	34	2	10	14	2	1	0	4	0	0	0	3	0	4	1	1	2	.412	.351
San Diego	.286	8	37	35	7	10	21	5	0	2	8	0	0	0	2	0	4	0	1	0	.600	.324
Chicago	.267	8	33	30	4	8	15	1	0	2	6	0	0	0	3	1	8	0	0	2	.500	.333
Cincinnati	.263	5	22	19	2	5	8	0	0	1	3	0	0	0	3	1	5	0	1	1	.421	.364
Atlanta	.258	8	37	31	3	8	10	2	0	0	4	0	0	2	4	0	12	0	0	0	.323	.378
Pittsburgh	.250	5	22	20	2	5	8	0	0	1	5	0	0	0	2	0	5	0	0	0	.400	.318
Colorado	.208	6	24	24	1	5	6	1	0	0	0	0	0	0	0	0	8	0	0	0	.250	.208
New York	.194	8	32	31	1	6	9	0	0	1	4	0	0	0	1	0	5	1	1	0	.290	.219
Houston	.185	6	29	27	2	5	11	3	0	1	3	0	1	0	1	0	8	0	0	1	.407	.207
San Francisco	.167	5	24	24	3	4	5	1	0	0	3	0	0	0	0	0	5	0	0	0	.208	.167
Milwaukee	.156	8	40	32	5	5	6	1	0	0	5	0	0	0	8	1	11	0	0	3	.188	.325
Los Angeles	.143	8	35	28	7	4	5	1	0	0	6	0	1	0	6	0	8	2	0	0	.179	.345
Florida	.133	8	32	30	1	4	8	1	0	1	1	0	0	0	2	0	6	1	0	0	.267	.188
Montreal	.133	8	30	30	0	4	4	0	0	0	0	0	0	0	0	0	4	0	0	1	.133	.133
Totals	.221	112	491	447	47	99	151	20	1	10	58	0	2	4	38	3	98	5	4	10	.337	.287

TOP DESIGNATED HITTERS

Minimum 15 at-bats. *Lefthanded batter. †Switch-hitter.

Player, Team	Avg.	G	TPA	AB	R	H	TB	2B	3B	HR	RBI	SH	SF	HP	BB	IBB	SO	SB	CS	GDP	Slg.	OBP
Jordan, Kevin, Phi.	.303	8	36	33	5	10	12	2	0	0	3	0	0	1	2	0	3	0	0	0	.364	.361
Jaha, John, Mil.	.172	8	36	29	2	5	6	1	0	0	5	0	0	0	7	1	8	0	0	3	.207	.333
Livingstone, Scott, Mon.*	.053	5	19	19	0	1	1	0	0	0	0	0	0	0	0	0	3	0	0	0	.053	.053
Rodriguez, Henry, Chi.*	.211	5	21	19	3	4	10	0	0	2	4	0	0	0	2	1	6	0	0	2	.526	.286
Vaughn, Greg, S.D.	.389	4	20	18	6	7	16	3	0	2	7	0	0	0	2	0	2	0	0	0	.889	.450
Jackson, Ryan, Fla.*	.118	5	18	17	0	2	3	1	0	0	0	0	0	0	1	0	4	0	0	0	.176	.167
Clark, Dave, Hou.*	.133	4	16	15	1	2	4	2	0	0	0	0	0	0	1	0	4	0	0	0	.267	.188
Piazza, Mike, N.Y.	.267	4	16	15	1	4	7	0	0	1	2	0	0	0	1	0	1	0	0	0	.467	.313

ALL DESIGNATED HITTERS

*Lefthanded batter. †Switch-hitter.

Player, Team	Avg.	G	TPA	AB	R	H	TB	2B	3B	HR	RBI	SH	SF	HP	BB	IBB	SO	SB	CS	GDP	Slg.	OBP
Abbott, Kurt, Col.	.000	1	4	4	0	0	0	0	0	0	0	0	0	0	0	0	4	0	0	0	.000	.000
Alexander, Manny, Chi.	.375	2	8	8	1	3	4	1	0	0	2	0	0	0	0	0	2	0	0	0	.500	.375
Alou, Moises, Hou.	.250	1	4	4	1	1	4	0	0	1	1	0	0	0	0	0	2	0	0	0	1.000	.250
Bautista, Danny, Atl.	.500	1	2	2	0	1	1	0	0	0	1	0	0	0	0	0	0	0	0	0	.500	.500
Benard, Marvin, S.F.*	.000	2	6	6	0	0	0	0	0	0	0	0	0	0	0	0	1	0	0	0	.000	.000
Benitez, Yamil, Ari.	.286	2	8	7	1	2	5	0	0	1	3	0	0	1	0	0	0	0	0	0	.714	.375
Berry, Sean, Hou.	.000	1	3	3	0	0	0	0	0	0	0	0	0	0	0	0	1	0	0	1	.000	.000
Bichette, Dante, Col.	.000	1	4	4	0	0	0	0	0	0	0	0	0	0	0	0	1	0	0	0	.000	.000
Biggio, Craig, Hou.	.500	1	5	4	0	2	3	1	0	0	2	0	1	0	0	0	0	0	0	0	.750	.400
Bogar, Tim, Hou.	.000	1	1	1	0	0	0	0	0	0	0	0	0	0	0	0	0	0	0	0	.000	.000
Brede, Brent, Ari.*	.667	1	3	3	1	2	2	0	0	0	0	0	0	0	0	0	1	0	0	0	.667	.667
Cangelosi, John, Fla.†	.000	1	2	1	0	0	0	0	0	0	0	0	0	0	1	0	0	0	0	0	.000	.500
Castillo, Alberto, N.Y.	.000	1	1	1	0	0	0	0	0	0	0	0	0	0	0	0	0	0	0	0	.000	.000
Clark, Dave, Hou.*	.133	4	16	15	1	2	4	2	0	0	0	0	0	0	1	0	4	0	0	0	.267	.188
Colbrunn, Greg, Col.	.500	3	6	6	0	3	4	1	0	0	0	0	0	0	0	0	1	0	0	0	.667	.500
Eisenreich, Jim, L.A.*	.143	2	9	7	2	1	1	0	0	0	0	0	0	0	2	0	2	0	0	0	.143	.333
Floyd, Cliff, Fla.*	.167	3	12	12	1	2	5	0	0	1	1	0	0	0	0	0	2	1	0	0	.417	.167
Franco, Matt, N.Y.*	.000	2	7	7	0	0	0	0	0	0	0	0	0	0	0	0	3	0	0	0	.000	.000
Galarraga, Andres, Atl.	.143	2	10	7	0	1	1	0	0	0	1	0	0	2	1	0	5	0	0	0	.143	.400
Greene, Willie, Cin.*	.200	1	5	5	1	1	4	0	0	1	1	0	0	0	0	0	2	0	0	0	.800	.200
Gwynn, Tony, S.D.*	.231	3	13	13	1	3	5	2	0	0	0	0	0	0	0	0	1	0	0	0	.385	.231
Hamelin, Bob, Mil.*	.000	1	1	1	0	0	0	0	0	0	0	0	0	0	0	0	1	0	0	0	.000	.000
Hardtke, Jason, Chi.†	.500	1	3	2	0	1	1	0	0	0	0	0	0	0	1	0	0	0	0	0	.500	.667
Harris, Lenny, Cin.*	.500	1	6	6	0	3	3	0	0	0	1	0	0	0	0	0	1	0	1	0	.500	.500
Hayes, Charlie, S.F.	.200	2	10	10	1	2	2	0	0	0	1	0	0	0	0	0	3	0	0	0	.200	.200
Howard, Thomas, L.A.*	.000	1	0	0	1	0	0	0	0	0	0	0	0	0	0	0	0	0	0	0	.000	.000
Hunter, Brian, St.L.	.250	1	4	4	0	1	1	0	0	0	0	0	0	0	0	0	2	0	0	0	.250	.250
Huskey, Butch, N.Y.	.400	1	5	5	0	2	2	0	0	0	2	0	0	0	0	0	0	1	1	0	.400	.400
Jackson, Darrin, Mil.	.000	2	0	0	1	0	0	0	0	0	0	0	0	0	0	0	0	0	0	0	.000	.000
Jackson, Ryan, Fla.*	.118	5	18	17	0	2	3	1	0	0	0	0	0	0	1	0	4	0	0	0	.176	.167
Jaha, John, Mil.	.172	8	36	29	2	5	6	1	0	0	5	0	0	0	7	1	8	0	0	3	.207	.333
Jones, Chris, S.F.	.250	2	8	8	2	2	3	1	0	0	2	0	0	0	0	0	1	0	0	0	.375	.250
Jordan, Brian, St.L.	.385	3	14	13	2	5	7	2	0	0	2	0	0	0	1	0	0	0	0	1	.538	.429
Jordan, Kevin, Phi.	.303	8	36	33	5	10	12	2	0	0	3	0	0	1	2	0	3	0	0	0	.364	.361
Karros, Eric, L.A.	.000	2	9	6	0	0	0	0	0	0	0	0	0	0	3	0	2	0	0	0	.000	.333
Konerko, Paul, L.A.	.200	3	12	10	3	2	3	1	0	0	4	0	1	0	1	0	2	0	0	0	.300	.250
Lankford, Ray, St.L.*	.000	1	4	3	0	0	0	0	0	0	0	0	0	0	1	0	1	0	0	0	.000	.250
Livingstone, Scott, Mon.*	.053	5	19	19	0	1	1	0	0	0	0	0	0	0	0	0	3	0	0	0	.053	.053
Lockhart, Keith, Atl.*	.250	2	9	8	1	2	3	1	0	0	0	0	0	0	1	0	2	0	0	0	.375	.333
Lopez, Javy, Atl.	.250	1	4	4	0	1	1	0	0	0	1	0	0	0	0	0	1	0	0	0	.250	.250
Martin, Al, Pit.*	.000	2	5	5	0	0	0	0	0	0	0	0	0	0	0	0	0	0	0	0	.000	.000

Player, Team	Avg.	G	TPA	AB	R	H	TB	2B	3B	HR	RBI	SH	SF	HP	BB	IBB	SO	SB	CS	GDP	Slg.	OBP
May, Derrick, Mon.*	.143	2	7	7	0	1	1	0	0	0	0	0	0	0	0	0	1	0	0	0	.143	.143
McGee, Willie, St.L.†	.286	3	15	14	0	4	6	0	1	0	2	0	0	0	1	0	1	1	1	1	.429	.333
Miller, Damian, Ari.	.500	2	2	2	0	1	1	0	0	0	0	0	0	0	0	0	0	0	0	0	.500	.500
Mouton, James, S.D.	.000	1	0	0	0	0	0	0	0	0	0	0	0	0	0	0	0	0	1	0	.000	.000
Newfield, Marc, Mil.	.000	2	2	2	0	0	0	0	0	0	0	0	0	0	0	0	2	0	0	0	.000	.000
Nieves, Melvin, Cin.†	.125	3	11	8	1	1	1	0	0	0	1	0	0	0	3	1	2	0	0	1	.125	.364
Perez, Eddie, Atl.	.000	1	4	3	1	0	0	0	0	0	0	0	0	0	1	0	1	0	0	0	.000	.250
Piazza, Mike, N.Y.	.267	4	16	15	1	4	7	0	0	1	2	0	0	0	1	0	1	0	0	0	.467	.313
Pride, Curtis, Atl.*	.429	2	8	7	1	3	4	1	0	0	1	0	0	0	1	0	3	0	0	0	.571	.500
Robertson, Mike, Ari.*	.000	2	4	4	0	0	0	0	0	0	0	0	0	0	0	0	1	0	0	0	.000	.000
Rodriguez, Henry, Chi.*	.211	5	21	19	3	4	10	0	0	2	4	0	0	0	2	1	6	0	0	2	.526	.286
Smith, Mark, Pit.	.385	3	14	13	2	5	8	0	0	1	5	0	0	0	1	0	5	0	0	0	.615	.429
Stinnett, Kelly, Ari.	.333	1	4	3	0	1	1	0	0	0	0	0	0	0	1	0	0	0	0	0	.333	.500
Sweeney, Mark, S.D.*	.000	1	4	4	0	0	0	0	0	0	1	0	0	0	0	0	1	0	0	0	.000	.000
Tatum, Jimmy, N.Y.	.000	1	3	3	0	0	0	0	0	0	0	0	0	0	0	0	1	0	0	0	.000	.000
Valentin, Jose, Mil.†	.000	1	1	0	1	0	0	0	0	0	0	0	0	0	1	0	0	0	0	0	.000	1.000
Vander Wal, John, Col.*	.333	3	6	6	1	2	2	0	0	0	0	0	0	0	0	0	2	0	0	0	.333	.333
Vaughn, Greg, S.D.	.389	4	20	18	6	7	16	3	0	2	7	0	0	0	2	0	2	0	0	0	.889	.450
Walker, Larry, Col.*	.000	1	4	4	0	0	0	0	0	0	0	0	0	0	0	0	0	0	0	0	.000	.000
Ward, Turner, Pit.†	.000	1	3	2	0	0	0	0	0	0	0	0	0	0	1	0	0	0	0	0	.000	.333
White, Derrick, Chi.	.000	1	1	1	0	0	0	0	0	0	0	0	0	0	0	0	0	0	0	0	.000	.000
White, Rondell, Mon.	.500	1	4	4	0	2	2	0	0	0	0	0	0	0	0	0	0	0	0	1	.500	.500
Woodall, Brad, Mil.†	.000	1	0	0	1	0	0	0	0	0	0	0	0	0	0	0	0	0	0	0	.000	.000
Young, Eric, L.A.	.200	1	5	5	1	1	1	0	0	0	1	0	0	0	0	0	2	2	0	0	.200	.200

The following designated hitters, each of whom appeared in at least one game, had no plate appearances, runs scored or stolen base attempts: Martinez, Manny, Pittsburgh (2); Ordonez, Rey, New York; Sefcik, Kevin, Philadelphia; Veras, Quilvio, San Diego.

PINCH-HITTING

TEAM

Team	Avg.	G	TPA	AB	R	H	TB	2B	3B	HR	RBI	SH	SF	HP	BB	IBB	SO	SB	CS	GDP	Slg.	OBP
Chicago	.254	133	262	228	30	58	100	8	2	10	44	5	1	1	27	3	66	1	2	3	.439	.335
Montreal	.245	119	225	200	14	49	65	10	0	2	33	1	6	2	16	2	47	2	0	5	.325	.299
Atlanta	.243	126	242	214	28	52	76	9	0	5	23	2	1	3	22	2	55	3	2	3	.355	.321
St. Louis	.235	129	251	226	33	53	95	10	1	10	36	1	0	0	24	3	58	4	1	4	.420	.308
Philadelphia	.232	132	255	224	24	52	78	11	0	5	30	5	2	5	19	0	56	2	0	1	.348	.304
Milwaukee	.226	136	258	226	18	51	79	7	0	7	36	1	0	1	30	0	66	0	1	9	.350	.319
Colorado	.224	136	311	268	38	60	106	17	1	9	52	5	2	2	34	0	86	0	2	5	.396	.314
New York	.224	134	294	255	24	57	84	11	2	4	37	1	6	0	32	7	69	1	0	5	.329	.304
San Francisco	.223	124	224	202	20	45	81	6	0	10	38	1	1	1	19	1	49	0	1	1	.401	.291
Los Angeles	.219	124	227	201	24	44	64	9	1	3	16	6	0	1	19	1	53	3	0	8	.318	.290
Florida	.209	132	275	244	17	51	64	4	0	3	17	2	1	2	26	1	60	1	0	5	.262	.283
Cincinnati	.205	139	286	244	29	50	68	10	1	2	31	0	4	1	37	4	69	1	0	5	.279	.308
Pittsburgh	.202	120	196	173	16	35	54	7	0	4	21	3	3	4	13	0	48	2	0	6	.312	.269
Houston	.188	117	227	202	19	38	53	7	1	2	18	2	1	2	20	2	70	2	0	7	.262	.267
San Diego	.177	134	271	231	18	41	57	8	1	2	27	4	6	2	28	2	56	2	2	5	.247	.266
Arizona	.173	133	251	225	14	39	51	3	0	3	24	0	0	4	22	0	70	0	0	5	.227	.259
Totals	.218	2068	4055	3563	366	775	1175	137	10	81	483	39	34	31	388	28	978	24	11	77	.330	.297

INDIVIDUAL
TOP PINCH-HITTERS

Minimum 20 at-bats. *Lefthanded batter. †Switch-hitter.

Player, Team	Avg.	G	TPA	AB	R	H	TB	2B	3B	HR	RBI	SH	SF	HP	BB	IBB	SO	SB	CS	GDP	Slg.	OBP
Colbrunn, Greg, Col.-Atl.	.364	51	50	44	4	16	19	3	0	0	11	0	0	1	5	0	12	0	1	0	.432	.440
Alexander, Manny, Chi.	.360	27	27	25	2	9	12	0	0	1	4	0	0	0	2	1	9	0	1	0	.480	.407
May, Derrick, Mon.*	.353	39	38	34	0	12	14	2	0	0	2	0	0	0	4	0	5	0	0	1	.412	.421
Newfield, Marc, Mil.	.333	40	39	36	2	12	18	3	0	1	7	0	0	0	3	0	8	0	0	3	.500	.385
Lampkin, Tom, St.L*	.304	29	26	23	4	7	14	1	0	2	2	0	0	0	3	1	1	0	0	1	.609	.385
Reed, Jeff, Col.*	.300	36	36	30	6	9	17	2	0	2	10	0	1	1	4	0	9	0	0	1	.567	.389
Houston, Tyler, Chi.*	.300	23	22	20	6	6	12	0	0	2	4	1	0	0	1	0	6	0	0	0	.600	.333
Harris, Lenny, Cin.-N.Y.*	.300	48	46	40	2	12	15	3	0	0	2	1	0	0	5	2	3	0	0	4	.375	.340
Myers, Greg, S.D.*	.300	24	23	20	1	6	9	3	0	0	3	0	0	0	3	1	3	0	0	1	.450	.391
Mabry, John, St.L*	.296	31	30	27	6	8	17	3	0	2	8	0	0	0	3	1	6	0	0	0	.630	.367
Brown, Brant, Chi.*	.286	25	22	21	0	6	7	1	0	0	4	0	0	1	0	7	1	0	0	.333	.318
Jordan, Kevin, Phi.	.278	57	56	54	5	15	24	3	0	2	10	0	0	1	1	0	8	0	0	0	.444	.304
Cedeno, Roger, L.A.†	.276	31	31	29	6	8	13	3	1	0	5	0	0	0	2	0	11	0	0	1	.448	.323
Amaro, Ruben Jr., Phi.†	.275	56	56	51	3	14	18	4	0	0	6	0	2	0	3	0	9	0	0	0	.353	.304
Pratt, Todd, N.Y.	.273	24	23	22	2	6	9	3	0	0	6	0	0	0	1	0	8	0	0	0	.409	.304
Ward, Turner, Pit.†	.273	37	37	33	4	9	16	1	0	2	6	0	0	1	3	0	8	0	0	1	.485	.351
Benard, Marvin, S.F.*	.273	45	45	44	3	12	13	1	0	0	7	0	0	0	1	0	9	0	0	0	.295	.289

ALL PINCH-HITTERS

*Lefthanded batter. †Switch-hitter.

Player, Team	Avg.	G	TPA	AB	R	H	TB	2B	3B	HR	RBI	SH	SF	HP	BB	IBB	SO	SB	CS	GDP	Slg.	OBP
Abbott, Kurt, Col.	.375	19	19	16	5	6	15	3	0	2	8	0	1	0	2	0	3	0	0	0	.938	.421
Abreu, Bobby, Phi.*	.125	10	10	8	0	1	1	0	0	0	0	0	0	0	2	0	4	1	0	0	.125	.300
Agbayani, Benny, N.Y.	.000	1	1	1	0	0	0	0	0	0	0	0	0	0	0	0	1	0	0	0	.000	.000
Alexander, Manny, Chi.	.360	27	27	25	2	9	12	0	0	1	4	0	0	0	2	1	9	0	1	0	.480	.407
Alfonzo, Edgardo, N.Y.	.000	2	2	1	0	0	0	0	0	0	1	0	0	0	1	0	1	0	0	0	.000	.500
Allensworth, Jermaine, Pit-NY.	.250	9	9	8	2	2	2	0	0	0	0	0	0	0	1	0	2	0	0	0	.250	.333
Alou, Moises, Hou.	.000	6	6	5	0	0	0	0	0	0	0	0	0	0	1	1	2	0	0	0	.000	.167
Amaro, Ruben Jr., Phi.†	.275	56	56	51	3	14	18	4	0	0	6	0	2	0	3	0	9	0	0	0	.353	.304
Anderson, Marlon, Phi.*	.333	6	6	6	2	2	6	1	0	1	2	0	0	0	0	0	2	0	0	0	1.000	.333
Andrews, Shane, Mon.	.000	4	4	4	0	0	0	0	0	0	0	0	0	0	0	0	1	0	0	0	.000	.000
Arias, Alex, Phi.	.154	16	16	13	0	2	2	0	0	0	1	1	0	0	2	0	5	0	0	0	.154	.267
Arias, George, S.D.	.500	5	4	4	1	2	5	0	0	1	1	0	0	0	0	0	0	0	0	0	1.250	.500
Aurilia, Rich, S.F.	1.000	2	2	2	0	2	2	0	0	0	0	0	0	0	0	0	0	0	0	0	1.000	1.000
Ausmus, Brad, Hou.	.000	3	3	0	0	0	0	0	0	0	0	1	0	0	2	0	0	0	0	0	.000	1.000
Baerga, Carlos, N.Y.†	.333	7	7	6	0	2	2	0	0	0	3	0	1	0	0	0	0	0	0	0	.333	.286
Bagwell, Jeff, S.F.	1.000	1	1	1	0	1	1	0	0	0	1	0	0	0	0	0	0	0	0	0	1.000	1.000
Ball, Jeff, S.F.	.000	1	1	1	0	0	0	0	0	0	0	0	0	0	0	0	0	0	0	0	.000	.000
Banks, Brian, Mil.†	.333	18	18	15	3	5	9	1	0	1	5	0	0	0	3	0	5	0	0	0	.600	.444
Barrett, Michael, Mon.	.000	2	2	2	0	0	0	0	0	0	0	0	0	0	0	0	0	0	0	0	.000	.000
Barry, Jeff, Col.†	.167	6	6	6	1	1	1	0	0	0	0	0	0	0	0	0	3	0	0	0	.167	.167
Bates, Jason, Col.†	.222	38	38	36	5	8	10	2	0	0	3	0	0	0	2	0	13	0	0	1	.278	.263
Batista, Tony, Ari.	.125	28	28	24	3	3	6	0	0	1	3	0	0	0	4	0	9	0	0	1	.250	.250
Bautista, Danny, Atl.	.259	27	27	27	4	7	11	1	0	1	1	0	0	0	0	0	7	0	0	0	.407	.259
Becker, Rich, N.Y.*	.214	16	16	14	2	3	4	1	0	0	2	0	0	0	2	0	7	1	0	0	.286	.313
Bell, Derek, Hou.	.000	3	3	3	0	0	0	0	0	0	0	0	0	0	0	0	2	0	0	0	.000	.000
Bell, Jay, Ari.	.250	4	4	4	0	1	1	0	0	0	1	0	0	0	0	0	1	0	0	0	.250	.250
Belliard, Ronnie, Mil.	.200	5	5	5	0	1	1	0	0	0	0	0	0	0	0	0	1	0	0	0	.200	.200
Beltre, Adrian, L.A.	.000	3	3	2	0	0	0	0	0	0	0	0	0	0	1	0	2	0	0	0	.000	.333
Benard, Marvin, S.F.*	.273	45	45	44	3	12	13	1	0	0	7	0	0	0	1	0	9	0	0	0	.295	.289
Benes, Andy, Ari.	.000	1	1	1	0	0	0	0	0	0	0	0	0	0	0	0	0	0	0	0	.000	.000

Player, Team	Avg.	G	TPA	AB	R	H	TB	2B	3B	HR	RBI	SH	SF	HP	BB	IBB	SO	SB	CS	GDP	Slg.	OBP
Benitez, Yamil, Ari.	.065	35	35	31	2	2	5	0	0	1	3	0	0	1	3	0	14	0	0	1	.161	.171
Berg, Dave, Fla.	.429	17	17	14	1	6	7	1	0	0	2	0	0	0	3	0	5	0	0	0	.500	.529
Berry, Sean, Hou.	.235	20	20	17	3	4	7	0	0	1	3	0	0	0	3	0	5	0	0	0	.412	.350
Bichette, Dante, Col.	.500	4	4	4	0	2	2	0	0	0	0	0	0	0	0	0	0	0	0	0	.500	.500
Bieser, Steve, Pit.*	.300	12	12	10	2	3	4	1	0	0	1	0	0	0	2	0	2	0	0	0	.400	.417
Biggio, Craig, Hou.	.000	1	1	0	1	0	0	0	0	0	0	0	0	1	0	0	0	0	0	0	.000	1.000
Blauser, Jeff, Chi.	.308	14	14	13	0	4	6	0	1	0	1	0	0	0	1	0	1	0	0	0	.462	.357
Bogar, Tim, Hou.	.000	7	7	4	0	0	0	0	0	0	0	1	0	1	1	0	3	0	0	0	.000	.333
Bonds, Barry, S.F.*	1.000	2	2	1	0	1	2	1	0	0	0	0	0	0	1	0	0	0	0	0	2.000	1.000
Bonilla, Bobby, Fla.-L.A.†	.000	5	5	5	0	0	0	0	0	0	1	0	0	0	0	0	0	0	0	0	.000	.000
Boone, Aaron, Cin.	.143	7	7	7	0	1	1	0	0	0	0	0	0	0	0	0	1	0	0	0	.143	.143
Boone, Bret, Cin.	.000	2	2	2	0	0	0	0	0	0	0	0	0	0	0	0	0	0	0	0	.000	.000
Brede, Brent, Ari.*	.211	41	41	38	1	8	9	1	0	0	2	0	0	0	3	0	5	0	0	1	.237	.268
Brogna, Rico, Phi.*	.000	3	3	3	0	0	0	0	0	0	0	0	0	0	0	0	1	0	0	0	.000	.000
Brown, Adrian, Pit.†	.000	3	3	3	0	0	0	0	0	0	0	0	0	0	0	0	0	0	0	0	.000	.000
Brown, Brant, Chi.*	.286	25	22	21	0	6	7	1	0	0	4	0	0	0	1	0	7	1	0	0	.333	.318
Brown, Emil, Pit.	.000	3	3	3	0	0	0	0	0	0	0	0	0	0	0	0	2	0	0	0	.000	.000
Burks, Ellis, Col.-S.F.	.000	4	4	3	0	0	0	0	0	0	0	0	0	0	1	0	1	0	0	1	.000	.250
Burnitz, Jeromy, Mil.*	.000	3	3	2	0	0	0	0	0	0	0	0	0	0	1	0	0	0	0	0	.000	.333
Cabrera, Orlando, Mon.	.000	1	1	1	0	0	0	0	0	0	0	0	0	0	0	0	1	0	0	0	.000	.000
Caminiti, Ken, S.D.†	.250	5	5	4	1	1	2	1	0	0	2	0	0	0	1	0	0	0	0	0	.500	.400
Cangelosi, John, Fla.†	.237	72	72	59	6	14	17	0	0	1	2	1	0	0	12	0	10	1	0	2	.288	.366
Carter, Joe, S.F.	.154	14	14	13	2	2	8	0	0	2	6	0	0	0	1	0	2	0	0	0	.615	.214
Casey, Sean, Cin.*	.154	15	15	13	1	2	2	0	0	0	2	0	0	0	2	1	3	0	0	0	.154	.267
Castillo, Alberto, N.Y.	.500	2	2	2	0	1	1	0	0	0	1	0	0	0	0	0	0	0	0	0	.500	.500
Castro, Juan, L.A.	.000	6	6	5	0	0	0	0	0	0	0	0	1	0	0	0	0	0	0	0	.000	.000
Cedeno, Roger, L.A.†	.276	31	31	29	6	8	13	3	1	0	5	0	0	0	2	0	11	0	0	1	.448	.323
Cianfrocco, Archi, S.D.	.000	11	11	11	0	0	0	0	0	0	0	0	0	0	0	0	5	0	0	0	.000	.000
Cirillo, Jeff, Mil.	.500	2	2	2	1	1	1	0	0	0	0	0	0	0	0	0	0	0	0	0	.500	.500
Clark, Dave, Hou.*	.262	72	67	65	4	17	20	3	0	0	1	0	0	0	2	0	23	0	0	2	.308	.284
Clayton, Royce, St.L.	1.000	3	3	1	2	1	1	0	0	0	1	0	0	0	2	0	0	0	0	0	1.000	1.000
Clemente, Edgard, Col.	.500	2	2	2	0	1	1	0	0	0	0	0	0	0	0	0	0	0	0	0	.500	.500
Colbrunn, Greg, Col.-Atl.	.364	51	50	44	4	16	19	3	0	0	11	0	0	1	5	0	12	0	1	0	.432	.440
Collier, Lou, Pit.	.000	2	2	0	0	0	0	0	0	0	0	0	0	0	2	0	0	0	0	0	.000	1.000
Cora, Alex, L.A.*	.000	5	5	3	1	0	0	0	0	0	0	2	0	0	0	0	0	0	0	0	.000	.000
Counsell, Craig, Fla.*	.250	5	5	4	0	1	1	0	0	0	0	0	0	0	1	0	1	0	0	0	.250	.400
Cromer, Tripp, L.A.	.167	6	6	6	1	1	4	0	0	1	1	0	0	0	0	0	2	0	0	0	.667	.167
Cruz, Jacob, S.F.*	.000	3	3	3	0	0	0	0	0	0	0	0	0	0	0	0	2	0	0	0	.000	.000
Daubach, Brian, Fla.*	.250	6	6	4	0	1	2	1	0	0	1	0	0	1	1	0	3	0	0	0	.500	.500
Delgado, Wilson, S.F.†	.000	5	5	4	1	0	0	0	0	0	0	1	0	0	1	0	1	0	0	0	.000	.200
Dellucci, David, Ari.*	.273	15	15	11	3	3	3	0	0	0	2	0	0	2	2	0	3	0	0	0	.273	.467
DeRosa, Mark, Atl.	.500	2	2	2	1	1	1	0	0	0	0	0	0	0	0	0	1	0	0	0	.500	.500
DeShields, Delino, St.L*	.300	14	13	10	4	3	8	0	1	1	3	0	0	0	3	0	3	2	0	0	.800	.462
Devereaux, Mike, L.A.	.200	5	5	5	0	1	1	0	0	0	1	0	0	0	0	0	0	0	0	1	.200	.200
Diaz, Alex, S.F.†	.143	14	14	14	1	2	3	1	0	0	3	0	0	0	0	0	4	0	0	0	.214	.143
Diaz, Edwin, Ari.	.000	1	1	1	0	0	0	0	0	0	0	0	0	0	0	0	0	0	0	0	.000	.000
Dreifort, Darren, L.A.	.000	1	1	0	0	0	0	0	0	0	0	0	0	0	1	0	0	0	0	0	.000	1.000
Drew, J.D., St.L*	.500	4	4	4	0	2	2	0	0	0	3	0	0	0	0	0	2	0	0	0	.500	.500
Dunston, Shawon, S.F.	.235	18	18	17	2	4	8	1	0	1	3	0	0	1	0	0	4	0	1	0	.471	.278
Dunwoody, Todd, Fla.*	.000	12	12	11	0	0	0	0	0	0	0	0	0	0	1	0	2	0	0	0	.000	.083
Echevarria, Angel, Col.	.500	11	11	10	2	5	5	0	0	0	3	0	0	0	1	0	0	0	1	0	.500	.545
Eisenreich, Jim, Fla.-L.A.*	.146	57	55	48	4	7	11	1	0	1	4	0	0	0	7	1	13	0	0	2	.229	.255
Eusebio, Tony, Hou.	.071	15	15	14	0	1	2	1	0	0	1	0	0	0	1	0	5	0	0	1	.143	.133
Everett, Carl, Hou.†	.182	11	11	11	1	2	4	0	1	0	1	0	0	0	0	0	5	1	0	0	.364	.182
Fabregas, Jorge, Ari.-N.Y.*	.125	18	16	16	1	2	2	0	0	0	4	0	0	0	0	0	4	0	0	1	.125	.125
Finley, Steve, S.D.*	.000	7	7	6	0	0	0	0	0	0	0	0	0	0	1	0	1	0	0	0	.000	.143
Floyd, Cliff, Fla.*	.400	5	5	5	0	2	3	1	0	0	1	0	0	0	0	0	0	0	0	0	.600	.400
Fordyce, Brook, Cin.	.000	5	5	4	1	0	0	0	0	0	0	0	0	0	1	0	3	0	0	0	.000	.200
Fox, Andy, Ari.*	.154	15	15	13	1	2	2	0	0	0	0	0	0	0	2	0	6	0	0	0	.154	.267
Franco, Matt, N.Y.*	.255	70	68	55	6	14	20	3	0	1	7	0	1	0	12	5	10	0	0	2	.364	.382
Frias, Hanley, Ari.†	.125	8	8	8	1	1	4	0	0	1	2	0	0	0	0	0	3	0	0	1	.500	.125
Fullmer, Brad, Mon.*	.333	4	3	3	1	1	2	1	0	0	2	0	0	0	0	0	2	0	0	0	.667	.333
Gaetti, Gary, St.L-Chi.	.200	10	10	10	2	2	5	0	0	1	2	0	0	0	0	0	2	0	0	0	.500	.200
Galarraga, Andres, Atl.	.500	2	2	2	0	1	1	0	0	0	0	0	0	0	0	0	0	0	0	0	.500	.500
Gant, Ron, St.L	.375	19	19	16	5	6	13	1	0	2	7	0	0	0	3	0	4	0	0	1	.813	.474
Garcia, Freddy Ad., Pit.	.250	5	5	4	0	1	1	0	0	0	2	0	1	0	0	0	1	0	0	1	.250	.200
Garcia, Guillermo, Cin.	.000	2	2	2	0	0	0	0	0	0	0	0	0	0	0	0	1	0	0	0	.000	.000
Garcia, Karim, Ari.*	.214	14	14	14	1	3	4	1	0	0	2	0	0	0	0	0	4	0	0	0	.286	.214
Gilbert, Shawn, N.Y.-St.L	.250	5	4	4	0	1	1	0	0	0	0	0	0	0	0	0	2	1	0	0	.250	.250
Gilkey, Bernard, N.Y.-Ari.	.000	8	8	5	1	0	0	0	0	0	0	0	0	0	3	0	2	0	0	1	.000	.375
Giovanola, Ed, S.D.*	.056	27	25	18	1	1	3	0	1	0	1	3	0	0	4	0	2	0	1	0	.167	.227
Gomez, Chris, S.D.	.000	2	2	1	0	0	0	0	0	0	0	0	0	0	1	0	0	0	0	0	.000	.500
Goodwin, Curtis, Col.*	.000	24	24	20	1	0	0	0	0	0	0	2	0	0	2	0	9	0	0	0	.000	.091
Grace, Mark, Chi.*	.500	3	3	2	0	1	2	1	0	0	2	0	0	0	1	1	0	0	0	0	1.000	.667
Graffanino, Tony, Atl.	.160	30	30	25	3	4	6	2	0	0	1	0	0	2	3	0	7	0	1	0	.240	.300
Greene, Willie, Cin.*	.333	14	13	12	4	4	8	1	0	1	3	0	0	0	1	0	2	0	0	0	.667	.385
Grissom, Marquis, Mil.	.333	8	8	6	0	2	3	1	0	0	2	0	0	0	2	0	2	0	1	0	.500	.500
Guerrero, Vladimir, Mon.	.000	2	2	1	0	0	0	0	0	0	1	0	1	0	0	0	0	0	0	0	.000	.000
Guerrero, Wilton, L.A.†	.333	19	19	18	2	6	7	1	0	0	2	0	0	0	1	0	6	0	0	0	.389	.368
Guillen, Jose, Pit.	.500	2	2	2	1	1	4	0	0	1	1	0	0	0	0	0	0	0	0	0	2.000	.500
Guillen, Ozzie, Atl.*	.273	13	13	11	1	3	3	0	0	0	1	0	1	0	1	0	1	0	0	0	.273	.333
Gutierrez, Ricky, Hou.	1.000	4	4	2	1	2	3	1	0	0	1	0	0	0	2	1	0	0	0	0	1.500	1.000
Gwynn, Tony, S.D.*	.167	9	9	6	0	1	1	0	0	0	2	0	2	0	1	1	1	0	0	1	.167	.222
Hamelin, Bob, Mil.*	.222	64	60	54	6	12	25	1	0	4	7	0	0	0	6	0	14	0	0	2	.463	.300

Player, Team	Avg.	G	TPA	AB	R	H	TB	2B	3B	HR	RBI	SH	SF	HP	BB	IBB	SO	SB	CS	GDP	Slg.	OBP
Hamilton, Darryl, S.F.-Col.*....	.200	7	7	5	1	1	1	0	0	0	0	0	0	0	2	0	0	0	0	0	.200	.429
Hamilton, Joey, S.D.	.000	1	1	1	0	0	0	0	0	0	0	0	0	0	0	0	0	0	0	0	.000	.000
Haney, Todd, N.Y.	.000	3	3	2	0	0	0	0	0	0	0	0	0	0	1	0	0	0	0	0	.000	.333
Hardtke, Jason, Chi.†............	.167	12	12	12	0	2	2	0	0	0	1	0	0	0	0	0	5	0	0	0	.167	.167
Harris, Lenny, Cin.-N.Y.*	.300	48	46	40	2	12	15	3	0	0	2	1	0	0	5	2	3	0	0	4	.375	.378
Hayes, Charlie, S.F.	.227	24	24	22	2	5	11	0	0	2	5	0	1	0	1	0	5	0	0	0	.500	.250
Helms, Wes, Atl.	.000	3	3	3	0	0	0	0	0	0	0	0	0	0	0	0	2	0	0	0	.000	.000
Helton, Todd, Col.*	.091	14	14	11	0	1	2	1	0	0	2	0	0	0	3	0	5	0	0	1	.182	.286
Henley, Bob, Mon.................	.333	7	7	6	0	2	2	0	0	0	1	0	0	0	1	0	0	0	0	1	.333	.429
Hernandez, Carlos, S.D.	.077	13	13	13	1	1	2	1	0	0	2	0	0	0	0	0	3	0	0	1	.154	.077
Hernandez, Jose, Chi.	.455	12	12	11	2	5	10	2	0	1	1	1	0	0	0	0	3	0	0	0	.909	.455
Hernandez, Livan, Fla............	.000	2	2	2	0	0	0	0	0	0	0	0	0	0	0	0	1	0	0	0	.000	.000
Hidalgo, Richard, Hou...........	.400	5	5	5	1	2	2	0	0	0	0	0	0	0	0	0	0	0	0	0	.400	.400
Hill, Glenallen, Chi...............	.308	16	16	13	4	4	10	0	0	2	7	0	0	0	3	1	5	0	0	0	.769	.438
Holbert, Ray, Atl.-Mon.	.500	2	2	2	0	1	1	0	0	0	0	0	0	0	0	0	0	0	0	0	.500	.500
Hollandsworth, Todd, L.A.*	.333	3	3	3	1	1	4	0	0	1	1	0	0	0	0	0	1	0	0	0	1.333	.333
Houston, Tyler, Chi.*	.300	23	22	20	6	6	12	0	0	2	4	1	0	0	1	0	6	0	0	0	.600	.333
Howard, David, St.L†	.000	4	4	4	0	0	0	0	0	0	0	0	0	0	0	0	2	0	0	0	.000	.000
Howard, Thomas, L.A.*	.190	23	21	21	2	4	5	1	0	0	1	0	0	0	0	0	3	1	0	2	.238	.190
Howell, Jack, Hou.*	.273	13	12	11	2	3	4	1	0	0	3	0	0	0	1	0	4	0	0	1	.364	.333
Hubbard, Mike, Mon.	.286	7	7	7	1	2	3	1	0	0	0	0	0	0	0	0	4	0	0	0	.429	.286
Hubbard, Trenidad, L.A.	.261	27	27	23	1	6	8	2	0	0	0	0	0	1	3	0	8	2	0	0	.348	.370
Hudler, Rex, Phi.	.143	16	16	14	1	2	3	1	0	0	1	0	0	0	2	0	6	0	0	0	.214	.250
Hughes, Bobby, Mil...............	.231	13	13	13	2	3	6	0	0	1	2	0	0	0	0	0	6	0	0	1	.462	.231
Hundley, Todd, N.Y.†............	.154	17	16	13	2	2	5	0	0	1	1	0	0	0	3	0	7	0	0	0	.385	.313
Hunter, Brian R., St.L...........	.241	31	31	29	6	7	13	3	0	1	2	1	0	0	1	0	6	0	1	2	.448	.267
Huskey, Butch, N.Y...............	.077	16	14	13	1	1	2	1	0	0	2	0	1	0	0	0	2	0	0	0	.154	.071
Incaviglia, Pete, Hou.............	.111	10	10	9	0	1	2	1	0	0	2	0	0	0	1	0	4	0	0	0	.222	.200
Jackson, Damian, Cin.	.000	1	1	1	0	0	0	0	0	0	0	0	0	0	0	0	1	0	0	0	.000	.000
Jackson, Darrin, Mil..............	.267	17	17	15	0	4	4	0	0	0	5	0	0	0	2	0	4	0	0	0	.267	.353
Jackson, Ryan, Fla.*	.194	38	37	36	3	7	7	0	0	0	1	0	0	0	1	0	13	0	0	0	.194	.216
Jaha, John, Mil.	.000	9	9	8	0	0	0	0	0	0	0	0	0	0	1	0	7	0	0	0	.000	.111
Javier, Stan, S.F.†................	.222	20	20	18	1	4	5	1	0	0	2	0	0	0	2	1	4	0	0	1	.278	.300
Jefferies, Gregg, Phi.†	.333	6	6	6	1	2	2	0	0	0	1	0	0	0	0	0	1	1	0	0	.333	.333
Jenkins, Geoff, Mil.*	.111	11	11	9	1	1	1	0	0	0	1	0	0	0	2	0	3	0	0	1	.111	.273
Jensen, Marcus, Mil.†............	.000	1	1	1	0	0	0	0	0	0	0	0	0	0	0	0	1	0	0	0	.000	.000
Johnson, Brian, S.F.	.000	5	5	5	0	0	0	0	0	0	0	0	0	0	0	0	2	0	0	0	.000	.000
Johnson, Charles, L.A.	.667	3	3	3	0	2	3	1	0	0	0	0	0	0	0	0	0	0	0	0	1.000	.667
Johnson, Lance, Chi.*	.250	8	8	8	1	2	2	0	0	0	1	0	0	0	0	0	0	0	0	0	.250	.250
Johnson, Russ, Hou.	.000	3	3	3	0	0	0	0	0	0	0	0	0	0	0	0	0	0	0	0	.000	.000
Jones, Andruw, Atl.	.000	3	3	1	2	0	0	0	0	0	0	0	0	0	2	0	1	0	0	0	.000	.667
Jones, Chipper, Atl.†.............	.000	1	1	1	0	0	0	0	0	0	0	0	0	0	0	0	0	0	0	0	.000	.000
Jones, Chris, Ari.-S.F............	.120	28	28	25	2	3	4	1	0	0	2	0	0	0	3	0	11	0	0	1	.160	.214
Jordan, Brian, St.L...............	.286	7	7	7	0	2	3	1	0	0	0	0	0	0	0	0	1	0	0	0	.429	.286
Jordan, Kevin, Phi...............	.278	57	56	54	5	15	24	3	0	2	10	0	0	1	1	0	8	0	0	0	.444	.304
Joyner, Wally, S.D.*	.300	10	10	10	1	3	4	1	0	0	1	0	0	0	0	0	1	0	0	0	.400	.300
Karros, Eric, L.A..................	.000	1	1	1	0	0	0	0	0	0	0	0	0	0	0	0	1	0	0	0	.000	.000
Kelly, Pat, St.L....................	.000	11	11	11	0	0	0	0	0	0	0	0	0	0	0	0	5	0	0	0	.000	.000
Kendall, Jason, Pit.	.000	5	5	3	0	0	0	0	0	0	0	0	2	0	0	0	0	0	0	0	.000	.400
Kent, Jeff, S.F.	.000	2	2	2	0	0	0	0	0	0	0	0	0	0	0	0	0	0	0	0	.000	.000
Kile, Darryl, Col.	.000	2	2	1	0	0	0	0	0	0	0	1	0	0	0	0	0	0	0	0	.000	.000
Kirby, Wayne, N.Y.*	.375	9	9	8	2	3	5	0	1	0	0	0	0	0	1	0	2	0	0	0	.625	.444
Klassen, Danny, Ari..............	.000	1	1	1	0	0	0	0	0	0	0	0	0	0	0	0	1	0	0	0	.000	.000
Klesko, Ryan, Atl.*	.000	5	5	4	0	0	0	0	0	0	0	0	0	0	1	1	0	0	0	0	.000	.000
Konerko, Paul, L.A.-Cin.........	.125	11	11	8	0	1	1	0	0	0	1	0	1	0	2	0	3	0	0	0	.125	.273
Kotsay, Mark, Fla.*...............	.462	13	13	13	2	6	9	0	0	1	3	0	0	0	0	0	2	0	0	0	.692	.462
Laker, Tim, Pit.....................	.444	10	10	9	1	4	7	0	0	1	1	0	0	0	1	0	1	0	0	0	.778	.500
Lampkin, Tom, St.L*.............	.304	29	26	23	4	7	14	1	0	2	2	0	0	0	3	1	1	0	0	1	.609	.385
Langston, Mark, S.D.	.000	1	1	0	0	0	0	0	0	0	0	1	0	0	0	0	0	0	0	0	.000	.000
Lankford, Ray, St.L*	.154	16	16	13	2	2	5	0	0	1	2	0	0	0	3	0	6	0	0	0	.385	.313
Lansing, Mike, Col.	.000	1	1	1	0	0	0	0	0	0	0	0	0	0	0	0	1	0	0	0	.000	.000
Larkin, Barry, Cin.	.000	3	3	1	1	0	0	0	0	0	1	0	0	0	2	0	0	0	0	0	.000	.667
Lee, Derrek, Fla...................	.071	16	16	14	0	1	1	0	0	0	0	0	0	0	2	0	6	0	0	2	.071	.188
Leskanic, Curtis, Col.	.000	1	1	1	0	0	0	0	0	0	0	0	0	0	0	0	0	0	0	0	.000	.000
Levis, Jesse, Mil.*	.000	9	9	7	0	0	0	0	0	0	0	0	0	0	2	0	1	0	0	1	.000	.222
Lewis, Mark, Phi..................	.333	3	3	3	1	1	4	0	0	1	2	0	0	0	0	0	2	0	0	0	1.333	.333
Leyritz, Jim, S.D..................	.200	19	18	15	0	3	3	0	0	0	1	0	0	1	2	0	4	0	0	1	.200	.333
Lieberthal, Mike, Phi.	.333	6	6	6	1	2	5	0	0	1	4	0	0	0	0	0	3	0	0	0	.833	.333
Liriano, Nelson, Col.†............	.000	8	7	7	0	0	0	0	0	0	0	0	0	0	0	0	2	0	0	0	.000	.000
Livingstone, Scott, Mon.*	.268	54	48	41	1	11	15	4	0	0	8	0	3	0	4	2	6	1	0	0	.366	.313
Lockhart, Keith, Atl.*	.333	19	19	18	2	6	7	1	0	0	1	0	0	0	1	0	1	1	0	0	.389	.368
LoDuca, Paul, L.A.................	.000	4	4	4	0	0	0	0	0	0	0	0	0	0	0	0	0	0	0	0	.000	.000
Lombard, George, Atl.*	.500	3	2	2	1	1	4	0	0	1	1	0	0	0	0	0	1	0	0	0	2.000	.500
Lopez, Javy, Atl.	.143	9	9	7	0	1	1	0	0	0	1	0	0	1	1	1	2	0	1	2	.143	.222
Lopez, Luis M., N.Y.†............	.158	43	43	38	3	6	6	0	0	0	3	0	1	0	4	0	11	0	0	0	.158	.233
Loretta, Mark, Mil.	.167	20	20	18	0	3	4	1	0	0	4	0	0	1	1	0	6	0	0	1	.222	.250
Lowery, Terrell, Chi.	.000	6	5	2	1	0	0	0	0	0	0	0	0	0	3	0	2	0	0	0	.000	.600
Luke, Matt, L.A.*	.231	31	28	26	4	6	10	1	0	1	4	0	0	0	2	0	6	0	0	1	.385	.286
Mabry, John, St.L*	.296	31	30	27	6	8	17	3	0	2	8	0	0	0	3	1	6	0	0	0	.630	.367
Magee, Wendell Jr., Phi.	.000	1	1	1	0	0	0	0	0	0	0	0	0	0	0	0	0	0	0	0	.000	.000
Manwaring, Kirt, Col.	.000	6	6	2	1	0	0	0	0	0	0	0	2	0	2	0	1	0	1	0	.000	.500
Marrero, Eli, St.L.................	.000	9	9	7	0	0	0	0	0	0	1	0	0	0	2	0	0	0	0	0	.000	.222
Martin, Al, Pit.*	.250	12	12	12	1	3	3	0	0	0	0	0	0	0	0	0	5	2	0	1	.250	.250
Martinez, Greg, Mil.†	.000	2	2	1	0	0	0	0	0	0	0	0	0	0	1	0	1	0	0	0	.000	.500

Player, Team	Avg.	G	TPA	AB	R	H	TB	2B	3B	HR	RBI	SH	SF	HP	BB	IBB	SO	SB	CS	GDP	Slg.	OBP
Martinez, Manny, Pit.	.125	8	8	8	0	1	2	1	0	0	1	0	0	0	0	0	4	0	0	0	.250	.125
Martinez, Ramon E., S.F.	.500	4	4	2	0	1	1	0	0	0	0	1	0	0	1	0	0	0	0	0	.500	.667
Martinez, Sandy, Chi.*	.214	18	18	14	2	3	4	1	0	0	0	0	0	1	3	0	5	0	0	0	.286	.389
Matheny, Mike, Mil.	.000	1	1	1	0	0	0	0	0	0	0	0	0	0	0	0	0	0	0	0	.000	.000
Maxwell, Jason, Chi.	.333	5	4	3	1	1	4	0	0	1	2	1	0	0	0	0	2	0	0	0	1.333	.333
May, Derrick, Mon.*	.353	39	38	34	0	12	14	2	0	0	2	0	0	0	4	0	5	0	0	1	.412	.421
Mayne, Brent, S.F.*	.400	12	12	10	0	4	5	1	0	0	2	0	0	0	2	0	1	0	0	0	.500	.500
McEwing, Joe, St.L.	.000	5	5	5	0	0	0	0	0	0	0	0	0	0	0	0	1	0	0	0	.000	.000
McGee, Willie, St.L†	.179	45	43	39	2	7	7	0	0	0	3	0	0	0	4	1	13	1	0	0	.179	.256
McGuire, Ryan, Mon.*	.118	21	20	17	2	2	2	0	0	0	1	0	0	0	3	0	8	0	0	0	.118	.250
McGwire, Mark, St.L.	.667	3	3	3	2	2	6	1	0	1	2	0	0	0	0	0	0	0	0	0	2.000	.667
McRae, Brian, N.Y.†	.111	9	9	9	0	1	2	1	0	0	0	0	0	0	0	0	2	0	0	0	.222	.111
Meluskey, Mitch, Hou.†	.000	6	6	5	0	0	0	0	0	0	0	0	0	0	1	0	3	0	0	1	.000	.167
Merced, Orlando, Chi.*	.375	10	10	8	2	3	6	0	0	1	5	0	1	0	1	0	1	0	0	2	.750	.400
Metcalfe, Mike, L.A.	.000	1	1	1	0	0	0	0	0	0	0	0	0	0	0	0	0	0	0	0	.000	.000
Meulens, Hensley, Ari.	.000	3	3	3	0	0	0	0	0	0	0	0	0	0	0	0	3	0	0	0	.000	.000
Mieske, Matt, Chi.	.192	32	31	26	2	5	7	2	0	0	5	1	0	0	4	0	6	0	0	0	.269	.300
Millar, Kevin, Fla.	.000	1	1	0	0	0	0	0	0	0	0	0	0	0	1	0	0	0	0	0	.000	1.000
Miller, Damian, Ari.	.200	10	10	10	0	2	2	0	0	0	0	0	0	0	0	0	4	0	0	0	.200	.200
Milliard, Ralph, N.Y.	.000	1	1	1	0	0	0	0	0	0	0	0	0	0	0	0	1	0	0	0	.000	.000
Mirabelli, Doug, S.F.	1.000	1	1	1	1	1	4	0	0	1	2	0	0	0	0	0	0	0	0	0	4.000	1.000
Montgomery, Ray, Hou.	.400	5	5	5	2	2	2	0	0	0	0	0	0	0	0	0	1	0	0	0	.400	.400
Moore, Trey, Mon.*	.000	1	1	1	0	0	0	0	0	0	0	0	0	0	0	0	1	0	0	0	.000	.000
Morandini, Mickey, Chi.*	.333	6	6	3	1	1	1	0	0	0	1	0	0	0	3	0	0	0	0	0	.333	.667
Mordecai, Mike, Mon.	.000	11	10	10	0	0	0	0	0	0	0	0	0	0	0	0	1	0	0	2	.000	.000
Mouton, James, S.D.	.167	14	14	12	0	2	2	0	0	0	1	0	0	0	2	0	3	0	0	0	.167	.286
Mueller, Bill, S.F.†	.143	7	7	7	1	1	4	0	0	1	2	0	0	0	0	0	2	0	0	0	.571	.143
Myers, Greg, S.D.*	.300	24	23	20	1	6	9	3	0	0	3	0	0	0	3	1	3	0	0	1	.450	.391
Newfield, Marc, Mil.	.333	40	39	36	2	12	18	3	0	1	7	0	0	0	3	0	8	0	0	3	.500	.385
Nieves, Jose, Chi.	.000	1	1	0	0	0	0	0	0	0	0	0	0	1	0	0	0	0	0	0	.000	.000
Nieves, Melvin, Cin.†	.220	60	60	50	3	11	14	3	0	0	6	0	1	0	9	0	20	0	0	0	.280	.333
Nilsson, David, Mil.*	.273	14	13	11	0	3	3	0	0	0	0	0	1	0	1	0	2	0	0	0	.273	.333
Nunnally, Jon, Cin.*	.000	10	10	6	1	0	0	0	0	0	0	0	0	0	4	0	1	0	0	1	.000	.400
Olerud, John, N.Y.*	.400	6	6	5	0	2	3	1	0	0	0	0	0	0	1	1	0	0	0	0	.600	.500
Oliver, Darren, St.L.	.000	1	1	1	0	0	0	0	0	0	0	0	0	0	0	0	0	0	0	0	.000	.000
Ordaz, Luis, St.L.	.000	2	2	2	0	0	0	0	0	0	0	0	0	0	0	0	0	0	0	0	.000	.000
Ordonez, Rey, N.Y.	.000	1	1	1	0	0	0	0	0	0	0	0	0	0	0	0	1	0	0	0	.000	.000
Orie, Kevin, Chi.	.167	7	7	6	1	1	1	0	0	0	1	0	0	0	1	0	2	0	1	1	.167	.286
Osik, Keith, Pit.	.143	8	7	7	1	1	1	0	0	0	0	0	0	0	0	0	3	0	0	1	.143	.143
Owens, Eric, Mil.	.222	10	10	9	0	2	2	0	0	0	1	0	0	0	1	0	1	0	0	1	.222	.300
Pagnozzi, Tom, St.L	.333	9	9	9	0	3	3	0	0	0	0	0	0	0	0	0	3	0	0	0	.333	.333
Paquette, Craig, N.Y.	.000	2	2	2	0	0	0	0	0	0	0	0	0	0	0	0	1	0	0	0	.000	.000
Payton, Jay, N.Y.	.500	6	5	4	0	2	2	0	0	0	0	0	0	0	1	0	0	0	0	0	.500	.600
Pena, Angel, L.A.	.333	3	3	3	0	1	1	0	0	0	0	0	0	0	0	0	1	0	0	0	.333	.333
Perez, Eddie, Atl.	.250	10	10	8	0	2	2	0	0	0	1	0	0	0	2	0	2	0	0	0	.250	.400
Perez, Eduardo, Cin.	.200	42	42	35	5	7	9	2	0	0	6	0	1	1	5	0	16	0	0	0	.257	.310
Perez, Neifi, Col.†	.000	2	2	2	0	0	0	0	0	0	0	0	0	0	0	0	0	0	0	0	.000	.000
Perez, Robert, Mon.	.259	28	28	27	3	7	7	0	0	0	4	0	1	0	0	0	8	0	0	0	.259	.250
Petagine, Roberto, Cin.*	.429	17	17	14	4	6	9	1	1	0	2	0	0	0	3	0	1	1	0	0	.643	.529
Phillips, J.R., Hou.*	.105	21	21	19	2	2	5	0	0	1	4	0	0	0	2	0	6	0	0	1	.263	.190
Phillips, Tony, N.Y.†	.667	3	3	3	1	2	2	0	0	0	0	0	0	0	0	0	0	0	0	0	.667	.667
Piazza, Mike, Fla.-N.Y.	.600	7	7	5	1	3	7	1	0	1	5	0	1	0	1	0	1	0	0	0	1.400	.571
Polanco, Placido, St.L.	.167	6	6	6	0	1	1	0	0	0	1	0	0	0	0	0	1	0	0	0	.167	.167
Polcovich, Kevin, Pit.	.143	8	8	7	1	1	1	0	0	0	0	0	0	0	1	0	3	0	0	0	.143	.250
Powell, Dante, S.F.	1.000	2	2	1	1	1	4	0	0	1	1	0	0	0	1	0	0	0	0	0	4.000	1.000
Pratt, Todd, N.Y.	.273	24	23	22	2	6	9	3	0	0	6	0	0	0	1	0	8	0	0	0	.409	.304
Pride, Curtis, Atl.*	.184	45	43	38	4	7	11	1	0	1	1	1	0	1	3	0	12	2	0	0	.289	.262
Prince, Tom, L.A.	.500	6	6	4	2	2	2	0	0	0	0	0	0	0	2	0	0	0	0	0	.500	.667
Ramirez, Aramis, Pit.	.000	1	1	1	0	0	0	0	0	0	0	0	0	0	0	0	1	0	0	0	.000	.000
Reed, Jeff, Col.*	.300	36	36	30	6	9	17	2	0	2	10	0	1	1	4	0	9	0	0	1	.567	.389
Reese, Pokey, Cin.	.000	3	3	3	0	0	0	0	0	0	0	0	0	0	0	0	1	0	0	0	.000	.000
Relaford, Desi, Phi.†	.333	4	4	3	0	1	2	1	0	0	2	1	0	0	0	0	0	0	0	0	.667	.333
Renteria, Edgar, Fla.	.250	4	4	4	0	1	1	0	0	0	1	0	0	0	0	0	2	0	0	0	.250	.250
Rios, Armando, S.F.*	.500	6	6	4	3	2	8	0	0	2	3	0	0	0	2	0	2	0	0	0	2.000	.667
Rivera, Ruben, S.D.	.222	10	10	9	1	2	2	0	0	0	0	0	0	0	1	0	4	2	0	0	.222	.300
Robertson, Mike, Ari.*	.200	10	10	10	0	2	2	0	0	0	0	0	0	0	0	0	1	0	0	0	.200	.200
Rodriguez, Henry, Chi.*	.250	11	10	8	0	2	3	1	0	0	1	0	0	0	2	0	5	0	0	0	.375	.400
Rolen, Scott, Phi.	.000	1	1	1	0	0	0	0	0	0	0	0	0	0	0	0	1	0	0	0	.000	.000
Romero, Mandy, S.D.†	.000	2	2	1	0	0	0	0	0	0	0	0	0	0	1	0	0	0	0	0	.000	.500
Roskos, John, Fla.	.111	9	9	9	1	1	1	0	0	0	0	0	0	0	0	0	4	0	0	0	.111	.111
Sanchez, Rey, S.F.	.429	9	9	7	1	3	3	0	0	0	1	0	0	0	2	0	0	0	0	0	.429	.556
Sanders, Reggie, Cin.	.286	7	7	7	0	2	2	0	0	0	0	0	0	0	0	0	2	0	0	0	.286	.286
Sanford, Chance, Pit.*	.000	8	8	7	1	0	0	0	0	0	0	0	0	0	1	0	2	0	1	0	.000	.125
Santangelo, F.P., Mon.†	.429	10	10	7	2	3	3	0	0	0	4	0	0	1	2	0	1	1	0	0	.429	.600
Sefcik, Kevin, Phi.	.167	42	42	30	6	5	5	0	0	0	3	0	4	5	0	0	7	0	0	1	.167	.359
Seguignol, Fernando, Mon.†	1.000	1	1	1	1	1	1	0	0	0	0	0	0	0	0	0	0	0	0	0	1.000	1.000
Servais, Scott, Chi.	.000	15	14	13	1	0	0	0	0	0	0	0	0	0	1	0	0	0	0	0	.000	.071
Sheets, Andy, S.D.	.000	8	8	8	0	0	0	0	0	0	0	0	0	0	0	0	4	0	1	0	.000	.000
Sheffield, Gary, Fla.-L.A.	.250	4	4	4	0	1	1	0	0	0	0	0	0	0	0	0	0	0	0	1	.250	.250
Shumpert, Terry, Col.	.235	19	19	17	3	4	7	0	0	1	2	0	0	0	2	0	6	0	0	0	.412	.316
Simon, Randall, Atl.*	.000	3	3	3	0	0	0	0	0	0	0	0	0	0	0	0	1	0	0	0	.000	.000
Smith, Mark, Pit.	.167	27	27	24	2	4	6	2	0	0	1	0	1	1	1	0	5	0	0	0	.250	.222
Snow, J.T., S.F.†	.000	9	9	7	0	0	0	0	0	0	0	0	0	0	2	0	3	0	0	0	.000	.222
Spiers, Bill, Hou.*	.000	23	23	20	1	0	0	0	0	0	1	0	1	0	2	0	6	1	0	1	.000	.087

Player, Team	Avg.	G	TPA	AB	R	H	TB	2B	3B	HR	RBI	SH	SF	HP	BB	IBB	SO	SB	CS	GDP	Slg.	OBP
Stankiewicz, Andy, Ari............	.208	26	26	24	1	5	5	0	0	0	1	0	0	1	1	0	4	0	0	0	.208	.269
Stinnett, Kelly, Ari.	.167	8	8	6	0	1	1	0	0	0	2	0	0	0	2	0	4	0	0	0	.167	.375
Stovall, DaRond, Mon.†...........	.286	14	14	14	2	4	8	1	0	1	4	0	0	0	0	0	4	0	0	1	.571	.286
Strange, Doug, Pit.†...............	.182	38	38	33	1	6	8	2	0	0	6	3	1	0	1	0	9	0	0	1	.242	.200
Strittmatter, Mark, Col............	.000	1	1	1	0	0	0	0	0	0	0	0	0	0	0	0	0	0	0	0	.000	.000
Stynes, Chris, Cin.	.313	17	17	16	3	5	5	0	0	0	3	0	0	0	1	0	0	0	0	1	.313	.353
Sweeney, Mark, S.D.*	.194	76	73	62	6	12	16	1	0	1	8	0	3	1	7	0	18	0	0	1	.258	.274
Tarasco, Tony, Cin.*	.125	10	10	8	3	1	4	0	0	1	4	0	0	0	2	0	2	0	0	0	.500	.300
Tatum, Jim, N.Y.	.188	20	19	16	1	3	8	0	1	1	5	0	2	0	1	0	7	0	0	0	.500	.211
Taubensee, Eddie, Cin.*	.071	15	15	14	1	1	1	0	0	0	0	0	0	0	1	1	6	0	0	0	.071	.133
Tomko, Brett, Cin.	.000	1	1	1	0	0	0	0	0	0	0	0	0	0	0	0	1	0	0	0	.000	.000
Tucker, Michael, Atl.*	.357	17	17	14	4	5	8	0	0	1	2	0	0	0	3	0	3	0	0	0	.571	.471
Valdes, Pedro, Chi.*	.143	8	7	7	1	1	3	0	1	0	1	0	0	0	0	0	0	0	0	0	.429	.143
Valentin, Jose, Mil.†..............	.100	15	14	10	2	1	1	0	0	0	1	0	0	0	4	0	4	0	0	0	.100	.357
Vander Wal, John, Col.-S.D.*...	.212	82	78	66	11	14	32	7	1	3	14	0	0	0	12	0	20	0	0	0	.485	.333
Vaughn, Greg, S.D.	.000	3	3	2	1	0	0	0	0	0	1	0	0	0	1	0	1	0	0	0	.000	.333
Veras, Quilvio, S.D.†.............	.000	7	7	5	1	0	0	0	0	0	1	0	1	0	1	0	1	0	0	0	.000	.143
Veres, Dave, Col.	.000	1	1	1	0	0	0	0	0	0	0	0	0	0	0	0	0	0	0	0	.000	.000
Vidro, Jose, Mon.†................	.143	26	26	21	0	3	4	1	0	0	2	1	1	1	2	0	5	0	0	0	.190	.240
Vina, Fernando, Mil.*	.000	1	1	1	0	0	0	0	0	0	0	0	0	0	0	0	0	0	0	0	.000	.000
Vizcaino, Jose, L.A.†.............	.000	2	2	1	1	0	0	0	0	0	0	0	1	0	0	0	0	0	0	0	.000	.000
Walker, Larry, Col.*	.250	8	8	8	2	2	6	1	0	1	4	0	0	0	0	0	4	0	0	0	.750	.250
Ward, Daryle, Hou.*	.333	4	4	3	1	1	1	0	0	0	1	0	0	0	1	0	2	0	0	0	.333	.500
Ward, Turner, Pit.†................	.273	37	37	33	4	9	16	1	0	2	6	0	0	1	3	0	8	0	0	1	.485	.351
Watkins, Pat, Cin.	.111	11	11	9	0	1	1	0	0	0	1	0	1	0	1	0	2	0	0	0	.111	.182
Wehner, John, Fla.	.182	24	23	22	2	4	4	0	0	0	0	0	0	0	1	0	3	0	0	0	.182	.217
Wengert, Don, S.D.	.000	1	1	1	0	0	0	0	0	0	0	0	0	0	0	0	1	0	0	0	.000	.000
White, Derrick, Chi.-Col.	.059	18	17	17	1	1	4	0	0	1	2	0	0	0	0	0	9	0	0	0	.235	.059
White, Devon, Ari.†................	1.000	3	3	2	0	2	2	0	0	0	2	0	0	0	1	0	0	0	0	0	1.000	1.000
Widger, Chris, Mon.	.500	2	2	2	1	1	4	0	0	1	4	0	0	0	0	0	0	0	0	0	2.000	.500
Wilkins, Rick, N.Y.*	.000	1	1	1	0	0	0	0	0	0	0	0	0	0	0	0	0	0	0	0	.000	.000
Williams, Eddie, S.D.	.400	10	10	10	1	4	4	0	0	0	2	0	0	0	0	0	2	0	0	0	.400	.400
Williams, Gerald, Atl.	.207	33	33	29	4	6	12	3	0	1	9	0	0	0	4	0	9	0	0	1	.414	.303
Williams, Matt, Ari.	.000	5	5	4	0	0	0	0	0	0	1	0	0	0	1	0	2	0	0	0	.000	.200
Wilson, Preston, N.Y.-Fla.	.000	8	8	7	1	0	0	0	0	0	0	0	0	1	0	0	3	0	0	0	.000	.125
Womack, Tony, Pit.*	.000	2	2	2	0	0	0	0	0	0	0	0	0	0	0	0	1	0	0	0	.000	.000
Woodall, Brad, Mil.†	.500	2	2	2	1	1	1	0	0	0	1	0	0	0	0	0	1	0	0	0	.500	.500
Young, Dmitri, Cin.†..............	.000	8	8	8	0	0	0	0	0	0	0	0	0	0	0	0	3	0	0	0	.000	.000
Young, Eric, L.A.	.000	3	3	1	0	0	0	0	0	0	0	2	0	0	0	0	0	0	0	0	.000	.000
Young, Kevin, Pit.	.500	2	2	2	0	1	1	0	0	0	0	0	0	0	0	0	1	0	0	0	.500	.500
Zaun, Gregg, Fla.†................	.190	23	23	21	0	4	4	0	0	0	1	1	0	0	1	0	0	0	0	1	.190	.227
Zeile, Todd, Fla.	.000	2	2	1	0	0	0	0	0	0	0	0	0	0	1	0	0	0	0	0	.000	.500
Zuber, Jon, Phi.*	.200	29	29	25	4	5	6	1	0	0	1	0	0	0	4	0	6	0	0	0	.240	.310

PINCH-HITTERS WITH TWO OR MORE TEAMS

Player, Team	Avg.	G	TPA	AB	R	H	TB	2B	3B	HR	RBI	SH	SF	HP	BB	IBB	SO	SB	CS	GDP	Slg.	OBP
Allensworth, Jermaine, Pit.	.000	4	4	3	1	0	0	0	0	0	0	0	0	0	1	0	1	0	0	0	.000	.250
Allensworth, Jermaine, N.Y.	.400	5	5	5	1	2	2	0	0	0	0	0	0	0	0	0	1	0	0	0	.400	.400
Bonilla, Bobby, Fla.†.............	.000	3	3	3	0	0	0	0	0	0	1	0	0	0	0	0	0	0	0	0	.000	.000
Bonilla, Bobby, L.A.†.............	.000	2	2	2	0	0	0	0	0	0	0	0	0	0	0	0	0	0	0	0	.000	.000
Burks, Ellis, Col.	.000	3	3	3	0	0	0	0	0	0	0	0	0	0	0	0	1	0	0	1	.000	.000
Burks, Ellis, S.F.	.000	1	1	0	0	0	0	0	0	0	0	0	0	0	1	0	0	0	0	0	.000	1.000
Colbrunn, Greg, Col.	.346	32	31	26	2	9	11	2	0	0	6	0	0	1	4	0	6	0	1	0	.423	.452
Colbrunn, Greg, Atl.	.389	19	19	18	2	7	8	1	0	0	5	0	0	0	1	0	6	0	0	0	.444	.421
Eisenreich, Jim, Fla.*	.154	14	14	13	1	2	6	1	0	1	3	0	0	0	1	0	4	0	0	0	.462	.214
Eisenreich, Jim, L.A.*	.143	43	41	35	3	5	5	0	0	0	1	0	0	0	6	1	9	0	0	2	.143	.268
Fabregas, Jorge, Ari.*	.125	9	8	8	0	1	1	0	0	0	1	0	0	0	0	0	2	0	0	0	.125	.125
Fabregas, Jorge, N.Y.*	.125	9	8	8	1	1	1	0	0	0	3	0	0	0	0	0	2	0	0	1	.125	.125
Gaetti, Gary, St.L.	.143	7	7	7	0	1	1	0	0	0	1	0	0	0	0	0	1	0	0	0	.143	.143
Gaetti, Gary, Chi.	.333	3	3	3	2	1	4	0	0	1	1	0	0	0	0	0	1	0	0	0	1.333	.333
Gilbert, Shawn, N.Y.	.000	2	2	2	0	0	0	0	0	0	0	0	0	0	0	0	1	0	0	0	.000	.000
Gilbert, Shawn, St.L.	.500	3	2	2	0	1	1	0	0	0	0	0	0	0	0	0	1	1	0	0	.500	.500
Gilkey, Bernard, N.Y.	.000	6	6	4	1	0	0	0	0	0	1	0	0	0	2	0	1	0	0	1	.000	.333
Gilkey, Bernard, Ari.	.000	2	2	1	0	0	0	0	0	0	0	0	0	0	1	0	1	0	0	0	.000	.500
Hamilton, Darryl, S.F.*	.000	3	3	3	0	0	0	0	0	0	0	0	0	0	0	0	0	0	0	0	.000	.000
Hamilton, Darryl, Col.*	.500	4	4	2	1	1	1	0	0	0	0	0	0	0	2	0	0	0	0	0	.500	.750
Harris, Lenny, Cin.*	.333	32	31	27	2	9	12	3	0	0	2	0	0	0	4	2	2	0	0	3	.444	.419
Harris, Lenny, N.Y.*	.231	16	15	13	0	3	3	0	0	0	0	1	0	0	1	0	1	0	0	1	.231	.286
Holbert, Ray, Atl.	1.000	1	1	1	0	1	1	0	0	0	0	0	0	0	0	0	0	0	0	0	1.000	1.000
Holbert, Ray, Mon.	.000	1	1	1	0	0	0	0	0	0	0	0	0	0	0	0	0	0	0	0	.000	.000
Jones, Chris, Ari.	.273	13	13	11	1	3	4	1	0	0	2	0	0	0	2	0	3	0	0	1	.364	.385
Jones, Chris, S.F.	.000	15	15	14	1	0	0	0	0	0	0	0	0	0	1	0	8	0	0	0	.000	.067
Konerko, Paul, L.A.	.250	5	5	4	0	1	1	0	0	0	0	0	0	0	1	0	2	0	0	0	.250	.400
Konerko, Paul, Cin.	.000	6	6	4	0	0	0	0	0	0	1	0	0	0	1	0	1	0	0	0	.000	.167
Piazza, Mike, Fla.	.000	1	1	0	0	0	0	0	0	0	1	0	1	0	0	0	0	0	0	0	.000	.000
Piazza, Mike, N.Y.	.600	6	6	5	1	3	7	1	0	1	4	0	0	0	1	0	0	0	0	0	1.400	.667
Sheffield, Gary, Fla.	.333	3	3	3	0	1	1	0	0	0	0	0	0	0	0	0	1	0	0	0	.333	.333
Sheffield, Gary, L.A.	.000	1	1	1	0	0	0	0	0	0	0	0	0	0	0	0	0	0	0	0	.000	.000
Vander Wal, John, Col.*	.204	67	64	54	9	11	28	6	1	3	14	0	0	0	10	0	18	0	0	0	.519	.328
Vander Wal, John, S.D.*..........	.250	15	14	12	2	3	4	1	0	0	0	0	0	0	2	0	2	0	0	0	.333	.333
White, Derrick, Chi.	.100	11	10	10	1	1	4	0	0	1	2	0	0	0	0	0	5	0	0	0	.400	.100
White, Derrick, Col.	.000	7	7	7	0	0	0	0	0	0	0	0	0	0	0	0	4	0	0	1	.000	.000
Wilson, Preston, N.Y.	.000	1	1	1	0	0	0	0	0	0	0	0	0	0	0	0	1	0	0	0	.000	.000
Wilson, Preston, Fla.	.000	7	7	6	1	0	0	0	0	0	0	0	0	1	0	0	2	0	0	0	.000	.143

PITCHING

TEAM

Team	W	L	Pct.	ERA	G	ShO	Rel.	Sv.	IP	H	TBF	R	ER	HR	SH	SF	HB	BB	IBB	SO	WP	Bk.
Atlanta	106	56	.654	3.25	162	23	354	45	1438.2	1291	5967	581	520	117	59	27	35	467	37	1232	51	3
Houston	102	60	.630	3.50	162	11	340	44	1471.1	1435	6214	620	572	147	52	41	42	465	25	1187	50	5
San Diego	98	64	.605	3.63	162	11	369	59	1454.2	1384	6151	635	587	139	75	29	49	501	45	1217	63	6
New York	88	74	.543	3.76	162	16	399	46	1458.0	1381	6161	645	609	152	64	42	68	532	59	1129	40	11
Los Angeles	83	79	.512	3.81	162	10	342	44	1447.1	1332	6168	678	612	135	72	38	56	587	26	1178	46	9
Pittsburgh	69	93	.426	3.91	163	10	395	41	1449.0	1433	6217	718	629	147	64	50	31	530	53	1112	45	14
San Francisco	89	74	.546	4.18	163	6	433	44	1477.0	1457	6362	739	686	171	80	46	52	562	68	1089	58	3
St. Louis	83	79	.512	4.31	163	10	428	44	1469.2	1513	6392	782	703	151	92	45	54	558	38	972	42	14
Montreal	65	97	.401	4.38	162	5	443	39	1427.0	1448	6207	783	695	156	77	50	57	533	39	1017	50	12
Cincinnati	77	85	.475	4.44	162	8	366	44	1441.1	1400	6206	760	711	170	74	44	52	573	42	1098	60	7
Chicago	90	73	.552	4.47	163	7	449	56	1477.1	1528	6472	792	733	180	62	46	48	575	48	1207	48	14
Milwaukee	74	88	.457	4.63	162	2	416	39	1451.0	1538	6325	812	746	188	82	44	61	550	29	1063	48	7
Arizona	65	97	.401	4.63	162	6	368	37	1432.1	1463	6151	812	737	188	80	40	41	489	32	908	52	14
Philadelphia	75	87	.463	4.64	162	10	385	32	1463.0	1476	6339	808	754	188	73	43	54	544	27	1176	73	5
Colorado	77	85	.475	4.99	162	5	406	36	1432.2	1583	6277	855	794	174	62	43	63	562	17	951	47	9
Florida	54	108	.333	5.18	162	3	420	24	1449.2	1617	6553	923	834	182	95	56	58	715	61	1016	62	10
Totals	1295	1299	.499	4.23	1298	143	6313	675	23240.0	23279	100162	11943	10922	2585	1163	684	821	8743	646	17552	835	143

NOTE—Totals for earned runs for several clubs do not agree with composite total for all pitchers of each respective club due to instances in which provisions of Section 10.18(i) of the Scoring Rules were applied. The following differences are to be noted: New York pitchers add to 611; San Francisco pitchers add to 687; St. Louis pitchers add to 706; Montreal pitchers add to 696; Chicago pitchers add to 738; Arizona pitchers add to 738; Colorado pitchers add to 796; Florida pitchers add to 838.

INDIVIDUAL

TOP QUALIFIERS FOR EARNED-RUN AVERAGE TITLE

Minimum 162 innings. *Throws lefthanded.

Pitcher, Team	W	L	Pct.	ERA	G	GS	CG	ShO	GF	Sv.	IP	H	TBF	R	ER	HR	SH	SF	HB	BB	IBB	SO	WP	Bk.
Maddux, Greg, Atl.	18	9	.667	2.22	34	34	9	5	0	0	251.0	201	987	75	62	13	15	5	7	45	10	204	4	0
Brown, Kevin, S.D.	18	7	.720	2.38	36	35	7	3	0	0	257.0	225	1032	77	68	8	13	3	10	49	4	257	10	0
Leiter, Al, N.Y.*	17	6	.739	2.47	28	28	4	2	0	0	193.0	151	789	55	53	8	6	2	11	71	2	174	4	1
Glavine, Tom, Atl.*	20	6	.769	2.47	33	33	4	3	0	0	229.1	202	934	67	63	13	6	2	2	74	2	157	3	0
Daal, Omar, Ari.*	8	12	.400	2.88	33	23	3	1	4	0	162.2	146	664	60	52	12	9	6	3	51	3	132	0	1
Smoltz, John, Atl.	17	3	.850	2.90	26	26	2	2	0	0	167.2	145	681	58	54	10	4	2	4	44	2	173	3	1
Hermanson, Dustin, Mon.	14	11	.560	3.13	32	30	1	0	0	0	187.0	163	768	80	65	21	9	3	3	56	3	154	4	3
Harnisch, Pete, Cin.	14	7	.667	3.14	32	32	2	1	0	0	209.0	176	854	79	73	24	8	5	6	64	4	157	4	1
Schilling, Curt, Phi.	15	14	.517	3.25	35	35	15	2	0	0	268.2	236	1089	101	97	23	14	7	6	61	3	300	12	1
Cordova, Francisco, Pit.	13	14	.481	3.31	33	33	3	2	0	0	220.1	204	921	91	81	22	9	3	6	69	5	157	1	1
Ashby, Andy, S.D.	17	9	.654	3.34	33	33	5	1	0	0	226.2	223	939	90	84	23	8	5	7	58	8	151	7	0
Hampton, Mike, Hou.*	11	7	.611	3.36	32	32	1	1	0	0	211.2	227	917	92	79	18	7	7	5	81	1	137	4	2
Wood, Kerry, Chi.	13	6	.684	3.40	26	26	1	1	0	0	166.2	117	699	69	63	14	2	4	11	85	1	233	6	3
Reed, Rick, N.Y.	16	11	.593	3.48	31	31	2	1	0	0	212.1	208	845	84	82	30	8	5	6	29	2	153	1	0
Reynolds, Shane, Hou.	19	8	.704	3.51	35	35	3	1	0	0	233.1	257	989	99	91	25	5	7	2	53	2	209	5	0

DEPARTMENTAL LEADERS: W—Glavine, Atl., 20; L—Kile, Col., 17; G—Beck, Chi., 81; GS—Brown, S.D., Kile, Col., Reynolds, Hou., Schilling, Phi., 35; CG—Schilling, Phi., 15; ShO—Maddux, Atl., 5; GF—Beck, Chi., 70; Sv.—Hoffman, S.D., 53; IP—Schilling, Phi., 268; H—Hernandez, Fla., 265; TBF—Schilling, Phi., 1089; R—Astacio, Col., 160; ER—Astacio, Col., 145; HR—Anderson, Ari., Astacio, Col., 39; SH—Estes, S.F., Kile, Col., Maddux, Atl., 15; SF—Park, L.A., 10; HB—Astacio, Col., 17; BB—Hamilton, S.D., 106; IBB—Tavarez, S.F., 11; SO—Schilling, Phi., 300; WP—Schmidt, Pit., 15; BK—Anderson, Ari., 6.

ALL PITCHERS

*Throws lefthanded.

Pitcher, Team	W	L	Pct.	ERA	G	GS	CG	ShO	GF	Sv.	IP	H	TBF	R	ER	HR	SH	SF	HB	BB	IBB	SO	WP	Bk.
Acevedo, Juan, St.L	8	3	.727	2.56	50	9	0	0	29	15	98.1	83	394	30	28	7	8	1	4	29	2	56	3	0
Adams, Terry, Chi.	7	7	.500	4.33	63	0	0	0	15	1	72.2	72	330	39	35	7	3	3	1	41	3	73	4	3
Adamson, Joel, Ari.*	0	3	.000	8.22	5	5	0	0	0	0	23.0	25	104	21	21	5	1	1	3	11	0	14	0	0
Alfonseca, Antonio, Fla.	4	6	.400	4.08	58	0	0	0	27	8	70.2	75	316	36	32	10	7	6	3	33	9	46	1	0
Anderson, Brian, Ari.*	12	13	.480	4.33	32	32	2	1	0	0	208.0	221	845	109	100	39	8	3	4	24	2	95	3	6
Ashby, Andy, S.D.	17	9	.654	3.34	33	33	5	1	0	0	226.2	223	939	90	84	23	8	5	7	58	8	151	7	0
Astacio, Pedro, Col.	13	14	.481	6.23	35	34	0	0	0	0	209.1	245	938	160	145	39	12	3	17	74	0	170	2	0
Aybar, Manny, St.L	6	6	.500	5.98	20	14	0	0	1	0	81.1	90	369	58	54	6	4	1	2	42	1	57	2	0
Bailey, Cory, S.F.	0	0	.000	2.70	5	0	0	0	1	0	3.1	2	13	1	1	1	0	0	1	0	2	0	0
Banks, Willie, Ari.	1	2	.333	3.09	33	0	0	0	8	1	43.2	34	188	21	15	2	4	1	1	25	2	32	4	1
Barrios, Manuel, Fla.-L.A.	0	0	.000	2.45	3	0	0	0	1	0	3.2	4	17	1	1	1	0	0	0	4	0	1	0	0
Batista, Miguel, Mon.	3	5	.375	3.80	56	13	0	0	12	0	135.0	141	598	66	57	12	7	5	6	65	7	92	6	1
Beck, Rod, Chi.	3	4	.429	3.02	81	0	0	0	70	51	80.1	86	349	33	27	11	2	5	2	20	4	81	2	0
Beech, Matt, Phi.*	3	9	.250	5.15	21	21	0	0	0	0	117.0	126	531	78	67	19	4	2	4	63	2	113	8	0
Belinda, Stan, Cin.	4	8	.333	3.23	40	0	0	0	24	1	61.1	46	254	23	22	7	7	1	1	28	6	57	3	0
Beltran, Rigo, N.Y.*	0	0	.000	3.38	7	0	0	0	0	0	8.0	6	33	3	3	1	0	1	0	4	0	5	0	0
Benes, Andy, Ari.	14	13	.519	3.97	34	34	1	0	0	0	231.1	221	979	111	102	25	11	8	6	74	3	164	9	1
Bennett, Shayne, Mon.	5	5	.500	5.50	62	0	0	0	11	1	91.2	97	417	61	56	8	9	6	6	45	3	59	3	1
Bere, Jason, Cin.	3	2	.600	4.12	9	7	0	0	2	0	43.2	39	184	20	20	3	0	2	1	20	0	31	1	0
Bergman, Sean, Hou.	12	9	.571	3.72	31	27	1	0	1	0	172.0	183	733	81	71	20	3	5	42	3	100	8	1
Blair, Willie, Ari.-N.Y.	5	16	.238	4.98	34	25	0	0	2	0	175.1	188	750	101	97	31	14	4	4	61	2	92	6	0
Boehringer, Brian, S.D.	5	2	.714	4.36	56	1	0	0	18	0	76.1	75	347	38	37	10	5	1	4	45	4	67	1	0
Bohanon, Brian, N.Y.-L.A.*	7	11	.389	2.67	39	18	2	0	4	0	151.2	121	626	56	45	13	7	2	11	57	2	111	3	0
Borland, Toby, Phi.	0	0	.000	5.00	6	0	0	0	3	0	9.0	8	39	5	5	1	1	0	0	9	2	0	0
Boskie, Shawn, Mon.	1	3	.250	9.17	5	5	0	0	0	0	17.2	34	90	21	18	5	1	1	2	4	1	10	0	0

Pitcher, Team	W	L	Pct.	ERA	G	GS	CG	ShO	GF	Sv.	IP	H	TBF	R	ER	HR	SH	SF	HB	BB	IBB	SO	WP	Bk.
Bottalico, Ricky, Phi.	1	5	.167	6.44	39	0	0	0	28	6	43.1	54	206	31	31	7	1	2	1	25	5	27	2	0
Bottenfield, Kent, St.L.	4	6	.400	4.44	44	17	0	0	11	4	133.2	128	578	72	66	13	11	3	4	57	3	98	3	2
Brantley, Jeff, St.L.	0	5	.000	4.44	48	0	0	0	33	14	50.2	40	209	26	25	12	5	3	1	18	3	48	1	0
Brewer, Billy, Phi.*	0	1	.000	108.00	2	0	0	0	0	0	0.1	3	6	4	4	0	0	0	0	2	0	0	0	0
Brock, Chris, S.F.	0	0	.000	3.90	13	0	0	0	4	0	27.2	31	120	13	12	3	2	0	0	7	1	19	0	0
Brow, Scott, Ari.	1	0	1.000	7.17	17	0	0	0	5	0	21.1	22	98	17	17	2	2	1	0	14	2	13	0	0
Brown, Kevin, S.D.	18	7	.720	2.38	36	35	7	3	0	0	257.0	225	1032	77	68	8	13	3	10	49	4	257	10	0
Brownson, Mark, Col.	1	0	1.000	4.73	2	2	1	1	0	0	13.1	16	57	7	7	2	0	0	1	2	0	8	0	0
Brunson, Will, L.A.*	0	1	.000	11.57	2	0	0	0	1	0	2.1	3	11	3	3	0	0	0	0	2	0	1	0	0
Bruske, Jim, L.A.-S.D.	3	0	1.000	3.53	39	0	0	0	11	1	51.0	57	229	22	20	3	0	0	3	23	3	35	3	0
Bullinger, Kirk, Mon.	1	0	1.000	9.00	8	0	0	0	1	0	7.0	14	35	8	7	1	0	0	0	0	0	2	0	1
Busby, Mike, St.L.	5	2	.714	4.50	26	2	0	0	7	0	46.0	45	202	23	23	3	3	2	5	15	0	33	3	0
Butler, Adam, Atl.*	0	1	.000	10.80	8	0	0	0	1	0	5.0	5	28	7	6	1	2	1	1	6	1	7	1	0
Byrd, Paul, Atl.-Phi.	5	2	.714	2.68	9	8	2	1	0	0	57.0	45	233	19	17	6	2	1	0	18	1	39	2	0
Cabrera, Jose, Hou.	0	0	.000	8.31	3	0	0	0	1	0	4.1	7	19	4	4	0	0	0	0	1	1	1	0	0
Cather, Mike, Atl.	2	2	.500	3.92	36	0	0	0	11	0	41.1	39	173	21	18	7	4	2	2	12	1	33	0	0
Charlton, Norm, Atl.*	2	0	1.000	1.38	13	0	0	0	8	1	13.0	7	53	2	2	0	1	1	1	8	0	6	2	0
Chen, Bruce, Atl.*	2	0	1.000	3.98	4	4	0	0	0	0	20.1	23	91	9	9	3	1	0	1	9	1	17	0	0
Chouinard, Bobby, Mil.-Ari.	0	2	.000	4.14	27	2	0	0	9	0	41.1	46	181	24	19	5	4	2	0	11	2	27	5	0
Christiansen, Jason, Pit.*	3	3	.500	2.51	60	0	0	0	19	6	64.2	51	269	22	18	2	5	1	0	27	7	71	3	0
Clark, Mark, Chi.	9	14	.391	4.84	33	33	2	1	0	0	213.2	236	918	116	115	23	12	6	4	48	4	161	5	2
Clement, Matt, S.D.	2	0	1.000	4.61	4	2	0	0	0	0	13.2	15	62	8	7	0	2	0	0	7	1	13	2	0
Clontz, Brad, L.A.-N.Y.	2	0	1.000	6.08	20	0	0	0	6	0	23.2	19	101	16	16	4	0	0	2	12	4	16	0	0
Cook, Dennis, N.Y.*	8	4	.667	2.38	73	0	0	0	18	1	68.0	60	286	21	18	5	3	3	3	27	4	79	1	1
Cooke, Steve, Cin.*	1	0	1.000	1.50	1	1	0	0	0	0	6.0	4	23	1	1	0	0	1	0	0	3	0	0	0
Cordova, Francisco, Pit.	13	14	.481	3.31	33	33	3	2	0	0	220.1	204	921	91	81	22	9	6	3	69	5	157	1	1
Corey, Bryan, Ari.	0	0	.000	9.00	3	0	0	0	2	0	4.0	6	20	4	4	1	1	0	1	2	0	1	0	0
Croushore, Rick, St.L.	0	3	.000	4.97	41	0	0	0	15	8	54.1	44	243	31	30	6	2	1	4	29	2	47	6	0
Cunnane, Will, S.D.	0	0	.000	6.00	3	0	0	0	1	0	3.0	4	14	2	2	1	0	0	0	1	1	0	0	0
Daal, Omar, Ari.*	8	12	.400	2.88	33	23	3	1	4	0	162.2	146	664	60	52	12	9	6	3	51	3	132	0	1
Darensbourg, Vic, Fla.*	0	7	.000	3.68	59	0	0	0	11	0	71.0	52	287	29	29	5	3	3	0	30	6	74	4	0
Darwin, Danny, S.F.	8	10	.444	5.51	33	25	0	0	2	0	148.2	176	660	97	91	23	12	3	3	49	4	81	4	0
DeHart, Rick, Mon.*	0	0	.000	4.82	26	0	0	0	6	1	28.0	34	134	22	15	3	3	1	0	13	1	14	1	1
DeJean, Mike, Col.	3	1	.750	3.03	59	1	0	0	9	2	74.1	78	307	29	25	4	4	4	1	24	1	27	3	0
De Los Santos, Valerio, Mil.*	0	0	.000	2.91	13	0	0	0	3	0	21.2	11	75	7	7	4	0	0	0	2	0	18	1	0
Dempster, Ryan, Fla.	1	5	.167	7.08	14	11	0	0	1	0	54.2	72	272	47	43	6	5	6	9	38	1	35	5	0
Dessens, Elmer, Pit.	2	6	.250	5.67	43	5	0	0	8	0	74.2	90	332	50	47	10	4	3	0	25	2	43	1	0
DiPoto, Jerry, Col.	3	4	.429	3.53	68	0	0	0	51	19	71.1	61	295	31	28	8	2	2	3	25	3	49	7	0
Dodd, Robert, Phi.*	1	0	1.000	7.20	4	0	0	0	3	0	5.0	7	25	6	4	1	0	2	1	1	0	4	1	1
Dreifort, Darren, L.A.	8	12	.400	4.00	32	26	1	1	0	0	180.0	171	752	84	80	12	11	6	10	57	2	168	9	0
Edmondson, Brian, Atl.-Fla.	4	4	.500	3.91	53	0	0	0	13	0	76.0	76	334	38	33	10	5	3	3	37	5	40	5	0
Elarton, Scott, Hou.	2	1	.667	3.32	28	2	0	0	7	2	57.0	40	227	21	21	5	1	1	1	20	0	56	1	0
Eldred, Cal, Mil.	4	8	.333	4.80	23	23	0	0	0	0	133.0	157	602	82	71	14	5	3	4	61	3	86	6	0
Embree, Alan, Atl.-Ari.*	4	2	.667	4.19	55	0	0	0	16	1	53.2	56	237	32	25	7	4	1	1	23	0	43	3	0
Estes, Shawn, S.F.*	7	12	.368	5.06	25	25	1	1	0	0	149.1	150	661	89	84	14	15	4	5	80	6	136	6	1
Eversgerd, Bryan, St.L.*	0	0	.000	9.00	8	0	0	0	2	0	6.0	9	31	7	6	1	0	2	1	2	0	4	0	0
Fontenot, Joe, Fla.	0	7	.000	6.33	8	8	0	0	0	0	42.2	56	204	34	30	5	3	1	5	20	1	24	6	0
Ford, Ben, Ari.	0	0	.000	9.90	8	0	0	0	2	0	10.0	13	49	12	11	2	0	0	2	3	0	5	1	0
Fossas, Tony, Chi.*	0	0	.000	9.00	3	0	0	0	1	0	4.0	8	26	4	4	1	0	0	0	6	0	6	0	0
Foster, Kevin, Chi.	0	0	.000	16.20	3	0	0	0	1	0	3.1	8	20	6	6	1	0	2	0	2	0	3	0	0
Fox, Chad, Mil.	1	4	.200	3.95	49	0	0	0	12	0	57.0	56	242	27	25	4	6	0	1	20	0	64	5	0
Franco, John, N.Y.*	0	8	.000	3.62	61	0	0	0	54	38	64.2	66	289	28	26	4	4	5	4	29	7	59	2	0
Frascatore, John, St.L.	3	4	.429	4.14	69	0	0	0	15	0	95.2	95	415	48	44	11	4	1	3	36	3	49	2	0
Gaetti, Gary, St.L.	0	0	.000	0.00	1	0	0	0	1	0	1.0	2	5	0	0	0	0	0	0	0	0	0	0	0
Gardner, Mark, S.F.	13	6	.684	4.33	33	33	4	2	0	0	212.0	203	886	106	102	29	6	7	6	65	5	151	5	1
Glauber, Keith, Cin.	0	0	.000	2.35	3	0	0	0	2	0	7.2	6	31	2	2	0	0	2	0	1	0	4	2	0
Glavine, Tom, Atl.*	20	6	.769	2.47	33	33	4	3	0	0	229.1	202	934	67	63	13	6	2	2	74	2	157	3	0
Gomes, Wayne, Phi.	9	6	.600	4.24	71	0	0	0	16	1	93.1	94	408	48	44	9	5	1	3	35	4	86	6	0
Gonzalez, Gabe, Fla.*	0	0	.000	9.00	3	0	0	0	1	0	1.0	1	5	1	1	0	0	0	1	1	0	0	0	0
Gonzalez, Jeremi, Chi.	7	7	.500	5.32	20	20	1	1	0	0	110.0	124	493	72	65	13	5	2	3	41	5	70	2	3
Gonzalez, Lariel, Col.	0	0	.000	0.00	1	0	0	0	1	0	3.0	0	3	0	0	0	0	0	0	0	0	0	0	0
Grace, Mike, Phi.	4	7	.364	5.48	21	15	0	0	1	0	90.1	116	418	61	55	10	7	1	8	30	1	46	1	1
Graves, Danny, Cin.	2	1	.667	3.32	62	0	0	0	35	8	81.1	76	340	31	30	6	2	5	2	28	4	44	4	0
Green, Tyler, Phi.	6	12	.333	5.03	27	27	0	0	0	0	159.1	142	699	97	89	23	5	6	9	85	1	113	8	0
Grzanich, Mike, Hou.	0	0	.000	18.00	1	0	0	0	1	0	1.0	1	6	2	2	0	0	1	0	2	0	1	0	0
Guthrie, Mark, L.A.*	2	1	.667	3.50	53	0	0	0	11	0	54.0	56	241	26	21	3	5	0	2	24	1	45	2	0
Halama, John, Hou.*	1	1	.500	5.85	6	6	0	0	0	0	32.1	37	147	21	21	3	0	3	4	2	13	0	21	2	1
Hall, Darren, L.A.	0	3	.000	10.32	11	0	0	0	2	0	11.1	17	56	14	13	2	0	1	1	5	0	8	0	0
Hamilton, Joey, S.D.	13	13	.500	4.27	34	34	0	0	0	0	217.1	220	958	113	103	15	13	6	8	106	10	147	4	0
Hammond, Chris, Fla.*	0	2	.000	6.59	3	3	0	0	0	0	13.2	20	67	11	10	3	2	1	8	0	8	0	0
Hampton, Mike, Hou.*	11	7	.611	3.36	32	32	1	1	0	0	211.2	227	917	92	79	18	7	7	5	81	1	137	4	2
Haney, Chris, Chi.*	0	0	.000	7.20	5	0	0	0	1	0	5.0	3	19	4	4	2	0	0	0	1	0	4	0	0
Harnisch, Pete, Cin.	14	7	.667	3.14	32	32	2	1	0	0	209.0	176	854	79	73	24	8	5	6	64	4	157	4	1
Harris, Lenny, Cin.	0	0	.000	0.00	1	0	0	0	1	0	1.0	0	3	0	0	0	0	0	0	0	0	0	0	0
Harris, Reggie, Hou.	0	0	.000	6.00	6	0	0	0	1	0	6.0	6	26	4	4	1	0	1	0	2	0	2	0	0
Hartgraves, Dean, S.F.*	0	0	.000	9.53	5	0	0	0	1	0	5.2	10	32	7	6	1	0	2	0	4	0	4	1	0
Henderson, Rod, Mil.	0	0	.000	9.82	2	0	0	0	1	0	3.2	5	17	4	4	2	0	0	1	0	0	1	0	0
Henriquez, Oscar, Fla.	0	0	.000	8.55	15	0	0	0	4	0	20.0	26	100	22	19	4	0	2	1	12	0	19	1	0
Henry, Doug, Hou.	2	8	.200	3.04	59	0	0	0	25	2	71.0	55	296	25	24	9	3	3	0	35	5	59	7	0
Heredia, Felix, Fla.-Chi.*	3	3	.500	5.06	71	2	0	0	18	2	58.2	57	268	39	33	2	1	2	1	38	3	54	6	1
Hermanson, Dustin, Mon.	14	11	.560	3.13	32	30	1	0	0	0	187.0	163	768	80	65	21	9	3	3	56	3	154	4	3
Hernandez, Livan, Fla.	10	12	.455	4.72	33	33	9	0	0	0	234.1	265	1040	133	123	37	8	5	6	104	8	162	4	3

Pitcher, Team	W	L	Pct.	ERA	G	GS	CG	ShO	GF	Sv.	IP	H	TBF	R	ER	HR	SH	SF	HB	BB	IBB	SO	WP	Bk.
Hershiser, Orel, S.F.	11	10	.524	4.41	34	34	0	0	0	0	202.0	200	887	105	99	22	12	5	13	85	7	126	12	0
Hitchcock, Sterling, S.D.*	9	7	.563	3.93	39	27	2	1	3	1	176.1	169	743	83	77	29	9	3	9	48	2	158	11	1
Hoffman, Trevor, S.D.	4	2	.667	1.48	66	0	0	0	61	53	73.0	41	274	12	12	2	3	0	1	21	2	86	8	0
Hudek, John, N.Y.-Cin.	5	6	.455	3.09	58	0	0	0	23	0	64.0	50	289	27	22	8	5	5	4	47	4	68	1	0
Hudson, Joe, Mil.	0	0	.000	162.00	1	0	0	0	0	0	0.1	2	7	6	6	0	0	1	0	4	1	0	0	0
Hutton, Mark, Cin.	1	0	1.000	7.41	10	2	0	0	2	0	17.0	24	87	14	14	2	0	0	1	17	0	3	1	0
Jimenez, Jose, St.L	3	0	1.000	2.95	4	3	0	0	0	0	21.1	22	94	8	7	0	1	1	0	8	0	12	0	0
Johnson, Mike, Mon.	0	2	.000	14.73	2	2	0	0	0	0	7.1	16	40	12	12	4	0	0	1	2	0	4	0	0
Johnson, Randy, Hou.*	10	1	.909	1.28	11	11	4	4	0	0	84.1	57	329	12	12	4	0	1	3	26	1	116	0	0
Johnstone, John, S.F.	6	5	.545	3.07	70	0	0	0	13	0	88.0	72	370	32	30	10	4	5	1	38	8	86	4	0
Jones, Doug, Mil.	3	4	.429	5.17	46	0	0	0	34	12	54.0	65	239	32	31	15	3	3	4	11	1	43	0	0
Jones, Bobby J., N.Y.	9	9	.500	4.05	30	30	0	0	0	0	195.1	192	804	94	88	23	4	7	8	53	2	115	2	2
Jones, Bobby M., Col.*	7	8	.467	5.22	35	20	1	0	1	0	141.1	153	630	87	82	12	9	6	6	66	0	109	4	1
Jordan, Ricardo, Cin.*	1	0	1.000	3.53	6	0	0	0	0	0	3.1	4	21	9	9	2	0	1	0	7	0	1	0	0
Judd, Mike, L.A.	0	0	.000	15.09	7	0	0	0	3	0	11.1	19	63	19	19	4	2	0	1	9	1	14	0	0
Juden, Jeff, Mil.	7	11	.389	5.53	24	24	2	0	0	0	138.1	149	629	91	85	20	9	7	10	66	0	109	6	0
Karchner, Matt, Chi.	3	1	.750	5.14	29	0	0	0	3	0	28.0	30	132	18	16	6	2	0	2	14	2	22	1	0
Karl, Scott, Mil.*	10	11	.476	4.40	33	33	0	0	0	0	192.1	219	843	104	94	21	14	3	4	66	4	102	6	0
Kile, Darryl, Col.	13	17	.433	5.20	36	35	4	1	1	0	230.1	257	1020	141	133	28	15	8	7	96	4	158	12	0
King, Curtis, St.L	2	0	1.000	3.53	36	0	0	0	11	2	51.0	50	218	20	20	5	2	2	3	20	4	28	0	0
Kline, Steve, Mon.*	3	6	.333	2.76	78	0	0	0	18	1	71.2	62	319	25	22	4	1	2	3	41	7	76	5	0
Klingenbeck, Scott, Cin.	1	3	.250	5.96	4	4	0	0	0	0	22.2	26	102	17	15	6	2	1	1	7	0	13	0	0
Krivda, Rick, Cin.*	0	2	.000	11.28	16	1	0	0	1	0	26.1	41	138	34	33	7	3	1	3	19	1	19	1	1
Kroon, Marc, S.D.-Cin.	0	0	.000	9.39	6	0	0	0	4	0	7.2	7	38	8	8	0	0	0	1	9	0	6	2	1
Kubenka, Jeff, L.A.*	1	0	1.000	0.96	6	0	0	0	2	0	9.1	4	40	1	1	0	2	1	0	8	0	10	1	0
Langston, Mark, S.D.*	4	6	.400	5.86	22	16	0	0	0	0	81.1	107	380	55	53	11	5	4	1	41	1	56	3	1
Lankford, Frank, L.A.	0	2	.000	5.95	12	0	0	0	9	1	19.2	23	89	13	13	2	0	0	2	7	0	7	1	0
Larkin, Andy, Fla.	3	8	.273	9.64	17	14	0	0	0	0	74.2	101	373	87	80	12	5	2	4	55	3	43	3	0
Lawrence, Sean, Pit.*	1	2	.667	7.32	7	3	0	0	0	0	19.2	25	92	16	16	4	0	2	0	10	0	12	1	0
Leiter, Al, N.Y.*	17	6	.739	2.47	28	28	4	2	0	0	193.0	151	789	55	53	8	6	2	11	71	2	174	4	1
Leiter, Mark, Phi.	7	5	.583	3.55	69	0	0	0	50	23	88.2	67	378	36	35	8	9	4	8	47	5	84	5	0
Leskanic, Curtis, Col.	6	4	.600	4.40	66	0	0	0	20	0	75.2	75	332	37	37	9	0	0	1	40	2	55	3	1
Lieber, Jon, Pit.	8	14	.364	4.11	29	28	2	0	1	1	171.0	182	731	93	78	23	7	4	3	40	4	138	0	3
Ligtenberg, Kerry, Atl.	3	2	.600	2.71	75	0	0	0	56	30	73.0	51	290	24	22	6	1	1	0	24	1	79	3	0
Lima, Jose, Hou.	16	8	.667	3.70	33	33	3	1	0	0	233.1	229	950	100	96	34	11	5	7	32	1	169	4	0
Loaiza, Esteban, Pit.	6	5	.545	4.52	21	14	0	0	3	0	91.2	96	394	50	46	13	5	7	3	30	1	53	1	2
Loewer, Carlton, Phi.	7	8	.467	6.09	21	21	1	0	0	0	122.2	154	549	86	83	18	5	8	3	39	1	58	4	0
Loiselle, Rich, Pit.	2	7	.222	3.44	54	0	0	0	43	19	55.0	56	258	26	21	2	5	1	2	36	9	48	0	0
Looper, Braden, St.L.	0	1	.000	5.40	4	0	0	0	3	0	3.1	5	16	4	2	1	0	1	0	4	0	4	1	0
Lowe, Sean, St.L	0	3	.000	15.19	4	1	0	0	2	0	5.1	11	31	9	9	1	1	0	0	5	0	2	0	0
Ludwick, Eric, Fla.	1	4	.200	7.44	13	6	0	0	0	0	32.2	46	159	31	27	7	2	2	0	17	1	27	2	0
Maddux, Greg, Atl.	18	9	.667	2.22	34	34	9	5	0	0	251.0	201	987	75	62	13	15	5	7	45	10	204	4	0
Maddux, Mike, Mon.	3	4	.429	3.72	51	0	0	0	20	1	55.2	50	228	24	23	3	3	3	1	15	1	33	3	1
Magnante, Mike, Hou.*	4	7	.364	4.88	48	0	0	0	20	2	51.2	56	237	28	28	2	3	1	4	26	4	39	3	0
Maloney, Sean, L.A.	0	1	.000	4.97	11	0	0	0	2	0	12.2	13	57	7	7	2	1	0	2	5	0	11	1	0
Mantei, Matt, Fla.	3	4	.429	2.96	42	0	0	0	23	9	54.2	38	224	19	18	1	3	4	7	23	3	63	0	0
Manuel, Barry, Ari.	1	0	1.000	7.47	13	0	0	0	3	0	15.2	17	79	14	13	5	0	0	1	14	3	12	0	0
Martinez, Javier, Pit.	1	0	1.000	4.83	37	0	0	0	13	0	41.0	39	199	32	22	5	1	3	4	34	1	42	5	0
Martinez, Dennis, Atl.	4	6	.400	4.45	53	5	1	1	11	2	91.0	109	396	53	45	8	2	3	3	19	5	62	2	0
Martinez, Ramon, L.A.	7	3	.700	2.83	15	15	1	0	0	0	101.2	76	418	41	32	8	2	3	3	41	1	91	2	0
McCurry, Jeff, Pit.	1	3	.250	6.52	16	0	0	0	8	0	19.1	24	87	14	14	4	2	1	1	9	0	11	0	0
McElroy, Chuck, Col.*	6	4	.600	2.90	78	0	0	0	27	2	68.1	68	281	23	22	3	0	3	0	24	0	61	0	0
McMichael, Greg, N.Y.-L.A.-N.Y.	5	4	.556	4.10	64	0	0	0	19	2	68.0	81	317	39	31	9	6	4	3	35	10	55	6	1
Meadows, Brian, Fla.	11	13	.458	5.21	31	31	1	0	0	0	174.1	222	772	106	101	20	14	4	3	46	3	88	5	1
Medina, Rafael, Fla.	2	6	.250	6.01	12	12	0	0	0	0	67.1	76	327	50	45	8	5	4	3	52	3	49	5	0
Mercedes, Jose, Mil.	2	2	.500	6.75	7	5	0	0	0	0	32.0	42	146	25	24	5	1	2	1	9	1	11	0	0
Mercker, Kent, St.L*	11	11	.500	5.07	30	29	0	0	1	0	161.2	199	716	99	91	11	10	9	3	53	4	72	6	4
Mesa, Jose, S.F.	5	3	.625	3.52	32	0	0	0	18	0	30.2	30	139	14	12	1	4	0	0	18	2	28	8	0
Miceli, Dan, S.D.	10	5	.667	3.22	67	0	0	0	18	2	72.2	64	302	28	26	6	3	2	1	27	4	70	5	1
Michalak, Chris, Ari.*	0	0	.000	11.81	5	0	0	0	2	0	5.1	9	29	7	7	1	0	1	0	4	0	5	0	0
Miller, Kurt, Chi.	0	0	.000	0.00	3	0	0	0	0	0	4.0	3	15	0	0	0	0	0	0	0	0	4	0	0
Miller, Trevor, Hou.*	2	0	1.000	3.04	37	1	0	0	15	1	53.1	57	235	21	18	4	0	1	0	20	1	30	1	0
Millwood, Kevin, Atl.	17	8	.680	4.08	31	29	3	1	1	0	174.1	175	748	86	79	18	8	3	3	56	3	163	6	1
Mlicki, Dave, N.Y.-L.A.	8	7	.533	4.57	30	30	3	1	0	0	181.1	188	789	102	92	23	8	7	7	63	5	117	10	0
Moore, Trey, Mon.*	2	5	.286	5.02	13	11	0	0	1	0	61.0	78	277	37	34	5	1	3	1	17	3	35	2	0
Morgan, Mike, Chi.	0	1	.000	7.15	5	5	0	0	0	0	22.2	30	112	21	18	8	3	0	1	15	1	10	0	0
Morman, Alvin, S.F.*	0	1	.000	5.14	9	0	0	0	3	0	7.0	8	32	4	4	4	0	0	0	3	0	7	0	0
Morris, Matt, St.L	7	5	.583	2.53	17	17	2	1	0	0	113.2	101	468	37	32	8	6	1	3	42	6	79	3	0
Mulholland, Terry, Chi.*	6	5	.545	2.89	70	6	0	0	14	3	112.0	100	476	49	36	7	5	3	4	39	7	72	4	0
Mullins, Gregory, Mil.*	0	0	.000	0.00	2	0	0	0	1	0	1.0	1	5	0	0	0	0	0	1	0	0	1	0	0
Munoz, Mike, Col.*	2	2	.500	5.66	40	0	0	0	13	0	41.1	53	189	32	26	2	1	1	1	16	2	24	1	0
Myers, Mike, Mil.*	2	2	.500	2.70	70	0	0	0	14	1	50.0	44	211	19	15	5	4	2	6	22	1	40	2	1
Myers, Randy, S.D.*	1	3	.250	6.28	21	0	0	0	15	6	14.1	15	64	10	10	2	2	0	0	7	1	9	2	0
Myers, Rodney L., Chi.	0	0	.000	7.00	10	0	0	0	3	0	18.0	20	82	14	14	3	0	0	0	6	0	15	1	0
Neagle, Denny, Atl.*	16	11	.593	3.55	32	31	5	2	0	0	210.1	196	861	91	83	25	7	3	6	60	3	165	6	1
Nen, Robb, S.F.	7	7	.500	1.52	78	0	0	0	67	40	88.2	59	357	21	15	4	2	1	25	5	110	3	0
Nitkowski, C.J., Hou.*	3	3	.500	3.77	43	0	0	0	11	3	59.2	49	262	27	25	3	5	2	3	44	3	1
Nomo, Hideo, L.A.-N.Y.	6	12	.333	4.92	29	28	3	0	0	0	157.1	130	687	88	86	19	8	5	4	94	2	167	13	4
Nunez, Vladimir, Ari.	0	0	.000	10.13	4	0	0	0	2	0	5.1	7	25	6	6	0	0	0	0	2	0	2	0	1
Nye, Ryan, Phi.	0	0	.000	27.00	1	0	0	0	1	0	1.0	3	6	3	3	0	0	0	0	0	0	0	0	0
Ojala, Kirt, Fla.*	2	7	.222	4.42	41	13	1	0	4	0	125.0	128	554	71	59	14	10	2	4	59	4	75	6	0
Oliver, Darren, St.L*	4	4	.500	4.26	10	10	0	0	0	0	57.0	64	256	31	27	7	5	2	0	23	1	29	1	3

Pitcher, Team	W	L	Pct.	ERA	G	GS	CG	ShO	GF	Sv.	IP	H	TBF	R	ER	HR	SH	SF	HB	BB	IBB	SO	WP	Bk.
Olson, Gregg, Ari.	3	4	.429	3.01	64	0	0	0	49	30	68.2	56	281	25	23	4	3	1	1	25	1	55	2	0
Ortiz, Russ, S.F.	4	4	.500	4.99	22	13	0	0	3	0	88.1	90	394	51	49	11	5	4	4	46	1	75	3	0
Osborne, Donovan, St.L.*	5	4	.556	4.09	14	14	1	1	0	0	83.2	84	358	42	38	11	3	4	1	22	2	60	1	0
Osuna, Antonio, L.A.	7	1	.875	3.06	54	0	0	0	25	6	64.2	50	272	26	22	8	2	2	2	32	0	72	1	0
Painter, Lance, St.L.*	4	0	1.000	3.99	65	0	0	0	9	1	47.1	42	207	24	21	5	4	2	4	28	3	39	2	0
Pall, Donn, Fla.	0	1	.000	5.13	23	0	0	0	11	0	33.1	42	141	19	19	5	3	1	1	7	2	26	2	0
Park, Chan Ho, L.A.	15	9	.625	3.71	34	34	2	0	0	0	220.2	199	946	101	91	16	11	10	11	97	1	191	6	2
Parris, Steve, Cin.	6	5	.545	3.73	18	16	1	1	0	0	99.0	89	421	44	41	9	7	1	4	32	3	77	1	1
Patrick, Bronswell, Mil.	4	1	.800	4.69	32	3	0	0	8	0	78.2	83	334	43	41	9	4	3	0	29	1	49	2	0
Patterson, Bob, Chi.*	1	1	.500	7.52	33	0	0	0	4	1	20.1	36	107	20	17	2	1	2	0	12	3	17	0	0
Pavano, Carl, Mon.	6	9	.400	4.21	24	23	0	0	0	0	134.2	130	580	70	63	18	5	6	8	43	1	83	1	0
Perez, Carlos, Mon.-L.A.*	11	14	.440	3.59	34	34	7	2	0	0	241.0	244	1009	109	96	21	14	3	3	63	4	128	7	1
Perez, Odalis, Atl.*	0	1	.000	4.22	10	0	0	0	0	0	10.2	10	45	5	5	1	0	0	4	0	5	0	0
Perez, Yorkis, Phi.*	0	2	.000	3.81	57	0	0	0	7	0	52.0	40	221	23	22	3	2	3	0	25	0	42	7	0
Peters, Chris, Pit.*	8	10	.444	3.47	39	21	1	0	7	1	148.0	142	630	63	57	13	4	5	3	55	4	103	4	1
Petkovsek, Mark, St.L.	7	4	.636	4.77	48	10	0	0	7	0	105.2	131	476	63	56	9	9	3	8	36	3	55	1	1
Pickett, Ricky, Ari.*	0	0	.000	81.00	2	0	0	0	0	0	0.2	3	9	6	6	0	0	0	0	4	0	2	1	0
Pisciotta, Marc, Chi.	1	2	.333	4.09	43	0	0	0	12	0	44.0	44	206	21	20	4	1	1	2	32	3	31	6	0
Plunk, Eric, Mil.	1	2	.333	3.69	26	0	0	0	7	1	31.2	33	143	14	13	3	1	2	3	15	1	36	1	0
Politte, Cliff, St.L.	2	3	.400	6.32	8	8	0	0	0	0	37.0	45	172	32	26	6	3	1	1	18	0	22	2	1
Poole, Jim Ri., S.F.*	1	3	.250	5.29	26	0	0	0	8	0	32.1	38	140	20	19	5	4	1	0	9	5	16	2	0
Portugal, Mark, Phi.	10	5	.667	4.44	26	26	3	0	0	0	166.1	186	704	88	82	26	8	2	4	32	2	104	4	0
Powell, Jay, Fla.-Hou.	7	7	.500	3.23	62	0	0	0	35	7	70.1	58	302	28	26	6	3	1	3	37	9	62	1	0
Powell, Jeremy, Mon.	1	5	.167	7.92	7	6	0	0	1	0	25.0	27	112	25	22	5	2	2	4	11	0	14	0	0
Priest, Eddie, Cin.*	0	1	.000	10.50	2	2	0	0	0	0	6.0	12	29	8	7	2	0	1	0	1	0	1	0	0
Pulsipher, Bill, N.Y.-Mil.*	4	4	.429	5.10	26	11	0	0	2	0	72.1	86	320	41	41	8	4	1	31	4	1	51	2	2
Radinsky, Scott, L.A.*	6	6	.500	2.63	62	0	0	0	30	13	61.2	63	264	21	18	5	6	2	4	20	1	45	0	3
Raggio, Brady, St.L.	1	1	.500	15.43	4	1	0	0	2	0	7.0	22	43	12	12	1	0	1	1	3	0	3	0	0
Ramirez, Roberto, S.D.*	0	1	1.000	6.14	21	0	0	0	4	0	14.2	12	70	13	10	4	1	0	0	12	1	17	3	1
Rath, Gary, L.A.*	0	0	.000	10.80	3	0	0	0	1	0	3.1	3	15	4	4	1	0	0	2	0	4	0	0
Rath, Fred, Col.	0	0	.000	1.69	2	0	0	0	1	0	5.1	6	23	1	1	0	1	2	0	2	0	0	0	0
Reed, Rick, N.Y.	16	11	.593	3.48	31	31	2	1	0	0	212.1	208	845	84	82	30	8	5	6	29	2	153	1	0
Reed, Steve, S.F.	2	1	.667	1.48	50	0	0	0	14	1	54.2	30	213	10	9	4	2	0	4	19	5	50	0	0
Remlinger, Mike, Cin.*	8	15	.348	4.82	35	28	1	1	0	0	164.1	164	727	96	88	23	12	7	5	87	1	144	11	1
Reyes, Carlos, S.D.	2	2	.500	3.58	22	0	0	0	8	1	27.2	23	109	11	11	4	2	1	2	6	0	24	0	1
Reyes, Dennis, L.A.-Cin.*	3	5	.375	4.54	19	10	0	0	4	0	67.1	62	300	36	34	3	7	2	1	47	5	77	6	1
Reyes, Al, Mil.	5	1	.833	3.95	50	0	0	0	13	0	57.0	55	253	26	25	9	2	1	31	1	58	2	0
Reynolds, Shane, Hou.	19	8	.704	3.51	35	35	3	1	0	0	233.1	257	986	99	91	25	5	7	3	53	2	209	5	0
Reynoso, Armando, N.Y.	7	3	.700	3.82	11	11	0	0	0	0	68.1	64	292	31	29	4	4	1	5	32	3	40	2	2
Rincon, Ricardo, Pit.*	0	2	.000	2.91	60	0	0	0	27	14	65.0	50	272	31	21	6	1	2	0	29	2	64	2	0
Ritz, Kevin, Col.	0	2	.000	11.00	2	2	0	0	0	0	9.0	17	46	11	11	1	0	0	1	2	0	3	1	0
Rocker, John, Atl.*	1	3	.250	2.13	47	0	0	0	16	2	38.0	22	156	10	9	4	3	0	3	22	4	42	6	0
Rodriguez, Felix, Ari.	0	2	.000	6.14	43	0	0	0	23	5	44.0	44	207	31	30	5	4	3	1	29	1	36	5	2
Rodriguez, Rich, S.F.*	0	1	1.000	3.70	68	0	0	0	11	2	65.2	69	278	28	27	7	2	2	0	20	5	44	3	0
Rojas, Mel, N.Y.	5	2	.714	6.05	50	0	0	0	19	2	58.0	68	262	39	39	9	4	2	3	30	5	41	2	0
Roque, Rafael, Mil.*	4	2	.667	4.88	9	9	0	0	0	0	48.0	42	206	28	26	9	1	4	1	24	0	34	3	1
Rueter, Kirk, S.F.*	16	9	.640	4.36	33	33	1	0	0	0	187.2	193	806	100	91	27	5	8	7	57	3	102	6	0
Ryan, Ken, Phi.	0	0	.000	4.37	17	1	0	0	6	0	22.2	21	108	12	11	1	2	1	20	1	16	4	0
Saipe, Mike, Col.	0	1	.000	10.80	2	2	0	0	0	0	10.0	22	54	12	12	5	1	0	2	0	0	2	0	0
Sanchez, Jesus, Fla.*	7	9	.438	4.47	35	29	0	0	1	0	173.0	178	765	98	86	18	12	4	9	1	2	137	8	5
Sanders, Scott, S.D.	3	1	.750	4.11	23	0	0	0	7	0	30.2	33	131	20	14	5	4	0	5	1	26	1	0
Scanlan, Bob, Hou.	0	1	.000	3.08	27	0	0	0	9	0	26.1	24	118	12	9	4	3	3	1	13	0	9	5	0
Schilling, Curt, Phi.	15	14	.517	3.25	35	35	15	2	0	0	268.2	236	1089	101	97	23	14	7	6	61	3	300	12	0
Schmidt, Jason, Pit.	11	14	.440	4.07	33	33	0	0	0	0	214.1	228	916	106	97	24	10	3	4	71	3	158	15	1
Schourek, Pete, Hou.*	7	6	.538	4.52	15	15	0	0	0	0	80.0	82	354	43	40	10	5	4	4	36	0	59	5	0
Seanez, Rudy, Atl.	4	1	.800	2.75	34	0	0	0	8	2	36.0	25	148	13	11	2	1	1	16	0	50	2	0
Shaw, Jeff, Cin.-L.A.	3	8	.273	2.12	73	0	0	0	69	48	85.0	75	339	22	20	8	5	2	1	19	5	55	0	0
Silva, Jose, Pit.	6	7	.462	4.40	18	18	1	0	0	0	100.1	104	425	55	49	7	5	5	1	30	2	64	2	2
Small, Aaron, Ari.	3	1	.750	3.69	23	0	0	0	6	0	31.2	32	130	14	13	5	2	1	8	1	14	0	0
Smith, Pete J., S.D.	3	2	.600	4.78	10	8	0	0	2	0	43.1	45	193	23	23	5	1	2	3	18	1	36	2	0
Smith, Travis, Mil.	0	0	.000	0.00	1	0	0	0	1	0	2.0	1	7	0	0	0	0	0	0	1	0	0	0	0
Smoltz, John, Atl.	17	3	.850	2.90	26	26	2	0	0	0	167.2	145	681	58	54	10	4	2	4	44	2	173	3	1
Sodowsky, Clint, Ari.	3	6	.333	5.68	45	6	0	0	10	0	77.2	86	357	56	49	5	5	2	7	39	5	42	4	2
Speier, Justin, Chi.-Fla.	0	3	.000	8.71	19	0	0	0	10	0	20.2	27	99	20	20	7	2	1	0	13	1	17	3	0
Spencer, Stan, S.D.	1	0	1.000	4.70	6	5	0	0	0	0	30.2	29	124	16	16	5	0	1	4	0	31	0	0
Spradlin, Jerry, Phi.	4	4	.500	3.53	69	0	0	0	20	1	81.2	63	319	34	32	9	4	2	2	20	1	76	6	1
Springer, Russ, Ari.-Atl.	5	4	.556	4.10	48	0	0	0	14	0	52.2	51	232	26	24	4	2	1	1	30	4	56	5	0
Stanifer, Rob, Fla.	2	4	.333	5.63	38	0	0	0	11	1	48.0	54	222	33	30	5	2	3	0	22	2	30	1	0
Steenstra, Kennie, Chi.	0	0	.000	10.80	4	0	0	0	1	0	3.1	7	18	4	4	2	0	0	1	0	4	0	0
Stephenson, Garrett, Phi.	0	2	.000	9.00	6	6	0	0	0	0	23.0	31	118	24	23	3	1	0	19	0	17	0	1
Stevens, Dave, Chi.	2	2	.333	4.74	31	0	0	0	13	0	38.0	42	169	20	20	6	1	1	17	5	31	1	1
Stoops, Jim, Col.	1	0	1.000	2.25	3	0	0	0	1	0	4.0	5	17	1	1	0	0	1	3	0	0	0	0
Stottlemyre, Todd, St.L.	9	9	.500	3.51	23	23	3	0	0	0	161.1	146	674	74	63	20	7	3	4	51	0	147	4	2
Sullivan, Scott, Cin.	5	5	.500	5.21	67	0	0	0	13	1	102.0	98	440	62	59	14	3	4	9	36	4	86	4	0
Suppan, Jeff, Ari.	1	7	.125	6.68	13	13	1	0	0	0	66.0	82	299	55	49	12	3	2	1	21	1	39	2	0
Tabaka, Jeff, Pit.*	2	2	.500	3.02	37	0	0	0	9	0	50.2	37	212	19	17	6	2	2	5	22	4	40	1	0
Tam, Jeff, N.Y.	1	1	.500	6.28	15	0	0	0	5	0	14.1	13	60	10	10	2	0	0	2	4	1	8	0	0
Tapani, Kevin, Chi.	19	9	.679	4.85	35	34	2	2	0	0	219.0	244	945	120	118	30	11	9	5	62	4	136	7	0
Tavarez, Julian, S.F.	5	3	.625	3.80	60	0	0	0	12	1	85.1	96	374	43	36	5	3	8	36	11	52	1	1
Telemaco, Amaury, Chi.-Ari.	7	10	.412	3.91	43	18	0	0	5	0	148.2	150	637	75	65	18	8	6	4	46	2	78	7	0
Telford, Anthony, Mon.	3	6	.333	3.86	77	0	0	0	24	1	91.0	85	398	45	39	9	10	4	4	36	1	59	8	1
Thompson, Mark, Col.	1	2	.333	7.71	6	6	0	0	0	0	23.1	36	116	22	20	8	2	2	5	12	0	14	1	0

1998 N.L. STATISTICS Pitching

Pitcher, Team	W	L	Pct.	ERA	G	GS	CG	ShO	GF	Sv.	IP	H	TBF	R	ER	HR	SH	SF	HB	BB	IBB	SO	WP	Bk.
Thomson, John, Col.	8	11	.421	4.81	26	26	2	0	0	0	161.0	174	680	86	86	21	8	5	2	49	0	106	4	2
Thurman, Mike, Mon.	4	5	.444	4.70	14	13	0	0	1	0	67.0	60	287	38	35	7	2	4	3	26	2	32	3	0
Tomko, Brett, Cin.	13	12	.520	4.44	34	34	1	0	0	0	210.2	198	887	111	104	22	12	2	7	64	3	162	9	1
Trachsel, Steve, Chi.	15	8	.652	4.46	33	33	1	0	0	0	208.0	204	894	107	103	27	9	7	8	84	5	149	3	2
Urbina, Ugueth, Mon.	6	3	.667	1.30	64	0	0	0	59	34	69.1	37	272	11	10	2	2	1	0	33	2	94	3	2
Valdes, Ismael, L.A.	11	10	.524	3.98	27	27	2	2	0	0	174.0	171	745	82	77	17	5	3	2	66	4	122	4	2
Valdes, Marc, Mon.	1	3	.250	7.43	20	4	0	0	3	0	36.1	41	169	34	30	6	1	2	1	21	2	28	4	0
Valdez, Efrain, Ari.*	0	0	.000	4.15	6	0	0	0	2	0	4.1	7	20	2	2	2	0	0	0	1	0	2	0	0
Van Poppel, Todd, Pit.	1	2	.333	5.36	18	7	0	0	3	0	47.0	53	208	32	28	4	3	2	0	18	3	32	5	3
VanRyn, Ben, Chi.-S.D.*	0	1	.000	5.06	15	0	0	0	3	0	10.2	12	55	6	6	0	0	1	2	10	0	7	1	0
Vazquez, Javier, Mon.	5	15	.250	6.06	33	32	0	0	1	0	172.1	196	764	121	116	31	9	4	11	68	2	139	2	0
Veres, Dave, Col.	3	1	.750	2.83	63	0	0	0	26	8	76.1	67	319	26	24	6	0	2	2	27	2	74	2	2
Wagner, Paul, Mil.	1	5	.167	7.11	13	9	0	0	1	0	55.2	67	261	49	44	10	5	2	1	31	1	37	3	0
Wagner, Billy, Hou.*	4	3	.571	2.70	58	0	0	0	50	30	60.0	46	247	19	18	6	4	0	0	25	1	97	2	0
Wainhouse, David, Col.	1	0	1.000	4.91	10	0	0	0	3	0	11.0	15	51	6	6	1	0	0	2	5	0	3	1	0
Wall, Donne, S.D.	5	4	.556	2.43	46	1	0	0	14	1	70.1	50	287	20	19	6	4	2	1	32	2	56	3	1
Weathers, David, Cin.-Mil.	6	5	.545	4.91	44	9	0	0	9	0	110.0	130	492	69	60	6	6	2	3	41	3	94	7	2
Weaver, Eric, L.A.	2	0	1.000	0.93	7	0	0	0	4	0	9.2	5	35	1	1	1	1	0	0	6	0	5	0	0
Weber, Neil, Ari.*	0	0	.000	11.57	4	0	0	0	0	0	2.1	5	15	3	3	0	0	0	0	3	0	4	0	0
Welch, Mike, Phi.	0	2	.000	8.27	10	2	0	0	0	0	20.2	26	94	19	19	7	1	0	2	7	0	15	0	0
Wendell, Turk, N.Y.	5	1	.833	2.93	66	0	0	0	17	4	76.2	62	319	25	25	4	2	1	2	33	9	58	1	0
Wengert, Don, S.D.-Chi.	1	5	.167	5.26	31	6	0	0	9	1	63.1	76	288	38	37	10	1	0	3	28	0	46	1	0
White, Gabe, Cin.*	5	5	.500	4.01	69	3	0	0	29	9	98.2	86	404	46	44	17	2	2	1	27	6	83	3	0
Whiteside, Matt, Phi.	1	1	.500	8.50	10	0	0	0	1	0	18.0	27	85	18	17	6	0	0	0	5	0	14	0	1
Wickman, Bob, Mil.	6	9	.400	3.72	72	0	0	0	51	25	82.1	79	357	38	34	5	10	3	4	39	2	71	1	0
Wilkins, Marc, Pit.	0	0	.000	3.52	16	0	0	0	6	0	15.1	13	67	6	6	1	0	1	2	9	2	17	1	1
Williams, Mike, Pit.	4	2	.667	1.94	37	1	0	0	9	0	51.0	39	204	12	11	1	1	2	0	16	4	59	3	0
Williams, Todd, Cin.	0	1	.000	7.71	6	0	0	0	2	0	9.1	15	50	8	8	1	0	0	0	6	0	4	0	0
Winchester, Scott, Cin.	3	6	.333	5.81	16	16	1	0	0	0	79.0	101	359	56	51	12	2	2	4	27	2	40	3	0
Winston, Darrin, Phi.*	2	2	.500	6.12	27	0	0	0	5	1	25.0	31	114	18	17	7	2	0	2	6	0	11	1	0
Witt, Bobby, St.L	2	5	.286	4.94	17	5	0	0	8	0	47.1	55	217	32	26	7	4	1	2	20	1	28	1	1
Wohlers, Mark, Atl.	0	1	.000	10.18	27	0	0	0	17	8	20.1	18	113	23	23	2	1	0	1	33	0	22	7	0
Wolcott, Bob, Ari.	1	3	.250	7.09	6	6	0	0	0	0	33.0	32	141	27	26	7	1	0	0	13	1	21	1	0
Wood, Kerry, Chi.	13	6	.684	3.40	26	26	1	1	0	0	166.2	117	699	69	63	14	2	4	11	85	1	233	6	3
Woodall, Brad, Mil.*	7	9	.438	4.96	31	20	0	0	4	0	138.0	145	594	81	76	25	7	2	6	47	4	85	3	0
Woodard, Steve, Mil.	10	12	.455	4.18	34	26	0	0	2	0	165.2	170	692	83	77	19	2	4	9	33	4	135	3	2
Wright, Jamey, Col.	9	14	.391	5.67	34	34	1	0	0	0	206.1	235	919	143	130	24	8	6	11	95	3	86	6	3
Yoshii, Masato, N.Y.	6	8	.429	3.93	29	29	1	0	0	0	171.2	166	724	79	75	22	9	4	6	53	5	117	5	1
Young, Tim, Mon.*	0	0	.000	6.00	10	0	0	0	0	0	6.0	6	29	4	4	0	1	0	0	4	0	7	0	0

COMBINATION SHUTOUTS: **Arizona (4)**—Anderson and Rodriguez; Benes and Valdez; Benes and Olson; Benes, Embree and Olson. **Atlanta (9)**—Maddux and Cather; Glavine, Cather and Ligtenberg; Neagle, Martinez and Ligtenberg; Maddux and Ligtenberg; Millwood, O. Perez and Charlton; Glavine, Neagle, Millwood, Charlton and Ligtenberg; Neagle, Martinez, Rocker and Ligtenberg; Chen, Seanez and Charlton; Smoltz, Charlton, Springer and Seanez. **Chicago (2)**—Tapani and Beck; Wood, Mulholland and Beck. **Cincinnati (5)**—Weathers and Shaw; Harnisch, Belinda and Williams; Reyes, Hudek and White; Bere, Remlinger and Hudek; Parris and White. **Colorado (3)**—Thomson and McElroy; Astacio, McElroy and DiPoto; Kile and Veres. **Florida (3)**—Sanchez, Heredia and Powell; Meadows, Darensbourg and Edmondson; Sanchez, Mantei, Edmondson, Darensbourg and Stanifer. **Houston (4)**—Bergman and Miller; Hampton and Wagner; Reynolds and Nitkowski; Reynolds, Powell and Wagner. **Los Angeles (4)**—Martinez and Radinsky; Dreifort and Shaw; Dreifort, Radinsky and Shaw; Bohanon and Shaw. **Milwaukee (2)**—Roque and Plunk; Pulsipher, Fox, Myers, Plunk and Wickman. **Montreal (5)**—Moore, Maddux and Urbina; Hermanson and Maddux; Powell, Maddux and Telford; Hermanson, Kline and Urbina; Pavano, Young, Maddux, DeHart, Telford and Urbina. **New York (13)**—Yoshii, McMichael and Rojas; Jones, McMichael, Cook, J. Franco, Rojas and Wendell; Leiter, McMichael and Hudek; Leiter, Wendell and Hudek; Reed and Hudek; Jones and J. Franco; Leiter, McMichael and Cook; Reed and J. Franco; Nomo, Tam and Rojas; Reynoso and Cook; Blair, Cook and J. Franco; Leiter and Wendell; Reynoso, Wendell and J. Franco;. **Philadelphia (7)**—Portugal and Leiter; Schilling and Leiter; Beech, Gomes and Leiter; Green, Perez and Spradlin; Schilling, Gomes, Perez and Leiter; Portugal, Gomes and Leiter; Portugal, Perez and Gomes. **Pittsburgh (8)**—Cordova, Wilkins and Loiselle; Schmidt and Christiansen; Silva, Rincon and Loiselle; Lieber and Rincon; Loaiza and Rincon; Lieber and Christiansen; Schmidt, Dessens and Rincon; Cordova and Rincon. **St. Louis (8)**—Stottlemyre, Painter, Frascatore and Looper; Osborne, Acevedo and Bottenfield; Stottlemyre and Brantley; Acevedo, Painter and Brantley; Petkovsek and Bottenfield; Petkovsek, King and Painter; Osborne and Acevedo; Morris, Busby and Acevedo. **San Diego (6)**—Smith, Reyes, Wengert and Hitchcock; Langston and Wall; Hamilton and Hoffman; Brown, R. Myers, Miceli and Hoffman; Hamilton, R. Myers and Hoffman; Hamilton and Hoffman. **San Francisco (3)**—Hershiser and Nen; Darwin and Nen; Estes, Reed and Nen.

PITCHERS WITH TWO OR MORE TEAMS

Pitcher, Team	W	L	Pct.	ERA	G	GS	CG	ShO	GF	Sv.	IP	H	TBF	R	ER	HR	SH	SF	HB	BB	IBB	SO	WP	Bk.
Barrios, Manuel, Fla.	0	0	.000	3.38	2	0	0	0	0	0	2.2	4	13	1	1	1	0	0	0	2	0	1	0	0
Barrios, Manuel, L.A.	0	0	.000	0.00	1	0	0	0	1	0	1.0	0	4	0	0	0	0	0	0	2	0	0	0	0
Blair, Willie, Ari.	4	15	.211	5.34	23	23	0	0	0	0	146.2	165	634	91	87	27	11	3	3	51	2	71	5	0
Blair, Willie, N.Y.	1	1	.500	3.14	11	2	0	0	2	0	28.2	23	116	10	10	4	3	1	1	10	0	21	1	0
Bohanon, Brian, N.Y.*	2	4	.333	3.15	25	4	0	0	4	0	54.1	47	230	21	19	4	2	0	6	21	2	39	1	0
Bohanon, Brian, L.A.*	5	7	.417	2.40	14	14	2	0	0	0	97.1	74	396	35	26	9	5	2	5	36	0	72	2	0
Bruske, Jim, L.A.	3	0	1.000	3.48	35	0	0	0	10	1	44.0	47	195	18	17	2	0	0	3	19	1	31	3	0
Bruske, Jim, S.D.	0	0	.000	3.86	4	0	0	0	1	0	7.0	10	34	4	3	1	0	0	0	4	2	4	0	0
Byrd, Paul, Atl.	0	0	.000	13.50	1	0	0	0	0	0	2.0	4	11	3	3	0	0	0	0	1	0	1	0	0
Byrd, Paul, Phi.	5	2	.714	2.29	8	8	2	1	0	0	55.0	41	222	16	14	6	2	1	0	17	1	38	2	0
Chouinard, Bobby, Mil.	0	0	.000	3.00	1	0	0	0	0	0	3.0	5	12	1	1	0	0	1	0	0	0	1	0	0
Chouinard, Bobby, Ari.	0	2	.000	4.23	26	2	0	0	9	0	38.1	41	169	23	18	5	4	1	0	11	2	26	5	0
Clontz, Brad, L.A.	2	0	1.000	5.66	18	0	0	0	6	0	20.2	15	87	13	13	3	0	0	2	10	4	14	0	0
Clontz, Brad, N.Y.	0	0	.000	9.00	2	0	0	0	0	0	3.0	4	14	3	3	1	0	0	0	2	0	2	0	0
Edmondson, Brian, Atl.	0	1	.000	4.32	10	0	0	0	3	0	16.2	14	73	10	8	2	0	0	0	8	1	8	4	0
Edmondson, Brian, Fla.	4	3	.571	3.79	43	0	0	0	10	0	59.1	62	261	28	25	8	5	3	3	29	4	32	1	0
Embree, Alan, Atl.*	1	0	1.000	4.34	20	0	0	0	5	0	18.2	23	87	14	9	2	1	1	0	10	0	19	0	0
Embree, Alan, Ari.*	3	2	.600	4.11	35	0	0	0	11	1	35.0	33	150	18	16	5	3	0	1	13	0	24	3	0
Heredia, Felix, Fla.*	0	3	.000	5.49	41	2	0	0	12	2	41.0	38	194	30	25	1	1	2	1	32	2	38	5	1
Heredia, Felix, Chi.*	3	0	1.000	4.08	30	0	0	0	6	0	17.2	19	74	9	8	1	0	0	0	6	1	16	1	0
Hudek, John, N.Y.	1	4	.200	4.00	28	0	0	0	15	0	27.0	23	123	13	12	2	3	2	2	19	3	28	0	0
Hudek, John, Cin.	4	2	.667	2.43	30	0	0	0	8	0	37.0	27	166	14	10	6	2	3	2	28	1	40	1	0

Pitcher, Team	W	L	Pct.	ERA	G	GS	CG	ShO	GF	Sv.	IP	H	TBF	R	ER	HR	SH	SF	HB	BB	IBB	SO	WP	Bk.
Kroon, Marc, S.D.	0	0	.000	0.00	2	0	0	0	2	0	2.1	0	8	0	0	0	0	0	0	1	0	2	0	0
Kroon, Marc, Cin.	0	0	.000	13.50	4	0	0	0	2	0	5.1	7	30	8	8	0	0	0	1	8	0	4	2	1
McMichael, Greg, L.A.	0	1	.000	4.40	12	0	0	0	1	1	14.1	17	66	8	7	1	3	1	1	6	3	11	1	0
McMichael, Greg, N.Y.	5	3	.625	4.02	52	0	0	0	18	1	53.2	64	251	31	24	8	3	2	3	29	7	44	5	1
Mlicki, Dave, N.Y.	1	4	.200	5.68	10	10	1	0	0	0	57.0	68	264	38	36	8	2	3	5	25	4	39	4	0
Mlicki, Dave, L.A.	7	3	.700	4.05	20	20	2	1	0	0	124.1	120	525	64	56	15	6	4	2	38	1	78	6	0
Nomo, Hideo, L.A.	2	7	.222	5.05	12	12	2	0	0	0	67.2	57	295	39	38	8	2	2	3	38	0	73	4	1
Nomo, Hideo, N.Y.	4	5	.444	4.82	17	16	1	0	0	0	89.2	73	392	49	48	11	6	3	1	56	2	94	9	3
Perez, Carlos, Mon.*	7	10	.412	3.75	23	23	3	0	0	0	163.1	177	690	79	68	12	11	3	3	33	3	82	5	1
Perez, Carlos, L.A.*	4	4	.500	3.24	11	11	4	2	0	0	77.2	67	319	30	28	9	3	0	0	30	1	46	2	0
Powell, Jay, Fla.	4	4	.500	4.21	33	0	0	0	26	3	36.1	36	165	19	17	5	3	1	2	22	6	24	1	0
Powell, Jay, Hou.	3	3	.500	2.38	29	0	0	0	9	4	34.0	22	137	9	9	1	0	0	1	15	3	38	0	0
Pulsipher, Bill, N.Y.*	0	0	.000	6.91	15	1	0	0	1	0	14.1	23	68	11	11	2	1	0	0	5	1	13	0	0
Pulsipher, Bill, Mil.*	3	4	.429	4.66	11	10	0	0	1	0	58.0	63	252	30	30	6	3	4	1	26	3	38	2	2
Reyes, Dennis, L.A.*	0	4	.000	4.71	11	3	0	0	4	0	28.2	27	130	17	15	1	3	1	0	20	4	33	1	1
Reyes, Dennis, Cin.*	3	1	.750	4.42	8	7	0	0	0	0	38.2	35	170	19	19	2	4	1	1	27	1	44	5	0
Shaw, Jeff, Cin.	2	4	.333	1.81	39	0	0	0	35	23	49.2	40	192	11	10	2	4	2	1	12	4	29	0	0
Shaw, Jeff, L.A.	1	4	.200	2.55	34	0	0	0	34	25	35.1	35	147	11	10	6	1	0	0	7	1	26	0	0
Speier, Justin, Chi.	0	0	.000	13.50	1	0	0	0	0	0	1.1	2	7	2	2	0	0	0	0	1	0	2	1	0
Speier, Justin, Fla.	0	3	.000	8.38	18	0	0	0	10	0	19.1	25	92	18	18	7	2	1	0	12	1	15	2	0
Springer, Russ, Ari.	4	3	.571	4.13	26	0	0	0	13	0	32.2	29	140	16	15	4	0	0	1	14	1	37	3	0
Springer, Russ, Atl.	1	1	.500	4.05	22	0	0	0	1	0	20.0	22	92	10	9	0	2	1	0	16	3	19	2	0
Telemaco, Amaury, Chi.	1	1	.500	3.90	14	0	0	0	4	0	27.2	23	118	12	12	5	0	0	0	13	0	18	3	0
Telemaco, Amaury, Ari.	6	9	.400	3.94	27	18	0	0	1	0	121.0	127	519	63	53	13	8	6	4	33	2	60	4	0
VanRyn, Ben, Chi.*	0	0	.000	3.38	9	0	0	0	2	0	8.0	9	39	3	3	0	0	1	1	6	0	6	0	0
VanRyn, Ben, S.D.*	0	1	.000	10.13	6	0	0	0	1	0	2.2	3	16	3	3	0	0	0	1	4	0	1	1	0
Weathers, David, Cin.	2	4	.333	6.21	16	9	0	0	0	0	62.1	86	294	47	43	3	4	1	1	27	2	51	5	1
Weathers, David, Mil.	4	1	.800	3.21	28	0	0	0	9	0	47.2	44	198	22	17	3	2	1	2	14	1	43	2	1
Wengert, Don, S.D.	0	0	.000	5.93	10	0	0	0	3	1	13.2	21	64	9	9	2	0	0	0	5	0	5	0	0
Wengert, Don, Chi.	1	5	.167	5.07	21	6	0	0	6	0	49.2	55	224	29	28	8	1	0	3	23	0	41	1	0

FIELDING

TEAM

Team	Pct.	G	PO	A	E	TC	DP	PB	Team	Pct.	G	PO	A	E	TC	DP	PB
Atlanta	.985	162	4316	1681	91	6088	139	13	Cincinnati	.980	162	4324	1563	122	6009	142	10
San Francisco ...	.984	163	4431	1806	101	6338	157	13	Florida	.979	162	4349	1738	129	6216	177	18
Arizona	.984	162	4297	1721	100	6118	125	6	Los Angeles	.978	162	4342	1731	134	6207	154	8
Chicago	.984	163	4432	1622	101	6155	107	7	St. Louis	.978	163	4409	1781	142	6332	160	6
New York	.984	162	4374	1672	101	6147	151	11	Pittsburgh	.977	163	4347	1698	140	6185	161	14
Colorado	.984	162	4298	1795	102	6195	193	9	Montreal	.975	162	4281	1688	155	6124	127	18
San Diego	.983	162	4364	1727	104	6195	155	17	Totals	.981	1298	69720	27513	1850	99083	2415	188
Houston	.983	162	4414	1782	108	6304	144	9									
Philadelphia	.982	162	4389	1747	110	6246	131	15									
Milwaukee	.982	162	4353	1761	110	6224	192	14									

TRIPLE PLAYS: Los Angeles, New York, Philadelphia, San Francisco.

INDIVIDUAL

FIRST BASEMEN

NOTE: All caps denotes fielding-percentage leader based on 81 games for catchers, 108 for all other non-pitchers and 162 innings for pitchers. *Throws lefthanded.

Player, Team	Pct.	G	PO	A	E	TC	DP
Arias, George, S.D.	1.000	1	4	0	0	4	1
Bagwell, Jeff, Hou.	.995	147	1239	128	7	1374	115
Ball, Jeff, S.F.	1.000	1	10	0	0	10	1
Banks, Brian, Mil.	1.000	2	8	0	0	8	0
Brede, Brent, Ari.*	.984	12	58	5	1	64	4
Brogna, Rico, Phi.*	.996	151	1238	141	5	1384	103
Brown, Brant, Chi.*	1.000	7	32	2	0	34	2
Carter, Joe, S.F.	.990	16	87	8	1	96	5
Casey, Sean, Cin.	.994	86	643	36	4	683	65
Cianfrocco, Archi, S.D.	1.000	19	91	11	0	102	11
Cirillo, Jeff, Mil.	1.000	6	50	13	0	63	8
Colbrunn, Greg, Col.-Atl.	.993	36	271	25	2	298	20
Daubach, Brian, Fla.	1.000	4	23	1	0	24	4
DeShields, Delino, St.L.	.000	1	0	0	0	0	0
Echevarria, Angel, Col.	1.000	4	20	2	0	22	3
Eisenreich, Jim, Fla.-L.A.*	.975	19	73	4	2	79	12
Fox, Andy, Ari.	1.000	12	104	6	0	110	7
Franco, Matt, N.Y.	1.000	14	68	4	0	72	3
Fullmer, Brad, Mon.	.985	137	1070	79	17	1166	81
Gaetti, Gary, St.L.	1.000	3	15	0	0	15	2
Galarraga, Andres, Atl.	.992	149	1218	81	11	1310	114
Garcia, Freddy, Pit.	.964	4	25	2	1	28	2
Grace, Mark, Chi.*	.994	156	1279	122	8	1409	82
Guillen, Ozzie, Atl.	1.000	1	2	0	0	2	0
Hamelin, Bob, Mil.*	.992	51	230	7	2	239	22
Harris, Lenny, N.Y.	1.000	1	1	0	0	1	0
Hayes, Charlie, S.F.	.995	45	347	34	2	383	37
Helton, Todd, Col.*	.995	146	1164	146	7	1317	156
Hernandez, Carlos, S.D.	1.000	1	1	0	0	1	0
Hernandez, Jose, Chi.	1.000	3	19	1	0	20	2
Houston, Tyler, Chi.	1.000	7	32	2	0	34	1
Howell, Jack, Hou.	1.000	10	63	6	0	69	3
Hudler, Rex, Phi.	1.000	1	8	1	0	9	0
Hunter, Brian, St.L.*	1.000	10	23	1	0	24	2
Jackson, Ryan, Fla.*	.973	44	300	21	9	330	30
Jaha, John, Mil.	.994	57	441	23	3	467	57
Jordan, Kevin, Phi.	1.000	24	158	15	0	173	16
Joyner, Wally, S.D.*	.993	127	985	81	7	1073	101
Karros, Eric, L.A.	.991	136	1150	110	12	1272	122
Kent, Jeff, S.F.	1.000	1	1	0	0	1	0
Klesko, Ryan, Atl.*	.981	7	48	4	1	53	4
Konerko, Paul, L.A.-Cin.	.996	30	208	21	1	230	9
Kotsay, Mark, Fla.*	1.000	3	3	1	0	4	0
Laker, Tim, Pit.	1.000	4	33	1	0	34	4
Lampkin, Tom, St.L.	1.000	2	5	0	0	5	0
Larkin, Stephen, Cin.*	1.000	1	6	0	0	6	0
Lee, Derrek, Fla.	.993	132	950	114	8	1072	116
Lee, Travis, Ari.*	.998	146	1269	100	3	1372	104
Leyritz, Jim, S.D.	.993	20	134	8	1	143	12
Livingstone, Scott, Mon.	.917	3	10	1	1	12	4
Loretta, Mark, Mil.	.992	70	353	23	3	379	41
Luke, Matt, L.A.*	1.000	18	64	13	0	77	5
Mabry, John, St.L.	1.000	16	93	11	0	104	8
Marrero, Eli, St.L.	1.000	2	1	1	0	2	0
McGee, Willie, St.L.	1.000	1	2	2	0	4	0
McGuire, Ryan, Mon.*	.980	78	275	25	6	306	18

Player, Team	Pct.	G	PO	A	E	TC	DP
McGwire, Mark, St.L.	.992	151	1326	97	12	1435	128
Miller, Damian, Ari.	1.000	1	0	1	0	1	0
Mordecai, Mike, Mon.	1.000	1	2	0	0	2	0
Nilsson, David, Mil.	.984	49	355	21	6	382	43
Olerud, John, N.Y.*	.996	157	1258	116	5	1379	119
Paquette, Craig, N.Y.	1.000	2	3	0	0	3	0
Perez, Eddie, Atl.	.938	8	15	0	1	16	1
Perez, Eduardo, Cin.	.985	51	290	45	5	340	35
Petagine, Roberto, Cin.*	1.000	15	46	4	0	50	4
Phillips, J.R., Hou.*	.962	12	70	6	3	79	7
Pratt, Todd, N.Y.	1.000	3	11	0	0	11	1
Roskos, John, Fla.	1.000	1	1	0	0	1	0
Seguignol, Fernando, Mon.	1.000	7	44	5	0	49	3
Servais, Scott, Chi.	1.000	1	2	1	0	3	0
Sheets, Andy, S.D.	1.000	2	9	0	0	9	2
Simon, Randall, Atl.*	1.000	4	36	1	0	37	3
Smith, Mark, Pit.	1.000	6	30	4	0	34	3
Snow, J.T., S.F.*	.999	136	1040	94	1	1135	99
Spehr, Tim, N.Y.	1.000	1	2	0	0	2	0
Spiers, Bill, Hou.	1.000	7	34	1	0	35	1
Strange, Doug, Pit.	1.000	3	2	1	0	3	0
Sweeney, Mark, S.D.*	.993	21	128	5	1	134	11
Tatum, Jim, N.Y.	1.000	9	32	1	0	33	1
Vander Wal, John, Col.-S.D.*	1.000	5	22	3	0	25	1
Williams, Eddie, S.D.	1.000	7	47	3	0	50	3
Young, Dmitri, Cin.	.994	44	304	22	2	328	25
Young, Kevin, Pit.	.994	157	1334	80	8	1422	139
Zeile, Todd, L.A.	1.000	1	2	0	0	2	0
Zuber, Jon, Phi.*	1.000	4	15	1	0	16	1

TRIPLE PLAYS: Brogna, Phi.; Hayes, S.F.; Olerud, N.Y.

FIRST BASEMEN WITH TWO OR MORE TEAMS

Player, Team	Pct.	G	PO	A	E	TC	DP
Colbrunn, Greg, Col.	.992	27	216	21	2	239	18
Colbrunn, Greg, Atl.	1.000	9	55	4	0	59	2
Eisenreich, Jim, Fla.*	.965	10	53	2	2	57	7
Eisenreich, Jim, L.A.*	1.000	9	20	2	0	22	5
Konerko, Paul, L.A.	.995	23	170	15	1	186	8
Konerko, Paul, Cin.	1.000	7	38	6	0	44	1
Vander Wal, John, Col.*	1.000	2	8	1	0	9	0
Vander Wal, John, S.D.*	1.000	3	14	2	0	16	1

SECOND BASEMEN

Player, Team	Pct.	G	PO	A	E	TC	DP
Abbott, Kurt, Col.	1.000	7	13	17	0	30	3
Alexander, Manny, Chi.	.979	27	43	51	2	96	11
Anderson, Marlon, Phi.	.978	9	14	30	1	45	6
Arias, Alex, Phi.	1.000	1	1	0	0	1	0
Baerga, Carlos, N.Y.	.986	144	289	340	9	638	97
Bates, Jeff, Col.	.974	17	13	24	1	38	4
Batista, Tony, Ari.	.994	41	71	84	1	156	23
Bell, David, St.L.	1.000	1	0	2	0	2	1
Bell, Jay, Ari.	.985	15	28	38	1	67	7
Belliard, Ronnie, Mil.	.000	1	0	0	0	0	0
Berg, Dave, Fla.	1.000	27	55	48	0	103	13
Biggio, Craig, Hou.	.980	159	318	431	15	764	92
Bogar, Tim, Hou.	1.000	11	10	14	0	24	4
Boone, Aaron, Cin.	.000	1	0	0	1	1	0
Boone, Bret, Cin.	.988	156	329	416	9	754	100

Player, Team	Pct.	G	PO	A	E	TC	DP
Cabrera, Orlando, Mon.	.970	28	59	72	4	135	16
Castillo, Luis, Fla.	.970	44	117	113	7	237	34
Castro, Juan, L.A.	.984	38	47	73	2	122	22
Cianfrocco, Archi, S.D.	1.000	3	3	1	0	4	1
Cora, Alex, L.A.	1.000	4	4	8	0	12	3
Counsell, Craig, Fla.	.991	104	237	299	5	541	72
DeShields, Delino, St.L.	.983	111	247	273	9	529	66
Diaz, Edwin, Ari.	.938	3	7	8	1	16	2
Dunston, Shawon, S.F.	1.000	1	0	1	0	1	1
Fox, Andy, Ari.	.982	60	103	118	4	225	23
Frias, Hanley, Ari.	1.000	3	6	5	0	11	2
Gaetti, Gary, St.L.	.000	1	0	0	0	0	0
Gilbert, Shawn, St.L.	1.000	2	1	0	0	1	0
Giovanola, Ed, S.D.	.992	36	45	78	1	124	12
Graffanino, Tony, Atl.	.971	93	139	226	11	376	41
Guerrero, Wilton, L.A.-Mon.	.972	84	156	197	10	363	41
Guillen, Ozzie, Atl.	1.000	2	1	5	0	6	1
Haney, Todd, N.Y.	.000	1	0	0	0	0	0
Harris, Lenny, N.Y.	1.000	2	1	0	0	1	0
Hernandez, Jose, Chi.	1.000	2	2	4	0	6	1
Holbert, Ray, Mon.	1.000	1	2	3	0	5	0
Howard, David, St.L.	1.000	19	37	49	0	86	5
Hubbard, Mike, Mon.	.000	1	0	0	0	0	0
Johnson, Russ, Hou.	1.000	1	2	2	0	4	0
Jordan, Kevin, Phi.	.966	22	32	54	3	89	12
Kelly, Pat, St.L.	.964	41	79	108	7	194	18
Kent, Jeff, S.F.	.972	134	278	404	20	702	87
Klassen, Danny, Ari.	.964	29	60	74	5	139	16
Lansing, Mike, Col.	.987	153	345	425	10	780	116
Lewis, Mark, Phi.	.978	140	276	437	16	729	74
Liriano, Nelson, Col.	1.000	3	4	2	0	6	1
Lockhart, Keith, Atl.	.984	97	130	250	6	386	56
Lopez, Luis, N.Y.	.975	50	74	85	4	163	16
Loretta, Mark, Mil.	1.000	13	12	15	0	27	5
Malloy, Marty, Atl.	1.000	10	16	22	0	38	4
Martinez, Ramon E., S.F.	1.000	14	15	20	0	35	7
Maxwell, Jason, Chi.	1.000	1	0	1	0	1	0
McEwing, Joe, St.L.	1.000	6	9	10	0	19	3
Metcalfe, Mike, L.A.	.000	1	0	0	0	0	0
Milliard, Ralph, N.Y.	.833	5	3	2	1	6	0
Morandini, Mickey, Chi.	.993	152	267	404	5	676	70
Mordecai, Mike, Mon.	.980	21	17	32	1	50	7
Mueller, Bill, S.F.	.968	10	16	14	1	31	4
Ordaz, Luis, St.L.	1.000	1	2	3	0	5	1
Owens, Eric, Mil.	.500	4	1	0	1	2	0
Polanco, Placido, St.L.	.982	14	34	21	1	56	10
Polcovich, Kevin, Pit.	1.000	15	15	37	0	52	9
Reese, Pokey, Cin.	1.000	3	6	9	0	15	3
Sanchez, Rey, S.F.	.991	36	36	76	1	113	18
Sanford, Chance, Pit.	.500	1	1	0	1	2	0
Santangelo, F.P., Mon.	.983	35	47	71	2	120	7
Sefcik, Kevin, Phi.	1.000	1	1	0	0	1	0
Sheets, Andy, S.D.	.975	22	38	39	2	79	7
Shumpert, Terry, Col.	1.000	6	2	14	0	16	3
Spiers, Bill, Hou.	.958	9	10	13	1	24	2
Stankiewicz, Andy, Ari.	.994	61	62	94	1	157	17
Strange, Doug, Pit.	1.000	9	17	18	0	35	6
Stynes, Chris, Cin.	1.000	11	15	22	0	37	4
Veras, Quilvio, S.D.	.987	131	258	405	9	672	89
Vidro, Jose, Mon.	.975	56	77	121	5	203	25
Vina, Fernando, Mil.	.986	158	404	468	12	884	135
Walker, Larry, Col.	.000	1	0	0	0	0	0
Womack, Tony, Pit.	.978	152	304	450	17	771	104
Young, Eric, L.A.	.976	113	225	304	13	542	67
Zaun, Gregg, Fla.	1.000	1	0	1	0	1	0

TRIPLE PLAYS: Lewis, Phi.; Young, L.A.

SECOND BASEMEN WITH TWO OR MORE TEAMS

Player, Team	Pct.	G	PO	A	E	TC	DP
Guerrero, Wilton, L.A.	.968	32	53	67	4	124	16
Guerrero, Wilton, Mon.	.975	52	103	130	6	239	25

THIRD BASEMEN

Player, Team	Pct.	G	PO	A	E	TC	DP
Abbott, Kurt, Col.	1.000	3	2	1	0	3	0
Alexander, Manny, Chi.	.963	19	8	18	1	27	1
Alfonzo, Edgar, N.Y.	.976	144	117	248	9	374	20
Andrews, Shane, Mon.	.954	147	95	322	20	437	28
Arias, Alex, Phi.	1.000	5	0	1	0	1	0
Arias, George, S.D.	.933	14	5	23	2	30	2
Banks, Brian, Mil.	.000	1	0	0	0	0	0

Player, Team	Pct.	G	PO	A	E	TC	DP
Barrett, Michael, Mon.	.714	3	0	5	2	7	0
Bates, Jeff, Col.	.000	3	0	0	0	0	0
Batista, Tony, Ari.	.974	15	9	28	1	38	1
Bell, David, St.L.	1.000	4	1	2	0	3	0
Beltre, Adrian, L.A.	.925	74	31	130	13	174	13
Berg, Dave, Fla.	.953	25	19	42	3	64	2
Berry, Sean, Hou.	.953	87	55	150	10	215	13
Bogar, Tim, Hou.	.909	11	4	6	1	11	1
Bonilla, Bobby, Fla.-L.A.	.915	85	58	125	17	200	14
Boone, Aaron, Cin.	.950	52	37	97	7	141	7
Booty, Josh, Fla.	.833	7	4	11	3	18	1
Caminiti, Ken, S.D.	.931	126	77	207	21	305	16
Castilla, Vinny, Col.	.970	162	110	316	13	439	39
Castro, Juan, L.A.	.923	12	5	7	1	13	2
Cianfrocco, Archi, S.D.	.875	13	7	14	3	24	0
Cirillo, Jeff, Mil.	.976	149	99	340	11	450	45
Fox, Andy, Ari.	.973	26	23	48	2	73	4
Franco, Matt, N.Y.	1.000	13	5	18	0	23	2
Frias, Hanley, Ari.	1.000	2	0	1	0	1	0
Gaetti, Gary, St.L-Chi.	.983	119	71	221	5	297	17
Garcia, Freddy, Pit.	.949	47	28	102	7	137	9
Gilbert, Shawn, N.Y.	.000	1	0	0	0	0	0
Giovanola, Ed, S.D.	.965	37	11	44	2	57	2
Graffanino, Tony, Atl.	1.000	1	0	0	0	0	0
Greene, Willie, Cin.	.936	76	48	128	12	188	20
Guillen, Ozzie, Atl.	1.000	1	1	1	0	2	0
Hardtke, Jason, Chi.	1.000	7	0	3	0	3	0
Harris, Lenny, N.Y.	.929	10	2	11	1	14	1
Hayes, Charlie, S.F.	.989	46	22	67	1	90	6
Helms, Wes, Atl.	.750	4	1	2	1	4	0
Hernandez, Jose, Chi.	.958	72	45	114	7	166	4
Houston, Tyler, Chi.	.875	12	1	13	2	16	1
Howard, David, St.L.	1.000	14	3	3	0	6	0
Howell, Jack, Hou.	1.000	2	1	5	0	6	0
Hubbard, Trenidad, L.A.	1.000	1	0	0	0	0	0
Johnson, Russ, Hou.	1.000	5	1	7	0	8	0
Jones, Chipper, Atl.	.971	158	105	290	12	407	28
Jordan, Brian, St.L.	1.000	1	0	1	0	1	0
Jordan, Kevin, Phi.	.929	6	5	8	1	14	1
Kinkade, Mike, N.Y.	.000	1	0	0	0	0	0
Konerko, Paul, L.A.-Cin.	.976	20	7	33	1	41	1
Lansing, Mike, Col.	1.000	1	0	0	0	0	0
Leyritz, Jim, S.D.	1.000	1	3	0	0	3	0
Livingstone, Scott, Mon.	.938	17	6	24	2	32	0
Lockhart, Keith, Atl.	.000	1	0	0	0	0	0
Lopez, Luis, N.Y.	1.000	11	1	12	0	13	2
Loretta, Mark, Mil.	1.000	22	18	33	0	51	9
Mabry, John, St.L.	.914	38	18	46	6	70	1
Millar, Kevin, Fla.	.833	2	2	3	1	6	1
Mordecai, Mike, Mon.	.889	11	3	5	1	9	0
Mueller, Bill, S.F.	.952	137	83	273	18	374	32
Ordaz, Luis, St.L.	.000	2	0	0	0	0	0
Orie, Kevin, Chi.-Fla.	.952	105	88	207	15	310	12
Osik, Keith, Pit.	.964	7	9	18	1	28	4
Paquette, Craig, N.Y.	1.000	4	2	2	0	4	1
Perez, Eduardo, Cin.	1.000	1	0	2	0	2	0
Polcovich, Kevin, Pit.	1.000	8	2	17	0	19	1
Ramirez, Aramis, Pit.	.941	71	29	114	9	152	13
Reese, Pokey, Cin.	.985	32	20	45	1	66	7
Rolen, Scott, Phi.	.970	159	135	319	14	468	28
Sanford, Chance, Pit.	.900	5	4	5	1	10	2
Santangelo, F.P., Mon.	1.000	1	0	0	0	0	0
Sefcik, Kevin, Phi.	.500	2	1	0	1	2	0
Sheets, Andy, S.D.	.909	23	8	12	2	22	2
Spiers, Bill, Hou.	.966	99	57	170	8	235	9
Strange, Doug, Pit.	.940	42	25	54	5	84	3
Stynes, Chris, Cin.	.946	22	9	26	2	37	3
Tatis, Fernando, St.L.	.928	55	35	120	12	167	7
Tatum, Jim, N.Y.	1.000	3	2	2	0	4	0
Vidro, Jose, Mon.	.900	7	4	5	1	10	2
Walker, Larry, Col.	.000	1	0	0	0	0	0
Wehner, John, Fla.	1.000	8	2	10	0	12	0
Williams, Matt, Ari.	.972	134	99	282	11	392	18
Zeile, Todd, L.A.-Fla.	.957	105	68	175	11	254	13

TRIPLE PLAY: Bonilla, L.A.

THIRD BASEMEN WITH TWO OR MORE TEAMS

Player, Team	Pct.	G	PO	A	E	TC	DP
Bonilla, Bobby, Fla.	.922	26	18	41	5	64	6
Bonilla, Bobby, L.A.	.912	59	40	84	12	136	8
Gaetti, Gary, St.L.	.985	83	47	153	3	203	15
Gaetti, Gary, Chi.	.979	36	24	68	2	94	2

Player, Team	Pct.	G	PO	A	E	TC	DP
Konerko, Paul, L.A.	.952	11	5	15	1	21	1
Konerko, Paul, Cin.	1.000	9	2	18	0	20	0
Orie, Kevin, Chi.	.966	57	39	101	5	145	7
Orie, Kevin, Fla.	.939	48	49	106	10	165	5
Zeile, Todd, L.A.	.929	40	25	53	6	84	2
Zeile, Todd, Fla.	.971	65	43	122	5	170	11

SHORTSTOPS

Player, Team	Pct.	G	PO	A	E	TC	DP
Abbott, Kurt, Col.	1.000	7	4	6	0	10	2
Alexander, Manny, Chi.	.964	50	37	71	4	112	15
Alfonzo, Edgar, N.Y.	.000	1	0	0	0	0	0
Arias, Alex, Phi.	.985	38	43	86	2	131	10
Aurilia, Rich, S.F.	.979	120	154	313	10	477	71
Bates, Jeff, Col.	.833	3	2	3	1	6	2
Batista, Tony, Ari.	.971	34	43	93	4	140	13
Bell, Jay, Ari.	.971	138	196	399	18	613	77
Belliard, Rafael, Atl.	.952	7	7	13	1	21	4
Beltre, Adrian, L.A.	1.000	2	1	1	0	2	0
Berg, Dave, Fla.	.933	17	16	40	4	60	8
Blauser, Jeff, Chi.	.965	106	129	255	14	398	36
Bogar, Tim, Hou.	.989	55	49	127	2	178	16
Boone, Aaron, Cin.	.000	1	0	0	0	0	0
Cabrera, Orlando, Mon.	.984	52	63	124	3	190	20
Castilla, Vinny, Col.	.000	1	0	0	0	0	0
Castro, Juan, L.A.	.954	47	43	102	7	152	29
Clayton, Royce, St.L.	.970	89	140	286	13	439	53
Collier, Lou, Pit.	.960	107	148	287	18	453	56
Cora, Alex, L.A.	.956	21	22	21	2	45	6
Delgado, Wilson, S.F.	1.000	6	3	6	0	9	2
DeRosa, Mark, Atl.	1.000	4	1	1	0	2	0
Dunston, Shawon, S.F.	.938	9	11	4	1	16	0
Frias, Hanley, Ari.	1.000	2	3	4	0	7	0
Giovanola, Ed, S.D.	.000	1	0	0	0	0	0
Gomez, Chris, S.D.	.980	143	180	397	12	589	93
Gonzalez, Alex, Fla.	.978	25	29	58	2	89	17
Graffanino, Tony, Atl.	1.000	2	0	1	0	1	0
Greene, Willie, Cin.	.800	2	1	3	1	5	1
Grudzielanek, Mark, Mon.-L.A.	.954	156	230	455	33	718	90
Guerrero, Wilton, L.A.	.947	14	12	24	2	38	6
Guillen, Ozzie, Atl.	.977	71	93	160	6	259	25
Gutierrez, Ricky, Hou.	.976	141	215	404	15	634	82
Hernandez, Jose, Chi.	.963	45	53	104	6	163	19
Holbert, Ray, Atl.	.952	7	6	14	1	21	3
Howard, David, St.L.	.953	16	12	29	2	43	4
Jackson, Damian, Cin.	.972	10	14	21	1	36	3
Kelly, Pat, St.L.	1.000	2	0	1	0	1	0
Larkin, Barry, Cin.	.979	145	207	361	12	580	79
Liriano, Nelson, Col.	1.000	1	0	2	0	2	0
Lopez, Luis, N.Y.	.933	39	36	47	6	89	17
Loretta, Mark, Mil.	.986	56	67	144	3	214	39
Milliard, Ralph, N.Y.	.000	1	0	0	0	0	0
Mordecai, Mike, Mon.	.953	30	16	45	3	64	6
Nieves, Jose, Chi.	.000	1	0	0	0	0	0
Nunez, Abraham, Pit.	.930	23	33	60	7	100	12
Ordaz, Luis, St.L.	.945	54	68	154	13	235	34
Ordonez, Rey, N.Y.	.975	151	265	401	17	683	82
Perez, Neifi, Col.	.975	162	272	516	20	808	127
Polanco, Placido, St.L.	.952	28	38	81	6	125	18
Polcovich, Kevin, Pit.	.916	54	59	159	20	238	32
Reese, Pokey, Cin.	.873	18	24	24	7	55	7
Relaford, Desi, Phi.	.960	137	189	380	24	593	72
Renteria, Edgar, Fla.	.966	129	194	372	20	586	93
Sanchez, Rey, S.F.	.977	76	106	185	7	298	33
Sanford, Chance, Pit.	1.000	1	0	1	0	1	0
Sheets, Andy, S.D.	.964	39	41	94	5	140	18
Spiers, Bill, Hou.	.000	2	0	0	0	0	0
Stynes, Chris, Cin.	1.000	2	1	2	0	3	1
Tatis, Fernando, St.L.	1.000	3	1	3	0	4	0
Valentin, Jose, Mil.	.963	139	173	370	21	564	69
Vizcaino, Jose, L.A.	.985	66	89	172	4	265	33
Weiss, Walt, Atl.	.967	96	97	257	12	366	63
Womack, Tony, Pit.	1.000	2	1	1	0	2	0

TRIPLE PLAYS: Arias, Phi.; Aurilia, S.F.; Ordonez, N.Y.; Vizcaino, L.A.

SHORTSTOPS WITH TWO OR MORE TEAMS

Player, Team	Pct.	G	PO	A	E	TC	DP
Grudzielanek, Mark, Mon.	.950	105	152	283	23	458	56
Grudzielanek, Mark, L.A.	.962	51	78	172	10	260	34

OUTFIELDERS

Player, Team	Pct.	G	PO	A	E	TC	DP
Abbott, Kurt, Col.	.929	9	13	0	1	14	0
Abreu, Bobby, Phi.	.973	146	272	17	8	297	0
Agbayani, Benny, N.Y.	1.000	9	6	0	0	6	0
Alexander, Manny, Chi.	1.000	1	1	0	0	1	0
Allensworth, Jermaine, Pit.-N.Y.	.983	97	167	4	3	174	2
Alou, Moises, Hou.	.980	154	232	11	5	248	2
Amaro, Ruben, Phi.	1.000	51	26	3	0	29	0
Banks, Brian, Mil.	.500	1	0	1	1	2	0
Barry, Jeff, Col.	1.000	10	20	1	0	21	0
Bautista, Danny, Atl.	.959	58	47	0	2	49	0
Becker, Rich, N.Y.*	.984	41	56	4	1	61	0
Bell, Derek, Hou.	.973	154	281	8	8	297	3
Benard, Marvin, S.F.*	.982	79	109	1	2	112	1
Benitez, Yamil, Ari.	.972	62	101	4	3	108	1
Bichette, Dante, Col.	.965	156	289	14	11	314	6
Bieser, Steve, Pit.	.000	1	0	0	0	0	0
Bonds, Barry, S.F.*	.984	155	301	2	5	308	0
Bonilla, Bobby, L.A.	.941	12	16	0	1	17	0
Brede, Brent, Ari.*	.964	58	78	2	3	83	1
Brown, Adrian, Pit.	.977	38	83	3	2	88	2
Brown, Brant, Chi.*	.963	102	180	1	7	188	0
Brown, Emil, Pit.	1.000	10	21	2	0	23	0
Burks, Ellis, Col.-S.F.	.979	139	276	6	6	288	0
Burnitz, Jeromy, Mil.	.972	161	306	10	9	325	3
Cangelosi, John, Fla.*	.969	45	62	1	2	65	0
Carter, Joe, S.F.	1.000	17	15	0	0	15	0
Cedeno, Roger, L.A.	.978	77	86	4	2	92	1
Cianfrocco, Archi, S.D.	1.000	3	2	0	0	2	0
Clark, Dave, Hou.	.885	22	22	1	3	26	0
Clemente, Edgard, Col.	.857	7	6	0	1	7	0
Colbrunn, Greg, Col.-Atl.	1.000	6	8	0	0	8	0
Dellucci, David, Ari.*	.987	117	230	3	3	236	3
Devereaux, Mike, L.A.	1.000	5	9	1	0	10	0
Diaz, Alex, S.F.	1.000	21	28	2	0	30	0
Drew, J.D., St.L	1.000	11	19	1	0	20	1
Dunston, Shawon, S.F.	.900	6	9	0	1	10	0
Dunwoody, Todd, Fla.*	.989	111	273	9	3	285	4
Echevarria, Angel, Col.	1.000	4	3	0	0	3	0
Eisenreich, Jim, Fla.-L.A.*	.977	32	42	1	1	44	0
Everett, Carl, Hou.	.987	123	296	12	4	312	3
Finley, Steve, S.D.*	.981	157	351	12	7	370	6
Floyd, Cliff, Fla.	.974	146	251	10	7	268	1
Fox, Andy, Ari.	.976	48	77	3	2	82	0
Franco, Matt, N.Y.	.923	13	11	1	1	13	0
Frank, Mike, Cin.*	1.000	28	60	1	0	61	0
Gaetti, Gary, St.L.	.000	1	0	0	0	0	0
Gant, Ron, St.L.	.971	104	162	4	5	171	0
Garcia, Karim, Ari.*	.975	103	191	6	5	202	1
Gibson, Derrick, Col.	.929	7	11	2	1	14	0
Gilkey, Bernard, N.Y.-Ari.	.989	104	170	12	2	184	1
Glanville, Doug, Phi.	.995	158	360	14	2	376	3
Goodwin, Curtis, Col.*	.983	91	118	1	2	121	0
Greene, Willie, Cin.	1.000	28	43	1	0	44	0
Grissom, Marquis, Mil.	.991	137	317	8	3	328	3
Guerrero, Vladimir, Mon.	.951	157	323	9	17	349	3
Guerrero, Wilton, L.A.	.857	7	6	0	1	7	0
Guillen, Jose, Pit.	.968	151	283	16	10	309	4
Gwynn, Tony, S.D.*	.993	116	142	5	1	148	0
Hamilton, Darryl, S.F.-Col.	.997	144	297	5	1	303	1
Hammonds, Jeffrey, Cin.	.985	25	64	3	1	68	1
Haney, Todd, N.Y.	.000	1	0	0	0	0	0
Hardtke, Jason, Chi.	.000	1	0	0	0	0	0
Harris, Lenny, Cin.-N.Y.	.968	97	117	5	4	126	0
Hernandez, Jose, Chi.	1.000	54	74	3	0	77	0
Hidalgo, Richard, Hou.	.978	72	131	3	3	137	1
Hill, Glenallen, Chi.	.984	34	59	3	1	63	0
Hollandsworth, Todd, L.A.*	.957	51	87	1	4	92	0
Hollins, Damon, Atl.-L.A.*	1.000	7	7	0	0	7	0
Howard, David, St.L.	1.000	2	1	1	0	2	1
Howard, Thomas, L.A.	1.000	29	33	2	0	35	0
Hubbard, Trenidad, L.A.	.991	81	110	3	1	114	0
Hudler, Rex, Phi.	1.000	9	19	0	0	19	0
Hughes, Bobby, Mil.	1.000	3	1	0	0	1	0
Hundley, Todd, N.Y.	.898	34	42	2	5	49	0
Hunter, Brian, St.L.*	.938	25	43	2	3	48	1
Huskey, Butch, N.Y.	.978	103	166	8	4	178	1
Incaviglia, Pete, Hou.	1.000	3	3	0	0	3	0
Jackson, Damian, Cin.	1.000	3	6	0	0	6	0
Jackson, Darrin, Mil.	.982	94	106	3	2	111	0
Jackson, Ryan, Fla.*	.976	32	41	0	1	42	0

1998 N.L. STATISTICS *Fielding*

Player, Team	Pct.	G	PO	A	E	TC	DP
Javier, Stan, S.F.	.986	121	217	0	3	220	1
Jefferies, Gregg, Phi.	.994	121	168	7	1	176	0
Jenkins, Geoff, Mil.	.968	81	115	6	4	125	2
Johnson, Brian, S.F.	1.000	1	1	0	0	1	0
Johnson, Lance, Chi.*	.975	78	154	5	4	163	2
Jones, Andruw, Atl.	.995	159	413	20	2	435	6
Jones, Chris, Ari.-S.F.	.956	37	42	1	2	45	0
Jones, Terry, Mon.	.988	60	161	4	2	167	3
Jordan, Brian, St.L.	.970	141	284	11	9	304	6
Kelly, Pat, St.L.	.000	3	0	0	0	0	0
Kirby, Wayne, N.Y.	1.000	19	15	1	0	16	1
Klesko, Ryan, Atl.*	.994	120	147	9	1	157	1
Konerko, Paul, L.A.-Cin.	1.000	18	20	0	0	20	0
Kotsay, Mark, Fla.*	.984	145	347	20	6	373	2
Lampkin, Tom, St.L.	1.000	5	1	0	0	1	0
Lankford, Ray, St.L.*	.986	145	338	7	5	350	2
Leyritz, Jim, S.D.	.000	1	0	0	0	0	0
Little, Mark, St.L.	1.000	7	11	0	0	11	0
Lombard, George, Atl.	1.000	2	2	0	0	2	0
Lopez, Luis, N.Y.	.923	9	12	0	1	13	0
Loretta, Mark, Mil.	.000	1	0	0	0	0	0
Lowery, Terrell, Chi.	.929	22	13	0	1	14	0
Luke, Matt, L.A.*	.990	63	97	6	1	104	0
Mabry, John, St.L.	.971	80	95	7	3	105	3
Magee, Wendell, Phi.	.941	19	31	1	2	34	0
Martin, Al, Pit.*	.985	114	192	6	3	201	1
Martinez, Greg, Mil.	.000	6	0	0	0	0	0
Martinez, Manny, Pit.	.989	62	92	0	1	93	0
May, Derrick, Mon.	.984	48	57	3	1	61	1
McEwing, Joe, St.L.	1.000	3	1	0	0	1	0
McGee, Willie, St.L.	.938	88	100	6	7	113	1
McGuire, Ryan, Mon.*	.981	46	51	1	1	53	0
McRae, Brian, N.Y.	.987	154	302	8	4	314	3
Merced, Orlando, Chi.	1.000	4	3	0	0	3	0
Meulens, Hensley, Ari.	1.000	4	6	1	0	7	0
Mieske, Matt, Chi.	.974	62	36	1	1	38	0
Miller, Damian, Ari.	.000	2	0	0	0	0	0
Mondesi, Raul, L.A.	.980	148	284	6	6	296	1
Montgomery, Ray, Hou.	1.000	2	1	0	0	1	0
Mouton, James, S.D.	.969	33	30	1	1	32	0
Newfield, Marc, Mil.	.962	55	73	3	3	79	0
Nieves, Melvin, Cin.	1.000	25	31	1	0	32	0
Nilsson, David, Mil.	.963	37	50	2	2	54	0
Nunnally, Jon, Cin.	.956	70	126	5	6	137	0
Owens, Eric, Mil.	1.000	16	13	2	0	15	0
Paquette, Craig, N.Y.	.000	1	0	0	0	0	0
Payton, Jay, N.Y.	1.000	9	6	1	0	7	0
Perez, Eduardo, Cin.	1.000	1	1	0	0	1	0
Perez, Robert, Mon.	.852	29	20	3	4	27	0
Petagine, Roberto, Cin.*	1.000	15	28	0	0	28	0
Phillips, J.R., Hou.*	1.000	6	2	0	0	2	0
Phillips, Tony, N.Y.	.967	51	86	2	3	91	0
Powell, Dante, S.F.	1.000	8	2	0	0	2	0
Pride, Curtis, Atl.	1.000	22	41	0	0	41	0
Rios, Armando, S.F.*	1.000	5	5	0	0	5	0
Rivera, Ruben, S.D.	.973	91	104	3	3	110	0
Rodriguez, Henry, Chi.*	.996	114	215	7	1	223	1
Sanders, Reggie, Cin.	.978	131	263	4	6	273	0
Santangelo, F.P., Mon.	.983	92	164	6	3	173	0
Sefcik, Kevin, Phi.	.989	60	87	1	1	89	0
Seguignol, Fernando, Mon.	1.000	9	21	0	0	21	0
Sheffield, Gary, Fla.-L.A.	.991	126	217	9	2	228	4
Smith, Mark, Pit.	.977	24	42	0	1	43	0
Sosa, Sammy, Chi.	.975	159	334	14	9	357	2
Stovall, DaRond, Mon.*	.925	47	35	2	3	40	0
Stynes, Chris, Cin.	1.000	80	123	4	0	127	2
Sweeney, Mark, S.D.*	1.000	34	37	0	0	37	0
Tarasco, Tony, Cin.	1.000	7	10	0	0	10	0
Tatum, Jim, N.Y.	1.000	4	6	0	0	6	0
Tucker, Michael, Atl.	.995	118	194	5	1	200	1
Valdes, Pedro, Chi.*	1.000	7	10	0	0	10	0
Vander Wal, John, Col.-S.D.*	1.000	30	28	2	0	30	0
Vaughn, Greg, S.D.	.993	151	270	5	2	277	1
Walker, Larry, Col.	.984	123	236	8	4	248	2
Ward, Turner, Pit.	.983	97	163	7	3	173	2
Watkins, Pat, Cin.	.971	77	98	1	3	102	0
Wehner, John, Fla.	1.000	23	25	2	0	27	0
White, Derrick, Chi.-Col.	1.000	3	1	0	0	1	0
White, Devon, Ari.	.987	144	371	3	5	379	0
White, Rondell, Mon.	.996	96	261	7	1	269	3
Williams, Gerald, Atl.	.970	120	158	2	5	165	0
Wilson, Preston, N.Y.-Fla.	.958	18	23	0	1	24	0

Player, Team	Pct.	G	PO	A	E	TC	DP
Womack, Tony, Pit.	1.000	5	4	0	0	4	0
Young, Dmitri, Cin.	.940	105	154	3	10	167	0
Zuber, Jon, Phi.*	1.000	5	7	0	0	7	0

TRIPLE PLAY: McRae, Chi.

OUTFIELDERS WITH TWO OR MORE TEAMS

Player, Team	Pct.	G	PO	A	E	TC	DP
Allensworth, Jermaine, Pit.	.980	66	145	4	3	152	2
Allensworth, Jermaine, N.Y.	1.000	31	22	0	0	22	0
Burks, Ellis, Col.	.975	98	187	5	5	197	0
Burks, Ellis, S.F.	.989	41	89	1	1	91	0
Colbrunn, Greg, Col.	1.000	5	6	0	0	6	0
Colbrunn, Greg, Atl.	1.000	1	2	0	0	2	0
Eisenreich, Jim, Fla.*	1.000	8	9	0	0	9	0
Eisenreich, Jim, L.A.*	.971	24	33	1	1	35	0
Gilkey, Bernard, N.Y.	.992	77	121	9	1	131	1
Gilkey, Bernard, Ari.	.981	27	49	3	1	53	0
Hamilton, Darryl, S.F.	1.000	96	194	4	0	198	1
Hamilton, Darryl, Col.	.990	48	103	1	1	105	0
Harris, Lenny, Cin.	.929	32	37	2	3	42	0
Harris, Lenny, N.Y.	.988	65	80	3	1	84	0
Hollins, Damon, Atl.*	1.000	3	2	0	0	2	0
Hollins, Damon, L.A.*	1.000	4	5	0	0	5	0
Jones, Chris, Ari.	1.000	8	11	0	0	11	0
Jones, Chris, S.F.	.941	29	31	1	2	34	0
Konerko, Paul, L.A.	1.000	11	12	0	0	12	0
Konerko, Paul, Cin.	1.000	7	8	0	0	8	0
Sheffield, Gary, Fla.	.986	37	68	3	1	72	2
Sheffield, Gary, L.A.	.994	89	149	6	1	156	2
Vander Wal, John, Col.*	1.000	25	21	2	0	23	0
Vander Wal, John, S.D.*	1.000	5	7	0	0	7	0
White, Derrick, Chi.	1.000	1	0	0	0	0	0
White, Derrick, Col.	1.000	2	1	0	0	1	0
Wilson, Preston, N.Y.	.909	7	10	0	1	11	0
Wilson, Preston, Fla.	1.000	11	13	0	0	13	0

CATCHERS

Player, Team	Pct.	G	PO	A	E	TC	DP	PB
Ausmus, Brad, Hou.	.992	124	850	58	7	915	10	4
Banks, Brian, Mil.	1.000	5	4	0	0	4	0	0
Barrett, Michael, Mon.	.963	3	22	4	1	27	1	0
Bennett, Gary, Phi.	1.000	9	50	2	0	52	0	0
Castillo, Alberto, N.Y.	.990	35	193	15	2	210	3	1
Colbrunn, Greg, Col.	.000	1	0	0	0	0	0	0
Davis, Ben, S.D.	1.000	1	2	0	0	2	0	0
Estalella, Bobby, Phi.	.988	47	321	12	4	337	0	5
Eusebio, Tony, Hou.	.992	54	352	19	3	374	2	4
Fabregas, Jorge, Ari.-N.Y.	.991	53	290	36	3	329	4	2
Fordyce, Brook, Cin.	.978	54	288	20	7	315	3	0
Garcia, Guillermo, Cin.	.988	11	74	6	1	81	1	2
Henley, Bob, Mon.	.995	35	189	14	1	204	1	3
Hernandez, Carlos, S.D.	.992	122	794	53	7	854	6	13
Houston, Tyler, Chi.	.993	63	418	21	3	442	4	3
Hubbard, Mike, Mon.	1.000	24	83	4	0	87	1	1
Hughes, Bobby, Mil.	.995	72	397	29	2	428	5	6
Hundley, Todd, N.Y.	1.000	2	18	2	0	20	0	0
Jensen, Marcus, Mil.	1.000	1	1	0	0	1	0	0
Johnson, Brian, S.F.	.994	95	590	33	4	627	4	7
Johnson, Charles, Fla.-L.A.	.992	131	908	60	8	976	11	6
Kendall, Jason, Pit.	.992	144	1015	58	9	1082	10	9
Knorr, Randy, Fla.	.989	15	82	7	1	90	2	4
Laker, Tim, Pit.	1.000	1	2	0	0	2	0	0
Lampkin, Tom, St.L.	.986	62	331	19	5	355	5	4
Levis, Jesse, Mil.	1.000	14	83	2	0	85	0	1
Leyritz, Jim, S.D.	.987	24	139	11	2	152	1	1
Lieberthal, Mike, Phi.	.988	83	607	41	8	656	5	5
LoDuca, Paul, L.A.	1.000	4	18	2	0	20	1	1
Lopez, Javy, Atl.	.995	128	978	68	5	1051	6	11
Manwaring, Kirt, Col.	.988	108	528	48	7	583	6	8
Marrero, Eli, St.L.	.991	73	426	30	4	460	3	1
Martinez, Sandy, Chi.	.985	33	185	7	3	195	1	1
Matheny, Mike, Mil.	.987	107	570	45	8	623	9	6
Mayne, Brent, S.F.	.991	88	493	39	5	537	5	6
Meluskey, Mitch, Hou.	1.000	3	9	0	0	9	1	0
Miller, Damian, Ari.	.986	46	255	26	4	285	2	5
Mirabelli, Doug, S.F.	.974	10	34	4	1	39	0	0
Myers, Greg, S.D.	.987	52	276	29	4	309	4	2
Nilsson, David, Mil.	.970	7	31	1	1	33	0	1
Osik, Keith, Pit.	1.000	26	143	12	0	155	1	4
Pagnozzi, Tom, St.L.	.982	44	259	17	5	281	5	1
Parent, Mark, Phi.	.987	34	211	15	3	229	5	5

Player, Team	Pct.	G	PO	A	E	TC	DP	PB
Pena, Angel, L.A.	1.000	4	26	2	0	28	0	1
Perez, Eddie, Atl.	.997	45	275	29	1	305	2	2
Perez, Neifi, Col.	.000	1	0	0	0	0	0	0
Piazza, Mike, L.A.-Fla.-N.Y.	.990	140	984	85	11	1080	7	5
Pratt, Todd, N.Y.	.973	16	67	4	2	73	1	2
Prince, Tom, L.A.	1.000	32	175	16	0	191	2	1
Redmond, Mike, Fla.	.992	37	216	25	2	243	3	3
Reed, Jeff, Col.	.986	99	452	27	7	486	4	1
Romero, Mandy, S.D.	.963	6	24	2	1	27	0	1
Servais, Scott, Chi.	.994	110	652	47	4	703	6	3
Spehr, Tim, N.Y.	1.000	21	118	10	0	128	1	1
Stinnett, Kelly, Ari.	.984	86	458	37	8	503	3	1
Strittmatter, Mark, Col.	1.000	3	10	1	0	11	1	0
Tatum, Jim, N.Y.	1.000	4	11	3	0	14	0	0
Taubensee, Eddie, Cin.	.988	126	776	44	10	830	5	8
Widger, Chris, Mon.	.983	123	752	64	14	830	12	14
Wilkins, Rick, N.Y.	.957	4	21	1	1	23	0	0
Zaun, Gregg, Fla.	.986	88	531	48	8	587	12	10

TRIPLE PLAY: Pratt, N.Y.

CATCHERS WITH TWO OR MORE TEAMS

Player, Team	Pct.	G	PO	A	E	TC	DP	PB
Fabregas, Jorge, Ari.	.996	41	228	30	1	259	2	0
Fabregas, Jorge, N.Y.	.971	12	62	6	2	70	2	2
Johnson, Charles, Fla.	.990	31	193	10	2	205	2	1
Johnson, Charles, L.A.	.992	100	715	50	6	771	9	5
Piazza, Mike, L.A.	.993	37	277	25	2	304	1	0
Piazza, Mike, Fla.	.968	4	27	3	1	31	1	0
Piazza, Mike, N.Y.	.989	99	680	57	8	745	5	5

PITCHERS

Player, Team	Pct.	G	PO	A	E	TC	DP
Acevedo, Juan, St.L.	.960	50	6	18	1	25	0
Adams, Terry, Chi.	.850	63	4	13	3	20	0
Adamson, Joel, Ari.*	.800	5	0	4	1	5	0
Alfonseca, Antonio, Fla.	.909	58	4	6	1	11	1
Anderson, Brian, Ari.*	.966	32	11	46	2	59	4
Ashby, Andy, S.D.	.980	33	14	35	1	50	4
Astacio, Pedro, Col.	1.000	35	22	31	0	53	3
Aybar, Manny, St.L	1.000	20	8	8	0	16	0
Bailey, Cory, S.F.	.000	5	0	0	0	0	0
Banks, Willie, Ari.	1.000	33	7	6	0	13	0
Barrios, Manuel, Fla.-L.A.	.000	3	0	0	0	0	0
Batista, Miguel, Mon.	.969	56	10	21	1	32	1
Beck, Rod, Chi.	1.000	81	8	11	0	19	1
Beech, Matt, Phi.*	1.000	21	0	13	0	13	2
Belinda, Stan, Cin.	.857	40	2	10	2	14	1
Beltran, Rigo, N.Y.*	1.000	7	0	1	0	1	0
Benes, Andy, Ari.	1.000	34	23	25	0	48	2
Bennett, Shayne, Mon.	1.000	62	4	14	0	18	1
Bere, Jason, Cin.	1.000	9	1	5	0	6	0
Bergman, Sean, Hou.	.968	31	16	14	1	31	0
Blair, Willie, Ari.-N.Y.	.978	34	10	35	1	46	3
Boehringer, Brian, S.D.	1.000	56	7	8	0	15	0
Bohanon, Brian, N.Y.-L.A.*	.960	39	10	38	2	50	3
Borland, Toby, Fla.	1.000	6	0	1	0	1	0
Boskie, Shawn, Mon.	.800	5	0	4	1	5	0
Bottalico, Ricky, Phi.	1.000	39	5	6	0	11	1
Bottenfield, Kent, St.L.	1.000	44	3	27	0	30	0
Brantley, Jeff, St.L.	1.000	48	4	0	0	4	0
Brewer, Billy, Phi.*	.000	2	0	0	0	0	0
Brock, Chris, S.F.	.750	13	1	2	1	4	0
Brow, Scott, Ari.	.857	17	5	1	1	7	0
Brown, Kevin, S.D.	.973	36	31	41	2	74	2
Brownson, Mark, Col.	1.000	2	1	0	0	1	0
Brunson, Will, L.A.*	.000	2	0	0	0	0	0
Bruske, Jim, L.A.-S.D.	1.000	39	2	3	0	5	0
Bullinger, Kirk, Mon.	1.000	8	0	3	0	3	0
Busby, Mike, St.L.	1.000	26	3	4	0	7	1
Butler, Adam, Atl.*	.000	8	0	0	1	0	0
Byrd, Paul, Atl.-Phi.	.909	9	3	7	1	11	1
Cabrera, Jose, Hou.	1.000	3	0	1	0	1	0
Cather, Mike, Atl.	.875	36	0	7	1	8	0
Charlton, Norm, Atl.*	1.000	13	2	2	0	4	0
Chen, Bruce, Atl.*	1.000	4	0	1	0	1	0
Chouinard, Bobby, Mil.-Ari.	1.000	27	3	4	0	7	0
Christiansen, Jason, Pit.*	.875	60	2	5	1	8	0
Clark, Mark, Chi.	1.000	33	11	24	0	35	0
Clement, Matt, S.D.	.000	4	0	0	0	0	0
Clontz, Brad, L.A.-N.Y.	.667	20	1	1	1	3	0
Cook, Dennis, N.Y.*	.917	73	2	9	1	12	1
Cooke, Steve, Cin.*	1.000	1	0	1	0	1	0
Cordova, Francisco, Pit.	.977	33	12	30	1	43	1
Corey, Bryan, Ari.	1.000	3	0	1	0	1	0
Croushore, Rick, St.L	1.000	41	2	13	0	15	0
Cunnane, Will, S.D.	1.000	3	0	1	0	1	0
Daal, Omar, Ari.*	.975	33	6	33	1	40	2
Darensbourg, Vic, Fla.*	1.000	59	1	6	0	7	0
Darwin, Danny, S.F.	.944	33	10	24	2	36	1
DeHart, Rick, Mon.*	1.000	26	7	6	0	13	0
DeJean, Mike, Col.	1.000	59	6	6	0	12	3
De Los Santos, Valerio, Mil.*	1.000	13	0	2	0	2	0
Dempster, Ryan, Fla.	1.000	14	2	12	0	14	2
Dessens, Elmer, Pit.	.929	43	4	9	1	14	0
DiPoto, Jerry, Col.	1.000	68	3	7	0	10	2
Dodd, Robert, Phi.*	.000	4	0	0	0	0	0
Dreifort, Darren, L.A.	.938	32	18	42	4	64	4
Edmondson, Brian, Atl.-Fla.	.889	53	7	9	2	18	0
Elarton, Scott, Hou.	1.000	28	4	4	0	8	1
Eldred, Cal, Mil.	.913	23	9	12	2	23	4
Embree, Alan, Atl.-Ari.*	1.000	55	3	5	0	8	1
Estes, Shawn, S.F.*	.943	25	6	27	2	35	0
Eversgerd, Bryan, St.L.*	1.000	8	2	1	0	3	0
Fontenot, Joe, Fla.	1.000	8	4	9	0	13	1
Ford, Ben, Ari.	.500	8	0	1	1	2	0
Fossas, Tony, Chi.*	1.000	8	0	1	0	1	0
Foster, Kevin, Chi.	.000	3	0	0	0	0	0
Fox, Chad, Mil.	1.000	49	3	5	0	8	0
Franco, John, N.Y.*	1.000	61	4	16	0	20	2
Frascatore, John, St.L	.917	69	11	11	2	24	1
Gaetti, Gary, St.L	.000	1	0	0	0	0	0
Gardner, Mark, S.F.	1.000	33	14	33	0	47	2
Glauber, Keith, Cin.	.000	3	0	0	0	0	0
Glavine, Tom, Atl.*	.984	33	11	50	1	62	3
Gomes, Wayne, Phi.	.950	71	13	6	1	20	0
G. Gonzalez, Gabe, Phi.*	1.000	3	0	1	0	1	0
Gonzalez, Jeremi, Chi.	.950	20	6	13	1	20	0
Gonzalez, Lareil, Col.	.000	1	0	0	0	0	0
Grace, Mike, Phi.	1.000	21	1	11	0	12	0
Graves, Danny, Cin.	.917	62	7	15	2	24	0
Green, Tyler, Phi.	.875	27	12	16	4	32	1
Grzanich, Mike, Hou.	.000	1	0	0	0	0	0
Guthrie, Mark, L.A.*	.923	53	3	9	1	13	0
Halama, John, Hou.*	1.000	6	2	5	0	7	0
Hall, Darren, L.A.	1.000	11	3	0	0	3	0
Hamilton, Joey, S.D.	.938	34	15	30	3	48	3
Hammond, Chris, Fla.*	1.000	3	0	0	0	0	0
Hampton, Mike, Hou.*	.938	32	11	49	4	64	7
Haney, Chris, Chi.*	1.000	5	0	1	0	1	0
Harnisch, Pete, Cin.	1.000	32	20	18	0	38	4
Harris, Lenny, Cin.	.000	1	0	0	0	0	0
Harris, Reggie, Hou.	1.000	6	1	0	0	1	0
Hartgraves, Dean, S.F.*	1.000	5	0	0	0	0	0
Henderson, Rod, Mil.	.000	2	0	0	0	0	0
Henriquez, Oscar, Fla.	.000	15	0	0	0	0	0
Henry, Doug, Hou.	1.000	59	4	4	0	8	1
Heredia, Felix, Fla.-Chi.*	.875	71	4	3	1	8	0
Hermanson, Dustin, Mon.	.915	32	18	25	4	47	3
Hernandez, Livan, Fla.	1.000	33	15	35	0	50	3
Hershiser, Orel, S.F.	.983	34	21	36	1	58	3
Hitchcock, Sterling, S.D.*	1.000	39	6	17	0	23	2
Hoffman, Trevor, S.D.	1.000	66	3	4	0	7	1
Hudek, John, N.Y.-Cin.	1.000	58	3	7	0	10	0
Hudson, Joe, Mil.	.000	1	0	0	0	0	0
Hutton, Mark, Cin.	1.000	10	3	4	0	7	1
Jimenez, Jose, St.L.	1.000	4	0	5	0	5	0
Johnson, Mike, Mon.	1.000	2	0	1	0	1	0
Johnson, Randy, Hou.*	.889	11	1	7	1	9	1
Johnstone, John, S.F.	1.000	70	8	5	0	13	0
Jones, Doug, Mil.	.917	46	4	7	1	12	1
Jones, Bobby J., N.Y.	.961	30	14	35	2	51	3
Jones, Bobby M., Col.*	.897	35	8	18	3	29	0
Jordan, Ricardo, Col.*	1.000	6	1	0	0	1	0
Judd, Mike, L.A.	1.000	7	0	4	0	4	0
Juden, Jeff, Mil.	.958	24	8	15	1	24	1
Karchner, Matt, Chi.	1.000	29	1	5	0	6	0
Karl, Scott, Mil.*	.947	33	12	38	0	50	3
Kile, Darryl, Col.	.947	36	22	32	3	57	1
King, Curtis, St.L.	1.000	36	10	9	0	19	1
Kline, Steve, Mon.*	.929	78	3	10	1	14	0
Klingenbeck, Scott, Cin.	1.000	4	4	3	0	7	0
Krivda, Rick, Cin.*	1.000	16	1	3	0	4	0
Kroon, Marc, S.D.-Cin.	1.000	6	0	3	0	3	0

Player, Team	Pct.	G	PO	A	E	TC	DP
Kubenka, Jeff, L.A.*	.750	6	0	3	1	4	0
Langston, Mark, S.D.*	.947	22	2	16	1	19	1
Lankford, Frank, L.A.	1.000	12	6	8	0	14	0
Larkin, Andy, Fla.	1.000	17	4	11	0	15	1
Lawrence, Sean, Pit.*	1.000	7	0	2	0	2	0
Leiter, Al, N.Y.*	1.000	28	4	18	0	22	0
Leiter, Mark, Phi.	.952	69	12	8	1	21	2
Leskanic, Curtis, Col.	1.000	66	5	9	0	14	0
Lieber, Jon, Pit.	1.000	29	12	17	0	29	1
Ligtenberg, Kerry, Atl.	.600	75	1	2	2	5	0
Lima, Jose, Hou.	.949	33	24	32	3	59	3
Loaiza, Esteban, Pit.	1.000	21	10	18	0	28	3
Loewer, Carlton, Phi.	.955	21	6	15	1	22	0
Loiselle, Rich, Pit.	1.000	54	2	10	0	12	0
Looper, Braden, St.L.	.000	4	0	0	0	0	0
Lowe, Sean, St.L	1.000	4	1	1	0	2	0
Ludwick, Eric, Fla.	.857	13	2	4	1	7	1
Maddux, Greg, Atl.	.959	34	31	63	4	98	5
Maddux, Mike, Mon.	1.000	51	3	10	0	13	0
Magnante, Mike, Hou.*	1.000	48	6	17	0	23	0
Maloney, Sean, L.A.	1.000	11	2	2	0	4	1
Mantei, Matt, Fla.	1.000	42	4	5	0	9	1
Manuel, Barry, Ari.	1.000	13	1	0	0	1	0
Martinez, Javier, Pit.	.667	37	2	0	1	3	0
Martinez, Dennis, Atl.	.957	53	6	16	1	23	2
Martinez, Ramon, L.A.	1.000	15	11	17	0	28	1
McCurry, Jeff, Pit.	1.000	16	1	3	0	4	0
McElroy, Chuck, Col.*	1.000	78	0	6	0	6	2
McMichael, Greg, NY-LA-NY	1.000	64	5	16	0	21	1
Meadows, Brian, Fla.	.975	31	18	21	1	40	2
Medina, Rafael, Fla.	1.000	12	5	4	0	9	2
Mercedes, Jose, Mil.	1.000	7	0	3	0	3	0
Mercker, Kent, St.L*	.935	30	3	26	2	31	0
Mesa, Jose, S.F.	.667	32	1	1	1	3	0
Miceli, Dan, S.D.	1.000	67	4	3	0	7	1
Michalak, Chris, Ari.*	.000	5	0	0	0	0	0
Miller, Kurt, Chi.	.000	3	0	0	0	0	0
Miller, Trever, Hou.*	1.000	37	4	6	0	10	0
Millwood, Kevin, Atl.	.962	31	9	16	1	26	1
Mlicki, Dave, N.Y.-L.A.	.977	30	21	22	1	44	1
Moore, Trey, Mon.*	1.000	13	6	10	0	16	0
Morgan, Mike, Chi.	1.000	5	2	5	0	7	2
Morman, Alvin, S.F.*	1.000	9	0	1	0	1	0
Morris, Matt, St.L	.955	17	4	17	1	22	5
Mulholland, Terry, Chi.*	.810	70	7	10	4	21	1
Mullins, Gregory, Mil.*	.000	2	0	0	0	0	0
Munoz, Mike, Col.*	1.000	40	3	6	0	9	1
Myers, Mike, Mil.*	.875	70	3	11	2	16	4
Myers, Randy, S.D.*	1.000	21	0	2	0	2	0
Myers, Rodney, Chi.	1.000	12	0	2	0	2	0
Neagle, Denny, Atl.*	1.000	32	4	20	0	24	0
Nen, Robb, S.F.	.923	78	4	8	1	13	1
Nitkowski, C.J., Hou.*	1.000	43	1	10	0	11	2
Nomo, Hideo, L.A.-N.Y.	1.000	29	10	14	0	24	0
Nunez, Vladimir, Ari.	.000	4	0	0	0	0	0
Nye, Ryan, Phi.	.000	1	0	0	0	0	0
Ojala, Kirt, Fla.*	.917	41	9	24	3	36	4
Oliver, Darren, St.L*	1.000	10	0	12	0	12	1
Olson, Gregg, Ari.	1.000	64	4	7	0	11	0
Ortiz, Russ, S.F.	.957	22	9	13	1	23	2
Osborne, Donovan, St.L*	.813	14	5	8	3	16	2
Osuna, Antonio, L.A.	.917	54	3	8	1	12	1
Painter, Lance, St.L*	1.000	65	6	12	0	18	1
Pall, Donn, Fla.	1.000	23	3	5	0	8	0
Park, Chan Ho, L.A.	.923	34	20	28	4	52	5
Parris, Steve, Cin.	1.000	18	5	21	0	26	0
Patrick, Bronswell, Mil.	1.000	32	2	7	0	9	0
Patterson, Bob, Chi.*	1.000	33	0	2	0	2	0
Pavano, Carl, Mon.	.933	24	15	13	2	30	1
Perez, Carlos, Mon.-L.A.*	1.000	34	11	44	0	55	3
Perez, Odalis, Atl.*	1.000	10	0	1	0	1	0
Perez, Yorkis, Phi.*	.909	57	3	7	1	11	0
Peters, Chris, Pit.*	.864	39	3	16	3	22	2
Petkovsek, Mark, St.L.	.950	48	8	11	1	20	1
Pickett, Ricky, Ari.*	.000	2	0	0	0	0	0
Pisciotta, Marc, Chi.	1.000	43	2	5	0	7	1
Plunk, Eric, Mil.	.000	26	0	0	0	0	0
Politte, Cliff, St.L	.875	8	3	4	1	8	0
Poole, Jim, S.F.*	1.000	26	4	4	0	8	0
Portugal, Mark, Phi.	.932	26	24	17	3	44	2
Powell, Jay, Fla.-Hou.	1.000	62	8	5	0	13	0
Powell, Jeremy, Mon.	1.000	7	2	3	0	5	0

Player, Team	Pct.	G	PO	A	E	TC	DP
Priest, Eddie, Cin.*	.000	2	0	0	0	0	0
Pulsipher, Bill, N.Y.-Mil.*	1.000	26	1	12	0	13	0
Radinsky, Scott, L.A.*	.917	62	2	9	1	12	0
Raggio, Brady, St.L.	1.000	4	1	1	0	2	1
Ramirez, Roberto, S.D.*	1.000	21	0	1	0	1	0
Rath, Gary, L.A.*	.000	3	0	0	0	0	0
Rath, Fred, Col.	.000	2	0	0	0	0	0
Reed, Rick, N.Y.	.980	31	12	38	1	51	2
Reed, Steve, S.F.	.875	50	1	6	1	8	0
Remlinger, Mike, Cin.*	.920	35	7	16	2	25	1
Reyes, Carlos, S.D.	1.000	22	2	4	0	6	0
Reyes, Dennis, L.A.-Cin.*	.813	19	1	12	3	16	0
Reyes, Al, Mil.	.800	50	2	6	2	10	1
Reynolds, Shane, Hou.	.970	35	24	40	2	66	9
Reynoso, Armando, N.Y.	.967	11	5	24	1	30	2
Rincon, Ricardo, Pit.*	.857	60	3	9	2	14	2
Ritz, Kevin, Col.	1.000	2	2	3	0	5	0
Rocker, John, Atl.*	1.000	47	1	6	0	7	0
Rodriguez, Felix, Ari.	1.000	43	1	12	0	13	0
Rodriguez, Rich, S.F.*	.952	68	9	11	1	21	0
Rojas, Mel, N.Y.	.944	50	6	11	1	18	1
Roque, Rafael, Mil.*	1.000	9	3	10	0	13	1
Rueter, Kirk, S.F.*	.962	33	12	39	2	53	2
Ryan, Ken, Phi.	1.000	17	1	4	0	5	0
Saipe, Mike, Col.	1.000	2	2	2	0	4	0
Sanchez, Jesus, Fla.*	.952	35	6	34	2	42	4
Sanders, Scott, S.D.	.889	23	5	3	1	9	0
Scanlan, Bob, Hou.	.833	27	4	1	1	6	0
Schilling, Curt, Phi.	.962	35	18	33	2	53	3
Schmidt, Jason, Pit.	.920	33	7	16	2	25	2
Schourek, Pete, Hou.*	1.000	15	1	7	0	8	0
Seanez, Rudy, Atl.	1.000	34	3	1	0	4	0
Shaw, Jeff, Cin.-L.A.	.897	73	8	18	3	29	0
Silva, Jose, Pit.	1.000	18	3	18	0	21	1
Small, Aaron, Ari.	1.000	23	1	1	0	2	0
Smith, Pete, S.D.	1.000	10	3	5	0	8	2
Smith, Travis, Mil.	.000	1	0	0	0	0	0
Smoltz, John, Atl.	1.000	26	12	20	0	32	2
Sodowsky, Clint, Ari.	.941	45	4	12	1	17	1
Speier, Justin, Chi.-Fla.	1.000	19	0	2	0	2	0
Spencer, Stan, S.D.	1.000	6	1	1	0	2	0
Spradlin, Jerry, Phi.	1.000	69	8	8	0	16	1
Springer, Russ, Ari.-Atl.	.800	48	2	2	1	5	0
Stanifer, Rob, Fla.	.900	38	5	4	1	10	0
Steenstra, Kennie, Chi.	.000	4	0	0	0	0	0
Stephenson, Garrett, Phi.	1.000	6	3	1	0	4	0
Stevens, Dave, Chi.	1.000	31	1	1	0	2	0
Stoops, Jim, Col.	1.000	3	1	1	0	2	1
Stottlemyre, Todd, St.L.	.976	23	18	22	1	41	2
Sullivan, Scott, Cin.	.952	67	9	11	1	21	1
Suppan, Jeff, Ari.	1.000	13	6	15	0	21	1
Tabaka, Jeff, Pit.*	.917	37	1	10	1	12	1
Tam, Jeff, N.Y.	1.000	15	3	1	0	4	0
Tapani, Kevin, Chi.	1.000	35	11	31	0	42	1
Tavarez, Julian, S.F.	.933	60	4	10	1	15	1
Telemaco, Amaury, Chi.-Ari.	.943	41	13	20	2	35	0
Telford, Anthony, Mon.	.958	77	5	18	1	24	1
Thompson, Mark, Col.	1.000	6	2	2	0	4	0
Thomson, John, Col.	1.000	26	15	15	0	30	3
Thurman, Mike, Mon.	1.000	14	1	12	0	13	0
Tomko, Brett, Cin.	.976	34	14	26	1	41	1
Trachsel, Steve, Chi.	.966	33	23	34	2	59	1
Urbina, Ugueth, Mon.	1.000	64	2	3	0	5	0
Valdes, Ismael, L.A.	.973	27	12	24	1	37	1
Valdes, Marc, Mon.	1.000	20	3	6	0	9	0
Valdez, Efrain, Ari.*	1.000	6	1	1	0	2	0
Van Poppel, Todd, Pit.	1.000	18	1	2	0	3	0
VanRyn, Ben, Chi.-S.D.*	1.000	15	1	0	0	1	0
Vazquez, Javier, Mon.	1.000	33	12	24	0	36	3
Veres, Dave, Col.	1.000	63	7	11	0	18	0
Wagner, Paul, Mil.	1.000	13	3	7	0	10	1
Wagner, Billy, Hou.*	.800	58	2	2	1	5	0
Wainhouse, David, Col.	1.000	10	2	4	0	6	2
Wall, Donne, S.D.	1.000	46	4	10	0	14	2
Weathers, David, Cin.-Mil.	1.000	44	5	14	0	19	1
Weaver, Eric, L.A.	1.000	7	0	1	0	1	0
Weber, Neil, Ari.*	.000	4	0	0	0	0	0
Welch, Mike, Phi.	1.000	10	2	2	0	4	1
Wendell, Turk, N.Y.	.944	66	5	12	1	18	0
Wengert, Don, S.D.-Chi.	1.000	31	2	7	0	9	1
White, Gabe, Cin.*	1.000	69	4	12	0	16	0
Whiteside, Matt, Phi.	1.000	10	2	2	0	4	0

Player, Team	Pct.	G	PO	A	E	TC	DP
Wickman, Bob, Mil.	.920	72	10	13	2	25	1
Wilkins, Marc, Pit.	1.000	16	0	1	0	1	0
Williams, Mike, Pit.	.929	37	0	13	1	14	0
Williams, Todd, Cin.	1.000	6	0	1	0	1	0
Winchester, Scott, Cin.	1.000	16	6	8	0	14	1
Winston, Darrin, Phi.*	1.000	27	2	3	0	5	0
Witt, Bobby, St.L	1.000	17	3	9	0	12	2
Wohlers, Mark, Atl.	1.000	27	3	1	0	4	0
Wolcott, Bob, Ari.	.833	6	3	2	1	6	1
Wood, Kerry, Chi.	1.000	26	4	9	0	13	1
Woodall, Brad, Mil.*	.939	31	5	26	2	33	4
Woodard, Steve, Mil.	.960	34	9	15	1	25	0
Wright, Jamey, Col.	.964	34	18	36	2	56	5
Yoshii, Masato, N.Y.	.919	29	14	20	3	37	2
Young, Tim, Mon.*	1.000	10	0	2	0	2	0

TRIPLE PLAY: Dreifort, L.A.

PITCHERS WITH TWO OR MORE TEAMS

Player, Team	Pct.	G	PO	A	E	TC	DP
Barrios, Manuel, Fla.	.000	2	0	0	0	0	0
Barrios, Manuel, L.A.	.000	1	0	0	0	0	0
Blair, Willie, Ari.	.975	23	10	29	1	40	3
Blair, Willie, N.Y.	1.000	11	0	6	0	6	0
Bohanon, Brian, N.Y.*	.957	25	6	16	1	23	1
Bohanon, Brian, L.A.*	.963	14	4	22	1	27	2
Bruske, Jim, L.A.	1.000	35	2	3	0	5	0
Bruske, Jim, S.D.	.000	4	0	0	0	0	0
Byrd, Paul, Atl.	.000	1	0	0	0	0	0
Byrd, Paul, Phi.	.909	8	3	7	1	11	1
Chouinard, Bobby, Mil.	1.000	1	0	1	0	1	0
Chouinard, Bobby, Ari.	1.000	26	3	3	0	6	0
Clontz, Brad, L.A.	.500	18	0	1	1	2	0
Clontz, Brad, N.Y.	1.000	2	1	0	0	1	0
Edmondson, Brian, Atl.	1.000	10	2	4	0	6	0
Edmondson, Brian, Fla.	.833	43	5	5	2	12	0
Embree, Alan, Atl.*	1.000	20	1	4	0	5	1

Player, Team	Pct.	G	PO	A	E	TC	DP
Embree, Alan, Ari.*	1.000	35	2	1	0	3	0
Heredia, Felix, Fla.*	1.000	41	3	3	0	6	0
Heredia, Felix, Chi.*	.500	30	1	0	1	2	0
Hudek, John, N.Y.	1.000	28	1	5	0	6	0
Hudek, John, Cin.	1.000	30	2	2	0	4	0
Kroon, Marc, S.D.	.000	2	0	0	0	0	0
Kroon, Marc, Cin.	1.000	4	0	3	0	3	0
McMichael, Greg, N.Y.	1.000	52	4	9	0	13	1
McMichael, Greg, L.A.	1.000	12	1	7	0	8	0
Mlicki, Dave, N.Y.	.933	10	6	8	1	15	0
Mlicki, Dave, L.A.	1.000	20	15	14	0	29	0
Nomo, Hideo, L.A.	1.000	12	6	2	0	8	0
Nomo, Hideo, N.Y.	1.000	17	4	12	0	16	0
Perez, Carlos, Mon.*	1.000	23	6	30	0	36	1
Perez, Carlos, L.A.*	1.000	11	5	14	0	19	2
Powell, Jay, Fla.	1.000	33	6	4	0	10	0
Powell, Jay, Hou.	1.000	29	2	1	0	3	0
Pulsipher, Bill, N.Y.*	1.000	15	0	5	0	5	0
Pulsipher, Bill, Mil.*	1.000	11	1	7	0	8	0
Reyes, Dennis, L.A.*	.778	11	1	6	2	9	0
Reyes, Dennis, Cin.*	.857	8	0	6	1	7	0
Shaw, Jeff, Cin.	.867	39	4	9	2	15	0
Shaw, Jeff, L.A.	.929	34	4	9	1	14	0
Speier, Justin, Chi.	.000	1	0	0	0	0	0
Speier, Justin, Fla.	1.000	18	0	2	0	2	0
Springer, Russ, Ari.	.667	26	2	0	1	3	0
Springer, Russ, Atl.	1.000	22	0	2	0	2	0
Telemaco, Amaury, Chi.	1.000	14	2	5	0	7	0
Telemaco, Amaury, Ari.	.929	27	11	15	2	28	0
VanRyn, Ben, Chi.*	1.000	9	1	0	0	1	0
VanRyn, Ben, S.D.*	.000	6	0	0	0	0	0
Weathers, David, Cin.	1.000	16	4	7	0	11	0
Weathers, David, Mil.	1.000	28	1	7	0	8	1
Wengert, Don, S.D.	1.000	10	0	1	0	1	0
Wengert, Don, Chi.	1.000	21	2	6	0	8	1

MISCELLANEOUS

SHUTOUT GAMES

Read across for wins, down for losses.

Team	St.L.	Atl.	Hou.	N.Y.	S.D.	L.A.	Chi.	Phi.	Col.	Cin.	S.F.	Pit.	Fla.	Mon.	Ari.	Mil.	A.L.	W	L	Pct.
St. Louis	..	0	1	1	0	1	0	0	0	1	0	1	0	1	2	1	1	10	2	.833
Atlanta	0	..	1	2	1	1	0	1	1	1	2	3	2	1	3	1	3	23	6	.793
Houston	0	0	..	1	0	0	0	1	0	1	0	3	0	2	0	1	2	11	6	.647
New York	1	0	0	..	0	0	2	4	0	1	0	2	1	2	0	1	2	16	9	.640
San Diego	0	1	0	0	..	1	0	2	0	0	1	0	0	0	3	2	1	11	7	.611
Los Angeles	0	1	0	0	0	..	0	1	2	2	1	1	0	0	1	0	1	10	9	.526
Chicago	0	1	1	0	0	1	..	0	0	0	1	0	0	1	1	1	0	7	7	.500
Philadelphia	0	1	1	0	0	1	1	..	0	0	0	1	0	0	2	1	2	10	11	.476
Colorado	0	0	1	1	1	0	0	0	..	0	1	0	0	1	0	0	0	5	6	.455
Cincinnati	0	0	0	1	0	0	0	1	0	..	0	0	0	2	2	2	0	8	10	.444
San Francisco	0	0	0	0	0	1	1	0	0	0	..	0	2	1	0	0	1	6	8	.429
Pittsburgh	1	0	0	1	2	0	1	0	1	1	1	..	0	1	0	1	0	10	14	.417
Florida	0	0	0	0	2	0	0	1	0	0	0	0	..	0	0	0	0	3	6	.333
Montreal	0	0	0	1	0	1	0	0	1	0	1	0	1	..	0	0	0	5	13	.278
Arizona	0	1	0	0	0	1	1	0	0	1	0	1	0	0	..	0	1	6	16	.273
Milwaukee	0	0	0	0	0	0	0	0	1	0	0	0	0	1	..	0	2	11	.154
A.L. clubs	0	1	1	1	1	1	1	0	1	1	0	2	0	2	0	0	..	..	..	..
Lost	2	6	6	9	7	9	7	11	6	10	8	14	6	13	16	11	..	143	141	.504

N.L. shutouts vs. A.L. clubs (14): Arizona vs. Texas; Atlanta vs. Baltimore, Tampa Bay and Toronto; Houston vs. Kansas City and Minnesota; Los Angeles vs. Oakland; New York N.L. vs. Boston and Tampa Bay; Philadelphia vs. Baltimore and Tampa Bay; St. Louis vs. Kansas City; San Diego vs. Seattle; San Francisco vs. Texas.

HOME RECORD

Read across for home wins, down for road losses.

Team	Atl.	Hou.	S.D.	Chi.	S.F.	L.A.	St.L.	N.Y.	Col.	Pit.	Phi.	Cin.	Mon.	Mil.	Ari.	Fla.	A.L.	W	L	Pct.
Atlanta	..	1	4	3	4	6	2	6	2	3	5	2	4	4	3	4	3	56	25	.691
Houston	3	..	2	3	4	1	3	3	4	4	3	5	2	6	2	5	5	55	26	.679
San Diego	2	3	..	2	4	4	4	4	4	1	5	6	2	2	6	2	3	54	27	.667
Chicago	3	1	1	..	5	4	4	3	2	5	2	3	6	3	3	3	3	51	31	.622
San Francisco	0	1	2	1	..	4	3	4	3	6	2	5	5	2	4	3	4	49	32	.605
Los Angeles	1	4	3	3	4	..	2	1	3	4	3	3	5	4	4	1	3	48	33	.593
St. Louis	2	4	1	5	2	4	..	1	2	5	3	2	5	3	5	2	2	48	34	.585
New York	3	1	2	2	2	2	4	..	4	4	3	4	2	3	3	3	5	47	34	.580
Colorado	1	4	3	1	4	3	2	1	..	2	1	3	3	3	3	5	3	42	39	.519
Pittsburgh	2	1	3	3	2	3	4	3	3	..	0	4	2	2	0	5	3	40	40	.500
Philadelphia	3	2	0	2	0	1	3	1	2	5	..	2	3	3	5	5	3	40	41	.494
Cincinnati	1	3	1	2	1	2	4	1	1	3	3	..	3	3	2	6	3	39	42	.481
Montreal	4	1	2	2	2	3	2	4	2	1	2	1	..	1	5	3	4	39	42	.481
Milwaukee	0	2	2	3	4	2	1	1	4	3	4	2	4	..	1	3	2	38	43	.469
Arizona	1	3	3	2	3	2	1	1	3	3	1	0	1	4	..	3	3	34	47	.420
Florida	3	2	3	2	0	2	0	2	2	2	5	0	2	0	1	..	5	31	50	.383
A.L. clubs	2	1	5	6	1	3	6	4	5	2	4	1	6	2	3	5	..	..	..	..
Lost on road	31	34	37	42	42	46	45	40	46	53	46	43	55	45	50	58	..	711	586	.548

HOME RECORDS IN INTERLEAGUE GAMES

Team	Bal.	Bos.	N.Y.	T.B.	Tor.	Team	Chi.	Cle.	Det.	K.C.	Min.	Team	Ana.	Oak.	Sea.	Tex.
Atlanta	..	1-2	0-2	..	2-1	Chicago	3-0	0-2	..	..	..	Arizona	1-2	..	2-1	0-2
Florida	..	1-2	..	2-0	2-1	Cincinnati	..	1-2	..	0-2	2-1	Colorado	..	2-1	..	1-2
Montreal	3-0	..	1-2	..	0-2	Houston	2-1	..	..	2-1	1-1	Los Angeles	1-1	2-1	..	..
New York	2-0	..	1-2	2-1	..	Milwaukee	..	1-2	1-2	..	..	San Diego	2-1	..	1-1	..
Philadelphia	1-2	1-1	..	1-2	..	Pittsburgh	0-2	..	1-2	..	2-1	San Francisco	..	0-2	2-1	2-1
						St. Louis	..	..	1-1	1-2	..					

ROAD RECORD

Read across for road wins, down for home losses.

Team	Atl.	Hou.	S.D.	N.Y.	S.F.	Chi.	Cin.	Mil.	St.L.	L.A.	Phi.	Col.	Ari.	Pit.	Mon.	Fla.	A.L.	W	L	Pct.
Atlanta	..	3	1	3	3	0	5	3	4	2	3	3	5	4	2	3	6	50	31	.617
Houston	2	..	3	2	2	4	3	3	2	2	4	1	3	5	5	1	5	47	34	.580
San Diego	2	1	..	1	4	2	5	4	2	3	3	3	3	3	2	3	3	44	37	.543
New York	0	3	2	..	2	3	2	5	2	3	5	2	2	0	2	4	4	41	40	.506
San Francisco	2	2	2	1	..	2	2	2	4	2	4	2	3	1	1	6	4	40	42	.488
Chicago	3	3	4	1	2	..	3	3	0	0	1	5	4	3	1	4	2	39	42	.481
Cincinnati	1	0	0	2	1	3	..	3	4	3	1	3	3	2	5	3	4	38	43	.469
Milwaukee	2	0	1	0	1	3	3	..	2	2	0	3	2	3	2	6	6	36	45	.444
St. Louis	1	3	2	2	3	2	1	5	..	1	3	4	2	0	1	3	2	35	45	.438
Los Angeles	0	2	2	2	2	2	1	1	2	..	2	3	4	3	0	4	5	35	46	.432
Philadelphia	1	0	1	3	2	4	3	2	0	3	..	2	2	3	4	1	4	35	46	.432
Colorado	2	2	2	2	3	1	2	1	1	3	4	..	3	4	1	1	1	35	46	.432
Arizona	0	1	0	3	2	3	4	2	1	2	1	3	..	3	1	3	2	31	50	.383
Pittsburgh	0	1	2	2	0	0	3	3	2	2	1	1	3	..	5	1	3	29	53	.354

Team	Atl.	Hou.	S.D.	N.Y.	S.F.	Chi.	Cin.	Mil.	St.L.	L.A.	Phi.	Col.	Ari.	Pit.	Mon.	Fla.	A.L.	W	L	Pct.
Montreal	2	1	2	4	1	0	0	2	1	1	3	0	2	1	..	4	2	26	55	.321
Florida	2	1	1	3	0	0	0	0	4	2	1	1	1	1	3	..	3	23	58	.284
A.L. clubs	5	3	2	3	4	2	5	4	3	2	5	3	5	5	4	3	..	..	..	..
Lost at home	25	26	27	34	32	31	42	43	34	33	41	39	47	40	42	50	..	584	713	.450

PITCHING AGAINST EACH CLUB

ARIZONA—65-97

Pitcher	Atl. W-L	Chi. W-L	Cin. W-L	Col. W-L	Fla. W-L	Hou. W-L	L.A. W-L	Mil. W-L	Mon. W-L	N.Y. W-L	Phi. W-L	Pit. W-L	St.L. W-L	S.D. W-L	S.F. W-L	A.L. W-L	Total W-L
Adamson, J.	0-0	0-0	0-0	0-0	0-1	0-0	0-0	0-0	0-0	0-0	0-0	0-0	0-0	0-1	0-0	0-0	0-3
Anderson, B.	0-1	0-1	1-1	2-1	0-0	1-0	1-1	1-1	1-2	1-0	0-1	1-1	0-0	0-2	2-0	1-1	12-13
Banks, W.	0-0	0-0	0-0	0-1	0-0	0-0	0-0	1-0	0-0	0-0	0-0	0-0	0-1	0-0	0-0	0-0	1-2
Benes, A.	1-1	1-0	2-1	1-1	0-0	0-1	1-2	1-1	1-0	0-1	1-1	1-0	1-1	0-1	2-0	1-2	14-13
Blair, W.	0-2	1-1	0-1	1-1	0-0	0-1	1-1	0-1	0-1	0-0	0-0	1-0	0-2	0-2	0-1	0-1	4-15
Brow, S.	0-0	0-0	0-0	0-0	1-0	0-0	0-0	0-0	0-0	0-0	0-0	0-0	0-0	0-0	0-0	0-0	1-0
Chouinard, B.	0-0	0-0	0-0	0-0	0-0	0-0	0-0	0-0	0-0	0-1	0-0	0-0	0-0	0-0	0-0	0-0	0-1
Corey, B.	0-0	0-0	0-0	0-0	0-0	0-0	0-0	0-0	0-0	0-0	0-0	0-0	0-0	0-0	0-0	0-0	0-0
Daal, O.	0-2	1-1	1-1	1-1	1-0	0-2	1-0	0-0	0-0	1-1	0-2	1-1	0-0	0-0	0-1	1-0	8-12
Embree, A.	0-0	0-0	0-0	0-0	0-0	1-1	0-1	0-0	0-0	0-0	1-0	0-0	0-0	0-0	0-0	1-0	3-2
Ford, B.	0-0	0-0	0-0	0-0	0-0	0-0	0-0	0-0	0-0	0-0	0-0	0-0	0-0	0-0	0-0	0-0	0-0
Manuel, B.	0-0	0-0	0-0	0-0	1-0	0-0	0-0	0-0	0-0	0-0	0-0	0-0	0-0	0-0	0-0	0-0	1-0
Michalak, C.	0-0	0-0	0-0	0-0	0-0	0-0	0-0	0-0	0-0	0-0	0-0	0-0	0-0	0-0	0-0	0-0	0-0
Nunez, V.	0-0	0-0	0-0	0-0	0-0	0-0	0-0	0-0	0-0	0-0	0-0	0-0	0-0	0-0	0-0	0-0	0-0
Olson, G.	0-0	0-0	0-0	0-1	0-0	0-0	0-0	0-0	0-0	1-0	0-1	0-0	0-0	1-0	1-2	0-0	3-4
Pickett, R.	0-0	0-0	0-0	0-0	0-0	0-0	0-0	0-0	0-0	0-0	0-0	0-0	0-0	0-0	0-0	0-0	0-0
Rodriguez, F.	0-0	0-1	0-0	0-0	0-0	0-0	0-0	0-0	0-0	0-0	0-0	0-0	0-0	0-1	0-0	0-0	0-2
Small, A.	0-0	0-0	0-0	1-0	0-0	0-0	0-0	1-0	0-0	0-0	0-0	1-0	0-0	0-1	0-0	0-0	3-1
Sodowsky, C.	0-0	0-0	0-1	0-0	1-0	0-0	0-0	0-0	0-1	0-0	0-0	0-1	0-2	0-0	0-0	1-1	3-6
Springer, R.	0-1	0-0	0-0	0-0	1-0	0-0	0-1	0-0	0-1	0-0	0-0	0-0	1-0	1-0	0-0	0-1	4-3
Suppan, J.	0-0	0-1	0-0	0-0	0-1	0-0	0-1	0-0	0-0	0-0	0-1	1-0	0-0	0-1	0-2	0-0	1-7
Telemaco, A.	0-1	1-2	0-0	0-0	1-0	2-0	0-2	0-2	0-0	0-2	1-1	0-0	0-0	1-0	0-0	0-1	6-9
Valdez, E.	0-0	0-0	0-0	0-0	0-0	0-0	0-0	0-0	0-0	0-0	0-0	0-0	0-0	0-0	0-0	0-0	0-0
Weber, N.	0-0	0-0	0-0	0-0	0-0	0-0	0-0	0-0	0-0	0-0	0-0	0-0	0-0	0-0	0-0	0-0	0-0
Wolcott, B.	0-0	1-0	0-0	0-0	0-0	0-0	0-0	0-0	0-0	0-1	0-0	0-0	0-0	0-0	0-0	0-1	1-3
Totals	1-8	5-7	4-5	6-6	6-2	4-5	4-8	6-3	2-7	4-5	2-7	6-3	2-7	3-9	5-7	5-8	65-97

INTERLEAGUE BREAKDOWN: Daal 1-0, Sodowsky 0-1, Wolcott 0-1 vs. Angels; Anderson 1-0, Benes 0-1, Springer 0-1 vs. A's; Benes 0-1, Embree 1-0, Sodowsky 1-0 vs. Mariners; Anderson 0-1, Benes 1-0, Blair 0-1, Telemaco 0-1 vs. Rangers.

ATLANTA—106-56

Pitcher	Ari. W-L	Chi. W-L	Cin. W-L	Col. W-L	Fla. W-L	Hou. W-L	L.A. W-L	Mil. W-L	Mon. W-L	N.Y. W-L	Phi. W-L	Pit. W-L	St.L. W-L	S.D. W-L	S.F. W-L	A.L. W-L	Total W-L
Butler, A.	0-0	0-0	0-0	0-0	0-0	0-0	0-0	0-1	0-0	0-0	0-0	0-0	0-0	0-0	0-0	0-0	0-1
Byrd, P.	0-0	0-0	0-0	0-0	0-0	0-0	0-0	0-0	0-0	0-0	0-0	0-0	0-0	0-0	0-0	0-0	0-0
Cather, M.	1-0	0-0	0-0	0-0	0-0	0-0	0-0	0-1	0-0	0-1	0-0	0-0	1-0	0-0	0-0	0-0	2-2
Charlton, N.	0-0	0-0	0-0	0-0	0-0	0-0	0-0	0-0	0-0	0-0	0-0	0-0	0-0	0-0	0-0	0-0	0-0
Chen, B.	1-0	0-0	0-0	0-0	1-0	0-0	0-0	0-0	0-0	0-0	0-0	0-0	0-0	0-0	0-0	0-0	2-0
Edmondson, B.	0-0	0-1	0-0	0-0	0-0	0-0	0-0	0-0	0-0	0-0	0-0	0-0	0-0	0-0	0-0	0-0	0-1
Embree, A.	0-0	0-0	0-0	0-0	0-0	0-0	0-0	0-0	0-0	0-0	0-0	0-0	0-0	0-0	0-0	1-0	1-0
Glavine, T.	3-0	1-0	0-0	0-0	0-2	1-0	1-0	2-0	1-0	1-1	3-0	1-0	2-0	1-1	1-2	2-0	20-6
Ligtenberg, K.	1-0	0-0	0-0	0-0	0-0	0-1	0-0	1-0	0-0	0-0	0-1	0-0	0-0	0-0	0-0	0-0	3-2
Maddux, G.	0-1	1-1	2-0	1-1	1-1	0-1	2-0	2-0	1-1	1-0	0-1	2-0	0-1	0-1	2-0	3-0	18-9
Martinez, D.	0-0	0-0	0-0	0-1	0-0	0-0	1-0	0-0	1-0	0-0	1-1	0-0	0-2	0-0	1-0	0-2	4-6
Millwood, K.	0-0	1-1	0-1	2-1	1-0	0-1	2-0	0-1	2-1	0-0	1-0	2-0	1-0	1-1	1-0	1-1	17-8
Neagle, D.	1-0	0-2	1-0	2-0	1-1	2-0	2-1	0-0	1-1	2-0	1-0	0-2	1-0	0-1	1-0	1-3	16-11
Perez, O.	0-0	0-0	0-0	0-0	0-1	0-0	0-0	0-0	0-0	0-0	0-0	0-0	0-0	0-0	0-0	0-0	0-1
Rocker, J.	0-0	0-1	0-0	0-0	0-0	0-0	0-0	0-1	0-1	0-0	0-0	0-0	1-0	0-0	0-0	0-0	1-3
Seanez, R.	0-0	0-0	2-0	0-0	0-0	0-0	0-0	0-0	0-0	1-1	0-0	0-0	0-0	0-0	0-0	0-0	4-1
Smoltz, J.	1-0	0-0	2-0	0-0	3-0	1-2	1-0	1-0	1-0	2-0	1-0	2-0	0-0	2-0	0-0	0-1	17-3
Springer, R.	0-0	0-0	0-1	0-0	0-0	0-0	0-0	0-0	0-0	0-0	0-0	0-0	0-0	0-0	0-0	1-0	1-1
Wohlers, M.	0-0	0-0	0-0	0-0	0-0	0-0	0-0	0-0	0-1	0-0	0-0	0-0	0-0	0-0	0-0	0-0	0-1
Totals	8-1	3-6	7-2	5-3	7-5	4-5	8-1	7-2	6-6	9-3	8-4	7-2	6-3	5-4	7-2	9-7	106-56

INTERLEAGUE BREAKDOWN: Maddux 1-0, Millwood 1-0, Neagle 0-1 vs. Orioles; Embree 1-0, Martinez 0-1, Neagle 0-1 vs. Red Sox; Glavine 1-0, Martinez 0-1, Millwood 0-1, Neagle 0-1 vs. Yankees; Glavine 1-0, Maddux 0-1, Smoltz 0-1 vs. Blue Jays; Maddux 1-0, Neagle 1-0, Springer 1-0 vs. Devil Rays.

CHICAGO—90-73

Pitcher	Ari. W-L	Atl. W-L	Cin. W-L	Col. W-L	Fla. W-L	Hou. W-L	L.A. W-L	Mil. W-L	Mon. W-L	N.Y. W-L	Phi. W-L	Pit. W-L	St.L. W-L	S.D. W-L	S.F. W-L	A.L. W-L	Total W-L
Adams, T.	1-0	1-1	0-0	0-0	1-0	0-0	0-1	1-0	1-1	0-1	1-0	0-0	1-0	0-0	0-1	0-2	7-7
Beck, R.	0-0	1-0	0-0	0-0	0-0	0-1	0-0	2-1	0-0	0-0	0-1	0-0	0-0	0-0	0-0	0-1	3-4
Clark, M.	0-2	0-1	1-1	0-2	1-1	2-2	0-1	1-0	2-0	0-0	0-1	1-0	0-0	0-2	0-1	1-0	9-14
Fossas, T.	0-0	0-0	0-0	0-0	0-0	0-0	0-0	0-0	0-0	0-0	0-0	0-0	0-0	0-0	0-0	0-0	0-0
Foster, K.	0-0	0-0	0-0	0-0	0-0	0-0	0-0	0-0	0-0	0-0	0-0	0-0	0-0	0-0	0-0	0-0	0-0
Gonzalez, J.	0-0	0-0	0-1	0-0	1-0	0-0	1-1	0-0	0-0	0-3	1-1	0-1	1-0	0-0	1-0	2-0	7-7
Haney, C.	0-0	0-0	0-0	0-0	0-0	0-0	0-0	0-0	0-0	0-0	0-0	0-0	0-0	0-0	0-0	0-0	0-0
Heredia, F.	0-0	0-0	1-0	0-0	0-0	0-0	0-0	0-0	0-0	0-0	0-0	0-0	1-0	1-0	0-0	0-0	3-0
Karchner, M.	0-0	0-0	1-0	0-0	0-0	1-0	0-0	0-0	0-0	0-0	0-0	1-0	0-1	0-0	0-0	0-0	3-1
Miller, K.	0-0	0-0	0-0	0-0	0-0	0-0	0-0	0-0	0-0	0-0	0-0	0-0	0-0	0-0	0-0	0-0	0-0
Morgan, M.	0-0	0-0	0-0	0-0	0-0	0-0	0-0	0-0	0-0	0-0	0-0	0-0	0-0	0-0	0-0	0-0	0-0
Mulholland, T.	0-0	0-0	0-1	1-0	1-0	0-1	0-0	1-0	1-0	0-0	0-1	0-2	1-0	0-0	1-0	0-0	6-5
Myers, R.	0-0	0-0	0-0	0-0	0-0	0-0	0-0	0-0	0-0	0-0	0-0	0-0	0-0	0-0	0-0	0-0	0-0
Patterson, B.	0-0	0-0	0-0	0-0	1-0	0-0	0-0	0-0	0-0	0-0	0-0	0-0	0-0	0-0	0-0	0-0	1-1
Pisciotta, M.	0-0	0-0	0-0	0-0	0-0	0-0	0-1	0-0	0-0	0-0	0-0	1-0	0-0	0-0	0-0	0-1	1-2
Speier, J.	0-0	0-0	0-0	0-0	0-0	0-0	0-0	0-0	0-0	0-0	0-0	0-0	0-0	0-0	0-0	0-0	0-0

Pitcher	Ari. W-L	Atl. W-L	Cin. W-L	Col. W-L	Fla. W-L	Hou. W-L	L.A. W-L	Mil. W-L	Mon. W-L	N.Y. W-L	Phi. W-L	Pit. W-L	St.L. W-L	S.D. W-L	S.F. W-L	A.L. W-L	Total W-L
Steenstra, K.	0-0	0-0	0-0	0-0	0-0	0-0	0-0	0-0	0-0	0-0	0-0	0-0	0-0	0-0	0-0	0-0	0-0
Stevens, D.	0-0	0-0	0-0	0-0	0-0	0-0	0-0	0-0	0-0	0-0	0-0	1-1	0-1	0-0	0-0	0-0	1-2
Tapani, K.	1-1	2-1	0-1	2-0	0-1	0-1	1-0	0-1	2-0	2-0	0-1	4-0	0-0	2-0	2-1	1-1	19-9
Telemaco, A.	0-0	0-0	0-0	0-0	0-0	0-0	0-0	0-0	0-0	0-0	0-0	0-0	0-1	1-0	0-0	0-0	1-1
Trachsel, S.	2-0	1-0	0-0	3-0	1-0	0-1	1-0	1-1	1-0	1-1	0-1	0-0	1-2	1-0	2-0	0-2	15-8
VanRyn, B.	0-0	0-0	0-0	0-0	0-0	0-0	0-0	0-0	0-0	0-0	0-0	0-0	0-0	0-0	0-0	0-0	0-0
Wengert, D.	1-1	0-0	0-1	0-0	0-0	0-1	0-0	0-1	0-0	0-0	0-0	0-0	0-1	0-0	0-0	0-0	1-5
Wood, K.	2-1	1-0	3-0	1-0	1-0	1-0	1-1	0-1	0-1	1-0	1-0	0-0	1-0	0-0	0-0	0-1	13-6
Totals	7-5	6-3	6-5	7-2	7-2	4-7	4-5	6-6	7-2	4-5	3-6	8-3	4-7	5-4	7-3	5-8	90-73

INTERLEAGUE BREAKDOWN: Gonzalez 1-0, Mulholland 1-0, Tapani 1-0 vs. White Sox; Adams 0-1, Tapani 0-1 vs. Indians; Adams 0-1, Pisciotta 0-1 vs. Tigers; Beck 0-1, Gonzalez 1-0, Trachsel 0-1 vs. Royals; Clark 1-0, Trachsel 0-1, Wood 0-1 vs. Twins.

CINCINNATI—77-85

Pitcher	Ari. W-L	Atl. W-L	Chi. W-L	Col. W-L	Fla. W-L	Hou. W-L	L.A. W-L	Mil. W-L	Mon. W-L	N.Y. W-L	Phi. W-L	Pit. W-L	St.L. W-L	S.D. W-L	S.F. W-L	A.L. W-L	Total W-L
Belinda, S.	0-0	0-1	0-0	0-1	0-0	0-0	0-1	0-0	0-1	0-1	1-1	2-1	0-0	0-0	1-1	0-0	4-8
Bere, J.	0-1	0-0	1-0	0-0	0-0	0-1	0-0	0-0	1-0	0-0	0-0	1-0	0-0	0-0	0-0	0-0	3-2
Cooke, S.	0-0	0-0	0-0	0-0	0-0	0-0	0-0	0-0	0-0	0-0	0-0	0-0	1-0	0-0	0-0	0-0	1-0
Glauber, K.	0-0	0-0	0-0	0-0	0-0	0-0	0-0	0-0	0-0	0-0	0-0	0-0	0-0	0-0	0-0	0-0	0-0
Graves, D.	0-0	0-0	0-0	0-0	0-0	0-0	1-0	0-0	0-0	0-0	0-1	1-0	0-0	0-0	0-0	0-0	2-1
Harnisch, P.	0-1	0-0	2-0	1-1	0-0	0-1	1-0	2-1	1-0	1-0	1-0	1-1	2-0	0-1	0-1	2-0	14-7
Harris, L.	0-0	0-0	0-0	0-0	0-0	0-0	0-0	0-0	0-0	0-0	0-0	0-0	0-0	0-0	0-0	0-0	0-0
Hudek, J.	1-0	1-0	1-0	0-0	1-0	0-0	0-0	0-0	0-0	0-0	0-0	0-1	0-1	0-0	0-0	0-0	4-2
Hutton, M.	0-0	0-0	0-0	0-0	0-0	0-0	0-0	0-0	0-1	0-0	0-0	0-0	0-0	0-0	0-0	0-0	0-1
Jordan, R.	0-0	0-0	0-0	1-0	0-0	0-0	0-0	0-0	0-0	0-0	0-0	0-0	0-0	0-0	0-0	0-0	1-0
Klingenbeck, S.	0-1	0-0	0-0	0-0	0-0	1-0	0-0	0-0	0-0	0-0	0-0	0-0	0-0	0-0	0-2	1-0	1-3
Krivda, R.	0-0	0-1	0-0	0-0	0-0	0-1	0-0	0-0	0-0	0-0	0-0	0-0	0-0	0-0	0-0	0-0	0-2
Kroon, M.	0-0	0-0	0-0	0-0	0-0	0-0	0-0	0-0	0-0	0-0	0-0	0-0	0-0	0-0	0-0	0-0	0-0
Parris, S.	1-0	0-1	1-0	0-0	1-0	0-1	0-1	0-1	2-0	0-0	0-1	0-0	0-0	0-0	0-0	1-0	6-5
Priest, E.	0-0	0-0	0-0	0-0	0-0	0-0	0-0	0-0	0-0	0-0	0-0	0-0	0-0	0-1	0-0	0-0	0-1
Remlinger, M.	1-1	0-2	0-1	1-1	0-0	1-0	0-1	1-2	1-0	1-0	0-0	0-1	1-1	0-2	0-1	0-2	8-15
Reyes, D.	0-0	0-0	0-0	0-0	2-0	0-0	0-0	1-0	0-0	0-0	0-0	0-1	0-0	0-0	0-0	0-0	3-1
Shaw, J.	0-0	0-0	0-0	0-0	0-0	0-1	1-0	0-0	0-0	0-1	0-0	0-0	0-2	0-0	1-0	0-0	2-4
Sullivan, S.	0-0	1-1	0-0	0-0	1-0	0-0	0-0	0-0	0-0	1-1	0-0	0-0	1-0	0-2	1-0	0-1	5-5
Tomko, B.	2-0	0-0	0-2	0-1	2-0	1-1	1-1	1-1	1-0	0-1	1-0	1-2	1-0	0-2	0-1	2-0	13-12
Weathers, D.	0-0	0-1	0-1	0-1	0-0	0-1	0-0	0-0	1-0	0-0	0-0	0-0	0-0	0-0	0-0	0-0	2-4
White, G.	0-0	0-0	0-2	0-0	0-0	0-0	1-0	1-0	0-1	0-1	0-0	2-0	0-1	0-0	1-0	0-0	5-5
Williams, T.	0-0	0-0	0-0	0-0	0-0	0-0	0-0	0-0	0-0	0-0	0-1	0-0	0-0	0-0	0-0	0-0	0-1
Winchester, S.	0-0	0-0	0-0	1-0	1-0	0-1	0-0	0-0	0-0	0-0	0-0	0-1	0-0	0-0	0-0	1-0	3-6
Totals	5-4	2-7	5-6	4-5	9-0	3-8	5-4	6-5	8-1	3-6	4-5	5-7	8-3	1-11	2-7	7-6	77-85

INTERLEAGUE BREAKDOWN: Tomko 1-0, Winchester 0-1 vs. White Sox; Harnisch 1-0, Klingenbeck 0-1, Remlinger 0-1 vs. Indians; Harnisch 1-0, Parris 1-0, White 1-0 vs. Tigers; Klingenbeck 0-1, Remlinger 0-1 vs. Royals; Shaw 1-0, Sullivan 0-1, Tomko 1-0 vs. Twins.

COLORADO—77-85

Pitcher	Ari. W-L	Atl. W-L	Chi. W-L	Cin. W-L	Fla. W-L	Hou. W-L	L.A. W-L	Mil. W-L	Mon. W-L	N.Y. W-L	Phi. W-L	Pit. W-L	St.L. W-L	S.D. W-L	S.F. W-L	A.L. W-L	Total W-L
Astacio, P.	1-1	0-1	1-1	1-2	1-0	1-1	0-0	1-1	2-0	0-3	0-1	1-0	0-1	1-1	2-0	1-1	13-14
Brownson, M.	0-0	0-0	0-0	0-0	0-0	1-0	0-0	0-0	0-0	0-0	0-0	0-0	0-0	0-0	0-0	0-0	1-0
DeJean, M.	0-0	0-0	0-0	0-0	0-0	0-0	2-0	0-0	0-0	0-0	0-0	0-0	0-1	0-0	1-0	0-0	3-1
DiPoto, J.	0-0	0-0	0-0	0-0	1-0	0-0	0-2	0-0	0-0	0-0	0-0	0-0	0-0	0-0	1-0	1-2	3-4
Gonzalez, L.	0-0	0-0	0-0	0-0	0-0	0-0	0-0	0-0	0-0	0-0	0-0	0-0	0-0	0-0	0-0	0-0	0-0
Jones, B.	0-1	0-0	1-0	2-0	0-0	0-0	1-1	0-0	0-0	0-2	1-1	1-0	0-0	1-1	0-1	0-1	7-8
Kile, D.	1-1	1-2	0-1	0-1	1-0	0-1	1-1	0-1	2-0	2-0	2-0	0-2	1-1	1-2	1-2	0-2	13-17
Leskanic, C.	0-0	0-0	0-0	1-0	1-2	0-0	0-0	0-0	1-0	0-0	1-0	0-0	0-0	1-1	0-0	0-0	6-4
McElroy, C.	1-0	0-0	0-0	0-0	2-0	1-0	0-0	0-1	0-0	0-1	0-1	0-0	1-0	0-0	1-1	0-0	6-4
Munoz, M.	0-1	0-0	0-1	0-0	0-0	0-0	1-0	0-0	0-0	0-0	0-0	0-0	0-0	0-0	1-0	1-0	2-2
Rath, F.	0-0	0-0	0-0	0-0	0-0	0-0	0-0	0-0	0-0	0-0	0-0	0-0	0-0	0-0	0-0	0-0	0-0
Ritz, K.	0-0	0-0	0-0	0-0	0-0	0-0	0-0	0-1	0-0	0-0	0-0	0-1	0-0	0-0	0-0	0-0	0-2
Saipe, M.	0-0	0-0	0-0	0-0	0-0	0-0	0-0	0-0	0-0	0-0	0-0	0-0	0-0	0-0	0-0	0-1	0-1
Stoops, J.	0-0	0-0	0-0	0-0	0-0	0-0	0-0	0-0	0-0	0-0	0-0	0-0	0-0	1-0	0-0	0-0	1-0
Thompson, M.	0-0	0-1	0-0	0-0	0-1	1-0	0-0	0-0	0-0	0-0	0-0	0-0	0-0	0-0	0-0	0-0	1-2
Thomson, J.	2-0	0-1	0-3	0-1	0-0	1-1	0-0	0-1	1-1	0-0	2-0	1-1	0-1	0-0	0-1	0-1	8-11
Veres, D.	0-0	0-0	0-0	0-0	0-0	0-0	0-1	0-0	1-0	1-0	0-0	0-0	0-0	0-0	0-0	0-0	3-1
Wainhouse, D.	1-0	0-0	0-0	0-0	0-0	0-0	0-0	0-0	0-0	0-0	0-0	0-0	0-0	0-0	0-0	0-0	1-0
Wright, J.	0-2	2-0	0-1	1-0	0-0	0-1	1-2	2-2	1-1	0-0	0-1	1-1	0-2	1-1	0-0	0-0	9-14
Totals	6-6	3-5	2-7	5-4	6-3	6-5	6-6	4-7	7-2	3-6	5-4	5-4	3-6	5-7	7-5	4-8	77-85

INTERLEAGUE BREAKDOWN: DiPoto 0-1, Jones 0-1, Kile 0-1 vs. Angels; DeJean 1-0, DiPoto 0-1, Munoz 1-0 vs. A's; Astacio 1-0, Kile 0-1, Saipe 0-1 vs. Mariners; Astacio 0-1, DiPoto 1-0, Thomson 0-1 vs. Rangers.

FLORIDA—54-108

Pitcher	Ari. W-L	Atl. W-L	Chi. W-L	Cin. W-L	Col. W-L	Hou. W-L	L.A. W-L	Mil. W-L	Mon. W-L	N.Y. W-L	Phi. W-L	Pit. W-L	St.L. W-L	S.D. W-L	S.F. W-L	A.L. W-L	Total W-L
Alfonseca, A.	0-1	0-0	0-0	0-0	0-0	0-0	0-0	0-2	1-0	0-0	1-2	0-0	1-0	0-1	0-0	1-0	4-6
Barrios, M.	0-0	0-0	0-0	0-0	0-0	0-0	0-0	0-0	0-0	0-0	0-0	0-0	0-0	0-0	0-0	0-0	0-0
Darensbourg, V.	0-3	0-0	0-0	0-0	0-0	0-0	0-0	0-0	0-1	0-0	0-1	0-0	0-0	0-2	0-0	0-0	0-7
Dempster, R.	1-2	0-0	0-2	0-0	0-0	0-0	0-0	0-0	0-0	0-0	0-1	0-0	0-0	0-0	0-0	0-0	1-5
Edmondson, B.	0-0	0-0	0-0	0-0	0-0	0-0	0-0	1-1	1-0	0-0	0-0	0-0	0-0	0-2	2-0	0-0	4-3
Fontenot, J.	0-0	0-1	0-0	0-0	0-0	0-0	0-0	0-1	0-0	0-1	0-0	0-1	0-0	0-0	0-3	0-0	0-7
Gonzalez, G.	0-0	0-0	0-0	0-0	0-0	0-0	0-0	0-0	0-0	0-0	0-0	0-0	0-0	0-0	0-0	0-0	0-0
Hammond, C.	0-0	0-0	0-0	0-0	0-0	0-1	0-0	0-0	0-0	0-0	0-0	0-1	0-0	0-0	0-0	0-0	0-2
Henriquez, O.	0-0	0-0	0-0	0-0	0-0	0-0	0-0	0-0	0-0	0-0	0-0	0-0	0-0	0-0	0-0	0-0	0-0
Heredia, F.	0-0	0-0	0-2	0-0	0-0	0-0	0-0	0-1	0-0	0-0	0-0	0-0	0-0	0-0	0-0	0-0	0-3
Hernandez, L.	0-1	0-2	1-1	0-1	0-0	1-2	0-1	0-2	0-1	1-0	2-0	1-0	0-1	1-0	0-0	3-0	10-12
Larkin, A.	0-1	0-0	0-0	0-1	0-1	1-1	1-0	0-0	0-0	0-1	0-0	1-0	0-0	0-1	0-2	0-0	3-8

Pitcher	Ari. W-L	Atl. W-L	Chi. W-L	Cin. W-L	Col. W-L	Hou. W-L	L.A. W-L	Mil. W-L	Mon. W-L	N.Y. W-L	Phi. W-L	Pit. W-L	St.L. W-L	S.D. W-L	S.F. W-L	A.L. W-L	Total W-L
Ludwick, E.	1-0	0-0	0-0	0-0	0-0	0-1	0-0	0-0	0-1	0-0	0-0	0-1	0-0	0-0	0-1	0-0	1-4
Mantei, M.	0-0	1-0	0-0	0-2	0-1	0-0	0-0	0-0	0-0	2-0	0-0	0-0	0-0	0-0	0-1	0-0	3-4
Meadows, B.	1-0	1-0	1-0	0-1	1-0	0-1	0-2	0-1	1-2	1-3	2-0	0-2	1-0	1-1	0-0	1-0	11-13
Medina, R.	0-0	0-1	0-0	0-1	0-1	0-0	0-0	0-0	1-1	0-0	0-1	0-1	1-0	0-0	0-0	0-0	2-6
Ojala, K.	0-0	1-2	0-0	0-1	0-0	0-1	0-0	0-0	1-1	0-0	0-0	0-0	0-0	0-1	0-0	0-1	2-7
Pall, D.	0-0	0-0	0-0	0-1	0-0	0-0	0-0	0-0	0-0	0-0	0-0	0-0	0-0	0-0	0-0	0-0	0-1
Powell, J.	0-0	0-0	0-1	0-0	2-0	0-0	0-0	0-1	0-0	0-0	0-0	1-1	0-0	1-0	0-0	0-1	4-4
Sanchez, J.	0-0	2-1	0-0	0-0	0-0	1-0	2-0	0-0	0-1	0-2	1-0	0-0	1-1	1-0	0-1	0-2	7-9
Speier, J.	0-0	0-0	0-0	0-0	0-1	0-0	0-1	0-0	0-0	0-0	0-0	0-0	0-0	0-1	0-0	0-0	0-3
Stanifer, R.	0-0	0-0	0-1	0-1	0-1	0-0	1-1	0-0	0-0	0-0	1-0	0-0	0-0	0-0	0-0	0-0	2-4
Totals	3-8	5-7	2-7	0-9	3-6	3-6	4-5	0-9	5-7	5-7	6-6	3-6	4-5	4-5	0-9	7-6	54-108

INTERLEAGUE BREAKDOWN: Edmondson 1-0, Fontenot 0-1, Hernandez 1-0 vs. Orioles; Dempster 1-0, Fontenot 0-1, Sanchez 0-1 vs. Red Sox; Dempster 0-1, Fontenot 0-1, Sanchez 0-1 vs. Yankees; Edmondson 1-0, Hernandez 1-0, Powell 0-1 vs. Blue Jays; Alfonseca 1-0, Dempster 0-1, Hernandez 1-0, Meadows 1-0 vs. Devil Rays.

HOUSTON—102-60

Pitcher	Ari. W-L	Atl. W-L	Chi. W-L	Cin. W-L	Col. W-L	Fla. W-L	L.A. W-L	Mil. W-L	Mon. W-L	N.Y. W-L	Phi. W-L	Pit. W-L	St.L. W-L	S.D. W-L	S.F. W-L	A.L. W-L	Total W-L
Bergman, S.	1-0	1-1	0-0	2-0	0-2	2-1	0-1	1-0	1-0	0-1	0-1	0-0	0-2	1-0	2-0	1-0	12-9
Cabrera, J.	0-0	0-0	0-0	0-0	0-0	0-0	0-0	0-0	0-0	0-0	0-0	0-0	0-0	0-0	0-0	0-0	0-0
Elarton, S.	0-0	0-1	1-0	0-0	0-0	0-0	0-0	1-0	0-0	0-0	0-0	0-0	0-0	0-0	0-0	0-0	2-1
Grzanich, M.	0-0	0-0	0-0	0-0	0-0	0-0	0-0	0-0	0-0	0-0	0-0	0-0	0-0	0-0	0-0	0-0	0-0
Halama, J.	0-0	0-0	0-0	0-0	0-0	0-0	0-0	1-0	0-0	0-0	0-0	0-0	0-0	0-1	0-0	0-1	1-2
Hampton, M.	1-1	1-1	0-0	1-0	2-1	0-1	1-0	0-1	0-0	1-0	1-0	2-0	0-1	0-1	0-0	1-0	11-7
Harris, R.	0-0	0-0	0-0	0-0	0-0	0-0	0-0	0-0	0-0	0-0	0-0	0-0	0-0	0-0	0-0	0-0	0-0
Henry, D.	0-0	1-0	0-0	0-0	1-1	0-0	1-0	0-0	2-0	0-1	1-0	0-0	0-0	0-0	1-0	1-0	8-2
Johnson, R.	0-0	1-0	1-0	1-0	0-0	0-0	0-0	1-0	0-0	0-0	1-1	3-0	2-0	0-0	0-0	0-0	10-1
Lima, J.	0-1	0-1	3-0	0-1	1-0	1-0	0-2	3-0	1-0	1-0	1-0	2-1	0-0	0-0	2-0	1-2	16-8
Magnante, M.	0-1	0-0	0-0	1-0	0-0	0-1	0-0	1-1	1-1	1-1	0-0	0-0	0-1	0-0	0-1	0-1	4-7
Miller, T.	0-0	0-0	0-0	0-0	0-0	0-0	0-0	0-0	0-0	0-0	0-0	0-0	1-0	1-0	0-0	0-0	2-0
Nitkowski, C.J.	0-0	0-0	0-0	1-0	0-0	0-0	0-0	0-0	1-0	0-0	0-0	0-0	1-1	0-1	0-1	0-0	3-3
Powell, J.	0-0	1-0	0-2	0-0	0-0	0-0	0-0	0-0	0-1	0-0	0-0	0-0	1-0	0-0	0-0	0-0	3-3
Reynolds, S.	2-0	0-0	1-2	0-2	1-0	2-1	1-1	1-0	1-0	0-0	3-0	2-0	1-1	1-1	0-0	3-0	19-8
Scanlan, B.	0-0	0-0	0-0	0-0	0-0	0-0	0-0	0-1	0-0	0-0	0-0	0-0	0-0	0-0	0-0	0-0	0-1
Schourek, P.	0-1	0-0	0-0	1-0	0-1	1-0	0-0	1-0	0-1	0-0	0-0	0-1	0-1	2-0	0-0	2-1	7-6
Wagner, B.	1-0	0-0	1-0	1-0	0-0	0-0	0-0	0-0	0-0	0-0	0-0	0-1	0-0	0-0	0-1	1-0	4-3
Totals	5-4	5-4	7-4	8-3	5-6	6-3	4-5	9-2	7-2	5-4	7-2	9-2	5-7	5-4	6-3	10-4	102-60

INTERLEAGUE BREAKDOWN: Bergman 1-0, Lima 0-1, Schourek 1-0 vs. White Sox; Magnante 0-1, Reynolds 1-0, Wagner 1-0 vs. Indians; Hampton 1-0, Henry 1-0, Schourek 1-0 vs. Tigers; Lima 1-0, Reynolds 1-0, Schourek 0-1 vs. Royals; Lima 0-1, Reynolds 1-0 vs. Twins.

LOS ANGELES—83-79

Pitcher	Ari. W-L	Atl. W-L	Chi. W-L	Cin. W-L	Col. W-L	Fla. W-L	Hou. W-L	Mil. W-L	Mon. W-L	N.Y. W-L	Phi. W-L	Pit. W-L	St.L. W-L	S.D. W-L	S.F. W-L	A.L. W-L	Total W-L
Barrios, M.	0-0	0-0	0-0	0-0	0-0	0-0	0-0	0-0	0-0	0-0	0-0	0-0	0-0	0-0	0-0	0-0	0-0
Bohanon, B.	0-0	0-0	0-0	0-0	1-0	1-0	1-0	0-0	0-0	0-1	1-0	1-1	0-1	0-3	0-1	0-0	5-7
Brunson, W.	0-0	0-0	0-0	0-0	0-0	0-0	0-0	0-0	0-0	0-0	0-0	0-0	0-0	0-0	0-0	0-1	0-1
Bruske, J.	0-0	0-0	0-0	1-0	0-0	0-0	1-0	0-0	0-0	0-0	0-0	0-0	0-0	0-0	0-0	1-0	3-0
Clontz, B.	0-0	0-0	1-0	0-0	0-0	0-0	0-0	0-0	0-0	0-0	0-0	1-0	0-0	0-0	0-0	0-0	2-0
Dreifort, D.	1-1	0-2	0-0	1-0	0-1	0-1	1-1	0-0	2-1	0-0	0-1	0-1	0-1	0-0	1-2	2-0	8-12
Guthrie, M.	0-0	0-1	1-0	0-0	0-0	0-0	0-0	0-0	0-0	0-0	0-0	1-0	0-0	0-0	0-0	0-0	2-1
Hall, D.	0-0	0-0	0-0	0-1	0-0	0-0	0-1	0-0	0-0	0-0	0-0	0-0	0-0	0-0	0-0	0-0	0-3
Judd, M.	0-0	0-0	0-0	0-0	0-0	0-0	0-0	0-0	0-0	0-0	0-0	0-0	0-0	0-0	0-0	0-0	0-0
Kubenka, J.	1-0	0-0	0-0	0-0	0-0	0-0	0-0	0-0	0-0	0-0	0-0	0-0	0-0	0-0	0-0	0-0	1-0
Lankford, F.	0-0	0-0	0-0	0-0	0-0	0-0	0-1	0-0	0-0	0-0	0-0	0-1	0-0	0-0	0-0	0-0	0-2
Maloney, S.	0-0	0-0	0-0	0-0	0-0	0-0	0-0	0-0	0-0	0-0	0-0	0-0	0-1	0-0	0-0	0-0	0-1
Martinez, R.	1-0	0-0	0-0	1-0	0-0	1-0	0-0	1-0	0-0	0-0	0-0	1-0	1-1	0-0	0-0	0-1	7-3
McMichael, G.	0-0	0-0	0-0	0-0	0-0	0-0	0-0	0-0	0-0	0-0	0-0	0-0	0-0	0-0	0-0	0-1	0-1
Mlicki, D.	0-1	0-1	0-0	0-2	2-0	0-0	0-0	1-0	2-0	0-1	0-0	0-0	0-0	2-0	0-0	0-0	7-3
Nomo, H.	0-1	0-0	0-0	0-2	0-1	0-0	0-1	1-0	1-1	0-0	0-0	0-1	0-0	0-0	0-0	1-0	2-7
Osuna, A.	0-0	0-0	0-0	0-0	0-0	1-0	0-1	1-0	0-0	1-0	0-0	1-0	0-0	1-0	0-0	1-0	7-1
Park, C. H.	2-1	0-1	1-1	0-0	0-2	1-1	1-0	1-0	0-0	0-1	2-0	2-1	0-0	3-1	1-0	2-0	15-9
Perez, C.	1-0	0-1	0-0	0-0	1-0	0-0	1-0	0-1	0-1	1-0	0-0	0-0	0-0	0-0	0-1	0-1	4-4
Radinsky, S.	0-0	1-0	0-0	0-0	1-1	1-0	1-0	0-0	0-0	0-1	0-1	1-1	0-0	1-1	1-0	0-0	6-6
Rath, G.	0-0	0-0	0-0	0-0	0-0	0-0	0-0	0-0	0-0	0-0	0-0	0-0	0-0	0-0	0-0	0-0	0-0
Reyes, D.	0-0	0-0	0-0	0-1	0-0	0-0	0-0	0-0	0-0	0-0	0-0	0-0	0-1	0-0	0-1	0-1	0-4
Shaw, J.	0-0	0-1	0-0	0-0	0-0	0-0	1-0	0-3	0-0	0-0	0-0	0-0	0-0	0-0	0-0	0-0	1-4
Valdes, I.	2-0	0-1	2-1	1-1	0-1	1-0	0-1	1-0	0-1	0-0	1-0	1-0	0-1	0-1	0-2	1-1	11-10
Weaver, E.	0-0	0-0	0-0	0-0	0-0	0-0	1-0	0-0	0-0	0-0	0-0	0-0	1-0	0-0	0-0	0-0	2-0
Totals	8-4	1-8	5-4	4-5	6-6	5-4	6-3	5-4	5-4	3-5	5-4	7-5	4-5	5-7	6-6	8-5	83-79

INTERLEAGUE BREAKDOWN: Brunson 0-1, McMichael 0-1, Osuna 1-0, Reyes 0-1 vs. Angels; Martinez 0-1, Park 1-0, Valdes 1-0 vs. A's; Bruske 1-0, Dreifort 1-0, Valdes 0-1 vs. Mariners; Dreifort 1-0, Park 1-0, Radinsky 1-0 vs. Rangers.

MILWAUKEE—74-88

Pitcher	Ari. W-L	Atl. W-L	Chi. W-L	Cin. W-L	Col. W-L	Fla. W-L	Hou. W-L	L.A. W-L	Mon. W-L	N.Y. W-L	Phi. W-L	Pit. W-L	St.L. W-L	S.D. W-L	S.F. W-L	A.L. W-L	Total W-L
Chouinard, B.	0-0	0-0	0-0	0-0	0-0	0-0	0-0	0-0	0-0	0-0	0-0	0-0	0-0	0-0	0-0	0-0	0-0
De Los Santos, V.	0-0	0-0	0-0	0-0	0-0	0-0	0-0	0-0	0-0	0-0	0-0	0-0	0-0	0-0	0-0	0-0	0-0
Eldred, C.	0-1	0-1	0-1	0-1	0-0	1-0	0-1	0-1	0-0	0-1	0-1	0-1	0-0	0-0	0-0	3-0	4-8
Fox, C.	0-1	0-0	1-0	0-1	0-0	0-0	0-1	0-0	0-0	0-0	0-0	0-0	0-0	0-0	0-0	0-0	1-4
Henderson, R.	0-0	0-0	0-0	0-0	0-0	0-0	0-0	0-0	0-0	0-0	0-0	0-0	0-0	0-0	0-0	0-0	0-0
Hudson, J.	0-0	0-0	0-0	0-0	0-0	0-0	0-0	0-0	0-0	0-0	0-0	0-0	0-0	0-0	0-0	0-0	0-0
Jones, D.	0-0	0-0	0-1	0-0	0-0	0-0	0-0	1-0	0-0	0-0	0-1	0-1	1-0	1-1	0-0	3-4
Juden, J.	1-1	0-2	0-0	0-0	0-1	1-0	1-0	1-0	0-1	1-1	0-1	1-1	0-1	0-0	0-0	1-2	7-11
Karl, S.	0-1	0-0	0-0	2-1	1-0	1-0	0-1	1-0	2-0	0-0	1-1	1-0	0-4	0-1	1-1	0-1	10-11

All records below are shown as W-L.

Pitcher	Ari.	Atl.	Chi.	Cin.	Col.	Fla.	Hou.	L.A.	Mon.	N.Y.	Phi.	Pit.	St.L.	S.D.	S.F.	A.L.	Total
Mercedes, J.	0-0	0-0	0-0	0-0	0-0	0-0	0-0	1-1	0-0	0-0	0-0	0-0	0-0	0-1	1-0	0-0	2-2
Mullins, G.	0-0	0-0	0-0	0-0	0-0	0-0	0-0	0-0	0-0	0-0	0-0	0-0	0-0	0-0	0-0	0-0	0-0
Myers, M.	0-0	1-0	0-0	0-0	0-0	0-0	0-0	0-0	0-0	0-0	1-0	0-0	0-0	0-0	0-0	0-1	2-2
Patrick, B.	0-0	0-0	2-0	0-0	1-0	0-0	0-0	0-0	0-0	0-1	0-0	0-0	0-0	0-0	0-0	1-0	4-1
Plunk, E.	0-0	0-0	1-0	0-0	0-0	0-0	0-0	0-1	0-0	0-0	0-0	0-0	0-1	0-0	0-0	0-0	1-2
Pulsipher, B.	0-0	0-0	0-1	1-0	1-1	0-0	0-1	0-1	0-0	0-0	0-0	0-0	0-0	1-0	0-0	0-0	3-4
Reyes, A.	0-0	0-0	1-1	0-0	1-0	2-0	0-0	1-0	0-0	0-0	0-0	0-0	0-0	0-0	0-0	0-0	5-1
Roque, R.	1-0	0-0	0-0	0-0	0-0	0-0	0-0	0-0	0-0	0-0	1-0	0-1	1-1	0-0	0-0	0-0	4-2
Smith, T.	0-0	0-0	0-0	0-0	0-0	0-0	0-0	0-0	0-0	0-0	0-0	0-0	0-0	0-0	0-0	0-0	0-0
Wagner, P.	0-0	0-1	0-0	0-0	0-0	0-0	0-0	0-1	0-1	0-0	0-0	0-0	0-1	1-1	0-0	0-0	1-5
Weathers, D.	0-0	0-0	0-0	0-0	0-1	0-0	0-0	0-0	1-0	0-0	2-0	0-0	1-0	0-0	0-0	0-0	4-1
Wickman, B.	0-1	0-1	0-1	0-0	0-0	1-0	1-0	0-1	2-1	0-2	0-1	0-0	0-0	0-1	1-0	1-0	6-9
Woodall, B.	1-1	0-1	1-1	1-1	1-1	0-0	0-1	0-0	0-0	0-1	0-0	1-0	0-0	0-0	0-0	1-1	7-9
Woodard, S.	0-0	1-1	0-0	1-2	1-0	2-0	0-3	0-0	0-0	0-0	1-1	1-1	2-1	0-1	0-0	1-1	10-12
Totals	3-6	2-7	6-6	5-6	7-4	9-0	2-9	4-5	6-3	1-8	4-5	6-5	3-8	3-6	5-4	8-6	74-88

INTERLEAGUE BREAKDOWN: Juden 1-0, Myers 0-1, Woodall 1-0 vs. White Sox; Eldred 1-0, Juden 0-1, Woodall 0-1 vs. Indians; Eldred 1-0, Karl 0-1, Woodard 0-1 vs. Tigers; Juden 0-1, Patrick 1-0, Wickman 1-0 vs. Royals; Eldred 1-0, Woodard 1-0 vs. Twins.

MONTREAL—65-97

Pitcher	Ari.	Atl.	Chi.	Cin.	Col.	Fla.	Hou.	L.A.	Mil.	N.Y.	Phi.	Pit.	St.L.	S.D.	S.F.	A.L.	Total
Batista, M.	0-0	2-1	0-1	0-0	0-0	0-0	0-1	1-0	0-0	0-0	0-0	0-1	0-0	0-0	0-0	0-1	3-5
Bennett, S.	2-0	0-0	0-0	0-0	0-0	0-0	0-1	0-0	0-2	2-0	0-1	0-0	0-1	1-0	0-0	0-0	5-5
Boskie, S.	0-0	1-0	0-0	0-0	0-0	0-1	0-0	0-0	0-0	0-0	0-0	0-1	0-0	0-0	0-0	0-1	1-3
Bullinger, K.	0-0	0-0	0-0	0-0	0-0	0-0	0-0	0-0	0-0	0-0	0-0	0-0	1-0	0-0	0-0	0-0	1-0
DeHart, R.	0-0	0-0	0-0	0-0	0-0	0-0	0-0	0-0	0-0	0-0	0-0	0-0	0-0	0-0	0-0	0-0	0-0
Hermanson, D.	3-0	1-0	0-0	0-1	0-1	3-0	0-1	0-0	0-2	0-1	0-1	0-1	1-0	2-0	1-1	2-2	14-11
Johnson, M.	0-0	0-1	0-0	0-0	0-0	0-0	0-1	0-0	0-0	0-0	0-0	0-0	0-0	0-0	0-0	0-0	0-2
Kline, S.	0-0	0-0	1-0	0-1	0-1	1-0	0-0	1-1	0-0	0-0	0-1	0-0	0-1	0-0	0-1	0-1	3-6
Maddux, M.	0-0	1-0	0-0	0-1	1-0	0-0	0-1	0-0	0-0	2-0	0-2	0-1	0-0	0-1	0-0	0-1	3-4
Moore, T.	0-0	0-0	0-1	0-1	1-0	0-0	0-1	0-0	1-0	0-0	0-0	0-1	0-0	0-1	0-1	0-0	2-5
Pavano, C.	0-0	0-0	0-1	0-0	0-0	0-1	1-0	0-0	0-0	2-1	1-1	1-0	0-1	0-2	0-0	1-2	6-9
Perez, C.	0-0	0-2	0-1	0-0	1-0	1-1	1-0	0-0	0-0	2-1	1-1	0-1	0-1	0-0	1-0	0-3	7-10
Powell, J.	0-1	0-0	0-1	0-1	0-1	0-0	0-0	1-1	0-0	0-0	0-0	0-0	0-0	0-0	0-0	0-0	1-5
Telford, A.	0-0	0-0	0-0	0-0	0-1	0-1	1-1	0-0	1-1	0-1	0-1	0-0	0-0	0-0	0-0	1-0	3-6
Thurman, M.	0-0	0-1	0-0	0-1	0-1	1-1	0-0	0-1	1-0	0-0	0-0	0-0	0-0	0-0	0-0	1-0	4-5
Urbina, U.	0-0	1-0	0-0	1-0	0-1	1-1	0-0	0-0	1-0	1-0	0-1	2-0	0-0	0-0	0-0	1-0	6-3
Valdes, M.	0-0	0-0	0-2	0-0	0-0	0-0	0-1	0-0	0-0	0-0	0-0	0-0	0-0	0-0	0-0	1-0	1-3
Vazquez, J.	2-1	0-1	0-1	0-2	0-1	1-0	0-0	0-1	0-1	0-1	1-0	0-1	0-1	0-1	0-3	1-0	5-15
Young, T.	0-0	0-0	0-0	0-0	0-0	0-0	0-0	0-0	0-0	0-0	0-0	0-0	0-0	0-0	0-0	0-0	0-0
Totals	7-2	6-6	2-7	1-8	2-7	7-5	2-7	4-5	3-6	8-4	5-7	2-7	3-6	4-4	3-6	6-10	65-97

INTERLEAGUE BREAKDOWN: Hermanson 1-0, Pavano 1-0, Vazquez 1-0 vs. Orioles; Hermanson 0-1, Pavano 0-1, Perez 0-1 vs. Red Sox; Hermanson 0-1, Perez 0-1, Valdes 1-0 vs. Yankees; Batista 0-1, Boskie 0-1, Pavano 0-1, Perez 0-1 vs. Blue Jays; Hermanson 1-0, Kline 0-1, Telford 1-0 vs. Devil Rays.

NEW YORK—88-74

Pitcher	Ari.	Atl.	Chi.	Cin.	Col.	Fla.	Hou.	L.A.	Mil.	Mon.	Phi.	Pit.	St.L.	S.D.	S.F.	A.L.	Total
Beltran, R.	0-0	0-0	0-0	0-0	0-0	0-0	0-0	0-0	0-0	0-0	0-0	0-0	0-0	0-0	0-0	0-0	0-0
Blair, W.	0-0	0-0	0-0	0-0	0-0	0-0	0-0	0-0	1-0	0-0	0-0	0-1	0-0	0-0	0-0	0-0	1-1
Bohanon, B.	0-1	0-1	0-0	1-0	0-0	1-1	0-0	0-0	0-0	0-0	0-0	0-1	0-0	0-0	0-0	0-0	2-4
Clontz, B.	0-0	0-0	0-0	0-0	0-0	0-0	0-0	0-0	0-0	0-0	0-0	0-0	0-0	0-0	0-0	0-0	0-0
Cook, D.	0-0	0-0	1-0	0-0	0-1	0-0	1-0	1-0	2-0	0-1	0-0	0-0	0-2	1-0	0-0	2-0	8-4
Franco, J.	0-0	0-1	0-1	0-0	0-0	0-1	0-1	0-1	0-0	0-2	0-0	0-1	0-0	0-0	0-0	0-0	0-8
Hudek, J.	0-0	0-0	0-0	0-1	0-0	0-1	0-0	0-1	0-0	0-0	0-0	0-0	0-0	0-0	0-0	1-1	1-4
Jones, B.	1-0	0-1	0-0	2-1	0-1	1-0	0-0	0-0	1-0	0-2	0-0	0-1	1-0	1-0	0-1	2-2	9-9
Leiter, A.	0-1	1-1	2-0	1-0	1-0	2-0	1-0	1-0	1-0	1-0	3-1	0-0	1-0	0-1	0-1	2-1	17-6
McMichael, G.	0-0	1-0	0-0	0-0	0-0	0-0	0-1	1-0	0-0	0-0	1-0	1-0	0-1	0-1	0-0	1-0	5-3
Mlicki, D.	1-0	0-0	0-1	0-0	0-0	0-0	0-1	0-0	0-1	0-0	0-0	0-1	0-0	0-0	0-0	0-0	1-4
Nomo, H.	0-1	0-0	0-0	0-0	0-1	0-0	1-0	0-0	0-0	1-1	0-0	0-1	1-0	1-0	0-0	0-0	4-5
Pulsipher, B.	0-0	0-0	0-0	0-0	0-0	0-0	0-0	0-0	0-0	0-0	0-0	0-0	0-0	0-0	0-0	0-0	0-0
Reed, R.	1-0	0-2	1-2	0-0	2-0	1-1	0-1	2-0	1-0	1-1	1-1	1-1	2-0	0-0	1-1	2-1	16-11
Reynoso, A.	1-0	0-1	1-0	0-0	1-0	0-0	0-0	1-0	0-1	0-0	1-0	1-0	0-1	0-0	0-0	0-0	7-3
Rojas, M.	1-0	0-0	0-0	1-0	1-0	0-0	0-0	0-0	1-0	0-0	0-0	1-0	0-1	0-0	0-0	0-0	5-2
Tam, Jeff	0-0	0-0	0-0	0-0	0-0	0-0	0-1	0-0	0-0	0-0	1-0	0-0	0-0	0-0	0-0	0-0	1-1
Wendell, T.	0-0	1-0	0-0	0-0	0-0	0-0	0-0	0-0	1-0	0-0	1-0	0-0	0-1	1-1	0-0	0-0	5-1
Yoshii, M.	0-1	0-2	0-0	1-1	1-0	2-0	0-0	0-1	0-0	0-1	0-0	1-1	1-0	0-0	0-0	0-1	6-8
Totals	5-4	3-9	5-4	6-3	6-3	7-5	4-5	5-3	8-1	4-8	8-4	4-5	6-3	4-5	4-5	9-7	88-74

INTERLEAGUE BREAKDOWN: Cook 1-0, Hudek 1-0, Jones 0-1, Reed 1-0 vs. Orioles; Jones 1-0, Leiter 1-0, Yoshii 0-1 vs. Red Sox; Cook 1-0, Jones 0-1, Leiter 0-1 vs. Yankees; Jones 1-0, Reed 0-1, Rojas 0-1 vs. Blue Jays; Hudek 0-1, Leiter 1-0, Reed 1-0 vs. Devil Rays.

PHILADELPHIA—75-87

Pitcher	Ari.	Atl.	Chi.	Cin.	Col.	Fla.	Hou.	L.A.	Mil.	Mon.	N.Y.	Pit.	St.L.	S.D.	S.F.	A.L.	Total
Beech, M.	0-0	0-0	0-1	0-0	0-0	0-0	0-2	1-1	0-0	0-0	0-1	1-0	0-1	0-1	0-0	1-2	3-9
Borland, T.	0-0	0-0	0-0	0-0	0-0	0-0	0-0	0-0	0-0	0-0	0-0	0-0	0-0	0-0	0-0	0-0	0-0
Bottalico, R.	0-1	0-0	0-0	0-0	0-0	1-1	0-0	0-0	0-1	0-0	0-1	0-0	0-0	0-0	0-1	0-0	1-5
Brewer, B.	0-0	0-1	0-0	0-0	0-0	0-0	0-0	0-0	0-0	0-0	0-0	0-0	0-0	0-0	0-0	0-0	0-1
Byrd, P.	0-0	0-0	0-0	0-0	1-0	0-0	1-0	0-1	0-0	1-0	1-0	1-0	0-0	0-1	0-0	0-0	5-2
Dodd, R.	0-0	0-0	0-0	0-0	0-0	0-0	0-0	0-0	0-0	0-0	0-0	0-0	1-0	0-0	0-0	0-0	1-0
Gomes, W.	0-0	0-0	0-0	0-0	0-1	1-0	1-0	0-0	2-1	3-1	0-0	0-0	0-1	0-0	0-1	2-1	9-6
Grace, M.	1-0	0-1	1-0	0-1	0-2	1-0	0-1	0-0	0-0	0-0	0-0	1-1	0-0	0-0	1-0		4-7
Green, T.	1-0	1-2	1-0	1-1	0-0	0-2	1-0	0-3	0-0	0-3	0-0	0-0	1-1	0-0	2-0		6-12
Leiter, M.	0-0	0-0	0-0	1-1	1-0	2-0	0-2	0-0	0-0	1-0	0-0	0-0	1-1	1-0	0-1		7-5
Loewer, C.	0-0	0-2	1-0	0-0	1-1	0-0	0-0	1-0	0-0	0-1	1-1	0-0	0-0	0-2	1-1		7-8

Pitcher	Ari. W-L	Atl. W-L	Chi. W-L	Cin. W-L	Col. W-L	Fla. W-L	Hou. W-L	L.A. W-L	Mil. W-L	Mon. W-L	N.Y. W-L	Pit. W-L	St.L. W-L	S.D. W-L	S.F. W-L	A.L. W-L	Total W-L
Nye, R.	0-0	0-0	0-0	0-0	0-0	0-0	0-0	0-0	0-0	0-0	0-0	0-0	0-0	0-0	0-0	0-0	0-0
Perez, Y.	0-0	0-0	0-0	0-0	0-0	0-0	0-1	0-0	0-0	0-0	0-0	0-0	0-0	0-0	0-1	0-0	0-2
Portugal, M.	1-1	0-0	0-1	1-0	1-0	0-0	0-0	1-0	0-0	1-1	2-0	2-0	0-1	0-1	0-0	1-0	10-5
Ryan, K.	0-0	0-0	0-0	0-0	0-0	0-0	0-0	0-0	0-0	0-0	0-0	0-0	0-0	0-0	0-0	0-0	0-0
Schilling, C.	3-0	2-1	1-0	0-1	0-0	0-2	0-1	1-0	2-1	2-2	0-1	2-0	1-0	0-3	1-0	0-2	15-14
Spradlin, J.	0-0	1-0	1-1	2-0	0-0	0-0	0-0	0-0	0-0	0-1	0-0	0-0	0-1	0-0	0-0	0-1	4-4
Stephenson, G.	0-0	0-1	0-0	0-0	0-1	0-0	0-0	0-0	0-0	0-0	0-0	0-0	0-0	0-0	0-0	0-0	0-2
Welch, M.	0-0	0-0	0-0	0-0	0-0	0-0	0-1	0-0	0-0	0-0	0-0	0-0	0-0	0-0	0-1	0-0	0-2
Whiteside, M.	0-0	0-0	0-0	0-0	0-0	0-0	0-0	0-0	0-0	0-0	0-0	0-0	0-0	1-1	0-0	0-0	1-1
Winston, D.	1-0	0-0	1-0	0-0	0-0	0-0	0-0	0-0	0-0	0-0	0-0	0-1	0-0	0-0	0-0	0-1	2-2
Totals	7-2	4-8	6-3	5-4	4-5	6-6	2-7	4-5	5-4	7-5	4-8	8-1	3-6	1-8	2-6	7-9	75-87

INTERLEAGUE BREAKDOWN: Beach 1-0, Leiter 0-1, Winston 0-1 vs. Orioles; Beach 0-1, Gomez 1-0, Loewer 1-0, Portugal 1-0 vs. Red Sox; Beech 0-1, Loewer 0-1, Spradlin 0-1 vs. Yankees; Gomes 1-0, Green 1-0, Schilling 0-1 vs. Blue Jays; Gomes 0-1, Green 1-0, Schilling 0-1 vs. Devil Rays.

PITTSBURGH—69-93

Pitcher	Ari. W-L	Atl. W-L	Chi. W-L	Cin. W-L	Col. W-L	Fla. W-L	Hou. W-L	L.A. W-L	Mil. W-L	Mon. W-L	N.Y. W-L	Phi. W-L	St.L. W-L	S.D. W-L	S.F. W-L	A.L. W-L	Total W-L
Christiansen, J.	0-0	0-0	0-0	1-0	1-0	0-1	0-1	0-1	0-0	1-0	0-0	0-0	0-0	0-0	0-0	0-0	3-3
Cordova, F.	0-2	1-1	1-1	1-1	0-1	0-0	1-2	0-1	2-0	2-0	0-3	0-3	3-0	1-0	1-1	0-0	13-14
Dessens, E.	0-0	0-0	0-0	1-0	0-0	0-0	0-1	0-1	1-1	0-0	0-0	0-0	0-0	0-1	0-1	0-1	2-6
Lawrence, S.	1-0	0-0	0-1	0-0	0-0	0-0	0-0	0-0	0-0	0-0	0-0	0-0	0-0	0-0	0-0	0-0	2-1
Lieber, J.	0-1	0-2	1-0	0-0	0-2	2-0	0-0	0-1	1-0	1-1	0-1	0-1	0-1	1-0	0-2	1-2	8-14
Loaiza, E.	0-1	1-0	0-0	0-0	1-0	0-2	0-0	0-1	1-0	0-0	0-0	0-1	0-0	0-0	3-0	0-0	6-5
Loiselle, R.	0-0	0-0	1-1	0-1	0-0	1-0	0-0	0-0	0-1	0-0	0-0	0-2	0-0	0-1	0-1	0-0	2-7
Martinez, J.	0-0	0-0	0-0	0-0	0-0	0-0	0-1	0-0	0-0	0-0	0-0	0-0	0-0	0-0	0-0	0-0	0-1
McCurry, J.	0-0	0-0	0-0	1-0	0-1	0-0	0-1	0-0	0-0	0-0	0-0	0-0	0-0	0-0	0-0	0-0	1-3
Peters, C.	0-1	0-1	0-1	1-0	1-0	0-0	0-0	1-0	1-1	1-2	1-0	0-0	0-0	0-1	0-0	1-2	8-10
Rincon, R.	0-0	0-0	0-0	0-1	0-0	0-0	0-0	0-1	0-0	0-0	0-0	0-0	0-0	0-0	0-0	0-0	0-2
Schmidt, J.	1-0	0-2	0-2	1-1	1-1	0-0	0-2	0-1	1-1	1-1	0-0	0-0	2-1	2-0	0-0	0-2	11-14
Silva, J.	0-0	0-1	0-1	1-1	0-0	1-0	1-0	0-1	0-0	0-0	0-0	0-1	0-1	1-0	1-1	1-0	6-7
Tabaka, J.	1-1	0-0	0-0	0-0	0-0	0-0	0-0	0-0	1-0	0-0	0-0	0-0	0-1	0-0	0-0	0-0	2-2
Van Poppel, T.	0-0	0-0	0-0	0-0	0-0	1-0	0-1	0-0	0-0	0-0	0-0	0-1	0-0	0-0	0-0	0-0	1-2
Wilkins, M.	0-0	0-0	0-0	0-0	0-0	0-0	0-0	0-0	0-0	0-0	0-0	0-0	0-0	0-0	0-0	0-0	0-0
Williams, M.	0-0	0-0	0-0	0-0	0-0	0-0	0-0	2-0	1-0	1-0	0-0	0-0	0-0	0-0	0-0	0-0	4-2
Totals	3-6	2-7	3-8	7-5	4-5	6-3	2-9	5-7	5-6	7-2	5-4	1-8	6-5	5-4	2-7	6-7	69-93

INTERLEAGUE BREAKDOWN: Dessens 0-1, Schmidt 0-1 vs. White Sox; Lieber 1-0, Loaiza 1-0, Peters 0-1 vs. Indians; Lieber 0-1, Loaiza 1-0, Peters 0-1 vs. Tigers; Lieber 0-1, Peters 1-0 vs. Royals; Loaiza 1-0, Schmidt 0-1, Silva 1-0 vs. Twins.

ST. LOUIS—83-79

Pitcher	Ari. W-L	Atl. W-L	Chi. W-L	Cin. W-L	Col. W-L	Fla. W-L	Hou. W-L	L.A. W-L	Mil. W-L	Mon. W-L	N.Y. W-L	Phi. W-L	Pit. W-L	S.D. W-L	S.F. W-L	A.L. W-L	Total W-L
Acevedo, J.	0-0	1-1	1-0	1-0	0-0	0-1	2-0	2-0	0-0	0-0	0-1	1-0	0-0	0-0	0-0	1-1	8-3
Aybar, M.	1-0	0-0	0-0	1-0	0-0	0-1	0-0	0-0	1-0	0-0	0-1	1-0	1-0	0-1	0-1	0-2	6-6
Bottenfield, K.	0-0	0-1	1-1	0-0	0-0	0-0	1-0	0-0	0-0	0-0	0-0	0-0	0-0	2-1	0-2	0-1	4-6
Brantley, J.	0-1	0-0	0-0	0-0	0-0	0-0	0-1	0-2	0-0	0-0	0-0	0-0	0-0	0-1	0-0	0-0	0-5
Busby, M.	1-0	0-0	0-0	0-0	1-1	0-0	0-0	0-0	1-0	1-1	0-0	1-0	0-0	0-0	0-0	0-0	5-2
Croushore, R.	0-0	0-1	0-0	0-1	0-0	0-0	0-0	0-1	0-0	0-0	0-0	0-0	0-0	0-0	0-0	0-0	0-3
Eversgerd, B.	0-0	0-0	0-0	0-0	0-0	0-0	0-0	0-0	0-0	0-0	0-0	0-0	0-0	0-0	0-0	0-0	0-0
Frascatore, J.	0-0	0-0	0-0	0-2	0-0	0-0	0-0	0-0	1-0	1-0	1-0	0-0	0-0	0-2	0-0	0-0	3-4
Gaetti, G.	0-0	0-0	0-0	0-0	0-0	0-0	0-0	0-0	0-0	0-0	0-0	0-0	0-0	0-0	0-0	0-0	0-0
Jimenez, J.	0-0	0-0	0-0	0-0	0-0	0-0	0-0	1-0	0-0	1-0	0-0	1-0	0-0	0-0	0-0	0-0	3-0
King, C.	0-0	0-0	0-0	0-0	0-0	1-0	0-0	0-0	0-0	0-0	0-0	0-0	0-0	1-0	0-0	0-0	2-0
Looper, B.	0-0	0-0	0-0	0-0	0-0	0-0	0-0	0-0	0-0	0-0	0-0	0-0	0-1	0-0	0-0	0-0	0-1
Lowe, S.	0-0	0-0	0-0	0-0	0-0	0-0	0-0	0-0	0-0	0-0	0-0	0-0	0-1	0-1	0-1	0-0	0-3
Mercker, K.	0-0	1-0	1-1	0-1	2-0	2-0	1-0	1-1	1-0	0-0	0-0	1-1	0-2	1-1	0-2	0-1	11-11
Morris, M.	0-0	0-1	0-0	0-0	0-0	1-0	1-1	0-0	2-0	0-0	1-1	0-0	1-1	1-0	0-0	0-0	7-5
Oliver, D.	0-0	0-0	2-0	0-0	0-0	1-0	0-2	0-0	1-1	0-0	0-0	0-0	0-0	0-0	0-0	0-0	4-4
Osborne, D.	0-1	0-0	0-0	1-0	0-0	0-0	0-1	0-0	0-0	2-1	0-0	1-1	0-0	0-0	0-0	0-0	5-4
Painter, L.	0-0	0-0	0-0	0-0	0-0	0-0	1-0	0-0	0-0	0-0	0-0	1-0	0-0	1-0	1-0	0-0	4-0
Petkovsek, M.	2-0	1-0	1-1	0-0	0-0	0-0	0-0	1-1	0-0	0-0	0-0	0-0	1-0	0-0	0-0	0-2	7-4
Politte, C.	0-0	0-1	0-0	0-0	0-0	1-0	0-0	0-0	0-0	0-1	0-1	1-0	0-0	0-0	0-0	0-0	2-3
Raggio, B.	1-0	0-0	0-0	0-0	0-0	0-1	0-0	0-0	0-0	0-0	0-0	0-0	0-0	0-0	0-0	0-0	1-1
Stottlemyre, T.	2-0	0-0	0-1	0-2	1-1	0-0	0-1	1-0	1-0	1-0	0-0	0-2	0-1	0-1	2-0		9-9
Witt, B.	0-0	0-1	1-0	0-2	0-0	0-0	0-0	0-0	0-0	0-0	0-0	0-0	0-1	0-0	1-0	0-0	2-5
Totals	7-2	3-6	7-4	3-8	6-3	5-4	7-5	5-4	8-3	6-3	3-6	6-3	5-6	3-6	5-7	4-9	83-79

INTERLEAGUE BREAKDOWN: Lowe 0-1, Painter 1-0, Petkovsek 0-1 vs. White Sox; Aybar 0-1, Petkovsek 0-1 vs. Indians; Bottenfield 0-1, Stottlemyre 1-0 vs. Tigers; Acevedo 1-0, Aybar 0-1, Mercker 0-1 vs. Royals; Bottenfield 0-1, Stottlemyre 1-0 vs. Twins.

SAN DIEGO—98-64

Pitcher	Ari. W-L	Atl. W-L	Chi. W-L	Cin. W-L	Col. W-L	Fla. W-L	Hou. W-L	L.A. W-L	Mil. W-L	Mon. W-L	N.Y. W-L	Phi. W-L	Pit. W-L	St.L. W-L	S.F. W-L	A.L. W-L	Total W-L
Ashby, A.	2-1	2-0	2-0	3-1	1-1	0-1	1-0	2-0	0-0	1-0	0-2	0-0	0-1	1-0	2-1	0-1	17-9
Boehringer, B.	0-0	0-0	1-0	1-0	0-0	0-0	0-0	0-0	0-0	0-1	1-0	1-0	1-0	0-0	0-1	0-0	5-2
Brown, K.	1-0	1-0	0-2	2-0	2-0	0-1	0-0	1-1	1-0	1-1	1-0	2-0	0-2	2-0	2-0	2-0	18-7
Bruske, J.	0-0	0-0	0-0	0-0	0-0	0-0	0-0	0-0	0-0	0-0	0-0	0-0	0-0	0-0	0-0	0-0	0-0
Clement, M.	1-0	0-0	0-0	0-0	1-0	0-0	0-0	0-0	0-0	0-0	0-0	0-0	0-0	0-0	0-0	0-0	2-0
Cunnane, W.	0-0	0-0	0-0	0-0	0-0	0-0	0-0	0-0	0-0	0-0	0-0	0-0	0-0	0-0	0-0	0-0	0-0
Hamilton, J.	2-0	1-2	0-1	3-0	1-1	1-0	0-2	2-1	0-1	1-0	0-1	1-0	0-1	1-0	1-0	0-2	13-13
Hitchcock, S.	0-1	0-0	0-0	0-0	0-0	1-1	0-1	0-0	3-0	0-1	0-0	1-0	1-0	1-0	1-2	0-0	9-7
Hoffman, T.	0-0	0-0	0-1	1-0	0-0	0-0	0-1	0-0	1-0	0-0	0-1	1-0	0-0	0-0	0-0	0-0	4-2
Kroon, M.	0-0	0-0	0-0	0-0	0-0	0-0	0-0	0-0	0-0	0-0	0-0	0-0	0-0	0-0	0-0	0-0	0-0
Langston, M.	0-0	0-1	0-0	0-0	1-0	0-0	1-0	0-1	0-1	0-0	0-0	1-1	0-1	1-0			4-6
Miceli, D.	1-0	0-0	1-1	0-0	0-0	1-1	1-1	0-1	0-1	0-0	2-0	1-0	0-0	1-0	2-1		10-5
Myers, R.	0-1	0-0	0-0	0-0	0-1	0-0	0-0	0-0	0-0	0-0	1-0	0-0	0-0	0-1	0-0		1-3

Pitcher	Ari. W-L	Atl. W-L	Chi. W-L	Cin. W-L	Col. W-L	Fla. W-L	Hou. W-L	L.A. W-L	Mil. W-L	Mon. W-L	N.Y. W-L	Phi. W-L	Pit. W-L	St.L. W-L	S.F. W-L	A.L. W-L	Total W-L
Ramirez, R.	0-0	0-0	0-0	0-0	0-0	0-0	0-0	0-0	0-0	0-0	0-0	0-0	0-0	0-0	1-0	0-0	1-0
Reyes, C.	0-0	0-0	0-0	0-0	0-0	0-0	0-0	0-1	0-0	0-1	0-0	0-0	1-0	1-0	0-0	0-0	2-2
Sanders, S.	0-0	0-0	0-0	0-0	1-1	1-0	0-0	1-0	0-0	0-0	0-0	0-0	0-0	0-0	0-0	0-0	3-1
Smith, P.	1-0	0-0	0-0	0-0	0-0	1-0	0-0	0-0	1-0	0-0	0-0	0-0	0-1	0-1	0-0	0-0	3-2
Spencer, S.	0-0	0-0	0-0	0-0	0-0	0-0	0-0	0-0	0-0	0-0	0-0	1-0	0-0	0-0	0-0	0-0	1-0
VanRyn, B.	0-0	0-1	0-0	0-0	0-0	0-0	0-0	0-0	0-0	0-0	0-0	0-0	0-0	0-0	0-0	0-0	0-1
Wall, D.	1-0	0-1	0-0	1-0	0-0	0-0	1-0	0-1	0-0	1-0	0-1	1-0	0-0	0-0	0-0	0-1	5-4
Wengert, D.	0-0	0-0	0-0	0-0	0-0	0-0	0-0	0-0	0-0	0-0	0-0	0-0	0-0	0-0	0-0	0-0	0-0
Totals	9-3	4-5	4-5	11-1	7-5	5-4	4-5	7-5	6-3	4-4	5-4	8-1	4-5	6-3	8-4	6-7	98-64

INTERLEAGUE BREAKDOWN: Brown 1-0, Hamilton 0-1, Hitchcock 1-0 vs. Angels; Brown 1-0, Hitchcock 0-1, Miceli 0-1 vs. A's; Ashby 0-1, Hamilton 0-1, Langston 1-0, Miceli 1-0 vs. Mariners; Hitchcock 0-1, Miceli 1-0, Wall 0-1 vs. Rangers.

SAN FRANCISCO—89-74

Pitcher	Ari. W-L	Atl. W-L	Chi. W-L	Cin. W-L	Col. W-L	Fla. W-L	Hou. W-L	L.A. W-L	Mil. W-L	Mon. W-L	N.Y. W-L	Phi. W-L	Pit. W-L	St.L. W-L	S.D. W-L	A.L. W-L	Total W-L
Bailey, C.	0-0	0-0	0-0	0-0	0-0	0-0	0-0	0-0	0-0	0-0	0-0	0-0	0-0	0-0	0-0	0-0	0-0
Brock, C.	0-0	0-0	0-0	0-0	0-0	0-0	0-0	0-0	0-0	0-0	0-0	0-0	0-0	0-0	0-0	0-0	0-0
Darwin, D.	1-1	1-1	1-0	1-0	0-0	0-0	0-0	0-1	0-0	1-1	1-0	1-0	0-1	0-1	0-3	1-0	8-10
Estes, S.	1-2	0-0	0-1	1-0	0-1	0-1	0-0	1-2	0-1	1-0	0-0	0-0	1-1	0-1	1-1	0-2	7-12
Gardner, M.	1-0	1-0	0-1	2-0	0-0	1-0	0-1	1-1	0-0	0-2	1-0	2-0	1-0	0-1	2-0	2-0	13-6
Hartgraves, D.	0-0	0-0	0-0	0-0	0-0	0-0	0-0	0-0	0-0	0-0	0-0	0-0	0-0	0-0	0-0	0-0	0-0
Hershiser, O.	1-1	0-1	1-0	1-0	1-1	1-0	0-0	2-1	1-2	0-0	1-1	0-0	1-0	1-0	0-1	0-2	11-10
Johnstone, J.	1-0	0-0	0-0	0-0	2-1	0-0	0-0	1-0	0-1	0-1	0-0	0-0	0-0	0-1	0-1	1-0	6-5
Mesa, J.	0-1	0-1	1-0	1-0	0-0	1-0	0-0	0-0	0-0	0-1	2-0	0-0	0-0	0-1	0-1	0-0	5-3
Morman, A.	0-0	0-0	0-0	0-0	0-1	0-0	0-0	0-0	0-0	0-0	0-0	0-0	0-0	0-0	0-0	0-0	0-1
Nen, R.	0-0	0-1	0-1	0-0	0-2	1-0	1-1	0-0	0-0	0-0	0-1	1-1	1-0	1-0	0-0	2-0	7-7
Ortiz, R.	0-0	0-0	0-2	0-1	0-0	0-0	0-0	1-0	0-0	0-0	2-0	0-1	1-0	0-0	0-0	0-0	4-4
Poole, J.	0-0	0-0	0-0	0-1	0-0	0-0	0-0	1-0	0-0	0-0	0-0	0-0	0-0	1-0	0-0	0-1	1-3
Reed, S.	0-0	0-0	0-0	0-0	0-0	0-0	1-0	0-0	1-0	0-0	0-0	0-0	0-0	0-1	0-0	0-0	2-1
Rodriguez, R.	1-0	0-0	0-0	0-0	2-0	0-0	0-0	0-0	0-0	0-0	0-0	0-0	0-0	1-0	0-0	0-0	4-0
Rueter, K.	1-0	0-3	0-0	1-0	1-1	1-0	1-2	0-0	2-0	3-0	0-1	1-0	1-0	1-1	1-0	2-0	16-9
Tavarez, J.	0-0	0-0	0-1	0-0	1-0	0-0	0-0	1-0	0-0	0-0	0-0	0-0	0-0	1-1	2-0	0-0	5-3
Totals	7-5	2-7	3-7	7-2	5-7	9-0	3-6	6-6	4-5	6-3	5-4	6-2	7-2	7-5	4-8	8-5	89-74

INTERLEAGUE BREAKDOWN: Estes 0-1, Nen 1-0, Rueter 1-0 vs. Angels; Estes 0-1, Gardner 1-0, Poole 0-1, Rueter 1-0 vs. A's; Darwin 1-0, Hershiser 0-1, Johnstone 1-0 vs. Mariners; Gardner 1-0, Hershiser 0-1, Nen 1-0 vs. Rangers.

HOME RUNS BY PARKS

	At Ari.	At Atl.	At Chi.	At Cin.	At Col.	At Fla.	At Hou.	At L.A.	At Mil.	At Mon.	At N.Y.	At Phi.	At Pit.	At St.L.	At S.D.	At S.F.	At A.L. Parks	Totals 1998	1997	HR Allow.
Arizona	82	3	6	5	11	4	2	3	4	6	5	5	1	9	4	5	4	159	....	188
Atlanta	4	104	3	9	9	9	6	2	4	4	10	8	9	7	3	11	13	215	174	117
Chicago	8	7	111	5	13	8	4	2	12	4	3	2	3	4	7	9	10	212	127	180
Cincinnati	7	2	10	66	8	2	3	5	6	5	4	2	4	4	0	5	5	138	142	170
Colorado	11	4	1	0	111	2	7	3	5	7	7	9	3	1	4	4	4	183	239	174
Florida	4	2	1	5	8	52	4	2	3	2	6	6	4	6	3	2	4	114	136	182
Houston	5	4	11	7	8	3	82	4	6	6	4	3	3	5	3	3	9	166	133	147
Los Angeles	9	7	8	1	5	7	3	78	3	0	3	4	4	12	4	3	8	159	174	135
Milwaukee	5	5	15	1	4	10	3	6	68	2	1	3	10	4	2	5	8	152	135	188
Montreal	4	5	4	3	2	9	3	6	4	65	6	5	5	4	4	7	7	147	172	156
New York	3	0	3	0	2	4	8	6	3	2	66	9	2	3	8	5	12	136	153	152
Philadelphia	2	0	5	7	4	3	4	4	3	4	0	68	3	4	1	2	12	126	116	188
Pittsburgh	3	0	4	8	2	0	3	2	2	3	2	5	58	8	2	1	4	107	129	147
St. Louis	3	1	8	4	7	8	9	2	13	4	7	12	6	113	9	7	10	223	144	151
San Diego	6	4	2	12	5	3	4	5	12	5	3	6	5	2	79	8	6	167	152	139
San Francisco	7	3	3	5	6	12	5	9	0	1	2	5	2	6	4	84	7	161	172	171
A.L. clubs	13	11	4	11	7	6	3	4	8	11	5	8	2	4	5	11	....	113	104	....
1998 Totals	176	162	199	149	212	142	153	143	160	131	134	160	124	196	142	172	123	2565	....	2585
1997 Totals	....	131	185	164	245	128	115	161	148	150	145	142	145	127	*171	159	....	....		†2163

*There were actually 170 home runs hit at San Diego in 1997. The totals include one home run by the Cardinals at Aloha Stadium, Honolulu, Hawaii. †The 1997 N.L. total excludes Milwaukee.

AT ARIZONA (176):

Arizona (82)—Lee 12, White 11, Bell 11, Williams 11, Batista 9, Stinnett 5, Fox 5, Garcia 4, Benitez 4, Klassen 3, Miller 2, Olson 1, Gilkey 1, Brede 1, Dellucci 1, Frias 1. **Atlanta (4)**—Lopez 2, Klesko 1, Williams 1. **Chicago (8)**—Grace 3, Sosa 3, Rodriguez 1, Brown 1. **Cincinnati (7)**—B. Larkin 3, Konerko 2, Sanders 1, Casey 1. **Colorado (11)**—Castilla 5, Bichette 2, Reed 1, Burks 1, Colbrunn 1, Lansing 1. **Florida (4)**—Floyd 1, Zaun 1, Lee 1, Kotsay 1. **Houston (5)**—Alou 2, Berry 1, Bagwell 1, Bell 1. **Los Angeles (9)**—Mondesi 3, Bonilla 1, Sheffield 1, Vizcaino 1, Karros 1, Young 1, Hubbard 1. **Milwaukee (5)**—Nilsson 2, Burnitz 1, Hamelin 1, Cirillo 1. **Montreal (4)**—Fullmer 1, Andrews 1, V. Guerrero 1. **Philadelphia (2)**—Parent 1, Brogna 1. **Pittsburgh (3)**—Garcia 1, Kendall 1, M. Martinez 1. **St. Louis (3)**—McGwire 1, Clayton 1, Jordan 1. **San Diego (6)**—Vaughn 2, Gwynn 1, Leyritz 1, Rivera 1, Sheets 1. **San Francisco (7)**—Johnson 2, Mueller 2, Dunston 1, Bonds 1, Snow 1. **Anaheim (7)**—Hollins 2, Erstad 2, Fielder 1, Walbeck 1, Anderson 1. **Seattle (5)**—Griffey 2, Wilson 1, Davis 1, Rodriguez 1. **Texas (1)**—McLemore 1.

AT ATLANTA (162):

Arizona (3)—Lee 2, Batista 1. **Atlanta (104)**—Lopez 18, C. Jones 17, Galarraga 16, A. Jones 16, Tucker 10, Klesko 8, Williams 5, Lockhart 4, E. Perez 3, Graffanino 3, Bautista 2, Guillen 1, Pride 1. **Chicago (7)**—Sosa 3, Alexander 2, Blauser 1, Tapani 1. **Cincinnati (2)**—Greene 1, Young 1. **Colorado (4)**—Castilla 3, Walker 1. **Florida (2)**—Orie 1, Lee 1. **Houston (4)**—Biggio 2, Berry 1, Bagwell 1. **Los Angeles (7)**—Karros 3, Zeile 2, Sheffield 1, Vizcaino 1. **Milwaukee (5)**—Burnitz 3, Vina 1, Cirillo 1. **Montreal (4)**—White 2, Andrews 1, C. Perez 1, Stovall 1. **St. Louis (1)**—Lankford 1. **San Diego (4)**—Gwynn 2, G. Myers 1, Vaughn 1, Gomez 1. **San Francisco (3)**—Aurilia 2, Bonds 1. **Boston (4)**—Valentin 2, Vaughn 1, Buford 1. **New York (2)**—O'Neill 1, Curtis 1. **Toronto (5)**—Green 2, Canseco 1, Delgado 1, Gonzalez 1.

AT CHICAGO (199):

Arizona (6)—Fox 2, Batista 2, White 1, Williams 1. **Atlanta (3)**—Galarraga 1, C. Jones 1, Pride 1. **Chicago (111)**—Sosa 35, Rodriguez 16, Hernandez 11, Brown 10, Grace 7, Hill 6, Servais 5, Gaetti 4, Morandini 4, Houston 4, Wood 2, Johnson 1, Merced 1, Alexander 1, Mieske 1, White 1, Orie 1, Maxwell 1. **Cincinnati (10)**—B. Boone 3, B. Larkin 2, Nunnally 2, Sanders 1, Petagine 1, Young 1. **Colorado (1)**—Helton 1. **Florida (1)**—Zeile 1. **Houston (11)**—Biggio 5, Alou 2, Ausmus 2, Spiers 1, Everett 1. **Los Angeles (8)**—Zeile 1, Karros 1, Piazza 1, Mondesi 1, Hubbard 1, Hollandsworth 1, Castro 1, Luke 1. **Milwaukee (15)**—Burnitz 4, Hughes 3, Jaha 2, Valentin 2, Cirillo 2, Loretta 1, Jenkins 1. **Montreal (4)**—V. Guerrero 2, Grudzielanek 1, Widger 1. **New York (3)**—Olerud 1, McRae 1, Huskey 1. **Philadelphia (5)**—Abreu 2, Jefferies 1, Brogna 1, Rolen 1. **Pittsburgh (4)**—Ward 1, Young 1, Martin 1, Collier 1. **St. Louis (8)**—McGwire 4, DeShields 4, Lankford 1, Jordan 1, Mabry 1. **San Diego (2)**—Caminiti 1, Sweeney 1. **San Francisco (3)**—Bonds 1, Kent 1, Mueller 1. **Chicago A.L. (2)**—O'Brien 1, Ordonez 1. **Cleveland (2)**—Fryman 1, Bell 1.

AT CINCINNATI (149):

Arizona (5)—Bell 2, Batista 2, White 1. **Atlanta (9)**—A. Jones 4, Galarraga 2, Williams 1, Lopez 1, Graffanino 1. **Chicago (5)**—Sosa 2, Gaetti 1, Grace 1, Hernandez 1. **Cincinnati (66)**—B. Boone 13, B. Larkin 8, Taubensee 8, Greene 8, Sanders 7, Fordyce 3, Stynes 3, Young 3, Casey 3, Nunnally 2, A. Boone 2, Nieves 1, Tarasco 1, Perez 1, Petagine 1, Watkins 1, Garcia 1. **Florida (5)**—Cangelosi 1, Johnson 1, Lee 1, Jackson 1, A. Gonzalez 1. **Houston (7)**—Biggio 1, Spiers 1, Alou 1, Bagwell 1, Bell 1, Bogar 1, Phillips 1. **Los Angeles (1)**—Mondesi 1. **Milwaukee (1)**—Burnitz 1. **Montreal (3)**—V. Guerrero 2, W. Guerrero 1. **Philadelphia (7)**—Rolen 3, Brogna 2, Jordan 1, Relaford 1. **Pittsburgh (8)**—Young 4, Kendall 2, Womack 1, Garcia 1. **St. Louis (4)**—Lankford 1, Jordan 1, Tatis 1, Drew 1. **San Diego (12)**—Vaughn 4, Gwynn 3, Finley 2, Joyner 1, Caminiti 1, Rivera 1. **San Francisco (5)**—Bonds 2, Johnson 2, Mueller 1. **Cleveland (3)**—Fryman 1, Burba 1, Thome 1. **Kansas City (5)**—Damon 2, Mack 1, King 1, Conine 1. **Minnesota (3)**—Steinbach 1, Merced 1, Lawton 1.

AT COLORADO (212):

Arizona (11)—Garcia 4, Stinnett 2, Lee 2, White 1, Bell 1, Williams 1. **Atlanta (9)**—Galarraga 2, C. Jones 2, A. Jones 2, Lopez 1, Lockhart 1, Tucker 1. **Chicago (13)**—Hernandez 4, Grace 2, Sosa 2, Gaetti 1, Hill 1, Rodriguez 1, Trachsel 1, Brown 1. **Cincinnati (8)**—B. Boone 2, Perez 2, Stynes 2, B. Larkin 1, Konerko 1. **Colorado (111)**—Castilla 26, Bichette 17, Walker 17, Helton 13, Burks 8, Lansing 7, Reed 6, Perez 6, Vander Wal 3, Hamilton 2, Abbott 2, Manwaring 1, Colbrunn 1, Goodwin 1, Echevarria 1. **Florida (8)**—Floyd 3, Bonilla 1, Zaun 1, Orie 1, Kotsay 1, Jackson 1. **Houston (8)**—Bagwell 3, Alou 2, Biggio 1, Spiers 1, Bell 1. **Los Angeles (5)**—Karros 4, Sheffield 1. **Milwaukee (4)**—Matheny 1, Cirillo 1, Loretta 1, Jenkins 1. **Montreal (2)**—V. Guerrero 1, Henley 1. **New York (2)**—Piazza 1, Alfonzo 1. **Philadelphia (4)**—Abreu 2, Glanville 1, Estalella 1. **Pittsburgh (2)**—Martin 1, Guillen 1. **St. Louis (7)**—McGee 2, Lampkin 2, McGwire 1, Lankford 1, Jordan 1. **San Diego (5)**—Finley 2, Joyner 1, Caminiti 1, Leyritz 1. **San Francisco (6)**—Javier 2, Carter 1, Bonds 1, Hayes 1, Kent 1. **Oakland (2)**—Roberts 1, Grieve 1. **Texas (5)**—Gonzalez 2, Clark 1, Kelly 1, Cedeno 1.

AT FLORIDA (142):

Arizona (4)—Williams 3, Lee 1. **Atlanta (9)**—Williams 2, C. Jones 2, Galarraga 1, Lopez 1, E. Perez 1, Helms 1, Lombard 1. **Chicago (8)**—Rodriguez 2, Grace 1, Sosa 1, Hernandez 1, Alexander 1, Houston 1, Orie 1. **Cincinnati (2)**—Watkins 1, Garcia 1. **Colorado (2)**—Castilla 1, Lansing 1. **Florida (52)**—Floyd 10, Sheffield 6, Johnson 5, Kotsay 5, Lee 4, Bonilla 3, Jackson 3, Zeile 2, Zaun 2, Counsell 2, Renteria 2, Dunwoody 2, Eisenreich 1, Orie 1, Berg 1, Wilson 1, Redmond 1, A. Gonzalez 1. **Houston (3)**—Berry 1, Bell 1, Everett 1. **Los Angeles (7)**—Mondesi 2, Sheffield 1, Zeile 1, Hubbard 1, Hollandsworth 1, Beltre 1. **Milwaukee (10)**—Valentin 3, Vina 2, Burnitz 2, Jackson 1, Grissom 1, Hughes 1. **Montreal (9)**—Andrews 3, Widger 2, V. Guerrero 2, May 1, Fullmer 1. **New York (4)**—McRae 1, Gilkey 1, Piazza 1, Huskey 1. **Philadelphia (3)**—Lieberthal 1, Abreu 1, Estalella 1. **St. Louis (8)**—McGwire 4, Gant 1, Mercker 1, Lankford 1, Jordan 1. **San Diego (3)**—Vaughn 2, Joyner 1. **San Francisco (12)**—Bonds 3, Kent 2, Aurilia 2, Mueller 2, Carter 1, Hayes 1, Mayne 1. **Boston (1)**—Jefferson 1. **Tampa Bay (1)**—Sorrento 1. **Toronto (4)**—Canseco 2, Fernandez 1, Delgado 1.

AT HOUSTON (153):

Arizona (2)—Stinnett 1, Batista 1. **Atlanta (6)**—Lopez 2, E. Perez 2, Klesko 1, C. Jones 1. **Chicago (4)**—Sosa 2, Blauser 1, Houston 1. **Cincinnati (3)**—B. Larkin 1, Petagine 1, Casey 1. **Colorado (7)**—Burks 2, Reed 1, Bichette 1, Castilla 1, Perez 1, Helton 1. **Florida (4)**—Zeile 1, Floyd 1, Lee 1, Berg 1. **Houston (82)**—Bagwell 20, Alou 19, Bell 12, Biggio 10, Berry 7, Everett 5, Hidalgo 3, Ausmus 2, Howell 1, Spiers 1, Eusebio 1, Gutierrez 1. **Los Angeles (3)**—Sheffield 1, Vizcaino 1, Mondesi 1. **Milwaukee (3)**—Grissom 1, Nilsson 1, Banks 1. **Montreal (3)**—Andrews 1, Grudzielanek 1, Fullmer 1. **New York (8)**—Piazza 2, Olerud 1, Baerga 1, Hundley 1, McRae 1, Huskey 1, Ordonez 1. **Philadelphia (4)**—Estalella 2, Zuber 1, Abreu 1. **Pittsburgh (3)**—Ward 1, Garcia 1, Allensworth 1. **St. Louis (9)**—McGwire 2, DeShields 2, Gaetti 1, Gant 1, Lankford 1, Hunter 1, Jordan 1. **San Diego (4)**—Vaughn 2, Gwynn 1, G. Myers 1. **San Francisco (5)**—Hayes 2, Bonds 1, Kent 1, Johnson 1. **Chicago A.L. (2)**—O'Brien 1, Belle 1. **Minnesota (1)**—Steinbach 1.

AT LOS ANGELES (143):

Arizona (3)—Fabregas 1, Benitez 1, Brede 1. **Atlanta (2)**—Galarraga 2. **Chicago (2)**—Sosa 1, Hernandez 1. **Cincinnati (5)**—B. Boone 2, B. Larkin 1, Sanders 1, Young 1. **Colorado (3)**—Walker 2, Abbott 1. **Florida (2)**—Lee 1, Dunwoody 1. **Houston (4)**—Alou 2, Bagwell 1, Everett 1. **Los Angeles (78)**—Mondesi 13, Karros 9, Johnson 9, Young 7, Luke 7, Bonilla 5, Sheffield 5, Piazza 5, Beltre 5, Hubbard 2, Grudzielanek 2, Cedeno 2, Konerko 2, Zeile 1, Howard 1, Dreifort 1, Hollandsworth 1, Nomo 1. **Milwaukee (6)**—Grissom 2, Valentin 1, Burnitz 1, Owens 1, Jenkins 1. **Montreal (6)**—V. Guerrero 2, Fullmer 2, Andrews 1, Widger 1. **New York (6)**—Alfonzo 2, Harris 1, Olerud 1, Baerga 1, Piazza 1. **Philadelphia (4)**—Jefferies 2, Rolen 1, Estalella 1. **Pittsburgh (2)**—Martin 1, Kendall 1. **St. Louis (2)**—Gaetti 1, Jordan 1. **San Diego (5)**—Caminiti 3, Gwynn 1, Hamilton 1. **San Francisco (9)**—Kent 3, Burks 2, Rios 2, Javier 1, Mayne 1. **Anaheim (2)**—Fielder 1, DiSarcina 1. **Oakland (2)**—Blowers 1, Giambi 1.

AT MILWAUKEE (160):

Arizona (4)—White 1, Bell 1, Benitez 1, Miller 1. **Atlanta (4)**—Galarraga 2, C. Jones 1, A. Jones 1. **Chicago (12)**—Sosa 4, Rodriguez 3, Hernandez 2, Johnson 1, Grace 1, Servais 1. **Cincinnati (6)**—Weathers 1, B. Boone 1, Greene 1, Nunnally 1, Young 1, Casey 1. **Cleveland (4)**—Dunston 1, Thome 1, M. Ramirez 1, Bell 1. **Colorado (5)**—Castilla 2, Manwaring 1, Hamilton 1, Lansing 1. **Florida (3)**—Floyd 1, Zaun 1, Redmond 1. **Houston (6)**—Bagwell 2, Hidalgo 2, Alou 1, Berry 1. **Los Angeles (3)**—Piazza 3. **Milwaukee (68)**—Burnitz 17, Valentin 7, Nilsson 6, Cirillo 6, Hamelin 5, Matheny 4, Hughes 4, Jenkins 4, Loretta 3, Jackson 2, Grissom 2, Jaha 2, Vina 2, Newfield 2, Woodall 1, Patrick 1. **Montreal (8)**—Andrews 2, V. Guerrero 2, May 1, White 1, Mordecai 1, Grudzielanek 1. **New York (3)**—Olerud 2, Huskey 1. **Philadelphia (3)**—Rolen 2, Sefcik 1. **Pittsburgh (2)**—Young 1, Guillen 1. **St. Louis (13)**—Gant 3, McGwire 2, Lankford 2, Gaetti 1, Kelly 1, Jordan 1, Mabry 1, Tatis 1, Aybar 1. **San Diego (12)**—Vaughn 4, Caminiti 2, Sheets 2, Gwynn 1, Joyner 1, Veras 1, Rivera 1. **Detroit (4)**—Higginson 2, Clark 2.

AT MONTREAL (131):

Arizona (6)—White 1, Bell 1, Meulens 1, Batista 1, Dellucci 1, Lee 1. **Atlanta (4)**—Lopez 2, Tucker 1, A. Jones 1. **Chicago (4)**—Rodriguez 2, Sosa 1, Brown 1. **Cincinnati (5)**—Sanders 1, B. Boone 1, Perez 1, Young 1, Casey 1. **Colorado (7)**—Helton 3, Burks 1, Bichette 1, Castilla 1, Vander Wal 1. **Florida (2)**—Knorr 1, Counsell 1. **Houston (6)**—Everett 3, Alou 2, Bell 1. **Milwaukee (2)**—Jaha 1, Vina 1. **Montreal (65)**—V. Guerrero 19, Andrews 12, White 9, Widger 6, Grudzielanek 3, Fullmer 3, Santangelo 2, Cabrera 2, Seguignol 2, May 1, Mordecai 1, R. Perez 1, Hubbard 1, Jones 1, McGuire 1, Henley 1. **New York (2)**—Harris 1, McRae 1. **Philadelphia (4)**—Rolen 2, Lewis 1, Lieberthal 1. **Pittsburgh (3)**—Young 2, Ward 1. **St. Louis (4)**—Gant 3, McGwire 1. **San Diego (5)**—Caminiti 2, Gwynn 1, G. Myers 1, Vaughn 1. **San Francisco (1)**—Dunston 1. **Baltimore (2)**—Palmeiro 1, Anderson 1, Hoiles 1. **New York A.L. (5)**—Martinez 2, Brosius 2, Williams 1. **Toronto (3)**—Stanley 1, Sprague 1, Delgado 1.

AT NEW YORK (134):

Arizona (5)—White 1, Bell 1, Williams 1, Stinnett 1, Lee 1. **Atlanta (10)**—Galarraga 3, A. Jones 3, Klesko 2, C. Jones 1, Malloy 1. **Chicago (3)**—Blauser 1, Sosa 1, Rodriguez 1. **Cincinnati (4)**—Nunnally 2, B. Larkin 1, Nieves 1. **Colorado (7)**—Burks 2, Castilla 2, Walker 1, Hamilton 1, Perez 1. **Florida (6)**—Floyd 2, Zeile 1, Orie 1, Dunwoody 1, Kotsay 1. **Houston (4)**—Alou 1, Bell 1, Everett 1, Ausmus 1. **Los Angeles (3)**—Mondesi 2, Karros 1. **Milwaukee (1)**—Nilsson 1. **Montreal (6)**—V. Guerrero 2, May 1, White 1, Santangelo 1, Henley 1. **New York (66)**—Olerud 13, McRae 12, Piazza 10, Alfonzo 8, Huskey 4, Phillips 3, Baerga 3, Becker 3, Harris 2, Tatum 2, Reed 1, Hundley 1, Gilkey 1, Pratt 1, Lopez 1, M. Franco 1. **Pittsburgh (2)**—Garcia 1, Ramirez 1. **St. Louis (7)**—McGwire 3, Jordan 3, Gant 1. **San Diego (3)**—Joyner 2, Gwynn 1. **San Francisco (2)**—Hayes 1, Kent 1. **Baltimore (2)**—Surhoff 1, Alomar 1. **New York A.L. (3)**—O'Neill 1, Martinez 1, Brosius 1.

AT PHILADELPHIA (160):

Arizona (5)—White 2, Fox 1, Batista 1, Lee 1. **Atlanta (8)**—Galarraga 4, Klesko 1, Lopez 1, C. Jones 1, Pride 1. **Chicago (2)**—Sosa 1, Brown 1. **Cincinnati (2)**—Greene 1, Young 1. **Colorado (9)**—Helton 4, Walker 2, Burks 1, Castilla 1, Lansing 1. **Florida (6)**—Lee 3, Zeile 1, Johnson 1, Counsell 1. **Houston (3)**—Alou 1, Berry 1, Bell 1. **Los Angeles (4)**—Sheffield 1, Karros 1, Mondesi 1, Johnson 1. **Milwaukee (3)**—Jaha 1, Burnitz 1, Hughes 1. **Montreal (5)**—May 1, White 1, V. Guerrero 1, Fullmer 1, Barrett 1. **New York (9)**—Huskey 2, Alfonzo 2, Baerga 1, McRae 1, Gilkey 1, Piazza 1, Allensworth 1. **Philadelphia (68)**—Rolen 19, Brogna 11, Abreu 10, Lieberthal 5, Lewis 4, Relaford 4, Jefferies 3, Glanville 3, Estalella 3, Sefcik 2, Amaro 1, Arias 1, Jordan 1, Anderson 1. **Pittsburgh (5)**—Young 1, Martin 1, Kendall 1, Nunez 1, Ramirez 1. **St. Louis (12)**—McGwire 4, Gaetti 3, Gant 3, DeShields 1, Jordan 1. **San Diego (6)**—Caminiti 3, Finley 1, Rivera 1, Sheets 1. **San Francisco (5)**—Kent 2, Bonds 1, Burks 1, Snow 1. **Baltimore (3)**—Carter 1, Palmeiro 1, Surhoff 1. **Boston (3)**—Valentin 1, Buford 1, Garciaparra 1. **Tampa Bay (2)**—McGriff 1, Sorrento 1.

AT PITTSBURGH (124):

Arizona (1)—Batista 1. **Atlanta (9)**—Galarraga 3, Klesko 3, C. Jones 2, Lopez 1. **Chicago (3)**—Sosa 2, Morandini 1. **Cincinnati (4)**—B. Boone 1, Greene 1, Stynes 1, Young 1. **Colorado (3)**—Bichette 1, Shumpert 1, Wright 1. **Florida (4)**—Lee 3, Floyd 1. **Houston (3)**—Hidalgo 2, Bagwell 1. **Los Angeles (4)**—Bonilla 1, Zeile 1, Karros 1, Mondesi 1. **Milwaukee (10)**—Burnitz 3, Valentin 2, Grissom 1, Nilsson 1, Jaha 1, Newfield 1, Loretta 1. **Montreal (5)**—White 2, Widger 1, Fullmer 1, Stovall 1. **New York (2)**—Piazza 1, Huskey 1. **Philadelphia (58)**—Young 15, Guillen 10, Ward 6, Kendall 6, Martin 5, M. Martinez 5, Ramirez 3, Womack 2, Garcia 2, Allensworth 1, Smith 1, Collier 1. **St. Louis (6)**—McGwire 2, Lankford 1, Clayton 1, Jordan 1, Tatis 1. **San Diego (5)**—Vaughn 2, Joyner 1, Hernandez 1, Sheets 1. **San Francisco (2)**—Bonds 1, Mayne 1. **Chicago A.L. (1)**—Durham 1. **Detroit (1)**—Gonzalez 1.

AT ST. LOUIS (196):

Arizona (9)—Williams 3, Stinnett 2, White 1, Bell 1, Benitez 1, Lee 1. **Atlanta (7)**—Galarraga 2, Lopez 2, A. Jones 2, Klesko 1. **Chicago (4)**—Gaetti 1, Sosa 1, Hernandez 1, Houston 1. **Cincinnati (4)**—Young 3, Taubensee 1. **Colorado (1)**—Helton 1. **Florida (6)**—Knorr 1, Floyd 1, Orie 1, Lee 1, Kotsay 1, A. Gonzalez 1. **Houston (5)**—Bagwell 2, Gutierrez 1, Everett 1, Phillips 1. **Los Angeles (12)**—Luke 3, Sheffield 2, Mondesi 2, Zeile 1, Howard 1, Cromer 1, Johnson 1, Hubbard 1. **Milwaukee (4)**—Cirillo 2, Jackson 1, Nilsson 1. **Montreal (4)**—Andrews 2, Santangelo 1, Cabrera 1. **New York (3)**—Hundley 1, Piazza 1, Fabregas 1. **Philadelphia (4)**—Lewis 1, Brogna 1, Glanville 1, Rolen 1. **Pittsburgh (8)**—Garcia 3, Young 1, Martin 1, Laker 1, Kendall 1, Guillen 1. **St. Louis (113)**—McGwire 38, Lankford 20, Gant 14, Jordan 9, Tatis 5, Lampkin 4, Mabry 4, Drew 4, DeShields 3, Kelly 3, Howard 2, Hunter 2, Marrero 2, Gaetti 1, Clayton 1, Polanco 1. **San Diego (2)**—Gwynn 1, Caminiti 1. **San Francisco (5)**—Kent 2, Bonds 1, Snow 1, Johnson 1, Mueller 1. **Detroit (4)**—Alvarez 2, Clark 1, Bako 1.

AT SAN DIEGO (142):

Arizona (4)—Bell 1, Benes 1, Benitez 1, Lee 1. **Atlanta (3)**—Williams 1, C. Jones 1, Lockhart 1. **Chicago (7)**—Sosa 2, Gaetti 1, Hill 1, Grace 1, Morandini 1, Hernandez 1. **Colorado (4)**—Castilla 2, Vander Wal 1, Helton 1. **Florida (3)**—Renteria 1, Castillo 1, Kotsay 1. **Houston (3)**—Alou 2, Bagwell 1. **Los Angeles (4)**—Sheffield 1, Karros 1, Mondesi 1, Castro 1. **Milwaukee (2)**—Burnitz 1, Jenkins 1. **Montreal (4)**—V. Guerrero 2, Hermanson 1, Widger 1. **New York (8)**—Piazza 2, Alfonzo 2, Harris 1, Baerga 1, McRae 1, Huskey 1. **Philadelphia (1)**—Jefferies 1. **Pittsburgh (2)**—Martin 2. **St. Louis (9)**—McGwire 3, Gaetti 2, Pagnozzi 1, Lankford 1, Clayton 1, Jordan 1. **San Diego (79)**—Vaughn 23, Caminiti 14, Finley 8, Hernandez 7, Gwynn 5, Veras 5, Joyner 4, Gomez 3, Rivera 2, Sheets 2, G. Myers 1, Leyritz 1, Cianfrocco 1, Sweeney 1, Giovanola 1, Arias 1. **San Francisco (4)**—Bonds 1, Sanchez 1, Kent 1, Benard 1. **Anaheim (4)**—Fielder 2, Anderson 1, Nevin 1. **Seattle (1)**—Griffey 1.

AT SAN FRANCISCO (172):

Arizona (5)—White 1, Bell 1, Garcia 1, Fox 1, Dellucci 1. **Atlanta (11)**—Galarraga 2, Lopez 2, C. Jones 2, Colbrunn 1, Bautista 1, Lockhart 1, Tucker 1, A. Jones 1. **Chicago (9)**—Rodriguez 3, Sosa 2, Blauser 1, Grace 1, Servais 1, Houston 1. **Cincinnati (5)**—Sanders 2, Taubensee 1, B. Boone 1, Greene 1. **Colorado (5)**—Reed 1, Burks 1, Hamilton 1, Lansing 1. **Florida (2)**—Floyd 1, Orie 1. **Houston (3)**—Bell 2, Berry 1. **Los Angeles (3)**—Sheffield 1, Mondesi 1, Hubbard 1. **Milwaukee (5)**—Grissom 1, Valentin 1, Burnitz 1, Matheny 1, Jenkins 1. **Montreal (7)**—Grudzielanek 2, Widger 2, Mordecai 1, Andrews 1, W. Guerrero 1. **New York (5)**—Piazza 2, Harris 1, Olerud 1, Castillo 1. **Philadelphia (2)**—Brogna 1, Magee 1. **Pittsburgh (1)**—Young 1. **St. Louis (7)**—Gaetti 2, Marrero 2, McGee 1, Jordan 1, Mabry 1. **San Diego (8)**—Vaughn 6, Caminiti 1, Finley 1. **San Francisco (84)**—Bonds 21, Kent 17, Snow 9, Hayes 7, Johnson 7, Carter 5, Aurilia 5, Burks 3, Jones 2, Benard 2, Javier 1, Dunston 1, Hamilton 1, Mueller 1, Mirabelli 1, Powell 1, Ortiz 1. **Oakland (2)**—Stairs 1, Giambi 1. **Seattle (4)**—Hill 1, Griffey 1, Davis 1, Rodriguez 1. **Texas (5)**—Clark 2, Gonzalez 1, Haselman 1, Tatis 1.

HISTORY

All-time results

Award winners

Hall of Fame

Team by team

ALL-TIME RESULTS

AMERICAN LEAGUE CHAMPIONS

Year	Team	Manager
1901	Chicago	Clark Griffith
1902	Philadelphia	Connie Mack
1903	Boston	Jimmy Collins
1904	Boston	Jimmy Collins
1905	Philadelphia	Connie Mack
1906	Chicago	Fielder Jones
1907	Detroit	Hugh Jennings
1908	Detroit	Hugh Jennings
1909	Detroit	Hugh Jennings
1910	Philadelphia	Connie Mack
1911	Philadelphia	Connie Mack
1912	Boston	Jake Stahl
1913	Philadelphia	Connie Mack
1914	Philadelphia	Connie Mack
1915	Boston	Bill Carrigan
1916	Boston	Bill Carrigan
1917	Chicago	Pants Rowland
1918	Boston	Ed Barrow
1919	Chicago	Kid Gleason
1920	Cleveland	Tris Speaker
1921	New York	Miller Huggins
1922	New York	Miller Huggins
1923	New York	Miller Huggins
1924	Washington	Bucky Harris
1925	Washington	Bucky Harris
1926	New York	Miller Huggins
1927	New York	Miller Huggins
1928	New York	Miller Huggins
1929	Philadelphia	Connie Mack
1930	Philadelphia	Connie Mack
1931	Philadelphia	Connie Mack
1932	New York	Joe McCarthy
1933	Washington	Joe Cronin
1934	Detroit	Mickey Cochrane
1935	Detroit	Mickey Cochrane
1936	New York	Joe McCarthy
1937	New York	Joe McCarthy
1938	New York	Joe McCarthy
1939	New York	Joe McCarthy
1940	Detroit	Del Baker
1941	New York	Joe McCarthy
1942	New York	Joe McCarthy
1943	New York	Joe McCarthy
1944	St. Louis	Luke Sewell
1945	Detroit	Steve O'Neill
1946	Boston	Joe Cronin
1947	New York	Bucky Harris
1948	Cleveland*	Lou Boudreau
1949	New York	Casey Stengel
1950	New York	Casey Stengel
1951	New York	Casey Stengel
1952	New York	Casey Stengel
1953	New York	Casey Stengel
1954	Cleveland	Al Lopez
1955	New York	Casey Stengel
1956	New York	Casey Stengel
1957	New York	Casey Stengel
1958	New York	Casey Stengel
1959	Chicago	Al Lopez
1960	New York	Casey Stengel
1961	New York	Ralph Houk
1962	New York	Ralph Houk
1963	New York	Ralph Houk
1964	New York	Yogi Berra
1965	Minnesota	Sam Mele
1966	Baltimore	Hank Bauer
1967	Boston	Dick Williams
1968	Detroit	Mayo Smith
1969	Baltimore (East Division)	Earl Weaver
1970	Baltimore (East Division)	Earl Weaver
1971	Baltimore (East Division)	Earl Weaver
1972	Oakland (West Division)	Dick Williams
1973	Oakland (West Division)	Dick Williams
1974	Oakland (West Division)	Al Dark
1975	Boston (East Division)	Darrell Johnson
1976	New York (East Division)	Billy Martin
1977	New York (East Division)	Billy Martin
1978	New York (East Division)	Billy Martin, Bob Lemon
1979	Baltimore (East Division)	Earl Weaver
1980	Kansas City (West Division)	Jim Frey
1981	New York (East Division)	Gene Michael, Bob Lemon
1982	Milwaukee (East Division)	Buck Rodgers, Harvey Kuenn
1983	Baltimore (East Division)	Joe Altobelli
1984	Detroit (East Division)	Sparky Anderson
1985	Kansas City (West Division)	Dick Howser
1986	Boston (East Division)	John McNamara
1987	Minnesota (West Division)	Tom Kelly
1988	Oakland (West Division)	Tony La Russa
1989	Oakland (West Division)	Tony La Russa
1990	Oakland (West Division)	Tony La Russa
1991	Minnesota (West Division)	Tom Kelly
1992	Toronto (East Division)	Cito Gaston
1993	Toronto (East Division)	Cito Gaston
1994	None†	
1995	Cleveland (Central Division)	Mike Hargrove
1996	New York (East Division)	Joe Torre
1997	Cleveland (Central Division)	Mike Hargrove
1998	New York (East Division)	Joe Torre

*Defeated Boston in one-game playoff. †New York finished the strike-shortened season with the league's best record.

NATIONAL LEAGUE CHAMPIONS

Year	Team	Manager
1876	Chicago	Albert Spalding
1877	Boston	Harry Wright
1878	Boston	Harry Wright
1879	Providence	George Wright
1880	Chicago	Adrian Anson
1881	Chicago	Adrian Anson
1882	Chicago	Adrian Anson
1883	Boston	John Morrill
1884	Providence	Frank Bancroft
1885	Chicago	Adrian Anson
1886	Chicago	Adrian Anson
1887	Detroit	William Watkins
1888	New York	James Mutrie
1889	New York	James Mutrie
1890	Brooklyn	William McGunnigle
1891	Boston	Frank Selee
1892	Boston	Frank Selee
1893	Boston	Frank Selee
1894	Baltimore	Edward Hanlon
1895	Baltimore	Edward Hanlon
1896	Baltimore	Edward Hanlon
1897	Boston	Frank Selee
1898	Boston	Frank Selee
1899	Brooklyn	Edward Hanlon
1900	Brooklyn	Edward Hanlon
1901	Pittsburgh	Fred Clarke
1902	Pittsburgh	Fred Clarke
1903	Pittsburgh	Fred Clarke
1904	New York	John McGraw
1905	New York	John McGraw
1906	Chicago	Frank Chance
1907	Chicago	Frank Chance

Year	Team	Manager	Year	Team	Manager
1908—Chicago	Frank Chance		1956—Brooklyn	Walter Alston	
1909—Pittsburgh	Fred Clarke		1957—Milwaukee	Fred Haney	
1910—Chicago	Frank Chance		1958—Milwaukee	Fred Haney	
1911—New York	John McGraw		1959—Los Angeles‡	Walter Alston	
1912—New York	John McGraw		1960—Pittsburgh	Danny Murtaugh	
1913—New York	John McGraw		1961—Cincinnati	Fred Hutchinson	
1914—Boston	George Stallings		1962—San Francisco§	Al Dark	
1915—Philadelphia	Pat Moran		1963—Los Angeles	Walter Alston	
1916—Brooklyn	Wilbert Robinson		1964—St. Louis	Johnny Keane	
1917—New York	John McGraw		1965—Los Angeles	Walter Alston	
1918—Chicago	Fred Mitchell		1966—Los Angeles	Walter Alston	
1919—Cincinnati	Pat Moran		1967—St. Louis	Red Schoendienst	
1920—Brooklyn	Wilbert Robinson		1968—St. Louis	Red Schoendienst	
1921—New York	John McGraw		1969—New York (East Division)	Gil Hodges	
1922—New York	John McGraw		1970—Cincinnati (West Division)	Sparky Anderson	
1923—New York	John McGraw		1971—Pittsburgh (East Division)	Danny Murtaugh	
1924—New York	John McGraw		1972—Cincinnati (West Division)	Sparky Anderson	
1925—Pittsburgh	Bill McKechnie		1973—New York (East Division)	Yogi Berra	
1926—St. Louis	Rogers Hornsby		1974—Los Angeles (West Division)	Walter Alston	
1927—Pittsburgh	Donie Bush		1975—Cincinnati (West Division)	Sparky Anderson	
1928—St. Louis	Bill McKechnie		1976—Cincinnati (West Division)	Sparky Anderson	
1929—Chicago	Joe McCarthy		1977—Los Angeles (West Division)	Tommy Lasorda	
1930—St. Louis	Gabby Street		1978—Los Angeles (West Division)	Tommy Lasorda	
1931—St. Louis	Gabby Street		1979—Pittsburgh (East Division)	Chuck Tanner	
1932—Chicago	Charlie Grimm		1980—Philadelphia (East Division)	Dallas Green	
1933—New York	Bill Terry		1981—Los Angeles (West Division)	Tommy Lasorda	
1934—St. Louis	Frank Frisch		1982—St. Louis (East Division)	Whitey Herzog	
1935—Chicago	Charlie Grimm		1983—Philadelphia (East Division)	Pat Corrales, Paul Owens	
1936—New York	Bill Terry		1984—San Diego (West Division)	Dick Williams	
1937—New York	Bill Terry		1985—St. Loius (East Division)	Whitey Herzog	
1938—Chicago	Gabby Hartnett		1986—New York (East Division)	Dave Johnson	
1939—Cincinnati	Bill McKechnie		1987—St. Louis (East Division)	Whitey Herzog	
1940—Cincinnati	Bill McKechnie		1988—Los Angeles (West Division)	Tommy Lasorda	
1941—Brooklyn	Leo Durocher		1989—San Francisco (West Division)	Roger Craig	
1942—St. Louis	Billy Southworth		1990—Cincinnati (West Division)	Lou Piniella	
1943—St. Louis	Billy Southworth		1991—Atlanta (West Division)	Bobby Cox	
1944—St. Louis	Billy Southworth		1992—Atlanta (West Division)	Bobby Cox	
1945—Chicago	Charlie Grimm		1993—Philadelphia (East Division)	Jim Fregosi	
1946—St. Louis*	Eddie Dyer		1994—None∞		
1947—Brooklyn	Burt Shotton		1995—Atlanta (East Division)	Bobby Cox	
1948—Boston	Billy Southworth		1996—Atlanta (East Division)	Bobby Cox	
1949—Brooklyn	Burt Shotton		1997—Florida (East Division)	Jim Leyland	
1950—Philadelphia	Eddie Sawyer		1998—San Diego (West Division)	Bruce Bochy	
1951—New York†	Leo Durocher				
1952—Brooklyn	Charlie Dressen				
1953—Brooklyn	Charlie Dressen				
1954—New York	Leo Durocher				
1955—Brooklyn	Walter Alston				

*Defeated Brooklyn, two games to none, in playoff for pennant
†Defeated Brooklyn, two games to one, in playoff for pennant.
‡Defeated Milwaukee, two games to none, in playoff for pennant.
§Defeated Los Angeles, two games to one, in playoff for pennant.
∞Montreal finished the strike-shortened season with the league's best record.

WORLD SERIES

Year	Winner	Loser	Games	Year	Winner	Loser	Games
1903—Boston A.L.	Pittsburgh N.L.	5-3		1927—New York A.L.	Pittsburgh, N.L.	4-0
1904—No Series				1928—New York A.L.	St. Louis N.L.	4-0
1905—New York N.L.	Philadelphia A.L.	4-1		1929—Philadelphia A.L.	Chicago N.L.	4-1
1906—Chicago A.L.	Chicago N.L.	4-2		1930—Philadelphia A.L.	St. Louis N.L.	4-2
1907—Chicago N.L.	Detroit A.L.	*4-0		1931—St. Louis N.L.	Philadelphia A.L.	4-3
1908—Chicago N.L.	Detroit A.L.	4-1		1932—New York A.L.	Chicago N.L.	4-0
1909—Pittsburgh N.L.	Detroit A.L.	4-3		1933—New York N.L.	Washington A.L.	4-1
1910—Philadelphia A.L.	Chicago N.L.	4-1		1934—St. Louis N.L.	Detroit A.L.	4-3
1911—Philadelphia A.L.	New York N.L.	4-2		1935—Detroit A.L.	Chicago N.L.	4-2
1912—Boston A.L.	New York N.L.	*4-3		1936—New York A.L.	New York N.L.	4-2
1913—Philadelphia A.L.	New York N.L.	4-1		1937—New York A.L.	New York N.L.	4-1
1914—Boston N.L.	Philadelphia A.L.	4-0		1938—New York A.L.	Chicago N.L.	4-0
1915—Boston A.L.	Philadelphia N.L.	4-1		1939—New York A.L.	Cincinnati N.L.	4-0
1916—Boston A.L.	Brooklyn N.L.	4-1		1940—Cincinnati N.L.	Detroit A.L.	4-3
1917—Chicago A.L.	New York N.L.	4-2		1941—New York A.L.	Brooklyn N.L.	4-1
1918—Boston A.L.	Chicago N.L.	4-2		1942—St. Louis N.L.	New York A.L.	4-1
1919—Cincinnati N.L.	Chicago A.L.	5-3		1943—New York A.L.	St. Louis N.L.	4-1
1920—Cleveland A.L.	Brooklyn N.L.	5-2		1944—St. Louis N.L.	St. Louis A.L.	4-2
1921—New York N.L.	New York A.L.	5-3		1945—Detroit A.L.	Chicago N.L.	4-3
1922—New York N.L.	New York A.L.	*4-0		1946—St. Louis N.L.	Boston A.L.	4-3
1923—New York A.L.	New York N.L.	4-2		1947—New York A.L.	Brooklyn, N.L.	4-3
1924—Washington A.L.	New York N.L.	4-3		1948—Cleveland A.L.	Boston N.L.	4-2
1925—Pittsburgh N.L.	Washington A.L.	4-3		1949—New York A.L.	Brooklyn N.L.	4-1
1926—St. Louis N.L.	New York A.L.	4-3		1950—New York A.L.	Philadelphia N.L.	4-0

Year	Winner	Loser	Games
1951—New York A.L.	New York N.L.	4-2
1952—New York A.L.	Brooklyn N.L.	4-3
1953—New York A.L.	Brooklyn N.L.	4-2
1954—New York N.L.	Cleveland A.L.	4-0
1955—Brooklyn N.L.	New York A.L.	4-3
1956—New York A.L.	Brooklyn N.L.	4-3
1957—Milwaukee N.L.	New York A.L.	4-3
1958—New York A.L.	Milwaukee N.L.	4-3
1959—Los Angeles N.L.	Chicago A.L.	4-2
1960—Pittsburgh N.L.	New York A.L.	4-3
1961—New York A.L.	Cincinnati N.L.	4-1
1962—New York A.L.	San Francisco N.L.	4-3
1963—Los Angeles N.L.	New York A.L.	4-0
1964—St. Louis N.L.	New York A.L.	4-3
1965—Los Angeles N.L.	Minnesota A.L.	4-3
1966—Baltimore A.L.	Los Angeles N.L.	4-0
1967—St. Louis N.L.	Boston A.L.	4-3
1968—Detroit A.L.	St. Louis N.L.	4-3
1969—New York N.L.	Baltimore A.L.	4-1
1970—Baltimore A.L.	Cincinnati N.L.	4-1
1971—Pittsburgh N.L.	Baltimore A.L.	4-3
1972—Oakland A.L.	Cincinnati N.L.	4-3
1973—Oakland A.L.	New York N.L.	4-3
1974—Oakland A.L.	Los Angeles N.L.	4-1
1975—Cincinnati N.L.	Boston A.L.	4-3

Year	Winner	Loser	Games
1976—Cincinnati N.L.	New York A.L.	4-0
1977—New York A.L.	Los Angeles N.L.	4-2
1978—New York A.L.	Los Angeles N.L.	4-2
1979—Pittsburgh N.L.	Baltimore A.L.	4-3
1980—Philadelphia N.L.	Kansas City A.L.	4-2
1981—Los Angeles N.L.	New York A.L.	4-2
1982—St. Louis N.L.	Milwaukee A.L.	4-3
1983—Baltimore A.L.	Philadelphia N.L.	4-1
1984—Detroit A.L.	San Diego N.L.	4-1
1985—Kansas City A.L.	St. Louis N.L.	4-3
1986—New York N.L.	Boston A.L.	4-3
1987—Minnesota A.L.	St. Louis N.L.	4-3
1988—Los Angeles N.L.	Oakland A.L.	4-1
1989—Oakland A.L.	San Francisco N.L.	4-0
1990—Cincinnati N.L.	Oakland A.L.	4-0
1991—Minnesota A.L.	Atlanta N.L.	4-3
1992—Toronto A.L.	Atlanta N.L.	4-2
1993—Toronto A.L.	Philadelphia N.L.	4-2
1994—No Series		
1995—Atlanta N.L.	Cleveland A.L.	4-2
1996—New York A.L.	Atlanta N.L.	4-2
1997—Florida N.L.	Cleveland A.L.	4-3
1998—New York A.L.	San Diego N.L.	4-0

*Includes tie game.

DIVISION SERIES

AMERICAN LEAGUE

Year	Winner (Division)	Loser (Division)	Games
1981—New York (East)	Milwaukee (East)	3-2
Oakland (West)	Kansas City (West)	3-0
1995—Cleveland (Central)	Boston (East)	3-0
Seattle (West)	New York* (East)	3-2
1996—New York (East)	Texas (West)	3-1
Baltimore (East)*	Cleveland (Central)	3-1
1997—Baltimore (East)	Seattle (West)	3-1
Cleveland (Central)	New York (East)*	3-2
1998—New York (East)	Texas (West)	3-0
Cleveland (Central)	Boston (East)*	3-1

NATIONAL LEAGUE

Year	Winner (Division)	Loser (Division)	Games
1981—Montreal (East)	Philadelphia (East)	3-2
Los Angeles (West)	Houston (West)	3-2
1995—Atlanta (East)	Colorado* (West)	3-1
Cincinnati (Central)	Los Angeles (West)	3-0
1996—Atlanta (East)	Los Angeles (West)*	3-0
St. Louis (Central)	San Diego (West)	3-0
1997—Atlanta (East)	Houston (Central)	3-0
Florida (East)*	San Francisco (West)	3-0
1998—Atlanta (East)	Chicago (Central)*	3-0
San Diego (West)	Houston (Central)	3-1

*Wild-card team.

CHAMPIONSHIP SERIES

AMERICAN LEAGUE

Year	Winner (Division)	Loser (Division)	Games
1969—Baltimore (East)	Minnesota (West)	3-0
1970—Baltimore (East)	Minnesota (West)	3-0
1971—Baltimore (East)	Oakland (West)	3-0
1972—Oakland (West)	Detroit (East)	3-2
1973—Oakland (West)	Baltimore (East)	3-2
1974—Oakland (West)	Baltimore (East)	3-1
1975—Boston (East)	Oakland (West)	3-0
1976—New York (East)	Kansas City (West)	3-2
1977—New York (East)	Kansas City (West)	3-2
1978—New York (East)	Kansas City (West)	3-1
1979—Baltimore (East)	California (West)	3-1
1980—Kansas City (West)	New York (East)	3-0
1981—New York (East)	Oakland (West)	3-0
1982—Milwaukee (East)	California (West)	3-2
1983—Baltimore (East)	Chicago (West)	3-1
1984—Detroit (East)	Kansas City (West)	3-0
1985—Kansas City (West)	Toronto (East)	4-3
1986—Boston (East)	California (West)	4-3
1987—Minnesota (West)	Detroit (East)	4-1
1988—Oakland (West)	Boston (East)	4-0
1989—Oakland (West)	Toronto (East)	4-1
1990—Oakland (West)	Boston (East)	4-0
1991—Minnesota (West)	Toronto (East)	4-1
1992—Toronto (East)	Oakland (West)	4-2
1993—Toronto (East)	Chicago (West)	4-2
1994—No series		
1995—Cleveland (Central)	Seattle (West)	4-2

Year	Winner (Division)	Loser (Division)	Games
1996—New York (East)	Baltimore (East)*	4-1
1997—Cleveland (Central)	Baltimore (East)	4-2
1998—New York (East)	Cleveland (Central)	4-2

NATIONAL LEAGUE

Year	Winner (Division)	Loser (Division)	Games
1969—New York (East)	Atlanta (West)	3-0
1970—Cincinnati (West)	Pittsburgh (East)	3-0
1971—Pittsburgh (East)	San Francisco (West)	3-1
1972—Cincinnati (West)	Pittsburgh (East)	3-2
1973—New York (East)	Cincinnati (West)	3-2
1974—Los Angeles (West)	Pittsburgh (East)	3-1
1975—Cincinnati (West)	Pittsburgh (East)	3-0
1976—Cincinnati (West)	Philadelphia (East)	3-0
1977—Los Angeles (West)	Philadelphia (East)	3-1
1978—Los Angeles (West)	Philadelphia (East)	3-1
1979—Pittsburgh (East)	Cincinnati (West)	3-0
1980—Philadelphia (East)	Houston (West)	3-2
1981—Los Angeles (West)	Montreal (East)	3-2
1982—St. Louis (East)	Atlanta (West)	3-0
1983—Philadelphia (East)	Los Angeles (West)	3-1
1984—San Diego (West)	Chicago (East)	3-2
1985—St. Louis (East)	Los Angeles (West)	4-2
1986—New York (East)	Houston (West)	4-2
1987—St. Louis (East)	San Francisco (West)	4-3
1988—Los Angeles (West)	New York (East)	4-3
1989—San Francisco (West)	Chicago (East)	4-1
1990—Cincinnati (West)	Pittsburgh (East)	4-2

Year	Winner (Division)	Loser (Division)	Games	Year	Winner (Division)	Loser (Division)	Games
1991—Atlanta (West)		Pittsburgh (East)	4-3	1996—Atlanta (East)		St. Louis (Central)	4-3
1992—Atlanta (West)		Pittsburgh (East)	4-3	1997—Florida (East)*		Atlanta (East)	4-2
1993—Philadelphia (East)		Atlanta (West)	4-2	1998—San Diego (West)		Atlanta (East)	4-2
1994—No series				*Wild-card team.			
1995—Atlanta (East)		Cincinnati (Central)	4-0				

ALL-STAR GAME

Date	Site	Score (Winner)	Winning pitcher (Losing pitcher)	Winning manager (Losing manager)	Att.
7-6-33	Comiskey Park Chicago	4-2 (A.L.)	Lefty Gomez, Yankees (Bill Hallahan, Cardinals)	Connie Mack, Athletics (John McGraw, Giants)	47,595
7-10-34	Polo Grounds New York	9-7 (A.L.)	Mel Harder, Indians (Van Mungo, Dodgers)	Joe Cronin, Senators (Bill Terry, Giants)	48,363
7-8-35	Municipal Stadium Cleveland	4-1 (A.L.)	Lefty Gomez, Yankees (Bill Walker, Cardinals)	Mickey Cochrane, Tigers (Frankie Frisch, Cardinals)	69,831
7-7-36	Braves Field Boston	4-3 (N.L.)	Dizzy Dean, Cardinals (Lefty Grove, Red Sox)	Charlie Grimm, Cubs (Joe McCarthy, Yankees)	25,556
7-7-37	Griffith Stadium Washington	8-3 (A.L.)	Lefty Gomez, Yankees (Dizzy Dean, Cardinals)	Joe McCarthy, Yankees (Bill Terry, Giants)	31,391
7-6-38	Crosley Field Cincinnati	4-1 (N.L.)	Johnny Vander Meer, Reds (Lefty Gomez, Yankees)	Bill Terry, Giants (Joe McCarthy, Yankees)	27,067
7-11-39	Yankee Stadium New York	3-1 (A.L.)	Tommy Bridges, Tigers (Bill Lee, Cubs)	Joe McCarthy, Yankees (Gabby Hartnett, Cubs)	62,892
7-9-40	Sportsman's Park St. Louis	4-0 (N.L.)	Paul Derringer, Reds (Red Ruffing, Yankees)	Bill McKechnie, Reds (Joe Cronin, Red Sox)	32,373
7-8-41	Briggs Stadium Detroit	7-5 (A.L.)	Ed Smith, White Sox (Claude Passeau, Cubs)	Del Baker, Tigers (Bill McKechnie, Reds)	54,674
7-6-42	Polo Grounds New York	3-1 (A.L.)	Spud Chandler, Yankees (Mort Cooper, Cardinals)	Joe McCarthy, Yankees (Leo Durocher, Dodgers)	34,178
7-13-43	Shibe Park Philadelphia	5-3 (A.L.)	Dutch Leonard, Senators (Mort Cooper, Cardinals)	Joe McCarthy, Yankees (Billy Southworth, Cardinals)	31,938
7-11-44	Forbes Field Pittsburgh	7-1 (N.L.)	Ken Raffensberger, Phillies (Tex Hughson, Red Sox)	Billy Southworth, Cardinals (Joe McCarthy, Yankees)	29,589
1945	No game played.				
7-9-46	Fenway Park Boston	12-0 (A.L.)	Bob Feller, Indians (Claude Passeau, Cubs)	Steve O'Neill, Tigers (Charlie Grimm, Cubs)	34,906
7-8-47	Wrigley Field Chicago	2-1 (A.L.)	Frank Shea, Yankees (Johnny Sain, Braves)	Joe Cronin, Red Sox (Eddie Dyer, Cardinals)	41,123
7-13-48	Sportsman's Park St. Louis	5-2 (A.L.)	Vic Raschi, Yankees (Johnny Schmitz, Cubs)	Bucky Harris, Yankees (Leo Durocher, Dodgers)	34,009
7-12-49	Ebbets Field Brooklyn	11-7 (A.L.)	Virgil Trucks, Tigers (Don Newcombe, Dodgers)	Lou Boudreau, Indians (Billy Southworth, Braves)	32,577
7-11-50	Comiskey Park Chicago	4-3* (N.L.)	Ewell Blackwell, Reds (Ted Gray, Tigers)	Burt Shotton, Dodgers (Casey Stengel, Yankees)	46,127
7-10-51	Briggs Stadium Detroit	8-3 (N.L.)	Sal Maglie, Giants (Ed Lopat, Yankees)	Eddie Sawyer, Phillies (Casey Stengel, Yankees)	52,075
7-8-52	Shibe Park Philadelphia	3-2† (N.L.)	Bob Rush, Cubs (Bob Lemon, Indians)	Leo Durocher, Giants (Casey Stengel, Yankees)	32,785
7-14-53	Crosley Field Cincinnati	5-1 (N.L.)	Warren Spahn, Braves (Allie Reynolds, Yankees)	Chuck Dressen, Dodgers (Casey Stengel, Yankees)	30,846
7-13-54	Municipal Stadium Cleveland	11-9 (A.L.)	Dean Stone, Senators (Gene Conley, Braves)	Casey Stengel, Yankees (Walter Alston, Dodgers)	68,751
7-12-55	Milwaukee Co. Stadium Milwaukee	6-5‡ (N.L.)	Gene Conley, Braves (Frank Sullivan, Red Sox)	Leo Durocher, Giants (Al Lopez, Indians)	45,643
7-10-56	Griffith Stadium Washington	7-3 (N.L.)	Bob Friend, Pirates (Billy Pierce, White Sox)	Walter Alston, Dodgers (Casey Stengel, Yankees)	28,843
7-9-57	Busch Stadium St. Louis	6-5 (A.L.)	Jim Bunning, Tigers (Curt Simmons, Phillies)	Casey Stengel, Yankees (Walter Alston, Dodgers)	30,693
7-8-58	Memorial Stadium Baltimore	4-3 (A.L.)	Early Wynn, White Sox (Bob Friend, Pirates)	Casey Stengel, Yankees (Fred Haney, Braves)	48,829
7-7-59	Forbes Field Pittsburgh	5-4 (N.L.)	Johnny Antonelli, Giants (Whitey Ford, Yankees)	Fred Haney, Braves (Casey Stengel, Yankees)	35,277
8-3-59	Memorial Coliseum Los Angeles	5-3 (A.L.)	Jerry Walker, Orioles (Don Drysdale, Dodgers)	Casey Stengel, Yankees (Fred Haney, Braves)	55,105
7-11-60	Municipal Stadium Kansas City	5-3 (N.L.)	Bob Friend, Pirates (Bill Monbouquette, Red Sox)	Walter Alston, Dodgers (Al Lopez, White Sox)	30,619
7-13-60	Yankee Stadium New York	6-0 (N.L.)	Vernon Law, Pirates (Whitey Ford, Yankees)	Walter Alston, Dodgers (Al Lopez, White Sox)	38,362
7-11-61	Candlestick Park San Francisco	5-4§ (N.L.)	Stu Miller, Giants (Hoyt Wilhelm, Orioles)	Danny Murtaugh, Pirates (Paul Richards, Orioles)	44,115
7-31-61	Fenway Park Boston	1-1 (tie)		Paul Richards, Orioles (A.L.) Danny Murtaugh, Pirates (N.L.)	31,851
7-10-62	District of Col. Stad. Washington	3-1 (N.L.)	Juan Marichal, Giants (Camilo Pascual, Twins)	Fred Hutchinson, Reds (Ralph Houk, Yankees)	45,480

HISTORY All-time results

– 311 –

Date	Site	Score (Winner)	Winning pitcher (Losing pitcher)	Winning manager (Losing manager)	Att.
7-30-62	Wrigley Field Chicago	9-4 (A.L.)	Ray Herbert, White Sox (Art Mahaffey, Phillies)	Ralph Houk, Yankees (Fred Hutchinson, Reds)	38,359
7-9-63	Municipal Stadium Cleveland	5-3 (N.L.)	Larry Jackson, Cubs (Jim Bunning, Tigers)	Alvin Dark, Giants (Ralph Houk, Yankees)	44,160
7-7-64	Shea Stadium New York	7-4 (N.L.)	Juan Marichal, Giants (Dick Radatz, Red Sox)	Walter Alston, Dodgers (Al Lopez, White Sox)	50,850
7-13-65	Metropolitan Stadium Bloomington, Minn.	6-5 (N.L.)	Sandy Koufax, Dodgers (Sam McDowell, Indians)	Gene Mauch, Phillies (Al Lopez, White Sox)	46,706
7-12-66	Busch Stadium St. Louis	2-1§ (N.L.)	Gaylord Perry, Giants (Pete Richert, Senators)	Walter Alston, Dodgers (Sam Mele, Twins)	49,936
7-11-67	Anaheim Stadium Anaheim, Calif.	2-1∞ (N.L.)	Don Drysdale, Dodgers (Jim Hunter, Athletics)	Walter Alston, Dodgers (Hank Bauer, Orioles)	46,309
7-9-68	Astrodome Houston	1-0 (N.L.)	Don Drysdale, Dodgers (Luis Tiant, Indians)	Red Schoendienst, Cardinals (Dick Williams, Red Sox)	48,321
7-23-69	R.F.K. Stadium Washington	9-3 (N.L.)	Steve Carlton, Cardinals (Mel Stottlemyre, Yankees)	Red Schoendienst, Cardinals (Mayo Smith, Tigers)	45,259
7-14-70	Riverfront Stadium Cincinnati	5-4‡ (N.L.)	Claude Osteen, Dodgers (Clyde Wright, Angels)	Gil Hodges, Mets (Earl Weaver, Orioles)	51,838
7-13-71	Tiger Stadium Detroit	6-4 (A.L.)	Vida Blue, Athletics (Dock Ellis, Pirates)	Earl Weaver, Orioles (Sparky Anderson, Reds)	53,559
7-25-72	Atlanta Stadium Atlanta	4-3§ (N.L.)	Tug McGraw, Mets (Dave McNally, Orioles)	Danny Murtaugh, Pirates (Earl Weaver, Orioles)	53,107
7-24-73	Royals Stadium Kansas City	7-1 (N.L.)	Rick Wise, Cardinals (Bert Blyleven, Twins)	Sparky Anderson, Reds (Dick Williams, Athletics)	40,849
7-23-74	Three Rivers Stadium Pittsburgh	7-2 (N.L.)	Ken Brett, Pirates (Luis Tiant, Red Sox)	Yogi Berra, Mets (Dick Williams, Athletics)	50,706
7-15-75	Milwaukee Co. Stadium Milwaukee	6-3 (N.L.)	Jon Matlack, Mets (Jim Hunter, Yankees)	Walter Alston, Dodgers (Alvin Dark, Athletics)	51,480
7-13-76	Veterans Stadium Philadelphia	7-1 (N.L)	Randy Jones, Padres (Mark Fidrych, Tigers)	Sparky Anderson, Reds (Darrell Johnson, Red Sox)	63,974
7-19-77	Yankee Stadium New York	7-5 (N.L.)	Don Sutton, Dodgers (Jim Palmer, Orioles)	Sparky Anderson, Reds (Billy Martin, Yankees)	56,683
7-11-78	San Diego Stadium San Diego	7-3 (N.L.)	Bruce Sutter, Cubs (Rich Gossage, Yankees)	Tommy Lasorda, Dodgers (Billy Martin, Yankees)	51,549
7-17-79	Kingdome Seattle	7-6 (N.L.)	Bruce Sutter, Cubs (Jim Kern, Rangers)	Tommy Lasorda, Dodgers (Bob Lemon, Yankees)	58,905
7-8-80	Dodger Stadium Los Angeles	4-2 (N.L.)	Jerry Reuss, Dodgers (Tommy John, Yankees)	Chuck Tanner, Pirates (Earl Weaver, Orioles)	56,088
8-9-81	Municipal Stadium Cleveland	5-4 (N.L.)	Vida Blue, Giants (Rollie Fingers, Brewers)	Dallas Green, Phillies (Jim Frey, Royals)	72,086
7-13-82	Olympic Stadium Montreal	4-1 (N.L.)	Steve Rogers, Expos (Dennis Eckersley, Red Sox)	Tommy Lasorda, Dodgers (Billy Martin, Athletics)	59,057
7-6-83	Comiskey Park Chicago	13-3 (A.L.)	Dave Stieb, Blue Jays (Mario Soto, Reds)	Harvey Kuenn, Brewers (Whitey Herzog, Cardinals)	43,801
7-10-84	Candlestick Park San Francisco	3-1 (N.L.)	Charlie Lea, Expos (Dave Stieb, Blue Jays)	Paul Owens, Phillies (Joe Altobelli, Orioles)	57,756
7-16-85	Metrodome Minneapolis	6-1 (N.L.)	LaMarr Hoyt, Padres (Jack Morris, Tigers)	Dick Williams, Padres (Sparky Anderson, Tigers)	54,960
7-15-86	Astrodome Houston	3-2 (A.L.)	Roger Clemens, Red Sox (Dwight Gooden, Mets)	Dick Howser, Royals (Whitey Herzog, Cardinals)	45,774
7-14-87	Oak.-Alameda Co. Col. Oakland	2-0▲ (N.L.)	Lee Smith, Cubs (Jay Howell, Athletics)	Dave Johnson, Mets (John McNamara, Red Sox)	49,671
7-12-88	Riverfront Stadium Cincinnati	2-1 (A.L.)	Frank Viola, Twins (Dwight Gooden, Mets)	Tom Kelly, Twins (Whitey Herzog, Cardinals)	55,837
7-11-89	Anaheim Stadium Anaheim, Calif.	5-3 (A.L.)	Nolan Ryan, Rangers (John Smoltz, Braves)	Tony La Russa, Athletics (Tommy Lasorda, Dodgers)	64,036
7-10-90	Wrigley Field Chicago	2-0 (A.L.)	Bret Saberhagen, Royals (Jeff Brantley, Giants)	Tony La Russa, Athletics (Roger Craig, Giants)	39,071
7-9-91	SkyDome Toronto	4-2 (A.L.)	Jimmy Key, Blue Jays (Dennis Martinez, Expos)	Tony La Russa, Athletics (Lou Piniella, Reds)	52,383
7-14-92	Jack Murphy Stadium San Diego	13-6 (A.L.)	Kevin Brown, Rangers (Tom Glavine, Braves)	Tom Kelly, Twins (Bobby Cox, Braves)	59,372
7-13-93	Oriole Park at Camden Yards, Baltimore	9-3 (A.L.)	Jack McDowell, White Sox (John Burkett, Giants)	Cito Gaston, Blue Jays (Bobby Cox, Braves)	48,147
7-12-94	Three Rivers Stadium Pittsburgh	8-7§ (N.L.)	Doug Jones, Phillies (Jason Bere, White Sox)	Jim Fregosi, Phillies (Cito Gaston, Blue Jays)	59,568
7-11-95	Ballpark in Arlington Arlington, Texas	3-2 (N.L.)	Heathcliff Slocumb, Phillies (Steve Ontiveros, A's)	Felipe Alou, Expos (Buck Showalter, Yankees)	50,920
7-9-96	Veterans Stadium Philadelphia	6-0 (N.L.)	John Smoltz, Braves (Charles Nagy, Indians)	Bobby Cox, Braves (Mike Hargrove, Indians)	62,670
7-8-97	Jacobs Field Cleveland	3-1 (A.L.)	Jose Rosado, Royals (Shawn Estes, Giants)	Joe Torre, Yankees (Bobby Cox, Braves)	44,916
7-7-98	Coors Field Colorado	13-8 (A.L.)	Bartolo Colon, Indians (Ugueth Urbina, Expos)	Mike Hargrove, Indians (Jim Leyland, Marlins)	51,267

*14 innings. †5 innings (rain). ‡12 innings. §10 innings. ∞15 innings. ▲13 innings.

AWARD WINNERS

AMERICAN LEAGUE

Year	Player	Team	Pos.	Points
1929—Al Simmons	Philadelphia	OF	40
1930—Joe Cronin	Washington	SS	52
1931—Lou Gehrig	New York	1B	40
1932—Jimmie Foxx	Philadelphia	1B	46
1933—Jimmie Foxx	Philadelphia	1B	49
1934—Lou Gehrig	New York	1B	51
1935—Hank Greenberg	Detroit	1B	64
1936—Lou Gehrig	New York	1B	55
1937—Charley Gehringer	Detroit	2B	78
1938—Jimmie Foxx	Boston	1B	304
1939—Joe DiMaggio	New York	OF	280
1940—Hank Greenberg	Detroit	OF	292
1941—Joe DiMaggio	New York	OF	291
1942—Joe Gordon	New York	2B	270
1943—Spud Chandler	New York	P	246
1944—Bobby Doerr	Boston	2B	
1945—Eddie Mayo	Detroit	2B	

NATIONAL LEAGUE

Year	Player	Team	Pos.	Points
1929—No selection			
1930—Bill Terry	New York	1B	47
1931—Chuck Klein	Philadelphia	OF	40
1932—Chuck Klein	Philadelphia	OF	46
1933—Carl Hubbell	New York	P	64
1934—Dizzy Dean	St. Louis	P	57
1935—Arky Vaughan	Pittsburgh	SS	42
1936—Carl Hubbell	New York	P	61
1937—Joe Medwick	St. Louis	OF	70
1938—Ernie Lombardi	Cincinnati	C	229
1939—Bucky Walters	Cincinnati	P	303
1940—Frank McCormick	Cincinnati	1B	274
1941—Dolf Camilli	Brooklyn	1B	300
1942—Mort Cooper	St. Louis	P	263
1943—Stan Musial	St. Louis	OF	267
1944—Marty Marion	St. Louis	SS	
1945—Tommy Holmes	Boston	OF	

AMERICAN LEAGUE

Year	Player	Team	Pos.
1944—Bobby Doerr	Boston	2B
	Hal Newhouser	Detroit	P
1945—Eddie Mayo	Detroit	2B
	Hal Newhouser	Detroit	P
1946—No selections		
1947—No selections		
1948—Lou Boudreau	Cleveland	SS
	Bob Lemon	Cleveland	P
1949—Ted Williams	Boston	OF
	Ellis Kinder	Boston	P
1950—Phil Rizzuto	New York	SS
	Bob Lemon	Cleveland	P
1951—Ferris Fain	Philadelphia	1B
	Bob Feller	Cleveland	P
1952—Luke Easter	Cleveland	1B
	Bobby Shantz	Philadelphia	P
1953—Al Rosen	Cleveland	3B
	Bob Porterfield	Washington	P
1954—Bobby Avila	Cleveland	2B
	Bob Lemon	Cleveland	P
1955—Al Kaline	Detroit	OF
	Whitey Ford	New York	P
1956—Mickey Mantle	New York	OF
	Billy Pierce	Chicago	P
1957—Ted Williams	Boston	OF
	Billy Pierce	Chicago	P
1958—Jackie Jensen	Boston	OF
	Bob Turley	New York	P
1959—Nellie Fox	Chicago	2B
	Early Wynn	Chicago	P
1960—Roger Maris	New York	OF
	Chuck Estrada	Baltimore	P
1961—Roger Maris	New York	OF
	Whitey Ford	New York	P
1962—Mickey Mantle	New York	OF
	Dick Donovan	Cleveland	P
1963—Al Kaline	Detroit	OF
	Whitey Ford	New York	P
1964—Brooks Robinson	Baltimore	3B
	Dean Chance	Los Angeles	P
1965—Tony Oliva	Minnesota	OF
	Jim Grant	Minnesota	P
1966—Frank Robinson	Baltimore	OF
	Jim Kaat	Minnesota	P

NATIONAL LEAGUE

Year	Player	Team	Pos.
1944—Marty Marion	St. Louis	SS
	Bill Voiselle	New York	P
1945—Tommy Holmes	Boston	OF
	Hank Borowy	Chicago	P
1946—No selections		
1947—No selections		
1948—Stan Musial	St. Louis	OF-1B
	Johnny Sain	Boston	P
1949—Enos Slaughter	St. Louis	OF
	Howard Pollet	St. Louis	P
1950—Ralph Kiner	Pittsburgh	OF
	Jim Konstanty	Philadelphia	P
1951—Stan Musial	St. Louis	OF
	Preacher Roe	Brooklyn	P
1952—Hank Sauer	Chicago	OF
	Robin Roberts	Philadelphia	P
1953—Roy Campanella	Brooklyn	C
	Warren Spahn	Milwaukee	P
1954—Willie Mays	New York	OF
	Johnny Antonelli	New York	P
1955—Duke Snider	Brooklyn	OF
	Robin Roberts	Philadelphia	P
1956—Hank Aaron	Milwaukee	OF
	Don Newcombe	Brooklyn	P
1957—Stan Musial	St. Louis	1B
	Warren Spahn	Milwaukee	P
1958—Ernie Banks	Chicago	SS
	Warren Spahn	Milwaukee	P
1959—Ernie Banks	Chicago	SS
	Sam Jones	San Francisco	P
1960—Dick Groat	Pittsburgh	SS
	Vern Law	Pittsburgh	P
1961—Frank Robinson	Cincinnati	OF
	Warren Spahn	Milwaukee	P
1962—Maury Wills	Los Angeles	SS
	Don Drysdale	Los Angeles	P
1963—Hank Aaron	Milwaukee	OF
	Sandy Koufax	Los Angeles	P
1964—Ken Boyer	St. Louis	3B
	Sandy Koufax	Los Angeles	P
1965—Willie Mays	San Francisco	OF
	Sandy Koufax	Los Angeles	P
1966—Roberto Clemente	Pittsburgh	OF
	Sandy Koufax	Los Angeles	P

HISTORY Award winners

Year	Player	Team	Pos.	Year	Player	Team	Pos.
1967—	Carl Yastrzemski	Boston	OF	1967—	Orlando Cepeda	St. Louis	1B
	Jim Lonborg	Boston	P		Mike McCormick	San Francisco	P
1968—	Ken Harrelson	Boston	OF	1968—	Pete Rose	Cincinnati	OF
	Denny McLain	Detroit	P		Bob Gibson	St. Louis	P
1969—	Harmon Killebrew	Minnesota	1B-3B	1969—	Willie McCovey	San Francisco	1B
	Denny McLain	Detroit	P		Tom Seaver	New York	P
1970—	Harmon Killebrew	Minnesota	3B	1970—	Johnny Bench	Cincinnati	C
	Sam McDowell	Cleveland	P		Bob Gibson	St. Louis	P
1971—	Tony Oliva	Minnesota	OF	1971—	Joe Torre	St. Louis	3B
	Vida Blue	Oakland	P		Ferguson Jenkins	Chicago	P
1972—	Dick Allen	Chicago	1B	1972—	Billy Williams	Chicago	OF
	Wilbur Wood	Chicago	P		Steve Carlton	Philadelphia	P
1973—	Reggie Jackson	Oakland	OF	1973—	Bobby Bonds	San Francisco	OF
	Jim Palmer	Baltimore	P		Ron Bryant	San Francisco	P
1974—	Jeff Burroughs	Texas	OF	1974—	Lou Brock	St. Louis	OF
	Jim Hunter	Oakland	P		Mike Marshall	Los Angeles	P
1975—	Fred Lynn	Boston	OF	1975—	Joe Morgan	Cincinnati	2B
	Jim Palmer	Baltimore	P		Tom Seaver	New York	P
1976—	Thurman Munson	New York	C	1976—	George Foster	Cincinnati	OF
	Jim Palmer	Baltimore	P		Randy Jones	San Diego	P
1977—	Rod Carew	Minnesota	1B	1977—	George Foster	Cincinnati	OF
	Nolan Ryan	California	P		Steve Carlton	Philadelphia	P
1978—	Jim Rice	Boston	OF	1978—	Dave Parker	Pittsburgh	OF
	Ron Guidry	New York	P		Vida Blue	San Francisco	P
1979—	Don Baylor	California	OF	1979—	Keith Hernandez	St. Louis	1B
	Mike Flanagan	Baltimore	P		Joe Niekro	Houston	P
1980—	George Brett	Kansas City	3B	1980—	Mike Schmidt	Philadelphia	3B
	Steve Stone	Baltimore	P		Steve Carlton	Philadelphia	P
1981—	Tony Armas	Oakland	OF	1981—	Andre Dawson	Montreal	OF
	Jack Morris	Detroit	P		Fernando Valenzuela	Los Angeles	P
1982—	Robin Yount	Milwaukee	SS	1982—	Dale Murphy	Atlanta	OF
	Dave Stieb	Toronto	P		Steve Carlton	Philadelphia	P
1983—	Cal Ripken Jr.	Baltimore	SS	1983—	Dale Murphy	Atlanta	OF
	LaMarr Hoyt	Chicago	P		John Denny	Philadelphia	P
1984—	Don Mattingly	New York	1B	1984—	Ryne Sandberg	Chicago	2B
	Willie Hernandez	Detroit	P		Rick Sutcliffe	Chicago	P
1985—	Don Mattingly	New York	1B	1985—	Willie McGee	St. Louis	OF
	Bret Saberhagen	Kansas City	P		Dwight Gooden	New York	P
1986—	Don Mattingly	New York	1B	1986—	Mike Schmidt	Philadelphia	3B
	Roger Clemens	Boston	P		Mike Scott	Houston	P
1987—	George Bell	Toronto	OF	1987—	Andre Dawson	Chicago	OF
	Jimmy Key	Toronto	P		Rick Sutcliffe	Chicago	P
1988—	Jose Canseco	Oakland	OF	1988—	Andy Van Slyke	Pittsburgh	OF
	Frank Viola	Minnesota	P		Orel Hershiser	Los Angeles	P
1989—	Ruben Sierra	Texas	OF	1989—	Kevin Mitchell	San Francisco	OF
	Bret Saberhagen	Kansas City	P		Mark Davis	San Diego	P
1990—	Cecil Fielder	Detroit	1B	1990—	Barry Bonds	Pittsburgh	OF
	Bob Welch	Oakland	P		Doug Drabek	Pittsburgh	P
1991—	Cal Ripken Jr.	Baltimore	SS	1991—	Barry Bonds	Pittsburgh	OF
	Roger Clemens	Boston	P		Tom Glavine	Atlanta	P

PITCHER OF THE YEAR

AMERICAN LEAGUE

Year	Pitcher	Team
1992—	Dennis Eckersley	Oakland
1993—	Jack McDowell	Chicago
1994—	Jimmy Key	New York
1995—	Randy Johnson	Seattle
1996—	Pat Hentgen	Toronto
1997—	Roger Clemens	Toronto
1998—	Roger Clemens	Toronto

NATIONAL LEAGUE

Year	Pitcher	Team
1992—	Greg Maddux	Chicago
1993—	Greg Maddux	Atlanta
1994—	Greg Maddux	Atlanta
1995—	Greg Maddux	Atlanta
1996—	John Smoltz	Atlanta
1997—	Pedro Martinez	Montreal
1998—	Kevin Brown	San Diego

ROOKIE OF THE YEAR

1946—Combined selection—Del Ennis, Philadelphia N.L., OF
1947—Combined selection—Jackie Robinson, Brooklyn N.L., 1B
1948—Combined selection—Richie Ashburn, Philadelphia N.L., OF

AMERICAN LEAGUE

Year	Player	Team	Pos.
1949—	Roy Sievers	St. Louis	OF
1950—	Whitey Ford	New York	P
1951—	Minnie Minoso	Chicago	OF
1952—	Clint Courtney	St. Louis	C

NATIONAL LEAGUE

Year	Player	Team	Pos.
1949—	Don Newcombe	Brooklyn	P
1950—	Combined A.L.-N.L. selection		
1951—	Willie Mays	New York	OF
1952—	Joe Black	Brooklyn	P

Year	Player	Team	Pos.
1953—Harvey Kuenn	Detroit	SS
1954—Bob Grim	New York	P
1955—Herb Score	Cleveland	P
1956—Luis Aparicio	Chicago	SS
1957—Tony Kubek	New York	IF-OF
(No pitcher named)		
1958—Albie Pearson	Washington	OF
Ryne Duren	New York	P
1959—Bob Allison	Washington	OF
1960—Ron Hansen	Baltimore	SS
1961—Dick Howser	Kansas City	SS
Don Schwall	Boston	P
1962—Tom Tresh	New York	OF-SS
1963—Pete Ward	Chicago	3B
Gary Peters	Chicago	P
1964—Tony Oliva	Minnesota	OF
Wally Bunker	Baltimore	P
1965—Curt Blefary	Baltimore	OF
Marcelino Lopez	California	P
1966—Tommie Agee	Chicago	OF
Jim Nash	Kansas City	P
1967—Rod Carew	Minnesota	2B
Tom Phoebus	Baltimore	P
1968—Del Unser	Washington	OF
Stan Bahnsen	New York	P
1969—Carlos May	Chicago	OF
Mike Nagy	Boston	P
1970—Roy Foster	Cleveland	OF
Bert Blyleven	Minnesota	P
1971—Chris Chambliss	Cleveland	1B
Bill Parsons	Milwaukee	P
1972—Carlton Fisk	Boston	C
Dick Tidrow	Cleveland	P
1973—Al Bumbry	Baltimore	OF
Steve Busby	Kansas City	P
1974—Mike Hargrove	Texas	1B
Frank Tanana	California	P
1975—Fred Lynn	Boston	OF
Dennis Eckersley	Cleveland	P
1976—Butch Wynegar	Minnesota	C
Mark Fidrych	Detroit	P
1977—Mitchell Page	Oakland	OF
Dave Rozema	Detroit	P
1978—Paul Molitor	Milwaukee	2B
Rich Gale	Kansas City	P
1979—Pat Putnam	Texas	1B
Mark Clear	California	P
1980—Joe Charboneau	Cleveland	OF
Britt Burns	Chicago	P
1981—Rich Gedman	Boston	C
Dave Righetti	New York	P
1982—Cal Ripken Jr.	Baltimore	SS-3B
Ed Vande Berg	Seattle	P
1983—Ron Kittle	Chicago	OF
Mike Boddicker	Baltimore	P
1984—Alvin Davis	Seattle	1B
Mark Langston	Seattle	P
1985 Ozzie Guillen	Chicago	SS
Teddy Higuera	Milwaukee	P
1986—Jose Canseco	Oakland	OF
Mark Eichhorn	Toronto	P
1987—Mark McGwire	Oakland	1B
Mike Henneman	Detroit	P
1988—Walt Weiss	Oakland	SS
Bryan Harvey	California	P
1989—Craig Worthington	Baltimore	3B
Tom Gordon	Kansas City	P
1990—Sandy Alomar Jr.	Cleveland	C
Kevin Appier	Kansas City	P
1991—Chuck Knoblauch	Minnesota	2B
Juan Guzman	Toronto	P
1992—Pat Listach	Milwaukee	SS
Cal Eldred	Milwaukee	P
1993—Tim Salmon	California	OF
Aaron Sele	Boston	P
1994—Bob Hamelin	Kansas City	DH
Brian Anderson	California	P

Year	Player	Team	Pos.
1953—Jim Gilliam	Brooklyn	2B
1954—Wally Moon	St. Louis	OF
1955—Bill Virdon	St. Louis	OF
1956—Frank Robinson	Cincinnati	OF
1957—Ed Bouchee	Philadelphia	1B
Jack Sanford	Philadelphia	P
1958—Orlando Cepeda	San Francisco	1B
Carlton Willey	Milwaukee	P
1959—Willie McCovey	San Francisco	1B
1960—Frank Howard	Los Angeles	OF
1961—Billy Williams	Chicago	OF
Ken Hunt	Cincinnati	P
1962—Ken Hubbs	Chicago	2B
1963—Pete Rose	Cincinnati	2B
Ray Culp	Philadelphia	P
1964—Dick Allen	Philadelphia	3B
Billy McCool	Cincinnati	P
1965—Joe Morgan	Houston	2B
Frank Linzy	San Francisco	P
1966—Tommy Helms	Cincinnati	3B
Don Sutton	Los Angeles	P
1967—Lee May	Cincinnati	1B
Dick Hughes	St. Louis	P
1968—Johnny Bench	Cincinnati	C
Jerry Koosman	New York	P
1969—Coco Laboy	Montreal	3B
Tom Griffin	Houston	P
1970—Bernie Carbo	Cincinnati	OF
Carl Morton	Montreal	P
1971—Earl Williams	Atlanta	C
Reggie Cleveland	St. Louis	P
1972—Dave Rader	San Francisco	C
Jon Matlack	New York	P
1973—Gary Matthews	San Francisco	OF
Steve Rogers	Montreal	P
1974—Greg Gross	Houston	OF
John D'Acquisto	San Francisco	P
1975—Gary Carter	Montreal	OF-C
John Montefusco	San Francisco	P
1976—Larry Herndon	San Francisco	OF
Butch Metzger	San Diego	P
1977—Andre Dawson	Montreal	OF
Bob Owchinko	San Diego	P
1978—Bob Horner	Atlanta	3B
Don Robinson	Pittsburgh	P
1979—Jeff Leonard	Houston	OF
Rick Sutcliffe	Los Angeles	P
1980—Lonnie Smith	Philadelphia	OF
Bill Gullickson	Montreal	P
1981—Tim Raines	Montreal	OF
Fernando Valenzuela	Los Angeles	P
1982—Johnny Ray	Pittsburgh	2B
Steve Bedrosian	Atlanta	P
1983—Darryl Strawberry	New York	OF
Craig McMurtry	Atlanta	P
1984—Juan Samuel	Philadelphia	2B
Dwight Gooden	New York	P
1985—Vince Coleman	St. Louis	OF
Tom Browning	Cincinnati	P
1986—Robby Thompson	San Francisco	2B
Todd Worrell	St. Louis	P
1987—Benito Santiago	San Diego	C
Mike Dunne	Pittsburgh	P
1988—Mark Grace	Chicago	1B
Tim Belcher	Los Angeles	P
1989—Jerome Walton	Chicago	OF
Andy Benes	San Diego	P
1990—David Justice	Atlanta	OF
Mike Harkey	Chicago	P
1991—Jeff Bagwell	Houston	1B
Al Osuna	Houston	P
1992—Eric Karros	Los Angeles	1B
Tim Wakefield	Pittsburgh	P
1993—Mike Piazza	Los Angeles	C
Kirk Rueter	Montreal	P
1994—Raul Mondesi	Los Angeles	OF
Steve Trachsel	Chicago	P

Year	Player	Team	Pos.	Year	Player	Team	Pos.
1995—Garret Anderson	California	OF		1995—Chipper Jones	Atlanta	3B	
Julian Tavarez	Cleveland	P		Hideo Nomo	Los Angeles	P	
1996—Derek Jeter	New York	SS		1996—Jason Kendall	Pittsburgh	C	
James Baldwin	Chicago	P		Alan Benes	St. Louis	P	
1997—Nomar Garciaparra	Boston	SS		1997—Scott Rolen	Philadelphia	3B	
Jason Dickson	Anaheim	P		Matt Morris	St. Louis	P	
1998—Ben Grieve	Oakland	OF		1998—Todd Helton	Colorado	1B	
Rolando Arrojo	Tampa Bay	P		Kerry Wood	Chicago	P	

FIREMAN OF THE YEAR

AMERICAN LEAGUE

Year	Pitcher	Team
1960—Mike Fornieles	Boston
1961—Luis Arroyo	New York
1962—Dick Radatz	Boston
1963—Stu Miller	Baltimore
1964—Dick Radatz	Boston
1965—Eddie Fisher	Chicago
1966—Jack Aker	Kansas City
1967—Minnie Rojas	California
1968—Wilbur Wood	Chicago
1969—Ron Perranoski	Minnesota
1970—Ron Perranoski	Minnesota
1971—Ken Sanders	Milwaukee
1972—Sparky Lyle	New York
1973—John Hiller	Detroit
1974—Terry Forster	Chicago
1975—Rich Gossage	Chicago
1976—Bill Campbell	Minnesota
1977—Bill Campbell	Boston
1978—Rich Gossage	New York
1979—Mike Marshall	Minnesota
Jim Kern	Texas
1980—Dan Quisenberry	Kansas City
1981—Rollie Fingers	Milwaukee
1982—Dan Quisenberry	Kansas City
1983—Dan Quisenberry	Kansas City
1984—Dan Quisenberry	Kansas City
1985—Dan Quisenberry	Kansas City
1986—Dave Righetti	New York
1987—Dave Righetti	New York
Jeff Reardon	Minnesota
1988—Dennis Eckersley	Oakland
1989—Jeff Russell	Texas
1990—Bobby Thigpen	Chicago
1991—Dennis Eckersley	Oakland
Bryan Harvey	California
1992—Dennis Eckersley	Oakland
1993—Jeff Montgomery	Kansas City
1994—Lee Smith	Baltimore
1995—Jose Mesa	Cleveland
1996—John Wetteland	New York
1997—Mariano Rivera	New York
1998—Tom Gordon	Boston

NATIONAL LEAGUE

Year	Pitcher	Team
1960—Lindy McDaniel	St. Louis
1961—Stu Miller	San Francisco
1962—Roy Face	Pittsburgh
1963—Lindy McDaniel	Chicago
1964—Al McBean	Pittsburgh
1965—Ted Abernathy	Chicago
1966—Phil Regan	Los Angeles
1967—Ted Abernathy	Cincinnati
1968—Phil Regan	L.A.-Chicago
1969—Wayne Granger	Cincinnati
1970—Wayne Granger	Cincinnati
1971—Dave Giusti	Pittsburgh
1972—Clay Carroll	Cincinnati
1973—Mike Marshall	Montreal
1974—Mike Marshall	Los Angeles
1975—Al Hrabosky	St. Louis
1976—Rawly Eastwick	Cincinnati
1977—Rollie Fingers	San Diego
1978—Rollie Fingers	San Diego
1979—Bruce Sutter	Chicago
1980—Rollie Fingers	San Diego
Tom Hume	Cincinnati
1981—Bruce Sutter	St. Louis
1982—Bruce Sutter	St. Louis
1983—Al Holland	Philadelphia
Lee Smith	Chicago
1984—Bruce Sutter	St. Louis
1985—Jeff Reardon	Montreal
1986—Todd Worrell	St. Louis
1987—Steve Bedrosian	Philadelphia
1988—John Franco	Cincinnati
1989—Mark Davis	San Diego
1990—John Franco	New York
1991—Lee Smith	St. Louis
1992—Doug Jones	Houston
Lee Smith	St. Louis
1993—Randy Myers	Chicago
1994—John Franco	New York
1995—Randy Myers	Chicago
1996—Trevor Hoffman	San Diego
1997—Jeff Shaw	Cincinnati
1998—Trevor Hoffman	San Diego

MAJOR LEAGUE PLAYER OF THE YEAR

Year	Player	Team	Year	Player	Team	Year	Player	Team
1936—Carl Hubbell	New York N.L.		1949—Ted Williams	Boston A.L.		1962—Maury Wills	Los Angeles N.L.
1937—Johnny Allen	Cleveland A.L.		1950—Phil Rizzuto	New York A.L.		Don Drysdale	Los Angeles N.L.
1938—Johnny Vander Meer	Cincinnati N.L.		1951—Stan Musial	St. Louis N.L.		1963—Sandy Koufax	Los Angeles N.L.
1939—Joe DiMaggio	New York A.L.		1952—Robin Roberts	Philadelphia N.L.		1964—Ken Boyer	St. Louis N.L.
1940—Bob Feller	Cleveland A.L.		1953—Al Rosen	Cleveland A.L.		1965—Sandy Koufax	Los Angeles N.L.
1941—Ted Williams	Boston A.L.		1954—Willie Mays	New York N.L.		1966—Frank Robinson	Baltimore A.L.
1942—Ted Williams	Boston A.L.		1955—Duke Snider	Brooklyn N.L.		1967—Carl Yastrzemski	Boston A.L.
1943—Spud Chandler	New York A.L.		1956—Mickey Mantle	New York A.L.		1968—Denny McLain	Detroit A.L.
1944—Marty Marion	St. Louis N.L.		1957—Ted Williams	Boston A.L.		1969—Willie McCovey	San Francisco N.L.
1945—Hal Newhouser	Detroit A.L.		1958—Bob Turley	New York A.L.		1970—Johnny Bench	Cincinnati N.L.
1946—Stan Musial	St. Louis N.L.		1959—Early Wynn	Chicago A.L.		1971—Joe Torre	St. Louis N.L.
1947—Ted Williams	Boston A.L.		1960—Bill Mazeroski	Pittsburgh N.L.		1972—Billy Williams	Chicago N.L.
1948—Lou Boudreau	Cleveland A.L.		1961—Roger Maris	New York A.L.		1973—Reggie Jackson	Oakland A.L.

Year	Player	Team	Year	Player	Team	Year	Player	Team
1974—Lou Brock	St. Louis N.L.		1983—Cal Ripken Jr.	Baltimore A.L.		1992—Gary Sheffield	San Diego N.L.	
1975—Joe Morgan	Cincinnati N.L.		1984—Ryne Sandberg	Chicago N.L.		1993—Frank Thomas	Chicago A.L.	
1976—Joe Morgan	Cincinnati N.L.		1985—Don Mattingly	New York A.L.		1994—Jeff Bagwell	Houston N.L.	
1977—Rod Carew	Minnesota A.L.		1986—Roger Clemens	Boston A.L.		1995—Albert Belle	Cleveland A.L.	
1978—Ron Guidry	New York A.L.		1987—George Bell	Toronto A.L.		1996—Alex Rodriguez	Seattle A.L.	
1979—Willie Stargell	Pittsburgh N.L.		1988—Orel Hershiser	Los Angeles N.L.		1997—Ken Griffey Jr.	Seattle A.L.	
1980—George Brett	Kansas City A.L.		1989—Kevin Mitchell	San Francisco N.L.		1998—Sammy Sosa	Chicago N.L.	
1981—Fernando Valenzuela	Los Angeles N.L.		1990—Barry Bonds	Pittsburgh N.L.				
1982—Robin Yount	Milwaukee A.L.		1991—Cal Ripken Jr.	Baltimore A.L.				

MAJOR LEAGUE MANAGER OF THE YEAR

Year	Manager	Team	Year	Manager	Team	Year	Manager	Team
1936—Joe McCarthy	New York A.L.		1962—Bill Rigney	Los Angeles A.L.		1987—Sparky Anderson	Detroit A.L.	
1937—Bill McKechnie	Boston N.L.		1963—Walter Alston	Los Angeles N.L.			Buck Rodgers	Montreal N.L.
1938—Joe McCarthy	New York A.L.		1964—Johnny Keane	St. Louis N.L.		1988—Tony La Russa	Oakland A.L.	
1939—Leo Durocher	Brooklyn N.L.		1965—Sam Mele	Minnesota A.L.			Tom Lasorda	L.A. N.L. (tie)
1940—Bill McKechnie	Cincinnati N.L.		1966—Hank Bauer	Baltimore A.L.			Jim Leyland	Pit. N.L. (tie)
1941—Billy Southworth	St. Louis N.L.		1967—Dick Williams	Boston A.L.		1989—Frank Robinson	Baltimore A.L.	
1942—Billy Southworth	St. Louis N.L.		1968—Mayo Smith	Detroit A.L.			Don Zimmer	Chicago N.L.
1943—Joe McCarthy	New York A.L.		1969—Gil Hodges	New York N.L.		1990—Jeff Torborg	Chicago A.L.	
1944—Luke Sewell	St. Louis A.L.		1970—Danny Murtaugh	Pittsburgh N.L.			Jim Leyland	Pittsburgh N.L.
1945—Ossie Bluege	Washington A.L.		1971—Charlie Fox	San Francisco N.L.		1991—Tom Kelly	Minnesota A.L.	
1946—Eddie Dyer	St. Louis N.L.		1972—Chuck Tanner	Chicago A.L.			Bobby Cox	Atlanta N.L.
1947—Bucky Harris	New York A.L.		1973—Gene Mauch	Montreal N.L.		1992—Tony La Russa	Oakland A.L.	
1948—Bill Meyer	Pittsburgh N.L.		1974—Bill Virdon	New York A.L.			Jim Leyland	Pittsburgh N.L.
1949—Casey Stengel	New York A.L.		1975—Darrell Johnson	Boston A.L.		1993—Johnny Oates	Baltimore A.L.	
1950—Red Rolfe	Detroit A.L.		1976—Danny Ozark	Philadelphia N.L.			Bobby Cox	Atlanta N.L.
1951—Leo Durocher	New York N.L.		1977—Earl Weaver	Baltimore A.L.		1994—Buck Showalter	New York A.L.	
1952—Eddie Stanky	St. Louis N.L.		1978—George Bamberger	Milwaukee A.L.			Felipe Alou	Montreal N.L.
1953—Casey Stengel	New York A.L.		1979—Earl Weaver	Baltimore A.L.		1995—Mike Hargrove	Cleveland A.L.	
1954—Leo Durocher	New York N.L.		1980—Bill Virdon	Houston N.L.			Don Baylor	Colorado N.L.
1955—Walter Alston	Brooklyn N.L.		1981—Billy Martin	Oakland A.L.		1996—Johnny Oates	Texas A.L.	
1956—Birdie Tebbetts	Cincinnati N.L.		1982—Whitey Herzog	St. Louis N.L.			Bruce Bochy	San Diego N.L.
1957—Fred Hutchinson	St. Louis N.L.		1983—Tony La Russa	Chicago A.L.		1997—Dave Johnson	Baltimore A.L.	
1958—Casey Stengel	New York A.L.		1984—Jim Frey	Chicago N.L.			Dusty Baker	San Fran. N.L.
1959—Walter A.L.ston	Los Angeles N.L.		1985—Bobby Cox	Toronto A.L.		1998—Joe Torre	New York A.L.	
1960—Danny Murtaugh	Pittsburgh N.L.		1986—John McNamara	Boston A.L.			Bruce Bochy	San Diego N.L.
1961—Ralph Houk	New York A.L.			Hal Lanier	Houston N.L.				

MAJOR LEAGUE EXECUTIVE OF THE YEAR

Year	Executive	Team	Year	Executive	Team	Year	Executive	Team
1936—Branch Rickey	St. Louis N.L.		1957—Frank Lane	St. Louis N.L.		1978—Spec Richardson	San Francisco N.L.	
1937—Ed Barrow	New York A.L.		1958—Joe Brown	Pittsburgh N.L.		1979—Hank Peters	Baltimore A.L.	
1938—Warren Giles	Cincinnati N.L.		1959—Buzzie Bavasi	L.A. N.L.		1980—Tal Smith	Houston N.L.	
1939—Larry MacPhail	Brooklyn N.L.		1960—George Weiss	New York A.L.		1981—John McHale	Montreal N.L.	
1940—Walter Briggs Sr.	Detroit A.L.		1961—Dan Topping	New York A.L.		1982—Harry Dalton	Milwaukee A.L.	
1941—Ed Barrow	New York A.L.		1962—Fred Haney	Los Angeles A.L.		1983—Hank Peters	Baltimore A.L.	
1942—Branch Rickey	St. Louis N.L.		1963—Bing Devine	St. Louis N.L.		1984—Dallas Green	Chicago N.L.	
1943—Clark Griffith	Washington A.L.		1964—Bing Devine	St. Louis N.L.		1985—John Schuerholz	Kansas City A.L.	
1944—Bill DeWitt	St. Louis A.L.		1965—Cal Griffith	Minnesota A.L.		1986—Frank Cashen	New York N.L.	
1945—Phil Wrigley	Chicago N.L.		1966—Lee MacPhail	Commissioner's Office		1987—Al Rosen	San Francisco N.L.	
1946—Tom Yawkey	Boston A.L.		1967—Dick O'Connell	Boston A.L.		1988—Fred Claire	Los Angeles N.L.	
1947—Branch Rickey	Brooklyn N.L.		1968—Jim Campbell	Detroit A.L.		1989—Roland Hemond	Baltimore A.L.	
1948—Bill Veeck	Cleveland A.L.		1969—John Murphy	New York N.L.		1990—Bob Quinn	Cincinnati N.L.	
1949—Bob Carpenter	Philadelphia N.L.		1970—Harry Dalton	Baltimore A.L.		1991—Andy MacPhail	Minnesota A.L.	
1950—George Weiss	New York A.L.		1971—Cedric Tallis	Kansas City A.L.		1992—Dan Duquette	Montreal N.L.	
1951—George Weiss	New York A.L.		1972—Roland Hemond	Chicago A.L.		1993—Lee Thomas	Philadelphia N.L.	
1952—George Weiss	New York A.L.		1973—Bob Howsam	Cincinnati N.L.		1994—John Hart	Cleveland A.L.	
1953—Lou Perini	Milwaukee N.L.		1974—Gabe Paul	New York A.L.		1995—John Hart	Cleveland A.L.	
1954—Horace Stoneham	New York N.L.		1975—Dick O'Connell	Boston A.L.		1996—Doug Melvin	Texas A.L.	
1955—Walter O'Malley	Brooklyn N.L.		1976—Joe Burke	Kansas City A.L.		1997—Cam Bonifay	Pittsburgh N.L.	
1956—Gabe Paul	Cincinnati N.L.		1977—Bill Veeck	Chicago A.L.		1998—Gerry Hunsicker	Houston N.L.	

HISTORY *Award winners*

1957
MAJORS
P— Bobby Shantz, New York A.L.
C— Sherm Lollar, Chicago A.L.
1B— Gil Hodges, Brooklyn N.L.
2B— Nellie Fox, Chicago A.L.
3B— Frank Malzone, Boston A.L.
SS— Roy McMillan, Cincinnati N.L.
OF— Minnie Minoso, Chicago A.L.
OF— Willie Mays, New York N.L.
OF— Al Kaline, Detroit A.L.

1958
AMERICAN LEAGUE
P— Bobby Shantz, New York
C— Sherm Lollar, Chicago
1B— Vic Power, Cleveland
2B— Frank Bolling, Detroit
3B— Frank Malzone, Boston
SS— Luis Aparicio, Chicago
OF— Norm Siebern, New York
OF— Jimmy Piersall, Boston
OF— Al Kaline, Detroit

NATIONAL LEAGUE
P— Harvey Haddix, Cincinnati
C— Del Crandall, Milwaukee
1B— Gil Hodges, Los Angeles
2B— Bill Mazeroski, Pittsburgh
3B— Ken Boyer, St. Louis
SS— Roy McMillan, Cincinnati
OF— Frank Robinson, Cincinnati
OF— Willie Mays, San Francisco
OF— Hank Aaron, Milwaukee

1959
AMERICAN LEAGUE
P— Bobby Shantz, New York
C— Sherm Lollar, Chicago
1B— Vic Power, Cleveland
2B— Nellie Fox, Chicago
3B— Frank Malzone, Boston
SS— Luis Aparicio, Chicago
OF— Minnie Minoso, Cleveland
OF— Al Kaline, Detroit
OF— Jackie Jensen, Boston

NATIONAL LEAGUE
P— Harvey Haddix, Pittsburgh
C— Del Crandall, Milwaukee
1B— Gil Hodges, Los Angeles
2B— Charley Neal, Los Angeles
3B— Ken Boyer, St. Louis
SS— Roy McMillan, Cincinnati
OF— Jackie Brandt, San Francisco
OF— Willie Mays, San Francisco
OF— Hank Aaron, Milwaukee

1960
AMERICAN LEAGUE
P— Bobby Shantz, New York
C— Earl Battey, Washington
1B— Vic Power, Cleveland
2B— Nellie Fox, Chicago
3B— Brooks Robinson, Baltimore
SS— Luis Aparicio, Chicago
OF— Minnie Minoso, Chicago
OF— Jim Landis, Chicago
OF— Roger Maris, New York

NATIONAL LEAGUE
P— Harvey Haddix, Pittsburgh
C— Del Crandall, Milwaukee
1B— Bill White, St. Louis
2B— Bill Mazeroski, Pittsburgh
3B— Ken Boyer, St. Louis
SS— Ernie Banks, Chicago
OF— Wally Moon, Los Angeles
OF— Willie Mays, San Francisco
OF— Hank Aaron, Milwaukee

1961
AMERICAN LEAGUE
P— Frank Lary, Detroit
C— Earl Battey, Minnesota
1B— Vic Power, Cleveland
2B— Bobby Richardson, New York
3B— Brooks Robinson, Baltimore
SS— Luis Aparicio, Chicago
OF— Al Kaline, Detroit
OF— Jimmy Piersall, Cleveland
OF— Jim Landis, Chicago

NATIONAL LEAGUE
P— Bobby Shantz, Pittsburgh
C— John Roseboro, Los Angeles
1B— Bill White, St. Louis
2B— Bill Mazeroski, Pittsburgh
3B— Ken Boyer, St. Louis
SS— Maury Wills, Los Angeles
OF— Willie Mays, San Francisco
OF— Roberto Clemente, Pittsburgh
OF— Vada Pinson, Cincinnati

1962
AMERICAN LEAGUE
P— Jim Kaat, Minnesota
C— Earl Battey, Minnesota
1B— Vic Power, Minnesota
2B— Bobby Richardson, New York
3B— Brooks Robinson, Baltimore
SS— Luis Aparicio, Chicago
OF— Jim Landis, Chicago
OF— Mickey Mantle, New York
OF— Al Kaline, Detroit

NATIONAL LEAGUE
P— Bobby Shantz, St. Louis
C— Del Crandall, Milwaukee
1B— Bill White, St. Louis
2B— Ken Hubbs, Chicago
3B— Jim Davenport, San Francisco
SS— Maury Wills, Los Angeles
OF— Willie Mays, San Francisco
OF— Roberto Clemente, Pittsburgh
OF— Bill Virdon, Pittsburgh

1963
AMERICAN LEAGUE
P— Jim Kaat, Minnesota
C— Elston Howard, New York
1B— Vic Power, Minnesota
2B— Bobby Richardson, New York
3B— Brooks Robinson, Baltimore
SS— Zoilo Versalles, Minnesota
OF— Al Kaline, Detroit
OF— Carl Yastrzemski, Boston
OF— Jim Landis, Chicago

NATIONAL LEAGUE
P— Bobby Shantz, St. Louis
C— Johnny Edwards, Cincinnati
1B— Bill White, St. Louis
2B— Bill Mazeroski, Pittsburgh
3B— Ken Boyer, St. Louis
SS— Bobby Wine, Philadelphia
OF— Willie Mays, San Francisco
OF— Roberto Clemente, Pittsburgh
OF— Curt Flood, St. Louis

1964
AMERICAN LEAGUE
P— Jim Kaat, Minnesota
C— Elston Howard, New York
1B— Vic Power, Los Angeles
2B— Bobby Richardson, New York
3B— Brooks Robinson, Baltimore
SS— Luis Aparicio, Baltimore
OF— Al Kaline, Detroit

OF— Jim Landis, Chicago
OF— Vic Davalillo, Cleveland

NATIONAL LEAGUE
P— Bobby Shantz, Philadelphia
C— Johnny Edwards, Cincinnati
1B— Bill White, St. Louis
2B— Bill Mazeroski, Pittsburgh
3B— Ron Santo, Chicago
SS— Ruben Amaro, Philadelphia
OF— Willie Mays, San Francisco
OF— Roberto Clemente, Pittsburgh
OF— Curt Flood, St. Louis

1965
AMERICAN LEAGUE
P— Jim Kaat, Minnesota
C— Bill Freehan, Detroit
1B— Joe Pepitone, New York
2B— Bobby Richardson, New York
3B— Brooks Robinson, Baltimore
SS— Zoilo Versalles, Minnesota
OF— Al Kaline, Detroit
OF— Tom Tresh, New York
OF— Carl Yastrzemski, Boston

NATIONAL LEAGUE
P— Bob Gibson, St. Louis
C— Joe Torre, Atlanta
1B— Bill White, St. Louis
2B— Bill Mazeroski, Pittsburgh
3B— Ron Santo, Chicago
SS— Leo Cardenas, Cincinnati
OF— Willie Mays, San Francisco
OF— Roberto Clemente, Pittsburgh
OF— Curt Flood, St. Louis

1966
AMERICAN LEAGUE
P— Jim Kaat, Minnesota
C— Bill Freehan, Detroit
1B— Joe Pepitone, New York
2B— Bobby Knoop, California
3B— Brooks Robinson, Baltimore
SS— Luis Aparicio, Baltimore
OF— Al Kaline, Detroit
OF— Tommie Agee, Chicago
OF— Tony Oliva, Minnesota

NATIONAL LEAGUE
P— Bob Gibson, St. Louis
C— John Roseboro, Los Angeles
1B— Bill White, Philadelphia
2B— Bill Mazeroski, Pittsburgh
3B— Ron Santo, Chicago
SS— Gene Alley, Pittsburgh
OF— Willie Mays, San Francisco
OF— Curt Flood, St. Louis
OF— Roberto Clemente, Pittsburgh

1967
AMERICAN LEAGUE
P— Jim Kaat, Minnesota
C— Bill Freehan, Detroit
1B— George Scott, Boston
2B— Bobby Knoop, California
3B— Brooks Robinson, Baltimore
SS— Jim Fregosi, California
OF— Carl Yastrzemski, Boston
OF— Paul Blair, Baltimore
OF— Al Kaline, Detroit

NATIONAL LEAGUE
P— Bob Gibson, St. Louis
C— Randy Hundley, Chicago
1B— Wes Parker, Los Angeles
2B— Bill Mazeroski, Pittsburgh
3B— Ron Santo, Chicago

SS— Gene Alley, Pittsburgh
OF— Roberto Clemente, Pittsburgh
OF— Curt Flood, St. Louis
OF— Willie Mays, San Francisco

1968
AMERICAN LEAGUE
P— Jim Kaat, Minnesota
C— Bill Freehan, Detroit
1B— George Scott, Boston
2B— Bobby Knoop, California
3B— Brooks Robinson, Baltimore
SS— Luis Aparicio, Chicago
OF— Mickey Stanley, Detroit
OF— Carl Yastrzemski, Boston
OF— Reggie Smith, Boston

NATIONAL LEAGUE
P— Bob Gibson, St. Louis
C— Johnny Bench, Cincinnati
1B— Wes Parker, Los Angeles
2B— Glenn Beckert, Chicago
3B— Ron Santo, Chicago
SS— Dal Maxvill, St. Louis
OF— Willie Mays, San Francisco
OF— Roberto Clemente, Pittsburgh
OF— Curt Flood, St. Louis

1969
AMERICAN LEAGUE
P— Jim Kaat, Minnesota
C— Bill Freehan, Detroit
1B— Joe Pepitone, New York
2B— Dave Johnson, Baltimore
3B— Brooks Robinson, Baltimore
SS— Mark Belanger, Baltimore
OF— Paul Blair, Baltimore
OF— Mickey Stanley, Detroit
OF— Carl Yastrzemski, Boston

NATIONAL LEAGUE
P— Bob Gibson, St. Louis
C— Johnny Bench, Cincinnati
1B— Wes Parker, Los Angeles
2B— Felix Millan, Atlanta
3B— Clete Boyer, Atlanta
SS— Don Kessinger, Chicago
OF— Roberto Clemente, Pittsburgh
OF— Curt Flood, St. Louis
OF— Pete Rose, Cincinnati

1970
AMERICAN LEAGUE
P— Jim Kaat, Minnesota
C— Ray Fosse, Cleveland
1B— Jim Spencer, California
2B— Dave Johnson, Baltimore
3B— Brooks Robinson, Baltimore
SS— Luis Aparicio, Chicago
OF— Mickey Stanley, Detroit
OF— Paul Blair, Baltimore
OF— Ken Berry, Chicago

NATIONAL LEAGUE
P— Bob Gibson, St. Louis
C— Johnny Bench, Cincinnati
1B— Wes Parker, Los Angeles
2B— Tommy Helms, Cincinnati
3B— Doug Rader, Houston
SS— Don Kessinger, Chicago
OF— Roberto Clemente, Pittsburgh
OF— Tommie Agee, New York
OF— Pete Rose, Cincinnati

1971
AMERICAN LEAGUE
P— Jim Kaat, Minnesota
C— Ray Fosse, Cleveland
1B— George Scott, Boston
2B— Dave Johnson, Baltimore
3B— Brooks Robinson, Baltimore

SS— Mark Belanger, Baltimore
OF— Paul Blair, Baltimore
OF— Amos Otis, Kansas City
OF— Carl Yastrzemski, Boston

NATIONAL LEAGUE
P— Bob Gibson, St. Louis
C— Johnny Bench, Cincinnati
1B— Wes Parker, Los Angeles
2B— Tommy Helms, Cincinnati
3B— Doug Rader, Houston
SS— Bud Harrelson, New York
OF— Roberto Clemente, Pittsburgh
OF— Bobby Bonds, San Francisco
OF— Willie Davis, Los Angeles

1972
AMERICAN LEAGUE
P— Jim Kaat, Minnesota
C— Carlton Fisk, Boston
1B— George Scott, Milwaukee
2B— Doug Griffin, Boston
3B— Brooks Robinson, Baltimore
SS— Ed Brinkman, Detroit
OF— Paul Blair, Baltimore
OF— Bobby Murcer, New York
OF— Ken Berry, California

NATIONAL LEAGUE
P— Bob Gibson, St. Louis
C— Johnny Bench, Cincinnati
1B— Wes Parker, Los Angeles
2B— Felix Millan, Atlanta
3B— Doug Rader, Houston
SS— Larry Bowa, Philadelphia
OF— Roberto Clemente, Pittsburgh
OF— Cesar Cedeno, Houston
OF— Willie Davis, Los Angeles

1973
AMERICAN LEAGUE
P— Jim Kaat, Chicago
C— Thurman Munson, New York
1B— George Scott, Milwaukee
2B— Bobby Grich, Baltimore
3B— Brooks Robinson, Baltimore
SS— Mark Belanger, Baltimore
OF— Paul Blair, Baltimore
OF— Amos Otis, Kansas City
OF— Mickey Stanley, Detroit

NATIONAL LEAGUE
P— Bob Gibson, St. Louis
C— Johnny Bench, Cincinnati
1B— Mike Jorgensen, Montreal
2B— Joe Morgan, Cincinnati
3B— Doug Rader, Houston
SS— Roger Metzger, Houston
OF— Bobby Bonds, San Francisco
OF— Cesar Cedeno, Houston
OF— Willie Davis, Los Angeles

1974
AMERICAN LEAGUE
P— Jim Kaat, Chicago
C— Thurman Munson, New York
1B— George Scott, Milwaukee
2B— Bobby Grich, Baltimore
3B— Brooks Robinson, Baltimore
SS— Mark Belanger, Baltimore
OF— Paul Blair, Baltimore
OF— Amos Otis, Kansas City
OF— Joe Rudi, Oakland

NATIONAL LEAGUE
P— Andy Messersmith, Los Angeles
C— Johnny Bench, Cincinnati
1B— Steve Garvey, Los Angeles
2B— Joe Morgan, Cincinnati
3B— Doug Rader, Houston

SS— Dave Concepcion, Cincinnati
OF— Cesar Cedeno, Houston
OF— Cesar Geronimo, Cincinnati
OF— Bobby Bonds, San Francisco

1975
AMERICAN LEAGUE
P— Jim Kaat, Chicago
C— Thurman Munson, New York
1B— George Scott, Milwaukee
2B— Bobby Grich, Baltimore
3B— Brooks Robinson, Baltimore
SS— Mark Belanger, Baltimore
OF— Paul Blair, Baltimore
OF— Joe Rudi, Oakland
OF— Fred Lynn, Boston

NATIONAL LEAGUE
P— Andy Messersmith, Los Angeles
C— Johnny Bench, Cincinnati
1B— Steve Garvey, Los Angeles
2B— Joe Morgan, Cincinnati
3B— Ken Reitz, St. Louis
SS— Dave Concepcion, Cincinnati
OF— Cesar Cedeno, Houston
OF— Cesar Geronimo, Cincinnati
OF— Garry Maddox, Philadelphia

1976
AMERICAN LEAGUE
P— Jim Palmer, Baltimore
C— Jim Sundberg, Texas
1B— George Scott, Milwaukee
2B— Bobby Grich, Baltimore
3B— Aurelio Rodriguez, Detroit
SS— Mark Belanger, Baltimore
OF— Joe Rudi, Oakland
OF— Dwight Evans, Boston
OF— Rick Manning, Cleveland

NATIONAL LEAGUE
P— Jim Kaat, Philadelphia
C— Johnny Bench, Cincinnati
1B— Steve Garvey, Los Angeles
2B— Joe Morgan, Cincinnati
3B— Mike Schmidt, Philadelphia
SS— Dave Concepcion, Cincinnati
OF— Cesar Cedeno, Houston
OF— Cesar Geronimo, Cincinnati
OF— Garry Maddox, Philadelphia

1977
AMERICAN LEAGUE
P— Jim Palmer, Baltimore
C— Jim Sundberg, Texas
1B— Jim Spencer, Chicago
2B— Frank White, Kansas City
3B— Graig Nettles, New York
SS— Mark Belanger, Baltimore
OF— Juan Beniquez, Texas
OF— Carl Yastrzemski, Boston
OF— Al Cowens, Kansas City

NATIONAL LEAGUE
P— Jim Kaat, Philadelphia
C— Johnny Bench, Cincinnati
1B— Steve Garvey, Los Angeles
2B— Joe Morgan, Cincinnati
3B— Mike Schmidt, Philadelphia
SS— Dave Concepcion, Cincinnati
OF— Cesar Geronimo, Cincinnati
OF— Garry Maddox, Philadelphia
OF— Dave Parker, Pittsburgh

1978
AMERICAN LEAGUE
P— Jim Palmer, Baltimore
C— Jim Sundberg, Texas
1B— Chris Chambliss, New York
2B— Frank White, Kansas City
3B— Graig Nettles, New York

SS— Mark Belanger, Baltimore
OF— Fred Lynn, Boston
OF— Dwight Evans, Boston
OF— Rick Miller, California

NATIONAL LEAGUE
P— Phil Niekro, Atlanta
C— Bob Boone, Philadelphia
1B— Keith Hernandez, St. Louis
2B— Dave Lopes, Los Angeles
3B— Mike Schmidt, Philadelphia
SS— Larry Bowa, Philadelphia
OF— Garry Maddox, Philadelphia
OF— Dave Parker, Pittsburgh
OF— Ellis Valentine, Montreal

1979
AMERICAN LEAGUE
P— Jim Palmer, Baltimore
C— Jim Sundberg, Texas
1B— Cecil Cooper, Milwaukee
2B— Frank White, Kansas City
3B— Buddy Bell, Texas
SS— Rick Burleson, Boston
OF— Dwight Evans, Boston
OF— Sixto Lezcano, Milwaukee
OF— Fred Lynn, Boston

NATIONAL LEAGUE
P— Phil Niekro, Atlanta
C— Bob Boone, Philadelphia
1B— Keith Hernandez, St. Louis
2B— Manny Trillo, Philadelphia
3B— Mike Schmidt, Philadelphia
SS— Dave Concepcion, Cincinnati
OF— Garry Maddox, Philadelphia
OF— Dave Parker, Pittsburgh
OF— Dave Winfield, San Diego

1980
AMERICAN LEAGUE
P— Mike Norris, Oakland
C— Jim Sundberg, Texas
1B— Cecil Cooper, Milwaukee
2B— Frank White, Kansas City
3B— Buddy Bell, Texas
SS— Alan Trammell, Detroit
OF— Fred Lynn, Boston
OF— Dwayne Murphy, Oakland
OF— Willie Wilson, Kansas City

NATIONAL LEAGUE
P— Phil Niekro, Atlanta
C— Gary Carter, Montreal
1B— Keith Hernandez, St. Louis
2B— Doug Flynn, New York
3B— Mike Schmidt, Philadelphia
SS— Ozzie Smith, San Diego
OF— Andre Dawson, Montreal
OF— Garry Maddox, Philadelphia
OF— Dave Winfield, San Diego

1981
AMERICAN LEAGUE
P— Mike Norris, Oakland
C— Jim Sundberg, Texas
1B— Mike Squires, Chicago
2B— Frank White, Kansas City
3B— Buddy Bell, Texas
SS— Alan Trammell, Detroit
OF— Dwayne Murphy, Oakland
OF— Dwight Evans, Boston
OF— Rickey Henderson, Oakland

NATIONAL LEAGUE
P— Steve Carlton, Philadelphia
C— Gary Carter, Montreal
1B— Keith Hernandez, St. Louis
2B— Manny Trillo, Philadelphia
3B— Mike Schmidt, Philadelphia
SS— Ozzie Smith, San Diego
OF— Andre Dawson, Montreal

OF— Garry Maddox, Philadelphia
OF— Dusty Baker, Los Angeles

1982
AMERICAN LEAGUE
P— Ron Guidry, New York
C— Bob Boone, California
1B— Eddie Murray, Baltimore
2B— Frank White, Kansas City
3B— Buddy Bell, Texas
SS— Robin Yount, Milwaukee
OF— Dwight Evans, Boston
OF— Dave Winfield, New York
OF— Dwayne Murphy, Oakland

NATIONAL LEAGUE
P— Phil Niekro, Atlanta
C— Gary Carter, Montreal
1B— Keith Hernandez, St. Louis
2B— Manny Trillo, Philadelphia
3B— Mike Schmidt, Philadelphia
SS— Ozzie Smith, St. Louis
OF— Andre Dawson, Montreal
OF— Dale Murphy, Atlanta
OF— Garry Maddox, Philadelphia

1983
AMERICAN LEAGUE
P— Ron Guidry, New York
C— Lance Parrish, Detroit
1B— Eddie Murray, Baltimore
2B— Lou Whitaker, Detroit
3B— Buddy Bell, Texas
SS— Alan Trammell, Detroit
OF— Dwight Evans, Boston
OF— Dave Winfield, New York
OF— Dwayne Murphy, Oakland

NATIONAL LEAGUE
P— Phil Niekro, Atlanta
C— Tony Pena, Pittsburgh
1B— Keith Hernandez, St.L.-N.Y.
2B— Ryne Sandberg, Chicago
3B— Mike Schmidt, Philadelphia
SS— Ozzie Smith, St. Louis
OF— Andre Dawson, Montreal
OF— Dale Murphy, Atlanta
OF— Willie McGee, St. Louis

1984
AMERICAN LEAGUE
P— Ron Guidry, New York
C— Lance Parrish, Detroit
1B— Eddie Murray, Baltimore
2B— Lou Whitaker, Detroit
3B— Buddy Bell, Texas
SS— Alan Trammell, Detroit
OF— Dwight Evans, Boston
OF— Dave Winfield, New York
OF— Dwayne Murphy, Oakland

NATIONAL LEAGUE
P— Joaquin Andujar, St. Louis
C— Tony Pena, Pittsburgh
1B— Keith Hernandez, New York
2B— Ryne Sandberg, Chicago
3B— Mike Schmidt, Philadelphia
SS— Ozzie Smith, St. Louis
OF— Dale Murphy, Atlanta
OF— Bob Dernier, Chicago
OF— Andre Dawson, Montreal

1985
AMERICAN LEAGUE
P— Ron Guidry, New York
C— Lance Parrish, Detroit
1B— Don Mattingly, New York
2B— Lou Whitaker, Detroit
3B— George Brett, Kansas City
SS— Alfredo Griffin, Oakland
OF— Gary Pettis, California
OF— Dave Winfield, New York

OF— Dwight Evans, Boston (tie)
    Dwayne Murphy, Oakland (tie)

NATIONAL LEAGUE
P— Rick Reuschel, Pittsburgh
C— Tony Pena, Pittsburgh
1B— Keith Hernandez, New York
2B— Ryne Sandberg, Chicago
3B— Tim Wallach, Montreal
SS— Ozzie Smith, St. Louis
OF— Willie McGee, St. Louis
OF— Dale Murphy, Atlanta
OF— Andre Dawson, Montreal

1986
AMERICAN LEAGUE
P— Ron Guidry, New York
C— Bob Boone, California
1B— Don Mattingly, New York
2B— Frank White, Kansas City
3B— Gary Gaetti, Minnesota
SS— Tony Fernandez, Toronto
OF— Gary Pettis, California
OF— Jesse Barfield, Toronto
OF— Kirby Puckett, Minnesota

NATIONAL LEAGUE
P— Fernando Valenzuela, Los Angeles
C— Jody Davis, Chicago
1B— Keith Hernandez, New York
2B— Ryne Sandberg, Chicago
3B— Mike Schmidt, Philadelphia
SS— Ozzie Smith, St. Louis
OF— Tony Gwynn, San Diego
OF— Dale Murphy, Atlanta
OF— Willie McGee, St. Louis

1987
AMERICAN LEAGUE
P— Mark Langston, Seattle
C— Bob Boone, California
1B— Don Mattingly, New York
2B— Frank White, Kansas City
3B— Gary Gaetti, Minnesota
SS— Tony Fernandez, Toronto
OF— Jesse Barfield, Toronto
OF— Kirby Puckett, Minnesota
OF— Dave Winfield, New York

NATIONAL LEAGUE
P— Rick Reuschel, Pit.-S.F.
C— Mike LaValliere, Pittsburgh
1B— Keith Hernandez, New York
2B— Ryne Sandberg, Chicago
3B— Terry Pendleton, St. Louis
SS— Ozzie Smith, St. Louis
OF— Eric Davis, Cincinnati
OF— Tony Gwynn, San Diego
OF— Andre Dawson, Chicago

1988
AMERICAN LEAGUE
P— Mark Langston, Seattle
C— Bob Boone, California
1B— Don Mattingly, New York
2B— Harold Reynolds, Seattle
3B— Gary Gaetti, Minnesota
SS— Tony Fernandez, Toronto
OF— Kirby Puckett, Minnesota
OF— Devon White, California
OF— Gary Pettis, Detroit

NATIONAL LEAGUE
P— Orel Hershiser, Los Angeles
C— Benito Santiago, San Diego
1B— Keith Hernandez, New York
2B— Ryne Sandberg, Chicago
3B— Tim Wallach, Montreal
SS— Ozzie Smith, St. Louis
OF— Andy Van Slyke, Pittsburgh
OF— Eric Davis, Cincinnati
OF— Andre Dawson, Chicago

1989
AMERICAN LEAGUE
P— Bret Saberhagen, Kansas City
C— Bob Boone, Kansas City
1B— Don Mattingly, New York
2B— Harold Reynolds, Seattle
3B— Gary Gaetti, Minnesota
SS— Tony Fernandez, Toronto
OF— Kirby Puckett, Minnesota
OF— Devon White, California
OF— Gary Pettis, Detroit

NATIONAL LEAGUE
P— Ron Darling, New York
C— Benito Santiago, San Diego
1B— Andres Galarraga, Montreal
2B— Ryne Sandberg, Chicago
3B— Terry Pendleton, St. Louis
SS— Ozzie Smith, St. Louis
OF— Andy Van Slyke, Pittsburgh
OF— Tony Gwynn, San Diego
OF— Eric Davis, Cincinnati

1990
AMERICAN LEAGUE
P— Mike Boddicker, Boston
C— Sandy Alomar Jr., Cleveland
1B— Mark McGwire, Oakland
2B— Harold Reynolds, Seattle
3B— Kelly Gruber, Toronto
SS— Ozzie Guillen, Chicago
OF— Ken Griffey Jr., Seattle
OF— Ellis Burks, Boston
OF— Gary Pettis, Texas

NATIONAL LEAGUE
P— Greg Maddux, Chicago
C— Benito Santiago, San Diego
1B— Andres Galarraga, Montreal
2B— Ryne Sandberg, Chicago
3B— Tim Wallach, Montreal
SS— Ozzie Smith, St. Louis
OF— Barry Bonds, Pittsburgh
OF— Andy Van Slyke, Pittsburgh
OF— Tony Gwynn, San Diego

1991
AMERICAN LEAGUE
P— Mark Langston, California
C— Tony Pena, Boston
1B— Don Mattingly, New York
2B— Roberto Alomar, Toronto
3B— Robin Ventura, Chicago
SS— Cal Ripken, Baltimore
OF— Ken Griffey Jr., Seattle
OF— Kirby Puckett, Minnesota
OF— Devon White, Toronto

NATIONAL LEAGUE
P— Greg Maddux, Chicago
C— Tom Pagnozzi, St. Louis
1B— Will Clark, San Francisco
2B— Ryne Sandberg, Chicago
3B— Matt Williams, San Francisco
SS— Ozzie Smith, St. Louis
OF— Barry Bonds, Pittsburgh
OF— Andy Van Slyke, Pittsburgh
OF— Tony Gwynn, San Diego

1992
AMERICAN LEAGUE
P— Mark Langston, California
C— Ivan Rodriguez, Texas
1B— Don Mattingly, New York
2B— Roberto Alomar, Toronto
3B— Robin Ventura, Chicago

SS— Cal Ripken, Baltimore
OF— Ken Griffey Jr., Seattle
OF— Kirby Puckett, Minnesota
OF— Devon White, Toronto

NATIONAL LEAGUE
P— Greg Maddux, Chicago
C— Tom Pagnozzi, St. Louis
1B— Mark Grace, Chicago
2B— Jose Lind, Pittsburgh
3B— Terry Pendleton, Atlanta
SS— Ozzie Smith, St. Louis
OF— Barry Bonds, Pittsburgh
OF— Andy Van Slyke, Pittsburgh
OF— Larry Walker, Montreal

1993
AMERICAN LEAGUE
P— Mark Langston, California
C— Ivan Rodriguez, Texas
1B— Don Mattingly, New York
2B— Roberto Alomar, Toronto
3B— Robin Ventura, Chicago
SS— Omar Vizquel, Seattle
OF— Ken Griffey Jr., Seattle
OF— Kenny Lofton, Cleveland
OF— Devon White, Toronto

NATIONAL LEAGUE
P— Greg Maddux, Atlanta
C— Kirt Manwaring, San Francisco
1B— Mark Grace, Chicago
2B— Robby Thompson, San Fran.
3B— Matt Williams, San Francisco
SS—Jay Bell, Pittsburgh
OF— Barry Bonds, San Francisco
OF— Marquis Grissom, Montreal
OF— Larry Walker, Montreal

1994
AMERICAN LEAGUE
P— Mark Langston, California
C— Ivan Rodriguez, Texas
1B— Don Mattingly, New York
2B— Roberto Alomar, Toronto
3B— Wade Boggs, New York
SS— Omar Vizquel, Cleveland
OF— Ken Griffey Jr., Seattle
OF— Kenny Lofton, Cleveland
OF— Devon White, Toronto

NATIONAL LEAGUE
P— Greg Maddux, Atlanta
C— Tom Pagnozzi, St. Louis
1B— Jeff Bagwell, Houston
2B— Craig Biggio, Houston
3B— Matt Williams, San Francisco
SS— Barry Larkin, Cincinnati
OF— Barry Bonds, San Francisco
OF— Marquis Grissom, Montreal
OF— Darren Lewis, San Francisco

1995
AMERICAN LEAGUE
P— Mark Langston, California
C— Ivan Rodriguez, Texas
1B— J.T. Snow, California
2B— Roberto Alomar, Toronto
3B— Wade Boggs, New York
SS— Omar Vizquel, Cleveland
OF— Ken Griffey Jr., Seattle
OF— Kenny Lofton, Cleveland
OF— Devon White, Toronto

NATIONAL LEAGUE
P— Greg Maddux, Atlanta
C— Charles Johnson, Florida

1B— Mark Grace, Chicago
2B— Craig Biggio, Houston
3B— Ken Caminiti, San Diego
SS— Barry Larkin, Cincinnati
OF— Raul Mondesi, Los Angeles
OF— Marquis Grissom, Atlanta
OF— Steve Finley, San Diego

1996
AMERICAN LEAGUE
P— Mike Mussina, Baltimore
C— Ivan Rodriguez, Texas
1B— J.T. Snow, California
2B— Roberto Alomar, Baltimore
3B— Robin Ventura, Chicago
SS— Omar Vizquel, Cleveland
OF— Jay Buhner, Seattle
OF— Ken Griffey Jr., Seattle
OF— Kenny Lofton, Cleveland

NATIONAL LEAGUE
P— Greg Maddux, Atlanta
C— Charles Johnson, Florida
1B— Mark Grace, Chicago
2B— Craig Biggio, Houston
3B— Ken Caminiti, San Diego
SS— Barry Larkin, Cincinnati
OF— Barry Bonds, San Francisco
OF— Marquis Grissom, Atlanta
OF— Steve Finley, San Diego

1997
AMERICAN LEAGUE
P— Mike Mussina, Baltimore
C— Ivan Rodriguez, Texas
1B— Rafael Palmeiro, Baltimore
2B— Chuck Knoblauch, Minnesota
3B— Matt Williams, Cleveland
SS— Omar Vizquel, Cleveland
OF— Jim Edmonds, Anaheim
OF— Ken Griffey Jr., Seattle
OF— Bernie Williams, New York

NATIONAL LEAGUE
P— Greg Maddux, Atlanta
C— Charles Johnson, Florida
1B— J.T. Snow, San Francisco
2B— Craig Biggio, Houston
3B— Ken Caminiti, San Diego
SS— Rey Ordonez, New York
OF— Barry Bonds, San Francisco
OF— Raul Mondesi, Los Angeles
OF— Larry Walker, Colorado

1998
AMERICAN LEAGUE
P— Mike Mussina, Baltimore
C— Ivan Rodriguez, Texas
1B— Rafael Palmeiro, Baltimore
2B— Roberto Alomar, Baltimore
3B— Robin Ventura, White Sox
SS— Omar Vizquel, Cleveland
OF— Jim Edmonds, Anaheim
OF— Ken Griffey Jr., Seattle
OF— Bernie Williams, New York

NATIONAL LEAGUE
P— Greg Maddux, Atlanta
C— Charles Johnson, Fla.-L.A.
1B— J.T. Snow, San Francisco
2B— Bret Boone, Cincinnati
3B— Scott Rolen, Philadelphia
SS— Rey Ordonez, New York
OF— Barry Bonds, San Francisco
OF— Andruw Jones, Atlanta
OF— Larry Walker, Colorado

1980

AMERICAN LEAGUE
1B— Cecil Cooper, Milwaukee
2B— Willie Randolph, New York
3B— George Brett, Kansas City
SS— Robin Yount, Milwaukee
OF— Ben Oglivie, Milwaukee
OF— Al Oliver, Texas
OF— Willie Wilson, Kansas City
C— Lance Parrish, Detroit
DH— Reggie Jackson, New York

NATIONAL LEAGUE
1B— Keith Hernandez, St. Louis
2B— Manny Trillo, Philadelphia
3B— Mike Schmidt, Philadelphia
SS— Garry Templeton, St. Louis
OF— Dusty Baker, Los Angeles
OF— Andre Dawson, Montreal
OF— George Hendrick, St. Louis
C— Ted Simmons, St. Louis
P— Bob Forsch, St. Louis

1981

AMERICAN LEAGUE
1B— Cecil Cooper, Milwaukee
2B— Bobby Grich, California
3B— Carney Lansford, Boston
SS— Rick Burleson, California
OF— Rickey Henderson, Oakland
OF— Dwight Evans, Boston
OF— Dave Winfield, New York
C— Carlton Fisk, Chicago
DH— Al Oliver, Texas

NATIONAL LEAGUE
1B— Pete Rose, Philadelphia
2B— Manny Trillo, Philadelphia
3B— Mike Schmidt, Philadelphia
SS— Dave Concepcion, Cincinnati
OF— Andre Dawson, Montreal
OF— George Foster, Cincinnati
OF— Dusty Baker, Los Angeles
C— Gary Carter, Montreal
P— Fernando Valenzuela, Los Angeles

1982

AMERICAN LEAGUE
1B— Cecil Cooper, Milwaukee
2B— Damaso Garcia, Toronto
3B— Doug DeCinces, California
SS— Robin Yount, Milwaukee
OF— Dave Winfield, New York
OF— Willie Wilson, Kansas City
OF— Reggie Jackson, California
C— Lance Parrish, Detroit
DH— Hal McRae, Kansas City

NATIONAL LEAGUE
1B— Al Oliver, Montreal
2B— Joe Morgan, San Francisco
3B— Mike Schmidt, Philadelphia
SS— Dave Concepcion, Cincinnati
OF— Dale Murphy, Atlanta
OF— Pedro Guerrero, Los Angeles
OF— Leon Durham, Chicago
C— Gary Carter, Montreal
P— Don Robinson, Pittsburgh

1983

AMERICAN LEAGUE
1B— Eddie Murray, Baltimore
2B— Lou Whitaker, Detroit
3B— Wade Boggs, Boston
SS— Cal Ripken Jr., Baltimore
OF— Jim Rice, Boston
OF— Dave Winfield, New York
OF— Lloyd Moseby, Toronto

C— Lance Parrish, Detroit
DH— Don Baylor, New York

NATIONAL LEAGUE
1B— George Hendrick, St. Louis
2B— Johnny Ray, Pittsburgh
3B— Mike Schmidt, Philadelphia
SS— Dickie Thon, Houston
OF— Andre Dawson, Montreal
OF— Dale Murphy, Atlanta
OF— Jose Cruz, Houston
C— Terry Kennedy, San Diego
P— Fernando Valenzuela, Los Angeles

1984

AMERICAN LEAGUE
1B— Eddie Murray, Baltimore
2B— Lou Whitaker, Detroit
3B— Buddy Bell, Texas
SS— Cal Ripken Jr., Baltimore
OF— Tony Armas, Boston
OF— Jim Rice, Boston
OF— Dave Winfield, New York
C— Lance Parrish, Detroit
DH— Andre Thornton, Cleveland

NATIONAL LEAGUE
1B— Keith Hernandez, New York
2B— Ryne Sandberg, Chicago
3B— Mike Schmidt, Philadelphia
SS— Garry Templeton, San Diego
OF— Dale Murphy, Atlanta
OF— Jose Cruz, Houston
OF— Tony Gwynn, San Diego
C— Gary Carter, Montreal
P— Rick Rhoden, Pittsburgh

1985

AMERICAN LEAGUE
1B— Don Mattingly, New York
2B— Lou Whitaker, Detroit
3B— George Brett, Kansas City
SS— Cal Ripken Jr., Baltimore
OF— Rickey Henderson, New York
OF— Dave Winfield, New York
OF— George Bell, Toronto
C— Carlton Fisk, Chicago
DH— Don Baylor, New York

NATIONAL LEAGUE
1B— Jack Clark, St. Louis
2B— Ryne Sandberg, Chicago
3B— Tim Wallach, Montreal
SS— Hubie Brooks, Montreal
OF— Willie McGee, St. Louis
OF— Dale Murphy, Atlanta
OF— Dave Parker, Cincinnati
C— Gary Carter, New York
P— Rick Rhoden, Pittsburgh

1986

AMERICAN LEAGUE
1B— Don Mattingly, New York
2B— Frank White, Kansas City
3B— Wade Boggs, Boston
SS— Cal Ripken Jr., Baltimore
OF— George Bell, Toronto
OF— Kirby Puckett, Minnesota
OF— Jesse Barfield, Toronto
C— Lance Parrish, Detroit
DH— Don Baylor, Boston

NATIONAL LEAGUE
1B— Glenn Davis, Houston
2B— Steve Sax, Los Angeles
3B— Mike Schmidt, Philadelphia
SS— Hubie Brooks, Montreal
OF— Tony Gwynn, San Diego

OF— Tim Raines, Montreal
OF— Dave Parker, Cincinnati
C— Gary Carter, New York
P— Rick Rhoden, Pittsburgh

1987

AMERICAN LEAGUE
1B— Don Mattingly, New York
2B— Lou Whitaker, Detroit
3B— Wade Boggs, Boston
SS— Alan Trammell, Detroit
OF— George Bell, Toronto
OF— Dwight Evans, Boston
OF— Kirby Puckett, Minnesota
C— Matt Nokes, Detroit
DH— Paul Molitor, Milwaukee

NATIONAL LEAGUE
1B— Jack Clark, St. Louis
2B— Juan Samuel, Philadelphia
3B— Tim Wallach, Montreal
SS— Ozzie Smith, St. Louis
OF— Andre Dawson, Chicago
OF— Eric Davis, Cincinnati
OF— Tony Gwynn, San Diego
C— Benito Santiago, San Diego
P— Bob Forsch, St. Louis

1988

AMERICAN LEAGUE
1B— George Brett, Kansas City
2B— Julio Franco, Cleveland
3B— Wade Boggs, Boston
SS— Alan Trammell, Detroit
OF— Kirby Puckett, Minnesota
OF— Jose Canseco, Oakland
OF— Mike Greenwell, Boston
C— Carlton Fisk, Chicago
DH— Paul Molitor, Milwaukee

NATIONAL LEAGUE
1B— Andres Galarraga, Montreal
2B— Ryne Sandberg, Chicago
3B— Bobby Bonilla, Pittsburgh
SS— Barry Larkin, Cincinnati
OF— Darryl Strawberry, New York
OF— Andy Van Slyke, Pittsburgh
OF— Kirk Gibson, Los Angeles
C— Benito Santiago, San Diego
P— Tim Leary, Los Angeles

1989

AMERICAN LEAGUE
1B— Fred McGriff, Toronto
2B— Julio Franco, Texas
3B— Wade Boggs, Boston
SS— Cal Ripken Jr., Baltimore
OF— Kirby Puckett, Minnesota
OF— Ruben Sierra, Texas
OF— Robin Yount, Milwaukee
C— Mickey Tettleton, Baltimore
DH— Harold Baines, Chi.-Tex.

NATIONAL LEAGUE
1B— Will Clark, San Francisco
2B— Ryne Sandberg, Chicago
3B— Howard Johnson, New York
SS— Barry Larkin, Cincinnati
OF— Kevin Mitchell, San Francisco
OF— Tony Gwynn, San Diego
OF— Eric Davis, Cincinnati
C— Craig Biggio, Houston
P— Don Robinson, San Francisco

1990

AMERICAN LEAGUE
1B— Cecil Fielder, Detroit
2B— Julio Franco, Texas

3B— Kelly Gruber, Toronto
SS— Alan Trammell, Detroit
OF— Rickey Henderson, Oakland
OF— Jose Canseco, Oakland
OF— Ellis Burks, Boston
C— Lance Parrish, California
DH— Dave Parker, Milwaukee

NATIONAL LEAGUE
1B— Eddie Murray, Los Angeles
2B— Ryne Sandberg, Chicago
3B— Matt Williams, San Francisco
SS— Barry Larkin, Cincinnati
OF— Barry Bonds, Pittsburgh
OF— Bobby Bonilla, Pittsburgh
OF— Darryl Strawberry, New York
C— Benito Santiago, San Diego
P— Don Robinson, San Francisco

1991
AMERICAN LEAGUE
1B— Cecil Fielder, Detroit
2B— Julio Franco, Texas
3B— Wade Boggs, Boston
SS— Cal Ripken Jr., Baltimore
OF— Jose Canseco, Oakland
OF— Joe Carter, Toronto
OF— Ken Griffey Jr., Seattle
C— Mickey Tettleton, Detroit
DH— Frank Thomas, Chicago

NATIONAL LEAGUE
1B— Will Clark, San Francisco
2B— Ryne Sandberg, Chicago
3B— Howard Johnson, New York
SS— Barry Larkin, Cincinnati
OF— Barry Bonds, Pittsburgh
OF— Bobby Bonilla, Pittsburgh
OF— Ron Gant, Atlanta
C— Benito Santiago, San Diego
P— Tom Glavine, Atlanta

1992
AMERICAN LEAGUE
1B— Mark McGwire, Oakland
2B— Roberto Alomar, Toronto
3B— Edgar Martinez, Seattle
SS— Travis Fryman, Detroit
OF— Joe Carter, Toronto
OF— Juan Gonzalez, Texas
OF— Kirby Puckett, Minnesota
C— Mickey Tettleton, Detroit
DH— Dave Winfield, Toronto

NATIONAL LEAGUE
1B— Fred McGriff, San Diego
2B— Ryne Sandberg, Chicago
3B— Gary Sheffield, San Diego
SS— Barry Larkin, Cincinnati
OF— Barry Bonds, Pittsburgh
OF— Andy Van Slyke, Pittsburgh
OF— Larry Walker, Montreal
C— Darren Daulton, Philadelphia
P— Dwight Gooden, New York

1993
AMERICAN LEAGUE
1B— Frank Thomas, Chicago
2B— Carlos Baerga, Cleveland

3B— Wade Boggs, New York
SS— Cal Ripken Jr., Baltimore
OF— Albert Belle, Cleveland
OF— Juan Gonzalez, Texas
OF— Ken Griffey Jr., Seattle
C— Mike Stanley, New York
DH— Paul Molitor, Toronto

NATIONAL LEAGUE
1B— Fred McGriff, S.D.-Atl.
2B— Robby Thompson, San Fran.
3B— Matt Williams, San Francisco
SS— Jay Bell, Pittsburgh
OF— Barry Bonds, San Francisco
OF— Lenny Dykstra, Philadelphia
OF— David Justice, Atlanta
C— Mike Piazza, Los Angeles
P— Orel Hershiser, Los Angeles

1994
AMERICAN LEAGUE
1B— Frank Thomas, Chicago
2B— Carlos Baerga, Cleveland
3B— Wade Boggs, New York
SS— Cal Ripken Jr., Baltimore
OF— Albert Belle, Cleveland
OF— Ken Griffey Jr., Seattle
OF— Kirby Puckett, Minnesota
C— Ivan Rodriguez, Texas
DH— Julio Franco, Chicago

NATIONAL LEAGUE
1B— Jeff Bagwell, Houston
2B— Craig Biggio, Houston
3B— Matt Williams, San Francisco
SS— Wil Cordero, Montreal
OF— Moises Alou, Montreal
OF— Barry Bonds, San Francisco
OF— Tony Gwynn, San Diego
C— Mike Piazza, Los Angeles
P— Mark Portugal, San Francisco

1995
AMERICAN LEAGUE
1B— Mo Vaughn, Boston
2B— Chuck Knoblauch, Minnesota
3B— Gary Gaetti, Kansas City
SS— John Valentin, Boston
OF— Albert Belle, Cleveland
OF— Tim Salmon, California
OF— Manny Ramirez, Cleveland
C— Ivan Rodriguez, Texas
DH— Edgar Martinez, Seattle

NATIONAL LEAGUE
1B— Eric Karros, Los Angeles
2B— Craig Biggio, Houston
3B— Vinny Castilla, Colorado
SS— Barry Larkin, Cincinnati
OF— Dante Bichette, Colorado
OF— Tony Gwynn, San Diego
OF— Sammy Sosa, Chicago
C— Mike Piazza, Los Angeles
P— Tom Glavine, Atlanta

1996
AMERICAN LEAGUE
1B— Mark McGwire, Oakland
2B— Roberto Alomar, Baltimore

3B— Jim Thome, Cleveland
SS— Alex Rodriguez, Seattle
OF— Albert Belle, Cleveland
OF— Juan Gonzalez, Texas
OF— Ken Griffey Jr., Seattle
C— Ivan Rodriguez, Texas
DH— Paul Molitor, Minnesota

NATIONAL LEAGUE
1B— Andres Galarraga, Colorado
2B— Eric Young, Colorado
3B— Ken Caminiti, San Diego
SS— Barry Larkin, Cincinnati
OF— Barry Bonds, San Francisco
OF— Ellis Burks, Colorado
OF— Gary Sheffield, Florida
C— Mike Piazza, Los Angeles
P— Tom Glavine, Atlanta

1997
AMERICAN LEAGUE
1B— Tino Martinez, New York
2B— Chuck Knoblauch, Minnesota
3B— Matt Williams, Cleveland
SS— Nomar Garciaparra, Boston
OF— Juan Gonzalez, Texas
OF— Ken Griffey Jr., Seattle
OF— David Justice, Cleveland
C— Ivan Rodriguez, Texas
DH— Edgar Martinez, Seattle

NATIONAL LEAGUE
1B— Jeff Bagwell, Houston
2B— Craig Biggio, Houston
3B— Vinny Castilla, Colorado
SS— Jeff Blauser, Atlanta
OF— Barry Bonds, San Francisco
OF— Tony Gwynn, San Diego
OF— Larry Walker, Colorado
C— Mike Piazza, Los Angeles
P— John Smoltz, Atlanta

1998
AMERICAN LEAGUE
1B— Rafael Palmeiro, Baltimore
2B— Damion Easley, Detroit
3B— Dean Palmer, Kansas City
SS— Alex Rodriguez, Seattle
OF— Juan Gonzalez, Texas
OF— Ken Griffey Jr., Seattle
OF— Albert Belle, Chicago
C— Ivan Rodriguez, Texas
DH— Jose Canseco, Toronto

NATIONAL LEAGUE
1B— Mark McGwire, St. Louis
2B— Craig Biggio, Houston
3B— Vinny Castilla, Colorado
SS— Barry Larkin, Cincinnati
OF— Sammy Sosa, Chicago
OF— Moises Alou, Houston
OF— Greg Vaughn, San Diego
C— Mike Piazza, L.A.-Fla.-N.Y.
P— Tom Glavine, Atlanta

MAJOR LEAGUE ALL-STAR TEAMS

1925
1B— Jim Bottomley, St. Louis N.L.
2B— Rogers Hornsby, St. Louis N.L.
SS— Glenn Wright, Pittsburgh N.L.
3B— Pie Traynor, Pittsburgh N.L.
OF— Kiki Cuyler, Pittsburgh N.L.
OF— Max Carey, Pittsburgh N.L.
OF— Goose Goslin, Washington A.L.
C— Mickey Cochrane, Phil. A.L.
P— Walter Johnson, Washington A.L.
P— Ed Rommel, Philadelphia A.L.
P— Dazzy Vance, Brooklyn N.L.

1926
1B— George Burns, Cleveland A.L.
2B— Rogers Hornsby, St. Louis N.L.
SS— Joe Sewell, Cleveland A.L.
3B— Pie Traynor, Pittsburgh N.L.
OF— Goose Goslin, Washington A.L.

OF— John Mostil, Chicago A.L.
OF— Babe Ruth, New York A.L.
C— Bob O'Farrell, St. Louis N.L.
P— Herb Pennock, New York A.L.
P— George Uhle, Cleveland A.L.
P— Grover Alexander, St. Louis N.L.

1927

1B— Lou Gehrig, New York A.L.
2B— Rogers Hornsby, New York N.L.
SS— Travis Jackson, New York N.L.
3B— Pie Traynor, Pittsburgh N.L.
OF— Babe Ruth, New York A.L.
OF— Al Simmons, Philadelphia A.L.
OF— Paul Waner, Pittsburgh N.L.
C— Gabby Hartnett, Chicago N.L.
P— Charley Root, Chicago N.L.
P— Ted Lyons, Chicago A.L.

1928

1B— Lou Gehrig, New York A.L.
2B— Rogers Hornsby, Boston N.L.
SS— Travis Jackson, New York N.L.
3B— Fred Lindstrom, New York N.L.
OF— Babe Ruth, New York A.L.
OF— Heinie Manush, St. Louis A.L.
OF— Paul Waner, Pittsburgh N.L.
C— Mickey Cochrane, Phil. A.L.
P— Lefty Grove, Philadelphia A.L.
P— Waite Hoyt, New York A.L.

1929

1B— Jimmie Foxx, Philadelphia A.L.
2B— Rogers Hornsby, Chicago N.L.
SS— Travis Jackson, New York N.L.
3B— Pie Traynor, Pittsburgh, N.L.
OF— Al Simmons, Philadelphia A.L.
OF— Hack Wilson, Chicago N.L.
OF— Babe Ruth, New York A.L.
C— Mickey Cochrane, Phil. A.L.
P— Lefty Grove, Philadelphia A.L.
P— Burleigh Grimes, Pittsburgh N.L.

1930

1B— Bill Terry, New York N.L.
2B— Frank Frisch, St. Louis N.L.
SS— Joe Cronin, Washington A.L.
3B— Fred Lindstrom, New York N.L.
OF— Al Simmons, Philadelphia A.L.
OF— Hack Wilson, Chicago N.L.
OF— Babe Ruth, New York A.L.
C— Mickey Cochrane, Phil. A.L.
P— Lefty Grove, Philadelphia A.L.
P— Wes Ferrell, Cleveland A.L.

1931

1B— Lou Gehrig, New York A.L.
2B— Frank Frisch, St. Louis N.L.
SS— Joe Cronin, Washington A.L.
3B— Pie Traynor, Pittsburgh A.L.
OF— Al Simmons, Philadelphia A.L.
OF— Earl Averill, Cleveland A.L.
OF— Babe Ruth, New York A.L.
C— Mickey Cochrane, Phil. A.L.
P— Lefty Grove, Philadelphia A.L.
P— George Earnshaw, Phil. A.L.

1932

1B— Jimmie Foxx, Philadelphia A.L.
2B— Tony Lazzeri, New York A.L.
SS— Joe Cronin, Washington A.L.
3B— Pie Traynor, Pittsburgh N.L.
OF— Lefty O'Doul, Brooklyn N.L.
OF— Earl Averill, Cleveland A.L.
OF— Chuck Klein, Philadelphia N.L.
C— Bill Dickey, New York A.L.
P— Lefty Grove, Philadelphia A.L.
P— Lon Warneke, Chicago N.L.

1933

1B— Jimmie Foxx, Philadelphia A.L.
2B— Charley Gehringer, Detroit A.L.

SS— Joe Cronin, Washington A.L.
3B— Pie Traynor, Pittsburgh N.L.
OF— Al Simmons, Chicago A.L.
OF— Wally Berger, Boston N.L.
OF— Chuck Klein, Philadelphia N.L.
C— Bill Dickey, New York A.L.
P— Alvin Crowder, Washington A.L.
P— Carl Hubbell, New York N.L.

1934

1B— Lou Gehrig, New York A.L.
2B— Charley Gehringer, Detroit A.L.
SS— Joe Cronin, Washington A.L.
3B— Mike Higgins, Philadelphia A.L.
OF— Al Simmons, Chicago A.L.
OF— Earl Averill, Cleveland A.L.
OF— Mel Ott, New York N.L.
C— Mickey Cochrane, Detroit A.L.
P— Lefty Gomez, New York A.L.
P— Schoolboy Rowe, Detroit A.L.
P— Dizzy Dean, St. Louis N.L.

1935

1B— Hank Greenberg, Detroit A.L.
2B— Charley Gehringer, Detroit A.L.
SS— Arky Vaughan, Pittsburgh N.L.
3B— Pepper Martin, St. Louis N.L.
OF— Joe Medwick, St. Louis N.L.
OF— Doc Cramer, Philadelphia A.L.
OF— Mel Ott, New York N.L.
C— Mickey Cochrane, Detroit A.L.
P— Carl Hubbell, New York N.L.
P— Dizzy Dean, St. Louis N.L.

1936

1B— Lou Gehrig, New York A.L.
2B— Charley Gehringer, Detroit A.L.
SS— Luke Appling, Chicago A.L.
3B— Mike Higgins, Philadelphia A.L.
OF— Joe Medwick, St. Louis N.L.
OF— Earl Averill, Cleveland A.L.
OF— Mel Ott, New York N.L.
C— Bill Dickey, New York A.L.
P— Carl Hubbell, New York N.L.
P— Dizzy Dean, St. Louis N.L.

1937

1B— Lou Gehrig, New York A.L.
2B— Charley Gehringer, Detroit A.L.
SS— Dick Bartell, New York N.L.
3B— Red Rolfe, New York A.L.
OF— Joe Medwick, St. Louis N.L.
OF— Joe DiMaggio, New York A.L.
OF— Paul Waner, Pittsburgh N.L.
C— Gabby Hartnett, Chicago N.L.
P— Carl Hubbell, New York N.L.
P— Red Ruffing, New York A.L.

1938

1B— Jimmie Foxx, Boston A.L.
2B— Charley Gehringer, Detroit A.L.
SS— Joe Cronin, Boston A.L.
3B— Red Rolfe, New York A.L.
OF— Joe Medwick, St. Louis N.L.
OF— Joe DiMaggio, New York A.L.
OF— Mel Ott, New York N.L.
C— Bill Dickey, New York A.L.
P— Red Ruffing, New York A.L.
P— Lefty Gomez, New York A.L.
P— Johnny Vander Meer, Cin. N.L.

1939

1B— Jimmie Foxx, Boston A.L.
2B— Joe Gordon, New York A.L.
SS— Joe Cronin, Boston A.L.
3B— Red Rolfe, New York A.L.
OF— Joe Medwick, St. Louis N.L.
OF— Joe DiMaggio, New York A.L.
OF— Ted Williams, Boston A.L.
C— Bill Dickey, New York A.L.
P— Red Ruffing, New York A.L.
P— Bob Feller, Cleveland A.L.
P— Bucky Walters, Cincinnati N.L.

1940

1B— Frank McCormick, Cincinnati N.L.
2B— Joe Gordon, New York A.L.
SS— Luke Appling, Chicago A.L.
3B— Stan Hack, Chicago N.L.
OF— Hank Greenberg, Detroit A.L.
OF— Joe DiMaggio, New York A.L.
OF— Ted Williams, Boston A.L.
C— Harry Danning, New York N.L.
P— Bob Feller, Cleveland A.L.
P— Bucky Walters, Cincinnati N.L.
P— Paul Derringer, Cincinnati N.L.

1941

1B— Dolf Camilli, Brooklyn N.L.
2B— Joe Gordon, New York A.L.
SS— Cecil Travis, Washington A.L.
3B— Stan Hack, Chicago N.L.
OF— Ted Williams, Boston A.L.
OF— Joe DiMaggio, New York A.L.
OF— Pete Reiser, Brooklyn N.L.
C— Bill Dickey, New York A.L.
P— Bob Feller, Cleveland A.L.
P— Whitlow Wyatt, Brooklyn N.L.
P— Thornton Lee, Chicago A.L.

1942

1B— Johnny Mize, New York N.L.
2B— Joe Gordon, New York A.L.
SS— Johnny Pesky, Boston A.L.
3B— Stan Hack, Chicago N.L.
OF— Ted Williams, Boston A.L.
OF— Joe DiMaggio, New York A.L.
OF— Enos Slaughter, St. Louis N.L.
C— Mickey Owen, Brooklyn N.L.
P— Mort Cooper, St. Louis N.L.
P— Tiny Bonham, New York A.L.
P— Tex Hughson, Boston A.L.

1943

1B— Rudy York, Detroit A.L.
2B— Billy Herman, Brooklyn N.L.
SS— Luke Appling, Chicago A.L.
3B— Billy Johnson, New York A.L.
OF— Dick Wakefield, Detroit A.L.
OF— Stan Musial, St. Louis N.L.
OF— Bill Nicholson, Chicago N.L.
C— Walker Cooper, St. Louis N.L.
P— Spud Chandler, New York A.L.
P— Mort Cooper, St. Louis N.L.
P— Rip Sewell, Pittsburgh N.L.

1944

1B— Ray Sanders, St. Louis N.L.
2B— Bobby Doerr, Boston A.L.
SS— Marty Marion, St. Louis N.L.
3B— Bob Elliott, Pittsburgh N.L.
OF— Stan Musial, St. Louis N.L.
OF— Dick Wakefield, Detroit A.L.
OF— Dixie Walker, Brooklyn, N.L.
C— Walker Cooper, St. Louis N.L.
P— Hal Newhouser, Detroit A.L.
P— Mort Cooper, St. Louis N.L.
P— Dizzy Trout, Detroit A.L.

1945

1B— Phil Cavarretta, Chicago N.L.
2B— George Stirnweiss, N.Y. A.L.
SS— Marty Marion, St. Louis N.L.
3B— Whitey Kurowski, St. Louis N.L.
OF— Tommy Holmes, Boston N.L.
OF— Andy Pafko, Chicago N.L.
OF— Goody Rosen, Brooklyn N.L.
C— Paul Richards, Detroit A.L.
P— Hal Newhouser, Detroit A.L.
P— Boo Ferriss, Boston A.L.
P— Hank Borowy, Chicago N.L.

1946

1B— Stan Musial, St. Louis N.L.
2B— Bobby Doerr, Boston A.L.
SS— Johnny Pesky, Boston A.L.

3B— George Kell, Detroit A.L.
OF— Ted Williams, Boston A.L.
OF— Dom DiMaggio, Boston A.L.
OF— Enos Slaughter, St. Louis N.L.
C— Aaron Robinson, New York A.L.
P— Hal Newhouser, Detroit A.L.
P— Bob Feller, Cleveland A.L.
P— Boo Ferriss, Boston A.L.

1947
1B— Johnny Mize, New York N.L.
2B— Joe Gordon, Cleveland A.L.
SS— Lou Boudreau, Cleveland A.L.
3B— George Kell, Detroit A.L.
OF— Ted Williams, Boston A.L.
OF— Joe DiMaggio, New York A.L.
OF— Ralph Kiner, Pittsburgh N.L.
C— Walker Cooper, New York N.L.
P— Ewell Blackwell, Cincinnati N.L.
P— Bob Feller, Cleveland A.L.
P— Ralph Branca, Brooklyn N.L.

1948
1B— Johnny Mize, New York N.L.
2B— Joe Gordon, Cleveland A.L.
SS— Lou Boudreau, Cleveland A.L.
3B— Bob Elliott, Boston N.L.
OF— Ted Williams, Boston A.L.
OF— Joe DiMaggio, New York A.L.
OF— Stan Musial, St. Louis N.L.
C— Birdie Tebbetts, Boston A.L.
P— Johnny Sain, Boston N.L.
P— Bob Lemon, Cleveland A.L.
P— Harry Brecheen, St. Louis N.L.

1949
1B— Tommy Henrich, New York A.L.
2B— Jackie Robinson, Brooklyn N.L.
SS— Phil Rizzuto, New York A.L.
3B— George Kell, Detroit A.L.
OF— Ted Williams, Boston A.L.
OF— Stan Musial, St. Louis N.L.
OF— Ralph Kiner, Pittsburgh N.L.
C— Roy Campanella, Brooklyn N.L.
P— Mel Parnell, Boston A.L.
P— Ellis Kinder, Boston A.L.
P— Joe Page, New York A.L.

1950
1B— Walt Dropo, Boston A.L.
2B— Jackie Robinson, Brooklyn N.L.
SS— Phil Rizzuto, New York A.L.
3B— George Kell, Detroit A.L.
OF— Stan Musial, St. Louis N.L.
OF— Ralph Kiner, Pittsburgh N.L.
OF— Larry Doby, Cleveland A.L.
C— Yogi Berra, New York A.L.
P— Vic Raschi, New York A.L.
P— Bob Lemon, Cleveland A.L.
P— Jim Konstanty, Phil. N.L.

1951
1B— Ferris Fain, Philadelphia A.L.
2B— Jackie Robinson, Brooklyn N.L.
SS— Phil Rizzuto, New York A.L.
3B— George Kell, Detroit A.L.
OF— Stan Musial, St. Louis N.L.
OF— Ted Williams, Boston A.L.
OF— Ralph Kiner, Pittsburgh N.L.
C— Roy Campanella, Brooklyn N.L.
P— Sal Maglie, New York N.L.
P— Preacher Roe, Brooklyn N.L.
P— Allie Reynolds, New York A.L.

1952
1B— Ferris Fain, Philadelphia A.L.
2B— Jackie Robinson, Brooklyn N.L.
SS— Phil Rizzuto, New York A.L.
3B— George Kell, Boston A.L.
OF— Stan Musial, St. Louis N.L.
OF— Hank Sauer, Chicago N.L.
OF— Mickey Mantle, New York A.L.

C— Yogi Berra, New York A.L.
P— Robin Roberts, Philadelphia N.L.
P— Bobby Shantz, Philadelphia A.L.
P— Allie Reynolds, New York A.L.

1953
1B— Mickey Vernon, Washington A.L.
2B— Red Schoendienst, St. Louis N.L.
SS— Pee Wee Reese, Brooklyn N.L.
3B— Al Rosen, Cleveland A.L.
OF— Stan Musial, St. Louis N.L.
OF— Duke Snider, Brooklyn N.L.
OF— Carl Furillo, Brooklyn N.L.
C— Roy Campanella, Brooklyn N.L.
P— Robin Roberts, Philadelphia N.L.
P— Warren Spahn, Milwaukee N.L.
P— Bob Porterfield, Washington A.L.

1954
1B— Ted Kluszewski, Cincinnati N.L.
2B— Bobby Avila, Cleveland A.L.
SS— Alvin Dark, New York N.L.
3B— Al Rosen, Cleveland A.L.
OF— Willie Mays, New York N.L.
OF— Stan Musial, St. Louis N.L.
OF— Duke Snider, Brooklyn N.L.
C— Yogi Berra, New York A.L.
P— Bob Lemon, Cleveland A.L.
P— Johnny Antonelli, New York N.L.
P— Robin Roberts, Philadelphia N.L.

1955
1B— Ted Kluszewski, Cincinnati N.L.
2B— Nellie Fox, Chicago A.L.
SS— Ernie Banks, Chicago N.L.
3B— Ed Mathews, Milwaukee N.L.
OF— Duke Snider, Brooklyn N.L.
OF— Ted Williams, Boston A.L.
OF— Al Kaline, Detroit A.L.
C— Roy Campanella, Brooklyn N.L.
P— Robin Roberts, Philadelphia N.L.
P— Don Newcombe, Brooklyn N.L.
P— Whitey Ford, New York A.L.

1956
1B— Ted Kluszewski, Cincinnati N.L.
2B— Nellie Fox, Chicago A.L.
SS— Harvey Kuenn, Detroit A.L.
3B— Ken Boyer, St. Louis N.L.
OF— Mickey Mantle, New York A.L.
OF— Hank Aaron, Milwaukee N.L.
OF— Ted Williams, Boston A.L.
C— Yogi Berra, New York A.L.
P— Don Newcombe, Brooklyn N.L.
P— Whitey Ford, New York A.L.
P— Billy Pierce, Chicago A.L.

1957
1B— Stan Musial, St. Louis N.L.
2B— Red Schoendienst, N.Y.-Mil. N.L.
SS— Gil McDougald, New York A.L.
3B— Ed Mathews, Milwaukee N.L.
OF— Mickey Mantle, New York A.L.
OF— Ted Williams, Boston A.L.
OF— Willie Mays, New York N.L.
C— Yogi Berra, New York A.L.
P— Warren Spahn, Milwaukee N.L.
P— Billy Pierce, Chicago N.L.
P— Jim Bunning, Detroit A.L.

1958
1B— Stan Musial, St. Louis N.L.
2B— Nellie Fox, Chicago A.L.
SS— Ernie Banks, Chicago N.L.
3B— Frank Thomas, Pittsburgh N.L.
OF— Ted Williams, Boston A.L.
OF— Willie Mays, San Francisco N.L.
OF— Hank Aaron, Milwaukee N.L.
C— Del Crandall, Milwaukee N.L.
P— Bob Turley, New York A.L.
P— Warren Spahn, Milwaukee N.L.
P— Bob Friend, Pittsburgh N.L.

1959
1B— Orlando Cepeda, S.F. N.L.
2B— Nellie Fox, Chicago A.L.
SS— Ernie Banks, Chicago N.L.
3B— Ed Mathews, Milwaukee N.L.
OF— Minnie Minoso, Cleveland A.L.
OF— Willie Mays, San Francisco N.L.
OF— Hank Aaron, Milwaukee N.L.
C— Sherm Lollar, Chicago A.L.
P— Early Wynn, Chicago A.L.
P— Sam Jones, San Francisco N.L.
P— Johnny Antonelli, S.F. N.L.

1960
1B— Bill Skowron, New York A.L.
2B— Bill Mazeroski, Pittsburgh N.L.
SS— Ernie Banks, Chicago N.L.
3B— Ed Mathews, Milwaukee N.L.
OF— Minnie Minoso, Chicago A.L.
OF— Willie Mays, San Francisco N.L.
OF— Roger Maris, New York A.L.
C— Del Crandall, Milwaukee N.L.
P— Vernon Law, Pittsburgh N.L.
P— Warren Spahn, Milwaukee N.L.
P— Ernie Broglio, St. Louis N.L.

1961
AMERICAN LEAGUE
1B— Norm Cash, Detroit
2B— Bobby Richardson, New York
SS— Tony Kubek, New York
3B— Brooks Robinson, Baltimore
OF— Mickey Mantle, New York
OF— Roger Maris, New York
OF— Rocky Colavito, Detroit
C— Elston Howard, New York
P— Whitey Ford, New York
P— Frank Lary, Detroit

NATIONAL LEAGUE
1B— Orlando Cepeda, San Francisco
2B— Frank Bolling, Milwaukee
SS— Maury Wills, Los Angeles
3B— Ken Boyer, St. Louis
OF— Willie Mays, San Francisco
OF— Frank Robinson, Cincinnati
OF— Roberto Clemente, Pittsburgh
C— Smoky Burgess, Pittsburgh
P— Joey Jay, Cincinnati
P— Warren Spahn, Milwaukee

1962
AMERICAN LEAGUE
1B— Norm Siebern, Kansas City
2B— Bobby Richardson, New York
SS— Tom Tresh, New York
3B— Brooks Robinson, Baltimore
OF— Leon Wagner, Los Angeles
OF— Mickey Mantle, New York
OF— Al Kaline, Detroit
C— Earl Battey, Minnesota
P— Ralph Terry, New York
P— Dick Donovan, Cleveland

NATIONAL LEAGUE
1B— Orlando Cepeda, San Francisco
2B— Bill Mazeroski, Pittsburgh
SS— Maury Wills, Los Angeles
3B— Ken Boyer, St. Louis
OF— Tommy Davis, Los Angeles
OF— Willie Mays, San Francisco
OF— Frank Robinson, Cincinnati
C— Del Crandall, Milwaukee
P— Don Drysdale, Los Angeles
P— Bob Purkey, Cincinnati

1963
AMERICAN LEAGUE
1B— Joe Pepitone, New York
2B— Bobby Richardson, New York
SS— Luis Aparicio, Baltimore

3B— Frank Malzone, Boston
OF— Carl Yastrzemski, Boston
OF— Albie Pearson, Los Angeles
OF— Al Kaline, Detroit
C— Elston Howard, New York
P— Whitey Ford, New York
P— Gary Peters, Chicago

NATIONAL LEAGUE
1B— Bill White, St. Louis
2B— Jim Gilliam, Los Angeles
SS— Dick Groat, St. Louis
3B— Ken Boyer, St. Louis
OF— Tommy Davis, Los Angeles
OF— Willie Mays, San Francisco
OF— Hank Aaron, Milwaukee
C— John Edwards, Cincinnati
P— Sandy Koufax, Los Angeles
P— Juan Marichal, San Francisco

1964
AMERICAN LEAGUE
1B— Dick Stuart, Boston
2B— Bobby Richardson, New York
SS— Jim Fregosi, Los Angeles
3B— Brooks Robinson, Baltimore
OF— Harmon Killebrew, Minnesota
OF— Mickey Mantle, New York
OF— Tony Oliva, Minnesota
C— Elston Howard, New York
P— Dean Chance, Los Angeles
P— Gary Peters, Chicago

NATIONAL LEAGUE
1B— Bill White, St. Louis
2B— Ron Hunt, New York
SS— Dick Groat, St. Louis
3B— Ken Boyer, St. Louis
OF— Billy Williams, Chicago
OF— Willie Mays, San Francisco
OF— Roberto Clemente, Pittsburgh
C— Joe Torre, Milwaukee
P— Sandy Koufax, Los Angeles
P— Jim Bunning, Philadelphia

1965
AMERICAN LEAGUE
1B— Fred Whitfield, Cleveland
2B— Bobby Richardson, New York
SS— Zoilo Versalles, Minnesota
3B— Brooks Robinson, Baltimore
OF— Carl Yastrzemski, Boston
OF— Jimmie Hall, Minnesota
OF— Tony Oliva, Minnesota
C— Earl Battey, Minnesota
P— Jim Grant, Minnesota
P— Mel Stottlemyre, New York

NATIONAL LEAGUE
1B— Willie McCovey, San Francisco
2B— Pete Rose, Cincinnati
SS— Maury Wills, Los Angeles
3B— Deron Johnson, Cincinnati
OF— Willie Stargell, Pittsburgh
OF— Willie Mays, San Francisco
OF— Hank Aaron, Milwaukee
C— Joe Torre, Milwaukee
P— Sandy Koufax, Los Angeles
P— Juan Marichal, San Francisco

1966
AMERICAN LEAGUE
1B— Boog Powell, Baltimore
2B— Bobby Richardson, New York
SS— Luis Aparicio, Baltimore
3B— Brooks Robinson, Baltimore
OF— Frank Robinson, Baltimore
OF— Al Kaline, Detroit
OF— Tony Oliva, Minnesota
C— Paul Casanova, Washington
P— Jim Kaat, Minnesota
P— Earl Wilson, Detroit

NATIONAL LEAGUE
1B— Felipe Alou, Atlanta
2B— Pete Rose, Cincinnati
SS— Gene Alley, Pittsburgh
3B— Ron Santo, Chicago
OF— Willie Stargell, Pittsburgh
OF— Willie Mays, San Francisco
OF— Roberto Clemente, Pittsburgh
C— Joe Torre, Atlanta
P— Sandy Koufax, Los Angeles
P— Juan Marichal, San Francisco

1967
AMERICAN LEAGUE
1B— Harmon Killebrew, Minnesota
2B— Rod Carew, Minnesota
SS— Jim Fregosi, California
3B— Brooks Robinson, Baltimore
OF— Carl Yastrzemski, Boston
OF— Al Kaline, Detroit
OF— Frank Robinson, Baltimore
C— Bill Freehan, Detroit
P— Jim Lonborg, Boston
P— Earl Wilson, Detroit

NATIONAL LEAGUE
1B— Orlando Cepeda, St. Louis
2B— Bill Mazeroski, Pittsburgh
SS— Gene Alley, Pittsburgh
3B— Ron Santo, Chicago
OF— Hank Aaron, Atlanta
OF— Jim Wynn, Houston
OF— Roberto Clemente, Pittsburgh
C— Tim McCarver, St. Louis
P— Mike McCormick, San Francisco
P— Ferguson Jenkins, Chicago

1968
AMERICAN LEAGUE
1B— Boog Powell, Baltimore
2B— Rod Carew, Minnesota
SS— Luis Aparicio, Chicago
3B— Brooks Robinson, Baltimore
OF— Ken Harrelson, Boston
OF— Willie Horton, Detroit
OF— Frank Howard, Washington
C— Bill Freehan, Detroit
P— Dave McNally, Baltimore
P— Denny McLain, Detroit

NATIONAL LEAGUE
1B— Willie McCovey, San Francisco
2B— Tommy Helms, Cincinnati
SS— Don Kessinger, Chicago
3B— Ron Santo, Chicago
OF— Billy Williams, Chicago
OF— Curt Flood, St. Louis
OF— Pete Rose, Cincinnati
C— Johnny Bench, Cincinnati
P— Bob Gibson, St. Louis
P— Juan Marichal, San Francisco

1969
AMERICAN LEAGUE
1B— Boog Powell, Baltimore
2B— Rod Carew, Minnesota
SS— Rico Petrocelli, Boston
3B— Harmon Killebrew, Minnesota
OF— Frank Howard, Washington
OF— Paul Blair, Baltimore
OF— Reggie Jackson, Oakland
C— Bill Freehan, Detroit
RHP— Denny McLain, Detroit
LHP— Mike Cuellar, Baltimore

NATIONAL LEAGUE
1B— Willie McCovey, San Francisco
2B— Glenn Beckert, Chicago
SS— Don Kessinger, Chicago
3B— Ron Santo, Chicago
OF— Cleon Jones, New York

OF— Matty Alou, Pittsburgh
OF— Hank Aaron, Atlanta
C— Johnny Bench, Cincinnati
RHP— Tom Seaver, New York
LHP— Steve Carlton, St. Louis

1970
AMERICAN LEAGUE
1B— Boog Powell, Baltimore
2B— Dave Johnson, Baltimore
SS— Luis Aparicio, Chicago
3B— Harmon Killebrew, Minnesota
OF— Frank Howard, Washington
OF— Reggie Smith, Boston
OF— Tony Oliva, Minnesota
C— Ray Fosse, Cleveland
RHP— Jim Perry, Minnesota
LHP— Sam McDowell, Cleveland

NATIONAL LEAGUE
1B— Willie McCovey, San Francisco
2B— Glenn Beckett, Chicago
SS— Don Kessinger, Chicago
3B— Tony Perez, Cincinnati
OF— Billy Williams, Chicago
OF— Bobby Tolan, Cincinnati
OF— Hank Aaron, Atlanta
C— Johnny Bench, Cincinnati
RHP— Bob Gibson, St. Louis
LHP— Jim Merritt, Cincinnati

1971
AMERICAN LEAGUE
1B— Norm Cash, Detroit
2B— Cookie Rojas, Kansas City
SS— Leo Cardenas, Minnesota
3B— Brooks Robinson, Baltimore
OF— Merv Rettenmund, Baltimore
OF— Bobby Murcer, New York
OF— Tony Oliva, Minnesota
C— Bill Freehan, Detroit
RHP— Jim Palmer, Baltimore
LHP— Vida Blue, Oakland

NATIONAL LEAGUE
1B— Lee May, Cincinnati
2B— Glenn Beckett, Chicago
SS— Bud Harrelson, New York
3B— Joe Torre, St. Louis
OF— Willie Stargell, Pittsburgh
OF— Willie Davis, Los Angeles
OF— Hank Aaron, Atlanta
C— Manny Sanguillen, Pittsburgh
RHP— Ferguson Jenkins, Chicago
LHP— Steve Carlton, St. Louis

1972
AMERICAN LEAGUE
1B— Dick Allen, Chicago
2B— Rod Carew, Minnesota
SS— Luis Aparicio, Boston
3B— Brooks Robinson, Baltimore
OF— Joe Rudi, Oakland
OF— Bobby Murcer, New York
OF— Richie Scheinblum, Kansas City
C— Carlton Fisk, Boston
RHP— Gaylord Perry, Cleveland
LHP— Wilbur Wood, Chicago

NATIONAL LEAGUE
1B— Willie Stargell, Pittsburgh
2B— Joe Morgan, Cincinnati
SS— Chris Speier, San Francisco
3B— Ron Santo, Chicago
OF— Billy Williams, Chicago
OF— Cesar Cedeno, Houston
OF— Roberto Clemente, Pittsburgh
C— Johnny Bench, Cincinnati
RHP— Ferguson Jenkins, Chicago
LHP— Steve Carlton, Philadelphia

1973
AMERICAN LEAGUE
1B— John Mayberry, Kansas City
2B— Rod Carew, Minnesota
SS— Bert Campaneris, Oakland
3B— Sal Bando, Oakland
OF— Reggie Jackson, Oakland
OF— Amos Otis, Kansas City
OF— Bobby Murcer, New York
C— Thurman Munson, New York
RHP— Jim Palmer, Baltimore
LHP— Ken Holtzman, Oakland

NATIONAL LEAGUE
1B— Tony Perez, Cincinnati
2B— Dave Johnson, Atlanta
SS— Bill Russell, Los Angeles
3B— Darrell Evans, Atlanta
OF— Bobby Bonds, San Francisco
OF— Cesar Cedeno, Houston
OF— Pete Rose, Cincinnati
C— Johnny Bench, Cincinnati
RHP— Tom Seaver, New York
LHP— Ron Bryant, San Francisco

1974
AMERICAN LEAGUE
1B— Dick Allen, Chicago
2B— Rod Carew, Minnesota
SS— Bert Campaneris, Oakland
3B— Sal Bando, Oakland
OF— Joe Rudi, Oakland
OF— Paul Blair, Baltimore
OF— Jeff Burroughs, Texas
C— Thurman Munson, New York
DH— Tommy Davis, Baltimore
RHP— Jim Hunter, Oakland
LHP— Mike Cuellar, Baltimore

NATIONAL LEAGUE
1B— Steve Garvey, Los Angeles
2B— Joe Morgan, Cincinnati
SS— Dave Concepcion, Cincinnati
3B— Mike Schmidt, Philadelphia
OF— Lou Brock, St. Louis
OF— Jim Wynn, Los Angeles
OF— Richie Zisk, Pittsburgh
C— Johnny Bench, Cincinnati
RHP— Andy Messersmith, Los Angeles
LHP— Don Gullett, Cincinnati

1975
AMERICAN LEAGUE
1B— John Mayberry, Kansas City
2B— Rod Carew, Minnesota
SS— Toby Harrah, Texas
3B— Graig Nettles, New York
OF— Jim Rice, Boston
OF— Fred Lynn, Boston
OF— Reggie Jackson, Oakland
C— Thurman Munson, New York
DH— Willie Horton, Detroit
RHP— Jim Palmer, Baltimore
LHP— Jim Kaat, Chicago

NATIONAL LEAGUE
1B— Steve Garvey, Los Angeles
2B— Joe Morgan, Cincinnati
SS— Larry Bowa, Philadelphia
3B— Bill Madlock, Chicago
OF— Greg Luzinski, Philadelphia
OF— Al Oliver, Pittsburgh
OF— Dave Parker, Pittsburgh
C— Johnny Bench, Cincinnati
RHP— Tom Seaver, New York
LHP— Randy Jones, San Diego

1976
AMERICAN LEAGUE
1B— Chris Chambliss, New York
2B— Bobby Grich, Baltimore

3B— George Brett, Kansas City
SS— Mark Belanger, Baltimore
OF— Joe Rudi, Oakland
OF— Mickey Rivers, New York
OF— Reggie Jackson, Baltimore
C— Thurman Munson, New York
DH— Hal McRae, Kansas City
RHP— Jim Palmer, Baltimore
LHP— Frank Tanana, California

NATIONAL LEAGUE
1B— Willie Montanez, S.F.-Atl.
2B— Joe Morgan, Cincinnati
3B— Mike Schmidt, Philadelphia
SS— Dave Concepcion, Cincinnati
OF— George Foster, Cincinnati
OF— Cesar Cedeno, Houston
OF— Ken Griffey, Cincinnati
C— Bob Boone, Philadelphia
RHP— Don Sutton, Los Angeles
LHP— Randy Jones, San Diego

1977
AMERICAN LEAGUE
1B— Rod Carew, Minnesota
2B— Willie Randolph, New York
3B— Graig Nettles, New York
SS— Rick Burleson, Boston
OF— Jim Rice, Boston
OF— Larry Hisle, Minnesota
OF— Bobby Bonds, California
C— Carlton Fisk, Boston
DH— Hal McRae, Kansas City
RHP— Nolan Ryan, California
LHP— Frank Tanana, California

NATIONAL LEAGUE
1B— Steve Garvey, Los Angeles
2B— Joe Morgan, Cincinnati
3B— Mike Schmidt, Philadelphia
SS— Garry Templeton, St. Louis
OF— George Foster, Cincinnati
OF— Dave Parker, Pittsburgh
OF— Greg Luzinski, Philadelphia
C— Ted Simmons, St. Louis
RHP— Rick Reuschel, Chicago
LHP— Steve Carlton, Philadelphia

1978
AMERICAN LEAGUE
1B— Rod Carew, Minnesota
2B— Frank White, Kansas City
3B— Graig Nettles, New York
SS— Robin Yount, Milwaukee
OF— Jim Rice, Boston
OF— Larry Hisle, Milwaukee
OF— Fred Lynn, Boston
C— Jim Sundberg, Texas
DH— Rusty Staub, Detroit
RHP— Jim Palmer, Baltimore
LHP— Ron Guidry, New York

NATIONAL LEAGUE
1B— Steve Garvey, Los Angeles
2B— Dave Lopes, Los Angeles
3B— Pete Rose, Cincinnati
SS— Larry Bowa, Philadelphia
OF— George Foster, Cincinnati
OF— Dave Parker, Pittsburgh
OF— Jack Clark, San Francisco
C— Ted Simmons, St. Louis
RHP— Gaylord Perry, San Diego
LHP— Vida Blue, San Francisco

1979
AMERICAN LEAGUE
1B— Cecil Cooper, Milwaukee
2B— Bobby Grich, California
3B— George Brett, Kansas City
SS— Roy Smalley, Minnesota
OF— Jim Rice, Boston

OF— Fred Lynn, Boston
OF— Ken Singleton, Baltimore
C— Darrell Porter, Kansas City
DH— Don Baylor, California
RHP— Jim Kern, Texas
LHP— Mike Flanagan, Baltimore

NATIONAL LEAGUE
1B— Keith Hernandez, St. Louis
2B— Dave Lopes, Los Angeles
3B— Mike Schmidt, Philadelphia
SS— Garry Templeton, St. Louis
OF— Dave Kingman, Chicago
OF— Omar Moreno, Pittsburgh
OF— Dave Winfield, San Diego
C— Ted Simmons, St. Louis
RHP— Joe Niekro, Houston
LHP— Steve Carlton, Philadelphia

1980
AMERICAN LEAGUE
1B— Cecil Cooper, Milwaukee
2B— Willie Randolph, New York
3B— George Brett, Kansas City
SS— Robin Yount, Milwaukee
OF— Ben Oglivie, Milwaukee
OF— Al Bumbry, Baltimore
OF— Reggie Jackson, New York
DH— Reggie Jackson, New York
C— Rick Cerone, New York
RHP— Steve Stone, Baltimore
LHP— Tommy John, New York

NATIONAL LEAGUE
1B— Keith Hernandez, St. Louis
2B— Manny Trillo, Philadelphia
3B— Mike Schmidt, Philadelphia
SS— Garry Templeton, St. Louis
OF— Dusty Baker, Los Angeles
OF— Cesar Cedeno, Houston
OF— George Hendrick, St. Louis
C— Gary Carter, Montreal
RHP— Jim Bibby, Pittsburgh
LHP— Steve Carlton, Philadelphia

1981
AMERICAN LEAGUE
1B— Cecil Cooper, Milwaukee
2B— Bobby Grich, California
3B— Buddy Bell, Texas
SS— Rick Burleson, California
OF— Rickey Henderson, Oakland
OF— Dwayne Murphy, Oakland
OF— Tony Armas, Oakland
C— Jim Sundberg, Texas
DH— Richie Zisk, Seattle
RHP— Jack Morris, Detroit
LHP— Ron Guidry, New York

NATIONAL LEAGUE
1B— Pete Rose, Philadelphia
2B— Manny Trillo, Philadelphia
3B— Mike Schmidt, Philadelphia
SS— Dave Concepcion, Cincinnati
OF— George Foster, Cincinnati
OF— Andre Dawson, Montreal
OF— Pedro Guerrero, Los Angeles
C— Gary Carter, Montreal
RHP— Tom Seaver, Cincinnati
LHP— Fernando Valenzuela, Los Angeles

1982
AMERICAN LEAGUE
1B— Cecil Cooper, Milwaukee
2B— Damaso Garcia, Toronto
3B— Doug DeCinces, California
SS— Robin Yount, Milwaukee
OF— Dave Winfield, New York
OF— Gorman Thomas, Milwaukee
OF— Dwight Evans, Boston
C— Lance Parrish, Detroit

DH— Hal McRae, Kansas City
RHP— Dave Stieb, Toronto
LHP— Geoff Zahn, California

NATIONAL LEAGUE
1B— Al Oliver, Montreal
2B— Manny Trillo, Philadelphia
3B— Mike Schmidt, Philadelphia
SS— Ozzie Smith, St. Louis
OF— Lonnie Smith, St. Louis
OF— Dale Murphy, Atlanta
OF— Pedro Guerrero, Los Angeles
C— Gary Carter, Montreal
RHP— Steve Rogers, Montreal
LHP— Steve Carlton, Philadelphia

1983
AMERICAN LEAGUE
1B— Eddie Murray, Baltimore
2B— Lou Whitaker, Detroit
3B— Wade Boggs, Boston
SS— Cal Ripken, Baltimore
OF— Jim Rice, Boston
OF— Dave Winfield, New York
OF— Lloyd Moseby, Toronto
C— Carlton Fisk, Chicago
DH— Greg Luzinski, Chicago
RHP— LaMarr Hoyt, Chicago
LHP— Ron Guidry, New York

NATIONAL LEAGUE
1B— George Hendrick, St. Louis
2B— Glenn Hubbard, Atlanta
3B— Mike Schmidt, Philadelphia
SS— Dickie Thon, Houston
OF— Dale Murphy, Atlanta
OF— Andre Dawson, Montreal
OF— Tim Raines, Montreal
C— Tony Pena, Pittsburgh
RHP— John Denny, Philadelphia
LHP— Larry McWilliams, Pittsburgh

1984
AMERICAN LEAGUE
1B— Don Mattingly, New York
2B— Lou Whitaker, Detroit
3B— Buddy Bell, Texas
SS— Cal Ripken, Baltimore
OF— Tony Armas, Boston
OF— Dwight Evans, Boston
OF— Dave Winfield, New York
C— Lance Parrish, Detroit
DH— Dave Kingman, Oakland
RHP— Mike Boddicker, Baltimore
LHP— Willie Hernandez, Detroit

NATIONAL LEAGUE
1B— Keith Hernandez, New York
2B— Ryne Sandberg, Chicago
3B— Mike Schmidt, Philadelphia
SS— Ozzie Smith, St. Louis
OF— Dale Murphy, Atlanta
OF— Jose Cruz, Houston
OF— Tony Gwynn, San Diego
C— Gary Carter, Montreal
RHP— Rick Sutcliffe, Chicago
LHP— Mark Thurmond, San Diego

1985
AMERICAN LEAGUE
1B— Don Mattingly, New York
2B— Damaso Garcia, Toronto
3B— Wade Boggs, Boston
SS— Cal Ripken, Baltimore
OF— Rickey Henderson, New York
OF— Harold Baines, Chicago
OF— Phil Bradley, Seattle
C— Carlton Fisk, Chicago
DH— Don Baylor, New York
RHP— Bret Saberhagen, Kansas City
LHP— Ron Guidry, New York

NATIONAL LEAGUE
1B— Keith Hernandez, New York
2B— Tom Herr, St. Louis
3B— Tim Wallach, Montreal
SS— Ozzie Smith, St. Louis
OF— Dave Parker, Cincinnati
OF— Willie McGee, St. Louis
OF— Dale Murphy, Atlanta
C— Gary Carter, New York
RHP— Dwight Gooden, New York
LHP— John Tudor, St. Louis

1986
AMERICAN LEAGUE
1B— Don Mattingly, New York
2B— Tony Bernazard, Cleveland
3B— Wade Boggs, Boston
SS— Tony Fernandez, Toronto
OF— Jim Rice, Boston
OF— George Bell, Toronto
OF— Kirby Puckett, Minnesota
C— Rich Gedman, Boston
DH— Don Baylor, Boston
RHP— Roger Clemens, Boston
LHP— Teddy Higuera, Milwaukee

NATIONAL LEAGUE
1B— Keith Hernandez, New York
2B— Steve Sax, Los Angeles
3B— Mike Schmidt, Philadelphia
SS— Ozzie Smith, St. Louis
OF— Tim Raines, Montreal
OF— Tony Gwynn, San Diego
OF— Dave Parker, Cincinnati
C— Gary Carter, New York
RHP— Mike Scott, Houston
LHP— Fernando Valenzuela, Los Angeles

1987
AMERICAN LEAGUE
1B— Don Mattingly, New York
2B— Willie Randolph, New York
3B— Wade Boggs, Boston
SS— Alan Trammell, Detroit
OF— George Bell, Toronto
OF— Kirby Puckett, Minnesota
OF— Dwight Evans, Boston
C— Matt Nokes, Detroit
DH— Paul Molitor, Milwaukee
RHP— Roger Clemens, Boston
LHP— Jimmy Key, Toronto

NATIONAL LEAGUE
1B— Jack Clark, St. Louis
2B— Juan Samuel, Philadelphia
3B— Tim Wallach, Montreal
SS— Ozzie Smith, St. Louis
OF— Andre Dawson, Chicago
OF— Tony Gwynn, San Diego
OF— Eric Davis, Cincinnati
C— Benito Santiago, San Diego
RHP— Rick Sutcliffe, Chicago
LHP— Zane Smith, Atlanta

1988
AMERICAN LEAGUE
1B— George Brett, Kansas City
2B— Johnny Ray, California
3B— Wade Boggs, Boston
SS— Alan Trammell, Detroit
OF— Kirby Puckett, Minnesota
OF— Mike Greenwell, Boston
OF— Jose Canseco, Oakland
C— Ernie Whitt, Toronto
DH— Harold Baines, Chicago
RHP— Dave Stewart, Oakland
LHP— Frank Viola, Minnesota

NATIONAL LEAGUE
1B— Will Clark, San Francisco
2B— Ryne Sandberg, Chicago

3B— Bobby Bonilla, Pittsburgh
SS— Barry Larkin, Cincinnati
OF— Darryl Strawberry, New York
OF— Andy Van Slyke, Pittsburgh
OF— Kevin McReynolds, New York
C— Mike LaValliere, Pittsburgh
RHP— Orel Hershiser, Los Angeles
LHP— Danny Jackson, Cincinnati

1989
AMERICAN LEAGUE
1B— Fred McGriff, Toronto
2B— Julio Franco, Texas
3B— Carney Lansford, Oakland
SS— Cal Ripken, Baltimore
OF— Ruben Sierra, Texas
OF— Kirby Puckett, Minnesota
OF— Robin Yount, Milwaukee
C— Mickey Tettleton, Baltimore
DH— Harold Baines, Chi.-Tex.
RHP— Bret Saberhagen, Kansas City
LHP— Chuck Finley, California

NATIONAL LEAGUE
1B— Will Clark, San Francisco
2B— Ryne Sandberg, Chicago
3B— Howard Johnson, New York
SS— Shawon Dunston, Chicago
OF— Tony Gwynn, San Diego
OF— Kevin Mitchell, San Francisco
OF— Eric Davis, Cincinnati
C— Benito Santiago, San Diego
RHP— Mike Scott, Houston
LHP— Mark Davis, San Diego

1990
AMERICAN LEAGUE
1B— Cecil Fielder, Detroit
2B— Julio Franco, Texas
3B— Kelly Gruber, Toronto
SS— Alan Trammell, Detroit
OF— Rickey Henderson, Oakland
OF— Jose Canseco, Oakland
OF— Ellis Burks, Boston
C— Carlton Fisk, Chicago
DH— Dave Parker, Milwaukee
RHP— Bob Welch, Oakland
LHP— Chuck Finley, California

NATIONAL LEAGUE
1B— Eddie Murray, Los Angeles
2B— Ryne Sandberg, Chicago
3B— Matt Williams, San Francisco
SS— Barry Larkin, Cincinnati
OF— Barry Bonds, Pittsburgh
OF— Bobby Bonilla, Pittsburgh
OF— Darryl Strawberry, New York
C— Mike Scioscia, Los Angeles
RHP— Doug Drabek, Pittsburgh
LHP— Frank Viola, New York

1991
AMERICAN LEAGUE
1B— Cecil Fielder, Detroit
2B— Julio Franco, Texas
3B— Wade Boggs, Boston
SS— Cal Ripken, Baltimore
OF— Jose Canseco, Oakland
OF— Joe Carter, Toronto
OF— Ken Griffey Jr., Seattle
C— Mickey Tettleton, Detroit
RHP— Roger Clemens, Boston
LHP— Jim Abbott, California

NATIONAL LEAGUE
1B— Will Clark, San Francisco
2B— Ryne Sandberg, Chicago
3B— Terry Pendleton, Atlanta
SS— Barry Larkin, Cincinnati
OF— Barry Bonds, Pittsburgh
OF— Bobby Bonilla, Pittsburgh

OF— Ron Gant, Atlanta
C— Benito Santiago, San Diego
RHP— Jose Rijo, Cincinnati
LHP— Tom Glavine, Atlanta

1992
AMERICAN LEAGUE
1B— Mark McGwire, Oakland
2B— Roberto Alomar, Toronto
3B— Edgar Martinez, Seattle
SS— Travis Fryman, Detroit
OF— Joe Carter, Toronto
OF— Mike Devereaux, Baltimore
OF— Kirby Puckett, Minnesota
C— Mickey Tettleton, Detroit
RHP— Jack McDowell, Chicago
LHP— Dave Fleming, Seattle

NATIONAL LEAGUE
1B— Fred McGriff, San Diego
2B— Ryne Sandberg, Chicago
3B— Gary Sheffield, San Diego
SS— Barry Larkin, Cincinnati
OF— Barry Bonds, Pittsburgh
OF— Andy Van Slyke, Pittsburgh
OF— Larry Walker, Montreal
C— Darren Daulton, Philadelphia
RHP— Greg Maddux, Chicago
LHP— Tom Glavine, Atlanta

1993
AMERICAN LEAGUE
1B— Frank Thomas, Chicago
2B— Carlos Baerga, Cleveland
3B— Travis Fryman, Detroit
SS— Cal Ripken Jr., Baltimore
OF— Albert Belle, Cleveland
OF— Juan Gonzalez, Texas
OF— Ken Griffey Jr., Seattle
C— Mike Stanley, New York
DH— Paul Molitor, Toronto
RHP— Jack McDowell, Chicago
LHP— Jimmy Key, New York

NATIONAL LEAGUE
1B— Fred McGriff, S.D.-Atl.
2B— Robby Thompson, San Francisco
3B— Matt Williams, San Francisco
SS— Jay Bell, Pittsburgh
OF— Barry Bonds, San Francisco
OF— Lenny Dykstra, Philadelphia
OF— David Justice, Atlanta
C— Mike Piazza, Los Angeles
RHP— Greg Maddux, Atlanta
LHP— Steve Avery, Atlanta

1994
AMERICAN LEAGUE
1B— Frank Thomas, Chicago
2B— Chuck Knoblauch, Minnesota
3B— Wade Boggs, New York
SS— Cal Ripken Jr., Baltimore

OF— Albert Belle, Cleveland
OF— Ken Griffey Jr., Seattle
OF— Kirby Puckett, Minnesota
C— Ivan Rodriguez, Texas
DH— Paul Molitor, Toronto
RHP— David Cone, Kansas City
LHP— Jimmy Key, New York

NATIONAL LEAGUE
1B— Jeff Bagwell, Houston
2B— Craig Biggio, Houston
3B— Matt Williams, San Francisco
SS— Barry Larkin, Cincinnati
OF— Moises Alou, Montreal
OF— Barry Bonds, San Francisco
OF— Tony Gwynn, San Diego
C— Mike Piazza, Los Angeles
RHP— Greg Maddux, Atlanta
LHP— Danny Jackson, Philadelphia

1995
AMERICAN LEAGUE
1B— Mo Vaughn, Boston
2B— Carlos Baerga, Cleveland
3B— Jim Thome, Cleveland
SS— Cal Ripken Jr., Baltimore
OF— Albert Belle, Cleveland
OF— Tim Salmon, California
OF— Jim Edmonds, California
C— Ivan Rodriguez, Texas
DH— Edgar Martinez, Seattle
RHP— Mike Mussina, Baltimore
LHP— Randy Johnson, Seattle

NATIONAL LEAGUE
1B— Eric Karros, Los Angeles
2B— Craig Biggio, Houston
3B— Vinny Castilla, Colorado
SS— Barry Larkin, Cincinnati
OF— Reggie Sanders, Cincinnati
OF— Dante Bichette, Colorado
OF— Sammy Sosa, Chicago
C— Mike Piazza, Los Angeles
RHP— Greg Maddux, Atlanta
LHP— Pete Schourek, Cincinnati

1996
AMERICAN LEAGUE
1B— Mark McGwire, Oakland
2B— Roberto Alomar, Baltimore
3B— Jim Thome, Cleveland
SS— Alex Rodriguez, Seattle
OF— Albert Belle, Cleveland
OF— Juan Gonzalez, Texas
OF— Ken Griffey Jr., Seattle
C— Ivan Rodriguez, Texas
DH— Paul Molitor, Minnesota
RHP— Pat Hentgen, Toronto
LHP— Andy Pettitte, New York

NATIONAL LEAGUE
1B— Jeff Bagwell, Houston
2B— Eric Young, Colorado

3B— Ken Caminiti, San Diego
SS— Barry Larkin, Cincinnati
OF— Barry Bonds, San Francisco
OF— Ellis Burks, Colorado
OF— Gary Sheffield, Florida
C— Mike Piazza, Los Angeles
RHP— John Smoltz, Atlanta
LHP— Al Leiter, Florida

1997
AMERICAN LEAGUE
1B— Tino Martinez, New York
2B— Chuck Knoblauch, Minnesota
3B— Matt Williams, Cleveland
SS— Nomar Garciaparra, Boston
OF— Ken Griffey Jr., Seattle
OF— David Justice, Cleveland
OF— Tim Salmon, Anaheim
C— Ivan Rodriguez, Texas
DH— Edgar Martinez, Seattle
RHP— Roger Clemens, Toronto
LHP— Randy Johnson, Seattle

NATIONAL LEAGUE
1B— Jeff Bagwell, Houston
2B— Craig Biggio, Houston
3B— Vinny Castillo, Colorado
SS— Jeff Blauser, Atlanta
OF— Barry Bonds, San Francisco
OF— Tony Gwynn, San Diego
OF— Larry Walker, Colorado
C— Mike Piazza, Los Angeles
RHP— Pedro Martinez, Montreal
LHP— Denny Neagle, Atlanta

1998
AMERICAN LEAGUE
1B— Rafael Palmeiro, Baltimore
2B— Roberto Alomar, Baltimore
3B— Scott Brosius, New York
SS— Alex Rodriguez, Seattle
OF— Ken Griffey Jr., Seattle
OF— Juan Gonzalez, Texas
OF— Albert Belle, Chicago
C— Ivan Rodriguez, Texas
DH— Jose Canseco, Toronto
RHP— Pedro Martinez, Boston
LHP— David Wells, New York

NATIONAL LEAGUE
1B— Mark McGwire, St. Louis
2B— Craig Biggio, Houston
3B— Vinny Castillo, Colorado
SS— Barry Larkin, Cincinnati
OF— Sammy Sosa, Chicago
OF— Moises Alou, Houston
OF— Greg Vaughn, San Diego
C— Mike Piazza, L.A.-Fla.-N.Y.
RHP— Kevin Brown, San Diego
LHP— Tom Glavine, Atlanta

MINOR LEAGUE PLAYER OF THE YEAR

Year	Player, Team, League
1936	John Vander Meer, Durham, Piedmont
1937	Charlie Keller, Newark, International
1938	Fred Hutchinson, Seattle, Pacific Coast
1939	Lou Novikoff, Tulsa, Texas; Los Angeles, Pacific Coast
1940	Phil Rizzuto, Kansas City, American Association
1941	John Lindell, Newark, International
1942	Dick Barrett, Seattle, Pacific Coast
1943	Chet Covington, Scranton, Eastern
1944	Rip Collins, Albany, Eastern
1945	Gil Coan, Chattanooga, Southern
1946	Sibby Sisti, Indianapolis, American Association
1947	Hank Sauer, Syracuse, International
1948	Gene Woodling, San Francisco, Pacific Coast

Year	Player, Team, League
1949	Orie Arntzen, Albany, Eastern
1950	Frank Saucier, San Antonio, Texas
1951	Gene Conley, Hartford, Eastern
1952	Bill Skowron, Kansas City, American Association
1953	Gene Conley, Toledo, American Association
1954	Herb Score, Indianapolis, American Association
1955	John Murff, Dallas, Texas
1956	Steve Bilko, Los Angeles, Pacific Coast
1957	Norm Siebern, Denver, American Association
1958	Jim O'Toole, Nashville, Southern
1959	Frank Howard, Victoria-Spokane
1960	Willie Davis, Spokane, Pacific Coast
1961	Howie Koplitz, Birmingham, Southern

Year	Player, Team, League	Year	Player, Team, League
1962	Bob Bailey, Columbus, International	1982	Ron Kittle, Edmonton, Pacific Coast
1963	Don Buford, Indianapolis, International	1983	Kevin McReynolds, Las Vegas, Pacific Coast
1964	Mel Stottlemyre, Richmond, International	1984	Alan Knicely, Wichita, American Association
1965	Joe Foy, Toronto, International	1985	Jose Canseco, Hunt., Southern-Tac., Pacific Coast
1966	Mike Epstein, Rochester, International	1986	Tim Pyznarski, Las Vegas, Pacific Coast
1967	Johnny Bench, Buffalo, International	1987	Randy Milligan, Tidewater, International
1968	Merv Rettenmund, Rochester, International	1988	Sandy Alomar Jr., Las Vegas, Pacific Coast
1969	Danny Walton, Oklahoma City, American Association		Gary Sheffield, Denver, American Association (tie)
1970	Don Baylor, Rochester, International	1989	Sandy Alomar Jr., Las Vegas, Pacific Coast
1971	Bobby Grich, Rochester, International	1990	Jose Offerman, Albuquerque, Pacific Coast
1972	Tom Paciorek, Albuquerque, Pacific Coast	1991	Pedro Martinez, Albuquerque, Pacific Coast
1973	Steve Ontiveros, Phoenix, Pacific Coast	1992	Tim Salmon, Edmonton, Pacific Coast
1974	Jim Rice, Pawtucket, International	1993	Cliff Floyd, Harrisburg, Eastern
1975	Hector Cruz, Tulsa, American Association	1994	Derek Jeter, Tampa, Florida State; Albany, Eastern;
1976	Pat Putnam, Asheville, Western Carolina		Columbus, International
1977	Ken Landreaux, S.L.C., Pacific Coast; El Paso, Texas	1995	Karim Garcia, Albuquerque, Pacific Coast
1978	Champ Summers, Indianapolis, American Association	1996	Vladimir Guerrero, West Palm Beach, Florida State;
1979	Mark Bomback, Vancouver, Pacific Coast		Harrisburg, Eastern
1980	Tim Raines, Denver, American Association	1997	Ben Grieve, Huntsville, Southern; Edmonton, Pacific Coast
1981	Mike Marshall, Albuquerque, Pacific Coast	1998	Gabe Kapler, Jacksonville, Southern

MINOR LEAGUE MANAGER OF THE YEAR

Year	Manager, Team, League	Year	Manager, Team, League
1936	Al Sothoron, Milwaukee, American Association	1968	Jack Tighe, Toledo, International
1937	Jake Flowers, Salisbury, Eastern Shore	1969	Clyde McCullough, Tidewater, International
1938	Paul Richards, Atlanta, Southern	1970	Tom Lasorda, Spokane, Pacific Coast
1939	Bill Meyer, Kansas City, American Association	1971	Del Rice, Salt Lake City, Pacific Coast
1940	Larry Gilbert, Nashville, Southern	1972	Hank Bauer, Tidewater, International
1941	Burt Shotton, Columbus, American Association	1973	Joe Morgan, Charleston, International
1942	Eddie Dyer, Columbus, American Association	1974	Joe Altobelli, Rochester, International
1943	Nick Cullop, Columbus, American Association	1975	Joe Frazier, Tidewater, International
1944	Al Thomas, Baltimore, International	1976	Vern Rapp, Denver, American Association
1945	Lefty O'Doul, San Francisco, Pacific Coast	1977	Tommy Thompson, Arkan., Texas
1946	Clay Hopper, Montreal, International	1978	Les Moss, Evansville, American Association
1947	Nick Cullop, Milwaukee, American Association	1979	Vern Benson, Syracuse, International
1948	Casey Stengel, Oakland, Pacific Coast	1980	Hal Lanier, Springfield, American Association
1949	Fred Haney, Hollywood, Pacific Coast	1981	Del Crandall, Albuquerque, Pacific Coast
1950	Rollie Hemsley, Columbus, American Association	1982	George Scherger, Indianapolis, American Association
1951	Charlie Grimm, Milwaukee, American Association	1983	Bill Dancy, Reading, Eastern
1952	Luke Appling, Memphis, Southern	1984	Bob Rodgers, Indianapolis, American Association
1953	Bobby Bragan, Hollywood, Pacific Coast	1985	Jim Fregosi, Louisville, American Association
1954	Kerby Farrell, Indianapolis, American Association	1986	Joe Sparks, Indianapolis, American Association
1955	Bill Rigney, Minneapolis, American Association	1987	Terry Collins, Albuquerque, Pacific Coast
1956	Kerby Farrell, Indianapolis, American Association	1988	Joe Sparks, Indianapolis, American Association
1957	Ben Geraghty, Wichita, American Association	1989	Bob Bailor, Syracuse, International
1958	Cal Ermer, Birmingham, Southern	1990	Sal Rende, Omaha, American Association
1959	Pete Reiser, Victoria, Texas	1991	Chris Chambliss, Greenville, Southern
1960	Mel McGaha, Toronto, International	1992	Grady Little, Greenville, Southern
1961	Kerby Farrell, Buffalo, International	1993	Jim Tracy, Harrisburg, Eastern
1962	Ben Geraghty, Jacksonville, International	1994	Mike Jirschele, Wilmington, Carolina
1963	Rollie Hemsley, Indianapolis, International	1995	Pete Mackanin, Ottawa, International
1964	Harry Walker, Jacksonville, International	1996	John Mizerock, Wilmington, Carolina
1965	Grady Hatton, Oklahoma City, Pacific Coast	1997	Marv Foley, Rochester, International
1966	Bob Lemon, Seattle, Pacific Coast	1998	Doug Davis, Columbia, South Atlantic
1967	Bob Skinner, San Diego, Pacific Coast		

MINOR LEAGUE EXECUTIVE OF THE YEAR (HIGHER CLASSIFICATIONS, 1936-1992)

(Restricted to Class AAA starting in 1963)

Year	Executive, Team, League	Year	Executive, Team, League
1936	Earl Mann, Atlanta, Southern	1952	Jack Cooke, Toronto, International
1937	Robert LaMotte, Savannah, Sally	1953	Richard Burnett, Dallas, Texas
1938	Louis McKenna, St. Paul, American Association	1954	Edward Stumpf, Indianapolis, American Association
1939	Bruce Dudley, Louisville, American Association	1955	Dewey Soriano, Seattle, Pacific Coast
1940	Roy Hamey, Kansas City, American Association	1956	Robert Howsam, Denver American Association
1941	Emil Sick, Seattle, Pacific Coast	1957	John Stiglmeier, Buffalo, International
1942	Bill Veeck, Milwaukee, American Association	1958	Edward Glennon, Birmingham, Southern
1943	Clarence Rowland, Los Angeles, Pacific Coast	1959	Edward Leishman, Salt Lake City, Pacific Coast
1944	William Mulligan, Seattle, Pacific Coast	1960	Ray Winder, Little Rock, Southern
1945	Bruce Dudley, Louisville, American Association	1961	Elten Schiller, Omaha, American Association
1946	Earl Mann, Atlanta, Southern	1962	George Sisler Jr., Rochester, International
1947	William Purnhage, Waterloo, I.I.I.	1963	Lewis Matlin, Hawaii, Pacific Coast
1948	Edward Glennon, Birmingham, Southern	1964	Edward Leishman, San Diego, Pacific Coast
1949	Ted Sullivan, Indianapolis, American Association	1965	Harold Cooper, Columbus, International
1950	Clearnce (Brick) Laws, Oakland, Pacific Coast	1966	John Quinn Jr., Hawaii, Pacific Coast
1951	Robert Howsam, Denver, West	1967	Hillman Lyons, Richmond, International

Year	Executive, Team, League		Year	Executive, Team, League
1968—Gabe Paul Jr., Tulsa, Pacific Coast			1981—Pat McKernan, Albuquerque, Pacific Coast	
1969—Bill Gardner, Louisville, International			1982—A. Ray Smith, Louisville, American Association	
1970—Dick King, Wichita, American Association			1983—A. Ray Smith, Louisville, American Association	
1971—Carl Steinfeldt Jr., Rochester, International			1984—Mike Tamburro, Pawtucket, International	
1972—Don Labbruzzo, Evansville, American Association			1985—Patty Cox Hampton, Oklahoma City, American Association	
1973—Merle Miller, Tucson, Pacific Coast			1986—Bob Goughan, Rochester, International	
1974—John Carbray, Sacramento, Pacific Coast			1987—Stu Kehoe, Vancouver, Pacific Coast	
1975—Stan Naccarato, Tacoma, Pacific Coast			1988—Bob Rich, Buffalo, American Association	
1976—Art Teece, Salt Lake City, Pacific Coast			1989—Larry Schmittou, Nashville, American Association	
1977—George Sisler Jr., Columbus, International			1990—Greg Corns, Phoenix, Pacific Coast	
1978—Willie Sanchez, Albuquerque, Pacific Coast			1991—Tom Maloney, Denver, American Association	
1979—George Sisler Jr., Columbus, International			1992—Lou Schwechheimer, Pawtucket, International	
1980—Jim Burris, Denver, American Association				

MINOR LEAGUE EXECUTIVE OF THE YEAR (LOWER CLASSIFICATIONS, 1950-1990)

(Separate awards for Class AA and Class A started in 1963; for Short Class A in 1988)

Year	Executive, Team, League		Year	Executive, Team, League
1950—H. Cooper, Hutchinson, Western Association			1975—Jim Paul, El Paso, Texas	
1951—O. W. (Bill) Hayes, Triple, B.S.			Cordy Jensen, Eugene, Northwest	
1952—Hillman Lyons, Danville, MOV			1976—Woodrow Reid, Chattanooga, Southern	
1953—Carl Roth, Peoria, I.I.I.			Don Buchheister, Cedar Rapids, Midwest	
1954—James Meagham, Cedar Rapids, I.I.I.			1977—Jim Paul, El Paso, Texas	
1955—John Petrakis, Dubuque, MOV			Harry Pells, Quad Cities, Midwest	
1956—Marvin Milkes, Fresno, California			1978—Larry Schmittou, Nashville, Southern	
1957—Richard Wagner, Lincoln, West.			Dave Hersh, Appleton, Midwest	
1958—Gerald Waring, Macon, Sally			1979—Bill Rigney Jr., Midland, Texas	
1959—Clay Dennis, Des Moines, I.I.I.			Tom Romenesko, Greensboro, W.C.	
1960—Hubert Kittle, Yakima, Northwest			1980—Frances Crockett, Charlotte, Southern	
1961—David Steele, Fresno, California			Tom Romenesko, Greensboro, W.C.	
1962—John Quinn Jr., San Jose, California			1981—Allie Prescott, Memphis, Southern	
1963—Hugh Finnerty, Tulsa, Texas			Dan Overstreet, Hagerstown, Caro.	
Ben Jewell, M. Valley, Pioneer			1982—Art Clarkson, Birmingham, Southern	
1964—Glynn West, Birmingham, Southern			Bob Carruesco, Stockton, California	
James Bayens, Rock Hill, W. Carolina			1983—Edward Kenney, New Britain, Eastern	
1965—Dick Butler, Dallas-Ft. Worth, Texas			Terry Reynolds, Vero Beach, Florida State	
Ken. Blackman, Quad Cities, Midwest			1984—Bruce Baldwin, Greenville, Southern	
1966—Tom Fleming, Evansville, Southern			Dave Tarrolly, Beloit, Midwest	
Cappy Harada, Lodi, California			1985—Ben Bernard, Albany-Colonie, Eastern	
1967—Robert Quinn, Reading, Eastern			Pete Vonachen, Peoria, Midwest	
Pat Williams, Spar'burg, W.C.			1986—Bill Davidson, Midland, Texas	
1968—Phil Howser, Charlotte, Southern			Rob Dlugozima, Durham, Carolina	
Merle Miller, Burlington, Midwest			1987—Joe Preseren, Tulsa, Texas	
1969—Charlie Blaney, Albuquerque, Texas			Skip Weisman, Greensboro, South Atlantic	
Bill Gorman, Visalia, California			1988—Bill Valentine, Arkansas, Texas	
1970—Carl Sawatski, Arkansas, Texas			Dennis Bastien, Charleston (W.Va.), South Atlantic	
Bob Williams, Bakersfield, California			Bob Beban, Eugene, Northwest	
1971—Miles Wolff, Savannah, Dixie Association			1989—Chuck Domino, Reading, Eastern	
Ed Holtz, Appleton, Midwest			John Baxter, South Bend, Midwest	
1972—John Begzos, S. Antonio, Texas			Bill Pereira, Boise, Northwest	
Bob Piccinini, Modesto, California			1990—Joe Preseren, Tulsa, Texas	
1973—Dick Kravitz, Jacksonville, Southern			Dan Chapman, Stockton, California	
Fritz Colschen, Clinton, Midwest			Dave Baggott, Salt Lake City, Pioneer	
1974—Jim Paul, El Paso, Texas				
Bing Russell, Portland, Northwest				

HISTORY *Award winners*

MINOR LEAGUE EXECUTIVE OF THE YEAR

Year	Executive, Team, League		Year	Executive, Team, League
1993—Todd Vander Woude, Harrisburg, Eastern (AA)			1996—Wayne Hodes, Trenton, Eastern (AA)	
1994—Scott Lane, West Michigan, Midwest (A)			1997—Andy Milovich, Erie, New York-Pennsylvania (A)	
1995—Jack and Mary Cain, Portland, Northwest (A)			1998—Chuck Domino, Reading, Eastern (AA)	

BASEBALL WRITERS' ASSOCIATION OF AMERICA
MOST VALUABLE PLAYER

AMERICAN LEAGUE

Year	Player	Team	Pos.	Points
1931—Lefty Grove	Philadelphia	P	78
1932—Jimmie Foxx	Philadelphia	1B	75
1933—Jimmie Foxx	Philadelphia	1B	74
1934—Mickey Cochrane	Detroit	C	67
1935—Hank Greenberg	Detroit	1B	*80
1936—Lou Gehrig	New York	1B	73

NATIONAL LEAGUE

Year	Player	Team	Pos.	Points
1931—Frank Frisch	St. Louis	2B	65
1932—Chuck Klein	Philadelphia	OF	78
1933—Carl Hubbell	New York	P	77
1934—Dizzy Dean	St. Louis	P	78
1935—Gabby Hartnett	Chicago	C	75
1936—Carl Hubbell	New York	P	60

Year	Player	Team	Pos.	Points	Year	Player	Team	Pos.	Points
1937—Charley Gehringer	Detroit	2B	78		1937—Joe Medwick	St. Louis	OF	70	
1938—Jimmie Foxx	Boston	1B	305		1938—Ernie Lombardi	Cincinnati	C	229	
1939—Joe DiMaggio	New York	OF	280		1939—Bucky Walters	Cincinnati	P	303	
1940—Hank Greenberg	Detroit	OF	292		1940—Frank McCormick	Cincinnati	1B	274	
1941—Joe DiMaggio	New York	OF	291		1941—Dolf Camilli	Brooklyn	1B	300	
1942—Joe Gordon	New York	2B	270		1942—Mort Cooper	St. Louis	P	263	
1943—Spud Chandler	New York	P	246		1943—Stan Musial	St. Louis	OF	267	
1944—Hal Newhouser	Detroit	P	236		1944—Marty Marion	St. Louis	SS	190	
1945—Hal Newhouser	Detroit	P	236		1945—Phil Cavarretta	Chicago	1B	279	
1946—Ted Williams	Boston	OF	224		1946—Stan Musial	St. Louis	1B	319	
1947—Joe DiMaggio	New York	OF	202		1947—Bob Elliott	Boston	3B	205	
1948—Lou Boudreau	Cleveland	SS	324		1948—Stan Musial	St. Louis	OF	303	
1949—Ted Williams	Boston	OF	272		1949—Jackie Robinson	Brooklyn	2B	264	
1950—Phil Rizzuto	New York	SS	284		1950—Jim Konstanty	Philadelphia	P	286	
1951—Yogi Berra	New York	C	184		1951—Roy Campanella	Brooklyn	C	243	
1952—Bobby Shantz	Philadelphia	P	280		1952—Hank Sauer	Chicago	OF	226	
1953—Al Rosen	Cleveland	3B	*336		1953—Roy Campanella	Brooklyn	C	297	
1954—Yogi Berra	New York	C	230		1954—Willie Mays	New York	OF	283	
1955—Yogi Berra	New York	C	218		1955—Roy Campanella	Brooklyn	C	226	
1956—Mickey Mantle	New York	OF	*336		1956—Don Newcombe	Brooklyn	P	223	
1957—Mickey Mantle	New York	OF	233		1957—Hank Aaron	Milwaukee	OF	239	
1958—Jackie Jensen	Boston	OF	233		1958—Ernie Banks	Chicago	SS	283	
1959—Nellie Fox	Chicago	2B	295		1959—Ernie Banks	Chicago	SS	232½	
1960—Roger Maris	New York	OF	225		1960—Dick Groat	Pittsburgh	SS	276	
1961—Roger Maris	New York	OF	202		1961—Frank Robinson	Cincinnati	OF	219	
1962—Mickey Mantle	New York	OF	234		1962—Maury Wills	Los Angeles	SS	209	
1963—Elston Howard	New York	C	248		1963—Sandy Koufax	Los Angeles	P	237	
1964—Brooks Robinson	Baltimore	3B	269		1964—Ken Boyer	St. Louis	3B	243	
1965—Zoilo Versalles	Minnesota	SS	275		1965—Willie Mays	San Francisco	OF	224	
1966—Frank Robinson	Baltimore	OF	*280		1966—Roberto Clemente	Pittsburgh	OF	218	
1967—Carl Yastrzemski	Boston	OF	275		1967—Orlando Cepeda	St. Louis	1B	*280	
1968—Denny McLain	Detroit	P	*280		1968—Bob Gibson	St. Louis	P	242	
1969—Harmon Killebrew	Minnesota	1B-3B	294		1969—Willie McCovey	San Francisco	1B	265	
1970—Boog Powell	Baltimore	1B	234		1970—Johnny Bench	Cincinnati	C	326	
1971—Vida Blue	Oakland	P	268		1971—Joe Torre	St. Louis	3B	318	
1972—Dick Allen	Chicago	1B	321		1972—Johnny Bench	Cincinnati	C	263	
1973—Reggie Jackson	Oakland	OF	*336		1973—Pete Rose	Cincinnati	OF	274	
1974—Jeff Burroughs	Texas	OF	248		1974—Steve Garvey	Los Angeles	1B	270	
1975—Fred Lynn	Boston	OF	326		1975—Joe Morgan	Cincinnati	2B	321½	
1976—Thurman Munson	New York	C	304		1976—Joe Morgan	Cincinnati	2B	311	
1977—Rod Carew	Minnesota	1B	273		1977—George Foster	Cincinnati	OF	291	
1978—Jim Rice	Boston	OF	352		1978—Dave Parker	Pittsburgh	OF	320	
1979—Don Baylor	California	OF	347		1979—Willie Stargell	Pittsburgh	1B	216	
					Keith Hernandez	St. Louis	1B	216	
1980—George Brett	Kansas City	3B	335		1980—Mike Schmidt	Philadelphia	3B	*336	
1981—Rollie Fingers	Milwaukee	P	319		1981—Mike Schmidt	Philadelphia	3B	321	
1982—Robin Yount	Milwaukee	SS	385		1982—Dale Murphy	Atlanta	OF	283	
1983—Cal Ripken Jr.	Baltimore	SS	322		1983—Dale Murphy	Atlanta	OF	318	
1984—Willie Hernandez	Detroit	P	306		1984—Ryne Sandberg	Chicago	2B	326	
1985—Don Mattingly	New York	1B	367		1985—Willie McGee	St. Louis	OF	280	
1986—Roger Clemens	Boston	P	339		1986—Mike Schmidt	Philadelphia	3B	287	
1987—George Bell	Toronto	OF	332		1987—Andre Dawson	Chicago	OF	269	
1988—Jose Canseco	Oakland	OF	*392		1988—Kirk Gibson	Los Angeles	OF	272	
1989—Robin Yount	Milwaukee	OF	256		1989—Kevin Mitchell	San Francisco	OF	314	
1990—Rickey Henderson	Oakland	OF	317		1990—Barry Bonds	Pittsburgh	OF	331	
1991—Cal Ripken Jr.	Baltimore	SS	318		1991—Terry Pendleton	Atlanta	3B	274	
1992—Dennis Eckersley	Oakland	P	306		1992—Barry Bonds	Pittsburgh	OF	304	
1993—Frank Thomas	Chicago	1B	*392		1993—Barry Bonds	San Francisco	OF	372	
1994—Frank Thomas	Chicago	1B	372		1994—Jeff Bagwell	Houston	1B	*392	
1995—Mo Vaughn	Boston	1B	308		1995—Barry Larkin	Cincinnati	SS	281	
1996—Juan Gonzalez	Texas	OF	290		1996—Ken Caminiti	San Diego	3B	*392	
1997—Ken Griffey Jr.	Seattle	OF	*392		1997—Larry Walker	Colorado	OF	359	
1998—Juan Gonzalez	Texas	OF	357		1998—Sammy Sosa	Chicago	OF	438	

*Unanimous selection.

CY YOUNG MEMORIAL AWARD

Year	Pitcher	Team	Votes	Year	Pitcher	Team	Votes
1956—Don Newcombe	Brooklyn	10		1966—Sandy Koufax	Los Angeles N.L.	*20	
1957—Warren Spahn	Milwaukee	15		1967—A.L.—Jim Lonborg	Boston	18	
1958—Bob Turley	New York A.L.	5		N.L.—Mike McCormick	San Francisco	18	
1959—Early Wynn	Chicago A.L.	13		1968—A.L.—Denny McLain	Detroit	*20	
1960—Vernon Law	Pittsburgh	8		N.L.—Bob Gibson	St. Louis	*20	
1961—Whitey Ford	New York A.L.	9		1969—A.L.—Denny McLain	Detroit	10	
1962—Don Drysdale	Los Angeles N.L.	14		Mike Cuellar	Baltimore	10	
1963—Sandy Koufax	Los Angeles N.L.	*20		N.L.—Tom Seaver	New York	23	
1964—Dean Chance	Los Angeles A.L.	17		1970—A.L.—Jim Perry	Minnesota	55	
1965—Sandy Koufax	Los Angeles N.L.	*20		N.L.—Bob Gibson	St. Louis	118	

Year	Pitcher	Team	Votes	Year	Pitcher	Team	Votes
1971—A.L.—Vida Blue	Oakland		98	1986—A.L.—Roger Clemens	Boston		*140
N.L.—Fergie Jenkins	Chicago		97	N.L.—Mike Scott	Houston		98
1972—A.L.—Gaylord Perry	Cleveland		64	1987—A.L.—Roger Clemens	Boston		124
N.L.—Steve Carlton	Philadelphia		*120	N.L.—Steve Bedrosian	Philadelphia		57
1973—A.L.—Jim Palmer	Baltimore		88	1988—A.L.—Frank Viola	Minnesota		138
N.L.—Tom Seaver	New York		71	N.L.—Orel Hershiser	Los Angeles		*120
1974—A.L.—Jim Hunter	Oakland		90	1989—A.L.—Bret Saberhagen	Kansas City		138
N.L.—Mike Marshall	Los Angeles		96	N.L.—Mark Davis	San Diego		107
1975—A.L.—Jim Palmer	Baltimore		98	1990—A.L.—Bob Welch	Oakland		107
N.L.—Tom Seaver	New York		98	N.L.—Doug Drabek	Pittsburgh		118
1976—A.L.—Jim Palmer	Baltimore		108	1991—A.L.—Roger Clemens	Boston		119
N.L.—Randy Jones	San Diego		96	N.L.—Tom Glavine	Atlanta		110
1977—A.L.—Sparky Lyle	New York		56½	1992—A.L.—Dennis Eckersley	Oakland		107
N.L.—Steve Carlton	Philadelphia		*104	N.L.—Greg Maddux	Chicago		112
1978—A.L.—Ron Guidry	New York		*140	1993—A.L.—Jack McDowell	Chicago		124
N.L.—Gaylord Perry	San Diego		116	N.L.—Greg Maddux	Atlanta		119
1979—A.L.—Mike Flanagan	Baltimore		136	1994—A.L.—David Cone	Kansas City		108
N.L.—Bruce Sutter	Chicago		72	N.L.—Greg Maddux	Atlanta		*140
1980—A.L.—Steve Stone	Baltimore		100	1995—A.L.—Randy Johnson	Seattle		136
N.L.—Steve Carlton	Philadelphia		118	N.L.—Greg Maddux	Atlanta		*140
1981—A.L.—Rollie Fingers	Milwaukee		126	1996—A.L.—Pat Hentgen	Toronto		110
N.L.—Fernando Valenzuela	Los Angeles		70	N.L.—John Smoltz	Atlanta		136
1982—A.L.—Pete Vuckovich	Milwaukee		87	1997—A.L.—Roger Clemens	Toronto		134
N.L.—Steve Carlton	Philadelphia		112	N.L.—Pedro Martinez	Montreal		134
1983—A.L.—LaMarr Hoyt	Chicago		116	1998—A.L.—Roger Clemens	Toronto		140
N.L.—John Denny	Philadelphia		103	N.L.—Tom Glavine	Atlanta		99
1984—A.L.—Willie Hernandez	Detroit		88	*Unanimous selection.			
N.L.—Rick Sutcliffe	Chicago		*120				
1985—A.L.—Bret Saberhagen	Kansas City		127				
N.L.—Dwight Gooden	New York		*120				

ROOKIE OF THE YEAR

1947—Combined selection—Jackie Robinson, Brooklyn N.L., 1B
1948—Combined selection—Alvin Dark, Boston N.L., SS

AMERICAN LEAGUE

NATIONAL LEAGUE

Year	Player	Team	Pos.	Votes	Year	Player	Team	Pos.	Votes
1949—Roy Sievers	St. Louis	OF	10		1949—Don Newcombe	Brooklyn	P	21	
1950—Walt Dropo	Boston	1B	15		1950—Sam Jethroe	Boston	OF	11	
1951—Gil McDougald	New York	3B	13		1951—Willie Mays	New York	OF	18	
1952—Harry Byrd	Philadelphia	P	9		1952—Joe Black	Brooklyn	P	19	
1953—Harvey Kuenn	Detroit	SS	23		1953—Jim Gilliam	Brooklyn	2B	11	
1954—Bob Grim	New York	P	15		1954—Wally Moon	St. Louis	OF	17	
1955—Herb Score	Cleveland	P	18		1955—Bill Virdon	St. Louis	OF	15	
1956—Luis Aparicio	Chicago	SS	22		1956—Frank Robinson	Cincinnati	OF	*24	
1957—Tony Kubek	New York	IF-OF	23		1957—Jack Sanford	Philadelphia	P	16	
1958—Albie Pearson	Washington	OF	14		1958—Orlando Cepeda	San Francisco	1B	*†21	
1959—Bob Allison	Washington	OF	18		1959—Willie McCovey	San Francisco	1B	*24	
1960—Ron Hansen	Baltimore	SS	22		1960—Frank Howard	Los Angeles	OF	12	
1961—Don Schwall	Boston	P	7		1961—Billy Williams	Chicago	OF	10	
1962—Tom Tresh	New York	OF-SS	13		1962—Ken Hubbs	Chicago	2B	19	
1963—Gary Peters	Chicago	P	10		1963—Pete Rose	Cincinnati	2B	17	
1964—Tony Oliva	Minnesota	OF	19		1964—Dick Allen	Philadelphia	3B	18	
1965—Curt Blefary	Baltimore	OF	12		1965—Jim Lefebvre	Los Angeles	2B	13	
1966—Tommie Agee	Chicago	OF	16		1966—Tommy Helms	Cincinnati	3B	12	
1967—Rod Carew	Minnesota	2B	19		1967—Tom Seaver	New York	P	11	
1968—Stan Bahnsen	New York	P	17		1968—Johnny Bench	Cincinnati	C	10½	
1969—Lou Piniella	Kansas City	OF	9		1969—Ted Sizemore	Los Angeles	2B	14	
1970—Thurman Munson	New York	C	23		1970—Carl Morton	Montreal	P	11	
1971—Chris Chambliss	Cleveland	1B	11		1971—Earl Williams	Atlanta	C	18	
1972—Carlton Fisk	Boston	C	*24		1972—Jon Matlack	New York	P	19	
1973—Al Bumbry	Baltimore	OF	13½		1973—Gary Matthews	San Francisco	OF	11	
1974—Mike Hargrove	Texas	1B	16½		1974—Bake McBride	St. Louis	OF	16	
1975—Fred Lynn	Boston	OF	23		1975—John Montefusco	San Francisco	P	12	
1976—Mark Fidrych	Detroit	P	22		1976—Butch Metzger	San Diego	P	11	
					Pat Zachry	Cincinnati	P	11	
1977—Eddie Murray	Baltimore	DH-1B	12½		1977—Andre Dawson	Montreal	OF	10	
1978—Lou Whitaker	Detroit	2B	21		1978—Bob Horner	Atlanta	3B	12½	
1979—John Castino	Minnesota	3B	7		1979—Rick Sutcliffe	Los Angeles	P	20	
Alfredo Griffin	Toronto	SS	7						
1980—Joe Charboneau	Cleveland	OF	103		1980—Steve Howe	Los Angeles	P	80	
1981—Dave Righetti	New York	P	127		1981—Fernando Valenzuela	Los Angeles	P	107	
1982—Cal Ripken	Baltimore	SS-3B	132		1982—Steve Sax	Los Angeles	2B	63	
1983—Ron Kittle	Chicago	OF	104		1983—Darryl Strawberry	New York	OF	109	
1984—Alvin Davis	Seattle	1B	134		1984—Dwight Gooden	New York	P	118	
1985—Ozzie Guillen	Chicago	SS	101		1985—Vince Coleman	St. Louis	OF	*120	
1986—Jose Canseco	Oakland	OF	110		1986—Todd Worrell	St. Louis	P	118	

HISTORY *Award winners*

Year	Player	Team	Pos.	Votes	Year	Player	Team	Pos.	Votes
1987—Mark McGwire	Oakland	1B	*140		1987—Benito Santiago	San Diego	C	*120
1988—Walt Weiss	Oakland	SS	103		1988—Chris Sabo	Cincinnati	3B	79
1989—Gregg Olson	Baltimore	P	136		1989—Jerome Walton	Chicago	OF	116
1990—Sandy Alomar Jr.	Cleveland	C	*140		1990—Dave Justice	Atlanta	OF	118
1991—Chuck Knoblauch	Minnesota	2B	136		1991—Jeff Bagwell	Houston	1B	118
1992—Pat Listach	Milwaukee	SS	122		1992—Eric Karros	Los Angeles	1B	116
1993—Tim Salmon	California	OF	*140		1993—Mike Piazza	Los Angeles	C	*140
1994—Bob Hamelin	Kansas City	DH	134		1994—Raul Mondesi	Los Angeles	OF	*140
1995—Marty Cordova	Minnesota	3B	105		1995—Hideo Nomo	Los Angeles	P	118
1996—Derek Jeter	New York	SS	*140		1996—Todd Hollandsworth	Los Angeles	OF	105
1997—Nomar Garciaparra	Boston	SS	*140		1997—Scott Rolen	Philadelphia	3B	*140
1998—Ben Grieve	Oakland	OF	130		1998—Kerry Wood	Chicago	P	128

*Unanimous selection. †Three writers did not vote.

MANAGER OF THE YEAR

AMERICAN LEAGUE | NATIONAL LEAGUE

Year	Manager	Team	Points	Year	Manager	Team	Points
1983—Tony La Russa	Chicago	17		1983— Tommy Lasorda	Los Angeles	10
1984—Sparky Anderson	Detroit	96		1984— Jim Frey	Chicago	101
1985—Bobby Cox	Toronto	104		1985— Whitey Herzog	St. Louis	86
1986—John McNamara	Boston	95		1986— Hal Lanier	Houston	108
1987—Sparky Anderson	Detroit	90		1987— Buck Rodgers	Montreal	92
1988—Tony La Russa	Oakland	103		1988— Tommy Lasorda	Los Angeles	101
1989—Frank Robinson	Baltimore	125		1989— Don Zimmer	Chicago	118
1990—Jeff Torborg	Chicago	128		1990— Jim Leyland	Pittsburgh	99
1991—Tom Kelly	Minnesota	138		1991— Bobby Cox	Atlanta	96
1992—Tony La Russa	Oakland	132		1992— Jim Leyland	Pittsburgh	109
1993—Gene Lamont	Chicago	72		1993— Dusty Baker	San Francisco	105
1994—Buck Showalter	New York	132		1994— Felipe Alou	Montreal	138
1995—Lou Piniella	Seattle	86		1995— Don Baylor	Colorado	122
1996—Johnny Oates	Texas	89		1996— Bruce Bochy	San Diego	76
Joe Torre	New York	89				
1997—Dave Johnson	Baltimore	88		1997— Dusty Baker	San Francisco	110
1998—Joe Torre	New York	128		1998— Larry Dierker	Houston	102

EARLY MOST VALUABLE PLAYER AWARDS

CHALMERS AWARD

AMERICAN LEAGUE | NATIONAL LEAGUE

Year	Player	Team	Pos.	Points	Year	Player	Team	Pos.	Points
1911—Ty Cobb	Detroit	OF	64		1911—Frank Schulte	Chicago	OF	29
1912—Tris Speaker	Boston	OF	59		1912—Larry Doyle	New York	2B	48
1913—Walter Johnson	Washington	P	54		1913—Jake Daubert	Brooklyn	1B	50
1914—Eddie Collins	Philadelphia	2B	63		1914—Johnny Evers	Boston	2B	50

LEAGUE AWARDS

AMERICAN LEAGUE | NATIONAL LEAGUE

Year	Player	Team	Pos.	Points	Year	Player	Team	Pos.	Points
1922—George Sisler	St. Louis	1B	59		1922—No selection			
1923—Babe Ruth	New York	OF	64		1923—No selection			
1924—Walter Johnson	Washington	P	55		1924—Dazzy Vance	Brooklyn	P	74
1925—Roger Peckinpaugh	Washington	SS	45		1925—Rogers Hornsby	St. Louis	2B	73
1926—George Burns	Cleveland	1B	63		1926—Bob O'Farrell	St. Louis	C	79
1927—Lou Gehrig	New York	1B	56		1927—Paul Waner	Pittsburgh	OF	72
1928—Mickey Cochrane	Philadelphia	C	53		1928—Jim Bottomley	St. Louis	1B	76
1929—No selection					1929—Rogers Hornsby	Chicago	2B	60

HALL OF FAME

ROSTER OF MEMBERS

Name	Des.*	Elec. year	Votes rec.†	Votes cast‡	% of vote	Teams as player
Aaron, Hank	P	1982	406	415	97.8	Milwaukee NL, Atlanta NL, Milwaukee AL
Alexander, Grover C.	P	1938	212	262	80.9	Philadelphia NL, Chicago NL, St. Louis NL
Alston, Walter	M	1983	CV	—	—	St. Louis NL
Anson, Cap	P	1939	C1	—	—	Chicago NL
Aparicio, Luis	P	1984	341	403	84.6	Chicago AL, Baltimore AL, Boston AL
Appling, Luke	P	1964	189	225	84	Chicago AL
Ashburn, Richie	P	1995	CV	—	—	Philadelphia NL, Chicago NL, New York NL
Averill, Earl	P	1975	CV	—	—	Cleveland AL, Detroit AL, Boston AL
Baker, Home Run	P	1955	CV	—	—	Philadelphia AL, New York AL
Bancroft, Dave	P	1971	CV	—	—	Philadelphia NL, New York NL, Boston NL, Brooklyn NL
Banks, Ernie	P	1977	321	383	83.8	Chicago NL
Barlick, Al	U	1989	CV	—	—	
Barrow, Ed	E	1953	CV	—	—	
Beckley, Jake	P	1971	CV	—	—	Pittsburgh NL, Pittsburgh PL, New York NL, Cincinnati NL, St. Louis NL
Bell, Cool Papa	P	1974	SCNL	—	—	Negro Leagues
Bench, Johnny	P	1989	431	447	96.4	Cincinnati NL
Bender, Chief	P	1953	CV	—	—	Philadelphia AL, Philadelphia NL, Chicago AL
Berra, Yogi	P	1972	339	396	85.6	New York AL, New York NL
Bottomley, Jim	P	1974	CV	—	—	St. Louis NL, Cincinnati NL, St. Louis AL
Boudreau, Lou	P	1970	232	300	77.3	Cleveland AL, Boston AL
Bresnahan, Roger	P	1945	C2	—	—	Washington NL, Chicago NL, Baltimore AL, New York NL, St. Louis NL
Brett, George	P	1999	488	497	98.2	Kansas City AL
Brock, Lou	P	1985	315	395	79.7	Chicago NL, St. Louis NL
Brouthers, Dan	P	1945	C2	—	—	Troy NL, Buffalo NL, Detroit NL, Boston NL, Boston PL, Boston AA, Brooklyn NL, Baltimore NL, Louisville NL, Philadelphia NL, New York NL
Brown, Three Finger	P	1949	C2	—	—	St. Louis NL, Chicago NL, Cincinnati NL
Bulkeley, Morgan	E	1937	CC	—	—	
Bunning, Jim	P	1996	CV	—	—	Detroit AL, Philadelphia NL, Pittsburgh NL, Los Angeles NL
Burkett, Jesse	P	1946	C2	—	—	New York NL, Cleveland NL, St. Louis NL, St. Louis AL, Boston AL
Campanella, Roy	P	1969	270	340	79.4	Brooklyn NL
Carew, Rod	P	1991	401	447	89.7	Minnesota AL, California AL
Carey, Max	P	1961	CV	—	—	Pittsburgh NL, Brooklyn NL
Carlton, Steve	P	1994	436	455	95.8	St. Louis NL, Philadelphia NL, San Francisco NL, Chicago AL, Cleveland AL, Minnesota AL
Cartwright, Alexander	O	1938	CC	—	—	
Chadwick, Henry	O	1938	CC	—	—	
Chance, Frank	P	1946	C2	—	—	Chicago NL, New York AL
Chandler, Happy	E	1982	CV	—	—	
Charleston, Oscar	P	1976	SCNL	—	—	Negro Leagues
Chesbro, Jack	P	1946	C2	—	—	Pittsburgh NL, New York AL, Boston AL
Clarke, Fred	P	1945	C2	—	—	Louisville NL, Pittsburgh NL
Clarkson, John	P	1963	CV	—	—	Worcester NL, Chicago NL, Boston AL, Cleveland NL
Clemente, Roberto	P	1973	393	424	92.7	Pittsburgh NL
Cobb, Ty	P	1936	222	226	98.2	Detroit AL, Philadelphia AL
Cochrane, Mickey	P	1947	128	161	79.5	Philadelphia AL, Detroit AL
Collins, Eddie	P	1939	213	274	77.7	Philadelphia AL, Chicago AL
Collins, Jimmy	P	1945	C2	—	—	Boston NL, Louisville NL, Boston AL, Philadelphia AL
Combs, Earle	P	1970	CV	—	—	New York AL
Comiskey, Charley	F/P	1939	C1	—	—	St. Louis AA, Chicago PL, Cincinnati NL
Conlan, Jocko	U	1974	CV	—	—	Chicago AL
Connolly, Tommy	U	1953	CV	—	—	
Connor, Roger	P	1976	CV	—	—	Troy NL, New York NL, New York PL, Philadelphia NL, St. Louis NL
Coveleski, Stan	P	1969	CV	—	—	Philadelphia AL, Cleveland AL, Washington AL, New York AL
Crawford, Sam	P	1957	CV	—	—	Cincinnati NL, Detroit AL
Cronin, Joe	P	1956	152	193	78.8	Pittsburgh NL, Washington AL, Boston AL
Cummings, Candy	P	1939	C1	—	—	Hartford NL, Cincinnati NL
Cuyler, Kiki	P	1968	CV	—	—	Pittsburgh NL, Chicago NL, Cincinnati NL, Brooklyn NL
Dandridge, Ray	P	1987	CV	—	—	Negro Leagues
Davis, George S.	P	1998	CV	—	—	Cleveland NL, New York NL, Chicago AL
Day, Leon	P	1995	CV	—	—	Negro Leagues
Dean, Dizzy	P	1953	209	264	79.2	St. Louis NL, Chicago NL, St. Louis AL
Delahanty, Ed	P	1945	C2	—	—	Philadelphia NL, Cleveland PL, Washington AL
Dickey, Bill	P	1954	202	252	80.2	New York AL
Dihigo, Martin	P	1977	SCNL	—	—	Negro Leagues
DiMaggio, Joe	P	1955	223	251	88.8	New York AL

HISTORY *Hall of Fame*

Name	Des.*	Elec. year	Votes rec.†	Votes cast‡	% of vote	Teams as player
Doby, Larry	P	1998	CV	—	—	Cleveland AL, Chicago AL, Detroit AL
Doerr, Bobby	P	1986	CV	—	—	Boston AL
Drysdale, Don	P	1984	316	403	78.4	Brooklyn NL, Los Angeles NL
Duffy, Hugh	P	1945	C2	—	—	Chicago NL, Chicago PL, Boston AA, Boston NL, Milwaukee AL, Philadelphia NL
Durocher, Leo	M	1994	CV	—	—	New York AL, Cincinnati NL, St. Louis NL, Brooklyn NL
Evans, Billy	U	1973	CV	—	—	
Evers, Johnny	P	1946	C2	—	—	Chicago NL, Boston NL, Philadelphia NL, Chicago AL
Ewing, Buck	P	1939	C1	—	—	Troy NL, New York NL, New York PL, Cleveland NL, Cincinnati NL
Faber, Red	P	1964	CV	—	—	Chicago AL
Feller, Bob	P	1962	150	160	93.8	Cleveland AL
Ferrell, Rick	P	1984	CV	—	—	St. Louis AL, Boston AL, Washington AL
Fingers, Rollie	P	1992	349	430	81.2	Oakland AL, San Diego NL, Milwaukee AL
Flick, Elmer	P	1963	CV	—	—	Philadelphia NL, Philadelphia AL, Cleveland AL
Ford, Whitey	P	1974	284	365	77.8	New York AL
Foster, Bill	P	1996	CV	—	—	Negro Leagues
Foster, Rube	P	1981	CV	—	—	Negro Leagues
Fox, Nellie	P	1997	CV	—	—	Philadelphia AL, Chicago AL, Houston NL
Foxx, Jimmie	P	1951	179	226	79.2	Philadelphia AL, Boston AL, Chicago NL, Philadelphia NL
Frick, Ford	E	1970	CV	—	—	
Frisch, Frank	P	1947	136	161	84.5	New York NL, St. Louis NL
Galvin, Pud	P	1965	CV	—	—	Buffalo NL, Pittsburgh AA, Pittsburgh NL, Pittsburgh PL, St. Louis NL
Gehrig, Lou	P	1939	SE	—	—	New York AL
Gehringer, Charley	P	1949	159	187	85.0	Detroit AL
Gibson, Bob	P	1981	337	401	84.0	St. Louis NL
Gibson, Josh	P	1972	SCNL	—	—	Negro Leagues
Giles, Warren	E	1979	CV	—	—	
Gomez, Lefty	P	1972	CV	—	—	New York AL, Washington AL
Goslin, Goose	P	1968	CV	—	—	Washington AL, St. Louis AL, Detroit AL
Greenberg, Hank	P	1956	164	193	85.0	Detroit AL, Pittsburgh NL
Griffith, Clark	M	1946	C2	—	—	St. Louis AA, Boston AA, Chicago NL, Chicago AL, New York AL, Cincinnati NL, Washington AL
Grimes, Burleigh	P	1964	CV	—	—	Pittsburgh NL, Brooklyn NL, New York NL, Boston NL, St. Louis NL, Chicago NL, New York AL
Grove, Lefty	P	1947	123	161	76.4	Philadelphia AL, Boston AL
Hafey, Chick	P	1971	CV	—	—	St. Louis NL, Cincinnati NL
Haines, Jesse	P	1970	CV	—	—	Cincinnati NL, St. Louis NL
Hamilton, Billy	P	1961	CV	—	—	Kansas City AA, Philadelphia NL, Boston NL
Hanlon, Ned	M	1996	CV	—	—	Cleveland NL, Detroit NL, Pittsburgh NL, Pittsburgh PL, Baltimore NL
Harridge, Will	E	1972	CV	—	—	
Harris, Bucky	M	1975	CV	—	—	Washington AL, Detroit AL
Hartnett, Gabby	P	1955	195	251	77.7	Chicago NL, New York NL
Heilmann, Harry	P	1952	203	234	86.8	Detroit AL, Cincinnati NL
Herman, Billy	P	1975	CV	—	—	Chicago NL, Brooklyn NL, Boston NL, Pittsburgh NL
Hooper, Harry	P	1971	CV	—	—	Boston AL, Chicago AL
Hornsby, Rogers	P	1942	182	233	78.1	St. Louis NL, New York NL, Boston NL, Chicago NL, St. Louis AL
Hoyt, Waite	P	1969	CV	—	—	New York NL, Boston AL, New York AL, Detroit AL, Philadelphia AL, Brooklyn NL, Pittsburgh NL
Hubbard, Cal	U	1976	CV	—	—	
Hubbell, Carl	P	1947	140	161	87.0	New York NL
Huggins, Miller	M	1964	CV	—	—	Cincinnati NL, St. Louis NL
Hulbert, William	F	1995	CV	—	—	
Hunter, Catfish	P	1987	315	413	76.3	Kansas City AL, Oakland AL, New York AL
Irvin, Monte	P	1973	SCNL	—	—	New York NL, Chicago NL, Negro Leagues
Jackson, Reggie	P	1993	396	423	93.6	Kansas City AL, Oakland AL, Baltimore AL, New York AL, California AL
Jackson, Travis	P	1982	CV	—	—	New York NL
Jenkins, Ferguson	P	1991	334	447	74.7	Philadelphia NL, Chicago NL, Texas AL, Boston AL
Jennings, Hugh	P	1945	C2	—	—	Louisville AA, Louisville NL, Baltimore NL, Brooklyn NL, Philadelphia NL, Detroit AL
Johnson, Ban	E	1937	CC	—	—	
Johnson, Judy	P	1975	SCNL	—	—	Negro Leagues
Johnson, Walter	P	1936	189	226	83.6	Washington AL
Joss, Addie	P	1978	CV	—	—	Cleveland AL
Kaline, Al	P	1980	340	385	88.3	Detroit AL
Keefe, Tim	P	1964	CV	—	—	Troy NL, New York AA, New York NL, New York PL, Philadelphia NL
Keeler, Willie	P	1939	207	274	75.5	New York NL, Brooklyn, NL, Baltimore NL, New York AL
Kell, George	P	1983	CV	—	—	Philadelphia AL, Detroit AL, Boston AL, Chicago AL, Baltimore AL
Kelley, Joe	P	1971	CV	—	—	Boston NL, Pittsburgh NL, Baltimore NL, Brooklyn NL, Baltimore AL, Cincinnati NL

Name	Des.*	Elec. year	Votes rec.†	Votes cast‡	% of vote	Teams as player
Kelly, George	P	1973	CV	—	—	New York NL, Pittsburgh NL, Cincinnati NL, Chicago NL, Brooklyn NL
Kelly, Mike	P	1945	C2	—	—	Cincinnati NL, Chicago NL, Boston NL, Boston PL, Cincinnati AA, Boston AA, New York NL
Killebrew, Harmon	P	1984	335	403	83.1	Washington AL, Minnesota AL, Kansas City AL
Kiner, Ralph	P	1975	273	362	75.4	Pittsburgh NL, Chicago NL, Cleveland AL
Klein, Chuck	P	1980	CV	—	—	Philadelphia NL, Chicago NL, Pittsburgh NL
Klem, Bill	U	1953	CV	—	—	
Koufax, Sandy	P	1972	344	396	86.9	Brooklyn NL, Los Angeles NL
Lajoie, Nap	P	1937	168	201	83.6	Philadelphia NL, Philadelphia AL, Cleveland AL
Landis, Kenesaw M.	E	1944	C2	—	—	
Lasorda, Tom	M	1997	CV	—	—	Brooklyn NL, Kansas City AL
Lazzeri, Tony	P	1991	CV	—	—	New York AL, Chicago NL, Brooklyn NL, New York NL
Lemon, Bob	P	1976	305	388	78.6	Cleveland AL
Leonard, Buck	P	1972	SCNL	—	—	Negro Leagues
Lindstrom, Fred	P	1976	CV	—	—	New York NL, Pittsburgh NL, Chicago NL, Brooklyn NL
Lloyd, John Henry	P	1977	SCNL	—	—	Negro Leagues
Lombardi, Ernie	P	1986	CV	—	—	Brooklyn NL, Cincinnati NL, Boston NL, New York NL
Lopez, Al	M	1977	CV	—	—	Brooklyn NL, Boston NL, Pittsburgh NL, Cleveland AL
Lyons, Ted	P	1955	217	251	86.5	Chicago AL
Mack, Connie	M	1937	CC	—	—	Washington NL, Buffalo PL, Pittsburgh NL
MacPhail, Larry	E	1978	CV	—	—	
MacPhail, Lee	E	1998	CV	—	—	
Mantle, Mickey	P	1974	322	365	88.2	New York AL
Manush, Heinie	P	1964	CV	—	—	Detroit AL, St. Louis AL, Washington AL, Boston AL, Brooklyn NL, Pittsburgh NL
Maranville, Rabbit	P	1954	209	252	82.9	Boston NL, Pittsburgh NL, Chicago NL, Brooklyn NL, St. Louis NL
Marichal, Juan	P	1983	313	374	83.7	San Francisco NL, Boston AL, Los Angeles NL
Marquard, Rube	P	1971	CV	—	—	New York NL, Brooklyn NL, Cincinnati NL, Boston NL
Mathews, Eddie	P	1978	301	379	79.4	Boston NL, Milwaukee NL, Atlanta NL, Houston NL, Detroit AL
Mathewson, Christy	P	1936	205	226	90.7	New York NL, Cincinnati NL
Mays, Willie	P	1979	409	432	94.7	New York (Giants)NL, San Francisco NL, New York (Mets)NL
McCarthy, Joe	M	1957	CV	—	—	
McCarthy, Tommy	P	1946	C2	—	—	Boston UA, Boston NL, Philadelphia NL, St. Louis AA, Brooklyn NL
McCovey, Willie	P	1986	346	425	81.4	San Francisco NL, San Diego NL, Oakland AL
McGinnity, Joe	P	1946	C2	—	—	Baltimore NL, Brooklyn NL, Baltimore AL, New York NL
McGowan, Bill	U	1992	CV	—	—	
McGraw, John	M	1937	CC	—	—	Baltimore AA, Baltimore NL, St. Louis NL, Baltimore AL, New York NL
McKechnie, Bill	M	1962	CV	—	—	Pittsburgh NL, Boston NL, New York AL, New York NL, Cincinnati
Medwick, Joe	P	1968	240	283	84.8	St. Louis NL, Brooklyn NL, New York NL, Boston NL
Mize, Johnny	P	1981	CV	—	—	St. Louis NL, New York NL, New York AL
Morgan, Joe	P	1990	363	444	81.8	Houston NL, Cincinnati NL, San Francisco NL, Philadelphia NL, Oakland AL
Musial, Stan	P	1969	317	340	93.2	St. Louis NL
Newhouser, Hal	P	1992	CV	—	—	Detroit AL, Cleveland AL
Nichols, Kid	P	1949	C2	—	—	Boston NL, St. Louis NL, Philadelphia NL
Niekro, Phil	P	1997	380	473	80.3	Milwaukee NL, Atlanta NL, New York AL, Cleveland AL, Toronto AL
O'Rourke, Jim	P	1945	C2	—	—	Boston NL, Providence NL, Buffalo NL, New York NL, Washington NL, New York PL
Ott, Mel	P	1951	197	226	87.2	New York NL
Paige, Satchel	P	1971	SCNL	—	—	Cleveland AL, St. Louis AL, Kansas City AL, Negro Leagues
Palmer, Jim	P	1990	411	444	92.6	Baltimore AL
Pennock, Herb	P	1948	94	121	77.7	Philadelphia AL, Boston AL, New York AL
Perry, Gaylord	P	1991	342	447	76.5	San Francisco NL, Cleveland AL, Texas AL, San Diego NL, New York AL, Atlanta NL, Seattle AL, Kansas City AL
Plank, Eddie	P	1946	C2	—	—	Philadelphia AL, St. Louis AL
Radbourn, Hoss	P	1939	C1	—	—	Buffalo NL, Providence NL, Boston NL, Boston PL, Cincinnati NL
Reese, Pee Wee	P	1984	CV	—	—	Brooklyn NL, Los Angeles NL
Rice, Sam	P	1963	CV	—	—	Washington AL, Cleveland AL
Rickey, Branch	E	1967	CV	—	—	St. Louis AL, New York AL
Rixey, Eppa	P	1963	CV	—	—	Philadelphia NL, Cincinnati NL
Rizzuto, Phil	P	1994	CV	—	—	New York AL
Roberts, Robin	P	1976	337	388	86.9	Philadelphia NL, Baltimore AL, Houston NL, Chicago NL
Robinson, Brooks	P	1983	344	374	92.0	Baltimore AL
Robinson, Frank	P	1982	370	415	89.2	Cincinnati NL, Baltimore AL, Los Angeles NL, California AL, Cleveland AL

– 337 –

Name	Des.*	Elec. year	Votes rec.†	Votes cast‡	% of vote	Teams as player
Robinson, Jackie	P	1962	124	160	77.5	Brooklyn NL
Robinson, Wilbert	M	1945	C2	—	—	Philadelphia AA, Baltimore AA, Baltimore NL, St. Louis NL, Baltimore AL
Rogan, Bullet Joe	P	1998	CV	—	—	
Roush, Edd	P	1962	CV	—	—	Chicago AL, New York NL, Cincinnati NL
Ruffing, Red	P	1967	266	306	86.9	Boston AL, New York AL, Chicago AL
Rusie, Amos	P	1977	CV	—	—	Indianapolis NL, New York NL, Cincinnati NL
Ruth, Babe	P	1936	215	226	95.1	Boston AL, New York AL, Boston NL
Ryan, Nolan	P	1999	491	497	98.8	New York NL, California AL, Houston NL, Texas AL
Schalk, Ray	P	1955	CV	—	—	Chicago AL, New York NL
Schmidt, Mike	P	1995	444	460	96.5	Philadelphia NL
Schoendienst, Red	P	1989	CV	—	—	St. Louis NL, New York (Giants) NL, Milwaukee NL
Seaver, Tom	P	1992	425	430	98.8	New York NL, Cincinnati NL, Chicago AL, Boston AL
Sewell, Joe	P	1977	CV	—	—	Cleveland AL, New York AL
Simmons, Al	P	1953	199	264	75.4	Philadelphia AL, Chicago AL, Detroit AL, Washington AL, Boston NL, Cincinnati NL, Boston AL
Sisler, George	P	1939	235	274	85.8	St. Louis AL, Washington AL, Boston NL
Slaughter, Enos	P	1985	CV	—	—	St. Louis NL, New York AL, Kansas City AL, Milwaukee NL
Snider, Duke	P	1980	333	385	86.5	Brooklyn NL, Los Angeles NL, New York NL, San Francisco NL
Spahn, Warren	P	1973	316	380	83.2	Boston NL, Milwaukee NL, New York NL, San Francisco NL
Spalding, Al	P	1939	C1	—	—	Chicago NL
Speaker, Tris	P	1937	165	201	82.1	Boston AL, Cleveland AL, Washington AL, Philadelphia AL
Stargell, Willie	P	1988	352	427	82.4	Pittsburgh NL
Stengel, Casey	M	1966	CV	—	—	Brooklyn NL, Pittsburgh NL, Philadelphia NL, New York NL, Boston NL
Sutton, Don	P	1998	386	473	81.6	Los Angeles NL, Houston NL, Milwaukee AL, Oakland AL, California AL
Terry, Bill	P	1954	195	252	77.4	New York NL
Thompson, Sam	P	1974	CV	—	—	Detroit NL, Philadelphia NL, Detroit AL
Tinker, Joe	P	1946	C2	—	—	Chicago NL, Cincinnati NL
Traynor, Pie	P	1948	93	121	76.9	Pittsburgh NL
Vance, Dazzy	P	1955	205	251	81.7	Pittsburgh NL, New York AL, Brooklyn NL, St. Louis NL, Cincinnati NL
Vaughan, Arky	P	1985	CV	—	—	Pittsburgh NL, Brooklyn NL
Veeck, Bill	E	1991	CV	—	—	
Waddell, Rube	P	1946	C2	—	—	Louisville NL, Pittsburgh NL, Chicago NL, Philadelphia AL, St. Louis AL
Wagner, Honus	P	1936	215	226	95.1	Louisville NL, Pittsburgh NL
Wallace, Bobby	P	1953	CV	—	—	Cleveland NL, St. Louis NL, St. Louis AL
Walsh, Ed	P	1946	C2	—	—	Chicago AL, Boston AL
Waner, Lloyd	P	1967	CV	—	—	Pittsburgh NL, Boston NL, Cincinnati NL, Philadelphia NL, Brooklyn NL
Waner, Paul	P	1952	195	234	83.3	Pittsburgh NL, Brooklyn NL, Boston NL, New York AL
Ward, John Montgomery	P	1964	CV	—	—	Providence NL, New York NL, Brooklyn PL, Brooklyn NL
Weaver, Earl	M	1996	CV	—	—	
Weiss, George	E	1971	CV	—	—	
Welch, Mickey	P	1973	CV	—	—	Troy NL, New York NL
Wells, Willie	P	1997	CV	—	—	
Wheat, Zack	P	1959	CV	—	—	Brooklyn NL, Philadelphia AL
Wilhelm, Hoyt	P	1985	331	395	83.8	New York NL, St. Louis NL, Cleveland AL, Baltimore AL, Chicago AL California AL, Atlanta NL, Chicago NL, Los Angeles NL
Williams, Billy	P	1987	354	413	85.7	Chicago NL, Oakland AL
Williams, Ted	P	1966	282	302	93.4	Boston AL
Willis, Vic	P	1995	CV	—	—	Boston NL, Pittsburgh NL, St. Louis NL
Wilson, Hack	P	1979	CV	—	—	New York NL, Chicago NL, Brooklyn NL, Philadelphia NL
Wright, George	M	1937	CC	—	—	Boston NL, Providence NL
Wright, Harry	M	1953	CV	—	—	Boston NL
Wynn, Early	P	1972	301	396	76.0	Washington AL, Cleveland AL, Chicago AL
Yastrzemski, Carl	P	1989	423	447	94.6	Boston AL
Yawkey, Tom	E	1980	CV	—	—	
Young, Cy	P	1937	153	201	76.1	Cleveland NL, St. Louis NL, Boston AL, Cleveland AL, Boston NL
Youngs, Ross	P	1972	CV	—	—	New York NL
Yount, Robin	P	1999	385	497	77.5	Milwaukee AL

*Designation for which he was honored. Abbreviations: E—executive; F—founder; M—manager; O—organizer; P—player; U—umpire.
†Where an abbreviation is listed rather than a vote total, the enshrinee was selected by one of the following groups: Centennial Commission (CC), committee of old-time players and writers (C1), committee on old-timers (C2), Committee on Veterans (CV), special election by Baseball Writers' Association of America (SE) or Special Committee on Negro Leagues (SCNL).
‡Votes cast by eligible members of the Baseball Writers' Association of America.
League abbreviations: AA—American Association; AL—American League; NL—National League; PL—Players League; UA—Union Association.

TEAM BY TEAM
AMERICAN LEAGUE

ANAHEIM ANGELS
YEARLY FINISHES

Year	Position	W	L	Pct.	*GB	Manager	Attendance
1961†	8th	70	91	.435	38 1/2	Bill Rigney	603,510
1962†	3rd	86	76	.531	10	Bill Rigney	1,144,063
1963†	9th	70	91	.435	34	Bill Rigney	821,015
1964†	5th	82	80	.506	17	Bill Rigney	760,439
1965†	7th	75	87	.463	27	Bill Rigney	566,727
1966‡	6th	80	82	.494	18	Bill Rigney	1,400,321
1967‡	5th	84	77	.522	7 1/2	Bill Rigney	1,317,713
1968‡	8th	67	95	.414	36	Bill Rigney	1,025,956

WEST DIVISION

Year	Position	W	L	Pct.	*GB	Manager	Attendance
1969‡	3rd	71	91	.438	26	Bill Rigney, Lefty Phillips	758,388
1970‡	3rd	86	76	.531	12	Lefty Phillips	1,077,741
1971‡	4th	76	86	.469	25 1/2	Lefty Phillips	926,373
1972‡	5th	75	80	.484	18	Del Rice	744,190
1973‡	4th	79	83	.488	15	Bobby Winkles	1,058,206
1974‡	6th	68	94	.420	22	Bobby Winkles, Dick Williams	917,269
1975‡	6th	72	89	.447	25 1/2	Dick Williams	1,058,163
1976‡	4th (tied)	76	86	.469	14	Dick Williams, Norm Sherry	1,006,774
1977‡	5th	74	88	.457	28	Norm Sherry, Dave Garcia	1,432,633
1978‡	2nd (tied)	87	75	.537	5	Dave Garcia, Jim Fregosi	1,755,386
1979‡	1st§	88	74	.543	+3	Jim Fregosi	2,523,575
1980‡	6th	65	95	.406	31	Jim Fregosi	2,297,327
1981‡	4th/7th	51	59	.464	∞	Jim Fregosi, Gene Mauch	1,441,545
1982‡	1st§	93	69	.574	+3	Gene Mauch	2,807,360
1983‡	5th (tied)	70	92	.432	29	John McNamara	2,555,016
1984‡	2nd (tied)	81	81	.500	3	John McNamara	2,402,997
1985‡	2nd	90	72	.556	1	Gene Mauch	2,567,427
1986‡	1st§	92	70	.568	+5	Gene Mauch	2,655,872
1987‡	6th (tied)	75	87	.463	10	Gene Mauch	2,696,299
1988‡	4th	75	87	.463	29	Cookie Rojas	2,340,925
1989‡	3rd	91	71	.562	8	Doug Rader	2,647,291
1990‡	4th	80	82	.494	23	Doug Rader	2,555,688
1991‡	7th	81	81	.500	14	Doug Rader, Buck Rodgers	2,416,236
1992‡	5th (tied)	72	90	.444	24	Buck Rodgers	2,065,444
1993‡	5th (tied)	71	91	.438	23	Buck Rodgers	2,057,460
1994‡	4th	47	68	.409	5	Buck Rodgers, Marcel Lachemann	1,512,622
1995‡	2nd	78	67	.538	1	Marcel Lachemann	1,748,680
1996‡	4th	70	91	.435	19 1/2	Marcel Lachemann, John McNamara, Joe Maddon	1,820,521
1997	2nd	84	78	.519	6	Terry Collins	1,767,330
1998	2nd	85	77	.525	3	Terry Collins	2,519,210

*Games behind winner. †Los Angeles Angels through September 1, 1965. ‡California Angels through 1996. §Lost championship series. ∞First half 31-29; second half 20-30.

MANAGERIAL RECORDS

Terry Collins 169-155, Jim Fregosi 237-249, Dave Garcia 60-66, Marcel Lachemann 161-170, Joe Maddon 8-14, Gene Mauch 379-332, John McNamara 161-191, Lefty Phillips 222-225, Doug Rader 232-216, Del Rice 75-80, Bill Rigney 625-707, Buck Rodgers 179-223, Cookie Rojas 75-87, Norm Sherry 76-71, Dick Williams 147-194, Bobby Winkles 109-127.

BALTIMORE ORIOLES
YEARLY FINISHES

Year	Position	W	L	Pct.	*GB	Manager	Attendance
1901†	8th	48	89	.350	35 1/2	Hugh Duffy	139,034
1902‡	2nd	78	58	.574	5	Jimmy McAleer	272,283
1903‡	6th	65	74	.468	26 1/2	Jimmy McAleer	380,405
1904‡	6th	65	87	.428	29	Jimmy McAleer	318,108
1905‡	8th	54	99	.354	40 1/2	Jimmy McAleer	339,112
1906‡	5th	76	73	.510	16	Jimmy McAleer	389,157
1907‡	6th	69	83	.454	24	Jimmy McAleer	419,025
1908‡	4th	83	69	.546	6 1/2	Jimmy McAleer	618,947
1909‡	7th	61	89	.407	36	Jimmy McAleer	366,274
1910‡	8th	47	107	.305	57	John O'Connor	249,889
1911‡	8th	45	107	.296	56 1/2	Bobby Wallace	207,984

Year	Position	W	L	Pct.	*GB	Manager	Attendance
1912‡	7th	53	101	.344	53	Bobby Wallace, George Stovall	214,070
1913‡	8th	57	96	.373	39	George Stovall, Branch Rickey	250,330
1914‡	5th	71	82	.464	28 1/2	Branch Rickey	244,714
1915‡	6th	63	91	.409	39 1/2	Branch Rickey	150,358
1916‡	5th	79	75	.513	12	Fielder Jones	335,740
1917‡	7th	57	97	.370	43	Fielder Jones	210,486
1918‡	5th	58	64	.475	15	Fielder Jones, Jimmy Austin, Jimmy Burke	122,076
1919‡	5th	67	72	.482	20 1/2	Jimmy Burke	349,350
1920‡	4th	76	77	.497	21 1/2	Jimmy Burke	419,311
1921‡	3rd	81	73	.526	17 1/2	Lee Fohl	355,978
1922‡	2nd	93	61	.604	1	Lee Fohl	712,918
1923‡	5th	74	78	.487	24	Lee Fohl, Jimmy Austin	430,296
1924‡	4th	74	78	.487	17	George Sisler	533,349
1925‡	3rd	82	71	.536	15	George Sisler	462,898
1926‡	7th	62	92	.403	29	George Sisler	283,986
1927‡	7th	59	94	.336	50 1/2	Dan Howley	247,879
1928‡	3rd	82	72	.532	19	Dan Howley	339,497
1929‡	4th	79	73	.520	26	Dan Howley	280,697
1930‡	6th	64	90	.416	38	Bill Killefer	152,088
1931‡	5th	63	91	.409	45	Bill Killefer	179,126
1932‡	6th	63	91	.409	44	Bill Killefer	112,558
1933‡	8th	55	96	.364	43 1/2	Bill Killefer, Allen Sothoron, Rogers Hornsby	88,113
1934‡	6th	67	85	.441	33	Rogers Hornsby	115,305
1935‡	7th	65	87	.428	28 1/2	Rogers Hornsby	80,922
1936‡	7th	57	95	.375	44 1/2	Rogers Hornsby	93,267
1937‡	8th	46	108	.299	56	Rogers Hornsby, Jim Bottomley	123,121
1938‡	7th	55	97	.362	44	Gabby Street	130,417
1939‡	8th	43	111	.279	64 1/2	Fred Haney	109,159
1940‡	6th	67	87	.435	23	Fred Haney	239,591
1941‡	6th (tied)	70	84	.455	31	Fred Haney, Luke Sewell	176,240
1942‡	3rd	82	69	.543	19 1/2	Luke Sewell	255,617
1943‡	6th	72	80	.474	25	Luke Sewell	214,392
1944‡	1st	89	65	.578	+1	Luke Sewell	508,644
1945‡	3rd	81	70	.536	6	Luke Sewell, Zack Taylor	482,986
1946‡	7th	66	88	.429	38	Luke Sewell, Zack Taylor	526,435
1947‡	8th	59	95	.383	38	Muddy Ruel	320,474
1948‡	6th	59	94	.386	37	Zack Taylor	335,546
1949‡	7th	53	101	.344	44	Zack Taylor	270,936
1950‡	7th	58	96	.377	40	Zack Taylor	247,131
1951‡	8th	52	102	.338	46	Zack Taylor	293,790
1952‡	7th	64	90	.416	31	Rogers Hornsby, Marty Marion	518,796
1953‡	8th	54	100	.351	46 1/2	Marty Marion	297,238
1954	7th	54	100	.351	57	Jimmie Dykes	1,060,910
1955	7th	57	97	.370	39	Paul Richards	852,039
1956	6th	69	85	.448	28	Paul Richards	901,201
1957	5th	76	76	.500	21	Paul Richards	1,029,581
1958	6th	74	79	.484	17 1/2	Paul Richards	829,991
1959	6th	74	80	.481	20	Paul Richards	891,926
1960	2nd	89	65	.578	8	Paul Richards	1,187,849
1961	3rd	95	67	.586	14	Paul Richards, Luman Harris	951,089
1962	7th	77	85	.475	19	Billy Hitchcock	790,254
1963	4th	86	76	.531	18 1/2	Billy Hitchcock	774,343
1964	3rd	97	65	.599	2	Hank Bauer	1,116,215
1965	3rd	94	68	.580	8	Hank Bauer	781,649
1966	1st	97	63	.606	+9	Hank Bauer	1,203,366
1967	6th (tied)	76	85	.472	15 1/2	Hank Bauer	955,053
1968	2nd	91	71	.562	12	Hank Bauer, Earl Weaver	943,977

EAST DIVISION

Year	Position	W	L	Pct.	*GB	Manager	Attendance
1969	1st§	109	53	.673	+19	Earl Weaver	1,058,168
1970	1st§	108	54	.667	+15	Earl Weaver	1,057,069
1971	1st§	101	57	.639	+12	Earl Weaver	1,023,037
1972	3rd	80	74	.519	5	Earl Weaver	899,950
1973	1st∞	97	65	.599	+8	Earl Weaver	958,667
1974	1st∞	91	71	.562	+2	Earl Weaver	962,572
1975	2nd	90	69	.566	4 1/2	Earl Weaver	1,002,157
1976	2nd	88	74	.543	10 1/2	Earl Weaver	1,058,609
1977	2nd (tied)	97	64	.602	2 1/2	Earl Weaver	1,195,769
1978	4th	90	71	.559	9	Earl Weaver	1,051,724
1979	1st§	102	57	.642	+8	Earl Weaver	1,681,009
1980	2nd	100	62	.617	3	Earl Weaver	1,797,438
1981	2nd/4th	59	46	.562	▲	Earl Weaver	1,024,652
1982	2nd	94	68	.580	1	Earl Weaver	1,613,031
1983	1st§	98	64	.605	+6	Joe Altobelli	2,042,071
1984	5th	85	77	.525	19	Joe Altobelli	2,045,784
1985	4th	83	78	.516	16	Joe Altobelli, Earl Weaver	2,132,387

Year	Position	W	L	Pct.	*GB	Manager	Attendance
1986	7th	73	89	.451	22 1/2	Earl Weaver	1,973,176
1987	6th	67	95	.414	31	Cal Ripken Sr.	1,835,692
1988	7th	54	107	.335	34 1/2	Cal Ripken Sr., Frank Robinson	1,660,738
1989	2nd	87	75	.537	2	Frank Robinson	2,535,208
1990	5th	76	85	.472	11 1/2	Frank Robinson	2,415,189
1991	6th	67	95	.414	24	Frank Robinson, Johnny Oates	2,552,753
1992	3rd	89	73	.549	7	Johnny Oates	3,567,819
1993	3rd (tied)	85	77	.525	10	Johnny Oates	3,644,965
1994	2nd	63	49	.563	6 1/2	Johnny Oates	2,535,359
1995	3rd	71	73	.493	15	Phil Regan	3,098,475
1996	2nd◆■∞	88	74	.543	4	Dave Johnson	3,646,950
1997	1st◆∞	98	64	.605	+2	Dave Johnson	3,711,132
1998	4th	79	83	.488	35	Ray Miller	3,685,194

*Games behind winner. †Milwaukee Brewers. ‡St. Louis Browns. §Won championship series. ∞Lost championship series. ▲First half 31-23; second half 28-23. ◆Wild-card playoff qualifier. ■Won division series.

MANAGERIAL RECORDS

Joe Altobelli 212-167, Jimmy Austin 29-38, Hank Bauer 407-318, Jim Bottomley 21-56, Jimmy Burke 172-180, Hugh Duffy 48-89, Jimmie Dykes 54-100, Lee Fohl 226-183, Fred Haney 125-227, Lum Harris 17-10, Billy Hitchcock 163-161, Rogers Hornsby 255-381, Dan Howley 220-239, Dave Johnson 186-138, Fielder Jones 158-196, Bill Killefer 224-329, Marty Marion 96-161, Jimmy McAleer 551-632, Ray Miller 79-83, Johnny Oates 291-270, Jack O'Connor 47-107, Phil Regan 71-73, Paul Richards 517-539, Branch Rickey 139-179, Cal Ripken Sr. 67-101, Frank Robinson 230-285, Luke Sewell 432-410, George Sisler 218-241, Al Sothoron 2-6, George Stovall 91-158, Gabby Street 55-97, Zack Taylor 235-410, Bobby Wallace 57-134, Earl Weaver 1,481-1,060.

BOSTON RED SOX
YEARLY FINISHES

Year	Position	W	L	Pct.	*GB	Manager	Attendance
1901	2nd	79	57	.581	4	Jimmy Collins	289,448
1902	3rd	77	60	.562	6 1/2	Jimmy Collins	348,567
1903	1st	91	47	.659	+14 1/2	Jimmy Collins	379,338
1904	1st	95	59	.617	+1 1/2	Jimmy Collins	623,295
1905	4th	78	74	.513	16	Jimmy Collins	468,828
1906	8th	49	105	.318	45 1/2	Jimmy Collins, Chick Stahl	410,209
1907	7th	59	90	.396	32 1/2	George Huff, Bob Unglaub, Deacon McGuire	436,777
1908	5th	75	79	.487	15 1/2	Deacon McGuire, Fred Lake	473,048
1909	3rd	88	63	.583	9 1/2	Fred Lake	668,965
1910	4th	81	72	.529	22 1/2	Patsy Donovan	584,619
1911	5th	78	75	.510	24	Patsy Donovan	503,961
1912	1st	105	47	.691	+14	Jake Stahl	597,096
1913	4th	79	71	.527	15 1/2	Jake Stahl, Bill Carrigan	437,194
1914	2nd	91	62	.595	8 1/2	Bill Carrigan	481,359
1915	1st	101	50	.669	+2 1/2	Bill Carrigan	539,885
1916	1st	91	63	.591	+2	Bill Carrigan	496,397
1917	2nd	90	62	.592	9	Jack Barry	387,856
1918	1st	75	51	.595	+2 1/2	Ed Barrow	249,513
1919	6th	66	71	.482	20 1/2	Ed Barrow	417,291
1920	5th	72	81	.471	25 1/2	Ed Barrow	402,445
1921	5th	75	79	.487	23 1/2	Hugh Duffy	279,273
1922	8th	61	93	.396	33	Hugh Duffy	259,184
1923	8th	61	91	.401	37	Frank Chance	229,668
1924	7th	67	87	.435	25	Lee Fohl	448,556
1925	8th	47	105	.309	49 1/2	Lee Fohl	267,782
1926	8th	46	107	.301	44 1/2	Lee Fohl	285,155
1927	8th	51	103	.331	59	Bill Carrigan	305,275
1928	8th	57	96	.373	43 1/2	Bill Carrigan	396,920
1929	8th	58	96	.377	48	Bill Carrigan	394,620
1930	8th	52	102	.338	50	Heinie Wagner	444,045
1931	6th	62	90	.408	45	Shano Collins	350,975
1932	8th	43	111	.279	64	Shano Collins, Marty McManus	182,150
1933	7th	63	86	.423	34 1/2	Marty McManus	268,715
1934	4th	76	76	.500	24	Bucky Harris	610,640
1935	4th	78	75	.510	16	Joseph Cronin	558,568
1936	6th	74	80	.481	28 1/2	Joe Cronin	626,895
1937	5th	80	72	.526	21	Joe Cronin	559,659
1938	2nd■	88	61	.591	9 1/2	Joe Cronin	646,459
1939	2nd	89	62	.589	17	Joe Cronin	573,070
1940	4th (tied)	82	72	.532	8	Joe Cronin	716,234
1941	2nd	84	70	.545	17	Joe Cronin	718,497
1942	2nd	93	59	.612	9	Joe Cronin	730,340
1943	7th	68	84	.447	29	Joe Cronin	358,225
1944	4th	77	77	.500	12	Joe Cronin	506,975
1945	7th	71	83	.461	17 1/2	Joe Cronin	603,794
1946	1st	104	50	.675	+12	Joe Cronin	1,416,944
1947	3rd	83	71	.539	14	Joe Cronin	1,427,315

Year	Position	W	L	Pct.	*GB	Manager	Attendance
1948	2nd†	96	59	.619	1	Joe McCarthy	1,558,798
1949	2nd	96	58	.623	1	Joe McCarthy	1,596,650
1950	3rd	94	60	.610	4	Joe McCarthy, Steve O'Neill	1,344,080
1951	3rd	87	67	.565	11	Steve O'Neill	1,312,282
1952	6th	76	78	.494	19	Lou Boudreau	1,115,750
1953	4th	84	69	.549	16	Lou Boudreau	1,026,133
1954	4th	69	85	.448	42	Lou Boudreau	931,127
1955	4th	84	70	.545	12	Pinky Higgins	1,203,200
1956	4th	84	70	.545	13	Pinky Higgins	1,137,158
1957	3rd	82	72	.532	16	Pinky Higgins	1,181,087
1958	3rd	79	75	.513	13	Pinky Higgins	1,077,047
1959	5th	75	79	.487	19	Pinky Higgins, Billy Jurges	984,102
1960	7th	65	89	.422	32	Billy Jurges, Pinky Higgins	1,129,866
1961	6th	76	86	.469	33	Pinky Higgins	850,589
1962	8th	76	84	.475	19	Pinky Higgins	733,080
1963	7th	76	85	.472	28	Johnny Pesky	942,642
1964	8th	72	90	.444	27	Johnny Pesky, Billy Herman	883,276
1965	9th	62	100	.383	40	Billy Herman	652,201
1966	9th	72	90	.444	26	Billy Herman, Pete Runnels	811,172
1967	1st	92	70	.568	+1	Dick Williams	1,727,832
1968	4th	86	76	.531	17	Dick Williams	1,940,788

EAST DIVISION

Year	Position	W	L	Pct.	*GB	Manager	Attendance
1969	3rd	87	75	.537	22	Dick Williams, Eddie Popowski	1,833,246
1970	3rd	87	75	.537	21	Eddie Kasko	1,595,278
1971	3rd	85	77	.525	18	Eddie Kasko	1,678,732
1972	2nd	85	70	.548	$^{1}/_{2}$	Eddie Kasko	1,441,718
1973	2nd	89	73	.549	8	Eddie Kasko	1,481,002
1974	3rd	84	78	.519	7	Darrell Johnson	1,556,411
1975	1st‡	95	65	.594	+4 $^{1}/_{2}$	Darrell Johnson	1,748,587
1976	3rd	83	79	.512	15 $^{1}/_{2}$	Darrell Johnson, Don Zimmer	1,895,846
1977	2nd (tied)	97	64	.602	2 $^{1}/_{2}$	Don Zimmer	2,074,549
1978	2nd§	99	64	.607	1	Don Zimmer	2,320,643
1979	3rd	91	69	.569	11 $^{1}/_{2}$	Don Zimmer	2,353,114
1980	4th	83	77	.519	19	Don Zimmer, Johnny Pesky	1,956,092
1981	5th/2nd (tied)	59	49	.546	∞	Ralph Houk	1,060,379
1982	3rd	89	73	.549	6	Ralph Houk	1,950,124
1983	6th	78	84	.481	20	Ralph Houk	1,782,285
1984	4th	86	76	.531	18	Ralph Houk	1,661,618
1985	5th	81	81	.500	18 $^{1}/_{2}$	John McNamara	1,786,633
1986	1st‡	95	66	.590	+5 $^{1}/_{2}$	John McNamara	2,147,641
1987	5th	78	84	.481	20	John McNamara	2,231,551
1988	1st▲	89	73	.549	+1	John McNamara, Joe Morgan	2,464,851
1989	3rd	83	79	.512	6	Joe Morgan	2,510,012
1990	1st▲	88	74	.543	+2	Joe Morgan	2,528,986
1991	2nd (tied)	84	78	.519	7	Joe Morgan	2,562,435
1992	7th	73	89	.451	23	Butch Hobson	2,468,574
1993	5th	80	82	.494	15	Butch Hobson	2,422,021
1994	4th	54	61	.470	17	Butch Hobson	1,775,818
1995	1st◆	86	58	.597	+7	Kevin Kennedy	2,164,410
1996	3rd	85	77	.525	7	Kevin Kennedy	2,315,231
1997	4th	78	84	.481	20	Jimy Williams	2,226,136
1998	2nd◆	92	70	.568	22	Jimy Williams	2,343,947

*Games behind winner. †Lost pennant playoff. ‡Won championship series. §Lost division playoff. ∞First half 30-26; second half 29-23. ▲Lost championship series. ◆Lost division series.

MANAGERIAL RECORDS

Ed Barrow 213-203, Jack Barry 90-62, Lou Boudreau 229-232, Bill Carrigan 489-500, Frank Chance 61-91, Jimmy Collins 455-376, Shano Collins 73-134, Joe Cronin 1,071-916, Patsy Donovan 159-147, Hugh Duffy 136-172, Lee Fohl 160-299, Bucky Harris 76-76, Billy Herman 128-182, Pinky Higgins 560-556, Butch Hobson 207-232, Ralph Houk 312-282, George Huff 2-6, Darrell Johnson 220-188, Billy Jurges 59-63, Eddie Kasko 346-295, Kevin Kennedy 171-135, Fred Lake 110-80, Joe McCarthy 223-145, Deacon McGuire 98-123, Marty McManus 95-153, John McNamara 297-273, Joe Morgan 301-262, Steve O'Neill 150-99, Johnny Pesky 147-179, Eddie Popowski 5-4, Pete Runnels 8-8, Chick Stahl 14-26, Jake Stahl 144-88, Bob Unglaub 9-20, Heinie Wagner 52-102, Dick Williams 260-217, Jimy Williams 170-154, Don Zimmer 411-304.

CHICAGO WHITE SOX
YEARLY FINISHES

Year	Position	W	L	Pct.	*GB	Manager	Attendance
1901	1st	83	53	.610	+4	Clark Griffith	354,350
1902	4th	74	60	.552	8	Clark Griffith	337,898
1903	7th	60	77	.438	30 $^{1}/_{2}$	Nixey Callahan	286,183
1904	3rd	89	65	.578	6	Nixey Callahan, Fielder Jones	557,123

Year	Position	W	L	Pct.	*GB	Manager	Attendance
1905	2nd	92	60	.605	2	Fielder Jones	687,419
1906	1st	93	58	.616	+3	Fielder Jones	585,202
1907	3rd	87	64	.576	5 1/2	Fielder Jones	666,307
1908	3rd	88	64	.579	1 1/2	Fielder Jones	636,096
1909	4th	78	74	.513	20	Billy Sullivan	478,400
1910	6th	68	85	.444	35 1/2	Hugh Duffy	552,084
1911	4th	77	74	.510	24	Hugh Duffy	583,208
1912	4th	78	76	.506	28	Nixey Callahan	602,241
1913	5th	78	74	.513	17 1/2	Nixey Callahan	644,501
1914	6th (tied)	70	84	.455	30	Nixey Callahan	469,290
1915	3rd	93	61	.604	9 1/2	Pants Rowland	539,461
1916	2nd	89	65	.578	2	Pants Rowland	679,923
1917	1st	100	54	.649	+9	Pants Rowland	684,521
1918	6th	57	67	.460	17	Pants Rowland	195,081
1919	1st	88	52	.629	+3 1/2	Kid Gleason	627,186
1920	2nd	96	58	.623	2	Kid Gleason	833,492
1921	7th	62	92	.403	36 1/2	Kid Gleason	543,650
1922	5th	77	77	.500	17	Kid Gleason	602,860
1923	7th	69	85	.448	30	Kid Gleason	573,778
1924	8th	66	87	.431	25 1/2	Johnny Evers	606,658
1925	5th	79	75	.513	18 1/2	Eddie Collins	832,231
1926	5th	81	72	.529	9 1/2	Eddie Collins	710,339
1927	5th	70	83	.458	29 1/2	Ray Schalk	614,423
1928	5th	72	82	.468	29	Ray Schalk, Lena Blackburne	494,152
1929	7th	59	93	.388	46	Lena Blackburne	426,795
1930	7th	62	92	.403	40	Donie Bush	406,123
1931	8th	56	97	.366	51	Donie Bush	403,550
1932	7th	49	102	.325	56 1/2	Lew Fonseca	233,198
1933	6th	67	83	.447	31	Lew Fonseca	397,789
1934	8th	53	99	.349	47	Lew Fonseca, Jimmie Dykes	236,559
1935	5th	74	78	.487	19 1/2	Jimmie Dykes	470,281
1936	3rd	81	70	.536	20	Jimmie Dykes	440,810
1937	3rd	86	68	.558	16	Jimmie Dykes	589,245
1938	6th	65	83	.439	32	Jimmie Dykes	338,278
1939	4th	85	69	.552	22 1/2	Jimmie Dykes	594,104
1940	4th (tied)	82	72	.532	8	Jimmie Dykes	660,336
1941	3rd	77	77	.500	24	Jimmie Dykes	677,077
1942	6th	66	82	.446	34	Jimmie Dykes	425,734
1943	4th	82	72	.532	16	Jimmie Dykes	508,962
1944	7th	71	83	.461	18	Jimmie Dykes	563,539
1945	6th	71	78	.477	15	Jimmie Dykes	657,981
1946	5th	74	80	.481	30	Jimmie Dykes, Ted Lyons	983,403
1947	6th	70	84	.455	27	Ted Lyons	876,948
1948	8th	51	101	.336	44 1/2	Ted Lyons	777,844
1949	6th	63	91	.409	34	Jack Onslow	937,151
1950	6th	60	94	.390	38	Jack Onslow, Red Corriden	781,330
1951	4th	81	73	.526	17	Paul Richards	1,328,234
1952	3rd	81	73	.526	14	Paul Richards	1,231,675
1953	3rd	89	65	.578	11 1/2	Paul Richards	1,191,353
1954	3rd	94	60	.610	17	Paul Richards, Marty Marion	1,231,629
1955	3rd	91	63	.591	5	Marty Marion	1,175,684
1956	3rd	85	69	.552	12	Marty Marion	1,000,090
1957	2nd	90	64	.584	8	Al Lopez	1,135,668
1958	2nd	82	72	.532	10	Al Lopez	797,451
1959	1st	94	60	.610	+5	Al Lopez	1,423,144
1960	3rd	87	67	.565	10	Al Lopez	1,644,460
1961	4th	86	76	.531	23	Al Lopez	1,146,019
1962	5th	85	77	.525	11	Al Lopez	1,131,562
1963	2nd	94	68	.580	10 1/2	Al Lopez	1,158,848
1964	2nd	98	64	.605	1	Al Lopez	1,250,053
1965	2nd	95	67	.586	7	Al Lopez	1,130,519
1966	4th	83	79	.512	15	Eddie Stanky	990,016
1967	4th	89	73	.549	3	Eddie Stanky	985,634
1968	8th (tied)	67	95	.414	36	Eddie Stanky, Al Lopez	803,775

WEST DIVISION

Year	Position	W	L	Pct.	*GB	Manager	Attendance
1969	5th	68	94	.420	29	Al Lopez, Don Gutteridge	589,546
1970	6th	56	106	.346	42	Don Gutteridge, Chuck Tanner	495,355
1971	3rd	79	83	.488	22 1/2	Chuck Tanner	833,891
1972	2nd	87	67	.565	5 1/2	Chuck Tanner	1,177,318
1973	5th	77	85	.475	17	Chuck Tanner	1,302,527
1974	4th	80	80	.500	9	Chuck Tanner	1,149,596
1975	5th	75	86	.466	22 1/2	Chuck Tanner	750,802
1976	6th	64	97	.398	25 1/2	Paul Richards	914,945
1977	3rd	90	72	.556	12	Bob Lemon	1,657,135

Year	Position	W	L	Pct.	*GB	Manager	Attendance
1978	5th	71	90	.441	20½	Bob Lemon, Larry Doby	1,491,100
1979	5th	73	87	.456	14	Don Kessinger, Tony La Russa	1,280,702
1980	5th	70	90	.438	26	Tony La Russa	1,200,365
1981	3rd/6th	54	52	.509	†	Tony La Russa	946,651
1982	3rd	87	75	.537	6	Tony La Russa	1,567,787
1983	1st‡	99	63	.611	+20	Tony La Russa	2,132,821
1984	5th (tied)	74	88	.457	10	Tony La Russa	2,136,988
1985	3rd	85	77	.525	6	Tony La Russa	1,669,888
1986	5th	72	90	.444	20	Tony La Russa, Jim Fregosi	1,424,313
1987	5th	77	85	.475	8	Jim Fregosi	1,208,060
1988	5th	71	90	.441	32½	Jim Fregosi	1,115,749
1989	7th	69	92	.429	29½	Jeff Torborg	1,045,651
1990	2nd	94	68	.580	9	Jeff Torborg	2,002,357
1991	2nd	87	75	.537	8	Jeff Torborg	2,934,154
1992	3rd	86	76	.531	10	Gene Lamont	2,681,156
1993	1st‡	94	68	.580	+8	Gene Lamont	2,581,091

CENTRAL DIVISION

Year	Position	W	L	Pct.	*GB	Manager	Attendance
1994	1st	67	46	.593	+1	Gene Lamont	1,697,398
1995	3rd	68	76	.472	32	Gene Lamont, Terry Bevington	1,609,773
1996	2nd	85	77	.525	14½	Terry Bevington	1,676,403
1997	2nd	80	81	.497	6	Terry Bevington	1,864,782
1998	2nd	80	82	.494	9	Jerry Manuel	1,391,146

*Games behind winner. †First half 31-22; second half 23-30. ‡Lost championship series.

MANAGERIAL RECORDS

Terry Bevington 222-214, Lena Blackburne 99-133, Donie Bush 118-189, Nixey Callahan 309-329, Eddie Collins 160-147, Red Corriden 52-72, Larry Doby 37-50, Hugh Duffy 145-159, Jimmie Dykes 899-940, Johnny Evers 66-87, Lew Fonseca 120-196, Jim Fregosi 193-226, Kid Gleason 392-364, Clark Griffith 157-113, Don Gutteridge 109-172, Fielder Jones 426-293, Don Kessinger 46-60, Tony La Russa 522-510, Gene Lamont 258-210, Bob Lemon 124-112, Al Lopez 840-650, Ted Lyons 185-245, Jerry Manuel 80-82, Marty Marion 179-138, Jack Onslow 71-133, Paul Richards 406-362, Pants Rowland 339-247, Ray Schalk 102-125, Eddie Stanky 206-197, Billy Sullivan 78-74, Chuck Tanner 401-414, Jeff Torborg 250-235.

CLEVELAND INDIANS

YEARLY FINISHES

Year	Position	W	L	Pct.	*GB	Manager	Attendance
1901	7th	54	82	.397	29	James McAleer	131,380
1902	5th	69	67	.507	14	Bill Armour	275,395
1903	3rd	77	63	.550	15	Bill Armour	311,280
1904	4th	86	65	.570	7½	Bill Armour	264,749
1905	5th	76	78	.494	19	Nap Lajoie	316,306
1906	3rd	89	64	.582	5	Nap Lajoie	325,733
1907	4th	85	67	.559	8	Nap Lajoie	382,046
1908	2nd	90	64	.584	½	Nap Lajoie	422,242
1909	6th	71	82	.464	27½	Nap Lajoie, Deacon McGuire	354,627
1910	5th	71	81	.467	32	Deacon McGuire	293,456
1911	3rd	80	73	.523	22	Deacon McGuire, George Stovall	406,296
1912	5th	75	78	.490	30½	Harry Davis, J.L. Birmingham	336,844
1913	3rd	86	66	.566	9½	J.L. Birmingham	541,000
1914	8th	51	102	.333	48½	J.L. Birmingham	185,997
1915	7th	57	95	.375	44½	J.L. Birmingham, Lee Fohl	159,285
1916	6th	77	77	.500	14	Lee Fohl	492,106
1917	3rd	88	66	.571	12	Lee Fohl	477,298
1918	2nd	73	54	.575	2½	Lee Fohl	295,515
1919	2nd	84	55	.604	3½	Lee Fohl, Tris Speaker	538,135
1920	1st	98	56	.636	+2	Tris Speaker	912,832
1921	2nd	94	60	.610	4½	Tris Speaker	748,705
1922	4th	78	76	.507	16	Tris Speaker	528,145
1923	3rd	82	71	.536	16½	Tris Speaker	558,856
1924	6th	67	86	.438	24½	Tris Speaker	481,905
1925	6th	70	84	.455	27½	Tris Speaker	419,005
1926	2nd	88	66	.571	3	Tris Speaker	627,426
1927	6th	66	87	.431	43½	Jack McAllister	373,138
1928	7th	62	92	.403	39	Roger Peckinpaugh	375,907
1929	3rd	81	71	.533	24	Roger Peckinpaugh	536,210
1930	4th	81	73	.536	21	Roger Peckinpaugh	528,657
1931	4th	78	76	.506	30	Roger Peckinpaugh	483,027
1932	4th	87	65	.572	19	Roger Peckinpaugh	468,953
1933	4th	75	76	.497	23½	Roger Peckinpaugh, Walter Johnson	387,936
1934	3rd	85	69	.552	16	Walter Johnson	391,338

Year	Position	W	L	Pct.	*GB	Manager	Attendance
1935	3rd	82	71	.536	12	Walter Johnson, Steve O'Neill	397,615
1936	5th	80	74	.519	22 1/2	Steve O'Neill	500,391
1937	4th	83	71	.539	19	Steve O'Neill	564,849
1938	3rd	86	66	.566	13	Ossie Vitt	652,006
1939	3rd	87	67	.565	20 1/2	Ossie Vitt	563,926
1940	2nd	89	65	.578	1	Ossie Vitt	902,576
1941	4th (tied)	75	79	.487	26	Roger Peckinpaugh	745,948
1942	4th	75	79	.487	28	Lou Boudreau	459,447
1943	3rd	82	71	.536	15 1/2	Lou Boudreau	438,894
1944	5th (tied)	72	82	.468	17	Lou Boudreau	475,272
1945	5th	73	72	.503	11	Lou Boudreau	558,182
1946	6th	68	86	.442	36	Lou Boudreau	1,057,289
1947	4th	80	74	.519	17	Lou Boudreau	1,521,978
1948	1st†	97	58	.626	+1	Lou Boudreau	2,620,627
1949	3rd	89	65	.578	8	Lou Boudreau	2,233,771
1950	4th	92	62	.597	6	Lou Boudreau	1,727,464
1951	2nd	93	61	.604	5	Al Lopez	1,704,984
1952	2nd	93	61	.604	2	Al Lopez	1,444,607
1953	2nd	92	62	.597	8 1/2	Al Lopez	1,069,176
1954	1st	111	43	.721	+8	Al Lopez	1,335,472
1955	2nd	93	61	.604	3	Al Lopez	1,221,780
1956	2nd	88	66	.571	9	Al Lopez	865,467
1957	6th	76	77	.497	21 1/2	Kerby Farrell	722,256
1958	4th	77	76	.503	14 1/2	Bobby Bragan, Joe Gordon	663,805
1959	2nd	89	65	.578	5	Joe Gordon	1,497,976
1960	4th	76	78	.494	21	Joe Gordon, Jimmie Dykes	950,985
1961	5th	78	83	.484	30 1/2	Jimmie Dykes	725,547
1962	6th	80	82	.494	16	Mel McGaha	716,076
1963	5th (tied)	79	83	.488	25 1/2	Birdie Tebbetts	562,507
1964	6th (tied)	79	83	.488	20	Birdie Tebbetts	653,293
1965	5th	87	75	.537	15	Birdie Tebbetts	934,786
1966	5th	81	81	.500	17	Birdie Tebbetts, George Strickland	903,359
1967	8th	75	87	.463	17	Joe Adcock	662,980
1968	3rd	86	75	.534	16 1/2	Alvin Dark	857,994

EAST DIVISION

Year	Position	W	L	Pct.	*GB	Manager	Attendance
1969	6th	62	99	.385	46 1/2	Alvin Dark	619,970
1970	5th	76	86	.469	32	Alvin Dark	729,752
1971	6th	60	102	.370	43	Alvin Dark, John Lipon	591,361
1972	5th	72	84	.462	14	Ken Aspromonte	626,354
1973	6th	71	91	.438	26	Ken Aspromonte	615,107
1974	4th	77	85	.475	14	Ken Aspromonte	1,114,262
1975	4th	79	80	.497	15 1/2	Frank Robinson	977,039
1976	4th	81	78	.509	16	Frank Robinson	948,776
1977	5th	71	90	.441	28 1/2	Frank Robinson, Jeff Torborg	900,365
1978	6th	69	90	.434	29	Jeff Torborg	800,584
1979	6th	81	80	.503	22	Jeff Torborg, Dave Garcia	1,011,644
1980	6th	79	81	.494	23	Dave Garcia	1,033,827
1981	6th/5th	52	51	.504	‡	Dave Garcia	661,395
1982	6th (tied)	78	84	.481	17	Dave Garcia	1,044,021
1983	7th	70	92	.432	28	Mike Ferraro, Pat Corrales	768,941
1984	6th	75	87	.463	29	Pat Corrales	734,079
1985	7th	60	102	.370	39 1/2	Pat Corrales	655,181
1986	5th	84	78	.519	11 1/2	Pat Corrales	1,471,805
1987	7th	61	101	.377	37	Pat Corrales, Doc Edwards	1,077,898
1988	6th	78	84	.481	11	Doc Edwards	1,411,610
1989	6th	73	89	.451	16	Doc Edwards, John Hart	1,285,542
1990	4th	77	85	.475	11	John McNamara	1,225,240
1991	7th	57	105	.352	34	John McNamara, Mike Hargrove	1,051,863
1992	4th (tied)	76	86	.469	20	Mike Hargrove	1,224,274
1993	6th	76	86	.469	19	Mike Hargrove	2,177,908

CENTRAL DIVISION

Year	Position	W	L	Pct.	*GB	Manager	Attendance
1994	2nd	66	47	.584	1	Mike Hargrove	1,995,174
1995	1st§∞	100	44	.694	+30	Mike Hargrove	2,842,745
1996	1st▲	99	62	.615	+14 1/2	Mike Hargrove	3,318,174
1997	1st§∞	86	75	.534	+6	Mike Hargrove	3,404,750
1998	1st§◆	89	73	.549	+9	Mike Hargrove	3,467,299

*Games behind winner. †Won pennant playoff. ‡First half 26-24; second half 26-27. §Won division series. ∞Won championship series. ▲Lost division series. ◆Lost championship series.

MANAGERIAL RECORDS

Joe Adcock 75-87, Bill Armour 232-195, Ken Aspromonte 220-260, Joe Birmingham 170-191, Lou Boudreau 728-649, Bobby Bragan 31-36, Pat Corrales 280-355, Alvin Dark 266-321, Harry Davis 54-71, Jimmie Dykes 103-115, Doc Edwards 173-207, Kerby Farrell 76-77, Mike Ferraro 40-60, Lee Fohl 327-310, Dave Garcia 247-244, Joe Gordon 184-151, Mike Hargrove 624-526, John Hart 8-11, Walter Johnson 179-168, Nap Lajoie 377-309, Johnny Lipon 18-41, Al Lopez 570-354, Jimmy McAleer 54-82, Jack McCallister 66-87, Mel McGaha 80-82, Deacon McGuire 91-117, John McNamara 102-137, Steve O'Neill 199-168, Roger Peckinpaugh 490-481, Frank Robinson 186-189, Tris Speaker 617-520, George Stovall 74-62, George Strickland 15-24, Birdie Tebbetts 269-298, Jeff Torborg 157-201, Oscar Vitt 262-198.

DETROIT TIGERS
YEARLY FINISHES

Year	Position	W	L	Pct.	*GB	Manager	Attendance
1901	3rd	74	61	.548	8 1/2	George Stallings	259,430
1902	7th	52	83	.385	30 1/2	Frank Dwyer	189,469
1903	5th	65	71	.478	25	Ed Barrow	224,523
1904	7th	62	90	.408	32	Ed Barrow, Bobby Lowe	177,796
1905	3rd	79	74	.516	15 1/2	Bill Armour	193,384
1906	6th	71	78	.477	21	Bill Armour	174,043
1907	1st	92	58	.613	+1 1/2	Hughey Jennings	297,079
1908	1st	90	63	.588	+ 1/2	Hughey Jennings	436,199
1909	1st	98	54	.645	+3 1/2	Hughey Jennings	490,490
1910	3rd	86	68	.558	18	Hughey Jennings	391,288
1911	2nd	89	65	.578	13 1/2	Hughey Jennings	484,988
1912	6th	69	84	.451	36 1/2	Hughey Jennings	402,870
1913	6th	66	87	.431	30	Hughey Jennings	398,502
1914	4th	80	73	.523	19 1/2	Hughey Jennings	416,225
1915	2nd	100	54	.649	2 1/2	Hughey Jennings	476,105
1916	3rd	87	67	.565	4	Hughey Jennings	616,772
1917	4th	78	75	.510	21 1/2	Hughey Jennings	457,289
1918	7th	55	71	.437	20	Hughey Jennings	203,719
1919	4th	80	60	.571	8	Hughey Jennings	643,805
1920	7th	61	93	.396	37	Hughey Jennings	579,650
1921	6th	71	82	.464	27	Ty Cobb	661,527
1922	3rd	79	75	.513	15	Ty Cobb	861,206
1923	2nd	83	71	.539	16	Ty Cobb	911,377
1924	3rd	86	68	.558	6	Ty Cobb	1,015,136
1925	4th	81	73	.526	16 1/2	Ty Cobb	820,766
1926	6th	79	75	.513	12	Ty Cobb	711,914
1927	4th	82	71	.536	27 1/2	George Moriarty	773,716
1928	6th	68	86	.442	33	George Moriarty	474,323
1929	6th	70	84	.455	36	Bucky Harris	869,318
1930	5th	75	79	.487	27	Bucky Harris	649,450
1931	7th	61	93	.396	47	Bucky Harris	434,056
1932	5th	76	75	.503	29 1/2	Bucky Harris	397,157
1933	5th	75	79	.487	25	Del Baker	320,972
1934	1st	101	53	.656	+7	Mickey Cochrane	919,161
1935	1st	93	58	.616	+3	Mickey Cochrane	1,034,929
1936	2nd	83	71	.539	19 1/2	Mickey Cochrane	875,948
1937	2nd	89	65	.578	13	Mickey Cochrane	1,072,276
1938	4th	84	70	.545	16	Mickey Cochrane, Del Baker	799,557
1939	5th	81	73	.526	26 1/2	Del Baker	836,279
1940	1st	90	64	.584	+1	Del Baker	1,112,693
1941	4th (tied)	75	79	.487	26	Del Baker	684,915
1942	5th	73	81	.474	30	Del Baker	580,087
1943	5th	78	76	.506	20	Steve O'Neill	606,287
1944	2nd	88	66	.571	1	Steve O'Neill	923,176
1945	1st	88	65	.575	+1 1/2	Steve O'Neill	1,280,341
1946	2nd	92	62	.597	12	Steve O'Neill	1,722,590
1947	2nd	85	69	.552	12	Steve O'Neill	1,398,093
1948	5th	78	76	.506	18 1/2	Steve O'Neill	1,743,035
1949	4th	87	67	.565	10	Red Rolfe	1,821,204
1950	2nd	95	59	.617	3	Red Rolfe	1,951,474
1951	5th	73	81	.474	25	Red Rolfe	1,132,641
1952	8th	50	104	.325	45	Red Rolfe, Fred Hutchinson	1,026,846
1953	6th	60	94	.390	40 1/2	Fred Hutchinson	884,658
1954	5th	68	86	.442	43	Fred Hutchinson	1,079,847
1955	5th	79	75	.513	17	Bucky Harris	1,181,838
1956	5th	82	72	.532	15	Bucky Harris	1,051,182
1957	4th	78	76	.506	20	Jack Tighe	1,272,346
1958	5th	77	77	.500	15	Jack Tighe, Bill Norman	1,098,924

Year	Position	W	L	Pct.	*GB	Manager	Attendance
1959	4th	76	78	.494	18	Bill Norman, Jimmie Dykes	1,221,221
1960	6th	71	83	.461	26	Jimmie Dykes, Billy Hitchcock, Joe Gordon	1,167,669
1961	2nd	101	61	.623	8	Bob Scheffing	1,600,710
1962	4th	85	76	.528	10 1/2	Bob Scheffing	1,207,881
1963	5th (tied)	79	83	.488	25 1/2	Bob Scheffing, Charlie Dressen	821,952
1964	4th	85	77	.525	14	Charlie Dressen	816,139
1965	4th	89	73	.549	13	Charlie Dressen, Bob Swift	1,029,645
1966	3rd	88	74	.543	10	Charlie Dressen, Bob Swift, Frank Skaff	1,124,293
1967	2nd	91	71	.562	1	Mayo Smith	1,447,143
1968	1st	103	59	.636	+12	Mayo Smith	2,031,847

EAST DIVISION

Year	Position	W	L	Pct.	*GB	Manager	Attendance
1969	2nd	90	72	.556	19	Mayo Smith	1,577,481
1970	4th	79	83	.488	29	Mayo Smith	1,501,293
1971	2nd	91	71	.562	12	Billy Martin	1,591,073
1972	1st†	86	70	.551	+ 1/2	Billy Martin	1,892,386
1973	3rd	85	77	.525	12	Billy Martin, Joe Schultz	1,724,146
1974	6th	72	90	.444	19	Ralph Houk	1,243,080
1975	6th	57	102	.358	37 1/2	Ralph Houk	1,058,836
1976	5th	74	87	.460	24	Ralph Houk	1,467,020
1977	4th	74	88	.457	26	Ralph Houk	1,359,856
1978	5th	86	76	.531	13 1/2	Ralph Houk	1,714,893
1979	5th	85	76	.528	18	Les Moss, Dick Tracewski, Sparky Anderson	1,630,929
1980	5th	84	78	.519	19	Sparky Anderson	1,785,293
1981	4th/2nd (tied)	60	49	.550	‡	Sparky Anderson	1,149,144
1982	4th	83	79	.512	12	Sparky Anderson	1,636,058
1983	2nd	92	70	.568	6	Sparky Anderson	1,829,636
1984	1st§	104	58	.642	+15	Sparky Anderson	2,704,794
1985	3rd	84	77	.522	15	Sparky Anderson	2,286,609
1986	3rd	87	75	.537	8 1/2	Sparky Anderson	1,899,437
1987	1st†	98	64	.605	+2	Sparky Anderson	2,061,830
1988	2nd	88	74	.543	1	Sparky Anderson	2,081,162
1989	7th	59	103	.364	30	Sparky Anderson	1,543,656
1990	3rd	79	83	.488	9	Sparky Anderson	1,495,785
1991	2nd	84	78	.519	7	Sparky Anderson	1,641,661
1992	6th	75	87	.463	21	Sparky Anderson	1,423,963
1993	3rd (tied)	85	77	.525	10	Sparky Anderson	1,971,421
1994	5th	53	62	.461	18	Sparky Anderson	1,184,783
1995	4th	60	84	.417	26	Sparky Anderson	1,180,979
1996	5th	53	109	.327	39	Buddy Bell	1,168,610
1997	3rd	79	83	.488	19	Buddy Bell	1,365,157

CENTRAL DIVISION

Year	Position	W	L	Pct.	*GB	Manager	Attendance
1998	5th	65	97	.401	24	Buddy Bell, Larry Parrish	1,409,391

*Games behind winner. †Lost championship series. ‡First half 31-26; second half 29-23. §Won championship series.

MANAGERIAL RECORDS

Sparky Anderson 1,431-1,248, Bill Armour 150-152, Del Baker 392-336, Ed Barrow 97-117, Buddy Bell 184-277, Ty Cobb 479-444, Mickey Cochrane 379-278, Chuck Dressen 221-189, Frank Dwyer 52-83, Jimmie Dykes 118-115, Joe Gordon 26-31, Bucky Harris 516-557, Ralph Houk 366-443, Fred Hutchinson 155-235, Hugh Jennings 1,131-972, Bobby Lowe 30-44, Billy Martin 248-204, George Moriarty 150-157, Les Moss 27-26, Bill Norman 58-64, Steve O'Neill 509-414, Larry Parrish 13-12, Red Rolfe 278-256, Bob Scheffing 210-173, Joe Schultz 14-14, Frank Skaff 40-39, Mayo Smith 363-285, George Stallings 74-61, Bob Swift 56-43, Jack Tighe 99-104.

KANSAS CITY ROYALS
YEARLY FINISHES

WEST DIVISION

Year	Position	W	L	Pct.	*GB	Manager	Attendance
1969	4th	69	93	.429	28	Joe Gordon	902,414
1970	4th (tied)	65	97	.401	33	Charlie Metro, Bob Lemon	693,047
1971	2nd	85	76	.528	16	Bob Lemon	910,784
1972	4th	76	78	.494	16 1/2	Bob Lemon	707,656
1973	2nd	88	74	.543	6	Jack McKeon	1,345,341
1974	5th	77	85	.475	13	Jack McKeon	1,173,292
1975	2nd	91	71	.562	7	Jack McKeon, Whitey Herzog	1,151,836
1976	1st†	90	72	.556	+2 1/2	Whitey Herzog	1,680,265
1977	1st†	102	60	.630	+8	Whitey Herzog	1,852,603
1978	1st†	92	70	.568	+5	Whitey Herzog	2,255,493
1979	2nd	85	77	.525	3	Whitey Herzog	2,261,845
1980	1st‡	97	65	.599	+14	Jim Frey	2,288,714
1981	5th/1st∞	50	53	.485	§	Jim Frey, Dick Howser	1,279,403

HISTORY *Team by team*

Year	Position	W	L	Pct.	*GB	Manager	Attendance
1982	2nd	90	72	.556	3	Dick Howser	2,284,464
1983	2nd	79	83	.488	20	Dick Howser	1,963,875
1984	1st‡	84	78	.519	+3	Dick Howser	1,810,018
1985	1st‡	91	71	.562	+1	Dick Howser	2,162,717
1986	3rd (tied)	76	86	.469	16	Dick Howser, Mike Ferraro	2,320,794
1987	2nd	83	79	.512	2	Billy Gardner, John Wathan	2,392,471
1988	3rd	84	77	.522	19 1/2	John Wathan	2,350,181
1989	2nd	92	70	.568	7	John Wathan	2,477,700
1990	6th	75	86	.466	27 1/2	John Wathan	2,244,956
1991	6th	82	80	.506	13	John Wathan, Hal McRae	2,161,537
1992	5th (tied)	72	90	.444	24	Hal McRae	1,867,689
1993	3rd	84	78	.519	10	Hal McRae	1,934,578

CENTRAL DIVISION

Year	Position	W	L	Pct.	*GB	Manager	Attendance
1994	3rd	64	51	.557	4	Hal McRae	1,400,494
1995	2nd	70	74	.486	30	Bob Boone	1,233,530
1996	5th	75	86	.466	24	Bob Boone	1,435,997
1997	5th	67	94	.416	19	Bob Boone, Tony Muser	1,517,638
1998	3rd	72	89	.447	16 1/2	Tony Muser	1,494,875

*Games behind winner. †Lost championship series. ‡Won championship series. §First half 20-30; second half 30-23. ∞Lost division series.

MANAGERIAL RECORDS

Bob Boone 181-206, Mike Ferraro 36-38, Jim Frey 127-105, Billy Gardner 62-64, Joe Gordon 69-93, Whitey Herzog 410-304, Dick Howser 404-365, Bob Lemon 207-218, Jack McKeon 215-205, Hal McRae 286-277, Charlie Metro 19-33, Tony Muser 103-137, John Wathan 288-270.

MINNESOTA TWINS
YEARLY FINISHES

Year	Position	W	L	Pct.	*GB	Manager	Attendance
1901†	6th	61	72	.459	20 1/2	Jimmy Manning	161,661
1902†	6th	61	75	.449	22	Tom Loftus	188,158
1903†	8th	43	94	.314	47 1/2	Tom Loftus	128,878
1904†	8th	38	113	.251	55 1/2	Patsy Donovan	131,744
1905†	7th	64	87	.421	29 1/2	Jake Stahl	252,027
1906†	7th	55	95	.367	37 1/2	Jake Stahl	129,903
1907†	8th	49	102	.325	43 1/2	Joe Cantillon	221,929
1908†	7th	67	85	.441	22 1/2	Joe Cantillon	264,252
1909†	8th	42	110	.276	56	Joe Cantillon	205,199
1910†	7th	66	85	.437	36 1/2	Jimmy McAleer	254,591
1911†	7th	64	90	.416	38 1/2	Jimmy McAleer	244,884
1912†	2nd	91	61	.599	14	Clark Griffith	350,663
1913†	2nd	90	64	.584	6 1/2	Clark Griffith	325,831
1914†	3rd	81	73	.526	19	Clark Griffith	243,888
1915†	4th	85	68	.556	17	Clark Griffith	167,332
1916†	7th	76	77	.497	14 1/2	Clark Griffith	177,265
1917†	5th	74	79	.484	25 1/2	Clark Griffith	89,682
1918†	3rd	72	56	.563	4	Clark Griffith	182,122
1919†	7th	56	84	.400	32	Clark Griffith	234,096
1920†	6th	68	84	.447	29	Clark Griffith	359,260
1921†	4th	80	73	.523	18	George McBride	456,069
1922†	6th	69	85	.448	25	Clyde Milan	458,552
1923†	4th	75	78	.490	23 1/2	Donie Bush	357,406
1924†	1st	92	62	.597	+2	Bucky Harris	534,310
1925†	1st	96	55	.636	+8 1/2	Bucky Harris	817,199
1926†	4th	81	69	.540	8	Bucky Harris	551,580
1927†	3rd	85	69	.552	25	Bucky Harris	528,976
1928†	4th	75	79	.487	26	Bucky Harris	378,501
1929†	5th	71	81	.467	34	Walter Johnson	355,506
1930†	2nd	94	60	.610	8	Walter Johnson	614,474
1931†	3rd	92	62	.597	16	Walter Johnson	492,657
1932†	3rd	93	61	.604	14	Walter Johnson	371,396
1933†	1st	99	53	.651	+7	Joe Cronin	437,533
1934†	7th	66	86	.434	34	Joe Cronin	330,074
1935†	6th	67	86	.438	27	Bucky Harris	255,011
1936†	4th	82	71	.536	20	Bucky Harris	379,525
1937†	6th	73	80	.477	28 1/2	Bucky Harris	397,799
1938†	5th	75	76	.497	23 1/2	Bucky Harris	522,694
1939†	6th	65	87	.428	41 1/2	Bucky Harris	339,257

Year	Position	W	L	Pct.	*GB	Manager	Attendance
1940†	7th	64	90	.416	26	Bucky Harris	381,241
1941†	6th (tied)	70	84	.455	31	Bucky Harris	415,663
1942†	7th	62	89	.411	39½	Bucky Harris	403,493
1943†	2nd	84	69	.549	13½	Ossie Bluege	574,694
1944†	8th	64	90	.416	25	Ossie Bluege	525,235
1945†	2nd	87	67	.565	1½	Ossie Bluege	652,660
1946†	4th	76	78	.494	28	Ossie Bluege	1,027,216
1947†	7th	64	90	.416	33	Ossie Bluege	850,758
1948†	7th	56	97	.366	40	Joe Kuhel	795,254
1949†	8th	50	104	.325	47	Joe Kuhel	770,745
1950†	5th	67	87	.435	31	Bucky Harris	699,697
1951†	7th	62	92	.403	36	Bucky Harris	695,167
1952†	5th	78	76	.506	17	Bucky Harris	699,457
1953†	5th	76	76	.500	23½	Bucky Harris	595,594
1954†	6th	66	88	.429	45	Bucky Harris	503,542
1955†	8th	53	101	.344	43	Chuck Dressen	425,238
1956†	7th	59	95	.383	38	Chuck Dressen	431,647
1957†	8th	55	99	.357	43	Chuck Dressen, Cookie Lavagetto	457,079
1958†	8th	61	93	.396	31	Cookie Lavagetto	475,288
1959†	8th	63	91	.409	31	Cookie Lavagetto	615,372
1960†	5th	73	81	.474	24	Cookie Lavagetto	743,404
1961	7th	70	90	.438	38	Cookie Lavagetto, Sam Mele	1,256,723
1962	2nd	91	71	.562	5	Sam Mele	1,433,116
1963	3rd	91	70	.565	13	Sam Mele	1,406,652
1964	6th (tied)	79	83	.488	20	Sam Mele	1,207,514
1965	1st	102	60	.630	+7	Sam Mele	1,463,258
1966	2nd	89	73	.549	9	Sam Mele	1,259,374
1967	2nd (tied)	91	71	.562	1	Sam Mele, Cal Ermer	1,483,547
1968	7th	79	83	.488	24	Cal Ermer	1,143,257

WEST DIVISION

Year	Position	W	L	Pct.	*GB	Manager	Attendance
1969	1st‡	97	65	.599	+9	Billy Martin	1,349,328
1970	1st‡	98	64	.605	+9	Bill Rigney	1,261,887
1971	5th	74	86	.463	26½	Bill Rigney	940,858
1972	3rd	77	77	.500	15½	Bill Rigney, Frank Quilici	797,901
1973	3rd	81	81	.500	13	Frank Quilici	907,499
1974	3rd	82	80	.506	8	Frank Quilici	662,401
1975	4th	76	83	.478	20½	Frank Quilici	737,156
1976	3rd	85	77	.525	5	Gene Mauch	715,394
1977	4th	84	77	.522	17½	Gene Mauch	1,162,727
1978	4th	73	89	.451	19	Gene Mauch	787,878
1979	4th	82	80	.506	6	Gene Mauch	1,070,521
1980	3rd	77	84	.478	19½	Gene Mauch, Johnny Goryl	769,206
1981	7th/4th	41	68	.376	§	Johnny Goryl, Billy Gardner	469,090
1982	7th	60	102	.370	33	Billy Gardner	921,186
1983	5th (tied)	70	92	.432	29	Billy Gardner	858,939
1984	2nd (tied)	81	81	.500	3	Billy Gardner	1,598,422
1985	4th (tied)	77	85	.475	14	Billy Gardner, Ray Miller	1,651,814
1986	6th	71	91	.438	21	Ray Miller, Tom Kelly	1,255,453
1987	1st∞	85	77	.525	+2	Tom Kelly	2,081,976
1988	2nd	91	71	.562	13	Tom Kelly	3,030,672
1989	5th	80	82	.494	19	Tom Kelly	2,277,438
1990	7th	74	88	.457	29	Tom Kelly	1,751,584
1991	1st∞	95	67	.586	+8	Tom Kelly	2,293,842
1992	2nd	90	72	.556	6	Tom Kelly	2,482,428
1993	5th (tied)	71	91	.438	23	Tom Kelly	2,048,673

CENTRAL DIVISION

Year	Position	W	L	Pct.	*GB	Manager	Attendance
1994	4th	53	60	.469	14	Tom Kelly	1,398,565
1995	5th	56	88	.389	44	Tom Kelly	1,057,667
1996	4th	78	84	.481	21½	Tom Kelly	1,437,352
1997	4th	68	94	.420	18½	Tom Kelly	1,411,064
1998	4th	70	92	.432	19	Tom Kelly	1,165,980

*Games behind winner. †Washington Senators (original club). ‡Lost championship series. §First half 17-39; second half 24-29. ∞Won championship series.

MANAGERIAL RECORDS

Ossie Bluege 375-394, Donie Bush 75-78, Joe Cantillon 158-297, Joe Cronin 165-139, Patsy Donovan 38-113, Chuck Dressen 116-212, Cal Ermer 145-129, Billy Gardner 268-353, Johnny Goryl 34-38, Clark Griffith 693-646, Bucky Harris 1,336-1,416, Walter Johnson 350-264, Tom Kelly 923-977, Joe Kuhel 106-201, Cookie Lavagetto 271-384, Tom Loftus 104-169, Jimmy Manning 61-72, Billy Martin 97-65, Gene Mauch 378-394, Jimmy McAleer 130-175, George McBride 80-73, Sam Mele 524-436, Clyde Milan 69-85, Ray Miller 109-130, Frank Quilici 280-287, Bill Rigney 208-184, Jake Stahl 119-182.

Year	Position	W	L	Pct.	*GB	Manager	Attendance
1901†	5th	68	65	.511	13 1/2	John McGraw	141,952
1902	8th	50	88	.362	34	John McGraw, Wilbert Robinson	174,606
1903	4th	72	62	.537	17	Clark Griffith	211,808
1904	2nd	92	59	.609	1 1/2	Clark Griffith	438,919
1905	6th	71	78	.477	21 1/2	Clark Griffith	309,100
1906	2nd	90	61	.596	3	Clark Griffith	434,709
1907	5th	70	78	.473	21	Clark Griffith	350,020
1908	8th	51	103	.331	39 1/2	Clark Griffith, Kid Elberfeld	305,500
1909	5th	74	77	.490	23 1/2	George Stallings	501,000
1910	2nd	88	63	.583	14 1/2	George Stallings, Hal Chase	355,857
1911	6th	76	76	.500	25 1/2	Hal Chase	302,444
1912	8th	50	102	.329	55	Harry Wolverton	242,194
1913	7th	57	94	.377	38	Frank Chance	357,551
1914	6th (tied)	70	84	.455	30	Frank Chance, Roger Peckinpaugh	359,477
1915	5th	69	83	.454	32 1/2	Bill Donovan	256,035
1916	4th	80	74	.519	11	Bill Donovan	469,211
1917	6th	71	82	.464	28 1/2	Bill Donovan	330,294
1918	4th	60	63	.488	13 1/2	Miller Huggins	282,047
1919	3rd	80	59	.576	7 1/2	Miller Huggins	619,164
1920	3rd	95	59	.617	3	Miller Huggins	1,289,422
1921	1st	98	55	.641	+4 1/2	Miller Huggins	1,230,696
1922	1st	94	60	.610	+1	Miller Huggins	1,026,134
1923	1st	98	54	.645	+16	Miller Huggins	1,007,066
1924	2nd	89	63	.586	2	Miller Huggins	1,053,533
1925	7th	69	85	.448	30	Miller Huggins	697,267
1926	1st	91	63	.591	+3	Miller Huggins	1,027,095
1927	1st	110	44	.714	+19	Miller Huggins	1,164,015
1928	1st	101	53	.656	+2 1/2	Miller Huggins	1,072,132
1929	2nd	88	66	.571	18	Miller Huggins, Art Fletcher	960,148
1930	3rd	86	68	.558	16	Bob Shawkey	1,169,233
1931	2nd	94	59	.614	13 1/2	Joe McCarthy	912,437
1932	1st	107	47	.695	+13	Joe McCarthy	962,320
1933	2nd	91	59	.607	7	Joe McCarthy	728,014
1934	2nd	94	60	.610	7	Joe McCarthy	854,682
1935	2nd	89	60	.597	3	Joe McCarthy	657,508
1936	1st	102	51	.667	+19 1/2	Joe McCarthy	976,913
1937	1st	102	52	.662	+13	Joe McCarthy	998,148
1938	1st	99	53	.651	+9 1/2	Joe McCarthy	970,916
1939	1st	106	45	.702	+17	Joe McCarthy	859,785
1940	3rd	88	66	.571	2	Joe McCarthy	988,975
1941	1st	101	53	.656	+17	Joe McCarthy	964,722
1942	1st	103	51	.669	+9	Joe McCarthy	988,251
1943	1st	98	56	.636	+13 1/2	Joe McCarthy	645,006
1944	3rd	83	71	.539	6	Joe McCarthy	822,864
1945	4th	81	71	.533	6 1/2	Joe McCarthy	881,846
1946	3rd	87	67	.565	17	Joe McCarthy, Bill Dickey, Johnny Neun	2,265,512
1947	1st	97	57	.630	+12	Bucky Harris	2,178,937
1948	3rd	94	60	.610	2 1/2	Bucky Harris	2,373,901
1949	1st	97	57	.630	+1	Casey Stengel	2,281,676
1950	1st	98	56	.636	+3	Casey Stengel	2,081,380
1951	1st	98	56	.636	+5	Casey Stengel	1,950,107
1952	1st	95	59	.617	+2	Casey Stengel	1,629,665
1953	1st	99	52	.656	+8 1/2	Casey Stengel	1,537,811
1954	2nd	103	51	.669	8	Casey Stengel	1,475,171
1955	1st	96	58	.623	+3	Casey Stengel	1,490,138
1956	1st	97	57	.630	+9	Casey Stengel	1,491,784
1957	1st	98	56	.636	+8	Casey Stengel	1,497,134
1958	1st	92	62	.597	+10	Casey Stengel	1,428,438
1959	3rd	79	75	.513	15	Casey Stengel	1,552,030
1960	1st	97	57	.630	+8	Casey Stengel	1,627,349
1961	1st	109	53	.673	+8	Ralph Houk	1,747,725
1962	1st	96	66	.593	+5	Ralph Houk	1,493,574
1963	1st	104	57	.646	+10 1/2	Ralph Houk	1,308,920
1964	1st	99	63	.611	+1	Yogi Berra	1,305,638
1965	6th	77	85	.475	25	Johnny Keane	1,213,552
1966	10th	70	89	.440	26 1/2	Johnny Keane, Ralph Houk	1,124,648
1967	9th	72	90	.444	20	Ralph Houk	1,259,514
1968	5th	83	79	.512	20	Ralph Houk	1,185,666

EAST DIVISION

Year	Position	W	L	Pct.	*GB	Manager	Attendance
1969	5th	80	81	.497	28 1/2	Ralph Houk	1,067,996
1970	2nd	93	69	.574	15	Ralph Houk	1,136,879

Year	Position	W	L	Pct.	*GB	Manager	Attendance
1971	4th	82	80	.506	21	Ralph Houk	1,070,771
1972	4th	79	76	.510	6½	Ralph Houk	966,328
1973	4th	80	82	.494	17	Ralph Houk	1,262,103
1974	2nd	89	73	.549	2	Bill Virdon	1,273,075
1975	3rd	83	77	.519	12	Bill Virdon, Billy Martin	1,288,048
1976	1st‡	97	62	.610	+10½	Billy Martin	2,012,434
1977	1st‡	100	62	.617	+2½	Billy Martin	2,103,092
1978	1st§‡	100	63	.613	+1	Billy Martin, Bob Lemon	2,335,871
1979	4th	89	71	.556	13½	Bob Lemon, Billy Martin	2,537,765
1980	1st∞	103	59	.636	+3	Dick Howser	2,627,417
1981	1st/6th◆‡	59	48	.551	▲	Gene Michael, Bob Lemon	1,614,533
1982	5th	79	83	.488	16	Bob Lemon, Gene Michael, Clyde King	2,041,219
1983	3rd	91	71	.562	7	Billy Martin	2,257,976
1984	3rd	87	75	.537	17	Yogi Berra	1,821,815
1985	2nd	97	64	.602	2	Yogi Berra, Billy Martin	2,214,587
1986	2nd	90	72	.556	5½	Lou Piniella	2,268,030
1987	4th	89	73	.549	9	Lou Piniella	2,427,672
1988	5th	85	76	.528	3½	Billy Martin, Lou Piniella	2,633,701
1989	5th	74	87	.460	14½	Dallas Green, Bucky Dent	2,170,485
1990	7th	67	95	.414	21	Bucky Dent, Stump Merrill	2,006,436
1991	5th	71	91	.438	20	Stump Merrill	1,863,733
1992	4th (tied)	76	86	.469	20	Buck Showalter	1,748,733
1993	2nd	88	74	.543	7	Buck Showalter	2,416,965
1994	1st	70	43	.619	+6½	Buck Showalter	1,675,556
1995	2nd◆▼	79	65	.549	7	Buck Showalter	1,705,263
1996	1st■‡	92	70	.568	+4	Joe Torre	2,250,877
1997	2nd◆▼	96	66	.593	2	Joe Torre	2,580,325
1998	1st■‡	114	48	.704	+22	Joe Torre	2,949,734

*Games behind winner. †Baltimore Orioles. ‡Won championship series. §Won pennant playoff. ∞Lost championship series. ▲First half 34-22; second half 25-26. ◆Wild-card playoff qualifier. ■Won division series. ▼Lost division series.

MANAGERIAL RECORDS

Yogi Berra 192-148, Frank Chance 117-168, Hal Chase 86-80, Bucky Dent 36-53, Bill Dickey 57-48, Bill Donovan 220-239, Kid Elberfeld 27-71, Art Fletcher 6-5, Dallas Green 56-65, Clark Griffith 419-370, Bucky Harris 191-117, Ralph Houk 944-806, Dick Howser 103-59, Miller Huggins 1,067-719, Johnny Keane 81-101, Clyde King 29-33, Bob Lemon 99-73, Billy Martin 501-385, Joe McCarthy 1,460-867, John McGraw 94-96, Stump Merrill 120-155, Gene Michael 92-76, Johnny Neun 8-6, Roger Peckinpaugh 10-10, Lou Piniella 224-193, Wilbert Robinson 24-57, Bob Shawkey 86-68, Buck Showalter 311-268, George Stallings 152-136, Casey Stengel 1,149-696, Joe Torre 302-184, Bill Virdon 142-124, Harry Wolverton 50-102.

OAKLAND ATHLETICS
YEARLY FINISHES

Year	Position	W	L	Pct.	*GB	Manager	Attendance
1901†	4th	74	62	.544	9	Connie Mack	206,329
1902†	1st	83	53	.610	+5	Connie Mack	442,473
1903†	2nd	75	60	.556	14½	Connie Mack	420,078
1904†	5th	81	70	.536	12½	Connie Mack	512,294
1905†	1st	92	56	.622	+2	Connie Mack	554,576
1906†	4th	78	67	.538	12	Connie Mack	489,129
1907†	2nd	88	57	.607	1½	Connie Mack	625,581
1908†	6th	68	85	.444	22	Connie Mack	455,062
1909†	2nd	95	58	.621	3½	Connie Mack	674,915
1910†	1st	102	48	.680	+14½	Connie Mack	588,905
1911†	1st	101	50	.669	+13½	Connie Mack	605,749
1912†	3rd	90	62	.592	15	Connie Mack	517,653
1913†	1st	96	57	.627	+6½	Connie Mack	571,896
1914†	1st	99	53	.651	+8½	Connie Mack	346,641
1915†	8th	43	109	.283	58½	Connie Mack	146,223
1916†	8th	36	117	.235	54½	Connie Mack	184,471
1917†	8th	55	98	.359	44½	Connie Mack	221,432
1918†	8th	52	76	.406	24	Connie Mack	177,926
1919†	8th	36	104	.257	52	Connie Mack	225,209
1920†	8th	48	106	.312	50	Connie Mack	287,888
1921†	8th	53	100	.346	45	Connie Mack	344,430
1922†	7th	65	89	.422	29	Connie Mack	425,356
1923†	6th	69	83	.454	29	Connie Mack	534,122
1924†	5th	71	81	.467	20	Connie Mack	531,992
1925†	2nd	88	64	.579	8½	Connie Mack	869,703
1926†	3rd	83	67	.553	6	Connie Mack	714,308
1927†	2nd	91	63	.591	19	Connie Mack	605,529
1928†	2nd	98	55	.641	2½	Connie Mack	689,756
1929†	1st	104	46	.693	+18	Connie Mack	839,176
1930†	1st	102	52	.662	+8	Connie Mack	721,663
1931†	1st	107	45	.704	+13½	Connie Mack	627,464
1932†	2nd	94	60	.610	13	Connie Mack	405,500

Year	Position	W	L	Pct.	*GB	Manager	Attendance
1933†	3rd	79	72	.523	19 1/2	Connie Mack	297,138
1934†	5th	68	82	.453	31	Connie Mack	305,847
1935†	8th	58	91	.389	34	Connie Mack	233,173
1936†	8th	53	100	.346	49	Connie Mack	285,173
1937†	7th	54	97	.358	46 1/2	Connie Mack	430,733
1938†	8th	53	99	.349	46	Connie Mack	385,357
1939†	7th	55	97	.362	51 1/2	Connie Mack	395,022
1940†	8th	54	100	.351	36	Connie Mack	432,145
1941†	8th	64	90	.416	37	Connie Mack	528,894
1942†	8th	55	99	.357	48	Connie Mack	423,487
1943†	8th	49	105	.318	49	Connie Mack	376,735
1944†	5th (tied)	72	82	.468	17	Connie Mack	505,322
1945†	8th	52	98	.347	34 1/2	Connie Mack	462,631
1946†	8th	49	105	.318	55	Connie Mack	621,793
1947†	5th	78	76	.506	19	Connie Mack	911,566
1948†	4th	84	70	.545	12 1/2	Connie Mack	945,076
1949†	5th	81	73	.526	16	Connie Mack	816,514
1950†	8th	52	102	.338	46	Connie Mack	309,805
1951†	6th	70	84	.455	28	Jimmie Dykes	465,469
1952†	4th	79	75	.513	16	Jimmie Dykes	627,100
1953†	7th	59	95	.383	41 1/2	Jimmie Dykes	362,113
1954†	8th	51	103	.331	60	Ed Joost	304,666
1955‡	6th	63	91	.409	33	Lou Boudreau	1,393,054
1956‡	8th	52	102	.338	45	Lou Boudreau	1,015,154
1957‡	7th	59	94	.386	38 1/2	Lou Boudreau, Harry Craft	901,067
1958‡	7th	73	81	.474	19	Harry Craft	925,090
1959‡	7th	66	88	.429	28	Harry Craft	963,683
1960‡	8th	58	96	.377	39	Bob Elliot	774,944
1961‡	9th (tied)	61	100	.379	47 1/2	Joe Gordon, Hank Bauer	683,817
1962‡	9th	72	90	.444	24	Hank Bauer	635,675
1963‡	8th	73	89	.451	31 1/2	Ed Lopat	762,364
1964‡	10th	57	105	.352	42	Ed Lopat, Mel McGaha	642,478
1965‡	10th	59	103	.364	43	Mel McGaha, Haywood Sullivan	528,344
1966‡	7th	74	86	.463	23	Alvin Dark	773,929
1967‡	10th	62	99	.385	29 1/2	Alvin Dark, Luke Appling	726,639
1968	6th	82	80	.506	21	Bob Kennedy	837,466

WEST DIVISION

Year	Position	W	L	Pct.	*GB	Manager	Attendance
1969	2nd	88	74	.543	9	Hank Bauer, John McNamara	778,232
1970	2nd	89	73	.549	9	John McNamara	778,355
1971	1st§	101	60	.627	+16	Dick Williams	914,993
1972	1st∞	93	62	.600	+5 1/2	Dick Williams	921,323
1973	1st∞	94	68	.580	+6	Dick Williams	1,000,763
1974	1st∞	90	72	.556	+5	Alvin Dark	845,693
1975	1st§	98	64	.605	+7	Alvin Dark	1,075,518
1976	2nd	87	74	.540	2 1/2	Chuck Tanner	780,593
1977	7th	63	98	.391	38 1/2	Jack McKeon, Bobby Winkles	495,599
1978	6th	69	93	.426	23	Bobby Winkles, Jack McKeon	526,999
1979	7th	54	108	.333	34	Jim Marshall	306,763
1980	2nd	83	79	.512	14	Billy Martin	842,259
1981	1st/2nd◆§	64	45	.587	▲	Billy Martin	1,304,054
1982	5th	68	94	.420	25	Billy Martin	1,735,489
1983	4th	74	88	.457	25	Steve Boros	1,294,941
1984	4th	77	85	.475	7	Steve Boros, Jackie Moore	1,353,281
1985	4th (tied)	77	85	.475	14	Jackie Moore	1,334,599
1986	3rd (tied)	76	86	.469	16	Jackie Moore, Tony La Russa	1,314,646
1987	3rd	81	81	.500	4	Tony La Russa	1,678,921
1988	1st∞	104	58	.642	+13	Tony La Russa	2,287,335
1989	1st∞	99	63	.611	+7	Tony La Russa	2,667,225
1990	1st∞	103	59	.636	+9	Tony La Russa	2,900,217
1991	4th	84	78	.519	11	Tony La Russa	2,713,493
1992	1st§	96	66	.593	+6	Tony La Russa	2,494,160
1993	7th	68	94	.420	26	Tony La Russa	2,035,025
1994	2nd	51	63	.447	1	Tony La Russa	1,242,692
1995	4th	67	77	.465	11 1/2	Tony La Russa	1,174,310
1996	3rd	78	84	.481	12	Art Howe	1,148,380
1997	4th	65	97	.401	25	Art Howe	1,264,218
1998	4th	74	88	.457	14	Art Howe	1,232,339

*Games behind winner. †Philadelphia Athletics. ‡Kansas City Athletics. §Lost championship series. ∞Won championship series. ▲First half 37-23; second half 27-22. ◆Won division series.

MANAGERIAL RECORDS

Luke Appling 10-30, Hank Bauer 187-226, Steve Boros 94-112, Lou Boudreau 151-260, Harry Craft 162-196, Alvin Dark 314-291, Jimmie Dykes 198-254, Bob Elliott 58-96, Joe Gordon 26-33, Art Howe 217-269, Eddie Joost 51-103, Bob Kennedy 82-80, Tony La Russa 695-614, Eddie Lopat 90-124, Connie Mack 3,582-3,814, Jim Marshall 54-108, Billy Martin 215-218, Mel McGaha 45-91, Jack McKeon 71-105, John McNamara 97-78, Jackie Moore 163-190, Haywood Sullivan 54-82, Chuck Tanner 87-74, Dick Williams 288-190, Bobby Winkles 61-86.

SEATTLE MARINERS
YEARLY FINISHES

WEST DIVISION

Year	Position	W	L	Pct.	*GB	Manager	Attendance
1977	6th	64	98	.395	38	Darrell Johnson	1,338,511
1978	7th	56	104	.350	35	Darrell Johnson	877,440
1979	6th	67	95	.414	21	Darrell Johnson	844,447
1980	7th	59	103	.364	38	Darrell Johnson, Maury Wills	836,204
1981	6th/5th	44	65	.404	†	Maury Wills, Rene Lachemann	636,276
1982	4th	76	86	.469	17	Rene Lachemann	1,070,404
1983	7th	60	102	.370	39	Rene Lachemann, Del Crandall	813,537
1984	5th (tied)	74	88	.457	10	Del Crandall, Chuck Cottier	870,372
1985	6th	74	88	.457	17	Chuck Cottier	1,128,696
1986	7th	67	95	.414	25	Chuck Cottier, Marty Martinez, Dick Williams	1,029,045
1987	4th	78	84	.481	7	Dick Williams	1,134,255
1988	7th	68	93	.422	35 1/2	Dick Williams, Jim Snyder	1,022,398
1989	6th	73	89	.451	26	Jim Lefebvre	1,298,443
1990	5th	77	85	.475	26	Jim Lefebvre	1,509,727
1991	5th	83	79	.512	12	Jim Lefebvre	2,147,905
1992	7th	64	98	.395	32	Bill Plummer	1,651,398
1993	4th	82	80	.506	12	Lou Piniella	2,051,853
1994	3rd	49	63	.438	2	Lou Piniella	1,104,206
1995	1st‡§	79	66	.545	+1	Lou Piniella	1,643,203
1996	2nd	85	76	.528	4 1/2	Lou Piniella	2,723,850
1997	1st∞	90	72	.556	+6	Lou Piniella	3,192,237
1998	3rd	76	85	.472	11 1/2	Lou Piniella	2,644,166

*Games behind winner. †First half 21-36; second half 23-29. ‡Won division series. §Lost championship series. ∞Lost division series.

MANAGERIAL RECORDS

Chuck Cottier 98-120, Del Crandall 93-141, Darrell Johnson 226-362, Rene Lachemann 140-180, Jim Lefebvre 233-253, Lou Piniella 461-442, Bill Plummer 64-98, Jimmy Snyder 45-60, Dick Williams 159-192, Maury Wills 26-56.

TAMPA BAY DEVIL RAYS
YEARLY FINISHES

EAST DIVISION

Year	Position	W	L	Pct.	*GB	Manager	Attendance
1998	5th	63	99	.389	51	Larry Rothschild	2,506,023

*Games behind winner.

MANAGERIAL RECORDS

Larry Rothschild 63-99.

TEXAS RANGERS
YEARLY FINISHES

Year	Position	W	L	Pct.	*GB	Manager	Attendance
1961†	9th (tied)	61	100	.379	47 1/2	Mickey Vernon	597,287
1962†	10th	60	101	.373	35 1/2	Mickey Vernon	729,775
1963†	10th	56	106	.346	48 1/2	Mickey Vernon, Gil Hodges	535,604
1964†	9th	62	100	.383	37	Gil Hodges	600,106
1965†	8th	70	92	.432	32	Gil Hodges	560,083
1966†	8th	71	88	.447	25 1/2	Gil Hodges	576,260
1967†	6th (tied)	76	85	.472	15 1/2	Gil Hodges	770,863
1968†	10th	65	96	.404	37 1/2	Jim Lemon	546,661

EAST DIVISION

Year	Position	W	L	Pct.	*GB	Manager	Attendance
1969†	4th	86	76	.531	23	Ted Williams	918,106
1970†	6th	70	92	.432	38	Ted Williams	824,789
1971†	5th	63	96	.396	38 1/2	Ted Williams	655,156

WEST DIVISION

Year	Position	W	L	Pct.	*GB	Manager	Attendance
1972	6th	54	100	.351	38 1/2	Ted Williams	662,974
1973	6th	57	105	.352	37	Whitey Herzog, Del Wilber, Billy Martin	686,085
1974	2nd	84	76	.525	5	Billy Martin	1,193,902
1975	3rd	79	83	.488	19	Billy Martin, Frank Lucchesi	1,127,924

Year	Position	W	L	Pct.	*GB	Manager	Attendance
1976	4th (tied)...............76		86	.469	14	Frank Lucchesi...1,164,982
1977	2nd.........................94		68	.580	8	Frank Lucchesi, Eddie Stanky, Connie Ryan, Billy Hunter 1,250,722
1978	2nd (tied)...............87		75	.537	5	Billy Hunter, Pat Corrales...1,447,963
1979	3rd.........................83		79	.512	5	Pat Corrales..1,519,671
1980	4th 76		85	.472	20 1/2	Pat Corrales..1,198,175
1981	2nd/3rd.................57		48	.543	‡	Don Zimmer..850,076
1982	6th.........................64		98	.395	29	Don Zimmer, Darrell Johnson.........................1,154,432
1983	3rd.........................77		85	.475	22	Doug Rader...1,363,469
1984	7th.........................69		92	.429	14 1/2	Doug Rader...1,102,471
1985	7th.........................62		99	.385	28 1/2	Doug Rader, Bobby Valentine.........................1,112,497
1986	2nd.........................87		75	.537	5	Bobby Valentine...1,692,002
1987	6th (tied)...............75		87	.463	10	Bobby Valentine...1,763,053
1988	6th.........................70		91	.435	33 1/2	Bobby Valentine...1,581,901
1989	4th.........................83		79	.512	16	Bobby Valentine...2,043,993
1990	3rd.........................83		79	.512	20	Bobby Valentine...2,057,911
1991	3rd.........................85		77	.525	10	Bobby Valentine...2,297,720
1992	4th.........................77		85	.475	19	Bobby Valentine, Toby Harrah.......................2,198,231
1993	2nd.........................86		76	.531	8	Kevin Kennedy...2,244,616
1994	1st.........................52		62	.456	+1	Kevin Kennedy...2,503,198
1995	3rd§.......................74		70	.514	4 1/2	Johnny Oates..1,985,910
1996	1st§.......................90		72	.556	+4 1/2	Johnny Oates..2,889,020
1997	3rd.........................77		85	.475	13	Johnny Oates..2,945,228
1998	1st§.......................88		74	.543	+3	Johnny Oates..2,927,409

*Games behind winner. †Washington Senators (second club). ‡First half 33-22; second half 24-26. §Lost division series.

MANAGERIAL RECORDS

Pat Corrales 160-164, Toby Harrah 32-44, Whitey Herzog 47-91, Gil Hodges 321-444, Billy Hunter 146-108, Darrell Johnson 26-40, Kevin Kennedy 138-138, Jim Lemon 65-96, Frank Lucchesi 142-149, Billy Martin 137-141, Johnny Oates 329-301, Doug Rader 155-200, Connie Ryan 2-4, Eddie Stanky 1-0, Bobby Valentine 581-605, Mickey Vernon 135-227, Del Wilber 1-0, Ted Williams 273-364, Don Zimmer 95-106.

TORONTO BLUE JAYS
YEARLY FINISHES

EAST DIVISION

Year	Position	W	L	Pct.	*GB	Manager	Attendance
1977	7th 54		107	.335	45 1/2	Roy Hartsfield...1,701,052
1978	7th 59		102	.366	40	Roy Hartsfield...1,562,585
1979	7th 53		109	.327	50 1/2	Roy Hartsfield...1,431,651
1980	7th 67		95	.414	36	Bobby Mattick...1,400,327
1981	7th/7th..................37		69	.349	†	Bobby Mattick...755,083
1982	6th (tied)...............78		84	.481	17	Bobby Cox..1,275,978
1983	4th.........................89		73	.549	9	Bobby Cox..1,930,415
1984	2nd.........................89		73	.549	15	Bobby Cox..2,110,009
1985	1st‡.......................99		62	.615	+2	Bobby Cox..2,468,925
1986	4th.........................86		76	.531	9 1/2	Jimy Williams..2,455,477
1987	2nd.........................96		66	.593	2	Jimy Williams..2,778,429
1988	3rd (tied)...............87		75	.537	2	Jimy Williams..2,595,175
1989	1st‡.......................89		73	.549	+2	Jimy Williams, Cito Gaston...........................3,375,883
1990	2nd.........................86		76	.531	2	Cito Gaston...3,885,284
1991	1st‡.......................91		71	.562	+7	Cito Gaston...4,001,527
1992	1st§.......................96		66	.593	+4	Cito Gaston...4,028,318
1993	1st§.......................95		67	.586	+7	Cito Gaston...4,057,947
1994	3rd.........................55		60	.478	16	Cito Gaston...2,907,933
1995	5th.........................56		88	.389	30	Cito Gaston...2,826,483
1996	4th.........................74		88	.457	18	Cito Gaston...2,559,573
1997	5th.........................76		86	.469	22	Cito Gaston, Mel Queen 2,589,297
1998	3rd 88		74	.543	26	Tim Johnson..2,454,183

*Games behind winner. †First half 16-42; second half 21-27. ‡Lost championship series. §Won championship series.

MANAGERIAL RECORDS

Bobby Cox 355-292, Cito Gaston 702-650, Roy Hartsfield 166-318, Tim Johnson 88-74, Bobby Mattick 104-164, Mel Queen 4-1, Jimy Williams 281-241.

NATIONAL LEAGUE

ARIZONA DIAMONDBACKS
YEARLY FINISHES

WEST DIVISION

Year	Position	W	L	Pct.	*GB	Manager	Attendance
1998	5th	65	97	.401	33	Buck Showalter	3,600,412

*Games behind winner.

MANAGERIAL RECORDS

Buck Showalter 65-97.

ATLANTA BRAVES
YEARLY FINISHES

Year	Position	W	L	Pct.	*GB	Manager	Attendance
1901†	5th	69	69	.500	20 1/2	Frank Selee	146,502
1902†	3rd	73	64	.533	29	Al Buckenberger	116,960
1903†	6th	58	80	.420	32	Al Buckenberger	143,155
1904†	7th	55	98	.359	51	Al Buckenberger	140,694
1905†	7th	51	103	.331	54 1/2	Fred Tenney	150,003
1906†	8th	49	102	.325	66 1/2	Fred Tenney	143,280
1907†	7th	58	90	.392	47	Fred Tenney	203,221
1908†	6th	63	91	.409	36	Joe Kelley	253,750
1909†	8th	45	108	.294	65 1/2	Frank Bowerman, Harry Smith	195,188
1910†	8th	53	100	.346	50 1/2	Fred Lake	149,027
1911†	8th	44	107	.291	54	Fred Tenney	116,000
1912†	8th	52	101	.340	52	Johnny Kling	121,000
1913†	5th	69	82	.457	31 1/2	George Stallings	208,000
1914†	1st	94	59	.614	+10 1/2	George Stallings	382,913
1915†	2nd	83	69	.546	7	George Stallings	376,283
1916†	3rd	89	63	.586	4	George Stallings	313,495
1917†	6th	72	81	.471	25 1/2	George Stallings	174,253
1918†	7th	53	71	.427	28 1/2	George Stallings	84,938
1919†	6th	57	82	.410	38 1/2	George Stallings	167,401
1920†	7th	62	90	.408	30	George Stallings	162,483
1921†	4th	79	74	.516	15	Fred Mitchell	318,627
1922†	8th	53	100	.346	39 1/2	Fred Mitchell	167,965
1923†	7th	54	100	.351	41 1/2	Fred Mitchell	227,802
1924†	8th	53	100	.346	40	Dave Bancroft	117,478
1925†	5th	70	83	.458	25	Dave Bancroft	313,528
1926†	7th	66	86	.434	22	Dave Bancroft	303,598
1927†	7th	60	94	.390	34	Dave Bancroft	288,685
1928†	7th	50	103	.327	44 1/2	Jack Slattery, Rogers Hornsby	227,001
1929†	8th	56	98	.364	43	Emil Fuchs	372,351
1930†	6th	70	84	.455	22	Bill McKechnie	464,835
1931†	7th	64	90	.416	37	Bill McKechnie	515,005
1932†	5th	77	77	.500	13	Bill McKechnie	507,606
1933†	4th	83	71	.539	9	Bill McKechnie	517,803
1934†	4th	78	73	.517	16	Bill McKechnie	303,205
1935†	8th	38	115	.248	61 1/2	Bill McKechnie	232,754
1936†	6th	71	83	.461	21	Bill McKechnie	340,585
1937†	5th	79	73	.520	16	Bill McKechnie	385,339
1938†	5th	77	75	.507	12	Casey Stengel	341,149
1939†	7th	63	88	.417	32 1/2	Casey Stengel	285,994
1940†	7th	65	87	.428	34 1/2	Casey Stengel	241,616
1941†	7th	62	92	.403	38	Casey Stengel	263,680
1942†	7th	59	89	.399	44	Casey Stengel	285,332
1943†	6th	68	85	.444	36 1/2	Casey Stengel	271,289
1944†	6th	65	89	.422	40	Bob Coleman	208,691
1945†	6th	67	85	.441	30	Bob Coleman, Del Bissonette	374,178
1946†	4th	81	72	.529	15 1/2	Billy Southworth	969,673
1947†	3rd	86	68	.558	8	Billy Southworth	1,277,361
1948†	1st	91	62	.595	+6 1/2	Billy Southworth	1,455,439
1949†	4th	75	79	.487	22	Billy Southworth	1,081,795
1950†	4th	83	71	.539	8	Billy Southworth	944,391
1951†	4th	76	78	.494	20 1/2	Billy Southworth, Tommy Holmes	487,475
1952†	7th	64	89	.418	32	Tommy Holmes, Charlie Grimm	281,278
1953‡	2nd	92	62	.597	13	Charlie Grimm	1,826,397

Year	Position	W	L	Pct.	*GB	Manager	Attendance
1954‡	3rd	89	65	.578	8	Charlie Grimm	2,131,388
1955‡	2nd	85	69	.552	13½	Charlie Grimm	2,005,836
1956‡	2nd	92	62	.597	1	Charlie Grimm, Fred Haney	2,046,331
1957‡	1st	95	59	.617	+8	Fred Haney	2,215,404
1958‡	1st	92	62	.597	+8	Fred Haney	1,971,101
1959‡	2nd§	86	70	.551	2	Fred Haney	1,749,112
1960‡	2nd	88	66	.571	7	Chuck Dressen	1,497,799
1961‡	4th	83	71	.539	10	Chuck Dressen, Birdie Tebbetts	1,101,441
1962‡	5th	86	76	.531	15½	Birdie Tebbetts	766,921
1963‡	6th	84	78	.519	15	Bobby Bragan	773,018
1964‡	5th	88	74	.543	5	Bobby Bragan	910,911
1965‡	5th	86	76	.531	11	Bobby Bragan	555,584
1966	5th	85	77	.525	10	Bobby Bragan, Billy Hitchcock	1,539,801
1967	7th	77	85	.475	24½	Billy Hitchcock, Ken Silvestri	1,389,222
1968	5th	81	81	.500	16	Lum Harris	1,126,540

WEST DIVISION

Year	Position	W	L	Pct.	*GB	Manager	Attendance
1969	1st∞	93	69	.574	+3	Lum Harris	1,458,320
1970	5th	76	86	.469	26	Lum Harris	1,078,848
1971	3rd	82	80	.506	8	Lum Harris	1,006,320
1972	4th	70	84	.455	25	Lum Harris, Eddie Mathews	752,973
1973	5th	76	85	.472	22½	Eddie Mathews	800,655
1974	3rd	88	74	.543	14	Eddie Mathews, Clyde King	981,085
1975	5th	67	94	.416	40½	Clyde King, Connie Ryan	534,672
1976	6th	70	92	.432	32	Dave Bristol	818,179
1977	6th	61	101	.377	37	Dave Bristol, Ted Turner	872,464
1978	6th	69	93	.426	26	Bobby Cox	904,494
1979	6th	66	94	.413	23½	Bobby Cox	769,465
1980	4th	81	80	.503	11	Bobby Cox	1,048,411
1981	4th/5th	50	56	.472	▲	Bobby Cox	535,418
1982	1st∞	89	73	.549	+1	Joe Torre	1,801,985
1983	2nd	88	74	.543	3	Joe Torre	2,119,935
1984	2nd (tied)	80	82	.494	12	Joe Torre	1,724,892
1985	5th	66	96	.407	29	Eddie Haas, Bobby Wine	1,350,137
1986	6th	72	89	.447	23½	Chuck Tanner	1,387,181
1987	5th	69	92	.429	20½	Chuck Tanner	1,217,402
1988	6th	54	106	.338	39½	Chuck Tanner, Russ Nixon	848,089
1989	6th	63	97	.394	28	Russ Nixon	984,930
1990	6th	65	97	.401	26	Russ Nixon, Bobby Cox	980,129
1991	1st◆	94	68	.580	+1	Bobby Cox	2,140,217
1992	1st◆	98	64	.605	+8	Bobby Cox	3,077,400
1993	1st∞	104	58	.642	+1	Bobby Cox	3,884,725

EAST DIVISION

Year	Position	W	L	Pct.	*GB	Manager	Attendance
1994	2nd	68	46	.596	6	Bobby Cox	2,539,240
1995	1st■◆	90	54	.625	+21	Bobby Cox	2,561,831
1996	1st■◆	96	66	.593	+8	Bobby Cox	2,901,242
1997	1st■∞	101	61	.623	+9	Bobby Cox	3,464,488
1998	1st■◆	106	56	.654	+18	Bobby Cox	3,361,350

*Games behind winner. †Boston Braves. ‡Milwaukee Braves. §Lost pennant playoff. ∞Lost championship series. ▲First half 25-29; second half 25-27. ◆Won championship series. ■Won division series.

MANAGERIAL RECORDS

Dave Bancroft 249-363, Del Bissonette 25-34, Frank Bowerman 23-55, Bobby Bragan 310-287, Dave Bristol 131-192, Al Buckenberger 186-242, Bob Coleman 107-140, Bobby Cox 1,063-853, Chuck Dressen 159-124, Emil Fuchs 56-98, Charlie Grimm 341-285, Eddie Haas 50-71, Fred Haney 341-231, Lum Harris 379-373, Billy Hitchcock 110-100, Tommy Holmes 61-69, Rogers Hornsby 39-83, Joe Kelley 63-91, Clyde King 96-101, Johnny Kling 52-101, Fred Lake 53-100, Eddie Mathews 149-161, Bill McKechnie 560-666, Fred Mitchell 186-274, Russ Nixon 130-216, Connie Ryan 9-18, Frank Selee 69-69, Ken Silvestri 0-3, Jack Slattery 11-20, Harry Smith 22-53, Billy Southworth 424-358, George Stallings 579-597, Casey Stengel 394-516, Chuck Tanner 153-208, Birdie Tebbetts 98-89, Fred Tenney 202-402, Joe Torre 257-229, Ted Turner 0-1, Bobby Wine 16-25.

CHICAGO CUBS

YEARLY FINISHES

Year	Position	W	L	Pct.	*GB	Manager	Attendance
1901	6th	53	86	.381	37	Tom Loftus	205,071
1902	5th	68	69	.496	34	Frank Selee	263,700
1903	3rd	82	56	.594	8	Frank Selee	386,205
1904	2nd	93	60	.608	13	Frank Selee	439,100
1905	3rd	92	61	.601	13	Frank Selee, Frank Chance	509,900

Year	Position	W	L	Pct.	*GB	Manager	Attendance
1906	1st	116	36	.763	+20	Frank Chance	654,300
1907	1st	107	45	.704	+17	Frank Chance	422,550
1908	1st	99	55	.643	+1	Frank Chance	665,325
1909	2nd	104	49	.680	6 1/2	Frank Chance	633,480
1910	1st	104	50	.675	+13	Frank Chance	526,152
1911	2nd	92	62	.597	7 1/2	Frank Chance	576,000
1912	3rd	91	59	.607	11 1/2	Frank Chance	514,000
1913	3rd	88	65	.575	13 1/2	Johnny Evers	419,000
1914	4th	78	76	.506	16 1/2	Hank O'Day	202,516
1915	4th	73	80	.477	17 1/2	Roger Bresnahan	217,058
1916	5th	67	86	.438	26 1/2	Joe Tinker	453,685
1917	5th	74	80	.481	24	Fred Mitchell	360,218
1918	1st	84	45	.651	+10 1/2	Fred Mitchell	337,256
1919	3rd	75	65	.536	21	Fred Mitchell	424,430
1950	5th (tied)	75	79	.487	18	Fred Mitchell	480,783
1921	7th	64	89	.418	30	Johnny Evers, Bill Killefer	410,107
1922	5th	80	74	.519	13	Bill Killefer	542,283
1923	4th	83	71	.539	12 1/2	Bill Killefer	703,705
1924	5th	81	72	.529	12	Bill Killefer	716,922
1925	8th	68	86	.442	27 1/2	Bill Killefer, Rabbit Maranville, George Gibson	622,610
1926	4th	82	72	.532	7	Joe McCarthy	885,063
1927	4th	85	68	.556	8 1/2	Joe McCarthy	1,159,168
1928	3rd	91	63	.591	4	Joe McCarthy	1,143,740
1929	1st	98	54	.645	+10 1/2	Joe McCarthy	1,485,166
1930	2nd	90	64	.584	2	Joe McCarthy, Rogers Hornsby	1,463,624
1931	3rd	84	70	.545	17	Rogers Hornsby	1,086,422
1932	1st	90	64	.584	+4	Rogers Hornsby, Charlie Grimm	974,688
1933	3rd	86	68	.558	6	Charlie Grimm	594,112
1934	3rd	86	65	.570	8	Charlie Grimm	707,525
1935	1st	100	54	.649	+4	Charlie Grimm	692,604
1936	2nd (tied)	87	67	.565	5	Charlie Grimm	699,370
1937	2nd	93	61	.604	3	Charlie Grimm	895,020
1938	1st	89	63	.586	+2	Charlie Grimm, Gabby Hartnett	951,640
1939	4th	84	70	.545	13	Gabby Hartnett	726,663
1940	5th	75	79	.487	25 1/2	Gabby Hartnett	534,878
1941	6th	70	84	.455	30	Jimmy Wilson	545,159
1942	6th	68	86	.442	38	Jimmy Wilson	590,872
1943	5th	74	79	.484	30 1/2	Jimmy Wilson	508,247
1944	4th	75	79	.487	30	Jimmy Wilson, Charlie Grimm	640,110
1945	1st	98	56	.636	+3	Charlie Grimm	1,036,386
1946	3rd	82	71	.536	14 1/2	Charlie Grimm	1,342,970
1947	6th	69	85	.448	25	Charlie Grimm	1,364,039
1948	8th	64	90	.416	27 1/2	Charlie Grimm	1,237,792
1949	8th	61	93	.396	36	Charlie Grimm, Frankie Frisch	1,143,139
1950	7th	64	89	.418	26 1/2	Frankie Frisch	1,165,944
1951	8th	62	92	.403	34 1/2	Frankie Frisch, Phil Cavarretta	894,415
1952	5th	77	77	.500	19 1/2	Phil Cavarretta	1,024,826
1953	7th	65	89	.422	40	Phil Cavarretta	763,658
1954	7th	64	90	.416	33	Stan Hack	748,183
1955	6th	72	81	.471	26	Stan Hack	875,800
1956	8th	60	94	.390	33	Stan Hack	720,118
1957	7th (tied)	62	92	.403	33	Bob Scheffing	670,629
1958	5th (tied)	72	82	.468	20	Bob Scheffing	979,904
1959	5th (tied)	74	80	.481	13	Bob Scheffing	858,255
1960	7th	60	94	.390	35	Charlie Grimm, Lou Boudreau	809,770
1961	7th	64	90	.416	29	Vedie Himsl, Harry Craft, Elvin Tappe, Lou Klein	673,057
1962	9th	59	103	.364	42 1/2	Charlie Metro, Elvin Tappe, Lou Klein	609,802
1963	7th	82	80	.506	17	Bob Kennedy	979,551
1964	8th	76	86	.469	17	Bob Kennedy	751,647
1965	8th	72	90	.444	25	Bob Kennedy, Lou Klein	641,361
1966	10th	59	103	.364	36	Leo Durocher	635,891
1967	3rd	87	74	.540	14	Leo Durocher	977,226
1968	3rd	84	78	.519	13	Leo Durocher	1,043,409

EAST DIVISION

Year	Position	W	L	Pct.	*GB	Manager	Attendance
1969	2nd	92	70	.568	8	Leo Durocher	1,674,993
1970	2nd	84	78	.519	5	Leo Durocher	1,642,705
1971	3rd (tied)	83	79	.512	14	Leo Durocher	1,653,007
1972	2nd	85	70	.548	11	Leo Durocher, Whitey Lockman	1,299,163
1973	5th	77	84	.478	5	Whitey Lockman	1,351,705
1974	6th	66	96	.407	22	Whitey Lockman, Jim Marshall	1,015,378
1975	5th (tied)	75	87	.463	17 1/2	Jim Marshall	1,034,819
1976	4th	75	87	.463	26	Jim Marshall	1,026,217
1977	4th	81	81	.500	20	Herman Franks	1,439,834
1978	3rd	79	83	.488	11	Herman Franks	1,525,311
1979	5th	80	82	.494	18	Herman Franks, Joe Amalfitano	1,648,587

Year	Position	W	L	Pct.	*GB	Manager	Attendance
1980	6th	64	98	.395	27	Preston Gomez, Joe Amalfitano	1,206,776
1981	6th/5th	38	65	.369	†	Joe Amalfitano	565,637
1982	5th	73	89	.451	19	Lee Elia	1,249,278
1983	5th	71	91	.438	19	Lee Elia, Charlie Fox	1,479,717
1984	1st‡	96	65	.596	+6 1/2	Jim Frey	2,104,219
1985	4th	77	84	.478	23 1/2	Jim Frey	2,161,534
1986	5th	70	90	.438	37	Jim Frey, John Vukovich, Gene Michael	1,859,102
1987	6th	76	85	.472	18 1/2	Gene Michael, Frank Lucchesi	2,035,130
1988	4th	77	85	.475	24	Don Zimmer	2,089,034
1989	1st‡	93	69	.574	+6	Don Zimmer	2,491,942
1990	4th	77	85	.475	18	Don Zimmer	2,243,791
1991	4th	77	83	.481	20	Don Zimmer, Joe Altobelli, Jim Essian	2,314,250
1992	4th	78	84	.481	18	Jim Lefebvre	2,126,720
1993	4th	84	78	.519	13	Jim Lefebvre	2,653,763

CENTRAL DIVISION

Year	Position	W	L	Pct.	*GB	Manager	Attendance
1994	5th	49	64	.434	16 1/2	Tom Trebelhorn	1,845,208
1995	3rd	73	71	.507	12	Jim Riggleman	1,918,265
1996	4th	76	86	.469	12	Jim Riggleman	2,219,110
1997	5th§	68	94	.420	16	Jim Riggleman	2,190,308
1998	2nd§	90	73	.552	12 1/2	Jim Riggleman	2,623,000

*Games behind winner. †First half 15-37; second half 23-28. ‡Lost championship series.

MANAGERIAL RECORDS

Joe Amalfitano 66-116, Lou Boudreau 54-83, Roger Bresnahan 73-80, Phil Cavarretta 169-213, Frank Chance 753-379, Harry Craft 7-9, Leo Durocher 535-526, Lee Elia 127-158, Jim Essian 59-63, Johnny Evers 130-121, Charlie Fox 17-22, Herman Franks 238-241, Jim Frey 196-182, Frank Frisch 141-196, George Gibson 12-14, Preston Gomez 38-52, Charlie Grimm 946-784, Stan Hack 196-265, Gabby Hartnett 203-176, Vedie Himsl 10-21, Rogers Hornsby 141-114, Roy Johnson 0-1, Bob Kennedy 182-198, Bill Killefer 299-292, Lou Klein 65-83, Jim Lefebvre 162-162, Whitey Lockman 157-162, Tom Loftus 53-86, Frank Lucchesi 8-17, Rabbit Maranville 23-30, Jim Marshall 175-218, Joe McCarthy 442-321, Charlie Metro 43-69, Gene Michael 114-124, Fred Mitchell 308-269, Hank O'Day 78-76, Jim Riggleman 307-324, Bob Scheffing 208-254, Frank Selee 295-223, Elvin Tappe 46-69, Joe Tinker 67-86, Tom Trebelhorn 49-64, John Vukovich 1-1, Jimmy Wilson 213-258, Don Zimmer 265-259.

CINCINNATI REDS
YEARLY FINISHES

Year	Position	W	L	Pct.	*GB	Manager	Attendance
1901	8th	52	87	.374	38	Bid McPhee	205,728
1902	4th	70	70	.500	33 1/2	Bid McPhee, Frank Bancroft, Joe Kelley	217,300
1903	4th	74	65	.532	16 1/2	Joe Kelley	351,680
1904	3rd	88	65	.575	18	Joe Kelley	391,915
1905	5th	79	74	.516	26	Joe Kelley	313,927
1906	6th	64	87	.424	51 1/2	Ned Hanlon	330,056
1907	6th	66	87	.431	41 1/2	Ned Hanlon	317,500
1908	5th	73	81	.474	26	John Ganzel	399,200
1909	4th	77	76	.503	33 1/2	Clark Griffith	424,643
1910	5th	75	79	.487	29	Clark Griffith	380,622
1911	6th	70	83	.458	29	Clark Griffith	300,000
1912	4th	75	78	.490	29	Hank O'Day	344,000
1913	7th	64	89	.418	37 1/2	Joe Tinker	258,000
1914	8th	60	94	.390	34 1/2	Buck Herzog	100,791
1915	7th	71	83	.461	20	Buck Herzog	218,878
1916	7th (tied)	60	93	.392	33 1/2	Buck Herzog, Christy Mathewson	255,846
1917	4th	78	76	.506	20	Christy Mathewson	269,056
1918	3rd	68	60	.531	15 1/2	Christy Mathewson, Heinie Groh	163,009
1919	1st	96	44	.686	+9	Pat Moran	532,501
1920	3rd	82	71	.536	10 1/2	Pat Moran	568,107
1921	6th	70	83	.458	24	Pat Moran	311,227
1922	2nd	86	68	.558	7	Pat Moran	493,754
1923	2nd	91	63	.591	4 1/2	Pat Moran	575,063
1924	4th	83	70	.542	10	Jack Hendricks	437,707
1925	3rd	80	73	.523	15	Jack Hendricks	464,920
1926	2nd	87	67	.565	2	Jack Hendricks	672,987
1927	5th	75	78	.490	18 1/2	Jack Hendricks	442,164
1928	5th	78	74	.513	16	Jack Hendricks	490,490
1929	7th	66	88	.429	33	Jack Hendricks	295,040
1930	7th	59	95	.383	33	Dan Howley	386,727
1931	8th	58	96	.377	43	Dan Howley	263,316
1932	8th	60	94	.390	30	Dan Howley	356,950
1933	8th	58	94	.382	33	Donie Bush	218,281
1934	8th	52	99	.344	42	Bob O'Farrell, Chuck Dressen	206,773

– 358 –

Year	Position	W	L	Pct.	*GB	Manager	Attendance
1935	6th	68	85	.444	31 1/2	Chuck Dressen	448,247
1936	5th	74	80	.481	18	Chuck Dressen	466,245
1937	8th	56	98	.364	40	Chuck Dressen, Bobby Wallace	411,221
1938	4th	82	68	.547	6	Bill McKechnie	706,756
1939	1st	97	57	.630	+4 1/2	Bill McKechnie	981,443
1940	1st	100	53	.654	+12	Bill McKechnie	850,180
1941	3rd	88	66	.571	12	Bill McKechnie	643,513
1942	4th	76	76	.500	29	Bill McKechnie	427,031
1943	2nd	87	67	.565	18	Bill McKechnie	379,122
1944	3rd	89	65	.578	16	Bill McKechnie	409,567
1945	7th	61	93	.396	37	Bill McKechnie	290,070
1946	6th	67	87	.435	30	Bill McKechnie	715,751
1947	5th	73	81	.474	21	Johnny Neun	899,975
1948	7th	64	89	.418	27	Johnny Neun, Bucky Walters	823,386
1949	7th	62	92	.403	35	Bucky Walters	707,782
1950	6th	66	87	.431	24 1/2	Luke Sewell	538,794
1951	6th	68	86	.442	28 1/2	Luke Sewell	588,268
1952	6th	69	85	.448	27 1/2	Luke Sewell, Rogers Hornsby	604,197
1953	6th	68	86	.442	37	Rogers Hornsby, Buster Mills	548,086
1954	5th	74	80	.481	23	Birdie Tebbetts	704,167
1955	5th	75	79	.487	23 1/2	Birdie Tebbetts	693,662
1956	3rd	91	63	.591	2	Birdie Tebbetts	1,125,928
1957	4th	80	74	.519	15	Birdie Tebbetts	1,070,850
1958	4th	76	78	.494	16	Birdie Tebbetts, Jimmie Dykes	788,582
1959	5th (tied)	74	80	.481	13	Mayo Smith, Fred Hutchinson	801,289
1960	6th	67	87	.435	28	Fred Hutchinson	663,486
1961	1st	93	61	.604	+4	Fred Hutchinson	1,117,603
1962	3rd	98	64	.605	3 1/2	Fred Hutchinson	982,085
1963	5th	86	76	.531	13	Fred Hutchinson	858,805
1964	2nd (tied)	92	70	.549	1	Fred Hutchinson, Dick Sisler	862,466
1965	4th	89	73	.549	8	Dick Sisler	1,047,824
1966	7th	76	84	.475	18	Don Heffner, Dave Bristol	742,958
1967	4th	87	75	.537	14 1/2	Dave Bristol	958,300
1968	4th	83	79	.512	14	Dave Bristol	733,354

WEST DIVISION

Year	Position	W	L	Pct.	*GB	Manager	Attendance
1969	3rd	89	73	.549	4	Dave Bristol	987,991
1970	1st†	102	60	.630	+14 1/2	Sparky Anderson	1,803,568
1971	4th (tied)	79	83	.488	11	Sparky Anderson	1,501,122
1972	1st‡	95	59	.617	+10 1/2	Sparky Anderson	1,611,459
1973	1st‡	99	63	.611	+3 1/2	Sparky Anderson	2,017,601
1974	2nd	98	64	.605	4	Sparky Anderson	2,164,307
1975	1st†	108	54	.667	+20	Sparky Anderson	2,315,603
1976	1st†	102	60	.630	+10	Sparky Anderson	2,629,708
1977	2nd	88	74	.543	10	Sparky Anderson	2,519,670
1978	2nd	92	69	.571	2 1/2	Sparky Anderson	2,532,497
1979	1st‡	90	71	.559	+1 1/2	John McNamara	2,356,933
1980	3rd	89	73	.549	3 1/2	John McNamara	2,022,450
1981	2nd/2nd	66	42	.611	§	John McNamara	1,093,730
1982	6th	61	101	.377	28	John McNamara, Russ Nixon	1,326,528
1983	6th	74	88	.457	17	Russ Nixon	1,190,419
1984	5th	70	92	.432	22	Vern Rapp, Pete Rose	1,275,887
1985	2nd	89	72	.553	5 1/2	Pete Rose	1,834,619
1986	2nd	86	76	.531	10	Pete Rose	1,692,432
1987	2nd	84	78	.519	6	Pete Rose	2,185,205
1988	2nd	87	74	.540	7	Pete Rose	2,072,528
1989	5th	75	87	.463	17	Pete Rose, Tommy Helms	1,979,320
1990	1st†	91	71	.562	+5	Lou Piniella	2,400,892
1991	5th	74	88	.457	20	Lou Piniella	2,372,377
1992	2nd	90	72	.556	8	Lou Piniella	2,315,946
1993	5th	73	89	.451	31	Tony Perez, Dave Johnson	2,453,232

CENTRAL DIVISION

Year	Position	W	L	Pct.	*GB	Manager	Attendance
1994	1st	66	48	.579	+1/2	Dave Johnson	1,897,681
1995	1st∞‡	85	59	.590	+9	Dave Johnson	1,837,649
1996	3rd	81	81	.500	7	Ray Knight	1,861,428
1997	3rd	76	86	.469	8	Ray Knight, Jack McKeon	1,785,788
1998	4th	77	85	.475	25	Jack McKeon	1,793,679

*Games behind winner. †Won championship series. ‡Lost championship series. §First half 35-21; second half 31-21. ∞Won division series.

MANAGERIAL RECORDS

Sparky Anderson 863-586, Frank Bancroft 9-7, Dave Bristol 298-265, Donie Bush 58-94, Chuck Dressen 214-282, Jimmie Dykes 24-17, John Ganzel 73-81, Clark Griffith 222-238, Heinie Groh 7-3, Ned Hanlon 130-174, Don Heffner 37-46, Tommy Helms 14-21, Jack Hendricks 469-450, Buck Herzog 165-226, Rogers Hornsby 91-106, Dan Howley 177-285, Fred Hutchinson 443-372, Dave Johnson 204-172, Joe Kelley 275-230, Ray Knight 124-137, Christy Mathewson 164-176, Bill McKechnie 747-632, Jack McKeon 110-115, John McNamara 279-244, Bid McPhee 79-124, Buster Mills 4-4, Pat Moran 425-329, Johnny Neun 117-137, Russ Nixon 101-131, Hank O'Day 75-78, Bob O'Farrell 30-60, Tony Perez 20-24, Lou Piniella 255-231, Vern Rapp 51-70, Pete Rose 426-388, Luke Sewell 176-234, Dick Sisler 121-94, Mayo Smith 35-45, Birdie Tebbetts 372-357, Joe Tinker 64-89, Bobby Wallace 5-20, Bucky Walters 81-123.

COLORADO ROCKIES
YEARLY FINISHES

WEST DIVISION

Year	Position	W	L	Pct.	*GB	Manager	Attendance
1993	6th	67	95	.414	37	Don Baylor	4,483,350
1994	3rd	53	64	.453	6 1/2	Don Baylor	3,281,511
1995	2nd†‡	77	67	.535	1	Don Baylor	3,390,037
1996	3rd	83	79	.512	8	Don Baylor	3,891,014
1997	3rd	83	79	.512	7	Don Baylor	3,888,453
1998	4th	77	85	.475	21	Don Baylor	3,789,347

*Games behind winner. †Wild-card playoff qualifier. ‡Lost division series.

MANAGERIAL RECORDS

Don Baylor 440-469.

FLORIDA MARLINS
YEARLY FINISHES

EAST DIVISION

Year	Position	W	L	Pct.	*GB	Manager	Attendance
1993	6th	64	98	.395	33	Rene Lachemann	3,064,847
1994	5th	51	64	.443	23 1/2	Rene Lachemann	1,937,467
1995	4th	67	76	.469	22 1/2	Rene Lachemann	1,700,466
1996	3rd	80	82	.494	16	Rene Lachemann, John Boles	1,746,767
1997	2nd†‡§	92	70	.568	9	Jim Leyland	2,364,387
1998	5th	54	108	.333	52	Jim Leyland	1,750,395

*Games behind winner. †Wild-card playoff qualifier. ‡Won division series. §Won championship series.

MANAGERIAL RECORDS

John Boles 40-35, Rene Lachemann 222-285, Jim Leyland 146-178.

HOUSTON ASTROS
YEARLY FINISHES

Year	Position	W	L	Pct.	*GB	Manager	Attendance
1962†	8th	64	96	.400	36 1/2	Harry Craft	924,456
1963†	9th	66	96	.407	33	Harry Craft	719,502
1964†	9th	66	96	.407	27	Harry Craft, Luman Harris	725,773
1965	9th	65	97	.401	32	Luman Harris	2,151,470
1966	8th	72	90	.444	23	Grady Hatton	1,872,108
1967	9th	69	93	.426	32 1/2	Grady Hatton	1,348,303
1968	10th	72	90	.444	25	Grady Hatton, Harry Walker	1,312,887

WEST DIVISION

Year	Position	W	L	Pct.	*GB	Manager	Attendance
1969	5th	81	81	.500	12	Harry Walker	1,442,995
1970	4th	79	83	.488	23	Harry Walker	1,253,444
1971	4th (tied)	79	83	.488	11	Harry Walker	1,261,589
1972	2nd	84	69	.549	10 1/2	Harry Walker, Leo Durocher, Salty Parker	1,469,247
1973	4th	82	80	.506	17	Leo Durocher, Preston Gomez	1,394,004
1974	4th	81	81	.500	21	Preston Gomez	1,090,728
1975	6th	64	97	.398	43 1/2	Preston Gomez, Bill Virdon	858,002
1976	3rd	80	82	.494	22	Bill Virdon	886,146
1977	3rd	81	81	.500	17	Bill Virdon	1,109,560
1978	5th	74	88	.457	21	Bill Virdon	1,126,145
1979	2nd	89	73	.549	1 1/2	Bill Virdon	1,900,312
1980	1st‡§	93	70	.571	+1	Bill Virdon	2,278,217

Year	Position	W	L	Pct.	*GB	Manager	Attendance
1981	3rd/1st▲	61	49	.555	∞	Bill Virdon	1,321,282
1982	5th	77	85	.475	12	Bill Virdon, Bob Lillis	1,558,555
1983	3rd	85	77	.525	6	Bob Lillis	1,351,962
1984	2nd (tied)	80	82	.494	12	Bob Lillis	1,229,862
1985	3rd (tied)	83	79	.512	12	Bob Lillis	1,184,314
1986	1st§	96	66	.593	+10	Hal Lanier	1,734,276
1987	3rd	76	86	.469	14	Hal Lanier	1,909,902
1988	5th	82	80	.506	12 1/2	Hal Lanier	1,933,505
1989	3rd	86	76	.531	6	Art Howe	1,834,908
1990	4th (tied)	75	87	.463	16	Art Howe	1,310,927
1991	6th	65	97	.401	29	Art Howe	1,196,152
1992	4th	81	81	.500	17	Art Howe	1,211,412
1993	3rd	85	77	.525	19	Art Howe	2,084,546

CENTRAL DIVISION

Year	Position	W	L	Pct.	*GB	Manager	Attendance
1994	2nd	66	49	.574	1/2	Terry Collins	1,561,136
1995	2nd	76	68	.528	9	Terry Collins	1,363,801
1996	2nd	82	80	.506	6	Terry Collins	1,975,888
1997	1st▲	84	78	.519	+5	Larry Dierker	2,046,781
1998	1st▲	102	60	.630	+12 1/2	Larry Dierker	2,450,451

*Games behind winner. †Houston Colt .45s. ‡Won division playoff. §Lost championship series. ∞First half 28-29; second half 33-20. ▲Lost division series.

MANAGERIAL RECORDS

Terry Collins 224-197, Harry Craft 191-280, Larry Dierker 186-138, Leo Durocher 98-95, Preston Gomez 128-161, Lum Harris 70-105, Grady Hatton 164-221, Art Howe 392-418, Hal Lanier 254-232, Bob Lillis 276-261, Bill Virdon 544-522, Harry Walker 355-353.

LOS ANGELES DODGERS
YEARLY FINISHES

Year	Position	W	L	Pct.	*GB	Manager	Attendance
1901†	3rd	79	57	.581	9 1/2	Ned Hanlon	189,200
1902†	2nd	75	63	.543	27 1/2	Ned Hanlon	199,868
1903†	5th	70	66	.515	19	Ned Hanlon	224,670
1904†	6th	56	97	.366	50	Ned Hanlon	214,600
1905†	8th	48	104	.316	56 1/2	Ned Hanlon	227,924
1906†	5th	66	86	.434	50	Patsy Donovan	227,400
1907†	5th	65	83	.439	40	Patsy Donovan	312,500
1908†	7th	53	101	.344	46	Patsy Donovan	275,600
1909†	6th	55	98	.359	55 1/2	Harry Lumley	321,300
1910†	6th	64	90	.416	40	Bill Dahlen	279,321
1911†	7th	64	86	.427	33 1/2	Bill Dahlen	269,000
1912†	7th	58	95	.379	46	Bill Dahlen	243,000
1913†	6th	65	84	.436	34 1/2	Bill Dahlen	347,000
1914†	5th	75	79	.487	19 1/2	Wilbert Robinson	122,671
1915†	3rd	80	72	.526	10	Wilbert Robinson	297,766
1916†	1st	94	60	.610	+2 1/2	Wilbert Robinson	447,747
1917†	7th	70	81	.464	26 1/2	Wilbert Robinson	221,619
1918†	5th	57	69	.452	25 1/2	Wilbert Robinson	83,831
1919†	5th	69	71	.493	27	Wilbert Robinson	360,721
1920†	1st	93	61	.604	+7	Wilbert Robinson	808,722
1921†	5th	77	75	.507	16 1/2	Wilbert Robinson	613,245
1922†	6th	76	78	.494	17	Wilbert Robinson	498,856
1923†	6th	76	78	.494	19 1/2	Wilbert Robinson	564,666
1924†	2nd	92	62	.597	1 1/2	Wilbert Robinson	818,883
1925†	6th (tied)	68	85	.444	27	Wilbert Robinson	659,435
1926†	6th	71	82	.464	17 1/2	Wilbert Robinson	650,819
1927†	6th	65	88	.425	28 1/2	Wilbert Robinson	637,230
1928†	6th	77	76	.503	17 1/2	Wilbert Robinson	664,863
1929†	6th	70	83	.458	28 1/2	Wilbert Robinson	731,886
1930†	4th	86	68	.558	6	Wilbert Robinson	1,097,339
1931†	4th	79	73	.520	21	Wilbert Robinson	753,133
1932†	3rd	81	73	.526	9	Max Carey	681,827
1933†	6th	65	88	.425	26 1/2	Max Carey	526,815
1934†	6th	71	81	.467	23 1/2	Casey Stengel	434,188
1935†	5th	70	83	.458	29 1/2	Casey Stengel	470,517
1936†	7th	67	87	.435	25	Casey Stengel	489,618
1937†	6th	62	91	.405	33 1/2	Burleigh Grimes	482,481
1938†	7th	69	80	.463	18 1/2	Burleigh Grimes	663,087
1939†	3rd	84	69	.549	12 1/2	Leo Durocher	955,668

Year	Position	W	L	Pct.	*GB	Manager	Attendance
1940†	2nd	88	65	.575	12	Leo Durocher	975,978
1941†	1st	100	54	.649	+2½	Leo Durocher	1,214,910
1942†	2nd	104	50	.675	2	Leo Durocher	1,037,765
1943†	3rd	81	72	.529	23½	Leo Durocher	661,739
1944†	7th	63	91	.409	42	Leo Durocher	605,905
1945†	3rd	87	67	.565	11	Leo Durocher	1,059,220
1946†	2nd‡	96	60	.615	2	Leo Durocher	1,796,824
1947†	1st	94	60	.610	+5	Clyde Sukeforth, Burt Shotton	1,807,526
1948†	3rd	84	70	.545	7½	Leo Durocher, Burt Shotton	1,398,967
1949†	1st	97	57	.630	+1	Burt Shotton	1,633,747
1950†	2nd	89	65	.578	2	Burt Shotton	1,185,896
1951†	2nd‡	97	60	.618	1	Chuck Dressen	1,282,628
1952†	1st	96	57	.627	+4½	Chuck Dressen	1,088,704
1953†	1st	105	49	.682	+13	Chuck Dressen	1,163,419
1954†	2nd	92	62	.597	5	Walter Alston	1,020,531
1955†	1st	98	55	.641	+13½	Walter Alston	1,033,589
1956†	1st	93	61	.604	+1	Walter Alston	1,213,562
1957†	3rd	84	70	.545	11	Walter Alston	1,028,258
1958	7th	71	83	.461	21	Walter Alston	1,845,556
1959	1st§	88	68	.564	+2	Walter Alston	2,071,045
1960	4th	82	72	.532	13	Walter Alston	2,253,887
1961	2nd	89	65	.578	4	Walter Alston	1,804,250
1962	2nd‡	102	63	.618	1	Walter Alston	2,755,184
1963	1st	99	63	.611	+6	Walter Alston	2,538,602
1964	6th (tied)	80	82	.494	13	Walter Alston	2,228,751
1965	1st	97	65	.599	+2	Walter Alston	2,553,577
1966	1st	95	67	.586	+1½	Walter Alston	2,617,029
1967	8th	73	89	.451	28½	Walter Alston	1,664,362
1968	7th	76	86	.469	21	Walter Alston	1,581,093

WEST DIVISION

Year	Position	W	L	Pct.	*GB	Manager	Attendance
1969	4th	85	77	.525	8	Walter Alston	1,784,527
1970	2nd	87	74	.540	14½	Walter Alston	1,697,142
1971	2nd	89	73	.549	1	Walter Alston	2,064,594
1972	3rd	85	70	.548	10½	Walter Alston	1,860,858
1973	2nd	95	66	.590	3½	Walter Alston	2,136,192
1974	1st∞	102	60	.630	+4	Walter Alston	2,632,474
1975	2nd	88	74	.543	20	Walter Alston	2,539,349
1976	2nd	92	70	.568	10	Walter Alston, Tommy Lasorda	2,386,301
1977	1st∞	98	64	.605	+10	Tommy Lasorda	2,955,087
1978	1st∞	95	67	.586	+2½	Tommy Lasorda	3,347,845
1979	3rd	79	83	.488	11½	Tommy Lasorda	2,860,954
1980	2nd▲	92	71	.564	1	Tommy Lasorda	3,249,287
1981	1st/4th•∞	63	47	.573	◆	Tommy Lasorda	2,381,292
1982	2nd	88	74	.543	1	Tommy Lasorda	3,608,881
1983	1st▼	91	71	.562	+3	Tommy Lasorda	3,510,313
1984	4th	79	83	.488	13	Tommy Lasorda	3,134,824
1985	1st▼	95	67	.586	+5½	Tommy Lasorda	3,264,593
1986	5th	73	89	.451	23	Tommy Lasorda	3,023,208
1987	4th	73	89	.451	17	Tommy Lasorda	2,797,409
1988	1st∞	94	67	.584	+7	Tommy Lasorda	2,980,262
1989	4th	77	83	.481	14	Tommy Lasorda	2,944,653
1990	2nd	86	76	.531	5	Tommy Lasorda	3,002,396
1991	2nd	93	69	.574	1	Tommy Lasorda	3,348,170
1992	6th	63	99	.389	35	Tommy Lasorda	2,473,266
1993	4th	81	81	.500	23	Tommy Lasorda	3,170,392
1994	1st	58	56	.509	+3½	Tommy Lasorda	2,279,355
1995	1st@	78	66	.542	+1	Tommy Lasorda	2,766,251
1996	2nd■@	90	72	.556	1	Tommy Lasorda, Bill Russell	3,188,454
1997	2nd	88	74	.543	2	Bill Russell	3,319,504
1998	3rd	83	79	.512	15	Bill Russell, Glenn Hoffman	3,089,201

*Games behind winner. †Brooklyn Dodgers. ‡Lost pennant playoff. §Won pennant playoff. ∞Won championship series. ▲Lost division playoff. ◆First half 36-21; second half 27-26. ■Wild-card playoff qualifier. ▼Lost championship series. •Won division series. @Lost division series.

MANAGERIAL RECORDS

Walter Alston 2,040-1,613, Max Carey 146-161, Bill Dahlen 251-355, Patsy Donovan 184-270, Chuck Dressen 298-166, Leo Durocher 738-565, Burleigh Grimes 131-171, Ned Hanlon 328-387, Glenn Hoffman 47-41, Tommy Lasorda 1,599-1,439, Harry Lumley 55-98, Wilbert Robinson 1,375-1,341, Bill Russell 173-149, Burt Shotton 326-215, Casey Stengel 208-251, Clyde Sukeforth 2-0.

MILWAUKEE BREWERS
YEARLY FINISHES

AMERICAN LEAGUE WEST DIVISION

Year	Position	W	L	Pct.	*GB	Manager	Attendance
1969†	6th	64	98	.395	33	Joe Schultz	677,944
1970	4th	65	97	.401	33	Dave Bristol	933,690
1971	6th	69	92	.429	32	Dave Bristol	731,531

AMERICAN LEAGUE EAST DIVISION

Year	Position	W	L	Pct.	*GB	Manager	Attendance
1972	6th	65	91	.417	21	Dave Bristol, Del Crandall	600,440
1973	5th	74	88	.457	23	Del Crandall	1,092,158
1974	5th	76	86	.469	15	Del Crandall	955,741
1975	5th	68	94	.420	28	Del Crandall	1,213,357
1976	6th	66	95	.410	32	Alex Grammas	1,012,164
1977	6th	67	95	.414	33	Alex Grammas	1,114,938
1978	3rd	93	69	.574	6 1/2	George Bamberger	1,601,406
1979	2nd	95	66	.590	8	George Bamberger	1,918,343
1980	3rd	86	76	.531	17	George Bamberger, Buck Rodgers	1,857,408
1981	3rd/1st§	62	47	.569	‡	Buck Rodgers	878,432
1982	1st∞	95	67	.586	+1	Buck Rodgers, Harvey Kuenn	1,978,896
1983	5th	87	75	.537	11	Harvey Kuenn	2,397,131
1984	7th	67	94	.416	36 1/2	Rene Lachemann	1,608,509
1985	6th	71	90	.441	28	George Bamberger	1,360,265
1986	6th	77	84	.478	18	George Bamberger, Tom Trebelhorn	1,265,041
1987	3rd	91	71	.562	7	Tom Trebelhorn	1,909,244
1988	3rd (tied)	87	75	.537	2	Tom Trebelhorn	1,923,238
1989	4th	81	81	.500	8	Tom Trebelhorn	1,970,735
1990	6th	74	88	.457	14	Tom Trebelhorn	1,752,900
1991	4th	83	79	.512	8	Tom Trebelhorn	1,478,729
1992	2nd	92	70	.568	4	Phil Garner	1,857,314
1993	7th	69	93	.426	26	Phil Garner	1,688,080

AMERICAN LEAGUE CENTRAL DIVISION

Year	Position	W	L	Pct.	*GB	Manager	Attendance
1994	5th	53	62	.461	15	Phil Garner	1,268,399
1995	4th	65	79	.451	35	Phil Garner	1,087,560
1996	3rd	80	82	.494	19 1/2	Phil Garner	1,327,155
1997	3rd	78	83	.484	8	Phil Garner	1,444,027

NATIONAL LEAGUE CENTRAL DIVISION

Year	Position	W	L	Pct.	*GB	Manager	Attendance
1998	5th	74	88	.457	28	Phil Garner	1,811,548

*Games behind winner. †Seattle Pilots. ‡First half 31-25; second half 31-22. §Lost division series. ∞Won championship series.

MANAGERIAL RECORDS

George Bamberger 377-351, Dave Bristol 144-209, Del Crandall 271-338, Phil Garner 511-557, Alex Grammas 133-190, Harvey Kuenn 160-118, Rene Lachemann 67-94, Buck Rodgers 124-102, Joe Schultz 64-98, Tom Trebelhorn 422-397.

MONTREAL EXPOS
YEARLY FINISHES

EAST DIVISION

Year	Position	W	L	Pct.	*GB	Manager	Attendance
1969	6th	52	110	.321	48	Gene Mauch	1,212,608
1970	6th	73	89	.451	16	Gene Mauch	1,424,683
1971	5th	71	90	.441	25 1/2	Gene Mauch	1,290,963
1972	5th	70	86	.449	26 1/2	Gene Mauch	1,142,145
1973	4th	79	83	.488	3 1/2	Gene Mauch	1,246,863
1974	4th	79	82	.491	8 1/2	Gene Mauch	1,019,134
1975	5th (tied)	75	87	.463	17 1/2	Gene Mauch	908,292
1976	6th	55	107	.340	46	Karl Kuehl, Charlie Fox	646,704
1977	5th	75	87	.463	26	Dick Williams	1,433,757
1978	4th	76	86	.469	14	Dick Williams	1,427,007
1979	2nd	95	65	.594	2	Dick Williams	2,102,173
1980	2nd	90	72	.556	1	Dick Williams	2,208,175
1981	3rd/1st‡§	60	48	.556	†	Dick Williams, Jim Fanning	1,534,564
1982	3rd	86	76	.531	6	Jim Fanning	2,318,292

Year	Position	W	L	Pct.	*GB	Manager	Attendance
1983	3rd	82	80	.506	8	Bill Virdon	2,320,651
1984	5th	78	83	.484	18	Bill Virdon, Jim Fanning	1,606,531
1985	3rd	84	77	.522	16 1/2	Buck Rodgers	1,502,494
1986	4th	78	83	.484	29 1/2	Buck Rodgers	1,128,981
1987	3rd	91	71	.562	4	Buck Rodgers	1,850,324
1988	3rd	81	81	.500	20	Buck Rodgers	1,478,659
1989	4th	81	81	.500	12	Buck Rodgers	1,783,533
1990	3rd	85	77	.525	10	Buck Rodgers	1,373,087
1991	6th	71	90	.441	26 1/2	Buck Rodgers, Tom Runnells	934,742
1992	2nd	87	75	.537	9	Tom Runnells, Felipe Alou	1,669,077
1993	2nd	94	68	.580	3	Felipe Alou	1,641,437
1994	1st	74	40	.649	+6	Felipe Alou	1,276,250
1995	5th	66	78	.458	24	Felipe Alou	1,309,618
1996	2nd	88	74	.543	8	Felipe Alou	1,616,709
1997	4th	78	84	.481	23	Felipe Alou	1,497,609
1998	4th	65	97	.401	41	Felipe Alou	914,717

*Games behind winner. †First half 30-25; second half 30-23. ‡Won division series. §Lost championship series.

MANAGERIAL RECORDS

Felipe Alou 535-496, Jim Fanning 116-103, Charlie Fox 12-22, Karl Kuehl 43-85, Gene Mauch 499-627, Buck Rodgers 520-499, Tom Runnells 68-81, Bill Virdon 146-147, Dick Williams 380-347.

NEW YORK METS
YEARLY FINISHES

Year	Position	W	L	Pct.	*GB	Manager	Attendance
1962	10th	40	120	.250	60 1/2	Casey Stengel	922,530
1963	10th	51	111	.315	48	Casey Stengel	1,080,108
1964	10th	53	109	.327	40	Casey Stengel	1,732,597
1965	10th	50	112	.309	47	Casey Stengel, Wes Westrum	1,768,389
1966	9th	66	95	.410	28 1/2	Wes Westrum	1,932,693
1967	10th	61	101	.377	40 1/2	Wes Westrum, Salty Parker	1,565,492
1968	9th	73	89	.451	24	Gil Hodges	1,781,657

EAST DIVISION

Year	Position	W	L	Pct.	*GB	Manager	Attendance
1969	1st†	100	62	.617	+8	Gil Hodges	2,175,373
1970	3rd	83	79	.512	6	Gil Hodges	2,697,479
1971	3rd (tied)	83	79	.512	14	Gil Hodges	2,266,680
1972	3rd	83	73	.532	13 1/2	Yogi Berra	2,134,185
1973	1st†	82	79	.509	+1 1/2	Yogi Berra	1,912,390
1974	5th	71	91	.438	17	Yogi Berra	1,722,209
1975	3rd (tied)	82	80	.506	10 1/2	Yogi Berra, Roy McMillan	1,730,566
1976	3rd	86	76	.531	15	Joe Frazier	1,468,754
1977	6th	64	98	.395	37	Joe Frazier, Joe Torre	1,066,825
1978	6th	66	96	.407	24	Joe Torre	1,007,328
1979	6th	63	99	.389	35	Joe Torre	788,905
1980	5th	67	95	.414	24	Joe Torre	1,192,073
1981	5th/4th	41	62	.398	‡	Joe Torre	704,244
1982	6th	65	97	.401	27	George Bamberger	1,323,036
1983	6th	68	94	.420	22	George Bamberger, Frank Howard	1,112,774
1984	2nd	90	72	.556	6 1/2	Dave Johnson	1,842,695
1985	2nd	98	64	.605	3	Dave Johnson	2,761,601
1986	1st†	108	54	.667	+21 1/2	Dave Johnson	2,767,601
1987	2nd	92	70	.568	3	Dave Johnson	3,034,129
1988	1st§	100	60	.625	+15	Dave Johnson	3,055,445
1989	2nd	87	75	.537	6	Dave Johnson	2,918,710
1990	2nd	91	71	.562	4	Dave Johnson, Bud Harrelson	2,732,745
1991	5th	77	84	.478	20 1/2	Bud Harrelson, Mike Cubbage	2,284,484
1992	5th	72	90	.444	24	Jeff Torborg	1,779,534
1993	7th	59	103	.364	38	Jeff Torborg, Dallas Green	1,873,183
1994	3rd	55	58	.487	18 1/2	Dallas Green	1,151,471
1995	2nd (tied)	69	75	.479	21	Dallas Green	1,273,183
1996	4th	71	91	.438	25	Dallas Green, Bobby Valentine	1,588,323
1997	3rd	88	74	.543	13	Bobby Valentine	1,766,174
1998	2nd	88	74	.543	18	Bobby Valentine	2,287,942

*Games behind winner. †Won championship series. ‡First half 17-34; second half 24-28. §Lost championship series.

MANAGERIAL RECORDS

George Bamberger 81-127, Yogi Berra 292-296, Mike Cubbage 3-4, Joe Frazier 101-106, Dallas Green 229-283, Bud Harrelson 145-129, Gil Hodges 339-309, Frank Howard 52-64, Davey Johnson 595-417, Roy McMillan 26-27, Salty Parker 4-7, Casey Stengel 175-404, Jeff Torborg 85-115, Joe Torre 286-420, Bobby Valentine 188-167, Wes Westrum 142-237.

YEARLY FINISHES

Year	Position	W	L	Pct.	*GB	Manager	Attendance
1901	2nd	83	57	.593	7 1/2	Bill Shettsline	234,937
1902	7th	56	81	.409	46	Bill Shettsline	112,066
1903	7th	49	86	.363	39 1/2	Chief Zimmer	151,729
1904	8th	52	100	.342	53 1/2	Hugh Duffy	140,771
1905	4th	83	69	.546	21 1/2	Hugh Duffy	317,932
1906	4th	71	82	.464	45 1/2	Hugh Duffy	294,680
1907	3rd	83	64	.565	21 1/2	Bill Murray	341,216
1908	4th	83	71	.539	16	Bill Murray	420,660
1909	5th	74	79	.484	36 1/2	Bill Murray	303,177
1910	4th	78	75	.510	25 1/2	Red Dooin	296,597
1911	4th	79	73	.520	19 1/2	Red Dooin	416,000
1912	5th	73	79	.480	30 1/2	Red Dooin	250,000
1913	2nd	88	63	.583	12 1/2	Red Dooin	470,000
1914	6th	74	80	.481	20 1/2	Red Dooin	138,474
1915	1st	90	62	.592	+7	Pat Moran	449,898
1916	2nd	91	62	.595	2 1/2	Pat Moran	515,365
1917	2nd	87	65	.572	10	Pat Moran	354,428
1918	6th	55	68	.447	26	Pat Moran	122,266
1919	8th	47	90	.343	47 1/2	Jack Coombs, Gavvy Cravath	240,424
1920	8th	62	91	.405	30 1/2	Gavvy Cravath	330,998
1921	8th	51	103	.331	43 1/2	Bill Donovan, Kaiser Wilhelm	273,961
1922	7th	57	96	.373	35 1/2	Kaiser Wilhelm	232,471
1923	8th	50	104	.325	45 1/2	Art Fletcher	228,168
1924	7th	55	96	.364	37	Art Fletcher	299,818
1925	6th (tied)	68	85	.444	27	Art Fletcher	304,905
1926	8th	58	93	.384	29 1/2	Art Fletcher	240,600
1927	8th	51	103	.331	43	Stuffy McInnis	305,420
1928	8th	43	109	.283	51	Burt Shotton	182,168
1929	5th	71	82	.464	27 1/2	Burt Shotton	281,200
1930	8th	52	102	.338	40	Burt Shotton	299,007
1931	6th	66	88	.429	35	Burt Shotton	284,849
1932	4th	78	76	.506	12	Burt Shotton	268,914
1933	7th	60	92	.395	31	Burt Shotton	156,421
1934	7th	56	93	.376	37	Jimmy Wilson	169,885
1935	7th	64	89	.418	35 1/2	Jimmy Wilson	205,470
1936	8th	54	100	.351	38	Jimmy Wilson	249,219
1937	7th	61	92	.399	34 1/2	Jimmy Wilson	212,790
1938	8th	45	105	.300	43	Jimmy Wilson, Hans Lobert	166,111
1939	8th	45	106	.298	50 1/2	Doc Prothro	277,973
1940	8th	50	103	.327	50	Doc Prothro	207,177
1941	8th	43	111	.279	57	Doc Prothro	231,401
1942	8th	42	109	.278	62 1/2	Hans Lobert	230,183
1943	7th	64	90	.416	41	Bucky Harris, Fred Fitzsimmons	466,975
1944	8th	61	92	.399	43 1/2	Fred Fitzsimmons	369,586
1945	8th	46	108	.299	52	Fred Fitzsimmons, Ben Chapman	285,057
1946	5th	69	85	.448	28	Ben Chapman	1,045,247
1947	7th (tied)	62	92	.403	32	Ben Chapman	907,332
1948	6th	66	88	.429	25 1/2	Ben Chapman, Dusty Cooke, Eddie Sawyer	767,429
1949	3rd	81	73	.526	16	Eddie Sawyer	819,698
1950	1st	91	63	.591	+2	Eddie Sawyer	1,217,035
1951	5th	73	81	.474	23 1/2	Eddie Sawyer	937,658
1952	4th	87	67	.565	9 1/2	Eddie Sawyer, Steve O'Neill	775,417
1953	3rd (tied)	83	71	.539	22	Steve O'Neill	853,644
1954	4th	75	79	.487	22	Steve O'Neill, Terry Moore	738,991
1955	4th	77	77	.500	21 1/2	Mayo Smith	922,886
1956	5th	71	83	.461	22	Mayo Smith	934,798
1957	5th	77	77	.500	19	Mayo Smith	1,146,230
1958	8th	69	85	.448	23	Mayo Smith, Eddie Sawyer	931,110
1959	8th	64	90	.416	23	Eddie Sawyer	802,815
1960	8th	59	95	.383	36	Eddie Sawyer, Andy Cohen, Gene Mauch	862,205
1961	8th	47	107	.305	46	Gene Mauch	590,039
1962	7th	81	80	.503	20	Gene Mauch	762,034
1963	4th	87	75	.537	12	Gene Mauch	907,141
1964	2nd (tied)	92	70	.568	1	Gene Mauch	1,425,891
1965	6th	85	76	.528	11 1/2	Gene Mauch	1,166,376
1966	4th	87	75	.537	8	Gene Mauch	1,108,201
1967	5th	82	80	.506	19 1/2	Gene Mauch	828,888
1968	7th (tied)	76	86	.469	21	Gene Mauch, George Myatt, Bob Skinner	664,546

HISTORY Team by team

Year	Position	W	L	Pct.	*GB	Manager	Attendance
1969	5th	63	99	.389	37	Bob Skinner, George Myatt	519,414
1970	5th	73	88	.453	15 1/2	Frank Lucchesi	708,247
1971	6th	67	95	.414	30	Frank Lucchesi	1,511,223
1972	6th	59	97	.378	37 1/2	Frank Lucchesi, Paul Owens	1,343,329
1973	6th	71	91	.438	11 1/2	Danny Ozark	1,475,934
1974	3rd	80	82	.494	8	Danny Ozark	1,808,648
1975	2nd	86	76	.531	6 1/2	Danny Ozark	1,909,233
1976	1st†	101	61	.623	+9	Danny Ozark	2,480,150
1977	1st†	101	61	.623	+5	Danny Ozark	2,700,070
1978	1st†	90	72	.556	+1 1/2	Danny Ozark	2,583,389
1979	4th	84	78	.519	14	Danny Ozark, Dallas Green	2,775,011
1980	1st‡	91	71	.562	+1	Dallas Green	2,651,650
1981	1st/3rd∞	59	48	.551	§	Dallas Green	1,638,752
1982	2nd	89	73	.549	3	Pat Corrales	2,376,394
1983	1st‡	90	72	.556	+6	Pat Corrales, Paul Owens	2,128,339
1984	4th	81	81	.500	15 1/2	Paul Owens	2,062,693
1985	5th	75	87	.463	26	John Felske	1,830,350
1986	2nd	86	75	.534	21 1/2	John Felske	1,933,335
1987	4th (tied)	80	82	.494	15	John Felske, Lee Elia	2,100,110
1988	6th	65	96	.404	35 1/2	Lee Elia, John Vukovich	1,990,041
1989	6th	67	95	.414	26	Nick Leyva	1,861,985
1990	4th (tied)	77	85	.475	18	Nick Leyva	1,992,484
1991	3rd	78	84	.481	20	Nick Leyva, Jim Fregosi	2,050,012
1992	6th	70	92	.432	26	Jim Fregosi	1,927,448
1993	1st‡	97	65	.599	+3	Jim Fregosi	3,137,674
1994	4th	54	61	.470	20 1/2	Jim Fregosi	2,290,971
1995	2nd (tied)	69	75	.479	21	Jim Fregosi	2,043,598
1996	5th	67	95	.414	29	Jim Fregosi	1,801,677
1997	5th	68	94	.420	33	Terry Francona	1,490,638
1998	3rd	75	87	.463	31	Terry Francona	1,715,702

*Games behind winner. †Lost championship series. ‡Won championship series. §First half 34-21; second half 25-27. ∞Lost division series.

MANAGERIAL RECORDS

Ben Chapman 197-277, Andy Cohen 1-0, Dusty Cooke 6-6, Jack Coombs 18-44, Pat Corrales 132-115, Gavvy Cravath 91-137, Bill Donovan 31-71, Red Dooin 392-370, Hugh Duffy 206-251, Lee Elia 111-142, John Felske 190-194, Fred Fitzsimmons 102-179, Art Fletcher 231-378, Terry Francona 143-181, Jim Fregosi 431-463, Dallas Green 169-130, Bucky Harris 40-53, Nick Leyva 148-189, Hans Lobert 42-111, Frank Lucchesi 166-233, Gene Mauch 645-684, Stuffy McInnis 51-103, Terry Moore 35-42, Pat Moran 323-257, Bill Murray 240-214, George Myatt 21-35, Steve O'Neill 182-140, Paul Owens 161-158, Danny Ozark 594-510, Doc Prothro 138-320, Eddie Sawyer 390-424, Bill Shettsline 139-138, Burt Shotton 370-549, Bob Skinner 92-123, Mayo Smith 264-281, John Vukovich 5-4, Kaiser Wilhelm 77-128, Jimmy Wilson 280-477, Chief Zimmer 49-86.

PITTSBURGH PIRATES
YEARLY FINISHES

Year	Position	W	L	Pct.	*GB	Manager	Attendance
1901	1st	90	49	.647	+7 1/2	Fred Clarke	251,955
1902	1st	103	36	.741	+27 1/2	Fred Clarke	243,826
1903	1st	91	49	.650	+6 1/2	Fred Clarke	326,855
1904	4th	87	66	.569	19	Fred Clarke	340,615
1905	2nd	96	57	.627	9	Fred Clarke	369,124
1906	3rd	93	60	.608	23 1/2	Fred Clarke	394,877
1907	2nd	91	63	.591	17	Fred Clarke	319,506
1908	2nd	98	56	.636	1	Fred Clarke	382,444
1909	1st	110	42	.724	+6 1/2	Fred Clarke	534,950
1910	3rd	86	67	.562	17 1/2	Fred Clarke	436,586
1911	3rd	85	69	.552	14 1/2	Fred Clarke	432,000
1912	2nd	93	58	.616	10	Fred Clarke	384,000
1913	4th	78	71	.523	21 1/2	Fred Clarke	296,000
1914	7th	69	85	.448	25 1/2	Fred Clarke	139,620
1915	5th	73	81	.474	18	Fred Clarke	225,743
1916	6th	65	89	.422	29	Jimmy Callahan	289,132
1917	8th	51	103	.331	47	Jimmy Callahan, Honus Wagner, Hugo Bezdek	192,807
1918	4th	65	60	.520	17	Hugo Bezdek	213,610
1919	4th	71	68	.511	24 1/2	Hugo Bezdek	276,810
1920	4th	79	75	.513	14	George Gibson	429,037
1921	2nd	90	63	.588	4	George Gibson	701,567
1922	3rd (tied)	85	69	.552	8	George Gibson, Bill McKechnie	523,675
1923	3rd	87	67	.565	8 1/2	Bill McKechnie	611,082
1924	3rd	90	63	.588	3	Bill McKechnie	736,883

Year	Position	W	L	Pct.	*GB	Manager	Attendance
1925	1st	95	58	.621	+8 1/2	Bill McKechnie	804,354
1926	3rd	84	69	.549	4 1/2	Bill McKechnie	798,542
1927	1st	94	60	.610	+1 1/2	Donie Bush	869,720
1928	4th	85	67	.559	9	Donie Bush	495,070
1929	2nd	88	65	.575	10 1/2	Donie Bush, Jewel Ens	491,377
1930	5th	80	74	.519	12	Jewel Ens	357,795
1931	5th	75	79	.487	26	Jewel Ens	260,392
1932	2nd	86	68	.558	4	George Gibson	287,262
1933	2nd	87	67	.565	5	George Gibson	288,747
1934	5th	74	76	.493	19 1/2	George Gibson, Pie Traynor	322,622
1935	4th	86	67	.562	13 1/2	Pie Traynor	352,885
1936	4th	84	70	.545	8	Pie Traynor	372,524
1937	3rd	86	68	.558	10	Pie Traynor	459,679
1938	2nd	86	64	.573	2	Pie Traynor	641,033
1939	6th	68	85	.444	28 1/2	Pie Traynor	376,734
1940	4th	78	76	.506	22 1/2	Frankie Frisch	507,934
1941	4th	81	73	.526	19	Frankie Frisch	482,241
1942	5th	66	81	.449	36 1/2	Frankie Frisch	448,897
1943	4th	80	74	.519	25	Frankie Frisch	604,278
1944	2nd	90	63	.588	14 1/2	Frankie Frisch	498,740
1945	4th	82	72	.532	16	Frankie Frisch	604,694
1946	7th	63	91	.409	34	Frankie Frisch, Spud Davis	749,962
1947	7th (tied)	62	92	.403	32	Billy Herman, Bill Burwell	1,283,531
1948	4th	83	71	.539	8 1/2	Billy Meyer	1,517,021
1949	6th	71	83	.461	26	Billy Meyer	1,499,435
1950	8th	57	96	.373	33 1/2	Billy Meyer	1,166,267
1951	7th	64	90	.416	32 1/2	Billy Meyer	980,590
1952	8th	42	112	.273	54 1/2	Billy Meyer	686,673
1953	8th	50	104	.325	55	Fred Haney	572,757
1954	8th	53	101	.344	44	Fred Haney	475,494
1955	8th	60	94	.390	38 1/2	Fred Haney	469,397
1956	7th	66	88	.429	27	Bobby Bragan	949,878
1957	7th (tied)	62	92	.403	33	Bobby Bragan, Danny Murtaugh	850,732
1958	2nd	84	70	.545	8	Danny Murtaugh	1,311,988
1959	4th	78	76	.506	9	Danny Murtaugh	1,359,917
1960	1st	95	59	.617	+7	Danny Murtaugh	1,705,828
1961	6th	75	79	.487	18	Danny Murtaugh	1,199,128
1962	4th	93	68	.578	8	Danny Murtaugh	1,090,648
1963	8th	74	88	.457	25	Danny Murtaugh	783,648
1964	6th (tied)	80	82	.494	13	Danny Murtaugh	759,496
1965	3rd	90	72	.556	7	Harry Walker	909,279
1966	3rd	92	70	.568	3	Harry Walker	1,196,618
1967	6th	81	81	.500	20 1/2	Harry Walker, Danny Murtaugh	907,012
1968	6th	80	82	.494	17	Larry Shepard	693,485

EAST DIVISION

Year	Position	W	L	Pct.	*GB	Manager	Attendance
1969	3rd	88	74	.543	12	Larry Shepard, Alex Grammas	769,369
1970	1st††	89	73	.549	+5	Danny Murtaugh	1,341,947
1971	1st‡	97	65	.599	+7	Danny Murtaugh	1,501,132
1972	1st†	96	59	.619	+11	Bill Virdon	1,427,460
1973	3rd	80	82	.494	2 1/2	Bill Virdon, Danny Murtaugh	1,319,913
1974	1st†	88	74	.543	+1 1/2	Danny Murtaugh	1,110,552
1975	1st†	92	69	.571	+6 1/2	Danny Murtaugh	1,270,018
1976	2nd	92	70	.568	9	Danny Murtaugh	1,025,945
1977	2nd	96	66	.593	5	Chuck Tanner	1,237,349
1978	2nd	88	73	.547	1 1/2	Chuck Tanner	964,106
1979	1st‡	98	64	.605	+2	Chuck Tanner	1,435,454
1980	3rd	83	79	.512	8	Chuck Tanner	1,646,757
1981	4th/6th	46	56	.451	§	Chuck Tanner	541,789
1982	4th	84	78	.519	8	Chuck Tanner	1,024,106
1983	2nd	84	78	.519	6	Chuck Tanner	1,225,916
1984	6th	75	87	.463	21 1/2	Chuck Tanner	773,500
1985	6th	57	104	.354	43 1/2	Chuck Tanner	735,900
1986	6th	64	98	.395	44	Jim Leyland	1,000,917
1987	4th (tied)	80	82	.494	15	Jim Leyland	1,161,193
1988	2nd	85	75	.531	15	Jim Leyland	1,866,713
1989	5th	74	88	.457	19	Jim Leyland	1,374,141
1990	1st††	95	67	.586	+4	Jim Leyland	2,049,908
1991	1st††	98	64	.605	+14	Jim Leyland	2,065,302
1992	1st††	96	66	.593	+9	Jim Leyland	1,829,395
1993	5th	75	87	.463	22	Jim Leyland	1,650,593

Year	Position	W	L	Pct.	*GB	Manager	Attendance
1994	3rd (tied)	53	61	.465	13	Jim Leyland	1,222,520
1995	5th	58	86	.403	27	Jim Leyland	905,517
1996	5th	73	89	.451	15	Jim Leyland	1,332,150
1997	2nd	79	83	.488	5	Gene Lamont	1,657,022
1998	6th	69	93	.426	33	Gene Lamont	1,560,950

*Games behind winner. †Lost championship series. ‡Won championship series. §First half 25-23; second half 21-33.

MANAGERIAL RECORDS

Hugo Bezdek 166-187, Bobby Bragan 102-155, Bill Burwell 1-0, Donie Bush 246-178, Jimmy Callahan 85-129, Fred Clarke 1,343-909, Spud Davis 1-2, Jewel Ens 176-167, Frank Frisch 539-528, George Gibson 401-330, Alex Grammas 4-1, Fred Haney 163-299, Billy Herman 61-92, Gene Lamont 148-176, Jim Leyland 851-863, Bill McKechnie 409-293, Billy Meyer 317-452, Danny Murtaugh 1,115-950, Larry Shepard 164-155, Chuck Tanner 711-685, Pie Traynor 457-406, Bill Virdon 163-128, Honus Wagner 1-4, Harry Walker 224-184.

ST. LOUIS CARDINALS
YEARLY FINISHES

Year	Position	W	L	Pct.	*GB	Manager	Attendance
1901	4th	76	64	.543	14 1/2	Patsy Donovan	379,988
1902	6th	56	78	.418	44 1/2	Patsy Donovan	226,417
1903	8th	43	94	.314	46 1/2	Patsy Donovan	226,538
1904	5th	75	79	.487	31 1/2	Kid Nichols	386,750
1905	6th	58	96	.377	47 1/2	Kid Nichols, Jimmy Burke, Matt Robison	292,800
1906	7th	52	98	.347	63	John McCloskey	283,770
1907	8th	52	101	.340	55 1/2	John McCloskey	185,377
1908	8th	49	105	.318	50	John McCloskey	205,129
1909	7th	54	98	.355	56	Roger Bresnahan	299,982
1910	7th	63	90	.412	40 1/2	Roger Bresnahan	355,668
1911	5th	75	74	.503	22	Roger Bresnahan	447,768
1912	6th	63	90	.412	41	Roger Bresnahan	241,759
1913	8th	51	99	.340	49	Miller Huggins	203,531
1914	3rd	81	72	.529	13	Miller Huggins	256,099
1915	6th	72	81	.471	18 1/2	Miller Huggins	252,666
1916	7th (tied)	60	93	.392	33 1/2	Miller Huggins	224,308
1917	3rd	82	70	.539	15	Miller Huggins	288,491
1918	8th	51	78	.395	33	Jack Hendricks	110,599
1919	7th	54	83	.394	40 1/2	Branch Rickey	167,059
1920	5th (tied)	75	79	.487	18	Branch Rickey	326,836
1921	3rd	87	66	.569	7	Branch Rickey	384,773
1922	3rd (tied)	85	69	.552	8	Branch Rickey	536,998
1923	5th	79	74	.516	16	Branch Rickey	338,551
1924	6th	65	89	.422	28 1/2	Branch Rickey	272,885
1925	4th	77	76	.503	18	Branch Rickey, Rogers Hornsby	404,959
1926	1st	89	65	.578	+2	Rogers Hornsby	668,428
1927	2nd	92	61	.601	1 1/2	Bob O'Farrell	749,340
1928	1st	95	59	.617	+2	Bill McKechnie	761,574
1929	4th	78	74	.513	20	Bill McKechnie, Billy Southworth	399,887
1930	1st	92	62	.597	+2	Gabby Street	508,501
1931	1st	101	53	.656	+13	Gabby Street	608,535
1932	6th (tied)	72	82	.468	18	Gabby Street	279,219
1933	5th	82	71	.536	9 1/2	Gabby Street, Frankie Frisch	256,171
1934	1st	95	58	.621	+2	Frankie Frisch	325,056
1935	2nd	96	58	.623	4	Frankie Frisch	506,084
1936	2nd (tied)	87	67	.565	5	Frankie Frisch	448,078
1937	4th	81	73	.526	15	Frankie Frisch	430,811
1938	6th	71	80	.470	17 1/2	Frankie Frisch, Mike Gonzalez	291,418
1939	2nd	92	61	.601	4 1/2	Ray Blades	400,245
1940	3rd	84	69	.549	16	Ray Blades, Mike Gonzalez, Billy Southworth	324,078
1941	2nd	97	56	.634	2 1/2	Billy Southworth	633,645
1942	1st	106	48	.688	+2	Billy Southworth	553,552
1943	1st	105	49	.682	+18	Billy Southworth	517,135
1944	1st	105	49	.682	+14 1/2	Billy Southworth	461,968
1945	2nd	95	59	.617	3	Billy Southworth	594,630
1946	1st†‡	98	58	.628	+2	Eddie Dyer	1,061,807
1947	2nd	89	65	.578	5	Eddie Dyer	1,247,913
1948	2nd	85	69	.552	6 1/2	Eddie Dyer	1,111,440
1949	2nd	96	58	.623	1	Eddie Dyer	1,430,676
1950	5th	78	75	.510	12 1/2	Eddie Dyer	1,093,411
1951	3rd	81	73	.526	15 1/2	Marty Marion	1,013,429
1952	3rd	88	66	.571	8 1/2	Eddie Stanky	913,113
1953	3rd (tied)	83	71	.539	22	Eddie Stanky	880,242
1954	6th	72	82	.468	25	Eddie Stanky	1,039,698

Year	Position	W	L	Pct.	*GB	Manager	Attendance
1955	7th	68	86	.442	30 1/2	Eddie Stanky, Harry Walker	849,130
1956	4th	76	78	.494	17	Fred Hutchinson	1,029,773
1957	2nd	87	67	.565	8	Fred Hutchinson	1,183,575
1958	5th (tied)	72	82	.468	20	Fred Hutchinson, Stan Hack	1,063,730
1959	7th	71	83	.461	16	Solly Hemus	929,953
1960	3rd	86	68	.558	9	Solly Hemus	1,096,632
1961	5th	80	74	.519	13	Solly Hemus, Johnny Keane	855,305
1962	6th	84	78	.519	17 1/2	Johnny Keane	953,895
1963	2nd	93	69	.574	6	Johnny Keane	1,170,546
1964	1st	93	69	.574	+1	Johnny Keane	1,143,294
1965	7th	80	81	.497	16 1/2	Red Schoendienst	1,241,201
1966	6th	83	79	.512	12	Red Schoendienst	1,712,980
1967	1st	101	60	.627	+10 1/2	Red Schoendienst	2,090,145
1968	1st	97	65	.599	+9	Red Schoendienst	2,011,167

EAST DIVISION

Year	Position	W	L	Pct.	*GB	Manager	Attendance
1969	4th	87	75	.537	13	Red Schoendienst	1,682,783
1970	4th	76	86	.469	13	Red Schoendienst	1,629,736
1971	2nd	90	72	.556	7	Red Schoendienst	1,604,671
1972	4th	75	81	.481	21 1/2	Red Schoendienst	1,196,894
1973	2nd	81	81	.500	1 1/2	Red Schoendienst	1,574,046
1974	2nd	86	75	.534	1 1/2	Red Schoendienst	1,838,413
1975	3rd (tied)	82	80	.506	10 1/2	Red Schoendienst	1,695,270
1976	5th	72	90	.444	29	Red Schoendienst	1,207,079
1977	3rd	83	79	.512	18	Vern Rapp	1,659,287
1978	5th	69	93	.426	21	Vern Rapp, Jack Krol, Ken Boyer	1,278,215
1979	3rd	86	76	.531	12	Ken Boyer	1,627,256
1980	4th	74	88	.457	17	Ken Boyer, Jack Krol, Whitey Herzog, Red Schoendienst	1,385,147
1981	2nd/2nd	59	43	.578	‡	Whitey Herzog	1,010,247
1982	1st§	92	70	.568	+3	Whitey Herzog	2,111,906
1983	4th	79	83	.488	11	Whitey Herzog	2,317,914
1984	3rd	84	78	.519	12 1/2	Whitey Herzog	2,037,448
1985	1st§	101	61	.623	+3	Whitey Herzog	2,637,563
1986	3rd	79	82	.491	28 1/2	Whitey Herzog	2,471,974
1987	1st§	95	67	.586	+3	Whitey Herzog	3,072,122
1988	5th	76	86	.469	25	Whitey Herzog	2,892,799
1989	3rd	86	76	.531	7	Whitey Herzog	3,080,980
1990	6th	70	92	.432	25	Whitey Herzog, Red Schoendienst, Joe Torre	2,573,225
1991	2nd	84	78	.519	14	Joe Torre	2,448,699
1992	3rd	83	79	.512	13	Joe Torre	2,418,483
1993	3rd	87	75	.537	10	Joe Torre	2,844,328

CENTRAL DIVISION

Year	Position	W	L	Pct.	*GB	Manager	Attendance
1994	3rd (tied)	53	61	.465	13	Joe Torre	1,866,544
1995	4th	62	81	.434	22 1/2	Joe Torre, Mike Jorgensen	1,756,727
1996	1st∞▲	88	74	.543	+6	Tony La Russa	2,654,718
1997	4th	73	89	.451	11	Tony La Russa	2,634,014
1998	3rd	83	79	.512	19	Tony La Russa	3,194,092

*Games behind winner. †Won pennant playoff. ‡First half 30-20; second half 29-23. §Won championship series. ∞Won division series. ▲Lost championship series.

MANAGERIAL RECORDS

Ray Blades 106-85, Ken Boyer 166-190, Roger Bresnahan 255-352, Jimmy Burke 17-32, Patsy Donovan 175-236, Eddie Dyer 446-325, Frank Frisch 458-354, Mike Gonzalez 9-13, Stan Hack 3-7, Solly Hemus 190-192, Jack Hendricks 51-78, Whitey Herzog 835-739, Rogers Hornsby 153-116, Miller Huggins 346-415, Fred Hutchinson 232-220, Mike Jorgensen 42-54, Johnny Keane 317-249, Tony La Russa 244-242, Marty Marion 81-73, John McCloskey 153-304, Bill McKechnie 129-88, Kid Nichols 94-108, Bob O'Farrell 92-61, Vern Rapp 89-90, Branch Rickey 458-485, Stanley Robison 22-35, Red Schoendienst 1,028-944, Billy Southworth 620-346, Eddie Stanky 260-238, Gabby Street 312-242, Joe Torre 351-354, Harry Walker 51-67.

SAN DIEGO PADRES
YEARLY FINISHES

WEST DIVISION

Year	Position	W	L	Pct.	*GB	Manager	Attendance
1969	6th	52	110	.321	41	Preston Gomez	512,970
1970	6th	63	99	.389	39	Preston Gomez	643,679
1971	6th	61	100	.379	28 1/2	Preston Gomez	557,513
1972	6th	58	95	.379	36 1/2	Preston Gomez, Don Zimmer	644,273
1973	6th	60	102	.370	39	Don Zimmer	611,826
1974	6th	60	102	.370	42	John McNamara	1,075,399

Year	Position	W	L	Pct.	*GB	Manager	Attendance
1975	4th	71	91	.438	37	John McNamara	1,281,747
1976	5th	73	89	.451	29	John McNamara	1,458,478
1977	5th	69	93	.426	29	John McNamara, Bob Skinner, Alvin Dark	1,376,269
1978	4th	84	78	.519	11	Roger Craig	1,670,107
1979	5th	68	93	.422	22	Roger Craig	1,456,967
1980	6th	73	89	.451	19 1/2	Jerry Coleman	1,139,026
1981	6th/6th	41	69	.373	†	Frank Howard	519,161
1982	4th	81	81	.500	8	Dick Williams	1,607,516
1983	4th	81	81	.500	10	Dick Williams	1,539,815
1984	1st†	92	70	.568	+12	Dick Williams	1,983,904
1985	3rd (tied)	83	79	.512	12	Dick Williams	2,210,352
1986	4th	74	88	.457	22	Steve Boros	1,805,716
1987	6th	65	97	.401	25	Larry Bowa	1,454,061
1988	3rd	83	78	.516	11	Larry Bowa, Jack McKeon	1,506,896
1989	2nd	89	73	.549	3	Jack McKeon	2,009,031
1990	4th (tied)	75	87	.463	16	Jack McKeon, Greg Riddoch	1,856,396
1991	3rd	84	78	.519	10	Greg Riddoch	1,804,289
1992	3rd	82	80	.506	16	Greg Riddoch, Jim Riggleman	1,722,102
1993	7th	61	101	.377	43	Jim Riggleman	1,375,432
1994	4th	47	70	.402	12 1/2	Jim Riggleman	953,857
1995	3rd	70	74	.486	8	Bruce Bochy	1,041,805
1996	1st§	91	71	.562	+1	Bruce Bochy	2,187,886
1997	4th	76	86	.469	14	Bruce Bochy	2,089,333
1998	1st∞	98	64	.605	+9 1/2	Bruce Bochy	2,555,901

*Games behind winner. †First half 23-33; second half 18-36. ‡Won championship series. §Lost division series. ∞Won division series.

MANAGERIAL RECORDS

Bruce Bochy 335-295, Steve Boros 74-88, Larry Bowa 81-127, Jerry Coleman 73-89, Roger Craig 152-171, Alvin Dark 49-65, Preston Gomez 180-316, Frank Howard 41-69, Jack McKeon 193-164, John McNamara 224-310, Greg Riddoch 200-194, Jim Riggleman 112-179, Dick Williams 337-311, Don Zimmer 114-190.

SAN FRANCISCO GIANTS
YEARLY FINISHES

Year	Position	W	L	Pct.	*GB	Manager	Attendance
1901†	7th	52	85	.380	37	George Davis	297,650
1902†	8th	48	88	.353	53 1/2	Horace Fogel, Heinie Smith, John McGraw	302,875
1903†	2nd	84	55	.604	6 1/2	John McGraw	579,530
1904†	1st	106	47	.693	+13	John McGraw	609,826
1905†	1st	105	48	.686	+9	John McGraw	552,700
1906†	2nd	96	56	.632	20	John McGraw	402,850
1907†	4th	82	71	.536	25 1/2	John McGraw	538,350
1908†	2nd (tied)	98	56	.636	1	John McGraw	910,000
1909†	3rd	92	61	.601	18 1/2	John McGraw	783,700
1910†	2nd	91	63	.591	13	John McGraw	511,785
1911†	1st	99	54	.647	+7 1/2	John McGraw	675,000
1912†	1st	103	48	.682	+10	John McGraw	638,000
1913†	1st	101	51	.664	+12 1/2	John McGraw	630,000
1914†	2nd	84	70	.545	10 1/2	John McGraw	364,313
1915†	8th	69	83	.454	21	John McGraw	391,850
1916†	4th	86	66	.566	7	John McGraw	552,056
1917†	1st	98	56	.636	+10	John McGraw	500,264
1918†	2nd	71	53	.573	10 1/2	John McGraw	256,618
1919†	2nd	87	53	.621	9	John McGraw	708,857
1920†	2nd	86	68	.558	7	John McGraw	929,609
1921†	1st	94	59	.614	+4	John McGraw	773,477
1922†	1st	93	61	.604	+7	John McGraw	945,809
1923†	1st	95	58	.621	+4 1/2	John McGraw	820,780
1924†	1st	93	60	.608	+1 1/2	John McGraw	844,068
1925†	2nd	86	66	.566	8 1/2	John McGraw	778,993
1926†	5th	74	77	.490	13 1/2	John McGraw	700,362
1927†	3rd	92	62	.597	2	John McGraw	858,190
1928†	2nd	93	61	.604	2	John McGraw	916,191
1929†	3rd	84	67	.556	13 1/2	John McGraw	868,806
1930†	3rd	87	67	.565	5	John McGraw	868,714
1931†	2nd	87	65	.572	13	John McGraw	812,163
1932†	6th (tied)	72	82	.468	18	John McGraw, Bill Terry	484,868
1933†	1st	91	61	.599	+5	Bill Terry	604,471
1934†	2nd	93	60	.608	2	Bill Terry	730,851
1935†	3rd	91	62	.595	8 1/2	Bill Terry	748,748
1936†	1st	92	62	.597	+5	Bill Terry	837,952

Year	Position	W	L	Pct.	*GB	Manager	Attendance
1937†	1st	95	57	.625	+3	Bill Terry	926,887
1938†	3rd	83	67	.553	5	Bill Terry	799,633
1939†	5th	77	74	.510	18 1/2	Bill Terry	702,457
1940†	6th	72	80	.474	27 1/2	Bill Terry	747,852
1941†	5th	74	79	.484	25 1/2	Bill Terry	763,098
1942†	3rd	85	67	.559	20	Mel Ott	779,621
1943†	8th	55	98	.359	49 1/2	Mel Ott	466,095
1944†	5th	67	87	.435	38	Mel Ott	674,083
1945†	5th	78	74	.513	19	Mel Ott	1,016,468
1946†	8th	61	93	.396	36	Mel Ott	1,219,873
1947†	4th	81	73	.526	13	Mel Ott	1,600,793
1948†	5th	78	76	.506	13 1/2	Mel Ott, Leo Durocher	1,459,269
1949†	5th	73	81	.474	24	Leo Durocher	1,218,446
1950†	3rd	86	68	.558	5	Leo Durocher	1,008,876
1951†‡	1st‡	98	59	.624	+1	Leo Durocher	1,059,539
1952†	2nd	92	62	.597	4 1/2	Leo Durocher	984,940
1953†	5th	70	84	.455	35	Leo Durocher	811,518
1954†	1st	97	57	.630	+5	Leo Durocher	1,155,067
1955†	3rd	80	74	.519	18 1/2	Leo Durocher	824,112
1956†	6th	67	87	.435	26	Bill Rigney	629,179
1957†	6th	69	85	.448	26	Bill Rigney	653,923
1958	3rd	80	74	.519	12	Bill Rigney	1,272,625
1959	3rd	83	71	.539	4	Bill Rigney	1,422,130
1960	5th	79	75	.513	16	Bill Rigney, Tom Sheehan	1,795,356
1961	3rd	85	69	.552	8	Alvin Dark	1,390,679
1962	1st‡	103	62	.624	+1	Alvin Dark	1,592,594
1963	3rd	88	74	.543	11	Alvin Dark	1,571,306
1964	4th	90	72	.556	3	Alvin Dark	1,504,364
1965	2nd	95	67	.586	2	Herman Franks	1,546,075
1966	2nd	93	68	.578	1 1/2	Herman Franks	1,657,192
1967	2nd	91	71	.562	10 1/2	Herman Franks	1,242,480
1968	2nd	88	74	.543	9	Herman Franks	837,220

WEST DIVISION

Year	Position	W	L	Pct.	*GB	Manager	Attendance
1969	2nd	90	72	.556	3	Clyde King	873,603
1970	3rd	86	76	.531	16	Clyde King, Charlie Fox	740,720
1971	1st§	90	72	.556	+1	Charlie Fox	1,106,043
1972	5th	69	86	.445	26 1/2	Charlie Fox	647,744
1973	3rd	88	74	.543	11	Charlie Fox	834,193
1974	5th	72	90	.444	30	Charlie Fox, Wes Westrum	519,987
1975	3rd	80	81	.497	27 1/2	Wes Westrum	522,919
1976	4th	74	88	.457	28	Bill Rigney	626,868
1977	4th	75	87	.463	23	Joe Altobelli	700,056
1978	3rd	89	73	.549	6	Joe Altobelli	1,740,477
1979	4th	71	91	.438	19 1/2	Joe Altobelli, Dave Bristol	1,456,402
1980	5th	75	86	.466	17	Dave Bristol	1,096,115
1981	5th/3rd	56	55	.505	∞	Frank Robinson	632,274
1982	3rd	87	75	.537	2	Frank Robinson	1,200,948
1983	5th	79	83	.488	12	Frank Robinson	1,251,530
1984	6th	66	96	.407	26	Frank Robinson, Danny Ozark	1,001,545
1985	6th	62	100	.383	33	Jim Davenport, Roger Craig	818,697
1986	3rd	83	79	.512	13	Roger Craig	1,528,748
1987	1st§	90	72	.556	+6	Roger Craig	1,917,168
1988	4th	83	79	.512	11 1/2	Roger Craig	1,785,297
1989	1st▲	92	70	.568	+3	Roger Craig	2,059,701
1990	3rd	85	77	.525	6	Roger Craig	1,975,528
1991	4th	75	87	.463	19	Roger Craig	1,737,478
1992	5th	72	90	.444	26	Roger Craig	1,561,987
1993	2nd	103	59	.636	1	Dusty Baker	2,606,354
1994	2nd	55	60	.478	3 1/2	Dusty Baker	1,704,608
1995	4th	67	77	.465	11	Dusty Baker	1,241,500
1996	4th	68	94	.420	23	Dusty Baker	1,413,922
1997	1st◆	90	72	.556	+2	Dusty Baker	1,690,869
1998	2nd	89	74	.546	9 1/2	Dusty Baker	1,925,634

*Games behind winner. †New York Giants. ‡Won pennant playoff. §Lost championship series. ∞First half 27-32; second half 29-23. ▲Won championship series. ◆Lost division series.

MANAGERIAL RECORDS

Joe Altobelli 225-239, Dusty Baker 472-436, Dave Bristol 85-98, Roger Craig 586-566, Alvin Dark 366-277, Jim Davenport 56-88, George Davis 52-85, Leo Durocher 637-523, Horace Fogel 18-23, Charlie Fox 348-327, Herman Franks 367-280, Clyde King 109-95, John McGraw 2,604-1,801, Mel Ott 464-530, Danny Ozark 24-32, Bill Rigney 406-430, Frank Robinson 264-277, Tom Sheehan 46-50, Heinie Smith 5-27, Bill Terry 823-661, Wes Westrum 118-129.

MINOR LEAGUES

Farm systems

International League

Mexican League

Pacific Coast League

Eastern League

Southern League

Texas League

California League

Carolina League

Florida State League

Midwest League

New York-Pennsylvania League

Northwest League

South Atlantic League

Appalachian League

Arizona League

Gulf Coast League

Pioneer League

Minor league index

FARM SYSTEMS

AMERICAN LEAGUE

ANAHEIM (6): AAA—Edmonton. AA—Erie. A—Boise, Cedar Rapids, Lake Elsinore. Rookie—Butte.
BALTIMORE (6): AAA—Rochester. AA—Bowie. A—Delmarva, Frederick. Rookie—Bluefield, Gulf Coast Orioles.
BOSTON (6): AAA—Pawtucket. AA—Trenton. A—Augusta, Lowell, Sarasota. Rookie—Gulf Coast Red Sox.
CHICAGO (6): AAA—Charlotte. AA—Birmingham. A—Burlington, Winston-Salem. Rookie—Bristol, Tucson White Sox.
CLEVELAND (6): AAA—Buffalo. AA—Akron. A—Columbus, Kinston, Mahoning Valley. Rookie—Burlington.
DETROIT (6): AAA—Toledo. AA—Jacksonville. A—Lakeland, Oneonta, West Michigan. Rookie—Gulf Coast Tigers.
KANSAS CITY (6): AAA—Omaha. AA—Wichita. A—Charleston (WV), Spokane, Wilmington. Rookie—Gulf Coast Royals.
MINNESOTA (6): AAA—Salt Lake. AA—New Britain. A—Fort Myers, Quad City. Rookie—Elizabethton, Gulf Coast Twins.
NEW YORK (6): AAA—Columbus. AA—Norwich. A—Greensboro, Tampa, Watertown. Rookie—Gulf Coast Yankees.
OAKLAND (6): AAA—Vancouver. AA—Midland. A—Modesto, Southern Oregon, Visalia. Rookie—Phoenix A's.
SEATTLE (6): AAA—Tacoma. AA—New Haven. A—Everett, Lancaster, Wisconsin. Rookie—Peoria Mariners.
TAMPA BAY (7): AAA—Durham. AA—Orlando. A—Charleston (SC), Hudson Valley, St. Petersburg. Rookie—Gulf Coast Devil Rays, Princeton.
TEXAS (6): AAA—Oklahoma. AA—Tulsa. A—Charlotte, Savannah. Rookie—Gulf Coast Rangers, Pulaski.
TORONTO (6): AAA—Syracuse. AA—Knoxville. A—Dunedin, Hagerstown, St. Catharines. Rookie—Medicine Hat.

NATIONAL LEAGUE

ARIZONA (6): AAA—Tucson. AA—El Paso. A—High Desert, South Bend. Rookie—Missoula, Peoria (AZ) Diamondbacks.
ATLANTA (7): AAA—Richmond. AA—Greenville. A—Jamestown, Macon, Myrtle Beach. Rookie—Danville, Gulf Coast Braves.
CHICAGO (6): AAA—Iowa. AA—West Tenn. A—Daytona Beach, Eugene, Lansing. Rookie—Mesa Cubs.
CINCINNATI (5): AAA—Indianapolis. AA—Chattanooga. A—Clinton, Rockford. Rookie—Billings.
COLORADO (6): AAA—Colorado Springs. AA—Carolina. A—Asheville, Portland (OR), Salem. Rookie—Mesa Rockies.
FLORIDA (6): AAA—Calgary. AA—Portland (ME). A—Brevard County, Kane County, Utica. Rookie—Gulf Coast Marlins.
HOUSTON (6): AAA—New Orleans. AA—Jackson. A—Auburn, Kissimmee, Michigan. Rookie—Martinsville.
LOS ANGELES (6): AAA—Albuquerque. AA—San Antonio. A—San Bernardino, Vero Beach, Yakima. Rookie—Great Falls.
MILWAUKEE (6): AAA—Louisville. AA—Huntsville. A—Beloit, Stockton. Rookie—Helena, Ogden.
MONTREAL (6): AAA—Ottawa. AA—Harrisburg. A—Fayetteville, Jupiter, Vermont. Rookie—Gulf Coast Expos.
NEW YORK (7): AAA—Norfolk. AA—Binghamton. A—Capital City, Pittsfield, St. Lucie. Rookie—Gulf Coast Mets, Kingsport.
PHILADELPHIA (6): AAA—Scranton/Wilkes-Barre. AA—Reading. A—Batavia, Clearwater, Piedmont. Rookie—Gulf Coast Phillies.
PITTSBURGH (6): AAA—Nashville. AA—Altoona. A—Hickory, Lynchburg, Williamsport. Rookie—Gulf Coast Pirates.
ST. LOUIS (6): AAA—Memphis. AA—Arkansas. A—New Jersey, Peoria (IL), Potomac. Rookie—Johnson City.
SAN DIEGO (6): AAA—Las Vegas. AA—Mobile. A—Fort Wayne, Rancho Cucamonga. Rookie—Idaho Falls, Peoria (AZ) Padres.
SAN FRANCISCO (5): AAA—Fresno. AA—Shreveport. A—Bakersfield, Salem-Keizer, San Jose.

INTERNATIONAL LEAGUE

LEAGUE OFFICE

President
Randy Mobley

Address
55 S. High St., Suite 202
Dublin, OH 43017

Phone
614-791-9300

TEAMS

BUFFALO BISONS

General manager
Mike Buczkowski
Manager
Jeff Datz
Ballpark (capacity, surface)
North AmeriCare Park (21,050, grass)
Affiliation
Indians
Address
P.O. Box 450
Buffalo, NY 14205
Phone
716-846-2003

CHARLOTTE KNIGHTS

V.P./general manager
Marty Steele
Manager
Tom Spencer
Ballpark (capacity, surface)
Knights Castle (10,005, grass)
Affiliation
White Sox
Address
P.O. Box 1207
Fort Mill, SC 29716-1207
Phone
803-548-8050

COLUMBUS CLIPPERS

General manager
Ken Schnacke
Manager
Trey Hillman
Ballpark (capacity, surface)
Cooper Stadium (15,000, grass)
Affiliation
Yankees
Address
1155 W. Mound St.
Columbus, OH 43223
Phone
614-462-5250

DURHAM BULLS

General manager
Peter Anlyan
Manager
Peter Anlyan
Ballpark (capacity, surface)
Durham Bulls Athletic Park
(10,000, grass)
Affiliation
Devil Rays
Address
409 Blackwell St.
Durham, NC 27702
Phone
919-687-6500

INDIANAPOLIS INDIANS

President/CEO
Max Schumacher
General manager
Cal Burleson
Manager
Dave Miley
Ballpark (capacity, surface)
Victory Field (15,000, grass)
Affiliation
Reds
Address
501 W. Maryland St.
Indianapolis, IN 46225
Phone
317-269-3545

LOUISVILLE RIVERBATS

General manager
Dale Owens
Manager
Gary Allenson
Ballpark (capacity, surface)
Cardinal Stadium (33,000, artificial)
Affiliation
Brewers
Address
P.O. Box 36407
Louisville, KY 40233
Phone
502-367-9121

NORFOLK TIDES

General manager
Dave Rosenfield
Manager
John Gibbons
Ballpark (capacity, surface)
Harbor Park (12,059, grass)
Affiliation
Mets
Address
150 Park Ave.
Norfolk, VA 23510
Phone
757-622-2222

OTTAWA LYNX

Director of baseball operations
To be announced
Manager
Jeff Cox
Ballpark (capacity, surface)
Jetform Park (10,332, grass)
Affiliation
Expos
Address
300 Coventry Rd.
Ottawa, Ontario K1K 4P5
Phone
613-747-5969

PAWTUCKET RED SOX

General manager
Lou Schwechheimer
Manager
Gary Jones
Ballpark (capacity, surface)
McCoy Stadium (10,000, grass)
Affiliation
Red Sox
Address
P.O. Box 2365
Pawtucket, RI 02861
Phone
401-724-7303

RICHMOND BRAVES

General manager
Bruce Baldwin
Manager
Randy Ingle
Ballpark (capacity, surface)
The Diamond (12,156, grass)
Affiliation
Braves
Address
P.O. Box 6667
Richmond, VA 23230
Phone
804-359-4444

ROCHESTER RED WINGS

General manager
Dan Mason
Manager
Dave Machemer
Ballpark (capacity, surface)
Frontier Field (22,844, grass)
Affiliation
Orioles
Address
1 Morrie Silver Way
Rochester, NY 14608
Phone
716-454-1001

SCRANTON/WILKES-BARRE RED BARONS

General manager
Rick Muntean
Manager
Marc Bombard
Ballpark (capacity, surface)
Lackawanna County Stadium (10,982,
artificial)
Affiliation
Phillies
Address
P.O. Box 3449
Scranton, PA 18505
Phone
570-969-2255

SYRACUSE SKY CHIEFS

General manager
John Simone
Manager
Terry Bevington
Ballpark (capacity, surface)
P&C Stadium (11,100, artificial)
Affiliation
Blue Jays

Address
One Tex Simone
Syracuse, NY 13208
Phone
315-474-7833

TOLEDO MUD HENS

General manager
Gene Cook
Manager
Gene Roof

Ballpark (capacity, surface)
Ned Skeldon Stadium (10,025, grass)
Affiliation
Tigers
Address
P.O. Box 6212
Toledo, OH 43614
Phone
419-893-9483

1998 FINAL STANDINGS

EASTERN DIVISION

Team	W	L	T	Pct.	GB
Buffalo (Indians)	81	62	0	.566	....
Syracuse (Blue Jays)	80	62	0	.563	0.5
Pawtucket (Red Sox)	77	64	1	.546	3.0
Rochester (Orioles)	70	74	0	.486	11.5
Ottawa (Expos)	69	74	0	.483	12.0
Scranton/Wilkes-Barre (Phillies)	67	75	0	.472	13.5

NORTHERN DIVISION

Team	W	L	T	Pct.	GB
Louisville (Brewers)	77	67	0	.535	....
Indianapolis (Reds)	76	67	0	.531	0.5
Columbus (Yankees)	67	77	0	.465	10.0
Toledo (Tigers)	52	89	1	.369	23.5

SOUTHERN DIVISION

Team	W	L	T	Pct.	GB
Durham (Devil Rays)	80	64	0	.556	....
Norfolk (Mets)	70	72	0	.493	9.0
Charlotte (Marlins)	70	73	0	.490	9.5
Richmond (Braves)	64	80	0	.444	16.0

COMPOSITE

Team	Buf.	Syr.	Dur.	Paw.	Lou.	Ind.	Nor.	Char.	Roch.	Ott.	SWB	Col.	Rich.	Tol.	W	L	T	Pct.	GB
Buffalo (Indians)	....	8	3	7	3	6	5	5	9	10	12	5	3	5	81	62	0	.566	....
Syracuse (Blue Jays)	8	....	6	8	4	4	3	5	4	9	13	5	5	6	80	62	0	.563	0.5
Durham (Devil Rays)	5	2	....	3	9	10	6	10	6	2	4	7	9	7	80	64	0	.556	1.5
Pawtucket (Red Sox)	9	7	5	....	4	3	3	5	11	8	7	3	6	6	77	64	0	.546	3.0
Louisville (Brewers)	5	4	3	4	....	5	7	8	5	5	3	10	6	12	77	67	0	.535	4.5
Indianapolis (Reds)	2	4	2	5	11	....	5	7	4	2	5	11	8	10	76	67	0	.531	5.0
Norfolk (Mets)	3	4	10	5	5	7	....	4	4	4	4	5	8	7	70	72	0	.493	10.5
Charlotte (Marlins)	3	3	6	3	4	5	12	....	4	3	3	6	9	9	70	73	0	.490	11.0
Rochester (Orioles)	7	12	2	5	3	4	4	4	....	8	8	4	5	4	70	74	0	.486	11.5
Ottawa (Expos)	6	7	6	8	3	5	4	5	8	....	6	3	4	4	69	74	0	.483	12.0
Scranton/Wilkes-Barre (Phillies)	3	3	4	9	5	3	4	4	8	10	....	4	4	6	67	75	0	.472	13.5
Columbus (Yankees)	3	3	5	5	6	5	7	6	4	5	4	....	6	8	67	77	0	.465	14.5
Richmond (Braves)	5	3	7	2	6	4	8	7	3	4	4	6	....	5	64	80	0	.444	17.5
Toledo (Tigers)	3	2	5	0	4	6	4	3	4	4	2	8	7	....	52	89	0	.369	28.0

Major league affiliations in parentheses.

PLAYOFFS: Buffalo defeated Syracuse, three games to none; Durham defeated Louisville, three games to none; Buffalo defeated Durham, three games to two to win league championship.

REGULAR-SEASON ATTENDANCE: Buffalo, 768,749; Charlotte, 299,664; Columbus, 488,674; Durham, 491,391; Indianapolis, 659,237; Louisville, 412,398; Norfolk, 479,222; Ottawa, 224,371; Pawtucket, 475,659; Richmond, 528,230; Rochester, 515,436; Scranton/Wilkes-Barre, 406,735; Syracuse, 420,488; Toledo, 311,652. Total—6,481,906. Playoffs (11games)—41,513. Class AAA All-Star Game at Norfolk, Va.—11,049.

MANAGERS: Buffalo, Jeff Datz; Charlotte, Fredi Gonzalez; Columbus, Stump Merrill; Durham, Bill Evers; Indianapolis, Dave Miley; Louisville, Gary Allenson; Norfolk, Rick Dempsey; Ottawa, Pat Kelly; Pawtucket, Ken Macha; Richmond, Jeff Cox; Rochester, Marv Foley; Scranton/Wilkes-Barre, Mark Bombard; Syracuse, Terry Bevington; Toledo, Gene Roof.

ALL-STAR TEAM: 1B—Roberto Petagine, Indianapolis; 2B—Ron Belliard, Louisville; 3B Scott McClain, Durham; SS—Jolbert Cabrera, Buffalo; OF—Allen Battle, Ottawa; Brian Daubach, Charlotte; Alex Ramirez, Buffalo; C—Einer Diaz, Buffalo; DH—Willis Otanez, Rochester; Utility—Todd Haney, Norfolk; Starting pitcher—Shannon Withem, Syracuse; Relief pitcher—Todd Williams; Indianapolis; Most Valuable Player—Roberto Petagine, Indianapolis; Most Valuable Pitcher—Shannon Withem, Syracuse; Rookie of the Year—Marlon Anderson, Scranton/Wilkes-Barre; Manager of the Year—Ken Macha, Pawtucket.

1998 BATTING
TEAM

Team	Avg.	G	TPA	AB	R	H	TB	2B	3B	HR	RBI	SH	SF	HP	BB	IBB	SO	SB	CS	GDP	LOB	ShO	Slg.	OBP
Buffalo	.282	143	5616	4942	837	1394	2319	253	27	206	781	23	42	55	554	23	900	94	55	110	1028	4	.469	.358
Louisville	.277	144	5551	4886	792	1354	2198	259	54	159	735	47	36	63	519	22	1009	190	73	109	986	5	.450	.352
Pawtucket	.275	142	5442	4724	763	1297	2124	224	21	187	708	26	47	52	593	19	949	132	73	124	1009	4	.450	.359
Durham	.274	144	5581	4872	787	1335	2134	275	22	160	729	46	39	43	581	22	906	148	80	102	1025	8	.438	.354
Indianapolis	.273	143	5466	4836	787	1322	2157	299	28	160	724	31	49	43	587	19	1018	77	42	99	1059	4	.446	.354
Scranton/W.-B.	.273	142	5541	4877	746	1332	2190	282	42	164	695	39	48	52	525	23	932	110	48	118	1018	4	.449	.347
Columbus	.273	144	5581	4972	726	1355	2181	278	46	152	675	26	41	47	495	18	941	103	49	130	1008	5	.439	.341
Rochester	.272	144	5459	4897	703	1331	2030	261	39	120	655	26	39	54	443	11	834	104	49	102	993	9	.415	.336
Charlotte	.271	143	5415	4783	739	1297	2088	274	29	153	696	37	36	60	499	19	1016	106	60	119	971	6	.437	.345

Team	Avg.	G	TPA	AB	R	H	TB	2B	3B	HR	RBI	SH	SF	HP	BB	IBB	SO	SB	CS	GDP	LOB	ShO	Slg.	OBP
Norfolk	.268	142	5453	4757	661	1274	1912	238	35	110	607	48	40	44	564	19	841	129	64	114	1065	6	.402	.348
Syracuse	.263	142	5306	4682	653	1231	2035	250	31	164	607	35	31	52	506	20	963	111	59	119	981	5	.435	.339
Toledo	.260	142	5263	4752	595	1237	1848	229	32	106	531	32	31	51	397	12	885	141	44	110	974	14	.389	.322
Richmond......	.256	144	5341	4733	607	1211	1842	244	27	111	567	41	39	54	474	29	977	94	45	127	977	9	.389	.328
Ottawa............	.255	143	5312	4686	600	1194	1729	239	34	76	550	54	39	51	482	15	935	165	59	105	1003	12	.369	.328

INDIVIDUAL

TOP QUALIFIERS FOR BATTING CHAMPIONSHIP

Minimum 389 plate appearances. *Lefthanded batter. †Switch-hitter.

Player, Team	Avg.	G	TPA	AB	R	H	TB	2B	3B	HR	RBI	SH	SF	HP	BB	IBB	SO	SB	CS	GDP	Slg.	OBP
Haney, Todd, Nor.	.345	117	506	440	84	152	202	33	4	3	51	5	1	5	55	1	44	11	2	13	.459	.423
Petagine, Roberto, Ind.*	.331	102	443	363	79	120	224	30	1	24	109	0	7	3	70	6	71	3	1	14	.617	.436
Lovullo, Torey, Buf.†	.326	92	393	328	66	107	183	17	4	17	65	1	9	1	54	1	32	3	3	9	.558	.413
Belliard, Ronnie, Lou.	.321	133	589	507	114	163	255	36	7	14	73	1	4	8	69	2	77	33	12	17	.503	.408
Cabrera, Jolbert, Buf.	.318	129	585	494	94	157	213	24	1	10	45	8	2	13	68	0	71	25	15	10	.431	.412
Daubach, Brian, Char.*	.316	140	600	497	102	157	315	45	4	35	124	0	7	15	80	9	114	9	3	15	.634	.421
Decker, Steve, Nor.	.314	102	416	354	55	111	168	21	0	12	60	0	4	4	54	2	49	0	2	13	.475	.406
Diaz, Einar, Buf.	.313	115	444	415	62	130	181	21	3	8	63	0	2	6	21	3	33	3	3	8	.436	.354
Nixon, Trot, Paw.*	.310	135	509	97	158	261	26	4	23	74	0	7	5	76	6	81	26	13	10	.513	.400
Matos, Francisco, Dur.-Col. ...	.310	108	435	407	55	126	162	20	5	2	47	2	2	3	21	0	41	5	3	17	.398	.346
Abad, Andy, Paw.*	.307	111	445	365	71	112	180	18	1	16	66	4	5	3	68	2	70	10	6	7	.493	.415
Anderson, Marlon, S./W.B.* ..	.306	136	620	575	104	176	284	32	14	16	86	5	5	7	28	1	77	24	12	11	.494	.343
Battle, Allen, Ott.	.304	132	541	454	72	138	206	31	2	11	68	2	6	8	71	3	81	34	5	13	.454	.403
Lowell, Mike, Col.	.304	126	558	510	79	155	273	34	3	26	99	0	5	6	37	2	85	4	0	10	.535	.355
Flores, Jose, S./W.B.	.301	98	405	345	53	104	144	18	2	6	34	7	2	2	49	1	45	12	6	7	.417	.389

DEPARTMENTAL LEADERS: G—Doster, 141; AB—Doster, 579; R—Ron Belliard, 114; H— Anderson, 176; TB—Daubach, 315; 2B—Daubach, 45; 3B—Anderson, 14; HR—Daubach, 35; RBI—Daubach, 124; SH—Gregory Martinez, 10; SF—Doster, 10; HP—Daubach, Krause, 15 each; BB—Lennon, 87; IBB—Daubach, 9; SO—Hiatt, 146; SB—Pose, 47; CS—J. Cabrera, L. Castillo, 15 each; GIDP—Simon, 22; Slg.—Daubach, .634; OBP—Petagine, .436.

ALL PLAYERS

*Lefthanded batter. †Switch-hitter.

Player, Team	Avg.	G	TPA	AB	R	H	TB	2B	3B	HR	RBI	SH	SF	HP	BB	IBB	SO	SB	CS	GDP	Slg.	OBP
Abad, Andy, Paw.*	.307	111	445	365	71	112	180	18	1	16	66	4	5	3	68	2	70	10	6	7	.493	.415
Agbayani, Benny, Nor.	.283	90	378	322	43	91	154	20	5	11	53	0	3	3	50	2	58	16	6	5	.478	.381
Almanzar, Richard, Tol.	.209	104	343	306	36	64	85	16	1	1	16	4	2	3	28	0	30	11	7	8	.278	.280
Alvarez, Gabe, Tol.	.273	67	283	249	37	68	145	15	1	20	58	0	3	1	30	0	60	3	1	7	.582	.350
Anderson, Marlon, S./W.B.* ..	.306	136	620	575	104	176	284	32	14	16	86	5	5	7	28	1	77	24	12	11	.494	.343
Angeli, Doug, S./W.B.	.178	42	131	118	12	21	28	4	0	1	10	2	1	2	8	0	36	1	1	3	.237	.240
Arnold, Jamie, Rich.	1.000	9	4	1	0	1	1	0	0	0	1	3	0	0	0	0	0	0	0	0	1.000	1.000
Arntzen, Brian, Ott.	.231	5	13	13	0	3	3	0	0	0	0	0	0	0	0	0	4	0	0	0	.231	.231
Arroyo, Luis, Nor.*	.000	8	1	1	0	0	0	0	0	0	0	0	0	0	0	0	1	0	0	0	.000	.000
Ashby, Chris, Col.	.091	5	14	11	0	1	1	0	0	0	0	1	0	0	3	0	6	0	0	0	.091	.286
Ashley, Billy, Paw.	.271	63	256	218	40	59	113	12	0	14	51	0	2	1	35	0	72	1	0	5	.518	.371
Aucoin, Derek, Nor.	.000	3	1	1	0	0	0	0	0	0	0	0	0	0	0	0	1	0	0	0	.000	.000
Aven, Bruce, Buf.	.200	5	21	15	4	3	7	1	0	1	1	0	0	0	6	0	5	3	0	0	.467	.429
Azuaje, Jesus, Nor.	.212	10	36	33	1	7	10	3	0	0	1	1	0	0	2	0	6	0	0	3	.303	.257
Bady, Ed, Ott.†	.154	5	16	13	0	2	2	0	0	0	0	0	0	0	3	0	5	0	0	0	.154	.313
Baez, Kevin, Ind.	.263	49	159	137	21	36	44	5	0	1	12	2	1	0	19	0	26	0	1	6	.321	.350
Bako, Paul, Tol.*	.292	13	50	48	5	14	22	3	1	1	6	0	1	0	1	0	13	0	0	1	.458	.300
Banks, Brian, Lou.†	.291	85	355	299	58	87	170	18	1	21	66	0	2	2	52	3	72	14	3	5	.569	.397
Barker, Kevin, Lou.*	.276	124	506	463	59	128	231	26	4	23	96	0	4	3	36	1	97	2	5	11	.499	.330
Barrios, Manny, Char.	1.000	18	2	1	1	1	1	0	0	0	0	0	0	0	1	0	0	0	0	0	1.000	1.000
Barron, Tony, S./W.B.	.272	102	421	375	60	102	181	23	1	18	62	0	2	5	39	3	83	7	4	15	.483	.347
Bartee, Kimera, Tol.†	.247	51	233	215	24	53	69	10	0	2	13	0	0	2	16	1	42	6	3	2	.321	.305
Battle, Allen, Ott.	.304	132	541	454	72	138	206	31	2	11	68	2	6	8	71	3	81	34	5	13	.454	.403
Beamon, Trey, Tol.*	.237	56	240	207	31	49	64	6	0	3	18	0	3	2	28	0	38	16	2	2	.309	.329
Beasley, Ray, Rich.	.000	2	2	1	0	0	0	0	0	0	0	0	1	0	0	0	0	0	0	0	.000	.000
Beck, Greg, Lou.	.000	10	8	6	0	0	0	0	0	0	0	2	0	0	0	0	4	0	0	0	.000	.000
Belk, Tim, Tol.	.267	84	314	292	40	78	126	19	1	9	34	0	1	3	18	1	55	5	0	6	.432	.315
Bell, Juan, Syr.†	.211	12	41	38	4	8	14	4	1	0	1	1	0	1	1	0	6	0	0	1	.368	.250
Bell, Mike, Nor.	.182	17	53	44	6	8	15	1	0	2	8	1	0	1	7	0	7	0	0	3	.341	.302
Belliard, Rafael, Rich.	.140	13	44	43	6	6	9	0	0	1	2	1	0	0	0	0	6	0	0	2	.209	.140
Belliard, Ronnie, Lou.	.321	133	589	507	114	163	255	36	7	14	73	1	4	8	69	2	77	33	12	17	.503	.408
Bellinger, Clay, Col.	.224	115	442	397	35	89	140	20	2	9	40	1	4	5	35	2	79	6	3	10	.353	.293
Beltran, Rigo, Nor.*	.313	37	17	16	2	5	6	1	0	0	3	1	0	0	0	3	0	0	0	0	.375	.313
Bennett, Gary, S./W.B.	.255	86	315	282	33	72	120	18	0	10	40	2	4	2	25	0	41	0	0	6	.426	.316
Benz, Jake, Ott.*	.400	25	6	5	1	2	3	1	0	0	0	0	0	0	1	0	1	0	0	0	.600	.400
Berry, Mike, Col.	.287	25	101	87	7	25	34	6	0	1	9	0	4	0	10	0	14	0	2	2	.391	.347
Betts, Todd, Buf.*	.229	14	44	35	5	8	17	3	0	2	6	0	1	0	8	0	7	0	0	0	.486	.364
Betzsold, James, Buf.	.244	74	242	209	36	51	93	10	1	10	27	0	6	0	27	0	72	4	4	3	.445	.347
Bierek, Kurt, Col.*	.300	14	55	50	8	15	25	5	1	1	8	0	0	0	5	0	8	0	0	2	.500	.364
Blosser, Greg, Dur.*	.253	115	453	371	78	94	192	23	0	25	72	1	6	2	73	3	114	10	5	4	.518	.374
Blum, Geoffrey, Ott.†	.174	8	27	23	1	4	4	0	0	0	1	0	0	0	3	0	6	0	0	0	.174	.269
Bocachica, Hiram, Ott.	.195	12	48	41	5	8	13	3	1	0	5	0	0	1	6	0	14	2	0	1	.317	.313
Bogle, Bryan, Roch.	.267	10	31	30	5	8	13	2	0	1	4	0	0	1	0	0	8	0	0	0	.433	.290
Bolton, Rod, Ind.	.103	29	35	29	2	3	4	1	0	0	2	4	1	0	1	0	12	0	1	1	.138	.129
Boone, Aaron, Ind.	.241	87	377	332	56	80	121	18	1	7	38	0	6	8	31	2	71	17	5	6	.364	.316
Booty, Josh, Char.	.142	38	136	127	9	18	30	3	0	3	11	0	2	0	7	2	44	0	1	5	.236	.184
Borbon, Pedro, Rich.*	1.000	20	1	1	1	1	1	0	0	0	0	0	0	0	0	0	0	0	0	0	1.000	1.000

Player, Team	Avg.	G	TPA	AB	R	H	TB	2B	3B	HR	RBI	SH	SF	HP	BB	IBB	SO	SB	CS	GDP	Slg.	OBP
Borland, Toby, Char.	.000	19	4	3	0	0	0	0	0	0	0	1	0	0	0	1	0	0	0	.000	.000
Borrero, Richie, Paw.	.176	6	18	17	3	3	3	0	0	0	0	0	0	0	1	0	5	0	0	1	.176	.222
Boskie, Shawn, Ott.	.111	13	13	9	0	1	1	0	0	0	0	2	0	0	2	0	4	0	0	0	.111	.273
Bottalico, Ricky, S./W.B.*	.000	10	1	1	0	0	0	0	0	0	0	0	0	0	0	0	0	0	0	0	.000	.000
Bowers, Brent, Nor.*	.244	82	304	275	36	67	96	8	3	5	31	3	5	0	21	0	59	17	6	6	.349	.292
Brannan, Ryan, S./W.B.	.000	16	1	1	0	0	0	0	0	0	0	0	0	0	0	0	1	0	0	0	.000	.000
Branson, Jeff, Buf.*	.261	12	51	46	5	12	18	4	1	0	2	0	0	0	5	1	9	0	0	0	.391	.333
Briggs, Anthony, Rich.	.000	28	22	22	0	0	0	0	0	0	0	0	0	0	0	0	9	0	0	0	.000	.000
Brito, Jorge, Lou.	.284	77	269	232	34	66	110	17	0	9	36	4	3	8	22	0	61	3	1	4	.474	.362
Brown, Kevin, Syr.	.625	2	8	8	2	5	7	2	0	0	0	0	0	0	0	0	2	0	0	0	.875	.625
Brumfield, Jacob, Char.	.167	95	268	227	24	38	60	13	0	3	25	1	2	4	34	0	41	7	1	6	.264	.285
Bryant, Pat, Paw.	.224	75	302	259	43	58	92	8	1	8	26	1	4	5	33	0	63	13	5	5	.355	.319
Bucchieri, Jim, Dur.	.305	106	388	351	51	107	145	14	3	6	34	6	0	5	25	1	28	37	13	11	.413	.360
Buckley, Travis, Rich.	.000	4	1	1	0	0	0	0	0	0	0	0	0	0	0	0	1	0	0	0	.000	.000
Bullard, Jason, Rich.	.333	36	3	3	0	1	1	0	0	0	0	0	0	0	0	0	0	0	0	0	.333	.333
Bunch, Mel, Ott.	.167	25	14	12	1	2	4	0	1	0	2	2	0	0	0	0	3	0	0	0	.333	.167
Burton, Darren, S./W.B.†	.266	117	458	394	56	105	186	21	3	18	64	2	3	6	53	1	83	9	0	10	.472	.354
Butler, Adam, Rich.*	.222	48	11	9	1	2	5	0	0	1	1	2	0	0	0	0	3	0	0	1	.556	.222
Butler, Rich, Dur.*	.297	38	172	145	28	43	75	8	0	8	35	0	3	2	22	3	24	6	2	1	.517	.390
Byrd, Paul, Rich.	.087	17	24	23	1	2	3	1	0	0	1	1	0	0	0	0	5	0	0	0	.130	.087
Cabrera, Jolbert, Buf.	.318	129	585	494	94	157	213	24	1	10	45	8	2	13	68	0	71	25	15	10	.431	.412
Cabrera, Orlando, Ott.	.232	66	307	272	31	63	80	9	4	0	26	2	5	0	28	0	27	19	9	8	.294	.298
Candelaria, Ben, Syr.*	.247	69	279	251	28	62	100	13	2	7	32	0	3	2	23	2	68	2	0	5	.398	.312
Cardona, Javier, Tol.	.191	47	176	162	12	31	50	4	0	5	16	4	0	1	9	1	32	0	0	3	.309	.238
Carey, Todd, Paw.-Nor.*	.255	109	369	329	34	84	137	22	2	9	39	1	3	0	35	1	70	5	6	4	.416	.324
Carlyle, Ken, Rich.	.050	30	21	20	0	1	1	0	0	0	0	0	0	0	1	0	8	0	0	0	.050	.095
Carpenter, Bubba, Col.*	.227	63	237	198	28	45	84	14	2	7	24	2	0	1	36	2	48	3	2	9	.424	.349
Carver, Steve, S./W.B.*	.304	8	25	23	3	7	12	2	0	1	4	0	0	0	2	0	10	0	1	0	.522	.360
Casanova, Raul, Tol.†	.257	50	197	171	17	44	73	8	0	7	26	0	1	3	22	1	28	0	1	6	.427	.350
Casey, Sean, Ind.*	.326	27	110	95	14	31	44	8	1	1	13	0	0	1	14	1	10	0	0	0	.463	.418
Castillo, Alberto, Nor.	.184	21	60	49	4	9	14	2	0	1	6	0	0	0	11	2	12	0	0	0	.286	.333
Castillo, Luis, Char.†	.287	100	462	380	74	109	124	11	2	0	15	4	2	0	75	1	68	41	15	6	.326	.403
Catalanotto, Frank, Tol.*	.333	28	129	105	20	35	59	6	3	4	28	1	2	7	14	0	21	0	0	2	.562	.438
Cather, Mike, Rich.	.000	11	1	1	0	0	0	0	0	0	0	0	0	0	0	0	1	0	0	0	.000	.000
Chancey, Bailey, Nor.†	.000	2	2	2	0	0	0	0	0	0	0	0	0	0	0	0	2	0	0	0	.000	.000
Chavez, Raul, Ott.	.226	11	37	31	2	7	7	0	0	0	1	1	0	0	5	0	5	0	0	1	.226	.333
Chen, Bruce, Rich.†	.000	4	3	1	0	0	0	0	0	0	0	1	0	0	1	0	0	0	0	0	.000	.500
Chouinard, Bobby, Lou.	.200	7	6	5	1	1	1	0	0	0	0	1	0	0	0	0	4	0	0	0	.200	.333
Christopherson, Eric, Nor.	.186	37	120	97	7	18	27	4	1	1	13	3	2	0	18	0	20	1	1	1	.278	.308
Clapinski, Chris, Char.†	.269	100	364	312	53	84	131	18	1	9	35	7	1	5	39	0	53	11	3	7	.420	.359
Clark, Howie, Roch.*	.232	30	104	95	13	22	37	4	1	3	8	0	0	0	9	0	11	1	2	2	.389	.298
Clontz, Brad, Nor.	.000	28	4	4	1	0	0	0	0	0	0	0	0	0	0	0	3	0	0	0	.000	.000
Clyburn, Danny, Roch.	.286	84	363	322	58	92	157	21	1	14	54	0	3	4	34	0	72	11	5	9	.488	.358
Cole, Jason, Ott.	.000	13	4	4	0	0	0	0	0	0	0	0	0	0	0	0	2	0	0	0	.000	.000
Coleman, Michael, Paw.	.253	93	379	340	47	86	141	13	0	14	37	3	1	8	27	0	92	12	9	4	.415	.322
Colon, Dennis, Nor.*	.269	51	183	160	18	43	50	7	0	0	9	1	0	1	21	0	21	1	2	3	.313	.357
Coquillette, Trace, Ott.	.254	74	281	252	30	64	99	14	0	7	40	2	3	7	17	1	38	3	3	9	.393	.315
Corbin, Archie, Char.	.000	34	4	3	1	0	0	0	0	0	0	0	0	0	0	0	0	0	0	0	.000	.250
Corey, Mark, Ind.	.000	1	2	2	0	0	0	0	0	0	0	0	0	0	0	0	1	0	0	0	.000	.000
Cornelius, Reid, Char.	.182	8	12	11	1	2	3	1	0	0	0	1	0	0	0	0	5	0	0	0	.273	.182
Cornett, Brad, Lou.	.000	12	11	8	0	0	0	0	0	0	0	3	0	0	0	0	7	0	0	0	.000	.000
Cortes, David, Rich.	.000	29	4	3	0	0	0	0	0	0	0	0	0	0	1	0	1	0	0	0	.000	.250
Costo, Tim, Syr.	.296	101	396	365	45	108	172	18	2	14	55	1	2	2	26	0	72	1	2	7	.471	.344
Cox, Darron, Dur.	.302	84	314	278	45	84	129	16	1	9	35	8	0	5	23	0	41	2	2	6	.464	.366
Cox, Steve, Dur.*	.253	119	495	430	64	109	175	23	2	13	67	2	5	2	56	6	100	3	4	9	.407	.339
Crowell, Jim, Ind.	.000	1	1	1	0	0	0	0	0	0	0	0	0	0	0	0	1	0	0	0	.000	.000
Cruz, Deivi, Tol.	.111	2	11	9	1	1	2	1	0	0	2	0	0	0	2	0	3	0	0	0	.222	.273
Cruz, Ivan, Col.*	.265	56	236	204	34	54	103	10	0	13	36	0	1	2	29	3	44	0	0	6	.505	.360
Cruz, Jacob, Buf.*	.331	43	184	169	32	56	107	8	2	13	36	0	1	1	13	0	26	2	3	3	.633	.380
Cruz, Jose, Syr.†	.298	40	174	141	29	42	79	14	1	7	23	0	1	0	32	0	32	8	4	2	.560	.425
Dalesandro, Mark, Syr.	.268	45	182	164	25	44	85	9	1	10	30	0	1	5	12	1	20	1	0	3	.518	.335
Darden, Tony, Nor.	.000	1	1	0	0	0	0	0	0	0	0	0	0	0	1	0	0	0	0	0	.000	1.000
Daubach, Brian, Char.*	.316	140	600	497	102	157	315	45	4	35	124	0	7	15	80	9	114	9	3	15	.634	.421
Davis, Chili, Col.†	.364	6	27	22	4	8	9	1	0	0	3	0	1	4	3	0	3	0	0	0	.409	.481
Davis, James, Ind.	.200	19	51	50	4	10	15	2	0	1	4	0	0	0	1	0	12	0	0	0	.300	.216
Dawkins, Walt, S./W.B.	.269	42	120	108	15	29	44	6	0	3	14	1	1	1	9	0	23	2	1	3	.407	.328
DeCinces, Tim, Roch.*	.095	7	23	21	1	2	3	1	0	0	0	0	0	0	2	0	6	0	0	0	.143	.174
Decker, Steve, Nor.	.314	102	416	354	55	111	168	21	0	12	60	0	4	4	54	2	49	0	2	13	.475	.406
Dedrick, Jim, Rich.†	1.000	26	1	1	0	1	1	0	0	0	0	0	0	0	0	0	0	0	0	0	1.000	1.000
DeHart, Rick, Ott.	.000	38	1	1	0	0	0	0	0	0	0	0	0	0	0	0	1	0	0	0	.000	.000
Delgado, Alex, Syr.	.234	82	319	286	22	67	99	14	0	6	28	3	1	4	25	3	39	2	0	15	.346	.304
Delgado, Carlos, Syr.*	.571	2	9	7	4	4	9	2	0	1	6	0	0	2	0	0	0	0	0	1	1.286	.667
De Los Santos, Eddy, Dur.	.273	4	12	11	2	3	5	2	0	0	2	0	0	1	0	0	6	0	0	0	.455	.333
Dempster, Ryan, Char.	.286	5	9	7	0	2	2	0	0	0	0	1	0	1	0	0	3	0	0	0	.286	.375
Depastino, Joe, Paw.	.242	9	34	33	1	8	9	1	0	0	4	0	0	1	0	0	8	1	1	1	.273	.265
DeSilva, John, Ott.	.000	7	3	2	0	0	0	0	0	0	0	0	0	0	1	0	1	0	0	0	.000	.333
Devarez, Cesar, Dur.	.267	38	125	116	11	31	52	5	2	4	20	0	0	1	8	0	24	4	2	3	.448	.320
Diaz, Eddy, Lou.-Paw.	.257	119	465	416	61	107	162	24	2	9	53	1	3	6	39	2	39	13	6	12	.389	.328
Diaz, Einar, Buf.	.313	115	444	415	62	130	181	21	3	8	63	0	2	6	21	3	33	3	3	8	.436	.354
Dodd, Robert, S./W.B.*	.000	42	2	2	0	0	0	0	0	0	0	0	0	0	0	0	0	0	0	0	.000	.000
Dodson, Bo, Roch.*	.276	116	456	387	57	107	161	26	2	8	48	0	2	5	62	1	65	5	2	6	.416	.382
Donato, Dan, Dur.*	.229	17	41	35	5	8	13	2	0	1	2	0	0	2	4	0	5	0	0	0	.371	.341

CLASS AAA International League

Player, Team	Avg.	G	TPA	AB	R	H	TB	2B	3B	HR	RBI	SH	SF	HP	BB	IBB	SO	SB	CS	GDP	Slg.	OBP
Donnelly, Brendan, Ind.	.000	19	4	4	0	0	0	0	0	0	0	0	0	0	0	0	4	0	0	0	.000	.000
Doster, David, S./W.B.	.276	141	645	579	79	160	254	38	4	16	84	1	10	4	51	2	80	23	6	14	.439	.334
Dotel, Octavio, Nor.	.038	17	31	26	3	1	1	0	0	0	0	3	0	0	2	0	11	0	0	0	.038	.107
Dunbar, Matt, Lou.*	.000	50	1	1	0	0	0	0	0	0	0	0	0	0	0	0	1	0	0	0	.000	.000
Dunn, Todd, Lou.	.382	10	36	34	5	13	19	3	0	1	1	0	0	2	0	0	10	0	2	1	.559	.417
Dunwoody, Todd, Char.*	.304	28	118	102	20	31	61	6	3	6	22	0	0	4	12	0	28	4	2	2	.598	.398
Ebert, Derrin, Rich.	.231	29	32	26	3	6	7	1	0	0	1	5	0	0	1	0	4	0	0	4	.269	.259
Eenhoorn, Robert, Nor.	.233	94	361	330	34	77	116	12	3	7	38	6	3	0	22	3	44	0	5	14	.352	.279
Eischen, Joey, Ind.*	.000	61	3	2	0	0	0	0	0	0	0	0	0	1	0	0	0	0	0	0	.000	.333
Ellis, Robert, Lou.	.063	30	20	16	2	1	1	0	0	0	1	2	0	0	2	0	8	0	0	1	.063	.167
Encarnacion, Juan, Tol.	.287	92	399	356	55	102	149	17	3	8	41	0	4	10	29	1	85	24	4	9	.419	.353
Estalella, Bobby, S./W.B.	.281	76	312	242	49	68	135	14	1	17	49	0	2	2	66	0	49	0	0	13	.558	.436
Estrada, Osmani, Char.	.259	8	30	27	3	7	8	1	0	0	3	0	0	2	1	0	4	0	0	0	.296	.333
Evans, Tom, Syr.	.300	109	459	400	57	120	199	32	1	15	55	0	1	8	50	1	74	11	7	13	.498	.388
Falteisek, Steve, Ott.	.190	35	24	21	1	4	4	0	0	0	1	2	0	0	1	0	7	0	0	0	.190	.227
Faries, Paul, Tol.	.290	122	518	458	65	133	167	21	5	1	36	8	1	5	46	0	54	33	7	12	.365	.361
Fernandez, Jose, Ott.	.267	21	67	60	8	16	22	4	1	0	4	1	1	0	5	0	14	3	1	2	.367	.318
Fernandez, Osvaldo, Nor.*	.000	2	1	1	0	0	0	0	0	0	0	0	0	0	0	0	1	0	0	0	.000	.000
Figga, Mike, Col.	.280	123	499	461	57	129	243	30	3	26	95	0	1	2	35	4	109	2	2	15	.527	.333
Fiore, Tony, S./W.B.	.200	41	5	5	0	1	1	0	0	0	0	0	0	0	0	0	2	0	0	0	.200	.200
Fithian, Grant, Col.	.111	5	11	9	1	1	3	0	1	0	0	0	0	0	2	0	1	0	0	1	.333	.273
Flaherty, John, Dur.	.130	6	25	23	1	3	4	1	0	0	2	0	1	0	1	0	5	0	0	1	.174	.160
Flores, Jose, S./W.B.	.301	98	405	345	53	104	144	18	2	6	34	7	2	2	49	1	45	12	6	7	.417	.389
Forbes, P.J., Roch.	.293	116	513	460	74	135	196	37	3	6	52	8	3	5	36	1	54	10	2	15	.426	.349
Fordyce, Brook, Ind.	.250	6	25	24	4	6	13	1	0	2	3	0	0	0	1	0	2	0	0	1	.542	.280
Foster, Jim, Roch.	.235	43	174	153	22	36	60	9	0	5	26	0	1	2	18	1	22	3	1	5	.392	.322
Franco, Matt, Nor.*	.368	5	22	19	2	7	8	1	0	0	1	0	0	0	3	0	1	2	0	1	.421	.455
Frank, Mike, Ind.*	.341	22	95	88	8	30	34	4	0	0	13	0	0	0	7	0	9	1	0	3	.386	.389
Freel, Ryan, Syr.	.229	37	151	118	19	27	37	4	0	2	12	0	3	4	26	0	16	9	4	3	.314	.377
Fyhrie, Mike, Nor.	.375	26	26	24	4	9	10	1	0	0	0	0	0	0	2	0	7	0	0	1	.417	.423
Garcia, Guillermo, Ind.	.254	93	357	334	48	85	162	20	0	19	60	1	0	0	22	1	81	0	2	9	.485	.301
Garcia, Jesse, Roch.	.294	44	175	160	20	47	61	6	4	0	18	2	3	3	7	0	22	7	5	3	.381	.329
Garcia, Luis, Tol.	.258	114	422	407	37	105	141	19	4	3	31	3	3	1	8	0	59	3	2	11	.346	.272
Garcia, Omar, Ind.	.412	7	18	17	2	7	10	0	0	1	3	0	0	0	1	0	2	0	0	0	.588	.444
Gardiner, Mike, Char.	.167	14	15	12	0	2	2	0	0	0	1	2	0	0	1	0	3	0	0	0	.167	.231
Geisler, Phil, Char.*	.161	14	34	31	2	5	6	1	0	0	1	0	0	0	3	0	13	0	0	1	.194	.235
Gibralter, Steve, Ind.	.257	68	239	226	34	58	111	12	4	11	31	0	1	2	10	0	66	1	2	3	.491	.293
Gilbert, Shawn, Nor.	.271	39	153	133	21	36	50	8	0	2	12	0	2	2	16	1	28	7	2	2	.376	.353
Giles, Brian, Buf.*	.239	13	52	46	5	11	19	2	0	2	7	0	0	0	6	0	8	0	0	2	.413	.327
Glass, Chip, Col.*	.200	8	15	15	2	3	4	1	0	0	2	0	0	0	0	0	1	0	0	1	.267	.200
Glauber, Keith, Ind.	.000	4	6	4	0	0	0	0	0	0	0	2	0	0	0	0	1	0	0	0	.000	.000
Goldsmith, Gary, Tol.	.000	46	1	1	0	0	0	0	0	0	0	0	0	0	0	0	0	0	0	0	.000	.000
Gomez, Rudy, Col.	.205	67	272	234	34	48	76	6	2	6	25	1	4	7	26	0	37	5	5	2	.325	.299
Gonzalez, Alex, Char.	.277	108	466	422	71	117	187	20	10	10	51	8	2	6	28	2	80	4	7	6	.443	.330
Gonzalez, Gabe, Char.*	.125	57	10	8	1	1	1	0	0	0	0	1	0	0	1	0	4	0	0	0	.125	.222
Grace, Mike, S./W.B.	.125	12	10	8	0	1	1	0	0	0	0	2	0	0	0	0	6	0	0	0	.125	.125
Grebeck, Brian, Syr.	.333	1	3	3	0	1	1	0	0	0	0	0	0	0	0	0	0	0	0	0	.333	.333
Greene, Charlie, Roch.	.212	77	267	250	23	53	75	10	0	4	28	5	0	3	9	0	54	1	1	4	.300	.248
Greene, Rick, Lou.	.000	58	1	1	0	0	0	0	0	0	0	0	0	0	0	0	1	0	0	0	.000	.000
Gresham, Kris, Tol.	.243	12	37	37	5	9	14	2	0	1	4	0	0	0	0	0	15	0	0	0	.378	.243
Grundt, Ken, Char.*	1.000	16	1	1	0	1	1	0	0	0	0	0	0	0	0	0	0	0	0	0	1.000	1.000
Guerra, Mark, Nor.	.000	18	3	3	0	0	0	0	0	0	0	0	0	0	0	0	1	0	0	0	.000	.000
Hammond, Chris, Char.*	.143	5	9	7	0	1	1	0	0	0	1	1	0	0	1	0	3	0	0	0	.143	.250
Hanel, Marcus, Rich.	.212	29	97	85	9	18	21	3	0	0	7	0	1	0	11	2	23	0	0	0	.247	.299
Haney, Todd, Nor.	.345	117	506	440	84	152	202	33	4	3	51	5	1	5	55	1	44	11	2	13	.459	.423
Hastings, Lionel, Char.	.242	104	289	265	40	64	81	10	2	1	21	2	0	3	19	0	55	4	3	4	.306	.300
Hawblitzel, Ryan, Char.	.217	20	25	23	3	5	8	0	0	1	4	1	0	0	1	0	5	0	0	0	.348	.250
Hawkins, Kraig, Dur.	.261	6	23	23	2	6	6	0	0	0	1	0	0	0	0	0	2	1	0	0	.261	.261
Held, Dan, S./W.B.	.266	119	446	398	64	106	185	28	3	15	57	2	3	9	34	4	102	2	3	9	.465	.336
Helms, Wes, Rich.	.275	125	503	451	56	124	192	27	1	13	75	0	4	13	35	2	103	6	2	11	.426	.342
Henderson, Rod, Lou.	.118	22	20	17	2	2	2	0	0	0	2	3	0	0	0	0	5	0	0	0	.118	.118
Henley, Bob, Ott.	.246	37	142	126	13	31	51	6	1	4	20	1	2	1	12	0	34	1	1	3	.405	.312
Henriquez, Oscar, Char.	.000	26	1	1	0	0	0	0	0	0	0	0	0	0	0	0	1	0	0	0	.000	.000
Henry, Santiago, Syr.	.194	62	233	216	20	42	67	8	1	5	25	4	1	2	10	0	55	4	5	2	.310	.236
Herrera, Jose, Syr.*	.273	118	516	473	72	129	198	21	6	12	40	6	4	1	32	1	60	27	12	11	.419	.318
Hiatt, Phil, Buf.	.247	119	503	453	81	112	224	19	0	31	74	2	3	4	41	1	146	4	1	16	.494	.313
Holbert, Ray, Rich.-Ott.	.307	87	302	267	39	82	113	17	4	2	25	4	0	0	31	3	67	10	5	2	.423	.379
Holifield, Rick, Rich.*	.231	70	223	186	27	43	65	9	5	1	11	0	0	3	34	2	52	15	2	4	.349	.359
Hollins, Damon, Rich.	.264	119	486	436	61	115	186	26	3	13	48	1	4	0	45	2	85	10	2	16	.427	.330
Holman, Craig, S./W.B.†	.000	6	6	5	1	0	0	0	0	0	0	0	0	0	1	0	3	0	0	0	.000	.167
Hubbard, Mike, Ott.	.229	20	74	70	9	16	21	5	0	0	8	0	1	0	3	0	13	0	0	3	.300	.257
Huckaby, Ken, Col.	.208	36	115	101	13	21	29	3	1	1	10	3	0	0	11	0	14	0	2	3	.287	.286
Hudler, Rex, Buf.	.194	11	43	36	4	7	8	1	0	0	2	1	0	2	4	0	10	0	0	1	.222	.310
Hulse, David, Paw.*	.329	21	87	85	9	28	41	6	2	1	13	0	0	0	2	0	18	3	1	4	.482	.345
Hundley, Todd, Nor.†	.433	10	44	30	9	13	26	1	0	4	15	0	0	0	14	1	10	0	0	0	.867	.614
Hunter, Scott, Nor.	.143	7	27	21	2	3	3	0	0	0	3	1	0	2	3	0	5	1	2	1	.143	.308
Hurst, Jimmy, Paw.	.286	103	422	360	61	103	176	11	1	20	67	1	0	1	59	1	98	22	9	17	.489	.388
Huskey, Butch, Nor.	.250	2	9	8	0	2	2	0	0	0	3	0	1	0	0	0	1	0	0	0	.250	.222
Hutton, Mark, Ind.	.063	16	18	16	0	1	1	0	0	0	0	2	0	0	0	0	5	0	0	0	.063	.063
Hyers, Tim, Char.*	.280	85	330	300	50	84	131	22	2	7	52	0	2	1	27	3	41	0	3	6	.437	.339
Ibarra, Jesse, Tol.†	.229	81	303	271	22	62	100	9	1	9	38	0	2	0	30	0	65	1	1	9	.369	.304
Isom, Johnny, Roch.	.225	39	162	142	13	32	42	4	0	2	13	0	0	2	18	0	31	2	0	1	.296	.321

Player, Team	Avg.	G	TPA	AB	R	H	TB	2B	3B	HR	RBI	SH	SF	HP	BB	IBB	SO	SB	CS	GDP	Slg.	OBP
Jackson, Damian, Ind.	.261	131	596	517	102	135	209	36	10	6	49	3	4	10	62	0	125	25	10	2	.404	.349
Jackson, Gavin, Paw.	.238	67	242	206	21	49	64	4	1	3	24	2	4	3	27	0	40	3	2	5	.311	.329
Jackson, Ryan, Char.*	.380	13	54	50	5	19	29	4	0	2	11	0	0	0	4	0	14	2	0	1	.580	.426
Jacobsen, Joe, Char.	.333	9	5	3	1	1	1	0	0	0	0	0	0	0	2	0	1	0	0	0	.333	.600
Jarvis, Kevin, Ind.†	.000	2	1	1	0	0	0	0	0	0	0	0	0	0	0	0	0	0	0	0	.000	.000
Jenkins, Geoff, Lou.*	.330	55	236	215	38	71	110	10	4	7	52	0	2	5	14	3	39	1	1	6	.512	.381
Jensen, Marcus, Lou.†	.226	74	264	230	29	52	95	13	0	10	33	0	0	1	33	1	64	0	3	5	.413	.326
Jeter, Derek, Col.	.400	1	5	5	2	2	4	2	0	0	0	0	0	0	0	0	2	0	0	0	.800	.400
Jimenez, D'Angelo, Col.†	.256	91	398	344	55	88	139	19	4	8	51	1	5	1	46	0	67	6	6	7	.404	.341
Johns, Keith, Paw.	.228	96	367	329	31	75	113	12	1	8	38	1	5	4	28	0	82	2	6	10	.343	.292
Johnson, Earl, Tol.†	.251	105	389	362	44	91	120	10	8	1	24	7	1	0	19	0	65	20	6	4	.331	.288
Johnson, Mark, Ind.*	.300	116	428	357	65	107	208	33	1	22	75	0	3	0	68	3	82	2	2	10	.583	.409
Johnson, Mike, Ott.*	.158	18	22	19	2	3	3	0	0	0	1	1	1	0	1	0	4	0	0	0	.158	.190
Jones, Terry, Ott.	.237	81	320	278	36	66	77	3	4	0	21	8	2	0	32	1	48	35	6	8	.277	.314
Jordan, Ricardo, Ind.*	.000	37	6	5	1	0	0	0	0	0	0	0	0	0	1	0	3	0	0	0	.000	.167
Kelly, Mike, Dur.	.083	4	16	12	2	1	1	0	0	0	0	0	0	0	4	0	5	0	0	1	.083	.313
Kelly, Pat, Syr.	.282	80	346	291	58	82	161	22	3	17	39	8	2	6	39	2	60	18	6	4	.553	.376
Keyser, Brian, Ind.	.083	42	17	12	1	1	1	0	0	0	2	2	1	0	2	0	4	0	0	0	.083	.200
Kieschnick, Brooks, Dur.*	.130	7	27	23	4	3	7	1	0	1	2	0	0	0	4	0	8	0	1	2	.304	.259
Kingsale, Eugene, Roch.†	.218	18	61	55	3	12	15	1	1	0	2	1	0	1	4	0	8	3	3	3	.273	.283
Kinkade, Mike, Lou.-Nor.	.300	110	472	416	69	125	190	29	6	8	64	2	4	11	39	1	76	16	3	12	.457	.372
Kirby, Wayne, Nor.*	.309	42	186	162	32	50	79	8	3	5	23	1	0	2	21	1	18	11	5	1	.488	.395
Klingenbeck, Scott, Ind.	.125	11	8	8	1	1	1	0	0	0	0	0	0	0	0	0	3	0	0	0	.125	.125
Knorr, Randy, Char.	.328	68	240	201	30	66	102	15	0	7	39	0	4	1	34	0	41	1	2	3	.507	.421
Konerko, Paul, Ind.	.327	39	174	150	25	49	81	8	0	8	39	0	3	2	19	0	18	1	0	8	.540	.402
Krause, Scott, Lou.	.292	117	455	390	71	114	221	25	2	26	82	3	1	15	46	3	104	11	4	16	.567	.387
Laker, Tim, Dur.	.239	40	164	134	36	32	72	7	0	11	26	0	1	1	28	1	32	1	1	4	.537	.372
Lamb, David, Roch.†	.298	48	201	178	24	53	65	7	1	1	16	1	2	3	17	1	25	1	5	4	.365	.365
Landry, Todd, Nor.	.063	9	18	16	2	1	2	1	0	0	2	0	0	0	2	0	4	0	0	1	.125	.167
Larkin, Andy, Char.	.000	11	5	5	0	0	0	0	0	0	0	0	0	0	0	0	5	0	0	0	.000	.000
LaRue, Jason, Ind.	.235	15	56	51	5	12	16	4	0	0	5	0	1	0	4	1	8	0	1	2	.314	.286
Lawrence, Chip, Roch.	.300	13	37	30	1	9	10	1	0	0	2	0	0	0	7	0	6	0	0	0	.333	.432
Ledee, Ricky, Col.*	.283	96	424	360	70	102	182	21	1	19	41	1	5	4	54	5	108	7	2	7	.506	.378
Lee, Derek, Roch.*	.283	107	415	364	63	103	180	17	3	18	57	0	2	0	49	0	61	5	6	12	.495	.371
Lennon, Pat, Syr.	.290	126	529	438	87	127	238	22	4	27	95	0	2	2	87	3	121	12	4	21	.543	.408
Lilly, Ted, Ott.*	.000	7	6	6	0	0	0	0	0	0	0	0	0	0	0	0	1	0	0	0	.000	.000
Lindstrom, David, Tol.	.000	1	3	3	0	0	0	0	0	0	0	0	0	0	0	0	1	0	0	0	.000	.000
Liniak, Cole, Paw.	.261	112	480	429	65	112	196	31	1	17	59	4	3	5	39	1	71	4	4	11	.457	.328
Listach, Pat, Buf.-S./W.B.†	.219	88	346	306	50	67	86	8	4	1	23	4	0	4	32	1	69	17	5	2	.281	.301
Lobaton, Jose, Col.	.143	6	7	7	0	1	2	1	0	0	0	0	0	0	0	0	2	0	0	1	.286	.143
Loewer, Carlton, S./W.B.†	.125	12	18	16	1	2	2	0	0	0	2	2	0	0	0	0	6	0	0	0	.125	.125
Long, Joey, Ott.	.000	34	3	3	1	0	0	0	0	0	0	0	0	0	0	0	0	0	0	0	.000	.000
Lopez, Luis, Syr.	.220	11	48	41	6	9	12	0	0	1	3	0	1	0	6	0	6	0	0	2	.293	.313
Lopez, Mickey, Lou.†	.250	3	6	4	1	1	1	0	0	0	0	0	0	0	2	1	0	0	0	0	.250	.500
Lovullo, Torey, Buf.†	.326	92	393	328	66	107	183	17	4	17	65	1	9	1	54	1	32	3	3	9	.558	.413
Lowell, Mike, Col.	.304	126	558	510	79	155	273	34	3	26	99	0	5	6	37	2	85	4	0	10	.535	.355
Lucca, Lou, Char.	.290	112	417	397	47	115	180	32	0	11	51	0	2	5	13	2	75	2	6	10	.453	.319
Ludwick, Eric, Char.	.200	8	5	5	0	1	1	0	0	0	0	0	0	0	0	0	1	0	0	0	.200	.200
Lukachyk, Rob, Ott.*	.234	73	253	222	34	52	84	13	2	5	25	2	0	7	22	0	52	13	0	2	.378	.323
Luzinski, Ryan, Roch.	.000	4	13	12	0	0	0	0	0	0	0	1	0	1	0	0	3	0	0	1	.000	.000
Lydy, Scott, Roch.	.136	20	72	66	3	9	17	5	0	1	8	0	1	1	4	0	15	1	0	2	.258	.194
Maduro, Calvin, S./W.B.	.259	28	32	27	4	7	8	1	0	0	2	4	1	0	0	0	11	1	0	0	.296	.250
Magdaleno, Ricky, Rich.	.293	73	275	249	32	73	101	11	1	5	29	1	2	0	23	1	63	1	3	3	.406	.350
Magee, Wendell, S./W.B.	.290	126	561	507	86	147	263	30	7	24	72	0	5	3	46	3	102	7	7	11	.519	.349
Mahoney, Mike, Rich.	.212	71	248	208	26	44	69	10	0	5	28	6	5	5	24	3	49	1	1	10	.332	.302
Makarewicz, Scott, Char.	.163	16	52	49	3	8	15	4	0	1	5	0	0	0	3	0	11	0	1	1	.306	.212
Malloy, Marty, Rich.*	.290	124	549	483	75	140	192	25	3	7	54	5	4	5	51	2	65	20	7	12	.398	.361
Maness, Dwight, Nor.	.100	6	10	10	1	1	1	0	0	0	0	0	0	0	0	0	4	2	0	0	.100	.100
Manto, Jeff, Buf.	.311	62	270	209	46	65	145	11	0	23	63	0	2	1	58	0	48	4	2	2	.694	.459
Manzanillo, Josias, Nor.	.100	13	12	10	0	1	1	0	0	0	0	1	0	0	1	0	5	0	0	0	.100	.182
Marine, Del, Ind.	.267	5	15	15	2	4	9	0	1	1	1	0	0	0	0	0	3	0	0	0	.600	.267
Martin, Chris, Dur.	.259	131	532	448	71	116	170	26	2	8	49	7	5	8	62	1	80	19	11	9	.379	.356
Martinez, Gabby, Col.	.237	36	139	131	17	31	36	3	1	0	8	2	1	1	4	0	22	5	3	6	.275	.263
Martinez, Greg, Lou.†	.261	115	437	376	65	98	136	4	11	4	25	10	0	0	51	0	80	43	7	3	.362	.349
Martinez, Jesus, Ind.*	.154	22	14	13	0	2	2	0	0	0	0	1	0	0	0	0	7	0	0	0	.154	.154
Martinez, Pablo, Lou.-Rich.†.	.243	78	247	222	25	54	67	5	1	2	12	2	2	1	20	3	41	7	5	5	.302	.306
Marx, Tim, Ind.	.154	20	62	52	5	8	10	0	1	0	6	2	1	0	7	1	13	0	0	1	.192	.250
Mateo, Jose, Rich.†	.143	6	8	7	0	1	1	0	0	0	0	0	0	0	1	0	3	0	0	0	.143	.250
Matos, Francisco, Dur.-Col.	.310	108	435	407	55	126	162	20	5	2	47	2	2	3	21	0	41	5	3	17	.398	.346
Maxcy, Brian, Nor.	.500	28	5	4	1	2	2	0	0	0	1	0	0	0	0	0	0	0	0	0	.500	.500
May, Derrick, Ott.*	.377	21	83	69	16	26	50	6	0	6	21	0	0	1	13	0	7	0	1	0	.725	.482
McClain, Scott, Dur.	.299	126	544	472	91	141	278	35	0	34	109	1	3	2	66	5	113	6	2	9	.589	.385
McGraw, Tom, Ott.*	.200	32	7	5	0	1	1	0	0	0	0	2	0	0	0	0	1	0	0	0	.200	.200
McKeel, Walt, Paw.	.288	48	192	170	26	49	73	10	1	4	26	0	1	1	21	0	27	1	2	8	.429	.370
McMillon, Billy, S./W.B.*	.258	77	307	267	42	69	126	16	1	13	38	0	3	3	34	1	59	6	3	6	.472	.345
Medina, Rafael, Char.	.000	11	4	3	0	0	0	0	0	0	0	1	0	0	0	0	3	0	0	1	.000	.000
Melhuse, Adam, Syr.†	.289	12	46	38	4	11	17	3	0	1	7	0	1	0	7	0	6	0	0	4	.447	.391
Mendoza, Carlos, Dur.*	.269	51	224	201	32	54	62	8	0	0	11	5	1	1	16	0	29	9	9	5	.308	.324
Mendoza, Reynol, Char.	.227	24	23	22	4	5	6	1	0	0	2	1	0	0	0	0	8	0	0	0	.273	.227
Mercedes, Henry, Ind.	.125	8	17	16	1	2	2	0	0	0	0	0	0	0	1	0	5	0	0	1	.125	.176
Merloni, Lou, Paw.	.386	27	113	88	17	34	63	3	1	8	22	1	0	8	16	0	13	2	2	2	.716	.518
Millan, Adan, S./W.B.	.130	8	29	23	5	3	7	1	0	1	3	0	0	1	5	0	7	0	0	0	.304	.310

Player, Team	Avg.	G	TPA	AB	R	H	TB	2B	3B	HR	RBI	SH	SF	HP	BB	IBB	SO	SB	CS	GDP	Slg.	OBP
Millar, Kevin, Char.	.326	14	58	46	14	15	30	3	0	4	15	0	1	2	9	0	7	1	0	3	.652	.448
Miller, David, Buf.*	.267	115	485	415	56	111	161	19	2	9	54	4	3	2	61	3	72	6	8	10	.388	.362
Miller, Orlando, Roch.	.294	37	157	143	21	42	63	4	1	5	25	0	0	5	9	0	31	3	1	1	.441	.357
Milliard, Ralph, Nor.	.259	127	513	417	73	108	185	24	4	15	52	5	2	8	79	0	59	17	6	4	.444	.385
Mimbs, Mark, Nor.*	.100	15	13	10	3	1	1	0	0	0	0	0	0	0	3	0	4	0	0	1	.100	.308
Minor, Blas, Lou.	.000	3	2	2	0	0	0	0	0	0	0	0	0	0	0	0	0	0	0	0	.000	.000
Mitchell, Keith, Paw.	.313	63	260	211	55	66	117	15	0	12	45	0	4	1	44	2	37	3	3	5	.555	.427
Mix, Greg, Rich.	.071	28	17	14	2	1	1	0	0	0	0	2	0	0	1	0	6	0	0	0	.071	.133
Moore, Trey, Ott.*	.000	3	1	1	0	0	0	0	0	0	0	0	0	0	0	0	1	0	0	0	.000	.000
Mora, Melvin, Nor.	.179	11	35	28	5	5	6	1	0	0	2	2	0	0	5	0	7	0	0	0	.214	.303
Morales, Eric, Nor.	.000	1	1	1	0	0	0	0	0	0	0	0	0	0	0	0	0	0	0	0	.000	.000
Mordecai, Mike, Ott.	.227	6	25	22	2	5	7	2	0	0	1	0	0	0	3	0	3	0	0	1	.318	.320
Morel, Ramon, Ott.	.200	12	6	5	0	1	1	0	0	0	0	1	0	0	0	0	2	0	0	0	.200	.200
Morman, Russ, Dur.	.283	98	405	367	48	104	162	26	1	10	67	0	3	3	32	0	65	0	1	13	.441	.343
Mosquera, Julio, Syr.	.213	28	105	94	10	20	32	6	0	2	4	1	1	4	5	0	12	1	0	2	.340	.279
Mottola, Chad, Ind.	.417	5	16	12	2	5	8	0	0	1	2	0	0	0	4	0	0	0	2	0	.667	.563
Mouton, Lyle, Roch.	.321	37	152	137	23	44	78	9	2	7	32	0	0	2	13	0	31	1	1	8	.569	.388
Mummau, Rob, Syr.	.429	3	7	7	0	3	4	1	0	0	2	0	0	0	0	0	1	0	0	0	.571	.429
Murphy, Mike, Roch.	.379	8	32	29	3	11	14	0	0	1	2	0	0	3	0	0	7	1	1	0	.483	.438
Murray, Glenn, Ind.	.198	42	139	126	20	25	43	6	0	4	16	0	0	0	13	0	47	1	2	0	.341	.273
Natal, Bob, Dur.-Char.	.273	72	250	231	31	63	110	12	1	11	43	1	2	3	13	0	33	2	1	11	.476	.317
Nicholas, Darrell, Lou.	.294	130	548	497	87	146	226	28	8	12	64	0	6	5	40	0	113	31	13	4	.455	.349
Nieves, Melvin, Ind.†	.283	15	62	53	10	15	25	4	0	2	13	0	0	0	9	0	11	0	0	0	.472	.387
Niles, Drew, Char.†	.265	16	57	49	5	13	17	1	0	1	5	0	1	1	6	0	12	0	1	1	.347	.351
Nix, James, Lou.	.000	27	1	1	0	0	0	0	0	0	0	0	0	0	0	0	0	0	0	0	.000	.000
Nixon, Trot, Paw.*	.310	135	597	509	97	158	261	26	4	23	74	0	7	5	76	6	81	26	13	10	.513	.400
Norris, Joe, Ind.	.000	4	1	1	0	0	0	0	0	0	0	0	0	0	0	0	1	0	0	0	.000	.000
Nunnally, Jon, Ind.*	.252	79	346	290	53	73	128	18	2	11	53	1	6	2	47	0	71	7	4	3	.441	.354
Nye, Ryan, S./W.B.	.105	23	20	19	1	2	2	0	0	0	2	0	0	0	1	0	7	0	0	0	.105	.150
Olmeda, Jose, Rich.†	.271	111	408	373	41	101	136	17	3	4	34	1	3	2	29	1	55	7	7	7	.365	.324
Ortiz, Nick, Ott.	.094	12	39	32	1	3	4	1	0	0	0	1	0	0	6	0	10	0	0	0	.125	.237
Otanez, Willis, Roch.	.285	124	537	481	87	137	246	24	2	27	100	1	8	6	41	6	104	1	0	8	.511	.343
Otero, Ricky, Roch.†	.288	87	381	354	53	102	151	25	6	4	45	0	3	3	21	1	30	10	5	4	.427	.331
Owens, Eric, Lou.	.335	77	292	254	48	85	119	11	4	5	40	0	4	0	34	0	30	21	6	7	.469	.408
Owens, Jayhawk, Ind.	.297	16	41	37	5	11	21	4	0	2	8	0	0	4	1	0	17	0	0	1	.568	.366
Pachot, John, Ott.	.227	100	368	344	33	78	104	18	1	2	39	3	3	3	15	1	45	2	2	13	.302	.263
Pall, Donn, Char.	.000	29	1	1	0	0	0	0	0	0	0	0	0	0	0	0	1	0	0	0	.000	.000
Paquette, Craig, Nor.	.279	15	63	61	11	17	29	1	1	3	14	0	1	0	1	0	13	2	1	2	.475	.286
Parker, Rick, Nor.	.244	90	288	246	38	60	102	11	2	9	31	1	1	5	35	1	43	13	6	6	.415	.348
Parris, Steve, Ind.	.222	13	19	18	2	4	5	1	0	0	1	1	0	0	0	0	7	0	0	0	.278	.222
Pasqualicchio, Mike, Lou.	.000	1	1	1	0	0	0	0	0	0	0	0	0	0	0	0	0	0	0	0	.000	.000
Patrick, Bronswell, Lou.	.000	6	9	7	0	0	0	0	0	0	0	0	2	0	0	0	2	0	0	0	.000	.000
Patterson, John, Dur.†	.301	25	78	73	12	22	33	5	0	2	11	1	0	1	3	0	12	1	1	0	.452	.338
Pavano, Carl, Ott.	.000	3	2	2	0	0	0	0	0	0	0	0	0	0	0	0	2	0	0	0	.000	.000
Payton, Jay, Nor.	.261	82	350	322	45	84	130	14	4	8	30	1	0	1	26	0	50	12	7	5	.404	.318
Perez, Odalki, Rich.*	.000	13	1	1	0	0	0	0	0	0	0	0	0	0	0	0	0	0	0	0	.000	.000
Perez, Santiago, Lou.†	.271	36	142	133	18	36	55	4	3	3	14	2	1	0	6	0	31	6	3	3	.414	.300
Perez, Tomas, Syr.†	.252	116	426	404	40	102	134	15	4	3	37	4	0	0	18	0	67	4	7	10	.332	.284
Perry, Chan, Buf.	.224	13	57	49	8	11	15	4	0	0	3	0	0	2	6	0	10	1	0	0	.306	.333
Perry, Herbert, Dur.	.294	5	18	17	1	5	9	4	0	0	1	0	0	1	0	0	2	0	0	2	.529	.333
Petagine, Roberto, Ind.*	.331	102	443	363	79	120	224	30	1	24	109	0	7	3	70	6	71	3	1	14	.617	.436
Phillips, Tony, Syr.†	.250	10	47	32	7	8	12	1	0	1	4	0	0	0	15	0	10	2	1	0	.375	.489
Pierce, Kirk, S./W.B.	.077	4	19	13	2	1	1	0	0	0	0	2	0	1	3	0	2	0	0	0	.077	.294
Plantier, Phil, Nor.*	.143	2	7	7	0	1	1	0	0	0	1	0	0	0	0	0	1	0	0	0	.143	.143
Pose, Scott, Col.*	.297	133	559	489	78	145	197	23	10	3	46	7	4	6	53	0	72	47	14	8	.403	.370
Post, Dave, Ott.	.300	93	365	330	59	99	144	23	2	6	35	1	0	6	28	1	50	7	7	5	.436	.365
Powell, Alonzo, Syr.	.229	15	56	48	8	11	21	1	0	3	9	0	0	1	7	0	12	0	1	2	.438	.339
Pozo, Arquimedez, Paw.	.305	90	378	348	53	106	172	20	5	12	51	0	3	5	22	1	44	4	2	12	.494	.352
Pratt, Todd, Nor.	.356	35	139	118	16	42	69	6	0	7	30	1	1	4	15	0	19	2	0	4	.585	.442
Pride, Curtis, Rich.*	.244	21	93	78	11	19	29	2	1	2	6	0	0	0	15	0	17	8	0	3	.372	.366
Priest, Eddie, Ind.	.000	6	7	6	1	0	0	0	0	0	0	0	0	0	1	0	4	0	0	0	.000	.143
Probst, Alan, Syr.	.333	12	35	33	2	11	15	1	0	1	4	0	0	0	2	0	6	0	0	2	.455	.371
Pulsipher, Bill, Nor.*	.308	14	13	13	3	4	4	0	0	0	0	0	0	0	0	0	2	0	0	0	.308	.308
Raleigh, Matt, Nor.	.000	4	4	4	0	0	0	0	0	0	0	0	0	0	0	0	3	0	0	0	.000	.000
Ramirez, Alex, Buf.	.299	121	546	521	94	156	295	21	8	34	103	0	4	5	16	4	101	6	4	11	.566	.324
Ramirez, Angel, Col.	.315	57	212	197	36	62	96	12	2	6	26	1	0	2	12	0	41	4	2	7	.487	.360
Ramirez, Hector, Char.	.000	55	6	5	0	0	0	0	0	0	0	0	0	0	0	0	3	0	0	0	.000	.000
Ramirez, Roberto, Roch.	.268	13	44	41	5	11	11	0	0	0	3	0	1	1	1	0	10	0	1	0	.268	.302
Ratliff, Jon, Rich.	.056	29	24	18	2	1	1	0	0	0	0	6	0	0	0	0	7	0	0	1	.056	.056
Redmond, Mike, Char.	.241	18	61	58	4	14	22	2	0	2	7	0	2	1	0	0	3	0	0	3	.379	.246
Reed, Brandon, Tol.	.500	39	2	2	0	1	1	0	0	0	0	0	0	0	0	0	0	0	0	0	.500	.500
Reese, Nate, Char.	.375	3	9	8	1	3	6	0	0	1	1	0	0	0	1	0	3	0	0	0	.750	.444
Reyes, Alberto, Lou.	.000	3	1	1	0	0	0	0	0	0	0	0	0	0	0	0	0	0	0	0	.000	.000
Reyes, Dennis, Ind.	.500	4	2	2	0	1	1	0	0	0	0	0	0	0	0	0	0	0	0	0	.500	.500
Reynoso, Armando, Nor.	.000	2	3	2	0	0	0	0	0	0	0	0	1	0	0	0	0	0	0	0	.000	.000
Rigsby, Randy, Char.*	.214	4	15	14	1	3	3	0	0	0	0	0	0	1	0	0	4	0	0	0	.214	.267
Ripken, Billy, Tol.	.316	5	21	19	3	6	7	1	0	0	1	0	0	0	2	0	0	0	0	0	.368	.381
Roberts, Bip, Tol.†	.263	6	22	19	2	5	5	0	0	0	0	0	0	1	2	1	4	2	0	0	.263	.364
Roberts, David, Buf.*	.133	5	16	15	2	2	2	0	0	0	2	0	1	0	0	0	3	2	0	0	.133	.125
Robinson, Kerry, Dur.*	.302	58	268	242	28	73	91	7	4	1	28	2	1	0	23	0	30	18	11	1	.376	.361
Rocker, John, Rich.	.000	9	2	2	0	0	0	0	0	0	0	0	0	0	0	0	1	0	0	0	.000	.000
Rodriguez, Frankie, Lou.	.000	47	12	11	0	0	0	0	0	0	0	0	1	0	0	0	2	0	0	0	.000	.000

CLASS AAA International League

Player, Team	Avg.	G	TPA	AB	R	H	TB	2B	3B	HR	RBI	SH	SF	HP	BB	IBB	SO	SB	CS	GDP	Slg.	OBP
Rodriguez, Luis, Syr.	.133	5	17	15	1	2	2	0	0	0	2	1	1	0	0	0	6	0	0	0	.133	.125
Rodriguez, Steve, Ott.	.280	75	256	232	24	65	81	11	1	1	28	5	1	3	15	1	34	6	7	5	.349	.331
Romero, Mandy, Paw.†	.331	45	169	139	20	46	75	5	0	8	27	2	4	0	24	6	15	0	0	1	.540	.419
Roque, Rafael, Lou.*	.167	9	6	6	1	1	1	0	0	0	0	0	0	0	0	0	2	0	0	0	.167	.167
Rosario, Mel, Roch.†	.248	34	121	113	10	28	41	4	0	3	10	0	1	1	6	0	24	5	2	1	.363	.289
Rose, Pete, Ind.*	.278	43	144	133	19	37	55	7	1	3	13	0	1	2	8	0	10	1	0	2	.414	.326
Roskos, John, Char.	.284	115	465	416	54	118	173	23	1	10	62	0	3	3	43	0	84	0	4	15	.416	.353
Ruffin, Johnny, Lou.-Nor.	.154	52	13	13	0	2	2	0	0	0	0	0	0	0	0	0	7	0	0	1	.154	.154
Sadler, Al, Lou.	.000	25	1	1	0	0	0	0	0	0	0	0	0	0	0	0	0	0	0	0	.000	.000
Sadler, Donnie, Paw.	.221	36	159	131	25	29	42	5	1	2	10	1	1	0	26	0	23	11	1	1	.321	.348
Samuels, Scott, Ott.*	.234	43	115	94	15	22	36	4	2	2	15	1	1	0	19	1	24	4	3	2	.383	.360
Sanders, Anthony, Syr.	.191	60	236	209	23	40	65	9	2	4	19	3	1	3	20	1	65	5	2	3	.311	.270
Santangelo, F.P., Ott.†	.250	2	9	8	1	2	2	0	0	0	1	0	0	1	0	0	3	0	0	0	.250	.333
Santiago, Benito, Syr.	.227	5	23	22	0	5	7	2	0	0	2	0	0	0	1	0	3	0	0	1	.318	.261
Sauerbeck, Scott, Nor.	.120	27	27	25	0	3	3	0	0	0	0	0	2	0	0	0	11	0	0	0	.120	.120
Saunders, Chris, Ott.	.274	131	537	478	58	131	188	26	2	9	58	0	5	7	46	1	98	1	1	10	.393	.343
Sauveur, Rich, Ind.*	1.000	7	1	1	1	1	4	0	1	2	0	0	0	0	0	0	0	0	0	0	4.000	1.000
Schall, Gene, Rich.	.300	100	392	340	60	102	190	22	0	22	73	0	6	9	37	3	80	1	3	5	.559	.378
Scott, Darryl, S./W.B.	.000	33	4	3	0	0	0	0	0	0	0	0	0	0	1	0	1	0	0	0	.000	.250
Scutaro, Marcos, Buf.	.231	8	27	26	3	6	9	3	0	0	4	1	0	0	0	0	2	0	0	0	.346	.231
Seefried, Tate, Ott.*	.184	38	132	114	10	21	33	3	0	3	12	0	1	0	17	0	37	0	1	4	.289	.288
Seguignol, Fernando, Ott.†	.257	32	124	109	16	28	54	8	0	6	16	1	1	1	12	0	43	0	0	1	.495	.333
Selby, William, Buf.*	.254	97	375	334	45	85	150	23	0	14	52	0	3	0	38	7	50	3	0	6	.449	.328
Sexson, Richie, Buf.	.297	89	402	344	58	102	187	20	1	21	74	0	5	3	50	2	68	1	2	11	.544	.386
Short, Rick, Roch.	.176	13	40	34	3	6	10	1	0	1	4	0	1	1	4	0	4	0	0	0	.294	.275
Siddall, Joe, Tol.*	.240	43	144	129	16	31	48	5	0	4	16	2	0	2	11	0	42	2	1	2	.372	.310
Sierra, Ruben, Nor.†	.259	28	124	108	16	28	42	5	0	3	19	0	3	0	13	2	18	3	0	4	.389	.331
Silvestri, Dave, Dur.	.277	129	557	480	74	133	192	31	2	8	56	6	6	4	61	1	73	12	9	7	.400	.359
Simon, Randall, Rich.*	.256	126	514	484	52	124	185	20	1	13	70	0	4	2	24	3	62	4	4	22	.382	.292
Simons, Mitch, Roch.	.216	59	213	190	21	41	56	8	2	1	16	1	1	1	20	0	16	7	2	4	.295	.292
Singleton, Chris, Col.*	.254	121	460	413	55	105	160	17	10	6	45	7	4	4	27	0	78	9	3	7	.387	.304
Smart, J.D., Ott.	.000	6	7	6	0	0	0	0	0	0	0	1	0	0	0	0	0	0	0	0	.000	.000
Smith, Dwight, Roch.*	.174	20	80	69	5	12	14	2	0	0	8	0	4	0	7	0	20	2	0	1	.203	.238
Smith, Ira, Tol.	.241	91	297	274	28	66	90	18	0	2	23	2	2	2	17	1	50	8	5	8	.328	.288
Smith, Travis, Lou.	.091	12	12	11	0	1	1	0	0	0	0	1	0	0	0	0	3	0	0	0	.091	.091
Snusz, Chris, S./W.B.	.111	3	9	9	0	1	2	1	0	0	0	0	0	0	0	0	2	0	0	1	.222	.111
Sojo, Luis, Col.	.217	6	24	23	1	5	7	2	0	0	2	0	0	0	1	0	1	1	0	1	.304	.250
Soliz, Steve, Buf.	.223	39	128	112	14	25	31	6	0	0	9	1	1	3	11	0	23	1	1	6	.277	.307
Spehr, Tim, Nor.	1.000	1	1	1	0	1	1	0	0	0	0	0	0	0	0	0	0	0	0	0	1.000	1.000
Spencer, Shane, Col.	.322	87	388	342	66	110	195	29	1	18	67	0	2	3	41	0	59	1	3	8	.570	.397
Stanifer, Rob, Char.	.000	21	5	4	0	0	0	0	0	0	0	1	0	0	0	0	0	0	0	0	.000	.000
Steed, Rick, Nor.	.250	13	8	8	1	2	4	0	1	0	3	0	0	0	0	0	1	0	0	0	.500	.250
Steph, Rod, Ind.	.000	3	1	1	0	0	0	0	0	0	0	0	0	0	0	0	0	0	0	0	.000	.000
Stephenson, Garrett, S./W.B. ..	.000	13	13	12	0	0	0	0	0	0	0	1	0	0	0	0	5	0	0	0	.000	.000
Stewart, Scott, Nor.	.000	9	8	7	0	0	0	0	0	0	0	1	0	0	0	0	2	0	0	0	.000	.000
Stovall, DaRond, Ott.†	.227	44	173	150	15	34	67	7	1	8	22	1	1	0	21	1	51	6	2	6	.447	.320
Swann, Pedro, Tol.*	.291	120	468	419	56	122	199	28	2	15	66	1	4	3	41	4	74	6	3	11	.475	.355
Tam, Jeff, Nor.	.000	45	3	2	0	0	0	0	0	0	0	1	0	0	0	0	1	0	0	0	.000	.000
Tamargo, John, Nor.†	.000	3	9	8	0	0	0	0	0	0	0	0	0	0	1	0	3	0	0	0	.000	.111
Tarasco, Tony, Ind.*	.313	90	367	319	53	100	169	19	1	16	45	2	2	1	43	1	46	3	2	4	.530	.395
Tavarez, Jesus, Roch.†	.280	102	401	364	62	102	134	17	6	1	30	5	3	2	27	0	59	22	3	4	.368	.331
Tebbs, Nate, Paw.†	.281	17	62	57	7	16	18	2	0	0	4	2	0	0	3	0	13	5	2	0	.316	.317
Tejero, Fausto, Rich.	.224	77	250	223	19	50	76	14	0	4	26	1	2	3	21	2	48	1	2	6	.341	.294
Thomas, Evan, S./W.B.	.500	2	4	4	0	2	2	0	0	0	0	0	0	0	0	0	1	0	0	0	.500	.500
Thomas, Greg, Buf.*	.091	4	12	11	1	1	2	1	0	0	2	0	0	0	1	0	5	0	0	1	.182	.167
Thurman, Mike, Ott.	.000	19	14	11	0	0	0	0	0	0	0	3	0	0	0	0	2	0	0	0	.000	.154
Thurston, Jerrey, Ott.	.033	13	34	30	2	1	1	0	0	0	0	0	0	0	4	0	15	0	0	0	.033	.147
Timmons, Ozzie, Ind.	.263	117	364	327	46	86	149	21	3	12	36	2	2	4	29	0	65	2	2	7	.456	.329
Tinsley, Lee, Ott.†	.216	51	207	185	25	40	59	9	2	2	19	3	2	1	16	0	43	13	2	2	.319	.279
Tomberlin, Andy, Tol.-Rich.* ..	.285	53	186	151	25	43	68	5	1	6	19	0	1	11	23	1	44	2	2	3	.450	.414
Torres, Jaime, Col.	.164	16	58	55	2	9	10	1	0	0	3	0	0	0	3	0	7	0	0	3	.182	.207
Trammell, Bubba, Dur.	.290	57	256	217	46	63	123	12	0	16	48	0	1	0	38	1	42	6	1	2	.567	.396
Troilo, Jason, Col.	.143	8	15	14	0	2	2	0	0	0	1	0	0	0	1	0	7	0	0	0	.143	.200
Troutman, Keith, S./W.B.	.000	43	2	1	0	0	0	0	0	0	0	0	0	0	1	0	1	0	0	0	.000	.500
Utting, Andy, Roch.†	.278	5	20	18	4	5	9	1	0	1	3	0	0	0	2	0	5	0	0	1	.500	.350
Valdez, Efrain, Nor.*	.000	18	1	1	0	0	0	0	0	0	0	0	0	0	1	0	0	0	0	0	.000	.000
Valdez, Trovin, Ott.	.278	5	18	18	3	5	8	1	1	0	1	0	0	0	0	0	2	1	1	0	.444	.278
VanEgmond, Tim, Lou.	.095	24	22	21	0	2	3	1	0	0	0	1	0	0	0	0	6	0	0	1	.143	.136
Vidro, Jose, Ott.†	.289	63	267	235	35	68	92	14	2	2	32	1	3	4	24	1	25	5	2	4	.391	.361
Villafuerte, Brandon, Char.	.000	10	1	1	0	0	0	0	0	0	0	0	0	0	0	0	0	0	0	0	.000	.000
Villano, Mike, Char.	.125	13	8	8	1	1	2	1	0	0	0	0	0	0	0	0	2	0	0	1	.250	.125
Vinas, Julio, Roch.	.352	62	216	199	26	70	111	15	4	6	40	1	2	1	12	0	30	2	1	3	.558	.388
Wagner, Paul, Lou.-Rich.	.333	11	4	3	1	1	1	0	0	0	0	1	0	0	0	0	0	0	0	0	.333	.333
Walker, Mike, Ind.	.000	78	7	7	0	0	0	0	0	0	0	0	0	0	0	0	6	0	0	0	.000	.000
Wallace, Derek, Nor.	.333	54	3	3	1	1	1	0	0	0	0	0	0	0	0	0	0	0	0	1	.333	.333
Warner, Mike, Rich.*	.220	96	370	322	42	71	115	16	5	6	27	1	0	0	47	1	85	7	5	2	.357	.320
Waszgis, B.J., Paw.	.202	66	241	208	31	42	78	9	0	9	41	4	3	0	26	0	52	2	4	7	.375	.287
Watkins, Pat, Ind.	.378	44	206	188	37	71	94	12	1	3	24	1	1	1	15	0	26	8	3	5	.500	.424
Wehner, John, Char.	.325	30	90	83	12	27	37	1	0	3	15	1	0	2	4	0	16	5	1	5	.446	.371
Welch, Mike, S./W.B.*	.200	31	6	5	0	1	1	0	0	0	1	0	0	0	1	0	2	0	0	0	.200	.333
Whatley, Gabe, Rich.*	.265	135	539	475	64	126	200	36	4	10	54	3	3	5	53	2	93	11	4	15	.421	.343
Wilcox, Luke, Dur.*	.225	43	169	151	17	34	51	11	0	2	17	0	1	1	16	0	27	0	0	6	.338	.302

Player, Team	Avg.	G	TPA	AB	R	H	TB	2B	3B	HR	RBI	SH	SF	HP	BB	IBB	SO	SB	CS	GDP	Slg.	OBP
Wilkins, Rick, Nor.*	.259	45	176	158	17	41	59	13	1	1	20	0	4	0	14	1	37	1	0	3	.373	.313
Williams, Jason, Ind.	.266	119	494	406	60	108	141	25	1	2	45	5	7	6	70	2	63	5	2	10	.347	.376
Williams, Jimmy, Char.*	.143	19	8	7	0	1	1	0	0	0	1	1	0	0	0	0	3	0	0	0	.143	.143
Williamson, Antone, Lou.*	.204	29	117	103	11	21	37	8	1	2	19	0	1	0	13	0	19	0	0	4	.359	.291
Williamson, Scott, Ind.	.000	5	3	0	0	0	0	0	0	0	0	0	0	0	3	0	0	0	0	0	.000	1.000
Wilson, Brandon, Buf.	.273	98	378	337	53	92	136	19	2	7	53	2	3	4	32	0	56	15	5	5	.404	.340
Wilson, Enrique, Buf.†	.281	56	245	221	40	62	87	13	0	4	23	3	2	0	19	0	21	8	3	6	.394	.335
Wilson, Paul, Nor.	.000	7	9	6	1	0	0	0	0	0	1	1	1	0	1	0	3	0	0	0	.000	.125
Wilson, Preston, Nor.-Char.	.273	112	473	429	80	117	233	30	4	26	86	0	5	3	36	0	143	15	7	8	.543	.330
Wilson, Vance, Nor.	.260	46	167	154	18	40	55	3	0	4	16	3	0	1	9	0	29	0	3	5	.357	.305
Winchester, Scott, Ind.	.333	6	4	3	0	1	1	0	0	0	1	0	1	0	0	0	1	0	0	0	.333	.250
Winn, Randy, Dur.†	.285	29	142	123	25	35	47	5	2	1	16	4	0	0	15	0	24	10	4	1	.382	.362
Witt, Kevin, Syr.*	.273	126	521	455	71	124	219	20	3	23	67	1	5	7	53	6	124	3	3	5	.481	.354
Wolf, Randy, S./W.B.*	.346	24	27	26	2	9	10	1	0	0	3	1	0	0	0	0	4	1	0	0	.385	.346
Wood, Jason, Tol.	.278	46	187	169	24	47	77	9	0	7	29	0	1	1	16	1	30	0	0	5	.456	.342
Woodall, Brad, Lou.*	.333	5	5	3	0	1	1	0	0	0	1	2	0	0	0	0	0	0	0	0	.333	.333
Woodward, Chris, Syr.	.200	25	94	85	9	17	29	6	0	2	6	2	0	0	7	0	20	1	1	4	.341	.261
Wunsch, Kelly, Lou.*	.000	9	15	12	1	0	0	0	0	0	0	0	0	1	2	0	6	0	0	0	.000	.200
Yarnall, Ed, Char.*	.000	15	10	9	0	0	0	0	0	0	0	1	0	0	0	0	2	0	0	1	.000	.000
Young, Tim, Ott.*	.000	20	3	3	0	0	0	0	0	0	0	0	0	0	0	0	2	0	0	0	.000	.000
Zosky, Eddie, Lou.	.245	90	278	257	36	63	101	12	1	8	35	4	1	1	15	2	47	1	3	3	.393	.288
Zuber, Jon, S./W.B.*	.325	80	335	280	47	91	134	23	4	4	56	1	6	2	45	7	34	0	0	8	.479	.414

GRAND SLAMS: Manto, 3; Barker, Ja. Cruz, Daubach, Lennon, Petagine, 2 each; Abad, G. Alvarez, Angeli, Banks, G. Bennett, Blosser, Brito, Brumfield, R. Butler, Coquillette, Jose Cruz, Dodson, Eenhoorn, Evans, Foster, A. Gonzalez, Hiatt, Knorr, Lowell, May, McClain, Merloni, Millar, D. Miller, Murray, Otanez, Nunnally, C. Owens, Schall, Seguignol, R. Sexson, Spencer, Tejero, Preston Wilson, Winn, 1 each.

AWARDED FIRST BASE ON CATCHER'S INTERFERENCE: Singleton, 5 (Bako, Banks, Brito, Marx 2); C. Martin 2 (Romero, A. Castillo); Milliard 2 (Mahoney, Knorr); Bucceri (Tejero); L. Castillo (Brito); Carey (Pachot); Daubach (Troilo); Forbes (Wilkins); J. Hurst (Knorr); Jimenez (Cardona); Saunders (Brito); Zuber (Pachot).

PLAYERS WITH TWO OR MORE TEAMS

Player, Team	Avg.	G	TPA	AB	R	H	TB	2B	3B	HR	RBI	SH	SF	HP	BB	IBB	SO	SB	CS	GDP	Slg.	OBP
Carey, Todd, Paw.*	.205	28	90	83	10	17	33	4	0	4	10	0	1	0	5	0	13	2	0	1	.398	.247
Carey, Todd, Nor.*	.272	81	279	246	24	67	104	18	2	5	29	1	2	0	30	1	57	3	6	3	.423	.349
Diaz, Eddy, Lou.	.238	86	314	277	31	66	98	15	1	5	40	1	3	5	28	2	27	8	5	5	.354	.316
Diaz, Eddy, Paw.	.295	33	151	139	30	41	64	9	1	4	13	0	0	1	11	0	12	5	1	7	.460	.351
Holbert, Ray, Rich.	.000	1	3	1	1	0	0	0	0	0	0	0	0	0	2	0	1	0	0	0	.000	.667
Holbert, Ray, Ott.	.308	86	299	266	38	82	113	17	4	2	25	4	0	0	29	3	66	10	5	2	.425	.376
Kinkade, Mike, Lou.	.309	80	336	291	57	90	147	24	6	7	46	1	2	6	36	1	52	10	2	7	.505	.394
Kinkade, Mike, Nor.	.280	30	136	125	12	35	43	5	0	1	18	1	2	5	3	0	24	6	1	5	.344	.319
Listach, Pat, Buf.†	.216	33	113	102	23	22	29	3	2	0	11	0	0	2	9	1	22	3	1	1	.284	.292
Listach, Pat, S./W.B.†	.221	55	233	204	27	45	57	5	2	1	12	4	0	2	23	0	47	14	4	1	.279	.306
Martinez, Pablo, Lou.†	.237	63	209	186	22	44	56	4	1	2	9	2	2	1	18	3	31	6	3	5	.301	.304
Martinez, Pablo, Rich.†	.278	15	38	36	3	10	11	1	0	0	3	0	0	0	2	0	10	1	2	0	.306	.316
Matos, Francisco, Dur.	.237	32	119	114	13	27	35	2	3	0	14	2	1	1	1	0	15	2	1	4	.307	.248
Matos, Francisco, Col.	.338	76	316	293	42	99	127	18	2	2	33	0	1	2	20	0	26	3	2	13	.433	.383
Natal, Bob, Dur.	.267	4	17	15	0	4	5	1	0	0	4	1	0	0	0	0	1	0	1	.333	.250
Natal, Bob, Col.	.273	68	233	216	31	59	105	11	1	11	39	0	1	3	13	0	33	1	1	10	.486	.322
Ruffin, Johnny, Lou.	.000	35	5	5	0	0	0	0	0	0	0	0	0	0	0	0	2	0	0	1	.000	.000
Ruffin, Johnny, Nor.	.250	17	8	8	0	2	2	0	0	0	0	0	0	0	0	0	5	0	0	0	.250	.250
Tomberlin, Andy, Tol.*	.340	14	59	47	13	16	26	2	1	2	4	0	0	4	8	0	15	1	1	0	.553	.475
Tomberlin, Andy, Rich.*	.260	39	127	104	12	27	42	3	0	4	15	0	1	7	15	1	29	1	1	3	.404	.386
Wagner, Paul, Lou.	.500	3	3	2	1	1	1	0	0	0	0	1	0	0	0	0	1	0	0	0	.500	.500
Wagner, Paul, Rich.	.000	8	1	1	0	0	0	0	0	0	0	0	0	0	0	0	1	0	0	0	.000	.000
Wilson, Preston, Nor.	.247	18	77	73	9	18	28	5	1	1	9	0	1	1	2	0	22	1	1	2	.384	.273
Wilson, Preston, Char.	.278	94	396	356	71	99	205	25	3	25	77	0	4	2	34	0	121	14	6	6	.576	.341

1998 PITCHING
TEAM

Team	W	L	Pct.	ERA	G	CG	ShO	Sv.	IP	H	TBF	R	ER	HR	SH	SF	HB	BB	IBB	SO	WP	Bk.
Syracuse	80	62	.563	3.68	142	10	9	42	1231.2	1150	5220	567	503	124	25	33	65	496	27	860	55	4
Norfolk	70	72	.493	4.07	142	6	9	34	1241.2	1248	5397	669	561	117	50	39	40	511	18	1043	57	4
Ottawa	69	74	.483	4.25	143	3	6	45	1233.1	1263	5424	680	582	147	34	31	76	529	15	906	59	7
Rochester	70	74	.486	4.31	144	6	9	33	1253.2	1173	5342	679	600	156	22	42	56	513	7	984	61	7
Louisville	77	67	.535	4.44	144	2	7	38	1263.2	1294	5556	702	623	145	40	28	55	531	24	945	65	5
Indianapolis	76	67	.531	4.46	143	3	9	36	1242.0	1262	5459	713	616	130	49	37	62	564	20	886	90	5
Richmond	64	80	.444	4.51	144	4	7	32	1247.0	1320	5435	702	625	125	43	43	36	487	15	968	77	4
Durham	80	64	.556	4.51	144	6	7	31	1260.1	1332	5481	706	632	137	24	29	51	467	23	961	62	7
Buffalo	81	62	.566	4.51	143	5	4	34	1260.0	1350	5550	734	632	139	33	34	51	491	17	973	74	8
Pawtucket	77	64	.546	4.62	142	5	6	35	1230.1	1290	5361	701	632	178	34	46	49	459	30	967	81	5
Columbus	67	77	.465	4.85	144	8	5	38	1278.0	1366	5701	774	688	156	29	42	40	599	8	975	59	3
Scranton/W.-B.	67	75	.472	4.89	142	17	8	33	1254.0	1373	5505	751	681	140	44	51	47	452	25	926	48	4
Charlotte	70	73	.490	5.26	143	9	6	42	1235.0	1384	5515	807	722	162	48	48	33	542	32	863	58	8
Toledo	52	89	.369	5.37	142	8	6	29	1214.0	1359	5481	811	724	172	36	54	60	578	10	849	75	11

TOP QUALIFIERS FOR EARNED-RUN AVERAGE TITLE

Minimum 115 innings.*Lefthanded pitcher.

Pitcher, Team	W	L	Pct.	ERA	G	GS	CG	ShO	GF	Sv.	IP	H	TBF	R	ER	HR	SH	SF	HB	BB	IBB	SO	WP	Bk.
Burrows, Terry, Roch.*	9	6	.600	2.92	29	15	1	0	3	0	132.1	104	531	49	43	8	1	7	2	42	0	112	2	1
Eiland, Dave, Dur.	13	5	.722	2.99	28	28	2	1	0	0	171.2	177	693	70	57	13	0	4	1	27	1	112	2	0
Jacome, Jason, Buf.*	14	2	.875	3.26	24	24	2	0	0	0	154.2	161	642	62	56	13	2	2	3	38	0	109	5	1
Withem, Shannon, Syr.	17	5	.773	3.27	28	27	4	2	1	0	189.2	176	781	72	69	14	4	5	10	58	2	113	2	0
Henderson, Rod, Ott.-Lou.	11	6	.647	3.47	28	19	1	0	2	0	132.1	123	559	62	51	7	3	1	4	51	0	80	1	0
Halladay, Roy, Syr.	9	5	.643	3.79	21	21	1	1	0	0	116.1	107	500	52	49	11	2	2	8	53	3	71	9	0
Bolton, Rod, Ind.	12	11	.522	3.81	29	29	1	1	0	0	177.0	166	746	82	75	15	3	2	5	64	1	117	6	1
Sauerbeck, Scott, Nor.*	7	13	.350	3.93	27	27	2	0	0	0	160.1	178	701	82	70	8	7	2	3	68	1	119	8	2
Manzanillo, Josias, Dur.-Nor.	11	10	.524	3.98	32	26	1	0	3	2	163.0	170	712	92	72	17	3	5	8	61	0	133	6	0
Nye, Ryan, S./W.B.	9	6	.600	4.05	23	22	3	2	0	0	140.0	139	595	73	63	8	4	2	7	49	2	118	7	2
Romano, Mike, Syr.	8	6	.571	4.14	27	13	1	0	7	1	117.1	131	516	66	54	13	0	2	4	53	3	69	6	0
Bennett, Joel, Roch.-S./W.B.	11	2	.846	4.17	26	22	1	0	0	0	149.0	150	640	75	69	15	2	4	3	62	2	134	3	0
Pena, Juan, Paw.	8	10	.444	4.38	24	23	1	1	0	0	139.2	141	606	73	68	17	4	2	8	51	3	146	14	2
VanEgmond, Tim, Lou.	6	11	.353	4.44	24	20	0	0	1	0	131.2	132	569	72	65	23	5	2	9	45	2	99	6	1
Ebert, Derrin, Rich.*	9	9	.500	4.51	29	29	0	0	0	0	163.2	195	710	94	82	14	5	3	3	49	1	88	4	0

DEPARTMENTAL LEADERS: W—Withem, 17; L—Drumright, 19; Pct.—Jacome, .875; G—M. Walker, 78; GS—Carlyle, 30; CG—Loewer, 5; ShO—Loewer, Nye, Withem, 2 each; GF—Batchelor, Eichhorn, Fleetham, T. Williams, 45 each; Sv.—T. Williams, 26; IP—Withem, 189.2; H—Maduro, 211; TBF—Maduro, 799; R—Drumright, 130; ER—Drumright, 119; HR—Farrell, 31; SH—Carlyle, 10; SF—Drumright, 13; HB—Drews, 16; BB—Drumright, 94; IBB—Green, Nunez, 7 each; SO—Pena, 146; WP—Wohlers, 17; BK—J. Martinez, 3.

ALL PITCHERS

*Lefthanded pitcher.

Pitcher, Team	W	L	Pct.	ERA	G	GS	CG	ShO	GF	Sv.	IP	H	TBF	R	ER	HR	SH	SF	HB	BB	IBB	SO	WP	Bk.
Alberro, Jose, Col.	8	10	.444	4.52	46	13	1	0	20	5	127.1	123	570	76	64	14	3	4	7	69	0	91	10	1
Aldred, Scott, Dur. *	2	4	.333	5.35	7	7	0	0	0	0	35.1	44	161	26	21	3	0	2	4	14	0	19	4	0
Almanzar, Carlos, Syr.	3	6	.333	2.31	30	0	0	0	19	10	50.2	44	211	21	13	7	1	1	4	13	2	53	2	0
Alvarez, Wilson, Dur. *	0	0	.000	3.86	1	1	0	0	0	0	4.2	4	19	2	2	0	0	0	0	2	0	6	0	0
Andujar, Luis, Syr.	3	2	.600	2.12	20	0	0	0	14	8	34.0	23	130	9	8	5	2	0	4	6	0	24	2	1
Arnold, Jamie, Rich.	1	0	1.000	9.58	9	2	0	0	2	1	20.2	30	102	22	22	1	1	3	1	17	1	10	3	0
Arroyo, Luis, Nor. *	0	0	.000	6.75	8	0	0	0	5	0	8.0	11	41	7	6	1	0	1	1	7	0	7	0	0
Aucoin, Derek, Nor.	0	0	.000	0.00	3	0	0	0	1	0	4.0	3	15	0	0	0	0	0	0	0	0	5	1	0
Avery, Steve, Paw. *	0	2	.000	5.56	3	3	0	0	0	0	11.1	9	53	9	7	2	3	2	1	9	0	6	0	0
Baez, Kevin, Ind.	0	0	.000	0.00	2	0	0	0	2	0	2.0	1	8	0	0	0	0	0	1	0	0	0	0	0
Barkley, Brian, Paw. *	7	9	.438	4.91	23	23	1	0	0	0	139.1	161	609	81	76	22	3	10	7	50	4	88	5	2
Baron, Jim, Col. *	1	5	.167	6.09	8	7	1	0	1	0	44.1	54	196	32	30	7	0	2	1	19	0	28	3	0
Barrios, Manny, Char.	2	0	1.000	3.70	18	1	0	0	6	0	24.1	19	98	10	10	3	0	1	9	2	0	22	0	0
Batchelor, Rich, Buf.	4	4	.500	3.39	57	0	0	0	45	22	58.1	58	263	26	22	3	2	0	4	25	1	64	7	1
Beasley, Ray, Rich. *	0	0	.000	4.50	2	0	0	0	1	0	6.0	8	28	3	3	0	2	0	0	2	0	6	0	0
Beck, Greg, Lou.	4	3	.571	5.67	10	8	1	0	0	0	46.0	49	204	31	29	8	3	2	2	16	0	37	2	0
Belk, Tim, Tol.	0	0	.000	18.00	3	0	0	0	3	0	3.0	4	18	6	6	3	0	0	0	5	0	1	2	0
Bellinger, Clay, Col.	0	0	.000	0.00	1	0	0	0	0	0	0.1	1	3	0	0	0	0	0	0	1	0	0	0	0
Beltran, Rigo, Nor. *	6	5	.545	4.29	36	11	0	0	7	1	94.1	104	418	51	45	16	2	1	40	1	98	5	1
Bennett, Joel, Roch.-S./W.B.	11	2	.846	4.17	26	22	1	0	0	0	149.0	150	640	75	69	15	2	4	3	62	2	134	3	0
Benz, Jake, Ott. *	1	5	.167	5.84	25	3	0	0	8	1	49.1	63	230	34	32	8	3	1	2	24	2	40	3	0
Blais, Mike, Paw.	0	1	.000	7.71	2	0	0	0	1	0	2.1	4	12	2	2	0	1	0	2	1	0	0	0	0
Blomdahl, Ben, Buf.	2	3	.400	4.76	35	2	0	0	6	1	70.0	83	303	43	37	12	1	3	2	17	1	42	0	0
Blood, Darin, Roch.	3	2	.600	2.48	6	6	1	1	0	0	32.2	24	131	11	9	2	0	0	5	13	0	14	1	0
Bolton, Rod, Ind.	12	11	.522	3.81	29	29	1	1	0	0	177.0	166	746	82	75	15	3	2	5	64	1	117	6	1
Borbon, Pedro, Rich. *	0	1	.000	5.70	20	0	0	0	1	0	23.2	29	106	17	15	1	0	0	2	8	0	15	0	0
Borland, Toby, S./W.B.-Char.	3	2	.600	3.47	32	0	0	0	14	6	49.1	47	210	20	19	4	0	2	2	24	1	41	5	1
Borowski, Joe, Col.	3	3	.500	2.93	45	0	0	0	10	4	73.2	66	320	25	24	6	3	4	2	39	1	67	3	0
Boskie, Shawn, Ott.	5	7	.417	4.55	13	13	0	0	0	0	87.0	100	375	48	44	7	0	2	5	21	1	51	5	0
Bottalico, Ricky, S./W.B.	0	1	.000	2.92	10	5	0	0	3	1	12.1	8	54	4	4	1	1	1	9	0	4	1	0
Bradley, Ryan, Col.	3	3	.500	6.19	3	3	0	0	0	0	16.0	15	72	13	11	4	0	0	13	0	12	1	0
Brannan, Ryan, S./W.B.	1	1	.500	7.56	16	0	0	0	12	2	16.2	21	88	18	14	0	1	1	3	13	2	12	3	0
Briggs, Anthony, Rich.	7	10	.412	5.33	28	21	0	0	5	0	121.2	125	536	82	72	16	1	4	1	57	0	91	9	1
Brow, Scott, Col.	3	2	.600	5.46	30	3	0	0	8	0	59.1	74	273	42	36	8	2	3	1	26	0	35	3	0
Bruske, Jim, Col.	0	0	.000	1.17	4	0	0	0	3	1	7.2	7	31	1	1	0	0	0	2	0	9	0	0
Buckley, Travis, Rich.	1	2	.333	3.79	4	3	0	0	1	0	19.0	21	82	11	8	2	0	2	1	4	0	7	0	0
Buddie, Mike, Col.	5	0	1.000	2.74	26	0	0	0	12	4	42.2	35	170	15	13	0	1	1	1	15	0	30	2	0
Bullard, Jason, Rich.	1	2	.333	4.91	36	0	0	0	13	0	55.0	56	235	36	30	3	1	2	3	22	0	48	14	0
Bullinger, Kirk, Ott.	0	0	.000	1.06	13	0	0	0	4	3	17.0	16	72	2	2	0	1	0	0	6	1	7	0	0
Bunch, Mel, Ott.	6	6	.500	4.59	25	19	0	0	2	0	104.0	101	456	58	53	17	3	3	11	48	0	99	7	2
Burrows, Terry, Roch. *	9	6	.600	2.92	29	15	1	0	3	0	132.1	104	531	49	43	8	1	7	2	42	0	112	2	1
Butler, Adam, Rich. *	3	7	.300	3.60	48	4	0	0	34	14	100.0	96	427	41	40	9	6	6	6	28	1	92	3	1
Byrd, Paul, Rich.	5	3	.625	3.69	17	17	2	0	0	0	102.1	92	424	44	42	9	2	2	36	2	84	3	1
Callaway, Michael, Dur.	5	3	.625	4.53	9	8	0	0	0	0	47.2	49	209	27	24	6	1	0	1	17	0	19	2	0
Carlson, Dan, Dur.	3	5	.375	6.35	19	11	0	0	3	0	63.2	87	316	52	48	8	1	1	3	28	0	59	4	1
Carlyle, Ken, Rich.	6	12	.333	5.17	30	30	0	0	0	0	156.2	206	701	104	90	22	10	4	2	46	1	76	2	0
Cather, Mike, Rich.	0	1	.000	5.87	11	0	0	0	2	0	15.1	22	72	12	10	1	2	0	0	6	0	10	2	0
Charlton, Norm, Rich. *	0	0	.000	0.00	2	0	0	0	1	0	2.0	2	8	0	0	0	0	0	0	1	0	4	0	0
Checo, Robinson, Paw.	6	2	.750	4.56	11	10	0	0	0	0	53.1	48	233	30	27	9	0	2	5	26	1	46	4	0
Chen, Bruce, Rich. *	2	1	.667	1.88	4	4	0	0	0	0	24.0	17	104	5	5	2	1	1	19	0	29	1	0
Chouinard, Bobby, Lou. *	2	1	.667	4.93	7	7	0	0	0	0	42.0	52	192	31	23	5	1	1	0	15	0	33	1	1
Clontz, Brad, Nor.	2	4	.333	3.43	28	0	0	0	7	0	42.0	43	185	26	16	4	0	1	1	16	3	49	2	0
Cole, Jason, Ott.	2	0	1.000	3.80	13	0	0	0	3	1	21.1	21	93	9	9	3	0	1	1	13	0	14	0	0

Pitcher, Team	W	L	Pct.	ERA	G	GS	CG	ShO	GF	Sv.	IP	H	TBF	R	ER	HR	SH	SF	HB	BB	IBB	SO	WP	Bk.
Converse, Jim, Roch.	2	8	.200	4.90	33	6	0	0	13	1	82.2	86	365	51	45	12	0	4	0	40	0	74	7	0
Cooke, Steve, Ind. *	0	1	.000	37.80	2	2	0	0	0	0	1.2	3	13	7	7	0	0	0	0	5	0	0	0	0
Coppinger, Rocky, Roch.	8	3	.727	3.50	14	13	1	0	1	0	87.1	80	379	38	34	11	2	3	3	43	1	64	0	0
Corbin, Archie, Char.	2	2	.500	2.59	34	0	0	0	12	3	48.2	25	212	15	14	2	1	2	0	46	1	55	7	0
Corey, Mark, Ind.	0	1	.000	4.50	1	1	1	0	0	0	6.0	4	24	3	3	1	1	0	0	3	0	2	0	0
Cornelius, Reid, Char.	3	2	.600	4.01	8	8	1	1	0	0	49.1	50	215	25	22	5	2	0	2	13	2	31	0	0
Cornett, Brad, Lou.	3	3	.500	3.65	12	8	0	0	0	0	61.2	64	256	30	25	9	4	1	2	14	0	34	1	0
Corsi, Jim, Paw.	0	0	.000	0.00	1	1	0	0	0	0	2.0	3	8	0	0	0	0	0	0	0	0	1	0	0
Cortes, David, Rich.	3	3	.500	2.82	29	0	0	0	17	4	44.2	37	181	15	14	2	3	1	0	14	3	46	1	0
Crow, Dean, Tol.	2	0	1.000	1.48	24	0	0	0	21	10	24.1	21	97	8	4	1	1	1	1	3	0	12	0	0
Crowell, Jim, Ind. *	0	0	.000	6.75	1	1	0	0	0	0	4.0	7	19	3	3	0	0	0	0	0	0	2	0	0
Cummings, John, Buf.-Paw. *	0	5	.000	6.16	10	8	0	0	1	0	38.0	46	170	28	26	3	1	0	3	12	0	17	2	0
Curtis, Chris, Roch.	2	6	.250	7.67	18	7	0	0	1	0	54.0	68	244	48	46	12	3	1	4	21	0	23	3	1
Daniels, John, Dur.	2	0	1.000	1.86	4	0	0	0	1	1	9.2	4	34	2	2	1	0	1	0	3	0	9	1	0
Darwin, David, Tol. *	1	0	1.000	1.29	1	1	1	0	0	0	7.0	4	25	1	1	1	0	0	1	0	0	5	0	0
Dedrick, Jim, Rich.	2	3	.400	5.30	26	0	0	0	17	0	37.1	36	160	24	22	4	0	2	0	15	3	27	2	0
Dempster, Ryan, Char.	3	1	.750	3.27	5	5	1	0	0	0	33.0	33	137	14	12	4	0	2	1	12	1	24	2	0
DeHart, Rick, Ott. *	7	1	.875	3.23	38	0	0	0	18	4	53.0	46	220	19	19	5	1	0	2	17	2	48	1	0
De Los Santos, Valerio, Lou. *	0	0	.000	3.60	5	0	0	0	2	0	5.0	4	19	2	2	0	0	0	0	0	0	0	0	0
DeSilva, John, Ott.	4	2	.667	2.61	7	7	0	0	0	0	48.1	42	191	15	14	5	1	2	2	12	0	25	1	1
Dixon, Tim, Ott. *	0	0	.000	5.89	9	0	0	0	5	0	18.1	22	84	15	12	2	0	1	0	7	0	13	3	0
Dodd, Robert, S./W.B. *	4	1	.800	3.24	42	0	0	0	16	6	41.2	37	177	15	15	4	2	1	1	19	2	41	0	0
Dodson, Bo, Roch. *	0	0	.000	0.00	3	0	0	0	2	0	3.0	1	10	0	0	0	0	0	0	1	0	0	1	0
Donnelly, Brendan, Ind.	4	1	.800	2.65	19	1	0	0	6	0	37.1	29	157	16	11	3	1	0	3	16	3	39	2	0
Dotel, Octavio, Nor.	8	6	.571	3.45	17	16	1	0	0	0	99.0	82	424	47	38	9	6	2	2	43	1	118	9	1
Dougherty, Tony, Buf.	0	0	.000	3.00	1	0	0	0	0	0	3.0	4	15	4	1	0	0	0	0	2	0	1	0	0
Drews, Matt, Tol.	5	17	.227	6.57	27	27	1	0	0	0	149.1	175	702	120	109	26	5	11	16	78	1	86	15	2
Driskill, Travis, Buf.	0	0	.000	9.00	1	1	0	0	0	0	6.0	9	28	6	6	0	0	0	0	1	0	5	0	0
Drumright, Mike, Tol.	4	19	.174	6.95	29	27	1	0	1	0	154.0	188	733	130	119	21	3	13	7	94	0	91	16	1
Dunbar, Matt, Lou. *	1	3	.250	6.14	50	0	0	0	18	0	55.2	74	281	47	38	6	1	1	7	32	1	45	5	1
Duran, Roberto, Tol. *	0	0	.000	27.00	1	0	0	0	0	0	0.2	1	5	2	2	0	0	0	0	2	0	1	0	0
Duvall, Mike, Dur. *	5	3	.625	3.22	32	9	1	0	5	0	72.2	74	314	31	26	3	0	1	2	32	3	55	5	0
Ebert, Derrin, Rich. *	9	9	.500	4.51	29	29	0	0	0	0	163.2	195	710	94	82	14	5	3	3	49	1	88	4	0
Eckersley, Dennis, Paw.	0	0	.000	4.50	2	0	0	0	0	0	2.0	2	8	1	1	1	0	0	0	0	0	2	0	0
Eichhorn, Mark, Dur.	5	3	.625	3.88	53	0	0	0	45	18	58.0	59	239	27	25	7	9	2	4	11	2	44	0	0
Eiland, Dave, Dur.	13	5	.722	2.99	28	28	2	1	0	0	171.2	177	693	70	57	13	0	4	1	27	1	112	2	0
Eischen, Joey, Ind. *	2	5	.286	4.54	61	0	0	0	18	2	73.1	73	326	42	37	9	7	3	4	29	3	60	7	0
Ellis, Robert, Lou.	10	10	.500	5.63	30	28	0	0	0	0	150.1	171	693	103	94	21	7	2	8	78	1	79	13	0
Erdos, Todd, Col.	3	2	.600	4.62	39	0	0	0	33	16	48.2	52	216	27	25	4	1	3	2	20	0	50	2	0
Escobar, Kelvim, Syr.	2	2	.500	3.77	13	10	0	0	2	1	59.2	51	253	26	25	7	1	1	4	24	0	64	3	0
Estrada, Horacio, Lou. *	0	0	.000	3.00	2	2	0	0	0	0	12.0	10	50	4	4	1	0	0	0	5	0	4	0	0
Falteisek, Steve, Ott.	10	11	.476	5.46	34	22	1	0	1	0	161.2	186	719	110	98	17	4	4	11	59	1	83	10	0
Farrell, Jim, Paw.	14	8	.636	5.51	28	25	2	1	0	0	163.1	176	709	106	100	31	2	5	5	52	0	142	8	1
Fernandez, Jared, Paw.	1	1	.500	4.74	5	2	0	0	2	0	24.2	26	107	16	13	5	0	2	3	7	0	15	4	0
Fernandez, Osvaldo, Nor. *	0	1	.000	5.40	2	0	0	0	1	0	3.1	6	17	2	2	0	1	0	1	2	0	2	1	0
Fesh, Sean, S./W.B. *	0	0	.000	3.00	8	0	0	0	1	0	6.0	3	25	2	2	0	0	0	1	4	1	4	0	0
Fiore, Tony, S./W.B.	4	7	.364	4.47	41	7	0	0	12	1	94.2	92	418	53	47	4	3	3	1	52	1	71	6	0
Fleetham, Ben, Ott.	4	2	.667	3.49	55	0	0	0	45	25	56.2	49	258	26	22	3	3	0	0	42	0	65	5	0
Fleming, Dave, Paw.-Roch. *	1	1	.500	6.58	8	4	0	0	3	0	26.0	29	122	21	19	6	0	0	1	16	0	7	0	0
Flener, Huck, Buf. *	7	3	.700	6.68	14	8	0	0	3	0	60.2	73	278	52	45	12	3	1	0	26	1	35	2	0
Fletcher, Paul, Syr.	3	4	.429	2.70	48	0	0	0	32	6	73.1	65	312	29	22	4	2	4	2	28	2	53	7	0
Florie, Bryce, Tol.	0	0	.000	0.00	1	1	0	0	0	0	4.0	0	12	0	0	0	0	0	0	0	0	3	0	0
Flury, Pat, Paw.	0	0	.000	5.64	17	0	0	0	5	0	22.1	23	100	15	14	3	1	0	0	16	0	22	4	0
Fontenot, Joe, Char.	0	1	.000	12.00	1	1	0	0	0	0	3.0	4	15	4	4	1	0	0	0	2	0	0	0	0
Frey, Steve, Paw. *	4	2	.667	3.88	50	0	0	0	16	2	62.2	66	270	29	27	6	4	4	1	22	4	42	3	0
Fussell, Chris, Roch.	5	2	.714	3.99	10	10	0	0	0	0	58.2	50	249	30	26	4	1	3	5	28	0	51	5	0
Fyhrie, Mike, Nor.	3	7	.300	6.64	24	17	0	0	3	0	100.1	115	461	83	74	12	2	8	5	45	1	60	4	0
Gaillard, Eddie, Dur.	2	0	1.000	7.65	18	0	0	0	1	0	20.0	27	98	18	17	5	0	1	3	11	0	21	3	0
Gallaher, Kevin, Roch.	2	6	.250	7.55	13	8	0	0	2	0	39.1	32	196	40	33	5	1	2	2	43	0	28	6	0
Garces, Rich, Paw.	0	1	.000	5.40	7	0	0	0	7	3	8.1	6	33	5	5	1	1	0	0	2	1	10	1	0
Gardiner, Mike, Char.	5	7	.417	6.01	14	14	1	0	0	0	88.1	107	397	63	59	17	1	2	1	34	1	53	1	0
Glauber, Keith, Ind.	1	3	.250	9.00	4	4	0	0	0	0	16.0	20	78	17	16	1	3	2	1	14	0	15	3	0
Goldsmith, Gary, Tol.	0	1	.000	5.26	46	0	0	0	14	1	78.2	83	339	47	46	16	1	4	3	29	2	50	5	0
Gonzalez, Gabe, Char. *	3	9	.250	5.48	57	4	0	0	13	2	87.0	101	412	67	53	3	8	7	1	53	5	41	2	1
Gooden, Dwight, Buf.	1	2	.333	9.00	4	4	0	0	0	0	16.0	23	74	16	16	5	0	0	0	7	0	18	1	0
Grace, Mike, S./W.B.	3	6	.333	5.04	11	10	2	0	0	0	75.0	92	327	44	42	8	9	3	5	18	1	39	2	0
Grahe, Joe, Col.	4	2	.667	4.53	12	5	1	0	2	0	43.2	42	185	23	22	4	0	1	3	11	1	22	4	1
Graterol, Beiker, Syr.	9	2	.818	4.59	16	16	0	0	0	0	96.0	103	422	55	49	10	1	1	12	32	1	62	3	1
Graves, Danny, Ind.	1	0	1.000	1.93	13	0	0	0	2	0	14.0	15	58	3	3	0	0	0	0	3	0	11	1	0
Greene, Rick, Lou.	6	6	.500	3.51	58	0	0	0	44	18	66.2	73	302	31	26	6	2	1	3	33	7	44	2	0
Greisinger, Seth, Tol.	3	4	.429	2.91	10	10	0	0	0	0	58.2	50	247	21	19	5	1	1	5	22	0	37	3	2
Grimsley, Jason, Buf.	6	3	.667	3.76	52	0	0	0	8	0	88.2	76	393	40	37	10	2	3	6	57	3	68	14	0
Grundt, Ken, Char. *	2	0	1.000	5.91	16	0	0	0	4	1	21.1	23	98	15	14	1	4	0	1	15	0	12	0	0
Guerra, Mark, Nor.	2	1	.667	6.46	18	0	0	0	8	0	30.2	40	142	24	22	6	2	3	1	14	1	19	0	0
Halladay, Roy, Syr.	9	5	.643	3.79	21	21	1	1	0	0	116.1	107	500	52	49	11	2	2	8	53	3	71	9	0
Hammond, Chris, Char. *	1	3	.250	4.82	5	5	0	0	0	0	28.0	35	129	17	15	2	3	1	0	14	2	22	0	0
Harriger, Denny, Tol.	5	12	.294	4.55	22	22	4	1	0	0	142.1	151	603	78	72	15	4	5	2	48	0	87	2	0
Harris, D.J., Syr.	1	4	.200	3.98	25	1	0	0	11	0	40.2	40	172	20	18	6	1	1	1	21	1	25	2	0
Harris, Gene, Nor.	0	0	.000	12.00	2	0	0	0	0	0	3.0	3	15	4	4	0	0	0	0	4	0	3	0	0
Harrison, Tommy, Rich.	2	0	1.000	4.50	2	2	0	0	0	0	10.0	9	41	5	5	0	0	0	0	3	0	11	0	0
Hastings, Lionel, Char.	0	0	.000	0.00	1	0	0	0	1	0	0.2	1	3	0	0	0	0	0	0	0	0	1	0	0
Hawblitzel, Ryan, Char.	8	5	.615	5.59	20	19	0	0	0	0	103.0	133	437	68	64	20	2	2	2	14	0	72	3	0

Pitcher, Team	W	L	Pct.	ERA	G	GS	CG	ShO	GF	Sv.	IP	H	TBF	R	ER	HR	SH	SF	HB	BB	IBB	SO	WP	Bk.
Heflin, Bronson, S./W.B.	0	0	.000	7.20	10	0	0	0	2	0	10.0	12	49	10	8	3	0	0	0	7	0	9	1	0
Henderson, Rod, Ott.-Lou.	11	6	.647	3.47	28	19	1	0	2	0	132.1	123	559	62	51	7	3	1	4	51	0	80	1	0
Henderson, Ryan, Nor.	0	0	.000	11.25	3	0	0	0	0	0	4.0	6	23	5	5	0	0	0	0	6	0	2	0	0
Henriquez, Oscar, Char.	1	0	1.000	2.56	26	0	0	0	19	11	31.2	29	134	12	9	3	0	1	2	12	0	37	4	0
Heredia, Wilson, Col.	4	7	.364	6.90	23	14	0	0	2	0	88.2	111	419	78	68	21	3	3	3	49	0	70	3	0
Hernandez, Orlando, Col.	6	0	1.000	3.83	7	7	0	0	0	0	42.1	41	182	19	18	2	2	1	5	17	0	59	1	0
Hernandez, Santos, Dur.	2	0	1.000	4.84	53	0	0	0	10	2	80.0	88	343	45	43	11	0	2	3	21	2	60	8	0
Holman, Craig, S./W.B.	1	3	.250	4.75	6	6	0	0	0	0	30.1	36	129	17	16	4	1	2	0	9	0	20	1	0
Horsman, Vincent, Roch. *	0	0	.000	2.92	6	0	0	0	2	0	12.1	13	48	5	4	2	0	0	1	0	8	0	0
Hudson, Joe, Paw.-Lou.	3	2	.600	4.65	55	0	0	0	27	10	60.0	70	279	39	31	4	2	3	2	28	4	36	4	0
Hurst, Bill, Tol.	0	1	.000	11.42	12	0	0	0	2	0	17.1	21	90	22	22	3	3	0	0	17	0	13	6	0
Hutton, Mark, Ind.	4	6	.400	4.43	16	16	0	0	0	0	83.1	91	370	50	41	7	3	4	5	37	0	47	4	0
Jacobs, Ryan, Rich. *	0	0	.000	18.69	2	0	0	0	0	0	4.1	9	28	9	9	1	0	0	0	6	0	1	1	0
Jacobsen, Joe, Char.	1	3	.250	5.95	9	8	0	0	0	0	42.1	64	191	29	28	8	3	0	0	7	0	17	1	0
Jacome, Jason, Buf. *	14	2	.875	3.26	24	24	2	0	0	0	154.2	161	642	62	56	13	2	2	3	38	0	109	5	1
Janzen, Marty, Col.	5	6	.455	5.77	16	12	1	0	0	0	68.2	78	318	48	44	8	0	3	1	38	0	54	6	0
Jarvis, Kevin, Ind.	1	0	1.000	9.00	2	2	0	0	0	0	7.0	10	32	7	7	3	0	0	0	1	0	5	2	0
Jerzembeck, Mike, Col.	4	9	.308	4.87	24	24	0	0	0	0	140.1	158	624	82	76	20	1	1	3	55	1	107	4	1
Johns, Doug, Roch. *	0	1	.000	1.69	2	2	0	0	0	0	10.2	7	45	3	2	2	0	0	2	6	0	4	0	0
Johns, Keith, Paw.	0	0	.000	0.00	1	0	0	0	1	0	1.0	0	6	0	0	0	0	1	2	0	0	0	0	0
Johnson, Craig, Tol.	1	0	1.000	5.40	1	1	0	0	0	0	5.0	6	22	4	3	1	0	0	1	1	0	1	0	0
Johnson, Dane, Syr.-Char.	2	0	1.000	3.24	9	0	0	0	6	3	8.1	8	34	3	3	1	0	0	6	0	4	0	0
Johnson, Jason, Dur.	1	0	1.000	2.92	2	2	0	0	0	0	12.1	6	44	4	4	2	0	0	2	0	14	0	0
Johnson, Mike, Ott.	4	9	.308	4.29	18	18	1	0	0	0	109.0	105	473	63	52	20	3	4	8	38	0	88	4	1
Jordan, Ricardo, Ind.-Col. *	4	4	.500	3.86	42	11	0	0	6	0	95.2	98	428	54	41	12	2	4	3	50	2	74	1	0
Karp, Ryan, Dur. *	2	6	.250	5.30	36	5	1	0	11	1	73.0	76	314	44	43	9	2	1	1	31	2	64	6	0
Karsay, Steve, Buf.	6	4	.600	3.76	16	14	0	0	0	0	79.0	89	342	39	33	5	0	1	3	15	0	63	2	0
Kaufman, Brad, Col.	1	2	.333	7.20	3	3	0	0	0	0	15.0	17	72	15	12	3	1	0	0	12	0	13	0	0
Keagle, Greg, Tol.	5	3	.625	4.63	15	14	0	0	0	0	81.2	94	365	48	42	12	1	2	6	32	0	61	1	2
Kelley, Rich, Roch. *	1	3	.250	5.45	15	3	0	0	4	1	38.0	34	156	28	23	6	4	1	1	17	0	24	2	1
Keyser, Brian, Ind.	6	6	.500	4.62	41	13	0	0	4	0	117.0	131	522	69	60	13	4	4	2	56	3	66	6	0
Kline, Steve, Ott. *	0	0	.000	0.00	2	0	0	0	0	0	2.2	1	8	0	0	0	0	0	0	0	0	1	0	0
Klingenbeck, Scott, Ind.	6	2	.750	2.86	10	10	0	0	0	0	63.0	57	249	26	20	7	1	2	0	10	0	50	0	0
Koch, Billy, Syr.	0	1	.000	14.29	2	2	0	0	0	0	5.2	9	31	9	9	1	0	1	0	5	0	9	0	1
Kroon, Marc, Ind.	3	2	.600	5.63	39	0	0	0	9	1	46.1	39	219	29	29	6	1	2	5	47	0	36	14	0
Lankford, Frank, Col.	5	9	.357	5.07	15	15	3	0	0	0	94.0	110	413	60	53	12	3	0	1	32	0	58	3	0
Larkin, Andy, Char.	4	1	.800	6.37	11	10	0	0	0	0	53.2	55	246	39	38	8	2	4	32	2	41	2	0
LeRoy, John, Dur.	0	1	.000	27.00	4	0	0	0	1	0	4.0	11	27	12	12	1	0	0	0	5	0	1	0	0
Lewis, Richie, Roch. *	5	7	.417	5.01	21	21	2	0	0	0	124.0	107	526	77	69	17	1	3	7	42	0	131	10	0
Lilly, Ted, Ott. *	2	2	.500	4.85	7	7	0	0	0	0	39.0	45	182	28	21	8	1	1	0	19	0	49	0	0
Loewer, Carlton, S./W.B.	7	3	.700	2.87	12	12	5	2	0	0	94.0	89	385	34	30	5	5	2	5	22	0	69	3	0
Long, Joey, Ott. *	2	4	.333	4.40	34	1	0	0	12	0	47.0	53	216	27	23	6	3	0	3	24	2	41	4	0
Looney, Brian, Col. *	4	4	.500	4.47	41	10	0	0	7	0	92.2	97	424	52	46	13	3	5	1	52	2	63	3	0
Lopez, Albie, Dur.	0	0	.000	0.00	2	0	0	0	0	0	3.0	4	13	0	0	0	0	0	0	1	0	2	0	0
Ludwick, Eric, Char.	1	3	.250	3.71	8	8	0	0	0	0	26.2	25	118	17	11	1	1	0	1	13	0	26	3	0
Lukasiewicz, Mark, Syr. *	2	2	.500	3.40	22	4	0	0	3	1	47.2	38	201	18	18	8	0	3	24	1	30	3	0
Maduro, Calvin, S./W.B.	12	9	.571	5.98	28	27	4	1	0	0	177.2	211	799	123	118	28	4	6	2	68	1	120	3	1
Maeda, Kats, Col.	0	1	.000	2.51	13	0	0	0	9	0	14.1	13	62	5	4	1	1	0	0	8	1	16	2	0
Mahay, Ron, Paw. *	3	1	.750	4.17	23	1	0	0	8	3	41.0	37	179	20	19	8	0	2	0	19	2	41	3	0
Mantei, Matt, Char.	1	2	.333	5.51	16	0	0	0	8	3	16.1	11	76	10	10	2	0	2	0	18	1	25	2	0
Manzanillo, Josias, Dur.-Nor.	11	10	.524	3.98	32	26	1	0	3	2	163.0	170	712	92	72	17	3	5	8	61	0	133	6	0
Martin, Tom, Buf. *	3	1	.750	6.00	41	0	0	0	0	0	36.0	46	167	25	24	4	1	1	3	13	0	35	1	0
Martinez, Jesus, Ind. *	7	6	.538	6.85	22	18	0	0	0	0	93.1	119	425	78	71	10	4	4	5	42	0	39	7	3
Martinez, Pedro, Tol. *	2	5	.286	3.79	58	1	0	0	31	8	71.1	72	310	38	30	8	4	3	1	31	2	49	1	1
Mathews, Terry, Roch.	0	1	.000	3.00	1	1	0	0	0	0	3.0	4	15	1	1	0	0	0	2	0	4	0	0
Matthews, Mike, Buf. *	9	6	.600	4.63	24	23	0	0	1	0	130.1	137	577	79	67	19	4	1	5	68	1	86	5	2
Maxcy, Brian, Nor.	3	0	1.000	2.74	28	0	0	0	5	0	49.1	49	228	25	15	3	1	1	4	27	0	39	4	0
McGraw, Tom, Ott. *	5	6	.455	3.73	32	10	0	0	8	2	82.0	79	358	38	34	6	4	2	3	36	2	43	2	0
Medina, Rafael, Char.	4	2	.667	3.90	11	9	3	1	1	0	57.2	53	245	27	25	8	0	2	2	26	1	41	4	1
Mendoza, Reynol, Char.	5	10	.333	6.19	24	18	1	0	1	0	125.0	163	583	101	86	18	5	6	5	57	3	59	3	2
Mimbs, Mark, Nor. *	9	2	.818	2.08	15	15	1	1	0	0	103.2	74	410	30	24	8	6	2	0	26	3	92	1	0
Mimbs, Mike, Col. *	0	2	.000	6.33	12	3	0	0	2	0	27.0	26	134	23	19	5	1	0	24	0	19	5	0
Minor, Blas, Lou.	1	0	1.000	5.00	3	1	0	0	1	0	9.0	10	39	6	5	0	0	1	0	2	0	9	0	0
Mix, Greg, Rich.	2	4	.333	2.92	28	2	0	0	13	2	64.2	52	268	24	21	8	1	2	4	19	0	59	1	0
Montgomery, Steve, Roch.	4	6	.400	4.40	51	4	0	0	29	8	88.0	79	364	50	43	14	3	3	0	24	2	66	3	0
Moore, Marcus, Buf.	3	5	.375	5.66	11	7	0	0	3	0	47.2	41	220	35	30	9	1	2	2	41	1	43	2	0
Moore, Trey, Ott. *	1	1	.500	5.54	3	3	0	0	0	0	13.0	18	59	8	8	1	0	4	0	8	1	0
Morel, Ramon, Ott.	4	3	.571	5.12	12	12	1	0	0	0	65.0	60	275	38	37	11	0	3	5	30	1	29	1	0
Morman, Alvin, Buf. *	0	0	.000	0.00	2	0	0	0	2	0	2.0	3	8	0	0	0	0	0	0	4	0	0
Mullins, Greg, Lou. *	3	1	.750	3.55	61	0	0	0	39	18	66.0	57	279	26	26	5	2	2	23	2	86	2	1
Munoz, Bobby, Roch.	3	1	.750	1.06	44	0	0	0	34	19	59.1	40	228	9	7	5	1	1	5	13	0	46	4	0
Munro, Peter, Paw.-Syr.	7	9	.438	5.06	26	25	0	0	0	0	151.1	169	663	91	85	17	4	5	6	58	4	117	12	0
Nichting, Chris, Buf.	8	6	.571	4.39	43	5	0	0	17	1	96.1	104	428	54	47	9	6	4	3	37	4	97	11	1
Niebla, Ruben, Ott. *	0	1	.000	5.11	6	0	0	0	3	0	12.1	20	58	12	7	4	0	0	4	0	7	0	0
Nix, James, Lou.	2	2	.500	7.01	27	1	0	0	8	0	34.2	43	169	28	27	4	2	1	0	24	2	28	1	0
Norris, Joe, Ind.	1	1	.500	5.40	4	2	0	0	0	0	10.0	13	48	10	6	3	0	1	6	0	7	0	0
Nunez, Maximo, Dur.	3	6	.333	5.00	58	0	0	0	32	5	63.0	67	292	39	35	9	5	1	5	40	7	53	5	1
Nye, Ryan, S./W.B.	9	6	.600	4.05	23	23	2	0	0	0	140.0	139	595	73	63	8	4	2	7	49	2	118	7	2
Ogea, Chad, Buf.	1	2	.667	3.61	9	9	1	0	0	0	42.1	42	178	19	17	2	1	1	4	5	0	34	1	0
Ontiveros, Steve, Roch.	5	1	.833	3.68	16	14	0	0	2	1	80.2	77	333	35	33	10	2	2	2	25	0	64	1	0
Osteen, Gavin, Roch. *	1	2	.333	3.96	44	0	0	0	18	2	72.2	74	310	37	32	10	1	2	3	25	0	46	4	2
Pacheco, Alexander, Dur.	0	0	.000	4.50	1	0	0	0	1	0	2.0	1	7	1	1	0	0	0	0	0	0	2	0	0

Pitcher, Team	W	L	Pct.	ERA	G	GS	CG	ShO	GF	Sv.	IP	H	TBF	R	ER	HR	SH	SF	HB	BB	IBB	SO	WP	Bk.
Pall, Donn, Char.	1	2	.333	4.15	29	0	0	0	25	14	34.2	33	147	17	16	1	2	2	0	10	0	33	1	0
Parris, Steve, Ind.	6	1	.857	3.84	13	13	1	1	0	0	84.1	74	347	38	36	8	2	3	1	26	1	102	6	0
Pasqualicchio, Mike, Lou. *	0	0	.000	3.00	1	1	0	0	0	0	6.0	6	25	2	2	1	0	0	0	4	0	5	0	0
Patrick, Bronswell, Lou.	3	1	.750	4.30	6	6	0	0	0	0	37.2	43	167	21	18	6	0	1	1	9	0	28	3	0
Pavano, Carl, Ott.	1	0	1.000	2.41	3	3	0	0	0	0	18.2	12	75	5	5	1	0	0	5	7	0	14	1	0
Pena, Juan, Paw.	8	10	.444	4.38	24	23	1	1	0	0	139.2	141	606	73	68	17	4	2	8	51	3	146	14	2
Pennington, Brad, Dur. *	4	4	.500	4.86	45	6	0	0	11	1	100.0	77	442	55	54	12	0	3	6	65	0	125	8	1
Perez, Odaliz, Rich. *	1	2	.333	2.96	13	0	0	0	10	3	24.1	26	100	8	4	1	0	0	7	1	2	22	2	0
Perez, Yorkis, S./W.B. *	0	0	.000	0.00	4	1	0	0	0	0	4.1	2	17	1	0	0	0	1	1	0	0	3	0	0
Person, Robert, Syr.	3	3	.500	2.29	20	6	1	0	12	6	59.0	38	238	17	15	9	1	1	1	29	2	55	3	0
Peterson, Kyle, Lou.	1	0	1.000	7.94	1	1	0	0	0	0	5.2	8	27	5	5	0	0	0	2	0	4	0	0
Ponson, Sidney, Roch.	1	0	1.000	0.00	1	1	0	0	0	0	5.0	4	20	0	0	0	0	0	0	1	0	3	0	0
Poole, Jim, Buf. *	1	0	1.000	0.87	13	0	0	0	4	0	10.1	6	40	3	1	0	0	0	1	2	0	16	0	0
Post, Dave, Ott.	0	0	.000	0.00	2	0	0	0	2	0	2.1	1	11	0	0	0	0	0	3	0	0	0	0	0
Powell, Brian, Tol.	0	0	.000	0.00	1	1	0	0	0	0	7.0	5	27	0	0	0	0	0	0	0	0	7	0	0
Priest, Eddie, Ind.-Buf. *	7	6	.538	4.87	22	22	0	0	0	0	122.0	139	537	75	66	16	4	1	3	35	1	65	4	0
Pulido, Carlos, Nor. *	0	0	.000	1.69	3	0	0	0	1	0	5.1	6	22	1	1	1	0	0	0	0	0	6	0	0
Pulsipher, Bill, Nor. *	7	5	.583	3.96	14	14	1	0	0	0	86.1	91	378	50	38	12	2	0	2	41	1	58	8	0
Purdy, Shawn, Rich.	3	1	.750	1.83	16	1	0	0	4	0	34.1	27	140	9	7	2	1	2	6	8	1	20	1	0
Rakers, Jason, Buf.	8	6	.571	4.57	21	21	1	0	0	0	126.0	134	542	70	64	13	2	6	8	38	0	89	7	1
Ramirez, Hector, Char.	3	3	.500	6.75	55	0	0	0	21	3	86.2	106	385	68	65	15	3	4	0	30	1	50	8	0
Ratliff, Jon, Rich. *	12	13	.480	4.94	29	29	2	0	0	0	151.1	167	671	90	83	18	4	9	4	65	0	143	9	0
Reed, Brandon, Tol.	5	7	.417	5.98	39	17	0	0	6	0	117.1	159	540	84	78	17	4	4	5	46	1	70	2	0
Rekar, Bryan, Dur.	0	1	.000	3.27	3	3	0	0	0	0	11.0	10	44	4	4	3	0	0	0	2	0	9	0	0
Resz, Greg, Col.	3	3	.500	4.92	12	9	0	0	0	0	53.0	53	235	35	29	4	2	3	2	23	0	31	0	0
Reyes, Alberto, Lou.	0	1	.000	8.31	3	2	0	0	0	0	4.1	5	20	5	4	1	0	1	0	2	0	5	0	0
Reyes, Dennis, Ind. *	2	0	1.000	3.00	4	4	0	0	0	0	24.0	20	100	10	8	1	0	0	0	14	0	27	5	0
Reynoso, Armando, Nor.	0	2	.000	10.61	2	2	0	0	0	0	9.1	14	45	11	11	1	1	0	1	4	1	8	1	0
Rhodes, Arthur, Roch. *	0	0	.000	4.50	1	1	0	0	0	0	2.0	3	10	1	1	0	0	0	1	0	1	0	0
Ricken, Ray, Col.	0	3	.000	7.32	4	3	1	0	1	1	19.2	24	88	17	16	5	0	2	0	11	0	17	1	0
Roberts, Willis, Tol.	3	3	.500	4.61	39	0	0	0	16	2	54.2	63	248	33	28	4	3	1	2	28	2	40	4	1
Rocker, John, Rich. *	1	1	.500	1.42	9	0	0	0	4	1	19.0	13	81	4	3	1	1	0	0	10	0	22	1	1
Rodriguez, Frankie, Lou.	4	3	.571	3.77	47	3	0	0	10	2	90.2	88	385	39	38	11	2	1	4	38	3	88	6	1
Rodriguez, Nerio, Roch.	1	4	.200	5.47	5	5	0	0	0	0	24.2	24	108	16	15	6	1	1	1	10	0	19	0	1
Rodriguez, Steve, Ott.	0	0	.000	3.00	3	0	0	0	3	0	3.0	3	12	1	1	0	0	0	0	1	0	2	0	0
Romano, Mike, Syr.	8	6	.571	4.14	27	13	1	0	7	1	117.1	131	516	66	54	13	0	2	4	53	3	69	6	0
Roque, Rafael, Lou. *	5	2	.714	3.62	9	8	0	0	0	0	49.2	42	207	21	20	2	2	2	4	19	1	43	1	0
Rose, Brian, Paw.	0	3	.000	7.64	6	6	0	0	0	0	17.2	24	84	19	15	5	0	2	4	10	0	17	0	0
Rose, Scott, Col.	2	0	1.000	3.75	29	0	0	0	10	2	36.0	43	161	18	15	1	0	1	0	17	0	27	0	0
Ruebel, Matt, Dur. *	9	6	.600	4.74	24	23	1	1	0	0	129.0	141	569	73	68	17	0	3	5	45	1	87	2	0
Ruffcorn, Scott, Ind.	6	2	.750	8.65	23	0	0	0	2	0	34.1	44	186	35	33	7	3	2	8	37	2	28	7	0
Ruffin, Johnny, Lou.-Nor.	6	3	.667	2.91	52	5	0	0	13	0	99.0	71	423	42	32	6	4	2	1	68	3	97	8	0
Rumer, Tim, Dur. *	7	2	.778	7.34	26	0	0	0	11	0	38.0	49	180	34	31	4	1	1	2	18	2	27	1	2
Ryan, Ken, S./W.B.	1	0	1.000	0.00	6	0	0	0	3	1	8.0	7	34	0	0	0	1	0	3	0	9	0	0
Sackinsky, Brian, Roch.	0	2	.000	6.46	7	2	0	0	4	0	15.1	22	70	12	11	0	1	0	0	4	0	9	1	1
Sadler, Al, Lou.	2	2	.500	5.40	25	0	0	0	6	0	33.1	29	149	21	20	6	2	2	1	18	1	39	4	0
Sager, A.J., Tol.	1	2	.333	3.00	14	0	0	0	5	1	24.0	27	107	8	8	1	1	1	0	13	1	16	0	0
Santana, Marino, Tol.	6	3	.667	2.90	44	0	0	0	24	7	68.1	44	277	30	22	10	1	4	1	34	1	94	10	2
Santos, Victor, Tol.	1	2	.333	11.05	5	3	0	0	1	0	14.2	24	80	22	18	5	0	0	1	10	0	12	0	0
Sauerbeck, Scott, Nor. *	7	13	.350	3.93	27	27	2	0	0	0	160.1	178	701	82	70	8	7	2	3	68	1	119	8	2
Sauveur, Rich, Ind. *	0	0	.000	3.00	7	0	0	0	2	1	9.0	9	40	8	3	2	0	1	4	0	6	0	0
Schmitt, Todd, Ott.-Tol.	1	1	.500	6.35	45	0	0	0	19	5	51.0	45	234	40	36	7	2	3	14	51	1	54	10	1
Schrenk, Steve, Paw.	8	3	.727	2.82	34	0	0	0	6	1	60.2	60	265	27	19	8	4	2	2	23	1	45	6	0
Scott, Darryl, Ott.-S./W.B.	4	6	.400	4.59	41	0	0	0	25	12	51.0	49	225	30	26	9	2	3	1	20	1	44	3	0
Seanez, Rudy, Rich.	2	0	1.000	1.29	16	0	0	0	13	7	21.0	13	85	9	3	1	0	1	0	7	1	33	1	0
Sexton, Jeff, Nor.	0	0	.000	4.07	21	0	0	0	5	1	24.1	25	111	16	11	1	2	3	1	15	1	15	3	2
Shelby, Anthony, Col. *	2	2	.500	3.19	23	5	0	0	3	0	48.0	47	205	19	17	1	1	2	4	13	0	39	2	0
Shouse, Brian, Paw. *	2	0	1.000	2.90	22	1	0	0	15	6	31.0	21	121	11	10	7	1	1	0	7	0	25	0	0
Shuey, Paul, Buf.	0	0	.000	2.51	11	0	0	0	4	2	14.1	11	61	4	4	0	0	1	0	6	0	22	1	0
Sievert, Mark, Syr.	7	6	.538	4.13	21	18	0	0	3	1	96.0	92	423	48	44	8	1	4	4	59	2	37	7	1
Sinclair, Steve, Syr. *	3	1	.750	2.17	43	1	0	0	16	3	49.2	37	204	15	12	2	1	2	1	23	2	45	0	0
Smart, J.D., Ott.	2	3	.400	4.89	6	6	0	0	0	0	35.0	34	149	22	19	3	2	2	2	11	0	16	0	0
Smith, Travis, Lou.	4	6	.400	5.32	12	11	0	0	0	0	67.2	77	296	44	40	9	3	4	2	25	1	36	3	0
Snyder, Matt, Roch.	2	1	.667	3.66	12	0	0	0	5	0	19.2	17	79	9	8	3	0	0	1	6	0	13	0	0
Springer, Dennis, Dur.	3	2	.400	2.87	5	5	0	0	0	0	37.2	34	157	13	12	1	1	1	1	15	0	23	1	0
Stanifer, Rob, Char.	4	2	.667	4.31	21	1	0	0	10	4	39.2	39	166	20	19	1	1	5	1	13	2	29	1	0
Steed, Rick, Nor.	3	7	.300	4.36	13	9	0	0	2	0	53.2	56	239	34	26	4	1	1	3	29	1	35	3	0
Steph, Rod, Roch.-Ind.	4	4	.500	3.45	17	2	0	0	7	0	31.1	36	129	15	12	6	0	0	2	5	1	25	2	0
Stephenson, Garrett, S./W.B.	1	8	.111	5.25	13	11	2	0	1	0	73.2	81	314	49	43	15	0	5	2	16	0	48	1	0
Stewart, Scott, Nor. *	0	6	.000	6.62	9	9	0	0	0	0	51.2	60	235	43	38	12	3	2	1	22	0	32	0	0
Stieb, Dave, Syr.	5	4	.556	2.73	9	9	2	0	0	0	66.0	44	252	23	20	5	4	4	2	17	1	47	2	0
Stull, Everett, Roch.	1	4	.200	8.86	21	7	0	0	6	0	42.2	49	222	44	42	9	0	3	5	45	0	39	6	0
Tam, Jeff, Nor.	3	3	.500	1.83	45	0	0	0	24	11	64.0	42	239	14	13	3	2	3	6	6	0	54	0	0
Tatis, Ramon, Dur. *	1	3	.250	3.67	19	9	0	0	4	2	61.1	66	267	29	25	5	1	2	3	24	2	44	4	1
Taylor, Kerry, Tol.	8	10	.444	5.77	26	17	1	0	3	0	112.1	140	528	84	72	18	3	2	8	59	0	93	4	0
Taylor, Scott, Roch.	1	1	.500	11.37	3	0	0	0	1	0	6.1	9	37	8	8	1	1	1	3	8	1	3	1	0
Tessmer, Jay, Col.	1	1	.500	0.49	12	0	0	0	11	5	18.1	8	64	2	1	1	0	1	1	1	0	14	0	0
Thomas, Evan, S./W.B.	0	1	.000	8.00	2	2	0	0	0	0	9.0	9	42	8	8	1	0	0	6	0	5	0	0
Thompson, Chris, Paw.	0	0	.000	3.00	2	0	0	0	0	0	3.0	3	12	1	1	0	0	1	1	0	3	1	0
Thurman, Mike, Ott.	7	7	.500	3.41	19	19	0	0	0	0	105.2	107	464	50	40	13	2	2	2	49	0	76	5	2
Tolar, Kevin, Ind. *	0	1	.000	10.43	19	0	0	0	3	0	14.2	21	82	18	17	3	1	0	0	17	1	19	3	0
Trlicek, Rick, Nor.	2	2	.500	6.08	19	0	0	0	10	3	26.2	30	118	20	18	5	1	3	1	12	0	21	0	0

Pitcher, Team	W	L	Pct.	ERA	G	GS	CG	ShO	GF	Sv.	IP	H	TBF	R	ER	HR	SH	SF	HB	BB	IBB	SO	WP	Bk.
Troutman, Keith, S./W.B.	6	3	.667	4.24	43	0	0	0	10	0	80.2	80	351	44	38	13	2	5	3	31	3	78	6	0
Turgeon, Dave, Roch.	1	1	.500	3.18	4	2	0	0	1	0	17.0	15	65	6	6	1	0	2	0	4	1	9	0	0
Turrentine, Rich, Nor.	0	0	.000	1.42	5	0	0	0	5	1	6.1	4	22	1	1	0	0	0	0	2	0	9	0	0
Valdez, Carlos, Paw.	4	3	.571	4.10	37	5	0	0	8	0	74.2	74	321	38	34	12	2	2	4	22	2	75	6	0
Valdez, Efrain, Nor. *	1	0	1.000	3.92	18	0	0	0	10	1	20.2	23	92	9	9	0	1	0	3	10	0	15	1	0
Valera, Julio, Col.	1	2	.333	6.38	8	2	0	0	2	0	18.1	19	79	13	13	7	1	0	0	7	2	12	1	0
VanEgmond, Tim, Lou.	6	11	.353	4.44	24	20	0	0	1	0	131.2	132	569	72	65	23	5	2	9	45	2	99	6	1
VanRyn, Ben, Syr. *	2	1	.667	3.51	30	0	0	0	7	2	41.0	34	164	16	16	3	1	3	0	13	1	30	0	0
Veras, Dario, Paw.	2	0	1.000	3.72	23	0	0	0	21	7	29.0	30	124	12	12	4	1	1	0	11	3	27	0	0
Villafuerte, Brandon, Char.	1	0	1.000	6.35	10	0	0	0	1	0	11.1	15	55	8	8	2	1	0	1	8	0	9	1	0
Villano, Mike, Char.	3	5	.375	7.69	13	10	0	0	1	0	59.2	82	277	55	51	14	1	4	3	18	0	47	3	2
Villone, Ron, Buf. *	2	2	.500	2.01	23	0	0	0	20	7	22.1	20	98	11	5	2	1	1	0	11	1	28	0	0
Wade, Terrell, Dur. *	1	1	.500	4.58	4	4	0	0	0	0	19.2	21	92	12	10	1	0	0	1	12	1	14	0	0
Wagner, Paul, Lou.-Rich.	2	0	1.000	5.19	11	3	0	0	1	0	26.0	28	112	16	15	3	1	0	0	8	0	15	1	0
Walker, Mike, Ind.	4	8	.333	3.17	78	3	0	0	40	6	102.1	86	448	49	36	6	9	3	13	48	2	63	6	0
Walker, Pete, Paw.	1	4	.200	5.94	22	0	0	0	6	0	33.1	34	145	26	22	8	2	1	0	17	1	19	1	0
Wallace, Derek, Nor.	5	2	.714	3.88	54	0	0	0	44	16	60.1	58	265	31	26	3	3	3	1	27	3	50	4	0
Wasdin, John, Paw.	1	0	1.000	3.00	4	2	0	0	2	0	12.0	11	52	6	4	0	0	1	0	5	0	10	1	0
Wehner, John, Char.	0	0	.000	0.00	1	0	0	0	1	0	1.0	0	3	0	0	0	0	0	0	1	1	0	0	0
Welch, Mike, S./W.B.	3	4	.429	5.97	31	6	0	0	9	2	75.1	98	342	56	50	5	8	3	6	17	6	32	1	0
West, David, Paw. *	5	0	1.000	1.13	17	0	0	0	11	3	24.0	19	106	4	3	1	0	0	2	12	1	23	1	0
White, Rick, Dur.	4	2	.667	4.22	9	9	1	0	0	0	53.1	63	230	29	25	3	1	1	3	11	0	31	3	0
Whiteside, Matt, S./W.B.	1	4	.200	6.48	30	1	0	0	20	5	33.1	47	151	24	24	4	1	0	0	7	0	21	1	0
Williams, Jimmy, Buf.-Char. *	4	10	.286	5.87	34	12	0	0	7	0	79.2	101	369	60	52	13	3	3	1	41	3	71	11	0
Williams, Shad, Col.	0	1	.000	12.75	5	1	0	0	0	0	12.0	24	66	19	17	1	0	1	1	8	0	10	0	0
Williams, Todd, Ind.	0	3	.000	2.31	53	0	0	0	45	26	58.1	54	243	19	15	0	2	2	3	24	2	35	5	1
Williamson, Scott, Ind.	0	0	.000	3.48	5	5	0	0	0	0	20.2	20	87	9	8	2	0	0	1	9	0	17	0	0
Wilson, Paul, Nor.	4	1	.800	4.42	7	7	0	0	0	0	38.2	42	168	19	19	2	3	0	2	9	0	30	1	0
Winchester, Scott, Ind.	3	2	.600	6.67	6	5	0	0	0	0	29.2	39	134	23	22	7	0	0	1	8	0	12	2	0
Winston, Darrin, S./W.B. *	0	2	.000	9.51	16	2	0	0	4	0	23.2	40	119	27	25	6	0	2	1	10	0	18	2	0
Withem, Shannon, Syr.	17	5	.773	3.27	28	27	4	2	1	0	189.2	176	781	72	69	14	4	5	10	58	2	113	2	0
Wohlers, Mark, Rich.	0	3	.000	20.43	16	0	0	0	1	0	12.1	21	91	28	28	5	0	0	0	36	0	16	17	0
Wolf, Randy, S./W.B. *	9	7	.563	4.62	24	23	1	0	0	0	148.0	167	650	88	76	16	2	10	4	48	4	118	6	1
Woodall, Brad, Lou. *	1	1	.500	3.90	5	5	0	0	0	0	30.0	32	135	19	13	3	0	0	0	15	0	27	4	0
Wunsch, Kelly, Lou. *	3	1	.750	3.83	9	8	0	0	0	0	51.2	53	220	23	22	6	0	1	3	15	0	36	2	0
Yarnall, Ed, Char. *	4	5	.444	6.20	15	13	2	0	0	0	69.2	79	331	60	48	11	5	3	3	39	4	47	2	1
Yennaco, Jay, Paw.-Syr.	3	5	.375	5.64	18	17	2	0	0	0	99.0	132	440	70	62	10	2	2	3	26	3	61	5	0
Young, Anthony, Buf.	2	3	.400	6.34	9	6	1	1	1	0	38.1	39	171	32	27	2	2	2	3	18	1	12	1	0
Young, Ray, Roch.	0	2	.000	8.03	5	1	0	0	1	1	12.1	18	59	11	11	2	1	0	0	6	0	10	0	0
Young, Tim, Ott. *	1	1	.500	2.03	20	0	0	0	10	2	26.2	26	119	14	6	1	0	0	1	12	2	34	0	0
Zosky, Eddie, Lou.	0	0	.000	0.00	1	0	0	0	1	0	0.1	1	2	0	0	0	0	0	0	0	0	1	0	0

COMBINATION SHUTOUTS: **Buffalo (3)**—Karsay-Villone, Ogea-Moore, Rakers-Grimsley-Poole-Batchelor. **Charlotte (4)**—Mendoza-Pail, Villano-Henriques, Hawblitzel-Ramirez-Barrios-Mantei, Ludwick-Williams-Borland-Henriquez. **Columbus (5)**—Orlando Hernandez-Erdos, Heredia-Borowski-Shelby, Lankford-Looney, Grahe-Tessmer, Jerzembeck-Ricken. **Durham (5)**—Aldred-Pennington, Eiland-Eichhorn, Ruebel-Karp-Hernandez, Duvall-Gaillard-Pennington-Nunez, Duvall-Gaillard-Eichhorn. **Indianapolis (7)**—Klingenbeck-Graves-Todd Williams, Bolton-Kroon-Eischen, Klingenbeck-Eischen-Williams, Klingenbeck-Kroon, Parris-Walker, Bolton-Walker, Bolton-Eischen-Steph. **Norfolk (8)**—Pulsipher-Trlicek-Wallace, Mimbs-Wallace, Sauerbeck-Beltran, Steed-Clontz-Beltran-Wallace, Manzanillo-Beltran-Wallace, Steed-Beltran, Wilson-Maxcy-Wallace, Wilson-Tam. **Louisville (7)**—Ruffin-Travis Smith-Dunbar-Mullins, VanEgmond-Nix-Greene, Cornett-Mullins, Roque-Rodriguez, Henderson-Mullins, VanEgmond-Mullins, Henderson-Greene. **Ottawa (6)**—Faltisek-Schmitt-Long, Boskie-Schmitt, Thurman-DeHart-Bunch-McGraw, Thurman-DeHart, Boskie-Fleetham, Moore-Falteisek-Fleetham. **Pawtucket (4)**—Checo-Hudson-Valdez-Shouse, Pena-Shouse-Frey, Yennaco-Frey-Shouse, Pena-Schrenk-Mahay. **Richmond (7)**—Harrison-Purdy-Bullard-Cortez, Ratliff-Butler, Byrd-Seanez, Briggs-Butler, Carlyle-Mix-Wohlers-Dedrick, Chen-Wohlers-Borbon, Ratliff-Perez. **Rochester (8)**—Ponson-Kelley, Bennett-Converse-Kelley-Munoz, Bennett-Montgomery, Montgomery-Taylor-Burrows, Ontiveros-Sackinsky, Burrows-Montgomery, Burrows-Munoz, Coppinger-Stull. **Scranton/Wilkes-Barre (3)**—Welch-Whiteside-Scott, Grace-Scott, Holman-Ryan-Fiore. **Syracuse (6)**—Person-Sievert, Sievert-Andujar, Stieb-Sinclair, Sinclair-Harris-VanRyn-Almanzar-Fletcher, Withem-Almanzar, Withem-Person. **Toledo (5)**—Drews-Santana, Greisinger-Crow, Greisinger-Crow, Powell-Sager-Roberts-Martinez, Reed-Martinez.

NO-HIT GAME: Pena, Pawtucket, defeated Durham, 5-0, July 22.

PITCHERS WITH TWO OR MORE TEAMS

Pitcher, Team	W	L	Pct.	ERA	G	GS	CG	ShO	GF	Sv.	IP	H	TBF	R	ER	HR	SH	SF	HB	BB	IBB	SO	WP	Bk.
Bennett, Joel, Roch.	10	0	1.000	3.64	18	15	1	0	0	0	101.1	99	425	46	41	9	2	3	2	37	1	99	3	0
Bennett, Joel, S./W.B.	1	2	.333	5.29	8	7	0	0	0	0	47.2	51	215	29	28	6	0	1	1	25	1	35	0	0
Borland, Toby, S./W.B.	0	2	.000	5.68	13	0	0	0	8	5	12.2	14	52	8	8	1	0	1	1	3	0	15	1	0
Borland, Toby, Char.	3	0	1.000	2.70	19	0	0	0	6	1	36.2	33	158	12	11	3	0	1	1	21	1	26	4	1
Cummings, John, Buf. *	0	1	.000	5.79	21	0	0	0	7	0	18.2	25	88	15	12	3	1	0	1	4	0	15	2	0
Cummings, John, Paw. *	0	5	.000	6.16	10	8	0	0	1	0	38.0	46	170	28	26	3	1	0	3	12	0	17	2	0
Fleming, Dave, Paw. *	1	1	.500	7.58	4	4	0	0	0	0	19.0	21	90	18	16	5	0	0	0	13	0	4	0	0
Fleming, Dave, Roch. *	0	0	.000	3.86	4	0	0	0	3	0	7.0	8	32	3	3	1	0	0	1	3	0	3	0	0
Henderson, Rod, Ott.	0	1	.000	9.00	6	0	0	0	1	0	11.0	23	66	17	11	3	1	0	0	12	0	12	0	0
Henderson, Rod, Lou.	11	5	.688	2.97	22	19	1	0	1	0	121.1	100	493	45	40	4	2	1	4	39	0	68	1	0
Hudson, Joe, Paw.	2	2	.500	4.53	46	0	0	0	26	10	47.2	57	222	32	24	3	2	2	0	23	3	32	4	0
Hudson, Joe, Lou.	1	0	1.000	5.11	9	0	0	0	1	0	12.1	13	57	7	7	1	0	1	2	5	1	4	0	0
Johnson, Dane, Syr.	1	0	1.000	3.18	7	0	0	0	5	3	5.2	5	23	2	2	0	0	0	0	5	0	4	0	0
Johnson, Dane, Char.	1	0	1.000	3.38	2	0	0	0	1	0	2.2	3	11	1	1	1	0	0	0	1	0	0	0	0
Jordan, Ricardo, Ind. *	2	4	.333	3.49	37	6	0	0	6	0	69.2	70	309	39	27	8	2	3	2	33	2	52	1	0
Jordan, Ricardo, Col. *	2	0	1.000	4.85	5	5	0	0	0	0	26.0	28	119	15	14	4	0	1	1	17	0	22	0	0
Manzanillo, Josias, Dur.	7	6	.538	4.64	19	14	0	0	2	1	85.1	93	377	57	44	12	0	1	4	30	0	61	3	0
Manzanillo, Josias, Nor.	4	4	.500	3.24	13	12	1	0	1	1	77.2	77	335	35	28	5	3	4	4	31	0	72	3	0
Munro, Peter, Paw.	5	4	.556	4.05	18	17	0	0	0	0	106.2	111	450	49	48	10	2	5	4	35	2	75	8	0
Munro, Peter, Syr.	2	5	.286	7.46	8	8	0	0	0	0	44.2	58	213	42	37	7	2	0	2	23	2	42	4	0
Priest, Eddie, Ind. *	4	1	.800	4.76	6	6	0	0	0	0	34.0	36	147	19	18	6	2	0	1	7	0	21	2	0
Priest, Eddie, Buf. *	3	5	.375	4.91	16	16	0	0	0	0	88.0	103	390	56	48	10	2	1	2	28	1	44	2	0
Ruffin, Johnny, Lou.	5	3	.625	3.00	35	2	0	0	11	0	60.0	40	262	27	20	4	2	0	1	48	2	57	7	0
Ruffin, Johnny, Nor.	1	0	1.000	2.77	17	3	0	0	2	0	39.0	31	161	15	12	2	2	2	0	20	1	40	1	0

Pitcher, Team	W	L	Pct.	ERA	G	GS	CG	ShO	GF	Sv.	IP	H	TBF	R	ER	HR	SH	SF	HB	BB	IBB	SO	WP	Bk.
Schmitt, Todd, Ott.	1	1	.500	3.31	30	0	0	0	13	5	32.2	18	148	15	12	2	1	1	13	25	1	34	6	1
Schmitt, Todd, Tol.	0	0	.000	11.78	15	0	0	0	6	0	18.1	27	106	25	24	5	1	2	1	26	0	20	4	0
Scott, Darryl, Ott.	0	1	.000	3.09	8	0	0	0	2	2	11.2	12	53	6	4	1	1	0	5	0	7	0	0
Scott, Darryl, S./W.B.	4	5	.444	5.03	33	0	0	0	23	10	39.1	37	172	24	22	8	1	2	1	15	1	37	3	0
Steph, Rod, Roch.	3	4	.429	3.32	14	0	0	0	6	0	21.2	25	87	11	8	4	0	0	2	2	1	17	1	0
Steph, Rod, Ind.	1	0	1.000	3.72	3	2	0	0	0	0	9.2	11	42	4	4	2	0	0	0	3	0	8	1	0
Wagner, Paul, Lou.	1	0	1.000	8.76	3	3	0	0	0	0	12.1	17	58	12	12	3	0	0	0	5	0	6	1	0
Wagner, Paul, Rich.	1	0	1.000	1.98	8	0	0	0	1	0	13.2	11	54	4	3	0	1	0	3	0	9	0	0
Williams, Jimmy, Buf. *	0	5	.000	7.43	15	3	0	0	4	0	26.2	38	133	27	22	5	0	1	0	17	1	28	7	0
Williams, Jimmy, Char. *..............	4	5	.444	5.09	19	9	0	0	3	0	53.0	63	236	33	30	8	3	2	1	24	2	43	4	0
Yennaco, Jay, Paw.	3	2	.600	5.82	11	11	1	0	0	0	60.1	77	266	43	39	6	1	1	0	16	1	34	5	0
Yennaco, Jay, Syr.	0	3	.000	5.35	7	6	1	0	0	0	38.2	55	174	27	23	4	1	1	3	10	2	27	0	0

1998 FIELDING
TEAM

Team	Pct.	G	PO	A	E	TC	DP	PB	Team	Pct.	G	PO	A	E	TC	DP	PB
Syracuse	.981	142	3695	1560	102	5357	156	6	Norfolk	.973	142	3725	1501	146	5372	158	15
Durham	.980	144	3781	1504	110	5395	117	18	Louisville..........	.973	144	3791	1571	150	5512	137	14
Rochester	.977	144	3761	1495	126	5382	135	17	Toledo	.973	142	3642	1427	142	5211	132	8
Scranton/W.-B. .	.976	142	3762	1511	132	5405	119	6	Charlotte	.972	143	3705	1639	155	5499	144	10
Ottawa	.975	143	3700	1467	130	5297	137	14	Columbus	.972	144	3834	1654	160	5648	133	16
Richmond	.974	144	3741	1449	141	5331	139	10	Buffalo..............	.969	143	3780	1472	170	5422	122	16
Indianapolis.......	.973	143	3726	1684	149	5559	165	15	TRIPLE PLAYS: None.								
Pawtucket	.973	142	3691	1429	143	5263	121	12									

INDIVIDUAL

FIRST BASEMEN

NOTE: All caps denotes fielding-percentage leader based on 72 games for catchers, 96 for all other non-pitchers or 144 innings for pitchers. *Throws lefthanded.

Player, Team	Pct.	G	PO	A	E	TC	DP
Abad, Andy, Paw.*........................	.993	86	683	64	5	752	65
Agbayani, Benny, Nor.	1.000	4	36	0	0	36	5
Arntzen, Brian, Ott.	1.000	1	1	0	0	1	0
Ashby, Chris, Col.	1.000	2	13	1	0	14	2
Ashley, Billy, Paw.	.980	25	187	12	4	203	18
Banks, Brian, Lou.	.990	10	84	11	1	96	10
Barker, Kevin, Lou.*	.992	112	949	73	8	1030	88
Barron, Tony, S./W.B.	.987	9	70	8	1	79	6
Belk, Tim, Ind.	.987	79	683	26	9	718	61
Bellinger, Clay, Col.	.993	44	264	14	2	280	23
Bennett, Gary, S./W.B.	1.000	2	1	0	0	1	0
Betzsold, James, Buf.	.907	8	32	7	4	43	3
Bierek, Kurt, Col.	.983	13	111	6	2	119	12
Carey, Todd, Paw.-Nor.	.992	36	230	25	2	257	28
Carpenter, Bubba, Col.*	.992	30	244	19	2	265	22
Casey, Sean, Ind.	.991	25	205	10	2	217	23
Catalanotto, Frank, Tol.	.984	19	106	14	2	122	8
Clark, Howie, Roch.	1.000	10	83	3	0	86	5
Colon, Dennis, Nor.*	1.000	23	205	15	0	220	26
Costo, Tim, Syr.	.997	41	347	26	1	374	34
Cox, Darron, Dur.	1.000	1	4	0	0	4	0
Cox, Steve, Dur.*	.994	117	1010	62	7	1079	84
Cruz, Ivan, Col.*	.991	53	502	39	5	546	45
Daubach, Brian, Char.	.996	25	236	18	1	255	26
Decker, Steve, Nor.	.994	70	580	46	4	630	65
Delgado, Carlos, Syr.	1.000	2	22	2	0	24	5
Diaz, Eddy, Lou.	1.000	2	20	1	0	21	5
Dodson, Bo, Roch.*	.990	112	885	69	10	964	87
Donato, Dan, Dur.	1.000	3	27	1	0	28	2
Faries, Paul, Tol.	.988	11	82	3	1	86	5
Fernandez, Jose, Ott.	1.000	4	25	3	0	28	6
Figga, Mike, Col.	.983	5	53	4	1	58	5
Foster, Jim, Roch.	1.000	6	38	5	0	43	5
Franco, Matt, Nor.	1.000	1	9	1	0	10	2
Garcia, Guillermo, Ind.	1.000	3	22	1	0	23	1
Garcia, Omar, Ind.	1.000	2	18	0	0	18	2
Hanel, Marcus, Rich.	1.000	1	8	0	0	8	0
Held, Dan, S./W.B.	.990	108	941	60	10	1011	82
Hiatt, Phil, Buf.	.988	73	593	57	8	658	64
Hudler, Rex, Buf.	1.000	1	7	0	0	7	1
Hyers, Tim, Char.*	.994	47	336	25	2	363	31
Ibarra, Jesse, Tol.	.969	38	261	21	9	291	33
Jackson, Ryan, Char.*	1.000	5	53	5	0	58	5
Jensen, Marcus, Lou.	1.000	2	3	1	0	4	1
Johns, Keith, Paw.	1.000	9	33	3	0	36	3
Johnson, Mark, Ind.*	.993	52	410	36	3	449	50
Kieschnick, Brooks, Dur.	.909	2	10	0	1	11	0
Kinkade, Mike, Lou.-Nor.	.994	19	148	15	1	164	15

Player, Team	Pct.	G	PO	A	E	TC	DP
Lopez, Luis, Syr.	1.000	1	2	0	0	2	0
Lovullo, Torey, Buf.	1.000	9	38	2	0	40	1
Lowell, Mike, Col.	.976	4	38	3	1	42	1
Lukachyk, Rob, Ott.	.997	39	315	24	1	340	22
Manto, Jeff, Buf.	1.000	34	273	20	0	293	35
Matos, Francisco, Col.	1.000	2	16	2	0	18	4
McKeel, Walt, Paw.	.989	13	85	4	1	90	4
Millar, Kevin, Char.	1.000	4	28	3	0	31	2
Mitchell, Keith, Paw.	1.000	1	6	0	0	6	0
Morman, Russ, Dur.	1.000	23	199	16	0	215	18
Nixon, Trot, Paw.*	1.000	1	1	0	0	1	0
Otanez, Willis, Roch.	.963	4	26	0	1	27	3
Pachot, John, Ott.	.981	14	93	8	2	103	11
Parker, Rick, Nor.	.913	7	20	1	2	23	3
Payton, Jay, Nor.	.976	25	227	16	6	249	23
Perry, Chan, Buf.	.971	7	65	3	2	70	1
Perry, Herbert, Dur.	1.000	3	19	2	0	21	3
Petagine, Roberto, Ind.*	.994	68	633	53	4	690	76
Post, Dave, Ott.	1.000	40	282	35	0	317	26
Pratt, Todd, Nor.	1.000	5	28	0	0	28	1
Rigsby, Randy, Char.*	1.000	2	20	1	0	21	2
Rose, Pete, Ind.	.960	4	21	3	1	25	3
Roskos, John, Char.	.994	76	644	38	4	686	64
Saunders, Chris, Ott.	.989	41	317	28	4	349	40
Schall, Gene, Rich.	.991	26	188	21	2	211	23
Seefried, Tate, Ott.	.985	17	122	7	2	131	14
Seguignol, Fernando, Ott.	1.000	2	10	2	0	12	1
Sexson, Richie, Buf.	1.000	21	141	22	0	163	8
Short, Rick, Roch.	1.000	1	8	0	0	8	1
Siddall, Joe, Tol.	1.000	6	23	2	0	25	1
Silvestri, Dave, Dur.	1.000	4	21	2	0	23	1
Simon, Randall, Rich.*	.989	118	981	51	11	1043	95
Spencer, Shane, Col.	.991	12	107	7	1	115	9
Tejero, Fausto, Rich.	1.000	3	20	3	0	23	3
Thurston, Jerrey, Ott.	1.000	1	2	1	0	3	0
Vinas, Julio, Roch.	.993	22	136	5	1	142	15
Waszgis, B.J., Paw.	1.000	4	14	2	0	16	1
Whatley, Gabe, Rich.	1.000	1	7	0	0	7	1
Wilkins, Rick, Nor.	.943	6	30	3	2	35	4
Williamson, Antone, Lou.	.982	11	104	5	2	111	12
WITT, Kevin, Syr.	.996	102	941	68	4	1013	105
Wood, Jason, Tol.	.987	11	70	5	1	76	8
Zuber, Jon, S./W.B.*	1.000	31	245	20	0	265	21

TRIPLE PLAY: Abad.

FIRST BASEMEN WITH TWO OR MORE TEAMS

Player, Team	Pct.	G	PO	A	E	TC	DP
Carey, Todd, Paw.	.988	22	154	10	2	166	14
Carey, Todd, Nor.	1.000	14	76	15	0	91	14
Kinkade, Mike, Lou.	.993	17	137	13	1	151	15
Kinkade, Mike, Nor.	1.000	2	11	2	0	13	0

CLASS AAA International League

– 389 –

SECOND BASEMEN

Player, Team	Pct.	G	PO	A	E	TC	DP
Almanzar, Richard, Tol.	.967	92	194	271	16	481	65
Anderson, Marlon, S./W.B.	.959	135	262	391	28	681	86
Azuaje, Jesus, Nor.	1.000	2	5	3	0	8	0
Baez, Kevin, Ind.	.962	24	55	72	5	132	24
Bell, Juan, Syr.	1.000	2	4	5	0	9	2
Belliard, Ronnie, Lou.	.978	130	228	401	14	643	98
Bellinger, Clay, Col.	.963	13	21	31	2	54	11
Berry, Mike, Col.	1.000	1	0	2	0	2	0
Blum, Geoffrey, Ott.	1.000	6	18	12	0	30	5
Boone, Aaron, Ind.	.941	7	18	14	2	34	6
Branson, Jeff, Buf.	1.000	6	16	11	0	27	4
Buccheri, Jim, Dur.	.986	17	30	38	1	69	3
Cabrera, Jolbert, Buf.	1.000	1	1	1	0	2	0
Cabrera, Orlando, Ott.	.955	21	42	63	5	110	14
Carey, Todd, Paw.	1.000	1	1	3	0	4	1
Castillo, Luis, Char.	.970	100	232	281	16	529	72
Catalanotto, Frank, Tol.	1.000	16	25	29	0	54	7
Clapinski, Chris, Char.	.978	11	19	25	1	45	6
Clark, Howie, Roch.	.929	7	14	12	2	28	6
Coquillette, Trace, Ott.	.982	46	110	103	4	217	25
Diaz, Eddy, Lou.-Paw.	.959	21	39	55	4	98	13
Doster, David, S./W.B.	1.000	9	18	26	0	44	3
Eenhoorn, Robert, Nor.	1.000	1	1	4	0	5	1
Faries, Paul, Tol.	.990	43	85	121	2	208	27
Flores, Jose, S./W.B.	.909	2	2	8	1	11	1
Forbes, P.J., Roch.	.990	84	170	231	4	405	48
Freel, Ryan, Syr.	.969	8	14	17	1	32	3
Garcia, Jesse, Roch.	.969	44	102	145	8	255	44
Garcia, Luis, Tol.	1.000	1	3	4	0	7	2
Gilbert, Shawn, Nor.	1.000	2	2	1	0	3	1
Gomez, Rudy, Col.	.984	66	128	179	5	312	43
Grebeck, Brian, Syr.	1.000	1	2	6	0	8	1
Haney, Todd, Nor.	1.000	14	26	39	0	65	14
Hastings, Lionel, Char.	.964	37	75	112	7	194	24
Henry, Santiago, Syr.	.973	40	70	112	5	187	20
Holbert, Ray, Ott.	1.000	4	2	4	0	6	1
Hudler, Rex, Buf.	.917	3	6	5	1	12	2
Jackson, Gavin, Paw.	.973	32	39	70	3	112	17
Jimenez, D'Angelo, Col.	1.000	3	6	5	0	11	2
Kelly, Pat, Syr.	.977	79	133	211	8	352	58
Lamb, David, Roch.	1.000	3	6	7	0	13	1
Listach, Pat, Buf.	1.000	19	37	40	0	77	4
Lobaton, Jose, Col.	1.000	6	3	7	0	10	1
Lopez, Mickey, Lou.	1.000	1	1	1	0	2	0
Lovullo, Torey, Buf.	.959	14	40	31	3	74	9
Magdaleno, Ricky, Rich.	.900	3	3	6	1	10	1
Malloy, Marty, Rich.	.977	123	206	351	13	570	75
Martin, Chris, Dur.	.667	1	3	1	2	6	0
Martinez, Gabby, Col.	1.000	4	7	9	0	16	2
Martinez, Pablo, Rich.	1.000	3	7	7	0	14	1
Matos, Francisco, Dur.-Col.	.988	89	145	255	5	405	40
Merloni, Lou, Paw.	.974	10	11	26	1	38	7
Milliard, Ralph, Nor.	.980	125	276	373	13	662	93
Mora, Melvin, Nor.	.833	2	4	1	1	6	0
Mordecai, Mike, Ott.	1.000	2	3	5	0	8	2
Niles, Drew, Char.	1.000	1	1	2	0	3	1
Olmeda, Jose, Rich.	1.000	14	22	36	0	58	11
Ortiz, Nick, Col.	1.000	5	17	8	0	25	1
Parker, Rick, Nor.	1.000	1	2	2	0	4	0
Patterson, John, Dur.	.961	16	28	46	3	77	13
Perez, Santiago, Lou.	1.000	1	0	1	0	1	0
Perez, Tomas, Syr.	.978	17	38	52	2	92	11
Phillips, Tony, Syr.	1.000	1	4	2	0	6	0
Post, Dave, Ott.	.930	12	21	32	4	57	6
Pozo, Arquimedez, Paw.	.963	53	121	138	10	269	37
Rodriguez, Steve, Ott.	.972	31	46	57	3	106	15
Sadler, Donnie, Paw.	.975	32	67	92	4	163	14
Scutaro, Marcos, Buf.	.938	7	12	18	2	32	4
Selby, William, Buf.	.950	5	10	9	1	20	5
Silvestri, Dave, Dur.	.976	97	159	256	10	425	59
Simons, Mitch, Roch.	.930	11	21	19	3	43	1
Sojo, Luis, Col.	1.000	1	1	1	0	2	0
Tamargo, John, Nor.	.846	3	5	6	2	13	1
Tavarez, Jesus, Roch.	1.000	1	1	1	0	2	0
Tebbs, Nate, Paw.	1.000	11	24	19	0	43	4
Vidro, Jose, Ott.	.981	30	73	79	3	155	21
Whatley, Gabe, Rich.	1.000	5	6	14	0	20	1
WILLIAMS, Jason, Ind.	.984	116	223	341	9	573	88
Wilson, Brandon, Buf.	.974	52	122	136	7	265	28
Wilson, Enrique, Buf.	.974	48	102	126	6	234	33
Zosky, Eddie, Lou.	.974	10	15	23	1	39	7

TRIPLE PLAYS: Castillo, Pozo.

SECOND BASEMEN WITH TWO OR MORE TEAMS

Player, Team	Pct.	G	PO	A	E	TC	DP
Diaz, Eddy, Lou.	.920	11	18	28	4	50	7
Diaz, Eddy, Paw.	1.000	10	21	27	0	48	6
Matos, Francisco, Dur.	.990	23	38	64	1	103	10
Matos, Francisco, Col.	.987	66	107	191	4	302	30

THIRD BASEMEN

Player, Team	Pct.	G	PO	A	E	TC	DP
Almanzar, Richard, Tol.	.933	7	3	11	1	15	0
Alvarez, Gabe, Tol.	.923	67	38	142	15	195	14
Azuaje, Jesus, Nor.	1.000	3	5	6	0	11	1
Baez, Kevin, Ind.	.938	6	6	9	1	16	1
Banks, Brian, Lou.	.933	8	4	10	1	15	2
Bell, Mike, Nor.	.667	14	2	16	9	27	2
Bellinger, Clay, Col.	.955	23	10	53	3	66	2
Berry, Mike, Col.	.905	8	4	15	2	21	0
Betts, Todd, Buf.	.833	8	3	17	4	24	3
Boone, Aaron, Ind.	.942	77	45	213	16	274	21
Booty, Josh, Char.	.919	37	20	94	10	124	7
Branson, Jeff, Buf.	1.000	7	4	18	0	22	4
Carey, Todd, Nor.	.873	49	18	78	14	110	6
Clapinski, Chris, Char.	.956	28	20	66	4	90	7
Clark, Howie, Roch.	1.000	1	1	1	0	2	0
Coquillette, Trace, Ott.	.912	22	15	37	5	57	4
Costo, Tim, Syr.	1.000	3	3	5	0	8	0
Dalesandro, Mark, Syr.	.889	12	3	13	2	18	1
Decker, Steve, Nor.	.667	3	0	2	1	3	0
Diaz, Eddy, Lou.-Paw.	.913	52	34	81	11	126	6
Donato, Dan, Dur.	1.000	4	2	1	0	3	0
Doster, David, S./W.B.	.951	134	87	283	19	389	20
Estrada, Osmani, Char.	.929	6	3	10	1	14	0
Evans, Tom, Syr.	.955	108	89	208	14	311	15
Faries, Paul, Tol.	.981	33	32	69	2	103	10
Fernandez, Jose, Ott.	.833	11	10	15	5	30	3
Flores, Jose, S./W.B.	.967	10	11	18	1	30	1
Forbes, P.J., Roch.	.973	16	6	30	1	37	1
Franco, Matt, Nor.	1.000	2	4	3	0	7	1
Garcia, Guillermo, Ind.	1.000	2	0	4	0	4	1
Garcia, Luis, Tol.	.786	6	3	8	3	14	0
Gilbert, Shawn, Nor.	1.000	3	0	2	0	2	0
Haney, Todd, Nor.	.919	41	22	69	8	99	13
Hastings, Lionel, Char.	.818	7	10	8	4	22	0
Helms, Wes, Rich.	.952	124	75	220	15	310	24
Henry, Santiago, Syr.	.926	10	2	23	2	27	1
Holbert, Ray, Ott.	.952	6	6	14	1	21	0
Hudler, Rex, Buf.	.750	4	1	5	2	8	0
Johns, Keith, Paw.	1.000	2	1	4	0	5	0
Kinkade, Mike, Lou.-Nor.	.925	81	67	166	19	252	17
Konerko, Paul, Ind.	.957	39	21	68	4	93	8
Lamb, David, Roch.	.875	4	2	5	1	8	1
Lawrence, Chip, Roch.	1.000	1	1	2	0	3	1
Liniak, Cole, Paw.	.939	106	86	192	18	296	13
Lopez, Luis, Syr.	.964	9	4	23	1	28	0
Lopez, Mickey, Lou.	1.000	1	0	1	0	1	0
Lovullo, Torey, Buf.	.895	74	36	135	20	191	16
Lowell, Mike, Col.	.946	118	76	277	20	373	23
Lucca, Lou, Char.	.937	67	60	148	14	222	17
Magdaleno, Ricky, Rich.	.667	1	2	0	1	3	0
Manto, Jeff, Buf.	.923	10	9	15	2	26	0
Martin, Chris, Dur.	1.000	2	0	1	0	1	0
Matos, Francisco, Col.	1.000	1	3	3	0	6	0
McClain, Scott, Dur.	.963	125	73	241	12	326	20
Melhuse, Adam, Syr.	1.000	2	2	5	0	7	0
Millar, Kevin, Char.	.846	11	6	16	4	26	1
Mora, Melvin, Nor.	.857	5	2	4	1	7	0
Natal, Bob, Dur.-Char.	1.000	3	1	6	0	7	0
Olmeda, Jose, Rich.	.929	7	4	9	1	14	3
OTANEZ, Willis, Roch.	.968	116	91	240	11	342	17
Owens, Eric, Lou.	.920	33	16	53	6	75	4
Paquette, Craig, Nor.	.906	10	3	26	3	32	0
Parker, Rick, Nor.	.333	2	0	1	2	3	1
Post, Dave, Ott.	1.000	4	1	5	0	6	0
Pozo, Arquimedez, Paw.	.879	9	7	22	4	33	1
Ripken, Billy, Tol.	1.000	4	3	12	0	15	1
Rodriguez, Steve, Ott.	.833	3	4	6	2	12	0
Rose, Pete, Ind.	.955	26	19	44	3	66	7
Saunders, Chris, Ott.	.956	83	55	162	10	227	11
Scutaro, Marcos, Buf.	1.000	1	0	1	0	1	0
Selby, William, Buf.	.963	26	17	62	3	82	4
Short, Rick, Roch.	1.000	12	8	19	0	27	0
Silvestri, Dave, Dur.	.980	18	14	34	1	49	2
Tebbs, Nate, Paw.	.778	4	3	4	2	9	0

Player, Team	Pct.	G	PO	A	E	TC	DP
Timmons, Ozzie, Ind.	1.000	1	1	0	0	1	0
Torres, Jaime, Col.	1.000	1	1	1	0	2	0
Vidro, Jose, Ott.	.955	23	18	45	3	66	6
Whatley, Gabe, Rich.	.917	17	8	25	3	36	4
Williamson, Antone, Lou.	.833	14	18	22	8	48	3
Wilson, Brandon, Buf.	.940	25	11	36	3	50	1
Wood, Jason, Tol.	.947	28	16	38	3	57	5
Zosky, Eddie, Lou.	.922	28	8	39	4	51	4

TRIPLE PLAY: Liniak.

THIRD BASEMEN WITH TWO OR MORE TEAMS

Player, Team	Pct.	G	PO	A	E	TC	DP
Diaz, Eddy, Lou.	.899	31	16	46	7	69	6
Diaz, Eddy, Paw.	.930	21	18	35	4	57	0
Kinkade, Mike, Lou.	.916	53	46	107	14	167	12
Kinkade, Mike, Nor.	.941	28	21	59	5	85	5
Natal, Bob, Dur.	1.000	1	0	4	0	4	0
Natal, Bob, Char.	1.000	2	1	2	0	3	0

SHORTSTOPS

Player, Team	Pct.	G	PO	A	E	TC	DP
Angeli, Doug, S./W.B.	.954	35	44	100	7	151	26
Azuaje, Jesus, Nor.	.938	4	4	11	1	16	3
Baez, Kevin, Ind.	.909	10	13	27	4	44	7
Bell, Juan, Syr.	.923	9	17	31	4	52	9
Belliard, Rafael, Rich.	.980	13	20	28	1	49	4
Belliard, Ronnie, Lou.	1.000	2	3	7	0	10	2
Bellinger, Clay, Col.	.946	27	36	87	7	130	14
Blum, Geoffrey, Ott.	1.000	2	1	3	0	4	1
Boone, Aaron, Ind.	.962	7	9	16	1	26	3
Cabrera, Jolbert, Buf.	.954	121	212	350	27	589	69
Cabrera, Orlando, Ott.	.967	45	80	127	7	214	24
Carey, Todd, Paw.-Nor.	.962	12	18	32	2	52	12
Clapinski, Chris, Char.	.958	23	22	70	4	96	11
Cruz, Deivi, Tol.	1.000	2	2	7	0	9	1
De Los Santos, Eddy, Dur.	1.000	4	2	11	0	13	0
Diaz, Eddy, Lou.-Paw.	.932	20	24	58	6	88	13
Doster, David, S./W.B.	.833	1	2	3	1	6	1
Eenhoorn, Robert, Nor.	.968	92	140	285	14	439	62
Estrada, Osmani, Char.	1.000	1	0	3	0	3	1
Faries, Paul, Tol.	.992	31	44	74	1	119	14
Flores, Jose, S./W.B.	.965	84	105	227	12	344	41
Forbes, P.J., Roch.	.974	20	31	44	2	77	14
Garcia, Luis, Tol.	.956	108	152	280	20	452	58
Gilbert, Shawn, Nor.	.967	9	8	21	1	30	4
Gonzalez, Alex, Char.	.960	107	161	322	20	503	74
Haney, Todd, Nor.	.942	33	41	73	7	121	17
Hastings, Lionel, Char.	.875	7	11	10	3	24	5
Henry, Santiago, Syr.	.950	11	15	23	2	40	6
Holbert, Ray, Rich.-Ott.	.967	76	127	192	11	330	45
Jackson, Damian, Ind.	.938	130	227	434	44	705	101
Jackson, Gavin, Paw.	.955	36	48	99	7	154	21
Jeter, Derek, Col.	.875	1	4	3	1	8	1
Jimenez, D'Angelo, Col.	.944	87	144	297	26	467	61
Johns, Keith, Paw.	.964	88	136	263	15	414	57
Lamb, David, Roch.	.965	40	61	104	6	171	31
Lawrence, Chip, Roch.	.900	12	14	22	4	40	4
Listach, Pat, Buf.-S./W.B.	.950	35	38	94	7	139	20
Lowell, Mike, Col.	1.000	2	0	3	0	3	0
Lucca, Lou, Char.	1.000	1	1	3	0	4	0
Magdaleno, Ricky, Rich.	.910	58	77	156	23	256	34
Martin, Chris, Dur.	.953	128	194	349	27	570	78
Martinez, Gabby, Col.	.906	27	39	67	11	117	13
Martinez, Pablo, Lou.-Rich.	.940	62	69	164	15	248	34
Mateo, Jose, Rich.	1.000	2	0	2	0	2	0
Matos, Francisco, Col.	1.000	2	1	3	0	4	1
McClain, Scott, Dur.	1.000	1	2	1	0	3	1
Merloni, Lou, Paw.	.979	15	16	30	1	47	3
Miller, Orlando, Nor.	.939	35	61	77	9	147	20
Milliard, Ralph, Nor.	1.000	1	1	0	0	1	0
Mordecai, Mike, Ott.	.958	4	6	17	1	24	3
Niles, Drew, Char.	.921	15	23	47	6	76	11
Olmeda, Jose, Rich.	.935	77	128	229	25	382	43
Ortiz, Nick, Ott.	.955	6	6	15	1	22	3
Paquette, Craig, Nor.	.944	4	4	13	1	18	3
Perez, Santiago, Lou.	.963	34	67	90	6	163	18
PEREZ, Tomas, Syr.	.977	99	167	385	13	565	86
Post, Dave, Ott.	1.000	4	4	7	0	11	2
Rodriguez, Steve, Ott.	.884	16	18	43	8	69	11
Sadler, Donnie, Paw.	1.000	4	6	12	0	18	2
Silvestri, Dave, Dur.	.969	18	29	33	2	64	5
Simons, Mitch, Roch.	.929	47	58	138	15	211	19

Player, Team	Pct.	G	PO	A	E	TC	DP
Sojo, Luis, Col.	.958	4	8	15	1	24	5
Wilson, Brandon, Buf.	.850	17	26	42	12	80	8
Wilson, Enrique, Buf.	1.000	6	6	15	0	21	3
Wood, Jason, Tol.	.973	8	13	23	1	37	2
Woodward, Chris, Syr.	.961	25	29	69	4	102	15
Zosky, Eddie, Lou.	.961	49	74	149	9	232	33

TRIPLE PLAY: Gonzalez.

SHORTSTOPS WITH TWO OR MORE TEAMS

Player, Team	Pct.	G	PO	A	E	TC	DP
Carey, Todd, Paw.	1.000	4	6	8	0	14	4
Carey, Todd, Nor.	.947	8	12	24	2	38	8
Diaz, Eddy, Lou.	.948	18	21	52	4	77	13
Diaz, Eddy, Paw.	.818	2	3	6	2	11	0
Holbert, Ray, Rich.	.833	1	2	3	1	6	0
Holbert, Ray, Ott.	.969	75	125	189	10	324	45
Listach, Pat, Buf.	1.000	1	2	0	0	2	0
Listach, Pat, S./W.B.	.949	34	36	94	7	137	20
Martinez, Pablo, Lou.	.937	56	68	156	15	239	33
Martinez, Pablo, Rich.	1.000	6	1	8	0	9	1

OUTFIELDERS

Player, Team	Pct.	G	PO	A	E	TC	DP
Abad, Andy, Paw.*	1.000	27	43	2	0	45	0
Agbayani, Benny, Nor.	.967	78	115	4	4	123	0
Angeli, Doug, S./W.B.	1.000	1	3	0	0	3	0
Ashley, Billy, Paw.	1.000	6	11	0	0	11	0
Bady, Ed, Ott.	1.000	5	10	1	0	11	1
Banks, Brian, Lou.	.979	30	45	2	1	48	0
Barker, Kevin, Lou.*	.889	9	8	0	1	9	0
Barron, Tony, S./W.B.	.982	57	102	7	2	111	1
Bartee, Kimera, Tol.	1.000	47	124	6	0	130	1
Battle, Allen, Ott.	.974	125	253	5	7	265	2
Beamon, Trey, Tol.	.950	46	92	3	5	100	1
Belk, Tim, Tol.	1.000	1	1	0	0	1	0
Bellinger, Clay, Col.	1.000	10	11	0	0	11	0
Betzsold, James, Buf.	.970	52	90	6	3	99	1
Blosser, Greg, Buf.*	.954	91	130	15	7	152	2
Bocachica, Hiram, Ott.	1.000	11	23	1	0	24	1
Bogle, Bryan, Roch.	.917	8	10	1	1	12	0
Bowers, Brent, Nor.	1.000	79	160	2	0	162	0
Brumfield, Jacob, Char.	.958	80	107	6	5	118	1
Bryant, Pat, Paw.	.986	71	140	4	2	146	0
Buccheri, Jim, Dur.	1.000	71	124	4	0	128	0
Burton, Darren, S./W.B.	.963	106	200	8	8	216	1
Butler, Rich, Dur.	.953	36	60	1	3	64	0
Cabrera, Jolbert, Buf.	1.000	7	22	1	0	23	1
Candelaria, Ben, Syr.	.967	65	79	8	3	90	2
Carpenter, Bubba, Col.*	.983	33	56	3	1	60	1
Carver, Steve, S./W.B.	1.000	6	8	0	0	8	0
Clapinski, Chris, Char.	1.000	34	47	1	0	48	0
Clyburn, Danny, Roch.	.970	72	125	4	4	133	0
Coleman, Michael, Paw.	.978	88	173	9	4	186	1
Colon, Dennis, Nor.*	1.000	16	17	0	0	17	0
Cox, Steve, Dur.*	1.000	2	1	0	0	1	0
Cruz, Ivan, Col.*	1.000	1	1	0	0	1	0
Cruz, Jacob, Col.	.949	43	70	5	4	79	0
Cruz, Jose, Syr.	.991	40	99	7	1	107	0
Dalesandro, Mark, Syr.	1.000	8	12	0	0	12	0
Daubach, Brian, Char.	.986	104	126	10	2	138	1
Dawkins, Walt, S./W.B.	.952	28	37	3	2	42	0
Diaz, Eddy, Lou.	.969	15	28	3	1	32	0
Dodson, Bo, Roch.*	1.000	1	1	0	0	1	0
Dunn, Todd, Lou.	1.000	4	6	0	0	6	0
Dunwoody, Todd, Char.*	.987	28	76	2	1	79	1
Encarnacion, Juan, Tol.	.973	91	168	10	5	183	3
Fernandez, Jose, Ott.	1.000	3	1	0	0	1	0
Franco, Matt, Nor.	.600	2	3	0	2	5	0
Frank, Mike, Ind.*	.979	22	44	2	1	47	1
Freel, Ryan, Syr.	.957	28	43	2	2	47	0
Geisler, Phil, Char.*	1.000	11	21	1	0	22	1
Gibralter, Steve, Ind.	.975	62	116	2	3	121	1
Gilbert, Shawn, Nor.	.974	25	36	2	1	39	0
Giles, Brian, Buf.*	.947	10	18	0	1	19	0
Glass, Chip, Col.*	1.000	4	8	2	0	10	1
Haney, Todd, Nor.	.974	27	37	1	1	39	0
Hastings, Lionel, Char.	.982	27	50	4	1	55	0
Hawkins, Kraig, Dur.	1.000	6	17	0	0	17	0
Herrera, Jose, Syr.*	.988	115	241	8	3	252	3
Hiatt, Phil, Buf.	1.000	3	8	0	0	8	0
Holifield, Rick, Rich.*	.953	51	100	2	5	107	1
Hollins, Damon, Rich.*	.980	113	233	8	5	246	2

Player, Team	Pct.	G	PO	A	E	TC	DP
Hudler, Rex, Buf.	1.000	3	2	1	0	3	0
Hulse, David, Paw.*	1.000	7	11	0	0	11	0
Hundley, Todd, Nor.	1.000	6	4	0	0	4	0
Hunter, Scott, Nor.	1.000	7	9	0	0	9	0
Hurst, Jimmy, Paw.	.947	78	150	11	9	170	2
Hyers, Tim, Char.*	1.000	46	61	1	0	62	0
Isom, Johnny, Roch.	.983	37	54	3	1	58	0
Jackson, Damian, Ind.	1.000	1	3	1	0	4	0
Jackson, Ryan, Char.*	1.000	4	4	1	0	5	0
Jenkins, Geoff, Lou.	.979	50	90	3	2	95	1
JOHNSON, Earl, Tol.	.992	104	246	11	2	259	3
Johnson, Mark, Ind.*	.944	26	33	1	2	36	0
Jones, Terry, Ott.	.980	79	193	5	4	202	2
Kelly, Mike, Dur.	.923	4	12	0	1	13	0
Kieschnick, Brooks, Dur.	1.000	5	11	0	0	11	0
Kingsale, Eugene, Roch.	1.000	16	38	2	0	40	2
Kirby, Wayne, Nor.	.987	40	71	5	1	77	0
Krause, Scott, Lou.	.963	94	151	4	6	161	0
Lamb, David, Roch.	1.000	2	5	0	0	5	0
Landry, Todd, Nor.*	1.000	4	8	0	0	8	0
Ledee, Ricky, Col.*	.971	79	132	1	4	137	0
Lee, Derek, Roch.	.968	53	90	1	3	94	0
Lennon, Pat, Syr.	.947	80	132	11	8	151	1
Listach, Pat, Buf.-S./W.B.	.968	14	27	3	1	31	2
Lucca, Lou, Char.	.964	37	50	4	2	56	0
Lukachyk, Rob, Ott.	.962	30	47	4	2	53	0
Lydy, Scott, Roch.	.976	15	40	0	1	41	0
Magdaleno, Ricky, Roch.	1.000	6	12	0	0	12	0
Magee, Wendell, S./W.B.	.966	124	302	7	11	320	1
Maness, Dwight, Nor.	1.000	3	4	0	0	4	0
Martinez, Greg, Lou.	.991	104	219	5	2	226	1
May, Derrick, Ott.	.960	16	23	1	1	25	0
McMillon, Billy, S./W.B.*	.986	70	133	9	2	144	2
Mendoza, Carlos, Dur.*	.954	49	99	5	5	109	0
Miller, David, Buf.*	.985	115	251	5	4	260	1
Mitchell, Keith, Paw.	.989	41	79	8	1	88	1
Mora, Melvin, Nor.	1.000	4	2	1	0	3	0
Mottola, Chad, Ind.	1.000	5	7	2	0	9	1
Mouton, Lyle, Roch.	.983	28	56	1	1	58	0
Murphy, Mike, Roch.	1.000	7	16	1	0	17	0
Murray, Glenn, Ind.	.981	32	50	1	1	52	0
Nicholas, Darrell, Lou.	.953	114	213	11	11	235	1
Nieves, Melvin, Ind.	.950	12	19	0	1	20	0
Nixon, Trot, Paw.*	.956	126	230	11	11	252	3
Nunnally, Jon, Ind.	.951	77	146	8	8	162	0
Olmeda, Jose, Rich.	1.000	8	16	1	0	17	0
Otanez, Willis, Roch.	1.000	2	5	0	0	5	0
Otero, Ricky, Roch.*	.995	87	187	5	1	193	1
Owens, Eric, Lou.	.973	39	69	4	2	75	0
Paquette, Craig, Nor.	1.000	1	2	0	0	2	0
Parker, Rick, Nor.	.974	69	103	9	3	115	2
Payton, Jay, Nor.	.989	50	88	4	1	93	2
Perry, Chan, Buf.	1.000	2	6	0	0	6	0
Petagine, Roberto, Ind.*	.944	20	32	2	2	36	0
Phillips, Tony, Syr.	.933	9	13	1	1	15	0
Pose, Scott, Col.	.983	103	158	11	3	172	0
Post, Dave, Ott.	.974	32	36	2	1	39	1
Powell, Alonzo, Syr.	.950	13	17	2	1	20	1
Pratt, Todd, Nor.	.929	7	11	2	1	14	0
Pride, Curtis, Rich.	1.000	14	28	1	0	29	1
Ramirez, Alex, Buf.	.963	109	224	7	9	240	1
Ramirez, Angel, Col.	.932	39	65	4	5	74	0
Ramirez, Roberto, Roch.	.964	12	26	1	1	28	0
Rigsby, Randy, Char.*	1.000	1	2	0	0	2	0
Roberts, David, Buf.*	1.000	5	12	1	0	13	0
Robinson, Kerry, Dur.*	.987	57	146	3	2	151	0
Rodriguez, Steve, Ott.	1.000	23	32	0	0	32	0
Roskos, John, Char.	1.000	1	3	0	0	3	0
Samuels, Scott, Ott.	.977	25	40	2	1	43	0
Sanders, Anthony, Syr.	.993	60	145	6	1	152	0
Santangelo, F.P., Ott.	1.000	1	2	0	0	2	0
Schall, Gene, Rich.	1.000	43	55	2	0	57	0
Seguignol, Fernando, Ott.	.971	27	34	0	1	35	0
Selby, William, Buf.	1.000	16	18	3	0	21	0
Sexson, Richie, Buf.	.978	69	129	7	3	139	2
Siddall, Joe, Tol.	1.000	2	2	0	0	2	0
Sierra, Ruben, Nor.	1.000	26	50	1	0	51	0
Singleton, Chris, Col.*	.974	117	251	10	7	268	2
Smith, Dwight, Roch.	.923	6	11	1	1	13	0
Smith, Ira, Tol.	.983	66	111	3	2	116	0
Spencer, Shane, Col.	.968	66	118	4	4	126	0
Stovall, DaRond, Ott.*	.962	40	74	2	3	79	1
Swann, Pedro, Tol.	.985	77	131	2	2	135	0
Tarasco, Tony, Ind.	1.000	70	101	3	0	104	1
Tavarez, Jesus, Roch.	.974	99	182	3	5	190	0
Tebbs, Nate, Paw.	1.000	2	3	0	0	3	0
Thomas, Greg, Buf.*	1.000	2	4	0	0	4	0
Timmons, Ozzie, Ind.	.986	95	133	5	2	140	1
Tinsley, Lee, Ott.	.975	43	76	3	2	81	0
Tomberlin, Andy, Tol.-Rich.*	.955	39	62	2	3	67	0
Trammell, Bubba, Dur.	.983	57	110	5	2	117	0
Valdez, Trovin, Ott.	1.000	3	4	0	0	4	0
Warner, Mike, Rich.*	.991	89	210	9	2	221	3
Watkins, Pat, Ind.	.981	44	98	5	2	105	3
Wehner, John, Char.	.939	21	29	2	2	33	0
Whatley, Gabe, Rich.	.991	107	207	14	2	223	2
Wilcox, Luke, Dur.	1.000	41	98	4	0	102	1
Wilson, Preston, Nor.-Char.	.975	109	224	10	6	240	0
Winn, Randy, Dur.	.966	29	55	1	2	58	0
Witt, Kevin, Syr.	1.000	18	32	0	0	32	0
Zosky, Eddie, Lou.	1.000	1	2	0	0	2	0
Zuber, Jon, S./W.B.*	1.000	47	83	3	0	86	0

TRIPLE PLAY: Wilson.

OUTFIELDERS WITH TWO OR MORE TEAMS

Player, Team	Pct.	G	PO	A	E	TC	DP
Listach, Pat, Buf.	.941	8	15	1	1	17	1
Listach, Pat, S./W.B.	1.000	6	12	2	0	14	1
Tomberlin, Andy, Tol.*	.867	11	12	1	2	15	0
Tomberlin, Andy, Rich.*	.981	28	50	1	1	52	0
Wilson, Preston, Nor.	.958	18	44	2	2	48	0
Wilson, Preston, Char.	.979	91	180	8	4	192	0

CATCHERS

Player, Team	Pct.	G	PO	A	E	TC	DP	PB
Arntzen, Brian, Ott.	1.000	3	13	2	0	15	0	0
Bako, Paul, Tol.	.988	13	75	5	1	81	0	0
Banks, Brian, Lou.	.976	16	111	10	3	124	1	3
Bennett, Gary, S./W.B.	.998	69	424	35	1	460	3	1
Borrero, Richie, Paw.	.944	6	29	5	2	36	2	0
Brito, Jorge, Lou.	.991	71	405	35	4	444	2	8
Brown, Kevin, Syr.	1.000	2	7	1	0	8	0	0
Cardona, Javier, Tol.	.983	46	262	31	5	298	4	3
Casanova, Raul, Tol.	.973	45	295	35	9	339	5	3
Castillo, Alberto, Nor.	.991	17	110	6	1	117	1	3
Chavez, Raul, Ott.	1.000	11	71	15	0	86	2	2
Christopherson, Eric, Nor.	.989	30	167	13	2	182	3	4
Cox, Darron, Dur.	.984	80	546	57	10	613	3	4
Dalesandro, Mark, Syr.	.980	10	45	3	1	49	0	0
Davis, James, Ind.	.976	17	73	7	2	82	1	1
DeCinces, Tim, Roch.	1.000	7	49	2	0	51	2	0
Decker, Steve, Nor.	.975	24	146	12	4	162	2	1
Delgado, Alex, Syr.	.987	79	547	53	8	608	7	0
Depastino, Joe, Paw.	1.000	9	47	3	0	50	0	0
Devarez, Cesar, Dur.	.991	36	205	27	2	234	1	8
Diaz, Einar, Buf.	.986	112	791	70	12	873	7	11
Donato, Dan, Dur.	1.000	7	26	1	0	27	0	1
Estalella, Bobby, S./W.B.	.990	67	469	25	5	499	3	4
Figga, Mike, Col.	.988	100	680	59	9	748	4	16
Fithian, Grant, Col.	.947	4	17	1	1	19	0	0
Flaherty, John, Dur.	1.000	3	23	4	0	27	0	0
Fordyce, Brook, Ind.	1.000	6	28	4	0	32	1	1
Foster, Jim, Roch.	.991	31	198	23	2	223	3	1
GARCIA, Guillermo, Ind.	.990	86	559	65	6	630	9	11
Greene, Charlie, Roch.	.988	77	517	55	7	579	6	3
Gresham, Kris, Tol.	.961	8	47	2	2	51	0	0
Hanel, Marcus, Rich.	.994	25	146	17	1	164	0	3
Henley, Bob, Ott.	.990	30	176	22	2	200	1	5
Hubbard, Mike, Ott.	.992	19	121	8	1	130	1	3
Huckaby, Ken, Col.	.978	34	201	21	5	227	2	0
Hundley, Todd, Nor.	.952	3	18	2	1	21	0	1
Jensen, Marcus, Lou.	.994	68	441	33	3	477	2	3
Knorr, Randy, Char.	.977	58	349	25	9	383	4	1
Laker, Tim, Dur.	.991	32	197	19	2	218	3	5
LaRue, Jason, Ind.	1.000	14	83	11	0	94	1	1
Lindstrom, David, Tol.	1.000	1	9	0	0	9	0	0
Luzinski, Ryan, Roch.	.950	4	18	1	1	20	0	1
Mahoney, Mike, Rich.	.984	65	379	44	7	430	2	3
Makarewicz, Scott, Char.	.967	15	82	5	3	90	1	2
Marine, Del, Tol.	.964	5	27	0	1	28	0	0
Marx, Tim, Ind.	.965	18	74	9	3	86	0	1
McKeel, Walt, Paw.	.980	36	220	23	5	248	0	6
Melhuse, Adam, Syr.	.960	8	41	7	2	50	0	1
Mercedes, Henry, Ind.	.944	5	13	4	1	18	0	0

Player, Team	Pct.	G	PO	A	E	TC	DP	PB
Millan, Adan, S./W.B.	1.000	6	42	0	0	42	0	1
Mosquera, Julio, Syr.	1.000	28	145	20	0	165	2	1
Natal, Bob, Char.	.982	59	342	37	7	386	3	3
Owens, Jayhawk, Ind.	.989	16	83	7	1	91	0	0
Pachot, John, Ott.	.986	76	475	69	8	552	8	3
Pierce, Kirk, S./W.B.	.923	4	34	2	3	39	0	0
Pratt, Todd, Nor.	.988	10	76	6	1	83	2	1
Probst, Alan, Syr.	.984	11	62	1	1	64	1	2
Redmond, Mike, Char.	1.000	18	101	20	0	121	5	2
Reese, Nate, Char.	1.000	3	20	2	0	22	0	2
Rodriguez, Luis, Syr.	1.000	5	28	2	0	30	1	1
Romero, Mandy, Paw.	.991	38	311	27	3	341	4	3
Rosario, Mel, Roch.	.984	26	172	18	3	193	3	7
Santiago, Benito, Syr.	1.000	4	19	1	0	20	0	0
Siddall, Joe, Tol.	.988	32	150	17	2	169	2	2
Snusz, Chris, S./W.B.	1.000	1	0	1	0	1	0	0
Soliz, Steve, Buf.	.984	39	215	27	4	246	1	5
Tejero, Fausto, Rich.	.983	63	483	42	9	534	10	4
Thurston, Jerrey, Ott.	.971	12	65	2	2	69	1	1
Torres, Jaime, Col.	.990	14	88	8	1	97	0	0
Troilo, Jason, Col.	.923	8	30	6	3	39	0	0
Utting, Andy, Roch.	1.000	5	35	2	0	37	0	2
Vinas, Julio, Roch.	1.000	5	35	2	0	37	0	3
Waszgis, B.J., Paw.	.984	62	386	32	7	425	5	3
Wilkins, Rick, Nor.	.995	26	201	12	1	214	2	0
Wilson, Vance, Nor.	.990	44	348	29	4	381	5	5

PITCHERS

Player, Team	Pct.	G	PO	A	E	TC	DP
Alberro, Jose, Col.	.971	46	9	25	1	35	1
Aldred, Scott, Dur.*	1.000	7	1	5	0	6	0
Almanzar, Carlos, Syr.	1.000	30	0	2	0	2	1
Alvarez, Wilson, Dur.*	1.000	1	0	1	0	1	0
Andujar, Luis, Syr.	1.000	20	4	1	0	5	0
Arnold, Jamie, Rich.	1.000	9	0	3	0	3	0
Arroyo, Luis, Nor.*	.500	8	1	0	1	2	0
Aucoin, Derek, Nor.	1.000	3	0	1	0	1	0
Avery, Steve, Paw.*	1.000	3	0	1	0	1	0
Barkley, Brian, Paw.*	.935	23	17	26	3	46	2
Baron, Jim, Col.*	1.000	8	0	8	0	8	0
Barrios, Manny, Char.	1.000	18	3	1	0	4	0
Batchelor, Rich, Buf.	.909	57	3	7	1	11	0
Beasley, Ray, Rich.*	1.000	2	0	3	0	3	0
Beck, Greg, Lou.	.833	10	6	4	2	12	1
Belk, Tim, Tol.	1.000	3	0	1	0	1	0
Beltran, Rigo, Nor.*	.778	36	4	10	4	18	0
Bennett, Joel, Roch.-S./W.B.	.966	26	12	16	1	29	1
Benz, Jake, Ott.*	.950	25	3	16	1	20	1
Blais, Mike, Paw.	1.000	2	0	1	0	1	0
Blomdahl, Ben, Buf.	1.000	35	3	8	0	11	0
Blood, Darin, Roch.	.889	6	2	6	1	9	2
Bolton, Rod, Ind.	.929	29	15	24	3	42	3
Borbon, Pedro, Rich.*	1.000	20	0	3	0	3	2
Borland, Toby, S./W.B.-Char.	1.000	32	5	6	0	11	0
Borowski, Joe, Col.	1.000	45	6	7	0	13	2
Boskie, Shawn, Ott.	.941	13	7	9	1	17	0
Bottalico, Ricky, S./W.B.	1.000	10	1	1	0	2	0
Bradley, Ryan, Col.	.400	3	1	1	3	5	0
Brannan, Ryan, S./W.B.	1.000	16	0	3	0	3	0
Briggs, Anthony, Rich.	.923	28	6	6	1	13	0
Brow, Scott, Col.	.882	30	5	10	2	17	2
Buckley, Travis, Rich.	1.000	4	0	1	0	1	1
Buddie, Mike, Col.	1.000	26	2	5	0	7	0
Bullard, Jason, Rich.	1.000	36	4	7	0	11	1
Bullinger, Kirk, Ott.	.833	13	2	3	1	6	0
Bunch, Mel, Ott.	1.000	25	4	7	0	11	3
Burrows, Terry, Roch.*	.963	29	8	18	1	27	1
Butler, Adam, Rich.*	.889	48	2	6	1	9	0
Byrd, Paul, Rich.	1.000	17	7	9	0	16	1
Callaway, Michael, Dur.	.875	9	4	3	1	8	1
Carlson, Dan, Dur.	1.000	19	5	9	0	14	1
Carlyle, Ken, Rich.	.947	30	11	25	2	38	0
Cather, Mike, Rich.	1.000	11	1	2	0	3	0
Charlton, Norm, Rich.*	1.000	2	0	2	0	2	0
Checo, Robinson, Paw.	.875	11	1	6	1	8	0
Chen, Bruce, Rich.*	1.000	4	1	5	0	6	0
Chouinard, Bobby, Lou.	1.000	7	4	5	0	9	0
Clontz, Brad, Nor.	1.000	28	0	4	0	4	0
Cole, Jason, Ott.	1.000	13	2	4	0	6	0
Converse, Jim, Roch.	1.000	33	4	8	0	12	0
Coppinger, Rocky, Roch.	.923	14	3	9	1	13	1
Corbin, Archie, Char.	.833	34	3	2	1	6	0
Cornelius, Reid, Char.	.923	8	3	9	1	13	0
Cornett, Brad, Lou.	1.000	12	6	10	0	16	0
Cortes, David, Rich.	1.000	29	1	6	0	7	1
Crow, Dean, Tol.	.750	24	0	3	1	4	0
Crowell, Jim, Ind.*	1.000	1	0	2	0	2	0
Cummings, John, Buf.-Paw.*	1.000	31	2	9	0	11	0
Curtis, Chris, Roch.	.929	18	1	12	1	14	0
Daniels, John, Dur.	1.000	4	1	2	0	3	0
Darwin, David, Tol.*	1.000	1	0	1	0	1	0
Dedrick, Jim, Rich.	1.000	26	2	10	0	12	1
DeHart, Rick, Ott.*	1.000	38	4	3	0	7	0
De Los Santos, Valerio, Lou.*	1.000	5	0	1	0	1	0
Dempster, Ryan, Char.	1.000	5	1	9	0	10	0
DeSilva, John, Ott.	.923	7	4	8	1	13	0
Dixon, Tim, Ott.*	1.000	9	0	2	0	2	0
Dodd, Robert, S./W.B.*	1.000	42	1	4	0	5	0
Donnelly, Brendan, Ind.	.800	19	2	2	1	5	0
Dotel, Octavio, Nor.	.875	17	2	12	2	16	0
Dougherty, Tony, Buf.	1.000	1	1	0	0	1	0
Drews, Matt, Tol.	.840	27	5	16	4	25	0
Drumright, Mike, Tol.	.909	29	9	21	3	33	0
Dunbar, Matt, Lou.*	1.000	50	7	8	0	15	0
Duvall, Mike, Dur.*	.882	32	3	12	2	17	1
Ebert, Derrin, Rich.*	.914	29	9	23	3	35	3
Eichhorn, Mark, Dur.	.957	53	3	19	1	23	1
EILAND, Dave, Dur.	1.000	28	12	47	0	59	4
Eischen, Joey, Ind.*	.895	61	7	10	2	19	0
Ellis, Robert, Lou.	.957	30	16	28	2	46	4
Erdos, Todd, Col.	1.000	39	2	2	0	4	0
Escobar, Kelvim, Syr.	.857	13	3	3	1	7	0
Estrada, Horacio, Lou.*	1.000	2	0	1	0	1	0
Falteisek, Steve, Ott.	.978	34	15	30	1	46	3
Farrell, Jim, Paw.	.931	28	15	12	2	29	1
Fernandez, Jared, Paw.	1.000	5	0	3	0	3	0
Fiore, Tony, S./W.B.	.967	41	13	16	1	30	2
Fleetham, Ben, Ott.	1.000	55	4	5	0	9	0
Fleming, Dave, Paw.-Roch.*	.889	8	3	5	1	9	2
Flener, Huck, Buf.*	.933	14	3	11	1	15	1
Fletcher, Paul, Syr.	.944	48	3	14	1	18	1
Florie, Bryce, Tol.	1.000	1	1	1	0	2	0
Flury, Pat, Paw.	.500	17	0	1	1	2	0
Fontenot, Joe, Char.	1.000	1	0	1	0	1	0
Frey, Steve, Paw.*	.958	50	6	17	1	24	1
Fussell, Chris, Roch.	1.000	10	4	4	0	8	0
Fyhrie, Mike, Nor.	.950	24	8	11	1	20	0
Gaillard, Eddie, Dur.	1.000	18	2	4	0	6	1
Gallaher, Kevin, Roch.	.769	13	2	8	3	13	1
Garces, Rich, Paw.	1.000	7	0	1	0	1	0
Gardiner, Mike, Char.	.947	14	6	12	1	19	1
Glauber, Keith, Ind.	1.000	4	2	5	0	7	0
Goldsmith, Gary, Tol.	.900	46	4	5	1	10	1
Gonzalez, Gabe, Char.*	.974	57	1	36	1	38	1
Gooden, Dwight, Buf.	1.000	4	1	2	0	3	1
Grace, Mike, S./W.B.	.933	11	1	13	1	15	0
Grahe, Joe, Col.	1.000	12	1	13	0	14	0
Graterol, Beiker, Syr.	1.000	16	4	6	0	10	1
Graves, Danny, Ind.	1.000	13	1	5	0	6	1
Greene, Rick, Lou.	1.000	58	5	9	0	14	2
Greisinger, Seth, Tol.	1.000	10	0	12	0	12	0
Grimsley, Jason, Buf.	.895	52	8	9	2	19	1
Grundt, Ken, Char.*	1.000	16	2	4	0	6	0
Guerra, Mark, Nor.	.923	18	5	7	1	13	0
Halladay, Roy, Syr.	1.000	21	11	9	0	20	1
Hammond, Chris, Char.*	1.000	5	2	10	0	12	0
Harriger, Denny, Tol.	.970	22	7	25	1	33	0
Harris, D.J., Syr.	1.000	25	2	1	0	3	0
Hawblitzel, Ryan, Char.	.952	20	6	14	1	21	0
Heflin, Bronson, S./W.B.	1.000	10	2	2	0	4	0
Henderson, Rod, Ott.-Lou.	.897	28	10	16	3	29	0
Henriquez, Oscar, Char.	1.000	26	1	2	0	3	0
Heredia, Wilson, Dur.	.938	23	5	10	1	16	0
Hernandez, Orlando, Col.	1.000	7	1	12	0	13	1
Hernandez, Santos, Dur.	1.000	53	5	6	0	11	0
Holman, Craig, S./W.B.	1.000	6	2	6	0	8	0
Horsman, Vincent, Roch.*	1.000	55	1	7	0	8	0
Hudson, Joe, Paw.-Lou.	1.000	55	1	7	0	8	0
Hurst, Bill, Tol.	1.000	12	3	1	0	4	0
Hutton, Mark, Ind.	.818	16	1	8	2	11	1
Jacobsen, Joe, Char.	.778	9	3	4	2	9	0
Jacome, Jason, Buf.*	.967	24	14	15	1	30	0
Janzen, Marty, Col.	.900	16	4	5	1	10	0
Jarvis, Kevin, Ind.	1.000	2	1	1	0	2	0

CLASS AAA International League

Player, Team	Pct.	G	PO	A	E	TC	DP
Jerzembeck, Mike, Col.	.960	24	10	14	1	25	0
Johns, Doug, Roch.*	1.000	2	0	2	0	2	0
Johns, Keith, Paw.	1.000	1	0	1	0	1	0
Johnson, Craig, Tol.	1.000	1	1	1	0	2	0
Johnson, Dane, Syr.-Char.	1.000	9	1	2	0	3	2
Johnson, Jason, Dur.	1.000	2	0	3	0	3	0
Johnson, Mike, Ott.	.871	18	12	15	4	31	3
Jordan, Ricardo, Ind.-Col.*	.889	42	1	15	2	18	2
Karp, Ryan, Dur.*	1.000	36	2	9	0	11	2
Karsay, Steve, Buf.	.952	16	8	12	1	21	0
Kaufman, Brad, Col.	.667	3	0	2	1	3	0
Keagle, Greg, Tol.	.933	15	3	11	1	15	1
Kelley, Rich, Roch.*	.727	15	1	7	3	11	1
Keyser, Brian, Ind.	.970	41	7	25	1	33	2
Kline, Steve, Ott.*	1.000	2	0	2	0	2	0
Klingenbeck, Scott, Ind.	1.000	11	6	3	0	9	0
Koch, Billy, Syr.	1.000	2	0	1	0	1	0
Kroon, Marc, Ind.	1.000	39	1	3	0	4	0
Lankford, Frank, Col.	1.000	15	7	20	0	27	1
Larkin, Andy, Char.	1.000	11	3	6	0	9	1
Lewis, Richie, Roch.	.969	21	11	20	1	32	2
Lilly, Ted, Ott.*	.750	7	2	4	2	8	0
Loewer, Carlton, S./W.B.	.935	12	9	20	2	31	1
Long, Joey, Ott.*	1.000	34	3	7	0	10	0
Looney, Brian, Col.*	.870	41	7	13	3	23	0
Ludwick, Eric, Char.	1.000	8	3	2	0	5	0
Lukasiewicz, Mark, Syr.*	1.000	22	3	3	0	6	1
Maduro, Calvin, S./W.B.	.977	28	17	25	1	43	3
Maeda, Kats, Col.	1.000	13	0	2	0	2	0
Mahay, Ron, Paw.*	.800	23	0	8	2	10	0
Manzanillo, Josias, Dur.-Nor.	.867	32	8	18	4	30	0
Martin, Tom, Buf.*	1.000	41	2	3	0	5	0
Martinez, Jesus, Ind.*	.952	22	1	19	1	21	2
Martinez, Pedro, Tol.*	1.000	58	2	9	0	11	1
Mathews, Terry, Roch.	1.000	1	1	0	0	1	0
Matthews, Mike, Buf.*	.906	24	5	24	3	32	0
Maxcy, Brian, Nor.	1.000	28	4	4	0	8	0
McGraw, Tom, Ott.*	.952	32	7	13	1	21	1
Medina, Rafael, Char.	1.000	11	3	7	0	10	0
Mendoza, Reynol, Char.	.860	24	6	31	6	43	3
Mimbs, Mark, Nor.*	.938	15	9	21	2	32	3
Mimbs, Mike, Col.*	.600	12	1	2	2	5	0
Minor, Blas, Lou.	1.000	3	0	1	0	1	0
Mix, Greg, Rich.	.750	28	2	1	1	4	0
Montgomery, Steve, Roch.	.929	51	3	10	1	14	0
Moore, Marcus, Buf.	.889	11	3	5	1	9	1
Moore, Trey, Ott.*	1.000	3	0	1	0	1	0
Morel, Ramon, Ott.	1.000	12	1	8	0	9	0
Mullins, Greg, Lou.*	.889	61	3	5	1	9	0
Munoz, Bobby, Roch.	1.000	44	2	16	0	18	0
Munro, Peter, Paw.-Syr.	.979	26	20	27	1	48	1
Nichting, Chris, Dur.	.778	43	4	10	4	18	0
Niebla, Ruben, Ott.*	1.000	6	0	2	0	2	1
Nix, James, Lou.	1.000	27	3	6	0	9	0
Norris, Joe, Ind.	.000	4	0	0	1	1	0
Nunez, Maximo, Dur.	1.000	58	1	9	0	10	0
Nye, Ryan, S./W.B.	.969	23	12	19	1	32	2
Ogea, Chad, Buf.	1.000	9	4	4	0	8	0
Ontiveros, Steve, Roch.	1.000	16	5	16	0	21	1
Osteen, Gavin, Roch.*	.920	44	5	18	2	25	2
Pacheco, Alexander, Dur.	1.000	1	0	1	0	1	0
Pall, Donn, Char.	1.000	29	1	6	0	7	1
Parris, Steve, Ind.	1.000	13	5	8	0	13	0
Patrick, Bronswell, Lou.	1.000	6	5	4	0	9	0
Pavano, Carl, Ott.	1.000	3	0	4	0	4	0
Pena, Juan, Paw.	.933	24	6	8	1	15	0
Pennington, Brad, Dur.*	1.000	45	2	5	0	7	1
Perez, Odaliz, Rich.*	1.000	13	2	5	0	7	3
Perez, Yorkis, S./W.B.*	1.000	4	0	1	0	1	0
Person, Robert, Syr.	.917	20	4	7	1	12	0
Peterson, Kyle, Lou.	1.000	1	0	3	0	3	0
Ponson, Sidney, Roch.	1.000	1	0	1	0	1	0
Poole, Jim, Buf.*	1.000	13	1	2	0	3	1
Powell, Brian, Tol.	1.000	1	1	2	0	3	0
Priest, Eddie, Ind.-Buf.*	.926	22	7	18	2	27	0
Pulsipher, Bill, Nor.*	1.000	14	4	10	0	14	2
Purdy, Shawn, Rich.	.857	16	1	5	1	7	0
Rakers, Jason, Buf.	.955	21	9	12	1	22	0
Ramirez, Hector, Char.	1.000	55	5	9	0	14	0
Ratliff, Jon, Rich.	.842	29	6	10	3	19	1
Reed, Brandon, Tol.	.750	39	1	8	3	12	0
Rekar, Bryan, Dur.	1.000	3	0	1	0	1	0

Player, Team	Pct.	G	PO	A	E	TC	DP
Resz, Greg, Col.	.750	12	2	7	3	12	0
Reyes, Dennis, Ind.*	.875	4	1	6	1	8	1
Reynoso, Armando, Nor.	1.000	2	1	3	0	4	0
Ricken, Ray, Col.	.500	4	0	2	2	4	0
Roberts, Willis, Tol.	.917	39	2	9	1	12	1
Rocker, John, Rich.*	1.000	9	0	4	0	4	0
Rodriguez, Frankie, Lou.	.963	47	9	17	1	27	0
Rodriguez, Nerio, Roch.	1.000	5	0	4	0	4	0
Rodriguez, Steve, Ott.	1.000	3	1	0	0	1	0
Romano, Mike, Syr.	1.000	27	7	15	0	22	1
Roque, Rafael, Lou.*	1.000	9	3	8	0	11	1
Rose, Brian, Paw.	1.000	6	2	2	0	4	0
Rose, Scott, Col.	1.000	29	1	5	0	6	0
Ruebel, Matt, Dur.*	1.000	24	3	17	0	20	0
Ruffcorn, Scott, Ind.	1.000	23	3	5	0	8	0
Ruffin, Johnny, Lou.-Nor.	.955	52	7	14	1	22	2
Rumer, Tim, Dur.*	1.000	26	3	5	0	8	0
Ryan, Ken, S./W.B.	1.000	6	1	2	0	3	0
Sackinsky, Brian, Roch.	.800	7	2	2	1	5	0
Sadler, Al, Lou.	1.000	25	3	2	0	5	0
Sager, A.J., Tol.	1.000	14	3	1	0	4	0
Santana, Marino, Tol.	.875	44	1	6	1	8	0
Santos, Victor, Tol.	.500	5	0	1	1	2	0
Sauerbeck, Scott, Nor.*	.970	27	8	24	1	33	5
Sauveur, Rich, Ind.*	1.000	7	0	5	0	5	1
Schmitt, Todd, Ott.-Tol.	1.000	45	3	4	0	7	0
Schrenk, Steve, Paw.	.889	34	2	6	1	9	0
Scott, Darryl, Ott.-S./W.B.	.875	41	2	5	1	8	0
Seanez, Rudy, Rich.	1.000	16	0	1	0	1	0
Sexton, Jeff, Buf.	1.000	21	1	4	0	5	0
Shelby, Anthony, Col.*	1.000	23	3	7	0	10	0
Shouse, Brian, Paw.*	1.000	22	2	2	0	4	0
Sievert, Mark, Syr.	.944	21	4	13	1	18	5
Sinclair, Steve, Syr.*	1.000	43	5	5	0	10	0
Smart, J.D., Ott.	.833	6	3	2	1	6	0
Smith, Travis, Lou.	1.000	12	6	11	0	17	0
Snyder, Matt, Roch.	1.000	12	0	2	0	2	1
Springer, Dennis, Dur.	1.000	5	1	4	0	5	0
Stanifer, Rob, Char.	1.000	21	3	3	0	6	0
Steed, Rick, Nor.	1.000	13	6	7	0	13	0
Steph, Rod, Roch.-Ind.	1.000	17	1	3	0	4	0
Stephenson, Garrett, S./W.B.	1.000	13	4	9	0	13	0
Stewart, Scott, Nor.*	1.000	9	1	4	0	5	0
Stieb, Dave, Syr.	.955	9	6	15	1	22	1
Stull, Everett, Roch.	1.000	21	2	3	0	5	1
Tam, Jeff, Nor.	.944	45	1	16	1	18	0
Tatis, Ramon, Dur.*	.909	19	1	9	1	11	0
Taylor, Kerry, Tol.	.938	26	8	7	1	16	1
Taylor, Scott, Roch.	1.000	3	0	3	0	3	1
Tessmer, Jay, Col.	1.000	12	2	2	0	4	0
Thomas, Evan, S./W.B.	1.000	2	0	2	0	2	0
Thurman, Mike, Ott.	1.000	19	3	12	0	15	1
Tolar, Kevin, Ind.*	1.000	19	0	4	0	4	0
Trlicek, Rick, Nor.	1.000	19	1	5	0	6	0
Troutman, Keith, S./W.B.	.750	43	1	5	2	8	0
Turgeon, Dave, Roch.	1.000	4	3	2	0	5	0
Turrentine, Rich, Nor.	1.000	5	0	2	0	2	0
Valdez, Carlos, Paw.	1.000	37	3	11	0	14	0
Valdez, Efrain, Nor.*	1.000	18	0	3	0	3	0
Valera, Julio, Col.	1.000	8	1	1	0	2	0
VanEgmond, Tim, Lou.	1.000	24	10	12	0	22	0
VanRyn, Ben, Syr.*	1.000	30	2	6	0	8	0
Veras, Dario, Paw.	.750	23	2	1	1	4	0
Villano, Mike, Char.	1.000	13	2	5	0	7	1
Villone, Ron, Buf.*	.714	23	1	4	2	7	0
Wagner, Paul, Lou.-Rich.	1.000	11	1	4	0	5	0
Walker, Mike, Ind.	1.000	78	18	25	0	43	3
Walker, Pete, Paw.	1.000	22	1	7	0	8	0
Wallace, Derek, Nor.	.857	54	4	2	1	7	0
Wasdin, John, Paw.	1.000	4	1	0	0	1	0
Wehner, John, Char.	1.000	1	0	1	0	1	1
Welch, Mike, S./W.B.	1.000	31	6	12	0	18	0
West, David, Paw.*	.667	17	0	2	1	3	0
White, Rick, Dur.	1.000	9	1	12	0	13	0
Whiteside, Matt, S./W.B.	.857	30	2	4	1	7	0
Williams, Jimmy, Buf.-Char.*	.889	34	9	15	3	27	0
Williams, Shad, Col.	1.000	5	0	3	0	3	1
Williams, Todd, Ind.	.962	53	6	19	1	26	2
Williamson, Scott, Ind.	1.000	5	0	1	0	1	0
Wilson, Paul, Nor.	1.000	7	2	8	0	10	1
Winchester, Scott, Ind.	1.000	6	7	0	0	7	0
Winston, Darrin, S./W.B.*	1.000	16	2	2	0	4	1

Player, Team	Pct.	G	PO	A	E	TC	DP
Withem, Shannon, Syr.	1.000	28	16	24	0	40	3
Wohlers, Mark, Rich.	1.000	16	1	0	0	1	0
Wolf, Randy, S./W.B.*	.962	24	7	18	1	26	2
Woodall, Brad, Lou.*	1.000	5	0	3	0	3	0
Wunsch, Kelly, Lou.*	.923	9	5	7	1	13	0
Yarnall, Ed, Char.*	.842	15	4	12	3	19	1
Yennaco, Jay, Paw.-Syr.	.857	18	4	8	2	14	1
Young, Anthony, Buf.	.625	9	4	1	3	8	0
Young, Tim, Ott.*	1.000	20	1	3	0	4	0

Player, Team	Pct.	G	PO	A	E	TC	DP
Johnson, Dane, Syr.	1.000	7	1	1	0	2	2
Johnson, Dane, Char.	1.000	2	0	1	0	1	0
Jordan, Ricardo, Ind.*	.929	37	0	13	1	14	1
Jordan, Ricardo, Col.*	.750	5	1	2	1	4	1
Manzanillo, Josias, Dur.	.905	19	7	12	2	21	0
Manzanillo, Josias, Nor.	.778	13	1	6	2	9	0
Munro, Peter, Paw.	1.000	18	16	18	0	34	1
Munro, Peter, Syr.	.929	8	4	9	1	14	0
Priest, Eddie, Ind.*	.857	6	0	6	1	7	0
Priest, Eddie, Buf.*	.950	16	7	12	1	20	0
Ruffin, Johnny, Lou.	1.000	35	4	7	0	11	0
Ruffin, Johnny, Nor.	.909	17	3	7	1	11	2
Schmitt, Todd, Ott.	1.000	30	2	4	0	6	0
Schmitt, Todd, Tol.	1.000	15	1	0	0	1	0
Scott, Darryl, Ott.	1.000	8	1	2	0	3	0
Scott, Darryl, S./W.B.	.800	33	1	3	1	5	0
Steph, Rod, Roch.	1.000	14	0	2	0	2	0
Steph, Rod, Ind.	1.000	3	1	1	0	2	0
Wagner, Paul, Lou.	1.000	3	0	2	0	2	0
Wagner, Paul, Rich.	1.000	8	1	2	0	3	0
Williams, Jimmy, Buf.*	.857	15	1	5	1	7	0
Williams, Jimmy, Char.*	.900	19	8	10	2	20	0
Yennaco, Jay, Paw.	.833	11	3	2	1	6	1
Yennaco, Jay, Syr.	.875	7	1	6	1	8	0

PITCHERS WITH TWO OR MORE TEAMS

Player, Team	Pct.	G	PO	A	E	TC	DP
Bennett, Joel, Roch.	.952	18	6	14	1	21	1
Bennett, Joel, S./W.B.	1.000	8	6	2	0	8	0
Borland, Toby, S./W.B.	1.000	13	1	2	0	3	0
Borland, Toby, Char.	1.000	19	4	4	0	8	0
Cummings, John, Buf.*	1.000	21	0	4	0	4	0
Cummings, John, Paw.	1.000	10	2	5	0	7	0
Fleming, Dave, Paw.*	.800	4	1	3	1	5	0
Fleming, Dave, Roch.*	1.000	4	2	2	0	4	2
Henderson, Rod, Ott.	.750	6	2	1	1	4	0
Henderson, Rod, Lou.	.920	22	8	15	2	25	0
Hudson, Joe, Paw.	1.000	46	1	5	0	6	0
Hudson, Joe, Lou.	1.000	9	0	2	0	2	0

The following players did not have any fielding statistics at the position indicated or appeared only as a designated hitter, pinch-hitter, or pinch-runner: Aven, dh; Baez, p; M. Bell, 1b; Bellinger, c, p; Bruske, p; Castillo, of; Chancey, ph; Cooke, p; D. Coquillette, of; Corey, p; Corsi, p; Cox, 1b; Dardin, p; C. Davis, dh; Dodson, p; Driskill, p; Duran, p; Eckersley, p; O. Fernandez, p; Fesh, p; Gresham, 3b; G. Harris, p; Harrison, p; Hastings, p; Held, 3b; Henderson, p; Hiatt, 3b; Huskey, dh; Jacobs, p; LeRoy, p; Listach, 3b; A. Lopez; Makarewicz, of; Mantei, p; McKeel, 3b; Merloni, 3b; Morales, of; Mormon, p; Mummau, 3b; Pasqualicchio, p; Plantier, dh; Post, p; Pulido, p; Raleigh, ph; A. Reyes, p; Rhodes, p; L. Roberts, dh; Shuey, p; Siddall, 3b; Silvestri, p; Spehr, ph; Tejero, of; C. Thompson,p; Villafuerte, p; Wade, p; R. Young, p; Zosky, p.

LEAGUE CHAMPIONS

Year	Team	Pct.
1884—	Trenton	.520
1885—	Syracuse	.584
1886—	Utica	.646
1887—	Toronto	.644
1888—	Syracuse	.723
1889—	Detroit	.649
1890—	Detroit	.617
1891—	Buffalo (reg. season)	.727
	Buffalo (supplemental)	.680
1892—	Providence	.615
	Binghamton*	.667
1893—	Erie	.606
1894—	Providence	.696
1895—	Springfield	.687
1896—	Providence	.602
1897—	Syracuse	.632
1898—	Montreal	.586
1899—	Rochester	.624
1900—	Providence	.616
1901—	Rochester	.642
1902—	Toronto	.669
1903—	Jersey City	.742
1904—	Buffalo	.657
1905—	Providence	.638
1906—	Buffalo	.607
1907—	Toronto	.619
1908—	Baltimore	.593
1909—	Rochester	.596
1910—	Rochester	.601
1911—	Rochester	.645
1912—	Toronto	.595
1913—	Newark	.625
1914—	Providence	.617
1915—	Buffalo	.632
1916—	Buffalo	.586
1917—	Toronto	.604
1918—	Toronto	.693
1919—	Baltimore	.671
1920—	Baltimore	.719
1921—	Baltimore	.717
1922—	Baltimore	.689
1923—	Baltimore	.677
1924—	Baltimore	.709
1925—	Baltimore	.633
1926—	Toronto	.657
1927—	Buffalo	.667
1928—	Rochester	.549
1929—	Rochester	.613
1930—	Rochester	.629
1931—	Rochester	.601
1932—	Newark	.649
1933—	Newark	.622
	Buffalo (4th)†	.494
1934—	Newark	.608
	Toronto (3rd)†	.559
1935—	Montreal	.597
	Syracuse (2nd)†	.565
1936—	Buffalo‡	.610
1937—	Newark‡	.717
1938—	Newark‡	.684
1939—	Jersey City	.582
	Rochester (2nd)†	.556
1940—	Rochester	.611
	Newark (2nd)†	.594
1941—	Newark	.649
	Montreal (2nd)†	.584
1942—	Newark	.601
	Syracuse (3rd)†	.513
1943—	Toronto	.625
	Syracuse (3rd)†	.536
1944—	Baltimore‡	.553
1945—	Montreal	.621
	Newark (2nd)†	.582
1946—	Montreal‡	.649
1947—	Jersey City	.610
	Syracuse (3rd)†	.575
1948—	Montreal‡	.614
1949—	Buffalo	.584
	Montreal (3rd)†	.545
1950—	Rochester	.609
	Baltimore (3rd)†	.556
1951—	Montreal‡	.617
1952—	Montreal	.629
	Rochester (3rd)†	.619
1953—	Rochester	.630
	Montreal (2nd)†	.586
1954—	Toronto	.630
	Syracuse (4th)§	.510
1955—	Montreal	.617
	Rochester (4th)†	.497
1956—	Toronto	.566
	Rochester (2nd)†	.553
1957—	Toronto	.575
	Buffalo (2nd)†	.571
1958—	Montreal‡	.588
1959—	Buffalo	.582
	Havana (3rd)†	.523
1960—	Toronto‡	.649
1961—	Columbus	.597
	Buffalo (3rd)†	.559
1962—	Jacksonville	.610
	Atlanta (3rd)†	.539
1963—	Syracuse∞	.533
	Indianapolis‡	.562
1964—	Jacksonville	.589
	Rochester (4th)†	.532
1965—	Columbus	.582
	Toronto (3rd)†	.556
1966—	Rochester	.565
	Toronto (2nd-tied)†	.558
1967—	Richmond	.574
	Toledo (3rd)†	.525
1968—	Toledo	.565
	Jacksonville (4th)†	.514
1969—	Tidewater	.563
	Syracuse (3rd)†	.536
1970—	Syracuse‡	.600
1971—	Rochester‡	.614
1972—	Louisville	.563
	Tidewater (3rd)†	.545
1973—	Charleston	.586
	Pawtuckets†	.534
1974—	Memphis	.613
	Rochester ∞‡	.611
1975—	Tidewater‡	.610
1976—	Rochester	.638
	Syracuse (2nd)†	.590
1977—	Pawtucket	.571
	Charleston (2nd)‡	.557
1978—	Charleston	.607
	Richmond (4th)†	.511
1979—	Columbus‡	.612
1980—	Columbus‡	.593
1981—	Columbus‡	.633
1982—	Richmond	.590
	Tidewater (3rd)†	.540
1983—	Columbus	.593
	Tidewater (4th)†	.511
1984—	Columbus	.590
	Pawtucket (4th)†	.536

CLASS AAA *International League*

Year	Team	Pct.	Year	Team	Pct.	Year	Team	Pct.
1985—	Syracuse	.564	1991—	Columbus◆	.590	1996—	Columbus◆	.599
	Tidewater (4th)†	.540		Pawtucket	.552		Rochester	.511
1986—	Richmond‡	.571	1992—	Columbus◆	.660	1997—	Rochester◆	.589
1987—	Tidewater	.579		Scr. W.B.	.592		Columbus	.556
	Columbus†	.550	1993—	Charlotte◆	.610	1998—	Buffalo■	.566
1988—	Rochester◆	.546		Rochester	.525			
	Tidewater	.546	1994—	Richmond◆	.567			
1989—	Syracuse	.572		Pawtucket	.549			
	Richmond◆	.555	1995—	Norfolk	.606			
1990—	Rochester◆	.614		Ottawa◆	.507			
	Columbus	.596						

*Won split-season playoff. †Won four-team playoff. ‡Won championship and four-team playoff. §Defeated Havana in game to decide fourth place, then won four-team playoff. ∞League was divided into Northern, Southern divisions. ▲League divided into American, National divisions. ◆League divided into Eastern, Western divisions; won playoffs. ■League divided into Eastern, Northern and Southern divisions; won four-team playoff. (NOTE—Known as Eastern League in 1884, New York State League in 1885, International League in 1886-87, International Association in 1888, International League in 1889-90, Eastern Association in 1891 and Eastern League from 1892 until 1912.)

CLASS AAA *International League*

MEXICAN LEAGUE

1998 FINAL STANDINGS

FIRST HALF

NORTHERN ZONE

Team	W	L	T	Pct.	GB
Monterrey	39	23	0	.629	....
Monclova	39	23	0	.629	....
Torreon	26	36	0	.419	13.0
Nuevo Laredo	25	37	0	.403	14.0
Saltillo	25	37	0	.403	14.0
Reynosa	24	38	0	.387	15.0

CENTRAL ZONE

Team	W	L	T	Pct.	GB
Mexico City Reds	41	21	0	.661	....
Mexico City Tigers	36	25	1	.590	4.5
Oaxaca	35	27	0	.565	6.0
Aguascalientes	34	28	0	.548	7.0
Cordoba	16	46	0	.258	25.0

SOUTHERN ZONE

Team	W	L	T	Pct.	GB
Tabasco	39	23	0	.629	....
Cancun	31	30	1	.508	7.5
Campeche	30	32	0	.484	9.0
Yucatan	29	33	0	.468	10.0
Chetumal	26	36	0	.419	13.0

SECOND HALF

NORTHERN ZONE

Team	W	L	T	Pct.	GB
Monterrey	41	16	1	.719	....
Monclova	36	23	1	.610	6.0
Torreon	29	31	0	.483	13.5
Reynosa	27	31	2	.466	14.5
Saltillo	25	32	2	.439	16.0
Nuevo Laredo	25	34	1	.424	17.0

CENTRAL ZONE

Team	W	L	T	Pct.	GB
Mexico City Reds	40	20	0	.667	....
Mexico City Tigers	36	23	0	.610	3.5
Oaxaca	33	23	1	.589	5.0
Aguascalientes	23	35	1	.397	16.0
Cordoba	21	37	1	.362	18.0

SOUTHERN ZONE

Team	W	L	T	Pct.	GB
Cancun	31	26	2	.544	....
Yucatan	28	30	1	.483	3.5
Tabasco	27	31	2	.466	4.5
Chetumal	25	31	1	.446	5.5
Campeche	17	41	0	.293	14.5

COMPOSITE

NORTHERN ZONE

Team	W	L	T	Pct.	GB
Monterrey	80	39	1	.672	....
Monclova	75	46	1	.620	6.0
Torreon	55	67	0	.451	26.5
Reynosa	51	69	2	.425	29.5
Saltillo	50	69	2	.420	30.0
Nuevo Laredo	50	71	1	.413	31.0

CENTRAL ZONE

Team	W	L	T	Pct.	GB
Mexico City Reds	81	41	0	.664	....
Mexico City Tigers	72	48	1	.600	8.0
Oaxaca	68	50	1	.576	11.0
Aguascalientes	57	63	1	.475	23.0
Cordoba	37	83	1	.308	43.0

SOUTHERN ZONE

Team	W	L	T	Pct.	GB
Tabasco	66	54	2	.550	....
Cancun	62	56	3	.525	3.0
Yucatan	57	63	1	.475	9.0
Chetumal	51	67	1	.432	14.0
Campeche	47	73	0	.392	19.0

PLAYOFFS—Monterrey defeated Yucatan, four games to none; Oaxaca defeated Mexico City Reds, four games to two; Mexico City Tigers defeated Tabasco, four games to two; Monclova defeated Cancun, four games to two, in the first round; Oaxaca defeated Monterrey, four games to three; Monclova defeated Mexico City Tigers, four games to three, in the second round; Oaxaca defeated Monclova, four games to none, in final series to capture league championship.

(Compiled by Ana Luisa Perea Talarico, League Statistician, Mexico, D.F.)

1998 BATTING

TEAM

Team	Avg.	G	TPA	AB	R	H	TB	2B	3B	HR	RBI	SH	SF	HP	BB	IBB	SO	SB	CS	GDP	LOB	ShO	Slg.	OBP
Mexico	.322	122	4950	4276	802	1375	1937	217	33	93	729	37	46	43	548	46	473	62	33	150	1020	1	.453	.400
Monterrey	.305	120	4841	4082	672	1243	1739	199	21	85	608	92	34	33	600	53	513	132	42	104	1036	4	.426	.395
Oaxaca	.304	119	4759	3996	735	1215	1695	198	30	74	660	65	51	39	608	46	487	67	41	124	963	6	.424	.397
Torreon	.292	122	4795	4129	609	1205	1658	206	38	57	534	77	34	43	512	35	550	89	29	139	978	3	.402	.373
Aguascalientes	.292	121	4657	3993	642	1164	1640	163	53	69	565	81	32	45	506	31	546	65	48	120	918	7	.411	.375
M.C. Tigers	.290	121	4838	4170	647	1210	1736	180	56	78	585	91	51	42	484	58	604	102	45	104	970	4	.416	.366
Saltillo	.281	121	4841	4112	582	1156	1477	151	22	42	534	90	31	31	577	26	465	69	45	119	1050	6	.359	.371
Nuevo Laredo	.281	122	4808	4086	536	1147	1534	156	24	61	480	74	34	49	565	32	413	47	39	148	1069	4	.375	.372
Monclova	.280	122	4831	4020	635	1124	1576	197	18	73	572	86	55	39	631	48	582	91	36	121	1004	4	.392	.378
Tabasco	.276	122	4579	4011	507	1106	1459	164	24	47	453	93	42	40	393	41	466	84	46	123	898	6	.364	.343
Chetumal	.272	119	4396	3829	455	1043	1304	149	23	22	400	85	31	35	416	41	371	74	45	122	885	10	.341	.347
Reynosa	.267	122	4638	4033	488	1077	1438	161	43	38	431	71	25	39	470	43	675	46	59	128	926	10	.357	.347
Cordoba	.258	121	4514	3887	429	1003	1272	134	27	27	375	87	34	31	475	41	558	69	52	119	933	13	.327	.341
Yucatan	.258	121	4553	3942	485	1017	1361	138	28	50	441	78	41	34	458	37	513	93	51	97	869	10	.345	.337
Cancun	.256	121	4490	3901	459	997	1326	151	20	46	412	83	23	28	455	37	482	55	36	136	879	12	.340	.336
Campeche	.255	120	4484	3924	407	999	1268	141	25	26	358	110	24	33	393	31	519	41	31	105	897	16	.323	.326

TOP QUALIFIERS FOR BATTING CHAMPIONSHIP

Minimum 329 plate appearances.

Player, Team	Avg.	G	TPA	AB	R	H	TB	2B	3B	HR	RBI	SH	SF	HP	BB	IBB	SO	SB	CS	GDP	Slg.	OBP
Flores, Miguel, Mont.	.381	100	457	399	87	152	204	32	4	4	67	6	3	1	48	4	26	32	6	13	.511	.446
Polonia, Luis, Tig.	.381	86	416	357	82	136	206	15	14	9	63	3	4	0	52	8	31	36	9	5	.577	.455
Espinoza, Ramon, Mex.	.379	121	575	533	114	202	264	31	5	7	62	3	5	8	26	4	36	16	10	24	.495	.413
Alvarez, Hector, Oax.	.366	108	499	435	87	159	201	25	4	3	47	5	3	2	54	1	45	4	4	14	.462	.435
Castellano, Pedro O., Mex.	.354	97	442	387	71	137	211	31	2	13	101	2	7	6	40	2	47	5	2	14	.545	.416
Carrillo, Matias, Tig.	.352	114	514	435	76	153	232	27	5	14	88	2	5	3	69	13	34	8	2	11	.533	.439
Rojas, Homar, Oax.	.352	103	435	386	73	136	212	33	2	13	92	6	9	4	30	1	21	2	2	7	.549	.396
Carter, Michael, Lar.-Tor.	.351	113	521	476	72	167	210	21	5	4	42	4	2	5	34	3	38	35	13	7	.441	.398
Durazo, Erubiel, Mont.	.350	119	527	420	84	147	240	32	2	19	98	1	2	5	99	8	71	4	3	9	.571	.477
Jones, Ron, Sal.	.349	120	536	441	59	154	213	26	0	11	86	0	2	2	91	7	44	0	0	13	.483	.461
Sherman, Darrell, Monc.	.347	97	445	320	84	111	133	7	3	3	29	3	7	9	106	7	26	36	4	2	.416	.511
Paez, Raul, Mex.	.341	95	341	279	62	95	130	15	1	6	55	2	3	2	55	6	37	1	4	10	.466	.448
Magallanes, Ever, Mont.	.337	93	432	356	67	120	157	20	4	3	32	14	2	2	58	7	29	11	9	12	.441	.431
Diaz, Luis Fernando, Agua.	.331	102	402	338	62	112	179	28	6	9	73	3	5	1	55	7	51	2	6	10	.530	.421
Martinez, Ray, Mex.	.330	119	549	440	99	145	243	31	2	21	83	2	4	4	69	4	59	3	4	20	.552	.422
Azocar, Oscar, Che.	.330	117	491	445	54	147	179	28	2	0	71	4	4	2	36	10	8	6	5	15	.402	.380

DEPARTMENTAL LEADERS: G—Aganza, Tellez, 122; AB—R. Espinoza, 533; R—R. Espinoza, 114; H—R. Espinoza, 202; TB—R. Espinoza, 264; 2B—Aganza, 36; 3B—Polonia, 14; HR—Smith, 29; RBI—Barrera, 110; SH—A. Castro, 24; SF—E. Jimenez, B. Rodriguez, 9; HP—Fentanes, 12; BB—Villanueva, 117; IBB—Velazquez, Villanueva, 16; SO—Bustillos, 88; SB—J.J. Munoz, 44; CS—L. Arredondo, 16; GIDP—Ortiz, Tellez, 26; Slg.—Smith .606; OBP—Durazo, .477.

ALL PLAYERS

Player, Team	Avg.	G	TPA	AB	R	H	TB	2B	3B	HR	RBI	SH	SF	HP	BB	IBB	SO	SB	CS	GDP	Slg.	OBP
Abrego, Jesus, Rey.	.272	113	431	334	48	91	120	14	3	3	35	8	1	6	82	9	56	4	6	5	.359	.423
Acuna, Jose Luis, Tor.	.167	29	52	42	12	7	7	0	0	0	1	2	0	1	7	0	11	3	1	1	.167	.300
Aganza, Ruben, Monc.	.278	122	528	439	78	122	205	36	1	15	88	7	6	5	71	8	51	4	2	10	.467	.380
Aguilar, Enrique, Cor.	.251	102	353	307	23	77	94	11	3	0	26	10	0	3	33	4	29	1	3	10	.306	.329
Aguilar, Mario, Cam.	.333	1	4	3	1	1	1	0	0	0	0	0	0	0	1	0	0	0	0	0	.333	.500
Aguilera, Antonio, Can.	.229	110	455	376	41	86	103	10	2	1	24	16	3	2	58	7	71	6	4	12	.274	.333
Aguilera, Armando, Sal.	.286	102	360	315	31	90	102	10	1	0	38	13	1	2	29	1	36	1	2	12	.324	.349
Almeida, Shammar, Agua.	.250	14	19	12	3	3	4	1	0	0	2	0	0	1	6	0	4	0	0	0	.333	.526
Alvarez, Hector, Oax.	.366	108	499	435	87	159	201	25	4	3	47	5	3	2	54	1	45	4	4	14	.462	.435
Alvarez, Heriberto, Cam.	.184	27	55	49	4	9	12	3	0	0	4	1	0	0	5	0	12	0	0	2	.245	.259
Amaro, Gerardo, Rey.	.197	69	193	173	15	34	43	3	3	0	13	6	1	0	13	0	46	1	2	11	.249	.251
Arano, Eloy, Che.-Mex.	.313	104	397	364	39	114	130	8	4	0	30	5	0	2	26	4	33	13	4	8	.357	.362
Arano, Wilfrido, Lar.	.318	108	379	321	36	102	131	19	2	2	43	2	2	6	48	6	15	3	5	6	.408	.414
Armenta, Fernando, Cor.	.206	47	115	102	10	21	28	2	1	1	12	1	0	0	12	1	35	0	2	3	.275	.289
Armenta, Guillermo, Mex.-Che.	.314	74	269	245	41	77	87	8	1	0	18	3	1	2	18	2	19	6	8	5	.355	.365
Arredondo, Hernan, Can.	.136	13	25	22	1	3	4	1	0	0	1	1	0	0	2	0	7	1	0	2	.182	.208
Arredondo, Jesus, Agua.	.293	118	495	396	80	116	128	9	0	1	46	13	1	6	79	1	39	10	5	13	.323	.417
Arredondo, Luis, Yuc.	.315	119	529	441	74	139	175	15	9	1	32	9	2	1	76	8	63	39	16	4	.397	.415
Arvizu, Javier, Can.	.286	74	243	182	27	52	63	8	0	1	20	6	1	1	53	6	35	1	0	4	.346	.447
Attwell, Sergio, Monc.-Cam.	.243	48	132	115	13	28	33	3	1	0	9	3	2	0	12	0	25	2	0	2	.287	.310
Avila, Roberto, Cor.	.274	31	72	62	6	17	18	1	0	0	3	3	0	1	6	0	10	1	1	3	.290	.348
Avila, Ruben, Tor.	.262	99	407	370	36	97	123	12	1	4	53	4	3	2	28	1	34	0	1	19	.332	.315
Avilez, L. Alejandro, Sal.	.191	29	57	47	11	9	9	0	0	0	4	1	0	2	7	1	15	3	0	0	.191	.321
Azocar, Oscar, Che.	.330	117	491	445	54	147	179	28	2	0	71	4	4	2	36	10	8	6	5	15	.402	.380
Barrera, Nelson, Oax.	.321	111	454	389	76	125	203	31	1	15	110	5	7	6	47	7	37	2	0	15	.522	.396
Beltran, Gerardo, Cor.	.100	10	25	20	2	2	2	0	0	0	1	0	1	0	4	0	1	2	0	1	.100	.240
Beltran, Juan, Cam.	.133	6	16	15	0	2	4	0	1	0	1	1	0	0	0	0	5	0	0	0	.267	.133
Bojorquez, Victor, Rey.	.301	110	440	409	53	123	161	24	7	0	33	7	1	2	21	0	57	7	5	9	.394	.337
Briggs, Stoney, Che.-Cor.	.239	70	289	251	39	60	93	5	2	8	31	2	3	2	31	2	48	21	2	7	.371	.324
Bruno, Julio, Tab.	.302	119	498	467	44	141	171	16	1	4	60	4	7	1	19	4	56	3	5	18	.366	.326
Bryant, Scott, Can.	.295	56	242	217	23	64	84	15	1	1	32	1	2	1	21	4	30	2	4	8	.387	.357
Bustillos, Luis, Rey.	.234	112	456	380	46	89	113	9	6	1	23	13	1	4	58	0	88	6	15	7	.297	.341
Cabrera, Alexander, Tig.	.317	116	522	451	83	143	246	26	7	21	83	0	7	11	53	13	77	4	3	19	.545	.397
Camacho, Reginaldo, Rey.	.222	96	315	288	17	64	84	7	2	3	38	6	2	1	18	2	66	3	0	10	.292	.269
Campos, Oscar, Can.	.000	2	3	3	0	0	0	0	0	0	0	0	0	0	0	0	1	0	0	0	.000	.000
Canizales, Juan Carlos, Mont.	.291	94	392	350	49	102	127	20	1	1	38	4	1	0	37	6	58	2	4	14	.363	.358
Carrasco, Ernesto, Lar.	.260	104	431	373	46	97	134	21	5	2	41	14	5	0	39	0	32	4	3	21	.359	.326
Carrillo, Matias, Tig.	.352	114	514	435	76	153	232	27	5	14	88	2	5	3	69	13	34	8	2	11	.533	.439
Carter, Michael, Lar.-Tor.	.351	113	521	476	72	167	210	21	5	4	42	4	2	5	34	3	38	35	13	7	.441	.398
Castaneda, Hector, Cor.	.302	98	367	295	35	89	128	18	0	7	49	3	3	2	64	5	50	1	1	11	.434	.426
Castaneda, Rafael, Oax.	.313	113	463	383	61	120	158	16	2	6	69	7	3	4	66	5	31	1	1	16	.413	.417
Castellano, Pedro O., Mex.	.354	97	442	387	71	137	211	31	2	13	101	2	7	6	40	2	47	5	2	14	.545	.416
Castillo, Juan, Oax.-Rey.	.250	19	86	68	11	17	18	1	0	0	7	5	1	1	11	0	16	1	1	3	.265	.358
Castro, Arnoldo, Can.	.281	117	511	442	52	124	157	15	3	4	36	24	3	0	42	1	31	6	4	19	.355	.341
Castro, Domingo, Agua.-Tig.	.222	9	12	9	2	2	2	0	0	0	1	0	1	1	1	0	4	0	0	0	.222	.364
Cazares, Rosario, Sal.	.000	1	0	0	1	0	0	0	0	0	0	0	0	0	0	0	0	0	0	0	.000	.000
Cazarin, Manuel, Can.	.207	112	437	406	39	84	112	16	0	4	30	6	2	6	17	1	24	5	0	23	.276	.248
Cedillo, Said, Can.	.100	8	12	10	1	1	1	0	0	0	0	2	0	0	0	0	4	0	0	1	.100	.250
Cervantes, Ivan, Rey.	.155	40	121	110	10	17	17	0	0	0	5	1	0	2	8	0	21	1	1	3	.155	.225
Cervantes, Refugio, Lar.	.244	50	81	78	5	19	23	4	0	0	7	1	2	0	0	1	0	1	5	.295	.254
Cervera, Francisco, Cam.	.258	60	239	198	22	51	74	5	3	4	24	2	2	3	34	4	27	3	2	2	.374	.371
Chamberlain, Wes, Cor.	.256	35	154	129	14	33	47	7	2	1	14	0	5	5	15	1	20	2	0	3	.364	.344
Chan, Armando, Monc.	.256	31	104	86	8	22	28	4	1	0	12	4	1	1	12	0	11	0	2	3	.326	.350
Chance, Tony, Monc.	.318	41	186	157	38	50	87	14	1	7	36	0	2	2	25	3	38	2	0	4	.554	.414

Player, Team	Avg.	G	TPA	AB	R	H	TB	2B	3B	HR	RBI	SH	SF	HP	BB	IBB	SO	SB	CS	GDP	Slg.	OBP
Cisneros, Ventura, Rey.	.133	10	16	15	1	2	4	0	1	0	0	0	0	0	1	0	3	1	0	0	.267	.188
Clark, Tim, Sal.-Yuc.	.277	67	283	242	35	67	103	15	3	5	39	1	3	1	36	3	30	0	2	3	.426	.369
Claudio, O. Patricio, Tab.	.275	119	524	443	73	122	169	17	9	4	45	9	5	1	66	5	69	32	12	5	.381	.367
Cobos, Rogelio, Cam.	.220	73	227	200	21	44	61	9	1	2	17	9	1	1	16	0	41	1	2	4	.305	.280
Cole, Alex, Che.-Mont.	.279	88	394	326	48	91	109	8	2	2	33	6	5	7	50	3	35	29	7	8	.334	.381
Coronado, Jorge, Oax.	.500	1	3	2	0	1	1	0	0	0	0	0	0	0	1	0	0	0	0	0	.500	.667
Cruz, Luis Alfonso, Rey.	.280	93	381	328	33	92	109	9	1	2	36	6	4	4	39	5	31	1	3	12	.332	.360
Cruz, Marco A., Tor.	.239	60	185	155	17	37	52	7	1	2	19	10	1	4	15	0	22	1	1	8	.335	.320
Cuevas, Jorge, Agua.	.312	65	157	138	37	43	64	4	4	3	17	0	2	5	12	1	43	0	1	3	.464	.382
De La Cruz, Hector, Che.	.255	64	256	216	28	55	75	7	2	3	22	1	3	1	35	1	24	13	6	4	.347	.357
De Lima, Rafael, Cor.	.304	112	484	408	61	124	155	21	2	2	45	5	3	0	68	10	58	10	3	10	.380	.401
Diaz, Luis Fernando, Agua.	.331	102	402	338	62	112	179	28	6	9	73	3	5	1	55	7	51	2	6	10	.530	.421
Diaz, Pedro, Agua.	.214	45	111	98	11	21	30	3	3	0	8	0	2	0	11	1	15	2	0	2	.306	.288
Diaz, Remigio, Mont.	.301	115	462	396	63	119	143	14	2	2	36	20	2	1	43	1	13	23	2	11	.361	.369
Dominguez, J. David, Can.	.264	115	422	360	33	95	136	21	1	6	39	3	1	1	57	3	50	1	1	9	.378	.365
Duran, Felipe, Oax.	.261	64	170	153	25	40	51	8	0	1	16	5	1	2	9	0	13	2	2	4	.333	.309
Durazo, Erubiel, Mont.	.350	119	527	420	84	147	240	32	2	19	98	1	2	5	99	8	71	4	3	9	.571	.477
Elvira, Honorio, Tab.	.000	5	5	5	0	0	0	0	0	0	0	0	0	0	0	0	3	0	0	1	.000	.000
Elvira, Narciso, Mont.	.000	1	3	3	0	0	0	0	0	0	0	0	0	0	0	0	0	0	0	0	.000	.000
Escalante, Marcelo, Sal.	.250	31	80	72	10	18	22	4	0	0	8	4	0	0	4	0	13	0	0	4	.306	.289
Esparza, Emerson, Monc.	.000	1	4	4	0	0	0	0	0	0	0	0	0	0	0	0	0	0	0	0	.000	.000
Espino, Daniel, Mont.	.322	46	100	87	9	28	36	2	3	0	11	2	1	5	5	0	13	1	0	1	.414	.388
Espino, Omar, Lar.	.211	71	189	147	23	31	48	5	0	4	19	3	3	4	32	0	40	1	1	4	.327	.360
Espinoza, E. Javier, Sal.-Can.	.197	74	212	173	14	34	42	6	1	0	13	4	1	1	33	3	25	4	1	5	.243	.327
Espinoza, Jose Manuel, Lar.	.276	100	372	326	38	90	112	10	6	0	27	6	1	5	34	1	40	2	6	11	.344	.352
Espinoza, Ramon, Mex.	.379	121	575	533	114	202	264	31	5	7	62	3	5	8	26	4	36	16	10	24	.495	.413
Esquer, Ramon, Oax.	.315	115	535	425	94	134	180	17	4	7	59	7	7	4	92	5	44	13	7	16	.424	.436
Estrada, Hector, Monc.	.272	113	440	386	41	105	163	15	2	13	65	4	6	4	40	7	49	2	0	11	.422	.342
Estrella, Isaac, Lar.	.345	17	35	29	9	10	13	3	0	0	4	0	0	0	6	0	9	2	2	0	.448	.457
Facundo, Armando, Tab.	.176	29	82	74	5	13	15	2	0	0	5	2	1	0	5	0	6	4	1	2	.203	.225
Felix, Jesus Arturo, Yuc.	.294	25	61	51	6	15	22	2	1	1	6	2	1	1	6	0	4	1	1	2	.431	.373
Felix, Jose Domingo, Tab.	.275	26	109	91	15	25	37	6	0	2	13	0	0	0	18	3	11	0	0	4	.407	.394
Felix, Junior, Yuc.-Tor.	.316	118	508	418	73	132	224	27	4	19	90	2	6	7	75	15	67	12	5	8	.536	.423
Felix, Lauro, Oax.	.212	58	233	170	23	36	41	3	1	0	14	5	2	1	55	1	40	4	3	1	.241	.404
Fentanes, Oscar, Tab.	.297	118	479	434	58	129	177	19	1	9	61	1	5	12	27	5	45	3	3	21	.408	.351
Fernandez, Daniel, Mex.	.318	87	416	346	73	110	137	8	8	1	40	5	1	2	62	3	31	3	1	9	.396	.423
Figueroa, Federico, Cam.	.000	8	11	11	1	0	0	0	0	0	0	0	0	0	0	0	0	0	0	1	.000	.000
Figueroa, Fernando, Tor.	.000	1	0	0	1	0	0	0	0	0	0	0	0	0	0	0	0	0	0	0	.000	.000
Figueroa, Marcos, Cor.	.218	45	135	119	10	26	27	1	0	0	9	6	2	1	7	0	22	1	2	5	.227	.264
Figueroa, Ricardo, Cam.	.098	23	46	41	0	4	4	0	0	0	2	4	0	0	1	0	18	0	0	0	.098	.119
Flores, Ignacio, Tor.	.000	1	1	1	0	0	0	0	0	0	0	0	0	0	0	0	1	0	0	0	.000	.000
Flores, Miguel, Mont.	.381	100	457	399	87	152	204	32	4	4	67	6	3	1	48	4	26	32	6	13	.511	.446
Fornes, Daniel, Rey.	.351	20	59	57	8	20	25	3	1	0	5	0	0	0	2	0	6	0	1	0	.439	.373
Franco, Manuel, Che.	.000	3	3	3	0	0	0	0	0	0	0	0	0	0	0	0	1	0	0	0	.000	.000
Gainer, Jay, Agua.-Oax.	.273	115	486	410	65	112	199	18	9	17	83	2	6	1	67	9	88	4	3	13	.485	.372
Gama, Ricardo, Yuc.	.300	32	119	100	16	30	34	4	0	0	11	2	4	1	12	0	10	1	0	3	.340	.368
Gamez, Francisco, Mont.	.000	1	0	0	0	0	0	0	0	0	0	0	0	0	0	0	0	0	0	0	.000	.000
Garcia, Carlos Miguel, Tab.	.094	19	40	32	4	3	3	0	0	0	2	0	0	0	8	1	4	0	0	2	.094	.275
Garcia, Cornelio, Tor.	.372	68	327	269	50	100	125	5	7	2	29	4	1	2	51	4	28	18	5	6	.465	.474
Garcia, Hector, Mont.	.283	76	259	223	30	63	79	5	4	1	20	8	3	2	23	1	19	11	2	3	.354	.351
Garcia, Heriberto, Che.	.274	108	452	394	49	108	119	11	0	0	25	15	3	2	38	1	23	8	5	19	.302	.339
Garcia, Omar, Che.-Can.	.276	93	375	333	43	92	104	10	1	0	27	1	5	2	34	9	21	5	2	14	.312	.342
Garza, Gerardo, Lar.	.275	111	412	357	45	98	122	10	1	4	38	6	3	4	42	2	34	1	3	7	.342	.355
Garzon, R. Eliseo, Tig.	.253	85	312	261	28	66	85	7	0	4	34	6	5	4	36	0	37	2	3	9	.326	.346
Gastelum, Carlos, Che.-Tab.	.192	79	180	167	8	32	35	3	0	0	11	8	1	0	4	0	14	0	0	9	.210	.209
Gastelum, Sergio Omar, Tig.	.308	113	490	429	71	132	165	19	4	2	46	16	3	8	34	2	32	12	6	11	.385	.367
Gavia, Jesus, Cor.-Yuc.	.202	80	204	188	13	38	46	6	1	0	11	2	5	6	3	0	21	0	3	10	.245	.233
Gomez, Heber, Tab.	.276	111	420	377	42	104	129	16	3	1	38	15	5	5	18	0	45	6	4	13	.342	.314
Gonzalez, Denio, Tab.	.301	116	476	359	74	108	190	23	1	19	61	0	3	5	109	10	55	2	5	9	.529	.466
Gonzalez, Fernando, Rey.	.000	8	15	14	1	0	0	0	0	0	0	0	0	1	0	0	3	0	0	0	.000	.067
Gonzalez, Jesus, Cam.-Monc.	.277	56	233	195	24	54	75	16	1	1	20	6	1	1	30	1	24	5	3	4	.385	.374
Gonzalez, Jose, Tor.-Yuc.	.268	112	462	392	69	105	155	21	4	7	56	1	2	1	66	1	75	28	8	13	.395	.373
Gonzalez, Roman, Cor.	.233	63	177	159	12	37	40	3	0	0	12	3	1	4	10	0	33	0	3	5	.252	.293
Gordon, Keith, Can.	.228	14	59	57	6	13	22	3	3	0	12	0	0	1	1	0	12	1	0	0	.386	.254
Gregg, Tommy, Mex.	.321	102	461	389	78	125	177	19	3	9	82	0	8	3	61	6	37	15	0	14	.455	.410
Guerrero, Francisco, Monc.	.218	88	339	275	29	60	67	7	0	0	17	14	4	4	42	0	53	9	3	9	.244	.326
Guerrero, Jaime, Che.	.227	51	157	141	10	32	38	4	1	0	9	5	0	0	11	1	20	1	0	3	.270	.283
Guerrero, Jose, Can.	.236	31	60	55	2	13	13	0	0	0	2	2	0	1	2	0	8	0	0	1	.236	.276
Guizar, Hector, Cam.-Monc.	.246	112	451	399	49	98	115	17	0	0	34	21	4	0	27	0	30	4	3	14	.288	.291
Guzman, Marco A., Cam.	.231	60	165	143	13	33	43	10	0	0	12	5	0	0	17	0	15	0	0	4	.301	.313
Hazlet, Steve, Cor.	.170	12	50	47	2	8	12	1	0	1	3	1	0	0	2	0	5	0	2	1	.255	.204
Hernandez, B. Cesar, Tor.	.000	8	7	7	1	0	0	0	0	0	0	0	0	0	0	0	3	0	0	0	.000	.000
Hernandez, Cesar, Yuc.	.257	42	175	167	18	43	57	5	3	1	11	1	1	0	6	0	21	6	3	3	.341	.282
Hernandez, Julio Cesar, Lar.	.256	118	424	363	38	93	111	11	2	1	45	16	2	2	41	0	36	0	1	13	.306	.333
Hernandez, Miguel, Che.	.236	58	83	72	6	17	20	3	0	0	8	2	0	1	8	0	6	0	1	2	.278	.321
Hurtado, Hector, Tor.	.258	80	259	236	18	61	82	10	1	3	30	8	2	1	12	1	46	2	0	8	.347	.295
Hyzdu, Adam, Mont.	.327	29	128	110	20	36	54	3	0	5	22	1	2	1	14	0	17	7	1	2	.491	.402
Iturbe, Pedro, Tig.	.251	103	382	338	49	85	125	11	7	5	36	12	4	2	26	4	52	6	4	5	.370	.305
Jimenez, Eduardo, Mex.	.295	112	491	366	76	108	198	26	2	20	85	0	9	1	115	12	58	3	1	16	.541	.456
Jimenez, G. Alfonso, Can.	.250	37	151	128	14	32	41	7	1	0	11	2	1	0	20	1	10	2	3	3	.320	.349
Jones, Ron, Sal.	.349	120	536	441	59	154	213	26	0	11	86	0	2	2	91	7	44	0	0	13	.483	.461
Leal, Guadalupe, Cam.	.300	88	311	280	25	84	114	16	1	4	31	2	1	4	24	6	27	1	3	6	.407	.362

Player, Team	Avg.	G	TPA	AB	R	H	TB	2B	3B	HR	RBI	SH	SF	HP	BB	IBB	SO	SB	CS	GDP	Slg.	OBP
Leyva, German, Sal.	.270	107	452	378	58	102	142	11	4	7	55	12	8	5	49	1	18	4	2	11	.376	.355
Linares, Rigoberto, Cor.	.233	10	31	30	1	7	8	1	0	0	1	0	0	0	1	0	5	2	0	2	.267	.258
Longmire, Tony, Yuc.	.209	25	104	91	8	19	26	4	0	1	12	0	1	2	10	3	19	5	0	0	.286	.298
Lopez, Fabian, Oax.	.285	82	229	207	29	59	82	9	4	2	31	7	2	0	13	0	11	0	1	5	.396	.324
Lopez, Gonzalo, Monc.	.283	48	175	159	19	45	53	6	1	0	20	2	0	0	14	1	18	0	3	9	.333	.341
Lopez, Jose Dionisio, Tor.	.000	2	1	1	1	0	0	0	0	0	0	0	0	0	0	0	0	0	0	0	.000	.000
Loredo, Jorge Luis, Cam.	.215	92	317	289	29	62	77	6	0	3	22	9	1	2	16	0	59	1	1	8	.266	.260
Luque, Raul, Tab.	.000	4	4	3	0	0	0	0	0	0	0	0	0	1	0	0	2	0	0	0	.000	.250
Lydy, Scott, Oax.	.329	28	106	76	22	25	28	0	0	1	7	0	3	1	26	2	15	2	1	0	.368	.491
Machiria, Pablo, Agua.	.262	105	421	386	31	101	152	18	9	5	47	7	3	3	22	3	32	0	3	18	.394	.304
Magallanes, Ever, Mont.	.337	93	432	356	67	120	157	20	4	3	32	14	2	2	58	7	29	11	9	12	.441	.431
Magallanes, Roberto, Mex.-Can.	.254	88	365	319	38	81	121	15	2	7	39	2	1	2	41	1	70	7	0	12	.379	.342
Magana, Gabriel, Yuc.	.000	4	3	3	1	0	0	0	0	0	0	0	0	0	0	0	2	0	0	0	.000	.000
Magana, Raul, Yuc.	.000	2	1	1	0	0	0	0	0	0	0	0	0	0	0	0	1	0	0	0	.000	.000
Malpica, Enrique, Che.	.218	47	120	101	13	22	26	2	1	0	7	6	2	1	10	0	12	0	0	3	.257	.289
Marcano, Raul, Che.	.307	25	109	101	13	31	41	5	1	1	15	1	3	1	3	0	7	1	1	5	.406	.324
Marrero, Orestes, Yuc.-Sal.	.253	97	433	379	63	96	161	22	5	11	63	2	3	1	48	3	70	4	1	8	.425	.336
Marrujo, Hector, Tab.	.235	13	37	34	3	8	8	0	0	0	4	0	1	0	2	0	4	1	1	1	.235	.270
Martinez, Abel, Can.	.254	56	128	118	16	30	31	1	0	0	12	4	0	1	5	0	19	6	3	5	.263	.290
Martinez, Enrique, Agua.	.294	96	382	320	49	94	126	14	6	2	32	12	2	3	45	0	47	9	5	8	.394	.384
Martinez, Grimaldo, Monc.	.259	103	475	382	56	99	117	12	3	0	42	19	6	2	66	0	32	7	4	20	.306	.366
Martinez, Luis C., Sal.	.262	34	70	65	8	17	19	2	0	0	4	3	0	0	2	0	10	0	1	2	.292	.284
Martinez, Raul, Che.	.322	50	140	121	13	39	49	4	0	2	13	5	1	4	9	0	8	1	0	5	.405	.385
Martinez, Ray, Mex.	.330	119	519	440	99	145	243	31	4	21	83	2	4	4	69	4	59	3	4	20	.552	.422
Mashore, Justine, Che.	.245	14	55	49	7	12	12	0	0	0	1	0	0	1	5	0	15	2	0	5	.245	.327
Mata, Noe, Che.	.190	21	27	21	4	4	6	0	1	0	2	1	0	0	5	0	5	0	0	0	.286	.346
Medina, J. Ramon, Cam.-Monc.	.235	111	452	392	44	92	118	15	4	1	38	7	2	4	47	2	75	4	4	9	.301	.321
Meggers, Mike, Agua.-Che.	.275	75	298	251	31	69	132	14	2	15	54	2	1	1	43	8	47	0	2	3	.526	.382
Mendez, Roberto Carlos, Oax.	.267	117	503	389	82	104	150	23	4	5	59	1	2	3	108	10	64	23	6	16	.386	.428
Mendoza, Omar, Lar.	.222	11	11	9	1	2	2	0	0	0	3	0	0	0	2	0	3	0	0	0	.222	.364
Mere, Pedro, Che.	.227	102	340	295	25	67	86	16	0	1	33	13	1	8	23	2	49	1	3	7	.292	.300
Meza, Alfredo, Mont.	.247	103	335	295	27	73	79	6	0	0	29	17	2	3	18	1	24	6	2	10	.268	.296
Meza, Gonzalo, Mex.	.279	57	137	122	22	34	44	4	3	0	6	1	1	0	13	0	10	2	2	2	.361	.346
Michel, Domingo, Cam.-Yuc.	.278	114	485	385	65	107	164	19	1	12	62	2	4	0	94	5	46	5	3	7	.426	.416
Minjarez, Francisco, Tig.-Agua.	.185	53	75	65	17	12	12	0	0	0	3	3	0	0	7	0	13	0	0	1	.185	.264
Montalvo, Ivan Vladimir, Tig.	.257	67	284	241	40	62	93	13	3	4	42	4	4	0	35	6	59	1	0	3	.386	.346
Montanez, M. Daniel, Can.	.176	35	37	34	8	6	6	0	0	0	1	1	0	0	2	0	7	1	0	1	.176	.222
Morales, Florentino, Lar.	.253	86	273	233	33	59	65	2	2	0	18	6	2	1	31	1	31	3	2	4	.279	.341
Morejon, Oswaldo, Yuc.	.241	104	376	340	34	82	87	5	0	0	22	13	1	2	20	0	25	10	6	16	.256	.287
Moreno, David, Tab.	.143	14	15	14	1	2	3	1	0	0	1	0	0	0	0	0	3	1	0	0	.214	.143
Moreno, Leonardo, Oax.	.302	73	230	205	27	62	70	4	2	0	27	8	3	4	10	1	18	2	3	8	.341	.342
Morones, Martin, Che.	.293	95	316	270	38	79	103	6	6	2	37	3	4	3	36	2	30	8	2	10	.381	.377
Mulligan, Sean, Cor.	.257	31	128	113	10	29	37	3	1	1	12	1	1	2	11	1	19	0	1	2	.327	.331
Munoz, Jose, Rey.	.325	115	509	431	82	140	198	25	12	3	60	7	3	3	65	10	36	11	8	17	.459	.414
Munoz, Jose De Jesus, Sal.	.305	106	476	393	84	120	147	9	6	2	43	4	0	2	77	4	45	44	14	4	.374	.422
Munoz, Miguel, Rey.	.000	1	4	4	0	0	0	0	0	0	0	0	0	0	0	0	0	0	0	0	.000	.000
Munoz, Noe, Mex.	.280	81	306	271	32	76	89	11	1	0	50	3	2	4	26	0	25	2	0	12	.328	.350
Nava, Lipson, Can.	.500	2	4	4	0	2	4	2	0	0	2	0	0	0	0	0	1	0	0	0	1.000	.500
Nunez, Jose Juan, Oax.	.000	1	2	2	0	0	0	0	0	0	0	0	0	0	0	0	1	0	0	0	.000	.000
Ochoa, Ariel, Cam.	.171	19	46	35	3	6	6	0	0	0	1	1	0	2	8	0	13	0	0	0	.171	.356
Ochoa, Edgar, Agua.	.169	42	84	77	4	13	15	2	0	0	6	1	0	0	6	0	19	0	1	3	.195	.229
Ojeda, Miguel, Mex.	.288	68	266	236	39	68	100	11	3	5	34	5	1	3	21	3	34	3	3	4	.424	.352
Olvera, Sergio, Monc.-Cam.	.240	49	161	150	11	36	42	2	2	0	12	4	1	3	3	0	12	3	4	4	.280	.268
Orantes, Ramon, Agua.	.313	109	445	402	60	126	168	12	3	8	51	5	1	5	32	2	54	4	3	18	.418	.370
Orozco, Carlos, Agua.	.000	5	5	4	0	0	0	0	0	0	0	0	0	0	1	0	1	0	0	0	.000	.200
Ortega, Antonio, Oax.	.290	57	146	131	12	38	45	4	0	1	14	2	0	0	13	1	23	0	1	6	.344	.354
Ortiz, Alejandro, Lar.	.280	112	465	396	53	111	152	13	2	8	45	5	2	4	58	4	36	0	1	26	.384	.376
Osuna, Hector, Yuc.	.205	63	178	156	6	32	40	5	0	1	16	9	0	2	11	0	21	0	0	4	.256	.266
Pacho, Carlos, Yuc.	.167	43	74	66	4	11	14	1	1	0	5	4	0	1	3	0	9	0	0	4	.212	.214
Pacho, Juan Jose, Yuc.	.253	118	473	396	54	100	111	7	2	0	29	14	4	1	58	0	32	4	4	13	.280	.346
Paez, Raul, Mex.	.341	95	341	279	62	95	130	15	1	6	55	2	3	2	55	6	37	1	4	10	.466	.448
Pagano, Scott, Can.-Agua.	.248	34	153	133	23	33	36	1	1	0	8	3	0	4	13	2	12	6	4	4	.271	.333
Parra, Frank, Cor.	.270	97	417	381	55	103	152	13	9	6	39	6	2	1	27	3	66	13	11	14	.399	.319
Patron, Damian, Oax.	.000	4	7	7	0	0	0	0	0	0	0	0	0	0	0	0	0	0	0	0	.000	.000
Payro, Edison, Can.	.281	118	480	406	55	114	129	9	3	0	41	11	0	0	63	5	58	7	10	10	.318	.377
Pecorilli, Aldo, Cam.	.333	33	133	117	12	39	57	9	0	3	18	0	1	0	15	3	13	1	0	1	.487	.406
Peguero, Julio, Can.-Tab.	.301	99	422	375	52	113	142	14	3	3	33	6	3	2	36	1	30	21	7	9	.379	.363
Pegues, Ron, Sal.	.288	39	164	146	24	42	60	6	0	4	24	1	0	1	16	1	26	2	2	5	.411	.362
Pena, Carlos, Yuc.	.265	31	79	68	6	18	19	1	0	0	5	3	0	1	7	0	13	0	0	3	.279	.342
Pena, Luis Alberto, Che.	.274	68	122	106	8	29	35	6	0	0	18	4	0	1	11	2	25	0	1	4	.330	.347
Pennyfeather, William, Rey.	.253	24	98	83	12	21	31	4	0	2	10	3	1	1	10	0	23	2	2	4	.373	.337
Perez, Alfredo, Lar.	.259	51	136	116	13	30	39	6	0	1	10	2	0	2	16	0	12	0	0	2	.336	.358
Perez, Francisco, Mex.-Oax.	.284	74	229	204	26	58	78	8	0	4	32	4	4	2	15	5	32	3	4	2	.382	.333
Perez, Juan Luis, Tor.	.224	27	57	49	5	11	14	3	0	0	2	5	0	0	3	1	10	0	0	1	.286	.269
Perez, Noel, Sal.	.308	7	15	13	1	4	4	0	0	0	2	0	0	0	2	0	2	0	0	0	.308	.400
Pinto, V. Placido, Monc.	.200	24	40	35	1	7	8	1	0	0	2	4	0	0	1	0	8	0	0	0	.229	.222
Polonia, Luis, Tig.	.381	86	416	357	82	136	206	15	14	9	63	3	4	0	52	8	31	36	9	5	.577	.455
Pough, Clyde C., Oax.	.227	57	237	194	47	44	74	7	1	7	33	0	2	6	35	1	36	6	3	5	.381	.359
Pulido, Jesus, Yuc.	.000	3	3	2	0	0	0	0	0	0	0	1	0	0	0	0	1	0	0	0	.000	.000
Quintero, Alan, Yuc.	.267	102	367	330	27	88	110	11	4	1	36	5	5	4	23	2	36	2	5	6	.333	.318
Quintero, Edgar, Mont.	.246	61	146	118	19	29	47	3	0	5	17	2	2	1	23	1	24	1	2	4	.398	.368
Quintero, Guillermo, Mont.	.209	60	116	91	12	19	21	2	0	0	7	9	1	1	14	0	17	3	1	1	.231	.318

Player, Team	Avg.	G	TPA	AB	R	H	TB	2B	3B	HR	RBI	SH	SF	HP	BB	IBB	SO	SB	CS	GDP	Sig.	OBP
Quintero, Victor, Yuc.	.000	2	1	1	0	0	0	0	0	0	0	0	0	0	0	0	0	0	0	1	.000	.000
Quiroz, Jose Julian, Che.	.250	5	4	4	1	1	1	0	0	0	0	0	0	0	0	0	0	0	0	0	.250	.250
Ramirez, Efren, Agua.-Che.	.226	31	82	62	6	14	15	1	0	0	5	5	1	3	11	0	10	0	0	1	.242	.364
Ramirez, Enrique, Can.	.292	119	444	404	45	118	133	10	1	1	30	9	4	1	26	0	26	4	2	9	.329	.333
Ramirez, Jesus, Che.	.235	95	288	255	25	60	68	6	1	0	14	5	1	1	26	2	14	3	7	4	.267	.307
Ramirez, Roberto, Agua.	.320	116	500	450	77	144	199	23	4	8	84	2	6	2	40	9	47	7	7	9	.442	.373
Ramon, Reyes, Tab.	.275	103	352	316	36	87	110	17	3	0	35	8	4	0	24	9	44	7	3	8	.348	.323
Ratliff, Darryl, Cam.	.289	38	165	142	14	41	50	3	3	0	14	4	1	2	16	2	19	5	3	6	.352	.366
Raven, Luis, Monc.	.349	40	179	149	28	52	80	14	1	4	34	1	2	1	26	2	26	2	1	5	.537	.444
Renteral, Jose M., Cor.	.100	10	23	20	1	2	2	0	0	0	1	1	0	0	2	0	6	0	1	0	.100	.182
Resendez, Carlos, Monc.	.182	12	22	22	2	4	8	1	0	1	3	0	0	0	0	0	6	0	0	1	.364	.182
Riley, Marquis, Agua.	.379	17	78	66	13	25	27	2	0	0	7	2	0	0	10	0	9	4	2	0	.409	.461
Rivera, Jesus Manuel, Tab.	.000	2	1	0	0	0	0	0	0	0	0	0	0	0	1	0	0	0	0	0	.000	1.000
Roa, Hector, Mex.-Cam.	.294	75	334	299	57	88	111	9	1	4	42	7	1	9	18	3	24	9	3	11	.371	.352
Robles, Gerardo, Oax.	.150	22	21	20	5	3	3	0	0	0	2	0	0	0	1	0	5	0	0	0	.150	.190
Robles, Javier, Tig.	.288	90	377	333	47	96	140	23	3	5	40	3	4	1	36	3	34	11	6	11	.420	.356
Robles, Juan Jose, Cor.	.220	78	234	209	17	46	56	10	0	0	12	6	1	2	16	0	26	1	0	5	.268	.281
Robles, Ricardo, Can.	.210	24	78	62	7	13	18	2	0	1	6	4	0	3	9	0	17	0	0	4	.290	.338
Robles, Trinidad, Tig.	.225	99	390	334	42	75	109	6	2	8	40	10	6	3	37	0	61	8	1	8	.326	.303
Rodriguez, Armando, Tig.	.289	73	237	197	28	57	72	13	1	0	30	3	3	2	32	0	35	3	2	5	.365	.389
Rodriguez, Aurelio Jr., Tab.	.200	26	74	70	5	14	15	1	0	0	4	1	0	1	2	0	10	0	1	2	.214	.233
Rodriguez, Boi, Monc.	.280	99	441	364	61	102	148	22	0	8	57	0	9	2	66	10	71	14	4	9	.407	.385
Rodriguez, Fernando, Tor.	.318	116	500	434	55	138	199	19	6	10	85	5	7	10	44	6	59	2	1	12	.459	.388
Rodriguez, Hector Jesus, Mex.	.263	17	40	38	3	10	10	0	0	0	4	1	0	0	1	0	5	0	1	2	.263	.282
Rojas, Francisco, Tab.	.133	31	48	45	3	6	8	2	0	0	1	0	0	1	2	0	5	0	0	0	.178	.188
Rojas, Homar, Oax.	.352	103	435	386	73	136	212	33	2	13	92	6	9	4	30	1	21	2	2	7	.549	.396
Romero, Marco Antonio, Yuc.	.212	48	159	137	14	29	37	5	0	1	15	1	3	3	15	1	24	1	0	6	.270	.297
Romero, Oscar, Monc.	.284	110	472	387	61	110	145	14	0	7	51	5	4	4	72	8	43	5	6	14	.375	.398
Rubio, Ortiz Sergio, Yuc.	.219	44	74	64	8	14	15	1	0	0	6	3	1	2	4	0	13	0	1	0	.234	.282
Ruiz, Juan De Dios, Yuc.-Cor.	.280	109	444	393	46	110	131	14	2	1	40	6	5	3	37	2	25	2	4	4	.333	.342
Saenz, Ricardo, Monc.	.322	78	325	286	44	92	157	21	1	14	58	1	4	3	31	2	54	0	3	9	.549	.389
Salas, Heriberto, Tor.	.290	102	448	393	66	114	157	24	5	3	34	6	2	3	44	2	50	9	2	11	.399	.364
Salinas, Rogelio, Yuc.	.200	11	22	20	1	4	8	1	0	1	4	0	0	1	1	0	3	0	0	0	.400	.273
Sanchez, Armando, Mont.	.257	43	52	35	3	9	9	0	0	0	7	1	1	0	15	3	3	0	0	2	.257	.471
Sanchez, Gerardo, Lar.	.293	115	516	444	63	130	176	16	0	10	69	4	3	9	56	0	43	1	2	14	.396	.381
Sanchez, Orlando, Mont.	.206	24	43	34	5	7	7	0	0	0	1	3	0	0	6	0	7	1	1	0	.206	.325
Sanchez, Raul, Can.	.135	81	208	178	25	24	31	5	1	0	12	7	2	1	20	0	40	2	3	5	.174	.224
Sanchez, Roque, Cam.	.256	89	328	305	27	78	89	7	2	0	25	7	3	3	10	1	18	5	1	7	.292	.283
Sandoval, Jose Luis, Mex.	.281	105	427	385	53	108	155	19	2	8	68	6	2	3	31	1	50	2	2	11	.403	.337
Sandoval, Octavio Augusto, Tig.	.217	78	231	203	22	44	51	3	2	0	13	8	4	3	13	0	57	4	2	4	.251	.269
Santana, Ivan, Tab.	.270	28	81	74	6	20	23	3	0	0	5	3	0	1	3	0	3	0	0	6	.311	.308
Santana, Mario, Mont.	.167	5	6	6	0	1	1	0	0	0	0	0	0	0	0	0	1	0	0	0	.167	.167
Saucedo, Roberto, Mont.	.223	62	144	121	9	27	41	5	0	3	15	1	1	2	19	0	16	0	0	3	.339	.336
Serrano, Jorge, Lar.	.000	1	0	0	0	0	0	0	0	0	0	0	0	0	0	0	0	0	0	0	.000	.000
Sherman, Darrell, Monc.	.347	97	445	320	84	111	133	7	3	3	29	3	7	9	106	7	26	36	4	2	.416	.511
Sievers, Carlos, Yuc.	.167	37	47	42	5	7	13	0	0	2	8	0	0	0	5	1	5	0	0	2	.310	.255
Smith, Charles, Mont.	.318	104	458	396	69	126	240	25	1	29	108	0	3	6	53	2	72	2	1	9	.606	.404
Soriano, Ricardo, Tor.	.250	29	93	84	13	21	27	3	0	1	3	0	0	1	8	0	13	1	0	2	.321	.323
Soto, Antonio, Can.	.000	1	1	1	0	0	0	0	0	0	0	0	0	0	0	0	0	0	0	0	.000	.000
Soto, Daniel, Oax.	.200	1	5	5	1	1	1	0	0	0	0	0	0	0	0	0	1	0	0	0	.200	.200
Soto, Saul, Rey.	.255	86	319	290	30	74	85	8	0	1	20	2	2	5	18	1	36	3	3	12	.293	.308
Stark, Matt, Tor.	.408	53	230	174	36	71	106	14	0	7	35	1	2	7	46	8	2	0	1	9	.609	.541
Suarez, Luis Mauricio, Tig.	.316	104	363	323	46	102	137	8	6	5	51	9	0	1	30	8	44	4	3	9	.424	.376
Tejeda, Arturo, Lar.	.059	18	20	17	1	1	1	0	0	0	1	0	1	0	2	0	2	0	0	1	.059	.150
Tellez, Alonso, Rey.	.294	122	504	456	41	134	194	22	1	12	57	0	4	1	43	9	52	0	6	26	.425	.353
Tiquet, Lazaro, Tab.	.288	43	116	104	13	30	40	4	0	2	11	3	0	1	8	1	15	2	0	1	.385	.345
Torres, Eduardo, Sal.	.216	37	134	111	9	24	24	0	0	0	11	1	0	2	20	3	14	1	0	4	.216	.346
Torres, Raymundo, Yuc.	.214	12	34	28	1	6	6	0	0	0	5	0	0	1	5	0	14	0	0	1	.214	.353
Trapaga, Julio Miguel, Tig.	.221	75	271	226	30	50	66	9	2	1	17	11	2	3	29	1	38	3	4	3	.292	.315
Tredaway, Chard, Yuc.	.269	104	440	390	44	105	142	20	1	5	52	6	2	0	42	5	49	3	2	7	.364	.339
Valdez, Edgar, Tor.	.000	6	4	3	0	0	0	0	0	0	0	0	0	0	1	0	0	0	0	0	.000	.250
Valdez, Emmanuel, Tig.	.167	6	6	6	0	1	1	0	0	0	0	0	0	0	0	0	1	0	0	1	.167	.167
Valdez, Francisco J., Tab.	.287	75	273	244	28	70	89	9	2	2	30	10	3	8	8	1	15	2	2	4	.365	.327
Valdez, Jesus, Cam.	.294	108	423	385	30	113	135	8	7	0	36	16	3	2	17	0	31	1	0	18	.351	.324
Valdez, Ramon, Cor.	.241	87	318	257	32	62	70	4	2	0	15	10	1	0	50	3	33	11	8	4	.272	.367
Valencia, Carlos, Sal.-Tab.	.277	76	242	213	17	59	75	11	1	1	27	5	4	0	20	0	16	0	2	7	.352	.333
Valenzuela, Armando, Sal.	.223	59	204	188	21	42	47	5	0	0	18	3	2	0	11	0	25	1	3	8	.250	.264
Valenzuela, Eduardo, Sal.	.274	71	228	190	19	52	56	1	0	1	14	10	1	0	27	1	23	0	2	7	.295	.362
Valenzuela, Horacio, Sal.	.270	68	188	163	14	44	64	9	1	3	23	1	0	1	23	3	16	2	1	7	.393	.364
Valenzuela, Irving, Monc.	.271	47	140	118	26	32	41	6	0	1	13	9	0	0	13	0	21	3	1	2	.347	.344
Valenzuela, Saul, Can.	.000	1	0	0	1	0	0	0	0	0	0	0	0	0	0	0	0	0	0	0	.000	.000
Valle, Cosme, Rey.	.207	44	125	111	8	23	31	6	1	0	13	3	1	1	9	0	23	2	0	5	.279	.270
Valle, Jorge Luis, Tor.	.318	113	452	400	66	127	187	27	6	7	53	6	2	3	41	0	49	4	3	17	.468	.383
Valle, Jose Luis, Cor.	.251	95	389	343	26	86	100	10	2	0	32	17	2	0	27	2	29	2	3	15	.292	.304
Valle, Roberto, Tor.	.167	6	11	6	3	1	1	0	0	0	3	0	1	1	3	0	1	0	2	0	.167	.455
Valrie, Kerry, Yuc.	.221	24	107	95	15	21	30	3	0	2	6	0	0	0	9	0	17	2	3	3	.316	.280
Vazquez, Felipe, Mex.	.192	24	28	26	3	5	5	0	0	0	1	0	0	1	1	0	4	0	0	0	.192	.250
Vazquez, P. Jorge Daniel, Monc.	.286	16	37	35	8	10	12	2	0	0	4	0	1	0	1	0	13	0	0	3	.343	.297
Vega, Edgar, Agua.	.313	103	353	297	43	93	119	8	6	2	38	13	3	3	37	1	45	3	3	9	.401	.391
Vega, Jorge, Agua.	.250	1	4	4	0	1	2	1	0	0	1	0	0	0	0	0	1	0	0	1	.500	.250
Vela, Manuel, Rey.	.230	50	92	74	15	17	19	2	0	0	10	2	0	1	15	0	17	2	1	1	.257	.367
Velazquez, Guillermo, Mont.	.301	117	521	425	85	128	187	23	0	12	80	0	5	0	91	16	76	2	1	9	.440	.420

Player, Team	Avg.	G	TPA	AB	R	H	TB	2B	3B	HR	RBI	SH	SF	HP	BB	IBB	SO	SB	CS	GDP	Slg.	OBP
Velez, Manuel, Tab.	.264	91	362	307	33	81	92	9	1	0	34	22	5	1	27	1	29	0	1	12	.300	.321
Verdugo, Hugo, Sal.	.222	2	9	9	0	2	2	0	0	0	0	0	0	0	0	0	1	0	0	0	.222	.222
Verdugo, Sostenes, Yuc.	.391	17	24	23	4	9	9	0	0	0	2	0	0	0	1	0	1	0	0	0	.391	.417
Verdugo, Vicente, Sal.	.293	110	487	393	56	115	137	15	2	1	50	14	6	3	71	0	27	0	8	12	.349	.400
Villanueva, Hector, Lar.	.301	117	497	372	61	112	192	20	0	20	56	0	5	3	117	16	41	0	2	19	.516	.467
Villarreal, Alejandro, Lar.	.245	80	282	237	32	58	86	10	0	6	29	7	1	6	31	0	19	3	0	10	.363	.345
Villarreal, Antonio, Yuc.	.000	1	4	3	0	0	0	0	0	0	0	0	0	0	1	0	1	0	0	0	.000	.250
Villarreal, Salvador, Rey.	.185	49	74	65	9	12	12	0	0	0	4	1	0	0	8	0	23	0	1	0	.185	.274
Villegas, Fernando, Sal.	.275	88	337	291	39	80	105	14	1	3	24	5	1	1	39	2	40	3	5	5	.361	.361
Villegas, Francisco, Sal.	.083	3	13	12	0	1	1	0	0	0	1	0	0	0	1	0	3	0	0	1	.083	.154
Villegas, Jose Angel, Agua.	.000	1	5	4	0	0	0	0	0	0	0	0	0	1	0	0	2	0	0	0	.000	.200
Vizcarra, Marco Antonio, Sal. ..	.272	105	379	316	53	86	90	4	0	0	27	13	3	9	38	0	23	4	2	10	.285	.363
Vizcarra, Roberto, Agua.	.297	118	517	445	78	132	195	17	5	12	67	10	2	4	56	2	29	19	8	11	.438	.379
Voita, Sam, Che.	.273	4	13	11	0	3	3	0	0	0	2	1	0	0	1	0	0	1	0	0	.273	.333
Whiten, Mark, Che.	.382	41	176	131	38	50	80	15	0	5	26	0	1	0	44	3	17	5	1	4	.611	.534
Wong, Julian, Che.-Agua.	.255	72	189	149	25	38	55	10	2	1	19	5	1	5	29	0	28	0	1	3	.369	.391
Yan, Julian, Rey.	.312	110	464	394	59	123	191	25	5	11	69	4	4	7	55	7	81	2	5	7	.485	.402
Yuriar, Jesus, Cor.-Yuc.	.197	47	148	127	10	25	29	2	1	0	8	2	0	1	18	2	9	2	3	5	.228	.301
Zambrano, Roberto, Can.	.295	112	472	383	63	113	205	22	2	22	87	0	5	6	78	14	38	2	2	15	.535	.417
Zamudio, Rafael, Tor.	.287	92	309	261	37	75	104	16	2	3	41	9	5	0	34	2	53	4	1	4	.398	.363
Zavala, Marco, Tig.	.500	1	4	2	0	1	1	0	0	0	1	2	0	0	0	0	0	0	0	0	.500	.500
Zazueta, Juan Carlos, Tor.	.262	91	371	324	43	85	97	12	0	0	25	10	1	4	32	0	21	2	2	12	.299	.335
Zazueta, Mauricio, Tor.	.284	114	473	405	57	115	166	19	4	8	60	6	4	2	56	4	62	8	1	15	.410	.370

GRAND SLAMS: Durazo 4; Smith 3; Diaz, Rojas, 2 each; Aganza, Ru. Avila, Barrera, R. Castaneda, P. Castellano, Chance, Estrada, Ju. Felix, Garza, E. Jimenez, Mendez, Michel, J. Munoz, Raven, T. Robles, B. Rodriguez, F. Rodriguez, Saenz, J. Sandoval, Suarez, Yan, M. Zazueta

AWARDED FIRST BASE ON CATCHER'S INTERFERENCE: Cazarin 2 (Vega, Garzon); A. Quintero (Villanueva); Parra (Cobos); E. Vega (Castaneda); Morones (Santana).

PLAYERS WITH TWO OR MORE TEAMS

Player, Team	Avg.	G	TPA	AB	R	H	TB	2B	3B	HR	RBI	SH	SF	HP	BB	IBB	SO	SB	CS	GDP	Slg.	OBP
Arano, Eloy, Che.	.300	63	243	217	27	65	79	8	3	0	16	3	0	2	21	3	17	8	3	3	.364	.367
Arano, Eloy, Mex.	.333	41	154	147	12	49	51	0	1	0	14	2	0	0	5	1	16	5	1	5	.347	.355
Armenta, Guillermo, Mex.	.348	39	121	112	22	39	43	4	0	0	13	0	1	1	7	2	5	0	1	1	.384	.388
Armenta, Guillermo, Che.	.286	35	148	133	19	38	44	4	1	0	5	3	0	1	11	0	14	6	7	4	.331	.345
Attwell, Sergio, Monc.	.214	12	34	28	4	6	8	0	1	0	2	1	0	0	5	0	6	0	0	0	.286	.333
Attwell, Sergio, Cam.	.253	36	98	87	9	22	25	3	0	0	7	2	2	0	7	0	19	2	0	2	.287	.302
Briggs, Stoney, Che.	.205	24	94	83	8	17	24	1	0	2	8	2	0	0	9	0	14	3	0	2	.289	.283
Briggs, Stoney, Cor.	.256	46	195	168	31	43	69	4	2	6	23	0	3	2	22	2	34	18	2	5	.411	.344
Carter, Michael, Lar.	.349	89	420	384	54	134	166	12	4	4	35	4	2	5	25	2	31	28	9	7	.432	.394
Carter, Michael, Tor.	.359	24	101	92	18	33	44	9	1	0	7	0	0	0	9	1	7	7	4	0	.470	.416
Castillo, Juan, Oax.	.340	13	58	47	10	16	17	1	0	0	7	3	1	1	6	0	9	1	1	3	.362	.418
Castillo, Juan, Rey.	.048	6	28	21	1	1	1	0	0	0	0	2	0	0	5	0	7	0	0	0	.048	.231
Castro, Domingo, Agua.	.000	2	0	0	0	0	0	0	0	0	0	0	0	0	0	0	0	0	0	0	.000	.000
Castro, Domingo, Tig.	.222	7	12	9	2	2	2	0	0	0	0	1	0	1	1	0	4	0	0	0	.222	.364
Clark, Tim, Sal.	.339	15	68	62	9	21	32	6	1	1	16	0	0	0	6	0	8	0	1	2	.516	.397
Clark, Tim, Yuc.	.256	52	215	180	26	46	71	9	2	4	23	1	3	1	30	3	22	0	1	1	.394	.360
Cole, Alex, Che.	.286	34	144	119	14	34	42	1	2	1	13	3	2	4	16	0	9	3	0	6	.353	.383
Cole, Alex, Mont.	.275	54	250	207	34	57	67	7	0	1	20	3	3	3	34	3	26	26	7	2	.324	.381
Espinoza, E. Javier, Sal.	.178	18	55	45	5	8	9	1	0	0	3	2	0	0	8	0	8	0	0	0	.200	.302
Espinoza, E. Javier, Can.	.203	56	157	128	9	26	33	5	1	0	10	2	1	1	25	3	17	4	1	5	.258	.335
Felix, Junior, Yuc.	.310	91	389	323	57	100	175	21	3	16	71	2	5	5	54	11	51	11	5	6	.542	.411
Felix, Junior, Tor.	.337	27	119	95	16	32	49	6	1	3	19	0	1	2	21	4	16	1	0	2	.516	.462
Gainer, Jay, Agua.	.249	57	222	185	27	46	87	9	4	8	36	0	3	1	33	3	39	2	1	7	.470	.360
Gainer, Jay, Oax.	.293	58	264	225	38	66	112	9	5	9	47	2	3	0	34	6	49	2	2	6	.498	.382
Garcia, Omar, Che.	.254	67	273	244	29	62	72	8	1	0	20	1	4	0	24	7	16	4	2	10	.295	.316
Garcia, Omar, Can.	.337	26	102	89	14	30	32	2	0	0	7	0	1	2	10	2	5	1	0	4	.360	.412
Gastelum, Carlos, Che.	.203	40	84	79	2	16	17	1	0	0	4	3	1	0	1	0	4	0	0	5	.215	.210
Gastelum, Carlos, Tab.	.182	39	96	88	6	16	18	2	0	0	7	5	0	0	3	0	10	0	0	4	.205	.209
Gavia, Jesus, Cor.	.225	53	113	102	6	23	26	3	0	0	7	1	4	3	3	0	13	0	2	4	.255	.259
Gavia, Jesus, Yuc.	.174	27	91	86	7	15	20	3	1	0	4	1	1	3	0	0	8	0	1	6	.233	.200
Gonzalez, Jesus, Cam.	.321	31	132	106	13	34	47	10	0	1	10	4	1	1	20	1	12	3	2	2	.443	.430
Gonzalez, Jesus, Monc.	.225	25	101	89	11	20	28	6	1	0	10	2	0	0	10	0	12	2	1	2	.315	.303
Gonzalez, Jose, Tor.	.250	93	388	328	58	82	120	20	3	4	36	1	2	0	57	1	61	26	6	12	.366	.359
Gonzalez, Jose, Yuc.	.359	19	74	64	11	23	35	1	1	3	20	0	0	1	9	0	14	2	2	1	.547	.446
Guizar, Hector, Cam.	.229	70	273	245	26	56	69	13	0	0	25	12	3	0	13	0	20	1	2	8	.282	.264
Guizar, Hector, Monc.	.273	42	178	154	23	42	46	4	0	0	9	9	1	0	14	0	10	3	1	6	.299	.331
Magallanes, Roberto, Mex.	.421	5	21	19	7	8	9	1	0	0	2	0	0	0	2	0	2	0	0	0	.474	.476
Magallanes, Roberto, Can.	.243	83	344	300	31	73	112	14	2	7	37	2	1	2	39	1	68	7	0	12	.373	.333
Marrero, Orestes, Yuc.	.214	15	61	56	5	12	20	2	0	2	3	1	0	0	4	1	12	0	0	2	.357	.267
Marrero, Orestes, Sal.	.260	82	372	323	58	84	141	20	5	9	60	1	3	1	44	2	58	4	1	6	.437	.348
Medina, J. Ramon, Cam.	.231	68	295	255	31	59	76	10	2	1	18	6	0	2	32	2	41	2	3	6	.298	.322
Medina, J. Ramon, Monc.	.241	43	157	137	13	33	42	5	2	0	20	1	2	2	15	0	34	2	1	3	.307	.321
Meggers, Mike, Yuc.	.283	33	132	106	19	30	65	3	1	10	26	1	0	0	25	1	23	0	1	2	.613	.420
Meggers, Mike, Che.	.269	42	166	145	12	39	67	11	1	5	28	1	1	1	18	7	24	0	1	1	.462	.352
Michel, Domingo, Cam.	.293	73	309	246	39	72	96	10	1	4	29	2	1	0	60	4	28	0	2	6	.390	.430
Michel, Domingo, Yuc.	.252	41	176	139	26	35	68	9	0	8	33	0	3	0	34	1	18	5	1	1	.489	.392
Minjarez, Francisco, Tig.	.200	8	27	25	2	5	5	0	0	0	1	1	0	0	1	0	8	0	0	0	.200	.231
Minjarez, Francisco, Agua.	.175	45	48	40	15	7	7	0	0	0	2	2	0	0	6	0	5	0	1	1	.175	.283
Olvera, Sergio, Monc.	.000	7	9	8	0	0	0	0	0	0	0	1	0	0	0	0	5	0	0	0	.000	.111
Olvera, Sergio, Cam.	.254	42	152	142	11	36	42	2	2	0	12	4	1	3	2	0	10	3	4	4	.296	.277
Pagano, Scott, Can.	.222	21	95	81	14	18	21	1	1	0	4	2	0	1	11	2	5	3	3	2	.259	.323
Pagano, Scott, Agua.	.288	13	58	52	9	15	15	0	0	0	2	1	0	3	2	0	7	3	1	2	.288	.351

Player, Team	Avg.	G	TPA	AB	R	H	TB	2B	3B	HR	RBI	SH	SF	HP	BB	IBB	SO	SB	CS	GDP	Slg.	OBP
Peguero, Julio, Can.	.100	3	12	10	0	1	1	0	0	0	0	0	0	0	2	0	3	0	0	0	.100	.250
Peguero, Julio, Tab.	.307	96	410	365	52	112	141	14	3	3	33	6	3	2	34	1	27	21	7	9	.386	.366
Perez, Francisco, Mex.	.240	8	28	25	1	6	6	0	0	0	4	0	1	1	1	0	2	0	0	0	.240	.286
Perez, Francisco, Oax.	.291	66	201	179	25	52	72	8	0	4	28	4	3	1	14	5	30	3	4	2	.402	.340
Ramirez, Efren, Agua.	.240	25	67	50	4	12	13	1	0	0	4	5	1	3	8	0	9	0	0	0	.260	.371
Ramirez, Efren, Che.	.167	6	15	12	2	2	2	0	0	0	1	0	0	0	3	0	1	0	0	1	.167	.333
Roa, Hector, Mex.	.321	40	182	159	35	51	67	7	0	3	26	5	1	4	13	2	15	2	1	7	.421	.384
Roa, Hector, Cam.	.264	35	152	140	22	37	44	2	1	1	16	2	0	5	5	1	9	7	2	4	.314	.313
Ruiz, Juan De Dios, Yuc.	.192	9	29	26	1	5	7	2	0	0	1	0	0	0	3	0	2	1	0	0	.269	.276
Ruiz, Juan De Dios, Cor.	.286	100	415	367	45	105	124	12	2	1	39	6	5	3	34	2	23	1	4	4	.338	.347
Valencia, Carlos, Sal.	.283	56	170	152	14	43	53	8	1	0	23	2	4	0	12	0	11	0	1	6	.349	.327
Valencia, Carlos, Tab.	.262	20	72	61	5	16	22	3	0	1	4	3	0	0	8	0	5	0	1	1	.361	.348
Wong, Julian, Che.	.308	20	37	26	5	8	10	2	0	0	5	1	0	1	9	0	3	0	0	0	.385	.500
Wong, Julian, Agua.	.244	52	152	123	20	30	45	8	2	1	14	4	1	4	20	0	25	0	1	3	.366	.365
Yuriar, Alcaraz Jesus, Cor. ..	.197	22	80	71	4	14	17	1	1	0	6	1	0	0	8	1	6	2	3	3	.239	.278
Yuriar, Alcaraz Jesus, Yuc. ...	.196	25	68	56	6	11	12	1	0	0	2	1	0	1	10	1	3	0	0	2	.214	.328

1998 PITCHING

TEAM

Team	W	L	Pct.	ERA	G	CG	ShO	Sv.	IP	H	TBF	R	ER	HR	SH	SF	HB	BB	IBB	SO	WP	Bk.
Tabasco............	66	54	.550	2.97	122	11	5	31	1062.1	986	3920	420	351	41	88	33	31	431	50	386	30	3
Yucatan	57	63	.475	3.29	121	9	3	23	1061.2	1082	3983	461	388	38	102	48	33	413	44	458	39	1
M.C. Reds	81	41	.664	3.47	122	12	3	26	1067.1	1062	4027	482	412	44	69	25	31	485	16	565	47	4
Monterrey	80	39	.672	3.58	120	6	4	31	1065.0	1023	3970	461	424	42	66	20	27	528	25	731	40	0
Cancun	62	56	.525	3.58	121	22	5	36	1051.2	1058	3963	486	418	82	78	22	38	400	15	467	44	3
Monclova	75	46	.620	3.74	122	11	4	42	1079.1	1119	4075	503	449	65	69	40	30	438	43	489	35	4
Campeche	47	73	.392	3.91	120	20	4	16	1046.1	1065	3907	549	454	38	102	35	42	584	52	524	80	2
Chetumal	51	67	.432	4.25	119	7	5	27	1013.2	1119	3893	540	479	41	90	40	45	413	42	405	36	5
Reynosa	51	69	.425	4.26	122	12	1	26	1066.2	1170	4119	620	505	57	81	30	36	597	22	580	79	4
M.C. Tigers........	72	48	.600	4.42	121	5	2	28	1083.0	1188	4134	603	532	60	89	40	54	557	40	563	50	4
Nuevo Laredo	50	71	.413	4.56	122	8	4	19	1058.2	1208	4105	620	536	69	82	38	35	529	46	568	80	7
Torreon.............	55	67	.451	4.81	122	15	2	25	1062.2	1181	4097	679	568	50	74	41	52	594	38	516	70	5
Saltillo..............	50	69	.420	4.91	121	12	2	19	1059.0	1207	4101	672	578	58	88	40	43	625	62	540	77	2
Oaxaca	68	50	.576	4.95	119	12	3	31	1031.0	1167	3996	669	567	67	65	38	36	500	32	547	61	7
Aguascalientes ..	57	63	.475	4.97	121	6	1	30	1027.2	1249	4096	669	567	76	59	47	30	497	62	423	63	4
Cordoba	37	83	.308	5.07	121	19	3	19	1027.0	1197	4005	656	579	60	98	51	41	500	57	455	54	5

INDIVIDUAL

TOP QUALIFIERS FOR EARNED-RUN AVERAGE TITLE

Minimum 98 innings.

Pitcher, Team	W	L	Pct.	ERA	G	GS	CG	ShO	Rel.	Sv.	IP	H	TBF	R	ER	HR	SH	SF	HB	BB	IBB	SO	WP	Bk.
Moreno, Angel, Yuc.	13	6	.684	1.96	27	26	4	2	1	0	183.1	152	752	52	40	3	6	2	5	74	1	112	4	1
Elvira, Narciso, Mont.	16	4	.800	2.00	24	24	0	0	0	0	157.2	130	643	41	35	5	11	0	4	54	1	114	2	0
Hernandez, M. Martin, Can. ..	10	6	.625	2.01	18	18	8	1	0	0	134.1	100	534	34	30	11	8	2	2	41	1	65	2	1
Ruiz, Cecilio, Tab.	15	7	.682	2.22	26	25	4	3	1	1	162.0	149	650	51	40	3	19	1	3	33	1	54	2	0
Young, Ray, Sal.	9	4	.692	2.33	15	15	7	2	0	0	108.0	86	451	39	28	1	9	1	0	58	3	105	10	0
Lopez, Jonas, Agua.-Yuc.-Tab. ..	9	3	.750	2.45	26	18	1	1	8	3	121.0	107	498	41	33	2	7	6	1	39	2	22	2	0
Bernal, Manuel, Mex.	12	5	.706	2.52	23	23	4	3	0	0	164.0	154	684	55	46	7	15	2	8	47	5	75	5	0
Osuna, Ricardo, Tab.	9	6	.600	2.54	25	24	2	0	1	0	159.1	136	660	58	45	7	8	2	4	63	5	52	6	0
Rodriguez, Salvador, Yuc. ..	9	6	.600	2.72	21	20	3	0	1	0	145.1	136	619	53	44	5	17	4	9	52	4	49	4	0
Campos, Francisco, Cam.	13	6	.684	2.88	27	27	8	2	0	0	206.1	193	856	74	66	8	10	6	3	66	7	130	8	1
Manzanillo, Ravelo, Cam.	13	10	.565	2.94	27	26	10	2	1	0	199.0	164	855	79	65	5	19	2	8	118	2	144	20	0
Soto, Fernando, Can.	12	7	.632	2.95	24	24	7	3	0	0	180.0	210	765	75	59	10	13	3	9	30	2	66	4	2
Rios, Jesus, Monc.	16	6	.727	3.00	24	24	6	2	0	0	177.0	156	728	65	59	8	10	5	6	62	4	93	4	0
Lopez, Emiglio, Tab.	9	7	.563	3.01	23	22	2	1	1	0	134.1	139	567	52	45	2	13	2	7	34	6	41	1	0
Diaz, Rafael, Mont.	14	4	.778	3.02	25	25	4	3	0	0	176.0	146	737	61	59	4	8	4	2	91	5	117	4	0

DEPARTMENTAL LEADERS: W—Elvira, Rios, 16; L—H. Heredia, 14; Pct.—Cuervo, .917; G—E. Neri, 67; GS—Campos, 27; CG—Manzanillo, Orozco, 10; ShO—A. Acosta, Bernal, R. Diaz, Ruiz, F. Soto, 3; Rel.—E. Neri, 66; Sv.—Metoyer, Solarte, 32; IP—Campos, 206.1; H—F. Soto, 210; TBF—Campos, 856; R—D. Perez, 111; ER—D. Perez, 99; HR—Carrasco, J. Lara, 17; SH—Orozco, 21; SF—Atilano, Mig. Garcia, R. Rodriguez, Saldana, 8; HB—Palafox, 16; BB—Manzanillo, 118; IBB—P. Reyes, 15; SO—Manzanillo, 144; WP—Manzanillo, 20; BK—Quintanilla, 4.

ALL PITCHERS

Pitcher, Team	W	L	Pct.	ERA	G	GS	CG	ShO	Rel.	Sv.	IP	H	TBF	R	ER	HR	SH	SF	HB	BB	IBB	SO	WP	Bk.
Acosta, Aaron, Lar.	12	5	.706	3.38	23	23	4	3	0	0	149.1	147	649	66	56	5	11	4	5	73	7	101	13	0
Acosta, Gerardo, Mex.-Oax. ..	5	4	.556	4.74	35	3	0	0	32	1	74.0	72	338	44	39	4	4	2	6	54	5	27	4	0
Adam, David, Tig.	4	6	.400	4.39	18	16	0	0	2	0	98.1	104	423	52	48	4	6	2	7	37	0	40	5	0
Aguilar, Jose Miguel, Tab.	1	3	.250	3.68	38	0	0	0	38	1	29.1	31	126	14	12	1	2	2	0	8	1	15	1	0
Aguilar, Mario, Cam.	0	4	.000	4.28	20	3	0	0	17	0	33.2	32	160	23	16	2	2	2	1	31	2	16	6	0
Aguilera, Edgar, Rey.	1	0	1.000	1.35	4	0	0	0	4	0	6.2	6	31	2	1	0	0	0	0	8	0	1	3	0
Aguirre, Gaudencio, Tab.	4	10	.286	3.60	63	2	0	0	61	23	90.0	82	382	40	36	7	8	1	3	48	10	45	3	1
Alicea, Miguel, Lar.	4	3	.571	6.18	25	0	0	0	25	8	27.2	36	121	19	19	4	1	1	0	7	2	13	0	0
Almeida, Rousell, Lar.	0	0	.000	5.84	12	0	0	0	12	0	12.1	14	62	11	8	0	2	1	1	11	2	9	4	0
Alvarez, Antonio, Monc.	1	1	.500	8.74	8	1	0	0	7	0	11.1	17	53	12	11	2	0	0	0	7	0	7	0	0
Alvarez, Cesar Octavio, Mex. ..	3	2	.600	1.98	5	5	2	0	0	0	41.0	33	167	12	9	1	4	0	1	14	0	19	0	0
Alvarez, Juan Jesus, Tab.	10	7	.588	3.21	24	23	0	0	1	0	145.2	149	640	65	52	7	12	3	6	62	7	59	2	0
Alvarez, Victor, Mex.	3	4	.429	3.62	22	12	0	0	9	2	79.2	80	365	39	32	3	7	2	3	49	2	36	3	3
Alvarez, Jose Carlos, Tab.-Can. ..	0	1	.000	8.64	8	0	0	0	8	0	8.1	18	48	11	8	3	1	1	2	4	2	1	1	0
Angulo, Luis Arturo, Sal.	2	4	.333	5.88	35	6	0	0	29	2	59.2	70	305	42	39	1	6	2	3	66	2	30	7	0

Pitcher, Team	W	L	Pct.	ERA	G	GS	CG	ShO	Rel.	Sv.	IP	H	TBF	R	ER	HR	SH	SF	HB	BB	IBB	SO	WP	Bk.
Antunez, Martin, Cor.	0	0	.000	54.00	1	0	0	0	1	0	0.2	2	6	4	4	0	0	1	0	2	0	1	2	0
Aponte, Eduardo, Can.	0	3	.000	8.05	3	3	0	0	0	0	19.0	25	84	17	17	3	1	0	0	4	1	8	0	0
Arano, Ramon, Cor.	0	0	.000	3.18	1	1	0	0	0	0	5.2	10	25	2	2	0	1	0	2	0	3	0	0
Arias, Joel De Jesus, Tor.	0	0	.000	13.50	2	0	0	0	2	0	4.0	6	24	6	6	0	0	1	1	4	0	2	1	0
Armenta, Alejandro, Tig.	2	5	.286	4.50	16	11	0	0	5	1	68.0	80	311	39	34	4	5	1	1	39	0	43	4	0
Atilano, Juan Carlos, Oax.	3	2	.600	6.46	49	0	0	0	49	4	54.1	53	251	48	39	5	8	8	3	44	3	36	5	0
Avilez, L. Alejandro, Sal.	0	0	.000	4.50	2	0	0	0	2	0	2.0	3	10	2	1	0	0	0	0	0	0	2	0	0
Ayala, Luis Ignacio, Sal.	7	8	.467	5.62	47	4	0	0	43	7	83.1	105	381	52	52	2	10	1	4	45	13	29	3	0
Azocar, Oscar, Che.	0	0	.000	9.00	1	0	0	0	1	0	1.0	2	5	1	1	1	0	0	0	0	0	1	0	0
Badorek, Mike, Tig.	1	0	1.000	4.50	3	3	0	0	0	0	14.0	19	62	8	7	0	0	0	1	4	0	7	0	0
Baez, Sixto, Oax.	5	5	.500	4.34	53	0	0	0	53	18	58.0	57	250	31	28	3	5	1	3	30	5	30	4	1
Barfield, John, Lar.-Tor.	2	3	.400	4.50	19	0	0	0	19	2	24.0	28	114	15	12	1	3	2	1	18	3	7	3	0
Barrera, Sigfrido, Tig.	0	0	.000	4.00	10	0	0	0	10	0	9.0	14	49	4	4	1	0	0	1	11	0	5	0	0
Barron, Avelino, Cam.	2	5	.286	4.50	31	2	0	0	29	0	52.0	48	233	31	26	2	7	5	2	36	2	17	4	0
Beltran, Alonso, Lar.-Tig.	9	7	.563	5.88	32	16	0	0	16	2	98.0	102	456	73	64	5	8	6	4	68	2	69	4	1
Bernal, Manuel, Mex.	12	5	.706	2.52	23	23	4	3	0	0	164.0	154	684	55	46	7	15	2	8	47	5	75	5	0
Blancas, Rigoberto, Tab.	1	1	.500	5.28	11	1	0	0	10	0	15.1	13	74	9	9	1	1	2	0	14	0	7	2	0
Bronson, Heflin, Sal.	0	3	.000	6.94	6	3	0	0	3	0	23.1	31	109	20	18	2	2	1	0	14	0	12	1	0
Brosnan, Jason, Tig.	1	2	.333	4.75	7	6	0	0	1	0	30.1	32	135	16	16	2	3	0	0	17	0	17	0	0
Bryant, Scott, Can.	0	0	.000	0.00	1	0	0	0	1	0	1.0	0	5	0	0	0	0	0	0	2	0	1	0	0
Burgos, John, Lar.	3	10	.231	4.35	31	11	1	0	20	2	93.0	120	429	54	45	7	11	4	1	38	3	50	4	0
Cabrales, Gabriel, Cor.-Agua.	2	1	.667	2.73	38	0	0	0	38	2	62.2	71	269	23	19	3	5	3	1	22	7	24	3	0
Camacho, Adrian, Tab.	0	1	.000	9.53	3	0	0	0	3	0	5.2	8	31	6	6	1	0	0	0	7	0	1	0	0
Camara, Pedro J., Cor.	3	4	.429	5.40	38	3	0	0	35	2	50.0	59	238	37	30	0	2	2	1	37	3	38	3	0
Campillo, Jorge, Tig.	6	2	.750	5.11	24	7	1	0	17	0	68.2	76	327	43	39	6	10	5	1	55	3	42	7	1
Campos, Francisco, Cam.	13	6	.684	2.88	27	27	8	2	0	0	206.1	193	856	74	66	8	10	6	3	66	7	130	8	1
Cano, Jose, Yuc.	1	2	.333	2.66	4	4	0	0	0	0	23.2	24	101	15	7	4	2	2	0	9	0	10	2	0
Cantuja, Coso, Tor.	0	0	.000	36.00	1	0	0	0	1	0	1.0	3	9	4	4	0	0	1	0	3	0	2	0	0
Carranza, D. Javier, Can.	8	7	.533	3.78	24	16	1	1	8	1	104.2	112	467	56	44	8	12	0	5	55	2	54	7	0
Carrasco, Alejandro, Oax.	11	7	.611	4.77	34	20	2	1	14	0	143.1	174	640	93	76	17	2	2	5	45	1	66	3	0
Castaneda, Aurelio, Agua.-Che.	4	6	.400	5.67	29	13	0	0	16	0	101.2	130	467	68	64	6	9	7	10	41	2	35	4	1
Castellanos, Hugo, Cam.	0	0	.000	11.74	8	2	0	0	6	0	7.2	11	49	11	10	0	0	2	0	15	0	8	4	0
Cazares, Rosario, Sal.	6	4	.600	4.52	44	2	0	0	42	6	69.2	80	303	40	35	4	5	4	2	31	4	42	1	0
Cazares, Tomas, Monc.	5	7	.417	4.45	20	14	1	0	6	0	83.0	77	371	48	41	1	2	4	2	52	2	36	3	1
Cecera, Jose Isabel, Monc.	7	1	.875	3.29	25	14	1	1	11	0	98.1	86	407	38	36	8	6	1	1	38	3	45	3	1
Cedeno, Bus, Tor.	3	4	.429	6.04	12	10	0	0	2	0	44.2	56	214	37	30	1	4	0	2	33	1	16	1	1
Cerros, Juan, Rey.	3	7	.300	3.26	48	0	0	0	48	10	82.1	72	350	37	30	2	9	1	3	41	6	35	4	0
Chapa, Javier, Cam.	0	2	.000	14.46	9	2	0	0	7	0	9.1	17	55	16	15	1	1	0	1	11	0	6	1	0
Compres, Fidel, Yuc.	0	1	.000	3.00	5	0	0	0	5	1	6.0	5	27	2	2	0	0	1	5	0	1	1	1	0
Cota, Marino, Oax.	7	3	.700	3.79	31	12	2	0	19	0	102.0	123	458	55	43	4	4	3	4	38	1	66	10	1
Couoh, Enrique, Tig.-Yuc.	5	8	.385	4.84	36	15	0	0	21	3	111.2	123	501	60	60	7	9	3	4	47	3	53	7	0
Cruz, Javier, Mex.	8	4	.667	4.04	35	7	0	0	28	6	75.2	73	330	39	34	3	5	2	3	33	1	50	4	0
Cruz, Luis M., Tig.	0	0	.000	5.94	12	0	0	0	12	0	16.2	21	76	11	11	2	0	1	0	10	0	10	2	1
Cruz, Rafael, Che.	0	2	.000	6.75	5	1	0	0	4	0	8.0	11	42	9	6	1	0	0	0	7	0	2	0	0
Cruz, M. Juan Diego, Yuc.	0	0	.000	7.71	7	0	0	0	7	0	4.2	7	22	4	4	0	0	0	2	0	3	1	0
Cuervo, Bernardo, Tig.	11	1	.917	3.73	21	12	3	1	9	1	94.0	92	388	42	39	4	5	3	4	32	3	27	2	0
De La Fuente, Julian, Rey.	5	2	.714	4.99	38	5	2	0	33	0	70.1	66	339	50	39	5	2	4	0	66	1	46	12	1
De La Hoya, Javier, Cor.	0	3	.000	8.71	5	4	0	0	1	0	20.2	34	106	25	20	3	1	1	1	12	2	16	3	0
Del Toro, Miguel, Mex.	9	4	.692	3.82	39	10	0	0	29	5	92.0	81	394	41	39	3	8	1	3	44	0	56	4	0
Delfin, Adolfo, Oax.	0	0	.000	6.23	3	0	0	0	3	0	4.1	5	21	4	3	0	0	0	1	2	0	2	0	0
Delgado, Tim, Sal.	2	2	.500	5.76	7	4	1	0	3	0	25.0	29	119	16	16	3	2	2	15	2	14	0	1
Diaz, Alejandro, Che.	2	5	.286	2.75	46	1	0	0	45	0	88.1	81	378	29	27	2	8	5	6	32	6	31	2	0
Diaz, Cesar, Len.	0	0	.000	6.14	7	0	0	0	7	0	7.1	10	33	5	5	2	0	1	1	2	0	3	1	0
Diaz, Marcos, Tor.	3	1	.750	3.00	19	2	0	0	17	0	33.0	25	141	12	11	1	3	5	1	23	1	11	2	0
Diaz, Rafael, Mont.	14	4	.778	3.02	25	25	4	3	0	0	176.0	146	737	61	59	4	8	4	2	91	5	117	4	0
Dominguez, David, Rey.	1	0	1.000	4.58	8	2	0	0	6	0	19.2	21	100	15	10	2	0	0	3	21	0	7	5	0
Dominguez, Herminio, Cam.	1	3	.000	5.04	13	1	0	0	13	2	25.0	22	105	18	14	1	3	1	0	8	0	7	0	0
Dorame, Randey, Rey.	6	13	.316	4.03	24	23	2	1	1	0	131.2	143	593	73	59	12	9	3	5	73	1	71	3	1
Duarte, Miguel Eduardo, Sal.	0	4	.000	5.96	25	6	0	0	19	0	54.1	76	264	43	36	4	5	8	0	31	2	19	9	0
Duncan, Calvin, Cor.	1	5	.167	7.15	13	8	0	0	5	1	39.0	58	193	36	31	2	2	0	1	22	2	23	3	0
Elguezabal., Octavio, Agua.	0	1	.000	3.10	11	1	0	0	10	0	20.1	13	88	10	7	0	1	2	1	17	1	9	3	0
Elvira, Narciso, Mont.	16	4	.800	2.00	24	24	0	0	0	0	157.2	130	643	41	35	5	11	0	4	54	1	114	2	0
Enriquez, Martin, Sal.	3	9	.250	4.43	20	20	2	0	0	0	105.2	116	483	62	52	9	10	2	6	51	4	56	8	0
Esparza, Emerson, Monc.	0	0	.000	2.45	8	0	0	0	8	0	11.0	11	51	5	3	1	0	0	1	7	0	1	2	0
Espinoza, Mario, Che.	0	0	.000	4.50	1	0	0	0	1	0	2.0	2	8	1	1	0	0	0	0	2	0	0	0	0
Esquer, Mercedes, Mont.	4	3	.571	3.62	16	15	1	1	1	0	79.2	90	341	36	32	2	4	2	0	25	1	51	2	0
Fajardo, Hector, Monc.	0	1	.000	14.21	3	3	0	0	0	0	6.1	13	37	10	10	1	0	1	0	7	0	2	1	0
Federico, Gustavo, Agua.	5	3	.625	3.80	35	1	0	0	34	5	45.0	40	189	22	19	0	3	4	2	22	3	13	1	0
Felix, Antonio, Tor.	0	0	.000	0.00	1	0	0	0	1	0	2.1	1	11	1	0	0	0	0	3	0	0	0	0
Figueroa, Fernando, Tor.	4	8	.333	5.82	18	16	4	0	2	0	94.1	113	434	72	61	7	11	5	2	47	2	35	5	0
Flores, Armando, Tab.	0	0	.000	6.00	2	0	0	0	2	0	3.0	2	12	0	2	0	0	0	1	0	2	0	0
Flores, Ignacio, Tor.	6	6	.500	2.87	49	2	0	0	47	17	87.2	82	384	36	28	4	11	5	44	13	58	10	1
Fontes, Agustin, Can.	5	3	.625	3.55	32	6	0	0	26	0	71.0	84	307	34	28	4	8	5	2	18	0	32	1	0
Fornes, Daniel, Rey.	0	0	.000	10.80	2	0	0	0	2	0	5.0	15	32	7	6	0	0	0	4	0	1	1	1
Franklin, Jay, Cor.	0	1	.000	19.29	1	1	0	0	0	0	2.1	7	16	5	5	0	0	0	2	0	2	0	0
Fregoso, Raul, Can.	0	0	.000	0.00	2	0	0	0	2	0	1.0	1	7	0	0	0	0	1	0	1	0	0	1	0
Galvez, Randy, Can.	13	4	.765	3.60	24	24	3	0	0	0	150.0	158	640	71	60	4	3	1	52	1	83	7	0
Galvez, Rosario, Agua.	3	1	.750	4.38	50	2	0	0	47	1	63.2	68	292	35	31	6	1	0	1	40	1	33	1	1
Gamez, Francisco, Mont.	5	5	.500	3.49	58	0	0	0	58	0	69.2	75	311	29	27	0	9	3	4	35	1	52	4	0
Garcia, Andres, Can.	0	0	.000	9.39	10	0	0	0	9	0	7.2	7	45	10	8	1	0	1	0	15	0	1	4	0
Garcia, Carlos, Mex.	2	1	.667	5.74	17	0	0	0	17	0	31.1	37	144	21	20	3	1	1	0	15	0	11	1	0
Garcia, Jose, Tig.	9	4	.692	2.72	52	0	0	0	52	2	82.2	75	351	37	25	1	10	3	4	32	13	31	2	1

Pitcher, Team	W	L	Pct.	ERA	G	GS	CG	ShO	Rel.	Sv.	IP	H	TBF	R	ER	HR	SH	SF	HB	BB	IBB	SO	WP	Bk.
Garcia, Manuel, Tig.	1	1	.500	9.00	8	0	0	0	8	0	9.0	14	51	10	9	1	1	0	3	7	1	3	1	0
Garcia, Jose Luis, Tig.	4	5	.444	4.66	59	7	0	0	52	2	87.0	101	377	50	45	7	11	2	4	24	5	47	3	0
Garcia, Adolfo, Cam.	1	1	.500	3.18	2	2	0	0	0	0	11.1	7	50	5	4	0	3	0	1	8	3	2	0	0
Garcia, Francisco, Mex.	0	0	.000	0.00	2	0	0	0	2	0	1.0	0	6	0	0	0	0	0	3	0	1	2	0	
Garcia, R. Miguel, Cor.	3	9	.250	5.92	38	6	1	0	32	1	92.2	127	441	67	61	4	12	8	5	44	12	38	2	0
Garibaldi, Cecilio, Tig.	0	0	.000	7.56	8	0	0	0	8	0	8.1	10	47	7	7	1	1	2	3	14	2	1	1	0
Garibay, Daniel, Tig.	10	2	.833	3.37	26	24	2	1	2	0	155.0	143	678	65	58	7	7	5	5	86	1	112	6	0
Garibay, Roberto, Tab.-Sal.	1	1	.500	4.05	15	1	0	0	14	0	33.1	35	144	15	15	3	2	2	0	14	2	7	4	0
Garibay, Salvador, Cam.-Lar.	2	4	.333	4.91	43	0	0	0	43	0	51.1	57	231	33	28	1	5	2	1	26	4	20	9	0
Garza, Roberto J., Lar.	5	8	.385	6.55	46	8	0	0	38	1	88.0	123	416	72	64	6	5	4	4	37	2	31	4	0
Gomez, Martin, Cor.	1	2	.333	4.48	30	0	0	0	30	0	70.1	71	308	39	35	7	6	5	1	36	8	22	2	0
Gonzalez, Gilberto, Tor.	5	7	.417	5.42	26	14	2	1	12	0	86.1	93	405	60	52	3	2	1	4	70	3	36	8	0
Gonzalez, Victor M., Che.	2	2	.500	7.91	32	3	0	0	29	0	52.1	81	264	48	46	4	5	4	1	31	3	18	4	0
Gonzalez, M. Arturo, Mont.	7	5	.583	5.04	17	16	0	0	1	0	80.1	115	367	53	45	6	7	1	3	19	1	30	3	0
Gracia, Edmundo, Sal.	1	1	.500	12.86	9	1	0	0	8	0	14.0	29	84	23	20	0	2	1	0	17	1	5	3	0
Grajales, Norberto, Tor.	3	7	.300	4.62	37	0	0	0	37	3	78.0	97	351	47	40	1	8	4	4	23	3	31	1	1
Gray, Denis, Tor.	0	2	.000	15.32	6	5	0	0	1	0	12.1	19	77	22	21	0	2	0	0	20	0	11	1	0
Guereca, Guillermo, Oax.	0	0	.000	27.00	1	0	0	0	1	0	0.2	2	5	3	2	0	0	0	0	0	0	1	0	0
Guerrero, Omar, Rey.	2	4	.333	4.09	11	9	0	0	2	0	66.0	73	305	34	30	4	6	3	0	40	2	15	2	0
Heredia, Hector, Agua.	6	14	.300	5.87	23	23	1	1	0	0	118.0	157	549	89	77	12	9	5	3	44	5	46	7	0
Heredia,, Julian, Mex.	4	4	.500	4.89	33	0	0	0	33	11	35.0	37	171	21	19	2	5	2	2	27	5	33	5	0
Hernandez, Fernando, Mont.	12	3	.800	3.54	31	17	1	0	14	1	114.1	86	507	45	45	3	5	2	0	90	1	106	6	0
Hernandez, Jose M., Monc.	12	7	.632	3.60	26	26	2	1	0	0	177.1	200	759	77	71	12	12	5	3	55	1	70	2	0
Hernandez, Julio, Sal.-Cor.	1	4	.200	9.13	17	8	1	1	9	0	47.1	72	242	54	48	5	3	3	1	37	3	14	1	0
Hernandez, Manuel, Agua.	0	5	.000	5.04	6	6	0	0	0	0	30.1	33	137	25	17	4	1	2	1	13	2	12	2	0
Hernandez, M. Martin, Can.	10	6	.625	2.01	18	18	8	1	0	0	134.1	100	534	34	30	11	8	2	2	41	1	65	2	1
Herrera, Alberto, Lar.	0	0	.000	3.24	9	1	0	0	8	0	16.2	21	86	12	6	2	0	0	1	19	0	16	3	0
Herrera, Calixto, Monc.	1	0	1.000	4.02	25	0	0	0	25	4	31.1	34	142	17	14	0	1	0	0	21	3	18	3	2
Herrera, Enrique, Tab.	2	5	.286	2.08	45	0	0	0	45	4	56.1	46	241	15	13	1	3	4	1	31	7	28	5	1
Huber, Jeff, Agua.	4	0	1.000	4.64	15	0	0	0	15	3	21.1	113	0.311	90	15	11	0	0	0	10	1	5	2	
Huerta, Luis Enrique, Lar.	8	6	.571	4.19	25	24	0	0	1	0	148.1	165	644	76	69	6	11	4	8	46	4	83	4	0
Huerta, Francisco, Che.	0	0	.000	0.00	1	1	0	0	0	0	4.2	3	16	0	0	0	0	0	0	1	0	0		
Hurst, Jonathan, Agua.-Sal.	1	1	.500	3.71	17	0	0	0	17	5	17.0	15	77	10	7	1	3	0	1	9	5	12	0	0
Izabal, Luis, Can.	0	0	.000	5.11	9	0	0	0	9	0	12.1	7	54	9	7	1	0	1	1	10	3	1	0	
Jimenez, German, Lar.	2	5	.286	4.31	20	13	0	0	7	0	64.2	83	299	41	31	6	7	4	1	33	3	14	4	0
Jimenez, Isaac, Che.	3	0	1.000	1.80	11	2	0	0	9	0	25.0	24	100	5	5	1	1	2	0	9	0	12	0	0
Jimenez, Jesus, Tor.	0	0	.000	3.24	11	0	0	0	11	0	8.1	7	43	5	3	0	1	1	0	11	0	3	1	0
Lara, Hugo, Che.	5	12	.294	4.17	27	24	3	1	3	0	138.0	157	609	78	64	6	14	4	10	43	4	54	1	1
Lara, Jorge, Sal.	6	10	.375	4.96	27	21	0	0	6	0	139.2	168	636	88	77	17	9	7	6	58	7	49	1	0
Larryl, Mitchel, Oax.	0	0	.000	6.75	4	1	0	0	3	0	5.1	5	33	5	4	0	1	0	0	12	1	3	1	0
Leal, Gerardo, Monc.	2	1	.667	4.70	10	6	0	0	4	0	38.1	40	175	23	20	4	1	3	2	23	0	14	1	0
Leon, Juan Antonio, Tor.	0	1	.000	7.78	17	0	0	0	17	0	19.2	31	100	18	17	1	0	2	1	13	1	9	1	0
Lewis, Greg, Cor.	2	2	.500	3.14	5	4	1	0	1	0	28.2	25	115	11	10	2	0	1	0	13	0	12	1	0
Lizarraga, Andres, Lar.	0	6	.000	5.60	33	5	0	0	28	0	53.0	75	261	38	33	4	6	1	0	32	4	6	3	0
Llanes, Emeterio, Yuc.	0	2	.000	2.92	10	0	0	0	10	0	12.1	12	55	5	4	0	2	0	0	8	2	4	1	0
Loaiza, Sabino, Cam.	5	11	.313	4.21	24	22	1	0	2	0	128.1	142	566	72	60	4	11	5	4	70	3	42	7	0
Lopez, Emiglio, Tab.	9	7	.563	3.01	23	22	2	1	1	0	134.1	139	567	52	45	2	13	2	7	34	6	41	1	0
Lopez, Javier, Che.	0	0	.000	27.00	2	0	0	0	2	0	1.1	3	12	4	4	0	0	0	1	4	1	2	0	0
Lopez, Jesus Nain, Oax.	3	3	.500	3.61	56	1	0	0	55	4	42.1	35	183	24	17	4	6	3	1	27	2	21	5	1
Lopez, Jonas, Agua.-Yuc.-Tab.	9	3	.750	2.45	26	18	1	1	8	3	121.0	107	498	41	33	2	7	6	1	39	2	22	2	0
Lopez, Jose Dionisio, Tor.	4	3	.571	4.82	34	3	0	0	31	0	65.1	71	301	40	35	3	1	1	2	49	1	20	4	0
Lopez, Juan Jose, Cam.	0	2	.000	2.67	20	1	0	0	19	4	27.0	29	122	9	8	1	2	1	1	14	4	9	2	0
Lopez, Raymundo, Tor.	1	0	1.000	5.85	11	1	0	0	10	0	20.0	23	98	17	13	4	0	1	1	12	0	8	1	0
Lopez, Rodrigo, Mex.	10	6	.625	3.35	26	26	1	0	0	0	163.2	165	710	73	61	9	12	2	4	79	0	95	6	0
Lopez, Garza R., Tor.	0	0	.000	0.00	1	0	0	0	1	0	1.0	0	3	0	0	0	0	0	0	0	0	1	0	0
Luevano, Juan, Che.	6	3	.667	3.36	35	13	2	2	22	4	88.1	88	379	35	33	3	7	1	3	39	4	34	4	1
Manrique, Alberto, Mont.	0	2	.000	8.61	25	1	0	0	24	0	38.2	44	195	38	37	2	4	1	3	36	5	24	3	0
Manzanillo, Ravelo, Cam.	13	10	.565	2.94	27	26	10	2	1	0	199.0	164	855	79	65	5	19	2	8	118	2	144	20	0
Marquez, Isidro, Tig.	11	6	.647	3.21	58	0	0	0	58	16	73.0	94	337	35	26	1	9	3	7	25	5	40	1	0
Martinez, Cesar, Mont.	0	0	.000	2.84	4	0	0	0	4	0	6.1	7	27	3	2	0	0	0	0	4	0	3	0	0
Martinez, Cesar, Tor.	5	4	.556	2.98	25	10	4	1	15	1	81.2	81	347	38	27	4	5	1	4	30	1	43	5	1
Martinez, Jose, Tab.	0	0	.000	0.00	2	0	0	0	2	0	1.0	1	6	0	0	0	0	0	0	2	0	1	0	0
Medina, Alonso, Sal.	0	0	.000	10.80	5	0	0	0	5	0	8.1	13	44	10	10	1	0	0	1	6	0	4	0	1
Melendez, Nestor, Rey.	5	2	.714	4.11	49	1	0	0	48	3	61.1	60	287	38	28	4	8	1	1	44	1	52	9	0
Mendez, Luis Fernando, Yuc.	3	4	.429	3.07	13	13	0	0	0	0	67.1	63	284	25	23	2	6	4	5	28	2	31	1	0
Metoyer, Tony, Can.	3	4	.429	2.29	53	0	0	0	53	32	63.0	35	257	19	16	2	8	1	1	32	2	53	3	0
Meza, Joel, Monc.	0	0	.000	7.20	4	0	0	0	4	0	5.0	5	22	4	4	0	1	0	0	3	2	1	0	0
Miranda, Luis Cesar, Yuc.	6	5	.545	3.18	57	0	0	0	57	15	68.0	77	307	28	24	3	13	3	3	24	6	28	3	0
Mo, Sanford Maredith, Agua.	5	7	.417	4.04	20	19	0	0	1	0	118.0	136	554	72	53	8	8	6	6	75	7	54	8	1
Montano, Francisco, Monc.-Tor.	2	2	.500	6.81	11	10	0	0	1	0	39.2	53	193	40	30	0	3	2	1	20	3	18	2	0
Montemayor, Humberto, Mont.	3	4	.429	3.96	28	9	0	0	19	0	75.0	71	339	39	33	5	4	1	4	48	1	39	4	0
Mora, Eleazar, Che.	9	9	.500	3.92	23	22	1	1	0	0	128.2	152	552	69	56	4	4	3	2	29	1	38	5	1
Morales, Luis Fernando, Che.	1	0	1.000	3.86	18	2	0	0	16	0	35.0	31	150	15	15	2	1	0	1	18	0	17	2	0
Moreno, Angel, Yuc.	13	6	.684	1.96	27	26	4	2	1	0	183.1	152	752	52	40	3	6	2	5	74	1	112	4	1
Moreno, Claudio, Mex.	1	0	1.000	5.03	18	0	0	0	18	1	39.1	48	190	25	22	1	0	2	0	28	0	25	5	0
Moreno, Jesus, Agua.	0	0	.000	6.75	6	3	0	0	3	0	14.2	18	65	12	11	5	0	0	0	5	0	3	0	0
Morenoleo, Bardo, Oax.	7	1	.500	5.48	24	22	1	1	2	0	120.0	151	546	82	73	8	3	3	2	56	1	89	7	0
Murillo, Felipe, Monc.	6	4	.600	2.54	40	0	0	0	40	6	56.2	55	232	20	16	2	8	5	0	15	7	12	3	0
Muroz, Leonardo, Mont.	3	1	.750	4.93	24	0	0	0	24	0	38.1	49	184	24	21	5	4	1	0	28	2	20	6	0
Munoz, Miguel, Rey.	4	8	.273	4.20	24	23	1	0	1	0	139.1	174	611	75	65	9	6	7	6	32	2	46	2	0
Munoz, Pablo, Can.	0	0	.000	9.53	13	0	0	0	13	0	5.2	12	34	6	6	3	1	0	0	6	0	4	1	0
Munoz, Pablo R., Oax.	0	1	.000	5.22	22	1	0	0	21	0	29.1	28	134	22	17	3	4	0	0	23	2	9	1	1

Pitcher, Team	W	L	Pct.	ERA	G	GS	CG	ShO	Rel.	Sv.	IP	H	TBF	R	ER	HR	SH	SF	HB	BB	IBB	SO	WP	Bk.
Navarro, Jose Felix, Tig.	4	4	.500	4.26	31	8	0	0	23	0	93.0	120	421	52	44	4	11	4	3	40	3	40	4	0
Navarro, Luis, Yuc.	1	8	.111	4.79	26	12	0	0	14	0	94.0	121	418	58	50	3	11	7	2	30	2	24	7	0
Neri, Braulio, Tab.-Agua.-Sal.	0	1	.000	2.70	23	0	0	0	23	0	23.1	23	117	7	7	2	2	2	0	23	2	17	5	0
Neri, Eduardo, Che.	5	7	.417	5.60	67	1	0	0	66	1	64.1	75	299	47	40	3	10	1	1	39	6	25	2	0
Nieblas, Omar Enrique, Tab.	0	2	.000	11.00	8	1	0	0	7	0	9.0	11	45	14	11	1	0	2	0	8	1	1	0	0
Nieves, Ernesto, Agua.	0	0	.000	2.70	10	0	0	0	10	0	10.0	11	52	4	3	0	1	0	2	10	4	5	4	1
Nunez, Javier, Sal.	1	1	.500	2.76	15	1	1	0	14	0	29.1	17	126	10	9	0	1	3	2	20	4	19	5	0
Nunez, I. Jose Juan, Cam.	0	0	.000	8.53	4	0	0	0	4	0	6.1	12	38	9	6	0	1	2	0	4	1	5	1	0
Nunez, G. Jose Juan, Oax.	3	1	.750	4.67	21	2	0	0	19	0	34.2	40	152	21	18	2	2	0	1	13	1	13	2	2
Ochoa, Pablo Joel, Rey.	3	9	.250	5.02	33	15	2	0	18	1	136.1	145	646	91	76	6	8	0	4	109	1	80	15	0
Ojeda, Ramon, Sal.	1	2	.333	4.62	25	4	0	0	21	0	50.2	74	230	30	26	3	0	3	1	15	0	19	1	0
Olague, Jesus, Mont.	1	1	.500	8.02	10	3	0	0	7	0	21.1	29	103	20	19	2	2	0	1	14	1	9	0	0
Orea, Flavio Cesar, Tor.	3	1	.750	3.42	35	1	0	0	34	2	76.1	66	318	35	29	3	2	4	1	34	2	45	3	0
Orozco, Jaime, Cor.	9	13	.409	3.50	23	21	10	1	2	1	157.0	155	646	68	61	9	21	5	4	29	4	44	3	2
Ortega, Raul, Yuc.	0	0	.000	3.00	15	0	0	0	15	1	9.0	5	42	4	3	0	0	1	0	10	4	5	0	0
Ortega, Roberto, Cor.	2	6	.250	5.47	18	16	1	0	2	0	79.0	88	382	54	48	5	9	5	0	69	0	47	9	0
Osuna, Ricardo, Tab.	9	6	.600	2.54	25	24	2	0	1	0	159.1	136	660	58	45	7	8	2	4	63	5	52	6	0
Osuna, Roberto, Yuc.	0	1	.000	4.91	7	0	0	0	7	2	7.1	7	38	6	4	0	1	1	0	6	1	5	1	0
Palacios, Israel, Rey.	0	0	.000	5.40	4	0	0	0	4	0	8.1	8	40	5	5	1	1	0	0	7	0	8	1	0
Palacios, Vicente, Mont.	7	2	.778	1.18	61	0	0	0	61	25	76.1	61	301	11	10	1	1	2	1	21	2	71	1	0
Palafox, Juan Manuel, Tor.	9	11	.450	4.46	25	25	3	0	0	0	153.1	182	691	96	76	8	10	5	16	57	3	65	9	1
Parra, Julio Cesar, Tig.-Lar.	2	2	.500	3.12	35	0	0	0	35	3	49.0	47	213	21	17	3	1	4	2	26	2	41	6	1
Parra, Milton Ramon, Cor.	0	0	.000	7.20	15	1	0	0	14	0	20.0	21	96	16	16	1	2	3	4	15	2	6	7	0
Perez, Dario, Oax.	13	5	.722	5.57	28	24	3	1	4	3	160.0	194	725	111	99	10	10	7	6	69	4	93	10	0
Perez, Leonardo, Agua.	6	6	.500	5.94	25	20	1	0	5	1	113.2	154	537	81	75	14	5	5	1	53	2	55	8	1
Perez, Vladimir, Rey.	7	3	.700	3.05	44	0	0	0	44	14	65.0	60	272	25	22	1	8	4	2	21	4	52	2	0
Pera, Joel, Agua.	0	0	.000	9.53	2	0	0	0	2	0	5.2	12	31	6	6	0	0	0	0	2	0	3	2	0
Pera, Joel Eduardo, Tor.	1	0	1.000	5.06	4	0	0	0	4	0	5.1	5	24	4	3	0	0	0	0	5	1	4	0	0
Pimentel, Roberto, Tab.	3	0	1.000	2.73	36	1	0	0	35	0	52.2	51	231	18	16	0	8	4	3	27	4	24	0	0
Powell, Dennis, Mont.	4	2	.667	1.59	56	0	0	0	56	5	68.0	50	269	14	12	0	7	2	3	22	3	60	3	0
Pulido, Raymundo, Cam.	1	4	.200	4.85	14	5	0	0	9	0	39.0	41	185	26	21	1	5	1	4	28	2	25	6	0
Purata, Julio, Rey.	4	6	.400	3.72	14	14	1	0	0	0	75.0	91	361	41	31	2	9	1	3	45	0	45	3	0
Quintanilla, Enrique, Lar.	4	12	.250	4.48	28	21	2	0	7	0	130.2	140	572	73	65	12	11	2	5	56	3	69	5	4
Quintero, Simon, Tor.	0	0	.000	0.00	1	0	0	0	1	0	0.0	2	2	0	0	0	0	0	0	0	0	0	0	0
Quiroz, Aaron, Che.	4	5	.444	6.14	14	13	0	0	1	0	55.2	62	248	43	38	3	4	1	3	27	0	35	6	1
Quiroz, Jose Julian, Che.	0	0	.000	1.71	20	0	0	0	20	0	21.0	24	95	5	4	0	0	3	2	10	2	11	1	0
Quirones, Enrique, Yuc.	7	8	.467	3.26	22	22	2	1	0	0	132.1	141	552	51	48	5	11	6	0	28	0	61	3	0
Ramirez, Roberto, Mex.	5	0	1.000	3.06	6	6	0	0	0	0	35.1	33	138	12	12	0	0	1	0	6	0	23	2	0
Ramos, Jorge, Can.	0	0	.000	8.44	5	0	0	0	5	0	5.1	11	26	5	5	2	0	0	0	2	0	0	0	0
Raygoza, V. Martin, Can.	4	3	.571	3.12	14	13	1	0	1	0	86.2	94	363	33	30	7	8	1	3	20	2	31	1	0
Renteria, Hilario, Can.	3	4	.429	3.91	12	8	0	0	4	0	53.0	68	228	26	23	2	1	3	0	14	0	20	1	0
Retes, Lorenzo, Cam.	0	3	.000	5.89	23	3	0	0	20	0	44.1	58	206	34	29	2	10	2	0	27	1	10	5	0
Reyes, Mario, Cor.	0	0	.000	4.50	2	0	0	0	2	0	6.0	5	29	3	3	0	0	0	1	4	0	4	0	0
Reyes, Nathanael, Mex.	1	2	.333	3.86	36	0	0	0	36	0	23.1	22	112	15	10	1	0	1	2	21	1	17	0	0
Reyes, Pablo, Cam.	7	8	.467	3.89	52	1	0	0	51	10	83.1	85	377	39	36	1	12	1	3	55	15	47	7	0
Reyes, Flavio, Cor.	3	2	.600	5.95	36	0	0	0	36	2	39.1	40	175	26	26	2	5	2	3	18	2	16	2	1
Rios, Jesus, Monc.	16	6	.727	3.00	24	24	6	2	0	0	177.0	156	728	65	59	8	10	5	6	62	4	93	4	0
Rivera, Francisco, Tor.	0	0	13.50		1	0	0	0	1	0	1.1	3	10	2	2	0	0	0	3	0	1	1	0	
Rivera, Oscar, Che.	1	3	.250	3.86	11	2	0	0	9	0	23.1	27	105	10	10	0	3	1	2	12	2	11	4	0
Rivera, E. Paul, Sal.-Can.	1	0	1.000	4.43	23	0	0	0	23	1	22.1	16	44	15	11	5	0	0	0	11	0	8	2	0
Rodriguez, Manuel, Cor.	0	4	.000	6.00	26	4	0	0	22	0	51.0	68	256	38	34	4	3	4	4	38	3	23	3	1
Rodriguez, Raul, Monc.	12	7	.632	3.73	26	26	1	0	0	0	183.1	201	787	85	76	9	10	8	7	62	7	90	4	0
Rodriguez, Salvador, Yuc.	9	6	.600	2.72	21	20	3	0	1	0	145.1	136	619	53	44	5	17	4	9	52	4	49	4	0
Rojo, Oscar, Cam.	1	3	.250	6.43	25	2	0	0	23	0	42.0	47	195	35	30	3	5	0	3	29	3	7	0	0
Romero, Alejandro, Mex.	8	5	.615	3.10	24	9	2	0	15	0	93.0	90	400	38	32	6	7	5	1	40	0	28	2	1
Romero, Jose Juan, Cor.	1	8	.111	4.87	43	0	0	0	43	12	68.1	78	318	44	37	1	12	2	6	33	6	32	5	1
Romo, Ricardo, Mont.	2	0	1.000	3.80	5	5	0	0	0	0	23.2	18	93	10	10	3	0	0	0	10	0	8	0	0
Rubio, Miguel, Mont.	1	1	.500	9.12	16	1	0	0	15	0	25.2	36	129	26	26	3	1	1	0	23	1	20	2	0
Ruiz, Cecilio, Tab.	15	7	.682	2.22	26	25	4	3	1	1	162.0	149	650	51	40	3	19	1	3	33	1	54	2	0
Saenz, Alfredo, Tor.-Agua.	2	2	.333	7.85	25	3	0	0	21	2	28.2	44	160	37	25	3	0	1	1	23	2	9	2	0
Salcedo, Jose, Sal.	0	1	.000	27.00	1	1	0	0	0	0	1.1	5	10	4	4	0	1	0	1	1	0	0	0	0
Saldara, Edgardo, Yuc.	6	5	.545	3.43	37	5	0	0	32	1	76.0	75	322	34	29	6	5	8	2	31	3	34	2	0
Sanchez, Efrain, Oax.-Cam.	2	9	.182	3.51	30	14	1	0	16	1	95.0	110	434	48	37	3	7	4	5	48	5	26	5	0
Sanchez, Hector, Agua.	8	11	.421	5.02	26	24	4	0	2	1	143.1	170	628	89	80	13	6	4	4	39	14	48	1	0
Sanchez, Pablo, Sal.	4	3	.571	3.99	19	13	0	0	6	0	94.2	97	440	52	42	2	7	4	6	66	1	45	5	0
Sanchez, P. Alejandro, Can.	1	0	1.000	2.87	30	0	0	0	30	0	53.1	37	215	18	17	4	4	2	1	22	0	26	2	0
Sandoval, Guillermo, Sal.	4	7	.364	6.26	36	11	1	0	25	0	92.0	109	450	75	64	2	11	1	3	70	10	43	11	0
Segura, Jose, Sal.	0	1	.000	3.38	5	0	0	0	5	1	5.1	2	25	2	2	0	1	0	3	1	3	0	0	
Serrano, Jorge, Lar.	0	0	.000	4.05	8	2	0	0	6	0	26.2	25	120	12	12	1	3	1	2	18	1	4	2	0
Sierra, Abel, Oax.-Che.	0	0	.000	8.49	13	3	0	0	10	0	23.1	35	120	24	22	1	2	2	1	20	1	7	0	0
Sinohui, David, Agua.	6	3	.667	1.90	37	0	0	0	37	11	52.0	50	237	14	11	0	7	3	2	30	8	31	6	0
Smith, Chuk, Tor.	4	0	1.000	3.08	12	9	2	0	3	0	61.1	54	282	28	21	2	4	1	5	44	1	59	12	0
Solarte, Jose, Monc.	6	3	.667	3.59	60	0	0	0	60	32	67.2	61	284	29	27	5	9	4	3	24	7	38	1	0
Solis, Ricardo, Cor.	7	9	.438	4.04	23	23	0	0	0	0	129.1	158	565	67	58	11	12	2	0	37	3	36	1	0
Sombra, Francisco, Agua.	3	2	.600	6.88	46	6	0	0	39	2	60.2	83	287	48	45	2	4	5	1	35	4	32	6	0
Soriano, Ricardo, Tor.	0	0	.000	0.00	1	0	0	0	1	0	0.2	0	2	0	0	0	0	0	0	1	0	0	0	0
Soto, Cruz A., Can.	9	9	.500	3.12	37	13	5	0	23	2	121.1	100	493	47	42	6	10	0	5	79	3	69	8	0
Soto, Daniel, Oax.	0	0	.000	6.23	7	0	0	0	7	0	8.2	10	46	9	6	2	0	1	2	7	0	6	2	0
Soto, Fernando, Can.	12	7	.632	2.95	24	24	7	3	0	0	180.0	210	765	75	59	10	13	3	9	30	2	66	4	2
Sulu, Mario, Cam.	1	2	.333	3.61	19	6	0	0	13	0	42.1	54	212	24	17	2	3	4	4	24	4	26	3	1
Taylor, Thomas, Tor.	0	1	.000	9.00	6	0	0	0	6	0	7.0	8	37	8	7	0	0	2	0	10	0	4	1	0
Tejeda, Felix, Che.	5	9	.357	4.51	20	19	1	1	1	0	101.2	123	455	57	51	5	8	4	1	34	1	34	1	0

Pitcher, Team	W	L	Pct.	ERA	G	GS	CG	ShO	Rel.	Sv.	IP	H	TBF	R	ER	HR	SH	SF	HB	BB	IBB	SO	WP	Bk.
Turgeon, Dave, Rey.	7	8	.467	3.88	18	18	4	0	0	0	125.1	139	542	67	54	7	8	6	5	39	1	87	7	0
Uribe, Juan Carlos, Yuc.	1	0	1.000	4.76	25	0	0	0	25	0	39.2	47	182	21	21	1	8	3	2	18	3	24	2	0
Valdez, Armando, Che.	4	4	.500	2.45	52	1	0	0	52	22	69.2	45	280	24	19	1	10	3	3	36	10	42	1	0
Valdez, Carlos, Yuc.	0	0	.000	0.00	3	0	0	0	3	0	1.2	3	10	0	0	0	0	0	0	2	0	2	0	0
Valdez, R. Rodolfo, Monc.	5	2	.714	4.38	25	7	0	0	18	0	61.2	68	270	31	30	8	4	0	3	21	2	34	4	0
Valencia, Jorge, Monc.	1	4	.200	3.86	23	0	0	0	23	0	42.0	53	191	25	18	1	4	2	1	18	4	18	1	0
Valenzuela, G. Saul, Can.	6	10	.375	5.84	22	20	0	0	2	0	114.0	134	497	80	74	14	4	4	7	42	1	25	6	0
Valenzuela, U. Jesus P., Oax.	0	0	.000	0.00	2	0	0	0	2	0	3.1	1	12	0	0	0	0	1	0	2	0	1	0	0
Valera, Julio, Mont.	1	2	.333	7.79	4	4	0	0	0	0	17.1	26	85	15	15	2	0	0	2	9	0	9	0	0
Valerio, Julio Cesar, Monc.	1	2	.333	3.10	37	1	0	0	36	1	29.0	41	145	12	10	3	3	2	1	20	3	9	2	0
Vargas, Ignacio, Yuc.	4	10	.286	5.56	30	13	0	0	17	1	90.2	115	418	65	56	3	10	2	2	42	9	25	4	0
Vargas, Joel, Tab.	3	2	.600	3.56	29	7	1	0	22	0	68.1	51	300	33	27	3	4	5	1	48	3	33	3	1
Vazquez, Adrian, Cam.	1	2	.333	4.00	4	4	0	0	0	0	18.0	16	85	11	8	1	2	0	2	14	0	15	2	0
Vazquez, Vicenty Marcos, Oax. .	5	4	.556	5.08	13	10	1	0	3	1	67.1	73	300	44	38	3	4	4	2	35	4	21	6	1
Vega, Obed, Lar.	2	2	.500	5.18	40	3	1	1	37	2	74.2	81	347	48	43	12	3	1	3	50	4	64	11	0
Velazquez, Ernesto, Yuc.-Tor. ...	2	1	.667	3.67	26	0	0	0	26	0	41.2	40	172	19	17	2	2	4	1	16	4	13	1	0
Velazquez, Israel, Cor.	4	11	.267	4.09	22	22	3	0	0	0	123.1	123	551	68	56	5	7	7	10	56	7	78	7	0
Verdugo, Hugo, Sal.	0	1	.000	6.17	8	2	0	0	6	0	11.2	13	55	9	8	1	1	0	1	8	1	7	3	0
Viano, Jacob, Tig.	0	1	.000	9.00	3	2	0	0	1	0	7.0	8	44	7	7	0	0	1	0	15	0	3	1	0
Villarreal, Antonio, Tor.	4	8	.333	4.47	18	18	0	0	0	0	88.2	101	386	52	44	7	8	1	2	30	1	35	3	0
Villegas, Jose Angel, Agua.	8	5	.615	5.19	39	14	0	0	25	1	104.0	139	475	71	60	3	6	5	3	42	3	35	5	0
Wagner, Hector, Oax.	8	6	.571	3.56	22	21	3	0	1	0	136.2	137	578	62	54	5	9	4	3	50	1	65	2	0
Williams, Jeff, Sal.	2	2	.500	4.78	5	5	0	0	0	0	26.1	30	126	19	14	1	4	0	1	18	2	10	3	0
Young, Ray, Sal.	9	4	.692	2.33	15	15	7	2	0	0	108.0	86	451	39	28	1	9	1	0	58	3	105	10	0
Zamudio, Armando, Lar.	0	0	.000	9.00	5	0	0	0	5	0	4.0	6	22	4	4	0	0	1	0	4	0	1	2	1
Zamudio, Jeovanni, Rey.	4	7	.364	5.40	21	12	0	0	9	0	73.1	97	346	55	44	2	7	0	4	42	3	33	9	1
Zavala, Marco, Tig.	0	1	.000	5.59	27	3	0	0	24	0	29.0	27	145	21	18	3	0	3	1	38	3	22	3	1

COMBINATION SHUTOUTS: A total of 70 combination shutouts were pitched in the Mexican League in 1998. Yucatan led the league with 11.
NO-HIT GAMES: Orozco, Cordoba, defeated Aguascalientes, 5-0, June 26; Vega, Nuevo Laredo, defeated Saltillo, 7-0, August 4.

PITCHERS WITH TWO OR MORE TEAMS

Pitcher, Team	W	L	Pct.	ERA	G	GS	CG	ShO	Rel.	Sv.	IP	H	TBF	R	ER	HR	SH	SF	HB	BB	IBB	SO	WP	Bk.
Acosta, Gerardo, Mex.	2	0	1.000	3.35	20	0	0	0	20	1	43.0	37	186	20	16	3	0	2	3	27	1	13	1	0
Acosta, Gerardo, Oax.	3	4	.429	6.68	15	3	0	0	12	0	31.0	35	152	24	23	1	4	0	3	27	4	14	3	0
Alvarez, Jose Carlos, Tab.	0	1	.000	20.25	2	0	0	0	2	0	1.1	6	12	3	3	2	1	0	1	1	1	0	0	0
Alvarez, Jose Carlos, Can.	0	0	.000	6.43	6	0	0	1	6	0	7.0	12	36	8	5	1	0	1	1	3	1	1	1	0
Barfield, John, Lar.	2	2	.500	4.76	12	0	0	0	12	1	17.0	20	80	12	9	0	1	0	0	12	3	3	2	0
Barfield, John, Tor.	0	1	.000	3.86	7	0	0	1	7	1	7.0	8	34	3	3	1	2	2	1	6	0	4	1	0
Beltran, Alonso, Lar.	4	5	.444	5.46	19	9	0	1	10	2	56.0	58	257	39	34	1	5	4	1	37	2	44	4	1
Beltran, Alonso, Tig.	5	2	.714	6.43	13	7	0	0	6	0	42.0	44	199	34	30	4	3	2	3	31	0	25	0	0
Cabrales, Gabriel, Cor.	0	0	.000	2.70	4	0	0	0	4	0	6.2	10	35	3	2	0	0	0	1	0	2	0	0
Cabrales, Gabriel, Agua.	2	1	.667	2.73	34	0	0	1	34	2	56.0	61	234	20	17	3	5	3	1	21	7	22	3	0
Castaneda, Aurelio, Agua.	0	0	.000	13.50	6	0	0	0	6	0	9.1	16	52	14	14	2	1	2	1	8	0	3	.1	0
Castaneda, Aurelio, Che.	4	6	.400	4.87	23	13	0	1	10	0	92.1	114	415	54	50	4	8	5	9	33	2	32	3	1
Couoh, Enrique, Tig.	3	6	.333	5.52	22	15	0	0	7	2	88.0	101	397	58	54	6	6	2	4	32	1	39	7	0
Couoh, Enrique, Yuc.	2	2	.500	2.28	14	0	0	3	14	1	23.2	22	104	6	6	1	3	1	0	15	2	14	0	0
Garibay, Roberto, Tab.	0	0	.000	4.41	10	0	0	0	10	0	16.1	17	72	8	8	3	2	0	0	9	2	2	3	0
Garibay, Roberto, Sal.	1	1	.500	3.71	5	1	0	0	4	0	17.0	18	72	7	7	0	0	2	0	5	0	5	1	0
Garibay, Salvador, Cam.	0	1	.000	9.28	8	0	0	0	8	0	10.2	18	56	14	11	1	1	1	0	6	0	3	4	0
Garibay, Salvador, Lar.	2	3	.400	3.76	35	0	0	1	35	0	40.2	39	175	19	17	0	4	1	1	20	4	17	5	0
Hernandez, Julio, Sal.	0	1	.000	6.97	3	1	0	0	2	0	10.1	12	48	11	8	1	0	0	1	7	0	2	0	0
Hernandez, Julio, Cor.	1	3	.250	9.73	14	7	1	0	7	0	37.0	60	194	43	40	4	3	3	0	30	3	12	1	0
Hurst, Jonathan, Agua.	0	1	.000	8.10	7	0	0	0	7	1	6.2	9	30	6	6	1	1	0	0	2	1	2	0	0
Hurst, Jonathan, Sal.	1	0	1.000	0.87	10	0	0	0	10	4	10.1	6	47	4	1	0	2	0	1	7	4	10	0	0
Lopez, Jonas, Agua.	0	1	.000	8.44	1	1	0	0	0	0	5.1	8	26	5	5	0	0	0	2	0	3	1	0
Lopez, Jonas, Yuc.	0	0	.000	2.16	2	1	0	0	1	0	8.1	13	40	3	2	0	1	0	4	0	2	0	0
Lopez, Jonas, Tab.	9	2	.818	2.18	23	16	1	1	7	3	107.1	86	432	33	26	2	6	6	1	33	2	17	1	0
Montano, Francisco, Monc.	0	0	.000	0.00	1	1	0	0	0	0	1	4	4	3	0	0	0	0	3	0	0	1	0
Montano, Francisco, Tor.	2	2	.500	6.81	11	10	0	0	1	0	39.2	53	193	40	30	0	3	2	1	20	3	18	2	0
Neri, Braulio, Tab.	0	0	.000	0.00	6	0	0	0	6	0	5.1	6	23	0	0	0	0	0	0	3	0	3	1	0
Neri, Braulio, Agua.	0	0	.000	0.00	5	0	0	0	5	0	4.2	4	28	0	0	0	0	0	1	10	3	0	0
Neri, Braulio, Sal.	0	1	.000	4.73	12	0	0	0	12	0	13.1	13	66	7	7	2	1	0	2	10	2	11	4	0
Parra, Julio Cesar, Tig.	0	0	.000	10.24	14	0	0	0	14	0	9.2	13	52	12	11	2	0	1	2	9	0	9	2	0
Parra, Julio Cesar, Lar.	2	2	.500	1.37	21	0	0	1	21	3	39.1	34	161	9	6	1	1	3	0	17	2	32	4	1
Rivera, E. Paul, Sal.	0	0	.000	4.00	9	0	0	0	9	0	9.0	7	40	7	4	2	0	0	0	6	0	2	1	0
Rivera, E. Paul, Can.	1	0	1.000	4.73	14	0	0	0	14	1	13.1	9	54	8	7	3	0	0	5	0	6	1	0
Saenz, Alfredo, Yuc.	0	1	.000	14.73	3	2	0	0	1	0	3.2	5	22	6	6	0	0	0	7	1	3	0	0
Saenz, Alfredo, Agua.	1	1	.500	6.84	22	1	0	0	21	2	25.0	39	138	31	19	3	0	1	1	16	1	6	2	0
Sanchez, Efrain, Oax.	0	2	.000	6.75	14	0	0	1	14	1	14.2	19	68	13	11	0	2	0	9	1	5	0	0
Sanchez, Efrain, Cam.	2	7	.222	2.91	16	14	1	0	2	0	80.1	96	346	35	26	3	5	4	5	39	4	21	5	0
Sierra, Abel, Oax.	0	0	.000	12.19	8	2	0	0	6	0	10.1	20	59	16	14	0	1	0	10	1	3	0	0
Sierra, Abel, Che.	0	0	.000	5.54	5	1	0	0	4	0	13.0	15	61	8	8	1	1	2	1	10	0	4	0	0
Velazquez, Ernesto, Yuc.	2	1	.667	3.50	21	0	0	3	21	0	36.0	36	151	16	14	2	2	4	1	15	4	9	1	0
Velazquez, Ernesto, Tor.	0	0	.000	4.76	5	0	0	0	5	0	5.2	4	21	3	3	0	0	0	1	0	4	0	0
Villarreal, Antonio, Tor.	2	7	.222	5.69	13	13	0	0	0	0	61.2	82	277	41	39	7	5	1	1	23	1	23	1	0
Villarreal, Antonio, Yuc.	2	1	.667	1.67	5	5	0	1	0	0	27.0	19	109	11	5	0	3	0	1	7	0	12	2	0

TEAM

Team	Pct.	G	PO	A	E	TC	DP	PB	Team	Pct.	G	PO	A	E	TC	DP	PB
Monterrey	.983	120	3195	1383	81	4659	117	3	Torreon	.971	122	3188	1572	143	4903	159	11
M.C. Reds	.978	122	3202	1511	106	4819	132	9	Saltillo	.970	121	3177	1480	144	4801	140	11
Monclova	.977	122	3239	1407	108	4754	142	9	Cordoba	.970	121	3080	1290	133	4503	119	2
M.C. Tigers	.977	121	3249	1469	113	4831	161	8	Aguascalientes	.968	121	3083	1425	149	4657	135	7
Chetumal	.977	119	3041	1413	105	4559	114	7	Oaxaca	.968	119	3093	1465	150	4708	173	7
Tabasco	.976	122	3187	1512	116	4815	106	1	Campeche	.968	120	3139	1461	152	4752	131	11
Cancun	.976	121	3155	1446	114	4715	138	10	Reynosa	.967	122	3200	1461	161	4822	139	14
Nuevo Laredo	.974	122	3176	1353	122	4651	145	14									
Yucatan	.973	121	3185	1453	128	4766	112	12									

TRIPLE PLAYS: Campeche 2, Monclova 2, Oaxaca, Tabasco, Torreon, Yucatan.

INDIVIDUAL

Note: Fielding statistics for multiple-team players are not broken down by teams. Teams listed in fielding are last clubs played by fielders.

FIRST BASEMEN

Player, Team	Pct.	G	PO	A	E	TC	DP
Aganza, Ruben, Monc.	.994	115	1067	72	7	1146	114
Almeida, Shammar, Agua.	1.000	5	15	2	0	17	1
Arano, Wilfrido, Lar.	1.000	1	3	0	0	3	0
Arvizu, Javier, Cor.	.988	69	548	44	7	599	60
Avila, Roberto, Cor.	.986	16	67	6	1	74	8
Avila, Ruben, Tor.	.987	87	843	52	12	907	95
Avilez, L. Alejandro, Sal.	1.000	7	21	4	0	25	3
Azocar, Oscar, Che.	.991	97	944	67	9	1020	86
Beltran, Gerardo, Cor.	1.000	3	26	1	0	27	3
Bryant, Scott, Can.	.989	32	327	26	4	357	35
Cabrera, Alexander, Tig.	.994	115	1103	88	7	1198	144
Carrillo, Matias, Tig.	1.000	3	11	0	0	11	1
Castaeda, Rafael, Oax.	.968	4	28	2	1	31	8
Castareda, Hector, Cor.	.990	22	177	12	2	191	13
Castellano, Pedro O., Mex.	.993	55	518	49	4	571	60
Cervantes, Ivan, Rey.	1.000	1	0	1	0	1	0
Cervantes, Refugio, Lar.	.977	6	41	1	1	43	2
Chamberlain, Wes, Cor.	.974	18	132	15	4	151	14
Clark, Tim, Yuc.	.987	62	569	61	8	638	54
Cobos, Rogelio, Cam.	1.000	1	1	0	0	1	0
Diaz, Luis Fernando, Agua.	.979	8	43	3	1	47	2
Durazo, Erubiel, Mont.	1.000	21	192	11	0	203	12
Espino, Daniel, Mont.	1.000	3	10	2	0	12	1
Espino, Omar, Lar.	1.000	11	41	2	0	43	7
Espinoza, E. Javier, Can.	1.000	2	8	1	0	9	1
Espinoza, Ramon, Mex.	1.000	1	6	0	0	6	0
Fornes, Daniel, Rey.	1.000	6	44	1	0	45	6
Gainer, Jay, Agua.	.992	98	921	83	8	1012	107
Garcia, Omar, Can.	.992	25	223	13	2	238	22
Gavia, Jesus, Yuc.	1.000	10	45	2	0	47	7
Gonzalez, Denio, Tab.	.993	82	840	64	6	910	59
Gonzalez, Jesus, Monc.	.986	9	63	5	1	69	12
Gregg, Tommy, Mex.	1.000	10	77	8	0	85	10
Guerrero, Jaime, Che.	1.000	2	4	0	0	4	1
Harrera, Nelson, Oax.	1.000	5	41	5	0	46	4
Hazlet, Steve, Cor.	1.000	7	58	7	0	65	5
Iturbe Salas, Pedro, Tig.	1.000	4	21	2	0	23	2
Leyva, German, Sal.	1.000	9	58	3	0	61	7
Lopez, Gonzalo, Monc.	1.000	1	7	0	0	7	1
Loredo, Jorge Luis, Cam.	1.000	1	10	0	0	10	2
Lydy, Scott, Oax.	1.000	2	9	3	0	12	1
Machiria, Pablo, Agua.	.988	67	612	26	8	646	60
Magallanes, Roberto, Can.	.975	23	222	11	6	239	23
Marrero, Orestes, Sal.	.982	52	360	31	7	398	41
Meggers, Mike, Che.	1.000	2	18	1	0	19	1
Michel, Domingo, Yuc.	.995	106	1005	56	5	1066	91
Minjarez, Francisco, Agua.	1.000	1	2	0	0	2	1
Munoz, Jose, Rey.	.985	8	62	4	1	67	7
Ochoa, Ariel, Cam.	1.000	2	2	0	0	2	0
Ochoa, Edgar, Agua.	.947	3	16	2	1	19	1
Ojeda, Miguel, Mex.	1.000	13	53	10	0	63	4
Orantes, Ramon, Agua.	.991	15	99	6	1	106	11
Ortega, Antonio, Oax.	1.000	1	1	0	0	1	0
Ortiz, Alejandro, Lar.	.995	43	343	22	2	367	39
Paez, Raul, Mex.	.997	66	562	43	2	607	48
Payro, Edison, Can.	1.000	3	22	0	0	22	2
Pecorilli, Aldo, Cam.	.990	11	89	11	1	101	11
Peguero, Julio, Tab.	.990	31	285	23	3	311	13
Pena, Luis A., Che.	1.000	4	8	1	0	9	1
Perez, Francisco, Oax.	.929	2	12	1	1	14	0
Pough, Clyde C., Oax.	.992	55	484	38	4	526	74

Player, Team	Pct.	G	PO	A	E	TC	DP
Ramon, Reyes, Tab.	.980	5	45	3	1	49	3
Ravem, Luis, Monc.	1.000	7	61	7	0	68	7
Robles, Gerardo, Oax.	1.000	1	0	2	0	2	0
Robles, Ricardo, Can.	1.000	4	39	4	0	43	4
Rodriguez, Armando, Tig.	.978	5	41	4	1	46	2
Rojas, Francisco, Tab.	1.000	26	116	10	0	126	12
Romero, Marco Antonio, Yuc.	.992	28	248	6	2	256	28
Salinas, Rogelio, Yuc.	1.000	5	26	1	0	27	2
Sanchez, Gerardo, Lar.	.994	41	293	33	2	328	36
Sanchez, Roque, Cam.	1.000	6	52	1	0	53	4
Saucedo, Roberto, Mont.	1.000	1	2	0	0	2	1
Sievers, Carlos, Yuc.	1.000	2	1	1	0	2	1
Smith, Charles, Mont.	.989	12	83	10	1	94	11
Stark, Matt, Tor.	.933	1	13	1	1	15	3
Tejeda, Arturo, Lar.	1.000	4	7	0	0	7	0
Torres, Eduardo, Sal.	1.000	3	15	2	0	17	1
Tredaway, Chard, Yuc.	.968	4	28	2	1	31	2
Valdez, Jesus, Cam.	.993	33	271	28	2	301	32
Valdez, Ramon, Cor.	1.000	1	2	0	0	2	0
Valdez IIa, Emmanuel, Tig.	1.000	1	4	0	0	4	0
Valenzuela, Armando, Sal.	1.000	2	11	0	0	11	1
Valenzuela, Eduardo, Sal.	.990	23	181	9	2	192	13
Valenzuela, Horacio, Sal.	.992	48	370	22	3	395	44
Vazquez, P. Jorge Daniel, Mont.	1.000	1	4	1	0	5	0
VELAZQUEZ, Guillermo, Mont.	.999	91	812	78	1	891	81
Velez, Manuel, Tab.	1.000	1	2	0	0	2	0
Villanueva, Hector, Lar.	1.000	37	311	18	0	329	40
Villarreal, Alejandro, Lar.	1.000	1	4	0	0	4	0
Yan, Julian, Rey.	.990	111	1067	77	12	1156	116
Young, Ray, Sal.	1.000	1	3	0	0	3	2
Zambrano, Roberto, Can.	.998	58	559	25	1	585	57
Zamudio, Rafael, Tor.	.991	42	306	22	3	331	37
Zazueta, Juan Carlos, Tor.	1.000	11	85	10	0	95	4

TRIPLE PLAYS: Aganza, Clark, Gainer, Michel, Zamudio.

SECOND BASEMEN

Player, Team	Pct.	G	PO	A	E	TC	DP
Arano, Eloy, Mex.	.968	45	107	103	7	217	28
Armenta, Guillermo, Che.	.980	36	84	112	4	200	24
Arredondo, Hernan, Can.	.944	7	6	11	1	18	2
Avila, Roberto, Cor.	.971	7	13	21	1	35	11
Bustillos, Luis, Rey.	.964	26	51	56	4	111	16
Carrasco, Ernesto, Lar.	.983	65	169	178	6	353	49
Castellano, Pedro O., Mex.	.978	42	85	135	5	225	23
Castro, Domingo, Tig.	1.000	3	7	5	0	12	2
Castro Acosta, Arnoildo, Can.	.987	116	333	357	9	699	86
Diaz, Pedro, Agua.	1.000	1	1	2	0	3	0
Escalante, Marcelo, Sal.	1.000	1	2	1	0	3	0
Esquer, Ramon, Oax.	.962	115	318	394	28	740	126
Estrella, Isaac, Lar.	.882	7	16	14	4	34	4
Facundo Zapot, Armando, Tab.	.971	24	31	71	3	105	16
Felix, Jesus Arturo, Yuc.	1.000	1	1	1	0	2	1
Flores, Miguel, Mont.	.977	97	268	253	12	533	62
Gama, Ricardo, Yuc.	.984	31	99	90	3	192	23
Garcia, Carlos Miguel, Tab.	.952	7	10	10	1	21	2
Gastelum, Sergio Omar, Tig.	.952	50	164	151	16	331	41
Gonzalez Garcia, Roman, Cor.	.976	49	117	84	5	206	23
Guerrero, Jaime, Che.	1.000	2	4	5	0	9	0
Hernandez, B. Cesar, Tor.	1.000	1	0	1	0	1	0
Iturbe, Pedro, Tig.	1.000	1	1	1	0	2	0
Linares, Rigoberto, Cor.	1.000	11	23	27	0	50	3
Lopez, Fabian, Oax.	.941	13	29	19	3	51	11

Player, Team	Pct.	G	PO	A	E	TC	DP
Lopez, Gonzalo, Monc.	.917	6	11	11	2	24	3
Loredo, Jorge Luis, Cam.	.961	47	142	131	11	284	36
Marrujo, Hector, Tab.	1.000	2	4	9	0	13	1
Martinez, Abel, Can.	.900	2	4	5	1	10	2
Martinez, Grimaldo, Monc.	.987	102	300	293	8	601	92
Martinez, Luis C., Sal.	.986	16	28	41	1	70	8
Mendoza, Omar, Lar.	1.000	1	1	1	0	2	1
MERE, Pedro, Che.	.988	93	252	261	6	519	65
Minjarez, Francisco, Agua.	.947	11	11	7	1	19	2
Montaaez, M. Daniel, Can.	1.000	4	5	7	0	12	3
Morales, Florentino, Lar.	.972	76	168	147	9	324	42
Morejon, Oswaldo, Yuc.	.979	95	241	270	11	522	60
Munoz, Jose, Rey.	.984	99	247	316	9	572	75
Parra, Frank, Cor.	.958	75	197	193	17	407	55
Perez, Alfredo, Cam.	.976	19	34	47	2	83	6
Quintero, Alan, Yuc.	1.000	1	2	0	0	2	0
Quintero, Guillermo, Mont.	.970	25	43	54	3	100	18
Ramirez, Jesus, Che.	1.000	1	5	0	0	5	0
Rivera Tapia, Jesus Manuel, Tab.	1.000	2	0	1	0	1	0
Roa, Hector, Cam.	.970	73	212	234	14	460	63
Robles, Gerardo, Oax.	1.000	2	1	0	0	1	0
Robles Acura, Trinidad, Tig.	1.000	4	7	5	0	12	1
Rodriguez, Hector Jesus, Mex.	1.000	1	3	6	0	9	2
Rodriguez, Jr. Aurelio, Tab.	1.000	13	39	37	0	76	5
Sanchez, Armando, Mont.	1.000	8	5	6	0	11	0
Sanchez, Orlando, Mont.	1.000	11	22	20	0	42	5
Sanchez, Roque, Cam.	.989	33	84	102	2	188	32
Soto, Saul, Rey.	1.000	2	9	2	0	11	1
Trapaga, Julio Miguel, Tig.	.969	75	193	208	13	414	70
Valenzuela, Irving, Monc.	.964	20	58	50	4	112	8
Valle, Jorge Luis, Tor.	1.000	1	0	3	0	3	0
Valle, Roberto, Tor.	1.000	1	1	2	0	3	1
Vela, Manuel, Rey.	1.000	9	17	28	0	45	5
Velez, Manuel, Tab.	.983	86	240	279	9	528	57
Verdugo, Sostenes, Yuc.	1.000	5	3	3	0	6	0
Verdugo, Vicente, Sal.	.980	110	302	329	13	644	91
Villarreal, Alejandro, Lar.	1.000	1	4	1	0	5	0
Vizcarra, Marco Antonio, Sal.	.932	15	19	22	3	44	8
Vizcarra, Roberto, Agua.	.981	109	286	339	12	637	92
Wong, Julian, Che.	.990	22	47	52	1	100	14
Zazueta, Juan Carlos, Tor.	.982	12	24	31	1	56	5
Zazueta, Mauricio, Tor.	.983	113	315	424	13	752	118

TRIPLE PLAYS: G. Martinez 2, Esquer, Roa, Morejon.

THIRD BASEMEN

Player, Team	Pct.	G	PO	A	E	TC	DP
Aguilar, Enrique, Cor.	.936	37	23	80	7	110	8
Arano, Eloy, Mex.	.947	48	38	105	8	151	5
Armenta, Guillermo, Che.	.885	8	8	15	3	26	1
Arredondo, Hernan, Can.	1.000	2	0	1	0	1	1
Avila, Roberto, Cor.	1.000	2	2	0	0	2	0
Avilez, L. Alejandro, Sal.	.833	4	1	4	1	6	0
Beltran, Juan, Cam.	.000	2	0	0	1	1	1
Bojorquez, Victor, Rey.	1.000	1	2	0	0	2	0
Bruno Marte, Julio, Tab.	.943	119	89	289	23	401	14
Bryant, Scott, Can.	.921	10	7	28	3	38	3
Camacho, Reginaldo, Rey.	.921	88	66	157	19	242	18
Carrasco, Ernesto, Lar.	.960	32	35	60	4	99	10
Castaneda, Rafael, Oax.	.941	109	100	251	22	373	33
Castellano, Pedro O., Mex.	1.000	4	0	6	0	6	0
Cedillo, Said, Can.	1.000	6	1	4	0	5	0
Cervera, Francisco, Cam.	.927	44	41	111	12	164	11
Cruz, Luis Alfonso, Rey.	1.000	1	1	0	0	1	0
De La Cruz, Hector, Che.	1.000	1	0	1	0	1	0
Diaz, Pedro, Agua.	.926	31	14	49	5	68	2
Estrella, Isaac, Lar.	.778	1	1	6	2	9	1
Felix, Junior, Tor.	1.000	1	2	2	0	4	0
Figueroa, Federico, Cam.	1.000	3	1	4	0	5	1
Garcia, Carlos Miguel, Tab.	1.000	2	0	1	0	1	1
Gastelum, Sergio Omar, Tig.	.971	9	8	25	1	34	1
Guerrero, Francisco, Monc.	1.000	11	8	11	0	19	2
Guerrero, Jaime, Che.	.963	38	25	80	4	109	8
Hernandez, Cesar, Yuc.	1.000	1	2	0	0	2	0
Hyzdu, Adam, Mont.	.333	1	1	0	2	3	1
Jimenez, Alfonso, Che.	.961	36	31	91	5	127	9
Leyva, German, Sal.	.924	102	86	204	24	314	23
Lopez, Fabian, Oax.	.947	15	7	29	2	38	3
Lopez, Gonzalo, Monc.	1.000	4	3	5	0	8	1
Loredo, Jorge Luis, Cam.	.933	25	21	63	6	90	7
Magallanes, Ever, Mont.	.954	94	95	196	14	305	21
Magallanes, Roberto, Can.	.950	42	25	108	7	140	11
Malpica, Enrique, Che.	.906	42	34	81	12	127	11

Player, Team	Pct.	G	PO	A	E	TC	DP
Marcano, Raul, Che.	1.000	1	1	1	0	2	0
Marrujo, Hector, Tab.	1.000	1	1	1	0	2	0
Martinez, Abel, Can.	.917	36	20	46	6	72	5
Martinez, Enrique, Agua.	1.000	1	1	0	0	1	0
Martinez, Ray, Mex.	.948	119	92	251	19	362	20
Meggers, Mike, Che.	1.000	1	0	3	0	3	0
Minjarez, Francisco, Agua.	.900	17	11	16	3	30	3
Montalvo, Ivan Vladimir, Tig.	.953	66	82	140	11	233	15
Montanez, M. Daniel, Can.	1.000	2	2	1	0	3	0
Morejon, Oswaldo, Yuc.	1.000	5	0	8	0	8	0
Munoz, Jose, Rey.	.881	13	11	26	5	42	0
Nava, Lipson, Can.	.333	1	0	1	2	3	0
Orantes, Ramon, Agua.	.922	90	64	171	20	255	28
Ortiz, Alejandro, Lar.	.964	35	33	47	3	83	9
Parra, Frank, Cor.	1.000	2	0	2	0	2	0
Pecorilli, Aldo, Cam.	.895	8	6	11	2	19	0
Perez, Alfredo, Cam.	.800	17	9	23	8	40	1
Perez, Juan Luis, Tor.	1.000	7	7	8	0	15	1
Quintero, Guillermo, Mont.	.923	9	1	11	1	13	1
Ramirez, Jesus, Che.	1.000	1	2	0	0	2	0
Roa, Hector, Cam.	.833	3	1	9	2	12	1
Robles, Trinidad, Tig.	.960	51	39	130	7	176	17
Rodriguez, Hector Jesus, Mex.	1.000	4	1	8	0	9	0
Rodriguez, Jr. Aurelio, Tab.	.900	3	2	7	1	10	0
Rojas, Francisco, Tab.	1.000	2	0	5	0	5	0
Romero, Oscar, Monc.	.946	111	112	241	20	373	24
RUIZ, Juan De Dios, Cor.	.955	90	63	212	13	288	25
Sanchez, Armando, Mont.	.857	8	4	8	2	14	1
Sanchez, Gerardo, Lar.	1.000	1	0	1	0	1	0
Sanchez, Orlando, Mont.	1.000	6	4	4	0	8	1
Sanchez, Roque, Cam.	.957	24	28	61	4	93	3
Saucedo, Roberto, Mont.	1.000	1	1	0	0	1	0
Smith, Charles, Mont.	.946	22	13	40	3	56	11
Tredaway, Chard, Yuc.	.910	103	83	252	33	368	20
Valdez, Ramon, Cor.	1.000	1	1	0	0	1	0
Valle, Cosme, Rey.	.887	35	25	69	12	106	4
Valle, Jorge Luis, Tor.	.944	83	77	194	16	287	26
Velez, Manuel, Tab.	.929	4	4	9	1	14	1
Verdugo, Sostenes, Yuc.	.667	3	0	4	2	6	0
Villarreal, Alejandro, Lar.	.932	69	60	118	13	191	11
Villarreal, Salvador, Rey.	1.000	1	0	1	0	1	0
Vizcarra, Marco Antonio, Sal.	.975	38	32	84	3	119	7
Wong, Julian, Che.	1.000	15	5	23	0	28	2
Zazueta, Juan Carlos, Tor.	.949	36	26	85	6	117	17

TRIPLE PLAYS: Romero, Sanchez, Tredaway.

SHORTSTOPS

Player, Team	Pct.	G	PO	A	E	TC	DP
Arano, Eloy, Mex.	.926	7	8	17	2	27	4
Arano, Wilfrido, Lar.	1.000	1	1	0	0	1	0
Armenta, Guillermo, Che.	.983	27	28	89	2	119	13
Arredondo, Jesus, Agua.	.962	118	206	409	24	639	79
Avilez, L Alejandro, Sal.	.932	14	23	32	4	59	10
Beltran, Juan, Cam.	.933	3	4	10	1	15	2
Bustillos, Luis, Rey.	.955	90	190	296	23	509	68
Carrasco, Ernesto, Lar.	.906	15	18	30	5	53	9
Castareda, Rafael, Oax.	1.000	1	1	3	0	4	0
Castro, Domingo, Tig.	1.000	3	0	2	0	2	1
Cervantes, Ivan, Rey.	.884	37	55	97	20	172	21
Cervera, Francisco, Cam.	.902	8	13	24	4	41	3
Claudio, O. Patricio, Tab.	1.000	1	2	0	0	2	0
Diaz, Pedro, Agua.	1.000	2	2	0	0	2	0
Diaz, Remigio, Mont.	.978	115	178	365	12	555	59
Duran, Felipe, Oax.	.945	63	75	148	13	236	42
Felix, Jesus Arturo, Yuc.	.915	17	18	36	5	59	3
Felix Reza, Lauro, Oax.	.904	52	80	164	26	270	45
Garcia, Carlos Miguel, Tab.	.913	6	8	13	2	23	0
GARCIA, Heriberto, Che.	.980	107	183	351	11	545	64
Gomez, Heber, Tab.	.951	111	181	377	29	587	65
Gonzalez, Roman, Cor.	.750	1	0	3	1	4	0
Guerrero, Francisco, Monc.	.970	78	128	265	12	405	55
Guerrero, Jaime, Che.	1.000	5	9	11	0	20	2
Guizar, Hector, Monc.	.948	111	227	392	34	653	83
Hernandez, B.Cesar, Tor.	.900	2	3	6	1	10	0
Hernandez, Julio Cesar, Lar.	.945	118	218	361	34	613	83
Jimenez, Alfonso, Can.	1.000	1	1	5	0	6	1
Jones, Ron, Sal.	.800	1	4	4	2	10	0
Lopez, Fabian, Oax.	.943	35	38	77	7	122	23
Loredo, Jorge Luis, Cam.	1.000	2	2	3	0	5	0
Magara, Gabriel, Yuc.	1.000	4	1	2	0	3	0
Marrujo, Hector, Tab.	.889	5	3	5	1	9	0
Martinez, Abel, Can.	1.000	1	2	1	0	3	1

Player, Team	Pct.	G	PO	A	E	TC	DP
Martinez, Enrique, Agua.	1.000	1	3	0	0	3	0
Martinez, Luis C., Sal.	.985	12	21	46	1	68	9
Mendoza, Omar, Lar.	1.000	1	0	1	0	1	0
Minjarez, Francisco, Agua.	1.000	5	0	3	0	3	0
Montarez, M. Daniel, Can.	1.000	12	6	7	0	13	0
Morales, Florentino, Lar.	1.000	1	3	0	0	3	0
Morejon, Oswaldo, Yuc.	1.000	1	0	1	0	1	0
Olvera, Sergio, Cam.	.957	43	77	101	8	186	20
Orantes, Ramon, Agua.	1.000	1	0	3	0	3	0
Pacho, Juan Jose, Yuc.	.971	118	207	387	18	612	71
Parra, Frank, Cor.	.953	12	15	26	2	43	2
Patron, Damian, Oax.	1.000	4	4	4	0	8	2
Perez, Alfredo, Cam.	1.000	12	7	21	0	28	2
Quintero, Edgar, Mont.	1.000	1	0	1	0	1	0
Quintero, Guillermo, Mont.	.925	16	11	26	3	40	2
Ramirez Ulloa, Enrique, Can.	.957	119	205	373	26	604	78
Robles, Gerardo, Oax.	1.000	5	4	2	0	6	2
Robles Acura, Javier, Tig.	.966	87	164	291	16	471	70
Robles Acura, Trinidad, Tig.	.985	40	68	130	3	201	34
Rodriguez, Jr. Aurelio, Tab.	.870	6	7	13	3	23	0
Ruiz Lara, Juan De Dios, Cor.	.940	17	42	52	6	100	8
Salas, Heriberto, Tor.	.957	101	175	365	24	564	85
Sanchez, Armando, Mont.	1.000	1	0	1	0	1	0
Sanchez, Orlando, Mont.	1.000	4	1	2	0	3	0
Sanchez, Roque, Cam.	1.000	1	1	2	0	3	0
Sandoval, Jose Luis, Mex.	.964	105	187	373	21	581	79
Trapaga, Julio Miguel, Tig.	1.000	1	0	1	0	1	0
Valenzuela, Armando, Sal.	.961	52	85	163	10	258	36
Valenzuela, Irving, Monc.	.962	9	8	17	1	26	3
Valle, Jorge Luis, Tor.	.942	19	40	58	6	104	14
Valle, Jose Luis, Cor.	.948	93	171	271	24	466	57
Valle, Roberto, Tor.	.333	2	1	0	2	3	0
Vela, Manuel, Rey.	.810	22	12	22	8	42	4
Velez, Manuel, Tab.	.833	1	3	2	1	6	0
Verdugo, Sostenes, Yuc.	.944	8	7	10	1	18	0
Villarreal, Alejandro, Lar.	1.000	1	2	1	0	3	0
Vizcarra, Marco Antonio, Sal.	.966	58	91	165	9	265	38
Vizcarra, Roberto, Agua.	1.000	1	2	1	0	3	0
Wong, Julian, Che.	.893	13	7	18	3	28	3
Zazueta, Juan Carlos, Tor.	.935	7	9	20	2	31	4

TRIPLE PLAYS: Guizar, Jor. Valle.

OUTFIELDERS

Player, Team	Pct.	G	PO	A	E	TC	DP
Abrego, Jesus, Rey.	.943	75	124	8	8	140	0
Acura, Jose Luis, Tor.	1.000	19	18	1	0	19	0
Aguilar, Mario, Cam.	1.000	1	2	0	0	2	0
Aguilera, Antonio, Cam.	.977	100	158	10	4	172	2
Aguilera, Armando, Sal.	1.000	5	8	0	0	8	0
Alvarez, Hector, Oax.	.981	108	240	14	5	259	2
Alvarez, Heriberto, Cam.	1.000	7	8	2	0	10	1
Amaro, Gerardo, Rey.	.991	60	104	10	1	115	2
Arano, Wilfrido, Lar.	.982	97	151	15	3	169	3
Armenta, Fernando, Yuc.	.981	25	49	3	1	53	0
Arredondo, Luis, Yuc.	.974	119	244	14	7	265	2
Attwell, Sergio, Cam.	.975	42	71	6	2	79	1
Bojorquez, Victor, Rey.	.973	107	201	16	6	223	4
Briggs, Stoney, Cor.	.983	71	169	6	3	178	1
Bruno, Julio, Tab.	1.000	1	1	0	0	1	0
Bryant, Scott, Can.	1.000	1	1	0	0	1	0
Cabrera, Alexander, Tig.	1.000	1	2	0	0	2	0
Canizales, Juan Carlos, Mont.	.963	70	98	6	4	108	0
Carrillo, Matias, Tig.	.991	110	213	7	2	222	0
Carter, Michael, Tor.	.965	112	232	17	9	258	3
Castillo, Juan, Rey.	.917	13	11	0	1	12	0
Castillo, Juan, Rey.	1.000	6	10	0	0	10	0
Chamberlain, Wes, Cor.	.968	16	30	0	1	31	0
Chan, Armando, Monc.	1.000	14	24	1	0	25	1
Chance, Tony, Monc.	.990	41	94	4	1	99	0
CLAUDIO, Patricio, Tab.	.994	116	310	7	2	319	2
Cole, Alex, Mont.	.979	87	178	6	4	188	1
Cruz, Luis Alfonso, Rey.	.941	92	161	16	11	188	3
Cuevas, Jorge, Agua.	.955	54	82	2	4	88	0
De La Cruz, Hector, Che.	.944	52	95	6	6	107	0
De Lima, Rafael, Cor.	.960	107	189	5	8	202	0
Diaz, Luis Fernando, Agua.	.971	84	134	2	4	140	0
Dominguez, J. David, Can.	.972	74	134	7	4	145	3
Durazo, Erubiel, Mont.	1.000	63	107	4	0	111	0
Escalante, Marcelo, Sal.	1.000	26	46	3	0	49	0
Espino, Daniel, Mont.	1.000	27	20	1	0	21	0
Espino, Omar, Lar.	.958	48	61	7	3	71	3
Espinoza, E. Javier, Can.	1.000	67	110	3	0	113	0

Player, Team	Pct.	G	PO	A	E	TC	DP
Espinoza, Jose M., Lar.	.988	86	165	6	2	173	0
Espinoza, Ramon, Mex.	.976	121	226	13	6	245	2
Felix, Jesus Arturo, Yuc.	1.000	1	2	0	0	2	0
Felix, Jose Domingo, Tab.	.964	15	26	1	1	28	0
Felix, Junior, Tor.	.972	55	97	8	3	108	2
Fentanes, Oscar, Tab.	.956	105	188	8	9	205	1
Fernandez, Daniel, Mex.	.986	86	196	8	3	207	1
Figueroa, Federico, Cam.	1.000	4	3	1	0	4	0
Figueroa, Marcos, Cor.	.983	32	58	1	1	60	0
Figueroa, Ricardo, Cam.	1.000	1	3	1	0	4	0
Fornes, Daniel, Rey.	1.000	11	16	2	0	18	1
Garcia, Cornelio, Tor.	.965	64	107	2	4	113	0
Garcia, Francisco, Mex.	1.000	1	2	0	0	2	0
Garcia, Hector, Mont.	.983	70	109	4	2	115	1
Garcia, Omar, Can.	.967	21	28	1	1	30	0
Gastelum, Sergio Omar, Tig.	.986	33	69	3	1	73	1
Gonzalez, Jose, Yuc.	.953	105	238	13	11	262	1
Gordon, Keith, Can.	1.000	13	20	0	0	20	0
Grego, Tommy, Mex.	.975	44	75	4	2	81	1
Hazlet, Steve, Cor.	1.000	5	9	0	0	9	0
Hernandez, Cesar, Yuc.	.959	42	105	12	5	122	3
Hyzdu, Adam, Mont.	1.000	31	74	6	0	80	0
Iturbe, Pedro, Tig.	.981	90	145	11	3	159	0
Jimenez, Eduardo, Mex.	.973	66	103	4	3	110	0
Leal, Guadalupe, Cam.	.962	71	119	8	5	132	3
Longmire, Tony, Yuc.	1.000	6	14	0	0	14	0
Lopez, Fabian, Oax.	1.000	5	3	0	0	3	0
Lopez, Gonzalo, Monc.	1.000	33	65	4	0	69	0
Loredo, Jorge Luis, Cam.	1.000	3	1	0	0	1	0
Luque Gonzalez, Raul, Tab.	1.000	2	3	0	0	3	0
Lydy, Scott, Oax.	1.000	23	28	0	0	28	0
Machiria, Pablo, Agua.	1.000	22	25	1	0	26	0
Magana, Raul, Yuc.	1.000	1	1	0	0	1	0
Marcano, Raul, Che.	.955	11	21	0	1	22	0
Marrero, Orestes, Sal.	.989	64	84	4	1	89	1
Martinez, Abel, Can.	1.000	5	5	0	0	5	0
Martinez, Enrique, Agua.	.970	63	121	9	4	134	2
Mashore, Justine, Che.	.946	15	34	1	2	37	0
Mata, Noe, Che.	1.000	17	21	1	0	22	0
Medina, Jose Ramon, Monc.	.962	109	236	18	10	264	2
Meggers, Mike, Che.	.975	64	112	4	3	119	1
Mendez, Roberto Carlos, Oax.	.962	117	194	6	8	208	2
Meza, Gonzalo, Mex.	.981	53	53	0	1	54	0
Minjarez, Francisco, Agua.	.667	5	1	1	1	3	0
Montarez, M. Daniel, Can.	1.000	2	1	0	0	1	0
Moreno, David, Tab.	1.000	11	10	0	0	10	0
Moreno, Leonardo, Oax.	.983	68	109	5	2	116	2
Morones, Martin, Che.	.946	78	118	4	7	129	2
Mulligan, Sean, Cor.	.954	29	60	2	3	65	2
Munoz, Jose De Jesus, Sal.	.966	105	262	19	10	291	4
Ochoa, Ariel, Cam.	1.000	3	1	0	0	1	0
Ojeda, Miguel, Mex.	.958	18	22	1	1	24	0
Olvera, Sergio, Cam.	1.000	3	1	0	0	1	0
Orozco, Carlos, Agua.	1.000	4	1	0	0	1	0
Ortega, Antonio, Oax.	1.000	8	4	0	0	4	0
Pagano, Scott, Can.	.951	33	72	6	4	82	3
Parra, Frank, Cor.	1.000	12	28	2	0	30	1
Payro, Edison, Can.	.977	114	244	14	6	264	2
Peguero, Julio, Tab.	1.000	68	149	8	0	157	2
Pegues, Ron, Sal.	.948	38	54	1	3	58	1
Pena, Luis A., Che.	1.000	1	2	0	0	2	0
Pennyteather, Will, Rey.	.974	22	36	2	1	39	0
Perez, Francisco, Oax.	.962	56	73	2	3	78	0
Perez, Juan Luis, Tor.	1.000	3	2	0	0	2	0
Polonia, Luis, Tig.	.962	42	73	2	3	78	1
Quintero, Alan, Yuc.	.979	76	139	3	3	145	0
Quintero, Edgar, Mont.	.979	39	43	3	1	47	0
Quintero, Guillermo, Mont.	.857	6	6	0	1	7	0
Ramirez, Jesus, Che.	.980	79	140	8	3	151	0
Ramirez, Roberto, Agua.	.946	117	263	19	16	298	5
Ramon, Reyes, Tab.	.978	50	84	7	2	93	1
Ratliff, Darryl, Cam.	.989	37	89	1	1	91	0
Renteral,, Jose M., Cor.	1.000	7	8	0	0	8	0
Riley, Marquis, Agua.	1.000	17	31	0	0	31	0
Robles, Gerardo, Oax.	1.000	2	1	0	0	1	0
Rodriguez, Boi, Monc.	.976	66	116	4	3	123	1
Rodriguez, Fernando, Cor.	.965	105	181	12	7	200	3
Rodriguez, Hector Jesus, Mex.	1.000	4	1	0	0	1	0
Rubio, Sergio, Yuc.	.964	40	51	2	2	55	0
Saenz, Ricardo, Monc.	.970	69	119	9	4	132	2
Sanchez, Gerardo, Lar.	.972	77	134	7	4	145	4
Sanchez, Raul, Can.	.949	76	125	5	7	137	2

Player, Team	Pct.	G	PO	A	E	TC	DP
Sandoval, Octavio Augusto, Tig.	.981	69	99	5	2	106	2
Santana, Ivan, Tab.	1.000	1	2	0	0	2	0
Sherman, Darrell, Monc.	.977	94	249	1	6	256	0
Sievers, Carlos, Yuc.	1.000	2	1	0	0	1	0
Smith, Charles, Mont.	.972	52	66	4	2	72	0
Soriano, Ricardo, Tor.	1.000	19	25	1	0	26	0
Suarez, Luis Mauricio, Tig.	.933	62	81	3	6	90	0
Tejeda, Arturo, Lar.	1.000	9	6	1	0	7	0
Tellez, Alonso, Rey.	1.000	1	4	0	0	4	0
Tiquet, Lazaro, Tab.	.750	11	6	0	2	8	0
Torreseduardo, Eduardo, Sal.	.984	33	56	4	1	61	0
Valdez, Jesus, Cam.	.953	66	117	6	6	129	0
Valdez, Ramon, Cor.	.972	78	199	8	6	213	0
Valencia, Carlos, Tab.	.989	68	89	5	1	95	1
Valenzuela, Irving, Monc.	.933	7	13	1	1	15	0
Valle, Jorge Luis, Tor.	1.000	9	9	1	0	10	0
Valrie, Kerry, Yuc.	.983	24	55	2	1	58	0
Vazquez, P. Jorge Daniel, Monc.	1.000	16	28	2	0	30	0
Vega, Jorge, Agua.	1.000	1	3	0	0	3	0
Villarreal, Alejandro, Lar.	1.000	1	2	0	0	2	0
Villarreal, Salvador, Rey.	.962	32	24	1	1	26	0
Villegas, Fernando, Sal.	.956	87	124	7	6	137	2
Whiten, Mark, Che.	.973	41	71	2	2	75	0
Yuriar, Jesus, Yuc.	.990	42	92	4	1	97	0
Zambrano, Roberto, Can.	.852	32	45	1	8	54	0
Zamudio, Rafael, Tor.	.955	48	58	5	3	66	1

TRIPLE PLAYS: An. Aguilera, Saenz.

CATCHERS

Player, Team	Pct.	G	PO	A	E	TC	DP	PB
Abrego, Jesus, Rey.	.984	31	168	20	3	191	3	4
Aguilera, Armando, Sal.	.966	93	418	72	17	507	7	6
Castareda, Hector, Cor.	.986	41	134	7	2	143	1	0
CAZARIN, Castro Manuel, Can. .	.996	111	463	85	2	550	5	9
Cervantes, Refugio, Lar.	.985	28	56	9	1	66	0	1
Cisneros, Ventura, Rey.	1.000	8	20	2	0	22	1	1
Cobos, Rogelio, Cam.	.981	69	301	54	7	362	5	6
Cruz, Marco A., Tor.	.991	58	194	24	2	220	1	5
Elvira, Honorio, Tab.	1.000	5	2	0	0	2	0	0
Estrada, Hector, Monc.	.978	112	441	56	11	508	10	5
Figueroa, Ricardo, Cam.	1.000	22	59	6	0	65	0	3
Garza, Gerardo, Lar.	.987	111	540	73	8	621	13	14
Garzon, R. Eliseo, Tig.	.979	79	381	38	9	428	3	2
Gastelum, Carlos, Tab.	.978	75	239	34	6	279	2	3
Gavia, Jesus, Yuc.	.968	60	214	27	8	249	0	1
Gonzalez, Fernando, Rey.	.958	8	22	1	1	24	0	0
Guerrero, Q. Jose, Cam.	1.000	27	54	3	0	57	1	1
Guzman, Marco A., Cam.	.968	58	206	36	8	250	5	2
Hernandez, Miguel, Che.	.969	55	107	16	4	127	2	0
Hurtado, Hector, Yuc.	.974	77	311	31	9	351	1	6
Martinez, Raul, Che.	.980	71	205	36	5	246	1	2
Meza, Alfredo, Mont.	.995	103	589	61	3	653	4	0
Munoz, Noe, Mex.	.985	80	368	30	6	404	2	3
Ochoa, Edgar, Agua.	.921	37	74	8	7	89	1	3
Ojeda, Miguel, Mex.	.991	51	197	32	2	231	3	5
Ortega, Antonio, Oax.	.976	34	141	21	4	166	2	1
Osuna, Hector, Yuc.	.991	63	205	21	2	228	2	6
Pacho, Carlos, Yuc.	.967	41	97	20	4	121	1	2
Pena, Carlos, Yuc.	.965	30	97	12	4	113	2	4
Pena, Luis A., Che.	1.000	2	1	0	0	1	0	0
Perez, Juan Luis, Tor.	.973	12	29	7	1	37	3	0
Perez, Noel, Tab.	1.000	6	13	1	0	14	0	2
Pinto, V. Placido, Monc.	.980	24	41	7	1	49	2	3
Pulido, Jesus, Yuc.	1.000	1	1	0	0	1	0	0
Ramirez, Efren, Agua.	.982	30	92	16	2	110	2	0
Ramirez, Jesus, Che.	1.000	2	4	0	0	4	0	0
Ramon, Reyes, Tab.	1.000	3	4	1	0	5	0	0
Resendez, Carlos, Monc.	1.000	12	39	2	0	41	0	1
Robles, Juan Jose, Cor.	.976	74	263	27	7	297	2	1
Rodriguez, Armando, Tig.	.988	60	223	31	3	257	4	5
Rojas, Homar, Oax.	.988	95	423	52	6	481	11	6
Santana, Ivan, Tab.	.954	27	94	9	5	108	0	0
Santana, Mario, Mont.	1.000	5	8	0	0	8	0	0
Saucedo, Roberto, Mont.	.995	51	166	16	1	183	3	3
Soriano, Ricardo, Tor.	1.000	1	1	0	0	1	0	0
Soto, Saul, Rey.	.976	84	403	44	11	458	8	9
Valdez, Francisco J., Tab.	.984	74	214	38	4	256	7	0
Valdez Avila, Emmanuel, Tig.	1.000	1	1	0	0	1	0	1
Valenzuela, Eduardo, Sal.	.975	39	143	10	4	157	3	2
Valle, Jorge Luis, Tor.	1.000	1	1	0	0	1	0	0
Vazquez, Felipe, Mex.	1.000	22	49	5	0	54	1	1
Vega, Edgar, Agua.	.963	90	321	40	14	375	4	4

Player, Team	Pct.	G	PO	A	E	TC	DP	PB
Villanueva, Hector, Lar.	.971	8	26	7	1	34	0	0
Voita, Sam, Che.	.909	3	8	2	1	11	0	2

TRIPLE PLAYS: Cobos, Estrada.

PITCHERS

Player, Team	Pct.	G	PO	A	E	TC	DP
Acosta, Aaron, Lar.	.971	23	6	27	1	34	2
Acosta, Gerardo, Oax.	.950	35	5	14	1	20	2
Adam, David, Tig.	.857	18	1	11	2	14	1
Aguilar, Jose Miguel, Tab.	1.000	38	4	6	0	10	0
Aguilar, Mario, Cam.	1.000	20	1	4	0	5	0
Aguilera, Edgar, Rey.	1.000	4	1	1	0	2	0
Aguirre, Gaudencio, Tab.	1.000	63	8	18	0	26	0
Alicea, Miguel, Lar.	1.000	25	1	3	0	4	0
Almeida, Rousell, Lar.	1.000	12	1	2	0	3	0
Alvarez, Antonio, Monc.	1.000	8	0	1	0	1	0
Alvarez, Cesar Octavio, Mex.	1.000	5	2	7	0	9	0
Alvarez, Juan Jesus, Tab.	1.000	24	4	25	0	29	1
Alvarez, Victor, Mex.	.909	22	4	16	2	22	2
Angulo, Luis Arturo, Sal.	.947	35	2	16	1	19	1
Aponte, Eduardo, Can.	1.000	3	2	3	0	5	0
Arano, Ramon, Cor.	1.000	1	0	1	0	1	0
Armenta, Alejandro, Tig.	.889	16	2	6	1	9	0
Atilano, Juan Carlos, Oax.	.933	49	6	8	1	15	2
Ayala, Luis Ignacio, Sal.	.969	47	8	23	1	32	3
Azocar, Oscar, Che.	1.000	1	0	1	0	1	0
Badorek, Mike, Tig.	1.000	3	0	1	0	1	0
Baez, Sixto, Oax.	1.000	53	3	19	0	22	2
Barfield, John D., Tor.	1.000	19	4	5	0	9	0
Barron, Avelino, Cam.	1.000	31	1	11	0	12	1
Beltran, Alonso, Tig.	1.000	32	6	16	0	22	1
Bernal, Manuel, Mex.	.959	23	17	30	2	49	3
Blancas, Rigoberto, Tab.	1.000	11	0	4	0	4	0
Bronson, Heflin, Sal.	1.000	6	3	2	0	5	0
Brosnan, Jason, Tig.	1.000	7	0	10	0	10	0
Cabrales, Gabriel, Agua.	1.000	38	2	11	0	13	1
Camara, Pedro J., Cor.	1.000	37	3	8	0	11	0
Campillo, Jorge, Tig.	1.000	24	3	9	0	12	0
Campos, Francisco, Cam.	.935	27	13	45	4	62	4
Cano, Jose, Yuc.	.857	4	1	5	1	7	0
Carranza, D. Javier, Can.	.926	24	4	21	2	27	3
Carrasco, Alejandro, Oax.	1.000	34	8	16	0	24	0
Castaaeda, Aurelio, Che.	.962	29	4	21	1	26	1
Castellanos, Hugo, Lar.	1.000	8	1	2	0	3	0
Cazares, Rosario, Sal.	.941	44	4	12	1	17	0
Cazares, Tomas, Monc.	1.000	20	2	14	0	16	0
Cecena, Jose Isabel, Monc.	1.000	25	6	16	0	22	2
Cedero, Blas, Tor.	1.000	12	2	8	0	10	0
Cerros, Juan, Rey.	.933	48	3	11	1	15	3
Chapa, Javier, Cam.	1.000	9	1	4	0	5	0
Cota, Marino, Oax.	.962	31	11	14	1	26	1
Couoh, Enrique, Yuc.	1.000	36	7	15	0	22	3
Cruz, Javier, Mex.	1.000	35	4	6	0	10	0
Cruz, Luis M., Tig.	1.000	12	1	2	0	3	0
Cuervo, Bernardo, Tig.	.889	21	3	13	2	18	1
De La Fuente, Julian, Rey.	.857	38	1	5	1	7	0
De La Hoya, Javier, Cor.	.889	5	5	3	1	9	0
Del Toro, Miguel, Mex.	.900	39	2	16	2	20	0
Delfin, Adolfo, Oax.	1.000	3	0	1	0	1	0
Delgado, Tim, Sal.	1.000	7	1	2	0	3	0
Diaz, Alejandro, Che.	1.000	46	7	20	0	27	1
Diaz, Marcos, Tor.	1.000	19	0	5	0	5	0
Diaz, Rafael, Mont.	.940	25	15	48	4	67	2
Dominguez, David, Rey.	1.000	8	1	1	0	2	0
Dominguez, Herminio, Cam.	.909	13	2	8	1	11	0
Dorame, Randey, Rey.	.966	24	5	23	1	29	0
Duarte, Miguel Eduardo, Sal.	1.000	25	6	12	0	18	1
Duncan, Calvin, Cor.	.929	13	5	8	1	14	0
Elguezabal, Octavio, Agua.	.800	11	0	4	1	5	1
Elvira, Narciso, Mont.	.970	24	7	25	1	33	0
Enriquez, Martin, Sal.	.885	20	4	19	3	26	0
Esparza, Emerson, Monc.	1.000	8	0	2	0	2	0
Espinoza, Martin, Sal.	1.000	1	0	1	0	1	0
Esquer, Mercedes, Mont.	1.000	16	2	16	0	18	1
Federico, Gustavo, Agua.	1.000	35	2	10	0	12	0
Figueroa, Fernando, Tor.	.971	18	7	26	1	34	1
Flores, Ignacio, Tor.	.935	49	6	23	2	31	2
Fontes, Agustin, Can.	.938	32	3	12	1	16	1
Fornes, Daniel, Rey.	1.000	9	0	2	0	2	0
Franklin, Jay, Cor.	1.000	1	1	0	0	1	0
Galvez, Randy, Mex.	.944	24	13	21	2	36	
Galvez, Rosario, Yuc.	1.000	50	0	9	0	9	

CLASS AAA Mexican League

Player, Team	Pct.	G	PO	A	E	TC	DP
Gamez, Francisco, Mont.	.917	58	7	15	2	24	0
Garcia, Adolfo, Cam.	1.000	2	0	5	0	5	1
Garcia, Andres, Can.	1.000	10	1	2	0	3	0
Garcia, Carlos, Mex.	1.000	17	1	6	0	7	0
Garcia, Jose, Tig.	1.000	53	4	17	0	21	1
Garcia, Manuel, Tig.	1.000	8	1	2	0	3	0
Garcia, R. Miguel, Cor.	1.000	38	5	28	0	33	0
Garcia Cruz, Jose Luis, Tig.	.955	59	5	16	1	22	0
Garibaldi, Cecilio, Tig.	1.000	8	0	2	0	2	0
Garibay, Daniel, Tig.	.966	26	4	24	1	29	1
Garibay, Roberto, Sal.	1.000	15	0	4	0	4	0
Garibay, Salvador, Lar.	1.000	43	5	6	0	11	2
Garza, Roberto J., Lar.	.950	46	4	15	1	20	3
Gomez, Martin, Cor.	.938	30	6	9	1	16	0
Gonzalez, Gilberto, Tor.	.857	26	6	12	3	21	0
Gonzalez, M. Arturo, Mont.	1.000	17	4	17	0	21	1
Gonzalez, Victor M., Che.	.900	32	3	6	1	10	0
Gracia, Edmundo, Sal.	1.000	9	0	1	0	1	0
Grajales, Norberto, Tor.	1.000	37	8	22	0	30	2
Gray, Denis, Tor.	1.000	6	2	2	0	4	0
Guerrero, Omar, Rey.	1.000	11	4	9	0	13	0
Heredia, Hector, Agua.	.964	23	7	20	1	28	0
Heredia, Julian, Mex.	.750	31	2	4	2	8	1
Hernandez, Fernando, Mont.	.950	31	3	16	1	20	2
Hernandez, Jose Manuel, Monc.	.971	26	7	27	1	35	1
Hernandez, Julio, Cor.	1.000	17	4	8	0	12	1
Hernandez, M. Martin, Can.	.947	18	1	17	1	19	2
Hernandez, Manuel, Agua.	.875	6	3	4	1	8	0
Herrera, Alberto, Lar.	1.000	9	3	1	0	4	0
Herrera, Calixto, Monc.	1.000	25	0	4	0	4	1
Herrera, Enrique, Tab.	1.000	45	5	12	0	17	3
Huber, Jeff, Agua.	1.000	15	4	3	0	7	0
Huerta, Luis Enrique, Lar.	.918	25	12	33	4	49	0
Hurst, Jonathan, Sal.	1.000	17	4	3	0	7	0
Izabal, Luis Alberto, Can.	1.000	9	2	1	0	3	0
Jimenez, German, Lar.	.955	20	3	18	1	22	1
Jimenez, Isaac, Che.	.833	11	1	5	1	6	0
Jimenez, Jesus, Tor.	.750	11	1	2	1	4	0
Lara, Hugo, Che.	.946	27	10	25	2	37	2
Larajorge, Jorge, Sal.	.917	27	7	15	2	24	0
Larryl, Mitchel, Oax.	1.000	4	0	3	0	3	0
Leal, Gerardo, Monc.	1.000	10	3	2	0	5	1
Leon, Juan Antonio, Tor.	1.000	17	0	1	0	1	1
Lewis, Greg, Cor.	1.000	5	1	7	0	8	0
Lizarraga, Andres, Lar.	.929	33	4	9	1	14	0
Llanes, Emeterio, Yuc.	1.000	10	0	2	0	2	0
Loaiza, Sabino, Cam.	.933	24	6	22	2	30	1
Lopez, Emigdio, Tab.	1.000	23	7	24	0	31	2
Lopez, Jesus Nain, Oax.	.909	58	3	7	1	11	1
Lopez, Jonas, Tab.	.962	26	2	23	1	26	0
Lopez, Jose Dionisio, Tor.	.933	34	4	10	1	15	2
Lopez, Juan Jose, Cam.	.909	20	2	8	1	11	2
Lopez, Raymundo, Tor.	1.000	11	0	5	0	5	0
LOPEZ, Rodrigo, Mex.	1.000	26	11	35	0	46	1
Luevano, Juan, Che.	1.000	35	5	9	0	14	1
Manrique, Alberto, Mont.	1.000	25	2	4	0	6	0
Manzanillo, Ravelo, Cam.	.943	27	6	27	2	35	1
Marquez, Isidro, Tig.	.957	58	3	19	1	23	1
Martinez, Cesar, Tor.	.933	25	3	11	1	15	0
Martinez, Cesar, Mont.	1.000	4	0	2	0	2	0
Medina, Alonso, Sal.	1.000	5	1	1	0	2	0
Melendez, Nestor, Rey.	.938	49	1	14	1	16	1
Mendez, Luis Fernando, Yuc.	1.000	13	5	14	0	19	2
Metoyer, Tony, Can.	.923	53	4	8	1	13	0
Meza, Joel, Monc.	1.000	4	0	3	0	3	0
Miranda, Julio Cesar, Yuc.	1.000	57	12	11	0	23	1
Mo, Sanford Maredith, Agua.	.950	20	7	12	1	20	1
Montano, Francisco, Tor.	.800	11	3	5	2	10	0
Montemayor, Humberto, Mont.	1.000	28	9	10	0	19	1
Mora, Eleazar, Che.	1.000	23	3	33	0	36	1
Morales, Luis Fernando, Che.	1.000	18	1	6	0	7	0
Moreno, Angel, Yuc.	.976	27	5	35	1	41	1
Moreno, Claudio, Mex.	.857	18	3	3	1	7	2
Moreno, Jesus, Agua.	1.000	6	0	5	0	5	0
Morenoleo, Bardo, Oax.	.957	24	6	16	1	23	2
Muaoz, Leonardo, Mont.	1.000	24	0	6	0	6	0
Munoz, Miguel, Rey.	1.000	24	6	24	0	30	2
Munoz, Pablo R., Oax.	.833	22	3	2	1	6	0
Murillo, Felipe, Monc.	.875	40	1	13	2	16	1
Muroz, Pablo, Cam.	1.000	13	0	2	0	2	0
Navarro, Jose Felix, Tig.	1.000	31	6	25	0	31	2
Navarro, Luis, Yuc.	.920	26	10	13	2	25	1

Player, Team	Pct.	G	PO	A	E	TC	DP
Neri, Braulio, Sal.	1.000	23	1	4	0	5	0
Neri, Eduardo, Che.	.909	67	3	17	2	22	1
Nieblas, Omar Enrique, Tab.	1.000	8	0	1	0	1	0
Nieves, Ernesto, Agua.	.500	10	0	1	1	2	0
Nunez, Jose Juan, Oax.	.800	21	2	2	1	5	0
Nurez, Javier, Sal.	1.000	15	0	6	0	6	0
Nurez, Jose Juan, Cam.	1.000	4	0	1	0	1	0
Ochoa, Pablo Joel, Rey.	.960	33	5	19	1	25	0
Ojeda, Ramon, Sal.	1.000	25	0	3	0	3	0
Olague, Jesus, Mont.	1.000	10	1	1	0	2	0
Orea, Cesar, Tor.	1.000	35	8	6	0	14	0
Orozco, Jaime, Cor.	.959	23	13	34	2	49	0
Ortega, Raul, Yuc.	.500	15	0	1	1	2	0
Ortega, Roberto, Cor.	1.000	18	5	14	0	19	1
Osuna, Ricardo, Tab.	1.000	25	11	19	0	30	2
Osuna, Roberto, Yuc.	1.000	7	1	0	0	1	0
Palacios, Vicente, Mont.	.900	61	3	6	1	10	0
Palafox, Juan Manuel, Tor.	.878	25	9	27	5	41	1
Parra, Julio, Lar.	.778	35	1	6	2	9	0
Parra, Milton Ramon, Cor.	1.000	15	1	2	0	3	0
Pena, Joel, Agua.	1.000	2	1	0	0	1	0
Perez, Dario, Oax.	1.000	28	11	31	0	42	2
Perez, Leonardo, Agua.	.895	25	3	14	2	19	0
Perez, Vladimir, Rey.	1.000	44	3	12	0	15	2
Pimentel, Roberto, Tab.	1.000	36	1	8	0	9	0
Powell, Dennis, Mont.	.938	56	2	13	1	16	1
Pulido, Raymundo, Cam.	1.000	14	4	8	0	12	0
Purata, Julio, Rey.	1.000	14	2	23	0	25	3
Quintanilla, Enrique, Lar.	.972	28	10	25	1	36	3
Quiroz, Aaron, Che.	1.000	14	6	11	0	17	0
Quiroz, Jose Julian, Che.	1.000	20	0	4	0	4	0
QuixONes, Enrique, Yuc.	.964	22	7	20	1	28	4
Ramirez, Roberto, Mex.	.929	6	5	8	1	14	1
Raygoza, V. Martin, Can.	.905	14	3	16	2	21	1
Renteria, Hilario, Can.	1.000	10	2	10	0	12	1
Retes, Lorenzo, Cam.	1.000	23	0	6	0	6	0
Reyes, Flavio, Cor.	1.000	36	1	5	0	6	1
Reyes, Nathanael, Mex.	.889	36	1	7	1	9	0
Reyes, Pablo, Cam.	.950	52	6	13	1	20	1
Rios, Jesus, Monc.	.917	24	14	19	3	36	2
Rivera, Oscar, Che.	1.000	11	0	6	0	6	1
Rivera, Paul, Can.	1.000	23	4	4	0	8	1
Rodriguez, Manuel, Cor.	1.000	26	1	1	0	2	0
Rodriguez, Raul, Monc.	.961	26	10	39	2	51	1
Rodriguez, Salvador, Yuc.	1.000	21	8	18	0	26	0
Rojo, Oscar, Cam.	1.000	25	4	7	0	11	2
Romero, Alejandro, Mex.	.957	24	6	16	1	23	0
Romero Lopez, Juan Jose, Cor.	1.000	43	6	13	0	19	0
Romo, Ricardo, Mont.	1.000	5	2	2	0	4	1
Rubio, Miguel, Mont.	1.000	16	2	1	0	3	0
Ruiz, Cecilio, Tab.	.963	26	3	23	1	27	1
Saenz, Alfredo, Agua.	1.000	25	0	5	0	5	0
Saldaaa, Edgardo, Yuc.	.941	37	3	13	1	17	1
Sanchez, Alejandro, Can.	1.000	30	3	17	0	20	1
Sanchez, Efrain, Cam.	.889	30	8	16	3	27	3
Sanchez, Hector, Agua.	.956	26	10	33	2	45	0
Sanchez, Pablo, Sal.	.889	19	4	20	3	27	3
Sandoval, Guillermo, Sal.	.957	36	9	13	1	23	1
Segura, Jose, Sal.	1.000	5	0	1	0	1	0
Serrano, Jorge, Lar.	1.000	8	5	3	0	8	0
Sierra, Abel, Che.	1.000	13	2	4	0	6	0
Sinohui, David, Agua.	.933	37	3	11	1	15	1
Smith, Chuk, Tor.	1.000	12	3	8	0	11	0
Solarte, Jose, Monc.	.933	60	1	13	1	15	1
Solis, Ricardo, Cor.	.972	23	11	24	1	36	0
Sombra, Francisco, Agua.	1.000	46	3	15	0	18	1
Soto, Cruz A., Can.	.976	37	8	32	1	41	3
Soto Martinez, Fernando, Can.	.971	24	6	27	1	34	1
Sulu, Mario, Cam.	.875	19	1	6	1	8	0
Surgosjohn, John, Lar.	1.000	31	3	14	0	17	1
Tejeda, Felix, Che.	.957	20	3	19	1	23	1
Turgeon, Dave, Rey.	1.000	18	8	23	0	31	0
Uribe, Juan Carlos, Yuc.	1.000	25	1	8	0	9	0
Valdez, Armando, Che.	.958	52	3	20	1	24	0
Valdez, R. Rodolfo, Monc.	1.000	25	1	5	0	6	1
Valencia, Jorge, Monc.	.900	23	3	6	1	10	0
Valenzuela, G. Saul, Can.	.933	22	10	18	2	30	4
Valera, Julio, Can.	1.000	4	0	1	0	1	0
Valerio, Julio Cesar, Monc.	1.000	37	0	6	0	6	1
Vargas, Ignacio, Yuc.	.895	30	6	11	2	19	1
Vargaslarajoel, Joel, Tab.	1.000	29	4	13	0	17	0
Vazquez, Adrian, Cam.	.889	4	2	6	1	9	1

Player, Team	Pct.	G	PO	A	E	TC	DP
Vazquez, Vicenty Marcos, Oax.	1.000	13	10	12	0	22	0
Vega Velarde, Obed, Lar.	.933	40	3	11	1	15	0
Velazquez, Ernesto, Tor.	1.000	26	1	1	0	2	0
Velazquez, Israel, Cor.	1.000	22	8	17	0	25	0
Verdugo, Hugo, Sal.	1.000	8	2	2	0	4	0
Viand, Jacob, Tig.	1.000	3	0	1	0	1	0
Villarreal, Antonio, Yuc.	1.000	18	7	19	0	26	2

Player, Team	Pct.	G	PO	A	E	TC	DP
Villegas, Jose Angel, Agua.	1.000	39	9	24	0	33	5
Wagner, Hector, Oax.	.952	22	17	23	2	42	3
Williams, Jeff, Sal.	.875	5	3	4	1	8	0
Young, Ray, Sal.	.852	15	9	14	4	27	2
Zamudio, Jeovanni, Rey.	1.000	21	8	19	0	27	2
Zavala, Marco, Tig.	1.000	27	2	5	0	7	0

LEAGUE CHAMPIONS

Year	Team	Pct.
1955—	Mexico City Tigers*	.539
1956—	Mexico City Reds	.692
1957—	Yucatan	.567
	Mex. C. Reds (2nd)†	.550
1958—	Nuevo Laredo	.625
1959—	Poza Rica	.575
	Mex. C. Reds (3rd)†	.507
1960—	Mexico City Tigers	.538
1961—	Veracruz	.575
1962—	Monterrey	.592
1963—	Puebla	.606
1964—	Mexico City Reds	.586
1965—	Mexico City Tigers	.590
1966—	Mexico City Tigers‡	.614
	Mexico City Reds	.571
1967—	Jalisco	.607
1968—	Mexico City Reds	.586
1969—	Reynosa	.591
1970—	Aguila§	.580
	Mexico City Reds	.607
1971—	Jalisco§	.558
	Saltillo	.593
1972—	Saltillo	.636
	Cordoba§	.541
1973—	Saltillo	.656
	Mexico City Reds∞	.590

Year	Team	Pct.
1974—	Jalisco	.627
	Mexico City Reds∞	.551
1975—	Tampico∞	.541
	Cordoba	.649
1976—	Mexico City Reds∞	.543
	Union Laguna	.547
1977—	Mexico City Reds	.623
	Nuevo Laredo∞	.507
1978—	Aguascalientes∞	.589
	Union Laguna	.523
1979—	Saltillo	.704
	Puebla∞	.628
1980—	No champion▲	
1981—	Mexico City Reds	.615
	Reynosa	.492
1982—	Ciudad Juarez∞	.570
	Mexico City Tigers	.508
1983—	Campeche♦	.614
	Ciudad Juarez	.535
1984—	Yucatan♦	.560
	Ciudad Juarez	.509
1985—	Mexico City Reds♦	.606
	Nuevo Laredo	.5275
1986—	Puebla♦	.682
	Monclova	.598

Year	Team	Pct.
1987—	Mexico City Reds♦	.605
	Monterrey	.536
1988—	Mexico City Reds♦	.646
	Nuevo Laredo	.602
1989—	Nuevo Laredo♦	.621
	Yucatan	.539
1990—	Nuevo Laredo	.618
	Leon♦	.565
1991—	Monterrey♦	.683
	Mexico City Reds	.627
1992—	Mexico City Tigers♦	.594
	Nuevo Laredo	.538
1993—	Nuevo Laredo	.589
	Tabasco♦	.528
1994—	Mexico City Red Devils♦	.646
	Monterrey Sultans	.608
1995—	Mexico City Red Devils	.708
	Monterrey Sultans♦	.570
1996—	Monterrey Sultans	.713
	Mexico City Reds♦	.619
1997—	Mexico City Red Devils	.686
	Mexico City Tigers■	.658
1998—	Monterrey	.672
	Oaxaca■	.576

*Defeated Nuevo Laredo, two games to none, in playoff for pennant. †Won four-team playoff. ‡Won split-season playoff. §League divided into Northern, Southern divisions; won two-team playoff. ∞League divided into Northern, Southern zones; sub-divided into Eastern, Western divisions, won eight-team playoff. ▲ A players strike on July 1 forced the cancellation of the regular season and playoff schedule. ♦ League divided into Northern, Southern zones; four clubs from each zone qualified for postseason play. Won final series for league championship. ■ League divided into Northern, Central and Southern zones; played split season, with top eight teams qualifying for playoffs. Won final series for league championship.

PACIFIC COAST LEAGUE

LEAGUE OFFICE

President
Branch Rickey

Address
1631 Mesa Ave.
Colorado Springs, CO 80906

Phone
719-636-3399

TEAMS

ALBUQUERQUE DUKES
General manager
Pat McKernan
Manager
Mike Scioscia
Ballpark (capacity, surface)
Albuquerque Sports Stadium (10,510, grass)
Affiliation
Dodgers
Address
Avenida Cesar Chavez SE
Albuquerque, NM 87106
Phone
505-243-1791

CALGARY CANNONS
Vice president, baseball operations
John Traub
Manager
Lynn Jones
Ballpark (capacity, surface)
Burn Stadium (8,000, grass)
Affiliation
Marlins
Address
2255 Crowchild Trail N.W.
Calgary, Alberta T2M 4S7
Phone
403-284-1111

COLORADO SPRINGS SKY SOX
General manager/president
Robert Goughan
Manager
Bill Hayes
Ballpark (capacity, surface)
Sky Sox Stadium (9,000, grass)
Affiliation
Rockies
Address
4385 Tutt Blvd.
Colorado Springs, CO 80922
Phone
719-597-1449

EDMONTON TRAPPERS
President/general manager
Mel Kowalchuk
Manager
Carney Lansford
Ballpark (capacity, surface)
Teluf Field (10,000; artificial infield, grass outfield)
Affiliation
Angels
Address
10233 96th Ave.
Edmonton, Alberta T5K 0A5

Phone
403-429-2934

FRESNO GRIZZLIES
Vice president/general manager
Derek Leistra
Manager
Ron Roenicke
Ballpark (capacity, surface)
Beinden Field (6,500, grass)
Affiliation
Giants
Address
1231 N Street
Fresno, CA 93721
Phone
209-442-1994

IOWA CUBS
General manager
Sam Bernabe
Manager
Terry Kennedy
Ballpark (capacity, surface)
Sec Taylor Stadium (10,500, grass)
Affiliation
Cubs
Address
350 SW 1 St.
Des Moines, IA 50309
Phone
515-243-6111

LAS VEGAS STARS
General manager
Don Logan
Manager
Mike Ramsey
Ballpark (capacity, surface)
Cashman Field (9,370, grass)
Affiliation
Padres
Address
850 Las Vegas Blvd. N
Las Vegas, NV 89101
Phone
702-386-7200

MEMPHIS REDBIRDS
President/general manager
Allie Prescott
Manager
Gaylen Pitts
Ballpark (capacity, surface)
Tim McCarver Stadium (8,700; artificial infield, grass outfield)
Affiliation
Cardinals
Address
800 Home Run Lane
Memphis, TN 38104

Phone
901-721-6000

NASHVILLE SOUNDS
General manager
Jeff Sedivy
Manager
Trent Jewett
Ballpark (capacity, surface)
Greer Stadium (11,500, grass)
Affiliation
Pirates
Address
534 Chestnut Street
Nashville, TN 37203
Phone
615-242-4371

NEW ORLEANS ZEPHYRS
General manager
Dan Hanrahan
Manager
Tony Pena
Ballpark (capacity, surface)
Zephyr Field (11,000, grass)
Affiliation
Astros
Address
6000 Airline Drive
Metairie, LA 70003
Phone
504-734-5155

OKLAHOMA REDHAWKS
General Manager
Tim O'Toole
Manager
Greg Biagini
Ballpark (capacity, surface)
Southwestern Bell Bricktown Ball Park (13,066, grass)
Affiliation
Rangers
Address
2 South Mickey Mantle
Oklahoma City, OK 73104
Phone
405-218-1000

OMAHA GOLDEN SPIKES
Vice president/general manager
Bill Gorman
Manager
Ron Johnson
Ballpark (capacity, surface)
Omaha's Rosenblatt Stadium (23,000, grass)
Affiliation
Royals
Address
1202 Bert Murphy Drive
Omaha, NE 68107

CLASS AAA Pacific Coast League

Phone
402-734-2550

SALT LAKE BUZZ
Assistant general manager
Dorsena Picknell
Manager
Phil Roof
Ballpark (capacity, surface)
Franklin-Covey Field (15,500, grass)
Affiliation
Twins
Address
P.O. Box 4108
Salt Lake City, UT 84110
Phone
801-485-3800

TACOMA RAINIERS
Executive vice president
Mel Taylor

Manager
Dave Myers
Ballpark (capacity, surface)
Cheney Stadium (10,106, grass)
Affiliation
Mariners
Address
P.O. Box 11087
Tacoma, WA 98411
Phone
252-752-7707

TUCSON SIDEWINDERS
General manager
Mike Feder
Manager
Chris Speier
Ballpark (capacity, surface)
Tucson Electric Park (11,000, grass)
Affiliation
Diamondbacks

Address
P.O. Box 27045
Tucson, AZ 85716
Phone
520-434-1021

VANCOUVER CANADIANS
Vice president/general manager
Gary Arthur
Manager
Mike Quade
Ballpark (capacity, surface)
Nat Bailey Stadium (6,500, grass)
Affiliation
Athletics
Address
4601 Ontario St.
Vancouver, B.C. V5V 3H4
Phone
604-872-5232

1998 FINAL STANDINGS
COMPOSITE

Team	Iowa	Fres.	Cal.	S.L.	Oma.	N.O.	Tac.	Edm.	Okla.	Mem.	L.V.	Nash.	Alb.	Tuc.	C.S.	Van.	W	L	T	Pct.	GB
Iowa (Cubs)	....	5	5	4	11	4	4	4	7	3	3	6	10	5	11	3	85	59	0	.590	....
Fresno (Giants)	3	....	3	6	6	2	2	4	3	5	9	6	7	12	6	7	81	62	0	.566	3.5
Calgary (White Sox)	3	5	....	6	3	5	5	7	4	4	3	5	6	5	5	15	81	62	0	.566	3.5
Salt Lake (Twins)	4	10	2	....	3	6	4	4	2	5	9	5	6	9	6	4	79	64	0	.552	5.5
Omaha (Royals)	5	2	5	5	....	4	3	6	4	5	3	4	11	5	12	5	79	64	0	.552	5.5
New Orleans (Astros)	4	6	2	2	4	....	5	6	8	7	6	6	3	6	5	6	76	66	0	.535	8.0
Tacoma (Mariners)	4	6	11	4	5	3	....	7	4	2	5	4	4	4	6	8	77	67	0	.535	8.0
Edmonton (Athletics)	4	4	9	4	1	2	9	....	4	4	5	5	4	4	7	10	76	67	0	.531	8.5
Oklahoma (Rangers)	1	5	4	6	4	8	4	4	....	9	4	8	4	5	5	3	74	70	0	.514	11.0
Memphis (Cardinals)	5	3	4	3	3	9	6	4	7	....	6	6	4	6	5	3	74	70	0	.514	11.0
Las Vegas (Padres)	5	7	5	6	5	2	3	3	4	2	....	4	6	9	5	4	70	72	0	.493	14.0
Nashville (Pirates)	2	2	3	3	4	9	4	3	8	10	4	....	3	3	6	6	67	76	0	.469	17.5
Albuquerque (Dodgers)	6	1	2	2	5	5	4	4	4	4	2	5	....	4	7	6	61	82	0	.427	23.5
Tucson (D'backs)	3	4	3	7	3	2	4	4	3	2	6	5	3	....	2	6	57	85	0	.401	27.0
Colo. Springs (Rockies)	5	2	3	2	4	3	2	1	3	3	3	5	9	6	....	4	55	89	0	.382	30.0
Vancouver (Angels)	5	0	1	4	3	2	8	6	5	5	4	2	2	2	4	....	53	90	0	.371	31.5

Major league affiliations in parentheses.

PLAYOFFS: New Orleans defeated Iowa two games to one; Calgary defeated Fresno three games to two; New Orleans defeated Calgary three games to two to win league championship; New Orleans defeated Buffalo three games to one to win inaugural AAA World Series.

REGULAR-SEASON ATTENDANCE: Albuquerque, 308,993; Calgary, 296,047; Colorado Springs, 220,281; Edmonton, 410,414; Fresno, 359,076; Iowa, 420,713; Las Vegas 336,005; Memphis, 395,592; Nashville, 323,068; New Orleans, 519,584; Oklahoma, 491,036; Omaha, 401,264; Salt Lake, 554,719; Tacoma, 337,623; Tucson, 300,460; Vancouver, 284,935. Total—5,959,104. Playoffs (13 games)—57,258. Class AAA All-Star Game at Norfolk, Va.—11,049.

MANAGERS: Albuquerque, Glenn Hoffman (through June 21), Jon Debus (June 22 through 26) and Ron Roenicke (June 27 through end of season); Calgary, Tom Spencer; Colorado Springs, Paul Zuvella; Edmonton, Mike Quade; Fresno, Jim Davenport; Iowa, Terry Kennedy; Las Vegas, Jerry Royster; Memphis, Gaylen Pitts; Nashville, Trent Jewett; New Orleans, John Tamargo; Oklahoma, Greg Biagini; Omaha, Ron Johnson; Salt Lake, Phil Roof; Tacoma, Dave Myers; Tucson, Chris Speier; Vancouver, Mitch Seoane. Managerial record of team with more than one manager: Albuquerque, Hoffman, 27-41; Debus, 1-4; Roenicke, 33-37.

ALL-STAR TEAM: 1B—Mario Valdez, Calgary; 2B—Dave Hajek, Las Vegas; 3B—George Arias, Las Vegas; SS—Scott Sheldon, Oklahoma; OF—Jeremy Giambi, Omaha; OF—Armando Rios, Fresno; OF—Derrick White, Iowa-Colorado Springs; C—Mitch Meluskey, New Orleans; DH—Chris Hatcher, Omaha; RHP—Kurt Miller, Iowa; LHP—John Halama, New Orleans; RP—Bart Evans, Omaha; Most Valuable Player—Chris Hatcher, Omaha; Rookie of the Year—Jeremy Giambi, Omaha; Manager of the Year—Terry Kennedy, Iowa.

1998 BATTING
TEAM

Team	Avg.	G	TPA	AB	R	H	TB	2B	3B	HR	RBI	SH	SF	HP	BB	IBB	SO	SB	CS	GDP	LOB	ShO	Slg.	OBP
New Orleans	.291	142	5508	4823	779	1402	2164	275	26	145	718	53	44	58	530	36	847	77	40	138	1044	7	.449	.365
Las Vegas	.288	142	5502	4950	772	1424	2294	336	33	156	729	29	50	55	418	22	1055	96	46	111	989	6	.463	.347
Salt Lake	.284	143	5441	4852	787	1380	2163	285	33	144	733	38	37	59	455	20	1017	136	63	98	968	4	.446	.351
Albuquerque	.284	143	5402	4790	709	1362	2045	256	47	111	656	71	47	54	440	18	854	195	85	111	960	6	.427	.348
Omaha	.283	143	5423	4819	766	1364	2311	254	24	215	728	32	43	43	486	24	966	117	61	131	966	1	.480	.351
Colo. Springs	.281	144	5531	4937	779	1387	2160	277	47	134	705	42	35	49	468	18	958	66	53	137	1009	11	.438	.347
Tucson	.281	142	5479	4891	700	1373	2066	255	45	116	641	27	50	66	445	17	936	70	35	131	1041	5	.422	.346
Memphis	.280	144	5676	5000	773	1402	2185	302	35	137	711	30	50	90	506	18	1077	62	43	120	1097	3	.437	.354
Iowa	.280	144	5585	4900	849	1370	2344	290	18	216	802	35	34	71	545	31	1058	53	46	122	999	1	.478	.358
Edmonton	.278	143	5517	4816	767	1338	2137	297	32	146	713	17	39	46	599	9	1002	91	49	127	1075	7	.444	.361

Team	Avg.	G	TPA	AB	R	H	TB	2B	3B	HR	RBI	SH	SF	HP	BB	IBB	SO	SB	CS	GDP	LOB	ShO	Slg.	OBP
Fresno	.278	143	5523	4832	815	1342	2187	243	25	184	742	60	36	59	536	38	911	106	45	103	987	7	.453	.355
Calgary	.277	143	5500	4829	806	1337	2158	289	23	162	745	46	54	75	496	22	895	100	41	121	996	4	.447	.350
Nashville	.271	143	5379	4769	699	1292	2090	251	32	161	651	38	32	73	467	9	1051	117	63	102	1005	5	.438	.343
Tacoma	.270	144	5576	4935	734	1330	2078	310	27	128	666	38	38	64	501	30	951	80	60	131	1032	4	.421	.342
Memphis	.266	144	5436	4836	675	1285	1965	287	39	105	621	59	27	38	476	23	851	103	74	99	976	13	.406	.335
Vancouver	.261	143	5266	4727	571	1236	1909	256	39	113	533	40	45	53	401	11	965	102	65	108	947	11	.404	.323

INDIVIDUAL

TOP QUALIFIERS FOR BATTING CHAMPIONSHIP

Minimum 389 plate appearances. *Lefthanded batter. †Switch-hitter.

Player, Team	Avg.	G	TPA	AB	R	H	TB	2B	3B	HR	RBI	SH	SF	HP	BB	IBB	SO	SB	CS	GDP	Slg.	OBP
Giambi, Jeremy, Oma.*	.372	96	394	325	68	121	206	21	2	20	66	2	4	6	57	8	64	8	5	4	.634	.469
Brinkley, Darryl, Nash.	.355	114	413	372	57	132	188	23	3	9	51	0	1	13	27	2	53	10	8	9	.505	.416
Meluskey, Mitch, N.O.†	.353	121	490	397	76	140	232	41	0	17	71	0	5	3	85	10	59	2	0	15	.584	.465
White, Derrick, Iowa-C.S.	.343	88	390	332	72	114	200	22	2	20	86	0	4	6	48	3	62	6	6	7	.602	.431
Valdez, Mario, Cal.*	.330	123	527	448	86	148	240	32	0	20	81	0	4	12	60	3	102	1	2	14	.536	.420
Franklin, Micah, Iowa†	.329	118	435	359	74	118	235	26	2	29	95	0	4	13	59	8	72	5	3	10	.655	.437
Hajek, Dave, L.V.	.328	130	578	539	85	177	240	45	3	4	63	3	12	1	23	0	46	14	6	13	.445	.350
Latham, Chris, S.L.†	.324	97	438	377	81	122	184	21	4	11	51	4	0	1	56	4	99	29	5	5	.488	.412
LoDuca, Paul, Alb.	.319	126	528	451	69	144	204	30	3	8	58	7	6	5	59	2	40	19	7	20	.452	.399
Ryan, Rob, Tuc.*	.317	116	472	394	71	125	198	18	2	17	66	0	5	10	63	3	61	9	3	5	.503	.419
McCarty, Dave, Tac.	.317	108	467	398	73	126	193	30	2	11	52	1	2	6	59	3	85	9	6	15	.485	.411
Stahoviak, Scott, S.L.*	.316	111	452	399	71	126	225	33	6	18	82	0	7	1	45	4	94	5	2	9	.564	.381
Saenz, Olmedo, Cal.	.313	124	540	466	89	146	262	29	0	29	102	0	7	22	45	3	49	3	3	16	.562	.394
Martinez, Ramon E., Fres.	.313	98	415	364	58	114	181	21	2	14	59	4	7	2	38	3	42	0	3	12	.497	.375
Stoner, Mike, Tuc.	.312	106	428	394	46	123	166	22	3	5	49	0	3	4	27	4	52	3	0	10	.421	.360

DEPARTMENTAL LEADERS: G—Quinlan, 137; AB—Hajek, Quinlan, 539; R—W. Johnson, 95; H—Hajek, 177; TB—Hatcher, 313; 2B—Rohrmeier, 51; 3B—E. Diaz, 12; HR—Hatcher, 46; RBI—Arias, 119; SH—C. Wilson, 9; SF—Hajek, 12; HP—Saenz, 22; BB—W. Johnson, 90; IBB—Meluskey, 10; SO—Quinlan, 155; SB—Frazier, 42; CS—W. Romero, 15; GIDP—LoDuca, 20; Slg.—M. Franklin, .655; OBP—Giambi, .469.

ALL PLAYERS

*Lefthanded batter. †Switch-hitter.

Player, Team	Avg.	G	TPA	AB	R	H	TB	2B	3B	HR	RBI	SH	SF	HP	BB	IBB	SO	SB	CS	GDP	Slg.	OBP
Abbott, Kurt, Edm.	.400	7	31	25	5	10	18	2	0	2	4	0	0	0	6	0	8	0	1	1	.720	.516
Acevedo, Juan, Mem.	.000	2	1	1	0	0	0	0	0	0	0	0	0	0	0	0	1	0	0	0	.000	.000
Alexander, Chad, N.O.	.400	2	5	5	1	2	2	0	0	0	2	0	0	0	0	0	2	0	0	0	.400	.400
Allen, Dusty, L.V.	.267	87	331	292	42	78	149	21	1	16	45	0	4	4	31	0	80	0	2	5	.510	.341
Allison, Brad, Tuc.	.000	4	7	6	1	0	0	0	0	0	0	0	0	0	1	0	3	0	0	0	.000	.143
Almanza, Armando, Mem.*	.500	31	2	2	1	1	2	1	0	0	0	0	0	0	0	0	1	0	0	0	1.000	.500
Alston, Garvin, C.S.	.000	45	1	1	1	0	0	0	0	0	0	0	0	0	0	0	0	0	0	0	.000	.000
Alvarez, Tavo, Nash.	.313	15	18	16	3	5	9	1	0	1	3	2	0	0	0	0	5	0	0	0	.563	.313
Anderson, Cliff, Alb.*	.232	48	150	142	16	33	55	6	2	4	24	0	0	1	7	1	23	3	0	1	.387	.273
Anderson, Jimmy, Nash.*	.048	36	24	21	0	1	1	0	0	0	0	3	0	0	0	0	4	0	0	0	.048	.048
Anthony, Eric, Alb.*	.303	59	226	189	34	57	100	9	2	10	26	0	1	1	36	3	43	3	3	2	.532	.414
Arias, George, L.V.	.308	114	482	435	73	134	283	33	4	36	119	0	5	5	37	2	108	0	1	9	.651	.365
Arocha, Rene, N.O.	.235	11	19	17	2	4	7	1	1	0	2	2	0	0	0	0	2	0	0	1	.412	.235
Arrandale, Matt, Mem.	.250	23	4	4	0	1	1	0	0	0	0	0	0	0	0	0	2	0	0	0	.250	.250
Aybar, Manny, Mem.	.143	14	15	14	1	2	2	0	0	0	0	0	1	0	0	0	3	0	0	0	.143	.143
Bailey, Cory, Fres.	.000	58	9	7	0	0	0	0	0	0	0	0	0	2	0	0	0	0	0	0	.000	.000
Ball, Jeff, Fres.	.296	124	520	456	81	135	227	29	0	21	80	0	1	8	55	6	86	5	2	18	.498	.381
Barberie, Bret, Okla.†	.305	133	583	502	70	153	215	36	4	6	55	3	6	15	57	3	85	3	3	11	.428	.388
Barker, Tim, C.S.	.266	78	285	252	31	67	80	10	0	1	27	6	1	1	25	0	43	5	6	4	.317	.333
Barkett, Andy, Okla.*	.314	80	293	255	38	80	119	17	5	4	36	0	3	0	35	2	43	3	4	6	.467	.392
Barndollar, Jeff, Tuc.	.000	1	1	1	0	0	0	0	0	0	0	0	0	0	0	0	0	0	0	0	.000	.000
Barnes, Brian, Mem.*	.105	37	24	19	1	2	2	0	0	0	0	0	4	0	1	0	9	0	0	0	.105	.150
Barrios, Manny, Alb.	.000	20	3	2	1	0	0	0	0	0	0	0	0	1	0	0	2	0	0	0	.000	.000
Barry, Jeff, C.S.†	.261	100	404	349	55	91	146	19	6	8	55	0	2	7	46	3	52	5	1	6	.418	.356
Bates, Jason, C.S.†	.324	49	202	182	37	59	85	9	1	5	20	1	1	1	17	0	31	1	2	4	.467	.383
Baughman, Justin, Van.	.297	54	246	222	35	66	84	10	4	0	15	5	2	4	13	0	28	26	8	7	.378	.344
Bautista, Juan, Tuc.	.150	9	24	20	1	3	3	0	0	0	1	0	1	1	2	0	5	0	0	2	.150	.250
Beckett, Robbie, C.S.	.500	21	2	2	0	1	1	0	0	0	0	0	0	0	0	0	2	0	0	0	.500	.500
Bellhorn, Mark, Edm.†	.249	87	378	309	57	77	135	20	4	10	44	0	1	6	62	0	90	6	2	8	.437	.384
Beltre, Esteban, S.L.	.278	133	558	510	84	142	180	24	4	2	49	5	4	0	39	0	109	26	11	7	.353	.330
Benson, Kris, Nash.	.042	28	27	24	1	1	1	0	0	0	0	0	0	2	0	0	17	0	0	0	.042	.080
Berblinger, Jeff, Tac.	.238	109	424	390	48	93	134	19	2	6	38	4	0	8	22	1	59	11	7	5	.344	.293
Berkman, Lance, N.O.†	.271	17	73	59	14	16	38	4	0	6	13	0	0	2	12	1	16	0	0	1	.644	.411
Berryhill, Damon, Edm.†	.257	21	88	74	8	19	28	9	0	0	14	0	4	0	10	1	13	0	0	3	.378	.330
Betten, Randy, Van.	.100	10	13	10	1	1	2	1	0	0	2	0	1	0	2	0	2	1	1	1	.200	.231
Bieser, Steve, Mem.*	.257	82	259	206	30	53	75	11	4	1	24	4	6	10	33	1	30	13	2	4	.364	.376
Blais, Mike, N.O.	.000	2	1	1	0	0	0	0	0	0	0	0	0	0	0	0	0	0	0	0	.000	.000
Blanco, Henry, Alb.	.269	48	158	134	19	36	59	11	0	4	23	0	2	0	22	1	27	2	0	5	.440	.367
Blood, Darin, Fres.†	.385	19	18	13	4	5	11	0	0	2	4	3	0	0	2	0	3	0	0	0	.846	.467
Bocachica, Hiram, Alb.	.238	26	121	101	16	24	45	7	1	4	16	1	0	6	13	1	24	5	3	1	.446	.358
Bolick, Frank, Van.†	.264	75	301	269	40	71	124	10	2	13	29	0	2	2	28	1	47	0	1	5	.461	.336
Bolton, Tom, Nash.*	.000	3	1	1	0	0	0	0	0	0	0	0	0	0	0	0	0	0	0	0	.000	.000
Bonds, Bobby, Fres.	.160	18	25	25	6	4	10	0	0	2	3	0	0	0	5	0	9	0	0	0	.400	.160
Boston, D.J., C.S.*	.284	41	122	109	22	31	42	6	1	1	8	1	0	1	11	1	19	0	2	4	.385	.355
Bourgeois, Steve, C.S.	.348	39	23	23	1	8	10	2	0	0	2	0	0	0	0	0	0	0	0	0	.435	.348

CLASS AAA Pacific Coast League

Player, Team	Avg.	G	TPA	AB	R	H	TB	2B	3B	HR	RBI	SH	SF	HP	BB	IBB	SO	SB	CS	GDP	Slg.	OBP
Boyd, Jason, Tuc.	1.000	15	1	1	1	1	1	0	0	0	0	0	0	0	0	0	0	0	0	0	1.000	1.000
Bradshaw, Terry, Oma.*	.264	105	352	295	61	78	129	12	0	13	35	1	1	4	51	2	52	12	6	2	.437	.379
Brede, Brent, Tuc.*	.313	29	118	96	16	30	46	8	1	2	16	0	1	0	21	0	20	2	1	3	.479	.432
Bridges, Kary, Iowa*	.215	64	195	181	25	39	51	10	1	0	14	0	2	1	11	0	12	0	2	4	.282	.262
Briggs, Stoney, Iowa	.250	2	4	4	1	1	1	0	0	0	1	0	0	0	0	0	0	0	0	0	.250	.250
Brinkley, Darryl, Nash.	.355	114	413	372	57	132	188	23	3	9	51	0	1	13	27	2	53	10	8	9	.505	.416
Brito, Luis, Nash.†	.231	9	28	26	3	6	6	0	0	0	0	0	0	0	2	0	3	0	0	1	.231	.286
Brito, Tilson, Tuc.	.259	42	157	143	20	37	57	12	1	2	12	3	1	2	8	0	29	0	1	5	.399	.305
Brock, Chris, Fres.	.263	17	28	19	3	5	7	2	0	0	4	5	0	0	4	0	1	0	0	0	.368	.391
Brock, Tarrik, Tac.*	.245	24	105	94	14	23	34	2	3	1	14	1	1	0	9	0	28	5	0	0	.362	.308
Brohawn, Troy, Fres.*	.200	30	26	25	1	5	6	1	0	0	0	0	0	0	1	0	4	0	0	1	.240	.231
Brown, Adrian, Nash.†	.289	85	347	311	58	90	121	12	5	3	27	6	2	0	28	1	38	25	7	7	.389	.346
Brown, Brant, Iowa*	.364	3	11	11	1	4	4	0	0	0	0	0	0	0	0	0	6	0	0	0	.364	.364
Brown, Randy, Nash.	.184	14	54	49	8	9	13	1	0	1	6	0	1	0	4	0	15	1	1	1	.265	.241
Brown, Roosevelt, Iowa*	.333	1	3	3	0	1	2	1	0	0	2	0	0	0	0	0	0	0	0	0	.667	.333
Brownson, Mark, C.S.*	.048	23	25	21	0	1	1	0	0	0	0	3	0	0	1	0	10	0	0	1	.048	.091
Brundage, David, Tac.*	.000	1	2	1	1	0	0	0	0	0	0	1	0	0	0	0	0	0	0	0	.000	.500
Brunson, Will, Alb.*	.154	34	19	13	0	2	2	0	0	0	0	6	0	0	0	0	5	0	1	0	.154	.154
Buchanan, Brian, S.L.	.278	133	547	500	74	139	225	29	3	17	82	1	1	9	36	1	90	14	2	7	.450	.337
Buhner, Jay, Tac.	.500	2	7	4	2	2	4	2	0	0	2	0	1	0	2	0	2	0	0	0	1.000	.571
Burke, Jamie, Van.	.216	61	185	162	16	35	47	6	0	2	14	2	2	6	13	0	25	0	1	7	.290	.295
Burke, John, C.S.*	.000	7	1	1	0	0	0	0	0	0	0	0	0	0	0	0	0	0	0	0	.000	.000
Butler, Rob, N.O.*	.274	70	249	223	21	61	77	11	1	1	29	5	2	1	17	1	19	2	2	12	.345	.325
Buxbaum, Danny, Van.	.320	27	105	100	10	32	42	4	0	2	17	0	2	1	2	0	17	0	1	3	.420	.333
Byrdak, Tim, Oma.*	1.000	27	1	1	0	1	1	0	0	0	1	0	0	0	0	0	0	0	0	0	1.000	1.000
Byrne, Earl, Iowa*	.000	10	8	8	0	0	0	0	0	0	0	0	0	0	0	0	3	0	1	0	.000	.000
Canale, George, Nash.*	.232	46	161	151	10	35	58	8	0	5	29	0	2	0	8	1	36	0	1	1	.384	.267
Candaele, Casey, Nash.-N.O.†	.283	110	403	368	54	104	134	16	4	2	40	1	2	1	31	3	53	3	1	15	.364	.338
Canizaro, Jay, Fres.	.226	45	125	106	23	24	52	6	2	6	14	0	1	1	17	1	23	0	1	3	.491	.336
Carr, Jeremy, Oma.	.292	49	202	178	40	52	87	14	3	5	23	2	2	1	19	1	31	19	5	3	.489	.360
Carvajal, Jovino, Van.†	.267	115	418	389	47	104	152	20	5	6	34	5	3	1	20	2	72	20	11	8	.391	.303
Castleberry, Kevin, Iowa*	.327	23	60	55	11	18	25	2	1	1	6	0	0	0	5	0	10	1	1	1	.455	.383
Castro, Juan, C.S.	.000	1	1	1	0	0	0	0	0	0	0	0	0	0	0	0	0	0	0	0	.000	.000
Chamberlain, Wes, Okla.	.365	27	109	96	16	35	57	7	0	5	21	0	2	4	7	2	12	0	1	1	.594	.422
Charles, Frank, Fres.	.500	4	11	10	2	5	8	0	0	1	1	0	0	0	1	0	2	0	0	0	.800	.545
Chavez, Eric, Edm.*	.325	47	209	194	38	63	114	18	0	11	40	0	2	1	12	0	32	2	3	4	.588	.364
Chavez, Raul, Tac.	.223	76	267	233	27	52	70	6	0	4	34	2	6	4	22	4	41	1	2	7	.300	.294
Cholowsky, Dan, C.S.	.243	104	379	342	44	83	126	15	2	8	39	3	3	3	28	1	72	4	2	13	.368	.303
Christenson, Ryan, Edm.	.261	22	104	88	17	23	34	6	1	1	7	0	1	0	15	0	24	4	1	1	.386	.365
Christopherson, Eric, Cal.	.352	21	64	54	12	19	38	2	1	5	14	2	1	0	7	1	7	0	0	0	.704	.419
Cianfrocco, Archi, L.V.	.283	38	139	127	15	36	64	8	1	6	16	0	0	1	11	0	35	3	1	2	.504	.345
Clement, Matt, L.V.	.000	27	31	21	1	0	0	0	0	0	1	8	0	1	1	0	8	0	0	0	.000	.087
Clemente, Edgard, C.S.	.252	135	543	493	79	124	225	21	7	22	82	1	5	4	40	0	117	5	5	6	.456	.310
Clemons, Chris, Tuc.	.067	20	15	15	0	1	1	0	0	0	0	0	0	0	0	0	7	0	0	0	.067	.067
Cline, Pat, Iowa	.281	122	475	424	52	119	184	22	2	13	60	1	5	9	36	4	59	2	3	14	.434	.346
Clontz, Brad, Alb.	.000	6	1	1	0	0	0	0	0	0	0	0	0	0	0	0	1	0	0	0	.000	.000
Colbert, Craig, L.V.	.167	5	18	18	0	3	4	1	0	0	2	0	0	0	0	0	3	0	0	0	.222	.167
Cole, Victor, Iowa*	.000	38	4	2	1	0	0	0	0	0	0	1	0	0	1	0	1	0	0	0	.000	.333
Coleman, Vince, Mem.†	.316	20	87	76	15	24	34	5	1	1	5	1	0	0	10	0	11	8	4	0	.447	.395
Conine, Jeff, Oma.	.000	2	9	9	0	0	0	0	0	0	0	0	0	0	0	0	3	0	0	0	.000	.000
Cookson, Brent, Tuc.	.360	36	121	100	24	36	66	12	0	6	19	0	1	2	18	0	26	0	0	1	.660	.463
Coolbaugh, Mike, C.S.	.277	108	425	386	62	107	194	35	2	16	75	2	4	1	32	0	93	0	3	13	.503	.331
Cora, Alex, Alb.*	.264	81	326	299	42	79	121	17	5	5	45	6	3	3	15	1	38	10	7	1	.405	.303
Corey, Bryan, Tuc.	.133	42	17	15	1	2	2	0	0	0	0	0	0	0	2	0	10	0	0	0	.133	.235
Cornelius, Reid, Tuc.	.455	19	15	11	1	5	6	1	0	0	1	4	0	0	0	0	5	0	0	0	.545	.455
Cornett, Brad, Tuc.	.000	6	4	3	0	0	0	0	0	0	0	1	0	0	0	0	3	0	0	0	.000	.000
Crabtree, Robbie, Fres.	.000	3	1	0	0	0	0	0	0	0	0	1	0	0	0	0	0	0	0	0	.000	.000
Cradle, Rickey, Tac.	.290	82	327	297	53	86	149	25	1	12	53	0	2	4	24	1	76	9	5	4	.502	.349
Crawford, Carlos, Nash.	.000	8	4	4	1	0	0	0	0	0	0	0	0	0	0	0	1	0	0	0	.000	.000
Cromer, D.T., Edm.*	.294	125	545	504	75	148	232	30	3	16	85	0	4	4	32	3	93	12	6	9	.460	.338
Cromer, Tripp, Alb.	.333	12	32	30	3	10	17	1	0	2	5	0	1	0	1	0	5	0	1	0	.567	.344
Cruz, Fausto, Van.	.262	117	464	420	47	110	160	26	6	4	43	7	7	2	28	2	76	7	4	4	.381	.306
Cruz, Jacob, Fres.*	.298	89	399	342	60	102	179	17	3	18	62	2	1	8	46	2	57	12	5	9	.523	.393
Cuevas, Trent, Alb.	.333	5	20	18	3	6	7	1	0	0	4	1	1	0	0	0	1	0	0	0	.389	.316
Cuyler, Milt, Okla.†	.000	2	8	6	0	0	0	0	0	0	0	0	0	0	2	0	4	0	1	0	.000	.250
Daal, Omar, Tuc.*	.000	1	1	1	0	0	0	0	0	0	0	0	0	0	0	0	0	0	0	0	.000	.000
Dandridge, Brad, Alb.	.182	15	37	33	5	6	9	3	0	0	4	0	0	1	3	0	5	0	0	0	.273	.270
Darwin, Jeff, Fres.	.000	56	2	2	0	0	0	0	0	0	0	0	0	0	0	0	2	0	0	0	.000	.000
Dascenzo, Doug, L.V.†	.192	7	32	26	5	5	6	1	0	0	2	0	1	0	5	0	2	2	0	0	.231	.313
Decker, Steve, Nash.	.129	18	67	62	5	8	17	3	0	2	4	0	0	0	5	0	14	0	0	4	.274	.194
De La Maza, Roland, Oma.	.143	34	7	7	1	1	1	0	0	0	0	0	0	0	0	0	4	0	0	0	.143	.143
Delgado, Wilson, Fres.†	.277	127	575	512	87	142	204	22	2	12	63	4	4	3	52	2	92	9	5	6	.398	.345
Dellucci, David, Tuc.*	.306	17	78	72	17	22	35	4	3	1	11	0	1	0	5	0	8	4	0	2	.486	.346
Demetral, Chris, Okla.*	.299	57	183	157	26	47	65	6	0	4	16	4	2	0	20	0	31	3	2	1	.414	.374
Dessens, Elmer, Nash.	.000	6	8	6	0	0	0	0	0	0	0	2	0	0	0	0	3	0	0	0	.000	.000
Devereaux, Mike, L.V.	.267	34	129	120	19	32	50	10	1	2	12	0	0	0	9	1	13	1	0	6	.417	.318
Diaz, Alex, Fres.†	.179	11	43	39	2	7	7	0	0	0	2	1	1	0	2	0	5	1	3	3	.179	.214
Diaz, Edwin, Tuc.	.263	131	548	510	61	134	195	31	12	2	49	2	5	4	27	0	105	9	6	9	.382	.302
Dishington, Nate, Mem.*	.265	60	232	200	30	53	100	15	1	10	34	0	0	8	24	1	88	1	1	2	.500	.366
Doman, Roger, Nash.	.000	7	2	1	0	0	0	0	0	0	0	0	0	0	0	0	0	0	0	0	.000	.000
Drew, J.D., Mem.*	.316	26	102	79	15	25	41	8	1	2	13	0	0	1	22	0	18	1	3	1	.519	.471
Dye, Jermaine, Oma.	.299	41	180	157	29	47	89	6	0	12	35	1	2	1	19	0	29	7	0	8	.567	.374

Player, Team	Avg.	G	TPA	AB	R	H	TB	2B	3B	HR	RBI	SH	SF	HP	BB	IBB	SO	SB	CS	GDP	Slg.	OBP
Echevarria, Angel, C.S.	.326	85	320	301	50	98	168	21	2	15	60	0	2	3	14	0	47	0	1	8	.558	.359
Edge, Tim, Nash.	.250	49	155	144	20	36	56	4	2	4	16	3	0	1	7	0	34	2	2	3	.389	.289
Edsell, Geoff, Van.*	.000	57	1	1	0	0	0	0	0	0	0	0	0	0	0	0	1	0	0	0	.000	.000
Elarton, Scott, N.O.	.133	14	21	15	1	2	3	1	0	0	1	5	0	0	1	0	0	0	0	0	.200	.188
Ellis, Kevin, Iowa.	.205	27	45	44	5	9	9	0	0	0	2	0	0	0	1	0	13	1	0	2	.205	.222
Encarnacion, Angelo, Van.	.240	8	25	25	3	6	8	2	0	0	2	0	0	0	0	0	2	0	1	1	.320	.240
Escamilla, Roman, Oma.	.000	1	1	1	0	0	0	0	0	0	0	0	0	0	0	0	1	0	0	0	.000	.000
Estrada, Osmani, Okla.	.354	15	56	48	17	17	22	2	0	1	3	2	0	1	5	0	2	1	0	1	.458	.426
Evans, Dave, Nash.	.000	7	1	1	0	0	0	0	0	0	0	0	0	0	0	0	0	0	0	0	.000	.000
Evans, Jason, Cal.†	.252	127	486	424	62	107	155	27	6	3	52	7	4	2	49	2	96	10	4	7	.366	.330
Fabregas, Jorge, Tuc.*	.250	6	23	20	2	5	6	1	0	0	3	0	0	0	3	0	1	0	0	2	.300	.348
Farmer, Michael, C.S.†	.176	32	36	34	7	6	10	2	1	0	3	2	0	0	0	0	13	0	0	1	.294	.176
Farnsworth, Kyle, Iowa†	.273	18	25	22	2	6	6	0	0	0	0	3	0	0	0	0	9	0	0	0	.273	.273
Fasano, Sal, Oma.	.214	4	15	14	1	3	7	1	0	1	2	0	0	0	1	0	4	0	1	1	.500	.267
Feliz, Pedro, Fres.	.429	3	8	7	1	3	7	1	0	1	3	0	0	0	1	0	0	0	0	1	1.000	.500
Ferguson, Jeff, S.L.	.206	81	263	223	35	46	63	6	1	3	20	3	0	13	24	0	42	7	2	7	.283	.319
Figueroa, Nelson, Tuc.†	.167	8	14	12	2	2	3	1	0	0	1	1	0	0	1	0	4	0	0	1	.250	.231
Finn, John, Cal.	.311	45	178	148	31	46	60	9	1	1	11	4	1	5	20	0	9	3	2	6	.405	.408
Flores, Ignacio, Alb.	.118	17	17	17	0	2	3	1	0	0	0	0	0	0	0	0	8	0	0	1	.176	.118
Florez, Tim, Tuc.	.282	77	253	227	31	64	80	5	1	3	23	0	5	3	18	1	49	4	2	10	.352	.336
Ford, Ben, Tuc.	.000	48	2	2	0	0	0	0	0	0	0	0	0	0	0	0	2	0	0	0	.000	.000
Foster, Kevin, Iowa.	.385	17	15	13	1	5	9	1	0	1	4	0	1	0	1	0	5	0	0	0	.692	.400
Franklin, Micah, Iowa†	.329	118	435	359	74	118	235	26	2	29	95	0	4	13	59	8	72	5	3	10	.655	.437
Frazier, Lou, Cal.†	.270	101	461	397	81	107	181	26	3	14	50	2	2	3	57	1	84	42	8	2	.456	.364
Frias, Hanley, Tuc.†	.289	63	282	253	32	73	94	10	4	1	21	2	3	0	24	0	41	16	7	4	.372	.346
Frontera, Chad, Fres.	.000	5	6	5	0	0	0	0	0	0	0	1	0	0	0	0	2	0	0	0	.000	.000
Fultz, Aaron, Fres.*	.000	10	1	0	0	0	0	0	0	0	0	1	0	0	0	0	0	0	0	0	.000	.000
Garcia, Carlos, Van.	.255	44	172	161	18	41	56	6	0	3	15	0	1	2	8	1	22	2	5	2	.348	.297
Garcia, Freddy, Nash.	.270	88	358	326	52	88	186	24	4	22	55	0	3	4	25	0	89	0	2	12	.571	.327
Garcia, Freddy, N.O.	.333	2	3	3	0	1	2	1	0	0	1	0	0	0	0	0	0	0	0	0	.667	.333
Garcia, Karim, Tuc.*	.311	27	122	106	21	33	71	4	2	10	27	0	1	0	15	1	24	5	1	2	.670	.393
Gazarek, Marty, Iowa.	.256	88	261	238	33	61	89	16	0	4	16	2	0	5	16	0	38	4	3	5	.374	.317
Geisler, Phil, Nash.-N.O.*	.211	28	63	57	4	12	14	2	0	0	4	0	1	0	5	1	20	0	1	1	.246	.270
Giambi, Jeremy, Oma.*	.372	96	394	325	68	121	206	21	2	20	66	2	4	6	57	8	64	8	5	4	.634	.469
Giard, Ken, Nash.	.000	15	3	3	0	0	0	0	0	0	0	0	0	0	0	0	2	0	0	0	.000	.000
Gibbs, Kevin, Alb.†	.125	2	10	8	1	1	1	0	0	0	1	0	0	0	2	0	1	0	0	0	.125	.300
Gibson, Derrick, C.S.	.292	126	537	497	84	145	213	20	3	14	81	0	2	3	35	2	110	14	6	17	.429	.341
Gil, Benji, Cal.	.248	128	516	460	80	114	190	24	5	14	69	5	6	4	41	2	90	11	4	9	.413	.311
Gilbert, Shawn, Mem.	.269	62	254	216	37	58	98	15	2	7	32	0	3	6	29	1	53	7	4	3	.454	.366
Giovanola, Ed, L.V.*	.333	4	17	15	4	5	5	0	0	0	1	0	0	0	2	0	3	0	1	0	.333	.412
Gipson, Charles, Tac.	.241	75	314	278	39	67	87	16	2	0	11	3	0	6	27	1	50	14	11	17	.313	.322
Glassey, Josh, Alb.*	.125	6	9	8	1	1	2	1	0	0	1	0	0	0	1	0	3	1	0	0	.250	.222
Glaus, Troy, Van.	.306	59	243	219	33	67	131	16	0	16	42	0	0	3	21	0	55	3	2	1	.598	.374
Glinatsis, George, C.S.	.000	20	14	12	0	0	0	0	0	0	0	2	0	0	0	0	7	0	0	0	.000	.000
Gonzales, Rene, Cal.-Okla.	.217	77	296	240	28	52	74	10	0	4	23	3	2	3	47	0	38	1	3	11	.308	.349
Gonzalez, Jimmy, L.V.	.238	51	180	160	22	38	62	9	0	5	21	1	2	1	15	1	44	1	0	1	.388	.303
Gray, Dennis, Iowa*	.000	9	1	1	0	0	0	0	0	0	0	0	0	0	0	0	0	0	0	0	.000	.000
Green, Scarborough, Mem.†..	.198	26	90	81	11	16	21	5	0	0	2	1	0	0	8	1	22	1	4	2	.259	.270
Greene, Todd, Van.	.278	30	125	108	16	30	63	12	0	7	20	0	2	3	12	0	17	1	0	2	.583	.360
Grijak, Kevin, Nash.*	.286	67	255	227	32	65	127	17	0	15	40	1	1	3	23	0	34	1	4	8	.559	.358
Grilli, Jason, Fres.	.000	8	10	9	0	0	0	0	0	0	0	1	0	0	0	0	5	0	0	0	.000	.000
Grundy, Phil, Oma.	.286	16	7	7	0	2	2	0	0	0	0	0	0	0	0	0	0	0	0	0	.286	.286
Grzanich, Mike, N.O.	.500	34	3	2	1	1	1	0	0	0	1	1	0	0	0	0	1	0	0	0	.500	.500
Gubanich, Creighton, L.V.	.291	86	331	292	48	85	164	22	0	19	70	0	6	3	30	3	85	1	1	4	.562	.356
Guerrero, Wilton, Alb.	.298	30	133	121	15	36	46	3	2	1	10	2	0	1	9	0	12	11	3	2	.380	.351
Guiel, Aaron, L.V.*	.311	60	218	183	33	57	95	15	4	5	31	1	2	4	28	2	51	5	1	4	.519	.410
Guillen, Carlos, N.O.-Tac.†	.279	124	522	466	75	130	198	19	5	13	55	7	4	5	40	1	78	4	6	6	.425	.340
Gutierrez, Jim, N.O.	.375	27	9	8	0	3	4	1	0	0	1	1	0	0	0	0	1	0	0	1	.500	.375
Guzman, Edwards, Fres.*	.305	102	356	325	50	99	143	17	0	9	48	3	1	3	24	4	47	1	0	4	.440	.347
Hajek, Dave, L.V.	.328	130	578	539	85	177	240	45	3	4	63	3	12	1	23	0	46	14	6	13	.445	.350
Halama, John, N.O.*	.214	17	22	14	2	3	4	1	0	0	1	5	1	0	2	0	6	0	0	0	.286	.294
Hale, Chip, Mem.*	.268	132	480	411	60	110	155	21	0	8	66	4	3	0	62	4	37	1	3	11	.377	.361
Hall, Joe, Okla.	.253	24	98	87	6	22	32	5	1	1	15	0	1	3	7	0	13	0	0	3	.368	.327
Halperin, Mike, Nash.*	.000	11	1	1	0	0	0	0	0	0	0	0	0	0	0	0	1	0	0	0	.000	.000
Halter, Shane, Oma.	.309	22	107	97	15	30	41	6	1	1	13	4	0	0	6	1	15	4	1	2	.423	.350
Hansell, Greg, Oma.	1.000	47	1	1	0	1	1	0	0	0	0	0	0	0	0	0	0	0	0	0	1.000	1.000
Hansen, Jed, Oma.	.278	127	476	417	63	116	197	19	7	16	56	4	7	4	44	0	125	17	9	7	.472	.347
Hardtke, Jason, Iowa†	.288	91	375	333	67	96	151	20	1	11	53	1	2	4	35	1	46	7	7	7	.453	.361
Harris, Reggie, N.O.	.000	51	1	1	0	0	0	0	0	0	0	0	0	0	0	0	1	0	0	0	.000	.000
Hartgraves, Dean, Fres.*	.500	38	5	4	3	2	5	0	0	1	1	0	0	0	1	0	0	0	0	0	1.250	.600
Hartman, Ron, Tuc.	.269	126	469	448	54	118	166	21	0	9	55	3	3	3	22	0	53	1	3	11	.379	.307
Hatcher, Chris, Oma.	.309	126	516	485	84	150	313	21	2	46	106	0	3	3	25	3	125	8	6	9	.645	.345
Heiserman, Rick, Mem.	.000	40	2	2	0	0	0	0	0	0	0	0	0	0	0	0	1	0	0	0	.000	.000
Helfand, Eric, Van.*	.400	2	8	5	2	2	2	0	0	0	1	0	0	0	3	0	1	0	0	0	.400	.625
Hemmings, Scot, L.V.	.125	3	9	8	0	1	1	0	0	0	0	1	0	0	0	0	3	0	0	0	.125	.222
Hemphill, Bret, Van.†	.252	47	167	155	16	39	65	10	2	4	12	0	0	0	12	0	33	0	1	4	.419	.305
Herges, Matt, Alb.*	.125	35	9	8	0	1	1	0	0	0	1	0	0	0	0	0	0	0	0	0	.125	.125
Hermansen, Chad, Nash.	.258	126	515	458	81	118	238	26	5	28	78	0	3	4	50	0	152	21	4	3	.520	.334
Hernandez, Carlos, N.O.	.298	134	535	494	64	147	177	23	2	1	54	7	1	12	21	3	81	29	11	10	.358	.341
Hernandez, Fernando, Tuc.	.000	3	3	3	0	0	0	0	0	0	0	0	0	0	0	0	2	0	0	0	.000	.000
Herrick, Jason, Van.*	.217	59	216	207	17	45	77	8	3	6	19	2	1	2	4	0	65	0	4	2	.372	.238
Hidalgo, Richard, N.O.	.167	10	27	24	0	4	6	2	0	0	1	0	0	0	3	0	2	0	0	3	.250	.259

Player, Team	Avg.	G	TPA	AB	R	H	TB	2B	3B	HR	RBI	SH	SF	HP	BB	IBB	SO	SB	CS	GDP	Slg.	OBP
Holbert, Aaron, Tac.	.314	56	247	229	38	72	111	12	0	9	31	2	1	3	12	0	40	6	6	3	.485	.355
Horn, Jeff, S.L.	.306	24	87	72	14	22	30	5	0	1	6	2	0	1	12	0	18	1	2	0	.417	.412
Horne, Tyrone, Mem.*	.364	3	12	11	1	4	5	1	0	0	1	0	0	0	1	0	4	0	0	0	.455	.417
Horsman, Brent, L.V.*	.500	1	2	2	1	1	1	0	0	0	0	0	0	0	0	0	1	0	0	0	.500	.500
Hosey, Steve, Oma.	.300	3	12	10	2	3	6	0	0	1	1	0	0	0	2	0	2	1	0	1	.600	.417
Howard, Matt, Fres.*	.278	117	464	406	70	113	140	21	0	2	36	6	2	10	40	3	34	10	6	8	.345	.356
Hubbard, Trenidad, Alb.	.300	11	36	30	6	9	18	0	0	3	5	0	0	1	5	0	5	2	1	1	.600	.417
Huckaby, Ken, Tac.	.224	16	54	49	4	11	13	2	0	0	1	0	0	0	5	0	6	0	0	2	.265	.296
Huisman, Rick, Fres.	.333	44	3	3	1	1	2	1	0	0	0	0	0	0	0	0	1	0	0	0	.667	.333
Hunter, Brian, Cal.	.097	11	37	31	1	3	4	1	0	0	6	0	2	2	2	1	9	0	0	1	.129	.189
Hunter, Torii, S.L.	.337	26	97	92	15	31	50	7	0	4	20	2	1	1	1	0	13	2	2	3	.543	.347
Huson, Jeff, Tuc.*	.305	27	88	82	7	25	34	4	1	1	12	0	1	0	5	0	14	0	2	0	.415	.352
Hutchins, Norm, Van.*	.207	7	33	29	4	6	9	0	0	1	3	0	1	1	2	0	9	1	2	0	.310	.273
Hyers, Tim, Tuc.*	.222	19	32	27	7	6	10	1	0	1	5	0	0	0	5	0	5	1	0	2	.370	.344
Hyzdu, Adam, Tuc.	.340	34	118	100	21	34	55	7	1	4	14	1	2	0	15	0	23	0	1	2	.550	.419
Ibanez, Raul, Tac.*	.216	52	216	190	24	41	69	8	1	6	25	0	2	0	24	2	47	1	1	3	.363	.301
Iglesias, Mike, Alb.	.077	39	17	13	0	1	1	0	0	0	1	3	0	0	1	0	4	0	0	0	.077	.143
Incaviglia, Pete, N.O.	.324	76	326	281	57	91	172	10	1	23	66	0	2	9	34	0	63	11	3	9	.612	.411
Ingram, Garey, Alb.	.302	108	421	377	60	114	173	25	5	8	58	7	2	5	30	1	69	20	6	7	.459	.360
Jean, Domingo, C.S.	.000	36	3	3	0	0	0	0	0	0	0	0	0	0	0	0	3	0	0	0	.000	.000
Jennings, Robin, Iowa*	.248	81	338	298	57	74	149	23	2	16	62	1	0	6	33	1	49	4	4	9	.500	.335
Jensen, Ryan, Fres.	.500	2	2	2	0	1	1	0	0	0	0	0	0	0	0	0	0	0	0	0	.500	.500
Jimenez, Miguel, Iowa	.000	7	1	0	0	0	0	0	0	0	0	0	0	0	1	0	0	0	0	0	.000	1.000
Johnson, Brian, Fres.	.316	5	20	19	4	6	13	1	0	2	3	0	0	0	1	0	5	0	0	1	.684	.350
Johnson, Keith, Alb.	.232	82	275	254	32	59	84	5	1	6	26	6	1	4	10	0	51	6	3	4	.331	.271
Johnson, Russ, N.O.	.309	122	558	453	95	140	193	28	2	7	52	4	6	5	90	2	64	11	11	10	.426	.424
Jones, Chris, Fres.	.267	25	67	60	11	16	32	1	3	3	8	1	0	0	6	0	12	2	1	0	.533	.333
Jones, Dax, N.O.	.275	31	93	80	17	22	31	2	2	1	10	0	1	0	12	0	9	1	1	4	.388	.366
Jones, Jack, Alb.	.232	15	59	56	7	13	19	1	1	1	7	0	1	0	2	0	13	1	1	3	.339	.271
Jorgensen, Randy, Tac.*	.233	81	280	253	27	59	83	13	1	3	26	3	3	0	21	4	42	0	0	7	.328	.289
Judd, Mike, Alb.	.211	17	20	19	2	4	5	1	0	0	0	0	0	1	0	0	6	0	0	0	.263	.211
Kaufman, Brad, L.V.	.152	23	33	33	2	5	6	1	0	0	1	0	0	0	0	0	17	0	0	1	.182	.152
Kennedy, Adam, Mem.*	.305	74	325	305	36	93	141	22	7	4	41	5	2	1	12	0	42	15	4	3	.462	.331
King, Ray, Iowa*	.000	37	1	0	0	0	0	0	0	0	0	0	0	1	0	0	0	0	0	0	.000	.000
Kirby, Wayne, Mem.*	.282	58	244	227	36	64	100	15	3	5	32	2	0	0	15	1	33	10	2	2	.441	.326
Kirgan, Chris, C.S.	.322	26	90	87	12	28	43	6	0	3	15	0	0	0	3	1	16	0	0	4	.494	.344
Klassen, Danny, Tuc.	.292	73	311	281	47	82	141	25	2	10	47	0	5	6	19	1	54	6	2	11	.502	.344
Klingenbeck, Scott, Nash.	.750	6	4	4	0	3	3	0	0	0	2	0	0	0	0	0	1	0	0	0	.750	.750
Kmak, Joe, Oma.	.222	24	71	63	6	14	23	3	0	2	9	1	0	0	7	0	8	0	0	3	.365	.300
Konerko, Paul, Alb.	.379	24	101	87	16	33	61	10	0	6	26	0	3	0	11	0	12	0	0	3	.701	.436
Koskie, Corey, S.L.*	.301	135	574	505	91	152	272	32	5	26	105	0	10	8	51	4	104	15	7	17	.539	.368
Kramer, Tom, C.S.	.286	49	7	7	1	2	2	0	0	0	0	0	0	0	0	0	2	0	0	0	.286	.286
Kubenka, Jeff, Alb.	.000	29	6	5	0	0	0	0	0	0	0	0	0	0	1	0	4	0	0	0	.000	.167
Kubinski, Tim, Edm.*	.000	57	1	1	0	0	0	0	0	0	0	0	0	0	0	0	1	0	0	0	.000	.000
Laker, Tim, Nash.	.355	44	177	152	30	54	105	16	1	11	34	0	1	3	21	0	26	1	0	6	.691	.441
LaRocca, Greg, L.V.	.309	95	339	304	55	94	150	22	5	8	39	2	2	12	19	0	48	7	4	3	.493	.371
Latham, Chris, S.L.†	.324	97	438	377	81	122	184	21	4	11	51	4	0	1	56	4	99	29	5	5	.488	.412
Lawrence, Sean, Nash.*	.045	26	24	22	1	1	2	1	0	0	0	2	0	0	0	0	13	0	0	0	.091	.045
Leach, Jalal, Fres.*	.354	35	139	130	23	46	85	8	2	9	26	0	1	0	8	1	26	3	2	1	.654	.388
LeCroy, Matt, S.L.	.308	3	13	13	2	4	11	1	0	2	4	0	0	0	0	0	7	0	0	0	.846	.308
Leius, Scott, Oma.	.298	71	280	258	40	77	132	10	0	15	46	0	3	2	17	0	30	7	3	14	.512	.343
Lesher, Brian, Edm.	.300	99	410	360	62	108	174	31	1	11	60	0	2	2	46	1	96	3	4	11	.483	.380
Lewis, Marc, S.L.	.293	119	473	444	61	130	205	31	1	14	68	3	2	1	23	0	64	10	11	16	.462	.328
Lewis, T.R., Okla.	.252	53	233	206	37	52	82	12	3	4	27	0	1	5	21	0	32	4	3	3	.398	.335
Lidle, Kevin, C.S.	.267	5	17	15	2	4	7	1	0	1	0	0	0	1	1	0	8	0	0	0	.467	.353
Liefer, Jeff, Cal.*	.258	8	33	31	3	8	14	3	0	1	10	0	0	0	2	0	12	0	0	1	.452	.303
Lilly, Ted, Alb.*	.000	5	5	5	0	0	0	0	0	0	0	0	0	0	0	0	3	0	0	0	.000	.000
Liriano, Nelson, C.S.†	.315	87	332	286	44	90	133	16	3	7	44	0	4	3	39	2	42	8	10	12	.465	.398
Little, Mark, Okla.-Mem.	.291	88	378	337	67	98	159	23	7	8	52	0	7	12	22	1	70	9	9	4	.472	.349
LoDuca, Paul, Alb.	.319	126	528	451	69	144	204	30	3	8	58	7	6	5	59	2	40	19	7	20	.452	.399
Lomon, Kevin, L.V.	.167	30	23	18	0	3	3	0	0	0	3	0	0	0	2	0	7	0	0	0	.167	.250
Long, Ryan, Oma.	.203	18	69	59	6	12	26	2	0	4	8	0	0	2	8	0	13	0	0	0	.441	.319
Looper, Braden, Mem.	.000	40	1	1	0	0	0	0	0	0	0	0	0	0	0	0	0	0	0	0	.000	.000
Lopez, Johann, N.O.	.143	45	7	7	0	1	2	1	0	0	0	0	0	0	0	0	4	0	0	0	.286	.143
Lopez, Mendy, Oma.	.179	60	217	195	18	35	52	6	1	3	14	3	0	1	18	0	44	2	3	0	.267	.252
Lovingier, Kevin, Mem.*	.000	39	2	2	0	0	0	0	0	0	0	0	0	0	0	0	1	0	0	0	.000	.000
Lowe, Sean, Mem.	.200	26	37	30	1	6	9	1	1	0	1	4	0	0	3	0	5	0	0	0	.300	.273
Lowery, Terrell, Iowa	.297	65	278	246	41	73	125	14	1	12	49	1	2	2	27	0	63	5	2	10	.508	.368
Luebbers, Larry, Mem.	.120	29	32	25	4	3	8	2	0	1	4	4	0	0	3	0	4	0	0	1	.320	.214
Luuloa, Keith, Van.	.333	8	35	30	4	10	11	1	0	0	3	0	1	0	4	0	3	1	1	1	.367	.400
Machado, Robert, Cal.	.264	66	269	239	31	63	94	19	0	4	27	5	2	3	20	0	33	2	2	9	.393	.326
Maddox, Garry, Tuc.*	.264	81	291	269	36	71	104	13	4	4	18	0	1	3	15	0	57	4	3	6	.387	.309
Makarewicz, Scott, N.O.	.167	4	12	12	1	2	2	0	0	0	1	0	0	0	0	0	4	0	0	0	.167	.167
Maldonado, Carlos, Tac.	.000	3	9	9	0	0	0	0	0	0	0	0	0	0	0	0	1	0	0	0	.000	.000
Maloney, Sean, Alb.	.000	26	2	2	0	0	0	0	0	0	0	0	0	0	0	0	1	0	0	0	.000	.000
Manuel, Barry, Van.	.500	23	3	2	0	1	2	1	0	0	1	0	0	0	1	0	0	0	0	0	1.000	.667
Marrero, Eli, Mem.	.238	32	144	130	22	31	57	5	0	7	21	0	1	0	13	1	23	5	4	3	.438	.306
Marrero, Kenny, Tuc.	.667	34	3	3	1	2	2	0	0	0	0	0	0	0	0	0	0	0	0	0	.667	.667
Martinez, Felix, Oma.†	.250	51	186	164	27	41	61	8	3	2	16	5	1	1	15	0	40	6	2	1	.372	.315
Martinez, Manny, Nash.	.240	22	82	75	12	18	26	5	0	1	6	0	0	0	7	0	20	5	3	1	.347	.305
Martinez, Ramon E., Fres.	.313	98	415	364	58	114	181	21	2	14	59	4	7	2	38	3	42	0	3	12	.497	.375
Martins, Eric, Edm.	.279	39	139	129	14	36	53	8	0	3	16	0	1	0	9	1	22	1	0	2	.411	.324

Player, Team	Avg.	G	TPA	AB	R	H	TB	2B	3B	HR	RBI	SH	SF	HP	BB	IBB	SO	SB	CS	GDP	Slg.	OBP
Mashore, Damon, Van.	.273	42	164	143	19	39	52	7	0	2	15	2	0	1	18	0	28	1	1	2	.364	.358
Maxwell, Jason, Iowa.............	.298	124	548	483	86	144	235	40	3	15	60	1	4	8	52	1	93	8	1	6	.487	.373
Mayes, Craig, Fres.*	.277	34	112	101	14	28	38	4	0	2	16	1	1	0	9	2	14	0	1	1	.376	.333
McAffee, Josh, Tuc.	.000	1	1	1	0	0	0	0	0	0	0	0	0	0	0	0	0	0	0	1	.000	.000
McCall, Rod, Iowa*	.252	114	431	361	78	91	200	19	0	30	70	0	2	4	64	5	151	0	2	4	.554	.369
McCarty, Dave, Tac.	.317	108	467	398	73	126	193	30	2	11	52	1	2	6	59	3	85	9	6	15	.485	.411
McDonald, Jason, Edm.† ...	.233	12	58	43	12	10	19	1	1	2	5	0	0	0	15	0	11	7	0	0	.442	.431
McDonald, Keith, Mem.	.318	58	184	170	21	54	83	8	0	7	22	2	0	2	10	2	30	1	1	2	.488	.363
McEwing, Joe, Mem.	.334	78	355	329	52	110	172	30	7	6	46	1	1	3	21	0	39	11	10	4	.523	.379
McKay, Cody, Edm.*	.228	19	69	57	6	13	16	3	0	0	5	2	0	3	7	0	5	1	0	2	.281	.343
Meacham, Rusty, Mem.-Nash. .	.143	53	7	7	0	1	1	0	0	0	0	0	0	0	0	0	1	0	0	0	.143	.143
Meier, Dan, Tuc.*	.207	10	31	29	5	6	9	3	0	0	2	0	1	0	1	0	9	0	0	1	.310	.226
Mejia, Roberto, Mem.	.240	49	185	175	23	42	75	5	2	8	25	1	2	2	5	0	42	10	5	3	.429	.266
Melendez, Dan, Alb.*	.280	77	241	207	24	58	76	10	1	2	30	3	2	1	28	1	37	3	2	5	.367	.366
Melo, Juan, L.V.†	.272	130	500	467	61	127	173	26	1	6	47	2	3	4	24	2	91	9	8	15	.370	.311
Meluskey, Mitch, N.O.†........	.353	121	490	397	76	140	232	41	0	17	71	0	5	3	85	10	59	2	0	15	.584	.465
Mendez, Carlos, Oma.	.272	50	186	173	23	47	66	13	0	2	18	0	2	1	10	0	24	3	0	4	.382	.312
Menechino, Frankie, Edm.	.278	106	461	378	72	105	160	11	7	10	40	2	1	10	70	1	75	9	10	11	.423	.403
Menhart, Paul, L.V.	.200	49	6	5	2	1	1	0	0	0	1	0	0	0	1	0	4	0	0	0	.200	.333
Mercedes, Henry, Fres.	.216	27	107	88	17	19	34	5	2	2	11	3	0	1	15	0	28	0	0	3	.386	.337
Meulens, Hensley, Tuc.-Cal. ..	.254	78	311	276	48	70	136	17	2	15	40	0	3	2	30	0	69	2	1	13	.493	.328
Michalak, Chris, Tuc.*...........	.000	30	13	10	1	0	0	0	0	0	0	2	0	0	1	0	6	0	0	0	.000	.091
Mieske, Matt, Iowa	.255	35	120	106	17	27	53	5	0	7	19	0	1	3	10	0	27	0	0	6	.500	.333
Milacki, Bob, N.O.	.091	29	37	33	2	3	6	1	1	0	2	2	0	0	2	0	10	0	0	2	.182	.143
Miller, Damian, Tuc.	.349	18	76	63	14	22	31	7	1	0	11	0	2	2	9	1	9	0	0	2	.492	.434
Miller, Kurt, Iowa	.294	28	38	34	2	10	14	1	0	1	6	3	0	0	1	0	5	0	0	1	.412	.314
Miller, Orlando, Oma.-N.O.	.269	68	242	212	31	57	83	16	2	2	24	0	3	2	25	1	57	2	0	7	.392	.347
Miller, Ryan, N.O.	.294	8	19	17	4	5	6	1	0	0	3	0	0	1	1	0	3	1	0	0	.353	.368
Miller, Travis, S.L.	.000	34	1	1	0	0	0	0	0	0	0	0	0	0	0	0	0	0	0	0	.000	.000
Mintz, Steve, Nash.*	.000	57	6	4	1	0	0	0	0	0	0	1	0	0	1	0	3	0	0	0	.000	.200
Mirabelli, Doug, Fres.	.260	85	324	265	45	69	124	12	2	13	53	3	1	3	52	6	55	2	0	9	.468	.386
Mitchell, Donovan, N.O.*	.282	49	115	103	16	29	45	5	1	3	15	1	1	1	9	0	19	2	3	3	.437	.342
Mitchell, Kevin, Edm.	.348	6	24	23	4	8	10	2	0	0	1	0	0	0	1	0	2	0	1	0	.435	.375
Mlicki, Doug, Mem.	.000	24	6	5	0	0	0	0	0	0	0	1	0	0	0	0	2	0	0	0	.000	.000
Molina, Ben, Van.	.293	49	191	184	13	54	68	9	1	1	22	1	1	0	5	0	14	1	1	6	.370	.311
Molina, Izzy, Edm.	.241	86	328	303	29	73	116	15	2	8	38	1	3	4	17	0	60	3	0	16	.383	.287
Molitor, Paul, S.L.	.500	2	10	10	0	5	6	1	0	0	0	0	0	0	0	0	0	0	0	1	.600	.500
Monahan, Shane, Tac.*	.249	69	302	277	32	69	99	8	5	4	33	4	2	0	19	3	47	6	4	3	.357	.295
Montgomery, Ray, N.O.	.290	75	305	272	42	79	126	18	1	9	45	0	4	3	26	0	48	4	2	8	.463	.354
Moore, Brandon, Cal.	.209	86	270	244	37	51	63	4	1	2	19	3	1	2	20	1	30	5	3	6	.258	.273
Moore, Joel, C.S.*	.200	12	12	10	1	2	2	0	0	0	2	1	0	0	1	0	5	0	0	0	.200	.273
Morales, Willie, Edm.	.194	73	262	242	25	47	75	13	0	5	30	1	1	1	17	0	47	0	1	8	.310	.249
Morenz, Shea, L.V.*	.297	13	40	37	5	11	19	5	0	1	6	0	0	2	1	0	9	0	0	2	.514	.350
Moreta, Ramon, Alb.	.370	8	29	27	5	10	15	1	2	0	3	0	1	0	1	0	9	2	2	0	.556	.379
Moriarty, Mike, S.L.	.224	64	187	161	21	36	57	8	2	3	19	2	1	1	22	0	39	2	1	1	.354	.319
Morman, Alvin, Fres.	.000	4	1	1	0	0	0	0	0	0	0	0	0	0	0	0	1	0	0	0	.000	.000
Morris, Matt, Mem.	.500	4	3	2	0	1	1	0	0	0	0	1	0	0	0	0	0	0	0	0	.500	.500
Mottola, Chad, Okla.	.265	74	278	257	29	68	89	13	1	2	22	0	2	1	18	1	49	8	3	7	.346	.313
Mouton, James, L.V.	.354	50	211	192	38	68	103	17	3	4	31	0	1	1	17	0	31	15	1	9	.536	.408
Munoz, Juan, Mem.*	.268	117	435	399	54	107	146	17	5	4	44	5	2	0	29	5	58	9	4	9	.366	.316
Murphy, Mike, Okla.	.216	24	81	74	10	16	17	1	0	0	5	1	0	0	6	0	23	3	1	1	.230	.275
Murray, Calvin, Fres.	.233	33	103	90	16	21	35	3	1	3	5	1	0	0	12	0	18	3	1	2	.389	.324
Murray, Heath, L.V.*	.080	27	29	25	0	2	2	0	0	0	0	2	0	0	1	0	9	0	0	0	.080	.115
Myers, Greg, L.V.*	.556	3	9	9	0	5	5	0	0	0	1	0	0	0	0	0	0	0	0	0	.556	.556
Myers, Rod, Iowa*	.218	30	116	101	15	22	28	4	1	0	10	1	2	0	12	0	25	4	4	3	.277	.296
Myers, Rodney, Iowa	.350	33	22	20	4	7	9	2	0	0	1	2	0	0	0	0	7	1	0	0	.450	.350
Neal, Mike, N.O.	.231	30	101	91	13	21	27	4	1	0	6	1	1	6	2	0	16	0	0	1	.297	.290
Neel, Troy, Van.*	.244	14	60	45	9	11	27	1	0	5	13	0	2	4	9	0	10	0	0	4	.600	.400
Neill, Mike, Edm.*	.302	99	445	371	72	112	168	18	4	10	48	6	1	2	65	0	91	6	5	12	.453	.408
Nevers, Tom, Van.	.202	30	95	89	7	18	21	0	0	1	4	0	1	0	5	0	18	1	0	3	.236	.242
Newman, Alan, L.V.*	.000	63	3	3	0	0	0	0	0	0	0	0	0	0	0	0	3	0	0	0	.000	.000
Newson, Warren, Okla.*	.307	111	470	398	75	122	208	21	1	21	75	1	5	0	66	4	106	7	5	11	.523	.401
Nieves, Jose, Iowa	.253	19	77	75	7	19	23	4	0	0	4	0	0	0	2	0	11	1	1	2	.307	.273
Nitkowski, C.J., N.O.*	.200	5	5	5	0	1	1	0	0	0	0	0	0	0	0	0	2	0	0	0	.200	.200
Norman, Les, Okla.	.305	100	414	380	64	116	182	32	2	10	51	5	3	9	17	0	79	6	2	8	.479	.347
Norton, Chris, Van.	.209	43	168	148	14	31	57	11	0	5	17	0	1	1	18	0	46	0	0	4	.385	.298
Nunez, Abraham, Nash.†	.249	94	413	366	50	91	108	12	3	3	32	2	1	5	39	0	73	16	8	9	.322	.328
Nunez, Vladimir, N.O.	.143	31	16	14	0	2	2	0	0	0	2	2	0	0	0	0	5	0	0	1	.143	.143
Obando, Sherman, C.S.	.293	55	169	140	23	41	77	12	0	8	28	0	2	2	25	1	26	3	0	3	.550	.402
Ogden, Jamie, S.L.*	.250	94	293	272	29	68	102	16	0	6	32	3	0	2	16	0	65	4	2	7	.375	.297
O'Neal, Troy, Tuc.	.229	55	142	118	15	27	35	5	0	1	14	1	0	9	14	0	33	0	2	4	.297	.355
Ontiveros, Steve, Mem.	.000	3	2	2	0	0	0	0	0	0	0	0	0	0	0	0	0	0	0	0	.000	.000
Ordaz, Luis, Mem.	.290	59	236	214	29	62	93	9	2	6	35	4	1	1	16	0	20	3	3	6	.435	.341
Orie, Kevin, Iowa	.370	24	106	92	27	34	69	8	0	9	24	0	0	2	12	1	15	1	0	3	.750	.453
Ortiz, David, S.L.*	.243	11	40	37	5	9	18	3	0	2	6	0	0	0	3	0	9	0	0	0	.486	.300
Ortiz, Hector, Oma.	.225	63	203	191	17	43	50	7	0	0	12	2	0	1	9	0	26	0	0	10	.262	.264
Ortiz, Luis, Oma.	.304	44	148	138	27	42	70	13	0	5	22	0	0	0	10	1	11	0	2	6	.507	.351
Ortiz, Russ, Fres.	.143	10	8	7	0	1	1	0	0	0	0	0	0	0	0	0	2	0	0	0	.143	.143
Osborne, Donovan, Mem.*	.000	1	3	2	0	0	0	0	0	0	0	1	0	0	0	0	1	0	0	0	.000	.000
Owens, Jayhawk, S.L.	.205	52	179	161	19	33	51	9	0	3	16	2	1	2	13	0	63	1	2	1	.317	.271
Palmeiro, Orlando, Van.*	.300	43	168	140	21	42	64	13	3	1	29	8	4	0	16	0	10	3	1	2	.457	.363
Patzke, Jeff, Nash.†	.299	104	421	361	48	108	145	16	0	7	48	2	1	9	48	0	74	5	6	6	.402	.394

Player, Team	Avg.	G	TPA	AB	R	H	TB	2B	3B	HR	RBI	SH	SF	HP	BB	IBB	SO	SB	CS	GDP	Slg.	OBP
Pearsall, J.J., Alb.*	.000	8	3	3	0	0	0	0	0	0	0	0	0	0	0	0	1	0	0	1	.000	.000
Pearson, Eddie, Cal.†	.291	99	382	354	32	103	147	21	1	7	53	0	5	1	22	5	63	1	2	13	.415	.330
Pegues, Steve, C.S.	.333	24	72	72	6	24	34	4	0	2	7	0	0	0	0	0	14	1	0	2	.472	.333
Pellow, Kit, Oma.	.185	14	58	54	8	10	19	3	0	2	6	0	2	0	2	0	19	2	0	1	.352	.207
Pendleton, Terry, Oma.†	.360	7	29	25	2	9	16	4	0	1	6	0	0	0	4	0	3	0	0	2	.640	.448
Peters, Don, Tuc.	.000	13	1	1	0	0	0	0	0	0	0	0	0	0	0	0	1	0	0	0	.000	.000
Petersen, Chris, Iowa	.234	118	424	389	54	91	135	16	2	8	41	5	2	7	21	3	100	2	4	12	.347	.284
Peterson, Charles, Nash.	.000	8	9	9	0	0	0	0	0	0	0	0	0	0	0	0	4	0	0	0	.000	.000
Phillips, J.R., N.O.*	.302	56	249	225	51	68	149	18	0	21	60	0	2	1	21	2	65	1	1	4	.662	.361
Phillips, Jason, Nash.	.091	5	12	11	0	1	1	0	0	0	0	0	1	0	0	0	4	0	0	0	.091	.091
Phillips, Randy, Fres.	.133	9	15	15	0	2	2	0	0	0	1	0	0	0	0	0	4	0	0	0	.133	.133
Pickford, Kevin, Nash.*	.111	13	20	18	0	2	2	0	0	0	1	2	0	0	0	0	6	0	0	1	.111	.111
Pierzynski, A.J., S.L.*	.255	59	220	208	29	53	85	7	2	7	30	2	1	0	9	2	24	3	1	4	.409	.284
Pisciotta, Marc, Iowa	1.000	28	1	1	0	1	2	1	0	0	1	0	0	0	0	0	0	0	0	0	2.000	1.000
Plantenberg, Erik, Fres.†	.000	53	7	7	0	0	0	0	0	0	0	0	0	0	0	0	5	0	0	0	.000	.000
Poe, Charles, L.V.	.277	118	426	393	56	109	162	25	2	8	43	0	1	6	26	1	81	6	2	11	.412	.331
Polanco, Placido, Mem.	.280	70	270	246	36	69	93	19	1	1	21	4	1	3	16	1	15	6	3	8	.378	.331
Politte, Cliff, Mem.	.100	10	12	10	1	1	1	0	0	0	0	2	0	0	0	0	2	0	0	0	.100	.100
Porter, Bo, Iowa	.364	4	15	11	2	4	5	1	0	0	3	0	0	0	4	0	4	1	2	0	.455	.533
Powell, Dante, Fres.	.230	134	540	448	83	103	168	17	3	14	52	3	4	14	71	1	138	41	9	6	.375	.350
Prieto, Ariel, Edm.	.000	10	1	1	0	0	0	0	0	0	0	0	0	0	0	0	0	0	0	0	.000	.000
Prieto, Chris, L.V.*	.304	92	394	352	65	107	143	18	6	2	35	1	0	1	40	1	48	20	11	4	.406	.377
Prieto, Rick, L.V.†	.266	32	94	79	15	21	29	6	1	0	8	0	1	2	12	0	22	4	2	0	.367	.372
Pritchett, Chris, Van.*	.259	104	419	374	42	97	141	21	1	7	41	3	5	0	37	3	72	2	2	14	.377	.322
Quinlan, Tom, Okla.	.278	137	608	539	75	150	237	33	3	16	97	1	6	19	43	0	155	4	0	14	.440	.349
Quire, Jeremy, Tuc.	.222	4	9	9	0	2	3	1	0	0	0	0	0	0	0	0	3	0	0	0	.333	.222
Radmanovich, Ryan, Tac.*	.300	110	456	397	73	119	201	33	2	15	65	5	7	1	46	3	83	2	4	6	.506	.368
Raggio, Brady, Mem.	.156	27	34	32	0	5	6	1	0	0	3	2	0	0	0	0	6	0	0	0	.188	.156
Rain, Steve, Iowa	.077	29	14	13	1	1	1	0	0	0	0	1	0	0	0	0	4	0	0	0	.077	.077
Ramirez, Aramis, Nash.	.274	47	198	168	19	46	71	10	0	5	18	0	2	4	24	0	28	0	2	3	.423	.374
Ramirez, Roberto, L.V.	.000	26	2	2	0	0	0	0	0	0	0	0	0	0	0	0	2	0	0	0	.000	.000
Ramos, Edgar, N.O.	.200	13	11	10	0	2	2	0	0	0	0	1	0	0	0	0	5	0	0	0	.200	.200
Ramos, Ken, S.L.-N.O.*	.287	102	329	286	34	82	112	13	1	5	41	3	2	1	35	3	37	3	1	4	.392	.364
Randolph, Steve, Tuc.*	.000	17	2	2	0	0	0	0	0	0	0	0	0	0	0	0	2	0	0	0	.000	.000
Rath, Fred, C.S.	.500	23	2	2	0	1	1	0	0	0	0	0	0	0	0	0	1	0	0	0	.500	.500
Rath, Gary, Alb.*	.276	28	32	29	2	8	9	1	0	0	6	3	0	0	0	0	8	1	0	0	.310	.276
Reyes, Dennis, Alb.	.286	7	7	7	0	2	2	0	0	0	0	0	0	0	0	0	0	0	0	0	.286	.286
Reyes, Jose, Nash.	.667	1	3	3	0	2	3	1	0	0	0	0	0	0	0	0	1	0	0	0	1.000	.667
Richardson, Brian, Alb.	.146	11	44	41	5	6	9	0	0	1	5	0	0	0	3	0	10	0	0	1	.220	.205
Richardson, Scott, Alb.	.296	108	382	348	59	103	158	21	2	10	52	1	5	3	25	1	63	19	4	12	.454	.344
Ricken, Ray, L.V.	.000	3	2	2	0	0	0	0	0	0	0	0	0	0	0	0	1	0	0	0	.000	.000
Riggs, Adam, Alb.	.371	44	196	170	30	63	94	13	3	4	25	1	1	3	21	1	29	12	6	1	.553	.446
Rios, Armando, Fres.*	.301	125	512	445	85	134	237	23	1	26	103	4	5	3	55	4	73	17	5	9	.533	.378
Ritz, Kevin, C.S.	.500	4	4	4	0	2	2	0	0	0	0	0	0	0	0	0	1	0	0	0	.500	.500
Rivera, Luis, N.O.	.232	33	92	82	17	19	26	2	1	1	7	1	0	0	9	0	8	2	1	2	.317	.308
Rivera, Roberto, N.O.*	.333	54	3	3	0	1	2	1	0	0	0	0	0	0	0	0	0	0	0	0	.667	.333
Rivera, Ruben, L.V.	.144	30	117	104	9	15	27	3	0	3	11	0	2	0	11	0	42	4	0	3	.260	.222
Roa, Joe, Fres.	.100	27	37	30	4	3	7	1	0	1	3	6	0	0	1	0	12	0	0	1	.233	.129
Roach, Peter, Alb.*	.500	21	2	2	0	1	1	0	0	0	0	0	0	0	0	0	0	0	0	0	.500	.500
Roberge, J.P., Alb.	.303	136	518	475	83	144	206	30	1	10	67	2	5	5	31	1	64	22	6	17	.434	.349
Roberson, Kevin, Cal.†	.271	119	487	431	84	117	234	36	0	27	97	1	7	11	37	1	128	5	1	5	.543	.340
Robertson, Mike, Tuc.*	.273	111	454	411	49	112	171	14	3	13	70	0	3	7	33	1	56	1	0	15	.416	.335
Rodriguez, Steve, Alb.	.227	7	29	22	6	5	10	2	0	1	3	1	0	1	5	2	4	1	0	0	.455	.393
Rogers, Kevin, Fres.*	.250	14	4	4	1	1	4	0	0	1	1	0	0	0	0	0	1	0	0	0	1.000	.250
Rohrmeier, Dan, Tac.	.286	135	574	507	93	145	275	51	2	25	104	0	1	7	59	4	109	0	4	20	.542	.368
Romero, Mandy, L.V.†	.290	40	153	131	25	38	70	8	0	8	22	1	0	1	20	1	25	0	1	9	.534	.388
Romero, Willie, Alb.	.285	114	442	403	50	115	172	21	3	10	61	4	5	5	25	2	68	23	15	14	.427	.331
Ronan, Marc, N.O.*	.244	51	141	123	7	30	38	5	0	1	10	0	0	1	17	2	25	0	0	3	.309	.340
Rooney, Mike, Tuc.	.333	3	5	3	0	1	1	0	0	0	0	0	0	0	0	0	2	0	0	0	.333	.333
Root, Derek, N.O.*	.000	1	2	2	0	0	0	0	0	0	0	0	0	0	0	0	2	0	0	0	.000	.000
Rose, Pete, Nash.*	.208	28	77	72	8	15	19	1	0	1	12	1	1	0	3	0	13	0	0	3	.264	.237
Rossiter, Mike, L.V.	.500	31	2	2	0	1	1	0	0	0	0	0	1	0	0	0	1	0	0	0	.500	.500
Rossy, Rico, Tac.	.286	56	238	210	33	60	102	18	0	8	36	2	0	0	26	2	36	1	1	7	.486	.364
Rupp, Brian, Mem.	.234	112	241	209	26	49	61	10	1	0	24	3	0	0	29	0	32	5	5	11	.292	.328
Rupp, Chad, S.L.	.291	115	489	413	78	120	211	25	3	20	89	1	8	6	61	4	105	8	3	3	.511	.383
Russo, Paul, N.O.	.254	93	309	268	33	68	121	15	1	12	44	3	4	4	30	1	55	0	0	10	.451	.333
Ryan, Matt, Nash.	.111	51	9	9	0	1	1	0	0	0	0	0	0	0	0	0	2	0	0	0	.111	.111
Ryan, Rob, Tuc.*	.317	116	472	394	71	125	198	18	2	17	66	0	5	10	63	3	61	9	3	5	.503	.419
Saenz, Olmedo, Cal.	.313	124	540	466	89	146	262	29	0	29	102	0	7	22	45	3	49	3	3	16	.562	.394
Sagmoen, Marc, Okla.*	.268	113	448	403	61	108	188	26	6	14	65	3	3	4	35	0	86	6	2	7	.467	.330
Saipe, Mike, C.S.	.240	24	27	25	3	6	9	1	1	0	1	2	0	0	0	0	5	0	0	0	.360	.240
Saitta, Rich, Alb.	.063	5	16	16	1	1	1	0	0	0	0	0	0	0	0	0	5	0	0	0	.063	.063
Salkeld, Roger, N.O.	.000	38	6	4	1	0	0	0	0	0	0	0	0	2	0	0	0	0	0	0	.000	.000
Sanders, Scott, L.V.	.167	15	7	6	0	1	1	0	0	0	0	1	0	0	0	0	1	0	0	1	.167	.167
Sanford, Chance, Nash.*	.259	27	97	81	17	21	42	7	1	4	21	0	0	0	16	0	12	0	1	1	.519	.381
Saylor, Jamie, N.O.*	.364	4	11	11	3	4	9	0	1	1	3	0	0	0	0	0	3	0	0	0	.818	.364
Scanlan, Bob, N.O.	.000	14	9	7	0	0	0	0	0	0	0	0	0	2	0	0	0	3	0	0	0	.000	.000
Scarsone, Steve, Van.	.270	115	451	407	50	110	202	24	4	20	55	0	3	7	34	0	112	4	2	10	.496	.335
Schroeffel, Scott, C.S.†	.000	1	1	1	0	0	0	0	0	0	0	0	0	0	0	0	0	0	0	0	.000	.000
Sealy, Scot, Tac.	.270	62	206	178	18	48	73	10	0	5	28	1	2	8	17	0	54	0	2	4	.410	.356
Secrist, Reed, Mem.*	.215	75	249	214	34	46	74	10	0	6	29	0	3	1	31	1	57	1	2	3	.346	.313
Seitzer, Brad, Tac.	.300	129	559	474	74	142	221	35	1	14	68	2	6	9	68	5	65	4	3	13	.466	.393

CLASS AAA Pacific Coast League

Player, Team	Avg.	G	TPA	AB	R	H	TB	2B	3B	HR	RBI	SH	SF	HP	BB	IBB	SO	SB	CS	GDP	Slg.	OBP
Sell, Chip, Alb.*	.316	37	149	136	22	43	49	2	2	0	10	1	1	0	11	0	23	9	6	1	.360	.365
Sexton, Chris, C.S.	.284	132	545	462	88	131	171	22	6	2	43	6	4	1	72	2	67	7	3	17	.370	.378
Shave, Jon, S.L.	.338	90	370	317	63	107	141	20	1	4	41	5	1	13	34	1	46	8	9	7	.445	.422
Sheaffer, Danny, Mem.	.213	25	70	61	10	13	24	2	0	3	10	0	0	0	9	0	8	0	0	4	.393	.314
Sheff, Chris, Edm.	.299	120	475	402	74	120	182	24	4	10	55	0	1	5	67	0	82	17	5	13	.453	.404
Sheldon, Scott, Okla.	.256	131	564	493	74	126	252	31	4	29	96	0	6	3	62	3	143	2	2	7	.511	.339
Shoemaker, Stephen, C.S.*	.167	15	14	12	1	2	2	0	0	0	0	2	0	0	0	0	5	0	0	0	.167	.167
Shumpert, Terry, C.S.	.306	97	420	376	66	115	196	29	8	12	50	4	1	4	35	4	59	11	11	11	.521	.370
Sikorski, Brian, N.O.	.375	19	18	16	5	6	6	0	0	0	1	0	0	0	2	0	5	0	0	0	.375	.444
Silva, Jose, Nash.	.000	3	3	3	0	0	0	0	0	0	0	0	0	0	0	0	1	0	0	0	.000	.000
Simmons, Brian, Cal.†	.290	94	403	355	72	103	171	21	4	13	51	3	3	1	41	1	82	10	6	6	.482	.363
Simons, Mitch, Tac.	.233	47	202	180	27	42	58	6	2	2	21	2	1	4	15	0	23	10	1	5	.322	.305
Sisco, Steve, Oma.	.280	109	405	371	58	104	184	20	0	20	58	5	3	0	26	1	58	4	6	11	.496	.325
Slusarski, Joe, N.O.	.000	31	3	3	0	0	0	0	0	0	0	0	0	0	0	0	1	0	0	0	.000	.000
Smith, Bubba, Tuc.	.148	9	34	27	3	4	7	0	0	1	6	0	1	0	6	2	7	0	0	1	.259	.294
Smith, Demond, Cal.†	.059	5	18	17	0	1	1	0	0	0	0	0	0	0	1	0	6	0	0	0	.059	.111
Smith, Jeff, S.L.*	.254	23	73	67	9	17	20	3	0	0	2	2	0	0	4	0	13	0	0	2	.299	.296
Smith, Mark, Nash.	.355	24	108	93	18	33	69	10	1	8	30	0	1	3	11	1	20	3	1	1	.742	.435
Snow, Casey, Alb.†	.200	7	26	20	2	4	6	2	0	0	2	0	1	1	4	0	7	0	0	0	.300	.346
Soderstrom, Steve, Fres.	.148	25	30	27	3	4	5	1	0	0	3	2	1	0	0	0	11	0	0	0	.185	.143
Sodowsky, Clint, Tuc.*	.000	2	3	2	0	0	0	0	0	0	0	1	0	0	0	0	2	0	0	0	.000	.000
Speier, Justin, Iowa	.000	45	2	1	0	0	0	0	0	0	0	0	0	0	1	0	1	0	0	0	.000	.500
Spencer, Stan, L.V.	.222	22	30	27	1	6	6	0	0	0	2	1	0	0	2	0	7	0	0	0	.222	.276
Spiezio, Scott, Edm.†	.231	5	16	13	3	3	7	1	0	1	4	0	0	0	3	0	2	0	0	0	.538	.375
Stahoviak, Scott, S.L.*	.316	111	452	399	71	126	225	33	6	18	82	0	7	1	45	4	94	5	2	9	.564	.381
Stankiewicz, Andy, Tuc.	.300	5	21	20	1	6	6	0	0	0	2	0	0	1	0	0	0	0	0	1	.300	.333
Staton, T.J., Nash.*	.242	62	206	186	28	45	71	8	0	6	21	0	1	3	15	0	55	5	4	3	.382	.307
Steed, Dave, Alb.	.278	57	166	151	18	42	63	7	1	4	21	0	2	2	11	0	39	0	1	5	.417	.331
Steenstra, Kennie, Iowa	.094	25	35	32	1	3	4	1	0	0	3	2	0	0	1	0	11	0	0	0	.125	.121
Stefanski, Mike, Mem.	.265	95	332	298	34	79	118	19	1	6	44	5	2	4	23	4	42	1	2	11	.396	.324
Stevens, Dave, Iowa	.000	26	6	4	0	0	0	0	0	0	0	2	0	0	0	0	2	0	0	0	.000	.000
Stevens, Lee, Okla.*	.333	3	12	12	2	4	7	0	0	1	1	0	0	0	0	0	2	0	0	0	.583	.333
Steverson, Todd, Mem.	.192	66	219	182	17	35	61	8	0	6	21	0	2	0	35	0	57	4	2	4	.335	.320
Stewart, Andy, Oma.	.345	8	31	29	5	10	17	4	0	1	6	0	0	1	1	0	1	0	1	3	.586	.387
Stone, Ricky, Alb.	.000	18	19	18	1	0	0	0	0	0	0	1	0	0	0	0	10	2	0	0	.000	.000
Stoner, Mike, Tuc.	.312	106	428	394	46	123	166	22	3	5	49	0	3	4	27	4	52	3	0	10	.421	.360
Strittmatter, Mark, C.S.	.278	87	301	255	32	71	110	15	3	6	38	2	2	12	30	1	48	0	0	6	.431	.378
Stuckenschneider, Eric, Alb.	.309	71	326	269	50	83	137	13	10	7	28	5	4	4	44	0	50	18	7	2	.509	.408
Suppan, Jeff, Tuc.	.188	17	18	16	2	3	4	1	0	0	0	2	0	0	0	0	2	0	0	0	.250	.188
Swartzbaugh, Dave, Iowa	.136	42	26	22	2	3	3	0	0	0	0	4	0	0	0	0	7	0	0	0	.136	.136
Sweet, Jon, Nash.*	.163	17	49	43	4	7	11	1	0	1	4	1	1	2	2	0	9	0	0	1	.256	.229
Taulbee, Andy, Fres.	.000	1	2	2	0	0	0	0	0	0	0	0	0	0	0	0	0	0	0	0	.000	.000
Tavarez, Julian, Fres.*	1.000	1	1	1	0	1	1	0	0	0	1	0	0	0	0	0	0	0	0	0	1.000	1.000
Taylor, Jamie, C.S.*	.275	27	71	69	9	19	31	6	0	2	11	1	0	0	1	0	18	0	0	2	.449	.286
Taylor, Scott, N.O.	.143	9	9	7	0	1	1	0	0	0	0	2	0	0	0	0	2	0	0	0	.143	.143
Tejada, Miguel, Edm.	.000	1	4	3	0	0	0	0	0	0	0	0	0	0	1	0	1	0	0	1	.000	.250
Thobe, Steve, Nash.	.000	7	11	11	0	0	0	0	0	0	0	0	0	0	0	0	2	0	0	0	.000	.000
Thompson, Jason, L.V.*	.271	58	209	192	21	52	78	15	1	3	17	0	1	0	16	1	49	3	3	2	.406	.325
Thurman, Gary, Van.	.220	58	209	182	24	40	53	6	2	1	16	3	0	4	20	0	42	8	1	5	.291	.311
Thurston, Jerry, Van.	.160	9	28	25	0	4	5	1	0	0	1	0	0	0	3	0	8	0	0	0	.200	.250
Tinsley, Lee, Van.†	.180	24	103	89	5	16	25	4	1	1	8	1	1	2	10	1	28	6	1	4	.281	.275
Tolar, Kevin, Nash.	.000	7	1	1	0	0	0	0	0	0	0	0	0	0	0	0	1	0	0	0	.000	.000
Tollberg, Brian, L.V.	.136	33	24	22	0	3	4	1	0	0	1	2	0	0	0	0	9	0	0	1	.182	.136
Torrealba, Yorvit, Fres.	.182	4	12	11	1	2	3	1	0	0	1	0	0	0	1	1	4	0	0	0	.273	.250
Toth, Dave, Cal.	.232	72	281	246	31	57	87	12	0	6	30	4	4	3	24	0	44	3	2	11	.354	.303
Tremie, Chris, Okla.	.223	78	281	247	35	55	65	10	0	0	12	4	1	5	24	0	47	1	1	12	.263	.303
Truby, Chris, N.O.	.412	5	18	17	6	7	13	1	1	1	1	0	0	0	1	0	3	1	0	0	.765	.444
Turner, Chris, Oma.	.300	67	244	200	32	60	79	14	1	1	16	1	1	3	39	2	36	6	3	4	.395	.420
Turner, Matt, Oma.	.143	42	8	7	0	1	1	0	0	0	2	0	0	0	1	0	3	0	0	0	.143	.250
Tuttle, Dave, Tuc.	.200	10	5	5	0	1	2	1	0	0	0	0	0	0	0	0	1	0	0	0	.400	.200
Tyler, Brad, Edm.*	.267	131	498	430	68	115	201	24	4	18	75	0	6	0	62	1	107	10	1	1	.467	.355
Tyler, Josh, Fres.	.000	3	4	3	0	0	0	0	0	0	0	0	0	0	1	0	1	0	0	0	.000	.250
Underwood, Jake, Tac.	.000	1	1	1	0	0	0	0	0	0	0	0	0	0	0	0	1	0	0	0	.000	.000
Unroe, Tim, Iowa	.173	39	117	104	9	18	26	5	0	1	9	1	2	0	10	0	30	1	0	5	.250	.241
Urbani, Thomas, Mem.*	.154	8	14	13	1	2	3	1	0	0	1	1	0	0	0	0	4	0	0	0	.231	.154
Valdes, Pedro, Iowa*	.314	65	258	229	49	72	135	12	0	17	40	0	2	0	27	3	38	2	1	6	.590	.384
Valdez, Efrain, Tuc.*	.000	28	5	5	0	0	0	0	0	0	0	0	0	0	0	0	2	0	0	0	.000	.000
Valdez, Mario, Cal.*	.330	123	527	448	86	148	240	32	0	20	81	0	4	12	60	3	102	1	2	14	.536	.420
Vavrek, Mike, C.S.*	.143	10	17	14	3	2	2	0	0	0	2	2	0	0	1	0	5	0	0	0	.143	.200
Velandia, Jorge, Edm.	.287	128	541	488	64	140	195	35	1	6	57	5	5	6	37	0	52	8	6	19	.400	.341
Velarde, Randy, Van.	.250	4	18	16	0	4	6	2	0	0	2	0	0	1	1	0	4	1	1	0	.375	.333
Vicente, Audo, Tuc.†	.143	4	8	7	0	1	1	0	0	0	0	0	0	1	0	0	6	0	0	0	.143	.250
Vitiello, Joe, Oma.	.285	103	428	376	44	107	185	20	2	18	71	0	7	6	39	2	68	0	0	19	.492	.355
Voigt, Jack, Edm.-Okla.	.333	38	162	138	20	46	76	12	0	6	22	0	1	1	22	0	34	1	3	1	.551	.426
Wainhouse, David, C.S.*	.000	38	3	2	0	0	0	0	0	0	0	0	0	0	1	0	1	0	0	0	.000	.333
Wallace, Kent, N.O.*	1.000	7	1	1	0	1	1	0	0	0	0	0	0	0	0	0	0	0	0	0	1.000	1.000
Ward, Daryle, N.O.*	.305	116	511	463	78	141	243	31	1	23	96	0	4	2	41	7	78	2	0	17	.525	.361
Warner, Ron, Mem.	.270	116	419	370	57	100	152	29	1	7	38	1	2	4	42	0	68	3	5	6	.411	.349
Wathan, Dusty, Tac.	.294	19	61	51	6	15	18	1	1	0	8	2	0	2	6	0	10	0	0	4	.353	.393
Weaver, Eric, Alb.	.200	46	5	5	0	1	1	0	0	0	1	0	0	0	0	0	1	0	0	0	.200	.200
Weber, Neil, Tuc.*	.167	46	14	12	3	2	2	0	0	0	0	1	0	0	1	0	6	0	0	0	.167	.231
Weibl, Clint, Mem.	.000	1	1	1	0	0	0	0	0	0	0	0	0	0	0	0	0	0	0	0	.000	.000

Player, Team	Avg.	G	TPA	AB	R	H	TB	2B	3B	HR	RBI	SH	SF	HP	BB	IBB	SO	SB	CS	GDP	Slg.	OBP
Wengert, Don, Iowa	.000	9	11	8	0	0	0	0	0	0	0	2	0	0	1	0	1	0	0	0	.000	.111
West, David, N.O.*	.000	20	4	4	0	0	0	0	0	0	0	0	0	0	0	0	3	0	0	0	.000	.000
White, Derrick, Iowa-C.S.	.343	88	390	332	72	114	200	22	2	20	86	0	4	6	48	3	62	6	6	7	.602	.431
Whitmore, Darrell, Nash.*	.309	105	355	311	58	96	180	19	1	21	50	0	2	6	36	1	87	3	4	5	.579	.389
Wiegandt, Scott, Nash.*	.000	11	1	1	0	0	0	0	0	0	0	0	0	0	0	0	1	0	0	0	.000	.000
Williams, Eddie, L.V.	.336	90	353	307	69	103	187	24	0	20	77	0	7	6	33	7	66	1	1	6	.609	.402
Williams, Jeff, Alb.	.100	22	30	20	3	2	3	1	0	0	2	7	0	0	3	0	11	0	0	0	.150	.217
Williams, Keith, Fres.	.292	113	378	353	47	103	187	23	2	19	68	1	4	2	18	1	74	0	1	4	.530	.326
Williams, Matt, Tuc.	.200	2	5	5	0	1	1	0	0	0	0	0	0	0	0	0	0	0	0	0	.200	.200
Williams, Mike, Nash.	.000	16	4	3	0	0	0	0	0	0	0	1	0	0	0	0	1	0	0	0	.000	.000
Williams, Reggie, Van.†	.282	100	435	373	58	105	155	25	5	5	39	1	2	6	53	2	98	13	12	2	.416	.378
Wilson, Craig, Cal.	.306	120	486	432	67	132	197	21	1	14	69	9	5	3	37	1	41	4	2	13	.456	.361
Wilson, Gary, Nash.-S.L.	.000	39	6	4	1	0	0	0	0	0	0	0	0	0	2	0	2	0	0	0	.000	.333
Wilson, Tom, Tuc.	.303	111	421	370	59	112	171	17	3	12	54	0	3	7	41	3	81	3	1	10	.462	.380
Wimmer, Chris, Nash.	.341	47	143	135	18	46	55	6	0	1	14	1	1	1	5	1	19	5	2	5	.407	.366
Witasick, Jay, Edm.	.000	27	3	3	0	0	0	0	0	0	1	0	0	0	0	0	2	0	0	0	.000	.000
Wolcott, Bob, Tuc.	.207	25	31	29	2	6	7	1	0	0	2	2	0	0	0	0	3	0	0	0	.241	.207
Wood, Jason, Edm.	.280	80	352	307	52	86	160	20	0	18	73	0	6	2	37	1	71	1	1	5	.521	.355
Wood, Kerry, Iowa	.000	1	2	1	0	0	0	0	0	0	0	1	0	0	0	0	0	0	0	0	.000	.000
Woods, Ken, Fres.	.364	23	48	44	9	16	21	5	0	0	5	1	0	1	2	1	8	0	0	1	.477	.404
Woodson, Kerry, C.S.	.375	43	9	8	0	3	3	0	0	0	0	1	0	0	0	0	2	0	0	0	.375	.375
Worrell, Steve, Iowa*	.000	18	1	1	0	0	0	0	0	0	0	0	0	0	0	0	1	0	0	0	.000	.000
Wright, Ron, Nash.	.214	17	67	56	6	12	15	3	0	0	9	0	1	1	9	0	18	0	0	2	.268	.328
Wrona, Rick, Okla.	.277	100	328	300	46	83	115	15	1	5	35	4	1	8	15	3	56	1	3	12	.383	.327
Young, Ernie, Oma.	.327	79	332	297	58	97	178	13	1	22	55	0	1	5	29	2	68	6	4	8	.599	.395
Zinter, Alan, Iowa‡	.310	129	500	419	82	130	224	23	1	23	81	0	3	3	75	1	116	3	5	10	.535	.416

GRAND SLAMS: Gilbert, Jennings, Roberge, M. Robertson, Simmons, Velandia, 1 each.

AWARDED FIRST BASE ON CATCHER'S INTERFERENCE: Maddox 3 (R. Chavez, J. Gonzalez, Cline); Valdez 3 (I. Molina, O'Neal, Tremie); Ramos 2 (Cholowsky, Marrero); Butler (LoDuca); Cromer (Wrona); J. Gonzalez (I. Molina); R. Gonzalez (A. Romero); McCarty (Morales); Staton (Meluskey); Ward (B. Molina).

PLAYERS WITH TWO OR MORE TEAMS

Player, Team	Avg.	G	TPA	AB	R	H	TB	2B	3B	HR	RBI	SH	SF	HP	BB	IBB	SO	SB	CS	GDP	Slg.	OBP
Candaele, Casey, Nash.†	.272	44	162	147	18	40	52	5	2	1	15	1	0	1	13	1	19	1	1	3	.354	.335
Candaele, Casey, N.O.†	.290	66	241	221	36	64	82	11	2	1	25	0	2	0	18	2	34	2	0	12	.371	.340
Geisler, Phil, Nash.*	.286	5	8	7	1	2	2	0	0	0	0	0	0	0	1	0	4	0	0	0	.286	.375
Geisler, Phil, N.O.*	.200	23	55	50	3	10	12	2	0	0	4	0	1	0	4	1	16	0	1	1	.240	.255
Gonzales, Rene, Cal.	.205	15	58	44	4	9	10	1	0	0	1	1	0	1	11	0	8	0	0	1	.227	.375
Gonzales, Rene, Okla.	.219	62	238	196	24	43	64	9	0	4	22	2	2	2	36	0	30	1	3	10	.327	.343
Guillen, Carlos, N.O.†	.291	100	420	374	67	109	171	18	4	12	51	6	4	5	31	1	61	3	4	5	.457	.350
Guillen, Carlos, Tac.†	.228	24	102	92	8	21	27	1	1	1	4	1	0	0	9	0	17	1	2	1	.293	.297
Little, Mark, Okla.	.296	69	305	274	58	81	133	20	4	8	46	0	5	10	16	0	60	9	6	4	.485	.351
Little, Mark, Mem.	.270	19	73	63	9	17	26	3	3	0	6	0	2	2	6	1	10	0	3	0	.413	.342
Meacham, Rusty, Mem.	.000	38	3	3	0	0	0	0	0	0	0	0	0	0	0	0	1	0	0	0	.000	.000
Meacham, Rusty, Nash.	.250	15	4	4	0	1	1	0	0	0	0	0	0	0	0	0	0	0	0	0	.250	.250
Meulens, Hensley, Tuc.	.250	76	303	268	45	67	126	16	2	13	37	0	3	2	30	0	67	2	1	12	.470	.327
Meulens, Hensley, Cal.	.375	2	8	8	3	3	10	1	0	2	3	0	0	0	0	0	2	0	0	1	1.250	.375
Miller, Orlando, Oma.	.246	39	132	114	16	28	44	10	0	2	15	0	2	1	15	1	32	1	0	5	.386	.333
Miller, Orlando, N.O.	.296	29	110	98	15	29	39	6	2	0	9	0	1	1	10	0	25	1	0	2	.398	.364
Ramos, Ken, S.L.*	.261	18	77	69	6	18	27	4	1	1	11	1	0	0	6	0	13	1	1	1	.391	.320
Ramos, Ken, N.O.*	.295	84	252	217	28	64	85	9	0	4	30	2	2	1	29	3	24	2	0	3	.392	.378
Voigt, Jack, Edm.	.324	18	76	68	10	22	40	6	0	4	11	0	0	0	8	0	15	1	2	0	.588	.395
Voigt, Jack, Okla.	.343	20	86	70	10	24	36	6	0	2	11	0	1	1	14	0	19	0	1	1	.514	.453
White, Derrick, Iowa	.363	66	295	251	57	91	166	17	2	18	76	0	2	4	38	3	48	4	5	4	.661	.451
White, Derrick, C.S.	.284	22	95	81	15	23	34	5	0	2	10	0	2	2	10	0	14	2	1	3	.420	.368
Wilson, Gary, Nash.	.000	29	5	3	1	0	0	0	0	0	0	0	0	0	2	0	2	0	0	0	.000	.400
Wilson, Gary, S.L.	.000	10	1	1	0	0	0	0	0	0	0	0	0	0	0	0	0	0	0	0	.000	.000

1998 PITCHING

TEAM

Team	W	L	Pct.	ERA	G	CG	ShO	Sv.	IP	H	TBF	R	ER	HR	SH	SF	HB	BB	IBB	SO	WP	Bk.
Memphis	74	70	.514	3.89	144	4	11	43	1266.2	1298	5375	611	548	140	45	26	42	406	18	1034	44	11
Vancouver	53	90	.371	4.33	143	16	6	31	1233.0	1264	5424	680	593	119	48	35	77	529	5	894	80	13
Tacoma	77	67	.535	4.37	144	8	8	42	1274.2	1274	5591	698	619	141	37	45	71	576	17	1009	41	5
Oklahoma	74	70	.514	4.45	144	9	6	32	1270.0	1351	5447	721	628	138	24	39	65	419	11	938	67	8
Fresno	81	62	.566	4.52	143	7	7	39	1247.2	1322	5378	692	626	164	54	33	59	395	21	1011	55	8
Edmonton	76	67	.531	4.54	143	10	6	37	1232.1	1298	5317	698	622	142	28	54	55	404	21	919	53	9
New Orleans	76	66	.535	4.70	142	10	5	43	1232.2	1310	5390	726	644	132	44	44	53	450	22	945	55	6
Iowa	85	59	.590	4.84	144	8	7	36	1257.0	1313	5501	749	676	150	54	34	33	522	9	1053	87	9
Salt Lake	79	64	.552	4.89	143	7	10	34	1234.1	1371	5452	750	671	142	31	41	42	459	23	969	74	15
Albuquerque	61	82	.427	4.91	143	6	3	30	1236.1	1423	5507	780	674	154	41	33	47	492	13	1030	69	11
Omaha	79	64	.552	4.94	143	6	6	46	1235.1	1399	5454	772	678	177	28	39	58	420	28	834	38	4
Las Vegas	70	72	.493	4.95	142	5	3	38	1246.2	1320	5577	771	686	127	46	39	3	570	35	1107	81	10
Calgary	81	62	.566	4.97	143	8	6	35	1242.1	1410	5536	764	686	165	30	46	59	504	19	919	59	16
Nashville	67	76	.469	4.98	143	2	6	44	1221.1	1345	5442	776	676	152	63	44	47	484	52	852	82	8
Tucson	57	85	.401	5.35	142	4	4	20	1236.2	1437	5603	850	735	167	40	41	64	502	28	922	74	15
Colo. Springs	55	89	.382	5.88	144	6	1	25	1228.2	1489	5715	947	803	163	42	68	78	637	24	958	63	13

TOP QUALIFIERS FOR EARNED-RUN AVERAGE TITLE

Minimum 115 innings. *Lefthanded pitcher.

Pitcher, Team	W	L	Pct.	ERA	G	GS	CG	ShO	GF	Sv.	IP	H	TBF	R	ER	HR	SH	SF	HB	BB	IBB	SO	WP	Bk.
Raggio, Brady, Mem.	8	9	.471	3.07	24	23	2	1	0	0	152.1	156	616	57	52	11	3	3	4	31	0	100	4	1
Baptist, Travis, S.L.*	8	5	.615	3.12	21	21	1	0	0	0	135.2	128	559	53	47	12	3	0	4	41	1	98	7	1
Lowe, Sean, Mem.	12	8	.600	3.18	25	21	0	0	0	0	153.0	147	637	57	54	17	6	1	4	61	1	114	2	0
Halama, John, N.O.*	12	3	.800	3.20	17	17	4	1	0	0	121.0	118	488	48	43	11	3	4	1	36	1	86	3	3
Brock, Chris, Fres.	11	3	.786	3.29	17	17	2	0	0	0	115.0	111	483	47	42	11	5	2	11	33	2	112	8	1
Clark, Terry, Okla.	12	5	.706	3.38	30	24	2	0	2	1	165.1	156	680	72	62	8	2	5	12	35	0	95	4	1
Barnes, Brian, Mem.*	7	5	.583	3.58	35	21	0	0	6	0	140.2	138	593	66	56	15	3	4	7	39	1	154	5	0
Wilson, Trevor, Van.*	5	9	.357	3.62	21	21	4	1	0	0	141.2	130	604	67	57	14	1	2	11	59	0	94	6	4
Heredia, Gil, Edm.	10	8	.556	3.67	29	19	6	1	7	1	144.2	154	595	69	59	13	5	8	2	18	3	99	2	1
Swartzbaugh, Dave, Iowa	14	5	.737	3.73	42	14	0	0	5	1	137.2	114	571	61	57	16	8	8	3	50	1	109	7	0
Barber, Brian, Oma.	8	4	.667	3.75	22	22	2	1	0	0	136.2	114	568	63	57	24	4	3	53	0	100	0	1	
Robertson, Rich, Van.*	11	12	.478	3.81	27	27	2	0	0	0	175.0	171	744	85	74	14	5	5	8	68	0	123	9	0
Miller, Kurt, Iowa	14	3	.824	3.81	28	27	2	0	0	0	167.2	153	711	77	71	13	4	5	3	77	0	145	6	0
Milacki, Bob, N.O.	10	8	.556	3.84	29	28	2	0	0	0	189.2	199	804	96	81	18	1	6	8	51	1	104	5	0
Witasick, Jay, Edm.	11	7	.611	3.87	27	26	2	1	1	0	149.0	126	621	74	64	19	2	6	7	49	0	155	5	1

DEPARTMENTAL LEADERS: W—K. Miller, Swartzbaugh, 14 each; L—W. King, 13; Pct.—Aybar, 1.000; G—Newman, 63; GS—Luebbers, 29; CG—G. Heredia, 6; ShO—Luebbers, Pickett, 2 each; GF—Chavez, 51; Sv.—B. Evans, 27; IP—Milacki, 189.2; H—Milacki, 199; TBF—Milacki, 804; R—Harrison, 116; ER—Harrison, 108; HR—Pratt, 29; SH—Anderson, Brohawn, 11 each; SF—Farmer, 11; HB—Clement, 30; BB—Hinchliffe, 88; IBB—Ryan, Turner, 8 each; SO—Clement, 160; WP—Lomon, 19; BK—Byrne, Pratt, 5 each.

ALL PITCHERS

*Lefthanded pitcher.

Pitcher, Team	W	L	Pct.	ERA	G	GS	CG	ShO	GF	Sv.	IP	H	TBF	R	ER	HR	SH	SF	HB	BB	IBB	SO	WP	Bk.
Abbott, Jim, Cal. *	2	2	.500	2.61	5	5	1	0	0	0	31.0	31	126	9	9	1	1	0	1	9	0	20	2	0
Abbott, Paul, Tac.	1	0	1.000	1.20	3	3	0	0	0	0	15.0	9	56	2	2	2	0	0	0	5	0	20	0	0
Abbott, Todd, Edm.	0	0	.000	0.00	3	0	0	0	2	0	4.2	3	17	0	0	0	0	0	1	0	4	0	0	
Acevedo, Juan, Mem.	0	0	.000	0.00	2	2	0	0	0	0	8.2	5	31	0	0	0	0	0	1	0	6	0	0	
Adams, Terry, Iowa	0	0	.000	0.00	3	0	0	0	0	0	4.0	1	16	1	0	0	0	0	3	0	5	1	0	
Adams, Willie, Edm.	0	0	.000	12.27	2	2	0	0	0	0	3.2	8	20	5	5	2	0	0	1	0	1	0	0	
Almanza, Armando, Mem. *	3	1	.750	3.03	31	0	0	0	9	1	35.2	35	163	18	12	1	1	1	0	19	1	45	6	2
Alston, Garvin, C.S.	2	4	.333	6.45	44	0	0	0	17	5	67.0	85	313	53	48	12	1	2	1	32	3	69	2	2
Alvarez, Juan, Van. *	1	1	.500	5.02	18	0	0	0	5	0	14.1	14	65	9	8	2	0	0	8	0	12	0	1	
Alvarez, Tavo, Nash.	3	5	.375	4.83	15	15	1	0	0	0	85.2	101	377	57	46	12	6	7	1	22	2	58	3	0
Anderson, Jimmy, Nash. *	9	10	.474	5.02	35	17	0	0	3	0	123.2	144	570	87	69	8	11	5	4	72	6	63	13	1
Andujar, Luis, Cal.	3	3	.500	6.26	13	9	0	0	0	0	50.1	62	226	38	35	8	0	1	5	15	1	46	0	0
Appier, Kevin, Oma.	3	2	.600	7.03	6	6	0	0	0	0	32.0	41	148	25	25	7	0	0	12	1	22	1	0	
Arocha, Rene, N.O.	5	4	.556	5.45	11	11	0	0	0	0	66.0	86	296	47	40	11	2	1	2	19	2	44	3	0
Arrandale, Matt, Mem.	5	2	.714	6.43	23	0	0	0	9	0	28.0	36	128	22	20	3	4	0	9	3	10	1	0	
Aybar, Manny, Mem.	10	0	1.000	2.60	13	13	0	0	0	0	83.0	62	324	24	24	7	3	2	3	17	0	63	1	4
Babineaux, Darrin, Alb.	0	0	.000	4.50	3	0	0	0	1	0	4.0	4	16	2	2	2	0	0	0	0	4	0	0	
Bailes, Scott, Okla. *	0	0	.000	0.00	1	0	0	0	1	0	1.1	2	6	0	0	0	0	0	0	2	0	0		
Bailey, Cory, Fres.	7	2	.778	2.47	57	0	0	0	25	10	94.2	79	375	31	26	4	1	2	3	18	4	76	4	2
Baptist, Travis, S.L. *	8	5	.615	3.12	21	21	1	0	0	0	135.2	128	559	53	47	12	3	0	4	41	1	98	7	1
Barber, Brian, Oma.	8	4	.667	3.75	22	22	2	1	0	0	136.2	114	568	63	57	24	4	3	53	0	100	0	1	
Barker, Richie, Iowa	3	1	.750	4.84	16	0	0	0	5	0	22.1	31	106	14	12	2	2	0	5	1	21	4	0
Barker, Tim, C.S.	0	0	.000	0.00	2	0	0	0	0	0	2.0	0	8	0	0	0	0	0	2	0	1	0	0	
Barndollar, Jeff, Tuc.	0	1	.000	9.00	1	1	0	0	0	0	4.0	7	25	4	4	1	0	0	4	2	2	1	1	
Barnes, Brian, Mem. *	7	5	.583	3.58	35	21	0	0	6	0	140.2	138	593	66	56	15	3	4	7	39	1	154	5	0
Barrios, Manny, Alb.	1	3	.250	6.00	20	2	0	0	7	0	36.0	47	170	25	24	7	1	1	2	15	0	33	4	0
Barry, Jeff, C.S.	0	0	.000	0.00	1	0	0	0	1	1	1.0	3	6	1	0	0	0	0	0	1	0	0		
Bautista, Jose, Cal.	3	3	.500	3.92	35	0	0	0	26	15	41.1	52	181	24	18	7	1	2	2	4	0	23	0	0
Beckett, Robbie, C.S. *	0	0	.000	9.00	21	0	0	0	10	0	26.0	35	137	27	26	4	0	3	1	28	0	28	3	1
Beirne, Kevin, Cal.	0	0	.000	4.50	2	2	0	0	0	0	8.0	12	38	5	4	1	1	1	4	0	6	0	0	
Beltre, Esteban, S.L.	0	0	.000	0.00	1	0	0	0	1	0	0.1	1	3	1	0	0	0	0	0	0	0	0	0	
Benson, Kris, Nash.	8	10	.444	5.37	28	28	1	1	0	0	156.0	162	689	102	93	26	5	6	5	50	5	129	9	0
Bertotti, Mike, Cal. *	3	2	.600	5.94	43	6	0	0	16	3	80.1	90	383	56	53	10	3	6	4	50	0	64	8	0
Berumen, Andres, Tac.	2	2	.500	6.93	9	8	0	0	0	0	37.2	39	187	37	29	6	2	2	2	30	1	31	6	0
Bevil, Brian, Oma.	1	0	1.000	1.38	10	0	0	0	2	0	13.0	10	55	2	2	1	0	0	1	4	1	19	2	0
Blais, Mike, N.O.	0	0	.000	0.00	2	0	0	0	1	0	2.2	1	10	0	0	0	0	0	1	0	1	0	0	
Blood, Darin, Fres.	4	5	.444	4.66	19	19	1	0	0	0	114.0	138	496	63	59	6	2	7	37	0	63	3	0	
Bluma, Jaime, Oma.	0	1	.000	6.28	14	0	0	0	9	2	14.1	19	67	13	10	4	0	1	0	7	2	8	0	0
Bolton, Tom, Nash. *	1	1	.500	10.38	3	1	0	0	2	0	4.1	8	23	5	5	0	0	0	2	1	3	0	0
Bonanno, Rob, Van.	0	3	.000	7.53	3	3	0	0	0	0	14.1	23	69	12	12	3	0	0	5	0	6	0	0
Bones, Ricky, S.L.-Oma.	6	3	.667	4.65	11	11	0	0	0	0	62.0	60	270	36	32	10	1	3	3	29	2	49	2	0
Bonilla, Denny, Tac. *	0	0	.000	11.81	2	0	0	0	0	0	5.1	11	26	7	7	1	0	0	0	4	2	0	0	
Bourgeois, Steve, C.S.	5	7	.417	5.57	38	13	0	0	7	1	114.2	154	531	82	71	14	4	3	5	62	5	87	8	0
Bovee, Mike, Van.	3	12	.200	5.59	48	8	1	1	13	1	95.0	109	436	61	59	6	7	3	6	50	4	76	4	0
Bowers, Shane, S.L.	9	7	.563	5.89	33	16	2	0	2	0	110.0	137	498	76	72	18	1	1	1	40	0	101	6	0
Boyd, Jason, Tuc.	2	2	.500	6.23	15	0	0	0	3	0	21.2	28	109	22	15	4	0	1	14	1	13	0	1	
Bradford, Chad, Cal.	4	1	.800	1.94	29	0	0	0	10	0	51.0	50	205	12	11	3	0	1	1	11	2	27	2	2
Brewer, Ryan, Oma.	0	0	.000	0.00	1	0	0	0	1	0	2.0	0	7	0	0	0	0	0	0	0	0	0	0	
Brock, Chris, Fres.	11	3	.786	3.29	17	17	2	0	0	0	115.0	111	483	47	42	11	5	2	11	33	2	112	8	1
Brohawn, Troy, Fres. *	10	8	.556	5.25	30	19	0	0	4	0	121.1	144	528	75	71	18	11	5	3	36	1	87	8	0
Brosnan, Jason, Van. *	0	0	.000	3.46	10	0	0	0	4	0	13.0	13	55	6	5	2	0	0	5	0	11	3	0
Brownson, Mark, C.S.	6	8	.429	5.34	21	21	3	0	0	0	124.2	131	542	85	74	22	5	8	14	37	0	82	2	3
Brunson, Will, Alb. *	5	8	.385	4.65	34	15	1	0	5	2	120.0	135	520	69	62	11	5	3	4	40	1	100	3	1

Pitcher, Team	W	L	Pct.	ERA	G	GS	CG	ShO	GF	Sv.	IP	H	TBF	R	ER	HR	SH	SF	HB	BB	IBB	SO	WP	Bk.
Bruske, Jim, L.V.	0	1	.000	6.00	5	0	0	0	4	1	6.0	8	25	4	4	1	0	0	0	1	0	2	0	0
Bullinger, Jim, Tac.	8	7	.533	5.05	20	16	0	0	2	0	101.2	106	459	64	57	13	1	1	8	58	1	73	4	0
Burke, John, C.S.	1	0	1.000	9.00	6	0	0	0	1	0	7.0	5	31	7	7	0	0	0	0	5	0	8	0	0
Busby, Mike, Mem.	0	0	.000	3.38	7	2	0	0	2	0	8.0	5	29	3	3	1	0	1	0	2	0	5	1	0
Butcher, Mike, Van.	1	4	.200	4.91	37	1	0	0	9	0	58.2	71	281	37	32	9	3	4	6	33	0	50	5	0
Byrdak, Tim, Oma. *	2	1	.667	2.45	26	0	0	0	8	1	36.2	31	161	13	10	3	4	0	2	20	0	32	2	0
Byrne, Earl, Iowa*	3	3	.500	6.34	10	9	0	0	0	0	49.2	54	226	37	35	8	1	1	0	29	0	34	3	5
Cabrera, Jose, N.O.	0	0	.000	5.40	5	0	0	0	2	1	5.0	2	19	3	3	2	0	0	1	1	0	6	1	1
Cadaret, Greg, Van. *	2	1	.667	0.00	9	0	0	0	3	1	10.0	4	36	2	0	0	1	0	3	0	12	1	0
Canale, George, Nash.	0	1	.000	0.00	1	0	0	0	1	0	2.0	2	9	2	0	0	0	0	0	0	0	1	0	0
Carroll, Dave, Edm. *	0	1	.000	12.54	7	0	0	0	2	0	9.1	22	55	16	13	2	0	0	1	5	0	11	1	0
Caruso, Gene, Nash. *	0	0	.000	0.00	2	0	0	0	1	0	2.0	2	9	0	0	0	0	0	2	1	2	0	0	0
Casian, Larry, Cal. *	4	1	.800	3.63	43	0	0	0	12	4	52.0	53	216	22	21	5	2	1	1	16	2	44	3	0
Castillo, Carlos, Cal.	1	1	.500	9.00	2	2	0	0	0	0	8.0	12	40	8	8	4	0	0	0	4	0	4	0	0
Chavez, Anthony, Van.	1	4	.200	2.63	53	0	0	0	51	22	51.1	44	218	20	15	5	4	2	6	17	0	42	0	0
Cholowsky, Dan, C.S.	0	0	.000	2.00	7	0	0	0	6	0	9.0	6	35	2	2	1	0	0	3	0	2	0	0
Chouinard, Bobby, Tuc.	0	0	.000	4.26	4	0	0	0	3	1	6.1	6	25	3	3	1	0	0	0	0	6	1	0
Christopherson, Eric, Cal. *	0	0	.000	9.00	1	0	0	0	1	0	1.0	3	5	1	1	0	0	1	0	0	0	0	0	0
Clark, Terry, Okla.	12	5	.706	3.38	30	24	2	0	2	1	165.1	156	680	72	62	8	2	5	12	35	0	95	4	1
Clement, Matt, L.V.	10	9	.526	3.98	27	27	1	0	0	0	171.2	157	763	94	76	12	4	4	30	85	2	160	18	2
Clemons, Chris, Tuc.	3	9	.250	6.15	20	19	0	0	1	0	86.1	103	410	69	59	13	2	4	9	44	0	79	2	0
Clontz, Brad, Alb.	1	2	.333	7.71	6	0	0	0	2	0	7.0	11	38	10	6	2	0	0	0	5	0	12	3	0
Cloude, Ken, Tac.	0	1	.000	6.75	1	1	0	0	0	0	4.0	4	16	3	3	1	0	0	1	0	4	0	0
Cole, Victor, Iowa	2	2	.500	3.74	38	2	0	0	6	0	67.1	77	296	35	28	4	3	1	1	25	0	69	7	1
Connelly, Steve, Edm.	6	0	1.000	3.79	55	0	0	0	27	13	76.0	64	310	34	32	7	1	2	2	24	2	62	5	0
Converse, Jim, Okla.	0	0	.000	5.14	4	0	0	0	2	1	7.0	8	31	5	4	3	0	0	0	2	0	4	0	0
Corbin, Archie, L.V.	0	0	.000	27.00	6	0	0	0	1	0	4.1	7	36	16	13	0	1	0	3	13	0	3	3	0
Corey, Bryan, Tuc.	4	6	.400	5.44	39	10	0	0	14	2	87.2	116	401	61	53	14	1	2	6	24	0	50	2	2
Cornelius, Reid, Tuc.	4	7	.364	5.94	19	16	0	0	0	0	94.0	108	412	70	62	16	2	2	3	26	1	65	3	2
Cornett, Brad, Tuc.	1	2	.333	7.86	6	6	0	0	0	0	26.1	44	127	25	23	6	1	2	0	6	0	12	1	0
Cortes, David, C.S.	1	0	1.000	7.71	6	0	0	0	3	0	7.0	14	37	6	6	0	0	0	2	0	5	0	0
Crabtree, Robbie, Fres.	0	0	.000	11.57	3	1	0	0	2	0	4.2	8	26	7	6	1	0	0	1	2	0	10	0	0
Crawford, Carlos, Nash.	2	2	.500	6.18	8	5	0	0	0	0	27.2	25	125	23	19	7	0	1	2	15	0	11	2	1
Croushore, Rick, Mem.	0	3	.000	4.71	23	0	0	0	9	2	28.2	21	115	16	15	3	1	0	1	9	0	40	2	0
Cruz, Nelson, Cal.	10	6	.625	5.33	35	18	2	1	4	0	126.2	159	571	85	75	18	2	5	11	40	1	101	5	1
Cumberland, Chris, S.L. *	3	2	.600	5.93	17	1	1	1	4	0	30.1	37	142	21	20	2	3	1	1	18	1	19	5	3
Cunnane, Will, L.V.	1	2	.333	5.25	33	0	0	0	9	4	36.0	45	171	26	21	1	2	2	3	19	4	30	2	0
Daal, Omar, Tuc. *	0	0	.000	3.00	1	1	0	0	0	0	3.0	3	13	2	1	0	0	0	1	0	4	0	0
Dale, Carl, Edm.	5	3	.625	4.08	11	11	1	1	0	0	64.0	64	276	31	29	12	1	2	6	26	0	41	3	0
Daniels, David, Nash.	0	0	.000	0.00	2	0	0	0	1	0	1.0	0	4	0	0	0	0	0	0	2	0	1	0	0
Darwin, Jeff, Fres.	2	6	.250	6.79	56	0	0	0	45	34	54.1	69	239	44	41	8	1	2	3	10	1	45	2	0
De La Maza, Roland, Oma.	9	6	.600	5.36	31	16	0	0	5	0	131.0	169	587	83	78	22	1	6	38	2	82	4	0
De La Rosa, Maximo, Tac.	2	1	.667	3.38	9	0	0	0	8	0	10.2	6	45	4	4	0	0	3	1	8	0	4	0	0
Dessens, Elmer, Nash.	3	1	.750	3.30	6	5	0	0	0	0	30.0	32	127	12	11	2	2	1	1	6	1	13	0	0
Dickson, Jason, Van.	2	1	.667	1.78	4	4	0	0	0	0	25.1	26	100	5	5	2	2	0	1	4	0	18	0	1
Diorio, Mike, N.O.	4	2	.667	5.22	21	0	0	0	8	2	29.1	38	134	24	17	3	2	1	1	11	4	14	1	0
Dixon, Bubba, L.V. *	3	3	.500	5.92	38	0	0	0	16	2	51.2	60	244	38	34	4	3	5	8	32	3	42	2	0
Dollar, Toby, Alb.	0	1	.000	4.70	7	0	0	0	3	0	7.2	14	45	10	4	1	0	1	0	5	0	3	1	0
Doman, Roger, Nash.	0	0	.000	9.22	7	1	0	0	2	0	13.2	16	65	14	14	4	0	2	1	6	0	9	2	0
Dougherty, Jim, Edm.	2	1	.667	3.75	45	0	0	0	26	6	57.2	57	254	24	24	7	2	1	2	33	4	45	1	0
Edsell, Geoff, Van.	4	8	.333	4.17	56	0	0	0	27	4	69.0	63	305	45	32	8	3	4	5	33	1	64	6	0
Elarton, Scott, N.O.	9	4	.692	4.01	14	14	2	1	0	0	92.0	71	383	42	41	6	0	3	4	41	3	100	3	0
Estes, Shawn, Fres. *	1	0	1.000	1.80	1	1	0	0	0	0	5.0	3	19	1	1	1	0	0	0	3	0	6	0	0
Evans, Bart, Oma.	3	1	.750	2.53	49	0	0	0	40	27	57.0	50	236	18	16	4	2	0	2	22	2	54	3	0
Evans, Dave, Nash.	0	2	.000	8.49	7	1	0	0	4	0	11.2	19	67	12	11	2	2	0	3	8	1	8	4	0
Everly, Bill, Alb.	0	1	.000	27.00	2	0	0	0	0	0	2.0	6	13	6	6	2	0	0	0	1	0	1	0	0
Eversgerd, Bryan, Mem. *	2	5	.286	3.34	49	0	0	0	17	0	56.2	51	238	25	21	9	1	0	1	20	1	50	2	1
Farmer, Michael, C.S. *	7	7	.500	5.61	28	23	0	0	2	0	126.2	173	608	107	79	19	7	11	7	56	5	74	6	1
Farnsworth, Kyle, Iowa	5	9	.357	6.93	18	18	0	0	0	0	102.2	129	469	88	79	18	5	7	2	36	0	79	4	1
Figueroa, Nelson, Tuc.	2	2	.500	3.70	7	7	0	0	0	0	41.1	46	180	22	17	8	0	2	2	16	1	29	1	0
Flores, Ignacio, Alb.	4	10	.286	7.11	17	17	0	0	0	0	88.2	113	415	72	70	16	0	3	1	48	1	63	10	0
Florez, Tim, Tuc.	0	0	.000	135.00	2	0	0	0	1	0	0.1	4	6	5	5	1	0	0	0	1	0	0	0	0
Ford, Ben, Tuc.	2	5	.286	4.35	48	0	0	0	36	13	68.1	68	313	41	33	6	3	3	33	5	63	7	1	0
Fordham, Tom, Cal. *	4	2	.667	3.02	9	9	0	0	0	0	56.2	38	225	21	19	6	1	3	0	26	0	39	3	0
Fossas, Tony, Iowa-Okla. *	0	1	.000	4.63	14	0	0	0	8	0	11.2	16	53	8	6	0	1	0	0	6	1	5	0	0
Foster, Kevin, Iowa	5	6	.455	6.85	17	11	1	1	4	0	67.0	74	300	52	51	19	1	2	0	38	0	75	5	0
Franklin, Ryan, Tac.	5	6	.455	4.51	34	16	1	0	10	1	127.2	148	561	75	64	18	4	8	10	32	2	90	0	0
Frontera, Chad, Fres.	1	2	.333	3.66	4	4	0	0	0	0	19.2	15	80	8	8	2	0	0	2	8	0	13	2	0
Fultz, Aaron, Fres. *	0	0	.000	5.06	10	0	0	0	3	0	16.0	22	68	10	9	2	0	0	2	1	13	1	0	0
Gajkowski, Steve, Tac.	3	3	.500	2.57	53	0	0	0	44	24	73.2	60	299	23	21	8	2	2	2	20	3	61	0	0
Gandarillas, Gus, S.L.	4	5	.444	5.27	53	1	0	0	24	4	70.0	88	322	47	41	4	1	2	0	24	5	42	9	0
Garcia, Freddy, N.O.-Tac. *	4	4	.500	3.64	7	7	0	0	0	0	47.0	44	193	19	19	8	0	2	0	14	0	43	2	1
Giard, Ken, Nash.	1	2	.333	5.71	15	0	0	0	5	0	17.1	17	82	12	11	3	0	1	0	12	0	16	0	0
Glinatsis, George, C.S.	2	9	.182	6.33	20	15	1	0	1	0	91.0	109	433	75	64	19	0	2	13	48	2	85	6	0
Granger, Jeff, Okla. *	4	8	.333	4.67	32	19	0	0	6	1	129.0	160	574	80	67	10	4	7	2	38	1	94	10	0
Gray, Dennis, Iowa*	0	0	.000	6.23	9	0	0	0	4	0	13.0	9	57	9	9	1	1	0	1	10	0	8	5	0
Grijak, Kevin, Nash.	0	0	.000	27.00	1	0	0	0	1	0	1.0	4	9	3	3	0	0	0	0	2	0	0	0	0
Grilli, Jason, Fres.	2	3	.400	5.14	8	8	0	0	0	0	42.0	49	193	30	24	7	1	0	1	5	18	0	37	1	1
Grundy, Phil, Oma.	6	4	.600	4.69	14	14	0	0	0	0	80.2	87	353	50	42	10	2	6	3	26	0	60	0	1
Grzanich, Mike, N.O.	1	2	.333	2.27	34	0	0	0	16	5	39.2	27	165	13	10	2	2	3	3	21	0	39	5	0
Gutierrez, Jim, N.O.	1	4	.200	6.44	27	0	0	0	8	0	43.1	70	208	36	31	7	1	2	13	1	25	3	0	
Halama, John, N.O. *	12	3	.800	3.20	17	17	4	1	0	0	121.0	118	488	48	43	11	3	4	3	16	1	86	3	3

- 425 -

Pitcher, Team	W	L	Pct.	ERA	G	GS	CG	ShO	GF	Sv.	IP	H	TBF	R	ER	HR	SH	SF	HB	BB	IBB	SO	WP	Bk.
Hale, Chip, Mem.	0	1	.000	0.00	1	0	0	0	1	0	0.0	3	4	1	1	0	0	0	0	1	0	0	0	0
Halperin, Mike, Nash. *	0	2	.000	5.79	11	0	0	0	5	0	14.0	17	67	9	9	2	1	0	1	9	1	10	0	0
Hansell, Greg, Edm.-Oma.	8	3	.727	2.69	59	0	0	0	32	13	83.2	76	344	27	25	7	0	1	6	18	4	75	4	0
Hanson, Erik, Van.	5	5	.500	4.50	14	14	2	1	0	0	82.0	82	353	43	41	7	4	2	3	36	0	60	6	0
Harikkala, Tim, Tac.	2	3	.400	4.89	18	4	1	1	9	1	57.0	74	257	32	31	6	1	1	1	13	0	44	0	0
Harris, Jeff, S.L.	8	0	1.000	5.91	25	0	0	0	18	3	32.0	38	148	24	21	4	3	3	0	19	4	24	3	0
Harris, Pep, Van.	1	0	1.000	2.84	2	0	0	0	1	1	6.1	4	25	2	2	0	0	0	0	3	0	7	1	0
Harris, Reggie, N.O.	2	3	.400	4.44	51	0	0	0	41	23	52.2	38	221	27	26	7	2	0	0	28	3	53	2	0
Harrison, Brian, Oma.	9	10	.474	6.41	25	25	1	0	0	0	151.2	193	685	116	108	23	2	8	13	42	1	73	1	1
Hartgraves, Dean, Fres. *	2	3	.400	3.97	38	1	0	0	11	3	70.1	67	295	35	31	8	2	5	1	19	4	64	1	0
Hartman, Ron, Tuc.	0	0	.000	5.79	2	0	0	0	1	0	4.2	7	24	3	3	1	0	0	2	2	0	1	0	0
Hasselhoff, Derek, Cal.	2	0	1.000	6.63	13	0	0	0	5	0	19.0	23	89	15	14	3	1	1	1	8	0	24	0	1
Hatcher, Chris, Oma.	0	1	.000	9.00	1	0	0	0	1	0	1.0	1	6	1	1	0	0	0	0	3	0	0	0	0
Haught, Gary, Edm.	1	0	1.000	7.55	19	0	0	0	2	0	31.0	43	147	27	26	6	0	3	3	14	0	20	2	0
Haynie, Jason, Nash. *	0	2	.000	9.19	3	3	0	0	0	0	15.2	24	76	18	16	3	0	1	2	7	0	6	2	0
Heathcott, Mike, Cal.	9	6	.600	5.04	39	13	1	0	10	1	109.0	113	483	65	61	12	2	4	5	51	2	77	8	0
Heflin, Bronson, Mem.	0	0	.000	9.00	2	0	0	0	0	0	2.0	2	8	2	2	1	0	0	1	0	0	1	0	0
Heiserman, Rick, Mem.	2	3	.400	4.02	40	0	0	0	16	6	40.1	54	185	21	18	2	2	1	2	14	1	28	1	0
Herbert, Russ, Cal.	9	10	.474	5.06	28	28	2	0	0	0	163.2	182	728	100	92	25	3	6	10	74	0	147	5	1
Heredia, Gil, Edm.	10	8	.556	3.67	29	19	6	1	7	1	144.2	154	595	69	59	13	5	8	2	18	3	99	2	1
Heredia, Julian, Nash.	0	0	.000	5.14	4	0	0	0	2	0	7.0	7	28	4	4	1	0	1	0	2	0	6	1	0
Herges, Matt, Alb.	3	5	.375	5.71	34	8	0	0	9	0	88.1	115	406	64	56	9	6	4	5	37	1	75	4	0
Hernandez, Fernando, Tuc.	0	1	.000	15.30	3	2	0	0	0	0	10.0	23	55	17	17	5	1	1	0	1	0	13	2	0
Hernandez, Xavier, Okla.	0	0	.000	1.35	5	0	0	0	1	0	6.2	5	28	1	1	0	0	0	1	1	0	9	2	0
Hinchliffe, Brett, Tac.	10	8	.556	4.00	25	25	2	1	0	0	159.2	132	681	80	71	22	1	5	4	88	2	100	4	2
Holdridge, David, Tac.	7	5	.583	3.31	42	0	0	0	17	7	70.2	55	299	28	26	2	6	2	7	34	5	73	3	1
Holtz, Mike, Van. *	0	0	.000	1.74	10	0	0	0	5	2	10.1	10	48	4	2	1	0	0	1	6	0	18	0	0
Holzemer, Mark, Edm. *	1	1	.500	3.23	30	0	0	0	8	6	39.0	41	168	15	14	2	3	4	3	11	1	27	2	0
Howard, Matt, Fres.	0	0	.000	0.00	1	0	0	0	1	0	0.2	1	4	0	0	0	0	1	0	1	0	1	0	0
Howry, Bobby, Cal.	1	2	.333	3.41	23	0	0	0	11	5	31.2	25	130	12	12	2	2	0	2	10	3	22	4	0
Hubbs, Dan, Alb.	1	2	.333	6.86	13	0	0	0	4	0	19.2	23	92	16	15	4	1	0	0	12	2	25	3	0
Huisman, Rick, Fres.	2	6	.250	5.38	44	0	0	0	17	0	72.0	65	309	43	43	18	0	2	1	34	2	80	4	0
Hurst, Jonathan, Okla.	1	2	.333	6.98	7	2	0	0	1	0	19.1	29	92	16	15	3	0	2	2	4	0	10	1	0
Hyers, Tim, Tuc. *	1	0	1.000	9.00	1	0	0	0	0	0	1.0	2	7	1	1	0	0	0	0	2	0	1	0	0
Hyzdu, Adam, Tuc.	0	0	.000	0.00	1	0	0	0	1	0	1.0	0	4	0	0	0	0	0	1	0	0	1	0	0
Iglesias, Mike, Alb.	7	1	.875	3.67	39	9	0	0	6	0	95.2	112	419	43	39	9	4	4	2	29	2	57	2	0
Jacobsen, Joe, Van.	0	0	.000	2.70	2	0	0	0	0	0	3.1	3	14	1	1	0	0	1	0	0	0	0	0	0
Jean, Domingo, C.S.	3	2	.600	5.48	36	0	0	0	12	0	47.2	64	226	33	29	5	1	7	3	25	1	38	4	0
Jensen, Ryan, Fres.	0	0	.000	4.76	2	1	0	0	0	0	5.2	4	25	5	3	2	0	1	0	4	0	6	0	0
Jimenez, Miguel, Iowa.	0	1	.000	10.13	7	1	0	0	2	0	10.2	15	54	12	12	2	0	0	1	7	0	7	5	1
Johnson, Barry, Okla.-Tuc.	2	9	.182	6.67	36	8	1	0	10	1	89.0	112	399	78	66	15	2	1	4	26	1	64	4	0
Johnson, Jonathan, Okla.	6	6	.500	4.90	19	18	1	0	1	1	112.0	109	474	66	61	15	0	4	11	32	0	94	6	2
Jones, Marcus, Edm.	2	0	1.000	2.53	2	2	0	0	0	0	10.2	14	50	7	3	1	0	0	5	4	0	4	1	0
Judd, Mike, Alb.	5	7	.417	4.56	17	17	3	1	0	0	94.2	98	424	62	48	17	4	2	6	44	0	77	6	3
Juelsgaard, Jarod, Tac.	5	5	.500	5.60	28	21	0	0	3	0	125.1	131	574	91	78	13	4	4	9	73	0	89	5	1
Kaufman, Brad, L.V.	9	9	.500	6.39	23	22	0	0	0	0	118.1	148	559	90	84	12	2	3	6	65	0	83	8	0
Kennison, Kyle, Tac.	0	0	.000	0.00	1	0	0	0	1	0	0.1	0	1	0	0	0	0	0	0	0	0	0	0	0
King, Bill, Edm.	8	13	.381	6.56	24	22	0	0	1	0	120.2	162	553	95	88	20	1	3	7	42	0	57	4	2
King, Curt, Mem.	0	1	.000	2.10	27	0	0	0	18	12	25.2	31	110	6	6	1	3	0	2	6	1	23	2	0
King, Ray, Iowa*	1	3	.250	5.01	37	0	0	0	7	2	32.1	36	143	20	18	4	1	0	0	15	1	26	4	0
Klingenbeck, Scott, Nash.	2	2	.500	6.14	6	6	0	0	0	0	29.1	45	137	24	20	3	2	2	2	7	0	15	0	1
Knight, Brandon, Okla.	0	7	.000	9.74	16	12	0	0	0	0	64.2	100	315	75	70	16	0	2	1	29	0	52	9	1
Kolb, Dan, Okla.	0	0	.000	0.00	1	0	0	0	1	0	1.0	1	5	0	0	0	0	0	1	0	0	0	0	0
Kramer, Tom, C.S.	3	6	.333	4.60	48	3	0	0	20	9	78.1	76	340	44	40	9	2	3	3	34	1	67	2	0
Kubenka, Jeff, Alb. *	2	5	.286	2.45	28	0	0	0	22	9	40.1	32	163	11	11	1	1	3	0	12	2	40	1	0
Kubinski, Tim, Edm. *	6	5	.545	4.54	57	1	0	0	23	2	75.1	77	321	40	38	8	2	3	3	22	3	54	3	1
Lagarde, Joe, Alb.	1	1	.500	3.10	14	0	0	0	8	2	20.1	16	87	7	7	1	1	0	3	7	0	18	3	0
Lawrence, Sean, Nash. *	12	9	.571	5.02	26	26	0	0	0	0	147.0	153	634	86	82	20	7	2	6	57	1	126	4	1
Laxton, Brett, Edm.	2	4	.333	6.60	8	8	0	0	0	0	46.1	45	204	35	34	6	3	1	5	24	2	21	7	0
Levine, Alan, Okla.	1	3	.250	4.73	12	7	0	0	4	1	53.1	51	223	33	28	7	1	1	2	17	0	30	1	0
Leyva, Julian, Edm.	0	1	.000	0.00	1	0	0	0	1	0	3.0	3	13	0	0	1	0	0	0	3	0	0	0	0
Lidle, Cory, Tuc.	0	0	.000	0.00	1	1	0	0	0	0	4.2	2	18	0	0	0	0	0	0	0	0	2	0	0
Lilly, Ted, Alb. *	1	3	.250	4.94	5	5	0	0	0	0	31.0	39	135	20	17	3	0	0	9	0	25	1	2	
Linton, Douglas, S.L.	4	4	.500	5.99	18	14	0	0	2	0	79.2	106	348	57	53	19	1	3	1	14	1	60	5	2
Lira, Felipe, Tac.	6	8	.429	4.26	20	20	2	1	0	0	129.0	142	560	69	61	10	6	6	11	42	0	88	2	0
Loiselle, Rich, Nash.	0	0	.000	0.00	4	0	0	0	3	2	5.0	3	18	0	0	0	0	0	0	0	0	6	0	0
Lomon, Kevin, L.V.	2	9	.182	5.15	30	17	0	0	3	0	124.0	128	551	78	71	13	4	3	8	62	2	118	19	1
Looper, Braden, Mem.	2	3	.400	3.10	40	0	0	0	32	20	40.2	43	177	16	14	3	2	1	2	13	1	43	3	0
Lopez, Johann, N.O.	7	2	.778	5.60	45	6	0	0	7	0	80.1	84	357	52	50	11	6	1	2	28	1	77	3	0
Lorraine, Andrew, Tac. *	7	4	.636	4.82	52	4	0	0	10	2	80.1	93	359	44	43	10	3	2	3	36	2	70	2	0
Lovingier, Kevin, Mem. *	5	1	.833	3.05	39	0	0	0	8	0	59.0	38	245	22	20	7	3	0	2	33	0	63	2	1
Lowe, Sean, Mem.	12	8	.600	3.18	25	21	0	0	0	0	153.0	147	637	57	54	17	6	1	4	61	1	114	2	0
Luebbers, Larry, Mem.	11	11	.500	4.10	29	29	2	2	0	0	173.1	183	732	96	79	23	5	2	7	47	1	110	2	0
Lundquist, David, Cal.	3	0	1.000	3.60	12	0	0	0	6	0	15.0	14	64	6	6	0	0	2	1	7	0	12	1	0
Maloney, Sean, Alb.	3	2	.600	4.63	26	0	0	0	23	9	35.0	38	150	21	18	6	1	0	1	8	1	38	4	0
Manning, David, Okla.	0	0	.000	1.00	6	0	0	0	4	1	9.0	11	36	1	1	1	0	0	0	0	0	9	0	0
Manuel, Barry, Tuc.	3	2	.600	2.61	23	0	0	0	12	0	41.1	28	170	12	12	2	0	2	16	2	40	1	1	
Manwiller, Tim, Edm.	1	0	1.000	0.82	2	0	0	0	1	0	11.0	8	39	1	1	0	0	1	0	2	0	10	0	0
Marrero, Kenny, Tuc.	4	2	.667	5.33	34	1	0	0	8	0	54.0	60	254	39	32	4	2	1	2	39	1	45	9	0
Martines, Jason, Tuc.	0	0	.000	0.00	1	0	0	0	0	0	1.1	0	6	0	0	0	0	0	0	2	0	2	0	0
Mathews, Del, Nash. *	1	0	1.000	10.50	4	0	0	0	0	0	6.0	8	33	8	7	1	0	1	0	6	0	4	2	0
Mathews, Terry, Edm.	2	2	.500	4.57	13	8	0	0	1	1	43.1	47	186	22	22	9	1	0	3	11	0	33	2	0

Pitcher, Team	W	L	Pct.	ERA	G	GS	CG	ShO	GF	Sv.	IP	H	TBF	R	ER	HR	SH	SF	HB	BB	IBB	SO	WP	Bk.
Maxcy, Brian, Mem.	1	1	.500	18.00	3	0	0	0	0	0	4.0	8	21	8	8	1	0	0	1	1	0	4	0	0
McCarthy, Greg, Tac. *	1	2	.333	4.19	19	0	0	0	6	1	19.1	15	95	14	9	2	1	1	2	22	0	24	4	0
McCurry, Jeff, Nash.	2	5	.286	4.96	40	0	0	0	35	23	45.1	45	193	26	25	9	4	0	0	15	6	34	2	0
McDill, Allen, Oma. *	6	4	.600	2.39	61	0	0	0	22	4	60.1	54	246	22	16	4	3	0	0	24	3	62	0	1
McDowell, Jack, Van.	0	0	.000	6.00	1	1	0	0	0	0	3.0	4	14	2	2	0	0	0	0	2	0	0	1	0
McMullen, Mike, Fres.	1	0	1.000	5.40	2	0	0	0	0	0	3.1	2	14	2	2	0	0	0	0	2	0	2	0	0
McNichol, Brian, Iowa*	0	0	.000	7.71	1	1	0	0	0	0	7.0	12	31	6	6	2	0	0	0	1	0	5	0	0
Meacham, Rusty, Mem.-Nash. .	3	3	.500	4.50	53	2	0	0	16	5	82.0	103	366	44	41	11	2	3	3	23	6	81	5	0
Meier, Dan, Tuc. *	1	0	1.000	2.70	2	0	0	0	2	0	3.1	3	14	2	1	1	0	0	0	0	0	2	0	0
Menhart, Paul, L.V.	7	6	.538	5.34	49	2	0	0	16	4	64.0	79	310	45	38	10	4	3	5	39	6	50	3	2
Michalak, Chris, Tuc. *	3	8	.273	5.03	29	9	0	0	6	0	73.1	91	326	47	41	11	2	5	4	29	3	50	4	3
Milacki, Bob, N.O.	10	8	.556	3.84	29	28	2	0	0	0	189.2	199	804	96	81	18	1	6	8	51	1	104	5	0
Miller, Kurt, Iowa	14	3	.824	3.81	28	27	2	0	0	0	167.2	153	711	77	71	13	4	5	3	77	0	145	6	0
Miller, Travis, S.L. *	3	4	.429	4.84	34	2	0	0	15	9	57.2	60	262	33	31	3	3	2	1	31	1	65	4	0
Mimbs, Mike, Van. *	1	1	.500	4.70	19	0	0	0	5	0	23.0	25	106	12	12	1	2	0	1	14	0	18	4	0
Mintz, Steve, Nash.	4	4	.500	5.45	56	0	0	0	18	1	72.2	85	334	48	44	7	4	4	3	32	2	45	3	0
Mlicki, Doug, Oma.-Mem.	2	6	.250	5.00	31	10	0	0	4	0	66.2	77	289	42	37	12	3	2	1	26	4	30	1	1
Molina, Izzy, Edm.	0	0	.000	27.00	1	0	0	0	1	0	1.0	2	6	3	3	1	0	0	0	2	0	0	0	0
Montgomery, Matt, Alb.	0	0	.000	0.00	3	0	0	0	3	2	3.0	0	11	0	0	0	1	0	1	2	0	3	0	0
Moody, Eric, Okla.	6	6	.500	3.38	45	6	0	0	29	12	101.1	112	436	51	38	9	2	4	6	23	4	73	4	1
Moore, Joel, C.S.	2	5	.286	6.72	12	12	0	0	0	0	65.2	78	302	54	49	7	3	3	6	31	0	46	3	1
Morman, Alvin, Fres. *	2	0	1.000	4.15	4	1	0	0	1	0	4.1	7	19	2	2	1	0	0	0	0	0	3	1	0
Morris, Matt, Mem.	1	1	1.000	4.50	4	4	0	0	0	0	14.0	16	60	8	7	1	0	0	0	4	0	11	1	0
Morse, Paul, Alb.	1	1	.500	3.00	2	2	0	0	0	0	15.0	8	59	5	5	1	0	1	3	6	0	11	0	0
Murray, Heath, L.V. *	9	11	.450	4.99	27	27	3	0	0	0	162.1	191	726	103	90	13	9	5	8	62	3	121	6	3
Myers, Jimmy, Okla.	7	1	.875	2.02	41	0	0	0	22	9	62.1	56	252	20	14	4	2	1	3	20	3	24	0	1
Myers, Rodney, Iowa	7	5	.583	3.91	33	13	2	1	17	11	101.1	84	429	47	44	10	5	2	5	45	1	86	6	0
Naulty, Dan, S.L.	1	0	1.000	6.75	5	0	0	0	2	0	5.1	8	24	4	4	0	0	0	0	2	0	5	0	0
Neal, Billy, Alb.	0	0	.000	4.66	6	0	0	0	5	1	9.2	11	40	5	5	1	0	2	1	2	0	6	1	0
Nelson, Chris, Edm.	0	1	.000	14.46	4	1	0	0	0	0	9.1	16	51	16	15	2	2	2	0	8	1	4	0	0
Newman, Alan, L.V. *	3	3	.500	3.30	63	0	0	0	23	7	76.1	58	332	29	28	2	5	3	3	50	3	76	6	0
Nina, Elvin, Edm.	0	0	.000	0.00	1	0	0	0	0	0	0.1	1	4	0	0	0	1	0	0	2	1	0	1	0
Nitkowski, C.J., N.O. *	0	1	.000	6.00	5	3	0	0	1	1	15.0	22	75	12	10	1	1	0	2	7	0	18	2	0
Nunez, Vladimir, Tuc.	4	4	.500	4.91	31	13	1	0	8	2	95.1	103	422	58	52	12	2	4	7	37	0	78	5	0
Ohme, Kevin, S.L. *	4	3	.571	5.01	51	0	0	0	23	6	82.2	90	361	48	46	5	3	4	6	31	3	47	3	1
Oleksik, George, Tuc.	0	0	.000	22.09	2	0	0	0	1	0	3.2	8	22	9	9	0	0	0	3	1	1	1	0
Oliver, Darren, Okla. *	0	0	.000	0.00	1	1	0	0	0	0	5.0	2	18	0	0	0	0	1	0	1	0	6	0	0
O'Neal, Troy, Tuc.	0	0	.000	27.00	1	0	0	0	0	0	2.0	7	18	10	6	2	0	0	1	2	0	0	1	0
Ontiveros, Steve, Mem.	0	1	.000	8.38	3	3	0	0	0	0	9.2	14	45	11	9	1	0	0	0	2	0	10	0	1
Ortiz, Russ, Fres.	3	1	.750	1.60	10	10	0	0	0	0	50.2	35	209	10	9	3	5	1	4	22	0	59	1	0
Osborne, Donovan, Mem. *	0	0	.000	6.23	1	1	0	0	0	0	4.1	5	19	4	3	2	0	0	0	0	0	6	0	0
Paniagua, Jose, Tac.	3	1	.750	2.77	44	0	0	0	18	5	68.1	66	292	25	21	2	4	4	4	22	1	61	0	0
Parque, Jim, Cal. *	2	3	.400	3.94	8	8	0	0	0	0	48.0	49	213	26	21	7	0	1	1	25	0	31	1	3
Patterson, Danny, Okla.	0	0	.000	4.50	1	0	0	0	0	0	2.0	4	11	1	1	0	0	0	1	0	2	0	0
Pavlas, Dave, Tuc.-Edm.	2	4	.333	3.80	35	3	0	0	18	2	66.1	66	285	34	28	7	0	4	2	17	2	49	2	0
Pearsall, J.J., Alb. *	1	1	.500	6.23	8	0	0	0	4	1	13.0	16	62	10	9	1	1	1	1	8	0	8	1	0
Perez, Juan, Edm. *	3	4	.429	3.12	24	0	0	0	9	1	40.1	35	168	17	14	3	0	1	1	18	2	37	0	0
Perisho, Matt, Okla. *	8	5	.615	3.89	15	15	1	0	0	0	90.1	91	394	41	39	6	2	3	6	42	0	60	6	1
Perkins, Dan, S.L.	5	0	1.000	4.82	7	7	1	0	0	0	46.2	48	205	30	25	8	0	2	2	20	1	33	2	0
Peters, Don, Tuc.	1	1	.500	7.59	13	0	0	0	5	0	21.1	27	96	18	18	8	1	2	0	7	1	4	3	0
Petersen, Chris, Iowa	0	0	.000	4.50	2	0	0	0	2	0	2.0	1	8	1	1	0	0	1	0	1	0	0	0	0
Phillips, Jason, Nash.	2	0	1.000	2.59	5	5	0	0	0	0	31.1	38	136	10	9	3	3	0	1	12	0	21	3	0
Phillips, Randy, Fres.	4	2	.667	5.32	9	8	0	0	0	0	44.0	56	194	30	26	10	3	1	1	8	0	45	0	0
Pickett, Ricky, Fres.-Tuc.-Okla.* .	7	7	.500	4.32	34	10	2	2	9	1	91.2	82	420	51	44	9	5	1	0	75	1	94	4	0
Pickford, Kevin, Nash. *	6	1	.857	3.49	13	12	0	0	0	0	80.0	84	336	33	31	7	4	2	0	20	2	59	4	0
Pisciotta, Marc, Iowa	3	5	.375	6.46	28	0	0	0	24	8	30.2	34	140	24	22	4	3	1	2	16	1	29	4	0
Plantenberg, Erik, Fres. *	4	5	.444	4.42	53	1	0	0	17	1	77.1	78	356	45	38	6	6	3	5	43	4	67	10	2
Politte, Cliff, Mem.	1	4	.200	7.64	10	10	0	0	0	0	50.2	71	244	46	43	10	3	2	0	24	0	42	3	0
Powell, John, Okla.	0	1	.000	8.41	11	0	0	0	6	1	20.1	24	94	21	19	6	1	0	2	5	0	20	0	0
Pratt, Rich, Cal. *	6	12	.333	6.29	29	23	1	0	4	0	133.0	191	615	112	93	29	3	5	4	44	3	76	1	5
Price, Jamey, Edm.	0	0	.000	1.29	2	2	0	0	0	0	7.0	6	26	1	1	0	0	0	0	0	0	6	0	0
Prieto, Ariel, Edm.	5	1	.833	2.56	10	10	1	0	0	0	52.2	47	212	20	15	3	0	2	0	12	0	50	3	1
Raggio, Brady, Mem.	8	9	.471	3.07	24	23	2	1	0	0	152.1	156	616	57	52	11	3	3	4	31	0	100	4	1
Rain, Steve, Iowa	4	6	.400	6.68	29	14	1	0	4	0	103.2	118	487	86	77	14	6	2	7	64	0	83	16	0
Ramirez, Roberto, L.V. *	1	1	.500	2.43	26	1	0	0	7	2	29.2	23	120	14	8	2	1	0	2	10	2	33	2	0
Ramos, Edgar, N.O.	2	3	.400	5.31	12	12	0	0	0	0	57.2	71	263	44	34	4	2	2	5	19	0	42	2	1
Randolph, Steve, Tuc. *	1	3	.250	3.18	17	1	0	0	3	0	22.2	16	99	11	8	1	0	2	0	19	2	23	3	0
Rath, Fred, S.L.-C.S.	6	3	.667	4.80	50	0	0	0	36	12	60.0	72	265	33	32	6	2	2	4	23	1	35	7	0
Rath, Gary, Alb. *	9	7	.563	4.52	28	24	1	0	3	1	157.1	184	687	91	79	17	5	1	4	52	1	119	2	0
Rawitzer, Kevin, Oma. *	4	5	.444	4.80	10	10	0	0	0	0	60.0	72	269	42	32	7	1	3	2	25	1	37	4	0
Redman, Mark, S.L. *	6	7	.462	5.53	19	18	0	0	1	0	99.1	111	446	75	61	13	2	5	5	41	1	88	3	3
Reichert, Dan, Oma.	1	1	.500	4.67	3	3	0	0	0	0	17.1	14	68	10	9	2	0	2	1	2	0	11	1	0
Reyes, Carlos, L.V.	0	0	.000	0.00	1	0	0	0	0	0	1.2	1	6	0	0	0	0	0	0	0	0	2	0	0
Reyes, Dennis, Alb. *	1	4	.200	1.44	7	7	1	1	0	0	43.2	31	176	13	7	5	0	0	1	18	0	58	1	0
Ricken, Ray, L.V.	0	1	.000	10.05	3	3	0	0	0	0	14.1	18	71	17	16	3	0	1	0	10	0	16	2	0
Rigby, Brad, Edm.	5	6	.455	5.94	13	13	0	0	0	0	69.2	86	310	52	46	5	2	6	3	17	0	34	3	1
Rincon, Ricardo, Nash. *	0	0	.000	0.00	1	0	0	0	0	0	1.0	0	3	0	0	0	0	0	0	1	0	0	0	0
Rios, Danny, N.O.	6	7	.462	5.63	25	18	2	0	4	1	123.0	159	563	90	77	14	2	4	6	41	0	51	6	0
Ritchie, Todd, S.L.	1	3	.250	4.15	36	0	0	0	18	6	60.2	55	271	38	28	5	2	4	4	31	3	62	2	0
Ritz, Kevin, C.S.	0	2	.000	8.31	4	4	0	0	0	0	17.1	25	90	23	16	2	2	3	1	9	0	7	0	0
Rivera, Roberto, N.O. *	5	4	.556	2.45	54	0	0	0	21	5	62.1	59	254	22	17	5	10	3	1	15	3	38	1	0
Rizzo, Todd, Cal. *	7	3	.700	6.75	50	0	0	0	19	6	72.0	102	358	62	54	6	3	3	3	39	3	58	10	1

Pitcher, Team	W	L	Pct.	ERA	G	GS	CG	ShO	GF	Sv.	IP	H	TBF	R	ER	HR	SH	SF	HB	BB	IBB	SO	WP	Bk.
Roa, Joe, Fres.	12	9	.571	5.17	27	27	2	1	0	0	162.0	192	702	102	93	26	9	2	4	32	0	97	3	2
Roach, Peter, Alb. *	0	0	.000	8.22	19	0	0	0	5	0	15.1	20	73	17	14	3	3	0	0	10	0	12	2	0
Roberts, Chris, Edm. *	0	4	.000	5.86	18	8	0	0	2	0	50.2	55	234	39	33	5	3	3	5	28	0	44	5	1
Robertson, Rich, Van. *	11	12	.478	3.81	27	27	2	0	0	0	175.0	171	744	85	74	14	5	5	8	68	0	123	9	0
Rodriguez, Felix, Tuc.	0	0	.000	9.00	1	0	0	0	0	0	1.0	1	6	1	1	0	0	0	0	2	0	0	0	0
Rodriguez, Frank, S.L.	5	7	.417	4.67	16	16	2	1	0	0	96.1	97	419	53	50	9	3	3	5	35	0	79	7	1
Rogers, Kevin, Fres. *	1	1	.500	7.36	14	1	0	0	6	0	18.1	23	84	15	15	5	0	0	0	8	1	15	2	0
Rooney, Mike, Tuc.	0	2	.000	4.60	3	3	0	0	0	0	15.2	20	74	10	8	3	2	0	2	9	1	6	0	0
Root, Derek, N.O. *	1	0	1.000	2.84	1	1	0	0	0	0	6.1	3	24	2	2	1	0	0	0	3	0	4	1	0
Rossiter, Mike, L.V.	2	2	.500	4.39	31	0	0	0	13	2	41.0	44	185	20	20	2	1	2	7	17	3	34	0	0
Rusch, Glendon, Oma. *	1	1	.500	7.98	3	3	0	0	0	0	14.2	20	72	18	13	4	1	1	1	6	0	14	0	0
Ryan, Matt, Nash.	4	3	.571	4.17	51	6	0	0	10	3	86.1	85	384	50	40	2	5	1	6	36	8	41	17	1
Sabel, Erik, Tuc.	1	0	1.000	8.71	7	0	0	0	1	0	10.1	17	53	10	10	0	2	1	1	5	1	7	1	0
Saier, Matt, Oma.	2	4	.333	8.32	9	9	0	0	0	0	48.2	73	232	46	45	13	1	2	2	16	0	25	0	0
Saipe, Mike, C.S.	5	11	.313	5.16	24	24	2	0	0	0	139.2	167	632	96	80	19	3	5	8	51	1	124	4	2
Salkeld, Roger, N.O.	3	6	.333	5.79	37	11	0	0	9	2	82.1	82	391	57	53	8	4	6	3	64	1	79	9	0
Sampson, Benj, S.L. *	10	7	.588	5.14	28	28	0	0	0	0	161.0	198	726	99	92	24	4	6	2	52	0	132	8	4
Sanders, Scott, L.V.	1	2	.333	3.44	15	3	0	0	6	3	36.2	34	151	14	14	2	2	1	2	13	3	43	0	0
Santiago, Jose, Oma.	0	0	.000	7.04	4	0	0	0	2	1	7.2	10	40	9	6	0	1	0	1	5	2	4	1	0
Sauveur, Rich, Nash. *	1	4	.200	1.81	46	0	0	0	20	10	44.2	34	178	15	9	0	2	2	1	17	4	43	2	0
Scanlan, Bob, N.O.	5	4	.556	6.46	14	12	1	0	0	0	61.1	90	295	50	44	6	3	5	2	24	0	35	2	0
Schmidt, Jeff, Van.	0	1	.000	6.60	18	0	0	0	3	0	30.0	47	152	31	22	5	1	0	3	11	0	16	9	2
Schoeneweis, Scott, Van. *	11	8	.579	4.50	27	27	2	0	0	0	180.0	188	787	102	90	18	6	5	9	59	0	133	9	1
Schroeffel, Scott, C.S.	0	0	.000	7.36	1	0	0	0	0	0	3.2	4	16	3	3	1	0	1	0	3	0	3	1	0
Seelbach, Chris, Tac.	1	0	1.000	6.17	6	0	0	0	4	0	11.2	13	53	9	8	5	0	0	0	2	0	10	0	0
Serafini, Dan, S.L. *	2	4	.333	3.71	9	8	0	0	1	0	53.1	56	233	29	22	4	0	0	3	21	0	39	4	0
Shoemaker, Stephen, C.S.	2	7	.222	9.05	15	12	0	0	1	0	62.2	80	325	68	63	7	1	4	2	63	1	56	6	1
Sikorski, Brian, N.O.	5	8	.385	5.79	15	14	1	0	0	0	84.0	86	371	57	54	9	2	4	6	32	1	64	2	1
Silva, Jose, Nash.	0	0	.000	4.82	3	3	0	0	0	0	9.1	10	40	5	5	2	0	0	4	0	6	0	2
Simas, Bill, Cal.	1	0	1.000	0.00	5	0	0	0	4	1	9.0	3	33	1	0	0	0	0	2	1	11	0	0
Slusarski, Joe, N.O.	1	4	.200	5.11	31	0	0	0	10	2	49.1	53	209	31	28	6	2	1	4	9	1	32	1	0
Small, Mark, Okla.	4	4	.500	4.60	15	6	0	0	4	0	47.0	53	206	30	24	4	1	3	4	13	1	42	8	0
Smith, Dan, Okla.	0	0	.000	6.00	1	1	0	0	0	0	6.0	6	25	4	4	2	1	0	1	0	0	0	0	0
Smith, Lee, N.O.	1	1	.500	6.97	10	0	0	0	7	2	10.1	14	49	8	8	2	0	0	0	4	0	11	0	0
Snyder, John, Cal.	7	3	.700	4.36	15	15	1	0	0	0	97.0	112	429	49	47	11	5	2	5	34	1	63	2	2
Soderstrom, Steve, Fres.	11	4	.733	4.05	25	23	2	0	1	1	137.2	133	580	71	62	20	2	3	7	39	0	96	4	0
Sodowsky, Clint, Tuc.	0	1	.000	3.86	2	2	0	0	0	0	9.1	11	42	4	4	0	0	0	3	0	7	0	1
Sparks, Steve, Van.	0	0	.000	2.89	4	4	2	0	0	0	28.0	23	114	11	9	2	1	3	1	6	0	19	2	0
Speier, Justin, Iowa	3	3	.500	5.05	45	0	0	0	33	12	51.2	52	226	31	29	10	3	0	5	19	1	49	6	0
Spencer, Sean, Tac. *	2	0	1.000	4.85	9	0	0	0	3	1	13.0	10	56	7	7	0	0	0	1	7	0	16	1	0
Spencer, Stan, L.V.	12	6	.667	3.93	22	22	0	0	0	0	137.1	120	570	67	60	17	3	3	5	42	2	136	6	1
Steed, Dave, Alb.	0	0	.000	27.00	1	0	0	0	1	0	1.0	5	8	4	3	1	0	1	0	1	0	0	0	0
Steenstra, Kennie, Iowa	11	5	.688	4.38	25	24	1	1	0	0	148.0	171	639	84	72	16	6	3	1	36	1	104	0	0
Stein, Blake, Edm.	3	1	.750	3.47	5	4	0	0	0	0	23.1	22	104	13	9	1	1	0	0	11	0	31	1	0
Steph, Rod, Oma.	2	0	1.000	6.92	17	1	0	0	3	0	26.0	32	123	26	20	8	0	0	3	8	0	14	1	0
Stevens, Dave, Iowa	4	1	.800	3.08	26	0	0	0	10	2	49.2	41	198	19	17	2	0	0	16	1	39	1	0
Stone, Ricky, Alb.	5	5	.500	5.38	18	16	0	0	0	0	105.1	120	465	69	63	13	2	1	3	41	0	85	9	1
Stoops, Jim, C.S.	1	0	1.000	1.23	11	0	0	0	6	1	14.2	6	58	6	2	0	0	2	1	8	0	17	0	0
Strittmatter, Mark, C.S.	0	0	.000	36.00	1	0	0	0	1	0	1.0	6	8	4	4	0	0	0	0	2	0	0	0	0
Sturtze, Tanyon, Okla.	3	1	.750	3.34	13	3	0	0	1	0	35.0	33	154	13	13	3	1	1	3	18	0	31	1	0
Suppan, Jeff, Tuc.	4	3	.571	3.63	13	12	0	0	0	0	67.0	75	292	29	27	4	1	0	3	17	1	62	4	0
Suzuki, Mac, Tac.	9	10	.474	4.37	28	21	2	1	1	0	131.2	130	578	70	64	19	2	3	5	70	1	117	8	0
Swartzbaugh, Dave, Iowa	14	5	.737	3.73	42	14	0	0	5	1	137.2	114	571	61	57	16	8	3	5	50	1	109	7	0
Tabaka, Jeff, Nash. *	0	1	.000	7.71	4	0	0	0	2	0	4.2	9	24	4	4	0	2	1	0	4	0	4	0	0
Taulbee, Andy, Fres.	0	1	.000	12.60	1	1	0	0	0	0	5.0	9	25	7	7	1	0	0	2	0	2	0	0
Tavarez, Julian, Fres.	0	0	.000	19.29	1	0	0	0	0	0	2.1	6	13	5	5	0	0	0	1	0	0	1	0	0
Taylor, Jamie, C.S.	0	0	.000	0.00	2	0	0	0	2	0	2.0	2	9	0	0	0	0	0	1	0	1	0	0
Taylor, Scott, N.O.	0	2	.000	9.10	9	6	0	0	1	0	28.2	40	141	29	29	6	1	1	3	19	0	20	1	0
Telgheder, Dave, Edm.	1	2	.333	7.31	3	3	0	0	0	0	16.0	26	74	14	13	2	0	1	0	3	0	9	0	1
Theodile, Robert, Cal.	0	2	.000	7.68	17	5	0	0	5	0	38.2	36	178	35	33	7	0	1	1	31	0	24	4	0
Thobe, Steve, Nash.	0	0	.000	4.50	2	0	0	0	2	0	2.0	1	8	1	1	0	0	1	1	0	2	0	0
Thomas, Larry, Okla. *	3	0	1.000	4.40	11	0	0	0	7	0	14.1	16	60	7	7	1	0	1	2	12	0	14	0	0
Thompson, Mark, C.S.	0	1	.000	18.90	1	1	0	0	0	0	3.1	10	19	7	7	3	0	0	0	1	0	0	1	0
Tolar, Kevin, Nash. *	0	0	.000	6.00	1	0	0	0	0	0	3.0	2	14	2	2	0	0	0	4	0	1	1	0
Tollberg, Brian, L.V.	6	6	.500	6.38	33	15	1	0	7	3	110.0	138	492	85	78	21	2	2	12	27	2	109	0	1
Turner, Matt, Oma.	1	5	.167	6.41	41	4	0	0	17	2	78.2	96	365	63	56	10	1	4	5	28	8	69	6	0
Tuttle, Dave, Tuc.	1	2	.333	6.84	10	3	0	0	3	0	26.1	32	125	20	20	2	2	1	2	16	1	8	0	0
Twiggs, Greg, Iowa*	2	0	1.000	4.15	7	0	0	0	3	0	8.2	12	42	6	4	0	0	0	6	1	4	0	0
Urbani, Thomas, Mem. *	2	3	.400	3.96	7	6	0	0	1	0	36.1	38	154	17	16	3	1	2	2	12	0	17	0	0
Valdez, Efrain, Tuc. *	1	4	.200	4.37	28	2	0	0	10	0	57.2	59	247	31	28	5	5	2	3	18	1	41	7	1
Van Landingham, Bill, Van.	0	6	.000	11.23	9	8	0	0	0	0	33.2	48	189	46	42	2	1	4	44	0	12	6	3
Van Poppel, Todd, Okla.	5	5	.500	3.72	15	13	2	0	0	0	87.0	88	370	44	36	11	0	2	1	25	0	69	3	1
Vavrek, Mike, C.S. *	2	6	.250	8.26	10	9	0	0	1	0	44.2	62	227	50	41	8	3	4	1	34	0	41	5	0
Venafro, Mike, Okla. *	0	0	.000	6.35	13	0	0	0	4	0	17.0	19	82	12	12	3	0	2	10	0	15	1	0
Veras, Dario, L.V.	2	1	.667	3.79	31	0	0	0	27	9	35.2	36	153	15	15	5	0	2	11	0	29	4	0
Verplancke, Joe, Tuc.	1	0	1.000	0.00	1	0	0	0	0	0	3.1	2	14	2	0	0	0	0	0	2	0	3	1	0
Wainhouse, David, C.S.	2	3	.400	3.60	38	0	0	0	30	4	50.0	47	214	25	20	4	3	2	3	23	0	44	1	1
Walker, Jamie, Oma. *	5	1	.833	2.70	7	7	0	0	0	0	46.2	57	198	15	14	3	2	1	2	11	1	21	1	0
Wall, Donne, L.V.	2	0	1.000	4.80	3	3	0	0	0	0	15.0	11	62	8	8	2	0	1	1	8	0	12	0	0
Wallace, Kent, N.O.	0	0	.000	10.57	7	0	0	0	6	0	7.2	16	41	10	9	2	0	0	0	1	0	7	0	0
Washburn, Jarrod, Van. *	4	4	.444	4.32	14	14	2	0	0	0	91.2	91	402	44	44	7	5	1	5	43	0	66	5	0
Watkins, Scott, Okla. *	6	1	.857	3.26	38	0	0	0	22	2	49.2	44	214	19	18	6	2	1	3	22	1	50	5	0

Pitcher, Team	W	L	Pct.	ERA	G	GS	CG	ShO	GF	Sv.	IP	H	TBF	R	ER	HR	SH	SF	HB	BB	IBB	SO	WP	Bk.
Watson, Allen, Van. *	0	1	.000	4.50	1	1	0	0	0	0	6.0	6	26	3	3	1	0	0	0	2	0	8	1	0
Weaver, Eric, Alb.	2	5	.286	5.55	46	0	0	0	26	3	61.2	65	277	41	38	7	2	2	3	32	2	63	2	0
Weber, Neil, Tuc. *	5	9	.357	5.11	46	11	1	0	6	1	112.2	116	508	82	64	17	5	3	4	55	0	79	12	1
Weibl, Clint, Mem.	0	1	.000	6.35	1	1	0	0	0	0	5.2	6	24	5	4	0	0	0	0	2	0	2	2	0
Wengert, Don, Iowa	3	1	.750	4.58	9	9	1	0	0	0	53.0	58	227	30	27	2	3	1	1	14	0	48	1	1
West, David, N.O. *	1	1	.500	2.56	19	2	0	0	3	0	31.2	26	136	11	9	2	0	0	1	22	0	33	3	0
Wiegandt, Scott, Nash. *	0	1	.000	6.35	11	0	0	0	1	0	11.1	12	54	10	8	2	0	0	1	9	0	6	2	0
Wilkins, Marc, Nash.	1	0	1.000	10.38	5	0	0	0	1	0	4.1	3	21	5	5	1	0	0	1	3	0	4	1	0
Williams, Jeff, Alb. *	8	8	.500	4.98	21	21	0	0	0	0	121.0	160	556	87	67	14	3	3	6	49	0	93	6	4
Williams, Mike, Nash.	0	2	.000	5.59	16	4	0	0	6	1	37.0	36	163	25	23	11	3	1	1	14	2	34	3	0
Williams, Shad, Van.	1	4	.200	3.18	14	10	1	0	1	0	68.0	65	281	30	24	9	2	0	1	18	0	29	2	1
Wilson, Gary, Nash.-S.L.	3	6	.333	6.04	39	5	0	0	8	1	82.0	101	374	62	55	15	1	3	5	27	7	52	1	1
Wilson, Tom, Tuc.	0	0	.000	0.00	1	0	0	0	1	0	1.0	0	4	0	0	0	0	0	0	0	0	1	0	0
Wilson, Trevor, Van. *	5	9	.357	3.62	21	21	4	1	0	0	141.2	130	604	67	57	14	1	2	11	59	0	94	6	4
Witasick, Jay, Edm. *	11	7	.611	3.87	27	26	2	1	1	0	149.0	126	621	74	64	19	2	6	7	49	0	155	5	1
Wojciechowski, Steve, S.L. *	0	2	.000	6.55	9	1	0	0	1	0	11.0	13	52	10	8	0	0	1	0	7	0	6	1	0
Wolcott, Bob, Tuc.	8	6	.571	5.18	23	21	2	1	0	0	128.2	156	551	79	74	13	4	3	4	26	1	100	0	1
Wolff, Bryan, L.V.	0	0	.000	6.75	9	0	0	0	5	1	10.2	14	50	8	8	5	2	0	0	5	0	8	0	0
Wood, Kerry, Iowa	1	0	1.000	0.00	1	1	0	0	0	0	5.0	1	17	0	0	0	0	0	0	2	0	11	0	0
Woodson, Kerry, C.S.	6	10	.375	5.48	42	7	0	0	4	0	93.2	110	436	72	57	5	6	3	7	64	4	51	6	1
Worrell, Steve, Iowa*	0	0	.000	4.20	18	0	0	0	5	0	15.0	25	75	9	7	3	2	0	1	4	0	14	2	0
Young, Danny, Iowa*	0	0	.000	0.00	2	0	0	0	1	0	2.0	1	7	0	0	0	0	0	0	1	0	1	0	0

COMBINATION SHUTOUTS: Albuquerque (1)—Barrios-Iglesias-Rath. Calgary (5)—Theodile-Bradford-Rizzo-Heathcott, Cruz-Rizzo, Heathcott-Bautista-Howry, Fordham-Theodile, Abbott-Heathcott-Cruz-Bertotti. Colorado Springs (1)—Bourgeois-Kramer. Edmonton (3)—Roberts-Connelly-Dougherty-Hansell, King-Holzemer-Connelly, Dale-Kubinski-Dougherty. Fresno (5)—Ortiz-Huisman-Plantenberg-Darwin, Brohawn-Bailey-Darwin, Frontera-Huisman-Bailey, Ortiz-Bailey, Roa-Hartgraves-Darwin. Iowa (4)—Steenstra-Worrell-Speier, Wengert-Foster, Wengert-Stevens, Steenstra-Myers. Las Vegas (3)—Clement-Menhart, Murray-Ramirez-Veras, Spencer-Rossiter-Cunnane-Dixon. Memphis (8)—Luebbers-King, Aybar-Croushore-Looper-King, Raggio-Croushore-Looper, Luebbers-Looper, Aybar-Milcki-Almanza-Heiserman, Aybar-Lovingier-Eversgerd-Milcki-Heiserman, Milcki-Lovingier-Eversgerd-Looper, Raggio-Lovingier-Milcki-Almanza. Nashville (5)—Lawrence-McCurry, Crawford-Sauveur-Ryan-McCurry, Ryan-Sauveur-Mintz-McCurry, Lawrence-Mintz-McCurry, Dessens-Anderson-Ryan-Sauveur. New Orleans (3)—Salkeld-Lopez-Smith-Harris, Ramos-Lopez-Smith, Sikorski-Rivera. Oklahoma (4)—Perisho-Clark-Levine, Clark-Moody, Small-Myers, Clark-Moody. Omaha (5)—Grundy-McDill-Evans, Harrison-Evans, De La Maza-Bevil, Grundy-Byrdak, Reichert-Byrdak. Salt Lake (8)—Baptist-Gandarillas-Naulty, Bones-Ritchie-Bowers-Rath, Bowers-Miller-Rath, Baptist-Ohme-Ritchie, Baptist-Miller, Redman-Rath-Miller, Sampson-Ohme-Harris, Sampson-Wilson-Harris. Tacoma (4)—Suzuki-McCarthy, Bullinger-Holdridge, Abbott-Harikkala, Garcia-Gajkowski-De La Rosa. Tucson (3)—Michalak-Martines-Corey-Ford, Figueroa-Ford, Figueroa-Manuel. Vancouver (2)—Robertson-Butcher-Chavez, Hanson-Holtz.

NO-HIT GAMES: None.

PITCHERS WITH TWO OR MORE TEAMS

Pitcher, Team	W	L	Pct.	ERA	G	GS	CG	ShO	GF	Sv.	IP	H	TBF	R	ER	HR	SH	SF	HB	BB	IBB	SO	WP	Bk.
Bones, Ricky, S.L.	5	1	.833	3.42	8	8	0	0	0	0	47.1	41	200	20	18	5	1	3	3	19	1	41	1	0
Bones, Ricky, Oma.	1	2	.333	8.59	3	3	0	0	0	0	14.2	19	70	16	14	5	0	0	0	10	1	8	1	0
Fossas, Tony, Iowa*	0	0	.000	3.60	10	0	0	0	5	0	5.0	10	26	4	2	0	0	0	2	0	2	0	0
Fossas, Tony, Okla. *	0	1	.000	5.40	4	0	0	0	3	0	6.2	6	27	4	4	0	1	0	0	4	1	3	0	0
Garcia, Freddy, N.O.	0	0	.000	3.14	2	2	0	0	0	0	14.1	14	56	5	5	2	0	0	0	13	0	13	2	0
Garcia, Freddy, Tac.	3	1	.750	3.86	5	5	0	0	0	0	32.2	30	137	14	14	6	0	0	2	13	0	30	0	1
Hansell, Greg, Edm.	0	0	.000	1.23	13	0	0	0	10	6	14.2	13	60	2	2	1	0	0	1	3	1	16	0	0
Hansell, Greg, Oma.	8	3	.727	4.30	46	0	0	0	22	7	69.0	63	284	35	33	6	0	1	5	15	3	59	4	0
Johnson, Barry, Okla.	8	2	.800	6.63	31	7	1	0	10	1	77.1	96	343	66	57	13	2	1	3	21	0	54	3	0
Johnson, Barry, Tuc.	0	1	.000	6.94	5	1	0	0	1	0	11.2	16	56	12	9	2	0	0	1	5	1	10	1	0
Meacham, Rusty, Mem.	1	2	.333	5.16	38	0	0	0	10	2	52.1	68	235	30	30	9	1	3	3	15	3	56	3	0
Meacham, Rusty, Nash.	2	1	.667	3.34	15	2	0	0	6	3	29.2	35	131	14	11	2	1	0	0	8	3	25	2	0
Mlicki, Doug, Oma.	1	1	.500	4.26	7	2	0	0	2	0	12.2	15	51	6	6	3	0	0	0	2	0	9	0	0
Mlicki, Doug, Mem.	1	5	.167	5.17	24	8	0	0	2	0	54.0	62	238	36	31	9	3	2	1	24	4	21	1	1
Pavlas, Dave, Tuc.	0	2	.000	8.64	9	0	0	0	8	1	8.1	15	46	11	8	3	0	1	1	5	1	8	0	0
Pavlas, Dave, Edm.	2	2	.500	3.10	26	3	0	0	10	1	58.0	51	239	23	20	4	0	3	1	12	1	41	2	0
Pickett, Ricky, Fres. *	1	1	.500	3.86	5	0	0	0	3	0	7.0	6	42	4	3	1	0	0	0	14	1	11	0	0
Pickett, Ricky, Okla. *	6	6	.500	3.71	24	10	2	2	5	1	80.0	69	349	39	33	7	2	1	0	52	0	78	3	0
Pickett, Ricky, Tuc. *	0	0	.000	15.43	5	0	0	0	1	0	4.2	7	29	8	8	1	0	0	0	9	0	5	1	0
Rath, Fred, S.L.	1	2	.333	4.55	27	0	0	0	22	8	31.2	35	133	16	16	4	1	0	2	8	0	15	3	0
Rath, Fred, C.S.	5	1	.833	5.08	23	0	0	0	14	4	28.1	37	132	17	16	2	1	2	2	15	1	20	4	0
Wilson, Gary, Nash.	3	5	.375	5.98	29	3	0	0	6	1	58.2	77	274	46	39	12	1	2	3	22	6	39	0	1
Wilson, Gary, S.L.	0	1	.000	6.17	12	0	0	0	2	0	23.1	24	100	16	16	3	0	1	2	5	1	13	1	0

1998 FIELDING
TEAM

Team	Pct.	G	PO	A	E	TC	DP	PB	Team	Pct.	G	PO	A	E	TC	DP	PB
Memphis	.978	144	3800	1580	121	5501	157	5	Omaha	.974	143	3706	1453	140	5299	138	5
Iowa	.978	144	3771	1495	121	5387	138	26	Salt Lake	.973	143	3703	1535	146	5384	134	11
Fresno	.976	143	3743	1449	126	5318	133	13	New Orleans	.973	142	3698	1468	144	5310	144	19
Edmonton	.976	143	3697	1512	127	5336	151	9	Tacoma	.971	144	3824	1523	159	5506	166	8
Oklahoma	.976	144	3810	1599	132	5541	136	13	Nashville	.970	143	3664	1532	159	5355	130	12
Calgary	.976	143	3727	1516	131	5374	143	19	Colo. Springs	.969	144	3686	1511	168	5365	152	14
Vancouver	.974	143	3699	1488	138	5325	156	13	Tucson	.968	142	3710	1464	171	5345	137	14
Albuquerque	.974	143	3709	1575	141	5425	132	12									
Las Vegas	.974	142	3740	1521	141	5402	157	30									

TRIPLE PLAYS: Albuquerque, New Orleans, Vancouver.

CLASS AAA Pacific Coast League

FIRST BASEMEN

NOTE: All caps denotes fielding-percentage leader based on 72 games for catchers, 96 for all other non-pitchers and 144 innings for pitchers. *Throws lefthanded.

Player, Team	Pct.	G	PO	A	E	TC	DP
Allen, Dusty, L.V.	.988	36	299	21	4	324	38
Anthony, Eric, Alb.*	.986	8	64	4	1	69	7
Arias, George, L.V.	1.000	4	28	2	0	30	1
BALL, Jeff, Fres.	.994	115	917	62	6	985	85
Barkett, Andy, Okla.*	.994	73	612	33	4	649	60
Barry, Jeff, C.S.	1.000	1	7	0	0	7	2
Bellhorn, Mark, Edm.	1.000	1	2	0	0	2	1
Berryhill, Damon, Edm.	1.000	1	2	0	0	2	0
Betten, Randy, Van.	1.000	2	6	0	0	6	1
Bolick, Frank, Van.	.927	4	35	3	3	41	2
Boston, D.J., C.S.*	.992	36	224	28	2	254	24
Brede, Brent, Tuc.*	.900	3	9	0	1	10	0
Brown, Brant, Iowa*	1.000	1	2	0	0	2	0
Burke, Jamie, Van.	.857	1	6	0	1	7	1
Buxbaum, Danny, Van.	1.000	23	180	11	0	191	27
Canale, George, Nash.	.991	28	213	15	2	230	18
Cholowsky, Dan, C.S.	1.000	10	70	10	0	80	8
Cianfrocco, Archi, L.V.	.980	11	91	9	2	102	10
Coolbaugh, Mike, C.S.	.986	24	127	16	2	145	16
Cromer, D.T., Edm.*	.988	115	1015	89	13	1117	113
Dishington, Nate, Mem.	.981	39	295	19	6	320	30
Dye, Jermaine, Oma.	1.000	4	31	1	0	32	6
Echevarria, Angel, C.S.	.985	48	363	25	6	394	44
Edge, Tim, Nash.	1.000	2	1	0	0	1	0
Ellis, Kevin, Iowa	1.000	1	7	1	0	8	1
Estrada, Osmani, Okla.	1.000	3	20	3	0	23	5
Florez, Tim, Tuc.	.987	12	77	0	1	78	10
Garcia, Freddy, Nash.	.976	21	147	16	4	167	15
Geisler, Phil, E.D.*	1.000	1	1	0	0	1	0
Giambi, Jeremy, Oma.*	.909	1	10	0	1	11	0
Gonzales, Rene, Okla.	.993	18	127	6	1	134	13
Greene, Todd, Van.	.988	9	75	5	1	81	7
Grijak, Kevin, Nash.	.990	55	458	37	5	500	46
Gubanich, Creighton, L.V.	1.000	8	59	3	0	62	7
Hale, Chip, Mem.	.997	40	314	26	1	341	35
Hall, Joe, Okla.	1.000	13	94	8	0	102	9
Halter, Shane, Oma.	1.000	3	23	2	0	25	3
Hartman, Ron, Tuc.	.980	12	91	8	2	101	17
Hatcher, Chris, Oma.	.981	8	48	3	1	52	2
Hosey, Steve, Oma.	1.000	2	2	0	0	2	0
Huckaby, Ken, Tac.	1.000	1	1	0	0	1	0
Hunter, Brian, Cal.*	1.000	2	8	0	0	8	0
Hyers, Tim, Tuc.*	1.000	2	4	0	0	4	1
Jennings, Robin, Iowa*	1.000	3	6	0	0	6	1
Jorgensen, Randy, Tac.*	.995	69	536	48	3	587	65
Kirgan, Chris, C.S.	.979	24	174	14	4	192	22
Konerko, Paul, Alb.	1.000	9	32	0	0	32	7
Laker, Tim, Alb.	.984	14	114	13	2	129	11
Lesher, Brian, Edm.*	.976	16	120	3	3	126	15
Lewis, T.R., Okla.	.988	25	232	11	3	246	16
Liefer, Jeff, Cal.	1.000	2	19	3	0	22	0
LoDuca, Paul, Alb.	.988	21	142	16	2	160	9
Mayes, Craig, Fres.	1.000	2	6	1	0	7	1
McCall, Rod, Iowa	.987	84	681	57	10	748	74
McCarty, Dave, Tac.*	.997	41	305	25	1	331	41
McDonald, Keith, Mem.	.933	3	13	1	1	15	2
Meier, Dan, Tuc.*	.984	8	58	3	1	62	6
Melendez, Dan, Alb.*	1.000	67	507	37	0	544	50
Mendez, Carlos, Oma.	1.000	30	250	13	0	263	27
Meulens, Hensley, Tuc.	.958	3	19	4	1	24	5
Molina, Izzy, Edm.	.964	3	24	3	1	28	4
Morales, Willie, Edm.	1.000	4	29	1	0	30	4
Munoz, Juan, Mem.*	.975	4	38	1	1	40	2
Neal, Mike, N.O.	1.000	3	16	2	0	18	1
Neel, Troy, Van.	.992	13	106	12	1	119	14
Norton, Chris, Van.	1.000	5	33	2	0	35	5
Obando, Sherman, C.S.	.990	24	196	8	2	206	16
Ogden, Jamie, S.L.*	.989	14	80	9	1	90	6
Ortiz, David, S.L.*	.966	9	76	10	3	89	8
Ortiz, Luis, Oma.	1.000	13	72	4	0	76	5
Pearson, Eddie, Cal.	1.000	12	83	8	0	91	8
Phillips, J.R., N.O.*	.995	45	349	22	2	373	30
Pritchett, Chris, Van.	.988	88	739	55	10	804	80
Richardson, Scott, Alb.	1.000	8	58	1	0	59	3

Player, Team	Pct.	G	PO	A	E	TC	DP
Rios, Armando, Fres.*	1.000	3	27	5	0	32	1
Roberge, J.P., Alb.	.994	45	334	21	2	357	28
Robertson, Mike, Tuc.*	.993	107	862	55	6	923	79
Rohrmeier, Dan, Tac.	.989	41	319	40	4	363	45
Romero, Mandy, L.V.	1.000	4	31	2	0	33	3
Rose, Pete, Nash.	.990	15	95	5	1	101	11
Rupp, Brian, Mem.	.990	74	365	41	4	410	38
Rupp, Chad, S.L.	.991	59	517	31	5	553	59
Russo, Paul, N.O.	.992	61	447	46	4	497	46
Sagmoen, Marc, Okla.*	.973	20	135	8	4	147	12
Scarsone, Steve, Van.	1.000	1	12	0	0	12	1
Sealy, Scot, Tac.	1.000	1	3	0	0	3	0
Secrist, Reed, Mem.	.974	20	143	6	4	153	14
Seitzer, Brad, Tac.	1.000	2	11	1	0	12	2
Sell, Chip, Alb.	.905	3	17	2	2	21	4
Shave, Jon, S.L.	1.000	2	13	2	0	15	2
Sheaffer, Danny, Mem.	1.000	9	54	8	0	62	4
Sisco, Steve, Oma.	1.000	8	51	1	0	52	5
Smith, Bubba, Tuc.	1.000	3	20	0	0	20	1
Smith, Mark, Nash.	1.000	7	62	5	0	67	6
Stahoviak, Scott, S.L.	.995	67	548	55	3	606	50
Steed, Dave, Alb.	1.000	15	116	10	0	126	15
Stefanski, Mike, Mem.	1.000	5	16	1	0	17	1
Stevens, Lee, Okla.*	1.000	1	12	1	0	13	1
Stewart, Andy, Oma.	1.000	2	2	0	0	2	0
Taylor, Jamie, C.S.	1.000	3	17	0	0	17	3
Thobe, Steve, Nash.	1.000	5	33	5	0	38	3
Thompson, Jason, L.V.*	.995	46	356	31	2	389	36
Unroe, Tim, Iowa	1.000	5	18	0	0	18	1
Valdez, Mario, Cal.	.987	117	1002	75	14	1091	107
Vitiello, Joe, Oma.	.992	89	735	51	6	792	79
Voigt, Jack, Edm.-Okla.	.988	9	76	5	1	82	2
Ward, Daryle, N.O.*	.979	54	376	45	9	430	48
Warner, Ron, Mem.	.984	9	56	7	1	64	8
White, Derrick, Iowa-C.S.	1.000	7	55	4	0	59	8
Williams, Eddie, L.V.	.990	46	352	28	4	384	47
Williams, Keith, Fres.	.988	34	245	12	3	260	23
Wilson, Craig, Cal.	1.000	18	123	5	0	128	17
Wilson, Tom, Tuc.	.969	13	88	6	3	97	9
Wright, Ron, Nash.	.986	16	125	11	2	138	9
Wrona, Rick, Okla.	.990	15	86	9	1	96	5
Zinter, Alan, Iowa	.992	66	451	25	4	480	44

TRIPLE PLAYS: Phillips, Pritchett.

FIRST BASEMEN WITH TWO OR MORE TEAMS

Player, Team	Pct.	G	PO	A	E	TC	DP
Voigt, Jack, Edm.	.984	7	59	4	1	64	1
Voigt, Jack, Okla.	1.000	2	17	1	0	18	1
White, Derrick, Iowa	1.000	6	46	3	0	49	7
White, Derrick, C.S.	1.000	1	9	1	0	10	1

SECOND BASEMEN

Player, Team	Pct.	G	PO	A	E	TC	DP
Anderson, Cliff, Alb.	.979	9	20	26	1	47	7
Barberie, Bret, Okla.	.982	110	229	321	10	560	67
Barker, Tim, C.S.	.990	59	114	181	3	298	46
Bates, Jason, C.S.	.952	10	7	13	1	21	1
Baughman, Justin, Van.	.985	46	124	140	4	268	41
Bellhorn, Mark, Edm.	.994	34	63	110	1	174	24
Berblinger, Jeff, Tac.	.953	57	103	163	13	279	39
Betten, Randy, Van.	.800	1	3	1	1	5	1
Bieser, Steve, Nash.	.840	4	12	9	4	25	1
Bridges, Kary, Iowa	.971	23	24	42	2	68	6
Brito, Tilson, Tac.	.957	23	45	67	5	117	25
Brown, Randy, Nash.	1.000	1	2	0	0	2	0
Candaele, Casey, Nash.-N.O.	.961	27	53	69	5	127	16
Canizaro, Jay, Fres.	.981	25	42	60	2	104	17
Castleberry, Kevin, Iowa	.956	11	13	30	2	45	7
Cholowsky, Dan, C.S.	.714	4	1	4	2	7	0
Cianfrocco, Archi, L.V.	1.000	1	3	3	0	6	1
Coolbaugh, Mike, C.S.	1.000	2	3	5	0	8	2
Cora, Alex, Alb.	.667	1	2	0	1	3	0
Cruz, Fausto, Van.	.974	19	31	43	2	76	10
Demetral, Chris, Okla.	.980	21	47	52	2	101	13
Diaz, Edwin, Tuc.	.961	108	229	293	21	543	68
Estrada, Osmani, Okla.	.902	7	15	22	4	41	4
Ferguson, Jeff, S.L.	.954	67	108	164	13	285	39

Player, Team	Pct.	G	PO	A	E	TC	DP
Finn, John, Cal.	1.000	23	47	58	0	105	18
Florez, Tim, Tuc.	.979	13	20	26	1	47	4
Frias, Hanley, Tuc.	1.000	1	0	1	0	1	1
Garcia, Carlos, Van.	.929	4	7	6	1	14	1
Gilbert, Shawn, Mem.	1.000	3	6	9	0	15	2
Gipson, Charles, Tac.	.964	11	26	27	2	55	12
Gonzales, Rene, Cal.-Okla.	.965	13	22	33	2	57	9
Guerrero, Wilton, Alb.	.989	21	44	49	1	94	13
Guillen, Carlos, Tac.	.982	24	49	63	2	114	16
Hajek, Dave, L.V.	.972	126	260	368	18	646	99
Hale, Chip, Mem.	.993	70	114	164	2	280	47
Hall, Joe, Okla.	.857	1	2	4	1	7	0
Halter, Shane, Oma.	1.000	3	4	3	0	7	1
Hansen, Jed, Oma.	.957	119	202	336	24	562	75
Hardtke, Jason, Iowa	.951	17	28	50	4	82	12
Hermansen, Chad, Nash.	.842	7	17	15	6	38	3
HERNANDEZ, Carlos, N.O.	.983	124	243	336	10	589	81
Holbert, Aaron, Tac.	.966	17	37	49	3	89	12
Howard, Matt, Fres.	.955	26	53	75	6	134	14
Huson, Jeff, Tuc.	1.000	8	13	21	0	34	2
Ingram, Garey, Alb.	.985	30	49	81	2	132	21
Johnson, Keith, Alb.	1.000	1	1	2	0	3	2
Johnson, Russ, N.O.	.977	10	21	22	1	44	7
Jones, Jack, Alb.	1.000	2	1	2	0	3	0
Kennedy, Adam, Mem.	.961	14	30	43	3	76	11
Klassen, Danny, Tuc.	.991	21	49	67	1	117	22
LaRocca, Greg, L.V.	.969	24	46	49	3	98	12
Leius, Scott, Oma.	1.000	1	1	4	0	5	2
Lidle, Kevin, C.S.	1.000	1	0	1	0	1	0
Liriano, Nelson, C.S.	.977	40	61	110	4	175	23
Luuloa, Keith, Van.	1.000	6	16	17	0	33	9
Martinez, Felix, Oma.	1.000	2	5	6	0	11	2
Martinez, Ramon E., Fres.	.982	97	209	280	9	498	57
Martins, Eric, Edm.	.933	4	7	7	1	15	2
Maxwell, Jason, Iowa	.975	104	208	265	12	485	68
McEwing, Joe, Mem.	1.000	1	2	0	0	2	0
Menechino, Frankie, Edm.	.979	74	133	192	7	332	48
Miller, Orlando, Oma.	.950	4	9	10	1	20	4
Moore, Brandon, Cal.	.992	79	175	206	3	384	54
Moriarty, Mike, S.L.	.964	37	59	100	6	165	28
Neal, Mike, N.O.	.929	7	14	12	2	28	3
Nevers, Tom, Van.	.944	9	11	23	2	36	3
Ordaz, Luis, Mem.	1.000	1	1	0	0	1	0
Ortiz, Luis, Oma.	1.000	1	1	1	0	2	0
Patzke, Jeff, Nash.	.975	101	209	306	13	528	74
Petersen, Chris, Iowa	.778	2	0	7	2	9	0
Polanco, Placido, Mem.	.989	58	98	174	3	275	41
Riggs, Adam, Alb.	.954	44	82	125	10	217	28
Rivera, Luis, N.O.	1.000	7	7	14	0	21	5
Roberge, J.P., Alb.	.954	34	69	77	7	153	19
Rodriguez, Steve, Alb.	.960	5	9	15	1	25	4
Rose, Pete, Nash.	1.000	3	0	1	0	1	0
Rossy, Rico, Tac.	1.000	3	4	10	0	14	3
Saitta, Rich, Alb.	1.000	5	9	11	0	20	3
Sanford, Chance, Nash.	.974	10	15	23	1	39	5
Scarsone, Steve, Van.	.967	60	116	144	9	269	38
Seitzer, Brad, Tac.	1.000	2	2	7	0	9	1
Sexton, Chris, C.S.	1.000	3	3	3	0	6	1
Shave, Jon, S.L.	.973	63	107	149	7	263	28
Shumpert, Terry, C.S.	.990	44	95	109	2	206	24
Simons, Mitch, Tac.	.969	15	26	37	2	65	8
Sisco, Steve, Oma.	.981	28	52	53	2	107	18
Spiezio, Scott, Edm.	.889	4	5	3	1	9	1
Stankiewicz, Andy, Tuc.	1.000	3	11	9	0	20	3
Stewart, Andy, Oma.	.750	1	2	1	1	4	1
Tyler, Brad, Edm.	.970	14	32	32	2	66	11
Unroe, Tim, Iowa	1.000	2	1	4	0	5	1
Velarde, Randy, Van.	1.000	3	3	7	0	10	0
Warner, Ron, Mem.	1.000	9	10	27	0	37	6
Williams, Reggie, Van.	1.000	2	1	4	0	5	1
Wilson, Craig, Cal.	.987	57	116	119	3	238	30
Wimmer, Chris, Nash.	1.000	14	14	12	0	26	3
Wood, Jason, Edm.	.983	21	46	69	2	117	20
Woods, Ken, Fres.	.800	3	5	3	2	10	1

TRIPLE PLAYS: Hernandez, Roberge, Scarsone.

SECOND BASEMEN WITH TWO OR MORE TEAMS

Player, Team	Pct.	G	PO	A	E	TC	DP
Candaele, Casey, Nash.	.963	20	46	57	4	107	10
Candaele, Casey, N.O.	.950	7	7	12	1	20	6
Gonzales, Rene, Cal.	1.000	1	0	1	0	1	0
Gonzales, Rene, Okla.	.964	12	22	32	2	56	9

THIRD BASEMEN

Player, Team	Pct.	G	PO	A	E	TC	DP
Anderson, Cliff, Alb.	.934	25	15	42	4	61	2
Arias, George, L.V.	.947	106	70	232	17	319	29
Ball, Jeff, Fres.	.842	6	2	14	3	19	5
Barberie, Bret, Okla.	.667	1	0	2	1	3	0
Barker, Tim, C.S.	.857	7	0	6	1	7	0
Barry, Jeff, C.S.	1.000	3	2	1	0	3	0
Bates, Jason, C.S.	.914	20	10	22	3	35	1
Bautista, Juan, Tuc.	1.000	1	0	1	0	1	0
Bellhorn, Mark, Edm.	.919	44	27	86	10	123	9
Berblinger, Jeff, Tac.	.842	22	18	30	9	57	2
Bolick, Frank, Van.	.970	29	21	76	3	100	9
Bridges, Kary, Iowa	.967	26	11	48	2	61	6
Burke, Jamie, Van.	.950	9	8	30	2	40	7
Canale, George, Nash.	1.000	1	0	1	0	1	0
Candaele, Casey, N.O.	.964	18	11	43	2	56	3
Castleberry, Kevin, Iowa	1.000	3	3	4	0	7	0
Chavez, Eric, Edm.	.935	46	34	66	7	107	8
Cholowsky, Dan, C.S.	.950	11	4	15	1	20	1
Cianfrocco, Archi, L.V.	.964	12	7	20	1	28	1
Coolbaugh, Mike, C.S.	.901	86	54	165	24	243	19
Cuevas, Trent, Alb.	1.000	5	4	9	0	13	2
Diaz, Edwin, Tuc.	.919	15	6	28	3	37	3
Estrada, Osmani, Okla.	1.000	1	0	3	0	3	0
Evans, Jason, Cal.	.500	1	0	1	1	2	0
Feliz, Pedro, Fres.	1.000	1	0	2	0	2	0
Finn, John, Cal.	1.000	12	4	18	0	22	0
Florez, Tim, Tuc.	.933	14	6	22	2	30	0
Franklin, Micah, Iowa	.800	5	1	7	2	10	0
Frias, Hanley, Tuc.	.950	6	3	16	1	20	2
Garcia, Freddy, Nash.	.921	67	38	137	15	190	9
Gilbert, Shawn, Mem.	.916	50	38	93	12	143	14
Giovanola, Ed, L.V.	.941	4	1	15	1	17	1
Gipson, Charles, Tac.	.955	11	5	16	1	22	2
Glaus, Troy, Van.	.932	58	46	131	13	190	12
Gonzales, Rene, Cal.-Okla.	.936	17	9	35	3	47	1
Gonzalez, Jimmy, L.V.	1.000	1	0	1	0	1	0
Grundy, Phil, Oma.	1.000	1	0	5	0	5	1
Gubanich, Creighton, L.V.	.857	6	4	14	3	21	3
Guiel, Aaron, L.V.	1.000	1	0	1	0	1	0
Guzman, Edwards, Fres.	.931	79	60	128	14	202	17
Hale, Chip, Mem.	.733	5	3	8	4	15	0
Hall, Joe, Okla.	1.000	4	1	14	0	15	0
Halter, Shane, Oma.	.900	2	4	5	1	10	0
Hardtke, Jason, Iowa	.944	66	40	94	8	142	7
Hartman, Ron, Tuc.	.906	103	62	170	24	256	13
Hosey, Steve, Oma.	1.000	1	1	2	0	3	0
Howard, Matt, Fres.	.985	67	36	99	2	137	7
Huson, Jeff, Tuc.	.909	3	2	8	1	11	0
Ingram, Garey, Alb.	.934	23	9	48	4	61	1
Johnson, Keith, Alb.	.926	40	15	73	7	95	4
JOHNSON, Russ, N.O.	.962	110	50	204	10	264	19
Jones, Jack, Alb.	.800	3	1	3	1	5	1
Konerko, Paul, Alb.	1.000	1	0	1	0	1	0
Koskie, Corey, S.L.	.935	131	83	250	23	356	21
LaRocca, Greg, L.V.	.941	26	8	40	3	51	3
Leius, Scott, Oma.	.928	61	35	106	11	152	10
Liriano, Nelson, C.S.	.897	23	6	29	4	39	4
Lopez, Mendy, Oma.	1.000	1	1	0	0	1	0
LoDuca, Paul, Alb.	.733	13	4	7	4	15	2
Luuloa, Keith, Van.	1.000	1	1	5	0	6	0
Martins, Eric, Edm.	.750	2	1	2	1	4	0
McEwing, Joe, Mem.	1.000	2	0	6	0	6	0
McKay, Cody, Edm.	1.000	1	2	1	0	3	0
Mejia, Roberto, Mem.	.938	45	26	110	9	145	8
Meulens, Hensley, Tuc.	1.000	2	1	7	0	8	2
Miller, Orlando, Oma.-N.O.	.983	23	7	51	1	59	5
Miller, Ryan, N.O.	1.000	1	1	5	0	6	1
Moriarty, Mike, S.L.	.833	7	3	12	3	18	0
Neal, Mike, N.O.	.926	9	6	19	2	27	2
Nevers, Tom, Van.	.741	8	2	18	7	27	2
Orie, Kevin, Iowa	.960	24	7	41	2	50	2
Ortiz, Luis, Oma.	.889	8	5	19	3	27	2
Pellow, Kit, Oma.	.919	14	13	21	3	37	1
Pendleton, Terry, Oma.	1.000	2	1	2	0	3	1
Quinlan, Tom, Okla.	.940	124	96	278	24	398	31
Ramirez, Aramis, Nash.	.932	46	33	77	8	118	8
Richardson, Brian, Alb.	1.000	4	4	11	0	15	1
Richardson, Scott, Alb.	.571	3	2	2	3	7	0
Rivera, Luis, N.O.	1.000	6	1	4	0	5	0
Roberge, J.P., Alb.	.924	53	25	96	10	131	6
Rodriguez, Steve, Alb.	1.000	1	1	1	0	2	0

Player, Team	Pct.	G	PO	A	E	TC	DP
Rose, Pete, Nash.	.875	8	3	11	2	16	0
Rupp, Brian, Mem.	.958	17	7	16	1	24	4
Russo, Paul, N.O.	1.000	3	1	0	0	1	0
Saenz, Olmedo, Cal.	.937	113	75	235	21	331	24
Sanford, Chance, Nash.	1.000	6	6	7	0	13	0
Scarsone, Steve, Van.	.912	42	22	92	11	125	9
Secrist, Reed, Mem.	1.000	1	0	1	0	1	0
Seitzer, Brad, Tac.	.915	115	67	214	26	307	24
Sexton, Chris, C.S.	1.000	2	1	3	0	4	0
Shave, Jon, S.L.	.800	14	2	14	4	20	2
Sheaffer, Danny, Mem.	1.000	2	0	1	0	1	0
Shumpert, Terry, C.S.	1.000	7	3	7	0	10	1
Sisco, Steve, Oma.	.968	43	31	60	3	94	4
Smith, Bubba, Tuc.	1.000	8	6	12	0	18	0
Smith, Mark, Nash.	.889	5	4	12	2	18	0
Stewart, Andy, Oma.	1.000	1	0	1	0	1	0
Taylor, Jamie, C.S.	1.000	14	7	20	0	27	3
Truby, Chris, N.O.	.917	5	4	7	1	12	3
Turner, Chris, Oma.	1.000	1	1	0	0	1	0
Tyler, Brad, Edm.	.846	10	5	17	4	26	3
Unroe, Tim, Iowa	.984	29	14	49	1	64	8
Vicente, Audo, Tuc.	1.000	1	0	3	0	3	0
Vitiello, Joe, Oma.	.800	4	3	5	2	10	0
Warner, Ron, Mem.	.965	41	29	80	4	113	10
Williams, Matt, Tuc.	1.000	2	0	1	0	1	0
Wilson, Craig, Cal.	.949	26	6	31	2	39	4
Wilson, Tom, Tuc.	.750	1	1	2	1	4	0
Wimmer, Chris, Nash.	1.000	21	7	36	0	43	4
Wood, Jason, Edm.	.949	41	23	89	6	118	9
Woods, Ken, Fres.	.947	8	9	9	1	19	1
Wrona, Rick, Okla.	1.000	2	0	1	0	1	0
Zinter, Alan, Iowa	.857	9	3	9	2	14	0

TRIPLE PLAY: R. Johnson.

THIRD BASEMEN WITH TWO OR MORE TEAMS

Player, Team	Pct.	G	PO	A	E	TC	DP
Gonzales, Rene, Cal.	1.000	1	0	5	0	5	0
Gonzales, Rene, Okla.	.929	16	9	30	3	42	1
Miller, Orlando, Oma.	.982	22	7	49	1	57	5
Miller, Orlando, N.O.	1.000	1	0	2	0	2	0

SHORTSTOPS

Player, Team	Pct.	G	PO	A	E	TC	DP
Abbott, Kurt, Edm.	.846	6	9	13	4	26	4
Anderson, Cliff, Alb.	.964	15	15	38	2	55	6
Bates, Jason, C.S.	.926	22	30	45	6	81	16
Baughman, Justin, Van.	.950	8	12	26	2	40	6
Bautista, Juan, Tuc.	.870	6	9	11	3	23	2
Bellhorn, Mark, Edm.	1.000	3	3	9	0	12	2
Beltre, Esteban, S.L.	.967	124	173	388	19	580	79
Betten, Randy, Van.	1.000	1	2	2	0	4	0
Brito, Luis, Nash.	.925	8	13	24	3	40	4
Brito, Tilson, Tac.	.891	18	43	55	12	110	21
Brown, Randy, Nash.	.947	13	19	35	3	57	7
Candaele, Casey, Nash.-N.O.	.922	18	21	50	6	77	11
Canizaro, Jay, Fres.	1.000	1	0	3	0	3	1
Cianfrocco, Archi, L.V.	1.000	1	2	1	0	3	0
Cora, Alex, Alb.	.959	80	124	270	17	411	54
Cromer, Tripp, Alb.	.952	8	3	17	1	21	2
Cruz, Fausto, Van.	.964	84	123	252	14	389	57
Delgado, Wilson, Fres.	.962	126	205	373	23	601	76
Demetral, Chris, Okla.	1.000	7	10	15	0	25	5
Diaz, Edwin, Tuc.	.889	8	12	20	4	36	9
Estrada, Osmani, Okla.	.900	2	2	7	1	10	2
Florez, Tim, Tuc.	.893	15	20	47	8	75	12
Frias, Hanley, Tuc.	.957	55	89	155	11	255	38
Garcia, Carlos, Van.	.949	39	71	97	9	177	25
Gil, Benji, Cal.	.943	117	160	319	29	508	69
Gilbert, Shawn, Mem.	1.000	1	0	2	0	2	0
Gipson, Charles, Tac.	.947	15	29	42	4	75	11
Gonzales, Rene, Okla.	.968	15	22	38	2	62	5
Guillen, Carlos, N.O.	.943	97	145	287	26	458	65
Halter, Shane, Oma.	.971	15	32	36	2	70	9
Hansen, Jed, Oma.	.862	10	8	17	4	29	3
Hernandez, Carlos, N.O.	.906	8	6	23	3	32	6
Holbert, Aaron, Tac.	.939	36	68	100	11	179	26
Howard, Matt, Fres.	.957	16	21	45	3	69	9
Huson, Jeff, Tuc.	.906	13	23	25	5	53	6
Ingram, Garey, Alb.	.667	1	1	1	1	3	1
Johnson, Keith, Alb.	.973	42	54	127	5	186	26
Johnson, Russ, N.O.	1.000	3	5	9	0	14	2
Jones, Jack, Alb.	1.000	10	11	32	0	43	9

Player, Team	Pct.	G	PO	A	E	TC	DP
Kennedy, Adam, Mem.	.976	61	98	182	7	287	43
Klassen, Danny, Tuc.	.968	51	79	135	7	221	29
LaRocca, Greg, L.V.	.963	22	31	48	3	82	14
Leius, Scott, Oma.	1.000	1	1	0	0	1	1
Liriano, Nelson, C.S.	.882	5	4	11	2	17	1
Lopez, Mendy, Oma.	.960	57	70	167	10	247	37
Luuloa, Keith, Van.	1.000	1	1	0	0	1	0
Martinez, Felix, Oma.	.934	42	69	129	14	212	33
Martinez, Ramon E., Fres.	.000	1	0	0	1	1	0
Martins, Eric, Edm.	.833	1	1	4	1	6	1
Maxwell, Jason, Iowa	.946	22	29	41	4	74	11
McEwing, Joe, Mem.	1.000	1	3	4	0	7	0
Melo, Juan, L.V.	.965	127	214	360	21	595	91
Miller, Orlando, Oma.-N.O.	.941	34	41	86	8	135	20
Moore, Brandon, Cal.	1.000	3	7	10	0	17	1
Moriarty, Mike, S.L.	.948	23	33	59	5	97	12
Neal, Mike, N.O.	1.000	5	2	13	0	15	3
Nevers, Tom, Van.	.929	14	19	33	4	56	11
Nieves, Jose, Iowa	.960	19	35	61	4	100	16
Nunez, Abraham, Nash.	.953	94	155	274	21	450	63
Ordaz, Luis, Mem.	.952	58	103	174	14	291	35
Patzke, Jeff, Nash.	1.000	2	0	3	0	3	0
PETERSEN, Chris, Iowa	.985	113	167	347	8	522	78
Polanco, Placido, Mem.	.944	9	15	19	2	36	5
Rivera, Luis, N.O.	.854	10	14	21	6	41	6
Rossy, Rico, Tac.	.950	51	90	138	12	240	43
Sanford, Chance, Nash.	.882	4	4	11	2	17	0
Saylor, Jamie, N.O.	.857	2	1	5	1	7	0
Sexton, Chris, C.S.	.957	126	212	346	25	583	81
Shave, Jon, S.L.	.875	8	11	17	4	32	5
Sheldon, Scott, Okla.	.959	123	162	397	24	583	76
Shumpert, Terry, C.S.	1.000	5	5	13	0	18	6
Simons, Mitch, Tac.	.934	28	42	71	8	121	15
Sisco, Steve, Oma.	.967	26	30	58	3	91	7
Tejada, Miguel, Edm.	1.000	1	0	5	0	5	0
Velandia, Jorge, Edm.	.974	126	203	428	17	648	93
Vicente, Audo, Tuc.	1.000	2	2	2	0	4	2
Warner, Ron, Mem.	.919	18	25	54	7	86	13
Wilson, Craig, Cal.	.969	33	32	92	4	128	22
Wimmer, Chris, Nash.	.926	14	18	32	4	54	10
Wood, Jason, Edm.	.960	7	7	17	1	25	3

SHORTSTOPS WITH TWO OR MORE TEAMS

Player, Team	Pct.	G	PO	A	E	TC	DP
Candaele, Casey, Nash.	.919	17	21	47	6	74	10
Candaele, Casey, N.O.	1.000	1	0	3	0	3	1
Miller, Orlando, Oma.	.949	9	9	28	2	39	5
Miller, Orlando, N.O.	.938	25	32	58	6	96	15

OUTFIELDERS

Player, Team	Pct.	G	PO	A	E	TC	DP
Alexander, Chad, N.O.	1.000	2	3	0	0	3	0
Allen, Dusty, N.O.	1.000	47	45	1	0	46	0
Anderson, Jimmy, Nash.*	1.000	1	1	0	0	1	0
Anthony, Eric, Alb.*	1.000	40	55	6	0	61	0
Barker, Tim, C.S.	.000	4	0	0	1	1	0
Barry, Jeff, C.S.	.955	93	181	12	9	202	3
Berkman, Lance, N.O.*	1.000	17	30	0	0	30	0
Betten, Randy, Van.	1.000	3	5	1	0	6	0
Bieser, Steve, Nash.	1.000	13	23	2	0	25	0
Bocachica, Hiram, Alb.	.976	25	80	2	2	84	1
Bolick, Frank, Van.	.929	14	26	0	2	28	0
Bonds, Bobby, Fres.	1.000	3	1	0	0	1	0
Boston, D.J., C.S.*	1.000	1	1	0	0	1	0
Bradshaw, Terry, Oma.	.955	91	162	7	8	177	1
Brede, Brent, Tuc.*	1.000	26	48	6	0	54	0
Brinkley, Darryl, Nash.	.987	86	154	3	2	159	0
Brock, Tarrik, Tac.*	1.000	24	59	1	0	60	0
Brown, Adrian, Nash.	.977	80	204	7	5	216	0
Brown, Brant, Iowa*	1.000	2	3	0	0	3	0
Buchanan, Brian, S.L.	.969	122	244	6	8	258	3
Butler, Rob, N.O.*	.958	67	135	3	6	144	1
Candaele, Casey, N.O.	.984	44	63	0	1	64	0
Canizaro, Jay, Fres.	1.000	4	7	1	0	8	0
Carr, Jeremy, Oma.	.984	46	118	5	2	125	0
Carvajal, Jovino, Van.	.982	103	214	7	4	225	2
Chamberlain, Wes, Okla.	1.000	16	24	2	0	26	1
Cholowsky, Dan, C.S.	.818	9	8	1	2	11	0
Christenson, Ryan, Edm.	1.000	22	56	2	0	58	1
Christopherson, Eric, Cal.	1.000	1	1	0	0	1	0
Cianfrocco, Archi, L.V.	.941	10	15	1	1	17	0
Clemente, Edgard, C.S.	.968	128	262	8	9	279	3

Player, Team	Pct.	G	PO	A	E	TC	DP
Coleman, Vince, Mem.	.882	20	14	1	2	17	0
Conine, Jeff, Oma.	1.000	1	2	0	0	2	0
Cookson, Brent, Tuc.	1.000	29	50	0	0	50	0
Coolbaugh, Mike, C.S.	1.000	1	3	0	0	3	0
Cradle, Rickey, Tac.	1.000	73	143	5	0	148	2
Cromer, D.T., Edm.*	.600	5	3	0	2	5	0
Cruz, Fausto, Van.	.972	13	32	3	1	36	1
Cruz, Jacob, Fres.*	.963	86	152	5	6	163	0
Cuyler, Milt, Okla.	1.000	2	3	0	0	3	0
Dascenzo, Doug, L.V.*	1.000	7	12	0	0	12	0
De La Maza, Roland, Oma.	1.000	2	2	0	0	2	0
Dellucci, David, Tuc.*	1.000	17	38	0	0	38	0
Demetral, Chris, Okla.	1.000	20	33	1	0	34	0
Devereaux, Mike, L.V.	.980	28	47	2	1	50	0
Diaz, Alex, Fres.	.818	7	8	1	2	11	0
Drew, J.D., Mem.	.966	25	54	3	2	59	1
Dye, Jermaine, Oma.	.989	36	88	3	1	92	1
Echevarria, Angel, C.S.	.980	34	45	3	1	49	0
Ellis, Kevin, Iowa	1.000	2	3	2	0	5	1
Evans, Jason, Cal.	.986	120	199	6	3	208	0
Finn, John, Cal.	.867	11	13	0	2	15	0
Florez, Tim, Tuc.	1.000	2	1	0	0	1	0
Franklin, Micah, Iowa	.980	94	141	4	3	148	0
Frazier, Lou, Cal.	.969	73	153	3	5	161	0
Garcia, Karim, Tuc.*	.958	27	67	1	3	71	1
Gazarek, Marty, Iowa	.974	76	142	10	4	156	2
Geisler, Phil, Nash.-N.O.*	.913	20	21	0	2	23	0
Giambi, Jeremy, Oma.*	.982	67	103	8	2	113	2
Gibbs, Kevin, Alb.	1.000	2	4	0	0	4	0
Gibson, Derrick, C.S.	.945	122	211	11	13	235	3
Gil, Benji, Cal.	.500	2	1	0	1	2	0
Gilbert, Shawn, Mem.	1.000	13	21	2	0	23	0
Gipson, Charles, Tac.	.955	40	82	3	4	89	2
Gonzales, Rene, Cal.	.938	12	15	0	1	16	0
Green, Scarborough, Mem.	1.000	25	48	1	0	49	1
Greene, Todd, Van.	1.000	4	7	1	0	8	0
Grundy, Phil, Oma.	1.000	1	1	0	0	1	0
Guerrero, Wilton, Alb.	1.000	8	11	0	0	11	0
Guiel, Aaron, L.V.	.946	50	60	10	4	74	1
Hall, Joe, Okla.	.833	5	5	0	1	6	0
Halter, Shane, Oma.	1.000	1	1	0	0	1	0
Hansen, Jed, Oma.	1.000	1	1	0	0	1	0
Hatcher, Chris, Oma.	.962	79	147	4	6	157	0
Hemmings, Scot, L.V.	.667	3	3	1	2	6	0
Hermansen, Chad, Nash.	.961	114	191	6	8	205	0
Herrick, Jason, Van.*	.991	57	102	4	1	107	1
Hidalgo, Richard, N.O.	1.000	9	17	0	0	17	0
Hosey, Steve, Oma.	1.000	2	5	1	0	6	0
Hubbard, Trenidad, Alb.	1.000	10	13	1	0	14	0
Hunter, Brian, Cal.*	1.000	9	18	2	0	20	0
Hunter, Torii, S.L.	.966	24	55	1	2	58	0
Huson, Jeff, Tuc.	1.000	1	1	0	0	1	0
Hutchins, Norm, Van.*	1.000	7	12	0	0	12	0
Hyers, Tim, Tuc.*	1.000	10	7	0	0	7	0
Hyzdu, Adam, Tuc.	.974	27	38	0	1	39	0
Ibanez, Raul, Tac.	.988	42	78	2	1	81	0
Incaviglia, Pete, N.O.	.955	48	62	1	3	66	0
Ingram, Garey, Alb.	1.000	54	60	1	0	61	0
Jennings, Robin, Iowa*	.962	79	123	5	5	133	2
Johnson, Brian, Fres.	1.000	5	10	0	0	10	0
Johnson, Keith, Alb.	1.000	1	1	0	0	1	0
Jones, Chris, Fres.	.944	13	17	0	1	18	0
Jones, Dax, N.O.	.960	27	46	2	2	50	2
Kirby, Wayne, Mem.	.975	58	113	4	3	120	2
Konerko, Paul, Alb.	.912	21	29	2	3	34	0
LaRocca, Greg, L.V.	.864	19	19	0	3	22	0
Latham, Chris, S.L.	.959	93	201	8	9	218	2
Leach, Jalal, Fres.*	.932	28	52	3	4	59	0
Lesher, Brian, Edm.*	.982	72	104	3	2	109	0
Lewis, Marc, S.L.	.984	113	171	8	3	182	1
Lewis, T.R., Okla.	.909	18	20	0	2	22	0
Liefer, Jeff, Cal.	1.000	4	7	0	0	7	0
Little, Mark, Okla.-Mem.	.990	83	194	6	2	202	1
Long, Ryan, Oma.	1.000	15	35	0	0	35	0
Lowery, Terrell, Iowa	.994	62	155	5	1	161	0
Maddox, Garry, Tuc.	.973	71	143	2	4	149	0
Martinez, Manny, Nash.	.943	20	31	2	2	35	1
Martins, Eric, Edm.	1.000	6	5	0	0	5	0
Mashore, Damon, Van.	.985	37	62	4	1	67	2
McCarty, Dave, Tac.*	.992	62	125	7	1	133	1
McDonald, Jason, Edm.	1.000	12	37	3	0	40	2
McEwing, Joe, Mem.	.981	75	138	14	3	155	3
Meulens, Hensley, Tuc.-Cal.	.915	49	72	3	7	82	0
Mieske, Matt, Iowa	.950	28	35	3	2	40	0
Mitchell, Donovan, N.O.	1.000	38	60	2	0	62	2
Monahan, Shane, Tac.	.993	64	141	1	1	143	0
Montgomery, Ray, N.O.	.976	73	156	4	4	164	2
Morenz, Shea, L.V.	1.000	11	16	1	0	17	1
Moreta, Ramon, Alb.	1.000	8	16	1	0	17	0
Mottola, Chad, Okla.	.953	72	118	5	6	129	0
Mouton, James, L.V.	.983	45	57	2	1	60	0
Munoz, Juan, Mem.*	.985	109	180	15	3	198	3
Murphy, Mike, Okla.	1.000	14	19	0	0	19	0
Murray, Calvin, Fres.	1.000	18	27	1	0	28	0
Myers, Rod, Oma.*	.986	29	67	4	1	72	1
Neal, Mike, N.O.*	1.000	2	10	0	0	10	0
Neill, Mike, Edm.	.971	96	165	5	5	175	1
Newson, Warren, Okla.*	.982	74	104	4	2	110	0
Norman, Les, Okla.	.987	80	144	11	2	157	3
Ogden, Jamie, S.L.*	.990	64	92	5	1	98	0
Palmeiro, Orlando, Van.	1.000	39	70	4	0	74	1
Pegues, Steve, C.S.	1.000	15	27	0	0	27	0
Peterson, Charles, Nash.	1.000	3	1	0	0	1	0
Phillips, J.R., N.O.*	.944	18	32	2	2	36	0
Poe, Charles, L.V.	.977	101	163	6	4	173	0
Porter, Bo, Iowa	1.000	3	6	0	0	6	0
Powell, Dante, Fres.	.976	132	284	2	7	293	0
Prieto, Chris, L.V.*	.969	91	174	12	6	192	2
Prieto, Rick, L.V.	1.000	24	25	2	0	27	0
Radmanovich, Ryan, Tac.	.982	97	164	4	3	171	1
Ramos, Ken, S.L.-N.O.*	.974	84	141	7	4	152	1
Richardson, Scott, Alb.	.972	77	100	5	3	108	2
Rios, Armando, Fres.*	.966	117	187	10	7	204	2
Rivera, Ruben, L.V.	1.000	30	53	2	0	55	0
Roberge, J.P., Alb.	1.000	7	6	0	0	6	0
Roberson, Kevin, Cal.	.980	115	236	9	5	250	3
Rohrmeier, Dan, Tac.	.952	40	58	1	3	62	0
Romero, Willie, Alb.	.964	108	181	6	7	194	2
Ryan, Rob, Tuc.*	.983	110	224	3	4	231	0
Sagmoen, Marc, Okla.*	.989	91	172	9	2	183	3
Sanford, Chance, Nash.	1.000	3	4	0	0	4	0
Saylor, Jamie, L.V.	1.000	1	2	0	0	2	0
Scarsone, Steve, Van.	1.000	1	1	0	0	1	0
Secrist, Reed, Mem.	.981	42	49	3	1	53	1
Sell, Chip, Alb.	1.000	31	60	2	0	62	0
Sexton, Chris, C.S.	1.000	1	3	0	0	3	0
Shave, Jon, S.L.	1.000	9	16	1	0	17	0
Sheff, Chris, Edm.	.993	118	262	10	2	274	3
Sheldon, Scott, Okla.	1.000	2	1	0	0	1	0
Shumpert, Terry, C.S.	.955	35	38	4	2	44	1
Simmons, Brian, Cal.	.967	92	197	6	7	210	0
Simons, Mitch, Tac.	1.000	1	2	0	0	2	0
Sisco, Steve, Oma.	.973	17	35	1	1	37	0
Smith, Demond, Cal.	1.000	3	4	0	0	4	0
Smith, Mark, Nash.	1.000	11	17	0	0	17	0
Stahoviak, Scott, S.L.	1.000	8	17	1	0	18	1
Staton, T.J., Nash.*	.945	56	102	2	6	110	0
Steverson, Todd, Mem.	.951	47	53	5	3	61	2
Stoner, Mike, Tuc.	.969	98	152	5	5	162	0
Stuckenschneider, Eric, Alb.	.993	71	131	2	1	134	0
Taylor, Jamie, C.S.	1.000	2	2	0	0	2	0
Thurman, Gary, Van.	.977	50	82	3	2	87	1
Tinsley, Lee, Van.	.977	22	39	3	1	43	0
Turner, Chris, Oma.	1.000	4	6	0	0	6	0
TYLER, Brad, Edm.	1.000	101	181	10	0	191	1
Unroe, Tim, Iowa	1.000	3	4	0	0	4	0
Valdes, Pedro, Iowa*	.965	60	106	3	4	113	0
Valdez, Mario, Cal.	.500	2	1	0	1	2	0
Voigt, Jack, Edm.-Okla.	.971	22	33	1	1	35	0
Ward, Daryle, N.O.*	.965	63	106	3	4	113	1
Warner, Ron, Mem.	.967	41	55	3	2	60	0
White, Derrick, Iowa-C.S.	.980	78	142	7	3	152	0
Whitmore, Darrell, Nash.	.960	70	96	1	4	101	0
Williams, Keith, Fres.	.929	47	63	2	5	70	0
Williams, Reggie, Van.	.991	95	220	9	2	231	2
Wilson, Craig, Cal.	1.000	2	2	1	0	3	0
Wilson, Tom, Tuc.	1.000	3	1	0	0	1	0
Wood, Jason, Edm.	.938	11	15	0	1	16	0
Young, Ernie, Oma.	.989	75	174	10	2	186	3
Zinter, Alan, Iowa	.909	5	9	1	1	11	0

TRIPLE PLAYS: Montgomery, Richardson.

OUTFIELDERS WITH TWO OR MORE TEAMS

Player, Team	Pct.	G	PO	A	E	TC	DP
Geisler, Phil, Nash.*	1.000	5	4	0	0	4	0
Geisler, Phil, N.O.*	.895	15	17	0	2	19	0
Little, Mark, Okla.	.994	64	161	6	1	168	1
Little, Mark, Mem.	.971	19	33	0	1	34	0
Meulens, Hensley, Tuc.	.914	47	71	3	7	81	0
Meulens, Hensley, Cal.	1.000	2	1	0	0	1	0
Ramos, Ken, S.L.*	1.000	17	19	1	0	20	0
Ramos, Ken, N.O.*	.970	67	122	6	4	132	1
Voigt, Jack, Edm.	1.000	6	8	0	0	8	0
Voigt, Jack, Okla.	.963	16	25	1	1	27	0
White, Derrick, Iowa	.975	59	111	5	3	119	0
White, Derrick, C.S.	1.000	19	31	2	0	33	0

CATCHERS

Player, Team	Pct.	G	PO	A	E	TC	DP	PB
Allison, Brad, Tuc.	1.000	4	14	1	0	15	0	0
Berryhill, Damon, Edm.	1.000	5	39	2	0	41	0	0
Bieser, Steve, Nash.	.993	54	284	21	2	307	0	3
Blanco, Henry, Alb.	.985	31	243	20	4	267	0	4
Burke, Jamie, Van.	.993	51	264	18	2	284	2	8
Charles, Frank, Fres.	.963	3	24	2	1	27	0	0
Chavez, Raul, Tac.	.990	74	523	70	6	599	12	2
Cholowsky, Dan, C.S.	.984	70	442	42	8	492	5	10
Christopherson, Eric, Cal.	.983	18	107	9	2	118	0	2
Cianfrocco, Archi, L.V.	1.000	1	1	0	0	1	0	0
Cline, Pat, Iowa	.987	112	806	50	11	867	3	18
Dandridge, Brad, Alb.	.933	6	26	2	2	30	0	0
Decker, Steve, Nash.	1.000	18	119	10	0	129	2	1
Edge, Tim, Nash.	.992	40	232	22	2	256	0	3
Ellis, Kevin, Iowa	1.000	4	7	1	0	8	0	0
Encarnacion, Angelo, Van.	.977	8	39	3	1	43	0	0
Fabregas, Jorge, Tuc.	1.000	5	28	3	0	31	1	2
Fasano, Sal, Oma.	1.000	4	26	1	0	27	1	0
Gonzalez, Jimmy, L.V.	.985	48	313	24	5	342	7	8
Greene, Todd, Van.	1.000	4	15	1	0	16	2	0
Gubanich, Creighton, L.V.	.991	68	507	43	5	555	2	16
Guzman, Edwards, Fres.	1.000	5	20	3	0	23	0	2
Helfand, Eric, Van.	1.000	2	4	1	0	5	0	0
Hemphill, Bret, Van.	.988	40	226	15	3	244	5	3
Horn, Jeff, S.L.	.994	23	148	9	1	158	0	1
Huckaby, Ken, Tac.	1.000	15	90	4	0	94	0	2
Kmak, Joe, Oma.	1.000	21	121	6	0	127	1	0
Laker, Tim, Nash.	.989	30	163	13	2	178	4	4
LeCroy, Matt, S.L.	1.000	2	6	0	0	6	0	0
Lidle, Kevin, C.S.	1.000	5	35	4	0	39	0	2
LoDuca, Paul, Alb.	.984	91	596	69	11	676	2	6
Machado, Robert, Cal.	.987	61	409	39	6	454	4	5
Makarewicz, Scott, N.O.	1.000	4	22	1	0	23	0	0
Maldonado, Carlos, Tac.	.933	3	14	0	1	15	0	0
Marrero, Eli, Mem.	.991	27	195	17	2	214	2	1
Mayes, Craig, Fres.	.989	30	173	13	2	188	2	2
McDonald, Keith, Mem.	1.000	32	189	15	0	204	3	1
McKay, Cody, Edm.	1.000	3	16	0	0	16	0	0
Meluskey, Mitch, N.O.	.987	108	702	49	10	761	8	17
Mendez, Carlos, Oma.	1.000	10	35	2	0	37	1	0
Mercedes, Henry, Fres.	.995	27	187	16	1	204	1	4
Miller, Damian, Tuc.	.973	18	95	15	3	113	0	2
Mintz, Steve, Nash.	1.000	1	3	2	0	5	0	0
MIRABELLI, Doug, Fres.	.9954	83	605	50	3	658	11	4
Molina, Ben, Oma.	.986	44	316	24	5	345	2	1
Molina, Izzy, Edm.	.981	77	525	42	11	578	6	6
Morales, Willie, Edm.	.988	64	357	39	5	401	2	3
Myers, Greg, L.V.	1.000	3	16	1	0	17	0	0
O'Neal, Troy, Tuc.	.972	45	224	19	7	250	3	1
Ortiz, Hector, Oma.	.978	62	318	30	8	356	4	5
Owens, Jayhawk, S.L.	.994	47	323	16	2	341	4	4
Pierzynski, A.J., S.L.	.983	59	366	30	7	403	3	5
Quire, Jeremy, Tuc.	1.000	3	9	1	0	10	0	0
Reyes, Jose, Nash.	1.000	1	2	0	0	2	0	0
Romero, Mandy, L.V.	.977	32	276	27	7	310	4	6
Ronan, Marc, N.O.	.985	46	252	18	4	274	4	2
Russo, Paul, N.O.	1.000	1	4	0	0	4	0	0
Sealy, Scot, Tac.	.994	47	290	23	2	315	1	3
Sheaffer, Danny, Mem.	1.000	6	38	3	0	41	0	0
Sisco, Steve, Oma.	.000	1	0	0	1	1	0	0
Smith, Jeff, S.L.	.994	22	145	9	1	155	2	1
Snow, Casey, Alb.	1.000	2	17	0	0	17	0	0
Steed, Dave, Alb.	.989	28	165	23	2	190	1	2
Stefanski, Mike, Mem.	.993	85	629	55	5	689	10	3
Stewart, Andy, Oma.	1.000	6	34	6	0	40	0	0
Strittmatter, Mark, C.S.	.991	81	504	53	5	562	4	2

Player, Team	Pct.	G	PO	A	E	TC	DP	PB
Sweet, Jon, Nash.	.986	15	66	7	1	74	1	1
Thurston, Jerrey, Van.	1.000	9	52	0	0	52	0	1
Torrealba, Yorvit, Fres.	1.000	4	22	0	0	22	0	1
Toth, Dave, Cal.	.992	68	423	52	4	479	8	12
Tremie, Chris, Okla.	.9945	78	498	45	3	546	4	2
Turner, Chris, Oma.	.992	55	331	20	3	354	1	1
Wathan, Dusty, Tac.	.993	19	134	15	1	150	1	1
Wilson, Tom, Tuc.	.981	94	565	48	12	625	5	9
Wrona, Rick, Okla.	.977	85	461	45	12	518	8	11
Zinter, Alan, Iowa	.989	39	262	19	3	284	4	8

PITCHERS

Player, Team	Pct.	G	PO	A	E	TC	DP
Abbott, Jim, Cal.*	1.000	5	2	6	0	8	0
Abbott, Paul, Tac.	1.000	3	0	2	0	2	0
Abbott, Todd, Edm.	1.000	3	1	1	0	2	1
Adams, Terry, Iowa	1.000	3	1	0	0	1	0
Almanza, Armando, Mem.*	.500	31	0	1	1	2	0
Alston, Garvin, C.S.	.923	44	5	7	1	13	0
Alvarez, Juan, Van.*	1.000	18	2	5	0	7	0
Alvarez, Tavo, Nash.	.957	15	2	20	1	23	0
Anderson, Jimmy, Nash.*	.944	35	12	39	3	54	2
Andujar, Luis, Cal.	.800	13	7	1	2	10	0
Appier, Kevin, Oma.	.800	6	1	3	1	5	0
Arocha, Rene, N.O.	1.000	11	1	12	0	13	1
Arrandale, Matt, Mem.	1.000	23	4	5	0	9	0
Aybar, Manny, Mem.	1.000	13	8	7	0	15	0
Bailes, Scott, Okla.*	1.000	1	0	1	0	1	0
Bailey, Cory, Fres.	.962	57	11	14	1	26	3
Baptist, Travis, S.L.*	.944	21	8	26	2	36	5
Barber, Brian, Oma.	.913	22	7	14	2	23	0
Barker, Richie, Iowa	1.000	16	0	5	0	5	1
Barndollar, Jeff, Tuc.	.000	1	0	0	1	1	0
Barnes, Brian, Mem.*	.960	35	7	17	1	25	3
Barrios, Manny, Alb.	1.000	20	1	6	0	7	0
Barry, Jeff, C.S.	1.000	1	0	1	0	1	0
Bautista, Jose, Cal.	.889	35	4	4	1	9	0
Beckett, Robbie, C.S.*	1.000	21	1	3	0	4	0
Beirne, Kevin, Cal.	1.000	2	0	1	0	1	0
Benson, Kris, Nash.	.969	38	15	16	1	32	0
Bertotti, Mike, Cal.*	.905	43	8	11	2	21	0
Berumen, Andres, Tac.	1.000	9	3	10	0	13	0
Bevil, Brian, Oma.	1.000	10	1	1	0	2	0
Blais, Mike, N.O.	1.000	2	1	2	0	3	0
Blood, Darin, Fres.	.900	19	7	20	3	30	6
Bluma, Jaime, Oma.	1.000	14	1	3	0	4	0
Bolton, Tom, Nash.*	1.000	3	1	2	0	3	0
Bonanno, Rob, Van.	1.000	3	2	0	0	2	0
Bones, Ricky, S.L.-Oma.	1.000	11	2	9	0	11	0
Bourgeois, Steve, C.S.	.971	38	12	21	1	34	7
Bovee, Mike, Van.	.950	48	7	12	1	20	0
Bowers, Shane, S.L.	.833	33	11	4	3	18	0
Boyd, Jason, Tuc.	.857	15	3	3	1	7	0
Bradford, Chad, Cal.	1.000	29	3	11	0	14	0
Brock, Chris, Fres.	.867	17	12	14	4	30	0
Brohawn, Troy, Fres.*	.935	30	4	25	2	31	2
Brosnan, Jason, Van.*	1.000	10	0	2	0	2	0
Brownson, Mark, C.S.	.971	21	11	22	1	34	0
Brunson, Will, Alb.*	1.000	34	7	26	0	33	0
Bullinger, Jim, Tac.	.971	20	10	24	1	35	0
Burke, John, C.S.	1.000	6	1	1	0	2	0
Butcher, Mike, Van.	.875	37	2	5	1	8	0
Byrdak, Tim, Oma.*	1.000	26	2	10	0	12	0
Byrne, Earl, Iowa*	1.000	10	1	11	0	12	1
Cabrera, Jose, N.O.	1.000	5	2	0	0	2	0
Cadaret, Greg, Van.*	1.000	9	1	0	0	1	0
Canale, George, Nash.	1.000	1	0	1	0	1	0
Casian, Larry, Cal.*	1.000	43	4	12	0	16	3
Castillo, Carlos, Cal.	1.000	2	2	0	0	2	0
Chavez, Anthony, Van.	.800	53	3	5	2	10	0
Cholowsky, Dan, C.S.	1.000	7	0	1	0	1	0
Chouinard, Bobby, Tuc.	1.000	4	0	1	0	1	0
Clark, Terry, Okla.	.971	30	12	21	1	34	1
Clement, Matt, L.V.	.800	27	12	20	8	40	1
Clemons, Chris, Tuc.	.889	20	7	9	2	18	2
Clontz, Brad, Alb.	1.000	6	0	1	0	1	0
Cloude, Ken, Tac.	1.000	1	0	1	0	1	0
Cole, Victor, Iowa	.923	38	1	11	1	13	0
Connelly, Steve, Edm.	1.000	55	4	9	0	13	1
Corbin, Archie, L.V.	.000	6	0	0	1	1	0
Corey, Bryan, Tuc.	.882	39	4	11	2	17	1
Cornelius, Reid, Tuc.	.935	19	6	23	2	31	2

Player, Team	Pct.	G	PO	A	E	TC	DP
Cornett, Brad, Tuc.	.833	6	1	4	1	6	1
Crawford, Carlos, Nash.	1.000	8	2	2	0	4	0
Croushore, Rick, Mem.	1.000	23	0	2	0	2	0
Cruz, Nelson, Cal.	.917	35	6	27	3	36	1
Cumberland, Chris, S.L.*	1.000	17	1	9	0	10	0
Cunnane, Will, L.V.	1.000	33	0	4	0	4	1
Dale, Carl, Edm.	1.000	11	1	4	0	5	0
Darwin, Jeff, Fres.	1.000	56	0	2	0	2	1
De La Maza, Roland, Oma.	.964	31	9	18	1	28	2
De La Rosa, Maximo, Tac.	1.000	9	1	4	0	5	0
Dessens, Elmer, Nash.	1.000	6	3	7	0	10	0
Dickson, Jason, Van.	1.000	4	3	2	0	5	1
Diorio, Mike, N.O.	1.000	21	1	4	0	5	0
Dixon, Bubba, L.V.*	1.000	38	4	6	0	10	0
Dougherty, Jim, Edm.	1.000	45	1	17	0	18	1
Edsell, Geoff, Van.	.870	56	6	14	3	23	1
Elarton, Scott, N.O.	.882	14	4	11	2	17	0
Estes, Shawn, Fres.*	1.000	1	0	1	0	1	0
Evans, Bart, Oma.	1.000	49	4	8	0	12	0
Evans, Dave, Nash.	1.000	7	0	3	0	3	0
Eversgerd, Bryan, Mem.*	.955	49	7	14	1	22	2
Farmer, Michael, C.S.*	.875	28	3	11	2	16	1
Farnsworth, Kyle, Iowa	1.000	18	7	13	0	20	1
Figueroa, Nelson, Tuc.	1.000	7	4	10	0	14	2
Flores, Ignacio, Alb.	.957	17	10	12	1	23	1
Ford, Ben, Tuc.	.857	48	6	6	2	14	1
Fordham, Tom, Cal.*	.933	9	5	9	1	15	1
Fossas, Tony, Iowa-Okla.*	1.000	14	0	3	0	3	1
Foster, Kevin, Iowa	.889	17	1	7	1	9	1
Franklin, Ryan, Tac.	.946	35	11	24	2	37	1
Frontera, Chad, Fres.	1.000	4	0	1	0	1	0
Fultz, Aaron, Fres.*	1.000	10	1	0	0	1	0
Gajkowski, Steve, Tac.	1.000	53	3	13	0	16	1
Gandarillas, Gus, S.L.	1.000	53	10	11	0	21	0
Garcia, Freddy, N.O.-Tac.	1.000	7	5	4	0	9	1
Giard, Ken, Nash.	1.000	15	2	1	0	3	0
Glinatsis, George, C.S.	.857	20	4	8	2	14	0
Granger, Jeff, Okla.*	.964	32	9	18	1	28	1
Gray, Dennis, Iowa*	1.000	9	1	2	0	3	0
Grilli, Jason, Fres.	1.000	8	2	2	0	4	0
Grundy, Phil, Oma.	.875	14	3	4	1	8	0
Grzanich, Mike, N.O.	.833	34	3	2	1	6	0
Gutierrez, Jim, N.O.	.889	27	2	6	1	9	0
Halama, John, N.O.*	.971	17	11	23	1	35	0
Halperin, Mike, Nash.*	1.000	11	2	0	0	2	0
Hansell, Greg, Edm.-Oma.	1.000	59	8	2	0	10	0
Hanson, Erik, Van.	.941	14	4	12	1	17	2
Harikkala, Tim, Tac.	1.000	18	3	4	0	7	1
Harris, Jeff, S.L.	.889	25	3	5	1	9	3
Harris, Pep, Van.	1.000	2	0	2	0	2	0
Harris, Reggie, N.O.	.778	51	4	3	2	9	1
Harrison, Brian, Oma.	1.000	25	10	13	0	23	1
Hartgraves, Dean, Fres.*	1.000	38	3	11	0	14	0
Hartman, Ron, Tuc.	1.000	2	0	1	0	1	0
Hasselhoff, Derek, Cal.	.833	13	2	3	1	6	0
Haught, Gary, Edm.	1.000	19	3	3	0	6	0
Haynie, Jason, Nash.*	1.000	3	0	3	0	3	0
Heathcott, Mike, Cal.	.955	39	3	18	1	22	1
Heflin, Bronson, Mem.	1.000	2	1	0	0	1	0
Heiserman, Rick, Mem.	1.000	40	3	5	0	8	0
Herbert, Russ, Cal.	.977	28	14	28	1	43	4
Heredia, Gil, Edm.	.951	29	14	25	2	41	0
Herges, Matt, Alb.	.875	34	10	11	3	24	1
Hernandez, Fernando, Tuc.	1.000	3	0	1	0	1	0
Hernandez, Xavier, Okla.	1.000	5	0	1	0	1	0
Hinchliffe, Brett, Tac.	.778	25	9	5	4	18	1
Holdridge, David, Tac.	.920	42	7	16	2	25	2
Holtz, Mike, Van.*	1.000	10	0	1	0	1	0
Holzemer, Mark, Edm.*	1.000	30	2	4	0	6	0
Howry, Bobby, Cal.	1.000	23	0	7	0	7	0
Hubbs, Dan, Alb.	1.000	13	3	1	0	4	0
Huisman, Rick, Fres.	1.000	44	0	5	0	5	0
Hurst, Jonathan, Okla.	1.000	7	2	4	0	6	0
Iglesias, Mike, Alb.	.750	39	4	2	2	8	0
Jacobsen, Joe, Van.	1.000	2	2	0	0	2	0
Jean, Domingo, C.S.	.875	36	6	1	1	8	1
Jensen, Ryan, Fres.	1.000	2	0	1	0	1	0
Jimenez, Miguel, Iowa	.667	7	0	2	1	3	0
Johnson, Barry, Okla.	1.000	31	4	9	0	13	0
Johnson, Jonathan, Okla.	.880	19	5	17	3	25	2
Jones, Marcus, Edm.	.500	2	0	1	1	2	0
Judd, Mike, Alb.	1.000	17	9	17	0	26	1
Juelsgaard, Jarod, Tac.	.844	28	9	18	5	32	1
Kaufman, Brad, L.V.	1.000	23	7	5	0	12	1
King, Bill, Edm.	.864	24	7	12	3	22	1
King, Curt, Mem.	1.000	27	3	4	0	7	2
King, Ray, Iowa*	.800	37	3	5	2	10	0
Klingenbeck, Scott, Nash.	1.000	6	2	10	0	12	0
Knight, Brandon, Okla.	.833	16	2	8	2	12	0
Kramer, Tom, C.S.	.895	48	6	11	2	19	1
Kubenka, Jeff, Alb.*	1.000	28	2	7	0	9	0
Kubinski, Tim, Edm.*	1.000	57	5	13	0	18	1
Lagarde, Joe, Alb.	1.000	14	0	3	0	3	0
Lawrence, Sean, Nash.*	.882	26	3	12	2	17	0
Laxton, Brett, Edm.	1.000	8	8	8	0	16	1
Levine, Alan, Okla.	.875	12	5	2	1	8	2
Lidle, Cory, Tuc.	1.000	1	1	2	0	3	0
Lilly, Ted, Alb.*	.833	5	2	3	1	6	1
Linton, Douglas, S.L.	.917	18	5	6	1	12	0
Lira, Felipe, Tac.	.971	20	12	21	1	34	1
Loiselle, Rich, Nash.	1.000	4	0	1	0	1	0
Lomon, Kevin, L.V.	.957	30	8	14	1	23	0
Looper, Braden, Mem.	1.000	40	0	5	0	5	0
Lopez, Johann, N.O.	1.000	45	5	10	0	15	0
Lorraine, Andrew, Tac.*	.889	52	4	12	2	18	3
Lovingier, Kevin, Mem.*	1.000	39	0	6	0	6	1
Lowe, Sean, Mem.	1.000	25	6	22	0	28	0
Luebbers, Larry, Mem.	.957	29	13	31	2	46	2
Lundquist, David, Cal.	1.000	12	1	0	0	1	0
Maloney, Sean, Alb.	1.000	26	0	4	0	4	0
Manuel, Barry, Tuc.	1.000	23	1	9	0	10	0
Manwiller, Tim, Edm.	1.000	2	0	2	0	2	0
Marrero, Kenny, Tuc.	.917	34	3	8	1	12	0
Mathews, Del, Nash.*	1.000	4	2	0	0	2	0
Mathews, Terry, Edm.	1.000	13	1	3	0	4	0
Maxcy, Brian, Mem.	1.000	3	1	1	0	2	0
McCarthy, Greg, Tac.*	1.000	19	1	1	0	2	0
McCurry, Jeff, Nash.	.929	40	5	8	1	14	0
McDill, Allen, Oma.*	1.000	61	2	6	0	8	0
McDowell, Jack, Van.	1.000	1	0	1	0	1	0
McMullen, Mike, Fres.	1.000	2	1	0	0	1	0
McNichol, Brian, Iowa*	1.000	1	1	0	0	1	0
Meacham, Rusty, Mem.-Nash.	.941	53	7	9	1	17	0
Menhart, Paul, L.V.	.870	49	6	14	3	23	3
Michalak, Chris, Tuc.*	1.000	29	3	25	0	28	1
MILACKI, Bob, N.O.	1.000	29	21	30	0	51	3
Miller, Kurt, Iowa	.967	28	5	24	1	30	4
Miller, Travis, S.L.*	1.000	34	3	8	0	11	0
Mimbs, Mike, Van.*	1.000	19	1	2	0	3	0
Mintz, Steve, Nash.	.875	56	4	10	2	16	1
Mlicki, Doug, Oma.-Mem.	.944	31	7	10	1	18	1
Montgomery, Matt, Alb.	1.000	3	0	1	0	1	0
Moody, Eric, Okla.	.955	45	6	15	1	22	0
Moore, Joel, C.S.	.813	12	5	8	3	16	2
Morman, Alvin, Fres.*	1.000	4	0	1	0	1	0
Morris, Matt, Mem.	1.000	4	1	0	0	1	0
Morse, Paul, Alb.	1.000	2	0	1	0	1	0
Murray, Heath, L.V.*	1.000	27	7	20	0	27	0
Myers, Jimmy, Okla.	.947	41	4	14	1	19	2
Myers, Rodney, Iowa	.938	33	5	25	2	32	2
Naulty, Dan, S.L.	1.000	5	2	0	0	2	0
Neal, Billy, Alb.	.500	6	1	0	1	2	0
Nelson, Chris, Edm.	1.000	4	0	2	0	2	0
Newman, Alan, L.V.*	.850	63	5	12	3	20	1
Nina, Elvin, Edm.	1.000	1	0	1	0	1	0
Nitkowski, C.J., N.O.*	.667	5	0	2	1	3	0
Nunez, Vladimir, Tuc.	.917	31	3	8	1	12	1
Ohme, Kevin, S.L.*	1.000	51	3	17	0	20	2
Oleksik, George, Tuc.	1.000	2	0	2	0	2	0
Oliver, Darren, Okla.*	1.000	1	1	0	0	1	0
Ontiveros, Steve, Mem.	.500	3	1	0	1	2	0
Ortiz, Russ, Fres.	1.000	10	2	9	0	11	0
Paniagua, Jose, Tac.	1.000	44	5	9	0	14	1
Parque, Jim, Cal.*	1.000	8	2	10	0	12	0
Pavlas, Dave, Edm.	1.000	26	2	7	0	9	0
Pearsall, J.J., Alb.*	.750	8	1	2	1	4	0
Perez, Juan, Edm.*	.667	24	1	1	1	3	0
Perisho, Matt, Okla.*	1.000	15	5	13	0	18	0
Perkins, Dan, S.L.	1.000	7	3	3	0	6	0
Peters, Don, Tuc.	1.000	13	1	7	0	8	1
Phillips, Jason, Nash.	.900	5	4	5	1	10	0
Phillips, Randy, Fres.	1.000	9	2	2	0	4	0
Pickett, Ricky, Fres.-Tuc.-Okla.*	.714	34	4	6	4	14	1
Pickford, Kevin, Nash.*	1.000	13	4	11	0	15	0

Player, Team	Pct.	G	PO	A	E	TC	DP
Pisciotta, Marc, Iowa	1.000	28	2	4	0	6	0
Plantenberg, Erik, Fres.*	1.000	53	6	13	0	19	0
Politte, Cliff, Mem.	1.000	10	6	8	0	14	0
Powell, John, Okla.	1.000	11	1	6	0	7	0
Pratt, Rich, Cal.*	.944	29	13	21	2	36	1
Price, Jamey, Edm.	1.000	2	1	0	0	1	0
Prieto, Ariel, Edm.	.833	10	3	12	3	18	2
Raggio, Brady, Mem.	.968	24	16	14	1	31	4
Rain, Steve, Iowa	.957	29	5	17	1	23	4
Ramirez, Roberto, L.V.*	1.000	26	2	4	0	6	0
Ramos, Edgar, N.O.	.818	12	9	9	4	22	2
Randolph, Steve, Tuc.*	.800	17	1	3	1	5	1
Rath, Fred, S.L.-CSP	.889	50	1	7	1	9	2
Rath, Gary, Alb.*	1.000	28	2	29	0	31	1
Rawitzer, Kevin, Oma.*	1.000	10	6	14	0	20	1
Redman, Mark, S.L.*	.864	19	6	13	3	22	2
Reichert, Dan, Oma.	.750	3	1	2	1	4	0
Reyes, Dennis, Alb.*	.750	7	1	5	2	8	0
Ricken, Ray, L.V.	.667	3	2	0	1	3	0
Rigby, Brad, Edm.	.727	13	3	5	3	11	0
Rincon, Ricardo, Nash.*	1.000	1	0	1	0	1	0
Rios, Dan, Oma.	.947	25	4	14	1	19	2
Ritchie, Todd, S.L.	.917	36	2	9	1	12	0
Ritz, Kevin, C.S.	1.000	4	2	3	0	5	0
Rivera, Roberto, N.O.*	.882	54	5	10	2	17	2
Rizzo, Todd, Cal.*	.867	50	1	12	2	15	1
Roa, Joe, Fres.	.979	27	10	37	1	48	1
Roach, Peter, Alb.*	.500	19	0	1	1	2	0
Roberts, Chris, Edm.*	.889	18	2	6	1	9	0
Robertson, Rich, Van.*	1.000	27	8	20	0	28	1
Rodriguez, Frank, S.L.	.938	16	13	17	2	32	1
Rogers, Kevin, Fres.*	1.000	14	0	2	0	2	0
Rooney, Mike, Tuc.	1.000	3	0	2	0	2	0
Root, Derek, N.O.*	1.000	1	1	0	0	1	0
Rossiter, Mike, L.V.	1.000	31	3	5	0	8	1
Rusch, Glendon, Oma.*	.500	3	0	1	1	2	0
Ryan, Matt, Nash.	.905	51	4	15	2	21	1
Sabel, Erik, Tuc.	1.000	7	0	1	0	1	0
Saier, Matt, Oma.	1.000	9	6	8	0	14	1
Saipe, Mike, C.S.	.917	24	7	15	2	24	1
Salkeld, Roger, N.O.	.909	37	4	6	1	11	0
Sampson, Benj, S.L.*	.974	28	10	28	1	39	0
Sanders, Scott, L.V.	1.000	15	4	5	0	9	1
Santiago, Jose, Oma.	1.000	4	0	1	0	1	0
Sauveur, Rich, Nash.*	1.000	46	3	9	0	12	1
Scanlan, Bob, N.O.	.929	14	7	6	1	14	0
Schmidt, Jeff, Van.	1.000	18	2	2	0	4	0
Schoeneweis, Scott, Van.*	.968	27	6	24	1	31	3
Seelbach, Chris, Tac.	1.000	6	0	1	0	1	0
Serafini, Dan, S.L.*	.846	9	2	9	2	13	1
Shoemaker, Stephen, C.S.	.769	15	6	4	3	13	0
Sikorski, Brian, N.O.	1.000	15	8	10	0	18	0
Silva, Jose, Nash.	1.000	3	2	2	0	4	0
Simas, Bill, Cal.	1.000	5	0	2	0	2	0
Slusarski, Joe, N.O.	1.000	31	4	7	0	11	0
Small, Mark, Okla.	1.000	15	2	6	0	8	0
Smith, Dan, Okla.	1.000	1	1	1	0	2	0
Smith, Lee, N.O.	1.000	10	2	0	0	2	0
Snyder, John, Cal.	.958	15	5	18	1	24	2
Soderstrom, Steve, Fres.	1.000	25	5	6	0	11	1
Sparks, Steve, Van.	1.000	4	5	3	0	8	0
Speier, Justin, Iowa	.875	45	2	5	1	8	0
Spencer, Sean, Tac.*	1.000	9	0	2	0	2	0
Spencer, Stan, L.V.	.929	22	11	15	2	28	0
Steenstra, Kennie, Iowa	.917	25	9	24	3	36	0
Stein, Blake, Edm.	1.000	5	2	3	0	5	0
Steph, Rod, Oma.	.500	17	1	1	2	4	0
Stevens, Dave, Iowa	.923	26	5	7	1	13	1
Stone, Ricky, Alb.	.900	18	6	12	2	20	2
Stoops, Jim, C.S.	1.000	11	1	0	0	1	0
Sturtze, Tanyon, Okla.	1.000	13	2	1	0	3	1
Suppan, Jeff, Tuc.	1.000	13	7	8	0	15	1
Suzuki, Mac, Tac.	.960	28	10	14	1	25	2
Swartzbaugh, Dave, Iowa	1.000	42	6	22	0	28	1
Tavarez, Julian, Fres.	1.000	1	0	1	0	1	0
Taylor, Scott, N.O.	1.000	9	1	5	0	6	1
Telgheder, Dave, Edm.	1.000	3	2	1	0	3	1
Theodile, Robert, Cal.	1.000	17	1	2	0	3	0
Thomas, Larry, Okla.*	1.000	11	1	1	0	2	0
Thompson, Mark, C.S.	1.000	1	1	0	0	1	0
Tolar, Kevin, Nash.*	1.000	1	1	0	0	1	0
Tollberg, Brian, L.V.	1.000	33	1	8	0	9	1
Turner, Matt, Oma.	1.000	41	7	8	0	15	0
Tuttle, Dave, Tuc.	1.000	10	1	2	0	3	0
Twiggs, Greg, Iowa*	1.000	7	0	3	0	3	0
Urbani, Thomas, Mem.*	1.000	7	1	9	0	10	1
Valdez, Efrain, Tuc.*	1.000	28	3	23	0	26	0
Van Landingham, Bill, Van.	.833	9	3	2	1	6	1
Van Poppel, Todd, Okla.	1.000	15	3	13	0	16	0
Vavrek, Mike, C.S.*	.889	10	3	5	1	9	0
Venafro, Mike, Okla.*	.857	13	0	6	1	7	0
Veras, Dario, L.V.	1.000	31	2	4	0	6	0
Verplancke, Joe, Tuc.	1.000	1	0	1	0	1	0
Wainhouse, David, C.S.	1.000	38	2	8	0	10	1
Walker, Jamie, Oma.*	1.000	7	2	8	0	10	0
Wall, Donne, L.V.	.750	3	2	1	1	4	0
Wallace, Kent, N.O.	1.000	7	0	1	0	1	0
Washburn, Jarrod, Van.*	.875	14	4	10	2	16	1
Watkins, Scott, Okla.*	1.000	38	2	11	0	13	0
Weaver, Eric, Alb.	1.000	46	7	6	0	13	1
Weber, Neil, Tuc.*	.909	46	2	8	1	11	0
Weibl, Clint, Mem.	1.000	1	0	1	0	1	0
Wengert, Don, Iowa	1.000	9	7	10	0	17	1
West, David, N.O.*	1.000	19	0	3	0	3	0
Wiegandt, Scott, Nash.*	1.000	11	0	2	0	2	0
Wilkins, Marc, Nash.	1.000	5	0	1	0	1	0
Williams, Jeff, Alb.*	.912	21	5	26	3	34	3
Williams, Mike, Nash.	1.000	16	0	6	0	6	0
Williams, Shad, Van.	1.000	14	5	10	0	15	1
Wilson, Gary, Nash.-S.L.	.947	39	8	10	1	19	2
Wilson, Trevor, Van.*	.969	21	13	18	1	32	4
Witasick, Jay, Edm.	.857	27	7	5	2	14	0
Wojciechowski, Steve, S.L.*	1.000	9	2	1	0	3	0
Wolcott, Bob, Tuc.	.964	23	6	21	1	28	2
Wolff, Bryan, L.V.	1.000	9	0	1	0	1	0
Woodson, Kerry, C.S.	.895	42	8	26	4	38	4
Worrell, Steve, Iowa*	.833	6	2	4	1	7	0

PITCHERS WITH TWO OR MORE TEAMS

Player, Team	Pct.	G	PO	A	E	TC	DP
Bones, Ricky, S.L.	1.000	8	2	6	0	8	0
Bones, Ricky, Oma.	1.000	3	0	3	0	3	0
Fossas, Tony, Iowa	1.000	10	0	1	0	1	1
Fossas, Tony, Okla.	1.000	4	0	2	0	2	0
Garcia, Freddy, N.O.	1.000	2	1	1	0	2	0
Garcia, Freddy, Tac.	1.000	5	4	3	0	7	1
Hansell, Greg, Edm.	1.000	13	2	1	0	3	0
Hansell, Greg, Oma.	1.000	46	6	1	0	7	0
Meacham, Rusty, Mem.	1.000	38	4	5	0	9	0
Meacham, Rusty, Nash.	.875	15	3	4	1	8	0
Mlicki, Doug, Oma.	1.000	7	0	5	0	5	0
Mlicki, Doug, Mem.	.923	24	7	5	1	13	1
Pickett, Ricky, Fres.	.750	5	1	2	1	4	0
Pickett, Ricky, Tuc.	.000	5	0	0	1	1	0
Pickett, Ricky, Okla.	.778	24	3	4	2	9	1
Rath, Fred, S.L.	1.000	27	0	4	0	4	1
Rath, Fred, C.S.	.800	23	1	3	1	5	1
Wilson, Gary, Nash.	.929	29	7	6	1	14	1
Wilson, Gary, S.L.	1.000	10	1	4	0	5	1

The following players did not have any fielding statistics at the positions indicated or appeared only as a designated hitter, pinch-hitter or pinch-runner: Alston, 3b; Acevedo, p; Adams, p; Babineaux, p; Bailey, of; T. Barker, p; Barnes, of; Juan Bautista, ss; Beltre, p; Berblinger, of; Bonilla, p; Brewer, p; Bridges, of; Briggs, of; Brito, 2b; Ro. Brown, dh; Brundage, dh; Bruske, p; Buhner, of; Buske, p; Busby, p; Byrdak, p; Canale, p; Candaele, 3b; Carr, 2b; Carroll, p; Caruso, p; Castro, ph; Colbert, dh, ph; Cholowsky, ss; Christopherson, p; Converse, p; Cortes, p; Crabtree, p; Daal,p; Dandridge, of; Daniels, p; Dollar, p; Doman, p; Escamilla, ph; Everly, p; Florez, p; F. Garcia, of; Glassey, c; Grijak, p; Hajek, ss; Hale, p; Hatcher, p; J. Heredia, p; Horne, dh; Horsman, of; Howard, c, p; Hyers, p; Hyzdu, p; B. Johnson, p; Kennison, p; Kirgan, of; Kolb, p; Kramer, of; Leyva, p; Manning, p; Martines, p; M. Martinez, 2b; McAffee, ph; Meier, of; Meluskey, ph; Michalak, of; O. Miller, p; K. Mitchel, dh; Molina, of, p; Molitor, dh; Mouton, 2b; Obando, of; O'Neal, p; Osborne, p; Patterson, p; Pavlos, p; Petersen, p; Quinlan, 2b; A. Ramirez, ss; L. Rivera, of; Robertson, of; Rupp, of; Felix Rodriguez, p; Schroeffel, p; Sealy, 3b; Secrist, c; Sheaffer, of; Stefanski, 3b; Sodowski, p; Steed, p; Steverson, 1b; Stritmatter, p; Tabaka, p; Taulbee, p; J. Taylor, p; Thobe, p; J. Thompson, p; J. Tyler, ph; Underwood, c; Watson, p; Tom Wilson, p; K. Wood, p; Woods, of, ss; Wrona, of; D. Young, p.

LEAGUE CHAMPIONS

Year	Team	Pct.	Year	Team	Pct.	Year	Team	Pct.
1903—	Los Angeles	.630	1940—	Seattle‡	.629	1975—	Salt Lake City	.556
1904—	Tacoma	.589	1941—	Seattle‡	.598		Hawaii•	.611
	Tacoma§	.571	1942—	Sacramento	.590	1976—	Salt Lake City	.625
	Los Angeles§	.571		Seattle (3rd)†	.539		Hawaii•	.531
1905—	Tacoma	.583	1943—	Los Angeles	.710	1977—	Phoenix•	.579
	Los Angeles*	.604		S. Francisco (2nd)†	.574		Hawaii	.541
1906—	Portland	.657	1944—	Los Angeles	.586	1978—	Tacoma††	.584
1907—	Los Angeles	.608		S. Francisco (3rd)†	.509		Albuquerque††	.557
1908—	Los Angeles	.585	1945—	Portland	.622	1979—	Albuquerque	.581
1909—	San Francisco	.623		S. Francisco (4th)†	.525		Salt Lake City‡‡	.541
1910—	Portland	.567	1946—	San Francisco‡	.628	1980—	Albuquerque	.578
1911—	Portland	.589	1947—	Los Angeles▲	.567		Hawaii	.539
1912—	Oakland	.591	1948—	Oakland‡	.606	1981—	Albuquerque*	.712
1913—	Portland	.559	1949—	Hollywood‡	.583		Tacoma	.561
1914—	Portland	.574	1950—	Oakland	.590	1982—	Albuquerque*	.594
1915—	San Francisco	.570	1951—	Seattle‡	.593		Spokane	.545
1916—	Los Angeles	.601	1952—	Hollywood	.606	1983—	Albuquerque	.594
1917—	San Francisco	.561	1953—	Hollywood	.589		Portland*	.528
1918—	Vernon	.569	1954—	San Diego■	.604	1984—	Hawaii	.621
	Los Angeles (2nd)◆	.548	1955—	Seattle	.552		Edmonton*	.486
1919—	Vernon	.613	1956—	Los Angeles	.637	1985—	Vancouver*	.522
1920—	Vernon	.556	1957—	San Francisco	.601		Phoenix	.563
1921—	Los Angeles	.574	1958—	Phoenix	.578	1986—	Vancouver	.616
1922—	San Francisco	.638	1959—	Salt Lake City	.552		Las Vegas*	.563
1923—	San Francisco	.617	1960—	Spokane	.601	1987—	Calgary	.596
1924—	Seattle	.545	1961—	Tacoma	.630		Albuquerque*	.542
1925—	San Francisco	.643	1962—	San Diego	.604	1988—	Vancouver	.599
1926—	Los Angeles	.599	1963—	Spokane	.620		Las Vegas*	.529
1927—	Oakland	.615		Oklahoma City•	.632	1989—	Albuquerque	.563
1928—	San Francisco*	.630	1964—	Arkansas	.609		Vancouver*	.514
	Sacramento∞	.626		San Diego•	.576	1990—	Albuquerque*	.641
	San Francisco∞	.626	1965—	Oklahoma City	.628		Edmonton	.553
1929—	Mission	.643		Portland	.547	1991—	Albuquerque	.580
	Hollywood*	.592	1966—	Seattle•	.561		Tucson*	.564
1930—	Los Angeles	.576		Tulsa	.578	1992—	Colorado Springs*	.596
	Hollywood*	.650	1967—	San Diego•	.574		Portland	.576
1931—	Hollywood	.626		Spokane	.541	1993—	Portland	.608
	San Francisco*	.608	1968—	Tulsa•	.642		Tucson*	.580
1932—	Portland	.587		Spokane	.586	1994—	Albuquerque*	.597
1933—	Los Angeles	.610	1969—	Tacoma•	.589		Vancouver	.542
1934—	Los Angeles▼	.786		Eugene	.603	1995—	Salt Lake	.549
	Los Angeles▼	.689	1970—	Spokane•	.644		Colorado Springs*	.538
1935—	Los Angeles	.648		Hawaii	.671	1996—	Edmonton*	.592
	San Francisco*	.608	1971—	Salt Lake City	.534		Phoenix	.479
1936—	Portland‡	.549		Tacoma	.545	1997—	Phoenix	.615
1937—	Sacramento	.573	1972—	Albuquerque	.622		Edmonton*	.556
	San Diego (3rd)†	.545		Eugene	.534	1998—	Iowa	.590
1938—	Los Angeles	.590	1973—	Tucson	.583		New Orleans†	.535
	Sacramento (3rd)†	.537		Spokane•	.563			
1939—	Seattle	.589	1974—	Spokane•	.549			
	Sacramento (4th)†	.500		Albuquerque	.535			

*Won split-season playoff. †Won four-team playoff. ‡Won pennant and four-team playoff. §Tied for second-half title with Tacoma winning playoff. ∞Tied for second-half title, with Sacramento winning playoff. ▲Ended regular season in tie with San Francisco and won one-game playoff for pennant, then won four-club playoff. ◆Won playoff from first-place Vernon and awarded championship. ■Defeated Hollywood in one-game playoff for pennant. ▼Won both halves, no playoff. •League was divided into Northern, Southern divisions in 1963, 1969-70-71, and Eastern, Western divisions in 1964 through 1968 and 1972 through 1977, won two-team playoff. ††League divided into Eastern and Western divisions, Tacoma and Albuquerque declared co-champions following cancellation of four-team playoff due to continuing rain and wet grounds. ‡‡Won second-half title and defeated Hawaii in four-team playoff.

CLASS AAA Pacific Coast League

EASTERN LEAGUE

LEAGUE OFFICE

President
Bill Troubh

Address
P.O. Box 9711
Portland, ME 04104

Phone
207-761-2700

TEAMS

AKRON AEROS
General manager/vice president
Jeff Auman
Manager
Joel Skinner
Ballpark (capacity, surface)
Canal Park (8,900, grass)
Affiliation
Indians
Address
300 S. Main St.
Akron, OH 44308
Phone
330-253-5151

ALTOONA CURVE
General manager
Sal Baglieri
Manager
Marty Brown
Ballpark (capacity, surface)
To be announced (6,122, grass)
Affiliation
Pirates
Address
P.O. Box 1029
Altoona, PA 16603
Phone
814-943-5400

BINGHAMTON METS
General manager
R.C. Reuteman
Manager
Doug Davis
Ballpark (capacity, surface)
Binghamton Municipal Stadium (6,064, grass)
Affiliation
Mets
Address
P.O. Box 598
Binghamton, NY 13902
Phone
607-723-6387

BOWIE BAYSOX
General manager
Jon Danos
Manager
Joe Ferguson
Ballpark (capacity, surface)
Prince George's Stadium (10,000, grass)
Affiliation
Orioles
Address
4101 NE Crain Highway
Bowie, MD 20716
Phone
301-805-6000

ERIE SEAWOLVES
General manager
Keith Hallal
Manager
Garry Templeton
Ballpark (capacity, surface)
Jerry Uht Park (6,000, grass)
Affiliation
Angels
Address
110 E. 10th Street
Erie, PA 16501
Phone
814-456-1300

HARRISBURG SENATORS
General manager
Todd Vander Woude
Manager
Doug Sisson
Ballpark (capacity, surface)
RiverSide Stadium (6,300, grass)
Affiliation
Expos
Address
P.O. Box 15757
Harrisburg, PA 17105
Phone
717-231-4444

NEW BRITAIN ROCK CATS
General manager
Gerry Berthiaume
Manager
John Russell
Ballpark (capacity, surface)
New Britain Stadium (6,146, grass)
Affiliation
Twins
Address
P.O. Box 1718
New Britain, CT 06050
Phone
860-224-8383

NEW HAVEN RAVENS
General manager
Chris Canetti
Manager
Dan Rowan
Ballpark (capacity, surface)
Yale Field (6,200, grass)
Affiliation
Mariners
Address
252 Derby Ave.
West Haven, CT 06516
Phone
1-800-728-3671

NORWICH NAVIGATORS
General manager
Brian Mahoney
Manager
Lee Mazzilli
Ballpark (capacity, surface)
Dodd Stadium (6,000, grass)
Affiliation
Yankees
Address
14 Stott Ave.
Norwich, CT 06360
Phone
860-887-7962

PORTLAND SEA DOGS
General manager
Charles Eshbach
Manager
Frank Cacciatore
Ballpark (capacity, surface)
Hadlock Field (6,000, grass)
Affiliation
Marlins
Address
P.O. Box 636
Portland, ME 04104
Phone
207-874-9300

READING PHILLIES
General manager
Chuck Domino
Manager
Gary Varsho
Ballpark (capacity, surface)
Municipal Memorial Stadium (8,500, grass)
Affiliation
Phillies
Address
P.O. Box 15050
Reading, PA 19612
Phone
610-375-8469

TRENTON THUNDER
General manager
Wayne Hodes
Manager
DeMarlo Hale
Ballpark (capacity, surface)
Mercer County Waterfront Park (6,300, grass)
Affiliation
Red Sox
Address
One Thunder Road
Trenton, NJ 08611
Phone
609-394-8326

CLASS AA *Eastern League*

1998 FINAL STANDINGS

NORTHERN DIVISION

Team	W	L	T	Pct.	GB
New Britain (Twins)	83	59	0	.585	....
Binghamton (Mets)	82	60	0	.577	1.0
Portland (Marlins)	66	75	0	.468	16.5
Norwich (Yankees)	66	76	0	.475	17.0
New Haven (Rockies)	59	83	0	.415	24.0

SOUTHERN DIVISION

Team	W	L	T	Pct.	GB
Akron (Indians)	81	60	0	.574	....
Harrisburg (Expos)	73	69	0	.514	8.5
Trenton (Red Sox)	71	70	0	.504	10.0
Bowie (Orioles)	71	71	0	.500	10.5
Reading (Phillies)	56	85	0	.397	25.0

COMPOSITE

Team	N.B.	Bing.	Akr.	Har.	Tren.	Bow.	Por.	Nor.	N.H.	Read.	W	L	T	Pct.	GB
New Britain (Twins)	....	8	9	6	10	9	9	11	12	9	83	59	0	.585	...
Binghamton (Mets)	10	....	3	8	10	10	11	11	9	10	82	60	0	.577	1.0
Akron (Indians)	5	11	....	10	8	11	6	11	7	12	81	60	0	.574	1.5
Harrisburg (Expos)	8	6	8	....	8	8	6	9	7	13	73	69	0	.514	10.0
Trenton (Red Sox)	4	4	9	10	....	10	7	7	10	10	71	70	0	.504	11.5
Bowie (Orioles)	5	4	7	10	8	....	9	5	11	12	71	71	0	.500	12.0
Portland (Marlins)	9	7	8	8	7	5	....	9	8	5	66	75	0	.468	16.5
Norwich (Yankees)	7	7	3	5	7	9	9	....	12	7	66	76	0	.465	17.0
New Haven (Rockies)	6	9	7	7	4	3	10	6	....	7	59	83	0	.415	24.0
Reading (Phillies)	5	4	6	5	8	6	8	7	7	....	56	85	0	.397	26.5

Major league affiliations in parentheses.

PLAYOFFS: Harrisburg defeated Akron three games to one; New Britain defeated Binghamton three games to one; Harrisburg defeated New Britain three games to one to win league championship.

REGULAR-SEASON ATTENDANCE: Akron, 521,122; Binghamton, 216,191; Bowie, 400,058; Harrisburg, 259,381; New Britain, 181,643; New Haven, 197,342; Norwich, 243,817; Portland, 398,800; Reading, 414,658; Trenton, 457,344. Total—3,290,356. Playoffs (12 games)—36,656. Class AA All-Star Game at New Haven, Conn.—6,248.

MANAGERS: Akron, Joel Skinner; Binghamton, John Gibbons; Bowie, Joe Ferguson; Harrisburg, Rick Sweet; New Britain, John Russell; New Haven, Tim Blackwell; Norwich, Trey Hillman; Portland, Lynn Jones; Reading, Al LeBoeuf; Trenton, Demarlo Hale.

ALL-STAR TEAM: 1B—Calvin Pickering, Bowie; 2B—Marcos Scutaro, Akron; 3B—Jose Fernandez, Harrisburg; SS—Cristian Guzman, New Britain; C—Michael Barrett, Harrisburg; OF—Jacque Jones, New Britain; Scott Hunter, Binghamton; Dernell Stenson, Trenton; DH—Doug Mientkiewicz, New Britain; RHP—Mike Lincoln, New Britain; LHP—Mike Kusiewicz, New Haven; RP—Brent Stentz, New Britain; Player of the Year—Calvin Pickering, Bowie; Pitcher of the Year—Brent Stentz, New Britain; Rookie of the Year—Calvin Pickering, Bowie; Manager of the Year—John Gibbons, Binghamton.

1998 BATTING

TEAM

Team	Avg.	G	TPA	AB	R	H	TB	2B	3B	HR	RBI	SH	SF	HP	BB	IBB	SO	SB	CS	GDP	LOB	ShO	Slg.	OBP
New Britain	.273	142	5366	4803	670	1310	1948	297	25	97	594	48	33	48	434	23	882	123	71	97	1010	10	.406	.337
Akron	.271	141	5552	4865	758	1317	2103	258	42	148	682	35	42	48	562	24	1075	123	56	94	1075	5	.432	.349
Bowie	.269	142	5318	4642	686	1248	1883	201	28	126	628	48	24	74	530	30	951	88	56	118	1030	4	.406	.351
Harrisburg	.266	142	5229	4631	667	1233	1980	251	35	142	610	62	31	73	432	29	920	157	61	97	925	1	.428	.336
Binghamton	.264	142	5338	4691	660	1239	1820	221	36	96	598	53	50	59	485	24	980	148	75	94	979	7	.388	.337
Portland	.260	141	5299	4684	634	1219	1861	217	34	119	589	43	37	43	492	16	1101	78	43	103	995	7	.397	.334
Norwich	.259	142	5312	4659	621	1206	1784	224	27	100	557	32	43	55	523	18	1007	146	74	114	1027	9	.383	.338
Trenton	.257	141	5361	4725	647	1214	1945	247	20	148	595	51	40	74	471	18	1042	72	63	91	980	12	.412	.331
New Haven	.253	142	5203	4630	578	1171	1732	227	17	100	530	54	34	25	460	34	898	121	77	117	910	12	.374	.322
Reading	.251	141	5305	4720	582	1184	1807	227	36	108	548	50	29	36	470	21	1036	66	40	117	963	14	.383	.322

INDIVIDUAL

TOP QUALIFIERS FOR BATTING CHAMPIONSHIP

Minimum 383 plate appearances. *Lefthanded batter. †Switch-hitter.

Player, Team	Avg.	G	TPA	AB	R	H	TB	2B	3B	HR	RBI	SH	SF	HP	BB	IBB	SO	SB	CS	GDP	Slg.	OBP
Mientkiewicz, Doug, N.B.*	.323	139	611	502	96	162	255	45	0	16	88	0	7	6	96	7	58	11	4	6	.508	.432
Barrett, Michael, Har.	.320	120	488	453	78	145	238	32	2	19	87	2	4	2	27	5	43	7	6	16	.525	.358
Scutaro, Marcos, Akr.	.316	124	529	462	68	146	218	27	6	11	62	4	6	10	47	0	71	33	16	8	.472	.387
Hunter, Scott, Bing.	.314	130	550	487	80	153	226	25	3	14	65	1	8	7	47	2	75	39	15	6	.464	.377
Pickering, Calvin, Bow.*	.309	139	599	488	93	151	276	28	2	31	114	0	2	11	98	16	119	4	6	20	.566	.434
Stumberger, Darren, Akr.	.301	139	616	545	83	164	237	39	2	10	76	1	8	5	56	0	79	1	2	15	.435	.366
Jones, Jacque, N.B.*	.299	134	566	518	78	155	263	39	3	21	85	4	3	4	37	8	134	18	11	4	.508	.349
Brown, Vick, Nor.	.298	102	399	352	62	105	143	14	3	6	34	1	0	6	40	0	75	35	10	7	.406	.379
Long, Terrence, Bing.*	.297	130	523	455	69	135	223	20	10	16	58	0	4	2	62	6	105	23	11	8	.490	.380
Fernandez, Jose, Har.	.295	104	420	369	59	109	189	27	1	17	58	1	5	9	36	3	73	16	6	3	.512	.368
Morgan, Scott, Akr.	.294	119	524	456	95	134	248	31	4	25	89	0	4	8	56	1	124	4	5	9	.544	.378
Perry, Mike, Nor.	.293	107	460	399	52	117	198	35	2	14	63	0	5	3	53	1	58	8	2	8	.496	.376
Raynor, Mark, Read.	.293	100	424	379	43	111	128	9	4	0	31	4	3	0	38	0	33	7	2	7	.338	.355
Veras, Wilton, Tren.	.291	126	502	470	70	137	220	27	4	16	67	6	5	6	15	1	66	5	4	14	.468	.319
Ashby, Chris, Nor.	.285	126	514	448	65	125	182	24	0	11	53	0	4	7	65	3	99	17	3	12	.416	.383

DEPARTMENTAL LEADERS: G—Bates, Guzman, 140 each; AB—Cey, 569; R—Mientkiewicz, 96; H—Stumberger, 164; TB—Pickering, 276; 2B—Mientkiewicz, 45; 3B—Long, 10; HR—Pickering, 31; RBI—Pickering, 114; SH—Guzman, 17; SF—S. Hunter, Stumberger, 8 each; HP—Chamblee, 16; BB—Pickering, 98; IBB—Pickering, 16; SO—Minor, 152; SB—Monds, 41; CS—McDonald, 22; GIDP—Pickering, 20; Slg.—Pickering, .566; OBP—Pickering, .434.

ALL PLAYERS

*Lefthanded batter. †Switch-hitter.

Player, Team	Avg.	G	TPA	AB	R	H	TB	2B	3B	HR	RBI	SH	SF	HP	BB	IBB	SO	SB	CS	GDP	Slg.	OBP
Adolfo, Carlos, Har.	.192	40	144	130	10	25	36	5	0	2	16	1	3	1	9	1	33	3	0	4	.277	.245
Alcantara, Israel, Read.	.310	53	223	203	36	63	124	12	2	15	44	0	1	2	17	2	37	0	1	9	.611	.368
Allen, Chad, N.B.	.262	137	568	504	70	132	201	31	7	8	82	1	5	6	51	0	78	21	9	19	.399	.334
Almonte, Wady, Bow.	.048	7	26	21	2	1	4	0	0	1	2	0	0	1	4	0	9	0	0	2	.190	.231
Amador, Manny, Read.†	.252	35	114	103	12	26	41	10	1	1	11	1	1	0	9	1	20	0	0	5	.398	.310
Angeli, Doug, Read.	.232	65	254	233	27	54	79	14	1	3	18	3	0	1	17	0	46	3	1	1	.339	.287
Arroyo, Luis, Bing.*	.000	57	2	1	0	0	0	0	0	0	0	0	0	0	1	0	1	0	0	0	.000	.500
Arteaga, Ivan, Bing.*	.000	23	5	4	0	0	0	0	0	0	0	1	0	0	0	0	2	0	0	0	.000	.000
Arteaga, J.D., Bing.*	.111	21	20	18	2	2	2	0	0	0	0	2	0	0	0	0	5	0	0	0	.111	.111
Ashby, Chris, Nor.	.285	126	514	438	65	125	182	24	0	11	53	0	4	7	65	3	99	17	3	12	.416	.383
Azuaje, Jesus, Bing.	.276	110	455	384	66	106	151	22	1	7	52	7	5	4	52	0	48	15	1	8	.393	.364
Bady, Ed, Har.†	.252	58	141	123	19	31	37	4	1	0	2	3	0	0	15	0	30	10	2	1	.301	.333
Baker, Jason, Har.	.300	25	13	10	1	3	6	0	0	1	1	2	0	0	1	0	1	0	0	0	.600	.364
Barnes, John, Tren.-N.B.	.273	120	511	451	62	123	189	22	1	14	44	2	5	4	49	3	56	4	9	13	.419	.346
Barnett, Marty, Read.	.000	5	2	1	0	0	0	0	0	0	0	1	0	0	0	0	0	0	0	0	.000	.000
Barrett, Michael, Har.	.320	120	488	453	78	145	238	32	2	19	87	2	4	2	27	5	43	7	6	16	.525	.358
Bates, Fletcher, Port.†	.274	140	587	537	67	147	213	23	5	11	60	1	1	2	46	2	118	19	6	4	.397	.333
Bell, Mike, Bing.	.265	78	320	275	47	73	131	14	1	14	56	0	6	2	35	1	50	3	5	5	.476	.346
Benz, Jake, Har.*	.000	17	4	4	0	0	0	0	0	0	1	0	0	0	0	0	1	0	0	0	.000	.000
Bergeron, Peter, Har.*	.246	34	153	134	22	33	49	8	4	0	9	2	0	0	17	0	26	8	3	0	.366	.331
Berry, Mike, Nor.	.293	107	460	399	50	117	198	35	2	14	63	0	5	3	53	1	58	8	2	8	.496	.376
Betances, Junior, Akr.	.283	76	298	269	41	76	114	10	5	6	31	2	0	2	25	1	54	11	2	4	.424	.348
Betts, Todd, Akr.*	.270	91	388	318	55	86	161	18	3	17	46	0	2	4	64	5	71	1	0	7	.506	.397
Bierek, Kurt, Nor.*	.235	95	401	344	44	81	137	13	2	13	61	0	2	3	50	1	61	0	1	8	.398	.336
Billingsley, Brent, Port.*	.158	28	24	19	2	3	3	0	0	0	0	3	0	0	2	0	8	0	0	0	.158	.238
Blum, Geoffrey, Har.†	.309	39	162	139	25	43	79	12	3	6	21	2	0	4	17	0	24	2	1	3	.568	.400
Bocachica, Hiram, Har.	.264	80	331	296	39	78	116	18	4	4	27	2	1	11	21	2	61	20	8	1	.392	.334
Bogle, Bryan, Bow.	.254	21	72	67	12	17	32	3	0	4	16	0	1	1	3	0	19	0	0	1	.478	.292
Booty, Josh, Port.	.202	71	273	247	28	50	94	8	3	10	39	1	4	1	20	0	74	1	1	10	.381	.261
Borland, Toby, Read.	.000	8	1	1	0	0	0	0	0	0	0	0	0	0	0	0	1	0	0	0	.000	.000
Borrero, Richie, Tren.	.247	51	179	162	21	40	64	6	0	6	24	7	0	4	6	0	32	3	3	2	.395	.291
Bost, Heath, N.H.	.000	41	2	0	0	0	0	0	0	0	0	1	0	0	1	0	0	0	0	0	.000	1.000
Brannan, Ryan, Read.	.500	41	4	2	0	1	1	0	0	0	0	1	0	0	1	0	1	0	0	0	.500	.667
Branyan, Russell, Akr.*	.294	43	199	163	35	48	113	11	3	16	46	0	1	0	35	4	58	1	1	2	.693	.417
Brester, Jason, N.H.*	.500	5	3	2	0	1	2	1	0	0	0	0	0	0	1	0	0	0	0	0	1.000	.667
Brown, Vick, Nor.	.298	102	399	352	62	105	143	14	3	6	34	1	0	6	40	0	75	35	10	7	.406	.379
Bryant, Pat, Tren.	.295	26	103	88	17	26	40	5	0	3	14	1	2	0	12	0	20	3	3	4	.455	.373
Budzinski, Mark, Akr.*	.262	127	535	478	68	125	186	21	5	10	62	4	2	1	50	2	125	12	8	9	.389	.331
Burger, Rob, Read.	.417	33	14	12	1	5	9	1	0	1	3	1	0	0	1	0	2	0	0	0	.750	.462
Burgus, Travis, Port.*	.000	38	1	1	0	0	0	0	0	0	0	0	0	0	0	0	1	0	0	0	.000	.000
Camilli, Jason, Har.	.111	6	21	18	1	2	2	0	0	0	1	0	0	0	3	0	5	0	0	0	.111	.238
Campos, Jesus, Har.	.259	83	285	263	23	68	91	11	0	4	30	9	5	1	7	0	18	13	3	9	.346	.275
Carroll, Jamey, Har.	.253	75	312	261	43	66	83	11	3	0	20	5	0	5	41	0	29	11	5	4	.318	.365
Carvajal, Jhonny, Har.	.260	112	387	338	37	88	108	12	4	0	21	8	1	6	34	5	69	4	6	12	.320	.333
Carver, Steve, Read.*	.260	127	528	458	63	119	199	17	0	21	88	0	4	2	64	8	108	0	3	12	.434	.350
Castro, Ramon, Port.	.250	31	98	88	9	22	34	3	0	3	11	0	2	0	8	0	21	0	0	3	.386	.306
Cey, Dan, N.B.	.251	136	616	569	82	143	199	28	2	8	50	3	1	3	40	0	95	23	7	13	.350	.303
Chambless, James, Tren.	.241	136	577	489	71	118	208	33	3	17	65	6	4	16	62	1	144	9	5	2	.425	.343
Chancey, Bailey, Bing.†	.146	25	55	48	1	7	9	2	0	0	2	0	1	6	0	18	0	0	6	.188	.255
Chevalier, Virgil, Tren.	.274	32	125	117	19	32	49	7	2	2	16	3	1	0	4	0	17	2	2	2	.419	.295
Clark, Howie, Bow.*	.286	88	309	276	37	79	122	16	0	9	45	0	1	3	29	2	42	1	1	7	.442	.359
Clark, Tim, Bow.*	.316	52	199	174	28	55	95	10	0	10	39	0	1	1	23	1	40	1	1	2	.546	.397
Coggin, David, Read.	.125	20	18	16	0	2	2	0	0	0	1	2	0	0	0	0	4	0	0	1	.125	.125
Cole, Jason, Har.	.000	22	2	1	0	0	0	0	0	0	0	0	1	0	0	0	1	0	0	0	.000	.000
Colon, Dennis, Bing.*	.285	69	284	256	40	73	108	14	3	5	37	0	2	1	25	3	16	5	1	7	.422	.349
Conner, Decomba, Bow.	.250	65	232	208	31	52	76	5	2	5	27	7	1	0	16	0	42	10	3	1	.365	.302
Cook, Hayward, Port.	.178	30	78	73	13	13	26	5	1	2	5	0	0	1	4	0	30	0	0	1	.356	.231
Coquillette, Trace, Har.	.332	49	209	187	40	62	99	10	0	9	23	0	1	6	15	0	41	10	3	2	.529	.397
Costello, Brian, Read.	.150	45	127	120	7	18	29	6	1	1	7	0	0	0	7	0	44	2	0	1	.242	.197
Crane, Todd, Read.	.074	9	32	27	2	2	5	0	0	1	2	0	0	3	2	0	7	1	1	1	.185	.219
Cromer, Brandon, Port.*	.223	122	439	391	51	87	155	13	5	15	47	1	4	0	43	0	89	3	2	12	.396	.297
Darden, Tony, Bing.	.288	107	361	320	38	92	128	19	4	3	36	0	6	10	25	2	57	5	6	7	.400	.352
Davis, Chili, Nor.†	.243	11	47	37	2	9	15	3	0	1	5	0	0	1	9	3	7	0	0	4	.405	.404
Davis, Jason, Read.*	.000	45	12	10	1	0	0	0	0	0	0	0	0	0	2	0	2	0	0	0	.000	.167
Davis, Tommy, Bow.	.280	37	149	132	12	37	51	11	0	1	15	0	1	3	13	2	27	0	0	1	.386	.356
Dawkins, Walt, Read.	.255	49	186	161	24	41	65	16	1	2	19	1	3	4	17	0	29	1	4	12	.404	.335
DeCinces, Tim, Bow.*	.333	5	19	18	5	6	10	1	0	1	4	0	0	0	1	0	5	0	0	0	.556	.368
Delahoya, Javier, Bow.	.000	7	1	1	0	0	0	0	0	0	0	0	0	0	0	0	0	0	0	0	.000	.000
De Leon, Jorge, Tren.	.291	29	96	86	11	25	32	7	0	0	10	5	0	0	5	0	3	2	1	5	.372	.330
Dempster, Ryan, Port.	.000	7	8	6	0	0	0	0	0	0	0	0	0	2	0	0	4	0	0	0	.000	.250
Dennis, Les, Nor.	.247	32	119	93	12	23	30	5	1	0	13	2	0	0	24	0	20	2	2	5	.323	.402
Depastino, Joe, Tren.	.295	73	306	275	34	81	127	16	0	10	43	0	2	1	28	5	51	3	0	4	.462	.359
Derosso, Tony, Tren.	.107	9	31	28	3	3	6	0	0	1	3	0	1	0	2	0	12	0	0	1	.214	.161
DeWitt, Scott, Port.	.000	50	3	2	0	0	0	0	0	0	0	0	0	0	1	0	0	0	0	0	.000	.000
Dixon, Tim, Har.*	.000	37	2	2	0	0	0	0	0	0	0	0	0	0	0	0	1	0	0	0	.000	.000
Dotel, Octavio, Bing.	.000	10	5	5	0	0	0	0	0	0	0	0	0	0	0	0	1	0	0	0	.000	.000
Duncan, Geoff, Port.	.500	42	2	2	0	1	1	0	0	0	0	0	0	0	0	0	0	0	0	0	.500	.500
Durocher, Jayson, Har.	.000	10	1	0	0	0	0	0	0	0	0	0	0	0	1	0	0	0	0	0	.000	.000
Emmons, Scott, Nor.	.172	48	165	145	12	25	34	6	0	1	5	0	2	4	14	0	43	2	1	4	.234	.261

Player, Team	Avg.	G	TPA	AB	R	H	TB	2B	3B	HR	RBI	SH	SF	HP	BB	IBB	SO	SB	CS	GDP	Slg.	OBP
Epperson, Chad, Tren.†	.253	109	434	383	53	97	173	27	2	15	57	3	4	6	38	2	129	2	8	6	.452	.327
Evans, Keith, Har.	.100	20	11	10	0	1	1	0	0	0	0	1	0	0	0	0	3	0	0	0	.100	.100
Everson, Darin, Tren.*	.273	9	39	33	4	9	12	3	0	0	2	0	0	1	5	0	5	0	0	0	.364	.385
Felston, Anthony, N.B.*	.222	12	56	45	5	10	12	2	0	0	5	1	1	3	6	0	10	2	1	0	.267	.345
Fernandez, Jared, Tren.	.000	36	1	1	0	0	0	0	0	0	0	0	0	0	0	0	0	0	0	0	.000	.000
Fernandez, Jose, Har.	.295	104	420	369	59	109	189	27	1	17	58	1	5	9	36	3	73	16	6	3	.512	.368
Fernandez, Osvaldo, Bing.*	.000	7	1	1	0	0	0	0	0	0	0	0	0	0	0	0	0	0	0	0	.000	.000
Feuerstein, Dave, N.H.	.275	133	540	505	61	139	180	13	5	6	51	7	2	2	23	0	56	18	11	15	.356	.308
Figueroa, Nelson, Bing.†	.176	21	22	17	4	3	3	0	0	0	3	4	0	0	1	0	3	0	0	0	.176	.222
Fithian, Grant, Nor.	.230	39	141	126	13	29	47	6	0	4	14	0	1	0	14	0	39	0	0	1	.373	.312
Fontenot, Joe, Port.	.455	7	13	11	3	5	5	0	0	0	2	0	0	1	1	0	2	0	0	0	.455	.538
Fonville, Chad, N.H.†	.249	54	217	189	26	47	49	2	0	0	9	2	2	1	23	0	24	16	5	7	.259	.330
Forster, Scott, Har.	.000	25	10	7	0	0	0	0	0	0	1	2	0	0	1	0	4	0	0	0	.000	.125
Fortin, Troy, N.B.	.183	23	67	60	3	11	15	4	0	0	6	0	0	2	5	0	13	0	0	2	.250	.269
Foster, Jim, Bow.	.240	66	257	221	24	53	85	17	0	5	33	0	0	5	31	1	38	1	1	6	.385	.346
Francia, David, Read.*	.238	68	289	269	29	64	93	12	4	3	20	3	2	2	13	0	41	6	7	3	.346	.276
Fraser, Joe, N.B.	.204	16	55	49	6	10	15	5	0	0	4	2	0	1	3	0	8	0	0	0	.306	.264
Funaro, Joe, Port.	.285	95	379	340	54	97	130	10	4	5	28	2	2	3	32	1	44	9	6	8	.382	.350
Gambill, Chad, N.H.	.191	50	176	152	16	29	41	3	0	3	9	1	1	1	21	0	53	3	2	4	.270	.291
Garcia, Amaury, Port.	.270	137	606	544	79	147	217	19	6	13	62	14	1	2	45	0	126	23	15	7	.399	.328
Garcia, Jesse, Bow.	.283	86	299	258	46	73	94	13	1	2	20	6	0	1	34	1	37	12	3	3	.364	.369
Garcia, Vicente, N.H.	.217	128	504	424	59	92	149	24	0	11	29	6	1	6	67	6	68	7	6	10	.351	.331
Garland, Tim, Bow.	.262	59	200	164	18	43	59	4	3	2	8	7	0	4	25	2	24	8	7	8	.360	.373
Gibralter, David, Tren.	.260	100	424	385	48	100	161	16	0	15	61	1	6	7	25	2	91	2	3	5	.418	.312
Giudice, John, N.H.	.250	61	229	212	26	53	81	11	1	5	31	2	2	2	11	0	55	2	3	4	.382	.291
Glass, Chip, Nor.*	.283	120	481	424	61	120	146	8	3	4	56	8	7	2	40	2	78	15	6	5	.344	.342
Glinatsis, George, N.H.	.000	12	3	2	0	0	0	0	0	0	0	0	0	0	1	0	2	0	0	0	.000	.333
Gomez, Rudy, Nor.	.312	46	208	189	31	59	82	10	2	3	20	0	0	2	17	0	28	8	6	9	.434	.375
Gonzales, Jose, N.H.	.000	2	2	2	0	0	0	0	0	0	0	0	0	0	0	0	2	0	0	0	.000	.000
Gooch, Arnold, Bing.	.138	27	32	29	1	4	4	0	0	0	0	1	0	2	0	0	16	0	0	1	.138	.194
Goodell, Steve, Port.	.186	48	150	118	13	22	31	6	0	1	11	2	0	4	26	1	35	0	1	3	.263	.351
Grifol, Pedro, Bing.	.223	116	430	394	34	88	115	18	0	3	57	2	5	1	28	4	72	2	2	12	.292	.273
Gross, Rafael, Akr.	.069	25	68	58	6	4	4	0	0	0	3	1	1	2	6	0	21	4	3	0	.069	.179
Guerra, Mark, Bing.	.000	30	3	3	0	0	0	0	0	0	0	0	0	0	0	0	3	0	0	0	.000	.000
Guiliano, Matt, Read.	.226	126	495	439	47	99	154	15	2	12	44	6	1	4	45	4	102	2	4	16	.351	.303
Gulan, Mike, Port.	.306	46	172	160	24	49	84	16	2	5	23	0	1	1	10	0	40	3	2	6	.525	.349
Gunderson, Shane, N.B.	.161	23	78	62	8	10	19	0	0	3	14	1	1	2	12	0	11	0	0	2	.306	.312
Gutierrez, Rick, Akr.	.194	12	36	31	6	6	7	1	0	0	2	0	0	0	5	0	4	0	0	1	.226	.306
Guzman, Cristian, N.B.†	.277	140	606	566	68	157	199	29	5	1	40	17	1	1	21	1	111	23	14	13	.352	.304
Hackman, Luther, N.H.	.133	28	16	15	2	2	3	1	0	0	1	1	0	0	0	0	8	0	0	0	.200	.133
Hairston, Jerry, Bow.	.326	55	249	221	42	72	105	12	3	5	37	2	1	5	20	0	25	6	4	5	.475	.393
Hamilton, Joe, Tren.*	.174	30	104	92	10	16	28	3	0	3	10	1	0	0	11	1	33	1	3	2	.304	.262
Hammonds, Jeffrey, Bow.	.333	3	9	6	4	2	2	0	0	0	0	0	0	1	2	0	2	3	1	0	.333	.556
Harris, Brian, Read.†	.250	11	46	40	5	10	12	0	1	0	4	0	1	0	5	0	7	0	1	0	.300	.326
Harriss, Robin, Akr.	.111	15	56	45	3	5	7	2	0	0	2	2	0	0	9	1	21	1	0	2	.156	.259
Hayes, Heath, Akr.	.207	91	360	329	36	68	117	14	1	11	46	2	3	2	24	1	95	2	3	7	.356	.263
Henderson, Ryan, Bing.	.000	29	2	2	0	0	0	0	0	0	0	0	0	0	0	0	1	0	0	0	.000	.000
Hinds, Rob, Nor.	.226	38	120	106	17	24	34	4	0	2	8	3	2	1	8	0	27	4	1	4	.321	.282
Houser, Kyle, N.H.	.234	101	343	312	29	73	78	5	0	0	32	6	4	1	20	1	38	5	3	14	.250	.279
Huelsmann, Mike, Akr.†	.100	9	26	20	4	2	5	0	0	1	1	1	0	1	4	0	9	1	0	0	.250	.280
Huff, Larry, Read.	.338	40	162	136	26	46	78	7	2	7	25	1	1	5	19	0	15	10	2	4	.574	.435
Hunter, Scott, Bing.	.314	130	550	487	80	153	226	25	3	14	65	1	8	7	47	2	75	39	15	6	.464	.377
Hunter, Torii, N.B.	.282	82	338	308	42	87	135	24	3	6	32	4	3	4	19	1	64	11	9	2	.438	.329
Isom, Johnny, Bow.	.240	93	362	325	47	78	131	12	1	13	39	2	2	4	29	0	72	1	3	18	.403	.308
Jackson, Gavin, Tren.	.244	50	189	168	12	41	50	7	1	0	17	1	2	0	18	0	21	3	1	5	.298	.314
Jacobsen, Joe, Port.	1.000	3	1	1	0	1	1	0	0	0	0	0	0	0	0	0	0	0	0	0	1.000	1.000
Jarrett, Link, N.H.†	.238	107	352	324	18	77	89	8	2	0	26	3	1	1	23	5	31	4	10	10	.275	.289
Jean, Domingo, N.H.	.000	12	3	1	0	0	0	0	0	0	0	2	0	0	0	0	1	0	0	0	.000	.000
Jimenez, D'Angelo, Nor.†	.270	40	182	152	21	41	57	6	2	2	21	2	1	2	25	1	26	5	5	3	.375	.378
Johnson, J.J., N.B.	.256	101	400	371	54	95	159	19	3	13	48	1	1	2	25	0	103	5	5	7	.429	.306
Johnson, Mark, Port.	.059	26	18	17	1	1	1	0	0	0	0	0	0	0	1	0	5	0	0	0	.059	.111
Johnson, Mike, Har.*	.000	7	6	5	1	0	0	0	0	0	0	0	0	1	0	0	1	0	0	0	.000	.167
Jones, Jacque, N.B.*	.299	134	566	518	78	155	263	39	5	21	85	4	3	4	37	4	134	18	11	4	.508	.349
Jones, Jaime, Port.*	.281	123	499	438	58	123	180	27	0	10	63	0	3	3	55	3	118	4	1	11	.411	.363
Keel, David, Nor.*	.178	36	145	118	12	21	36	6	0	3	19	0	2	1	24	0	31	0	3	5	.305	.317
Key, Jeff, Read.*	.196	63	243	224	24	44	73	8	0	7	24	3	1	1	14	2	69	6	0	4	.326	.246
Kingsale, Eugene, Bow.†	.262	111	501	427	69	112	136	11	5	1	34	10	4	12	48	1	79	29	12	6	.319	.350
Kirgan, Chris, N.H.	.272	114	479	427	63	116	214	32	0	22	79	0	5	3	44	8	105	2	1	9	.501	.340
Knupfer, Jason, Read.	.218	63	231	193	27	42	53	7	2	0	15	4	4	3	27	1	46	2	1	7	.275	.317
Kofler, Eric, Nor.*	.240	7	29	25	3	6	7	1	0	0	4	0	0	0	4	0	3	0	0	1	.280	.345
Kuilan, Hector, Port.	.252	31	114	107	8	27	37	4	0	2	14	3	2	0	2	0	9	3	0	1	.346	.261
Kusiewicz, Mike, N.H.	.184	27	43	38	2	7	9	2	0	0	2	3	0	0	2	0	10	0	0	1	.237	.225
Lamb, David, Bow.†	.303	66	274	241	29	73	91	10	1	2	25	4	1	1	27	1	33	1	3	6	.378	.374
Landry, Todd, Bing.	.274	118	474	430	54	118	173	22	3	9	62	1	2	4	37	1	77	3	1	11	.402	.336
Lawrence, Chip, Bow.	.250	6	12	12	0	3	4	1	0	0	1	0	0	0	0	0	4	0	0	0	.333	.250
Leese, Brandon, Port.	.176	20	20	17	2	3	6	0	0	1	1	0	0	0	3	0	4	0	0	0	.353	.176
Lidle, Kevin, N.H.	.143	11	39	35	5	5	13	2	0	2	5	1	0	0	3	0	13	0	0	0	.371	.211
Light, Tal, N.H.	.166	57	199	181	15	30	53	9	1	4	24	3	2	0	13	1	62	1	4	5	.293	.219
Lobaton, Jose, Nor.	.254	52	196	177	16	45	64	14	1	1	21	3	4	2	10	0	36	2	2	1	.362	.295
Long, Terrence, Bing.*	.297	130	523	455	69	135	223	20	10	16	58	0	4	2	62	6	105	23	11	8	.490	.380
Lopez, Jose, Bing.	.275	92	356	327	47	90	145	23	1	10	51	0	3	8	18	2	91	7	3	8	.443	.326
Luzinski, Ryan, Bow.	.240	72	266	233	25	56	80	3	0	7	23	1	0	2	20	0	72	3	3	5	.343	.306

Player, Team	Avg.	G	TPA	AB	R	H	TB	2B	3B	HR	RBI	SH	SF	HP	BB	IBB	SO	SB	CS	GDP	Slg.	OBP
Lyons, Mike, Bing.	.000	29	1	1	0	0	0	0	0	0	0	0	0	0	0	0	1	0	0	0	.000	.000
Maness, Dwight, Bing.-Tren. .	.244	112	479	406	63	99	166	15	5	14	42	9	3	10	51	0	108	18	11	8	.409	.340
Marsters, Brandon, Read.	.231	38	156	143	9	33	44	4	2	1	7	0	1	1	11	0	34	0	1	5	.308	.288
Martinez, Eddy, Bow.	.286	5	16	14	1	4	4	0	0	0	1	1	0	0	1	0	3	0	0	0	.286	.333
Martinez, Rafael, Tren.*	.204	15	56	49	5	10	13	3	0	0	3	0	0	1	6	0	13	0	0	1	.265	.304
Martinez, Ramiro, Har.*	.250	10	4	4	1	1	1	0	0	0	0	0	0	0	0	0	3	0	0	0	.250	.250
Matos, Luis, Bow.	.263	5	20	19	2	5	8	0	0	1	3	0	0	0	1	0	1	1	1	1	.421	.300
McCommon, Jason, Har.-Bow. .	.200	30	6	5	2	1	4	0	0	1	1	0	0	0	1	0	0	0	0	0	.800	.200
McDonald, Donzell, Nor.†	.253	134	565	495	80	125	177	20	7	6	36	7	4	4	55	1	127	35	22	7	.358	.330
McDonald, John, Akr.	.230	132	580	514	68	118	146	18	2	2	43	11	6	6	43	0	61	17	6	7	.284	.293
McLamb, Brian, Nor.†	.179	62	210	196	18	35	48	10	0	1	11	1	0	2	10	0	67	2	3	2	.245	.226
Mientkiewicz, Doug, N.B.*	.323	139	611	502	96	162	255	45	0	16	88	0	7	6	96	1	58	11	4	6	.508	.432
Millan, Adan, Read.	.297	61	226	195	18	58	105	18	1	9	42	0	3	0	28	0	36	1	1	6	.538	.381
Minor, Ryan, Bow.	.250	138	569	521	73	130	207	20	3	17	71	0	1	13	34	2	152	2	3	13	.397	.311
Mitchell, Keith, Tren.	.195	12	50	41	4	8	16	2	0	2	7	0	1	0	8	0	5	0	0	1	.390	.320
Mitchell, Scott, Har.	.158	32	21	19	1	3	3	0	0	0	1	1	0	0	1	0	5	0	0	0	.158	.200
Moeller, Chad, N.B.	.235	58	215	187	21	44	72	10	0	6	23	1	0	3	24	0	41	2	1	4	.385	.332
Molina, Gabe, Bow.	.000	47	1	1	0	0	0	0	0	0	0	0	0	0	0	0	0	0	0	0	.000	.000
Monds, Wonderful, N.H.	.280	122	498	453	76	127	192	32	3	9	58	5	3	4	33	1	105	41	12	5	.424	.333
Moore, Joel, N.H.*	.111	13	9	9	0	1	1	0	0	0	0	0	0	0	0	0	5	0	0	0	.111	.111
Moraga, David, Har.*	.000	19	2	2	0	0	0	0	0	0	0	0	0	0	0	0	1	0	0	0	.000	.000
Morales, Eric, Bing.	.138	39	122	109	9	15	18	3	0	0	4	3	1	0	9	0	29	0	1	3	.165	.202
Morales, Francisco, Har.	.215	96	348	311	25	67	107	11	1	9	45	0	2	5	30	4	86	1	1	12	.344	.293
Morales, Stephen, Port.†	.300	3	10	10	0	3	3	0	0	0	3	0	0	0	0	0	2	0	0	1	.300	.300
Morenz, Shea, Nor.*	.252	116	458	409	51	103	172	18	3	15	52	2	6	10	31	4	109	7	5	7	.421	.316
Morgan, Scott, Akr.	.294	119	524	456	95	134	248	31	4	25	89	0	4	8	56	1	124	4	5	9	.544	.378
Moriarty, Mike, N.B.	.286	38	136	112	22	32	52	8	0	4	15	3	1	3	17	0	16	0	4	1	.464	.391
Moss, Rick, N.B.*	.280	65	217	193	17	54	69	9	0	2	25	4	0	0	20	0	20	0	0	4	.358	.347
Moyle, Mike, Akr.	.301	39	153	133	19	40	57	5	0	4	23	0	1	2	17	0	27	1	0	9	.429	.386
Mucker, Kelcey, N.B.*	.296	71	259	226	22	67	96	14	0	5	27	2	5	3	23	0	31	1	0	10	.425	.362
Mull, Blaine, Port.	.111	9	10	9	1	1	1	0	0	0	1	1	0	0	0	0	3	0	0	0	.111	.111
Murray, Dan, Bing.	.077	28	40	26	2	2	2	0	0	0	2	7	0	0	7	0	11	0	0	0	.077	.273
Neubart, Garrett, Bing.	.275	109	421	363	58	100	125	10	3	3	37	7	5	12	34	0	65	29	8	4	.344	.353
Newstrom, Doug, N.H.*	.284	102	377	331	38	94	132	21	1	5	24	3	2	0	41	4	53	7	5	7	.399	.361
Niebla, Ruben, Har.*	.000	24	5	3	0	0	0	0	0	0	0	1	0	1	0	0	1	0	0	0	.000	.250
Norton, Chris, Port.	.353	22	80	68	12	24	48	4	1	6	19	0	0	0	12	0	17	0	0	1	.706	.450
Nyari, Pete, Read.	.000	53	2	2	0	0	0	0	0	0	0	0	0	0	0	0	2	0	0	0	.000	.000
Ojeda, Augie, Bow.†	.256	73	299	254	36	65	82	10	2	1	19	5	1	3	36	0	30	0	3	5	.323	.354
Ortiz, Nick, Har.-Tren.	.252	95	341	294	35	74	116	17	2	7	33	10	2	3	32	0	64	2	3	10	.395	.329
Paez, Israel, N.B.†	.220	62	177	164	26	36	42	4	1	0	13	1	0	1	11	0	34	5	3	1	.256	.273
Pageler, Mick, Port.	.000	60	3	2	0	0	0	0	0	0	0	0	0	0	1	0	2	0	0	0	.000	.333
Parker, Christian, Har.	.250	38	14	12	1	3	7	1	0	1	3	1	0	0	1	0	3	0	0	0	.583	.308
Paronto, Chad, Bow.	.000	8	1	1	0	0	0	0	0	0	0	0	0	0	0	0	1	0	0	0	.000	.000
Pegues, Steve, N.H.	.286	17	53	49	6	14	19	2	0	1	2	0	0	0	4	1	11	2	1	0	.388	.340
Peoples, Daniel, Akr.	.279	60	254	222	30	62	105	19	0	8	32	0	2	1	29	1	61	1	1	7	.473	.362
Perez, Danny, Bow.	.216	22	83	74	8	16	21	3	1	0	6	0	1	0	8	0	12	1	0	3	.284	.289
Perry, Chan, Akr.	.281	54	227	203	36	57	93	17	2	5	27	0	1	0	23	1	43	3	2	2	.458	.352
Petrick, Ben, N.H.	.238	106	411	349	52	83	164	21	3	18	50	0	3	3	56	1	89	7	7	5	.470	.345
Phelps, Tommy, Har.*	.200	12	10	10	0	2	2	0	0	0	2	0	0	0	0	0	4	0	0	0	.200	.200
Pickering, Calvin, Bow.*	.309	139	599	488	93	151	276	28	2	31	114	0	2	11	98	16	119	4	6	20	.566	.434
Pierce, Kirk, Read.	.253	80	313	265	31	67	97	12	0	6	29	2	1	4	41	2	63	0	0	6	.366	.360
Pierzynski, A.J., N.B.*	.297	59	227	212	30	63	83	11	0	3	17	2	1	2	10	4	25	0	2	4	.392	.333
Polanco, Enohel, Bing.	.241	26	87	79	10	19	23	4	0	0	5	1	0	0	7	2	27	1	1	1	.291	.302
Pond, Simon, Har.*	.000	2	4	3	0	0	0	0	0	0	0	0	0	0	1	0	1	0	0	0	.000	.250
Post, Dave, Har.	.345	19	66	58	9	20	28	3	1	1	9	0	0	1	7	0	3	1	1	0	.483	.424
Powell, Jeremy, Har.	.111	22	21	18	1	2	6	1	0	1	1	2	0	0	1	0	9	0	0	1	.333	.158
Price, Tom, N.H.*	.167	38	6	6	0	1	1	0	0	0	0	0	0	0	0	0	1	0	0	1	.167	.167
Pumphrey, Ken, Bing.	.333	3	3	3	1	1	1	0	0	0	0	0	0	0	0	0	2	0	0	0	.333	.333
Raifstanger, John, Tren.	.159	20	50	44	4	7	12	2	0	1	7	0	0	0	6	0	13	0	0	2	.273	.260
Raleigh, Matt, Bing.	.200	47	172	140	22	28	52	6	0	6	28	0	2	1	29	0	60	1	4	1	.371	.337
Ramirez, Angel, Nor.	.261	24	94	92	7	24	35	5	0	2	14	0	1	1	0	0	19	0	0	6	.380	.266
Ramirez, Peto, Akr.	.184	15	62	49	4	9	16	1	0	2	8	2	1	0	10	0	17	0	0	0	.327	.317
Ramirez, Roberto, Bow.	.286	6	23	21	4	6	9	0	0	1	1	0	0	0	2	0	5	0	0	1	.429	.348
Randall, Scott, N.H.	.133	29	35	30	2	4	4	0	0	0	2	4	0	0	1	0	6	0	0	2	.133	.161
Raynor, Mark, Read.	.293	100	424	379	43	111	128	9	4	0	31	4	3	0	38	0	33	7	2	7	.338	.355
Rector, Bobby, Port.	.000	14	1	1	0	0	0	0	0	0	0	0	0	0	0	0	1	0	0	0	.000	.000
Redmond, Mike, Port.	.321	8	33	28	7	9	16	4	0	1	7	1	0	2	2	0	2	0	0	2	.571	.406
Reeves, Glenn, Port.	.253	53	238	190	40	48	62	7	2	1	18	1	5	5	37	1	42	5	3	3	.326	.380
Rennhack, Mike, N.H.†	.308	52	208	182	27	56	82	15	1	3	32	0	3	0	23	0	31	4	3	8	.451	.380
Richards, Mark, Port.	.000	40	6	5	0	0	0	0	0	0	0	0	0	0	1	0	2	0	0	0	.000	.167
Richardson, Brian, N.H.	.100	6	21	20	1	2	2	0	0	0	2	0	0	0	1	0	4	1	0	2	.100	.143
Ritz, Kevin, N.H.	.500	3	2	2	0	1	1	0	0	0	0	0	0	0	0	0	0	0	0	0	.500	.500
Rivero, Eddie, Read.*	.273	69	221	205	23	56	90	15	2	5	31	0	0	0	16	0	57	0	0	2	.439	.326
Roberts, David, Akr.*	.361	56	269	227	49	82	123	10	5	7	33	5	1	1	35	5	30	28	6	3	.542	.447
Robertson, Ryan, Port.*	.260	98	358	308	31	80	115	14	0	7	47	0	4	2	44	2	62	0	1	8	.373	.352
Rodgers, Bobby, Port.	.200	14	10	10	0	2	3	1	0	0	0	0	0	0	0	0	3	0	0	0	.300	.200
Rodriguez, Sammy, Bing.	.125	3	9	8	2	1	1	0	0	0	1	0	0	0	1	0	0	0	0	0	.125	.222
Rodriguez, Victor, Port.	.284	66	249	222	28	63	86	9	1	4	19	4	0	5	18	0	26	5	4	7	.387	.331
Rolison, Nate, Port.*	.277	131	561	484	80	134	221	35	2	16	83	0	6	7	64	6	150	5	0	9	.457	.365
Rosario, Mel, Bow.†	.269	39	145	130	22	35	63	5	4	5	25	1	2	3	9	0	31	2	1	3	.485	.326
Royster, Aaron, Read.	.256	112	489	430	67	110	166	27	4	7	55	0	0	2	57	1	117	3	1	13	.386	.346
Salamon, John, N.H.	.000	53	3	3	0	0	0	0	0	0	0	0	0	0	0	0	1	0	0	0	.000	.000

Player, Team	Avg.	G	TPA	AB	R	H	TB	2B	3B	HR	RBI	SH	SF	HP	BB	IBB	SO	SB	CS	GDP	Slg.	OBP
Samuels, Scott, Har.*	.276	20	66	58	9	16	31	3	0	4	11	0	0	1	7	0	13	4	1	1	.534	.364
Sanchez, Yuri, Bing.*	.259	93	366	316	47	82	119	14	7	3	26	11	0	4	35	1	95	11	7	4	.377	.341
Sapp, Damian, Tren.	.242	28	103	91	9	22	42	5	0	5	10	0	0	3	9	0	35	0	0	2	.462	.330
Schwab, Chris, Har.	.000	3	5	4	0	0	0	0	0	0	0	0	0	0	1	0	3	0	0	0	.000	.200
Scutaro, Marcos, Akr.	.316	124	529	462	68	146	218	27	6	11	62	4	6	10	47	0	71	33	16	8	.472	.387
Seguignol, Fernando, Har.†	.288	80	317	281	54	81	169	13	0	25	69	0	1	6	29	4	77	6	1	6	.601	.366
Selby, William, Akr.*	.390	20	82	77	15	30	48	7	1	3	10	0	1	3	1	0	11	0	0	0	.623	.415
Shoemaker, Stephen, N.H.* ...	.308	15	15	13	2	4	5	1	0	0	1	1	0	0	1	0	2	0	1	0	.385	.357
Short, Rick, Bow.	.230	34	105	87	12	20	30	4	0	2	18	1	4	0	13	0	18	0	0	2	.345	.317
Shumaker, Anthony, Read.* ...	.080	30	30	25	1	2	3	1	0	0	1	3	0	0	2	0	9	0	0	0	.120	.148
Smart, J.D., Har.	.091	14	12	11	0	1	1	0	0	0	1	0	0	0	1	0	0	0	0	0	.091	.167
Smith, Hut, Read.	.000	22	4	2	0	0	0	0	0	0	0	1	0	0	1	0	2	0	0	0	.000	.333
Smith, Jeff, N.B.*	.274	27	93	84	11	23	37	11	0	1	12	1	2	1	5	2	21	0	0	3	.440	.315
Snusz, Chris, Read.	.321	12	31	28	6	9	11	2	0	0	1	0	0	3	0	0	6	0	0	0	.393	.387
Steed, Rick, Bing.	.500	9	6	6	0	3	3	0	0	0	1	0	0	0	0	0	2	0	0	0	.500	.500
Stenson, Dernell, Tren.*	.257	138	608	505	90	130	225	21	1	24	71	1	4	14	84	3	135	5	3	6	.446	.376
Stevens, Kris, Read.	.143	25	25	21	0	3	3	0	0	0	1	3	0	0	1	0	8	0	0	1	.143	.182
Stevenson, Rodney, Har.	.000	37	2	1	0	0	0	0	0	0	0	1	0	0	0	0	0	0	0	0	.000	.000
Stewart, Scott, Bing.	.176	24	18	17	1	3	3	0	0	0	1	1	0	0	0	0	2	0	0	2	.176	.176
Stowers, Chris, Har.*	.269	134	566	510	86	137	229	31	5	17	66	3	3	8	42	2	109	24	7	7	.449	.332
Stumberger, Darren, Akr.	.301	139	616	545	83	164	237	39	2	10	76	1	8	5	56	0	79	1	2	15	.435	.366
Taveras, Frank, Akr.*	.500	2	5	4	2	2	2	0	0	0	0	0	0	0	1	0	1	0	0	0	.500	.600
Taylor, Adam, Akr.	.200	3	12	10	0	2	2	0	0	0	1	0	1	0	1	0	6	0	0	0	.200	.250
Taylor, Jamie, N.H.*	.336	86	349	304	48	102	157	22	0	11	53	1	3	0	41	6	43	1	2	7	.516	.411
Taylor, Reggie, Read.*	.273	79	353	337	49	92	133	14	6	5	22	0	2	2	12	0	73	22	10	2	.395	.300
Tebbs, Nate, Tren.†	.256	104	437	394	44	101	132	21	2	2	31	3	1	3	36	0	63	14	13	10	.335	.323
Tejera, Michael, Port.*	.059	20	19	17	0	1	1	0	0	0	0	2	0	0	0	0	2	0	0	0	.059	.059
Thomas, Evan, Read.	.269	25	31	26	2	7	10	0	0	1	3	5	0	0	0	0	6	0	0	0	.385	.269
Thomas, Greg, Akr.*	.217	64	247	226	34	49	91	6	3	10	37	0	0	2	18	1	75	2	1	2	.403	.280
Torres, Jaime, Nor.	.275	81	290	262	30	72	107	9	1	8	35	0	2	2	24	2	31	4	2	12	.408	.338
Townsend, Dave, Port.	.000	11	2	1	0	0	0	0	0	0	0	1	0	0	0	0	1	0	0	0	.000	.000
Tracy, Andrew, Har.*	.227	62	242	211	33	48	96	12	3	10	33	0	3	4	24	3	62	1	2	5	.455	.314
Troilo, Jason, Nor.	.159	23	77	69	8	11	19	5	0	1	7	3	0	1	4	0	22	0	0	1	.275	.216
Tucker, Jon, Har.*	.278	25	98	79	13	22	38	7	0	3	16	1	0	0	18	0	18	0	0	1	.481	.412
Twiggs, Greg, Bow.	.000	31	1	1	0	0	0	0	0	0	0	0	0	0	0	0	0	0	0	0	.000	.000
Uchiyama, Tomoyuki, Read.*.	.000	43	14	9	1	0	0	0	0	0	0	5	0	0	0	0	6	0	0	0	.000	.000
Utting, Andy, Bow.†	.250	5	2	4	1	1	1	0	0	0	0	0	0	0	1	0	1	1	0	0	.250	.400
Valdez, Trovin, Har.	.256	54	130	121	16	31	47	8	1	2	10	3	0	0	6	0	21	14	2	3	.388	.291
Vardijan, Dan, Port.	1.000	19	1	1	0	1	1	0	0	0	0	0	0	0	0	0	0	0	0	0	1.000	1.000
Vasquez, Leo, Bing.*	.000	14	2	1	1	0	0	0	0	0	0	0	0	0	1	0	1	0	0	0	.000	.500
Vavrek, Mike, N.H.*	.158	19	22	19	2	3	3	0	0	0	1	1	0	0	2	0	9	0	0	0	.158	.238
Veniard, Jay, Bing.*	.500	11	2	2	1	1	2	1	0	0	0	0	0	0	0	0	1	0	0	0	1.000	.500
Veras, Wilton, Tren.	.291	126	502	470	70	137	220	27	4	16	67	6	5	6	15	1	66	5	4	14	.468	.319
Villafuerte, Brandon, Port.	.000	30	6	6	0	0	0	0	0	0	0	0	0	0	0	0	3	0	0	0	.000	.000
Werth, Jayson, Bow.	.158	5	21	19	2	3	5	2	0	0	1	0	0	0	2	0	6	1	0	0	.263	.238
White, Walt, Bow.	.271	70	227	203	23	55	86	9	2	6	25	2	2	4	16	0	53	1	1	5	.424	.333
Whitley, Matt, N.H.	.211	14	44	38	2	8	8	0	0	0	7	1	0	1	4	0	9	0	1	1	.211	.302
Whitlock, Brian, Akr.	.077	9	28	26	1	2	3	1	0	0	2	0	1	0	1	0	11	0	0	0	.115	.107
Williams, Bernie, Nor.†	.545	3	14	11	6	6	14	2	0	2	5	0	1	0	2	0	1	0	0	1	1.273	.571
Wolf, Randy, Read.*	.000	4	5	5	1	0	0	0	0	0	0	0	0	0	0	0	3	0	0	0	.000	.000
Woods, Brian, N.H.*	.000	31	1	1	0	0	0	0	0	0	0	0	0	0	0	0	0	0	0	0	.000	.000
Yarnall, Ed, Bing.*	.333	7	5	3	1	1	1	0	0	0	0	0	0	0	2	0	2	0	0	0	.333	.600
Zorrilla, Julio, Bing.†	.250	27	79	68	7	17	18	1	0	0	4	3	1	0	7	0	13	1	4	2	.265	.316

GRAND SLAMS: Bierek, Branyan, Budzinski, Gibralter, 2 each; Alcantara, Allen, Barrett, Bates, Booty, T. Clark, Coquillette, A. Garcia, Gunderson, Hamilton, Hayes, Jamie Jones, Long, J. McDonald, Morgan, Peoples, Raleigh, Short, Stumberger, Tracy, White, 1 each.

AWARDED FIRST BASE ON CATCHER'S INTERFERENCE: Azuaje 3 (Newstrom, Torres, Robertson); M. Bell 2 (Snusz, Depastino); Bierek 2 (Grifol 2); Allen (Depastino); Feuerstein (F. Morales); McLamb (E. Morales); Stumberger (Depastino); G. Thomas (T. Davis).

PLAYERS WITH TWO OR MORE TEAMS

Player, Team	Avg.	G	TPA	AB	R	H	TB	2B	3B	HR	RBI	SH	SF	HP	BB	IBB	SO	SB	CS	GDP	Slg.	OBP
Barnes, John, Tren.	.274	100	429	380	53	104	164	18	0	14	36	2	4	3	40	3	47	3	8	11	.432	.344
Barnes, John, N.B.	.268	20	82	71	9	19	25	4	1	0	8	0	1	1	9	0	9	1	1	2	.352	.354
Maness, Dwight, Bing.	.237	27	110	93	15	22	34	3	0	3	10	1	0	2	14	0	28	3	5	4	.366	.349
Maness, Dwight, Tren.	.246	85	369	313	48	77	132	12	5	11	32	8	3	8	37	0	80	15	6	4	.422	.338
McCommon, Jason, Har.	.500	6	2	2	2	1	4	0	0	1	1	0	0	0	0	0	0	0	0	0	2.000	.500
McCommon, Jason, Bow.	.000	24	4	3	0	0	0	0	0	0	0	1	0	0	0	0	2	0	0	0	.000	.000
Ortiz, Nick, Har.	.270	56	192	163	18	44	77	11	2	6	24	7	2	2	18	0	37	2	3	7	.472	.346
Ortiz, Nick, Tren.	.229	39	149	131	17	30	39	6	0	1	9	3	0	1	14	0	27	0	0	3	.298	.308

1998 PITCHING
TEAM

Team	W	L	Pct.	ERA	G	CG	ShO	Sv.	IP	H	TBF	R	ER	HR	SH	SF	HB	BB	IBB	SO	WP	Bk.
Binghamton.......	82	60	.577	3.34	142	8	13	43	1248.0	1151	5264	553	463	106	38	40	31	468	28	1142	54	11
Akron..............	81	60	.574	3.72	141	10	8	45	1251.0	1206	5349	601	517	105	47	37	60	492	20	872	68	13
New Britain	83	59	.585	3.87	142	5	12	51	1240.1	1227	5263	611	534	120	42	26	41	425	12	1056	71	6
Harrisburg........	73	69	.514	3.89	142	6	8	39	1215.2	1180	5195	603	526	117	50	37	64	455	24	865	66	5
New Haven	59	83	.415	4.23	142	11	7	31	1226.0	1234	5410	677	576	113	66	46	74	510	9	979	108	8
Trenton..........	71	70	.504	4.23	141	5	10	41	1244.1	1255	5334	670	585	114	50	34	43	470	40	971	79	4
Portland	66	75	.468	4.29	141	6	6	36	1220.1	1245	5387	691	582	135	68	23	61	530	35	1082	79	5

Team	W	L	Pct.	ERA	G	CG	ShO	Sv.	IP	H	TBF	R	ER	HR	SH	SF	HB	BB	IBB	SO	WP	Bk.
Norwich	66	76	.465	4.35	142	11	4	41	1216.0	1327	5393	702	588	108	35	40	48	470	30	969	74	8
Bowie	71	71	.500	4.50	142	8	7	36	1196.2	1176	5156	678	598	136	23	43	53	481	13	970	69	14
Reading	56	85	.397	4.55	141	6	6	30	1241.0	1340	5544	717	628	130	57	37	60	558	26	986	76	12

INDIVIDUAL

TOP QUALIFIERS FOR EARNED-RUN AVERAGE TITLE

Minimum 114 innings. *Lefthanded pitcher.

Pitcher, Team	W	L	Pct.	ERA	G	GS	CG	ShO	GF	Sv.	IP	H	TBF	R	ER	HR	SH	SF	HB	BB	IBB	SO	WP	Bk.
Kusiewicz, Mike, N.H.*	14	7	.667	2.32	27	26	2	0	0	0	178.2	161	740	59	46	4	12	6	16	35	0	151	9	1
Arteaga, J.D., Bing.*	8	7	.533	2.80	21	18	0	0	0	0	119.0	122	495	48	37	8	6	5	5	25	1	97	2	0
Brower, Jim, Akr.	13	5	.722	3.01	23	23	2	2	0	0	155.2	142	630	60	52	9	4	3	7	38	0	91	5	0
Powell, Jeremy, Har.	9	7	.563	3.01	22	22	1	0	0	0	131.2	115	546	54	44	13	7	2	9	37	0	77	6	1
Murray, Dan, Bing.	11	6	.647	3.18	27	27	1	1	0	0	164.1	153	681	64	58	13	3	2	8	54	2	159	5	0
Lincoln, Mike, N.B.	15	7	.682	3.22	26	26	1	0	0	0	173.1	180	720	80	62	13	8	5	5	35	0	109	5	0
Shumaker, Anthony, Read.*	7	10	.412	3.35	38	21	1	1	9	2	166.2	152	689	75	62	20	9	7	4	44	2	129	3	0
Thomas, Evan, Read.	8	5	.615	3.35	24	24	3	3	0	0	158.1	180	676	66	59	12	3	5	4	44	2	134	3	1
Sanders, Frankie, Akr.	11	8	.579	3.48	29	29	2	1	0	0	186.1	175	781	82	72	15	8	6	11	71	0	108	6	0
Parker, Christian, Har.	6	6	.500	3.48	36	16	0	0	8	5	126.2	124	550	66	49	9	6	2	10	47	3	73	8	0
Ramsay, Robert, Tren.*	12	6	.667	3.49	27	27	1	1	0	0	162.2	137	659	67	63	10	5	5	3	50	1	166	8	3
Evans, Keith, Har.	8	9	.471	3.56	20	20	1	0	0	0	124.0	133	520	59	49	13	6	2	8	30	2	76	2	0
Billingsley, Brent, Port.*	6	13	.316	3.74	28	28	0	0	0	0	171.0	172	741	90	71	24	5	2	6	70	2	183	17	1
Mitchell, Scott, Har.	9	3	.750	3.80	32	17	2	1	5	2	135.0	136	558	58	57	13	3	6	6	37	1	81	0	0
Randall, Scott, N.H.	10	14	.417	3.83	29	29	7	2	0	0	202.0	210	863	102	86	14	9	10	9	62	1	135	10	1

DEPARTMENTAL LEADERS: W—Lincoln, 15; L—Gooch, Mark Johnson, Randall, 14 each; Pct.—Duncan, .818; G—Urso, 69; GS—Bell, Cressend, Randall, Sanders, 29 each; CG—Randall, 7; ShO—Thomas, 3; GF—Stentz, 53; Sv.—Stentz, 43; IP—Randall, 202.0; H—Randall, 210; TBF—Randall, 863; R—Jackman, Randall, 102 each; ER—Stevens, 94; HR—Billingsley, Vavrek, 24 each; SH—Kusiewicz, 12; SF—Randall, 10; HB—Kusiewicz, 16; BB—Baker, Sanders, 71 each; IBB—Urso, 8; SO—Billingsley, 183; WP—Salamon, 22; BK—S. Stewart, 4.

ALL PITCHERS

*Lefthanded pitcher.

Pitcher, Team	W	L	Pct.	ERA	G	GS	CG	ShO	GF	Sv.	IP	H	TBF	R	ER	HR	SH	SF	HB	BB	IBB	SO	WP	Bk.
Arroyo, Luis, Bing.*	1	5	.167	2.58	57	0	0	0	16	3	66.1	59	280	30	19	1	5	2	1	26	3	78	4	1
Arteaga, Ivan, Bing.	2	1	.667	4.74	23	4	0	0	6	1	49.1	57	219	28	26	6	1	3	1	20	2	40	0	1
Arteaga, J.D., Bing.*	8	7	.533	2.80	21	18	0	0	0	0	119.0	122	495	48	37	8	6	5	5	25	1	97	2	0
Atkins, Ross, Akr.	7	8	.467	4.19	40	5	0	0	23	10	77.1	73	332	39	36	9	2	3	5	31	1	38	4	2
Aucoin, Derek, Bing.	0	0	.000	6.75	12	0	0	0	5	0	16.0	16	75	12	12	3	0	0	1	15	1	18	0	0
Azuaje, Jesus, Bing.	0	0	.000	0.00	2	0	0	0	0	0	2.0	1	7	0	0	0	0	0	0	0	0	2	0	0
Bady, Ed, Har.	0	0	.000	2.08	4	0	0	0	4	0	4.1	3	17	1	1	1	0	0	0	2	0	2	0	0
Baker, Jason, Har.	4	10	.286	5.64	25	20	0	0	2	0	103.0	95	476	69	65	18	1	3	8	71	1	88	11	1
Barbao, Joe, Read.	0	1	.000	11.85	10	0	0	0	2	0	13.2	20	71	18	18	3	2	1	1	13	2	8	3	0
Barnett, Marty, Read.	0	3	.000	6.20	5	5	0	0	0	0	24.2	31	116	17	17	5	0	1	2	13	0	21	0	1
Baron, Jim, Nor.*	6	4	.600	2.33	23	12	4	1	6	0	96.2	99	403	35	25	2	2	2	0	20	0	69	4	0
Bautista, Jose, Nor.	0	2	.000	15.12	3	3	0	0	0	0	8.1	17	49	16	14	5	0	1		4	0	4	0	0
Beale, Chuck, Tren.	5	3	.625	3.26	43	0	0	0	14	1	69.0	54	284	31	25	9	3	3	3	31	7	39	4	0
Beckett, Robbie, N.H.*	2	1	.667	5.11	22	0	0	0	8	0	24.2	20	121	14	14	3	1	0	3	23	0	36	5	0
Bell, Jason, N.B.	8	11	.421	4.67	29	29	2	0	0	0	169.2	148	694	90	88	21	3	2	5	61	1	166	4	2
Benz, Jake, Har.*	3	1	.750	1.08	16	0	0	0	7	4	33.1	19	133	5	4	2	1	1	1	11	3	31	0	0
Betances, Junior, Akr.	0	0	.000	0.00	1	0	0	0	1	0	1.0	1	5	0	0	0	0	0	1	0	0	0	0	0
Betancourt, Rafael, Tren.	0	0	.000	6.75	7	0	0	0	3	0	9.1	9	42	7	7	0	1	0	0	3	0	9	0	0
Beverlin, Jason, Nor.	3	5	.375	3.67	25	9	0	0	8	1	81.0	68	343	34	33	5	2	4	3	38	0	86	6	1
Billingsley, Brent, Port.*	6	13	.316	3.74	28	28	0	0	0	0	171.0	172	741	90	71	24	5	2	6	70	2	183	17	1
Blais, Mike, Tren.	2	1	.667	3.95	22	0	0	0	11	2	27.1	36	125	14	12	2	1	0	1	10	4	14	3	0
Borland, Toby, Read.	1	3	.250	9.64	8	0	0	0	8	3	9.1	18	51	12	10	4	1	0	5	10	5	13	1	0
Bost, Heath, N.H.	4	2	.667	3.30	41	0	0	0	14	2	46.1	43	193	20	17	2	5	0	4	11	0	48	3	1
Bradley, Ryan, Nor.	2	0	1.000	1.44	3	3	1	1	0	0	25.0	8	89	6	4	1	0	0	0	8	0	25	0	0
Brammer, J.D., Akr.	1	0	1.000	5.23	11	0	0	0	4	3	20.2	21	95	12	12	3	0	1	1	10	1	23	4	2
Brannan, Ryan, Read.	5	4	.556	3.56	41	0	0	0	26	6	55.2	55	254	31	22	5	5	2	4	29	3	42	4	1
Brester, Jason, N.H.*	2	0	1.000	1.59	5	4	0	0	0	0	22.2	22	97	7	4	0	1	0	1	7	0	15	3	1
Brittan, Corey, Bing.	1	1	.500	3.86	9	0	0	0	0	0	9.1	9	40	4	4	0	1	0	4	0		5	3	0
Brower, Jim, Akr.	13	5	.722	3.01	23	23	2	2	0	0	155.2	142	630	60	52	9	4	3	7	38	0	91	5	0
Brown, Jamie, Akr.	1	0	1.000	2.57	1	1	0	0	0	0	7.0	5	28	2	2	1	0	0	1	1	0	5	0	0
Burger, Rob, Read.	3	11	.214	6.03	33	19	1	0	10	0	115.0	119	529	88	77	21	3	8	9	69	1	102	10	1
Burgus, Travis, Port.*	2	1	.667	1.89	38	0	0	0	14	1	57.0	45	242	16	12	4	4	0	1	29	3	56	6	0
Calmus, Lance, Akr.	2	5	.286	5.50	23	2	0	0	6	0	52.1	55	238	34	32	7	1	4	7	28	0	23	4	1
Camp, Jared, Akr.	6	2	.750	3.78	18	16	0	0	2	0	85.2	84	364	37	36	8	3	5	5	31	0	42	2	1
Censale, Silvio, Read.*	0	0	.000	1.93	4	0	0	0	2	0	4.2	4	22	2	1	0	0	0	3	0		2	3	0
Chapman, Walker, N.B.	1	3	.250	3.86	23	2	0	0	4	0	49.0	47	204	22	21	5	3	1	1	18	1	38	4	0
Cho, Jin Ho, Tren.	5	2	.714	2.19	13	13	1	1	0	0	74.0	59	299	21	18	4	3	4	3	19	2	62	0	0
Clark, Howie, Bow.	0	0	.000	4.50	1	0	0	0	0	0	2.0	2	10	1	1	0	0	0	1	1	0	1	0	0
Clark, Tim, Bow.*	0	0	.000	0.00	1	0	0	0	1	0	1.0	1	4	0	0	0	0	0	0	1	0	1	0	0
Cobb, Trevor, N.B.*	6	9	.400	5.06	27	23	1	0	2	0	133.1	160	596	81	75	17	1	2	10	49	0	87	10	1
Coggin, David, Read.	4	8	.333	4.14	20	20	0	0	0	0	108.2	106	477	58	50	8	2	2	8	62	1	65	14	0
Cole, Jason, Har.	2	2	.500	3.42	22	0	0	0	17	0	23.2	28	107	9	9	2	1	3	1	14	3	15	4	1
Converse, Jim, Bow.	0	0	.000	7.20	1	1	0	0	0	0	5.0	9	23	4	4	1	0	0	3	0		6	1	0
Coppinger, Rocky, Bow.	2	2	.500	4.35	7	6	0	0	0	0	31.0	26	128	18	15	4	2	1	1	11	0	30	0	1
Cormier, Rheal, Akr.*	0	0	.000	6.52	3	3	0	0	0	0	9.2	15	45	7	7	3	0	1	2	0		6	1	0
Costa, Tony, Read.	0	0	.000	47.25	3	0	0	0	2	0	1.1	6	15	8	7	0	0	0	0	5	0	1	0	0
Crawford, Paxton, Tren.	6	5	.545	4.17	22	20	1	0	0	0	108.0	104	457	53	50	8	3	1	6	39	1	82	7	0
Cressend, Jack, Tren.	10	11	.476	4.34	29	29	1	1	0	0	149.1	168	646	86	72	13	10	2	5	55	0	130	6	0

Pitcher, Team	W	L	Pct.	ERA	G	GS	CG	ShO	GF	Sv.	IP	H	TBF	R	ER	HR	SH	SF	HB	BB	IBB	SO	WP	Bk.
Cumberland, Chris, N.B. *	3	4	.429	2.63	37	2	0	0	10	1	54.2	44	220	24	16	1	1	2	0	17	2	48	6	0
Curtis, Chris, Bow.	0	2	.000	6.95	12	1	0	0	3	0	22.0	27	97	18	17	3	0	0	0	11	0	11	2	0
Davis, Jason, Read. *	6	8	.429	4.82	45	10	0	0	11	1	104.2	116	488	68	56	8	5	1	8	55	3	81	6	2
De La Cruz, Fernando, Tren. ...	0	0	.000	0.00	3	0	0	0	2	1	3.2	3	15	0	0	0	0	0	0	1	0	3	1	0
De La Cruz, Francisco, Nor. ...	0	2	.000	7.71	2	2	0	0	0	0	4.2	8	31	13	4	2	0	1	1	4	0	5	0	0
Delahoya, Javier, Bow.	4	1	.800	3.82	6	4	1	0	1	0	30.2	32	126	13	13	4	0	0	2	7	1	33	0	0
De Los Santos, Luis, Nor.	2	6	.250	4.90	13	13	2	0	0	0	79.0	97	360	49	43	4	1	3	7	23	2	51	4	0
Dempster, Ryan, Port.	4	3	.571	3.22	7	7	0	0	0	0	44.2	34	180	20	16	8	3	0	3	15	0	33	1	0
De Paula, Sean, Akr.	1	1	.500	4.76	8	1	0	0	1	0	17.0	16	81	10	9	0	1	1	0	15	0	17	3	0
Deschenes, Marc, Akr.	4	6	.400	3.88	47	0	0	0	26	5	58.1	52	259	36	25	4	2	4	0	34	6	52	5	0
DeWitt, Scott, Port. *	4	4	.500	4.53	50	3	0	0	13	1	59.2	61	278	35	30	7	2	3	4	36	0	64	4	1
Dixon, Tim, Har. *	2	5	.286	3.88	37	0	0	0	15	2	58.0	58	249	29	25	5	3	2	1	16	2	52	4	0
Dotel, Octavio, Bing.	4	2	.667	1.97	10	10	2	1	0	0	68.2	41	261	19	15	4	1	1	0	24	1	82	0	1
Dougherty, Tony, Akr.	6	5	.545	3.07	43	0	0	0	25	5	76.1	68	328	29	26	5	7	1	2	36	3	60	4	0
Doyle, Tom, N.H. *	0	0	.000	0.00	6	0	0	0	4	0	5.1	2	20	0	0	0	0	1	0	2	0	0	0	0
Drabek, Doug, Bow.	0	0	.000	0.00	1	1	0	0	0	0	5.0	0	16	0	0	0	0	0	0	1	0	3	0	0
Driskill, Travis, Akr.	3	0	1.000	3.42	5	4	0	0	1	0	26.1	27	109	12	10	4	0	1	1	7	0	16	0	0
Duncan, Geoff, Port.	9	2	.818	2.83	42	0	0	0	29	11	57.1	39	242	21	18	2	1	6	31	5	74	5	1	
Durocher, Jayson, Har.	0	1	.000	3.97	10	0	0	0	4	1	11.1	10	48	8	5	0	1	1	0	6	0	12	1	0
Dykhoff, Radhames, Bow. * ...	3	7	.300	4.71	38	8	0	0	9	1	93.2	83	411	51	49	10	2	3	4	52	1	98	3	0
Eibey, Scott, Bow. *	1	1	.500	4.21	24	0	0	0	8	0	36.1	40	159	20	17	5	0	1	0	14	0	29	1	1
Einertson, Darrell, Nor.	3	1	.750	1.02	17	0	0	0	5	0	35.1	23	142	7	4	1	3	0	1	10	3	33	2	0
Estes, Eric, Bow.	5	2	.714	4.38	9	9	1	0	0	0	49.1	53	208	28	24	6	0	0	1	8	0	29	6	0
Evans, Dave, Bow.	1	1	.500	1.96	14	0	0	0	6	0	18.1	17	84	9	4	1	1	1	5	6	0	26	2	0
Evans, Keith, Har.	8	9	.471	3.56	20	20	1	0	0	0	124.0	133	520	59	49	13	6	2	8	30	2	76	2	0
Fernandez, Jared, Tren.	3	7	.300	5.25	36	7	0	0	10	1	118.1	132	527	80	69	8	8	3	3	51	3	70	15	1
Fernandez, Osvaldo, Bing. *	0	1	.000	4.05	7	1	0	0	1	0	13.1	10	56	7	6	1	1	2	2	6	0	16	2	0
Fesh, Sean, Read. *	3	1	.750	1.36	31	0	0	0	23	9	33.0	19	140	8	5	1	1	5	19	1	41	1	2	
Figueroa, Nelson, Bing.	12	3	.800	4.66	21	21	3	2	0	0	123.2	133	531	73	64	19	2	1	0	44	2	116	1	1
Flener, Huck, Akr. *	3	3	.500	1.85	12	10	3	2	1	0	73.0	57	289	18	15	2	2	0	3	22	0	51	5	3
Flury, Pat, Tren.	0	0	.000	1.66	26	0	0	0	24	16	30.2	24	122	6	6	2	0	0	0	11	1	37	3	0
Fontenot, Joe, Port.	3	1	.750	3.08	7	7	0	0	0	0	38.0	37	167	16	13	1	2	1	4	13	1	31	3	0
Forster, Scott, Har. *	7	3	.700	4.87	25	11	0	0	5	0	77.2	90	360	50	42	8	2	1	6	47	1	54	5	0
Fussell, Chris, Bow.	3	7	.300	4.26	18	18	0	0	0	0	93.0	87	413	54	44	13	1	6	4	52	1	84	4	0
Gallaher, Kevin, Bow.	2	0	1.000	5.06	9	0	0	0	6	0	16.0	12	77	9	9	0	1	0	0	17	1	18	5	0
Garza, Alberto, Akr.	3	0	1.000	3.86	4	4	1	0	0	0	21.0	24	95	12	9	1	0	1	1	9	0	19	0	0
Glinatsis, George, N.H.	1	2	.333	4.10	12	2	0	0	4	2	37.1	32	157	17	17	2	2	0	3	9	0	41	4	0
Gonzalez, Lariel, N.H.	0	4	.000	4.19	58	0	0	0	45	22	58.0	46	255	30	27	5	3	3	3	40	2	63	11	0
Gooch, Arnold, Bing.	11	14	.440	3.90	27	27	2	1	0	0	163.2	164	705	92	71	15	5	5	1	60	4	116	14	0
Gourdin, Tom, N.B.	8	4	.667	4.21	47	0	0	0	27	0	66.2	81	317	53	46	15	2	1	2	39	1	62	11	0
Guerra, Mark, Bing.	3	3	.500	2.83	30	2	0	0	21	12	41.1	38	171	17	13	5	1	2	1	30	0	0		
Hackman, Luther, N.H.	3	12	.200	5.44	28	23	1	0	2	0	139.0	169	640	102	84	18	7	7	10	54	1	90	10	2
Harris, Jeff, N.B.	1	0	1.000	1.66	10	0	0	0	11	5	38.0	21	138	7	7	3	1	1	0	5	0	40	0	1
Henderson, Ryan, Bing.	1	3	.000	3.35	29	0	0	0	16	4	40.1	34	173	18	15	2	1	1	0	20	3	39	3	1
Heredia, Maximo, Bow.	1	1	.500	6.23	5	4	0	0	0	0	13.0	18	56	9	9	2	0	0	1	2	0	7	0	0
Heredia, Wilson, Nor.	2	3	.400	5.57	5	5	0	0	0	0	32.1	31	139	22	20	4	0	2	1	9	1	31	1	1
Hernandez, Francis, Har.	3	3	.500	4.76	21	0	0	0	4	0	34.0	34	155	22	18	2	0	4	1	20	1	19	2	2
Jacobsen, Joe, Port.	1	0	1.000	1.69	3	0	0	0	2	0	5.1	4	19	1	1	1	0	0	0	0	0	3	0	0
Janzen, Marty, Nor.	1	7	.125	7.07	39	11	7	1	0	2	34.2	42	168	28	15	3	2	3	2	19	1	38	2	0
Jean, Domingo, N.H.	2	2	.500	7.00	12	5	0	0	4	1	27.0	30	131	21	21	1	2	0	1	19	0	17	3	1
Johnson, Barry, Nor.	1	0	1.000	3.75	7	0	0	0	3	0	12.0	13	53	6	5	1	1	0	5	0	12	1	0	
Johnson, Mark, Port.	5	14	.263	4.62	26	26	2	0	0	0	142.1	147	615	89	73	12	8	2	4	60	4	120	7	0
Johnson, Mike, Har.	3	2	.600	6.95	7	7	0	0	0	0	33.2	35	148	27	26	9	1	0	2	10	0	38	4	0
Kamieniecki, Scott, Bow.	1	0	1.000	4.76	3	3	0	0	0	0	11.1	13	49	6	6	1	0	0	0	5	0	5	1	0
Kawabata, Kyle, Read.	1	0	1.000	3.68	7	0	0	0	3	0	7.1	14	37	8	3	1	0	0	0	2	0	2	1	0
Kelley, Rich, Bow. *	8	2	.800	3.71	18	13	0	0	1	0	85.0	80	355	38	35	12	1	3	2	34	2	56	2	2
Kohlmeier, Ryan, Bow.	4	4	.500	6.12	42	0	0	0	28	7	50.0	52	219	37	34	13	1	1	3	16	1	56	2	1
Kusiewicz, Mike, N.H. *	14	7	.667	2.32	27	26	2	0	0	0	178.2	161	740	59	46	4	12	6	16	35	0	151	9	1
Lail, Denny, Nor.	0	0	.000	5.40	8	0	0	0	0	0	10.0	15	49	6	6	1	0	0	7	2	9	0	0	
Landry, Todd, Bing. *	0	0	.000	0.00	4	0	0	0	4	0	3.1	3	13	0	0	0	0	0	0	4	1	0		
Lane, Aaron, Bow. *	1	1	.500	6.26	15	0	0	0	6	0	23.0	29	107	19	16	2	0	2	4	14	1	11	4	0
Leese, Brandon, Port.	2	7	.364	4.13	20	20	0	0	0	0	126.1	137	544	70	58	16	11	1	5	37	1	94	2	0
Lidle, Kevin, N.H.	0	1	.000	27.00	1	0	0	0	1	0	2.0	4	14	6	6	1	0	0	0	3	0	2	0	0
Lincoln, Mike, N.B.	15	7	.682	3.22	26	26	1	0	0	0	173.1	180	720	80	62	13	8	5	5	35	0	109	5	0
Lisio, Joe, Nor.	1	0	1.000	0.00	1	0	0	0	0	0	1.0	1	5	0	0	0	1	0	0	1	0	1	0	0
Lyons, Mike, Bing.	4	1	.800	3.29	29	0	0	0	9	5	38.1	37	166	16	14	2	1	1	2	15	2	32	2	0
Maeda, Kats, Nor.	1	3	.250	7.71	28	0	0	0	10	1	37.1	44	186	36	32	4	1	0	31	2	27	5	0	
Mahaffey, Alan, N.B. *	2	3	.400	4.47	34	1	0	0	13	0	52.1	62	236	27	26	6	3	1	0	17	1	61	0	0
Marquez, Robert, Har.	0	0	.000	3.00	4	0	0	0	1	0	6.0	4	22	2	2	0	0	0	0	5	0	0		
Martinez, Ramiro, Har. *	0	2	.000	7.40	10	3	0	0	2	0	24.1	40	124	22	20	0	1	1	2	16	0	10	2	1
Martinez, Willie, Bow.	9	7	.563	4.38	26	26	2	1	0	0	154.0	169	661	92	75	15	6	2	6	44	0	117	10	1
Mathews, Terry, Bow.	1	0	1.000	6.00	1	1	0	0	0	0	3.0	3	12	2	2	1	0	0	0	0	0	1	0	0
Mays, Jarrod, Akr.	1	0	1.000	5.47	15	0	0	0	4	0	26.1	25	117	19	16	2	1	1	1	12	1	15	1	1
Mays, Joe, N.B.	5	3	.625	4.99	11	10	0	0	0	0	57.2	63	258	40	32	4	2	3	1	21	0	45	2	1
McCommon, Jason, Har.-Bow. .	9	8	.529	4.24	29	19	2	0	4	1	133.2	121	558	67	63	18	4	5	4	48	1	80	6	0
McCrary, Scott, Bing.	1	0	1.000	0.00	1	0	0	0	1	0	6.0	1	21	0	0	0	1	0	0	5	0	8	1	0
McCurtain, Paul, Port.	0	0	.000	5.40	1	0	0	0	0	0	1.2	2	8	1	1	0	2	0	0	1	0	2	1	0
Medina, Carlos, Bow. *	1	0	1.000	0.00	1	1	0	0	0	0	5.0	1	16	0	0	0	0	0	0	2	0	5	0	0
Mejia, Javier, Read.	0	0	.000	12.96	8	0	0	0	2	0	8.1	15	53	12	12	3	0	0	0	13	0	8	2	0
Merrick, Brett, Akr. *	1	1	.500	6.00	12	0	0	0	2	0	12.0	12	59	9	8	2	0	1	0	10	1	8	4	0
Miadich, Bart, Tren.	1	6	.143	5.96	22	8	0	0	4	1	54.1	66	253	39	36	4	1	2	5	26	1	33	3	0
Mitchell, Larry, Bow.	0	0	.000	9.64	4	1	0	0	1	0	4.2	6	29	5	5	0	0	0	0	11	0	2	0	0

Pitcher, Team	W	L	Pct.	ERA	G	GS	CG	ShO	GF	Sv.	IP	H	TBF	R	ER	HR	SH	SF	HB	BB	IBB	SO	WP	Bk.
Mitchell, Scott, Har.	9	3	.750	3.80	32	17	2	1	5	2	135.0	136	558	58	57	13	3	6	6	37	1	81	0	0
Molina, Gabe, Bow.	3	2	.600	3.36	47	0	0	0	38	24	61.2	48	256	24	23	5	3	1	1	27	0	75	5	1
Moore, Joel, N.H.	4	6	.400	3.89	13	12	0	0	0	0	81.0	84	348	42	35	7	1	2	1	26	0	69	3	0
Moore, Marcus, Akr.	2	5	.286	4.50	23	12	0	0	10	6	82.0	78	370	49	41	10	4	1	2	54	2	90	6	2
Moraga, David, Har. *	1	4	.200	4.95	19	4	0	0	5	1	40.0	42	182	27	22	3	2	1	3	22	2	23	5	0
Morales, Eric, Bing.	0	0	.000	18.00	1	0	0	0	1	0	1.0	3	6	2	2	1	0	0	0	0	0	0	0	0
Mota, Guillermo, Har.	2	0	1.000	1.06	12	0	0	0	9	4	17.0	10	60	2	2	0	0	0	0	2	0	19	2	0
Mucker, Kelcey, N.B.	0	0	.000	18.00	1	0	0	0	1	0	1.0	4	7	2	2	1	0	0	0	0	0	0	0	0
Mull, Blaine, Port.	0	3	.000	6.82	9	6	0	0	1	0	31.2	40	155	35	24	7	2	1	2	17	0	24	4	0
Murray, Dan, Bing.	11	6	.647	3.18	27	27	1	1	0	0	164.1	153	681	64	58	13	3	2	8	54	2	159	5	0
Narcisse, Tyrone, Nor.	1	0	1.000	5.23	29	0	0	0	16	1	53.1	61	247	38	31	6	0	2	4	26	1	43	11	0
Niebla, Ruben, Har. *	0	2	.000	4.60	24	1	0	0	3	1	43.0	45	178	23	22	5	1	6	1	6	0	30	4	0
Niedermaier, Brad, N.B.	0	0	.000	5.00	8	1	0	0	2	0	9.0	14	45	5	5	1	0	0	4	0	8	1	0
Nyari, Pete, Read.	1	7	.125	5.29	53	0	0	0	21	3	64.2	87	312	41	38	8	4	0	3	37	5	54	5	1
Ortiz, Nick, Har.	0	0	.000	0.00	1	0	0	0	0	0	1.0	1	5	0	0	0	0	0	1	0	0	0	0	0
Pageler, Mick, Port.	5	5	.500	4.62	60	0	0	0	32	13	76.0	73	336	40	39	8	2	2	6	32	5	67	5	1
Parker, Christian, Har.	6	6	.500	3.48	36	16	0	0	8	5	126.2	124	550	66	49	9	6	2	10	47	3	73	8	0
Paronto, Chad, Bow.	1	3	.250	5.80	8	7	0	0	1	1	35.2	38	165	30	23	1	0	1	3	23	0	28	4	0
Perez, Yorkis, Read. *	0	0	.000	0.00	1	1	0	0	0	0	1.0	0	3	0	0	0	0	0	0	1	0	0	0	0
Perkins, Dan, N.B.	13	5	.722	3.98	20	19	1	1	0	0	117.2	140	508	64	52	8	3	3	3	31	1	79	6	0
Phelps, Tommy, Har. *	5	4	.556	3.62	12	10	0	0	0	0	59.2	57	247	29	24	5	4	3	0	26	0	26	2	0
Phillips, Ben, Nor.	1	1	.500	4.94	16	0	0	0	6	0	23.2	19	102	13	13	2	1	3	2	16	1	22	2	0
Pontes, Dan, Bing.	3	2	.600	2.93	49	0	0	0	21	5	55.1	52	245	20	18	5	2	6	4	24	0	48	3	0
Powell, Jeremy, Har.	9	7	.563	3.01	22	22	1	0	0	0	131.2	115	546	54	44	13	7	2	9	37	0	77	6	1
Price, Tom, N.H. *	4	6	.400	3.67	38	4	0	0	12	1	68.2	85	292	33	28	8	5	5	3	7	0	36	2	0
Pumphrey, Ken, Bing.	1	0	1.000	4.50	3	2	0	0	0	0	8.0	10	36	4	4	0	0	0	3	0	6	0	0
Radlosky, Rob, N.B.	10	3	.769	4.02	27	19	0	0	0	0	132.0	127	552	61	59	16	6	2	6	38	0	117	7	0
Raifstanger, John, Tren.	0	0	.000	9.00	1	0	0	0	1	0	1.0	2	5	1	1	1	0	0	0	0	0	0	0	0
Rakers, Jason, Akr.	3	1	.750	2.59	5	5	0	0	0	0	31.1	35	130	10	9	2	2	1	0	7	0	27	2	0
Ramsay, Robert, Tren. *	12	6	.667	3.49	27	27	1	1	0	0	162.2	137	659	67	63	10	5	5	3	50	1	166	8	3
Randall, Scott, N.H.	10	14	.417	3.83	29	29	7	2	0	0	202.0	210	863	102	86	14	9	10	9	62	1	135	10	1
Rector, Bobby, Port.	1	1	.500	10.45	14	1	0	0	6	0	20.2	31	105	27	24	6	4	0	2	10	2	15	2	0
Redman, Mark, N.B. *	4	2	.667	1.52	8	8	0	0	0	0	47.1	40	190	11	8	3	1	0	3	17	0	51	1	1
Resz, Greg, Nor.	4	0	1.000	2.83	19	3	0	0	3	0	47.2	46	200	20	15	4	1	1	2	11	1	47	0	1
Richards, Mark, Port.	3	8	.273	5.38	40	7	0	0	19	5	75.1	96	360	54	45	4	4	3	3	43	5	56	5	0
Ricken, Ray, Nor.	5	4	.556	4.55	14	14	0	0	0	0	87.0	90	374	46	44	9	1	1	4	35	2	95	11	0
Riske, David, Akr.	0	0	.000	9.00	2	0	0	0	1	1	3.0	1	11	0	0	0	0	0	0	1	0	5	0	0
Ritz, Kevin, N.H.	1	2	.333	3.71	3	3	1	0	0	0	17.0	17	65	7	7	3	0	1	3	0	14	0	0
Rodgers, Bobby, Port.	6	5	.545	3.73	14	14	2	1	0	0	82.0	68	339	37	34	8	5	3	3	28	0	72	2	1
Rodriguez, Nerio, Bow.	0	1	.000	4.50	2	2	0	0	0	0	4.0	6	18	2	2	0	0	0	0	7	0	0	0
Rogers, Jason, Bow. *	4	3	.571	3.20	38	0	0	0	17	3	56.1	40	223	22	20	2	2	1	4	20	0	46	3	1
Romero, J.C., N.B. *	6	3	.667	2.19	51	1	0	0	14	2	78.0	48	324	28	19	3	6	2	4	43	3	79	13	0
Rose, Brian, Tren.	3	5	.375	3.90	24	0	0	0	6	2	32.1	39	150	16	14	2	5	3	0	16	5	23	0	0
Rose, Scott, Nor.	2	2	.500	6.14	26	0	0	0	19	5	36.2	49	167	26	25	2	2	2	0	16	6	22	1	0
Sackinsky, Brian, Bow.	0	0	.000	0.00	1	1	0	0	0	0	1.0	0	3	0	0	0	0	0	0	0	0	0	0	0
St. Pierre, Bob, Nor.	4	2	.667	4.03	24	0	0	0	6	0	38.0	46	175	23	17	1	1	3	3	15	1	26	1	0
Salamon, John, N.H.	2	3	.400	5.63	53	0	0	0	17	1	72.0	65	351	48	45	8	4	2	7	66	2	72	22	0
Sanders, Frankie, Akr.	11	8	.579	3.48	29	29	2	1	0	0	186.1	175	781	82	72	15	8	6	11	71	0	108	6	0
Schlomann, Brett, Nor.	9	9	.500	5.61	30	17	0	0	1	0	122.0	148	565	92	76	20	3	3	5	52	0	69	6	1
Scott, Darryl, Read.	0	1	.000	3.27	8	0	0	0	5	2	11.0	7	43	4	4	2	1	0	0	2	0	13	1	0
Sekany, Jason, Tren.	10	10	.500	5.21	28	28	1	0	0	0	148.2	151	643	101	86	21	4	5	5	57	0	113	14	0
Sexton, Jeff, Akr.	4	2	.667	1.57	27	0	0	0	19	11	57.1	41	232	12	10	2	2	0	3	19	3	49	2	0
Shelby, Anthony, Nor. *	0	0	.000	0.00	1	0	0	0	0	0	2.0	1	7	0	0	0	0	0	1	0	1	1	0
Shepherd, Alvie, Bow.	0	2	.000	3.32	6	3	0	0	0	0	19.0	13	79	8	7	3	0	1	0	14	0	12	0	1
Shoemaker, Stephen, N.H.	3	5	.375	4.89	15	15	0	0	0	0	84.2	69	390	60	46	7	6	3	5	63	0	85	4	0
Shuey, Paul, Akr.	0	0	.000	54.00	1	0	0	0	0	0	0.1	3	5	2	2	0	0	0	1	0	0	0	0
Shumaker, Anthony, Read. *	7	10	.412	3.35	38	21	1	1	9	2	166.2	152	689	75	62	20	9	7	4	44	2	129	3	0
Smart, J.D., Har.	3	5	.375	2.45	14	11	2	0	2	1	77.0	67	311	23	21	2	3	1	3	18	0	47	3	1
Smetana, Steve, Tren. *	2	3	.400	4.46	49	0	0	0	30	12	76.2	88	336	40	38	9	2	1	1	23	4	51	1	0
Smith, Hut, Bow.-Read.	2	9	.182	5.83	28	13	0	0	8	2	92.2	116	418	66	60	13	4	7	3	26	2	39	5	3
Snyder, Matt, Bow.	9	6	.600	4.35	22	20	4	1	0	0	120.0	127	510	66	58	14	1	3	4	30	0	116	6	3
Steed, Rick, Bing.	2	3	.400	2.74	9	7	0	0	1	0	46.0	37	186	14	14	2	1	2	0	18	2	30	2	0
Steinmetz, Earl, Bow.	0	0	.000	0.00	1	0	0	0	0	0	0.1	2	4	0	0	0	0	0	0	1	0	0	0	0
Stentz, Brent, N.B.	1	2	.333	1.98	57	0	0	0	53	43	59.0	44	244	13	13	3	2	1	1	28	2	65	1	0
Stevens, Kris, Read. *	8	11	.421	5.77	25	24	1	1	0	0	146.2	163	658	99	94	9	10	4	3	70	0	113	6	2
Stevenson, Rodney, Har.	5	0	1.000	4.35	37	0	0	0	23	8	39.1	32	168	19	19	3	2	2	2	18	5	47	1	0
Stewart, Rachaad, Bow. *	0	4	.000	10.80	5	5	0	0	0	0	20.0	27	96	25	24	3	0	3	1	11	1	7	2	1
Stewart, Scott, Bing. *	8	5	.615	3.70	24	13	0	0	3	2	90.0	91	382	44	37	12	4	2	1	29	2	65	2	4
Tebbs, Nate, Tren.	0	0	.000	0.00	1	0	0	0	0	0	1.0	0	3	0	0	0	0	0	0	0	0	1	0	0
Tejera, Michael, Port. *	9	5	.643	4.11	18	18	2	2	0	0	107.1	113	466	55	49	15	3	1	4	36	2	97	4	0
Tessmer, Jay, Nor.	3	4	.429	1.09	45	0	0	0	44	29	49.2	50	208	8	6	0	3	0	0	13	5	57	0	1
Thomas, Evan, Read.	8	5	.615	3.35	24	24	3	3	0	0	158.1	180	676	66	59	12	3	5	4	44	2	134	3	1
Towers, Josh, Bow.	2	1	.667	3.50	9	0	0	0	0	0	18.0	20	80	9	7	1	0	0	2	4	0	7	1	0
Townsend, Dave, Port.	0	0	1.000	6.26	11	2	0	0	2	0	23.0	35	115	18	16	3	2	1	1	11	0	9	0	0
Turrentine, Rich, Bing.	1	2	.333	2.93	28	0	0	0	23	10	30.2	15	125	10	10	3	2	0	1	17	0	55	5	1
Tweedlie, Brad, Tren.	1	2	.333	5.93	35	0	0	0	12	2	41.0	47	197	33	27	6	1	2	4	27	2	29	3	0
Twiggs, Greg, Bow. *	4	4	.500	4.12	31	7	0	0	7	0	74.1	85	321	43	34	5	3	0	23	2	59	6	0
Uchiyama, Tomoyuki, Read. *	5	6	.455	3.94	43	5	0	0	7	1	118.2	129	529	55	52	12	7	5	7	49	4	96	8	0
Urso, Sal, Tren. *	8	6	.571	4.13	69	0	0	0	18	3	83.1	86	354	45	38	7	2	0	2	32	8	86	8	0
Valera, Julio, Nor.	4	0	.000	6.91	5	5	1	0	0	0	27.1	30	124	23	21	4	3	0	3	12	0	17	3	1
Vardijan, Dan, Port.	1	1	.500	7.85	19	0	0	0	3	0	28.2	34	143	26	25	4	2	1	2	22	3	15	7	0
Vasquez, Leo, Bing. *	1	1	.500	4.60	14	2	0	0	2	1	29.1	28	140	16	15	1	2	1	2	25	0	28	3	0

Pitcher, Team	W	L	Pct.	ERA	G	GS	CG	ShO	GF	Sv.	IP	H	TBF	R	ER	HR	SH	SF	HB	BB	IBB	SO	WP	Bk.
Vavrek, Mike, N.H. *	5	12	.294	5.49	19	19	0	0	0	0	114.2	142	530	83	70	24	3	4	4	49	0	70	11	0
Veniard, Jay, Bing. *	1	0	1.000	3.94	11	0	0	0	2	0	16.0	17	73	10	7	3	0	1	0	10	2	16	1	0
Viano, Jake, Akr.	1	2	.333	7.80	9	0	0	0	1	1	15.0	24	75	17	13	3	0	1	2	7	1	10	0	1
Villafuerte, Brandon, Port.	0	2	.000	4.97	30	0	0	0	11	1	54.1	68	262	35	30	3	6	0	4	33	2	52	3	0
White, Walt, Port.	0	0	.000	0.00	3	0	0	0	3	0	2.2	2	11	0	0	0	0	1	0	1	0	0	0	0
Whitlock, Brian, Akr.	0	0	.000	9.00	1	0	0	0	0	0	1.0	2	6	1	1	0	0	0	0	1	0	0	0	0
Whitten, Casey, Akr. *	0	0	.000	0.00	1	0	0	0	1	0	1.0	1	4	0	0	0	0	0	0	0	0	0	0	0
Williams, Matt, Nor. *	8	11	.421	4.60	31	28	2	0	0	0	160.1	186	719	93	82	14	3	7	4	66	2	112	8	2
Williams, Shad, Nor.	4	2	.667	4.29	9	8	0	0	0	0	42.0	55	188	22	20	4	2	0	2	11	0	18	2	0
Wolf, Randy, Read. *	2	0	1.000	1.44	4	4	0	0	0	0	25.0	15	92	4	4	0	0	0	1	4	0	33	0	0
Woods, Brian, N.H.	1	3	.250	3.15	31	0	0	0	15	2	34.1	23	154	15	12	4	3	2	2	22	1	29	7	0
Yarnall, Ed, Bing.-Port. *	9	0	1.000	1.02	9	9	0	0	0	0	62.0	29	236	10	7	2	1	1	2	21	0	67	2	1
Yennaco, Jay, Tren.	3	3	.500	4.86	9	9	0	0	0	0	53.2	50	217	30	29	8	1	3	2	19	1	23	3	0
Yeskie, Nate, N.B.	0	0	.000	16.20	1	1	0	0	0	0	1.2	4	10	3	3	0	0	0	0	2	0	1	0	0
Young, Tim, Har. *	3	3	.500	3.79	26	0	0	0	19	3	35.2	28	146	17	15	3	5	0	1	10	0	52	1	0
Zancanaro, Dave, Nor. *	3	4	.429	4.70	16	13	0	0	2	0	69.0	80	300	42	36	9	2	1	3	23	0	49	3	0
Zolecki, Mike, N.H.	1	1	.500	9.28	8	0	0	0	5	0	10.2	10	49	11	11	3	1	0	0	8	0	6	1	1

COMBINATION SHUTOUTS: **Akron (2)**—Flener-Deschenes, Camp-Sexton. **Binghamton (8)**—Dotel-Arroyo-Henderson, Yarnall-Pontes-Arroyo-Turrentine, Yarnall-Arroyo-Pontes-Turrentine, Dotel-Arroyo-Henderson-Stewart, Yarnall-Pontes, Murray-Henderson-Arroyo-Turrentine, Stewart-Arteaga, Gooch-Lyons-Arroyo. **Bowie (6)**—Fussell-Shepherd-Eibey-Molina-Kohlmeier, Estes-Shepherd-Dykhoff-Molina, Twiggs-Eibey-Molina, McCommon-Molina-Kohlmeier, Kelley-Rogers-Twiggs, Medina-Paronto. **Harrisburg (7)**—Powell-Benz, Parker-Smart, Smart-Dixon, Evans-Mitchell, Powell-Mitchell, Evans-Dixon-Stevenson, Forster-Parker. **New Britain (10)**—Cobb-Radlosky-Mahaffey-Harris-Gourdin, Redman-Gourdin-Harris-Stentz, Lincoln-Romero-Cumberland, Redman-Cumberland-Stentz, Cumberland-Harris, Perkins-Harris, Bell-Cumberland-Romero, Radlosky-Cumberland-Harris, Bell-Chapman-Romero-Gourdin, Bell-Stentz. **New Haven (5)**—Kusiewicz-Glinatsis, Vavrek-Bost, Kusiewicz-Salamon-Gonzalez, Kusiewicz-Bost, Shoemaker-Bost-Gonzalez. **Norwich (2)**—Zancanaro-Tessmer, Ricken-Tessmer. **Portland (3)**—Dempster-DeWitt-Jacobsen, Billingsley-Duncan-Burgus-Pageler, Johnson-Pageler. **Reading (1)**—Stevens-Nyari. **Trenton (7)**—Cressend-Urso-Tweedlie, Crawford-Blais-Urso, Cressend-Urso-Smetana, Fernandez-Rose-Flury, Cressend-Urso-Flury, Cho-Urso-Flury, Cressend-Urso-Flury.

NO-HIT GAMES: None.

PITCHERS WITH TWO OR MORE TEAMS

Pitcher, Team	W	L	Pct.	ERA	G	GS	CG	ShO	GF	Sv.	IP	H	TBF	R	ER	HR	SH	SF	HB	BB	IBB	SO	WP	Bk.
McCommon, Jason, Har.	1	0	1.000	3.72	6	0	0	0	3	1	9.2	8	40	4	4	1	0	0	0	6	1	7	1	0
McCommon, Jason, Bow.	8	8	.500	4.28	23	19	2	0	1	0	124.0	113	518	63	59	17	4	5	4	42	0	73	5	0
Smith, Hut, Bow.	0	3	.000	6.90	6	5	0	0	1	0	30.0	32	129	23	23	5	0	2	5	6	0	12	2	1
Smith, Hut, Read.	2	6	.250	5.31	22	6	0	0	7	2	62.2	84	289	43	37	8	4	3	2	20	2	27	3	2
Yarnall, Ed, Bing. *	7	0	1.000	0.39	7	7	0	0	0	0	46.2	20	177	5	2	0	1	1	1	17	0	52	1	1
Yarnall, Ed, Port. *	2	0	1.000	2.93	2	2	0	0	0	0	15.1	9	59	5	5	2	1	0	1	4	0	15	1	0

1998 FIELDING
TEAM

Team	Pct.	G	PO	A	E	TC	DP	PB	Team	Pct.	G	PO	A	E	TC	DP	PB
Akron	.978	141	3753	1536	118	5407	142	17	Bowie	.973	142	3590	1358	139	5087	112	25
New Britain	.973	142	3721	1521	143	5385	146	8	New Haven	.971	142	3678	1536	158	5372	121	20
Harrisburg	.973	142	3647	1541	142	5330	138	19	Portland	.968	141	3661	1491	169	5321	137	18
Trenton	.973	141	3733	1560	145	5438	124	42	Norwich	.967	142	3648	1420	174	5242	83	15
Binghamton	.973	142	3744	1511	145	5400	128	14	TRIPLE PLAY: Norwich.								
Reading	.973	141	3723	1518	147	5388	137	26									

INDIVIDUAL

FIRST BASEMEN

NOTE: All caps denotes fielding-percentage leader based on 71 games for catchers, 95 for all other non-pitchers and 142 innings for pitchers. *Throws lefthanded.

Player, Team	Pct.	G	PO	A	E	TC	DP
Alcantara, Israel, Read.	.980	15	139	8	3	150	13
Ashby, Chris, Nor.	.971	21	150	18	5	173	8
Azuaje, Jesus, Bing.	1.000	1	1	0	0	1	0
Bierek, Kurt, Nor.	.989	94	731	72	9	812	56
Blum, Geoffrey, Har.	1.000	1	5	0	0	5	0
Bogle, Bryan, Bow.	1.000	1	11	0	0	11	2
Carver, Steve, Read.	.988	82	697	69	9	775	75
Chevalier, Virgil, Tren.	1.000	12	74	4	0	78	8
Clark, Howie, Bow.	1.000	8	12	0	0	12	0
Clark, Tim, Bow.*	.981	7	49	2	1	52	4
Colon, Dennis, Bing.*	.987	27	212	17	3	232	18
Davis, Tommy, Bow.	1.000	7	56	3	0	59	6
Depastino, Joe, Tren.	1.000	1	1	0	0	1	0
Emmons, Scott, Nor.	.988	10	77	7	1	85	2
Epperson, Chad, Tren.	.994	17	152	12	1	165	10
Everson, Darin, Tren.	1.000	6	56	4	0	60	5
Fernandez, Jose, Har.	.983	7	55	2	1	58	4
Fithian, Grant, Nor.	1.000	3	31	0	0	31	1
Fortin, Troy, N.B.	1.000	5	26	1	0	27	4
Fraser, Joe, N.B.	1.000	2	9	0	0	9	0
Gibralter, David, Tren.	.990	90	837	44	9	890	70
Gomez, Rudy, Nor.	1.000	3	24	1	0	25	0
Goodell, Steve, Port.	1.000	1	2	0	0	2	0
Gunderson, Shane, N.B.	1.000	1	2	1	0	3	0
Jarrett, Link, N.H.	1.000	1	5	1	0	6	0

Player, Team	Pct.	G	PO	A	E	TC	DP
Kirgan, Chris, N.H.	.985	111	988	72	16	1076	86
Kofler, Eric, Nor.*	1.000	6	35	3	0	38	2
Landry, Todd, Bing.*	.992	89	765	60	7	832	78
Martinez, Rafael, Tren.*	.976	15	111	10	3	124	11
McLamb, Brian, Nor.	.968	8	56	5	2	63	5
Mientkiewicz, Doug, N.B.	.991	137	1169	92	12	1273	116
Millan, Adan, Read.	1.000	11	105	4	0	109	11
Morales, Francisco, Har.	.984	16	116	9	2	127	17
Mucker, Kelcey, N.B.	1.000	4	16	1	0	17	6
Newstrom, Doug, N.H.	.988	25	228	16	3	247	21
Norton, Chris, Port.	.951	6	56	2	3	61	5
Perry, Chan, Akr.	1.000	4	29	5	0	34	5
Pickering, Calvin, Bow.*	.983	128	1063	60	20	1143	90
Pond, Simon, Har.	1.000	1	7	2	0	9	0
Post, Dave, Har.	1.000	7	43	1	0	44	4
Raifstanger, John, Tren.	1.000	2	6	2	0	8	1
Raleigh, Matt, Bing.	.990	31	279	22	3	304	18
Rivero, Eddie, Read.*	.987	34	286	23	4	313	26
Robertson, Ryan, Port.	1.000	4	30	4	0	34	1
Rolison, Nate, Port.	.989	131	1081	85	13	1179	116
Sapp, Damian, Tren.	1.000	2	12	1	0	13	2
Seguignol, Fernando, Har.	.983	59	485	50	9	544	38
STUMBERGER, Darren, Akr.	.992	135	1197	116	10	1323	124
Taylor, Jamie, N.B.	1.000	5	44	4	0	48	4
Thomas, Greg, Akr.*	1.000	4	19	0	0	19	3
Tracy, Andrew, Har.	.988	52	476	36	6	518	53
Tucker, Jon, Har.*	.989	13	83	8	1	92	10
TRIPLE PLAY: Bierek.							

SECOND BASEMEN

Player, Team	Pct.	G	PO	A	E	TC	DP
Azuaje, Jesus, Bing.	.990	66	104	195	3	302	42
Bady, Ed, Har.	1.000	1	2	1	0	3	0
Bell, Mike, Bing.	.957	54	84	114	9	207	20
Betances, Junior, Akr.	.948	18	29	44	4	77	10
Blum, Geoffrey, Har.	.971	9	13	20	1	34	4
Brown, Vick, Nor.	.954	98	178	254	21	453	37
Camilli, Jason, Har.	1.000	5	5	15	0	20	3
Carroll, Jamey, Har.	.962	54	98	152	10	260	42
Carvajal, Johnny, Har.	.978	12	13	31	1	45	9
Cey, Dan, N.B.	.967	135	246	373	21	640	97
Chamblee, James, Tren.	.974	131	247	352	16	615	92
Clark, Howie, Bow.	1.000	8	10	16	0	26	2
Coquillette, Trace, Har.	.973	45	61	121	5	187	20
Cromer, Brandon, Port.	1.000	1	1	0	0	1	0
Darden, Tony, Bing.	1.000	16	15	40	0	55	5
Dennis, Les, Nor.	.904	10	20	27	5	52	7
Fonville, Chad, N.H.	.945	12	20	32	3	55	5
Garcia, Amaury, Port.	.960	136	287	355	27	669	93
Garcia, Jesse, Bow.	.978	83	128	190	7	325	42
Garcia, Vicente, N.H.	.967	121	247	344	20	611	78
Gomez, Rudy, Nor.	1.000	17	41	53	0	94	8
Guiliano, Matt, Read.	.987	34	69	87	2	158	26
Gutierrez, Rick, Akr.	.978	10	17	28	1	46	9
Hairston, Jerry, Bow.	.984	54	109	133	4	246	34
Harris, Brian, Read.	.969	11	31	31	2	64	7
Hinds, Rob, Nor.	.957	16	21	24	2	47	2
Huff, Larry, Read.	.957	5	9	13	1	23	1
Jarrett, Link, N.H.	.965	12	19	36	2	57	7
Knupfer, Jason, Read.	.981	54	116	146	5	267	39
Lawrence, Chip, Bow.	1.000	3	2	4	0	6	0
McLamb, Brian, Nor.	.895	4	7	10	2	19	2
Moriarty, Mike, N.B.	.955	5	4	17	1	22	3
Ortiz, Nick, Har.	1.000	22	37	69	0	106	16
Paez, Israel, N.B.	1.000	6	6	16	0	22	6
Polanco, Enohel, Bing.	.667	2	0	2	1	3	0
Post, Dave, Har.	1.000	4	3	10	0	13	2
Raifstanger, John, Tren.	.571	1	2	2	3	7	0
Raynor, Mark, Read.	.957	43	82	117	9	208	30
Rodriguez, Victor, Port.	1.000	2	2	5	0	7	2
Sanchez, Yuri, Bing.	.750	2	1	2	1	4	0
SCUTARO, Marcos, Akr.	.977	118	244	339	14	597	85
Selby, William, Akr.	1.000	1	3	5	0	8	1
Short, Rick, Bow.	.909	9	5	5	1	11	1
Tebbs, Nate, Tren.	.964	12	22	32	2	56	5
White, Walt, Port.	1.000	6	14	15	0	29	5
Zorrilla, Julio, Bing.	.915	20	25	50	7	82	8

TRIPLE PLAY: Brown.

THIRD BASEMEN

Player, Team	Pct.	G	PO	A	E	TC	DP
Alcantara, Israel, Read.	.875	10	6	15	3	24	3
Amador, Manny, Read.	.846	15	10	23	6	39	3
Barrett, Michael, Har.	.932	34	18	64	6	88	9
Bell, Mike, Bing.	.938	18	8	22	2	32	0
Berry, Mike, Nor.	.927	103	59	157	17	233	12
Betances, Junior, Akr.	.952	43	25	75	5	105	7
Betts, Todd, Akr.	.972	58	48	93	4	145	11
Blum, Geoffrey, Har.	1.000	15	11	35	0	46	4
Booty, Josh, Port.	.931	68	43	159	15	217	20
Branyan, Russell, Akr.	.932	41	24	72	7	103	7
Clark, Howie, Bow.	.700	5	2	5	3	10	1
Coquillette, Trace, Har.	.600	1	0	3	2	5	1
Cromer, Brandon, Port.	.904	38	23	80	11	114	6
Darden, Tony, Bing.	.946	55	21	85	6	112	6
DeCinces, Tim, Bow.	.667	1	0	2	1	3	0
Dennis, Les, Nor.	.714	1	3	2	2	7	0
Fernandez, Jose, Har.	.916	85	64	165	21	250	13
Fraser, Joe, N.B.	.968	14	8	22	1	31	2
Funaro, Joe, Port.	1.000	2	1	3	0	4	1
Gibralter, David, Tren.	.778	5	4	10	4	18	1
Gomez, Rudy, Nor.	.917	4	6	5	1	12	0
Goodell, Steve, Port.	.818	7	2	7	2	11	2
Gross, Rafael, Akr.	1.000	1	0	1	0	1	0
Guiliano, Matt, Read.	.940	15	13	34	3	50	6
Gulan, Mike, Port.	.892	27	15	43	7	65	4
Huff, Larry, Read.	.972	36	29	74	3	106	9
Jarrett, Link, N.H.	.949	28	9	65	4	78	7
Knupfer, Jason, Read.	.889	2	2	6	1	9	1
Light, Tal, N.H.	.877	37	18	89	15	122	6
Lopez, Jose, Bing.	.896	79	36	163	23	222	7
McLamb, Brian, Nor.	.934	39	26	59	6	91	4
Millan, Adan, Read.	.860	17	10	39	8	57	3
Minor, Ryan, Bow.	.928	135	89	245	26	360	27
Moriarty, Mike, N.B.	.922	32	23	71	8	102	5
Moss, Rick, N.B.	.936	62	28	104	9	141	13
Ojeda, Augie, Bow.	.929	5	4	9	1	14	2
Ortiz, Nick, Har.	.933	11	4	24	2	30	2
Paez, Israel, N.B.	.861	45	26	67	15	108	6
Post, Dave, Har.	1.000	3	5	7	0	12	2
Raleigh, Matt, Bing.	.929	4	1	12	1	14	1
Raynor, Mark, Read.	.943	49	41	92	8	141	5
Richardson, Brian, N.H.	.800	3	1	7	2	10	1
Selby, William, Akr.	.900	3	4	5	1	10	1
Short, Rick, Bow.	.667	3	1	1	1	3	0
Taylor, Jamie, N.H.	.954	69	51	156	10	217	16
Tebbs, Nate, Tren.	.897	13	9	26	4	39	1
VERAS, Wilton, Tren.	.952	125	100	259	18	377	25
White, Walt, Port.	1.000	4	3	8	0	11	2
Whitley, Matt, N.H.	.905	8	4	15	2	21	0
Whitlock, Brian, Akr.	1.000	1	0	1	0	1	0

SHORTSTOPS

Player, Team	Pct.	G	PO	A	E	TC	DP
Angeli, Doug, Read.	.977	62	82	178	6	266	45
Azuaje, Jesus, Bing.	.982	39	54	114	3	171	21
Betances, Junior, Akr.	.952	6	4	16	1	21	2
Blum, Geoffrey, Har.	.983	15	19	39	1	59	9
Camilli, Jason, Har.	1.000	1	1	1	0	2	1
Carroll, Jamey, Har.	.932	23	40	56	7	103	14
CARVAJAL, Jhonny, Har.	.977	96	141	278	10	429	66
Chamblee, James, Tren.	1.000	1	0	1	0	1	1
Cromer, Brandon, Port.	.902	15	18	37	6	61	8
De Leon, Jorge, Tren.	.968	29	43	79	4	126	16
Dennis, Les, Nor.	.901	18	24	49	8	81	3
Funaro, Joe, Port.	.952	57	109	167	14	290	35
Garcia, Jesse, Bow.	.818	7	3	6	2	11	0
Gomez, Rudy, Nor.	.885	18	29	40	9	78	5
Guiliano, Matt, Read.	.952	80	105	213	16	334	41
Guzman, Cristian, N.B.	.952	140	211	426	32	669	95
Hairston, Jerry, Bow.	.667	1	0	2	1	3	0
Hinds, Rob, Nor.	.871	7	10	17	4	31	3
Houser, Kyle, N.H.	.956	94	138	273	19	430	49
Jackson, Gavin, Tren.	.972	50	86	155	7	248	31
Jarrett, Link, N.H.	.952	56	77	122	10	209	25
Jimenez, D'Angelo, Nor.	.938	40	62	119	12	193	24
Lamb, David, Bow.	.946	65	73	171	14	258	30
Lawrence, Chip, Bow.	1.000	3	1	4	0	5	0
Lobaton, Jose, Nor.	.941	50	61	116	11	188	13
Martinez, Eddy, Bow.	.917	5	5	6	1	12	2
McDonald, John, Akr.	.966	132	242	407	23	672	91
McLamb, Brian, Nor.	.944	10	12	22	2	36	4
Moriarty, Mike, N.B.	1.000	1	1	2	0	3	1
Ojeda, Augie, Bow.	.966	69	91	190	10	291	34
Ortiz, Nick, Har.-Tren.	.928	53	87	144	18	249	28
Paez, Israel, N.B.	1.000	4	4	9	0	13	1
Polanco, Enohel, Bing.	.930	23	39	54	7	100	12
Post, Dave, Har.	1.000	1	1	3	0	4	0
Raynor, Mark, Read.	1.000	2	2	6	0	8	3
Rodriguez, Victor, Port.	.954	56	74	156	11	241	34
Sanchez, Yuri, Bing.	.960	89	113	222	14	349	62
Scutaro, Marcos, Akr.	.950	7	7	12	1	20	3
Tebbs, Nate, Tren.	.954	31	36	88	6	130	15
White, Walt, Port.	.935	18	30	42	5	77	8
Whitley, Matt, N.H.	1.000	4	2	7	0	9	1

TRIPLE PLAY: Gomez.

SHORTSTOPS WITH TWO OR MORE TEAMS

Player, Team	Pct.	G	PO	A	E	TC	DP
Ortiz, Nick, Har.	.941	15	22	42	4	68	7
Ortiz, Nick, Tren.	.923	38	65	102	14	181	21

OUTFIELDERS

Player, Team	Pct.	G	PO	A	E	TC	DP
Adolfo, Carlos, Har.	.958	34	64	4	3	71	0
Alcantara, Israel, Read.	.875	4	7	0	1	8	0
Allen, Chad, N.B.	.980	133	185	11	4	200	2
Almonte, Wady, Bow.	.929	7	12	1	1	14	1
Angeli, Doug, Read.	1.000	4	4	0	0	4	0
Ashby, Chris, Nor.	.969	93	145	11	5	161	1
Azuaje, Jesus, Bing.	1.000	4	1	0	0	1	0
Bady, Ed, Har.	1.000	39	65	1	0	66	1
Barnes, John, Tren.-N.B.	.984	111	173	8	3	184	2

CLASS AA Eastern League

Player, Team	Pct.	G	PO	A	E	TC	DP
Bates, Fletcher, Port.	.962	139	266	9	11	286	2
Bell, Mike, Bing.	.889	6	8	0	1	9	0
Bergeron, Peter, Har.	1.000	32	67	5	0	72	1
Betances, Junior, Akr.	1.000	1	3	0	0	3	0
Bocachica, Hiram, Har.	.946	72	171	4	10	185	3
Bogle, Bryan, Bow.	.977	19	41	1	1	43	1
Bryant, Pat, Tren.	.979	24	45	2	1	48	0
BUDZINSKI, Mark, Akr.*	.989	126	270	6	3	279	1
Campos, Jesus, Har.	.970	76	129	1	4	134	0
Carver, Steve, Read.	.940	28	45	2	3	50	0
Chancey, Bailey, Bing.	1.000	12	14	0	0	14	0
Chevalier, Virgil, Tren.	.857	11	12	0	2	14	0
Clark, Howie, Bow.	.963	55	76	3	3	82	1
Colon, Dennis, Bing.*	.984	34	56	4	1	61	0
Conner, Decomba, Bow.	.984	61	118	2	2	122	0
Cook, Hayward, Port.	.944	17	17	0	1	18	0
Costello, Brian, Read.	.972	32	67	3	2	72	1
Crane, Todd, Read.	.857	9	17	1	3	21	0
Cromer, Brandon, Port.	.982	64	106	2	2	110	0
Darden, Tony, Bing.	1.000	19	24	2	0	26	1
Dawkins, Walt, Read.	.978	45	82	6	2	90	2
Derosso, Tony, Tren.	1.000	3	1	0	0	1	0
Epperson, Chad, Tren.	1.000	6	6	0	0	6	0
Felston, Anthony, N.B.*	.913	12	21	0	2	23	0
Feuerstein, Dave, N.H.	.986	128	199	10	3	212	2
Fonville, Chad, N.H.	1.000	32	47	1	0	48	0
Francia, David, Read.*	.993	67	142	8	1	151	3
Funaro, Joe, Port.	1.000	6	6	0	0	6	0
Gambill, Chad, N.H.	.958	39	63	6	3	72	1
Garcia, Jesse, Bow.	1.000	1	2	0	0	2	0
Garland, Tim, Bow.	1.000	55	108	2	0	110	0
Giudice, John, N.H.	.980	59	94	6	2	102	0
Glass, Chip, Nor.*	.984	107	235	12	4	251	0
Goodell, Steve, Port.	1.000	14	27	2	0	29	1
Gross, Rafael, Akr.	1.000	20	35	1	0	36	1
Gulan, Mike, Port.	1.000	3	1	0	0	1	0
Hamilton, Joe, Tren.	.982	29	55	1	1	57	0
Hammonds, Jeffrey, Bow.	1.000	3	3	0	0	3	0
Hinds, Rob, Nor.	1.000	2	3	0	0	3	0
Houser, Kyle, N.H.	1.000	1	0	1	0	1	0
Huelsmann, Mike, Akr.	1.000	8	11	1	0	12	0
Hunter, Scott, Bing.	.979	120	220	9	5	234	3
Hunter, Torii, N.B.	.989	82	168	8	2	178	2
Isom, Johnny, Bow.	.994	92	151	12	1	164	5
Jarrett, Link, N.H.	1.000	2	1	0	0	1	0
Johnson, J.J., N.B.	.973	46	68	3	2	73	1
Jones, Jacque, N.B.*	.968	129	288	12	10	310	2
Jones, Jaime, Port.*	.949	106	141	7	8	156	0
Keel, David, Nor.	1.000	5	4	0	0	4	0
Key, Jeff, Read.	.969	59	93	2	3	98	0
Kingsale, Eugene, Bow.	.980	111	279	9	6	294	4
Kofler, Eric, Nor.*	1.000	2	3	1	0	4	0
Landry, Todd, Bing.*	1.000	16	9	0	0	9	0
Light, Tal, N.H.	.900	12	8	1	1	10	0
Long, Terrence, Bing.	.958	128	218	9	10	237	2
Maness, Dwight, Bing.-Tren.	.970	108	248	13	8	269	3
Matos, Luis, Bow.	.833	5	4	1	1	6	1
McDonald, Donzell, Nor.	.976	128	312	8	8	328	1
Mientkiewicz, Doug, N.B.	1.000	3	2	0	0	2	0
Mitchell, Keith, Tren.	1.000	10	22	1	0	23	0
Monds, Wonderful, N.H.	.956	116	251	7	12	270	1
Morenz, Shea, Nor.	.988	82	158	3	2	163	1
Morgan, Scott, Akr.	.976	110	201	4	5	210	2
Mucker, Kelcey, N.B.	1.000	11	19	0	0	19	0
Neubart, Garrett, Bing.	.971	95	160	9	5	174	1
Newstrom, Doug, N.H.	.857	3	6	0	1	7	0
Pegues, Steve, N.H.	1.000	10	10	1	0	11	0
Peoples, Daniel, Akr.	.973	45	71	2	2	75	1
Perez, Danny, Bow.	1.000	19	24	0	0	24	0
Perry, Chan, Akr.	.976	27	37	4	1	42	1
Petrick, Ben, N.H.	1.000	1	2	0	0	2	0
Pickering, Calvin, Bow.*	.714	6	5	0	2	7	0
Post, Dave, Har.	1.000	3	1	1	0	2	0
Raifstanger, John, Tren.	1.000	4	7	0	0	7	0
Ramirez, Angel, Nor.	.900	17	26	1	3	30	0
Ramirez, Roberto, Bow.	1.000	6	5	0	0	5	0
Reeves, Glenn, Port.	1.000	50	79	5	0	84	0
Rennhack, Mike, N.H.	.972	41	66	3	2	71	0
Rivero, Eddie, Read.*	1.000	7	9	0	0	9	0
Roberts, David, Akr.*	.992	56	124	4	1	129	0
Royster, Aaron, Read.	.970	99	159	5	5	169	1
Samuels, Scott, Har.	.933	11	13	1	1	15	0
Schwab, Chris, Har.*	1.000	1	2	0	0	2	0
Seguignol, Fernando, Har.	1.000	16	18	0	0	18	0
Selby, William, Akr.	1.000	15	25	0	0	25	0
Short, Rick, Bow.	1.000	12	23	0	0	23	0
Stenson, Dernell, Tren.*	.975	131	218	15	6	239	1
Stowers, Chris, Har.*	.984	132	243	10	4	257	1
Taveras, Frank, Akr.	1.000	2	5	0	0	5	0
Taylor, Jamie, N.H.	1.000	1	2	0	0	2	0
Taylor, Reggie, Read.	.944	77	164	6	10	180	1
Tebbs, Nate, Tren.	.991	49	100	6	1	107	0
Thomas, Greg, Akr.*	1.000	37	66	4	0	70	1
Tracy, Andrew, Har.	1.000	1	5	0	0	5	0
Tucker, Jon, Har.*	1.000	13	15	1	0	16	0
Valdez, Trovin, Akr.	.935	34	29	0	2	31	0
White, Walt, Port.	.944	33	48	3	3	54	0
Williams, Bernie, Nor.	1.000	3	5	0	0	5	0

SHORTSTOPS WITH TWO OR MORE TEAMS

Player, Team	Pct.	G	PO	A	E	TC	DP
Barnes, John, Tren.	.979	94	134	6	3	143	1
Barnes, John, N.B.	1.000	17	39	2	0	41	1
Maness, Dwight, Bing.	.953	25	39	2	2	43	0
Maness, Dwight, Tren.	.973	83	209	11	6	226	3

CATCHERS

Player, Team	Pct.	G	PO	A	E	TC	DP	PB
Barrett, Michael, Har.	.989	83	499	49	6	554	5	6
Borrero, Richie, Tren.	.981	49	338	32	7	377	4	11
Castro, Ramon, Tren.	.946	12	82	5	5	92	0	1
Chevalier, Virgil, Tren.	.909	2	9	1	1	11	0	0
Davis, Tommy, Bow.	.969	23	150	7	5	162	0	9
Depastino, Joe, Tren.	.986	56	368	53	6	427	6	14
Emmons, Scott, Nor.	.983	34	210	22	4	236	2	6
Epperson, Chad, Tren.	.993	19	135	13	1	149	0	5
Fithian, Grant, Nor.	.988	23	140	18	2	160	2	2
Fortin, Troy, N.B.	.982	14	97	10	2	109	2	1
Foster, Jim, Bow.	.990	25	177	18	2	197	3	1
Gonzales, Jose, N.H.	1.000	2	10	0	0	10	0	0
Grifol, Pedro, Bing.	.990	114	897	81	10	988	11	6
Harriss, Robin, Akr.	.984	15	113	9	2	124	2	2
Hayes, Heath, Akr.	.988	85	507	59	7	573	1	7
Kuilan, Hector, Port.	.988	30	227	26	3	256	3	4
Lidle, Kevin, N.H.	.986	10	59	10	1	70	1	1
Luzinski, Ryan, Bow.	.993	61	371	45	3	419	0	6
Marsters, Brandon, Read.	.986	38	254	25	4	283	3	9
Millan, Adan, Read.	.994	24	153	11	1	165	2	6
Moeller, Chad, N.B.	.987	55	414	25	6	445	6	4
Morales, Eric, Bing.	.988	38	232	25	3	260	2	7
Morales, Francisco, Har.	.993	64	396	45	3	444	2	13
Morales, Stephen, Port.	1.000	3	16	3	0	19	0	0
Moyle, Mike, Akr.	.995	27	173	18	1	192	2	3
Newstrom, Doug, N.H.	.981	55	391	32	8	431	5	9
Norton, Chris, Port.	.980	14	90	9	2	101	0	4
Petrick, Ben, N.H.	.991	86	534	43	5	582	2	10
Pierce, Kirk, Read.	.987	74	561	61	8	630	3	11
Pierzynski, A.J., N.B.	.996	57	409	37	2	448	3	2
Ramirez, Peto, Bing.	.963	15	93	12	4	109	1	4
Redmond, Mike, Port.	.983	8	53	6	1	60	0	1
Robertson, Ryan, Port.	.989	85	630	68	8	706	8	8
Rodriguez, Sammy, Bing.	1.000	2	19	1	0	20	0	1
Rosario, Mel, Bow.	.973	35	216	38	7	261	3	8
Sapp, Damian, Tren.	.962	22	132	21	6	159	0	12
Smith, Jeff, N.B.	.994	23	151	15	1	167	1	1
Snusz, Chris, Read.	.979	7	39	7	1	47	0	0
Taylor, Adam, Akr.	.905	3	17	2	2	21	0	1
TORRES, Jaime, Nor.	.993	76	526	59	4	589	3	6
Troilo, Jason, Nor.	.957	23	124	9	6	139	0	1
Utting, Andy, Bow.	1.000	1	2	0	0	2	0	0
Werth, Jayson, Bow.	1.000	5	49	4	0	53	1	1

PITCHERS

Player, Team	Pct.	G	PO	A	E	TC	DP
Arroyo, Luis, Bing.*	.813	57	5	8	3	16	0
Arteaga, Ivan, Bing.	1.000	23	4	5	0	9	1
Arteaga, J.D., Bing.*	.970	21	8	24	1	33	2
Atkins, Ross, Akr.	.941	40	7	9	1	17	0
Aucoin, Derek, Bing.	1.000	12	2	2	0	4	1
Baker, Jason, Har.	.733	25	6	5	4	15	0
Barbao, Joe, Read.	1.000	10	0	2	0	2	0
Barnett, Marty, Read.	1.000	5	1	3	0	4	0
Baron, Jim, Nor.*	.926	23	6	19	2	27	2
Bautista, Jose, Nor.	1.000	3	1	1	0	2	0

CLASS AA Eastern League

Player, Team	Pct.	G	PO	A	E	TC	DP
Beale, Chuck, Tren.	1.000	43	4	14	0	18	1
Beckett, Robbie, N.H.*	1.000	22	1	1	0	2	0
Bell, Jason, N.B.	1.000	29	13	25	0	38	1
Benz, Jake, Har.*	.875	16	3	4	1	8	0
Betances, Junior, Akr.	1.000	1	0	1	0	1	0
Betancourt, Rafael, Tren.	1.000	7	1	1	0	2	0
Beverlin, Jason, Nor.	.941	25	5	11	1	17	1
Billingsley, Brent, Port.*	.893	28	7	18	3	28	2
Blais, Mike, Tren.	1.000	22	1	7	0	8	0
Borland, Toby, Read.	1.000	8	1	3	0	4	0
Bost, Heath, N.H.	1.000	41	3	7	0	10	2
Bradley, Ryan, Nor.	.667	3	0	2	1	3	0
Brammer, J.D., Akr.	.667	11	1	1	1	3	0
Brannan, Ryan, Read.	1.000	41	2	11	0	13	0
Brester, Jason, N.H.*	1.000	5	4	3	0	7	0
Brittan, Corey, Bing.	1.000	9	0	1	0	1	0
Brower, Jim, Akr.	.982	23	25	30	1	56	4
Brown, Jamie, Akr.	1.000	1	1	0	0	1	0
Burger, Rob, Read.	.933	33	12	16	2	30	0
Burgus, Travis, Port.*	1.000	38	3	9	0	12	0
Calmus, Lance, Akr.	1.000	23	3	8	0	11	1
Camp, Jared, Akr.	.909	18	4	6	1	11	0
Censale, Silvio, Read.*	1.000	4	0	1	0	1	0
Chapman, Walker, N.B.	1.000	23	3	8	0	11	2
Cho, Jin Ho, Tren.	1.000	13	3	11	0	14	0
Cobb, Trevor, N.B.*	.900	27	8	19	3	30	1
Coggin, David, Read.	.895	20	12	22	4	38	3
Cole, Jason, Har.	1.000	22	2	8	0	10	1
Converse, Jim, Bow.	1.000	1	0	2	0	2	0
Coppinger, Rocky, Bow.	.857	7	1	5	1	7	0
Cormier, Rheal, Akr.*	1.000	3	1	4	0	5	0
Crawford, Paxton, Tren.	1.000	22	8	13	0	21	2
Cressend, Jack, Tren.	1.000	29	10	21	0	31	0
Cumberland, Chris, N.B.*	.933	37	5	9	1	15	0
Curtis, Chris, Bow.	1.000	12	2	5	0	7	0
Davis, Jason, Read.*	.969	45	11	20	1	32	1
De La Cruz, Fernando, Tren.	1.000	3	0	2	0	2	0
De La Cruz, Francisco, Nor.	1.000	2	0	1	0	1	0
Delahoya, Javier, Bow.	1.000	6	3	3	0	6	1
De Los Santos, Luis, Nor.	1.000	13	8	13	0	21	0
Dempster, Ryan, Port.	1.000	7	7	11	0	18	2
De Paula, Sean, Akr.	1.000	8	0	2	0	2	0
Deschenes, Marc, Akr.	.778	47	2	5	2	9	1
DeWitt, Scott, Port.*	1.000	50	4	9	0	13	1
Dixon, Tim, Har.*	.867	37	5	8	2	15	0
Dotel, Octavio, Bing.	.933	10	4	10	1	15	0
Dougherty, Tony, Akr.	.867	43	4	9	2	15	0
Doyle, Tom, N.H.*	1.000	6	1	2	0	3	0
Drabek, Doug, Bow.	1.000	1	1	1	0	2	0
Driskill, Travis, Akr.	1.000	5	0	3	0	3	0
Duncan, Geoff, Port.	1.000	42	3	4	0	7	1
Durocher, Jayson, Har.	1.000	10	0	1	0	1	0
Dykhoff, Radhames, Bow.*	.875	38	2	12	2	16	2
Eibey, Scott, Bow.*	1.000	24	2	2	0	4	0
Einertson, Darrell, Nor.	1.000	17	0	9	0	9	0
Estes, Eric, Bow.	.500	9	3	9	0	12	0
Evans, Dave, Bow.	.500	14	0	1	1	2	0
Evans, Keith, Har.	.963	20	6	20	1	27	3
FERNANDEZ, Jared, Tren.	1.000	36	10	29	0	39	1
Fernandez, Osvaldo, Bing.*	1.000	7	0	4	0	4	0
Fesh, Sean, Read.*	.938	31	1	14	1	16	1
Figueroa, Nelson, Bing.	.966	21	9	19	1	29	1
Flener, Huck, Akr.*	1.000	12	7	19	0	26	1
Flury, Pat, Tren.	1.000	26	0	5	0	5	0
Fontenot, Joe, Tren.	.917	7	3	8	1	12	0
Forster, Scott, Har.*	.929	25	5	8	1	14	2
Fussell, Chris, Bow.	.889	18	4	12	2	18	0
Gallaher, Kevin, Bow.	1.000	9	1	2	0	3	0
Garza, Alberto, Akr.	1.000	4	0	2	0	2	0
Glinatsis, George, N.H.	1.000	12	1	5	0	6	0
Gonzalez, Lariel, N.H.	1.000	58	4	4	0	8	0
Gooch, Arnold, Bing.	.912	27	20	32	5	57	1
Gourdin, Tom, N.B.	.850	47	7	10	3	20	0
Guerra, Mark, Bing.	1.000	30	2	2	0	4	0
Hackman, Luther, N.H.	.946	28	9	26	2	37	1
Harris, Jeff, N.B.	1.000	26	0	6	0	6	1
Henderson, Ryan, Bing.	1.000	29	2	6	0	8	0
Heredia, Maximo, Bow.	.750	5	1	2	1	4	0
Heredia, Wilson, Nor.	1.000	5	4	5	0	9	0
Hernandez, Francis, Bow.	1.000	21	4	3	0	7	0
Jacobsen, Joe, Port.	1.000	3	1	0	0	1	0
Janzen, Marty, Nor.	.900	11	6	3	1	10	0
Jean, Domingo, N.H.	1.000	12	2	2	0	4	0
Johnson, Barry, Nor.	1.000	7	0	2	0	2	0
Johnson, Mark, Port.	.963	26	11	15	1	27	2
Johnson, Mike, Har.	1.000	7	4	3	0	7	0
Kamieniecki, Scott, Bow.	1.000	3	1	3	0	4	0
Kawabata, Kyle, Read.	1.000	7	1	1	0	2	0
Kelley, Rich, Bow.*	1.000	18	5	19	0	24	0
Kohlmeier, Ryan, Bow.	1.000	42	1	1	0	2	0
Kusiewicz, Mike, N.H.*	.932	27	8	33	3	44	1
Lail, Denny, Nor.	1.000	8	3	4	0	7	1
Lane, Aaron, Bow.*	1.000	15	1	13	0	14	1
Leese, Brandon, Port.	.944	20	9	25	2	36	3
Lidle, Kevin, N.H.	1.000	1	0	1	0	1	0
Lincoln, Mike, N.B.	.983	26	17	42	1	60	3
Lisio, Joe, Nor.	1.000	1	0	1	0	1	0
Lyons, Mike, Bing.	.778	29	3	4	2	9	0
Maeda, Kats, Nor.	1.000	28	3	8	0	11	0
Mahaffey, Alan, N.B.*	1.000	34	1	5	0	6	0
Marquez, Robert, Har.	1.000	4	2	1	0	3	0
Martinez, Ramiro, Har.*	.800	10	0	4	1	5	0
Martinez, Willie, Akr.	.909	26	20	30	5	55	3
Mathews, Terry, Bow.	1.000	1	0	2	0	2	1
Mays, Jarrod, Akr.	1.000	15	5	5	0	10	0
Mays, Joe, N.B.	1.000	11	4	3	0	7	0
McCommon, Jason, Har.-Bow.	.968	29	12	18	1	31	1
McCrary, Scott, Bing.	1.000	1	2	0	0	2	0
Mejia, Javier, Read.	1.000	8	0	2	0	2	0
Merrick, Brett, Akr.*	1.000	12	1	3	0	4	0
Miadich, Bart, Tren.	.833	22	6	4	2	12	0
Mitchell, Larry, Bow.	1.000	4	0	1	0	1	0
Mitchell, Scott, Har.	.977	32	18	24	1	43	2
Molina, Gabe, Bow.	.833	47	3	7	2	12	1
Moore, Joel, N.H.	1.000	13	2	11	0	13	1
Moore, Marcus, Akr.	.875	23	7	7	2	16	0
Moraga, David, Har.*	.917	19	4	7	1	12	1
Mota, Guillermo, Har.	1.000	12	1	2	0	3	0
Mull, Blaine, Port.	.909	9	2	8	1	11	0
Murray, Dan, Bing.	.957	27	14	31	2	47	4
Narcisse, Tyrone, Nor.	.833	29	3	7	2	12	0
Niebla, Ruben, Har.*	.800	24	0	4	1	5	0
Nyari, Pete, Read.	.813	53	4	9	3	16	2
Pageler, Mick, Port.	.917	60	5	6	1	12	0
Parker, Christian, Har.	.938	36	13	32	3	48	1
Paronto, Chad, Bow.	.500	8	1	0	1	2	0
Perkins, Dan, N.B.	.938	20	8	22	2	32	1
Phelps, Tommy, Har.*	.889	12	3	5	1	9	1
Phillips, Ben, Nor.	1.000	16	1	2	0	3	0
Pontes, Dan, Bing.	1.000	49	6	3	0	9	0
Powell, Jeremy, Har.	.917	22	17	16	3	36	1
Price, Tom, N.H.*	1.000	38	4	10	0	14	0
Pumphrey, Ken, Bing.	1.000	3	1	4	0	5	0
Radlosky, Rob, N.B.	1.000	27	4	13	0	17	0
Rakers, Jason, Akr.	.800	5	0	4	1	5	1
Ramsay, Robert, Tren.*	.892	27	7	26	4	37	0
Randall, Scott, N.H.	.970	29	25	39	2	66	3
Rector, Bobby, Port.	1.000	14	4	3	0	7	1
Redman, Mark, N.B.*	.929	8	3	10	1	14	0
Resz, Greg, Nor.	.900	19	4	5	1	10	0
Richards, Mark, Port.	1.000	40	6	12	0	18	2
Ricken, Ray, Nor.	.950	14	2	17	1	20	3
Riske, David, Akr.	1.000	2	0	1	0	1	0
Ritz, Kevin, N.H.	1.000	3	0	1	0	1	0
Rodgers, Bobby, Port.	.923	14	5	7	1	13	0
Rogers, Jason, Bow.*	1.000	38	2	6	0	8	0
Romero, J.C., N.B.*	.920	51	6	17	2	25	0
Rose, Brian, Tren.	1.000	24	3	5	0	8	0
Rose, Scott, Nor.	1.000	26	2	11	0	13	0
St. Pierre, Bob, Nor.	.900	24	6	3	1	10	0
Salamon, John, N.H.	.700	53	1	6	3	10	0
Sanders, Frankie, Akr.	.981	29	19	32	1	52	3
Schlomann, Brett, Nor.	.889	30	11	29	5	45	1
Scott, Darryl, Read.	1.000	8	0	2	0	2	0
Sekany, Jason, Tren.	.938	28	7	23	2	32	2
Sexton, Jeff, Akr.	.857	27	2	10	2	14	0
Shelby, Anthony, Nor.*	1.000	1	0	1	0	1	0
Shepherd, Alvie, Bow.	1.000	6	1	5	0	6	0
Shoemaker, Stephen, N.H.	.944	15	11	6	1	18	0
Shumaker, Anthony, Read.*	.972	38	11	24	1	36	3
Smart, J.D., Har.	1.000	14	8	13	0	21	0
Smetana, Steve, Tren.*	.955	49	6	15	1	22	1
Smith, Hut, Bow.-Read.	.864	28	6	13	3	22	3
Snyder, Matt, Bow.	1.000	22	5	11	0	16	1

Player, Team	Pct.	G	PO	A	E	TC	DP
Steed, Rick, Bing.	1.000	9	4	4	0	8	0
Stentz, Brent, N.B.	1.000	57	2	7	0	9	0
Stevens, Kris, Read.*	1.000	25	4	22	0	26	3
Stevenson, Rodney, Har.	1.000	37	3	3	0	6	0
Stewart, Rachaad, Bow.*	1.000	5	0	3	0	3	0
Stewart, Scott, Bing.*	.889	24	3	13	2	18	0
Tejera, Michael, Port.*	1.000	18	4	21	0	25	0
Tessmer, Jay, Nor.	.923	45	5	7	1	13	3
Thomas, Evan, Read.	1.000	24	13	9	0	22	2
Towers, Josh, Bow.	1.000	5	2	3	0	5	0
Townsend, Dave, Port.	1.000	11	0	2	0	2	0
Turrentine, Rich, Bing.	1.000	28	0	6	0	6	1
Tweedlie, Brad, Tren.	1.000	35	4	9	0	13	1
Twiggs, Greg, Bow.*	1.000	31	2	10	0	12	1
Uchiyama, Tomoyuki, Read.	1.000	43	12	24	0	36	1
Urso, Sal, Tren.*	.892	69	6	27	4	37	0
Valera, Julio, Tren.	1.000	5	2	5	0	7	0
Vardijan, Dan, Port.	1.000	19	1	7	0	8	0
Vasquez, Leo, Bing.*	1.000	14	0	6	0	6	1
Vavrek, Mike, N.H.*	.889	19	6	10	2	18	2
Veniard, Jay, Bing.*	.667	11	0	2	1	3	1

Player, Team	Pct.	G	PO	A	E	TC	DP
Viano, Jake, Akr.	1.000	9	1	0	0	1	0
Villafuerte, Brandon, Port.	.938	30	6	9	1	16	1
White, Walt, Port.	1.000	3	0	1	0	1	0
Williams, Matt, Nor.*	.977	31	8	34	1	43	1
Williams, Shad, Nor.	1.000	9	6	6	0	12	0
Wolf, Randy, Read.*	1.000	4	3	8	0	11	0
Woods, Brian, N.H.	.875	31	1	6	1	8	0
Yarnall, Ed, Bing.-Port.*	1.000	9	0	12	0	12	1
Yennaco, Jay, Tren.	1.000	9	3	3	0	6	0
Young, Tim, Har.*	1.000	26	1	4	0	5	0
Zancanaro, Dave, Nor.*	1.000	16	8	10	0	18	0
Zolecki, Mike, N.H.	1.000	8	1	3	0	4	0

PITCHERS WITH TWO OR MORE TEAMS

Player, Team	Pct.	G	PO	A	E	TC	DP
McCommon, Jason, Har.	1.000	6	1	3	0	4	1
McCommon, Jason, Bow.	.963	23	11	15	1	27	0
Smith, Hut, Bow.	.800	6	1	3	1	5	0
Smith, Hut, Read.	.882	22	5	10	2	17	3
Yarnall, Ed, Bing.*	1.000	7	0	9	0	9	1
Yarnall, Ed, Port.*	1.000	2	0	3	0	3	0

The following players did not have any fielding statistics at the positions indicated ar appeared only as a designated hitter, pinch-hitter or pinch-runner: Azuaje, p; Bady, p; Betts, 1b; Bierek, of; Chamblee, of; H. Clark, p; T. Clark, p; Costa, p; DeCinces, of; Gibralter, of; Grifol, of; Landry, p; Luzinski, of; McCurtain, p; Medina, p; E. Morales, p; Mucker, p; Niedermaier, p; Ortiz, p; Y. Perez, p; Raifstanger, 3b, c, p; N. Rodriguez, p; S. Rodriguez, 1b; Sackinsky, p; Shuey, p; Steinmetz, p; Tebbs, p; C. Thomas, dh; Whitlock, p, of; Whitten, p; Yeskie, p.

LEAGUE CHAMPIONS

Year	Team	Pct.
1923—	Williamsport	.661
1924—	Williamsport	.654
1925—	York§	.583
	Williamsport§	.583
1926—	Scranton	.627
1927—	Harrisburg	.630
1928—	Harrisburg	.603
1929—	Binghamton	.597
1930—	Wilkes-Barre	.572
1931—	Harrisburg	.597
1932—	Wilkes-Barre	.561
1933—	Binghamton	.690
1934—	Binghamton	.694
	Williamsport*	.603
1935—	Scranton	.657
	Binghamton*	.580
1936—	Scranton*	.609
	Elmira	.629
1937—	Elmira†	.622
1938—	Binghamton	.622
	Elmira (3rd)‡	.522
1939—	Scranton†	.571
1940—	Scranton	.568
	Binghamton (2nd)‡	.554
1941—	Wilkes-Barre	.630
	Elmira (3rd)‡	.514
1942—	Albany	.600
	Scranton (2nd)‡	.593
1943—	Scranton	.630
	Elmira (2nd)‡	.568
1944—	Hartford	.723
	Binghamton (4th)‡	.474
1945—	Utica	.615
	Albany (3rd)‡	.564
1946—	Scranton†	.691
1947—	Utica†	.652
1948—	Scranton†	.636
1949—	Albany	.664
	Binghamton (4th)‡	.500
1950—	Wilkes-Barre‡	.652
1951—	Wilkes-Barre‡	.612
	Scranton (2nd)†	.562

Year	Team	Pct.
1952—	Albany	.603
	Binghamton (2nd)‡	.562
1953—	Reading	.682
	Binghamton (2nd)‡	.636
1954—	Wilkes-Barre	.576
	Albany (3rd)‡	.540
1955—	Reading	.613
	Allentown (2nd)‡	.565
1956—	Schenectady†	.609
1957—	Binghamton	.607
	Reading (3rd)‡	.529
1958—	Lancaster∞	.568
	Binghamton (6th)‡	.493
1959—	Springfield†	.607
1960—	Williamsport▲	.551
	Springfield (3rd)▲	.496
1961—	Springfield	.612
1962—	Williamsport	.593
	Elmira (2nd)‡	.514
1963—	Charleston	.593
1964—	Elmira	.586
1965—	Pittsfield	.607
1966—	Elmira	.633
1967—	Binghamton◆	.586
	Elmira	.532
1968—	Pittsfield	.604
	Reading (2nd)‡	.579
1969—	York	.640
1970—	Waterbury■	.560
	Reading■	.553
1971—	Three Rivers	.569
	Elmira▼	.561
1972—	West Haven▼	.600
	Three Rivers	.559
1973—	Reading▼	.551
	Pittsfield	.551
1974—	Thetford Miners (2nd)•	.536
	Pittsfield (2nd)	.496
1975—	Reading	.613
	Bristol*	.587
1976—	Three Rivers	.601
	West Haven††	.576

Year	Team	Pct.
1977—	West Haven‡‡	.623
	Three Rivers	.551
1978—	Reading	.642
	Bristol*	.580
1979—	West Haven§§	.597
1980—	Holyoke*	.561
	Waterbury	.540
1981—	Glens Falls	.615
	Bristol*	.577
1982—	West Haven*	.614
	Lynn	.590
1983—	Lynn	.554
	New Britain‡	.518
1984—	Waterbury	.543
	Vermont‡	.536
1985—	Albany	.540
	Vermont‡	.514
1986—	Reading	.566
	Vermont‡	.554
1987—	Pittsfield	.630
	Harrisburg‡	.550
1988—	Glens Falls	.584
	Albany‡	.522
1989—	Albany‡	.657
	Harrisburg	.522
1990—	Albany	.568
	London‡	.547
1991—	Harrisburg	.621
	Albany‡	.543
1992—	Canton/Akron	.580
	Binghamton‡	.572
1993—	Harrisburg‡	.681
	Canton/Akron	.543
1994—	Harrisburg	.633
	Binghamton‡	.582
1995—	New Haven	.556
	Reading‡	.514
1996—	Portland	.589
	Harrisburg‡	.521
1997—	Harrisburg‡	.606
	Portland	.556
1998—	New Britain	.585
	Harrisburg‡	.514

*Won split-season playoff. †Won championship and four-team playoff. ‡Won four-team playoff. §Tied for pennant, York winning playoff. ∞League was divided into Northern, Southern divisions and played a split season; Lancaster was overall season leader. ▲Playoff finals canceled after one game because of rain with Williamsport and Springfield declared playoff co-champions. ◆League was divided into Eastern, Western divisions; Binghamton won playoff. ■Tied for pennant, Waterbury winning playoff. ▼League was divided into American, National divisions; won playoff. •League was divided into American and National divisions; won four-team playoff. ††League was divided into Northern, Southern divisions, won playoff. ‡‡League was divided into New England and Canadian-American divisions; won playoff. §§Won both halves of split season (no playoffs). (NOTE—Known as New York-Pennsylvania League prior to 1938.)

CLASS AA Eastern League

SOUTHERN LEAGUE

LEAGUE OFFICE

President/secretary-treasurer
Arnold Fielkow

Address
1 Depot St., Suite 300
Marietta, GA 30060

Phone
770-428-4749

TEAMS

BIRMINGHAM BARONS
General manager
Tony Ensor
Manager
Chris Cron
Ballpark (capacity, surface)
Hoover Metropolitan Stadium
(10,800, grass)
Affiliation
White Sox
Address
P.O. Box 360007
Birmingham, AL 35236
Phone
205-988-3200

CAROLINA MUDCATS
General manager
Joe Kremer
Manager
Jay Loviglio
Ballpark (capacity, surface)
Five County Stadium (4,500, grass)
Affiliation
Rockies
Address
P.O. Drawer 1218
Zebulon, NC 27597
Phone
919-269-2287

CHATTANOOGA LOOKOUTS
President
J. Frank Burke
General manager
Rich Mozingo
Manager
Phillip Wellman
Ballpark (capacity, surface)
Historic Engel Stadium (7,500, grass)
Affiliation
Reds
Address
P.O. Box 11002
Chattanooga, TN 37401
Phone
423-267-2208

GREENVILLE BRAVES
General manager
Steve DeSalvo

Manager
Paul Runge
Ballpark (capacity, surface)
Greenville Municipal Stadium (7,027,
grass)
Affiliation
Braves
Address
P.O. Box 16683
Greenville, SC 29606
Phone
864-299-3456

HUNTSVILLE STARS
President/general manager
Don Mincher
Manager
Darrell Evans
Ballpark (capacity, surface)
Joe W. Davis Stadium (10,400, grass)
Affiliation
Brewers
Address
P.O. Box 2769
Huntsville, AL 35804
Phone
256-882-2562

JACKSONVILLE SUNS
Vice president/general manager
Peter Bragan Jr.
Manager
Dave Anderson
Ballpark (capacity, surface)
Wolfson Park (8,200, grass)
Affiliation
Tigers
Address
P.O. Box 4756
Jacksonville, FL 32201
Phone
904-358-2846

KNOXVILLE SMOKIES
General manager
Dan Rajkowski
Manager
Omar Malave
Ballpark (capacity, surface)
Bill Meyer Stadium (6,412, grass)
Affiliation
Blue Jays

Address
633 Jessamine St.
Knoxville, TN 37917
Phone
423-637-9494

MOBILE BAYBEARS
General manager
Tom Simmons
Manager
Mike Basso
Ballpark (capacity, surface)
Hank Aaron Stadium (6,000, grass)
Affiliation
Padres
Address
P.O. Box 161663
Mobile, AL 36616
Phone
334-476-2287

ORLANDO RAYS
General manager
Tom Ramsberger
Manager
To be announced
Ballpark (capacity, surface)
Tinker Field (6,102, grass)
Affiliation
Devil Rays
Address
287 S. Tampa Ave.
Orlando, FL 32805
Phone
407-245-2827

WEST TENN DIAMOND JAXX
Assistant general manager
Brian Cheever
Manager
Dave Trembley
Ballpark (capacity, surface)
Pringles Park (6,000, grass)
Affiliation
Cubs
Address
4 Fun Place
Jackson, TN 38305
Phone
901-664-2020

CLASS AA *Southern League*

– 452 –

1998 FINAL STANDINGS

FIRST HALF

EAST DIVISION

Team	W	L	T	Pct.	GB
Jacksonville (Tigers)	48	22	0	.686	....
Orlando (Mariners)	32	38	0	.457	16.0
Knoxville (Blue Jays)	32	38	0	.457	16.0
Carolina (Pirates)	31	39	0	.443	17.0
Greenville (Braves)	30	40	0	.429	18.0

WEST DIVISION

Team	W	L	T	Pct.	GB
Mobile (Padres)	42	28	0	.600	....
Huntsville (Athletics)	40	30	0	.572	2.0
West Tenn (Cubs)	38	32	0	.543	4.0
Birmingham (White Sox)	32	38	0	.457	10.0
Chattanooga (Reds)	25	45	0	.357	17.0

SECOND HALF

EAST DIVISION

Team	W	L	T	Pct.	GB
Knoxville (Blue Jays)	39	31	0	.557	....
Jacksonville (Tigers)	38	32	0	.543	1.0
Greenville (Braves)	37	32	0	.536	1.5
Orlando (Mariners)	35	33	0	.515	3.0
Carolina (Pirates)	28	41	0	.406	10.5

WEST DIVISION

Team	W	L	T	Pct.	GB
Mobile (Padres)	44	26	0	.629	....
Chattanooga (Reds)	40	28	0	.588	3.0
Huntsville (Athletics)	32	38	0	.457	12.0
West Tenn (Cubs)	28	42	0	.400	16.0
Birmingham (White Sox)	26	44	0	.371	18.0

COMPOSITE

Team	Mob.	Jax.	Hun.	Knox.	Orl.	Gre.	W.T.	Chat.	Car.	Birm.	W	L	T	Pct.	GB
Mobile (Padres)	....	7	8	9	8	11	13	7	11	12	86	54	0	.614	....
Jacksonville (Tigers)	9	....	11	8	11	10	7	10	11	9	86	54	0	.614	....
Huntsville (Athletics)	7	5	....	9	13	7	8	9	9	5	72	68	0	.514	14.0
Knoxville (Blue Jays)	6	7	6	....	10	11	6	8	8	9	71	69	0	.507	15.0
Orlando (Cubs)	6	5	3	6	....	7	12	9	9	10	67	71	0	.486	18.0
Greenville (Braves)	5	5	8	5	9	....	9	7	8	11	67	72	0	.482	18.5
West Tenn (Cubs)	3	9	8	10	4	6	....	10	7	9	66	74	0	.471	20.0
Chattanooga (Reds)	9	6	7	8	3	8	6	....	9	9	65	73	0	.471	20.0
Carolina (Pirates)	5	4	7	7	7	7	8	6	....	8	59	80	0	.424	26.5
Birmingham (White Sox)	4	6	10	7	6	5	5	7	8	....	58	82	0	.414	28.0

Carolina's home games played in Zebulon, N.C.; West Tenn's home games played in Jackson, Tenn.

Major league affiliations in parentheses.

PLAYOFFS—Jacksonville defeated Knoxville three games to none; Mobile defeated Huntsville three games to none; Mobile defeated Jacksonville three games to one to win league championship.

REGULAR-SEASON ATTENDANCE: Birmingham, 298,054; Carolina, 230,768; Chattanooga, 230,475; Greenville, 269,525; Huntsville, 257,915; Jacksonville, 254,882; Knoxville, 122,886; Mobile, 271,002; Orlando, 144,126; West Tenn, 313,775. Total—2,393,408; Playoffs (10 games)—21,700. Class AA All-Star Game at New Haven, Conn.—6,248.

MANAGERS: Birmingham, Dave Huppert; Carolina, Jeff Banister; Chattanooga, Mark Berry; Greenville, Randy Ingle; Huntsville, Jeffrey Leonard; Jacksonville, Dave Anderson; Knoxville, Omar Malave; Mobile, Mike Ramsey; Orlando, Dan Rohn; West Tenn, Dave Trembley.

ALL-STAR TEAM: 1B—Mike Mitchell, Mobile; 2B—Jose Macias, Jacksonville; 3B—Eric Chavez, Huntsville; SS—Jose Nieves, West Tenn; OF—Gabe Kapler, Jacksonville; Emil Brown, Carolina; George Lombard, Greenville; Mike Darr, Mobile; DH—Robert Fick, Jacksonville; C—Ben Davis, Mobile; Utility—John Powers, Mobile; RHP—Kevin Beirne, Birmingham; LHP—Bruce Chen, Greenville; RP—Sean Spencer, Orlando; Most Valuable Player—Gabe Kapler, Jacksonville; Most Outstanding Pitcher—Bruce Chen, Greenville; Hustler of the Year—Nick Presto, Chattanooga; Manager of the Year—Mike Ramsey, Mobile.

1998 BATTING

TEAM

Team	Avg.	G	TPA	AB	R	H	TB	2B	3B	HR	RBI	SH	SF	HP	BB	IBB	SO	SB	CS	GDP	LOB	ShO	Slg.	OBP
Jacksonville	.290	140	5587	4878	882	1416	2230	323	46	133	828	23	68	56	562	22	908	105	41	82	1055	4	.457	.366
Knoxville	.276	140	5402	4701	795	1298	2085	280	39	143	735	42	45	42	572	11	866	121	76	98	980	3	.444	.357
Huntsville	.272	140	5504	4647	810	1266	1992	248	23	144	748	55	48	69	685	17	965	161	79	114	1050	4	.429	.371
Carolina	.271	140	5358	4626	706	1255	1882	239	35	106	626	43	53	59	571	25	911	125	66	119	1036	4	.407	.355
Mobile	.270	140	5599	4858	794	1312	2025	284	39	117	730	34	35	42	630	22	976	124	41	96	1112	8	.417	.357
Birmingham	.266	140	5307	4648	670	1235	1845	226	30	108	625	42	36	52	529	16	893	99	61	126	984	10	.397	.345
Greenville	.264	139	5361	4668	676	1232	1937	263	26	130	613	53	43	60	537	31	1036	146	87	115	968	5	.415	.345
West Tenn	.263	140	5392	4698	696	1236	1816	238	48	82	623	42	41	58	553	24	964	183	96	111	978	12	.387	.345
Chattanooga	.261	138	5322	4687	663	1222	1862	255	41	101	596	39	53	33	510	14	1007	67	54	109	997	6	.397	.334
Orlando	.256	138	5399	4652	691	1192	1757	213	41	90	626	34	50	68	595	15	883	116	73	103	1056	6	.378	.346

INDIVIDUAL

TOP QUALIFIERS FOR BATTING CHAMPIONSHIP

Minimum 378 plate appearances. *Lefthanded batter. †Switch-hitter.

Player, Team	Avg.	G	TPA	AB	R	H	TB	2B	3B	HR	RBI	SH	SF	HP	BB	IBB	SO	SB	CS	GDP	Slg.	OBP
LaRue, Jason, Chat.	.365	105	446	386	71	141	238	39	8	14	82	1	9	10	40	0	60	4	3	13	.617	.429
Brown, Emil, Car.	.330	123	536	466	89	154	231	31	2	14	67	0	9	11	50	2	71	24	7	12	.496	.401
Chavez, Eric, Hun.*	.328	88	384	335	66	110	205	27	1	22	86	3	3	1	42	4	61	12	4	6	.612	.402
Kapler, Gabe, Jack.	.322	139	629	547	113	176	319	47	6	28	146	0	11	5	66	5	93	6	4	6	.583	.393
Villalobos, Carlos, Jack.	.320	128	561	497	96	159	251	34	2	18	80	0	6	3	55	2	85	8	0	16	.505	.387
Fick, Robert, Jack.*	.318	130	601	515	101	164	277	47	6	18	114	0	9	6	71	6	83	8	4	8	.538	.401
Mitchell, Mike, Mob.*	.318	134	574	509	72	162	243	32	2	15	97	0	3	1	61	1	95	0	0	7	.477	.390
Lopez, Luis, Knox.	.313	119	519	450	70	141	215	27	1	15	85	0	8	3	58	3	55	0	2	18	.478	.389

Player, Team	Avg.	G	TPA	AB	R	H	TB	2B	3B	HR	RBI	SH	SF	HP	BB	IBB	SO	SB	CS	GDP	Slg.	OBP
Darr, Mike, Mob.*	.310	132	596	523	105	162	229	41	4	6	90	1	5	5	62	2	79	28	8	18	.438	.385
Smith, Demond, Birm.†	.308	84	383	321	75	99	151	23	7	5	30	4	4	6	48	1	67	25	14	2	.470	.404
Lombard, George, Gre.*	.308	122	507	422	84	130	229	25	4	22	65	5	4	5	71	10	140	35	5	2	.543	.410
Macias, Jose, Jack.†	.305	128	573	511	82	156	240	28	10	12	71	3	3	4	52	2	46	6	9	4	.470	.372
Powers, John, Mob.*	.303	127	566	476	92	144	215	27	4	12	52	4	2	8	76	1	76	9	6	8	.452	.406
Salzano, Jerry, Gre.	.302	101	382	324	48	98	144	19	3	7	49	2	2	8	46	1	67	14	8	8	.444	.400
Lee, Carlos, Birm.	.302	138	594	549	77	166	266	33	2	21	106	0	2	2	39	2	55	11	5	32	.485	.350
Gonzalez, Manny, Birm.†	.302	102	407	371	51	112	146	24	2	2	35	8	1	4	23	0	52	9	7	11	.394	.348

DEPARTMENTAL LEADERS: G—Inglin, Kapler, 139 each; AB—C. Lee, 549; R—Kapler, 113; H—Kapler, 176; TB—Kapler, 319; 2B—Fick, Kapler, 47 each; 3B—Porter, 11; HR—Kapler, 28; RBI—Kapler, 146; SH—Peeples, 17; SF—Kapler, 11; HP—R. Hernandez, 19; BB—M. Johnson, 105; IBB—Lombard, 10; SO—Ingram, 169; SB—Porter, 50; CS—Eaglin, 19; GIDP—C. Lee, 32; Slg.—LaRue, .617; OBP—M. Johnson, .443.

ALL PLAYERS
*Lefthanded batter. †Switch-hitter.

Player, Team	Avg.	G	TPA	AB	R	H	TB	2B	3B	HR	RBI	SH	SF	HP	BB	IBB	SO	SB	CS	GDP	Slg.	OBP
Ah Yat, Paul, Car.	.000	13	12	9	0	0	0	0	0	0	0	1	0	0	2	0	4	0	0	0	.000	.182
Alcantara, Israel, Orl.	.236	15	65	55	8	13	26	4	0	3	18	0	3	0	7	0	15	0	1	0	.473	.308
Allen, Dusty, Mob.	.253	42	189	154	30	39	75	10	4	6	42	0	2	1	32	1	26	1	0	3	.487	.381
Allen, Marlon, Chat.	.234	87	346	312	36	73	105	14	0	6	33	1	2	2	29	0	91	1	5	7	.337	.301
Anderson, Bill, Mob.	.000	13	5	3	0	0	0	0	0	0	0	0	0	0	2	0	0	0	0	0	.000	.400
Ardoin, Danny, Hun.	.248	109	439	363	67	90	159	21	0	16	62	6	1	7	62	0	87	8	4	10	.438	.367
Arnold, Jamie, Gre.	.333	33	8	6	1	2	5	0	1	0	1	4	1	1	0	0	3	0	0	0	.833	.286
Arroyo, Bronson, Car.	.200	23	17	15	1	3	5	2	0	0	1	1	0	0	1	0	8	0	0	0	.333	.250
Asche, Mike, Car.	.259	65	254	212	44	55	86	14	4	3	26	1	1	3	37	0	45	15	6	2	.406	.373
Averette, Robert, Chat.	.167	14	13	12	0	2	2	0	0	0	0	1	0	0	0	0	2	0	0	1	.167	.167
Baez, Kevin, Chat.	.256	49	210	180	30	46	56	10	0	0	22	1	2	1	26	1	27	0	1	6	.311	.349
Balfe, Ryan, Mob.†	.232	23	77	69	9	16	29	5	1	2	11	0	0	0	8	0	10	1	0	3	.420	.312
Barker, Glen, Jack.†	.280	110	526	453	95	127	186	29	6	6	54	7	5	4	57	1	120	31	7	1	.411	.362
Barker, Richie, W.T.	.000	51	3	3	0	0	0	0	0	0	0	0	0	0	0	0	2	0	0	0	.000	.000
Bass, Jayson, Gre.†	.227	86	279	233	27	53	80	10	1	5	18	6	2	1	37	1	60	11	6	2	.343	.333
Battle, Howard, Birm.-Gre.	.312	91	376	330	47	103	171	31	2	11	55	0	5	2	39	2	58	3	2	12	.518	.383
Bautista, Danny, Gre.	.333	2	7	6	1	2	5	0	0	1	2	0	0	0	1	1	1	0	0	0	.833	.429
Bautista, Juan, Birm.	.255	120	451	420	46	107	137	13	1	5	34	6	3	4	18	1	98	6	12	18	.326	.290
Beasley, Tony, Car.	.286	6	8	7	2	2	3	1	0	0	1	0	0	1	0	2	0	0	0	.429	.375
Berry, Jason, Hun.	.000	14	1	1	0	0	0	0	0	0	0	0	0	0	0	0	1	0	0	0	.000	.000
Blake, Casey, Knox.	.372	45	199	172	41	64	108	15	4	7	38	0	3	2	22	0	25	10	0	6	.628	.442
Borbon, Pedro, Gre.*	.000	16	1	1	0	0	0	0	0	0	0	0	0	0	0	0	1	0	0	0	.000	.000
Bowers, Brent, Knox.*	.280	27	124	107	19	30	43	5	1	2	12	1	0	0	16	1	18	9	1	3	.402	.374
Bowie, Micah, Gre.*	.208	30	29	24	1	5	5	0	0	0	4	2	0	0	3	0	6	0	0	0	.208	.296
Bowles, Justin, Hun.*	.277	74	319	274	50	76	129	21	4	10	48	4	3	1	37	0	60	2	1	11	.471	.362
Bream, Scott, Jack.†	.291	58	237	206	30	60	91	16	3	3	36	2	3	1	25	0	41	3	1	3	.442	.366
Bridges, Kary, W.T.*	.306	48	216	196	30	60	69	7	1	0	21	1	1	0	18	1	9	6	4	4	.352	.363
Briones, Chris, Mob.	.000	2	3	3	0	0	0	0	0	0	0	0	0	0	0	0	1	0	0	0	.000	.000
Brito, Luis, Car.†	.292	7	24	24	4	7	8	1	0	0	1	0	0	0	0	0	3	1	0	0	.333	.292
Brock, Tarrik, Orl.*	.277	111	443	372	76	103	190	28	7	15	65	1	5	6	59	4	110	17	9	2	.511	.380
Brooks, Ramy, Car.	.263	19	65	57	7	15	24	3	0	2	5	1	0	0	7	0	17	0	1	1	.421	.344
Brown, Chad, Car.*	.000	24	1	1	0	0	0	0	0	0	0	0	0	0	0	0	0	0	0	0	.000	.000
Brown, Emil, Car.	.330	123	536	466	89	154	231	31	2	14	67	0	9	11	50	2	71	24	7	12	.496	.401
Brown, Randy, Car.	.292	80	289	257	39	75	126	18	6	7	35	3	2	5	22	1	77	9	5	4	.490	.357
Brown, Roosevelt, W.T.*	.263	42	176	160	20	42	71	11	0	6	24	0	1	2	13	1	30	3	1	6	.444	.324
Buhner, Shawn, Orl.	.241	99	402	348	48	84	132	14	2	10	49	4	0	3	47	0	98	1	3	15	.379	.337
Byrne, Earl, W.T.*	.000	15	13	11	0	0	0	0	0	0	0	0	0	0	2	0	6	0	0	1	.000	.154
Candelaria, Ben, Knox.*	.333	36	168	156	33	52	96	8	3	10	31	1	1	1	9	0	31	0	3	2	.615	.371
Cardenas, Johnny, Birm.	.200	17	57	55	3	11	13	2	0	0	8	1	0	0	1	0	8	0	0	1	.236	.214
Cardona, Javier, Jack.	.331	46	181	163	31	54	84	16	1	4	40	0	2	1	15	1	29	0	0	6	.515	.387
Carlyle, Buddy, Mob.*	.111	27	37	36	1	4	5	1	0	0	0	0	0	0	1	0	8	0	0	1	.139	.135
Carroll, Dave, Hun.	.000	20	1	1	0	0	0	0	0	0	0	0	0	0	0	0	0	0	0	0	.000	.000
Caruso, Gene, Car.*	.000	3	1	0	1	0	0	0	0	0	0	0	0	0	1	0	0	0	0	0	.000	1.000
Castleberry, Kevin, W.T.*	.285	44	177	151	26	43	57	9	1	1	15	2	3	0	21	0	19	7	4	4	.377	.366
Castro, Jose, Hun.†	.163	55	176	147	24	24	38	4	2	2	16	2	0	2	25	0	48	12	1	4	.259	.293
Chavez, Eric, Hun.*	.328	88	384	335	66	110	205	27	1	22	86	3	3	1	42	4	61	12	4	6	.612	.402
Chen, Bruce, Gre.†	.000	24	25	20	0	0	0	0	0	0	0	2	0	0	3	0	7	0	0	0	.000	.130
Clark, Brady, Chat.	.270	64	258	222	41	60	81	13	1	2	16	1	0	4	31	0	34	12	4	11	.365	.370
Clifford, Jim, Orl.*	.000	1	1	1	0	0	0	0	0	0	0	0	0	0	0	0	0	0	0	0	.000	.000
Cole, Victor, W.T.*	.000	19	1	1	0	0	0	0	0	0	0	0	0	0	0	0	0	0	0	0	.000	.000
Cordero, Wil, Birm.	.286	11	42	35	6	10	18	2	0	2	11	0	0	0	7	0	3	0	0	1	.514	.405
Corey, Mark, Chat.	.000	6	4	4	0	0	0	0	0	0	0	0	0	0	0	0	2	0	0	0	.000	.000
Corn, Chris, Car.	.143	8	13	7	2	1	1	0	0	0	2	3	0	0	3	0	4	0	0	0	.143	.400
Cotton, John, W.T.*	.292	90	347	319	46	93	152	14	3	13	53	0	5	4	19	1	68	10	3	3	.476	.334
Crowell, Jim, Chat.	.333	5	3	3	0	1	1	0	0	0	0	0	0	0	0	0	2	0	0	0	.333	.333
Cruz, Charlie, Gre.*	.000	49	5	3	1	0	0	0	0	0	0	1	0	0	1	0	2	0	0	0	.000	.250
Curl, John, Mob.*	.275	104	404	363	47	100	174	22	2	16	66	0	1	0	40	1	108	6	1	4	.479	.347
Curtis, Kevin, W.T.	.161	22	70	62	6	10	16	1	1	1	10	0	0	2	6	0	17	0	0	1	.258	.257
Daniels, David, Car.	.000	35	1	1	0	0	0	0	0	0	0	0	0	0	0	0	1	0	0	0	.000	.000
Darr, Mike, Mob.†	.310	132	596	523	105	162	229	41	4	6	90	1	5	5	62	2	79	28	8	18	.438	.385
Dascenzo, Doug, Mob.†	.391	12	26	23	5	9	9	0	0	0	2	0	0	0	3	0	2	2	0	0	.391	.462
Davis, Ben, Mob.†	.286	116	489	433	65	124	199	29	2	14	75	1	7	6	42	3	60	4	2	11	.460	.352
Davis, James, Chat.	.294	37	138	126	11	37	48	5	0	2	12	2	0	2	8	0	21	0	0	4	.381	.346
Davis, Kane, Car.	.200	18	12	10	0	2	2	0	0	0	1	1	0	0	1	0	8	0	0	0	.200	.273
Dean, Chris, Orl.†	.197	62	244	203	26	40	60	12	1	2	22	2	3	4	32	1	39	3	3	2	.296	.314
De Los Santos, Mariano, Car.	.000	10	1	1	0	0	0	0	0	0	0	0	0	0	0	0	1	0	0	0	.000	.000

Player, Team	Avg.	G	TPA	AB	R	H	TB	2B	3B	HR	RBI	SH	SF	HP	BB	IBB	SO	SB	CS	GDP	Slg.	OBP
Delgado, Jose, Gre.†	.125	21	75	64	3	8	14	3	0	1	5	0	0	0	11	0	7	2	2	2	.219	.253
DeRosa, Mark, Gre.	.267	125	533	461	67	123	177	26	2	8	49	5	2	5	60	2	57	7	13	18	.384	.356
Doman, Roger, Car.	.000	10	5	5	0	0	0	0	0	0	0	0	0	0	0	0	3	0	0	0	.000	.000
Donato, Dan, Orl.*	.333	4	15	12	1	4	4	0	0	0	1	0	0	0	3	0	1	0	0	1	.333	.467
Doughty, Brian, Mob.	.250	17	5	4	0	1	1	0	0	0	0	1	0	0	0	0	1	0	0	0	.250	.250
Downs, Brian, Birm.	.297	10	44	37	3	11	12	1	0	0	3	1	2	2	2	0	7	0	0	1	.324	.349
Drumheller, Al, Mob.	.091	51	12	11	0	1	1	0	0	0	2	0	0	0	1	0	1	0	0	0	.091	.167
Dubose, Brian, Jack.*	.236	46	179	165	30	39	72	10	1	7	25	0	0	1	13	1	39	4	0	3	.436	.296
Dubose, Eric, Hun.*	1.000	15	1	1	0	1	1	0	0	0	0	0	0	0	0	0	0	0	0	0	1.000	1.000
Duncan, Courtney, W.T.*	.105	29	24	19	0	2	2	0	0	0	1	3	0	0	2	0	12	0	0	0	.105	.190
Eaglin, Mike, Gre.	.256	129	570	492	84	126	179	22	2	9	47	10	4	13	51	1	107	30	19	11	.364	.339
Eddie, Steve, Chat.	.290	134	577	520	70	151	217	30	3	10	81	4	9	1	43	3	84	3	3	16	.417	.340
Ellis, Kevin, W.T.	.172	12	30	29	3	5	8	0	0	1	2	0	0	0	1	0	3	0	0	1	.276	.200
Encarnacion, Mario, Hun.	.272	110	425	357	70	97	161	15	2	15	61	3	1	4	60	1	123	11	8	9	.451	.382
Espada, Josue, Hun.	.255	51	198	161	29	41	53	7	1	1	22	5	1	4	27	0	15	7	4	4	.329	.373
Estes, Eric, Mob.	.100	17	12	10	1	1	1	0	0	0	1	1	0	0	1	0	2	0	0	0	.100	.182
Etler, Todd, Chat.	.000	46	3	3	0	0	0	0	0	0	0	0	0	0	0	0	1	0	0	0	.000	.000
Evans, Dave, Car.	.000	26	8	6	0	0	0	0	0	0	0	2	0	0	0	0	4	0	0	0	.000	.000
Faggett, Ethan, Mob.*	.247	54	186	162	22	40	53	2	1	3	25	3	2	3	16	1	40	7	1	4	.327	.321
Farnsworth, Kyle, W.T.†	.294	13	20	17	2	5	5	0	0	0	2	1	0	1	1	0	9	0	0	2	.294	.368
Farris, Mark, Car.*	.273	111	416	373	49	102	140	18	1	6	38	0	2	3	38	5	74	3	3	10	.375	.344
Fick, Robert, Jack.*	.318	130	601	515	101	164	277	47	6	18	114	0	9	6	71	6	83	8	4	8	.538	.401
Figueroa, Luis, Car.†	.249	117	435	350	54	87	102	9	3	0	24	10	2	2	71	3	46	6	5	12	.291	.376
Finn, John, Birm.	.274	44	189	146	37	40	57	6	1	3	15	3	2	4	34	0	12	4	4	3	.390	.419
Forkerway, Trey, W.T.	.197	57	182	152	13	30	35	2	0	1	6	9	0	0	21	0	28	4	2	2	.230	.295
Foster, Kevin, W.T.	.000	2	1	0	0	0	0	0	0	0	0	0	1	0	0	0	0	0	0	0	.000	.000
Frank, Mike, Chat.*	.325	58	255	231	43	75	131	12	4	12	43	0	3	1	19	1	28	5	2	3	.567	.374
Freel, Ryan, Knox.	.286	66	293	252	47	72	107	17	3	4	36	3	4	1	33	0	32	18	9	3	.425	.366
Freeman, Ricky, W.T.	.270	106	428	370	67	100	171	18	4	15	76	0	4	9	45	3	50	7	5	7	.462	.360
Freire, Alejandro, Jack.	.275	129	554	494	79	136	214	30	0	16	78	1	9	17	33	1	83	3	1	16	.433	.336
Furniss, Eddy, Car.*	.136	16	50	44	1	6	7	1	0	0	3	0	2	0	4	0	13	0	0	1	.159	.200
Gama, Rick, Mob.	.221	49	174	149	21	33	47	7	2	1	17	1	1	0	23	0	16	3	1	5	.315	.324
Garcia, Al, W.T.†	.000	25	10	10	0	0	0	0	0	0	0	0	0	0	0	0	4	0	0	0	.000	.000
Garrison, Webster, Hun.	.271	104	352	295	47	80	128	15	0	11	51	1	4	1	51	0	56	1	3	5	.434	.376
Gazarek, Marty, W.T.	.328	21	80	64	14	21	32	4	2	1	11	0	1	2	13	1	10	6	2	3	.500	.450
Giard, Ken, Car.	.000	42	1	1	0	0	0	0	0	0	0	0	0	0	0	0	0	0	0	0	.000	.000
Gibralter, Steve, Chat.	.269	17	75	67	8	18	25	4	0	1	4	1	0	1	6	0	13	1	0	3	.373	.338
Gissell, Chris, W.T.	.000	1	1	1	0	0	0	0	0	0	0	0	0	0	0	0	1	0	0	0	.000	.000
Glauber, Keith, Chat.	.000	2	1	1	0	0	0	0	0	0	0	0	0	0	0	0	0	0	0	0	.000	.000
Gonzalez, Jimmy, Mob.	.294	26	98	85	14	25	51	8	0	6	17	0	0	0	13	0	22	0	0	1	.600	.388
Gonzalez, Manny, Birm.†	.302	102	407	371	51	112	146	24	2	2	35	8	1	4	23	0	52	9	7	11	.394	.348
Gonzalez, Ricky, Birm.	.219	23	84	73	5	16	18	2	0	0	11	3	1	0	7	0	18	0	0	2	.247	.284
Gonzalez, Wikleman, Mob.	.388	22	85	67	20	26	47	9	0	4	26	0	2	2	14	0	4	0	0	1	.701	.494
Goodell, Steve, Gre.	.278	5	22	18	7	5	15	1	0	3	6	0	0	1	3	0	3	0	0	1	.833	.409
Grigsby, Benji, W.T.	.500	35	4	2	2	1	1	0	0	0	1	0	0	0	2	0	1	0	0	0	.500	.750
Grijak, Kevin, Car.*	.349	41	171	146	29	51	86	8	0	9	33	0	3	4	18	2	15	1	0	4	.589	.427
Guevara, Giomar, Orl.	.333	14	54	45	13	15	22	5	1	0	6	1	0	0	8	0	11	0	0	3	.489	.434
Gunther, Kevin, Hun.	.000	45	1	1	0	0	0	0	0	0	0	0	0	0	0	0	0	0	0	0	.000	.000
Guthrie, David, Chat.†	.192	67	225	203	23	39	52	5	4	0	9	3	0	3	16	0	58	1	1	3	.256	.261
Guzman, Domingo, Mob.	.000	12	7	7	0	0	0	0	0	0	0	0	0	0	0	0	7	0	0	0	.000	.000
Hall, Ronnie, W.T.	.207	46	154	135	15	28	35	7	0	0	12	0	0	2	16	0	38	1	2	4	.259	.301
Harrison, Adonis, Orl.*	.230	58	226	191	35	44	63	6	2	3	21	1	1	3	30	0	30	6	4	2	.330	.342
Haverbusch, Kevin, Car.	.375	46	184	168	28	63	82	10	0	3	29	0	0	3	13	1	20	1	3	3	.488	.429
Hawkins, Kraig, Orl.	.283	51	225	184	37	52	59	3	2	0	13	1	0	1	39	1	31	12	5	1	.321	.411
Haynie, Jason, Car.*	.000	17	10	8	0	0	0	0	0	0	0	1	0	0	1	0	5	0	0	0	.000	.111
Hazlett, Steve, Mob.-Orl.	.199	66	241	206	29	41	75	12	5	4	28	0	1	3	31	1	66	0	2	3	.364	.311
Heller, Brad, Birm.	.364	6	12	11	1	4	4	0	0	0	0	0	0	1	0	0	2	0	0	0	.364	.417
Hernaiz, Juan, Jack.	.251	99	408	382	60	96	154	21	2	11	58	1	6	3	16	0	93	8	2	4	.403	.283
Hernandez, Alexander, Car.*	.259	115	504	452	62	117	177	22	7	8	48	5	6	0	41	2	81	11	4	12	.392	.317
Hernandez, Elvin, Car.	.154	27	13	13	0	2	2	0	0	0	1	0	0	0	0	0	5	0	0	0	.154	.154
Hernandez, Ramon, Hun.	.296	127	563	479	83	142	213	24	1	15	98	2	6	19	57	2	61	4	5	15	.445	.389
Hills, Rich, Orl.	.236	124	514	440	54	104	132	19	0	3	51	2	9	7	56	1	66	1	2	16	.300	.326
Holbert, Aaron, Orl.	.287	68	283	251	46	72	104	13	5	3	34	4	1	5	22	0	41	10	14	3	.414	.355
Horner, Jim, Orl.	.219	73	289	247	29	54	92	9	1	9	36	1	5	3	33	0	59	2	1	5	.372	.313
Hunter, Rich, Chat.	.250	7	7	4	1	1	1	0	0	0	0	2	0	0	1	0	0	0	0	0	.250	.400
Hurst, Doug, Chat.	.000	44	9	9	0	0	0	0	0	0	0	0	0	0	0	0	3	0	0	0	.000	.000
Ibarra, Jesse, Jack.†	.100	13	35	30	1	3	4	1	0	0	1	0	0	0	5	1	14	0	0	1	.133	.229
Inglin, Jeff, Birm.	.245	139	585	494	75	121	227	22	6	24	100	0	9	4	78	1	101	3	2	12	.460	.347
Ingram, Darron, Chat.	.232	125	516	466	62	108	198	21	9	17	65	0	7	0	43	1	169	4	3	8	.425	.293
Jacobs, Ryan, Gre.	.455	36	14	11	0	5	8	1	1	0	2	3	0	0	0	0	3	0	0	0	.727	.455
Jasco, Elinton, Car.	.240	8	27	25	3	6	10	0	2	0	2	0	0	0	2	0	4	0	1	0	.400	.296
Jenkins, Corey, Birm.	.154	7	28	26	3	4	5	1	0	0	1	0	0	0	2	0	17	0	0	0	.192	.214
Jennings, Robin, W.T.*	.000	2	6	6	0	0	0	0	0	0	0	0	0	0	0	0	2	0	0	0	.000	.000
Jimenez, Miguel, W.T.	.500	12	3	2	0	1	1	0	0	0	0	0	0	1	0	0	1	0	0	0	.500	.667
Johnson, Adam, Gre.*	.253	121	464	411	67	104	188	21	3	19	77	0	7	4	42	6	71	7	7	10	.457	.323
Johnson, Mark, Birm.*	.283	117	494	382	68	108	158	17	3	9	59	0	1	6	105	0	72	0	1	5	.414	.443
Jones, Ryan, Knox.	.250	109	461	408	50	102	156	21	0	11	51	0	3	5	44	0	79	4	4	6	.382	.328
Jorgensen, Randy, Orl.*	.385	7	31	26	4	10	13	3	0	0	10	0	0	1	4	0	3	0	0	2	.500	.484
Joseph, Terry, W.T.-Mob.	.221	76	287	240	44	53	74	8	2	3	24	5	0	13	29	0	58	9	8	6	.308	.337
Kapler, Gabe, Jack.	.322	139	629	547	113	176	319	47	6	28	146	0	11	5	66	5	93	6	4	6	.583	.393
Katz, Jason, Gre.†	.091	18	40	33	3	3	3	0	0	0	5	0	1	0	6	0	12	2	0	2	.091	.225
Kaufman, Brad, Mob.	.200	5	5	5	1	1	1	0	0	0	1	0	0	0	0	0	1	0	0	0	.200	.200

Player, Team	Avg.	G	TPA	AB	R	H	TB	2B	3B	HR	RBI	SH	SF	HP	BB	IBB	SO	SB	CS	GDP	Slg.	OBP
King, Ray, W.T.*	.000	25	3	2	0	0	0	0	0	0	0	1	0	0	0	0	2	0	0	0	.000	.000
Kolb, Brandon, Mob.	.000	21	9	7	0	0	0	0	0	0	0	0	0	0	2	0	4	0	0	0	.000	.222
Lackey, Steve, Jack.	.324	12	39	34	6	11	12	1	0	0	3	0	0	0	5	0	5	0	0	0	.353	.410
Larkin, Stephen, Chat.*	.228	80	296	267	33	61	94	22	1	3	31	1	4	1	23	0	52	3	4	7	.352	.288
LaRue, Jason, Chat.	.365	105	446	386	71	141	238	39	8	14	82	1	9	10	40	0	60	4	3	13	.617	.429
LeBlanc, Eric, Chat.*	.333	23	11	9	1	3	6	0	0	1	3	1	0	0	1	0	3	0	0	0	.667	.400
Lee, Carlos, Birm.	.302	138	594	549	77	166	266	33	2	21	106	0	2	2	39	2	55	11	5	32	.485	.350
Liefer, Jeff, Birm.*	.291	127	541	471	84	137	245	33	6	21	89	0	1	9	60	6	125	1	2	9	.520	.381
Linebarger, Keith, W.T.	.333	50	4	3	0	1	1	0	0	0	0	1	0	0	0	0	1	0	0	0	.333	.333
Lombard, George, Gre.*	.308	122	507	422	84	130	229	25	4	22	65	5	4	5	71	10	140	35	5	2	.543	.410
Long, Garrett, Car.	.296	28	110	98	14	29	32	3	0	0	8	0	0	1	11	1	27	1	0	6	.327	.373
Lopez, Luis, Knox.	.313	119	519	450	70	141	215	27	1	15	85	0	8	3	58	3	55	0	2	18	.478	.389
Lopez, Rodrigo, Mob.	.000	4	4	1	0	0	0	0	0	0	0	2	0	0	1	0	1	0	0	0	.000	.500
Luderer, Brian, Hun.	.289	17	43	38	4	11	14	1	1	0	5	1	0	1	3	0	7	0	0	1	.368	.357
Lyons, Curt, Chat.	.000	3	1	0	0	0	0	0	0	0	0	1	0	0	0	0	0	0	0	0	.000	.000
Macias, Jose, Jack.†	.305	128	573	511	82	156	240	28	10	12	71	3	3	4	52	2	46	6	9	4	.470	.372
MacRae, Scott, Chat.	.273	49	14	11	2	3	4	1	0	0	0	0	0	0	3	0	6	0	0	0	.364	.429
Mahoney, Mike, Gre.	.216	20	79	74	3	16	24	5	0	1	6	0	2	2	1	0	20	1	1	1	.324	.241
Mallard, Randi, Chat.	.182	13	12	11	2	2	2	0	0	0	2	0	1	0	0	0	3	0	0	0	.182	.167
Manning, Brian, Birm.	.186	12	47	43	2	8	9	1	0	0	2	0	0	2	2	0	8	0	0	2	.209	.255
Manning, Nate, W.T.	.193	16	60	57	5	11	12	1	0	0	6	0	0	1	2	0	14	0	2	2	.211	.233
Manzano, Adrian, Gre.	.250	39	4	4	1	1	2	1	0	0	0	0	0	0	0	0	3	0	0	0	.500	.500
Marcinczyk, T.R., Hun.	.269	131	568	501	90	135	242	25	2	26	88	0	7	9	51	3	127	2	6	15	.483	.343
Marine, Del, Jack.	.316	44	178	155	25	49	70	8	2	3	25	0	2	1	20	0	20	0	0	1	.452	.393
Marn, Kevin, Chat.	.361	20	42	36	8	13	16	3	0	0	4	0	1	0	5	0	8	2	0	0	.444	.429
Martins, Eric, Hun.	.303	70	286	234	45	71	97	15	1	3	24	10	1	6	34	1	32	6	4	8	.415	.404
Mathews, Del, Car.*	.500	22	2	2	0	1	2	1	0	0	1	0	0	0	0	0	1	0	0	0	1.000	.500
Mathis, Joe, Orl.*	.251	104	431	395	49	99	139	18	5	4	41	2	4	3	27	0	84	12	11	6	.352	.301
Matos, Pascual, Gre.	.249	99	361	338	40	84	138	16	1	12	58	3	2	4	14	2	102	4	1	9	.408	.285
Matthews, Gary, Mob.†	.307	72	313	254	62	78	122	15	4	7	51	0	3	1	55	2	50	11	1	6	.480	.428
McConnell, Sam, Car.*	.000	2	2	1	0	0	0	0	0	0	0	0	0	0	1	0	0	0	0	0	.000	.500
McDonald, Jason, Hun.†	.300	7	28	20	9	6	14	2	0	2	4	0	0	0	8	0	6	4	0	0	.700	.500
McGlinchy, Kevin, Gre.	.000	6	3	3	0	0	0	0	0	0	0	0	0	0	0	0	2	0	0	0	.000	.000
McKay, Cody, Hun.*	.286	9	29	21	5	6	9	0	0	1	1	0	0	2	6	0	5	0	0	0	.429	.483
McKinnon, Sandy, Birm.	.200	57	230	200	21	40	51	8	0	1	18	6	3	2	19	1	41	11	3	1	.255	.272
McNabb, Buck, W.T.*	.294	124	446	385	62	113	162	21	5	6	48	1	3	6	51	4	61	22	13	10	.421	.382
McNichol, Brian, W.T.*	.133	29	32	30	4	4	6	2	0	0	4	1	0	0	1	0	12	0	0	0	.200	.161
Melhuse, Adam, Knox.†	.300	76	310	240	56	72	139	22	0	15	43	0	0	0	70	1	39	4	4	6	.579	.458
Mendoza, Carlos, Orl.*	.338	35	166	139	27	47	59	3	3	1	19	4	0	4	19	0	18	16	2	6	.424	.432
Meyers, Chad, W.T.	.270	77	356	293	63	79	93	14	0	0	26	1	0	4	58	0	43	37	9	5	.317	.397
Micucci, Mike, W.T.*	.290	53	156	138	20	40	53	11	1	0	21	0	0	1	17	3	18	0	0	3	.384	.372
Millette, Joe, W.T.	.000	1	4	3	0	0	0	0	0	0	0	0	0	0	1	0	0	0	0	1	.000	.000
Mitchell, Derek, Jack.	.221	128	507	421	58	93	124	21	2	2	54	4	8	6	68	1	94	6	3	9	.295	.332
Mitchell, Mike, Mob.*	.318	134	574	509	72	162	243	32	2	15	97	0	3	1	61	1	95	0	0	7	.477	.390
Mix, Greg, Gre.	.000	22	1	0	0	0	0	0	0	0	0	0	0	0	1	0	0	0	0	0	.000	1.000
Molina, Jose, W.T.	.222	109	368	320	33	71	89	10	1	2	28	10	3	3	32	1	74	1	5	10	.278	.296
Moore, Kerwin, Hun.†	.214	116	444	341	63	73	96	12	4	1	35	5	6	4	88	0	97	43	14	1	.282	.376
Morris, Warren, Car.*	.331	44	179	151	28	50	79	8	3	5	30	0	3	1	24	1	34	5	2	2	.523	.419
Mosquera, Julio, Knox.	.279	12	48	43	4	12	13	1	0	0	8	0	1	0	4	0	7	0	0	0	.302	.333
Mummau, Rob, Knox.	.291	39	160	141	28	41	59	5	2	3	28	3	3	2	11	0	24	4	1	3	.418	.344
Murray, Glenn, Chat.	.249	60	265	217	35	54	96	16	1	8	31	0	3	3	42	0	67	3	3	1	.442	.374
Neill, Mike, Hun.*	.257	12	40	35	1	9	14	5	0	0	2	1	0	0	4	1	13	0	0	0	.400	.333
Nelson, Bry, W.T.†	.284	32	115	102	10	29	45	6	2	2	18	0	1	0	12	2	12	4	2	5	.441	.357
Nelson, Chris, Hun.†	.000	28	1	0	0	0	0	0	0	0	0	1	0	0	0	0	0	0	0	0	.000	1.000
Nelson, Joe, Gre.	.111	45	10	9	1	1	1	0	0	0	0	0	0	0	1	0	0	0	0	1	.111	.200
Nevers, Tom, Chat.	.217	58	245	221	30	48	86	9	4	7	31	4	1	2	17	3	53	1	0	6	.389	.278
Newhan, David, Mob.*	.261	121	564	491	89	128	196	26	3	12	45	2	1	2	68	1	110	27	8	8	.399	.353
Newman, Eric, Mob.	.150	27	25	20	2	3	3	0	0	0	2	2	0	0	3	0	3	0	0	1	.150	.261
Nicholson, Kevin, Mob.†	.215	132	550	488	64	105	153	27	3	5	52	5	6	3	47	7	114	9	5	10	.314	.285
Nieves, Jose, W.T.	.290	82	338	314	42	91	152	27	5	8	39	2	3	1	18	0	55	17	10	9	.484	.327
Norris, Dax, Gre.	.231	63	220	199	30	46	79	15	0	6	26	1	1	4	15	0	43	1	2	7	.397	.297
Norton, Phillip, W.T.†	.143	19	18	14	2	2	2	0	0	0	0	1	0	0	3	0	4	0	0	0	.143	.294
Nunez, Raymond, W.T.	.307	78	246	225	27	69	109	15	2	7	45	1	3	1	16	2	62	3	4	8	.484	.351
Nunez, Sergio, Birm.	.244	115	487	435	57	106	117	8	0	1	32	8	3	3	38	0	59	26	7	10	.269	.307
O'Connor, Brian, Car.*	.143	14	15	14	3	2	2	0	0	0	1	0	0	0	1	0	8	0	0	0	.143	.200
O'Dell, Jake, Hun.	.000	27	3	2	0	0	0	0	0	0	0	1	0	0	0	0	1	0	0	0	.000	.333
Ojeda, Miguel, Car.	.155	18	64	58	4	9	14	2	0	1	4	2	0	1	3	0	12	0	0	0	.241	.210
Olszewski, Eric, Gre.*	1.000	24	1	1	0	1	2	1	0	0	0	0	0	0	0	0	0	0	0	0	2.000	1.000
Ortiz, Santos, Hun.	.277	94	415	354	70	98	144	24	2	6	55	6	2	5	48	0	63	22	8	6	.407	.369
Patel, Manny, W.T.*	.200	7	18	15	1	3	4	1	0	0	1	0	1	0	2	0	5	1	1	0	.267	.278
Paul, Andy, Chat.	.000	17	2	2	0	0	0	0	0	0	0	0	0	0	0	0	0	0	0	0	.000	.000
Peeples, Michael, Knox.	.251	118	453	395	58	99	142	16	3	7	42	17	3	2	36	0	62	20	10	5	.359	.314
Pendergrass, Tyrone, Gre.†	.125	5	18	16	3	2	2	0	0	0	0	0	0	0	2	0	4	1	0	0	.125	.222
Perez, Odaliz, Gre.*	.130	23	28	23	2	3	6	0	0	1	3	5	0	0	0	0	4	0	0	0	.261	.130
Peterson, Charles, Car.	.267	86	323	296	41	79	122	17	1	8	40	2	1	0	24	2	53	16	9	12	.412	.321
Phillips, Jason, Car.	.118	25	25	17	2	2	2	0	0	0	2	6	0	0	2	0	4	0	0	0	.118	.211
Pickford, Cody, Car.*	.444	13	9	9	3	4	8	1	0	1	2	0	0	0	0	0	1	0	0	0	.889	.444
Polidor, Wil, Birm.†	.231	31	108	104	8	24	24	0	0	0	4	1	0	2	1	0	15	0	0	7	.231	.252
Porter, Bo, W.T.	.289	125	560	464	91	134	212	26	11	10	68	3	5	6	82	4	117	50	17	9	.457	.399
Powers, John, Mob.*	.303	127	566	476	92	144	215	27	4	12	52	4	2	8	76	1	76	9	6	8	.452	.406
Presto, Nick, Chat.	.249	128	566	481	75	120	154	22	0	4	35	9	2	0	74	1	52	20	18	5	.320	.348
Priest, Eddie, Chat.	.500	4	3	2	0	1	1	0	0	0	0	0	0	0	1	0	1	0	0	0	.500	.667
Prieto, Rick, Mob.†	.239	72	242	218	30	52	77	9	2	4	25	0	0	3	21	1	49	9	2	0	.353	.314

Player, Team	Avg.	G	TPA	AB	R	H	TB	2B	3B	HR	RBI	SH	SF	HP	BB	IBB	SO	SB	CS	GDP	Slg.	OBP
Probst, Alan, Knox.	.261	79	302	261	53	68	120	22	0	10	44	1	3	2	35	0	81	2	1	7	.460	.349
Ramirez, Joel, Orl.	.258	20	68	62	7	16	19	3	0	0	8	0	1	1	4	0	8	0	0	1	.306	.309
Reed, Chris, Chat.	.000	20	1	1	0	0	0	0	0	0	0	0	0	0	0	0	1	0	0	0	.000	.000
Reyes, Jose, Car.	.189	11	38	37	5	7	15	0	1	2	7	0	0	0	1	0	9	1	1	2	.405	.211
Riedling, John, Chat.	.100	24	12	10	0	1	1	0	0	0	0	1	0	0	1	0	6	0	0	0	.100	.182
Rivers, Jonathan, Knox.	.268	91	361	302	51	81	135	19	4	9	49	3	1	8	47	1	62	20	13	8	.447	.380
Rivette, Scott, Hun.†	.000	35	1	1	0	0	0	0	0	0	0	0	0	0	0	0	1	0	0	0	.000	.000
Roberts, David, Jack.*	.326	69	342	279	71	91	130	14	5	5	42	3	4	3	53	1	59	21	9	4	.466	.434
Roberts, Lonell, Gre.†	.291	47	196	182	26	53	78	9	5	2	17	0	2	0	11	0	42	4	4	2	.429	.328
Robinson, Kerry, Orl.*	.269	72	342	309	45	83	106	7	5	2	26	4	2	0	27	0	28	28	9	6	.343	.325
Rodriguez, Luis, Knox.	.412	8	24	17	6	7	9	0	1	0	1	0	0	0	7	0	5	1	0	1	.529	.583
Rodriguez, Tony, Orl.	.220	13	44	41	5	9	9	0	0	0	3	0	0	0	3	0	6	0	0	1	.220	.273
Rose, Ted, Chat.*	.300	29	31	30	4	9	20	3	1	2	9	1	0	0	0	0	4	0	0	2	.667	.300
Rossiter, Mike, Mob.	.000	22	4	2	0	0	0	0	0	0	0	1	0	0	1	0	0	0	0	0	.000	.333
Ruffcorn, Scott, Chat.	.000	10	1	1	0	0	0	0	0	0	0	0	0	0	0	0	1	0	0	0	.000	.000
Rumfield, Toby, Gre.	.290	125	517	462	61	134	196	32	0	10	66	1	8	3	43	1	67	9	4	17	.424	.349
Runion, Tony, Car.	1.000	7	1	1	1	1	2	1	0	0	1	0	0	0	0	0	0	0	0	0	2.000	1.000
Rust, Brian, Gre.	.257	95	307	265	43	68	116	19	1	9	39	1	2	4	35	2	93	10	1	5	.438	.350
Ryan, Jason, W.T.†	.095	30	23	21	1	2	2	0	0	0	0	1	0	1	0	8	0	0	0	.095	.136
Salzano, Jerry, Gre.	.302	101	382	324	48	98	144	19	3	7	49	2	2	8	46	1	67	14	8	8	.444	.400
Sanchez, Marcos, Mob.†	.182	7	24	22	4	4	10	1	1	1	4	0	0	0	2	0	13	1	0	1	.455	.250
Sanders, Anthony, Knox.	.400	6	27	25	9	10	24	2	0	4	9	0	0	0	2	0	6	0	1	0	.960	.444
Sanders, Tracy, Car.*	.234	113	451	342	69	80	168	18	2	22	70	0	7	5	97	2	86	3	4	6	.491	.404
Schutz, Carl, Gre.*	.000	33	3	3	0	0	0	0	0	0	0	0	0	0	0	0	1	0	0	0	.000	.000
Secrist, Reed, Knox.*	.240	15	54	50	9	12	24	4	1	2	8	0	0	0	4	1	14	0	0	2	.480	.296
Seefried, Tate, Birm.*	.238	66	264	231	21	55	81	14	0	4	36	0	1	0	32	2	61	0	1	4	.351	.330
Skett, Will, Knox.	.250	65	266	236	33	59	93	13	6	3	33	4	2	4	20	0	63	4	8	3	.394	.317
Skrmetta, Matt, Mob.†	.000	51	5	4	0	0	0	0	0	0	0	1	0	0	0	0	2	0	0	0	.000	.000
Slemmer, Dave, Hun.	.250	49	198	176	24	44	59	6	0	3	20	1	1	0	20	1	30	3	1	3	.335	.325
Smith, Demond, Birm.†	.308	84	383	321	75	99	151	23	7	5	30	4	4	6	48	1	67	25	14	2	.470	.404
Smith, Keilan, Jack.	.000	39	1	0	0	0	0	0	0	0	0	0	0	0	1	0	0	0	0	0	.000	1.000
Smoltz, John, Gre.	.000	3	1	0	0	0	0	0	0	0	0	0	1	0	0	0	0	0	0	0	.000	.000
Solano, Fausto, Knox.	.240	85	331	288	49	69	125	22	2	10	38	4	2	3	34	0	53	4	4	5	.434	.324
Sollmann, Scott, Jack.*	.077	30	36	26	4	2	2	0	0	0	1	2	0	1	7	0	4	1	1	0	.077	.294
Sorg, Jay, Chat.*	.227	88	299	264	27	60	83	8	3	3	28	1	3	0	31	3	56	1	2	5	.314	.305
Staton, T.J., Car.*	.300	63	253	223	37	67	107	17	1	7	48	0	2	3	25	1	52	6	4	5	.480	.375
Steinmann, Scott, Orl.*	.173	18	61	52	7	9	11	2	0	0	2	1	0	1	7	0	12	0	1	0	.212	.283
Stidham, Phil, Chat.	1.000	5	1	1	0	1	1	0	0	0	0	0	0	0	0	0	0	0	0	0	1.000	1.000
Strange, Doug, Car.†	.357	4	16	14	4	5	5	0	0	0	0	0	0	0	2	0	1	0	0	0	.357	.438
Stromsborg, Ryan, Knox.	.237	81	314	283	44	67	101	9	2	7	28	2	1	1	27	1	65	7	5	4	.357	.304
Sullivan, Brendan, Mob.	.000	35	1	1	0	0	0	0	0	0	0	0	0	0	0	0	1	0	0	0	.000	.000
Sweet, Jon, Car.*	.227	77	277	238	24	54	73	11	1	2	44	4	8	7	20	0	18	1	2	6	.307	.297
Tejada, Miguel, Hun.	.327	15	59	52	9	17	29	6	0	2	7	1	2	0	4	0	8	1	0	2	.558	.362
Temple, Jason, Car.	.000	20	1	1	0	0	0	0	0	0	0	0	0	0	0	0	1	0	0	0	.000	.000
Thobe, Steve, Car.	.156	52	179	154	15	24	37	7	0	2	15	0	3	2	20	2	45	2	1	11	.240	.257
Thobe, Tom, Chat.*	1.000	18	1	1	2	1	1	0	0	0	0	0	0	0	0	0	0	0	0	0	1.000	1.000
Thompson, Andy, Knox.	.285	125	543	481	74	137	216	33	2	14	88	0	5	3	54	2	69	8	3	10	.449	.357
Thompson, Karl, Orl.	.125	2	9	8	1	1	1	0	0	0	0	0	0	0	1	0	2	0	0	0	.125	.222
Tidwell, Dave, Chat.	.204	47	156	137	12	28	41	5	1	2	22	1	3	0	15	0	37	3	4	2	.299	.277
Tinoco, Luis, Orl.	.267	20	86	75	9	20	26	3	0	1	12	0	0	0	11	0	8	0	0	3	.347	.360
Tolar, Kevin, Car.	.000	43	3	3	0	0	0	0	0	0	0	0	0	0	0	0	1	0	0	1	.000	.000
Tollberg, Brian, Mob.	.286	6	8	7	1	2	2	0	0	0	2	1	0	0	0	0	2	0	0	0	.286	.286
Torres, Paul, Orl.	.276	123	538	457	57	126	185	19	2	12	73	3	7	3	67	1	63	3	3	12	.405	.367
Towle, Justin, Chat.	.284	56	177	148	25	42	68	9	1	5	25	0	3	1	25	1	31	3	0	5	.459	.384
Trippy, Joe, Gre.*	.217	64	208	175	19	38	45	4	0	1	9	3	0	3	27	0	33	2	8	7	.257	.332
Tucci, Pete, Knox.	.291	38	158	141	25	41	77	7	4	7	36	0	2	2	13	0	29	3	2	2	.546	.354
Unroe, Tim, W.T.	.241	16	65	54	6	13	19	6	0	0	9	0	1	2	8	0	20	0	0	0	.352	.354
Valette, Ramon, W.T.	.218	36	112	101	11	22	34	5	2	1	9	0	2	0	9	0	25	0	0	1	.337	.277
Van De Weg, Ryan, Mob.	.000	6	1	1	0	0	0	0	0	0	0	0	0	0	0	0	0	0	0	0	.000	.000
Vaz, Roberto, Hun.*	.295	131	530	457	54	135	187	18	5	8	62	4	10	3	56	4	63	23	16	14	.409	.369
Viera, Rob, Chat.	.400	5	16	15	1	6	7	1	0	0	2	0	0	1	0	0	3	0	0	0	.467	.438
Villalobos, Carlos, Jack.	.320	128	561	497	96	159	251	34	2	18	80	0	6	3	55	2	85	8	0	16	.505	.387
Villegas, Ismael, Gre.	.313	40	16	16	0	5	5	0	0	0	0	0	0	0	0	0	5	0	1	0	.313	.313
Walters, Brett, Mob.	.250	14	14	12	1	3	6	0	0	1	3	2	0	0	0	0	5	0	0	0	.500	.250
Warner, Mike, Gre.*	.256	23	97	78	12	20	34	6	1	2	5	1	0	1	17	2	19	3	3	1	.436	.396
Wathan, Dusty, Orl.	.256	69	282	234	32	60	76	10	0	2	21	2	2	15	28	2	39	3	1	8	.325	.369
Whittaker, Jerry, Birm.	.239	57	218	205	21	49	92	12	2	9	26	1	1	1	9	0	65	3	3	5	.449	.273
Wilcox, Luke, Orl.*	.287	88	381	331	57	95	175	23	3	17	69	0	6	5	39	5	54	2	3	6	.529	.365
Williams, Juan, W.T.*	.223	70	229	188	31	42	72	9	6	3	36	0	1	1	39	1	63	1	6	6	.383	.358
Williamson, Scott, Chat.	.125	18	19	16	3	2	2	0	0	0	1	1	0	0	2	0	10	0	0	0	.125	.222
Wilson, Craig, Car.	.331	45	168	148	20	49	75	11	0	5	21	0	2	4	14	0	32	4	1	2	.507	.399
Wilson, Todd, Orl.	.203	18	72	64	5	13	17	4	0	0	7	1	0	1	6	0	15	0	0	1	.266	.282
Wimmer, Chris, Car.	.271	59	249	218	28	59	71	7	1	1	20	1	6	4	20	0	32	15	8	6	.326	.335
Wolff, Bryan, Mob.	.000	33	24	20	0	0	0	0	0	0	0	2	0	0	2	0	11	0	0	0	.000	.091
Woodward, Chris, Knox.	.245	73	288	253	36	62	83	12	0	3	27	3	3	3	26	1	47	3	5	4	.328	.319
Worrell, Steve, W.T.*	1.000	32	2	2	1	2	2	0	0	0	0	0	0	0	0	0	0	0	0	0	1.000	1.000
Wright, Scott, Chat.	.000	26	1	0	0	0	0	0	0	0	0	0	0	0	1	0	0	0	0	0	.000	1.000
Zuleta, Julio, W.T.	.295	40	155	139	18	41	56	9	0	2	20	0	3	3	10	0	30	0	1	3	.403	.348

GRAND SLAMS: Arcoin, Curl, 3 each; Freeman, Liefer, Lombard, Marcinczyk, 2 each; Bowles, Carcona, Chavez, Encarnacion, Faggett, Fick, Frank, Harrison, Horner, Inglin, Kapler, L. Lopes, Mathis, Murray, Nevers, Salzano, Seefried, Skett, Solano, 1 each.

AWARDED FIRST BASE ON CATCHER'S INTERFERENCE: Lee 2 (Fick 2); Frank (Cardona); Hall (Horner); Jones (Cardona); Martins (Molina); Nicholson (Molina); L. Roberts (J. Davis); Torres (Cardona); Wathan (Probst); Whittaker (Fick).

Player, Team	Avg.	G	TPA	AB	R	H	TB	2B	3B	HR	RBI	SH	SF	HP	BB	IBB	SO	SB	CS	GDP	Slg.	OBP
Battle, Howard, Birm.	.179	12	45	39	6	7	14	4	0	1	5	0	2	0	4	0	7	0	0	0	.359	.244
Battle, Howard, Gre.	.330	79	331	291	41	96	157	27	2	10	50	0	3	2	35	2	51	3	2	12	.540	.402
Hazlett, Steve, Mob.	.229	34	112	96	16	22	38	7	3	1	9	0	1	1	15	1	24	0	1	2	.396	.339
Hazlett, Steve, Orl.	.173	32	129	110	13	19	37	5	2	3	19	0	1	2	16	0	42	0	1	1	.336	.287
Joseph, Terry, W.T.	.220	37	137	118	24	26	36	2	1	2	11	1	0	7	11	0	28	3	3	3	.305	.324
Joseph, Terry, Mob.	.221	39	150	122	20	27	38	6	1	1	13	4	0	6	18	0	30	6	5	3	.311	.349

1998 PITCHING

TEAM

Team	W	L	Pct.	ERA	G	CG	ShO	Sv.	IP	H	TBF	R	ER	HR	SH	SF	HB	BB	IBB	SO	WP	Bk.
Mobile	86	54	.614	3.85	140	9	9	35	1247.1	1173	5314	616	533	95	48	37	43	489	10	1048	62	8
West Tenn	66	74	.471	3.99	140	7	4	31	1236.2	1226	5371	660	548	96	51	37	58	525	26	1073	70	14
Greenville	67	72	.482	4.42	139	4	7	36	1235.1	1225	5483	711	607	120	54	50	33	645	24	1097	95	11
Chattanooga	65	73	.471	4.51	138	1	7	23	1218.1	1241	5406	706	610	88	31	53	42	629	41	837	81	14
Jacksonville	86	54	.614	4.57	140	8	8	36	1231.1	1243	5384	710	625	130	26	48	62	524	6	831	56	10
Orlando	67	71	.486	4.91	138	4	8	35	1215.0	1293	5372	759	663	136	36	48	56	508	8	897	70	13
Knoxville	71	69	.507	4.91	140	3	4	35	1210.2	1330	5425	781	661	120	37	50	46	563	27	840	61	8
Huntsville	72	68	.514	4.96	140	4	4	36	1220.1	1331	5594	833	673	125	34	68	80	646	21	931	91	14
Carolina	59	80	.424	5.19	139	4	6	25	1193.2	1298	5361	780	688	136	49	33	62	545	17	863	91	10
Birmingham	58	82	.414	5.20	140	7	5	31	1205.2	1304	5532	827	696	108	41	54	57	670	17	992	101	13

INDIVIDUAL

TOP QUALIFIERS FOR EARNED-RUN AVERAGE TITLE

Minimum 112 innings. *Lefthanded pitcher.

Pitcher, Team	W	L	Pct.	ERA	G	GS	CG	ShO	GF	Sv.	IP	H	TBF	R	ER	HR	SH	SF	HB	BB	IBB	SO	WP	Bk.
Wolff, Bryan, Mob.	9	3	.750	2.29	33	14	3	2	7	0	133.2	90	527	40	34	7	5	2	4	43	2	134	4	1
Chen, Bruce, Gre.*	13	7	.650	3.29	24	23	1	0	0	0	139.1	106	572	57	51	12	8	5	5	48	0	164	6	0
Laxton, Brett, Hun.	11	4	.733	3.40	21	21	0	0	0	0	129.2	109	570	64	49	4	3	6	10	79	0	82	8	0
Carlyle, Buddy, Chat.-Mob.	14	7	.667	3.43	28	28	2	1	0	0	188.2	185	783	80	72	13	8	3	7	46	0	100	4	1
Beirne, Kevin, Birm.	13	9	.591	3.44	26	26	2	1	0	0	167.1	142	702	77	64	12	6	6	6	87	2	153	4	2
Bowie, Micah, Gre.*	11	6	.647	3.48	30	29	1	0	0	0	163.0	132	676	73	63	12	7	2	6	64	0	160	7	3
Norton, Phillip, W.T.*	6	6	.500	3.52	19	19	1	1	0	0	120.1	118	515	60	47	11	4	3	5	50	1	119	6	1
McNichol, Brian, W.T.*	12	9	.571	3.72	28	26	4	1	0	0	179.0	170	753	88	74	14	5	6	7	62	5	168	9	1
Bruner, Clay, Jack.	10	6	.625	3.79	28	28	1	0	0	0	171.0	173	739	90	72	15	4	6	6	66	0	91	8	2
Perez, Odaliz, Gre.*	6	5	.545	4.02	23	21	0	0	0	0	132.0	127	558	67	59	15	3	3	2	53	2	143	4	1
Seelbach, Chris, Orl.	8	3	.727	4.03	23	21	0	0	0	0	116.0	103	500	63	52	5	4	4		52	0	106	6	1
Vining, Ken, Birm.*	10	12	.455	4.07	29	28	1	0	0	0	172.2	187	793	103	78	8	5	5	4	91	1	133	16	0
Duncan, Courtney, W.T.	7	9	.438	4.26	29	29	0	0	0	0	162.2	141	730	89	77	7	9	7	14	108	5	157	9	2
McBride, Chris, Knox.	10	5	.667	4.40	35	21	1	0	5	2	155.1	185	681	102	76	18	4	11	6	37	1	90	1	0
MacRae, Scott, Chat.	9	4	.692	4.43	49	5	0	0	6	0	113.2	105	492	70	56	5	3	2	3	56	2	67	10	0

DEPARTMENTAL LEADERS: W—Borkowski, 16; L—Phillips, J. Ryan, 13 each; Pct.—Powell, .833; G—Barker, Skrmetta, 51 each; GS—Bowie, Duncan, Rose, 29 each; CG—McNichol, Olsen, 4 each; ShO—Harikkala, Wolff, 2 each; GF—Sak, 43; Sv.—Spencer, 18; IP—Carlyle, 188.2; H—Luce, 218; TBF—Vining, 793; R—Melendez, 104; ER—Luce, 95; HR—Borkowski, 25; SH—C. Duncan, 9; SF—McBride, 11; HB—Melendez, 15; BB—C. Duncan, 108; IBB—Reed, 6; SO—McNichol, 168; WP—Bennett, 18; BK—D'Amico, 5.

ALL PITCHERS

*Lefthanded pitcher.

Pitcher, Team	W	L	Pct.	ERA	G	GS	CG	ShO	GF	Sv.	IP	H	TBF	R	ER	HR	SH	SF	HB	BB	IBB	SO	WP	Bk.
Abbott, Jim, Birm.*	2	3	.400	5.40	8	8	0	0	0	0	41.2	53	198	33	25	2	0	2	1	21	0	35	5	0
Ah Yat, Paul, Car.*	5	5	.500	3.63	13	13	1	0	0	0	84.1	84	362	43	34	10	1	3	2	21	0	60	6	0
Ambrose, John, Birm.	9	12	.429	5.18	31	22	0	0	3	0	140.2	156	641	90	81	18	2	4	13	69	2	103	14	2
Anderson, Bill, Mob.	3	0	1.000	2.30	13	6	0	0	0	0	43.0	32	177	12	11	3	1	0	0	23	0	39	2	1
Anderson, Jason, Hun.*	1	1	.500	5.29	3	3	1	1	0	0	17.0	16	80	15	10	2	1	0	2	11	1	14	1	1
Anderson, Matt, Jack.	1	0	1.000	0.60	13	0	0	0	12	10	15.0	7	56	1	1	1	2	0	0	5	0	11	1	0
Arnold, Jamie, Gre.	1	4	.200	4.43	32	6	0	0	7	1	83.1	93	387	51	41	12	2	1	3	46	2	48	12	0
Arroyo, Bronson, Car.	9	8	.529	5.46	23	22	1	0	0	0	127.0	158	573	91	77	18	4	6	3	51	0	90	7	0
Averette, Robert, Chat.	5	8	.385	5.11	14	14	0	0	0	0	81.0	97	355	51	46	6	2	3	3	36	2	32	2	0
Baez, Benito, Hun.*	3	8	.273	5.80	34	17	0	0	11	0	122.2	161	579	92	79	12	3	5	4	64	0	83	7	1
Bale, John, Knox.*	0	0	.000	6.75	3	0	0	0	0	0	1.1	1	5	1	1	1	0	0	0	0	0	0	0	0
Barker, Richie, W.T.	2	5	.286	2.68	51	0	0	0	42	16	53.2	51	227	22	16	3	4	0	2	17	0	23	1	1
Beasley, Tony, Car.	0	0	.000	9.00	1	0	0	0	1	0	1.0	3	6	1	1	0	0	1	0	0	0	0	0	0
Beirne, Kevin, Birm.	13	9	.591	3.44	26	26	2	1	0	0	167.1	142	702	77	64	12	6	6	6	87	2	153	4	2
Bennett, Tom, Hun.	1	1	.500	10.16	28	0	0	0	14	3	33.2	19	188	41	38	2	1	3	4	67	1	43	18	1
Berry, Jason, Hun.	2	0	1.000	4.22	13	0	0	0	6	0	21.1	26	94	11	10	2	1	1	1	5	1	18	3	0
Bonilla, Denny, Orl.*	2	3	.400	5.06	37	0	0	0	11	0	69.1	81	322	44	39	7	2	5	6	34	1	66	3	0
Borbon, Pedro, Gre.*	0	0	.000	4.74	16	0	0	0	2	0	19.0	21	91	14	10	2	1	1	2	14	0	10	0	0
Borkowski, Dave, Jack.	16	7	.696	4.63	28	28	3	1	0	0	178.2	204	775	99	92	25	2	7	10	54	0	97	10	2
Bowie, Micah, Gre.*	11	6	.647	3.48	30	29	1	0	0	0	163.0	132	676	73	63	12	7	2	6	64	0	160	7	3
Bradford, Chad, Birm.	1	1	.500	2.60	10	0	0	0	7	1	17.1	13	72	6	5	2	0	0	0	8	0	14	2	0
Briggs, Anthony, Gre.	1	0	1.000	5.68	6	0	0	0	3	0	12.2	12	55	9	8	0	1	0		8	0	10	6	0
Brooks, Antone, Gre.*	6	3	.667	3.55	26	0	0	0	7	1	38.0	42	168	16	15	1	3	4	1	19	0	37	2	0
Brown, Chad, Knox.-Car.*	0	4	.000	6.95	29	4	0	0	10	0	45.1	59	226	35	35	2	0	1	5	30	1	31	4	0
Brown, Darold, W.T.*	0	0	.000	4.50	6	0	0	0	3	0	8.0	8	35	4	4	1	0	1	0	5	0	5	1	1
Bruner, Clay, Jack.	10	6	.625	3.79	28	28	1	0	0	0	171.0	173	739	90	72	15	4	6	6	66	0	91	8	2
Bullard, Jason, Gre.*	1	1	.500	1.06	17	0	0	0	15	10	17.0	9	66	3	2	0	1	0		8	1	13	0	0
Bussa, Todd, Car.	0	2	.000	11.74	6	0	0	0	5	0	7.2	11	43	12	10	0	0	0	2	7	0	6	1	0

CLASS AA Southern League

Pitcher, Team	W	L	Pct.	ERA	G	GS	CG	ShO	GF	Sv.	IP	H	TBF	R	ER	HR	SH	SF	HB	BB	IBB	SO	WP	Bk.
Buteaux, Shane, Birm.	0	1	.000	5.68	13	1	0	0	3	0	25.1	36	125	28	16	1	2	3	1	11	0	12	5	1
Byrne, Earl, W.T. *	5	5	.500	4.83	15	15	0	0	0	0	85.2	80	366	50	46	11	2	1	3	36	1	94	4	1
Callahan, Damon, Chat.	0	0	.000	0.00	2	0	0	0	2	0	3.0	1	12	0	0	0	0	0	0	3	1	0	1	0
Callaway, Michael, Orl.	5	6	.455	4.42	18	17	0	0	0	0	89.2	103	407	56	44	8	1	1	4	44	0	57	7	2
Carlyle, Buddy, Chat.-Mob.	14	7	.667	3.43	28	28	2	1	0	0	188.2	185	783	80	72	13	8	3	7	46	0	100	4	1
Carmona, Rafael, Orl.	0	3	.000	14.29	4	4	0	0	0	0	11.1	18	57	18	18	4	1	0	1	6	0	11	2	2
Carroll, Dave, Hun. *	1	0	1.000	2.38	20	0	0	0	7	3	34.0	26	141	9	9	0	0	2	3	13	1	34	0	0
Caruso, Gene, Car. *	0	1	.000	11.12	3	0	0	0	2	0	5.2	10	30	8	7	0	1	0	1	2	0	8	0	0
Castro, Jose, Hun.	0	0	.000	9.00	1	0	0	0	1	0	1.0	2	5	1	1	0	0	1	0	0	0	0	0	0
Chantres, Carlos, Birm.	2	4	.333	5.81	20	5	0	0	7	1	52.2	58	251	35	34	5	6	6	0	42	1	49	3	0
Chen, Bruce, Gre. *	13	7	.650	3.29	24	23	1	0	0	0	139.1	106	572	57	51	12	8	5	5	48	0	164	6	0
Chrysler, Clint, Orl. *	0	0	.000	3.86	3	0	0	0	2	0	4.2	4	19	2	2	0	0	0	0	1	0	6	0	0
Cole, Victor, W.T.	2	2	.500	2.40	19	0	0	0	2	0	30.0	26	127	12	8	1	1	1	1	11	1	31	2	0
Cordero, Francisco, Jack.	1	1	.500	4.86	17	0	0	0	15	8	16.2	19	79	12	9	1	1	1	1	9	0	18	0	0
Corey, Mark, Chat.	0	4	.000	8.20	6	6	0	0	0	0	26.1	32	127	25	24	6	1	2	2	16	1	6	0	0
Corn, Chris, Car.	2	2	.500	5.48	8	7	0	0	1	0	46.0	61	207	31	28	8	0	0	2	14	0	26	4	0
Crawford, Carlos, Car.	0	0	.000	6.55	6	0	0	0	2	0	11.0	17	53	8	8	1	0	0	2	3	0	9	1	0
Crowell, Jim, Chat. *	0	4	.000	8.51	5	5	0	0	0	0	24.1	38	129	27	23	2	0	3	0	17	0	10	2	2
Cruz, Charlie, Gre. *	3	3	.500	3.33	49	1	0	0	16	4	73.0	80	315	33	27	6	4	3	1	31	3	57	5	1
D'Amico, Jeff, Hun.	5	5	.500	7.67	24	8	0	0	4	0	61.0	77	295	57	52	12	1	6	3	34	0	46	6	5
Dace, Derek, Jack. *	5	3	.625	4.16	40	0	0	0	15	3	67.0	51	277	32	31	8	0	2	2	29	0	48	2	0
Dale, Carl, Hun.	1	1	.500	4.61	3	3	0	0	0	0	13.2	13	60	7	7	2	0	2	0	8	0	10	0	0
Daniels, David, Car.	4	3	.571	2.97	35	0	0	0	32	16	39.1	34	163	15	13	0	1	3	2	16	1	37	2	2
Daniels, John, Orl.	1	2	.333	5.30	11	0	0	0	3	0	18.2	14	82	12	11	4	0	3	2	9	3	19	0	0
Darwin, David, Jack. *	12	6	.667	5.35	24	23	2	1	1	0	139.2	152	612	94	83	22	3	2	6	52	0	76	2	2
Davenport, Joe, Birm.	3	2	.600	7.22	26	0	0	0	15	1	38.2	54	202	36	31	2	1	4	2	30	0	22	5	0
Davey, Tom, Knox.	5	3	.625	3.87	48	9	0	0	32	16	76.2	70	348	35	33	2	3	2	3	52	0	78	9	1
Davis, Kane, Car.	1	11	.083	9.24	18	16	0	0	0	0	74.0	102	362	84	76	12	4	0	7	38	2	39	10	1
Davis, Keith, Jack.	0	0	.000	0.00	1	0	0	0	1	0	0.0	1	1	0	0	0	0	0	0	0	0	0	0	0
Davis, Tim, Orl. *	1	1	.500	2.45	14	5	0	0	2	1	22.0	18	86	9	6	2	0	2	1	4	0	19	3	0
De La Rosa, Maximo, Orl.	6	4	.600	3.03	42	0	0	0	29	8	62.1	47	260	23	21	2	4	4	3	24	1	51	5	0
Delgado, Danny, Orl.	0	0	.000	0.00	1	0	0	0	1	0	1.0	0	3	0	0	0	0	0	0	0	0	0	0	0
Della Ratta, Pete, Hun.	1	0	1.000	11.25	5	0	0	0	2	0	8.0	21	49	12	10	2	0	1	0	4	2	3	0	0
De Los Santos, Mariano, Car. .	1	2	.333	5.59	10	1	0	0	4	1	19.1	13	82	12	12	0	0	1	1	12	0	15	3	0
Dillinger, John, Car.	0	1	.000	14.29	4	0	0	0	0	0	5.2	11	32	9	9	4	1	0	2	4	0	4	0	0
Dixon, Bubba, Mob. *	0	3	.000	5.27	9	0	0	0	3	0	13.2	15	65	12	8	1	0	1	0	9	1	6	1	0
Doman, Roger, Car.-Knox.	3	2	.600	5.76	32	1	0	0	11	0	50.0	55	219	35	32	8	5	3	2	18	0	26	2	0
Donnelly, Brendan, Chat.	2	5	.286	2.98	38	0	0	0	35	13	45.1	43	203	16	15	4	1	1	3	24	5	47	8	0
Doughty, Brian, Mob.	0	0	.000	5.45	17	0	0	0	2	0	38.0	62	189	33	23	3	1	2	2	8	0	19	1	0
Doyle, Tom, Chat. *	0	1	.000	10.13	9	0	0	0	5	0	10.2	13	56	12	12	1	1	1	0	14	0	9	2	1
Drumheller, Al, Mob. *	5	4	.556	3.51	50	6	0	0	21	4	97.1	75	412	43	38	5	5	5	2	49	0	118	4	0
Dubose, Eric, Hun. *	7	6	.538	2.70	14	14	1	1	0	0	83.1	86	363	37	25	2	3	4	7	34	1	66	4	0
Duncan, Courtney, W.T.	7	9	.438	4.26	29	29	0	0	0	0	162.2	141	730	89	77	7	9	7	14	108	5	157	9	2
Dunham, Pat, Orl.	2	6	.250	4.95	10	9	0	0	0	0	56.1	52	245	33	31	8	1	2	1	32	0	34	2	2
Durkovic, Peter, Jack. *	2	1	.667	5.69	37	0	0	0	14	0	68.0	69	311	47	43	8	4	5	7	35	1	36	1	1
Eddie, Steve, Chat.	0	0	.000	36.00	1	0	0	0	1	0	1.0	6	13	8	4	0	0	0	0	3	0	1	1	0
Enochs, Chris, Hun.	9	10	.474	4.74	26	26	0	0	0	0	148.0	159	660	101	78	12	2	6	9	64	2	100	5	0
Estes, Eric, Mob.	7	4	.636	5.30	17	16	0	0	0	0	88.1	117	403	61	52	8	1	2	3	31	1	72	4	0
Etler, Todd, Chat.	6	0	1.000	1.92	46	0	0	0	21	5	65.2	61	276	21	14	1	2	1	3	21	2	58	3	0
Evans, Dave, Car.	5	4	.556	5.24	26	3	0	0	6	0	56.2	56	254	36	33	8	3	1	0	30	1	52	8	3
Farley, Joe, Birm. *	1	2	.333	11.15	6	1	0	0	0	0	15.1	20	78	19	19	0	2	0	2	15	1	7	1	0
Farnsworth, Kyle, W.T. *	8	2	.800	2.77	13	13	0	0	0	0	81.1	70	330	32	25	6	2	3	1	21	0	73	2	2
Fitzgerald, Brian, Orl. *	0	0	.000	2.08	2	0	0	0	1	1	4.1	5	18	1	1	0	0	0	0	1	0	4	0	0
Flach, Jason, Gre.	0	0	.000	0.00	1	0	0	0	0	0	1.1	3	7	0	0	0	0	0	0	0	0	4	0	0
Foster, Kevin, W.T.	1	0	1.000	2.25	2	0	0	0	0	0	4.0	5	17	1	1	0	0	0	0	1	0	5	0	0
Garcia, Al, W.T.	4	5	.444	4.96	25	10	0	0	3	0	78.0	89	334	47	43	2	5	1	6	16	1	39	0	2
Giard, Ken, Car.	6	5	.545	2.62	42	0	0	0	25	6	58.1	33	246	24	17	4	8	3	3	37	4	56	4	0
Giron, Isabel, Knox.	1	1	.500	3.82	6	5	0	0	0	0	35.1	29	145	15	15	5	0	1	0	13	1	35	3	0
Gissell, Chris, W.T.	0	1	.000	13.50	1	1	0	0	0	0	4.0	5	21	7	6	2	0	0	0	4	2	4	0	0
Glauber, Keith, Chat.	1	1	.500	4.00	2	2	0	0	0	0	9.0	3	35	4	4	1	0	0	0	6	0	5	0	0
Glover, Gary, Knox.	5	6	.455	6.75	8	8	0	0	0	0	37.1	41	183	36	28	2	1	3	3	28	0	14	2	0
Gordon, Mike, Knox.	8	2	.800	5.02	44	12	0	0	11	0	113.0	123	521	82	63	13	1	5	3	64	5	95	7	0
Graterol, Beiker, Knox.	5	6	.455	5.24	12	12	0	0	0	0	67.0	76	287	46	39	8	1	4	5	22	0	52	0	0
Grigsby, Benji, W.T.	2	3	.400	4.31	32	1	0	0	9	0	48.0	58	223	35	23	8	5	0	0	17	2	29	5	0
Grijak, Kevin, Car.	0	0	.000	27.00	1	0	0	0	1	0	1.0	4	8	3	3	1	0	0	0	1	0	1	0	0
Gryboski, Kevin, Orl.	0	0	.000	9.00	2	0	0	0	0	0	5.0	8	23	5	5	1	0	0	0	1	0	4	2	0
Gunther, Kevin, Hun.	3	5	.375	5.64	45	0	0	0	36	12	67.0	107	332	66	42	8	2	2	5	20	0	40	5	1
Guzman, Domingo, Mob.	5	2	.714	4.50	12	8	0	0	2	1	48.0	51	217	34	24	7	3	0	3	26	0	39	8	0
Halperin, Mike, Car.-Knox. *	5	1	.833	2.88	36	0	0	0	14	2	50.0	45	212	16	16	0	1	1	3	25	1	35	2	0
Hammack, Brandon, W.T.	3	0	1.000	2.45	21	0	0	0	9	3	25.2	14	103	7	7	1	0	0	0	16	0	22	2	0
Harikkala, Tim, Orl.	5	7	.417	4.53	15	15	3	2	0	0	103.1	112	429	56	52	9	5	2	7	14	0	55	0	0
Harris, D.J., Knox.	4	2	.667	2.77	22	0	0	0	8	2	48.2	52	203	17	15	1	1	1	0	24	1	31	3	0
Hartshorn, Ty, Knox.	7	6	.538	5.18	19	19	0	0	0	0	107.2	133	483	74	62	15	3	1	2	43	0	55	2	0
Harville, Chad, Hun.	0	0	.000	2.45	12	0	0	0	10	8	14.2	6	63	4	4	0	0	1	3	13	1	24	1	0
Haynie, Jason, Car. *	5	3	.625	3.50	17	15	0	0	0	0	79.2	82	338	37	31	8	2	2	4	28	2	44	3	0
Hernandez, Elvin, Car.	3	6	.333	5.72	27	13	0	0	1	0	102.1	127	462	73	65	14	0	3	2	31	0	67	5	0
Hiljus, Erik, Jack.	2	3	.400	3.70	42	0	0	0	17	2	65.2	49	280	31	27	7	2	3	0	35	0	85	4	0
Hudson, Tim, Hun.	10	9	.526	4.54	22	22	3	0	0	0	134.2	136	603	84	68	13	7	8	13	71	2	104	13	1
Hunter, Rich, Chat.	1	3	.250	5.97	7	6	0	0	0	0	34.2	37	157	28	23	5	3	2	1	17	1	15	3	1
Hurst, Bill, Jack.	0	0	.000	23.14	3	0	0	0	2	0	2.1	4	19	6	6	0	0	0	2	6	0	3	0	0
Hurst, Doug, Chat.	8	4	.667	3.84	44	5	0	0	11	1	89.0	85	366	41	38	9	3	3	3	38	5	37	3	2
Jacobs, Ryan, Gre. *	6	9	.400	5.35	35	15	0	0	7	0	101.0	104	478	73	60	14	3	8	2	72	3	74	12	1

CLASS AA Southern League

Pitcher, Team	W	L	Pct.	ERA	G	GS	CG	ShO	GF	Sv.	IP	H	TBF	R	ER	HR	SH	SF	HB	BB	IBB	SO	WP	Bk.
Janicki, Pete, Orl.	0	1	.000	10.80	12	0	0	0	8	0	18.1	24	92	24	22	5	0	2	2	12	0	13	7	0
Jimenez, Miguel, W.T.	1	3	.250	4.75	26	0	0	0	7	0	30.1	30	139	18	16	1	0	2	0	18	0	32	7	2
Kaufman, Brad, Mob.	1	0	1.000	1.11	5	5	0	0	0	0	24.1	18	96	3	3	0	2	0	2	8	0	21	1	0
Kaufman, John, Orl. *	0	5	.000	6.66	7	6	0	0	0	0	24.1	34	115	25	18	6	0	0	1	9	0	17	1	0
Kelly, Jeff, Car. *	0	0	.000	0.00	1	0	0	0	0	0	1.0	1	5	0	0	0	0	0	1	0	0	0	0	0
Kelly, John, Orl.	1	4	.200	5.23	9	8	0	0	0	0	41.1	51	188	29	24	7	1	1	2	18	0	32	3	2
Kimsey, Keith, Jack.	0	0	.000	22.50	3	0	0	0	1	0	4.0	10	26	10	10	1	0	2	1	3	0	3	0	0
King, Ray, W.T. *	1	2	.333	2.43	25	0	0	0	8	3	29.2	23	121	9	8	1	1	1	1	10	0	26	2	0
Kjos, Ryan, Hun.	1	0	1.000	5.40	9	0	0	0	2	0	13.1	9	62	8	8	2	1	1	2	12	0	7	1	0
Kolb, Brandon, Mob.	4	3	.571	4.50	21	6	0	0	4	1	62.0	46	274	33	31	4	3	3	1	40	0	58	6	0
Lakman, Jason, Birm.	0	10	.000	7.96	15	15	0	0	0	0	72.1	89	352	70	64	15	1	3	8	40	0	79	6	2
Lawrence, Clint, Knox. *	1	2	.333	6.84	7	7	0	0	0	0	25.0	31	131	24	19	4	0	0	0	23	2	16	2	1
Laxton, Brett, Hun.	11	4	.733	3.40	21	21	0	0	0	0	129.2	109	570	64	49	4	3	6	10	79	0	82	8	0
LeBlanc, Eric, Chat.	4	3	.571	3.93	23	7	0	0	6	0	66.1	56	286	33	29	5	1	4	1	38	0	49	7	1
Lee, Jeremy, Knox.	0	1	.000	3.38	10	0	0	0	5	0	16.0	16	70	6	6	1	0	2	1	3	0	7	1	0
LeRoy, John, Orl.	1	0	1.000	6.45	12	0	0	0	3	0	22.1	22	97	17	16	5	0	0	0	10	0	12	1	0
Linebarger, Keith, W.T.	3	3	.500	5.31	50	0	0	0	19	2	59.1	79	274	38	35	5	2	2	4	24	1	45	4	0
Lopez, Rodrigo, Mob.	3	0	1.000	1.40	4	4	2	1	0	0	25.2	21	101	11	4	1	0	1	0	4	0	20	0	0
Luce, Robert, Orl.	12	7	.632	5.09	27	26	1	0	1	0	168.0	218	741	103	95	20	2	2	6	49	0	73	1	0
Lukasiewicz, Mark, Knox. *	0	0	.000	1.93	5	0	0	0	2	1	9.1	6	33	2	2	0	0	0	0	1	0	16	0	0
Lundquist, David, Birm.	1	1	.500	3.29	33	0	0	0	21	10	41.0	28	165	15	15	1	2	1	2	15	1	41	1	0
Lyons, Curt, Chat.	0	1	.000	9.00	3	3	0	0	0	0	7.0	6	35	7	7	0	0	0	1	8	0	10	0	0
MacRae, Scott, Chat.	9	4	.692	4.43	49	5	0	0	6	0	113.2	105	492	70	56	5	3	2	3	56	2	67	10	0
Mallard, Randi, Chat.	1	4	.200	4.33	13	12	0	0	0	0	60.1	65	294	37	29	3	1	1	3	58	1	34	7	1
Manon, Julio, Orl.	0	2	.000	6.10	13	0	0	0	5	0	20.2	22	96	19	14	3	0	1	0	9	0	22	3	0
Manzano, Adrian, Gre.	1	5	.167	4.92	39	5	0	0	24	8	64.0	72	293	43	35	7	6	4	1	29	5	57	3	0
Marte, Damaso, Orl. *	7	6	.538	5.27	22	20	0	0	0	0	121.1	136	541	82	71	14	2	6	2	47	0	99	6	2
Mathews, Del, Car. *	2	0	1.000	2.34	22	0	0	0	8	1	42.1	36	180	14	11	2	3	0	3	17	0	36	1	0
McBride, Chris, Knox.	10	5	.667	4.40	35	21	1	0	5	2	155.1	185	681	102	76	18	4	11	6	37	1	90	1	0
McClellan, Sean, Knox.	3	5	.375	3.62	24	3	0	0	10	4	49.2	31	209	23	20	5	1	2	1	33	0	44	2	1
McConnell, Sam, Car. *	0	1	.000	4.50	2	1	0	0	0	0	12.0	15	53	7	6	2	1	1	0	3	0	5	0	0
McGlinchy, Kevin, Gre.	1	1	.500	5.18	6	6	0	0	0	0	33.0	35	144	19	19	5	1	1	1	15	1	20	0	0
McNichol, Brian, W.T. *	12	9	.571	3.72	28	26	4	1	0	0	179.0	170	753	88	74	14	5	6	7	62	5	168	9	1
Mears, Chris, Orl.	0	1	.000	9.64	1	1	0	0	0	0	4.2	8	24	5	5	0	0	0	0	2	0	4	0	0
Meiners, Doug, Knox.	7	6	.538	4.73	43	9	1	0	12	1	110.1	133	504	68	58	7	5	6	6	45	3	58	4	0
Melendez, Dave, Jack.	9	6	.600	5.06	25	25	0	0	0	0	153.0	166	685	104	86	16	1	8	15	61	0	83	8	0
Miller, Matt, Jack. *	3	7	.300	7.04	13	13	0	0	0	0	61.1	70	297	49	48	6	0	2	2	50	1	49	3	1
Mitchell, Larry, Birm.	0	0	.000	63.00	2	0	0	0	0	0	1.0	4	12	7	7	0	0	1	0	5	0	0	3	0
Mix, Greg, Gre.	1	1	.500	5.04	22	0	0	0	9	2	25.0	32	119	19	14	2	0	3	0	11	0	18	3	0
Montane, Ivan, Orl.	0	0	.000	11.57	2	0	0	0	0	0	2.1	3	12	3	3	0	0	0	0	2	0	0	0	0
Nelson, Chris, Hun.	3	4	.429	6.45	28	10	0	0	6	0	83.2	111	397	70	60	21	1	3	4	39	1	62	7	3
Nelson, Erick, Gre. *	1	2	.333	9.82	4	0	0	0	1	0	11.0	14	53	13	12	3	0	1	1	6	2	3	1	0
Nelson, Joe, Gre.	6	9	.400	4.98	45	12	1	1	15	2	108.1	124	506	76	60	9	8	4	5	69	2	74	11	1
Newman, Eric, Mob.	9	12	.429	5.59	27	25	1	1	0	0	140.0	152	632	100	87	14	5	9	6	71	1	120	17	0
Newton, Geronimo, Orl. *	4	1	.800	5.53	21	1	0	0	2	0	40.2	45	188	27	25	3	2	2	3	22	1	28	0	0
Nichols, Jamie, Birm.	0	0	.000	7.50	5	1	0	0	2	0	12.0	15	57	11	10	3	0	0	0	8	0	12	0	0
Norton, Phillip, W.T. *	6	6	.500	3.52	19	19	1	1	0	0	120.1	118	515	60	47	11	4	3	5	50	1	119	6	1
Nunez, Maximo, Orl.	2	0	1.000	0.77	6	0	0	0	5	2	11.2	5	43	1	1	0	1	1	0	4	1	14	2	0
O'Connor, Brian, Car. *	2	4	.333	8.25	14	13	0	0	0	0	64.1	86	318	65	59	11	3	2	3	53	1	41	12	0
O'Dell, Jake, Hun.	2	5	.286	5.17	27	9	0	0	6	0	78.1	84	347	54	45	8	3	6	3	30	3	69	2	0
Olsen, Jason, Birm.	8	10	.444	4.69	28	28	4	0	0	0	159.1	188	709	95	83	19	4	3	5	53	3	134	6	1
Olszewski, Eric, Gre.	1	3	.250	7.18	24	0	0	0	5	1	31.1	26	154	27	25	4	0	2	0	37	0	31	3	2
Paul, Andy, Chat.	0	1	.000	6.04	17	1	0	0	8	0	25.1	26	121	18	17	1	1	3	2	16	1	30	2	0
Pena, Jesus, Birm. *	0	2	.000	3.86	22	0	0	0	12	2	23.1	20	100	12	10	3	2	1	0	10	0	28	2	2
Perez, Juan, Hun. *	3	2	.600	2.45	27	0	0	0	19	8	36.2	29	157	13	10	3	3	2	1	16	4	37	2	1
Perez, Odaliz, Gre. *	6	5	.545	4.02	23	21	0	0	0	0	132.0	127	558	67	59	15	3	3	2	53	2	143	4	1
Phillips, Jason, Car.	7	13	.350	4.71	25	25	1	1	0	0	151.0	161	663	89	79	14	8	1	9	52	3	114	10	3
Pickford, Kevin, Car. *	5	1	.833	3.90	13	8	1	0	2	0	57.2	48	228	26	25	7	1	0	3	15	1	43	2	0
Pineiro, Joel, Orl.	1	0	1.000	5.40	1	1	0	0	0	0	5.0	7	22	4	3	0	0	1	0	2	0	2	0	0
Powell, Brian, Jack.	10	2	.833	3.07	14	14	2	1	0	0	93.2	84	379	37	32	5	0	3	4	24	0	51	3	2
Priest, Eddie, Chat. *	1	2	.333	1.73	4	4	0	0	0	0	26.0	15	105	6	5	1	1	0	0	10	1	29	1	0
Probst, Alan, Knox.	0	0	.000	27.00	1	0	0	0	0	0	1.0	4	8	3	3	0	0	0	0	1	0	0	0	0
Puffer, Brandon, Chat.	0	0	.000	3.12	7	0	0	0	4	0	8.2	2	32	3	3	2	0	0	1	3	0	6	0	0
Reed, Chris, Chat.	1	1	.500	5.25	20	0	0	0	5	0	36.0	41	169	25	21	3	2	2	0	25	6	13	2	0
Ricketts, Chad, W.T.	0	2	.000	3.52	13	0	0	0	11	6	15.1	19	65	7	6	0	0	1	1	4	2	13	1	0
Riedling, John, Chat.	3	10	.231	5.00	24	20	0	0	1	0	102.2	112	475	70	57	10	1	5	4	60	5	86	5	0
Rincon, Ricardo, Car. *	0	0	.000	6.00	2	0	0	0	2	0	3.0	5	16	2	2	1	1	0	0	2	0	1	0	0
Rivette, Scott, Hun.-Knox.	6	5	.545	4.52	42	0	0	0	11	2	77.2	82	353	50	39	7	1	6	5	39	1	57	6	0
Roberts, Willis, Jack.	3	1	.750	2.19	12	2	0	0	5	0	24.2	21	105	10	6	0	2	0	3	10	1	15	1	0
Rose, Ted, Chat.	11	10	.524	4.60	29	29	1	0	0	0	168.1	191	745	97	86	12	1	6	6	66	3	108	6	4
Rossiter, Mike, Mob.	2	0	1.000	1.79	22	0	0	0	3	0	45.1	34	185	10	9	2	1	0	1	11	0	46	1	0
Ruffcorn, Scott, Chat.	3	0	1.000	1.38	10	0	0	0	5	0	13.0	8	51	3	2	2	1	0	0	6	0	9	1	0
Runion, Tony, Car.	1	2	.333	4.82	7	0	0	0	6	0	9.1	11	47	7	5	0	1	0	0	7	1	11	1	1
Ryan, Jason, W.T.	3	13	.188	4.88	30	25	2	0	3	0	147.2	172	661	97	80	20	7	4	10	57	3	121	10	1
Ryan, Robert, Chat. *	1	0	1.000	2.20	16	0	0	0	6	4	16.1	13	67	4	4	0	1	1	0	6	0	21	0	0
Sak, James, Mob.	2	5	.286	5.14	45	0	0	0	43	16	49.0	33	212	29	28	3	0	2	1	36	3	56	5	0
Santos, Victor, Jack.	4	2	.667	4.17	6	6	0	0	0	0	36.2	40	159	20	17	2	1	3	1	15	1	37	1	0
Scheffer, Aaron, Orl.	1	0	1.000	2.20	19	0	0	0	11	5	32.2	23	132	8	8	3	2	0	0	13	0	33	1	1
Schutz, Carl, Gre.-W.T. *	2	4	.333	4.33	46	0	0	0	16	4	52.0	47	247	36	25	3	4	2	0	50	3	43	9	0
Secoda, Jason, Birm.	2	3	.400	6.34	39	0	0	0	20	1	65.1	78	307	50	46	6	2	4	2	39	2	45	7	1
Seelbach, Chris, Orl.	8	3	.727	4.03	23	21	0	0	0	0	116.0	103	500	63	52	5	4	6	4	52	0	106	6	1

Pitcher, Team	W	L	Pct.	ERA	G	GS	CG	ShO	GF	Sv.	IP	H	TBF	R	ER	HR	SH	SF	HB	BB	IBB	SO	WP	Bk.
Shaw, Curtis, Car. *	0	1	.000	9.95	3	1	0	0	2	0	6.1	10	35	8	7	0	0	0	0	6	0	2	0	0
Shumate, Jacob, Gre.	0	1	.000	15.43	2	0	0	0	0	0	2.1	3	13	4	4	0	0	0	0	4	0	1	1	0
Skrmetta, Matt, Mob.	9	2	.818	3.35	51	0	0	0	16	0	78.0	66	323	32	29	9	5	2	2	31	1	77	1	3
Skuse, Nick, Jack.	4	6	.400	4.76	49	0	0	0	39	13	62.1	54	268	34	33	7	0	1	1	30	1	74	4	0
Smith, Andy, Hun.	0	0	.000	10.13	7	0	0	0	2	0	10.2	15	54	13	12	2	2	1	1	8	1	10	1	0
Smith, Brian, Knox.	4	2	.667	4.06	42	0	0	0	15	7	71.0	72	307	39	32	7	2	4	3	25	3	50	2	0
Smith, Cam, Orl.	1	3	.250	4.62	23	1	0	0	8	0	39.0	32	186	27	20	6	3	3	6	32	0	49	9	0
Smith, Keilan, Jack.	4	3	.571	3.64	39	1	0	0	10	0	71.2	69	316	34	29	6	4	3	1	40	1	54	8	0
Smoltz, John, Gre.	0	1	.000	2.57	3	3	0	0	0	0	14.0	11	54	4	4	2	0	0	0	3	0	16	2	0
Spencer, Sean, Orl. *	2	1	.667	2.95	37	0	0	0	32	18	42.2	33	178	18	14	3	3	1	1	18	1	43	5	1
Stevenson, Jason, Knox.	6	10	.375	5.43	22	22	1	0	0	0	134.1	159	600	88	81	16	7	2	6	51	4	98	9	3
Stidham, Phil, Chat.	1	0	1.000	9.75	5	0	0	0	1	0	12.0	20	65	13	13	1	2	0	1	10	1	6	0	0
Sullivan, Brendan, Mob.	1	3	.333	1.85	35	0	0	0	29	13	39.0	28	153	8	8	1	1	1	3	16	1	24	2	0
Temple, Jason, Car.	0	0	.000	10.27	20	0	0	0	6	0	23.2	23	131	29	27	4	0	2	4	36	0	11	6	0
Theodile, Robert, Birm.	0	1	.000	7.56	8	0	0	0	4	0	16.2	18	85	18	14	1	2	1	2	16	0	17	0	0
Thobe, Tom, Chat. *	1	0	1.000	7.50	17	0	0	0	8	0	24.0	32	116	20	20	1	0	2	0	14	0	11	1	0
Thompson, John, Orl.	3	4	.429	6.87	19	3	0	0	6	0	38.0	43	172	31	29	5	2	3	1	20	0	11	1	0
Tolar, Kevin, Car. *	1	2	.333	2.22	42	0	0	0	15	1	48.2	35	211	12	12	1	4	1	2	33	0	48	1	0
Tollberg, Brian, Mob.	3	2	.600	2.41	6	6	1	0	0	0	41.0	31	152	11	11	3	1	0	1	4	0	45	0	1
Torres, Paul, Orl.	0	0	.000	9.00	2	0	0	0	2	0	1.0	3	7	1	1	0	0	1	0	0	0	0	0	0
Tucker, Julien, Birm.	4	6	.400	6.82	34	5	0	0	7	3	66.0	77	318	66	50	2	1	3	5	45	0	47	10	1
Van De Weg, Ryan, Mob.	2	3	.400	9.74	6	4	0	0	0	0	20.1	37	104	24	22	2	1	0	3	10	0	6	1	1
Vaz, Roberto, Hun. *	0	0	.000	9.00	1	0	0	0	1	0	1.0	1	4	1	1	0	0	0	0	0	0	0	0	0
Veniard, Jay, Knox. *	0	1	.000	9.58	11	0	0	0	4	0	10.1	10	51	12	11	2	1	0	0	12	1	7	2	2
Villegas, Ismael, Gre.	7	6	.538	5.28	40	17	1	0	11	3	124.1	134	567	78	73	11	3	3	3	71	1	120	11	2
Vining, Ken, Birm. *	10	12	.455	4.07	29	28	1	0	0	0	172.2	187	793	103	78	8	5	5	4	91	1	133	16	0
Vizcaino, Luis, Hun.	3	2	.600	4.66	7	7	0	0	0	0	38.2	43	182	27	20	8	0	3	3	22	0	26	2	0
Walters, Brett, Mob.	7	3	.700	4.91	14	13	0	0	1	0	77.0	86	329	43	42	9	5	4	2	23	0	51	0	0
Ward, Bryan, Birm. *	2	3	.400	2.36	29	0	0	0	24	12	42.0	33	187	19	11	0	2	3	1	25	3	40	5	0
Westfall, Allan, Orl.	2	1	.667	6.88	8	0	0	0	2	0	17.0	19	87	13	13	3	0	0	3	16	0	13	0	0
Wilkins, Marc, Car.	0	0	.000	4.50	2	0	0	0	1	0	2.0	1	7	1	1	1	0	0	0	0	0	4	0	0
Williamson, Scott, Chat.	4	5	.444	3.78	18	18	0	0	0	0	100.0	85	420	49	42	4	2	6	3	46	4	105	13	2
Winkelsas, Joe, Gre.	0	0	.000	4.15	4	0	0	0	1	0	4.1	3	20	2	2	0	0	0	0	4	0	3	0	0
Wohlers, Mark, Gre.	0	0	.000	0.00	1	1	0	0	0	0	1.0	1	5	1	0	0	1	0	1	0	1	0	0	0
Wolff, Bryan, Mob.	9	3	.750	2.29	33	14	3	2	7	0	133.2	90	527	40	34	7	5	2	4	43	2	134	4	1
Woods, Brian, Birm.	0	0	.000	11.45	7	0	0	0	4	0	11.0	15	60	15	14	4	0	1	1	10	0	10	3	0
Worrell, Steve, W.T. *	5	1	.833	3.66	32	0	0	0	10	1	32.0	40	151	14	13	1	1	4	2	15	1	37	0	0
Wright, Scott, Chat.	2	1	.667	2.68	26	0	0	0	12	0	43.2	42	184	15	13	3	1	5	2	12	0	30	1	0
Young, Danny, W.T. *	0	2	.000	3.67	23	1	0	0	4	0	27.0	22	114	13	11	1	2	0	1	15	0	20	2	0
Young, Joe, Knox.	2	7	.222	9.68	11	9	0	0	0	0	40.0	52	201	51	43	8	2	1	4	32	1	31	7	0
Zolecki, Mike, Birm.	0	0	.000	4.50	8	0	0	0	4	0	24.0	20	118	22	21	4	1	4	2	29	1	15	3	1

COMBINATION SHUTOUTS: **Birmingham (4)**—Olsen-Tucker-Ward, Vining-Tucker, Beirne-Secoda, Beirne-Lundquist. **Carolina (5)**—Pickford-Evans-Giard, Phillips-Giard, Phillips-Tolar-Daniels, Hanie-Matthews-Daniels, Davis-Matthews-Delossantos. **Chattanooga (7)**—Rose-Paul, Rose-Stidham-Etler, Williamson-Donnelly, Hurst-Etler, Rose-Hurst, Williamson-MacRae-Puffer, Glauber-MacRae-Etler. **Greenville (6)**—Villegas-Brooks, Chen-Nelson-Cruz-Brooks-Manzano, Bowie-Borbon-Manzano, Chen-Schutz-Borbon-Cruz, Bowie-Nelson, Bowie-Winkelsas-Bullard. **Huntsville (2)**—DuBose-Carroll, Hudson-D'Amico-Harville. **Jacksonville (5)**—Darwin-Hiljus, Smith-Hiljus-Skuse, Miller-Durkovic, Bruner-Hiljus, Borkowski-Smith-Skuse. **Knoxville (4)**—Gordon-Meiners-Davey, Davey-Halperin, McBride-Smith, Gordon-McClellan-Halperin. **Mobile (4)**—Kaufman-Drumheller-Wolff, Anderson-Rossiter-Sak, Wolff-Drumheller-Sullivan, Lopez-Estes-Doughty-Skrmetta. **Orlando (6)**—Kelly-Newton-Nunez, Seelbach-Spencer, Seelbach-Scheffer-Spencer, Luce-Scheffer-Spencer, Marte-LeRoy, Luce-Davis. **West Tenn (2)**—Norton-Barker, McNichol-Jimenez-Young-Barker.

NO-HIT GAMES: None.

PITCHERS WITH TWO OR MORE TEAMS

Pitcher, Team	W	L	Pct.	ERA	G	GS	CG	ShO	GF	Sv.	IP	H	TBF	R	ER	HR	SH	SF	HB	BB	IBB	SO	WP	Bk.
Brown, Chad, Knox. *	0	2	.000	14.85	5	4	0	0	0	0	13.1	29	82	22	22	2	0	0	1	13	0	10	1	0
Brown, Chad, Car. *	0	2	.000	3.66	24	0	0	0	10	0	32.0	30	144	13	13	0	0	1	4	17	1	21	3	0
Carlyle, Buddy, Chat.	0	1	.000	5.40	1	1	0	0	0	0	5.0	6	20	3	3	0	0	0	0	0	0	3	0	0
Carlyle, Buddy, Mob.	14	6	.700	3.38	27	27	2	1	0	0	183.2	179	763	77	69	13	8	3	7	46	0	97	4	1
Doman, Roger, Car.	0	1	.000	7.40	10	1	0	0	2	0	20.2	29	90	20	17	5	2	2	0	8	0	12	1	0
Doman, Roger, Knox.	3	1	.750	4.60	22	0	0	0	9	0	29.1	26	121	15	15	3	3	1	2	10	0	14	1	0
Halperin, Mike, Car. *	0	0	.000	0.00	1	0	0	0	0	0	0.2	1	4	0	0	0	0	0	0	1	0	0	0	0
Halperin, Mike, Knox. *	5	1	.833	2.92	35	0	0	0	14	2	49.1	44	208	16	16	0	1	1	3	24	1	35	2	0
Rivette, Scott, Hun.	6	4	.600	4.61	35	0	0	0	9	2	68.1	75	309	46	35	7	0	4	5	32	0	53	5	0
Rivette, Scott, Knox.	0	0	.000	3.86	7	0	0	0	2	0	9.1	7	44	4	4	0	1	2	0	7	1	4	1	0
Schutz, Carl, Gre. *	1	3	.250	5.59	33	0	0	0	13	4	37.0	41	182	29	23	3	3	2	0	32	2	33	6	0
Schutz, Carl, W.T. *	1	1	.500	1.20	13	0	0	0	3	0	15.0	6	65	7	2	1	0	0	0	18	1	10	3	0

1998 FIELDING

TEAM

Team	Pct.	G	PO	A	E	TC	DP	PB
Jacksonville	.974	140	3694	1518	139	5351	141	9
Mobile	.974	140	3742	1458	140	5340	128	11
Orlando	.973	138	3645	1437	141	5223	127	23
Chattanooga	.972	138	3655	1507	150	5312	156	35
West Tenn	.969	140	3710	1445	166	5321	98	30
Greenville	.968	139	3706	1450	169	5325	129	18
Knoxville	.968	140	3632	1542	170	5344	135	9
Carolina	.967	139	3581	1506	171	5258	145	23
Birmingham	.967	140	3617	1446	175	5238	119	22
Huntsville	.965	140	3661	1566	187	5414	142	22

TRIPLE PLAYS: None.

CLASS AA *Southern League*

INDIVIDUAL

FIRST BASEMEN

NOTE: All caps denotes fielding-percentage leader based on 70 games for catchers, 93 for all other non-pitchers and 140 innings for pitchers. *Throws lefthanded.

Player, Team	Pct.	G	PO	A	E	TC	DP
Alcantara, Israel, Orl.	1.000	3	17	3	0	20	1
Allen, Dusty, Mob.	1.000	6	28	1	0	29	1
Allen, Marlon, Chat.	.985	81	703	66	12	781	83
Ardoin, Danny, Hun.	.500	1	2	0	2	4	0
Battle, Howard, Birm.	.947	2	16	2	1	19	4
Bream, Scott, Jack.	1.000	3	19	3	0	22	3
Buhner, Shawn, Orl.	.990	72	646	35	7	688	64
Cordero, Wil, Birm.	.989	10	81	9	1	91	7
Cotton, John, W.T.	1.000	18	140	11	0	151	9
Curl, John, Mob.	1.000	21	150	10	0	160	17
Curtis, Kevin, W.T.	1.000	2	3	0	0	3	1
Downs, Brian, Birm.	.974	5	35	3	1	39	4
Dubose, Brian, Jack.	1.000	3	23	2	0	25	4
Farris, Mark, Car.	1.000	26	215	9	0	224	22
Fick, Robert, Jack.	1.000	7	45	6	0	51	5
Freeman, Ricky, W.T.	.989	85	695	42	8	745	52
Freire, Alejandro, Jack.	.987	125	1050	113	15	1178	109
Furniss, Eddy, Car.*	.990	14	93	11	1	105	9
Garrison, Webster, Hun.	1.000	4	35	4	0	39	5
Gonzalez, Jimmy, Mob.	1.000	2	5	1	0	6	0
Grijak, Kevin, Car.	.969	17	146	9	5	160	12
Hernandez, Ramon, Hun.	.970	22	183	10	6	199	16
Ibarra, Jesse, Jack.	.960	5	21	3	1	25	2
Johnson, Adam, Gre.*	.955	7	39	3	2	44	6
Johnson, Mark, Birm.	1.000	1	6	0	0	6	1
Jones, Ryan, Knox.	.988	66	606	50	8	664	66
Jorgensen, Randy, Orl.*	.956	5	42	1	2	45	4
Kapler, Gabe, Jack.	1.000	1	2	0	0	2	0
LaRue, Jason, Chat.	.947	2	18	0	1	19	4
Liefer, Jeff, Birm.	.987	100	753	59	11	823	68
Long, Garrett, Car.	1.000	1	3	3	0	6	0
Lopez, Luis, Knox.	.995	61	529	42	3	574	49
Marcinczyk, T.R., Hun.	.985	110	957	71	16	1044	103
Marine, Del, Jack.	.974	5	31	6	1	38	1
Mathis, Joe, Mob.	1.000	1	1	0	0	1	0
McKay, Cody, Hun.	1.000	4	29	0	0	29	3
Melhuse, Adam, Knox.	.979	16	123	15	3	141	6
MITCHELL, Mike, Mob.	.990	121	963	91	11	1065	102
Molina, Jose, W.T.	.833	1	5	0	1	6	0
Norris, Dax, Gre.	.960	5	23	1	1	25	2
Nunez, Raymond, W.T.	.985	20	127	8	2	137	10
Polidor, Wil, Birm.	1.000	3	7	0	0	7	0
Rumfield, Toby, Gre.	.985	114	867	64	14	945	77
Rust, Brian, Gre.	.989	25	160	12	2	174	18
Salzano, Jerry, Gre.	.973	5	36	0	1	37	5
Sanders, Tracy, Car.	.985	79	686	38	11	735	77
Secrist, Reed, Knox.	1.000	1	5	0	0	5	0
Seefried, Tate, Birm.	.991	24	207	19	2	228	20
Slemmer, Dave, Hun.	1.000	4	24	2	0	26	2
Sorg, Jay, Chat.	.996	62	512	44	2	558	58
Thobe, Steve, Car.	.989	14	78	8	1	87	11
Torres, Paul, Orl.	.981	44	351	17	7	375	25
Vaz, Roberto, Hun.*	.950	3	19	0	1	20	2
Wathan, Dusty, Orl.	1.000	14	104	12	0	116	12
Wilson, Todd, Orl.	1.000	7	34	7	0	41	6
Zuleta, Julio, Birm.	.991	32	203	18	2	223	19

SECOND BASEMEN

Player, Team	Pct.	G	PO	A	E	TC	DP
Asche, Mike, Car.	1.000	2	2	2	0	4	0
Baez, Kevin, Chat.	1.000	1	1	4	0	5	1
Battle, Howard, Gre.	1.000	1	1	1	0	2	0
Beasley, Tony, Car.	1.000	2	2	2	0	4	1
Bream, Scott, Jack.	1.000	9	15	21	0	36	5
Bridges, Kary, W.T.	.984	32	58	68	2	128	14
Brito, Luis, Car.	.875	1	1	6	1	8	1
Brown, Randy, Car.	1.000	10	24	26	0	50	6
Castleberry, Kevin, W.T.	.967	18	19	40	2	61	7
Castro, Jose, Hun.	.900	3	2	7	1	10	0
Cotton, John, W.T.	1.000	9	9	22	0	31	5
Dean, Chris, Orl.	.964	61	115	176	11	302	38
Delgado, Jose, Gre.	.984	12	28	32	1	61	10
Eaglin, Mike, Gre.	.961	124	258	329	24	611	71
Eddie, Steve, Chat.	1.000	9	16	23	0	39	6
Figueroa, Luis, Car.	.982	29	72	92	3	167	27
Finn, John, Birm.	1.000	13	30	25	0	55	6

Player, Team	Pct.	G	PO	A	E	TC	DP
Forkerway, Trey, W.T.	1.000	1	1	0	0	1	0
Freel, Ryan, Knox.	1.000	7	14	22	0	36	2
Gama, Rick, Mob.	.985	28	59	69	2	130	15
Garrison, Webster, Hun.	.969	34	68	89	5	162	22
Guevara, Giomar, Orl.	1.000	2	5	8	0	13	6
Harrison, Adonis, Orl.	.960	58	95	147	10	252	35
Hazlett, Steve, Orl.	1.000	2	0	4	0	4	1
Hills, Rich, Orl.	.960	10	15	9	1	25	3
Holbert, Aaron, Orl.	1.000	7	19	21	0	40	9
Jasco, Elinton, Car.	.897	6	12	14	3	29	2
Katz, Jason, Gre.	1.000	3	5	4	0	9	2
Lackey, Steve, Jack.	.964	6	12	15	1	28	5
MACIAS, Jose, Jack.	.977	127	246	354	14	614	85
Martins, Eric, Hun.	.989	37	72	105	2	179	30
Meyers, Chad, W.T.	.934	73	154	173	23	350	43
Morris, Warren, Car.	.964	40	87	100	7	194	29
Mummau, Rob, Knox.	.979	8	20	27	1	48	5
Nevers, Tom, Chat.	.947	5	8	10	1	19	4
Newhan, David, Mob.	.974	112	226	306	14	546	72
Nieves, Jose, W.T.	1.000	1	0	1	0	1	0
Nunez, Sergio, Birm.	.963	115	236	344	22	602	80
Ortiz, Santos, Hun.	.965	60	107	172	10	289	40
Patel, Manny, W.T.	.960	7	12	12	1	25	2
Peeples, Michael, Knox.	.966	109	195	323	18	536	62
Polidor, Wil, Birm.	.938	16	25	36	4	65	8
Powers, John, Mob.	1.000	4	13	5	0	18	2
Presto, Nick, Chat.	.970	128	287	370	20	677	95
Ramirez, Joel, Orl.	.909	4	5	5	1	11	0
Rodriguez, Tony, Orl.	.964	7	9	18	1	28	3
Rumfield, Toby, Gre.	1.000	1	0	2	0	2	0
Rust, Brian, Gre.	1.000	1	0	1	0	1	0
Salzano, Jerry, Gre.	.864	7	9	10	3	22	2
Slemmer, Dave, Hun.	.960	21	41	54	4	99	8
Solano, Fausto, Knox.	.959	18	28	43	3	74	12
Unroe, Tim, W.T.	1.000	1	2	2	0	4	0
Valette, Ramon, W.T.	.956	17	16	27	2	45	7
Wimmer, Chris, Car.	.989	55	119	143	3	265	42

THIRD BASEMEN

Player, Team	Pct.	G	PO	A	E	TC	DP
Alcantara, Israel, Orl.	.750	1	2	1	1	4	0
Allen, Marlon, Chat.	.000	1	0	0	1	1	0
Balfe, Ryan, Mob.	.903	12	7	21	3	31	3
Battle, Howard, Birm.-Gre.	.923	71	41	127	14	182	16
Blake, Casey, Knox.	.913	45	27	89	11	127	8
Bream, Scott, Jack.	.979	15	12	35	1	48	4
Bridges, Kary, W.T.	.977	22	8	34	1	43	1
Brown, Randy, Car.	.947	7	4	14	1	19	1
Castleberry, Kevin, W.T.	1.000	8	2	14	0	16	2
Castro, Jose, Hun.	.898	13	9	35	5	49	1
Chavez, Eric, Hun.	.935	79	54	146	14	214	13
Cotton, John, W.T.	.877	29	17	47	9	73	4
Donato, Dan, Orl.	.818	2	3	6	2	11	0
EDDIE, Steve, Chat.	.956	110	86	215	14	315	27
Farris, Mark, Car.	.905	82	57	153	22	232	3
Finn, John, Birm.	.950	7	7	12	1	20	2
Forkerway, Trey, W.T.	1.000	4	0	7	0	7	0
Garrison, Webster, Hun.	.969	35	28	67	3	98	8
Guthrie, David, Chat.	.963	16	10	16	1	27	3
Haverbusch, Kevin, Car.	.871	41	26	89	17	132	8
Hills, Rich, Orl.	.911	18	9	32	4	45	1
LaRue, Jason, Chat.	1.000	4	2	7	0	9	1
Lee, Carlos, Birm.	.902	127	99	223	35	357	16
Lopez, Luis, Knox.	1.000	29	19	50	0	69	4
Luderer, Brian, Hun.	1.000	1	1	0	0	1	0
Manning, Nate, W.T.	.841	16	10	27	7	44	4
Marcinczyk, T.R., Hun.	.912	11	9	22	3	34	1
McKay, Cody, Hun.	1.000	3	1	6	0	7	0
Millette, Joe, W.T.	.667	1	2	0	1	3	0
Mummau, Rob, Knox.	.943	17	10	23	2	35	2
Nelson, Bry, W.T.	.899	28	25	46	8	79	9
Nevers, Tom, Chat.	.750	2	2	4	2	8	0
Newhan, David, Mob.	1.000	3	3	4	0	7	0
Nunez, Raymond, W.T.	.900	34	16	47	7	70	2
Polidor, Wil, Birm.	.917	4	2	9	1	12	1
Powers, John, Mob.	.941	111	65	204	17	286	10
Prieto, Rick, Mob.	.789	7	1	14	4	19	3
Rust, Brian, Gre.	.944	56	37	98	8	143	16
Salzano, Jerry, Gre.	.863	30	19	50	11	80	3

Player, Team	Pct.	G	PO	A	E	TC	DP
Slemmer, Dave, Hun.	.853	12	10	19	5	34	3
Solano, Fausto, Knox.	1.000	3	0	3	0	3	0
Sorg, Jay, Chat.	.854	18	10	25	6	41	1
Strange, Doug, Car.	1.000	4	1	5	0	6	2
Stromsborg, Ryan, Knox.	.895	10	5	12	2	19	1
Thobe, Steve, Car.	.949	15	15	22	2	39	4
Thompson, Andy, Knox.	.814	44	24	72	22	118	8
Torres, Paul, Orl.	.920	65	50	123	15	188	15
Unroe, Tim, W.T.	.865	15	15	30	7	52	1
Valette, Ramon, W.T.	.867	6	4	9	2	15	2
Villalobos, Carlos, Jack.	.928	126	94	267	28	389	22
Wilson, Todd, Orl.	.950	8	4	15	1	20	0

THIRD BASEMEN WITH TWO OR MORE TEAMS

Player, Team	Pct.	G	PO	A	E	TC	DP
Battle, Howard, Birm.	1.000	3	2	1	0	3	0
Battle, Howard, Gre.	.922	68	39	126	14	179	16
Hazlett, Steve, Mob.	.974	15	8	29	1	38	1
Hazlett, Steve, Orl.	.571	3	1	3	3	7	0

SHORTSTOPS

Player, Team	Pct.	G	PO	A	E	TC	DP
Baez, Kevin, Chat.	.950	46	67	140	11	218	31
Battle, Howard, Gre.	1.000	7	7	11	0	18	2
Bautista, Juan, Birm.	.943	120	173	342	31	546	76
Bream, Scott, Jack.	.957	10	19	26	2	47	5
Brito, Luis, Car.	.905	5	5	14	2	21	4
Brown, Randy, Car.	.967	53	85	147	8	240	38
Castleberry, Kevin, W.T.	.833	11	11	14	5	30	3
Castro, Jose, Hun.	.930	31	33	99	10	142	20
Delgado, Jose, Gre.	.875	3	2	5	1	8	1
DeROSA, Mark, Gre.	.964	125	195	338	20	553	76
Eddie, Steve, Chat.	.818	4	1	8	2	11	0
Espada, Josue, Hun.	.951	46	57	116	9	182	23
Figueroa, Luis, Car.	.943	90	128	267	24	419	56
Finn, John, Birm.	.961	12	11	38	2	51	7
Forkerway, Trey, W.T.	.971	51	60	106	5	171	17
Freel, Ryan, Knox.	.938	2	5	10	1	16	2
Goodell, Steve, Gre.	1.000	5	2	16	0	18	4
Guevara, Giomar, Orl.	.911	13	14	37	5	56	6
Guthrie, David, Chat.	.959	50	78	130	9	217	26
Hills, Rich, Orl.	.925	50	65	133	16	214	30
Holbert, Aaron, Orl.	.965	62	95	178	10	283	35
Lackey, Steve, Jack.	.920	3	6	17	2	25	3
Martins, Eric, Hun.	.929	39	39	92	10	141	20
McKay, Cody, Hun.	1.000	1	1	1	0	2	0
Mitchell, Derek, Jack.	.953	128	205	383	29	617	87
Mummau, Rob, Knox.	.904	9	15	32	5	52	6
Nelson, Bry, W.T.	1.000	7	1	4	0	5	2
Nevers, Tom, Chat.	.927	48	57	145	16	218	33
Newhan, David, Mob.	1.000	1	0	3	0	3	0
Nicholson, Kevin, Mob.	.937	130	201	363	38	602	80
Nieves, Jose, W.T.	.934	81	130	210	24	364	31
Ortiz, Santos, Hun.	.901	35	52	102	17	171	21
Polidor, Wil, Birm.	.972	9	15	20	1	36	6
Powers, John, Mob.	.961	11	13	36	2	51	7
Ramirez, Joel, Orl.	.928	17	19	45	5	69	5
Rodriguez, Tony, Orl.	.917	7	9	13	2	24	2
Salzano, Jerry, Gre.	1.000	3	3	10	0	13	1
Solano, Fausto, Knox.	.931	60	96	186	21	303	28
Tejada, Miguel, Hun.	.922	13	18	41	5	64	16
Torres, Paul, Orl.	1.000	1	1	3	0	4	0
Valette, Ramon, W.T.	.949	12	12	25	2	39	5
Wimmer, Chris, Car.	1.000	2	1	3	0	4	0
Woodward, Chris, Knox.	.971	72	145	220	11	376	59

OUTFIELDERS

Player, Team	Pct.	G	PO	A	E	TC	DP
Alcantara, Israel, Orl.	1.000	2	3	0	0	3	0
Allen, Dusty, Mob.	.951	38	56	2	3	61	0
Ardoin, Danny, Hun.	1.000	2	3	1	0	4	0
Asche, Mike, Car.	.964	54	99	7	4	110	1
BARKER, Glen, Jack.	1.000	109	307	16	0	323	7
Bass, Jayson, Gre.	.968	79	150	3	5	158	1
Bautista, Danny, Gre.	1.000	2	6	0	0	6	0
Bowers, Brent, Knox.	.981	27	48	3	1	52	0
Bowles, Justin, Hun.*	.969	69	118	6	4	128	2
Bream, Scott, Jack.	1.000	16	45	0	0	45	0
Brock, Tarrik, Orl.*	.989	95	173	11	2	186	3
Brooks, Ramy, Chat.	1.000	1	1	0	0	1	0
Brown, Emil, Car.	.972	108	199	10	6	215	0
Brown, Randy, Car.	1.000	2	1	0	0	1	0

Player, Team	Pct.	G	PO	A	E	TC	DP
Brown, Roosevelt, W.T.	.956	41	61	4	3	68	0
Candelaria, Ben, Knox.	.938	36	58	3	4	65	0
Castleberry, Kevin, W.T.	1.000	11	6	2	0	8	0
Castro, Jose, Hun.	1.000	5	4	0	0	4	0
Clark, Brady, Chat.	.993	57	149	3	1	153	2
Cotton, John, W.T.	.977	36	40	2	1	43	0
Curl, John, Mob.	.949	60	90	4	5	99	1
Curtis, Kevin, W.T.	.889	8	8	0	1	9	0
Darr, Mike, Mob.	.979	129	261	13	6	280	2
Dascenzo, Doug, Mob.*	1.000	7	9	1	0	10	0
Dubose, Brian, Jack.	.935	24	28	1	2	31	0
Eaglin, Mike, Gre.	1.000	1	2	0	0	2	0
Eddie, Steve, Chat.	1.000	21	40	1	0	41	1
Encarnacion, Mario, Hun.	.969	94	181	8	6	195	1
Faggett, Ethan, Mob.*	.932	42	66	2	5	73	0
Fick, Robert, Jack.	1.000	1	2	0	0	2	0
Finn, John, Birm.	1.000	2	2	0	0	2	0
Frank, Mike, Chat.*	.985	51	127	3	2	132	1
Freel, Ryan, Knox.	.982	55	108	3	2	113	2
Freeman, Ricky, W.T.	1.000	19	28	0	0	28	0
Garrison, Webster, Hun.	.958	25	21	2	1	24	1
Gazarek, Marty, W.T.	1.000	20	38	5	0	43	1
Gibralter, Steve, Chat.	.968	15	29	1	1	31	1
Gonzalez, Manny, Birm.	.959	95	169	18	8	195	1
Hall, Ronnie, W.T.	.932	41	62	7	5	74	1
Hawkins, Kraig, Orl.	.972	47	98	5	3	106	0
Hazlett, Steve, Mob.-Orl.	1.000	28	47	3	0	50	0
Hernaiz, Juan, Jack.	.935	80	124	6	9	139	0
Hernandez, Alexander, Car.*	.955	110	217	15	11	243	4
Hills, Rich, Orl.	1.000	3	4	0	0	4	0
Inglin, Jeff, Birm.	.986	115	204	10	3	217	1
Ingram, Darron, Chat.	.986	115	203	5	3	211	2
Jenkins, Corey, Birm.	.857	7	6	0	1	7	0
Jennings, Robin, W.T.*	1.000	2	1	0	0	1	0
Johnson, Adam, Gre.*	.979	91	184	2	4	190	0
Joseph, Terry, W.T.-Mob.	.976	64	122	2	3	127	0
Kapler, Gabe, Jack.	.984	139	292	12	5	309	3
Katz, Jason, Gre.	1.000	7	13	0	0	13	0
Larkin, Stephen, Chat.*	.947	70	123	3	7	133	1
Liefer, Jeff, Birm.	1.000	10	10	1	0	11	0
Lombard, George, Gre.	.947	119	170	8	10	188	1
Long, Garrett, Car.	.915	26	42	1	4	47	0
Manning, Brian, Birm.	.933	8	14	0	1	15	0
Marn, Kevin, Chat.	.929	10	13	0	1	14	0
Mathis, Joe, Orl.	.991	93	216	5	2	223	2
Matthews, Gary, Mob.	.995	68	184	8	1	193	2
McDonald, Jason, Hun.	1.000	5	10	1	0	11	0
McKinnon, Sandy, Birm.	.966	56	106	6	4	116	2
McNabb, Buck, W.T.	.979	107	181	9	4	194	0
Melhuse, Adam, Knox.	1.000	2	4	0	0	4	0
Mendoza, Carlos, Orl.*	.964	25	53	1	2	56	0
Moore, Kerwin, Hun.	.961	103	192	7	8	207	2
Mummau, Rob, Knox.	1.000	4	4	1	0	5	0
Murray, Glenn, Chat.	.956	53	87	0	4	91	0
Neill, Mike, Hun.*	1.000	9	21	1	0	22	1
Pendergrass, Tyrone, Gre.	.889	5	8	0	1	9	0
Peterson, Charles, Car.	.944	75	126	9	8	143	5
Porter, Bo, W.T.	.989	125	258	10	3	271	0
Prieto, Rick, Mob.	.985	51	64	2	1	67	0
Rivers, Jonathan, Knox.	.982	87	152	10	3	165	2
Roberts, David, Jack.*	1.000	49	105	1	0	106	0
Roberts, Lonell, Gre.	.981	44	98	3	2	103	1
Robinson, Kerry, Orl.*	1.000	63	135	5	0	140	1
Salzano, Jerry, Gre.	.943	45	65	1	4	70	0
Sanders, Anthony, Knox.	1.000	6	15	3	0	18	1
Secrist, Reed, Knox.	1.000	5	7	1	0	8	0
Skett, Will, Knox.	.960	64	116	3	5	124	1
Slemmer, Dave, Hun.	.963	16	22	4	1	27	0
Smith, Demond, Birm.	.979	83	185	4	4	193	2
Sollmann, Scott, Jack.*	1.000	10	24	1	0	25	0
Staton, T.J., Car.*	.988	55	78	4	1	83	0
Stromsborg, Ryan, Knox.	.992	61	128	3	1	132	0
Thobe, Steve, Car.	1.000	5	6	1	0	7	0
Thompson, Andy, Knox.	.967	63	114	3	4	121	0
Tidwell, Dave, Chat.	.969	42	92	2	3	97	2
Tinoco, Luis, Orl.	1.000	15	23	2	0	25	0
Trippy, Joe, Gre.*	.978	48	83	6	2	91	2
Tucci, Pete, Knox.	.957	38	64	2	3	69	0
Vaz, Roberto, Hun.*	.962	125	218	9	9	236	0
Warner, Mike, Gre.*	1.000	20	42	0	0	42	0
Whittaker, Jerry, Birm.	.978	52	128	5	3	136	0
Wilcox, Luke, Orl.	.987	70	141	10	2	153	1
Williams, Juan, W.T.	.969	42	58	4	2	64	1

OUTFIELDERS WITH TWO OR MORE TEAMS

Player, Team	Pct.	G	PO	A	E	TC	DP
Hazlett, Steve, Mob.	1.000	12	18	1	0	19	0
Hazlett, Steve, Orl.	1.000	16	29	2	0	31	0
Joseph, Terry, W.T.	.977	28	42	0	1	43	0
Joseph, Terry, Mob.	.976	36	80	2	2	84	0

CATCHERS

Player, Team	Pct.	G	PO	A	E	TC	DP	PB
Ardoin, Danny, Hun.	.985	85	555	86	10	651	8	15
Asche, Mike, Car.	1.000	1	1	0	0	1	0	0
Briones, Chris, Mob.	1.000	2	3	0	0	3	0	0
Brooks, Ramy, Chat.	.977	15	72	13	2	87	2	5
Cardenas, Johnny, Birm.	1.000	17	105	12	0	117	1	2
Cardona, Javier, Jack.	.976	41	208	33	6	247	4	0
Davis, Ben, Mob.	.994	115	920	76	6	1002	7	10
Davis, James, Chat.	.979	35	208	23	5	236	1	8
Ellis, Kevin, W.T.	.983	10	54	5	1	60	1	2
Fick, Robert, Jack.	.983	79	493	39	9	541	4	5
Gonzalez, Jimmy, Mob.	.988	13	74	6	1	81	0	1
Gonzalez, Ricky, Birm.	.984	23	170	13	3	186	2	1
Gonzalez, Wikleman, Mob.	1.000	13	65	7	0	72	0	0
Heller, Brad, Birm.	.950	5	17	2	1	20	0	0
Hernandez, Ramon, Hun.	.987	51	341	32	5	378	0	6
Horner, Jim, Orl.	.989	71	515	45	6	566	6	14
Johnson, Mark, Birm.	.990	103	717	65	8	790	4	19
LaRue, Jason, Chat.	.985	92	526	83	9	618	4	21
Luderer, Brian, Hun.	.977	8	40	3	1	44	0	1
Mahoney, Mike, Gre.	.987	18	140	14	2	156	1	2
Marine, Del, Jack.	.987	28	146	11	2	159	1	4
Matos, Pascual, Gre.	.981	95	690	99	15	804	11	12
McKay, Cody, Hun.	1.000	1	7	3	0	10	0	0
Melhuse, Adam, Knox.	.977	54	297	36	8	341	4	4
Micucci, Mike, W.T.	.985	51	300	29	5	334	1	7
Molina, Jose, W.T.	.991	104	739	108	8	855	2	21
Mosquera, Julio, Knox.	.983	8	51	7	1	59	0	2
Mummau, Rob, Knox.	1.000	1	1	0	0	1	0	0
Norris, Dax, Gre.	.984	32	219	29	4	252	2	3
Ojeda, Miguel, Car.	.991	18	108	8	1	117	2	2
Probst, Alan, Knox.	.982	75	445	54	9	508	7	3
Reyes, Jose, Car.	.974	11	68	6	2	76	2	1
Rodriguez, Luis, Knox.	1.000	6	34	4	0	38	0	0
Rumfield, Toby, Gre.	1.000	6	32	2	0	34	1	1
Sanchez, Marcos, Mob.	.960	4	23	1	1	25	0	0
Secrist, Reed, Knox.	.947	5	35	1	2	38	0	0
Sorg, Jay, Chat.	1.000	1	1	0	0	1	0	0
Steinmann, Scott, Orl.	1.000	16	89	9	0	98	1	5
SWEET, Jon, Car.	.996	74	423	56	2	481	5	4
Thobe, Steve, Car.	1.000	17	104	11	0	115	1	9
Thompson, Karl, Orl.	1.000	8	8	2	0	10	0	0
Viera, Rob, Chat.	1.000	4	29	2	0	31	0	1
Wathan, Dusty, Orl.	.997	55	331	21	1	353	2	4
Wilson, Craig, Car.	.995	32	185	13	1	199	0	7

PITCHERS

Player, Team	Pct.	G	PO	A	E	TC	DP
Abbott, Jim, Birm.*	.846	8	4	7	2	13	0
Ah Yat, Paul, Car.*	.800	13	2	6	2	10	0
Ambrose, John, Birm.	.967	31	9	20	1	30	0
Anderson, Bill, Mob.	1.000	13	4	6	0	10	0
Anderson, Jason, Hun.*	.667	3	1	1	1	3	0
Anderson, Matt, Jack.	1.000	13	1	1	0	2	0
Arnold, Jamie, Gre.	.871	32	14	13	4	31	1
Arroyo, Bronson, Car.	1.000	23	9	17	0	26	1
Averette, Robert, Chat.	1.000	14	7	9	0	16	0
Baez, Benito, Hun.*	1.000	34	6	18	0	24	2
Barker, Richie, W.T.	.929	51	3	10	1	14	0
Beirne, Kevin, Birm.	.926	26	13	37	4	54	1
Bennett, Tom, Hun.	1.000	28	4	4	0	8	1
Berry, Jason, Hun.	.750	13	0	3	1	4	0
Bonilla, Denny, Orl.*	.938	37	5	10	1	16	1
Borbon, Pedro, Gre.*	1.000	16	2	6	0	8	1
Borkowski, Dave, Jack.	1.000	28	18	18	0	36	2
Bowie, Micah, Gre.*	.963	30	4	22	1	27	1
Bradford, Chad, Birm.	1.000	10	1	6	0	7	0
Briggs, Anthony, Gre.	1.000	6	3	3	0	6	0
Brooks, Antone, Gre.*	1.000	26	6	8	0	14	3
Brown, Chad, Knox.-Car.*	1.000	29	4	2	0	6	0
Brown, Darold, W.T.*	1.000	6	1	0	0	1	0
Bruner, Clay, Jack.	.923	28	34	26	5	65	2
Bullard, Jason, Gre.	1.000	17	0	2	0	2	0
Buteaux, Shane, Birm.	.875	13	4	3	1	8	0
Byrne, Earl, W.T.*	.938	15	3	12	1	16	0

Player, Team	Pct.	G	PO	A	E	TC	DP
Callaway, Michael, Orl.	.941	18	7	9	1	17	0
Carlyle, Buddy, Chat.-Mob.	.944	28	15	36	3	54	4
Carmona, Rafael, Orl.	1.000	4	0	1	0	1	0
Carroll, Dave, Hun.*	1.000	20	1	3	0	4	0
Caruso, Gene, Car.*	1.000	3	1	0	0	1	0
Chantres, Carlos, Birm.	.818	20	5	4	2	11	0
Chen, Bruce, Gre.*	.762	24	6	10	5	21	0
Cole, Victor, W.T.	1.000	19	2	5	0	7	1
Cordero, Francisco, Jack.	.800	17	2	2	1	5	0
Corey, Mark, Chat.	1.000	6	2	4	0	6	0
Corn, Chris, Car.	1.000	8	2	8	0	10	0
Crawford, Carlos, Car.	.500	6	1	0	1	2	0
Crowell, Jim, Chat.*	1.000	5	1	1	0	2	0
Cruz, Charlie, Gre.*	1.000	49	1	11	0	12	0
Dace, Derek, Jack.*	.929	40	6	7	1	14	0
Dale, Carl, Hun.	1.000	3	2	1	0	3	0
D'Amico, Jeff, Hun.	1.000	24	2	5	0	7	0
Daniels, David, Car.	.923	35	3	9	1	13	2
Daniels, John, Orl.	.750	11	0	3	1	4	0
Darwin, David, Jack.*	.971	24	10	23	1	34	5
Davenport, Joe, Birm.	1.000	26	0	3	0	3	0
Davey, Tom, Knox.	.944	48	3	14	1	18	1
Davis, Kane, Car.	1.000	18	2	13	0	15	0
Davis, Tim, Orl.*	.875	14	3	4	1	8	1
De La Rosa, Maximo, Orl.	1.000	42	6	10	0	16	1
De Los Santos, Mariano, Car.	1.000	10	1	2	0	3	0
Dixon, Bubba, Mob.*	.667	9	0	2	1	3	0
Doman, Roger, Car.-Knox.	.941	32	1	15	1	17	2
Donnelly, Brendan, Chat.	1.000	38	2	4	0	6	0
Doughty, Brian, Mob.	.889	17	1	7	1	9	0
Doyle, Tom, Chat.*	1.000	9	1	4	0	5	1
Drumheller, Al, Mob.*	.944	50	6	11	1	18	0
Dubose, Eric, Hun.*	.963	14	11	15	1	27	2
Duncan, Courtney, W.T.	.915	29	13	30	4	47	1
Dunham, Pat, Orl.	1.000	10	4	2	0	6	0
Durkovic, Peter, Jack.*	1.000	37	2	7	0	9	0
Enochs, Chris, Hun.	.920	26	11	12	2	25	0
Estes, Eric, Mob.	.941	17	6	10	1	17	0
Etler, Todd, Chat.	1.000	46	9	9	0	18	0
Evans, Dave, Car.	1.000	26	2	7	0	9	0
Farley, Joe, Birm.*	1.000	6	0	5	0	5	0
Farnsworth, Kyle, W.T.	1.000	13	8	10	0	18	0
Fitzgerald, Brian, Orl.*	1.000	2	1	0	0	1	0
Foster, Kevin, W.T.	1.000	2	1	0	0	1	0
Garcia, Al, W.T.	.968	25	2	28	1	31	0
Giard, Ken, Car.	1.000	42	3	9	0	12	2
Giron, Isabel, Knox.	1.000	6	1	4	0	5	0
Gissell, Chris, W.T.	.000	1	0	0	1	1	0
Glauber, Keith, Chat.	1.000	2	0	1	0	1	0
Glover, Gary, Knox.	.933	8	6	8	1	15	1
Gordon, Mike, Knox.	.903	44	10	18	3	31	2
Graterol, Beiker, Knox.	.909	12	3	7	1	11	1
Grigsby, Benji, W.T.	.944	32	5	12	1	18	1
Gunther, Kevin, Hun.	.941	45	6	10	1	17	2
Guzman, Domingo, Mob.	.889	12	2	6	1	9	1
Halperin, Mike, Knox.*	1.000	35	4	15	0	19	1
Hammack, Brandon, W.T.	1.000	21	0	4	0	4	0
Harikkala, Tim, Orl.	1.000	15	7	17	0	24	2
Harris, D.J., Knox.	1.000	22	3	1	0	4	0
Hartshorn, Ty, Orl.	.964	19	11	16	1	28	1
Harville, Chad, Hun.	1.000	12	1	0	0	1	0
Haynie, Jason, Car.*	.857	17	4	14	3	21	0
Hernandez, Elvin, Car.	.920	27	7	16	2	25	0
Hiljus, Erik, Jack.	1.000	42	6	4	0	10	0
Hudson, Tim, Hun.	.840	22	6	15	4	25	0
Hunter, Rich, Chat.	.778	7	0	7	2	9	0
Hurst, Doug, Chat.	1.000	44	6	15	0	21	1
Jacobs, Ryan, Gre.*	.920	35	5	18	2	25	2
Jimenez, Miguel, W.T.	1.000	26	2	5	0	7	0
Kaufman, Brad, Mob.	1.000	5	2	3	0	5	0
Kaufman, John, Orl.*	.800	7	0	4	1	5	0
Kelly, Jeff, Car.*	1.000	1	1	0	0	1	0
Kelly, John, Orl.	.929	9	2	11	1	14	1
King, Ray, W.T.*	1.000	25	5	10	0	15	0
Kjos, Ryan, Hun.	1.000	9	1	2	0	3	0
Kolb, Brandon, Mob.	.824	21	6	8	3	17	1
Lakman, Jason, Birm.	.909	15	7	3	1	11	0
Lawrence, Clint, Knox.*	.889	7	3	5	1	9	1
Laxton, Brett, Hun.	1.000	21	14	16	0	30	2
Lee, Jeremy, Knox.	1.000	10	0	1	0	1	0
LeBlanc, Eric, Chat.	.826	23	8	11	4	23	0
LeRoy, John, Orl.	1.000	12	2	3	0	5	0
Linebarger, Keith, W.T.	1.000	50	6	2	0	8	0

Player, Team	Pct.	G	PO	A	E	TC	DP
Lopez, Rodrigo, Mob.	1.000	4	2	8	0	10	1
Luce, Robert, Orl.	.952	27	10	30	2	43	3
Lukasiewicz, Mark, Knox.*	1.000	5	0	1	0	1	0
Lundquist, David, Birm.	1.000	33	3	4	0	7	1
Lyons, Curt, Chat.	1.000	3	0	1	0	1	0
MacRae, Scott, Chat.	1.000	49	10	10	0	20	1
Mallard, Randi, Chat.	.913	13	6	15	2	23	2
Manon, Julio, Orl.	.500	13	1	1	2	4	0
Manzano, Adrian, Gre.	1.000	39	5	8	0	13	0
Marte, Damaso, Orl.*	.947	22	5	13	1	19	1
Mathews, Del, Car.*	.900	22	4	14	2	20	0
McBride, Chris, Knox.	.943	35	11	22	2	35	4
McClellan, Sean, Knox.	1.000	24	1	7	0	8	2
McConnell, Sam, Car.*	.750	2	0	3	1	4	0
McGlinchy, Kevin, Gre.	1.000	6	1	1	0	2	0
McNichol, Brian, W.T.*	.926	28	7	18	2	27	1
Mears, Chris, Orl.	1.000	1	1	0	0	1	0
Meiners, Doug, Knox.	.969	43	13	18	1	32	1
Melendez, Dave, Jack.	.953	25	19	22	2	43	5
Miller, Matt, Jack.*	1.000	13	6	5	0	11	1
Mix, Greg, Gre.	1.000	22	0	3	0	3	0
Nelson, Chris, Hun.	.786	28	2	9	3	14	0
Nelson, Joe, Gre.	.917	45	11	22	3	36	0
Newman, Eric, Mob.	.964	27	7	20	1	28	1
Newton, Geronimo, Orl.*	1.000	21	0	9	0	9	1
Nichols, Jamie, Birm.	1.000	5	1	4	0	5	0
Norton, Phillip, W.T.*	1.000	19	5	23	0	28	0
Nunez, Maximo, Orl.	1.000	6	1	3	0	4	0
O'Connor, Brian, Car.*	.909	14	1	9	1	11	1
O'Dell, Jake, Hun.	1.000	27	4	13	0	17	1
Olsen, Jason, Birm.	1.000	28	12	22	0	34	2
Olszewski, Eric, Gre.	1.000	24	2	6	0	8	0
Paul, Andy, Chat.	1.000	17	4	2	0	6	0
Pena, Jesus, Birm.*	.833	22	1	4	1	6	1
Perez, Juan, Hun.*	.857	27	1	5	1	7	0
Perez, Odaliz, Gre.*	.947	23	1	17	1	19	1
Phillips, Jason, Car.	.941	25	13	35	3	51	2
Pickford, Kevin, Car.*	.889	13	2	6	1	9	1
Powell, Brian, Jack.	.905	14	8	11	2	21	1
Priest, Eddie, Chat.*	1.000	4	0	4	0	4	0
Puffer, Brandon, Chat.	1.000	7	0	2	0	2	0
Reed, Chris, Chat.	1.000	20	3	10	0	13	1
Ricketts, Chad, W.T.	1.000	13	2	2	0	4	1
Riedling, John, Chat.	.913	24	10	11	2	23	0
Rincon, Ricardo, Car.*	1.000	2	0	1	0	1	0
Rivette, Scott, Hun.-Knox.	1.000	42	2	7	0	9	1
Roberts, Willis, Jack.	1.000	12	2	7	0	9	0
Rose, Ted, Chat.	.909	29	11	19	3	33	2
Rossiter, Mike, Mob.	1.000	22	4	2	0	6	0
Ruffcorn, Scott, Chat.	1.000	10	1	0	0	1	0
Runion, Tony, Car.	1.000	7	0	1	0	1	0
RYAN, Jason, W.T.	1.000	30	11	35	0	46	0
Ryan, Robert, Chat.*	1.000	16	0	5	0	5	0
Sak, James, Mob.	1.000	45	4	3	0	7	0
Santos, Victor, Jack.	1.000	6	0	4	0	4	0
Scheffer, Aaron, Orl.	.800	19	1	3	1	5	0
Schutz, Carl, Gre.-W.T.*	1.000	46	1	10	0	11	0
Secoda, Jason, Birm.	.938	39	6	9	1	16	0
Seelbach, Chris, Orl.	.909	23	5	15	2	22	1
Shaw, Curtis, Car.*	1.000	3	0	2	0	2	0
Shumate, Jacob, Gre.	1.000	2	0	1	0	1	0
Skrmetta, Matt, Mob.	.889	51	2	6	1	9	1
Skuse, Nick, Jack.	1.000	49	1	3	0	4	1
Smith, Andy, Hun.	1.000	7	0	1	0	1	0
Smith, Brian, Knox.	1.000	42	4	6	0	10	0
Smith, Cam, Orl.	.750	23	1	2	1	4	0
Smith, Keilan, Jack.	1.000	39	5	7	0	12	1
Smoltz, John, Atl.	1.000	3	1	2	0	3	0
Spencer, Sean, Orl.*	1.000	37	2	6	0	8	0
Stevenson, Jason, Knox.	.933	33	6	22	2	30	2
Stidham, Phil, Chat.	1.000	5	1	2	0	3	1
Sullivan, Brendan, Mob.	1.000	35	3	12	0	15	2
Temple, Jason, Car.	.400	20	1	1	3	5	0
Theodile, Robert, Birm.	.857	8	3	3	1	7	0
Thobe, Tom, Chat.*	1.000	17	4	4	0	8	0
Thompson, John, Orl.	1.000	19	0	8	0	8	1
Tolar, Kevin, Orl.*	1.000	42	0	8	0	8	0
Tollberg, Brian, Mob.	.875	6	2	5	1	8	0
Tucker, Julien, Birm.	.688	34	3	8	5	16	2
Van De Weg, Ryan, Mob.	1.000	6	3	4	0	7	0
Veniard, Jay, Knox.*	1.000	11	0	5	0	5	0
Villegas, Ismael, Gre.	.955	40	10	11	1	22	3
Vining, Ken, Birm.*	.806	29	6	19	6	31	0
Vizcaino, Luis, Hun.	1.000	7	2	5	0	7	0
Walters, Brett, Mob.	.938	14	6	9	1	16	1
Ward, Bryan, Birm.*	.875	29	0	7	1	8	0
Westfall, Allan, Orl.	1.000	8	1	2	0	3	0
Williamson, Scott, Chat.	.952	18	10	10	1	21	1
Winkelsas, Joe, Gre.	.667	4	2	0	1	3	0
Wolff, Bryan, Mob.	.941	33	14	18	2	34	2
Woods, Brian, Birm.	1.000	7	1	0	0	1	0
Worrell, Steve, W.T.*	1.000	32	0	2	0	2	0
Young, Danny, W.T.*	1.000	23	0	4	0	4	0
Young, Joe, Knox.	.800	11	4	4	2	10	2

PITCHERS WITH TWO OR MORE TEAMS

Player, Team	Pct.	G	PO	A	E	TC	DP
Brown, Chad, Knox.*	1.000	5	1	0	0	1	0
Brown, Chad, Car.*	1.000	24	3	2	0	5	0
Carlyle, Buddy, Chat.	1.000	1	1	1	0	2	1
Carlyle, Buddy, Birm.	.942	27	14	35	3	52	3
Doman, Roger, Car.	1.000	10	0	5	0	5	0
Doman, Roger, Knox.	.917	22	1	10	1	12	2
Rivette, Scott, Hun.	1.000	35	2	5	0	7	1
Rivette, Scott, Knox.	1.000	7	0	2	0	2	0
Schutz, Carl, Gre.*	1.000	33	0	6	0	6	0
Schutz, Carl, W.T.*	1.000	13	1	4	0	5	0

The following players did not have any fielding statistics at the positions indicated or appeared only as a designated hitter, pinch-hitter or pinch-runner: Baez, 3b; Bale, p; Beasley, p; Bennett, of; Bussa, p; Callahan, p; Castro, p; Chrystler, p; J. Davis, 1b; K. Davis, p; D. Delgado, p; Della Rata, p; Dillinger, p; Donato, 1b; Eddie, p; Ellis, of; Flach, p; Grijak, p; Gryboski, p; Gunther, 3b; Halperin, p; B. Hurst, p; Janicki, p; Kimsey, p; Luderer, of; L. Mitchel, p; Montane, p; Martins, of; McKay, of; Mosquera, of; E. Nelson, p; Ortiz, of; Pineiro, p; Probst, p; L. Rodriguez, of; T. Sanders, of; Steinmann, 1b, 3b; Torres, p; Towle, dh, ph; Vaz, p; Wilkins, p; Wohlers, p; Wright, p; Zolecki, p.

LEAGUE CHAMPIONS

Year	Team	Pct.
1904—	Macon	.598
1905—	Macon	.625
1906—	Savannah	.637
1907—	Charleston	.620
1908—	Jacksonville	.694
1909—	Chattanooga*	.738
	Augusta	.702
1910—	Columbus	.588
1911—	Columbus*	.681
	Columbia	.710
1912—	Jacksonville*	.679
	Columbus	.632
1913—	Savannah	.754
	Savannah	.593
1914—	Savannah*	.667
	Albany	.650
1915—	Macon	.588
	Columbus*	.686
1916—	Augusta*	.617
	Columbia	.631
1917—	Charleston	.741
	Columbia*	.667
1918—	Did not operate.	
1919—	Columbia	.585
1920—	Columbia	.633
1921—	Columbia	.642
1922—	Charleston	.625
1923—	Charlotte*	.653
	Macon	.580
1924—	Augusta	.612
1925—	Spartanburg	.620
1926—	Greenville	.662
1927—	Greenville	.622
1928—	Asheville	.664
1929—	Asheville	.605
	Knoxville*	.634
1930—	Greenville*	.620
	Macon	.643
1931-35—	Did not operate.	
1936—	Jacksonville	.652
	Columbus*	.650
1937—	Columbus	.572
	Savannah (3rd)†	.565
1938—	Savannah	.574
	Macon (2nd)†	.570
1939—	Columbus	.601
	Augusta (2nd)†	.597
1940—	Savannah	.627
	Columbus (2nd)†	.583
1941—	Macon	.643
	Columbia (2nd)†	.636
1942—	Charleston	.620
	Macon (2nd)†	.585
1943-45—	Did not operate.	

Year	Team	Pct.
1946—	Columbus	.568
	Augusta (4th)†	.547
1947—	Columbus	.575
	Savannah (2nd)†	.563
1948—	Charleston	.572
	Greenville (3rd)†	.549
1949—	Macon‡	.623
1950—	Macon‡	.588
1951—	Montgomery	.607
1952—	Columbia	.649
	Montgomery (3rd)†	.558
1953—	Jacksonville	.679
	Savannah (2nd)†	.571
1954—	Jacksonville	.593
	Savannah (2nd)†	.571
1955—	Columbia	.636
	Augusta (3rd)†	.543
1956—	Jacksonville‡	.621
1957—	Augusta	.636
	Charlotte (2nd)†	.562
1958—	Augusta	.550
	Macon (3rd)†	.500
1959—	Knoxville	.557
	Gastonia (4th)†	.504
1960—	Columbia	.597
	Savannah (3rd)†	.561
1961—	Asheville	.635
1962—	Savannah	.662
	Macon (3rd)†	.576
1963—	Augusta*	.661
	Lynchburg	.662
1964—	Lynchburg	.579

Year	Team	Pct.
1965—	Columbus	.572
1966—	Mobile	.629
1967—	Birmingham	.604
1968—	Asheville	.614
1969—	Charlotte	.579
1970—	Columbus	.569
1971—	Did not operate as league—clubs were members of Dixie Association.	
1972—	Asheville	.583
	Montgomery§	.561
1973—	Montgomery§	.580
	Jacksonville	.559
1974—	Jacksonville	.565
	Knoxville§	.533
1975—	Orlando	.587
	Montgomery§	.545
1976—	Montgomery∞	.591
	Orlando	.540
1977—	Montgomery∞	.628
	Jacksonville	.522
1978—	Knoxville∞	.611
	Savannah	.500
1979—	Columbus	.587
	Nashville∞	.576
1980—	Memphis	.576
	Charlotte∞	.500
1981—	Nashville	.566
	Orlando∞	.556
1982—	Jacksonville	.576
	Nashville∞	.535
1983—	Birmingham∞	.628
	Jacksonville	.531

Year	Team	Pct.
1984—	Charlotte∞	.510
	Knoxville	.483
1985—	Charlotte	.545
	Huntsville∞	.542
1986—	Huntsville	.553
	Columbus∞	.500
1987—	Charlotte	.586
	Birmingham∞	.476
1988—	Greenville	.604
	Chattanooga∞	.566
1989—	Birmingham∞	.615
	Greenville	.504
1990—	Orlando	.590
	Memphis∞	.507
1991—	Greenville	.611
	Orlando∞	.535
1992—	Greenville∞	.699
	Chattanooga	.629
1993—	Birmingham∞	.549
	Knoxville	.500
1994—	Huntsville∞	.587
	Carolina	.529
1995—	Carolina∞	.618
	Chattanooga	.580
1996—	Chattanooga	.579
	Jacksonville∞	.543
1997—	Huntsville	.554
	Greenville∞	.529
1998—	Mobile∞	.614
	Jacksonville	.614

*Won split season playoff. †Won four-club playoff. ‡Won championship and four-club playoff. §League was divided into Eastern and Western divisions; won play-off. ∞League was divided into Eastern and Western divisions and played split season; won playoff.

CLASS AA *Southern League*

TEXAS LEAGUE

LEAGUE OFFICE

President/treasurer
Tom Kayser

Address
2442 Facet Oak
San Antonio, TX 78232

Phone
210-545-5297

TEAMS

ARKANSAS TRAVELERS

General manager
Bill Valentine

Manager
Chris Maloney

Ballpark (capacity, surface)
Ray Winder Field (6,089, grass)

Affiliation
Cardinals

Address
P.O. Box 55066
Little Rock, AR 72215

Phone
501-664-1555

EL PASO DIABLOS

Vice president, administration & ticketing
Andrew Wheeler

Vice president, stadium operations
Rob Sesish

Manager
Don Wakamatsu

Ballpark (capacity, surface)
Cohen Stadium (9,765, grass)

Affiliation
Diamondbacks

Address
P.O. Drawer 4797
El Paso, TX 79914

Phone
915-755-2000

JACKSON GENERALS

General manager
Bill Blackwell

Manager
Jim Pankovits

Ballpark (capacity, surface)
Smith-Wills Stadium (5,200, grass)

Affiliation
Astros

Address
P.O. Box 4209
Jackson, MS 39296

Phone
601-981-4664

MIDLAND ROCKHOUNDS

General manager
Monty Hoppel

Manager
Tony DeFrancesco

Ballpark (capacity, surface)
Christensen Stadium (5,000, grass)

Affiliation
Athletics

Address
P.O. Box 51187
Midland, TX 79710

Phone
915-683-4251

SAN ANTONIO MISSIONS

General manager
Dave Oldham

Manager
To be announced

Ballpark (capacity, surface)
Nelson Wolf Stadium (6,300, grass)

Affiliation
Dodgers

Address
5757 Highway 90 West
San Antonio, TX 78227

Phone
210-675-7275

SHREVEPORT CAPTAINS

General manager
Daniel Robinson

Manager
Shane Turner

Ballpark (capacity, surface)
Fair Grounds Field (6,200, grass)

Affiliation
Giants

Address
P.O. Box 3448
Shreveport, LA 71133

Phone
318-636-5555

TULSA DRILLERS

Executive v.p./general manager
Chuck Lamson

Manager
Bobby Jones

Ballpark (capacity, surface)
Drillers Stadium (11,000, grass)

Affiliation
Rangers

Address
P.O. Box 4448
Tulsa, OK 74159

Phone
918-744-5998

WICHITA WRANGLERS

General manager
Trevor Hinz

Manager
John Mizerock

Ballpark (capacity, surface)
Lawrence-Dumont Stadium (6,067,
artificial infield, grass outfield)

Affiliation
Royals

Address
P.O. Box 1420
Wichita, KS 67201

Phone
316-267-3372

1998 FINAL STANDINGS

FIRST HALF

EAST DIVISION

Team	W	L	T	Pct.	GB
Arkansas (Cardinals)	42	26	0	.618	....
Jackson (Astros)	35	33	0	.515	7.0
Shreveport (Giants)	32	36	0	.471	10.0
Tulsa (Rangers)	28	40	0	.412	14.0

WEST DIVISION

Team	W	L	T	Pct.	GB
San Antonio (Dodgers)	38	30	0	.559	....
El Paso (Brewers)	35	33	0	.515	3.0
Midland (Angels)	33	35	0	.485	5.0
Wichita (Royals)	29	39	0	.426	9.0

SECOND HALF

EAST DIVISION

Team	W	L	T	Pct.	GB
Tulsa (Rangers)	50	22	0	.694	....
Arkansas (Cardinals)	38	34	0	.528	12.0
Jackson (Astros)	35	37	0	.486	15.0
Shreveport (Giants)	25	47	0	.347	25.0

WEST DIVISION

Team	W	L	T	Pct.	GB
Wichita (Royals)	46	26	0	.639	....
El Paso (Brewers)	34	38	0	.472	12.0
Midland (Angels)	31	41	0	.431	15.0
San Antonio (Dodgers)	29	43	0	.403	17.0

CLASS AA *Texas League*

COMPOSITE

Team	Ark.	Tul.	Wich.	Jac.	E.P.	S.A.	Mid.	Shre.	W	L	T	Pct.	G.B.
Arkansas (Cardinals)	....	16	3	21	7	8	6	19	80	60	0	.571	....
Tulsa (Rangers)	16	....	5	10	10	3	7	22	78	62	0	.557	2.0
Wichita (Royals)	9	5	....	9	17	15	16	4	75	65	0	.536	5.0
Jackson (Astros)	11	17	3	....	6	10	5	18	70	70	0	.500	10.0
El Paso (Brewers)	3	2	15	4	....	18	19	8	69	71	0	.493	11.0
San Antonio (Dodgers)	4	7	17	2	14	....	16	7	67	73	0	.479	13.0
Midland (Angels)	4	5	16	5	13	16	....	5	64	76	0	.457	16.0
Shreveport (Giants)	13	10	6	14	4	3	7	....	57	83	0	.407	23.0

Arkansas' home games played in Little Rock, Ark.

Major league affiliations in parentheses.

PLAYOFFS: Wichita defeated San Antonio three games to two; Tulsa defeated Arkansas three games to none; Tulsa defeated Wichita four games to three to win league championship.

REGULAR-SEASON ATTENDANCE: Arkansas, 190,987; El Paso, 296,609; Jackson, 110,595; Midland, 190,076; San Antonio, 387,715; Shreveport, 161,940; Tulsa, 345,097; Wichita, 155,353. Total—1,838,372; Playoffs (15 games)—35,607. Class AA All-Star Game in New Haven, Conn.—6,248.

MANAGERS: Arkansas, Chris Maloney; El Paso, Ed Romero; Jackson, Jim Pankovits; Midland, Don Long; San Antonio, Ron Roenicke (through June 26) and Lance Parrish (June 27 through end of season); Shreveport, Mike Hart; Tulsa, Bobby Jones; Wichita, John Mizerock. Managerial record of team with more than one manager: San Antonio, Roenicke 44-37, Parrish 23-36.

ALL-STAR TEAM: 1B—Danny Buxbaum, Midland; 2B—Carlos Febles, Wichita; 3B—Adrian Beltre, San Antonio; SS—Santiago Perez, El Paso; OF—Peter Bergeron, San Antonio; Lance Berkman, Jackson; Jason Conti, Tulsa; Tyrone Horne, Arkansas; Mark Quinn, Wichita; DH—Eddie Christian, Midland; C—Angel Pena, San Antonio; Utility—Keith Luuloa, Midland; RHP—Freddy Garcia, Jackson; RHP—Jose Jimenez, Arkansas; RHP—Jason Grilli, Shreveport; LHP—Ted Lilly, San Antonio; LHP—Steve Prihoda, Wichita; RP—Jose Santiago, Wichita; Most Valuable Player—Tyrone Horne, Arkansas; Pitcher of the Year—Jose Jimenez, Arkansas; Manager of the Year—Chris Maloney, Arkansas.

1998 BATTING

TEAM

Team	Avg.	G	TPA	AB	R	H	TB	2B	3B	HR	RBI	SH	SF	HP	BB	IBB	SO	SB	CS	GDP	LOB	ShO	Slg.	OBP
El Paso	.293	140	5550	4923	835	1442	2159	298	52	105	769	42	46	73	466	23	894	137	86	76	1037	2	.439	.360
Wichita	.291	140	5458	4766	857	1389	2308	293	37	184	786	48	50	61	533	21	832	111	59	125	978	4	.484	.367
Midland	.290	140	5536	4857	811	1408	2206	282	60	132	748	40	51	62	526	24	911	124	70	122	1035	3	.454	.363
Jackson	.278	140	5363	4782	724	1331	2134	262	23	165	664	51	28	54	448	25	898	90	64	110	983	4	.446	.345
Tulsa	.271	140	5469	4802	757	1300	2025	274	44	121	680	18	41	71	537	21	941	118	67	115	1033	5	.422	.350
San Antonio	.270	140	5362	4726	689	1274	1981	247	56	116	616	84	38	51	463	19	885	182	78	85	983	8	.419	.339
Arkansas	.267	140	5325	4632	787	1237	2016	264	46	141	716	41	44	49	559	34	1009	125	56	89	960	6	.435	.349
Shreveport	.251	140	5231	4645	574	1165	1764	229	32	102	540	37	39	53	457	20	874	102	54	113	967	11	.380	.322

INDIVIDUAL

TOP QUALIFIERS FOR BATTING CHAMPIONSHIP

Minimum 378 plate appearances. *Lefthanded batter. †Switch-hitter.

Player, Team	Avg.	G	TPA	AB	R	H	TB	2B	3B	HR	RBI	SH	SF	HP	BB	IBB	SO	SB	CS	GDP	Slg.	OBP
Quinn, Mark, Wich.	.349	100	432	372	82	130	216	26	6	16	84	0	7	10	43	1	54	4	1	5	.581	.424
Pena, Angel, S.A.	.335	126	542	483	81	162	264	32	2	22	105	3	2	6	48	3	80	9	5	7	.547	.401
Luuloa, Keith, Mid.	.334	130	579	479	85	160	274	43	10	17	102	2	16	7	75	5	54	6	5	15	.572	.419
Christian, Eddie, Mid.†	.333	105	455	400	80	133	195	39	4	5	49	0	2	3	49	4	61	13	11	6	.488	.407
Morris, Warren, Tul.*	.331	95	440	390	59	129	203	22	5	14	73	1	2	4	43	2	63	12	7	11	.521	.401
Febles, Carlos, Wich.	.326	126	531	432	110	141	229	28	9	14	52	5	3	11	80	1	70	51	16	6	.530	.441
Neal, Mike, Jack.	.326	103	386	341	53	111	193	27	2	17	70	1	1	4	39	0	80	4	4	7	.566	.400
Gonzalez, Raul, Wich.	.325	118	520	455	84	148	232	31	1	17	86	1	4	2	58	3	53	12	8	15	.510	.401
Andreopoulos, Alex, E.P.*	.321	113	447	377	72	121	188	35	1	10	93	2	5	9	54	4	31	2	3	9	.499	.413
Brown, Ray, Wich.*	.318	114	469	402	79	128	224	31	1	21	96	1	6	3	57	5	57	4	2	16	.557	.402
Bergeron, Peter, S.A.*	.317	109	489	416	81	132	189	17	8	8	54	9	1	2	61	1	69	33	9	2	.454	.406
Conti, Jason, Tul.*	.315	130	611	530	125	167	267	31	12	15	67	1	2	9	63	4	96	19	13	5	.504	.396
Iapoce, Anthony, E.P.†	.314	133	631	576	97	181	222	23	6	2	53	9	2	11	33	1	67	35	20	4	.385	.362
Hutchins, Norm, Mid.*	.312	99	414	394	74	123	193	20	10	10	50	0	1	4	14	0	84	32	10	8	.490	.341
Horne, Tyrone, Ark.*	.312	123	520	443	94	138	268	13	3	37	139	0	6	1	70	7	97	18	7	8	.605	.402

DEPARTMENTAL LEADERS: G—Clapp, 139; AB—Iapoce, 576; R—Conti, 125 H—Iapoce, 181; TB—Luuloa, 274; 2B—Luuloa, 43; 3B—S. Perez, 13; HR—Horne, 37; RBI—Horne, 139; SH—Harkrider, 12; SF—Luuloa, 16; HP—Kominek, 22; BB—Clapp, 86; IBB—Berkman, 10; SO—Abbott, 135; SB—Febles, 51; CS—Iapoce, 20; GIDP—Lariviere, 18; Slg.—Horne, .605; OBP—Febles, .441.

ALL PLAYERS

*Lefthanded batter. †Switch-hitter.

Player, Team	Avg.	G	TPA	AB	R	H	TB	2B	3B	HR	RBI	SH	SF	HP	BB	IBB	SO	SB	CS	GDP	Slg.	OBP
Abbott, Chuck, Mid.†	.263	132	579	525	74	138	183	21	9	2	62	8	4	4	38	0	135	66	9	18	.349	.315
Alexander, Chad, Jack.	.286	128	498	416	77	119	195	33	2	13	45	3	3	5	71	0	80	6	7	8	.469	.394
Alguacil, Jose, Shre.†	.206	43	112	97	13	20	28	3	1	1	6	5	0	1	9	1	15	3	2	2	.289	.280
Allen, Luke, S.A.*	.333	23	85	78	9	26	40	3	1	3	10	1	0	0	6	1	16	1	2	0	.513	.381
Almond, Greg, Ark.	.190	10	24	21	3	4	8	1	0	1	7	0	0	0	3	0	5	0	0	0	.381	.292
Amezcua, Adan, Jack.	.205	23	76	73	6	15	23	2	0	2	6	0	0	0	3	0	11	1	1	3	.315	.237
Anderson, Cliff, S.A.*	.210	29	109	100	13	21	32	3	1	2	9	4	1	3	1	0	17	0	0	1	.320	.238
Andreopoulos, Alex, E.P.*	.321	113	447	377	72	121	188	35	1	10	93	2	5	9	54	4	31	2	3	9	.499	.413
Babineaux, Darrin, S.A.	.000	39	11	9	0	0	0	0	0	0	0	2	0	0	0	0	6	0	0	0	.000	.000
Barker, Kevin, E.P.*	.306	20	92	85	14	26	47	6	0	5	14	0	2	2	3	0	21	2	1	2	.553	.337
Barkett, Andy, Tul.*	.268	43	186	157	23	42	61	11	1	2	31	0	1	1	27	0	22	0	0	2	.389	.376

Player, Team	Avg.	G	TPA	AB	R	H	TB	2B	3B	HR	RBI	SH	SF	HP	BB	IBB	SO	SB	CS	GDP	Slg.	OBP
Barnes, Larry, Mid.*	.273	69	278	245	29	67	109	16	4	6	35	2	2	1	28	3	54	4	2	5	.445	.348
Beck, Greg, E.P.	.118	30	18	17	1	2	3	1	0	0	1	0	0	0	1	0	4	0	0	0	.176	.167
Beltran, Carlos, Wich.†	.352	47	208	182	50	64	125	13	3	14	44	2	0	1	23	3	30	7	1	4	.687	.427
Beltre, Adrian, S.A.	.321	64	292	246	49	79	143	21	2	13	56	0	5	2	39	2	37	20	4	3	.581	.411
Benes, Adam, Ark.*	.000	12	2	1	1	0	0	0	0	0	0	0	0	0	1	0	1	0	0	0	.000	.500
Bergeron, Peter, S.A.*	.317	109	489	416	81	132	189	17	8	8	54	9	1	2	61	1	69	33	9	2	.454	.406
Berkman, Lance, Jack.†	.306	122	517	425	82	130	236	34	0	24	89	0	3	4	85	10	82	6	4	14	.555	.424
Bermudez, Manny, Shre.	.000	5	2	1	0	0	0	0	0	0	0	1	0	0	0	0	1	0	0	0	.000	.000
Betten, Randy, Mid.	.230	76	241	209	30	48	74	16	2	2	19	8	2	4	18	0	50	3	2	6	.354	.300
Blais, Mike, Jack.	.000	21	4	3	0	0	0	0	0	0	0	1	0	0	0	0	1	0	0	0	.000	.000
Blanco, Alberto, Jack.*	.267	12	15	15	3	4	4	0	0	0	0	0	0	0	0	0	7	0	0	0	.267	.267
Bland, Nate, S.A.*	.000	26	3	3	0	0	0	0	0	0	0	0	0	0	0	0	2	0	0	0	.000	.000
Bonds, Bobby, Shre.	.282	43	173	156	24	44	59	7	1	2	18	0	0	1	16	1	21	6	0	6	.378	.353
Brester, Jason, Shre.*	.050	19	23	20	0	1	1	0	0	0	0	1	0	0	2	0	9	0	0	0	.050	.136
Brown, Ray, Wich.*	.318	114	469	402	79	128	224	31	1	21	96	1	6	3	57	5	57	4	2	16	.557	.402
Brumbaugh, Cliff, Tul.	.259	132	549	483	65	125	206	34	1	15	76	3	5	4	54	5	77	1	3	12	.427	.335
Burke, Jamie, Mid.	.244	12	48	41	7	10	11	1	0	0	4	0	0	0	7	0	4	0	0	4	.268	.354
Buxbaum, Danny, Mid.	.330	76	329	297	58	98	172	19	2	17	53	2	2	0	28	3	33	1	1	8	.579	.385
Byington, Jimmie, Wich.	.167	26	85	66	12	11	12	1	0	0	5	2	1	1	15	0	19	1	2	2	.182	.325
Cameron, Ken, Ark.*†	.171	40	89	82	7	14	19	1	2	0	3	0	1	0	6	1	17	0	0	1	.232	.225
Cancel, Robinson, E.P.	.323	58	185	158	17	51	64	10	0	1	30	4	1	0	22	1	32	2	2	5	.405	.403
Canizaro, Jay, Shre.	.224	83	342	281	47	63	108	7	1	12	32	1	3	4	53	1	46	5	2	8	.384	.352
Castro, Ramon, Jack.	.256	48	185	168	27	43	73	6	0	8	25	0	0	4	13	2	31	0	1	3	.435	.324
Charles, Frank, Shre.	.287	108	440	411	49	118	195	39	1	12	66	0	5	6	18	0	93	0	2	10	.474	.323
Chavez, Carlos, E.P.	.000	54	5	5	0	0	0	0	0	0	0	0	0	0	0	0	3	0	0	0	.000	.000
Christian, Eddie, Mid.†	.333	105	455	400	80	133	195	39	4	5	49	0	2	3	49	4	61	13	11	6	.488	.407
Clapp, Stubby, Ark.*	.278	139	622	514	113	143	227	30	9	12	57	8	6	8	86	3	100	18	10	10	.442	.386
Collins, Sean, Tul.	.138	11	36	29	3	4	5	1	0	0	1	1	0	0	6	0	8	0	0	1	.172	.286
Conti, Jason, Tul.*	.315	130	611	530	125	167	267	31	12	15	67	1	2	9	63	4	96	19	13	5	.504	.396
Cooney, Kyle, S.A.	.250	1	4	4	1	1	1	0	0	0	0	0	0	0	0	0	0	0	0	0	.250	.250
Cornett, Brad, E.P.	.000	3	6	4	0	0	0	0	0	0	0	1	0	0	1	0	0	0	0	0	.000	.200
Corps, Edwin, Shre.	.125	46	11	8	0	1	1	0	0	0	0	1	0	1	1	0	4	0	0	0	.125	.300
Correa, Miguel, E.P.†	.279	136	574	537	75	150	225	26	5	13	89	2	5	3	27	1	98	11	8	6	.419	.315
Crabtree, Robbie, Shre.	.000	26	6	5	0	0	0	0	0	0	0	1	0	0	0	0	2	0	0	0	.000	.000
Crafton, Kevin, Ark.	.000	46	3	2	0	0	0	0	0	0	0	0	0	0	1	0	0	0	0	0	.000	.000
Curtis, Matt, Mid.†	.262	113	473	431	53	113	172	19	5	10	65	3	5	1	33	1	72	2	2	14	.399	.313
Dalton, Jed, Mid.	.295	80	307	258	43	76	103	11	2	4	34	3	4	4	38	0	48	7	5	8	.399	.388
Davis, Allen, S.A.*	.000	6	3	3	0	0	0	0	0	0	0	0	0	0	0	0	0	0	0	0	.000	.000
Davis, Glenn, S.A.†	.290	20	79	69	14	20	40	2	0	6	15	0	0	0	10	0	22	2	0	2	.580	.380
Dawsey, Jason, E.P.*	.333	6	3	3	1	1	1	0	0	0	0	0	0	0	0	0	0	0	0	0	.333	.333
De Los Santos, Valerio, E.P.*	.222	42	9	9	1	2	2	0	0	0	3	0	0	0	0	0	5	0	0	2	.222	.222
Demetral, Chris, Tul.*	.272	45	183	147	22	40	67	9	3	4	18	2	0	1	33	0	24	2	3	4	.456	.409
Denbow, Don, Shre.	.153	44	134	111	14	17	37	7	2	3	10	1	0	1	21	0	47	2	1	3	.333	.293
DeShields, Delino, Ark.*	.154	4	15	13	1	2	2	0	0	0	0	0	0	0	2	0	6	0	1	0	.154	.267
Deskins, Casey, S.A.	.063	22	18	16	0	1	1	0	0	0	0	0	1	0	1	0	8	0	0	0	.063	.167
Detmers, Kris, Ark.†	.069	27	34	29	2	2	2	0	0	0	2	2	0	0	3	0	15	0	0	0	.069	.156
Diaz, Freddie, Mid.†	.182	4	14	11	3	2	2	0	0	0	2	0	0	0	3	0	4	0	0	0	.182	.357
Diaz, Juan, S.A.	.266	56	205	188	26	50	102	13	0	13	30	0	0	2	15	1	45	0	0	4	.543	.327
Dilone, Juan, Shre.†	.207	36	126	111	13	23	47	8	2	4	16	1	1	3	10	2	35	3	1	4	.423	.288
Diorio, Mike, Jack.	.000	32	4	3	0	0	0	0	0	0	0	1	0	0	1	0	1	0	0	0	.000	.250
Dishington, Nate, Ark.*	.253	75	281	237	40	60	119	6	1	17	49	0	1	3	40	1	91	6	1	3	.502	.367
Dollar, Toby, S.A.	.059	23	23	17	0	1	1	0	0	0	0	3	0	0	3	0	7	0	0	0	.059	.200
Dransfeldt, Kelly, Tul.	.252	58	249	226	43	57	107	15	4	9	36	0	3	2	18	0	79	8	1	4	.473	.309
Drew, J.D., Ark.*	.328	19	81	67	18	22	42	3	1	5	11	0	0	1	13	1	15	2	1	0	.627	.444
Duffy, Jim, Jack.	.156	12	33	32	1	5	6	1	0	0	0	0	0	0	1	0	9	0	0	1	.188	.182
Duncan, Sean, Jack.*	.500	28	7	4	2	2	5	0	0	1	3	0	0	0	3	0	1	0	0	0	1.250	.714
Dunn, Todd, E.P.	.313	75	330	294	60	92	165	28	3	13	57	0	3	6	27	1	63	7	2	6	.561	.379
Durrington, Trent, Mid.†	.225	112	429	351	62	79	94	10	1	1	30	7	4	17	50	0	74	24	12	5	.268	.346
Encarnacion, Angelo, Mid.	.215	28	104	93	9	20	27	1	0	2	7	2	0	1	8	0	11	0	0	2	.290	.284
Escamilla, Roman, Wich.	.264	43	142	129	16	34	43	6	0	1	10	1	2	0	10	0	21	0	1	7	.333	.312
Estrada, Horacio, E.P.*	.111	8	11	9	1	1	1	0	0	0	1	0	0	0	1	0	1	0	0	0	.111	.200
Evans, Mike, Wich.*	.209	72	265	230	35	48	96	10	1	12	34	4	2	2	27	2	62	0	1	2	.417	.295
Faurot, Adam, E.P.	.297	101	270	249	27	74	94	13	2	1	39	6	2	4	9	2	49	10	3	5	.378	.330
Febles, Carlos, Wich.	.326	126	531	432	110	141	229	28	9	14	52	5	3	11	80	1	70	51	16	6	.530	.441
Feliz, Pedro, Shre.	.264	100	379	364	39	96	159	23	2	12	50	0	4	2	9	0	62	0	1	15	.437	.282
Frontera, Chad, Shre.	.000	8	10	10	0	0	0	0	0	0	0	0	0	0	0	0	2	0	0	0	.000	.000
Fultz, Aaron, Shre.*	.000	54	2	2	0	0	0	0	0	0	0	0	0	0	0	0	2	0	0	0	.000	.000
Gallaher, Kevin, E.P.	.000	7	1	1	0	0	0	0	0	0	0	0	0	0	0	0	0	0	0	0	.000	.000
Garcia, Freddy, Jack.	.000	19	27	21	1	0	0	0	0	0	1	4	0	1	1	0	9	0	0	0	.000	.043
Garcia, Miguel, S.A.	.200	27	11	10	0	2	2	0	0	0	1	0	0	0	1	0	5	0	1	0	.200	.273
Garcia, Ossie, Ark.	.245	94	220	200	32	49	65	10	3	0	24	1	2	4	13	1	35	10	6	5	.325	.301
Garland, Tim, Shre.	.263	55	217	194	24	51	64	6	2	1	16	2	2	4	15	1	24	15	5	3	.330	.326
Gil, Geronimo, S.A.	.290	75	260	241	27	70	111	17	3	6	29	2	2	0	15	0	43	2	1	8	.461	.329
Glaus, Troy, Mid.	.309	50	230	188	51	58	130	11	2	19	51	0	1	2	39	3	41	4	2	4	.691	.430
Glendenning, Mike, Shre.	.244	78	294	254	27	62	99	12	2	7	33	0	1	4	35	1	57	0	0	4	.390	.344
Goligoski, Jason, Tul.*	.218	65	228	202	21	44	52	4	2	0	10	1	1	3	21	0	44	0	2	3	.257	.300
Gonzalez, Raul, Wich.	.325	118	520	455	84	148	232	31	1	17	86	1	4	2	58	3	53	12	8	15	.510	.401
Goodwin, Joe, Tul.	.097	30	34	31	3	3	4	1	0	0	3	0	1	1	0	0	7	0	0	2	.129	.147
Graves, Bryan, Mid.	.224	29	105	85	8	19	25	3	0	1	6	1	1	2	16	0	18	0	1	5	.294	.356
Green, Chad, E.P.†	.000	7	7	6	0	0	0	0	0	0	0	0	0	0	1	0	3	0	0	0	.000	.143
Green, Scarborough, Ark.†	.360	18	81	75	16	27	37	2	1	2	9	0	0	0	6	0	12	9	2	0	.493	.407
Grilli, Jason, Shre.	.286	21	29	28	5	8	12	4	0	0	1	0	0	0	0	0	13	0	0	0	.429	.286

Player, Team	Avg.	G	TPA	AB	R	H	TB	2B	3B	HR	RBI	SH	SF	HP	BB	IBB	SO	SB	CS	GDP	Slg.	OBP
Groppuso, Mike, E.P.	.300	119	510	437	100	131	250	36	4	25	90	0	4	4	65	4	113	2	1	8	.572	.392
Grote, Jason, Shre.	.200	10	11	10	1	2	3	1	0	0	1	0	0	0	0	0	6	0	0	0	.300	.200
Gutierrez, Jim, Jack.	.000	8	4	4	0	0	0	0	0	0	0	0	0	0	0	0	2	0	0	1	.000	.000
Haas, Chris, Ark.*	.274	132	531	445	75	122	217	27	4	20	83	0	5	8	73	5	129	1	2	5	.488	.382
Hall, Yates, Ark.	.000	8	1	1	0	0	0	0	0	0	0	0	0	0	0	0	0	0	0	0	.000	.000
Hardge, Mike, Ark.	.293	106	407	355	60	104	156	24	2	8	66	1	5	3	43	2	78	8	8	7	.439	.369
Hardwick, Bubba, E.P.*	.000	32	4	4	0	0	0	0	0	0	0	0	0	0	0	0	1	0	0	0	.000	.000
Harkrider, Kip, S.A.*	.239	103	389	343	37	82	117	18	4	3	40	12	2	2	30	2	57	8	4	7	.341	.302
Herrick, Jason, Mid.*	.332	71	301	274	61	91	179	20	7	18	73	1	4	2	20	2	75	5	5	1	.653	.377
Hodges, Kevin, Jack.	.133	29	20	15	1	2	3	1	0	0	1	5	0	0	0	0	7	0	0	0	.200	.133
Hollins, Stacy, Shre.-E.P.	.214	28	15	14	1	3	4	1	0	0	2	0	1	0	0	0	6	0	0	0	.286	.200
Hommel, Brian, E.P.*	1.000	14	1	1	0	1	1	0	0	0	0	0	0	0	0	0	0	0	0	0	1.000	1.000
Hook, Chris, Shre.-Jack.	.000	30	10	6	0	0	0	0	0	0	0	0	0	2	0	0	2	0	0	0	.000	.250
Horne, Tyrone, Ark.*	.312	123	520	443	94	138	268	13	3	37	139	0	6	1	70	7	97	18	7	8	.605	.402
Huber, Jeff, E.P.	.000	9	4	4	0	0	0	0	0	0	0	0	0	0	0	0	3	0	0	0	.000	.000
Huntsman, Scott, E.P.	.667	52	3	3	0	2	2	0	0	0	0	0	0	0	0	0	1	0	0	0	.667	.667
Hutchins, Norm, Mid.*	.312	89	414	394	74	123	193	20	10	10	50	0	1	4	14	0	84	32	10	8	.490	.341
Hutzler, Jeff, Shre.	.000	2	1	1	0	0	0	0	0	0	0	0	0	0	0	0	1	0	0	0	.000	.000
Iapoce, Anthony, E.P.†	.314	133	631	576	97	181	222	23	6	2	53	9	2	11	33	1	67	35	20	4	.385	.362
Jarvis, Matt, Ark.	.000	56	3	2	0	0	0	0	0	0	0	0	0	0	1	0	0	0	0	0	.000	.333
Jimenez, Jose, Ark.	.086	26	40	35	2	3	3	0	0	0	1	4	0	0	1	0	16	0	0	1	.086	.111
Johnson, Keith, S.A.	.299	40	174	154	20	46	67	10	1	3	16	6	1	3	10	2	26	10	5	3	.435	.351
Johnson, Ric, Jack.	.200	23	84	80	5	16	16	2	0	0	2	0	0	1	3	0	9	0	1	2	.225	.238
Jones, Jack, S.A.	.226	77	278	248	36	56	88	9	4	5	28	3	3	6	18	0	69	3	4	4	.355	.291
Keith, Jeff, Shre.*	.000	10	2	1	0	0	0	0	0	0	0	0	1	0	0	0	0	0	0	0	.000	.000
Kennedy, Adam, Ark.*	.278	52	221	205	35	57	90	11	2	6	24	3	3	2	8	0	21	6	2	4	.439	.307
Kester, Tim, Jack.	.333	5	4	3	1	1	1	0	0	0	0	0	0	0	1	0	1	0	0	0	.333	.500
King, Brett, Shre.	.171	85	291	257	29	44	66	9	2	3	19	2	2	3	27	1	64	4	2	4	.257	.256
King, Cesar, Tul.	.222	90	357	316	40	70	99	16	2	3	39	3	6	2	30	2	68	1	1	10	.313	.288
Kirkreit, Daron, E.P.	.300	18	11	10	0	3	3	0	0	0	1	0	0	0	0	0	5	0	0	0	.300	.300
Kleiner, Stacy, Ark.	.258	99	373	333	44	86	134	28	1	6	57	3	1	3	33	2	79	1	2	5	.402	.330
Koeyers, Ramsey, Tul.	.250	55	181	164	25	41	55	2	0	4	18	0	0	4	13	1	45	1	0	8	.335	.320
Kominek, Toby, E.P.	.302	135	595	496	114	150	242	33	4	17	83	0	4	22	73	4	120	21	16	5	.488	.412
Kubenka, Jeff, S.A.	.000	9	1	0	1	0	0	0	0	0	0	0	0	0	1	0	0	0	0	0	.000	1.000
Lariviere, Jason, Ark.	.255	132	493	435	69	111	174	29	5	8	58	2	4	2	50	1	58	14	6	18	.400	.332
Leach, Jalal, Shre.*	.344	72	295	253	43	87	138	17	2	10	45	0	5	0	36	3	35	10	2	8	.545	.418
Levrault, Allen, E.P.	.200	12	12	10	1	2	4	0	1	0	1	1	0	0	1	0	2	0	0	0	.400	.273
Lewis, Anthony, Wich.*	.206	10	39	34	6	7	20	1	0	4	8	0	0	0	5	1	7	0	0	2	.588	.308
Lilly, Ted, S.A.*	.000	17	15	11	1	0	0	0	0	0	0	3	0	0	1	0	5	0	0	0	.000	.083
Linebrink, Scott, Shre.	.250	21	26	24	2	6	7	1	0	0	2	0	0	0	2	0	6	0	0	1	.292	.308
Logan, Marcus, Ark.	.174	28	28	23	2	4	4	0	0	0	4	3	0	0	2	0	7	0	0	1	.174	.240
Long, Ryan, Wich.	.255	67	269	247	32	63	100	14	1	7	29	1	1	3	17	1	50	2	2	10	.405	.310
Lopez, Mickey, E.P.†	.277	120	516	459	81	127	175	24	9	2	64	4	5	2	46	1	61	12	10	11	.381	.342
Lopez, Pedro, Jack.	.287	60	205	178	29	51	92	14	0	9	28	1	1	8	17	0	27	2	0	6	.517	.373
Lopez, Roberto, E.P.†	.271	73	229	199	24	54	74	15	1	1	26	1	3	4	22	0	24	8	5	1	.372	.351
Lovingier, Kevin, Ark.*	.000	19	4	3	1	0	0	0	0	0	0	0	0	0	1	0	1	0	0	0	.000	.250
Luuloa, Keith, Mid.	.334	130	579	479	85	160	274	43	10	17	102	2	16	7	75	5	54	6	5	15	.572	.419
Maddox, Garry, Jack.*	.351	25	101	94	20	33	49	3	2	3	14	0	0	0	5	0	20	3	2	0	.521	.384
Makarewicz, Scott, Jack.	.239	33	119	113	17	27	54	6	0	7	22	1	0	2	3	1	16	0	0	4	.478	.271
Malave, Jaime, S.A.	.255	28	63	55	3	14	22	5	0	1	4	2	0	0	6	1	10	0	0	2	.400	.328
Martin, Jeff, Shre.	.000	31	5	4	0	0	0	0	0	0	0	1	0	0	0	0	0	0	0	0	.000	.000
Marval, Raul, Shre.	.236	96	317	296	14	70	81	6	1	1	21	4	3	1	13	0	35	2	2	10	.274	.268
Masaoka, Onan, S.A.	.125	27	19	16	2	2	2	0	0	0	0	2	0	0	1	0	2	1	0	0	.125	.176
Mateo, Ruben, Tul.	.309	107	485	433	79	134	226	32	3	18	75	3	4	15	30	1	56	18	8	7	.522	.370
Mayes, Craig, Shre.*	.239	29	94	88	11	21	32	2	0	3	16	1	1	0	4	0	9	0	0	0	.364	.269
Mayo, Blake, S.A.	.000	13	1	1	0	0	0	0	0	0	0	0	0	0	0	0	0	0	0	0	.000	.000
McEwing, Joe, Ark.	.354	60	249	223	45	79	135	21	4	9	46	1	2	1	21	4	18	4	2	2	.605	.409
McKinley, Dan, Shre.*	.179	33	127	112	16	20	29	3	3	0	11	0	1	3	11	1	30	2	3	3	.259	.268
McMullen, Mike, Shre.	.000	52	5	4	0	0	0	0	0	0	0	1	0	0	0	0	1	0	0	1	.000	.000
McNally, Sean, Wich.	.263	98	366	319	43	84	129	21	3	6	44	2	5	1	39	0	86	2	4	9	.404	.344
Medrano, Tony, Wich.	.306	96	349	301	48	92	140	14	2	10	46	8	3	9	28	0	36	3	3	7	.465	.378
Mendez, Carlos, Wich.	.319	52	220	207	37	66	107	14	0	9	39	1	5	0	7	1	20	4	1	10	.517	.333
Metcalfe, Mike, S.A.	.282	57	249	213	35	60	84	5	5	3	19	3	2	1	30	1	24	19	15	3	.394	.370
Miller, Ryan, Jack.	.307	102	318	293	36	90	119	20	0	3	26	3	4	9	9	0	43	6	4	10	.406	.343
Miller, Wade, Jack.	.250	10	10	8	0	2	2	0	0	0	1	2	0	0	0	0	2	0	0	0	.250	.250
Minor, Damon, Shre.*	.239	81	327	289	39	69	124	11	1	14	52	0	2	6	30	1	51	1	0	5	.429	.321
Miranda, Tony, Wich.	.184	27	94	76	14	14	19	2	0	1	10	4	2	2	10	0	10	2	0	3	.250	.289
Mitchell, Dean, S.A.	.000	46	5	4	0	0	0	0	0	0	0	0	0	0	1	0	0	0	0	0	.000	.200
Mitchell, Donovan, Jack.*	.275	70	291	265	36	73	90	7	2	2	27	2	2	1	21	0	34	8	7	9	.340	.329
Molina, Ben, Mid.	.357	41	172	154	28	55	90	8	0	9	39	0	1	3	14	2	7	0	1	7	.584	.419
Morillo, Cesar, Shre.†	.111	10	19	18	1	2	2	0	0	0	2	0	0	1	0	0	3	0	0	1	.111	.158
Morris, Greg, Mid.	.274	31	133	106	13	29	43	6	1	2	12	0	1	4	22	0	14	1	0	1	.406	.414
Morris, Matt, Ark.	.000	1	1	1	0	0	0	0	0	0	0	0	0	0	0	0	1	0	0	0	.000	.000
Morris, Warren, Tul.*	.331	95	440	390	59	129	203	22	5	14	73	1	2	4	43	2	63	12	7	11	.521	.401
Mota, Tony, S.A.†	.243	59	239	222	20	54	82	10	6	2	22	2	3	0	12	1	36	16	8	6	.369	.278
Mottola, Chad, Tul.	.500	8	36	26	9	13	17	1	0	1	7	0	0	0	10	1	1	3	0	0	.654	.639
Mounce, Tony, Jack.*	.045	33	24	22	0	1	1	0	0	0	0	2	0	0	0	0	11	0	0	0	.045	.045
Munoz, Juan, Ark.*	.269	28	125	119	16	32	41	9	0	0	18	0	3	0	3	0	15	0	0	4	.345	.280
Murphy, Mike, Tul.	.250	58	227	196	26	49	73	8	2	4	22	0	2	2	27	1	56	6	2	8	.372	.344
Murray, Calvin, Shre.	.309	88	401	337	63	104	160	22	5	8	39	1	0	5	58	1	45	34	15	8	.475	.418
Myers, Rod, Wich.*	.224	41	178	143	19	32	55	11	0	4	21	3	2	0	30	1	31	8	1	0	.385	.354
Nathan, Joe, Shre.	.000	5	2	2	1	0	0	0	0	0	0	0	0	0	0	0	0	0	0	0	.000	.000

Player, Team	Avg.	G	TPA	AB	R	H	TB	2B	3B	HR	RBI	SH	SF	HP	BB	IBB	SO	SB	CS	GDP	Slg.	OBP
Neal, Billy, S.A.	.000	31	4	4	0	0	0	0	0	0	0	0	0	0	0	0	1	0	0	0	.000	.000
Neal, Mike, Jack.	.326	103	386	341	53	111	193	27	2	17	70	1	1	4	39	0	80	4	4	7	.566	.400
Nelson, Charles, S.A.*	.233	91	270	236	36	55	76	9	0	4	19	7	4	1	22	0	34	13	5	3	.322	.297
Nilsson, Dave, E.P.*	.294	5	19	17	4	5	8	3	0	0	5	0	0	0	2	0	1	0	0	0	.471	.368
Norris, Joe, E.P.	.000	40	3	2	0	0	0	0	0	0	0	0	0	0	1	0	1	0	0	0	.000	.333
Norton, Chris, Mid.	.317	17	70	60	10	19	32	1	0	4	12	0	0	1	9	0	23	0	0	1	.533	.414
Nussbeck, Mark, Ark.*	.077	10	13	13	0	1	1	0	0	0	1	0	0	0	0	0	5	0	0	0	.077	.077
O'Brien, Charlie, Mid.	.118	5	19	17	1	2	2	0	0	0	2	0	0	0	2	1	4	1	0	0	.118	.211
O'Malley, Paul, Jack.	.214	29	38	28	4	6	6	0	0	0	3	5	0	0	5	0	13	0	0	1	.214	.333
O'Neal, Troy, E.P.	.180	16	56	50	2	9	11	2	0	0	7	0	0	1	5	1	12	0	0	2	.220	.268
O'Neill, Doug, Tul.	.221	18	78	68	10	15	26	5	0	2	5	0	0	0	10	0	16	4	0	2	.382	.321
Oropesa, Eddie, Shre.*	.250	32	32	28	1	7	7	0	0	0	3	2	0	0	2	0	7	0	0	0	.250	.300
Ortiz, Hector, Wich.	.154	4	15	13	1	2	2	0	0	0	0	0	0	0	2	0	1	0	1	0	.154	.267
Osborne, Donovan, Ark.*	.200	5	7	5	2	1	1	0	0	0	1	1	1	0	0	0	1	0	0	0	.200	.167
Owens, Billy, Jack.†	.264	53	174	159	18	42	66	6	0	6	28	0	1	1	13	3	17	1	1	6	.415	.322
Pasqualicchio, Mike, E.P.	.111	10	9	9	0	1	1	0	0	0	0	0	0	0	0	0	5	0	0	0	.111	.111
Passini, Brian, E.P.*	.000	12	12	12	0	0	0	0	0	0	0	0	0	0	0	0	5	0	0	0	.000	.000
Pearsall, J.J., S.A.*	.000	46	4	3	0	0	0	0	0	0	0	0	0	0	1	0	2	0	0	0	.000	.250
Pellow, Kit, Wich.	.267	103	411	374	70	100	217	24	3	29	73	1	3	6	27	2	107	4	3	2	.580	.324
Pena, Angel, S.A.	.335	126	542	483	81	162	264	32	2	22	105	3	2	6	48	3	80	9	5	7	.547	.401
Perez, Jhonny, Jack.	.285	130	497	439	65	125	175	20	0	10	39	6	0	1	45	4	72	22	11	9	.399	.353
Perez, Richard, E.P.	.292	17	27	24	6	7	8	1	0	0	1	0	0	1	2	0	5	0	0	3	.333	.370
Perez, Santiago, E.P.†	.306	107	495	454	73	139	218	20	13	11	64	4	5	4	28	3	70	21	11	7	.480	.348
Peterson, Kyle, E.P.*	.000	7	4	3	0	0	0	0	0	0	0	1	0	0	0	0	1	0	0	0	.000	.000
Phair, Kelly, E.P.	.275	28	112	102	7	28	30	2	0	0	8	2	0	0	8	0	17	1	2	3	.294	.327
Phillips, Randy, Shre.	.263	17	24	19	3	5	7	2	0	0	6	3	0	0	2	0	6	0	0	0	.368	.333
Pimentel, Jose, S.A.	.203	90	306	271	34	55	79	4	4	4	24	11	1	6	17	0	59	16	7	6	.292	.264
Podsednik, Scott, Tul.*	.240	17	81	75	9	18	24	4	1	0	4	0	0	0	6	0	11	5	2	3	.320	.296
Politte, Cliff, Ark.	.125	10	17	16	1	2	3	1	0	0	1	0	1	0	0	0	4	0	0	0	.188	.125
Poor, Jeff, Shre.	.000	2	2	2	0	0	0	0	0	0	0	0	0	0	0	0	0	0	0	0	.000	.000
Priess, Matthew, Shre.	.000	2	2	1	0	0	0	0	0	0	0	0	0	0	1	0	0	0	0	0	.000	.500
Prieto, Alejandro, Wich.	.263	113	425	384	61	101	139	18	7	2	35	8	0	2	31	0	54	4	8	13	.362	.321
Prihoda, Steve, Wich.	.000	58	1	1	0	0	0	0	0	0	0	0	0	0	0	0	1	0	0	0	.000	.000
Prokopec, Luke, S.A.*	.500	5	3	2	1	1	4	0	0	1	1	1	0	0	0	0	1	0	0	0	2.000	.500
Quinn, Mark, Wich.	.349	100	432	372	82	130	216	26	6	16	84	0	7	10	43	1	54	4	1	5	.581	.424
Ramirez, Peto, Shre.	.250	12	31	24	1	6	9	3	0	0	3	0	2	0	5	0	7	0	0	2	.375	.355
Ramos, Edgar, Jack.	.200	17	10	10	0	2	2	0	0	0	0	0	0	0	0	0	4	0	0	0	.200	.200
Reed, Steve, Ark.	.105	32	20	19	1	2	3	1	0	0	0	1	0	0	0	0	7	0	0	1	.158	.105
Rennhack, Mike, E.P.†	.289	82	293	256	55	74	111	19	3	4	38	0	4	0	33	0	52	1	2	2	.434	.365
Ricabal, Dan, S.A.	.000	54	7	7	0	0	0	0	0	0	0	0	0	0	0	0	3	0	0	0	.000	.000
Richard, Chris, Ark.*	.202	28	100	89	7	18	31	5	1	2	17	0	1	1	9	0	10	0	1	1	.348	.280
Richards, Rowan, Tul.	.222	34	143	126	23	28	50	4	0	6	23	0	2	3	12	0	25	0	1	6	.397	.301
Rivera, Micky, Ark.	.194	64	117	108	11	21	33	7	1	1	5	1	1	1	6	1	18	0	4	4	.306	.241
Robles, Oscar, Jack.*	.200	4	7	5	0	1	1	0	0	0	0	0	1	0	1	1	1	0	0	0	.200	.333
Rodriguez, Frankie, E.P.	.000	4	1	0	0	0	0	0	0	0	0	0	0	0	1	0	0	0	0	0	.000	1.000
Rogers, Kevin, Shre.*	.000	14	1	1	0	0	0	0	0	0	0	0	0	0	0	0	0	0	0	0	.000	.000
Rolls, Damian, S.A.	.219	50	168	160	18	35	44	6	0	1	9	1	1	0	6	0	28	2	0	9	.275	.246
Root, Derek, Jack.*	.250	7	10	8	2	2	2	0	0	0	1	0	0	1	1	0	2	0	0	1	.250	.333
Roque, Rafael, E.P.*	.267	16	17	15	0	4	4	0	0	0	1	2	0	0	0	0	6	0	0	0	.267	.267
Sadler, Al, E.P.	.000	34	2	2	1	0	0	0	0	0	0	0	0	0	0	0	1	0	0	0	.000	.000
Sanchez, Victor, Jack.	.276	117	469	439	65	121	221	29	1	23	80	1	4	4	21	1	100	4	3	12	.503	.312
Sasser, Rob, Tul.	.281	111	485	417	57	117	170	25	2	8	62	1	4	3	60	0	98	18	12	11	.408	.372
Saylor, Jamie, Jack.*	.292	122	516	462	80	135	219	21	6	17	66	7	3	5	39	1	91	15	10	4	.474	.352
Schmidt, Dave, Ark.*	.268	66	214	183	23	49	71	11	1	3	15	2	1	2	26	5	47	0	0	6	.388	.363
Sell, Chip, S.A.*	.252	64	250	218	36	55	88	12	6	3	37	3	4	3	22	1	40	6	0	6	.404	.324
Sergio, Thomas, Tul.*	.256	11	43	39	7	10	13	1	1	0	0	0	0	0	4	0	1	0	0	0	.333	.326
Shirley, Al, Wich.†	.226	32	103	93	13	21	38	2	0	5	12	2	0	3	5	0	30	3	2	1	.409	.287
Sikorski, Brian, Jack.	.143	15	24	21	4	3	4	1	0	0	0	2	0	0	1	0	6	0	0	1	.190	.182
Simonton, Benji, Shre.	.280	45	182	161	19	45	69	7	1	5	19	0	1	1	19	1	44	5	0	3	.429	.357
Slusarski, Joe, Jack.	.000	9	3	2	0	0	0	0	0	0	0	0	0	0	1	0	1	0	0	0	.000	.333
Smiga, Jason, Tul.	.000	2	6	6	0	0	0	0	0	0	0	0	0	0	0	0	0	0	0	0	.000	.000
Smith, Eric, Jack.	1.000	6	1	1	0	1	1	0	0	0	0	0	0	0	0	0	0	0	0	0	1.000	1.000
Smith, Scott, Shre.	.333	7	16	15	3	5	5	0	0	0	1	0	1	0	0	0	4	0	0	1	.333	.313
Spivey, Junior, Tul.	.311	34	152	119	26	37	58	10	1	3	16	1	1	3	28	1	25	8	4	1	.487	.450
Stewart, Andy, Wich.	.338	85	335	305	45	103	165	26	0	12	58	2	4	5	19	0	33	0	2	11	.541	.381
Stone, Ricky, S.A.	.417	13	12	12	1	5	6	1	0	0	1	0	0	0	0	0	4	2	0	0	.500	.417
Stuckenschneider, Eric, S.A.	.277	72	340	282	60	78	117	16	7	3	22	2	3	9	44	1	47	16	3	3	.415	.388
Sturdivant, Marcus, Mid.*	.250	17	71	68	7	17	22	5	0	0	8	1	0	0	2	0	8	2	1	2	.324	.271
Taulbee, Andy, Shre.	.000	3	3	1	0	0	0	0	0	0	0	1	0	0	1	0	1	0	0	0	.000	.500
Taylor, Scott, Wich.	.000	14	1	1	0	0	0	0	0	0	0	0	0	0	0	0	0	0	0	0	.000	.000
Thurston, Jerrey, Mid.	.316	29	106	95	20	30	40	4	0	2	22	0	1	2	8	0	24	0	0	2	.421	.377
Tinsley, Lee, Mid.†	.262	11	44	42	2	11	17	4	1	0	5	0	0	0	2	0	7	3	1	0	.405	.295
Torrealba, Yorvit, Shre.	.235	59	222	196	18	46	53	7	0	0	13	3	1	4	18	3	30	0	5	3	.270	.311
Trammell, Gary, Jack.*	.251	110	338	315	42	79	106	9	3	4	24	1	0	2	22	2	49	4	5	3	.337	.300
Truby, Chris, Jack.	.289	80	337	308	46	89	167	20	5	16	63	0	5	4	20	0	50	8	3	5	.542	.335
Tucker, Jon, S.A.*	.297	100	408	360	46	107	175	34	2	10	64	1	3	3	41	2	74	3	5	6	.486	.371
Tyler, Josh, Shre.	.205	14	42	39	5	8	8	0	0	0	3	0	1	1	1	0	4	0	0	1	.205	.238
Vallone, Gar, Mid.†	.167	2	6	6	0	1	1	0	0	0	0	0	0	0	0	0	2	0	0	0	.167	.167
Van Rossum, Chris, Shre.*	.161	23	72	62	5	10	14	2	1	0	3	1	0	0	9	0	15	2	2	1	.226	.268
Verdugo, Jason, Shre.	.333	9	3	3	0	1	1	0	0	0	0	0	0	0	0	0	2	0	0	0	.333	.333
Vessel, Andrew, Tul.	.238	106	443	408	42	97	144	23	0	8	49	1	3	9	22	3	63	5	5	12	.353	.290
Wallace, Kent, Jack.*	.000	29	5	3	1	0	0	0	0	0	0	0	0	0	2	0	3	0	0	0	.000	.400

Player, Team	Avg.	G	TPA	AB	R	H	TB	2B	3B	HR	RBI	SH	SF	HP	BB	IBB	SO	SB	CS	GDP	Slg.	OBP
Walter, Mike, Jack.	.000	38	1	1	0	0	0	0	0	0	0	0	0	0	0	0	1	0	0	0	.000	.000
Weibl, Clint, Ark.	.179	25	33	28	3	5	7	2	0	0	3	3	0	0	2	0	12	0	0	0	.250	.233
Williams, Jeff, S.A.	.250	7	9	8	1	2	2	0	0	0	0	0	0	0	1	0	4	0	0	0	.250	.333
Windham, Mike, Ark.	.077	40	17	13	0	1	1	0	0	0	0	1	0	0	3	0	4	0	0	1	.077	.250
Woods, Ken, Shre.	.307	94	368	335	44	103	139	20	2	4	33	0	3	2	28	1	31	8	9	8	.415	.361
Woolf, Jason, Ark.†	.265	76	340	294	63	78	122	22	5	4	16	2	1	9	34	0	84	28	5	2	.415	.358
Wooten, Shawn, Mid.	.321	8	31	28	3	9	16	4	0	1	6	0	0	0	3	0	4	0	0	0	.571	.387
Wunsch, Kelly, E.P.*	.056	17	19	18	0	1	1	0	0	0	0	1	0	0	0	0	8	1	0	0	.056	.056
Zamora, Pete, S.A.*	.154	12	14	13	0	2	2	0	0	0	1	1	0	0	0	0	1	0	0	0	.154	.154
Zywica, Mike, Tul.	.280	58	242	214	40	60	98	15	4	5	45	0	4	5	19	0	56	7	3	3	.458	.347

GRAND SLAMS: Horne, 4; Berkman, D. Minor, 3 each; Dunn, Groppuso, LaRiviere, Mayes, Pena, 2 each; Abbott, Barnes, Beltran, Bergeron, Brown, Buxbaum, Clapp, Curtis, J. Diaz, Evans, Gonzalez, Haas, Hardge, Herrick, Hutchins, Kleiner, Kominek, Long, Mateo, McNally, W. Morris, M. Neal, Owens, Richards, Saylor, Stewart, Truby, Woods.

AWARDED FIRST BASE ON CATCHER'S INTERFERENCE: Conti (Pena 2, Castro 3, Charles), J. Perez (Charles 2, Kleiner, Cancel, Charles, Pena), 6 each; Maddox 2 (C. King, Graves), Christian (Castro), Hutchins (P. Lopes), Leach (Castro), McEwing (P. Lopes).

PLAYERS WITH TWO OR MORE TEAMS

Player, Team	Avg.	G	TPA	AB	R	H	TB	2B	3B	HR	RBI	SH	SF	HP	BB	IBB	SO	SB	CS	GDP	Slg.	OBP
Hollins, Stacy, Shre.	.000	18	8	8	0	0	0	0	0	0	0	0	0	0	0	0	3	0	0	0	.000	.000
Hollins, Stacy, E.P.	.500	10	7	6	1	3	4	1	0	0	2	0	1	0	0	0	3	0	0	0	.667	.429
Hook, Chris, Shre.	.000	15	1	1	0	0	0	0	0	0	0	0	0	0	0	0	1	0	0	0	.000	.000
Hook, Chris, Jack.	.000	15	9	5	0	0	0	0	0	0	0	2	0	0	2	0	4	0	0	0	.000	.286

1998 PITCHING

TEAM

Team	W	L	Pct.	ERA	G	CG	ShO	Sv.	IP	H	TBF	R	ER	HR	SH	SF	HB	BB	IBB	SO	WP	Bk.
Tulsa..................	78	62	.557	4.15	140	8	8	33	1235.2	1146	5298	648	570	126	23	38	47	540	10	963	86	13
San Antonio	67	73	.479	4.22	140	4	7	36	1229.1	1269	5374	698	576	108	34	45	51	477	10	927	76	10
Shreveport	57	83	.407	4.26	140	7	4	33	1217.1	1216	5340	668	576	113	58	39	74	531	49	959	85	12
Jackson	70	70	.500	4.28	140	4	1	35	1220.2	1186	5327	691	581	135	48	37	79	504	29	989	63	10
Arkansas	80	60	.571	4.64	140	3	7	35	1201.1	1313	5292	707	620	129	41	46	47	489	13	750	75	8
Midland	64	76	.457	5.32	140	18	5	26	1225.1	1431	5494	849	724	168	48	39	59	443	16	961	64	11
Wichita	75	65	.536	5.40	140	2	5	38	1213.1	1489	5529	861	728	161	59	49	60	470	38	799	70	9
El Paso	69	71	.493	5.73	140	4	6	29	1224.1	1496	5658	912	779	126	50	44	57	535	22	896	99	15

INDIVIDUAL

TOP QUALIFIERS FOR EARNED-RUN AVERAGE TITLE

Minimum 112 innings. *Lefthanded pitcher.

Pitcher, Team	W	L	Pct.	ERA	G	GS	CG	ShO	GF	Sv.	IP	H	TBF	R	ER	HR	SH	SF	HB	BB	IBB	SO	WP	Bk.
Jimenez, Jose, Ark.	15	6	.714	3.11	26	26	1	1	0	0	179.2	156	743	71	62	9	4	12	68	1	88	13	0
Garcia, Freddy, Jack.	6	7	.462	3.24	19	19	2	0	0	0	119.1	94	505	48	43	8	4	0	6	58	0	115	8	0
Glynn, Ryan, Tul.	9	6	.600	3.44	26	24	4	1	0	0	157.0	140	660	66	60	12	4	3	5	64	0	111	9	1
Oropesa, Eddie, Shre.*	7	11	.389	3.78	32	20	2	0	3	0	143.0	143	623	71	60	6	7	5	7	67	3	104	15	2
Grilli, Jason, Shre.	7	10	.412	3.79	21	21	3	0	0	0	123.1	113	511	60	52	11	6	3	4	37	0	100	6	3
Brester, Jason, Shre.*	2	8	.200	3.82	19	19	0	0	0	0	113.0	117	490	58	48	11	7	4	0	44	3	79	4	2
Beaumont, Matt, Mid.*	9	12	.429	4.20	34	18	1	0	6	1	128.2	124	583	81	60	10	5	4	10	67	1	107	3	3
Lee, Corey, Tul.*	10	9	.526	4.51	26	25	1	0	0	0	143.2	105	625	81	72	16	3	5	5	102	1	132	12	1
Prihoda, Steve, Wich.*	11	8	.579	4.72	58	3	0	0	16	3	122.0	140	528	76	64	18	9	7	9	23	7	85	7	1
Kolb, Dan, Tul.	12	11	.522	4.82	28	28	2	0	0	0	162.1	187	730	104	87	11	3	5	8	76	1	83	8	1
Detmers, Kris, Ark.*	9	10	.474	4.92	27	26	0	0	0	0	153.2	175	698	100	84	14	8	8	8	78	1	88	9	3
Linebrink, Scott, Shre.	10	8	.556	5.02	21	21	0	0	0	0	113.0	101	494	66	63	12	6	5	7	58	1	128	8	0
Ray, Ken, Wich.	10	5	.667	5.20	24	21	0	0	0	0	117.2	149	530	79	68	7	5	5	3	47	2	71	1	0
Gooding, Jason, Wich.*	5	7	.417	5.22	25	23	0	0	1	0	129.1	171	593	93	75	15	9	9	10	43	1	68	8	2
Pote, Lou, Mid.*	8	10	.444	5.31	32	19	6	1	7	0	154.1	194	700	110	91	18	5	6	6	54	1	117	8	0

DEPARTMENTAL LEADERS: W—Jimenez, 15; L—Beaumont, 12; Pct.—Mullen, .800; ERA—Jimenez, 3.11; G—Prihoda, 58; GS—Kolb, O'Malley 28 each; CG—Pote, 6; ShO—Several pitchers tied with 1 each; GF—Santiago, 41; Sv.—Santiago, 22; IP—Jimenez, 179.2; H—Cooper, 215; TBF—Cooper, 750; R—Cooper, 138; ER—Cooper, 128; HR—Cooper, 35; SH—Gooding, Prihoda, 9 each; SF—Gooding, Weibl, 9 each; HB—O'Malley, 23; BB—Lee, 102; IBB—Fultz, 10; SO—Cooper, 141; WP—Chavez, Hollins, Oropesa, 15 each; BK—Pasqualicchio, 7.

ALL PITCHERS

*Lefthanded pitcher.

Pitcher, Team	W	L	Pct.	ERA	G	GS	CG	ShO	GF	Sv.	IP	H	TBF	R	ER	HR	SH	SF	HB	BB	IBB	SO	WP	Bk.
Adam, Dave, Jack.	0	0	.000	2.08	3	0	0	0	0	0	4.1	2	18	1	1	0	0	0	0	3	0	5	0	0
Alguacil, Jose, Shre.	0	0	.000	27.00	1	0	0	0	1	0	1.0	5	9	3	3	0	0	0	1	0	0	0	0	0
Almanza, Armando, Ark. *	4	1	.800	3.31	28	0	0	0	16	8	32.2	27	140	13	12	2	0	0	2	18	0	46	4	0
Alvarez, Juan, Mid. *	3	4	.429	4.30	40	0	0	0	31	12	46.0	40	197	26	22	5	2	1	2	21	3	41	2	1
Appier, Kevin, Wich.	0	1	.000	6.00	1	1	0	0	0	0	6.0	8	25	4	4	1	0	0	2	0	1	0	0
Babineaux, Darrin, S.A.	5	4	.556	3.38	39	4	0	0	13	3	77.1	66	329	34	29	8	0	5	1	33	0	56	6	0
Bailes, Scott, Tul.*	0	1	.000	10.80	2	0	0	0	2	1	1.2	4	9	2	2	0	0	0	0	4	0	0	0
Beaumont, Matt, Mid. *	9	12	.429	4.20	34	18	1	0	6	1	128.2	124	583	81	60	10	5	4	10	67	1	107	3	3
Beck, Greg, E.P.	9	7	.563	6.70	30	15	0	0	5	0	98.0	135	452	80	73	14	2	3	8	24	2	76	7	0
Benes, Adam, Ark.	0	0	.000	6.06	12	0	0	0	6	0	16.1	21	73	12	11	2	1	2	1	2	1	8	2	0
Bermudez, Manny, Shre.	0	4	.000	7.56	5	2	1	0	0	0	25.0	33	117	23	21	6	0	2	3	11	0	16	1	1
Blais, Mike, Jack.	1	2	.333	3.08	21	0	0	0	6	0	38.0	40	162	15	13	3	0	3	8	0	37	0	0
Blanco, Alberto, Jack. *	4	4	.500	5.76	12	12	0	0	0	0	59.1	65	261	43	38	10	4	3	1	24	0	60	4	2
Bland, Nate, S.A. *	4	2	.667	2.78	26	0	0	0	5	0	45.1	56	203	21	14	0	0	2	2	14	0	34	3	0
Bluma, Jaime, Wich.	1	2	.333	5.37	39	0	0	0	18	0	62.0	67	291	49	37	10	1	0	4	35	6	38	5	0

Pitcher, Team	W	L	Pct.	ERA	G	GS	CG	ShO	GF	Sv.	IP	H	TBF	R	ER	HR	SH	SF	HB	BB	IBB	SO	WP	Bk.
Bonanno, Rob, Mid.	7	4	.636	4.05	14	14	2	0	0	0	100.0	108	414	48	45	20	2	2	5	16	0	56	0	1
Brantley, Jeff, Ark.	0	0	.000	0.00	2	0	0	0	0	0	1.2	0	6	0	0	0	0	1	0	1	0	3	0	0
Brester, Jason, Shre. *	2	8	.200	3.82	19	19	0	0	0	0	113.0	117	490	58	48	11	7	4	0	44	3	79	4	2
Brewer, Ryan, Wich.	3	0	1.000	4.00	20	0	0	0	6	1	36.0	47	161	16	16	3	2	1	0	12	3	30	3	0
Brosnan, Jason, Mid. *	3	0	1.000	6.20	16	0	0	0	6	0	24.2	32	120	20	17	7	0	2	1	13	1	24	1	0
Byington, Jimmie, Wich.	0	0	.000	27.00	1	0	0	0	1	0	1.0	2	8	3	3	0	0	1	1	2	0	0	0	0
Byrdak, Tim, Wich. *	3	5	.375	4.15	34	0	0	0	10	2	52.0	58	242	29	24	3	4	4	2	28	1	37	2	3
Calero, Kiko, Wich.	1	0	1.000	9.64	3	3	0	0	0	0	14.0	23	72	16	15	2	1	0	1	6	0	5	0	0
Chavez, Carlos, E.P.	3	5	.375	5.91	54	4	0	0	7	0	88.1	104	417	74	58	6	6	2	4	45	5	83	15	1
Cooper, Brian, Mid.	8	10	.444	7.13	32	24	5	0	4	1	161.2	215	750	138	128	35	5	6	9	59	1	141	7	0
Cornett, Brad, E.P.	0	2	.000	5.17	3	3	0	0	0	0	15.2	22	75	16	9	4	1	0	0	5	0	10	3	1
Corps, Edwin, Shre.	2	5	.286	3.90	46	5	0	0	11	1	92.1	94	396	47	40	13	5	4	2	32	4	42	8	0
Crabtree, Robbie, Shre.	2	0	1.000	1.67	26	0	0	0	13	4	54.0	30	205	11	10	4	1	0	2	16	2	56	2	0
Crafton, Kevin, Ark.	5	1	.833	3.23	46	0	0	0	13	1	55.2	52	227	23	20	8	3	2	0	7	0	44	2	0
Davis, Allen, S.A. *	2	2	.500	3.16	6	5	0	0	0	0	31.1	31	132	13	11	2	1	0	1	9	0	33	0	1
Dawsey, Jason, E.P. *	1	3	.250	7.96	6	6	0	0	0	0	31.2	34	147	29	28	4	1	2	2	22	1	19	1	0
Deakman, Josh, Mid.	3	4	.429	7.51	29	5	0	0	9	1	50.1	79	243	52	42	7	1	3	4	14	1	29	2	1
De La Cruz, Fernando, Mid.	0	0	.000	54.00	2	0	0	0	0	0	1.0	5	13	7	6	0	0	0	1	4	0	1	0	0
De Los Santos, Valerio, E.P. *	6	2	.750	3.92	42	4	0	0	32	10	66.2	81	305	34	29	2	5	3	1	25	1	62	5	1
Deskins, Casey, S.A. *	4	8	.333	4.87	22	16	0	0	2	0	94.1	118	425	68	51	12	4	6	9	22	2	64	1	0
Detmers, Kris, Ark. *	9	10	.474	4.92	27	26	0	0	0	0	153.2	175	698	100	84	14	8	8	8	78	1	88	9	3
Diorio, Mike, Jack.	2	3	.400	2.09	32	0	0	0	24	11	43.0	35	182	16	10	0	3	0	2	21	4	31	2	0
Dishington, Nate, Ark.	0	0	.000	0.00	1	0	0	0	0	0	0.0	0	1	0	0	0	0	0	0	1	0	0	0	0
Dollar, Toby, S.A.	6	11	.353	5.48	23	22	2	1	1	0	143.0	170	628	97	87	18	8	5	8	39	0	65	9	0
Duncan, Sean, Jack. *	3	1	.750	2.75	28	0	0	0	10	1	39.1	27	170	15	12	6	3	3	1	21	4	37	2	0
Elliott, Donnie, Tul.	1	1	.500	5.79	20	0	0	0	11	2	28.0	24	124	20	18	2	0	0	2	21	0	25	3	1
Estrada, Horacio, E.P. *	5	0	1.000	4.53	8	8	0	0	0	0	49.2	50	206	27	25	3	6	2	2	21	0	37	4	1
Etherton, Seth, Mid.	1	5	.167	6.14	9	7	1	0	1	0	48.1	57	211	36	33	9	3	2	1	12	0	35	1	1
Evans, Mike, Wich.	0	0	.000	9.00	1	0	0	0	1	0	1.0	2	6	1	1	0	0	0	0	1	0	0	0	0
Faurot, Adam, E.P.	0	0	.000	27.00	1	0	0	0	1	0	1.0	4	8	3	3	0	0	1	0	1	0	0	0	0
Flury, Pat, Wich.	1	1	.500	5.40	8	0	0	0	2	0	11.2	14	59	11	7	0	1	0	3	7	0	13	1	0
Frontera, Chad, Shre.	0	4	.000	4.30	8	8	0	0	0	0	37.2	52	185	24	18	3	2	1	6	27	1	28	2	0
Fultz, Aaron, Shre. *	5	7	.417	3.77	54	0	0	0	34	15	62.0	58	273	40	26	4	8	3	3	29	10	61	5	1
Gallaher, Kevin, E.P.	0	0	.000	29.25	5	0	0	0	2	0	4.0	2	33	13	13	1	0	0	2	18	0	3	1	0
Garcia, Freddy, Jack.	6	7	.462	3.24	19	19	2	0	0	0	119.1	94	505	48	43	8	4	0	6	58	0	115	8	0
Garcia, Miguel, S.A.	1	3	.250	4.27	26	7	0	0	7	0	65.1	65	289	36	31	4	1	0	5	31	0	39	3	0
Garcia, Ossie, Ark.	0	0	.000	27.00	1	0	0	0	1	0	0.2	3	6	2	2	0	0	0	0	1	0	0	0	0
Garrett, Hal, S.A.	2	1	.667	3.63	11	2	0	0	6	2	22.1	21	95	9	9	1	0	0	0	13	0	13	2	0
Glynn, Ryan, Tul.	9	6	.600	3.44	26	24	4	1	0	0	157.0	140	660	66	60	12	4	3	5	64	0	111	9	1
Gooding, Jason, Wich. *	5	7	.417	5.22	25	23	0	0	1	0	129.1	171	593	93	75	15	9	9	10	43	1	68	8	2
Grebe, Brett, Mid.	0	0	.000	4.32	10	0	0	0	2	0	16.2	18	76	11	8	1	1	1	1	8	0	12	4	0
Greene, Danny, Mid.	6	3	.667	4.82	37	0	0	0	18	3	56.0	61	256	34	30	5	5	1	2	32	6	59	5	1
Grilli, Jason, Shre.	7	10	.412	3.79	21	21	3	0	0	0	123.1	113	511	60	52	11	6	3	4	37	0	100	6	3
Groppuso, Mike, E.P.	0	1	.000	27.00	1	0	0	0	1	0	0.1	1	4	1	1	0	0	0	0	2	0	0	0	0
Grote, Jason, Shre.	2	5	.286	6.79	10	10	0	0	0	0	53.0	84	252	44	40	5	2	3	3	15	1	27	3	0
Grundy, Phil, Wich.	2	7	.222	8.11	18	14	0	0	2	1	81.0	117	396	86	73	21	6	1	6	49	1	60	6	0
Gutierrez, Jim, Jack.	2	1	.667	4.22	8	2	0	0	1	0	21.1	20	90	11	10	0	0	2	0	5	0	18	0	0
Hall, Darren, S.A.	0	0	.000	10.80	2	2	0	0	0	0	1.2	1	7	2	2	1	0	0	0	1	0	2	0	0
Hall, Yates, Ark.	0	0	.000	18.62	8	0	0	0	2	0	9.2	16	63	21	20	2	0	0	2	19	0	2	2	0
Hardwick, Bubba, E.P. *	3	3	.500	4.93	32	1	0	0	13	1	49.1	66	235	35	27	5	4	0	0	24	1	26	3	0
Heflin, Bronson, Ark.	0	1	.000	6.75	2	0	0	0	1	0	1.1	1	8	1	1	0	0	1	0	4	0	0	0	0
Heiserman, Rick, Ark.	0	3	.000	4.96	18	0	0	0	18	9	16.1	20	76	11	9	1	1	0	1	5	0	9	2	0
Henderson, Ryan, E.P.	2	0	1.000	3.68	20	0	0	0	11	5	22.0	22	105	14	9	0	0	0	3	13	2	20	2	0
Herges, Matt, S.A.	0	0	.000	0.00	3	0	0	0	0	0	6.0	3	21	0	0	0	0	0	0	2	0	3	0	0
Hernandez, Xavier, Tul.	0	0	.000	3.00	2	2	0	0	0	0	3.0	3	13	1	1	1	0	0	1	0	0	2	1	0
Hill, Jason, Mid. *	1	1	.500	4.91	48	0	0	0	17	2	66.0	68	311	44	36	5	4	0	7	38	1	53	2	1
Hill, Tyrone, Mid. *	0	2	.000	3.78	3	3	0	0	0	0	16.2	14	64	7	7	2	0	1	0	5	0	12	1	0
Hodges, Kevin, Jack.	4	5	.444	3.61	29	15	0	0	4	0	107.1	108	462	55	43	8	5	2	7	38	3	70	6	2
Hollins, Stacy, Shre.-E.P.	7	5	.583	5.79	28	12	0	0	3	1	98.0	113	458	75	63	14	4	4	11	53	3	60	15	0
Hommel, Brian, E.P. *	1	3	.250	7.41	14	0	0	0	4	0	17.0	23	85	17	14	2	0	1	0	14	0	16	3	1
Hook, Chris, Shre.-Jack.	4	5	.444	5.50	30	7	0	0	14	3	68.2	62	320	47	42	6	3	4	13	52	3	45	11	0
Huber, Jeff, Mid.-E.P. *	1	1	.500	7.71	16	2	0	0	2	1	23.1	45	122	24	20	5	1	1	0	6	1	17	5	0
Huntsman, Scott, E.P.	4	3	.571	8.35	52	0	0	0	12	3	74.1	106	353	71	69	12	1	4	4	31	2	49	5	1
Hurst, Jonathan, Tul.	0	1	.000	4.50	10	1	0	0	1	0	26.0	25	108	16	13	1	1	2	0	8	1	23	2	0
Hutzler, Jeff, Shre.	0	2	.000	5.91	2	2	0	0	0	0	10.2	13	47	7	7	1	0	0	1	2	1	10	0	0
Jacobsen, Joe, Mid.	2	1	.667	1.51	26	1	0	0	19	5	35.2	34	148	13	6	1	4	0	1	7	0	19	5	0
Jarvis, Matt, Ark. *	6	1	.857	4.10	56	0	0	0	32	15	59.1	55	258	30	27	2	2	0	3	30	2	46	3	0
Jimenez, Jose, Ark.	15	6	.714	3.11	26	26	1	1	0	0	179.2	156	743	71	62	9	6	4	12	68	1	88	13	0
Johnson, Gregory, Mid. *	0	0	.000	10.80	2	0	0	0	0	0	1.2	4	10	2	2	0	0	1	0	2	0	1	1	0
Juarbe, Ken, Tul. *	0	1	.000	5.65	7	1	0	0	0	0	14.1	16	69	10	9	2	0	1	0	11	0	13	1	2
Keith, Jeff, Shre. *	1	1	.500	8.59	10	0	0	0	5	0	22.0	26	109	23	21	4	0	2	0	20	1	15	2	0
Kester, Tim, Jack.	5	5	.500	4.19	55	0	0	0	26	6	86.0	90	364	47	40	13	5	2	6	19	5	51	0	0
Kirkreit, Daron, Wich.-E.P.	2	9	.182	6.37	28	20	0	0	2	0	111.2	155	532	91	79	10	7	5	5	55	1	54	11	1
Knight, Brandon, Tul.	6	6	.500	5.11	14	14	0	0	0	0	86.1	94	379	54	49	11	1	3	0	37	0	87	12	0
Kolb, Dan, Tul.	12	11	.522	4.82	28	28	2	0	0	0	162.1	187	730	104	87	11	3	5	8	76	1	83	8	1
Kubenka, Jeff, S.A. *	0	0	.000	7.00	9	0	0	0	6	0	9.0	10	47	11	7	2	0	1	1	7	0	10	3	1
Lee, Corey, Tul. *	10	9	.526	4.51	26	25	1	0	0	0	143.2	105	625	81	72	16	3	5	5	102	1	132	12	1
Levrault, Allen, E.P.	1	5	.167	5.89	11	11	0	0	0	0	62.2	77	281	51	41	7	2	2	1	17	0	46	1	1
Lilly, Ted, S.A. *	8	4	.667	3.30	17	17	0	0	0	0	111.2	114	471	50	41	8	1	2	1	37	0	96	4	3
Linebrink, Scott, Shre.	10	8	.556	5.02	21	21	0	0	0	0	113.0	101	494	66	63	12	6	5	7	58	1	128	8	0
Lisio, Joe, Tul.	0	0	.000	8.10	9	0	0	0	3	0	13.1	21	67	13	12	1	0	1	0	8	0	13	0	0
Lock, Dan, Jack. *	0	1	.000	11.25	16	0	0	0	7	1	12.0	15	71	17	15	1	1	1	1	19	2	13	2	0

Pitcher, Team	W	L	Pct.	ERA	G	GS	CG	ShO	GF	Sv.	IP	H	TBF	R	ER	HR	SH	SF	HB	BB	IBB	SO	WP	Bk.
Logan, Marcus, Ark.	7	7	.500	5.51	28	20	0	0	4	0	125.2	162	574	91	77	15	5	5	2	56	0	66	11	0
Lovingier, Kevin, Ark. *	1	0	1.000	2.63	19	0	0	0	6	0	24.0	20	104	9	7	2	0	0	0	13	1	26	3	0
Manning, David, Tul.	2	0	1.000	4.85	6	0	0	0	1	0	13.0	13	61	7	7	2	0	1	0	11	0	15	2	0
Martin, Jeff, Shre.	1	2	.333	3.03	31	1	0	0	7	0	59.1	53	246	23	20	4	3	0	2	17	2	43	4	1
Martinez, Jose, Tul.	2	2	.500	7.60	7	7	0	0	0	0	34.1	46	160	34	29	6	1	2	2	14	0	21	3	2
Masaoka, Onan, S.A. *	6	6	.500	5.32	27	20	1	1	2	1	110.0	114	500	79	65	11	2	5	6	63	0	94	3	1
Mayo, Blake, S.A.	2	1	.667	1.47	13	0	0	0	5	1	18.1	13	73	3	3	0	0	0	6	0	15	3	1
McDougal, Mike, Ark.	2	3	.400	4.94	24	0	0	0	8	1	31.0	45	143	21	17	7	0	2	2	5	1	16	1	0
McDowell, Jack, Mid.	0	1	.000	3.86	1	1	0	0	0	0	7.0	5	28	3	3	1	0	0	0	2	0	5	0	0
McEwing, Joe, Ark.	0	0	.000	27.00	1	0	0	0	1	0	1.0	3	7	3	3	0	0	0	1	0	1	0	0	0
McMullen, Mike, Shre.	6	4	.600	2.13	52	0	0	0	37	9	67.2	47	296	23	16	1	5	1	6	41	9	76	5	0
McNally, Sean, Wich.	0	0	.000	7.94	5	0	0	0	5	0	5.2	6	23	5	5	2	0	2	0	1	0	0	0	0
Mercedes, Jose, E.P.	0	0	.000	10.80	1	1	0	0	0	0	3.1	9	18	4	4	2	0	1	0	0	0	0	0	0
Michalak, Chris, Tul. *	1	2	.333	1.83	10	0	0	0	3	0	19.2	10	73	4	4	2	2	0	2	2	0	15	0	2
Miller, Eric, Wich.	1	0	1.000	5.70	18	0	0	0	6	0	23.2	36	118	22	15	3	0	0	1	13	2	20	3	0
Miller, Wade, Jack.	5	0	1.000	2.32	10	10	0	0	0	0	62.0	49	262	23	16	7	1	0	4	27	2	48	3	1
Minor, Blas, E.P.	1	3	.250	4.62	8	2	0	0	2	1	25.1	30	108	14	13	5	1	0	0	3	1	26	2	0
Mitchell, Dean, S.A.	2	5	.286	3.30	46	3	0	0	29	14	79.0	74	331	31	29	8	5	1	3	22	2	76	4	0
Montoya, Norm, Mid. *	2	3	.400	4.66	9	5	0	0	0	0	36.2	46	156	21	19	3	3	0	1	6	0	15	5	0
Moore, Bobby, Tul.	0	0	.000	0.00	1	0	0	0	1	0	1.0	0	3	0	0	0	0	0	0	0	0	2	0	0
Moreno, Orber, Wich.	0	1	.000	2.88	24	0	0	0	19	7	34.1	28	144	13	11	1	2	0	0	12	3	40	3	0
Morris, Matt, Ark.	0	0	.000	0.00	1	0	0	0	1	1	4.0	4	17	0	0	0	0	0	0	2	0	0	0	0
Mounce, Tony, Jack. *	6	6	.500	5.09	32	17	1	0	3	0	109.2	128	498	73	62	14	3	5	2	48	0	82	5	0
Mullen, Scott, Wich. *	8	2	.800	4.11	12	12	0	0	0	0	70.0	66	289	34	32	7	0	3	1	26	0	42	7	0
Nathan, Joe, Shre.	1	3	.250	8.80	4	4	0	0	0	0	15.1	20	74	15	15	4	0	2	9	0	10	0	0
Neal, Billy, S.A.	1	2	.333	4.66	31	0	0	0	11	0	48.1	58	225	31	25	2	0	1	3	22	2	27	10	0
Nix, James, E.P.	0	0	.000	14.09	8	0	0	0	2	0	7.2	20	47	14	12	1	0	0	0	6	0	11	2	0
Norris, Joe, E.P.	3	1	.750	6.66	40	0	0	0	21	3	52.2	51	256	46	39	8	2	6	5	48	1	41	7	0
Nussbeck, Mark, Ark.	4	2	.667	5.10	10	8	0	0	0	0	42.1	44	192	30	24	7	2	2	1	18	1	21	2	0
O'Malley, Paul, Jack.	11	10	.524	5.45	29	28	1	0	1	0	152.0	162	695	112	92	22	6	7	23	70	2	89	6	4
Oropesa, Eddie, Shre. *	7	11	.389	3.78	32	20	2	0	3	0	143.0	143	623	71	60	6	7	5	7	67	3	104	15	2
Ortiz, Ramon, Mid.	2	1	.667	5.55	7	7	0	0	0	0	47.0	50	202	31	29	10	1	2	1	16	0	53	3	1
Osborne, Donovan, Ark. *	2	0	1.000	4.26	5	5	0	0	0	0	19.0	16	76	9	9	2	0	0	0	3	0	21	0	0
Pasqualicchio, Mike, E.P. *	3	5	.375	7.65	10	9	0	0	1	0	42.1	61	211	39	36	3	0	1	2	26	1	31	2	7
Passini, Brian, E.P. *	4	5	.556	2.91	12	12	1	1	0	0	80.1	69	334	35	26	5	2	2	2	28	0	51	5	0
Patterson, Danny, Tul.	0	0	.000	4.50	2	1	0	0	1	0	4.0	3	14	2	2	1	0	0	0	0	0	4	0	0
Pearsall, J.J., S.A. *	6	5	.545	4.38	46	4	0	0	11	0	72.0	71	320	38	35	8	0	2	2	37	2	63	5	0
Pedraza, Rod, Tul.	3	2	.600	2.48	6	5	0	0	0	0	36.1	30	136	11	10	1	0	1	0	4	0	31	0	0
Perisho, Matt, Tul. *	0	0	.000	6.00	1	1	0	0	0	0	3.0	3	16	2	2	0	0	0	3	0	1	0	0
Peterson, Kyle, E.P.	3	2	.600	4.40	7	7	1	0	0	0	43.0	41	187	24	21	2	2	2	1	16	0	33	1	0
Phillips, Randy, Shre.	6	4	.600	3.97	17	17	1	0	0	0	95.1	95	412	44	42	11	2	3	10	30	3	68	3	2
Politte, Cliff, Ark.	5	3	.625	2.96	10	10	1	1	0	0	67.0	56	265	25	22	6	3	1	1	16	0	61	0	0
Pote, Lou, Mid.	8	10	.444	5.31	32	19	6	1	7	0	154.1	194	700	110	91	18	5	6	6	54	1	117	8	0
Powell, John, Tul.	2	4	.333	2.50	28	0	0	0	15	0	54.0	38	219	18	15	7	2	1	2	21	2	44	7	0
Prihoda, Steve, Wich. *	11	8	.579	4.72	58	3	0	0	16	3	122.0	140	528	76	64	18	9	7	9	23	7	85	7	1
Prokopec, Luke, S.A.	3	0	1.000	1.38	5	5	0	0	0	0	26.0	16	106	5	4	0	1	1	13	0	25	2	1
Ramos, Edgar, Jack.	2	4	.333	6.10	17	6	0	0	2	0	48.2	61	212	34	33	6	1	1	2	12	1	47	9	0
Rawitzer, Kevin, Wich. *	7	4	.636	5.08	14	14	2	0	0	0	85.0	94	379	52	48	13	3	5	3	28	0	54	4	1
Ray, Ken, Wich.	10	5	.667	5.20	24	21	0	0	0	0	117.2	149	530	79	68	7	5	5	3	47	2	71	1	0
Reed, Steve, Ark.	4	7	.364	6.03	32	17	0	0	0	0	116.1	163	529	92	78	18	5	8	3	31	1	53	6	2
Reichert, Dan, Wich.	1	4	.200	9.75	8	8	0	0	0	0	36.0	52	186	40	39	7	1	1	4	29	1	24	2	1
Rennhack, Mike, E.P.	0	0	.000	18.00	1	0	0	0	1	0	1.0	4	6	2	2	1	0	0	0	0	0	0	0	0
Ricabal, Dan, S.A.	2	9	.182	6.12	54	1	0	0	38	15	78.0	78	355	59	53	7	2	7	6	40	1	61	10	0
Rodriguez, Frankie, E.P.	0	0	.000	1.50	4	0	0	0	2	0	6.0	7	26	2	1	0	0	2	1	5	0	0
Rogers, Kevin, Shre. *	1	0	1.000	5.87	14	1	0	0	7	0	23.0	25	106	17	15	2	0	1	2	9	1	18	0	0
Root, Derek, Jack. *	4	1	.800	3.89	7	6	0	0	0	0	44.0	46	192	24	19	4	1	1	1	17	1	31	1	0
Roque, Rafael, E.P. *	5	6	.455	4.40	16	16	1	0	0	0	94.0	113	432	56	46	8	2	0	4	35	2	70	4	0
Sabel, Erik, Tul.	7	0	1.000	3.20	24	2	0	0	7	2	56.1	46	226	24	20	6	0	0	2	13	1	33	6	0
Sadler, Al, E.P.	1	0	1.000	4.12	34	0	0	0	17	6	43.2	44	186	20	20	2	1	1	1	12	1	37	3	0
Saier, Matt, Wich.	9	5	.643	5.16	18	18	0	0	0	0	103.0	127	463	70	59	14	3	3	5	28	1	80	8	1
Santiago, Jose, Wich.	3	4	.429	3.61	52	0	0	0	41	22	72.1	79	316	36	29	9	6	1	1	27	7	31	1	0
Sikorski, Brian, Jack.	6	4	.600	4.07	15	15	0	0	0	0	97.1	83	419	50	44	13	3	2	6	44	1	80	3	1
Slusarski, Joe, Jack.	2	2	.500	6.33	9	2	0	0	1	0	21.1	22	87	17	15	3	1	1	2	0	13	1	0
Smith, Dan, Tul.	13	9	.591	5.81	26	25	1	0	0	0	153.1	162	675	101	99	27	1	7	11	58	1	105	9	1
Smith, Eric, Jack.	1	0	1.000	5.59	6	0	0	0	2	0	9.2	9	42	6	6	0	0	0	5	1	11	1	0
Smith, Lee, Jack.	0	0	.000	0.00	2	0	0	0	2	0	2.0	1	7	0	0	0	0	0	0	0	0	5	0	0
Smith, Willie, Wich.	0	0	.000	10.80	4	0	0	0	2	0	5.0	8	27	6	6	0	0	0	1	4	0	3	1	0
Sollecito, Gabe, Tul.	1	0	1.000	1.93	5	0	0	0	3	0	9.1	5	39	3	2	0	0	1	4	0	10	2	0
Sparks, Steve, Mid.	0	4	.000	7.08	7	7	0	0	0	0	40.2	49	184	38	32	3	2	1	0	15	0	34	3	1
Steph, Rod, Wich.	0	0	.000	6.52	8	0	0	0	6	2	9.2	17	48	8	7	1	0	2	2	0	8	0	0
Stone, Ricky, S.A.	7	2	.778	3.84	13	13	1	1	0	0	82.0	76	336	40	35	7	5	1	1	26	0	69	6	0
Sturtze, Tanyon, Tul.	1	0	1.000	5.40	1	0	0	0	0	0	1.2	2	7	1	1	1	0	0	0	2	0	3	0	0
Taulbee, Andy, Shre.	0	1	.000	4.02	3	3	0	0	0	0	15.2	17	72	9	7	1	0	0	9	0	10	1	0
Taylor, Scott, Wich. *	7	3	.700	4.78	14	13	0	0	0	0	79.0	91	341	50	42	13	1	2	2	17	0	54	3	0
Toth, Robert, Wich.	0	3	.000	14.59	5	2	0	0	2	0	12.1	27	73	26	20	7	2	0	0	10	2	9	0	0
Turner, Matt, Wich.	1	0	1.000	0.00	1	0	0	0	1	0	5.2	8	27	2	0	0	0	0	0	2	0	3	0	0
Tuttle, Dave, Tul.	1	2	.333	2.69	36	2	0	0	13	4	73.2	73	316	30	22	4	0	2	5	29	0	47	2	0
Van Poppel, Todd, Tul.	0	0	.000	4.50	1	1	0	0	0	0	4.0	2	17	2	2	1	0	0	4	0	2	0	0
Venafro, Mike, Tul. *	3	4	.429	3.10	46	0	0	0	39	14	52.1	42	223	21	18	5	3	1	1	26	0	45	3	0
Verdugo, Jason, Shre.	1	2	.333	3.72	9	1	0	0	2	1	19.1	17	81	9	8	4	1	1	6	2	27	0	0
Wagner, Billy, Jack. *	0	0	.000	0.00	3	1	0	0	1	0	3.0	1	10	0	0	0	0	0	0	0	7	0	0
Wallace, Kent, Jack.	3	2	.600	2.54	29	0	0	0	19	11	49.2	37	195	17	14	4	2	2	2	11	0	51	2	0

Pitcher, Team	W	L	Pct.	ERA	G	GS	CG	ShO	GF	Sv.	IP	H	TBF	R	ER	HR	SH	SF	HB	BB	IBB	SO	WP	Bk.
Walter, Mike, Jack.	1	7	.125	4.66	38	0	0	0	23	3	48.1	48	223	31	25	7	3	2	5	22	3	55	4	0
Washburn, Jarrod, Mid. *	0	1	.000	6.23	1	1	0	0	0	0	8.2	13	40	8	6	2	1	0	0	2	0	8	0	0
Watkins, Scott, Tul. *	1	0	1.000	2.14	10	1	0	0	4	1	21.0	14	80	5	5	1	0	0	0	2	0	25	1	0
Watson, Allen, Mid. *	0	0	.000	2.25	1	1	0	0	0	0	4.0	6	19	2	1	0	0	1	1	1	0	3	1	0
Weibl, Clint, Ark.	12	10	.545	5.37	25	23	0	0	0	0	139.0	161	616	86	83	22	4	9	5	53	2	85	3	0
Welch, Travis, Ark.	1	1	.500	2.79	23	0	0	0	10	0	29.0	27	129	10	9	2	0	0	2	18	0	15	4	2
Williams, Jeff, S.A. *	3	0	1.000	2.59	7	7	0	0	0	0	41.2	43	182	19	12	3	1	3	0	13	1	35	1	1
Windham, Mike, Ark.	3	4	.429	5.09	40	5	1	0	12	0	76.0	86	341	47	43	8	1	1	2	41	2	49	8	1
Wise, Matt, Mid.	9	10	.474	5.42	27	27	3	1	0	0	167.2	195	735	111	101	23	4	5	6	46	0	131	9	0
Wunsch, Kelly, E.P. *	5	6	.455	5.95	17	17	1	1	0	0	101.1	127	469	81	67	11	4	3	9	31	0	70	7	0
Zamora, Pete, S.A. *	3	8	.273	4.46	12	12	0	0	0	0	66.2	71	299	52	33	6	4	3	1	27	0	47	1	1
Zimmerman, Jeff, Tul.	3	1	.750	1.29	41	0	0	0	28	9	63.0	38	249	16	9	3	2	0	3	20	3	67	3	2

COMBINATION SHUTOUTS: **Arkansas (5)**—Jimenez-Heiserman, Weibl-Lovingier, Logan-Jarvis, Osborne-Weibl-Crafton-Jarvis, Jimenez-McDougal. **El Paso (4)**—Estrada-Hardwick-Norris, Beck-Sadler-DeLosSantos, Passini-Nix-DeLosSantos, Chavez-Beck-Minor. **Jackson (1)**—O'Malley-Kester. **Midland (3)**—Etherton-Greene-Jacobsen, Montoya-Grebe-Jacobsen, Cooper-Jacobsen. **San Antonio (4)**—Garcia-Mitchel-Ricabal, Dollar-Pearsal-Mitchell, Prokopec-Ricabal-Mayo-Garrett, Davis-Pearsall-Garrett. **Shreveport (4)**—Phillips-Hollins-McMullen, Linebrink-Corps, Oropesa-Verdugo, Oropesa-Verdugo-Crabtree. **Tulsa (7)**—Glynn-Tuttle-Michalak, Lee-Zimmerman, Smith-Sabel, Smith-Zimmerman-Tuttle, Smith-Simmerman, Pedraza-Elliott, Kolb-Bailes. **Wichita (5)**—Rawitzer-Ray-Santiago, Mullen-Bluma-Santiago-Prihoda, Taylor-Prihoda, Ray-Prihoda-Santiago, Ray-Prihoda-Santiago.

NO-HIT GAME: Jimenez, Arkansas, defeated Shreveport, 6-0, August 27.

PITCHERS WITH TWO OR MORE TEAMS

Pitcher, Team	W	L	Pct.	ERA	G	GS	CG	ShO	GF	Sv.	IP	H	TBF	R	ER	HR	SH	SF	HB	BB	IBB	SO	WP	Bk.
Hollins, Stacy, Shre.	1	2	.333	6.46	18	3	0	0	3	1	46.0	54	222	40	33	6	2	0	7	29	2	29	9	0
Hollins, Stacy, E.P.	6	3	.667	5.19	10	9	0	0	0	0	52.0	59	236	35	30	8	2	4	4	24	1	31	6	0
Hook, Chris, Shre.	2	0	1.000	3.86	15	0	0	0	10	2	25.2	19	120	11	11	0	1	1	7	22	3	12	7	0
Hook, Chris, Jack.	2	5	.286	6.49	15	7	0	0	4	1	43.0	43	200	36	31	6	2	3	6	30	0	33	4	0
Huber, Jeff, Mid. *	0	0	.000	7.50	7	0	0	0	2	1	6.0	14	34	6	5	1	0	0	3	1	5	1	0	
Huber, Jeff, E.P. *	1	1	.500	7.79	9	2	0	0	0	0	17.1	31	88	18	15	4	1	1	0	3	0	12	4	0
Kirkreit, Daron, Wich.	1	3	.250	6.63	10	7	0	0	0	0	38.0	52	184	34	28	4	3	2	3	16	1	23	5	0
Kirkreit, Daron, E.P.	1	6	.143	6.23	18	13	0	0	2	0	73.2	103	348	57	51	6	4	3	2	39	0	31	6	1

1998 FIELDING

TEAM

Team	Pct.	G	PO	A	E	TC	DP	PB	Team	Pct.	G	PO	A	E	TC	DP	PB
Tulsa..................	.974	140	3707	1537	138	5382	148	23	San Antonio	.963	140	3688	1634	205	5527	118	19
Arkansas	.973	140	3604	1548	141	5293	161	12	Jackson..............	.961	140	3662	1582	210	5454	120	15
Shreveport	.971	140	3652	1598	157	5407	132	13	El Paso..............	.960	140	3673	1592	218	5483	145	16
Midland	.969	140	3676	1549	165	5390	113	24	TRIPLE PLAYS: Midland, Tulsa.								
Wichita	.964	140	3640	1567	196	5403	129	21									

INDIVIDUAL

FIRST BASEMEN

NOTE: All caps denotes fielding-percentage leader based on 70 games for catchers, 93 for all other non-pitchers and 140 innings for pitchers. *Throws lefthanded.

Player, Team	Pct.	G	PO	A	E	TC	DP
Barker, Kevin, E.P.*	.995	20	198	16	1	215	15
Barkett, Andy, Tul.*	.995	43	370	23	2	395	45
Barnes, Larry, Mid.*	.988	57	534	37	7	578	44
Betten, Randy, Mid.	1.000	3	9	2	0	11	0
Brown, Ray, Mid.	.978	110	986	57	23	1066	94
BRUMBAUGH, Cliff, Tul.	.990	97	850	64	9	923	86
Buxbaum, Danny, Mid.	.981	55	465	51	10	526	35
Cancel, Robinson, E.P.	.857	4	6	0	1	7	1
Charles, Frank, Shre.	.993	41	387	23	3	413	42
Curtis, Matt, Mid.	.800	2	4	0	1	5	0
Davis, Glenn, S.A.*	.993	16	133	15	1	149	16
Demetral, Chris, Tul.	1.000	1	1	0	0	1	0
Diaz, Juan, S.A.	.963	44	377	18	15	410	27
Dishington, Nate, Ark.	.982	64	540	47	11	598	63
Evans, Mike, Wich.	1.000	1	2	0	0	2	0
Gil, Geronimo, S.A.	.976	9	72	11	2	85	5
Goligoski, Jason, Tul.	1.000	1	10	0	0	10	0
Groppuso, Mike, E.P.	.995	52	375	37	2	414	55
Haas, Chris, Ark.	1.000	9	81	2	0	83	9
Hardge, Mike, Ark.	.983	52	396	20	7	423	41
Kleiner, Stacy, Ark.	1.000	2	15	2	0	17	2
Koeyers, Ramsey, Tul.	1.000	1	9	0	0	9	0
Kominek, Toby, Ark.	.980	66	602	31	13	646	52
Lariviere, Jason, Ark.	1.000	1	2	0	0	2	0
Lopez, Pedro, Jack.	1.000	1	1	0	0	1	0
Luuloa, Keith, Mid.	.982	23	198	20	4	222	16
McNally, Sean, Wich.	.986	33	249	25	4	278	11
Mendez, Carlos, Wich.	.976	9	74	6	2	82	9
Minor, Damon, Shre.*	.988	72	641	39	8	688	57
Morris, Greg, Mid.	1.000	3	14	0	0	14	0
Neal, Mike, Jack.	.986	6	70	2	1	73	2
Nilsson, Dave, E.P.	.975	5	32	7	1	40	4

Player, Team	Pct.	G	PO	A	E	TC	DP
Norton, Chris, Mid.	1.000	3	28	1	0	29	2
Owens, Billy, Ark.	.985	27	246	17	4	267	16
Rennhack, Mike, E.P.	.972	5	33	2	1	36	3
Richard, Chris, Ark.*	.986	24	202	8	3	213	28
Sanchez, Victor, Jack.	.979	103	893	83	21	997	76
Schmidt, Dave, Ark.	1.000	2	8	0	0	8	3
Sell, Chip, S.A.	1.000	4	35	4	0	39	3
Simonton, Benji, Shre.	1.000	16	154	5	0	159	11
Trammell, Gary, Jack.	1.000	2	14	2	0	16	1
Truby, Chris, Jack.	1.000	8	43	6	0	49	3
Tucker, Jon, S.A.*	.985	73	676	64	11	751	54
Tyler, Josh, Shre.	1.000	1	1	0	0	1	0
Woods, Ken, Shre.	1.000	15	122	8	0	130	12
Wooten, Shawn, Mid.	.967	3	24	5	1	30	2
TRIPLE PLAYS: Barnes, Brumbaugh.							

SECOND BASEMEN

Player, Team	Pct.	G	PO	A	E	TC	DP
Alguacil, Jose, Shre.	1.000	10	11	14	0	25	2
Anderson, Cliff, S.A.	.966	12	28	29	2	59	4
Betten, Randy, Mid.	.974	11	15	22	1	38	4
Canizaro, Jay, Shre.	.976	80	145	255	10	410	51
CLAPP, Stubby, Ark.	.978	137	332	436	17	785	113
Demetral, Chris, Tul.	1.000	4	8	8	0	16	1
DeShields, Delino, Mid.	1.000	3	6	5	0	11	1
Diaz, Freddie, Mid.	.857	2	2	4	1	7	2
Durrington, Trent, Mid.	.973	74	139	224	10	373	35
Faurot, Adam, E.P.	.922	15	23	24	4	51	3
Febles, Carlos, Wich.	.968	120	248	334	19	601	63
Goligoski, Jason, Tul.	.977	8	21	21	1	43	7
Harkrider, Kip, S.A.	.976	38	76	128	5	209	23
Johnson, Keith, S.A.	.714	2	2	3	2	7	0
Jones, Jack, S.A.	.952	10	17	23	2	42	7
Kennedy, Adam, Ark.	1.000	1	1	0	0	1	0
King, Brett, Shre.	.991	21	39	67	1	107	16
Lopez, Mickey, E.P.	.954	115	281	367	31	679	92

Player, Team	Pct.	G	PO	A	E	TC	DP
Lopez, Roberto, E.P.	.915	23	31	44	7	82	10
Luuloa, Keith, Mid.	.979	58	111	174	6	291	31
Medrano, Tony, Wich.	.971	31	49	84	4	137	20
Metcalfe, Mike, S.A.	.950	56	117	151	14	282	32
Miller, Ryan, Jack.	.961	38	50	72	5	127	14
Morris, Warren, Tul.	.964	88	179	274	17	470	63
Perez, Jhonny, Jack.	.966	67	130	181	11	322	37
Perez, Richard, E.P.	.938	3	5	10	1	16	3
Pimentel, Jose, S.A.	.960	26	47	72	5	124	17
Prieto, Alejandro, Wich.	1.000	2	5	5	0	10	2
Rivera, Micky, Ark.	.895	3	10	7	2	19	2
Robles, Oscar, Jack.	1.000	1	1	2	0	3	0
Sasser, Rob, Tul.	1.000	1	2	4	0	6	0
Saylor, Jamie, Jack.	.957	52	91	174	12	277	32
Sergio, Thomas, Tul.	.912	8	11	20	3	34	5
Spivey, Junior, Tul.	.980	34	62	84	3	149	18
Tyler, Josh, Shre.	1.000	2	6	12	0	18	3
Woods, Ken, Shre.	.980	38	87	106	4	197	19

TRIPLE PLAYS: Luuloa, Morris.

THIRD BASEMEN

Player, Team	Pct.	G	PO	A	E	TC	DP
Anderson, Cliff, S.A.	.926	12	6	19	2	27	1
Beltre, Adrian, S.A.	.910	58	41	130	17	188	5
Betten, Randy, Mid.	.923	11	5	19	2	26	2
Brumbaugh, Cliff, Tul.	.933	23	13	43	4	60	5
Burke, Jamie, Mid.	.870	12	4	16	3	23	0
Buxbaum, Danny, Mid.	.938	10	7	23	2	32	5
Clapp, Stubby, Ark.	1.000	1	0	2	0	2	0
Demetral, Chris, Tul.	1.000	4	4	8	0	12	0
Durrington, Trent, Mid.	.905	7	5	14	2	21	1
Faurot, Adam, E.P.	.915	50	38	92	12	142	11
FELIZ, Pedro, Shre.	.926	97	71	204	22	297	31
Glaus, Troy, Mid.	.925	48	34	101	11	146	12
Goligoski, Jason, Tul.	.867	3	1	12	2	15	1
Groppuso, Mike, E.P.	.929	67	40	131	13	184	16
Haas, Chris, Ark.	.926	112	65	209	22	296	28
Hardge, Mike, Ark.	.975	21	14	25	1	40	4
Johnson, Keith, S.A.	.927	14	6	32	3	41	4
Jones, Jack, S.A.	.909	8	3	7	1	11	2
King, Brett, Shre.	.971	13	9	24	1	34	2
Lopez, Roberto, E.P.	.894	41	16	68	10	94	10
Luuloa, Keith, Mid.	.951	30	21	76	5	102	5
Malave, Jaime, S.A.	.750	10	5	16	7	28	0
McNally, Sean, Wich.	.855	41	26	80	18	124	9
Medrano, Tony, Wich.	.981	34	16	35	1	52	2
Miller, Ryan, Jack.	.877	28	17	40	8	65	8
Morris, Greg, Mid.	.925	26	17	57	6	80	5
Neal, Mike, Jack.	.893	55	22	78	12	112	4
Pellow, Kit, Wich.	.904	90	62	184	26	272	21
Perez, Richard, E.P.	.714	3	0	5	2	7	2
Rivera, Micky, Ark.	.944	39	11	40	3	54	4
Rolls, Damian, S.A.	.947	48	38	124	9	171	7
Sasser, Rob, Tul.	.919	110	66	229	26	321	25
Trammell, Gary, Jack.	1.000	1	3	3	0	6	1
Truby, Chris, Jack.	.932	70	51	155	15	221	15
Tyler, Josh, Shre.	.923	9	9	15	2	26	0
Woods, Ken, Shre.	.898	33	16	63	9	88	6

SHORTSTOPS

Player, Team	Pct.	G	PO	A	E	TC	DP
ABBOTT, Chuck, Mid.	.955	132	195	337	25	557	70
Alguacil, Jose, Shre.	.946	19	18	35	3	56	7
Anderson, Cliff, S.A.	.947	5	4	14	1	19	3
Betten, Randy, Mid.	.932	8	12	29	3	44	4
Demetral, Chris, Tul.	.972	36	48	93	4	145	23
Dransfeldt, Kelly, Tul.	.950	58	81	184	14	279	30
Durrington, Trent, Mid.	1.000	1	0	2	0	2	0
Goligoski, Jason, Tul.	.963	49	101	160	10	271	36
Hardge, Mike, Ark.	1.000	1	0	4	0	4	1
Harkrider, Kip, S.A.	.949	63	86	176	14	276	34
Johnson, Keith, S.A.	.944	25	28	91	7	126	11
Jones, Jack, S.A.	.936	55	65	168	16	249	29
Kennedy, Adam, Ark.	.940	51	90	143	15	248	34
King, Brett, Shre.	.959	45	62	125	8	195	23
Lopez, Mickey, E.P.	.885	7	4	19	3	26	2
Luuloa, Keith, Mid.	.800	2	0	8	2	10	0
Marval, Raul, Shre.	.956	86	114	259	17	390	45
McEwing, Joe, Ark.	1.000	6	10	16	0	26	6
McNally, Sean, Wich.	1.000	2	3	4	0	7	1
Medrano, Tony, Wich.	.972	40	59	114	5	178	20
Miller, Ryan, Jack.	.920	20	18	51	6	75	13

Player, Team	Pct.	G	PO	A	E	TC	DP
Neal, Mike, Jack.	.915	34	48	70	11	129	19
Perez, Jhonny, Jack.	.911	55	84	141	22	247	28
Perez, Richard, E.P.	.800	5	3	5	2	10	1
Perez, Santiago, E.P.	.932	107	186	310	36	532	63
Phair, Kelly, E.P.	.927	28	56	83	11	150	20
Prieto, Alejandro, Wich.	.933	110	174	311	35	520	59
Rivera, Micky, Ark.	.949	14	21	35	3	59	7
Saylor, Jamie, Jack.	.955	51	52	141	9	202	22
Smiga, Jason, Tul.	.750	1	4	2	2	8	1
Woods, Ken, Shre.	.829	8	11	18	6	35	4
Woolf, Jason, Ark.	.946	75	116	235	20	371	50

TRIPLE PLAY: Goligoski.

OUTFIELDERS

Player, Team	Pct.	G	PO	A	E	TC	DP
Alexander, Chad, Jack.	.977	119	197	18	5	220	1
Allen, Luke, S.A.	.918	23	42	3	4	49	0
Beltran, Carlos, Wich.	.960	45	93	2	4	99	1
BERGERON, Peter, S.A.	.992	107	228	17	2	247	5
Berkman, Lance, Jack.*	.980	118	183	9	4	196	4
Betten, Randy, Mid.	.974	39	68	6	2	76	0
Bonds, Bobby, Shre.	.920	29	41	5	4	50	1
Brumbaugh, Cliff, Tul.	1.000	12	18	2	0	20	0
Byington, Jimmie, Wich.	1.000	23	52	1	0	53	0
Cameron, Ken, Ark.*	1.000	19	16	0	0	16	0
Christian, Eddie, Mid.*	.976	53	77	5	2	84	1
Clapp, Stubby, Ark.	1.000	2	1	0	0	1	0
Collins, Sean, Tul.	1.000	8	10	0	0	10	0
Conti, Jason, Tul.	.976	115	183	20	5	208	2
Correa, Miguel, E.P.	.957	131	238	7	11	256	1
Curtis, Matt, Mid.	.987	55	71	5	1	77	1
Dalton, Jed, Mid.	.971	74	126	6	4	136	2
Davis, Glenn, S.A.*	1.000	6	5	2	0	7	0
Denbow, Don, Shre.	.979	34	45	1	1	47	0
Dilone, Juan, Shre.	.963	31	50	2	2	54	0
Drew, J.D., Ark.	.980	18	46	2	1	49	0
Duffy, Jim, Jack.	1.000	9	13	0	0	13	0
Dunn, Todd, E.P.	.939	68	114	9	8	131	0
Durrington, Trent, Mid.	.980	28	47	1	1	49	0
Evans, Mike, Wich.	.978	32	44	1	1	46	0
Faurot, Adam, E.P.	1.000	6	3	1	0	4	0
Garcia, Ossie, Ark.	1.000	79	114	5	0	119	1
Garland, Tim, Shre.	.987	50	73	1	1	75	1
Gil, Geronimo, S.A.	.923	22	36	0	3	39	0
Glendenning, Mike, Shre.	.949	68	90	3	5	98	0
Gonzalez, Raul, Wich.	.957	102	191	11	9	211	3
Green, Scarborough, Ark.	1.000	18	44	1	0	45	0
Hardge, Mike, Ark.	.971	31	62	4	2	68	0
Herrick, Jason, Mid.*	.934	69	126	2	9	137	0
Horne, Tyrone, Ark.	.964	95	155	6	6	167	1
Hutchins, Norm, Mid.*	.961	88	191	4	8	203	0
Iapoce, Anthony, E.P.*	.973	133	279	8	8	295	1
Johnson, Ric, Jack.	.947	21	33	3	2	38	0
Kominek, Toby, E.P.	.975	66	110	7	3	120	1
Lariviere, Jason, Ark.	.977	128	239	11	6	256	1
Leach, Jalal, Shre.*	.976	66	120	4	3	127	1
Long, Ryan, Wich.	.968	56	113	7	4	124	0
Luuloa, Keith, Mid.	1.000	9	12	1	0	13	0
Maddox, Garry, Jack.	1.000	23	38	2	0	40	1
Mateo, Ruben, Tul.	.970	106	215	11	7	233	3
McEwing, Joe, Ark.	.992	50	120	9	1	130	1
McKinley, Dan, Shre.	.966	31	53	3	2	58	0
Miranda, Tony, Wich.	.938	23	30	0	2	32	0
Mitchell, Donavon, Jack.	.959	65	115	2	5	122	0
Mota, Tony, S.A.	.969	57	89	5	3	97	1
Mottola, Chad, Tul.	1.000	4	5	0	0	5	0
Munoz, Juan, Ark.*	1.000	28	47	2	0	49	1
Murphy, Mike, Tul.	1.000	16	28	1	0	29	0
Murray, Calvin, Shre.	.966	88	198	3	7	208	1
Myers, Rod, Wich.*	1.000	36	70	5	0	75	2
Neal, Mike, Jack.	1.000	4	6	0	0	6	0
Nelson, Charles, S.A.*	.980	49	95	5	2	102	0
O'Neill, Doug, Tul.	1.000	6	10	0	0	10	0
Pimentel, Jose, S.A.	.935	46	80	7	6	93	1
Podsednik, Scott, Tul.*	1.000	17	33	1	0	34	0
Prieto, Alejandro, Wich.	1.000	1	1	0	0	1	0
Quinn, Mark, Wich.	.955	89	157	11	8	176	4
Rennhack, Mike, E.P.	.976	27	41	0	1	42	0
Richards, Rowan, Tul.	1.000	4	9	0	0	9	0
Saylor, Jamie, Jack.	.971	22	30	4	1	35	1
Sell, Chip, S.A.	.984	38	60	3	1	64	1
Shirley, Al, Wich.	.940	29	58	5	4	67	1

Player, Team	Pct.	G	PO	A	E	TC	DP
Simonton, Benji, Shre.	1.000	24	35	0	0	35	0
Smith, Scott, Shre.	1.000	3	5	0	0	5	0
Stewart, Andy, Wich.	1.000	1	4	0	0	4	0
Stuckenschneider, Eric, S.A.	.968	71	114	6	4	124	1
Sturdivant, Marcus, Mid.*	.926	16	23	2	2	27	0
Tinsley, Lee, Mid.	.882	11	12	3	2	17	0
Trammell, Gary, Jack.	.944	65	95	6	6	107	0
Tucker, Jon, S.A.*	.971	18	32	2	1	35	0
Van Rossum, Chris, Shre.*	1.000	16	18	0	0	18	0
Vessel, Andrew, Tul.	.990	90	185	8	2	195	2
Zywica, Mike, Tul.	.980	51	92	5	2	99	2

CATCHERS

Player, Team	Pct.	G	PO	A	E	TC	DP	PB
Almond, Greg, Ark.	1.000	5	21	1	0	22	0	0
Amezcua, Adan, Jack.	.985	21	121	12	2	135	2	4
Andreopoulos, Alex, E.P.	.988	89	509	61	7	577	4	5
Cancel, Robinson, E.P.	.979	47	280	48	7	335	4	8
Castro, Ramon, Jack.	.974	48	329	40	10	379	2	5
Charles, Frank, Shre.	.976	57	402	46	11	459	6	5
Curtis, Matt, Mid.	.991	29	204	16	2	222	0	2
Encarnacion, Angelo, Mid.	.977	28	181	32	5	218	3	4
Escamilla, Roman, Wich.	.985	37	173	18	3	194	3	10
Evans, Mike, Wich.	.875	3	6	1	1	8	0	0
Gil, Geronimo, S.A.	.979	28	170	20	4	194	0	2
Goodwin, Joe, Tul.	1.000	10	61	3	0	64	2	0
Graves, Bryan, Mid.	.970	27	146	13	5	164	2	9
King, Cesar, Tul.	.988	89	585	73	8	666	12	18
Kleiner, Stacy, Ark.	.986	87	487	59	8	554	6	5
Koeyers, Ramsey, Tul.	.989	50	344	29	4	377	3	5
Lopez, Pedro, Jack.	.974	50	338	35	10	383	5	5
Makarewicz, Scott, Jack.	.992	33	221	19	2	242	3	1
Malave, Jaime, S.A.	.923	5	11	1	1	13	0	1
Mayes, Craig, Shre.	.991	20	100	10	1	111	1	2
Mendez, Carlos, Wich.	.994	33	164	16	1	181	2	1
Molina, Ben, Mid.	.988	33	233	21	3	257	2	7
Norton, Chris, Mid.	1.000	1	1	0	0	1	0	0
O'Brien, Charlie, Mid.	1.000	5	33	0	0	33	0	0
O'Neal, Troy, E.P.	.984	16	101	20	2	123	2	3
Ortiz, Hector, Wich.	.968	4	24	6	1	31	0	0
Pena, Angel, S.A.	.984	112	781	81	14	876	9	16
Poor, Jeff, Shre.	1.000	2	9	0	0	9	0	0
Ramirez, Peto, Shre.	.982	12	48	7	1	56	1	3
Schmidt, Dave, Ark.	.993	55	274	30	2	306	4	6
Sell, Chip, S.A.	1.000	4	4	0	0	4	0	0
STEWART, Andy, Wich.	.988	78	437	62	6	505	4	10
Thurston, Jerrey, Mid.	.990	28	187	20	2	209	2	2
Torrealba, Yorvit, Shre.	.996	58	397	70	2	469	4	3

PITCHERS

Player, Team	Pct.	G	PO	A	E	TC	DP
Almanza, Armando, Ark.*	1.000	28	0	5	0	5	2
Alvarez, Juan, Mid.*	.938	40	4	11	1	16	0
Babineaux, Darrin, S.A.	.941	39	9	7	1	17	0
Beaumont, Matt, Mid.*	.880	34	6	16	3	25	2
Beck, Greg, E.P.	.947	30	4	14	1	19	1
Benes, Adam, Ark.	1.000	12	1	3	0	4	1
Bermudez, Manny, Shre.	.800	5	0	4	1	5	0
Blais, Mike, Jack.	1.000	21	3	7	0	10	1
Blanco, Alberto, Jack.*	.885	12	6	17	3	26	1
Bland, Nate, S.A.*	.714	26	2	8	4	14	0
Bluma, Jaime, Mid.	1.000	39	6	10	0	16	0
BONANNO, Rob, Mid.	1.000	14	13	17	0	30	1
Brester, Jason, Shre.*	.792	19	4	15	5	24	0
Brewer, Ryan, Wich.	1.000	20	4	5	0	9	1
Brosnan, Jason, Mid.*	.667	16	0	2	1	3	1
Byrdak, Tim, Wich.*	1.000	34	2	12	0	14	1
Calero, Kiko, Wich.	1.000	3	1	1	0	2	0
Chavez, Carlos, E.P.	.826	54	6	13	4	23	1
Cooper, Brian, Mid.	.889	32	11	21	4	36	1
Cornett, Brad, E.P.	1.000	3	1	4	0	5	0
Corps, Edwin, Shre.	.882	46	4	11	2	17	0
Crabtree, Robbie, Shre.	1.000	26	3	9	0	12	0
Crafton, Kevin, Ark.	1.000	46	3	4	0	7	0
Davis, Allen, S.A.*	1.000	6	1	1	0	2	0
Dawsey, Jason, E.P.*	1.000	6	2	7	0	9	2
Deakman, Josh, Mid.	1.000	29	4	6	0	10	0
De Los Santos, Valerio, E.P.*	.917	42	3	8	1	12	1
Deskins, Casey, S.A.*	.880	22	6	16	3	25	1
Detmers, Kris, Ark.*	.920	27	3	20	2	25	3
Diorio, Mike, Jack.	.867	32	4	9	2	15	1
Dollar, Toby, S.A.	.977	23	9	34	1	44	3

Player, Team	Pct.	G	PO	A	E	TC	DP
Duncan, Sean, Jack.*	.846	28	6	5	2	13	1
Elliott, Donnie, Tul.	1.000	20	0	1	0	1	1
Estrada, Horacio, E.P.*	1.000	8	4	11	0	15	0
Etherton, Seth, Mid.	1.000	9	1	7	0	8	1
Flury, Pat, Wich.	1.000	8	1	3	0	4	0
Frontera, Chad, Shre.	1.000	8	5	8	0	13	0
Fultz, Aaron, Shre.*	.933	54	1	13	1	15	4
Garcia, Freddy, S.A.	.975	19	19	20	1	40	3
Garcia, Miguel, S.A.	.941	26	7	9	1	17	1
Garrett, Hal, S.A.	1.000	11	2	5	0	7	2
Glynn, Ryan, Tul.	.955	26	18	24	2	44	3
Gooding, Jason, Wich.*	.938	25	8	22	2	32	2
Grebe, Brett, Mid.	1.000	10	1	4	0	5	0
Greene, Danny, Mid.	1.000	37	1	10	0	11	1
Grilli, Jason, Shre.	.935	21	4	25	2	31	1
Grote, Jason, Shre.	1.000	10	1	7	0	8	0
Grundy, Phil, Wich.	.786	18	3	8	3	14	0
Gutierrez, Jim, Jack.	1.000	8	4	4	0	8	0
Hardwick, Bubba, E.P.*	.786	32	3	8	3	14	0
Heflin, Bronson, Mid.	1.000	2	0	1	0	1	0
Heiserman, Rick, Ark.	1.000	18	0	3	0	3	0
Henderson, Ryan, E.P.	1.000	20	1	4	0	5	0
Hernandez, Xavier, Tul.	1.000	2	1	1	0	2	0
Hill, Jason, Mid.*	1.000	48	4	12	0	16	0
Hill, Tyrone, Mid.*	1.000	3	1	5	0	6	0
Hodges, Kevin, Jack.	.875	29	8	20	4	32	1
Hollins, Stacy, Shre.-E.P.	1.000	28	6	17	0	23	1
Hommel, Brian, E.P.*	1.000	14	0	1	0	1	0
Hook, Chris, Shre.-Jack.	1.000	30	7	7	0	14	0
Huber, Jeff, Mid.-E.P.*	1.000	16	0	5	0	5	0
Huntsman, Scott, E.P.	.929	52	4	9	1	14	1
Hurst, Jonathan, Tul.	1.000	10	0	3	0	3	0
Hutzler, Jeff, Shre.	1.000	2	1	0	0	1	0
Jacobsen, Joe, Mid.	.889	26	3	5	1	9	0
Jarvis, Matt, Ark.*	1.000	56	5	12	0	17	3
Jimenez, Jose, Ark.	.965	26	9	46	2	57	3
Juarbe, Ken, Tul.*	.857	7	0	6	1	7	0
Keith, Jeff, Shre.*	1.000	10	2	2	0	4	0
Kester, Tim, Jack.	1.000	55	4	15	0	19	1
Kirkreit, Daron, Wich.-E.P.	.947	28	5	13	1	19	2
Knight, Brandon, Tul.	.917	14	5	6	1	12	0
Kolb, Dan, Tul.	.971	28	11	23	1	35	2
Lee, Corey, Tul.*	.885	26	10	13	3	26	2
Levrault, Allen, E.P.	.889	11	2	6	1	9	0
Lilly, Ted, S.A.*	.840	17	4	17	4	25	1
Linebrink, Scott, Shre.	.882	21	8	7	2	17	0
Lisio, Joe, Tul.	1.000	9	1	3	0	4	1
Lock, Dan, Jack.*	.750	16	1	2	1	4	0
Logan, Marcus, Ark.	1.000	28	4	15	0	19	0
Lovingier, Kevin, Ark.*	.750	19	0	3	1	4	0
Manning, David, Tul.	1.000	6	1	1	0	2	0
Martin, Jeff, Shre.	.909	31	3	7	1	11	0
Martinez, Jose, Tul.	1.000	7	1	2	0	3	0
Masaoka, Onan, S.A.*	.857	27	2	16	3	21	2
Mayo, Blake, S.A.	1.000	13	3	0	0	3	0
McDougal, Mike, Ark.	1.000	24	1	7	0	8	2
McMullen, Mike, Shre.	.813	52	3	10	3	16	1
McNally, Sean, Wich.	1.000	5	0	1	0	1	0
Mercedes, Jose, E.P.	1.000	1	0	1	0	1	0
Michalak, Chris, Tul.*	1.000	10	2	5	0	7	0
Miller, Eric, Wich.	1.000	18	1	0	0	1	0
Miller, Wade, Jack.	1.000	10	5	6	0	11	0
Minor, Blas, E.P.	1.000	8	0	3	0	3	0
Mitchell, Dean, S.A.	.947	46	6	12	1	19	0
Montoya, Norm, Mid.*	1.000	9	5	14	0	19	2
Moreno, Orber, Wich.	1.000	24	3	3	0	6	0
Mounce, Tony, Jack.*	.903	32	6	22	3	31	1
Mullen, Scott, Wich.*	1.000	12	4	9	0	13	1
Nathan, Joe, Shre.	1.000	4	1	2	0	3	0
Neal, Billy, S.A.	1.000	31	5	6	0	11	0
Norris, Joe, E.P.	.818	40	4	5	2	11	0
Nussbeck, Mark, Ark.	1.000	1	4	0	0	5	0
O'Malley, Paul, Jack.	.953	29	9	32	2	43	0
Oropesa, Eddie, Shre.*	.946	32	11	24	2	37	2
Ortiz, Ramon, Mid.	.923	7	3	9	1	13	0
Osborne, Donovan, Ark.*	1.000	5	1	2	0	3	1
Pasqualicchio, Mike, E.P.*	1.000	10	3	9	0	12	0
Passini, Brian, E.P.*	.909	12	3	7	1	11	1
Patterson, Danny, Tul.	1.000	2	0	1	0	1	0
Pearsall, J.J., S.A.*	1.000	46	7	8	0	15	0
Pedraza, Rod, Tul.	.875	6	2	5	1	8	0
Perisho, Matt, Tul.*	1.000	1	0	1	0	1	0

Player, Team	Pct.	G	PO	A	E	TC	DP
Peterson, Kyle, E.P.	1.000	7	3	8	0	11	0
Phillips, Randy, Shre.	.870	17	6	14	3	23	2
Politte, Cliff, Ark.	.941	10	2	14	1	17	2
Pote, Lou, Mid.	.912	32	15	16	3	34	1
Powell, John, Tul.	1.000	28	4	6	0	10	2
Prihoda, Steve, Wich.*	.971	58	6	27	1	34	0
Prokopec, Luke, S.A.	1.000	5	1	3	0	4	0
Ramos, Edgar, Jack.	.933	17	3	11	1	15	0
Rawitzer, Kevin, Wich.*	.957	14	5	17	1	23	0
Ray, Ken, Wich.	.958	24	4	19	1	24	0
Reed, Steve, Ark.	.824	32	3	11	3	17	0
Reichert, Dan, Wich.	.857	8	1	5	1	7	0
Rennhack, Mike, E.P.	1.000	1	1	0	0	1	0
Ricabal, Dan, S.A.	1.000	54	7	10	0	17	0
Rodriguez, Frankie, E.P.	1.000	4	1	1	0	2	0
Rogers, Kevin, Shre.*	1.000	14	0	1	0	1	0
Root, Derek, Jack.*	.700	7	1	6	3	10	0
Roque, Rafael, E.P.*	.914	16	9	23	3	35	0
Sabel, Erik, Tul.	.923	24	2	10	1	13	0
Sadler, Al, E.P.	1.000	34	2	3	0	5	0
Saier, Matt, Wich.	.875	18	6	8	2	16	0
Santiago, Jose, Wich.	.947	52	6	12	1	19	0
Sikorski, Brian, Jack.	.969	15	11	20	1	32	1
Slusarski, Joe, Jack.	1.000	9	7	3	0	10	0
Smith, Dan, Tul.	.933	26	16	12	2	30	0
Smith, Eric, Jack.	.667	6	1	1	1	3	0
Smith, Lee, Jack.	1.000	2	1	0	0	1	0
Smith, Willie, Wich.	.000	4	0	0	1	1	0
Sollecito, Gabe, Tul.	1.000	5	0	2	0	2	0
Sparks, Steve, Mid.	1.000	7	7	13	0	20	0
Steph, Rod, Wich.	1.000	8	0	1	0	1	0
Stone, Ricky, S.A.	.905	13	4	15	2	21	3

Player, Team	Pct.	G	PO	A	E	TC	DP
Taulbee, Andy, Shre.	.500	3	1	0	1	2	0
Taylor, Scott, Wich.	.950	14	6	13	1	20	4
Toth, Robert, Wich.	1.000	5	0	2	0	2	0
Turner, Matt, Wich.	1.000	1	2	0	0	2	0
Tuttle, Dave, Tul.	1.000	36	4	12	0	16	4
Van Poppel, Todd, Tul.	1.000	1	0	1	0	1	0
Venafro, Mike, Tul.*	.923	46	4	8	1	13	0
Verdugo, Jason, Shre.	1.000	9	0	3	0	3	0
Wallace, Kent, Jack.	.923	29	5	7	1	13	0
Walter, Mike, Jack.	.800	38	2	2	1	5	0
Watkins, Scott, Tul.*	1.000	10	2	1	0	3	0
Watson, Allen, Mid.*	1.000	1	0	1	0	1	0
Weibl, Clint, Ark.	1.000	25	9	17	0	26	2
Welch, Travis, Ark.	1.000	23	6	2	0	8	1
Williams, Jeff, S.A.*	1.000	7	3	5	0	8	0
Windham, Mike, Ark.	.920	40	10	13	2	25	0
Wise, Matt, Mid.	.971	27	16	18	1	35	0
Wunsch, Kelly, E.P.*	.870	17	6	14	3	23	0
Zamora, Pete, S.A.*	.800	12	1	15	4	20	1
Zimmerman, Jeff, Tul.	1.000	41	4	8	0	12	0

PITCHERS WITH TWO OR MORE TEAMS

Player, Team	Pct.	G	PO	A	E	TC	DP
Hollins, Stacy, Shre.	1.000	18	3	7	0	10	1
Hollins, Stacy, E.P.	1.000	10	3	10	0	13	0
Hook, Chris, Shre.	1.000	15	4	2	0	6	0
Hook, Chris, Jack.	1.000	15	3	5	0	8	0
Huber, Jeff, Mid.*	1.000	7	0	3	0	3	0
Huber, Jeff, E.P.*	1.000	9	0	2	0	2	0
Kirkreit, Daron, Wich.	.833	10	1	4	1	6	0
Kirkreit, Daron, E.P.	1.000	18	4	9	0	13	2

The following players did not have any fielding statistics at the positions indicated or appeared only as a designated hitter, pinch-hitter or pinch-runner: Adam, p; Alguacil, p; Appier, p; Bailes, p; Barnes, of; Brantley, p; Byington, p; Cancel, 3b; Cooney, dh; De La Cruz, p; Dishington, p; Evans, p; Faurot, p; Gallaher, p; O. Garcia, p; C. Green, ph; Groppuso, p; D. Hall, p; Y. Hall, p; Herges, p; G. Johnson, p; B. King, of; Kubenka, p; Lewis, dh, ph; McDowell, p; McEwing, p; Medrano, 1b; Moore, p; M. Morris, p; Nix, p; Pena, of; Priess, ph; Sturtze, p; Vallone, dh, ph; Wagner, p; Washburn, p; Woods, of.

LEAGUE CHAMPIONS

Year	Team	Pct.	Year	Team	Pct.	Year	Team	Pct.
1888—	Dallas	.671	1920—	Fort Worth	.703	1946—	Fort Worth	.656
1889—	Houston	.551		Fort Worth	.750		Dallas (2nd)§	.591
1890—	Galveston	.705	1921—	Fort Worth	.691	1947—	Houston‡	.623
1892—	Houston	.741		Fort Worth	.662	1948—	Fort Worth†	.601
	Houston	.613	1922—	Fort Worth	.694	1949—	Fort Worth	.649
1895—	Dallas	.754		Fort Worth	.711		Tulsa (2nd)§	.584
	Fort Worth*	.750	1923—	Fort Worth	.632	1950—	Beaumont	.595
1896—	Fort Worth	.757	1924—	Fort Worth	.689		San Antonio (4th)§	.513
	Houston*	.679		Fort Worth	.763	1951—	Houston‡	.619
	Galveston	.548	1925—	Fort Worth	.711	1952—	Dallas	.571
1897—	San Antonio†	.657		Dallas▲	.653		Shreveport (3rd)§	.522
	Galveston†	.717	1926—	Dallas	.574	1953—	Dallas‡	.571
1898—	League disbanded.		1927—	Wichita Falls	.654	1954—	Shreveport	.559
1899—	Galveston	.632	1928—	Houston*	.679		Houston (2nd)§	.553
	Galveston	.762		Wichita Falls	.731	1955—	Dallas	.581
1900-01—	Did not operate.		1929—	Dallas*	.588		Shreveport (3rd)§	.540
1902—	Corsicana	.866		Wichita Falls	.620	1956—	Houston	.623
	Corsicana	.682	1930—	Wichita Falls	.697	1957—	Dallas	.662
1903—	Paris-Waco	.615		Fort Worth*	.632		Houston (2nd)§	.630
	Dallas*	.648	1931—	Houston♦	.625	1958—	Fort Worth	.582
1904—	Corsicana*	.615		Houston	.734		Cor. Christi (3rd)§	.507
	Fort Worth	.800	1932—	Beaumont*	.640	1959—	Victoria	.589
1905—	Fort Worth	.545		Dallas	.727		Austin (2nd)§	.548
1906—	Fort Worth	.677	1933—	Houston	.623	1960—	Rio Grande Valley	.590
	Cleburne∞	.609		San Antonio (4th)§	.523		Tulsa (3rd)	.528
1907—	Austin	.629	1934—	Galveston‡	.579	1961—	Amarillo	.643
1908—	San Antonio	.664	1935—	Oklahoma City‡	.590		San Antonio (3rd)§	.532
1909—	Houston	.601	1936—	Dallas	.604	1962—	El Paso	.571
1910—	Dallas†	.586		Tulsa (3rd)§	.519		Tulsa (2nd)§	.550
	Houston†	.586	1937—	Oklahoma City	.635	1963—	San Antonio	.564
1911—	Austin	.575		Fort Worth (3rd)§	.535		Tulsa (3rd)§	.529
1912—	Houston	.626	1938—	Beaumont	.635	1964—	San Antonio‡	.607
1913—	Houston	.620	1939—	Houston	.606	1965—	Tulsa	.574
1914—	Houston†	.671		Fort Worth (4th)§	.540		Albuquerque■	.550
	Waco†	.671	1940—	Houston‡	.652	1966—	Arkansas	.579
1915—	Waco	.592	1941—	Houston	.673	1967—	Albuquerque	.557
1916—	Waco	.587		Dallas (4th)§	.519	1968—	Arkansas	.586
1917—	Dallas	.600	1942—	Beaumont	.605		El Paso■	.562
1918—	Dallas	.584		Shreveport (2nd)§	.576	1969—	Amarillo	.593
1919—	Shreveport*	.677	1943-44-45—	Did not operate.			Memphis■	.504
	Fort Worth	.651						

Year	Team	Pct.	Year	Team	Pct.	Year	Team	Pct.
1970—	Albuquerque◆	.615	1980—	Arkansas•	.596	1990—	San Antonio	.582
	Memphis	.507		San Antonio	.544		Shreveport•	.489
1971—	Did not operate as league—clubs		1981—	San Antonio	.571	1991—	Shreveport•	.632
	were members of Dixie Association.			Jackson•	.507		El Paso	.596
1972—	Alexandria	.600	1982—	El Paso	.559	1992—	Shreveport	.566
	El Paso■	.557		Tulsa•	.515		Wichita•	.515
1973—	San Antonio	.590	1983—	Jackson	.507	1993—	El Paso	.563
	Memphis■	.558		Beaumont•	.500		Jackson•	.541
1974—	Victoria■	.581	1984—	Beaumont	.654	1994—	El Paso•	.647
	El Paso	.555		Jackson•	.610		Jackson	.548
1975—	Lafayette▼	.558	1985—	El Paso	.632	1995—	Shreveport•	.652
	Midland▼	.604		Jackson•	.537		Midland	.485
1976—	Amarillo■	.600	1986—	El Paso•	.630	1996—	Jackson•	.547
	Shreveport	.515		Jackson	.533		Wichita	.500
1977—	El Paso	.600	1987—	Wichita•	.515	1997—	San Antonio•	.604
	Arkansas•	.485		Jackson	.515		Shreveport	.551
1978—	El Paso•	.593	1988—	El Paso	.552	1998—	Arkansas	.571
	Jackson	.567		Tulsa•	.522		Tulsa•	.557
1979—	Arkansas•	.571	1989—	Arkansas•	.585			
	Midland	.563		Wichita	.537			

*Won split-season playoff. †Won playoff for title. ‡Finished first and won four-club playoff. §Won four-club playoff. ∞Title to Cleburne by default. ▲Tied with Dallas in second half and won playoff for championship. ◆Tied with Beaumont at end of first half and won title in best-of-five series played as part of second-half schedule. ■League divided into Eastern, Western divisions; won two-team playoff. ▼League divided into Eastern, Western divisions; declared co-champions when playoffs were not completed. •League divided into Eastern and Western divisions and played split-season; won playoffs. NOTE—Championship awarded to winner of four-team play-off, 1933-51; first-place team and playoff winner co-champions, 1952-64.

CALIFORNIA LEAGUE

LEAGUE OFFICE

President
Joe Gagliardi
Address
2380 S. Bascom Ave., Suite 200
Campbell, CA 95008
Phone
408-369-8038

Teams (affiliation)
Bakersfield Blaze (Giants)
High Desert Mavericks (Diamondbacks)
Lake Elsinore Storm (Angels)
Lancaster Jethawks (Mariners)
Modesto A's (A's)
Rancho Cucamonga Quakes (Padres)

San Bernardino Stampede (Dodgers)
San Jose Giants (Giants)
Stockton Ports (Brewers)
Visalia Oaks (A's)

1998 FINAL STANDINGS

FIRST HALF

VALLEY DIVISION

Team	W	L	T	Pct.	GB
San Jose (Giants)	46	24	0	.657	....
Lancaster (Mariners)	40	30	0	.571	6.0
High Desert (Diamondbacks)	38	32	0	.543	8.0
Modesto (Athletics)	35	35	0	.500	11.0
Stockton (Brewers)	34	36	0	.486	12.0

FREEWAY DIVISION

Team	W	L	T	Pct.	GB
Rancho Cucamonga (Padres)	36	34	0	.514	....
Visalia (Athletics)	35	35	0	.500	1.0
Lake Elsinore (Angels)	35	35	0	.500	1.0
San Bernardino (Dodgers)	27	43	0	.386	9.0
Bakersfield (Giants)	24	46	0	.343	12.0

SECOND HALF

VALLEY DIVISION

Team	W	L	T	Pct.	GB
High Desert (Diamondbacks)	44	26	0	.629	....
Modesto (Athletics)	42	28	0	.600	2.0
Lancaster (Mariners)	38	32	0	.543	6.0
San Jose (Giants)	37	33	0	.529	7.0
Stockton (Brewers)	32	38	0	.457	12.0

FREEWAY DIVISION

Team	W	L	T	Pct.	GB
Rancho Cucamonga (Padres)	41	29	0	.586	....
Visalia (Athletics)	32	38	0	.457	9.0
Lake Elsinore (Angels)	31	39	0	.443	10.0
San Bernardino (Dodgers)	28	42	0	.400	13.0
Bakersfield (Giants)	25	45	0	.357	16.0

COMPOSITE

Team	S.J.	H.D.	Lan.	R.C.	Mod.	Vis.	Stoc.	L.E.	S.B.	Bak.	W	L	T	Pct.	GB
San Jose (Giants)	....	10	9	4	11	13	13	7	8	8	83	57	0	.593	....
High Desert (Diamondbacks)	10	....	8	10	4	10	6	11	13	10	82	58	0	.586	1.0
Lancaster (Mariners)	3	12	....	11	9	10	7	10	7	9	78	62	0	.557	5.0
Rancho Cucamonga (Padres)	8	2	9	....	8	4	7	12	13	14	77	63	0	.550	6.0
Modesto (Athletics)	9	8	11	4	....	6	10	10	6	13	77	63	0	.550	6.0
Visalia (Athletics)	7	2	2	8	6	....	11	5	13	13	67	73	0	.479	16.0
Stockton (Brewers)	7	6	5	5	10	9	....	5	7	12	66	74	0	.471	17.0
Lake Elsinore (Angels)	5	9	10	8	2	7	7	....	12	6	66	74	0	.471	17.0
San Bernardino (Dodgers)	4	7	5	7	6	7	5	8	....	6	55	85	0	.393	28.0
Bakersfield (Giants)	4	2	3	6	7	7	8	6	6	....	49	91	0	.350	34.0

Major league affiliations in parentheses.

High Desert played home games in Adelanto, Calif.

PLAYOFFS: Lake Elsinore defeated Visalia two games to none; High Desert defeated Lancaster two games to none; San Jose defeated High Desert three games to two; Rancho Cucamonga defeated Lake Elsinore three games to none; San Jose defeated Rancho Cucamonga three games to one to win league championship.

REGULAR-SEASON ATTENDANCE: Bakersfield, 78,027; High Desert, 151,245; Lake Elsinore, 287,005; Lancaster, 238,173; Modesto, 135,620; Rancho Cucamonga, 338,145; San Bernardino, 223,219; San Jose, 141,180; Stockton, 80,589; Visalia, 60,154. Total—1,733,357. Playoffs (16 games)—33,525. All-Star Game at Lancaster, Calif.—4,714.

MANAGERS: Bakersfield, Frank Reberger; High Desert, Don Wakamatsu; Lake Elsinore, Mario Mendoza; Lancaster, Rick Burleson; Modesto, Juan Navarette; Rancho Cucamonga, Mike Basso; San Bernardino, Mickey Hatcher (through June 24), Joe Vavra (June 25 through June 28) and Tim Wallach (June 29 through end of season); San Jose, Shane Turner; Stockton, Bernie Moncallo; Visalia, Tony Defrancesco. Managerial record of teams with more than one manager: San Bernardino, Hatcher 29-48, Vavra 2-2, Wallach 24-35.

ALL-STAR GAME: 1B—Cirilo Cruz, Lancaster; 2B—Adonis Harrison, Lancaster; 3B—Jarrod Patterson, High Desert; SS—Julius Matos, High Desert; OF—A.J. Johnson, Rancho Cucamonga; Jeff Davanon, Modesto; Juan Dilone, San Jose; C—Giuseppe Chiarmonte, San Jose; DH—Brendan Kingman, Lancaster; SP—Brad Penny, High Desert; SP—Tim Manwiller, Modesto; SP—Luke Prokopec, San Bernardino; RP—Jim Stoops, San Jose; Most Valuable Player—Brad Penny, High Desert; Pitcher of the Year—Brad Penny, High Desert; Rookie of the Year—Giuseppe Chiaramonte, San Jose; Manager of the Year—Don Wakamatsu, High Desert.

1998 BATTING

TEAM

Team	Avg.	G	TPA	AB	R	H	TB	2B	3B	HR	RBI	SH	SF	HP	BB	IBB	SO	SB	CS	GDP	LOB	ShO	Slg.	OBP
Lancaster	.285	140	5635	4882	909	1392	2138	293	57	113	802	27	50	70	606	23	1004	180	84	98	1057	3	.438	.369
High Desert	.276	140	5407	4804	779	1327	2087	260	64	124	706	20	41	51	491	13	1115	147	65	99	963	5	.434	.347
Visalia	.270	140	5473	4746	739	1282	1908	268	38	94	645	50	45	70	562	11	1136	147	80	107	1051	4	.402	.353
Modesto	.268	140	5492	4754	748	1276	1909	271	46	90	664	40	42	58	598	12	1174	180	83	94	1088	4	.402	.354
R. Cucamonga	.266	140	5438	4790	764	1276	1994	257	61	115	675	43	37	62	506	13	1129	88	57	106	992	9	.416	.342
Stockton	.266	140	5212	4697	601	1250	1723	251	24	58	524	47	40	68	360	22	789	103	58	114	946	10	.367	.325
San Jose	.261	140	5320	4710	704	1230	1852	245	31	105	622	35	42	43	490	11	1050	126	78	97	978	5	.393	.334
Lake Elsinore	.259	140	5407	4760	719	1232	1947	288	41	115	663	31	34	51	535	21	1128	107	65	101	993	10	.409	.337
Bakersfield	.250	140	5430	4837	642	1210	1781	238	27	93	559	38	25	65	465	10	1208	105	49	92	1036	15	.368	.323
S. Bernardino	.249	140	5189	4675	516	1166	1615	227	45	44	448	57	30	47	380	16	1034	164	112	71	925	12	.345	.310

TOP QUALIFIERS FOR BATTING CHAMPIONSHIP

Minimum 378 plate appearances. *Lefthanded batter. †Switch-hitter.

Player, Team	Avg.	G	TPA	AB	R	H	TB	2B	3B	HR	RBI	SH	SF	HP	BB	IBB	SO	SB	CS	GDP	Slg.	OBP
Kingman, Brendan, Lan.	.340	112	507	456	91	155	239	30	3	16	78	1	4	6	40	6	55	6	7	20	.524	.397
Patterson, Jarrod, H.D.*	.335	131	564	492	89	165	271	34	9	18	102	0	3	2	66	4	97	9	2	8	.551	.414
Cruz, Cirilo, Lan.	.311	134	618	546	86	170	233	40	1	7	104	1	7	8	56	3	122	2	2	12	.427	.379
Johnson, A.J., R.C.	.308	134	580	539	94	166	281	33	5	24	94	2	5	6	28	2	98	15	10	15	.521	.346
Barajas, Rod, H.D.	.303	113	481	442	67	134	229	26	0	23	81	0	7	7	25	2	81	1	1	13	.518	.345
McKinley, Dan, Bak.*	.301	94	425	379	58	114	156	16	4	6	44	4	2	10	30	2	84	19	6	8	.412	.366
Matos, Julius, H.D.	.301	111	479	439	70	132	179	27	4	4	60	7	8	2	23	0	40	19	13	9	.408	.333
Allen, Luke, S.F.*	.298	105	443	399	51	119	168	25	6	4	46	7	4	3	30	0	93	18	11	4	.421	.349
Regan, Jason, Lan.	.298	124	539	416	105	124	219	26	6	19	82	0	6	11	106	1	123	9	3	7	.526	.447
Russin, Tom, Vis.	.296	101	432	388	70	115	186	27	1	14	74	1	2	7	33	1	62	1	2	17	.479	.360
Saitta, Rich, S.F.	.296	121	509	446	62	132	178	17	7	5	51	4	4	3	52	1	92	23	17	6	.399	.370
Dewey, Jason, L.E.	.294	111	459	391	64	115	196	30	3	15	66	0	2	0	66	0	118	8	8	10	.501	.394
Wooten, Shawn, L.E.	.294	105	440	395	56	116	195	31	0	16	74	0	4	3	38	3	82	0	2	9	.494	.357
Lara, Eddie, Vis.†	.289	122	499	447	63	129	177	18	6	6	62	11	4	8	29	0	65	12	12	16	.396	.340
Bass, Jayson, Lan.*	.288	110	438	392	40	113	214	26	6	21	84	0	2	4	40	2	102	31	12	3	.546	.358
Piatt, Adam, Mod.	.288	133	589	500	91	144	250	40	3	20	107	1	8	0	80	1	99	20	6	15	.500	.381

DEPARTMENTAL LEADERS: G—Macalutas, 138; AB—Cruz, 546; R—Regan, 105; H—Cruz, 170; TB—A. Johnson, 281; 2B—Cruz, Piatt, 40 each; 3B—Adams, McClure, 11 each; HR—Flaherty, A. Johnson, 24 each; RBI—Piatt, 107; SH—Davillalo, 15; SF—Chiaramonte, 12; HP—Macalutas, 18; BB—Regan, 106; IBB—Klimek, 7; SO—Flaherty, 171; SB—Moreta, 46; CS—Moreta, 23; GIDP—Kingman, 20; Slg.—Jarrod Patterson, .551; OBP—Regan, .447.

ALL PLAYERS

*Lefthanded batter. †Switch-hitter.

Player, Team	Avg.	G	TPA	AB	R	H	TB	2B	3B	HR	RBI	SH	SF	HP	BB	IBB	SO	SB	CS	GDP	Slg.	OBP
Adams, John, H.D.	.267	76	330	303	50	81	155	19	11	11	43	0	1	2	24	2	98	8	3	6	.512	.324
Alfano, Jeff, Stoc.	.242	113	433	389	39	94	129	21	1	4	40	0	1	6	37	1	93	7	4	14	.332	.316
Alguacil, Jose, Bak.†	.250	61	254	228	25	57	78	11	2	2	23	7	0	8	11	0	45	3	0	6	.342	.308
Allen, Luke, S.F.*	.298	105	443	399	51	119	168	25	6	4	46	7	4	3	30	0	93	18	11	4	.421	.349
Allison, Brad, H.D.	.265	21	80	68	10	18	28	6	2	0	14	1	0	1	10	0	20	0	0	1	.412	.367
Auterson, Jeff, S.F.	.188	53	171	149	10	28	43	8	2	1	19	5	2	4	11	0	45	6	5	2	.289	.259
Baeza, Art, Bak.	.243	64	282	251	35	61	106	17	2	8	38	1	0	3	27	0	44	0	2	7	.422	.324
Barajas, Rod, H.D.	.303	113	481	442	67	134	229	26	0	23	81	0	7	7	25	2	81	1	1	13	.518	.345
Barnes, Larry, L.E.*	.246	51	206	183	32	45	81	11	2	7	33	0	1	2	22	2	49	2	0	3	.443	.330
Bass, Jayson, Lan.*	.288	110	438	392	40	113	214	26	6	21	84	0	2	4	40	2	102	31	12	3	.546	.358
Bautista, Juan, H.D.	.111	6	20	18	1	2	5	0	0	1	1	0	0	1	1	0	5	0	0	0	.278	.200
Bearden, Doug, Stoc.	.231	115	399	359	43	83	101	15	0	1	26	8	2	2	28	0	80	6	6	1	.281	.289
Bell, Ricky, S.F.	.232	133	511	483	38	112	151	18	3	5	50	3	3	6	16	0	99	6	9	11	.313	.264
Bertrand, Ben, S.J.	.196	13	49	46	3	9	12	3	0	0	3	0	0	0	3	0	13	0	0	1	.261	.245
Blanco, Henry, S.F.	.316	7	23	19	5	6	13	1	0	2	3	0	0	0	4	0	6	1	0	2	.684	.435
Bramlett, Jeff, S.F.	.196	67	183	148	22	29	44	8	2	1	15	0	1	2	27	0	62	5	2	2	.297	.326
Briones, Chris, R.C.	.198	33	93	91	6	18	32	5	0	3	12	0	1	1	0	0	26	0	1	3	.352	.215
Brown, Eric, Bak.	.214	5	14	14	1	3	3	0	0	0	1	0	0	0	0	0	7	0	1	0	.214	.214
Burrows, Mike, Lan.*	.162	27	86	74	7	12	13	1	0	0	5	0	1	0	11	0	22	4	4	1	.176	.267
Byas, Michael, S.J.†	.251	135	609	521	87	131	148	10	2	1	36	2	5	0	81	1	98	30	22	8	.284	.349
Byrnes, Eric, Vis.	.426	29	129	108	26	46	71	9	2	4	21	0	2	1	18	0	15	11	1	2	.657	.504
Calloway, Ron, H.D.*	.282	44	174	156	30	44	65	8	2	3	27	2	2	2	12	0	38	2	4	3	.417	.337
Camilo, Juan, Vis.*	.223	85	260	220	29	49	70	9	0	4	27	2	0	3	35	3	75	5	4	1	.318	.337
Campusano, Carlos, S.J.	.184	34	108	98	11	18	23	1	2	0	7	1	1	3	5	0	29	0	0	3	.235	.243
Cancel, Robinson, Stoc.	.188	11	36	32	3	6	7	1	0	0	2	0	0	0	4	0	8	2	1	1	.219	.278
Carmona, Cesarin, R.C.	.261	105	395	368	48	96	132	12	9	2	45	6	1	3	17	1	99	21	8	8	.359	.298
Casper, Brett, Bak.	.194	74	267	237	27	46	68	10	3	2	18	0	7	4	23	0	75	5	4	8	.287	.285
Castro, Jose, Mod.†	.218	57	229	197	23	43	67	11	5	1	18	0	1	3	28	1	66	10	3	2	.340	.323
Castro, Nelson, L.E.	.234	131	519	470	73	110	152	16	7	4	41	0	3	6	40	1	101	36	12	5	.323	.301
Cesar, Dionys, Vis.†	.281	130	567	501	87	141	212	34	8	7	54	6	3	1	56	2	98	31	12	6	.423	.333
Chiaramonte, Giuseppe, S.J. .	.273	129	565	502	87	137	242	33	3	22	87	0	12	4	47	4	139	5	2	7	.482	.333
Clark, Kevin, H.D.	.265	127	545	498	72	132	226	24	5	20	98	0	5	6	36	0	121	1	0	16	.454	.319
Clifton, Rodney, Mod.	.270	118	496	433	71	117	186	30	6	9	67	2	6	3	52	0	106	11	5	8	.430	.348
Colangelo, Mike, L.E.	.379	36	165	145	33	55	87	11	3	5	21	0	1	6	13	0	24	2	6	2	.600	.448
Colon, Jose, Stoc.	.263	50	178	156	20	41	63	8	1	4	21	3	1	2	16	0	34	2	3	4	.404	.337
Connors, Brett, Lan.	.287	27	107	101	17	29	60	11	1	6	26	0	1	2	3	0	16	0	0	1	.594	.318
Cosme, Caonabo, Mod.	.275	124	456	414	48	114	150	24	3	2	41	10	3	2	27	0	137	16	7	0	.362	.321
Cromer, Tripp, S.F.	.400	4	15	15	3	6	13	1	0	2	6	0	0	0	0	0	2	0	0	0	.867	.400
Crosby, Bubba, S.F.*	.216	56	223	199	25	43	56	9	2	0	14	4	3	0	17	0	38	3	5	3	.281	.274
Cruz, Cirilo, Lan.	.311	134	618	546	86	170	233	40	1	7	104	1	7	8	56	3	122	2	2	12	.427	.379
Cuntz, Casey, H.D.	.290	47	200	176	34	51	80	10	2	5	25	0	2	2	20	0	45	6	2	5	.455	.365
Darula, Bobby, Stoc.*	.289	18	55	45	10	13	22	4	1	1	8	1	0	1	8	1	6	2	0	1	.489	.407
Davalillo, David, L.E.	.264	125	551	493	66	130	165	26	3	1	49	15	1	2	39	1	71	4	2	14	.335	.320
DaVanon, Jeff, Mod.†	.336	84	367	301	66	101	141	17	4	5	60	0	1	1	59	1	69	33	10	4	.468	.439
Davis, Josh, Mod.	.250	51	147	124	13	31	37	3	0	1	10	4	1	2	16	0	34	4	0	2	.298	.343
Davis, Monty, Mod.	.304	78	311	280	48	85	131	16	3	8	44	3	2	3	23	0	45	11	5	10	.468	.360
Dean, Aaron, S.F.*	.167	40	110	102	6	17	26	6	0	1	6	0	1	1	7	0	31	2	1	1	.255	.218
Dean, Chris, Lan.†	.256	46	187	168	33	43	74	15	2	4	26	0	2	3	14	0	28	14	4	4	.440	.321
Deboer, Rob, Vis.	.279	125	527	409	83	114	186	25	1	15	66	1	3	17	97	3	157	6	5	5	.455	.433
Delgado, Reymundo, Bak.*..	.296	21	81	71	7	21	27	6	0	0	5	1	1	2	8	0	8	0	1	0	.380	.363
Denbow, Don, Bak.	.307	29	125	101	18	31	45	4	2	2	13	0	2	2	22	1	35	0	3	0	.446	.440
Dewey, Jason, L.E.	.294	111	459	391	64	115	196	30	3	15	66	0	2	0	66	0	118	8	8	10	.501	.394
Diaz, Freddie, L.E.†	.304	75	300	273	36	83	121	23	0	5	29	0	2	0	25	4	59	0	1	6	.443	.360

CLASS A California League

Player, Team	Avg.	G	TPA	AB	R	H	TB	2B	3B	HR	RBI	SH	SF	HP	BB	IBB	SO	SB	CS	GDP	Slg.	OBP
Dilone, Juan, S.J.†	.320	85	355	316	63	101	183	24	2	18	47	0	4	4	31	2	103	19	9	3	.579	.383
Dunn, Nathan, R.C.	.222	41	152	135	13	30	50	7	2	3	14	1	1	0	15	0	50	3	2	1	.370	.298
Dunn, Todd, Stoc.	.154	3	13	13	2	2	3	1	0	0	0	0	0	0	0	0	4	0	0	1	.231	.154
Elliott, David, Stoc.	.281	96	358	317	52	89	141	22	3	8	44	2	5	4	30	3	56	12	8	10	.445	.346
Espino, Fernando, Lan.	.317	17	52	41	5	13	20	3	2	0	10	3	1	2	5	0	10	1	1	2	.488	.408
Faircloth, Chad, Bak.-S.J.*	.248	102	372	351	44	87	120	16	4	3	32	1	1	2	17	0	90	13	5	5	.342	.286
Farris, Ed, Vis.*	.120	9	26	25	2	3	3	0	0	0	1	0	0	0	1	0	7	0	0	0	.120	.154
Filchner, Duane, Vis.*	.298	64	253	218	34	65	93	18	2	2	31	1	4	0	30	0	29	1	1	5	.427	.377
Flaherty, Tim, Bak.	.234	124	531	478	72	112	211	27	0	24	90	0	5	7	41	1	171	0	0	6	.441	.301
Flores, Javier, Vis.	.252	49	187	163	19	41	56	7	1	2	17	3	1	8	12	0	32	0	0	4	.344	.332
French, Anton, Lan.†	.268	106	426	380	77	102	144	11	8	5	42	5	6	2	33	3	72	41	8	0	.379	.325
Fuentes, Joel, S.J.-Bak.†	.288	40	161	146	19	42	56	5	0	3	19	0	0	2	13	0	40	0	3	0	.384	.354
Gallo, Ismael, S.F.*	.298	68	260	235	23	70	84	10	2	0	21	1	2	5	17	0	23	7	3	3	.357	.355
Gann, Jamie, H.D.	.221	59	231	217	25	48	80	8	3	6	25	0	1	5	8	0	59	9	4	4	.369	.264
Garcia, Juan, H.D.	.167	8	37	30	5	5	5	0	0	0	0	0	0	0	7	0	11	4	1	1	.167	.324
Geronimo, Cesar, L.E.	.203	85	288	266	32	54	71	9	1	2	24	2	1	4	15	0	56	6	2	9	.267	.255
Gillespie, Eric, L.E.*	.316	30	113	98	13	31	52	12	0	3	11	0	0	1	14	1	21	2	1	1	.531	.407
Glendenning, Mike, S.J.	.250	48	200	176	26	44	83	9	0	10	33	0	0	0	24	0	66	1	1	5	.472	.340
Gonzalez, Wikleman, R.C.	.288	75	324	292	51	84	142	24	2	10	59	0	4	2	26	1	54	0	0	6	.486	.346
Goudie, Jaime, S.F.	.183	49	194	175	16	32	43	5	3	0	4	2	1	5	11	1	36	4	2	6	.246	.250
Graves, Bryan, L.E.	.200	8	21	20	1	4	5	1	0	0	1	0	0	0	1	0	7	0	0	0	.250	.238
Green, Chad, Stoc.†	.344	40	166	151	30	52	69	13	2	0	17	1	1	1	12	3	22	22	5	2	.457	.394
Greene, Clay, Bak.	.217	52	205	175	26	38	41	3	0	0	9	1	0	1	28	0	51	13	8	1	.234	.328
Greene, Todd, L.E.	.227	12	49	44	9	10	15	2	0	1	6	0	1	0	4	0	7	1	0	1	.341	.286
Guerrero, Sergio, Stoc.	.275	40	139	120	10	33	40	4	0	1	15	3	2	2	12	0	5	1	2	3	.333	.346
Guevara, Giomar, Lan.	.246	19	76	61	15	15	19	4	0	0	3	0	0	1	14	0	20	1	1	1	.311	.395
Guiel, Jeff, L.E.*	.270	101	409	315	64	85	171	24	7	16	60	0	3	8	83	5	87	19	9	3	.543	.430
Gulseth, Mark, S.J.*	.283	119	529	467	72	132	201	38	2	9	75	1	3	6	50	2	67	2	2	11	.430	.357
Hagins, Steve, L.E.	.279	97	403	359	64	100	183	26	3	17	68	1	4	12	27	2	98	5	5	10	.510	.346
Ham, Kevin, L.E.	.215	105	404	353	43	76	115	15	6	4	57	6	5	2	38	0	101	3	4	6	.326	.291
Hardwick, Bubba, Stoc.*	.000	23	1	1	0	0	0	0	0	0	0	0	0	0	0	0	1	0	0	0	.000	.000
Harrison, Adonis, Lan.*	.337	69	313	258	63	87	122	21	4	2	35	1	2	2	49	0	48	24	14	4	.473	.444
Haynes, Larry, Lan.	.111	5	9	9	1	1	2	1	0	0	2	0	0	0	0	0	1	0	0	0	.222	.111
Haynes, Nathan, Mod.*	.252	125	574	507	89	128	158	13	7	1	41	6	2	4	54	2	139	42	18	10	.312	.328
Hudson, Bert, H.D.	.147	35	128	116	10	17	24	5	1	0	3	1	0	1	10	0	31	4	0	2	.207	.220
Illig, Brett, S.F.	.236	41	141	123	13	29	45	8	1	2	14	0	1	1	16	0	42	0	1	2	.366	.326
Itzoe, Josh, R.C.	.228	52	186	149	22	34	41	4	0	1	17	1	0	1	35	0	41	2	2	1	.275	.378
Jenkins, Dee, Sto.-Vis.*	.265	115	495	434	61	115	183	24	4	12	49	6	6	7	42	0	115	18	9	9	.422	.335
Johnson, A.J., R.C.	.308	134	580	539	94	166	281	33	5	24	94	2	5	6	28	2	98	15	10	15	.521	.346
Johnson, Patrick, L.E.	.000	4	7	6	0	0	0	0	0	0	0	0	0	0	1	0	2	0	0	0	.000	.143
Jones, Tim, Mod.*	.207	66	240	184	35	38	64	9	1	5	23	3	2	3	48	2	88	11	8	2	.348	.376
Joseph, Terry, R.C.	.214	13	60	56	6	12	15	1	1	0	5	1	1	1	1	0	16	1	3	0	.268	.237
Kane, Ryan, L.E.	.206	48	180	160	21	33	58	11	1	4	25	0	2	1	17	0	39	0	2	8	.363	.283
Karros, Eric, S.F.	.267	4	15	15	3	4	5	1	0	0	1	0	0	0	0	0	2	0	0	1	.333	.267
Kennedy, Gus, R.C.	.263	124	519	430	89	113	208	25	8	18	75	3	4	3	79	1	130	15	8	12	.484	.378
Kent, Robbie, R.C.	.269	116	510	457	65	123	172	22	3	7	59	8	5	7	33	0	81	2	1	15	.376	.326
Kingman, Brendan, Lan.	.340	112	507	456	91	155	239	30	3	16	78	1	4	6	40	6	55	6	7	20	.524	.397
Klimek, Josh, Stoc.*	.284	124	487	440	61	125	191	27	6	9	56	1	6	4	36	1	60	4	2	6	.434	.340
Koerner, Mike, Vis.*	.231	113	399	360	50	83	148	20	3	13	62	2	4	3	30	0	104	6	9	4	.411	.292
Lara, Eddie, Vis.†	.289	122	499	447	63	129	177	18	6	6	62	11	4	8	29	0	65	12	12	16	.396	.340
Leach, Nick, S.F.*	.235	131	521	469	49	110	162	30	2	6	48	2	1	5	44	4	96	6	11	6	.345	.306
Leyva, Julian, Mod.*	.000	29	1	1	0	0	0	0	0	0	0	0	0	0	0	0	0	0	0	0	.000	.000
Lindsey, Shawn, Bak.*	.333	10	32	27	6	9	11	2	0	0	2	0	0	0	5	0	6	1	2	0	.407	.438
Lopez, Jose, H.D.	.273	12	45	44	3	12	15	3	0	0	5	0	0	1	0	0	8	0	0	0	.341	.289
Loyd, Brian, R.C.	.305	87	374	318	55	97	130	19	1	4	35	2	2	10	42	1	45	1	4	8	.409	.401
Luderer, Brian, Mod.	.133	19	51	45	3	6	12	2	2	0	3	2	0	0	4	0	6	0	0	0	.267	.204
Macalutas, Jon, Stoc.	.285	138	592	527	72	150	199	31	0	6	59	2	5	18	40	1	52	6	8	16	.378	.353
Maddox, Garry, H.D.*	.625	2	10	8	3	5	10	2	0	1	4	0	1	0	1	1	1	0	0	2	1.250	.600
Magruder, Christopher, Bak.†	.304	22	105	92	21	28	38	7	0	1	4	0	0	0	13	1	16	3	0	2	.413	.390
Martin, Jared, H.D.†	.244	50	195	168	30	41	67	7	5	3	21	6	1	1	19	0	37	3	3	4	.399	.323
Martinez, Hipolito, Mod.	.226	111	387	340	51	77	131	21	3	9	52	1	1	5	40	0	112	11	10	5	.385	.316
Martinez, Tony, H.D.	.133	9	36	30	2	4	5	1	0	0	0	0	0	0	6	0	11	0	1	1	.167	.278
Mathis, Jared, Stoc.	.289	69	222	204	24	59	65	6	0	0	17	8	3	4	3	0	17	8	0	3	.319	.308
Matos, Julius, H.D.	.301	114	479	439	70	132	179	27	4	4	60	7	8	2	23	0	40	19	13	9	.408	.333
Mayes, Craig, S.J.*	.364	3	11	11	1	4	8	1	0	1	4	0	0	0	0	0	1	0	0	1	.727	.364
McAffee, Josh, H.D.	.222	4	13	9	3	2	3	1	0	0	2	0	0	2	2	0	5	0	0	0	.333	.462
McClure, Brian, R.C.*	.264	129	574	492	89	130	204	25	11	9	57	5	4	7	66	2	98	4	3	8	.415	.357
McCrotty, Will, S.F.	.221	103	368	344	20	76	103	18	0	3	29	6	2	3	11	0	69	1	2	7	.299	.250
McKay, Cody, Mod.*	.284	107	465	402	59	114	159	25	1	6	58	3	3	17	40	1	62	2	4	12	.396	.370
McKinley, Dan, S.F.	.301	94	425	379	58	114	156	16	4	6	44	4	2	10	30	2	84	19	6	8	.412	.366
Melendez, Angel, Bak.-S.J.	.266	66	233	214	26	57	87	12	0	6	32	1	1	1	15	0	45	5	1	5	.407	.316
Mendoza, Carlos, S.J.†	.214	110	398	365	36	78	91	7	3	0	20	12	0	1	19	0	64	11	8	10	.249	.255
Mensik, Todd, Mod.*	.274	111	447	379	56	104	176	26	2	14	59	2	1	2	63	2	103	1	4	2	.464	.380
Miller, Kevin, Mod.	.230	39	142	126	20	29	39	3	2	1	13	1	2	1	12	0	35	3	0	3	.310	.298
Minor, Damon, S.J.*	.284	48	207	176	26	50	83	10	1	7	36	0	1	2	28	0	40	0	1	1	.472	.386
Monzon, Jose, L.E.	.143	2	7	7	1	1	1	0	0	0	1	0	0	0	0	0	2	0	0	0	.143	.143
Moore, Mike, Lan.	.206	19	71	63	12	13	27	3	1	3	11	0	2	1	5	0	27	0	1	0	.429	.268
Moreta, Ramon, S.F.	.257	134	593	536	67	138	174	19	7	1	24	11	0	2	44	1	109	46	23	8	.325	.316
Morillo, Cesar, Bak.†	.184	14	43	38	3	7	7	0	0	0	6	1	1	0	3	0	10	0	0	1	.184	.238
Morimoto, Ken, S.F.†	.262	44	140	130	21	34	42	2	3	0	5	5	0	0	5	0	35	11	2	2	.323	.289
Morris, Greg, L.E.	.264	66	269	231	35	61	92	18	2	3	41	3	0	1	34	0	39	6	4	5	.398	.361
Mota, Pedro, S.J.-Bak.*	.204	30	115	108	10	22	28	4	1	0	6	1	0	0	6	0	31	4	2	0	.259	.246

Player, Team	Avg.	G	TPA	AB	R	H	TB	2B	3B	HR	RBI	SH	SF	HP	BB	IBB	SO	SB	CS	GDP	Slg.	OBP
Murphy, Nate, L.E.*	.167	40	130	120	15	20	37	2	0	5	10	1	0	0	9	1	46	5	2	2	.308	.225
Myers, Greg, R.C.*	.000	3	11	9	1	0	0	0	0	0	0	0	0	0	2	0	1	0	0	1	.000	.182
Neubart, Adam, H.D.	.326	39	159	141	24	46	67	7	4	2	21	2	2	5	9	0	35	4	2	3	.475	.382
Noriega, Ray, Vis.	.000	36	1	1	0	0	0	0	0	0	0	0	0	0	0	0	1	0	0	0	.000	.000
Otero, William, Bak.	.294	69	292	245	33	72	95	14	0	3	36	7	3	2	35	1	50	8	0	4	.388	.382
Paciorek, Pete, R.C.*	.277	137	561	481	82	133	224	28	6	17	86	6	6	4	63	3	135	8	7	4	.466	.361
Patterson, Jarrod, H.D.*	.335	131	564	492	89	165	271	34	9	18	102	0	3	2	66	4	97	9	2	8	.551	.414
Paulino, Jose, Mod.	.000	40	0	0	1	0	0	0	0	0	0	0	0	0	0	0	0	0	0	0	.000	.000
Pecci, Jay, Mod.†	.315	21	80	73	9	23	30	2	1	1	6	2	0	1	4	0	11	2	1	1	.411	.359
Pernalete, Marco, Bak.†	.232	73	207	190	19	44	50	6	0	0	12	4	0	2	11	0	52	5	1	1	.263	.281
Pernell, Brandon, R.C.	.200	44	140	125	18	25	47	8	4	2	7	2	0	2	11	0	39	1	2	0	.376	.275
Petrosian, Ara, Vis.	.000	19	1	1	0	0	0	0	0	0	0	0	0	0	0	0	1	0	0	0	.000	.000
Phair, Kelly, Stoc.	.265	70	269	238	42	63	90	18	0	3	27	2	1	3	25	0	47	4	2	9	.378	.341
Phoenix, Wynter, S.F.*	.248	110	361	318	38	79	122	16	3	7	47	3	2	3	35	2	67	20	11	2	.384	.327
Piatt, Adam, Mod.	.288	133	589	500	91	144	250	40	3	20	107	1	8	0	80	1	99	20	6	15	.500	.381
Poor, Jeff, Bak.	.208	26	87	77	6	16	24	5	0	1	4	0	0	0	10	0	15	0	0	5	.312	.299
Priess, Matthew, Bak.	.287	52	214	188	23	54	77	11	0	4	19	1	2	4	19	0	30	0	0	11	.410	.362
Prospero, Ted, Bak.	.241	65	213	199	27	48	72	7	1	5	23	2	0	1	11	0	48	7	3	4	.362	.284
Ramirez, Joel, Lan.	.255	53	212	184	34	47	68	9	0	4	31	2	5	5	16	0	23	8	2	5	.370	.324
Ramirez, Peto, Bak.	.202	28	96	89	5	18	36	6	0	4	15	1	0	0	6	0	28	1	0	1	.404	.253
Reeder, Cory, Stoc.	.224	44	128	116	12	26	43	5	0	4	10	0	1	0	11	0	41	0	0	3	.371	.289
Regan, James, Vis.	.298	124	539	416	105	124	219	26	6	19	82	0	6	11	106	1	123	9	3	7	.526	.447
Rexrode, Jackie, H.D.*	.341	53	257	208	51	71	87	5	4	1	23	0	3	0	46	0	42	19	1	2	.418	.455
Reynoso, Ben, R.C.	.213	63	166	150	19	32	46	4	2	2	14	5	0	1	10	0	37	2	0	5	.307	.267
Robinson, Adam, Vis.	.233	82	348	296	54	69	88	13	3	0	26	3	3	3	43	0	89	14	4	4	.297	.333
Rodriguez, Guillermo, S.J.	.000	1	1	1	0	0	0	0	0	0	0	0	0	0	0	0	0	0	0	0	.000	.000
Rodriguez, Juan, L.E.†	.216	62	224	194	23	42	60	7	1	3	20	2	2	2	24	0	58	4	3	1	.309	.306
Rodriguez, Miguel, Stoc.	.255	99	312	290	36	74	102	11	1	5	40	0	0	0	22	2	61	9	5	4	.352	.308
Rodriguez, Miguel, H.D.	.255	15	58	55	11	14	25	2	0	3	6	0	0	0	3	0	21	2	1	0	.455	.293
Romano, Scott, Mod.	.220	36	145	127	18	28	43	8	2	1	16	0	1	4	13	0	24	0	1	5	.339	.310
Rosario, Omar, Vis.*	.222	82	256	212	33	47	60	8	1	1	24	5	2	4	33	0	68	18	4	2	.283	.335
Russin, Tom, Vis.	.296	101	432	388	70	115	186	27	1	14	74	1	2	7	33	1	62	1	2	17	.479	.360
Sachse, Matt, Lan.*	.267	86	332	285	51	76	124	16	4	8	45	2	4	0	41	1	77	4	4	6	.435	.355
Saitta, Rich, S.F.	.296	121	509	446	62	132	178	17	7	5	51	4	4	3	52	1	92	23	17	6	.399	.370
Sanchez, Marcos, R.C.†	.306	56	157	144	30	44	76	10	2	6	24	1	0	2	10	1	47	1	0	8	.528	.359
Sandoval, Jhensy, H.D.	.276	107	421	398	49	110	149	20	2	5	53	1	3	4	15	0	129	10	10	7	.374	.307
Santiesteban, Francisco, Lan.	.240	46	173	146	22	35	56	5	2	4	21	3	0	3	21	0	25	4	3	2	.384	.347
Schaub, Greg, Stoc.	.267	134	496	479	45	128	166	24	1	4	52	5	6	3	3	0	75	9	5	19	.347	.273
Seal, Scott, R.C.*	.246	121	488	427	52	105	150	23	5	4	62	0	2	11	48	1	113	8	5	9	.351	.336
Simonton, Benji, S.J.	.320	89	359	300	59	96	180	28	4	16	69	0	2	4	53	0	100	4	2	4	.600	.426
Skeels, David, Vis.	.225	78	252	222	19	50	69	14	1	1	35	8	1	3	18	0	42	0	1	7	.311	.291
Slemmer, Dave, Vis.	.285	67	291	260	39	74	119	16	1	9	36	0	3	0	28	1	53	3	2	11	.458	.351
Smith, Scott, Bak.	.247	49	199	178	27	44	69	11	1	4	18	0	0	3	18	0	52	2	1	2	.388	.327
Snow, Casey, S.F.†	.281	99	379	335	44	94	134	24	2	4	42	3	3	4	34	6	75	5	6	2	.400	.351
Soriano, Fred, Bak.	.244	72	271	242	38	59	84	9	2	4	23	2	0	5	22	1	71	9	4	3	.347	.320
Soriano, Jose, Vis.	.300	86	333	290	55	87	125	13	5	5	28	2	3	3	35	1	49	26	17	2	.431	.378
Sosa, Nicolas, Vis.	.277	102	409	357	39	99	129	21	0	3	44	1	5	5	41	0	122	1	0	13	.361	.355
Spivey, Junior, H.D.	.281	79	353	285	64	80	119	14	5	5	35	0	1	3	64	0	61	34	12	4	.418	.416
Stewart, Paxton, L.E.*	.237	64	196	177	26	42	57	10	1	1	13	1	2	1	15	1	50	3	1	4	.322	.297
Sturdivant, Marcus, Lan.*	.262	29	119	107	19	28	42	8	3	0	9	1	1	2	8	0	13	8	3	1	.393	.322
Sweeney, Kevin, H.D.*	.267	98	399	333	59	89	147	25	3	9	38	0	4	0	60	5	73	6	3	9	.441	.385
Sykes, Jamie, H.D.	.168	36	145	125	13	21	39	5	2	3	16	0	1	0	19	0	33	5	2	1	.312	.276
Thompson, Karl, Lan.	.263	90	355	315	53	83	126	17	4	6	47	1	3	11	25	0	75	3	3	8	.400	.336
Thrower, Jake, R.C.†	.268	37	149	127	24	34	44	7	0	1	10	0	2	1	19	0	19	4	1	2	.346	.362
Tinoco, Luis, Lan.	.284	108	460	412	61	117	167	20	6	6	69	3	2	5	38	2	79	5	1	15	.405	.350
Tommasini, Kevin, Bak.-S.J.	.210	39	134	124	13	26	45	5	1	4	12	0	0	1	9	0	30	0	2	3	.363	.269
Torrealba, Yorvit, S.J.	.286	21	74	70	10	20	22	2	0	0	10	2	1	0	1	0	6	2	2	2	.314	.292
Tyler, Josh, S.J.-Bak.	.258	113	448	414	51	107	158	24	3	7	64	6	4	3	21	0	61	19	10	10	.382	.296
Valenti, Jon, Bak.	.245	113	436	371	52	91	134	23	1	6	35	2	5	1	57	2	65	2	2	10	.361	.343
Vallone, Gar, L.E.†	.143	4	8	7	0	1	1	0	0	0	1	0	1	0	0	0	2	0	0	0	.143	.125
Van Rossum, Chris, S.J.*	.248	65	237	214	33	53	74	9	3	2	15	1	1	4	17	0	55	10	2	6	.346	.314
Vazquez, Ramon, Lan.*	.276	121	557	468	77	129	169	26	4	2	72	4	1	2	81	5	66	15	11	6	.361	.384
Velarde, Randy, L.E.	.550	5	23	20	6	11	18	2	1	1	7	0	0	1	2	0	1	1	0	1	.900	.609
Wallace, Flint, Mod.	1.000	3	1	1	1	1	1	0	0	0	0	0	0	0	0	0	0	0	0	0	1.000	1.000
Walther, Chris, Stoc.	.279	115	456	419	52	117	154	20	4	3	50	6	2	8	21	2	41	2	2	7	.368	.324
Washam, Jason, Stoc.	.213	86	281	235	24	50	71	12	3	1	28	3	3	7	33	0	38	1	2	7	.302	.324
Webb, Kevin, L.E.	.212	14	37	33	7	7	14	1	0	2	5	0	0	4	0	0	9	0	0	2	.424	.297
Wells, Zach, Vis.	.210	49	163	143	9	30	45	6	3	1	14	0	3	0	17	0	52	0	3	2	.315	.288
Wilson, Keith, H.D.	.067	17	50	45	4	3	7	1	0	1	3	0	0	0	5	0	13	0	0	1	.156	.160
Wilson, Steve, S.F.	.229	15	36	35	0	8	9	1	0	0	3	1	0	0	0	0	12	0	0	1	.257	.229
Wolff, Mike, Mod.*	.291	102	367	320	46	93	134	21	1	6	46	0	3	7	35	2	38	3	1	7	.419	.370
Wooten, Shawn, L.E.	.294	105	440	395	56	116	195	31	0	16	74	0	4	3	38	3	82	0	2	9	.494	.357
Young, Travis, Bak.	.244	133	603	517	79	126	163	21	2	4	63	11	6	8	61	2	101	27	12	14	.315	.329
Zuniga, Tony, S.J.	.244	113	444	397	52	97	149	20	4	8	59	0	3	5	39	0	64	1	2	7	.375	.318

GRAND SLAMS: Adams, Koerner, Prospero, 2 each; Barnes, Calloway, Camilo, Clifton, Cruz, Flaherty, J. Fuentes, W. Gonzalez, Guiel, Itzoe, T. Jones, Kennedy, Kingman, Lara, H. Martinez, Melendez, Jarrod Patterson, Piatt, H. Ramirez, Regan, Fred Soriano, Jose Soriano, Wolff, 1 each.

AWARDED FIRST BASE ON CATCHER'S INTERFERENCE: Bramlett 5 (Dewey, Flaherty, Thompson, Skeels 2); Gulseth 2 (Barajas, Flores); Sweeney 2 (McCrotty, Flores); Wolff 2 (Dewey, Flores); Davalillo (Alfano); Harrison (Priess); N. Haynes (Reeder); Melendez (Skeels); Mendoza (McCrotty); Jarrod Patterson (Deboer); Paciorek (Alfano); Russin (Flaherty); Vazquez (Marcos Sanchez).

PLAYERS WITH TWO OR MORE TEAMS

Player, Team	Avg.	G	TPA	AB	R	H	TB	2B	3B	HR	RBI	SH	SF	HP	BB	IBB	SO	SB	CS	GDP	Slg.	OBP
Faircloth, Chad, Bak.*	.257	84	308	288	39	74	102	13	3	3	30	1	1	2	16	0	78	12	2	5	.354	.300
Faircloth, Chad, S.J.*	.206	18	64	63	5	13	18	3	1	0	2	0	0	0	1	0	12	1	1	0	.286	.219
Fuentes, Joel, S.J.†	.310	9	34	29	5	9	11	2	0	0	2	0	0	1	4	0	9	0	1	0	.379	.412
Fuentes, Joel, Bak.†	.282	31	127	117	14	33	45	3	0	3	17	0	0	1	9	0	31	0	2	0	.385	.339
Jenkins, Dee, Stoc.*	.271	50	191	166	24	45	67	8	1	4	12	2	1	3	19	0	48	6	3	3	.404	.354
Jenkins, Dee, Vis.*	.261	65	304	268	37	70	116	16	3	8	37	4	5	4	23	0	67	12	6	6	.433	.323
Melendez, Angel, Bak.	.213	12	48	47	4	10	14	1	0	1	4	0	0	0	1	0	11	1	0	1	.298	.229
Melendez, Angel, S.J.	.281	54	185	167	22	47	73	11	0	5	28	1	1	1	14	0	34	4	1	4	.437	.339
Mota, Pedro, S.J.*	.218	15	58	55	2	12	15	3	0	0	4	1	0	0	2	0	16	2	1	0	.273	.246
Mota, Pedro, Bak.*	.189	15	57	53	8	10	13	1	1	0	2	0	0	0	4	0	15	2	1	0	.245	.246
Tommasini, Kevin, Bak.	.212	33	109	99	12	21	37	5	1	3	11	0	0	1	9	0	26	0	1	1	.374	.284
Tommasini, Kevin, S.J.	.200	6	25	25	1	5	8	0	0	1	5	0	0	0	0	0	4	0	1	2	.320	.200
Tyler, Josh, S.J.	.247	50	209	194	24	48	65	10	2	1	21	3	2	0	10	0	29	7	8	8	.335	.282
Tyler, Josh, Bak.	.268	53	239	220	27	59	93	14	1	6	43	3	2	3	11	0	32	12	2	2	.423	.309

1998 PITCHING
TEAM

Team	W	L	Pct.	ERA	G	CG	ShO	Sv.	IP	H	TBF	R	ER	HR	SH	SF	HB	BB	IBB	SO	WP	Bk.
San Jose	83	57	.593	3.58	140	4	11	46	1225.2	1174	5191	567	488	77	38	26	63	396	4	1088	63	18
High Desert	82	58	.586	3.84	140	3	7	34	1235.2	1243	5326	676	527	113	31	35	43	439	10	1133	64	9
R. Cucamonga	77	63	.550	3.94	140	0	6	38	1231.0	1231	5375	661	539	82	31	48	65	513	4	1019	92	24
Modesto	77	63	.550	4.03	140	3	11	35	1229.0	1256	5402	692	551	72	46	37	57	499	22	1103	61	18
Stockton	66	74	.471	4.16	140	9	8	29	1218.2	1187	5397	686	563	87	43	39	67	593	11	1198	103	11
San Bernardino	55	85	.393	4.33	140	2	9	36	1236.0	1233	5451	735	594	85	53	44	48	535	18	1064	95	17
Visalia	67	73	.479	4.40	140	3	7	31	1225.2	1328	5403	746	599	101	42	43	53	438	23	1085	95	18
Lancaster	78	62	.557	4.61	140	3	10	33	1230.1	1290	5477	749	630	124	24	36	60	557	16	1181	98	21
Lake Elsinore	66	74	.471	4.73	140	11	5	36	1230.0	1357	5475	786	647	91	40	34	65	493	21	972	107	20
Bakersfield	49	91	.350	4.75	140	3	3	28	1229.0	1342	5526	823	649	117	40	44	64	526	19	924	101	20

INDIVIDUAL

TOP QUALIFIERS FOR EARNED-RUN AVERAGE TITLE
Minimum 112 innings. *Lefthanded pitcher.

Pitcher, Team	W	L	Pct.	ERA	G	GS	CG	ShO	GF	Sv.	IP	H	TBF	R	ER	HR	SH	SF	HB	BB	IBB	SO	WP	Bk.
Patterson, John, H.D.	8	7	.533	2.83	25	25	0	0	0	0	127.0	102	519	54	40	12	0	3	4	42	0	148	5	0
Penny, Brad, H.D.	14	5	.737	2.96	28	28	1	0	0	0	164.0	138	661	65	54	15	3	2	9	35	0	207	4	0
Manwiller, Tim, Mod.	13	6	.684	3.17	30	21	1	0	2	1	156.1	150	650	69	55	8	1	5	3	46	1	129	3	2
Nathan, Joe, S.J.	8	6	.571	3.32	22	22	0	0	0	0	122.0	100	506	51	45	13	1	1	10	48	0	118	1	0
Jensen, Ryan, Bak.	11	12	.478	3.37	29	27	0	0	1	0	168.1	162	726	89	63	14	6	1	8	61	3	164	10	2
Bierbrodt, Nick, H.D.*	8	7	.533	3.40	24	23	1	0	0	0	129.2	122	560	66	49	7	3	6	7	64	0	88	9	0
Knoll, Brian, S.J.	7	7	.500	3.45	42	6	1	1	15	3	114.2	135	490	47	44	4	3	3	5	21	0	109	5	0
Anderson, Jason, Mod.*	9	4	.692	3.46	28	24	1	1	2	0	145.2	147	612	67	56	5	5	4	2	53	0	110	5	1
Leyva, Julian, Mod.	11	7	.611	3.60	28	21	1	0	3	1	137.2	156	577	70	55	9	4	3	5	25	2	92	1	0
Iddon, Brent, R.C.	7	4	.636	3.63	32	19	0	0	4	1	139.0	149	602	67	56	10	4	6	9	40	0	110	4	1
Garcia, Jose, Stoc.	11	12	.478	3.67	28	28	1	0	0	0	169.1	147	749	89	69	12	3	9	10	91	1	167	16	0
Tucker, Ben, S.J.	5	5	.500	3.75	29	14	0	0	5	1	112.2	97	467	54	47	10	4	2	9	33	1	69	3	2
Gregg, Kevin, Mod.	8	7	.533	3.81	30	24	0	0	3	1	144.0	139	640	72	61	7	9	2	6	76	2	141	7	0
Jensen, Jared, Vis.	5	9	.357	4.00	31	24	0	0	5	1	148.2	161	629	87	66	16	5	6	1	40	1	112	10	0
Niles, Randy, Vis.	6	12	.333	4.07	31	22	0	0	2	0	148.1	144	648	92	67	12	11	4	11	54	3	103	9	5

DEPARTMENTAL LEADERS: W—Penny, 14; L—Morse, 14; Pct.—Andra, .800; G—Montgomery, 63; GS—Garcia, Middlebrook, Penny, 28 each; CG—Levrault, 4; ShO—Several players tied with 1 each; GF—Montgomery, 58; Sv.—Stoops, 31; IP—Garcia, 169.1; H—Holmes, 192; TBF—Garcia, 749; R—Morse, 110; ER—Morse, 90; HR—J. Jensen, Knott, 16 each; SH—Niles, 11; SF—Morse, Garcia, Middlebrook, 9 each; HB—Several players tied with 4 each; BB—Garcia, 91; IBB—Dellaratta, 6; SO—Penny, 207; WP—Rice, 21; BK—Malloy, 8.

ALL PITCHERS
*Lefthanded pitcher.

Pitcher, Team	W	L	Pct.	ERA	G	GS	CG	ShO	GF	Sv.	IP	H	TBF	R	ER	HR	SH	SF	HB	BB	IBB	SO	WP	Bk.
Abbott, Todd, Vis.	3	3	.500	7.13	34	0	0	0	11	0	48.0	71	245	47	38	6	3	4	2	21	2	49	10	1
Abreu, Oscar, Mod.	2	2	.500	7.78	34	0	0	0	15	1	56.2	56	287	51	49	5	2	1	10	54	0	68	9	1
Agosto, Stevenson, R.C.*	5	8	.385	6.08	23	23	0	0	0	0	108.0	132	505	83	73	14	4	6	3	68	0	91	15	4
Akin, Jay, Stoc.*	2	3	.400	2.96	44	0	0	0	15	2	85.0	95	371	33	28	6	5	2	2	34	2	75	3	0
Alejo, Nigel, Stoc.	2	3	.400	7.96	8	7	1	1	0	0	31.2	44	159	33	28	1	1	2	3	17	0	22	3	1
Anderson, Jason, Mod.*	9	4	.692	3.46	28	24	1	1	2	0	145.2	147	612	67	56	5	5	4	2	53	0	110	5	1
Andra, Jeff, S.J.*	8	2	.800	3.32	15	15	2	1	0	0	86.2	75	358	36	32	2	4	0	2	28	0	80	5	1
Andrews, Jeff, H.D.	1	1	.500	4.32	6	3	0	0	2	0	25.0	36	119	19	12	1	0	2	0	7	0	8	0	0
Avery, Paul, S.B.*	1	1	.500	3.05	5	4	0	0	0	0	20.2	21	95	12	7	2	2	1	0	12	0	16	4	0
Ayala, Julio, Lan.*	10	7	.588	4.45	25	25	1	1	0	0	139.2	166	634	91	69	14	5	8	1	44	1	129	15	2
Bailey, Phil, Bak.*	2	2	.500	5.74	20	0	0	0	9	0	31.1	40	154	22	20	1	1	0	1	23	2	27	4	0
Bane, Jaymie, L.E.*	0	0	.000	5.40	17	0	0	0	1	0	18.1	26	92	16	11	2	1	1	2	9	0	18	0	2
Bearden, Doug, Stoc.	0	0	.000	0.00	1	0	0	0	1	0	1.0	0	4	0	0	0	0	0	0	1	0	0	0	0
Bell, Scott, S.B.	2	1	.667	0.92	8	0	0	0	3	0	19.2	20	84	4	2	1	4	0	1	7	3	11	0	0
Bennett, Tom, Vis.	1	0	1.000	0.00	1	1	0	0	0	0	7.0	1	24	0	0	0	0	0	0	3	0	9	0	0
Bermudez, Manny, S.J.	7	11	.389	4.64	24	24	1	0	0	0	139.2	161	609	82	72	10	4	2	4	44	0	87	8	0
Berry, Jason, Vis.	0	0	.000	27.00	1	0	0	0	1	0	0.2	5	12	2	2	1	0	1	0	1	0	0	1	0
Bierbrodt, Nick, H.D.*	8	7	.533	3.40	24	23	1	0	0	0	129.2	122	560	66	49	7	3	6	7	64	0	88	9	0
Blumenstock, Brad, Mod.	2	2	.500	8.67	15	5	0	0	1	1	36.1	58	195	40	35	6	2	1	2	22	0	29	5	0
Bond, Jason, Lan.*	7	3	.700	4.46	20	16	1	1	1	1	80.2	87	360	53	40	9	1	1	1	38	0	95	6	1

Pitcher, Team	W	L	Pct.	ERA	G	GS	CG	ShO	GF	Sv.	IP	H	TBF	R	ER	HR	SH	SF	HB	BB	IBB	SO	WP	Bk.
Bramlett, Jeff, S.B.	0	0	.000	0.00	1	0	0	0	1	0	1.0	1	4	0	0	0	0	0	0	0	0	0	0	0
Bump, Nate, S.J.	6	1	.857	1.75	11	11	0	0	0	0	61.2	37	240	13	12	2	1	1	2	24	0	61	2	0
Burnside, Adrian, S.B.*	1	10	.091	7.81	21	12	0	0	2	0	78.1	97	381	79	68	6	5	6	8	48	0	65	8	0
Carmody, Brian, R.C.*	3	1	.750	2.20	8	8	0	0	0	0	49.0	42	193	14	12	0	0	1	1	9	0	48	3	0
Carmona, Rafael, Lan.	0	1	.000	6.23	4	4	0	0	0	0	13.0	12	55	10	9	1	0	0	0	5	0	11	0	2
Carroll, Dave, Mod.*	1	4	.200	3.03	22	0	0	0	11	4	32.2	34	156	21	11	1	2	1	2	22	2	29	1	0
Cervantes, Peter, S.B.	0	5	.000	5.54	30	7	0	0	8	0	65.0	79	295	48	40	6	2	3	2	22	0	57	5	0
Chung, Rocky, S.B.	1	2	.333	4.44	5	5	0	0	0	0	24.1	24	103	13	12	2	1	1	0	6	0	22	0	0
Cowsill, Brendon, L.E.	2	2	.500	6.53	17	0	0	0	9	2	30.1	38	138	22	22	2	1	3	1	13	2	22	3	0
Crabtree, Robbie, S.J.	6	1	.857	0.99	24	0	0	0	10	2	54.1	39	213	6	6	0	4	0	3	8	0	67	1	0
Crews, Jason, H.D.	7	7	.500	4.17	48	0	0	0	14	2	86.1	100	384	62	40	4	0	3	5	22	1	58	12	2
Crossan, Clayton, Stoc.	1	1	.500	9.64	17	0	0	0	5	0	18.2	32	97	21	20	2	0	1	3	11	0	8	2	0
Cummings, Ryan, L.E.	0	1	.000	5.40	1	1	0	0	0	0	5.0	5	23	3	3	0	0	0	2	3	0	4	1	0
Dale, Carl, Mod.	1	2	.333	2.37	3	3	0	0	0	0	19.0	15	74	6	5	1	0	0	3	2	0	14	0	0
Darrell, Tommy, L.E.	4	11	.267	5.71	21	16	0	0	2	0	97.2	120	465	76	62	7	2	2	11	44	3	56	14	4
Davis, Allen, S.B.*	1	2	.333	2.90	5	5	0	0	0	0	31.0	30	127	13	10	2	1	1	0	7	0	34	1	2
Dawsey, Jason, Stoc.*	4	2	.667	3.18	19	9	0	0	3	0	62.1	54	263	28	22	3	4	1	0	27	1	79	7	0
Deakman, Josh, L.E.	4	2	.667	2.22	9	0	0	0	5	1	24.1	25	101	6	6	1	2	0	2	4	1	13	1	0
Della Ratta, Pete, Vis.	5	1	.833	2.44	36	0	0	0	28	13	59.0	43	249	24	16	5	3	1	1	25	6	73	4	0
Derenches, Albert, Lan.*	0	0	.000	2.45	9	0	0	0	6	0	18.1	11	77	5	5	3	0	0	0	12	0	18	0	0
Diaz, Antonio, R.C.	0	1	1.000	4.41	17	0	0	0	8	2	34.2	36	144	17	17	5	0	1	0	6	0	23	4	0
Dodd, Scott, R.C.*	4	6	.400	3.68	43	0	0	0	11	3	66.0	65	295	35	27	3	2	1	2	41	3	59	9	1
Donaldson, Bo, L.E.	4	6	.400	3.77	54	3	0	0	42	20	76.1	65	340	38	32	7	5	3	9	40	4	99	12	4
Dotel, Melido, S.B.	0	1	.000	8.35	11	0	0	0	3	0	18.1	12	100	20	17	0	0	1	5	30	0	15	5	2
Doughty, Brian, R.C.	2	1	.667	2.56	16	2	0	0	3	1	31.2	29	134	14	9	2	1	1	3	8	0	23	2	2
Duarte, Renney, L.E.	6	7	.462	4.96	32	14	3	0	11	3	127.0	148	567	84	70	14	5	5	5	48	4	74	8	1
Dubose, Eric, Vis.*	6	1	.857	3.38	17	10	0	0	4	1	72.0	56	307	34	27	5	1	2	5	35	0	85	8	2
Dunham, Pat, Lan.	9	5	.643	3.46	17	17	0	0	0	0	104.0	97	442	48	40	8	0	3	8	41	0	88	4	6
Estes, Shawn, Bak.*	0	0	.000	0.00	1	1	0	0	0	0	4.1	3	17	0	0	0	0	0	1	0	0	5	0	0
Esteves, Jake, Bak.	0	2	.000	4.29	14	6	0	0	4	1	35.2	43	168	30	17	7	1	2	2	12	0	24	0	0
Estrella, Luis, S.J.	5	6	.455	4.75	36	2	0	0	12	2	72.0	79	315	41	38	5	3	1	2	27	0	57	9	1
Faust, Jason, Vis.*	1	2	.333	4.85	14	0	0	0	6	0	29.2	39	137	27	16	4	4	3	0	14	0	25	4	0
Fischer, Mike, S.B.	1	3	.250	4.56	12	12	0	0	0	0	51.1	57	229	35	26	6	0	2	1	15	0	38	2	3
Fitzgerald, Brian, Lan.*	1	2	.333	4.20	41	0	0	0	18	1	70.2	79	315	39	33	5	2	1	2	24	2	48	1	0
Flores, Pedro, S.B.*	2	4	.333	3.10	30	10	0	0	7	3	78.1	75	345	37	27	0	3	2	3	38	0	56	3	1
Foran, John, R.C.	3	2	.600	3.42	12	1	0	0	8	2	26.1	28	125	16	10	2	0	0	5	8	1	26	2	1
Frontera, Chad, Bak.	2	6	.250	5.40	11	11	0	0	0	0	53.1	63	246	39	32	4	2	2	7	23	0	29	6	2
Fuentes, Brian, Lan.*	7	7	.500	4.17	24	22	0	0	1	0	118.2	121	541	73	55	8	1	6	9	81	0	137	14	2
Gangemi, Joseph, L.E.*	0	5	.000	5.70	13	13	0	0	0	0	66.1	91	302	52	42	6	1	2	0	22	1	32	7	0
Garcia, Jose, Stoc.	11	12	.478	3.67	28	28	1	0	0	0	169.1	147	749	89	69	12	3	9	10	91	1	167	16	0
Gonzalez, Jose, Lan.	2	0	1.000	4.24	8	1	0	0	3	0	17.0	17	77	9	8	2	0	1	1	9	0	17	3	0
Gorrell, Chris, Vis.	3	5	.375	5.20	32	0	0	0	12	5	55.1	65	247	39	32	3	5	2	6	17	2	53	4	1
Greene, Danny, L.E.	1	0	1.000	2.19	11	0	0	0	10	6	12.1	9	48	3	3	0	0	0	1	1	0	22	2	0
Gregg, Kevin, Mod.	8	7	.533	3.81	30	24	0	0	3	1	144.0	139	640	72	61	7	9	2	6	76	2	141	7	0
Grieve, Tim, H.D.	4	2	.667	4.73	27	0	0	0	18	6	45.2	43	202	29	24	5	1	1	3	22	2	61	5	0
Grote, Jason, S.J.	7	2	.778	2.45	15	15	0	0	0	0	88.0	85	363	30	24	2	2	1	2	22	0	88	6	0
Gryboski, Kevin, S.J.	5	5	.500	2.65	37	3	0	0	18	5	85.0	75	351	35	25	4	1	2	4	31	1	73	3	0
Gulin, Lindsay, Lan.*	2	2	.500	5.84	9	0	0	0	3	0	24.2	32	118	17	16	3	0	0	1	15	0	18	1	2
Gunther, Kevin, Mod.	0	0	.000	1.80	4	0	0	0	3	2	5.0	4	18	2	1	0	0	0	0	0	0	4	0	0
Gutierrez, Javier, Stoc.	0	2	.000	19.29	5	0	0	0	1	0	4.2	4	30	10	10	1	0	0	1	11	0	5	4	0
Guzman, Domingo, R.C.	1	1	.500	3.74	4	4	0	0	0	0	21.2	22	91	11	9	1	0	1	1	6	0	16	3	0
Hall, Darren, S.B.	1	0	1.000	0.00	8	2	0	0	2	0	9.2	4	33	0	0	0	1	0	0	2	0	8	0	0
Hardwick, Bubba, Stoc.*	2	1	.667	1.61	22	0	0	0	16	4	22.1	17	100	9	4	0	1	2	0	14	0	26	2	0
Harriger, Mark, L.E.	5	5	.500	4.09	13	12	3	1	0	0	81.1	86	350	43	37	5	3	2	2	23	0	68	6	0
Harris, Pep, L.E.	0	1	.000	0.00	4	1	0	0	0	0	9.1	9	38	5	0	0	0	0	2	0	0	12	0	0
Harville, Chad, Vis.	4	3	.571	3.00	24	7	0	0	12	4	69.0	59	294	25	23	0	0	2	5	31	0	76	6	2
Hawkins, Al, Stoc.	3	4	.429	4.55	9	9	0	0	0	0	55.1	60	252	37	28	7	1	4	3	26	0	32	4	1
Helmer, Chad, Stoc.	6	7	.462	4.02	46	0	0	0	31	6	65.0	45	283	35	29	6	4	2	4	42	0	76	9	0
Herndon, Harry, R.C.	3	2	.600	3.40	6	6	0	0	0	0	39.2	37	165	18	15	5	2	2	2	13	0	29	1	0
Hill, Ken, L.E.	0	0	.000	6.75	1	1	0	0	0	0	4.0	5	21	4	3	0	0	1	0	5	0	2	1	0
Hinchliffe, Brett, Lan.	1	1	.500	1.59	3	3	0	0	0	0	17.0	8	62	5	3	2	0	0	0	5	0	26	1	0
Hite, Kevin, R.C.	4	0	1.000	3.02	30	0	0	0	25	12	41.2	36	166	16	14	2	0	3	0	8	1	45	4	0
Hollins, Stacy, Stoc.	0	0	.000	4.50	1	1	0	0	0	0	4.0	3	19	4	2	1	0	0	0	2	0	3	0	0
Holmes, Mike, Vis.	9	10	.474	4.14	31	24	2	1	4	0	152.0	192	657	86	70	14	2	1	7	21	3	98	8	1
Hudson, Tim, Mod.	4	0	1.000	1.67	8	5	0	0	2	0	37.2	19	150	10	7	0	2	0	2	18	0	48	2	1
Husted, Brent, S.B.	3	6	.333	3.60	49	0	0	0	20	1	85.0	77	360	41	34	6	4	2	2	24	4	68	6	0
Hutchings, Mark, Bak.	0	0	.000	6.30	6	0	0	0	4	0	10.0	8	47	7	7	1	0	0	1	7	0	6	0	0
Hutzler, Jeff, S.B.*	1	7	.125	5.71	51	0	0	0	21	3	80.1	96	372	64	51	7	6	2	4	31	4	34	6	0
Iddon, Brent, R.C.	7	4	.636	3.63	32	19	0	0	4	1	139.0	149	602	67	56	10	4	6	9	40	0	110	4	1
Jacob, Russell, H.D.	3	2	.600	4.41	31	7	0	0	4	1	67.1	78	310	42	33	2	2	1	2	26	0	64	7	0
Janicki, Pete, Lan.	2	3	.400	8.83	15	3	0	0	5	2	34.2	40	162	34	34	0	3	0	2	5	14	1	36	4	0
Jensen, Jared, Vis.	5	9	.357	4.00	31	24	0	0	5	1	148.2	161	629	87	66	16	5	6	1	40	1	112	10	0
Jensen, Ryan, Bak.	11	12	.478	3.37	29	27	0	0	1	0	168.1	162	726	89	63	14	6	1	8	61	3	164	10	2
Johnson, Eric, S.J.	0	0	.000	9.64	5	0	0	0	3	0	4.2	5	27	7	5	0	0	1	0	3	0	5	0	0
Johnson, Gregory, L.E.*	3	3	.500	4.28	37	1	0	0	13	0	75.2	78	323	40	36	9	5	1	1	23	3	63	5	1
Johnston, Doug, Stoc.	5	1	.833	2.69	9	9	1	0	0	0	60.1	47	240	20	18	3	0	1	5	26	0	54	1	2
Jones, Marcus, Vis.	7	9	.438	4.67	29	20	0	0	8	4	131.0	155	587	79	68	8	2	4	7	45	3	112	2	3
Joseph, Kevin, Bak.	9	4	.000	8.14	6	6	0	0	0	0	21.0	35	120	26	19	3	1	1	2	20	0	17	7	0
Kaye, Justin, Lan.	1	2	.333	6.82	16	0	0	0	7	0	30.1	37	139	24	23	4	2	1	0	13	2	34	9	0
Keith, Jeff, S.J.*	1	1	.500	3.77	23	0	0	0	13	0	28.2	28	133	16	12	2	4	1	6	16	1	29	2	0
Kelly, John, Lan.	4	4	.500	5.45	23	6	0	0	4	1	69.1	73	296	46	42	11	0	2	2	20	0	60	7	0
Kennison, Kyle, Lan.	2	1	.667	7.11	15	0	0	0	7	2	25.1	34	122	21	20	3	0	2	1	19	0	14	0	0

– 485 –

Pitcher, Team	W	L	Pct.	ERA	G	GS	CG	ShO	GF	Sv.	IP	H	TBF	R	ER	HR	SH	SF	HB	BB	IBB	SO	WP	Bk.
Kent, Robbie, R.C.	0	0	.000	0.00	1	0	0	0	1	0	1.0	1	4	0	0	0	0	0	0	0	0	0	0	0
Kimball, Andrew, Mod.	5	6	.455	4.44	42	8	0	0	24	12	97.1	113	440	62	48	7	3	8	6	29	5	96	6	2
Kiyono, Masashi, S.J.	2	5	.286	5.94	13	8	0	0	2	0	47.0	56	208	37	31	8	1	2	2	14	0	20	4	2
Knoll, Brian, S.J.	7	7	.500	3.45	42	6	1	1	15	3	114.2	135	490	47	44	4	3	3	5	21	0	109	5	0
Knott, Eric, H.D.*	12	7	.632	4.52	28	22	1	0	3	0	143.1	175	616	84	72	16	3	4	1	28	1	96	3	3
Koehler, Russ, Lan.	1	3	.250	7.06	10	0	0	0	2	0	21.2	29	106	17	17	3	0	0	1	11	2	21	3	1
Kolb, Brandon, R.C.	0	2	.000	3.05	4	4	0	0	0	0	20.2	14	92	8	7	3	0	0	1	18	0	16	0	1
Kramer, Matthew, S.B.	0	1	.000	6.00	8	0	0	0	6	0	12.0	13	49	8	8	1	0	1	0	1	0	8	1	0
Larreal, Guillermo, Bak.	1	1	.500	4.82	9	0	0	0	2	0	18.2	23	82	14	10	3	1	0	0	2	1	14	0	1
Lee, Derek, Stoc.*	5	9	.357	4.17	30	18	1	1	2	1	136.0	134	583	70	63	9	4	5	5	48	1	141	8	0
Levrault, Allen, Stoc.	9	3	.750	2.87	16	15	4	1	0	0	97.1	76	388	33	31	8	4	3	2	27	0	86	2	1
Leyva, Edgar, L.E.	8	5	.615	4.76	33	13	0	0	8	2	121.0	125	525	72	64	6	2	3	5	48	0	99	6	1
Leyva, Julian, Mod.	11	7	.611	3.60	28	21	1	0	3	1	137.2	156	577	70	55	9	4	3	5	25	2	92	1	0
Lidle, Cory, H.D.	0	0	.000	0.00	1	0	0	0	0	0	2.2	2	13	1	0	0	0	0	0	2	0	6	0	0
Lisio, Joe, H.D.	1	2	.333	5.87	11	0	0	0	3	0	15.1	19	79	11	10	1	1	0	2	11	1	17	1	0
Loiz, Niuman, Stoc.	0	0	.000	7.84	12	1	0	0	4	0	20.2	24	103	19	18	3	0	0	1	19	0	15	2	0
Luckert, Gabriel, Bak.	0	0	.000	16.20	2	0	0	0	2	0	1.2	5	12	3	3	0	0	0	1	1	0	1	1	0
Lynch, Ryan, R.C.*	3	3	.500	2.95	21	2	0	0	11	1	42.2	34	179	17	14	2	0	2	3	19	0	35	1	0
Macey, Fausto, Bak.	5	8	.385	5.28	17	15	1	0	1	0	87.0	114	381	63	51	14	2	2	4	20	0	72	6	4
Malerich, William, Bak.-S.J.*	3	3	.500	3.63	46	0	0	0	15	3	74.1	64	324	36	30	4	4	3	11	39	2	59	4	0
Malloy, Bill, S.J.	11	7	.611	4.88	41	15	0	0	10	4	125.1	132	550	81	68	10	5	4	4	42	1	103	10	8
Manwiller, Tim, Mod.	13	6	.684	3.17	30	21	1	0	2	1	156.1	150	650	69	55	8	1	5	3	46	1	129	3	2
Martines, Jason, H.D.	0	1	.000	7.59	5	0	0	0	1	0	10.2	16	50	10	9	3	1	2	0	3	0	7	1	0
Mateo, Julio, Lan.	0	0	.000	6.75	1	0	0	0	0	0	1.1	1	6	1	1	1	0	1	1	0	1	0	0	0
Maurer, Dave, R.C.*	5	2	.714	2.70	48	0	0	0	14	5	83.1	56	348	27	25	1	5	1	1	46	1	93	8	2
McCall, Travis, Mod.*	6	2	.750	1.84	20	0	0	0	16	4	29.1	17	112	7	6	2	1	1	3	10	1	25	1	1
McDonald, Matt, S.B.*	3	2	.600	4.59	24	0	0	0	4	0	49.0	50	232	36	25	2	3	2	2	32	2	55	9	2
McDowell, Jack, L.E.	1	0	1.000	9.00	1	1	0	0	0	0	5.0	7	22	5	5	1	0	0	0	0	0	4	0	0
Middlebrook, Jason, R.C.	10	12	.455	4.92	28	28	0	0	0	0	150.0	162	665	99	82	10	1	9	4	63	0	132	17	4
Mlodik, Kevin, Vis.	0	1	.000	12.00	4	0	0	0	1	0	3.0	9	19	5	4	0	0	0	0	2	0	1	3	0
Montgomery, Matt, S.B.	4	6	.400	3.19	63	0	0	0	58	26	79.0	69	331	31	28	6	4	3	1	27	4	81	5	1
Morse, Paul, S.B.	7	14	.333	5.27	30	26	0	0	2	0	153.2	160	696	110	90	13	6	9	6	77	0	116	17	2
Moskau, Ryan, S.B.*	3	3	.500	3.46	6	6	1	1	0	0	39.0	37	163	18	15	2	1	0	4	16	1	31	1	1
Nathan, Joe, S.J.	8	6	.571	3.32	22	22	0	0	0	0	122.0	100	506	51	45	13	1	1	10	48	0	118	1	0
Newton, Geronimo, Lan.*	3	0	1.000	3.13	19	0	0	0	10	2	31.2	30	141	15	11	2	1	0	0	21	0	30	5	0
Nickle, Douglas, L.E.	3	4	.429	4.48	11	10	1	0	0	0	66.1	68	285	40	33	3	0	1	3	25	0	69	13	1
Nielsen, Thomas, Bak.*	1	0	1.000	7.88	4	0	0	0	1	0	8.0	10	40	11	7	1	1	1	0	5	0	8	2	0
Niles, Randy, Vis.	6	12	.333	4.07	31	22	0	0	2	0	148.1	144	648	92	67	12	11	4	11	54	3	103	9	5
Nina, Elvin, Vis.	8	8	.500	4.49	30	21	1	1	5	0	130.1	135	583	77	65	9	2	6	5	62	1	131	13	2
Noriega, Ray, Vis.*	3	5	.375	6.18	36	6	0	0	10	2	71.1	91	328	55	49	8	2	4	2	24	1	77	6	0
Norris, Ben, H.D.*	2	2	.500	5.53	9	6	0	0	2	1	40.2	48	180	27	25	7	2	0	0	18	0	17	1	0
O'Dell, Jake, Vis.	3	1	.750	2.20	9	5	0	0	3	1	41.0	34	164	13	10	0	1	1	0	9	0	36	2	1
O'Reilly, John, Stoc.	5	6	.455	5.20	32	11	0	0	6	1	97.0	101	438	65	56	7	3	2	7	57	1	95	6	0
Oleksik, George, H.D.	3	3	.500	4.46	41	1	0	0	12	0	72.2	82	326	51	36	8	3	2	1	31	0	57	4	0
Paredes, Roberto, Stoc.	1	3	.250	3.86	43	0	0	0	27	11	46.2	54	222	30	20	1	2	2	2	27	1	47	16	0
Passini, Brian, Stoc.*	5	6	.455	3.60	15	15	1	0	0	0	90.0	83	375	39	36	7	4	1	3	31	0	91	4	0
Patterson, John, H.D.	8	7	.533	2.83	25	25	0	0	0	0	127.0	102	519	54	40	12	0	3	4	42	0	148	5	0
Paulino, Jose, Mod.	2	4	.333	5.53	38	0	0	0	13	1	70.0	79	321	57	43	4	3	2	0	28	3	53	2	3
Pena, Juan, Mod.*	3	2	.600	5.18	6	6	0	0	0	0	33.0	50	154	25	19	2	2	1	1	7	0	32	3	0
Penny, Brad, H.D.	14	5	.737	2.96	28	28	1	0	0	0	164.0	138	661	65	54	15	3	2	9	35	0	207	4	0
Perozo, Felix, L.E.	0	1	.000	2.25	10	0	0	0	6	2	12.0	11	52	4	3	1	1	1	0	6	0	12	2	0
Peters, Don, H.D.	0	1	.000	2.21	21	0	0	0	19	8	20.1	24	94	11	5	2	0	1	0	7	1	20	0	0
Peterson, Kyle, Stoc.	4	7	.364	3.55	17	17	0	0	0	0	96.1	99	430	54	38	4	6	1	8	33	0	109	5	5
Petrosian, Ara, Vis.	1	2	.333	9.82	19	0	0	0	8	2	29.1	40	152	36	32	9	1	2	0	24	0	24	3	0
Pineiro, Joel, Lan.	2	0	1.000	7.80	9	9	1	1	0	0	45.0	52	217	40	39	6	0	6	0	22	0	48	2	3
Prokopec, Luke, S.B.	8	5	.615	2.69	20	20	0	0	0	0	110.1	98	460	43	33	11	3	2	3	33	1	148	5	1
Puorto, Jamie, H.D.*	0	0	.000	7.71	1	0	0	0	0	0	2.1	4	11	2	2	0	0	0	0	1	0	2	0	0
Ramirez, Erasmo, Bak.*	1	1	.500	3.38	14	0	0	0	9	3	21.1	20	80	8	8	0	2	0	2	6	0	17	1	3
Randolph, Steve, H.D.*	4	4	.500	3.59	17	17	0	0	0	0	85.1	71	357	44	34	6	3	2	3	42	0	104	0	0
Regalado, Maximo, S.B.	3	3	.500	4.18	14	3	0	0	1	0	47.1	45	212	30	22	4	0	1	3	24	0	42	4	0
Rice, Nathan, Bak.*	3	8	.273	5.40	30	21	0	0	0	0	120.0	133	562	96	72	8	3	7	4	78	1	87	21	0
Riley, Michael, Bak.*	6	12	.333	4.50	40	15	2	0	7	2	128.0	130	555	73	64	8	3	3	0	58	1	110	9	1
Robertson, Doug, Vis.	2	1	.667	4.95	17	0	0	0	11	0	20.0	23	88	11	11	1	0	1	0	7	1	15	1	0
Rodriguez, Juan, L.E.*	0	0	.000	27.00	1	0	0	0	1	0	1.0	3	6	3	3	0	0	0	0	1	0	0	0	0
Rodriguez, Larry, H.D.	0	2	.000	5.08	6	5	0	0	0	0	28.1	29	116	19	16	5	1	1	0	5	0	15	1	1
Rogers, Kevin, Bak.*	0	0	.000	2.11	12	0	0	0	3	0	21.1	15	83	9	5	2	3	2	0	4	1	19	2	0
Rosado, Juan, Stoc.*	0	1	.000	7.65	21	0	0	0	9	4	20.0	27	113	23	17	2	0	1	3	23	2	21	3	0
Sabel, Erik, H.D.	0	0	.000	3.18	14	0	0	0	9	4	22.2	25	100	8	8	2	1	0	4	3	0	13	1	0
Sachse, Matt, Lan.*	0	0	.000	6.75	1	0	0	0	1	0	1.1	3	7	1	1	0	0	0	0	0	0	0	0	0
Sanchez, Martin, H.D.	3	0	1.000	3.05	35	0	0	0	32	11	44.1	36	189	16	15	7	3	1	3	21	1	35	7	1
Scheffer, Aaron, Lan.	2	2	.500	3.14	25	0	0	0	19	10	43.0	46	189	19	15	0	2	1	1	12	3	65	5	0
Schultz, Jeffrey, Mod.	0	1	.000	4.32	19	0	0	0	9	3	33.1	34	149	26	16	1	3	1	0	19	1	32	4	3
Scott, Tim, S.B.	0	1	.000	4.50	2	2	0	0	0	0	4.0	4	15	2	2	1	0	0	0	2	0	2	0	0
Skeels, David, Vis.	0	0	.000	5.40	7	0	0	0	7	0	10.0	8	40	7	6	1	0	0	0	3	0	6	1	0
Smith, Cam, Lan.	1	1	.500	2.50	8	0	0	0	3	2	18.0	11	81	7	5	1	0	3	0	13	0	32	4	0
Snow, Bert, Mod.	1	1	.500	3.12	2	2	0	0	0	0	8.2	12	46	8	3	1	0	1	0	6	0	12	1	0
Stark, Dennis, Lan.	1	2	.333	4.29	5	5	0	0	0	0	21.0	18	100	12	10	1	1	0	1	17	0	21	0	0
Stephens, Jason, L.E.	7	6	.538	4.10	35	13	1	1	6	0	123.0	128	534	72	56	7	6	2	6	47	3	89	11	1
Stockstill, Jason, L.E.*	8	5	.615	4.41	25	16	1	0	3	0	100.0	111	450	65	49	10	2	2	2	45	0	77	5	0
Stoops, Jim, S.J.	3	1	.667	0.98	45	0	0	0	43	31	55.1	28	222	7	6	0	0	3	0	25	0	96	1	0
Stover, C.D., S.B.	3	2	.600	4.57	13	3	0	0	0	0	41.1	45	180	23	21	5	1	1	2	11	0	26	1	0
Sullivan, Brendan, R.C.	3	2	.600	1.08	35	0	0	0	31	8	41.2	23	168	7	5	0	1	0	4	19	2	37	1	0

Pitcher, Team	W	L	Pct.	ERA	G	GS	CG	ShO	GF	Sv.	IP	H	TBF	R	ER	HR	SH	SF	HB	BB	IBB	SO	WP	Bk.
Sweeney, Brian, Lan.	6	0	1.000	3.63	17	4	0	0	3	0	52.0	41	211	26	21	6	0	1	1	21	1	48	2	1
Szymborski, Tom, R.C.	0	0	.000	5.59	15	1	0	0	4	0	29.0	48	147	24	18	2	4	3	2	14	0	8	2	1
Taczy, Craig, S.B.*	6	11	.353	5.85	35	16	1	0	6	0	124.2	155	582	102	81	8	6	4	1	66	2	83	15	0
Takahashi, Kurt, Bak.	0	0	.000	4.66	5	0	0	0	2	0	9.2	11	41	7	5	0	0	1	0	3	0	7	0	0
Taulbee, Andy, Bak.	3	4	.429	5.38	18	13	0	0	0	0	75.1	96	348	55	45	10	0	6	3	33	0	43	7	1
Thompson, John, Lan.	3	5	.375	7.09	10	10	0	0	0	0	47.0	61	221	45	37	9	2	2	4	20	1	26	1	0
Thurmond, Travis, Bak.	0	0	.000	0.00	2	0	0	0	0	0	6.0	0	24	0	0	0	0	0	0	5	0	7	0	0
Tokarse, Brian, L.E.	9	9	.500	5.74	22	22	2	0	0	0	125.1	150	553	93	80	7	1	2	9	42	0	97	6	4
Torres, Luis, R.C.	4	0	1.000	4.18	42	0	0	0	14	1	64.2	72	297	36	30	3	1	1	11	26	0	57	2	4
Travis, Jesse, Bak.	1	7	.125	6.08	50	6	0	0	31	9	80.0	96	378	66	54	11	1	3	5	33	2	58	11	3
Tucker, Ben, S.J.	5	5	.500	3.75	29	14	0	0	5	1	112.2	97	467	54	47	10	4	2	9	33	1	69	3	2
Tyler, Josh, Bak.	1	0	1.000	0.00	1	0	0	0	1	0	1.0	1	5	0	0	0	0	0	0	1	0	0	0	0
Urban, Jeffrey, S.J.*	4	0	1.000	3.52	4	4	0	0	0	0	23.0	27	103	13	9	2	2	1	3	5	0	23	2	0
Valdes, Ismael, S.B.	1	0	1.000	2.84	1	1	0	0	0	0	6.1	7	27	2	2	0	1	0	0	1	0	4	0	0
Valenti, Jon, Bak.	1	2	.333	7.08	9	2	0	0	4	0	20.1	26	100	21	16	5	0	0	0	13	0	11	1	0
Verdugo, Jason, Bak.-S.J.	6	6	.500	3.21	29	11	0	0	18	3	81.1	81	334	35	29	4	1	3	2	15	0	60	0	0
Verplancke, Joe, H.D.	10	4	.714	3.65	42	2	0	0	14	1	81.1	65	344	41	33	9	3	4	3	40	0	87	4	2
Vizcaino, Luis, Mod.	6	3	.667	2.74	23	16	0	0	2	0	102.0	72	421	39	31	5	1	4	5	43	1	108	6	4
Vogelsong, Ryan, S.J.	0	0	.000	7.58	4	4	0	0	0	0	19.0	23	83	16	16	3	1	2	1	4	0	26	2	4
Volkman, Keith, L.E.*	1	0	1.000	6.02	20	2	0	0	6	0	43.1	46	223	40	29	3	3	3	4	41	0	34	4	1
Waites, David, Mod.	1	2	.333	5.56	22	0	0	0	17	3	22.2	29	115	18	14	1	1	1	2	16	2	25	5	0
Walker, Kevin, R.C.*	11	7	.611	4.15	22	22	0	0	0	0	121.1	122	514	62	56	10	2	3	4	48	0	94	3	2
Wallace, Flint, Mod.	2	8	.200	5.04	32	5	0	0	13	1	60.2	68	277	38	34	7	5	2	4	22	2	55	0	0
Watson, Allen, L.E.*	1	0	1.000	0.00	1	1	0	0	0	0	5.0	3	17	0	0	0	0	1	0	6	0	4	0	0
Wells, Matt, Bak.	3	8	.273	4.50	40	6	0	0	15	5	104.0	107	472	63	52	9	4	7	8	46	3	70	3	3
Westfall, Allan, Lan.	4	3	.571	3.12	37	0	0	0	27	5	52.0	39	229	21	18	1	6	1	6	28	2	55	5	1
Wilson, Jeff, H.D.*	2	0	1.000	5.23	12	0	0	0	4	0	20.2	28	96	14	12	1	1	0	0	8	0	18	0	0
Witte, Dominic, R.C.	0	0	.000	4.91	7	0	0	0	6	2	11.0	14	47	6	6	0	0	0	1	6	1	6	1	0
Wolff, Mike, Mod.*	0	0	.000	36.00	1	0	0	0	1	0	1.0	4	8	4	4	0	0	0	0	1	0	1	0	0
Wooten, Greg, Lan.	2	2	.500	7.18	6	6	0	0	0	0	31.1	43	144	26	25	5	0	2	1	12	0	22	2	0
Workman, Widd, R.C.-S.B.	8	9	.471	5.02	21	21	0	0	0	0	113.0	119	521	91	63	7	4	8	8	54	0	72	10	1
Zamora, Pete, S.B.*	4	1	.800	2.09	25	5	0	0	15	6	81.2	43	321	21	19	1	5	1	4	33	0	77	3	2
Zapata, Juan, Stoc.	1	3	.250	6.69	25	0	0	0	10	3	35.0	41	178	34	26	4	1	0	5	26	2	46	3	1
Zerbe, Chad, S.J.*	2	0	1.000	3.35	23	0	0	0	12	1	37.2	37	159	16	14	3	0	1	3	12	0	28	1	0
Zimmerman, Jordan, Lan.*	0	1	.000	4.86	3	3	0	0	0	0	16.2	21	74	9	9	2	0	0	0	8	0	8	1	0

COMBINATION SHUTOUTS: **Bakersfield (3)**—Verdugo-Travis, Macey-Riley-Ramirez, Taulbee-Riley. **High Desert (7)**—Penny-Lisio-Verplancke-Sanchez, Patterson-Jacobs, Knott-Oleksik, Randolph-Grieve, Penny-Jacob-Oleksik, Penny-Oleksik-Peters, Penny-Grieve. **Lake Elsinore (3)**—Leyva-Greene, Volkman-Cowsill-Bane-Donaldson, Donaldson-Deakman-Johnson. **Lancaster (7)**—Stark-Koehler-Scheffer-Westfall, Bond-Fitzgerald-Kennison, Dunham-Westfall, Dunham-Gulin-Westfall, Fuentes-Fitzgerald-Scheffer, Bond-Newton-Janicki, Fuentes-Westfall. **Modesto (9)**—Hudson-Gregg, Gregg-Hudson, Gregg-Wallace, Hudson-Gregg-Waites, Manwiller-Anderson, Gregg-Kimball, Vizcaino-Paulino, Leyva-Paulino, Anderson-McCall-Kimball. **Rancho Cucamonga (6)**—Carmody-Doughty, Walker-Dodd, Agosto-Iddon, Walker-Szymborski, Workman-White, Walker-Maurer-Torres. **San Bernardino (8)**—Flores-Stover-McDonald-Montgomery, Prokopek-McDonald-Montgomery-Husted, Flores-Montgomery, Prokopek-Zamora, Prokopec-Husted-Montgomery, Prokopek-Hall-Montgomery, Regalado-Bell-Montgomery, Avery-Flores. **San Jose (9)**—Bermudez-Tucker, Grote-Crabtree-Stoops, Nathan-Keith, Andra-Crabtree, Bump-Malloy-Keith, Nathan-Zerbe-Stoops, Knoll-Keith-Kiyono-Stoops, Nathan-Malerich-Stoops, Kiyono-Malerich. **Stockton (5)**—Garcia-Levrault-Paredes, Dawsey-O'Reilly-Loiz, Levrault-Lee, O'Reilly-Akin-Zapata, Garcia-Hardwick-Helmer. **Visalia (5)**—Harville-O'Dell, Dubose-Della Ratta, Jensen-Holmes, Nina-Abbott, Niles-Della Ratta.
NO-HIT GAMES: None.

PITCHERS WITH TWO OR MORE TEAMS

Pitcher, Team	W	L	Pct.	ERA	G	GS	CG	ShO	GF	Sv.	IP	H	TBF	R	ER	HR	SH	SF	HB	BB	IBB	SO	WP	Bk.
Malerich, William, Bak.*	1	1	.500	4.71	26	0	0	0	5	1	42.0	36	184	22	22	3	2	1	7	25	1	35	4	0
Malerich, William, S.J.*	2	2	.500	2.23	20	0	0	0	10	2	32.1	28	140	14	8	1	2	2	4	14	1	24	0	0
Verdugo, Jason, Bak.	6	6	.500	3.25	28	11	0	0	17	3	80.1	79	329	35	29	4	1	3	2	15	0	59	0	0
Verdugo, Jason, S.J.	0	0	.000	0.00	1	0	0	0	1	0	1.0	2	5	0	0	0	0	0	0	0	0	1	0	0
Workman, Widd, R.C.	8	8	.500	4.67	20	20	0	0	0	0	108.0	109	494	84	56	7	4	7	8	52	0	71	10	1
Workman, Widd, S.B.	0	1	.000	12.60	1	1	0	0	0	0	5.0	10	27	7	7	0	0	1	0	2	0	1	0	0

1998 FIELDING

TEAM

Team	Pct.	G	PO	A	E	TC	DP	PB	Team	Pct.	G	PO	A	E	TC	DP	PB
San Jose	.974	140	3677	1627	141	5445	113	18	Visalia	.959	140	3677	1583	225	5485	133	27
Lancaster	.967	140	3691	1513	175	5379	108	13	High Desert	.958	140	3707	1558	229	5494	118	32
Lake Elsinore......	.966	140	3690	1617	186	5493	139	48	Modesto...........	.958	140	3687	1524	227	5438	117	33
R. Cucamonga ..	.965	140	3693	1535	187	5415	113	14	Bakersfield	.955	140	3687	1512	247	5446	132	34
San Bernardino .	.964	140	3708	1461	192	5361	121	33	TRIPLE PLAYS: Lake Elsinore, Rancho Cucamonga.								
Stockton...........	.961	140	3656	1382	202	5240	113	23									

INDIVIDUAL

FIRST BASEMEN

NOTE: All caps denotes fielding-percentage leader based on 70 games for catchers, 93 for all other non-pitchers and 140 innings for pitchers. *Throws lefthanded.

Player, Team	Pct.	G	PO	A	E	TC	DP
Allison, Brad, H.D.	1.000	1	6	0	0	6	0
Baeza, Art, Bak.	.992	64	578	66	5	649	65
Barnes, Larry, L.E.*	.987	50	451	17	6	474	40
Bramlett, Jeff, S.B.	.993	20	136	7	1	144	9
Clark, Kevin, H.D.	.978	95	807	70	20	897	62
Connors, Greg, Lan.	.959	7	67	3	3	73	5

Player, Team	Pct.	G	PO	A	E	TC	DP
Cruz, Cirilo, Lan.	.991	87	724	42	7	773	54
Davis, Monty, Mod.	1.000	2	2	0	0	2	0
Dean, Aaron, S.B.*	.985	11	64	1	1	66	5
Dean, Chris, Lan.	1.000	3	7	2	0	9	0
Delgado, Reymundo, Bak.*	1.000	3	21	4	0	25	1
Farris, Ed, Vis.	.875	3	21	0	3	24	2
Filchner, Duane, Vis.*	1.000	1	7	0	0	7	1
Flaherty, Tim, Bak.	.959	18	156	7	7	170	10
Greene, Todd, L.E.	.833	2	9	1	2	12	2
Gulseth, Mark, S.J.	.989	71	684	42	8	734	54

Player, Team	Pct.	G	PO	A	E	TC	DP
Hagins, Steve, L.E.	.818	1	9	0	2	11	1
Johnson, A.J., R.C.	1.000	2	14	0	0	14	1
Karros, Eric, S.B.	1.000	4	32	2	0	34	4
Kent, Robbie, R.C.	1.000	7	36	3	0	39	1
Kingman, Brendan, Lan.	.991	53	399	31	4	434	38
Leach, Nick, S.B.	.982	117	940	83	19	1042	89
Macalutas, Jon, Stoc.	.984	116	889	55	15	959	74
Martinez, Hipolito, Mod.	1.000	3	0	1	0	1	0
Martinez, Tony, H.D.	.857	1	6	0	1	7	0
McKay, Cody, Mod.	1.000	2	13	0	0	13	1
Mensik, Todd, Mod.*	.966	71	498	49	19	566	41
Minor, Damon, S.J.*	.987	44	413	36	6	455	29
Morris, Greg, L.E.	1.000	3	27	1	0	28	0
PACIOREK, Pete, R.C.*	.991	137	1198	78	12	1288	97
Patterson, Jarrod, H.D.	.992	42	342	28	3	373	39
Phair, Kelly, Stoc.	1.000	1	4	1	0	5	0
Ramirez, Joel, Lan.	1.000	1	3	0	0	3	0
Reeder, Cory, Stoc.	1.000	7	31	3	0	34	6
Rodriguez, Juan, L.E.	.964	6	24	3	1	28	2
Romano, Scott, Mod.	1.000	2	3	0	0	3	0
Rosario, Omar, Vis.*	.900	5	9	0	1	10	1
Russin, Tom, Vis.	.978	65	460	32	11	503	33
Sachse, Matt, Lan.*	1.000	1	3	0	0	3	0
Simonton, Benji, S.J.	.985	26	252	15	4	271	21
Slemmer, Dave, Vis.	.989	11	80	6	1	87	8
Sosa, Nicolas, Vis.	.984	82	680	57	12	749	76
Stewart, Paxton, L.E.	.988	15	82	3	1	86	11
Sweeney, Kevin, H.D.*	1.000	4	25	3	0	28	2
Tyler, Josh, Bak.	1.000	1	1	0	0	1	0
Valenti, Jon, Bak.	.980	23	186	14	4	204	17
Walther, Chris, Stoc.	.977	26	195	20	5	220	16
Wells, Zach, Bak.	.983	35	261	26	5	292	24
Wilson, Keith, H.D.	1.000	3	17	2	0	19	1
Wilson, Steve, S.B.	1.000	1	2	0	0	2	1
Wolff, Mike, Mod.*	.990	85	647	55	7	709	61
Wooten, Shawn, L.E.	.999	78	726	52	1	779	66

TRIPLE PLAYS: Barnes, Paciorek.

SECOND BASEMEN

Player, Team	Pct.	G	PO	A	E	TC	DP
Alguacil, Jose, Bak.	.958	54	100	129	10	239	34
Bautista, Juan, H.D.	.923	3	5	7	1	13	3
Bearden, Doug, Stoc.	.948	12	23	32	3	58	9
Castro, Jose, Mod.	.976	31	62	62	3	127	13
Cesar, Dionys, Vis.	.941	22	33	63	6	102	13
Cosme, Caonabo, Mod.	.953	62	138	169	15	322	39
Cromer, Tripp, S.B.	1.000	3	2	8	0	10	0
Cuntz, Casey, H.D.	1.000	3	4	9	0	13	2
DAVALILLO, David, L.E.	.976	124	240	380	15	635	77
Davis, Monty, Mod.	.968	34	73	77	5	155	15
Dean, Chris, Lan.	.982	43	61	100	3	164	20
Diaz, Freddie, L.E.	1.000	13	24	30	0	54	9
Fuentes, Joel, S.J.-Bak.	.942	27	64	66	8	138	12
Gallo, Ismael, S.B.	1.000	5	8	14	0	22	6
Goudie, Jaime, S.B.	.960	48	92	126	9	227	25
Guerrero, Sergio, Stoc.	.944	36	62	90	9	161	16
Guevara, Giomar, Lan.	.966	14	19	37	2	58	6
Harrison, Adonis, Lan.	.960	67	137	172	13	322	43
Jenkins, Dee, Stoc.-Vis.	.963	113	220	299	20	539	79
Kent, Robbie, R.C.	.944	6	9	8	1	18	2
Lara, Eddie, Vis.	.959	12	19	28	2	49	5
Martin, Jared, H.D.	.883	17	33	50	11	94	12
Mathis, Jared, Stoc.	.987	22	37	37	1	75	7
McClure, Brian, R.C.	.969	125	249	307	18	574	77
Morillo, Cesar, Bak.	1.000	1	2	5	0	7	0
Morimoto, Ken, S.B.	.937	38	79	85	11	175	19
Otero, William, Bak.	.938	26	59	63	8	130	21
Patterson, Jarrod, H.D.	1.000	1	2	0	0	2	0
Pernalete, Marco, Bak.	.943	26	40	42	5	87	11
Phair, Kelly, Stoc.	.969	41	63	94	5	162	17
Piatt, Adam, Mod.	1.000	2	0	2	0	2	0
Prospero, Ted, Bak.	.951	26	59	57	6	122	12
Ramirez, Joel, Lan.	.974	30	47	65	3	115	11
Regan, Jason, Lan.	.750	2	3	0	1	4	0
Rexrode, Jackie, H.D.	.935	42	98	118	15	231	24
Reynoso, Ben, R.C.	.933	11	10	18	2	30	3
Rodriguez, Juan, L.E.	1.000	2	2	3	0	5	0
Romano, Scott, Mod.	.930	22	38	55	7	100	11
Saitta, Rich, S.B.	.975	57	109	128	6	243	29
Slemmer, Dave, Vis.	.982	47	102	119	4	225	22
Spivey, Junior, H.D.	.947	75	144	210	20	374	47
Thrower, Jake, R.C.	.951	8	13	26	2	41	5

Player, Team	Pct.	G	PO	A	E	TC	DP
Tyler, Josh, S.J.-Bak.	1.000	6	8	14	0	22	3
Valenti, Jon, Bak.	1.000	1	1	3	0	4	0
Vallone, Gar, L.E.	1.000	1	2	3	0	5	0
Velarde, Randy, L.E.	.966	5	10	18	1	29	3
Wooten, Shawn, L.E.	1.000	1	2	6	0	8	4
Young, Travis, S.J.	.974	133	228	404	17	649	80

TRIPLE PLAY: McClure.

SECOND BASEMEN WITH TWO OR MORE TEAMS

Player, Team	Pct.	G	PO	A	E	TC	DP
Fuentes, Joel, S.J.	1.000	6	9	17	0	26	2
Fuentes, Joel, Bak.	.929	21	55	49	8	112	10
Jenkins, Dee, Stoc.	.954	48	81	105	9	195	25
Jenkins, Dee, Vis.	.968	65	139	194	11	344	54
Tyler, Josh, S.J.	1.000	2	3	5	0	8	1
Tyler, Josh, Bak.	1.000	4	5	9	0	14	2

THIRD BASEMEN

Player, Team	Pct.	G	PO	A	E	TC	DP
Alguacil, Jose, Bak.	.500	2	0	2	2	4	0
Bearden, Doug, Stoc.	.946	16	13	22	2	37	1
Bell, Ricky, S.B.	.928	133	76	270	27	373	22
Cesar, Dionys, Vis.	.859	69	38	121	26	185	13
Clark, Kevin, H.D.	.750	1	1	2	1	4	0
Connors, Greg, Lan.	1.000	2	0	8	0	8	0
Cuntz, Casey, H.D.	.875	29	9	47	8	64	4
Davis, Monty, Mod.	.700	4	2	5	3	10	1
Diaz, Freddie, L.E.	.939	51	40	130	11	181	19
Dunn, Nathan, R.C.	.836	36	18	79	19	116	8
Flores, Javier, Vis.	.778	14	7	21	8	36	1
Gillespie, Eric, L.E.	.800	11	6	30	9	45	1
Guerrero, Sergio, Stoc.	.500	3	1	0	1	2	0
Guevara, Giomar, Lan.	1.000	2	0	3	0	3	1
Gulseth, Mark, S.J.	1.000	1	1	1	0	2	0
Kane, Ryan, L.E.	.944	44	34	84	7	125	11
Kent, Robbie, R.C.	.933	93	66	156	16	238	12
Kingman, Brendan, Lan.	.923	24	13	59	6	78	9
Klimek, Josh, Stoc.	.898	85	55	129	21	205	11
Lara, Eddie, Vis.	.945	54	21	150	10	181	16
Luderer, Brian, Mod.	.667	1	1	1	1	3	0
Martin, Jared, H.D.	.962	19	8	43	2	53	7
Martinez, Tony, H.D.	1.000	3	3	4	0	7	0
McKay, Cody, Mod.	.857	16	6	18	4	28	2
Morillo, Cesar, Bak.	.824	6	5	9	3	17	0
Morris, Greg, L.E.	.908	39	28	91	12	131	7
Otero, William, Bak.	.727	4	1	7	3	11	2
Patterson, Jarrod, H.D.	.900	81	48	140	21	209	8
Phair, Kelly, Stoc.	1.000	8	7	13	0	20	1
Piatt, Adam, Mod.	.891	125	64	198	32	294	14
Prospero, Ted, Bak.	.814	17	12	23	8	43	2
Ramirez, Joel, Lan.	1.000	2	1	2	0	3	0
Ramirez, Peto, Bak.	.800	3	5	3	2	10	1
Reeder, Cory, Stoc.	.000	1	0	0	1	1	0
Regan, Jason, Lan.	.938	116	74	241	21	336	15
Rexrode, Jackie, H.D.	.842	11	8	24	6	38	2
Reynoso, Ben, R.C.	.923	13	1	11	1	13	0
Romano, Scott, Mod.	.909	5	4	6	1	11	1
Russin, Tom, Vis.	.722	8	1	12	5	18	2
Saitta, Rich, S.B.	.947	8	4	14	1	19	0
Slemmer, Dave, Vis.	1.000	10	3	16	0	19	1
Spivey, Junior, H.D.	1.000	2	1	6	0	7	0
Thrower, Jake, R.C.	.920	11	5	18	2	25	0
Tommasini, Kevin, S.J.	.875	3	1	6	1	8	0
Tyler, Josh, S.J.-Bak.	.946	83	70	177	14	261	13
Valenti, Jon, Bak.	.910	70	58	145	20	223	16
Vallone, Gar, L.E.	1.000	1	0	2	0	2	0
Walther, Chris, Stoc.	.877	43	38	69	15	122	7
Wooten, Shawn, L.E.	.750	5	1	5	2	8	0
ZUNIGA, Tony, H.D.	.942	104	51	210	16	277	15

THIRD BASEMEN WITH TWO OR MORE TEAMS

Player, Team	Pct.	G	PO	A	E	TC	DP
Tyler, Josh, S.J.	.957	35	26	84	5	115	6
Tyler, Josh, Bak.	.938	48	44	93	9	146	7

SHORTSTOPS

Player, Team	Pct.	G	PO	A	E	TC	DP
Alguacil, Jose, Bak.	.957	4	10	12	1	23	1
Bautista, Juan, H.D.	1.000	3	7	7	0	14	3
Bearden, Doug, Stoc.	.915	91	131	191	30	352	40
Campusano, Carlos, S.J.	.947	33	30	114	8	152	20
Carmona, Cesarin, R.C.	.919	102	127	336	41	504	53

Player, Team	Pct.	G	PO	A	E	TC	DP
Castro, Jose, Mod.	.908	29	36	82	12	130	16
Castro, Nelson, L.E.	.942	131	185	372	34	591	71
Cesar, Dionys, Vis.	.864	12	16	22	6	44	7
Cosme, Caonabo, Mod.	.908	62	87	149	24	260	31
Cuntz, Casey, H.D.	.961	15	25	48	3	76	11
Davalillo, David, L.E.	1.000	2	1	3	0	4	0
Diaz, Freddie, L.E.	.966	13	17	39	2	58	11
Fuentes, Joel, S.J.	1.000	1	3	1	0	4	0
Gallo, Ismael, S.B.	.922	61	69	179	21	269	32
Guevara, Giomar, Lan.	1.000	4	9	18	0	27	3
Illig, Brett, S.B.	.888	41	51	92	18	161	18
Kent, Robbie, R.C.	.926	6	8	17	2	27	2
Klimek, Josh, Stoc.	.882	20	28	54	11	93	13
Lara, Eddie, Vis.	.976	54	87	156	6	249	35
Martin, Jared, H.D.	.956	13	14	29	2	45	3
Mathis, Jared, Stoc.	.913	15	13	29	4	46	5
Matos, Julius, H.D.	.941	110	185	342	33	560	66
MENDOZA, Carlos, S.J.	.951	110	169	369	28	566	64
Miller, Kevin, Mod.	.959	37	54	135	8	197	26
Morillo, Cesar, Bak.	1.000	3	0	6	0	6	0
Otero, William, Bak.	.918	43	54	115	15	184	17
Pecci, Jay, Mod.	.950	21	39	75	6	120	17
Pernalete, Marco, Bak.	.912	40	54	101	15	170	16
Phair, Kelly, Stoc.	.974	30	42	71	3	116	12
Piatt, Adam, Mod.	1.000	3	3	5	0	8	0
Ramirez, Joel, Lan.	.883	17	26	42	9	77	9
Reynoso, Ben, R.C.	.948	40	62	101	9	172	25
Robinson, Adam, Vis.	.934	81	103	265	26	394	42
Saitta, Rich, S.B.	.929	46	84	140	17	241	29
Soriano, Fred, Bak.	.940	72	99	212	20	331	47
Spivey, Junior, H.D.	1.000	2	2	8	0	10	1
Thrower, Jake, R.C.	1.000	3	4	10	0	14	0
Vazquez, Ramon, Lan.	.944	121	150	368	31	549	57
Zuniga, Tony, S.J.	1.000	2	2	7	0	9	2

TRIPLE PLAY: N. Castro.

OUTFIELDERS

Player, Team	Pct.	G	PO	A	E	TC	DP
Adams, John, H.D.	.921	31	57	1	5	63	0
Alguacil, Jose, Bak.	1.000	2	1	0	0	1	0
Allen, Luke, S.B.	.971	105	190	8	6	204	1
Auterson, Jeff, S.B.	.959	51	68	2	3	73	0
Bass, Jayson, Lan.*	.944	74	95	7	6	108	2
Bramlett, Jeff, S.B.	1.000	14	20	0	0	20	0
Brown, Eric, Bak.	.000	1	0	0	1	1	0
Burrows, Mike, Lan.*	1.000	25	36	3	0	39	0
Byas, Michael, S.J.	.983	134	228	9	4	241	2
Byrnes, Eric, Vis.	.952	29	56	4	3	63	0
Calloway, Ron, H.D.*	.946	43	68	2	4	74	0
Camilo, Juan, Vis.	.930	82	103	4	8	115	1
Casper, Brett, Bak.	.941	72	107	5	7	119	1
Cesar, Dionys, Vis.	.941	28	29	3	2	34	0
Clifton, Rodney, Mod.	.960	109	184	9	8	201	2
Colangelo, Mike, L.E.	1.000	35	78	3	0	81	0
Colon, Jose, Stoc.	.976	45	78	3	2	83	1
Connors, Greg, Lan.	.333	5	1	0	2	3	0
Crosby, Bubba, S.B.*	.990	54	101	2	1	104	0
DaVanon, Jeff, Mod.	.902	73	112	7	13	132	1
Delgado, Reymundo, Bak.*	.950	12	17	2	1	20	1
Denbow, Don, Bak.	.959	25	44	3	2	49	1
Dewey, Jason, L.E.	1.000	1	1	0	0	1	0
Dilone, Juan, S.J.	.955	63	78	6	4	88	0
Dunn, Nathan, R.C.	1.000	2	4	0	0	4	0
Dunn, Todd, Stoc.	.500	2	1	0	1	2	0
Elliott, David, Stoc.	.958	94	149	9	7	165	0
Espino, Fernando, Lan.	.923	15	24	0	2	26	0
Faircloth, Chad, Bak.-S.J.	.947	90	155	6	9	170	2
Filchner, Duane, Vis.*	.975	45	37	2	1	40	0
Flaherty, Tim, Bak.	1.000	1	1	0	0	1	0
French, Anton, Lan.	.945	91	172	0	10	182	0
Fuentes, Joel, Lan.	1.000	1	1	0	0	1	0
Gann, Jamie, H.D.	.959	59	110	7	5	122	2
Garcia, Juan, H.D.	.938	8	15	0	1	16	0
Geronimo, Cesar, L.E.	.943	81	129	3	8	140	1
Gillespie, Eric, L.E.	1.000	6	10	0	0	10	0
Glendenning, Mike, S.J.	.959	48	66	4	3	73	0
Green, Chad, Stoc.	1.000	40	61	6	0	67	1
Greene, Clay, Bak.	.943	46	81	1	5	87	0
Guiel, Jeff, L.E.	.963	94	143	11	6	160	1
Ham, Kevin, L.E.	.941	103	173	19	12	204	4
Haynes, Larry, Lan.	1.000	4	4	0	0	4	0
Haynes, Nathan, Mod.*	.939	123	211	5	14	230	1

Player, Team	Pct.	G	PO	A	E	TC	DP
Hudson, Bert, H.D.	.917	35	43	1	4	48	0
Itzoe, Josh, R.C.	.949	29	36	1	2	39	0
Johnson, A.J., R.C.	.961	130	254	14	11	279	4
Jones, Tim, Mod.	.926	46	70	5	6	81	0
Joseph, Terry, R.C.	.958	13	23	0	1	24	0
KENNEDY, Gus, R.C.	.991	110	207	4	2	213	0
Kent, Robbie, R.C.	1.000	1	1	0	0	1	0
Kingman, Brendan, Lan.	1.000	15	17	0	0	17	0
Koerner, Mike, Vis.*	.989	108	163	11	2	176	1
Lindsey, Shawn, Bak.*	1.000	6	6	0	0	6	0
Maddox, Garry, H.D.	1.000	2	6	0	0	6	0
Magruder, Christopher, Bak.	1.000	22	48	2	0	50	0
Martinez, Hipolito, Mod.	.963	94	144	13	6	163	2
Mathis, Jared, Stoc.	1.000	24	17	1	0	18	0
McKinley, Dan, Bak.	.986	94	209	10	3	222	3
Melendez, Angel, Bak.-S.J.	.968	47	57	4	2	63	0
Moore, Mike, Lan.	1.000	16	21	0	0	21	0
Moreta, Ramon, S.B.	.962	132	313	16	13	342	3
Morris, Greg, L.E.	1.000	18	34	2	0	36	0
Mota, Pedro, S.J.-Bak.*	.977	29	39	4	1	44	0
Murphy, Nate, L.E.*	.982	26	50	4	1	55	0
Neubart, Adam, H.D.	.955	39	59	4	3	66	0
Patterson, Jarrod, H.D.	1.000	7	8	2	0	10	0
Pernell, Brandon, R.C.	.975	40	74	5	2	81	2
Phoenix, Wynter, S.B.*	.947	81	102	5	6	113	1
Ramirez, Peto, Bak.	.833	4	5	0	1	6	0
Rodriguez, Juan, L.E.	.954	55	79	4	4	87	2
Rodriguez, Miguel, Stoc.	.912	44	49	3	5	57	0
Rodriguez, Miguel, H.D.	.957	15	21	1	1	23	0
Rosario, Omar, Vis.*	.877	71	90	3	13	106	0
Russin, Tom, Vis.	.932	37	52	3	4	59	0
Sachse, Matt, Lan.*	.979	78	136	6	3	145	1
Saitta, Rich, S.B.	1.000	8	9	2	0	11	0
Sandoval, Jhensy, H.D.	.950	106	177	13	10	200	1
Schaub, Greg, Stoc.	.970	134	213	16	7	236	3
Seal, Scott, R.C.*	.963	117	166	16	7	189	0
Simonton, Benji, S.J.	.915	44	52	2	5	59	0
Skeels, David, Vis.	1.000	1	2	0	0	2	0
Smith, Scott, Bak.	.937	39	68	6	5	79	0
Soriano, Jose, Vis.	.974	78	138	9	4	151	3
Stewart, Paxton, L.E.	1.000	34	47	2	0	49	0
Sturdivant, Marcus, Lan.*	.981	27	51	1	1	53	0
Sweeney, Kevin, H.D.*	.974	54	69	5	2	76	0
Sykes, Jamie, H.D.	.966	35	50	6	2	58	1
Tinoco, Luis, Lan.	.910	96	132	10	14	156	0
Tommasini, Kevin, Bak.-S.J.	.921	25	34	1	3	38	0
Tyler, Josh, S.J.	.955	14	20	1	1	22	0
Valenti, Jon, Bak.	.923	9	11	1	1	13	0
Van Rossum, Chris, S.J.*	.979	57	87	6	2	95	1
Walther, Chris, Stoc.	1.000	55	81	7	0	88	2
Washam, Jason, Stoc.	.957	45	43	2	2	47	0
Wells, Zach, Bak.	1.000	2	1	0	0	1	0

TRIPLE PLAY: Seal.

OUTFIELDERS WITH TWO OR MORE TEAMS

Player, Team	Pct.	G	PO	A	E	TC	DP
Faircloth, Chad, Bak.	.941	72	122	6	8	136	2
Faircloth, Chad, S.J.	.971	18	33	0	1	34	0
Melendez, Angel, Bak.	1.000	12	17	1	0	18	0
Melendez, Angel, S.J.	.956	35	40	3	2	45	0
Mota, Pedro, S.J.*	.957	15	19	3	1	23	0
Mota, Pedro, Bak.*	1.000	14	20	1	0	21	0
Tommasini, Kevin, Bak.	.943	22	32	1	2	35	0
Tommasini, Kevin, S.J.	.667	3	2	0	1	3	0

CATCHERS

Player, Team	Pct.	G	PO	A	E	TC	DP	PB
Alfano, Jeff, Stoc.	.978	106	872	107	22	1001	7	18
Allison, Brad, H.D.	.996	20	200	22	1	223	1	2
Barajas, Rod, H.D.	.983	95	749	85	14	848	6	21
Bertrand, Ben, S.J.	1.000	13	77	10	0	87	1	7
Blanco, Henry, S.B.	1.000	4	17	3	0	20	0	0
Briones, Chris, R.C.	.992	20	105	13	1	119	3	2
Cancel, Robinson, Stoc.	.988	10	67	16	1	84	1	2
CHIARAMONTE, Giuseppe, S.J.	.990	105	826	71	9	906	5	11
Clark, Kevin, H.D.	.978	14	77	11	2	90	0	2
Connors, Greg, Lan.	.986	10	65	6	1	72	1	0
Darula, Bobby, Stoc.	1.000	1	1	0	0	1	0	0
Davis, Josh, Mod.	.987	50	267	42	4	313	1	10
Deboer, Rob, Vis.	.979	64	466	36	11	513	4	17
Dewey, Jason, L.E.	.981	83	598	62	13	673	2	30
Flaherty, Tim, Bak.	.984	79	492	51	9	552	7	15

Player, Team	Pct.	G	PO	A	E	TC	DP	PB
Flores, Javier, Vis.	.973	28	191	28	6	225	2	5
Gillespie, Eric, L.E.	1.000	1	2	0	0	2	0	0
Gonzalez, Wikleman, R.C.	.993	43	346	56	3	405	3	9
Graves, Bryan, L.E.	1.000	8	43	10	0	53	1	1
Hagins, Steve, L.E.	.968	51	287	46	11	344	3	17
Johnson, Patrick, L.E.	1.000	3	13	1	0	14	0	0
Kingman, Brendan, Lan.	1.000	10	83	10	0	93	0	0
Lopez, Jose, H.D.	.986	8	65	7	1	73	1	2
Loyd, Brian, R.C.	.977	72	495	50	13	558	2	1
Luderer, Brian, Mod.	.989	17	83	10	1	94	0	6
Mathis, Jared, Stoc.	.978	11	80	7	2	89	3	0
Mayes, Craig, S.J.	1.000	3	17	2	0	19	0	0
McAffee, Josh, H.D.	1.000	3	19	2	0	21	0	1
McCrotty, Will, S.B.	.985	102	772	84	13	869	5	27
McKay, Cody, Mod.	.990	93	761	92	9	862	8	17
Monzon, Jose, L.E.	1.000	2	15	4	0	19	1	0
Myers, Greg, R.C.	1.000	2	8	0	0	8	0	1
Poor, Jeff, Bak.	.983	19	105	11	2	118	0	2
Priess, Matthew, Bak.	.969	43	315	33	11	359	4	9
Ramirez, Peto, Bak.	.889	5	23	1	3	27	0	4
Reeder, Cory, Stoc.	.989	24	159	23	2	184	3	3
Rodriguez, Guillermo, S.J.	1.000	1	1	0	0	1	0	0
Rodriguez, Miguel, Stoc.	1.000	1	4	0	0	4	0	0
Sanchez, Marcos, R.C.	.959	21	83	11	4	98	1	1
Santiesteban, Francisco, Lan.	.994	42	313	39	2	354	0	3
Skeels, David, Vis.	.981	60	435	38	9	482	1	5
Snow, Casey, S.B.	.983	33	216	13	4	233	2	4
Thompson, Karl, Lan.	.987	90	719	63	10	792	6	10
Tommasini, Kevin, Bak.-S.J.	1.000	7	13	1	0	14	0	3
Torrealba, Yorvit, S.J.	.989	19	171	16	2	189	0	0
Tyler, Josh, Bak.	.857	3	9	3	2	14	1	1
Wilson, Keith, H.D.	1.000	9	34	4	0	38	0	4
Wilson, Steve, S.B.	1.000	12	64	2	0	66	0	2

TRIPLE PLAY: Loyd.

CATCHERS WITH TWO OR MORE TEAMS

Player, Team	Pct.	G	PO	A	E	TC	DP	PB
Tommasini, Kevin, Bak.	1.000	6	10	1	0	11	0	3
Tommasini, Kevin, S.J.	1.000	1	3	0	0	3	0	0

PITCHERS

Player, Team	Pct.	G	PO	A	E	TC	DP
Abbott, Todd, Vis.	.944	34	3	14	1	18	0
Abreu, Oscar, Mod.	.909	34	6	4	1	11	1
Agosto, Stevenson, R.C.*	.967	23	8	21	1	30	0
Akin, Jay, Stoc.*	.933	44	1	13	1	15	2
Alejo, Nigel, Stoc.	.889	8	3	5	1	9	0
Anderson, Jason, Mod.*	.927	28	8	43	4	55	1
Andra, Jeff, S.J.*	.941	15	3	13	1	17	0
Andrews, Jeff, H.D.	1.000	6	6	1	0	7	0
Avery, Paul, S.B.*	.667	5	1	1	1	3	0
Ayala, Julio, Lan.*	.867	25	6	20	4	30	1
Bailey, Phil, Bak.*	.875	20	1	6	1	8	0
Bane, Jaymie, L.E.*	1.000	17	0	1	0	1	0
Bearden, Doug, Stoc.	1.000	1	0	1	0	1	0
Bell, Scott, S.B.	1.000	8	4	3	0	7	0
Bennett, Tom, Vis.	1.000	1	1	1	0	2	0
Bermudez, Manny, S.J.	1.000	24	16	14	0	30	3
Bierbrodt, Nick, H.D.*	.925	24	7	30	3	40	2
Blumenstock, Brad, Mod.	.833	15	3	7	2	12	0
Bond, Jason, Lan.*	.882	20	6	9	2	17	0
Bump, Nate, S.J.	1.000	11	6	6	0	12	0
Burnside, Adrian, S.B.*	.833	21	3	12	3	18	1
Carmody, Brian, R.C.*	1.000	8	0	11	0	11	1
Carmona, Rafael, Lan.	1.000	4	0	3	0	3	0
Carroll, Dave, Mod.*	.889	22	1	7	1	9	0
Cervantes, Peter, S.B.	.923	30	5	7	1	13	2
Chung, Rocky, S.B.	1.000	5	0	4	0	4	0
Cowsill, Brendon, L.E.	1.000	17	1	8	0	9	1
Crabtree, Robbie, S.J.	1.000	24	2	14	0	16	0
Crews, Jason, H.D.	.862	48	12	13	4	29	1
Crossan, Clayton, Stoc.	.800	17	2	2	1	5	1
Cummings, Ryan, L.E.	1.000	1	0	1	0	1	1
Dale, Carl, Mod.	.857	3	0	6	1	7	0
Darrell, Tommy, L.E.	.850	21	8	9	3	20	0
Davis, Allen, S.B.*	1.000	5	3	2	0	5	0
Dawsey, Jason, Stoc.*	.875	19	3	4	1	8	0
Deakman, Josh, L.E.	.750	9	1	2	1	4	0
Della Ratta, Pete, Vis.	.750	36	5	7	4	16	1
Derenches, Albert, Lan.*	1.000	9	1	2	0	3	0
Diaz, Antonio, R.C.	1.000	17	3	4	0	7	0
Dodd, Scott, R.C.*	1.000	43	3	12	0	15	0
Donaldson, Bo, L.E.	.857	54	3	9	2	14	0
Dotel, Melido, S.B.	1.000	11	1	3	0	4	0
Doughty, Brian, R.C.	1.000	16	2	8	0	10	1
Duarte, Renney, L.E.	.906	32	11	18	3	32	1
Dubose, Eric, Vis.*	.875	17	4	10	2	16	0
Dunham, Pat, Lan.	.870	17	13	7	3	23	1
Estes, Shawn, Bak.*	.000	1	0	0	1	1	0
Esteves, Jake, Bak.	.750	14	3	3	2	8	0
Estrella, Luis, S.J.	.920	36	7	16	2	25	0
Faust, Jason, Vis.*	1.000	14	0	4	0	4	0
Fischer, Mike, S.B.	.857	12	5	7	2	14	0
Fitzgerald, Brian, Lan.*	.938	41	5	10	1	16	1
Flores, Pedro, S.B.*	.947	30	3	15	1	19	2
Foran, John, R.C.	.500	12	1	1	2	4	0
Frontera, Chad, Bak.	.875	11	5	9	2	16	1
Fuentes, Brian, Lan.*	.853	24	2	27	5	34	1
Gangemi, Joseph, L.E.*	1.000	13	6	6	0	12	0
GARCIA, Jose, Stoc.	1.000	28	14	33	0	47	2
Gorrell, Chris, Vis.	.800	32	2	10	3	15	0
Greene, Danny, L.E.	1.000	11	0	1	0	1	0
Gregg, Kevin, Mod.	.972	30	12	23	1	36	1
Grieve, Tim, H.D.	.933	27	4	10	1	15	0
Grote, Jason, S.J.	.857	15	6	12	3	21	1
Gryboski, Kevin, Lan.	1.000	37	5	11	0	16	0
Gulin, Lindsay, Lan.*	.900	9	1	3	0	4	1
Gunther, Kevin, Mod.	1.000	4	2	1	0	3	1
Guzman, Domingo, R.C.	.875	4	3	4	1	8	0
Hall, Darren, S.B.	1.000	8	0	2	0	2	1
Hardwick, Bubba, Stoc.*	.900	22	2	7	1	10	0
Harriger, Mark, L.E.	.846	13	3	8	2	13	0
Harris, Pep, L.E.	1.000	4	2	0	0	2	0
Harville, Chad, Vis.	1.000	24	6	9	0	15	1
Hawkins, Al, Stoc.	1.000	9	4	8	0	12	1
Helmer, Chad, Stoc.	.750	46	1	5	2	8	0
Herndon, Harry, R.C.	1.000	6	4	4	0	8	0
Hill, Ken, L.E.	.500	1	0	1	1	2	0
Hinchliffe, Brett, Lan.	1.000	3	1	5	0	6	2
Hite, Kevin, R.C.	1.000	30	0	5	0	5	0
Hollins, Stacy, Stoc.	1.000	1	0	1	0	1	0
Holmes, Mike, Vis.	.935	31	10	19	2	31	2
Hudson, Tim, Mod.	.917	8	3	8	1	12	0
Husted, Brent, S.B.	.913	49	7	14	2	23	1
Hutchings, Mark, Bak.	1.000	6	0	2	0	2	0
Hutzler, Jeff, Bak.	.963	51	8	18	1	27	2
Iddon, Brent, R.C.	.903	32	7	21	3	31	0
Jacob, Russell, H.D.	.895	31	5	12	2	19	0
Janicki, Pete, Lan.	1.000	15	4	3	0	7	0
Jensen, Jared, Vis.	.946	31	17	18	2	37	0
Jensen, Ryan, Bak.	.828	29	6	18	5	29	0
Johnson, Eric, S.J.	1.000	5	1	0	0	1	0
Johnson, Gregory, L.E.*	1.000	37	2	16	0	18	1
Johnston, Doug, Stoc.	1.000	9	3	5	0	8	0
Jones, Marcus, Vis.	1.000	29	6	17	0	23	1
Joseph, Kevin, Bak.	1.000	6	3	3	0	6	0
Kaye, Justin, Lan.	1.000	16	2	3	0	5	0
Keith, Jeff, S.J.*	.875	23	1	6	1	8	0
Kelly, John, Lan.	.950	23	8	11	1	20	0
Kennison, Kyle, Lan.	1.000	15	0	7	0	7	1
Kimball, Andrew, Mod.	.909	42	8	12	2	22	0
Kiyono, Masashi, S.J.	.833	13	6	4	2	12	0
Knoll, Brian, S.J.	1.000	42	6	22	0	28	2
Knott, Eric, H.D.*	.958	28	5	18	1	24	0
Koehler, Russ, L.E.	1.000	10	0	2	0	2	0
Kolb, Brandon, R.C.	.500	4	1	1	2	4	0
Kramer, Matthew, S.B.	1.000	8	2	0	0	2	0
Larreal, Guillermo, Bak.	.800	9	0	4	1	5	0
Lee, Derek, Stoc.*	.971	30	10	23	1	34	1
Levrault, Allen, Stoc.	.938	16	4	11	1	16	1
Leyva, Edgar, L.E.	.960	33	9	15	1	25	2
Leyva, Julian, Mod.	.967	28	9	20	1	30	1
Lisio, Joe, H.D.	1.000	11	1	5	0	6	1
Loiz, Niuman, Stoc.	1.000	12	1	1	0	2	0
Lynch, Ryan, R.C.*	1.000	21	2	9	0	11	0
Macey, Fausto, Bak.	.913	17	5	16	2	23	1
Malerich, William, Bak.-S.J.*	.950	46	8	11	1	20	1
Malloy, Bill, S.J.	.931	41	7	20	2	29	0
Manwiller, Tim, Mod.	.968	30	9	21	1	31	0
Martines, Jason, H.D.	1.000	5	0	1	0	1	0
Maurer, Dave, R.C.*	.950	48	6	13	1	20	0
McCall, Travis, Mod.*	1.000	20	1	4	0	5	0
McDonald, Matt, S.B.*	.900	24	1	8	1	10	1
McDowell, Jack, L.E.	1.000	1	0	1	0	1	0

Player, Team	Pct.	G	PO	A	E	TC	DP
Middlebrook, Jason, R.C.	.926	28	6	19	2	27	0
Mlodik, Kevin, Vis.	1.000	4	0	2	0	2	0
Montgomery, Matt, S.B.	1.000	63	6	12	0	18	1
Morse, Paul, S.B.	.953	30	14	27	2	43	3
Moskau, Ryan, S.B.*	1.000	6	5	6	0	11	2
Nathan, Joe, S.J.	.909	22	8	12	2	22	3
Newton, Geronimo, Lan.*	.857	19	3	3	1	7	1
Nickle, Douglas, L.E.	1.000	11	4	13	0	17	0
Nielsen, Thomas, Bak.*	1.000	4	1	2	0	3	0
Niles, Randy, Vis.	.941	31	7	25	2	34	1
Nina, Elvin, Vis.	.917	30	13	20	3	36	2
Noriega, Ray, Vis.*	.950	36	5	14	1	20	1
Norris, Ben, H.D.*	.889	9	4	4	1	9	1
O'Dell, Jake, Vis.	.778	9	4	3	2	9	0
Oleksik, George, H.D.	.963	41	7	19	1	27	0
O'Reilly, John, Stoc.	1.000	32	5	13	0	18	1
Paredes, Roberto, Stoc.	.769	43	1	9	3	13	1
Passini, Brian, Stoc.*	.938	15	6	9	1	16	1
Patterson, John, H.D.	.923	25	10	14	2	26	0
Paulino, Jose, Mod.	.917	38	4	7	1	12	0
Pena, Juan, Mod.*	1.000	6	0	4	0	4	0
Penny, Brad, H.D.	.893	28	8	17	3	28	0
Perozo, Felix, L.E.	1.000	10	1	0	0	1	0
Peters, Don, H.D.	1.000	21	2	2	0	4	0
Peterson, Kyle, Stoc.	.864	17	7	12	3	22	0
Petrosian, Ara, Vis.	.600	19	1	2	2	5	0
Pineiro, Joel, Lan.	1.000	9	4	8	0	12	0
Prokopec, Luke, S.B.	1.000	20	4	12	0	16	0
Puorto, Jamie, H.D.*	1.000	1	0	1	0	1	0
Ramirez, Erasmo, Bak.*	1.000	14	1	6	0	7	0
Randolph, Steve, H.D.*	.773	17	0	17	5	22	1
Regalado, Maximo, S.B.	1.000	14	6	1	0	7	0
Rice, Nathan, Bak.*	.844	30	5	22	5	32	0
Riley, Michael, Bak.*	1.000	40	11	22	0	33	1
Robertson, Doug, Vis.	1.000	17	1	5	0	6	0
Rodriguez, Larry, H.D.	.667	6	0	4	2	6	0
Rogers, Kevin, Bak.*	1.000	12	0	5	0	5	0
Rosado, Juan, Stoc.*	1.000	21	0	3	0	3	0
Sabel, Erik, H.D.	1.000	14	1	2	0	3	0
Sanchez, Martin, H.D.	.909	35	1	9	1	11	0
Scheffer, Aaron, Lan.	.900	25	1	8	1	10	1
Schultz, Jeffrey, Mod.	.778	19	4	3	2	9	0
Skeels, David, Vis.	1.000	7	4	0	0	4	0
Smith, Cam, Lan.	1.000	9	0	1	0	1	0
Snow, Bert, Mod.	1.000	2	0	1	0	1	0
Stark, Dennis, Lan.	.778	5	1	6	2	9	0

Player, Team	Pct.	G	PO	A	E	TC	DP
Stephens, Jason, L.E.	.778	35	1	20	6	27	2
Stockstill, Jason, L.E.*	.889	25	7	17	3	27	1
Stoops, Jim, S.J.	1.000	45	2	5	0	7	0
Stover, C.D., S.B.	1.000	13	0	3	0	3	0
Sullivan, Brendan, R.C.	.917	35	2	9	1	12	1
Sweeney, Brian, Lan.	1.000	17	5	4	0	9	0
Szymborski, Tom, R.C.	.900	15	2	7	1	10	0
Taczy, Craig, S.B.*	.933	35	10	18	2	30	0
Takahashi, Kurt, Bak.	.333	5	1	0	2	3	0
Taulbee, Andy, Bak.	.929	18	7	6	1	14	1
Thompson, John, Lan.	1.000	10	4	4	0	8	0
Thurmond, Travis, Bak.	1.000	2	1	0	0	1	0
Tokarse, Brian, L.E.	.912	22	9	22	3	34	2
Torres, Luis, R.C.	1.000	42	3	11	0	14	1
Travis, Jesse, Bak.	.900	50	3	6	1	10	0
Tucker, Ben, S.J.	1.000	29	8	26	0	34	2
Urban, Jeffrey, S.J.*	1.000	4	1	1	0	2	0
Valdes, Ismael, S.B.	1.000	1	2	3	0	5	0
Valenti, Jon, Bak.	1.000	9	1	3	0	4	0
Verdugo, Jason, Bak.	.857	28	4	2	1	7	1
Verplancke, Joe, H.D.	1.000	42	7	7	0	14	0
Vizcaino, Luis, Mod.	.955	23	9	12	1	22	0
Vogelsong, Ryan, S.J.	1.000	4	0	1	0	1	0
Volkman, Keith, L.E.*	1.000	20	0	4	0	4	0
Waites, David, Mod.	1.000	22	3	4	0	7	0
Walker, Kevin, R.C.*	.969	22	9	22	1	32	3
Wallace, Flint, Mod.	1.000	32	3	10	0	13	0
Watson, Allen, L.E.*	1.000	1	0	1	0	1	0
Wells, Matt, Bak.	.889	40	5	11	2	18	0
Westfall, Allan, Lan.	1.000	37	6	11	0	17	1
Wilson, Jeff, H.D.*	.667	12	0	2	1	3	0
Witte, Dominic, R.C.	1.000	7	0	2	0	2	0
Wooten, Greg, Lan.	.833	6	1	4	1	6	0
Workman, Widd, R.C.-S.B.	.960	21	10	14	1	25	2
Zamora, Pete, S.B.*	1.000	25	5	14	0	19	2
Zapata, Juan, Stoc.	1.000	25	1	2	0	3	0
Zerbe, Chad, S.J.*	1.000	23	2	6	0	8	0
Zimmerman, Jordan, Lan.*	1.000	3	0	3	0	3	0

PITCHERS WITH TWO OR MORE TEAMS

Player, Team	Pct.	G	PO	A	E	TC	DP
Malerich, William, Bak.*	.923	26	5	7	1	13	1
Malerich, William, S.J.*	1.000	20	3	4	0	7	0
Workman, Widd, R.C.	.957	20	9	13	1	23	2
Workman, Widd, S.B.	1.000	1	1	1	0	2	0

The following players did not have any fielding statistics at the positions indicated or appeared only as a designated hitter, pinch-hitter or pinch-runner: Berry, p; Bramlett, p; Gillespie, 2b; J. Gonzalez, p; Gutierrez, p; Kent, p; Lidle, p; Luckert, p; Mateo, p; Morimoto, ss; Otero, of; Priess, of; Prospero, of; J. Rodriguez, p; Miguel A. Rodriguez, ss; Sachse, p; Tyler, of, p, ss; Verdugo, p; Webb, dh, ph; Wolff, of, p.

LEAGUE CHAMPIONS

Year	Team	Pct.	Year	Team	Pct.	Year	Team	Pct.
1914—	Fresno	.571	1960—	Reno	.614	1974—	Fresno§	.607
1915—	Modesto	.857		Reno	.657		San Jose	.579
1916-40—	Did not operate.		1961—	Reno	.743	1975—	Reno	.614
1941—	Fresno	.643		Reno	.643		Reno	.614
	Santa Barbara (2nd)*	.597	1962—	San José§	.686	1976—	Salinas	.650
1942—	Santa Barbara†	.642		Reno	.587		Reno§	.547
1943-44-45—	Did not operate.		1963—	Modesto	.589	1977—	Salinas	.564
1946—	Stockton‡	.600		Stockton§	.687		Lodi§	.579
1947—	Stockton‡	.679	1964—	Fresno	.638	1978—	Visalia§	.698
1948—	Fresno	.607		Fresno	.600		Lodi	.607
	Santa Barbara (3rd)*	.529	1965—	San Jose	.586	1979—	San Jose§	.636
1949—	Bakersfield	.612		Stockton§	.614		Reno	.525
	San Jose (4th)*	.543	1966—	Modesto	.577	1980—	Stockton§	.638
1950—	Ventura	.607		Modesto	.671		Visalia	.507
	Modesto (2nd)*	.586	1967—	San Jose§	.676	1981—	Visalia	.621
1951—	Santa Barbara‡	.599		Modesto	.586		Lodi§	.521
1952—	Fresno‡	.629	1968—	San Jose	.629	1982—	Modesto§	.671
1953—	San Jose‡	.664		Fresno§	.623		Visalia	.586
1954—	Modesto‡	.623	1969—	Stockton§	.600	1983—	Visalia	.621
1955—	Stockton	.733		Visalia	.614		Redwood§	.529
	Fresno	.718	1970—	Bakersfield	.667	1984—	Modesto§	.597
1956—	Fresno§	.650		Bakersfield	.671		Bakersfield	.486
1957—	Visalia∞	.622	1971—	Visalia§	.583	1985—	Fresno§	.575
	Salinas (4th)*	.504		Fresno	.500		Stockton	.566
1958—	Fresno*	.639	1972—	Modesto§	.547	1986—	Palm Springs	.613
	Bakersfield	.672		Bakersfield	.629		Stockton§	.585
1959—	Bakersfield	.592	1973—	Lodi§	.657	1987—	Fresno§	.559
	Modesto§	.643		Bakersfield	.571		Reno	.535

CLASS A   California League

Year	Team	Pct.	Year	Team	Pct.	Year	Team	Pct.
1988—	Stockton	.657	1992—	Stockton§	.610	1996—	San Jose	.636
	Riverside§	.599		Visalia	.551		Lake Elsinore‡	.550
1989—	Stockton	.627	1993—	High Desert§	.620	1997—	High Desert▲	.593
	Bakersfield§	.577		Modesto	.529		San Bernardino	.486
1990—	Visalia	.638	1994—	Modesto	.706	1998—	San Jose▲	.593
	Stockton§	.582		Rancho Cucamonga§	.566		Rancho Cucamonga	.550
1991—	San Jose	.676	1995—	San Bernardino§	.612			
	High Desert§	.537		San Jose	.550			

*Won four-club playoff. †League disbanded June 28. ‡Won championship and four-club playoff. §Won split-season playoff. ∞Won both halves of split season. ▲Played split season and won six-club playoff.

CAROLINA LEAGUE

LEAGUE OFFICE

President/treasurer
John Hopkins
Address
P.O. Box 9503
Greensboro, NC 27429
Phone
910-691-9030

Teams (affiliation)
Frederick Keys (Orioles)
Kinston Indians (Indians)
Lynchburg Hillcats (Pirates)
Myrtle Beach Pelicans (Atlanta)
Prince William Cannons (Cardinals)
Salem Avalanche (Rockies)

Wilmington Blue Rocks (Royals)
Winston-Salem Warthogs (White Sox)

1998 FINAL STANDINGS
FIRST HALF

NORTHERN DIVISION

Team	W	L	T	Pct.	GB
Wilmington (Royals)	40	30	0	.571	....
Lynchburg (Pirates)	36	34	0	.514	4.0
Frederick (Orioles)	35	35	0	.500	5.0
Prince William (Cardinals)	29	40	0	.420	10.5

SOUTHERN DIVISION

Team	W	L	T	Pct.	GB
Winston-Salem (White Sox)	41	28	0	.594	....
Kinston (Indians)	36	34	0	.514	5.5
Danville (Braves)	31	39	0	.443	10.5
Salem (Rockies)	31	39	0	.443	10.5

SECOND HALF

NORTHERN DIVISION

Team	W	L	T	Pct.	GB
Wilmington (Royals)	46	24	0	.657	....
Prince William (Cardinals)	43	27	0	.614	3.0
Lynchburg (Pirates)	33	37	0	.471	13.0
Frederick (Orioles)	29	41	0	.414	17.0

SOUTHERN DIVISION

Team	W	L	T	Pct.	GB
Winston-Salem (White Sox)	38	32	0	.543	....
Kinston (Indians)	33	37	0	.471	5.0
Salem (Rockies)	31	39	0	.443	7.0
Danville (Braves)	27	43	0	.386	11.0

COMPOSITE

Team	Wil.	W.S.	P.W.	Lyn.	Kin.	Fred.	Sal.	Dan.	W	L	T	Pct.	GB
Wilmington (Royals)	....	10	11	11	12	14	14	14	86	54	0	.614	....
Winston-Salem (White Sox)	10	....	12	11	10	9	12	15	79	60	0	.568	6.5
Prince William (Cardinals)	9	7	....	10	8	13	13	12	72	67	0	.518	13.5
Lynchburg (Pirates)	9	9	10	....	13	8	6	14	69	71	0	.493	17.0
Kinston (Indians)	8	10	12	7	....	12	10	10	69	71	0	.493	17.0
Frederick (Orioles)	6	11	7	12	8	....	10	10	64	76	0	.457	22.0
Salem (Rockies)	6	8	7	14	10	10	....	7	62	78	0	.443	24.0
Danville (Braves)	6	5	8	6	10	10	13	....	58	82	0	.414	28.0

Major league affiliations in parentheses.

PLAYOFFS: Wilmington defeated Winston-Salem three games to one to win league championship.

REGULAR-SEASON ATTENDANCE: Danville, 74,737; Frederick, 301,760; Kinston, 143,309; Lynchburg, 113,145; Prince William, 220,145; Salem, 189,069; Wilmington, 320,540; Winston-Salem, 159,460. Total—1,522,165. Playoffs (4 games)—5,961. All-Star Game at Wilmington, Del.—5,227.

MANAGERS: Danville, Paul Runge; Frederick, Tommy Shields; Kinston, Mako Oliveras; Lynchburg, Jeff Richardson (Through August 18) and Jeff Livesey (August 19 through end of season); Prince William, Joe Cunningham; Salem, Jay Loviglio; Wilmington, Darrell Evans (through July 16), Kevin Long (July 17 through July 23) and Brian Poldberg (July 24 through end of season); Winston-Salem, Chris Cron. Managerial records of teams with more than one manager: Lynchburg, Richardson 61-60, Livesey 8-11; Wilmington, Evans 53-38, Long 6-1, Poldberg 27-15.

ALL-STAR TEAM: 1B—Chris Heintz, Winston-Salem; 2B—(tie) Emiliano Escandon, Wilmington and Doug Livingston, Salem; 3B—Joe Crede, Winston-Salem; SS—Brent Butler, Prince William; Utility INF—Juan Sosa, Salem; OF—Cordell Farley, Prince William; Rod Bair, Salem; Luis Saturria, Prince William; Utility OF—Dan Olson, Winston-Salem; C—Blake Barthol, Salem; DH—Jose Leon, Prince William; SP—Rich Ankiel, Prince William; RP—David Riske, Kinston; Most Valuable Player—Joe Crede, Winston-Salem; Pitcher of the Year—Rick Ankiel, Prince William; Manager of the Year—Chris Cron, Winston-Salem.

1998 BATTING
TEAM

Team	Avg.	G	TPA	AB	R	H	TB	2B	3B	HR	RBI	SH	SF	HP	BB	IBB	SO	SB	CS	GDP	LOB	ShO	Slg.	OBP
Prince William..	.269	139	5163	4659	651	1255	1854	264	37	87	590	41	48	72	343	16	1126	153	101	84	898	4	.398	.326
Winston-Salem..	.267	139	5236	4645	691	1240	1919	264	47	107	620	52	47	75	417	15	1061	141	83	92	915	6	.413	.334
Lynchburg	.262	140	5187	4643	607	1216	1854	259	35	103	549	36	37	59	412	14	1107	126	70	97	941	3	.399	.328
Salem	.260	140	5169	4624	616	1202	1740	243	29	79	539	53	39	57	396	23	933	187	83	101	892	8	.376	.323
Wilmington.....	.257	140	5297	4557	618	1169	1699	258	28	72	567	69	47	81	543	27	979	171	94	120	994	7	.373	.343
Frederick	.249	140	5192	4574	586	1138	1692	221	21	97	537	59	45	62	452	18	960	151	76	95	939	12	.370	.322
Kinston...........	.227	140	5126	4462	570	1012	1578	210	31	98	512	69	29	70	496	19	1124	121	82	58	920	16	.354	.312
Danville	.227	140	5029	4595	452	1041	1505	193	26	73	407	38	27	66	303	13	1095	114	78	90	845	18	.328	.283

CLASS A *Carolina League*

INDIVIDUAL

TOP QUALIFIERS FOR BATTING CHAMPIONSHIP

Minimum 378 plate appearances. *Lefthanded batter. †Switch-hitter.

Player, Team	Avg.	G	TPA	AB	R	H	TB	2B	3B	HR	RBI	SH	SF	HP	BB	IBB	SO	SB	CS	GDP	Slg.	OBP
Crede, Joe, W.S.	.315	137	568	492	92	155	253	32	3	20	88	0	11	12	53	3	98	9	7	10	.514	.387
Bair, Rod, Sal.	.299	114	468	425	62	127	203	42	5	8	60	0	5	13	24	3	64	12	6	11	.478	.351
Walker, Morgan, Lyn.	.298	105	404	373	46	111	177	24	0	14	68	0	7	2	22	0	92	1	0	10	.475	.334
Saturria, Luis, P.W.	.294	129	506	462	70	136	215	25	9	12	73	1	7	8	28	1	104	26	15	12	.465	.341
May, Freddy, Lyn.*	.292	126	520	466	64	136	182	23	4	5	42	0	3	0	51	2	112	26	16	12	.391	.360
Leon, Jose, P.W.	.291	124	504	436	77	127	227	31	3	21	74	2	4	9	53	4	137	5	3	6	.521	.376
Farley, Cordell, P.W.	.291	134	584	546	92	159	242	28	11	11	59	4	0	7	27	1	145	50	17	4	.443	.333
Barthol, Blake, Sal.	.290	122	503	441	56	128	202	37	2	11	68	4	5	7	46	5	94	5	3	2	.458	.363
Heintz, Chris, W.S.	.289	130	556	508	66	147	200	21	4	8	79	3	9	5	31	0	87	10	8	17	.394	.331
Butler, Brent, P.W.	.286	126	532	475	63	136	200	27	2	11	76	2	7	9	39	2	74	3	4	12	.421	.347
Christensen, McKay, W.S.*	.285	95	434	361	69	103	144	17	6	4	32	4	2	11	53	1	54	20	10	3	.399	.391
Huelsmann, Mike, Kin.†	.285	114	509	425	63	121	163	19	4	5	47	6	2	6	70	5	67	21	16	3	.384	.392
Cepeda, Jose, Wil.	.281	115	453	391	46	110	143	20	5	1	38	10	5	11	36	3	55	19	3	8	.366	.354
Rodriguez, Liu, W.S.†	.279	112	491	420	62	117	156	27	3	2	43	10	7	9	45	0	40	15	10	13	.371	.356
Hogan, Todd, P.W.	.278	123	523	485	79	135	171	24	3	2	45	4	7	7	20	1	116	26	19	7	.353	.312
Sosa, Juan, Sal.	.278	133	587	529	88	147	215	20	12	8	47	7	4	4	43	1	83	64	16	12	.406	.334

DEPARTMENTAL LEADERS: G—Crede, 137; AB—C. Farley, 546; R—Crede, C. Farley, 92 each; H—C. Farley, 159; TB—Crede, 253; 2B—Bair, 42; 3B—Sosa, 12; HR—Glavine, 22; RBI—Crede, 88; SH—Taft, 17; SF—Crede, 11; HP—Pointer, 17; BB—Escandon, 74; IBB—Several players tied at 5 each; SO—Pointer, 177; SB—Sosa, 64; CS—Hallmark, Hogan, Moore, 19 each; GIDP—Heintz, 17; Slg.—Leon, .521; OBP—Huelsmann, .392.

ALL PLAYERS

*Lefthanded batter. †Switch-hitter.

Player, Team	Avg.	G	TPA	AB	R	H	TB	2B	3B	HR	RBI	SH	SF	HP	BB	IBB	SO	SB	CS	GDP	Slg.	OBP
Albert, Rashad, W.S.	.273	18	58	55	10	15	26	0	4	1	10	2	0	0	1	0	16	3	1	1	.473	.286
Alley, Chip, Fred.†	.262	112	410	340	42	89	141	23	1	9	47	5	1	4	60	2	60	0	2	5	.415	.378
Alvarez, Carlos, Kin.	.212	10	40	33	3	7	10	0	0	1	4	0	1	2	4	0	11	2	0	0	.303	.325
Amado, Jose, Wil.	.263	70	273	236	34	62	93	17	1	4	28	1	2	10	24	2	28	6	5	11	.394	.353
Ametller, Jesus, Wil.	.313	101	374	358	52	112	144	29	0	1	38	6	5	3	2	0	29	4	6	8	.402	.318
Anderson, Blake, Sal.†	.254	68	222	197	22	50	65	10	1	1	18	0	1	1	23	2	50	2	1	4	.330	.333
Anderson, Franklin, Lyn.	.083	8	13	12	1	1	2	1	0	0	1	0	0	0	1	0	3	0	0	1	.167	.154
Anthony, Brian, Sal.*	.276	123	483	442	53	122	186	19	0	15	65	3	4	5	29	4	85	7	9	10	.421	.325
Antigua, Nilson, Lyn.	.000	3	3	3	0	0	0	0	0	0	0	0	0	0	0	0	0	0	0	0	.000	.000
Asche, Mike, Lyn.	.320	29	114	103	24	33	56	8	0	5	13	0	1	0	10	0	17	9	0	1	.544	.377
Bair, Rod, Sal.	.299	114	468	425	62	127	203	42	5	8	60	0	5	13	24	3	64	12	6	11	.478	.351
Barthol, Blake, Sal.	.290	122	503	441	56	128	202	37	2	11	68	4	5	7	46	5	94	5	3	2	.458	.363
Bass, Jayson, Dan.†	.158	10	39	38	3	6	9	1	1	0	1	0	0	1	0	0	12	2	1	0	.237	.179
Beltran, Carlos, Wil.†	.276	52	220	192	32	53	82	14	0	5	32	0	1	2	25	0	39	11	7	2	.427	.364
Benefield, Brian, Kin.	.220	71	300	259	44	57	85	9	2	5	34	4	2	4	31	1	50	8	4	1	.328	.311
Benham, Jason, Fred.*	.250	4	17	16	2	4	4	0	0	0	2	0	0	0	1	0	3	1	0	0	.250	.294
Berger, Brandon, Wil.	.222	110	408	338	53	75	123	18	3	8	50	7	5	5	53	1	94	13	3	11	.364	.332
Borges, Alex, Dan.	.108	21	40	37	0	4	4	0	0	0	1	1	0	0	2	0	15	1	0	3	.108	.154
Brito, Luis, Lyn.†	.239	12	47	46	4	11	13	2	0	0	1	0	0	0	1	0	7	0	0	2	.283	.255
Britt, Bryan, P.W.	.176	86	304	284	23	50	83	6	0	9	33	1	4	2	13	1	98	1	1	6	.292	.215
Brown, Dermal, Wil.*	.258	128	503	442	64	114	178	30	2	10	58	1	0	7	53	5	115	26	10	12	.403	.347
Bruce, Robert, Kin.	.188	55	164	149	11	28	38	4	0	2	15	2	2	7	4	0	45	3	2	2	.255	.241
Bryant, Chris, Fred.	.259	135	552	483	66	125	186	22	0	13	81	1	8	8	52	3	127	11	3	14	.385	.336
Bryant, Clint, Sal.	.241	123	475	436	46	105	143	12	1	8	31	4	2	5	23	1	73	7	7	12	.328	.285
Bryant, Matt, Lyn.	.277	51	194	177	20	49	64	7	1	2	13	0	0	0	17	0	38	1	1	5	.362	.340
Burke, Mark, Dan.*	.108	13	37	37	2	4	5	1	0	0	1	0	0	0	0	0	14	1	0	1	.135	.108
Butler, Brent, P.W.	.286	126	532	475	63	136	200	27	2	11	76	2	7	9	39	2	74	3	4	12	.421	.347
Byington, Jimmie, Wil.	.337	32	103	98	13	33	42	7	1	0	6	2	1	2	10	0	20	3	4	0	.429	.405
Cameron, Ken, P.W.*	.326	42	168	138	22	45	66	12	0	3	23	2	1	3	24	0	23	8	7	1	.478	.434
Casimiro, Carlos, Fred.	.236	131	514	478	44	113	199	23	9	15	61	4	6	1	25	2	98	10	7	16	.416	.273
Cepeda, Jose, Wil.*	.281	115	453	391	46	110	143	20	5	1	38	10	5	11	36	3	55	19	3	8	.366	.354
Christensen, McKay, W.S.*	.285	95	434	361	69	103	144	17	6	4	32	4	2	11	53	1	54	20	10	3	.399	.391
Coffee, Gary, Wil.	.191	16	60	47	4	9	10	1	0	0	4	0	1	1	11	2	20	2	0	0	.213	.350
Coffie, Ivanon, Fred.*	.256	130	537	473	62	121	192	19	2	16	75	3	9	3	48	2	109	17	12	11	.406	.323
Collier, Lou, Lyn.	.167	5	21	18	4	3	5	2	0	0	0	0	0	2	0	0	2	1	0	0	.278	.286
Connacher, Kevin, W.S.	.241	80	259	212	45	51	87	9	3	7	23	9	1	3	34	1	63	15	5	1	.410	.352
Conner, Decomba, Fred.	.298	32	134	121	16	36	53	7	2	2	11	1	0	2	10	0	21	10	5	2	.438	.361
Crede, Joe, W.S.	.315	137	568	492	92	155	253	32	3	20	88	0	11	12	53	3	98	9	7	10	.514	.387
Cruz, Edgar, Kin.	.152	9	33	33	1	5	7	2	0	0	3	0	0	0	0	0	9	0	0	0	.212	.152
Daedelow, Craig, Fred.	.270	40	144	122	12	33	40	4	0	1	15	6	0	1	15	0	18	2	0	0	.328	.355
Davis, Albert, Lyn.	.000	1	1	1	0	0	0	0	0	0	0	0	0	0	0	0	0	0	0	0	.000	.000
Davison, Ashanti, Fred.	.167	9	21	18	4	3	4	1	0	0	3	0	0	2	1	0	4	0	0	0	.222	.286
DeCinces, Tim, Fred.*	.267	110	440	374	50	100	173	25	0	16	64	1	2	4	59	2	90	3	4	8	.463	.371
Deck, Billy, P.W.*	.239	118	419	355	34	85	116	13	3	4	45	5	6	13	40	3	87	5	6	8	.327	.333
Delgado, Jose, Dan.†	.241	82	331	303	26	73	94	10	1	3	18	4	2	3	19	0	45	9	7	9	.310	.291
Dellaero, Jason, W.S.†	.208	121	463	428	45	89	148	23	3	10	49	3	2	5	25	2	147	12	4	5	.346	.259
Dent, Darrell, Fred.*	.246	131	519	456	65	112	133	19	1	0	24	13	3	4	43	1	95	33	16	4	.292	.314
Diaz, Maikell, Fred.	.213	13	49	47	3	10	10	0	0	0	4	1	0	1	0	0	10	1	1	3	.213	.229
DiPace, Danny, Wil.*	.122	16	49	41	5	5	5	0	0	0	2	0	0	1	7	0	20	0	0	2	.122	.265
Dorman, John, Kin.	.208	106	376	317	46	66	94	14	4	2	22	15	2	8	34	1	76	24	9	10	.297	.299
Downs, Brian, W.S.	.259	9	29	27	3	7	16	3	0	2	8	0	0	1	0	0	9	0	0	0	.593	.310
Duverge, Salvador, Sal.	.214	5	14	14	2	3	7	1	0	1	2	0	0	0	0	0	4	0	0	0	.500	.214
Eckelman, Alex, P.W.	.292	38	100	89	15	26	35	1	1	2	9	1	1	0	9	0	14	2	2	2	.393	.354

Player, Team	Avg.	G	TPA	AB	R	H	TB	2B	3B	HR	RBI	SH	SF	HP	BB	IBB	SO	SB	CS	GDP	Slg.	OBP
Escandon, Emiliano, Wil.†	.261	116	436	353	50	92	132	23	1	5	58	1	5	3	74	5	64	5	9	10	.374	.389
Falciglia, Tony, P.W.	.000	4	7	7	0	0	0	0	0	0	0	0	0	0	0	0	1	0	0	0	.000	.000
Farley, Cordell, P.W.	.291	134	584	546	92	159	242	28	11	11	59	4	0	7	27	1	145	50	17	4	.443	.333
Felix, Hersy, Wil.	.333	3	3	3	0	1	1	0	0	0	0	0	0	0	0	0	2	0	0	0	.333	.333
Feramisco, Derek, P.W.	.297	72	282	256	39	76	111	23	3	2	30	2	2	2	20	2	78	6	3	0	.434	.350
Figueroa, Franky, Fred.	.158	4	20	19	2	3	7	1	0	1	3	0	0	1	0	0	4	0	0	0	.368	.200
Fowler, Maleke, Fred.	.186	84	235	210	25	39	46	5	1	0	8	4	0	1	20	0	40	25	6	3	.219	.260
Furniss, Eddy, Lyn.*	.193	31	128	109	7	21	34	7	0	2	11	0	1	1	17	0	38	1	0	1	.312	.305
Gambill, Chad, Sal.	.248	41	156	145	12	36	51	9	0	2	16	0	1	1	9	0	38	0	0	6	.352	.295
Garavito, Eddy, Fred.†	.211	4	20	19	4	4	7	1	1	0	2	0	0	0	1	0	5	0	1	0	.368	.250
Garcia, Luis, W.S.	.270	106	412	389	49	105	166	29	1	10	58	2	5	3	13	1	68	8	5	6	.427	.295
Garland, Tim, Fred.	.263	11	45	38	4	10	11	1	0	0	5	1	1	2	3	0	5	6	1	0	.289	.341
Glavine, Mike, Kin.*	.219	125	484	398	61	87	178	23	1	22	76	2	6	5	73	4	117	1	4	4	.447	.342
Gomez, Ramon, W.S.	.218	43	141	124	21	27	36	5	2	0	10	3	0	2	12	1	36	13	3	1	.290	.297
Gonzalez, Jose, W.S.	.267	14	32	30	3	8	10	2	0	0	5	1	0	0	1	0	8	0	2	1	.333	.290
Gonzalez, Ricky, Kin.	.181	53	168	144	13	26	38	12	0	0	5	5	1	1	17	0	27	1	5	3	.264	.270
Goodell, Steve, Dan.	.298	54	228	198	21	59	92	14	2	5	20	4	3	6	17	1	42	3	4	5	.465	.366
Gross, Rafael, Kin.	.228	43	157	145	19	33	44	8	0	1	8	0	2	3	7	0	42	7	6	1	.303	.274
Gutierrez, Rick, Kin.	.294	4	18	17	2	5	9	1	0	1	2	0	0	0	1	0	3	0	1	0	.529	.333
Haad, Yamid, Lyn.	.254	88	323	299	32	76	103	8	2	5	34	4	4	3	13	0	54	1	7	11	.344	.288
Hage, Thomas, Fred.*	.288	45	180	163	15	47	65	12	0	2	27	0	3	2	12	1	27	0	0	1	.399	.339
Hairston, Jerry, Fred.	.283	80	337	293	56	83	126	22	3	5	33	1	3	12	28	3	32	13	7	4	.430	.366
Hallmark, Pat, Wil.	.272	103	426	364	59	99	135	19	1	5	35	6	5	5	46	0	71	33	19	6	.371	.357
Hamlin, Mark, Sal.	.270	57	226	200	29	54	96	16	1	8	36	0	0	7	19	1	57	0	2	5	.480	.354
Hammond, Joey, Fred.	.300	3	13	10	3	3	4	1	0	0	2	0	0	0	3	0	2	1	0	0	.400	.462
Harriss, Robin, Kin.	.227	44	154	132	19	30	36	6	0	0	11	3	1	2	16	1	36	1	3	4	.273	.318
Haverbusch, Kevin, Lyn.	.331	49	198	181	25	60	98	12	1	8	39	0	2	6	9	0	33	4	2	5	.541	.379
Heintz, Chris, W.S.	.289	130	556	508	66	147	200	21	4	8	79	3	9	5	31	0	87	10	8	17	.394	.331
Hessman, Mike, Dan.	.200	118	483	445	47	89	170	21	0	20	63	0	2	6	30	0	172	3	3	6	.382	.259
Hogan, Todd, P.W.	.278	123	523	485	79	135	171	24	3	2	45	4	7	7	20	1	116	26	19	7	.353	.312
Huelsmann, Mike, Kin.†	.285	114	509	425	63	121	163	19	4	5	47	6	2	6	70	5	67	21	16	3	.384	.392
Hundt, Bo, Lyn.†	.179	11	44	39	2	7	7	0	0	0	2	1	1	1	2	0	9	2	2	1	.179	.233
Hutchison, Bernard, Sal.	.201	101	351	293	44	59	77	8	2	2	23	12	3	3	40	1	88	37	13	4	.263	.301
Jackson, Jeff, Lyn.	.278	28	110	97	16	27	41	8	0	2	15	2	0	3	8	1	31	3	2	2	.423	.352
Jackson, Jeremy, Sal.*	.177	41	146	124	14	22	25	3	0	0	11	4	1	2	15	0	46	4	3	0	.202	.275
Jasco, Elinton, Lyn.	.250	14	35	32	8	8	9	1	0	0	1	1	0	0	2	0	6	1	2	0	.281	.294
Jimenez, Ruben, Kin.†	.230	66	213	187	22	43	63	8	3	2	23	6	0	4	16	0	42	8	6	1	.337	.304
Katz, Jason, Dan.†	.200	6	16	15	2	3	5	0	1	0	2	0	0	0	1	0	4	0	0	1	.333	.250
Keck, Brian, Sal.	.274	85	301	263	30	72	89	8	3	1	24	11	2	1	24	0	39	10	11	8	.338	.334
Kennedy, Adam, P.W.*	.261	17	75	69	9	18	24	6	0	0	7	0	1	0	5	0	12	5	2	1	.348	.307
Kent, Troy, Kin.	.240	101	361	329	33	79	116	20	1	5	33	2	2	5	23	1	84	2	3	4	.353	.298
Klee, Chuck, W.S.	.200	28	76	65	7	13	19	4	1	0	1	3	1	0	7	0	22	0	0	4	.292	.274
Konrady, Dennis, Kin.*	.236	127	506	419	70	99	155	17	3	11	49	8	5	5	69	2	59	6	5	8	.370	.347
Lawrence, Chip, Fred.	.221	48	113	104	9	23	24	1	0	0	6	5	0	0	4	0	24	0	2	3	.231	.250
Layne, Jason, Wil.*	.272	108	418	357	54	97	171	28	8	10	71	2	5	9	45	2	108	1	0	5	.479	.363
Leon, Jose, P.W.	.291	124	504	436	77	127	227	31	3	21	74	2	4	9	53	4	137	5	3	6	.521	.376
LeCronier, Jason, Fred.*	.208	54	166	154	12	32	50	4	1	4	14	1	2	1	8	0	52	0	1	2	.325	.248
Lidle, Kevin, Sal.	.119	31	62	59	6	7	17	4	0	2	7	0	0	0	3	0	14	0	0	2	.288	.161
Livingston, Doug, Sal.	.270	131	579	514	87	139	178	31	1	2	58	7	5	3	50	0	98	27	5	12	.346	.336
Long, Garrett, Lyn.	.282	91	364	309	46	87	139	29	1	7	43	0	3	3	49	2	83	7	2	8	.450	.382
Longueira, Tony, Wil.	.152	10	38	33	5	5	6	1	0	0	3	0	0	2	3	0	3	0	0	2	.182	.263
Lorenzana, Luis, Lyn.	.237	95	334	283	27	67	84	7	2	2	24	9	2	5	35	1	62	2	2	8	.297	.329
Lunar, Fernando, Dan.	.220	91	306	286	19	63	81	9	0	3	28	2	0	12	6	0	52	1	1	8	.283	.266
Mackowiak, Rob, Lyn.*	.274	86	319	292	30	80	125	24	6	3	31	4	2	4	17	0	65	6	3	4	.428	.321
Manning, Brian, W.S.	.272	80	298	265	32	72	109	15	2	6	39	0	2	9	20	2	48	6	10	9	.411	.341
Martine, Chris, P.W.	.186	96	329	279	29	52	71	13	0	2	25	5	3	4	38	0	77	2	6	4	.254	.290
Mateo, Jose, Dan.†	.221	74	252	217	22	48	56	8	0	0	10	7	1	0	27	0	57	13	14	1	.258	.306
May, Freddy, Lyn.*	.292	126	520	466	64	136	182	23	4	5	42	0	3	0	51	2	112	26	16	12	.391	.360
McDonald, Darnell, Fred.	.222	4	21	18	3	4	9	2	0	1	2	0	0	0	3	0	6	2	0	1	.500	.333
McKinnon, Sandy, W.S.	.262	45	166	149	18	39	52	8	1	1	15	3	0	2	12	0	37	3	2	2	.349	.325
McNeal, Pepe, P.W.	.209	57	179	163	17	34	55	7	1	4	17	4	0	3	9	0	54	0	1	3	.337	.263
Mejia, Miguel, Fred.	.196	49	158	138	15	27	34	4	0	1	8	5	4	2	9	0	43	7	3	2	.246	.248
Miranda, Tony, Wil.	.277	47	169	148	16	41	62	7	1	4	21	1	2	5	13	1	28	2	1	9	.419	.351
Miyake, Chris, Lyn.	.253	120	460	411	48	104	136	20	3	2	38	10	4	3	32	3	79	5	3	9	.331	.309
Mohr, Dustan, Kin.	.242	134	543	491	60	119	217	23	9	19	65	2	2	9	39	3	146	8	4	7	.442	.309
Moore, Kenderick, Wil.	.271	121	454	387	54	105	145	17	4	5	41	6	4	12	45	0	51	22	19	6	.375	.362
Morris, Bobby, Kin.*	.262	25	78	65	11	17	27	2	1	2	14	3	1	3	6	0	12	2	1	1	.415	.347
Mortimer, Mark, Dan.	.237	98	386	338	32	80	113	11	2	6	33	0	2	5	41	4	53	0	4	12	.334	.326
Ndungidi, Ntema, Fred.*	.000	1	2	2	0	0	0	0	0	0	0	0	0	0	0	0	1	0	0	0	.000	.000
Norris, Dax, Dan.	.326	28	104	92	9	30	53	12	1	3	21	0	3	2	7	1	15	1	2	1	.576	.375
Nunez, Abraham, Lyn.†	.222	5	21	18	2	4	5	1	0	0	2	0	0	0	3	0	1	1	0	2	.278	.333
Olson, Dan, W.S.*	.260	117	457	404	73	105	202	33	5	18	68	1	4	7	41	2	152	5	6	2	.500	.336
O'Toole, Bobby, Fred.	.138	14	32	29	1	4	4	0	0	0	0	1	0	0	2	0	12	0	0	0	.138	.194
Pagan, Carlos, Wil.	.218	77	226	202	24	44	76	11	0	7	27	3	2	0	19	0	48	1	3	10	.376	.283
Paul, Josh, W.S.	.255	123	496	444	66	113	180	20	7	11	63	7	2	5	38	2	91	20	8	11	.405	.319
Paz, Richard, Fred.	.245	40	171	143	31	35	54	10	0	3	8	3	0	4	21	0	22	6	3	3	.378	.357
Pena, Alex, Lyn.	.063	5	16	16	1	1	2	1	0	0	0	0	0	0	0	0	8	0	0	0	.125	.063
Pendergrass, Tyrone, Dan.†	.276	132	574	518	74	143	198	23	10	4	35	5	1	7	43	0	91	39	18	7	.382	.339
Phillips, Paul, Wil.	.400	2	6	5	0	2	2	0	0	0	2	0	1	0	0	0	1	0	0	0	.400	.333
Pointer, Corey, Lyn.	.224	118	446	375	70	84	169	25	3	18	46	1	0	17	53	2	177	12	10	2	.451	.346
Porzio, Mike, Dan.*	.000	26	2	2	0	0	0	0	0	0	0	0	0	0	0	0	2	0	0	0	.000	.000
Radcliff, Victor, Wil.	.226	41	140	137	14	31	43	6	0	2	19	0	0	0	3	0	34	5	1	6	.314	.243
Redman, Julian, Lyn.*	.257	131	566	525	70	135	199	26	10	6	46	3	5	1	32	2	73	36	16	5	.379	.298

Player, Team	Avg.	G	TPA	AB	R	H	TB	2B	3B	HR	RBI	SH	SF	HP	BB	IBB	SO	SB	CS	GDP	Slg.	OBP
Reyes, Jose, Lyn.	.222	18	60	54	11	12	25	4	0	3	9	0	0	2	4	0	17	2	0	0	.463	.300
Richard, Chris, P.W.*	.267	8	31	30	5	8	10	2	0	0	1	0	0	0	1	0	5	1	0	2	.333	.290
Rivera, Carlos, Lyn.*	.230	29	115	113	11	26	42	4	0	4	16	0	1	1	0	0	19	0	1	3	.372	.235
Rivera, Micky, P.W.	.000	7	6	6	1	0	0	0	0	0	0	0	0	0	0	0	4	0	1	0	.000	.000
Rivera, Roberto, Fred.	.333	3	7	6	1	2	5	0	0	1	1	0	0	0	1	1	0	0	0	0	.833	.429
Robinson, Adam, Kin.	.165	24	105	91	9	15	27	3	0	3	8	2	0	1	11	0	22	4	1	2	.297	.262
Robinson, Tony, Lyn.	.083	3	14	12	3	1	1	0	0	0	0	0	0	0	2	0	4	2	0	0	.083	.214
Rocha, Juan, Wil.	.250	16	44	40	5	10	11	1	0	0	3	0	0	0	4	0	7	1	1	2	.275	.318
Rodriguez, Liu, W.S.†	.279	112	491	420	62	117	156	27	3	2	43	10	7	9	45	0	40	15	16	-13	.371	.356
Rodriquez, Gary, Kin.*	.239	45	129	109	9	26	29	3	0	0	11	4	0	1	15	0	30	3	0	1	.266	.336
Ross, Jason, Dan.	.212	115	400	378	36	80	118	14	3	6	34	2	2	3	15	0	107	11	5	5	.312	.246
Rumfield, Brock, Fred.	.000	5	12	12	0	0	0	0	0	0	0	0	0	0	0	0	4	0	0	1	.000	.000
Russell, Jake, Kin.	.128	15	40	39	1	5	10	2	0	1	1	0	0	1	0	0	13	0	0	0	.256	.150
Saturria, Luis, P.W.	.294	129	506	462	70	136	215	25	9	12	73	1	7	8	28	1	104	26	15	12	.465	.341
Scharrer, Jim, Dan.	.193	115	430	409	28	79	120	23	0	6	31	0	3	1	17	1	118	1	5	9	.293	.226
Schmack, Brian, W.S.	.000	42	1	1	0	0	0	0	0	0	0	0	0	0	0	0	1	0	0	0	.000	.000
Sheppard, Greg, W.S.	.265	89	293	260	29	69	105	13	1	7	27	1	1	1	30	0	82	2	2	6	.404	.342
Short, Rick, Fred.	.308	59	251	221	36	68	100	14	0	6	28	1	3	8	18	1	29	3	2	12	.452	.376
Sosa, Juan, Sal.	.278	133	587	529	88	147	215	20	12	8	47	7	4	4	43	1	83	64	16	12	.406	.334
Stevenson, Chad, Dan.	.103	9	29	29	2	3	3	0	0	0	0	0	0	0	0	0	11	0	0	0	.103	.103
Stewart, Colin, Dan.	.333	4	16	12	3	4	4	0	0	0	1	0	0	1	3	0	2	4	1	0	.333	.500
Taft, Brett, Wil.	.257	121	466	405	55	104	138	25	0	3	31	17	3	4	37	2	79	18	6	10	.341	.323
Tanner, Paul, P.W.	.253	95	240	221	24	56	84	17	1	3	35	2	0	2	15	1	68	9	8	8	.380	.307
Taylor, Adam, Kin.	.167	7	20	18	2	3	6	0	0	1	3	0	0	0	2	0	8	0	1	0	.333	.250
Terhune, Mike, Dan.†	.220	107	397	368	44	81	99	9	0	3	26	6	2	4	17	0	67	8	5	13	.269	.261
Terrell, Jim, W.S.*	.455	3	11	11	1	5	10	3	1	0	2	0	0	0	0	0	2	0	0	0	.909	.455
Tomlinson, Goef, Wil.*	.279	38	152	136	15	38	48	8	1	0	16	2	0	0	14	2	26	2	2	3	.353	.347
Trippy, Joe, Dan.*	.189	31	126	106	8	20	22	2	0	0	5	4	1	4	11	1	22	10	4	2	.208	.287
Ullery, Dave, Wil.*	.193	74	240	202	16	39	53	5	0	3	22	10	5	2	21	2	66	1	1	5	.262	.270
Utting, Andy, Fred.†	.108	15	43	37	2	4	4	0	0	0	1	2	0	0	4	0	6	0	0	0	.108	.195
Valera, Willy, Kin.	.111	3	9	9	1	1	1	0	0	0	0	0	0	0	0	0	3	0	0	0	.111	.111
Wade, Michael, Fred.	.133	14	30	30	1	4	7	0	0	1	2	0	0	0	0	0	10	0	0	0	.233	.133
Walker, Morgan, Lyn.	.298	105	404	373	46	111	177	24	0	14	68	0	7	2	22	0	92	1	0	10	.475	.334
Walker, Shon, Lyn.*	.217	19	70	60	9	13	25	3	0	3	8	1	0	1	8	0	25	0	0	2	.417	.319
Warner, Bryan, Sal.*	.237	116	468	422	47	100	149	17	1	10	62	0	4	5	37	5	84	5	5	5	.353	.303
Whitaker, Chad, Kin.*	.215	127	490	455	46	98	153	25	0	10	48	0	0	1	34	1	148	16	10	6	.336	.271
Whitley, Matt, Sal.	.258	41	134	120	18	31	37	6	0	0	11	1	2	0	11	0	16	7	2	4	.308	.316
Whitlock, Brian, Kin.	.212	73	229	198	24	42	72	9	3	5	30	5	0	2	24	0	74	4	1	0	.364	.304
Williams, Glenn, Dan.	.215	134	519	470	40	101	156	26	1	9	44	3	3	6	37	3	132	1	3	5	.332	.279
Wilson, Craig, Lyn.	.269	61	247	219	26	59	111	12	2	12	45	0	1	5	22	1	53	2	1	3	.507	.348
Wong, Jerrod, Dan.	.239	81	315	297	34	71	103	9	4	5	33	0	2	5	10	2	62	6	1	2	.347	.274

GRAND SLAMS: Barthol, Casimiro, Escandon, Mohr, 2 each; B. Anderson, Anthony, Chris Bryant, Daedelow, DeCinces, Downs, Glavine, Haverbusch, Hessman, Layne, Lidle, May, Morris, Whitaker, 1 each.

AWARDED FIRST BASE ON CATCHER'S INTERFERENCE: Clint Bryant 5 (McNeal, Shepard, Martine, Heintz, Pagan); Christensen 3 (Harriss, Martine, Haad); Manning 2 (Konrady, Taylor); Bair (Shepard); Coffie (Paul); Wong (Martine).

1998 PITCHING

TEAM

Team	W	L	Pct.	ERA	G	CG	ShO	Sv.	IP	H	TBF	R	ER	HR	SH	SF	HB	BB	IBB	SO	WP	Bk.
Wilmington	86	54	.614	2.97	140	11	16	39	1239.2	1076	5142	491	409	66	65	37	70	405	29	1085	77	9
Kinston.............	69	71	.493	3.43	140	6	5	42	1209.1	1107	5066	556	461	96	54	36	65	401	25	1045	58	8
Danville...........	58	82	.414	3.51	140	6	10	37	1236.2	1165	5299	586	482	63	56	41	61	488	39	1190	62	3
Lynchburg........	69	71	.493	3.64	140	9	12	44	1219.1	1207	5159	602	493	96	42	38	65	368	13	1056	64	3
Winston-Salem .	79	60	.568	3.72	139	9	8	29	1218.0	1151	5184	609	503	91	43	39	86	411	8	1057	59	13
Frederick	64	76	.457	3.81	140	8	10	37	1217.1	1221	5201	634	515	99	56	46	53	419	14	981	96	6
Prince William...	72	67	.518	3.86	139	4	8	36	1204.0	1143	5076	625	517	101	50	42	56	380	12	952	69	8
Salem................	62	78	.443	4.45	140	11	5	30	1214.2	1203	5285	688	600	104	51	40	86	490	5	1019	88	10

INDIVIDUAL

TOP QUALIFIERS FOR EARNED-RUN AVERAGE TITLE

Minimum 112 innings. *Lefthanded pitcher.

Pitcher, Team	W	L	Pct.	ERA	G	GS	CG	ShO	GF	Sv.	IP	H	TBF	R	ER	HR	SH	SF	HB	BB	IBB	SO	WP	Bk.
Martin, Chandler, Sal.	12	7	.632	2.48	24	7	0	0	0	0	160.0	136	641	54	44	9	5	1	4	43	0	104	14	0
Porzio, Mike, Dan.-Sal.*	5	5	.500	2.58	33	18	1	0	8	2	139.1	114	557	54	40	13	6	3	3	42	5	141	2	0
France, Aaron, Lyn.	6	5	.545	2.72	26	20	0	0	2	0	129.0	99	529	51	39	9	3	1	12	45	0	110	7	0
Lineweaver, Aaron, Wil.	13	5	.722	2.79	26	26	5	2	0	0	168.0	136	685	62	52	5	12	3	14	54	3	116	8	1
Ankiel, Rich, P.W.*	9	6	.600	2.79	21	21	1	0	0	0	126.0	91	503	46	39	8	5	3	12	38	0	181	10	1
Bacsik, Mike, Kin.*	10	9	.526	2.88	27	27	1	0	0	0	165.2	147	667	64	53	17	5	4	4	37	3	128	4	0
McConnell, Sam, Lyn.*	8	5	.615	2.90	19	19	3	1	0	0	121.0	118	483	48	39	4	2	1	1	20	0	80	2	0
McGlinchy, Kevin, Dan.	9	8	.529	2.91	22	22	1	0	0	0	142.1	122	566	55	46	7	6	3	6	29	0	129	1	0
Durbin, Chad, Wil.	10	7	.588	2.93	26	26	0	0	0	0	147.2	126	624	57	48	10	5	7	8	59	3	162	13	1
Thorn, Todd, Wil.*	9	8	.529	3.13	26	24	4	2	0	0	149.1	128	604	60	52	12	7	9	7	28	2	103	5	3
McNatt, Josh, Fred.*	11	8	.579	3.15	27	26	3	1	0	0	157.1	141	661	78	55	10	8	4	5	70	2	118	17	3
Garza, Alberto, Kin.	4	8	.333	3.20	20	20	3	0	0	0	112.1	79	467	44	40	7	5	1	6	60	0	110	8	1
Chapman, Jake, Wil.*	13	9	.591	3.27	27	26	1	1	0	0	162.1	158	665	72	59	4	6	3	6	37	1	113	5	2
Bell, Rob, Dan.	7	9	.438	3.28	28	28	2	0	0	0	178.1	169	736	79	65	8	6	6	7	46	0	197	8	0
Towers, Josh, Fred.	8	7	.533	3.34	25	20	3	0	3	1	145.1	137	583	58	54	11	6	3	11	9	0	122	5	2

DEPARTMENTAL LEADERS: W—Chapman, Colmenares, Iglesias, Lineweaver, 13 each; L—Walls, 13; Pct.—Iglesias, .929; G—DeLeon, 57; GS—R. Bell, Colmenares, Lambert, 28 each; CG—C. Martin, 7; ShO—Ah Yat, 3; GF—D. Lee, 52; Sv.—Riske, 33; IP—R. Bell, 178.1; H—Colmenares, 187; TBF—R. Bell, 736; R—Colmenares, 96; ER—Colmenares, 90; HR—Bacsik, 17; SH—Lineweaver, 12; SF—Thorn, 9; HB—Lakman, 17; BB—Jacobs, 89; IBB—Milburn, Winkelsas, 8 each; SO—R. Bell, 197; WP—Jacobs, 19; BK—Daneker, 4.

ALL PITCHERS
*Lefthanded pitcher.

Pitcher, Team	W	L	Pct.	ERA	G	GS	CG	ShO	GF	Sv.	IP	H	TBF	R	ER	HR	SH	SF	HB	BB	IBB	SO	WP	Bk.
Abbott, Jim, W.S.*	2	1	.667	5.40	4	4	0	0	0	0	21.2	17	87	13	13	2	0	0	0	7	0	13	4	0
Ah Yat, Paul, Lyn.*	6	3	.667	2.73	14	14	4	3	0	0	102.1	95	410	40	31	9	1	3	4	13	2	77	2	0
Alvarado, Carlos, Lyn.	3	5	.375	5.61	13	10	0	0	1	0	59.1	69	274	48	37	10	4	2	3	24	0	52	6	0
Ankiel, Rich, P.W.*	9	6	.600	2.79	21	21	1	0	0	0	126.0	91	503	46	39	8	5	3	12	38	0	181	10	1
Avrard, Corey, P.W.	4	5	.444	5.06	31	11	0	0	6	0	80.0	67	345	57	45	9	2	6	3	50	0	52	5	0
Ayers, Mike, Lyn.*	3	3	.500	7.59	34	0	0	0	15	0	40.1	53	188	36	34	5	1	2	5	17	0	31	2	1
Bacsik, Mike, W.S.*	10	9	.526	2.88	27	27	1	0	0	0	165.2	147	667	64	53	17	5	4	4	37	3	128	4	0
Bailey, Roger, Sal.	0	2	.000	8.71	3	3	0	0	0	0	10.1	13	56	11	10	0	1	2	1	11	0	5	2	0
Baird, Brandon, Wil.*	6	2	.750	3.05	54	0	0	0	23	4	56.0	49	247	26	19	2	6	0	3	29	6	59	1	0
Bauer, Chuck, Lyn.	3	3	.500	4.41	12	8	0	0	1	0	49.0	70	218	33	24	1	1	2	2	8	1	29	1	0
Beasley, Ray, Dan.*	6	8	.429	3.56	54	0	0	0	20	8	55.2	54	241	26	22	3	3	2	3	24	4	55	2	1
Bell, Mike, Fred.*	7	4	.636	2.69	38	0	0	0	20	7	60.1	53	236	22	18	3	6	3	2	13	2	38	3	0
Bell, Rob, Dan.	7	9	.438	3.28	28	28	2	0	0	0	178.1	169	736	79	65	8	6	6	7	46	0	197	8	0
Benes, Adam, P.W.	1	0	1.000	1.35	10	0	0	0	1	0	13.1	12	58	6	2	1	0	0	0	4	0	9	0	0
Berger, Brandon, Wil.	0	0	.000	13.50	2	0	0	0	2	0	2.0	3	12	3	3	1	0	0	0	4	0	0	0	0
Bevel, Bobby, Sal.*	6	4	.600	2.26	51	0	0	0	26	3	91.2	72	373	26	23	4	2	3	4	24	0	92	5	1
Biddle, Rocky, W.S.	4	5	.444	4.57	16	16	0	0	0	0	82.2	92	382	55	42	7	0	4	5	45	0	72	5	1
Brammer, J.D., Kin.	3	2	.600	1.33	15	0	0	0	8	2	27.0	15	106	6	4	1	0	0	1	8	0	33	1	1
Brewer, Ryan, Wil.	3	1	.750	1.54	26	0	0	0	13	9	41.0	36	169	12	7	2	5	1	0	11	3	36	4	0
Brown, Jamie, Kin.	11	9	.550	3.81	27	27	2	0	0	0	172.2	162	717	91	73	12	3	11	3	44	1	148	4	2
Buirley, Matthew, Lyn.	1	0	1.000	6.97	13	0	0	0	3	0	20.2	26	108	22	16	1	2	2	2	15	0	21	4	0
Burke, John, Sal.	0	0	.000	1.13	2	0	0	0	0	0	8.0	3	32	1	1	1	0	0	0	7	0	8	0	0
Bussa, Todd, Lyn.	2	4	.333	2.25	35	0	0	0	25	14	48.0	45	205	16	12	2	1	2	2	23	3	54	3	0
Calero, Kiko, Wil.	7	3	.700	2.86	17	17	0	0	0	0	97.2	74	409	33	31	7	1	3	7	51	1	90	6	0
Calmus, Lance, Kin.	0	1	.000	6.75	7	1	0	0	2	0	12.0	14	56	12	9	1	0	0	0	7	0	10	1	0
Carter, Lance, Wil.	1	4	.200	3.29	28	1	0	0	11	5	52.0	50	217	21	19	5	5	3	4	14	1	61	4	0
Chacon, Shawn, Sal.	0	4	.000	5.30	12	12	0	0	0	0	56.0	53	258	35	33	5	3	2	6	31	0	54	8	1
Chantres, Carlos, W.S.	5	5	.500	3.77	13	13	1	0	0	0	88.1	71	370	43	37	10	3	6	8	41	0	86	5	0
Chapman, Jake, Wil.*	13	9	.591	3.27	27	26	1	1	0	0	162.1	158	665	72	59	4	6	3	6	37	1	113	5	2
Colmenares, Luis, Sal.	13	6	.684	5.05	28	28	1	0	0	0	160.1	187	716	96	90	16	5	3	11	63	0	117	8	0
Coogan, Patrick, P.W.	5	4	.556	5.47	14	14	0	0	0	0	74.1	94	340	55	46	7	3	4	4	25	0	57	5	2
Corey, Michael, Dan.	1	0	1.000	0.00	2	0	0	0	2	0	3.0	3	11	0	0	0	0	0	0	0	0	5	0	0
Corn, Chris, Lyn.	1	1	.500	1.09	7	3	0	0	2	0	24.2	20	98	6	3	1	2	1	1	7	0	25	2	0
Culp, Wes, Dan.	2	4	.333	5.37	37	0	0	0	15	0	57.0	67	286	42	34	3	4	5	8	43	5	33	5	0
Daedelow, Craig, Fred.	0	0	.000	0.00	1	0	0	0	1	0	0.1	1	1	0	0	0	0	0	0	0	0	0	0	0
Daneker, Pat, W.S.	5	0	1.000	2.04	7	7	2	0	0	0	53.0	51	210	13	12	3	2	0	2	5	1	43	1	4
Daniels, David, Lyn.	0	0	.000	1.47	14	0	0	0	12	9	18.1	9	65	3	3	2	1	0	0	3	0	19	0	0
Davenport, Joe, W.S.	2	0	1.000	1.38	20	0	0	0	15	2	26.0	25	106	9	4	0	0	1	2	4	0	26	3	0
De Leon, Jose, P.W.	3	9	.250	4.88	57	0	0	0	49	26	55.1	61	247	37	30	7	5	2	4	19	3	30	1	0
De Paula, Sean, Kin.	3	2	.600	2.36	28	1	0	0	14	1	49.2	50	226	20	13	0	2	1	3	18	3	59	6	0
Deschenes, Marc, Kin.	0	0	.000	0.00	1	0	0	0	1	0	1.0	0	4	0	0	0	0	0	1	0	2	0	0	
Dewitt, Matt, P.W.	6	9	.400	3.64	24	24	1	0	0	0	148.1	132	588	65	60	13	3	3	7	18	0	118	5	0
Dishman, Richard, Dan.	3	2	.600	1.86	20	11	0	0	6	2	77.1	54	308	20	16	1	3	1	3	28	0	85	3	0
Doyle, Tom, Sal.*	5	3	.625	4.26	18	5	0	0	2	0	57.0	50	237	38	27	4	1	1	7	21	1	49	5	1
Drew, Tim, Kin.	3	8	.273	5.20	15	15	0	0	0	0	90.0	105	392	58	52	9	3	5	5	31	1	67	5	2
Duff, Matt, Lyn.	4	5	.444	3.30	40	0	0	0	25	10	62.2	52	257	26	23	4	3	3	1	20	2	61	4	0
Durbin, Chad, Wil.	10	7	.588	2.93	26	26	0	0	0	0	147.2	126	624	57	48	10	5	7	8	59	3	162	13	1
Edwards, Jon, Kin.	5	0	1.000	2.70	21	0	0	0	3	0	33.1	31	140	10	10	1	3	0	1	14	0	28	1	0
Eibey, Scott, Fred.*	1	2	.333	3.86	21	0	0	0	5	1	35.0	47	152	17	15	3	4	1	0	8	0	20	3	0
Emiliano, Jamie, Lyn.	1	1	.500	3.52	4	0	0	0	1	0	7.2	9	36	3	3	0	0	1	0	5	0	6	1	0
Falkenborg, Brian, Fred.	5	5	.500	4.50	15	14	1	1	0	0	78.0	83	338	42	39	6	3	2	4	18	0	70	8	0
Farley, Joe, W.S.*	5	6	.455	4.99	21	19	1	0	0	0	119.0	126	521	73	66	14	2	4	3	55	0	70	6	3
Flach, Jason, Dan.	5	5	.500	3.14	37	11	0	0	7	1	106.0	110	453	43	37	5	6	4	6	31	4	108	6	0
Fogg, Josh, W.S.	0	1	.000	0.00	1	0	0	0	1	0	1.0	2	6	2	0	0	0	0	0	0	0	2	1	0
Forbes, Cameron, Fred.	2	3	.400	3.22	14	3	0	0	2	0	36.1	38	165	20	13	1	0	2	3	21	0	16	7	0
France, Aaron, Lyn.	5	5	.545	2.72	26	20	0	0	2	0	129.0	99	529	51	39	9	1	12	45	0	110	7	0
Garrett, Neil, Sal.	0	3	.000	5.40	12	9	0	0	0	0	45.0	55	201	28	27	8	1	3	5	11	0	27	0	2
Garza, Alberto, Kin.	4	8	.333	3.20	20	20	3	0	0	0	112.1	79	467	44	40	7	5	1	6	60	0	110	8	1
Geis, John, P.W.*	3	1	.750	4.35	32	0	0	0	13	0	39.1	49	170	24	19	3	5	4	0	10	1	27	2	0
Gonzalez, Edwin, Wil.	1	0	1.000	1.23	5	2	0	0	1	0	22.0	17	82	3	3	1	2	0	5	1	0	34	1	0
Gonzalez, Mike, Lyn.*	0	3	.000	6.67	7	7	0	0	0	0	28.1	40	131	21	21	5	0	1	3	13	0	22	1	0
Gross, Rafael, Kin.	0	0	.000	54.00	1	0	0	0	0	0	0.1	3	5	3	2	0	0	1	0	0	0	0	1	0
Guzman, Wilson, Lyn.*	0	1	.000	13.50	3	0	0	0	1	0	2.2	4	17	4	4	1	1	0	0	5	1	2	0	0
Hacen, Abraham, Fred.	7	10	.412	4.46	30	26	0	0	4	0	145.1	138	632	83	72	15	10	8	3	74	1	93	8	0
Hall, Yates, P.W.	1	1	.500	7.15	5	1	0	0	0	0	11.1	11	52	10	9	2	0	0	6	1	7	0	0	
Halla, Ryan, Lyn.	5	4	.556	3.70	40	0	0	0	13	0	56.0	51	238	27	23	5	8	3	2	22	1	51	1	1
Hamilton, Jimmy, Kin.*	4	6	.400	2.75	44	0	0	0	15	4	75.1	61	305	25	23	5	8	4	5	25	5	83	4	0
Hasselhoff, Derek, W.S.	0	0	.000	0.00	1	0	0	0	0	0	2.0	3	9	0	0	0	0	0	0	0	0	1	0	0
Heredia, Maximo, Fred.	1	3	.250	4.92	29	0	0	0	7	1	64.0	71	279	44	35	6	5	2	19	3	36	3	0	
Hernandez, Francis, Fred.	0	0	.000	5.79	5	0	0	0	4	0	4.2	4	21	3	3	1	0	1	0	3	0	3	0	0
Huffaker, Mike, P.W.	3	4	.429	5.91	53	0	0	0	14	0	67.0	78	302	50	44	12	5	2	6	23	0	49	7	0
Hughes, Mike, Kin.*	1	3	.250	4.95	9	4	0	0	2	0	36.1	45	161	26	20	8	4	1	0	8	2	27	4	0
Hunt, Jon, W.S.*	1	1	.500	9.00	6	0	0	0	3	0	8.0	11	35	8	8	1	0	0	0	3	0	2	0	0
Hutchinson, Chad, P.W.	2	0	1.000	2.79	5	5	0	0	0	0	29.0	20	118	12	9	1	1	1	11	0	31	0	2	
Iglesias, Mario, W.S.	13	1	.929	2.31	35	0	0	0	18	5	70.0	78	51	305	24	20	5	4	2	4	19	0	90	3	0

– 497 –

Pitcher, Team	W	L	Pct.	ERA	G	GS	CG	ShO	GF	Sv.	IP	H	TBF	R	ER	HR	SH	SF	HB	BB	IBB	SO	WP	Bk.
Izquierdo, Hansel, W.S.	0	0	.000	0.00	1	0	0	0	1	1	2.0	1	7	0	0	0	0	0	0	1	0	2	0	0
Jacobs, Dwayne, Dan.	5	10	.333	4.99	31	19	0	0	5	0	110.0	92	507	71	61	10	1	3	12	89	2	112	19	1
Jerue, Tristan, P.W.	3	3	.500	2.11	7	7	0	0	0	0	42.2	31	167	13	10	0	2	1	2	11	0	34	2	1
Karnuth, Jason, P.W.	8	1	.889	1.67	16	15	2	2	1	0	108.0	86	411	26	20	3	6	0	7	14	0	53	4	0
Kelly, Jeff, Lyn.*	0	4	.000	5.46	10	4	0	0	3	0	29.2	33	130	25	18	2	0	4	0	10	0	18	3	0
Kenady, Jake, Sal.*	0	2	.000	6.75	32	0	0	0	16	0	58.2	53	275	49	44	5	3	2	5	52	0	43	14	0
Key, Jimmy, Fred.*	1	0	1.000	3.00	1	1	0	0	0	0	6.0	4	22	2	2	2	0	0	0	2	0	6	0	0
Koeman, Matt, Kin.	0	0	.000	1.35	4	0	0	0	2	0	6.2	9	32	8	1	2	0	1	0	1	0	4	0	0
Kohlmeier, Ryan, Fred.	1	2	.333	7.45	9	0	0	0	9	5	9.2	10	44	9	8	1	0	2	1	3	0	15	0	1
Lakman, Jason, W.S.	3	2	.600	3.77	13	13	1	0	0	0	86.0	62	363	37	36	0	2	2	17	30	0	98	3	0
Lamber, Justin, Wil.*	2	2	.500	3.38	32	0	0	0	16	2	53.1	43	228	21	20	3	1	2	1	29	3	68	6	0
Lambert, Kris, Lyn.*	10	11	.476	3.59	28	28	1	0	0	0	160.2	161	677	79	64	14	6	5	13	44	0	145	5	0
Lane, Aaron, Fred.*	1	1	.500	2.70	5	1	0	0	3	1	13.1	9	51	5	4	0	1	0	1	7	0	6	1	0
Lawrence, Chip, Fred.	0	0	.000	0.00	1	0	0	0	1	0	1.0	0	4	0	0	0	0	0	0	1	0	0	0	0
Lee, Chris, Fred.	0	0	.000	4.50	2	0	0	0	1	0	4.0	3	16	2	2	1	0	0	0	2	0	4	0	0
Lee, David, Sal.	3	5	.375	3.77	54	0	0	0	52	25	57.1	57	244	26	24	2	4	4	3	15	1	54	3	1
LeCronier, Jason, Fred.	0	0	.000	0.00	1	0	0	0	1	0	0.2	0	3	0	0	0	0	0	0	1	0	1	0	0
Lidle, Kevin, Sal.	1	1	.500	8.64	10	0	0	0	1	0	16.2	22	86	16	16	0	1	1	0	15	1	6	1	0
Lineweaver, Aaron, Wil.	13	5	.722	2.79	26	26	5	2	0	0	168.0	136	685	62	52	5	12	3	14	54	3	116	8	1
Lundquist, David, W.S.	1	0	1.000	2.53	6	0	0	0	2	0	10.2	9	42	4	3	0	1	0	0	3	0	9	0	0
Macca, Chris, Sal.	0	1	.000	18.00	10	0	0	0	4	0	11.0	17	76	28	22	1	1	3	3	23	0	6	6	1
Mackey, Jason, Kin.*	0	0	.000	6.75	5	0	0	0	0	0	12.0	19	61	9	9	1	1	0	2	5	1	8	1	2
Marquis, Jason, Dan.	2	12	.143	4.87	22	22	1	0	0	0	114.2	120	500	65	62	3	4	3	6	41	0	135	7	0
Martin, Chandler, Sal.	12	7	.632	2.48	24	24	7	0	0	0	160.0	136	641	54	44	9	5	1	4	43	0	104	14	0
Martin, Jeff, Lyn.	0	0	.000	9.00	2	2	0	0	0	0	6.0	6	30	6	6	0	0	0	1	5	0	5	0	0
Mastrolonardo, David, Fred.	1	6	.143	5.01	48	0	0	0	37	15	55.2	59	251	34	31	7	1	4	1	29	1	69	4	0
Matcuk, Steve, Sal.	3	11	.214	4.71	18	15	1	0	1	0	99.1	107	420	59	52	12	4	4	12	18	0	69	4	0
Mays, Jarrod, Kin.	1	1	.500	1.59	4	4	0	0	0	0	17.0	12	68	6	3	1	0	1	0	7	1	10	0	0
McConnell, Sam, Lyn.*	8	5	.615	2.90	19	19	3	1	0	0	121.0	118	483	48	39	4	2	1	1	20	0	80	2	0
McDade, Neal, Lyn.	5	3	.625	3.30	25	11	0	0	6	3	90.0	87	369	35	33	7	3	3	5	20	0	74	5	1
McDougal, Mike, P.W.	3	0	1.000	2.81	17	2	0	0	3	0	32.0	38	132	11	10	4	1	0	1	2	0	28	1	0
McGlinchy, Kevin, Dan.	9	8	.529	2.91	22	22	1	0	0	0	142.1	122	566	55	46	7	6	3	6	29	0	129	1	0
McNatt, Josh, Fred.*	11	8	.579	3.15	27	26	3	1	0	0	157.1	141	661	78	55	10	8	4	5	70	2	118	17	3
Merrick, Brett, Kin.*	0	0	.000	9.00	2	0	0	0	1	0	2.0	3	10	2	2	1	0	0	0	1	0	0	0	0
Meyer, Jake, W.S.	0	1	.000	2.92	11	0	0	0	10	2	12.1	12	51	6	4	1	0	0	0	3	2	13	2	0
Milburn, Robert, Dan.*	0	2	.000	4.05	45	0	0	0	16	2	53.1	62	248	32	24	5	3	4	1	27	8	33	3	0
Montgomery, Greg, P.W.	6	1	.857	6.92	35	0	0	0	6	0	40.1	44	190	37	31	2	1	3	1	25	0	25	7	0
Moreno, Orber, Wil.	3	2	.600	0.82	23	0	0	0	17	7	33.0	8	115	3	3	1	1	0	0	10	1	50	1	0
Mullen, Scott, Wil.*	8	4	.667	2.21	14	14	1	1	0	0	85.2	68	344	28	21	4	3	1	7	25	0	56	3	1
Myette, Aaron, W.S.	4	2	.667	2.01	6	6	1	1	0	0	44.2	32	178	14	10	4	1	0	1	14	0	54	0	0
Navarro, Jason, P.W.*	6	7	.462	4.36	30	24	0	0	3	0	136.1	143	600	79	66	12	1	8	5	66	1	105	9	1
Negrette, Richard, Kin.	3	5	.375	2.88	28	0	0	0	11	0	50.0	32	208	22	16	3	3	3	4	27	1	41	5	0
Nelson, Erick, Dan.*	3	1	.750	2.61	10	8	0	0	0	0	41.1	42	172	17	12	2	0	2	0	11	0	38	2	1
Newell, Brett, Wil.	0	0	.000	9.90	10	0	0	0	5	0	10.0	17	53	11	11	2	0	1	0	6	0	5	2	0
Nichols, Jamie, W.S.	3	3	.500	5.50	19	4	0	0	9	0	54.0	71	240	34	33	5	1	2	2	11	0	39	3	0
Nussbeck, Mark, P.W.	3	6	.333	3.56	14	13	0	0	0	0	86.0	75	349	40	34	10	2	1	1	16	0	65	0	0
Ochsenfeld, Chris, W.S.*	0	0	.000	4.50	17	0	0	0	11	2	26.0	26	117	15	13	0	0	2	1	12	0	16	7	0
O'Connor, Brian, Lyn.*	6	2	.750	2.60	14	14	1	0	0	0	86.2	86	371	34	25	3	3	1	1	22	1	84	7	0
Olszewski, Tim, Fred.	3	4	.429	4.70	34	0	0	0	10	1	61.1	83	274	46	32	8	2	5	4	14	2	37	4	0
Onley, Shawn, Dan.	6	8	.429	3.86	44	2	1	0	16	2	93.1	89	412	48	40	4	7	3	2	47	2	77	3	0
Opipari, Mario, P.W.	5	5	.500	2.17	32	2	0	0	19	3	54.0	47	221	17	13	1	6	3	0	9	3	26	1	0
Paredes, Carlos, Wil.	4	0	1.000	3.97	37	0	0	0	20	5	45.1	53	215	29	20	0	4	0	4	24	3	46	8	0
Paronto, Chad, Fred.	7	6	.538	3.13	18	18	0	0	0	0	103.2	116	451	44	36	4	3	2	3	39	0	87	8	0
Parrish, John, Fred.*	4	4	.500	3.27	16	16	1	0	0	0	82.2	77	352	39	30	5	3	4	5	27	1	81	9	0
Paugh, Rick, Lyn.*	0	1	.000	2.92	14	0	0	0	3	0	12.1	14	53	4	4	2	0	0	0	4	0	8	1	0
Paulino, Arison, Lyn.	0	0	.000	14.73	2	0	0	0	0	0	3.2	6	19	6	6	2	0	0	1	3	0	5	0	0
Peguero, Americo, Fred.	0	1	.000	6.43	5	4	0	0	1	0	14.0	10	62	11	10	1	0	0	0	11	0	15	0	0
Pena, Jesus, W.S.*	3	4	.429	3.13	23	0	0	0	13	7	31.2	20	125	11	11	2	2	2	1	12	1	37	0	1
Pirkl, Greg, Kin.	2	0	1.000	2.73	14	0	0	0	9	0	26.1	23	111	10	8	2	0	1	1	7	1	26	3	0
Porzio, Mike, Dan.-Sal.*	5	5	.500	2.58	33	18	1	0	8	2	139.1	114	557	54	40	13	6	3	3	42	5	141	2	0
Quevedo, Ruben, Dan.	0	2	.000	3.58	6	6	0	0	0	0	32.2	28	143	22	13	2	1	2	3	13	1	35	2	0
Reichert, Dan, Wil.	2	0	1.000	3.21	2	2	0	0	0	0	14.0	13	55	5	5	0	0	0	0	4	0	10	5	0
Reichow, Bob, Kin.	0	0	.000	23.63	2	0	0	0	0	0	2.2	5	18	7	7	0	0	0	4	2	0	1	2	0
Richardson, Kasey, Fred.*	1	0	1.000	5.30	22	0	0	0	8	1	37.1	44	169	29	22	4	2	1	1	14	1	38	9	0
Rigdon, Paul, Kin.	11	7	.611	4.03	24	24	0	0	0	0	127.1	126	532	65	57	9	2	6	9	35	1	97	3	0
Riske, David, Kin.	1	1	.500	2.33	53	0	0	0	50	33	54.0	48	218	15	14	4	2	1	1	15	0	67	1	0
Roberts, Mark, W.S.	9	9	.500	3.92	27	25	2	1	0	0	165.1	165	706	88	72	15	6	8	10	50	1	142	6	0
Rogers, Jason, Fred.*	0	3	.000	3.98	17	0	0	0	3	0	20.1	19	87	12	9	2	1	0	2	7	0	19	2	0
Romero, Jordan, Fred.	2	5	.286	3.04	15	8	0	0	4	0	50.1	45	216	19	17	2	0	1	4	21	0	58	3	0
Romine, Jason, Sal.	1	2	.333	6.75	6	0	0	0	1	0	12.0	15	59	9	9	0	2	1	0	10	1	8	1	0
Rosa, Cristy, Sal.	1	2	.333	3.99	17	0	0	0	5	0	29.1	31	135	17	13	2	2	0	2	16	0	21	2	0
Runion, Tony, Lyn.	5	8	.385	3.00	36	0	0	0	15	4	57.0	49	239	21	19	5	4	1	6	20	2	72	7	0
Schmack, Brian, W.S.	5	5	.500	2.20	42	0	0	0	34	10	61.1	48	256	23	15	3	5	0	9	17	0	52	2	1
Schroeffel, Scott, Sal.	7	5	.583	4.74	38	1	0	0	12	2	81.2	86	368	53	43	11	3	3	5	31	1	91	6	1
Scott, Brian, W.S.	6	6	.500	4.93	19	19	0	0	0	0	100.1	116	462	70	55	9	5	4	9	43	0	76	2	3
Secoda, Jason, W.S.	2	0	1.000	1.59	6	0	0	0	4	0	11.1	8	43	2	2	0	1	0	0	2	1	8	1	0
Sims, Kenny, Fred.	0	0	.000	1.35	3	0	0	0	2	1	6.2	6	26	2	1	1	0	0	0	0	0	8	0	0
Spenser, Kaipo, Kin.	2	6	.250	3.76	13	13	0	0	0	0	67.0	74	286	30	28	6	2	0	7	23	0	31	2	0
Stein, Ethan, Wil.	4	4	.500	3.07	41	0	0	0	17	6	76.1	78	322	34	26	7	5	2	1	13	1	56	4	1
Steinmetz, Earl, Fred.	1	1	.500	3.13	13	0	0	0	5	0	23.0	23	101	13	8	3	1	0	1	6	1	20	2	0
Stepka, Tom, Sal.	1	3	.250	5.97	11	5	0	0	4	0	31.2	32	137	21	21	6	0	1	6	13	0	26	0	0
Stevenson, Chad, Dan.	0	0	.000	0.00	1	0	0	0	1	0	1.0	2	5	0	0	0	0	0	0	0	0	2	0	0

Pitcher, Team	W	L	Pct.	ERA	G	GS	CG	ShO	GF	Sv.	IP	H	TBF	R	ER	HR	SH	SF	HB	BB	IBB	SO	WP	Bk.
Stoops, Jim, Sal.	0	0	.000	0.00	3	0	0	0	1	0	4.1	2	16	0	0	0	1	0	0	1	0	8	0	0
Tapia, Rafael, Fred.	0	0	.000	0.00	1	0	0	0	0	0	1.0	1	4	0	0	0	0	0	0	0	0	1	0	0
Temple, Jason, Lyn.	1	0	1.000	7.36	6	0	0	0	2	0	11.0	14	50	11	9	2	1	2	0	5	0	11	1	0
Thompson, Mark, Sal.	0	0	.000	3.95	3	3	0	0	0	0	13.2	17	61	7	6	2	0	0	1	3	0	10	0	0
Thorn, Todd, Wil.*	9	8	.529	3.13	26	24	4	2	0	0	149.1	128	604	60	52	12	7	9	7	28	2	103	5	3
Towers, Josh, Fred.	8	7	.533	3.34	25	20	3	0	3	1	145.1	137	583	58	54	11	6	3	11	9	0	122	5	2
Tryon, Eric, Dan.*	0	0	.000	11.57	6	0	0	0	2	0	4.2	11	29	6	6	0	0	0	0	5	0	1	0	0
Viano, Jake, Kin.	3	0	1.000	1.54	14	0	0	0	10	1	23.1	14	93	4	4	2	1	0	1	10	2	21	2	0
Virchis, Adam, W.S.	5	6	.455	3.39	22	13	1	0	3	0	103.2	104	434	54	39	9	6	1	10	20	0	73	3	0
Wagner, Ken, Kin.	1	2	.333	3.00	10	0	0	0	6	1	21.0	15	88	8	7	0	3	2	1	10	2	18	0	0
Walls, Doug, Sal.	6	13	.316	4.47	27	26	2	0	1	0	159.0	145	677	91	79	10	11	5	9	63	0	169	7	2
Warner, Bryan, Sal.*	0	0	.000	0.00	3	0	0	0	2	0	1.2	1	8	0	0	0	0	0	0	2	0	0	0	0
Watson, Mark, Kin.*	0	1	.000	0.00	1	1	0	0	0	0	6.1	3	26	4	0	0	0	1	0	2	0	8	0	0
Welch, Travis, P.W.	0	1	.000	2.13	12	0	0	0	11	7	12.2	10	55	4	3	0	1	0	1	6	0	8	2	0
West, Adam, P.W.*	2	3	.400	5.25	43	0	0	0	13	0	48.0	54	228	36	28	3	1	2	1	27	3	47	8	1
Whitley, Curtis, W.S.*	0	1	.000	0.63	10	0	0	0	4	0	14.1	11	61	2	1	0	0	1	0	6	0	21	1	0
Whitlock, Brian, Kin.	0	0	.000	9.00	1	0	0	0	1	0	1.0	1	4	1	1	1	0	0	0	0	0	1	0	0
Whitten, Casey, Kin.*	1	0	1.000	3.18	9	3	0	0	1	0	17.0	11	65	6	6	3	0	1	0	7	1	17	1	0
Wilson, Kris, Wil.	0	3	.000	3.75	10	2	0	0	4	1	24.0	19	96	10	10	0	2	2	3	6	1	20	1	0
Winkelsas, Joe, Dan.	6	9	.400	2.22	50	0	0	0	36	22	69.0	66	298	26	17	3	7	0	3	24	8	53	0	0
Zolecki, Mike, W.S.	1	1	.500	4.30	8	0	0	0	5	0	14.2	17	68	9	7	1	2	1	1	8	2	6	1	0

COMBINATION SHUTOUTS: **Danville (10)**—Bell-Onley-Beasley, Jacobs-Porzio-Winkelsas, Porzio-Winkelsas, McGlinchy-Flach-Beasley-Winkelsas, Bell-Winkelsas-Beasley, McGlinchy-Jacobs, Flach-Beasley, Dishman-Milburn-Winkelsas, Dishman-Beasley-Winkelsas, Flach-Beasley. **Frederick (8)**—Paronto-Towers-Mastrolonardo, Paronto-Rogers-Towers, Falkenborg-Forbes-Rogers, McNatt-Mastrolonardo, Hacen-Rogers-Mastrolonardo, Paronto-Eibey-Hernandez, Romero-Heredia-Steinmetz-Mastrolonardo, Hacen-Eibey-Bell-Kohlmeier. **Kinston (5)**—Garza-De Paula, Bacsik-Brammer, Rigdon-Hamilton-Riske, Whitten-Hamilton-Riske, Brown-Negrete. **Lynchburg (8)**—O'Connor-Bussa-Ayers-Daniels, Martin-Runion-Bussa-Halla-Daniels, France-Runion-Daniels, France-Ayers-Runion-Daniels, O'Connor-Bussa, Gonzalez-Duff-Paugh-Bussa, Lambert-Runion, McConnell-Bussa. **Prince William (6)**—Ankiel-McDougal, Navarro-Huffaker-DeLeon, Ankiel-Opipari-DeLeon, Ankiel-Geis-Opipari-DeLeon, Jerue-Geis-Navarro, Karnuth-DeLeon. **Salem (5)**—Walls-Bevel-Lee, Martin-Lee, Martin-Bevel-Lee, Porzio-Bevel, Porzio-Bevel. **Wilmington (9)**—Mullen-Moreno, Calero-Carter-Moreno, Chapman-Brewer, Thorn-Paredes, Lineweaver-Carter, Calero-Lamber, Durbin-Baird-Lamber, Chapman-Paredes, Lineweaver-Stein. **Winston-Salem (6)**—Lakman-Nichols-Pena, Abbott-Iglesias, Chantres-Nichols, Roberts-Iglesias, Daneker-Schmack-Iglesias-Meyer, Myette-Whitley-Schmack.
NO-HIT GAMES: None.

PITCHERS WITH TWO OR MORE TEAMS

Pitcher, Team	W	L	Pct.	ERA	G	GS	CG	ShO	GF	Sv.	IP	H	TBF	R	ER	HR	SH	SF	HB	BB	IBB	SO	WP	Bk.
Porzio, Mike, Dan.*	3	2	.600	2.51	26	11	1	0	8	2	97.0	74	384	34	27	7	5	3	1	30	5	95	1	0
Porzio, Mike, Sal.*	2	3	.400	2.76	7	7	0	0	0	0	42.1	40	173	20	13	6	1	0	2	12	0	46	1	0

1998 FIELDING
TEAM

Team	Pct.	G	PO	A	E	TC	DP	PB	Team	Pct.	G	PO	A	E	TC	DP	PB
Salem	.972	140	3644	1541	147	5332	103	22	Frederick	.967	140	3652	1509	177	5338	137	29
Kinston	.972	140	3628	1435	144	5207	111	12	Danville	.967	140	3710	1376	175	5261	106	13
Prince William	.969	139	3612	1519	162	5293	113	11	Lynchburg	.966	140	3658	1477	178	5313	117	24
Winston-Salem	.969	139	3654	1469	164	5287	116	14									
Wilmington	.968	140	3719	1576	177	5472	130	30									

TRIPLE PLAYS: Lynchburg, Salem.

INDIVIDUAL

FIRST BASEMEN

NOTE: All caps denotes fielding-percentage leader based on 70 games for catchers, 93 for all other non-pitchers and 140 innings for pitchers. *Throws lefthanded.

Player, Team	Pct.	G	PO	A	E	TC	DP
Amado, Jose, Wil.	1.000	2	13	1	0	14	0
Anthony, Brian, Sal.	.990	118	1010	98	11	1119	80
Britt, Bryan, P.W.	.985	41	311	16	5	332	21
Bruce, Robert, Kin.	1.000	8	45	4	0	49	2
Bryant, Chris, Fred.	.988	82	679	60	9	748	68
Bryant, Clint, Sal.	1.000	1	1	1	0	2	0
Burke, Mark, Dan.*	1.000	2	19	3	0	22	0
Byington, Jimmie, Wil.	1.000	1	2	1	0	3	1
Cepeda, Jose, Wil.	.988	41	284	37	4	325	28
Coffee, Gary, Wil.	.974	7	74	2	2	78	5
Daedelow, Craig, Fred.	1.000	1	1	0	0	1	1
DeCinces, Tim, Fred.	1.000	15	111	7	0	118	9
Deck, Billy, P.W.*	.9931	114	929	87	7	1023	85
DiPace, Danny, Wil.	1.000	1	9	0	0	9	0
Downs, Brian, W.S.	1.000	2	16	3	0	19	1
Figueroa, Franky, Fred.	.972	4	35	0	1	36	3
Furniss, Eddy, Lyn.*	.977	30	243	17	6	266	14
GLAVINE, Mike, Kin.*	.9934	107	838	66	6	910	63
Goodell, Steve, Dan.	.985	15	121	10	2	133	6
Hage, Thomas, Fred.	.989	42	342	19	4	365	26
Heintz, Chris, W.S.	.989	101	785	80	10	875	63
Keck, Brian, Sal.	.992	28	230	12	2	244	14
Kent, Troy, Kin.	.992	34	239	17	2	258	27
Klee, Chuck, W.S.	1.000	10	53	3	0	56	5
Konrady, Dennis, Kin.	1.000	3	1	0	0	1	0
Lawrence, Chip, Fred.	1.000	2	4	0	0	4	0

Player, Team	Pct.	G	PO	A	E	TC	DP
Layne, Jason, Wil.	.990	95	808	70	9	887	78
Leon, Jose, P.W.	.964	3	25	2	1	28	1
Long, Garrett, Lyn.	.989	63	526	35	6	567	47
Mortimer, Mark, Dan.	.986	17	123	16	2	141	13
Olson, Dan, W.S.*	1.000	7	40	1	0	41	5
Rivera, Carlos, Lyn.*	.989	23	172	16	2	190	18
Scharrer, Jim, Dan.	.977	96	658	63	17	738	64
Sheppard, Greg, W.S.	.987	35	282	16	4	302	27
Short, Rick, Fred.	1.000	4	31	1	0	32	4
Ullery, Dave, Wil.	.982	7	53	1	1	55	6
Utting, Andy, Fred.	.971	5	28	6	1	35	8
Walker, Morgan, Lyn.*	.989	23	158	23	2	183	21
Whitlock, Brian, Kin.	1.000	5	24	1	0	25	3
Wilson, Craig, Lyn.	.966	7	52	4	2	58	5
Wong, Jerrod, Dan.*	.985	16	118	11	2	131	4

TRIPLE PLAYS: Anthony, Hage.

SECOND BASEMEN

Player, Team	Pct.	G	PO	A	E	TC	DP
Ametller, Jesus, P.W.	.962	88	121	209	13	343	44
Benefield, Brian, Kin.	.971	70	147	192	10	349	45
Bryant, Clint, Sal.	.941	4	10	6	1	17	2
Butler, Brent, P.W.	1.000	1	0	1	0	1	0
Byington, Jimmie, Wil.	1.000	2	2	1	0	3	0
Casimiro, Carlos, Fred.	.963	114	233	313	21	567	75
Cepeda, Jose, Wil.	.993	33	59	85	1	145	24
Connacher, Kevin, W.S.	.977	50	86	124	5	215	27
Delgado, Jose, Dan.	.920	5	11	12	2	25	3
Dorman, John, Kin.	.963	8	12	14	1	27	4
Eckelman, Alex, P.W.	1.000	19	23	33	0	56	5

– 499 –

Player, Team	Pct.	G	PO	A	E	TC	DP
Escandon, Emiliano, Wil.	.939	73	131	162	19	312	40
Garavito, Eddy, Fred.	.944	4	8	9	1	18	2
Gonzalez, Jose, W.S.	1.000	3	4	3	0	7	1
Gross, Rafael, Kin.	.667	1	1	1	1	3	0
Gutierrez, Rick, Kin.	1.000	1	2	2	0	4	1
Hairston, Jerry, Fred.	.972	14	27	43	2	72	10
Jasco, Elinton, Lyn.	.977	9	18	24	1	43	4
Jimenez, Ruben, Kin.	.970	34	48	80	4	132	19
Keck, Brian, Sal.	1.000	1	1	3	0	4	1
Kennedy, Adam, P.W.	.944	15	25	42	4	71	6
Klee, Chuck, W.S.	1.000	1	1	0	0	1	0
Konrady, Dennis, Kin.	1.000	1	1	1	0	2	1
Lawrence, Chip, Fred.	.938	9	15	15	2	32	4
Livingston, Doug, Sal.	.985	130	266	374	10	650	63
Longueira, Tony, Wil.	.750	2	3	0	1	4	1
Lorenzana, Luis, Lyn.	.975	89	158	236	10	404	56
Mateo, Jose, Dan.	1.000	3	0	1	0	1	0
Miyake, Chris, Lyn.	.980	45	90	107	4	201	23
Moore, Kenderick, Wil.	.951	53	99	132	12	243	22
Morris, Bobby, Kin.	.750	2	0	3	1	4	0
Nunez, Abraham, Lyn.	.800	1	1	3	1	5	1
Rivera, Micky, P.W.	1.000	2	2	4	0	6	1
Robinson, Tony, Lyn.	1.000	3	6	6	0	12	1
RODRIGUEZ, Liu, W.S.	.986	96	183	245	6	434	54
Short, Rick, Fred.	1.000	5	9	13	0	22	3
Tanner, Paul, P.W.	.953	50	72	69	7	148	20
Terhune, Mike, Dan.	1.000	12	17	21	0	38	7
Whitley, Matt, Sal.	1.000	5	7	15	0	22	3
Whitlock, Brian, Kin.	.971	36	51	85	4	140	15
Williams, Glenn, Dan.	.952	126	219	297	26	542	66

THIRD BASEMEN

Player, Team	Pct.	G	PO	A	E	TC	DP
Amado, Jose, Wil.	.915	69	46	149	18	213	14
Asche, Mike, Lyn.	.737	7	2	12	5	19	0
Benham, Jason, Fred.	.917	3	2	9	1	12	0
Bruce, Robert, Kin.	1.000	2	1	0	0	1	0
Bryant, Chris, Fred.	.778	7	3	4	2	9	1
Bryant, Clint, Sal.	.906	112	64	217	29	310	18
Bryant, Matt, Lyn.	.974	14	14	23	1	38	3
Butler, Brent, P.W.	.962	12	4	21	1	26	1
Byington, Jimmie, Wil.	.872	26	18	50	10	78	9
Casimiro, Carlos, Fred.	.959	14	9	38	2	49	2
Cepeda, Jose, Wil.	.950	39	21	74	5	100	8
Coffie, Ivanon, Fred.	.902	52	42	78	13	133	3
Connacher, Kevin, W.S.	.947	6	7	11	1	19	2
Crede, Joe, W.S.	.929	132	100	290	30	420	20
Daedelow, Craig, Fred.	.867	7	8	18	4	30	4
DeCinces, Tim, Fred.	.692	3	3	6	4	13	1
Diaz, Maikell, Fred.	1.000	9	2	14	0	16	1
Eckelman, Alex, P.W.	.929	14	2	24	2	28	1
Escandon, Emiliano, Wil.	.864	11	8	11	3	22	0
Gonzalez, Jose, W.S.	.800	5	3	1	1	5	0
Goodell, Steve, Dan.	1.000	4	5	2	0	7	0
Gross, Rafael, Kin.	.899	23	17	45	7	69	4
Gutierrez, Rick, Kin.	1.000	2	1	8	0	9	0
Hammond, Joey, Fred.	.909	3	2	8	1	11	1
Haverbusch, Kevin, Lyn.	.900	12	13	23	4	40	3
Heintz, Chris, W.S.	.636	5	2	5	4	11	0
HESSMAN, Mike, Dan.	.934	112	62	192	18	272	16
Hundt, Bo, Lyn.	.792	10	8	11	5	24	1
Jimenez, Ruben, Kin.	1.000	7	2	7	0	9	0
Keck, Brian, Sal.	.924	23	16	45	5	66	1
Kent, Troy, Kin.	.880	26	23	43	9	75	5
Klee, Chuck, W.S.	.833	3	1	4	1	6	0
Konrady, Dennis, Kin.	.932	82	45	119	12	176	9
Lawrence, Chip, Fred.	.818	12	1	8	2	11	0
Leon, Jose, P.W.	.933	117	76	257	24	357	24
Longueira, Tony, Wil.	.944	7	2	15	1	18	2
Mackowiak, Rob, Lyn.	.916	80	53	143	18	214	13
Miyake, Chris, Lyn.	.943	23	14	52	4	70	3
Pagan, Carlos, Wil.	.667	2	2	0	1	3	1
Paz, Richard, Fred.	.929	30	16	49	5	70	4
Rumfield, Brock, Fred.	.750	5	2	4	2	8	0
Short, Rick, Fred.	.905	10	7	12	2	21	1
Tanner, Paul, P.W.	.964	11	5	22	1	28	0
Terhune, Mike, Dan.	.877	27	10	40	7	57	9
Terrell, Jim, W.S.	.667	1	1	1	1	3	0
Valera, Willy, Kin.	.750	2	0	3	1	4	0
Whitley, Matt, Sal.	.941	8	3	13	1	17	1
Whitlock, Brian, Kin.	.886	19	10	29	5	44	2

SHORTSTOPS

Player, Team	Pct.	G	PO	A	E	TC	DP
Benham, Jason, Fred.	.500	1	1	2	3	6	2
Brito, Luis, Lyn.	.958	12	17	29	2	48	7
Bryant, Matt, Lyn.	.949	38	57	91	8	156	17
Butler, Brent, P.W.	.944	116	148	327	28	503	58
Casimiro, Carlos, Fred.	1.000	1	1	1	0	2	1
Cepeda, Jose, Wil.	.963	16	20	32	2	54	6
Coffie, Ivanon, Fred.	.949	50	86	136	12	234	39
Collier, Lou, Lyn.	.840	5	5	16	4	25	4
Daedelow, Craig, Fred.	.833	2	2	3	1	6	1
Delgado, Jose, Dan.	.921	34	62	55	10	127	12
Dellaero, Jason, W.S.	.914	121	183	306	46	535	63
Diaz, Maikell, Fred.	.929	3	5	8	1	14	0
DORMAN, John, Kin.	.963	98	143	277	16	436	54
Escandon, Emiliano, Wil.	.968	15	18	43	2	63	7
Gonzalez, Jose, W.S.	.909	3	4	6	1	11	0
Goodell, Steve, Dan.	.951	33	51	66	6	123	16
Gutierrez, Rick, Kin.	1.000	1	2	4	0	6	0
Hairston, Jerry, Fred.	.937	65	89	238	22	349	51
Haverbusch, Kevin, Lyn.	.908	32	54	85	14	153	19
Jimenez, Ruben, Kin.	.962	24	34	42	3	79	3
Keck, Brian, Sal.	.960	8	9	15	1	25	2
Kennedy, Adam, P.W.	.889	2	1	7	1	9	1
Klee, Chuck, W.S.	.867	15	16	23	6	45	4
Lawrence, Chip, Fred.	.953	18	14	27	2	43	2
Longueira, Tony, Wil.	1.000	2	4	3	0	7	0
Lorenzana, Luis, Lyn.	1.000	4	3	8	0	11	1
Mackowiak, Rob, Lyn.	1.000	1	1	0	0	1	0
Mateo, Jose, Dan.	.935	64	72	189	18	279	28
Miyake, Chris, Lyn.	.936	54	86	132	15	233	31
Nunez, Abraham, Lyn.	1.000	4	5	15	0	20	3
Paz, Richard, Fred.	.889	11	8	24	4	36	1
Robinson, Adam, Kin.	.940	24	24	54	5	83	14
Rodriguez, Liu, W.S.	.951	12	18	21	2	41	4
Sosa, Juan, Sal.	.944	122	196	328	31	555	60
Taft, Brett, Wil.	.955	119	157	348	24	529	64
Tanner, Paul, P.W.	.959	33	41	76	5	122	13
Terhune, Mike, Dan.	.919	17	27	41	6	74	6
Valera, Willy, Kin.	1.000	1	0	1	0	1	0
Whitley, Matt, Sal.	.974	14	23	51	2	76	11
Whitlock, Brian, Kin.	.944	5	4	13	1	18	1

TRIPLE PLAYS: Coffie, Sosa.

OUTFIELDERS

Player, Team	Pct.	G	PO	A	E	TC	DP
Albert, Rashad, W.S.	.944	15	34	0	2	36	0
Alvarez, Carlos, Kin.	1.000	9	5	0	0	5	0
Asche, Mike, Lyn.	.933	14	14	0	1	15	0
Bair, Rod, Sal.	.990	113	185	12	2	199	3
Bass, Jayson, Dan.	.957	10	22	0	1	23	0
Beltran, Carlos, Wil.	.983	50	109	4	2	115	1
Berger, Brandon, Wil.	.986	89	139	4	2	145	0
Borges, Alex, Dan.	1.000	2	1	0	0	1	0
Brown, Dermal, Wil.	.908	107	124	5	13	142	1
Bruce, Robert, Kin.	1.000	18	20	0	0	20	0
Bryant, Chris, Fred.	.947	50	70	2	4	76	0
Byington, Jimmie, Wil.	1.000	4	10	0	0	10	0
Cameron, Ken, P.W.*	.982	27	51	4	1	56	2
Christensen, McKay, W.S.*	.981	95	199	6	4	209	3
Conner, Decomba, Fred.	1.000	27	50	1	0	51	0
Daedelow, Craig, Fred.	1.000	18	25	3	0	28	0
Davis, Albert, Lyn.	1.000	1	1	0	0	1	0
Davison, Ashanti, Fred.	1.000	7	14	1	0	15	0
Deck, Billy, P.W.*	1.000	4	1	0	0	1	0
Delgado, Jose, Dan.	.909	15	17	3	2	22	1
Dent, Darrell, Fred.*	.985	131	259	6	4	269	3
Duverge, Salvador, Sal.	1.000	3	3	0	0	3	0
Escandon, Emiliano, Wil.	1.000	4	2	0	0	2	0
Farley, Cordell, P.W.	.954	130	215	13	11	239	0
Feramisco, Derek, P.W.	.917	14	21	1	2	24	0
Fowler, Maleke, Fred.	.956	73	101	7	5	113	1
Gambill, Chad, Sal.	.964	14	27	0	1	28	0
Garcia, Luis, W.S.	.983	100	165	7	3	175	1
Garland, Tim, Fred.	1.000	11	12	0	0	12	0
Gomez, Ramon, W.S.	.952	39	60	0	3	63	0
Goodell, Steve, Dan.	1.000	5	4	0	0	4	0
Gross, Rafael, Kin.	1.000	17	26	0	0	26	0
Hallmark, Pat, Wil.	.958	19	23	0	1	24	0
Hamlin, Mark, Sal.	.945	48	65	4	4	73	0
HOGAN, Todd, P.W.	.993	122	292	7	2	301	1
Huelsmann, Mike, Kin.	.968	113	237	7	8	252	1

Player, Team	Pct.	G	PO	A	E	TC	DP
Hutchison, Bernard, Sal.	.973	101	179	3	5	187	0
Jackson, Jeff, Lyn.	.895	22	32	2	4	38	0
Jackson, Jeremy, Sal.	.953	40	76	5	4	85	2
Katz, Jason, Dan.	1.000	4	12	0	0	12	0
Keck, Brian, Sal.	1.000	12	20	3	0	23	1
Klee, Chuck, W.S.	1.000	1	3	0	0	3	0
Lawrence, Chip, Fred.	1.000	4	6	0	0	6	0
LeCronier, Jason, Fred.	.943	45	48	2	3	53	0
Long, Garrett, Lyn.	1.000	14	16	4	0	20	1
Manning, Brian, W.S.	.980	58	93	5	2	100	1
Mateo, Jose, Dan.	1.000	6	7	0	0	7	0
May, Freddy, Lyn.*	.978	122	170	7	4	181	1
McDonald, Darnell, Fred.	1.000	4	8	0	0	8	0
McKinnon, Sandy, W.S.	1.000	43	52	2	0	54	1
Mejia, Miguel, Fred.	1.000	48	73	5	0	78	0
Miranda, Tony, Wil.	.984	38	59	2	1	62	0
Mohr, Dustan, Kin.	.968	119	203	10	7	220	2
Moore, Kenderick, Wil.	.990	68	97	2	1	100	1
Morris, Bobby, Kin.	1.000	2	2	0	0	2	0
Mortimer, Mark, Dan.	.920	22	21	2	2	25	0
Olson, Dan, W.S.*	.956	82	103	5	5	113	2
Pena, Alex, Lyn.	1.000	5	8	1	0	9	1
Pendergrass, Tyrone, Dan.	.984	129	300	7	5	312	0
Pointer, Corey, Lyn.	.950	110	223	6	12	241	2
Radcliff, Victor, Wil.	.971	35	63	3	2	68	1
Redman, Julian, Lyn.*	.971	131	263	7	8	278	0
Rivera, Roberto, Fred.	1.000	3	3	0	0	3	0
Rocha, Juan, Wil.	.933	11	14	0	1	15	0
Rodriguez, Gary, Kin.	.956	29	43	0	2	45	0
Ross, Jason, Dan.	.984	115	230	13	4	247	3
Saturria, Luis, P.W.	.943	127	235	11	15	261	3
Short, Rick, Fred.	.989	43	88	5	1	94	1
Stewart, Colin, Dan.	1.000	4	9	0	0	9	0
Tanner, Paul, P.W.	1.000	3	1	0	0	1	0
Terhune, Mike, Dan.	.982	35	53	2	1	56	0
Terrell, Jim, W.S.	1.000	2	3	1	0	4	0
Tomlinson, Goef, Wil.*	.955	33	63	0	3	66	0
Trippy, Joe, Dan.*	.981	31	45	7	1	53	0
Walker, Morgan, Lyn.*	.930	19	39	1	3	43	0
Warner, Bryan, Sal.*	.950	100	125	9	7	141	0
Whitaker, Chad, Kin.	.968	119	206	7	7	220	1
Whitlock, Brian, Kin.	1.000	11	16	1	0	17	0
Wong, Jerrod, Dan.*	.980	59	93	7	2	102	0

CATCHERS

Player, Team	Pct.	G	PO	A	E	TC	DP	PB
Alley, Chip, Fred.	.986	95	604	83	10	697	7	22
Anderson, Blake, Sal.	.984	28	170	16	3	189	1	1
Anderson, Franklin, Lyn.	.952	8	38	2	2	42	0	0
Antigua, Nilson, Lyn.	1.000	1	1	0	0	1	0	0
Barthol, Blake, Sal.	.989	101	760	81	9	850	1	17
Borges, Alex, Dan.	1.000	11	27	2	0	29	0	3
Bryant, Chris, Fred.	.750	1	3	0	1	4	0	0
Cruz, Edgar, Kin.	1.000	6	35	5	0	40	0	0
DeCinces, Tim, Fred.	.988	40	233	24	3	260	1	2
Downs, Brian, W.S.	1.000	4	25	3	0	28	0	0
Falciglia, Tony, P.W.	1.000	2	4	2	0	6	0	0
Felix, Hersy, Wil.	1.000	3	8	0	0	8	0	0
Gonzalez, Ricky, Kin.	.992	52	344	45	3	392	3	1
Haad, Yamid, Lyn.	.982	84	593	77	12	682	4	16
Hallmark, Pat, Wil.	.977	32	195	22	5	222	3	5
Harriss, Robin, Kin.	.987	44	354	32	5	391	1	5
Heintz, Chris, W.S.	.984	34	220	21	4	245	0	8
Konrady, Dennis, Kin.	.985	41	302	23	5	330	1	6
Lidle, Kevin, Dan.	.984	18	103	19	2	124	1	4
Lunar, Fernando, Dan.	.990	90	726	103	8	837	9	2
Martine, Chris, P.W.	.986	96	652	77	10	739	3	6
McNeal, Pepe, P.W.	.985	56	294	34	5	333	3	5
Mortimer, Mark, Dan.	.988	39	290	26	4	320	1	5
Norris, Dax, Dan.	.992	13	109	12	1	122	1	1
O'Toole, Bobby, Fred.	.982	9	49	5	1	55	0	1
Pagan, Carlos, Wil.	.985	72	491	50	8	549	4	13
PAUL, Josh, W.S.	.997	109	818	118	3	939	8	6
Phillips, Paul, Wil.	1.000	2	12	3	0	15	0	0
Reyes, Jose, Lyn.	.976	17	114	10	3	127	2	2
Russell, Jake, Kin.	1.000	6	16	1	0	17	0	0
Sheppard, Greg, W.S.	.778	3	6	1	2	9	0	0
Stevenson, Chad, Dan.	.975	9	74	5	2	81	0	2
Taylor, Adam, W.S.	.930	5	32	8	3	43	1	0
Ullery, Dave, Wil.	.995	62	381	55	2	438	6	12
Utting, Andy, Fred.	1.000	5	31	1	0	32	0	2
Wade, Michael, Fred.	.985	12	57	7	1	65	1	2
Wilson, Craig, Lyn.	.989	42	322	33	4	359	3	6

PITCHERS

Player, Team	Pct.	G	PO	A	E	TC	DP
Abbott, Jim, W.S.*	1.000	4	4	8	0	12	3
Ah Yat, Paul, Lyn.*	1.000	14	9	18	0	27	1
Alvarado, Carlos, Lyn.	.938	13	3	12	1	16	0
Ankiel, Rich, P.W.*	.926	21	5	20	2	27	0
Avrard, Corey, P.W.	1.000	31	3	3	0	6	1
Ayers, Mike, Lyn.*	1.000	34	1	7	0	8	1
Bacsik, Mike, Kin.*	.957	27	12	33	2	47	1
Bailey, Roger, Sal.	1.000	3	0	1	0	1	0
Baird, Brandon, Wil.*	.923	54	1	11	1	13	1
Bauer, Chuck, Lyn.	1.000	12	2	14	0	16	0
Beasley, Ray, Dan.*	1.000	54	5	13	0	18	0
Bell, Mike, Fred.*	1.000	38	10	18	0	28	1
Bell, Rob, Dan.	.837	28	14	22	7	43	1
Benes, Adam, P.W.	.750	10	2	1	1	4	1
Bevel, Bobby, Sal.*	.957	51	5	17	1	23	1
Biddle, Rocky, W.S.	.778	16	3	11	4	18	0
Brammer, J.D., Kin.	.500	15	0	1	1	2	0
Brewer, Ryan, Wil.	1.000	26	2	11	0	13	0
Brown, Jamie, Kin.	.943	27	10	23	2	35	1
Buirley, Matthew, Lyn.	1.000	13	3	4	0	7	0
Burke, John, Sal.	1.000	2	0	3	0	3	0
Bussa, Todd, Lyn.	1.000	35	5	9	0	14	1
Calero, Kiko, Wil.	.958	17	13	10	1	24	0
Calmus, Lance, Kin.	1.000	7	0	1	0	1	0
Carter, Lance, Wil.	.917	28	7	4	1	12	1
Chacon, Shawn, Sal.	.938	12	0	15	1	16	0
Chantres, Carlos, W.S.	1.000	13	7	8	0	15	1
Chapman, Jake, Wil.*	.964	27	13	40	2	55	1
Colmenares, Luis, Sal.	.885	28	19	27	6	52	0
Coogan, Patrick, P.W.	.917	14	2	9	1	12	0
Corn, Chris, Lyn.	1.000	7	1	5	0	6	1
Culp, Wes, Dan.	1.000	37	5	5	0	10	0
Daedelow, Craig, Fred.	1.000	1	0	1	0	1	0
Daneker, Pat, W.S.	1.000	7	4	10	0	14	2
Daniels, David, Lyn.	.833	14	2	3	1	6	1
Davenport, Joe, W.S.	.833	20	3	2	1	6	1
De Leon, Jose, P.W.	.909	57	3	7	1	11	1
De Paula, Sean, Kin.	1.000	28	1	8	0	9	0
Dewitt, Matt, P.W.	1.000	24	11	21	0	32	1
Dishman, Richard, Dan.	.920	20	7	16	2	25	0
Doyle, Tom, Sal.*	1.000	18	7	4	0	11	0
Drew, Tim, Kin.	.952	15	7	13	1	21	4
Duff, Matt, Lyn.	1.000	40	4	13	0	17	2
Durbin, Chad, Wil.	.913	26	7	14	2	23	0
Edwards, Jon, Kin.	.875	21	2	5	1	8	0
Eibey, Scott, Fred.*	.889	21	2	6	1	9	0
Emiliano, Jamie, Sal.	1.000	4	2	1	0	3	0
Falkenborg, Brian, Fred.	1.000	15	1	5	0	6	1
Farley, Joe, W.S.*	.968	21	6	24	1	31	0
Flach, Jason, Dan.	.957	37	12	10	1	23	0
Forbes, Cameron, Fred.	1.000	14	3	4	0	7	1
France, Aaron, Lyn.	.972	26	14	21	1	36	1
Garrett, Neil, Sal.	1.000	12	2	12	0	14	1
Garza, Alberto, Kin.	1.000	20	9	17	0	26	1
Geis, John, P.W.*	1.000	32	1	9	0	10	0
Gonzalez, Edwin, Wil.	.833	5	5	0	1	6	0
Gonzalez, Mike, Lyn.*	.857	7	1	5	1	7	2
Guzman, Wilson, Lyn.*	1.000	3	0	1	0	1	0
Hacen, Abraham, Fred.	.964	30	10	17	1	28	1
Hall, Yates, P.W.	1.000	5	1	1	0	2	0
Halla, Ryan, Lyn.	.800	40	2	6	2	10	0
Hamilton, Jimmy, Kin.*	1.000	44	3	12	0	15	0
Heredia, Maximo, Fred.	.826	29	5	14	4	23	3
Huffaker, Mike, P.W.	.917	53	4	7	1	12	0
Hughes, Mike, Kin.*	.818	9	2	7	2	11	0
Hunt, Jon, W.S.*	1.000	6	1	1	0	2	0
Hutchinson, Chad, P.W.	1.000	5	1	3	0	4	0
Iglesias, Mario, W.S.	1.000	35	5	7	0	12	0
Jacobs, Dwayne, Dan.	.783	31	7	11	5	23	2
Jerue, Tristan, P.W.	1.000	7	1	2	0	3	1
Karnuth, Jason, P.W.	.955	16	2	19	1	22	2
Kelly, Jeff, Lyn.*	1.000	10	2	2	0	4	0
Kenady, Jake, Sal.*	.667	32	1	5	3	9	0
Key, Jimmy, Fred.*	1.000	1	0	1	0	1	0
Lakman, Jason, W.S.	.941	13	7	9	1	17	0
Lamber, Justin, Wil.*	.889	32	4	4	1	9	0
Lambert, Kris, Lyn.*	.933	28	5	23	2	30	1
Lane, Aaron, Fred.*	1.000	5	1	5	0	6	0
Lee, David, Sal.	.889	54	7	1	1	9	0
Lidle, Kevin, Sal.	1.000	10	1	6	0	7	0
Lineweaver, Aaron, Wil.	.957	26	9	35	2	46	1

Player, Team	Pct.	G	PO	A	E	TC	DP
Lundquist, David, W.S.	1.000	6	0	1	0	1	0
Macca, Chris, Sal.	1.000	10	2	7	0	9	0
Mackey, Jason, Kin.*	1.000	5	1	2	0	3	0
Marquis, Jason, Dan.	1.000	22	7	12	0	19	0
MARTIN, Chandler, Sal.	1.000	24	21	36	0	57	1
Mastrolonardo, David, Fred.	.909	48	5	5	1	11	0
Matcuk, Steve, Sal.	.895	18	2	15	2	19	1
Mays, Jarrod, Kin.	1.000	4	2	2	0	4	0
McConnell, Sam, Lyn.*	1.000	19	3	24	0	27	2
McDade, Neal, Lyn.	.955	25	7	14	1	22	1
McDougal, Mike, P.W.	.857	17	1	5	1	7	0
McGlinchy, Kevin, Dan.	.962	22	9	16	1	26	4
McNatt, Josh, Fred.*	.907	27	8	31	4	43	2
Merrick, Brett, Kin.*	1.000	2	1	0	0	1	0
Meyer, Jake, W.S.	.500	11	0	1	1	2	0
Milburn, Robert, Dan.*	.905	45	6	13	2	21	2
Montgomery, Greg, P.W.	.800	35	2	6	2	10	1
Moreno, Orber, Wil.	1.000	23	1	2	0	3	0
Mullen, Scott, Wil.*	.969	14	9	22	1	32	5
Myette, Aaron, W.S.	1.000	6	2	4	0	6	0
Navarro, Jason, P.W.*	.917	30	2	20	2	24	0
Negrette, Richard, Kin.	.882	28	6	9	2	17	2
Nelson, Erick, Dan.*	.800	10	3	9	3	15	0
Newell, Brett, Wil.	.800	10	1	3	1	5	1
Nichols, Jamie, W.S.	.842	19	6	10	3	19	0
Nussbeck, Mark, P.W.	1.000	14	11	16	0	27	0
Ochsenfeld, Chris, W.S.*	1.000	17	1	4	0	5	0
O'Connor, Brian, Lyn.*	.952	14	2	18	1	21	0
Olszewski, Tim, Fred.	.900	34	2	7	1	10	0
Onley, Shawn, Dan.	.955	44	8	13	1	22	1
Opipari, Mario, P.W.	1.000	32	4	14	0	18	1
Paredes, Carlos, Wil.	.882	37	4	11	2	17	0
Paronto, Chad, Fred.	.897	18	8	18	3	29	1
Parrish, John, Fred.*	.905	16	7	12	2	21	0
Paugh, Rick, Lyn.*	.800	14	0	4	1	5	0
Pena, Jesus, W.S.*	1.000	23	2	4	0	6	0
Pirkl, Greg, Kin.	1.000	14	1	2	0	3	0
Porzio, Mike, Dan.-Sal.*	.938	33	5	25	2	32	2
Quevedo, Ruben, Dan.	.750	6	2	1	1	4	0
Reichert, Dan, Wil.	.833	2	1	4	1	6	0
Richardson, Kasey, Fred.*	.846	22	4	7	2	13	0

Player, Team	Pct.	G	PO	A	E	TC	DP
Rigdon, Paul, Kin.	.917	24	7	15	2	24	1
Riske, David, Kin.	1.000	53	3	9	0	12	1
Roberts, Mark, W.S.	.955	27	10	11	1	22	1
Rogers, Jason, Fred.*	1.000	17	1	1	0	2	0
Romero, Jordan, Fred.	1.000	15	3	3	0	6	0
Romine, Jason, Sal.	1.000	6	1	2	0	3	0
Rosa, Cristy, Sal.	1.000	17	1	4	0	5	0
Runion, Tony, Lyn.	1.000	36	2	12	0	14	0
Schmack, Brian, W.S.	.889	42	4	12	2	18	0
Schroeffel, Scott, Sal.	.955	38	5	16	1	22	1
Scott, Brian, W.S.	.909	19	10	10	2	22	1
Secoda, Jason, W.S.	1.000	6	2	3	0	5	0
Sims, Kenny, Fred.	1.000	3	1	1	0	2	0
Spenser, Kaipo, Kin.	1.000	13	1	10	0	11	0
Stein, Ethan, Wil.	.875	41	4	10	2	16	0
Steinmetz, Earl, Fred.	1.000	13	1	4	0	5	0
Stepka, Tom, Sal.	1.000	11	3	3	0	6	0
Tapia, Rafael, Fred.	1.000	1	1	0	0	1	0
Temple, Jason, Lyn.	1.000	6	0	1	0	1	0
Thompson, Mark, Sal.	.500	3	1	0	1	2	0
Thorn, Todd, Wil.*	.950	26	13	25	2	40	1
Towers, Josh, Fred.	.977	25	19	24	1	44	3
Tryon, Eric, Dan.*	.000	6	0	0	1	1	0
Viano, Jason, Wil.	1.000	14	0	5	0	5	1
Virchis, Adam, W.S.	.920	22	11	12	2	25	0
Wagner, Ken, Kin.	.833	10	2	3	1	6	0
Walls, Doug, Sal.	.974	27	12	26	1	39	0
Warner, Bryan, Sal.*	1.000	3	0	1	0	1	0
Watson, Mark, Kin.*	1.000	1	1	0	0	1	0
Welch, Travis, P.W.	1.000	12	1	4	0	5	0
West, Adam, P.W.*	.667	43	4	6	5	15	2
Whitley, Curtis, W.S.*	1.000	10	0	3	0	3	0
Whitten, Casey, Kin.*	.818	9	1	8	2	11	0
Wilson, Kris, Wil.	.833	10	2	3	1	6	0
Winkelsas, Joe, Dan.	1.000	50	8	11	0	19	0
Zolecki, Mike, W.S.	1.000	8	0	2	0	2	0

PITCHERS WITH TWO OR MORE TEAMS

Player, Team	Pct.	G	PO	A	E	TC	DP
Porzio, Mike, Dan.	.900	26	2	16	2	20	1
Porzio, Mike, Sal.	1.000	7	3	9	0	12	1

The following players did not have any fielding statistics at the positions indicated or appeared only as a designated hitter, pinch-hitter or pinch-runner: B. Anderson, of; Berger, p; M. Burke, of; Corey, p; Daedelow, 2b; DeCinces, 2b; Deschenes, 2b; Eckelman, of; Fogg, p; Gross, p; Hasselhoff, p; Haverbusch, 2b; Hernandez, p; Hogan, 1b; Hundt, of; Izquierdo, p; Jimenez, of; Karnuth, of; Koeman, of; Kohlmeier, p; Lawrence, p; LeCronier, p; C. Lee, p; Lidle, 2b; Mackowiak, 2b, of; J. Martin, p; Ndungidi, of; Paulino, p; Peguero, p; Radcliff, 3b; Reichow, p; Richard, dh; M. Rivera, ss; L. Rodriguez, 1b; Russell, 3b; Stevenson, p; Stoops, p; S. Walker, of; Whitaker, 3b; Whitlock, p.

LEAGUE CHAMPIONS

Year	Team	Pct.	Year	Team	Pct.	Year	Team	Pct.
1945—	Danville	.681	1963—	Kinston§	.538	1977—	Lynchburg	.591
1946—	Greensboro	.599		Greensboro§	.590		Peninsula‡	.556
	Raleigh (2nd)†	.563		Wilson (2nd)†	.535	1978—	Peninsula	.696
1947—	Burlington	.613	1964—	Kinston§	.572		Lynchburg†	.614
	Raleigh (3rd)†	.574		Winston-Salem§†	.590	1979—	Winston-Salem■	.607
1948—	Raleigh	.592	1965—	Peninsula§	.597	1980—	Peninsula‡	.714
	Martinsville (2nd)†	.570		Durham§	.580		Durham	.600
1949—	Danville	.601		Tidewater†	.528	1981—	Peninsula	.522
	Burlington (4th)†	.500	1966—	Kinston§	.547		Hagerstown‡	.507
1950—	Winston-Salem*	.693		Winston-Salem§	.586	1982—	Alexandria‡	.597
1951—	Durham	.600		Rocky Mount†	.533		Durham	.588
	Winston-Salem (2nd)†	.583	1967—	Durham∞(West.)	.536	1983—	Lynchburg‡	.691
1952—	Raleigh	.581		Raleigh (East.)	.542		Winston-Salem	.529
	Reidsville (4th)†	.536	1968—	Salem (West.)	.607	1984—	Lynchburg†	.645
1953—	Raleigh	.593		Ral-Dur (East.)	.597		Durham	.486
	Danville (2nd)†	.572		HP-Thom.▲(W.)	.493	1985—	Lynchburg	.679
1954—	Fayetteville*	.628	1969—	Rocky M (East.)	.569		Winston-Salem‡	.417
1955—	HP-Thomasville	.580		Salem (West.)	.542	1986—	Hagerstown	.655
	Danville (2nd)†	.533		Ral-Dur◆(East.)	.560		Winston-Salem‡	.594
1956—	HP-Thomasville	.591	1970—	Winston-Salem‡	.586	1987—	Salem‡	.576
	Fayetteville (4th)§	.523		Burlington	.597		Kinston	.536
1957—	Durham	.632	1971—	Peninsula‡	.647	1988—	Kinston§	.629
	HP-Thomasville	.622		Kinston	.623		Lynchburg	.486
1958—	Danville	.576	1972—	Salem‡	.657	1989—	Durham	.609
	Burlington (4th)†	.511		Burlington	.632		Prince William‡	.522
1959—	Raleigh	.600	1973—	Lynchburg	.588	1990—	Kinston	.652
	Wilson (2nd)†	.550		Winston-Salem‡	.557		Frederick‡	.544
1960—	Greensboro‡	.636	1974—	Salem	.671	1991—	Kinston‡	.645
	Burlington	.586		Salem	.582		Lynchburg	.482
1961—	Wilson	.594	1975—	Rocky Mount	.667	1992—	Lynchburg	.570
1962—	Durham	.636		Rocky Mount	.614		Peninsula‡	.536
	Wilson	.600	1976—	Winston-Salem	.618	1993—	Wilmington	.532
	Kinston (2nd)†	.593		Winston-Salem	.551		Winston-Salem‡	.514

Year	Team	Pct.	Year	Team	Pct.	Year	Team	Pct.
1994—	Wilmington‡	.681	1996—	Wilmington▼	.571	1998—	Wilmington▼	.614
	Winston-Salem	.555		Kinston	.551		Winston-Salem	.568
1995—	Wilmington	.601	1997—	Kinston	.621			
	Kinston‡	.591		Lynchburg†	.586			

*Won championship and four-club playoff. †Won four-club playoff. ‡Won split-season playoff. §League was divided into Eastern, Western divisions. ∞Won eight-club, two-division playoff. sWon eight-club, two-division playoff against Raleigh-Durham. ◆Won eight-club, two-division playoff against Burlington. ■Won both halves of split season (no playoffs). ▼League divided into Northern and Southern divisions and played a split-season, won playoffs.

FLORIDA STATE LEAGUE

LEAGUE OFFICE

President
Chuck Murphy

Address
P.O. Box 349
Daytona Beach, FL 32115

Phone
904-252-7479

Teams (affiliation)
Brevard County Manatees (Marlins)
Charlotte Rangers (Rangers)
Clearwater Phillies (Phillies)
Daytona Cubs (Cubs)
Dunedin Blue Jays (Blue Jays)
Fort Myers Miracle (Twins)
Jupiter Hammerheads (Expos)

Kissimmee Cobras (Astros)
Lakeland Tigers (Tigers)
St. Lucie Mets (Mets)
St. Petersburg Devil Rays (Devil Rays)
Sarasota Red Sox (Red Sox)
Tampa Yankees (Yankees)
Vero Beach Dodgers (Dodgers)

1998 FINAL STANDINGS

FIRST HALF

EAST DIVISION

Team	W	L	T	Pct.	GB
Jupiter (Expos)	40	30	0	.571	....
St. Lucie (Mets)	36	33	0	.522	3.5
Daytona (Cubs)	35	35	0	.500	5.0
Kissimmee (Astros)	30	40	0	.429	10.0
Vero Beach (Dodgers)	29	41	0	.414	11.0
Brevard County (Marlins)	18	52	0	.257	22.0

WEST DIVISION

Team	W	L	T	Pct.	GB
Charlotte (Rangers)	46	23	0	.667	....
Dunedin (Blue Jays)	43	27	0	.614	3.5
Clearwater (Phillies)	42	28	0	.600	4.5
Sarasota (Red Sox)	38	31	0	.551	8.0
Lakeland (Tigers)	38	32	0	.543	8.5
St. Petersburg (Devil Rays)	37	33	0	.529	9.5
Fort Myers (Twins)	30	39	0	.435	16.0
Tampa (Yankees)	26	44	0	.371	20.5

SECOND HALF

EAST DIVISION

Team	W	L	T	Pct.	GB
Jupiter (Expos)	40	30	0	.571	....
St. Lucie (Mets)	34	33	1	.507	4.5
Kissimmee (Astros)	34	35	0	.493	5.5
Daytona (Cubs)	32	38	0	.457	8.0
Vero Beach (Dodgers)	29	40	0	.420	10.5
Brevard County (Marlins)	25	45	0	.357	15.0

WEST DIVISION

Team	W	L	T	Pct.	GB
Tampa (Yankees)	46	23	0	.667	....
Clearwater (Phillies)	40	30	0	.571	6.5
Sarasota (Red Sox)	38	30	0	.559	7.5
Dunedin (Blue Jays)	39	31	0	.557	7.5
Charlotte (Rangers)	36	33	0	.522	10.0
Fort Myers (Twins)	35	34	1	.507	11.0
Lakeland (Tigers)	29	40	0	.420	17.0
St. Petersburg (Devil Rays)	27	42	0	.391	19.0

COMPOSITE

Team	Char.	Dun.	Cle.	Jup.	Sar.	Tam.	StL	Lak.	Day.	F.M.	StP	Kis.	V.B.	B.C.	W	L	T	Pct.	GB
Charlotte (Rangers)	....	6	6	3	5	9	4	7	4	12	8	6	5	7	82	56	0	.594	....
Dunedin (Blue Jays)	6	....	7	3	9	7	5	7	4	6	11	5	4	8	82	58	0	.586	1.0
Clearwater (Phillies)	6	9	....	4	8	8	6	7	4	9	9	3	5	4	82	58	0	.586	1.0
Jupiter (Expos)	5	5	4	....	2	4	6	5	8	6	7	8	11	9	80	60	0	.571	3.0
Sarasota (Red Sox)	6	3	4	6	....	5	4	8	5	8	7	8	5	7	76	61	0	.555	5.5
Tampa (Yankees)	3	7	6	4	7	....	2	6	7	7	9	6	3	5	72	67	0	.518	10.5
St. Lucie (Mets)	4	3	2	10	2	6	....	5	8	3	3	7	6	11	70	66	1	.515	11.0
Lakeland (Tigers)	9	5	5	3	8	5	3	....	4	3	6	5	4	7	67	72	0	.482	15.5
Daytona (Cubs)	4	4	4	6	3	1	8	4	....	5	1	7	8	12	67	73	0	.479	16.0
Fort Myers (Twins)	4	6	3	2	8	5	3	9	3	....	5	4	6	7	65	73	1	.471	17.0
St. Petersburg (Devil Rays)	4	3	5	1	5	7	5	6	7	7	....	4	5	5	64	75	0	.460	18.5
Kissimmee (Astros)	2	3	5	8	0	2	7	3	9	4	3	....	10	8	64	75	0	.460	18.5
Vero Beach (Dodgers)	2	4	3	5	3	5	10	4	6	2	3	4	....	7	58	81	0	.417	24.5
Brevard County (Marlins)	1	0	4	5	1	3	3	1	4	1	3	8	9	....	43	97	0	.307	40.0

Brevard County played home games in Melbourne, Fla.; Charlotte played home games in Port Charlotte, Fla.

Major league affiliations in parentheses.

PLAYOFFS: St. Lucie defeated Jupiter two games to none; Tampa defeated Charlotte two games to none; St. Lucie defeated Tampa three games to two to win league championship.

REGULAR-SEASON ATTENDANCE: Brevard County, 107,546; Charlotte, 43,659; Clearwater, 73,300; Daytona, 74,082; Dunedin, 60,485; Fort Myers, 107,110; Jupiter 94,155; Kissimmee, 41,941; Lakeland, 35,693; St. Lucie, 37,189; St. Petersburg, 87,181; Sarasota, 43,219; Tampa, 110,341; Vero Beach, 50,094. Total—965,995 Playoffs (9 games)—2,944. All-Star Game in Fort Myers—4,146.

MANAGERS: Brevard County, Rick Renteria; Charlotte, James Byrd; Clearwater, Bill Dancy; Daytona, Steve Roadcap; Dunedin, Rocket Wheeler; Fort Myers, Mike Boulanger; Jupiter, Doug Sisson; Kissimmee, Manny Acta; Lakeland, Mark Meleski; St. Lucie, Howie Freiling; St. Petersburg, Roy Silver; Sarasota, Bob Geren; Tampa, Lee Mazzilli, Vero Beach, John Shoemaker.

ALL-STAR TEAM: 1B—Shawn Gallagher, Charlotte; 2B—Brent Abernathy, Dunedin; 3B—Casey Blake, Dunedin; SS—Kelly Dransfeldt, Charlotte; Utility INF—David Eckstein, Sarasota; OF—Pete Tucci, Dunedin; Alex Sanchez, St. Petersburg; Mike Zywica, Charlotte; Utility OF—Julio Ramirez, Brevard County; C—Chad Moeller, Fort Myers; C—Victor Valencia, Tampa; DH—Tommy Peterman, Fort Myers; RHP—Billy Koch, Dunedin; RHP—Ken Pumphrey, St. Lucie; RHP—Mark Rutherford, Clearwater LHP—Doug Davis, Charlotte; RP—R.A. Dickey, Charlotte; RP—Kyle Kawabata, Clearwater; Most Valuable Player—Shawn Gallagher, Charlotte; Manager of the Year— Doug Sisson, Jupiter; Coach of the Year—Rocket Wheeler, Dunedin; Coach—James Byrd, Charlotte.

1998 BATTING

TEAM

Team	Avg.	G	TPA	AB	R	H	TB	2B	3B	HR	RBI	SH	SF	HP	BB	IBB	SO	SB	CS	GDP	LOB	ShO	Slg.	OBP
Dunedin	.284	140	5398	4797	763	1364	2076	291	23	125	684	54	44	54	449	13	1082	162	92	93	978	7	.433	.349
Daytona	.281	140	5545	4851	830	1361	2053	249	43	119	745	31	33	90	540	19	1000	167	69	105	1049	9	.423	.361
Charlotte	.277	138	5363	4699	800	1303	1977	262	41	110	710	32	65	49	518	14	915	271	109	78	943	2	.421	.351
Fort Myers	.273	139	5463	4840	704	1321	1874	217	27	94	631	54	40	49	480	34	863	222	86	99	1025	6	.387	.342
Clearwater	.273	140	5503	4829	758	1317	1919	250	47	86	668	46	59	88	481	21	803	163	80	108	1015	4	.397	.346
Tampa	.272	139	5375	4760	712	1297	1971	243	28	125	642	44	47	69	455	19	1009	128	59	92	993	6	.414	.342
St. Petersburg..	.269	139	5411	4827	629	1297	1791	222	31	70	569	34	51	36	463	23	857	118	71	111	1054	9	.371	.334
Kissimmee	.268	139	5306	4720	679	1265	1857	226	39	96	611	28	34	57	467	15	815	170	71	102	983	8	.393	.339
Lakeland	.267	139	5384	4767	717	1271	1866	224	34	101	644	36	43	57	481	14	960	145	70	86	1014	9	.391	.338
Sarasota	.264	137	5272	4607	711	1217	1805	237	33	95	626	31	37	74	523	17	1008	164	56	102	1013	7	.392	.346
St. Lucie	.254	137	5143	4593	623	1168	1712	211	30	91	557	51	38	67	394	12	977	147	84	87	914	5	.373	.320
Vero Beach	.252	139	5214	4635	573	1167	1713	196	28	98	506	36	36	42	465	15	967	134	67	101	1003	10	.370	.323
Jupiter	.250	140	5261	4676	638	1170	1705	239	19	86	555	38	48	58	441	15	968	162	80	81	940	4	.365	.320
Brevard County.	.234	140	5147	4582	484	1073	1472	150	33	61	433	39	34	56	436	12	969	156	68	94	980	12	.321	.306

INDIVIDUAL

TOP QUALIFIERS FOR BATTING CHAMPIONSHIP

Minimum 378 plate appearances. *Lefthanded batter. †Switch-hitter.

Player, Team	Avg.	G	TPA	AB	R	H	TB	2B	3B	HR	RBI	SH	SF	HP	BB	IBB	SO	SB	CS	GDP	Slg.	OBP
Blake, Casey, Dun.	.350	88	389	340	62	119	186	28	3	11	65	3	7	9	30	1	81	9	6	5	.547	.409
Zuleta, Julio, Day.	.344	94	422	366	69	126	201	25	1	16	86	1	5	15	35	1	59	6	3	12	.549	.418
Sanchez, Alex, St.P.*	.330	128	593	545	77	180	218	17	9	1	50	4	12	1	31	1	70	66	33	5	.400	.360
Tucci, Pete, Dun.	.329	92	394	356	72	117	222	30	3	23	76	2	2	5	29	0	97	8	5	6	.624	.385
Abernathy, Brent, Dun.	.328	124	548	485	85	159	206	36	1	3	65	12	6	1	44	0	38	35	13	11	.425	.381
Johnson, Nick, Tam.*	.317	92	393	303	69	96	163	14	1	17	58	0	3	19	68	3	76	1	4	5	.538	.466
Peterman, Tommy, Ft.M.*	.312	135	593	519	71	162	262	36	2	20	110	1	6	4	63	13	86	2	0	11	.505	.387
Lawrence, Joe, Dun.*	.308	125	569	454	102	140	216	31	6	11	44	5	1	4	105	2	88	15	12	11	.476	.441
Gallagher, Shawn, Char.	.308	137	603	520	111	160	283	37	4	26	121	0	10	7	66	3	116	18	6	5	.544	.386
Eckstein, David, Sar.	.306	135	615	503	99	154	200	29	4	3	58	1	2	22	87	3	51	45	16	8	.398	.428
Giles, Tim, Dun.*	.303	102	398	363	53	110	188	20	2	18	65	1	3	0	31	3	83	3	2	4	.518	.355
Lugo, Julio, Kis.	.303	128	570	509	81	154	223	20	14	7	62	6	2	4	49	3	72	51	18	13	.438	.367
Lamb, Michael, Char.†	.302	135	595	536	83	162	230	35	3	9	93	2	8	4	45	5	63	18	7	10	.429	.356
Wakeland, Chris, Lake.*	.302	131	567	487	82	147	237	36	4	15	89	4	5	5	66	4	111	19	13	4	.487	.387
Morris, Jeremy, Dun.	.301	124	502	445	69	134	200	25	1	13	72	2	6	1	48	1	96	11	3	8	.449	.366

DEPARTMENTAL LEADERS: G—Burnham, 139; AB—J. Ramirez, 559; R—Gallagher, 111; H—Sanchez, 180; TB—Gallagher, 283; 2B—Gallagher, 37; 3B—Lugo, 14; HR—Gallagher, 26; RBI—Gallagher, 121; SH—Davidson, 13; SF—Sanchez, 12; HP—Eckstein, 22; BB—J. Lawrence, 105; IBB—Peterman, 13; SO—Schwab, 175; SB—Felston, 86; CS—Sanchez, 33; GIDP—Espinal, 21; Slg.—Tucci, .624; OBP—N. Johnson, .466.

ALL PLAYERS

*Lefthanded batter. †Switch-hitter.

Player, Team	Avg.	G	TPA	AB	R	H	TB	2B	3B	HR	RBI	SH	SF	HP	BB	IBB	SO	SB	CS	GDP	Slg.	OBP
Abernathy, Brent, Dun.	.328	124	548	485	85	159	206	36	1	3	65	12	6	1	44	0	38	35	13	11	.425	.381
Abreu, Dennis, Day.	.260	127	577	535	87	139	176	21	5	2	58	8	0	3	31	0	133	23	14	14	.329	.304
Acevedo, Luis, Char.	.000	1	4	4	0	0	0	0	0	0	0	0	0	0	0	0	1	0	0	0	.000	.000
Adams, Jason, Kis.	.250	84	295	268	31	67	97	11	2	5	32	2	2	2	21	0	57	1	3	7	.362	.307
Adolfo, Carlos, Jup.	.269	88	379	334	51	90	149	16	2	13	44	3	1	4	37	0	80	10	8	6	.446	.348
Adriana, Sharnol, Dun.	.286	73	265	227	45	65	113	24	0	8	44	0	2	6	30	1	57	18	6	5	.498	.381
Airoso, Kurt, Lake.	.290	109	461	386	69	112	181	24	0	15	61	1	1	5	67	0	106	7	3	7	.469	.401
Alcantara, Israel, St.P.	.333	38	164	141	21	47	82	5	0	10	26	0	0	2	21	2	29	1	0	6	.582	.427
Allen, Buck, Cle.*	.000	47	1	0	0	0	0	0	0	0	0	1	0	0	0	0	0	0	0	0	.000	.000
Alleyne, Roberto, St.P.	.194	18	74	67	8	13	26	5	1	2	11	0	0	0	7	0	22	0	0	1	.388	.270
Alvarez, Julio, Lake.†	.000	9	15	13	2	0	0	0	0	0	0	0	0	0	2	0	5	0	0	1	.000	.133
Alvarez, Rafael, Ft.M.†	.292	110	445	391	54	114	150	20	2	4	38	5	3	1	45	8	51	19	8	5	.384	.364
Amador, Manny, Cle.†	.276	35	120	105	12	29	37	5	0	1	14	2	2	1	10	0	21	1	2	3	.352	.339
Amerson, Gordon, Tam.*	.211	6	21	19	2	4	5	1	0	0	1	0	0	1	1	0	4	0	0	1	.263	.286
Amezcua, Adan, Kis.	.275	72	294	262	40	72	117	9	1	8	35	1	2	7	22	0	43	2	0	8	.447	.345
Anderson, Christopher, St.P.	.143	10	15	14	2	2	2	0	0	0	3	0	0	1	0	0	8	0	0	0	.143	.200
Artzen, Brian, Jup.	.276	17	63	58	10	16	24	3	1	1	6	0	0	1	4	0	12	0	0	3	.414	.333
Arredondo, Hernando, St.P.	.189	25	94	90	14	17	24	4	0	1	4	2	0	0	2	0	18	0	0	4	.267	.207
August, Brian, Tam.	.159	22	72	63	7	10	11	1	0	0	1	1	1	1	6	0	16	1	0	4	.175	.239
Aylor, Brian, Tam.*	.268	17	60	56	8	15	25	4	0	2	6	1	0	1	2	1	23	4	0	1	.446	.305
Bady, Ed, Jup.†	.250	1	4	4	1	1	2	1	0	0	0	0	0	0	0	0	1	1	0	0	.500	.250
Barr, Tucker, Kis.	.253	57	208	182	25	46	80	10	0	8	31	0	1	2	23	0	39	0	2	2	.440	.341
Bautista, Rayner, Lake.	.236	32	119	110	11	26	32	4	1	0	15	2	1	0	6	0	36	0	0	2	.291	.274
Bazzani, Matt, Sar.	.200	2	5	5	0	1	3	0	1	0	1	0	0	0	0	0	3	0	0	1	.600	.200
Beamon, Trey, Lake.*	.500	2	9	6	2	3	3	0	0	0	0	0	0	0	3	0	0	0	0	0	.500	.667
Becker, Brian, St.P.	.283	129	547	492	64	139	198	27	4	8	63	0	8	4	43	1	116	1	1	14	.402	.340
Bell, Mike, St.L.	.349	18	82	63	11	22	34	5	2	1	14	2	5	2	8	2	10	2	1	1	.540	.410
Blake, Casey, Dun.*	.350	88	389	340	62	119	186	28	3	11	65	3	7	9	30	1	81	9	6	5	.547	.409
Blandford, Paul, Jup.	.211	12	47	38	9	8	12	1	0	1	7	0	1	0	7	0	7	0	0	1	.316	.326
Blum, Geoffrey, Jup.†	.276	17	75	58	13	16	22	6	0	0	5	2	1	1	13	1	14	1	0	0	.379	.411
Bolivar, Papo, Ft.M.	.264	126	523	489	59	129	163	15	2	5	45	3	1	1	29	1	104	14	11	14	.333	.306
Bradley, Milton, Jup.†	.287	67	299	261	55	75	106	14	1	5	34	1	2	5	30	2	42	17	9	3	.406	.369
Bravo, Danny, Jup.†	.155	24	83	71	5	11	12	1	0	0	3	0	2	2	8	0	14	1	1	0	.169	.253

Player, Team	Avg.	G	TPA	AB	R	H	TB	2B	3B	HR	RBI	SH	SF	HP	BB	IBB	SO	SB	CS	GDP	Slg.	OBP
Brett, Jason, St.L.	.333	2	7	6	1	2	2	0	0	0	1	0	1	0	0	0	1	0	0	0	.333	.286
Brown, Jason, V.B.	.228	85	301	267	23	61	86	13	0	4	27	3	1	4	26	1	60	0	0	9	.322	.305
Brown, Richard, Tam.*	.298	80	334	282	46	84	136	13	3	11	38	2	0	5	45	1	54	8	6	3	.482	.404
Brown, Roosevelt, Day.*	.344	68	271	244	49	84	136	15	5	9	43	0	2	2	23	3	46	3	2	6	.557	.402
Burnham, Gary, Cle.*	.296	139	597	513	93	152	229	33	10	8	70	0	7	14	63	8	76	10	4	9	.446	.384
Burns, Kevin, Kis.*	.270	128	547	470	69	127	216	24	4	19	81	0	3	5	69	5	124	11	3	8	.460	.367
Burrell, Patrick, Cle.	.303	37	161	132	29	40	70	7	1	7	30	0	2	0	27	2	22	2	0	3	.530	.416
Callahan, David, B.C.*	.333	5	22	21	3	7	8	1	0	0	4	0	0	1	0	0	4	0	0	1	.381	.364
Camilli, Jason, Jup.	.258	89	353	314	45	81	104	15	1	2	33	1	1	2	35	2	55	9	10	2	.331	.335
Camilo, Jose, B.C.*	.216	101	395	357	34	77	106	16	2	3	27	9	3	3	23	0	74	10	7	4	.297	.267
Capellan, Rene, Lake.	.230	55	212	200	24	46	57	6	1	1	22	1	1	4	6	0	18	1	4	7	.285	.265
Carey, Orlando, Tam.	.160	10	31	25	5	4	4	0	0	0	1	4	0	0	2	0	7	3	0	1	.160	.222
Carr, Dustin, St.P.	.256	138	608	516	85	132	183	23	5	6	52	8	3	11	70	4	86	11	4	9	.355	.355
Carreno, Jose, Jup.	.250	10	31	28	2	7	14	1	0	2	6	1	0	0	2	0	6	0	0	0	.500	.300
Carroll, Jamey, Jup.	.261	55	254	222	40	58	63	5	0	0	14	2	1	5	24	1	26	11	4	2	.284	.345
Cedeno, Jesus, Lake.	.238	84	317	286	41	68	101	14	2	5	39	3	3	4	21	1	66	1	3	5	.353	.296
Cedeno, Roger, V.B.†	.429	6	26	21	5	9	14	0	1	1	6	0	0	0	5	0	5	1	0	2	.667	.538
Chancey, Bailey, St.L.†	.232	54	215	168	33	39	44	5	0	0	10	5	0	6	36	0	34	27	3	3	.262	.386
Chatman, Karl, Jup.	.210	69	269	238	25	50	75	11	1	4	28	1	5	2	23	0	63	13	1	8	.315	.280
Chavera, Arnie, Kis.*	.301	84	318	269	46	81	134	17	0	12	50	1	5	8	35	2	64	0	0	5	.498	.391
Cheek, Shawn, Char.	.138	32	94	87	7	12	22	4	0	2	10	0	1	4	2	0	32	0	1	0	.253	.191
Chevalier, Virgil, Sar.	.327	81	362	327	59	107	161	22	4	8	59	1	6	1	27	3	59	13	4	5	.492	.374
Chiaffredo, Paul, Dun.	.234	89	321	290	34	68	99	19	0	4	41	6	3	6	16	0	68	1	3	8	.341	.286
Choi, Kyung, Sar.*	.271	63	209	181	25	49	73	10	1	4	23	1	4	3	17	0	32	7	0	5	.403	.337
Clapinski, Chris, B.C.†	.071	5	22	14	1	1	3	0	1	0	4	0	1	0	7	2	2	0	0	1	.214	.364
Colina, Roberto, St.P.*	.300	94	409	360	44	108	152	22	2	6	46	0	2	3	44	5	50	2	3	8	.422	.379
Collier, Lamonte, Cle.	.259	25	85	81	7	21	25	2	1	0	5	1	0	0	3	0	15	1	1	4	.309	.286
Collins, Francis, Cle.	.248	32	138	121	20	30	33	1	1	0	3	1	0	1	15	0	22	5	4	2	.273	.336
Colquitt, Jason, Lake.	.148	24	69	61	4	9	11	2	0	0	5	0	1	1	6	1	19	0	0	2	.180	.232
Conway, Scott, B.C.*	.167	9	27	24	3	4	5	1	0	0	0	0	0	1	2	0	5	0	0	0	.208	.259
Cook, Hayward, B.C.	.198	70	277	243	21	48	61	9	2	0	16	2	1	2	29	0	78	10	2	4	.251	.287
Cooley, Shannon, Cle.*	.218	19	62	55	3	12	16	1	0	1	6	2	1	0	4	0	10	1	0	1	.291	.267
Corps, Erick, St.P.†	.257	101	353	303	41	78	100	10	3	2	32	2	5	2	41	0	61	4	7	6	.330	.345
Cossins, Tim, Tam.	.223	30	100	94	6	21	30	6	0	1	6	2	1	0	3	0	14	0	0	4	.319	.245
Costello, Brian, Cle.	.243	36	150	136	20	33	51	7	1	3	15	2	2	2	8	1	41	4	2	1	.375	.291
Cotton, John, Day.*	.292	12	52	48	8	14	27	4	0	3	11	0	0	1	3	0	8	0	0	3	.563	.346
Crane, Todd, Cle.	.270	126	526	440	77	119	178	22	5	9	57	4	6	4	72	2	88	34	8	10	.405	.374
Cranford, Joey, Ft.M.	.224	75	287	254	41	57	102	15	3	8	39	4	0	2	26	0	58	6	1	3	.402	.301
Cruz, Deivi, Lake.	.000	2	9	9	0	0	0	0	0	0	1	0	0	0	0	0	1	0	0	0	.000	.000
Cuevas, Trent, V.B.	.259	92	352	324	42	84	124	21	2	5	41	2	1	3	22	1	52	3	0	11	.383	.311
Dallimore, Brian, Kis.	.254	62	269	240	34	61	74	11	1	0	19	4	1	5	19	0	42	7	5	6	.308	.321
Davidson, Cleatus, Ft.M.†	.241	130	591	527	97	127	159	12	7	2	45	13	3	3	45	0	99	44	16	6	.302	.303
Davis, Glenn, V.B.†	.237	102	453	376	63	89	167	14	2	20	63	0	5	2	70	1	106	13	4	7	.444	.355
De La Rosa, Tomas, Jup.	.251	117	446	390	56	98	131	22	1	3	43	10	3	6	37	0	61	27	7	5	.336	.323
Delgado, Carlos, Dun.*	.313	4	18	16	4	5	12	1	0	2	7	0	0	0	2	0	4	0	0	1	.750	.389
De Los Santos, Eddy, St.P.	.239	111	421	393	33	94	107	11	1	0	32	5	3	3	17	1	64	6	4	7	.272	.274
Dennis, Les, Tam.	.183	44	114	104	16	19	26	4	0	1	8	5	0	0	5	0	20	1	0	6	.250	.220
Derosso, Tony, Sar.	.308	4	16	13	1	4	7	3	0	0	5	0	0	0	3	1	1	0	0	0	.538	.438
Diaz, Juan, V.B.	.292	67	278	250	33	73	138	12	1	17	51	0	3	4	21	2	52	1	2	4	.552	.353
Donato, Dan, St.P.*	.310	43	184	171	21	53	68	12	0	1	25	0	3	0	10	1	22	1	1	5	.398	.342
Dransfeldt, Kelly, Char.	.322	67	282	245	46	79	150	17	0	18	76	0	6	2	29	1	67	7	2	4	.612	.390
Dubose, Brian, Lake.*	.314	69	303	258	45	81	136	7	3	14	48	0	4	2	39	2	51	8	3	5	.527	.403
Duffy, Jim, Kis.	.188	24	86	80	7	15	20	2	0	1	8	0	0	2	4	0	29	1	1	1	.250	.244
Eckstein, David, Sar.	.306	135	615	503	99	154	200	29	4	3	58	1	2	22	87	3	51	45	16	8	.398	.428
Ellis, John, Char.	.231	60	218	208	22	48	66	9	0	3	25	1	0	0	9	0	43	1	2	4	.317	.263
Elwood, Brad, Tam.	.333	3	4	3	1	1	1	0	0	0	1	1	0	0	0	0	0	0	0	0	.333	.333
Emmons, Scott, Tam.	.250	13	29	24	3	6	8	2	0	0	4	0	0	1	4	0	6	1	0	2	.333	.379
Encarnacion, Juan, Lake.	.250	4	19	16	4	4	6	0	1	0	4	0	0	1	2	0	4	4	0	0	.375	.368
Erickson, Corey, St.L.	.225	100	372	346	49	78	127	23	4	6	33	0	1	9	16	0	88	5	2	6	.367	.277
Escalona, Felix, Kis.	.000	3	4	4	0	0	0	0	0	0	0	0	0	0	0	0	1	0	0	0	.000	.000
Espinal, Juan, Sar.	.278	127	552	508	76	141	223	32	1	16	88	1	2	4	37	2	107	3	1	21	.439	.330
Estrada, Johnny, Cle.†	.222	37	126	117	8	26	34	8	0	0	13	2	2	0	5	0	7	0	0	2	.291	.250
Everson, Darin, Sar.*	.351	17	65	57	16	20	42	5	1	5	17	0	1	2	5	0	9	1	0	3	.737	.415
Faggett, Ethan, Sar.*	.279	62	271	233	42	65	91	12	1	4	25	7	3	3	25	1	55	13	5	3	.391	.352
Farraez, Jesus, Kis.	.242	44	148	132	18	32	39	2	1	1	11	1	0	1	14	0	36	4	0	3	.295	.320
Felston, Anthony, Ft.M.*	.279	114	532	427	74	119	127	8	0	0	43	10	6	6	83	2	65	86	26	5	.297	.398
Font, Franklin, Day.	.294	60	225	204	26	60	64	2	1	0	16	2	0	1	18	0	35	7	6	3	.314	.354
Forkerway, Trey, Day.	.149	35	83	74	9	11	18	2	1	1	11	0	1	0	8	0	6	0	1	1	.243	.229
Francia, David, Cle.*	.278	48	217	194	33	54	85	13	0	6	23	2	2	7	12	0	30	13	4	4	.438	.340
Fraser, Joe, Ft.M.	.267	34	124	101	25	27	41	3	1	3	13	3	2	3	15	1	12	3	1	2	.406	.372
Friedholm, Scott, St.P.	.200	10	17	15	2	3	4	1	0	0	1	0	0	0	2	0	3	0	0	0	.267	.294
Fuentes, Javier, Sar.	.275	82	300	251	45	69	97	14	1	4	29	1	0	7	38	1	38	5	2	5	.386	.385
Fuller, Aaron, Day.†	.295	79	361	292	63	86	129	17	7	4	36	2	2	1	64	1	50	18	4	3	.442	.421
Gainey, Bryon, St.L.*	.280	88	358	336	47	94	172	15	3	19	57	0	3	3	16	2	116	1	3	8	.512	.316
Gallagher, Shawn, Char.	.308	137	603	520	111	160	283	37	4	26	121	0	10	7	66	0	116	18	6	5	.544	.386
Garcia, Neil, St.P.†	.320	92	373	328	45	105	143	20	0	6	52	1	2	2	40	4	40	3	4	6	.436	.395
Garrett, Jason, B.C.	.216	62	244	222	16	48	64	5	1	3	25	1	2	2	17	0	55	1	3	7	.288	.276
Giles, Tim, Dun.*	.303	102	398	363	53	110	188	20	2	18	65	1	3	0	31	3	83	3	2	4	.518	.355
Glassey, Josh, V.B.*	.226	58	199	159	19	36	49	7	0	2	16	3	1	1	35	1	27	1	2	4	.308	.363
Gomera, Rafael, V.B.	.232	55	192	168	16	39	56	6	1	3	13	2	2	2	18	1	56	2	6	3	.333	.311
Goodwin, Joe, Char.	.385	10	31	26	5	10	13	3	0	0	4	0	0	1	4	0	2	0	1	1	.500	.484
Goudie, Jaime, V.B.	.322	35	133	115	15	37	49	7	1	1	8	2	1	3	12	1	24	7	4	3	.426	.397

Player, Team	Avg.	G	TPA	AB	R	H	TB	2B	3B	HR	RBI	SH	SF	HP	BB	IBB	SO	SB	CS	GDP	Slg.	OBP
Green, Kevin, B.C.	.176	22	55	51	5	9	13	1	0	1	5	0	0	0	4	0	19	3	0	0	.255	.236
Gresham, Kris, Jup.	.220	24	87	82	8	18	30	6	0	2	8	0	0	3	2	0	17	1	3	1	.366	.264
Guerrero, Pedro, Char.	.000	1	4	4	0	0	0	0	0	0	0	0	0	0	0	0	1	0	0	0	.000	.000
Guerrero, Rafael, St.P.	.226	76	273	252	23	57	77	9	1	3	18	4	1	1	15	2	32	1	4	8	.306	.271
Gunderson, Shane, Ft.M.	.268	42	180	149	25	40	71	12	2	5	20	4	1	3	23	1	42	3	2	1	.477	.375
Hacker, Steve, Ft.M.	.247	62	272	251	29	62	106	11	0	11	38	0	2	2	17	0	40	0	1	9	.422	.298
Hall, Noah, Jup.	.250	4	12	8	2	2	2	0	0	0	0	0	0	1	3	0	1	1	1	0	.250	.500
Hall, Ronnie, Day.	.000	1	4	4	0	0	0	0	0	0	0	0	0	0	0	0	3	0	0	0	.000	.000
Haltiwanger, Garrick, St.L.	.186	108	394	344	35	64	110	11	1	11	42	5	3	7	34	0	69	7	6	5	.320	.271
Haney, Todd, St.L.	.250	1	4	4	1	1	1	0	0	0	0	0	0	0	0	0	0	0	0	0	.250	.250
Harrell, Ken, Tam.	.125	18	32	32	3	4	5	1	0	0	3	0	0	0	0	0	8	2	1	0	.156	.125
Harris, Brian, Cle.†	.277	118	508	437	55	121	165	17	6	5	65	6	9	9	47	2	56	20	13	13	.378	.353
Harvey, Aaron, B.C.*	.286	3	9	7	3	2	2	0	0	0	1	1	0	0	1	0	1	2	0	0	.286	.375
Hawkins, Kraig, St.P.	.198	30	109	96	15	19	22	1	1	0	4	1	0	1	11	0	12	9	4	2	.229	.287
Heinrichs, Jon, B.C.	.285	128	534	470	63	134	191	17	2	12	64	0	8	6	50	3	68	21	6	7	.406	.356
Henley, Bob, Jup.	.340	13	58	50	10	17	26	3	0	2	14	0	1	2	5	1	5	1	1	3	.520	.414
Henry, Santiago, Dun.	.389	12	56	54	9	21	29	5	0	1	7	0	0	0	2	1	8	2	2	2	.537	.411
Hinds, Rob, Tam.	.250	27	125	100	15	25	36	4	2	1	9	0	1	3	21	0	25	6	5	0	.360	.392
Hubbard, Jeremy, Day.	.000	5	6	6	0	0	0	0	0	0	0	0	0	0	0	0	2	0	0	0	.000	.000
Huff, Brent, St.L.	.259	118	490	451	60	117	179	23	3	11	60	1	6	7	25	0	108	8	10	14	.397	.305
Huls, Steve, Ft.M.†	.211	74	252	223	30	47	53	3	0	1	25	4	3	2	20	0	43	3	5	7	.238	.278
Hundley, Todd, St.L.†	.214	12	54	42	4	9	14	2	0	1	6	0	0	0	12	1	8	0	1	1	.333	.389
Hyers, Matt, Kis.†	.182	10	28	22	4	4	5	1	0	0	2	1	0	1	4	0	3	0	1	0	.227	.333
Jasco, Elinton, Day.	.314	45	183	156	37	49	62	5	4	0	24	7	2	2	16	0	34	25	4	0	.397	.381
Jefferson, Reggie, Sar.*	.357	4	15	14	2	5	5	0	0	0	2	0	0	0	1	0	3	0	0	1	.357	.400
Jenkins, Corey, Sar.	.175	79	282	252	24	44	64	7	2	3	28	2	2	1	25	0	109	2	1	2	.254	.250
Johnson, Damon, Dun.	.278	94	363	338	48	94	127	17	2	4	32	1	2	5	17	1	98	16	9	6	.376	.320
Johnson, Gary, Day.	.232	116	481	413	61	96	144	12	0	12	55	1	4	10	53	3	101	10	2	7	.349	.331
Johnson, Nick, Tam.*	.317	92	393	303	69	96	163	14	1	17	58	0	3	19	68	3	76	1	4	5	.538	.466
Johnson, Ric, Kis.	.270	103	423	381	67	103	142	17	2	6	45	2	1	5	34	0	48	20	8	5	.373	.337
Jones, Aaron, Tam.*	.216	11	41	37	2	8	10	2	0	0	4	0	0	0	4	0	12	0	0	0	.270	.293
Jones, Jack, V.B.	.167	9	31	30	4	5	11	1	1	1	3	0	0	0	1	0	7	0	0	0	.367	.194
Jones, Jay, B.C.*	.221	74	281	262	15	58	75	8	0	3	25	2	3	1	13	3	34	1	3	12	.286	.258
Kane, Ryan, Tam.	.132	16	63	53	4	7	12	2	0	1	4	1	2	0	7	0	12	1	0	1	.226	.226
Kawabata, Kyle, Cle.	.000	53	1	1	0	0	0	0	0	0	1	0	0	0	0	0	0	0	0	0	.000	.000
Keel, David, Tam.*	.327	27	128	107	18	35	47	3	0	3	16	0	1	2	18	1	18	3	1	3	.439	.430
Kelleher, Pat, V.B.*	.263	58	217	194	20	51	63	7	1	1	12	3	1	2	17	2	38	8	3	6	.325	.327
Key, Jeff, Cle.*	.335	63	241	212	38	71	101	13	4	3	45	1	3	8	17	1	45	5	8	4	.476	.400
Kieschnick, Brooks, St.P.*	.248	28	117	105	15	26	47	6	0	5	18	0	1	0	11	0	18	0	0	4	.448	.316
Kiil, Harry, Cle.	.275	116	482	397	90	109	188	31	3	14	70	6	4	5	70	3	109	23	6	4	.474	.387
King, Brad, Day.	.293	84	317	276	49	81	101	17	0	1	37	2	2	7	30	0	37	5	6	11	.366	.375
Kleinz, Larry, B.C.	.288	88	380	320	48	92	138	23	1	7	34	1	5	7	46	0	51	1	0	8	.431	.384
Knowles, Eric, Tam.	.278	95	406	360	46	100	130	16	4	2	41	6	8	2	30	0	62	3	6	9	.361	.330
Kofler, Eric, Tam.*	.309	87	361	337	50	104	165	25	3	10	69	0	4	1	19	1	51	1	2	2	.490	.343
Kuilan, Hector, B.C.	.226	61	225	208	13	47	76	11	0	6	28	2	1	2	12	0	29	2	1	3	.365	.274
Lackey, Steve, Lake.	.284	102	464	415	68	118	147	14	3	3	39	9	5	4	31	0	73	19	7	7	.354	.336
Lamb, Michael, Char.†	.302	135	595	536	83	162	230	35	3	9	93	2	8	4	45	5	63	18	7	10	.429	.356
Lambert, Clark, St.L.	.000	3	8	8	0	0	0	0	0	0	0	0	0	0	0	0	2	0	0	1	.000	.000
Landry, Jacques, Lake.	.252	105	433	397	51	100	154	17	2	11	51	4	2	4	26	1	105	8	6	4	.388	.303
Langaigne, Selwyn, Dun.*	.261	128	523	475	52	124	131	7	0	0	38	7	2	2	37	0	73	21	17	12	.276	.316
Larned, Andrew, Sar.	.154	8	18	13	0	2	2	0	0	0	2	0	0	0	5	0	2	0	0	0	.154	.389
Lawrence, Joe, Dun.	.308	125	569	454	102	140	216	31	6	11	44	5	1	4	105	2	88	15	12	11	.476	.441
LeCronier, Jason, St.P.*	.231	36	110	104	13	24	39	4	1	3	21	1	1	0	4	0	31	1	2	3	.375	.257
LeCroy, Matt, Ft.M.	.305	51	231	200	32	61	108	9	1	12	51	0	6	4	21	1	35	2	1	7	.540	.372
Lemonis, Chris, Lake.*	.281	93	359	327	45	92	120	17	1	3	48	0	3	2	27	3	46	1	1	10	.367	.337
Leon, Donny, Tam.†	.291	100	418	385	54	112	168	24	1	10	59	1	2	7	23	1	64	0	0	9	.436	.341
Lindstrom, David, Lake.	.246	103	408	337	52	83	122	20	2	5	42	3	7	11	50	1	46	0	3	8	.362	.356
Lisanti, Bob, Day.	.100	12	11	10	1	1	1	0	0	0	1	0	0	0	1	0	4	0	0	0	.100	.182
Lobaton, Jose, Tam.	.254	33	140	130	21	33	51	4	1	4	15	3	1	2	4	0	32	4	1	2	.392	.285
Lomasney, Steve, Sar.	.239	122	521	443	74	106	196	22	1	22	63	1	2	16	59	3	145	13	4	7	.442	.348
Lopez, Felipe, Dun.†	.385	4	13	13	3	5	10	0	1	1	1	0	0	0	0	0	3	0	0	1	.769	.385
Lopiccolo, Jamie, Lake.	.291	106	474	440	52	128	202	32	3	12	77	0	5	5	24	0	85	7	3	13	.459	.331
Lough, Aaron, Ft.M.	.500	1	5	4	2	2	5	0	0	1	1	0	0	0	1	0	1	0	0	0	1.250	.600
Loyd, Brian, Dun.	.204	16	58	49	8	10	13	0	0	1	5	1	2	1	5	0	10	1	0	3	.265	.281
Lugo, Julio, Kis.	.303	128	570	509	81	154	223	20	14	7	62	6	2	4	49	3	72	51	18	13	.438	.367
Machado, Albenis, Jup.†	.125	3	8	8	1	1	3	0	1	0	0	0	0	0	0	0	1	0	0	0	.375	.125
Maduro, Remy, B.C.*	.263	65	225	198	17	52	59	7	0	0	12	0	0	6	21	1	31	0	0	5	.298	.351
Makarewicz, Scott, B.C.	.284	20	82	74	5	21	27	0	0	2	10	0	1	1	6	1	15	0	2	0	.365	.341
Malave, Jaime, V.B.	.270	28	99	89	12	24	44	6	1	4	9	0	0	0	10	0	16	1	0	1	.494	.343
Maloney, Jeff, Dun.†	.183	94	330	300	43	55	94	7	1	10	32	3	2	2	23	2	76	6	4	2	.313	.245
Manning, Nate, Day.	.269	108	469	427	61	115	188	23	1	16	71	2	4	10	26	5	89	2	4	13	.440	.323
Marine, Del, Lake.	.259	15	56	54	6	14	21	4	0	1	3	0	0	0	2	0	5	0	0	4	.389	.286
Marsh, Roy, Sar.	.277	109	412	357	63	99	129	13	7	1	35	4	4	4	43	0	56	27	9	8	.361	.358
Marsters, Brandon, Cle.	.283	76	289	265	33	75	107	12	1	6	39	4	2	2	16	0	41	2	1	4	.404	.326
Martinez, Gabby, Tam.	.319	44	175	166	26	53	78	8	1	5	24	1	0	3	5	2	20	21	6	5	.470	.351
Martinez, Rafael, Sar.*	.267	98	385	329	49	88	116	9	2	5	40	2	1	4	49	1	59	6	4	6	.353	.368
Mateo, Henry, Jup.†	.279	12	49	43	11	12	17	3	1	0	6	1	1	2	2	0	6	3	0	0	.395	.333
Mateo, Ruben, Char.	.000	1	4	4	0	0	0	0	0	0	1	0	0	0	0	0	1	0	0	0	.000	.000
McCrary, Scott, St.L.	1.000	37	1	1	0	1	1	0	0	0	0	0	0	0	0	0	0	0	0	0	1.000	1.000
McDonald, Donzell, Tam.†	.333	5	22	18	6	6	11	1	2	0	2	1	0	1	2	0	7	2	0	0	.611	.429
McNamara, Rusty, Cle.	.291	134	578	529	78	154	219	36	1	9	94	3	9	14	23	1	44	14	7	20	.414	.332
Mejia, Maximiliano, V.B.	.260	77	315	288	30	75	111	14	2	6	26	3	3	1	19	0	58	17	8	3	.385	.305

Player, Team	Avg.	G	TPA	AB	R	H	TB	2B	3B	HR	RBI	SH	SF	HP	BB	IBB	SO	SB	CS	GDP	Slg.	OBP
Mejia, Renato, B.C.	.195	32	121	113	9	22	26	1	0	1	11	1	1	0	6	0	40	1	1	4	.230	.233
Mendoza, Carlos, St.P.*	.313	8	40	32	6	10	12	2	0	0	8	2	1	1	4	0	3	4	2	0	.375	.395
Meran, Jorge, Lake.	.200	7	20	20	0	4	7	3	0	0	1	0	0	0	0	0	7	0	0	0	.350	.200
Meyers, Chad, Day.	.323	48	226	186	39	60	83	8	3	3	25	1	1	5	33	1	29	23	7	1	.446	.436
Moeller, Chad, Ft.M.	.327	66	288	254	37	83	127	24	1	6	39	0	0	3	31	4	37	2	3	8	.500	.406
Monroe, Craig, Char.	.242	132	550	472	73	114	205	26	7	17	76	0	7	3	66	0	102	50	13	15	.434	.334
Montilla, Miguel, Tam.	.125	10	20	16	2	2	3	1	0	0	0	0	0	0	4	0	6	0	0	1	.188	.300
Moore, Lacarlo, Lake.*	.290	28	109	100	17	29	36	3	2	0	13	0	0	2	7	0	17	7	3	1	.360	.349
Mora, Melvin, St.L.	.273	17	61	55	5	15	15	0	0	0	8	0	1	0	5	0	9	1	1	0	.273	.328
Mordecai, Mike, Jup.	.000	2	9	8	0	0	0	0	0	0	0	0	0	0	1	0	3	0	0	1	.000	.111
Morgan, Dave, Dun.	.229	28	85	70	9	16	35	4	0	5	15	0	2	1	12	0	16	0	1	3	.500	.341
Morimoto, Ken, V.B.†	.167	45	167	144	20	24	28	2	1	0	8	1	0	1	21	0	38	13	1	2	.194	.277
Morris, Jeremy, Tam.	.301	124	502	445	69	134	200	25	1	13	72	2	6	1	48	1	96	11	3	8	.449	.366
Moss, Rick, Ft.M.*	.313	41	188	160	18	50	60	7	0	1	19	1	0	3	24	0	17	0	0	3	.375	.412
Mota, Tony, V.B.†	.319	61	274	254	45	81	130	18	5	7	35	0	0	2	18	3	27	13	8	6	.512	.369
Mucker, Kelcey, Ft.M.*	.338	21	78	71	11	24	36	6	0	2	9	0	0	2	5	0	10	1	0	1	.507	.397
Murphy, Mike, Char.	.286	3	10	7	4	2	3	1	0	0	1	0	0	0	3	0	1	1	0	0	.429	.500
Myers, Adrian, Char.	.269	122	528	454	84	122	174	20	7	6	64	7	9	3	55	1	98	51	23	11	.383	.345
Newton, Kimani, V.B.	.280	62	202	168	26	47	67	3	1	5	13	3	1	1	29	0	35	10	3	2	.399	.387
Nunez, Jose, Jup.	.229	54	187	166	24	38	44	6	0	0	9	3	0	1	17	0	33	2	1	2	.265	.304
Nunnari, Talmadge, Jup.*	.294	56	237	201	18	59	79	14	0	2	34	0	6	0	30	1	39	1	2	2	.393	.376
Olmeda, Jose, Sar.†	.209	113	387	358	37	75	116	18	4	5	42	5	3	2	19	0	112	8	5	8	.324	.251
Ottavinia, Paul, Tam.*	.253	57	193	174	25	44	78	13	3	5	28	0	5	0	14	2	20	2	0	3	.448	.301
Owens-Bragg, Luke, St.P.†	.206	33	77	63	9	13	16	1	1	0	6	0	1	0	13	0	13	0	1	2	.254	.338
Owens, Billy, Kis.†	.182	10	37	33	4	6	12	0	0	2	4	0	0	0	4	0	7	0	0	5	.364	.270
Padilla, Roy, Sar.*	.255	109	400	365	46	93	125	17	3	3	53	3	2	2	28	1	66	12	2	11	.342	.310
Parker, Chris, Lake.	.176	7	18	17	0	3	3	0	0	0	0	0	0	0	1	0	6	0	0	0	.176	.222
Parsons, Jeff, St.L.-Kis.	.248	61	206	165	26	41	48	2	1	1	18	6	2	0	33	0	27	14	2	1	.291	.370
Patterson, John, St.P.†	.263	6	20	19	4	5	10	2	0	1	2	0	0	0	1	0	4	0	0	0	.526	.300
Patzke, Jeff, Dun.†	.290	20	71	62	10	18	18	0	0	0	4	0	0	0	9	0	18	0	1	0	.290	.380
Paulino, David, B.C.	.175	35	111	97	7	17	18	1	0	0	5	1	0	0	13	0	31	6	0	2	.186	.273
Payton, Jay, St.L.	.143	3	10	7	0	1	1	0	0	0	0	0	0	0	3	2	1	0	0	0	.143	.400
Pena, Carlos, Char.*	.273	7	25	22	1	6	7	1	0	0	3	0	0	1	2	0	8	0	1	0	.318	.320
Perry, Herbert, St.P.	.125	2	10	8	1	1	1	0	0	0	0	0	0	0	2	0	2	0	0	0	.125	.300
Peterman, Tommy, Ft.M.*	.312	135	593	519	71	162	262	36	2	20	110	1	6	4	63	13	86	2	0	11	.505	.387
Phillips, Jason, St.L.	.464	8	31	28	4	13	15	2	0	0	2	1	0	0	2	0	1	0	1	0	.536	.500
Piniella, Juan, Char.	.306	61	249	222	37	68	88	8	3	2	23	1	0	1	25	0	38	23	6	0	.396	.379
Podsednik, Scott, Char.*	.285	81	356	302	55	86	118	12	4	4	39	4	6	0	44	0	32	26	8	2	.391	.369
Polanco, Enohel, St.L.	.264	75	262	239	35	63	79	8	1	2	19	5	2	5	11	0	38	6	2	2	.331	.307
Pomierski, Joe, St.P.*	.236	112	437	390	47	92	158	28	1	12	67	2	5	0	40	1	90	3	1	9	.405	.303
Pond, Simon, Jup.*	.238	105	380	344	40	82	102	15	1	1	32	2	4	6	24	2	58	1	4	7	.297	.296
Prada, Nelson, Ft.M.	.241	41	141	133	11	32	41	6	0	1	11	1	0	3	4	0	21	0	0	5	.308	.279
Pratt, Todd, St.L.	.450	5	23	20	2	9	13	1	0	1	3	0	0	2	1	0	5	1	0	0	.650	.522
Pratt, Wes, Kis.	.254	19	74	67	9	17	22	2	0	1	10	0	1	0	6	0	12	1	3	2	.328	.311
Quatraro, Matthew, St.P.	.248	73	307	270	36	67	97	14	2	4	31	1	3	2	31	1	67	4	0	12	.359	.327
Raifstanger, John, Sar.	.255	43	180	145	23	37	61	12	0	4	24	1	1	0	33	1	37	4	3	3	.421	.391
Ramirez, Dan, St.L.	.271	123	520	469	65	127	163	17	2	5	54	5	10	6	3	32	0	93	27	19	9	.348	.318
Ramirez, Julio, B.C.	.279	135	613	559	90	156	239	20	12	13	58	3	2	4	45	2	147	71	27	3	.428	.328
Ramsey, Brad, Day.	.288	89	359	312	49	90	135	25	1	6	37	0	2	13	32	0	64	4	1	6	.433	.376
Raynor, Mark, Cle.	.247	23	101	93	19	23	29	1	1	1	10	0	1	0	7	0	12	1	1	2	.312	.297
Reding, Josh, Jup.	.250	4	12	12	2	3	4	1	0	0	2	0	0	0	0	0	3	0	1	0	.333	.250
Reeder, Jim, Kis.*	.228	73	253	228	32	52	69	11	3	0	24	0	4	6	15	2	30	7	1	4	.303	.289
Reese, Nate, St.L.	.175	11	44	40	3	7	15	2	0	2	7	1	0	0	3	0	9	0	0	2	.375	.233
Reyes, Dadny, B.C.†	.000	1	1	1	0	0	0	0	0	0	0	0	0	0	0	0	0	0	0	0	.000	.000
Reynoso, Ismael, B.C.	.216	72	259	231	25	50	64	4	2	2	19	2	1	4	21	0	50	6	2	4	.277	.292
Richards, Rowan, Char.	.274	57	227	212	32	58	83	14	1	3	22	0	1	3	11	1	48	5	8	3	.392	.317
Rico, Diego, Day.*	.276	108	427	366	70	101	158	22	7	7	58	2	3	5	51	2	76	18	7	7	.432	.369
Riggs, Eric, V.B.†	.248	61	257	230	30	57	84	12	3	3	17	3	1	0	23	0	46	3	4	1	.365	.315
Riley, Cash, V.B.	.226	124	473	434	47	98	143	16	1	9	42	0	3	5	31	1	125	12	9	10	.329	.283
Rivas, Luis, Ft.M.	.281	126	490	463	58	130	173	21	5	4	51	4	3	14	0	75	34	8	11	.374	.324
Rivera, Luis A., Jup.	.111	7	20	18	1	2	2	0	0	0	0	1	0	0	1	0	6	0	0	0	.111	.158
Rivera, Luis J., Jup.	.250	1	4	4	0	1	1	0	0	0	2	0	0	0	0	0	1	0	0	0	.250	.250
Rivers, Jonathan, Dun.	.200	5	21	20	0	4	6	2	0	0	4	0	0	0	1	0	5	2	1	1	.300	.238
Robles, Oscar, Kis.*	.271	66	251	207	31	56	65	7	1	0	24	2	1	3	38	0	14	6	2	1	.314	.390
Rodriguez, Felix, Tam.	.000	1	2	1	0	0	0	0	0	0	0	0	0	0	1	0	0	0	0	0	.000	.500
Rodriguez, Luis, Dun.	.291	67	217	196	34	57	84	15	0	4	41	5	4	2	10	0	39	11	2	3	.429	.325
Rodriguez, Mike, Dun.	.216	15	44	37	4	8	10	2	0	0	2	2	0	2	3	0	4	0	0	2	.270	.310
Rodriguez, Noel, Kis.	.245	15	60	53	6	13	19	3	0	1	8	0	0	2	5	0	3	0	0	2	.358	.333
Rodriguez, Sammy, St.L.	.257	53	180	152	20	39	56	9	1	2	24	4	2	2	20	0	36	3	1	1	.368	.349
Rojas, Mo, Sar.	.118	5	19	17	1	2	3	1	0	0	2	0	0	1	1	0	5	2	0	0	.176	.211
Rollins, Jimmy, Cle.†	.244	119	495	445	72	121	175	18	9	6	35	4	3	4	41	1	62	23	9	9	.354	.306
Rolls, Damian, V.B.	.244	73	294	266	28	65	74	9	0	0	30	1	2	2	23	0	43	13	3	6	.278	.349
Romano, Jason, Char.	.208	7	28	24	3	5	6	1	0	0	1	1	0	2	0	2	1	2	0	.250	.259
Rose, Mike, Kis.†	.226	18	71	62	9	14	27	4	0	3	9	1	0	0	8	0	14	1	0	2	.435	.314
Ruan, Wilken, V.B.	.167	5	19	18	2	3	3	0	0	0	0	1	0	0	0	0	3	2	0	0	.167	.211
Ruiz, Ramon, V.B.	.191	18	74	68	10	13	17	4	0	0	6	1	0	0	5	0	15	2	0	3	.250	.247
Runnells, T.J., Lake.	.182	6	22	22	3	4	5	1	0	0	1	0	0	0	0	0	6	0	0	1	.227	.182
Salinas, Trey, St.P.	.227	22	74	66	7	15	21	3	0	1	7	0	0	2	6	0	10	0	0	1	.318	.311
Samboy, Nelson, Kis.	.285	124	568	527	73	150	198	31	4	3	45	0	3	1	37	0	71	40	15	10	.376	.331
Samuel, Cody, Tam.	.338	47	178	154	27	52	85	15	0	6	32	0	1	3	20	2	44	0	0	7	.552	.421
Sanchez, Alex, St.P.*	.330	128	593	545	77	180	218	17	9	1	50	4	12	1	31	1	70	66	33	5	.400	.360
Sankey, Brian, V.B.*	.259	98	343	309	35	80	120	11	1	9	44	1	4	5	24	1	52	0	1	4	.388	.319

Player, Team	Avg.	G	TPA	AB	R	H	TB	2B	3B	HR	RBI	SH	SF	HP	BB	IBB	SO	SB	CS	GDP	Slg.	OBP
Santiago, Benito, Dun.	.162	11	40	37	4	6	10	1	0	1	5	0	0	0	3	0	9	3	0	1	.270	.225
Sapp, Damian, Sar.	.244	35	147	127	18	31	61	9	0	7	23	0	3	2	15	0	38	1	0	3	.480	.327
Sassanella, Jeremy, Lake.†	.000	1	3	3	0	0	0	0	0	0	0	0	0	0	0	0	2	0	0	0	.000	.000
Sasser, Rob, Char.	.308	4	16	13	1	4	6	2	0	0	3	0	0	0	3	0	5	1	0	1	.462	.438
Schaffer, Jake, Lake.	.248	102	433	395	56	98	156	19	3	11	48	2	2	3	31	1	90	4	4	4	.395	.306
Schifano, Anthony, B.C.	.234	91	330	304	28	71	85	3	4	1	14	4	0	6	14	0	46	8	1	11	.280	.281
Schneider, Brian, Jup.*	.272	82	327	302	32	82	105	12	1	3	30	0	2	1	22	1	38	4	4	9	.348	.321
Schroeder, John, Ft.M.*	.207	39	147	135	17	28	57	5	0	8	24	0	0	2	10	3	53	0	0	0	.422	.272
Schwab, Chris, Jup.	.215	120	478	433	56	93	183	19	1	23	48	2	2	1	40	0	175	7	6	6	.423	.282
Scioneaux, Damian, St.P.*	.185	18	59	54	4	10	10	0	0	0	1	1	0	0	4	0	8	1	0	0	.185	.241
Sergio, Thomas, Char.*	.294	112	517	453	90	133	192	30	7	5	39	4	4	10	46	1	59	33	10	6	.424	.368
Shuck, Jason, St.L.	.200	3	6	5	0	1	1	0	0	0	0	0	0	0	1	0	1	0	0	0	.200	.333
Shumpert, Derek, Tam.	.197	21	74	66	8	13	15	2	0	0	3	1	0	0	7	0	25	0	2	2	.227	.274
Skett, Will, Dun.	.325	37	143	123	25	40	64	8	2	4	25	1	1	3	15	0	43	6	2	3	.520	.408
Smiga, Jason, Char.	.303	26	72	66	7	20	21	1	0	0	5	0	0	0	6	0	11	2	2	2	.318	.361
Smith, Jeff, Ft.M.*	.348	6	25	23	4	8	10	2	0	0	1	0	0	1	1	0	2	1	0	1	.435	.400
Smith, Rod, Tam.†	.245	86	379	327	57	80	117	15	2	6	35	6	2	5	39	1	70	40	14	5	.358	.332
Snusz, Chris, Cle.	.196	19	60	56	6	11	12	1	0	0	6	1	1	1	1	0	9	0	0	0	.214	.220
Sojo, Luis, Tam.	.222	3	11	9	1	2	2	0	0	0	0	0	0	0	2	0	0	0	0	0	.222	.364
Solano, Danny, Char.	.260	84	319	262	46	68	86	15	0	1	30	9	4	2	42	0	54	9	6	3	.328	.361
Sollmann, Scott, Lake.*	.252	104	476	401	81	101	126	11	4	2	35	7	3	3	62	0	52	59	17	1	.314	.354
Speed, Dorian, Day.	.268	85	276	250	43	67	106	11	5	6	34	3	1	2	20	0	56	13	5	2	.424	.326
Spehr, Tim, St.L.	.184	14	51	38	7	7	12	2	0	1	6	0	1	3	9	0	16	0	0	0	.316	.373
Stevens, Tony, Ft.M.†	.286	3	7	7	0	2	2	0	0	0	1	0	0	0	0	0	0	0	0	0	.286	.286
Stone, Craig, Dun.	.267	104	385	356	44	95	164	29	2	12	53	3	3	3	20	2	125	3	6	1	.461	.309
Stromsborg, Ryan, Dun.	.250	30	117	108	12	27	38	5	0	2	12	2	1	1	5	0	28	1	0	2	.352	.287
Tamargo, John, St.L.†	.242	105	402	347	40	84	110	24	1	0	33	9	2	3	41	2	60	14	7	3	.317	.326
Taveras, Luis, Char.	.163	76	266	246	21	40	57	4	2	3	24	2	4	0	14	0	70	4	6	6	.232	.205
Taylor, Greg, Cle.†	.275	22	66	51	7	14	15	1	0	0	11	3	0	4	8	0	5	0	2	2	.294	.413
Tessmar, Tim, St.L.*	.271	106	412	377	48	102	141	21	3	4	54	0	1	2	32	2	72	11	4	11	.374	.330
Thames, Marcus, Tam.	.284	122	496	457	62	130	187	18	3	11	59	1	5	8	24	1	78	13	6	5	.409	.328
Thompson, Nick, Cle.	.274	59	203	186	24	51	69	10	1	2	23	0	2	7	8	0	40	3	3	6	.371	.325
Torres, Bernie, V.B.	.253	123	459	415	44	105	120	9	3	0	29	8	7	3	26	0	62	9	7	14	.289	.297
Tracy, Andrew, Jup.*	.267	71	298	251	37	67	118	16	1	11	53	0	5	3	39	3	69	6	4	3	.470	.366
Treanor, Matt, B.C.	.235	80	290	243	24	57	74	8	0	3	28	1	3	5	38	0	45	3	2	4	.305	.346
Truby, Chris, Kis.	.311	52	236	212	36	66	126	16	1	14	48	0	2	3	19	3	30	6	1	2	.594	.373
Tucci, Pete, Dun.	.329	92	394	356	72	117	222	30	3	23	76	2	5	5	29	0	97	8	5	6	.624	.385
Tyner, Jason, St.L.*	.303	50	222	201	30	61	69	2	3	0	16	3	0	1	17	0	20	15	11	3	.343	.361
Uccello, Jeff, Sar.	.229	36	117	109	11	25	30	2	0	1	7	1	1	0	6	0	21	2	0	2	.275	.267
Ugueto, Luis, B.C.†	.182	3	12	11	0	2	2	0	0	0	0	1	0	0	0	0	5	0	0	0	.182	.182
Valdez, Trovin, Jup.	.264	54	240	220	31	58	80	13	3	1	31	3	3	3	11	0	28	22	7	1	.364	.304
Valencia, Victor, Tam.	.224	122	449	411	53	92	160	18	1	16	43	5	4	3	26	2	139	0	1	4	.389	.273
Valent, Eric, Cle.*	.264	34	145	125	24	33	58	8	1	5	25	0	1	3	16	0	29	1	2	4	.464	.359
Valera, Yohanny, St.L.	.205	91	328	298	37	61	126	21	1	14	42	1	1	7	21	0	92	1	1	7	.423	.272
Vargas, Arias, Lake.	.143	3	10	7	2	1	3	0	1	0	2	0	0	1	2	0	3	0	0	0	.429	.400
Vasquez, Alejandro, Kis.*	.053	6	20	19	0	1	1	0	0	0	0	0	0	0	1	0	9	1	0	2	.053	.100
Vaughn, Lateef, Ft.M.	.288	22	65	59	9	17	21	2	1	0	8	1	1	1	3	0	12	2	3	0	.356	.328
Vazquez, Alex, Char.	.190	24	54	42	3	8	9	1	0	0	6	1	0	2	9	0	16	5	0	0	.214	.358
Velez, Jose, Kis.†	.277	98	356	329	38	91	117	11	3	3	42	3	4	0	18	0	30	6	7	12	.356	.311
Venghaus, Jeff, B.C.†	.181	116	440	375	38	68	92	10	4	2	23	6	2	5	52	0	91	10	8	6	.245	.288
Vieira, Scott, Day.	.370	15	67	54	11	20	29	6	0	1	13	0	1	3	9	0	12	3	0	1	.537	.478
Wakeland, Chris, Lake.*	.302	131	567	487	82	147	237	26	5	18	89	4	5	5	66	4	111	19	13	4	.487	.387
Walker, Ron, Day.	.286	100	410	357	57	102	196	20	1	24	78	0	0	7	46	1	80	5	2	11	.549	.378
Ware, Jeremy, Jup.	.246	127	533	492	51	121	192	35	3	10	64	4	7	7	23	1	102	21	5	16	.390	.285
Warren, Lance, V.B.*	.212	37	76	66	6	14	18	4	0	0	7	0	0	1	9	0	23	5	2	0	.273	.316
Warriax, Brandon, Char.	.125	5	17	16	2	2	2	0	0	0	1	0	0	0	1	0	5	0	0	1	.125	.176
Washington, Kelley, B.C.	.173	27	105	98	7	17	23	2	2	0	9	1	0	0	6	0	30	0	1	4	.235	.221
Wesemann, Jason, Cle.	.205	32	99	88	10	18	23	3	1	0	8	1	0	2	8	0	19	0	3	1	.261	.286
White, Walt, B.C.	.154	13	46	39	6	6	6	0	0	0	4	0	0	0	7	0	9	0	2	2	.154	.283
Williams, Bernie, Tam.†	.500	1	3	2	0	1	2	1	0	0	0	0	0	0	1	0	0	0	0	0	1.000	.667
Williams, Juan, Day.*	.200	17	80	65	15	13	20	4	0	1	8	0	0	1	14	1	23	2	1	2	.308	.350
Willis, Symmion, Dun.	.036	9	30	28	1	1	1	0	0	0	1	0	1	1	0	0	11	1	0	0	.036	.067
Wilson, Vance, St.L.	.063	4	16	16	0	1	1	0	0	0	0	0	0	0	0	0	5	0	0	0	.063	.063
Yedo, Carlos, Day.*	.223	56	238	206	26	46	79	10	1	7	43	0	3	2	27	1	53	0	0	2	.383	.315
Zamora, Junior, St.L.	.285	99	398	368	58	105	160	17	4	10	53	0	0	5	25	1	60	4	3	9	.435	.339
Zorrilla, Julio, St.L.†	.257	37	151	136	16	35	46	3	1	2	16	3	3	0	9	0	20	5	8	2	.338	.297
Zuleta, Julio, Day.	.344	94	422	366	69	126	201	25	1	16	86	1	5	5	35	1	59	6	3	12	.549	.418
Zywica, Mike, Char.	.381	68	296	252	67	96	156	21	3	11	49	0	4	6	34	2	40	16	5	4	.619	.459

GRAND SLAMS: Airoso 2, Becker, Blake, R. Cedeno, Colina, Cotton, Cranford, G. Davis, DeLaRosa, Delgado, Dubose, Everson, Hacker, Hinds, Heinrichs, Jenkins, Key, Lobaton, McNamara, Moeller, T. Mota, Piniella, Pomierski, Raifstanger, Reese, Schroeder, Valera, Wakeland, Yedo.

AWARDED FIRST ON CATCHER'S INTERFERENCE: Choi 3 (Glassey 2, Taveras); Fuentes 3 (Makarewicz, N. Thompson, Parker); Michael J. Bell [SLU] 2 (Glassey 2); Monroe 2 (Glassey, Larned); Schifano 2 (Donato, Chavera); Cranford (Chiaffredo); Velez 2 (King, Gresham); Airoso (Lomasney); Haltiwanger (Barr); Kleinz (Ramsey); M. Mejia (Marsters); M. Thomas (Quatraro).

PLAYERS WITH TWO OR MORE TEAMS

Player, Team	Avg.	G	TPA	AB	R	H	TB	2B	3B	HR	RBI	SH	SF	HP	BB	IBB	SO	SB	CS	GDP	Slg.	OBP
Parsons, Jeff, St.L.	.250	27	88	68	15	17	20	0	0	1	8	2	0	0	18	0	12	9	1	0	.294	.407
Parsons, Jeff, Kis.	.247	34	118	97	11	24	28	2	1	0	10	4	2	0	15	0	15	5	1	1	.289	.342

CLASS A *Florida State League*

TEAM

Team	W	L	Pct.	ERA	G	CG	ShO	Sv.	IP	H	TBF	R	ER	HR	SH	SF	HB	BB	IBB	SO	WP	Bk.
Jupiter	80	60	.571	3.34	140	5	11	35	1238.0	1184	5219	557	460	70	49	37	83	379	0	869	55	3
Charlotte	82	56	.594	3.40	138	6	6	54	1221.1	1154	5205	582	462	111	31	35	50	440	11	965	55	10
Dunedin	82	58	.586	3.81	140	7	12	43	1232.1	1197	5376	647	522	91	37	39	73	531	16	1074	80	11
St. Lucie	70	66	.515	3.84	137	1	9	34	1207.0	1178	5182	623	515	95	42	37	56	435	17	898	75	15
Clearwater	82	58	.586	3.92	140	5	5	43	1254.0	1383	5344	643	546	93	42	39	44	339	20	854	77	17
Tampa	72	67	.518	4.10	139	6	9	32	1223.2	1229	5451	725	557	76	44	46	49	567	52	1064	79	22
Lakeland	67	72	.482	4.16	139	9	5	36	1215.1	1259	5365	707	562	109	42	42	63	501	13	883	87	4
Kissimmee	64	75	.460	4.19	139	8	7	29	1211.2	1321	5390	698	564	103	36	38	66	482	29	889	73	16
Fort Myers	65	73	.471	4.21	139	3	3	28	1239.2	1363	5543	735	580	75	52	45	63	508	10	949	118	8
Sarasota	76	61	.555	4.24	137	16	11	37	1194.1	1199	5198	683	563	82	31	50	40	457	21	964	98	10
St. Petersburg	64	75	.460	4.28	139	3	6	32	1236.1	1259	5352	708	588	108	32	48	55	423	13	1019	74	10
Daytona	67	73	.479	4.50	140	6	1	28	1219.1	1328	5449	754	610	103	43	54	64	460	19	1004	85	9
Brevard County	43	97	.307	4.64	140	11	8	18	1199.2	1309	5372	765	618	100	35	57	94	532	11	814	79	10
Vero Beach	58	81	.417	4.96	139	6	5	26	1200.2	1228	5359	794	662	141	38	42	46	539	11	947	70	16

INDIVIDUAL

TOP QUALIFIERS FOR EARNED-RUN AVERAGE TITLE

Minimum 112 innings. *Lefthanded pitcher.

Pitcher, Team	W	L	Pct.	ERA	G	GS	CG	ShO	GF	Sv.	IP	H	TBF	R	ER	HR	SH	SF	HB	BB	IBB	SO	WP	Bk.
Rutherford, Mark, Cle.	8	5	.615	2.65	18	18	0	0	0	0	119.0	94	452	40	35	11	3	3	5	20	0	71	3	1
Martinez, Jose, Char.	7	5	.583	2.77	19	19	2	0	0	0	123.2	120	521	55	38	12	3	3	5	28	3	86	5	3
Armas, Tony, Jup.	12	8	.600	2.88	27	27	1	1	0	0	153.1	140	656	63	49	11	11	1	10	59	0	136	3	0
Cames, Aaron, B.C.	5	10	.333	3.12	27	25	1	0	1	0	152.2	134	657	73	53	11	3	3	15	59	0	161	6	3
Pumphrey, Ken, St.L.	10	6	.625	3.16	25	25	1	0	0	0	142.1	126	606	66	50	7	2	6	7	57	0	99	9	1
Hazlett, Andy, Sar.*	11	7	.611	3.19	30	22	4	2	1	1	160.2	154	662	76	57	4	7	3	25	2	135	3	1
Davis, Doug, Char.*	11	7	.611	3.24	27	27	1	1	0	0	155.1	129	665	69	56	8	1	3	13	74	0	173	8	0
Westbrook, Jake, Jup.	11	6	.647	3.26	27	27	2	0	0	0	171.0	169	720	70	62	11	5	3	11	60	0	79	4	0
Spiers, Corey, Ft.M.*	9	8	.529	3.33	24	24	1	0	0	0	151.1	172	650	70	56	7	2	5	6	38	0	98	7	1
Delgado, Ernie, Dun.	7	10	.412	3.64	44	9	2	1	13	1	118.2	119	532	57	48	5	6	1	6	59	4	97	6	2
Cook, Derrick, Char.	13	7	.650	3.66	26	26	1	1	0	0	167.1	170	710	81	68	13	8	2	5	64	1	111	13	1
Robertson, Jeromie, Kis.*	10	10	.500	3.70	28	28	2	0	0	0	175.0	185	740	83	72	13	5	7	53	3	131	5	6
Gagne, Eric, V.B.	9	7	.563	3.74	25	25	3	0	0	0	139.2	118	584	69	58	16	2	4	4	48	0	144	5	3
Spence, Cam, Tam.	9	5	.643	3.75	21	20	2	0	0	0	127.1	125	542	66	53	7	5	4	2	38	1	105	3	4
Koch, Billy, Dun.	14	7	.667	3.75	25	25	0	0	0	0	124.2	120	528	65	52	8	2	2	7	41	0	108	4	3

DEPARTMENTAL LEADERS: W—DeYoung, Koch, 14 each; L—M. Castillo, 15; Pct.—Enders, .909; G—Garza, 58; GS—Ashworth, Hooten, Jacquez, McKnight, Robertson, 28 each; CG—J. Garrett, Kim, 5 each; ShO—J. Garrett, Hazlett, Robbins, Root, 2 each; GF—Dickey, 54; Sv.—Dickey, 38; IP—Robertson, 175.0; H—Jacquez, 215; TBF—Jacquez, Robertson, 740 each; R—J. Garrett, 108; ER—J. Garrett, 90; HR—Manias, 27; SH—Armas, Fieldbinder, 11 each; SF—Manias, 11; HB—Nicholson, 20; BB—Kinney, 93; IBB—Cubillan, Dingman, 9 each; SO—D. Davis, 173; WP—Kinney, 25; BK—Robertson, Seo, 6 each.

ALL PITCHERS

*Lefthanded pitcher.

Pitcher, Team	W	L	Pct.	ERA	G	GS	CG	ShO	GF	Sv.	IP	H	TBF	R	ER	HR	SH	SF	HB	BB	IBB	SO	WP	Bk.
Adair, Derek, Cle.	7	3	.700	5.12	14	13	1	1	1	0	77.1	81	316	47	44	9	1	1	1	10	0	55	4	1
Adkins, Tim, Dun.*	0	1	.000	5.92	19	0	0	0	10	1	24.1	32	114	18	16	2	0	1	3	10	0	18	2	1
Allen, Buck, Cle.*	5	1	.833	4.69	47	5	0	0	14	1	78.2	93	341	43	41	11	5	2	3	23	2	39	8	0
Alvarez, Wilson, St.P.*	0	1	.000	27.00	1	1	0	0	0	0	1.2	5	12	5	5	1	0	0	0	2	0	2	0	0
Alvord, Aaron, Lake.	0	0	.000	7.20	1	1	0	0	0	0	5.0	7	24	4	4	2	0	0	0	4	0	1	1	0
Anderson, Matt, Lake.	1	0	1.000	0.69	17	0	0	0	13	3	26.0	18	108	4	2	0	2	1	0	8	0	34	2	0
Aquino, Julio, St.P.	1	3	.250	3.51	34	0	0	0	23	9	41.0	45	177	18	16	1	1	3	3	8	0	38	3	1
Armas, Tony, Jup.	12	8	.600	2.88	27	27	1	1	0	0	153.1	140	656	63	49	11	11	1	10	59	0	136	3	0
Armenta, Alfredo, St.P.*	1	2	.333	4.62	6	6	0	0	0	0	25.1	25	116	16	13	2	0	0	3	11	0	21	2	0
Arteaga, Ivan, St.L.	2	1	.667	5.27	9	0	0	0	3	0	15.2	13	64	10	9	1	1	1	0	7	1	8	1	1
Arteaga, J.D., St.L.*	2	0	1.000	2.89	15	2	0	0	1	0	37.1	37	154	15	12	1	4	0	0	7	0	28	1	1
Ashworth, Kym, Lake.*	6	11	.353	3.82	28	28	1	0	0	0	160.1	169	697	96	68	14	6	6	9	60	1	113	13	0
Aucoin, Derek, St.L.	1	0	1.000	8.38	8	0	0	0	4	0	9.2	10	46	9	9	1	0	1	4	4	0	13	5	0
Baker, Jason, Jup.*	0	1	.000	9.00	2	0	0	0	0	0	1.0	0	6	1	1	0	0	0	0	3	0	0	0	0
Bale, John, Dun.*	4	5	.444	4.64	24	9	0	0	5	4	66.0	68	290	39	34	5	3	5	4	23	1	78	6	1
Barnett, Marty, Dun.	0	1	.000	6.26	7	6	0	0	0	0	27.1	34	128	23	19	4	0	0	1	14	0	13	2	1
Bauder, Mike, Ft.M.*	5	6	.455	4.59	36	8	0	0	7	1	98.0	108	442	61	50	6	3	5	46	1	79	6	3
Bean, Seth, Ft.M.	0	0	.000	3.78	10	0	0	0	6	1	16.2	16	68	7	7	0	0	5	0	19	0	0		
Belitz, Todd, St.P.*	2	2	.500	5.04	7	7	0	0	0	0	44.2	39	188	28	25	3	2	3	2	14	0	40	2	0
Bell, Mike, Jup.*	0	1	.000	5.14	5	0	0	0	0	0	7.0	16	37	8	4	1	1	0	1	2	0	5	2	0
Bell, Scott, V.B.	1	1	.000	5.40	1	1	0	0	0	0	5.0	8	23	4	3	1	0	1	0	0	0	1	0	0
Benesh, Edward, St.P.	4	5	.444	4.79	38	4	0	0	4	1	77.0	86	337	50	41	4	2	0	2	22	1	65	6	0
Berger, Craig, St.L.	2	0	1.000	1.29	3	0	0	0	2	0	7.0	7	27	1	1	0	0	0	1	0	2	0	1
Betancourt, Rafael, Sar.	3	1	.750	3.54	20	0	0	0	4	2	28.0	22	111	12	11	2	1	0	0	6	0	33	0	0
Bettencourt, Justin, Lake.*	5	7	.417	4.04	30	13	0	0	7	1	104.2	106	477	57	47	6	6	7	4	62	0	86	12	0
Betti, Rich, Sar.*	1	2	.333	11.45	4	4	0	0	0	0	11.0	19	51	14	14	4	0	1	0	3	0	11	0	0
Beverlin, Jason, Tam.	1	3	.250	5.63	7	5	0	0	0	0	32.0	37	142	23	20	2	0	4	1	16	2	15	2	1
Blanco, Alberto, Kis.*	0	0	.000	6.35	2	2	0	0	0	0	11.1	12	50	9	8	1	1	0	3	0	13	1	0
Blank, Matt, Jup.*	5	1	.833	2.34	8	6	0	0	1	0	42.1	33	170	14	11	2	0	4	10	0	26	0	1
Bleazard, David, Dun.	1	0	1.000	4.26	14	0	0	0	0	0	19.0	20	88	14	9	1	0	2	11	0	20	4	1
Bogott, Kurt, Dun.*	0	0	.000	0.00	3	0	0	0	0	0	6.1	2	21	0	0	0	0	6	0	1	0	8	0	0
Bowers, Cedrick, St.P.*	5	9	.357	4.38	28	26	0	0	1	0	150.0	144	655	89	73	14	6	4	1	80	1	156	6	2
Bowles, Brian, Dun.	1	2	.333	3.33	9	2	1	0	0	0	27.0	32	126	13	10	2	1	1	1	16	0	17	1	1

Pitcher, Team	W	L	Pct.	ERA	G	GS	CG	ShO	GF	Sv.	IP	H	TBF	R	ER	HR	SH	SF	HB	BB	IBB	SO	WP	Bk.
Bradford, Josh, Dun.	4	4	.500	4.97	17	12	1	0	3	1	70.2	75	316	43	39	4	4	1	7	30	0	46	5	0
Bradley, Ryan, Tam.	7	4	.636	2.38	32	11	1	1	18	7	94.2	59	383	29	25	5	1	1	6	30	4	112	16	2
Braswell, Bryan, Kis.*	11	9	.550	3.95	27	26	2	1	0	0	159.2	176	698	92	70	22	3	3	4	48	0	118	7	2
Brittan, Corey, St.L.	4	2	.667	3.90	34	0	0	0	17	2	67.0	74	290	35	29	1	2	2	2	14	0	40	5	1
Brookens, Casey, Day.	3	3	.500	6.61	23	1	0	0	8	0	32.2	40	156	30	24	5	2	6	0	22	1	19	3	0
Brown, Chad, Dun.*	1	1	.500	2.30	3	2	0	0	0	0	15.2	13	64	8	4	0	2	0	0	3	0	10	0	0
Buchanan, Brian, Tam.*	0	1	.000	22.50	1	1	0	0	0	0	2.0	4	18	7	5	0	0	0	0	8	0	1	2	0
Buckles, Bucky, Char.	4	0	1.000	0.57	18	0	0	0	9	1	31.1	21	122	4	2	1	1	1	0	15	1	18	0	0
Bullinger, Kirk, Jup.	0	0	.000	5.40	8	0	0	0	1	0	10.0	9	42	7	6	1	0	0	0	2	0	12	2	0
Cames, Aaron, B.C.	5	10	.333	3.12	27	25	1	0	1	0	152.2	134	657	73	53	11	3	3	15	59	0	161	6	3
Cammack, Eric, St.L.	3	2	.600	2.02	29	0	0	0	24	11	35.2	22	142	12	8	2	0	1	0	14	2	53	0	0
Campos, David, B.C.*	0	0	.000	12.91	6	0	0	0	3	0	7.2	20	47	11	11	1	0	1	1	4	0	6	1	0
Cannon, Jon, Day.*	0	3	.000	3.73	7	7	1	0	0	0	31.1	37	142	22	13	1	2	2	0	12	0	28	1	0
Cannon, Kevan, Sar.*	5	1	.833	4.08	44	0	0	0	28	10	57.1	57	248	29	26	3	1	0	1	26	0	60	10	0
Capellan, Rene, Lake.	0	1	.000	27.00	1	0	0	0	1	0	0.1	1	3	1	1	0	1	0	0	1	0	0	0	0
Carrasco, Troy, Ft.M.*	0	4	.000	4.53	19	4	0	0	2	0	45.2	52	209	29	23	4	2	2	1	26	0	35	6	1
Castillo, Alberto, Tam.*	0	0	.000	13.50	12	0	0	0	3	0	11.1	14	75	17	17	2	1	2	3	25	1	11	5	2
Castillo, Frank, Lake.	1	0	1.000	0.00	1	1	0	0	0	0	5.0	2	18	0	0	0	1	0	1	0	0	4	0	0
Castillo, Marcos, V.B.	5	15	.250	4.99	25	25	2	0	0	0	139.0	141	614	95	77	14	5	6	9	47	0	77	6	3
Cepeda, Victor, Lake.	3	0	1.000	1.99	8	2	1	0	1	0	22.2	8	85	5	5	3	0	0	0	14	1	22	0	0
Chambers, Scott, V.B.*	3	1	.750	6.21	43	2	0	0	21	2	84.0	99	392	75	58	15	1	4	0	36	1	85	6	0
Chapman, Walker, Ft.M.	4	0	1.000	1.97	24	0	0	0	11	2	50.1	40	209	17	11	1	0	1	1	15	0	47	4	0
Checo, Robinson, Sar.	0	1	.000	9.00	1	1	0	0	0	0	2.0	3	10	2	2	0	0	0	0	1	0	4	0	0
Chiavacci, Ronald, Jup.	0	1	.000	2.35	4	0	0	0	1	1	7.2	5	29	2	2	0	2	0	2	2	0	5	0	0
Cho, Jin Ho, Sar.	3	1	.750	3.09	5	5	0	0	0	0	32.0	33	132	14	11	1	0	4	0	5	0	30	2	0
Choate, Randy, Tam.*	1	8	.111	5.27	13	13	0	0	0	0	70.0	83	316	57	41	6	4	1	3	22	2	55	2	0
Civit, Xavier, Jup.	0	0	.000	4.50	13	0	0	0	4	2	18.0	21	78	9	9	2	1	1	0	3	0	14	0	0
Clark, Chris, B.C.	2	3	.400	4.30	40	2	0	0	30	9	60.2	52	288	38	29	1	3	7	4	46	3	58	12	0
Cook, Derrick, Char.	13	7	.650	3.66	26	26	1	1	0	0	167.1	170	710	81	68	13	8	2	5	64	1	111	13	1
Corcoran, Tim, St.L.	0	0	.000	8.22	4	0	0	0	2	0	7.2	10	35	7	7	1	0	0	0	2	0	8	0	0
Cordero, Francisco, Lake.	0	0	.000	0.00	1	0	0	0	0	0	0.0	1	1	0	0	0	0	0	0	0	0	0	0	0
Correa, Elvis, V.B.	1	5	.167	6.57	42	2	0	0	12	1	86.1	118	413	71	63	11	5	4	2	42	2	54	9	1
Costa, Tony, Cle.	0	1	.000	8.25	6	2	0	0	1	0	12.0	9	56	11	11	0	1	2	0	14	0	5	8	4
Cubillan, Darwin, Tam.	9	2	.818	4.71	45	1	0	0	13	1	65.0	79	310	45	34	3	1	7	1	36	9	70	8	1
Daniel, Michael, Char.	0	2	.000	6.00	4	0	0	0	0	0	9.0	11	40	7	6	1	0	1	0	3	0	4	0	0
Daniels, John, St.P.	4	2	.667	1.77	34	0	0	0	33	19	40.2	31	170	12	8	3	3	1	4	11	1	46	4	1
Darley, Ned, Char.	0	0	.000	3.38	3	0	0	0	3	0	2.2	2	10	1	1	0	1	0	0	0	0	3	1	0
Davis, Doug, Char.*	11	7	.611	3.24	27	27	1	1	0	0	155.1	129	665	69	56	8	1	3	13	74	0	173	8	0
Davis, Keith, Lake.	3	3	.500	4.00	43	0	0	0	17	7	74.1	72	328	40	33	6	6	1	6	32	0	73	12	1
Day, Zach, Tam.	5	8	.385	5.49	18	17	0	0	0	0	100.0	142	479	89	61	5	3	2	6	32	4	69	5	0
DeJesus, Javier, Day.*	5	5	.500	5.23	43	1	0	0	14	0	53.1	63	249	34	31	7	3	2	2	24	1	55	2	0
De La Cruz, Andres, Tam.	0	0	.000	0.00	3	0	0	0	1	0	3.2	2	15	0	0	0	1	0	0	2	1	1	1	0
De La Cruz, Fernando, Sar.	0	0	.000	1.04	12	0	0	0	8	4	17.1	10	67	2	2	1	1	1	1	7	0	10	0	0
De La Cruz, Francisco, Tam.	5	6	.455	4.54	19	12	0	0	5	0	75.1	81	344	55	38	5	4	1	3	36	1	66	5	0
Delgado, Ernie, Dun.	7	10	.412	3.64	44	9	2	1	13	1	118.2	119	532	57	48	5	6	1	6	59	4	97	6	2
De Los Santos, Luis, Tam.	4	2	.667	4.19	10	10	1	0	0	0	66.2	69	280	40	31	2	3	2	3	11	0	33	5	1
DeYoung, Dan, Char.-B.C.	14	8	.636	4.59	26	26	2	0	0	0	155.0	167	660	88	79	16	4	7	6	43	0	71	4	1
Dickey, R.A., Char.	1	5	.167	3.30	57	0	0	0	54	38	60.0	58	260	31	22	9	4	1	0	22	3	53	3	2
Dingman, Craig, Tam.	5	4	.556	3.18	50	0	0	0	28	7	70.2	48	293	29	25	8	3	2	1	39	9	95	2	0
Downs, Scott, Day.*	8	9	.471	3.90	27	27	2	0	0	0	161.2	179	713	83	70	12	7	7	4	55	0	117	12	4
Duckworth, Brandon, Cle.	6	2	.750	3.74	9	9	1	1	0	0	53.0	64	235	25	22	2	2	1	1	22	0	46	4	0
uncan, Geoff, B.C.	1	3	.250	2.25	17	0	0	0	9	2	32.0	35	135	15	8	1	2	0	2	9	3	30	2	0
uncan, Sean, Kis.*	2	0	1.000	3.31	23	0	0	0	10	2	32.2	29	144	13	12	1	1	2	4	17	0	20	0	0
Duran, Roberto, Lake.*	0	0	.000	4.15	8	0	0	0	2	0	8.2	4	46	5	4	0	1	1	2	13	1	9	1	0
urocher, Jayson, Jup.	2	1	.667	4.21	23	0	0	0	12	5	36.1	47	162	21	17	3	1	2	1	8	0	27	4	0
uvall, Mike, St.P.*	0	0	.000	2.70	2	0	0	0	2	0	3.1	4	16	1	1	0	0	0	0	2	0	3	2	0
aton, Adam, Cle.	9	8	.529	4.44	24	23	1	0	0	0	131.2	152	578	68	65	9	3	5	5	47	1	89	9	1
hlers, Corey, B.C.	1	6	.143	4.37	45	0	0	0	16	1	90.2	91	386	50	44	13	2	2	3	26	0	54	3	2
nders, Trevor, St.P.*	10	1	.909	2.23	51	0	0	0	16	1	68.2	48	267	20	17	4	2	2	3	15	3	61	5	0
spinal, Jose, Day.	10	10	.500	4.73	28	22	0	0	3	0	144.2	165	641	95	76	16	6	3	6	50	1	117	10	0
vans, Keith, Jup.	5	2	.714	2.86	8	8	1	0	0	0	50.1	45	194	18	16	1	0	1	3	5	0	25	1	0
verly, Bill, V.B.	7	6	.538	4.57	49	4	0	0	30	3	106.1	108	464	65	54	12	6	5	9	31	2	59	2	2
eliciano, Pedro, V.B.*	2	5	.286	4.61	22	10	0	0	8	2	68.1	68	300	44	35	8	0	1	2	30	1	51	2	0
ennell, Barry, Day.*	2	2	.500	2.59	24	0	0	0	10	2	31.1	30	151	16	9	0	1	0	2	22	2	24	1	0
ereira, Ramon, Kis.	0	0	.000	0.00	1	0	0	0	0	0	0.0	2	3	3	3	0	0	0	0	1	0	0	0	0
eldbinder, Mick, Ft.M.	10	8	.556	4.73	35	21	0	0	4	1	137.0	171	614	99	72	14	11	6	4	44	1	64	9	0
sher, Louis, Day.	3	4	.429	4.66	49	1	0	0	14	1	65.2	50	283	40	34	4	5	6	5	38	2	54	11	0
ores, Randy, Tam.*	1	2	.333	6.46	5	5	0	0	0	0	23.2	28	115	23	17	2	2	2	1	16	2	15	0	4
olkers, Ken, Dun.	0	3	.000	8.40	9	0	0	0	5	0	15.0	23	77	16	14	2	1	2	1	9	3	13	1	0
orster, Scott, Jup.*	0	0	.000	9.00	6	0	0	0	1	0	8.0	9	38	10	8	0	0	1	1	5	0	7	2	0
oster, Kevin, Day.	0	0	.000	10.13	3	0	0	0	0	0	2.2	2	19	7	3	1	0	0	0	7	1	3	0	0
oster, Kris, V.B.	3	5	.375	6.79	24	6	0	0	7	1	53.0	59	249	45	40	8	2	1	1	27	0	52	6	5
owler, Blair, B.C.	3	6	.333	4.25	28	9	1	0	4	1	91.0	95	412	54	43	5	2	3	6	44	1	54	9	3
ranklin, Wayne, V.B.*	9	3	.750	3.53	48	0	0	0	26	10	86.2	81	369	43	34	7	3	5	2	26	0	78	3	2
agliano, Steve, B.C.	0	0	.000	4.85	8	0	0	0	3	0	13.0	15	63	12	7	3	1	0	1	10	0	7	1	1
agne, Eric, V.B.	9	7	.563	3.74	25	25	3	1	0	0	139.2	118	584	69	58	16	2	4	4	48	0	144	5	3
aillard, Eddie, St.P.	0	0	.000	0.00	1	1	0	0	0	0	2.0	1	7	0	0	0	0	0	0	0	0	2	0	0
arcia, Apostol, Lake.	5	8	.385	5.43	34	16	1	0	6	1	119.1	155	560	89	72	14	2	2	10	52	0	56	8	1
arcia, Gabe, Kis.	7	10	.412	5.36	30	23	1	0	3	0	141.0	178	652	98	84	15	1	5	5	62	3	93	14	0
arcia, Neil, St.P.	0	0	.000	0.00	1	0	0	0	1	0	0.1	0	1	0	0	0	0	0	0	0	0	0	0	0
ardner, Lee, St.P.	0	0	.000	0.00	3	0	0	0	1	0	4.0	3	15	0	0	0	0	0	0	1	0	2	0	0
arrett, Hal, V.B.	6	6	.500	4.97	20	20	1	0	0	0	112.1	111	506	75	62	11	1	3	7	57	0	86	10	0
arrett, Josh, Sar.	8	12	.400	5.21	26	25	5	2	0	0	155.1	182	692	108	90	17	3	5	14	40	1	68	4	1

Pitcher, Team	W	L	Pct.	ERA	G	GS	CG	ShO	GF	Sv.	IP	H	TBF	R	ER	HR	SH	SF	HB	BB	IBB	SO	WP	Bk.
Garvin, Robert, B.C.	1	2	.333	5.48	15	0	0	0	6	1	23.0	21	108	16	14	2	2	1	3	14	0	12	1	0
Garza, Chris, Ft.M.*	5	5	.500	2.74	58	0	0	0	43	14	82.0	73	358	33	25	3	9	4	4	46	3	63	9	0
Gaskill, Derek, St.L.	0	3	.000	2.89	7	1	0	0	3	0	18.2	16	75	6	6	2	2	2	0	3	0	21	3	0
Gissell, Chris, Day.	7	6	.538	4.17	22	21	1	0	0	0	136.0	149	597	80	63	12	3	5	11	38	1	123	7	0
Glover, Gary, Dun.	7	6	.538	4.28	19	18	0	0	0	0	109.1	117	484	66	52	8	1	6	7	36	0	88	11	1
Gonzalez, Dicky, St.L.	2	1	.667	3.09	8	8	0	0	0	0	46.2	46	193	22	16	8	1	0	1	13	0	23	1	0
Gorecki, Rick, St.P.	0	0	.000	0.00	1	1	0	0	0	0	4.2	4	19	0	0	0	0	0	0	1	0	7	0	0
Green, Jason, Kis.	2	5	.286	3.34	51	3	0	0	44	14	67.1	64	304	34	25	4	2	2	4	32	3	67	5	1
Grzanich, Mike, Kis.	1	1	.500	6.14	4	0	0	0	1	0	7.1	9	36	7	5	0	2	0	1	5	0	8	1	0
Gulin, Lindsay, St.L.*	1	1	.500	2.33	6	4	0	0	0	0	27.0	16	106	9	7	2	2	0	1	11	1	19	1	0
Hafer, Jeff, St.L.	3	3	.500	7.99	24	0	0	0	11	1	41.2	63	200	42	37	7	1	4	2	11	1	37	3	0
Hanson, Erik, Dun.	0	0	.000	2.25	1	1	0	0	0	0	4.0	4	18	1	1	0	0	0	0	2	0	5	0	0
Hart, Len, Day.*	3	3	.500	3.55	37	0	0	0	11	2	50.2	52	221	28	20	4	1	3	2	20	1	46	2	0
Hartshorn, Ty, Dun.	8	0	1.000	1.29	9	9	1	1	0	0	63.0	52	252	16	9	1	2	0	1	17	0	54	2	0
Hayden, Terry, Sar.*	1	2	.333	4.70	13	1	0	0	7	0	23.0	25	96	13	12	2	0	3	0	7	0	20	0	0
Hazlett, Andy, Sar.*	11	7	.611	3.19	30	22	4	2	1	1	160.2	154	662	76	57	4	2	7	3	25	2	135	3	1
Hendrickson, Mark, Dun.*	4	3	.571	2.37	16	5	0	0	1	1	49.1	44	207	16	13	2	2	2	0	26	1	38	2	0
Henry, Butch, Sar.*	0	1	.000	1.35	1	1	0	0	0	0	6.2	4	23	2	1	0	0	0	0	0	0	5	0	0
Herbison, Brett, St.L.	7	13	.350	5.15	26	25	0	0	0	0	146.2	165	649	93	84	10	7	7	9	52	2	94	10	0
Hernandez, Orlando, Tam.	1	1	.500	1.00	2	2	0	0	0	0	9.0	3	37	2	1	0	0	4	3	0	0	15	1	0
Hibbard, Billy, Dun.	0	0	.000	0.00	2	0	0	0	1	0	4.0	4	16	0	0	0	1	0	0	2	0	1	0	0
Hoff, Steve, B.C.-Day.*	5	11	.313	4.87	21	21	2	0	0	0	112.2	131	500	75	61	11	2	9	7	39	1	71	9	0
Holmes, Darren, Tam.	0	0	.000	4.50	2	1	0	0	0	0	2.0	4	11	2	1	0	0	0	0	6	0	0	0	0
Holt, Chris, Kis.	0	1	.000	9.00	1	1	0	0	0	0	4.0	6	20	4	4	0	0	0	4	0	1	1	0	0
Hooten, David, Ft.M.	9	11	.450	4.49	28	28	0	0	0	0	158.1	185	714	94	79	7	0	10	11	57	0	136	4	0
Hunter, Germaine, Sar.	0	0	.000	4.61	7	0	0	0	2	0	13.2	15	65	12	7	2	0	1	1	9	1	14	3	1
Hurst, Bill, Lake.	0	0	.000	0.00	2	0	0	0	1	0	4.0	2	13	0	0	0	0	0	0	0	0	0	0	0
Hurtado, Victor, B.C.	3	3	.500	3.87	18	18	1	1	0	0	100.0	105	427	57	43	12	1	7	6	23	0	59	3	0
Jacquez, Thomas, Cle.*	9	11	.450	4.30	29	28	2	1	0	0	169.2	215	740	102	81	12	6	9	3	31	3	108	5	4
James, Delvin, St.P.	0	0	.000	10.80	1	0	0	0	1	0	1.2	2	7	2	2	0	0	1	0	0	0	0	0	0
Jimenez, Jason, St.P.*	0	2	.000	8.53	13	0	0	0	8	0	19.0	24	97	20	18	3	0	2	3	10	2	15	3	1
Johnson, Jonathan, Char.	0	3	.000	4.63	3	3	0	0	0	0	11.2	10	51	6	6	2	0	1	2	4	0	11	0	0
Jones, Jay, B.C.	0	0	.000	3.38	2	0	0	0	2	0	2.2	2	10	1	1	0	0	0	0	0	0	2	0	0
Jones, Kiki, St.P.	1	0	1.000	6.00	6	0	0	0	2	0	9.0	7	37	7	6	1	0	0	3	6	1	1	1	0
Kaufman, John, St.P.*	7	5	.583	3.18	18	17	0	0	0	0	102.0	92	430	40	36	6	2	3	1	33	0	93	5	1
Kawabata, Kyle, Cle.	4	3	.571	2.64	53	0	0	0	50	33	64.2	63	270	25	19	3	6	1	4	16	2	49	3	1
Kershner, Jason, Cle.*	3	3	.500	4.01	41	8	0	0	11	3	94.1	108	405	57	42	8	1	3	6	25	0	65	8	0
Kessel, Kyle, St.L.*	2	7	.222	5.14	16	16	0	0	0	0	89.1	101	394	58	51	11	2	1	7	27	0	61	3	1
Kim, Sun, Sar.	12	8	.600	4.82	26	24	5	0	0	0	153.0	159	655	88	82	18	2	8	2	40	1	132	11	0
Kimsey, Keith, Lake.	6	1	.857	3.92	28	4	0	0	9	2	62.0	56	274	33	27	2	1	3	6	29	1	52	6	0
Kinney, Matt, Sar.-Ft.M.	12	8	.600	3.80	29	27	2	1	1	1	158.2	140	698	88	67	5	7	3	2	93	3	135	25	2
Knoll, Randy, Cle.	1	3	.250	6.20	5	5	0	0	0	0	20.1	31	101	17	14	6	0	1	0	11	0	14	1	0
Koch, Billy, Dun.	14	7	.667	3.75	25	25	0	0	0	0	124.2	120	528	65	52	8	2	2	7	41	0	108	4	3
LaChapelle, Yan, Dun.	11	8	.579	3.99	24	24	1	1	0	0	126.1	114	542	68	56	16	2	2	5	58	0	126	8	1
Lail, Denny, Tam.	4	0	1.000	4.07	31	0	0	0	13	1	48.2	44	211	24	22	3	1	2	1	25	0	46	4	1
Lara, Nelson, B.C.	2	5	.286	9.42	19	4	0	0	5	0	28.2	27	149	36	30	2	0	4	7	33	0	32	8	0
LaRosa, Tom, Ft.M.	2	3	.333	7.91	22	3	0	0	12	0	38.2	37	198	39	34	4	0	2	9	48	0	29	22	1
Lawrence, Clint, Dun.*	6	3	.667	4.91	20	12	1	1	4	1	84.1	107	391	54	46	6	1	0	5	41	0	55	10	0
Lee, Jeremy, Dun.	2	0	1.000	3.90	15	0	0	0	4	0	27.2	26	114	13	12	5	3	2	3	6	1	18	0	0
Leese, Brandon, B.C.	1	5	.167	5.70	8	8	0	0	0	0	47.1	63	209	36	30	3	1	1	2	7	0	30	2	0
Leon, Scott, St.P.	1	3	.250	4.46	16	4	0	0	3	0	36.1	33	161	23	18	2	0	2	4	17	0	22	3	1
LeRoy, John, St.P.	1	1	.500	4.58	11	0	0	0	3	0	17.2	18	75	9	9	1	3	0	2	6	0	17	0	0
Lisio, Joe, Tam.	2	3	.400	2.48	31	0	0	0	28	15	32.2	19	135	13	9	2	4	0	3	16	2	43	2	0
Lohrman, Dave, St.L.	2	3	.400	6.75	19	1	0	0	6	0	30.2	39	145	27	23	6	0	1	2	14	1	27	5	0
Lopez, Albie, St.P.	0	1	.000	18.00	1	1	0	0	0	0	1.0	2	5	2	2	1	0	0	0	0	0	1	0	0
Love, Farley, Kis.	0	0	.000	4.61	11	0	0	0	7	0	13.2	14	69	9	7	3	0	0	2	12	0	17	2	0
Love, Jeff, Kis.	3	2	.600	2.89	42	0	0	0	7	3	90.1	88	382	41	29	5	0	1	3	24	1	61	6	0
Lowe, Benny, Dun.	1	1	.500	1.93	9	0	0	0	2	0	9.1	8	46	5	2	0	1	2	6	0	13	1	0
Lukasiewicz, Mark, Dun.*	1	1	.500	0.84	9	0	0	0	1	0	10.2	7	42	2	1	0	0	4	0	8	0	0	0	0
Lynch, Jim, Kis.	5	2	.714	2.95	9	9	1	1	0	0	55.0	36	227	22	18	4	0	5	28	0	40	2	2	
Lyons, Jonathan, Sar.	1	0	1.000	4.50	7	0	0	0	2	0	12.0	15	54	7	6	2	0	0	2	0	14	0	0	
Lyons, Mike, St.L.	3	2	.600	0.89	28	0	0	0	23	9	40.2	28	172	12	4	0	2	1	3	14	2	27	2	2
Madison, Scott, St.P.*	2	0	1.000	5.36	27	0	0	0	11	0	42.0	53	186	28	25	2	1	3	0	20	1	18	2	0
Mairena, Oswaldo, Tam.*	1	5	.167	3.17	52	0	0	0	11	0	54.0	53	238	24	19	5	2	3	2	23	3	50	0	2
Maldonado, Esteban, Kis.	1	4	.200	6.98	28	0	0	0	12	1	38.2	51	193	37	30	3	3	0	1	26	7	24	2	1
Malko, Bryan, Ft.M.	0	1	.000	6.92	7	0	0	0	3	2	13.0	19	67	14	10	0	1	0	1	9	0	5	3	0
Maness, Chris, Cle.	0	1	.500	0.63	8	0	0	0	3	1	14.1	11	56	2	1	0	1	0	0	4	0	11	0	0
Manias, James, St.P.*	6	13	.316	5.58	30	21	0	0	3	0	137.0	167	618	99	85	27	3	11	9	37	0	79	7	0
Mann, Jim, Dun.	0	2	.000	3.04	51	0	0	0	47	25	50.1	31	206	19	17	4	0	2	24	1	59	2	0	
Manning, David, Char.	0	0	.000	0.00	7	0	0	0	2	0	8.1	4	36	4	0	1	0	0	6	0	11	0	0	
Manon, Julio, St.P.	5	5	.500	3.72	38	0	0	0	14	1	55.2	41	219	25	23	7	0	0	2	19	1	73	4	1
Markey, Barry, Day.	7	6	.538	4.81	43	9	0	0	15	3	106.2	119	473	62	57	6	5	7	10	31	5	59	4	0
Marquez, Robert, Jup.	5	4	.556	3.86	39	0	0	0	14	3	51.1	60	234	28	22	4	4	2	3	23	3	50	0	2
Marriott, Mike, B.C.	0	4	.000	7.64	5	5	0	0	0	0	17.2	23	94	20	15	1	1	1	3	19	0	11	3	0
Marsh, Roy, Sar.	0	0	.000	9.00	1	0	0	0	1	0	1.0	1	5	1	1	0	0	0	0	1	0	1	0	1
Martinez, Jose, Char.	7	5	.583	2.77	19	19	2	0	0	0	123.2	120	521	55	38	12	3	5	3	28	3	86	5	3
Martinez, Romulo, Lake.	6	3	.667	2.63	49	0	0	0	35	16	65.0	63	276	32	19	6	2	1	0	20	3	34	2	1
Mattes, Troy, Jup.	7	6	.538	3.07	17	10	0	0	2	0	73.1	73	307	33	25	8	4	1	9	3	0	42	2	1
Matz, Brian, Jup.*	1	2	.333	6.05	15	6	0	0	4	2	41.2	54	196	31	28	3	1	0	2	19	0	29	2	0
Mayo, Blake, V.B.	4	7	.364	2.94	32	7	0	0	21	5	82.2	70	356	35	27	7	8	2	1	48	4	53	4	0
Mays, Joe, Ft.M.	7	2	.778	3.04	16	15	0	0	0	0	94.2	101	409	45	32	7	5	2	5	23	0	83	4	0
McClellan, Sean, Dun.	4	0	1.000	2.21	24	0	0	0	14	6	57.0	34	223	14	14	3	1	0	3	10	0	73	2	0
McCrary, Scott, St.L.	8	4	.667	2.92	37	4	0	0	14	6	92.1	78	373	40	30	9	3	2	2	18	2	75	7	1

Pitcher, Team	W	L	Pct.	ERA	G	GS	CG	ShO	GF	Sv.	IP	H	TBF	R	ER	HR	SH	SF	HB	BB	IBB	SO	WP	Bk.
McEntire, Ethan, St.L.*	5	4	.556	2.94	22	12	0	0	3	0	85.2	85	388	38	28	5	4	0	1	58	1	52	1	0
McGarity, Jeremy, Char.	1	0	1.000	0.00	3	0	0	0	2	0	8.2	5	32	0	0	1	0	2	0	0	0	6	0	0
McKnight, Tony, Kis.	11	13	.458	4.67	28	28	0	0	0	0	154.1	191	701	101	80	12	4	3	9	50	2	104	12	2
McMullen, Jerry, Sar.*	3	1	.750	2.73	39	0	0	0	10	2	62.2	53	273	23	19	3	6	3	3	36	1	60	5	2
Mejia, Javier, Cle.	3	3	.500	4.05	32	0	0	0	8	1	46.2	40	191	22	21	2	3	1	1	19	1	39	6	0
Mendes, Jaime, Cle.	9	3	.750	3.58	48	0	0	0	15	3	65.1	74	281	34	26	4	6	3	2	15	3	48	2	1
Miadich, Bart, Sar.	3	2	.600	3.14	22	0	0	0	15	7	48.2	40	199	20	17	1	3	0	1	15	4	64	2	1
Miles, Chad, Lake.*	1	8	.111	5.55	42	1	0	0	17	2	61.2	67	297	43	38	9	2	3	3	38	2	65	4	1
Mills, Ryan, Ft.M.*	0	0	.000	1.80	2	2	0	0	0	0	5.0	2	20	3	1	0	0	0	0	1	0	3	3	0
Minaya, Pedro, B.C.	0	2	.000	14.46	3	3	0	0	0	0	9.1	20	51	17	15	3	0	0	0	7	1	6	0	1
Mitchell, Courtney, Cle.*	4	4	.500	3.36	55	0	0	0	17	1	77.2	93	342	37	29	3	3	1	3	19	3	61	1	3
Mobley, Kevin, Lake.	4	3	.571	4.76	34	8	1	1	10	2	79.1	80	345	44	42	9	0	3	5	36	2	58	4	0
Moore, Bobby, Char.	1	3	.250	5.23	38	1	0	0	21	6	74.0	86	335	45	43	14	2	2	2	27	1	51	3	0
Moore, Chris, B.C.	1	6	.143	8.03	8	8	0	0	0	0	24.2	32	123	25	22	6	0	1	3	23	0	9	1	0
Moraga, David, Jup.*	5	2	.714	2.80	25	0	0	0	11	0	45.0	37	180	22	14	2	5	2	1	9	0	38	3	0
Morris, Alex, B.C.	1	1	.500	8.33	23	0	0	0	14	1	27.0	35	145	27	25	1	0	0	7	26	0	13	3	0
Mota, Danny, Ft.M.	3	5	.375	2.85	19	4	0	0	9	0	47.1	45	206	21	15	3	1	3	0	22	0	49	6	1
Mota, Guillermo, Jup.	3	2	.600	0.66	20	0	0	0	13	2	41.0	18	149	6	3	0	2	1	2	6	0	27	0	0
Mota, Henry, Char.	5	3	.625	3.88	34	4	0	0	12	4	95.0	98	420	55	41	11	3	5	1	40	0	60	2	1
Mounce, Tony, Kis.*	1	2	.333	6.92	5	5	0	0	0	0	26.0	35	122	22	20	2	2	0	2	13	1	15	1	0
Mull, Blaine, B.C.	4	6	.400	4.32	16	16	3	1	0	0	100.0	114	424	53	48	6	2	7	5	32	0	65	1	0
Musgrave, Scott, Sar.*	2	3	.400	6.30	28	4	0	0	8	0	60.0	73	282	46	42	6	4	1	3	31	0	34	3	1
Nakamura, Mike, Ft.M.	1	3	.250	3.45	8	6	1	0	1	0	28.2	28	123	15	11	3	2	0	2	10	0	21	1	0
Narcisse, Tyrone, Tam.	0	0	.000	1.80	4	0	0	0	1	0	5.0	4	23	1	1	0	0	0	1	3	0	7	0	0
Nelson, Jeff, Tam.	0	0	.000	0.00	2	1	0	0	0	0	2.0	1	9	1	0	0	0	0	1	1	0	4	0	0
Nicholson, John, Jup.	10	7	.588	4.05	27	26	0	0	0	0	153.1	151	670	81	69	5	4	7	20	59	1	122	20	0
Niebla, Ruben, Jup.*	0	1	.000	1.19	13	0	0	0	3	0	22.2	15	90	8	3	1	0	1	1	5	0	22	1	0
Niedermaier, Brad, Kis.	4	2	.667	7.88	25	0	0	0	13	3	40.0	59	202	39	35	3	2	0	1	21	1	44	13	0
Norton, Phillip, Day.*	4	3	.571	3.27	10	10	0	0	0	0	66.0	57	275	30	24	4	1	1	2	26	1	54	4	1
Opipari, Mario, Ft.M.	0	1	.000	3.97	17	0	0	0	4	0	34.0	38	152	19	15	2	1	1	3	13	1	18	1	0
Ortega, Pablo, St.P.	5	9	.357	4.40	28	25	2	0	2	0	155.1	187	685	104	76	13	3	7	6	39	1	111	3	1
O'Shaughnessy, Jay, V.B.	4	9	.308	5.01	30	17	0	0	1	0	100.2	88	461	65	56	8	2	2	2	83	1	116	6	0
Palki, Jeromy, Ft.M.	0	4	.000	4.76	40	0	0	0	17	4	58.2	51	263	39	31	3	4	3	2	29	1	48	7	0
Paluk, Brian, V.B.	4	7	.364	6.27	35	10	0	0	6	2	99.0	118	458	79	69	19	3	4	6	43	0	58	8	0
Pascarella, Josh, Kis.	0	0	.000	2.45	2	0	0	0	0	0	3.2	7	22	3	1	1	0	0	0	2	0	0	0	0
Pavano, Carl, Jup.	0	0	.000	6.60	4	4	0	0	0	0	15.0	20	63	11	11	1	0	0	0	3	0	14	0	0
Pedraza, Rod, Char.	5	5	.500	3.16	15	8	0	0	1	0	68.1	54	273	30	24	6	0	1	2	15	0	55	3	0
Phelps, Tommy, Jup.*	2	2	.500	4.39	7	7	0	0	0	0	41.0	42	181	21	20	3	0	2	2	15	0	21	1	0
Phillips, Ben, Tam.	3	1	.750	1.73	23	0	0	0	3	1	41.2	22	183	12	8	2	1	2	2	36	3	51	5	0
Pineda, Isauro, Sar.	4	2	.667	5.23	10	9	0	0	0	0	41.1	43	185	30	24	1	1	6	0	20	0	22	5	0
Pipes, Joey, Kis.	2	1	.667	4.10	20	0	0	0	8	0	26.1	35	131	17	12	2	4	1	2	13	3	17	3	0
Poland, Trey, Char.*	8	5	.615	3.87	26	25	1	0	0	0	148.2	150	645	82	64	15	2	4	4	60	1	138	7	2
Pujals, Denis, St.P.	5	2	.714	2.85	42	0	0	0	9	1	72.2	73	308	30	23	1	2	1	2	22	2	46	2	0
Pumphrey, Ken, St.L.	10	6	.625	3.16	25	25	1	0	0	0	142.1	126	606	66	50	7	2	6	7	57	0	99	9	1
Quintal, Craig, Lake.	8	10	.444	5.43	21	21	2	1	0	0	127.2	169	568	91	77	14	4	7	6	23	1	59	3	0
Rahilly, Michael, Sar.	1	0	1.000	1.59	7	0	0	0	3	1	17.0	17	71	7	3	2	0	1	1	2	0	13	0	0
Rangel, Julio, Tam.	2	3	.400	5.15	10	7	0	0	2	0	43.2	47	208	30	25	5	1	2	1	30	2	31	3	1
Regalado, Maximo, V.B.	0	2	.000	6.75	4	4	0	0	0	0	16.0	17	78	15	12	3	0	0	1	13	0	14	1	0
Reitsma, Chris, Sar.	0	0	.000	2.84	8	8	0	0	0	0	12.2	12	55	6	4	0	0	1	0	5	0	9	0	0
Rekar, Bryan, St.P.	0	0	.000	0.69	4	4	0	0	0	0	13.0	6	45	2	1	0	0	0	0	2	0	15	1	0
Reynoso, Armando, St.L.	0	1	.000	3.75	4	4	0	0	0	0	12.0	14	51	6	5	2	0	0	0	1	0	6	1	0
Ricketts, Chad, Day.	2	1	.667	1.84	47	0	0	0	41	19	49.0	41	204	15	10	0	3	0	3	11	1	59	2	0
Rijo, Jose, Kis.	1	6	.143	3.15	48	0	0	0	20	5	74.1	70	319	34	26	5	4	6	8	30	2	46	3	1
Rizzo, Nick, B.C.	2	0	1.000	0.98	7	0	0	0	3	0	18.1	15	78	8	2	0	0	1	0	7	0	7	0	0
Robbins, Jake, Tam.	11	6	.647	3.84	26	25	2	2	0	0	152.1	167	674	83	65	5	5	6	5	72	2	87	4	1
Roberts, Grant, St.L.	4	5	.444	4.23	17	17	0	0	0	0	72.1	72	323	37	34	11	1	1	5	37	0	70	2	0
Robertson, Jeromie, Kis.*	10	10	.500	3.70	28	28	2	0	0	0	175.0	185	740	83	72	13	3	5	7	53	3	131	5	0
Rodgers, Bobby, B.C.	1	1	.500	4.08	7	7	0	0	0	0	35.1	34	143	17	16	2	2	1	1	7	0	35	1	0
Rogers, Brian, Tam.	0	0	.000	4.20	3	3	0	0	0	0	15.0	12	70	7	7	1	0	0	0	14	0	13	0	1
Romo, Greg, Lake.	5	5	.500	4.01	12	12	3	0	0	0	76.1	72	325	46	34	4	1	2	1	30	0	53	9	0
Root, Derek, Kis.*	5	4	.556	2.35	29	9	2	2	13	4	80.1	69	323	28	21	3	2	1	4	20	2	79	4	1
Roper, Chad, Ft.M.	0	7	.000	8.93	17	6	0	0	2	0	40.1	61	204	46	40	2	2	3	21	2	30	4	1	0
Rosario, Rafael, Lake.	0	3	.000	4.50	9	0	0	0	8	1	12.0	13	59	7	6	2	1	0	1	7	0	5	1	0
Rosario, Reynaldo, Lake.	0	0	.000	9.82	4	0	0	0	2	0	3.2	5	19	4	4	0	0	0	4	0	2	0	0
Rose, Brian, Sar.	0	2	.000	1.49	22	0	0	0	14	4	36.1	35	161	16	6	1	2	1	1	12	2	37	2	0
Rutherford, Mark, Cle.	8	5	.615	2.65	18	18	0	0	0	0	119.0	94	452	40	35	11	3	3	5	20	0	71	3	1
Ryan, Ken, Cle.	0	0	.000	3.00	4	4	0	0	0	0	9.0	5	34	3	3	0	0	1	3	0	10	1	0
St. Pierre, Bob, Tam.	0	0	.000	6.90	16	0	0	0	4	0	30.0	46	146	26	23	4	0	2	2	12	2	21	2	0
Saneaux, Francisco, Char.	3	1	.750	3.93	17	0	0	0	6	3	36.2	34	161	21	16	4	1	1	5	16	0	43	5	0
Santos, Victor, Lake.	5	2	.714	2.51	16	15	0	0	1	1	100.1	88	408	38	28	9	5	2	3	24	1	74	3	0
Saylor, Ryan, Jup.	2	4	.333	2.54	27	0	0	0	20	7	46.0	32	176	15	13	3	0	1	1	15	0	45	1	0
Schaffer, Trevor, Dun.	0	2	.000	4.65	47	0	0	0	21	2	69.2	58	325	48	36	5	3	6	13	48	4	45	4	0
Schaffner, Eric, Tam.	0	1	.000	5.40	7	0	0	0	2	0	11.2	17	58	8	7	1	0	2	0	4	1	6	0	1
Schourek, Pete, Kis.*	0	0	.000	1.08	2	1	0	0	0	0	8.1	8	38	1	1	0	2	0	1	4	0	9	0	0
Schultz, Eric, Char.	3	3	.500	4.38	6	5	1	0	0	0	24.2	24	109	13	12	1	0	1	1	11	0	13	2	0
Seale, Dustin, Dun.*	0	0	.000	0.00	2	0	0	0	1	0	3.0	2	13	1	0	0	0	0	0	3	0	1	0	0
Seo, Jae, St.L.	3	1	.750	2.31	8	7	0	0	0	0	35.0	26	141	13	9	2	2	0	3	10	0	37	1	6
Short, Barry, St.L.	2	3	.400	4.22	22	0	0	0	6	0	42.2	52	198	24	20	1	3	1	2	23	4	25	4	0
Simon, Benjamin, V.B.	1	2	.333	6.75	7	5	0	0	1	0	18.2	22	81	14	14	1	0	0	0	7	0	16	2	0
Smith, Brian, Dun.	1	0	1.000	3.38	4	0	0	0	2	2	10.2	8	42	4	4	0	0	0	3	1	9	0	0
Smith, Eric, Kis.	2	3	.400	6.35	9	4	0	0	2	0	28.1	37	136	22	20	3	0	1	1	16	1	14	2	0
Smith, Taylor, Dun.	0	0	.000	2.70	1	1	0	0	0	0	3.1	3	17	1	1	0	0	0	3	6	0	2	0	0
Sollecito, Gabe, Char.	5	2	.714	0.90	37	0	0	0	18	2	60.0	54	251	13	6	1	1	3	6	14	2	50	0	0

Pitcher, Team	W	L	Pct.	ERA	G	GS	CG	ShO	GF	Sv.	IP	H	TBF	R	ER	HR	SH	SF	HB	BB	IBB	SO	WP	Bk.
Sorzano, Ronnie, Day.	0	2	.000	6.64	23	0	0	0	13	1	42.0	50	195	35	31	4	1	3	6	17	2	31	4	1
Spear, Russell, Lake.	8	7	.533	4.73	18	17	0	0	0	0	97.0	101	434	68	51	9	1	3	6	44	0	78	6	0
Spence, Cam, Tam.	9	5	.643	3.75	21	20	2	0	0	0	127.1	125	542	66	53	7	5	4	2	38	1	105	3	4
Spiers, Corey, Ft.M.*	9	8	.529	3.33	24	24	1	0	0	0	151.1	172	650	70	56	7	2	5	6	38	0	98	7	1
Stachler, Eric, Kis.	0	2	.000	14.90	7	0	0	0	3	0	9.2	17	55	16	16	4	2	0	0	9	1	9	1	0
Stevens, Kris, Cle.*	2	2	.500	1.55	5	5	0	0	0	0	29.0	20	113	6	5	0	0	0	7	14	4	0	
Stevenson, Rodney, Jup.	0	1	.000	2.66	19	0	0	0	14	10	23.2	13	91	7	7	2	1	1	0	6	0	21	1	0
Stieb, Dave, Dun.	2	0	1.000	3.00	3	3	0	0	0	0	15.0	17	65	8	5	2	0	0	5	0	19	1	0
Strickland, Scott, Jup.	4	3	.571	3.39	22	11	0	0	7	2	69.0	64	282	28	26	5	4	2	1	20	0	51	0	1
Sturtze, Tanyon, Char.	0	1	.000	6.00	1	0	0	0	0	0	3.0	2	12	3	2	0	1	0	0	1	0	3	0	0
Taylor, Greg, Cle.	0	0	.000	0.00	1	0	0	0	0	0	1.0	3	3	0	0	0	0	0	0	0	1	0	0	
Tessmar, Tim, St.L.*	0	0	.000	27.00	1	0	0	0	1	0	1.0	3	9	3	3	0	0	0	3	0	1	1	0	
Teut, Nate, Day.*	5	3	.625	5.48	11	11	1	0	0	0	65.2	88	302	48	40	7	0	3	19	0	54	5	1	
Thompson, Chris, Sar.	5	2	.714	3.18	30	0	0	0	16	4	45.1	48	194	19	16	1	2	1	1	17	5	28	8	0
Thompson, Nick, Cle.	0	0	.000	0.00	1	0	0	0	1	0	1.0	0	3	0	0	0	0	0	0	0	0	0	0	
Townsend, Dave, B.C.	0	5	.000	5.94	12	11	1	0	0	0	50.0	63	241	40	33	4	3	0	38	0	30	5	0	
Tucker, Thomas, Jup.	1	1	.500	1.00	2	1	0	0	1	0	9.0	5	32	1	1	0	1	1	0	0	0	10	1	0
Turman, Jimmy, Jup.	3	2	.600	3.31	8	6	1	0	0	0	35.1	37	149	20	13	1	2	3	1	12	0	15	3	0
Valdes, Ismael, V.B.	0	0	.000	0.00	1	1	0	0	0	0	3.0	2	11	0	0	0	0	0	0	1	0	3	0	0
Van Gilder, Ryan, Jup.	1	1	.500	2.70	10	0	0	0	3	0	16.2	16	70	6	5	1	1	2	3	3	0	9	0	0
Vardijan, Dan, B.C.	2	0	1.000	3.00	8	0	0	0	5	0	12.0	15	56	4	4	0	1	1	2	4	0	8	2	0
Vargas, Claudio, B.C.	0	1	.000	4.66	2	2	0	0	0	0	9.2	15	46	5	5	1	1	0	0	4	0	9	0	0
Vasquez, Leo, St.L.*	3	2	.600	2.22	24	6	0	0	10	4	69.0	44	264	20	17	3	3	4	3	24	0	46	5	0
Veniard, Jay, St.L.	1	1	.500	1.80	12	0	0	0	6	1	15.0	8	59	5	3	0	0	1	2	6	0	10	3	0
Villafuerte, Brandon, B.C.	1	0	1.000	0.93	3	0	0	0	3	0	9.2	7	34	3	1	0	0	0	1	0	6	0	0	
Wade, Terrell, St.P.*	0	1	.000	3.60	3	3	0	0	0	0	15.0	12	66	8	6	2	0	1	1	7	0	16	1	0
Wagner, Matt, Jup.	0	0	.000	0.00	1	1	0	0	0	0	5.0	6	21	0	0	0	0	0	0	2	0	0	
Walker, Ron, Day.	0	0	.000	18.00	1	0	0	0	0	0	1.0	1	5	2	2	0	0	0	1	0	1	1	0	
Wallace, Jim, Kis.	0	0	.000	4.15	4	0	0	0	1	0	4.1	2	25	2	2	0	0	0	2	10	0	3	1	0
Welch, Robb, Sar.	4	6	.400	6.75	20	13	0	0	1	1	76.0	70	371	66	57	6	2	1	8	72	1	64	21	0
Wesemann, Jason, Cle.	0	0	.000	0.00	1	0	0	0	1	0	1.0	2	5	1	0	0	0	0	0	0	0	0	0	
Westbrook, Jake, Jup.	11	6	.647	3.26	27	27	2	0	0	0	171.0	169	720	70	62	11	5	3	11	60	0	79	4	0
White, Keith, Dun.	0	0	.000	10.80	3	0	0	0	2	0	3.1	7	16	4	4	2	0	0	1	0	1	0	0	
White, Matt, St.P.	4	8	.333	5.55	17	17	1	0	0	0	95.2	107	433	70	59	10	2	5	6	41	0	64	12	0
Whiteman, Greg, Cle.*	0	1	.000	9.00	2	2	0	0	0	0	8.0	15	38	8	8	1	1	0	1	2	0	8	0	0
Widerski, Jon, B.C.	0	3	.000	6.43	24	1	0	0	6	0	42.0	51	209	36	30	6	1	4	7	31	1	25	4	0
Wiggins, Scott, Tam.*	1	1	.500	1.87	11	5	0	0	3	0	33.2	19	136	12	7	1	2	0	0	17	1	36	2	0
Wilson, Paul, St.L.	0	1	.000	6.38	5	5	0	0	0	0	18.1	23	78	13	13	2	0	1	0	4	0	16	1	0
Wimberly, Larry, Cle.*	7	2	.778	3.63	14	10	0	0	1	0	72.0	77	293	30	29	4	0	4	3	12	0	66	0	0
Woodring, Jason, Jup.	1	1	.500	3.07	35	0	0	0	21	1	44.0	47	196	22	15	3	2	6	13	0	19	2	0
Wyckoff, Travis, B.C.*	4	5	.444	3.21	41	0	0	0	22	3	73.0	77	313	33	26	4	2	3	7	27	1	31	6	0
Yeager, Gary, Cle.	4	1	.800	3.44	41	2	0	0	12	0	81.0	102	363	42	31	4	0	2	4	25	4	44	8	0
Yeskie, Nate, Ft.M.	4	2	.667	3.30	14	11	1	0	2	0	62.2	74	273	27	23	4	2	0	5	16	0	39	3	0
Yoder, Jeff, Day.	7	9	.438	5.03	26	24	1	0	1	0	143.0	158	645	97	80	16	3	6	4	47	0	128	10	2
Young, Danny, Day.*	1	1	.500	5.19	7	0	0	0	3	0	8.2	9	42	5	5	0	0	0	8	0	6	1	0	
Young, Joe, Dun.	4	1	.800	4.63	8	8	0	0	0	0	44.2	50	201	34	23	8	0	4	2	22	0	43	2	1
Zimmerman, Jeff, Char.	2	1	.667	1.26	10	0	0	0	3	0	14.1	10	52	2	2	1	0	1	0	14	0	0	0	

COMBINATION SHUTOUTS: **Brevard County (5)**—Rodgers-Duncan-Clark, Cames-Fowler-Clark, Cames-Wyckoff, Mull-Ehlers, Cames-Ehlers. **Charlotte (4)**—Cook-Zimmerman-Dickey, Cook-Pedraza-Mota, Pedraza-Dickey, Cook-Moore. **Clearwater (2)**—Stephens-Kershner-Kawabata, Ryan-Adair. **Daytona (1)**—Downs-Fisher-Hart. **Dunedin (7)**—Koch-Bale, Koch-Lee-Adkins-Mann, Glover-Delgado-Mann, Koch-Delgado, Bradford-Hendrickson, Glover-Lukasiewicz-Mann, LaChapelle-Bale-Mann. **Fort Myers (3)**—Yeskie-Malko, Mota-Niedermaier, Spiers-Garza. **Jupiter (10)**—Evans-Niebla-Marquez-Mota, Nicholson-Niebla-Stevenson, Westbrook-Niebla-Civit, Mattes-Moraga-Woodring, Phelps-Moraga-Durocher, Strickland-Bullinger-Mota-Marquez, Westbrook-Saylor-Marquez, Blank-Matz, Westbrook-Woodring-Saylor, Tucker-Strickland. **Kissimmee (3)**—Robertson-Root, Robertson-Maldonado-Green, Root-Love-Green-Duncan-Smith. **Lakeland (1)**—Castillo-Santos. **St. Lucie (9)**—Seo-Arteaga-Hohrman-Lyons, Gulin-Arteaga-Hafer, Pumphrey-Lyons-Lohrman, Pumphrey-Brittan, Herbison-Lyons, McCrary-Brittan, Roberts-Short-Aucoin-Cammack, Roberts-McEntire-Veniard, Seo-Brittan. **St. Petersburg (6)**—Manias-Benesh-Enders-Daniels, Armenta-Benesh-Enders-Daniels, Kaufman-Aquino-Benesh, Faufman-Enders-Manon-Aquino, Kaufman-Benesh-Madison, Bowers-LeRoy-Daniels. **Sarasota (6)**—Kinney-McMullen-Rose, Garrett-Cannon, Garrett-McMullen-Rose, Hazlett-Betancourt-Thompson, Kim-Thompson-DeLaCruz, Betti-Cannon-Rose-Thompson. **Tampa (5)**—Robbins-Phillips-Bradley, Bradley-Lail, Bradley-Lail, Robbins-Cubillan-Lisio, Robbins-Mairena-Dingman. **Vero Beach (4)**—O'Shaughnessy-Mayo, O'Shaughnessy-Paluk-Mayo, O'Shaughnessy-Feliciano, O'Shaughnessy-Feliciano.

NO-HIT GAME: Bradley, Tampa, defeated Lakeland, 8-0, June 22.

PITCHERS WITH TWO OR MORE TEAMS

Pitcher, Team	W	L	Pct.	ERA	G	GS	CG	ShO	GF	Sv.	IP	H	TBF	R	ER	HR	SH	SF	HB	BB	IBB	SO	WP	Bk.
DeYoung, Dan, Char.	13	4	.765	4.02	20	20	0	0	0	0	118.2	112	500	60	53	11	1	6	2	39	0	62	3	1
DeYoung, Dan, B.C.	1	4	.200	6.44	6	6	2	0	0	0	36.1	55	160	28	26	5	3	1	4	4	0	9	1	0
Hoff, Steve, B.C.*	5	8	.385	4.11	15	15	2	0	0	0	85.1	93	364	50	39	7	2	6	5	27	1	45	4	0
Hoff, Steve, Day.*	0	3	.000	7.24	6	6	0	0	0	0	27.1	38	136	25	22	4	0	3	2	12	0	26	5	0
Kinney, Matt, Sar.	9	6	.600	4.01	22	20	2	1	1	0	121.1	109	536	70	54	5	5	2	2	75	3	96	19	2
Kinney, Matt, Ft.M.	3	2	.600	3.13	7	7	0	0	0	0	37.1	31	162	18	13	0	2	1	0	18	0	39	6	0

1998 FIELDING

TEAM

Team	Pct.	G	PO	A	E	TC	DP	PB	Team	Pct.	G	PO	A	E	TC	DP	PB
Clearwater	.971	140	3762	1686	161	5609	136	20	St. Petersburg	.964	139	3709	1369	191	5269	93	23
Jupiter	.969	140	3714	1645	171	5530	127	16	Kissimmee	.962	139	3635	1506	202	5343	121	26
St. Lucie	.969	137	3621	1623	170	5414	131	29	Vero Beach	.962	139	3602	1443	202	5247	100	33
Charlotte	.967	138	3664	1521	175	5360	116	40	Lakeland	.961	139	3646	1582	213	5441	114	24
Dunedin	.966	140	3697	1516	182	5395	133	25	Daytona	.956	140	3658	1480	234	5372	114	40
Fort Myers	.965	139	3719	1664	193	5576	140	38	Tampa	.956	139	3671	1461	236	5368	106	24
Sarasota	.965	137	3583	1399	181	5163	95	34	TRIPLE PLAYS: None.								
Brevard County	.964	140	3599	1441	186	5226	131	34									

FIRST BASEMEN

NOTE: All caps denotes fielding-percentage leader based on 70 games for catchers, 93 for all other non-pitchers and 140 innings for pitchers. *Throws lefthanded.

Player, Team	Pct.	G	PO	A	E	TC	DP
Adams, Jason, Kis.	.986	8	69	4	1	74	8
Adriana, Sharnol, Dun.	1.000	8	17	2	0	19	3
Alleyne, Roberto, Kis.	1.000	1	8	3	0	11	1
August, Brian, Tam.	1.000	2	12	1	0	13	3
Becker, Brian, St.P.	.992	113	916	101	8	1025	72
Brown, Jason, V.B.	1.000	4	20	1	0	21	0
BURNHAM, Gary, Cle.*	.994	114	1084	68	7	1159	109
Burns, Kevin, Kis.*	.987	127	1078	87	15	1180	93
Burrell, Patrick, Cle.	.995	22	202	13	1	216	14
Callahan, David, B.C.*	1.000	5	44	3	0	47	5
Chavera, Arnie, Kis.	1.000	2	7	0	0	7	1
Cheek, Shawn, Char.	.923	9	45	3	4	52	5
Chevalier, Virgil, Sar.	.982	14	102	8	2	112	5
Chiaffredo, Paul, Dun.	1.000	4	15	0	0	15	0
Colina, Roberto, St.P.*	.995	23	168	15	1	184	5
Conway, Scott, B.C.*	1.000	9	59	3	0	62	7
Corps, Erick, St.P.	1.000	2	4	0	0	4	1
Cossins, Tim, Tam.	.955	13	101	5	5	111	9
Davis, Glenn, V.B.*	.994	32	293	24	2	319	30
Delgado, Carlos, Dun.	1.000	2	13	0	0	13	0
Diaz, Juan, V.B.	.986	55	484	23	7	514	29
Dubose, Brian, Lake.	.990	69	623	48	7	678	52
Espinal, Juan, Sar.	1.000	1	2	0	0	2	1
Everson, Darin, Sar.	.984	16	124	3	2	129	5
Gainey, Bryon, St.L.	.980	76	707	39	15	761	58
Gallagher, Shawn, Char.	.984	128	1110	46	19	1175	95
Garrett, Jason, B.C.	.989	57	499	33	6	538	48
Giles, Tim, Dun.	.988	77	617	65	8	690	73
Glassey, Josh, V.B.	.923	3	11	1	1	13	2
Gunderson, Shane, Ft.M.	1.000	1	7	0	0	7	1
Hacker, Steve, Ft.M.	.984	14	118	7	2	127	11
Huff, Brent, St.L.	1.000	3	18	0	0	18	0
Huls, Steve, Ft.M.	1.000	2	6	0	0	6	0
Johnson, Gary, Day.	1.000	2	20	0	0	20	4
Johnson, Nick, Tam.*	.986	90	785	58	12	855	58
Jones, Aaron, Tam.*	.988	11	69	10	1	80	8
Jones, Jay, B.C.	.995	49	361	27	2	390	39
Knowles, Eric, Tam.	1.000	1	4	0	0	4	0
Kofler, Eric, Tam.*	.956	19	137	15	7	159	12
Lamb, Michael, Char.	.964	2	26	1	1	28	2
Lemonis, Chris, Lake.	.986	24	201	13	3	217	19
Lindstrom, David, Lake.	.976	9	77	6	2	85	6
Lomasney, Steve, Sar.	.971	3	31	3	1	35	0
Lopiccolo, Jamie, Lake.	.985	39	366	26	6	398	27
Manning, Nate, Day.	.978	26	172	9	4	185	15
Martinez, Rafael, Sar.*	.992	97	793	66	7	866	61
Mejia, Renato, B.C.	.971	23	191	12	6	209	19
Morgan, Dave, Dun.	1.000	2	20	2	0	22	0
Nunez, Jose, Jup.	1.000	3	18	3	0	21	4
Nunnari, Talmadge, Jup.*	.993	53	491	50	4	545	49
Owens, Billy, Kis.	1.000	3	23	1	0	24	2
Patzke, Jeff, Dun.	1.000	2	14	0	0	14	0
Pena, Carlos, Char.*	.977	4	41	2	1	44	6
Peterman, Tommy, Ft.M.*	.993	123	1156	80	9	1245	117
Pond, Simon, Jup.	.979	15	135	8	3	146	7
Pratt, Todd, St.L.	1.000	2	17	3	0	20	1
Quatraro, Matthew, St.P.	.961	6	47	2	2	51	6
Raifstanger, John, Sar.	1.000	4	18	3	0	21	2
Rodriguez, Luis, Dun.	1.000	4	7	1	0	8	1
Rodriguez, Mike, Dun.	1.000	2	18	0	0	18	0
Samuel, Cody, Tam.	1.000	12	69	4	0	73	6
Sankey, Brian, V.B.*	.984	53	382	39	7	428	31
Sapp, Damian, Sar.	.956	13	80	7	4	91	11
Schroeder, John, Ft.M.	1.000	3	20	3	0	23	3
Schwab, Chris, Jup.*	.923	2	22	2	2	26	1
Stone, Craig, Dun.	.982	65	443	62	9	514	39
Tessmar, Tim, St.L.*	.985	69	608	38	10	656	60
Tracy, Andrew, Jup.	.993	67	635	49	5	689	52
Treanor, Matt, B.C.	1.000	1	3	1	0	4	1
Uccello, Jeff, Sar.	1.000	1	3	0	0	3	0
Vieira, Scott, Day.	1.000	5	42	1	0	43	2
Walker, Ron, Day.	1.000	1	7	0	0	7	0
Ware, Jeremy, Jup.	.857	1	6	0	1	7	0
Wesemann, Jason, Cle.	1.000	10	54	5	0	59	6
Yedo, Carlos, Day.*	.977	37	314	21	8	343	25
Zuleta, Julio, Day.	.982	76	643	58	13	714	51

SECOND BASEMEN

Player, Team	Pct.	G	PO	A	E	TC	DP
Abernathy, Brent, Dun.	.973	123	240	338	16	594	67
Adams, Jason, Kis.	1.000	8	8	19	0	27	4
Adriana, Sharnol, Dun.	.980	10	19	30	1	50	10
Alvarez, Julio, Lake.	.875	3	3	4	1	8	1
Amador, Manny, Cle.	1.000	8	7	17	0	24	1
August, Brian, Tam.	.929	7	11	15	2	28	3
Bell, Mike, St.L.	.929	10	21	31	4	56	5
Blandford, Paul, Jup.	1.000	2	3	7	0	10	0
Blum, Geoffrey, Jup.	.984	13	26	36	1	63	8
Camilli, Jason, Jup.	.967	47	77	156	8	241	23
Capellan, Rene, Lake.	.908	37	59	99	16	174	16
Carr, Dustin, St.P.	.957	137	245	314	25	584	63
Carroll, Jamey, Jup.	.983	46	86	139	4	229	28
Clapinski, Chris, B.C.	1.000	1	1	4	0	5	0
Corps, Erick, St.P.	1.000	1	0	1	0	1	0
Cossins, Tim, Tam.	.750	1	1	2	1	4	0
Cranford, Joey, Ft.M.	.967	18	28	59	3	90	11
Cuevas, Trent, V.B.	.956	42	63	88	7	158	16
Dallimore, Brian, Kis.	.965	11	27	28	2	57	6
Davidson, Cleatus, Ft.M.	.967	125	320	403	25	748	98
Dennis, Les, Tam.	.945	18	21	31	3	55	7
ECKSTEIN, David, Sar.	.989	115	197	323	6	526	54
Erickson, Corey, St.L.	.972	41	83	123	6	212	32
Font, Franklin, Day.	.962	39	70	105	7	182	25
Forkerway, Trey, Day.	.961	21	35	39	3	77	8
Fuentes, Javier, Sar.	.935	26	38	49	6	93	11
Fuller, Aaron, Day.	.852	7	10	13	4	27	2
Goudie, Jaime, V.B.	.984	18	28	35	1	64	9
Guerrero, Pedro, Char.	1.000	1	1	3	0	4	0
Haney, Todd, St.L.	1.000	1	3	2	0	5	0
Harris, Brian, Cle.	.979	116	287	367	14	668	80
Henry, Santiago, Dun.	1.000	7	11	10	0	21	3
Hinds, Rob, Tam.	.917	27	68	76	13	157	13
Jasco, Elinton, Day.	.973	39	81	100	5	186	21
Jones, Jack, V.B.	.900	3	4	5	1	10	1
Knowles, Eric, Tam.	.967	7	7	22	1	30	2
Lackey, Steve, Lake.	.925	8	18	19	3	40	3
Lemonis, Chris, Lake.	1.000	7	13	13	0	26	3
Lobaton, Jose, Tam.	.977	8	18	25	1	44	7
Mateo, Henry, Jup.	1.000	11	23	24	0	47	9
McNamara, Rusty, Cle.	1.000	7	18	26	0	44	2
Meyers, Chad, Day.	.940	48	95	109	13	217	24
Montilla, Miguel, Tam.	1.000	2	1	4	0	5	1
Mora, Melvin, St.L.	1.000	8	12	29	0	41	4
Mordecai, Mike, Jup.	1.000	1	2	3	0	5	2
Morimoto, Ken, V.B.	.928	45	78	103	14	195	17
Myers, Adrian, Char.	1.000	1	2	1	0	3	0
Nunez, Jose, Jup.	.959	22	58	58	5	121	12
Owens-Bragg, Luke, St.P.	1.000	4	4	4	0	8	0
Parsons, Jeff, Kis.	.952	23	29	70	5	104	16
Patterson, John, St.P.	1.000	1	0	1	0	1	0
Patzke, Jeff, Dun.	.939	5	13	18	2	33	3
Paulino, David, B.C.	.962	17	30	46	3	79	11
Pond, Simon, Jup.	.778	4	2	5	2	9	0
Raifstanger, John, Sar.	.952	6	4	16	1	21	2
Raynor, Mark, Cle.	1.000	1	3	3	0	6	0
Reyes, Dadny, B.C.	1.000	1	0	2	0	2	0
Robles, Oscar, Kis.	.962	45	98	105	8	211	25
Rodriguez, Mike, Dun.	.857	1	1	5	1	7	1
Romano, Jason, Char.	.978	7	20	25	1	46	6
Runnells, T.J., Lake.	.923	6	10	14	2	26	2
Samboy, Nelson, Kis.	.960	59	135	174	13	322	41
Schaffer, Jake, Lake.	.970	84	169	252	13	434	55
Schifano, Anthony, B.C.	.968	10	30	30	2	62	9
Sergio, Thomas, Char.	.959	108	230	289	22	541	49
Shuck, Jason, St.L.	1.000	3	5	6	0	11	2
Smiga, Jason, Char.	.963	13	22	30	2	54	6
Smith, Rod, Tam.	.945	85	128	233	21	382	37
Solano, Danny, Char.	.963	16	32	47	3	82	16
Stevens, Tony, Ft.M.	1.000	2	1	2	0	3	0
Stromsborg, Ryan, Dun.	1.000	1	0	2	0	2	0
Tamargo, John, St.L.	.964	52	80	160	9	249	32
Taylor, Greg, Cle.	.984	13	18	43	1	62	8
Torres, Bernie, V.B.	.961	49	82	113	8	203	27
Vaughn, Lateef, Ft.M.	.917	2	3	8	1	12	2
Venghaus, Jeff, B.C.	.953	113	255	309	28	592	68
White, Walt, B.C.	1.000	1	5	4	0	9	2
Zorrilla, Julio, St.L.	.959	32	69	94	7	170	20

THIRD BASEMEN

Player, Team	Pct.	G	PO	A	E	TC	DP
Adams, Jason, Kis.	.888	37	12	67	10	89	4
Adriana, Sharnol, Dun.	.903	28	21	44	7	72	6
Alcantara, Israel, St.P.	.912	27	18	44	6	68	1
Amador, Manny, Cle.	.944	11	3	31	2	36	4
Arredondo, Hernando, St.P.	.892	20	18	40	7	65	1
August, Brian, Tam.	.952	8	5	15	1	21	1
Bell, Mike, St.L.	.833	2	2	3	1	6	0
Blake, Casey, Dun.	.939	86	64	183	16	263	16
Blandford, Paul, Jup.	.920	5	5	18	2	25	1
Blum, Geoffrey, Jup.	.889	2	3	5	1	9	1
Bravo, Danny, Jup.	.945	23	19	33	3	55	2
Brett, Jason, St.L.	1.000	2	0	7	0	7	0
Brown, Jason, V.B.	1.000	1	1	3	0	4	0
Camilli, Jason, Jup.	.948	26	15	58	4	77	6
Capellan, Rene, Lake.	1.000	3	1	1	0	2	0
Clapinski, Chris, B.C.	.000	1	0	0	1	1	0
Collier, Lamonte, Cle.	1.000	4	4	5	0	9	0
Corps, Erick, St.P.	.922	63	35	83	10	128	9
Cotton, John, Day.	.846	5	2	9	2	13	0
Cranford, Joey, Ft.M.	.895	35	19	58	9	86	3
Cuevas, Trent, V.B.	.857	41	18	72	15	105	8
Dallimore, Brian, Kis.	.956	52	39	113	7	159	12
Dennis, Les, Tam.	.889	6	5	3	1	9	1
Donato, Dan, St.P.	.966	9	10	18	1	29	4
Erickson, Corey, St.L.	.956	54	25	149	8	182	11
Escalona, Felix, Kis.	1.000	1	1	0	0	1	0
Espinal, Juan, Sar.	.914	125	78	218	28	324	15
Font, Franklin, Day.	.870	12	3	17	3	23	1
Forkerway, Trey, Day.	.667	7	2	2	2	6	0
Fraser, Joe, Ft.M.	.932	31	23	73	7	103	9
Fuentes, Javier, Sar.	.914	15	6	26	3	35	3
Garcia, Neil, St.P.	.884	15	12	26	5	43	1
Goudie, Jaime, V.B.	.903	15	5	23	3	31	0
Huls, Steve, Ft.M.	.931	54	29	119	11	159	9
Jones, Jack, V.B.	1.000	2	0	4	0	4	1
Kane, Ryan, Tam.	.867	16	3	23	4	30	2
King, Brad, Day.	.500	2	0	1	1	2	0
Kleinz, Larry, B.C.	.900	73	50	156	23	229	15
Knowles, Eric, Tam.	.917	13	6	27	3	36	6
LAMB, Michael, Char.	.931	132	98	304	30	432	19
Landry, Jacques, Lake.	.905	99	79	196	29	304	17
Lawrence, Joe, Dun.	1.000	4	0	10	0	10	0
Lemonis, Chris, Lake.	.879	40	33	91	17	141	3
Leon, Donny, Tam.	.890	99	61	166	28	255	10
Malave, Jaime, V.B.	1.000	2	0	3	0	3	0
Manning, Nate, Day.	.899	54	38	104	16	158	9
McNamara, Rusty, Cle.	.882	121	77	244	43	364	15
Montilla, Miguel, Tam.	.727	4	3	5	3	11	2
Moss, Rick, Ft.M.	.911	25	18	54	7	79	6
Nunez, Jose, Jup.	.889	22	11	37	6	54	2
Owens-Bragg, Luke, St.P.	.825	16	12	21	7	40	1
Parsons, Jeff, St.L.-Kis.	.875	7	0	14	2	16	3
Patzke, Jeff, Dun.	.909	4	0	10	1	11	1
Paulino, David, B.C.	1.000	2	0	3	0	3	0
Perry, Herbert, St.P.	.875	2	2	5	1	8	0
Pond, Simon, Jup.	.856	74	35	125	27	187	11
Raifstanger, John, Sar.	1.000	1	0	4	0	4	0
Raynor, Mark, Cle.	1.000	3	3	11	0	14	2
Reding, Josh, Jup.	1.000	3	2	6	0	8	3
Rico, Diego, Day.*	1.000	1	0	4	0	4	0
Robles, Oscar, Kis.	1.000	1	1	1	0	2	1
Rodriguez, Luis, Dun.	1.000	1	1	2	0	3	0
Rodriguez, Mike, Dun.	1.000	4	3	8	0	11	0
Rodriguez, Sammy, St.L.	.500	2	1	2	3	6	0
Rolls, Damian, V.B.	.951	73	65	187	13	265	12
Ruiz, Ramon, V.B.	.791	17	13	21	9	43	2
Salinas, Trey, St.P.	.714	3	2	3	2	7	0
Samboy, Nelson, Kis.	1.000	1	0	1	0	1	0
Sasser, Rob, Char.	1.000	3	2	9	0	11	1
Schifano, Anthony, B.C.	.969	63	55	131	6	192	16
Smiga, Jason, Char.	1.000	6	1	5	0	6	1
Stone, Craig, Dun.	.762	14	4	12	5	21	4
Stromsborg, Ryan, Dun.	.842	13	2	14	3	19	2
Tracy, Andrew, Dun.	1.000	2	3	2	0	5	0
Treanor, Matt, B.C.	1.000	1	1	2	0	3	1
Truby, Chris, V.B.	.951	51	45	130	9	184	16
Vaughn, Lateef, Ft.M.	.714	2	1	4	2	7	0
Venghaus, Jeff, B.C.	.667	1	0	2	1	3	0
Walker, Ron, Day.	.899	74	50	128	20	198	14
Warren, Lance, V.B.	1.000	4	0	2	0	2	0
Wesemann, Jason, Cle.	1.000	4	3	8	0	11	1
Zamora, Junior, St.L.	.916	80	57	204	24	285	18

THIRD BASEMEN WITH TWO OR MORE TEAMS

Player, Team	Pct.	G	PO	A	E	TC	DP
Parsons, Jeff, St.L.	.909	6	0	10	1	11	3
Parsons, Jeff, Kis.	.800	1	0	4	1	5	0

SHORTSTOPS

Player, Team	Pct.	G	PO	A	E	TC	DP
Abreu, Dennis, Day.	.912	125	192	386	56	634	66
Acevedo, Luis, Char.	1.000	1	2	1	0	3	1
Adams, Jason, Kis.	1.000	13	16	20	0	36	5
Adriana, Sharnol, Dun.	.967	14	17	41	2	60	10
Alvarez, Julio, Lake.	.760	4	7	12	6	25	2
Bautista, Rayner, Lake.	.906	32	47	88	14	149	21
Blum, Geoffrey, Jup.	1.000	2	2	8	0	10	0
Bravo, Danny, Jup.	1.000	2	2	3	0	5	1
Camilli, Jason, Jup.	.944	12	19	32	3	54	5
Carroll, Jamey, Jup.	.941	8	10	22	2	34	4
Clapinski, Chris, B.C.	1.000	1	1	4	0	5	0
Collier, Lamonte, Cle.	.928	16	15	49	5	69	7
Corps, Erick, St.P.	.889	31	50	78	16	144	15
Cruz, Deivi, Lake.	1.000	2	1	2	0	3	0
Cuevas, Trent, V.B.	1.000	14	14	21	0	35	4
Davidson, Cleatus, Ft.M.	.905	5	5	14	2	21	2
De La Rosa, Tomas, Jup.	.9516	117	208	382	30	620	69
De Los Santos, Eddy, St.P.	.927	111	154	303	36	493	40
Dennis, Les, Tam.	.950	19	20	37	3	60	6
Dransfeldt, Kelly, Char.	.941	66	100	205	19	324	38
Eckstein, David, Sar.	1.000	16	17	45	0	62	8
Font, Franklin, Day.	.935	14	16	42	4	62	2
Forkerway, Trey, Day.	.962	6	10	15	1	26	4
Fuentes, Javier, Sar.	.884	24	34	50	11	95	11
Henry, Santiago, Dun.	.926	5	9	16	2	27	7
Huls, Steve, Ft.M.	.932	12	17	38	4	59	12
Hyers, Matt, Kis.	.920	7	7	16	2	25	3
Jones, Jack, V.B.	.889	5	2	6	1	9	1
Kleinz, Larry, B.C.	1.000	1	3	4	0	7	1
Knowles, Eric, Tam.	.931	74	115	207	24	346	39
Lackey, Steve, Lake.	.929	95	146	310	35	491	46
Lawrence, Joe, Dun.	.912	120	163	335	48	546	66
Lobaton, Jose, Tam.	.920	23	34	46	7	87	10
Lopez, Felipe, Dun.	.692	4	2	7	4	13	1
Lugo, Julio, Kis.	.921	98	181	308	42	531	54
Machado, Albenis, Jup.	1.000	2	1	4	0	5	0
Martinez, Gabby, Tam.	.910	37	54	98	15	167	16
Montilla, Miguel, Tam.	.800	4	3	5	2	10	1
Mora, Melvin, St.L.	.957	6	8	14	1	23	6
Mordecai, Mike, Jup.	1.000	1	2	1	0	3	0
Nunez, Jose, Jup.	1.000	1	2	4	0	6	0
Olmeda, Jose, Sar.	.912	113	192	275	45	512	44
Owens-Bragg, Luke, St.P.	1.000	2	2	1	0	3	0
Parsons, Jeff, St.L.-Kis.	.918	25	32	58	8	98	8
Paulino, David, B.C.	.875	14	15	41	8	64	3
Polanco, Enohel, St.L.	.958	74	108	214	14	336	41
Raifstanger, John, Sar.	1.000	1	0	1	0	1	1
Reding, Josh, Jup.	1.000	1	3	2	0	5	1
Reynoso, Ismael, B.C.	.938	71	121	165	19	305	44
Riggs, Eric, V.B.	.943	59	104	178	17	299	30
Rivas, Luis, Ft.M.	.913	124	162	415	55	632	78
Robles, Oscar, Kis.	.929	21	26	39	5	70	11
ROLLINS, Jimmy, Cle.	.9517	119	192	380	29	601	76
Schaffer, Jake, Lake.	.877	13	22	35	8	65	8
Schifano, Anthony, B.C.	.924	17	19	42	5	66	9
Smiga, Jason, Char.	1.000	3	3	7	0	10	1
Sojo, Luis, Tam.	.923	3	4	8	1	13	2
Solano, Danny, Char.	.979	68	118	208	7	333	44
Stromsborg, Ryan, Dun.	.917	2	3	8	1	12	3
Tamargo, John, St.L.	.951	48	50	126	9	185	23
Taylor, Greg, Cle.	1.000	4	4	5	0	9	1
Torres, Bernie, V.B.	.935	75	104	185	20	309	28
Ugueto, Luis, B.C.	.857	3	5	7	2	14	0
Warriax, Brandon, Char.	.947	5	7	11	1	19	2
Washington, Kelley, B.C.	.901	27	37	72	12	121	16
Wesemann, Jason, Cle.	.952	9	17	23	2	42	6
White, Walt, B.C.	.927	11	17	34	4	55	2

SHORTSTOPS WITH TWO OR MORE TEAMS

Player, Team	Pct.	G	PO	A	E	TC	DP
Parsons, Jeff, St.L.	.922	17	26	45	6	77	6
Parsons, Jeff, Kis.	.905	8	6	13	2	21	2

OUTFIELDERS

Player, Team	Pct.	G	PO	A	E	TC	DP
Adolfo, Carlos, Jup.	.966	81	136	8	5	149	2
Airoso, Kurt, Lake.	.982	67	105	4	2	111	0
Alcantara, Israel, St.P.	.895	8	17	0	2	19	0
Alleyne, Roberto, Kis.	.921	17	32	3	3	38	0
Alvarez, Rafael, Ft.M.*	.985	102	184	12	3	199	2
Amerson, Gordon, Tam.*	1.000	4	4	0	0	4	0
Aylor, Brian, Tam.*	.895	11	16	1	2	19	0
Bady, Ed, Jup.	1.000	1	1	0	0	1	0
Beamon, Trey, Lake.	1.000	2	2	0	0	2	0
Bell, Mike, St.L.	1.000	6	6	0	0	6	0
Bolivar, Papo, Ft.M.	.962	124	193	10	8	211	0
Bradley, Milton, Jup.	.993	61	138	8	1	147	4
Brown, Richard, Tam.*	.960	56	94	3	4	101	1
Brown, Roosevelt, Day.	.982	64	106	4	2	112	3
Camilli, Jason, Jup.	1.000	3	5	1	0	6	1
Camilo, Jose, B.C.*	.987	88	144	8	2	154	1
Carey, Orlando, Tam.	.889	9	8	0	1	9	0
Cedeno, Jesus, Lake.	.988	82	156	8	2	166	2
Cedeno, Roger, Lake.	.933	6	14	0	1	15	0
Chancey, Bailey, St.L.	.971	41	65	3	2	70	0
Chatman, Karl, Jup.	.975	61	114	3	3	120	0
Chevalier, Virgil, Sar.	.962	18	25	0	1	26	0
Choi, Kyung, Sar.*	.968	36	60	1	2	63	0
Colina, Roberto, St.P.*	.882	15	15	0	2	17	0
Collier, Lamonte, Cle.	.800	4	8	0	2	10	0
Collins, Francis, Cle.	.984	29	54	6	1	61	1
Cook, Hayward, B.C.	.992	60	115	8	1	124	2
Cooley, Shannon, Cle.	1.000	12	15	2	0	17	0
Costello, Brian, Cle.	.965	32	52	3	2	57	0
Cotton, John, Day.	1.000	7	9	0	0	9	0
Crane, Todd, Cle.	.968	120	262	10	9	281	0
Cranford, Joey, Ft.M.	1.000	15	22	4	0	26	0
Davis, Glenn, V.B.*	.980	54	96	2	2	100	0
Derosso, Tony, Sar.	1.000	3	1	0	0	1	0
Duffy, Jim, Kis.	.977	23	38	4	1	43	0
Emmons, Scott, Tam.	1.000	1	3	0	0	3	0
Encarnacion, Juan, Lake.	1.000	4	7	1	0	8	0
Faggett, Ethan, Sar.*	.972	61	98	6	3	107	1
Farraez, Jesus, Kis.	.888	42	84	3	11	98	1
Felston, Anthony, Ft.M.*	.972	113	233	8	7	248	0
Francia, David, Cle.*	.968	46	89	3	3	95	0
Fuller, Aaron, Day.	.960	62	94	2	4	100	0
Gomera, Rafael, V.B.	.947	54	104	4	6	114	1
Green, Kevin, B.C.	.941	17	28	4	2	34	0
Guerrero, Rafael, St.P.	.980	73	141	5	3	149	1
Gunderson, Shane, Ft.M.	.955	39	60	3	3	66	2
Hall, Noah, Jup.	1.000	3	2	1	0	3	0
Hall, Ronnie, Day.	1.000	1	1	0	0	1	0
Haltiwanger, Garrick, St.L.*	.967	92	140	6	5	151	0
Harrell, Ken, Tam.	.889	2	8	0	1	9	0
Harvey, Aaron, B.C.	1.000	3	3	0	0	3	0
Hawkins, Kraig, St.P.	.983	29	58	1	1	60	0
Heinrichs, Jon, B.C.	.985	109	189	6	3	198	0
Huff, Brent, Cle.	.973	102	172	9	5	186	1
Hundley, Todd, St.L.	.900	9	17	1	2	20	0
Jasco, Elinton, Day.	.833	4	5	0	1	6	0
Jenkins, Corey, Sar.	.902	73	105	6	12	123	0
Johnson, Damon, Dun.	.994	91	147	7	1	155	2
Johnson, Gary, Day.	.979	113	227	11	5	243	2
Johnson, Ric, Kis.	.984	103	244	5	4	253	0
Keel, David, Tam.	1.000	2	3	1	0	4	0
Kelleher, Pat, V.B.	.940	43	77	2	5	84	0
Key, Jeff, Cle.	.988	53	82	3	1	86	1
Kieschnick, Brooks, St.P.	.889	25	24	0	3	27	0
Kiil, Harry, Lake.	.978	104	176	4	4	184	0
King, Brad, Day.	1.000	5	4	1	0	5	0
Kofler, Eric, Tam.*	1.000	58	91	8	0	99	2
Langaigne, Selwyn, Dun.*	.989	127	267	9	3	279	2
LeCronier, Jason, St.P.	1.000	35	50	2	0	52	0
Lopiccolo, Jamie, Lake.	.956	24	41	2	2	45	0
Maduro, Remy, B.C.	1.000	17	24	2	0	26	1
Maloney, Jeff, Dun.	1.000	46	73	3	0	76	0
Marsh, Roy, Sar.	.992	105	240	8	2	250	2
Mateo, Ruben, Char.	1.000	1	2	0	0	2	0
McDonald, Donzell, Tam.	1.000	5	14	0	0	14	0
McNamara, Rusty, Cle.	1.000	1	2	1	0	3	0
Mejia, Maximiliano, V.B.	.964	74	127	5	5	137	1
Mejia, Renato, B.C.	1.000	8	15	0	0	15	0
Mendoza, Carlos, St.P.*	1.000	8	20	1	0	21	0
Meyers, Chad, Day.	1.000	1	2	0	0	2	0
Monroe, Craig, Char.	.951	121	198	17	11	226	3
Moore, Lacarlo, Lake.	.984	28	56	4	1	61	1
Mora, Melvin, St.L.	1.000	1	1	0	0	1	0
Morris, Jeremy, Tam.	.963	113	173	7	7	187	1
Mota, Tony, V.B.	.984	54	118	3	2	123	0
Mucker, Kelcey, Ft.M.	.943	18	32	1	2	35	1
Myers, Adrian, Char.	.974	97	222	3	6	231	1
Newton, Kimani, V.B.	.989	53	86	1	1	88	0
Ottavinia, Paul, Tam.*	.954	41	62	0	3	65	0
Owens-Bragg, Luke, St.P.	1.000	4	5	0	0	5	0
Padilla, Roy, Sar.*	.968	107	232	7	8	247	2
Parsons, Jeff, St.L.-Kis.	1.000	3	5	0	0	5	0
Payton, Jay, St.L.	1.000	3	8	0	0	8	0
Peterman, Tommy, Ft.M.*	1.000	6	10	0	0	10	0
Piniella, Juan, Char.	.971	53	99	2	3	104	0
Podsednik, Scott, Char.*	.986	63	143	3	2	148	2
Pomierski, Joe, St.P.	.963	98	171	12	7	190	1
Pond, Simon, Jup.	1.000	1	1	0	0	1	0
Pratt, Todd, St.L.	1.000	1	1	0	0	1	0
Pratt, Wes, Kis.	.969	19	30	1	1	32	0
Quatraro, Matthew, St.P.	1.000	2	3	0	0	3	0
Raifstanger, John, Sar.	1.000	26	47	3	0	50	0
Ramirez, Dan, St.L.	.964	118	250	14	10	274	1
Ramirez, Julio, B.C.	.979	135	365	17	8	390	3
Reeder, Jim, Kis.	.969	68	121	6	4	131	1
Richards, Rowan, Char.	.929	10	13	0	1	14	0
Rico, Diego, Day.*	.968	101	176	5	6	187	2
Riley, Cash, V.B.	.938	100	163	4	11	178	1
Rivers, Jonathan, Dun.	1.000	5	7	0	0	7	0
Rodriguez, Luis, Dun.	1.000	7	10	1	0	11	0
Rodriguez, Mike, Dun.	1.000	6	7	0	0	7	0
Rodriguez, Noel, Kis.	.950	15	18	1	1	20	0
Rojas, Mo, Sar.	1.000	5	11	0	0	11	0
Ruan, Wilken, Jup.	1.000	5	8	0	0	8	0
Salinas, Trey, St.P.	1.000	7	10	0	0	10	0
Samboy, Nelson, Kis.	.952	57	111	7	6	124	0
Sanchez, Alex, St.P.*	.965	128	330	5	12	347	1
Sankey, Brian, V.B.*	1.000	6	2	1	0	3	0
Schwab, Chris, Jup.*	.977	48	80	4	2	86	2
Scioneaux, Damian, St.P.	.960	17	23	1	1	25	0
Shumpert, Derek, Tam.	.889	14	16	0	2	18	0
Skett, Will, Dun.	.982	33	53	3	1	57	1
Smiga, Jason, Char.	1.000	1	1	0	0	1	0
SOLLMANN, Scott, Lake.*	.996	96	238	6	1	245	2
Speed, Dorian, Day.	.986	80	137	3	2	142	0
Stevens, Tony, Ft.M.	1.000	1	1	0	0	1	0
Stromsborg, Ryan, Dun.	.966	16	24	4	1	29	0
Thames, Marcus, Tam.	.970	120	282	7	9	298	2
Thompson, Nick, Cle.	1.000	10	9	0	0	9	0
Tucci, Pete, Dun.	.955	91	139	9	7	155	2
Tyner, Jason, St.L.*	.976	49	80	0	2	82	0
Valdez, Trovin, Jup.	.935	50	80	6	6	92	0
Valent, Eric, Cle.*	1.000	34	57	6	0	63	0
Vasquez, Alejandro, Kis.*	.875	5	7	0	1	8	0
Vaughn, Lateef, Ft.M.	.900	12	27	0	3	30	0
Vazquez, Alex, Char.	.969	23	28	3	1	32	0
Velez, Jose, Kis.*	.977	95	167	3	4	174	0
Vieira, Scott, Day.	.909	9	10	0	1	11	0
Wakeland, Chris, Lake.*	.959	122	194	17	9	220	2
Ware, Jeremy, Jup.	.983	112	221	14	4	239	6
Warren, Lance, V.B.	.000	4	0	0	1	1	0
Williams, Bernie, Tam.	1.000	1	2	0	0	2	0
Williams, Juan, Day.	1.000	3	7	1	0	8	0
Willis, Symmion, Dun.	.929	9	13	0	1	14	0
Zywica, Mike, Char.	.990	64	100	3	1	104	1

OUTFIELDERS WITH TWO OR MORE TEAMS

Player, Team	Pct.	G	PO	A	E	TC	DP
Parsons, Jeff, St.L.	1.000	2	4	0	0	4	0
Parsons, Jeff, Kis.	1.000	1	1	0	0	1	0

CATCHERS

Player, Team	Pct.	G	PO	A	E	TC	DP	PB
Amezcua, Adan, Kis.	.972	66	422	58	14	494	5	11
Anderson, Christopher, St.P.	.944	8	17	0	1	18	0	1
Arntzen, Brian, Jup.	1.000	16	79	9	0	88	1	1
Barr, Tucker, Kis.	.976	48	298	25	8	331	4	7
Bazzani, Matt, Sar.	1.000	1	3	0	0	3	0	0
Brown, Jason, V.B.	.990	73	462	51	5	518	1	16
Carreno, Jose, Jup.	1.000	9	49	3	0	52	1	4
Chavera, Arnie, Kis.	.963	17	97	7	4	108	2	7
Cheek, Shawn, Char.	1.000	13	54	2	0	56	0	3
Chevalier, Virgil, Sar.	.991	17	104	11	1	116	2	6
Chiaffredo, Paul, Dun.	.986	84	621	64	10	695	9	8
Colquitt, Jason, Lake.	.959	24	106	11	5	122	0	6
Cossins, Tim, Tam.	.984	16	113	9	2	124	0	4
Donato, Dan, St.P.	.988	29	216	23	3	242	4	10

CLASS A Florida State League

Player, Team	Pct.	G	PO	A	E	TC	DP	PB
Ellis, John, Char.	.988	60	359	45	5	409	2	20
Elwood, Brad, Tam.	1.000	3	3	2	0	5	0	0
Emmons, Scott, Tam.	.983	13	56	2	1	59	0	5
Estrada, Johnny, Cle.	.979	36	200	32	5	237	2	6
Friedholm, Scott, St.P.	1.000	6	27	1	0	28	0	0
Garcia, Neil, St.P.	.993	60	399	43	3	445	1	7
Glassey, Josh, V.B.	.967	53	340	37	13	390	3	6
Goodwin, Joe, Char.	.957	8	42	3	2	47	0	2
Gresham, Kris, Jup.	.980	24	166	29	4	199	4	3
Harrell, Ken, Tam.	.938	9	29	1	2	32	0	2
Henley, Bob, Jup.	.986	10	63	8	1	72	0	1
Hubbard, Jeremy, Day.	1.000	4	6	0	0	6	0	0
Huls, Steve, Ft.M.	1.000	3	7	1	0	8	0	1
Isenia, Chairon, St.P.	1.000	1	1	0	0	1	0	0
Jones, Jay, B.C.	1.000	8	31	2	0	33	1	2
King, Brad, Day.	.978	75	465	72	12	549	8	17
Kuilan, Hector, B.C.	.987	55	320	57	5	382	6	12
Lambert, Clark, St.L.	1.000	2	9	2	0	11	0	0
Larned, Andrew, Sar.	.947	4	14	4	1	19	0	1
LeCroy, Matt, Ft.M.	.991	44	309	28	3	340	0	17
LINDSTROM, David, Lake.	.9931	95	627	96	5	728	4	12
Lisanti, Bob, Day.	.966	12	27	1	1	29	0	0
Lomasney, Steve, Sar.	.981	80	559	76	12	647	3	16
Lough, Aaron, Ft.M.	1.000	1	11	2	0	13	0	1
Loyd, Brian, Dun.	.992	15	107	11	1	119	1	2
Makarewicz, Scott, B.C.	.992	20	111	20	1	132	2	5
Malave, Jaime, V.B.	.982	24	146	20	3	169	0	11
Marine, Del, Lake.	.989	15	75	14	1	90	0	2
Marsters, Brandon, Cle.	.988	74	477	76	7	560	4	10
Meran, Jorge, Lake.	.979	7	41	6	1	48	0	2
Moeller, Chad, Ft.M.	.980	57	395	36	9	440	0	9
Morgan, Dave, Dun.	.933	3	10	4	1	15	0	2
Parker, Chris, Lake.	.950	7	34	4	2	40	0	1
Phillips, Jason, St.L.	1.000	8	48	3	0	51	0	1
Prada, Nelson, Ft.M.	.987	40	194	26	3	223	1	8
Pratt, Todd, St.L.	1.000	2	22	3	0	25	0	0
Quatraro, Matthew, St.P.	.976	49	382	32	10	424	4	5
Raifstanger, John, Sar.	1.000	1	1	0	0	1	0	0
Ramsey, Brad, Day.	.967	70	486	48	18	552	4	23
Reese, Nate, Cle.	.977	10	69	15	2	86	1	2
Rivera, Luis A., Jup.	.981	7	48	5	1	54	0	0
Rivera, Luis J., Jup.	1.000	1	7	1	0	8	0	0
Rodriguez, Felix, Tam.	1.000	1	3	0	0	3	0	0
Rodriguez, Luis, Dun.	.986	50	330	29	5	364	2	13
Rodriguez, Mike, Dun.	1.000	3	11	2	0	13	0	0
Rodriguez, Sammy, St.L.	.983	47	261	28	5	294	3	8
Rose, Mike, Kis.	.973	17	94	14	3	111	0	1
Salinas, Trey, St.P.	.818	3	8	1	2	11	0	0
Santiago, Benito, Dun.	1.000	5	19	6	0	25	1	0
Sapp, Damian, Sar.	.967	18	132	15	5	152	1	6
Schneider, Brian, Jup.	.981	76	483	81	11	575	2	7
Smith, Jeff, Ft.M.	.973	4	33	3	1	37	0	2
Snusz, Chris, Cle.	.979	17	87	7	2	96	0	0
Spehr, Tim, St.L.	.978	8	42	3	1	46	0	0
Taveras, Luis, Char.	.984	76	505	63	9	577	2	15
Thompson, Nick, Cle.	.942	23	123	8	8	139	0	4
Treanor, Matt, B.C.	.989	55	323	33	4	360	4	13
Uccello, Jeff, Sar.	.988	32	156	14	2	172	1	5
Valencia, Victor, Tam.	.980	122	861	92	19	972	7	18
Valera, Yohanny, St.L.	.9929	78	506	54	4	564	3	20
Vargas, Arias, Lake.	1.000	3	9	5	0	14	0	1
Vieira, Scott, Day.	1.000	2	10	0	0	10	0	0
Warren, Lance, V.B.	1.000	9	14	2	0	16	0	0
Wesemann, Jason, Ft.M.	.800	1	4	0	1	5	0	0
Wilson, Vance, St.L.	1.000	4	19	3	0	22	0	0

PITCHERS

Player, Team	Pct.	G	PO	A	E	TC	DP
Adair, Derek, Cle.	1.000	14	4	20	0	24	3
Adkins, Tim, Dun.*	1.000	19	3	3	0	6	0
Allen, Buck, Cle.*	1.000	47	1	26	0	27	0
Alvarez, Wilson, St.P.*	1.000	1	0	1	0	1	0
Anderson, Matt, Lake.	.000	17	0	0	1	1	0
Aquino, Julio, St.P.	1.000	34	7	4	0	11	0
Armas, Tony, Jup.	.907	27	18	21	4	43	0
Armenta, Alfredo, St.P.*	1.000	6	3	4	0	7	0
Arteaga, Ivan, St.L.	.500	9	0	2	2	4	0
Arteaga, J.D., St.L.*	.875	15	0	7	1	8	0
Ashworth, Kym, Lake.*	.942	28	7	42	3	52	2
Aucoin, Derek, St.L.	1.000	8	0	1	0	1	0
Bale, John, Dun.*	.692	24	2	7	4	13	0
Barnett, Marty, Cle.	.750	7	1	2	1	4	0
Bauder, Mike, Ft.M.*	.955	36	4	17	1	22	1
Bean, Seth, Ft.M.	.500	10	1	0	1	2	0
Belitz, Todd, St.P.*	1.000	7	3	5	0	8	0

Player, Team	Pct.	G	PO	A	E	TC	DP
Bell, Mike, Jup.*	1.000	5	0	2	0	2	0
Benesh, Edward, St.P.	.947	38	6	12	1	19	0
Berger, Craig, St.L.	1.000	3	0	3	0	3	0
Betancourt, Rafael, Sar.	1.000	20	0	4	0	4	0
Bettencourt, Justin, Lake.*	.957	30	4	18	1	23	1
Betti, Rich, Sar.*	1.000	4	0	4	0	4	1
Beverlin, Jason, Tam.	.875	7	4	3	1	8	0
Blanco, Alberto, Kis.*	1.000	2	1	4	0	5	0
Blank, Matt, Jup.*	1.000	8	3	10	0	13	1
Bleazard, David, Dun.	.800	14	2	2	1	5	0
Bogott, Kurt, Dun.*	1.000	3	0	1	0	1	0
Bowers, Cedrick, St.P.*	1.000	28	9	16	0	25	0
Bowles, Brian, Dun.	.875	9	2	5	1	8	0
Bradford, Josh, Dun.	.941	17	8	8	1	17	0
Bradley, Ryan, Tam.	1.000	32	6	8	0	14	1
Braswell, Bryan, Kis.*	.939	27	7	24	2	33	2
Brittan, Corey, St.L.	.875	34	1	13	2	16	0
Brookens, Casey, Day.	1.000	23	4	6	0	10	0
Brown, Chad, Dun.*	1.000	3	2	5	0	7	0
Buchanan, Brian, Tam.*	1.000	1	0	1	0	1	0
Buckles, Bucky, Char.	.778	18	1	6	2	9	2
Bullinger, Kirk, Jup.	1.000	8	2	1	0	3	0
Cames, Aaron, B.C.	.864	27	7	12	3	22	0
Cammack, Eric, St.L.	1.000	29	3	2	0	5	0
Campos, Jason, B.C.*	1.000	6	1	0	0	1	0
Cannon, Jon, Day.*	.900	7	4	5	1	10	0
Cannon, Kevan, Sar.*	.846	44	5	6	2	13	0
Carrasco, Troy, Ft.M.*	1.000	19	3	7	0	10	0
Castillo, Alberto, Tam.*	1.000	12	1	1	0	2	0
Castillo, Marcos, V.B.	.909	25	11	19	3	33	0
Cepeda, Victor, Lake.	1.000	8	2	4	0	6	0
Chambers, Scott, V.B.*	1.000	43	2	9	0	11	0
Chapman, Walker, Ft.M.	.917	24	3	8	1	12	0
Checo, Robinson, Sar.	1.000	1	0	1	0	1	0
Cho, Jin Ho, Sar.	.889	5	0	8	1	9	0
Choate, Randy, Tam.*	.885	13	6	17	3	26	0
Civit, Xavier, Jup.	1.000	13	0	1	0	1	0
Clark, Chris, B.C.	.833	40	4	6	2	12	0
Cook, Derrick, Char.	.828	26	6	18	5	29	1
Corcoran, Tim, St.L.	1.000	4	0	1	0	1	0
Correa, Elvis, V.B.	1.000	42	13	15	0	28	3
Costa, Tony, Cle.	1.000	6	2	0	0	2	0
Cubillan, Darwin, Tam.	.941	45	2	14	1	17	0
Daniel, Michael, Char.	1.000	4	0	2	0	2	0
Daniels, John, St.P.	1.000	34	0	8	0	8	0
Darley, Ned, Char.	1.000	3	0	2	0	2	0
Davis, Doug, Char.*	.941	27	4	28	2	34	3
Davis, Keith, Lake.	.875	43	1	6	1	8	0
Day, Zach, Tam.	.900	18	5	13	2	20	0
DeJesus, Javier, Day.*	.889	43	1	7	1	9	0
De La Cruz, Andres, Tam.	1.000	3	0	1	0	1	0
De La Cruz, Fernando, Sar.	1.000	12	0	2	0	2	0
De La Cruz, Francisco, Tam.	.875	19	4	10	2	16	0
Delgado, Ernie, Dun.	.897	44	9	17	3	29	0
De Los Santos, Luis, Tam.	.967	10	9	20	1	30	2
DeYoung, Dan, Char.-B.C.	.880	26	3	19	3	25	0
Dickey, R.A., Char.	.900	57	2	7	1	10	0
Dingman, Craig, Tam.	.909	50	5	5	1	11	0
Downs, Scott, Day.*	.957	27	13	31	2	46	0
Duckworth, Brandon, Cle.	1.000	9	6	10	0	16	1
Duncan, Geoff, B.C.	1.000	17	0	4	0	4	0
Duncan, Sean, Kis.*	1.000	23	1	7	0	8	1
Duran, Roberto, Lake.*	1.000	8	1	3	0	4	0
Durocher, Jayson, Jup.	1.000	23	1	1	0	2	0
Duvall, Mike, St.P.*	1.000	2	0	1	0	1	0
EATON, Adam, Cle.	1.000	24	15	22	0	37	4
Ehlers, Corey, B.C.	1.000	45	2	10	0	12	2
Enders, Trevor, St.P*	1.000	51	10	17	0	27	1
Espinal, Jose, Day.	.872	28	17	17	5	39	2
Evans, Keith, Jup.	.933	8	4	10	1	15	1
Everly, Bill, V.B.	.914	49	9	23	3	35	0
Feliciano, Pedro, V.B.*	.941	22	4	12	1	17	1
Fennell, Barry, Day.*	1.000	24	1	3	0	4	0
Fieldbinder, Mick, Ft.M.	.935	35	11	18	2	31	1
Fisher, Louis, Day.	.909	49	2	8	1	11	1
Flores, Randy, Tam.*	1.000	5	3	4	0	7	0
Folkers, Ken, Dun.	.500	9	0	1	1	2	0
Forster, Scott, Jup.*	.500	6	0	1	1	2	0
Foster, Kevin, Day.	1.000	3	0	1	0	1	0
Foster, Kris, V.B.	1.000	24	6	5	0	11	0
Fowler, Blair, B.C.	.800	28	8	8	4	20	1
Franklin, Wayne, V.B.*	.800	48	5	15	5	25	0
Gagliano, Steve, B.C.	1.000	8	0	2	0	2	0
Gagne, Eric, V.B.	.900	25	4	14	2	20	2
Garcia, Apostol, Lake.	.912	34	15	16	3	34	2

Player, Team	Pct.	G	PO	A	E	TC	DP	Player, Team	Pct.	G	PO	A	E	TC	DP
Garcia, Gabe, Kis.	1.000	30	4	10	0	14	0	Miadich, Bart, Sar.	.800	22	0	8	2	10	1
Gardner, Lee, St.P.	1.000	3	1	0	0	1	0	Miles, Chad, Lake.*	.875	42	5	9	2	16	0
Garrett, Hal, V.B.	.920	20	13	10	2	25	2	Minaya, Pedro, B.C.	1.000	3	1	1	0	2	1
Garrett, Josh, Sar.	.923	26	14	22	3	39	0	Mitchell, Courtney, Cle.*	1.000	55	4	10	0	14	0
Garvin, Robert, B.C.	.667	15	1	3	2	6	0	Mobley, Kevin, Lake.	1.000	34	1	5	0	6	0
Garza, Chris, Ft.M.*	.958	58	4	19	1	24	1	Moore, Bobby, Char.	1.000	38	4	16	0	20	0
Gaskill, Derek, St.L.	1.000	7	0	1	0	1	0	Moore, Chris, B.C.	.875	8	3	4	1	8	0
Gissell, Chris, Day.	.889	22	7	9	2	18	1	Moraga, David, Jup.*	1.000	25	6	10	0	16	2
Glover, Gary, Dun.	.968	19	18	12	1	31	0	Morris, Alex, B.C.	1.000	23	2	2	0	4	0
Gonzalez, Dicky, St.L.	1.000	8	5	7	0	12	1	Mota, Danny, Ft.M.	1.000	19	2	4	0	6	0
Gorecki, Rick, St.P.	1.000	1	2	0	0	2	0	Mota, Guillermo, Jup.	.800	20	2	2	1	5	0
Green, Jason, Kis.	.941	51	6	10	1	17	0	Mota, Henry, Char.	.923	34	2	10	1	13	2
Grzanich, Mike, Kis.	1.000	4	0	3	0	3	0	Mounce, Tony, Kis.*	1.000	5	0	5	0	5	0
Gulin, Lindsay, St.L.*	1.000	6	1	9	0	10	1	Mull, Blaine, B.C.	.950	16	7	12	1	20	2
Hafer, Jeff, St.L.	.909	24	3	7	1	11	0	Musgrave, Scott, Sar.*	1.000	28	3	7	0	10	1
Hanson, Erik, Dun.	1.000	1	0	1	0	1	0	Nakamura, Mike, Ft.M.	.667	8	0	6	3	9	0
Hart, Len, Day.*	1.000	37	4	10	0	14	2	Narcisse, Tyrone, Tam.	1.000	4	0	1	0	1	0
Hartshorn, Ty, Dun.	.929	9	8	5	1	14	2	Nicholson, John, Jup.	.953	27	19	22	2	43	2
Hayden, Terry, Sar.*	1.000	13	1	2	0	3	0	Niebla, Ruben, Jup.*	1.000	13	0	5	0	5	0
Hazlett, Andy, Sar.*	.978	30	11	33	1	45	0	Niedermaier, Brad, Ft.M.	.900	25	3	6	1	10	0
Hendrickson, Mark, Dun.*	1.000	16	5	7	0	12	0	Norton, Phillip, Day.*	.938	10	3	12	1	16	0
Herbison, Brett, St.L.	1.000	26	6	25	0	31	2	Opipari, Mario, Ft.M.	1.000	17	2	5	0	7	1
Hernandez, Orlando, Tam.	1.000	2	1	2	0	3	0	Ortega, Pablo, St.P.	.930	28	19	21	3	43	1
Hibbard, Billy, Dun.	1.000	2	1	0	0	1	0	O'Shaughnessy, Jay, V.B.	.938	30	5	10	1	16	0
Hoff, Steve, B.C.-Day.*	.955	21	4	17	1	22	3	Palki, Jeromy, Ft.M.	.909	40	4	6	1	11	1
Holt, Chris, Kis.	1.000	1	2	1	0	3	1	Paluk, Brian, V.B.	.920	35	7	16	2	25	0
Hooten, David, Ft.M.	.976	28	11	29	1	41	2	Pavano, Carl, Jup.	1.000	4	0	2	0	2	0
Hunter, Germaine, Sar.	1.000	7	1	1	0	2	0	Pedraza, Rod, Char.	1.000	15	2	16	0	18	2
Hurtado, Victor, B.C.	.895	18	7	10	2	19	1	Phelps, Tommy, Jup.*	1.000	7	0	6	0	6	0
Jacquez, Thomas, Cle.*	.974	29	10	28	1	39	1	Phillips, Ben, Tam.	.818	23	2	7	2	11	0
Jimenez, Jason, St.P.*	.778	13	1	6	2	9	0	Pineda, Isauro, Sar.	.889	10	4	4	1	9	0
Johnson, Jonathan, Char.	.500	3	0	1	1	2	0	Pipes, Joey, Kis.	1.000	20	1	1	0	2	0
Jones, Kiki, St.P.	1.000	6	2	0	0	2	0	Poland, Trey, Char.*	.815	26	4	18	5	27	0
Kaufman, John, St.P.*	1.000	18	3	8	0	11	1	Pujals, Denis, St.P.	.813	42	3	10	3	16	2
Kawabata, Kyle, Cle.	.900	53	3	15	2	20	1	Pumphrey, Ken, St.L.	.938	25	12	18	2	32	1
Kershner, Jason, Cle.*	.889	41	5	11	2	18	0	Quintal, Craig, Lake.	.970	21	8	24	1	33	2
Kessel, Kyle, St.L.*	.933	16	1	13	1	15	0	Rahilly, Michael, Sar.	1.000	7	0	1	0	1	0
Kim, Sun, Sar.	.958	26	12	11	1	24	0	Rangel, Julio, Tam.	.714	10	1	4	2	7	0
Kimsey, Keith, Lake.	1.000	28	2	3	0	5	0	Regalado, Maximo, V.B.	1.000	4	1	0	0	1	0
Kinney, Matt, Sar.-Ft.M.	.862	29	12	13	4	29	2	Reitsma, Chris, Sar.	1.000	8	0	1	0	1	0
Knoll, Randy, Cle.	.875	5	2	5	1	8	1	Rekar, Bryan, St.P.	1.000	4	2	0	0	2	0
Koch, Billy, Dun.	.941	25	14	18	2	34	3	Reynoso, Armando, St.L.	1.000	4	1	3	0	4	0
LaChapelle, Yan, Dun.	.871	24	16	11	4	31	2	Ricketts, Chad, Day.	.833	47	2	3	1	6	0
Lail, Denny, Tam.	1.000	31	5	11	0	16	1	Rijo, Jose, Kis.	.923	48	4	8	1	13	1
Lara, Nelson, B.C.	.200	19	0	1	4	5	0	Rizzo, Nick, B.C.	1.000	7	0	1	0	1	0
LaRosa, Tom, Ft.M.	.900	22	5	4	1	10	2	Robbins, Jake, Tam.	.911	26	15	26	4	45	1
Lawrence, Clint, Dun.*	.938	20	6	9	1	16	1	Roberts, Grant, St.L.	.923	17	4	8	1	13	0
Lee, Jeremy, Dun.	1.000	15	4	6	0	10	0	Robertson, Jeromie, Kis.*	.950	28	5	33	2	40	0
Leese, Brandon, B.C.	1.000	8	1	6	0	7	0	Rodgers, Bobby, B.C.	1.000	7	2	7	0	9	0
Leon, Scott, St.P.	1.000	16	2	7	0	9	2	Rogers, Brian, Lake.	1.000	3	0	2	0	2	0
LeRoy, John, St.P.	1.000	11	1	6	0	7	1	Romo, Greg, Lake.	.923	12	5	7	1	13	0
Lisio, Joe, Tam.	.800	31	1	3	1	5	0	Root, Derek, Kis.*	1.000	29	4	16	0	20	1
Lohrman, Dave, St.L.	.667	19	1	3	2	6	1	Roper, Chad, Ft.M.	.938	17	8	7	1	16	1
Love, Farley, Kis.	1.000	11	0	4	0	4	0	Rosario, Rafael, Lake.	1.000	9	0	2	0	2	1
Love, Jeff, Kis.	.813	42	3	10	3	16	2	Rosario, Reynaldo, Lake.	1.000	4	1	0	0	1	0
Lowe, Benny, Dun.*	.750	9	1	2	1	4	0	Rose, Brian, Sar.	1.000	22	2	4	0	6	0
Lukasiewicz, Mark, Dun.*	.000	9	0	0	1	1	0	Rutherford, Mark, Cle.	.917	18	8	14	2	24	4
Lynch, Jim, Kis.	.800	9	2	2	1	5	0	Ryan, Ken, Cle.	1.000	4	1	0	0	1	0
Lyons, Jonathan, Sar.	1.000	7	1	1	0	2	0	Saneaux, Francisco, Char.	1.000	17	0	9	0	9	0
Lyons, Mike, St.L.	.917	28	5	6	1	12	2	Santos, Victor, Lake.	.962	16	5	20	1	26	1
Madison, Scott, St.P.*	1.000	27	1	17	0	18	0	Saylor, Ryan, Jup.	1.000	27	2	5	0	7	0
Mairena, Oswaldo, Tam.*	1.000	52	2	5	0	7	0	Schaffer, Trevor, Dun.	1.000	47	10	9	0	19	1
Maldonado, Esteban, Kis.	.700	28	2	5	3	10	0	Schaffner, Eric, Tam.	1.000	7	0	1	0	1	0
Malko, Bryan, Ft.M.	1.000	7	0	3	0	3	0	Schourek, Pete, Kis.*	1.000	2	1	1	0	2	0
Maness, Chris, Cle.	1.000	8	2	2	0	4	0	Schultz, Eric, Char.	1.000	6	1	0	0	1	0
Manias, James, St.P.*	.926	30	8	17	2	27	0	Seo, Jae, St.L.	1.000	8	1	3	0	4	0
Mann, Jim, Dun.	.889	51	4	4	1	9	0	Short, Barry, St.L.	1.000	22	6	9	0	15	3
Manon, Julio, St.P.	1.000	38	4	9	0	13	1	Simon, Benjamin, V.B.	1.000	7	0	3	0	3	0
Markey, Barry, Day.	.923	43	11	25	3	39	3	Smith, Brian, Dun.	1.000	4	1	1	0	2	0
Marquez, Robert, Jup.	.929	39	4	9	1	14	0	Smith, Eric, Kis.	1.000	9	0	6	0	6	0
Marriott, Mike, B.C.	.200	5	0	1	4	5	0	Smith, Taylor, Dun.	1.000	1	0	1	0	1	0
Martinez, Jose, Char.	.889	19	5	11	2	18	1	Sollecito, Gabe, Char.	.864	37	5	14	3	22	0
Martinez, Romulo, Lake.	.850	49	9	8	3	20	1	Sorzano, Ronnie, Day.	.800	23	1	3	1	5	0
Mattes, Troy, Jup.	.938	17	7	8	1	16	1	Spear, Russell, Lake.	.880	18	14	8	3	25	1
Matz, Brian, Jup.*	1.000	15	1	6	0	7	0	Spence, Cam, Tam.	.917	21	7	15	2	24	0
Mayo, Blake, V.B.	.923	32	2	22	2	26	0	Spiers, Corey, Ft.M.*	1.000	24	6	27	0	33	0
Mays, Joe, Ft.M.	1.000	16	4	15	0	19	1	St. Pierre, Bob, Tam.	.909	16	3	7	1	11	0
McClellan, Sean, Dun.	.833	24	4	1	1	6	0	Stachler, Eric, Kis.	1.000	7	0	1	0	1	0
McCrary, Scott, St.L.	.950	37	5	14	1	20	1	Stevens, Kris, Cle.*	1.000	5	2	9	0	11	0
McEntire, Ethan, St.L.*	1.000	22	6	16	0	22	2	Stevenson, Rodney, Jup.	1.000	19	1	5	0	6	0
McGarity, Jeremy, Char.	1.000	3	0	2	0	2	0	Stieb, Dave, Dun.	1.000	3	1	2	0	3	0
McKnight, Tony, Kis.	.931	28	12	15	2	29	2	Strickland, Scott, Jup.	1.000	22	4	7	0	11	0
McMullen, Jerry, Sar.*	1.000	39	4	14	0	18	0	Sturtze, Tanyon, Char.	1.000	1	0	2	0	2	0
Mejia, Javier, Cle.	.800	32	0	8	2	10	1	Teut, Nate, Day.*	.929	11	3	10	1	14	0
Mendes, Jaime, Cle.	.941	48	3	13	1	17	0	Thompson, Chris, Sar.	1.000	30	3	4	0	7	2

CLASS A Florida State League

Player, Team	Pct.	G	PO	A	E	TC	DP
Townsend, Dave, B.C.	.833	12	2	3	1	6	1
Tucker, Thomas, Jup.	1.000	2	0	1	0	1	0
Turman, Jimmy, Jup.	.700	8	3	4	3	10	0
Valdes, Ismael, V.B.	1.000	1	0	1	0	1	1
Van Gilder, Ryan, Jup.	1.000	10	4	0	0	4	0
Vardijan, Dan, B.C.	1.000	8	1	2	0	3	0
Vargas, Claudio, B.C.	1.000	2	2	2	0	4	0
Vasquez, Leo, St.L.*	.920	24	4	19	2	25	2
Veniard, Jay, St.L.*	1.000	12	1	3	0	4	0
Villafuerte, Brandon, B.C.	1.000	3	0	2	0	2	0
Wade, Terrell, St.P.*	1.000	3	0	1	0	1	0
Wagner, Matt, Jup.	1.000	1	1	1	0	2	0
Welch, Robb, Sar.	.900	20	5	4	1	10	0
Westbrook, Jake, Jup.	.949	27	21	35	3	59	4
White, Matt, St.P.	.857	17	6	12	3	21	0
Whiteman, Greg, Cle.*	1.000	2	0	3	0	3	0
Widerski, Jon, B.C.	.800	24	4	4	2	10	0
Wiggins, Scott, Tam.*	.900	11	3	6	1	10	0
Wilson, Paul, St.L.	1.000	5	4	2	0	6	0
Wimberly, Larry, Cle.*	1.000	14	0	12	0	12	0
Woodring, Jason, Jup.	.786	35	4	7	3	14	0
Wyckoff, Travis, B.C.*	.882	41	2	13	2	17	2
Yeager, Gary, Cle.	1.000	41	5	17	0	22	0
Yeskie, Nate, Ft.M.	1.000	14	2	8	0	10	0
Yoder, Jeff, Day.	.960	26	9	15	1	25	0
Young, Joe, Dun.	.667	8	1	1	1	3	0
Zimmerman, Jeff, Char.	1.000	10	0	2	0	2	0

PITCHERS WITH TWO OR MORE TEAMS

Player, Team	Pct.	G	PO	A	E	TC	DP
DeYoung, Dan, Char.	.900	20	2	16	2	20	0
DeYoung, Dan, B.C.*	.800	6	1	3	1	5	0
Hoff, Steve, B.C.*	.938	15	2	13	1	16	3
Hoff, Steve, Day.*	1.000	6	2	4	0	6	0
Kinney, Matt, Sar.	.826	22	10	9	4	23	2
Kinney, Matt, Ft.M.	1.000	7	2	4	0	6	0

The following players did not have any fielding statistics at the positions indicated or appeared only as a designated hitter, pinch-hitter or pinch-runner: Adriana, of; R. Alvarez, ss; Alvord, p; Baker, p; S. Bell, p; Bravo, 2b; Burnham, of; Capellan, p; F. Castillo, p; Chiavacci, p; Corps, of; Fereira, p; Forkerway, of; Gaillard, p; N. Garcia, p; Glassey, of; Goudie, of; K. Green, 1b; B. Henry, p; Holmes, p; Huls, 2b; Hurst, p; James, p; Jefferson, dh; Jay Jones, p; King, 2b; A. Lopez, p; D. Manning, p; Markey, of; Marsh, p; Mills, p; Murphy, dh; Nelson, p; Pascarella, dh; Sassanella, dh; Seale, of; Schaffer, of; Sergio, of; Taylor, p; Tessmar, p; N. Thompson, p; Walker, of, p; Wallace, p; Wesemann, p; K. White, p; W. White, 3b; D. Young, p.

LEAGUE CHAMPIONS

Year	Team	Pct.
1919—	Sanford*	.605
	Orlando*	.703
1920—	Tampa	.654
	Tampa	.722
1921—	Orlando	.635
1922—	St. Petersburg	.503
	St. Petersburg	.618
1923—	Orlando	.667
	Orlando	.678
1924—	Lakeland	.695
	Lakeland	.683
1925—	St. Petersburg	.667
	Tampa†	.696
1926—	Sanford	.647
	Sanford	.623
1927—	Orlando†	.600
	Miami	.661
1928-35—	Did not operate.	
1936—	Gainesville	.542
	St. Augustine (4th)†	.492
1937—	Gainesville§	.616
1938—	Leesburg	.626
	Gainesville (2nd)‡	.615
1939—	Sanford§	.787
1940—	Daytona Beach	.619
	Orlando (4th)‡	.507
1941—	St. Augustine	.659
	Leesburg (4th)‡	.488
1942-45—	Did not operate.	
1946—	Orlando§	.681
1947—	St. Augustine	.625
	Gainesville (2nd)‡	.584
1948—	Orlando	.643
	Daytona Beach (2nd)‡	.616
1949—	Gainesville	.635
	St. Augustine (3rd)‡	.556
1950—	Orlando	.629
	DeLand (3rd)‡	.590
1951—	DeLand§	.643
1952—	DeLand∞	.704
	Palatka (3rd)‡	.569
1953—	Daytona Beach†	.657
	DeLand	.703
1954—	Jacksonville Beach	.629
	Lakeland†	.594
1955—	Orlando	.671
	Orlando	.643
1956—	Cocoa	.614
	Cocoa	.671
1957—	Palatka	.629
	Tampa†	.681
1958—	St. Petersburg	.732
	St. Petersburg	.681
1959—	Tampa	.591
	St. Petersburg†	.612
1960—	Lakeland	.731
	Palatka†	.614
1961—	Tampa†	.710
	Sarasota	.696
1962—	Sarasota	.689
	Fort Lauderdale†	.623
1963—	Sarasota	.645
	Sarasota	.667
1964—	Fort Lauderdale†	.629
	St. Petersburg	.594
1965—	Fort Lauderdale	.627
	Fort Lauderdale	.634
1966—	Leesburg†	.781
	St. Petersburg	.700
1967—	St. Petersburg▲	.691
	Orlando	.638
1968—	Miami	.613
	Orlando◆	.579
1969—	Miami■	.606
	Orlando	.606
1970—	Miami▼	.662
	St. Petersburg	.600
1971—	Miami▼	.667
	Daytona Beach	.586
1972—	Miami•	.562
	Daytona Beach	.606
1973—	St. Petersburg††	.575
	West Palm Beach	.580
1974—	West Palm Beach††	.598
	Fort Lauderdale	.626
1975—	St. Petersburg††	.652
	Miami	.581
1976—	Tampa	.559
	Lakeland††	.536
1977—	Lakeland††	.616
	West Palm Beach	.583
1978—	Lakeland	.565
	Miami§	.539
1979—	Fort Lauderdale	.643
	Winter Haven‡‡	.577
1980—	Daytona Beach	.628
	Fort Lauderdale††	.606
1981—	Fort Myers	.554
	Daytona Beach§§	.504
1982—	Fort Lauderdale§§	.621
	Tampa	.546
1983—	Daytona Beach	.634
	Vero Beach§§	.515
1984—	Tampa	.532
	Fort Lauderdale§§	.521
1985—	Fort Myers∞∞∞	.590
	Fort Lauderdale	.550
1986—	St. Petersburg∞∞∞	.647
	West Palm Beach	.593
1987—	Fort Lauderdale∞∞∞	.616
	Osceola	.576
1988—	Osceola	.606
	St. Lucie▲▲	.532
1989—	Port Charlotte▲▲	.540
	St. Petersburg	.540
1990—	West Palm Beach	.697
	Vero Beach▲▲	.585
1991—	Clearwater	.623
	West Palm Beach▲▲	.550
1992—	Sarasota	.639
	Lakeland◆◆	.530
1993—	St. Lucie	.600
	Clearwater§§	.556
1994—	Tampa§§	.606
	Brevard County	.561
1995—	Daytona§§	.644
	Fort Myers	.577
1996—	Tampa	.627
	St. Lucie§§	.534
1997—	St. Petersburg■ ■	.591
	Vero Beach	.511
1998—	Charlotte	.594
	St. Lucie■■	.515

*Split-season playoff abandoned after each team won three games. †Won split-season playoff. ‡Won four-club playoff. §Won championship and four-club playoff. ∞Won both halves of split season. ▲League divided into Eastern and Western divisions with split season. St. Petersburg and Orlando won both halves of split season; St. Petersburg won playoff. ◆League divided into Eastern and Western divisions. Miami won regular-season pennant on basis of highest won-lost percentage. Orlando won four-club playoff involving first two teams in each division. •League divided into Southern and Central divisions. Miami won playoff between division leaders. (NOTE—Pennant awarded to playoff winner in 1936.) ▼League divided into Eastern and Western divisions. Miami won regular-season pennant on basis of highest won-loss percentage, and also won four-club playoff involving first two teams in each division. ∞League divided into Eastern and Western divisions. Won four-club playoff involving first two teams in each division. ††League divided into Northern and Southern divisions. Won four-club playoff involving first two teams in each division. ‡‡League divided into Northern and Southern divisions. Same two clubs won both halves; won playoffs. §§Won split-season playoff. ∞∞∞League divided into Western, Central and Southern divisions. Won four-club playoff. ▲▲League divided into Eastern, Western and Central divisions; played split-season. Won six-club playoff. ◆◆League divided into Eastern, Western and Central divisions; played split-season. Won eight-club playoff. ■ ■League divided into East and West divisions and played split season; won four-club playoff.

MIDWEST LEAGUE

LEAGUE OFFICE

President
George H. Spelius
Address
P.O. Box 936
Beloit, WI 53512
Phone
608-364-1188

Teams (affiliation)
Beloit Snappers (Brewers)
Burlington Bees (White Sox)
Cedar Rapids Kernels (Angels)
Clinton Lumber Kings (Reds)
Fort Wayne Wizards (Padres)
Kane County Cougars (Marlins)
Lansing Lugnuts (Cubs)

Michigan Battle Cats (Astros)
Peoria Chiefs (Cardinals)
Quad City River Bandits (Twins)
Rockford (name to be announced) (Reds)
South Bend Silver Hawks
(Diamondbacks)
West Michigan Whitecaps (Tigers)
Wisconsin Timber Rattlers (Mariners)

1998 FINAL STANDINGS

FIRST HALF

EASTERN DIVISION

Team	W	L	T	Pct.	GB
West Michigan (Tigers)	43	29	0	.597	....
Fort Wayne (Twins)	41	31	0	.569	2.0
Lansing (Royals)	37	35	0	.514	6.0
Michigan (Red Sox)	36	36	0	.500	7.0
South Bend (Diamondbacks)	21	51	0	.292	22.0

CENTRAL DIVISION

Team	W	L	T	Pct.	GB
Wisconsin (Mariners)	39	30	0	.565	....
Kane County (Marlins)	36	36	0	.500	4.5
Beloit (Brewers)	35	36	0	.493	5.0
Peoria (Cardinals)	34	38	0	.472	6.5
Rockford (Cubs)	32	39	0	.451	8.0

WESTERN DIVISION

Team	W	L	T	Pct.	GB
Quad City (Astros)	40	31	0	.563	....
Cedar Rapids (Angels)	40	32	0	.556	0.5
Burlington (Reds)	36	36	0	.500	4.5
Clinton (Padres)	30	40	0	.429	9.5

SECOND HALF

EASTERN DIVISION

Team	W	L	T	Pct.	GB
Michigan (Red Sox)	43	25	0	.632	....
West Michigan (Tigers)	40	28	0	.588	3.0
Fort Wayne (Twins)	38	30	0	.559	5.0
Lansing (Royals)	34	34	0	.500	9.0
South Bend (Diamondbacks)	19	49	0	.279	24.0

CENTRAL DIVISION

Team	W	L	T	Pct.	GB
Rockford (Cubs)	39	29	0	.574	....
Peoria (Cardinals)	38	30	0	.559	1.0
Wisconsin (Mariners)	33	35	0	.485	6.0
Kane County (Marlins)	33	35	0	.485	6.0
Beloit (Brewers)	29	39	0	.426	10.0

WESTERN DIVISION

Team	W	L	T	Pct.	GB
Quad City (Astros)	37	31	0	.544	....
Clinton (Padres)	35	33	0	.515	2.0
Cedar Rapids (Angels)	31	37	0	.456	6.0
Burlington (Reds)	27	41	0	.397	10.0

COMPOSITE

Team	W.M.	Mch.	F.W.	Q.C.	Wis.	Peo.	Rck.	Lan.	C.R.	K.C.	Clin.	Bel.	Burl.	S.B.	W	L	T	Pct.	GB
West Michigan (Tigers)	....	8	10	4	4	6	5	10	5	5	4	6	4	12	83	57	0	.593	....
Michigan (Red Sox)	9	....	6	3	7	5	4	11	7	4	6	2	5	10	79	61	0	.564	4.0
Fort Wayne (Twins)	7	11	....	2	4	6	4	10	4	5	2	5	5	14	79	61	0	.564	4.0
Quad City (Astros)	4	5	6	....	5	3	4	2	12	3	12	5	9	7	77	62	0	.554	5.5
Wisconsin (Mariners)	4	1	4	2	....	10	10	3	4	12	4	10	4	4	72	65	0	.526	9.5
Peoria (Cardinals)	2	3	2	5	7	....	12	5	3	8	7	10	2	6	72	68	0	.514	11.0
Rockford (Cubs)	3	4	4	4	7	5	....	6	4	9	5	8	5	7	71	68	0	.511	11.5
Lansing (Royals)	7	6	7	6	5	3	2	....	5	3	4	5	4	14	71	69	0	.507	12.0
Cedar Rapids (Angels)	3	1	4	8	4	5	4	3	....	4	11	5	13	6	71	69	0	.507	12.0
Kane County (Marlins)	3	2	3	5	5	9	8	5	4	....	5	10	5	5	69	71	0	.493	14.0
Clinton (Padres)	4	4	6	8	2	1	3	4	9	3	....	2	14	5	65	73	0	.471	17.0
Beloit (Brewers)	2	6	3	3	7	7	8	3	3	7	6	....	4	5	64	75	0	.460	18.5
Burlington (Reds)	4	3	3	11	4	6	3	4	7	3	6	4	....	5	63	77	0	.450	20.0
South Bend (Diamondbacks)	5	7	3	1	4	2	1	3	2	3	3	3	3	....	40	100	0	.286	43.0

Quad City's home games played in Davenport, Iowa; Kane County's home games played in Geneva, Ill.; Michigan's home games played in Battle Creek, Mich. West Michigan's home games played in Comstock Park, Mich.

Major league affiliations in parentheses.

PLAYOFFS: Clinton defeated Quad City two games to one; Fort Wayne defeated Peoria two games to one; Rockford defeated Wisconsin two games to one; West Michigan defeated Michigan two games to one; Rockford defeated Fort Wayne two games to none; West Michigan defeated Clinton two games to none; West Michigan defeated Rockford three games to one to win league championship.

REGULAR-SEASON ATTENDANCE: Beloit, 61,108; Burlington, 60,492; Cedar Rapids, 128,742; Clinton, 44,401; Fort Wayne, 214,702; Kane County, 481,352; Lansing, 485,815; Michigan, 107,137; Peoria, 154,910; Quad City, 153,886; Rockford, 75,600; South Bend, 196,793; West Michigan, 500,083; Wisconsin, 227,306. Total— 2,892,327. Playoffs (20 games)—36,771. All-Star Game at Clinton, Iowa—2,572.

MANAGERS: Beloit, Don Money; Burlington, Phillip Wellman; Cedar Rapids, Garry Templeton; Clinton, Tom LeVasseur; Fort Wayne, Jose Marzan; Kane County, Juan Bustabad; Lansing, Bob Herold; Michigan, Billy Gardner, Jr.; Peoria, Jeff Shireman; Quad City, Mike Rojas; Rockford, Ruben Amaro; South Bend, Roly Dearmas; West Michigan, Bruce Fields; Wisconsin, Gary Varsho.

ALL-STAR TEAM: 1B—Ross Gload, Kane County; 2B—Jermaine Clark, Wisconsin; 3B—Matt Erickson, Kane County; SS—Pablo Ozuna, Peoria; OF—Juan LeBron, Lansing; Bucky Jacobsen, Beloit; Quincy Foster, Kane County; Rodney Lindsey, Clinton-West Michigan; C—Shea Hillenbrand, Michigan; DH—James Thomas, Quad City; LHP—Ryan Anderson, Wisconsin; RHP—Tristan Jerue, Peoria; LH Reliever—Brian Partenheimer, Michigan; RH Reliever—Gene Stechschulte, Peoria; Most Valuable Player—Pablo Ozuna, Peoria; Prospect of the Year—Pablo Ozuna, Peoria; Manager of the Year—Billy Gardner, Jr., Michigan.

CLASS A *Midwest League*

– 521 –

TEAM

Team	Avg.	G	TPA	AB	R	H	TB	2B	3B	HR	RBI	SH	SF	HP	BB	IBB	SO	SB	CS	GDP	LOB	ShO	Slg.	OBP
Peoria	.274	140	5380	4758	748	1302	1865	247	35	82	653	64	35	88	435	15	992	162	98	95	969	6	.392	.343
Fort Wayne	.271	140	5437	4734	742	1284	1938	280	52	90	650	39	36	95	533	15	1101	117	68	112	1047	8	.409	.354
Lansing	.261	140	5383	4735	695	1237	1877	247	63	89	607	41	39	72	496	18	989	207	77	89	998	2	.396	.338
Beloit	.261	139	5406	4735	659	1236	1783	232	18	93	586	72	35	82	482	22	1055	65	46	98	1071	7	.377	.337
Michigan	.260	140	5376	4720	685	1229	1781	232	31	86	595	32	44	81	499	11	957	92	58	104	1048	11	.377	.339
Kane County	.257	140	5308	4602	644	1182	1579	206	22	49	554	61	48	88	509	22	947	189	88	111	995	5	.343	.339
Wisconsin	.256	137	5192	4602	640	1180	1788	231	49	93	566	65	32	51	442	25	990	199	79	93	934	10	.389	.326
Rockford	.255	139	5203	4588	637	1172	1670	225	45	61	544	52	38	65	460	9	1112	203	79	91	946	11	.364	.329
Quad City	.253	139	5157	4627	657	1172	1738	230	30	92	584	43	24	51	412	21	992	197	108	91	848	9	.376	.320
W. Michigan	.251	140	5306	4705	660	1182	1677	250	40	55	572	47	46	65	445	14	1078	188	63	70	978	16	.356	.322
Burlington	.248	140	5120	4577	567	1137	1644	208	34	77	506	39	35	46	423	11	1123	181	80	79	919	11	.359	.316
Clinton	.239	138	5152	4495	592	1075	1552	211	34	66	509	31	30	78	518	15	1036	194	78	118	939	3	.345	.326
Cedar Rapids	.238	140	5306	4677	607	1112	1637	216	24	87	529	34	27	75	493	14	1031	183	95	84	971	9	.350	.319
South Bend	.237	140	5206	4599	537	1089	1535	204	31	60	484	27	45	48	487	16	1148	93	65	77	999	13	.334	.314

INDIVIDUAL

TOP QUALIFIERS FOR BATTING CHAMPIONSHIP

Minimum 378 plate appearances. *Lefthanded batter. †Switch-hitter.

Player, Team	Avg.	G	TPA	AB	R	H	TB	2B	3B	HR	RBI	SH	SF	HP	BB	IBB	SO	SB	CS	GDP	Slg.	OBP
Ozuna, Pablo, Peo.	.357	133	592	538	122	192	266	27	10	9	62	12	2	11	29	3	56	62	26	6	.494	.400
Hillenbrand, Shea, Mich.	.349	129	532	498	80	174	272	33	4	19	93	1	3	10	19	2	49	13	7	11	.546	.383
Erickson, Matt, K.C.*	.324	124	541	441	83	143	191	32	2	4	64	7	3	18	72	1	62	17	7	8	.433	.436
Clark, Jermaine, Wis.*	.324	123	512	448	81	145	213	24	13	6	55	4	1	2	57	4	64	40	14	3	.475	.402
Ryan, Mike, Ft.W.*	.318	113	465	412	68	131	194	24	6	9	72	3	5	1	44	2	92	7	4	8	.471	.381
Amrhein, Mike, Rock.	.317	121	501	457	61	145	208	34	1	9	87	3	3	8	30	1	47	7	4	20	.455	.367
Gload, Ross, K.C.*	.313	132	567	501	77	157	240	41	3	12	92	2	3	3	58	7	84	7	6	13	.479	.386
Kim, Dave, Peo.	.309	127	540	463	75	143	224	38	2	13	92	3	8	13	53	2	77	3	7	4	.484	.393
Valera, Ramon, Wis.†	.298	119	491	423	75	126	164	18	4	4	40	16	2	4	46	1	94	52	19	3	.388	.371
Zapata, Alexis, W.M.	.298	103	423	376	57	112	171	18	4	11	70	3	6	2	36	0	101	20	8	7	.455	.357
Bunkley, Antuan, W.M.	.297	129	553	492	74	146	202	32	0	8	91	0	7	7	47	2	64	4	2	8	.411	.362
Jacobsen, Buck, Bel.	.293	135	594	499	96	146	260	31	1	27	100	0	4	8	83	3	133	5	2	10	.521	.399
Bly, Derrick, Rock.	.292	135	561	490	64	143	209	40	7	4	65	2	4	7	58	1	147	10	5	6	.427	.372
Longueira, Tony, Lan.	.291	97	394	357	46	104	147	21	2	6	49	4	5	5	25	0	58	5	7	4	.412	.342
Randolph, Jaisen, Rock.	.289	128	547	491	78	142	181	18	9	1	33	9	2	5	40	2	113	32	21	4	.369	.348
MaCrory, Bob, Peo.	.289	123	561	488	86	141	163	13	3	1	62	16	3	7	47	1	70	40	15	10	.334	.358

DEPARTMENTAL LEADERS: G—Wesson, 138; AB—Franco, 551; R—Ozuna, 122; H—Ozuna, 192; TB—Hillenbrand, 272; 2B—Gload, 41; 3B—Clark, 13; HR—Jacobsen, 27; RBI—Jacobsen, 100; SH—Osilka, 18; SF—Wise, 9; HP—Melconian, 28; BB—Jacobsen, 83; IBB—Gload, 7; SO—Craig, 160; SB—Foster, 73; CS—Ozuna, 26; GIDP—Amrhein, 20; Slg.—Hillenbrand, .546; OBP—Erickson, .436.

ALL PLAYERS

*Lefthanded batter. †Switch-hitter.

Player, Team	Avg.	G	TPA	AB	R	H	TB	2B	3B	HR	RBI	SH	SF	HP	BB	IBB	SO	SB	CS	GDP	Slg.	OBP
Abreu, Nelson, Rock.	.264	89	309	269	38	71	117	13	6	7	41	7	1	1	31	1	59	8	6	7	.435	.341
Ahumada, Alejandro, Mich.	.277	111	430	390	45	108	134	22	2	0	35	3	4	8	25	0	91	4	7	9	.344	.330
Alevras, Chad, Mich.	.249	85	316	281	35	70	107	14	1	7	39	0	4	4	27	2	70	1	1	8	.381	.320
Alleyne, Roberto, Q.C.	.234	76	283	248	39	58	100	14	2	8	33	0	5	5	25	0	73	5	2	6	.403	.311
Allison, Brad, S.B.	.163	29	94	86	6	14	15	1	0	0	5	0	0	0	8	0	21	0	0	2	.174	.234
Amrhein, Mike, Rock.	.317	121	501	457	61	145	208	34	1	9	87	3	3	8	30	1	47	7	4	20	.455	.367
Arauz, Leobardo, Clin.†	.000	5	12	8	1	0	0	0	0	0	0	0	0	0	4	0	1	0	1	0	.000	.333
Arguellas, Rudy, C.R.†	.198	28	107	86	12	17	20	1	1	0	4	4	0	5	12	0	15	4	1	1	.233	.330
Baderdeen, Kevin, Burl.	.250	59	226	212	31	53	91	8	0	10	28	2	0	3	9	0	75	5	1	4	.429	.290
Baston, Stanley, Burl.	.140	19	67	57	3	8	8	0	0	0	2	0	1	0	9	0	23	1	3	0	.140	.254
Bautista, Jorge, K.C.	.261	84	321	272	33	71	112	16	2	7	50	0	6	3	40	1	63	3	4	9	.412	.355
Bautista, Juan, S.B.	.213	71	260	235	22	50	66	13	0	1	11	0	1	5	19	0	60	7	5	5	.281	.285
Beatriz, Ramy, Bel.*	.258	87	339	302	42	78	101	9	1	4	28	2	0	2	33	2	60	17	4	6	.334	.325
Betancourt, Oscar, C.R.	.206	92	370	339	33	70	92	13	0	3	32	0	1	4	26	0	62	1	2	11	.271	.270
Bevins, Andy, Peo.	.244	130	557	508	68	124	214	30	3	18	98	1	3	10	34	1	145	6	4	10	.421	.303
Bly, Derrick, Rock.	.292	135	561	490	64	143	209	40	7	4	65	2	4	7	58	1	147	10	5	6	.427	.372
Bolling, Kirk, S.B.	.189	44	162	143	18	27	43	4	0	4	21	0	1	4	14	1	49	2	1	3	.301	.278
Borrego, Ramon, Ft.W.†	.261	119	498	422	61	110	149	18	3	5	55	11	4	2	59	0	75	17	10	4	.353	.351
Brewer, Brad, C.R.	.188	28	81	69	12	13	16	0	0	1	8	0	0	1	11	0	18	0	0	0	.232	.309
Brito, Juan, Lan.	.245	63	234	212	16	52	59	7	0	0	22	1	2	2	17	0	41	2	2	6	.278	.305
Brock, J.J., S.B.	.260	91	391	354	45	92	123	19	3	2	21	6	2	3	26	1	75	4	8	10	.347	.314
Bunkley, Antuan, W.M.	.297	129	553	492	74	146	202	32	0	8	91	0	7	7	47	2	64	4	2	8	.411	.362
Burford, Kevin, Clin.*	.258	123	523	446	68	115	167	26	4	6	55	1	4	10	62	2	125	15	4	8	.374	.358
Burress, Andy, Burl.	.281	124	519	449	75	126	198	25	10	9	67	0	5	3	62	2	91	25	5	12	.441	.368
Bush, Ron, W.M.	.167	4	13	12	2	2	2	0	0	0	1	0	0	0	1	0	3	0	0	0	.167	.231
Caceres, Wilmy, Burl.†	.293	35	158	150	23	44	55	8	0	1	14	1	0	3	4	0	24	7	5	3	.367	.325
Caiazzo, Nick, Bel.	.287	127	545	505	56	145	190	22	1	7	71	2	6	9	23	2	77	3	1	15	.376	.326
Calloway, Ron, S.B.*	.263	69	282	251	29	66	91	12	2	3	33	1	3	2	25	1	50	6	5	3	.363	.331
Camp, Shawn, Clin.	.000	47	1	1	0	0	0	0	0	0	0	0	0	0	0	0	0	0	0	0	.000	.000
Campbell, Wylie, Burl.†	.269	75	287	234	33	63	71	8	0	0	20	11	2	6	34	1	35	18	3	3	.303	.373
Capista, Aaron, Mich.†	.261	127	508	471	58	123	173	25	5	5	68	2	6	6	23	0	47	5	3	16	.367	.300
Carter, Quincy, Rock.	.248	27	112	101	9	25	37	6	0	2	14	0	0	0	11	0	18	9	2	1	.366	.321

Player, Team	Avg.	G	TPA	AB	R	H	TB	2B	3B	HR	RBI	SH	SF	HP	BB	IBB	SO	SB	CS	GDP	Slg.	OBP
Caruso, Joe, Lan.	.269	120	496	417	73	112	176	23	7	9	60	1	5	13	60	1	61	24	9	9	.422	.374
Cathey, Joe, Q.C.†	.233	114	460	399	57	93	118	15	2	2	28	17	1	8	35	1	84	19	14	1	.296	.307
Chapman, Scott, Q.C.*	.238	82	295	277	28	66	97	14	1	5	28	2	1	6	9	1	67	7	5	12	.350	.276
Child, Casey, C.R.	.201	51	196	179	14	36	47	3	1	2	16	3	1	4	9	0	34	5	5	5	.263	.254
Clark, Jermaine, Wis.*	.324	123	512	448	81	145	213	24	13	6	55	4	1	2	57	4	64	40	14	3	.475	.402
Closser, J.D., S.B.†	.214	4	17	14	3	3	4	1	0	0	2	1	0	0	2	0	7	0	0	0	.286	.313
Coffee, Gary, Lan.	.284	83	347	285	52	81	140	21	7	8	44	0	3	4	55	2	91	5	2	4	.491	.403
Colangelo, Mike, C.R.	.277	22	98	83	13	23	43	8	0	4	8	0	1	2	12	1	16	5	1	0	.518	.378
Cole, Eric, Q.C.	.280	132	530	500	73	140	215	30	6	11	83	0	1	5	24	0	104	32	15	7	.430	.319
Colon, Jose, Bel.	.261	44	170	157	25	41	63	7	0	5	29	3	0	0	10	1	29	0	2	7	.401	.305
Connell, Gerald, Rock.	.168	82	282	256	22	43	65	11	1	3	17	0	1	2	23	0	84	7	0	10	.254	.241
Connors, Greg, Wis.	.283	94	393	364	45	103	176	31	3	12	57	0	5	1	22	0	95	8	8	5	.484	.321
Craig, Benny, Burl.†	.224	103	392	335	41	75	143	21	1	15	46	1	4	5	47	4	160	2	1	5	.427	.325
Cridland, Mark, Bel.*	.260	79	322	296	35	77	115	16	2	6	37	5	4	3	14	3	63	0	1	4	.389	.297
Cronin, Shane, Clin.	.253	112	420	380	34	96	121	16	0	3	46	2	3	7	28	1	47	6	1	13	.318	.313
Cuddyer, Mike, Ft.W.	.276	129	572	497	82	137	224	37	7	12	81	0	4	10	61	3	107	16	7	13	.451	.364
Cust, Jack, S.B.*	.242	16	68	62	5	15	18	3	0	0	4	0	1	0	5	1	20	0	1	0	.290	.294
Cutshall, Pat, Q.C.	.246	114	464	422	52	104	145	20	3	5	54	0	5	4	33	0	44	15	11	12	.344	.304
Darr, Ryan, Peo.	.289	12	42	38	7	11	17	2	2	0	2	1	0	1	2	0	10	0	1	0	.447	.341
Dawkins, Travis, Burl.	.264	102	409	367	52	97	119	7	6	1	30	2	2	1	37	0	60	37	10	10	.324	.332
Deardorff, Jeff, Bel.	.255	88	361	326	41	83	135	17	1	11	45	2	1	4	27	1	125	3	1	5	.414	.318
De Leon, Jorge, Mich.	.265	50	205	185	23	49	65	8	1	2	19	3	2	0	15	0	19	4	0	4	.351	.317
Delgado, Ariel, C.R.*	.234	133	556	509	54	119	167	25	4	5	67	1	4	2	40	1	105	24	13	14	.328	.290
Diaz, Angel, C.R.	.333	5	19	15	2	5	11	0	0	2	3	0	0	1	3	0	7	0	0	0	.733	.474
Diaz, Miguel, Peo.	.209	53	142	139	21	29	39	7	0	1	16	2	0	1	0	0	19	4	6	6	.281	.214
Dillon, Joe, Lan.	.261	73	308	268	37	70	136	17	2	15	43	4	0	0	36	1	57	9	2	6	.507	.349
DiPace, Danny, Lan.*	.265	20	64	49	11	13	17	1	0	1	7	0	2	2	11	1	14	1	0	1	.347	.406
Donaldson, Rhodney, K.C.*	.219	108	397	334	55	73	86	13	0	0	45	4	4	1	54	0	56	23	10	15	.257	.326
Dougherty, Jeb, C.R.	.252	107	473	425	62	107	131	12	3	2	42	6	4	12	26	0	69	40	8	5	.308	.310
Duffy, Jim, Q.C.	.260	37	134	123	16	32	49	8	0	3	17	1	0	1	9	1	34	5	0	3	.398	.316
Eady, Gerald, Wis.	.170	80	266	235	28	40	69	7	5	4	23	5	2	2	22	1	101	13	4	9	.294	.245
Eberwein, Kevin, Clin.	.296	65	283	247	42	73	129	20	3	10	38	2	2	6	26	0	66	4	2	6	.522	.374
Eckelman, Alex, Peo.	.327	16	57	52	7	17	26	4	1	1	11	0	0	0	5	0	9	0	2	0	.500	.386
Erickson, Matt, K.C.*	.324	124	541	441	83	143	191	32	2	4	64	7	3	18	72	1	62	17	7	8	.433	.436
Espino, Fernando, Wis.	.201	49	182	159	16	32	39	4	0	1	12	2	2	2	17	1	35	3	3	5	.245	.283
Feramisco, Derek, Peo.	.200	26	99	85	18	17	24	4	0	1	5	1	1	4	8	0	23	1	0	0	.282	.296
Figueroa, Luis, Wis.	.291	96	357	306	41	89	110	18	0	1	48	0	1	8	42	5	18	7	1	13	.359	.389
Fischer, Mark, Mich.	.253	102	419	379	52	96	143	19	2	8	50	0	3	1	36	2	93	9	6	5	.377	.317
Font, Franklin, Rock.	.270	66	267	237	34	64	73	5	2	0	15	4	1	5	20	0	39	25	6	5	.308	.338
Foster, Quincy, K.C.*	.253	134	616	545	90	138	172	14	10	0	37	8	4	8	51	4	114	73	19	7	.316	.324
Franco, Raul, K.C.	.287	132	596	551	81	158	188	24	0	2	51	12	7	2	24	2	52	15	12	8	.341	.315
Franks, Lance, Peo.	.000	58	0	0	0	0	0	0	0	0	0	0	0	0	0	0	0	0	1	0	.000	.000
Gancasz, Michael, Mich.	.261	26	56	46	7	12	15	1	1	0	3	0	1	4	5	0	17	0	0	0	.326	.375
Garrick, Matt, C.R.	.245	61	244	212	27	52	77	13	0	4	25	2	0	1	29	0	55	5	1	2	.363	.339
Gentry, Aaron, Peo.	.237	99	328	279	39	66	89	10	2	3	27	7	7	6	29	0	98	13	4	5	.319	.315
Gload, Ross, K.C.*	.313	132	567	501	77	157	240	41	3	12	92	2	3	3	58	7	84	7	6	13	.479	.386
Gonzalez, Santos, Clin.†	.201	89	310	274	31	55	76	9	3	2	21	5	1	3	27	1	71	16	7	7	.277	.279
Gordon, Brian, S.B.*	.280	126	493	468	46	131	190	23	6	8	61	0	7	4	14	2	100	6	4	5	.406	.302
Graham, Jess, Mich.*	.261	113	480	414	73	108	164	22	5	8	61	2	2	12	50	1	96	10	4	13	.396	.356
Green, Kevin, K.C.	.156	33	115	96	8	15	20	2	0	1	8	2	1	1	15	0	32	6	5	0	.208	.274
Grimmett, Ryan, W.M.	.228	113	491	412	68	94	128	11	10	1	33	13	3	8	55	3	123	48	14	3	.311	.328
Grubbs, Chris, Rock.	.156	39	115	96	8	15	20	3	1	0	1	0	0	4	15	0	38	0	1	1	.208	.296
Guerrero, Sergio, Bel.	.267	47	210	191	24	51	61	10	0	0	20	2	2	3	12	0	17	1	5	4	.319	.317
Guillen, Jose, Bel.†	.299	42	161	147	16	44	53	5	2	0	12	3	0	0	11	0	45	6	4	2	.361	.348
Guzman, Julio, S.B.	.196	17	63	56	6	11	14	0	0	1	4	0	0	3	4	0	25	2	0	1	.250	.286
Haas, Danny, Mich.*	.234	96	330	299	39	70	95	14	1	3	29	2	2	5	22	1	55	1	2	7	.318	.296
Habig, Keith, Mich.	.083	6	12	12	2	1	1	0	0	0	1	0	0	0	0	0	2	0	0	1	.083	.083
Halloran, Matt, Clin.	.224	123	510	459	48	103	133	21	3	1	42	5	3	10	33	0	92	19	12	15	.290	.289
Hamilton, Joe, Mich.*	.271	63	238	203	36	55	94	12	0	9	34	3	2	2	28	0	68	3	1	6	.463	.362
Hargrove, Harvey, Wis.	.241	121	512	449	68	108	193	26	7	15	62	7	3	8	45	2	118	21	7	7	.430	.319
Harper, Brandon, K.C.	.231	113	464	412	34	95	133	22	2	4	50	1	5	4	42	3	64	1	3	16	.323	.305
Harrison, Jamal, Ft.W.	.278	107	440	389	58	108	163	25	3	8	49	0	2	9	40	1	93	7	5	11	.419	.357
Haynes, Larry, Wis.	.231	5	14	13	4	3	3	0	0	0	0	0	0	0	1	0	2	1	0	1	.231	.286
Hill, Jeremy, Lan.	.240	86	313	288	25	69	95	12	1	4	37	4	2	4	15	1	75	4	1	8	.330	.285
Hillenbrand, Shea, Mich.	.349	129	532	498	80	174	272	33	4	19	93	1	3	10	19	2	49	13	7	11	.546	.383
Hinske, Eric, Rock.*	.450	6	26	20	8	9	16	4	0	1	4	0	1	0	5	0	6	1	0	0	.800	.538
Horsman, Brent, Clin.*	.240	67	225	208	25	50	70	9	1	3	18	0	0	2	15	0	49	10	6	7	.337	.298
Howard, Marcus, Mich.	.202	30	104	94	7	19	25	1	1	1	10	0	0	2	8	0	24	2	2	2	.266	.279
Hudson, Bert, S.B.	.210	80	297	271	35	57	94	13	3	6	32	1	3	1	21	0	82	1	0	4	.347	.267
Hunter, Johnny, Clin.	.226	116	497	407	65	92	149	17	5	10	42	1	3	4	82	3	116	36	9	5	.366	.359
Hunter, Travis, K.C.	.136	10	23	22	0	3	3	0	0	0	1	0	0	0	1	0	5	0	0	0	.136	.174
Hyers, Matt, Q.C.†	.238	58	145	122	22	29	37	6	1	0	15	2	0	1	20	0	28	8	5	2	.303	.350
Jacobsen, Buck, Bel.	.293	135	594	499	96	146	260	31	1	27	100	0	4	8	83	3	133	5	2	10	.521	.399
Jacomino, Mandy, W.M.*	.209	93	317	273	35	57	87	15	0	5	40	0	2	1	41	3	63	2	1	5	.319	.312
Jaha, John, Bel.	.000	2	7	4	1	0	0	0	0	0	0	0	0	1	2	0	2	0	0	0	.000	.429
James, Brandon, Bel.*	.223	81	303	269	34	60	99	13	1	8	33	3	0	0	31	2	82	2	5	6	.368	.303
Jasco, Elinton, Rock.	.279	12	46	43	8	12	13	1	0	0	3	0	1	0	2	0	12	2	3	0	.302	.304
Jaworowski, Aaron, Ft.W.*	.268	51	209	190	28	51	76	14	1	3	28	0	0	3	16	0	50	0	0	3	.400	.335
Jimenez, Felipe, Rock.	.221	120	425	367	46	81	103	11	4	1	36	11	2	15	28	0	126	36	11	7	.281	.301
Johnson, Duan, Wis.	.214	32	129	112	15	24	33	3	0	2	12	1	1	1	14	2	18	3	2	3	.295	.305
Johnson, Jason, Rock.	.241	76	264	232	35	56	79	6	1	5	22	0	4	7	21	0	43	13	5	1	.341	.318
Johnson, Patrick, C.R.	.230	47	174	148	16	34	44	4	0	2	20	1	0	4	21	0	26	2	3	5	.297	.341

Player, Team	Avg.	G	TPA	AB	R	H	TB	2B	3B	HR	RBI	SH	SF	HP	BB	IBB	SO	SB	CS	GDP	Slg.	OBP
Johnson, Rontrez, Mich.	.271	85	382	306	65	83	123	15	5	5	32	1	5	4	66	0	46	24	8	4	.402	.402
Jones, Keith, S.B.	.222	55	220	189	19	42	67	13	0	4	30	2	2	3	24	0	70	2	2	4	.354	.317
Keaveney, Jeff, Mich.	.252	112	452	373	61	94	163	24	0	15	54	0	5	9	65	3	104	0	2	10	.437	.372
Kim, Dave, Peo.	.309	127	540	463	75	143	224	38	2	13	92	3	8	13	53	2	77	3	7	4	.484	.389
King, Willie, Rock.*	.121	13	37	33	3	4	4	0	0	0	0	0	0	0	4	0	11	0	0	2	.121	.216
Kirby, Scott, Bel.	.203	107	418	359	51	73	120	19	2	8	40	5	1	6	47	0	109	5	4	7	.334	.305
Knight, Marcus, C.R.†	.239	97	401	364	38	87	132	19	1	8	51	1	1	11	24	0	59	5	6	4	.363	.305
Koerner, Pat, S.B.	.152	9	37	33	6	5	7	2	0	0	4	0	0	1	3	0	2	0	0	4	.212	.243
Kraus, Jake, Bel.	.314	86	329	271	47	85	123	18	1	6	42	2	3	7	46	1	33	0	0	7	.454	.422
Larson, Brandon, Burl.	.221	18	72	68	5	15	24	3	0	2	9	0	0	0	4	0	16	2	1	1	.353	.264
Lauterhahn, Dan, W.M.	.220	94	341	305	34	67	88	21	0	0	17	8	2	2	24	0	56	8	2	3	.289	.279
Lawrence, Mike, C.R.	.250	75	278	248	31	62	80	12	0	2	25	0	4	1	25	0	57	1	2	5	.323	.317
Lawrence, Tony, Clin.	.233	86	339	296	35	69	112	16	3	7	40	2	4	1	35	1	93	5	4	8	.378	.313
LeBron, Juan, Lan.	.251	121	513	442	70	111	206	26	9	17	84	1	5	8	57	5	129	18	11	11	.466	.344
LeCroy, Matt, Ft.W.	.276	64	269	225	33	62	108	17	1	9	40	0	2	8	34	1	45	0	0	9	.480	.387
Lee, Jason, Peo.*	.264	122	440	382	51	101	141	15	5	5	47	4	2	9	43	3	103	10	10	5	.369	.351
Leggett, Adam, C.R.†	.273	125	543	443	83	121	186	26	3	11	50	8	3	8	80	3	83	24	14	9	.420	.391
Leon, Carlos, Mich.†	.250	107	446	372	59	93	115	7	3	3	37	10	3	11	50	0	81	10	10	5	.309	.353
Lignitz, Jeremiah, W.M.*	.176	44	139	125	9	22	26	4	0	0	12	1	1	1	11	1	45	0	0	2	.208	.246
Lindsey, Rodney, Clin.-W.M.	.272	85	368	313	69	85	133	11	8	7	34	1	2	13	39	2	96	60	12	3	.425	.373
Lisanti, Bob, Rock.	.227	26	95	75	7	17	27	7	0	1	14	2	3	1	14	0	18	2	0	1	.360	.344
Liverziani, Claudio, Wis.*	.248	106	396	355	43	88	125	20	4	3	33	8	2	1	30	2	67	16	3	4	.352	.307
LoCurto, Gary, Mich.*	.186	60	222	188	20	35	43	8	0	0	15	2	1	0	31	0	52	1	3	2	.229	.300
Logan, Kyle, Q.C.*	.264	110	397	352	50	93	131	22	2	4	49	2	5	2	36	3	50	22	13	4	.372	.332
Longmire, Marcel, Rock.	.161	40	141	124	10	20	26	4	1	0	11	3	1	0	13	0	36	6	2	5	.210	.239
Longueira, Tony, Lan.	.291	97	396	357	46	104	147	21	2	6	49	4	5	5	25	0	58	5	7	8	.412	.342
Lopez, Jose, S.B.	.201	43	153	144	12	29	41	5	2	1	20	2	2	1	4	0	35	0	3	3	.285	.225
Lopez, Manny, Ft.W.	.273	115	442	395	62	108	154	17	4	7	53	3	1	3	38	2	80	6	4	15	.390	.341
Lopez, Omar, S.B.	.143	11	42	35	4	5	7	2	0	0	2	0	1	0	5	0	8	0	0	0	.200	.244
Lopez, Rafael, Wis.	.223	35	131	121	11	27	37	5	1	1	12	0	0	1	9	0	18	0	0	4	.306	.282
Maas, Steve, Lan.	.000	43	1	1	0	0	0	0	0	0	0	0	0	0	0	0	0	0	0	0	.000	.000
MaCrory, Bob, Peo.	.289	123	561	488	86	141	163	13	3	1	62	16	3	7	47	1	70	40	15	10	.334	.358
Maier, Taber, Peo.	.269	84	328	271	47	73	95	14	1	2	28	4	1	6	45	0	52	6	5	5	.351	.384
Maldonado, Carlos, Wis.	.174	7	25	23	4	4	4	0	0	0	1	0	0	0	2	0	1	0	0	1	.174	.240
Mansavage, Jay, Q.C.†	.216	85	293	268	31	58	77	16	0	1	19	5	1	0	19	3	67	13	2	4	.287	.267
Marchiano, Mike, Wis.	.288	117	501	444	62	128	205	29	3	14	74	0	4	6	47	3	72	13	5	10	.462	.361
Marino, Larry, Mich.	.180	53	164	139	15	25	31	3	0	1	13	2	0	1	22	0	26	0	0	0	.223	.296
Martin, Casey, C.R.	.247	97	381	336	40	83	133	18	1	10	46	0	4	5	36	6	97	3	2	4	.396	.325
Martin, Jared, S.B.†	.234	15	58	47	8	11	11	0	0	0	4	1	2	0	8	0	6	1	0	0	.234	.333
Martinez, Belvani, S.B.	.250	18	85	80	11	20	22	2	0	0	6	0	0	2	3	0	22	5	1	3	.275	.294
Martinez, Tony, S.B.	.220	24	102	82	13	18	25	1	0	2	15	0	2	1	17	1	18	0	0	2	.305	.353
Martinez, Victor, Wis.	.136	5	22	22	2	3	3	0	0	0	2	0	0	0	0	0	5	1	0	1	.136	.136
Matheny, Mike, Bel.	.250	2	9	8	1	2	3	1	0	0	2	0	0	0	1	0	3	0	0	0	.375	.333
Mathis, Jared, Bel.	.267	24	96	90	12	24	29	5	0	0	3	4	0	1	1	0	8	0	1	4	.322	.283
Maynard, Scott, Wis.	.174	81	271	236	29	41	57	8	1	2	17	3	2	0	30	0	70	4	4	6	.242	.265
McAffee, Josh, S.B.	.091	21	74	66	3	6	13	1	0	2	4	0	0	1	7	0	31	0	0	1	.197	.189
McConnell, Jason, Ft.W.†	.259	91	363	316	52	82	106	12	3	2	23	8	1	7	31	1	48	19	10	5	.335	.338
McDaniel, Ryan, Clin.	.183	41	103	93	12	17	19	2	0	0	5	0	0	1	9	0	34	3	0	5	.204	.262
McDaniels, Paul, Mich.*	.172	12	35	29	4	5	6	1	0	0	1	0	1	1	4	0	11	2	0	1	.207	.286
McHenry, Joe, Ft.W.*	.257	46	162	144	21	37	45	4	2	0	11	2	0	1	15	0	46	3	0	3	.313	.331
McKinney, Antonio, W.M.	.071	5	16	14	0	1	1	0	0	0	2	0	1	0	1	0	4	0	0	0	.071	.125
McNeal, Aaron, Q.C.	.284	112	407	370	54	105	164	15	1	14	61	1	0	5	31	2	112	3	3	12	.443	.347
Meadows, Tydus, Rock.	.291	35	154	134	35	39	65	5	0	7	24	0	1	4	15	1	32	6	1	1	.485	.377
Medina, Luis, Rock.	.194	10	39	36	2	7	9	2	0	0	1	0	0	1	2	0	6	1	0	4	.250	.256
Medosch, Keith, C.R.	.208	71	210	178	19	37	55	9	3	1	14	2	0	0	30	0	37	1	6	4	.309	.322
Medrano, Steve, Lan.†	.259	106	393	340	45	88	112	14	5	0	29	13	2	4	34	2	39	15	3	4	.329	.332
Meier, Dan, S.B.*	.179	22	67	56	7	10	13	3	0	0	5	0	0	0	11	0	20	0	0	1	.232	.313
Melconian, Alex, K.C.	.227	132	549	453	61	103	133	10	1	6	53	10	8	28	50	1	135	21	3	12	.294	.336
Melo, Ramon, Rock.	.333	11	39	33	7	11	15	1	0	1	5	2	1	0	3	0	9	4	0	0	.455	.378
Metzler, Rod, Lan.†	.251	88	366	323	45	81	112	17	4	2	34	4	0	3	36	0	77	17	6	2	.347	.331
Miles, Aaron, Q.C.†	.244	108	403	369	42	90	130	22	6	2	37	7	1	1	25	3	52	28	13	7	.352	.293
Montas, Ricardo, Lan.	.229	51	164	140	21	32	41	4	1	1	14	1	0	1	22	2	28	4	2	4	.293	.337
Montgomery, Andre, Burl.	.216	75	270	245	25	53	73	8	0	4	32	1	2	2	20	0	60	9	5	1	.298	.279
Moon, Brian, Bel.†	.256	118	523	438	62	112	137	20	1	1	54	9	7	23	46	4	62	0	1	9	.313	.352
Moore, Donnie, Bel.	.219	61	202	183	14	40	51	5	0	2	13	5	1	4	9	0	55	2	2	2	.279	.269
Mora, Juan, W.M.*	.231	88	331	308	33	71	105	15	5	3	38	5	1	3	14	0	103	7	3	3	.341	.270
Moreno, Jose, Wis.	.240	84	304	262	36	63	85	10	3	2	26	17	2	4	19	1	36	5	6	4	.324	.300
Murray, Doug, Q.C.*	.212	21	37	33	4	7	10	0	0	1	3	0	0	3	1	0	10	0	0	1	.303	.297
Newman, Howard, Burl.	.273	7	22	22	0	6	6	0	0	0	3	0	0	0	0	0	7	1	1	0	.273	.273
Nieves, Wilbert, Clin.	.255	115	446	380	47	97	128	22	0	3	55	4	6	7	47	4	69	7	9	16	.337	.343
Niles, Drew, K.C.†	.276	26	103	87	12	24	28	4	0	0	9	0	4	0	12	1	20	2	1	1	.322	.350
Nilsson, Dave, Bel.*	.417	4	15	12	3	5	11	3	0	1	7	0	1	0	2	0	0	0	0	1	.917	.467
Nunez, Abraham, S.B.†	.255	110	442	364	44	93	138	14	2	9	47	3	5	3	67	4	81	12	14	4	.379	.371
Nykoluk, Kevin, Peo.	.280	67	236	218	29	61	74	7	0	2	24	0	1	4	13	0	34	1	4	6	.339	.331
Ochoa, Javier, Q.C.	.000	5	8	7	1	0	0	0	0	0	0	0	0	0	1	0	2	0	0	0	.000	.125
Orndorff, Dave, Ft.W.	.261	99	434	380	68	99	145	20	4	6	47	3	0	7	44	0	91	30	12	5	.382	.348
Ortega, Bill, Peo.	.276	105	447	398	57	110	143	23	2	2	60	3	2	5	39	0	69	4	8	14	.359	.347
Osborne, Mark, S.B.*	.241	78	317	270	33	65	85	11	0	3	28	0	4	0	43	1	65	4	4	3	.315	.341
Osilka, Garret, Bel.	.260	127	590	492	74	128	181	26	3	7	32	18	5	10	65	1	118	18	11	3	.368	.355
Ozarowski, Rich, W.M.†	.261	92	341	299	47	78	110	22	2	2	27	4	2	4	32	1	49	5	4	5	.368	.338
Ozuna, Pablo, Peo.	.357	133	592	538	122	192	266	27	10	9	62	12	2	11	29	3	56	62	26	6	.494	.400
Pagan, Felix, Ft.W.	.276	69	266	225	36	62	110	21	3	7	40	1	3	2	34	0	56	2	1	5	.489	.371

Player, Team	Avg.	G	TPA	AB	R	H	TB	2B	3B	HR	RBI	SH	SF	HP	BB	IBB	SO	SB	CS	GDP	Slg.	OBP
Pagnozzi, Tom, Peo.	.125	4	14	8	2	1	1	0	0	0	1	0	0	0	6	0	1	0	0	0	.125	.500
Pena, Frankie, Ft.W.	.189	47	146	132	16	25	41	4	0	4	17	1	4	0	9	0	34	0	0	3	.311	.234
Philip-Guide, Sheldon, C.R.	.140	13	46	43	5	6	6	0	0	0	2	0	0	1	2	0	15	0	0	1	.140	.196
Pitts, Rick, Lan.	.229	85	275	249	33	57	73	5	4	1	21	5	4	3	13	1	62	22	6	2	.293	.271
Polonia, Israel, K.C.	.211	15	43	38	6	8	11	0	0	1	2	0	0	3	2	0	17	1	1	0	.289	.302
Price, Corey, Burl.†	.236	52	179	157	17	37	48	11	0	0	15	4	1	1	16	0	41	4	2	4	.306	.309
Quaccia, Luke, Peo.*	.279	131	496	437	68	122	188	31	1	11	67	3	2	8	46	5	88	4	2	15	.430	.357
Quire, Jeremy, S.B.	.192	57	189	177	11	34	46	9	0	1	17	0	2	4	6	0	44	0	0	8	.260	.233
Radcliff, Victor, Lan.	.261	66	291	253	42	66	104	15	4	5	33	0	4	8	26	0	53	12	5	5	.411	.344
Rakers, Jason, Clin.*	.256	55	209	172	20	44	62	6	3	2	21	3	0	6	28	1	53	5	2	5	.360	.379
Randolph, Jaisen, Rock.	.289	128	547	491	78	142	181	18	9	1	33	9	2	5	40	2	113	32	21	4	.369	.348
Reed, Brian, K.C.	.500	3	8	6	1	3	4	1	0	0	2	0	0	0	2	0	2	0	0	0	.667	.625
Reese, Nate, K.C.	.250	13	47	40	3	10	14	1	0	1	7	0	0	2	5	0	12	0	0	2	.350	.362
Restovich, Mike, Ft.W.	.444	11	49	45	9	20	29	5	2	0	6	0	0	0	4	0	12	0	0	1	.644	.490
Rexrode, Jackie, S.B.*	.291	50	225	175	33	51	62	7	2	0	7	3	1	1	45	1	31	22	3	1	.354	.437
Reynoso, Ismael, K.C.	.188	48	170	144	15	27	34	4	0	1	9	5	0	4	17	0	34	3	3	2	.236	.291
Rinne, Jim, S.B.	.273	18	68	55	10	15	19	4	0	0	5	1	0	0	12	0	17	1	2	1	.345	.403
Rios, Brian, W.M.	.265	100	375	343	44	91	120	18	1	3	46	3	3	3	23	2	60	5	4	6	.350	.315
Rios, Fernando, Burl.	.253	119	458	407	49	103	133	13	1	5	38	4	3	2	42	0	65	16	10	8	.327	.324
Rivas, Julio, K.C.	.000	1	1	1	0	0	0	0	0	0	0	0	0	0	0	0	0	0	0	0	.000	.000
Rivera, Francisco, Burl.*	.172	31	110	93	4	16	21	5	0	0	6	2	0	1	14	0	15	2	0	2	.226	.287
Rivera, Mike, W.M.	.275	108	426	403	40	111	178	34	3	9	67	1	5	2	15	0	68	0	2	8	.442	.301
Rodriguez, Miguel, S.B.	.232	29	108	99	12	23	35	9	0	1	8	0	0	2	7	0	32	3	2	0	.354	.296
Rodriguez, Wilfredo, Q.C.*	.000	28	0	0	0	0	0	0	0	0	0	0	0	0	0	0	0	0	1	0	.000	.000
Rogue, Francisco, Bel.	.163	15	51	49	2	8	8	0	0	0	3	2	0	0	0	0	10	0	0	2	.163	.163
Rojas, Christian, Burl.	.284	40	151	141	27	40	73	5	2	8	20	0	1	0	9	1	33	5	2	4	.518	.325
Roneberg, Brett, K.C.*	.271	68	270	240	35	65	81	7	0	3	35	3	1	1	25	0	50	2	5	11	.338	.341
Rosario, Ruben, Peo.	.000	12	0	0	0	0	0	0	0	0	0	0	0	0	0	0	0	1	0	0	.000	.000
Rose, Mike, Q.C.†	.303	88	324	267	48	81	119	13	2	7	40	3	1	1	52	3	56	10	8	5	.446	.417
Ruotsinoja, Jacob, Clin.*	.214	96	392	341	50	73	114	16	2	7	42	1	1	5	44	1	91	3	2	8	.334	.312
Rupert, Bryan, Peo.	.217	81	304	272	29	59	102	12	2	9	30	3	2	1	26	0	80	4	2	5	.375	.286
Rutherford, Daryl, Clin.	.148	23	91	81	11	12	13	1	0	0	3	0	0	2	8	0	9	7	2	1	.160	.242
Ryan, Mike, Ft.W.*	.318	113	465	412	68	131	194	24	6	9	72	3	5	1	44	2	92	7	4	8	.471	.381
Salazar, Juan, Rock.	.255	100	371	322	39	82	116	20	1	4	53	0	4	1	44	1	85	7	3	7	.360	.342
Sanchez, Wellington, Bel.	.248	39	162	137	23	34	43	5	2	0	15	5	0	1	19	2	24	3	2	4	.314	.344
Santana, Pedro, W.M.	.263	118	484	438	79	115	162	21	7	4	45	4	5	9	28	0	93	64	7	4	.370	.317
Santiago, Arnold, Rock.	.218	34	114	110	12	24	28	2	1	0	9	0	2	0	2	0	21	1	1	2	.255	.228
Santonocito, Justin, S.B.*	.170	47	160	153	13	26	35	2	2	1	9	2	1	2	2	0	43	0	2	3	.229	.190
Santos, Jose, K.C.	.188	32	142	117	17	22	41	9	2	2	12	1	0	3	21	2	49	5	1	0	.350	.326
Schaeffer, Jon, Ft.W.	.283	122	500	414	77	117	188	31	5	10	64	3	5	23	55	2	117	3	5	16	.454	.392
Schesser, Heath, W.M.	.207	93	368	323	48	67	83	14	1	0	19	3	3	6	33	0	67	1	1	6	.257	.290
Schmidt, Donnie, Wis.	.000	44	0	0	1	0	0	0	0	0	0	0	0	0	0	0	0	0	0	0	.000	.000
Schnabel, Matthew, K.C.*	.127	24	75	63	5	8	12	1	0	1	6	2	2	1	7	0	21	0	0	3	.190	.219
Schrager, Tony, Rock.	.251	50	218	167	38	42	74	12	1	6	19	3	2	3	43	1	32	3	2	4	.443	.409
Secoda, Joe, Peo.	.042	10	24	24	2	1	1	0	0	0	0	0	0	0	0	0	15	0	0	2	.042	.042
Serrano, Danny, C.R.†	.265	9	36	34	3	9	14	2	0	1	2	0	0	0	2	0	8	0	0	2	.412	.306
Shrum, Allen, Ft.W.	.059	6	17	17	0	1	1	0	0	0	0	0	0	0	0	0	8	0	0	0	.059	.059
Silvestre, Juan, Wis.	.252	106	434	401	44	101	176	20	5	15	56	2	2	7	22	1	98	7	2	9	.439	.301
Smith, Jason, Rock.*	.239	126	506	464	67	111	165	15	9	7	60	6	4	1	31	1	122	23	6	2	.356	.286
Smith, Nester, Ft.W.†	.258	115	472	414	59	107	163	18	7	8	53	3	3	14	38	2	103	7	8	10	.394	.339
Snellgrove, Clay, Clin.	.239	104	406	368	42	88	112	14	2	2	30	4	1	6	27	0	32	11	9	7	.304	.301
Sorg, Jay, Burl.*	.257	20	79	74	6	19	30	5	0	2	10	0	1	0	4	1	13	2	0	4	.405	.291
Steele, Alex, W.M.	.248	123	497	424	53	105	147	18	3	6	47	2	2	7	62	1	137	0	7	9	.347	.352
Steelmon, Wyley, S.B.*	.277	90	364	307	36	85	132	18	1	9	47	2	2	2	51	3	77	0	0	4	.430	.381
Stewart, Paxton, C.R.*	.200	9	34	30	4	6	8	2	0	0	2	0	0	0	4	0	4	4	1	1	.267	.294
Suarez, Marc, Burl.	.245	61	237	212	26	52	90	15	1	7	27	0	0	5	20	0	75	4	5	3	.425	.325
Sutton, Bruce, Ft.W.	.231	42	136	117	12	27	42	13	1	0	11	1	2	5	11	1	44	0	2	1	.359	.319
Sykes, Jamie, S.B.	.204	26	111	93	12	19	33	2	3	2	10	0	0	2	16	0	20	5	0	0	.355	.333
Taveras, Jose, S.B.	.191	26	79	68	7	13	17	2	1	0	6	2	1	0	8	0	22	0	0	1	.250	.273
Taveras, Jose, Lan.	.281	14	60	57	7	16	22	3	0	1	7	0	0	0	2	0	3	3	1	1	.386	.317
Tegland, Ron, Clin.	.206	13	40	34	4	7	11	1	0	1	7	0	1	1	4	0	12	0	1	0	.324	.300
Thoen, E.J., C.R.	.218	130	503	441	57	96	174	22	1	18	55	3	2	7	50	2	129	10	5	5	.395	.306
Thomas, Jim, Q.C.	.257	103	408	342	67	88	169	14	2	21	69	1	3	4	58	0	115	8	3	3	.494	.369
Thrower, Jake, Clin.†	.290	43	171	145	25	42	70	11	1	5	27	0	0	4	22	0	22	11	3	5	.483	.398
Tidwell, Dave, Burl.	.291	39	154	134	21	39	55	10	0	2	10	2	0	1	17	0	41	6	2	1	.410	.375
Tolentino, Juan, C.R.	.261	133	557	495	82	129	201	27	6	11	57	3	2	6	51	1	135	49	25	6	.406	.336
Tomlinson, Goef, Lan.*	.285	68	318	274	55	78	129	16	7	7	39	0	0	5	39	2	34	21	6	4	.471	.384
Torres, Rafael, Clin.	.272	42	152	136	18	37	49	7	1	1	15	0	1	2	13	0	32	3	2	1	.360	.342
Uccello, Jeff, Mich.	.220	21	46	41	4	9	12	3	0	0	1	1	0	1	3	0	6	3	2	0	.293	.289
Urquiola, Carlos, S.B.*	.319	39	179	166	28	53	69	8	4	0	16	0	2	1	10	0	15	10	8	1	.416	.358
Valera, Ramon, Wis.†	.298	119	491	423	75	126	164	18	4	4	40	16	2	4	46	1	94	52	19	3	.388	.371
Vasquez, Alejandro, Q.C.*	.114	18	37	35	2	4	7	0	0	1	5	0	0	2	1	0	4	0	1	1	.200	.162
Viera, Rob, Burl.	.278	33	122	115	11	32	46	6	1	2	13	0	0	2	5	0	26	0	0	3	.400	.320
Washington, Kelley, K.C.	.247	65	260	239	28	59	76	5	0	4	21	4	0	6	11	0	75	10	8	4	.318	.297
Welsh, Eric, Burl.*	.259	135	565	525	49	136	196	33	3	7	68	1	3	9	27	1	112	7	6	5	.373	.305
Wesson, Barry, Q.C.	.252	138	532	493	71	124	170	21	2	7	43	2	0	5	32	1	90	22	12	11	.345	.304
Williams, Jovany, Peo.	.215	54	175	158	20	34	58	10	1	4	21	4	1	2	10	0	43	3	1	2	.367	.269
Williams, Micah, Lan.	.241	77	296	270	43	65	87	8	4	2	19	3	0	5	18	0	55	33	10	3	.322	.300
Williams, Mike, Wis.	.143	27	89	84	8	12	14	2	0	0	4	1	1	1	2	0	40	1	1	2	.167	.170
Williams, Patrick, Wis.	.240	71	253	229	35	55	96	8	0	11	36	0	3	4	17	2	78	5	1	5	.419	.300
Willis, Dave, Lan.	.281	97	397	374	56	105	172	30	5	9	50	0	4	2	17	0	69	9	2	10	.460	.312
Wise, Dewayne, Burl.*	.224	127	554	496	61	111	150	15	9	2	44	7	9	1	41	1	111	27	17	4	.302	.280

CLASS A *Midwest League*

Player, Team	Avg.	G	TPA	AB	R	H	TB	2B	3B	HR	RBI	SH	SF	HP	BB	IBB	SO	SB	CS	GDP	Slg.	OBP
Yedo, Carlos, Rock.*	.290	9	36	31	6	9	20	5	0	2	10	0	0	0	5	0	8	0	0	1	.645	.389
Zapata, Alexis, W.M.	.298	103	423	376	57	112	171	18	4	11	70	3	6	2	36	0	101	20	8	7	.455	.357

GRAND SLAMS: LeBron, 3; Bevins, Delgado, Jacobsen, Orndorff, Rose, J. Thomas, 2 each; Alevras, Amrhein, Jo. Bautista, Duffy, Eberwein, Gload, Jimenez, K. Jones, T. Laurence, Marchiano, C. Martin, Miles, Moon, Pagan, Schrager, Zapata, 1 each.

AWARDED FIRST BASE ON CATCHER'S INTERFERENCE: Jimenez 2 (Suarez, F. Rivera); M. Lopes 2 (Nieves, Gancasz); Nieves 2 (Serrano, Brito); Bevins (Tegland); Connors (Rogue); Deardorff (Nieves); Hillenbrand (M. Rivera); T. Lawrence (Hillenbrand); Leggett (Chapman); O. Lopez (J. Hill); Maier (Longmire); Pagan (Allison); Pitts (Nieves).

PLAYERS WITH TWO OR MORE TEAMS

Player, Team	Avg.	G	TPA	AB	R	H	TB	2B	3B	HR	RBI	SH	SF	HP	BB	IBB	SO	SB	CS	GDP	Slg.	OBP
Lindsey, Rodney, Clin.	.271	40	177	155	32	42	66	4	4	4	17	1	1	3	17	1	54	36	4	2	.426	.352
Lindsey, Rodney, W.M.	.272	45	191	158	37	43	67	7	4	3	17	0	1	10	22	1	42	24	8	1	.424	.393

1998 PITCHING

TEAM

Team	W	L	Pct.	ERA	G	CG	ShO	Sv.	IP	H	TBF	R	ER	HR	SH	SF	HB	BB	IBB	SO	WP	Bk.
West Michigan ..	83	57	.593	3.01	140	13	14	36	1235.2	1056	5089	511	413	75	45	23	61	359	12	1177	58	11
Quad City	77	62	.554	3.44	139	10	14	36	1223.1	1002	5196	558	467	75	51	29	86	532	41	1057	78	23
Cedar Rapids.....	71	69	.507	3.51	140	21	13	26	1242.0	1132	5211	606	485	101	35	33	63	415	2	1033	116	11
Beloit..............	64	75	.460	3.80	139	11	9	32	1221.0	1242	5296	669	515	97	56	26	60	420	17	1041	77	5
Burlington	63	77	.450	3.81	140	15	8	30	1206.0	1135	5258	659	511	76	40	32	77	525	14	1059	127	9
Clinton............	65	73	.471	3.95	138	5	7	21	1198.2	1207	5220	668	526	67	44	46	75	459	20	1020	82	9
Rockford	71	68	.511	3.97	139	7	7	39	1210.1	1182	5259	643	534	72	41	34	70	524	14	939	98	12
Kane County	69	71	.493	3.98	140	6	11	31	1221.0	1220	5302	662	540	77	47	37	76	440	20	1093	72	9
Michigan	79	61	.564	3.98	140	2	7	46	1225.0	1243	5330	631	542	64	48	51	77	463	26	1025	75	8
Wisconsin	72	65	.526	3.98	137	1	5	34	1209.0	1156	5319	642	535	77	56	30	80	578	17	1274	87	19
Fort Wayne.......	79	61	.564	4.01	140	2	9	33	1226.2	1224	5396	678	546	69	45	36	60	477	21	1027	95	14
Lansing	71	69	.507	4.19	140	1	9	38	1233.2	1216	5379	673	574	76	45	46	73	516	3	991	102	9
Peoria.............	72	68	.514	4.30	140	3	3	37	1224.2	1222	5348	715	585	82	50	49	74	513	9	896	96	8
South Bend	40	100	.286	4.41	140	2	5	19	1195.0	1352	5345	755	585	72	44	40	53	413	12	919	122	11

INDIVIDUAL

TOP QUALIFIERS FOR EARNED-RUN AVERAGE TITLE
Minimum 112 innings. *Lefthanded pitcher.

Pitcher, Team	W	L	Pct.	ERA	G	GS	CG	ShO	GF	Sv.	IP	H	TBF	R	ER	HR	SH	SF	HB	BB	IBB	SO	WP	Bk.
Childers, Jason, Bel.	8	6	.571	1.92	34	14	1	0	4	0	117.0	104	477	48	25	8	6	2	1	22	2	110	7	2
Burnett, Allan, K.C.	10	4	.714	1.97	20	20	0	0	0	0	119.0	74	469	27	26	3	2	0	8	45	0	186	6	2
Harriger, Mark, Q.C.	8	4	.667	2.23	16	16	3	1	0	0	117.0	86	472	37	29	3	3	2	4	38	0	105	14	1
Shearn, Tom, Q.C.	7	7	.500	2.25	21	21	2	1	0	0	120.0	88	487	38	30	8	4	0	6	52	1	93	3	0
Corey, Mark, Burl.	12	6	.667	2.44	20	20	6	2	0	0	140.0	125	577	55	38	9	3	3	6	36	0	109	10	1
Fish, Steve, C.R.	10	4	.714	2.47	30	14	3	1	4	0	127.2	111	516	52	35	7	2	4	3	28	0	121	5	1
Jerue, Tristan, Peo.	12	4	.750	2.53	20	20	1	0	0	0	131.2	107	544	48	37	7	4	3	10	48	0	100	4	1
Guttormson, Rick, Clin.	10	7	.588	2.60	30	25	0	0	4	2	159.0	155	673	66	46	9	1	4	12	41	1	141	7	1
Johnson, Craig, W.M.	14	6	.700	2.79	26	26	3	2	0	0	164.2	146	658	66	51	14	2	4	9	22	0	116	4	1
Andrews, Jeff, S.B.	3	8	.273	2.85	20	17	0	0	2	0	123.0	130	524	62	39	4	4	3	2	28	2	68	7	1
Ireland, Eric, Q.C.	14	9	.609	2.88	29	28	6	2	1	0	206.0	172	860	80	66	15	5	4	15	71	2	191	7	3
Webb, Alan, W.M.*	10	7	.588	2.93	27	27	3	2	0	0	172.0	110	690	69	56	9	4	0	18	58	1	202	10	1
Thomas, Brad, Ft.W.*	11	8	.579	2.95	27	26	1	0	1	0	152.1	146	650	68	50	9	4	5	8	45	1	126	12	3
Herndon, Marty, Clin.	10	8	.556	2.99	21	21	3	1	0	0	132.1	119	543	49	44	4	3	6	8	34	0	101	2	0
Harris, Josh, Burl.	10	12	.455	3.05	27	27	6	2	0	0	177.1	166	735	82	60	6	2	6	9	45	0	169	12	1

DEPARTMENTAL LEADERS: W—Thomas, 15; L—Van Wormer, 15; Pct.—Johnston, .800; G—Messman, 63; GS—Ireland, Loux, 28 each; CG—Corey, Harris, Ireland, 6 each; ShO—Corey, Cowsill, Harris, Ireland, Johnson, Webb, 2 each; GF—Stechschulte, 51; Sv.—Stechschulte, 33; IP—Ireland, 206.0; H—Loux, 184; TBF—Ireland, 860; R—S. Norris, 103; ER—S. Norris, 86; HR—Stewart, 22; SH—Curtice, Jensen, J. Thomas, 9 each; SF—Carnes, 8; HB—Webb, 18; BB—S. Norris, 87; IBB—Hecht, 12; SO—Webb, 202; WP—Arnold, 21; BK—W. Rodriguez, 9.

ALL PITCHERS
*Lefthanded pitcher.

Pitcher, Team	W	L	Pct.	ERA	G	GS	CG	ShO	GF	Sv.	IP	H	TBF	R	ER	HR	SH	SF	HB	BB	IBB	SO	WP	Bk.
Abell, Antonio, Peo.	0	0	.000	5.16	16	0	0	0	9	0	22.2	20	107	13	13	1	1	2	3	21	0	15	4	0
Affeldt, Jeremy, Lan.*	0	3	.000	9.53	6	3	0	0	0	0	17.0	27	90	21	18	1	0	1	0	12	0	8	2	0
Akin, Aaron, K.C.	1	4	.200	3.66	12	10	0	0	0	0	51.2	50	228	28	21	3	1	2	5	20	0	41	2	2
Alexander, Jordy, Lan.*	4	2	.667	5.11	21	15	0	0	0	0	91.2	98	400	56	52	11	3	4	6	31	0	69	1	0
Almonte, Hector, K.C.	1	5	.167	3.95	43	0	0	0	41	21	43.1	51	200	22	19	5	1	1	19	0	51	3	2
Altman, Gene, Burl.	6	9	.400	4.49	25	24	1	0	0	0	130.1	129	558	73	65	11	4	2	4	48	0	108	6	2
Anderson, Ryan, Wis.*	6	5	.545	3.23	22	22	0	0	0	0	111.1	86	474	47	40	4	3	3	10	67	0	152	4	3
Andrews, Jeff, S.B.	3	8	.273	2.85	20	17	0	0	2	0	123.0	130	524	62	39	4	4	3	2	28	2	68	7	1
Ankiel, Rich, Peo.*	3	0	1.000	2.06	7	7	0	0	0	0	35.0	15	128	8	8	0	1	1	2	12	0	41	1	0
Appier, Kevin, Lan.	0	0	.000	2.25	1	1	0	0	0	0	4.0	4	17	1	1	0	0	0	2	0	0	5	0	0
Aragon, Angel, Clin.	6	8	.429	4.43	42	7	0	0	14	1	91.1	100	400	57	45	7	3	4	3	36	3	77	8	0
Arias, Rafael, Mich.	7	7	.500	5.09	34	12	0	0	3	1	109.2	130	486	68	62	8	2	7	6	31	0	69	6	0
Arnold, Neal, Peo.	7	15	.318	4.45	27	27	1	0	0	0	155.2	164	680	101	77	8	2	5	15	54	0	113	21	1
Bane, Jaymie, C.R.*	1	2	.333	3.75	19	0	0	0	8	0	24.0	21	105	15	10	1	0	3	12	0	18	2	1
Baston, Stanley, Burl.	0	0	.000	0.00	1	0	0	0	1	0	0.2	0	3	0	0	0	0	0	0	0	0	0	0	0
Bello, Emerson, Wis.	6	3	.667	3.28	43	0	0	0	17	4	82.1	73	355	39	30	1	5	4	8	35	0	78	6	2
Bieniasz, Derek, Wis.	2	1	.667	5.25	5	4	0	0	0	0	24.0	32	109	16	14	3	0	3	2	0	21	1	0
Bloomer, Chris, S.B.	2	6	.250	2.79	34	4	0	0	26	10	42.0	36	179	18	13	3	6	1	0	13	1	46	4	0
Booker, Chris, Rock.	1	2	.333	3.36	44	1	0	0	22	4	64.1	47	287	32	24	2	3	5	4	53	4	78	8	1

Pitcher, Team	W	L	Pct.	ERA	G	GS	CG	ShO	GF	Sv.	IP	H	TBF	R	ER	HR	SH	SF	HB	BB	IBB	SO	WP	Bk.
Borges, Reece, K.C.	1	2	.333	4.71	10	0	0	0	3	0	21.0	24	94	13	11	1	2	0	0	8	1	8	2	1
Brea, Lesli, Wis.	3	4	.429	2.76	49	0	0	0	34	12	58.2	47	260	26	18	1	3	1	2	40	2	86	5	0
Burnett, Allan, K.C.	10	4	.714	1.97	20	20	0	0	0	0	119.0	74	469	27	26	3	2	0	8	45	0	186	6	2
Byrd, Ben, Bel.	3	7	.300	3.79	39	2	0	0	11	1	76.0	83	338	49	32	8	8	0	1	25	2	62	5	0
Calero, Kiko, Lan.	1	0	1.000	3.78	4	4	0	0	0	0	16.2	19	76	7	7	1	0	0	2	7	0	10	1	1
Camp, Shawn, Clin.	3	5	.375	2.62	47	0	0	0	39	13	55.0	48	240	19	16	0	3	3	7	20	4	62	6	1
Carnes, Matt, Ft.W.	8	5	.615	5.37	47	10	1	0	18	5	104.0	119	473	74	62	5	8	8	7	36	5	92	8	1
Carter, Aaron, Lan.	5	4	.556	3.78	43	0	0	0	24	12	78.2	72	346	40	33	5	8	2	3	36	1	89	10	0
Carter, Lance, Lan.	3	1	.750	0.67	15	2	0	0	10	2	40.1	34	158	6	3	0	1	1	0	9	1	37	0	0
Caruso, Joe, Lan.	0	0	.000	27.00	1	0	0	0	1	0	1.0	5	9	3	3	1	0	0	0	1	0	0	0	0
Castillo, Jose, W.M.	0	1	.000	2.44	51	0	0	0	47	28	51.2	42	202	15	14	4	3	0	0	11	3	47	3	1
Cepeda, Wellington, S.B.	4	2	.667	3.88	40	0	0	0	23	2	60.1	66	271	35	26	4	1	1	1	20	1	47	8	0
Cervantes, Chris, S.B.*	2	2	.500	1.34	21	0	0	0	10	2	33.2	29	137	8	5	0	3	2	1	6	1	37	4	0
Childers, Jason, Bel.	8	6	.571	1.92	34	14	1	0	4	0	117.0	104	477	48	25	8	6	2	1	22	2	110	7	2
Childers, Matt, Bel.	3	7	.300	5.10	14	12	3	0	0	0	67.0	89	303	55	38	5	3	2	4	20	0	49	2	0
Chrysler, Clint, Wis.*	0	2	.000	5.33	17	0	0	0	4	1	27.0	33	123	19	16	1	2	1	1	9	1	30	2	0
Cisar, Mark, Mich.	1	1	.500	4.91	6	0	0	0	2	1	7.1	8	37	4	4	0	0	1	0	8	0	4	2	0
Comer, Scott, K.C.*	6	4	.600	2.87	15	14	2	0	1	0	97.1	91	395	42	31	13	1	2	4	9	0	85	0	0
Connors, Greg, Wis.	0	0	.000	45.00	1	0	0	0	1	0	1.0	5	8	5	5	1	0	0	0	1	0	0	0	0
Corey, Mark, Burl.	12	6	.667	2.44	20	20	6	2	0	0	140.0	125	577	55	38	9	3	3	6	36	0	109	10	1
Cosgrove, Mike, Ft.W.	5	0	1.000	1.34	44	0	0	0	30	7	53.2	46	218	11	8	1	0	2	2	11	1	42	2	1
Cowsill, Brendon, C.R.	7	3	.700	2.88	17	12	2	2	5	1	90.2	79	365	35	29	5	1	1	2	29	0	61	4	1
Cronin, Shane, Clin.	0	0	.000	18.00	1	0	0	0	1	0	1.0	4	9	6	2	2	0	1	0	1	0	1	1	0
Curtice, John, Mich.*	6	6	.500	3.37	25	25	1	0	0	0	133.2	96	572	61	50	7	9	5	8	79	0	146	14	3
Darrell, Tommy, C.R.	3	4	.429	4.05	9	9	3	0	0	0	66.2	68	281	35	30	7	0	3	2	17	0	44	7	0
Davies, Bob, Ft.W.	7	8	.467	3.69	34	23	0	0	4	3	127.0	121	558	62	52	6	2	2	8	52	3	114	3	1
Davis, Lance, Burl.*	4	2	.667	1.99	25	4	0	0	5	0	54.1	35	216	17	12	3	5	0	2	29	4	38	6	0
De La Cruz, Ynocencio, S.B.	3	2	.600	4.09	10	10	0	0	0	0	50.2	48	212	29	23	2	3	1	3	12	0	33	3	0
Delaney, Donovan, Lan.	0	4	.000	3.19	25	0	0	0	12	3	36.2	31	172	19	13	2	4	2	2	26	0	47	1	0
Delano, Michael, Rock.*	2	1	.667	5.40	5	5	0	0	0	0	23.1	23	109	17	14	2	0	1	0	17	0	20	4	1
Derenches, Albert, Wis.*	1	2	.333	6.07	17	0	0	0	6	2	29.2	38	139	24	20	1	2	1	1	13	0	29	4	0
Dobson, Dwayne, C.R.	4	7	.364	3.40	23	14	1	1	2	0	100.2	87	412	43	38	9	3	2	6	30	0	67	9	0
Dose, Gary, Ft.W.	1	2	.333	5.50	17	0	0	0	2	1	34.1	42	167	28	21	2	3	1	0	19	1	28	5	0
Douglass, Ryan, Lan.	4	8	.333	6.17	18	18	0	0	0	0	89.0	122	418	80	61	5	3	6	9	33	0	45	8	2
Duarte, Renney, C.R.	3	1	.750	0.56	4	4	2	0	0	0	32.0	17	119	7	2	1	0	0	1	1	0	28	0	0
Duchscherer, Justin, Mich.	7	12	.368	4.79	30	26	0	0	2	0	142.2	166	627	87	76	9	7	3	13	47	3	106	7	1
Fennell, Barry, Rock.*	2	0	1.000	0.64	17	0	0	0	9	6	28.1	14	110	2	2	0	1	0	2	12	0	25	3	0
Fish, Steve, C.R.	10	4	.714	2.47	30	14	3	1	4	0	127.2	111	516	52	35	7	2	4	3	28	0	121	5	1
Fleming, John, S.B.	0	1	.000	8.10	3	2	0	0	0	0	10.0	18	48	10	9	1	0	0	1	1	0	5	1	0
Fox, Chad, Bel.	0	1	.000	4.50	2	1	0	0	0	0	2.0	1	7	1	1	0	1	0	0	0	0	3	0	0
Franks, Lance, Peo.	4	6	.400	2.28	58	0	0	0	23	4	75.0	57	295	23	19	4	4	3	3	20	4	68	5	0
Gagliano, Steve, K.C.	1	1	.500	7.66	8	3	0	0	3	0	22.1	33	109	21	19	2	1	3	1	10	0	17	2	0
Gandy, Josh, Ft.W.*	4	7	.364	4.81	44	11	0	0	5	1	101.0	113	446	59	54	4	3	4	6	33	2	76	1	0
Garland, Jon, Rock.	4	7	.364	5.03	19	19	1	0	0	0	107.1	124	467	69	60	11	1	1	8	45	0	70	5	1
Geis, John, Peo.*	0	2	.000	2.96	23	0	0	0	6	0	27.1	21	115	15	9	2	3	1	1	10	0	21	2	0
Getz, Rod, Burl.	0	1	.000	7.07	13	1	0	0	4	0	14.0	21	80	14	11	2	1	1	6	14	0	15	2	0
Gissell, Chris, Rock.	3	0	1.000	0.80	5	5	0	0	0	0	33.2	27	138	8	3	0	1	1	1	15	0	23	1	0
Giuliano, Joe, Burl.	3	5	.375	3.87	44	1	0	0	10	0	81.1	78	363	41	35	6	1	3	11	35	4	65	9	1
Glauber, Keith, Burl.	0	1	.000	3.86	7	1	0	0	1	0	14.0	13	73	9	6	1	0	0	2	6	0	13	2	0
Goetz, Geoff, K.C.*	1	4	.200	4.64	9	9	0	0	0	0	42.2	44	189	22	22	4	1	1	2	24	1	36	5	0
Gonzales, Rick, Peo.	5	2	.714	3.14	28	0	0	0	4	0	43.0	43	187	16	15	3	5	2	3	14	1	24	2	3
Gonzalez, Edwin, Lan.	8	3	.727	3.40	23	22	0	0	0	0	127.0	120	530	57	48	5	5	3	7	39	0	106	7	1
Gonzalez, Jose, Wis.	7	4	.636	4.52	26	3	0	0	10	0	61.2	68	281	34	31	10	6	0	5	27	3	68	3	1
Good, Andy, S.B.	0	1	.000	3.00	2	0	0	0	1	0	6.0	7	28	4	2	0	0	0	2	1	0	6	0	1
Green, Steve, C.R.	2	6	.250	4.54	18	10	1	0	5	0	83.1	86	356	49	42	9	3	3	3	25	0	61	9	1
Grubbs, Chris, Rock.	0	0	.000	4.50	1	0	0	0	1	0	2.0	3	10	1	1	0	0	0	1	0	0	1	0	0
Gulin, Lindsay, Wis.*	1	3	.250	3.72	13	8	0	0	2	1	48.1	47	207	24	20	5	3	1	3	20	0	51	6	0
Guttormson, Rick, Clin.	10	7	.588	2.60	30	25	0	0	4	2	159.0	155	673	66	46	9	1	4	12	41	1	141	7	1
Guzman, Toribio, Peo.	1	0	1.000	7.16	13	0	0	0	2	0	16.1	20	91	19	13	2	0	1	3	15	0	7	4	1
Hamulack, Tim, Q.C.*	0	2	.000	3.24	52	0	0	0	14	0	58.1	58	253	23	21	3	3	2	3	26	3	52	5	1
Harrell, Scott, Burl.	2	0	1.000	4.02	31	0	0	0	8	0	47.0	34	209	23	21	2	1	0	1	33	0	57	10	0
Harriger, Mark, C.R.	8	4	.667	2.23	16	16	3	1	0	0	117.0	86	472	37	29	3	3	2	4	38	0	105	14	1
Harris, Josh, Burl.	10	12	.455	3.05	27	27	6	2	0	0	177.1	166	735	82	60	6	2	6	9	45	0	169	12	1
Hart, Damien, Burl.*	0	4	.000	3.41	19	2	0	0	8	1	34.1	37	152	27	13	3	2	0	1	15	1	24	5	2
Hawkins, Al, Bel.	6	3	.667	3.58	15	14	1	0	0	0	88.0	94	382	52	35	4	7	2	7	20	0	64	3	1
Hayden, Terry, Mich.*	2	2	.500	7.76	20	0	0	0	5	1	31.1	46	151	29	27	5	2	1	3	10	1	30	1	0
Hecht, Brian, Q.C.	3	6	.333	3.41	61	0	0	0	46	22	74.0	63	318	33	28	3	5	4	6	27	12	56	0	1
Henderson, Scott, K.C.	10	7	.588	2.99	40	1	0	0	19	4	81.1	64	337	29	27	2	4	2	4	27	7	96	2	0
Henriquez, Hector, K.C.*	0	5	.000	5.29	10	8	1	0	1	0	49.1	55	216	36	29	3	7	1	1	20	1	30	4	0
Herndon, Harry, Clin.	10	8	.556	2.99	21	21	3	1	0	0	132.1	119	543	59	44	3	4	5	8	34	0	101	2	0
Hill, Ken, C.R.	0	0	.000	1.23	2	2	0	0	0	0	7.1	7	28	1	1	0	0	0	0	1	0	6	0	0
Hill, Kendall, Ft.W.	5	3	.625	4.35	26	12	0	0	6	1	68.1	65	295	38	33	7	1	2	2	30	0	50	4	1
Hoard, Brent, Ft.W.*	2	1	.667	5.23	15	2	0	0	2	0	31.0	32	141	19	18	0	0	0	0	20	2	37	9	0
Hunter, Germaine, Mich.	2	0	1.000	1.19	22	0	0	0	9	2	30.1	23	120	5	4	0	0	1	0	14	1	31	1	0
Hunter, Johnny, Clin.	0	0	.000	0.00	1	0	0	0	1	0	0.1	0	2	0	0	0	0	0	0	1	0	0	0	0
Hurst, Doug, Burl.	1	2	.333	3.38	7	0	0	0	6	3	10.2	11	43	5	4	1	1	0	2	0	0	10	1	0
Incantalupo, Todd, Bel.*	3	8	.273	5.02	29	13	0	0	5	0	100.1	129	469	69	56	7	5	2	5	47	1	59	3	0
Ireland, Eric, Q.C.	14	9	.609	2.88	29	28	6	2	1	0	206.0	172	860	80	66	15	5	4	15	71	2	191	7	3
Jacobs, Jake, Ft.W.	2	4	.333	6.19	48	0	0	0	11	0	75.2	78	352	64	52	10	4	3	7	39	2	78	14	2
Jensen, Jason, S.B.*	4	11	.267	4.18	28	26	1	0	0	0	153.0	174	684	91	71	8	9	2	6	59	0	115	12	0
Jerue, Tristan, Peo.	12	4	.750	2.53	20	20	1	0	0	0	131.2	107	544	48	37	7	4	3	10	48	0	100	4	1
Johnson, Craig, W.M.	14	6	.700	2.79	26	26	3	2	0	0	164.2	146	658	66	51	14	2	4	9	22	0	116	4	1

Pitcher, Team	W	L	Pct.	ERA	G	GS	CG	ShO	GF	Sv.	IP	H	TBF	R	ER	HR	SH	SF	HB	BB	IBB	SO	WP	Bk.
Johnston, Doug, Bel.	8	2	.800	2.47	14	14	2	1	0	0	91.0	77	379	30	25	6	1	0	7	28	1	71	3	1
Jones, Charlie, S.B.	4	6	.400	4.23	39	5	0	0	9	1	87.1	79	377	52	41	7	1	6	2	36	2	86	17	0
Kaye, Justin, Wis.	6	2	.750	1.71	28	0	0	0	23	9	47.1	25	196	11	9	2	6	0	2	30	4	79	6	0
Kelley, Jason, Rock.	0	0	.000	3.78	9	0	0	0	2	0	16.2	9	71	8	7	0	1	1	0	13	1	14	2	0
Kendall, Phil, Bel.	5	9	.357	4.74	27	27	3	1	0	0	152.0	166	668	94	80	16	3	7	4	54	0	109	15	0
Key, Scott, Lan.	4	9	.308	2.95	38	0	0	0	24	7	91.2	68	386	37	30	4	7	4	8	40	0	74	9	0
Kirby, Scott, Bel.	0	0	.000	0.00	1	0	0	0	1	0	1.0	0	3	0	0	0	0	0	0	0	0	1	0	0
Kirst, Mark, Bel.	3	3	.500	3.48	24	0	0	0	14	2	41.1	38	177	17	16	1	1	1	5	12	1	44	6	0
Knotts, Gary, K.C.	8	8	.500	3.87	27	27	3	0	0	0	158.1	144	686	84	68	11	4	6	11	66	1	148	7	0
Koehler, Russ, Wis.	1	6	.143	4.79	17	10	0	0	2	0	73.1	85	327	45	39	9	0	1	5	23	1	49	5	2
Kramer, Aaron, Clin.	1	0	1.000	2.00	3	2	0	0	0	0	9.0	13	40	4	2	0	1	0	0	2	0	7	0	0
Krawczyk, Jack, Bel.	3	1	.750	4.69	19	3	0	0	5	0	40.1	37	165	23	21	3	2	0	1	11	1	42	0	0
Lanfranco, Otoniel, Peo.	7	1	.875	2.60	11	11	0	0	0	0	72.2	67	296	25	21	4	1	1	1	22	0	51	1	0
Lara, Nelson, Clin.	2	2	.500	6.14	10	4	0	0	2	0	29.1	29	141	23	20	1	1	2	7	23	0	21	4	1
Lawrence, Brian, Clin.	5	3	.625	2.80	12	12	2	0	0	0	80.1	67	323	34	25	5	2	1	4	13	0	79	0	0
Levan, Matt, K.C.*	1	7	.125	6.38	30	9	0	0	7	0	91.2	111	410	72	65	10	4	1	3	36	2	87	2	0
LeBlanc, Eric, Burl.	3	3	.500	3.02	19	6	0	0	5	0	56.2	51	237	25	19	1	1	3	4	20	0	41	6	0
Lidge, Bradley, Q.C.	0	1	.000	3.27	4	4	0	0	0	0	11.0	10	50	5	4	0	0	0	1	5	0	6	1	0
Lima, Cory, K.C.	3	3	.500	4.61	31	7	0	0	9	0	80.0	106	379	56	41	4	1	3	8	29	0	48	7	1
Lohse, Kyle, Rock.	13	8	.619	3.22	28	26	3	1	1	0	170.2	158	712	76	61	8	8	5	11	45	1	121	13	1
Lopez, Javier, S.B.*	2	4	.333	6.55	16	9	0	0	1	0	44.0	60	218	36	32	2	2	3	0	30	0	31	7	0
Loux, Shane, W.M.	7	13	.350	4.64	28	28	2	1	0	0	157.0	184	698	96	81	13	2	4	8	52	0	88	12	2
Love, Farley, Q.C.	4	2	.667	0.90	13	0	0	0	10	3	20.0	6	77	4	2	0	4	0	0	13	4	30	5	2
Lubozynski, Matt, C.R.*	2	0	1.000	2.53	19	0	0	0	6	1	21.1	17	80	10	6	6	0	0	1	5	0	12	0	0
Lynch, Jim, Q.C.	8	6	.571	3.39	20	17	0	0	1	0	101.0	80	438	47	38	4	2	4	13	58	1	97	9	2
Lynch, Ryan, Clin.*	0	2	.000	1.80	17	0	0	0	5	2	20.0	14	86	8	4	1	4	2	2	10	1	28	2	0
Lyons, Jonathan, Mich.	3	4	.429	2.77	41	0	0	0	17	3	65.0	63	294	29	20	2	7	3	7	27	4	57	3	0
Maas, Steve, Lan.	3	3	.500	3.77	43	0	0	0	32	12	71.2	71	318	33	30	5	1	2	3	31	0	59	12	0
Magers, Mathew, Rock.*	2	6	.250	2.60	50	0	0	0	18	5	52.0	57	236	26	15	0	4	1	1	32	2	31	1	1
Maier, Taber, Peo.	0	0	.000	9.00	2	0	0	0	2	0	2.0	2	10	2	2	0	0	0	1	2	0	0	0	0
Malko, Bryan, Ft.W.	8	3	.727	3.98	22	11	0	0	1	0	74.2	72	324	38	33	1	3	1	2	30	0	53	6	0
Mallard, Randi, Burl.	9	3	.750	3.38	14	13	2	0	0	0	82.2	79	356	41	31	3	2	1	1	32	0	71	6	1
Mallette, Brian, Bel.	2	1	.667	3.09	50	0	0	0	44	23	55.1	40	234	23	19	2	1	0	3	29	2	76	2	0
Mallory, Andrew, Rock.	2	7	.222	7.23	33	1	0	0	13	0	61.0	63	298	59	49	5	2	2	8	43	0	44	12	0
Mansavage, Jay, Q.C.	0	0	.000	0.00	1	0	0	0	1	0	1.1	1	6	0	0	0	0	0	0	0	0	1	0	0
Marriott, Mike, K.C.	2	4	.333	3.74	10	10	0	0	0	0	53.0	59	238	31	22	2	2	1	5	18	1	23	3	0
Marshall, Lee, Ft.W.	8	5	.615	5.19	46	12	0	0	9	1	104.0	133	481	74	60	5	1	2	5	33	1	71	9	2
Martines, Jason, S.B.	0	2	.000	3.51	21	0	0	0	16	0	33.1	33	148	16	13	1	0	1	1	15	0	31	4	1
Maynard, Scott, Wis.	0	0	.000	10.13	2	0	0	0	2	0	2.2	5	13	3	3	1	0	0	0	1	0	0	0	0
McCall, Travis, S.B.*	0	4	.000	7.33	15	2	0	0	3	0	27.0	37	126	26	22	1	2	0	2	5	2	21	3	1
McCarter, Jason, Q.C.	5	4	.556	4.61	47	0	0	0	15	4	70.1	59	317	41	36	4	7	2	5	39	5	55	6	0
McClaskey, Tim, K.C.	5	2	.714	4.26	34	2	0	0	18	2	74.0	87	326	45	35	5	4	5	16	3	70	4	0
McCutcheon, Mike, S.B.*	3	3	.500	3.65	13	6	0	0	4	0	49.1	53	214	30	20	2	2	1	0	22	0	32	8	2
McFerrin, Chris, Q.C.	0	2	.000	3.76	29	0	0	0	15	2	38.1	25	186	21	16	2	1	0	4	41	3	35	6	0
McGuire, Brandon, C.R.	0	2	.000	6.75	5	2	0	0	1	0	12.0	18	63	13	9	3	0	0	3	6	0	8	1	0
McLeary, Marty, Mich.	5	7	.417	4.16	37	7	0	0	11	0	88.2	99	396	58	41	4	1	3	5	35	2	54	5	1
Meche, Gil, Wis.	8	7	.533	3.44	26	26	0	0	0	0	149.0	136	643	77	57	9	2	3	5	63	0	168	12	2
Medina, Tomas, Lan.	3	2	.600	7.66	14	0	0	0	8	0	24.2	24	123	22	21	4	0	3	1	26	0	14	4	1
Mendoza, Hatuey, S.B.	0	4	.000	5.25	4	4	0	0	0	0	24.0	29	116	21	14	1	0	1	1	15	0	20	3	1
Mercedes, Carlos, Q.C.	8	12	.400	4.49	31	24	1	0	1	0	148.1	146	649	88	74	14	8	5	10	52	3	99	9	5
Messman, Joe, Q.C.	6	3	.667	3.08	63	0	0	0	16	5	87.2	70	359	36	30	2	2	3	4	33	4	74	9	0
Meyers, Mike, Rock.*	7	5	.583	3.36	17	16	0	0	0	0	85.2	75	363	37	32	3	2	0	3	32	2	86	5	1
Miller, Aaron, Ft.W.*	1	0	1.000	3.34	22	0	0	0	6	0	29.2	20	133	13	11	1	1	1	2	21	1	26	5	0
Miller, Ernie, C.R.*	3	2	.600	3.74	8	8	0	0	0	0	43.1	49	188	24	18	3	3	0	1	9	0	25	2	0
Miller, Matt, Peo.	3	1	.750	5.18	27	2	0	0	8	0	48.2	50	212	35	28	6	1	2	3	15	0	38	1	0
Miller, Matt, W.M.*	7	4	.636	1.52	14	14	3	1	0	0	95.0	59	366	20	16	1	5	0	4	26	0	102	4	1
Miller, Tom, Mich.*	0	0	.000	6.35	11	0	0	0	3	0	17.0	28	78	13	12	2	0	1	0	7	1	10	1	0
Montas, Ricardo, Lan.	0	0	.000	3.38	2	0	0	0	1	0	2.2	1	11	1	1	0	0	0	0	2	0	1	0	0
Moore, Griffin, Lan.	0	0	.000	18.00	1	0	0	0	1	0	1.0	3	6	2	2	0	0	0	0	0	0	1	0	0
Mota, Danny, Ft.W.	4	3	.571	2.25	25	0	0	0	20	7	32.0	24	135	14	8	2	3	0	2	8	1	39	1	1
Myers, Aaron, Bel.	4	5	.444	4.68	11	10	0	0	0	0	57.2	65	258	36	30	3	3	1	5	19	0	41	5	1
Myers, Taylor, Lan.	0	0	.000	3.60	1	1	0	0	0	0	5.0	5	21	3	2	0	0	0	1	0	1	0	0	0
Naff, Todd, Clin.	1	4	.200	4.11	42	4	0	0	12	1	85.1	94	396	53	39	5	1	4	3	55	0	51	12	0
Nakamura, Mike, Ft.W.	2	5	.286	3.26	29	9	0	0	6	1	80.0	82	347	41	29	8	4	3	3	29	0	70	4	2
Needham, Kevin, Burl.	2	5	.286	5.36	9	9	0	0	0	0	42.0	46	186	30	25	2	2	2	2	20	0	22	3	0
Nickle, Douglas, C.R.	8	4	.667	3.78	20	7	1	1	3	0	69.0	66	285	30	29	2	2	3	4	20	0	59	11	0
Noel, Todd, Rock.-K.C.	8	8	.500	4.41	23	21	1	0	0	0	126.2	128	543	70	62	2	4	3	8	54	0	96	12	1
Norris, Ben, S.B.*	1	5	.167	3.32	15	15	0	0	0	0	89.1	98	389	44	33	6	1	5	10	27	0	53	7	0
Norris, Stephen, Peo.*	9	8	.529	5.35	27	26	1	0	0	0	144.2	149	647	103	86	11	4	6	4	87	0	94	9	0
Norton, Jason, Mich.	3	1	.750	1.93	7	7	0	0	0	0	42.0	34	173	14	9	1	1	1	1	12	2	36	3	0
O'Dette, Rick, Mich.*	0	0	.000	9.00	1	1	0	0	0	0	2.0	0	11	2	2	0	0	0	0	6	0	2	1	0
Ohman, William, Rock.*	1	1	.500	4.44	4	4	0	0	0	0	24.1	25	104	13	12	3	2	0	2	7	0	21	1	0
Oiseth, Jon, Clin.*	3	6	.333	5.99	31	5	0	0	13	0	70.2	85	336	55	47	4	2	2	6	45	6	52	10	0
Ortega, Wilbert, Clin.*	4	2	.667	3.95	33	0	0	0	15	1	41.0	37	178	24	18	4	5	2	3	14	0	40	6	3
Palma, Ricardo, Rock.*	7	6	.538	4.46	21	19	0	0	0	0	103.0	114	451	59	51	6	6	3	4	36	0	65	9	1
Pamus, Javier, Lan.	0	2	.000	13.00	7	1	0	0	2	0	9.0	15	47	14	13	0	0	0	0	8	1	0	0	0
Parent, Jerry, Clin.	4	7	.364	5.51	29	8	0	0	8	0	78.1	77	356	54	48	5	4	6	6	47	3	67	8	1
Parker, Brandon, Wis.	7	6	.538	5.22	27	26	0	0	0	0	127.2	121	572	82	74	8	3	4	13	79	1	152	7	4
Partenheimer, Brian, Mich.*	7	5	.583	3.62	60	0	0	0	23	6	82.0	79	344	35	33	5	5	5	8	21	7	61	5	0
Pass, Jeff, S.B.*	0	0	.000	4.50	2	0	0	0	2	0	2.0	1	8	1	1	0	0	1	0	1	0	1	1	0
Pearson, Jason, K.C.*	0	0	.000	3.38	2	0	0	0	2	0	2.2	3	14	3	1	0	0	1	1	1	0	1	0	0
Pederson, Justin, Lan.	13	5	.722	3.45	30	27	0	0	1	0	154.0	132	644	66	59	9	3	5	11	62	0	119	10	2

Pitcher, Team	W	L	Pct.	ERA	G	GS	CG	ShO	GF	Sv.	IP	H	TBF	R	ER	HR	SH	SF	HB	BB	IBB	SO	WP	Bk.
Perozo, Felix, C.R.	0	3	.000	2.52	26	0	0	0	26	16	25.0	16	107	10	7	2	2	2	2	12	1	23	6	0
Perry, Tim, Clin.	1	3	.250	5.06	9	8	0	0	0	0	48.0	50	210	32	27	6	2	0	2	19	0	37	4	0
Persails, Mark, W.M.	11	5	.688	2.83	39	3	0	0	15	2	92.1	75	372	33	29	7	7	1	3	29	0	64	4	0
Peterson, Jay, Burl.	3	8	.273	6.18	16	15	0	0	0	0	62.2	60	296	52	43	7	1	1	6	49	0	62	11	0
Pettyjohn, Adam, W.M.*	4	2	.667	1.97	8	8	1	1	0	0	50.1	46	210	15	11	3	3	0	4	9	0	64	1	0
Pichardo, Carlos, Lan.	0	0	.000	13.50	5	0	0	0	1	0	6.0	11	34	9	9	2	0	1	2	2	0	3	1	0
Piersoll, Christopher, Rock.	2	0	1.000	3.92	27	4	1	0	11	2	59.2	52	251	28	26	8	1	0	4	20	0	55	3	0
Pineiro, Joel, Wis.	8	4	.667	3.19	16	16	1	0	0	0	96.0	92	401	40	34	8	3	2	3	28	1	84	3	1
Polanco, Elvis, Rock.	6	6	.500	5.82	26	7	0	0	6	0	68.0	81	319	50	44	5	3	4	5	40	0	51	6	2
Porter, Aaron, C.R.	0	0	.000	8.80	22	0	0	0	4	0	30.2	40	145	30	30	4	1	1	3	16	0	21	5	0
Priebe, Kevin, Bel.*	1	3	.250	2.15	43	0	0	0	15	2	54.1	43	241	17	13	3	8	0	2	37	4	63	2	0
Puorto, Jamie, S.B.*	3	8	.273	3.68	37	3	0	0	14	1	80.2	99	357	46	33	9	2	0	4	13	1	80	4	1
Putnicki, Billy, K.C.	6	3	.667	3.23	29	0	0	0	17	4	55.2	48	234	23	20	1	5	2	2	16	2	34	9	0
Rahilly, Michael, Mich.	2	0	1.000	8.84	12	1	0	0	2	0	18.1	25	87	18	18	2	1	0	0	9	0	19	4	0
Ramagli, Matt, Lan.	0	1	.000	3.18	3	0	0	0	0	0	5.2	8	29	6	2	0	0	0	0	5	0	2	0	0
Ramirez, Jose, W.M.*	4	5	.444	4.98	22	10	1	0	4	0	72.1	69	315	49	40	5	2	3	2	31	1	60	7	0
Rayborn, Kenny, Mich.	4	2	.667	4.56	17	8	0	0	5	0	49.1	62	217	27	25	5	1	3	1	13	0	34	8	0
Reichert, Dan, Lan.	1	1	.500	3.28	13	6	0	0	1	0	35.2	25	152	16	13	0	1	2	3	20	0	35	4	1
Ricks, Ron, C.R.	1	2	.333	3.00	12	4	0	0	3	0	36.0	34	152	13	12	2	2	0	0	10	0	29	2	1
Ridley, Brian, Q.C.*	0	0	.000	5.14	8	0	0	0	4	0	7.0	6	29	4	4	1	1	0	0	1	0	7	0	0
Riegert, Tim, Peo.*	1	0	1.000	4.34	31	0	0	0	9	0	37.1	31	157	21	18	3	1	2	1	24	0	21	5	1
Rincon, Juan, Ft.W.	6	4	.600	3.83	37	13	0	0	17	6	96.1	84	427	51	41	6	5	1	5	54	1	74	12	0
Rizzo, Nick, K.C.	3	2	.600	2.91	26	0	0	0	10	0	52.2	49	230	31	17	1	2	3	3	22	1	33	3	0
Rodriguez, Hector, C.R.	3	1	.750	2.57	33	0	0	0	14	1	56.0	32	232	23	16	6	4	1	6	31	1	75	8	1
Rodriguez, Jose, Peo.*	2	4	.333	4.58	40	0	0	0	12	0	39.1	47	191	32	20	0	6	1	2	19	1	30	3	0
Rodriguez, Larry, S.B.	0	2	.000	7.36	5	2	0	0	0	0	14.2	25	71	15	12	3	0	2	2	2	0	11	2	0
Rodriguez, Wilfredo, Q.C.*	11	5	.688	3.05	28	27	1	0	0	0	165.0	122	667	70	56	7	6	3	9	62	1	170	8	9
Romo, Greg, W.M.	7	4	.636	2.92	16	16	0	0	0	0	95.2	78	390	42	31	6	1	0	1	25	0	105	3	0
Rooney, Mike, S.B.	4	9	.308	5.20	21	20	1	0	1	0	105.2	122	474	75	61	6	2	7	7	35	0	72	2	1
Rosado, Juan, Bel.*	1	1	.500	3.95	14	2	0	0	3	0	27.1	29	120	14	12	2	0	0	2	11	0	24	3	0
Rosario, Ruben, Peo.	3	3	.500	6.97	12	1	0	0	3	0	20.2	21	108	19	16	2	1	1	1	24	0	24	4	1
Rupp, Michael, Mich.	6	1	.857	5.03	11	11	0	0	0	0	48.1	51	220	28	27	2	0	2	2	30	0	48	3	0
Ryan, Jeremy, Q.C.	1	0	1.000	3.27	3	2	0	0	0	0	11.0	6	42	4	4	3	0	0	0	3	0	8	0	0
Ryan, Pat, Clin.	3	5	.375	8.05	12	12	0	0	0	0	53.2	63	249	51	48	5	4	2	5	24	0	37	0	2
Sanchez, Martin, S.B.	1	0	1.000	8.74	9	0	0	0	8	2	11.1	14	53	11	11	3	1	0	0	3	0	14	2	0
Sanchez, Simon, S.B.	0	0	.000	4.85	3	2	0	0	1	0	13.0	18	59	7	7	2	1	1	0	3	0	8	0	0
Santana, Johan, Q.C.*	0	1	.000	9.45	2	1	0	0	0	0	6.2	14	36	7	7	1	2	0	0	3	0	6	1	0
Santana, Pedro, Mich.	5	3	.625	5.11	15	9	0	0	2	0	61.2	77	279	41	35	3	1	5	3	19	1	39	3	0
Santiago, Derek, K.C.	0	1	.000	24.00	2	1	0	0	0	0	3.0	9	21	9	8	2	0	0	0	1	0	6	3	0
Schmidt, Donnie, Wis.	3	4	.429	4.33	42	0	0	0	19	4	68.2	67	315	39	33	3	6	4	8	33	3	52	6	0
Schroeder, Chad, W.M.	5	3	.625	3.25	35	0	0	0	13	2	63.2	67	272	29	23	4	5	1	1	11	0	51	2	0
Schubmehl, Brian, Bel.	5	5	.500	2.49	50	0	0	0	17	3	72.1	51	295	25	20	4	5	2	2	29	1	79	6	0
Serrano, Wascar, Clin.	9	7	.563	3.22	26	26	0	0	0	0	156.2	150	663	74	56	6	6	4	6	54	1	143	7	0
Shearn, Tom, Q.C.	7	7	.500	2.25	21	21	2	1	0	0	120.0	88	487	38	30	8	4	0	6	52	1	93	3	0
Shepard, David, Burl.	1	4	.200	6.48	29	0	0	0	28	10	33.1	50	171	31	24	5	5	3	4	16	4	40	3	0
Sheredy, Kevin, Peo.	4	4	.500	3.97	13	13	0	0	0	0	68.0	75	304	38	30	6	6	4	4	24	0	39	13	0
Shibilo, Andy, Peo.	1	3	.250	8.51	7	7	0	0	0	0	30.2	42	143	30	29	2	1	4	3	11	0	22	0	0
Shields, Scot, C.R.	6	5	.545	3.65	58	0	0	0	38	7	74.0	62	311	33	30	5	5	2	8	29	0	81	9	1
Simpson, Allan, Wis.	3	5	.375	4.44	19	19	0	0	0	0	93.1	89	420	52	46	5	4	2	7	61	0	86	5	2
Sismondo, Bobby, W.M.*	0	3	.000	2.11	5	5	0	0	0	0	21.1	21	92	9	5	0	1	1	0	9	0	24	0	2
Smith, Brandon, Q.C.	3	1	.750	4.21	8	5	0	0	1	0	36.1	27	148	17	17	7	0	0	3	9	1	29	0	0
Smith, Matt, Lan.*	0	3	.000	3.81	9	3	0	0	3	0	26.0	21	108	12	11	2	1	1	0	14	0	19	2	0
Snyder, Bill, W.M.	3	1	.750	1.82	42	0	0	0	20	2	59.1	40	236	17	12	2	1	1	3	18	2	84	1	0
Solano, Francisco, Lan.	2	1	.667	2.91	4	4	0	0	0	0	21.2	17	93	8	7	2	0	1	1	14	0	16	0	0
Sorzano, Ronnie, Rock.	1	1	.500	5.68	9	0	0	0	6	2	12.2	25	68	11	8	0	0	0	0	8	1	9	2	0
Spiers, Corey, Ft.W.*	2	0	1.000	0.67	5	5	0	0	0	0	27.0	15	103	7	2	0	0	0	0	13	0	20	0	0
Stark, Zac, Wis.*	6	4	.600	4.31	44	2	0	0	10	1	77.1	79	348	43	37	3	5	1	2	37	0	71	8	2
Stechschulte, Gene, Peo.	4	8	.333	2.59	57	0	0	0	51	33	66.0	58	279	26	19	1	5	2	2	21	2	70	2	0
Stewart, Paul, Bel.	8	10	.444	4.90	26	25	1	0	0	0	143.1	164	633	99	78	22	1	4	9	45	1	114	8	0
Stumbo, Wes, Burl.	0	0	.000	3.86	6	0	0	0	1	0	9.1	7	41	7	4	1	1	0	1	5	0	7	3	0
Sullivan, Shane, Rock.	4	3	.571	3.66	41	0	0	0	15	2	71.1	67	306	31	29	6	2	2	4	32	1	56	4	1
Surridge, Lance, Mich.	3	3	.500	2.81	18	8	0	0	5	2	64.0	59	274	26	20	2	2	2	6	27	2	43	4	0
Taglienti, Jeff, Mich.	4	2	.667	1.89	57	0	0	0	49	30	76.1	54	303	19	16	0	3	2	3	17	2	111	3	0
Tank, Travis, Bel.	0	1	.000	4.00	4	1	0	0	2	1	9.0	12	46	6	4	1	0	1	0	4	0	7	1	0
Tejera, Michael, K.C.*	6	1	.857	2.77	10	10	0	0	0	0	55.1	44	218	20	17	3	3	1	2	13	0	47	2	0
Teut, Nate, Rock.*	8	5	.615	3.31	16	16	1	0	0	0	103.1	99	434	49	38	9	1	3	6	23	0	67	3	1
Therneau, Dave, Burl.	2	3	.400	3.86	7	6	0	0	1	0	39.2	36	166	17	17	3	2	0	0	17	0	42	4	0
Thomas, Brad, Ft.W.*	11	8	.579	2.95	27	26	1	0	1	0	152.1	146	650	68	50	9	4	5	8	45	1	126	12	3
Thomas, Joe, Mich.-Ft.W.*	15	8	.652	3.25	26	26	1	1	0	0	166.0	158	697	69	60	8	9	5	12	40	0	131	1	3
Thurman, Corey, Lan.	5	6	.455	3.61	14	11	0	0	2	0	62.1	47	261	31	25	6	0	1	4	30	0	61	10	0
Timm, Dan, Burl.	3	1	.750	5.74	34	1	0	0	15	1	58.0	50	278	43	37	1	1	0	7	47	0	62	19	1
Timmerman, Heath, C.R.	7	13	.350	4.30	27	27	4	1	0	0	161.1	170	708	100	77	20	4	6	7	61	0	132	14	0
Tribe, Byron, Mich.	0	0	.000	5.04	5	5	0	0	0	0	25.0	17	110	15	14	1	0	2	0	15	0	25	0	0
Ulloa, Enmanuel, Wis.	0	0	.000	1.80	3	0	0	0	0	0	5.0	4	20	1	1	0	1	1	0	1	0	5	0	0
Van Wormer, Marc, S.B.	3	15	.167	8.09	34	13	0	0	10	1	89.0	130	455	95	80	6	2	1	7	51	1	66	17	1
Verdugo, Orlando, Clin.	0	0	.000	2.70	6	0	0	0	3	1	10.0	7	41	3	3	1	0	0	0	3	0	20	1	0
Viator, Dustin, Clin.	3	6	.333	5.28	42	6	0	0	18	0	92.0	113	416	67	54	4	2	6	7	33	1	67	6	1
Viegas, Randy, W.M.*	4	1	.800	3.95	52	0	0	0	16	1	54.2	52	243	29	24	3	2	4	5	24	3	61	4	0
Volkman, Keith, C.R.*	3	6	.333	4.92	11	11	1	0	0	0	64.0	66	286	46	35	6	0	3	4	35	0	57	8	3
Wagner, Paul, Bel.	0	1	.000	7.20	1	1	0	0	0	0	5.0	7	21	4	4	0	0	1	1	0	0	3	1	0
Waligora, Tom, Rock.	0	4	.000	4.81	35	0	0	0	28	18	33.2	36	150	22	18	3	1	3	1	14	2	32	6	0
Walker, Kevin, Clin.*	2	0	1.000	1.23	2	2	0	0	0	0	14.2	11	59	2	2	0	0	0	1	7	0	10	2	0

CLASS A Midwest League

Pitcher, Team	W	L	Pct.	ERA	G	GS	CG	ShO	GF	Sv.	IP	H	TBF	R	ER	HR	SH	SF	HB	BB	IBB	SO	WP	Bk.
Wallace, Jim, Q.C.	0	0	.000	15.43	8	1	0	0	3	0	7.0	4	42	12	12	0	0	0	6	13	0	3	5	0
Ward, Monty, Lan.	0	0	.000	12.00	1	0	0	0	0	0	3.0	8	20	4	4	0	0	0	0	3	0	4	1	0
Weaver, Jeff, W.M.	1	0	1.000	1.38	2	2	0	0	0	0	13.0	8	46	3	2	1	1	1	0	0	0	21	1	0
Webb, Alan, W.M.*	10	7	.588	2.93	27	27	3	2	0	0	172.0	110	690	69	56	9	4	0	18	58	1	202	10	1
Wells, Bob, Wis.	0	1	.000	3.00	1	1	0	0	0	0	3.0	4	13	2	1	0	0	0	0	0	0	2	1	0
White, Matt, S.B.	0	0	.000	7.71	3	0	0	0	1	0	7.0	12	34	6	6	1	0	0	0	2	0	6	0	0
Whitesides, Johnny, Burl.	1	7	.125	5.06	18	10	0	0	3	0	58.2	70	277	46	33	4	1	4	2	29	0	42	6	0
Williamson, Jeremy, Lan.*	0	0	.000	8.31	9	0	0	0	5	0	13.0	18	69	12	12	0	1	1	2	12	0	7	3	0
Willis, Craig, Wis.	4	2	.667	2.91	13	0	0	0	5	0	21.2	20	95	13	7	1	2	1	2	8	1	11	3	0
Wilson, Jeff, S.B.*	1	5	.167	2.56	12	4	0	0	6	0	38.2	34	163	17	11	0	2	1	1	13	2	30	6	1
Wilson, Kris, Lan.	10	5	.667	3.53	18	18	1	0	0	0	117.1	119	470	50	46	7	3	3	3	15	0	74	2	0
Wingerd, Josh, Peo.	0	2	.000	7.87	29	5	0	0	6	0	50.1	77	238	50	44	7	0	4	1	7	0	30	6	0
Woodrum, Randy, Burl.*	0	1	0.000	5.33	13	0	0	0	6	0	27.0	25	122	17	16	2	2	1	1	20	0	24	1	0
Woodward, Finley, Peo.	6	5	.545	5.30	34	21	0	0	2	0	137.2	156	616	91	81	13	4	4	11	63	1	88	9	0
Wright, Scott, Burl.	0	1	.000	0.28	27	0	0	0	23	15	32.0	12	119	4	1	1	2	1	1	8	1	38	2	0
Yanz, Eric, Lan.	5	6	.455	5.42	34	4	0	0	11	2	81.1	91	371	57	49	2	4	3	4	39	1	78	12	1
Zamarripa, Mark, W.M.	6	2	.750	2.23	35	1	0	0	12	1	72.2	59	299	19	18	3	6	3	3	34	2	88	2	3
Zapata, Juan, Bel.	1	1	.500	2.61	16	0	0	0	7	0	20.2	13	80	7	6	2	1	1	1	7	1	20	5	0
Zyskowski, Garrett, Q.C.*	5	3	.625	3.67	14	9	0	0	1	0	54.0	45	232	28	22	1	1	2	1	24	1	45	4	0

COMBINATION SHUTOUTS: **Beloit (7)**—Johnston-Childers-Tank, Hawkins-Zapata, Kendall-Zapata-Mallette, Myers-Byrd-Priebe, Stewart-Priebe-Byrd, Krawczyk-Priebe-Schubmehl-Mallette, Childers-Mallette. **Burlington (4)**—Davis-Timm, Harris-Giuliano-Wright. Harris-Shepard, Corey-Giuliano-Shepard. **Cedar Rapids (6)**—Miller-Shields-Rodriguez, Harriger-Perozo, Dobson-Rodriguez, Nickle-Perozo, Cowsill-Shields, Volkman-Rodriguez-Bane-Perozo. **Clinton (6)**—Serrano-Naff-Camp, Guttormson-Lynch, Parent-Camp, Herndon-Camp, Serrano-Camp, Serrano-Naff-Viator. **Fort Wayne (9)**—Thomas-Marshall-Rincon, Spiers-Davies, Gandy-Nakamura-Marshall, Malko-Mota-Nakamura, Rincon-Marshall-Carnes, Davies-Malko-Gandy-Mota, Davies-Malko-Cosgrove, Thomas-Miller, Davies-Carnes-Miller-Cosgrove. **Kane County (11)**—Tejera-Henderson, Tejera-Borges-Almonte, Marriott-Henderson-Almonte, Burnett-Levan-Putnicki, Burnett-Almonte, Lima-Henderson, Knotts-Putnicki-Henderson, Burnett-Putnicki, Noel-Almonte, Burnett-Akin, Burnett-Henderson. **Lansing (9)**—Thurman-Carter-Maas, Gonzalez-Key, Gonzalez-Williamson, Wilson-Key, Douglass-Yanz, Pederson-Reichert-Key, Solano-Key, Yanz-Carter, Thurman-Delaney-Carter. **Michigan (6)**—Rupp-Taglienti, Rupp-Lyons-Taglienti, Norton-McLeary-Partenheimer, Surridge-Cisar-Taglienti, Duchscherer-Taglienti, Arias-Cisar. **Peoria (3)**—Jerue-Franks-Stechschulte, Woodward-Riegert-Franks, Jerue-Rodriguez-Franks-Stechschulte. **Quad City (11)**—Shearn-Love-Hecht, Shearn-Hamulack, Shearn-McCarter-Hamulack-Love, Lynch-Hamulack-Messman-Hecht, Shearn-McFerrin, Rodriguez-McCarter, Lynch-Messman, Shearn-Hamulack-Hecht-Messman-McFerrin, Ryan-Hamulack-Hecht, Zyskowski-Messman-Hamulack-Hecht, Ireland-Hamulack. **Rockford (6)**—Noel-Magers, Teut-Magers, Teut-Sullivan-Magers, Lohse-Magers-Waligora, Meyers-Waligora, Delano-Sullivan-Waligora. **South Bend (5)**—De La Cruz-Cepeda-Bloomer, Jensen-Van Wormer, Jensen-Jones-Cepeda, Lopez-Puorto-Sanchez, Puorto-Cervantes. **West Michigan (7)**—Romo-Snyder-Castillo, Johnson-Persails-Zamarripa, Romo-Viegas-Snyder, Sismondo-Persails-Schroeder-Viegas-Castillo, Webb-Viegas-Castillo, Ramirez-Persails, Johnson-Zamarripa. **Wisconsin (5)**—Pineiro-Stark-Brea, Anderson-Schmidt-Bello, Simpson-Chrysler-Brea-Bello, Anderson-Brea-Kaye, Parker-Derenches.

NO-HIT GAMES: None.

PITCHERS WITH TWO OR MORE TEAMS

Pitcher, Team	W	L	Pct.	ERA	G	GS	CG	ShO	GF	Sv.	IP	H	TBF	R	ER	HR	SH	SF	HB	BB	IBB	SO	WP	Bk.
Noel, Todd, Rock.	6	6	.500	4.03	16	16	1	0	0	0	89.1	83	375	45	40	1	2	2	5	37	0	70	10	1
Noel, Todd, K.C.	2	2	.500	5.30	7	5	0	0	0	0	37.1	45	168	25	22	1	2	1	3	17	0	26	2	0
Thomas, Joe, Mich.*	12	5	.706	3.25	20	20	1	1	0	0	130.1	126	551	52	47	6	6	4	11	36	0	100	1	3
Thomas, Joe, Ft.W.*	3	3	.500	3.28	6	6	0	0	0	0	35.2	32	146	17	13	2	3	1	1	4	0	31	0	0

1998 FIELDING
TEAM

Team	Pct.	G	PO	A	E	TC	DP	PB	Team	Pct.	G	PO	A	E	TC	DP	PB
Michigan	.970	140	3675	1415	160	5250	109	26	Peoria...............	.963	140	3674	1680	203	5557	145	32
Lansing	.968	140	3701	1544	171	5416	132	24	Fort Wayne ...	.962	140	3680	1586	210	5476	103	20
Wisconsin	.968	137	3627	1366	163	5156	98	31	Clinton.............	.962	138	3596	1527	205	5328	134	29
Quad City	.968	139	3670	1527	172	5369	113	15	Burlington	.960	140	3618	1480	212	5310	125	23
Cedar Rapids....	.968	140	3726	1640	178	5544	134	11	Beloit...............	.957	139	3663	1531	234	5428	106	14
West Michigan ..	.967	140	3707	1559	177	5443	125	17	South Bend	.952	140	3585	1619	263	5467	104	22
Kane County......	.966	140	3663	1508	183	5354	108	14	TRIPLE PLAYS: Michigan, Wisconsin.								
Rockford	.965	139	3631	1596	192	5419	135	24									

INDIVIDUAL

FIRST BASEMEN

NOTE: All caps denotes fielding-percentage leader based on 70 games for catchers, 93 for all other non-pitchers and 140 innings for pitchers. *Throws lefthanded.

Player, Team	Pct.	G	PO	A	E	TC	DP
Alevras, Chad, Mich.	.962	20	145	6	6	157	14
Alleyne, Roberto, Q.C.	.984	16	123	4	2	129	6
Allison, Brad, S.B.	1.000	1	2	0	0	2	0
Amrhein, Mike, Rock.	.989	33	236	23	3	262	22
Bautista, Jorge, K.C.	.979	10	84	9	2	95	5
Bautista, Juan, S.B.	1.000	3	10	0	0	10	2
Bevins, Andy, Peo.	.956	9	86	1	4	91	13
Bly, Derrick, Rock.	.980	27	185	8	4	197	25
Bunkley, Antuan, W.M.	.985	125	1113	78	18	1209	102
Caiazzo, Nick, Bel.	.976	36	314	12	8	334	19
Coffee, Gary, Lan.	.983	45	384	22	7	413	38
Connors, Greg, Wis.	.994	26	161	11	1	173	13
Craig, Benny, Burl.	.991	14	114	2	1	117	12
Cronin, Shane, Clin.	.991	112	988	72	10	1070	98
Cust, Jack, S.B.	.975	16	150	9	4	163	8
Delgado, Ariel, C.R.*	.988	128	1265	65	16	1346	114
Dillon, Joe, Lan.	.993	45	416	37	3	456	36
DiPace, Danny, Lan.	.989	12	86	3	1	90	7

Player, Team	Pct.	G	PO	A	E	TC	DP
Duffy, Jim, Q.C.	1.000	3	20	1	0	21	2
Eberwein, Kevin, Clin.	1.000	1	1	0	0	1	1
Gancasz, Michael, Mich.	.988	14	74	7	1	82	6
Gload, Ross, K.C.*	.989	129	1160	69	14	1243	89
Hamilton, Joe, Mich.	.976	21	188	15	5	208	9
Harrison, Jamal, Ft.W.	.982	51	462	36	9	507	33
Hillenbrand, Shea, Mich.	1.000	12	88	5	0	93	5
Hinske, Eric, Rock.	1.000	4	15	0	0	15	0
Hunter, Travis, K.C.	.938	3	14	1	1	16	0
Hyers, Matt, Q.C.	1.000	1	2	0	0	2	0
Jacobsen, Buck, Bel.	1.000	1	4	1	0	5	0
Jacomino, Mandy, W.M.	.971	7	34	0	1	35	2
James, Brandon, Bel.	.989	30	268	12	3	283	18
Jaworowski, Aaron, Ft.W.	.992	41	359	34	3	396	25
Johnson, Duan, Wis.	.983	16	109	8	2	119	14
Jones, Keith, S.B.	.980	10	91	7	2	100	7
Keaveney, Jeff, Mich.	.978	26	205	18	5	228	25
Koerner, Pat, S.B.	.933	4	38	4	3	45	4
Kraus, Jake, Bel.	.984	80	634	42	11	687	42
Lawrence, Tony, Clin.	.952	11	93	6	5	104	9
LIVERZIANI, Claudio, Wis.	.996	94	739	55	5	797	54
Longmire, Marcel, Rock.	.896	5	43	0	5	48	3

Player, Team	Pct.	G	PO	A	E	TC	DP
Longueira, Tony, Lan.	1.000	11	96	6	0	102	13
LoCurto, Gary, Mich.	.988	59	463	30	6	499	32
Martin, Casey, C.R.	.988	18	149	11	2	162	7
Martinez, Tony, S.B.	1.000	14	134	12	0	146	4
Maynard, Scott, Wis.	1.000	4	10	1	0	11	0
McNeal, Aaron, Q.C.	.988	102	850	69	11	930	70
Medina, Luis, Rock.	1.000	6	54	3	0	57	5
Meier, Dan, S.B.*	1.000	22	166	9	0	175	18
Montas, Ricardo, Lan.	.987	23	137	18	2	157	16
Nilsson, Dave, Bel.	1.000	3	23	1	0	24	1
Nykoluk, Kevin, Peo.	.981	17	97	4	2	103	11
Osborne, Mark, S.B.	.984	14	120	5	2	127	7
Pagan, Felix, Ft.W.	.978	5	39	6	1	46	2
Price, Corey, Burl.	1.000	2	1	0	0	1	0
Quaccia, Luke, Peo.	.991	130	1162	97	12	1271	117
Quire, Jeremy, S.B.	.981	6	46	5	1	52	2
Rakers, Jason, Clin.	.973	8	69	3	2	74	6
Rios, Brian, W.M.	.984	17	119	6	2	127	5
Ryan, Mike, Ft.W.	1.000	2	4	1	0	5	0
Salazar, Juan, Rock.	.994	54	419	41	3	463	46
Santiago, Arnold, Rock.	.981	28	234	23	5	262	17
Schaeffer, Jon, Ft.W.	.992	51	437	30	4	471	34
Snellgrove, Clay, Clin.	.983	17	108	5	2	115	8
Sorg, Jay, Burl.	1.000	4	32	1	0	33	2
Steelmon, Wyley, S.B.	.988	62	533	40	7	580	38
Taveras, Jose, S.B.	1.000	2	2	0	0	2	0
Thomas, Jim, Q.C.	.996	31	259	13	1	273	18
Uccello, Jeff, Mich.	1.000	6	26	0	0	26	4
Welsh, Eric, Burl.*	.987	125	1111	66	16	1193	104
Williams, Patrick, Wis.	.978	17	127	6	3	136	5
Willis, Dave, Lan.	1.000	17	109	10	0	119	13
Yedo, Carlos, Rock.*	1.000	8	66	9	0	75	7

TRIPLE PLAYS: Hillenbrand, Liverziani.

SECOND BASEMEN

Player, Team	Pct.	G	PO	A	E	TC	DP
Abreu, Nelson, Rock.	.871	17	18	36	8	62	6
Ahumada, Alejandro, Mich.	.942	26	45	52	6	103	13
Baston, Stanley, Burl.	1.000	2	2	5	0	7	0
Bautista, Juan, S.B.	.968	25	57	63	4	124	18
Borrego, Ramon, Ft.W.	.995	48	81	119	1	201	25
Brewer, Brad, C.R.	.974	9	18	20	1	39	5
Bush, Ron, W.M.	.875	2	5	2	1	8	1
Campbell, Wylie, Burl.	.986	68	112	168	4	284	40
Caruso, Joe, Lan.	.973	47	95	124	6	225	33
Clark, Jermaine, Wis.	.970	116	173	285	14	472	49
Connors, Greg, Wis.	.750	3	4	2	2	8	0
Cuddyer, Mike, Ft.W.	1.000	1	1	0	0	1	0
De Leon, Jorge, Mich.	.961	18	32	42	3	77	9
Eckelman, Alex, Peo.	1.000	4	4	9	0	13	4
Erickson, Matt, K.C.	.976	9	14	26	1	41	4
Figueroa, Luis, Wis.	1.000	1	1	1	0	2	0
Font, Franklin, Rock.	.961	66	142	204	14	360	55
Franco, Raul, K.C.	.973	131	251	356	17	624	66
Gentry, Aaron, Peo.	.974	7	14	23	1	38	7
Gonzalez, Santos, Clin.	.953	73	131	197	16	344	38
Guerrero, Sergio, Bel.	.968	45	107	134	8	249	29
Hyers, Matt, Q.C.	1.000	2	3	10	0	13	2
Jasco, Elinton, Rock.	.857	12	25	29	9	63	6
Kirby, Scott, Bel.	.931	20	50	45	7	102	10
Leggett, Adam, C.R.	.973	123	223	391	17	631	70
Leon, Carlos, Mich.	.965	107	209	254	17	480	55
Longueira, Tony, Lan.	.958	34	77	105	8	190	24
Maier, Taber, Peo.	1.000	10	20	24	0	44	4
Mansavage, Jay, Q.C.	.968	44	74	105	6	185	17
Marino, Larry, Mich.	.667	1	2	0	1	3	1
Martin, Jared, S.B.	1.000	7	8	19	0	27	0
Martinez, Victor, Wis.	1.000	1	0	3	0	3	0
Mathis, Jared, Bel.	1.000	11	17	30	0	47	5
MACRORY, Bob, Peo.	.973	122	279	372	18	669	97
McConnell, Jason, Ft.W.	.940	31	57	85	9	151	10
Medosch, Keith, C.R.	1.000	14	20	30	0	50	8
Metzler, Rod, Lan.	.957	66	146	163	14	323	40
Miles, Aaron, Q.C.	.945	100	200	277	28	505	53
Montgomery, Andre, Burl.	.955	56	98	155	12	265	32
Moreno, Jose, Wis.	1.000	1	1	1	0	2	0
Niles, Drew, K.C.	.500	1	0	1	1	2	0
Orndorff, Dave, Ft.W.	.947	69	131	175	17	323	30
Osilka, Garret, Bel.	.949	68	117	160	15	292	26
Ozarowski, Rich, W.M.	.961	26	52	70	5	127	11
Price, Corey, Burl.	.921	18	31	39	6	76	9
Rexrode, Jackie, S.B.	.943	49	110	137	15	262	28

Player, Team	Pct.	G	PO	A	E	TC	DP
Rios, Brian, W.M.	.933	3	5	9	1	15	2
Santana, Pedro, W.M.	.959	117	205	309	22	536	72
Santonocito, Justin, S.B.	.952	26	50	68	6	124	17
Schrager, Tony, Rock.	.964	50	79	111	7	197	26
Snellgrove, Clay, Clin.	.973	74	148	215	10	373	55
Urquiola, Carlos, S.B.	.923	39	74	81	13	168	18
Valera, Ramon, Wis.	.969	26	38	56	3	97	9

TRIPLE PLAY: Leon.

THIRD BASEMEN

Player, Team	Pct.	G	PO	A	E	TC	DP
Abreu, Nelson, Rock.	.928	30	12	52	5	69	6
Ahumada, Alejandro, Mich.	.932	81	38	153	14	205	8
Baderdeen, Kevin, Burl.	.872	51	35	108	21	164	15
Baston, Stanley, Burl.	.919	15	7	27	3	37	1
Bautista, Jorge, K.C.	.840	11	3	18	4	25	0
Bautista, Juan, S.B.	.938	13	11	50	4	65	4
Betancourt, Oscar, C.R.	.918	88	66	181	22	269	16
BLY, Derrick, Rock.	.945	117	62	245	18	325	19
Bolling, Kirk, S.B.	.844	39	20	72	17	109	4
Borrego, Ramon, Ft.W.	.818	27	13	50	14	77	0
Bush, Ron, W.M.	1.000	1	0	1	0	1	0
Campbell, Wylie, Burl.	.667	3	0	2	1	3	0
Caruso, Joe, Lan.	.930	71	49	123	13	185	8
Connors, Greg, Wis.	.977	23	10	33	1	44	1
Cutshall, Pat, Q.C.	.906	111	75	206	29	310	18
Darr, Ryan, Peo.	.917	12	10	23	3	36	0
Deardorff, Jeff, Bel.	.918	87	56	167	20	243	17
De Leon, Jorge, Mich.	.917	26	17	49	6	72	4
Dillon, Joe, Lan.	.911	13	8	33	4	45	3
Eberwein, Kevin, Clin.	.902	51	41	115	17	173	15
Eckelman, Alex, Peo.	.952	7	2	18	1	21	3
Erickson, Matt, K.C.	.935	102	68	204	19	291	14
Gentry, Aaron, Peo.	.891	77	44	152	24	220	20
Gordon, Brian, S.B.	1.000	1	0	1	0	1	0
Guerrero, Sergio, Bel.	1.000	1	1	1	0	2	0
Habig, Keith, Mich.	1.000	1	1	0	0	1	0
Hargrove, Harvey, Wis.	1.000	6	2	1	0	3	1
Hillenbrand, Shea, Mich.	.500	2	0	1	1	2	0
Hyers, Matt, Q.C.	.889	7	4	12	2	18	2
Johnson, Duan, Wis.	.000	1	0	0	1	1	0
Jones, Keith, S.B.	.876	29	13	65	11	89	3
Kirby, Scott, Bel.	.933	50	33	107	10	150	7
Larson, Brandon, Burl.	1.000	18	10	52	0	62	2
Lawrence, Mike, C.R.	.938	55	37	129	11	177	10
Longueira, Tony, Lan.	.750	6	3	12	5	20	2
Lopez, Jose, S.B.	.833	4	1	9	2	12	0
Lopez, Omar, S.B.	.935	11	5	24	2	31	3
Lopez, Rafael, Wis.	1.000	3	0	4	0	4	0
Maier, Taber, Peo.	.942	58	27	136	10	173	9
Mansavage, Jay, Q.C.	.963	30	12	65	3	80	4
Marino, Larry, Mich.	.974	52	25	86	3	114	8
Martin, Jared, S.B.	1.000	3	3	9	0	12	1
Martinez, Tony, S.B.	.739	6	6	11	6	23	0
Martinez, Victor, Wis.	.889	3	4	4	1	9	2
Mathis, Jared, Bel.	.600	2	1	2	2	5	0
Maynard, Scott, Wis.	.000	1	0	0	1	1	0
McConnell, Jason, Ft.W.	.667	5	2	4	3	9	0
Medina, Luis, Rock.	1.000	4	2	6	0	8	1
Medosch, Keith, C.R.	1.000	2	0	1	0	1	0
Melo, Ramon, Rock.	1.000	2	1	1	0	2	0
Montas, Ricardo, Lan.	1.000	24	17	43	0	60	2
Montgomery, Andre, Burl.	.848	11	9	19	5	33	2
Moreno, Jose, Wis.	.667	4	1	3	2	6	0
Ozarowski, Rich, W.M.	.923	4	1	11	1	13	3
Pagan, Felix, Ft.W.	.909	10	7	23	3	33	3
Price, Corey, Burl.	.907	31	24	54	8	86	8
Rakers, Jason, Clin.	.882	37	13	62	10	85	8
Rios, Brian, W.M.	.933	67	40	127	12	179	9
Ryan, Mike, Ft.W.	.907	109	85	227	32	344	13
Salazar, Juan, Rock.	.833	2	0	5	1	6	0
Santonocito, Justin, S.B.	.971	16	12	22	1	35	1
Santos, Jose, K.C.	.953	27	18	63	4	85	4
Schaeffer, Jon, Ft.W.	1.000	1	0	1	0	1	0
Schesser, Heath, W.M.	.893	76	33	150	22	205	6
Snellgrove, Clay, Clin.	.950	14	10	28	2	40	4
Sorg, Jay, Burl.	.933	15	10	32	3	45	1
Taveras, Jose, S.B.	.847	20	14	47	11	72	3
Thrower, Jason, Clin.	.925	41	29	69	8	106	8
Valera, Ramon, Wis.	.915	34	14	40	5	59	4
Willis, Dave, Lan.	.838	38	23	65	17	105	5

SHORTSTOPS

Player, Team	Pct.	G	PO	A	E	TC	DP
Abreu, Nelson, Rock.	.960	30	48	71	5	124	11
Ahumada, Alejandro, Mich.	.949	15	26	49	4	79	7
Bautista, Juan, S.B.	.912	29	43	92	13	148	9
Bly, Derrick, Rock.	1.000	1	1	1	0	2	0
Borrego, Ramon, Ft.W.	1.000	5	3	9	0	12	1
Brewer, Brad, C.R.	.951	16	20	38	3	61	6
Brock, J.J., S.B.	.929	91	145	302	34	481	45
Bush, Ron, W.M.	.800	1	0	4	1	5	0
Caceres, Wilmy, Burl.	.936	35	40	92	9	141	19
Capista, Aaron, Mich.	.956	126	188	329	24	541	58
Caruso, Joe, Lan.	.333	2	0	1	2	3	0
Cathey, Joe, Q.C.	.947	112	142	327	26	495	52
Connors, Greg, Wis.	1.000	1	0	1	0	1	0
Cuddyer, Mike, Ft.W.	.907	122	200	393	61	654	59
Dawkins, Travis, Burl.	.924	101	149	289	36	474	59
De Leon, Jorge, Mich.	1.000	5	5	16	0	21	3
Eckelman, Alex, Peo.	1.000	5	4	9	0	13	3
Erickson, Matt, K.C.	.944	4	5	12	1	18	3
Figueroa, Luis, Wis.	1.000	1	1	4	0	5	0
Gentry, Aaron, Peo.	.926	11	8	17	2	27	2
Gonzalez, Santos, Clin.	.943	15	22	28	3	53	9
Guillen, Jose, Bel.	.903	42	66	102	18	186	17
Halloran, Matt, Clin.	.931	123	180	335	38	553	66
Hyers, Matt, Q.C.	.968	35	41	81	4	126	13
Lauterhahn, Dan, W.M.	.933	94	120	283	29	432	58
Leon, Carlos, Mich.	1.000	1	1	1	0	2	1
Longueira, Tony, Lan.	.947	39	64	116	10	190	22
Maier, Taber, Peo.	.926	14	15	35	4	54	11
Mansavage, Jay, Q.C.	1.000	5	6	16	0	22	6
Martin, Jared, S.B.	.900	4	5	13	2	20	3
Martinez, Belvani, S.B.	.893	18	20	72	11	103	9
Martinez, Victor, Wis.	1.000	2	2	1	0	3	1
Mathis, Jared, Bel.	1.000	2	1	8	0	9	0
McConnell, Jason, Ft.W.	.882	17	17	50	9	76	5
Medosch, Keith, C.R.	.947	6	6	12	1	19	3
MEDRANO, Steve, Lan.	.969	106	164	328	16	508	67
Melo, Ramon, Rock.	.867	8	21	18	6	45	5
Montgomery, Andre, Burl.	.909	6	9	11	2	22	2
Moreno, Jose, Wis.	.913	76	103	180	27	310	37
Niles, Drew, K.C.	.981	12	15	37	1	53	6
Osilka, Garret, Bel.	.916	62	90	195	26	311	30
Ozarowski, Rich, W.M.	.929	47	59	124	14	197	24
Ozuna, Pablo, Peo.	.929	125	195	395	45	635	80
Polonia, Israel, K.C.	.887	14	14	33	6	53	4
Price, Corey, Burl.	.800	1	0	4	1	5	1
Reynoso, Ismael, K.C.	.934	48	158	158	16	242	25
Rios, Brian, W.M.	.885	8	4	19	3	26	3
Sanchez, Wellington, Bel.	.895	39	51	120	20	191	15
Santonocito, Justin, S.B.	.714	2	0	5	2	7	0
Smith, Jason, Rock.	.939	113	203	379	38	620	78
Snellgrove, Clay, Clin.	1.000	4	3	7	0	10	2
Thoen, E.J., C.R.	.931	127	186	367	41	594	80
Thrower, Jake, Clin.	.900	3	5	4	1	10	0
Valera, Ramon, Wis.	.910	68	99	153	25	277	22
Washington, Kelley, K.C.	.919	64	85	200	25	310	35

TRIPLE PLAYS: Capista, Valera.

OUTFIELDERS

Player, Team	Pct.	G	PO	A	E	TC	DP
Abreu, Nelson, Rock.	.972	20	31	4	1	36	1
Alleyne, Roberto, Q.C.	.980	38	50	0	1	51	0
Arauz, Leobardo, Clin.	1.000	5	7	0	0	7	0
Arguellas, Rudy, C.R.	.970	28	29	3	1	33	0
Baderdeen, Kevin, Burl.	1.000	7	9	0	0	9	0
Beatriz, Ramy, Bel.*	.925	85	141	8	12	161	0
Bevins, Andy, Peo.	.987	94	149	5	2	156	0
Borrego, Ramon, Ft.W.	.986	40	66	6	1	73	1
Burford, Kevin, Clin.*	.942	110	138	7	9	154	0
Burress, Andy, Burl.	.920	120	141	8	13	162	3
Calloway, Ron, S.B.*	.944	58	93	8	6	107	0
Carter, Quincy, Rock.	.935	17	28	1	2	31	1
Child, Casey, C.R.	.973	50	70	3	2	75	2
Colangelo, Mike, C.R.	.933	17	14	0	1	15	0
Cole, Eric, Q.C.	.973	131	207	8	6	221	2
Colon, Jose, Bel.	.939	40	73	4	5	82	2
Connell, Gerald, Rock.	.968	63	86	5	3	94	0
Connors, Greg, Wis.	.971	22	29	5	1	35	1
Craig, Benny, Burl.	.952	20	20	0	1	21	0
Cridland, Mark, Bel.	.931	79	112	10	9	131	1
Delgado, Ariel, C.R.*	1.000	5	5	1	0	6	0
Diaz, Miguel, Peo.	.980	48	96	1	2	99	0
Donaldson, Rhodney, K.C.	.933	84	135	5	10	150	0
Dougherty, Jeb, C.R.	.968	105	172	9	6	187	2
Duffy, Jim, Q.C.	.905	22	18	1	2	21	1
Eady, Gerald, Wis.	.948	76	105	4	6	115	1
Espino, Fernando, Wis.	.921	42	63	7	6	76	1
Feramisco, Derek, Peo.	.978	23	42	3	1	46	0
Fischer, Mark, Mich.	.953	95	177	5	9	191	0
Foster, Quincy, K.C.	.954	132	257	14	13	284	3
Gordon, Brian, S.B.	.975	115	149	8	4	161	0
Graham, Jess, Mich.*	.979	109	170	13	4	187	1
Green, Kevin, W.M.	.982	32	54	2	1	57	0
Grimmett, Ryan, W.M.	.980	112	188	7	4	199	1
Guerrero, Sergio, Bel.	1.000	1	1	0	0	1	0
Guzman, Julio, S.B.	.947	15	16	2	1	19	0
Haas, Danny, Mich.	.922	71	110	8	10	128	1
Habig, Keith, Mich.	1.000	3	2	0	0	2	0
Hamilton, Joe, Mich.	.985	41	62	2	1	65	0
Hargrove, Harvey, Wis.	.961	116	191	8	8	207	3
Haynes, Larry, Wis.	1.000	4	8	0	0	8	0
Hinske, Eric, Rock.	.667	4	4	0	2	6	0
Horsman, Brent, Clin.	.968	61	109	13	4	126	4
Howard, Marcus, Mich.	.980	29	49	1	1	51	0
Hudson, Bert, S.B.	.955	63	77	7	4	88	0
Hunter, Johnny, Clin.	.960	107	176	15	8	199	2
Jacobsen, Buck, Bel.	.967	132	227	9	8	244	1
James, Brandon, Bel.	1.000	23	35	1	0	36	0
Jimenez, Felipe, Rock.	.974	115	211	10	6	227	2
Johnson, Jason, Rock.	.964	52	72	8	3	83	2
Johnson, Rontrez, Mich.	.983	82	175	3	3	181	1
Kim, Dave, Peo.	.934	114	155	15	12	182	0
Kirby, Scott, Bel.	.913	21	21	0	2	23	0
Knight, Marcus, C.R.	.943	32	48	2	3	53	0
LeBron, Juan, Lan.	.960	114	184	10	8	202	1
Lee, Jason, Peo.	.944	112	194	9	12	215	2
Lindsey, Rodney, Clin.-W.M.	.963	84	151	4	6	161	0
LOGAN, Kyle, Q.C.	.993	106	137	5	1	143	2
Longmire, Marcel, Rock.	.974	24	37	0	1	38	0
Lopez, Manny, Ft.W.	.955	110	182	7	9	198	2
Marchiano, Mike, Wis.	.985	103	119	9	2	130	1
Martinez, Tony, S.B.	.889	3	8	0	1	9	0
Mathis, Jared, Bel.	1.000	8	13	2	0	15	0
McConnell, Jason, Ft.W.	.964	36	46	7	2	55	1
McDaniels, Paul, Mich.	1.000	12	22	0	0	22	0
McHenry, Joe, Ft.W.	.957	43	64	2	3	69	1
McKinney, Antonio, W.M.	1.000	5	8	0	0	8	0
Meadows, Tydus, Rock.	.950	33	54	3	3	60	0
Medosch, Keith, C.R.	.947	47	49	5	3	57	0
Melconian, Alex, K.C.	.955	102	121	6	6	133	0
Metzler, Rod, Lan.	.975	22	38	1	1	40	1
Moore, Donnie, Bel.	.953	58	80	2	4	86	0
Mora, Juan, W.M.*	.950	68	108	5	6	119	2
Nunez, Abraham, S.B.	.944	109	226	8	14	248	1
Orndorff, Dave, Ft.W.	1.000	20	20	0	0	20	0
Ortega, Bill, Peo.	.951	50	74	3	4	81	0
Ozarowski, Rich, W.M.	1.000	2	3	0	0	3	0
Pagan, Felix, Ft.W.	.931	30	26	1	2	29	0
Philip-Guide, Sheldon, C.R.	.947	11	18	0	1	19	0
Pitts, Rick, Lan.	.975	78	113	3	3	119	0
Radcliff, Victor, Lan.	.959	60	90	4	4	98	0
Randolph, Jaisen, Rock.	.974	121	222	6	6	234	1
Reed, Brian, K.C.	1.000	2	1	0	0	1	0
Restovich, Mike, Ft.W.	1.000	10	13	1	0	14	0
Rinne, Jim, S.B.	.967	17	27	2	1	30	0
Rios, Fernando, Burl.	.971	117	218	13	7	238	2
Rodriguez, Miguel, S.B.	.936	23	44	0	3	47	0
Rojas, Christian, Burl.	.963	15	24	2	1	27	0
Roneberg, Brett, K.C.*	.955	68	105	1	5	111	0
Rose, Mike, Q.C.	1.000	2	3	0	0	3	0
Ruotsinoja, Jacob, Clin.	.933	82	108	3	8	119	0
Rutherford, Daryl, Clin.	.966	23	26	2	1	29	0
Schaeffer, Jon, Ft.W.	1.000	4	1	0	0	1	0
Schnabel, Matthew, K.C.	.909	14	10	0	1	11	0
Secoda, Joe, Peo.	.750	6	6	0	2	8	0
Silvestre, Juan, Wis.	.949	70	98	13	6	117	2
Smith, Nester, Ft.W.	.979	113	180	5	4	189	0
Steele, Alex, W.M.	.985	122	184	14	3	201	2
Stewart, Paxton, C.R.	.857	6	11	1	2	14	0
Sutton, Bruce, Ft.W.	.957	41	60	6	3	69	3
Sykes, Jamie, S.B.	.943	26	46	4	3	53	1
Taveras, Jose, Lan.	.964	13	27	0	1	28	0
Tidwell, Dave, Burl.	.947	23	35	1	2	38	0
Tolentino, Juan, C.R.	.967	132	228	10	8	246	2

Player, Team	Pct.	G	PO	A	E	TC	DP
Tomlinson, Goef, Lan.*	.980	60	143	2	3	148	0
Torres, Rafael, Lan.	.944	30	32	2	2	36	0
Uccello, Jeff, Mich.	1.000	3	2	1	0	3	0
Vasquez, Alejandro, Q.C.*	1.000	10	9	1	0	10	1
Wesson, Barry, Q.C.	.986	138	271	15	4	290	3
Williams, Micah, Lan.	.979	61	91	2	2	95	0
Willis, Dave, Lan.	.926	14	24	1	2	27	0
Wise, Dewayne, Burl.*	.972	124	233	8	7	248	3
Zapata, Alexis, W.M.	.982	80	107	4	2	113	0

TRIPLE PLAY: Espino.

OUTFIELDERS WITH TWO OR MORE TEAMS

Player, Team	Pct.	G	PO	A	E	TC	DP
Lindsey, Rodney, Clin.	.949	40	72	2	4	78	0
Lindsey, Rodney, W.M.	.976	44	79	2	2	83	0

CATCHERS

Player, Team	Pct.	G	PO	A	E	TC	DP	PB
Alevras, Chad, Mich.	.984	49	331	32	6	369	4	4
Allison, Brad, S.B.	.971	28	180	24	6	210	1	4
Amrhein, Mike, Rock.	.992	72	419	52	4	475	2	9
Brito, Juan, Lan.	.989	63	454	65	6	525	3	8
Caiazzo, Nick, Bel.	.982	37	250	28	5	283	2	6
Chapman, Scott, Q.C.	.981	57	427	38	9	474	5	6
Closser, J.D., S.B.	1.000	3	22	1	0	23	0	2
Connors, Greg, Wis.	.991	29	200	17	2	219	1	2
Diaz, Angel, C.R.	1.000	1	2	0	0	2	0	0
Gancasz, Michael, Mich.	.981	12	50	2	1	53	0	1
Garrick, Matt, C.R.	.977	59	405	71	11	487	4	3
Grubbs, Chris, Rock.	.967	31	184	24	7	215	1	3
Harper, Brandon, K.C.	.983	110	900	72	17	989	8	11
Hill, Jeremy, Lan.	.986	85	554	78	9	641	4	16
Hillenbrand, Shea, Mich.	.981	87	612	58	13	683	5	20
Hunter, Travis, K.C.	1.000	3	13	0	0	13	0	1
Johnson, Patrick, C.R.	.991	44	289	39	3	331	2	7
Lawrence, Tony, Clin.	.987	32	218	17	3	238	2	11
LeCroy, Matt, Ft.W.	.997	51	344	35	1	380	2	6
Lignitz, Jeremiah, W.M.	.990	42	278	27	3	308	1	9
Lisanti, Bob, Rock.	.977	26	199	11	5	215	0	2
Longmire, Marcel, Rock.	.950	4	17	2	1	20	0	3
Lopez, Jose, S.B.	.987	36	272	30	4	306	0	5
Lopez, Rafael, Wis.	.987	30	285	10	4	299	1	9
Maldonado, Carlos, Wis.	.990	7	96	5	1	102	0	0
Mansavage, Jay, Q.C.	1.000	1	0	1	0	1	0	0
Martin, Casey, C.R.	.991	40	295	27	3	325	3	1
Matheny, Mike, Bel.	1.000	1	13	1	0	14	0	0
MAYNARD, Scott, Wis.	.996	77	653	59	3	715	4	16
McAffee, Josh, Clin.	.969	21	139	16	5	160	1	2
McDaniel, Ryan, Clin.	.978	34	153	24	4	181	1	8
Melconian, Alex, K.C.	.993	21	123	19	1	143	1	2
Moon, Brian, Bel.	.978	94	726	113	19	858	15	7
Murray, Doug, Q.C.	.988	20	76	8	1	85	0	3
Newman, Howard, Burl.	1.000	7	48	8	0	56	0	2
Nieves, Wilbert, Clin.	.982	90	665	82	14	761	11	10
Nykoluk, Kevin, Peo.	.983	29	156	15	3	174	1	4
Ochoa, Javier, Q.C.	1.000	5	21	1	0	22	0	0
Osborne, Mark, S.B.	.958	15	79	13	4	96	2	3
Ozarowski, Rich, W.M.	.000	1	0	0	1	1	0	0
Pagnozzi, Tom, Peo.	1.000	3	28	0	0	28	0	1
Pena, Frankie, Ft.W.	.985	44	236	32	4	272	3	7
Quire, Jeremy, S.B.	.996	47	246	34	1	281	2	6
Reese, Nate, K.C.	1.000	9	71	13	0	84	0	0
Rivera, Francisco, Burl.	.983	30	269	27	5	301	4	7
Rivera, Mike, W.M.	.990	106	889	108	10	1007	7	8
Rogue, Francisco, Bel.	.975	11	69	8	2	79	0	1
Rose, Mike, Q.C.	.988	81	565	67	8	640	5	6
Rupert, Bryan, Peo.	.974	73	425	57	13	495	0	11
Salazar, Juan, Rock.	.987	22	129	19	2	150	2	7
Schaeffer, Jon, Ft.W.	.998	57	419	33	1	453	1	5
Serrano, Danny, C.R.	.971	4	32	2	1	35	1	0
Shrum, Allen, Ft.W.	1.000	6	40	4	0	44	0	2
Sorg, Jay, Burl.	1.000	2	10	0	0	10	0	2
Suarez, Marc, Burl.	.980	55	404	44	9	457	1	4
Tegland, Ron, Clin.	.667	2	2	0	1	3	0	0
Uccello, Jeff, Mich.	1.000	9	63	5	0	68	1	1
Viera, Rob, Burl.	.956	25	158	16	8	182	1	5
Williams, Jovany, Peo.	.974	47	301	40	9	350	1	16
Williams, Mike, Burl.	.995	27	186	22	1	209	2	3
Williams, Patrick, Wis.	.962	13	67	9	3	79	1	4

PITCHERS

Player, Team	Pct.	G	PO	A	E	TC	DP
Abell, Antonio, Peo.	.833	16	2	3	1	6	0
Affeldt, Jeremy, Lan.*	.714	6	1	4	2	7	0
Akin, Aaron, K.C.	.917	12	3	8	1	12	0
Alexander, Jordy, Lan.*	1.000	21	5	11	0	16	1
Almonte, Hector, K.C.	1.000	43	1	3	0	4	0
Altman, Gene, Burl.	.943	25	10	23	2	35	1
Anderson, Ryan, Wis.*	.912	22	6	25	3	34	0
Andrews, Jeff, S.B.	.903	20	8	20	3	31	3
Ankiel, Rich, Peo.*	1.000	7	3	9	0	12	0
Appier, Kevin, Lan.	1.000	1	1	0	0	1	0
Aragon, Angel, Clin.	.963	42	12	14	1	27	1
Arias, Rafael, Mich.	1.000	34	7	11	0	18	1
ARNOLD, Neal, Peo.	1.000	27	10	30	0	40	2
Bane, Jaymie, C.R.*	1.000	19	0	8	0	8	0
Bello, Emerson, Wis.	.786	43	1	10	3	14	0
Bieniasz, Derek, Wis.	1.000	5	1	5	0	6	0
Bloomer, Chris, S.B.	.875	34	1	6	1	8	0
Booker, Chris, Rock.	1.000	44	1	7	0	8	1
Borges, Reece, K.C.	1.000	10	3	2	0	5	0
Brea, Lesli, Wis.	.889	49	2	6	1	9	0
Burnett, Allan, K.C.	.900	20	2	16	2	20	1
Byrd, Ben, Bel.	.864	39	1	18	3	22	1
Calero, Kiko, Lan.	1.000	4	1	4	0	5	0
Camp, Shawn, Clin.	1.000	47	4	5	0	9	0
Carnes, Matt, Ft.W.	1.000	47	8	29	0	37	1
Carter, Aaron, Lan.	.857	43	2	4	1	7	0
Carter, Lance, Lan.	.900	15	0	9	1	10	0
Castillo, Jose, W.M.	1.000	51	0	2	0	2	0
Cepeda, Wellington, S.B.	1.000	40	5	8	0	13	0
Cervantes, Chris, S.B.*	1.000	21	2	11	0	13	1
Childers, Jason, Bel.	.806	34	4	21	6	31	1
Childers, Matt, Bel.	1.000	14	4	14	0	18	1
Chrysler, Clint, Wis.*	.875	17	1	6	1	8	0
Cisar, Mark, Mich.	1.000	6	1	0	0	1	0
Comer, Scott, K.C.*	1.000	15	3	11	0	14	1
Corey, Mark, Burl.	.892	20	9	24	4	37	2
Cosgrove, Mike, Ft.W.	1.000	44	4	8	0	12	0
Cowsill, Brendon, C.R.	.962	17	6	19	1	26	3
Curtice, John, Mich.*	.800	25	6	10	4	20	0
Darrell, Tommy, C.R.	.857	9	3	9	2	14	1
Davies, Bob, Ft.W.	1.000	34	13	16	0	29	1
Davis, Lance, Burl.*	.950	25	2	17	1	20	1
De La Cruz, Ynocencio, S.B.	.900	10	3	6	1	10	0
Delaney, Donovan, Lan.	.750	25	1	5	2	8	0
Delano, Michael, Rock.*	1.000	5	0	1	0	1	0
Derenches, Albert, Wis.*	1.000	17	0	8	0	8	0
Dobson, Dwayne, C.R.	1.000	23	8	11	0	19	1
Dose, Gary, Ft.W.	.929	17	3	10	1	14	2
Douglass, Ryan, Lan.	.957	18	10	12	1	23	2
Duarte, Renney, C.R.	.750	4	1	5	2	8	0
Duchscherer, Justin, Mich.	.976	30	7	34	1	42	4
Fennell, Barry, Rock.*	1.000	17	2	9	0	11	0
Fish, Steve, C.R.	.875	30	4	17	3	24	0
Fleming, John, S.B.	1.000	3	1	2	0	3	1
Franks, Lance, Peo.	1.000	58	6	19	0	25	0
Gagliano, Steve, K.C.	1.000	8	0	3	0	3	1
Gandy, Josh, Ft.W.*	1.000	44	7	16	0	23	1
Garland, Jon, Rock.	.966	19	10	18	1	29	0
Geis, John, Peo.*	1.000	23	1	4	0	5	0
Getz, Rod, Burl.	.800	13	1	3	1	5	1
Gissell, Chris, Rock.	1.000	5	2	6	0	8	1
Giuliano, Joe, Burl.	.941	44	4	12	1	17	1
Glauber, Keith, Burl.	1.000	7	1	1	0	2	0
Goetz, Geoff, K.C.*	1.000	9	3	6	0	9	2
Gonzales, Rick, Peo.	.938	28	8	7	1	16	1
Gonzalez, Edwin, Lan.	.929	23	13	26	3	42	2
Gonzalez, Jose, Wis.	.900	26	4	14	2	20	0
Good, Andy, C.R.	.000	2	0	0	1	1	0
Green, Steve, C.R.	1.000	18	2	7	0	9	1
Gulin, Lindsay, Wis.*	.929	13	1	12	1	14	0
Guttormson, Rick, Clin.	.897	30	11	24	4	39	1
Guzman, Toribio, Peo.	.667	13	0	2	1	3	0
Hamulack, Tim, Q.C.*	.846	54	2	9	2	13	1
Harrell, Scott, Burl.	1.000	31	5	5	0	10	0
Harriger, Mark, C.R.	.966	16	6	22	1	29	3
Harris, Josh, Burl.	.909	27	12	38	5	55	3
Hart, Damien, Burl.*	.786	19	2	9	3	14	2
Hawkins, Al, Bel.	.913	15	5	16	2	23	0
Hayden, Terry, Mich.*	1.000	20	1	4	0	5	0
Hecht, Brian, Q.C.	.960	61	4	20	1	25	1
Henderson, Scott, K.C.	.955	40	7	14	1	22	2

Player, Team	Pct.	G	PO	A	E	TC	DP
Henriquez, Hector, K.C.*	.824	10	1	13	3	17	1
Herndon, Harry, Clin.	.959	21	11	36	2	49	1
Hill, Ken, C.R.	1.000	2	1	1	0	2	0
Hill, Kendall, Ft.W.	.750	26	4	5	3	12	0
Hoard, Brent, Ft.W.*	.889	15	2	6	1	9	0
Hunter, Germaine, Mich.	1.000	22	1	7	0	8	1
Incantalupo, Todd, Bel.*	.893	29	7	18	3	28	1
Ireland, Eric, Q.C.	.765	29	11	28	12	51	6
Jacobs, Jake, Ft.W.	.923	48	4	8	1	13	1
Jensen, Jason, S.B.*	.854	28	8	33	7	48	2
Jerue, Tristan, Peo.	.893	20	7	18	3	28	2
Johnson, Craig, W.M.	.953	26	15	26	2	43	2
Johnston, Doug, Bel.	1.000	14	5	12	0	17	0
Jones, Charlie, S.B.	.955	39	7	14	1	22	0
Kaye, Justin, Wis.	1.000	28	1	7	0	8	0
Kelley, Jason, Rock.	.750	9	2	1	1	4	0
Kendall, Phil, Bel.	.946	27	11	24	2	37	2
Key, Scott, Lan.	.842	38	5	11	3	19	0
Kirst, Mark, Bel.	.909	24	4	6	1	11	0
Knotts, Gary, K.C.	.978	27	11	33	1	45	1
Koehler, Russ, Wis.	.882	17	0	15	2	17	0
Kramer, Aaron, Clin.	1.000	3	0	1	0	1	0
Krawczyk, Jack, Bel.	1.000	19	2	7	0	9	1
Lanfranco, Otoniel, Peo.	1.000	11	3	16	0	19	2
Lara, Nelson, K.C.	.667	10	1	1	1	3	0
Lawrence, Brian, Clin.	.920	12	4	19	2	25	0
LeBlanc, Eric, Burl.	1.000	19	3	6	0	9	0
Levan, Matt, K.C.*	.952	30	3	17	1	21	0
Lidge, Bradley, Q.C.	1.000	4	1	3	0	4	0
Lima, Cory, K.C.	.900	31	6	12	2	20	0
Lohse, Kyle, Rock.	.955	28	15	27	2	44	1
Lopez, Javier, S.B.*	1.000	16	2	10	0	12	1
Loux, Shane, W.M.	.971	28	8	25	1	34	2
Love, Farley, Q.C.	.800	13	1	3	1	5	0
Lubozynski, Matt, C.R.*	1.000	19	5	10	0	15	1
Lynch, Jim, Q.C.	.875	20	10	11	3	24	1
Lynch, Ryan, Clin.*	1.000	17	2	2	0	4	0
Lyons, Jonathan, Mich.	1.000	41	5	6	0	11	0
Maas, Steve, Lan.	1.000	43	1	10	0	11	0
Magers, Mathew, Rock.*	.895	50	6	11	2	19	0
Malko, Bryan, Ft.W.	.929	22	5	8	1	14	0
Mallard, Randi, Burl.	.833	14	4	16	4	24	0
Mallette, Brian, Bel.	1.000	50	3	10	0	13	1
Mallory, Andrew, Rock.	.889	33	6	10	2	18	0
Marriott, Mike, K.C.	.818	10	1	8	2	11	0
Marshall, Lee, Ft.W.	.880	46	7	15	3	25	0
Martines, Jason, S.B.	1.000	21	0	2	0	2	0
Maynard, Scott, Wis.	1.000	2	0	1	0	1	0
McCall, Travis, S.B.*	.857	15	2	4	1	7	0
McCarter, Jason, Q.C.	1.000	47	7	7	0	14	0
McClaskey, Tim, K.C.	.938	34	8	7	1	16	0
McCutcheon, Mike, S.B.*	.850	13	5	12	3	20	1
McFerrin, Chris, Q.C.	.714	29	2	3	2	7	0
McGuire, Brandon, C.R.	1.000	5	0	3	0	3	0
McLeary, Marty, Mich.	1.000	37	6	19	0	25	0
Meche, Gil, Wis.	.975	26	11	28	1	40	2
Medina, Tomas, Lan.	1.000	14	2	3	0	5	0
Mendoza, Hatuey, S.B.	.750	4	0	3	1	4	0
Mercedes, Carlos, Q.C.	.929	31	9	30	3	42	1
Messman, Joe, Q.C.	.962	63	10	15	1	26	1
Meyers, Mike, Rock.	.923	17	1	11	1	13	0
Miller, Aaron, Ft.W.*	.900	22	4	5	1	10	0
Miller, Ernie, C.R.*	.875	8	2	12	2	16	0
Miller, Matt L., W.M.*	.941	14	1	15	1	17	0
Miller, Matt D., Peo.	1.000	27	3	3	0	6	0
Miller, Tom, Mich.*	1.000	11	1	1	0	2	0
Mota, Danny, Ft.W.	1.000	25	2	6	0	8	0
Myers, Aaron, Bel.	1.000	11	2	11	0	13	0
Myers, Taylor, Lan.	.500	1	0	1	1	2	0
Naff, Todd, Clin.	.947	42	6	12	1	19	1
Nakamura, Mike, Ft.W.	.882	29	2	13	2	17	0
Needham, Kevin, Burl.*	.867	9	0	13	2	15	1
Nickle, Douglas, C.R.	1.000	20	10	20	0	30	4
Noel, Todd, Rock.-K.C.	1.000	23	8	14	0	22	0
Norris, Ben, S.B.*	.968	15	5	25	1	31	1
Norris, Stephen, Peo.*	.935	27	5	38	3	46	1
Norton, Jason, Mich.	.900	7	3	6	1	10	0
Ohman, William, Rock.*	.857	4	1	5	1	7	1
Oiseth, Jon, Clin.*	.889	31	1	7	1	9	0
Ortega, Wilbert, Clin.*	.800	33	1	7	2	10	1
Palma, Ricardo, Rock.*	.923	21	3	21	2	26	2
Pamus, Javier, Lan.	1.000	7	0	3	0	3	0
Parent, Jerry, Clin.	.750	29	3	9	4	16	0
Parker, Brandon, Wis.	.912	27	7	24	3	34	0
Partenheimer, Brian, Mich.*	1.000	60	5	16	0	21	0
Pederson, Justin, Lan.	.913	30	5	16	2	23	0
Perozo, Felix, C.R.	1.000	26	2	6	0	8	0
Perry, Tim, Clin.	.941	9	5	11	1	17	1
Persails, Mark, W.M.	.923	39	9	15	2	26	3
Peterson, Jay, Burl.	.909	16	4	6	1	11	1
Pettyjohn, Adam, W.M.*	1.000	8	5	9	0	14	0
Piersoll, Christopher, Rock.	.857	27	2	4	1	7	0
Pineiro, Joel, Wis.	.917	16	6	16	2	24	2
Polanco, Elvis, Rock.	1.000	26	4	18	0	22	2
Porter, Aaron, C.R.	1.000	22	1	7	0	8	1
Priebe, Kevin, Bel.*	1.000	43	4	14	0	18	1
Puorto, Jamie, S.B.*	.964	37	5	22	1	28	0
Putnicki, Billy, K.C.	.867	29	3	10	2	15	1
Rahilly, Michael, Mich.	1.000	12	0	1	0	1	0
Ramagli, Matt, Lan.	1.000	3	0	2	0	2	1
Ramirez, Jose, W.M.*	.955	22	4	17	1	22	2
Rayborn, Kenny, Mich.	1.000	17	7	3	0	10	0
Reichert, Dan, Lan.	1.000	13	3	5	0	8	0
Ricks, Ron, C.R.	1.000	12	0	8	0	8	0
Ridley, Brian, Q.C.*	1.000	8	1	0	0	1	0
Riegert, Tim, Peo.*	.833	31	2	8	2	12	0
Rincon, Juan, Ft.W.	1.000	37	11	14	0	25	2
Rizzo, Nick, K.C.	1.000	26	7	9	0	16	2
Rodriguez, Hector, C.R.	.750	33	0	9	3	12	0
Rodriguez, Jose, Peo.*	1.000	40	1	3	0	4	0
Rodriguez, Larry, S.B.	.500	5	1	1	2	4	0
Rodriguez, Wilfredo, Q.C.*	.950	28	9	29	2	40	0
Romo, Greg, W.M.	1.000	16	6	14	0	20	1
Rooney, Mike, S.B.	.840	21	7	14	4	25	0
Rosado, Juan, Bel.*	.857	14	0	6	1	7	0
Rosario, Ruben, Peo.	1.000	12	1	2	0	3	0
Rupp, Michael, Mich.	1.000	11	2	4	0	6	0
Ryan, Jeremy, Q.C.	1.000	3	0	3	0	3	0
Ryan, Pat, Clin.	.857	12	3	9	2	14	1
Sanchez, Martin, S.B.	1.000	9	3	2	0	5	0
Sanchez, Simon, S.B.	1.000	3	2	0	0	2	0
Santana, Johan, Q.C.*	1.000	2	0	3	0	3	0
Santana, Pedro, Mich.	.917	15	3	8	1	12	0
Schmidt, Donnie, Wis.	1.000	42	8	15	0	23	2
Schroeder, Chad, W.M.	1.000	35	4	8	0	12	0
Schubmehl, Brian, Bel.	.941	50	6	10	1	17	1
Serrano, Wascar, Clin.	.930	26	8	32	3	43	0
Shearn, Tom, Q.C.	.958	21	5	18	1	24	1
Shepard, David, Burl.	1.000	29	1	3	0	4	0
Sheredy, Kevin, Peo.	.818	13	8	10	4	22	0
Shibilo, Andy, Peo.	.875	7	3	4	1	8	0
Shields, Scot, Clin.	.955	58	5	16	1	22	2
Simpson, Allan, Wis.	1.000	19	6	15	0	21	2
Sismondo, Bobby, W.M.*	.909	5	0	10	1	11	0
Smith, Brandon, Q.C.	1.000	8	0	4	0	4	1
Smith, Matt, Lan.*	1.000	10	2	3	0	5	0
Snyder, Bill, W.M.	.923	42	4	8	1	13	1
Solano, Francisco, Lan.	.333	4	0	1	2	3	0
Sorzano, Ronnie, Rock.	1.000	9	2	1	0	3	1
Spiers, Corey, Ft.W.*	1.000	5	2	8	0	10	0
Stark, Zac, Wis.*	1.000	44	3	13	0	16	2
Stechschulte, Gene, Peo.	1.000	57	4	8	0	12	1
Stewart, Paul, Bel.	1.000	26	7	16	0	23	1
Stumbo, Wes, Burl.	1.000	6	0	2	0	2	0
Sullivan, Shane, Rock.	1.000	41	4	10	0	14	0
Surridge, Lance, Mich.	1.000	18	4	10	0	14	1
Taglienti, Jeff, Mich.	1.000	57	5	8	0	13	1
Tank, Travis, Bel.	1.000	4	2	0	0	2	0
Tejera, Michael, K.C.*	1.000	10	7	10	0	17	0
Teut, Nate, Rock.*	.944	16	5	12	1	18	2
Therneau, Dave, Burl.	1.000	7	1	6	0	7	0
Thomas, Brad, Ft.W.*	.973	27	5	31	1	37	0
Thomas, Joe, Mich.-Ft.W.*	.919	26	8	26	3	37	1
Thurman, Corey, Lan.	.875	14	3	4	1	8	0
Timm, Dan, Burl.	.824	34	4	10	3	17	0
Timmerman, Heath, C.R.	.926	27	9	16	2	27	2
Tribe, Byron, Mich.	1.000	5	2	4	0	6	0
Ulloa, Enmanuel, Wis.	1.000	3	0	2	0	2	0
Van Wormer, Marc, S.B.	.765	34	4	9	4	17	0
Viator, Dustin, Clin.	.933	42	8	20	2	30	1
Viegas, Randy, W.M.*	.750	52	3	6	3	12	1
Volkman, Keith, C.R.*	.909	11	4	16	2	22	0
Wagner, Paul, Bel.	1.000	1	1	0	0	1	0
Waligora, Tom, Rock.	.889	35	2	6	1	9	0

Player, Team	Pct.	G	PO	A	E	TC	DP
Walker, Kevin, Clin.*	1.000	2	2	8	0	10	2
Wallace, Jim, Q.C.	1.000	8	1	1	0	2	0
Weaver, Jeff, W.M.	1.000	2	0	2	0	2	0
Webb, Alan, W.M.*	1.000	27	11	27	0	38	0
Wells, Bob, Wis.	1.000	1	2	0	0	2	0
White, Matt, S.B.	1.000	3	1	0	0	1	0
Whitesides, Johnny, Burl.	.900	18	4	5	1	10	0
Williamson, Jeremy, Lan.*	1.000	9	2	3	0	5	0
Willis, Craig, Wis.	1.000	13	0	4	0	4	0
Wilson, Jeff, S.B.*	.714	12	0	5	2	7	0
Wilson, Kris, Lan.	1.000	18	10	20	0	30	3
Wingerd, Josh, Peo.	1.000	29	2	6	0	8	0
Woodrum, Randy, Burl.*	.750	13	1	2	1	4	0

Player, Team	Pct.	G	PO	A	E	TC	DP
Woodward, Finley, Peo.	.975	34	12	27	1	40	4
Wright, Scott, Burl.	.833	27	1	4	1	6	0
Yanz, Eric, Lan.	.870	34	10	10	3	23	1
Zamarripa, Mark, W.M.	.900	35	3	15	2	20	2
Zapata, Juan, Bel.	.800	16	1	3	1	5	0
Zyskowski, Garrett, Q.C.*	1.000	14	2	9	0	11	0

PITCHERS WITH TWO OR MORE TEAMS

Player, Team	Pct.	G	PO	A	E	TC	DP
Noel, Todd, Rock.	1.000	16	4	8	0	12	0
Noel, Todd, K.C.	1.000	7	4	6	0	10	0
Thomas, Joe, Mich.*	.897	20	6	20	3	29	1
Thomas, Joe, Ft.W.*	1.000	6	2	6	0	8	0

The following players did not have any fielding statistics at the positions indicated or appeared only as a designated hitter, pinch-hitter, or pinch-runner: Baston, p; Jorge Bautista, of; Juan Bautista, of; Campbell 1b, ss; Caruso, p; Cathey, 3b; Clark, of; Conners, p; Cronin, p; Eckelman, of; Fox, p; Grubbs, p; Hudson, c; J. Bautista, p; Hurst, p; Jacomino, of; Jaha, dh; D. Johnson, c; King, dh; Kirby, p; Liverziani, of; Jose Lopez, of; Maier, p; Mansavage, p; C. Martin, of; Melo, 2b; Miles, 3b, of; Montas, p; G. Moore, p; Nykoluk, 3b; O'Dette, p; Pass, p; Pearson, p; Pichardo, p; Reese, of; Rivas, ph; D. Santiago, p; Verdugo, p; Ward, p.

LEAGUE CHAMPIONS

Year	Team	Pct.
1947—	Belleville	.667
	Belleville	.672
1948—	West Frankfort*	.708
1949—	Centralia	.627
	Paducah (4th)†	.454
1950—	Centralia‡	.675
1951—	Paris§	.700
	Danville (4th)†	.432
1952—	Danville∞	.685
	Decatur (3rd)†	.584
1953—	Decatur*	.576
1954—	Decatur	.587
	Danville (2nd)‡	.528
1955—	Dubuque*	.587
1956—	Paris▲	.656
	Dubuque	.603
1957—	Decatur▲	.683
	Clinton	.623
1958—	Michigan City	.623
	Waterloo◆	.613
1959—	Waterloo	.613
	Waterloo	.613
1960—	Waterloo	.629
	Waterloo	.677
1961—	Waterloo	.613
	Quincy◆	.594
1962—	Dubuque◆	.667
	Waterloo	.625
1963—	Clinton	.710
	Clinton	.629
1964—	Clinton	.667
	Fox Cities◆	.667
1965—	Burlington	.667
	Burlington	.677

Year	Team	Pct.
1966—	Fox Cities◆	.689
	Cedar Rapids	.762
1967—	Wisconsin Rapids	.685
	Appleton◆	.587
1968—	Decatur	.656
	Quad Cities◆	.648
1969—	Appleton	.648
	Appleton	.690
1970—	Quincy◆	.691
	Quad Cities	.581
1971—	Appleton	.642
	Quad Cities■	.548
1972—	Appleton	.598
	Danville■	.584
1973—	Wisconsin Rapids■	.562
	Danville	.537
1974—	Appleton	.593
	Danville■	.517
1975—	Waterloo■	.727
	Quad Cities	.624
1976—	Waterloo■	.600
	Cedar Rapids	.595
1977—	Waterloo	.580
	Burlington■	.511
1978—	Appleton■	.708
	Burlington	.500
1979—	Waterloo	.600
	Quad Cities■	.579
1980—	Waterloo■	.610
	Quad Cities	.532
1981—	Wausau■	.636
	Quad Cities	.570
1982—	Madison	.626
	Appleton▼	.579

Year	Team	Pct.
1983—	Appleton•	.635
	Springfield	.576
1984—	Appleton•	.640
	Springfield	.504
1985—	Kenosha▼	.568
	Peoria	.536
1986—	Springfield	.621
	Waterloo▼	.557
1987—	Springfield	.671
	Kenosha▼	.586
1988—	Cedar Rapids■	.621
	Kenosha	.579
1989—	South Bend■	.644
	Springfield	.541
1990—	Cedar Rapids	.657
	Quad City■	.579
1991—	Clinton■	.583
	Madison	.558
1992—	Quad City	.664
	Cedar Rapids■	.594
1993—	Clinton	.597
	South Bend■	.566
1994—	Rockford	.640
	Cedar Rapids■	.554
1995—	Beloit††	.633
	Michigan	.543
1996—	Wisconsin	.570
	West Michigan††	.558
1997—	Kane County	.507
	Lansing**	.504
1998—	West Michigan††	.593

*Won championship and four-club playoff. †Won four-club playoff. ‡Playoff finals canceled because of bad weather. §Won both halves of split season. ∞Won first half of split season and tied Paris for second-half title. ▲Won first-half title and four-team playoff. ◆Won split season playoff. ■League divided into Northern and Southern divisions and played split season. Playoff winner. ▼League divided into Northern, Central and Southern divisions. Playoff winner. •League divided into Northern, Central and Southern divisions; regular season and playoff winner. ††League divided into Eastern, Central and Western divisions; regular season and playoff winner. **League divided into Eastern, Central and Western divisions, playoff winner. (NOTE—Known as Illinois State League in 1947-48 and Mississippi-Ohio Valley League from 1949 through 1955.)

CLASS A Midwest League

NEW YORK-PENN LEAGUE

LEAGUE OFFICE

President
Bob Julian
Address
1629 Oneida St.
Utica, NY 13501
Phone
315-733-8036

Teams (affiliation)
Auburn Doubledays (Astros)
Batavia Muck Dogs (Phillies)
Hudson Valley Renegades (Devil Rays)
Jamestown Jammers (Braves)
Lowell Spinners (Red Sox)
Mahoning Valley Scrappers (Indians)
New Jersey Cardinals (Cardinals)

Oneonta Tigers (Tigers)
Pittsfield Mets (Mets)
St. Catharines Stompers (Blue Jays)
Utica Blue Sox (Marlins)
Vermont Expos (Expos)
Watertown Yankees (Yankees)
Williamsport Crosscutters (Pirates)

1998 FINAL STANDINGS

McNAMARA DIVISION

Team	W	L	T	Pct.	GB
Hudson Valley (Devil Rays)	50	26	0	.658	....
Vermont (Expos)	36	40	0	.474	14.0
Pittsfield (Mets)	35	41	0	.461	15.0
New Jersey (Cardinals)	34	41	0	.453	15.5
Lowell (Red Sox)	32	44	0	.421	18.0

PINCKNEY DIVISION

Team	W	L	T	Pct.	GB
Oneonta (Yankees)	45	31	0	.592	....
Auburn (Astros)	43	32	0	.573	1.5
Watertown (Indians)	42	34	0	.553	3.0
Williamsport (Cubs)	39	36	0	.520	5.5
Utica (Marlins)	35	41	0	.461	10.0

STEDLER DIVISION

Team	W	L	T	Pct.	GB
Batavia (Phillies)	43	33	0	.566	....
St. Catharines (Blue Jays)	38	38	0	.500	5.0
Jamestown (Tigers)	32	43	0	.427	10.5
Erie (Pirates)	26	50	0	.342	17.0

COMPOSITE

Team	H.V.	One.	Aub.	Bat.	Wat.	Wpt.	StC	Ver.	Uti.	Pit.	N.J.	Jam.	Low.	Erie	W	L	T	Pct.	GB
Hudson Valley (Devil Rays)	....	1	0	4	1	1	0	9	3	11	8	2	7	3	50	26	0	.658	....
Oneonta (Yankees)	1	....	7	3	6	4	6	1	8	1	2	2	1	3	45	31	0	.592	5.0
Auburn (Astros)	2	7	....	1	6	6	2	0	7	2	1	3	4	2	43	32	0	.573	6.5
Batavia (Phillies)	0	1	3	....	2	2	10	4	2	2	2	4	2	9	43	33	0	.566	7.0
Watertown (Indians)	1	6	4	2	....	9	2	3	7	2	1	2	1	2	42	34	0	.553	8.0
Williamsport (Cubs)	1	6	5	2	5	....	1	1	8	1	2	2	0	5	39	36	0	.520	10.5
St. Catharines (Blue Jays)	2	0	2	2	2	1	....	3	1	5	2	9	2	7	38	38	0	.500	12.0
Vermont (Expos)	3	1	2	2	1	1	3	....	0	6	6	2	7	2	36	40	0	.474	14.0
Utica (Marlins)	3	4	5	2	5	4	1	2	....	1	0	4	2	2	35	41	0	.461	15.0
Pittsfield (Mets)	1	1	0	2	0	1	1	6	1	....	8	3	8	3	35	41	0	.461	15.0
New Jersey (Cardinals)	4	0	1	0	1	2	2	6	2	4	....	4	8	8	34	41	0	.453	15.5
Jamestown (Tigers)	0	0	1	8	2	2	3	0	2	1	3	....	1	9	32	43	0	.427	17.5
Lowell (Red Sox)	5	1	0	2	1	2	2	5	0	4	4	3	....	3	32	44	0	.421	18.0
Erie (Pirates)	3	3	2	3	2	1	5	0	0	1	2	3	1	....	26	50	0	.342	24.0

Major league affiliations in parentheses.

Hudson Valley home games played in Fishkill, N.Y.; New Jersey home games played in Augusta, N.J.; Vermont home games played in Winooski, Vt.

PLAYOFFS: Auburn defeated Batavia two games to one; Oneonta defeated Hudson Valley two games to none; Auburn and Oneonta named co-New York-Penn League champions due to series being rained out.

REGULAR-SEASON ATTENDANCE: Auburn, 52,597; Batavia, 42,908; Erie, 187,743; Hudson Valley, 158,202; Jamestown, 60,481; Lowell, 174,020; New Jersey, 153,445; Oneonta, 57,200; Pittsfield, 84,323; St. Catharines, 55,787; Utica, 58,902; Vermont, 105,064; Watertown, 28,103; Williamsport, 60,718. Total—1,279,493. Playoffs (5 games)—7,300.

MANAGERS: Auburn, Lyle Yates: Batavia, Frank Klebe; Erie, Tracy Woodson; Hudson Valley, Charlie Montoyo; Jamestown, Tim Torricelli; Lowell, Dick Berardino; New Jersey, Jose Oquendo, Oneonta, Joe Arnold; Pittsfield, Roger Lafrancois; St. Catharines, Duane Larson; Utica, Ken Joyce; Vermont, Tony Barbone; Watertown, Ted Kubiak; Williamsport, Bob Ralston.

ALL-STAR TEAM: 1B—Eric Hinske, Williamsport; 2B—Keith Ginter, Auburn; 3B—(tie) Brooks Badeaux, Hudson Valley and Jared Sandberg, Hudson Valley; SS—Zach Sorensen, Watertown; Reserve INF—Rico Washington, Erie; OF—Christopher Connally, Williamsport; Sean Mahoney, Hudson Valley; Christian Rojas, Watertown; Angel Mendoza, Lowell; C—Paul Hoover, Hudson Valley; Matt Frick, Pittsfield; Kelly Ramos, Pittsfield; RHP—Geoff Geary, Batavia; Chris Reinike, Watertown; LHP—Brody Percell, Watertown; Darwin Peguero, Auburn; Adam Flohr, Hudson Valley; DH—Shayne Carnes, Batavia; Most Valuable Player—Brian August, Oneonta; Executive of the Year—Rob Fowler, Utica.

1998 BATTING

TEAM

Team	Avg.	G	TPA	AB	R	H	TB	2B	3B	HR	RBI	SH	SF	HP	BB	IBB	SO	SB	CS	GDP	LOB	ShO	Slg.	OBP
Hudson Valley	.273	76	3088	2683	452	732	1038	127	28	41	390	27	27	46	305	12	557	117	43	45	600	3	.387	.354
Oneonta	.268	76	2915	2563	417	687	968	121	35	30	366	11	19	34	288	2	580	85	35	49	551	5	.378	.347
Auburn	.267	75	2854	2468	414	659	991	150	22	46	367	11	28	46	301	8	591	101	50	45	518	3	.402	.354
St. Catharines	.255	76	2941	2564	389	655	994	134	20	55	336	21	19	42	295	5	631	86	37	33	565	4	.388	.340
Watertown	.254	76	2892	2495	395	634	961	132	27	47	342	10	22	36	329	14	546	103	43	40	550	2	.385	.347
Pittsfield	.251	76	2895	2629	364	659	972	113	28	48	317	16	21	30	199	6	600	97	35	34	505	5	.370	.308
Erie	.250	76	2971	2671	363	669	988	125	16	54	306	10	19	41	230	7	682	59	31	50	554	5	.370	.317
Williamsport	.250	75	2760	2433	359	609	883	118	24	36	318	16	25	51	235	6	549	111	45	39	479	4	.363	.326

Team	Avg.	G	TPA	AB	R	H	TB	2B	3B	HR	RBI	SH	SF	HP	BB	IBB	SO	SB	CS	GDP	LOB	ShO	Slg.	OBP
Vermont	.250	76	2810	2484	337	620	804	109	18	13	281	23	23	33	247	7	581	77	71	40	506	4	.324	.323
Batavia	.249	76	2902	2528	387	629	918	125	16	44	335	7	15	47	305	7	678	65	35	57	549	6	.363	.339
Utica	.245	76	2709	2424	325	594	825	99	15	34	278	21	9	32	223	8	607	65	44	49	466	7	.340	.316
Lowell	.244	76	2886	2570	330	628	941	146	19	43	288	32	15	48	221	0	641	36	14	54	548	6	.366	.314
Jamestown	.241	75	2867	2557	354	617	915	99	35	43	299	13	18	35	244	6	595	93	36	58	515	4	.358	.314
New Jersey	.231	75	2785	2443	309	565	765	91	20	23	263	28	26	52	236	4	631	137	49	42	495	9	.313	.309

INDIVIDUAL

TOP QUALIFIERS FOR BATTING CHAMPIONSHIP

Minimum 205 plate appearances. *Lefthanded batter. †Switch-hitter.

Player, Team	Avg.	G	TPA	AB	R	H	TB	2B	3B	HR	RBI	SH	SF	HP	BB	IBB	SO	SB	CS	GDP	Slg.	OBP
Pratt, Scott, Wat.*	.351	47	215	174	37	61	85	12	3	2	14	1	1	5	34	1	26	15	10	4	.489	.467
Mahoney, Sean, H.V.	.347	65	290	248	44	86	121	16	2	5	53	0	6	5	31	3	47	11	5	4	.488	.421
Carter, Charley, Aub.	.330	61	246	218	32	72	122	24	1	8	42	1	4	1	22	1	35	1	1	5	.560	.388
Washington, Rico, Erie*	.330	51	221	197	31	65	101	14	2	6	31	0	0	7	17	2	33	1	2	4	.513	.403
Carnes, M. Shayne, Bat.*	.329	66	271	237	52	78	111	15	0	6	38	0	1	4	29	1	48	3	0	7	.468	.410
August, Brian, One.	.318	70	285	242	48	77	124	22	2	7	67	1	2	5	35	1	38	5	2	4	.512	.412
Ginter, Keith, Aub.	.315	71	310	241	55	76	124	22	1	8	41	0	2	7	60	0	68	10	7	1	.515	.461
Brett, Jason, Pit.	.315	53	209	184	40	58	62	4	0	0	14	7	1	6	11	0	34	18	3	2	.337	.371
Darjean, John, One.	.314	64	249	226	43	71	94	9	4	2	23	4	0	1	18	0	42	16	5	1	.416	.367
Estevez, Domingo, St.C.†	.306	56	235	209	40	64	113	16	6	7	33	2	1	4	19	0	26	12	7	4	.541	.373
Butler, Garrett, H.V.†	.304	68	312	280	47	85	109	14	2	2	44	6	2	1	23	0	48	21	8	1	.389	.356
Goodson, Steven, H.V.*	.303	62	261	234	45	71	103	15	4	3	32	0	0	1	26	2	57	3	3	3	.440	.375
Sorensen, Zach, Wat.†	.300	53	237	200	38	60	95	7	8	4	26	2	0	0	35	0	35	14	4	2	.475	.404
Badeaux, Brooks, H.V.†	.300	68	308	267	48	80	100	9	4	1	36	7	2	3	29	0	47	11	4	4	.375	.372
Dina, Allen, Pit.	.299	68	308	278	47	83	124	16	5	5	39	1	4	1	24	0	34	18	5	1	.446	.352

DEPARTMENTAL LEADERS: G—Carek, Urquhart, 76 each; AB—Moreno, 286; R—Duncan, Ginter, 55 each; H—Mahoney, 86; TB—Sandberg, 133; 2B—C. Carter, 24; 3B—Sorensen, 8; HR—C. Rojas, Sandberg, 12 each; RBI—August, 67; SH—Badeaux, Brett, 7 each; SF—Frese, 7; HP—Freeman, 14; BB—Ginter, 60; IBB—Maraga, 5; SO—Duncan, 101; SB—Snead, 42; CS—Machado, 13; GIDP—Maxwell, 10; Slg.—C. Carter, .560; OBP—Pratt, .467.

ALL PLAYERS

*Lefthanded batter. †Switch-hitter.

Player, Team	Avg.	G	TPA	AB	R	H	TB	2B	3B	HR	RBI	SH	SF	HP	BB	IBB	SO	SB	CS	GDP	Slg.	OBP
Abreu, Miguel, Uti.	.176	58	134	125	13	22	27	2	0	1	9	2	0	1	6	0	44	1	1	1	.216	.220
Adams, Lawrence, St.C.	.000	3	8	8	0	0	0	0	0	0	0	0	0	0	0	0	6	0	0	1	.000	.000
Adeeb, Josh, Low.	.250	3	8	8	1	2	2	0	0	0	0	0	0	0	0	0	2	0	0	1	.250	.250
Adorno, Wilson, Erie†	.182	5	12	11	1	2	3	1	0	0	0	0	0	0	1	0	2	0	0	0	.273	.250
Alfonso, Eliezer, N.J.	.246	48	187	175	16	43	55	4	1	2	19	1	3	2	6	0	49	1	0	5	.314	.274
Anderson, Franklin, Erie	.146	19	50	48	3	7	10	3	0	0	2	0	0	0	2	0	17	1	0	0	.208	.180
Araujo, Danilo, N.J.	.212	32	101	85	18	18	21	1	1	0	9	2	1	0	13	0	24	21	4	0	.247	.313
Araujo, Victor, Erie	.238	17	65	63	9	15	23	2	0	2	9	0	0	1	1	0	18	1	0	0	.365	.262
August, Brian, One.	.318	70	285	242	48	77	124	22	2	7	67	1	2	5	35	1	38	5	2	4	.512	.412
Backe, Brandon, H.V.	.231	11	29	26	3	6	8	2	0	0	1	0	0	1	2	0	7	0	0	0	.308	.310
Badeaux, Brooks, H.V.†	.300	68	308	267	48	80	100	9	4	1	36	7	2	3	29	0	47	11	4	4	.375	.372
Barnett, Brian, St.C.	.296	48	169	152	22	45	63	8	2	2	16	1	1	0	15	0	41	4	1	0	.414	.357
Bautista, Rayner, Jam.	.207	60	243	222	27	46	65	5	4	2	15	1	0	2	18	1	67	11	2	4	.293	.273
Bender, Heath, Wat.*	.114	10	37	35	1	4	4	0	0	0	1	1	0	0	1	0	9	0	0	0	.114	.139
Benham, David, Low.	.275	41	142	131	17	36	54	12	0	2	6	1	0	3	7	0	23	1	0	4	.412	.326
Bernhardt, Jossephang, St.C.	.182	59	201	181	18	33	52	11	1	2	19	1	2	0	17	1	61	0	0	4	.287	.250
Besco, Derek, Jam.	.235	49	205	183	27	43	72	9	1	6	18	0	2	2	17	0	30	11	3	6	.393	.304
Beverly, Demetrius, Bat.	.256	29	95	82	8	21	32	8	0	1	13	0	0	2	11	0	34	0	0	4	.390	.358
Beverly, Shomari, Bat.	.207	9	30	29	2	6	7	1	0	0	1	0	0	0	1	0	9	0	1	0	.241	.233
Boles, Kevin, Wil.*	.206	20	35	34	2	7	8	1	0	0	3	0	0	1	1	0	11	0	0	1	.235	.229
Bone, Billy, Erie	.345	21	72	58	14	20	28	2	0	2	11	0	2	1	11	0	12	2	1	2	.483	.444
Bonilla, Elin, Bat.	.181	35	83	72	7	13	17	2	1	0	9	1	1	0	9	0	21	0	0	2	.236	.268
Boone, Matt, Jam.	.303	9	35	33	8	10	19	2	2	1	11	0	0	0	2	1	3	0	0	0	.576	.343
Bowring, Jason, Pit.	.228	55	205	180	23	41	74	15	0	6	30	2	2	3	18	1	43	4	1	0	.411	.305
Brett, Jason, Pit.	.315	53	209	184	40	58	62	4	0	0	14	7	1	6	11	0	34	18	3	2	.337	.371
Brown, Billy, St.C.	.275	72	328	280	41	77	104	12	3	3	34	2	2	5	39	0	51	27	12	2	.371	.371
Buckley, Brandon, Aub.	.224	26	89	76	5	17	21	4	0	0	9	0	0	0	12	0	13	0	1	2	.276	.330
Bundy, Ryan, St.C.	.196	47	169	148	20	29	59	6	3	6	16	0	1	7	13	0	55	2	2	1	.399	.290
Burkhart, Lance, Ver.	.295	16	60	44	13	13	19	4	1	0	5	1	1	1	13	0	13	0	0	0	.432	.458
Bush, Ron, Jam.	.290	53	214	200	23	58	83	9	2	4	23	2	0	1	11	0	31	4	2	4	.415	.330
Butler, Garrett, H.V.†	.304	68	312	280	47	85	109	14	2	2	44	6	2	1	23	0	48	21	8	1	.389	.356
Byrd, Brandon, Aub.	.207	32	131	121	12	25	36	2	0	3	12	0	3	1	5	0	50	0	0	4	.298	.238
Candelaria, Tito, One.*	.306	23	40	36	6	11	13	0	1	0	7	0	0	0	4	0	7	0	0	2	.361	.375
Carek, Mark, One.	.246	76	296	260	30	64	77	8	1	1	24	2	0	4	30	0	60	2	2	3	.296	.333
Carnes, M. Shayne, Bat.*	.329	66	271	237	52	78	111	15	0	6	38	0	1	4	29	1	48	3	0	7	.468	.410
Carter, Charley, Aub.	.330	61	246	218	32	72	122	24	1	8	42	1	4	1	22	1	35	1	1	5	.560	.388
Carter, Shannon, St.C.*	.262	24	67	61	8	16	22	3	0	1	7	1	0	1	4	0	14	2	0	1	.361	.318
Casillas, Uriel, Bat.	.224	60	265	219	37	49	70	9	0	4	31	3	4	7	32	0	47	3	2	4	.320	.336
Castri, Andrea, One.	.290	49	155	138	27	40	52	4	1	2	21	0	3	6	8	0	43	11	0	4	.377	.348
Chambliss, Russ, One.*	.080	29	27	25	4	2	2	0	0	0	0	0	2	0	1	0	12	1	1	1	.080	.111
Champagne, Andre, Pit.	.200	5	13	10	1	2	5	0	0	0	1	0	0	2	1	1	2	0	1	0	.500	.308
Clark, Greg, N.J.	.176	51	187	170	15	30	39	3	0	2	14	0	1	1	15	0	46	1	0	7	.229	.246
Cleto, Ambioris, Erie	.192	49	191	167	26	32	36	4	0	0	10	2	0	5	17	0	49	4	2	4	.216	.286
Cole, Brian, Pit.	.250	2	8	8	0	2	3	1	0	0	1	0	0	0	0	0	1	1	0	0	.375	.250
Connally, Christopher, Wil.	.298	56	231	198	38	59	107	13	4	9	43	1	2	5	25	1	37	5	3	3	.540	.387
Cotten, Jeremy, Erie	.153	22	80	72	5	11	20	3	0	2	5	0	0	0	8	0	30	0	0	3	.278	.238

Player, Team	Avg.	G	TPA	AB	R	H	TB	2B	3B	HR	RBI	SH	SF	HP	BB	IBB	SO	SB	CS	GDP	Slg.	OBP
Cronk, Brian, Erie†	.143	3	10	7	1	1	1	0	0	0	1	1	0	1	1	0	2	1	0	0	.143	.333
Cruz, Luis, H.V.	.222	63	258	230	36	51	82	4	3	7	32	6	1	2	19	1	46	4	5	7	.357	.286
Daggett, Jesse, Erie	.248	48	188	165	18	41	59	10	1	2	15	0	1	2	20	1	31	4	0	5	.358	.335
Da Luz, Craig, Jam.	.258	47	175	159	27	41	65	6	3	4	19	3	1	7	5	0	29	6	4	6	.409	.308
Dampeer, Kelly, Wat.	.277	68	269	235	33	65	83	11	2	1	25	1	3	4	26	1	49	11	8	4	.353	.354
Darjean, John, One.	.314	64	249	226	43	71	94	9	4	2	23	4	0	1	18	0	42	16	5	1	.416	.367
Davis, J.J., Erie	.270	52	220	196	25	53	93	12	2	8	39	0	2	2	20	1	54	4	1	3	.474	.341
Deitrick, Jeremy, Bat.	.132	16	62	53	6	7	13	1	1	1	7	0	1	1	6	2	16	0	2	0	.245	.230
De La Cruz, Henry, Wil.	.272	66	255	224	36	61	86	8	4	3	26	0	1	7	23	0	90	16	9	2	.384	.357
DeNure, Chip, Bat.	.242	48	169	157	13	38	55	6	1	3	22	2	1	5	4	0	39	6	2	5	.350	.281
Deshazer, Jeremy, Aub.†	.200	9	21	20	2	4	5	1	0	0	1	0	0	1	0	0	6	0	0	0	.250	.238
Diaz, Diogenes, Erie	.267	39	148	131	15	35	50	6	0	3	14	0	2	1	14	0	35	1	0	3	.382	.338
Dimmick, Josh, Aub.†	.275	13	45	40	5	11	15	4	0	0	6	1	0	0	3	0	8	0	0	1	.375	.326
Dina, Allen, Pit.	.299	68	308	278	47	83	124	16	5	5	39	1	4	1	24	0	34	18	5	1	.446	.352
Dito, Robert, Ver.	.286	4	12	7	2	2	3	1	0	0	0	1	0	1	3	0	2	0	0	0	.429	.545
Duncan, Carlos, Bat.	.264	71	311	276	55	73	119	23	4	5	43	0	6	0	29	1	101	13	4	3	.431	.347
Dunn, Ryan, Aub.*	.182	34	134	110	18	20	34	5	0	3	22	0	2	6	16	0	39	1	1	5	.309	.313
Eaddy, Deon, Wil.	.211	49	165	142	10	30	39	5	2	0	11	1	1	2	18	1	30	4	0	3	.275	.307
Elliott, Dawan, Erie*	.253	48	188	178	17	45	73	9	2	5	26	0	1	0	9	1	48	1	2	2	.410	.293
Ensberg, Morgan, Aub.	.230	59	250	196	39	45	72	10	1	5	31	0	2	6	46	1	51	15	3	5	.367	.388
Escalona, Felix, Aub.	.208	51	171	149	22	31	39	5	0	1	17	1	4	6	11	0	33	4	2	4	.262	.282
Estevez, Domingo, St.C.†	.306	56	235	209	40	64	113	16	6	7	33	2	1	4	19	0	26	12	7	4	.541	.373
Everett, Adam, Low.	.296	21	87	71	11	21	31	6	2	0	9	1	1	3	11	0	13	2	1	2	.437	.407
Falcon, Edwin, Low.	.225	64	242	213	21	48	72	13	1	3	32	2	0	2	25	0	70	1	0	4	.338	.313
Farnsworth, Troy, N.J.	.257	65	254	218	33	56	90	14	1	6	37	2	3	6	25	0	64	2	4	2	.413	.345
Fatheree, Danny, Aub.	.260	52	220	196	26	51	67	10	0	2	27	1	3	1	19	1	40	1	4	4	.342	.324
Feliz, Joselyn, Uti.	.208	32	99	96	8	20	32	6	0	2	12	1	0	0	2	0	26	0	0	2	.333	.224
Flores, Jose, Low.†	.147	49	128	116	17	17	22	5	0	0	2	4	0	1	7	0	31	2	1	1	.190	.202
Folkers, Brandon, N.J.*	.241	52	152	133	7	32	42	5	1	1	16	2	4	3	10	2	50	2	2	0	.316	.300
Forbes, Kevin, Ver.	.000	2	4	4	0	0	0	0	0	0	0	0	0	0	0	0	3	0	0	0	.000	.000
Forbush, Nate, Jam.†	.231	33	129	117	18	27	37	4	0	2	16	0	1	1	11	0	29	1	1	4	.316	.302
Foulds, Kalin, H.V.†	.197	20	81	71	14	14	19	3	1	0	3	3	0	1	6	0	7	7	0	0	.268	.269
Freeman, Brad, N.J.	.249	73	301	253	37	63	86	11	3	2	26	6	4	14	24	1	45	19	10	0	.340	.342
Frese, Nate, Wil.	.218	54	202	174	28	38	52	8	0	2	18	3	7	2	16	0	38	5	2	1	.299	.281
Frick, Matt, Uti.	.265	55	205	185	30	49	84	12	1	7	34	1	1	2	16	0	45	2	1	3	.454	.328
Ginter, Keith, Aub.	.315	71	310	241	55	76	124	22	1	8	41	0	2	7	60	0	68	10	7	1	.515	.461
Goodson, Steven, H.V.*	.303	62	261	234	45	71	103	15	4	3	32	0	0	1	26	2	57	3	3	3	.440	.375
Gordnier, Aaron, Wat.	.250	36	131	108	17	27	43	7	0	3	16	0	0	1	22	3	32	7	1	1	.398	.382
Green, Kevin, Uti.	.375	3	8	8	3	3	6	0	0	1	2	0	0	0	0	0	1	0	0	0	.750	.375
Greene, Alan, One.†	.252	70	283	254	35	64	89	11	4	2	39	0	2	1	26	0	62	8	4	6	.350	.322
Gregg, Neal, One.*	.217	58	189	161	22	35	65	10	4	4	23	2	0	6	20	0	49	3	2	4	.404	.326
Griffin, Matthew, Wil.	.256	64	242	207	32	53	76	11	0	4	29	4	0	7	24	0	33	13	5	1	.367	.353
Grindell, Nate, Wat.	.259	27	98	81	13	21	31	7	0	1	13	0	2	0	15	0	9	1	2	1	.383	.367
Groebner, Mark, Ver.	.253	36	115	95	12	24	28	2	1	0	14	2	1	2	15	0	28	1	1	1	.295	.363
Gross, Jeremy, One.	.200	11	12	10	1	2	3	1	0	0	0	0	0	0	2	0	6	0	0	0	.300	.333
Haley, Ryan, Wat.*	.333	1	4	3	1	1	1	0	0	0	0	0	0	0	1	0	0	0	0	0	.333	.500
Hammond, Jamie, Ver.	.233	30	94	86	7	20	22	2	0	0	12	0	0	3	5	0	17	3	3	1	.256	.298
Hargreaves, Brad, Wil.	.260	47	143	131	15	34	38	4	0	0	18	1	0	4	7	0	22	3	1	3	.290	.317
Hart, Keith, Low.	.273	41	171	165	14	45	66	12	0	3	30	0	2	1	3	0	34	0	1	6	.400	.287
Hazelton, Justin, Jam.	.172	27	102	87	9	15	22	3	2	0	7	0	0	0	15	0	40	1	0	0	.253	.294
Heine, Kyle, One.	.167	27	44	42	3	7	11	1	0	1	4	0	0	0	2	0	11	0	0	2	.262	.205
Hendricks, Jason, Ver.	.261	7	23	23	4	6	7	1	0	0	2	0	0	0	0	0	4	2	0	1	.304	.261
Hernandez, Jesus, Wat.*	.241	70	300	257	42	62	100	13	5	5	43	2	2	0	39	2	49	15	0	5	.389	.339
Hernandez, Michel, One.	.254	61	227	205	29	52	64	8	2	0	24	1	1	0	20	0	19	4	4	10	.312	.319
Heying, Scott, St.C.*	.261	46	132	115	15	30	36	6	0	0	13	3	1	1	12	0	19	1	1	4	.313	.333
Hill, Willy, Uti.*	.270	72	303	270	34	73	91	10	4	0	19	6	0	5	22	2	48	10	9	2	.337	.337
Hinske, Eric, Wil.*	.298	68	289	248	46	74	121	20	0	9	57	0	4	2	35	3	61	19	3	2	.488	.384
Hodges, Scott, Wil.*	.278	67	284	266	35	74	102	13	3	3	35	2	4	1	11	1	59	8	1	3	.383	.305
Honeycutt, Heath, Uti.	.241	68	276	245	40	59	92	8	2	7	33	0	0	6	25	2	67	11	2	4	.376	.326
Hook, Kevin, Ver.	.500	5	8	8	1	4	5	1	0	0	0	0	0	0	0	0	1	0	1	0	.625	.500
Hoover, Paul, H.V.	.283	73	326	269	51	76	110	20	1	4	37	0	6	11	39	3	44	26	3	5	.409	.388
Hubbard, Jeremy, Wil.	.167	12	33	30	4	5	6	1	0	0	3	0	0	0	3	0	4	0	0	2	.200	.212
Hubbel, Travis, St.C.	.125	10	19	16	1	2	3	1	0	0	1	0	0	0	3	0	9	0	0	0	.188	.263
Hummel, Dan, N.J.	.223	48	145	121	17	27	40	7	0	2	17	2	2	4	16	1	30	2	1	3	.331	.329
Hunt, Joe, Erie†	.244	58	241	217	30	53	59	6	0	0	11	0	2	0	22	0	42	12	7	1	.272	.311
Inge, Brandon, Jam.†	.230	51	215	191	24	44	80	10	1	8	29	0	1	6	17	1	53	8	8	4	.419	.312
Jackson, Brandon, St.C.	.263	57	195	171	30	45	53	5	0	1	11	4	0	2	18	0	26	6	0	5	.310	.340
James, Tony, Low.	.272	68	279	235	42	64	101	13	0	8	34	6	2	9	27	0	45	7	1	2	.430	.366
Johnson, Chadwick, Low.	.200	38	126	110	16	22	33	2	0	3	13	0	0	3	13	0	37	1	0	3	.300	.302
Jones, Aaron, One.*	.299	51	192	157	34	47	68	8	2	3	31	1	1	0	33	1	31	2	1	5	.433	.419
Jordan, Kevin, Aub.	.232	53	194	181	29	42	64	8	4	2	28	0	1	2	10	1	41	6	3	3	.354	.278
Jordan, Yustin, Erie	.000	2	7	6	0	0	0	0	0	0	0	0	0	0	1	0	4	0	0	0	.000	.143
Joyce, Jesse, Aub.	.306	41	156	144	27	44	67	9	4	2	19	2	0	1	9	1	26	4	1	1	.465	.351
Kane, Kevin, One.	.200	8	10	10	1	2	3	1	0	0	0	0	0	0	0	0	7	0	0	0	.300	.200
Kato, Takaaki, Wil.*	.253	58	183	154	19	39	51	10	1	0	19	0	4	1	24	1	30	1	1	3	.331	.350
Kelly, Chris, N.J.	.262	19	70	61	6	16	23	4	0	1	6	0	1	1	7	0	17	1	0	1	.377	.343
Kelly, Heath, Uti.	.232	34	109	95	14	22	27	3	1	0	10	1	1	3	9	0	29	1	1	3	.284	.315
Kidwell, Tommy, N.J.	.244	39	134	123	14	30	36	6	0	0	9	0	1	2	8	0	17	1	2	3	.293	.299
Kofler, Ed, H.V.	.000	16	0	0	0	0	0	0	0	0	0	0	0	0	0	0	0	0	0	0	.000	.000
Lambert, Clark, Pit.	.262	18	51	42	6	11	13	0	1	0	0	0	0	1	8	0	9	0	0	1	.310	.392
Lara, Felix, Erie*	.236	36	135	127	18	30	42	7	1	1	8	0	0	2	4	1	37	6	4	3	.331	.262

Player, Team	Avg.	G	TPA	AB	R	H	TB	2B	3B	HR	RBI	SH	SF	HP	BB	IBB	SO	SB	CS	GDP	Slg.	OBP
Larned, Andrew, Low.	.222	21	57	54	4	12	15	3	0	0	5	0	1	0	2	0	12	0	0	2	.278	.246
Law, Keith, Jam.	.171	33	117	105	11	18	28	5	1	1	11	1	1	0	10	0	23	3	2	6	.267	.241
Leahy, Bart, Uti.	.216	49	152	139	13	30	42	9	0	1	11	2	2	0	9	0	46	3	2	6	.302	.260
Lebron, Jesus, St.C.	.254	43	142	126	25	32	52	6	1	4	21	2	1	0	13	0	43	7	4	1	.413	.321
Ledesma, Philip, Low.	.202	54	151	129	17	26	38	4	1	2	12	4	0	4	13	0	35	4	2	1	.295	.295
Lee, Richard, St.C.	.286	23	93	77	14	22	40	6	0	4	17	0	1	4	11	0	17	1	0	0	.519	.398
Lentz, Ryan, Ver.*	.251	67	277	231	37	58	75	12	1	1	23	1	2	5	38	1	34	4	4	5	.325	.366
Llanos, Alex, H.V.*	.277	54	220	188	24	52	66	9	1	1	24	2	3	1	26	2	36	5	2	7	.351	.362
Longmire, Marcel, Wil.	.202	58	191	173	20	35	57	6	2	4	19	0	2	7	9	0	50	5	4	5	.329	.267
Lopez, Felipe, St.C.†	.373	19	86	83	14	31	43	5	2	1	11	0	0	0	3	0	14	4	2	1	.518	.395
Lucca, Tony, Uti.*	.239	42	128	109	12	26	39	7	0	2	13	1	2	1	15	1	20	1	0	5	.358	.331
Ludvigsen, Marc, Pit.*	.202	49	137	129	14	26	33	5	1	0	7	0	1	1	6	1	48	0	0	0	.256	.241
Machado, Albenis, Ver.†	.279	58	239	197	31	55	67	5	2	1	23	3	4	3	32	0	33	11	13	4	.340	.381
MacMillan, Chris, Wat.	.227	57	225	194	28	44	68	9	0	5	30	0	3	2	26	1	47	0	1	2	.351	.320
Maddox, Derrick, Bat.*	.114	29	85	70	7	8	10	2	0	0	3	0	0	2	13	0	32	0	2	2	.143	.271
Mahoney, Sean, H.V.	.347	65	290	248	44	86	121	16	2	5	53	0	6	5	31	3	47	11	5	4	.488	.421
Malave, Dennis, Wat.*	.250	6	20	20	1	5	8	0	0	1	6	0	0	0	0	0	4	2	1	0	.400	.250
Marn, Josh, H.V.	.207	29	95	82	11	17	19	2	0	0	8	0	0	2	11	0	19	0	1	2	.232	.316
Matranga, David, Aub.	.306	40	176	144	34	44	71	13	1	4	24	1	1	5	25	1	38	16	3	0	.493	.423
Maxwell, Keith, Erie.	.267	66	280	240	43	64	107	15	2	8	30	2	1	8	29	0	54	0	1	10	.446	.363
McDaniels, Paul, Low.*	.241	58	213	170	33	41	74	8	2	7	24	0	3	13	27	0	49	1	1	2	.435	.380
McGinnis, Ronald, Bat.	.146	31	110	103	7	15	24	3	0	2	10	0	1	2	4	0	41	0	1	5	.233	.191
McGrath, Sean, Pit.	.212	10	38	33	4	7	12	2	0	1	1	0	0	0	5	0	8	1	2	2	.364	.316
McKinley, Josh, Ver.†	.136	6	24	22	2	3	3	0	0	0	4	0	1	0	1	0	9	0	0	1	.136	.167
McKinney, Antonio, Jam.	.308	39	144	130	26	40	55	9	0	2	17	1	0	1	12	0	26	11	3	3	.423	.371
McNaughton, Troy, N.J.*	.255	53	183	157	27	40	58	7	4	1	14	3	1	2	20	0	45	6	5	4	.369	.344
Medina, Luis, Wil.	.184	36	120	114	14	21	23	2	0	0	9	0	0	3	3	0	19	4	2	3	.202	.225
Mejias, Oliver, Erie†	.258	11	34	31	2	8	9	1	0	0	4	1	1	0	1	0	8	0	0	2	.290	.273
Melo, Ramon, Wil.	.382	10	35	34	6	13	22	6	0	1	4	0	0	0	1	0	4	2	1	1	.647	.400
Mendoza, Angel, Low.	.297	69	274	256	29	76	110	20	4	2	36	4	4	1	9	0	70	7	3	4	.430	.319
Meran, Jorge, Jam.	.273	30	127	110	13	30	51	7	1	4	20	0	0	2	15	2	24	3	1	3	.464	.370
Michaels, Jason, Bat.	.268	67	281	235	45	63	116	14	3	11	49	0	2	4	40	3	69	4	2	5	.494	.381
Miller, Kenny, Pit.	.216	68	248	222	25	48	60	9	0	1	16	3	0	2	21	1	42	7	3	1	.270	.290
Miller, Travis, H.V.	.191	47	163	141	29	27	45	4	4	2	10	0	0	3	19	0	45	5	3	0	.319	.301
Molina, Jim, N.J.	.226	58	229	212	25	48	63	9	0	2	28	2	0	2	13	0	58	22	1	6	.297	.278
Moore, Lacarlo, Jam.*	.317	19	67	60	10	19	23	4	0	0	5	0	1	1	5	0	10	6	1	0	.383	.373
Moraga, Omar, Wat.*	.264	65	280	246	38	65	91	18	4	0	28	1	1	4	28	5	55	14	5	5	.370	.348
Morales, Stephen, Uti.†	.247	26	92	85	14	21	32	2	0	3	14	0	2	0	5	0	18	2	1	2	.376	.283
Moreno, Mikel, Wil.	.273	73	317	286	51	78	105	13	4	2	28	3	2	7	19	0	51	23	8	4	.367	.331
Morillo, Luis, St.C.*	.200	1	5	5	1	1	1	0	0	0	0	0	0	0	0	0	0	0	0	0	.200	.200
Mulvehill, Brandon, Pit.	.252	56	224	210	24	53	74	6	6	1	24	1	1	3	9	0	64	11	4	1	.352	.291
Myers, Tootie, Ver.	.240	73	312	271	33	65	86	15	3	0	24	3	3	6	29	0	86	14	7	5	.317	.324
Na, Jim, Ver.*	.210	43	137	119	12	25	33	4	2	0	12	0	0	3	14	0	40	4	7	0	.277	.309
Neal, Blaine, Uti.*	.190	53	146	121	13	23	27	4	0	0	13	0	0	2	23	0	32	2	1	7	.223	.329
Nicholson, Derek, Aub.*	.310	50	196	168	28	52	75	9	1	4	34	0	3	2	23	1	34	3	2	1	.446	.393
Nicolas, Jose, Erie	.248	66	273	242	33	60	92	8	3	6	35	2	3	4	22	1	85	6	5	3	.380	.317
Nieves, Juan, St.C.	.274	60	232	208	26	57	95	15	1	7	38	0	3	7	14	2	31	2	2	2	.457	.336
Nunez, Jose, N.J.	.216	55	175	162	17	35	48	6	2	1	14	1	0	3	9	0	22	5	4	4	.296	.270
Olivares, Teuris, One.	.277	73	304	271	44	75	114	15	6	4	43	0	5	2	26	0	60	14	7	5	.421	.339
Paciorek, Tom, Pit.	.107	8	28	28	5	3	3	0	0	0	0	0	0	0	0	0	7	0	0	0	.107	.107
Padgett, Matt, Uti.*	.219	71	271	247	31	54	77	9	1	4	39	1	1	0	22	0	73	4	3	3	.312	.281
Parker, Clark, Erie†	.235	8	20	17	4	4	5	1	0	0	1	0	0	0	3	0	4	1	1	0	.294	.350
Pass, Patrick, Uti.	.132	15	43	38	5	5	8	0	0	1	2	0	0	0	5	0	17	2	1	0	.211	.233
Patton, Barry, Wat.	.067	11	35	30	1	2	3	1	0	0	1	0	0	1	4	0	14	1	0	1	.100	.200
Payne, Ronald, Wil.*	.231	48	191	169	27	39	64	9	5	2	23	1	1	4	16	0	42	8	5	4	.379	.311
Pena, Rodolfo, Low.	.229	15	40	35	3	8	14	3	0	1	4	2	0	0	3	0	8	0	0	0	.400	.289
Peniche, Fray, Jam.	.206	11	37	34	3	7	10	0	0	1	4	0	2	0	1	0	10	0	1	1	.294	.216
Perez, Angelo, St.C.	.269	40	130	119	11	32	49	9	1	2	13	1	2	1	7	1	29	3	0	2	.412	.310
Perez, Edwin, Wat.	.119	12	45	42	6	5	6	1	0	0	3	0	0	0	3	0	9	2	1	1	.143	.178
Piercy, Brad, Ver.*	.235	68	282	264	39	62	81	8	1	3	31	1	2	1	14	2	71	8	7	4	.307	.274
Pigott, Anthony, H.V.	.250	9	17	16	3	4	5	1	0	0	3	0	0	0	1	0	2	1	0	1	.313	.294
Pittman, Thomas, Ver.	.212	58	241	222	27	47	72	13	0	4	30	0	3	16	2	0	67	2	5	7	.324	.274
Polk, Chad, St.C.†	.231	50	164	130	25	30	43	4	0	3	18	0	0	3	31	1	45	8	1	1	.331	.390
Polonia, Israel, Uti.	.301	45	168	146	23	44	66	6	2	4	22	0	0	5	17	0	47	3	5	1	.452	.393
Porter, Colin, Aub.*	.283	67	267	240	40	68	106	18	4	4	30	2	1	5	19	0	61	14	11	3	.442	.347
Powers, Jeff, Wat.*	.299	18	75	67	10	20	28	5	0	1	11	1	1	1	5	0	10	1	0	3	.418	.351
Pratt, Scott, Wat.*	.351	47	215	174	37	61	85	12	3	2	14	1	1	5	34	1	26	15	10	4	.489	.467
Puffinbarger, Rusty, Wat.	.167	12	35	24	6	4	6	2	0	0	4	0	0	4	7	0	6	0	0	0	.250	.429
Punto, Nicholas, Bat.†	.247	72	323	279	51	69	89	9	4	1	20	0	1	1	42	0	48	19	7	4	.319	.347
Quero, Pedro, Ver.	.289	73	303	273	40	79	92	8	1	1	30	4	3	1	22	1	45	7	12	4	.337	.341
Rachels, Wesley, Bat.	.301	41	153	133	19	40	45	5	0	0	16	0	0	2	18	0	15	2	1	6	.338	.392
Ramos, Kelly, Pit.†	.298	63	233	215	31	64	95	10	6	3	34	0	4	1	13	1	36	0	1	6	.442	.335
Rand, Ian, H.V.	.227	26	85	75	13	17	24	2	1	1	13	1	0	3	6	0	16	2	2	2	.320	.310
Rauls, Ian, Bat.*	.264	57	209	178	27	47	54	7	0	0	7	1	1	3	26	0	55	9	7	1	.303	.365
Ravelo, Manuel, Erie	.204	26	99	93	8	19	23	2	1	0	5	0	0	1	5	0	26	2	4	0	.247	.253
Reyes, Dadny, Uti.†	.100	4	10	10	0	1	1	0	0	0	0	0	0	0	0	0	4	0	0	1	.100	.100
Reyes, Deurys, Jam.*	.198	33	128	111	11	22	33	3	4	0	11	0	0	2	15	0	35	5	2	0	.297	.305
Rhodes, Dusty, One.*	.275	68	271	236	47	65	83	10	4	0	18	0	2	4	29	0	51	9	3	7	.352	.362
Ribaudo, Mike, Pit.	.307	39	139	137	12	42	59	8	0	3	24	0	1	1	0	0	26	3	5	3	.431	.309
Rich, Billy, Jam.	.271	62	263	225	42	61	95	9	5	5	34	0	4	6	28	0	44	7	3	7	.422	.361
Riggins, Auntwan, St.C.†	.167	5	13	12	1	2	2	0	0	0	0	0	0	0	1	0	3	0	0	0	.167	.231

Player, Team	Avg.	G	TPA	AB	R	H	TB	2B	3B	HR	RBI	SH	SF	HP	BB	IBB	SO	SB	CS	GDP	Slg.	OBP
Rigsby, Randy, Uti.*	.302	54	202	179	26	54	73	12	2	1	16	0	0	2	21	3	42	3	4	3	.408	.381
Rivera, Juan, One.	.278	6	19	18	2	5	8	0	0	1	3	0	0	1	0	4	1	1	0	.444	.316
Rivera, Luis J., Ver.	.211	33	116	109	10	23	30	5	1	0	7	1	1	2	3	0	26	0	3	3	.275	.243
Rodeheaver, Roger, Bat.	.143	28	82	70	9	10	14	2	1	0	5	0	0	1	11	0	25	0	0	1	.200	.268
Rodriguez, Pedro, Pit.*	.205	57	172	156	14	32	34	2	0	0	19	0	3	0	13	1	34	10	4	1	.218	.262
Rodriguez, Ronny, Low.	.083	5	15	12	3	1	1	0	0	0	1	0	0	0	3	0	5	0	0	1	.083	.267
Rojas, Christian, Wat.	.266	61	253	218	41	58	108	12	1	12	46	0	2	8	25	1	63	6	3	3	.495	.360
Rojas, Mo, Low.	.270	63	256	241	27	65	103	21	1	5	27	0	1	4	10	0	57	0	0	9	.427	.309
Roush, Ryan, Low.	.229	39	133	118	8	27	36	6	0	1	8	1	0	0	14	0	28	2	2	1	.305	.311
Runnells, T.J., Jam.	.238	63	265	239	31	57	70	8	1	1	25	4	3	1	18	1	47	2	0	5	.293	.291
Salazar, Jeremy, Bat.	.279	20	73	68	6	19	30	5	0	2	18	0	0	1	4	0	21	0	0	1	.441	.329
Sandberg, Jared, H.V.	.288	73	323	271	49	78	133	15	2	12	54	0	4	5	42	1	76	13	3	6	.491	.388
Santana, Osmany, Wat.*	.282	19	89	78	17	22	38	4	3	2	13	0	0	0	11	0	8	3	2	2	.487	.371
Santoro, Patrick, Low.	.247	55	217	190	24	47	72	7	6	2	19	0	1	0	26	0	54	4	0	3	.379	.336
Santos, Angel, Low.†	.245	28	113	102	19	25	34	4	1	1	12	2	0	0	9	0	12	2	1	4	.333	.306
Schmidt, Todd, N.J.†	.141	29	93	78	9	11	18	1	0	2	7	0	1	0	14	0	24	1	0	1	.231	.269
Schrager, Tony, Wil.	.192	8	31	26	4	5	5	0	0	0	3	0	0	0	5	0	9	3	1	0	.192	.323
Secoda, Joe, N.J.	.226	53	176	159	13	36	40	4	0	0	14	2	2	3	10	0	59	7	4	1	.252	.282
Silletti, Pete, St.C.†	.000	1	2	1	0	0	0	0	0	0	0	0	0	0	1	0	0	0	0	0	.000	.500
Skrehot, Shaun, Erie	.249	63	284	269	33	67	83	10	0	2	18	1	3	4	7	0	43	10	1	3	.309	.276
Smalls, Terrance, Uti.*	.275	43	110	102	14	28	29	1	0	0	6	1	0	2	5	0	13	10	4	0	.284	.321
Smetek, Peter, H.V.*	.091	19	39	33	1	3	5	2	0	0	2	0	0	1	4	0	18	1	0	0	.152	.211
Smith, Casey, Wat.	.186	67	248	226	22	42	59	6	1	3	23	0	3	4	15	0	65	4	0	5	.261	.246
Smith, Nate, N.J.	.245	42	164	143	17	35	46	5	3	0	17	4	2	2	13	0	27	4	1	2	.322	.313
Snead, Esix, N.J.†	.233	58	234	193	38	45	60	4	4	1	16	1	0	7	33	0	54	42	11	3	.311	.365
Snyder, Earl, Pit.	.252	71	288	262	39	66	109	8	1	11	40	0	1	2	23	0	60	0	1	6	.416	.316
Sorensen, Zach, Wat.†	.300	53	237	200	38	60	95	7	8	4	26	2	0	0	35	0	35	14	4	2	.475	.404
Stratton, Robert, Pit.	.226	34	135	124	18	28	59	5	4	6	18	0	0	0	11	0	55	3	2	2	.476	.289
Suriel, Miguel, H.V.	.258	60	254	225	27	58	77	7	3	2	35	2	3	6	18	0	35	6	4	3	.342	.325
Terni, Chaz, Low.	.255	46	182	165	22	42	60	7	1	3	14	2	0	3	12	0	38	2	1	4	.364	.317
Thompson, Sonny, Low.	.105	8	19	19	1	2	2	0	0	0	0	0	0	0	0	0	7	0	0	0	.105	.105
Thompson, Tyler, St.C.	.252	70	296	246	42	62	91	17	0	4	32	0	3	1	46	0	64	6	5	3	.370	.368
Tolbert, William (Alex), Erie* .	.086	12	38	35	3	3	7	1	0	1	3	0	0	0	3	0	13	0	0	1	.200	.158
Torres, Andres, Jam.†	.234	48	221	192	28	45	62	2	6	1	21	1	2	1	25	0	50	13	2	1	.323	.323
Umbria, Jose, St.C.	.237	32	111	97	14	23	25	2	0	0	13	4	0	1	9	0	22	0	0	1	.258	.308
Upshaw, Ryan, Wat.*	.257	70	296	257	43	66	104	17	0	7	39	1	4	2	32	0	56	7	5	1	.405	.339
Urquhart, Derick, Ver.*	.247	76	280	243	32	60	79	15	2	0	26	4	1	1	31	0	43	13	7	2	.325	.333
Valdez, Jerry, Bat.	.271	60	246	214	29	58	97	13	1	8	40	0	2	6	24	0	41	0	1	4	.453	.358
Valentine, Anthony, Pit.	.201	49	169	139	22	28	42	8	0	2	19	1	2	7	20	1	25	10	1	4	.302	.327
Vargas, Arias, Jam.	.214	48	181	159	16	34	45	4	2	1	13	0	1	2	19	0	44	1	1	4	.283	.304
Vento, Mike, One.	.304	43	169	148	25	45	63	9	3	1	23	0	2	5	14	0	28	8	3	1	.426	.379
Walker, Shon, Erie*	.337	27	115	101	24	34	64	8	2	6	28	0	1	0	13	0	35	2	0	1	.634	.409
Wallis, Michael, Wil.*	.202	38	99	89	7	18	23	1	2	0	5	2	0	0	7	0	18	0	0	1	.258	.260
Ware, Ryan, H.V.	.259	9	30	27	7	7	12	2	0	1	3	0	0	0	3	0	7	0	0	0	.444	.333
Warren, Christopher, Low.	.000	1	1	1	0	0	0	0	0	0	0	0	0	0	0	0	0	0	0	0	.000	.000
Washington, Dion, One.	.185	47	143	124	14	23	35	4	1	2	14	0	0	0	19	0	50	1	0	1	.282	.294
Washington, Rico, Erie*	.330	51	221	197	31	65	101	14	2	6	31	0	0	7	17	2	33	1	2	4	.513	.403
Wathan, Derek, Uti.†	.268	60	253	224	32	60	72	8	2	0	23	5	0	3	21	0	35	10	9	6	.321	.339
Whitlock, Kris, St.C.*	.185	45	144	119	21	22	48	2	0	8	23	0	1	5	19	0	51	0	0	0	.403	.319
Wigginton, Ty, Pit.	.239	70	290	272	39	65	111	14	4	8	29	1	0	1	16	0	72	11	2	4	.408	.284
Williams, Ricky, Bat.	.283	13	55	53	7	15	15	0	0	0	3	0	0	2	0	0	16	6	3	0	.283	.309
Wright, Bryan, Low.	.034	13	33	29	1	1	1	0	0	0	3	0	1	0	0	0	11	0	0	1	.034	.067
Yates, Chris, Aub.	.254	67	250	224	40	57	73	6	5	0	24	1	2	2	21	1	48	26	11	6	.326	.321

GRAND SLAMS: August, Joyce, 2 each; Bundy, Connally, Darjean, Davis, Denure, R. Dunn, Hart, Matranga, Michaels, Mulvehill, C. Rojas, Sandberg, Upshaw, Whitlock, 1 each.

AWARDED FIRST BASE ON CATCHER'S INTERFERENCE: Besco (Longmire); Byrd (M. Hernandez); Deitrick (Daggett); Dimmick (Daggett); Eadoy (Casey Smith); Hoover (M. Hernandez); Ledesma (Bundy); Hammond (Daggett); Sandberg (Burkhart); Smetek (Morales); Wallis (M. Hernandez).

1998 PITCHING

TEAM

Team	W	L	Pct.	ERA	G	CG	ShO	Sv.	IP	H	TBF	R	ER	HR	SH	SF	HB	BB	IBB	SO	WP	Bk.
Hudson Valley ...	50	26	.658	3.28	76	0	7	25	691.1	592	2918	325	252	31	22	19	50	245	5	693	76	9
Williamsport	39	36	.520	3.43	75	3	6	13	644.2	553	2734	310	246	28	16	23	21	303	5	539	45	11
Vermont	36	40	.474	3.65	76	1	7	14	653.0	591	2808	319	265	36	20	17	56	246	0	582	61	5
Watertown	42	34	.553	3.67	76	2	6	18	652.1	616	2799	326	266	45	13	21	39	250	11	641	48	9
New Jersey	34	41	.453	3.70	75	0	5	21	656.2	597	2849	361	270	29	19	20	40	261	1	659	48	17
Oneonta	45	31	.592	3.76	76	3	5	22	656.0	623	2844	349	274	36	20	20	31	264	4	574	44	16
Utica	35	41	.461	3.76	76	2	4	18	636.2	635	2733	330	266	42	19	12	34	217	8	525	37	14
Auburn	43	32	.573	3.83	75	1	6	20	646.1	585	2808	348	275	35	24	17	44	273	3	659	60	18
Batavia	43	33	.566	3.85	76	2	5	20	661.2	660	2816	340	283	30	13	16	29	188	2	599	55	6
Lowell	32	44	.421	4.29	76	0	3	18	663.0	685	2988	400	316	36	13	27	44	297	27	687	67	17
St. Catharines	38	38	.500	4.46	76	1	5	21	662.0	722	2947	428	328	52	16	18	49	293	2	606	56	13
Jamestown	32	43	.427	4.48	75	1	2	17	660.2	694	2922	404	329	38	12	24	27	278	2	603	79	22
Pittsfield	35	41	.461	4.60	76	1	2	20	672.1	734	2993	428	344	37	23	30	42	261	14	522	52	11
Erie	26	50	.342	5.61	76	0	4	11	673.1	763	3127	527	420	82	16	22	67	282	8	580	50	9

TOP QUALIFIERS FOR EARNED-RUN AVERAGE TITLE

Minimum 61 innings. *Lefthanded pitcher.

Pitcher, Team	W	L	Pct.	ERA	G	GS	CG	ShO	GF	Sv.	IP	H	TBF	R	ER	HR	SH	SF	HB	BB	IBB	SO	WP	Bk.
Geary, Geoffrey, Bat.	9	1	.900	1.60	16	15	1	1	1	0	95.1	78	368	20	17	6	3	0	0	14	0	101	3	0
Reinike, Chris, Wat.	10	2	.833	1.91	15	15	0	0	0	0	89.2	64	367	21	19	1	0	2	8	33	1	92	2	0
Hill, Terrance, Low.*	0	4	.000	2.00	19	7	0	0	6	0	63.0	60	282	28	14	2	0	2	2	33	3	61	6	0
Oswalt, Roy, Aub.	4	5	.444	2.18	11	11	0	0	0	0	70.1	49	289	24	17	3	1	2	3	31	0	67	2	1
Percell, Brody, Wat.*	9	2	.818	2.21	15	15	1	1	0	0	85.2	73	343	28	21	7	2	1	2	16	0	105	2	0
Lampley, Daniel, Low.	7	2	.778	2.39	13	11	0	0	2	0	64.0	51	275	25	17	4	0	2	9	22	0	95	7	2
Whiteley, Shad, One.	8	2	.800	2.44	14	14	1	0	0	0	81.0	53	335	30	22	0	3	1	5	39	0	85	6	5
Jodie, Brett, One.	7	6	.538	2.59	15	15	1	1	0	0	94.0	87	381	40	27	7	1	3	0	21	0	73	3	1
Flohr, Adam, H.V.*	5	1	.833	2.61	15	14	0	0	1	0	79.1	69	316	28	23	3	1	1	4	11	0	70	3	0
Peguero, Darwin, Aub.*	5	4	.556	2.80	20	6	0	0	5	0	64.1	53	278	30	20	3	3	1	1	31	0	86	8	4
James, Delvin, H.V.	7	4	.636	2.98	15	15	0	0	0	0	81.2	71	345	39	27	2	1	1	5	32	0	64	6	0
Whitney, Jacob, Aub.*	5	5	.500	2.98	18	13	0	0	2	0	84.2	92	365	42	28	5	1	0	5	16	0	64	4	4
Kofler, Ed, H.V.	6	3	.667	3.03	16	12	0	0	1	1	77.1	65	317	34	26	4	2	2	4	24	0	64	6	3
Weber, Brett, One.	4	1	.800	3.04	19	8	1	1	2	0	68.0	68	285	28	23	4	2	0	3	13	0	68	4	3
Padua, Geraldo, One.	8	0	1.000	3.14	15	14	0	0	0	0	86.0	79	362	40	30	3	1	2	9	29	0	75	2	1

DEPARTMENTAL LEADERS: W—Reinike, 10; L—Mangum, 9; Pct.—Padua, 1.000; G—Griffin, 35; GS—Alvord, 16; CG—Sams, 2; ShO—Several players tied at 1 each; GF—Gooden, Krug, 27 each; Sv.—Gooden, 17; IP—Geary, 95.1; H—Koutrouba, 109; TBF—Alvord, 402; R—Alvord, 57; ER—Alvord, 60; HR—Alvarado, 10; SH—Several players tied at 5 each; SF—Several players tied at 5 each; HB—Santana, 10; BB—Redding, 50; IBB—Flores, 5; SO—Percell, 105; WP—McGowan, 15; BK—Koutrouba, 9.

ALL PITCHERS

*Lefthanded pitcher.

Pitcher, Team	W	L	Pct.	ERA	G	GS	CG	ShO	GF	Sv.	IP	H	TBF	R	ER	HR	SH	SF	HB	BB	IBB	SO	WP	Bk.
Adorno, Wilson, Erie	0	0	.000	36.00	1	0	0	0	1	0	1.0	5	9	4	4	1	0	0	1	0	1	0	0	0
Agamennone, Brandon, Ver.	3	1	.750	1.42	9	3	0	0	0	0	31.2	19	124	6	5	1	0	1	1	11	0	30	0	0
Alvarado, David, Erie	0	3	.000	9.14	19	3	0	0	1	0	42.1	64	210	46	43	10	1	3	2	18	0	41	4	0
Alvord, Aaron, Jam.	5	6	.455	6.45	16	16	0	0	0	0	83.2	104	402	67	60	5	2	2	5	45	0	71	8	1
Aracena, Juan, Wat.	1	4	.200	2.84	18	0	0	0	17	6	25.1	21	103	8	8	2	1	0	0	7	1	22	1	0
Aramboles, Ricardo, One.	1	0	1.000	1.50	1	1	0	0	0	0	6.0	4	23	2	1	1	0	0	1	1	0	8	0	0
Arthurs, Shane, Ver.	4	4	.500	3.77	16	13	1	0	0	0	76.1	81	334	41	32	4	5	2	7	27	0	43	10	0
Avila, David, Uti.	1	1	.500	3.57	12	0	0	0	3	0	22.2	26	101	13	9	1	0	0	2	10	0	13	2	0
Bacci, Tony, Erie*	2	4	.333	5.34	6	6	0	0	0	0	30.1	25	131	24	18	6	0	1	2	10	0	23	3	0
Bair, Andy, Uti.*	1	2	.333	5.28	14	0	0	0	9	0	15.1	14	69	9	9	2	0	1	1	10	0	12	2	0
Barrett, Scott, Aub.*	2	4	.333	5.88	10	10	0	0	0	0	49.0	49	221	33	32	1	3	0	3	27	0	58	13	2
Bates, Casey, N.J.	1	2	.333	3.29	27	0	0	0	9	0	41.0	39	175	15	15	2	1	2	2	13	0	52	2	5
Behn, Brendan, Pit.*	3	5	.375	3.53	14	14	1	0	0	0	79.0	80	348	41	31	1	2	0	5	39	2	59	6	0
Beimel, Joe, Erie*	1	4	.200	6.32	17	6	0	0	3	0	47.0	56	220	39	33	6	3	1	5	22	0	37	3	1
Bellhorn, Todd, Pit.*	3	4	.429	3.56	15	12	0	0	0	0	68.1	69	291	31	27	3	3	1	3	20	0	60	6	2
Berger, Craig, Pit.	3	3	.500	2.32	23	0	0	0	17	5	50.1	54	221	21	13	1	3	1	3	11	0	43	4	0
Berthelot, Eric, Pit.*	0	3	.000	4.85	4	3	0	0	0	0	13.0	21	67	15	7	0	0	2	0	8	0	5	0	0
Blackmore, John, Aub.	5	2	.714	4.69	19	1	0	0	5	0	55.2	49	238	31	29	1	5	3	7	25	0	42	4	0
Bowring, Jason, Pit.	0	0	.000	0.00	1	0	0	0	1	0	1.0	0	4	0	0	0	0	0	0	0	0	0	0	0
Bravo, Franklin, Erie	2	4	.333	8.36	11	9	0	0	0	0	37.2	57	186	43	35	5	0	0	3	16	0	37	3	0
Bridges, Donald, Ver.	5	6	.455	4.90	13	13	0	0	0	0	68.0	71	311	42	37	2	2	2	8	37	0	43	8	0
Brito, Juan, Pit.*	3	0	1.000	9.31	10	0	0	0	3	0	19.1	21	90	20	20	1	1	2	3	9	2	7	2	0
Brown, Chris, Wil.	2	1	.667	2.97	28	0	0	0	8	0	39.1	35	162	14	13	3	0	1	0	18	0	31	1	2
Brown, Craig, Wat.*	1	2	.333	7.23	16	0	0	0	8	1	18.2	29	104	20	15	4	0	0	0	17	1	19	3	1
Bruback, Matthew, Wil.	2	7	.222	3.93	14	14	0	0	0	0	66.1	62	304	46	29	2	2	3	4	45	0	43	7	0
Buchanan, Brian, One.*	2	2	.500	4.15	15	5	0	0	3	0	34.2	34	157	16	16	0	0	0	2	25	0	32	4	1
Buirley, Matthew, Erie	1	1	.500	2.86	16	0	0	0	15	4	22.0	12	85	7	7	2	0	0	2	7	0	31	1	0
Buller, Sean, Jam.*	2	2	.500	6.03	13	5	0	0	4	0	37.1	42	167	30	25	3	0	2	1	12	0	26	1	0
Burchart, Kyle, Erie.	1	0	1.000	6.75	10	0	0	0	3	0	9.1	16	56	16	7	2	0	1	4	6	0	7	0	0
Carlson, Jeff, One.	1	0	1.000	4.28	18	0	0	0	10	0	33.2	33	148	19	16	1	0	0	2	13	1	21	0	0
Carpenter, Justin, One.	3	1	.750	5.19	28	0	0	0	14	4	26.0	22	114	18	15	1	3	0	2	16	0	11	3	0
Carr, Timothy, Pit.	3	5	.375	5.81	23	1	0	0	8	1	48.0	54	231	44	31	2	2	3	4	29	1	37	2	0
Carrasco, Danny, Wat.	1	1	.500	5.40	13	1	0	0	6	2	31.2	36	145	23	19	3	1	0	2	14	0	38	1	0
Casey, Joe, St.C.	1	2	.333	12.27	4	3	0	0	0	0	11.0	18	65	19	15	1	0	1	0	9	2	9	2	0
Castelli, Robert, Ver.	1	2	.333	2.70	23	2	0	0	10	1	36.2	35	161	16	11	1	1	0	3	21	0	44	3	0
Ciesla, Dave, Bat.*	0	1	.000	4.44	26	0	0	0	9	2	24.1	26	107	15	12	1	1	1	1	6	1	19	3	0
Cisar, Mark, Low.	2	1	.667	1.42	22	0	0	0	22	9	38.0	22	151	11	6	1	1	2	1	10	0	42	1	0
Clackum, Scott, Uti.	1	1	.500	1.50	20	0	0	0	19	10	24.0	16	93	5	4	0	0	0	1	5	2	28	0	0
Classen, Ender, Erie	0	1	.000	2.45	2	2	0	0	0	0	11.0	9	42	3	3	2	0	0	1	4	0	10	0	0
Coco, Pasqual, St.C.	3	7	.300	3.20	15	15	1	0	0	0	81.2	62	353	52	29	4	2	1	9	32	0	84	10	3
Cook, Andy, Pit.	5	3	.625	3.73	15	11	0	0	1	0	70.0	78	304	36	29	6	2	4	3	20	1	54	5	2
Cornejo, Jesse, H.V.*	6	1	.857	3.08	34	0	0	0	12	0	49.2	40	218	21	17	2	5	1	2	22	1	50	8	0
Cowan, Bobby, Uti.	1	0	1.000	2.76	17	1	0	0	6	0	32.2	29	129	11	10	2	2	1	5	0	26	0	0	0
Cummins, Jon, H.V.	0	0	.000	4.98	14	0	0	0	9	0	21.2	24	102	17	12	2	1	1	3	10	0	25	5	0
Dagley, Corey, Bat.	1	5	.167	4.86	18	5	0	0	4	0	50.0	53	210	31	27	3	1	1	3	11	0	37	1	0
Dant, Larry, Wil.	4	3	.571	4.12	26	0	0	0	4	0	39.1	41	174	23	18	2	4	1	1	16	0	29	2	1
Delano, Michael, Wil.*	4	1	.800	2.44	9	9	0	0	0	0	44.1	32	185	16	12	0	1	5	24	0	60	6	1	
Delatori, Keola, Wil.	2	2	.500	3.97	11	9	0	0	0	0	47.2	33	207	25	21	4	0	0	0	35	0	41	5	1
Dobson, Scott, Ver.	1	2	.333	7.52	17	0	0	0	6	0	20.1	17	109	22	17	1	0	6	23	0	22	9	2	
Donahoo, Matt, Low.*	0	3	.000	6.49	16	1	0	0	2	0	34.2	49	173	29	25	5	0	1	3	18	3	36	2	2
Donovan, Thomas, Bat.	2	2	.500	3.94	23	0	0	0	11	1	32.0	31	136	17	14	1	2	1	4	6	0	22	1	0
Drese, Ryan, Wat.	2	5	.286	4.07	9	9	0	0	0	0	42.0	40	179	21	19	1	0	2	3	14	0	40	4	0
Dunn, Keith, One.	0	0	.000	5.40	2	0	0	0	2	1	1.2	2	5	1	1	0	0	0	0	0	0	0	0	0

Pitcher, Team	W	L	Pct.	ERA	G	GS	CG	ShO	GF	Sv.	IP	H	TBF	R	ER	HR	SH	SF	HB	BB	IBB	SO	WP	Bk.
Erwin, Dave, Wat.	0	0	.000	7.20	3	0	0	0	2	0	5.0	6	23	4	4	1	0	0	1	1	0	7	0	0
Escobar, Ruben, Wat.	0	1	.000	3.70	14	0	0	0	2	0	24.1	20	96	12	10	0	0	3	0	6	0	14	3	0
Everett, Matt, Wat.	3	3	.500	2.33	16	0	0	0	11	0	19.1	16	89	7	5	1	0	1	1	12	3	24	2	0
Eversgerd, Randy, St.C.	4	2	.667	3.12	17	2	0	0	7	0	34.2	35	144	17	12	3	2	0	0	4	1	34	2	0
Farizo, Brad, Uti.	5	5	.500	4.04	14	14	1	0	0	0	82.1	96	361	43	37	6	2	1	1	21	0	47	4	0
Field, Nathan, Ver.	3	1	.750	3.09	25	0	0	0	16	2	35.0	32	150	16	12	1	1	0	3	11	0	39	5	1
Flohr, Adam, H.V.*	5	1	.833	2.61	15	14	0	0	1	0	79.1	69	316	28	23	3	1	1	4	11	0	70	3	0
Flores, Benito, Low.*	1	5	.167	4.68	20	4	0	0	7	3	42.1	46	199	26	22	2	1	1	1	20	5	47	6	2
Folkers, Brandon, N.J.*	0	0	.000	0.00	2	0	0	0	2	0	0.2	0	2	0	0	0	0	0	0	0	0	1	0	0
Frierson, Andrew, Ver.*	0	0	.000	3.86	2	0	0	0	1	0	4.2	5	20	2	2	2	1	0	0	1	0	4	0	0
Gagliano, Steve, Uti.	6	4	.600	3.31	13	12	1	0	0	0	68.0	67	292	33	25	4	2	1	1	27	1	66	5	1
Garcia, Wilson, N.J.	3	0	1.000	3.76	19	0	0	0	2	0	26.1	34	119	15	11	2	2	1	3	7	0	22	1	1
Garvin, Robert, Uti.	0	2	.000	5.50	5	3	0	0	0	0	18.0	24	83	12	11	1	0	1	0	8	0	6	0	0
Geary, Geoffrey, Bat.	9	1	.900	1.60	16	15	1	1	1	0	95.1	78	368	20	17	6	3	0	0	14	0	101	3	0
Gonzales, Rick, N.J.	0	0	.000	2.70	6	0	0	0	3	0	6.2	3	25	2	2	0	0	0	0	2	0	10	1	1
Gooden, Derek, N.J.	1	3	.250	1.71	29	0	0	0	27	17	31.2	22	124	11	6	0	1	1	0	9	0	30	3	0
Gourlay, Matthew, St.C.	5	1	.833	2.48	25	0	0	0	5	3	54.1	34	224	17	15	4	1	0	2	26	1	62	5	0
Gracesqui, Franklyn, St.C.*	1	0	1.000	6.61	11	0	0	0	9	0	16.1	16	81	12	12	2	0	0	3	12	0	19	5	2
Grammer, Ed, Bat.	0	0	.000	3.00	3	0	0	0	0	0	3.0	5	14	2	1	1	0	0	0	0	0	1	0	0
Gray, Michael, Erie	4	0	1.000	3.20	29	0	0	0	6	0	45.0	49	194	22	16	4	0	1	6	5	1	39	1	0
Gresko, Michael, Erie-Pit.*	1	0	1.000	13.50	14	0	0	0	5	0	19.1	39	119	33	29	1	1	1	3	21	1	19	5	1
Griffin, Kirk, N.J.	5	1	.833	1.63	35	0	0	0	8	4	49.2	32	208	23	9	4	3	1	3	15	0	51	3	0
Guillory, Dan, Wat.	1	0	1.000	3.00	3	0	0	0	1	0	6.0	4	26	2	2	0	1	1	3	1	5	0	1
Gunderson, Matthew, Wil.	0	0	.000	1.19	27	0	0	0	17	7	37.2	21	156	10	5	0	1	2	1	20	0	39	1	0
Gutierrez, Lazaro, Jam.*	2	2	.500	3.89	27	0	0	0	4	0	41.2	34	182	27	18	1	0	1	1	19	0	37	8	0
Gutshall, Eric, N.J.	0	1	.000	5.23	29	0	0	0	15	0	32.2	31	154	29	19	2	0	1	4	14	1	22	3	0
Guzman, Toribio, N.J.	1	4	.200	7.27	17	2	0	0	4	0	43.1	62	212	47	35	7	3	3	2	14	0	27	5	0
Hammons, Matt, Wil.	1	1	.500	4.24	3	3	0	0	0	0	17.0	13	69	8	8	1	0	0	1	7	0	14	2	0
Hancock, Joshua, Low.	0	1	.000	2.25	1	1	0	0	0	0	4.0	5	20	2	1	0	0	1	0	4	0	4	1	0
Harber, Ryan, Uti.*	2	6	.250	5.55	11	6	0	0	4	0	35.2	46	161	29	22	6	0	0	4	0	38	0	5
Harper, Travis, H.V.	6	2	.750	1.92	13	10	0	0	1	0	56.1	38	228	14	12	2	1	1	8	20	0	81	4	0
Heams, Shane, Jam.	2	2	.500	3.99	24	0	0	0	14	6	47.1	43	202	27	21	1	0	1	2	16	0	73	5	0
Held, Travis, N.J.	5	5	.500	4.05	14	14	0	0	0	0	73.1	71	307	42	33	3	1	3	6	18	0	65	3	3
Hertzel, Patrick, H.V.	5	3	.625	4.01	15	15	0	0	0	0	74.0	66	318	44	33	0	3	5	24	0	56	7	1
Hiles, Cary, Bat.	2	2	.500	2.97	25	0	0	0	23	10	30.1	27	134	11	10	0	0	1	13	0	45	4	1
Hill, Terrance, Low.*	0	4	.000	2.00	19	7	0	0	6	0	63.0	60	282	28	14	2	0	2	2	33	3	61	6	0
Hlodan, George, Erie	2	3	.400	6.05	20	8	0	0	4	1	58.0	82	275	44	39	3	3	6	15	0	31	2	0
Hostetler, Jim, Jam.	1	0	1.000	4.76	16	1	0	0	8	2	28.1	27	130	18	15	1	0	5	1	11	2	39	9	1
Hueda, Alejandro, St.C.	2	5	.286	6.26	11	8	0	0	1	0	41.2	51	195	38	29	6	2	4	3	18	0	25	3	0
Huggins, David, St.C.	7	5	.583	4.15	15	15	0	0	0	0	84.2	85	373	46	39	4	0	3	6	35	0	67	2	1
Hutchinson, Chad, N.J.	0	1	.000	3.52	3	3	0	0	0	0	15.1	15	67	7	6	0	0	2	4	0	20	0	0
Jackson, Brian, Wat.	0	0	.000	11.25	1	1	0	0	0	0	4.0	7	21	6	5	0	0	1	0	3	0	2	0	0
James, Delvin, H.V.	7	4	.636	2.98	15	15	0	0	0	0	81.2	71	345	39	27	2	1	1	5	32	0	64	6	0
Jimenez, Jason, H.V.*	5	2	.714	1.60	29	0	0	0	6	4	39.1	20	154	13	7	1	3	0	5	13	1	55	2	1
Jodie, Brett, One.	7	6	.538	2.59	15	15	1	1	0	0	94.0	87	381	40	27	7	1	3	0	21	0	73	3	1
Johnston, Michael, Erie*	0	0	.000	4.50	2	0	0	0	2	0	2.0	4	12	4	1	0	0	0	1	0	2	0	0
Julio, Jorge, Ver.	3	1	.750	2.57	7	7	0	0	0	0	42.0	30	173	12	12	1	1	1	3	15	0	52	1	1
Jupe, Eric, Uti.	0	3	.000	3.78	13	0	0	0	1	0	16.2	17	75	8	7	3	0	0	2	6	0	17	0	0
Kanovich, Jason, Ver.*	2	4	.333	3.44	20	5	0	0	6	0	49.2	42	210	24	19	2	0	3	4	17	0	41	3	0
Kearney, Ryan, Wat.	1	2	.333	1.57	20	1	0	0	8	3	46.0	39	188	16	8	1	4	1	1	10	1	45	2	1
Keisler, Randy, One.*	1	1	.500	7.45	6	2	0	0	1	1	9.2	14	51	10	8	0	0	3	0	7	1	11	0	0
Keller, Kris, Jam.	1	3	.250	3.27	27	0	0	0	24	8	33.0	29	141	12	12	3	1	2	1	16	0	41	3	0
Kingrey, Jarrod, St.C.	0	0	.000	0.48	25	0	0	0	24	16	37.2	21	148	7	2	1	1	0	0	17	0	58	5	1
Kloes, David, One.	1	2	.333	7.88	17	0	0	0	10	0	24.0	38	129	26	21	4	1	4	1	12	1	17	3	1
Knowles, Michael, One.	0	4	.000	5.73	5	5	0	0	0	0	22.0	22	106	18	14	1	2	2	1	16	0	12	1	1
Kofler, Ed, H.V.	6	3	.667	3.03	16	12	0	0	1	1	77.1	65	317	34	26	4	2	2	4	24	0	64	6	3
Koutrouba, Thomas, Jam.*	4	8	.333	4.76	15	14	1	1	1	0	85.0	109	375	54	45	6	3	4	0	29	0	64	5	9
Krug, Dustin, Wil.	1	1	.500	1.48	27	0	0	0	27	4	30.1	26	123	6	5	0	1	0	1	8	2	26	1	0
Kubes, Gregory, Bat.*	7	3	.700	3.23	15	12	0	0	0	0	75.1	72	303	33	27	1	3	2	0	23	0	79	4	3
Lampley, Daniel, Low.	7	2	.778	2.39	13	11	0	0	2	0	64.0	51	275	25	17	4	0	2	9	22	0	95	7	2
Lanfranco, Otoniel, N.J.	1	0	1.000	1.24	5	5	0	0	0	0	29.0	14	116	5	4	0	2	1	3	13	0	35	1	1
Langen, Brian, N.J.*	0	0	.000	7.64	20	0	0	0	6	0	17.2	30	94	21	15	0	1	1	2	11	0	12	6	0
Larned, Andrew, Low.	0	0	.000	0.00	1	0	0	0	1	0	1.0	0	3	0	0	0	0	0	0	0	0	1	0	0
Ledesma, Philip, Low.	0	0	.000	0.00	1	0	0	0	0	0	0.0	0	3	0	0	0	0	0	2	1	0	0	0	0
Linarelli, Tom, Low.	2	4	.333	7.06	18	6	0	0	4	0	51.0	78	261	51	40	5	3	5	2	28	4	44	3	2
Lovingood, Ray, Pit.*	0	2	.000	8.10	13	4	0	0	5	0	26.2	29	124	24	24	3	2	2	15	2	17	3	0
Lowery, Phil, Uti.*	2	1	.667	2.31	7	7	0	0	0	0	35.0	29	144	12	9	1	0	2	1	14	0	37	4	1
Luttig, Chris, Erie*	1	2	.333	3.60	27	0	0	0	14	4	30.0	30	132	16	12	2	2	0	1	10	2	39	2	1
Madson, William, Jam.	1	2	.333	2.26	16	7	0	0	3	0	55.2	47	225	17	14	3	2	1	3	17	0	46	6	0
Maleski, Eric, Wat.	0	0	.000	6.00	2	0	0	0	1	0	3.0	5	14	2	2	0	0	1	0	0	0	3	0	0
Mangum, Mark, Ver.	3	9	.250	4.46	14	12	0	0	1	1	70.2	78	303	39	35	3	2	2	6	15	0	59	4	0
Marietta, Ron, Wat.*	1	1	.500	5.09	11	11	0	0	0	0	53.0	55	240	35	30	8	1	1	9	26	0	41	6	3
Markwell, Diegomar, St.C.*	3	3	.500	5.54	17	5	0	0	3	0	52.0	61	251	39	32	2	0	2	3	35	0	40	7	1
Maroth, Mike, Low.*	2	3	.400	2.90	6	6	0	0	0	0	31.0	22	127	13	10	1	0	1	3	13	0	34	3	0
Matsko, Rich, Wat.	2	3	.400	8.59	20	0	0	0	8	1	36.2	43	169	37	35	2	1	0	1	24	1	41	5	0
Mattson, John, Pit.	6	4	.600	5.20	18	9	0	0	4	0	71.0	76	311	47	41	6	1	2	6	20	0	52	6	0
McBride, Jason, One.	0	1	.000	22.50	2	0	0	0	2	0	2.0	3	13	5	5	0	0	0	3	0	1	0	0
McCurtain, Paul, Uti.	0	1	.000	4.38	17	2	0	0	5	1	39.0	35	173	25	19	1	5	0	3	19	2	33	7	0
McGowan, Brian, Jam.	3	2	.600	7.45	18	0	0	0	7	0	29.0	35	136	27	24	1	0	0	2	23	0	24	15	0
Mejias, Oliver, Erie	0	0	.000	0.00	1	0	0	0	1	0	1.0	0	3	0	0	0	0	0	0	0	2	0	0
Miller, Tom, Low.*	2	4	.333	3.81	16	6	0	0	2	1	49.2	51	221	24	21	1	3	1	3	20	3	57	4	1
Molina, Primitivo, Low.	3	2	.600	1.96	15	0	0	0	7	2	23.0	21	94	6	5	0	2	1	1	6	2	16	0	0

Pitcher, Team	W	L	Pct.	ERA	G	GS	CG	ShO	GF	Sv.	IP	H	TBF	R	ER	HR	SH	SF	HB	BB	IBB	SO	WP	Bk.
Mondello, Peter, Bat.	1	0	1.000	13.50	4	0	0	0	2	0	4.0	7	23	7	6	1	0	1	1	4	1	2	2	0
Montilla, Felix, Erie	1	5	.167	6.28	27	1	0	0	9	1	38.2	53	187	33	27	6	2	2	2	14	2	32	3	0
Moore, Chris, Uti.	2	5	.286	3.66	13	13	0	0	0	0	66.1	55	285	34	27	6	0	3	4	36	0	48	3	0
Mowel, Mike, Low.	2	6	.250	4.46	15	13	0	0	2	0	66.2	65	285	39	33	3	1	2	3	20	2	46	6	0
Norton, Jason, Low.	1	1	.500	4.62	6	4	0	0	0	0	25.1	22	105	17	13	1	0	0	1	7	0	33	1	3
Novits, Carey, Wat.*	0	0	.000	3.38	5	2	0	0	1	0	10.2	11	43	4	4	1	1	1	0	2	0	9	1	0
Noyce, David, Uti.*	4	2	.667	3.52	17	0	0	0	5	2	30.2	23	128	15	12	1	4	1	4	11	1	28	1	1
O'Dette, Rick, Low.*	0	2	.000	11.34	9	1	0	0	2	0	16.2	14	98	23	21	1	0	1	2	32	0	16	8	0
Ohman, William, Wil.*	4	4	.500	6.46	10	7	0	0	0	0	39.0	39	167	32	28	6	0	3	1	13	0	35	7	0
Olsen, Kevin, Uti.	4	3	.571	2.60	21	4	0	0	8	2	45.0	37	181	21	13	3	1	0	1	10	1	56	1	1
Ortega, Franklin, N.J.	2	0	1.000	4.21	15	0	0	0	5	0	25.2	16	121	12	12	1	1	2	3	28	0	23	1	2
Oswalt, Roy, Aub.	4	5	.444	2.18	11	11	0	0	0	0	70.1	49	289	24	17	3	1	2	3	31	0	67	2	1
Padua, Geraldo, One.	8	0	1.000	3.14	15	14	0	0	0	0	86.0	79	362	40	30	3	1	2	3	29	0	75	2	1
Pascarella, Josh, Aub.	1	3	.250	8.42	15	3	0	0	5	0	31.0	48	157	32	29	3	2	0	1	16	0	20	3	0
Paulino, Arison, Erie	0	0	.000	12.00	2	0	0	0	0	0	3.0	6	16	6	4	1	0	1	0	1	0	3	0	0
Pavlovich, Tony, Erie	0	2	.000	1.64	8	0	0	0	3	1	11.0	6	42	3	2	1	0	0	0	2	0	17	0	0
Peguero, Darwin, Aub.*	5	4	.556	2.80	20	6	0	0	5	0	64.1	53	278	30	20	3	3	1	1	31	0	86	8	4
Percell, Brody, Wat.*	9	2	.818	2.21	15	15	1	1	0	0	85.2	73	343	28	21	7	2	1	2	16	0	105	2	0
Perez, Julio, Ver.	2	1	.667	2.70	12	0	0	0	5	2	23.1	21	101	10	7	1	0	0	3	6	0	29	4	1
Pettyjohn, Adam, Jam.	2	2	.500	2.86	4	4	0	0	0	0	22.0	21	93	10	7	0	1	2	2	4	0	24	1	1
Phillips, Matthew, Low.	4	4	.500	4.21	15	14	0	0	0	0	72.2	81	322	44	34	3	2	4	5	27	2	57	6	1
Pidgeon, Matt, Uti.	6	5	.545	3.78	14	14	0	0	0	0	78.2	86	335	41	33	5	1	2	9	22	0	55	6	3
Pilato, John, Bat.	4	4	.500	4.12	19	12	0	0	6	3	67.2	57	282	34	31	5	0	2	3	28	0	63	8	0
Pineda, Jairo, Aub.	0	0	.000	1.50	1	1	0	0	0	0	6.0	5	22	1	1	1	0	0	0	0	0	5	0	0
Pizarro, Melvin, Bat.*	0	0	.000	14.11	10	0	0	0	3	0	14.2	21	92	30	23	1	0	0	3	21	0	14	7	1
Place, Eric, St.C.*	4	5	.444	6.51	19	8	0	0	5	0	55.1	59	249	47	40	6	3	1	4	22	0	40	4	2
Powalski, Richard, Wil.*	1	2	.333	5.24	18	0	0	0	3	0	34.1	36	150	24	20	1	1	3	2	19	1	20	5	0
Prater, Andy, Erie	3	3	.500	5.76	18	11	0	0	3	0	59.1	60	280	44	38	8	0	2	9	30	1	44	0	1
Prather, Scott, N.J.*	4	6	.400	3.15	15	14	0	0	0	0	71.1	55	295	30	25	2	2	0	1	30	0	73	6	0
Princi, Peter, Pit.	1	3	.250	5.75	22	0	0	0	6	3	40.2	47	187	31	26	3	1	1	5	22	2	38	2	2
Prokop, Michael, Pit.	1	2	.333	2.74	26	0	0	0	20	7	42.2	42	178	18	13	3	1	3	1	8	1	36	2	1
Ramirez, Jose, Jam.*	1	0	1.000	0.00	1	0	0	0	0	0	4.0	4	15	0	0	0	0	0	0	1	0	5	1	0
Redding, Tim, Aub.	7	3	.700	4.52	16	15	0	0	1	1	73.2	49	323	44	37	2	2	3	7	50	0	98	10	4
Reinike, Chris, Wat.	10	2	.833	1.91	15	15	0	0	0	0	89.2	64	367	21	19	1	0	2	8	33	1	92	2	0
Rhea, Thad, Erie	4	4	.500	3.63	12	12	0	0	0	0	62.0	61	274	37	25	4	1	1	8	24	0	41	6	0
Ribaudo, Mike, Pit.	0	0	.000	0.00	1	0	0	0	1	0	1.0	1	6	2	0	0	0	0	1	0	0	0	0	0
Ridenour, Ryan, One.*	0	5	.000	9.38	13	6	0	0	1	0	31.2	47	160	34	33	6	1	1	7	12	0	22	6	1
Ridley, Brian, Aub.*	3	0	1.000	3.75	17	0	0	0	5	0	24.0	23	105	12	10	1	1	2	1	9	1	27	5	0
Roberts, Richard, Jam.*	3	7	.300	3.15	15	15	0	0	0	0	85.2	96	379	44	30	4	3	2	2	37	0	60	4	3
Rodriguez, Cristobal, Ver.	0	0	.000	4.91	6	2	0	0	0	0	14.2	6	66	8	8	1	0	1	2	14	0	14	1	0
Rodriguez, Jorge, One.	2	1	.667	3.34	20	0	0	0	5	0	32.1	31	142	18	12	1	1	0	1	18	0	34	5	1
Rogers, Brian, One.	2	2	.500	2.31	6	6	0	0	0	0	35.0	23	135	9	9	3	1	1	1	10	0	34	2	1
Rosario, Juan, H.V.	1	4	.200	7.53	22	2	0	0	4	1	34.2	39	161	33	29	2	1	2	6	20	0	27	7	1
Rosario, Rodrigo, Aub.	0	0	.000	0.00	2	0	0	0	2	0	2.0	0	9	0	0	0	0	0	0	3	0	2	1	0
Rosario, Ruben, N.J.	2	7	.222	5.11	16	9	0	0	1	0	49.1	33	216	33	28	2	0	2	5	37	0	63	6	2
Rupe, Ryan, H.V.	1	0	1.000	0.68	3	3	0	0	0	0	13.1	8	50	1	1	0	1	0	0	2	0	18	1	0
Saenz, Jason, Pit.*	2	3	.400	6.75	12	7	0	0	1	0	44.0	56	199	37	33	6	1	2	2	23	1	34	4	2
Sams, Aaron, Wil.*	6	5	.545	3.43	15	14	2	0	0	0	78.2	66	335	40	30	4	1	3	2	47	0	72	6	4
Sandoval, Marcos, St.C.	1	2	.333	6.15	16	4	0	0	3	1	41.0	33	185	32	28	4	1	0	7	22	0	39	3	1
Santana, Humberto, Pit.*	3	2	.600	3.30	14	13	0	0	0	0	71.0	69	295	32	26	2	2	5	1	18	1	60	4	2
Santana, Johan, Aub.*	7	5	.583	4.36	15	15	1	1	0	0	86.2	81	370	52	42	9	3	3	10	21	0	88	7	0
Satterfield, Jeremy, St.C.	0	1	.000	10.38	1	1	0	0	0	0	4.1	3	22	5	5	0	1	1	5	0	6	1	0
Schuldt, Matt, H.V.	3	2	.600	2.81	33	0	0	0	12	5	41.2	30	175	15	13	2	4	0	3	20	3	56	8	1
Seale, Dustin, St.C.*	2	0	1.000	4.99	21	0	0	0	9	0	39.2	41	184	28	22	5	1	2	3	19	0	43	2	0
Seaman, John, Uti.	0	0	.000	6.41	14	0	0	0	7	2	26.2	35	123	19	19	2	0	0	2	9	1	15	2	2
Seberino, Ronni, H.V.*	3	2	.600	4.15	22	5	0	0	1	0	52.0	47	223	29	24	2	1	5	2	24	0	61	12	2
Serrano, Elio, Bat.	3	2	.600	2.55	13	3	0	0	3	1	35.1	28	144	13	10	1	1	2	2	10	0	26	2	1
Serrano, Jim, Ver.	0	0	.000	1.17	7	0	0	0	7	5	7.2	3	28	1	1	0	0	0	0	1	0	12	1	0
Sessions, Doug, Aub.	1	0	1.000	2.30	26	0	0	0	24	14	31.1	22	125	10	8	2	2	1	0	10	0	41	0	1
Severino, Edy, St.C.	0	0	.000	2.25	2	0	0	0	0	0	4.0	1	15	1	1	1	0	0	0	3	0	5	0	0
Shaddix, Jeff, One.	4	1	.800	3.94	21	0	0	0	2	1	29.2	27	130	16	13	2	1	1	0	13	0	28	2	0
Shea, Galen, Jam.	0	1	.000	7.71	2	0	0	0	2	1	2.1	3	10	2	2	0	0	0	0	3	0	0	0	0
Sheldon, Kyle, Ver.	0	0	.000	2.33	21	0	0	0	16	2	27.0	17	107	8	7	2	1	2	4	0	32	4	0
Shibilo, Andy, N.J.	4	4	.500	3.45	9	9	0	0	0	0	47.0	51	202	21	18	2	1	0	3	8	0	54	0	1
Siciliano, Jess, Erie	0	0	.000	5.68	12	0	0	0	4	0	12.2	16	65	14	8	0	1	0	2	8	1	8	4	1
Silva, Carlos, Bat.	2	3	.400	6.35	9	7	0	0	0	0	45.1	61	206	37	32	4	0	1	2	9	0	27	2	0
Sismondo, Bobby, Jam.*	2	0	1.000	0.71	2	2	0	0	0	0	12.2	7	49	1	1	1	0	0	1	3	0	19	0	1
Slomkowski, Robert, Low.	3	0	1.000	9.39	22	0	0	0	13	3	30.2	42	150	38	32	5	0	3	3	12	1	32	6	4
Smetek, Peter, H.V.*	0	0	.000	1.69	4	0	0	0	4	0	5.1	6	23	2	1	0	0	0	0	1	0	7	2	0
Smith, Brandon, Aub.	0	1	.000	2.20	13	0	0	0	9	4	28.2	26	126	13	7	0	0	1	1	12	2	30	1	1
Smith, Clinton, Jam.	2	5	.286	5.64	12	8	0	0	1	0	44.2	47	207	36	28	4	0	0	3	27	0	44	7	3
Smith, Taylor, St.C.	4	5	.444	5.10	15	15	0	0	0	0	77.2	87	351	61	44	8	0	4	5	26	0	61	4	0
Sosa, Franklin, Jam.	0	1	.000	6.19	19	0	0	0	6	0	36.1	40	165	28	25	5	0	0	4	17	0	15	6	2
Sparks, Steve, Erie	2	7	.222	4.43	14	10	0	0	0	0	63.0	55	282	38	31	3	0	2	9	30	1	61	5	3
Spiegel, Mike, Wat.*	1	0	1.000	0.00	1	1	0	0	0	0	6.0	2	25	1	0	0	0	0	2	5	0	7	0	1
Stafford, Mike, St.C.*	1	0	1.000	1.38	14	0	0	0	8	1	26.0	22	107	7	4	1	2	0	1	6	0	14	1	2
Stemle, Steve, N.J.	3	3	.500	1.83	9	9	0	0	0	0	44.1	37	184	17	9	1	0	1	14	0	47	4	1
Sullivan, Peter, Aub.	1	0	1.000	4.88	17	0	0	0	14	1	24.0	28	117	17	13	3	1	0	4	14	0	20	1	1
Swinburnson, Tyler, Wat.	0	1	.000	5.01	17	0	0	0	8	4	32.1	30	149	21	18	1	0	2	1	23	1	29	8	0
Terwilliger, Rich, Aub.	0	0	.000	9.00	2	0	0	0	2	0	3.0	6	16	3	3	0	0	0	1	0	0	2	1	0
Tetz, Kristofer, Ver.	5	5	.500	3.79	17	11	0	0	3	1	76.0	76	322	41	32	8	3	1	3	19	0	51	4	0
Torres, Leonardo, Wil.*	1	2	.333	0.92	27	0	0	0	10	2	39.0	24	149	7	4	3	2	15	2	36	0	0

Pitcher, Team	W	L	Pct.	ERA	G	GS	CG	ShO	GF	Sv.	IP	H	TBF	R	ER	HR	SH	SF	HB	BB	IBB	SO	WP	Bk.
Tucker, Thomas, Ver.	3	1	.750	2.18	6	6	0	0	0	0	33.0	24	135	9	8	0	1	0	2	15	0	34	3	0
Vael, Rob, Wat.	4	3	.571	4.12	12	9	0	0	1	0	54.2	56	228	25	25	7	0	1	3	16	0	52	5	0
Vargas, Jose, Wat.	2	2	.500	1.45	5	5	1	0	0	0	31.0	28	127	14	5	1	1	1	2	7	0	22	2	0
Vega, Rene, Pit.*	1	0	1.000	1.69	2	0	0	0	1	0	5.1	2	19	1	1	0	0	0	0	1	0	6	0	0
Vogt, Robert, Erie*	0	4	.000	9.68	15	5	0	0	4	0	30.2	40	162	42	33	9	0	4	1	32	0	25	10	0
Vogtli, Robb, One.	1	2	.333	3.91	25	0	0	0	22	14	25.1	29	119	16	11	1	3	1	2	13	1	28	2	0
Waldron, Bradley, Ver.	1	1	.500	4.50	16	0	0	0	5	0	26.0	26	108	14	13	5	0	3	2	6	0	24	0	0
Walrond, Les, N.J.*	2	4	.333	4.01	13	10	0	0	0	0	51.2	52	228	31	23	1	1	2	0	24	0	52	3	0
Wamback, Trevor, Ver.	0	1	.000	6.10	3	2	0	0	1	0	10.1	8	46	8	7	2	0	0	1	4	0	7	1	0
Weaver, Jeff, Jam.	1	0	1.000	1.50	3	3	0	0	0	0	12.0	6	44	4	2	0	0	1	1	0	0	12	0	1
Weber, Brett, One.	4	1	.800	3.04	19	8	1	1	2	0	68.0	68	285	28	23	4	2	0	3	13	0	68	4	3
Wedel, Jeremy, Bat.	7	6	.538	4.38	16	15	1	0	0	0	88.1	102	376	48	43	3	1	2	3	15	0	65	11	0
Weslowski, Robert, Pit.	1	1	.500	11.05	2	2	0	0	0	0	7.1	10	40	11	9	0	0	1	2	5	0	3	2	0
Westmoreland, Ken, Bat.	3	1	.750	1.43	7	7	0	0	0	0	37.2	33	147	10	6	0	0	0	0	5	0	39	1	0
White, Matt, Wat.*	3	2	.600	4.28	6	6	0	0	0	0	27.1	31	120	19	13	4	0	2	2	11	1	24	1	2
Whiteley, Shad, One.	8	2	.800	2.44	14	14	1	0	0	0	81.0	53	335	30	22	0	3	1	5	39	0	85	6	5
Whitney, Jacob, Aub.*	5	5	.500	2.98	18	13	0	0	2	0	84.2	92	365	42	28	5	1	0	5	16	0	64	4	4
Wiedl, Andrew, Bat.*	2	2	.500	4.60	21	0	0	0	5	0	31.1	33	148	22	16	1	0	2	5	15	0	26	2	0
Williams, David, Erie*	2	2	.500	3.23	22	2	0	0	4	0	47.1	45	203	21	17	6	2	0	3	14	0	38	2	0
Williams, Larry, Erie	0	1	.000	13.50	2	1	0	0	0	0	3.1	7	20	5	5	0	1	0	0	3	0	3	0	1
Wood, Stanton, One.	0	0	.000	0.00	7	0	0	0	1	1	13.1	7	49	3	0	1	0	1	0	3	0	14	1	0
Wright, Christopher, H.V.	1	1	.500	2.30	31	0	0	0	23	14	47.0	44	197	17	12	3	0	1	2	9	0	41	2	0
Wuertz, Michael, Wil.	7	5	.583	3.44	14	14	1	0	0	0	86.1	79	359	36	33	4	3	2	0	19	0	59	1	2
Zallie, Chris, Low.*	3	2	.600	4.01	20	2	0	0	6	0	49.1	56	219	24	22	2	1	1	2	24	2	67	6	0
Zamarripa, Tony, Wil.	4	2	.667	3.97	17	5	0	0	3	0	45.1	46	194	23	20	1	0	3	0	17	0	34	1	0
Zipser, Mike, Bat.	0	1	.000	2.67	19	0	0	0	3	0	27.0	26	117	10	8	1	1	1	8	0	0	33	3	0
Zwemke, Bryan, H.V.	1	1	.500	7.50	12	0	0	0	2	0	18.0	25	91	18	15	3	1	1	1	13	0	18	3	0
Zyskowski, Garrett, Aub.*	2	0	1.000	0.00	5	0	0	0	0	0	12.0	5	47	4	0	1	0	1	0	8	0	9	0	0

COMBINATION SHUTOUTS: **Auburn (5)**—Redding-Peguero, Santana-Blackmore-Sessions, Whitney-Peguero, Redding-Peguero-Sullivan, Peguero-Pascarella-Redding. **Batavia (4)**—Kuber-Pilato, Wedel-Wiedl-Hiles, Gaery-Ciesla-Pilato, Geary-Hiles. **Erie (3)**—Rhea-Gray-Luttig, Prater-Williams-Gray-Buirley, Williams-Hlodin-Siciliano. **Hudson Valley (7)**—James-Kofler, Rupe-Jimenez, Hertzel-Wright-Jimenez-Schuldt, Harper-Seberino-Schuldt-Wright, Flohr-Rosario-Jimenez-Cummins, Harper-Cornejo-Schuldt-Wright, James-Jimenez-Flohr. **Jamestown (1)**—Smith-McGowan-Keller. **Lowell (3)**—Miller-Donahoo-Cisar, Lampley-Hill-Cisar, Lampley-Cisar. **New Jersey (5)**—Lanfranco-Griffin-Langen-Gooden, Lanfranco-Griffin-Langen-Gooden, Shibilo-Bates-Langen-Gooden, Prather-Garcia-Guzman, Hutchinson-Rosario-Garcia-Gooden. **Oneonta (3)**—Rogers-Vogtli, Padua-Carpenter, Whiteley-Rodriguez. **Pittsfield (2)**—Santana-Berger, Bellhorn-Prokop. **St. Catharines (5)**—Huggins-Gourlay-Marxwell, Gourlay-Kingrey, Huggins-Gourlay-Kingrey, Place-Gourlay-Eversgerd-Kingrey, Huggins-Gourlay. **Utica (4)**—Moore-Cowan-Olsen, Farizo-Jupe-Clackum, Olsen-Noyce-Clackum, Olsen-Noyce. **Vermont (7)**—Julio-Field-Serrano, Tetz-Mangum, Mangum-Kanovich-Sheldon-Serrano, Agamennone-Tetz-Waldron-Sheldon, Bridges-Kanovich-Field, Arthurs-Kanovich-Sheldon, Tetz-Sheldon. **Watertown (4)**—Marietta-Everett, Percell-Carrasco, Reinike-Escobar-Kearney, Reinike-Escobar-Everett. **Williamsport (6)**—Wuertz-Gunderson, Bruback-Dant-Gunderson, Wuertz-Gunderson, Ohman-Torres, Hammons-Torres-Krug, Wuertz-Torres.

NO-HIT GAMES: None.

PITCHERS WITH TWO OR MORE TEAMS

Pitcher, Team	W	L	Pct.	ERA	G	GS	CG	ShO	GF	Sv.	IP	H	TBF	R	ER	HR	SH	SF	HB	BB	IBB	SO	WP	Bk.
Gresko, Michael, Erie*	0	0	.000	23.82	5	0	0	0	0	0	5.2	14	41	16	15	1	0	0	1	9	0	8	1	1
Gresko, Michael, Pit.*	0	1	.000	9.22	9	0	0	0	5	0	13.2	25	78	17	14	0	1	1	2	12	1	11	4	0

1998 FIELDING

TEAM

Team	Pct.	G	PO	A	E	TC	DP	PB	Team	Pct.	G	PO	A	E	TC	DP	PB
Auburn	.966	75	1939	729	95	2763	59	26	Jamestown........	.957	75	1982	840	127	2949	54	23
Utica................	.965	76	1910	829	98	2837	62	13	Vermont	.957	76	1959	795	124	2878	60	25
Williamsport.......	.965	75	1934	771	98	2803	63	24	Pittsfield	.955	76	2017	870	135	3022	75	10
Watertown.........	.965	76	1957	769	100	2826	59	15	St. Catharines ...	.951	76	1986	793	143	2922	55	17
Oneonta...........	.963	76	1968	811	106	2885	62	14	Lowell	.948	76	1989	815	154	2958	43	17
New Jersey	.962	75	1970	720	105	2795	49	18	Erie	.945	76	2020	749	162	2931	58	22
Hudson Valley ...	.962	76	2074	837	115	3026	63	17	TRIPLE PLAYS: None.								
Batavia	.962	76	1985	841	112	2938	70	12									

INDIVIDUAL

FIRST BASEMEN

NOTE: All caps denotes fielding-percentage leader based on 38 games for catchers, 51 for all other non-pitchers and 76 innings for pitchers. *Throws lefthanded.

Player, Team	Pct.	G	PO	A	E	TC	DP
Adorno, Wilson, Erie	1.000	1	1	0	0	1	0
August, Brian, One.	.957	10	66	1	3	70	5
Bacci, Tony, Erie*	1.000	1	0	1	0	1	1
Bender, Heath, Wat.*	.988	10	78	5	1	84	5
Benham, David, Low.	.944	3	15	2	1	18	1
Besco, Derek, Jam.	.986	6	69	4	1	74	3
Byrd, Brandon, Aub.	.952	19	152	6	8	166	10
Carnes, M. Shayne, Bat.* .	.986	61	534	42	8	584	49
Carter, Charley, Aub.	.994	59	487	23	3	513	44
Castri, Andrea, One.	1.000	1	9	1	0	10	0
Daggett, Jesse, Erie	1.000	8	59	2	0	61	4
Da Luz, Craig, Jam.	.952	7	55	4	3	62	3
Dampeer, Kelly, Wat.	.986	17	134	6	2	142	9
Elliott, Dawan, Erie*	.947	15	103	4	6	113	7
Falcon, Edwin, Low.	.983	35	283	12	5	300	17
Farnsworth, Troy, N.J.	.963	21	146	9	6	161	9

Player, Team	Pct.	G	PO	A	E	TC	DP
Folkers, Brandon, N.J.*	.981	41	292	17	6	315	18
Forbush, Nate, Jam.	.984	19	178	9	3	190	16
Goodson, Steven, H.V.	.979	58	530	32	12	574	46
Gregg, Neal, One.	.988	49	384	21	5	410	30
Hart, Keith, Low.	.977	33	278	15	7	300	14
HINSKE, Eric, Wil.	.997	68	561	49	2	612	51
Hummel, Dan, N.J.	.989	28	172	14	2	188	14
Jones, Aaron, One.*	.989	30	255	27	3	285	21
Kato, Takaaki, Wil.	1.000	3	23	0	0	23	2
Law, Keith, Jam.	.960	8	69	3	3	75	3
Leahy, Bart, Uti.	1.000	1	1	0	0	1	0
Lee, Richard, St.C.	1.000	2	9	1	0	10	1
Longmire, Marcel, Wil.	.980	7	46	3	1	50	4
Lucca, Tony, Uti.*	.989	19	168	11	2	181	15
Ludvigsen, Marc, Pit.*	1.000	1	1	0	0	1	0
MacMillan, Chris, Wat.	.980	47	376	18	8	402	32
Marn, Josh, H.V.	1.000	7	67	8	0	75	4
Maxwell, Keith, Erie	.982	56	421	25	8	454	38
Na, Jim, Ver.	.981	16	94	7	2	103	8
Neal, Blaine, Uti.	.982	33	252	16	5	273	17

Player, Team	Pct.	G	PO	A	E	TC	DP
Nieves, Juan, St.C.	.984	33	216	23	4	243	21
Peniche, Fray, Jam.	1.000	11	75	3	0	78	3
Pittman, Thomas, Ver.	.979	58	490	25	11	526	37
Polk, Chad, St.C.	.935	11	40	3	3	46	3
Quero, Pedro, Ver.	.972	10	65	4	2	71	7
Rigsby, Randy, Uti.*	.985	36	298	22	5	325	28
Rodeheaver, Roger, Bat.	.989	23	169	10	2	181	17
Rojas, Mo, Low.	.987	9	69	6	1	76	5
Smith, Casey, Wat.	.963	4	24	2	1	27	2
Snyder, Earl, Pit.	.990	46	391	26	4	421	40
Suriel, Miguel, H.V.	1.000	12	97	7	0	104	8
Tolbert, William (Alex), Erie	1.000	5	47	1	0	48	1
Umbria, Jose, St.C.	1.000	11	83	5	0	88	9
Valentine, Anthony, Pit.	.988	39	323	18	4	345	29
Vargas, Arias, Jam.	.982	29	257	11	5	273	20
Walker, Shon, Erie*	.917	1	11	0	1	12	0
Whitlock, Mike, St.C.	.985	43	301	18	5	324	14

SECOND BASEMEN

Player, Team	Pct.	G	PO	A	E	TC	DP
Araujo, Danilo, N.J.	.974	24	31	44	2	77	6
Araujo, Victor, One.	.831	16	30	39	14	83	9
August, Brian, One.	.933	6	5	9	1	15	1
Backe, Brandon, H.V.	.800	2	2	2	1	5	0
Barnett, Brian, St.C.	.907	23	37	41	8	86	3
Bone, Billy, Erie	.970	16	26	38	2	66	11
Brett, Jason, Pit.	.915	25	46	62	10	118	11
Bush, Ron, Jam.	.966	20	33	52	3	88	13
Casillas, Uriel, Bat.	.958	51	87	143	10	240	36
Champagne, Andre, Pit.	.800	2	2	2	1	5	0
Cruz, Luis, H.V.	.959	63	125	154	12	291	40
Dampeer, Kelly, Wat.	.981	35	68	88	3	159	19
Eaddy, Deon, Wil.	1.000	1	2	1	0	3	0
Escalona, Felix, Aub.	1.000	8	7	12	0	19	1
Estevez, Domingo, St.C.	.935	39	79	80	11	170	19
Farnsworth, Troy, N.J.	.800	3	1	3	1	5	0
Foulds, Kalin, H.V.	1.000	5	7	9	0	16	0
GINTER, Keith, Aub.	.971	71	93	178	8	279	36
Griffin, Matthew, Wil.	.962	38	62	88	6	156	20
Hammond, Jamie, Ver.	.968	10	11	19	1	31	2
Heying, Scott, St.C.	.983	27	42	74	2	118	15
Hill, Willy, Uti.	.966	12	8	20	1	29	3
Hook, Kevin, Ver.	.000	1	0	0	1	1	0
Jackson, Brandon, St.C.	1.000	6	8	12	0	20	1
James, Tony, Low.	.967	48	98	107	7	212	17
Joyce, Jesse, Aub.	1.000	1	0	1	0	1	0
Kane, Kevin, One.	.667	5	0	2	1	3	0
Kelly, Heath, Uti.	.963	25	43	60	4	107	8
Kidwell, Tommy, N.J.	.949	38	65	84	8	157	18
Llanos, Alex, H.V.	1.000	8	13	19	0	32	7
McGrath, Sean, Pit.	.885	4	9	14	3	26	2
Mejias, Oliver, Erie	1.000	7	5	10	0	15	0
Melo, Ramon, Wil.	1.000	4	7	6	0	13	2
Moraga, Omar, Wat.	1.000	4	9	5	0	14	0
Moreno, Mikel, Wil.	.972	29	55	82	4	141	18
Myers, Tootie, Ver.	.936	70	144	162	21	327	36
Nunez, Jose, N.J.	.964	18	34	46	3	83	7
Olivares, Teuris, One.	.953	73	123	199	16	338	44
Parker, Clark, Erie	.840	5	4	17	4	25	4
Polonia, Israel, Uti.	.945	22	44	59	6	109	11
Powers, Jeff, Wat.	1.000	2	1	3	0	4	0
Pratt, Scott, Wat.	.966	36	53	88	5	146	17
Rachels, Wesley, Bat.	.983	26	50	63	2	115	18
Ravelo, Manuel, Erie	.849	15	26	19	8	53	5
Roush, Ryan, Low.	1.000	1	1	1	0	2	0
Runnells, T.J., Jam.	.960	58	118	143	11	272	21
Santoro, Patrick, Low.	.940	28	50	59	7	116	7
Santos, Angel, Low.	.969	8	16	15	1	32	4
Schrager, Tony, Wil.	.960	8	6	18	1	25	2
Skrehot, Shaun, Erie	.966	23	44	42	3	89	9
Smalls, Terrance, Uti.	.979	22	45	49	2	96	11
Ware, Ryan, H.V.	1.000	3	3	5	0	8	1
Washington, Rico, Erie	1.000	4	2	11	0	13	3
Wigginton, Ty, Pit.	.964	52	104	135	9	248	35

THIRD BASEMEN

Player, Team	Pct.	G	PO	A	E	TC	DP
Adorno, Wilson, Erie	.889	3	3	5	1	9	3
Anderson, Franklin, Erie	1.000	3	1	2	0	3	0
August, Brian, One.	.907	53	30	77	11	118	3
Barnett, Brian, St.C.	.824	16	9	33	9	51	1
Bernhardt, Jossephang, St.C.	.836	28	12	49	12	73	6

Player, Team	Pct.	G	PO	A	E	TC	DP
Bone, Billy, Erie	.889	5	3	5	1	9	0
Boone, Matt, Jam.	.700	4	3	4	3	10	0
Bowring, Jason, Pit.	.889	45	32	96	16	144	3
Brett, Jason, Pit.	.783	16	6	30	10	46	6
Bush, Ron, Jam.	.962	32	22	53	3	78	3
Casillas, Uriel, Bat.	.950	6	7	12	1	20	0
Castri, Andrea, One.	.817	38	23	44	15	82	1
Cotten, Jeremy, Erie	.714	12	6	14	8	28	1
Cronk, Brian, Erie	.875	3	2	5	1	8	0
Da Luz, Craig, Jam.	.931	36	21	100	9	130	6
Dampeer, Kelly, Wat.	.923	4	4	8	1	13	1
Darjean, John, One.	1.000	1	2	0	0	2	0
Duncan, Carlos, Bat.	.893	71	41	159	24	224	10
Eaddy, Deon, Wil.	.927	37	26	63	7	96	2
ENSBERG, Morgan, Aub.	.926	58	38	99	11	148	6
Escalona, Felix, Aub.	.667	3	3	3	3	9	0
Estevez, Domingo, St.C.	.750	1	2	1	1	4	1
Farnsworth, Troy, N.J.	.916	44	32	88	11	131	10
Feliz, Joselyn, Uti.	.625	1	1	4	3	8	0
Griffin, Matthew, Wil.	.909	14	8	22	3	33	5
Haley, Ryan, Wat.	1.000	1	10	0	0	10	0
Hammond, Jamie, Ver.	1.000	2	0	3	0	3	0
Hart, Keith, Low.	.667	4	2	0	1	3	0
Heying, Scott, St.C.	.923	7	2	10	1	13	1
Hodges, Scott, Ver.	.881	39	22	82	14	118	8
Honeycutt, Heath, Uti.	.898	65	36	140	20	196	9
Hoover, Paul, H.V.	1.000	1	1	0	0	1	0
Hubbel, Travis, St.C.	.667	7	1	5	3	9	0
Jackson, Brandon, St.C.	.882	18	8	22	4	34	5
Jordan, Yustin, Erie	.900	2	4	5	1	10	0
Joyce, Jesse, Aub.	.917	14	8	25	3	36	2
Kelly, Chris, N.J.	.810	9	5	12	4	21	0
Law, Keith, Jam.	.636	7	0	7	4	11	0
Lee, Richard, St.C.	.800	12	6	18	6	30	0
Lentz, Ryan, Ver.	.879	37	24	78	14	116	8
Llanos, Alex, H.V.	.846	6	5	6	2	13	1
MacMillan, Chris, Wat.	1.000	9	6	10	0	16	1
Maxwell, Keith, Erie	.000	1	0	0	1	1	0
McGrath, Sean, Pit.	1.000	3	2	7	0	9	0
Medina, Luis, Wil.	.810	36	24	44	16	84	5
Mejias, Oliver, Erie	1.000	3	2	4	0	6	0
Moraga, Omar, Wat.	.885	59	47	114	21	182	13
Nunez, Jose, N.J.	.903	29	15	50	7	72	3
Padgett, Matt, Uti.	.000	2	0	0	1	1	0
Perez, Edwin, Wat.	.929	4	4	9	1	14	0
Polk, Chad, St.C.	.867	4	0	13	2	15	0
Polonia, Israel, Uti.	.800	5	5	3	2	10	0
Ribaudo, Mike, Pit.	.667	1	2	4	3	9	1
Riggins, Auntwan, St.C.	.923	5	6	6	1	13	0
Rodriguez, Ronny, Low.	.786	4	2	9	3	14	3
Rojas, Mo, Low.	1.000	8	3	6	0	9	0
Sandberg, Jared, H.V.	.915	70	55	159	20	234	15
Santoro, Patrick, Low.	.615	9	5	11	10	26	1
Santos, Angel, Low.	.941	5	4	12	1	17	0
Skrehot, Shaun, Erie	.818	13	4	23	6	33	3
Smalls, Terrance, Uti.	.842	6	4	12	3	19	0
Suriel, Miguel, H.V.	1.000	2	1	3	0	4	1
Terni, Chaz, Low.	.917	46	36	96	12	144	5
Valentine, Anthony, Pit.	.810	8	2	15	4	21	2
Ware, Ryan, H.V.	1.000	2	2	6	0	8	0
Washington, Rico, Erie	.935	44	22	93	8	123	6
Wigginton, Ty, Pit.	.864	11	5	14	3	22	1
Wright, Bryan, Low.	.889	6	2	6	1	9	1

SHORTSTOPS

Player, Team	Pct.	G	PO	A	E	TC	DP
Backe, Brandon, H.V.	.833	3	3	2	1	6	1
Badeaux, Brooks, H.V.	.927	67	81	200	22	303	32
Bautista, Rayner, Jam.	.917	60	87	191	25	303	30
Bernhardt, Jossephang, St.C.	.920	32	48	67	10	125	10
Brett, Jason, Pit.	.938	10	12	33	3	48	3
Bush, Ron, Jam.	1.000	1	3	5	0	8	1
Carek, Mark, One.	.961	76	100	246	14	360	44
Casillas, Uriel, Bat.	.917	2	5	6	1	12	2
Champagne, Andre, Pit.	.923	2	3	9	1	13	1
Cleto, Ambioris, Erie	.932	48	89	157	18	264	24
DeNure, Chip, Bat.	.737	5	5	9	5	19	3
Eaddy, Deon, Wil.	.903	7	14	14	3	31	4
Ensberg, Morgan, Aub.	1.000	1	1	2	0	3	1
Escalona, Felix, Aub.	.939	39	69	100	11	180	23
Everett, Adam, Low.	.918	21	34	67	9	110	9
Foulds, Kalin, H.V.	.926	9	8	17	2	27	2

Player, Team	Pct.	G	PO	A	E	TC	DP
Freeman, Brad, N.J.	.926	73	97	178	22	297	22
Frese, Nate, Wil.	.958	53	88	163	11	262	32
Griffin, Matthew, Wil.	.930	14	31	22	4	57	6
Hammond, Jamie, Ver.	.944	19	28	56	5	89	8
Hook, Kevin, Ver.	1.000	3	4	8	0	12	2
Jackson, Brandon, St.C.	.924	36	39	95	11	145	10
James, Tony, Low.	.889	5	5	11	2	18	2
Kelly, Heath, Uti.	1.000	2	3	8	0	11	1
Law, Keith, Jam.	.897	17	27	51	9	87	7
Lopez, Felipe, St.C.	.895	18	21	56	9	86	13
Machado, Albenis, Ver.	.954	55	97	175	13	285	26
Matranga, David, Aub.	.943	40	43	122	10	175	17
McKinley, Josh, Ver.	1.000	3	3	7	0	10	0
Melo, Ramon, Wil.	1.000	5	9	6	0	15	2
Miller, Kenny, Pit.	.921	67	128	211	29	368	43
Nunez, Jose, N.J.	.875	9	9	12	3	24	2
Olivares, Teuris, One.	1.000	4	1	4	0	5	0
Perez, Edwin, Wat.	.871	7	8	19	4	31	5
Polonia, Israel, Uti.	.909	12	27	33	6	66	11
Powers, Jeff, Wat.	.923	15	12	48	5	65	6
Pratt, Scott, Wat.	1.000	2	4	5	0	9	1
Punto, Nicholas, Bat.	.924	71	107	222	27	356	45
Reyes, Dadny, Uti.	.917	3	4	7	1	12	0
Rodeheaver, Roger, Bat.	1.000	1	0	1	0	1	0
Roush, Ryan, Low.	.873	36	41	83	18	142	10
Santoro, Patrick, Low.	1.000	2	0	4	0	4	1
Santos, Angel, Low.	.868	16	20	46	10	76	4
Skrehot, Shaun, Erie	.890	28	45	76	15	136	13
Smalls, Terrance, Uti.	.875	2	4	3	1	8	1
Sorensen, Zach, Wat.	.951	52	71	160	12	243	25
Ware, Ryan, H.V.	1.000	2	2	6	0	8	0
WATHAN, Derek, Uti.	.964	59	78	162	9	249	29
Wright, Bryan, Low.	.786	6	5	17	6	28	2

OUTFIELDERS

Player, Team	Pct.	G	PO	A	E	TC	DP
Abreu, Miguel, Uti.	.958	55	63	6	3	72	0
Adeeb, Josh, Low.	1.000	3	2	2	0	4	0
August, Brian, One.	.800	5	4	0	1	5	0
Backe, Brandon, H.V.	1.000	5	7	0	0	7	0
Barnett, Brian, St.C.	1.000	4	5	0	0	5	0
Besco, Derek, Jam.	1.000	23	35	2	0	37	0
Beverly, Demetrius, Bat.	.897	23	26	0	3	29	0
Beverly, Shomari, Bat.	.952	9	18	2	1	21	0
Bonilla, Elin, Bat.	.974	30	35	2	1	38	0
Bowring, Jason, Pit.	1.000	1	2	0	0	2	0
Brown, Billy, St.C.	.957	66	84	4	4	92	2
Butler, Garrett, H.V.	.966	67	136	5	5	146	0
Carnes, M. Shayne, Bat.*	1.000	5	3	2	0	5	0
Carter, Shannon, St.C.*	.958	20	19	4	1	24	0
Chambliss, Russ, One.	1.000	19	15	0	0	15	0
Cole, Brian, Pit.	1.000	2	3	0	0	3	0
Connally, Christopher, Wil.	.959	54	63	8	3	74	1
Darjean, John, One.	.992	63	119	3	1	123	2
Davis, J.J., Erie	.932	51	95	1	7	103	0
De La Cruz, Henry, Wil.	.949	65	106	5	6	117	0
Deshazer, Jeremy, Aub.	1.000	7	7	0	0	7	0
DeNure, Chip, Bat.	1.000	43	53	3	0	56	1
Dina, Allen, Pit.	.955	68	141	8	7	156	1
Dunn, Ryan, Aub.	.964	17	23	4	1	28	1
Elliott, Dawan, Erie*	.911	28	48	3	5	56	0
Flores, Jose, Low.	.909	42	47	3	5	55	0
Folkers, Brandon, N.J.*	1.000	3	1	0	0	1	0
Forbes, Kevin, Ver.	1.000	2	2	0	0	2	0
Foulds, Kalin, H.V.	1.000	6	7	1	0	8	0
Gordnier, Aaron, Wat.	.958	28	22	1	1	24	0
Green, Kevin, Uti.	1.000	2	2	0	0	2	0
Greene, Alan, One.	.980	68	93	3	2	98	1
Grindell, Nate, Wat.	.976	21	39	1	1	41	0
Groebner, Mark, Ver.	.974	35	35	3	1	39	1
Hazelton, Justin, Jam.	.969	25	29	2	1	32	0
Hendricks, Jason, Ver.	1.000	6	7	1	0	8	0
Hernandez, Jesus, Wat.*	.956	70	123	7	6	136	1
Hill, Willy, Uti.	.970	61	90	6	3	99	1
Hunt, Joe, Erie	.914	54	114	3	11	128	1
Jordan, Kevin, Aub.	.921	36	34	1	3	38	0
Joyce, Jesse, Aub.	1.000	18	28	3	0	31	1
Kane, Kevin, One.	1.000	1	1	0	0	1	0
Lara, Felix, Erie*	.922	32	56	3	5	64	0
Leahy, Bart, Uti.	.957	42	43	2	2	47	1
Lebron, Jesus, St.C.	.988	42	82	2	1	85	0
Ledesma, Philip, Low.	.971	50	65	3	2	70	1

Player, Team	Pct.	G	PO	A	E	TC	DP
Longmire, Marcel, Wil.	1.000	5	7	2	0	9	0
Ludvigsen, Marc, Pit.*	.951	38	36	3	2	41	0
MacMillan, Chris, Wat.	1.000	1	1	0	0	1	0
Maddox, Derrick, Bat.	.933	11	12	2	1	15	0
Mahoney, Sean, H.V.	.966	61	82	3	3	88	0
Malave, Dennis, Wat.*	.882	6	15	0	2	17	0
Maxwell, Keith, Erie	.917	10	10	1	1	12	1
McDaniels, Paul, Low.	.912	51	43	9	5	57	1
McGrath, Sean, Pit.	1.000	3	1	0	0	1	0
McKinney, Antonio, Jam.	.918	31	43	2	4	49	0
McNaughton, Troy, N.J.*	.980	39	47	1	1	49	0
Mendoza, Angel, Low.	.946	68	102	4	6	112	0
Michaels, Jason, Bat.	.949	65	93	1	5	99	0
Miller, Travis, H.V.	.930	44	49	4	4	57	1
MOLINA, Jim, N.J.	1.000	57	93	6	0	99	0
Moore, Lacarlo, Jam.	1.000	16	23	1	0	24	0
Moreno, Mikel, Wil.	.986	36	68	5	1	74	0
Morillo, Luis, St.C.*	1.000	1	1	0	0	1	0
Mulvehill, Brandon, Pit.	.965	53	73	9	3	85	1
Na, Jim, Ver.	.963	23	26	0	1	27	0
Neal, Blaine, Uti.	1.000	1	2	0	0	2	0
Nicholson, Derek, Aub.	.941	38	61	3	4	68	0
Nicolas, Jose, Erie	.950	66	105	9	6	120	0
Nieves, Juan, St.C.	1.000	19	19	2	0	21	0
Paciorek, Tom, Pit.	1.000	8	8	1	0	9	0
Padgett, Matt, Uti.	.968	67	85	5	3	93	0
Pass, Patrick, Uti.	.913	12	18	3	2	23	2
Payne, Ronald, Wil.*	.980	48	97	2	2	101	0
Perez, Angelo, St.C.	1.000	38	66	4	0	70	0
Perez, Edwin, Wat.	1.000	1	1	0	0	1	0
Piercy, Brad, Ver.	.983	33	55	2	1	58	0
Pigott, Anthony, H.V.	1.000	6	6	1	0	7	0
Porter, Colin, Aub.*	.976	60	76	5	2	83	2
Quero, Pedro, Ver.	.893	65	68	7	9	84	0
Rand, Ian, H.V.	.879	24	26	3	4	33	0
Rauls, Ian, Bat.*	.978	51	84	3	2	89	0
Reyes, Deurys, Jam.*	.957	31	44	1	2	47	0
Rhodes, Dusty, One.	.980	68	90	8	2	100	1
Rich, Billy, Jam.	.938	59	80	11	6	97	3
Rigsby, Randy, Uti.*	1.000	16	23	1	0	24	0
Rivera, Juan, One.	1.000	6	3	1	0	4	0
Rodriguez, Pedro, Pit.*	.987	54	71	7	1	79	2
Rojas, Christian, Wat.	.968	59	89	3	3	95	2
Rojas, Mo, Low.	.925	42	45	4	4	53	1
Santana, Osmany, Wat.*	1.000	19	48	0	0	48	0
Secoda, Joe, N.J.	.976	48	77	4	2	83	1
Smetek, Peter, H.V.*	1.000	16	8	0	0	8	0
Smith, Nate, N.J.	.974	38	37	1	1	39	0
Snead, Esix, N.J.	.976	55	123	1	3	127	1
Snyder, Earl, Pit.	.974	24	36	2	1	39	0
Stratton, Robert, Pit.	1.000	4	5	0	0	5	0
Suriel, Miguel, H.V.	.976	32	36	4	1	41	0
Thompson, Sonny, Low.	1.000	6	7	1	0	8	0
Thompson, Tyler, St.C.	.989	63	89	4	1	94	1
Torres, Andres, Jam.	.944	46	80	5	5	90	0
Upshaw, Ryan, Wat.	.949	33	32	5	2	39	0
Urquhart, Derick, Ver.*	.983	76	164	5	3	172	1
Vento, Mike, One.	1.000	24	35	0	0	35	0
Walker, Shon, Erie*	1.000	1	4	1	0	5	0
Wallis, Michael, Wil.*	.983	35	55	2	1	58	0
Washington, Dion, One.	.857	13	10	2	2	14	1
Wigginton, Ty, Pit.	.500	4	2	0	2	4	0
Williams, Ricky, Bat.	1.000	12	17	1	0	18	0
Yates, Chris, Aub.*	.993	65	131	3	1	135	3

CATCHERS

Player, Team	Pct.	G	PO	A	E	TC	DP	PB
Alfonso, Eliezer, N.J.	.981	24	186	17	4	207	2	9
Anderson, Franklin, Erie	1.000	14	101	14	0	115	1	6
Benham, David, Low.	.977	30	228	25	6	259	2	8
Boles, Kevin, Wil.	1.000	11	33	2	0	35	0	1
Buckley, Brandon, Aub.	.986	26	198	17	3	218	1	8
Bundy, Ryan, St.C.	.972	43	313	40	10	363	2	7
Burkhart, Lance, Ver.	.967	12	77	12	3	92	3	5
Candelaria, Tito, One.	.977	19	77	7	2	86	0	4
Clark, Greg, N.J.	.990	43	347	41	4	392	5	8
Daggett, Jesse, Erie	.988	31	234	12	3	249	1	11
Dampeer, Kelly, Wat.	1.000	1	3	0	0	3	0	0
Deitrick, Jeremy, Bat.	.976	10	75	7	2	84	0	4
Diaz, Diogenes, Erie	.978	39	249	21	6	276	2	5
Dimmick, Josh, Aub.	1.000	9	56	2	0	58	0	1
Dito, Robert, Ver.	.969	4	28	3	1	32	0	0

Player, Team	Pct.	G	PO	A	E	TC	DP	PB
Falcon, Edwin, Low.	1.000	3	6	0	0	6	0	1
Fatheree, Danny, Aub.	.986	44	400	18	6	424	3	17
Feliz, Joselyn, Uti.	.985	17	115	15	2	132	1	5
Forbush, Nate, Jam.	1.000	8	68	12	0	80	1	2
FRICK, Matt, Uti.	.993	38	250	38	2	290	1	3
Gross, Jeremy, One.	1.000	3	7	0	0	7	0	0
Hargreaves, Brad, Wil.	.985	47	276	42	5	323	3	3
Heine, Kyle, One.	.962	23	70	6	3	79	1	5
Hernandez, Michel, One.	.981	59	409	57	9	475	6	8
Hoover, Paul, H.V.	.990	52	446	50	5	501	2	8
Hubbard, Jeremy, Wil.	1.000	11	71	6	0	77	0	1
Hummel, Dan, N.J.	1.000	7	37	2	0	39	0	1
Inge, Brandon, Jam.	.981	35	263	40	6	309	1	11
Johnson, Chadwick, Low.	.981	28	231	32	5	268	2	2
Lambert, Clark, Pit.	1.000	18	88	10	0	98	3	0
Larned, Andrew, Low.	.978	20	118	17	3	138	1	3
Longmire, Marcel, Wil.	.947	25	165	15	10	190	1	19
Marn, Josh, H.V.	1.000	18	115	9	0	124	0	3
McGinnis, Ronald, Bat.	.988	31	214	31	3	248	0	3
Meran, Jorge, Jam.	1.000	15	112	17	0	129	1	4
Morales, Stephen, Uti.	.984	26	161	22	3	186	0	5
Patton, Barry, Wat.	1.000	9	70	2	0	72	0	3
Pena, Rodolfo, Low.	.992	15	96	27	1	124	0	3
Piercy, Brad, Ver.	.981	33	234	26	5	265	2	8
Polk, Chad, St.C.	.974	19	142	9	4	155	0	5
Puffinbarger, Rusty, Wat.	.970	12	59	5	2	66	1	3
Ramos, Kelly, Pit.	.978	57	386	59	10	455	2	10
Rand, Ian, H.V.	1.000	1	1	0	0	1	0	0
Ribaudo, Mike, Pit.	.986	14	62	11	1	74	0	0
Rivera, Luis J., Ver.	.975	32	242	31	7	280	1	12
Salazar, Jeremy, Bat.	1.000	16	116	14	0	130	1	0
Schmidt, Todd, N.J.	.978	10	82	7	2	91	1	0
Silletti, Pete, St.C.	1.000	1	2	0	0	2	0	0
Smith, Casey, Wat.	.978	64	511	69	13	593	5	9
Suriel, Miguel, H.V.	.984	13	118	8	2	128	1	6
Umbria, Jose, St.C.	.988	22	152	9	2	163	3	5
Valdez, Jerry, Bat.	.986	25	187	25	3	215	1	5
Vargas, Arias, Jam.	.984	19	161	19	3	183	1	6
Washington, Rico, Erie	1.000	5	15	3	0	18	1	0

Player, Team	Pct.	G	PO	A	E	TC	DP
Cummins, Jon, H.V.	.000	14	0	0	1	1	0
Dagley, Corey, Bat.	.900	18	3	6	1	10	1
Dant, Larry, Wil.	.929	26	1	12	1	14	1
Delano, Michael, Wil.*	1.000	9	2	1	0	3	0
Delatori, Keola, Wil.	.778	11	2	5	2	9	0
Dobson, Scott, Ver.	.500	17	0	2	2	4	0
Donahoo, Matt, Low.*	1.000	16	0	5	0	5	0
Donovan, Thomas, Bat.	1.000	23	5	1	0	6	1
Drese, Ryan, Wat.	1.000	9	2	4	0	6	1
Escobar, Ruben, Wat.	.667	14	0	2	1	3	0
Everett, Matt, Wat.	1.000	16	0	1	0	1	0
Eversgerd, Randy, St.C.	1.000	17	0	5	0	5	0
Farizo, Brad, Uti.	.900	14	3	15	2	20	0
Field, Nathan, Ver.	.889	25	2	6	1	9	0
Flohr, Adam, H.V.*	1.000	15	3	17	0	20	1
Flores, Benito, Low.*	.875	20	1	13	2	16	0
Frierson, Andrew, Ver.*	1.000	2	0	1	0	1	0
Gagliano, Steve, Uti.	.947	13	5	13	1	19	2
Garcia, Wilson, N.J.	1.000	19	2	5	0	7	1
Garvin, Robert, Uti.	1.000	5	0	3	0	3	0
Geary, Geoffrey, Bat.	1.000	16	9	10	0	19	2
Gonzales, Rick, N.J.	1.000	6	1	0	0	1	0
Gooden, Derek, N.J.	1.000	29	3	11	0	14	0
Gourlay, Matthew, St.C.	.833	25	2	8	2	12	0
Gracesqui, Franklyn, St.C.*	1.000	11	0	2	0	2	0
Grammer, Ed, Bat.	1.000	3	0	1	0	1	0
Gray, Michael, Erie	1.000	29	3	3	0	6	0
Griffin, Kirk, N.J.	.917	35	2	9	1	12	0
Guillory, Dan, Wat.	1.000	3	1	2	0	3	0
Gunderson, Matthew, Wil.	1.000	27	3	4	0	7	0
Gutierrez, Lazaro, Jam.*	1.000	27	0	4	0	4	0
Gutshall, Eric, N.J.	1.000	29	2	2	0	4	0
Guzman, Toribio, N.J.	.818	17	4	5	2	11	0
Hammons, Matt, Wil.	1.000	3	0	5	0	5	0
Harber, Ryan, Uti.*	1.000	11	0	6	0	6	0
Harper, Travis, H.V.	1.000	13	4	7	0	11	1
Heams, Shane, Jam.	.700	24	3	4	3	10	0
Held, Travis, N.J.	.750	14	2	10	4	16	0
Hertzel, Patrick, H.V.	.760	15	4	15	6	25	0
Hiles, Cary, Bat.	.889	25	1	7	1	9	1
Hill, Terrance, Low.*	.909	19	3	7	1	11	2
Hlodan, George, Erie	1.000	20	1	8	0	9	0
Hostetler, Jim, Jam.	1.000	16	2	1	0	3	0
Hueda, Alejandro, St.C.	1.000	11	5	6	0	11	0
Huggins, David, St.C.	.846	15	14	8	4	26	1
Hutchinson, Chad, N.J.	.667	3	0	2	1	3	0
Jackson, Brian, Wat.	.000	1	0	0	1	1	0
James, Delvin, H.V.	1.000	15	3	9	0	12	1
Jimenez, Jason, H.V.*	.800	29	2	6	2	10	0
Jodie, Brett, One.	.923	15	4	8	1	13	2
Johnston, Michael, Erie*	1.000	2	0	1	0	1	0
Julio, Jorge, Ver.	1.000	7	2	4	0	6	0
Jupe, Eric, Uti.	1.000	13	0	2	0	2	0
Kanovich, Jason, Ver.*	1.000	20	1	6	0	7	0
Kearney, Ryan, Wat.	1.000	20	10	3	0	13	0
Keller, Kris, Jam.	1.000	27	3	0	0	3	0
Kingrey, Jarrod, St.C.	.875	25	2	5	1	8	1
Kloes, David, One.	.667	17	0	2	1	3	0
Knowles, Michael, One.	1.000	5	1	1	0	2	0
Kofler, Ed, H.V.	.947	16	4	14	1	19	0
Koutrouba, Thomas, Jam.*	.750	15	6	18	8	32	1
Krug, Dustin, Wil.	1.000	27	0	9	0	9	0
Kubes, Gregory, Bat.*	.957	15	7	15	1	23	1
Lampley, Daniel, Low.	.778	13	3	4	2	9	0
Lanfranco, Otoniel, N.J.	1.000	5	2	1	0	3	0
Langen, Brian, N.J.*	1.000	23	3	4	0	7	0
Linarelli, Tom, Low.	.875	18	1	6	1	8	0
Lovingood, Ray, Pit.*	1.000	13	1	1	0	2	1
Lowery, Phil, Uti.*	.778	7	0	7	2	9	1
Luttig, Chris, Erie*	.800	27	0	4	1	5	0
Madson, William, Jam.	.833	16	2	8	2	12	0
Maleski, Eric, Wat.	1.000	2	1	1	0	2	0
Mangum, Mark, Ver.	.929	14	5	8	1	14	1
Marietta, Ron, Wat.*	1.000	11	2	9	0	11	0
Markwell, Diegomar, St.C.*	.857	17	3	9	2	14	0
Maroth, Mike, Low.*	.818	6	1	8	2	11	1
Matsko, Rich, Wat.	1.000	20	1	6	0	7	0
Mattson, John, Pit.	.875	18	5	2	1	8	0
McCurtain, Paul, Uti.	1.000	17	2	8	0	10	0
McGowan, Brian, Jam.	1.000	18	3	4	0	7	0
Miller, Tom, Low.*	1.000	16	0	13	0	13	0
Molina, Primitivo, Low.	1.000	15	2	7	0	9	0

PITCHERS

Player, Team	Pct.	G	PO	A	E	TC	DP
Agamennone, Brandon, Ver.	1.000	9	2	3	0	5	0
Alvarado, David, Erie	1.000	19	2	3	0	5	0
Alvord, Aaron, Jam.	.917	16	0	11	1	12	1
Aracena, Juan, Wat.	1.000	18	2	3	0	5	0
Aramboles, Ricardo, One.	.500	1	0	1	1	2	0
Arthurs, Shane, Ver.	.889	16	6	10	2	18	1
Avila, David, Uti.	1.000	12	2	4	0	6	2
Bacci, Tony, Erie*	.500	6	0	2	2	4	0
Bair, Andy, Uti.*	1.000	14	1	5	0	6	0
Barrett, Scott, Aub.*	1.000	10	1	7	0	8	0
Bates, Casey, N.J.	1.000	27	2	5	0	7	0
Behn, Brendan, Pit.*	1.000	14	6	8	0	14	0
Beimel, Joe, Erie*	1.000	17	1	11	0	12	0
Bellhorn, Todd, Pit.*	1.000	15	3	11	0	14	1
Berger, Craig, Pit.	.818	23	2	7	2	11	0
Berthelot, Eric, Pit.*	1.000	4	1	2	0	3	0
Blackmore, John, Aub.	1.000	19	3	9	0	12	1
Bravo, Franklin, Erie	.889	11	2	6	1	9	0
Bridges, Donald, Ver.	.947	13	4	14	1	19	0
Brito, Juan, Pit.*	.800	10	0	4	1	5	0
Brown, Chris, Wil.	1.000	28	4	6	0	10	0
Brown, Craig, Wat.*	1.000	16	1	1	0	2	0
Bruback, Matthew, Wil.	.714	14	5	10	6	21	0
Buchanan, Brian, One.*	1.000	15	1	5	0	6	2
Buller, Sean, Jam.*	.875	13	0	7	1	8	1
Burchart, Kyle, Erie	1.000	10	1	1	0	2	0
Carlson, Jeff, One.	.867	18	3	10	2	15	0
Carpenter, Justin, One.	.750	28	1	2	1	4	0
Carr, Timothy, Pit.	.900	23	3	6	1	10	0
Carrasco, Danny, Wat.	.667	13	0	2	1	3	0
Casey, Joe, St.C.	.333	4	1	0	2	3	1
Castelli, Robert, Ver.	1.000	23	3	6	0	9	1
Ciesla, Dave, Bat.*	.800	26	0	4	1	5	0
Cisar, Mark, Low.	.750	22	0	6	2	8	0
Clackum, Scott, Uti.	1.000	20	0	4	0	4	0
Classen, Ender, Erie	1.000	2	0	1	0	1	0
Coco, Pasqual, St.C.	.667	15	1	5	3	9	0
Cook, Andy, Pit.	1.000	15	3	7	0	10	2
Cornejo, Jesse, H.V.*	.947	34	2	16	1	19	0
Cowan, Bobby, Uti.	1.000	17	2	7	0	9	1

CLASS A New York-Pennsylvania League

Player, Team	Pct.	G	PO	A	E	TC	DP
Mondello, Peter, Bat.	1.000	4	0	2	0	2	0
Montilla, Felix, Erie	1.000	27	0	4	0	4	0
Moore, Chris, Uti.	.933	13	5	9	1	15	1
Mowel, Mike, Low.	.900	15	7	11	2	20	0
Norton, Jason, Low.	1.000	6	1	4	0	5	0
Novits, Carey, Wat.*	1.000	5	1	3	0	4	1
Noyce, David, Uti.*	1.000	17	3	4	0	7	0
O'Dette, Rick, Low.*	1.000	9	2	2	0	4	0
Ohman, William, Wil.*	1.000	10	1	3	0	4	1
Olsen, Kevin, Uti.	.938	21	6	9	1	16	0
Ortega, Franklin, N.J.	1.000	15	2	1	0	3	0
Oswalt, Roy, Aub.	.882	11	3	12	2	17	4
Padua, Geraldo, One.	.840	15	6	15	4	25	1
Pascarella, Josh, Aub.	1.000	15	2	10	0	12	1
Pavlovich, Tony, Erie	1.000	8	1	1	0	2	0
Peguero, Darwin, Aub.*	.909	20	1	9	1	11	0
Percell, Brody, Wat.*	1.000	15	2	12	0	14	1
Perez, Julio, Ver.	1.000	12	3	2	0	5	0
Pettyjohn, Adam, Jam.*	1.000	4	3	2	0	5	0
Phillips, Matthew, Low.	1.000	15	6	12	0	18	0
PIDGEON, Matt, Uti.	1.000	14	5	18	0	23	1
Pilato, John, Bat.	1.000	19	3	9	0	12	0
Pineda, Jairo, Aub.	1.000	1	0	2	0	2	0
Place, Eric, St.C.*	.905	19	3	16	2	21	0
Powalski, Richard, Wil.*	1.000	18	1	12	0	13	0
Prater, Andy, Erie	.727	18	3	5	3	11	0
Prather, Scott, N.J.*	.846	15	3	8	2	13	1
Princi, Peter, Pit.	.889	22	1	7	1	9	1
Prokop, Michael, Pit.	.900	26	2	7	1	10	0
Redding, Tim, Aub.	.647	16	4	7	6	17	0
Reinike, Chris, Wat.	1.000	15	2	13	0	15	1
Rhea, Thad, Erie	.842	12	5	11	3	19	2
Ribaudo, Mike, Pit.	.500	1	0	1	1	2	0
Ridenour, Ryan, One.*	1.000	13	2	0	0	2	0
Ridley, Brian, Aub.*	1.000	17	1	4	0	5	0
Roberts, Richard, Jam.*	.958	15	3	20	1	24	2
Rodriguez, Cristobal, Ver.	1.000	6	1	0	0	1	0
Rodriguez, Jorge, One.	1.000	20	4	9	0	13	1
Rogers, Brian, One.	1.000	6	1	7	0	8	0
Rosario, Juan, H.V.	.800	22	3	5	2	10	1
Rosario, Ruben, N.J.	.923	16	5	7	1	13	0
Rupe, Ryan, H.V.	1.000	3	0	2	0	2	0
Saenz, Jason, Pit.*	1.000	12	4	2	0	6	1
Sams, Aaron, Wil.*	.929	15	3	10	1	14	1
Sandoval, Marcos, St.C.	.800	16	2	2	1	5	0
Santana, Humberto, Pit.*	1.000	14	3	16	0	19	1
Santana, Johan, Aub.*	.846	15	3	19	4	26	2
Schuldt, Matt, H.V.	1.000	33	0	3	0	3	0
Seale, Dustin, St.C.*	1.000	21	1	4	0	5	1
Seaman, John, Uti.	1.000	14	3	8	0	11	0
Seberino, Ronni, H.V.*	.750	22	2	10	4	16	0
Serrano, Elio, Bat.	1.000	13	4	3	0	7	0
Serrano, Jim, Ver.	.667	7	2	0	1	3	0
Sessions, Doug, Aub.	1.000	26	1	2	0	3	0
Shaddix, Jeff, One.	1.000	21	3	6	0	9	1
Sheldon, Kyle, Ver.	.750	21	2	1	1	4	0
Shibilo, Andy, N.J.	1.000	9	2	3	0	5	0
Siciliano, Jess, Erie	1.000	12	2	0	0	2	0
Silva, Carlos, Bat.	.667	9	0	2	1	3	1
Sismondo, Bobby, Jam.*	1.000	2	0	1	0	1	0
Slomkowski, Robert, Low.	.600	22	2	1	2	5	1
Smetek, Peter, H.V.*	1.000	4	0	1	0	1	0
Smith, Brandon, Aub.	.667	13	0	2	1	3	0
Smith, Clinton, Jam.	.857	12	1	5	1	7	0
Smith, Taylor, St.C.	1.000	15	7	12	0	19	2
Sosa, Franklin, Jam.	1.000	19	1	2	0	3	1
Sparks, Steve, Erie	.800	14	3	5	2	10	1
Spiegel, Mike, Wat.*	1.000	1	0	2	0	2	0
Stafford, Mike, St.C.*	.750	14	2	1	1	4	0
Stemle, Steve, N.J.	1.000	9	4	3	0	7	0
Sullivan, Peter, Aub.	.800	17	2	2	1	5	1
Swinburnson, Tyler, Wat.	.889	17	3	5	1	9	0
Tetz, Kristofer, Ver.	1.000	17	4	10	0	14	2
Torres, Leonardo, Wil.*	1.000	27	1	8	0	9	0
Tucker, Thomas, Ver.	1.000	6	1	6	0	7	0
Vael, Rob, Wat.	1.000	12	5	8	0	13	0
Vargas, Jose, Wat.	.778	5	1	6	2	9	0
Vega, Rene, Pit.*	1.000	2	1	0	0	1	0
Vogt, Robert, Erie*	1.000	15	1	3	0	4	1
Vogtli, Robb, One.	1.000	25	1	5	0	6	0
Walrond, Les, N.J.*	.818	13	2	7	2	11	0
Wamback, Trevor, Ver.	1.000	3	1	0	0	1	0
Weaver, Jeff, Jam.	.500	3	0	1	1	2	0
Weber, Brett, One.	.889	19	4	12	2	18	1
Wedel, Jeremy, Bat.	.917	16	9	13	2	24	1
Weslowski, Robert, Pit.	1.000	2	0	3	0	3	0
Westmoreland, Ken, Bat.	.889	7	3	5	1	9	0
White, Matt, Wat.*	1.000	6	1	5	0	6	0
Whiteley, Shad, One.	.813	14	5	8	3	16	0
Whitney, Jacob, Aub.*	.909	18	3	17	2	22	0
Wiedl, Andrew, Bat.*	.600	21	1	2	2	5	0
Williams, David, Erie*	1.000	22	3	12	0	15	2
Wood, Stanton, One.	1.000	7	1	2	0	3	1
Wright, Christopher, H.V.	.846	31	6	5	2	13	0
Wuertz, Michael, Wil.	.938	14	4	11	1	16	1
Zallie, Chris, Low.*	.833	20	1	4	1	6	1
Zamarripa, Tony, Wil.	.900	17	4	5	1	10	1
Zipser, Mike, Bat.	.750	19	2	1	1	4	0
Zwemke, Bryan, H.V.	1.000	12	2	4	0	6	0
Zyskowski, Garrett, Aub.*	.000	5	0	0	1	1	0

The following players did not have any fielding statistics at the positions indicated or appeared only as a designated hitter, pinch-hitter or pinch-runner: Adams, dh; ph; Adorno, p; Barnett, ss; Bowring, p; Buirley, p; Dunn, p; Erwin, p; Folkers, p; Gresko, p; Gross, p; Hancock, p; Heine, of; Honeycutt, of; T. James, 3b; C. Johnson; K. Jordan, 3b; Keisler, p; H. Kelly, of; Larned, p; Ledesma, p; Lucca, of; McBride, p; McGrath, ss; Mejias, p; Melo, of; Nicholson, 1b; Paulino, p; Pigott, 2b; Pizarro, p; Punto, 2b; Rachels, of; Ramirez, p; Ramos, 3b; Dadny Reyes, 3b; R. Rodriguez, ss; Rosario, p; Rousch, 3b; Satterfield, p; Severino, p; Shea, p; Suriel, 2b; Terwilliger, p; Valentine, of; Waldron, p; L. Williams, p; Warren, ph.

LEAGUE CHAMPIONS

Year	Team	Pct.	Year	Team	Pct.	Year	Team	Pct.
1939—	Olean*	.631	1954—	Corning*	.621	1968—	Auburn	.645
1940—	Olean*	.625	1955—	Hamilton*	.656		Oneonta (2nd)*	.558
1941—	Jamestown	.618	1956—	Wellsville*	.617	1969—	Oneonta	.662
	Bradford (2nd)†	.549	1957—	Wellsville	.632	1970—	Auburn	.623
1942—	Jamestown*	.672		Erie (2nd)†	.598	1971—	Oneonta	.662
1943—	Lockport	.591	1958—	Wellsville	.556	1972—	Niagara Falls	.686
	Wellsville (3rd)†	.532		Geneva (2nd)†	.548	1973—	Auburn	.667
1944—	Lockport	.608	1959—	Wellsville†	.635	1974—	Oneonta	.768
	Jamestown (2nd)†	.565	1960—	Erie	.643	1975—	Newark	.688
1945—	Batavia*	.677		Wellsville (2nd)†	.535		Newark	.714
1946—	Jamestown‡	.672	1961—	Geneva	.616	1976—	Elmira	.727
	Batavia‡	.672		Olean (4th)†	.512		Elmira	.703
1947—	Jamestown*	.690	1962—	Jamestown	.580	1977—	Oneonta▲	.671
1948—	Lockport*	.603		Auburn (3rd)†	.521		Batavia	.600
1949—	Bradford*	.635	1963—	Auburn	.585	1978—	Oneonta	.729
1950—	Hornell	.653		Batavia (3rd)†	.485		Geneva♦	.718
	Olean (2nd)†	.568	1964—	Auburn§	.622	1979—	Geneva	.725
1951—	Olean	.622	1965—	Binghamton	.677		Oneonta♦	.618
	Hornell (3rd)†	.568		Binghamton	.607	1980—	Oneonta▲	.662
1952—	Hamilton	.659	1966—	Auburn∞	.620		Geneva	.649
	Jamestown (2nd)†	.643		Binghamton	.646	1981—	Oneonta▲	.658
1953—	Jamestown*	.704	1967—	Auburn	.667		Jamestown	.649

Year	Team	Pct.	Year	Team	Pct.	Year	Team	Pct.
1982—	Oneonta	.566	1988—	Oneonta▲	.632	1994—	Auburn	.592
	Niagara Falls▲	.553		Jamestown	.618		New Jersey▼	.573
1983—	Utica▲	.649	1989—	Pittsfield	.697	1995—	Vermont	.645
	Newark	.649		Jamestown▲	.579		Watertown▼	.630
1984—	Newark	.622	1990—	Oneonta■	.667	1996—	Vermont▼	.649
	Little Falls▲	.587		Geneva	.662		St. Catharines	.579
1985—	Oneonta*	.705	1991—	Pittsfield	.662	1997—	Batavia	.635
	Auburn	.603		Jamestown■	.654		Pittsfield▼	.568
1986—	Oneonta◆	.766	1992—	Hamilton	.737	1998—	Hudson Valley	.658
	St. Catharines◆	.632		Geneva▼	.547		Oneonta††	.592
1987—	Geneva▲	.632	1993—	Niagara Falls▼	.603		Auburn††	.573
	Watertown	.579		Pittsfield	.533			

*Won championship and four-club playoff. †Won four-club playoff. ‡Jamestown and Batavia declared co-champions; Batavia defeated Jamestown in final of four-club playoff. §Won championship and two-club playoff. ∞Won split-season playoff. ▲League divided into Eastern and Western divisions; won playoff. League divided into Wrigley and Yawkey divisions; won playoff. ■League divided into Eastern, Western and Stedler divisions; won playoff. ▼League divided into McNamara, Pinckney and Stedler divisions; won playoff. ††Named co-champions due to final series being rained out. (NOTE—Known as Pennsylvania-Ontario-New York League from 1939 through 1956.)

NORTHWEST LEAGUE

LEAGUE OFFICE

President/treasurer
Bob Richmond
Address
P.O. Box 4941
Scottsdale, AZ 85261
Phone
602-483-8224

Teams (affiliation)
Boise Hawks (Angels)
Eugene Emeralds (Cubs)
Everett AquaSox (Mariners)
Portland Rockies (Rockies)
Salem-Keizer Volcanoes (Giants)
Southern Oregon Timberjacks (A's)

Spokane Indians (Royals)
Yakima Bears (Dodgers)

1998 FINAL STANDINGS

NORTH DIVISION

Team	W	L	T	Pct.	GB
Spokane (Royals)	47	29	0	.618	....
Boise (Angels)	47	29	0	.618	....
Everett (Mariners)	34	42	0	.447	13.0
Yakima (Dodgers)	32	44	0	.421	15.0

SOUTH DIVISION

Team	W	L	T	Pct.	GB
Southern Oregon (Athletics)	43	33	0	.566	....
Salem-Keizer (Giants)	43	33	0	.566	....
Portland (Rockies)	34	42	0	.447	9.0
Eugene (Braves)	24	52	0	.316	19.0

COMPOSITE

Team	Spo.	Boi.	S.O.	S.K.	Port.	Ever.	Yak.	Eug.	W	L	T	Pct.	GB
Spokane (Royals)	....	6	5	6	8	5	9	8	47	29	0	.618	....
Boise (Angels)	6	....	6	5	6	7	9	8	47	29	0	.618	....
Southern Oregon (Athletics)	5	4	....	5	8	7	5	9	43	33	0	.566	4.0
Salem-Keizer (Giants)	4	5	7	....	8	6	6	7	43	33	0	.566	4.0
Portland (Rockies)	2	4	4	4	....	5	6	9	34	42	0	.447	13.0
Everett (Mariners)	7	5	3	4	5	....	6	4	34	42	0	.447	13.0
Yakima (Dodgers)	3	3	5	4	4	6	....	7	32	44	0	.421	15.0
Eugene (Braves)	2	2	3	5	3	6	3	....	24	52	0	.316	23.0

Major league affiliations in parentheses.

Southern Oregon played home games in Medford, Ore.

PLAYOFFS: Salem-Keizer defeated Boise three games to none to win league championship.

REGULAR-SEASON ATTENDANCE: Boise, 152,496; Eugene, 136,310; Everett, 119,396; Portland, 184,172; Salem-Keizer, 133,980; Southern Oregon, 71,822; Spokane, 186,362; Yakima, 76,049. Total—1,060,587. Playoffs (3 games)—8,727.

MANAGERS: Boise, Tom Kotchman; Eugene, Jim Saul; Everett, Terry Pollreisz; Portland, Jim Eppard; Salem-Keizer, Keith Comstock; Southern Oregon, Greg Sparks; Spokane, Jeff Garber; Yakima, Tony Harris.

ALL-STAR TEAM: 1B—Jason Hart, Southern Oregon; 2B—Jason Huisman, Boise; 3B—Henry Calderon, Spokane; SS—Chone Figgins, Portland; OF—Jeremy Dodson, Spokane; Juan Pierre, Portland; Jake Weber, Everett; C—Paul Phillips, Spokane; DH—Bill Mott, Boise; LHP—(tie) Cary Ammons, Spokane and Jeff Hundley, Boise; RHP—(tie) Chris Mears, Everett and Sean Sedlack, Spokane; LHRP—Chris Demouy, Boise; RHP—Benji Miller, Salem-Keizer; Most Valuable Player—Jason Hart, Southern Oregon; Manager of the Year—Keith Comstock, Salem-Keizer.

1998 BATTING

TEAM

Team	Avg.	G	TPA	AB	R	H	TB	2B	3B	HR	RBI	SH	SF	HP	BB	IBB	SO	SB	CS	GDP	LOB	ShO	Slg.	OBP
Spokane	.283	76	3082	2623	474	741	1102	144	20	59	425	30	36	39	354	13	529	120	35	43	612	2	.420	.372
Salem-Keizer	.278	76	3038	2619	484	727	1083	114	49	48	421	14	29	39	337	9	537	139	53	36	574	3	.414	.365
S. Oregon	.264	76	3081	2617	495	692	1077	121	30	68	420	9	37	39	379	5	556	78	29	47	594	3	.412	.361
Portland	.264	76	2972	2638	375	697	910	109	19	22	316	35	20	29	250	7	501	98	31	46	588	3	.345	.332
Everett	.263	76	3040	2643	434	695	1062	143	16	64	363	14	23	31	329	13	652	98	37	54	597	4	.402	.349
Yakima	.259	76	2973	2605	372	675	944	129	18	35	319	28	29	35	276	6	542	92	42	47	577	2	.362	.334
Boise	.258	76	3048	2597	459	671	1049	149	14	67	405	14	21	68	348	8	586	68	22	49	613	2	.404	.358
Eugene	.256	76	2971	2634	367	675	989	122	18	52	324	18	20	53	246	8	610	109	40	43	576	3	.375	.330

INDIVIDUAL

TOP QUALIFIERS FOR BATTING CHAMPIONSHIP

Minimum 205 plate appearances. *Lefthanded batter. †Switch-hitter.

Player, Team	Avg.	G	TPA	AB	R	H	TB	2B	3B	HR	RBI	SH	SF	HP	BB	IBB	SO	SB	CS	GDP	Slg.	OBP
Pierre, Juan, Port.*	.352	64	290	264	55	93	106	9	2	0	30	4	1	2	19	0	11	38	9	3	.402	.399
Martinez, Victor, Ever.	.344	67	322	288	60	99	131	13	2	5	32	2	2	2	28	0	48	21	8	8	.455	.403
Weber, Jake, Ever.*	.338	75	352	275	75	93	150	20	2	11	52	2	3	5	67	3	42	14	7	3	.545	.471
Calderon, Henry, Spo.	.337	72	319	282	58	95	143	17	2	9	48	3	4	5	25	3	66	19	4	4	.507	.396
Dodson, Jeremy, Spo.*	.336	69	305	268	56	90	146	19	5	9	59	0	5	6	25	2	59	8	4	6	.545	.398
Clark, Douglas, S.K.*	.335	59	264	227	49	76	105	8	6	3	41	1	1	3	32	0	31	12	8	1	.463	.422
Magruder, Christopher, S.K.†	.333	47	226	177	43	59	86	8	5	3	18	2	2	8	37	1	21	14	7	2	.486	.464
Huisman, Jason, Boi.	.325	73	329	292	47	95	134	20	2	5	59	0	1	9	27	2	52	5	0	7	.459	.398
Ross, David, Yak.	.309	59	230	191	31	59	93	14	1	6	25	2	2	1	34	0	49	2	2	5	.487	.412
Phillips, Paul, Spo.	.308	59	257	234	55	72	100	12	2	4	25	0	1	4	18	0	19	12	1	2	.427	.366
Feliciano, Jesus, Yak.*	.305	73	343	302	47	92	101	7	1	0	26	2	4	3	32	0	37	34	10	4	.334	.372
Freitas, Jeremy, Spo.*	.305	54	225	197	31	60	100	19	0	7	45	0	2	2	24	1	39	0	2	1	.508	.382

Player, Team	Avg.	G	TPA	AB	R	H	TB	2B	3B	HR	RBI	SH	SF	HP	BB	IBB	SO	SB	CS	GDP	Slg.	OBP
Mott, Bill, Boi.*	.304	63	264	207	54	63	95	11	0	7	37	1	3	5	48	1	41	21	1	1	.459	.441
Luster, Jeremy, S.K.†	.304	51	209	181	32	55	92	13	3	6	48	0	3	2	23	1	30	6	4	3	.508	.383
Duck, Kevin, Port.*	.304	59	236	214	19	65	84	11	1	2	34	3	4	0	15	2	52	1	1	4	.393	.343

DEPARTMENTAL LEADERS: G—J. Hart, Weber, 75 each; AB—Feliciano, 302; R—Weber, 75; H—Martinez, 99; TB—J. Hart, 157; 2B—Auterson, 26; 3B—Hall, 8; HR—J. Hart, 20; RBI—J. Hart, 69; SH—Leon, 8; SF—J. Hart, 8; HP—Blakely, 22; BB—Weber, 67; IBB—Southall, 6; SO—Southall, 82; SB—Pierre, 38; CS—J. Simmons, 11; GIDP—Montas, 10; Slg.—Weber, .545; OBP—Weber, .471.

ALL PLAYERS

*Lefthanded batter. †Switch-hitter.

Player, Team	Avg.	G	TPA	AB	R	H	TB	2B	3B	HR	RBI	SH	SF	HP	BB	IBB	SO	SB	CS	GDP	Slg.	OBP
Alcala, Juan, Ever.	.163	29	109	104	6	17	24	2	1	1	7	0	0	0	5	0	25	1	1	2	.231	.202
Allen, Jeffrey, S.K.	.293	60	256	215	47	63	116	10	5	11	47	1	2	5	33	3	64	10	5	2	.540	.396
Alvarez, German, Eug.*	.224	23	95	76	9	17	21	4	0	0	14	0	1	0	18	0	11	4	0	2	.276	.368
Auterson, Jeff, Yak.	.266	74	324	290	43	77	129	26	4	6	53	2	2	4	26	0	72	9	5	6	.445	.332
Balbuena, Mike, Yak.	.167	24	56	48	4	8	12	1	0	1	7	1	1	0	6	0	13	0	0	0	.250	.255
Basabe, Jesus, S.O.	.265	60	241	204	44	54	106	6	2	14	40	0	1	10	26	1	71	5	3	1	.520	.373
Bertrand, Ben, S.K.	.105	8	22	19	0	2	3	1	0	0	1	0	0	0	3	0	8	0	0	1	.158	.227
Blakely, Darren, Boi.†	.277	71	328	267	50	74	110	9	6	5	33	1	4	22	34	3	69	9	3	2	.412	.398
Brignac, Junior, Eug.	.233	70	302	270	36	63	87	13	1	3	29	0	3	6	23	0	74	15	7	5	.322	.305
Byrnes, Eric, S.O.	.314	42	188	169	36	53	88	10	2	7	31	0	1	2	16	1	16	6	1	3	.521	.378
Calderon, Henry, Spo.	.337	72	319	282	58	95	143	17	2	9	48	3	4	5	25	3	66	19	4	4	.507	.396
Camilo, Juan, S.O.*	.343	31	136	108	25	37	63	8	3	4	29	0	5	1	22	0	32	5	2	0	.583	.441
Carroll, Mark, Ever.	.000	1	3	3	0	0	0	0	0	0	0	0	0	0	0	0	0	0	0	0	.000	.000
Casper, Brett, S.K.	.308	7	28	26	2	8	11	1	1	0	3	0	0	0	2	0	7	0	1	0	.423	.357
Castro, Al, Eug.†	.260	74	330	296	33	77	98	10	1	3	33	5	2	5	22	0	49	8	1	1	.331	.320
Castro, Juan, Port.	.237	39	150	139	19	33	47	6	1	2	18	0	0	2	9	0	37	1	0	7	.338	.293
Cheshier, Casey, Eug.	.253	55	204	190	22	48	77	7	2	6	23	0	0	5	9	0	51	5	1	2	.405	.304
Child, Casey, Boi.	.214	74	311	280	37	60	96	10	1	8	36	1	1	5	24	0	61	7	5	4	.343	.287
Christensen, Mike, Boi.	.262	70	308	286	47	75	124	22	0	9	47	1	2	1	18	2	63	1	0	9	.434	.306
Clark, Douglas, S.K.*	.335	59	264	227	49	76	105	8	6	3	41	1	1	3	32	0	31	12	8	1	.463	.422
Collins, Michael, Yak.	.284	18	75	67	5	19	21	2	0	0	2	3	0	1	4	0	6	2	6	0	.313	.333
Condon, Mike, Boi.	.234	33	117	94	19	22	32	7	0	1	11	2	0	5	16	0	15	0	1	4	.340	.374
Cosbey, Chris, S.O.*	.286	49	201	185	30	53	70	9	4	0	20	0	1	1	14	0	33	7	2	2	.378	.334
Cox, Brian, Eug.	.260	59	244	208	34	54	76	11	1	3	23	1	2	3	30	0	36	7	2	3	.365	.358
Croud, Will, Boi.†	.243	65	307	255	52	62	85	13	2	2	23	3	1	2	46	0	48	17	6	2	.333	.362
Curry, Mike, Spo.*	.251	67	284	227	53	57	72	8	2	1	25	2	6	3	46	2	41	30	7	1	.317	.376
Dean, Mike, S.K.	.279	52	208	183	29	51	74	7	5	2	34	1	3	2	19	1	51	13	4	2	.404	.348
Detienne, Dave, Yak.	.193	32	98	88	10	17	20	3	0	0	6	2	1	0	7	0	22	6	3	0	.227	.250
Diaz, Angel, Boi.	.200	3	13	10	3	2	5	0	0	1	1	0	0	0	3	0	4	0	1	0	.500	.385
Diaz, Michael, Boi.*	.221	32	102	86	20	19	23	2	1	0	11	0	0	0	16	0	16	4	2	0	.267	.343
DiPace, Danny, Spo.*	.274	44	139	113	12	31	60	11	0	6	34	0	4	4	18	1	28	0	0	1	.531	.381
Dodson, Jeremy, Spo.*	.336	69	305	268	56	90	146	19	5	9	59	0	5	6	25	2	59	8	4	6	.545	.398
Duck, Kevin, Port.*	.304	59	236	214	19	65	84	11	1	2	34	3	4	0	15	2	52	1	1	4	.393	.343
Duverge, Salvador, Port.	.231	16	65	52	13	12	19	4	0	1	9	1	0	2	10	1	12	1	0	2	.365	.375
Etheredge, Josh, Port.	.226	38	163	137	13	31	40	5	2	0	13	0	2	5	19	0	35	2	1	0	.292	.337
Ewan, Bry, Eug.	.219	56	235	210	26	46	75	9	1	6	33	1	2	2	20	0	72	0	2	4	.357	.291
Farris, Jeff, S.O.*	.154	15	61	52	5	8	13	2	0	1	3	0	1	0	8	0	26	1	0	4	.250	.262
Feliciano, Jesus, Yak.*	.305	73	343	302	47	92	101	7	1	0	26	2	4	3	32	0	37	34	10	4	.334	.372
Figgins, Desmond, Port.†	.283	69	302	269	41	76	94	9	3	1	26	6	1	2	24	0	56	25	4	3	.349	.345
Fox, Brian, Boi.*	.246	24	73	61	9	15	29	3	1	3	14	0	0	0	12	0	11	0	0	0	.475	.370
Franklin, Jason, Port.	.242	59	242	211	30	51	70	8	1	3	23	1	1	1	28	0	49	5	0	4	.332	.332
Frazier, Carlos, S.K.	.000	11	11	11	0	0	0	0	0	0	0	0	0	0	0	0	4	0	0	1	.000	.000
Freitas, Jeremy, Spo.*	.305	54	225	197	31	60	100	19	0	7	45	0	2	2	24	1	39	0	2	1	.508	.382
Fry, Ryan, Spo.	.233	47	168	146	25	34	68	8	3	6	28	2	1	3	16	1	40	1	2	0	.466	.319
Garcia, Ismael, Yak.	.284	41	116	102	20	29	41	4	1	2	15	1	1	1	10	0	22	1	0	1	.402	.351
Goelz, Jim, Yak.	.183	69	254	213	20	39	45	6	0	0	15	6	4	3	28	0	36	9	0	6	.211	.282
Gomez, Erick, Spo.*	.059	4	17	17	1	1	1	0	0	0	0	0	0	0	0	0	2	0	0	1	.059	.059
Gorr, Robb, Yak.	.264	66	276	254	43	67	95	9	2	5	35	2	4	1	15	2	33	2	1	4	.374	.303
Gorrie, Brad, S.O.	.242	55	245	198	46	48	64	7	3	1	20	0	3	1	43	0	42	15	5	5	.323	.376
Goudie, Jaime, Yak.	.275	35	148	138	15	38	50	8	2	0	16	2	2	0	6	0	16	6	1	5	.362	.301
Greer, Matt, Yak.	.286	19	52	49	7	14	17	1	1	0	8	0	0	0	3	0	16	1	0	0	.347	.327
Gregory, Rich, Eug.	.221	25	81	68	11	15	25	2	1	2	7	0	0	5	8	1	20	3	0	1	.368	.354
Hall, Justin, S.O.	.287	69	310	265	56	76	113	12	8	3	33	2	2	6	35	0	39	5	3	9	.426	.380
Hanseen, Tye, Eug.	.237	38	132	118	12	28	34	6	0	0	12	2	1	0	11	1	21	1	0	3	.288	.300
Hart, Corey, Spo.†	.242	58	211	157	25	38	53	6	0	3	21	2	0	2	50	0	38	8	4	1	.338	.431
Hart, Jason, S.O.	.258	75	342	295	58	76	157	19	1	20	69	0	8	3	36	2	67	0	1	9	.532	.336
Haynes, Larry, Ever.	.241	67	255	241	36	58	102	12	1	10	41	0	3	2	9	1	69	15	3	5	.423	.271
Herrera, Pedro, Spo.	.274	25	86	73	11	20	26	2	2	0	7	1	0	1	10	0	13	1	1	3	.356	.376
Hill, Jason, Boi.	.261	57	229	203	30	53	91	17	0	7	39	0	1	3	22	0	45	1	0	7	.448	.341
Hill, Steven, S.K.†	.263	55	202	186	40	49	63	4	1	0	24	0	2	4	10	0	24	18	4	3	.339	.312
Hood, Jay, Boi.	.197	41	162	132	20	26	41	6	0	3	19	0	2	5	23	0	22	1	1	2	.311	.333
Howe, Matthew, S.O.	.278	68	318	255	57	71	108	16	3	5	47	0	6	3	54	1	45	5	2	4	.424	.403
Huisman, Jason, Boi.	.325	73	329	292	47	95	134	20	2	5	59	0	1	9	27	2	52	5	0	7	.459	.398
Johnson, Erik, Port.	.274	51	206	186	30	51	84	12	0	7	30	1	1	1	17	0	26	0	0	6	.452	.337
Kelley, Casey, Boi.*	.224	55	195	161	31	36	70	13	0	7	37	0	2	0	32	0	64	1	0	3	.435	.349
Kellner, Ryan, Yak.	.273	19	58	55	6	15	21	1	1	1	5	0	0	2	1	0	22	0	0	1	.382	.310
Kenna, David, S.K.*	.000	5	5	3	0	0	0	0	0	0	0	0	0	0	2	0	1	0	0	0	.000	.400
Kuzmic, Craig, Ever.†	.280	54	227	186	36	52	97	14	2	9	47	0	3	5	33	3	55	3	1	3	.522	.390
Landaeta, Luis, Port.*	.297	29	121	111	19	33	40	3	2	0	12	0	0	2	8	1	16	4	4	2	.360	.355
Leon, Richy, Port.	.231	52	219	186	27	43	56	8	1	1	18	8	5	3	16	0	20	0	4	4	.301	.295
Ligons, Merrell, Spo.†	.279	51	220	179	34	50	63	7	3	0	29	5	3	5	28	1	41	15	2	3	.352	.386

Player, Team	Avg.	G	TPA	AB	R	H	TB	2B	3B	HR	RBI	SH	SF	HP	BB	IBB	SO	SB	CS	GDP	Slg.	OBP
Lindsey, Shawn, S.K.*	.277	30	119	101	21	28	33	0	1	1	6	0	1	0	17	0	22	7	2	0	.327	.378
Luderer, Brian, S.O.	.297	10	39	37	9	11	21	2	1	2	7	0	0	0	2	0	7	0	0	0	.568	.333
Luster, Jeremy, S.K.†	.304	51	209	181	32	55	92	13	3	6	48	0	3	2	23	1	30	6	4	3	.508	.383
Magruder, Christopher, S.K.†	.333	47	226	177	43	59	86	8	5	3	18	2	2	8	37	1	21	14	7	2	.486	.464
Mahoney, Ricardo, Port.	.255	50	210	188	22	48	61	8	1	1	23	2	2	1	17	1	41	1	1	4	.324	.317
Maldonado, Carlos, Ever.	.287	42	164	150	19	43	68	10	0	5	24	0	2	2	10	0	17	1	0	5	.453	.335
Maluchnik, Gregg, Eug.	.255	58	214	184	25	47	68	15	0	2	19	2	1	7	20	0	55	2	3	3	.370	.349
Martinez, Victor, Ever.	.344	67	322	288	60	99	131	13	2	5	32	2	2	2	28	0	48	21	8	8	.455	.403
Mattern, Erik, S.K.	.245	48	183	151	18	37	49	2	2	2	20	1	0	1	30	0	26	9	5	1	.325	.374
McCorkle, Shawn, Ever.*	.265	47	188	162	27	43	70	6	0	7	37	0	0	2	24	0	46	1	0	4	.432	.367
McDowell, Arturo, S.K.*	.221	47	208	172	32	38	45	3	2	0	18	3	0	4	29	0	46	13	2	2	.262	.346
Mercedes, Luis, S.K.	.000	4	6	6	0	0	0	0	0	0	1	0	0	0	0	0	3	0	0	0	.000	.000
Montas, Ricardo, Spo.	.303	63	250	211	45	64	77	10	0	1	27	4	4	1	30	1	28	10	1	10	.365	.386
Mota, Pedro, S.K.*	.118	8	20	17	0	2	3	1	0	0	0	0	0	0	3	0	4	0	1	0	.176	.250
Mott, Bill, Boi.*	.304	63	264	207	54	63	95	11	0	7	37	1	3	5	48	1	41	21	1	1	.459	.441
Newton, Kimani, Yak.	.245	41	160	147	19	36	56	6	1	4	18	1	0	0	12	0	29	7	2	4	.381	.302
Nieckula, Aaron, S.O.	.206	41	151	126	17	26	32	6	0	0	21	2	2	2	18	0	31	2	0	1	.254	.311
Nogowski, Brandon, S.O.*	.000	17	1	1	0	0	0	0	0	0	0	0	0	0	0	0	1	0	0	0	.000	.000
Nunez, Jose, Port.	.231	46	182	156	13	36	43	7	0	0	13	4	2	1	19	1	24	0	1	1	.276	.315
Oliver, Brian, Boi.	.259	17	66	54	6	14	19	3	1	0	5	3	0	1	8	0	6	0	1	4	.352	.365
Oliver, William, Boi.	.289	43	145	121	23	35	66	7	0	8	27	0	3	7	14	0	46	0	1	3	.545	.386
O'Neil, John, Boi.	.220	20	45	41	4	9	11	2	0	0	3	0	0	3	1	0	7	0	0	0	.268	.289
Oropeza, Asdrubal, Eug.	.287	28	120	108	20	31	55	6	0	6	24	0	1	0	11	1	31	0	0	2	.509	.350
Pacheco, Domingo, Ever.†	.262	35	120	107	16	28	34	3	0	1	12	1	1	2	8	0	24	6	0	2	.318	.322
Parker, Hubert, Ever.†	.187	69	265	214	33	40	49	7	1	0	13	6	2	1	42	0	60	14	6	5	.229	.320
Paterson, Joe, Yak.	.278	56	207	187	20	52	88	14	2	6	34	0	2	1	17	1	37	2	4	4	.471	.338
Pecci, Jay, S.O.†	.292	39	158	130	21	38	40	2	0	0	14	1	1	4	22	0	22	3	4	0	.308	.408
Phillips, Paul, Spo.	.308	59	257	234	55	72	100	12	2	4	25	0	1	4	18	0	19	12	1	2	.427	.366
Pierre, Juan, Port.*	.352	64	290	264	55	93	106	9	2	0	30	4	1	2	19	0	11	38	5	3	.402	.399
Pujols, Rafael, S.O.	.224	54	205	183	24	41	58	6	1	3	24	0	1	0	21	0	34	3	0	4	.317	.302
Ransom, Bryan, S.K.	.233	71	288	236	52	55	99	12	7	6	27	3	4	2	43	1	56	19	6	4	.419	.351
Rivera, Juan, Spo.	.157	19	59	51	6	8	9	1	0	0	6	1	0	0	7	0	19	0	0	1	.176	.259
Robinson, Brian, Ever.	.270	60	232	204	33	55	83	14	1	4	27	0	2	2	24	0	34	1	0	4	.407	.349
Rodriguez, Guillermo, S.K.	.250	1	4	4	0	1	1	0	0	0	0	0	0	0	0	0	1	0	1	0	.250	.250
Rosario, Melvin, Port.*	.224	61	241	210	30	47	55	4	2	0	17	4	1	0	26	1	52	12	4	1	.262	.308
Rosario, Omar, S.O.*	.257	29	119	101	18	26	39	4	0	3	13	1	0	2	15	0	26	5	2	0	.386	.364
Ross, David, Yak.	.309	59	230	191	31	59	93	14	1	6	25	2	2	1	34	0	49	2	2	5	.487	.412
Ruiz, Ramon, Yak.	.259	39	169	139	27	36	56	8	0	4	19	0	2	8	20	3	40	1	2	1	.403	.379
Ruiz, Willy, Spo.	.215	43	151	130	18	28	32	0	2	0	9	6	1	0	14	0	21	11	6	2	.246	.290
Salazar, Oscar, S.O.	.317	28	121	101	19	32	53	4	1	5	28	1	3	0	16	0	22	5	2	0	.525	.400
Sampson, Jacob, Yak.	.203	36	89	74	12	15	21	2	2	0	9	3	1	1	10	0	18	2	1	1	.284	.302
Sanchez, Manuel, Eug.*	.259	60	218	201	28	52	85	7	4	6	24	0	1	4	12	2	35	12	5	3	.423	.312
Schwieder, Nicholas, Boi.	.000	1	1	0	1	0	0	0	0	0	0	0	0	0	1	0	0	0	0	0	.000	1.000
Serrano, Sammy, S.K.	.288	48	205	191	41	55	96	12	1	9	40	1	4	0	9	1	36	2	1	4	.503	.314
Shackleford, Brian, Spo.*	.293	70	311	266	35	78	131	21	1	10	55	4	3	3	35	1	52	3	1	6	.492	.378
Simmons, Jerry, Eug.	.275	73	322	284	48	78	131	14	3	11	40	0	2	11	25	3	65	26	11	5	.461	.354
Slemmer, Ben, Spo.	.208	25	81	72	9	15	21	3	0	1	9	0	2	0	7	0	23	2	0	1	.292	.272
Smith, Sam, Port.	.207	11	88	82	10	17	27	5	1	1	11	1	0	1	4	0	23	1	0	0	.329	.253
Southall, Rick, Ever.*	.290	67	293	248	40	72	117	19	1	8	47	0	3	3	39	6	82	0	1	5	.472	.389
Stewart, Colin, Eug.	.265	60	235	204	29	54	69	7	1	2	23	2	3	4	22	0	33	12	3	6	.338	.343
Story-Harden, Thomari, Yak.	.188	49	159	128	19	24	29	5	0	0	15	0	3	9	19	0	48	1	0	4	.227	.327
Strickland, Gregory, Eug.*	.300	56	239	217	34	65	88	11	3	2	20	5	1	1	15	0	57	14	5	3	.406	.346
Summers, John, S.K.†	.303	56	240	211	33	64	84	13	2	1	38	1	1	3	24	1	48	5	0	6	.398	.381
Theodorou, Nick, Yak.†	.278	46	160	133	24	37	49	12	0	0	11	1	0	0	26	0	26	7	5	1	.368	.396
Thomas, Gary, S.O.	.203	61	246	207	30	42	52	8	1	0	21	2	2	4	31	0	42	11	2	5	.251	.316
Tommasini, Kevin, S.K.	.189	20	61	53	9	10	20	3	2	1	8	0	0	2	6	0	8	3	0	2	.377	.295
Torcato, Tony, S.K.*	.291	54	243	220	31	64	92	15	2	3	43	0	6	3	14	0	38	4	2	0	.418	.333
Underwood, Jake, Ever.	.200	15	40	40	2	8	12	4	0	0	3	0	0	0	0	0	11	0	0	0	.300	.200
Valderrama, Carlos, S.K.	.345	7	30	29	5	10	11	1	0	0	4	0	0	1	0	0	7	4	0	2	.379	.441
Wade, Bryn, Boi.	.234	14	53	47	6	11	18	4	0	1	3	2	1	0	3	0	16	1	0	1	.383	.275
Weber, Jake, Ever.*	.338	75	352	275	75	93	150	20	2	11	52	2	3	5	67	3	42	14	7	3	.545	.471
Whitehurst, Tom, Port.	.262	59	259	233	34	61	84	10	2	3	39	0	0	6	19	0	47	7	2	5	.361	.333
Williams, P.J., Ever.	.220	36	162	141	24	31	45	8	3	0	4	1	0	2	18	0	35	12	6	3	.319	.317
Woodward, Mattson, Ever.	.145	36	120	110	6	16	17	1	0	0	2	0	1	1	8	0	35	0	1	4	.155	.208
Wright, Steven, Ever.*	.077	4	16	13	1	1	1	0	0	0	0	0	0	0	3	0	5	0	0	0	.077	.250
Zambrano, Alan, Ever.†	.248	48	173	149	20	37	62	10	2	3	15	2	1	2	11	0	64	9	3	1	.395	.304

GRAND SLAMS: Freitas, Huisman, McCorkle, 2 each; Basebe, Duverge, Ewan, Fry, J. Hart, Salazar, Shackelford, Southall, Weber, Whitehurst, 1 each.

AWARDED FIRST BASE ON CATCHER'S INTERFERENCE: Dodson 2 (A. Diaz 2); I. Garcia (Phillips); Leon (Dean); Pacheco 2 (Kellner 2); Nieckula (Dean); Whitehurst (Alcala).

1998 PITCHING

TEAM

Team	W	L	Pct.	ERA	G	CG	ShO	Sv.	IP	H	TBF	R	ER	HR	SH	SF	HB	BB	IBB	SO	WP	Bk.
Spokane	47	29	.618	3.47	76	0	2	24	675.0	670	2995	357	260	32	17	20	30	301	15	648	48	20
Boise	47	29	.618	3.82	76	1	5	19	664.2	665	2914	371	282	59	15	21	38	237	11	534	57	11
S. Oregon	43	33	.566	4.48	76	0	3	24	669.0	717	3027	433	333	51	25	27	35	292	15	542	63	25
Portland	34	42	.447	4.65	76	1	1	14	666.0	688	3012	416	344	50	16	26	43	322	1	525	65	11
Salem-Keizer	43	33	.566	4.69	76	1	1	19	664.0	643	2970	425	346	60	21	25	49	316	5	610	74	22
Yakima	32	44	.421	4.75	76	0	3	21	671.0	695	3084	462	354	57	20	28	33	377	8	576	63	12
Everett	34	42	.447	4.87	76	1	2	15	669.0	727	3067	464	362	50	26	34	43	325	2	517	73	14
Eugene	24	52	.316	5.55	76	0	1	16	661.2	767	3142	532	408	56	22	36	62	349	12	561	68	23

TOP QUALIFIERS FOR EARNED-RUN AVERAGE TITLE

Minimum 61 innings. *Lefthanded pitcher.

Pitcher, Team	W	L	Pct.	ERA	G	GS	CG	ShO	GF	Sv.	IP	H	TBF	R	ER	HR	SH	SF	HB	BB	IBB	SO	WP	Bk.
Ammons, Cary, Spo.*	5	3	.625	1.70	15	14	0	0	0	0	74.1	56	298	23	14	4	3	1	1	32	0	83	8	1
Longo, Neil, Ever.	6	2	.750	2.26	16	11	0	0	2	0	75.2	67	310	31	19	0	2	1	2	23	0	48	8	0
Mears, Chris, Ever.	9	1	.900	2.74	15	15	1	0	0	0	98.2	86	411	39	30	6	2	4	5	33	0	67	2	5
Bridges, Douglas, Boi.*	6	2	.750	2.98	15	15	0	0	0	0	81.2	73	349	37	27	6	2	2	4	35	1	63	4	2
Difelice, Mark, Port.	4	6	.400	3.31	15	13	0	0	2	0	81.2	83	343	45	30	6	1	2	3	11	0	62	3	1
Hundley, Jeffrey, Boi.*	8	3	.727	3.40	16	16	0	0	0	0	92.2	77	376	42	35	7	1	4	2	27	1	89	7	2
Sedlacek, Shawn, Spo.	9	2	.818	3.45	16	13	0	0	0	0	86.0	89	371	43	33	2	1	4	6	18	0	62	4	5
Logowski, Brandon, S.O.*	4	4	.500	3.71	17	8	0	0	8	1	68.0	74	299	44	28	6	1	2	3	11	0	66	6	0
Ward, Monty, Spo.	6	1	.857	3.79	15	15	0	0	0	0	71.1	66	304	33	30	4	0	2	1	35	1	76	7	1
Gomes, Tony, Yak.	2	8	.200	4.09	16	11	0	0	2	1	72.2	76	321	53	33	6	0	4	4	34	0	52	11	2
Jones, Christopher, S.K.*	4	4	.556	4.13	14	13	0	0	0	0	72.0	76	304	40	33	6	3	3	4	17	0	60	4	1
Dobis, Jason, S.O.	7	4	.636	4.25	16	12	0	0	1	0	78.1	76	346	44	37	3	3	1	2	36	3	46	6	0
Vargas, Derrick, Port.*	4	4	.500	4.43	14	8	0	0	3	2	63.0	67	288	40	31	6	2	3	3	32	0	44	4	0
Leach, Mike, Boi.	4	2	.667	4.50	15	14	1	0	0	0	70.0	79	320	49	35	8	1	1	6	26	1	45	5	1
Emanuel, Brandon, Boi.	4	5	.444	4.59	15	15	0	0	0	0	80.1	96	356	59	41	8	0	1	8	21	1	42	4	0

DEPARTMENTAL LEADERS: W—Mears, Sedlacek, 9 each; L—Sylvester, 11; Pct.—Mears, .900; G—J. Lee, 31; GS—Hundley, Sylvester, 16 each; CG—Several players tied at 1; ShO—None; GF—Miller, 27; Sv.—Miller, 17; IP—Mears, 98.2; H—Bond, 99; TBF—Mears, 411; R—Torres, 72; ER—Torres, 49; HR—Brummitt, 10; SH—Mzias, Snow, Torres, 5 each; SF—Torres, 8; HB—Brummitt, 10; BB—Soto, 53; IBB—Bond, McDaniel, 4 each; SO—Hundley, 89; WP—Soto, 23; BK—Frachiseur, 7.

ALL PITCHERS

*Lefthanded pitcher.

Pitcher, Team	W	L	Pct.	ERA	G	GS	CG	ShO	GF	Sv.	IP	H	TBF	R	ER	HR	SH	SF	HB	BB	IBB	SO	WP	Bk.
Abreu, Winston, Eug.	0	4	.000	6.35	17	10	0	0	3	0	45.1	39	206	36	32	6	0	2	5	31	0	52	6	0
Ammons, Cary, Spo.*	5	3	.625	1.70	15	14	0	0	0	0	74.1	56	298	23	14	4	3	1	1	32	0	83	8	1
Avery, Paul, Yak.*	1	2	.667	4.24	9	3	0	0	1	0	23.1	23	105	12	11	2	0	0	0	15	0	16	3	0
Balbuena, Caleb, Ever.	0	0	.000	6.30	12	1	0	0	5	0	20.0	25	94	15	14	0	1	0	2	9	0	11	2	2
Balbuena, Mike, Yak.	0	0	.000	10.80	3	0	0	0	2	0	3.1	5	18	4	4	2	0	0	1	3	0	2	1	0
Barboza, Carlos, Port.	0	1	.000	2.92	14	0	0	0	4	0	24.2	26	113	12	8	0	0	2	0	14	0	10	3	2
Barnsby, Scott, Yak.	2	4	.333	5.01	26	3	0	0	10	1	50.1	63	235	37	28	3	2	2	2	22	2	35	5	0
Bautista, Francisco, Spo.	3	1	.750	3.71	22	0	0	0	9	1	28.2	22	131	21	12	1	1	1	4	16	1	19	2	2
Beaver, Greg, Ever.	4	0	1.000	7.20	9	6	0	0	0	0	25.0	33	125	28	20	3	0	2	2	12	0	16	5	0
Bell, Scott, Yak.	0	1	.000	2.39	11	2	0	0	1	0	37.2	35	161	19	10	2	2	3	0	16	2	37	2	1
Berroa, Oliver, Ever.	1	2	.333	4.23	11	2	0	0	2	0	27.2	23	129	15	13	2	1	2	4	20	0	21	3	0
Birrell, Simon, Eug.	1	0	1.000	9.59	13	0	0	0	5	0	25.1	32	131	30	27	2	0	3	22	2	24	5	1
Bond, Tommy, Boi.	6	6	.500	4.71	15	15	0	0	0	0	80.1	99	363	57	42	9	2	2	3	14	4	57	6	2
Bornyk, Matt, Yak.	5	3	.625	5.56	17	5	0	0	5	2	55.0	63	242	39	34	8	2	1	1	15	0	34	2	0
Bradley, Brian, Port.	3	4	.429	4.04	10	10	0	0	0	0	49.0	43	218	27	22	1	2	2	7	26	0	39	7	0
Bridenbaugh, Christian, Yak.* .	4	1	.800	5.13	17	4	0	0	4	1	47.1	47	218	29	27	7	2	3	2	24	0	28	1	0
Bridges, Douglas, Boi.*	6	2	.750	2.98	15	15	0	0	0	0	81.2	73	349	37	27	6	2	2	4	35	1	63	4	2
Brink, Jim, S.O.	3	0	1.000	4.31	24	1	0	0	17	11	56.1	63	241	32	27	4	1	2	1	16	2	43	2	2
Brummitt, Travis, Eug.	1	7	.125	7.08	17	6	0	0	3	1	54.2	73	279	60	43	10	2	1	10	32	1	34	2	4
Brunet, Michael, Boi.	0	0	.000	10.80	4	0	0	0	0	0	3.1	4	21	4	4	1	0	1	3	0	4	1	1
Bump, Nate, S.K.	0	0	.000	0.00	2	2	0	0	0	0	8.0	5	31	0	0	0	2	3	0	8	1	0
Burch, Matt, Spo.	3	2	.600	4.79	12	12	0	0	0	0	56.1	64	264	34	30	2	1	1	4	25	0	47	2	5
Burnside, Adrian, Yak.*	1	4	.200	4.05	8	6	0	0	1	0	33.1	27	156	21	15	0	1	2	2	30	0	34	8	1
Calandriello, Donato, S.O.*	1	0	1.000	3.71	6	0	0	0	1	1	17.0	19	75	8	7	1	4	3	0	8	2	15	1	0
Cameron, Ryan, Port.	0	6	.000	6.02	18	2	0	0	9	1	40.1	45	193	30	27	7	2	0	1	24	0	47	2	0
Caraccioli, Lance, Yak.*	0	5	.000	5.18	11	7	0	0	3	0	41.2	43	193	26	24	7	0	0	1	28	0	44	5	1
Carter, Justin, Port.*	1	1	.500	3.78	15	2	0	0	4	0	33.1	41	151	20	14	1	2	1	2	10	0	35	5	1
Casper, Michael, Spo.	3	2	.600	2.87	19	0	0	0	5	1	37.2	42	170	25	12	3	0	0	10	0	23	0	1
Chrysler, Clint, Ever.*	4	2	.667	2.12	24	0	0	0	20	9	34.0	30	156	11	8	2	1	1	2	18	0	44	5	0
Colyer, Stephen, Yak.*	2	2	.500	4.96	15	12	0	0	2	0	65.1	72	302	46	36	2	1	1	4	36	0	75	5	0
Connolly, Keith, S.K.	2	1	.667	4.79	21	0	0	0	8	0	35.2	34	156	22	19	5	0	1	3	14	1	38	7	0
Cook, Aaron, Port.	5	8	.385	4.88	15	15	1	0	0	0	79.1	87	364	50	43	8	1	1	7	39	0	38	7	0
Corey, Michael, Eug.	1	0	1.000	1.69	20	0	0	0	13	7	32.0	28	133	8	6	1	2	2	9	2	27	2	0
Crawford, Jeremy, S.O.*	0	0	.000	13.50	2	0	0	0	1	0	2.2	6	17	4	4	0	1	0	3	0	3	0	0
Davis, Allen, Yak.*	2	0	1.000	1.13	4	2	0	0	1	0	16.0	10	61	4	2	0	0	0	3	0	14	1	0
DeJesus, Tony, Ever.*	3	3	.500	5.71	19	3	0	0	7	0	41.0	44	199	34	26	6	1	4	28	0	46	6	0
Delgado, Danny, Ever.	0	0	.000	4.50	14	0	0	0	0	0	30.0	31	123	15	15	2	0	1	0	8	0	32	3	0
Demouy, Chris, Boi.*	5	1	.833	1.54	20	0	0	0	17	9	23.1	11	96	5	4	0	3	1	1	11	0	29	2	2
Derenches, Albert, Ever.*	1	0	1.000	6.19	9	0	0	0	4	1	16.0	19	79	15	11	3	0	2	1	12	0	16	0	0
Dickinson, Rodney, Eug.	3	0	1.000	3.16	13	0	0	0	5	0	25.2	17	113	11	9	0	0	2	2	18	2	21	2	1
Difelice, Mark, Port.	4	6	.400	3.31	15	13	0	0	2	0	81.2	83	343	45	30	6	1	2	3	11	0	62	3	1
Dobis, Jason, S.O.	7	4	.636	4.25	16	12	0	0	1	0	78.1	76	346	44	37	3	3	1	2	36	3	46	6	0
Dunning, Justin, Ever.	1	3	.250	6.60	13	9	0	0	1	0	46.1	53	228	40	34	4	0	1	5	30	0	46	10	0
Duprey, Pete, Ever.*	0	0	.000	3.38	2	0	0	0	1	0	2.2	3	14	1	1	0	1	3	1	1	0	0
Emanuel, Brandon, Boi.	4	5	.444	4.59	15	15	0	0	0	0	80.1	96	356	59	41	8	0	1	8	21	1	42	4	0
Esteves, Jake, S.K.	0	0	.000	2.25	1	1	0	0	0	0	4.0	1	15	1	1	0	1	0	5	0	0
Farley, Joseph, S.K.*	0	2	.000	8.74	3	3	0	0	0	0	11.1	12	50	12	11	3	0	0	6	0	6	1	0
Faust, Jason, S.O.*	2	0	1.000	1.42	7	0	0	0	6	0	12.2	9	53	3	2	1	0	0	3	0	17	3	0
Fields, Brian, S.K.*	1	1	.500	1.80	5	0	0	0	2	0	10.0	8	41	3	2	0	0	1	0	4	0	11	0	2
Frachiseur, Zachery, Eug.	5	4	.556	5.49	23	1	0	0	7	1	58.1	74	271	45	33	3	4	2	1	21	1	74	2	7
Garcia, Bryan, S.O.	2	3	.333	7.25	7	3	0	0	1	0	22.1	36	111	21	18	4	2	1	9	1	6	3	1
Garey, Dan, Ever.	0	1	.000	4.63	9	0	0	0	6	0	11.2	18	58	12	6	0	1	2	1	6	0	5	4	1
Garmong, Aaron, Eug.*	2	2	.500	4.44	24	2	0	0	13	6	46.2	50	218	28	23	1	3	0	3	33	2	24	2	3
Gilfillan, Jason, Spo.	0	0	.000	4.91	6	0	0	0	1	0	7.1	7	36	5	4	0	1	6	0	8	0	0

CLASS A *Northwest League*

Pitcher, Team	W	L	Pct.	ERA	G	GS	CG	ShO	GF	Sv.	IP	H	TBF	R	ER	HR	SH	SF	HB	BB	IBB	SO	WP	Bk.
Gilich, Denny, Boi.	1	1	.500	3.24	13	0	0	0	9	1	16.2	11	70	9	6	3	0	1	0	9	0	27	0	0
Gomes, Tony, Yak.	2	8	.200	4.09	16	11	0	0	2	1	72.2	76	321	53	33	6	0	4	4	34	0	52	11	2
Gonzalez, Armando, Port.	0	1	.000	3.21	5	0	0	0	3	0	14.0	14	57	6	5	1	0	1	1	3	0	8	1	0
Goodrich, Randy, S.K.	4	5	.444	5.20	17	10	0	0	1	0	62.1	74	274	43	36	5	0	3	4	17	1	38	2	3
Gordon, Kevin, Port.	2	2	.500	5.52	8	7	0	0	0	0	29.1	31	137	24	18	3	0	1	5	14	0	20	4	1
Harrell, Timothy, Yak.	5	3	.625	3.88	13	6	0	0	3	0	53.1	53	237	30	23	4	2	1	4	24	0	50	4	1
Harwas, Oliver, Boi.	1	3	.250	3.16	20	1	0	0	5	0	37.0	42	166	19	13	2	0	2	1	12	0	29	4	0
Hebert, Cedric, Yak.	1	1	.500	3.20	4	3	0	0	0	0	19.2	18	84	9	7	1	1	1	0	9	0	15	1	1
Hills, Mark, S.K.*	4	1	.800	5.03	11	10	0	0	0	0	48.1	47	219	28	27	4	1	1	3	27	0	34	4	0
Holden, Brian, Eug.*	3	4	.429	5.13	17	6	0	0	6	1	52.2	62	251	41	30	2	2	1	5	24	0	37	6	0
Hooper, Jimmy, Spo.	4	2	.667	2.78	17	0	0	0	4	1	35.2	39	159	14	11	1	1	1	1	17	1	36	1	2
Hudson, Luke, Port.	3	6	.333	4.74	15	15	0	0	0	0	79.2	68	361	46	42	8	1	4	4	51	0	82	8	3
Huller, Mike, S.K.*	1	1	.500	8.03	19	0	0	0	6	0	24.2	27	142	31	22	1	2	1	6	31	0	14	5	2
Hundley, Jeffrey, Boi.*	8	3	.727	3.40	16	16	0	0	0	0	92.2	77	376	42	35	7	1	4	2	27	1	89	7	2
Hutchings, Mark, S.K.	0	2	.000	5.02	8	0	0	0	3	0	14.1	13	70	12	8	2	0	1	0	15	1	10	2	2
Jackson, Chris, S.K.	1	1	.500	6.80	17	7	0	0	1	0	42.1	43	219	43	32	5	0	4	4	40	0	27	12	1
Jackson, Jeremy, Spo.*	0	1	.000	3.05	7	5	0	0	1	0	20.2	22	92	10	7	2	1	2	1	11	0	29	1	1
Jacobs, Gregory, Boi.*	3	2	.600	4.24	25	0	0	0	6	0	23.1	23	113	16	11	0	0	2	2	20	2	16	4	0
Johnson, David, Port.	0	0	.000	3.86	6	0	0	0	6	1	4.2	8	24	2	2	0	0	1	1	1	0	6	2	0
Johnson, Eric, S.K.	0	0	.000	6.35	5	2	0	0	0	0	11.1	11	59	8	8	1	0	0	1	13	0	8	5	0
Johnson, Jeremiah, Eug.	0	1	.000	5.68	7	1	0	0	3	0	6.1	8	33	6	4	0	0	3	1	4	0	3	1	0
Jones, Christopher, S.K.*	5	4	.556	4.13	14	13	0	0	0	0	72.0	76	304	40	33	6	3	3	4	17	0	60	4	1
Jones, Greg, Boi.	0	2	.000	4.93	22	0	0	0	3	1	34.2	37	152	22	19	3	2	1	3	13	0	28	3	0
Joseph, Kevin, S.K.	1	1	.500	4.36	23	0	0	0	0	0	43.1	36	194	25	21	3	1	3	5	27	0	37	8	1
Kawahara, Orin, Ever.	0	3	.000	5.67	17	0	0	0	2	0	33.1	43	161	27	21	1	1	1	2	17	0	26	4	1
Kennedy, Ryan, Port.	0	0	.000	36.00	1	0	0	0	0	0	1.0	3	7	4	4	0	0	0	0	1	0	2	0	0
Kenny, Seth, S.O.	0	0	.000	0.00	2	0	0	0	2	0	2.0	2	8	0	0	0	0	0	0	0	0	3	0	0
Kidd, Jake, Port.	1	0	1.000	7.46	20	0	0	0	11	3	35.0	49	177	33	29	3	2	1	2	26	0	20	2	0
Kirkpatrick, Brian, Port.	1	0	1.000	11.49	12	0	0	0	5	0	15.2	18	77	20	20	0	0	0	3	10	0	10	6	0
Kiyono, Masashi, S.K.	1	1	.500	4.00	2	2	0	0	0	0	9.0	10	41	7	4	1	0	0	1	3	0	6	0	1
Klein, Matt, S.O.	4	1	.800	4.15	16	2	0	0	8	3	47.2	56	222	25	22	3	2	1	3	22	2	43	4	5
Labitzke, Jesse, Port.*	4	3	.571	4.97	17	2	0	0	4	1	50.2	53	230	30	28	2	2	3	2	30	1	44	6	0
Lamattina, Ryan, Port.*	4	0	1.000	3.23	18	0	0	0	7	0	30.2	29	135	14	11	3	0	0	0	18	0	30	2	0
Leach, Mike, Boi.	4	2	.667	4.50	15	14	1	0	0	0	70.0	79	320	49	35	8	1	1	6	26	1	45	5	1
Lee, Garrett, Eug.	2	3	.400	6.32	9	9	0	0	0	0	47.0	56	216	41	33	7	1	2	7	11	1	47	1	2
Lee, Wayne, Spo.	3	4	.429	3.82	31	0	0	0	18	3	35.1	28	161	22	15	1	2	0	0	23	3	48	3	0
Longo, Neil, Ever.	6	2	.750	2.26	16	11	0	0	2	0	75.2	67	310	31	19	0	2	1	2	23	0	48	8	0
Looper, Aaron, Ever.	4	5	.444	6.86	14	14	0	0	0	0	59.0	72	272	52	45	8	4	0	2	31	0	40	6	1
Lubozynski, Matt, Boi.*	2	1	.667	1.63	9	0	0	0	2	1	27.2	17	103	5	5	1	1	1	0	7	0	21	2	0
Mahan, Dallas, Ever.*	0	0	.000	10.38	8	0	0	0	5	0	8.2	15	47	10	10	3	1	1	0	6	0	4	1	0
Maluchnik, Gregg, Eug.	0	0	.000	6.75	1	0	0	0	1	0	1.1	2	6	1	1	0	0	0	0	0	0	0	0	0
Mateo, Julio, Ever.	3	3	.500	4.70	28	0	0	0	13	4	38.1	40	170	25	20	6	3	2	2	17	1	37	6	0
Mazone, Brian, Eug.*	1	6	.143	5.53	20	9	0	0	5	0	68.1	91	314	50	42	8	3	4	2	27	0	32	1	1
McDaniel, Denton, Spo.*	1	5	.167	4.25	29	0	0	0	7	1	36.0	42	173	25	17	2	0	1	2	19	4	43	4	1
McGuire, Brandon, Boi.	0	0	.000	5.27	8	0	0	0	2	0	13.2	13	65	9	8	3	1	0	1	9	0	6	1	0
Mears, Chris, Ever.	9	1	.900	2.74	15	15	1	0	0	0	98.2	86	411	39	30	6	2	4	5	33	0	67	2	5
Miller, Benji, S.K.	4	3	.571	2.25	30	0	0	0	27	17	44.0	33	180	13	11	1	0	0	0	20	0	51	4	0
Montero, Alcantara, S.O.	2	3	.400	8.68	14	3	0	0	6	0	37.1	47	191	42	36	5	2	3	4	26	0	28	6	2
Moody, Jason, Yak.*	1	0	1.000	3.38	9	0	0	0	4	2	13.1	7	59	5	5	1	0	0	1	13	0	18	0	0
Moore, Brad, S.O.	1	1	.500	3.20	17	2	0	0	6	3	39.1	29	184	24	14	1	0	2	4	34	0	33	8	2
Morrison, Cody, Boi.	5	1	.833	1.78	30	0	0	0	20	6	35.1	25	154	10	7	0	1	0	3	16	0	40	9	1
Morrison, Robbie, Spo.	3	0	1.000	2.13	26	0	0	0	22	13	25.1	15	111	8	6	2	2	1	1	18	2	33	1	0
Moskau, Ryan, Yak.*	3	0	1.000	1.23	9	6	0	0	3	2	36.2	22	156	11	5	3	2	0	3	13	0	42	0	1
Mundy, Mike, Port.	2	0	1.000	2.25	21	0	0	0	17	6	24.0	16	94	9	6	1	1	2	1	5	0	19	2	2
Myers, Taylor, Spo.	0	0	.000	5.79	1	1	0	0	0	0	4.2	4	20	3	3	1	0	0	0	3	0	1	2	0
Nielsen, Thomas, S.K.*	5	1	.833	11.14	21	0	0	0	8	0	26.2	38	140	39	33	3	0	4	4	18	1	28	2	2
Nix, Wayne, S.O.	6	6	.500	5.32	16	15	0	0	1	0	71.0	76	319	56	42	7	0	2	1	37	0	56	10	2
Nogowski, Brandon, S.O.*	4	4	.500	3.71	17	8	0	0	8	1	68.0	74	299	44	28	6	1	2	3	11	0	66	6	0
Ojeda, Joseph, S.K.	0	0	.000	9.00	5	0	0	0	4	0	5.0	10	30	7	5	2	0	0	0	4	0	0	0	0
Oyler, Scott, S.O.	4	4	.500	3.48	22	0	0	0	14	3	54.1	53	243	28	21	5	1	4	5	29	3	42	5	2
Ozias, Todd, S.K.	3	4	.429	3.94	27	0	0	0	15	2	45.2	38	184	23	20	6	5	1	2	12	1	51	6	0
Pamus, Javier, Spo.	2	1	.667	5.20	12	4	0	0	0	0	36.1	40	169	30	21	2	1	1	3	16	1	33	3	1
Pena, Juan, S.O.*	1	2	.333	2.15	8	8	0	0	0	0	46.0	46	194	21	11	2	1	1	2	10	1	38	0	3
Penny, Tony, Spo.	2	2	.500	2.91	28	0	0	0	7	3	52.2	55	231	25	17	2	3	1	0	20	2	48	3	0
Petrosian, Ara, S.O.	0	0	.000	0.00	1	0	0	0	1	0	0.1	0	1	0	0	0	0	0	0	0	0	1	0	0
Pourron, Joe, Yak.	0	7	.000	6.32	25	4	0	0	15	10	47.0	50	225	43	33	5	3	4	3	30	2	33	4	0
Proctor, Scott, Yak.	0	1	.000	10.80	3	1	0	0	2	2	5.0	9	26	8	6	1	1	1	0	1	0	4	1	2
Ramirez, Erasmo, S.K.*	0	1	.000	3.72	9	2	0	0	0	0	19.1	19	81	11	8	3	1	0	1	2	0	23	0	0
Ramirez, Horacio, Eug.*	2	7	.222	6.31	16	8	0	0	3	0	55.2	84	273	51	39	4	3	6	4	17	0	39	4	2
Romero, John, Boi.	0	0	.000	5.93	10	0	0	0	6	0	13.2	24	72	12	9	4	0	1	0	6	0	8	1	0
Santos, Joshua, S.K.*	4	1	.800	4.04	11	11	1	0	0	0	49.0	50	224	28	22	2	3	0	7	19	0	57	7	5
Schultz, Jeffrey, S.O.	1	0	1.000	0.00	2	0	0	0	0	0	4.2	0	16	0	0	0	0	0	0	1	0	10	1	0
Sedlacek, Shawn, Spo.	9	2	.818	3.45	16	13	0	0	0	0	86.0	89	371	43	33	2	1	4	6	18	0	62	4	5
Simmons, Wendell, Yak.	2	2	.500	4.50	15	0	0	0	12	0	22.0	24	103	15	11	2	0	1	0	15	2	18	3	0
Snow, Bert, S.O.	1	3	.250	5.64	11	8	0	0	1	0	44.2	52	215	38	28	2	5	3	6	18	1	35	5	1
Sobkowiak, Scott, Eug.	3	2	.600	1.55	8	8	0	0	0	0	40.2	25	163	12	7	1	0	1	3	13	0	55	4	0
Sonnier, Shawn, Spo.	0	0	.000	1.35	7	0	0	0	3	1	6.2	7	27	1	1	0	0	0	0	1	0	10	1	0
Soto, Seferino, Eug.	1	0	1.000	9.09	20	0	0	0	5	0	34.2	44	205	46	35	4	1	3	5	53	0	28	23	1
Suarez, Luis, Boi.	0	0	.000	3.86	11	0	0	0	3	1	16.1	15	69	7	7	2	0	0	1	3	1	18	0	0
Suazo, Rigoberto, S.O.	0	0	.000	0.00	2	0	0	0	1	1	1.1	0	5	0	0	0	0	0	0	1	0	0	0	0
Sylvester, Billy, Eug.	0	11	.000	6.51	16	16	0	0	0	0	55.1	73	273	61	40	7	0	4	7	24	0	42	5	1
Thompson, Eric, S.O.	5	2	.714	4.45	13	12	0	0	0	0	56.2	60	252	34	28	7	2	0	3	25	0	51	2	5

Pitcher, Team	W	L	Pct.	ERA	G	GS	CG	ShO	GF	Sv.	IP	H	TBF	R	ER	HR	SH	SF	HB	BB	IBB	SO	WP	Bk.
Thornton, Matt, Ever.*	0	0	.000	27.00	2	0	0	0	0	0	1.1	1	8	4	4	0	0	0	0	3	0	0	0	0
Thurman, Corey, Spo.	3	3	.500	4.05	12	12	0	0	0	0	60.0	72	278	35	27	3	1	3	5	31	0	49	6	0
Torres, Melqui, Ever.	3	10	.231	6.07	16	15	0	0	1	1	72.2	92	356	72	49	4	5	8	6	40	0	41	7	1
Urban, Jeffrey, S.K.*	1	2	.333	4.98	5	3	0	0	0	0	21.2	21	95	14	12	1	2	0	0	8	0	22	2	0
Van Buren, Jermaine, Port.	0	0	.000	3.60	2	2	0	0	0	0	10.0	7	43	4	4	0	0	2	1	7	0	9	1	1
Vargas, Derrick, Port.*	4	4	.500	4.43	14	8	0	0	3	2	63.0	67	288	40	31	6	2	3	0	32	0	44	4	0
Vogelsong, Ryan, S.K.	6	1	.857	1.77	10	10	0	0	0	0	56.0	37	221	15	11	5	3	2	1	16	0	66	2	2
Voyles, Bradley, Eug.	0	0	.000	3.09	7	0	0	0	4	0	11.2	9	57	5	4	0	1	1	2	10	1	22	2	0
Wagner, Denny, S.O.	0	1	.000	18.00	2	2	0	0	0	0	4.0	11	26	9	8	0	0	0	0	3	0	5	1	0
Ward, Monty, Spo.	6	1	.857	3.79	15	15	0	0	0	0	71.1	66	304	33	30	4	0	2	1	35	1	76	7	1
Williams, Adam, S.K.*	0	0	.000	7.36	7	0	0	0	0	0	11.0	17	57	9	9	1	0	0	0	6	0	15	0	1
Williams, Joel, Yak.	0	1	.000	16.41	15	1	0	0	5	0	17.0	31	125	42	31	0	1	2	5	40	0	10	6	1
Williams, Kris, Boi.	2	0	1.000	5.52	10	0	0	0	2	0	14.2	19	69	9	9	2	1	1	2	5	0	12	4	0
Willis, Craig, Ever.	0	2	.000	5.33	12	0	0	0	4	0	27.0	32	127	18	16	0	2	2	0	9	0	16	1	3
Yates, Tyler, S.O.	0	0	.000	0.00	2	0	0	0	1	1	2.1	2	9	0	0	0	0	0	0	1	0	1	0	0

COMBINATION SHUTOUTS: **Boise (5)**—Bond-Jones-Lubozynski-Romero, Hundley-Lubozynski, Bridges-Jones-Harwas, Hundley-Morrison, Hundley-Morrison. **Eugene (1)**—Ramirez-Garmong. **Everett (2)**—Torres-Chrysler, Mears-Balbuena. **Portland (5)**—Defelice-Vargas, Cook-Lamattina-Johnson, Hudson-Kirkpatrick-Kidd, Cook-Lamattina-Mundy, Vargas-Cameron. **Salem-Keizer (1)**—Jones-Miller. **Southern Oregon (3)**—Moore-Dobis-Suazo-Brink, Snow-Brink, Nogowski-Brink. **Spokane (2)**—Ammons-Bautista-Lee, Pamus-Penny. **Yakima (3)**—Davis-Pourron, Colyer-Barnsby-Pourron, Burnside-Bornyk-Pourron.

NO-HIT GAMES: None.

1998 FIELDING

TEAM

Team	Pct.	G	PO	A	E	TC	DP	PB
Portland	.963	76	1998	823	109	2930	59	34
Salem-Keizer	.960	76	1992	813	118	2923	55	22
Everett	.957	76	2007	903	130	3040	56	34
Spokane	.957	76	2025	827	128	2980	57	24
Boise	.956	76	1994	934	134	3062	60	20
Yakima	.955	76	2013	791	133	2937	57	27
Southern Oregon	.952	76	2007	853	145	3005	53	18
Eugene	.943	76	1985	758	166	2909	65	17

TRIPLE PLAY: Salem-Keizer.

INDIVIDUAL

FIRST BASEMEN

NOTE: All caps denotes fielding-percentage leader based on 38 games for catchers, 51 for all other non-pitchers and 76 innings for pitchers. *Throws lefthanded.

Player, Team	Pct.	G	PO	A	E	TC	DP
Alvarez, German, Eug.*	.964	22	180	8	7	195	13
Balbuena, Mike, Yak.	1.000	1	2	0	0	2	0
Cheshier, Casey, Eug.	.967	26	195	9	7	211	24
DiPace, Danny, Port.	.955	8	60	4	3	67	5
Duck, Kevin, Port.*	.983	58	478	42	9	529	39
Etheredge, Josh, Port.	.989	10	88	6	1	95	7
Farris, Ed, S.O.	1.000	5	43	1	0	44	3
Fox, Brian, Boi.	1.000	2	16	0	0	16	1
Freitas, Jeremy, Spo.	.978	35	293	20	7	320	24
Gomez, Erick, Spo.	.969	4	28	3	1	32	1
GORR, Robb, Yak.	.989	64	515	46	6	567	44
Gregory, Rich, Eug.	.983	11	56	3	1	60	8
Hart, Jason, S.O.	.982	67	622	45	12	679	45
Huisman, Jason, Boi.	1.000	1	5	1	0	6	0
Johnson, Erik, Port.	.875	2	7	0	1	8	1
Kelley, Casey, Boi.	.986	53	452	28	7	487	35
Luster, Jeremy, S.K.	.988	46	375	28	5	408	35
Mahoney, Ricardo, Port.	.984	15	113	9	2	124	6
Maluchnik, Gregg, Eug.	.990	23	188	16	2	206	13
Martinez, Victor, Ever.	1.000	1	5	1	0	6	1
McCorkle, Shawn, Ever.	.979	34	320	11	7	338	18
Montas, Ricardo, Spo.	.980	36	266	21	6	293	18
Oliver, William, Boi.	.993	35	285	12	2	299	21
Pujols, Rafael, S.O.	.962	5	44	7	2	53	3
Robinson, Brian, Ever.	.984	15	116	6	2	124	9
Rosario, Omar, S.O.*	1.000	1	1	0	0	1	0
Shackleford, Brian, Spo.*	1.000	2	2	0	0	2	0
Story-Harden, Thomari, Eug.	.963	15	99	5	4	108	10
Summers, John, S.K.	.990	35	294	16	3	313	18
Woodward, Mattson, Ever.	.994	36	298	10	2	310	22

TRIPLE PLAY: Luster.

SECOND BASEMEN

Player, Team	Pct.	G	PO	A	E	TC	DP
Castro, Al, Eug.	.944	37	71	82	9	162	28
Collins, Michael, Yak.	.895	8	13	21	4	38	3
Condon, Mike, Boi.	.936	31	67	79	10	156	21
Franklin, Jason, Port.	.953	17	36	65	5	106	11
Garcia, Ismael, Yak.	.947	21	27	44	4	75	9
Goelz, Jim, Yak.	1.000	15	17	32	0	49	3
Gorrie, Brad, S.O.	.936	49	93	125	15	233	21
Goudie, Jaime, Yak.	.929	28	50	81	10	141	10
Hall, Justin, S.O.	.942	21	34	63	6	103	11
Hart, Corey, Spo.	.960	33	49	95	6	150	17
Hill, Steven, S.K.	.949	38	74	94	9	177	24
Hood, Jay, Boi.	.818	3	2	7	2	11	0
Huisman, Jason, Boi.	.962	33	71	106	7	184	16
Leon, Richy, Port.	.974	14	30	45	2	77	5
Ligons, Merrell, Spo.	.923	8	4	20	2	26	1
Martinez, Victor, Ever.	.955	27	54	95	7	156	9
Mattern, Erik, Ever.	.985	45	90	109	3	202	19
Montas, Ricardo, Spo.	1.000	5	6	6	0	12	0
Nunez, Jose, Port.	.969	45	84	135	7	226	22
Oliver, Brian, Boi.	1.000	2	4	6	0	10	2
Pacheco, Domingo, Ever.	.919	15	18	50	6	74	4
Ruiz, Willy, Spo.	.936	41	64	98	11	173	17
Salazar, Oscar, S.O.	.955	7	23	19	2	44	3
Sanchez, Manuel, Eug.	.920	48	87	98	16	201	22
Theodorou, Nick, Yak.	.952	23	35	64	5	104	17
Wade, Bryn, Boi.	.932	14	30	39	5	74	6
Zambrano, Alan, Ever.	.923	40	71	98	14	183	22

TRIPLE PLAY: Mattern.

THIRD BASEMEN

Player, Team	Pct.	G	PO	A	E	TC	DP
Balbuena, Mike, Yak.	.800	14	5	15	5	25	0
CALDERON, Henry, Spo.	.913	60	40	106	14	160	10
Castro, Al, Eug.	.879	31	17	41	8	66	4
Cheshier, Casey, Eug.	.641	16	9	16	14	39	4
Christensen, Mike, Boi.	.894	67	30	180	25	235	12
Detienne, Dave, Yak.	.800	23	9	19	7	35	1
Franklin, Jason, Port.	.878	39	25	76	14	115	7
Goelz, Jim, Yak.	.882	9	1	14	2	17	2
Goudie, Jaime, Yak.	.824	6	7	7	3	17	1
Hall, Justin, S.O.	.889	9	9	15	3	27	0
Hart, Corey, Spo.	.897	13	15	20	4	39	1
Hill, Steven, S.K.	.895	11	4	13	2	19	0
Howe, Matthew, S.O.	.894	58	41	120	19	180	4
Huisman, Jason, Boi.	.882	9	6	24	4	34	1
Kuzmic, Craig, Ever.	.846	27	12	54	12	78	5
Leon, Richy, Port.	.919	25	18	39	5	62	2
Martinez, Victor, Ever.	.938	19	10	35	3	48	2
Montas, Ricardo, Spo.	1.000	2	3	1	0	4	0
Oropeza, Asdrubal, Eug.	.887	28	24	70	12	106	13
Pacheco, Domingo, Ever.	1.000	2	2	2	0	4	0
Pujols, Rafael, S.O.	.000	1	0	0	1	1	0
Robinson, Brian, Ever.	.863	34	21	61	13	95	4
Ruiz, Ramon, Yak.	.915	39	30	67	9	106	9
Salazar, Oscar, S.O.	.813	10	6	20	6	32	0
Sanchez, Manuel, Eug.	.783	6	3	15	5	23	1

CLASS A *Northwest League*

Player, Team	Pct.	G	PO	A	E	TC	DP
Slemmer, Ben, Spo.	.875	7	4	10	2	16	0
Smith, Sam, Port.	.838	14	6	25	6	37	3
Summers, John, S.K.	.891	16	6	43	6	55	3
Tommasini, Kevin, S.K.	.600	3	2	1	2	5	0
Torcato, Tony, S.K.	.886	53	20	112	17	149	5
TRIPLE PLAY: Hill.							

SHORTSTOPS

Player, Team	Pct.	G	PO	A	E	TC	DP
Brignac, Junior, Eug.	.879	68	108	175	39	322	30
Calderon, Henry, Spo.	.912	14	20	32	5	57	7
Castro, Al, Eug.	.814	10	13	22	8	43	4
Collins, Michael, Yak.	.915	12	13	30	4	47	3
Detienne, Dave, Yak.	.900	11	15	30	5	50	5
FIGGINS, Desmond, Port.	.947	67	90	198	16	304	28
Goelz, Jim, Yak.	.946	52	96	132	13	241	29
Hall, Justin, S.O.	.922	34	33	120	13	166	20
Hill, Steven, S.K.	.933	6	4	10	1	15	0
Hood, Jay, Boi.	.910	37	43	108	15	166	15
Huisman, Jason, Boi.	.941	27	31	96	8	135	17
Leon, Richy, Port.	.945	12	13	39	3	55	9
Ligons, Merrell, Spo.	.907	44	67	128	20	215	20
Martinez, Victor, Ever.	.778	3	3	4	2	9	1
Mattern, Erik, S.K.	.875	2	1	6	1	8	1
Mercedes, Luis, S.K.	1.000	3	2	1	0	3	0
Montas, Ricardo, Spo.	.940	24	26	68	6	100	13
Oliver, Brian, Boi.	.919	15	15	42	5	62	8
Pacheco, Domingo, Ever.	.894	13	12	30	5	47	2
Parker, Hubert, Ever.	.938	67	95	222	21	338	37
Pecci, Jay, S.O.	.913	36	68	110	17	195	15
Ransom, Bryan, S.K.	.928	71	92	216	24	332	37
Salazar, Oscar, S.O.	.857	6	10	20	5	35	6
Sampson, Jacob, Yak.	.845	20	19	30	9	58	5

OUTFIELDERS

Player, Team	Pct.	G	PO	A	E	TC	DP
Allen, Jeffrey, S.K.	.991	55	111	4	1	116	0
Auterson, Jeff, Yak.	.955	73	122	6	6	134	1
Balbuena, Mike, Yak.	1.000	2	1	0	0	1	0
Basabe, Jesus, S.O.	.852	47	66	3	12	81	0
Blakely, Darren, Boi.	.971	70	134	1	4	139	0
Byrnes, Eric, S.O.	.986	40	67	2	1	70	0
Camilo, Juan, S.O.	.938	26	28	2	2	32	1
Casper, Brett, S.K.	1.000	7	8	0	0	8	0
Cheshier, Casey, Eug.	1.000	2	3	0	0	3	0
Child, Casey, S.K.	.991	74	110	3	1	114	0
Clark, Douglas, S.K.	.929	56	64	1	5	70	0
Cosbey, Chris, S.O.*	.988	44	75	5	1	81	0
Cox, Brian, Eug.	.977	59	125	2	3	130	1
Croud, Will, Boi.	.973	64	96	14	3	113	0
Curry, Mike, Spo.	.974	66	146	4	4	154	1
Diaz, Michael, Boi.*	.838	29	29	2	6	37	0
Dodson, Jeremy, Spo.	.968	64	86	6	3	95	1
Duverge, Salvador, Port.	.964	15	23	4	1	28	0
Etheredge, Josh, Port.	1.000	9	10	0	0	10	0
Feliciano, Jesus, Yak.*	.975	73	191	6	5	202	3
Frazier, Carlos, S.K.	1.000	10	3	0	0	3	0
Fry, Ryan, Spo.	1.000	44	62	3	0	65	0
Gregory, Rich, Eug.	.818	9	8	1	2	11	0
Haynes, Larry, Ever.	.963	62	125	4	5	134	0
Kuzmic, Craig, Ever.	.938	18	28	2	2	32	0
Landaeta, Luis, Port.*	.957	26	44	1	2	47	0
Lindsey, Shawn, S.K.*	.903	22	25	3	3	31	0
Magruder, Christopher, S.K.	.976	44	82	1	2	85	1
Martinez, Victor, Ever.	.929	23	49	3	4	56	1
McDowell, Arturo, S.K.*	.976	45	79	3	2	84	0
Mota, Pedro, S.K.*	.750	6	3	0	1	4	0
Mott, Bill, Boi.	1.000	1	1	0	0	1	0
Newton, Kimani, Yak.	.952	40	55	5	3	63	0
Pacheco, Domingo, Ever.	.000	1	0	0	1	1	0
Paterson, Joe, Yak.	1.000	39	50	3	0	53	0
Phillips, Paul, Spo.	.667	1	2	0	1	3	0
Pierre, Juan, Port.*	.955	64	100	5	5	110	0
Rosario, Melvin, Port.*	.962	61	146	7	6	159	3
Rosario, Omar, S.O.*	.896	25	39	4	5	48	1
SHACKLEFORD, Brian, Spo.*	1.000	67	91	6	0	97	1
Simmons, Jerry, Eug.	.953	71	116	5	6	127	0
Southall, Kirk, Ever.	.952	19	17	3	1	21	1
Stewart, Colin, Eug.	.990	50	96	8	1	105	2
Story-Harden, Thomari, Yak.	.500	7	1	2	3	6	0
Strickland, Gregory, Eug.*	.946	44	83	4	5	92	1
Theodorou, Nick, Yak.	1.000	12	9	1	0	10	0

Player, Team	Pct.	G	PO	A	E	TC	DP
Thomas, Gary, S.O.	.975	59	113	3	3	119	0
Valderrama, Carlos, S.K.	1.000	2	3	0	0	3	0
Weber, Jake, Ever.*	.978	75	131	4	3	138	2
Whitehurst, Tom, Port.	.974	57	112	1	3	116	0
Williams, P.J., Ever.	.977	36	78	8	2	88	0
Wright, Steven, Ever.*	1.000	4	3	2	0	5	0
Zambrano, Alan, Ever.	1.000	3	2	0	0	2	0

CATCHERS

Player, Team	Pct.	G	PO	A	E	TC	DP	PB
Alcala, Juan, Ever.	.994	28	155	14	1	170	0	19
Bertrand, Ben, S.K.	1.000	8	54	4	0	58	0	3
Carroll, Mark, Ever.	1.000	1	9	1	0	10	0	0
Castro, Juan, Port.	.984	29	173	11	3	187	1	15
Dean, Mike, S.K.	.969	35	281	32	10	323	1	9
Diaz, Angel, Boi.	.931	3	24	3	2	29	0	1
Ewan, Bry, Eug.	.989	12	80	11	1	92	0	6
Fox, Brian, Boi.	.984	21	115	12	2	129	0	4
Greer, Matt, Yak.	.978	18	82	8	2	92	0	11
Hanseen, Tye, Eug.	.986	36	246	28	4	278	0	3
Herrera, Pedro, Spo.	.968	22	173	11	6	190	0	3
Hill, Jason, Boi.	.977	48	313	32	8	353	1	9
JOHNSON, Erik, Port.	.990	39	282	18	3	303	1	16
Kellner, Ryan, Yak.	.950	13	86	10	5	101	0	3
Kenna, David, S.K.	1.000	3	4	0	0	4	0	0
Kuzmic, Craig, Ever.	.978	7	39	6	1	46	0	2
Luderer, Brian, S.O.	.979	7	39	7	1	47	0	2
Mahoney, Ricardo, Port.	.977	13	78	8	2	88	2	3
Maldonado, Carlos, Ever.	.984	39	250	52	5	307	1	11
Maluchnik, Gregg, Eug.	.982	32	245	32	5	282	1	8
Nieckula, Aaron, S.O.	.974	38	230	28	7	265	1	7
O'Neil, John, Boi.	.944	18	78	7	5	90	0	6
Phillips, Paul, Spo.	.980	49	377	62	9	448	5	13
Pujols, Rafael, S.O.	.975	44	281	36	8	325	2	9
Rivera, Juan, Spo.	.991	12	98	10	1	109	2	8
Rodriguez, Guillermo, S.K.	1.000	1	8	0	0	8	0	0
Ross, David, Yak.	.979	57	428	47	10	485	1	13
Schwieder, Nicholas, Boi.	1.000	1	1	0	0	1	0	0
Serrano, Sammy, S.K.	.978	34	254	19	6	279	0	7
Tommasini, Kevin, S.K.	1.000	5	9	0	0	9	0	3
Underwood, Jake, Ever.	.971	12	55	11	2	68	0	2

PITCHERS

Player, Team	Pct.	G	PO	A	E	TC	DP
Abreu, Winston, Eug.	1.000	17	1	4	0	5	0
Ammons, Cary, Spo.*	.917	15	3	19	2	24	1
Avery, Paul, Yak.*	1.000	9	2	2	0	4	0
Balbuena, Caleb, Ever.	1.000	12	0	5	0	5	1
Barboza, Carlos, Port.	1.000	14	2	0	0	2	0
Barnsby, Scott, Yak.	.833	26	3	2	1	6	0
Bautista, Francisco, Spo.	1.000	22	1	2	0	3	0
Beaver, Greg, Ever.	.800	9	0	4	1	5	0
Bell, Scott, Yak.	1.000	11	3	5	0	8	0
Berroa, Oliver, Ever.	1.000	11	1	1	0	2	0
Birrell, Simon, Eug.	.600	13	0	3	2	5	0
Bond, Tommy, Boi.	.897	15	6	20	3	29	4
Bornyk, Matt, Yak.	1.000	17	4	5	0	9	0
Bradley, Brian, Port.	.933	10	5	9	1	15	1
Bridenbaugh, Christian, Yak.*	.857	17	1	5	1	7	0
Bridges, Douglas, Boi.*	.947	15	2	16	1	19	2
Brink, Jim, S.O.	1.000	24	4	15	0	19	1
Brummitt, Travis, Eug.	1.000	17	3	12	0	15	1
Brunet, Michael, Boi.	1.000	4	0	1	0	1	0
Bump, Nate, S.K.	1.000	8	0	1	0	1	0
Burch, Matt, Spo.	.727	12	4	4	3	11	0
Burnside, Adrian, Yak.*	1.000	11	0	4	0	4	0
Calandriello, Donato, S.O.*	1.000	6	0	2	0	2	0
Cameron, Ryan, Port.	.900	18	2	7	1	10	0
Caraccioli, Lance, Yak.*	.889	11	2	6	1	9	0
Carter, Justin, Port.*	.933	15	2	12	1	15	1
Casper, Michael, Spo.	.750	19	0	6	2	8	0
Chrysler, Clint, Ever.*	1.000	24	2	3	0	5	0
Colyer, Stephen, Yak.*	1.000	15	3	5	0	8	0
Connolly, Keith, S.K.	1.000	21	1	1	0	2	1
Cook, Aaron, Port.	.923	15	9	15	2	26	1
Corey, Michael, Eug.	1.000	20	3	11	0	14	0
Crawford, Jeremy, S.O.*	1.000	2	0	1	0	1	0
Davis, Allen, Yak.*	1.000	4	0	3	0	3	1
DeJesus, Tony, Ever.*	1.000	19	2	3	0	5	0
Delgado, Danny, Ever.	1.000	14	1	5	0	6	0
Demouy, Chris, Boi.*	1.000	20	1	6	0	7	0
Derenches, Albert, Ever.*	1.000	9	0	2	0	2	0

Player, Team	Pct.	G	PO	A	E	TC	DP
Dickinson, Rodney, Eug.	1.000	13	2	2	0	4	0
Difelice, Mark, Port.	.875	15	1	6	1	8	1
Dobis, Jason, S.O.	1.000	16	6	17	0	23	1
Dunning, Justin, Ever.	.875	13	3	4	1	8	0
Emanuel, Brandon, Boi.	.947	15	7	11	1	19	2
Esteves, Jake, S.K.	1.000	1	0	1	0	1	0
Farley, Joseph, S.K.*	1.000	3	0	3	0	3	0
Faust, Jason, S.O.*	1.000	7	0	3	0	3	0
Fields, Brian, S.K.*	.500	9	1	0	1	2	0
Frachiseur, Zachery, Eug.	.833	23	3	7	2	12	0
Garcia, Bryan, S.O.	.833	7	2	3	1	6	0
Garey, Dan, Ever.	1.000	9	0	1	0	1	0
Garmong, Aaron, Eug.*	.947	24	2	16	1	19	0
Gilfillan, Jason, Spo.	1.000	6	1	0	0	1	0
Gilich, Denny, Boi.	1.000	13	1	1	0	2	0
Gomes, Tony, Yak.	.833	16	3	2	1	6	1
Gonzalez, Armando, Port.	1.000	5	2	2	0	4	0
Goodrich, Randy, S.K.	.882	17	5	10	2	17	0
Gordon, Kevin, Port.	1.000	8	2	5	0	7	0
Harrell, Timothy, Yak.	.929	13	7	6	1	14	0
Harwas, Oliver, Boi.	.889	20	2	6	1	9	0
Hebert, Cedric, Yak.	1.000	4	0	3	0	3	0
Hills, Mark, S.K.*	1.000	11	6	11	0	17	1
Holden, Brian, Eug.*	.909	17	2	8	1	11	0
Hooper, Jimmy, Port.	1.000	17	1	3	0	4	0
Hudson, Luke, Port.	1.000	15	4	5	0	9	0
Huller, Mike, S.K.*	.667	19	0	2	1	3	0
Hundley, Jeffrey, Boi.*	.939	16	5	26	2	33	0
Hutchings, Mark, S.K.	.667	8	0	2	1	3	0
Jackson, Chris, S.K.	.714	17	1	4	2	7	0
Jackson, Jeremy, Spo.*	1.000	7	2	3	0	5	0
Jacobs, Gregory, Boi.*	1.000	25	0	1	0	1	0
Johnson, David, Port.	.000	6	0	0	1	1	0
Johnson, Eric, S.K.	1.000	5	1	2	0	3	0
Johnson, Jeremiah, Eug.	1.000	7	1	1	0	2	1
Jones, Christopher, S.K.*	1.000	14	4	14	0	18	0
Jones, Greg, Boi.	1.000	22	4	7	0	11	1
Joseph, Kevin, S.K.	.889	23	3	5	1	9	0
Kawahara, Orin, Ever.	.778	17	2	5	2	9	1
Kidd, Jake, Port.	1.000	20	4	4	0	8	0
Kirkpatrick, Brian, Port.	1.000	12	2	0	0	2	0
Kiyono, Masashi, S.K.	1.000	2	0	2	0	2	0
Klein, Matt, S.O.	.900	16	3	6	1	10	0
Labitzke, Jesse, Port.*	1.000	17	2	6	0	8	0
Lamattina, Ryan, Port.*	.714	18	2	3	2	7	0
Leach, Mike, Boi.	.857	15	1	11	2	14	1
Lee, Garrett, Eug.	1.000	9	1	8	0	9	0
Lee, Wayne, Spo.	.833	31	3	2	1	6	0
Longo, Neil, Ever.	.968	16	5	25	1	31	3
Looper, Aaron, Ever.	.944	14	3	14	1	18	0
Lubozynski, Matt, Boi.*	1.000	9	2	11	0	13	0
Mahan, Dallas, Ever.*	1.000	8	0	3	0	3	1
Mateo, Julio, Ever.	1.000	28	2	3	0	5	0
Mazone, Brian, Eug.*	1.000	20	4	18	0	22	1
McDaniel, Denton, Spo.*	.750	29	1	2	1	4	0
McGuire, Brandon, Boi.	1.000	8	1	2	0	3	0
Mears, Chris, Ever.	1.000	15	3	13	0	16	1
Miller, Benji, S.K.	1.000	30	7	9	0	16	0
Montero, Alcantara, S.O.	.889	14	4	4	1	9	0
Moore, Brad, S.O.	1.000	17	5	4	0	9	2
Morrison, Cody, Boi.	.778	30	1	6	2	9	0
Morrison, Robbie, Spo.	1.000	26	2	4	0	6	0
Moskau, Ryan, Yak.*	1.000	9	4	7	0	11	0
Mundy, Mike, Port.	1.000	21	0	6	0	6	0
Myers, Taylor, Spo.	1.000	1	1	1	0	2	0
Nielsen, Thomas, S.K.*	.400	21	0	2	3	5	0
Nix, Wayne, S.O.	1.000	16	4	4	0	8	0
Nogowski, Brandon, S.O.*	1.000	17	6	7	0	13	0
Ojeda, Joseph, S.K.	1.000	5	0	1	0	1	0
Oyler, Scott, S.O.	.900	22	1	8	1	10	1
Ozias, Todd, S.K.	1.000	27	6	4	0	10	0
Pamus, Javier, Spo.	.778	12	3	4	2	9	2
Pena, Juan, S.O.*	1.000	8	1	8	0	9	0
Penny, Tony, Spo.	.765	28	3	10	4	17	1
Pourron, Joe, Yak.	.600	25	2	1	2	5	0
Ramirez, Erasmo, S.K.*	1.000	9	1	5	0	6	0
Ramirez, Horacio, Eug.*	.882	16	2	13	2	17	1
Romero, John, Boi.	1.000	10	0	2	0	2	0
Santos, Joshua, S.K.*	.833	11	2	8	2	12	2
SEDLACEK, Shawn, Spo.	1.000	16	7	19	0	26	2
Simmons, Wendell, Yak.	.833	15	0	5	1	6	1
Snow, Bert, S.O.	1.000	11	3	5	0	8	0
Sobkowiak, Scott, Eug.	1.000	8	3	3	0	6	1
Soto, Seferino, Eug.	.800	20	1	3	1	5	0
Suarez, Luis, Boi.	1.000	11	1	3	0	4	0
Suazo, Rigoberto, S.O.	1.000	2	0	1	0	1	0
Sylvester, Billy, Eug.	.857	16	4	2	1	7	0
Thompson, Eric, S.O.	1.000	13	3	9	0	12	1
Thurman, Corey, Spo.	.938	12	7	8	1	16	0
Torres, Melqui, Ever.	.880	16	4	18	3	25	1
Urban, Jeffrey, S.K.*	1.000	5	1	2	0	3	0
Van Buren, Jermaine, Port.	1.000	2	1	0	0	1	0
Vargas, Derrick, Port.*	.733	14	2	9	4	15	0
Vogelsong, Ryan, S.K.	.818	10	1	8	2	11	0
Voyles, Bradley, Eug.	.500	7	0	1	1	2	0
Ward, Monty, Spo.	.909	15	4	6	1	11	0
Williams, Adam, Yak.*	1.000	7	1	4	0	5	0
Williams, Joel, Yak.	.500	15	0	1	1	2	0
Williams, Kris, Boi.	.800	10	2	2	1	5	0
Willis, Craig, Ever.	1.000	12	1	5	0	6	0
Yates, Tyler, S.O.	1.000	2	0	1	0	1	0

The following players did not have any fielding statistics at the positions indicated or appeared only as a designated hitter, pinch-hitter or pinch-runner: G. Alvarez, of; Balbuena, p; Cheshier, 2b; Condon, 1b, ss; DiPace, of; Duprey, p; Franklin, 1b; C. Hart, ss; J. Hart, 3b; Kennedy, p; Kenny, p; Mercedes, 2b; Mahoney, of; Maluchnik, p, of; McCorkle, of; Moody, p; Nunez, ss; Petrosian, p; Proctor, p; Schultz, p; Sonnier, p; Theodorou, 1b; Thornton, p; Tommasini, 1b; Wagner, p.

LEAGUE CHAMPIONS

Year	Team	Pct.	Year	Team	Pct.	Year	Team	Pct.
1901—	Portland	.675	1922—	Calgary‡	.600	1954—	Vancouver*	.636
1902—	Butte	.608	1923-36	—Did not operate.			Lewiston	.629
1903—	Butte	.578	1937—	Wenatchee	.603	1955—	Salem	.646
1904—	Boise	.625		Tacoma*	.627		Eugene*	.639
1905—	Vancouver	.586	1938—	Yakima	.583	1956—	Yakima	.691
	Everett*	.667		Bellingham (2nd)†	.511		Yakima	.619
1906—	Tacoma	.600	1939—	Wenatchee	.601	1957—	Eugene	.576
1907—	Aberdeen	.625		Tacoma (2nd)†	.533		Wenatchee*	.647
1908—	Vancouver	.578	1940—	Spokane	.587	1958—	Lewiston	.621
1909—	Seattle	.653		Tacoma (4th)†	.500		Yakima*	.594
1910—	Spokane*	.596	1941—	Spokane	.669	1959—	Salem	.623
1911—	Vancouver	.628	1942—	Vancouver	.594		Yakima*	.563
1912—	Seattle	.600	1943-45	—Did not operate.		1960—	Yakima	.638
1913—	Vancouver	.600	1946—	Wenatchee	.622		Yakima	.562
1914—	Vancouver	.632	1947—	Vancouver	.566	1961—	Lewiston*	.621
1915—	Seattle	.564	1948—	Spokane	.614		Yakima	.600
1916—	Spokane	.622	1949—	Yakima	.660	1962—	Wenatchee*	.574
1917—	Great Falls	.592		Vancouver (2nd)†	.615		Tri-City	.580
1918—	Seattle	.588	1950—	Yakima	.613	1963—	Lewiston	.594
1919—	Seattle	.590	1951—	Spokane	.655		Yakima*	.613
1920—	Victoria	.600	1952—	Victoria	.631	1964—	Eugene	.636
1921—	Yakima	.710	1953—	Salem	.635		Yakima*	.611
	Yakima	.660		Spokane*	.590			

CLASS A   Northwest League

Year	Team	Pct.
1965—	Lewiston	.667
	Tri-City*	.681
1966—	Tri-City	.679
1967—	Medford	.607
1968—	Tri-City	.600
1969—	Rogue Valley	.633
1970—	Lewiston§	.538
	Coos Bay-No. Bend	.563
1971—	Tri-City§	.625
	Bend	.538
1972—	Lewiston§	.675
	Walla Walla	.513
1973—	Walla Walla∞	.638
	Portland	.563
1974—	Bellingham	.619
	Eugene▲	.571
1975—	Portland	.545
	Eugene◆	.684
1976—	Portland	.556
	Walla Walla◆	.639
1977—	Bellingham■	.618
	Portland	.667

Year	Team	Pct.
1978—	Grays Harbor▼	.671
	Eugene	.514
1979—	Central Oregon◆	.606
	Walla Walla	.571
1980—	Bellingham•	.643
	Eugene•	.529
1981—	Medford◆	.600
	Bellingham	.557
1982—	Medford	.757
	Salem◆	.486
1983—	Medford††	.735
	Bellingham	.588
1984—	Tri-Cities††	.622
	Medford	.608
1985—	Everett††	.541
	Eugene	.541
1986—	Bellingham††	.608
	Eugene	.608
1987—	Spokane▲	.711
	Everett	.653
1988—	Southern Oregon	.605
	Spokane◆	.553

Year	Team	Pct.
1989—	Southern Oregon	.600
	Spokane◆	.547
1990—	Boise	.697
	Spokane◆	.645
1991—	Boise◆	.658
	Yakima	.579
1992—	Bellingham◆	.566
	Bend	.566
1993—	Bellingham	.579
	Boise◆	.539
1994—	Yakima	.645
	Boise◆	.579
1995—	Boise◆	.640
	Bellingham	.566
1996—	Eugene	.645
	Yakima§	.526
1997—	Boise	.671
	Portland◆	.579
1998—	Spokane	.618
	Boise	.618
	Salem-Keizer◆	.566

*Won split-season playoff. †Won four-club playoff. ‡League disbanded June 18. §League divided into Northern and Southern divisions, declared champion under league rules. ∞League divided into Eastern and Western divisions, declared champion under league rules. ▲League divided into Eastern and Western divisions; won two-team playoff. ◆League divided into North and South divisions; won two-team playoff. ■League divided into Affiliate and Independent divisions; won two-team playoff. ▼Declared league champion after winning one-game playoff. Balance of playoff canceled due to rain and wet grounds. •Declared co-champion after winning one game. Balance of playoff canceled due to rain and wet grounds. ††League divided into Washington and Oregon divisions; won two-team playoff. (NOTE—Known as Pacific Northwest League 1901-02, Pacific National League 1903-04, Northwestern League 1905-18, Pacific Coast International League 1919-22 and Western International League 1937-54.)

CLASS A *Northwest League*

SOUTH ATLANTIC LEAGUE

LEAGUE OFFICE

President/secretary-treasurer
John Moss

Address
P.O. Box 38
Kings Mountain, NC 28086

Phone
704-739-3466

Teams (affiliation)
Asheville Tourists (Rockies)
Augusta Greenjackets (Red Sox)
Capital City Bombers (Mets)
Charleston (S.C.) Riverdogs (Devil Rays)
Charleston (W.Va.) Alley Cats (Royals)
Columbus Redstixx (Indians)
Delmarva Shorebirds (Orioles)

Cape Fear Crocks (Expos)
Greensboro Bats (Yankees)
Hagerstown Suns (Blue Jays)
Hickory Crawdads (Pirates)
Macon Braves (Braves)
Piedmont Bollweevils (Phillies)
Savannah Sand Gnats (Rangers)

1998 FINAL STANDINGS

FIRST HALF

NORTHERN DIVISION

Team	W	L	T	Pct.	GB
Hagerstown (Blue Jays)	44	26	0	.629	....
Cape Fear (Expos)	43	27	0	.614	1.0
Delmarva (Orioles)	42	29	0	.592	2.5
Charleston, W.Va. (Reds)	25	44	0	.362	18.5

CENTRAL DIVISION

Team	W	L	T	Pct.	GB
Columbia (Mets)	47	22	0	.681	....
Greensboro (Yankees)	37	33	0	.529	10.5
Piedmont (Phillies)	36	34	0	.514	11.5
Asheville (Rockies)	32	38	0	.457	15.5
Charleston, S.C. (Devil Rays)	31	39	0	.443	16.5
Hickory (White Sox)	25	44	0	.362	22.0

SOUTHERN DIVISION

Team	W	L	T	Pct.	GB
Augusta (Pirates)	35	36	0	.493	....
Savannah (Rangers)	35	36	0	.493	....
Macon (Braves)	30	40	0	.429	5.5
Columbus (Indians)	28	42	0	.400	6.5

SECOND HALF

NORTHERN DIVISION

Team	W	L	T	Pct.	GB
Delmarva (Orioles)	39	32	0	.549	....
Hagerstown (Blue Jays)	37	34	0	.521	2.0
Cape Fear (Expos)	37	34	0	.521	2.0
Charleston, W.Va. (Reds)	19	52	0	.268	20.0

CENTRAL DIVISION

Team	W	L	T	Pct.	GB
Columbia (Mets)	43	29	0	.597	....
Greensboro (Yankees)	42	30	0	.583	1.0
Piedmont (Phillies)	40	31	0	.563	2.5
Asheville (Rockies)	39	31	0	.557	3.0
Charleston, S.C. (Devil Rays)	36	35	0	.507	6.5
Hickory (White Sox)	31	40	0	.437	11.5

SOUTHERN DIVISION

Team	W	L	T	Pct.	GB
Macon (Braves)	39	32	0	.549	....
Augusta (Pirates)	33	38	0	.465	6.0
Columbus (Indians)	31	39	0	.443	7.5
Savannah (Rangers)	31	40	0	.437	8.0

COMPOSITE

Team	C'bia	Hag.	Del.	C.F.	Gbr.	Pied.	Ash.	Mac.	Aug.	CSC	Sav.	C'bus	Hic.	CWV	W	L	T	Pct.	GB
Columbia (Mets)	....	4	4	6	9	11	8	5	6	12	5	6	9	5	90	51	0	.638	....
Hagerstown (Blue Jays)	4	....	12	10	2	4	6	3	3	4	3	3	7	20	81	60	0	.574	9.0
Delmarva (Orioles)	4	14	....	16	5	3	3	1	4	4	2	4	5	16	81	61	0	.570	9.5
Cape Fear (Expos)	2	16	10	....	5	3	7	2	2	6	4	2	4	17	80	61	0	.567	10.0
Greensboro (Yankees)	7	6	3	3	....	8	8	4	5	10	5	4	9	7	79	63	0	.556	11.5
Piedmont (Phillies)	3	4	5	5	10	....	9	4	7	7	5	3	11	3	76	65	0	.539	14.0
Asheville (Rockies)	6	2	5	1	7	6	....	5	3	9	5	5	11	6	71	69	0	.507	18.5
Macon (Braves)	3	1	3	2	4	4	3	....	13	4	12	13	4	3	69	72	0	.489	21.0
Augusta (Pirates)	2	1	0	2	3	1	5	13	....	4	17	13	4	3	68	74	0	.479	22.5
Charleston, S.C. (Devil Rays)	6	4	4	2	5	8	6	4	4	....	4	4	10	6	67	74	0	.475	23.0
Savannah (Rangers)	3	1	2	0	3	3	14	9	4	4	....	17	5	2	66	76	0	.465	24.5
Columbus (Indians)	2	1	0	2	3	5	2	13	13	4	9	....	3	2	59	81	0	.421	30.5
Hickory (White Sox)	6	1	3	4	6	4	7	3	4	4	3	5	....	6	56	84	0	.400	33.5
Charleston, W.Va. (Reds)	5	3	10	8	1	5	2	1	1	2	2	2	2	....	44	96	0	.314	45.5

Major league affiliations in parentheses.

PLAYOFFS: Augusta defeated Macon two games to none; Hagerstown defeated Delmarva two games to none; Columbia defeated Piedmont two games to none; Greensboro defeated Cape Fear two games to none; Greensboro defeated Augusta two games to none; Columbia defeated Hagerstown two games to one; Columbia defeated Greensboro two games to one to win league championship.

REGULAR-SEASON ATTENDANCE: Asheville, 148,638; Augusta, 162,509; Cape Fear, 75,799; Charleston, S.C., 234,840; Charleston, W.Va., 91,219; Columbia, 141,138; Columbus, 94,241; Delmarva, 295,938; Greensboro, 160,465; Hagerstown, 109,932; Hickory, 193,258; Macon, 120,009; Piedmont, 125,653; Savannah, 130,509. Total—2,084,148. Playoffs (16 games)—15,918; All-Star Game at Charleston, S.C.—6,675.

MANAGERS: Asheville, Ron Gideon; Augusta, Marty Brown; Cape Fear, Luis Dorante; Charleston, S.C., Greg Mahlberg; Charleston, W.VA., Barry Lyons; Columbia, Doug Davis; Columbus, Eric Wedge; Delmarva, Dave Machemer; Greensboro, Tom Nieto; Hagerstown, Marty Pevey; Hickory, Mark Haley; Macon, Brian Snitker; Piedmont, Ken Oberkfell; Savannah, Paul Carey.

ALL-STAR TEAM: 1B—Matt Berger, Hickory; 2B—Marcus Giles, Macon; 3B—Mo Bruce, Columbia; SS—Jersen Perez, Columbia; OF—Alex Escobar, Columbia; Noah Hall, Cape Fear; Kory Dehaan, Augusta; Utility OF—Vernon Wells, Hagerstown; C—Toby Hall, Charleston, S.C.; DH—Bobby Cripps, Hagerstown; RHP—John Sneed, Hagerstown; LHP—Clayton Andrews, Hagerstown; Manager—Doug Davis, Columbia; Coach—Glenn Hubbard, Macon; Most Valuable Player—Marcus Giles, Macon; Most Valuable Pitcher—Clayton Andrews, Hagerstown; Most Outstanding Major League Prospect—Alex Escobar, Columbia; General Manager of the Year—Mark Schuster, Charleston, S.C.

CLASS A *South Atlantic League*

TEAM

Team	Avg.	G	TPA	AB	R	H	TB	2B	3B	HR	RBI	SH	SF	HP	BB	IBB	SO	SB	CS	GDP	LOB	ShO	Slg.	OBP
Columbia	.273	141	5442	4844	761	1324	2007	239	36	124	669	41	39	70	448	13	1278	295	82	48	1016	4	.414	.341
Piedmont	.273	141	5499	4856	704	1324	1819	243	27	66	627	57	35	67	484	15	949	146	55	115	1069	5	.375	.345
Cape Fear	.272	141	5238	4643	732	1261	1738	199	37	68	613	104	35	5	451	14	991	201	101	100	938	5	.374	.334
Hagerstown	.269	141	5315	4678	712	1258	1895	233	22	120	644	57	32	72	476	12	936	124	64	91	1010	9	.405	.343
Asheville	.266	140	5271	4676	696	1242	1859	242	21	111	605	64	32	72	427	6	1066	136	76	77	932	8	.398	.334
Hickory	.263	140	5361	4817	614	1269	1832	215	27	98	545	62	34	65	383	10	1080	156	92	112	977	9	.380	.324
Savannah	.260	142	5245	4675	701	1215	1846	198	50	111	602	26	33	60	451	7	1221	252	105	71	881	4	.395	.331
Delmarva	.258	142	5299	4680	678	1207	1736	217	45	74	602	48	57	82	432	10	1041	211	80	95	936	12	.371	.328
Macon	.258	141	5374	4726	770	1217	2031	245	25	173	693	23	51	80	494	7	1185	101	69	99	932	9	.430	.335
Columbus	.257	140	5367	4718	708	1211	1838	235	34	108	627	34	39	66	510	0	1148	133	58	77	1009	6	.390	.335
Augusta	.256	142	5367	4657	732	1190	1785	236	37	95	651	36	47	87	540	11	1089	202	105	84	991	8	.383	.341
Charleston, S.C.	.249	141	5334	4723	685	1177	1718	220	18	95	594	26	37	56	492	15	1040	92	62	108	947	8	.364	.325
Greensboro	.244	142	5266	4689	625	1144	1768	214	22	122	558	26	35	58	458	7	1309	84	49	96	936	5	.377	.317
Charleston, W.Va.	.234	140	4997	4497	515	1054	1494	208	17	66	452	34	28	63	375	5	1124	143	76	91	864	8	.332	.301

INDIVIDUAL

TOP QUALIFIERS FOR BATTING CHAMPIONSHIP

Minimum 383 plate appearances. *Lefthanded batter. †Switch-hitter.

Player, Team	Avg.	G	TPA	AB	R	H	TB	2B	3B	HR	RBI	SH	SF	HP	BB	IBB	SO	SB	CS	GDP	Slg.	OBP
Bruce, Mo, C'bia	.341	126	560	516	81	176	253	24	4	15	74	1	1	4	41	4	107	45	15	5	.490	.390
Terrell, Jim, Hick.*	.338	131	571	500	84	169	237	21	4	13	64	9	4	5	53	2	90	25	8	15	.474	.404
Giles, Marcus, Mac.	.329	135	604	505	111	166	321	38	3	37	108	0	3	10	85	4	103	12	5	15	.636	.433
Hall, Toby, C.S.C.	.321	105	427	377	59	121	166	25	1	6	50	0	6	5	39	2	32	3	7	15	.440	.386
Paz, Richard, Del.	.320	98	415	325	55	104	137	10	4	5	50	2	5	8	75	2	42	22	7	6	.422	.453
Hall, Noah, C.F.	.318	127	519	447	84	142	210	21	7	11	90	3	3	14	52	2	69	33	9	16	.470	.403
DeHaan, Kory, Aug.*	.314	132	567	475	85	149	228	39	8	8	75	8	7	8	69	3	114	33	13	4	.480	.404
Escobar, Alex, C'bia	.310	112	483	416	90	129	243	23	5	27	91	5	3	5	54	1	133	49	7	1	.584	.393
Velazquez, Jose, C.S.C.*	.308	111	476	413	71	127	184	20	2	11	64	0	4	4	55	6	70	0	2	4	.446	.391
Pena, Jose, Sav.	.305	125	490	466	68	142	192	22	5	6	66	2	2	3	17	0	91	40	16	14	.412	.332
Santos, Jose, Sav.	.299	107	443	381	78	114	206	17	6	21	76	0	3	8	51	2	119	26	7	7	.541	.391
Berger, Matt, Hick.	.299	126	530	469	72	140	242	30	0	24	94	1	8	2	50	6	111	3	2	14	.516	.363
Edwards, Michael, C'bus	.294	124	571	497	82	146	212	34	4	8	81	3	2	3	66	2	95	16	6	13	.427	.379
Terrell, Jeffrey, Pied.*	.291	118	469	392	71	114	141	15	6	0	47	6	3	6	62	1	55	18	7	9	.360	.393
Sears, Todd, Ash.*	.290	130	543	459	71	133	196	25	2	11	82	1	6	5	72	1	89	10	4	9	.427	.387

DEPARTMENTAL LEADERS: G—M. Young, 140; AB—McDonald, 528; R—Giles, 111; H—Bruce, 176; TB—Giles, 321; 2B—Dehaan, 39; 3B—Hamilton, Jersen Perez, 10 each; HR—Giles, 37; RBI—Giles, 108; SH—Mitchell, 17; SF—Garavito, 12; HP—X. Burns, 22; BB—Giles, 85; IBB—M. Berger, Velazquez, 6 each; SO—Brooks, 164; SB—Gutierrez, 60; CS—Freeman, 24; GIDP—Almonte, 17; Slg.—Giles, .636; OBP—Paz, .453.

ALL PLAYERS

*Lefthanded batter. †Switch-hitter.

Player, Team	Avg.	G	TPA	AB	R	H	TB	2B	3B	HR	RBI	SH	SF	HP	BB	IBB	SO	SB	CS	GDP	Slg.	OBP
Aalbers, Brady, C.W.Va.	.174	22	54	46	3	8	10	2	0	0	1	2	0	2	4	0	12	1	2	2	.217	.269
Adorno, Wilson, Aug.†	.188	11	35	32	3	6	10	1	0	1	5	1	0	1	1	0	11	0	0	0	.313	.235
Alamo, Efrain, Ash.	.247	130	526	494	67	122	195	25	0	16	62	3	0	4	25	0	141	18	12	9	.395	.289
Albaral, Randy, Hag.	.239	86	259	234	34	56	62	4	1	0	19	6	0	3	16	1	48	15	3	4	.265	.296
Albert, Rashad, Hick.	.259	106	419	390	48	101	145	18	4	6	39	5	2	8	14	0	96	23	11	5	.372	.297
Allison, Cody, C'bus*	.238	74	271	244	27	58	86	11	1	5	29	0	2	3	22	0	44	2	3	10	.352	.306
Almonte, Erick, Gre.	.209	120	491	450	53	94	125	13	0	6	33	7	2	3	29	0	121	6	2	17	.278	.260
Alvarez, Carlos, C'bus	.260	72	297	265	33	69	102	18	3	3	34	1	3	11	17	1	62	6	4	3	.385	.328
Alviso, Jerome, Ash.†	.276	134	524	486	64	134	184	30	1	6	41	10	3	7	18	0	60	11	11	6	.379	.309
Amerson, Gordon, Gre.*	.222	4	19	18	2	4	4	0	0	0	2	0	0	1	0	0	1	0	0	0	.222	.263
Anderson, Franklin, Aug.	.209	16	48	43	3	9	14	3	1	0	7	1	1	1	2	0	19	0	0	1	.326	.255
Arias, Rogelio, Ash.	.274	84	345	317	36	87	122	16	2	5	37	7	2	4	15	0	40	0	3	6	.385	.314
Aylor, Brian, Gre.*	.238	47	148	130	18	31	55	5	2	5	13	3	0	1	13	0	67	5	1	0	.423	.313
Baderdeen, Kevin, C.W.Va.	.180	31	96	89	10	16	25	3	0	2	7	0	2	1	4	0	36	2	4	3	.281	.219
Bagley, Lorenzo, Hag.	.259	111	410	359	53	93	162	20	2	15	75	0	4	8	39	0	97	2	1	12	.451	.341
Bain, Tyler, C.S.C.*	.133	4	17	15	3	2	2	0	0	0	2	0	0	0	2	0	4	1	0	1	.133	.235
Bennett, Ryan, C'bia	.286	57	198	175	20	50	64	6	1	2	20	3	1	1	18	0	49	2	0	3	.366	.354
Berger, Matt, Hick.	.299	126	530	469	72	140	242	30	0	24	94	1	8	2	50	6	111	3	2	14	.516	.363
Berns, Robert, C.S.C.	.268	130	546	474	71	127	186	26	0	11	62	1	5	11	55	2	98	1	3	13	.392	.354
Blakeney, Mo, C.F.†	.244	94	347	307	34	75	101	14	3	2	32	6	2	5	27	0	75	10	12	5	.329	.314
Borges, Elio, Hick.†	.212	22	58	52	7	11	14	3	0	0	7	2	1	1	2	0	18	2	1	2	.269	.250
Bradley, Milton, C.F.†	.302	75	314	281	54	85	132	21	4	6	50	3	3	4	23	1	57	13	6	7	.470	.360
Bravo, Danny, C.F.†	.277	101	398	343	48	95	127	12	4	4	44	14	1	8	32	2	65	7	10	11	.370	.352
Brooks, Anthony, Mac.	.255	133	547	502	74	128	201	26	4	13	55	6	5	10	24	0	164	17	15	4	.400	.299
Brown, Billy, Hag.	.264	44	171	148	22	39	53	8	0	2	19	1	0	3	19	0	38	12	5	2	.358	.359
Bruce, Mo, C'bia	.341	126	560	516	81	176	253	24	4	15	74	1	1	4	41	4	107	45	15	5	.490	.390
Bryant, Matt, Aug.	.299	59	211	177	24	53	65	4	1	2	18	2	4	2	26	0	29	1	5	3	.367	.388
Burke, Mark, Mac.*	.277	65	275	235	47	65	104	15	0	8	36	0	4	1	35	0	36	2	2	10	.443	.367
Burkhart, Lance, C.F.	.240	17	70	50	10	12	20	3	1	1	11	1	1	2	16	1	17	1	3	0	.400	.435
Burns, Pat, C'bia†	.264	128	545	477	77	126	185	25	2	10	61	0	3	16	49	3	132	16	2	6	.388	.350
Burns, Xavier, Aug.	.242	125	483	414	64	100	169	20	5	13	49	0	5	22	42	0	107	6	3	9	.408	.340
Butler, Allen, Gre.*	.269	125	528	469	70	126	211	26	1	19	81	2	5	2	50	2	139	4	3	9	.450	.344
Butler, Garrett, C.S.C.†	.246	45	181	171	28	42	58	7	3	1	25	2	1	1	6	0	29	8	3	4	.339	.274

Player, Team	Avg.	G	TPA	AB	R	H	TB	2B	3B	HR	RBI	SH	SF	HP	BB	IBB	SO	SB	CS	GDP	Slg.	OBP
Caceres, Wilmy, C.W.Va.†	.259	103	429	394	48	102	128	12	7	0	27	7	0	9	18	0	62	24	14	9	.325	.306
Caddell, Carl, C.W.Va.*	.000	15	1	1	0	0	0	0	0	0	0	0	0	0	0	0	1	0	0	0	.000	.000
Cameron, Troy, Mac.*	.222	133	550	472	70	105	194	20	3	21	65	3	4	5	66	1	162	4	3	9	.411	.322
Caradonna, Brett, Hick.*	.266	116	501	447	43	119	151	21	1	3	35	1	3	5	45	2	84	15	11	5	.338	.338
Carey, Orlando, Gre.	.128	34	87	78	11	10	11	1	0	0	2	0	0	1	8	0	27	1	1	1	.141	.218
Castillo, Geramel, Sav.†	.176	22	80	74	7	13	21	2	0	2	8	0	2	1	3	0	29	2	1	3	.284	.213
Castro, Martires, Sav.	.225	67	229	209	26	47	71	11	2	3	25	0	2	2	16	0	69	4	1	3	.340	.284
Charles, Curtis, Del.	.179	10	30	28	4	5	7	0	1	0	1	0	0	1	1	0	10	2	2	0	.250	.233
Chatman, Karl, C.F.	.335	65	259	221	41	74	115	11	3	8	41	7	1	4	26	1	58	12	4	7	.520	.413
Cheek, Shawn, Sav.	.273	18	59	55	7	15	24	4	1	1	5	0	0	1	3	0	16	1	0	0	.436	.322
Clark, Kirby, Pied.*	.292	86	353	322	46	94	145	29	2	6	63	0	4	1	26	3	84	2	0	16	.450	.343
Cloud, Casey, Aug.*	.220	36	115	91	10	20	22	2	0	0	13	1	2	2	19	0	24	0	0	1	.242	.360
Collier, Lamonte, Pied.	.318	45	185	154	21	49	67	11	2	1	30	4	2	1	24	0	38	4	3	5	.435	.409
Collins, Francis, Pied.	.314	81	361	306	48	96	107	9	1	0	18	7	1	5	42	1	49	14	4	2	.350	.404
Copeland, Brandon, C'bia	.241	105	417	345	58	83	145	23	0	13	48	4	4	12	52	2	130	17	4	3	.420	.356
Copley, Travis, C.W.Va.*	.232	59	236	211	26	49	69	8	0	4	21	1	2	1	21	2	59	6	2	5	.327	.302
Cordero, Willy, Sav.	.241	112	413	378	35	91	108	10	2	1	38	3	3	8	21	0	85	21	12	11	.286	.293
Cortez, Santos, Aug.	.105	6	22	19	2	2	2	0	0	0	2	0	0	1	2	0	3	0	0	1	.105	.227
Crespo, Cesar, C'bia†	.252	116	483	428	61	108	152	18	4	6	48	7	1	3	44	1	114	47	14	6	.355	.326
Cripps, Bobby, Hag.*	.265	123	480	423	64	112	222	17	3	29	88	5	4	7	41	3	123	2	3	7	.525	.337
Cruz, Edgar, C'bus	.247	107	440	396	59	98	173	27	0	16	65	0	3	7	34	3	97	1	0	8	.437	.316
Cruz, Geronimo, Sav.†	.000	9	23	23	2	0	0	0	0	0	0	2	0	0	0	0	6	2	0	0	.000	.000
Cruz, Luis, C.S.C.	.190	34	149	137	15	26	36	5	1	1	11	1	0	0	11	0	28	4	1	1	.263	.250
Darjean, John, Gre.	.190	23	93	84	9	16	22	2	2	0	8	2	1	0	6	0	11	6	4	0	.262	.242
Davis, J.J., Aug.	.198	30	109	106	11	21	39	6	0	4	11	0	0	0	3	0	24	1	1	4	.368	.222
Davison, Ashanti, Del.	.154	7	27	26	1	4	6	0	1	0	1	0	0	0	1	0	6	0	1	3	.231	.185
DeHaan, Kory, Aug.*	.314	132	567	475	85	149	228	39	8	8	75	8	7	8	69	3	114	33	13	4	.480	.404
Diaz, Diogenes, Aug.	.042	9	28	24	1	1	1	0	0	0	1	0	0	0	3	0	12	0	0	0	.042	.143
Diaz, Maikell, Del.	.243	59	200	169	26	41	65	7	4	3	24	6	1	4	20	0	40	4	2	1	.385	.335
Dina, Allen, C'bia	.375	2	8	8	1	3	5	2	0	0	3	0	0	0	0	0	1	0	0	0	.625	.375
Dominique, Bubba, Pied.	.282	133	591	514	82	145	255	38	0	24	102	0	4	12	61	4	97	0	2	9	.496	.369
Downs, Brian, Hick.	.278	91	355	331	35	92	134	15	0	9	39	2	2	3	17	0	68	2	4	8	.405	.317
Duncan, Carlos, Pied.	.198	32	129	111	20	22	38	3	2	3	12	1	1	1	15	0	47	8	1	2	.342	.297
Durham, Chad, Hick.	.233	117	527	480	57	112	133	7	4	2	34	11	1	6	29	0	74	33	16	5	.277	.281
Edwards, Michael, C'bus	.294	124	571	497	82	146	212	34	4	8	81	3	2	3	66	2	95	16	6	13	.427	.379
Elliott, Dawan, Aug.*	.050	8	22	20	1	1	2	1	0	0	2	0	0	0	2	0	8	0	0	1	.100	.136
Escobar, Alex, C'bia	.310	112	483	416	90	129	243	23	5	27	91	5	3	5	54	1	133	49	7	1	.584	.393
Espada, Angel, C'bia	.261	40	172	157	26	41	48	5	1	0	14	4	1	2	8	0	15	20	5	2	.306	.304
Estrada, Johnny, Pied.†	.310	77	317	303	33	94	133	14	2	7	44	0	3	5	6	1	19	0	1	11	.439	.331
Evans, Lee, Aug.†	.223	98	372	337	43	75	111	19	1	5	43	0	4	3	28	0	90	6	3	6	.329	.285
Ewan, Bry, Mac.	.212	19	69	66	4	14	19	2	0	1	9	0	1	0	2	0	27	1	0	1	.288	.232
Fajardo, Alejandro, Pied.	.280	115	518	457	83	128	169	24	1	5	46	12	4	1	44	1	88	38	4	6	.370	.342
Fauske, Josh, Hick.	.269	104	421	375	55	101	164	18	0	15	60	1	5	2	36	1	65	2	2	12	.437	.333
Figueroa, Franky, Del.	.276	137	554	515	61	142	218	29	4	13	94	0	11	14	14	1	113	8	0	15	.423	.307
Fisher, Anthony, Sav.	.269	122	524	458	86	123	193	24	5	12	39	3	3	7	52	1	104	35	16	5	.421	.350
Fitzgerald, Jason, C'bus*	.273	132	542	490	60	134	216	28	3	16	80	1	9	4	38	1	117	21	6	1	.441	.325
Folmar, Ryan, Ash.*	.000	5	16	14	0	0	0	0	0	0	0	0	0	1	1	0	11	0	0	0	.000	.125
Forbes, Kevin, C.F.	.256	58	235	211	24	54	78	10	1	4	28	0	5	4	15	0	59	5	3	4	.370	.311
Foulds, Kalin, C.S.C.†	.188	15	54	48	4	9	10	1	0	0	1	0	1	4	0	7	4	2	1	.208	.264
Fowler, Ben, C'bus†	.197	57	204	188	20	37	57	5	0	5	26	0	5	0	11	0	74	0	0	4	.303	.235
Freeman, Terrance, Aug.†	.254	122	507	398	84	101	123	16	3	0	31	3	1	21	84	0	69	47	24	7	.309	.409
Fritz, Jim, Pied.	.227	50	197	172	21	39	59	9	1	3	21	1	1	9	14	0	55	0	1	6	.343	.316
Furniss, Eddy, Aug.*	.465	24	112	86	32	40	74	7	0	9	31	0	2	0	24	1	20	1	1	2	.860	.571
Garavito, Eddy, Del.†	.247	135	546	481	81	119	182	20	8	9	66	4	12	5	44	3	93	25	15	9	.378	.310
Garcia, Douglas, Sav.*	.213	25	86	80	7	17	23	0	2	0	11	0	2	0	4	0	15	3	0	2	.288	.244
Garcia, Sandro, C.W.Va.	.216	104	402	366	43	79	108	15	1	4	35	8	3	2	23	1	59	9	5	7	.295	.264
Garrett, Scott, C.W.Va.	.175	52	183	171	10	30	33	3	0	0	14	1	0	1	10	0	58	1	0	8	.193	.225
Giles, Marcus, Mac.	.329	135	604	505	111	166	321	38	3	37	108	0	3	10	85	4	103	12	5	15	.636	.433
Giron, Alejandro, Pied.	.228	51	198	180	14	41	50	5	2	0	19	4	2	3	9	0	34	8	4	1	.278	.273
Gonzales, Jose, Ash.	.190	41	139	121	17	23	35	3	0	3	14	2	1	2	13	0	38	0	2	2	.289	.277
Gonzalez, Luis, C'bus	.272	101	367	320	48	87	112	14	1	3	32	10	1	3	28	0	63	10	3	5	.350	.345
Grabowski, Jason, Sav.*	.270	104	411	352	63	95	162	13	6	14	52	0	1	1	57	0	93	16	9	7	.460	.372
Guerrero, Rafael, C.S.C.	.220	25	102	91	11	20	29	3	0	2	12	0	2	1	8	1	17	1	0	1	.319	.284
Gutierrez, Victor, Aug.	.246	128	531	460	81	113	143	19	4	1	50	11	3	3	54	0	67	60	18	10	.311	.327
Guzman, Carlos, Pied.*	.285	74	250	228	29	65	75	10	0	0	26	4	1	1	16	0	46	8	13	6	.329	.333
Hafner, Travis, Sav.*	.237	123	484	405	62	96	167	15	4	16	84	0	5	6	68	2	139	7	3	8	.412	.351
Hairston, Jason, Mac.	.240	109	463	413	61	99	187	21	2	21	76	1	6	11	32	1	136	9	7	6	.453	.307
Hall, Noah, C.F.	.318	127	519	447	84	142	210	21	7	11	90	3	3	14	52	2	69	33	9	16	.470	.403
Hall, Toby, C.S.C.	.321	105	427	377	59	121	166	25	1	6	50	0	6	5	39	2	32	3	7	15	.440	.386
Haman, Mack, Del.	.000	2	6	6	0	0	0	0	0	0	0	0	0	0	0	0	4	0	0	0	.000	.000
Hamilton, Jon, C'bus*	.261	133	580	487	88	127	214	22	10	15	71	3	4	7	79	1	130	22	9	4	.439	.369
Hammond, Joey, Del.	.237	38	152	135	19	32	43	6	1	1	15	0	0	1	16	0	21	1	2	5	.319	.322
Harris, Kevin, Sav.	.163	27	89	86	12	14	23	1	1	2	9	1	1	0	1	0	39	5	0	0	.267	.170
Hayes, Chris, Hag.	.295	63	243	207	41	61	104	11	3	8	33	3	1	9	23	0	41	6	2	2	.502	.388
Hendricks, Jason, C.F.	.193	48	163	145	22	28	47	1	0	6	20	1	2	4	11	0	49	6	1	2	.324	.265
Hoch, Corey, Del.	.206	16	38	34	6	7	13	3	0	1	4	0	0	0	4	0	6	0	0	1	.382	.289
Hollins, Darontaye, Hick.	.220	45	165	150	17	33	50	6	1	3	13	2	0	3	10	0	40	7	6	3	.333	.282
Hook, Kevin, C.F.	.247	47	186	158	21	39	44	5	0	0	13	4	2	0	29	6	3	6	.278	.339
Hooper, Daren, Del.	.207	96	356	319	36	66	105	13	1	8	36	1	1	9	26	0	147	1	2	4	.329	.285
Hoover, Paul, C.S.C.	.290	40	151	124	24	36	57	10	1	3	19	0	5	22	1	29	2	1	0	.460	.417
Huff, Aubrey, C.S.C.*	.321	69	294	265	38	85	145	19	1	13	54	0	5	4	24	0	40	3	1	5	.547	.371
Hughes, Brian, Del.	.289	38	140	121	14	35	46	6	1	1	20	3	1	2	13	0	17	7	2	4	.380	.365

Player, Team	Avg.	G	TPA	AB	R	H	TB	2B	3B	HR	RBI	SH	SF	HP	BB	IBB	SO	SB	CS	GDP	Slg.	OBP
Hundt, Bo, Aug.†	.241	54	201	174	26	42	69	10	1	5	26	2	1	0	24	0	41	4	3	3	.397	.332
Izturis, Cesar, Hag.†	.262	130	447	413	56	108	126	13	1	1	38	9	2	2	20	0	43	20	9	5	.305	.297
Jackson, Jeremy, Ash.*	.285	92	391	361	57	103	155	16	3	10	52	3	0	3	24	1	88	13	10	4	.429	.335
James, Kenny, C.F.†	.253	114	496	451	73	114	136	10	3	2	32	12	1	11	21	0	68	41	6	6	.302	.302
Jaramillo, Frank, Sav.	.248	101	355	315	50	78	132	12	6	10	41	0	1	2	37	1	98	8	5	2	.419	.330
Joffrion, Jack, C.S.C.	.190	72	275	263	22	50	79	11	0	6	33	1	0	2	9	0	69	2	7	2	.300	.223
Johns, Michael, Ash.	.192	59	178	167	18	32	45	5	1	2	9	2	2	0	7	0	34	3	0	2	.269	.222
Johnson, Eric, Aug.	.237	23	83	76	9	18	25	4	0	1	12	0	0	2	5	0	24	2	2	1	.329	.301
Johnson, Jason, Pied.	.267	106	494	446	63	119	142	14	3	1	45	6	1	5	36	0	58	32	12	9	.318	.328
Johnson, Tom, C'bia	.232	89	342	306	54	71	112	16	5	5	40	3	3	3	27	0	87	22	7	1	.366	.298
Johnston, Clint, Aug.*	.154	20	15	13	2	2	2	0	0	0	0	0	0	0	2	0	7	0	0	0	.154	.267
Kelly, Kenneth, C.S.C.	.280	54	242	218	46	61	87	7	5	3	17	0	1	4	19	0	52	19	4	1	.399	.347
Kidd, Scott, Gre.	.274	126	525	468	74	128	209	30	4	17	58	2	6	5	44	1	118	9	6	10	.447	.338
Kilburg, Joe, C'bus*	.251	121	528	446	81	112	160	19	4	7	44	11	0	4	67	0	93	24	10	8	.359	.354
Klee, Chuck, Hick.	.190	49	172	163	11	31	48	7	2	2	18	2	1	0	6	0	42	1	1	6	.294	.218
Kopacz, Derek, Hick.	.149	13	52	47	3	7	9	2	0	0	8	1	0	1	3	0	19	0	0	1	.191	.216
Kurilla, Kevin, Pied.	.199	53	204	181	21	36	48	6	0	2	15	2	1	1	19	0	56	1	0	4	.265	.277
Lambert, Clark, C'bia	.130	11	25	23	3	3	3	0	0	0	1	0	0	1	1	0	6	0	0	0	.130	.200
Landaeta, Luis, Ash.*	.220	28	102	91	12	20	24	1	0	1	9	4	4	0	2	0	14	5	3	0	.264	.227
Lankford, Derrick, Aug.*	.278	127	528	457	72	127	226	25	4	22	89	0	7	5	59	5	119	8	5	11	.495	.362
Lara, Felix, Aug.*	.171	14	36	35	6	6	10	1	0	1	6	0	0	1	0	0	18	0	0	1	.286	.194
Lehr, Ryan, Mac.	.285	115	448	400	60	114	181	26	1	13	69	0	2	4	42	0	67	1	4	12	.453	.357
Lentz, Ryan, C.F.*	.333	3	13	9	6	3	7	1	0	1	3	0	1	3	0	2	0	0	0	.778	.538
Lina, Estivinson, Sav.	.212	73	236	217	22	46	64	8	2	2	12	2	0	5	12	0	72	2	3	1	.295	.269
Lindsey, John, Ash.	.275	126	516	472	59	130	199	21	3	14	73	3	2	15	24	2	114	2	4	11	.422	.329
Lopez-Cao, Mike, C.S.C.*	.250	14	30	24	2	6	6	0	0	0	4	0	1	1	4	0	4	2	0	0	.250	.367
Lundberg, David, Sav.†	1.000	50	1	1	1	1	1	0	0	0	0	0	0	0	0	0	0	0	0	0	1.000	1.000
Mackowiak, Rob, Aug.*	.243	25	85	70	16	17	24	4	0	1	8	1	0	1	13	0	19	4	2	2	.343	.369
Markray, Thad, C.W.Va.	.107	36	127	121	7	13	20	4	0	1	7	2	0	0	4	0	38	0	1	2	.165	.136
Marn, Kevin, C.W.Va.	.259	96	383	344	40	89	122	19	1	4	39	2	4	5	28	0	63	15	6	9	.355	.320
Martinez, Eddy, Del.	.263	113	412	361	46	95	119	16	1	2	39	13	3	2	33	0	66	21	7	9	.330	.326
Mateo, Henry, C.F.†	.276	114	488	416	72	115	157	20	5	4	41	15	4	13	40	2	111	22	16	5	.377	.355
Matos, Luis, Del.	.272	133	561	503	73	137	196	26	6	7	62	6	7	7	38	0	90	42	14	9	.390	.328
Maxwell, Keith, Aug.	.222	22	86	81	8	18	28	4	0	2	13	0	1	2	2	0	13	2	1	1	.346	.244
Maxwell, Vernon, Gre.	.234	104	463	418	53	98	137	10	7	5	35	1	4	8	32	0	121	11	2	5	.328	.299
McDonald, Darnell, Del.	.261	144	575	528	87	138	190	24	5	6	44	4	5	5	33	0	117	35	11	5	.360	.308
McGee, Tom, Del.	.268	50	139	123	16	33	44	5	0	2	14	2	2	3	9	0	23	4	2	2	.358	.322
McGrath, Sean, C'bia	.172	26	97	87	6	15	28	4	0	3	9	4	0	3	3	0	28	3	2	2	.322	.226
Medrano, Ryan, C.W.Va.	.227	115	418	361	54	82	122	19	0	7	30	1	0	6	50	0	73	6	2	9	.338	.331
Mejia, Juan, Pied.	.195	55	175	164	24	32	45	7	3	0	13	4	0	1	6	0	50	11	1	5	.274	.228
Mejias, Oliver, Aug.†	.219	36	104	96	11	21	27	1	1	1	10	3	0	0	5	0	27	1	2	3	.281	.257
Melian, Jackson, Gre.	.255	135	524	467	66	119	165	18	2	8	45	1	4	7	41	0	120	15	12	12	.353	.322
Messner, Jake, C'bus*	.167	25	85	78	9	13	24	2	0	3	13	0	2	0	5	0	21	3	1	0	.308	.212
Miller, Kenny, C'bia	.276	35	134	116	16	32	38	4	1	0	9	1	1	1	15	0	16	4	5	0	.328	.361
Mirizzi, Marc, Gre.†	.279	103	412	373	57	104	168	29	1	11	44	1	2	5	31	1	85	4	5	10	.450	.341
Mitchell, Andres, Ash.	.249	136	531	446	71	111	165	19	4	9	58	17	1	11	56	0	139	25	12	8	.370	.334
Montilla, Miguel, Gre.	.000	1	3	3	0	0	0	0	0	0	0	0	0	0	0	0	3	0	0	0	.000	.000
Moreno, Juan, C'bia	.285	113	476	435	69	124	178	22	1	10	51	0	2	3	36	0	98	31	8	4	.409	.342
Morillo, Luis, Hag.*	.253	38	99	87	13	22	29	3	2	0	9	2	0	0	10	0	17	1	3	1	.333	.330
Morrison, Greg, Hag.*	.276	123	473	434	59	120	188	19	2	15	72	0	3	8	28	5	61	4	7	7	.433	.330
Mortimer, Mark, Mac.	.298	28	114	94	21	28	50	7	0	5	26	0	0	2	18	0	11	1	0	2	.532	.421
Mounts, J.R., Hick.	.240	110	473	430	57	103	160	20	2	11	43	4	1	11	27	0	154	20	7	6	.372	.301
Munoz, Billy, C'bus*	.266	120	487	417	61	111	173	24	1	12	60	0	1	1	68	2	104	3	2	6	.415	.370
Neuberger, Scott, C.S.C.	.242	132	526	475	53	115	147	18	1	4	58	3	4	3	41	2	134	5	7	16	.309	.304
Newkirk, Jeff, Hick.*	.215	26	105	93	11	20	35	8	2	1	7	0	1	1	10	0	20	2	4	3	.376	.295
Newman, Howard, C.W.Va.	.182	3	11	11	1	2	5	0	0	1	2	0	0	0	0	0	5	0	0	0	.455	.182
Nicolas, Jose, Aug.	.196	55	175	153	23	30	47	6	1	3	15	0	1	2	19	0	54	2	4	1	.307	.291
Nieves, Juan, Hag.	.167	3	7	6	0	1	3	0	1	0	1	0	0	0	1	0	1	1	0	0	.500	.286
Nunez, Jorge, Hag.	.250	4	16	16	0	4	4	0	0	0	1	0	0	0	0	0	1	1	0	0	.250	.250
Nunnari, Talmadge, C.F.*	.304	79	333	289	51	88	112	18	0	2	51	0	0	1	42	2	44	4	4	5	.388	.395
O'Hearn, Brandon, C.W.Va.	.233	113	434	390	36	91	137	21	2	7	49	0	7	6	31	0	144	4	5	5	.351	.295
Oliver, Johnny, C.W.Va.	.224	115	440	416	33	93	149	23	0	11	57	0	1	1	22	0	109	11	8	10	.358	.264
Oropeza, Willie, C.F.	.229	57	220	192	22	44	54	5	1	1	18	6	2	3	17	1	44	2	4	3	.281	.299
Owens-Bragg, Luke, C.S.C.†.	.118	9	40	34	3	4	6	2	0	0	2	3	1	0	2	0	3	0	0	0	.176	.162
Pacheco, Juan, Del.	.000	1	4	3	1	0	0	0	0	0	0	0	0	0	1	0	3	0	0	0	.000	.250
Patton, Cory, C'bia	.266	55	180	154	32	41	48	4	1	0	14	3	2	1	20	0	43	18	5	1	.312	.350
Paxton, Chris, Del.*	.259	63	202	170	20	44	58	11	0	1	19	2	1	2	27	2	39	0	1	3	.341	.354
Paz, Richard, Del.	.320	98	415	325	55	104	137	10	4	5	56	2	5	8	75	2	42	22	7	6	.422	.453
Pena, Alex, Aug.	.253	90	320	292	47	74	106	15	1	5	26	1	3	0	24	0	69	7	5	8	.363	.307
Pena, Carlos, Sav.*	.325	30	130	117	22	38	70	14	0	6	20	0	1	4	8	0	25	3	2	0	.598	.385
Pena, Elvis, Ash.†	.287	115	521	428	93	123	173	24	4	6	48	7	2	14	70	2	85	41	12	5	.404	.332
Pena, Jose, Sav.	.305	125	490	466	68	142	192	22	5	6	66	2	2	3	17	0	91	40	16	14	.412	.332
Perez, Edwin, C'bus	.236	33	109	89	14	21	25	1	0	1	10	0	2	1	17	0	12	1	2	1	.281	.358
Perez, Jersen, C'bia	.279	120	525	488	72	136	195	18	10	7	64	5	11	3	18	0	128	14	4	6	.400	.302
Perez, Nestor, C.S.C.	.175	62	236	211	20	37	41	4	0	0	16	6	3	0	13	0	36	3	4	6	.194	.220
Perez, Richard, Del.	.114	23	39	35	6	4	4	0	0	0	4	1	1	0	2	0	12	0	0	0	.114	.158
Peters, Tony, Hag.	.303	104	358	327	58	99	143	12	1	10	35	3	0	3	25	0	72	15	7	8	.437	.354
Phelps, Josh, Hag.	.265	117	439	385	48	102	152	24	1	8	44	1	5	8	40	1	80	2	0	12	.395	.342
Phillips, Jason, C'bia	.271	69	281	251	36	68	100	15	1	5	37	1	1	5	23	1	35	5	2	3	.398	.343
Pigott, Anthony, C.S.C.	.170	29	103	100	9	17	28	3	1	2	11	0	1	0	2	0	26	0	1	1	.280	.184
Piniella, Juan, Sav.	.341	72	298	255	51	87	121	13	6	3	39	7	2	4	30	0	48	28	11	0	.475	.416
Pinto, Rene, Gre.	.227	109	408	365	31	83	110	25	1	0	40	2	1	8	32	0	87	2	5	11	.301	.303

– 562 –

Player, Team	Avg.	G	TPA	AB	R	H	TB	2B	3B	HR	RBI	SH	SF	HP	BB	IBB	SO	SB	CS	GDP	Slg.	OBP
Price, Corey, C.W.Va.†	.323	36	148	130	19	42	51	6	0	1	12	4	0	2	12	0	22	6	3	4	.392	.389
Pugh, Josh, Mac.	.231	40	151	134	20	31	40	7	1	0	11	1	1	1	14	0	38	0	0	2	.299	.307
Purkiss, Matt, Gre.*	.206	55	207	180	20	37	70	6	0	9	32	1	3	2	21	0	77	0	0	3	.389	.291
Reding, Josh, C.F.	.233	73	288	253	32	59	68	6	0	1	21	9	0	4	22	1	71	13	4	8	.269	.305
Reyes, Jose, Aug.	.261	25	75	69	10	18	35	2	3	3	9	0	0	0	6	0	15	0	1	0	.507	.320
Rivera, Carlos, Aug.*	.285	87	336	316	38	90	124	17	1	5	53	0	3	6	11	2	46	3	5	9	.392	.318
Rivera, Francisco, C.W.Va.*	.071	5	17	14	0	1	1	0	0	0	0	0	0	0	3	0	2	0	0	1	.071	.235
Rivera, Luis A., C.F.	.221	60	186	163	28	36	54	4	1	4	18	3	2	8	10	0	34	3	0	3	.331	.295
Rivera, Luis J., C.F.	.213	25	87	80	8	17	22	5	0	0	6	3	0	0	4	0	28	1	2	3	.275	.250
Rivera, Roberto, Del.	.238	110	427	390	55	93	145	21	5	7	50	3	5	4	25	1	99	17	4	5	.372	.288
Roach, Jason, C'bia	.277	98	414	375	55	104	187	27	1	18	70	0	3	6	30	0	121	2	1	5	.499	.338
Rodriguez, Hernandez, C.W.Va.	.282	85	349	323	53	91	121	18	0	4	28	3	1	4	18	0	53	24	6	4	.375	.327
Rodriguez, John, Gre.*	.252	119	479	408	64	103	159	18	4	10	49	0	3	4	64	1	93	14	3	7	.390	.357
Rodriguez, Mike, Hag.	.303	50	151	132	20	40	53	10	0	1	17	6	1	4	8	0	20	1	1	3	.402	.359
Rodriguez, Gary, C'bus*	.364	15	52	44	10	16	20	2	1	0	3	1	0	1	6	0	9	0	0	0	.455	.451
Romano, Jason, Sav.	.271	134	588	524	72	142	190	19	4	7	52	5	5	8	46	1	94	40	17	6	.363	.336
Rowand, Aaron, Hick.	.342	61	256	222	42	76	110	13	3	5	32	5	2	6	21	0	36	7	3	5	.495	.410
Salazar, Jeremy, Pied.	.285	41	186	158	20	45	61	10	0	2	19	0	1	4	23	0	39	1	0	3	.386	.387
Salinas, Trey, C.S.C.	.265	47	167	147	26	39	59	6	1	4	17	0	0	2	18	0	22	2	1	8	.401	.353
Samuel, Cody, Gre.	.200	14	57	50	7	10	13	0	0	1	3	0	0	2	5	0	23	0	1	0	.260	.298
Sanchez, Manuel, Mac.*	.174	13	55	46	5	8	14	1	1	1	4	0	1	1	7	0	5	1	1	0	.304	.291
Sanchez, Toby, C.W.Va.	.243	126	480	408	52	99	159	18	3	12	48	0	1	6	65	1	160	4	7	6	.390	.354
Sandberg, Jared, C.S.C.	.183	56	222	191	31	35	55	11	0	3	25	0	1	3	27	0	76	4	0	6	.288	.293
Sandoval, Danny, Hick.†	.230	126	480	430	43	99	115	12	2	0	30	14	2	5	29	0	88	13	15	10	.267	.285
Sandusky, Scott, C.F.	.286	53	205	189	16	54	62	5	0	1	19	5	0	0	11	0	54	3	1	3	.328	.325
Santos, Jose, Sav.	.299	107	443	381	78	114	206	17	6	21	76	0	3	8	51	2	119	26	7	7	.541	.391
Schneider, Brian, C.F.*	.299	38	159	134	33	40	72	7	2	7	30	4	2	3	16	1	9	6	3	3	.537	.381
Schwartzbauer, Brad, Ash.*	.269	107	413	346	55	93	149	24	1	10	57	2	6	3	56	0	80	4	1	2	.431	.370
Scioneaux, Damian, C.S.C.*	.248	72	317	270	44	67	93	9	4	3	26	1	1	1	42	0	44	16	9	11	.344	.350
Seabol, Scott, Gre.	.286	71	229	210	24	60	92	11	0	7	33	1	2	3	13	2	40	2	2	4	.438	.333
Sears, Todd, Ash.*	.290	130	543	459	71	133	196	26	2	11	82	1	6	5	72	1	89	10	4	9	.427	.387
Sienko, Ryan, Sav.	.174	17	50	46	5	8	11	3	0	0	4	0	0	0	4	0	20	0	0	0	.239	.240
Smothers, Stewart, Mac.	.204	139	572	506	61	103	153	17	3	9	60	7	8	5	46	1	145	17	12	9	.302	.273
Sosa, Jovanny, Aug.	.226	26	101	93	8	21	34	8	1	1	14	2	0	2	4	0	31	2	2	1	.366	.273
Soules, Ryan, Gre.*	.268	98	397	332	48	89	160	16	2	17	54	2	4	1	58	0	107	3	1	5	.482	.375
Spencer, Jeff, Mac.	.261	115	499	437	94	114	223	21	2	28	79	0	4	11	47	0	143	11	5	5	.510	.345
Stanton, Tom, C'bia*	.161	29	102	87	4	14	23	3	0	2	15	0	2	4	9	1	35	0	1	0	.264	.265
Staubach, Jeff, Gre.	.333	2	4	3	0	1	1	0	0	0	0	0	0	0	1	0	1	0	0	0	.333	.500
Stevenson, Chad, Mac.	.206	32	109	102	9	21	28	7	0	0	8	0	1	1	5	0	26	0	0	6	.275	.248
Strange, Mike, Hag.	.226	76	238	186	33	42	56	11	0	1	12	2	0	5	45	0	59	9	5	4	.301	.390
Suriel, Miguel, C.S.C.	.083	4	14	12	0	1	1	0	0	0	0	0	0	0	2	0	2	1	0	0	.083	.214
Sutton, Joe, Hick.*	.231	76	278	238	29	55	85	14	2	4	22	2	1	6	31	1	75	1	1	6	.357	.333
Taveras, Frank, C.W.Va.*	.260	84	297	281	31	73	104	12	2	5	33	1	2	3	10	0	71	1	5	5	.370	.291
Taylor, Corey, C.W.Va.	.214	54	207	173	28	37	60	8	3	3	19	1	2	7	24	0	46	15	4	1	.347	.330
Taylor, Greg, Pied.†	.216	66	243	218	24	47	56	9	0	0	21	5	3	3	14	0	46	1	1	7	.257	.269
Terrell, Jeffrey, Pied.*	.291	118	469	392	71	114	141	15	6	0	47	6	3	6	62	1	55	18	7	9	.360	.393
Terrell, Jim, Hick.*	.338	131	571	500	84	169	237	21	4	13	64	9	4	5	53	3	90	25	8	15	.474	.404
Thorpe, A.D., Mac.†	.268	128	584	519	94	139	174	21	4	2	34	4	5	13	43	0	70	21	15	10	.335	.336
Tidwell, Dave, C.W.Va.	.265	8	38	34	10	9	10	1	0	0	1	0	0	1	3	0	9	6	0	0	.294	.342
Tiller, Brad, C'bus	.165	38	119	103	21	17	19	2	0	0	5	1	0	2	13	0	36	3	0	1	.184	.271
Toomey, Chris, C.W.Va.	.237	18	64	59	5	14	20	3	0	1	4	2	0	2	1	0	21	1	1	2	.339	.274
Torrealba, Steve, Mac.	.273	67	239	209	28	57	97	10	0	10	37	1	6	3	20	0	31	3	0	7	.464	.336
Torres, Jason, Sav.*	.196	19	51	46	1	9	11	2	0	0	5	0	0	0	5	0	17	0	0	0	.239	.275
Trahan, Mike, C.S.C.	.240	80	357	317	45	76	120	17	0	9	37	2	0	3	35	0	74	6	4	6	.379	.321
Twombley, Dennis, Gre.	.188	40	140	133	13	25	50	4	0	7	21	1	1	1	4	0	45	1	1	2	.376	.216
Valent, Eric, Pied.*	.427	22	104	89	24	38	74	12	0	8	28	0	1	0	14	2	19	0	0	0	.831	.500
Valera, Willy, C'bus	.200	6	23	20	4	4	7	0	0	1	3	1	0	0	2	0	2	0	1	2	.350	.273
Van Iten, Bob, Pied.*	.260	121	525	461	60	120	154	18	2	4	58	1	2	8	53	2	69	0	1	14	.334	.345
Velazquez, Jose, C.S.C.*	.308	111	476	413	71	127	184	20	2	11	64	0	4	4	55	6	70	0	2	4	.446	.391
Vidal, Gilbert, Ash.	.298	76	305	275	42	82	124	21	0	7	42	0	2	2	25	0	43	2	1	9	.451	.359
Ware, Frank, C.S.C.	.268	26	94	82	12	22	23	1	0	0	4	2	0	1	9	1	21	2	2	1	.280	.348
Warriax, Brandon, Sav.	.209	51	206	187	24	39	56	8	0	3	14	3	0	0	16	0	41	9	2	2	.299	.271
Washington, Dion, Gre.	.120	16	57	50	5	6	6	0	0	0	1	0	0	1	6	0	23	1	0	0	.120	.228
Washington, Rico, Aug.*	.300	12	60	50	12	15	25	2	1	2	12	0	1	2	7	0	9	2	0	0	.500	.400
Wells, Vernon, Hag.	.285	134	562	509	86	145	217	35	2	11	65	1	2	1	49	1	84	13	8	8	.426	.348
Werth, Jayson, Del.	.265	120	476	408	71	108	158	20	3	8	53	1	2	15	50	0	92	21	6	14	.387	.364
Whitehead, Braxton, C.W.Va.	.248	116	451	408	33	101	137	24	0	4	48	0	5	6	32	1	79	6	5	4	.336	.308
Wilder, Paul, C.S.C.*	.197	76	318	264	48	52	100	9	0	13	39	0	1	8	43	0	118	3	3	2	.379	.326
Williams, Jewell, C'bus	.249	96	395	353	60	88	134	14	4	8	38	1	3	11	27	0	118	20	6	6	.380	.320
Williams, Mike, C.W.Va.	.222	12	30	27	4	6	7	1	0	0	3	0	0	1	2	0	13	2	1	0	.259	.300
Wilson, Travis, Mac.	.462	3	13	13	2	6	9	0	0	1	4	0	0	0	0	0	4	0	0	0	.692	.462
Young, Mike, Hag.	.282	140	598	522	86	147	238	33	5	16	87	7	7	7	55	1	96	16	8	12	.456	.354
Zapp, A.J., Mac.*	.260	20	83	73	9	19	36	6	1	3	12	0	0	2	8	0	18	1	0	1	.493	.349
Zech, Scott, C.F.	.286	102	373	304	53	87	120	20	2	3	45	9	4	13	43	0	48	13	8	3	.395	.393
Zepeda, Jesse, Hag.†	.231	105	365	290	39	67	83	7	0	3	29	11	3	4	57	0	56	5	2	4	.286	.362
Zweifel, Kent, Ash.	.286	64	224	194	43	49	93	11	0	11	43	1	1	9	19	0	44	1	1	4	.467	.314

GRAND SLAMS: Adorno, Almonte, Cameron, Collier, Copeland, Crespo, Cripps, 2; E. Cruz, Edwards, Fitzgerald, Giles, Hafner, Hall, Hairston, Hooper, Moreno, Neuberger, Peters, Purkiss, Sanchez, J. Spencer, Santos, Van Iten, Velazquez, R. Washington, Wells, Zech, Zepeda, 1 each.

AWARDED FIRST BASE ON CATCHER'S INTERFERENCE: Melian 4 (Arias, Fauske, Gonzales, J. Phelps); Fauske 2 (T. Hall, Bennett); Scioneaux 2 (Lina, Vidal); Wilder 2 (Fauske, Estrada); Aylor (Fritz); Caceres (Phelps); Fisher (Pugh); Giles (Lina); Izturis (Arias); Landaeta (Pinto); Nunnary (Downs); Vidal (Evans); Zweifel (T. Hall), 1 each.

TEAM

Team	W	L	Pct.	ERA	G	CG	ShO	Sv.	IP	H	TBF	R	ER	HR	SH	SF	HB	BB	IBB	SO	WP	Bk.
Hagerstown	81	60	.574	3.25	141	9	15	28	1209.1	1067	5098	567	437	69	45	40	90	438	18	1179	79	17
Columbia	90	51	.638	3.47	141	5	7	45	1240.0	1131	5290	619	478	80	51	29	68	468	7	1189	77	8
Greensboro	79	63	.556	3.60	142	10	9	41	1243.0	1192	5310	631	497	98	39	24	48	421	21	1228	76	14
Delmarva	81	61	.570	3.74	142	5	9	46	1235.2	1160	5253	598	513	91	64	29	45	505	17	1150	86	17
Piedmont	76	65	.539	3.83	141	11	11	43	1246.2	1294	5314	659	531	111	31	47	56	311	7	1060	70	14
Asheville	71	69	.507	3.98	140	11	4	30	1217.2	1294	5296	685	539	129	49	29	67	403	1	1146	72	10
Charleston (S.C.)	67	74	.475	4.04	141	3	9	29	1233.0	1242	5301	657	553	90	43	28	91	391	3	1085	103	19
Augusta	68	74	.479	4.15	142	5	5	33	1213.2	1150	5290	707	560	92	34	38	59	520	13	1209	87	25
Cape Fear	80	61	.567	4.17	141	6	10	29	1229.1	1202	5291	658	569	104	45	48	3	431	0	911	84	8
Hickory	56	84	.400	4.35	140	6	5	33	1246.2	1262	5478	761	602	122	47	36	70	508	12	1065	100	19
Savannah	66	76	.465	4.61	142	10	4	32	1218.2	1212	5436	742	624	108	36	49	89	541	1	1068	106	14
Macon	69	72	.489	4.62	141	3	3	32	1221.1	1246	5492	814	627	130	42	53	70	558	7	1186	157	20
Charleston (W.Va.)	44	96	.314	4.84	140	15	3	19	1179.0	1378	5303	769	634	76	74	45	70	433	21	868	89	15
Columbus	59	81	.421	4.87	140	4	6	26	1207.2	1264	5346	766	654	131	38	39	77	493	17	1114	111	16

INDIVIDUAL

TOP QUALIFIERS FOR EARNED-RUN AVERAGE TITLE

Minimum 114 innings. *Lefthanded pitcher.

Pitcher, Team	W	L	Pct.	ERA	G	GS	CG	ShO	GF	Sv.	IP	H	TBF	R	ER	HR	SH	SF	HB	BB	IBB	SO	WP	Bk.
Andrews, Clayton, Hag.*	10	7	.588	2.28	27	26	2	1	0	0	162.0	112	635	59	41	7	4	5	6	46	0	193	7	2
Reith, Brian, Gre.	6	7	.462	2.28	20	20	3	1	0	0	118.1	86	475	42	30	7	2	0	3	32	0	116	1	0
Belitz, Todd, C.S.C.*	6	4	.600	2.42	21	21	0	0	0	0	130.0	99	530	44	35	8	6	1	8	48	0	123	11	1
Giron, Isabel, Hag.	10	9	.526	2.49	21	21	4	3	0	0	126.1	110	517	57	35	11	6	3	7	27	1	129	7	2
Sneed, John, Hag.	16	2	.889	2.56	27	27	2	1	0	0	161.2	123	660	59	46	9	4	0	11	58	0	210	5	2
Blank, Matt, C.F.*	9	2	.818	2.61	21	21	2	2	0	0	134.2	121	539	45	39	6	4	2	9	24	0	114	1	1
Flores, Randy, Gre.*	12	7	.632	2.62	21	20	2	1	0	0	130.2	119	535	48	38	6	2	3	7	33	0	139	2	4
Spurgeon, Jay, Del.	11	3	.786	2.64	27	20	0	0	0	0	136.1	112	547	49	40	8	5	5	6	48	0	103	3	0
Dougherty, James, C'bia*	15	2	.882	2.74	20	20	1	1	0	0	134.2	112	547	51	41	8	4	3	4	50	0	107	5	0
Cutchins, Todd, C'bia*	9	5	.643	2.77	23	23	0	0	0	0	123.1	113	520	48	38	5	4	2	6	47	0	102	3	0
Duckworth, Brandon, Pied.	9	8	.529	2.80	21	21	5	3	0	0	147.2	116	577	58	46	10	1	5	7	24	0	119	8	2
McClellan, Matt, Hag.	8	7	.533	3.09	25	25	1	0	0	0	139.2	109	589	65	48	8	5	4	14	58	3	126	6	5
Daneker, Pat, Hick.	6	6	.500	3.15	17	17	2	0	0	0	117.0	115	474	50	41	14	2	0	1	16	0	95	2	6
Thompson, Travis, Ash.	6	7	.462	3.24	26	24	0	0	0	0	147.1	155	619	71	53	11	1	4	6	30	0	113	6	1
Lewis, Craig, Gre.	11	6	.647	3.37	28	26	3	0	1	0	173.2	170	721	77	65	16	6	2	3	34	1	178	8	4

DEPARTMENTAL LEADERS: W—Sneed, 16; L—Merrell, 15; Pct.—Sneed, .889; G—Black, 58; GS—Wheeler, 29; CG—Duckworth, Price, 5 each; ShO—Duckworth, Giron, 3 each; GF—Black, Brown, Reyes, 52 each; Sv.—Black, 34; IP—Shipp, 184.2; H—Shipp, 210; TBF—Shipp, 780; R—Izquierdo, 104; ER—Harrison, Wheeler, 89 each; HR—R. Price, 23; SH—Seifert, 12; SF—Quezada, 9; HB—Izquierdo, 22; BB—Izquierdo, 76; IBB—Wallace, 8; WP—Shumate, 39.

ALL PITCHERS

*Lefthanded pitcher.

Pitcher, Team	W	L	Pct.	ERA	G	GS	CG	ShO	GF	Sv.	IP	H	TBF	R	ER	HR	SH	SF	HB	BB	IBB	SO	WP	Bk.
Abbott, Jim, Hick.*	0	0	.000	2.25	1	1	0	0	0	0	4.0	3	15	1	1	0	0	0	0	2	0	2	0	0
Acevedo, Jose, C.W.Va.	9	9	.500	3.91	25	25	2	0	0	0	158.2	169	668	74	69	9	4	3	6	40	0	132	6	0
Achilles, Matt, Del.	8	7	.533	3.78	26	25	2	1	0	0	150.0	143	654	71	63	14	4	2	2	70	0	125	6	2
Agamennone, Brandon, C.F.	2	0	1.000	3.06	6	6	1	1	0	0	35.1	24	134	15	12	2	0	1	2	6	0	29	0	0
Allen, Rodney, Sav.	0	1	.000	3.15	4	3	0	0	0	0	20.0	21	88	11	7	0	0	0	2	4	0	18	1	0
Alvarado, Carlos, Aug.	4	4	.500	3.60	14	10	0	0	0	0	50.0	48	209	20	20	2	2	2	1	24	0	50	6	0
Andrews, Clayton, Hag.*	10	7	.588	2.28	27	26	2	1	0	0	162.0	112	635	59	41	7	4	5	6	46	0	193	7	2
Aracena, Juan, C'bus	0	1	.000	13.50	5	0	0	0	3	0	6.2	15	38	10	10	0	0	1	0	6	1	4	5	0
Averette, Robert, C.W.Va.	5	4	.556	2.79	14	14	3	0	0	0	84.0	84	355	38	26	2	6	3	2	26	0	68	4	1
Ayers, Mike, Aug.*	0	1	.000	17.47	4	0	0	0	1	0	5.2	11	37	13	11	0	0	1	0	6	1	6	3	0
Bacci, Tony, Aug.*	4	4	.500	3.81	27	1	0	0	0	0	49.2	39	221	33	21	4	1	3	1	34	1	51	3	1
Bailey, Roger, Ash.	0	0	.000	3.86	1	1	0	0	0	0	4.2	5	22	2	2	1	0	0	1	5	0	1	1	0
Bailie, Matt, Pied.	0	0	.000	0.00	2	0	0	0	0	0	2.1	3	13	0	0	0	0	0	3	0	0	2	0	0
Baker, Jason, C.F.*	1	0	1.000	9.72	5	0	0	0	2	0	8.1	11	45	9	9	0	1	1	2	8	0	2	2	0
Barry, Shawn, C'bia*	1	3	.250	2.76	53	0	0	0	39	19	62.0	42	273	27	19	5	6	2	1	38	4	93	6	1
Bass, Aaron, C.S.C.*	2	0	1.000	23.14	2	0	0	0	0	0	2.1	7	16	6	6	1	0	0	0	3	0	2	1	0
Bauer, Chuck, Aug.	2	1	.667	0.75	6	0	0	0	1	0	12.0	3	40	1	1	0	1	0	0	5	0	12	1	0
Bauer, Richard, Del.	5	8	.385	4.73	22	22	1	1	0	0	118.0	127	505	69	62	11	5	2	8	44	0	81	6	0
Bauldree, Joe, Mac.	1	0	1.000	4.05	29	0	0	0	12	3	53.1	49	238	30	24	8	2	1	11	19	0	53	9	1
Bausher, Andy, Aug.*	7	10	.412	4.43	24	21	2	0	0	0	109.2	112	480	69	54	5	2	3	9	36	0	119	4	2
Bautista, Martin, C'bus	1	4	.200	10.01	7	7	0	0	0	0	29.2	42	153	36	33	7	0	2	3	24	0	25	7	0
Becks, Ryan, C.F.*	11	6	.647	5.30	28	22	1	0	0	0	122.1	140	549	88	72	13	7	4	10	55	0	72	12	1
Behn, Brendan, C'bia*	0	0	.000	1.50	1	1	0	0	0	0	6.0	4	24	1	1	0	0	1	0	2	0	5	1	1
Beitey, Jason, Sav.	0	0	.000	9.00	1	1	0	0	0	0	4.0	3	22	7	4	1	0	2	0	5	1	1	1	0
Belitz, Todd, C.S.C.*	6	4	.600	2.42	21	21	0	0	0	0	130.0	99	530	44	35	8	6	1	8	48	0	123	11	1
Bello, Jilberto, Del.	1	0	1.000	4.50	3	0	0	0	1	0	4.0	6	18	2	2	1	0	0	2	0	4	1	1	0
Benoit, Joaquin, Sav.	4	3	.571	3.83	15	15	1	0	0	0	80.0	79	339	41	34	8	3	1	3	18	0	68	3	1
Berger, Craig, C'bia.	2	0	1.000	1.23	5	0	0	0	3	1	7.1	8	30	1	1	0	0	1	0	0	0	7	0	0
Black, Brett, Pied.	5	4	.556	2.18	58	0	0	0	52	34	66.0	55	264	19	16	5	0	0	0	17	0	88	1	0
Blakeney, Mo, C.F.	0	0	.000	0.00	1	0	0	0	0	0	1.0	0	6	0	0	0	0	0	0	3	0	0	0	0
Blank, Matt, C.F.*	9	2	.818	2.61	21	21	2	2	0	0	134.2	121	539	45	39	6	4	2	9	24	0	114	1	1
Blevins, Jeremy, Gre.	5	8	.385	4.81	24	23	0	0	0	0	119.2	121	545	80	64	5	4	5	6	66	0	110	10	1
Bond, Aaron, Sav.	10	10	.500	4.37	28	27	3	1	0	0	167.0	184	731	96	81	11	2	8	5	41	0	119	9	0
Borbon, Pedro, Mac.*	0	0	.000	9.00	3	0	0	0	1	0	3.0	4	14	3	3	1	0	0	0	3	0	3	0	0

Pitcher, Team	W	L	Pct.	ERA	G	GS	CG	ShO	GF	Sv.	IP	H	TBF	R	ER	HR	SH	SF	HB	BB	IBB	SO	WP	Bk.
Borne, Matt, Hick.	2	1	.667	8.86	15	0	0	0	4	1	21.1	36	113	24	21	2	1	3	4	11	1	16	6	0
Bowles, Brian, Hag.	2	4	.333	4.52	31	4	0	0	9	0	67.2	80	306	41	34	4	2	3	9	18	1	48	6	0
Box, John, C.S.C.*	7	2	.778	2.58	55	0	0	0	23	2	76.2	63	306	28	22	2	2	1	1	10	0	67	7	1
Brackeen, Colin, Hag.*	4	4	.500	2.45	37	0	0	0	18	0	55.0	46	230	18	15	0	1	1	7	19	1	61	7	0
Bravo, Franklin, Aug.	1	2	.333	4.47	20	5	0	0	4	0	46.1	44	215	27	23	8	0	2	2	30	0	43	2	2
Brazoban, Melvin, Sav.	3	6	.333	4.76	18	18	0	0	0	0	87.0	68	374	50	46	9	2	3	6	48	0	84	8	2
Brewer, Clint, C.W.Va.	0	7	.000	6.66	35	7	0	0	13	1	73.0	90	362	71	54	7	5	3	5	49	5	46	12	2
Brito, Juan, C'bia*	1	1	.500	3.80	13	0	0	0	6	1	23.2	21	104	14	10	0	2	1	2	10	0	17	0	1
Brown, Derek, Del.	3	4	.429	1.85	55	0	0	0	52	33	68.0	55	270	19	14	3	5	2	1	13	2	63	8	1
Brown, Elliot, C.S.C.	2	7	.222	4.96	40	15	0	0	5	0	107.0	123	475	72	59	10	1	5	10	40	1	59	8	1
Brueggemann, Dean, Ash.*	7	3	.700	2.48	41	0	0	0	18	4	69.0	60	284	28	19	3	3	1	1	28	1	92	5	0
Caddell, Carl, C.W.Va.*	0	0	.000	4.03	15	0	0	0	8	0	29.0	31	134	15	13	1	3	1	1	15	0	24	2	0
Cammack, Eric, C'bia	4	0	1.000	2.81	25	0	0	0	22	8	32.0	17	127	13	10	2	0	0	2	13	0	49	1	0
Cardona, Steve, Hick.	3	5	.375	4.59	44	0	0	0	28	6	64.2	57	276	35	33	4	7	3	0	28	4	65	9	2
Carrion, Jorge, Sav.	5	5	.500	5.65	15	13	1	0	1	1	73.1	71	342	51	46	6	3	1	9	51	0	38	8	1
Carter, Roger, C.S.C.	3	4	.429	4.92	13	9	0	0	0	0	53.0	47	244	34	29	8	1	2	9	31	0	46	8	0
Casey, Joe, Hag.	2	7	.222	4.66	22	16	0	0	1	0	77.1	84	346	53	40	6	6	3	6	41	2	62	4	1
Castillo, Alberto, Gre.*	0	0	.000	3.72	5	0	0	0	3	0	9.2	8	48	6	4	0	0	0	0	14	0	13	2	0
Choate, Randy, Gre.*	1	5	.167	3.00	8	8	1	0	0	0	39.0	46	165	21	13	1	1	0	0	7	0	32	3	0
Ciravolo, Jon, Mac.	1	2	.333	5.02	16	1	0	0	3	1	28.2	37	139	19	16	4	0	0	2	17	0	30	5	0
Civit, Xavier, C'bia	0	1	.000	9.00	3	0	0	0	1	0	6.0	10	30	6	6	1	0	0	2	2	0	6	0	0
Combs, Chris, Aug.	5	6	.455	3.25	33	12	0	0	10	3	97.0	100	422	51	35	8	4	5	6	28	0	76	8	1
Cook, O.J., Aug.	0	1	.000	3.11	47	0	0	0	38	17	46.1	34	200	17	16	2	3	0	2	29	1	54	8	2
Corcoran, Tim, C'bia	2	3	.400	2.61	20	1	0	0	10	4	48.1	43	204	21	14	4	1	1	5	15	0	38	3	0
Cotton, Joe, Pied.	6	8	.429	4.42	44	0	0	0	20	5	77.1	73	322	48	38	14	4	6	6	16	1	79	3	0
Crawford, Danny, Aug.	4	11	.267	4.68	20	18	1	1	1	0	109.2	120	460	67	57	9	3	4	2	15	0	71	3	0
Cremer, Rick, Gre.*	8	1	.889	2.50	13	13	0	0	0	0	79.1	56	316	28	22	5	1	3	2	25	1	79	3	1
Crowell, Jim, C.W.Va.*	0	4	.000	13.20	5	5	0	0	0	0	15.0	28	83	23	22	1	0	2	2	9	0	9	1	0
Cummins, Jon, C.S.C.	1	0	1.000	8.74	8	0	0	0	2	0	11.1	15	61	15	11	0	2	1	2	11	0	8	6	1
Currens, Tim, Hick.	1	2	.333	5.71	28	0	0	0	14	1	58.1	71	262	46	37	8	1	2	3	24	0	36	5	0
Cutchins, Todd, C'bia*	9	5	.643	2.77	23	23	0	0	0	0	123.1	113	520	48	38	5	4	2	6	47	0	102	3	0
Daneker, Pat, Hick.	6	6	.500	3.15	17	17	2	0	0	0	117.0	115	474	50	41	14	2	0	1	16	0	95	2	6
Danner, Andy, C.W.Va.	1	1	.500	6.06	21	0	0	0	10	2	35.2	48	173	30	24	2	2	2	3	15	2	30	3	0
Davis, Kane, Aug.	0	0	.000	6.00	2	2	0	0	0	0	9.0	9	36	6	6	0	1	1	0	3	0	6	2	0
Day, Zach, Gre.	1	2	.333	2.77	7	6	1	0	0	0	36.0	35	155	22	11	1	2	1	3	6	0	37	4	0
Deckard, Edward, C.S.C.	0	0	.000	7.04	3	0	0	0	1	0	7.2	13	36	7	6	0	0	0	0	3	0	2	2	0
De La Cruz, Francisco, Gre.	2	1	.667	3.98	5	3	0	0	1	0	20.1	15	83	9	9	3	0	1	1	10	1	18	0	1
Dishman, Richard, Mac.	1	1	.500	3.89	18	0	0	0	6	1	39.1	38	170	22	17	2	3	0	0	17	1	44	2	1
Dougherty, James, C'bia*	15	2	.882	2.74	20	20	1	1	0	0	134.2	112	547	51	41	8	4	3	4	50	0	107	5	0
Drew, Tim, C'bus	4	3	.571	3.79	13	13	0	0	0	0	71.1	68	311	43	30	5	0	4	6	26	0	64	5	2
Duckworth, Brandon, Pied.	9	8	.529	2.80	21	21	5	3	0	0	147.2	116	577	58	46	10	1	5	7	24	0	119	8	2
Duff, Matt, Aug.	0	1	1.000	3.00	10	0	0	0	3	9	9.0	8	42	3	3	1	0	0	1	4	0	12	0	0
Eason, Clay, Pied.	3	1	.750	3.72	34	2	0	0	11	0	65.1	53	271	32	27	8	1	5	2	22	0	67	4	0
Eavenson, Clay, Gre.	0	0	.000	4.50	1	0	0	0	1	0	4.0	5	19	4	2	0	1	0	1	0	0	2	1	0
Ellison, Jason, Gre.	4	6	.400	3.17	54	0	0	0	49	28	65.1	56	279	30	23	5	5	0	2	27	3	71	6	0
Embry, Byron, Mac.	2	5	.286	4.39	50	0	0	0	20	6	69.2	51	320	49	34	6	4	8	2	50	2	71	8	0
Emiliano, Jamie, Ash.	3	4	.429	3.50	41	0	0	0	38	18	43.2	56	208	22	17	2	4	1	5	21	0	35	1	0
Estrella, Leo, C'bia-Hag.	11	11	.500	4.05	25	25	3	0	0	0	149.0	154	635	85	67	10	9	6	11	36	1	124	3	2
Eversgerd, Randy, Hag.	3	1	.750	8.10	11	0	0	0	2	0	23.1	32	112	22	21	3	1	4	1	13	0	16	1	0
Felix, Miguel, Hick.	3	11	.214	6.47	21	19	1	0	0	0	97.1	111	468	90	70	10	1	1	6	64	0	86	13	1
Fenus, Justin, Pied.	10	8	.556	5.11	30	24	0	0	1	0	135.2	169	618	90	77	14	4	5	5	45	0	81	11	5
Fitzpatrick, Luke, Hick.*	2	0	1.000	3.14	20	0	0	0	5	0	28.2	37	136	14	10	2	0	3	1	16	1	31	2	1
Fleck, Will, Mac.	7	0	1.000	2.65	48	0	0	0	38	14	71.1	56	298	26	21	6	4	5	1	27	1	91	6	1
Fleming, Emar, Sav.	7	8	.467	4.84	37	21	1	0	4	1	139.1	145	626	88	75	19	2	3	14	61	0	133	8	3
Flores, Randy, Gre.*	12	7	.632	2.62	21	20	2	1	0	0	130.2	119	535	48	38	6	2	3	7	33	0	139	2	4
Fogg, Josh, Hick.	1	3	.250	2.18	8	8	0	0	0	0	41.1	36	173	17	10	4	1	0	1	13	0	29	1	1
Fontaine, Tom, Del.	0	2	.000	15.88	6	0	0	0	2	0	5.2	9	34	10	10	1	1	0	1	8	0	7	1	0
Frey, Christopher, Sav.	1	0	1.000	3.52	7	0	0	0	2	0	15.1	19	71	8	6	1	0	0	0	8	0	17	0	0
Garcia, Ariel, Hick.	0	6	.000	4.89	9	7	0	0	0	0	38.2	44	171	31	21	8	2	1	1	14	1	14	3	0
Garcia, Sandro, C.W.Va.	0	0	.000	22.50	1	0	0	0	1	0	2.0	4	12	5	5	0	0	0	0	2	0	1	1	0
Garcia, Sonny, Del.	2	0	1.000	2.52	4	4	1	0	0	0	25.0	17	100	9	7	2	2	0	1	9	0	21	5	1
Gardner, Lee, C.S.C.	0	3	.000	4.04	28	0	0	0	13	3	35.2	38	154	18	16	3	2	0	1	4	0	55	1	0
Gardner, Nathan, C.W.Va.	6	4	.600	3.97	45	0	0	0	25	6	77.0	89	352	41	34	6	7	2	3	33	3	64	8	0
Garland, Jon, Hick.	1	4	.200	5.40	5	5	0	0	0	0	26.2	36	126	20	16	2	1	2	2	13	0	19	2	0
Gaskill, Derek, C'bia	5	5	.500	5.47	29	7	0	0	16	0	82.1	83	360	55	50	8	4	1	7	30	0	95	11	0
Giron, Isabel, Hag.	10	9	.526	4.24	29	21	4	3	0	0	126.1	110	517	70	59	11	6	3	7	27	1	129	7	2
Goetz, Geoff, C'bia*	4	4	.556	3.96	15	15	0	0	0	0	77.1	68	336	45	34	3	0	1	6	37	0	68	12	1
Gonzalez, Armando, Ash.	0	3	.000	4.41	11	0	0	0	7	0	16.1	27	80	11	8	1	2	1	1	8	0	18	3	0
Gonzalez, Dicky, C'bia	10	3	.769	3.31	18	18	1	0	0	0	111.1	104	449	57	41	9	5	1	9	14	1	107	5	1
Gonzalez, Ignacio, C.S.C.	0	4	.000	6.39	30	0	0	0	10	0	49.1	70	243	40	35	4	2	2	6	22	0	40	4	1
Gonzalez, Mike, Aug.*	4	2	.667	2.84	11	9	0	0	0	0	50.2	43	221	24	16	2	1	1	7	26	0	72	3	4
Gorman, Pat, C'bia	5	5	.500	5.01	42	6	0	0	22	5	70.0	74	333	53	39	2	5	5	5	46	0	66	3	2
Grabow, John, Aug.*	6	3	.667	5.78	17	16	0	0	0	0	71.2	84	329	59	46	7	1	5	3	34	0	67	9	0
Greene, Ryan, Mac.	3	3	.500	2.89	22	0	0	0	6	2	37.1	40	160	19	12	4	2	0	0	6	1	46	3	0
Guillory, Dan, C'bus.	3	5	.375	3.48	10	0	0	0	3	0	33.2	26	136	14	13	5	6	1	1	9	2	33	1	3
Guy, Brad, Aug.	6	4	.600	3.02	56	0	0	0	24	4	86.1	75	363	39	29	7	6	0	4	26	4	94	10	3
Guzman, Wilson, Aug.*	6	3	.667	2.57	42	0	0	0	15	4	70.0	55	287	24	20	0	1	3	2	24	1	73	0	1
Hale, Mark, C.S.C.	0	0	.000	10.80	4	0	0	0	4	0	5.0	4	25	6	6	2	0	0	0	6	0	8	0	0
Halpin, Jeremy, Del.	9	5	.643	3.97	57	0	0	0	25	7	93.0	93	388	45	41	8	7	1	1	17	7	104	6	0
Hamilton, Jon, C'bus*	0	0	.000	0.00	1	0	0	0	0	0	1.0	1	5	0	0	0	0	0	0	0	0	0	0	0
Haring, Brett, C.W.Va.*	2	9	.182	3.32	38	13	2	0	15	4	108.1	123	457	48	40	6	8	3	2	26	1	91	5	0
Harrison, Scott, C'bus	5	12	.294	6.13	27	24	1	0	1	0	130.2	161	600	100	89	14	4	2	7	53	0	118	10	0

Pitcher, Team	W	L	Pct.	ERA	G	GS	CG	ShO	GF	Sv.	IP	H	TBF	R	ER	HR	SH	SF	HB	BB	IBB	SO	WP	Bk.
Heath, Woody, Hag.	11	3	.786	2.97	24	10	0	0	6	1	94.0	79	381	42	31	4	3	4	3	27	2	82	8	4
Hebson, Bryan, C.F.	4	5	.444	4.71	16	16	0	0	0	0	72.2	71	323	42	38	8	1	4	11	29	0	57	1	0
Hootselle, Jeff, Pied.*	1	0	1.000	6.34	24	0	0	0	15	0	38.1	40	187	32	27	4	0	3	1	28	1	40	5	0
Horgan, Joe, C'bus*	2	1	.667	2.38	22	1	0	0	9	0	34.0	19	134	9	9	3	0	0	0	21	0	27	7	0
Howard, Tom, C.S.C.*	3	3	.500	3.16	33	0	0	0	8	0	51.1	55	234	25	18	2	3	0	2	25	1	39	8	0
Huff, Tim, Hag.*	2	0	1.000	3.81	26	0	0	0	14	0	49.2	62	222	23	21	4	0	1	2	17	3	30	3	0
Huggins, David, Hag.	0	2	.000	7.98	12	0	0	0	11	2	14.2	16	77	15	13	0	2	1	3	14	0	13	3	0
Hughes, Mike, C'bus*	7	2	.778	3.74	18	9	0	0	3	1	74.2	81	330	38	31	6	1	4	5	22	1	86	2	0
Huntsman, Brandon, Del.	7	6	.538	3.94	23	17	0	0	0	0	98.1	114	447	59	43	5	6	2	5	53	1	71	7	0
Izquierdo, Hansel, Hick.	9	11	.450	4.37	28	27	2	1	1	0	175.0	159	771	104	85	14	6	2	22	76	0	186	15	1
James, Delvin, C.S.C.	2	0	1.000	5.40	7	0	0	0	2	0	8.1	12	40	5	5	0	0	2	1	2	0	8	0	0
Jaramillo, Frank, Sav.	0	0	.000	0.00	1	0	0	0	1	0	0.2	1	3	0	0	0	0	0	0	0	0	1	0	0
Johnson, David, Ash.	0	1	.000	2.70	17	0	0	0	11	0	20.0	15	97	14	6	0	0	0	2	22	0	26	6	0
Johnston, Clint, Aug.*	3	3	.500	2.75	16	11	0	0	1	0	59.0	42	243	20	18	4	0	2	2	32	0	68	3	1
Johnston, Sean, C'bia*	2	2	.500	3.35	11	11	0	0	0	0	53.2	54	239	28	20	2	2	1	5	31	0	42	6	0
Julio, Jorge, C.F.	2	2	.500	5.68	6	6	0	0	0	0	31.2	33	134	20	20	4	1	1	1	12	0	20	1	0
Kalinowski, Josh, Ash.*	12	10	.545	3.92	28	28	3	1	0	0	172.1	159	743	93	75	15	7	4	8	65	0	215	17	3
Kelly, Jeff, Aug.*	1	1	.500	7.50	18	3	0	0	4	0	42.0	54	192	41	35	5	2	2	2	16	1	36	2	0
Kertis, John, Sav.	2	3	.400	4.03	38	3	0	0	17	1	76.0	74	364	45	34	9	2	4	14	46	0	90	9	0
Key, Calvin, Pied.	5	7	.417	4.88	26	19	2	1	1	0	120.0	157	542	85	65	8	3	2	5	34	0	74	10	1
Kimbrell, Mike, C.S.C.*	1	1	.500	7.71	13	0	0	0	2	0	18.2	24	92	18	16	2	1	1	0	15	0	17	0	3
Kingrey, Jarrod, Hag.	0	1	.000	3.86	1	0	0	0	1	0	2.1	3	10	2	1	0	1	0	0	0	0	3	0	0
Koeman, Matt, C'bus	2	4	.333	5.40	31	1	0	0	7	1	55.0	59	250	36	33	7	2	3	5	24	1	57	4	0
Krall, Eric, Gre.*	0	1	.000	6.63	14	0	0	0	8	0	19.0	27	100	21	14	1	0	0	0	18	0	15	2	0
Kringen, Jake, Ash.*	6	8	.429	4.63	28	24	0	0	3	1	145.2	185	638	90	75	21	5	2	3	29	0	119	4	0
Lanzetta, Tobin, C.F.	4	4	.500	4.38	38	0	0	0	13	1	74.0	77	326	43	36	6	1	1	9	27	0	66	3	1
Lara, Yovanny, C.F.	2	5	.286	7.08	22	9	0	0	3	0	54.2	61	281	51	43	5	2	4	7	48	0	31	15	0
Layne, Roger, C'bus	2	0	1.000	2.49	4	4	0	0	0	0	25.1	12	91	7	7	3	0	0	1	4	0	28	2	0
Lee, Chris, Del.	3	0	1.000	3.79	19	0	0	0	8	1	35.2	27	150	17	15	5	0	0	3	4	0	39	2	1
Leon, Scott, C.S.C.	0	1	.000	4.24	5	2	0	0	0	0	17.0	15	73	9	8	2	0	0	3	4	0	15	2	1
Levy, Tye, C.W.Va.*	1	10	.091	5.95	34	7	0	0	10	1	81.2	109	374	65	54	8	6	1	2	28	0	54	1	2
Lewis, Craig, Gre.	11	6	.647	3.37	28	26	3	0	1	0	173.2	170	721	77	65	16	6	2	3	34	1	178	8	4
Lewis, Derrick, Mac.	5	6	.455	3.81	23	23	0	0	0	0	113.1	108	502	64	48	7	1	4	8	55	0	100	15	2
Lohrman, Dave, C'bia	3	1	.750	1.06	21	0	0	0	12	4	42.1	27	180	14	5	2	2	1	0	20	1	53	3	0
Lopez, Jose, Hick.	4	3	.571	4.50	33	0	0	0	26	5	46.0	43	192	23	23	9	1	1	2	16	1	33	3	0
Lovingood, Ray, C'bia*	1	1	.667	4.83	6	6	0	0	0	0	31.2	33	137	20	17	4	1	0	0	14	0	27	3	0
Lundberg, David, Sav.	6	9	.400	5.54	50	0	0	0	43	14	87.2	105	396	69	54	9	7	2	7	27	1	70	5	0
Luttig, Chris, Aug.*	0	0	.000	18.00	4	0	0	0	1	0	3.0	7	21	6	6	0	0	0	1	3	0	4	3	0
Maberry, Mark, C'bia	3	1	.750	2.05	12	0	0	0	0	0	22.0	19	87	5	5	1	1	0	1	7	0	26	1	0
Madison, Scott, C.S.C.*	4	2	.667	3.63	9	8	0	0	0	0	44.2	53	188	25	18	4	2	0	2	13	0	25	1	3
Manbeck, Mark, Pied.	1	4	.200	4.70	7	7	0	0	0	0	38.1	51	177	24	20	3	0	1	4	5	0	30	3	0
Marsonek, Sam, Sav.	0	0	.000	3.86	2	2	0	0	0	0	7.0	7	36	7	3	0	0	1	3	3	0	4	1	0
Martinez, Caleb, Pied.*	2	0	1.000	6.66	13	0	0	0	5	2	25.2	31	116	23	19	1	2	2	3	4	0	26	0	0
Matcuk, Steve, Ash.	1	3	.250	4.62	13	7	0	0	3	1	48.2	60	223	32	25	7	2	0	3	22	0	32	4	0
Mathys, Jason, Gre.	1	0	1.000	6.75	4	0	0	0	1	0	9.1	18	48	8	7	1	0	0	0	3	0	8	1	0
Matz, Brian, C.F.*	3	5	.375	2.83	17	16	0	0	0	0	98.2	75	391	35	31	5	4	1	3	28	0	63	11	0
McBride, Jason, Gre.	0	0	.000	11.48	7	0	0	0	3	0	13.1	24	74	21	17	3	0	1	1	10	0	11	1	0
McClellan, Matt, Hag.	7	7	.533	3.09	25	25	1	0	0	0	139.2	109	589	65	48	8	5	4	14	58	3	126	6	5
McConnell, Sam, Aug.*	4	3	.571	3.20	8	8	1	0	0	0	45.0	36	183	22	16	2	1	0	1	13	1	35	1	0
McEntire, Ethan, C'bia*	1	0	1.000	0.00	1	1	0	0	0	0	5.0	3	22	0	0	0	0	0	0	4	0	2	0	0
McNally, Andrew, C'bus.	2	2	.500	3.00	38	0	0	0	24	8	45.0	41	199	22	15	4	2	1	2	19	5	53	5	0
Medina, Carlos, Del.*	4	6	.400	3.79	22	11	0	0	5	0	80.2	70	343	41	34	7	10	3	6	39	1	85	5	3
Mejias, Oliver, Aug.	0	0	.000	.000	2	0	0	0	2	0	3.2	4	15	0	0	0	0	0	0	1	0	1	0	0
Merrell, Phil, C.W.Va.	5	15	.250	4.64	26	25	4	0	0	0	149.1	169	656	91	77	11	8	4	9	43	0	117	14	0
Meyer, Jake, Hick.	0	6	.000	3.21	35	0	0	0	24	11	56.0	58	244	30	20	5	2	1	0	22	1	47	7	0
Miller, Justin, Ash.	13	8	.619	3.69	27	27	3	1	0	0	163.1	177	705	89	67	14	4	3	15	40	0	142	5	0
Miller, Matt, Sav.	3	1	.750	2.29	17	0	0	0	10	3	35.1	25	137	9	9	2	0	2	0	10	0	46	2	0
Montero, Francisco, Pied.	5	8	.385	4.05	20	20	1	0	0	0	120.0	145	506	68	54	13	5	5	7	15	0	68	3	0
Murphy, Darren, Del.*	0	0	.000	4.32	5	0	0	0	2	0	8.1	11	39	4	4	0	1	0	0	4	0	4	2	0
Myette, Aaron, Hick.	9	4	.692	2.47	17	17	0	0	0	0	102.0	84	421	43	28	4	2	3	8	30	0	103	5	0
Nation, Joey, Mac.*	6	12	.333	5.03	29	28	1	0	0	0	143.0	179	640	102	80	15	6	6	1	39	0	141	10	0
Negrette, Richard, C'bus	1	3	.250	5.09	21	0	0	0	10	2	40.2	39	181	24	23	4	0	0	5	22	1	35	6	0
Nichols, Jamie, Hick.	0	1	.000	3.79	11	0	0	0	7	1	19.0	15	82	8	8	1	0	0	0	13	3	19	2	0
Obando, Omar, Gre.	2	0	1.000	4.60	21	0	0	0	8	2	29.1	29	123	15	15	3	3	1	2	9	2	24	1	0
O'Toole, Ryan, C.W.Va.	0	0	.000	11.81	4	0	0	0	2	0	5.1	9	36	10	7	0	0	1	9	0	2	2	0
Pacheco, Delvis, Mac.	7	4	.636	4.97	18	10	0	0	3	0	63.1	67	272	39	35	12	1	2	6	14	0	42	5	0
Pacheco, Enemecio, Ash.	0	0	.000	6.75	2	0	0	0	1	0	4.0	5	19	5	3	1	0	0	0	1	0	2	0	0
Peguero, Americo, Del.	2	1	.667	6.00	15	2	0	0	5	2	36.0	38	165	26	24	4	2	0	0	22	0	37	1	1
Pena, Alex, Aug.	0	0	.000	18.00	1	0	0	0	1	0	1.0	2	8	2	2	0	0	1	0	3	0	1	1	0
Perez, Elvis, Hick.*	0	1	.000	10.80	3	0	0	0	1	0	3.1	8	23	6	4	0	0	0	0	6	0	2	0	0
Perez, Julio, C'bus	0	1	.000	8.27	9	0	0	0	4	1	16.1	18	76	17	15	6	1	1	2	10	0	18	2	0
Perez, Julio, C.F.	1	1	.500	3.18	9	0	0	0	0	0	17.0	17	74	7	6	1	1	2	3	6	0	10	3	0
Perez, Norberto, Del.	5	2	.714	4.06	24	4	0	0	7	0	51.0	54	229	29	23	1	3	2	2	26	1	52	7	0
Petrosian, Ara, Ash.	0	3	.000	6.66	18	0	0	0	12	0	24.1	30	116	19	18	7	0	2	3	13	0	32	2	0
Phelps, Travis, C.S.C.	5	8	.385	4.85	18	18	0	0	0	0	91.0	100	401	54	49	4	1	3	35	0	96	7	0
Pirkl, Greg, C'bus	2	2	.500	3.33	26	0	0	0	24	7	27.0	22	111	10	10	0	1	0	6	1	29	1	0
Plummer, Raymond, C.F.*	0	2	.000	8.01	31	1	0	0	15	2	48.1	56	221	43	43	11	2	3	4	18	0	36	3	0
Presley, Kirk, C'bia	0	0	.000	3.00	3	0	0	0	1	0	6.0	7	29	5	2	0	0	0	4	0	6	0	0
Price, Chris, Ash.	1	3	.250	5.27	18	0	0	0	9	1	27.1	27	123	26	16	4	2	2	3	11	0	21	1	0
Price, Ryan, Ash.	10	7	.588	4.12	27	26	5	0	1	0	168.1	178	717	93	77	23	4	5	8	41	0	145	11	0
Puffer, Brandon, C.W.Va.	2	7	.222	6.93	29	0	0	0	12	1	50.2	68	242	45	39	4	2	1	7	23	4	36	5	0
Queen, Mike, C'bia*	1	0	1.000	3.38	2	2	0	0	0	0	8.0	4	32	4	3	0	0	1	0	4	0	9	1	0

Pitcher, Team	W	L	Pct.	ERA	G	GS	CG	ShO	GF	Sv.	IP	H	TBF	R	ER	HR	SH	SF	HB	BB	IBB	SO	WP	Bk.
Quevedo, Ruben, Mac.	11	3	.786	3.13	25	15	1	0	0	0	112.0	114	470	50	39	13	3	4	1	31	0	117	5	1
Quezada, Edward, C.F.	8	8	.500	4.10	30	19	2	1	1	0	138.1	136	592	72	63	12	5	9	12	51	0	82	5	1
Ramirez, Horacio, Mac.*	1	7	.125	5.86	12	12	0	0	0	0	55.1	70	249	50	36	8	2	3	2	16	0	38	2	0
Ramos, Fernando, Pied.	3	2	.600	3.35	26	0	0	0	13	2	48.1	41	192	19	18	4	1	1	0	12	2	53	1	0
Ramos, Juan, C.F.	4	4	.500	2.39	25	0	0	0	21	6	37.2	33	152	13	10	4	2	0	3	5	0	29	1	0
Reichow, Bob, C'bus	2	6	.250	5.83	39	4	0	0	15	0	78.2	108	381	69	51	8	2	3	9	31	3	46	13	1
Reith, Brian, Gre.	6	7	.462	2.28	20	20	3	1	0	0	118.1	86	475	42	30	7	2	0	3	32	0	116	1	0
Reyes, Eddy, C.S.C.	4	6	.400	2.19	56	0	0	0	52	24	61.2	60	255	23	15	2	2	1	3	12	1	49	6	0
Reynolds, Chris, C.S.C.	0	0	.000	2.70	2	0	0	0	1	0	3.1	2	15	1	1	1	0	0	1	2	0	5	0	0
Richardson, Kasey, Del.*	2	2	.500	2.68	16	3	0	0	8	2	40.1	23	156	13	12	2	3	1	3	11	1	47	5	1
Riggan, Jerrod, C'bia	4	1	.800	3.70	14	0	0	0	7	1	41.1	38	177	21	17	5	3	1	1	14	1	40	2	0
Riley, Matthew, Del.*	5	4	.556	1.19	16	14	0	0	0	0	83.0	42	324	19	11	0	2	1	0	44	0	136	9	3
Rivera, Luis, Mac.	5	5	.500	3.98	20	20	0	0	0	0	92.2	78	405	53	41	8	3	3	6	41	0	118	8	2
Rivera, Luis A., C.F.	0	0	.000	0.00	1	0	0	0	1	0	1.0	1	4	0	0	0	0	0	0	0	0	1	0	0
Roach, Jason, C'bia	0	0	.000	0.00	1	0	0	0	1	0	1.0	1	5	0	0	0	0	0	0	1	0	1	0	0
Robinson, Dustin, C.W.Va.	5	10	.333	4.47	25	24	2	0	0	0	141.0	153	616	85	70	13	6	8	9	44	1	92	7	1
Rogers, Brian, Gre.	2	1	.667	7.88	3	3	0	0	0	0	16.0	18	71	15	14	6	0	1	1	6	0	19	3	0
Romero, Jordan, Del.	4	5	.444	5.33	15	14	0	0	1	0	79.1	87	351	50	47	9	2	3	5	31	0	70	4	2
Rosa, Cristy, Ash.	3	2	.600	5.09	18	0	0	0	3	0	35.1	49	163	25	20	4	2	0	0	12	0	22	3	0
Rupe, Ryan, C.S.C.	6	1	.857	2.40	10	10	0	0	0	0	56.1	33	215	18	15	3	0	1	6	9	0	62	3	0
Ryan, Robert, C.W.Va.*	0	0	.000	2.08	3	0	0	0	3	2	4.1	1	15	1	1	0	1	0	0	1	0	5	1	0
Salley, Anthony, Hag.*	0	2	.000	4.58	20	0	0	0	7	0	39.1	40	177	24	20	3	3	1	3	22	1	30	9	0
Salyers, Jeremy, C.F.	4	4	.500	3.77	42	2	0	0	18	3	71.2	70	310	41	30	8	5	1	8	23	0	32	8	2
Santana, Humberto, C'bia*	0	1	.000	3.31	5	3	0	0	1	1	16.1	14	70	7	6	1	1	0	0	3	0	20	2	0
Sarmiento, Dan, C'bus*	1	1	.500	7.71	6	0	0	0	4	0	9.1	9	45	11	8	1	0	2	1	9	0	10	3	0
Saylor, Ryan, C.F.	4	1	.800	2.45	24	0	0	0	22	6	36.2	26	143	10	10	2	1	1	2	7	0	50	1	0
Scarce, Bubba, Mac.	4	4	.500	4.25	20	1	0	0	5	0	36.0	34	163	19	17	5	0	2	2	23	0	29	3	1
Schaffner, Eric, Gre.	5	2	.714	4.35	14	4	0	0	1	0	39.1	53	179	26	19	5	1	0	1	7	0	35	4	0
Schorzman, Steve, Hick.	2	2	.500	6.54	23	0	0	0	4	0	42.2	37	187	32	31	8	5	1	4	24	0	35	1	0
Schreiner, Jon, C.F.	2	0	1.000	1.80	3	0	0	0	1	0	10.0	9	42	2	2	0	0	2	1	6	0	4	0	0
Schurman, Ryan, Mac.	2	4	.333	4.34	17	9	1	0	1	0	64.1	64	286	43	31	9	2	3	5	26	0	53	6	2
Scott, Brian, Hick.	4	2	.667	2.79	6	6	0	0	0	0	38.2	33	164	16	12	3	3	1	1	11	0	38	2	1
Seabol, Scott, Gre.	0	0	.000	4.50	2	0	0	0	2	0	2.0	3	9	1	1	0	0	0	0	0	0	1	1	0
Seabury, Jaron, Hag.	2	1	.667	1.65	45	0	0	0	35	17	54.2	37	222	14	10	3	2	2	6	21	1	48	4	0
Seay, Bobby, C.S.C.*	1	7	.125	4.30	15	15	0	0	0	0	69.0	59	289	40	33	10	3	2	5	29	0	74	7	2
Seifert, Ryan, Ash.	7	6	.538	4.12	36	0	0	0	19	5	87.1	66	363	44	40	8	12	4	6	37	0	90	1	0
Sellers, Roger, C.W.Va.	0	1	.000	7.67	12	0	0	0	8	0	27.0	39	136	27	23	1	1	4	4	15	1	13	4	0
Sequea, Jacobo, C.W.Va.	3	5	.375	6.02	13	11	0	0	1	0	55.1	68	261	42	37	3	6	1	6	33	0	33	6	3
Serrano, Jim, C.F.	2	0	1.000	3.65	15	0	0	0	8	3	24.2	22	116	11	10	2	1	2	1	15	0	29	5	0
Shaw, Curtis, Aug.*	1	0	1.000	5.00	2	2	0	0	0	0	9.0	8	36	5	5	0	0	0	1	5	0	6	1	0
Sheldon, Kyle, C.F.	2	0	1.000	2.35	4	0	0	0	3	0	7.2	7	29	2	2	0	0	0	0	4	0	5	0	0
Shepard, David, C.W.Va.	2	8	.200	5.06	16	8	2	0	8	2	48.0	58	215	41	27	1	7	3	4	9	2	33	5	0
Shiell, Jason, Mac.	0	1	.000	4.50	4	3	0	0	0	0	8.0	7	32	4	4	2	0	0	0	1	0	8	1	0
Shipp, Kevin, Pied.	10	11	.476	3.46	28	28	3	0	0	0	184.2	210	780	99	71	20	4	7	5	26	0	142	8	4
Shourds, Anthony, Sav.	3	7	.300	4.10	37	0	0	0	17	3	74.2	60	326	39	34	4	5	3	6	34	0	68	6	0
Shumate, Jacob, Mac.	5	4	.556	6.75	44	0	0	0	10	0	50.2	44	280	54	38	5	2	3	13	75	0	65	39	1
Siciliano, Jess, Aug.	0	1	.000	7.36	5	0	0	0	3	0	3.2	5	22	4	3	2	0	1	0	5	0	6	1	0
Sido, Wilson, C'bus	2	0	1.000	2.55	4	4	0	0	0	0	24.2	17	101	7	7	1	0	0	3	8	1	27	0	1
Siegel, Justin, Sav.*	1	1	.500	1.17	7	0	0	0	1	0	15.1	7	60	3	2	0	1	0	1	10	0	11	0	0
Silva, Douglas, Sav.	3	4	.429	4.57	38	0	0	0	22	7	65.0	72	280	34	33	6	0	4	2	13	0	60	7	0
Silva, Troy, C'bus	4	3	.571	3.33	16	12	1	1	1	0	75.2	66	320	29	28	7	1	2	4	32	0	84	6	1
Smart, J.D., C.F.	3	0	1.000	2.45	3	1	0	0	0	0	11.0	7	39	3	3	1	0	0	0	0	0	12	1	0
Smith, Ryan, Sav.*	8	6	.571	7.07	35	7	0	0	11	1	84.0	90	410	77	66	8	2	6	6	66	0	88	24	2
Smoltz, John, Mac.	0	0	.000	3.60	2	2	0	0	0	0	10.0	7	40	4	4	1	0	0	0	1	0	14	1	0
Sneed, John, Hag.	16	2	.889	2.56	27	27	2	1	0	0	161.2	123	660	59	46	9	4	0	11	58	0	210	5	2
Solano, Manny, C.W.Va.	3	2	.600	3.21	18	1	0	0	9	0	33.2	38	156	17	12	1	2	2	4	13	2	18	3	1
Sparks, Steve, Aug.	0	1	.000	6.23	2	2	0	0	0	0	8.2	11	43	9	6	1	0	1	0	4	0	12	1	0
Spence, Cam, Gre.	3	2	.600	2.06	8	7	0	0	0	0	39.1	34	151	10	9	1	0	0	0	5	0	41	3	0
Spencer, Jeff, Mac.	0	0	.000	22.50	2	0	0	0	2	0	2.0	6	13	5	5	1	0	0	0	1	0	1	1	0
Spenser, Kaipo, C'bus	1	7	.125	6.22	11	11	0	0	0	0	55.0	66	264	49	38	11	3	2	4	32	0	36	4	0
Spiegel, Mike, C'bus*	5	6	.455	6.20	13	13	0	0	0	0	65.1	75	297	53	45	7	2	1	6	34	0	61	6	2
Spurgeon, Jay, Del.	11	3	.786	2.64	27	20	0	0	0	0	136.1	112	547	49	40	8	5	5	6	48	0	103	3	0
Spurling, Chris, Gre.	1	0	1.000	3.00	1	1	0	0	0	0	6.0	7	25	2	2	1	0	0	0	1	0	5	0	0
Stabile, Paul, Aug.*	5	7	.417	4.30	29	20	1	1	3	1	129.2	111	562	82	62	15	2	0	7	51	2	132	5	2
Stephens, John, Del.	1	2	.333	2.60	6	6	1	1	0	0	34.2	25	141	11	10	3	1	0	1	13	0	40	3	0
Stockstill, Jason, Hick.*	0	0	.000	5.79	10	0	0	0	5	3	14.0	13	64	10	9	3	1	0	1	11	0	8	2	0
Strickland, Scott, C.F.	0	3	.000	4.46	15	2	0	0	11	4	36.1	36	161	19	18	3	3	1	3	12	0	53	1	0
Tapia, Rafael, Del.	1	0	1.000	5.40	2	0	0	0	1	0	1.2	3	7	1	1	0	0	0	0	1	1	0	0	0
Taylor, Brien, Gre.*	0	1	.000	9.59	13	1	0	0	4	0	25.1	26	126	29	27	4	0	0	2	26	2	17	6	0
Tellez, Eloy, Hick.	0	0	.000	10.13	4	0	0	0	0	0	5.1	11	30	6	6	2	1	1	1	3	0	3	2	0
Temple, Jason, Aug.	0	2	.000	8.35	13	0	0	0	7	0	18.1	21	98	18	17	1	1	1	1	26	0	25	6	0
Theodile, Simeon, Del.	2	1	.667	6.48	19	0	0	0	10	0	25.0	30	118	19	18	3	0	0	1	11	0	21	3	1
Thieme, Richard, Mac.*	0	4	.000	8.29	16	6	0	0	3	0	33.2	41	175	43	31	1	3	2	7	28	0	19	7	2
Thompson, Doug, Ash.	0	0	.000	4.70	9	1	0	0	0	0	15.1	17	74	9	8	4	1	0	1	7	0	17	0	2
Thompson, Travis, Ash.	6	7	.462	3.24	26	24	0	0	0	0	147.1	155	619	71	53	11	1	4	6	36	0	113	6	1
Thomson, John, Ash.	1	0	1.000	0.00	2	2	0	0	0	0	9.0	5	32	1	0	0	0	0	0	1	0	12	1	0
Tilton, Ira, Pied.	4	4	.500	4.03	28	0	0	0	12	0	60.1	63	270	30	27	2	5	3	7	31	3	36	6	0
Tokarse, Brian, Hick.	0	1	.000	7.36	2	2	0	0	0	0	3.2	3	17	3	3	1	0	0	2	3	0	3	1	0
Turman, Jimmy, C.F.	8	5	.615	4.62	21	20	0	0	1	1	111.0	126	490	69	57	11	1	4	9	30	0	76	8	0
Turnbow, Mark, C'bus	6	5	.545	4.07	16	16	1	0	0	0	90.2	94	386	47	41	9	4	1	3	26	1	73	6	1
Tynan, Chris, Sav.	6	8	.429	4.40	21	21	1	0	0	0	116.2	113	529	69	57	11	2	8	3	74	0	95	10	3
Vael, Rob, C'bus	0	6	.000	10.29	9	9	0	0	0	0	42.0	65	206	51	48	10	2	3	1	21	0	35	5	0

CLASS A *South Atlantic League*

Pitcher, Team	W	L	Pct.	ERA	G	GS	CG	ShO	GF	Sv.	IP	H	TBF	R	ER	HR	SH	SF	HB	BB	IBB	SO	WP	Bk.
Valle, Yoiset, Gre.*	4	2	.667	4.18	33	1	0	0	6	1	51.2	53	234	27	24	3	1	0	8	24	0	55	6	1
Van Gilder, Ryan, C.F.	4	4	.500	3.02	30	0	0	0	13	4	44.2	43	190	18	15	0	4	4	3	14	0	35	2	0
Virchis, Adam, Hick.	1	3	.250	3.38	9	0	0	0	4	1	18.2	16	72	8	7	1	1	1	0	5	0	19	0	1
Wagner, Ken, C'bus	4	2	.667	2.51	33	0	0	0	10	3	71.2	55	293	25	20	2	4	2	4	20	0	92	5	0
Walker, Adam, Pied.*	9	0	1.000	2.04	15	15	0	0	0	0	84.0	60	337	21	19	2	2	1	3	21	0	114	7	1
Walker, Tyler, C'bia	5	5	.500	4.12	34	13	0	0	3	1	115.2	122	503	63	53	9	3	4	3	38	0	110	8	1
Wallace, Chris, Gre.	4	7	.364	3.02	54	0	0	0	24	8	89.1	89	389	43	30	4	10	6	5	26	8	79	7	3
Watson, Mark, C'bus*	4	4	.429	4.05	31	12	1	0	8	0	97.2	95	408	53	44	10	3	3	3	32	0	77	6	2
Weimer, Matt, Hag.	7	6	.538	2.85	48	0	0	0	29	8	72.2	62	308	31	23	3	2	2	8	26	2	59	5	0
Westmoreland, Ken, Pied.	3	0	1.000	1.93	5	5	0	0	0	0	32.2	27	142	11	7	3	0	1	0	17	0	41	0	0
Weymouth, Marty, Hick.	4	5	.444	4.34	31	14	0	0	10	3	112.0	125	499	74	54	7	3	5	7	32	0	99	9	0
Wheeler, Dan, C.S.C.	12	14	.462	4.43	29	29	3	1	0	0	181.0	206	763	96	89	16	7	6	11	29	0	136	4	0
White, Darell, Sav.	4	3	.571	4.22	13	11	3	1	2	1	70.1	68	302	38	33	6	2	5	5	25	0	53	4	0
White, Matt, C.S.C.	4	3	.571	3.82	12	12	0	0	0	0	75.1	72	316	41	32	1	3	5	2	21	0	59	10	1
Whitley, Curtis, Hick.*	4	8	.333	4.17	22	17	1	1	1	1	112.1	111	498	70	52	7	6	5	3	58	0	87	7	0
Wiggins, Scott, Gre.*	2	2	.500	2.98	14	4	0	0	6	1	42.1	37	171	17	14	4	0	2	1	11	0	56	0	0
Williams, Larry, Aug.	4	7	.364	5.05	35	2	0	0	9	0	67.2	65	305	45	38	7	2	0	4	38	1	77	3	3
Wise, William, Del.	6	3	.667	4.67	34	0	0	0	10	1	61.2	74	267	35	32	4	5	5	2	18	3	40	2	0
Wood, Stanton, Gre.	5	2	.714	3.90	31	2	0	0	14	1	64.2	57	269	29	28	13	2	1	0	20	3	67	1	0
Wrigley, Jase, Ash.	1	1	.500	5.74	13	0	0	0	5	1	15.2	18	70	11	10	3	0	0	1	4	0	12	1	1
Wyatt, Ben, Mac.*	4	6	.400	7.83	40	9	0	0	13	1	87.1	119	434	94	76	9	2	5	2	52	1	66	19	3
Yankosky, L. J., Mac.	4	1	.800	2.87	20	2	0	0	11	4	47.0	33	192	22	15	3	2	0	1	18	1	37	2	0
Young, Joe, Hag.	3	1	.750	5.31	7	7	0	0	0	0	39.0	38	173	23	23	4	1	3	1	18	0	42	2	0
Zambrano, Victor, C.S.C.	6	4	.600	3.38	48	2	0	0	15	0	77.1	72	330	32	29	5	5	0	12	20	1	89	7	1

COMBINATION SHUTOUTS: **Asheville (2)**—Kalinowski-Brueggemann-Emiliano, Kalinowski-Thompson-Wrigley. **Augusta (3)**—Shaw-Williams-Cook-Duff, Gonzalez-Guy-Cook, Bravo-Alvarado-Guy-Cook. **Cape Fear (6)**—Turman-Van Gilder-Lanzetta, Matz-Salyers-Lanzetta, Blank-Saylor, Matz-Saylor, Quezada-Lara-Saylor, Blank-Van Gilder. **Charleston, S.C. (8)**—Belitz-Zambrano-Box, Madison-Box-Reyes, Madison-Brown-Zambrano, Carter-Howard-Gonzalez, Belitz-Reyes, Belitz-Gardner-Reyes, Rupe-Brown-Box-Reyes, Phelps-Zambrano-Gardner. **Charleston, W.Va. (3)**—Averette-Gardner-Haring, Haring-Solano, Acevedo-Ryan. **Columbia (6)**—Gonzalez-Gorman, Goetz-Brito-Gaskill, Cutchins-Corcoran, Cutchins-Riggan, Walker-Corcoran-Barry, Gonzalez-Corcoran. **Columbus (5)**—Layne-Watson, Turnbow-McNally, Spiegel-Pirkl, Watson-Reichow-Horgan, Sido-Guillory. **Delmarva (6)**—Achilles-Brown, Spurgeon-Halpin, Achilles-Romero, Bauer-Lee, Spurgeon-Brown, Medina-Halpin. **Greensboro (7)**—Blevins-Schaffner-Wallace, Blevins-Wallace-Ellison, Flores-Obando, Flores-Wallace, Flores-Wallace, Reith-Wallace-Ellison, Wood-De La Cruz. **Hagerstown (10)**—Giron-Weimer-Seabury, Sneed-Huggins, Andrews-Weimer-Seabury, Heath-Casey-Weimer, Andrews-Salley-Huff, Sneed-Seabury, McClellan-Brackeen-Huff, Andrews-Weimer, Bowles-Huff, Estrella-Weimer. **Hickory (3)**—Myette-Currens, Myette-Meyer, Myette-Cardona-Lopez. **Macon (3)**—Ramirez-Wyatt-Dishman, Lewis-Fleck, Nation-Bauldree-Scarce. **Piedmont (7)**—Shipp-Fenus-Black, Walker-Black, Montero-Black, Duckworth-Black, Walker-Fenus-Eason-Ramos, Walker-Black, Walker-Ramos-Black. **Savannah (2)**—Carrion-Shourds, Tynan-Lundberg.

NO-HIT GAMES: Achilles, Delmarva, defeated Hagerstown, 5-0, April 27; Kalinowski, Asheville, defeated Charlestown, S.C., 5-0, August 26.

PITCHERS WITH TWO OR MORE TEAMS

Pitcher, Team	W	L	Pct.	ERA	G	GS	CG	ShO	GF	Sv.	IP	H	TBF	R	ER	HR	SH	SF	HB	BB	IBB	SO	WP	Bk.
Estrella, Leo, C'bia	10	8	.556	3.93	20	20	3	0	0	0	119.0	120	502	66	52	10	7	3	8	23	0	97	1	1
Estrella, Leo, Hag.	1	3	.250	4.50	5	5	0	0	0	0	30.0	34	133	19	15	0	2	3	3	13	1	27	2	1

1998 FIELDING

TEAM

Team	Pct.	G	PO	A	E	TC	DP	PB	Team	Pct.	G	PO	A	E	TC	DP	PB
Delmarva	.970	142	3707	1519	159	5385	131	22	Piedmont	.959	141	3740	1472	220	5432	125	26
Cape Fear	.968	141	3688	1587	175	5450	87	12	Savannah	.959	142	3656	1364	214	5234	107	28
Columbus	.966	140	3623	1504	181	5308	104	33	Hickory	.958	142	3740	1637	235	5612	118	40
Greensboro	.965	142	3729	1491	189	5409	106	21	Augusta	.958	142	3641	1397	223	5261	103	47
Hagerstown	.965	141	3628	1486	186	5300	124	30	Charleston (W.Va.)	.957	140	3537	1447	222	5206	127	21
Charleston (S.C.)	.965	141	3699	1521	191	5411	107	25	Macon	.946	141	3664	1282	284	5230	89	29
Asheville	.963	140	3653	1587	200	5440	130	24									
Columbia	.961	141	3718	1587	216	5521	136	19									

TRIPLE PLAYS: Charleston (W.Va.), Columbia, Macon, Savannah.

INDIVIDUAL

FIRST BASEMEN

NOTE: All caps denotes fielding-percentage leader based on 71 games for catchers, 95 for all other non-pitchers and 142 innings for pitchers. *Throws lefthanded.

Player, Team	Pct.	G	PO	A	E	TC	DP
Allison, Cody, C'bus	.994	20	151	9	1	161	13
Berger, Matt, Hick.	.984	94	876	62	15	953	73
Berns, Robert, C.S.C.*	.986	127	1094	109	17	1220	80
Blakeney, Mo, C.F.	.994	35	292	23	2	317	20
Bravo, Danny, C.F.	1.000	3	28	3	0	31	1
Burke, Mark, Mac.*	.976	39	303	23	8	334	20
Burns, Pat, C'bia*	.984	114	1026	78	18	1122	91
Cheek, Shawn, Sav.	.966	6	27	1	1	29	1
Clark, Kirby, Pied.	1.000	2	1	0	0	1	0
Copley, Travis, C.W.Va.	1.000	3	24	0	0	24	3
Cripps, Bobby, Hag.	1.000	3	9	1	0	10	1
Dominique, Bubba, Pied.	.997	34	298	25	1	324	24
Downs, Brian, Hick.	.988	7	76	6	1	83	6
Edwards, Michael, C'bus	1.000	3	19	1	0	20	2
Fauske, Josh, Hick.	.975	34	301	16	8	325	23
Figueroa, Franky, Del.	.987	137	1164	73	16	1253	111
Fisher, Anthony, Sav.	1.000	9	58	6	0	64	3
Furniss, Eddy, Aug.*	.990	12	97	5	1	103	11

Player, Team	Pct.	G	PO	A	E	TC	DP
Garrett, Scott, C.W.Va.	1.000	1	3	0	0	3	0
Grabowski, Jason, Sav.	1.000	1	98	3	0	101	6
Hafner, Travis, Sav.	.986	66	524	27	8	559	48
Hayes, Chris, Hag.	.964	24	127	8	5	140	18
Hoover, Paul, C.S.C.	1.000	1	1	0	0	1	0
Hundt, Bo, Hick.	1.000	5	27	5	0	32	3
Jaramillo, Frank, Sav.	.978	27	210	12	5	227	19
Klee, Chuck, Hick.	.875	1	7	0	1	8	0
Kopacz, Derek, Hick.	.955	7	63	1	3	67	5
Lankford, Derrick, Aug.	.986	59	441	38	7	486	27
Lehr, Jason, Mac.	.983	60	431	34	8	473	32
Lina, Estivinson, C.F.	1.000	4	28	2	0	30	4
Lindsey, John, Ash.	.9877	112	966	77	13	1056	85
Marn, Kevin, C.W.Va.	.969	19	145	11	5	161	14
Maxwell, Keith, Aug.	1.000	8	56	3	0	59	6
Mirizzi, Marc, Gre.	.984	15	114	11	2	127	7
Morrison, Greg, Hag.*	.987	106	816	65	12	893	76
Mortimer, Mark, Mac.	.978	18	119	15	3	137	9
Munoz, Billy, C'bus*	.985	117	981	74	16	1071	67
Nunnari, Talmadge, C.F.*	.992	74	656	59	6	721	38
O'Hearn, Brandon, C.W.Va.	1.000	2	14	0	0	14	2
Oropeza, Willie, C.F.	.994	23	163	9	1	173	8

Player, Team	Pct.	G	PO	A	E	TC	DP
Paxton, Chris, Del.	.988	15	74	9	1	84	5
Pena, Carlos, Sav.*	.986	28	196	16	3	215	12
Peters, Tony, Hag.	.913	7	40	2	4	46	0
Purkiss, Matt, Gre.	.982	35	310	11	6	327	24
Reyes, Jose, Aug.	1.000	3	6	0	0	6	0
Rivera, Carlos, Aug.*	.989	70	500	30	6	536	45
Rivera, Luis A., C.F.	1.000	19	137	4	0	141	9
Roach, Jason, C'bia	.988	25	224	20	3	247	29
Rodriguez, Mike, Hag.	.986	10	68	3	1	72	5
Salinas, Trey, C.S.C.	1.000	6	27	3	0	30	2
Samuel, Cody, Gre.	.952	14	116	3	6	125	11
Sanchez, Toby, C.W.Va.	.980	122	1047	58	23	1128	91
Schwartzbauer, Brad, Ash.	.982	29	253	19	5	277	30
Seabol, Scott, Gre.	1.000	7	43	4	0	47	4
Sienko, Ryan, Sav.	1.000	1	4	1	0	5	0
Soules, Ryan, Gre.	.987	75	685	50	10	745	52
Spencer, Jeff, Mac.	.981	9	49	3	1	53	4
Stanton, Tom, C'bia	1.000	3	29	2	0	31	2
Strange, Mike, Hag.	.956	17	101	8	5	114	13
Suriel, Miguel, C.S.C.	1.000	1	0	1	0	1	0
Taveras, Frank, C'bus	.990	13	92	8	1	101	11
Terrell, Jim, Hick.	1.000	2	9	0	0	9	0
VAN ITEN, Bob, Pied.	.9881	108	851	59	11	921	84
Velazquez, Jose, C.S.C.*	.989	11	82	6	1	89	7
Vidal, Gilbert, Ash.	1.000	4	19	0	0	19	2
Zapp, A.J., Mac.	.969	17	120	7	4	131	7

TRIPLE PLAYS: Lehr, Morrison, Roach.

SECOND BASEMEN

Player, Team	Pct.	G	PO	A	E	TC	DP
Alviso, Jerome, Ash.	.980	27	41	58	2	101	13
Bain, Tyler, C.S.C.	.857	4	6	6	2	14	1
Borges, Elio, Hick.	1.000	4	4	2	0	6	0
Bravo, Danny, C.F.	.989	18	40	49	1	90	10
Bruce, Mo, C'bia	.969	8	9	22	1	32	2
Bryant, Matt, Aug.	.986	18	29	39	1	69	7
Collier, Lamonte, Pied.	.500	1	0	1	1	2	0
Cordero, Willy, Sav.	.960	7	10	14	1	25	3
Crespo, Cesar, C'bia	.948	108	223	267	27	517	77
Cruz, Luis, C.S.C.	.943	34	58	75	8	141	14
Diaz, Maikell, Del.	1.000	4	6	8	0	14	1
Durham, Chad, Hick.	.961	117	203	370	23	596	72
Espada, Angel, C'bia	.875	9	9	26	5	40	6
Foulds, Kalin, C.S.C.	1.000	7	12	14	0	26	2
Freeman, Terrance, Aug.	.955	118	223	283	24	530	57
Garavito, Eddy, Del.	.973	131	300	347	18	665	84
Garcia, Sandro, C.W.Va.	.938	31	44	76	8	128	18
Giles, Marcus, Mac.	.954	127	229	294	25	548	53
Hammond, Joey, Del.	.833	3	2	3	1	6	1
Hook, Kevin, C.F.	.944	14	29	38	4	71	6
Izturis, Cesar, Hag.	1.000	2	7	2	0	9	1
Jaramillo, Frank, Sav.	.900	8	8	10	2	20	1
Johns, Michael, Ash.	1.000	5	5	12	0	17	3
Kidd, Scott, Gre.	.955	124	221	331	26	578	65
Kilburg, Joe, C'bus	.970	118	192	298	15	505	59
Klee, Chuck, Hick.	.944	3	4	13	1	18	3
Mateo, Henry, C.F.	.971	109	250	257	15	522	48
McGrath, Sean, C'bia	.965	17	30	52	3	85	9
Medrano, Ryan, C.W.Va.	.977	84	161	218	9	388	50
Mejia, Juan, Pied.	.946	25	48	58	6	112	8
Mejias, Oliver, Aug.	.925	12	18	31	4	53	5
Mirizzi, Marc, Gre.	.956	21	32	54	4	90	12
Owens-Bragg, Luke, C.S.C.	1.000	1	4	2	0	6	0
Paz, Richard, Del.	.972	10	9	26	1	36	6
Pena, Elvis, Ash.	.945	109	197	306	29	532	73
Perez, Edwin, C'bus	.933	7	8	6	1	15	0
Perez, Jersen, C'bia	.846	4	4	7	2	13	2
Price, Corey, C.W.Va.	.959	33	55	86	6	147	14
Romano, Jason, Sav.	.952	133	305	326	32	663	76
Sanchez, Manuel, Mac.	.818	3	4	5	2	11	0
Schwartzbauer, Brad, Ash.	.900	3	5	4	1	10	1
Strange, Mike, Hag.	1.000	8	8	10	0	18	1
Taveras, Frank, C'bus	.955	5	9	12	1	22	3
Taylor, Greg, Pied.	1.000	1	2	2	0	4	0
Terrell, Jeffrey, Pied.	.946	118	250	315	32	597	76
Terrell, Jim, Hick.	.948	20	37	54	5	96	15
Thorpe, A.D., Mac.	.982	14	19	35	1	55	3
Tiller, Brad, C'bus	.946	19	25	45	4	74	9
Trahan, Mike, C.S.C.	.948	80	144	200	19	363	45
Ware, Ryan, C.S.C.	.942	17	26	55	5	86	11
Washington, Rico, Aug.	1.000	3	1	3	0	4	1
YOUNG, Mike, Hag.	.978	128	196	302	11	509	75

Player, Team	Pct.	G	PO	A	E	TC	DP
Zech, Scott, C.F.	.964	6	16	11	1	28	0
Zepeda, Jesse, Hag.	.969	22	24	39	2	65	11

TRIPLE PLAYS: Crespo, Romano, Young.

THIRD BASEMEN

Player, Team	Pct.	G	PO	A	E	TC	DP
Albaral, Randy, Hag.	1.000	1	1	1	0	2	0
Baderdeen, Kevin, C.W.Va.	.860	21	13	36	8	57	6
Bennett, Ryan, C'bia	.750	1	0	3	1	4	0
Berger, Matt, Hick.	.926	28	23	64	7	94	3
Borges, Elio, Hick.	.811	14	3	27	7	37	1
Bravo, Danny, C.F.	.894	31	21	55	9	85	1
Bruce, Mo, C'bia	.939	92	83	212	19	314	24
Bryant, Matt, Aug.	.922	28	9	50	5	64	2
Burkhart, Lance, C.F.	1.000	2	0	4	0	4	0
Burns, Xavier, Aug.	.881	85	41	158	27	226	10
BUTLER, Allen, Gre.	.929	124	71	230	23	324	17
Cameron, Troy, Mac.	.830	61	39	88	26	153	10
Clark, Kirby, Pied.	.807	29	13	58	17	88	4
Copley, Travis, C.W.Va.	.914	37	24	61	8	93	2
Cordero, Willy, Sav.	1.000	2	2	1	0	3	0
Diaz, Maikell, Del.	.980	23	12	37	1	50	1
Dominique, Bubba, Pied.	.860	43	29	69	16	114	4
Duncan, Carlos, Pied.	.844	28	19	62	15	96	3
Edwards, Michael, C'bus	.904	114	77	216	31	324	14
Fritz, Jim, Pied.	.667	5	2	8	5	15	1
Garavito, Eddy, Del.	1.000	1	0	1	0	1	0
Garcia, Sandro, C.W.Va.	.860	46	27	59	14	100	6
Hafner, Travis, Sav.	.920	24	16	30	4	50	2
Hammond, Joey, Del.	.923	35	16	44	5	65	10
Hayes, Chris, Hag.	.892	35	18	73	11	102	11
Hoch, Corey, Del.	.833	7	2	8	2	12	0
Hoover, Paul, C.S.C.	.840	7	4	17	4	25	2
Huff, Aubrey, C.S.C.	.957	69	47	133	8	188	14
Hundt, Bo, Aug.	.917	19	14	30	4	48	1
Izturis, Cesar, Hag.	1.000	1	0	1	0	1	0
Jaramillo, Frank, Sav.	.930	18	14	26	3	43	5
Johns, Michael, Ash.	.958	13	8	15	1	24	1
Klee, Chuck, Hick.	.868	22	13	46	9	68	7
Kurilla, Kevin, Pied.	.908	40	35	74	11	120	6
Lehr, Ryan, Mac.	.780	41	20	58	22	100	1
Lentz, Ryan, C.F.	.938	3	3	12	1	16	1
Mackowiak, Rob, Aug.	1.000	4	3	2	0	5	0
Markray, Thad, C.W.Va.	.830	36	25	58	17	100	3
McGrath, Sean, C'bia	.800	5	5	7	3	15	0
Medrano, Ryan, C.W.Va.	1.000	6	3	8	0	11	0
Mejia, Juan, Pied.	.667	6	1	3	2	6	0
Mejias, Oliver, Aug.	.857	10	6	18	4	28	3
Mirizzi, Marc, Gre.	.929	15	7	32	3	42	4
Mortimer, Mark, Mac.	.500	2	0	1	1	2	0
Nunez, Jorge, Hag.	.833	4	2	3	1	6	0
Oropeza, Willie, C.F.	.841	29	16	42	11	69	1
Owens-Bragg, Luke, C.S.C.	.818	5	0	9	2	11	0
Paz, Richard, Del.	.943	88	68	163	14	245	13
Perez, Edwin, C'bus	.957	9	11	11	1	23	3
Perez, Jersen, C'bia	1.000	8	5	11	0	16	2
Price, Corey, C.W.Va.	1.000	4	2	7	0	9	0
Roach, Jason, C'bia	.865	40	17	73	14	104	7
Rodriguez, Mike, Hag.	1.000	1	0	1	0	1	0
Salinas, Trey, C.S.C.	.769	5	4	6	3	13	1
Sanchez, Manuel, Mac.	.750	5	4	8	4	16	0
Sandberg, Jared, C.S.C.	.862	56	43	94	22	159	9
Santos, Jose, Sav.	.891	104	72	197	33	302	22
Schwartzbauer, Brad, Ash.	.878	29	14	72	12	98	3
Seabol, Scott, Gre.	.846	10	4	18	4	26	0
Sears, Todd, Ash.	.888	106	49	197	31	277	18
Strange, Mike, Hag.	.928	42	17	86	8	111	6
Taveras, Frank, C'bus	.974	18	6	31	1	38	3
Terrell, Jim, Hick.	.905	84	59	161	23	243	8
Thorpe, A.D., Mac.	.889	36	34	54	11	99	5
Tiller, Brad, C'bus	1.000	5	1	10	0	11	0
Ware, Ryan, C.S.C.	1.000	1	1	1	0	2	0
Washington, Rico, Aug.	1.000	8	3	10	0	13	1
Wilson, Travis, Mac.	1.000	2	1	0	0	1	0
Zech, Scott, C.F.	.931	90	53	205	19	277	11
Zepeda, Jesse, Hag.	.934	82	39	146	13	198	20

TRIPLE PLAYS: Bruce, Zepeda.

SHORTSTOPS

Player, Team	Pct.	G	PO	A	E	TC	DP
Aalbers, Brady, C.W.Va.	.875	21	19	37	8	64	8
Almonte, Erick, Gre.	.911	120	176	307	47	530	61

Player, Team	Pct.	G	PO	A	E	TC	DP
Alviso, Jerome, Ash.	.947	110	182	370	31	583	67
Baderdeen, Kevin, C.W.Va.	1.000	1	1	2	0	3	0
Bravo, Danny, C.F.	.942	42	60	120	11	191	19
Bruce, Mo, C'bia	.929	3	2	11	1	14	2
Bryant, Matt, Aug.	.918	15	19	26	4	49	4
Caceres, Wilmy, C.W.Va.	.923	103	167	303	39	509	68
Cameron, Troy, Mac.	.852	70	96	135	40	271	24
Collier, Lamonte, Pied.	.892	44	73	117	23	213	33
Cordero, Willy, Sav.	.913	94	108	259	35	402	34
Crespo, Cesar, C'bia	1.000	1	1	4	0	5	0
Diaz, Maikell, Del.	.945	34	48	89	8	145	21
Duncan, Carlos, Pied.	.917	4	3	19	2	24	3
Espada, Angel, C'bia	.800	1	2	2	1	5	2
Foulds, Kalin, C.S.C.	.875	1	2	5	1	8	0
Gonzalez, Luis, C'bus	.940	101	137	301	28	466	58
Gutierrez, Victor, Aug.	.908	126	180	312	50	542	57
Hoch, Corey, Del.	.667	2	0	2	1	3	0
Hook, Kevin, C.F.	.906	31	36	89	13	138	13
Hoover, Paul, C.S.C.	1.000	2	1	9	0	10	1
IZTURIS, Cesar, Hag.	.951	129	183	376	29	588	71
Jaramillo, Frank, Sav.	1.000	6	7	11	0	18	0
Joffrion, Jack, C.S.C.	.937	72	88	196	19	303	36
Johns, Michael, Ash.	.931	37	49	113	12	174	18
Klee, Chuck, Hick.	.963	12	19	33	2	54	6
Kurilla, Kevin, Pied.	.969	14	14	48	2	64	7
Martinez, Eddy, Del.	.950	113	153	319	25	497	64
Mateo, Henry, C.F.	1.000	2	4	2	0	6	0
McGrath, Sean, C'bia	1.000	4	3	13	0	16	7
Medrano, Ryan, C.W.Va.	.945	26	33	53	5	91	15
Mejia, Juan, Pied.	.901	18	19	54	8	81	10
Mejias, Oliver, Aug.	.968	8	11	19	1	31	2
Miller, Kenny, C'bia	.910	35	47	104	15	166	20
Mirizzi, Marc, Gre.	.958	23	27	65	4	96	14
Owens-Bragg, Luke, C.S.C.	.789	4	3	12	4	19	2
Paz, Richard, Del.	1.000	1	1	2	0	3	0
Perez, Edwin, C'bus	.898	12	11	33	5	49	5
Perez, Jersen, C'bia	.941	100	138	312	28	478	61
Perez, Nestor, C.S.C.	.965	62	84	191	10	285	26
Price, Corey, C.W.Va.	1.000	1	3	4	0	7	1
Reding, Josh, C.F.	.942	73	117	259	23	399	31
Romano, Jason, Sav.	1.000	1	2	4	0	6	0
Sandoval, Danny, Hick.	.912	126	174	417	57	648	79
Taveras, Frank, C'bus	.943	22	26	57	5	88	5
Taylor, Greg, Pied.	.965	65	87	186	10	283	34
Terrell, Jim, Hick.	.938	7	10	20	2	32	2
Thorpe, A.D., Mac.	.905	73	110	187	31	328	26
Tiller, Brad, C'bus	.963	9	7	19	1	27	4
Valera, Willy, C'bus	.909	6	8	12	2	22	0
Ware, Ryan, C.S.C.	1.000	2	1	5	0	6	1
Warriax, Brandon, Sav.	.904	47	50	128	19	197	15
Young, Mike, Hag.	.967	24	20	39	2	61	10
Zepeda, Jesse, Hag.	1.000	2	1	0	0	1	0

TRIPLE PLAY: Thorpe.

OUTFIELDERS

Player, Team	Pct.	G	PO	A	E	TC	DP
Alamo, Efrain, Ash.	.968	129	171	13	6	190	5
Albaral, Randy, Hag.	.930	78	103	4	8	115	2
Albert, Rashad, Hick.	.973	97	175	7	5	187	1
Alvarez, Carlos, C'bus	.948	41	47	8	3	58	0
Amerson, Gordon, Gre.*	.714	4	5	0	2	7	0
Aylor, Brian, Gre.*	.933	41	55	1	4	60	1
Bagley, Lorenzo, Hag.	.964	81	103	3	4	110	1
Bennett, Ryan, C'bia	1.000	1	2	0	0	2	0
Blakeney, Mo, C.F.	.917	44	53	2	5	60	0
Bradley, Milton, C.F.	.968	52	87	5	3	95	1
Brooks, Anthony, Mac.	.953	133	308	13	16	337	3
Brown, Billy, Hag.	.935	44	56	2	4	62	0
Burns, Xavier, Aug.	1.000	17	27	1	0	28	0
Butler, Garrett, C.S.C.	.991	44	105	3	1	109	1
Caradonna, Brett, Hick.	.959	98	132	7	6	145	0
Carey, Orlando, Gre.	.962	28	45	5	2	52	0
Castillo, Geramel, Sav.	1.000	22	35	2	0	37	0
Castro, Martires, Sav.	.968	55	91	1	3	95	1
Charles, Curtis, Del.	1.000	8	7	1	0	8	0
Chatman, Karl, C.F.	.973	57	104	4	3	111	1
Collins, Francis, Pied.	.964	80	102	6	4	112	2
Copeland, Brandon, C'bia	.950	103	122	11	7	140	0
Cortez, Santos, Aug.	.875	6	7	0	1	8	0
Cruz, Geronimo, Sav.*	1.000	8	11	1	0	12	1
Darjean, John, Gre.	.970	19	32	0	1	33	0
Davis, J.J., Aug.	.923	21	35	1	3	39	0

Player, Team	Pct.	G	PO	A	E	TC	DP
Davison, Ashanti, Del.	1.000	7	7	0	0	7	0
DeHaan, Kory, Aug.	.984	126	244	7	4	255	1
Dina, Allen, C'bia	1.000	2	2	0	0	2	0
Elliott, Dawan, Aug.*	1.000	7	9	1	0	10	0
Escobar, Alex, C'bia	.941	101	186	5	12	203	1
Fajardo, Alejandro, Pied.	.968	114	264	12	9	285	2
Fisher, Anthony, Sav.	.989	115	249	9	3	261	1
Fitzgerald, Jason, C'bus*	.968	127	225	17	8	250	0
Forbes, Kevin, C.F.	.986	51	71	2	1	74	1
Foulds, Kalin, C.S.C.	1.000	5	10	1	0	11	0
Garcia, Douglas, Sav.*	1.000	6	12	0	0	12	0
Garcia, Sandro, C.W.Va.	1.000	16	20	5	0	25	0
Giron, Alejandro, Pied.	.957	47	84	4	4	92	0
Guerrero, Rafael, C.S.C.	.952	25	36	4	2	42	0
Guzman, Carlos, Pied.*	.984	68	113	10	2	125	1
Hafner, Travis, Sav.	1.000	1	2	0	0	2	0
Hairston, Jason, Mac.	.841	63	68	1	13	82	0
Hall, Noah, C.F.	.977	107	159	8	4	171	0
Hamilton, Jon, C'bus*	.980	131	236	14	5	255	1
Harris, Kevin, Sav.	.886	21	29	2	4	35	0
Hayes, Chris, Hag.	.900	7	9	0	1	10	0
Hendricks, Jason, C.F.	.981	30	47	4	1	52	1
Hollins, Darontaye, Hick.	.973	43	67	6	2	75	0
Hooper, Daren, Del.	.958	24	23	0	1	24	0
Hughes, Brian, Del.	.949	38	54	2	3	59	0
Hundt, Bo, Aug.	.927	25	30	8	3	41	1
Jackson, Jeremy, Ash.	.936	92	123	8	9	140	1
James, Kenny, C.F.	.969	95	211	7	7	225	1
Jaramillo, Frank, Sav.	.972	32	33	2	1	36	0
Johnson, Eric, Aug.	.914	22	31	1	3	35	0
Johnson, Jason, Pied.	.974	106	215	8	6	229	1
Johnson, Tom, C'bia	.949	84	159	7	9	175	1
Kelly, Kenneth, C.S.C.	.964	54	122	10	5	137	3
Landaeta, Luis, Ash.*	.975	27	36	3	1	40	1
Lankford, Derrick, Aug.	.917	18	21	1	2	24	0
Lara, Felix, Aug.*	1.000	12	18	1	0	19	0
Mackowiak, Rob, Aug.	.931	22	26	1	2	29	0
Marn, Kevin, C.W.Va.	.955	69	120	8	6	134	1
Matos, Luis, Del.	.964	131	254	12	10	276	4
Maxwell, Keith, Aug.	.941	12	16	0	1	17	0
Maxwell, Vernon, Gre.	.966	95	166	6	6	178	0
McDonald, Darnell, Del.	.940	119	167	5	11	183	0
Melian, Jackson, Gre.	.964	131	201	13	8	222	2
Messner, Jake, C'bus*	.750	8	6	0	2	8	0
Mirizzi, Marc, Gre.	1.000	3	7	0	0	7	0
MITCHELL, Andres, Ash.	.992	136	243	16	2	261	3
Moreno, Juan, C'bia	.914	102	108	9	11	128	1
Morillo, Luis, Hag.*	1.000	32	36	3	0	39	0
Morrison, Greg, Hag.*	.800	1	4	0	1	5	0
Mortimer, Mark, Mac.	1.000	2	6	0	0	6	0
Mounts, J.R., Hick.	.984	106	177	7	3	187	1
Neuberger, Scott, C.S.C.	.977	131	246	12	6	264	0
Newkirk, Jeff, Hick.*	.941	21	45	3	3	51	0
Nicolas, Jose, Aug.	.848	55	52	4	10	66	1
Nieves, Juan, Hag.	.667	2	1	1	1	3	0
Nunnari, Talmadge, C.F.*	.909	8	10	0	1	11	0
O'Hearn, Brandon, C.W.Va.	.951	95	159	17	9	185	5
Oliver, Johnny, C.W.Va.	.969	104	147	11	5	163	3
Patton, Cory, C'bia	.926	42	48	2	4	54	0
Pena, Alex, Aug.	.969	88	153	5	5	163	1
Pena, Carlos, Sav.*	1.000	1	1	0	0	1	0
Pena, Jose, Sav.	.951	109	161	13	9	183	3
Perez, Richard, Del.	.833	14	10	0	2	12	0
Peters, Tony, Hag.	.967	88	107	12	4	123	0
Pigott, Anthony, C.S.C.	.977	29	43	0	1	44	0
Piniella, Juan, Sav.	.985	71	126	5	2	133	0
Reyes, Jose, Aug.	.857	3	6	0	1	7	0
Rivera, Carlos, Aug.*	1.000	3	2	0	0	2	0
Rivera, Roberto, Del.	.959	104	149	14	7	170	5
Rodriguez, Hernandez, C.W.Va.	.979	83	177	9	4	190	3
Rodriguez, John, Gre.*	.958	103	129	7	6	142	1
Rodriguez, Mike, Hag.	1.000	19	17	1	0	18	0
Rodriguez, Gary, C'bus	.895	13	16	1	2	19	1
Rowand, Aaron, Hick.	.966	47	79	7	3	89	2
Scioneaux, Damian, C.S.C.	.973	71	135	7	4	146	0
Seabol, Scott, Gre.	1.000	18	25	0	0	25	0
Sienko, Ryan, Sav.	1.000	1	1	0	0	1	0
Smothers, Stewart, Mac.	.965	139	314	14	12	340	4
Sosa, Jovanny, Aug.	.833	19	34	1	7	42	0
Spencer, Jeff, Mac.	.980	90	136	9	3	148	1
Strange, Mike, Hag.	.667	4	2	0	1	3	0
Taveras, Frank, C'bus	.971	24	31	2	1	34	1

Player, Team	Pct.	G	PO	A	E	TC	DP
Taylor, Corey, C.W.Va.	.988	42	83	1	1	85	1
Terrell, Jim, Hick.	.952	18	20	0	1	21	0
Thorpe, A.D., Mac.	1.000	2	1	0	0	1	0
Tidwell, Dave, C.W.Va.	1.000	7	12	0	0	12	0
Tiller, Brad, C'bus	1.000	1	2	0	0	2	0
Toomey, Chris, C.W.Va.	.913	18	41	1	4	46	0
Valent, Eric, Pied.*	.952	21	38	2	2	42	1
Ware, Ryan, C.S.C.	1.000	3	3	1	0	4	0
Washington, Dion, Gre.	.667	6	2	0	1	3	0
Wells, Vernon, Hag.	.980	129	243	6	5	254	1
Wilder, Paul, C.S.C.	.963	68	71	7	3	81	2
Williams, Jewell, C'bus	.971	94	133	2	4	139	1
Zweifel, Kent, Ash.	.985	52	65	1	1	67	0

TRIPLE PLAY: Fisher.

CATCHERS

Player, Team	Pct.	G	PO	A	E	TC	DP	PB
Adorno, Wilson, Aug.	.915	8	40	3	4	47	0	1
Allison, Cody, C'bus	1.000	7	32	3	0	35	0	0
Anderson, Franklin, Aug.	.938	14	98	8	7	113	1	0
Arias, Rogelio, Ash.	.979	74	582	60	14	656	3	13
Bennett, Ryan, C'bia	.990	53	346	46	4	396	4	8
Bravo, Danny, C.F.	1.000	1	3	0	0	3	0	0
Burkhart, Lance, C.F.	1.000	7	37	7	0	44	0	0
Cheek, Shawn, Sav.	.989	12	83	4	1	88	0	3
Clark, Kirby, Pied.	.979	18	85	10	2	97	3	10
Cloud, Casey, Aug.	.978	26	168	12	4	184	0	8
Copley, Travis, C.W.Va.	.986	12	64	5	1	70	2	4
Cripps, Bobby, Hag.	.977	57	421	55	11	487	4	12
Cruz, Edgar, C'bus	.986	98	756	106	12	874	4	25
Diaz, Diogenes, Aug.	1.000	8	70	9	0	79	0	0
Downs, Brian, Hick.	.976	61	452	43	12	507	2	12
Estrada, Johnny, Pied.	.990	73	523	63	6	592	6	9
Evans, Lee, Aug.	.992	86	678	73	6	757	3	32
Ewan, Bry, Mac.	.968	13	83	8	3	94	1	3
Fauske, Josh, Hick.	.985	34	231	30	4	265	1	10
Folmar, Ryan, Ash.	1.000	2	19	3	0	22	0	0
Fowler, Ben, C'bus	.980	44	305	31	7	343	1	8
Fritz, Jim, Pied.	.967	23	139	6	5	150	1	4
Garrett, Scott, C.W.Va.	.993	40	243	22	2	267	1	6
Gonzales, Jose, Ash.	.989	40	314	39	4	357	0	5
Grabowski, Jason, Sav.	.989	60	480	47	6	533	5	8
Hall, Toby, C.S.C.	.979	102	749	84	18	851	4	6
Hoover, Paul, C.S.C.	.982	31	197	22	4	223	2	12
Hundt, Bo, Aug.	1.000	1	2	0	0	2	0	0
Lambert, Clark, C'bia	1.000	10	54	8	0	62	1	2
Lina, Estivinson, Sav.	.964	56	377	46	16	439	3	11
Lopez-Cao, Mike, C.S.C.	.969	9	29	2	1	32	0	0
McGee, Tom, Del.	.989	39	248	23	3	274	3	7
Mortimer, Mark, Mac.	.968	3	29	1	1	31	0	2
Newman, Howard, C.W.Va.	.955	3	21	0	1	22	1	1
Oropeza, Willie, C.F.	.988	11	68	12	1	81	0	2
Paxton, Chris, Del.	1.000	4	25	1	0	26	0	0
Peters, Tony, Hag.	1.000	1	1	0	0	1	0	0
Phelps, Josh, Hag.	.975	85	688	62	19	769	1	17
Phillips, Jason, C'bia	.994	68	575	52	4	631	5	5
PINTO, Rene, Gre.	.996	108	909	93	4	1006	2	16
Pugh, Josh, Mac.	.984	39	340	28	6	374	2	13
Reyes, Jose, Aug.	.993	14	125	18	1	144	1	6
Rivera, Francisco, C.W.Va.	1.000	2	14	2	0	16	0	0
Rivera, Luis A., C.F.	.994	31	139	14	1	154	0	4
Rivera, Luis J., C.F.	.987	24	139	17	2	158	0	2
Rodriguez, Mike, Hag.	.988	11	73	9	1	83	2	1
Salazar, Jeremy, Pied.	.995	40	347	36	2	385	1	3
Salinas, Trey, C.S.C.	1.000	11	106	9	0	115	1	3
Sandusky, Scott, C.F.	.980	49	283	53	7	343	5	2
Schneider, Brian, C.F.	.980	35	261	32	6	299	0	2
Seabol, Scott, Gre.	1.000	1	1	0	0	1	0	0
Sienko, Ryan, Sav.	.958	11	60	9	3	72	2	1
Stanton, Tom, C'bia	.991	23	192	20	2	214	0	4
Staubach, Jeff, Gre.	1.000	2	4	0	0	4	0	0
Stevenson, Chad, Mac.	.989	31	236	40	3	279	3	2
Suriel, Miguel, C.S.C.	.964	4	23	4	1	28	0	4
Sutton, Joe, Hick.	.985	56	403	51	7	461	3	18
Torrealba, Steve, Mac.	.988	62	500	58	7	565	3	9
Torres, Jason, Sav.	.982	19	99	8	2	109	1	5
Twombley, Dennis, Gre.	.997	38	286	34	1	321	0	5
Vidal, Gilbert, Ash.	.972	31	228	17	7	252	3	6
Washington, Rico, Aug.	1.000	1	6	3	0	9	1	0
Werth, Jayson, Del.	.991	111	863	131	9	1003	5	15
Whitehead, Braxton, C.W.Va.	.985	75	516	74	9	599	6	7
Williams, Mike, C.W.Va.	.966	11	47	10	2	59	1	3

TRIPLE PLAY: Lina.

PITCHERS

Player, Team	Pct.	G	PO	A	E	TC	DP
Abbott, Jim, Hick.*	1.000	1	0	4	0	4	0
Acevedo, Jose, C.W.Va.	.966	25	6	22	1	29	1
Achilles, Matt, Del.	.912	26	9	22	3	34	0
Agamennone, Brandon, C.F.	.833	6	1	4	1	6	1
Allen, Rodney, Sav.	.500	4	0	2	2	4	0
Alvarado, Carlos, Aug.	1.000	14	3	7	0	10	0
Andrews, Clayton, Hag.*	1.000	27	7	21	0	28	2
Averette, Robert, C.W.Va.	.960	14	9	15	1	25	0
Bacci, Tony, Aug.*	.769	27	3	7	3	13	1
Bailey, Roger, Ash.	1.000	1	1	1	0	2	0
Baker, Jason, C.F.*	1.000	5	0	2	0	2	0
Barry, Shawn, C'bia*	.833	52	3	7	2	12	1
Bauer, Chuck, Aug.	1.000	6	0	2	0	2	0
Bauer, Richard, Aug.	1.000	22	1	17	0	18	0
Bauldree, Joe, Mac.	.750	29	9	3	4	16	0
Bausher, Andy, Aug.*	.882	24	2	13	2	17	2
Bautista, Martin, C'bus	1.000	7	0	3	0	3	1
Becks, Ryan, C.F.*	.950	28	13	25	2	40	0
Beitey, Jason, Sav.	1.000	1	1	1	0	2	0
Belitz, Todd, C.S.C.*	.968	21	9	21	1	31	2
Benoit, Joaquin, Sav.	.929	15	5	8	1	14	1
Berger, Craig, C'bia	1.000	5	0	1	0	1	0
Black, Brett, Pied.	1.000	58	3	4	0	7	0
BLANK, Matt, C.F.*	1.000	21	15	27	0	42	1
Blevins, Jeremy, Gre.	.923	24	8	16	2	26	4
Bond, Aaron, Sav.	.955	28	6	15	1	22	1
Borne, Matt, Hick.	.667	15	1	1	1	3	0
Bowles, Brian, Hag.	1.000	31	4	13	0	17	1
Box, John, C.S.C.*	1.000	55	4	17	0	21	1
Brackeen, Colin, Hag.*	.867	37	2	11	2	15	1
Bravo, Franklin, Aug.	1.000	20	3	3	0	6	0
Brazoban, Melvin, Sav.	.933	18	8	6	1	15	0
Brewer, Clint, C.W.Va.	1.000	35	4	14	0	18	0
Brito, Juan, C'bia*	1.000	13	1	3	0	4	0
Brown, Derek, Del.	.950	55	4	15	1	20	0
Brown, Elliot, C.S.C.	.889	40	8	16	3	27	1
Brueggemann, Dean, Ash.*	1.000	41	4	20	0	24	0
Caddell, Carl, C.W.Va.*	.400	15	0	2	3	5	0
Cammack, Eric, C'bia	1.000	25	2	4	0	6	0
Cardona, Steve, Hick.	.889	44	6	10	2	18	0
Carrion, Jorge, Sav.	.955	15	7	14	1	22	1
Carter, Roger, C.S.C.	.833	13	1	4	1	6	0
Casey, Joe, Hag.	.917	22	8	14	2	24	0
Castillo, Alberto, Gre.*	1.000	5	0	1	0	1	0
Choate, Randy, Gre.*	.889	8	1	7	1	9	1
Ciravolo, Jon, Mac.	1.000	16	1	4	0	5	0
Combs, Chris, Aug.	.933	33	11	17	2	30	1
Cook, O.J., Aug.	1.000	47	6	2	0	8	1
Corcoran, Tim, C'bia	1.000	20	1	3	0	4	0
Cotton, Joe, Pied.	1.000	44	3	9	0	12	1
Crawford, Danny, Aug.	1.000	20	8	19	0	27	2
Cremer, Rick, Gre.*	1.000	13	2	17	0	19	0
Crowell, Jim, C.W.Va.*	1.000	5	1	3	0	4	0
Cummins, Jon, C.S.C.	.000	8	0	0	1	1	0
Currens, Tim, Hick.	1.000	28	5	5	0	10	1
Cutchins, Todd, C'bia*	.905	23	11	27	4	42	1
Daneker, Pat, Hick.	.953	17	9	32	2	43	0
Danner, Andy, C.W.Va.	.833	21	2	8	2	12	2
Davis, Kane, Aug.	1.000	2	0	1	0	1	0
Day, Zach, Gre.	1.000	7	1	6	0	7	0
Deckard, Edward, C.S.C.	1.000	3	1	1	0	2	0
De La Cruz, Francisco, Gre.	.857	5	2	4	1	7	0
Dishman, Richard, Mac.	.750	18	1	2	1	4	0
Dougherty, James, C'bia*	.967	20	4	25	1	30	1
Drew, Tim, C'bus	1.000	13	1	12	0	13	1
Duckworth, Brandon, Pied.	1.000	21	8	30	0	38	2
Duff, Matt, Aug.	1.000	10	0	2	0	2	0
Eason, Clay, Pied.	1.000	34	4	5	0	9	0
Ellison, Jason, Gre.	1.000	54	3	10	0	13	1
Embry, Byron, Mac.	.875	50	3	4	1	8	0
Emiliano, Jamie, Ash.	1.000	41	5	2	0	7	0
Estrella, Leo, C'bia-Hag.	.905	25	9	29	4	42	1
Eversgerd, Randy, Hag.	1.000	11	6	0	0	7	0
Felix, Miguel, Hick.	.893	21	7	18	3	28	1
Fenus, Justin, Pied.	.930	30	17	23	3	43	0
Fitzpatrick, Luke, Hick.*	1.000	20	3	6	0	9	1
Fleck, Will, Mac.	.818	48	0	9	2	11	1
Fleming, Emar, Sav.	.958	37	8	15	1	24	2
Flores, Randy, Gre.*	.974	21	8	29	1	38	3
Fogg, Josh, Hick.	1.000	8	3	2	0	5	0
Frey, Christopher, Sav.	1.000	7	0	2	0	2	0

CLASS A South Atlantic League

Player, Team	Pct.	G	PO	A	E	TC	DP
Garcia, Ariel, Hick.	1.000	9	1	6	0	7	0
Garcia, Sonny, Del.	1.000	4	2	8	0	10	0
Gardner, Lee, C.S.C.	.818	28	4	5	2	11	0
Gardner, Nathan, C.W.Va.	.952	45	6	14	1	21	2
Garland, Jon, Hick.	1.000	5	2	8	0	10	0
Gaskill, Derek, C'bia.	.857	29	3	9	2	14	2
Giron, Isabel, Hag.	.857	21	7	11	3	21	0
Goetz, Geoff, C'bia*.	.895	15	4	13	2	19	0
Gonzalez, Armando, Ash.	1.000	11	2	3	0	5	0
Gonzalez, Dicky, C'bia	.953	18	11	30	2	43	4
Gonzalez, Ignacio, C.S.C.	.952	30	7	13	1	21	1
Gonzalez, Mike, Aug.*	.800	11	0	8	2	10	0
Gorman, Pat, C'bia	.875	42	6	8	2	16	0
Grabow, John, Aug.*	.944	17	3	14	1	18	0
Greene, Ryan, Mac.	.875	22	3	4	1	8	1
Guillory, Dan, C'bia.	1.000	20	1	8	0	9	0
Guy, Brad, Aug.	.917	56	2	20	2	24	1
Guzman, Wilson, Aug.*	1.000	42	2	9	0	11	0
Halpin, Jeremy, Del.	.966	57	7	21	1	29	1
Hamilton, Jon, C'bus*	.000	1	0	0	1	1	0
Haring, Brett, C.W.Va.*	1.000	38	5	34	0	39	0
Harrison, Scott, C'bus	.857	27	11	13	4	28	0
Heath, Woody, Hag.	.962	24	7	18	1	26	3
Hebson, Bryan, C.F.	.929	16	5	8	1	14	0
Hootselle, Jeff, Pied.*	1.000	24	2	3	0	5	0
Horgan, Joe, C'bus*	.750	22	0	3	1	4	1
Howard, Tom, C.S.C.*	.929	33	3	10	1	14	0
Huff, Tim, Hag.*	.857	26	4	2	1	7	0
Huggins, David, Hag.	.600	12	0	3	2	5	0
Hughes, Mike, C'bus*	.923	18	3	9	1	13	0
Huntsman, Brandon, Del.	1.000	23	1	13	0	14	0
Izquierdo, Hansel, Hick.	.818	28	10	17	6	33	1
James, Delvin, C.S.C.	1.000	7	0	1	0	1	0
Johnson, David, Ash.	1.000	17	0	2	0	2	1
Johnston, Clint, Aug.*	1.000	16	2	5	0	7	0
Johnston, Sean, C'bia*	1.000	11	3	7	0	10	2
Julio, Jorge, C.F.	1.000	6	3	0	0	3	0
Kalinowski, Josh, Ash.*	.953	28	8	33	2	43	3
Kelly, Jeff, Aug.*	.800	18	2	6	2	10	0
Kertis, John, Sav.	.833	38	3	7	2	12	0
Key, Calvin, Pied.	.905	26	5	14	2	21	1
Kimbrell, Mike, C.S.C.*	.889	13	2	6	1	9	0
Kingrey, Jarrod, Hag.	.000	1	0	0	1	1	0
Koeman, Matt, C'bus	1.000	31	5	7	0	12	0
Krall, Eric, Gre.*	1.000	14	0	5	0	5	0
Kringen, Jake, Ash.*	.886	28	8	23	4	35	1
Lanzetta, Tobin, C.F.	.833	38	4	6	2	12	0
Lara, Yovanny, C.F.	1.000	22	1	7	0	8	0
Layne, Roger, C'bus.	1.000	4	4	1	0	5	0
Lee, Chris, Del.	.800	19	0	4	1	5	0
Leon, Scott, C.S.C.	1.000	5	1	1	0	2	1
Levy, Tye, C.W.Va.*	1.000	34	3	14	0	17	1
Lewis, Craig, Gre.	.902	28	9	28	4	41	1
Lewis, Derrick, Mac.	.833	23	6	14	4	24	0
Lohrman, Dave, C'bia	1.000	21	1	4	0	5	0
Lopez, Jose, Hick.	1.000	33	2	11	0	13	1
Lovingood, Ray, C'bia*	.800	6	1	3	1	5	0
Lundberg, David, Sav.	.947	50	5	13	1	19	1
Maberry, Mark, C'bia	1.000	12	2	3	0	5	2
Madison, Scott, C.S.C.*	.895	9	3	14	2	19	0
Manbeck, Mark, Pied.	.667	7	2	2	2	6	0
Marsonek, Sam, Sav.	.667	2	0	2	1	3	1
Martinez, Caleb, Pied.*	.875	13	3	4	1	8	1
Matcuk, Steve, Ash.	.957	13	7	15	1	23	2
Matz, Brian, C.F.*	1.000	17	5	16	0	21	0
McBride, Jason, Gre.	1.000	7	1	3	0	4	0
McClellan, Matt, Hag.	.860	25	19	18	6	43	1
McConnell, Sam, Aug.*	1.000	8	3	12	0	15	0
McNally, Andrew, C'bus	1.000	38	3	3	0	6	0
Medina, Carlos, Del.*	.923	22	1	11	1	13	0
Mejias, Oliver, Aug.	1.000	2	1	0	0	1	0
Merrell, Phil, C.W.Va.	.885	26	4	19	3	26	0
Meyer, Jake, Hick.	1.000	35	4	9	0	13	2
Miller, Justin, Ash.	.862	27	8	17	4	29	1
Miller, Matt, Sav.	1.000	17	2	6	0	8	0
Montero, Francisco, Pied.	.963	20	13	13	1	27	0
Myette, Aaron, Hick.	.842	17	7	9	3	19	0
Nation, Joey, Mac.*	.939	29	3	28	2	33	1
Negrette, Richard, C'bia	1.000	21	6	9	0	15	1
Nichols, Jamie, Hick.	.500	11	0	2	2	4	0
Obando, Omar, Gre.	.857	21	2	4	1	7	0
O'Toole, Ryan, C.W.Va.	.500	4	1	0	1	2	0
Pacheco, Delvis, Mac.	1.000	18	2	6	0	8	0
Pacheco, Enemecio, Ash.	1.000	2	0	1	0	1	0
Peguero, Americo, Del.	.800	15	1	3	1	5	0
Perez, Elvis, Hick.*	.500	3	0	1	1	2	0
Perez, Julio, C'bus	.800	9	1	3	1	5	1
Perez, Julio, C.F.	1.000	9	2	4	0	6	0
Perez, Norberto, Del.	.778	24	0	7	2	9	0
Petrosian, Ara, Ash.	.000	18	0	0	1	1	0
Phelps, Travis, C.S.C.	1.000	18	9	18	0	27	1
Pirkl, Greg, C'bus	.800	26	1	3	1	5	0
Plummer, Raymond, C.F.*	1.000	31	1	5	0	6	0
Presley, Kirk, C'bia.	1.000	3	0	1	0	1	0
Price, Chris, Ash.	.667	18	2	2	2	6	0
Price, Ryan, Ash.	.919	27	11	23	3	37	3
Puffer, Brandon, C.W.Va.	.625	29	3	7	6	16	0
Queen, Mike, C'bia*	1.000	2	1	1	0	2	0
Quevedo, Ruben, Mac.	.938	25	6	9	1	16	0
Quezada, Edward, C.F.	.875	30	5	16	3	24	2
Ramirez, Horacio, Mac.*	1.000	12	3	10	0	13	0
Ramos, Fernando, Pied.	.857	26	0	6	1	7	2
Ramos, Juan, C.F.	1.000	25	6	7	0	13	0
Reichow, Bob, C'bus	1.000	39	9	15	0	24	1
Reith, Brian, Gre.	.818	20	6	12	4	22	1
Reyes, Eddy, C.S.C.	1.000	56	4	8	0	12	0
Richardson, Kasey, Del.*	1.000	16	2	11	0	13	0
Riggan, Jerrod, C'bia	1.000	14	1	8	0	9	1
Riley, Matthew, Del.*	.750	16	1	11	4	16	0
Rivera, Luis, Mac.	.923	20	4	20	2	26	1
Rivera, Luis A., C.F.	1.000	1	0	1	0	1	0
Robinson, Dustin, C.W.Va.	.933	25	8	20	2	30	1
Rogers, Brian, Gre.	1.000	3	1	3	0	4	1
Romero, Jordan, Del.	.938	15	3	12	1	16	0
Rosa, Cristy, Ash.	1.000	18	3	8	0	11	1
Rupe, Ryan, C.S.C.	.941	10	9	7	1	17	1
Salley, Anthony, Hag.*	1.000	20	4	5	0	9	0
Salyers, Jeremy, C.F.	.857	42	6	12	3	21	0
Santana, Humberto, C'bia*	1.000	5	0	5	0	5	0
Sarmiento, Dan, C'bus*	.833	6	1	4	1	6	0
Saylor, Ryan, C.F.	.833	24	4	1	1	6	1
Scarce, Bubba, Mac.	.889	20	5	3	1	9	0
Schaffner, Eric, Gre.	1.000	14	3	9	0	12	1
Schorzman, Steve, Hick.	.800	23	3	5	2	10	1
Schurman, Ryan, Mac.	.850	17	4	13	3	20	1
Scott, Brian, Hick.	1.000	6	2	3	0	5	1
Seabury, Jaron, Hag.	1.000	45	2	7	0	9	1
Seay, Bobby, C.S.C.*	1.000	15	3	10	0	13	0
Seifert, Ryan, Ash.	1.000	36	5	17	0	22	1
Sellers, Roger, C.W.Va.	1.000	12	1	2	0	3	1
Sequea, Jacobo, C.W.Va.	.800	13	2	14	4	20	1
Serrano, Jim, C.F.	1.000	15	2	4	0	6	0
Shaw, Curtis, Aug.*	1.000	2	0	4	0	4	0
Sheldon, Kyle, C.F.	1.000	4	0	1	0	1	0
Shepard, David, C.W.Va.	.905	16	6	13	2	21	1
Shipp, Kevin, Pied.	.943	28	18	32	3	53	1
Shourds, Anthony, Sav.	.882	37	5	10	2	17	0
Shumate, Jacob, Mac.	.545	44	3	3	5	11	0
Siciliano, Jess, Aug.	.500	5	0	1	1	2	0
Sido, Wilson, C'bus	1.000	4	1	4	0	5	0
Siegel, Justin, Sav.*	1.000	7	1	9	0	10	1
Silva, Douglas, Sav.	1.000	38	1	7	0	8	1
Silva, Troy, C'bia	.778	16	4	10	4	18	0
Smart, J.D., C.F.	1.000	3	3	1	0	4	0
Smith, Ryan, Sav.*	.889	35	4	4	1	9	0
Sneed, John, Hag.	.920	27	8	15	2	25	2
Solano, Manny, C.W.Va.	.750	18	2	4	2	8	0
Sparks, Steve, Aug.	1.000	2	3	1	0	4	0
Spence, Cam, Gre.	1.000	8	0	11	0	11	0
Spencer, Jeff, Mac.	1.000	2	0	1	0	1	0
Spenser, Kaipo, C'bus	.923	11	3	9	1	13	1
Spiegel, Mike, C'bus*	.933	13	3	11	1	15	1
Spurgeon, Jay, Del.	.971	27	6	27	1	34	3
Spurling, Chris, Gre.	1.000	1	0	3	0	3	0
Stabile, Paul, Aug.*	.789	29	2	13	4	19	1
Stephens, John, Del.	.778	6	5	2	2	9	0
Stockstill, Jason, Hick.*	1.000	10	1	1	0	2	0
Strickland, Scott, C.F.	1.000	15	4	5	0	9	0
Tapia, Rafael, Del.	1.000	2	1	0	0	1	1
Taylor, Brien, Gre.*	.667	13	1	1	1	3	0
Tellez, Eloy, Hick.	1.000	4	0	1	0	1	0
Temple, Jason, Aug.	1.000	13	0	2	0	2	0
Theodile, Simeon, Del.	1.000	19	0	4	0	4	0
Thieme, Richard, Mac.*	.850	16	1	16	3	20	0

Player, Team	Pct.	G	PO	A	E	TC	DP
Thompson, Doug, Ash.	1.000	9	1	0	0	1	0
Thompson, Travis, Ash.	.939	26	16	15	2	33	3
Tilton, Ira, Pied.	.875	28	2	5	1	8	0
Tokarse, Brian, Hick.	1.000	2	1	0	0	1	0
Turman, Jimmy, C.F.	.926	21	9	16	2	27	3
Turnbow, Mark, C'bus	.933	17	8	20	2	30	0
Tynan, Chris, Sav.	.889	21	5	11	2	18	0
Vael, Rob, C'bus	.833	9	1	4	1	6	0
Valle, Yoiset, Gre.*	.833	33	2	8	2	12	0
Van Gilder, Ryan, C.F.	.944	30	6	11	1	18	0
Virchis, Adam, Hick.	1.000	9	1	9	0	10	0
Wagner, Ken, C'bus	.778	33	1	6	2	9	1
Walker, Adam, Pied.*	.833	15	1	4	1	6	0
Walker, Tyler, C'bia	.909	34	7	13	2	22	1
Wallace, Chris, Gre.	.917	54	4	18	2	24	0
Watson, Mark, C'bus*	.897	31	6	20	3	29	1
Weimer, Matt, Hag.	.917	48	8	14	2	24	1
Westmoreland, Ken, Pied.	.875	5	4	3	1	8	0
Weymouth, Marty, Hick.	.952	31	7	13	1	21	1

Player, Team	Pct.	G	PO	A	E	TC	DP
Wheeler, Dan, C.S.C.	.974	29	9	28	1	38	1
White, Darell, Sav.	.882	13	6	9	2	17	0
White, Matt, C.S.C.	.778	12	5	9	4	18	0
Whitley, Curtis, Hick.*	.875	22	3	11	2	16	0
Wiggins, Scott, Gre.*	1.000	14	1	13	0	14	0
Williams, Larry, Aug.	.857	35	3	9	2	14	1
Wise, William, Del.	.857	34	1	11	2	14	0
Wood, Stanton, Gre.	1.000	31	1	8	0	9	0
Wrigley, Jase, Ash.	1.000	13	3	2	0	5	1
Wyatt, Ben, Mac.*	.867	41	4	9	2	15	0
Yankosky, L. J., Mac.	.923	20	7	5	1	13	1
Young, Joe, Hag.	1.000	7	2	1	0	3	0
Zambrano, Victor, C.S.C.	.964	48	10	17	1	28	1

PITCHERS WITH TWO OR MORE TEAMS

Player, Team	Pct.	G	PO	A	E	TC	DP
Estrella, Leo, C'bia	.886	20	5	26	4	35	0
Estrella, Leo, Hag.	1.000	5	4	3	0	7	1

The following players did not have any fielding statistics at the positions indicated or appeared only as a designated hitter, pinch-hitter or pinch-runner: Albaral, 1b; Allison, ss; Aracena, p; Ayers, p; Baderdeen, of; Bagley, 2b; Bailie, p; Bass, p; Behn, p; Bello, p; Blakeney, p; Borbon, p; Civit, p; Eavenson, p; Fontaine, p; Sandro Garcia, p; Hale, p; Hamen, dh; C. Jaramillo, p; Lopez, 3b; Luttig, p; Mathys, p; McEntire, p; McGee, of; Montilla, dh; Moreno, 2b; Murphy, p; Pacheco, dh; A. Pena, p; J. Phelps, 3b, of; Reynolds, p; Roach, of, p; M. Rodriguez, ss; Ryan, p; Salinas, of; Santos, 2b; Schreiner, p; Seabol, p; Shiell, p; Smoltz, p; Strange, ss; C. Taylor, 1b; Thomson, p; Torrealba, 3b; R. Washington, ss; Ware, 1b; M. Young, of; Zepeda, 1b, of.

LEAGUE CHAMPIONS

Year	Team	Pct.
1948—	Lincolnton*	.627
1949—	Newton-Conover	.667
	Rutherford Co. (2nd)†	.627
1950—	Newton-Conover	.627
	Lenoir (2nd)†	.626
1951—	Morganton	.645
	Shelby (2nd)†	.604
1952—	Lincolnton	.649
	Shelby (2nd)†	.645
1953-59—	League inactive.	
1960—	Lexington	.707
	Salisbury (2nd)†	.650
1961—	Salisbury	.627
	Shelby (4th)†	.481
1962—	Statesville	.563
	Statesville	.700
1963—	Greenville†	.576
	Salisbury	.631
1964—	Rock Hill	.672
	Salisbury‡	.631
1965—	Salisbury	.641
	Rock Hill‡	.603
1966—	Spartanburg	.682
	Spartanburg	.767
1967—	Spartanburg	.730
	Spartanburg	.567
1968—	Spartanburg	.597
	Greenwood‡	.597
1969—	Greenwood‡	.587
	Shelby	.565

Year	Team	Pct.
1970—	Greenville	.576
	Greenville	.619
1971—	Greenwood	.631
	Greenwood	.759
1972—	Spartanburg‡	.788
	Greenville	.652
1973—	Spartanburg‡	.646
	Gastonia	.619
1974—	Gastonia	.606
	Gastonia	.672
1975—	Spartanburg	.543
	Spartanburg	.614
1976—	Asheville	.544
	Greenwood‡	.600
1977—	Greenwood	.557
	Gastonia‡	.590
1978—	Greenwood	.614
	Greenwood	.565
1979—	Greenwood‡	.565
	Spartanburg	.525
1980—	Greensboro	.590
	Charleston	.561
1981—	Greensboro‡	.695
	Greenwood	.549
1982—	Greensboro‡	.681
	Florence	.546
1983—	Columbia	.620
	Gastonia‡	.587
1984—	Charleston	.549
	Asheville‡	.510

Year	Team	Pct.
1985—	Florence‡	.599
	Greensboro	.540
1986—	Columbia‡	.682
	Asheville	.643
1987—	Asheville	.655
	Myrtle Beach‡	.597
1988—	Charleston (S.C.)	.616
	Spartanburg‡	.500
1989—	Gastonia	.657
	Augusta‡	.535
1990—	Columbia	.580
	Charleston (W.Va.)‡	.538
1991—	Charleston (W.Va.)	.648
	Columbia‡	.614
1992—	Columbia	.572
	Myrtle Beach‡	.522
1993—	Savannah‡	.662
	Greensboro	.603
1994—	Columbus	.630
	Savannah‡	.599
1995—	Piedmont	.586
	Augusta‡	.551
1996—	Delmarva	.585
	Savannah†	.511
1997—	Delmarva§	.543
	Greensboro	.536
1998—	Columbia§	.638
	Hagerstown	.574

*Won championship and four-club playoff. †Won four-club playoff. ‡Won split-season playoff. §Won split season, eight-club playoff. (NOTE—Known as Western Carolina League from 1948 through 1962 and known as Western Carolinas League through 1979.)

CLASS A *South Atlantic League*

APPALACHIAN LEAGUE

LEAGUE OFFICE

President
Lee Landers
Address
283 Deerchase Circle
Statesville, NC 28625
Phone
704-873-5300

Teams (affiliation)
Bluefield Orioles (Orioles)
Bristol White Sox (White Sox)
Burlington Indians (Indians)
Danville Braves (Braves)
Elizabethton Twins (Twins)
Johnson City Cardinals (Cardinals)

Kingsport Mets (Mets)
Martinsville (Name to be announced)
  (Astros)
Princeton Devil Rays (Devil Rays)
Pulaski Rangers (Rangers)

1998 FINAL STANDINGS

NORTH DIVISION

Team	W	L	T	Pct.	GB
Princeton (Devil Rays)	38	30	0	.559	....
Bluefield (Orioles)	33	34	0	.493	4.5
Martinsville (Phillies)	32	36	0	.471	6.0
Burlington (Indians)	31	36	0	.463	6.5
Danville (Braves)	30	38	0	.441	8.0

SOUTH DIVISION

Team	W	L	T	Pct.	GB
Bristol (White Sox)	42	24	0	.636	....
Elizabethton (Twins)	38	29	0	.567	4.5
Kingsport (Mets)	38	30	0	.559	5.0
Pulaski (Rangers)	29	37	0	.439	13.0
Johnson City (Cardinals)	25	42	0	.373	17.5

COMPOSITE

Team	Bri.	Eliz.	Pri.	King.	Blu.	Mar.	Burl.	Dan.	Pul.	J.C.	W	L	T	Pct.	GB
Bristol (White Sox)	....	5	4	8	4	5	4	4	4	4	42	24	0	.636	....
Elizabethton (Twins)	5	....	5	3	5	2	2	6	3	7	38	29	0	.567	4.5
Princeton (Devil Rays)	2	1	....	2	8	5	6	4	6	4	38	30	0	.559	5.0
Kingsport (Mets)	4	7	4	....	3	2	2	4	4	8	38	30	0	.559	5.0
Bluefield (Orioles)	2	1	4	3	....	3	3	7	7	3	33	34	0	.493	9.5
Martinsville (Phillies)	1	4	1	4	3	....	5	5	5	4	32	36	0	.471	11.0
Burlington (Indians)	2	3	4	4	3	5	....	3	3	4	31	36	0	.463	11.5
Danville (Braves)	2	0	2	2	3	5	9	....	3	4	30	38	0	.441	13.0
Pulaski (Rangers)	0	3	4	2	3	7	3	3	....	4	29	37	0	.439	13.0
Johnson City (Cardinals)	6	5	2	2	2	2	2	2	2	....	25	42	0	.373	17.5

Major league affiliations in parentheses.

PLAYOFFS—Bristol defeated Princeton two games to none to win league championship.

REGULAR-SEASON ATTENDANCE: Bluefield, 39,940; Bristol, 26,966; Burlington, 45,495; Danville, 50,711; Elizabethton, 10,665; Johnson City, 19,684; Kingsport, 49,579; Martinsville, 44,501; Princeton, 36,548; Pulaski, 8,812. Total—332,901. Playoffs (2 games)—1,731.

MANAGERS: Bluefield, Andy Etchebarren; Bristol, Nick Capra; Burlington, Joe Mikulik; Danville, Franklin Stubbs; Elizabethton, Jon Mathews; Johnson City, Steve Turco; Kingsport, Tim Foli; Martinsville, Greg Legg; Princeton, Dave Howard; Pulaski, Bruce Crabbe.

ALL-STAR TEAM: 1B—Nate Espy, Martinsville; 2B—Rafael Furcal, Danville; 3B—(tie) Paul Day, Burlington and Travis Wilson, Danville; SS—Jack Wilson, Johnson City; Utility INF—Kevin Hodge, Elizabethton; OF—Brian McMillin, Elizabethton; Michael Restovich, Elizabethton; Mario Valenzuela, Bristol; Utility OF—Brian Cole, Kingsport; C—Humberto Cota, Princeton; DH—Manny Lutz, Bristol; RHP—Gary Bohannon, Kingsport; LHP—Jeremy Robinson, Princeton; RP—James Lira, Princeton; Player of the Year—Michael Restovich, Elizabethton; Pitcher of the Year—Jeremy Robinson, Princeton; Manager of the Year—Nick Capra, Bristol.

1998 BATTING

TEAM

Team	Avg.	G	TPA	AB	R	H	TB	2B	3B	HR	RBI	SH	SF	HP	BB	IBB	SO	SB	CS	GDP	LOB	ShO	Slg.	OBP
Elizabethton	.289	67	2741	2336	462	676	1039	127	13	70	402	8	22	46	329	7	490	61	26	65	554	1	.445	.385
Bristol	.279	66	2661	2302	447	643	1022	117	17	76	390	22	20	35	282	6	477	100	28	42	476	1	.444	.364
Pulaski	.276	66	2542	2214	363	610	861	99	22	36	308	13	24	26	265	4	496	81	38	41	476	4	.389	.346
Burlington	.271	67	2500	2253	335	611	881	100	16	46	297	9	16	18	204	6	529	92	41	38	442	2	.391	.334
Princeton	.270	68	2649	2309	413	624	930	105	27	49	349	32	22	38	248	8	556	72	34	42	466	2	.403	.348
Kingsport	.268	68	2596	2287	386	614	960	126	35	50	330	36	19	42	212	4	439	90	50	31	425	4	.420	.339
Johnson City	.259	68	2564	2309	351	598	916	107	26	53	295	8	12	32	203	2	596	93	34	38	458	3	.397	.326
Danville	.256	68	2628	2297	359	589	833	114	17	32	294	11	16	38	266	4	563	151	45	39	506	4	.363	.341
Martinsville	.256	68	2642	2325	361	596	861	101	19	42	303	11	15	37	254	2	586	92	31	30	503	1	.370	.337
Bluefield	.256	67	2525	2230	331	571	834	90	19	45	283	11	20	27	237	4	473	70	40	40	455	4	.374	.332

INDIVIDUAL

TOP QUALIFIERS FOR BATTING CHAMPIONSHIP

Minimum 184 plate appearances. *Lefthanded batter. †Switch-hitter.

Player, Team	Avg.	G	TPA	AB	R	H	TB	2B	3B	HR	RBI	SH	SF	HP	BB	IBB	SO	SB	CS	GDP	Slg.	OBP
Wilson, Jack, J.C.†	.373	61	263	241	50	90	128	18	4	4	29	1	0	3	18	0	30	22	6	4	.531	.424
Day, Paul, Burl.	.362	60	251	229	33	83	124	16	2	7	45	0	3	2	17	0	39	10	0	6	.541	.406
Espy, Nate, Mar.	.361	66	287	227	50	82	143	20	1	13	56	1	4	4	51	1	55	2	2	4	.630	.479
Restovich, Mike, Eliz.	.355	65	305	242	68	86	147	20	1	13	64	0	0	9	54	0	58	5	2	10	.607	.489
Valenzuela, Mario, Bris.	.330	61	262	233	44	77	122	13	1	10	46	0	2	3	24	1	49	6	4	3	.524	.397
Furcal, Rafael, Dan.†	.328	66	309	268	56	88	111	15	4	0	23	1	1	3	36	0	29	60	15	2	.414	.412
Mann, Derek, Prin.*	.325	68	315	280	63	91	116	10	6	1	32	2	0	1	32	1	46	16	7	4	.414	.396
Wilson, Travis, Dan.	.323	65	291	269	48	87	149	25	5	9	48	0	1	4	17	1	54	16	5	5	.554	.371
Centile, Raul, Burl.†	.320	53	201	181	27	58	75	6	1	3	22	0	0	2	18	1	36	3	4	6	.414	.382

Player, Team	Avg.	G	TPA	AB	R	H	TB	2B	3B	HR	RBI	SH	SF	HP	BB	IBB	SO	SB	CS	GDP	Slg.	OBP
Fennell, Jason, Bris.†	.318	47	199	170	40	54	85	8	1	7	33	0	5	1	23	1	25	0	1	5	.500	.392
Ottevaere, Derek, Pul.	.314	54	233	204	32	64	90	11	3	3	40	1	4	4	20	0	41	5	1	4	.441	.379
Gonzalez, Jose, Bris.	.312	51	231	205	39	64	81	14	0	1	24	3	1	4	18	0	35	16	5	5	.395	.377
Beverly, Shomari, Mar.	.311	44	195	177	37	55	83	13	6	1	25	1	2	2	13	0	51	12	5	4	.469	.361
Nina, Amuarys, Pul.	.310	50	205	174	34	54	71	9	4	0	20	0	2	4	25	0	35	9	9	5	.408	.405
Cota, Humberto, Prin.	.310	67	287	245	48	76	142	13	4	15	61	1	3	6	32	1	59	4	4	3	.580	.399

DEPARTMENTAL LEADERS: G—Mann, 68; AB—Mann, 280; R—Restovich, 68; H—Mann, 91; TB—Lutz, 157; 2B—T. Wilson, 25; 3B—Cole, Newkirk, 8 each; HR—Lutz, 17; RBI—Restovich, 64; SH—Nestor Perez, 17; SF—Pursell, 8; HP—Milton, Restovich, 9 each; BB—Restovich, 54; IBB—Esquerra, 3; SO—Harris, 97; SB—Furcal, 60; CS—Furcal, 15; GIDP—G. Torres, 10; Slg.—Espy, .630; OBP—Restovich, .489.

ALL PLAYERS

*Lefthanded batter. †Switch-hitter.

Player, Team	Avg.	G	TPA	AB	R	H	TB	2B	3B	HR	RBI	SH	SF	HP	BB	IBB	SO	SB	CS	GDP	Slg.	OBP
Acevas, Jonathan, Bris.	.296	43	170	135	29	40	70	12	3	4	30	3	1	2	29	0	38	1	3	2	.519	.425
Acevedo, Carlos, Mar.	.237	64	262	249	31	59	79	11	3	1	25	0	0	1	12	0	32	6	6	2	.317	.275
Aldridge, Cory, Dan.*	.294	60	247	214	37	63	90	16	1	3	33	1	1	2	29	1	48	16	2	3	.421	.382
Allen, Troy, Dan.*	.271	63	271	236	32	64	90	17	0	3	32	0	1	2	32	2	63	2	2	3	.381	.362
Almonte, Claudio, Eliz.	.303	62	261	241	45	73	107	10	3	6	40	0	0	2	18	1	57	12	2	6	.444	.356
Alvarez, Jimmy, Eliz.	.219	46	195	155	32	34	50	8	4	0	14	2	2	3	33	0	37	6	2	4	.323	.363
Alvarez, Nelson, King.	.229	21	55	48	8	11	18	1	3	0	4	2	0	1	4	0	15	1	1	0	.375	.302
Arias, Jeison, Prin.	.247	54	192	170	29	42	65	8	0	5	26	3	2	2	15	1	53	6	0	7	.382	.312
Backe, Brandon, Prin.	.250	27	106	92	14	23	30	5	1	0	7	0	1	1	12	0	31	1	1	1	.326	.340
Ballard, Ryan, Prin.	.258	15	37	31	5	8	10	2	0	0	2	0	0	0	6	0	7	0	0	1	.323	.378
Banez, Marco, J.C.*	.197	38	146	137	18	27	32	1	2	0	7	0	0	1	8	0	26	3	2	2	.234	.247
Barlow, Marlon, Prin.*	.216	14	44	37	6	8	10	2	0	0	3	1	0	2	4	0	6	3	2	0	.270	.326
Bastardo, Angel, Burl.	.240	51	196	179	29	43	76	12	0	7	25	0	1	1	15	0	59	1	3	2	.425	.301
Batista, Carlos, Burl.	.234	54	212	205	15	48	77	8	0	7	35	1	1	3	2	0	66	2	0	3	.376	.251
Benham, Jason, Blue.*	.223	57	226	202	38	45	75	6	3	6	28	1	1	1	21	0	36	3	1	2	.371	.298
Beverly, Shomari, Mar.	.311	44	195	177	37	55	83	13	6	1	25	1	2	2	13	0	51	12	5	4	.469	.361
Bishop, Bennie, Mar.	.219	51	188	169	24	37	52	7	1	2	19	0	3	0	16	0	45	9	2	1	.308	.298
Bonilla, Juan, Blue.	.269	37	129	119	16	32	49	8	0	3	16	0	2	1	7	1	21	0	1	3	.412	.310
Boscan, Jean, Dan.	.218	51	211	170	35	37	52	3	0	4	24	1	1	2	37	0	44	2	3	4	.306	.342
Bowers, Jason, J.C.	.291	60	236	213	31	62	91	10	5	3	38	1	4	5	13	0	43	10	8	2	.427	.340
Brosam, Eric, Eliz.*	.254	36	129	114	10	29	40	5	0	2	14	1	2	2	10	1	35	0	1	4	.351	.320
Bushman, Jon, Mar.	.400	4	7	5	1	2	4	2	0	0	1	0	0	0	2	0	2	0	1	0	.800	.571
Caines, Franklyn, Mar.	.207	35	124	116	16	24	43	4	0	5	18	0	2	0	6	0	35	1	1	0	.371	.242
Carter, Shannon, Blue.*	.247	36	159	150	23	37	42	2	0	1	10	0	0	0	9	0	35	14	3	1	.280	.289
Carvajal, Ramon, J.C.†	.235	54	224	200	32	47	72	6	2	5	26	1	1	3	19	0	41	11	2	2	.360	.309
Castaneda, Cesar, Pul.	.265	56	232	200	33	53	80	9	0	6	26	2	4	5	21	1	52	1	1	3	.400	.343
Castillo, Geramel, Pul.†	.302	38	167	149	23	45	63	9	3	1	18	1	1	0	16	1	32	4	4	2	.423	.367
Centile, Raul, Burl.†	.320	53	201	181	27	58	75	6	1	3	22	0	0	2	18	1	36	3	4	6	.414	.388
Champagne, Andre, King.	.180	42	156	133	19	24	32	6	1	0	13	2	1	5	15	0	13	4	1	2	.241	.286
Chavez, Endy, King.*	.289	33	137	114	26	33	49	8	4	0	17	0	0	1	17	0	17	10	5	1	.430	.373
Chwan, Brian, Prin.*	.320	36	112	100	14	32	45	7	0	2	13	1	2	0	9	0	15	1	0	3	.450	.369
Cody, Brian, Mar.	.218	24	96	87	10	19	39	6	1	4	18	0	0	0	9	0	19	1	0	4	.448	.292
Cole, Brian, King.	.300	56	241	230	36	69	113	13	8	5	35	1	3	0	7	1	23	15	8	1	.491	.317
Collura, Todd, Eliz.	.205	28	96	88	14	18	27	6	0	1	10	0	1	4	3	0	29	0	0	3	.307	.260
Cota, Humberto, Prin.	.310	67	287	245	48	76	142	13	4	15	61	1	3	6	32	1	59	4	4	3	.580	.399
Davison, Ashanti, Blue.	.255	50	228	196	30	50	67	8	3	1	17	3	1	4	24	0	32	16	8	3	.342	.347
Day, Paul, Bur.	.362	60	251	229	33	83	124	16	2	7	45	0	3	2	17	0	39	10	0	6	.541	.406
Deitrick, Jeremy, Mar.	.292	8	28	24	5	7	7	0	0	0	5	0	0	1	3	0	5	0	1	0	.292	.393
Depippo, Jeff, Burl.	.209	39	134	115	16	24	33	6	0	1	9	0	1	6	10	0	33	0	2	3	.287	.303
Diaz, Maikell, Blue.	.300	11	46	40	4	12	13	1	0	0	6	0	2	0	4	0	6	2	1	0	.325	.348
Durick, Chad, King.	.190	11	46	42	6	8	15	2	1	1	6	0	0	1	3	0	11	0	2	1	.357	.261
Dyt, Darren, Pul.*	.304	59	232	207	31	63	96	9	3	6	27	2	0	1	22	1	52	4	2	7	.464	.374
Edgar, Jason, Pul.*	.291	45	189	151	28	44	56	8	2	0	16	2	1	3	32	0	20	9	2	2	.371	.422
Escalante, Jaime, Blue.†	.247	53	187	166	24	41	59	9	0	3	12	0	0	4	17	1	46	3	1	2	.355	.332
Escobar, Gustavo, J.C.	.236	43	143	127	16	30	49	7	0	4	17	0	1	1	14	0	25	4	3	0	.386	.315
Espino, Jose, J.C.	.236	47	181	165	29	39	69	3	0	9	25	1	0	2	13	0	52	7	3	3	.418	.300
Espy, Nate, Mar.	.361	66	287	227	50	82	143	20	1	13	56	1	4	4	51	1	55	2	2	4	.630	.479
Esquerra, Marques, Burl.†	.304	55	222	207	32	63	87	8	2	4	28	0	1	2	12	3	35	11	3	3	.420	.347
Fennell, Jason, Bris.†	.318	47	199	170	40	54	85	8	1	7	33	0	5	1	23	1	25	0	1	5	.500	.392
Furcal, Rafael, Dan.†	.328	66	309	268	56	88	111	15	4	0	23	1	1	3	36	0	29	60	15	2	.414	.412
Gallaher, T.T., Burl.	.236	43	139	106	19	25	33	3	1	1	7	3	0	0	30	0	22	4	4	1	.311	.404
Garcia, Douglas, Pul.*	.358	23	99	95	12	34	43	3	0	2	21	1	1	0	2	0	19	2	1	1	.453	.367
Garcia, Sandy, Prin.	.216	54	184	171	23	37	47	10	0	0	21	2	1	3	7	0	40	7	5	2	.275	.258
Gobbel, Gene, King.	.307	48	179	150	28	46	71	7	0	6	19	4	0	6	19	0	28	14	4	1	.473	.406
Gonzalez, Jose, Bris.	.312	51	231	205	39	64	81	14	0	1	24	3	1	4	18	0	35	16	5	5	.395	.377
Gooden, Carl, J.C.	.211	6	24	19	4	4	7	0	0	1	3	0	0	3	2	0	3	2	0	0	.368	.375
Grindell, Nate, Burl.	.244	14	43	41	6	10	15	2	0	1	7	0	0	0	2	0	6	0	0	0	.366	.279
Grummitt, Dan, King.	.264	44	131	106	25	28	47	3	2	4	19	1	1	8	15	0	39	2	1	2	.443	.392
Gunner, Chie, Prin.*	.293	41	135	116	22	34	52	3	3	3	16	0	0	2	17	2	30	3	1	1	.448	.393
Guzman, Juan, Blue.	.100	23	20	20	2	2	3	1	0	0	4	0	0	0	0	0	5	0	0	0	.150	.100
Guzman, Yorkis, King.	.318	42	141	132	20	42	72	5	5	5	26	2	1	1	5	0	23	5	1	1	.545	.345
Hage, Tom, Blue.*	.364	28	128	107	26	39	79	8	1	10	37	0	4	2	15	0	9	1	0	2	.738	.438
Haman, Mack, Blue.	.225	38	135	120	19	27	39	6	0	2	11	1	0	5	9	0	33	1	1	4	.325	.306
Hammond, Joey, Blue.	.388	31	143	129	23	50	58	5	0	1	16	0	1	1	12	0	15	4	2	4	.450	.441
Hankins, Ryan, Bris.	.255	50	229	188	40	48	93	4	1	13	38	3	2	0	36	1	47	4	1	5	.495	.372
Hannahan, Buzz, Mar.	.274	55	245	197	38	54	62	4	2	0	20	1	0	5	42	0	31	14	6	1	.315	.414
Harding, Todd, Burl.	.263	26	81	76	10	20	36	4	0	4	11	0	0	1	4	0	30	4	0	1	.474	.309
Harris, Kevin, Pul.	.224	60	248	232	37	52	89	7	3	8	35	1	3	1	10	0	97	25	4	5	.384	.256

Player, Team	Avg.	G	TPA	AB	R	H	TB	2B	3B	HR	RBI	SH	SF	HP	BB	IBB	SO	SB	CS	GDP	Slg.	OBP
Hawthorne, Kyle, Eliz.	.301	45	223	193	46	58	72	7	2	1	21	2	2	3	23	0	31	9	4	4	.373	.380
Hill, Bobby, King.*	.271	57	207	181	33	49	75	12	4	2	28	4	4	5	13	2	25	9	4	1	.414	.330
Hodge, Kevin, Eliz.	.289	55	228	194	37	56	110	16	1	12	54	0	3	2	29	1	55	4	4	2	.567	.382
Hyde, Brandon, Bris.	.372	27	123	94	21	35	59	9	0	5	26	0	0	8	21	0	20	0	1	3	.628	.520
Infante, Danny, Pul.	.243	46	190	169	24	41	64	12	1	3	19	1	0	2	18	0	52	1	2	1	.379	.323
Ishida, Takehito, Mar.	.182	10	23	22	3	4	6	0	1	0	1	0	0	0	1	0	6	1	0	1	.273	.217
Isturiz, Maicer, Burl.†	.290	55	236	217	33	63	81	8	2	2	33	2	0	0	17	0	32	16	6	4	.373	.342
Jackson, Chris, Burl.	.250	7	20	20	1	5	6	1	0	0	0	0	0	0	0	0	5	0	0	0	.300	.250
James, Drue, Dan.	.178	27	94	73	6	13	18	2	0	1	9	0	2	2	17	0	25	1	0	2	.247	.340
Jaramillo, Tony, Pul.*	.293	17	53	41	9	12	17	0	1	1	6	1	0	0	11	0	11	1	1	2	.415	.442
Jaworowski, Aaron, Eliz.*	.500	7	27	24	6	12	20	2	0	2	5	0	0	0	3	0	2	0	0	1	.833	.556
Jenkins, Brian, King.	.259	55	226	201	31	52	81	10	2	5	25	1	1	5	18	0	17	8	5	5	.403	.333
Jewson, Benjamin, Mar.	.261	35	140	119	19	31	38	4	0	1	11	1	0	4	16	0	48	0	1	1	.319	.367
Jhonson, Yoan, Mar.	.242	11	37	33	3	8	8	0	0	0	2	1	0	1	2	0	10	1	0	1	.242	.306
Johnson, Duane, Mar.†	.216	27	59	51	9	11	13	2	0	0	2	0	0	0	8	0	21	3	1	0	.255	.322
Johnson, Gabe, J.C.	.251	57	212	187	30	47	91	11	3	9	32	0	1	4	20	0	71	3	1	1	.487	.335
Johnson, Tony, King.†	.242	58	215	182	35	44	79	7	2	8	30	1	0	2	28	1	48	7	6	5	.434	.349
Jones, Jeremy, Pul.	.277	26	112	101	11	28	42	3	1	3	14	0	1	0	10	0	18	0	0	5	.416	.339
Jordan, Yustin, Eliz.	.257	20	77	74	14	19	24	2	0	1	3	0	0	0	3	0	20	2	0	1	.324	.286
Kennedy, Brian, Eliz.*	.317	26	102	82	11	26	33	4	0	1	16	0	3	2	15	2	18	0	2	5	.402	.422
Kerry, Bill, J.C.	.157	31	71	51	7	8	10	2	0	0	4	0	0	2	12	0	17	0	1	2	.196	.338
Kirkpatrick, Michael, Blue.*	.279	14	47	43	9	12	18	1	1	1	6	0	1	0	3	0	15	1	1	0	.419	.319
Koone, Chuck, Blue.†	.143	16	54	42	4	6	6	0	0	0	2	2	1	1	8	0	14	0	1	1	.143	.288
Kurtz, Justin, King.	.000	18	1	1	0	0	0	0	0	0	0	0	0	0	0	0	0	0	0	0	.000	.000
LaForest, Pierre Luc, Prin.*	.275	25	105	91	18	25	40	7	1	2	14	1	0	1	12	1	18	4	1	0	.440	.365
Lebron, Hector, Prin.*	.237	59	234	207	35	49	74	11	1	4	34	1	2	5	19	1	53	1	1	9	.357	.313
Ledbetter, Blake, J.C.	.262	37	140	122	15	32	54	8	1	4	21	0	2	3	13	1	37	1	0	5	.443	.343
Lemon, Tim, J.C.	.226	50	207	190	25	43	65	6	2	4	23	1	1	0	15	0	50	11	1	4	.342	.282
Lorenzo, Juan, Eliz.†	.261	44	189	176	33	46	74	8	1	6	23	1	2	3	7	0	17	4	1	3	.420	.298
Lutz, Manuel, Bris.*	.305	65	299	279	52	85	157	21	0	17	58	1	0	4	14	2	56	2	1	7	.563	.347
Malave, Dennis, Burl.*	.279	60	245	208	40	58	83	3	5	4	19	2	0	1	34	0	59	27	13	6	.399	.383
Mann, Derek, Prin.*	.325	68	315	280	63	91	116	10	6	1	32	2	0	1	32	1	46	16	7	4	.414	.396
Marchant, Nick, Mar.	.189	24	83	74	8	14	19	3	1	0	5	0	0	0	9	0	23	2	0	0	.257	.277
Marciniak, Dave, Eliz.	.296	54	242	189	46	56	78	8	1	4	26	1	2	3	47	0	32	5	1	5	.413	.440
Martin, Billy, King.	.308	61	244	214	43	66	106	19	0	7	42	0	2	6	22	0	58	1	1	5	.495	.385
Martin, Jason, Mar.	.233	18	49	43	9	10	11	1	0	0	3	0	0	1	5	0	8	2	0	1	.256	.327
Martin, Tommy, Blue.	.280	18	60	50	8	14	16	2	0	0	5	1	0	2	7	0	12	4	2	1	.320	.390
Massimo, Ryan, Dan.	.206	22	68	63	6	13	15	2	0	0	6	0	0	1	4	0	18	1	0	1	.238	.265
McArthur, Joe, Mar.	.214	38	143	126	18	27	48	2	2	5	17	1	2	6	8	0	56	0	0	1	.381	.289
McIntyre, Remer, J.C.	.231	41	111	104	17	24	25	1	0	0	9	0	0	0	7	0	40	6	2	1	.240	.279
McMillin, Brian, Eliz.	.352	36	155	122	30	43	71	10	0	6	39	0	2	4	27	0	22	8	3	4	.582	.477
Meadows, Mike, King.	.253	51	197	170	33	43	71	10	0	6	31	3	1	4	19	0	57	4	2	1	.418	.340
Medrano, Ricardo, Bris.†	.230	40	186	148	34	34	34	0	0	0	11	4	1	3	29	0	23	28	4	4	.230	.365
Meliah, David, Pul.	.262	48	202	183	21	48	71	8	0	5	28	1	3	2	13	1	26	5	3	0	.388	.313
Merriman, D. Terrell, Bris.*	.227	37	148	128	24	29	41	9	0	1	14	2	0	0	17	0	33	10	1	0	.320	.317
Milton, Prinz, Dan.	.255	58	238	220	24	56	73	5	0	4	33	1	1	9	7	0	77	10	2	4	.332	.304
Minges, Tyler, Burl.	.306	12	51	49	7	15	22	2	1	1	5	0	0	0	2	0	10	1	0	0	.449	.333
Moore, Frank, Prin.*	.118	8	20	17	3	2	2	0	0	0	1	1	0	0	2	0	9	0	0	0	.118	.211
Murch, Jeremy, Prin.*	.274	58	223	197	36	54	89	6	7	5	40	0	5	2	19	0	58	4	6	2	.452	.336
Ndungidi, Ntema, Blue.*	.295	59	246	210	26	62	103	10	5	7	35	0	0	1	35	2	52	6	5	3	.490	.398
Newkirk, Jeff, Bris.*	.266	59	258	222	40	59	95	8	8	4	33	4	2	3	27	0	32	19	1	3	.428	.350
Nina, Amuarys, Pul.	.310	50	205	174	34	54	71	9	4	0	20	0	2	4	25	0	35	9	9	5	.408	.405
Nolasco, Regino, Blue.	.233	66	234	215	27	50	63	7	3	0	26	1	1	2	15	0	40	12	5	4	.293	.288
Norrell, Troy, Mar.	.240	36	130	121	11	29	48	7	0	4	14	0	0	2	7	0	47	1	0	2	.397	.292
Ortega, Jose, J.C.	.233	46	139	133	16	31	47	11	1	1	9	0	1	1	4	0	34	3	0	1	.353	.259
Ottevaere, Derek, Pul.	.314	54	233	204	32	64	90	11	3	3	40	1	4	4	20	0	41	5	1	4	.441	.379
Pacheco, Juan, Blue.	.227	12	48	44	7	10	11	1	0	0	3	1	0	0	3	0	5	0	0	1	.250	.277
Paciorek, Tom, King.	.265	42	164	151	20	40	70	12	3	4	22	3	1	1	8	0	31	3	1	4	.464	.304
Padilla, Jorge, Mar.	.356	23	98	90	10	32	50	3	0	5	25	0	3	1	4	0	24	2	0	3	.556	.378
Perez, Nestor, Prin.	.258	66	300	244	41	63	70	7	0	0	25	17	3	3	33	1	29	13	8	2	.287	.350
Poulsen, Christopher, Dan.	.271	19	77	70	7	19	24	3	1	0	9	0	2	0	5	0	12	0	0	1	.343	.312
Proctor, Mark, King.	.263	14	40	38	3	10	13	0	0	1	4	0	0	1	1	0	9	0	3	0	.342	.300
Prosper, Gerard, King.*	.233	16	50	43	7	10	12	2	0	0	3	0	0	2	5	0	7	1	0	0	.279	.340
Pursell, Mike, Burl.*	.256	57	234	199	37	51	80	15	1	4	30	1	8	0	26	2	34	3	4	2	.402	.330
Ramirez, Edgar, Prin.	.254	53	224	205	31	52	91	11	2	8	35	1	2	2	14	0	63	7	3	2	.444	.305
Ramirez, Luis, Blue.	.187	46	174	150	16	28	46	5	2	3	20	0	5	2	17	0	50	1	3	5	.307	.270
Restovich, Mike, Eliz.	.355	65	305	242	68	86	147	20	1	13	64	0	0	9	54	0	58	5	2	10	.607	.489
Reyes, Ambiorix, Mar.†	.223	62	240	215	35	48	55	3	2	0	21	2	2	5	16	0	24	12	3	4	.256	.290
Rodriguez, Jose, J.C.*	.000	2	4	4	0	0	0	0	0	0	0	0	0	0	0	0	1	0	0	0	.000	.000
Rojas, Alejandro, Mar.†	.239	50	208	180	24	43	53	7	0	1	15	3	0	1	24	1	44	23	2	0	.294	.332
Roman, Junior, Bris.†	.222	7	33	27	8	6	6	0	0	0	1	0	0	2	4	0	6	0	3	0	.222	.364
Romano, Jimmie, Pul.	.188	11	35	32	5	6	6	0	0	0	4	0	0	1	2	0	5	1	2	1	.188	.257
Romero, Marty, Bris.	.239	19	78	71	9	17	37	2	0	6	19	0	0	1	6	0	21	1	0	0	.521	.308
Selander, Craig, Eliz.*	.286	36	141	119	23	34	65	4	0	9	33	0	1	0	21	2	20	1	1	0	.546	.390
Silva, Carlos, Burl.	.175	16	42	40	2	7	7	0	0	0	3	0	1	0	1	0	8	0	0	1	.175	.190
Stoffels, Alex, King.	.292	41	154	137	23	40	49	7	1	0	18	3	1	0	13	0	29	4	5	3	.358	.351
Suarez, Luis, Bris.	.253	59	227	198	35	50	60	5	1	1	25	2	5	0	22	0	40	7	1	3	.303	.320
Sutton, Bruce, Eliz.	.154	19	53	39	6	6	7	1	0	0	2	0	0	2	12	0	13	2	1	1	.179	.377
Taylor, Joshua, King.	.264	36	110	91	13	24	30	4	1	0	8	4	2	0	13	0	21	2	1	0	.330	.368
Thompson, Eric, Burl.*	.211	55	189	175	27	37	45	6	1	0	18	0	0	1	14	0	54	10	2	1	.257	.270
Torres, Gabriel, Eliz.	.248	46	186	161	19	40	59	7	0	4	25	1	1	4	19	0	23	1	2	10	.366	.341

Player, Team	Avg.	G	TPA	AB	R	H	TB	2B	3B	HR	RBI	SH	SF	HP	BB	IBB	SO	SB	CS	GDP	Slg.	OBP
Torres, Jason, Pul.*	.277	44	164	141	20	39	46	5	1	0	15	2	1	0	20	1	23	2	0	4	.326	.364
Torres, Reynaldo, J.C.	.286	44	162	147	19	42	63	12	0	3	20	1	0	3	11	0	53	1	2	3	.429	.348
Utting, Andy, Blue.†	.245	40	171	147	16	36	51	6	0	3	22	0	1	1	22	0	29	2	5	1	.347	.345
Valenzuela, Mario, Bris.	.330	61	262	233	44	77	122	13	1	10	46	0	2	3	24	1	49	6	4	3	.524	.397
Vasquez, Geraldo, J.C.	.145	31	75	62	11	9	17	2	3	0	5	0	1	0	12	0	21	5	1	1	.274	.280
Velazquez, Gil, King.	.103	12	35	29	2	3	4	1	0	0	4	3	1	0	2	0	7	2	0	0	.138	.156
Velazquez, Juan, Dan.†	.248	65	260	230	34	57	77	8	3	2	24	5	2	1	22	0	36	16	5	7	.335	.314
Ventura, Frankie, Burl.	.167	3	6	6	1	1	1	0	0	0	0	0	0	0	0	0	1	0	0	0	.167	.167
Villar, Jose, Dan.	.172	39	169	151	22	26	47	6	3	3	20	1	0	5	12	0	61	14	7	2	.311	.256
Vilorio, Leonel, Eliz.	.325	35	132	123	22	40	55	9	0	2	13	0	1	3	5	0	21	2	0	2	.447	.364
Wallace, Derek, Bris.	.221	54	221	204	32	45	82	12	2	7	32	0	1	4	12	1	52	6	2	2	.402	.276
Ward, Gregory, Dan.	.185	52	199	168	25	31	48	8	0	3	19	0	2	4	25	0	58	5	0	4	.286	.302
Warriax, Brandon, Pul.	.254	61	233	209	33	53	67	11	0	1	20	0	1	3	20	0	42	2	4	4	.321	.326
Wilson, Cliff, Blue.*	.225	23	90	80	13	18	36	4	1	4	11	1	0	0	9	0	20	0	0	2	.450	.303
Wilson, Jack, J.C.†	.373	61	263	241	50	90	128	18	4	4	29	1	0	3	18	0	30	22	6	4	.531	.424
Wilson, Travis, Dan.	.323	65	291	269	48	87	149	25	5	9	48	0	1	4	17	1	54	16	5	5	.554	.371
Wright, Corey, Pul.*	.278	39	181	133	41	37	56	4	3	3	26	2	1		45	0	23	14	4	2	.421	.459
Zydowsky, John, Dan.	.212	49	194	165	27	35	39	4	0	0	14	1	2	3	23	0	38	8	4	1	.236	.316

GRAND SLAMS: Almonte, Cody, Espino, Gallaher, Harris, Hill, Hodge, Isturiz, Jaramillo, Newkirk, G. Torres, 1 each.

AWARDED FIRST BASE ON CATCHER'S INTERFERENCE: Kerry 6 (G. Torres 3, Boscan, Stoffels, Romero); Depippo 2 (Acevas, G. Torres); Harris (Cota); T. Johnson 2 (Acevas, Cota); Lutz (Escalante); Medrano (G. Torres); Merriman (Cota).

1998 PITCHING

TEAM

Team	W	L	Pct.	ERA	G	CG	ShO	Sv.	IP	H	TBF	R	ER	HR	SH	SF	HB	BB	IBB	SO	WP	Bk.
Pulaski	29	37	.439	3.99	66	6	0	11	566.0	552	2437	339	251	51	18	9	31	181	4	485	41	11
Kingsport	38	30	.559	4.17	68	2	5	20	601.2	600	2637	346	279	49	19	16	28	228	5	568	59	12
Martinsville	32	36	.471	4.25	68	2	1	13	591.0	618	2624	365	279	49	17	21	25	211	6	481	67	18
Bluefield	33	34	.493	4.29	67	3	6	12	579.1	578	2529	342	276	45	9	22	27	211	4	549	57	12
Bristol	42	24	.636	4.46	66	5	2	17	589.2	632	2617	368	292	57	16	18	38	214	6	542	68	7
Princeton	38	30	.559	4.64	68	0	2	20	593.1	640	2631	383	306	38	17	20	36	248	3	505	62	15
Elizabethton	38	29	.567	5.03	67	0	5	12	576.2	604	2583	375	322	60	20	15	32	249	7	592	56	9
Burlington	31	36	.463	5.05	67	2	2	15	573.1	560	2625	409	322	31	13	23	46	353	2	545	85	29
Danville	30	38	.441	5.30	68	3	2	12	580.1	638	2648	412	342	41	17	15	38	307	1	475	66	15
Johnson City	25	42	.373	6.29	67	1	1	14	579.2	710	2731	469	405	78	15	27	38	298	9	463	64	15

INDIVIDUAL

TOP QUALIFIERS FOR EARNED-RUN AVERAGE TITLE

Minimum 54 innings. *Lefthanded pitcher.

Pitcher, Team	W	L	Pct.	ERA	G	GS	CG	ShO	GF	Sv.	IP	H	TBF	R	ER	HR	SH	SF	HB	BB	IBB	SO	WP	Bk.
Garcia, Sonny, Blue.	4	2	.667	2.04	12	8	0	0	2	0	57.1	39	226	15	13	2	0	2	1	19	0	77	3	4
German, Yon, King.*	6	5	.545	2.34	13	13	0	0	0	0	77.0	63	311	31	20	9	5	1	0	12	2	75	5	1
Bohannon, Gary, King.	6	3	.667	2.56	10	10	1	1	0	0	59.2	56	238	19	17	1	1	0	0	5	0	49	2	1
Suttles, Donnie, Burl.	5	3	.625	2.87	12	11	0	0	0	0	62.2	40	272	23	20	2	1	2	8	49	0	77	10	7
Theodile, Simeon, Blue.	2	5	.286	2.96	18	6	0	0	3	1	54.2	47	224	18	18	2	0	2	2	15	0	61	3	0
Robinson, Jeremy, Prin.*	6	2	.750	3.01	13	13	0	0	0	0	71.2	78	290	34	24	4	2	0	1	9	0	64	5	3
Stewart, John, Pul.*	4	4	.500	3.17	13	13	1	0	0	0	76.2	82	324	42	27	8	1	2	3	10	0	57	3	3
Jackson, Brian, Burl.	5	3	.625	3.21	12	12	1	0	0	0	70.0	66	299	29	25	5	4	0	7	23	0	61	3	1
Guzman, Ambiorix, Pul.	6	3	.667	3.24	9	9	2	0	0	0	66.2	59	259	30	24	9	2	0	1	7	0	46	1	1
Freeman, Kai, Bris.	6	2	.750	3.28	11	9	1	0	0	0	57.2	56	252	28	21	1	2	0	4	21	0	44	5	3
Murphy, Brian, Blue.	3	4	.429	3.32	14	6	3	1	5	0	57.0	65	248	29	21	3	3	3	2	7	1	41	0	0
Balfour, Grant, Eliz.	7	2	.778	3.36	13	13	0	0	0	0	77.2	70	327	36	29	7	0	2	5	27	0	75	6	0
Jacobson, Andrew, Bris.	4	3	.571	3.52	12	8	2	0	1	0	64.0	72	288	38	25	3	2	2	6	24	1	38	9	0
Fitts, Brian, Eliz.	5	3	.625	3.64	12	12	0	0	0	0	59.1	57	260	27	24	3	3	3	7	23	1	48	5	2
Kennedy, Joe, Prin.*	6	4	.600	3.74	13	13	0	0	0	0	67.1	66	282	37	28	5	1	2	3	26	0	44	4	2

DEPARTMENTAL LEADERS: W—Balfour, 7; L—Bautista, Boublis, Colon, Rayborn, Truitt, 7 each; Pct.—Encarnacion, Simpson, .857 each; G—Alcantara, 31; GS—R. Smith, Taylor, 14 each; CG—B. Murphy, 3; ShO—Several players tied at 1; GF—Bailie, Lira, 22; Sv.—Lira, 14; IP—Figueroa, Mendoza, 80.0 each; H—Colon, 92; TBF—Figueroa, 353; R—Standridge, 61; ER—Taylor, 50; HR—Figueroa, 14; SH—Fisher, German, Herndon, 5 each; SF—Christenson, 6; HB—Suttles, 8; BB—Suttles, 49; IBB—Driscoll, Viles, 3 each; SO—Figueroa, 102; WP—Rayborn, 14; Bk—Suttles, 7.

ALL PITCHERS

*Lefthanded pitcher.

Pitcher, Team	W	L	Pct.	ERA	G	GS	CG	ShO	GF	Sv.	IP	H	TBF	R	ER	HR	SH	SF	HB	BB	IBB	SO	WP	Bk.
Acosta, Luis, J.C.	0	0	.000	19.29	1	0	0	0	0	0	2.1	4	16	5	5	0	0	1	2	3	0	3	0	0
Alcantara, Alvin, J.C.*	1	1	.500	5.56	31	0	0	0	6	0	43.2	53	193	32	27	7	1	1	2	11	0	31	2	0
Almonte, Edwin, Bris.	3	0	1.000	3.38	8	3	0	0	1	0	26.2	29	113	14	10	3	0	1	1	4	0	26	2	0
Alvarez, Nelson, King.	0	0	.000	40.50	1	0	0	0	0	0	0.2	3	8	3	3	0	0	0	1	2	0	1	0	0
Backe, Brandon, Prin.	0	0	.000	0.00	1	0	0	0	1	0	2.0	0	9	0	0	0	0	0	0	3	0	3	0	0
Bailie, Matt, Mar.	4	2	.667	2.84	24	0	0	0	22	9	31.2	33	136	13	10	2	2	1	2	6	2	36	1	2
Baisley, Brad, Mar.	3	2	.600	3.58	7	7	0	0	0	0	27.2	27	113	12	11	2	0	1	2	4	0	14	2	0
Balfour, Grant, Eliz.	7	2	.778	3.36	13	13	0	0	0	0	77.2	70	327	36	29	7	0	2	5	27	0	75	6	0
Bautista, Martin, Burl.	3	7	.300	4.76	13	13	1	0	0	0	73.2	78	324	49	39	5	1	0	4	35	0	64	7	3
Bell, Heath, King.	1	0	1.000	2.54	12	0	0	0	11	8	46.0	40	189	15	13	5	1	2	2	11	0	61	4	0
Bello, Jilberto, Blue.	1	2	.333	5.01	26	0	0	0	21	10	32.1	22	135	18	18	3	0	1	2	14	0	43	7	2
Berck, Darrel, Burl.	2	1	.667	5.92	16	0	0	0	2	1	38.0	37	176	29	25	2	2	1	4	23	0	40	4	0
Birrell, Simon, Dan.	3	0	1.000	0.96	14	0	0	0	6	2	28.0	14	109	8	3	1	1	0	2	15	0	26	4	0
Blackmon, Kurt, Mar.	1	2	.333	4.12	16	5	0	0	2	1	43.2	51	196	26	20	3	1	2	2	17	0	26	4	1

Pitcher, Team	W	L	Pct.	ERA	G	GS	CG	ShO	GF	Sv.	IP	H	TBF	R	ER	HR	SH	SF	HB	BB	IBB	SO	WP	Bk.
Bohannon, Gary, King.	6	3	.667	2.56	10	10	1	1	0	0	59.2	56	238	19	17	1	1	0	0	5	0	49	2	1
Book, Jeremy, J.C.	3	3	.500	7.04	13	13	0	0	0	0	62.2	85	298	52	49	13	4	3	2	27	0	45	5	2
Boublis, Daniel, Pul.	4	7	.364	4.74	13	13	0	0	0	0	74.0	79	313	50	39	10	1	0	4	14	0	58	9	1
Bowers, Jason, Dan. *	1	0	1.000	9.31	13	0	0	0	9	0	19.1	32	103	23	20	0	0	1	0	14	0	9	4	2
Brito, Juan, King. *	0	2	.000	6.57	10	0	0	0	3	0	24.2	30	110	19	18	3	0	0	0	6	0	20	1	0
Brown, Michael, Prin.	1	2	.333	7.41	13	6	0	0	3	0	34.0	38	166	29	28	3	1	2	5	22	0	28	3	3
Butler, Andrew, Eliz.	2	1	.667	6.57	17	3	0	0	1	0	37.0	37	165	29	27	6	0	0	1	19	0	56	4	0
Casteel, Raymond, Blue.	5	3	.625	4.02	13	13	0	0	0	0	69.1	66	304	38	31	6	1	2	6	26	0	50	8	2
Castro, Rafael, Mar.	1	1	.500	6.75	14	1	0	0	3	0	21.1	37	112	22	16	3	0	0	2	9	2	14	1	1
Christenson, Ryan, J.C.	2	3	.400	3.59	18	5	0	0	2	0	52.2	50	228	28	21	5	0	6	3	20	0	38	5	0
Coleman, Billy, Eliz.	0	0	.000	2.40	8	0	0	0	4	0	15.0	12	57	4	4	0	0	1	0	3	0	16	0	0
Colon, Roman, Dan.	1	7	.125	5.77	13	13	0	0	0	0	73.1	92	336	59	47	7	1	0	2	28	0	53	11	0
Cummins, Jon, Prin.	1	1	.500	4.67	9	1	0	0	4	0	17.1	21	83	15	9	1	0	0	2	12	0	16	5	1
Daniel, Michael, Pul.	3	1	.750	3.64	10	2	1	0	4	1	29.2	29	122	12	12	5	0	1	0	8	1	27	0	1
Deckard, Edward, Prin.	0	0	.000	4.79	11	0	0	0	4	0	20.2	25	94	16	11	0	1	0	0	11	1	12	3	1
Dent, Doug, Dan.	5	3	.625	3.61	9	9	1	0	0	0	47.1	57	212	28	19	4	2	1	3	19	0	29	1	1
Dixon, Derek, Blue.	0	0	.000	27.00	2	0	0	0	1	0	1.1	1	8	4	4	0	0	0	2	1	0	2	0	0
Douglass, Sean, Blue.	2	2	.500	3.23	10	10	0	0	0	0	53.0	45	210	20	19	6	0	1	0	14	0	62	3	0
Driscoll, Randy, King.	4	1	.800	3.48	23	0	0	0	10	1	41.1	39	182	24	16	1	0	0	2	18	3	42	3	0
Duenas, Alain, Bris.	1	2	.333	7.48	6	3	0	0	1	0	21.2	37	103	19	18	8	0	1	1	3	0	14	1	0
Encarnacion, Orlando, King.	6	1	.857	4.58	13	13	1	0	0	0	70.2	73	301	39	36	9	2	1	7	25	0	40	7	0
Farmer, Jason, Burl.	0	0	.000	9.28	18	0	0	0	14	6	21.1	29	110	23	22	2	0	3	0	15	0	19	7	1
Felix, Miguel, Bris.	1	1	.500	4.57	5	4	0	0	0	0	21.2	20	100	16	11	2	1	1	4	15	0	23	3	0
Figueroa, Juan, Bris.	5	5	.500	5.06	13	13	2	1	0	0	80.0	87	353	58	45	14	2	3	4	22	0	102	4	1
Fischer, Eric, Bris.*	0	1	.000	6.35	4	0	0	0	3	0	5.2	9	29	5	4	1	0	0	1	0	0	5	0	0
Fisher, Peter, Eliz.	5	3	.625	5.16	12	12	0	0	0	0	66.1	82	290	43	38	9	5	1	3	9	0	57	2	2
Fitts, Brian, Eliz.	5	3	.625	3.64	12	12	0	0	0	0	59.1	57	260	27	24	3	3	3	7	23	1	48	5	2
Flock, Rick, Eliz.	1	1	.500	7.03	19	0	0	0	7	0	32.0	43	149	27	25	2	1	3	3	11	0	36	6	1
Frederick, Kevin, Eliz.	1	4	.200	4.25	17	0	0	0	10	1	29.2	28	130	21	14	4	1	0	0	10	1	46	4	0
Freeman, Kai, Bris.	6	2	.750	3.28	11	9	1	0	0	0	57.2	56	252	28	21	1	2	0	4	21	0	44	5	3
Gallardo, Stalin, Mar.	0	0	.000	2.25	2	0	0	0	1	0	4.0	6	19	3	1	1	0	0	0	1	0	4	0	0
Garcia, Ariel, Bris.	0	0	.000	11.12	3	2	0	0	0	0	5.2	10	27	9	7	1	0	0	1	0	0	4	1	0
Garcia, Sonny, Blue.	4	2	.667	2.04	12	8	0	0	2	0	57.1	39	226	15	13	2	0	2	1	19	0	77	3	4
Gargano, Mike, J.C.	1	5	.167	7.87	12	8	0	0	0	0	42.1	54	200	39	37	8	1	2	3	24	1	29	10	2
German, Yon, King. *	6	5	.545	2.34	13	13	0	0	0	0	77.0	63	311	31	20	9	5	1	0	12	2	75	5	1
Gobbel, Gene, King.	0	0	.000	13.50	1	0	0	0	1	0	2.0	3	12	3	3	0	0	0	3	0	0	3	0	1
Grammer, Ed, Mar.	4	1	.800	5.08	16	0	0	0	5	1	28.1	24	143	19	16	4	3	1	0	16	0	22	7	0
Gray, Michael, Dan. *	0	0	.000	4.23	20	1	0	0	13	4	27.2	27	125	15	13	0	2	1	1	11	0	41	3	2
Grummitt, Dan, Prin.	0	1	.000	13.50	1	0	0	0	1	0	0.2	2	4	1	1	0	0	0	0	0	0	0	0	0
Guzman, Ambiorix, Pul.	6	3	.667	3.24	9	9	2	0	0	0	66.2	59	259	30	24	9	2	0	1	7	0	46	1	1
Guzman, Juan, Blue.	1	2	.333	1.42	15	0	0	0	9	1	25.1	22	106	12	4	1	0	0	1	7	0	26	1	1
Guzman, Yorkis, King.	0	0	.000	0.00	1	0	0	0	1	0	0.1	0	1	0	0	0	0	0	0	0	0	0	0	0
Haines, Talley, Prin.	2	3	.400	5.19	27	1	0	0	9	2	43.1	54	197	32	25	4	0	1	2	17	0	37	5	1
Hand, Jon, J.C.	1	3	.250	3.52	29	0	0	0	9	3	38.1	42	165	24	15	2	0	1	8	0	0	35	4	4
Harden, Nathan, Dan.	0	0	.000	6.60	11	0	0	0	9	0	15.0	12	76	11	11	1	0	1	6	14	0	12	2	0
Hernandez, Mario, Burl.	1	0	1.000	6.89	13	0	0	0	8	0	15.2	16	78	12	12	1	0	0	1	10	0	17	4	5
Herndon, Eric, Dan.	1	3	.250	5.31	21	0	0	0	11	3	42.1	45	195	29	25	1	5	1	4	22	0	48	3	3
Hill, T.J., Prin.	0	1	.000	3.60	4	0	0	0	2	0	5.0	5	21	3	2	0	0	0	0	1	0	4	0	0
Holden, Brian, Dan. *	2	0	1.000	3.86	4	0	0	0	2	0	7.0	10	33	3	3	0	0	1	2	0	0	0	0	0
Holzbauer, Joseph, Dan.	1	0	1.000	4.73	17	0	0	0	0	0	26.2	27	126	17	14	1	1	1	3	24	1	24	11	0
Hopson, Craig, J.C.	4	3	.571	5.66	29	0	0	0	13	0	35.0	41	158	24	22	3	2	2	1	15	1	27	2	0
Hughes, Travis, Pul.	2	6	.250	3.89	22	3	0	0	17	2	41.2	30	188	25	18	2	0	0	4	25	1	48	8	3
Jackson, Brian, Burl.	5	3	.625	3.21	12	12	1	0	0	0	70.0	66	299	29	25	5	4	0	7	23	0	61	3	1
Jacobson, Andrew, Bris.	4	3	.571	3.52	12	8	2	0	1	0	64.0	72	288	38	25	3	2	2	6	24	1	38	9	0
Johnson, Solomon, Bris.*	2	2	.500	3.74	14	7	0	0	2	0	43.1	38	189	22	18	1	0	3	4	26	0	38	4	0
Johnson, Tony, King.	0	0	.000	27.00	1	0	0	0	1	0	1.0	4	8	3	3	0	0	0	0	1	0	2	0	0
Jones, Sean, Blue.	2	2	.667	9.76	14	6	0	0	3	0	39.2	62	203	49	43	6	1	2	2	20	0	30	6	0
Kane, Kyle, Bris.	1	0	1.000	5.32	13	0	0	0	3	0	23.2	34	115	21	14	3	1	2	3	8	0	17	6	0
Kennedy, Brian, Eliz.	0	1	.000	9.00	1	0	0	0	1	0	1.0	5	2	1	1	0	0	1	0	2	0	0	0	0
Kennedy, Joe, Prin. *	6	4	.600	3.74	13	13	0	0	0	0	67.1	66	282	37	28	5	1	2	3	26	0	44	4	7
Kerry, Bill, J.C.	0	0	.000	9.00	1	0	0	0	1	0	1.0	3	7	1	1	1	0	0	0	1	0	0	0	0
Koeth, Mark, Burl.	0	2	.000	10.73	20	0	0	0	10	1	27.2	45	151	40	33	1	0	3	3	22	0	14	9	2
Kosderka, Matthew, Pul.	3	6	.333	4.60	14	11	2	0	2	0	60.2	62	262	42	31	5	2	1	3	21	0	52	3	0
Krystofoski, Jay, King.	1	1	.500	4.76	8	0	0	0	4	0	11.1	11	52	10	6	0	0	1	2	5	0	11	1	1
Kurtz, Justin, King.	1	3	.250	5.91	17	2	0	0	6	1	35.0	47	171	25	23	1	2	0	2	21	0	37	9	2
Lamarsh, Robert, Pul. *	1	2	.333	5.28	11	2	0	0	4	0	29.0	35	133	22	17	1	0	0	11	0	0	28	0	0
Lambert, Jeremy, J.C.	4	4	.500	4.92	13	11	0	0	0	0	64.0	73	294	44	35	7	1	2	6	37	0	30	4	1
Lawson, Jarrod, Mar.	4	3	.571	4.04	13	13	0	0	0	0	62.1	65	273	40	28	3	2	2	4	26	0	38	1	3
Lira, James, Prin.	4	1	.800	3.75	29	0	0	0	22	14	36.0	36	161	18	15	3	2	1	1	19	2	51	3	0
Lopez, Jose, Bris.	2	0	1.000	3.12	5	0	0	0	3	1	8.2	10	39	6	3	0	1	1	0	3	0	4	1	0
Lowe, Matthew, King.	2	4	.333	6.42	13	8	0	0	2	0	40.2	50	198	40	29	5	0	0	4	21	0	31	6	1
Lutz, Manuel, Bris.	0	0	.000	0.00	1	0	0	0	1	0	1.0	3	3	0	0	0	0	0	0	0	0	1	0	0
MacGillivray, Monte, Prin. *	0	1	.000	9.42	10	0	0	0	2	0	14.1	18	72	16	15	1	0	0	2	13	0	8	2	0
Madson, Ryan, Mar.	3	3	.500	4.83	12	10	0	0	0	0	54.0	57	237	38	29	5	0	0	2	20	0	52	9	1
Maleski, Eric, Burl.	4	2	.667	2.05	19	0	0	0	15	5	44.0	37	174	17	10	0	0	0	10	2	47	8	1	
Maness, Chris, Mar.	2	2	.500	3.38	19	0	0	0	7	0	32.0	31	142	17	12	4	0	0	12	1	40	3	0	
Maness, Nicholas, King.	5	3	.625	4.48	13	13	0	0	0	0	64.1	68	289	41	32	7	2	5	1	30	0	76	7	1
Marifian, John, Mar. *	0	2	.000	3.99	16	1	0	0	3	0	29.1	25	129	20	13	0	0	1	1	14	0	31	8	2
Marr, Jason, J.C.	2	2	.500	2.12	25	0	0	0	20	10	34.0	23	142	11	8	3	1	0	2	10	1	36	5	0
Martinez, Alex, Mar.	1	3	.250	2.92	22	0	0	0	10	0	37.0	30	164	22	12	3	1	3	1	22	0	28	2	3
Matew, Francisco, J.C.	3	5	.375	9.42	18	6	1	0	4	0	43.0	66	212	49	45	5	1	1	2	15	1	42	4	3

Pitcher, Team	W	L	Pct.	ERA	G	GS	CG	ShO	GF	Sv.	IP	H	TBF	R	ER	HR	SH	SF	HB	BB	IBB	SO	WP	Bk.
McDermott, Ryan, Burl.	1	6	.143	8.51	12	8	0	0	3	0	37.0	36	190	44	35	4	0	2	6	36	0	21	5	0
McDonald, Jon, Prin. *	4	2	.667	2.61	25	0	0	0	3	0	38.0	34	164	14	11	1	1	0	3	19	0	35	2	1
McPadden, Mike, Burl.	0	5	.000	8.89	16	0	0	0	4	0	26.1	28	139	37	26	1	0	3	2	30	0	18	5	0
Mendoza, Geronimo, Bris.......	5	2	.714	3.83	13	13	0	0	0	0	80.0	78	350	40	34	5	2	1	4	30	0	70	6	0
Mikkola, Shaun, King.	0	0	.000	6.35	4	0	0	0	3	0	5.2	8	29	4	4	3	0	0	0	5	0	4	0	1
Montana, Joaquin, King.	0	0	.000	3.86	1	0	0	0	0	0	2.1	1	10	2	1	0	0	0	0	1	0	4	0	2
Moore, Eric, Pul.	0	4	.000	5.12	17	0	0	0	12	1	31.2	34	151	25	18	0	2	1	4	16	0	25	5	0
Morelock, Chris, Burl.	2	1	.667	4.01	16	1	0	0	5	1	33.2	36	165	31	15	3	1	2	2	28	0	29	4	2
Murch, Jeremy, Prin. *	0	0	.000	0.00	1	0	0	0	1	0	2.0	0	6	0	0	0	0	0	1	0	0	1	0	0
Murphy, Brian, Blue.	3	4	.429	3.32	14	6	3	1	5	0	57.0	65	248	29	21	3	3	3	2	7	1	41	0	0
Murphy, Darren, Blue. *	2	0	1.000	4.12	16	0	0	0	4	0	19.2	25	85	9	9	0	0	0	0	5	0	16	1	0
Myers, Gene, Blue.	0	2	.000	7.83	17	1	0	0	7	0	23.0	35	129	27	20	2	0	2	2	24	1	25	13	2
Norrell, Troy, Mar.	0	0	.000	0.00	1	0	0	0	1	0	0.2	2	4	0	0	0	0	0	0	0	0	0	0	0
Nunez, Franklin, Mar.	2	2	.500	2.49	6	4	0	0	0	0	25.1	23	109	10	7	0	0	2	8	0	19	2	3
Perez, Norberto, Blue.	1	1	.500	4.97	6	0	0	0	3	0	12.2	8	47	7	7	2	1	0	4	0	11	1	1
Perez, Pablo, Eliz.	3	5	.375	6.41	16	7	0	0	2	0	53.1	73	250	45	38	9	1	1	2	24	1	39	3	0
Phillips, Randy, Dan. *	1	2	.333	9.95	13	0	0	0	3	0	19.0	19	99	23	21	1	0	3	2	24	0	14	12	3
Ratliff, Craig, Blue.	0	0	.000	5.14	3	3	0	0	0	0	14.0	18	66	12	8	1	0	2	1	5	0	11	1	0
Rayborn, Kris, J.C. *	1	7	.125	11.06	10	10	0	0	0	0	35.0	40	191	48	43	5	1	3	5	47	0	26	14	2
Reynolds, Chris, Prin.	1	1	.500	4.86	22	1	0	0	7	1	37.0	38	168	25	20	0	1	2	3	15	0	37	5	0
Reynolds, Jacob, Burl.	1	4	.200	7.76	10	5	0	0	2	0	29.0	27	142	28	25	2	0	1	5	26	0	30	13	1
Rios, Romualdo, Pul.	1	2	.333	5.49	10	10	0	0	0	0	41.0	47	182	34	25	2	2	1	3	14	0	30	5	2
Rivera, Saul, Eliz.	3	3	.500	2.25	23	0	0	0	21	7	36.0	19	147	10	9	4	2	0	0	19	2	65	1	0
Rizo, Miguel, J.C.	0	2	.000	11.81	16	0	0	0	5	0	26.2	55	155	37	35	7	1	1	4	20	1	14	3	1
Roberts, Marquis, Prin. *	3	2	.600	5.59	8	8	0	0	0	0	37.0	49	174	30	23	6	2	1	4	12	0	27	1	2
Robinson, Jeremy, Prin. *.....	6	2	.750	3.01	13	13	0	0	0	0	71.2	78	290	34	24	4	2	0	1	9	0	64	5	3
Rodgers, Marcus, Bris.	3	0	1.000	4.18	18	0	0	0	5	1	28.0	11	107	14	13	1	0	0	1	10	0	39	2	1
Rosales, Rudy, Burl.	0	0	.000	13.50	1	0	0	0	1	0	2.0	6	14	3	3	0	0	0	1	1	0	0	0	0
Rose, Johnathan, Mar. *	3	0	1.000	3.99	22	0	0	0	8	2	38.1	29	166	22	17	4	2	1	3	11	0	48	7	0
Ruhl, Nathan, Prin.	1	1	.500	4.76	14	0	0	0	6	3	17.0	12	76	10	9	2	1	0	1	11	0	25	6	0
Ryba, Jason, Blue.	3	3	.500	5.24	12	9	0	0	0	0	46.1	46	217	36	27	6	0	3	4	25	0	41	4	0
Sabathia, C.C., Burl. *	1	0	1.000	4.50	5	5	0	0	0	0	18.0	20	83	14	9	1	0	1	1	8	0	35	1	1
Sanchez, Willmen, Burl. *	2	1	.667	4.82	8	4	0	0	1	1	28.0	25	118	16	15	2	1	3	2	13	0	26	1	1
Scarce, Bubba, Dan.	0	0	.000	0.00	2	0	0	0	2	2	3.0	1	12	0	0	0	0	0	2	0	3	0	0
Schaeffer, Mike, Pul. *	3	0	1.000	2.45	18	2	0	0	8	1	47.2	34	200	16	13	3	3	1	2	19	1	42	1	0
Schmidt, Pat, Dan. *	2	1	.667	5.59	12	0	0	0	5	0	19.1	14	86	14	12	2	2	0	2	15	0	16	1	0
Sheets, Matt, Eliz.	2	3	.400	9.00	14	8	0	0	2	0	42.0	52	220	47	42	4	2	1	2	37	0	39	7	1
Silva, Carlos, Mar.	1	4	.200	5.05	7	7	1	0	0	0	41.0	48	180	24	23	2	2	3	2	4	0	21	3	2
Simpson, Cory, Dan.	6	1	.857	5.02	14	6	1	1	4	1	52.0	47	224	29	29	6	0	0	2	34	0	44	2	0
Sims, Kenny, Blue.	5	3	.625	3.10	19	1	0	0	6	0	49.1	49	204	20	17	2	1	0	1	14	2	32	3	0
Smith, Jamie, Bris.	1	0	1.000	8.38	8	0	0	0	4	0	9.2	16	49	9	9	5	0	0	3	1	0	12	2	0
Smith, Robert, J.C. *	3	3	.500	5.18	14	14	0	0	0	0	64.1	85	305	47	37	9	2	3	2	34	1	65	2	0
Standridge, Jason, Prin.	4	4	.500	7.00	12	12	0	0	0	0	63.0	82	298	61	49	4	2	4	3	28	0	47	9	0
Stewart, John, Pul. *	4	4	.500	3.17	13	13	1	0	0	0	76.2	82	324	42	27	8	1	2	3	10	0	57	3	3
Sturdy, Tim, Eliz.	5	1	.833	4.00	12	12	0	0	0	0	69.2	65	302	38	31	4	1	2	6	27	0	46	8	1
Suggs, Willie, King.	0	5	.000	4.72	15	7	0	0	1	0	47.2	46	225	29	25	2	3	1	5	36	0	44	9	0
Suttles, Donnie, Burl.	5	3	.625	2.87	12	11	0	0	0	0	62.2	40	272	23	20	2	1	2	8	49	0	77	10	7
Tanaka, Masahiro, Mar.	0	0	.000	7.20	4	0	0	0	1	0	5.0	9	29	8	4	0	0	1	1	2	0	3	4	0
Tapia, Rafael, Blue.	0	2	.000	5.48	4	4	0	0	0	0	21.1	24	97	18	13	1	2	0	11	0	20	3	0
Taylor, Aaron, Dan.	3	6	.333	6.25	14	14	1	0	0	0	72.0	87	334	60	50	9	1	3	3	36	0	55	3	1
Tellez, Eloy, Bris.	4	2	.667	6.59	14	0	0	0	6	0	27.1	39	127	23	20	3	4	1	9	1	18	9	1
Theodile, Simeon, Blue.	2	5	.286	2.96	18	6	0	0	3	1	54.2	47	229	24	18	2	0	2	15	0	61	3	0
Truitt, Derrick, Dan.	0	7	.000	6.91	13	12	0	0	0	0	54.2	72	258	51	42	3	2	1	6	27	0	38	2	1
Turnbow, Derrick, Mar.	2	6	.250	5.01	13	13	1	0	0	0	70.0	66	300	44	39	7	3	5	1	26	1	45	5	0
Vallis, Jamie, Eliz. *	1	2	.333	5.68	21	0	0	0	12	1	25.1	28	126	20	16	4	1	1	1	19	1	24	8	1
Vega, Rene, King. *	3	2	.600	5.63	22	2	0	0	11	5	40.0	46	186	32	25	2	3	3	2	17	0	42	4	1
Victoria, Lester, Eliz. *	3	0	1.000	6.68	22	0	0	0	7	3	32.1	37	155	26	24	4	2	0	2	20	1	43	2	1
Vigeland, William, Pul.	0	1	.000	6.58	11	1	0	0	3	0	26.0	30	127	21	19	3	2	0	3	19	1	23	4	0
Viles, Jeff, J.C.	0	1	.000	6.62	27	0	0	0	8	1	34.0	36	162	28	25	4	0	1	2	24	3	42	2	1
Weaver, Joseph, Pul.	2	1	.667	1.74	17	0	0	0	10	5	41.1	31	176	20	8	3	3	2	4	17	0	49	2	1
Wheeler, David, King.	3	0	1.000	1.44	19	0	0	0	12	5	31.1	12	117	7	5	1	0	2	0	9	0	26	1	0
White, Matt, Burl. *	4	1	.800	1.94	8	8	0	0	0	0	46.1	34	190	14	10	0	2	2	0	24	0	47	4	0
Williams, Mike, Bris.	3	1	.750	3.49	24	0	0	0	18	9	38.2	28	162	16	15	1	1	0	5	16	1	43	4	1
Williams, Tom, Bris.	1	0	1.000	7.71	4	4	0	0	0	0	16.1	23	78	18	14	4	0	0	0	7	0	12	2	0
Willoughby, Justin, Dan. *	4	5	.444	4.03	13	13	0	0	0	0	73.2	87	320	42	33	5	0	2	1	20	0	53	7	2
Wilson, Cliff, Blue.	0	1	.000	12.00	1	0	0	0	1	0	3.0	4	15	4	4	0	1	0	1	0	0	1	0	0
Wilson, Mike, Mar.	1	3	.250	4.81	9	7	0	0	0	0	39.1	40	172	25	21	6	1	1	0	13	0	40	8	0
Wright, Barrett, Prin.	5	4	.556	4.28	13	13	0	0	0	0	73.2	79	315	41	35	4	3	4	4	23	0	54	7	1
Wright, Jason, Prin. *	0	0	.000	0.68	9	0	0	0	4	0	13.1	3	51	1	1	0	0	1	4	7	0	12	2	0
Wylie, Mitchell, Bris.	0	2	.000	3.30	20	0	0	0	14	6	30.0	34	133	12	11	1	0	2	0	11	2	32	7	0
Zachery, Nicholas, J.C. *.......	0	0	.000	0.00	1	0	0	0	0	0	0.2	0	5	0	0	0	0	0	1	2	0	0	0	0

COMBINATION SHUTOUTS: **Bluefield (5)**—Casteel-Bello, Garcia-Murphy-Bello, Garcia-Theodile-Bello, Douglass-Guzman-Perez, Sims-Ryba-Bello. **Bristol (1)**—Johnson-Kane-Smith. **Burlington (2)**—Sanchez-Berck-Koeth, Jackson-Farmer. **Danville (1)**—Truitt-Schmidt-Gray. **Elizabethton (5)**—Fitts-Victoria, Perez-Victoria-Rivera, Sturdy-Flock-Vallis, Fitts-Vallis, Balfour-Vallis. **Johnson City (1)**—Lambert-Marr. **Kingsport (4)**—Maness-Driscoll-Vega, German-Suggs-Kurtz-Krystofolski, Bohannon-Bell, German-Driscoll-Bell. **Martinsville (1)**—Baisley-Blackmon-Rose. **Princeton (2)**—Standridge-Lira-MacGillivray-Ruhl, Robinson-Reynolds-McDonald-Brown. **Pulaski (0)**—None.

NO-HIT GAMES: None.

TEAM

Team	Pct.	G	PO	A	E	TC	DP	PB	Team	Pct.	G	PO	A	E	TC	DP	PB
Princeton	.959	68	1780	811	111	2702	54	12	Pulaski	.953	66	1698	785	123	2606	51	18
Danville	.959	68	1741	778	108	2627	69	25	Elizabethton	.952	67	1730	719	123	2572	39	25
Bristol	.957	66	1769	736	113	2618	53	18	Kingsport	.952	68	1805	757	130	2692	55	25
Burlington	.954	67	1720	735	119	2574	60	32	Martinsville	.949	68	1773	808	138	2719	36	23
Bluefield	.953	67	1738	714	120	2572	36	23	TRIPLE PLAY: Danville.								
Johnson City	.953	67	1739	732	122	2593	48	25									

INDIVIDUAL

FIRST BASEMEN

NOTE: All caps denotes fielding-percentage leader based on 34 games for catchers, 45 for all other non-pitchers. *Throws lefthanded.

Player, Team	Pct.	G	PO	A	E	TC	DP
ALLEN, Troy, Dan.	.991	50	414	33	4	451	47
Alvarez, Jimmy, Eliz.	1.000	1	4	1	0	5	0
Banez, Marco, J.C.*	1.000	4	20	3	0	23	0
Bastardo, Angel, Burl.	.933	2	13	1	1	15	1
Batista, Carlos, Burl.	.984	53	464	24	8	496	44
Bonilla, Juan, Blue.	.993	16	130	11	1	142	9
Brosam, Eric, Eliz.	.986	35	273	16	4	293	18
Caines, Franklyn, Mar.	.981	15	100	4	2	106	6
Chwan, Brian, Prin.	1.000	1	4	0	0	4	1
Cota, Humberto, Prin.	1.000	1	11	0	0	11	0
Durick, Chad, King.	.971	4	30	3	1	34	5
Escalante, Jaime, Blue.	.951	5	37	2	2	41	1
Espy, Nate, Mar.	.988	57	554	38	7	599	23
Esquerra, Marques, Burl.	.950	3	18	1	1	20	1
Fennell, Jason, Bris.	1.000	1	8	0	0	8	2
Grindell, Nate, Burl.	1.000	2	13	0	0	13	1
Grummitt, Dan, Prin.	.993	20	126	7	1	134	8
Hage, Tom, Blue.	.985	28	254	7	4	265	15
Hyde, Brandon, Bris.	.750	1	3	0	1	4	0
Infante, Danny, Pul.	.978	46	446	34	11	491	37
Jaworowski, Aaron, Eliz.	1.000	6	60	5	0	65	3
Jenkins, Brian, King.	.987	9	69	6	1	76	3
Jordan, Yustin, Eliz.	.986	19	122	15	2	139	9
Lebron, Hector, Prin.	.989	59	476	52	6	534	41
Lorenzo, Juan, Eliz.	.989	13	82	10	1	93	2
Lutz, Manuel, Bris.	.980	65	614	39	13	666	45
Martin, Billy, King.	1.000	9	80	2	0	82	4
Martin, Jason, Mar.	1.000	1	3	0	0	3	1
Massimo, Ryan, Dan.	.953	17	116	7	6	129	10
Meadows, Mike, King.	.983	47	451	22	8	481	30
Ortega, Jose, J.C.	.980	33	232	16	5	253	15
Ottevaere, Derek, Pul.	.995	21	208	13	1	222	12
Paciorek, Tom, King.	.952	2	18	2	1	21	3
Pursell, Mike, Burl.	.956	11	83	4	4	91	10
Ramirez, Luis, Blue.	.923	2	12	0	1	13	1
Torres, Reynaldo, J.C.	.981	43	337	17	7	361	29
Utting, Andy, Blue.	.976	18	151	11	4	166	10
Viloria, Leonel, Eliz.	.933	3	10	4	1	15	1
Zydowsky, John, Dan.	1.000	7	40	3	0	43	8
TRIPLE PLAY: Massimo.							

SECOND BASEMEN

Player, Team	Pct.	G	PO	A	E	TC	DP
Alvarez, Jimmy, Eliz.	.971	9	15	19	1	35	6
Backe, Brandon, Prin.	1.000	1	3	3	0	6	0
Benham, Jason, Blue.	1.000	1	1	3	0	4	0
Carvajal, Ramon, J.C.	.909	39	63	116	18	197	21
Centile, Raul, Burl.	.935	43	84	117	14	215	19
Champagne, Andre, King.	.976	25	36	47	2	85	8
Edgar, Jason, Pul.	.960	41	64	130	8	202	24
Escobar, Gustavo, J.C.	.968	28	41	51	3	95	11
Esquerra, Marques, Burl.	.970	18	46	50	3	99	12
Furcal, Rafael, Dan.	.965	65	183	198	14	395	51
Gobbel, Gene, King.	1.000	11	17	35	0	52	5
Gonzalez, Jose, Bris.	.943	21	44	56	6	106	15
Grindell, Nate, Burl.	1.000	1	0	1	0	1	0
Hammond, Joey, Blue.	.963	29	61	95	6	162	14
Hankins, Ryan, Bris.	1.000	3	1	1	0	2	0
Hannahan, Buzz, Mar.	.950	24	42	73	6	121	7
Hawthorne, Kyle, Eliz.	.906	15	24	24	5	53	4
Hill, Bobby, Blue.	.921	28	57	60	10	127	17
Jaramillo, Tony, Pul.	.955	7	9	12	1	22	3
Lorenzo, Juan, Eliz.	.975	8	11	28	1	40	6

Player, Team	Pct.	G	PO	A	E	TC	DP
MANN, Derek, Prin.	.966	66	134	210	12	356	43
Marciniak, Dave, Eliz.	.933	37	66	88	11	165	12
Martin, Tommy, Blue.	.910	15	19	42	6	67	8
Massimo, Ryan, Dan.	.667	1	1	1	1	3	0
Medrano, Ricardo, Bris.	.978	40	79	97	4	180	18
Meliah, David, Pul.	.966	25	37	77	4	118	11
Nolasco, Regino, Blue.	.939	13	25	52	5	82	4
Pacheco, Juan, Blue.	.932	11	18	23	3	44	7
Ramirez, Edgar, Prin.	.500	1	1	1	2	4	0
Rojas, Alejandro, Mar.	.957	48	87	137	10	234	20
Roman, Junior, Bris.	.889	7	11	13	3	27	4
Silva, Carlos, Burl.	.956	14	16	27	2	45	4
Taylor, Joshua, King.	.887	16	18	29	6	53	4
Vasquez, Geraldo, J.C.	.973	7	14	22	1	37	5
Zydowsky, John, Dan.	.895	4	8	9	2	19	1
TRIPLE PLAY: Furcal.							

THIRD BASEMEN

Player, Team	Pct.	G	PO	A	E	TC	DP
Backe, Brandon, Prin.	.842	6	3	13	3	19	0
Benham, Jason, Blue.	.910	52	46	96	14	156	7
BOWERS, Jason, J.C.	.947	60	45	133	10	188	11
Caines, Franklyn, Mar.	.897	11	7	19	3	29	1
Castaneda, Cesar, Pul.	.878	56	27	124	21	172	7
Champagne, Andre, King.	.667	4	1	5	3	9	0
Day, Paul, Burl.	.892	48	37	87	15	139	6
Durick, Chad, King.	1.000	1	1	2	0	3	0
Escobar, Gustavo, J.C.	.769	3	2	8	3	13	2
Esquerra, Marques, Burl.	.889	15	7	33	5	45	0
Gobbel, Gene, King.	.737	4	4	10	5	19	1
Gonzalez, Jose, Bris.	.922	30	15	56	6	77	5
Hankins, Ryan, Bris.	.918	41	26	86	10	122	11
Hannahan, Buzz, Mar.	.915	28	22	64	8	94	6
Harding, Todd, Burl.	1.000	6	1	6	0	7	2
Hodge, Kevin, Eliz.	.913	45	29	86	11	126	2
Ishida, Takehito, Mar.	1.000	1	0	1	0	1	0
Jewson, Benjamin, Mar.	.782	27	21	47	19	87	1
Jordan, Yustin, Eliz.	.250	1	0	1	3	4	0
LaForest, Pierre Luc, Prin.	.870	18	16	31	7	54	1
Lorenzo, Juan, Eliz.	.813	9	3	23	6	32	3
Lutz, Manuel, Bris.	1.000	1	2	0	0	2	0
Mann, Derek, Prin.	1.000	1	0	1	0	1	0
Marciniak, Dave, Eliz.	.667	3	1	1	1	3	0
Martin, Billy, King.	.900	43	24	66	10	100	7
Martin, Jason, Mar.	.727	9	0	16	6	22	0
Martin, Tommy, Blue.	.667	1	1	1	1	3	0
Massimo, Ryan, Dan.	.600	1	1	2	2	5	0
Meliah, David, Pul.	.907	14	6	33	4	43	0
Pacheco, Juan, Blue.	.667	1	0	2	1	3	0
Proctor, Mark, King.	.941	14	12	20	2	34	2
Pursell, Mike, Burl.	.500	1	0	1	1	2	0
Ramirez, Edgar, Prin.	.863	47	28	79	17	124	8
Ramirez, Luis, Blue.	1.000	1	0	1	0	1	0
Taylor, Joshua, King.	1.000	9	1	8	0	9	1
Vasquez, Geraldo, J.C.	.870	14	9	11	3	23	0
Velazquez, Gil, King.	1.000	1	0	2	0	2	0
Vilorio, Leonel, Eliz.	.879	14	8	21	4	33	1
Wilson, Cliff, Blue.	.905	15	11	27	4	42	0
Wilson, Travis, Dan.	.936	65	55	150	14	219	13
Zydowsky, John, Dan.	1.000	2	2	10	0	12	0

SHORTSTOPS

Player, Team	Pct.	G	PO	A	E	TC	DP
Alvarez, Jimmy, Eliz.	.906	32	30	76	11	117	7
Backe, Brandon, Prin.	1.000	2	4	4	0	8	0
Benham, Jason, Blue.	.818	3	2	7	2	11	2
Centile, Raul, Burl.	.923	14	10	26	3	39	7

Player, Team	Pct.	G	PO	A	E	TC	DP
Champagne, Andre, King.	.885	8	7	16	3	26	2
Diaz, Maikell, Blue.	.900	11	14	31	5	50	3
Escobar, Gustavo, J.C.	.941	11	8	24	2	34	5
Esquerra, Marques, Burl.	.643	5	4	5	5	14	1
Gobbel, Gene, King.	.920	28	37	67	9	113	16
Gonzalez, Jose, Bris.	1.000	1	1	0	0	1	0
Hammond, Joey, Blue.	.714	2	2	3	2	7	1
Hankins, Ryan, Bris.	.806	8	2	23	6	31	2
Hannahan, Buzz, Mar.	1.000	4	5	9	0	14	0
Hawthorne, Kyle, Eliz.	.946	26	46	76	7	129	11
Hill, Bobby, King.	.924	24	32	89	10	131	12
Hodge, Kevin, Eliz.	1.000	1	3	2	0	5	0
Ishida, Takehito, Mar.	.933	7	6	8	1	15	0
Isturiz, Maicer, Burl.	.929	55	82	178	20	280	37
Lorenzo, Juan, Eliz.	.970	8	10	22	1	33	2
Massimo, Ryan, Dan.	1.000	1	0	1	0	1	0
Meliah, David, Pul.	.920	7	5	18	2	25	0
Nolasco, Regino, Blue.	.912	53	72	135	20	227	20
Pacheco, Juan, Blue.	.500	2	1	1	2	4	0
PEREZ, Nestor, Prin.	.976	66	116	208	8	332	43
Reyes, Ambiorix, Mar.	.942	62	72	205	17	294	23
Romero, Marty, Bris.	.600	1	1	2	2	5	1
Suarez, Luis, Bris.	.923	59	72	180	21	273	29
Taylor, Joshua, King.	.891	11	12	29	5	46	3
Vasquez, Geraldo, J.C.	.889	6	2	6	1	9	0
Velazquez, Gil, King.	.863	12	14	30	7	51	3
Velazquez, Juan, Dan.	.937	65	93	188	19	300	42
Warriax, Brandon, Pul.	.913	61	85	187	26	298	40
Wilson, Jack, J.C.	.940	60	85	164	16	265	18
Zydowsky, John, J.C.	.882	6	5	10	2	17	2
Milton, Prinz, Dan.	.915	46	69	6	7	82	0
Minges, Tyler, Burl.	.857	12	16	2	3	21	0
Murch, Jeremy, Prin.*	.904	55	62	4	7	73	0
Ndungidi, Ntema, Blue.	.875	48	54	2	8	64	0
NEWKIRK, Jeff, Bris.*	.981	59	103	3	2	108	0
Nina, Amuarys, Pul.	.987	37	72	2	1	75	0
Norrell, Troy, Mar.	.895	17	14	3	2	19	0
Ortega, Jose, J.C.	.944	14	15	2	1	18	0
Ottevaere, Derek, Pul.	.958	14	21	2	1	24	0
Paciorek, Tom, King.	.923	36	47	1	4	52	0
Padilla, Jorge, Mar.	.955	22	42	0	2	44	0
Prosper, Gerard, King.*	.929	15	13	0	1	14	0
Pursell, Mike, Burl.	.957	33	43	2	2	47	0
Ramirez, Edgar, Prin.	1.000	4	2	2	0	4	0
Ramirez, Luis, Blue.	.945	31	45	7	3	55	1
Restovich, Mike, Eliz.	.912	60	86	7	9	102	1
Selander, Craig, Eliz.	.941	30	41	7	3	51	0
Sutton, Bruce, Eliz.	1.000	6	6	1	0	7	0
Thompson, Eric, Burl.*	.957	53	82	7	4	93	1
Valenzuela, Mario, Bris.	.955	59	94	12	5	111	0
Ventura, Frankie, Burl.	1.000	3	1	0	0	1	0
Villar, Jose, Dan.	.951	39	74	3	4	81	1
Vilorio, Leonel, Eliz.	.889	8	7	1	1	9	1
Wallace, Derek, Bris.	.952	45	54	5	3	62	0
Ward, Gregory, Dan.	.962	39	49	1	2	52	0
Wright, Corey, Pul.*	.938	39	72	3	5	80	0
Zydowsky, John, Dan.	.963	31	51	1	2	54	0

OUTFIELDERS

Player, Team	Pct.	G	PO	A	E	TC	DP
Acevedo, Carlos, Mar.	.935	63	124	5	9	138	1
Aldridge, Cory, Dan.	.955	58	64	0	3	67	0
Almonte, Claudio, Eliz.	.930	60	104	3	8	115	1
Alvarez, Nelson, King.	1.000	1	1	0	0	1	0
Arias, Jeison, Prin.	.890	53	77	4	10	91	0
Backe, Brandon, Prin.	1.000	13	16	4	0	20	0
Banez, Marco, J.C.*	.961	34	45	4	2	51	0
Barlow, Marlon, Prin.	.933	14	13	1	1	15	0
Beverly, Shomari, Mar.	1.000	16	26	0	0	26	0
Bishop, Bennie, Mar.	.944	49	64	4	4	72	0
Caines, Franklyn, Mar.	1.000	4	5	0	0	5	0
Carter, Shannon, Blue.*	.946	36	67	3	4	74	0
Castillo, Geramel, Pul.	.923	34	44	4	4	52	1
Champagne, Andre, King.	.933	9	14	0	1	15	0
Chavez, Endy, J.C.	.941	16	29	3	2	34	1
Cole, Brian, King.	.966	55	82	4	3	89	1
Davison, Ashanti, Blue.	.965	50	80	3	3	86	0
Depippo, Jeff, Burl.	1.000	3	2	0	0	2	0
Durick, Chad, King.	1.000	3	1	0	0	1	0
Dyt, Darren, J.C.	.914	38	52	1	5	58	0
Escobar, Gustavo, J.C.	1.000	2	1	0	0	1	0
Espino, Jose, J.C.	.957	47	97	13	5	115	3
Esquerra, Marques, Burl.	1.000	3	3	0	0	3	0
Fennell, Jason, Bris.	1.000	4	6	0	0	6	0
Gallaher, T.T., Burl.	.923	42	51	9	5	65	1
Garcia, Douglas, Pul.*	.914	18	30	2	3	35	0
Garcia, Sandy, Prin.	.898	51	100	6	12	118	0
Gooden, Carl, J.C.	.929	6	12	1	1	14	0
Grindell, Nate, Burl.	1.000	8	8	0	0	8	0
Gunner, Chie, Mar.	.919	37	34	0	3	37	0
Guzman, Yorkis, King.	.947	15	17	1	1	19	0
Haman, Mack, Blue.	.958	25	46	0	2	48	0
Harding, Todd, Burl.	1.000	7	6	0	0	6	0
Harris, Kevin, Pul.	.855	58	55	4	10	69	0
Hill, Bobby, King.	1.000	3	1	0	0	1	0
Jenkins, Brian, King.	.923	38	47	1	4	52	1
Jhonson, Yoan, Mar.	.765	8	11	2	4	17	0
Johnson, Duane, Mar.	.926	22	23	2	2	27	0
Johnson, Tony, King.	.944	36	51	0	3	54	0
Kennedy, Brian, Eliz.	.867	8	13	0	2	15	0
Kirkpatrick, Michael, Blue.*	1.000	7	7	0	0	7	0
Koone, Chuck, Blue.	1.000	15	19	1	0	20	0
Lemon, Tim, J.C.	.903	50	88	5	10	103	0
Lorenzo, Juan, Eliz.	1.000	4	5	0	0	5	0
Malave, Dennis, Burl.*	.973	58	70	3	2	75	1
Marchant, Nick, Mar.	.962	23	24	1	1	26	0
McIntyre, Remer, J.C.	.929	39	61	4	5	70	0
McMillin, Brian, Eliz.	.962	35	48	2	2	52	0
Merriman, D. Terrell, Bris.*	.946	35	70	0	4	74	0

CATCHERS

Player, Team	Pct.	G	PO	A	E	TC	DP	PB
Acevas, Jonathan, Bris.	.979	43	334	47	8	389	2	13
Alvarez, Nelson, King.	.979	16	84	10	2	96	0	3
Ballard, Ryan, Prin.	.984	11	57	3	1	61	0	0
Bastardo, Angel, Burl.	.993	30	230	36	2	268	3	12
Bonilla, Juan, Blue.	1.000	13	82	15	0	97	0	7
Boscan, Jean, Prin.	.983	49	341	52	7	400	1	20
Chwan, Brian, Prin.	.977	18	70	14	2	86	0	2
Cody, Ryan, Mar.	.993	19	133	17	1	151	1	8
Collura, Todd, Eliz.	.983	23	157	12	3	172	0	10
Cota, Humberto, Prin.	.973	52	382	48	12	442	1	10
Deitrick, Jeremy, Mar.	.951	7	33	6	2	41	0	1
Depippo, Jeff, Burl.	.981	36	271	43	6	320	4	18
Escalante, Jaime, Blue.	.983	47	346	54	7	407	0	12
Guzman, Juan, Blue.	.976	8	37	3	1	41	0	3
Guzman, Yorkis, King.	.986	25	182	29	3	214	3	16
Hyde, Brandon, Bris.	.988	8	68	12	1	81	0	1
Jackson, Chris, Burl.	.978	5	40	5	1	46	0	2
James, Drue, Dan.	.993	23	135	16	1	152	1	5
Johnson, Gabe, J.C.	.977	38	236	22	6	264	3	13
Jones, Jeremy, Pul.	.968	18	132	21	5	158	0	2
Kerry, Bill, J.C.	.958	27	107	8	5	120	0	4
Ledbetter, Blake, J.C.	.973	24	135	10	4	149	1	8
McArthur, Joe, Mar.	.967	38	254	35	10	299	1	11
Norrell, Troy, Mar.	.984	11	55	8	1	64	1	3
Romano, Jimmie, Pul.	.953	10	73	9	4	86	0	3
Romero, Marty, Bris.	.980	17	135	15	3	153	2	4
STOFFELS, Alex, King.	.991	40	281	39	3	323	4	6
Sutton, Bruce, Eliz.	.942	8	42	7	3	52	1	3
Torres, Gabriel, Eliz.	.974	46	374	69	12	455	5	12
Torres, Jason, Pul.	.974	41	271	33	8	312	1	13
Utting, Andy, Blue.	.987	9	71	6	1	78	0	1

PITCHERS

Player, Team	Pct.	G	PO	A	E	TC	DP
Acosta, Luis, J.C.	1.000	1	1	0	0	1	0
Alcantara, Alvin, J.C.*	.857	31	1	5	1	7	0
Almonte, Edwin, Bris.	.833	8	2	3	1	6	0
Bailie, Matt, Mar.	1.000	24	3	9	0	12	1
Baisley, Brad, Mar.	1.000	7	3	4	0	7	1
Balfour, Grant, Eliz.	.920	13	9	14	2	25	0
Bautista, Martin, Burl.	1.000	13	2	10	0	12	2
Bell, Heath, King.	1.000	22	5	6	0	11	0
Bello, Jilberto, Blue.	1.000	26	3	3	0	6	0
Berck, Darrel, Burl.	.778	16	5	2	2	9	0
Birrell, Simon, Dan.	.500	14	0	1	1	2	0
Blackmon, Kurt, Mar.	.833	15	7	8	3	18	2
Bohannon, Gary, King.	1.000	10	4	17	0	21	2
Book, Jeremy, J.C.	1.000	13	2	11	0	13	1
Boublis, Daniel, Pul.	1.000	13	3	11	0	14	1
Bowers, Jason, Dan.*	.800	13	1	3	1	5	0
Brito, Juan, King.*	.857	10	0	6	1	7	0
Brown, Michael, Prin.	.818	13	7	2	2	11	0

Player, Team	Pct.	G	PO	A	E	TC	DP
Butler, Andrew, Eliz.	.800	17	1	3	1	5	0
Casteel, Raymond, Blue.	1.000	13	5	9	0	14	0
Castro, Rafael, Mar.	.500	14	1	1	2	4	0
Christenson, Ryan, J.C.	1.000	18	2	7	0	9	0
Coleman, Billy, Eliz.	1.000	8	0	3	0	3	0
Colon, Roman, Dan.	.875	13	3	11	2	16	0
Cummins, Jon, Prin.	.750	9	1	2	1	4	1
Daniel, Michael, Pul.	.750	10	1	2	1	4	0
Deckard, Edward, Prin.	1.000	11	2	2	0	4	0
Dent, Doug, Dan.	.875	9	2	5	1	8	0
Douglass, Sean, Blue.	1.000	10	0	4	0	4	0
Driscoll, Randy, King.	1.000	23	1	8	0	9	0
Duenas, Alain, Bris.	1.000	6	0	2	0	2	0
Encarnacion, Orlando, King.	.957	13	10	12	1	23	1
Farmer, Jason, Burl.	1.000	18	1	2	0	3	0
Felix, Miguel, Bris.	.833	5	1	4	1	6	1
Figueroa, Juan, Bris.	.722	13	2	11	5	18	0
Fisher, Peter, Eliz.	.850	12	9	8	3	20	0
Fitts, Brian, Eliz.	1.000	12	3	14	0	17	0
Flock, Rick, Eliz.	1.000	19	1	5	0	6	0
Frederick, Kevin, Eliz.	1.000	17	3	3	0	6	0
Freeman, Kai, Bris.	.824	11	4	10	3	17	1
Gallardo, Stalin, Mar.	1.000	2	0	2	0	2	0
Garcia, Sonny, Blue.	1.000	12	1	7	0	8	0
Gargano, Mike, J.C.	1.000	12	1	7	0	8	0
German, Yon, King.*	.920	13	5	18	2	25	1
Gobbel, Gene, King.	1.000	1	0	1	0	1	0
Grammer, Ed, Mar.	.750	16	1	5	2	8	0
Gray, Michael, Dan.*	.750	20	4	2	2	8	0
Guzman, Ambiorix, Pul.	1.000	9	5	10	0	15	0
Guzman, Juan, Blue.	1.000	15	1	1	0	2	0
Haines, Talley, Prin.	1.000	27	5	7	0	12	2
Hand, Jon, J.C.	1.000	29	3	9	0	12	1
Harden, Nathan, Dan.	1.000	11	0	2	0	2	0
Hernandez, Mario, Burl.	1.000	13	0	2	0	2	0
Herndon, Eric, Dan.	.938	21	5	10	1	16	1
Hill, T.J., Prin.	.500	4	1	0	1	2	0
Holden, Brian, Dan.*	1.000	4	0	1	0	1	0
Holzbauer, Joseph, Dan.	.833	17	3	2	1	6	0
Hopson, Craig, J.C.	1.000	29	2	3	0	5	0
Hughes, Travis, Pul.	1.000	22	1	6	0	7	0
Jackson, Brian, Burl.	.867	12	3	10	2	15	1
Jacobson, Andrew, Bris.	.938	12	1	14	1	16	1
Johnson, Solomon, Bris.*	1.000	14	2	4	0	6	1
Jones, Sean, Blue.	1.000	14	1	2	0	3	0
Kane, Kyle, Bris.	.750	13	1	2	1	4	0
Kennedy, Joe, Prin.*	.955	13	2	19	1	22	1
Koeth, Mark, Burl.	1.000	20	0	1	0	1	0
Kosderka, Matthew, Pul.	1.000	14	3	0	0	7	0
Krystofoski, Jay, King.	1.000	8	1	4	0	5	2
Kurtz, Justin, King.	.833	17	1	4	1	6	0
Lamarsh, Robert, Pul.*	1.000	11	1	5	0	6	0
Lambert, Jeremy, J.C.	.950	13	4	15	1	20	3
Lawson, Jarrod, Mar.	1.000	13	3	11	0	14	1
Lira, James, Prin.	1.000	29	4	5	0	9	1
Lopez, Jose, Bris.	1.000	5	0	3	0	3	0
Lowe, Matthew, King.	.889	13	1	7	1	9	1
MacGillivray, Monte, Prin.*	1.000	10	0	4	0	4	0
Madson, Ryan, Mar.	.842	12	5	11	3	19	1
Maleski, Eric, Burl.	.900	19	4	5	1	10	1
Maness, Chris, Mar.	.750	19	2	4	2	8	0
Maness, Nicholas, King.	.857	13	2	10	2	14	0
Marifian, John, Mar.*	.833	16	0	5	1	6	0
Marr, Jason, J.C.	1.000	25	3	6	0	9	0
Martinez, Alex, Mar.	.917	22	3	8	1	12	0
Matew, Francisco, J.C.	.909	18	4	6	1	11	0
McDermott, Ryan, Burl.	.667	12	1	3	2	6	1
McDonald, Jon, Prin.*	1.000	25	2	10	0	12	2
McPadden, Mike, Burl.	.500	16	0	1	1	2	0
Mendoza, Geronimo, Bris.	.947	13	4	14	1	19	0
Mikkola, Shaun, King.	1.000	4	0	1	0	1	0
Moore, Eric, Pul.	.833	17	6	4	2	12	0
Morelock, Chris, Burl.	.750	16	1	2	1	4	0
Murphy, Brian, Blue.	1.000	14	7	7	0	14	0
Murphy, Darren, Blue.*	1.000	16	0	4	0	4	0
Myers, Gene, Blue.	.444	17	1	3	5	9	0
Nunez, Franklin, Mar.	.800	6	1	3	1	5	0
Perez, Norberto, Blue.	1.000	6	0	4	0	4	0
Perez, Pablo, Eliz.	.824	16	4	10	3	17	0
Phillips, Randy, Dan.*	1.000	13	2	4	0	6	1
Ratliff, Craig, Blue.	.800	3	2	2	1	5	0
Rayborn, Kris, J.C.*	.636	10	1	6	4	11	0
Reynolds, Chris, Prin.	.900	22	3	6	1	10	0
Reynolds, Jacob, Burl.	1.000	10	0	2	0	2	1
Rios, Romualdo, Pul.	.933	10	7	7	1	15	0
Rivera, Saul, Eliz.	1.000	23	5	5	0	10	0
Rizo, Jason, Blue.	1.000	16	3	7	0	10	0
Roberts, Marquis, Prin.*	1.000	8	5	15	0	20	0
Robinson, Jeremy, Prin.*	.952	13	2	18	1	21	1
Rodgers, Marcus, Bris.	.714	18	3	2	2	7	1
Rose, Johnathan, Mar.*	.750	22	1	5	2	8	0
Ruhl, Nathan, Prin.	1.000	14	0	2	0	2	0
Ryba, Jason, Blue.	.833	12	1	4	1	6	0
Sanchez, Willmen, Burl.*	.667	8	0	2	1	3	0
Scarce, Bubba, Dan.	1.000	2	1	1	0	2	0
Schaeffer, Mike, Pul.*	1.000	18	2	4	0	6	0
Schmidt, Pat, Dan.*	1.000	12	1	2	0	3	1
Sheets, Matt, Eliz.	.909	14	6	4	1	11	0
Silva, Carlos, Mar.	1.000	7	4	8	0	12	0
Simpson, Cory, Dan.	.800	14	3	1	1	5	0
Sims, Kenny, Blue.	1.000	19	3	11	0	14	0
Smith, Robert, J.C.*	.900	14	2	7	1	10	0
Standridge, Jason, Prin.	1.000	12	5	10	0	15	0
Stewart, John, Pul.*	1.000	13	6	14	0	20	1
STURDY, Tim, Eliz.	1.000	12	6	17	0	23	3
Suggs, Willie, King.	.652	15	2	13	8	23	0
Suttles, Donnie, Burl.	1.000	12	4	11	0	15	0
Tapia, Rafael, Blue.	.800	4	1	3	1	5	0
Taylor, Aaron, Dan.	.850	14	4	13	3	20	1
Tellez, Eloy, Bris.	1.000	14	0	14	0	14	0
Theodile, Simeon, Blue.	1.000	18	1	5	0	6	1
Truitt, Derrick, Dan.	.857	13	4	14	3	21	0
Turnbow, Derrick, Mar.	.952	13	8	12	1	21	0
Vallis, Jamie, Eliz.*	1.000	21	0	3	0	3	0
Vega, Rene, King.*	.692	22	0	9	4	13	0
Victoria, Lester, Eliz.*	1.000	22	3	3	0	6	0
Vigeland, William, Pul.	1.000	11	2	6	0	8	1
Viles, Jeff, J.C.	.833	27	3	2	1	6	0
Weaver, Joseph, Pul.	1.000	17	4	4	0	8	0
Wheeler, David, King.	1.000	19	2	3	0	5	0
White, Matt, Burl.*	.857	8	1	11	2	14	0
Williams, Mike, Bris.	1.000	24	5	3	0	8	0
Willoughby, Justin, Dan.*	.917	13	7	15	2	24	2
Wilson, Cliff, Blue.	1.000	1	0	1	0	1	0
Wilson, Mike, Mar.	.800	9	4	8	3	15	0
Wright, Barrett, Prin.	1.000	13	5	12	0	17	0
Wright, Jason, Prin.	1.000	9	1	2	0	3	0
Wylie, Mitchell, Bris.	1.000	20	1	3	0	4	0

The following players did not have any statistics at the positions indicated or appeared only as a designated hitter, pinch-hitter or pinch-runner: N. Alvarez, p; Backe, p; Benham, of; Bohannon, c; Bushman, c; Cummins, of; Dixon, p; Edgar, ss, of; Espy, of; Fischer, p; A. Garcia, p; Grindell, ss; Grummitt, of, p; Y. Guzman, p; Harding, ss; Hodge, 1b, c; Ishida, 2b; James, of; Jewson, 2b; D. Johnson, 1b, of; G. Johnson, 1b; T. Johnson, p; B. Kennedy, p; Kerry, of; Lebron, of; Lutz, p; J. Martin, ss; T. Martin, of; Montada, p; Murch, p; F. Moore, ss; Norrell, ss, p; Poulsen, dh; Stoffels, of; R. Torres, of; Rodriguez, dh; Romero, 1b; Rosales, p; Sabathia, p; J. Smith, p; Tanaka, p; Vasquez, c; T. Williams, p; Zachery, p.

LEAGUE CHAMPIONS

Year	Team	Pct.
1921—	Greenville	.608
	Johnson City*	.627
1922—	Bristol	.557
1923—	Knoxville	.635
1924—	Knoxville*	.642
	Bristol	.607
1925—	Greenville	.667
1926-36—	Did not operate.	
1937—	Elizabethton	.559
	Pennington Gap*	.580
1938—	Elizabethton	.664
	Greenville (3rd)†	.571
1939—	Elizabethton‡	.597
1940—	Johnson City§	.726
	Elizabethton	.750
1941—	Johnson City	.614
	Elizabethton*	.661
1942—	Bristol	.667
	Bristol∞	.660
1943—	Bristol	.755
	Bristol▲	.617
1944—	Kingsport‡	.575
1945—	Kingsport‡	.670

Year	Team	Pct.	Year	Team	Pct.	Year	Team	Pct.
1946—	New River‡	.675	1968—	Marion	.583	1986—	Johnson City	.667
1947—	Pulaski	.648	1969—	Pulaski▼	.576		Pulaski•	.621
	New River (3rd)†	.516		Johnson City	.544	1987—	Burlington•	.729
1948—	Pulaski‡	.680	1970—	Bluefield	.638		Johnson City	.609
1949—	Bluefield‡	.721	1971—	Bluefield▼	.609	1988—	Kingsport•	.644
1950—	Bluefield	.600		Kingsport	.559		Burlington	.529
	Bluefield♦	.745	1972—	Bristol▼	.588	1989—	Elizabethton•	.691
1951—	Kingsport‡	.659		Covington	.586		Pulaski	.618
1952—	Johnson City	.595	1973—	Kingsport	.757	1990—	Elizabethton	.761
	Welch (3rd)†	.509	1974—	Bristol▼	.754	1991—	Pulaski•	.662
1953—	Welch*	.705		Bluefield	.536		Burlington	.597
	Johnson City	.672	1975—	Marion	.515	1992—	Elizabethton	.742
1954—	Bluefield‡	.619		Johnson City▼	.603		Bluefield•	.597
1955—	Salem■	.689	1976—	Johnson City▼	.714	1993—	Burlington•	.647
1956—	Did not operate.			Bluefield	.600		Elizabethton	.552
1957—	Bluefield	.701	1977—	Kingsport	.623	1994—	Princeton•	.621
1958—	Johnson City	.662	1978—	Elizabethton	.594		Johnson City	.618
1959—	Morristown	.603	1979—	Paintsville	.800	1995—	Bluefield	.754
1960—	Wytheville	.614	1980—	Paintsville	.657		Kingsport•	.727
1961—	Middlesboro	.591	1981—	Paintsville	.657	1996—	Kingsport	.716
1962—	Bluefield	.671	1982—	Bluefield▼	.681		Bluefield▼	.618
1963—	Bluefield	.652		Johnson City	.478	1997—	Pulaski	.632
1964—	Johnson City	.662	1983—	Paintsville	.653		Bluefield•	.580
1965—	Salem	.614	1984—	Elizabethton•	.580	1998—	Bristol•	.636
1966—	Marion	.623		Pulaski	.536		Princeton	.559
1967—	Bluefield	.627	1985—	Bristol††	.638			

*Won split-season playoff. †Won four-team playoff. ‡Won championship and four-team playoff. §Johnson City, first-half winner, won playoff involving six clubs. ∞Won both halves and defeated second-place Elizabethton in playoff. ▲Won both halves, but Erwin won four-team playoff. ♦Won both halves, but Bristol won two-club playoff. ■Salem and Johnson City declared playoff co-champions when weather forced cancellation of final series. ▼League was divided into Northern, Southern divisions; declared league champion based on highest won-lost percentage. •League was divided into North and South divisions; won playoff. ††Bristol declared league champion based on regular-season record.

ARIZONA LEAGUE

LEAGUE OFFICE

President/treasurer
Bob Richmond

Address
P.O. Box 4941
Scottsdale, AZ 85261

Phone
602-483-8224

Teams*
Athletics
Cubs
Diamondbacks
Mariners
Padres
Rockies
White Sox

*Teams play their games in Mesa, Peoria, Phoenix, Tucson and other Arizona sites to be announced.

1998 FINAL STANDINGS
COMPOSITE

Team	Roc.	Mar.	Cubs	Ath.	Dia.	Pad.	MAS	W.S.	W	L	T	Pct.	GB
Rockies	....	1	0	2	15	2	12	10	42	14	0	.750	....
Mariners	1	....	10	10	2	6	1	1	31	24	0	.564	10.5
Cubs	2	6	....	6	0	12	2	1	29	26	0	.527	12.5
Athletics	0	6	10	....	1	9	1	2	29	27	0	.518	13.0
Diamondbacks	1	0	1	1	....	1	11	9	24	31	0	.436	17.5
Padres	0	10	4	7	1	....	0	1	23	31	0	.426	18.0
Mex. League All-Stars (Indep.)	4	1	0	1	5	1	....	10	22	33	0	.400	19.5
White Sox	6	0	1	0	7	0	6	....	20	34	0	.370	21.0

Games played in Chandler, Mesa, Peoria and Scottsdale.

Club names are major league affiliations.

FORFEIT: Diamondbacks forfeited to Rockies, June 26 (Rockies won, 9-0).

PLAYOFFS: No playoffs scheduled.

REGULAR-SEASON ATTENDANCE: No total official attendance figures reported.

MANAGERS: Athletics, John Kuehl; Cubs, Nate Oliver; Diamondbacks, Mike Brumley; Mariners, Darrin Garner; Mexican All-Stars, Abelardo Vega; Padres, Randy Whisler; Rockies, P.J. Carey; White Sox, Tony Pena.

ALL-STAR TEAM: 1B—Rene Reyes, Rockies; 2B—Esteban German, Athletics; 3B—(tie) Shawn Garrett, Padres; David Kelton, Cubs; SS—Christian Berroa, Padres; DH—Rolando Garza, White Sox; C—Miguel Olivo, Athletics; OF—Rusty Keith, Athletics; Tydus Meadows, Cubs; Ernesto Medina, Mexican All-Stars; LHP—(tie) Yonder Linares, Cubs; Andrew Vanhekken, Mariners; RHP—Jermaine Van Buren, Rockies; LHR—Yonder Linares, Cubs; RHR—Enmanuel Ulloa, Mariners; Manager of the Year—P.J. Carey, Rockies; Most Valuable Player—Rene Reyes, Rockies.

1998 BATTING
TEAM

Team	Avg.	G	TPA	AB	R	H	TB	2B	3B	HR	RBI	SH	SF	HP	BB	IBB	SO	SB	CS	GDP	LOB	ShO	Slg.	OBP
Rockies	.302	56	2205	1939	364	585	809	82	26	30	296	8	22	47	189	5	432	124	56	33	415	0	.417	.374
White Sox	.280	54	2062	1803	302	505	708	92	15	27	247	10	9	27	213	7	441	85	53	43	362	2	.393	.363
Diamondbacks	.274	55	2133	1887	300	517	732	93	31	20	252	2	23	28	193	7	519	123	30	30	410	2	.388	.346
Padres	.269	54	2189	1897	313	510	688	101	25	9	245	12	23	44	213	9	503	103	44	23	422	2	.363	.352
Athletics	.263	55	2250	1907	353	502	720	92	33	20	285	13	24	38	268	3	459	97	38	41	432	6	.378	.361
Cubs	.262	55	2175	1898	330	498	768	108	30	34	275	9	16	55	453	2	453	86	43	22	395	1	.405	.346
Mex. All-Stars	.258	55	2131	1858	304	480	648	107	11	13	259	22	15	29	207	2	470	51	35	42	405	5	.349	.339
Mariners	.255	55	2181	1903	289	485	668	85	28	14	236	17	21	39	201	14	486	91	40	37	408	3	.351	.335

INDIVIDUAL

TOP QUALIFIERS FOR BATTING CHAMPIONSHIP
Minimum 151 plate appearances. *Lefthanded batter. †Switch-hitter.

Player, Team	Avg.	G	TPA	AB	R	H	TB	2B	3B	HR	RBI	SH	SF	HP	BB	IBB	SO	SB	CS	GDP	Slg.	OBP
Reyes, Rene, Rock.†	.429	49	201	177	40	76	108	9	4	5	39	0	1	15	8	1	15	16	7	5	.610	.493
Battersby, Eric, W.S.	.375	43	168	136	34	51	87	15	3	5	27	1	2	0	29	0	32	4	2	0	.640	.479
Garza, Rolando, W.S.	.354	53	230	206	41	73	97	11	2	3	33	1	1	4	18	2	35	17	7	7	.471	.415
Roman, Junior, W.S.†	.354	36	157	130	28	46	54	3	1	1	15	1	0	2	24	0	23	17	8	1	.415	.462
Clarke, Jason, Cubs†	.343	35	157	140	30	48	72	10	4	2	25	1	2	2	12	0	15	7	4	0	.514	.397
Garrett, Shawn, Pad.†	.333	49	206	186	36	62	79	13	2	0	29	0	1	3	16	0	36	5	3	3	.425	.393
Fernandez, Alex, Mar.*	.331	44	163	151	25	50	88	11	6	5	31	0	2	1	9	3	23	3	1	3	.583	.368
Valdez, Emmanuel, M.A.S.	.328	50	222	183	31	60	85	18	2	1	35	1	5	7	26	0	55	5	3	5	.464	.421
Freeman, Choo, Rock.	.320	40	169	147	35	47	65	3	6	1	24	0	3	4	15	0	25	14	1	2	.442	.391
Colina, Javier, Rock.	.320	44	195	169	28	54	82	6	2	6	39	1	4	3	18	0	30	9	4	5	.485	.387
Berroa, Cristian, Pad.†	.319	53	218	207	33	66	95	22	2	1	33	0	3	4	4	1	38	8	4	0	.459	.339
Keith, Rusty, Ath.	.318	48	208	179	37	57	92	18	4	3	39	1	6	2	20	0	21	6	3	4	.514	.382
Sanchez, Augustin, Rock.†	.318	45	205	170	40	54	83	15	4	2	27	3	4	2	26	1	28	13	8	1	.488	.406
Closser, J.D., Dia.†	.313	45	190	150	26	47	76	13	2	4	21	0	1	2	37	2	36	3	2	3	.507	.453
Olivo, Miguel, Ath.	.311	46	177	164	30	51	74	11	3	2	23	0	1	4	8	0	43	2	2	5	.451	.356

DEPARTMENTAL LEADERS: G—German, Medina, Munoz, Rincon, 55 each; AB—Rincon, 230; R—German, 52; H—R. Reyes, 76; TB—R. Reyes, 108; 2B—C. Berroa, 22; 3B—German, 10; HR—Colina, Kelton, 6 each; RBI—Colina, Keith, R. Reyes, 39 each; SH—Duenas, 7; SF—Keith, 6; HP—R. Reyes, 15; BB—Cosentino, 39; IBB—Fernandez, 3; SO—Curry, 88; SB—German, 40; CS—Vilorio, 10; GIDP—Medina, 7; Slg.—Battersby, .640; OBP—R. Reyes, .493.

ALL PLAYERS

*Lefthanded batter. †Switch-hitter.

Player, Team	Avg.	G	TPA	AB	R	H	TB	2B	3B	HR	RBI	SH	SF	HP	BB	IBB	SO	SB	CS	GDP	Slg.	OBP
Aguirregaviria, Frank, W.S. ...	.202	37	122	104	18	21	25	4	0	0	9	1	0	2	15	0	36	2	4	5	.240	.314
Aldrup, Morey, Cubs	.242	18	74	62	14	15	26	2	0	3	9	0	1	2	9	0	15	2	1	1	.419	.351
Ardizzone, Matt, Pad.†	.385	4	14	13	3	5	9	1	0	1	4	0	1	0	0	0	0	0	1	0	.692	.357
Arias, Francisco, M.A.S.	.265	54	236	204	37	54	71	12	1	1	22	3	3	5	21	1	34	13	4	3	.348	.343
Armenta, Cristian, M.A.S.	.302	53	224	205	42	62	92	20	2	2	27	1	0	4	14	0	42	4	7	4	.449	.359
Bass, Kevin, Cubs†	.147	23	82	75	8	11	17	1	1	1	8	0	0	1	6	0	22	1	3	0	.227	.220
Battersby, Eric, W.S.	.375	43	168	136	34	51	87	15	3	5	27	1	2	0	29	0	32	4	2	0	.640	.479
Beasley, Justin, Dia.	.231	3	14	13	1	3	4	1	0	0	1	0	0	0	1	0	2	0	0	0	.308	.286
Berroa, Cristian, Pad.†	.319	53	218	207	33	66	95	22	2	1	33	0	3	4	4	1	38	8	4	0	.459	.339
Betts, Dewayne, Ath.	.195	46	150	123	21	24	31	3	2	0	21	0	3	4	20	0	36	6	5	3	.252	.320
Borges, Elio, W.S.†	.000	1	1	1	0	0	0	0	0	0	0	0	0	0	0	0	0	0	0	0	.000	.000
Boykin, Paul, Pad.*	.300	43	207	180	37	54	76	6	8	0	20	2	1	1	22	2	39	24	4	1	.422	.377
Cabrera, Mayron, W.S.	.333	30	75	72	10	24	27	3	0	0	11	1	0	0	2	0	15	3	2	2	.375	.351
Canales, Joel, M.A.S.	.253	30	100	87	13	22	29	7	0	0	15	1	0	1	11	0	19	0	0	2	.333	.343
Carroll, Mark, Mar.	.180	31	111	89	13	16	23	5	1	0	5	0	3	1	18	0	24	1	0	4	.258	.315
Castillo, Ruben, Mar.	.213	26	87	75	8	16	16	0	0	0	6	2	0	0	10	0	23	2	1	1	.213	.306
Clark, Jamie, Mar.*	.222	32	102	81	14	18	25	3	2	0	13	1	1	0	19	0	30	2	0	1	.309	.366
Clarke, Jason, Cubs†	.343	35	157	140	30	48	72	10	4	2	25	1	2	2	12	0	15	7	4	0	.514	.397
Cline, Carlos, W.S.*	.263	39	136	118	9	31	37	6	0	0	12	0	1	1	16	0	39	4	3	3	.314	.353
Closser, J.D., Dia.†	.313	45	190	150	26	47	76	13	2	4	21	0	1	2	37	2	36	3	2	3	.507	.453
Colina, Javier, Rock.	.320	44	195	169	28	54	82	6	2	6	39	1	4	3	18	0	30	9	4	5	.485	.387
Conyer, Darryl, Dia.*	.216	26	123	102	20	22	35	1	6	0	12	0	4	0	17	1	46	18	2	0	.343	.317
Cook, Jon, Pad.	.259	46	193	162	34	42	53	6	1	1	18	0	2	9	20	1	40	18	6	1	.327	.368
Corbett, Heath, Dia.	.289	34	135	121	13	35	50	9	0	2	25	0	2	1	11	0	40	3	1	3	.413	.348
Corniel, Henry, Ath.	1.000	1	1	1	0	1	1	0	0	0	1	0	0	0	0	0	0	0	0	0	1.000	1.000
Cosentino, Tony, Pad.	.264	42	194	148	29	39	50	9	1	0	24	0	4	3	39	1	31	1	2	5	.338	.418
Cruz, Juan, Cubs	1.000	13	1	1	0	1	2	1	0	0	0	0	0	0	0	0	0	0	0	0	2.000	1.000
Curry, Jesse, Pad.*	.194	46	208	180	24	35	54	7	3	2	20	1	0	2	25	0	88	4	2	2	.300	.300
Declet, Miguel, Ath.	.222	17	51	45	6	10	10	0	0	0	6	1	0	1	4	0	12	1	0	2	.222	.300
De La Cruz, Jose, Ath.	.237	46	181	156	19	37	52	5	2	2	26	0	4	0	21	0	29	1	0	2	.333	.320
Delgado, Chris, W.S.	.302	38	150	129	28	39	66	12	0	5	25	0	0	1	20	0	30	6	1	1	.512	.400
Doakes, Schuyler, Mar.†	.309	39	152	136	24	42	54	8	2	0	12	2	1	3	10	0	23	10	7	1	.397	.367
Dorsett, Chris, Cubs	.309	20	67	55	14	17	28	5	0	2	18	0	3	0	9	1	8	1	0	1	.509	.388
Duenas, Manuel, M.A.S.	.222	51	200	162	20	36	45	6	0	1	25	7	2	5	24	0	54	2	1	4	.278	.337
Durango, Ariel, Mar.†	.269	24	79	67	16	18	29	3	1	2	10	3	0	3	6	0	18	7	5	0	.433	.355
Easter, J.J., Rock.	.262	22	69	61	11	16	18	2	0	0	5	0	0	0	8	0	20	9	2	0	.295	.348
Egly, John, Dia.†	.172	35	135	122	14	21	28	2	1	1	9	2	2	0	9	0	58	4	2	2	.230	.226
Encarnacion, Bernardo, Rock. .	.322	34	142	121	20	39	58	5	1	4	25	0	1	8	11	0	33	2	0	4	.479	.411
Espinoza, Efren, M.A.S.	.313	9	17	16	4	5	7	2	0	0	1	0	1	0	0	0	4	0	0	0	.438	.294
Estrella, Gorky, Mar.	.244	50	209	164	31	40	60	10	2	2	26	0	2	7	36	1	50	8	2	3	.366	.397
Fernandez, Alex, Mar.*	.331	44	163	151	25	50	88	11	6	5	31	0	2	1	9	3	23	3	1	3	.583	.368
Forbes, Matt, Ath.	.250	47	191	160	24	40	54	10	2	0	17	2	1	0	28	0	56	11	5	1	.338	.360
Freeman, Choo, Rock.	.320	40	169	147	35	47	65	3	6	1	24	0	3	4	15	0	25	14	1	2	.442	.391
Freeman, Corey, Mar.	.287	37	136	122	21	35	37	2	0	0	15	1	2	2	9	1	20	9	1	1	.303	.341
French, Ron, Pad.	.190	18	72	63	9	12	16	4	0	0	5	0	0	6	3	0	13	1	0	4	.254	.292
Fukuhara, Pete, Cubs	.286	49	217	182	37	52	77	16	0	3	36	1	3	6	25	0	23	5	7	2	.423	.384
Gann, Jamie, Dia.	.429	2	7	7	1	3	4	1	0	0	1	0	0	0	0	0	2	0	0	0	.571	.429
Garcia, Cip, Mar.	.194	30	112	98	10	19	29	6	2	0	11	0	2	0	12	1	23	1	2	4	.296	.277
Garcia, Tony, W.S.	.250	36	141	120	21	30	48	5	2	3	21	0	1	5	15	1	31	5	4	3	.400	.355
Garrett, Shawn, Pad.†	.333	49	206	186	36	62	79	13	2	0	29	0	1	3	16	0	36	5	3	3	.425	.393
Garza, Rolando, W.S.	.354	53	230	206	41	73	97	11	2	3	33	1	1	4	18	2	35	17	7	7	.471	.415
German, Esteban, Ath.	.307	55	242	202	52	62	91	3	10	2	28	2	1	4	33	0	43	40	8	1	.450	.413
German, Franklin, Cubs..........	.238	41	176	164	22	39	53	11	0	1	13	3	1	1	7	0	53	8	6	3	.323	.272
Gil, Ivan, M.A.S.†	.171	24	75	70	9	12	12	0	0	0	4	1	0	0	4	0	14	2	2	1	.171	.216
Goldbach, Jeff, Cubs.............	.265	38	149	136	22	36	63	11	2	4	25	0	0	2	11	0	41	5	2	1	.463	.329
Gomer, Jeramy, Cubs*	.000	11	0	0	0	0	0	0	0	0	0	1	0	0	0	0	0	0	0	0	.000	.000
Gonzalez, Franklin, Pad.	.276	19	84	76	12	21	30	2	2	1	11	0	0	1	7	0	18	7	1	0	.395	.345
Graffagnini, Keith, Mar.	.235	22	89	81	10	19	24	1	2	0	11	0	0	3	5	1	16	2	0	2	.296	.303
Guerrero, Joel, Pad.†	.232	37	135	112	10	26	29	3	0	0	6	4	0	0	19	0	41	11	8	0	.259	.344
Guiel, Aaron, Pad.*	.500	8	24	16	8	8	16	3	1	1	6	0	0	2	5	1	5	1	1	0	1.000	.667
Gutierrez, Said, Pad.	.253	28	104	91	13	23	29	4	1	0	14	0	1	5	7	0	26	3	2	0	.319	.337
Guzman, Javier, Rock.†	.292	17	51	48	4	14	16	2	0	0	4	0	0	0	3	0	21	4	0	1	.333	.333
Hall, Victor, Dia.*	.188	28	114	101	10	19	22	1	1	0	10	0	1	2	10	0	29	14	2	1	.218	.272
Heintzelman, Brian, Dia.	.289	15	45	38	6	11	14	0	0	1	10	0	0	2	5	0	11	1	1	0	.368	.400
Hernandez, Esteban, M.A.S. ..	.174	34	104	92	13	16	27	5	0	2	10	2	0	2	8	0	36	0	1	2	.293	.255
Hernandez, Orlando, Mar.	.286	31	103	91	8	26	30	2	1	0	11	1	1	3	7	1	26	3	1	2	.330	.353
Holliday, Matt, Rock.	.342	32	138	117	20	40	61	4	1	5	23	0	4	2	15	2	21	2	1	0	.521	.413
Joseph, Adolfo, Dia.	.331	28	131	124	31	41	66	8	4	3	28	0	1	2	4	0	39	10	0	0	.532	.359
Kail, Tom, Dia.	.265	26	110	102	13	27	37	2	4	0	13	0	2	1	5	0	18	2	2	0	.363	.300
Keith, Rusty, Ath.	.318	48	208	179	37	57	92	18	4	3	39	1	6	2	20	0	21	6	3	4	.514	.382
Kelton, Dave, Cubs...............	.265	50	207	181	39	48	83	7	5	6	29	0	1	2	23	0	58	16	3	2	.459	.353
Kent, Mat, Mar.*	.225	27	95	89	5	20	23	3	0	0	10	0	1	2	3	1	23	0	3	6	.258	.263
Knorr, Mario, Dia.*	.289	41	174	149	28	43	52	3	3	0	11	2	0	1	22	0	35	11	4	1	.349	.385
Koen, Nate, Cubs	.271	14	51	48	5	13	18	0	1	1	8	0	0	0	3	0	10	0	0	0	.375	.294
Lopez, Miguel, Dia.	.355	22	85	76	8	27	44	9	1	2	16	0	2	2	5	0	9	3	2	1	.579	.400
Lopez, Orlando, Mar.	.242	34	107	95	15	23	26	3	0	0	5	1	0	3	8	0	26	6	4	1	.274	.321
Lopez, Rafael, Mar.	.333	5	16	15	1	5	7	2	0	0	2	0	0	1	0	0	2	0	1	0	.467	.375
Lowe, Ernesto, W.S.	.225	29	104	80	11	18	23	2	0	1	11	1	1	3	18	0	21	6	2	1	.288	.382
Mack, Tony, Ath.	.252	43	156	127	20	32	51	8	1	3	17	1	1	10	17	0	44	2	2	1	.402	.381
Manuel, Marcellous, W.S.*	.299	44	151	137	29	41	69	11	1	5	26	1	0	0	13	1	19	5	3	7	.504	.360

Player, Team	Avg.	G	TPA	AB	R	H	TB	2B	3B	HR	RBI	SH	SF	HP	BB	IBB	SO	SB	CS	GDP	Slg.	OBP
Martinez, Daniel, Cubs†	.200	17	57	50	6	10	12	0	1	0	3	1	0	0	6	0	10	6	1	2	.240	.286
Martinez, Dionnar, Cubs†	.192	25	86	78	13	15	18	3	0	0	6	0	0	1	7	0	22	4	2	0	.231	.267
Mauck, Matt, Cubs*	.240	37	157	125	22	30	47	6	4	1	16	1	3	9	19	0	45	3	1	0	.376	.372
McCarty, Brock, Dia.	.226	43	159	146	19	33	42	4	1	1	15	0	1	1	11	1	43	16	4	4	.288	.283
Meadows, Tydus, Cubs	.367	27	117	98	25	36	61	8	4	3	26	0	0	2	17	1	17	6	5	1	.622	.470
Medina, Ernesto, M.A.S.	.277	55	246	220	39	61	82	11	2	2	38	2	2	2	20	0	42	7	4	7	.373	.340
Meier, Dan, Dia.*	.343	12	47	35	10	12	18	3	0	1	5	0	1	0	11	0	8	1	0	0	.514	.489
Morency, Vernand, Rock.	.213	24	74	61	11	13	13	0	0	0	3	0	0	1	12	0	17	3	1	2	.213	.351
Mosley, Kelly, W.S.	.230	32	96	87	14	20	23	1	1	0	3	0	0	3	6	0	30	3	3	2	.264	.302
Motley, Brittan, Pad.†	.242	27	112	91	15	22	33	6	1	1	11	3	1	1	13	1	36	5	2	0	.363	.275
Moye, Melvin, Dia.	.224	24	91	85	10	19	29	4	0	2	13	0	0	1	5	0	21	1	0	2	.341	.275
Munoz, Adan, M.A.S.	.254	55	226	201	28	51	75	12	0	4	28	0	1	1	23	0	61	4	2	6	.373	.332
Navarro, Ibrahim, Cubs	.282	31	130	117	18	33	53	7	2	3	13	1	0	2	10	0	28	2	0	3	.453	.404
Neal, Steve, Dia.*	.319	12	56	47	8	15	19	4	0	0	8	0	0	3	6	1	13	4	0	0	.404	.429
Neubart, Adam, Dia.	.158	6	23	19	6	3	5	2	0	0	0	0	0	1	3	0	2	1	0	0	.263	.304
Nielson, Bret, Mar.*	.233	40	142	120	16	28	50	6	5	2	20	1	2	1	18	2	58	5	1	0	.417	.333
Nixon, Justin, Ath.*	.160	40	111	81	20	13	21	3	1	1	11	2	1	2	23	0	42	3	4	5	.259	.355
Noboa, Joel, Cubs	.276	39	164	152	19	42	64	9	2	3	20	0	2	0	10	1	49	4	3	4	.421	.317
Olivo, Miguel, Ath.	.311	46	177	164	30	51	74	11	3	2	23	0	1	4	8	0	43	2	2	5	.451	.354
Paulino, Henry, Rock.	.253	24	83	79	16	20	21	1	0	0	8	0	0	0	4	0	17	2	6	3	.266	.289
Pena, Pelagio, Mar.	.304	18	48	46	5	14	20	2	2	0	3	0	0	2	0	0	11	0	1	2	.435	.333
Perez, Rafael, W.S.*	.263	40	132	118	19	31	49	4	4	2	18	1	0	2	10	1	47	5	6	0	.415	.331
Pinero, Juan, Cubs†	.264	51	241	201	38	53	77	13	4	1	18	1	1	12	26	0	30	15	7	5	.383	.379
Porter, Jamie, Ath.	.254	34	147	126	25	32	42	10	0	0	16	1	0	1	19	1	30	7	3	2	.333	.356
Proctor, Jerry, Dia.	.167	3	6	6	1	1	1	0	0	0	0	1	0	0	0	0	1	0	0	1	.167	.167
Quintana, Wilfredo, Mar.	.270	32	125	111	18	30	49	10	0	3	25	1	4	2	7	0	23	5	1	0	.441	.315
Rapp, Travis, W.S.	.243	18	45	37	5	9	14	5	0	0	3	1	0	1	6	1	15	0	1	0	.378	.364
Reed, Jeremy, Pad.	.212	17	56	52	2	11	12	1	0	0	5	0	2	0	2	0	20	1	0	4	.231	.232
Reyes, Rene, Rock.†	.429	49	201	177	40	76	108	9	4	5	39	0	1	15	8	1	15	16	7	5	.610	.493
Rincon, Isaias, M.A.S.	.235	55	256	230	32	54	65	9	1	0	27	1	0	1	24	0	70	9	5	5	.283	.310
Rivera, Jesus, M.A.S.*	.258	44	161	132	27	34	38	2	1	0	15	3	0	1	25	1	18	4	3	2	.288	.380
Robinson, Coby, Cubs	.205	26	97	83	7	17	26	4	1	1	7	0	0	10	4	0	27	1	0	0	.313	.320
Rodriguez, Mervin, W.S.	.283	23	60	53	8	15	16	1	0	0	7	0	1	2	4	1	16	1	1	2	.302	.350
Rohena, Omar, Cubs	.143	20	60	56	2	8	8	0	0	0	4	0	0	3	1	0	20	2	1	1	.143	.200
Roman, Junior, W.S.†	.354	36	157	130	28	46	54	3	1	1	15	1	0	2	24	0	23	17	8	1	.415	.462
Rosario, Felix, Mar.†	.233	33	80	73	12	17	18	1	0	0	7	1	0	4	2	0	22	9	4	0	.247	.291
Salazar, Oscar, Ath.	.324	26	115	102	29	33	56	7	5	2	18	0	0	1	12	0	15	4	1	1	.549	.400
Saldua, Luis, M.A.S.	.232	24	64	56	9	13	20	3	2	0	12	0	1	0	7	0	21	1	3	1	.357	.313
Samuel, Tomas, Rock.	.304	37	127	112	20	34	51	7	2	2	17	1	1	1	12	0	40	4	9	2	.455	.373
Sanchez, Augustin, Rock.†	.318	45	205	170	40	54	83	15	4	2	27	3	4	2	26	1	28	13	8	1	.488	.406
Santamarina, Juan, W.S.*	.200	41	177	165	15	33	43	4	0	2	20	0	2	1	9	0	36	3	1	6	.261	.243
Scheid, Jeremy, Ath.*	.283	53	239	191	31	54	76	8	1	4	35	0	5	5	38	2	32	5	1	5	.398	.406
Schmidt, Bryan, Pad.	.289	47	222	194	29	56	68	12	0	0	22	1	4	4	19	2	28	6	3	3	.351	.357
Schmidt, J.P., Ath.*	.196	38	122	107	18	21	23	2	0	0	14	2	0	2	11	0	26	6	2	2	.215	.283
Schneidmiller, Gary, Ath.	.241	38	158	141	21	34	45	4	2	1	13	1	1	2	13	0	30	3	2	1	.319	.312
Shipp, Charles, Cubs	.294	9	35	34	6	10	17	2	1	1	6	0	0	0	1	0	1	0	0	0	.500	.314
Simmons, Brian, W.S.†	.167	5	13	12	1	2	2	0	0	0	0	0	0	0	1	0	6	0	0	0	.167	.231
Smith, Sam, Rock.	.303	30	124	122	20	37	48	7	2	0	21	0	0	2	0	0	21	5	2	1	.393	.315
Sobet, Renato, Pad.	.209	30	119	110	15	23	33	1	3	1	15	0	2	1	6	0	40	4	2	0	.300	.250
Soriano, Rafael, Mar.	.167	32	122	108	17	18	22	4	0	0	6	2	1	6	11	1	34	5	3	1	.204	.250
Sosa, Jorge, Rock.†	.237	45	167	152	23	36	50	6	1	2	11	0	1	2	12	0	57	4	3	3	.329	.299
Stankiewicz, Andy, Dia.	.300	3	10	10	2	3	3	0	0	0	3	0	0	0	0	0	0	0	0	0	.300	.300
Tineo, Esmerlin, W.S.*	.214	32	106	98	11	21	28	5	1	0	6	1	0	0	7	0	15	4	5	3	.286	.267
Underwood, Jake, Mar.	.321	11	30	28	2	9	16	3	2	0	5	0	0	2	0	0	8	0	1	1	.571	.367
Uribe, Juan, Rock.	.277	40	168	148	25	41	52	5	3	0	17	3	2	3	12	0	25	8	1	1	.351	.339
Urquiola, Carlos, Dia.*	.618	9	42	34	14	21	32	3	4	0	10	0	0	3	5	0	5	13	1	0	.941	.690
Valdez, Emmanuel, M.A.S.	.328	50	222	183	31	60	85	18	2	1	35	1	5	7	26	0	55	5	3	5	.464	.421
Valera, Gregori, Dia.	.282	45	174	163	20	46	59	11	1	0	11	0	3	1	7	0	34	2	1	6	.362	.310
Vicente, Audo, Dia.†	.271	24	98	85	20	23	28	3	1	0	5	0	0	4	9	0	18	12	3	2	.329	.367
Vieira, Scott, Cubs	.500	4	14	12	2	6	10	1	0	1	4	0	0	0	2	0	0	0	0	0	.833	.571
Vilorio, Miguel, Rock.	.292	32	140	130	29	38	40	2	0	0	17	0	1	0	9	0	16	27	10	1	.308	.339
Weeks, Paul, Pad.	.313	7	25	16	4	5	6	1	0	0	2	1	1	1	6	0	4	4	3	0	.375	.500
Williams, George, Ath.†	.500	1	3	2	0	1	1	0	0	0	0	0	0	0	1	0	0	0	0	0	.500	.667
Williams, P.J., Mar.	.349	16	73	63	18	22	22	0	0	0	2	1	0	1	8	2	9	13	2	1	.349	.431
Winchester, Jeff, Rock.	.208	43	153	125	22	26	43	8	0	3	16	0	0	6	22	0	46	2	1	2	.344	.353

GRAND SLAMS: Nielson 2; C. Delgado, Goldbach, F. Gonzalez, Salazar, 1 each.

AWARDED FIRST BASE ON CATCHER'S INTERFERENCE: Motley 3 (Kent, Goldbach, Carroll); Nixon 2 (Mauck, Cosentino); Boykin (Mauck); Encarnacion (A. Garcia); Lowe (Pena); Motley (Kent); R. Perez (Heintzelman).

1998 PITCHING
TEAM

Team	W	L	Pct.	ERA	G	CG	ShO	Sv.	IP	H	TBF	R	ER	HR	SH	SF	HB	BB	IBB	SO	WP	Bk.
Mariners	31	24	.564	3.57	55	0	3	15	497.0	436	2168	270	197	18	12	10	39	213	2	576	62	27
Rockies	42	14	.750	3.73	56	2	6	21	489.1	454	2104	259	203	9	10	12	24	190	5	530	50	11
Padres	23	31	.426	4.55	54	0	3	8	484.1	503	2191	320	245	16	19	14	40	213	5	439	41	13
Cubs	29	26	.527	4.60	55	0	3	8	485.2	539	2227	336	248	13	17	22	35	231	16	419	52	23
Athletics	29	27	.518	4.71	56	0	2	15	491.1	520	2211	334	257	22	8	30	53	214	3	486	68	26
Diamondbacks	24	31	.436	4.85	55	0	3	11	471.0	522	2155	337	254	24	8	16	47	195	0	460	69	13
Mexican All-Stars	22	33	.400	4.99	55	2	1	7	468.2	522	2067	302	260	31	11	18	36	182	11	396	32	24
White Sox	20	34	.370	6.19	54	0	1	7	456.1	586	2212	397	314	34	15	26	33	243	7	437	49	27

TOP QUALIFIERS FOR EARNED-RUN AVERAGE TITLE
Minimum 45 innings. *Lefthanded pitcher.

Pitcher, Team	W	L	Pct.	ERA	G	GS	CG	ShO	GF	Sv.	IP	H	TBF	R	ER	HR	SH	SF	HB	BB	IBB	SO	WP	Bk.
Van Buren, Jermaine, Rock. ...	7	2	.778	2.22	12	11	1	1	0	0	65.0	42	256	20	16	2	0	0	3	22	0	92	3	2
Prouty, Scott, Mar.	3	2	.600	2.44	13	11	0	0	1	0	48.0	40	218	27	13	1	0	1	4	32	0	57	6	0
Trask, Cody, Rock.	6	1	.857	2.49	20	0	0	0	4	2	47.0	36	192	16	13	0	1	2	2	18	1	68	4	1
Linares, Yonder, Cubs*	7	2	.778	2.91	15	2	0	0	4	0	55.2	62	227	24	18	1	2	2	2	5	1	32	0	0
Colome, Jesus, Ath.	2	5	.286	3.18	12	11	0	0	0	0	56.2	47	229	27	20	1	0	1	6	16	0	62	5	3
Flores, Jorge, M.A.S. *	2	2	.500	3.40	18	3	0	0	10	2	50.1	52	206	22	19	4	2	2	5	7	3	53	1	3
Navarro, Joel, M.A.S.	4	4	.500	3.55	13	10	0	0	1	0	66.0	81	281	34	26	1	1	3	2	13	2	43	1	1
Little, Roger, Rock.	4	1	.800	3.80	14	8	0	0	0	0	47.1	50	212	30	20	1	1	1	1	18	0	46	4	1
De Paula, Julio, Rock.	5	5	.500	3.81	17	9	0	0	4	2	54.1	54	238	30	23	1	2	3	1	18	1	62	10	0
Pacheco, Enemecio, Rock.	5	0	1.000	3.99	12	11	0	0	0	0	58.2	51	240	31	26	1	0	2	3	17	0	59	3	1
Morel, Francis, Dia.	3	2	.600	4.13	15	6	0	0	6	0	56.2	64	245	32	26	1	2	2	3	17	0	41	2	3
Verdugo, Oswaldo, M.A.S.	2	2	.500	4.20	12	8	0	0	3	0	49.1	57	210	28	23	3	1	2	4	13	0	56	3	1
Garcia, Gerardo, M.A.S.	1	8	.111	4.86	15	9	0	0	3	0	46.1	49	203	30	25	3	0	0	4	27	0	47	6	5
Arias, Joel, M.A.S.	1	7	.125	5.48	18	4	0	0	5	1	46.0	50	212	33	28	3	1	4	3	20	3	27	0	0
Meyer, John, Pad.	2	5	.286	5.66	12	11	0	0	0	0	49.1	54	230	40	31	2	0	3	7	33	0	46	7	1

DEPARTMENTAL LEADERS: W—Linares, Van Buren, 7 each; L—G. Garcia, 8; Pct.—Trask, .857; G—Gomez, 29; GS—Caraballo, 13; CG—Angulo, 2; ShO—Several players tied at 1; GF—Gomez, 24; Sv.—Gomez, 12; IP—Navarro, 66.0; H—Caraballo, 90; TBF—Caraballo, 328; R—Caraballo, 71; ER—Caraballo, 53; HR—A. Simpson, 8; SH—Aguilera, Beltran, 4 each; SF—Caraballo, 7; HB—Carreras, Ruiz, 9 each; BB—Walton, 45; IBB—Hardcastle, 5; SO—Van Buren, 92; WP—Walton, 22; BK—Caraballo, 8.

ALL PITCHERS
*Lefthanded pitcher.

Pitcher, Team	W	L	Pct.	ERA	G	GS	CG	ShO	GF	Sv.	IP	H	TBF	R	ER	HR	SH	SF	HB	BB	IBB	SO	WP	Bk.
Abbott, Paul, Mar.	0	0	.000	0.00	1	0	0	0	0	0	3.0	1	12	0	0	0	0	0	1	0	0	6	0	0
Acosta, Jhon, Cubs	2	0	1.000	2.20	11	2	0	0	1	0	28.2	25	119	13	7	0	0	1	1	10	0	24	0	0
Adams, Willie, Mar.	0	1	.000	2.45	2	2	0	0	0	0	3.2	3	17	2	1	0	0	0	1	1	0	3	0	0
Aguilera, Edgar, M.A.S.	4	3	.571	6.06	11	8	0	0	3	0	35.2	39	174	29	24	4	4	2	3	22	1	39	5	2
Almonte, Edwin, W.S.	0	0	.000	0.93	5	0	0	0	2	0	9.2	6	37	5	1	0	0	1	1	0	0	6	0	0
Alvarez, Larry, Cubs	1	1	.500	5.54	10	0	0	0	2	0	26.0	24	114	17	16	2	2	0	3	8	1	15	4	0
Angulo, Victor, M.A.S. *	3	1	.750	4.76	11	5	2	0	0	0	39.2	36	174	21	21	2	1	0	2	25	0	23	4	1
Arias, Joel, M.A.S.	1	7	.125	5.48	18	4	0	0	5	1	46.0	50	212	33	28	3	1	4	3	20	3	27	0	0
Barcelo, Lorenzo, W.S.	0	1	.000	1.50	3	3	0	0	0	0	6.0	6	24	1	1	0	1	0	0	0	0	9	0	0
Barndollar, Jeff, Dia.	2	1	.667	4.01	9	6	0	0	1	0	42.2	43	185	22	19	2	1	1	4	15	0	46	5	2
Barnes, Pat, Mar. *	0	1	.000	7.94	3	0	0	0	1	0	5.2	6	29	5	5	0	0	1	0	5	0	6	3	0
Bartosh, Cliff, Pad. *	3	2	.600	3.48	13	5	0	0	0	0	44.0	43	190	23	17	2	1	2	4	16	0	43	4	0
Batista, Rafael, Mar.	1	1	.500	4.15	14	1	0	0	3	0	30.1	33	137	16	14	0	0	0	6	7	0	28	3	4
Battersby, Eric, W.S. *	0	0	.000	0.00	1	0	0	0	0	0	0.1	1	1	0	0	0	0	0	0	0	0	1	0	0
Batts, Nathan, Cubs*	3	2	.600	5.40	13	7	0	0	1	0	36.2	40	183	31	22	1	1	0	5	34	1	28	7	2
Bazzell, Shane, Ath.	4	2	.667	3.27	12	8	0	0	0	0	41.1	30	174	19	15	1	1	3	3	15	0	51	9	5
Bell, Casey, Pad.	4	1	.800	2.63	7	7	0	0	0	0	41.0	34	167	19	12	0	2	2	8	0	0	36	0	2
Beltran, Francis, Cubs	1	1	.500	5.55	12	5	0	0	4	0	35.2	49	165	23	22	1	4	2	2	14	1	26	1	1
Bennett, Tom, Ath.	1	2	.333	7.11	5	2	0	0	0	0	12.2	9	70	15	10	0	0	0	3	18	0	20	7	0
Berroa, Oliver, Mar.	0	1	.000	3.38	5	5	0	0	0	0	26.2	24	112	14	10	1	1	1	1	8	0	26	4	1
Bevis, P.J., Dia.	3	3	.500	5.96	14	9	0	0	1	0	45.1	55	205	39	30	6	0	0	5	10	0	48	7	0
Biddle, Rocky, W.S.	1	0	1.000	3.94	5	2	0	0	0	0	16.0	15	72	9	7	2	0	0	2	8	0	18	5	0
Bieniasz, Derek, Mar.	1	4	.200	9.00	5	4	0	0	0	0	15.0	26	74	18	15	1	1	0	4	1	0	12	0	1
Borne, Matt, W.S.	0	0	.000	4.50	2	0	0	0	0	0	4.0	3	20	3	2	0	1	0	1	4	0	3	0	0
Brown, Darold, Cubs*	0	0	.000	0.00	1	1	0	0	0	0	1.0	1	5	0	0	0	0	0	0	2	0	0	0	0
Brown, Tighe, W.S.	0	0	.000	4.26	5	0	0	0	2	0	6.1	7	33	8	3	1	0	0	1	4	0	10	1	1
Caraballo, Angel, W.S. *	3	5	.375	7.49	14	13	0	0	0	0	63.2	90	328	71	53	5	1	7	8	36	0	57	11	8
Carballo, Enrique, M.A.S.	1	0	1.000	2.11	12	0	0	0	5	0	21.1	17	86	6	5	1	0	0	3	7	1	19	3	1
Carreras, Marino, Mar. *	0	1	.000	3.38	10	8	0	0	0	0	37.1	27	179	25	14	1	2	5	9	30	0	43	6	4
Castillo, Adolfo, M.A.S.	0	0	.000	3.86	4	1	0	0	1	0	16.1	19	69	8	7	1	1	0	0	3	0	12	0	3
Colome, Jesus, Ath.	2	5	.286	3.18	12	11	0	0	0	0	56.2	47	229	27	20	1	0	1	6	16	0	62	5	3
Condrey, Clay, Pad.	0	1	.000	3.38	5	0	0	0	0	0	5.1	6	26	4	2	0	0	0	0	5	1	4	1	1
Conroy, Ken, Cubs	2	0	1.000	1.64	9	0	0	0	4	0	11.0	6	50	5	2	0	1	2	7	0	0	15	1	1
Corniel, Henry, Ath.	3	1	.750	3.11	17	0	0	0	5	0	37.2	36	158	16	13	3	1	2	4	9	0	30	2	0
Crawford, Jeremy, Ath. *	3	0	1.000	3.90	17	0	0	0	3	0	30.0	36	136	17	13	0	2	3	12	0	0	25	1	1
Crivello, Justin, Dia. *	0	2	.000	3.86	20	0	0	0	11	3	30.1	30	140	15	13	1	2	1	4	16	0	42	4	1
Cruz, Juan, Cubs	2	4	.333	6.10	12	5	0	0	0	0	41.1	61	210	48	28	2	1	5	3	14	0	36	8	3
D'Amico, Jeff, Ath.	0	0	.000	3.86	4	1	0	0	0	0	9.1	6	34	4	4	2	0	0	1	1	0	8	0	0
Darr, Jerry, Pad.	1	0	1.000	3.47	7	7	0	0	0	0	23.1	16	98	10	9	0	0	3	12	0	0	27	2	0
DeLeon, Bryan, Pad.	1	3	.250	7.52	16	0	0	0	7	0	26.1	39	135	27	22	1	1	0	3	13	1	18	3	0
Delgado, Danny, Mar.	2	1	.667	4.73	5	0	0	0	0	0	13.1	12	55	9	7	3	0	0	1	2	0	15	0	0
Deliza, Carlos, Pad.	1	1	.500	2.82	18	1	0	0	6	1	38.1	33	161	14	12	0	0	0	4	13	0	34	2	0
De Paula, Julio, Rock.	5	5	.500	3.81	17	9	0	0	4	2	54.1	54	238	30	23	1	2	3	1	18	1	62	10	0
Devine, Travis, Pad.	0	2	.000	18.00	2	2	0	0	0	0	2.0	6	14	5	4	0	0	0	1	0	0	3	0	1
Dowell, Brian, Pad.	3	2	.600	6.91	14	0	0	0	9	2	27.1	29	125	22	21	0	1	0	14	0	0	29	1	0
Duenas, Alain, W.S.	0	0	.000	2.25	6	0	0	0	5	0	8.0	6	34	2	2	0	0	0	2	0	0	11	0	1
Duprey, Pete, Mar. *	3	0	1.000	3.48	19	1	0	0	12	2	33.2	35	148	17	13	0	2	0	1	12	0	43	2	5
Ericks, Dave, Cubs	0	2	.000	4.29	11	0	0	0	2	0	21.0	23	104	19	10	0	1	3	17	4	0	15	2	4
Ferrand, Dario, W.S.	2	2	.500	4.60	16	0	0	0	5	1	31.1	49	142	18	16	2	0	1	0	4	0	19	0	3
Fischer, Eric, W.S. *	0	1	.000	5.20	8	8	0	0	0	0	27.2	30	129	18	16	3	0	0	1	14	0	31	2	3
Fleming, John, Dia.	0	0	.000	0.00	1	0	0	0	1	0	1.0	2	5	0	0	0	0	0	0	1	0	2	0	0
Flores, Jorge, M.A.S. *	2	2	.500	3.40	18	3	0	0	10	2	50.1	52	206	22	19	4	2	2	5	7	3	53	1	3
Fogg, Josh, W.S.	1	0	1.000	0.00	2	0	0	0	0	0	4.0	3	13	0	0	0	1	0	0	1	0	5	1	0

SUMMER CLASS A *Arizona League*

Pitcher, Team	W	L	Pct.	ERA	G	GS	CG	ShO	GF	Sv.	IP	H	TBF	R	ER	HR	SH	SF	HB	BB	IBB	SO	WP	Bk.
Freeman, Kai, W.S.	0	0	.000	4.50	1	0	0	0	0	0	2.0	1	8	1	1	0	1	0	1	0	2	1	0
Frias, Yovany, W.S.	1	1	.500	8.13	11	4	0	0	2	0	27.2	41	146	30	25	2	1	2	6	22	1	21	5	0
Garcia, Gerardo, M.A.S.	1	8	.111	4.86	15	9	0	0	3	0	46.1	49	203	30	25	3	0	0	4	27	0	47	6	5
Garner, Brandon, Rock.	3	0	1.000	4.29	13	7	0	0	1	0	35.2	33	154	18	17	0	0	1	1	15	0	28	6	3
German, Franklyn, Ath.	2	1	.667	6.13	14	12	0	0	0	0	54.1	69	249	43	37	5	1	5	7	18	0	46	5	3
Gomer, Jeramy, Cubs*	2	3	.400	5.45	11	9	0	0	0	0	36.1	44	156	27	22	2	0	4	2	9	0	39	3	0
Gomez, Diogenes, Rock.	1	0	1.000	2.55	29	0	0	0	24	12	35.1	30	141	15	10	0	1	0	1	11	1	28	4	0
Gonzalez, Martin, W.S.	0	1	.000	28.42	7	0	0	0	2	0	6.1	24	53	25	20	1	0	0	0	8	0	9	1	0
Good, Andy, Dia.	1	3	.250	4.28	9	8	0	0	0	0	33.2	46	152	25	16	1	0	1	2	7	0	25	3	0
Griman, Carlos, Dia.	0	1	.000	5.14	2	2	0	0	0	0	7.0	8	36	6	4	0	0	0	0	5	0	7	2	1
Guzman, Ricardo, M.A.S.	0	0	.000	7.94	11	0	0	0	3	0	22.2	28	102	21	20	4	0	2	5	8	0	13	3	0
Hammons, Matt, Cubs	0	1	.000	2.33	7	6	0	0	0	0	19.1	18	84	6	5	0	1	0	1	10	0	29	1	2
Hardcastle, John, Cubs*	0	2	.000	10.80	12	2	0	0	4	1	20.0	35	118	33	24	0	2	0	3	20	5	17	4	4
Hasselhoff, Derek, W.S.	0	0	.000	0.00	6	1	0	0	1	0	10.0	6	36	1	0	0	0	0	0	0	0	16	0	0
Hawkins, Ryan, Pad.	0	0	.000	0.00	1	0	0	0	0	0	2.0	0	8	0	0	0	0	0	1	0	0	2	0	1
Heintzelman, Brian, Dia.	0	0	.000	0.00	1	0	0	0	1	0	1.0	0	3	0	0	0	0	0	0	0	0	1	0	0
Herrera, Jose, Mar.	0	0	.000	1.93	4	0	0	0	1	0	9.1	5	38	3	2	0	0	0	6	0	10	3	0
Hessler, John, Rock.	4	0	1.000	4.50	16	0	0	0	4	1	28.0	23	124	21	14	0	1	0	4	16	0	13	3	0
Iannacone, Steve, Rock.	2	1	.667	6.21	15	0	0	0	6	1	29.0	35	137	25	20	2	0	2	2	18	1	31	4	1
Jimenez, Francisco, Dia.	3	4	.429	6.43	12	3	0	0	3	0	28.0	36	126	24	20	5	0	0	4	7	0	18	2	2
Jones, Keith, Dia.	0	0	.000	27.00	2	0	0	0	0	0	1.1	7	11	4	4	0	0	1	0	2	0	0	0	0
Kelley, Brenton, Dia.	0	2	.000	2.70	17	0	0	0	12	6	23.1	24	101	10	7	0	0	2	4	0	27	3	0
Kenny, Seth, Ath.	1	5	.167	3.03	13	6	0	0	5	3	35.2	46	165	25	12	1	0	4	3	8	0	35	2	3
Koplove, Mike, Dia.	0	0	.000	9.00	2	0	0	0	0	0	4.0	4	19	4	4	0	0	1	2	0	5	0	0
Kvasnicka, Jay, W.S.	0	2	.000	9.00	7	0	0	0	4	1	8.0	11	38	10	8	0	1	1	0	2	0	8	0	0
Linares, Yonder, Cubs*	7	2	.778	2.91	15	2	0	0	4	0	55.2	62	227	24	18	1	2	2	2	5	1	32	0	0
Little, Rodney, Rock.	2	2	.500	3.47	19	0	0	0	8	2	36.1	38	172	18	14	1	3	1	2	21	1	42	4	0
Little, Roger, Rock.	4	1	.800	3.80	14	8	0	0	0	0	47.1	50	212	30	20	1	1	1	1	18	0	46	4	1
Luque, Roger, Pad. *	2	1	.667	5.79	12	6	0	0	3	0	42.0	59	196	36	27	3	1	3	2	9	0	38	4	2
Mack, Tony, Ath.	0	0	.000	0.00	1	0	0	0	1	0	0.1	1	3	0	0	0	0	0	1	0	0	0	0
Mahan, Dallas, Mar. *	2	1	.667	0.47	7	0	0	0	2	1	19.1	12	75	2	1	0	1	0	1	4	1	20	0	0
Manuel, Barry, Dia.	0	0	.000	0.00	1	0	0	0	0	0	2.0	1	7	0	0	0	0	0	0	0	0	2	0	0
Manuel, Marcellous, W.S. *	1	0	1.000	9.00	1	1	0	0	0	0	5.0	8	27	5	5	2	0	0	0	4	0	8	1	0
Massimi, Matt, Mar. *	0	0	.000	3.86	9	0	0	0	1	1	11.2	8	47	5	5	0	1	0	1	2	0	13	1	0
Matos, Josue, Mar.	3	0	1.000	2.20	17	2	0	0	6	0	41.0	29	164	14	10	2	1	0	2	11	0	51	3	2
Medina, Alonso, M.A.S.	2	4	.333	9.23	19	2	0	0	7	1	26.1	38	132	30	27	0	2	1	6	16	0	24	3	1
Meeks, Eric, Ath.	2	1	.667	4.60	12	8	0	0	1	0	43.0	35	181	22	22	1	4	2	2	19	0	41	9	2
Mendoza, Hatuey, Dia.	2	3	.400	3.65	11	10	0	0	0	0	44.1	43	209	30	18	1	0	1	5	23	0	54	13	0
Meyer, John, Pad.	2	5	.286	5.66	12	11	0	0	0	0	49.1	54	230	40	31	2	0	3	7	33	0	46	7	1
Morel, Francis, Dia.	3	2	.600	4.13	15	6	0	0	6	0	56.2	64	245	32	26	1	2	2	3	17	0	41	2	3
Murphy, Matt, Cubs*	2	1	.667	3.67	14	2	0	0	8	2	27.0	29	122	11	11	0	0	1	3	0	37	2	3
Navarro, Joel, M.A.S.	4	4	.500	3.55	13	10	0	0	1	0	66.0	81	281	34	26	1	1	3	2	13	2	43	1	1
Negron, Jose, Ath.	1	0	1.000	6.00	7	1	0	0	1	0	15.0	19	72	11	10	1	0	4	2	7	0	15	2	1
Ohm, Joe, Cubs	1	1	.500	3.48	13	4	0	0	7	2	31.0	31	130	14	12	1	0	1	0	6	0	20	3	0
Orantes, Jaime, M.A.S.	1	2	.333	7.43	12	5	0	0	5	3	26.2	34	124	25	22	2	0	1	3	10	1	29	1	5
Pacheco, Enemecio, Rock.	5	0	1.000	3.99	12	11	0	0	0	0	58.2	51	240	31	26	1	0	2	3	17	0	59	3	1
Pass, Jeff, Dia. *	4	1	.800	8.78	16	0	0	0	7	1	26.2	27	135	31	26	3	0	0	2	26	0	28	8	1
Perez, Elvis, W.S. *	2	3	.400	6.75	14	8	0	0	1	0	48.0	60	225	38	36	3	1	0	5	33	0	42	9	0
Pitre, Diogenes, Ath.	0	3	.000	7.78	17	4	0	0	6	2	41.2	61	212	47	36	3	1	1	6	30	1	43	8	1
Precinal, Huilberto, Pad.	0	0	.000	6.23	5	0	0	0	2	0	4.1	5	22	3	3	1	0	0	5	0	4	1	1
Prinz, Bret, Dia.	0	0	.000	3.38	4	0	0	0	4	0	5.1	7	24	3	2	0	0	1	0	3	0	3	0	0
Prouty, Scott, Mar.	3	2	.600	2.44	13	11	0	0	1	0	48.0	40	218	27	13	1	0	1	4	32	0	57	6	0
Ramirez, Carlos, M.A.S.	0	0	.000	5.71	11	0	0	0	7	0	17.1	20	76	12	11	1	0	1	0	8	0	7	2	1
Reyes, Hipolito, W.S.	2	1	.667	6.65	14	1	0	0	6	1	21.2	33	109	21	16	2	2	0	1	13	2	16	3	6
Rhodes, Kendall, Dia.	2	1	.667	3.32	13	0	0	0	5	0	21.2	24	108	18	8	0	3	3	12	0	20	5	0
Robinson, Ken, Dia.	0	0	.000	0.00	1	1	0	0	0	0	2.0	0	6	0	0	0	0	0	0	0	0	0	0
Rodgers, Marcus, W.S.	0	0	.000	6.35	2	1	0	0	0	0	5.2	8	28	5	4	0	1	0	1	2	0	6	1	0
Rodriguez, Felix, Dia.	0	0	.000	4.15	3	2	0	0	0	0	4.1	3	18	4	2	0	0	0	1	2	0	5	0	0
Rohling, Stuart, W.S.	3	5	.375	8.06	13	6	0	0	1	0	44.2	63	234	51	40	4	2	5	2	30	0	41	5	1
Roney, Matt, Rock.	1	1	.500	5.80	9	9	1	0	0	0	40.1	50	187	31	26	1	0	3	11	0	49	4	2
Ruiz, Juan, Pad.	2	7	.222	5.98	13	12	0	0	0	0	55.2	58	262	45	37	4	2	3	9	24	0	38	5	1
Sanchez, Juan, Rock.	1	1	.500	3.86	8	0	0	0	3	1	9.1	11	42	4	4	0	0	1	5	0	10	1	0
Santana, Fausto, W.S.	0	2	.000	7.20	12	0	0	0	8	2	15.0	19	75	14	12	0	1	1	3	10	1	12	0	1
Silverio, Marcelino, Pad.	1	1	.500	4.03	18	0	0	0	3	1	38.0	35	170	22	17	2	2	1	24	0	38	1	0
Simpson, Allan, Mar.	1	0	1.000	0.96	3	0	0	0	1	1	9.1	8	37	2	1	1	0	3	0	12	0	0
Simpson, Andre, W.S.	3	6	.333	6.20	14	6	0	0	4	0	40.2	47	189	36	28	8	1	3	1	20	1	35	2	1
Smith, Jamie, W.S.	0	2	.000	7.27	5	0	0	0	2	0	8.2	14	48	9	7	0	0	0	3	4	1	16	0	1
Stark, Dennis, Mar.	0	0	.000	2.16	3	1	0	0	0	0	8.1	9	36	2	2	0	0	0	0	2	0	13	0	0
Stockman, Phil, Dia.	0	0	.000	0.00	1	0	0	0	0	0	0.1	0	3	0	0	0	0	0	2	0	1	0	0
Suazo, Rigoberto, Ath.	1	1	.500	7.97	12	0	0	0	4	1	20.1	21	98	22	18	0	1	3	14	0	22	7	2
Tauscher, Ryan, Ath. *	3	2	.600	5.13	17	0	0	0	6	2	26.1	26	124	23	15	1	1	3	15	1	27	1	1
Taylor, Tony, Ath.	4	2	.667	5.67	20	0	0	0	10	2	33.1	43	154	25	21	1	1	4	13	1	27	8	2
Thomas, Dave, Pad.	0	0	.000	4.64	18	0	0	0	12	0	21.1	24	110	19	11	0	2	0	1	17	0	19	5	2
Thomas, Drew, Pad.	2	5	.286	3.53	19	0	0	0	10	2	43.1	47	189	27	17	1	1	2	4	12	2	40	2	1
Thompson, Mark, Rock.	0	0	.000	0.00	1	1	0	0	0	0	3.0	1	9	0	0	0	0	0	0	0	2	0	0
Totten, Kris, Mar.	2	2	.500	4.55	15	0	0	0	6	3	31.2	31	141	19	16	3	2	1	0	13	0	33	2	3
Trask, Cody, Rock.	6	1	.857	2.49	20	0	0	0	4	2	47.0	36	192	16	13	0	1	2	18	1	68	4	1
Traylor, Chris, Mar. *	0	0	.000	5.79	13	0	0	0	0	0	9.1	6	37	6	6	1	0	4	1	9	0	2	0
Trejo, Francisco, Dia. *	2	5	.286	6.42	13	6	0	0	1	0	40.2	45	193	37	29	0	2	4	4	27	0	48	9	0
Ulloa, Enmanuel, Mar.	4	0	1.000	0.88	19	0	0	0	14	7	41.0	21	144	6	4	1	1	0	0	5	0	40	0	0
Valenzuela, Jose, M.A.S.	1	0	1.000	3.86	2	2	0	0	0	0	4.2	2	18	3	2	0	0	0	3	0	6	0	0
Van Buren, Jermaine, Rock.	7	2	.778	2.22	12	11	1	1	0	0	65.0	42	256	20	16	2	0	3	22	0	92	3	2

Pitcher, Team	W	L	Pct.	ERA	G	GS	CG	ShO	GF	Sv.	IP	H	TBF	R	ER	HR	SH	SF	HB	BB	IBB	SO	WP	Bk.
Vanhekken, Andrew, Mar. *	6	3	.667	4.43	11	8	0	0	0	0	40.2	34	179	23	20	1	0	0	2	18	0	55	7	1
Verdugo, Oswaldo, M.A.S.	2	2	.500	4.20	12	8	0	0	3	0	49.1	57	210	28	23	3	1	2	4	13	0	56	3	1
Verigood, Steve, Dia. *	0	1	.000	5.68	4	0	0	0	1	0	6.1	7	27	5	4	1	0	1	2	0	0	9	0	2
Vracar, Paul, Cubs	1	4	.200	7.56	13	5	0	0	0	0	25.0	25	130	29	21	1	1	2	6	23	0	21	6	1
Wagner, Denny, Ath.	2	1	.667	3.86	3	1	0	0	0	0	7.0	4	28	4	3	0	0	1	3	0	0	11	1	0
Waldrum, Kevin, Cubs	4	1	.800	4.67	16	0	0	0	11	1	27.0	27	122	19	14	1	2	3	1	12	0	23	5	1
Walton, Sam, Mar. *	3	6	.333	6.44	13	11	0	0	0	0	50.1	55	251	51	36	1	0	2	2	45	0	52	22	2
Watkins, Steve, Pad.	1	0	1.000	1.31	9	3	0	0	1	0	20.2	15	88	4	3	0	2	1	1	10	0	20	3	0
Whatley, Brannon, W.S.	1	2	.333	2.91	16	0	0	0	8	2	34.0	35	153	14	11	1	2	1	1	19	1	32	1	1
White, Matt, Dia.	2	1	.667	4.60	15	2	0	0	1	0	43.0	46	197	28	22	3	1	2	3	19	0	40	6	1
Williams, Randall, Cubs*	1	0	1.000	0.00	2	1	0	0	0	0	3.0	0	11	0	0	0	0	0	0	2	0	6	0	0
Williams, Tom, W.S.	0	0	.000	0.00	1	0	0	0	0	0	2.0	2	10	2	0	0	0	0	0	1	0	1	0	0
Yates, Tyler, Ath.	0	0	.000	3.91	15	0	0	0	8	2	23.0	28	107	12	10	0	0	0	1	14	0	20	1	2
Zambrano, Carlos, Cubs	0	1	.000	3.15	14	2	0	0	4	1	40.0	39	177	17	14	0	0	0	0	25	3	36	3	1
Zimmerman, Jordan, Mar. *	0	1	.000	3.00	5	3	0	0	1	0	12.0	14	55	6	4	1	0	0	2	7	0	11	0	0

COMBINATION SHUTOUTS: **Athletics (2)**—Bazzell-Negron-Yates, Bazzell-Corniel-Tauscher. **Cubs (3)**—Gomer-Hammons-Linares, Ohm-Beltran-Alvarez-Murphy, Beltran-Batts-Ohm. **Diamondbacks (3)**—Mendoza-Stockman-Crivello, Good-Morel-Kelley, Barndollar-Pass-Kelley. **Mariners (3)**—Zimmerman-Bieniasz-Mahan, Matos-Ulloa, Prouty-Simpson. **Mexican All-Stars (1)**—Aguilara-Flores. **Padres (3)**—Bell-Silverio-Luque, Luque-Deliza-Precinal, Watkins-Drew Thomas-Silverio. **Rockies (4)**—De Paula-Roger Little-Garner, Thompson-Van Buren-Gomez, De Paula-Trask, Garner-Rodney Little. **White Sox (0)**—None.

NO-HIT GAMES: None.

1998 FIELDING

TEAM

Team	Pct.	G	PO	A	E	TC	DP	PB
Mexican All-Stars	.961	55	1406	615	82	2103	37	15
Athletics	.957	56	1474	592	93	2159	44	34
Mariners	.949	55	1491	547	109	2147	31	36
Rockies	.947	56	1468	607	115	2190	48	18
Cubs	.947	55	1457	600	116	2173	53	29
Padres	.946	54	1453	498	111	2062	33	14
Diamondbacks	.934	55	1413	549	138	2100	47	15
White Sox	.929	54	1369	515	145	2029	41	10

TRIPLE PLAYS: None.

INDIVIDUAL

FIRST BASEMEN

NOTE: All caps denotes fielding-percentage leader based on 28 games for catchers, 37 for all other non-pitchers and 56 innings for pitchers. *Throws lefthanded.

Player, Team	Pct.	G	PO	A	E	TC	DP
Bass, Kevin, Cubs	.981	18	148	5	3	156	20
Battersby, Eric, W.S.*	1.000	2	9	1	0	10	1
Canales, Joel, M.A.S.	1.000	1	5	0	0	5	0
Cline, Carlos, W.S.*	.965	30	206	14	8	228	20
Closser, J.D., Dia.	.923	2	12	0	1	13	0
Colina, Javier, Rock.	1.000	2	8	0	0	8	2
Cosentino, Tony, Pad.	.975	9	71	7	2	80	3
Curry, Jesse, Pad.*	.979	46	392	28	9	429	27
De La Cruz, Jose, Ath.	.967	4	27	2	1	30	0
Delgado, Chris, W.S.	.973	26	164	15	5	184	16
Egly, John, Dia.	.992	16	122	6	1	129	10
Encarnacion, Bernardo, Rock.	.965	17	158	9	6	173	10
Estrella, Gorky, Mar.	.714	1	5	0	2	7	0
Garcia, Cip, Mar.	.980	17	133	15	3	151	11
Garza, Rolando, W.S.	.909	1	10	0	1	11	0
Graffagnini, Keith, Mar.	1.000	20	170	3	0	173	7
Heintzelman, Brian, Dia.	1.000	2	24	1	0	25	3
Keith, Rusty, Ath.	1.000	1	6	1	0	7	0
Koen, Nate, Cubs	.957	10	76	13	4	93	7
Martinez, Dionnar, Cubs	1.000	1	1	0	0	1	0
Mauck, Matt, Cubs	.994	19	158	7	1	166	15
Meier, Dan, Dia.*	1.000	11	72	10	0	82	6
Moye, Melvin, Dia.	.955	10	59	4	3	66	11
MUNOZ, Adan, M.A.S.	.9883	38	316	24	4	344	24
Neal, Steve, Dia.*	.962	11	91	9	4	104	13
Reyes, Rene, Rock.	.969	34	271	10	9	290	28
Rohena, Omar, Cubs	.990	12	93	2	1	96	5
Scheid, Jeremy, Ath.*	.9878	52	455	34	6	495	36
Smith, Sam, Rock.	1.000	8	61	4	0	65	4
Soriano, Rafael, Mar.	.984	23	163	20	3	186	10
Tineo, Esmerlin, W.S.*	1.000	1	3	1	0	4	0
Valdez, Emmanuel, M.A.S.	.983	18	163	14	3	180	10
Vicente, Audo, Dia.	.951	5	37	2	2	41	2
Vieira, Scott, Cubs	1.000	3	22	0	0	22	2

SECOND BASEMEN

Player, Team	Pct.	G	PO	A	E	TC	DP
Aguirregaviria, Frank, W.S.	.940	15	26	37	4	67	7
Aldrup, Morey, Cubs	.935	7	17	12	2	31	4
Ardizzone, Matt, Pad.	1.000	3	2	4	0	6	0
Armenta, Christian, M.A.S.	1.000	2	1	4	0	5	1
Berroa, Cristian, Pad.	1.000	2	2	1	0	3	0
Borges, Elio, W.S.	1.000	1	1	2	0	3	1
Clarke, Jason, Cubs	.963	18	43	61	4	108	17
Colina, Javier, Rock.	.918	10	17	28	4	49	3
Declet, Miguel, Ath.	.833	4	3	7	2	12	3
Doakes, Schuyler, Mar.	.943	32	36	64	6	106	11
Durango, Ariel, Mar.	.960	17	25	47	3	75	8
Garza, Rolando, W.S.	.918	14	36	31	6	73	4
German, Esteban, Dia.	.940	53	87	116	13	216	20
German, Franklin, Cubs	.946	24	49	73	7	129	16
Gil, Eric, M.A.S.	.951	20	37	41	4	82	6
Guerrero, Joel, Pad.	.981	12	23	28	1	52	3
Hernandez, Esteban, M.A.S.	1.000	1	2	0	0	2	0
Knorr, Mario, Dia.	.905	30	45	60	11	116	7
Lowe, Ernesto, W.S.	1.000	2	1	2	0	3	0
Martinez, Daniel, Cubs	.918	11	20	25	4	49	5
Moye, Melvin, Dia.	.909	6	10	10	2	22	2
Paulino, Henry, Rock.	.980	22	39	58	2	99	12
Rapp, Travis, W.S.	1.000	1	1	1	0	2	0
RIVERA, Jesus, M.A.S.	.960	39	81	112	8	201	23
Rodriguez, Mervin, W.S.	.836	16	19	27	9	55	1
Roman, Junior, W.S.	.932	12	35	33	5	73	9
Rosario, Felix, Mar.	.938	9	9	21	2	32	4
Salazar, Oscar, Ath.	1.000	5	10	8	0	18	3
Schmidt, Bryan, Pad.	.975	36	74	81	4	159	20
Schmidt, J.P., Ath.	.600	2	2	1	2	5	0
Stankiewicz, Andy, Dia.	1.000	3	5	8	0	13	2
Urquiola, Carlos, Dia.	.955	9	20	22	2	44	9
Vicente, Audo, Dia.	.955	10	20	22	2	44	6
Vilorio, Miguel, Rock.	.957	28	45	66	5	116	15
Weeks, Paul, Pad.	1.000	6	10	15	0	25	3

THIRD BASEMEN

Player, Team	Pct.	G	PO	A	E	TC	DP
Aguirregaviria, Frank, W.S.	.556	3	2	3	4	9	1
Aldrup, Morey, Cubs	.750	4	1	5	2	8	1
Armenta, Christian, M.A.S.	.909	7	4	16	2	22	1
Castillo, Ruben, Mar.	1.000	2	1	3	0	4	0
Colina, Javier, Rock.	.953	13	7	34	2	43	3
Declet, Miguel, Ath.	.857	7	5	7	2	14	0
De La Cruz, Jose, Ath.	.875	15	8	27	5	40	3
Delgado, Chris, W.S.	.818	3	3	6	2	11	0
Duenas, Manuel, M.A.S.	.898	50	26	80	12	118	3
Egly, John, Dia.	.809	19	11	27	9	47	2
ESTRELLA, Gorky, Mar.	.903	48	27	94	13	134	3
Garrett, Shawn, Pad.	.851	49	40	63	18	121	7
Garza, Rolando, W.S.	.889	9	3	13	2	18	1
German, Franklin, Cubs	.842	6	7	9	3	19	0
Holliday, Matt, Rock.	.851	24	11	46	10	67	2

Player, Team	Pct.	G	PO	A	E	TC	DP
Kelton, Dave, Cubs	.891	46	29	94	15	138	9
Mack, Tony, Ath.	.667	1	2	2	2	6	0
Moye, Melvin, Dia.	1.000	3	0	4	0	4	0
Noboa, Joel, Dia.	.805	37	23	72	23	118	3
Rosario, Felix, Mar.	.875	13	4	17	3	24	2
Salazar, Oscar, Ath.	.907	18	8	41	5	54	3
Santamarina, Juan, W.S.	.843	41	28	63	17	108	4
Schmidt, Bryan, Pad.	.824	9	2	12	3	17	0
Schmidt, J.P., Ath.	.892	14	13	20	4	37	1
Schneidmiller, Gary, Ath.	.944	6	4	13	1	18	1
Smith, Sam, Rock.	.875	21	9	33	6	48	2

SHORTSTOPS

Player, Team	Pct.	G	PO	A	E	TC	DP
ARIAS, Francisco, M.A.S.	.950	51	90	136	12	238	27
Berroa, Cristian, Pad.	.921	52	78	121	17	216	21
Castillo, Ruben, Mar.	.826	24	41	49	19	109	11
Clarke, Jason, Cubs	.833	4	3	12	3	18	2
Colina, Javier, Rock.	.894	18	26	50	9	85	9
Declet, Miguel, Ath.	.941	5	8	8	1	17	0
Espinoza, Efren, M.A.S.	1.000	6	6	10	0	16	2
Freeman, Corey, Mar.	.909	35	48	82	13	143	10
Garza, Rolando, W.S.	.893	31	51	66	14	131	19
Gil, Eric, M.A.S.	.875	3	1	6	1	8	1
Martinez, Daniel, Cubs	1.000	2	2	4	0	6	0
Martinez, Dionnar, Cubs	.848	23	18	49	12	79	9
Navarro, Ibrahim, Cubs	.911	31	48	95	14	157	23
Neubart, Adam, Dia.	.800	2	6	6	3	15	3
Rodriguez, Mervin, W.S.	.600	5	2	4	4	10	0
Roman, Junior, W.S.	.945	24	42	62	6	110	10
Salazar, Oscar, Ath.	.957	6	11	11	1	23	2
Schmidt, Bryan, Pad.	.692	5	1	8	4	13	1
Schmidt, J.P., Ath.	.916	20	26	50	7	83	9
Schneidmiller, Gary, Ath.	.912	31	45	90	13	148	14
Uribe, Juan, Rock.	.927	40	55	122	14	191	25
Valera, Gregori, Dia.	.937	45	88	135	15	238	30
Vicente, Audo, Dia.	.912	9	11	20	3	34	4

OUTFIELDERS

Player, Team	Pct.	G	PO	A	E	TC	DP
Aldrup, Morey, Cubs	1.000	6	12	0	0	12	0
Armenta, Christian, M.A.S.	.981	41	48	4	1	53	1
Bass, Kevin, Cubs	1.000	1	2	0	0	2	0
Battersby, Eric, W.S.*	.947	28	52	2	3	57	0
Betts, Dewayne, Ath.	.968	43	59	1	2	62	0
Boykin, Paul, Pad.	.972	42	62	7	2	71	0
Cabrera, Mayron, W.S.	.857	20	12	0	2	14	0
Canales, Joel, M.A.S.	1.000	14	9	2	0	11	0
Clark, Jamie, Mar.*	.953	28	39	2	2	43	1
Clarke, Jason, Cubs	.857	3	6	0	1	7	0
Conyer, Darryl, Dia.*	.889	22	39	1	5	45	0
Cook, Jon, Pad.	.954	45	100	3	5	108	0
Corbett, Heath, Dia.	.962	28	46	4	2	52	0
Easter, J.J., Rock.	1.000	18	19	1	0	20	1
Encarnacion, Bernardo, Rock.	1.000	9	5	0	0	5	0
Fernandez, Alex, Mar.*	.983	37	56	1	1	58	1
Forbes, Matt, Ath.	.922	39	43	4	4	51	0
Freeman, Choo, Rock.	.880	38	42	2	6	50	0
FUKUHARA, Pete, Cubs	.989	47	88	6	1	95	1
Gann, Jamie, Dia.	.750	2	3	0	1	4	0
German, Franklin, Cubs	1.000	2	7	0	0	7	0
Gonzalez, Franklin, Pad.	1.000	2	3	0	0	3	0
Guerrero, Joel, Pad.	.919	23	30	4	3	37	1
Guiel, Aaron, Pad.	1.000	8	11	0	0	11	0
Guzman, Javier, Rock.	.895	13	16	1	2	19	0
Hall, Victor, Dia.*	.957	23	41	4	2	47	1
Heintzelman, Brian, Dia.	1.000	4	4	0	0	4	0
Hernandez, Orlando, Mar.	.966	25	28	0	1	29	0
Joseph, Adolfo, Dia.	.767	23	22	1	7	30	1
Kail, Tom, Dia.	.923	17	24	0	2	26	0
Keith, Rusty, Ath.	.973	46	69	3	2	74	2
Knorr, Mario, Dia.	.900	7	8	1	1	10	0
Lopez, Orlando, Mar.	.927	29	33	5	3	41	0
Lowe, Ernesto, W.S.	.895	24	34	0	4	38	0
Mack, Tony, Ath.	.921	32	33	2	3	38	0
Manuel, Marcellous, W.S.*	.969	21	30	1	1	32	1
McCarty, Brock, Dia.	.977	38	43	0	1	44	0
Meadows, Tydus, Cubs	.939	26	40	6	3	49	0
Medina, Ernesto, M.A.S.	.933	55	88	10	7	105	0
Morency, Vernand, Rock.	.810	23	14	3	4	21	1
Mosley, Kelly, W.S.	.913	27	42	0	4	46	0
Motley, Brittan, Pad.	.930	26	37	3	3	43	1

Player, Team	Pct.	G	PO	A	E	TC	DP
Moye, Melvin, Dia.	1.000	6	5	2	0	7	0
Neubart, Adam, Dia.	1.000	4	3	0	0	3	0
Nielson, Bret, Mar.	.930	37	37	3	3	43	1
Nixon, Justin, Ath.*	.976	38	37	3	1	41	0
Olivo, Miguel, Ath.	1.000	2	1	0	0	1	0
Perez, Rafael, W.S.	.863	37	65	4	11	80	0
Pinero, Juan, Cubs	.951	48	77	0	4	81	0
Proctor, Jerry, Dia.	1.000	3	1	0	0	1	0
Quintana, Wilfredo, Mar.	.900	18	18	0	2	20	0
Rincon, Isaias, M.A.S.	.960	55	110	9	5	124	0
Robinson, Coby, Cubs	.970	24	30	2	1	33	0
Rohena, Omar, Cubs	.625	8	5	0	3	8	0
Saldua, Luis, M.A.S.	.750	3	3	0	1	4	0
Sanchez, Augustin, Rock.	.983	43	55	2	1	58	0
Shipp, Charles, Cubs	1.000	9	13	1	0	14	0
Simmons, Brian, W.S.	1.000	4	3	0	0	3	0
Sobet, Renato, Pad.	.942	29	42	7	3	52	0
Soriano, Rafael, Mar.	.846	8	10	1	2	13	0
Sosa, Jorge, Rock.	.928	43	60	4	5	69	1
Tineo, Esmerlin, W.S.*	.903	27	27	1	3	31	0
Williams, P.J., Mar.	1.000	14	22	1	0	23	0

CATCHERS

Player, Team	Pct.	G	PO	A	E	TC	DP	PB
Aguirregaviria, Frank, W.S.	.977	17	75	9	2	86	0	4
Beasley, Justin, Dia.	.969	3	27	4	1	32	0	1
CARROLL, Mark, Mar.	.990	30	271	29	3	303	0	12
Closser, J.D., Dia.	.967	37	311	38	12	361	2	10
Cosentino, Tony, Pad.	.980	19	178	17	4	199	2	8
De La Cruz, Jose, Ath.	.991	25	187	30	2	219	3	12
Dorsett, Chris, Cubs	.992	17	109	11	1	121	0	7
French, Ron, Pad.	.980	8	46	3	1	50	0	0
Garcia, Cip, Mar.	.833	1	9	1	2	12	0	0
Garcia, Tony, W.S.	.965	36	270	36	11	317	1	5
Goldbach, Jeff, Cubs	.952	27	173	26	10	209	0	8
Gutierrez, Said, Pad.	.952	24	162	16	9	187	2	5
Heintzelman, Brian, Dia.	.971	8	64	3	2	69	0	4
Hernandez, Esteban, M.A.S.	.968	33	199	40	8	247	1	7
Kent, Mat, Mar.	.991	15	105	7	1	113	0	11
Koen, Nate, Cubs	.955	3	20	1	1	22	0	2
Lopez, Miguel, Dia.	.964	10	88	19	4	111	1	0
Lopez, Rafael, Mar.	.966	3	25	3	1	29	0	3
Mauck, Matt, Cubs	.948	16	115	12	7	134	0	12
Munoz, Adam, M.A.S.	1.000	4	31	3	0	34	0	2
Olivo, Miguel, Ath.	.977	38	293	44	8	345	2	22
Pena, Pelagio, Mar.	.970	16	122	6	4	132	1	10
Rapp, Travis, W.S.	.964	14	92	16	4	112	0	1
Reed, Jeremy, Pad.	.911	11	66	6	7	79	0	1
Reyes, Rene, Rock.	.943	14	117	16	8	141	2	6
Samuel, Tomas, Rock.	.989	25	156	25	2	183	1	7
Underwood, Jake, Mar.	1.000	6	36	6	0	42	0	0
Valdez, Emmanuel, M.A.S.	.974	25	162	23	5	190	1	6
Winchester, Jeff, Rock.	.975	32	250	21	7	278	1	5

PITCHERS

Player, Team	Pct.	G	PO	A	E	TC	DP
Acosta, Jhon, Cubs	.750	11	2	1	1	4	0
Aguilera, Edgar, M.A.S.	.778	11	0	7	2	9	0
Almonte, Edwin, W.S.	1.000	5	0	1	0	1	0
Alvarez, Larry, Cubs	.833	10	0	5	1	6	0
Angulo, Victor, M.A.S.*	.889	11	4	4	1	9	0
Arias, Joel, M.A.S.	.800	18	0	8	2	10	0
Barcelo, Lorenzo, W.S.	1.000	3	0	1	0	1	0
Barndollar, Jeff, Dia.	.833	9	2	3	1	6	2
Bartosh, Cliff, Pad.*	.923	13	2	10	1	13	0
Batista, Rafael, Mar.	.750	14	0	3	1	4	0
Batts, Nathan, Cubs*	1.000	13	2	1	0	3	0
Bazzell, Shane, Ath.	1.000	12	1	8	0	9	0
Bell, Casey, Pad.	.923	7	5	7	1	13	1
Beltran, Francis, Cubs	1.000	12	2	5	0	7	0
Bennett, Tom, Ath.	1.000	5	1	2	0	3	0
Berroa, Oliver, Mar.	1.000	5	3	4	0	7	0
Bevis, P.J., Dia.	.900	14	1	8	1	10	1
Biddle, Rocky, W.S.	.750	5	0	3	1	4	0
Bieniasz, Derek, Mar.	1.000	5	1	5	0	6	0
Borne, Matt, W.S.	1.000	2	1	1	0	2	0
Brown, Tighe, W.S.	1.000	5	0	1	0	1	0
Caraballo, Angel, W.S.*	.867	14	5	8	2	15	0
Carballo, Enrique, M.A.S.	1.000	12	2	3	0	5	0
Carreras, Marino, Mar.*	.800	10	1	7	2	10	0
Castillo, Adolfo, M.A.S.	1.000	4	0	1	0	1	0
Colome, Jesus, Ath.	.909	12	4	6	1	11	0

Player, Team	Pct.	G	PO	A	E	TC	DP
Condrey, Clay, Pad.	1.000	5	1	0	0	1	0
Conroy, Ken, Cubs	1.000	9	0	2	0	2	0
Corniel, Henry, Ath.	1.000	17	3	4	0	7	0
Crawford, Jeremy, Ath.*	1.000	17	3	3	0	6	1
Crivello, Justin, Dia.*	.500	20	0	2	2	4	0
Cruz, Juan, Cubs	1.000	12	3	4	0	7	0
D'Amico, Jeff, Ath.	1.000	4	2	2	0	4	0
Darr, Jerry, Pad.	1.000	7	2	5	0	7	0
DeLeon, Bryan, Pad.	1.000	16	2	2	0	4	0
Delgado, Danny, Mar.	1.000	5	2	0	0	2	0
Deliza, Carlos, Pad.	1.000	18	1	6	0	7	1
De Paula, Julio, Rock.	.571	17	0	4	3	7	0
Devine, Travis, Pad.	1.000	2	0	1	0	1	0
Dowell, Brian, Pad.	.750	14	0	3	1	4	0
Duenas, Alain, W.S.	1.000	6	0	1	0	1	0
Duprey, Pete, Mar.*	.600	19	1	2	2	5	0
Ericks, Dave, Cubs	.500	11	0	1	1	2	0
Ferrand, Dario, W.S.	1.000	16	4	8	0	12	1
Fischer, Eric, W.S.*	.500	8	0	1	1	2	0
Flores, Jorge, M.A.S.*	.900	18	0	9	1	10	1
Fogg, Josh, W.S.	1.000	2	0	2	0	2	0
Freeman, Kai, W.S.	1.000	1	1	1	0	2	0
Frias, Yovany, W.S.	.500	11	1	1	2	4	0
Garcia, Gerardo, M.A.S.	.824	15	3	11	3	17	1
Garner, Brandon, Rock.	1.000	13	4	5	0	9	0
German, Franklyn, Ath.	1.000	14	2	6	0	8	0
Gomer, Jeramy, Cubs*	1.000	11	1	3	0	4	0
Gomez, Diogenes, Rock.	.923	29	2	10	1	13	0
Gonzalez, Martin, W.S.	1.000	7	2	0	0	2	0
Good, Andy, Dia.	.909	9	3	7	1	11	1
Griman, Carlos, Dia.	1.000	2	1	1	0	2	0
Guzman, Ricardo, M.A.S.	1.000	11	0	1	0	1	0
Hammons, Matt, Cubs.	1.000	7	1	2	0	3	0
Hardcastle, John, Cubs*	.714	12	3	2	2	7	0
Hasselhoff, Derek, W.S.	1.000	6	0	3	0	3	0
Hawkins, Ryan, Pad.	.000	1	0	0	1	1	0
Hessler, John, Rock.	1.000	16	1	8	0	9	0
Iannacone, Steve, Rock.	1.000	15	2	2	0	4	0
Kelley, Brenton, Dia.	.500	17	0	2	2	4	0
Kenny, Seth, Ath.	1.000	13	0	8	0	8	0
Koplove, Mike, Dia.	1.000	2	1	0	0	1	0
Kvasnicka, Jay, W.S.	1.000	7	1	0	0	1	0
Linares, Yonder, Cubs*	.941	15	0	16	1	17	1
Little, Rodney, Rock.	.857	19	4	2	1	7	0
Little, Roger, Rock.	.833	14	3	7	2	12	0
Luque, Roger, Pad.*	.800	12	0	8	2	10	0
Mahan, Dallas, Mar.*	1.000	7	0	5	0	5	0
Manuel, Barry, Dia.	1.000	1	0	2	0	2	0
Massimi, Matt, Mar.*	1.000	9	0	2	0	2	0
Matos, Josue, Mar.	1.000	17	1	6	0	7	2
Medina, Alonso, M.A.S.	1.000	19	1	2	0	3	0
Meeks, Eric, Ath.	1.000	12	4	5	0	9	1
Mendoza, Hatuey, Dia.	.933	11	8	6	1	15	2
Meyer, John, Pad.	.750	12	1	2	1	4	0
Morel, Francis, Dia.	.833	15	2	8	2	12	0
Murphy, Matt, Cubs*	1.000	14	2	8	0	10	0
NAVARRO, Joel, M.A.S.	1.000	13	7	15	0	22	0
Negron, Jose, Ath.	.500	7	1	0	1	2	0
Ohm, Joe, Cubs	.875	13	1	6	1	8	1
Orantes, Jaime, M.A.S.	1.000	12	3	7	0	10	0
Pacheco, Enemecio, Rock.	.889	12	2	14	2	18	1
Pass, Jeff, Dia.*	1.000	16	0	4	0	4	0
Perez, Elvis, W.S.*	.889	14	2	6	1	9	1
Pitre, Diogenes, Ath.	.571	17	2	2	3	7	0
Precinal, Huilberto, Pad.	1.000	5	0	1	0	1	0
Prinz, Bret, Dia.	1.000	4	2	1	0	3	0
Prouty, Scott, Mar.	.667	13	4	4	4	12	0
Ramirez, Carlos, M.A.S.	1.000	11	1	4	0	5	0
Reyes, Hipolito, W.S.	.714	14	1	4	2	7	1
Rhodes, Kendall, Dia.	.875	13	6	1	1	8	0
Rodgers, Marcus, W.S.	1.000	2	0	3	0	3	0
Rodriguez, Felix, Dia.	.000	3	0	0	1	1	0
Rohling, Stuart, W.S.	.833	13	3	7	2	12	1
Roney, Matt, Rock.	1.000	9	4	3	0	7	1
Ruiz, Juan, Pad.	.917	13	2	9	1	12	0
Sanchez, Juan, Rock.	1.000	8	1	0	0	1	0
Santana, Fausto, W.S.	1.000	12	2	2	0	4	2
Silverio, Marcelino, Pad.	.667	18	1	1	1	3	0
Simpson, Allan, Mar.	1.000	3	1	1	0	2	0
Simpson, Andre, W.S.	.857	14	1	5	1	7	0
Smith, Jamie, W.S.	.000	5	0	0	1	1	0
Suazo, Rigoberto, Ath.	1.000	12	5	4	0	9	0
Tauscher, Ryan, Ath.*	1.000	17	0	6	0	6	0
Taylor, Tony, Ath.	1.000	20	2	8	0	10	0
Thomas, Dave, Pad.	.714	18	3	2	2	7	0
Thomas, Drew, Pad.	.500	19	1	4	5	10	0
Thompson, Mark, Rock.	1.000	1	0	1	0	1	0
Totten, Kris, Mar.	1.000	15	1	5	0	6	0
Trask, Cody, Rock.	.769	20	2	8	3	13	1
Traylor, Chris, Mar.*	1.000	7	0	1	0	1	0
Trejo, Francisco, Dia.*	.714	13	1	4	2	7	0
Ulloa, Enmanuel, Mar.	.889	19	1	7	1	9	0
Valenzuela, Jose, M.A.S.	1.000	2	0	1	0	1	0
Van Buren, Jermaine, Rock.	.909	12	2	8	1	11	0
Vanhekken, Andrew, Mar.*	.800	11	1	3	1	5	0
Verdugo, Oswaldo, M.A.S.	1.000	12	3	8	0	11	0
Verigood, Steve, Dia.*	.750	4	0	3	1	4	1
Vracar, Paul, Cubs	.857	13	1	5	1	7	1
Wagner, Denny, Ath.	.500	3	0	1	1	2	0
Waldrum, Kevin, Cubs	1.000	16	2	3	0	5	1
Walton, Sam, Mar.*	.714	13	1	9	4	14	0
Watkins, Steve, Pad.	1.000	9	0	3	0	3	0
Whatley, Brannon, W.S.	1.000	16	1	6	0	7	0
White, Matt, Dia.	.600	15	1	2	2	5	1
Yates, Tyler, Ath.	1.000	15	2	2	0	4	0
Zambrano, Carlos, Cubs	.909	14	5	5	1	11	1
Zimmerman, Jordan, Mar.*	.600	5	0	3	2	5	0

The following players did not have any fielding statistics at the positions indicated or appeared only as a designated hitter, pinch-hitter or pinch-runner: Abbott, p; Adams, p; Barnes, p; Battersby, p; Brown, p; Cabrera, 3b; Cline, of; Fleming, p; Heintzelman, p; Herrera, p; Jimenez, p; Jones, p; Mack, p; M. Manuel, 1b, p; McCarthy, 2b; R. Perez, 1b; Porter, dh, ph; Rapp, 3b; Rivera, 1b; K. Robinson, p; S. Smith, 2b; Stark, p; Stockman, p; G. Williams, dh; R. Williams, p; T. Williams, p.

LEAGUE CHAMPIONS

Year	Team	Pct.	Year	Team	Pct.	Year	Team	Pct.
1988—	Peoria Brewers	.690	1992—	Scottsdale A's	.607	1996—	Padres	.643
1989—	Peoria Brewers	.732	1993—	Scottsdale A's	.636	1997—	Cubs	.618
1990—	Peoria Brewers	.679	1994—	Chandler Cardinals	.607	1998—	Rockies	.750
1991—	Scottsdale A's	.650	1995—	Scottsdale A's	.661			

SUMMER CLASS A *Arizona League*

GULF COAST LEAGUE

LEAGUE OFFICE

President
Tom Saffell
Address
1503 Clower Creek Dr., H-262
Sarasota, FL 34231
Phone
941-966-6407

Teams*
Braves
Devil Rays
Expos
Marlins
Mets
Orioles
Phillies
Pirates
Rangers
Red Sox

Royals
Tigers
Twins
Yankees
*Teams play their games in Bradenton, Dunedin, Fort Myers, Kissimmee, Lakeland, Melbourne, Orlando, Port Charlotte, Port St. Lucie, St. Petersburg, Sarasota, Tampa and West Palm Beach, Fla.

1998 FINAL STANDINGS

EASTERN DIVISION

Team	W	L	T	Pct.	GB
Marlins	38	22	0	.633	....
Expos	32	27	0	.542	5.5
Braves	25	35	0	.417	13.0
Mets	24	35	0	.407	13.5

NORTHERN DIVISION

Team	W	L	T	Pct.	GB
Devil Rays	36	24	0	.600	....
Yankees	34	26	0	.567	2.0
Tigers	28	32	0	.467	8.0
Astros	22	38	0	.367	14.0

WESTERN DIVISION

Team	W	L	T	Pct.	GB
Twins	34	26	0	.567	....
Rangers	34	26	0	.567	....
Royals	32	28	0	.533	2.0
Orioles	28	32	0	.467	6.0
Red Sox	27	33	0	.450	7.0
Pirates	25	35	0	.417	9.0

COMPOSITE

Team	Mar.	D.R.	Yan.	Twi.	Ran.	Exp.	Roy.	Tig.	Ori.	R.S.	Pir.	Brav.	Mets	Ast.	W	L	T	Pct.	GB
Marlins	....	0	0	0	0	12	0	0	0	0	0	12	14	0	38	22	0	.633	....
Devil Rays	0	....	12	0	0	0	0	10	0	0	0	0	0	14	36	24	0	.600	2.0
Yankees	0	8	....	0	0	0	0	13	0	0	0	0	0	13	34	26	0	.567	4.0
Twins	0	0	0	....	6	0	6	0	7	7	8	0	0	0	34	26	0	.567	4.0
Rangers	0	0	0	6	....	0	7	0	6	5	10	0	0	0	34	26	0	.567	4.0
Expos	8	0	0	0	0	....	0	0	0	0	0	15	9	0	32	27	0	.542	5.5
Royals	0	0	0	6	5	0	....	0	6	7	8	0	0	0	32	28	0	.533	6.0
Tigers	0	10	7	0	0	0	0	....	0	0	0	0	0	11	28	32	0	.467	10.0
Orioles	0	0	0	5	6	0	6	0	....	6	5	0	0	0	28	32	0	.467	10.0
Red Sox	0	0	0	5	7	0	5	0	6	....	4	0	0	0	27	33	0	.450	11.0
Pirates	0	0	0	4	2	0	4	0	7	8	....	0	0	0	25	35	0	.417	13.0
Braves	8	0	0	0	0	5	0	0	0	0	0	....	12	0	25	35	0	.417	13.0
Mets	6	0	0	0	0	10	0	0	0	0	0	8	....	0	24	35	0	.407	13.5
Astros	0	6	7	0	0	0	0	9	0	0	0	0	0	....	22	38	0	.367	16.0

Games played in Bradenton, Dunedin, Fort Myers, Melbourne, Osceola, Port Charlotte, St. Lucie County, Sarasota, Tampa and West Palm Beach, Fla.

Club names are major league affiliations.

FORFEIT: Braves forfeited to Marlins, August 22, second game (Marlins won, 9-0).

PLAYOFFS: Rangers defeated Twins one game to none; Devil Rays defeated Marlins one game to none; Rangers defeated Devil Rays two games to none to win league championship.

REGULAR-SEASON ATTENDANCE: No total attendance figures reported.

MANAGERS: Astros, Julio Linares; Braves, Rick Albert; Devil Rays, Bobby Ramos; Expos, Frank Kremblas; Marlins, Jon Deeble; Mets, John Stephenson; Orioles, Butch Davis; Pirates,Woody Huyke; Rangers, Darryl Kennedy; Red Sox, Luis Aguayo; Royals, Andre David; Tigers, Kevin Bradshaw; Twins, Steve Liddle; Yankees, Kenney Dominguez.

ALL-STAR TEAM: 1B—David Goodwin, Royals; 2B—Pedro Guerrero, Rangers; 3B—Matt Boone, Tigers; SS—Josh KcKinley, Expos; OF—Tonayne Brown, Red Sox; Richard Gomez, Tigers; Juan Rivera, Yankees; C—Allen Shrum, Twins; SP—Wes Anderson, Marlins; RP—Robert Quarnstrom, Rangers; Manager of the Year—Darryl Kennedy, Rangers.

1998 BATTING

TEAM

Team	Avg.	G	TPA	AB	R	H	TB	2B	3B	HR	RBI	SH	SF	HP	BB	IBB	SO	SB	CS	GDP	LOB	ShO	Slg.	OBP
Red Sox	.289	60	2304	2003	347	579	849	107	23	39	290	20	31	34	216	1	367	99	34	37	440	5	.424	.363
Tigers	.274	60	2341	2091	310	572	810	104	25	28	272	8	8	44	190	4	529	100	43	29	446	2	.387	.345
Royals	.262	60	2259	2015	271	527	715	92	6	28	235	14	18	24	188	2	405	60	19	44	463	5	.355	.329
Devil Rays	.258	60	2255	1999	322	516	770	103	29	31	269	13	20	42	181	5	492	79	48	28	377	1	.385	.330
Twins	.258	60	2223	1983	280	511	720	102	10	29	232	9	18	27	186	6	371	85	30	39	430	2	.363	.327
Marlins	.257	59	2146	1890	274	486	686	106	20	18	223	13	16	46	181	4	514	104	37	34	392	3	.363	.334
Yankees	.253	60	2251	1955	293	495	704	87	13	32	252	15	10	45	226	3	486	41	32	55	410	6	.360	.343

Team	Avg.	G	TPA	AB	R	H	TB	2B	3B	HR	RBI	SH	SF	HP	BB	IBB	SO	SB	CS	GDP	LOB	ShO	Slg.	OBP
Rangers	.251	60	2232	1937	275	486	680	90	16	24	220	27	18	45	205	5	426	53	44	37	413	4	.351	.334
Pirates	.250	60	2299	2064	294	517	791	101	19	45	255	9	21	37	168	7	471	90	20	34	422	1	.383	.315
Astros	.242	60	2268	2041	237	493	671	100	12	18	204	12	6	28	181	4	470	73	55	33	419	3	.329	.311
Orioles	.236	60	2282	1999	289	471	645	79	22	17	231	13	22	53	195	2	428	112	35	31	419	5	.323	.317
Mets	.230	59	2087	1898	222	436	634	86	23	22	189	14	12	45	118	3	420	50	26	35	355	8	.334	.289
Expos	.228	59	2025	1823	219	416	562	72	25	8	157	26	12	31	133	1	444	119	84	16	285	4	.308	.290
Braves	.228	59	2127	1907	202	434	640	104	15	24	170	9	8	34	169	6	491	58	41	28	386	8	.336	.301

INDIVIDUAL

TOP QUALIFIERS FOR BATTING CHAMPIONSHIP

Minimum 162 plate appearances. *Lefthanded batter. †Switch-hitter.

Player, Team	Avg.	G	TPA	AB	R	H	TB	2B	3B	HR	RBI	SH	SF	HP	BB	IBB	SO	SB	CS	GDP	Slg	OBP
Goodwin, David, Roy.	.367	48	205	177	26	65	97	20	0	4	33	1	2	5	20	1	33	0	0	2	.548	.441
Pena, Jose, R.S.	.344	48	183	160	28	55	85	12	3	4	21	1	0	8	14	0	33	6	5	2	.531	.423
Vasquez, Alejandro, Ast.*	.335	57	231	209	31	70	103	20	3	3	23	0	1	0	21	4	34	7	7	4	.493	.394
Rivera, Juan, Yan.	.333	57	238	210	43	70	117	9	1	12	45	0	1	1	26	2	27	8	5	10	.557	.408
Gomez, Richard, Tig.	.333	47	188	162	42	54	91	11	4	6	40	0	0	5	21	3	37	20	2	3	.562	.426
Rodriguez, Carlos, R.S.	.325	54	215	197	35	64	106	14	2	8	37	0	3	4	11	0	37	14	3	2	.538	.367
Brown, Tonayne, R.S.	.316	54	240	225	43	71	115	12	4	8	38	0	5	2	8	0	32	15	6	4	.511	.338
Ramirez, Charlie, Roy.	.305	50	211	200	27	61	74	9	2	0	23	2	1	1	7	0	35	13	5	6	.370	.330
Boone, Matt, Tig.	.293	49	202	191	28	56	90	11	4	5	29	0	1	1	9	1	42	3	2	2	.471	.327
Guerrero, Pedro, Rang.	.290	52	227	186	35	54	71	10	2	1	25	6	2	7	26	0	42	11	7	0	.382	.394
Medrano, Jesus, Mar.	.286	48	200	175	42	50	69	11	1	2	15	1	1	2	21	1	30	26	7	1	.394	.367
Jacobs, John, D.R.	.284	51	177	155	21	44	70	12	4	2	29	0	3	4	15	0	50	7	4	2	.452	.356
Turnquist, Tyler, Ast.	.283	56	237	219	31	62	88	15	4	1	29	0	0	4	14	0	23	6	5	7	.402	.338
Rix, Derek, R.S.*	.283	44	178	152	28	43	83	8	4	8	38	1	4	2	19	0	48	2	0	0	.546	.362
Garcia, Alfredo, Mets	.280	54	226	200	42	56	98	13	4	7	35	0	3	9	14	0	34	20	2	1	.490	.350

DEPARTMENTAL LEADERS: G—Quinones, 59; AB—Batista, Soler, 226 each; R—Soler, 47; H—T. Brown, 71; TB—J. Rivera, 117; 2B—Goodwin, Vasquez, 20 each; 3B—Soler, 7; HR—J. Rivera, 12; RBI—J. Rivera, 45; SH—Espinoza, P. Guerrero, 6 each; SF—A. Alvarez, T. Brown, Rumfield, 5 each; HP—Cubillan, 16; BB—Miqueas Rodriguez, 48; IBB—Vasquez, 4; SO—Reed, 70; SB—Reed, 40; CS—McKinley, Ruan, 13 each; GIDP—Quinones, 10; Slg.—Richard Gomez, .562; OBP—Miqueas Rodriguez, .466.

ALL PLAYERS

*Lefthanded batter. †Switch-hitter.

Player, Team	Avg.	G	TPA	AB	R	H	TB	2B	3B	HR	RBI	SH	SF	HP	BB	IBB	SO	SB	CS	GDP	Slg	OBP
Acevedo, Luis, Rang.	.000	1	4	2	1	0	0	0	0	0	0	0	0	0	2	0	0	0	0	0	.000	.500
Ackerman, Scott, Exp.	.263	18	68	57	9	15	19	1	0	1	7	1	0	1	9	0	12	0	2	0	.333	.373
Adorno, Wilson, Pir.†	.222	4	11	9	1	2	5	0	0	1	1	0	0	2	0	0	0	0	0	2	.556	.364
Aguila, Chris, Mar.	.269	51	193	171	29	46	76	12	3	4	29	1	0	2	19	1	49	6	2	4	.444	.349
Alfaro, Jason, Ast.	.242	47	191	178	20	43	54	8	0	1	18	2	0	0	11	0	24	5	5	5	.303	.286
Alou, Felipe, Roy.	.253	44	176	162	20	41	56	7	1	2	22	4	1	1	8	0	31	6	3	4	.346	.291
Altagen, Matthew, Tig.	.232	33	131	112	14	26	33	7	0	0	8	0	0	4	15	0	35	3	4	1	.295	.344
Alvarez, Antonio, Pir.	.247	50	212	190	27	47	74	13	1	4	29	1	5	3	13	1	24	19	1	4	.389	.299
Alvarez, Julio, Tig.†	.342	31	121	114	14	39	49	6	2	0	15	2	0	2	3	0	26	11	6	0	.430	.370
Alvarez, Nelson, Mets	.321	16	59	56	3	18	28	2	1	2	6	0	0	1	2	0	11	0	0	0	.500	.356
Amerson, Gordon, Yan.*	.270	13	47	37	6	10	14	1	0	1	7	0	0	0	10	0	15	4	1	1	.378	.426
Araujo, Victor, Pir.	.284	24	100	95	18	27	33	1	1	1	10	0	0	0	5	0	9	11	4	1	.347	.320
Aude, Rich, Exp.	.333	2	8	6	1	2	3	1	0	0	0	0	0	0	1	0	3	0	0	0	.500	.500
Ayres, Yancy, Roy.	.227	18	47	44	5	10	12	2	0	0	3	0	0	1	2	0	8	0	0	0	.273	.277
Baez, Ernies, Rang.†	.211	37	140	123	14	26	31	3	1	0	11	4	1	0	12	0	15	5	3	2	.252	.279
Bailey, Jeff, Mar.	.331	37	154	127	21	42	58	10	0	2	28	0	1	7	19	1	31	3	2	3	.457	.442
Batista, Angel, D.R.*	.212	57	252	226	35	48	72	11	2	3	23	2	1	4	19	0	67	10	8	2	.319	.284
Benham, David, R.S.	.364	6	25	22	3	8	14	3	0	1	3	0	0	1	2	0	1	0	0	0	.636	.440
Berrien, Samuel, Ori.*	.236	45	181	148	22	35	50	5	2	2	21	0	0	5	28	0	31	4	4	5	.338	.376
Betemit, Wilson, Brav.†	.220	51	193	173	23	38	69	8	4	5	16	0	0	0	20	0	49	6	5	1	.399	.301
Blum, Geoffrey, Exp.†	.167	5	19	18	0	3	6	1	1	0	1	0	0	0	1	0	4	0	0	0	.333	.211
Boone, Matt, Tig.	.293	49	202	191	28	56	90	11	4	5	29	0	1	1	9	1	42	3	2	2	.471	.327
Borjas, Henry, R.S.†	.242	42	152	124	20	30	33	3	0	0	8	5	3	2	18	0	26	5	3	1	.266	.340
Brazell, Craig, Mets*	.298	13	50	47	6	14	22	3	1	1	6	0	0	1	2	0	13	0	0	0	.468	.340
Bronowicz, Scott, Brav.*	.256	27	82	78	6	20	26	6	0	0	6	0	1	0	3	0	18	0	0	1	.333	.280
Brown, Andy, Yan.*	.229	36	150	131	19	30	48	5	2	3	24	0	1	2	16	0	38	0	3	3	.366	.320
Brown, Richard, Yan.*	.429	6	16	14	6	6	12	0	0	2	2	0	0	1	1	0	3	2	0	0	.857	.500
Brown, Tonayne, R.S.	.316	54	240	225	43	71	115	12	4	8	38	0	5	2	8	0	32	15	6	4	.511	.338
Bryan, Sean, Roy.*	.202	24	88	84	8	17	20	3	0	0	6	0	0	0	4	0	20	0	0	2	.238	.239
Buck, John, Ast.	.286	36	142	126	24	36	54	9	0	3	15	1	0	2	13	0	22	2	2	0	.429	.362
Burke, Paul, Brav.	.171	33	91	76	8	13	24	8	0	1	5	0	0	1	14	1	18	0	1	3	.316	.340
Burton, Willie, Pir.	.222	19	68	63	6	14	20	4	1	0	5	1	0	1	3	1	26	1	0	0	.317	.269
Bystrowski, Robert, Ast.	.149	41	156	134	20	20	31	5	0	2	14	0	3	3	16	0	37	8	4	1	.231	.250
Cabrera, Raymond, Ori.	.272	49	191	184	21	50	67	9	1	2	30	1	1	3	2	0	25	5	0	4	.364	.289
Callahan, David, Mar.*	.379	29	114	103	16	39	50	11	0	0	7	0	0	0	11	0	15	2	1	0	.485	.439
Calzado, Napolean, Ori.	.230	31	126	113	15	26	43	6	4	1	18	1	1	1	10	0	17	1	1	2	.381	.296
Cardona, Raynier, Pir.†	.215	22	75	65	4	14	20	1	1	1	5	0	0	2	8	0	13	3	1	3	.308	.320
Caridi, Tony, R.S.†	.136	13	25	22	1	3	4	1	0	0	0	2	0	0	1	0	7	0	0	0	.182	.174
Carpenter, Bubba, Yan.*	.235	5	19	17	3	4	11	0	2	1	7	0	0	0	2	0	2	0	0	0	.647	.316
Carrasco, Ricardo, Roy.	.247	54	216	182	33	45	83	9	1	9	33	0	3	4	27	0	49	0	0	7	.456	.352
Carreno, Jose, Exp.	.284	40	144	134	14	38	45	4	0	1	16	1	2	2	5	0	21	5	5	3	.336	.315
Carrillo, Robert, Ast.	.158	36	128	114	8	18	22	4	0	0	7	0	1	5	8	0	52	0	1	0	.193	.242
Casilla, Luis, Ast.	.212	25	71	66	2	14	17	3	0	0	10	0	0	0	5	0	20	1	3	0	.258	.268
Chourio, Jorjanis, Pir.	.218	26	84	78	8	17	23	3	0	1	11	0	1	3	2	1	21	4	0	0	.295	.262

SUMMER CLASS A *Gulf Coast League*

Player, Team	Avg.	G	TPA	AB	R	H	TB	2B	3B	HR	RBI	SH	SF	HP	BB	IBB	SO	SB	CS	GDP	Slg.	OBP
Clark, Tommy, Brav.	.130	33	103	92	10	12	17	2	0	1	8	2	0	1	8	0	40	2	1	1	.185	.208
Cleveland, Russell, Tig.	.215	31	93	79	5	17	20	3	0	0	4	0	0	3	11	0	27	1	4	1	.253	.333
Colina, Roberto, D.R.*	.364	3	11	11	0	4	5	1	0	0	2	0	0	0	0	0	1	0	0	0	.455	.364
Conway, Scott, Mar.*	.267	39	134	120	13	32	50	10	1	2	27	0	2	2	10	2	34	1	1	4	.417	.328
Cotten, Jeremy, Pir.	.314	24	99	86	13	27	52	4	0	7	22	0	2	2	9	0	29	1	0	1	.605	.384
Cronk, Brian, Pir.†	.233	27	107	90	11	21	36	4	1	3	10	0	2	3	12	1	26	1	0	2	.400	.336
Cruz, Ivan, Yan.*	.600	5	13	10	2	6	12	3	0	1	5	0	0	0	3	0	3	0	0	0	1.200	.692
Cruz, Rafael, Rang.	.233	41	149	129	20	30	34	1	0	1	7	0	0	5	14	0	26	0	1	1	.264	.331
Cubillan, Jose, Rang.†	.267	46	189	150	30	40	63	10	2	3	15	1	0	16	21	0	47	8	4	2	.420	.412
Daigle, Leo, Tig.	.308	36	148	133	19	41	56	8	2	1	24	0	2	3	10	0	19	2	1	1	.421	.365
Davison, Ashanti, Ori.	.214	4	17	14	2	3	3	0	0	0	1	0	0	1	2	0	2	4	0	0	.214	.353
De Aza, Modesto, Ast.	.238	42	167	151	25	36	50	9	1	1	12	1	0	1	14	0	51	23	5	1	.331	.307
De Caster, Yurendell, D.R.	.236	56	200	174	25	41	57	4	3	2	17	3	2	2	19	0	48	10	4	3	.328	.315
Degroote, Casey, Yan.*	.173	36	116	104	10	18	22	4	0	0	7	1	0	2	9	0	35	0	0	5	.212	.252
De Jesus, Wilmer, Exp.	.050	6	22	20	0	1	1	0	0	0	0	0	0	0	2	0	8	0	0	2	.050	.136
De La Rosa, Frank, Tig.	.259	32	121	112	17	29	40	8	0	1	13	1	1	0	7	0	24	1	2	5	.357	.300
De Los Santos, Eddy, Ast.	.135	27	79	74	3	10	12	2	0	0	8	0	0	1	4	0	32	1	2	3	.162	.190
Depastino, Joe, R.S.	.294	6	22	17	2	5	11	1	1	1	1	0	0	0	5	0	3	0	0	0	.647	.455
Derosso, Tony, R.S.	.467	4	16	15	4	7	9	2	0	0	3	0	0	0	1	0	3	0	0	0	.600	.500
Diaz, David, Pir.	.227	10	26	22	0	5	5	0	0	0	4	2	0	0	2	0	10	0	0	0	.227	.292
Dito, Robert, Exp.	.375	9	19	16	3	6	10	1	0	1	2	0	0	1	2	0	4	0	0	0	.625	.474
Dominguez, Luis, Ast.	.282	31	127	110	9	31	36	3	1	0	13	1	0	1	15	0	17	5	8	1	.327	.373
Donato, Gregorio, Brav.	.210	19	70	62	6	13	20	4	0	1	6	1	1	1	5	0	17	1	1	0	.323	.275
Dorrmann, Brian, Yan.	.254	41	153	130	18	33	42	9	0	0	11	3	1	6	13	0	10	2	3	1	.323	.347
Edge, Michael, Exp.	.168	35	110	101	10	17	20	1	1	0	5	1	0	3	5	0	42	8	3	0	.198	.229
Edwards, John, Twi.	.118	10	35	34	1	4	5	1	0	0	3	0	0	0	1	0	8	0	0	0	.147	.143
Elder, Rick, Ori.*	.340	29	121	106	19	36	58	5	4	3	26	0	3	0	12	0	20	3	2	0	.547	.397
Elorduy, Daniel, Brav.	.237	43	167	152	18	36	62	8	0	6	20	1	0	8	6	1	30	2	1	1	.408	.301
Erwin, Christopher, Rang.	.303	27	79	76	12	23	33	5	1	1	11	1	1	0	1	0	20	0	1	3	.434	.308
Espinoza, Andres, Exp.	.235	43	144	132	15	31	36	3	1	0	7	6	0	2	4	0	13	15	8	1	.273	.268
Felix, Hersy, Roy.	.260	48	199	173	23	45	65	5	0	5	25	0	3	2	21	0	34	0	1	4	.376	.342
Ferrand, Francisco, Mar.*	.263	36	130	114	14	30	46	5	4	1	11	0	2	1	13	0	26	2	2	2	.404	.338
Fischer, Mark, R.S.	.192	7	30	26	5	5	11	0	0	2	5	0	0	0	4	1	8	2	0	0	.423	.300
Foerter, Justin, Mar.*	.273	3	11	11	1	3	3	0	0	0	2	0	0	0	0	0	5	0	0	0	.273	.273
Fowler, David, Yan.	.188	39	113	101	11	19	29	3	2	1	9	0	0	3	9	0	47	3	2	3	.287	.274
Frawley, Scott, Brav.	.287	33	119	108	11	31	47	11	1	1	12	0	1	1	9	0	26	0	2	4	.435	.345
Fuentes, Omar, Yan.	.310	38	141	126	18	39	54	9	0	2	12	0	0	4	11	0	14	0	1	5	.429	.383
Gainey, Bryon, Mets*	.107	8	28	28	2	3	6	0	0	1	1	0	0	0	0	0	11	0	0	1	.214	.107
Galarraga, Luis, Mar.	.188	37	95	80	10	15	20	2	0	1	10	1	0	4	10	0	37	1	0	1	.250	.309
Garabito, Vianney, Yan.	.212	48	171	156	17	33	44	5	0	2	16	3	1	1	10	0	27	3	0	6	.282	.262
Garcia, Alfredo, Mets	.280	54	226	200	42	56	98	13	4	7	35	0	3	9	14	0	34	20	2	1	.490	.350
Garcia, Manuel, R.S.†	.204	18	55	49	5	10	13	3	0	0	2	2	1	1	2	0	10	2	0	1	.265	.245
Garcia, Rafael, Roy.	.213	20	70	61	6	13	16	3	0	0	7	0	0	0	9	0	15	7	1	0	.262	.314
Gettis, Byron, Roy.	.216	27	94	88	11	19	21	2	0	0	4	1	1	0	4	0	20	0	0	2	.239	.247
Gomez, Richard, Tig.	.333	47	188	162	42	54	91	11	4	6	40	0	0	5	21	3	37	20	2	3	.562	.426
Gonzalez, Felix, Exp.	.143	27	77	70	5	10	10	0	0	0	3	0	1	2	4	0	12	4	4	1	.143	.208
Goodwin, David, Roy.	.367	48	205	177	26	65	97	20	0	4	33	1	2	5	20	1	33	0	0	2	.548	.441
Graham, Tarik, Roy.	.167	33	82	66	13	11	14	1	1	0	5	0	0	5	11	0	27	5	0	1	.212	.329
Green, Richard, Ori.	.173	18	58	52	1	9	10	1	0	0	1	1	0	0	5	0	21	2	2	1	.192	.246
Gross, Jeremy, Yan.	1.000	1	1	1	1	1	1	0	0	0	0	0	0	0	0	0	0	0	0	0	1.000	1.000
Guerrero, Jason, D.R.	.077	14	19	13	3	1	1	0	0	0	1	0	1	0	5	0	3	0	1	0	.077	.316
Guerrero, Julio, R.S.	.207	39	162	145	21	30	34	4	0	0	13	2	0	4	11	0	21	12	1	6	.234	.281
Guerrero, Pedro, Rang.	.290	52	227	186	35	54	71	10	2	1	25	6	2	7	26	0	42	11	7	0	.382	.394
Gutierrez, Derrick, Ori.	.241	32	129	112	15	27	33	2	2	0	14	0	3	5	9	0	27	3	1	3	.295	.318
Gutierrez, Fernando, Ori.	.185	32	104	92	10	17	20	3	0	0	5	0	0	3	9	0	19	2	1	2	.217	.279
Guzman, Yorkis, Mets	.000	1	5	5	0	0	0	0	0	0	0	0	0	0	0	0	0	0	0	1	.000	.000
Hacker, Steve, Twi.	.208	6	26	24	5	5	8	0	0	1	3	0	0	0	2	0	2	0	0	0	.333	.269
Harts, Jeremy, Pir.†	.268	34	136	123	21	33	51	9	3	1	11	1	0	5	7	0	37	10	0	5	.415	.333
Hazelton, Justin, Tig.	.353	4	18	17	1	6	8	2	0	0	3	0	0	0	1	0	6	0	1	0	.471	.389
Heffernan, Christian, Brav.*	.280	38	92	82	13	23	35	5	2	1	10	0	1	0	9	0	21	5	3	2	.427	.348
Hendricks, Ian, Mets	.263	45	165	152	18	40	60	14	3	0	14	0	0	7	6	0	48	2	3	4	.395	.321
Henson, Drew, Yan.	.316	10	41	38	5	12	18	3	0	1	2	0	0	0	3	1	9	0	0	1	.474	.366
Hernandez, Jose, Pir.	.317	14	44	41	7	13	16	3	0	0	7	0	1	0	2	0	6	0	0	0	.390	.341
Hoch, Corey, Ori.	.353	19	79	68	9	24	34	8	1	0	11	0	2	2	7	0	10	3	1	0	.500	.418
Hopper, Norris, Roy.	.308	40	150	133	19	41	45	2	1	0	11	2	2	0	13	0	12	11	2	1	.338	.365
Hoshina, Koji, Exp.†	.167	6	21	18	3	3	4	1	0	0	0	0	0	1	2	0	5	2	3	0	.222	.286
Hughes, Brian, Ori.	.341	21	96	85	22	29	36	5	1	0	7	0	0	1	10	0	10	15	3	1	.424	.417
Hundley, Todd, Mets†	.000	1	4	2	0	0	0	0	0	0	0	0	0	0	2	0	1	0	0	0	.000	.500
Hunter, David, Mets*	.143	27	74	70	6	10	12	2	0	0	4	0	0	0	4	0	30	0	0	2	.171	.189
Isenia, Chairon, D.R.	.295	42	142	132	25	39	53	10	2	0	14	0	2	0	8	0	20	7	6	1	.402	.331
Jacobs, John, D.R.	.284	51	177	155	21	44	70	12	4	2	29	0	4	15	0	0	50	7	4	2	.452	.356
Jefferson, Dave, Exp.	.167	8	32	24	3	4	4	0	0	0	3	0	1	0	7	0	9	1	2	0	.167	.344
Jefferson, Reggie, R.S.*	.000	1	4	4	0	0	0	0	0	0	0	0	0	0	0	0	1	0	0	0	.000	.000
Jimenez, Carlos, Tig.	.250	47	206	188	29	47	58	9	1	0	18	0	1	2	15	0	48	7	2	2	.309	.311
Jimenez, Jonathan, Rang.	.270	13	46	37	5	10	12	2	0	0	8	0	3	1	5	0	11	1	0	1	.324	.348
Johnson, Eric, Pir.	.290	7	33	31	7	9	21	4	1	2	5	0	0	0	2	0	9	1	0	0	.677	.333
Johnson, Kareem, Twi.	.240	39	133	121	19	29	37	6	1	0	10	0	1	3	8	0	26	2	1	3	.306	.301
Jones, Andrew (A.J), Pir.	.186	30	116	97	11	18	24	4	1	0	7	1	2	0	16	0	23	4	0	0	.247	.296
Jones, Damien, Brav.*	.271	50	204	192	25	52	61	5	2	0	7	2	0	0	10	0	48	15	7	2	.318	.307
Kawabata, Kenichiro, R.S.†.	.252	39	128	107	16	27	33	4	1	0	10	3	1	0	17	0	24	10	5	1	.308	.352
Kieschnick, Brooks, D.R.*.	.500	3	13	12	4	6	13	1	0	2	8	0	0	0	1	0	0	0	0	1	1.083	.538
Koone, Chuck, Ori.†	.208	31	116	96	14	20	30	3	2	1	14	0	3	1	16	1	31	6	2	0	.313	.319
Lane, Ryan, Twi.	.292	18	70	65	9	19	32	5	1	2	10	1	0	0	4	0	13	2	1	1	.492	.333
Langerhans, Ryan, Brav.*	.277	43	168	148	15	41	65	10	4	2	19	0	1	0	19	1	38	2	5	0	.439	.357

Player, Team	Avg.	G	TPA	AB	R	H	TB	2B	3B	HR	RBI	SH	SF	HP	BB	IBB	SO	SB	CS	GDP	Slg.	OBP
Lara, Balmes, Tig.	.219	17	68	64	7	14	19	2	0	1	9	0	1	1	2	1	19	0	0	0	.297	.250
Larned, Andrew, R.S.	.125	2	9	8	1	1	1	0	0	0	0	0	0	0	1	0	1	1	0	0	.125	.222
Lauterhahn, Dan, Tig.	.273	3	12	11	1	3	3	0	0	0	0	0	0	0	1	0	2	1	0	0	.273	.333
Leon, Alfredo, Ori.	.071	9	30	28	3	2	2	0	0	0	1	0	1	0	1	0	4	0	0	1	.071	.100
Linares, Rodney, Ast.	.079	14	43	38	1	3	3	0	0	0	0	1	0	0	4	0	17	0	1	0	.079	.167
Liniak, Cole, R.S.	.000	2	9	8	1	0	0	0	0	0	0	0	0	1	0	0	1	0	0	0	.000	.111
Lopez, Guuillermo, Brav.	.179	23	65	56	2	10	12	2	0	0	4	0	1	3	5	0	18	1	1	0	.214	.277
Lopez, Jose, Mets†	.211	5	20	19	2	4	10	3	0	1	6	0	1	0	0	0	5	0	0	0	.526	.200
Lopez, Radhames, Ori.†	.204	14	58	49	4	10	11	1	0	0	3	1	0	1	7	0	13	2	0	2	.224	.316
Lough, Aaron, Twi.	.250	38	112	100	4	25	31	6	0	0	10	0	2	1	9	0	22	1	2	2	.310	.313
Louwsma, Chris, Mar.	.184	22	82	76	7	14	17	3	0	0	6	1	0	0	5	0	19	0	1	1	.224	.235
Lugo, Felix, Exp.†	.232	57	212	194	22	45	69	9	6	1	26	0	1	3	14	0	69	9	6	2	.356	.292
Lugo, Roberto, Mets*	.098	35	95	82	6	8	10	2	0	0	6	2	0	1	10	0	20	0	0	1	.122	.204
Mack, Antonio, Ori.	.181	40	140	127	18	23	28	2	0	1	9	4	0	0	9	0	46	4	4	1	.220	.235
Malinowski, Scott, Mets*	.260	35	111	104	10	27	32	5	0	0	6	1	1	0	5	0	9	0	0	3	.308	.291
Marciante, Frank, Rang.†	.310	37	146	129	17	40	52	9	0	1	16	1	0	2	14	0	17	1	2	3	.403	.386
Martin, Brian, D.R.	.255	46	179	153	24	39	62	11	0	4	24	2	0	6	18	0	57	0	2	1	.405	.356
Martin, Tommy, Ori.	.197	24	89	76	11	15	18	3	0	0	11	2	1	1	9	0	19	9	2	1	.237	.287
Massucco, Scott, Yan.	.244	26	94	86	10	21	27	1	1	1	9	1	0	1	6	0	15	2	0	2	.314	.301
McCorvey, Kenneth, Twi.	.222	44	129	117	11	26	38	9	0	1	8	1	1	0	10	1	41	5	0	2	.325	.281
McKeel, Walt, R.S.	.250	13	41	36	1	9	14	2	0	1	4	0	1	0	4	0	8	0	0	1	.389	.317
McKinley, Josh, Exp.†	.269	57	239	208	36	56	80	11	5	1	19	2	1	4	24	1	40	14	13	0	.385	.354
McLaughlin, Erik, Brav.	.100	19	54	50	1	5	7	2	0	0	1	0	0	0	4	1	26	1	1	1	.140	.167
Medrano, David, Rang.	.195	50	182	154	19	30	46	7	0	3	17	2	3	2	21	1	61	2	0	1	.299	.294
Medrano, Jesus, Mar.	.286	48	200	175	42	50	69	11	1	2	15	1	1	2	21	1	30	26	7	1	.394	.367
Mejia, Renato, Mar.	.250	47	155	136	16	34	46	4	1	2	21	1	3	5	10	0	37	6	3	5	.338	.318
Mendoza, Carlos, D.R. *	.444	6	25	18	6	8	9	1	0	0	4	0	1	1	5	0	3	3	1	1	.500	.560
Merloni, Lou, R.S.	.000	1	1	1	0	0	0	0	0	0	0	0	0	0	0	0	0	0	0	0	.000	.000
Meseberg, Michael, D.R.*	.059	5	17	17	0	1	1	0	0	0	1	0	0	0	0	0	6	1	0	0	.059	.059
Miller, Josh, Pir.*	.268	36	147	138	20	37	57	10	2	2	18	0	1	2	6	2	27	4	3	1	.413	.306
Monzon, Francisco, Ori.	.117	32	84	77	3	9	10	1	0	0	5	0	1	1	5	0	17	0	0	1	.130	.179
Moore, Frank, D.R.*	.303	39	104	99	13	30	43	4	3	1	9	0	0	1	4	1	15	7	1	5	.434	.337
Moore, Griffin, Roy.	.231	35	132	117	13	27	38	5	0	2	12	1	1	0	11	1	11	4	1	4	.325	.295
Mundo, Alberto, Brav.†	.201	44	185	169	14	34	44	4	0	2	17	0	1	2	13	1	35	7	0	1	.260	.265
Nanita, Emmanuel, Twi.	.232	42	143	125	22	29	41	6	3	0	9	0	0	4	14	0	19	5	2	1	.328	.329
Nelson, Reggie, Tig.	.193	43	163	135	22	26	27	1	0	0	8	0	0	2	26	0	25	22	5	1	.200	.331
Nettles, Jeff, Yan.	.125	12	29	24	1	3	4	1	0	0	1	0	0	0	5	0	4	0	1	1	.167	.276
Nowlin, Cody, Rang.*	.272	52	223	202	25	55	93	13	2	7	34	0	1	1	19	3	42	1	4	1	.460	.336
Nunez, Edward, Twi.*	.182	4	11	11	3	2	2	0	0	0	1	0	0	0	0	0	1	4	0	0	.182	.182
Nunez, Jose, Roy.	.263	46	171	156	22	41	56	6	0	3	15	1	2	0	12	0	27	0	0	4	.359	.312
Ochoa, Javier, Ast.	.212	34	108	85	7	18	22	2	1	0	6	2	1	6	14	0	15	1	2	0	.259	.358
Ojeda, Augie, Ori.†	.400	4	20	15	6	6	8	2	0	0	2	0	0	2	3	0	1	3	0	0	.533	.550
Oropeza, Asdrubal, Brav.	.268	35	144	127	18	34	52	10	1	2	13	0	0	4	13	0	27	4	1	3	.409	.354
Ortiz, Juan, Exp.	.229	49	187	170	24	39	55	7	3	1	15	3	1	1	12	0	31	16	11	2	.324	.283
Osborn, Jason, Mets	.245	19	60	53	3	13	15	2	0	0	4	2	1	3	1	0	12	0	0	1	.283	.293
Osorio, Issrael, D.R.	.229	34	122	109	18	25	48	5	0	6	20	0	2	3	8	0	34	1	0	4	.440	.295
Pacheco, Juan, Ori.	.267	31	129	116	20	31	45	6	1	2	11	0	1	3	9	0	17	5	3	2	.388	.333
Parker, Chris, Tig.	.282	33	121	103	13	29	46	5	0	4	17	1	0	7	10	0	35	0	3	2	.447	.383
Paulino, David, Mar.	.340	21	57	50	9	17	19	0	1	0	5	2	0	0	5	0	14	5	5	0	.380	.400
Paulino, Waren, Yan.*	.500	4	4	4	0	2	2	0	0	0	0	0	0	0	0	0	0	0	0	0	.500	.500
Pelfrey, Brice, Pir.	.189	41	186	164	20	31	34	3	0	0	13	0	2	8	12	0	29	5	2	2	.207	.274
Pellicciotta, Marc, Ast.	.209	36	120	110	14	23	32	3	0	2	12	2	0	0	8	0	20	3	0	4	.291	.263
Pena, Carlos, Rang.*	.400	2	8	5	1	2	2	0	0	0	0	0	0	0	3	0	1	1	1	1	.400	.625
Pena, Jose, R.S.	.344	48	183	160	28	55	85	12	3	4	21	1	0	8	14	0	33	6	5	2	.531	.423
Pena, Rodolfo, R.S.	.349	24	88	83	15	29	38	5	2	0	14	0	1	1	3	0	11	1	1	5	.458	.375
Pender, Darrell, Tig.	.279	38	153	129	27	36	51	3	3	1	15	1	0	7	16	0	44	16	3	3	.395	.388
Penna, Shaun, R.S.	.212	31	113	99	13	21	26	5	0	0	10	3	2	0	9	0	24	1	1	2	.263	.273
Perea, Carlos, Roy.	.250	36	132	116	11	29	29	0	0	0	7	2	0	1	13	0	20	4	4	3	.250	.331
Perich, Joshua, Mets	.233	35	125	116	8	27	41	4	2	2	13	0	1	0	8	1	32	0	1	0	.353	.280
Perry, Herbert, D.R.	.115	8	30	26	1	3	3	0	0	0	1	0	0	1	3	0	5	0	0	0	.115	.233
Player, David, Roy.*	.000	1	4	3	0	0	0	0	0	0	0	0	0	0	1	0	3	0	0	0	.000	.250
Pratt, Todd, Mets	.250	2	8	4	1	1	1	0	0	0	0	0	0	0	4	0	1	0	0	0	.250	.625
Pressley, Josh, D.R.*	.304	36	149	125	22	38	47	6	0	1	16	0	0	4	20	1	29	2	1	0	.376	.396
Pridie, Jon, Twi.	.217	31	113	106	10	23	32	6	0	1	15	0	0	1	6	0	24	0	1	7	.302	.265
Prieto, Jonathan, Pir.†	.302	34	150	129	22	39	50	7	2	0	16	2	1	0	18	0	19	7	6	0	.388	.385
Proctor, Mark, Mets	.184	20	52	49	3	9	14	1	2	0	2	1	0	0	2	0	5	0	3	2	.286	.216
Prosper, Gerard, Mets*	.241	11	34	29	5	7	7	0	0	0	0	0	1	0	4	0	7	0	1	0	.241	.333
Quinones, Marcus, Rang.†	.261	59	235	203	27	53	73	9	4	1	22	3	1	3	25	1	34	3	7	10	.360	.349
Raines, Timothy, Ori.	.244	59	242	197	40	48	66	7	4	1	13	3	0	12	30	1	53	37	4	0	.335	.373
Rains, Nick, Mets	.261	12	24	23	5	6	9	1	1	0	2	0	0	0	1	0	10	2	1	0	.391	.292
Ramirez, Anthony, Ast.*	.354	20	74	65	8	23	27	4	0	0	9	0	0	2	7	0	13	3	2	1	.415	.432
Ramirez, Charlie, Roy.	.305	50	211	200	27	61	74	9	2	0	23	2	1	1	7	0	35	13	5	6	.370	.330
Ramirez, Edgar, D.R.	.382	9	34	34	5	13	23	5	1	1	3	0	0	0	0	0	4	0	1	0	.676	.382
Ravelo, Manuel, Pir.	.253	24	100	95	11	24	32	1	2	1	7	0	2	0	3	0	17	9	1	1	.337	.270
Reding, Josh, Exp.	.375	2	8	8	2	3	4	1	0	0	0	0	0	0	0	0	3	1	1	1	.500	.375
Reed, Brian, Mar.	.246	56	246	211	35	52	78	13	5	1	14	1	2	6	26	0	70	40	8	4	.370	.343
Resendez, Carlos, Mar.	.214	6	16	14	0	3	3	0	0	0	2	0	1	0	1	0	6	0	0	0	.214	.250
Reyes, Dadny, Mar.†	.297	30	77	64	7	19	28	4	1	1	12	1	1	1	10	0	8	0	0	1	.438	.395
Rhodes, Nicholas, D.R.	.234	23	70	64	6	15	16	1	0	0	6	1	0	3	1	0	12	3	0	1	.250	.279
Rivas, Julio, Mar.	.148	13	30	27	1	4	4	0	0	0	3	0	0	1	2	0	11	0	0	0	.148	.233
Rivas, Justo, Brav.	.186	37	134	113	11	21	31	6	2	0	11	1	0	4	16	0	31	6	3	5	.274	.308
Rivera, Juan, Yan.	.333	57	238	210	43	70	117	9	1	12	45	0	1	0	26	2	27	8	5	10	.557	.408
Rix, Derek, R.S.*	.283	44	178	152	28	43	83	8	4	8	38	1	4	2	19	0	48	2	0	0	.546	.362
Rodriguez, Carlos, R.S.	.325	54	215	197	35	64	106	14	2	8	37	0	3	4	11	0	37	14	3	2	.538	.367

Player, Team	Avg.	G	TPA	AB	R	H	TB	2B	3B	HR	RBI	SH	SF	HP	BB	IBB	SO	SB	CS	GDP	Slg.	OBP
Rodriguez, Felix, Yan.	.320	11	27	25	3	8	9	1	0	0	6	1	0	0	1	0	4	0	0	1	.360	.346
Rodriguez, Junior, Yan.	.277	48	221	159	27	44	58	12	1	0	24	2	2	10	48	0	60	2	8	1	.365	.466
Rodriguez, Luis, Twi.†	.278	52	205	180	33	50	66	11	1	1	15	1	2	0	22	2	17	14	3	4	.367	.353
Rodriguez, Ronny, R.S.	.287	27	98	87	12	25	38	8	1	1	17	0	1	2	8	0	15	1	1	2	.437	.357
Rodriguez, Steve, Tig.	.246	36	151	130	19	32	54	6	2	4	20	2	0	3	16	0	33	2	2	5	.415	.342
Rollins, Antwon, Rang.	.210	53	230	210	23	44	54	5	1	1	16	2	3	3	11	0	60	8	8	4	.257	.256
Rosado, Omar, Exp.	.179	47	164	145	13	26	33	7	0	0	10	4	0	4	11	0	38	9	8	0	.228	.256
Ruan, Wilken, Exp.	.239	54	215	201	22	48	66	9	3	1	19	3	2	2	5	0	43	13	13	1	.328	.262
Rumfield, Brock, Ori.	.232	49	210	185	26	43	62	10	0	3	25	0	5	11	9	0	23	3	4	3	.335	.300
Ryan, Gregory, Rang.*	.240	53	213	183	27	44	63	9	2	2	22	4	2	5	19	0	16	8	3	6	.344	.325
Ryan, Kelvin, D.R.	.266	57	239	222	34	59	84	10	3	3	36	1	2	4	10	0	38	2	4	6	.378	.307
Saffer, Jon, Exp.*	.125	2	9	8	3	1	1	0	0	0	2	0	0	0	1	0	2	1	0	0	.125	.222
St. Pierre, Maxim, Tig.	.385	31	120	104	18	40	49	3	0	2	15	0	0	1	15	0	12	6	2	1	.471	.467
Sajiun, Joel, Twi.	.253	50	113	99	12	25	39	6	1	2	12	0	0	4	9	0	33	1	1	0	.394	.339
Salazar, Ruben, Twi.	.248	50	176	161	16	40	56	5	1	3	25	2	3	1	9	0	29	10	3	4	.348	.287
Samuel, Cody, Yan.	.429	2	8	7	3	3	7	1	0	1	2	0	0	0	1	0	0	0	0	0	1.000	.500
Sandberg, Eric, Twi.*	.316	35	134	114	17	36	53	8	0	3	18	0	0	2	18	2	17	4	2	4	.465	.418
Santana, Emmanuel, Roy.*	.326	16	51	46	7	15	27	6	0	2	10	0	1	1	3	0	9	0	0	1	.587	.373
Santana, Pedro, Yan.	.246	16	68	61	11	15	17	2	0	0	7	0	1	3	3	0	18	1	0	1	.279	.309
Santos, Angel, R.S.†	.351	23	93	77	14	27	34	5	1	0	13	1	2	0	13	0	10	7	3	1	.442	.435
Sassanella, Jeremy, Tig.†	.256	34	124	117	13	30	46	5	1	3	12	0	1	2	4	0	31	0	2	1	.393	.290
Seale, Marvin, Mets†	.220	37	146	132	24	29	43	4	5	0	7	1	0	3	10	0	40	11	3	2	.326	.290
Segura, Rolando, Pir.	.274	28	104	95	15	26	41	6	0	3	15	0	0	2	7	0	23	2	0	1	.432	.337
Sein, Javier, Yan.*	.260	43	144	123	17	32	45	8	1	1	21	1	0	5	15	0	33	0	1	5	.366	.364
Seo, Jae, Mets	.296	11	38	27	5	8	16	0	1	2	4	0	0	4	7	0	9	1	0	0	.593	.500
Shanks, James, Roy.	.264	42	166	144	21	38	47	9	0	0	13	0	1	3	18	0	26	10	1	3	.326	.355
Sheffield, Jeff, Yan.†	.244	20	45	41	2	10	11	1	0	0	4	1	1	0	2	0	18	0	0	0	.268	.273
Shrum, Allen, Twi.	.331	42	143	127	17	42	82	10	0	10	25	0	0	3	13	1	27	3	2	2	.646	.406
Shuck, Jason, Mets	.271	46	184	170	21	46	56	10	0	0	16	1	0	2	11	1	34	7	5	3	.329	.322
Shumpert, Derek, Yan.	.125	6	20	16	3	2	4	0	1	0	0	0	0	0	4	0	11	1	0	0	.250	.300
Smith, Ryan, Mets	.172	31	99	93	8	16	23	5	1	0	9	1	0	2	3	0	15	1	0	2	.247	.214
Smith, Toebius, Brav.	.152	20	56	46	6	7	8	1	0	0	0	1	0	1	8	0	17	0	2	2	.174	.241
Soler, Ramon, D.R.†	.252	58	264	226	47	57	81	7	7	1	19	4	2	5	27	0	48	23	11	1	.358	.342
Sosa, Jovanny, Pir.	.311	32	128	119	23	37	69	6	1	8	25	0	0	1	8	0	32	3	1	1	.580	.359
Southward, Deshawn, Twi.	.267	56	192	165	31	44	57	5	1	2	24	0	3	3	21	0	33	11	4	2	.345	.354
Stanton, Eric, Pir.	.191	25	96	89	8	17	27	7	0	1	6	0	0	0	7	0	19	0	0	4	.303	.250
Stevens, Tony, Twi.†	.257	52	202	187	30	48	66	7	1	3	12	1	1	2	11	0	19	3	7	1	.353	.303
Stratton, Robert, Mets	.261	12	49	46	4	12	22	1	0	3	13	0	1	0	2	1	15	1	0	0	.478	.286
Sziksai, Jeff, Yan.	.224	35	142	125	12	28	32	4	0	0	9	2	1	3	11	0	21	0	2	5	.256	.300
Taveras, Jose, Roy.	.222	7	29	27	4	6	10	1	0	1	4	0	0	0	2	0	11	0	0	0	.370	.276
Terni, Chaz, R.S.	.317	17	74	63	14	20	26	4	1	0	13	0	3	0	8	0	12	1	0	3	.413	.378
Tiburcio, Emigdio, Tig.†	.356	21	80	73	12	26	40	4	5	0	12	1	1	0	5	0	23	3	0	0	.548	.392
Tillis, Cameron, Roy.†	.154	3	13	13	1	2	3	1	0	0	1	0	0	0	0	0	4	0	0	0	.231	.154
Tolli, Barry, Tig.	.179	39	121	117	9	21	30	7	1	0	10	0	0	1	3	0	41	2	2	1	.256	.207
Torres, Franklin, Twi.	.276	50	203	174	32	48	54	6	0	0	24	2	4	3	20	0	29	15	1	5	.310	.353
Torres, Frederick, Rang.	.221	32	113	104	13	23	37	5	0	3	13	3	1	0	5	0	23	1	1	3	.356	.253
Torres, Luis, Brav.†	.243	48	184	169	15	41	57	13	0	1	13	1	0	8	6	1	26	6	7	1	.337	.301
Torres, Rommel, Pir.	.222	26	92	81	11	18	23	5	0	0	3	1	0	1	9	0	18	1	1	3	.284	.308
Tsujita, Osamu, D.R.*	.288	41	136	118	27	34	62	11	4	3	27	0	3	1	14	2	35	2	4	1	.525	.360
Tucker, Mamon, Ori.	.143	12	43	42	5	6	6	0	0	0	2	0	0	0	1	0	17	1	0	2	.143	.163
Turnquist, Tyler, Ast.	.283	56	237	219	31	62	88	15	4	1	29	0	0	4	14	0	23	6	5	7	.402	.338
Tyson, Torre, R.S.†	.322	36	151	118	29	38	53	9	0	2	18	0	0	3	30	0	8	8	4	3	.449	.470
Ugueto, Luis, Mar.†	.229	50	180	166	20	38	50	8	2	0	15	2	2	2	8	0	37	7	1	2	.301	.270
Valdez, Angel, Yan.	.232	47	185	168	34	39	57	5	2	3	19	0	1	3	13	0	61	11	5	4	.339	.297
Valdez, Darlin, Exp.	.000	5	11	11	0	0	0	0	0	0	0	0	0	0	0	0	3	0	0	0	.000	.000
Vann, Eric, Roy.†	.043	6	25	23	1	1	2	1	0	0	1	0	0	0	2	0	10	0	1	0	.087	.120
Van Pareren, Tim, Exp.†	.250	28	83	76	9	19	27	5	0	1	6	1	0	1	5	0	19	7	0	2	.355	.305
Vasquez, Alejandro, Ast.*	.335	57	231	209	31	70	103	20	2	3	23	0	1	0	21	4	34	7	7	4	.493	.394
Vazquez, Carlos, D.R.	.169	24	73	65	6	11	20	3	0	2	9	0	1	3	4	1	17	1	0	0	.308	.247
Vega, Jonathan, Ast.	.200	50	199	180	17	36	58	3	2	5	25	0	0	2	17	0	62	3	3	2	.322	.276
Velazquez, Gil, Mets	.186	33	111	97	7	18	21	3	0	0	7	3	1	2	8	0	10	2	1	1	.216	.259
Venales, Luis, Mar.	.154	27	71	65	7	10	13	1	1	0	4	0	1	3	2	0	26	0	0	2	.200	.211
Wade, Michael, Ori.	.118	7	19	17	3	2	5	0	0	1	1	0	0	0	2	0	5	0	1	0	.294	.211
Walker, Javon, Mar.	.222	32	105	90	15	20	29	3	0	2	9	0	1	9	5	0	38	4	3	2	.322	.324
Walker, Shon, Pir.*	.389	4	21	18	7	7	17	2	1	2	7	0	0	0	3	0	5	0	0	0	.944	.476
Warren, Christopher, R.S.	.298	32	131	114	23	34	49	2	2	3	16	0	2	3	12	0	20	4	0	3	.430	.374
Washington, Mo, Pir.	.206	39	151	136	19	28	49	4	1	5	13	0	1	2	12	1	49	4	0	2	.360	.278
Watkins, Thomas, Twi.	.219	33	84	73	8	16	21	5	0	0	8	1	1	0	9	0	11	5	0	1	.288	.301
Whitby, Corey, R.S.*	.386	18	61	44	13	17	19	0	1	0	6	0	2	0	15	0	3	7	1	0	.432	.525
Williams, Clyde, Roy.*	.238	57	235	206	25	49	69	10	5	0	16	4	3	3	19	0	63	14	5	1	.335	.302
Wilson, Vance, Mets	.357	10	30	28	5	10	21	5	0	2	9	0	1	0	1	0	5	0	1	2	.750	.367
Wright, Charles, Yan.*	.171	17	45	41	11	7	7	0	0	0	3	0	0	0	4	0	11	2	0	0	.171	.244
Wright, Corey, Yan.*	.273	11	51	44	6	12	16	2	1	0	3	0	0	0	7	0	11	3	2	0	.364	.373
Wright, Ron, Pir.	.600	3	13	10	4	6	12	0	0	2	5	0	0	0	2	0	0	0	0	0	1.200	.615
Yancy, Michael, Mets	.212	42	152	137	15	29	36	2	1	1	12	0	1	7	7	0	27	2	5	6	.263	.283
Zamora, Junior, Mets	.200	2	6	5	1	1	3	0	1	0	2	0	0	0	1	0	0	0	0	0	.600	.333
Zapata, Juan, Ast.	.275	50	195	182	17	50	62	10	1	0	3	2	0	1	10	0	31	5	5	3	.341	.316
Zapey, Winton, Mar.	.202	38	112	104	11	21	30	9	0	0	5	2	0	1	5	0	27	1	1	2	.288	.245
Zardis, Alex, Mets	.186	37	93	86	8	16	20	4	0	0	3	1	1	2	3	0	17	0	0	3	.233	.242
Zorrilla, Julio, Mets†	.211	10	39	38	4	8	8	0	0	0	2	0	0	0	1	0	4	1	0	0	.211	.231

GRAND SLAMS: Calzado, Carrasco, Goodwin, P. Guerrero, J. Rivera, Rix, Santana, Shrum, Jovanny Sosa, 1 each.

AWARDED FIRST BASE ON CATCHER'S INTERFERENCE: Moore 2 (F. Gutierrez, Monzon); Ruan 2 (Zapey 2); Cubillan (Lough); Rhodes (Buck); Rollins (Lough); Sajiun (R. Torres).

1998 PITCHING

TEAM

Team	W	L	Pct.	ERA	G	CG	ShO	Sv.	IP	H	TBF	R	ER	HR	SH	SF	HB	BB	IBB	SO	WP	Bk.
Marlins	38	22	.633	2.19	59	2	10	16	501.1	369	2007	178	122	14	15	8	29	149	5	540	47	4
Expos	32	27	.542	2.62	59	2	7	15	512.1	450	2122	207	149	19	15	9	39	110	0	442	27	5
Royals	32	28	.533	3.39	60	1	5	15	511.2	470	2205	250	193	26	19	19	39	194	3	429	49	7
Yankees	34	26	.567	3.42	60	0	3	21	521.0	496	2213	260	198	20	13	8	33	169	6	463	40	10
Rangers	34	26	.567	3.50	60	0	7	17	516.1	497	2187	250	201	31	10	19	35	150	1	441	35	12
Braves	25	35	.417	3.68	60	0	3	13	506.0	455	2112	250	207	16	21	16	46	151	2	468	38	9
Red Sox	27	33	.450	3.69	60	0	3	11	504.2	483	2196	288	207	34	14	18	27	181	4	466	45	9
Twins	34	26	.567	3.70	60	1	1	15	509.0	508	2229	271	209	23	13	18	33	176	7	402	52	9
Devil Rays	36	24	.600	3.89	60	1	4	11	522.1	522	2282	282	226	31	17	11	36	203	5	461	39	15
Mets	24	35	.407	3.91	59	3	3	13	497.2	498	2146	282	216	23	11	15	42	191	7	419	67	16
Astros	22	38	.367	4.25	60	3	3	10	531.1	537	2331	316	251	27	15	17	54	187	1	543	30	15
Tigers	28	32	.467	4.31	60	2	2	11	526.0	521	2290	304	252	31	3	8	36	219	4	510	45	6
Orioles	28	32	.467	4.57	60	0	5	13	523.1	564	2357	323	266	42	19	27	31	225	3	373	48	6
Pirates	25	35	.417	4.72	60	0	1	14	522.0	569	2430	373	274	26	17	27	55	232	5	357	71	27

INDIVIDUAL

TOP QUALIFIERS FOR EARNED-RUN AVERAGE TITLE

Minimum 48 innings. *Lefthanded pitcher.

Pitcher, Team	W	L	Pct.	ERA	G	GS	CG	ShO	GF	Sv.	IP	H	TBF	R	ER	HR	SH	SF	HB	BB	IBB	SO	WP	Bk.
Anderson, Wes, Mar.	5	2	.714	1.39	11	11	1	1	0	0	64.2	44	256	25	10	0	3	1	7	18	1	66	3	2
Bong, Jung, Brav. *	1	1	.500	1.49	11	10	0	0	0	0	48.1	31	181	9	8	2	1	1	6	14	0	56	7	3
Villanueva, Bill, Mar.	6	2	.750	1.88	11	11	0	0	0	0	57.1	46	227	14	12	0	1	0	8	13	0	54	2	0
McGinnis, Johnny, Brav.	2	6	.250	1.89	13	11	0	0	0	0	62.0	40	247	23	13	0	0	0	9	17	0	53	10	0
Chiavacci, Ronald, Exp.	6	3	.667	2.13	13	6	0	0	0	0	55.0	43	218	17	13	1	3	0	2	13	0	42	3	2
Spurling, Chris, Yan.	2	1	.667	2.28	13	6	0	0	2	1	51.1	57	219	21	13	3	0	2	11	0	44	2	0
Nunez, Jose, Mets*	3	7	.300	2.38	13	11	1	0	0	0	68.0	60	267	26	18	6	1	3	12	0	69	0	1
Weslowski, Robert, Mets	5	3	.625	2.54	11	10	1	1	0	0	60.1	59	248	25	17	2	1	2	2	20	0	37	4	1
Garcia, Rosman, Yan.	4	3	.571	2.55	12	12	0	0	0	0	67.0	70	284	38	19	1	3	0	3	9	0	47	1	2
Frazier, Bradley, Twi.	4	3	.571	2.61	9	9	0	0	0	0	51.2	51	220	17	15	1	0	1	5	13	1	40	6	0
Shields, Drew, Mar.	7	2	.778	2.63	13	11	1	0	0	1	65.0	48	262	24	19	3	4	2	4	19	1	65	10	1
Bechler, Steven, Ori.	2	4	.333	2.72	9	9	0	0	0	0	49.2	51	209	22	15	4	1	1	1	8	0	39	4	1
Affeldt, Jeremy, Roy. *	4	3	.571	2.89	12	9	0	0	0	0	56.0	50	241	24	18	1	3	0	8	24	0	67	7	0
Diaz, Luis, Tig.	2	2	.500	2.91	25	0	0	0	0	0	52.2	46	228	21	17	3	1	0	5	23	1	58	4	0
Ratliff, Craig, Ori.	5	4	.556	3.07	10	10	0	0	0	0	55.2	53	243	31	19	4	0	3	3	21	0	33	4	0

DEPARTMENTAL LEADERS: W—Marin, 8; L—Aguilar, Mayi, Jose Nunez, 7 each; Pct.—Marin, 1.000; G—Marin, 27; CG—Several players tied at 12; ShO—Several players tied at 1; GF—Quarnstrom, 21; Sv.—Dunn, Quarnstrom, 12 each; IP—Pineda, 73.1; H—Chisnall, 83; TBF—Pineda, 315; R—Chisnall, 54; ER—Aguilar, 46; HR—B. Diaz, 7; SH—Melson, 6; SF—G. Gonzalez, Hamilton, Mendez, E. Perez, 4 each; HB—Pineda, 10; BB—Marx, 39; IBB—Several players tied with 2 each; SO—Pineda, 83; WP—South, 17; BK—Aguilar, 7.

ALL PITCHERS

*Lefthanded pitcher.

Pitcher, Team	W	L	Pct.	ERA	G	GS	CG	ShO	GF	Sv.	IP	H	TBF	R	ER	HR	SH	SF	HB	BB	IBB	SO	WP	Bk.
Acosta, Alberto, Yan.	1	1	.500	3.38	8	6	0	0	0	0	29.1	20	123	13	11	2	0	0	2	17	0	27	0	0
Adam, Dave, D.R.	0	1	.000	4.50	1	1	0	0	0	0	2.0	3	9	1	1	0	0	0	0	0	0	1	0	0
Affeldt, Jeremy, Roy. *	4	3	.571	2.89	12	9	0	0	0	0	56.0	50	241	24	18	1	3	0	8	24	0	67	7	0
Aguilar, Edwin, Ast.	3	7	.300	7.86	14	9	1	0	0	1	52.2	69	254	49	46	5	2	0	7	31	0	60	5	7
Alvarez, Wilson, D.R. *	0	0	.000	0.00	1	1	0	0	0	0	3.0	2	11	0	0	0	0	0	1	0	0	4	0	0
Anderson, Antwoine, Mar. *	3	1	.750	1.35	15	0	0	0	10	3	33.1	23	128	6	5	1	0	1	0	8	0	37	3	1
Anderson, Wes, Mar.	5	2	.714	1.39	11	11	1	1	0	0	64.2	44	256	25	10	0	3	1	7	18	1	66	3	2
Andujar, Jesse, Exp.	1	2	.333	3.56	18	0	0	0	12	0	30.1	30	138	17	12	2	0	1	7	11	0	27	0	0
Appier, Kevin, Roy.	0	1	.000	2.70	1	1	0	0	0	0	3.1	3	16	3	1	0	0	1	0	1	0	2	0	0
Aramboles, Ricardo, Yan.	2	1	.667	2.93	10	9	0	0	0	0	40.0	33	160	14	13	0	2	1	1	13	0	44	2	2
Armstrong, Charles, D.R. *	1	0	1.000	6.00	14	0	0	0	4	0	15.0	16	73	11	10	0	0	0	14	0	18	0	0
Aucoin, Derek, Mets	0	0	.000	5.63	5	0	0	0	0	0	8.0	6	36	6	5	0	0	0	3	3	0	16	4	0
Backsmeyer, Justin, Rang.	0	0	.000	1.13	5	1	0	0	0	0	8.0	9	38	5	1	0	0	1	1	7	0	4	1	0
Baldassano, Joseph, Exp.	0	1	.000	0.92	14	0	0	0	13	4	19.2	11	85	4	2	0	1	1	3	15	0	24	6	0
Bazan, Juan, Pir.	1	0	1.000	2.93	8	0	0	0	3	0	15.1	11	62	7	5	1	0	0	7	0	9	1	0
Bechler, Steven, Ori.	2	4	.333	2.72	9	9	0	0	0	0	49.2	51	209	22	15	4	1	1	1	8	0	39	4	1
Beitey, Jason, Rang.	0	0	.000	0.00	5	0	0	0	2	1	9.0	5	37	0	0	0	0	0	3	3	0	7	0	0
Belcher, B.J., Rang.	0	0	.000	18.90	3	0	0	0	1	0	3.1	9	20	7	7	0	0	0	1	1	0	3	1	1
Bennett, Jeff, Pir.	2	4	.333	4.63	13	11	0	0	0	0	46.2	50	212	29	24	4	0	2	7	13	0	18	2	0
Betancourt, Rafael, R.S.	0	2	.000	7.20	4	3	0	0	0	0	5.0	6	22	5	4	1	0	1	0	1	0	4	1	1
Betti, Rich, R.S. *	0	1	.000	10.50	3	1	0	0	0	0	6.0	6	36	7	7	1	0	0	2	6	0	6	0	0
Bevil, Brian, Roy.	0	0	.000	2.25	3	3	0	0	0	0	4.0	4	19	2	1	0	0	0	2	0	7	1	0
Blake, Peter, Twi. *	1	5	.167	4.23	8	8	0	0	0	0	38.1	41	167	24	18	1	1	2	1	20	0	28	6	1
Bobbitt, Josh, Rang. *	2	1	.667	4.50	19	0	0	0	12	2	36.0	46	169	24	18	2	1	4	12	0	41	5	3
Bong, Jung, Brav. *	1	1	.500	1.49	11	10	0	0	0	0	48.1	31	181	9	8	2	1	1	6	14	0	56	7	3
Brewer, Dustin, Ori.	0	4	.000	5.90	14	9	0	0	0	0	50.1	64	232	36	33	3	1	3	0	25	0	29	3	0
Brito, Yorbis, Brav.	1	0	1.000	20.25	3	0	0	0	0	0	2.2	7	15	6	6	0	0	0	1	0	0	2	0	0
Buckles, Bucky, Rang.	0	0	.000	0.00	2	2	0	0	0	0	3.0	0	9	0	0	0	0	0	0	0	0	2	0	0
Bullinger, Kirk, Exp.	0	0	.000	0.00	2	2	0	0	0	0	4.0	2	14	0	0	0	0	0	0	0	0	7	0	0
Bullock, Jeremiah, Rang. *	1	6	.143	5.00	11	9	0	0	0	0	45.0	54	203	34	25	3	2	1	1	21	0	30	5	0
Bumatay, Mike, Pir. *	2	3	.400	3.18	13	5	0	0	2	1	39.2	46	188	29	14	1	2	3	4	16	0	37	4	2
Cadena, Nathan, R.S.	0	0	.000	3.60	4	0	0	0	1	0	5.0	3	20	2	2	0	0	0	1	0	5	2	1
Calvo, Jose, Ast.	0	2	.000	3.91	13	0	0	0	7	1	23.0	22	97	12	10	1	2	0	2	7	0	18	0	0

Pitcher, Team	W	L	Pct.	ERA	G	GS	CG	ShO	GF	Sv.	IP	H	TBF	R	ER	HR	SH	SF	HB	BB	IBB	SO	WP	Bk.
Campos, David, Mar. *	3	0	1.000	0.00	9	0	0	0	9	3	23.1	7	86	1	0	1	0	0	0	10	1	41	1	0
Centeno, Juan, Ast.	4	6	.400	3.79	21	0	0	0	10	0	40.1	59	194	35	17	1	0	2	3	5	1	27	2	1
Cepeda, Victor, Tig.	4	1	.800	3.00	18	2	0	0	8	1	45.0	31	178	18	15	1	0	1	2	11	0	49	3	0
Checketts, Andrew, R.S.	0	0	.000	0.00	2	0	0	0	1	0	2.0	2	12	0	0	0	0	0	1	2	0	5	0	0
Checo, Robinson, R.S.	1	0	1.000	3.00	3	3	0	0	0	0	9.0	9	37	5	3	1	0	0	1	0	0	13	0	0
Chiasson, Scott, Roy.	2	0	1.000	4.81	13	0	0	0	6	1	24.1	24	111	17	13	2	2	1	5	11	0	26	10	0
Chiavacci, Ronald, Exp.	6	3	.667	2.13	13	6	0	0	0	0	55.0	43	218	17	13	1	3	0	2	13	0	42	3	2
Chipperfield, Calvin, Tig.	3	2	.600	3.10	12	12	0	0	0	0	52.1	44	216	23	18	2	0	0	2	24	0	69	4	0
Chisnall, Wesley, Exp.	3	5	.375	6.19	13	11	0	0	0	0	56.2	83	274	54	39	3	1	2	9	6	0	39	6	0
Chivers, Jason, Mets*	3	5	.375	3.71	12	10	0	0	0	0	53.1	52	231	34	22	3	0	1	2	20	0	40	3	2
Classen, Ender, Pir.	1	5	.167	3.59	12	11	0	0	0	0	52.2	51	235	34	21	0	3	3	9	18	1	28	8	3
Cooke, Andrew, Twi. *	6	1	.857	1.29	17	2	0	0	4	2	42.0	33	169	10	6	1	2	1	1	5	0	42	2	4
Cornejo, Nate, Tig.	1	0	1.000	1.26	5	0	0	0	2	1	14.1	12	58	2	2	0	0	0	1	2	0	9	1	0
Craun, Robert, Mar.	0	1	.000	5.16	12	0	0	0	5	2	22.2	24	104	17	13	4	2	1	1	11	0	23	1	0
Crawford, Carlos, Pir.	1	1	.500	3.31	12	0	0	0	11	2	16.1	16	70	6	6	0	0	0	1	6	2	9	4	0
Curtis, Daniel, Brav.	2	1	.667	3.15	14	0	0	0	9	2	40.0	33	161	17	14	3	2	1	4	9	0	32	0	0
Dansby, Justin, Brav.	2	2	.500	5.64	15	0	0	0	12	1	22.1	29	110	15	14	1	3	0	2	14	1	23	3	1
Deckard, Edward, D.R.	1	0	1.000	1.13	4	0	0	0	2	1	8.0	7	31	1	1	0	0	0	1	1	0	1	1	0
De La Cruz, Andres, Yan.	6	2	.750	2.68	21	0	0	0	9	4	40.1	37	164	16	12	1	2	2	10	1	0	28	4	0
De La Cruz, Fernando, R.S.	0	0	.000	13.50	1	0	0	0	1	0	2.0	4	10	3	3	0	0	0	0	0	0	2	0	0
De La Cruz, Francisco, Yan.	1	1	.500	3.29	3	0	0	0	0	0	13.2	11	61	9	5	1	0	0	0	8	1	18	1	0
DeLaCruz, Juan, Pir.	1	4	.200	3.44	11	11	0	0	0	0	49.2	53	219	29	19	2	3	1	5	9	0	20	3	2
Denholm, Richard, Twi.	1	0	1.000	7.85	13	0	0	0	6	1	18.1	20	87	17	16	3	1	0	2	9	1	9	2	2
Dent, Doug, Brav.	0	2	.000	4.30	4	4	0	0	0	0	14.2	14	61	11	7	1	0	2	2	4	0	16	1	2
Diaz, Billy, Rang.	3	3	.500	4.28	13	5	0	0	1	0	48.1	51	195	26	23	7	0	2	5	5	0	29	0	1
Diaz, Luis, Tig.	2	2	.500	2.91	25	0	0	0	7	0	52.2	46	228	21	17	3	1	0	5	23	1	58	4	0
Dickson, Daniel, D.R. *	1	2	.333	5.30	14	3	0	0	0	0	18.2	29	94	17	11	1	0	0	2	5	0	17	0	0
Dito, Robert, Exp.	1	0	1.000	0.00	1	0	0	0	1	0	1.0	0	4	0	0	0	0	0	1	0	0	0	0	0
Dittfurth, Ryan, Rang.	3	2	.600	1.34	8	6	0	0	0	0	33.2	25	143	8	5	0	2	0	6	11	0	33	4	2
Douglass, Ryan, Roy.	0	3	.000	6.65	9	2	0	0	0	0	23.0	30	105	19	17	3	0	1	2	12	0	11	2	0
Dukeman, Gregory, Brav.	3	2	.600	2.32	18	0	0	0	15	7	31.0	26	126	10	8	3	2	0	8	0	0	19	3	1
Dunn, Keith, Yan.	0	2	.000	1.23	21	0	0	0	19	12	36.2	16	132	6	5	2	0	0	9	2	0	38	1	0
Earl, Ryan, Tig. *	0	0	.000	2.93	6	4	0	0	0	0	15.1	12	66	6	5	0	0	0	0	8	0	11	0	0
Eavenson, Clay, Yan.	3	4	.429	4.98	12	3	0	0	4	0	34.1	38	143	22	19	3	1	1	1	7	0	25	5	0
Ennis, John, Brav.	0	3	.000	4.62	8	2	0	0	2	0	25.1	30	113	16	13	0	1	0	2	6	1	18	1	0
Erickson, John, D.R.	3	2	.600	3.94	19	0	0	0	10	1	29.2	34	147	21	13	0	0	1	3	17	0	22	2	4
Erwin, Christopher, Rang.	0	0	.000	0.00	1	0	0	0	1	0	0.2	1	5	0	0	0	0	0	1	1	0	0	0	0
Escalona, Jesus, Ori.	1	1	.500	3.86	3	2	0	0	0	0	11.2	9	52	7	5	0	1	0	7	6	0	6	0	1
Espinal, Jose, Twi.	2	0	1.000	4.62	9	5	1	1	2	1	25.1	23	114	14	13	3	0	2	0	15	0	15	3	1
Fereira, Ramon, Ast.	1	1	.500	5.40	16	0	0	0	14	4	21.2	27	104	15	13	0	0	3	6	0	0	20	0	0
Figueroa, Carlos, Rang. *	6	1	.857	3.57	19	0	0	0	8	1	40.1	34	162	17	16	4	0	1	1	11	0	39	3	2
Fischer, Sean, Ori. *	4	3	.571	3.21	17	3	0	0	8	2	42.0	32	186	17	15	0	3	1	5	26	0	31	5	0
Flock, Rick, Twi.	0	0	.000	0.00	2	0	0	0	1	0	4.1	0	14	0	0	0	0	0	0	2	0	5	0	0
Foote, Joe, Twi.	6	3	.667	3.90	13	10	0	0	1	0	57.2	61	255	35	25	4	1	1	3	15	1	60	6	0
Frazier, Bradley, Twi.	4	3	.571	2.61	9	9	0	0	0	0	51.2	51	220	17	15	1	0	1	5	13	1	40	6	0
French, Eric, Roy.	0	0	.000	7.94	3	0	0	0	3	2	5.2	6	29	5	5	1	0	1	1	5	0	4	1	0
Frey, Christopher, Rang.	2	2	.500	2.79	10	7	0	0	1	1	42.0	34	177	19	13	1	0	3	3	10	0	45	4	1
Frierson, Andrew, Exp. *	3	1	.750	1.25	15	0	0	0	11	2	21.2	16	86	5	3	0	1	0	2	5	0	17	0	1
Gaillard, Eddie, D.R.	0	0	.000	0.00	2	0	0	0	0	0	4.0	0	13	0	0	0	0	1	0	5	0	5	0	0
Gamble, Jr., Jerome, R.S.	2	3	.400	4.43	11	6	0	0	1	1	42.2	33	187	24	21	4	0	1	5	19	0	49	5	1
Garces, Rich, R.S.	0	0	.000	3.27	7	7	0	0	0	0	11.0	11	43	4	4	0	0	0	0	0	0	8	0	2
Garcia, Rosman, Yan.	4	3	.571	2.55	12	12	0	0	0	0	67.0	70	284	38	19	1	3	0	3	9	0	47	1	2
Garff, Jeff, Rang.	0	0	.000	0.00	1	0	0	0	1	0	2.0	3	10	1	0	0	0	0	0	2	0	2	0	0
Garibaldi, Cecilio, D.R.	1	3	.250	5.06	22	0	0	0	16	5	26.2	30	116	16	15	2	1	3	1	9	1	20	2	0
George, Chris, Roy. *	0	1	.000	2.87	5	4	0	0	0	0	15.2	14	65	9	5	1	1	0	4	4	0	10	0	0
Getz, Cody, D.R. *	1	2	.333	3.86	16	0	0	0	3	2	21.0	20	92	11	9	2	3	0	0	11	0	19	1	0
Gilfillan, Jason, Roy.	1	1	.500	8.00	7	6	0	0	0	0	9.0	10	42	8	8	1	0	1	4	6	1	6	1	0
Glaser, Eric, R.S.	2	3	.400	4.18	15	1	0	0	12	5	32.1	28	137	19	15	3	2	0	12	1	0	29	1	0
Go, Ho, Pir.	2	3	.400	4.84	13	0	0	0	4	0	35.1	33	155	25	19	3	0	2	4	11	0	26	2	5
Gomez, Rafael, Mets	3	0	1.000	3.86	13	2	0	0	6	2	28.0	22	113	16	12	3	0	2	1	6	0	22	2	0
Gomez, Ricardo, Pir.	0	1	.000	5.87	9	0	0	0	4	0	15.1	23	79	12	10	1	0	0	0	9	0	12	1	3
Gonzalez, Giovanni, Pir.	2	1	.667	7.50	14	0	0	0	5	2	24.0	32	126	23	20	4	0	4	6	11	1	15	2	1
Good, Eric, Exp. *	1	2	.333	2.08	6	3	0	0	0	0	17.1	11	71	4	4	0	0	0	1	8	0	20	1	1
Gorecki, Rick, D.R.	0	0	.000	0.00	4	2	0	0	0	0	5.0	3	20	0	0	0	1	0	0	2	0	5	0	0
Graham, Frank, Mets	0	1	.000	4.09	3	2	0	0	0	0	11.0	6	47	5	5	0	0	0	3	5	0	14	1	1
Grantham, Ryan, Exp.	0	0	.000	0.00	1	0	0	0	0	0	1.0	0	3	0	0	0	0	0	0	0	0	0	0	0
Guerrero, Jason, D.R.	1	0	1.000	3.86	6	0	0	0	3	0	9.1	10	41	6	4	1	0	0	4	0	0	12	1	0
Guerrero, Junior, Roy.	4	4	.500	3.23	13	6	0	0	3	0	61.1	57	257	24	22	2	4	2	2	19	0	58	5	1
Guevara, Daniel, D.R. *	0	0	.000	5.40	4	0	0	0	0	0	3.1	4	17	3	2	0	0	0	0	2	0	5	0	0
Hafer, Jeff, Mets	0	0	.000	3.52	4	4	0	0	0	0	7.2	8	30	3	3	1	0	0	0	1	0	6	2	0
Haigler, Phil, Twi.	0	0	.000	1.54	3	1	0	0	0	0	11.2	9	41	2	2	0	0	0	0	4	0	6	0	0
Hamilton, Charles, Roy.	2	1	.667	4.38	15	0	0	0	7	0	24.2	25	118	22	12	0	1	4	1	15	1	19	4	4
Hancock, Joshua, R.S.	1	1	.500	3.38	5	1	0	0	0	0	13.1	9	51	5	5	1	2	0	3	0	0	21	0	0
Haney, Chris, Roy. *	1	0	1.000	0.00	1	1	0	0	0	0	2.1	2	11	2	0	0	0	0	0	1	0	1	0	0
Hardebeck, Jason, Pir. *	0	0	.000	4.15	2	0	0	0	0	0	4.1	5	20	2	2	0	0	0	0	3	0	4	2	0
Harris, Veon, Pir.	0	0	.000	6.08	7	0	0	0	3	0	13.1	13	65	12	9	0	0	2	12	0	0	16	3	3
Hebson, Bryan, Exp.	2	0	1.000	0.53	4	4	0	0	0	0	17.0	10	64	1	1	0	0	0	7	0	0	16	2	0
Hee, Aaron, Mets*	3	1	.750	3.19	18	1	0	0	8	0	31.0	34	136	14	11	1	2	0	1	11	2	30	8	1
Hernandez, Luis, D.R. *	3	2	.600	2.40	10	8	0	0	0	0	41.1	36	176	19	11	1	1	2	1	18	1	19	3	0
Hidalgo, Edgar, Rang.	2	1	.667	4.76	10	0	0	0	2	0	17.0	23	77	9	9	1	0	1	0	9	0	16	1	0
Hill, Ryan, Roy.	0	0	.000	0.00	5	0	0	0	0	0	5.0	3	24	1	0	0	0	0	0	7	0	4	3	0
Hill, T.J., D.R.	0	0	.000	2.25	7	1	0	0	2	0	12.0	10	48	4	3	1	0	0	1	3	0	8	0	0

Pitcher, Team	W	L	Pct.	ERA	G	GS	CG	ShO	GF	Sv.	IP	H	TBF	R	ER	HR	SH	SF	HB	BB	IBB	SO	WP	Bk.
Hostetler, Jim, Tig.	0	0	.000	3.38	2	0	0	0	1	0	2.2	3	12	1	1	0	0	0	1	0	0	2	1	0
Houle, Marc, Ori.	0	1	.000	6.43	9	0	0	0	5	3	14.0	17	68	11	10	2	0	2	2	7	1	11	1	0
Hunter, Germaine, R.S.	1	0	1.000	0.00	1	0	0	0	0	0	2.0	0	6	0	0	0	0	0	0	0	0	4	0	0
Huntsman, Brandon, Ori.	0	0	.000	0.00	1	1	0	0	0	0	1.2	0	6	0	0	0	0	0	0	1	0	3	0	0
Hurst, Bill, Tig.	0	0	.000	1.59	3	0	0	0	0	0	5.2	2	19	1	1	1	0	0	0	1	0	7	0	0
Janzen, Marty, Yan.	0	0	.000	0.00	1	1	0	0	0	0	3.0	1	10	0	0	0	0	0	0	0	0	5	0	0
Johnston, Michael, Pir. *	1	2	.333	3.34	13	3	0	0	3	0	29.2	28	127	17	11	1	2	2	0	10	0	17	5	1
Johnston, Rikki, Tig. *	2	4	.333	4.71	11	11	0	0	0	0	49.2	57	212	27	26	4	0	0	2	18	0	46	1	0
Kessel, Kyle, Mets*	1	1	.500	0.64	4	4	0	0	0	0	14.0	5	53	4	1	1	1	1	0	1	5	19	0	0
Kim, Jae, R.S.	0	1	.000	5.25	5	1	0	0	0	0	12.0	12	58	14	7	0	1	2	2	5	0	3	2	0
Klein, Cody, Yan. *	4	1	.800	5.23	17	0	0	0	4	1	20.2	19	94	13	12	1	1	0	3	11	0	20	2	1
Klepacki, Edward, Exp.	1	4	.200	3.13	9	6	1	0	1	0	37.1	39	161	20	13	1	0	3	4	3	0	23	2	0
Knowles, Michael, Yan.	2	1	.667	2.84	8	7	0	0	0	0	38.0	34	162	15	12	0	0	3	16	0	30	4	3
Krystofoski, Jay, Mets	0	0	.000	10.13	1	0	0	0	0	0	2.2	7	16	3	3	0	0	0	2	0	1	1	0
Lampley, Daniel, R.S.	1	0	1.000	0.00	1	0	0	0	1	0	3.1	1	12	0	0	0	0	0	3	1	0
Langston, David, Yan.	2	2	.500	5.74	15	0	0	0	7	0	31.1	45	147	21	20	1	2	1	3	9	2	26	1	0
Laroche, Jeff, Mar. *	0	1	.000	2.45	4	0	0	0	1	0	7.1	7	32	6	2	1	0	1	0	3	0	8	0	0
LaRosa, Tom, Twi.	0	2	.000	1.29	4	0	0	0	2	0	7.0	1	30	4	1	0	0	1	2	7	0	6	1	0
Ledden, Ryan, D.R.	0	3	.000	8.44	14	4	0	0	3	0	26.2	33	128	26	25	4	0	0	3	16	0	21	5	1
Lelless, Alexander, Brav.	4	0	1.000	4.41	14	0	0	0	8	2	32.2	32	136	16	16	1	1	0	4	8	0	21	0	0
Levesque, Benjamin, Pir.	2	2	.500	7.11	6	0	0	0	1	0	12.2	17	67	15	10	2	1	1	2	9	1	11	3	1
Lima, Frank, Tig.	5	3	.625	4.70	12	12	1	0	0	0	59.1	62	254	39	31	3	0	3	14	0	66	3	0
Lluberes, Alberto, Ori.	0	1	.000	9.00	2	0	0	0	2	0	3.0	5	14	4	3	0	0	1	0	0	2	2	0
Lopez, Carlos, Exp.	3	3	.500	2.89	14	1	0	0	5	3	37.1	33	153	16	12	2	2	0	2	5	0	22	1	1
Lopez, Gustavo, Mar.	1	3	.250	3.60	9	1	0	0	5	2	20.0	17	81	8	8	2	1	0	0	11	1	16	1	0
Love, Farley, Ast.	0	0	.000	4.50	1	0	0	0	0	0	2.0	2	8	1	1	0	0	0	0	1	0	1	0	0
Lugo, Roberto, Mets*	0	1	.000	10.80	1	0	0	0	1	0	1.2	2	10	2	2	0	0	0	0	3	1	3	0	1
Mancha, Tony, Roy.	3	1	.750	3.34	20	0	0	0	15	3	32.1	33	142	19	12	4	1	2	1	12	0	25	2	1
Mangieri, John, Mets	1	1	.500	6.61	16	1	0	0	8	1	31.1	35	145	29	23	0	0	1	8	20	0	15	6	3
Manning, David, Rang.	0	0	.000	5.40	3	3	0	0	0	0	5.0	6	22	3	3	0	1	1	0	1	0	2	1	0
Marichal, Rafael, Pir.	3	1	.750	2.08	18	0	0	0	18	6	30.1	26	130	14	7	1	2	0	6	0	30	1	0
Marin, Willy, D.R.	8	0	1.000	2.28	27	0	0	0	9	2	47.1	39	181	13	12	4	4	1	0	4	1	43	0	4
Maroth, Mike, R.S. *	1	1	.500	0.00	4	2	0	0	1	0	12.2	9	49	3	0	0	0	0	2	0	14	0	0
Marrero, Darwin, Exp.	1	1	.500	1.85	14	1	0	0	3	1	39.0	33	156	10	8	1	2	0	1	4	0	39	0	0
Marsonek, Sam, Rang.	0	0	.000	0.00	2	2	0	0	0	0	4.2	2	18	1	0	0	0	1	0	0	2	0	0
Martin, Jeff, Pir.	0	0	.000	0.00	1	0	0	0	0	0	1.0	4	7	2	0	0	0	0	0	0	0	0	0	0
Martinez, Anastacio, R.S.	2	3	.400	3.18	12	10	0	0	0	0	51.0	45	212	28	18	2	1	2	3	12	0	50	4	1
Martinez, Lionel, Brav.	0	0	.000	6.00	3	0	0	0	0	0	3.0	3	15	2	2	0	0	1	1	0	4	0	0
Martinez, Obispo, Brav.	1	1	.500	6.00	3	0	0	0	1	0	9.0	9	35	6	6	2	1	0	0	5	0	5	0	0
Marx, Tommy, Tig. *	1	3	.250	4.29	12	12	0	0	0	0	42.0	33	197	27	20	2	0	6	39	0	38	9	1
Mathys, Jason, Yan.	4	3	.571	4.22	12	0	0	0	3	2	21.1	19	92	11	10	0	0	0	2	7	0	21	3	0
Mayi, Leonardo, Brav. *	2	7	.222	3.67	12	12	0	0	0	0	56.1	63	231	29	23	3	2	1	2	9	0	54	2	0
McCormick, Terry, D.R. *	2	2	.500	3.86	11	9	0	0	0	0	46.2	46	205	24	20	3	2	3	21	0	56	4	1
McGill, Frankie, Rang.	3	1	.750	3.51	9	7	0	0	0	0	33.1	35	142	17	13	1	1	3	2	9	0	24	4	0
McGinnis, Johnny, Brav.	4	6	.250	1.89	13	11	0	0	0	0	62.0	40	247	23	13	0	0	9	17	0	53	10	0
McKoin, Heath, D.R. *	2	1	.667	5.95	10	3	0	0	1	0	19.2	21	90	15	13	2	1	1	11	0	16	1	0
Medrano, Juan, Roy.	4	3	.571	3.52	12	8	0	0	1	1	64.0	57	266	28	25	2	2	2	6	16	0	27	3	1
Melson, Nate, Twi.	5	1	.833	3.66	12	10	0	0	1	0	64.0	63	267	30	26	3	6	1	5	13	2	43	1	0
Mendez, David, Brav. *	2	2	.500	5.66	11	8	0	0	0	0	41.1	39	184	31	26	0	3	4	5	19	0	41	3	1
Mikkola, Shaun, Mets	1	4	.200	4.85	10	5	0	0	1	0	39.0	43	174	23	21	2	1	0	4	23	0	20	7	1
Miller, Aaron, Twi. *	0	0	.000	0.00	4	0	0	0	3	0	5.1	4	23	0	0	0	0	0	0	4	0	12	0	0
Miller, Greg, R.S. *	6	0	1.000	2.49	11	7	0	0	0	0	43.1	33	187	18	12	2	4	18	0	47	3	2
Minaya, Pedro, Mar.	4	0	1.000	1.00	11	9	0	0	1	0	45.0	27	168	8	5	0	0	9	0	61	4	0
Moon, Chang, Pir.	1	0	1.000	4.78	13	0	0	0	1	0	32.0	38	147	19	17	2	1	0	10	0	32	3	1
Morrobel, Juan, Pir. *	0	0	.000	1.35	3	0	0	0	1	0	6.2	2	28	1	1	0	0	1	5	0	7	0	0
Moses, Stephen, Mets	0	2	.000	4.35	14	0	0	0	7	2	20.2	16	89	11	10	0	0	3	14	0	18	13	1
Mott, Tom, Yan.	0	1	.000	4.66	5	0	0	0	3	0	9.2	12	44	5	5	0	0	1	0	5	1	6	2	0
Munoz, Marcos, Yan.	0	0	.000	3.00	2	1	0	0	1	0	3.0	4	14	1	1	0	0	0	1	0	1	1	0
Murphy, Brian, Ori.	0	0	.000	1.42	3	0	0	0	3	1	6.1	7	29	3	1	0	0	2	2	0	2	0	0
Nannini, Mike, Ast.	1	1	.500	1.49	8	6	1	1	0	0	36.1	23	140	6	6	0	0	0	13	0	39	0	0
Norris, Shon, R.S.	0	2	.000	2.25	15	0	0	0	12	5	24.0	22	105	10	6	0	1	1	9	0	14	2	0
Norton, Jason, R.S. *	1	1	.500	1.50	3	0	0	0	3	0	6.0	2	20	1	1	1	0	0	1	0	9	1	0
Nowakowski, Brian, Twi.	0	0	.000	4.50	13	1	0	0	7	0	20.0	25	92	13	10	1	0	1	5	1	6	6	0
Nunez, Jose, Mets*	3	7	.300	2.38	13	11	1	0	0	0	68.0	60	267	26	18	6	1	3	2	12	0	69	0	1
Oswalt, Roy, Ast.	1	1	.500	2.25	4	4	0	0	0	0	16.0	10	62	6	4	2	1	1	3	1	0	27	0	1
Otanez, Willis, R.S.	0	3	.000	5.59	13	2	0	0	7	0	29.0	27	128	21	18	1	1	2	0	11	0	30	4	0
Padilla, Juan, Twi.	1	1	.500	1.40	17	0	0	0	14	10	25.2	19	100	4	4	1	1	0	2	1	0	27	1	0
Palacios, Refugio, Mets	1	1	.500	7.71	5	3	1	0	1	0	14.0	23	73	17	12	1	0	1	3	7	0	10	1	0
Paugh, Rick, Pir. *	0	0	.000	5.68	4	1	0	0	2	0	6.1	10	27	4	4	1	0	0	1	0	5	0	0
Paz, Rolando, Ori.	0	0	.000	0.00	1	0	0	0	1	0	1.0	2	6	0	0	0	0	0	0	0	2	0	0
Pearson, Jason, Mar. *	4	0	1.000	1.57	11	3	0	0	5	2	34.1	28	134	8	6	0	0	1	5	0	36	2	0
Peguero, Kerbin, R.S. *	1	1	.500	2.55	9	0	0	0	1	0	17.2	13	75	8	5	0	1	1	0	11	0	9	2	0
Peguero, Radhame, D.R.	6	0	1.000	3.18	11	9	1	1	0	0	56.2	54	235	22	20	3	1	6	22	0	50	8	1
Perez, Carlos, Exp. *	1	0	1.000	0.00	1	0	0	0	1	0	5.0	5	20	2	0	1	0	0	1	1	0	2	0	0
Perez, Elvis, Brav.	0	0	.000	5.50	11	2	0	0	4	0	36.0	43	160	23	22	5	1	4	3	12	0	26	0	1
Perez, Randy, Ori. *	0	2	.000	4.50	8	0	0	0	5	2	24.0	29	104	13	12	1	3	1	0	7	2	17	1	0
Perich, Joshua, Mets	0	0	.000	0.00	1	0	0	0	1	0	1.0	0	3	0	0	0	0	0	0	0	0	1	0	0
Pichardo, Carlos, Roy.	0	0	.000	1.47	14	0	0	0	14	7	18.1	6	73	4	3	1	1	1	8	0	9	0	0
Pidgeon, Chip, Mets*	0	3	.000	9.00	16	0	0	0	8	0	25.0	34	123	27	25	1	1	1	3	13	1	21	7	1
Pineda, Isauro, R.S.	0	0	.000	3.38	4	0	0	0	1	0	13.1	11	55	7	5	1	0	0	5	0	16	1	1
Pineda, Jairo, Ast.	2	6	.250	3.93	12	12	1	0	0	0	73.1	74	315	45	32	4	2	3	10	17	0	83	3	3
Pipes, Joey, Ast.	0	0	.000	1.23	4	0	0	0	3	1	7.1	5	26	1	1	0	0	0	2	0	7	0	1

SUMMER CLASS A — Gulf Coast League

Pitcher, Team	W	L	Pct.	ERA	G	GS	CG	ShO	GF	Sv.	IP	H	TBF	R	ER	HR	SH	SF	HB	BB	IBB	SO	WP	Bk.
Pratt, Andrew, Rang. *	4	3	.571	3.86	12	8	0	0	1	0	56.0	49	225	25	24	4	1	3	1	14	0	49	0	1
Price, Kevin, D.R.	1	0	1.000	3.51	16	0	0	0	2	0	25.2	20	109	15	10	1	1	0	3	8	0	22	4	0
Pridie, Jon, Twi.	0	0	.000	6.75	1	0	0	0	0	0	1.1	2	8	1	1	0	0	0	0	2	0	1	0	0
Pruitt, Jason, Ori. *	4	3	.571	4.08	17	3	0	0	6	1	46.1	44	197	21	21	6	1	3	3	17	0	47	4	0
Quarnstrom, Robert, Rang. *..	4	1	.800	1.56	23	0	0	0	21	12	34.2	16	120	6	6	1	1	0	1	3	0	37	1	1
Ralston, Kris, Roy.	0	1	.000	4.50	2	0	0	0	0	0	2.0	5	11	3	1	0	0	0	0	0	0	2	0	0
Ramirez, Jose, Tig. *	0	1	.000	3.86	2	0	0	0	0	0	7.0	7	30	3	3	1	0	0	0	4	0	8	0	0
Rangel, Julio, Yan.	1	0	1.000	5.27	3	3	0	0	0	0	13.2	18	63	8	8	2	1	0	2	7	0	19	1	2
Ratliff, Craig, Ori.	5	4	.556	3.07	10	10	0	0	0	0	55.2	53	243	31	19	4	0	3	3	21	0	33	4	0
Reisinger, Justin, Yan.	0	1	.000	6.75	9	1	0	0	3	0	17.1	19	80	16	13	0	0	2	2	9	0	13	4	0
Ridenour, Jeffrey, Rang.	0	2	.000	3.53	18	0	0	0	8	0	43.1	48	192	23	17	2	2	1	1	18	0	29	4	0
Ridenour, Ryan, Yan. *	0	2	.000	3.00	4	4	0	0	0	0	15.1	7	70	10	9	0	0	1	2	13	0	17	3	0
Rivera, Homero, Tig. *	3	6	.333	5.34	16	7	1	0	4	2	57.1	64	250	40	34	6	0	1	3	17	1	53	5	3
Roberts, Marquis, D.R. *	1	0	1.000	0.00	3	2	0	0	0	0	9.0	1	29	0	0	0	0	0	2	1	0	8	0	0
Roberts, Mike, Rang.	2	0	1.000	3.00	3	2	0	0	0	0	12.0	10	44	4	4	1	0	0	1	0	0	10	0	0
Rodriguez, Cristobal, Exp.	1	1	.500	2.45	8	8	0	0	0	0	40.1	30	166	16	11	2	0	1	3	11	0	48	2	0
Rodriguez, Jose, D.R.	3	3	.500	4.26	12	11	0	0	0	0	63.1	77	283	38	30	5	1	1	7	12	2	61	4	3
Rodriguez, Marino, Mar. *	0	1	.000	0.91	12	2	0	0	5	3	29.2	20	117	8	3	0	0	0	2	9	0	30	5	0
Rodriguez, Tony, Yan.	1	0	1.000	1.29	6	0	0	0	4	0	7.0	4	33	1	1	0	0	0	2	8	0	10	5	0
Rojas, Frances, Twi. *	1	2	.333	3.42	13	0	0	0	4	0	23.2	21	105	13	9	3	0	0	2	9	0	17	5	0
Roller, Adam, R.S.	0	2	.000	4.85	15	2	0	0	3	1	39.0	51	194	31	21	3	1	1	2	22	1	27	10	1
Rondon, Gabriel, Mets	2	1	.667	0.50	8	1	0	0	5	3	18.0	10	71	2	1	0	2	1	2	1	1	17	0	1
Rosario, Rafael, Tig.	1	4	.200	9.35	22	0	0	0	10	2	43.1	62	213	49	45	5	0	2	5	18	0	29	8	1
Rosario, Reynaldo, Tig.	0	1	.000	1.99	10	0	0	0	2	1	22.2	21	99	8	5	1	0	1	2	15	1	17	0	0
Rosario, Rodrigo, Ast.	2	2	.500	4.12	13	12	0	0	1	0	67.2	61	286	36	31	6	1	2	4	30	0	65	4	1
Russo, Mike, Roy.	5	2	.714	3.48	18	0	0	0	8	1	33.2	31	147	16	13	4	2	2	3	15	2	37	2	0
Ryan, Jeremy, Ast.	1	0	1.000	1.69	4	4	0	0	0	0	16.0	7	58	4	3	0	0	0	2	0	0	18	2	0
Saneaux, Francisco, Ori.	2	0	1.000	3.45	3	3	0	0	0	0	15.2	15	68	6	6	0	0	0	0	8	0	10	2	0
Santana, Alfredo, Tig.	3	5	.375	4.21	22	0	0	0	20	4	36.1	40	166	26	17	2	2	1	3	12	1	32	3	1
Schmidt, Pat, Brav.*	1	1	.500	8.44	3	0	0	0	2	0	5.1	8	27	5	5	0	0	0	0	4	0	6	0	0
Schreiner, Jon, Exp.	1	1	.500	1.80	13	3	0	0	7	2	35.0	24	138	9	7	0	3	1	2	10	0	28	2	0
Schwager, Matthew, Ori.	0	2	.000	6.75	12	1	0	0	7	3	24.0	31	113	19	18	5	2	0	1	13	0	20	1	3
Sents, Marcus, Twi.	2	5	.286	6.43	9	9	0	0	0	0	35.0	36	169	33	25	0	0	2	2	28	0	24	3	0
Seo, Jae, Mets	0	0	.000	0.00	2	0	0	0	0	0	5.0	4	17	0	0	0	0	0	0	0	0	5	0	0
Sexton, Patrick, Mets	0	1	.000	6.23	10	0	0	0	8	5	13.0	16	62	13	9	1	0	0	1	7	1	10	1	0
Seybt, Paul, R.S.	1	2	.333	3.00	16	0	0	0	14	1	27.0	32	124	12	9	1	0	1	1	11	2	24	3	0
Shepherd, Alvie, Ori.	0	0	.000	4.76	3	3	0	0	0	0	5.2	7	26	3	3	2	0	0	0	3	0	4	0	0
Shields, Drew, Mar.	7	2	.778	2.63	13	11	1	0	1	0	65.0	48	262	24	19	3	4	2	4	19	1	65	10	1
Siciliano, Jess, Pir.	2	1	.667	13.50	4	0	0	0	1	0	4.2	7	27	8	7	0	0	0	1	4	0	1	2	0
Silverthorn, Will, R.S.*	4	4	.500	4.84	11	8	0	0	0	0	44.2	52	188	26	24	3	0	2	1	13	0	39	2	1
Smetek, Peter, D.R.*	0	0	.000	0.00	2	0	0	0	1	0	2.0	0	7	0	0	0	0	0	0	1	0	1	0	0
Smith, Eric, Pir.	0	1	.000	8.59	7	0	0	0	3	0	7.1	14	43	12	7	1	0	1	0	3	0	5	1	0
Solano, Alexander, R.S.	3	3	.500	3.51	12	6	0	0	1	1	51.1	65	236	35	20	5	2	2	3	17	0	35	1	0
Solano, Francisco, Roy.	1	3	.250	2.64	9	6	1	0	0	0	47.2	44	200	19	14	0	1	1	4	9	0	29	2	0
Sopkin, Josh, Roy.	0	0	.000	6.23	6	0	0	0	0	0	8.2	8	40	6	6	1	0	0	0	9	0	2	1	0
Sosa, Jorby, Yan.	1	1	.500	3.77	12	3	0	0	3	1	31.0	39	136	22	13	1	1	0	2	5	0	26	0	0
South, Carl, Pir.	0	0	.000	24.00	8	0	0	0	2	0	6.0	15	48	17	16	1	0	0	1	13	0	3	17	0
Spurling, Chris, Yan.	2	1	.667	2.28	13	6	0	0	2	1	51.1	57	219	21	13	3	0	2	2	11	0	44	2	0
Stanford, Derek, Ast.	2	4	.333	4.27	12	11	0	0	0	0	52.2	53	234	32	25	2	1	1	5	25	0	52	6	1
Stenger, Pat, Twi.	3	1	.750	3.86	13	4	0	0	2	1	35.0	57	168	26	15	1	0	2	3	5	0	23	3	1
Strange, Patrick, Mets	1	1	.500	1.42	4	4	0	0	0	0	19.0	18	79	3	3	0	0	0	1	7	0	19	0	0
Sturtze, Tanyon, Rang.	0	1	.000	7.71	3	3	0	0	0	0	7.0	12	37	7	6	1	0	0	0	4	0	10	0	0
Tapia, Rafael, Ori.	2	0	1.000	5.23	11	2	0	0	4	0	32.2	42	149	24	19	1	1	1	3	9	0	22	3	0
Targac, Matthew, Brav.*	2	2	.500	3.99	13	2	0	0	5	0	38.1	22	155	20	17	0	3	0	4	13	0	48	5	0
Terwilliger, Rich, Ast.	1	2	.333	4.45	12	0	0	0	6	1	28.1	34	134	16	14	0	1	1	2	12	0	31	4	0
Thomas, Gaige, Mar.	3	3	.500	2.55	15	6	0	0	8	1	42.1	24	175	20	12	1	1	0	3	21	1	53	12	1
Tomaszewski, Eliot, Ori.	0	1	.000	7.16	16	1	0	0	10	1	27.2	29	148	28	22	2	1	2	3	32	0	19	3	1
Torres, Elvin, Yan.	0	0	.000	3.60	2	0	0	0	1	0	5.0	3	19	2	2	2	0	0	0	1	0	2	0	0
Trinidad, Fernando, Ori.	1	0	1.000	4.50	3	0	0	0	2	0	6.0	4	29	3	3	0	1	2	1	6	0	1	0	0
Tucker, Thomas, Exp.	1	0	1.000	0.75	7	7	0	0	0	0	36.0	23	134	5	3	1	0	0	0	5	0	40	0	0
Turner, Kyle, Roy. *	6	1	.857	2.36	12	6	0	0	0	0	42.0	36	178	13	11	3	0	1	3	17	0	55	5	0
Turnquist, Tyler, Ast.	0	1	.000	11.57	1	0	0	0	0	0	2.1	3	11	3	3	1	1	0	0	1	0	4	0	0
Underhill, Ray, Twi.	2	0	1.000	2.53	14	1	0	0	6	0	21.1	18	92	9	6	1	1	1	1	8	0	13	1	0
Urbina, Ulmer, Exp.	0	0	.000	4.50	5	0	0	0	0	0	6.0	3	26	5	3	1	0	0	1	3	0	9	1	0
Ushiromatsu, Juei, Mets*	0	2	.000	4.85	16	0	0	0	4	0	26.0	39	123	19	14	1	0	3	2	11	1	27	7	2
Valdez, Domingo, Rang.	2	2	.500	3.09	10	5	0	0	0	0	32.0	24	142	15	11	3	0	0	3	16	0	27	1	0
Vallejo, Etanislao, Pir.	3	1	.750	3.71	13	6	0	0	0	0	34.0	31	156	19	14	0	2	3	5	22	0	26	5	0
Vargas, Claudio, Mar.	0	4	.000	4.08	5	4	0	0	0	0	28.2	24	117	15	13	1	0	0	3	7	0	27	2	0
Veras, Enger, D.R.	1	1	.500	6.75	5	4	0	0	0	0	16.0	19	79	14	12	1	0	0	1	12	0	19	1	0
Vianna, Marcel, Brav.	3	4	.429	2.51	12	8	0	0	1	1	46.2	35	190	17	13	0	1	1	2	13	0	49	3	0
Villanueva, Bill, Mar.	6	2	.750	1.88	11	11	0	0	0	0	57.1	46	227	14	12	1	0	0	8	13	0	54	2	0
Wallace, Jim, Ast.	1	1	.500	4.70	13	0	0	0	7	1	30.2	29	139	18	16	1	1	2	7	9	0	26	2	0
Walsh, Steven, Roy.	0	2	.000	1.88	9	8	0	0	0	0	28.2	22	110	6	6	1	1	0	2	4	0	28	0	0
Walter, Mike, Ast.	0	0	.000	0.00	3	0	0	0	1	1	4.0	2	15	0	0	0	0	0	0	1	0	6	0	0
Wamback, Trevor, Exp.	5	0	.833	2.47	12	7	1	0	3	1	43.2	39	176	16	12	2	1	1	2	20	0	33	1	0
Weslowski, Robert, Mets	5	3	.625	2.54	11	10	1	0	0	0	60.1	59	248	25	17	2	1	1	2	20	0	37	4	1
Wesolowski, David, Mar.	1	2	.333	4.55	12	1	0	0	7	0	27.2	30	120	18	14	1	1	0	0	5	0	23	1	0
Wheeler, Mike, Ast.	0	1	.000	3.60	4	0	0	0	1	0	5.0	8	24	2	2	0	0	0	0	2	0	5	1	0
White, James, Pir.	1	4	.200	2.51	12	12	0	0	0	0	38.2	44	192	37	31	1	2	1	6	30	0	26	2	5
Whitecotton, Billy, Ori.	4	2	.667	6.14	10	7	0	0	0	0	48.1	52	212	35	33	6	2	3	5	12	0	29	6	0
Whiteman, Mike, Tig. *	2	1	.667	5.31	12	0	0	0	0	0	20.1	19	92	13	12	0	0	0	1	13	0	16	3	0
Whitfield, Jacob, Twi. *	0	0	.000	13.50	7	0	0	0	3	0	8.0	10	51	14	12	0	0	0	5	10	0	12	4	0

Pitcher, Team	W	L	Pct.	ERA	G	GS	CG	ShO	GF	Sv.	IP	H	TBF	R	ER	HR	SH	SF	HB	BB	IBB	SO	WP	Bk.
Wiggins, Scott, Yan. *	0	0	.000	0.00	1	1	0	0	0	0	1.2	2	7	1	0	0	0	0	0	0	0	2	0	0
Wilkerson, Byron, Ast.	3	3	.500	4.67	18	2	0	0	5	0	52.0	49	230	35	27	4	3	3	5	24	0	54	1	0
Wojciechowski, Steve, Twi. *	0	0	.000	0.00	2	0	0	0	0	0	3.2	2	13	0	0	0	0	0	0	0	0	7	0	0
Wright, Jason, D.R.	0	2	.000	3.48	7	0	0	0	3	0	10.1	8	48	5	4	0	1	0	1	7	0	8	2	1
Yarno, Joshua, Ori.	3	4	.429	4.37	16	6	0	0	4	0	57.2	71	266	40	28	6	2	3	2	20	0	46	9	0

COMBINATION SHUTOUTS: **Astros (2)**—Stanford-Centeno-Wheeler-Fereira, Ryan-Walter-Terwilliger-Centeno. **Braves (3)**—Mendez-Vianna, Bong-Curtis, Mendez-Curtis. **Devil Rays (3)**—Alvarez-McCormick-Marin-Armstrong-Deckard, Gorecki-Roberts-Dickson-Garibaldi, McCormick-Peguero-Wright. **Expos (7)**—Tucker-Chisnall-Chiavacci-Frierson, Hebson-Good-Wamback, Good-Klepacki-Schreiner, Rodriguez-Klepacki-Frierson,Tucker-Schreiner-Frierson, Schreiner-Frierson-Andujar, Chiavacci-Good-Lopez-Andujar. **Marlins (9)**—Minaya-A. Anderson-Campos, W. Anderson-A. Anderson-A. Anderson-Rodriguez, Pearson-A. Anderson, Shields-LaRoche-Lopez, Minaya-Pearson, Villanueva-Campos, W. Anderson-Pearson, Villanueva-A. Anderson, Villanueva-Rodriguez-Campos. **Mets (2)**—Weslowski-Rondon-Moses, Kessel-Seo-Mangieri. **Orioles (5)**—Ratliff-Tomaszewski-Fischer, Bechler-Schwager-Tomaszewski, Ratliff-Pruitt, Yarno-Tomaszewski, Pruitt-Houle. **Pirates (1)**—White-Vallejo-Crawford. **Rangers (7)**—McGill-Hidalgo-Quarnstrom, Manning-Pratt, Manning-Dittforth-Frey, Valdez-Diaz-Figueroa, Dittforth-Backsmeyer-Beitey-Ridenour, Valdez-Backsmeyer-Quarnstrom, Dittforth-Ridenour-Bobbitt. **Red Sox (3)**—Gamble-Betancourt-Miller-Norris, Martinez-Seybt-Norris, Miller-Checketts-Cadena-Solano. **Royals (5)**—Walsh-Affeldt-Gilfillan-Chiasson-Medrano, Gilfillan-Affeldt-Russo-Pichardo, Walsh-Guerrero-Sopkin-Mancha, Affeldt-Mancha-Pichardo, Solano-Russo. **Tigers (2)**—Earl-Rosario-Diaz-Cepeda, Chipperfield-Cornejo. **Twins (0)**—None. **White Sox (0)**—None. **Yankees (3)**—Aramboles-Dunn, Garcia-Dunn, Spurling-Klein-Mathys-De La Cruz.

NO-HIT GAMES: None.

1998 FIELDING

TEAM

Team	Pct.	G	PO	A	E	TC	DP	PB	Team	Pct.	G	PO	A	E	TC	DP	PB
Yankees	.962	60	1563	647	87	2297	39	18	Tigers	.956	60	1578	634	103	2315	46	26
Marlins	.962	59	1504	653	86	2243	28	30	Devil Rays	.954	60	1567	664	107	2338	60	27
Expos	.961	59	1537	620	87	2244	34	12	Orioles	.953	60	1570	654	109	2333	54	21
Rangers	.961	60	1549	643	90	2282	43	19	Red Sox	.953	60	1514	628	106	2248	36	19
Braves	.958	59	1518	629	93	2240	40	14	Twins	.952	60	1527	704	113	2344	45	9
Mets	.958	59	1493	697	95	2285	41	18	Pirates	.936	60	1566	646	150	2362	48	22
Royals	.957	60	1535	621	97	2253	48	13									
Astros	.956	60	1594	584	100	2278	44	25									

TRIPLE PLAY: Pirates.

INDIVIDUAL

FIRST BASEMEN

NOTE: All caps denotes fielding-percentage leader based on 30 games for catchers, 40 for all other non-pitchers and 60 innings for pitchers. *Throws lefthanded.

Player, Team	Pct.	G	PO	A	E	TC	DP
Adorno, Wilson, Pir.	1.000		8	1	0	9	0
Alvarez, Antonio, Pir.	.986	9	69	4	1	74	6
Aude, Rich, Exp.	.909	1	9	1	1	11	0
Benham, David, R.S.	.968	3	28	2	1	31	3
Berrien, Samuel, Ori.*	.963	44	383	9	15	407	33
Borjas, Henry, R.S.	.971	8	64	3	2	69	2
Brazell, Craig, Mets	.968	4	29	1	1	31	2
Callahan, David, Mar.*	.988	27	227	21	3	251	9
Calzado, Napolean, Ori.	1.000	1	1	0	0	1	0
Carrasco, Ricardo, Roy.	.983	43	388	18	7	413	39
Carrillo, Robert, Ast.	.986	36	263	15	4	282	27
Casilla, Luis, Ast.	1.000	2	4	0	0	4	1
Colina, Roberto, D.R.*	1.000	1	4	0	0	4	1
Conway, Scott, Mar.*	.983	32	278	15	5	298	12
Cronk, Brian, Pir.	.977	27	238	15	6	259	18
Cruz, Ivan, Yan.*	1.000	4	18	0	0	18	4
Daigle, Leo, Tig.	.982	32	246	22	5	273	17
Elder, Rick, Ori.*	1.000	3	27	0	0	27	4
Elorduy, Daniel, Brav.	.986	41	331	29	5	365	22
Erwin, Christopher, Rang.	1.000	1	8	2	0	10	1
Foerter, Justin, Mar.	1.000	2	20	0	0	20	0
Frawley, Scott, Brav.	.972	12	101	4	3	108	9
Gainey, Bryon, Mets	.974	8	69	5	2	76	9
Garabito, Vianney, Yan.	.941	9	55	9	4	68	4
Goodwin, David, Roy.	.960	20	151	15	7	173	8
Hacker, Steve, Twi.	.983	6	55	3	1	59	6
Hoch, Corey, Ori.	1.000	9	60	3	0	63	8
Hunter, David, Mets*	.981	24	201	9	4	214	13
Isenia, Chairon, D.R.	1.000	1	7	0	0	7	1
Jacobs, John, D.R.	1.000	1	1	0	0	1	0
Kieschnick, Brooks, D.R.	1.000	2	11	0	0	11	0
Lane, Ryan, Twi.	.974	3	34	3	1	38	0
Lough, Aaron, Twi.	1.000	10	51	6	0	57	5
Lugo, Roberto, Mets*	.989	33	249	16	3	268	13
Marciante, Frank, Rang.	.972	15	129	8	4	141	11
McKeel, Walt, R.S.	1.000	1	6	1	0	7	0
Mejia, Renato, Mar.	1.000	4	15	2	0	17	1
Moore, Frank, D.R.	1.000	1	1	0	0	1	1
Oropeza, Asdrubal, Brav.	1.000	3	26	0	0	26	1
Osorio, Isrrael, D.R.	1.000	3	12	2	0	14	1
Pacheco, Juan, Ori.	1.000	1	1	1	0	2	0
Pena, Carlos, Rang.*	1.000	1	10	1	0	11	1
Pena, Rodolfo, R.S.	.955	8	63	1	3	67	4
Pressley, Josh, D.R.	.959	24	201	9	9	219	18
Pridie, Jon, Twi.	1.000	5	41	4	0	45	0
Proctor, Mark, Mets	.857	1	6	0	1	7	1
Rains, Nick, Mets	1.000	1	3	0	0	3	0
RIX, Derek, R.S.	.994	41	311	32	2	345	21
Rodriguez, Carlos, R.S.	.915	8	38	5	4	47	2
Rumfield, Brock, Ori.	1.000	3	27	0	0	27	2
Ryan, Gregory, Rang.*	.993	44	395	18	3	416	27
Samuel, Cody, Yan.	1.000	2	7	0	0	7	1
Sandberg, Eric, Twi.*	.976	32	271	12	7	290	15
Sassanella, Jeremy, Tig.	.992	31	233	21	2	256	25
Segura, Rolando, Pir.	1.000	1	6	0	0	6	0
Sein, Javier, Yan.	.997	39	319	12	1	332	17
Shrum, Allen, Twi.	.871	5	26	1	4	31	4
Stanton, Eric, Pir.	.985	24	183	12	3	198	16
Torres, Franklin, Twi.	.990	12	96	6	1	103	11
Torres, Luis, Brav.	1.000	4	43	4	0	47	6
Tsujita, Osamu, D.R.	.968	27	196	13	7	216	18
Tucker, Mamon, Ori.	1.000	3	23	3	0	26	1
Turnquist, Tyler, Ast.	.985	27	189	11	3	203	15
Valdez, Angel, Yan.	.980	16	144	3	3	150	10
Van Pareren, Tim, Exp.	1.000	3	22	3	0	25	1
Vazquez, Carlos, D.R.	.992	14	113	6	1	120	11
Wade, Michael, Ori.	1.000	2	19	2	0	21	2
Williams, Clyde, Exp.*	.983	56	505	19	9	533	31
Wright, Ron, Pir.	1.000	1	11	0	0	11	0
Zardis, Alex, Mets	1.000	1	1	0	0	1	0

SECOND BASEMEN

Player, Team	Pct.	G	PO	A	E	TC	DP
Alvarez, Antonio, Pir.	1.000	4	7	7	0	14	0
Alvarez, Julio, Tig.	.972	23	51	53	3	107	13
Araujo, Victor, Pir.	1.000	5	3	16	0	19	2
Blum, Geoffrey, Exp.	1.000	3	4	12	0	16	2
Borjas, Henry, R.S.	.945	23	36	50	5	91	10
De Aza, Modesto, Ast.	.937	39	72	76	10	158	20
De Caster, Yurendell, D.R.	.959	48	107	102	9	218	30
Dorrmann, Brian, Yan.	.991	24	48	62	1	111	10
Erwin, Christopher, Rang.	1.000	1	1	0	0	1	0
Garabito, Vianney, Yan.	.882	5	5	10	2	17	1
Garcia, Rafael, Roy.	1.000	4	5	7	0	12	2
Guerrero, Jason, D.R.	.941	4	7	9	1	17	1
Guerrero, Pedro, Rang.	.974	51	115	113	6	234	24
Gutierrez, Derrick, Ori.	.920	4	12	11	2	25	3
Hendricks, Jett, Mets	.953	10	18	23	2	43	1
Hopper, Norris, Roy.	.969	30	54	69	4	127	12
Lane, Ryan, Twi.	.900	5	5	4	1	10	2

Player, Team	Pct.	G	PO	A	E	TC	DP
Linares, Rodney, Ast.	1.000	3	2	4	0	6	0
Lopez, Radhames, Ori.	.917	14	29	26	5	60	4
Malinowski, Scott, Mets	.952	12	13	27	2	42	6
Martin, Tommy, Ori.	.952	12	30	30	3	63	8
Medrano, David, Rang.	1.000	9	22	15	0	37	1
MEDRANO, Jesus, Mar.	.984	44	75	115	3	193	7
Moore, Frank, D.R.	.957	13	19	25	2	46	4
Mundo, Alberto, Brav.	.968	34	53	67	4	124	12
Nelson, Reggie, Tig.	.954	30	67	58	6	131	16
Nunez, Jose, Roy.	.667	1	1	1	1	3	0
Oropeza, Asdrubal, Brav.	1.000	1	2	1	0	3	0
Pacheco, Juan, Ori.	.936	29	62	84	10	156	25
Paulino, David, Mar.	1.000	2	5	4	0	9	1
Pellicciotta, Marc, Ast.	.931	25	50	45	7	102	10
Perea, Carlos, Roy.	.942	32	50	79	8	137	19
Prieto, Jonathan, Pir.	.957	34	58	99	7	164	21
Ravelo, Manuel, Pir.	.938	22	42	64	7	113	10
Reyes, Dadny, Mar.	.982	19	25	30	1	56	9
Rodriguez, Luis, Twi.	.968	35	68	83	5	156	16
Rodriguez, Ronny, R.S.	.889	3	2	6	1	9	1
Rosado, Omar, Exp.	.950	44	68	124	10	202	15
Rumfield, Brock, Ori.	1.000	3	6	6	0	12	0
Salazar, Ruben, Twi.	1.000	3	1	5	0	6	0
Santos, Angel, R.S.	1.000	8	14	17	0	31	4
Shuck, Jason, Mets	.938	23	44	62	7	113	13
Stevens, Tony, Twi.	1.000	9	9	10	0	19	3
Sziksai, Jeff, Yan.	.957	35	67	68	6	141	12
Tiburcio, Emigdio, Tig.	.955	12	22	20	2	44	2
Torres, Franklin, Twi.	.908	19	37	52	9	98	13
Torres, Luis, Brav.	.971	28	60	76	4	140	17
Tyson, Torre, R.S.	.953	34	54	87	7	148	9
Van Pareren, Tim, Exp.	.981	13	27	24	1	52	8
Watkins, Thomas, Twi.	.867	6	5	8	2	15	2
Zardis, Alex, Mets	.875	10	15	27	6	48	6
Zorrilla, Julio, Mets	.974	10	11	26	1	38	5

THIRD BASEMEN

Player, Team	Pct.	G	PO	A	E	TC	DP
Aguila, Chris, Mar.	.850	41	17	68	15	100	6
Alvarez, Antonio, Pir.	.924	29	32	78	9	119	6
Alvarez, Julio, Tig.	.882	7	5	10	2	17	1
Boone, Matt, Tig.	.879	49	32	77	15	124	5
Borjas, Henry, R.S.	.818	10	4	14	4	22	0
Bronowicz, Scott, Brav.	1.000	1	1	1	0	2	0
Bryan, Sean, Roy.	.882	21	14	31	6	51	2
Calzado, Napolean, Ori.	.947	21	19	52	4	75	3
Cotten, Jeremy, Pir.	.774	16	7	17	7	31	0
De Caster, Yurendell, D.R.	.929	4	4	9	1	14	1
Degroote, Casey, Yan.	.806	17	7	22	7	36	1
De Los Santos, Eddy, Ast.	.769	4	1	9	3	13	1
Dominguez, Luis, Ast.	.907	27	19	49	7	75	3
Donato, Gregorio, Brav.	.821	14	10	22	7	39	0
Elorduy, Daniel, Brav.	.750	1	0	3	1	4	0
Erwin, Christopher, Rang.	.850	13	6	28	6	40	1
Garabito, Vianney, Yan.	.940	34	16	63	5	84	4
Hendricks, Ian, Mets	.871	29	28	53	12	93	3
Henson, Drew, Yan.	.951	10	12	27	2	41	2
Hoch, Corey, Ori.	1.000	4	3	9	0	12	1
Isenia, Chairon, D.R.	1.000	1	2	2	0	4	0
Jacobs, John, D.R.	.872	47	13	82	14	109	5
Jimenez, Carlos, Tig.	1.000	1	0	2	0	2	0
Jimenez, Jonathan, Rang.	.909	10	4	26	3	33	3
Lane, Ryan, Twi.	1.000	1	2	1	0	3	0
Leon, Alfredo, Ori.	1.000	2	3	0	0	3	0
Lopez, Jose, Mets	1.000	5	3	12	0	15	1
Louwsma, Chris, Mar.	.905	16	13	25	4	42	0
Lugo, Felix, Exp.	.896	56	34	104	16	154	7
Malinowski, Scott, Mets	.850	7	8	9	3	20	0
Martin, Tommy, Ori.	1.000	2	1	2	0	3	1
Medrano, David, Rang.	.929	39	20	85	8	113	9
Moore, Griffin, Roy.	1.000	1	1	0	0	1	0
Nettles, Jeff, Yan.	.933	4	5	9	1	15	0
Nunez, Jose, Roy.	.932	45	30	94	9	133	7
Oropeza, Asdrubal, Brav.	.918	31	28	62	8	98	4
Penna, Shaun, R.S.	.850	30	19	49	12	80	0
Perry, Herbert, D.R.	.900	4	1	8	1	10	2
Pridie, Jon, Twi.	.841	14	8	29	7	44	1
Proctor, Mark, Mets	.913	11	8	13	2	23	2
Quinones, Marcus, Rang.	1.000	1	0	4	0	4	0
Ramirez, Anthony, Ast.	.765	14	7	19	8	34	2
Ramirez, Edgar, D.R.	.821	8	5	18	5	28	4
Reyes, Dadny, Mar.	1.000	2	2	6	0	8	0

Player, Team	Pct.	G	PO	A	E	TC	DP
Rodriguez, Luis, Twi.	.875	3	2	5	1	8	0
Rumfield, Brock, Ori.	.902	36	24	77	11	112	10
SALAZAR, Ruben, Twi.	.940	44	30	126	10	166	9
Santos, Angel, R.S.	.933	5	3	11	1	15	1
Segura, Rolando, Pir.	.898	19	12	32	5	49	1
Shuck, Jason, Mets	.857	2	1	5	1	7	0
Terni, Chaz, R.S.	.887	17	13	34	6	53	3
Tiburcio, Emigdio, Tig.	.895	8	6	11	2	19	1
Torres, Franklin, Twi.	.952	7	7	13	1	21	2
Torres, Luis, Brav.	.929	14	10	29	3	42	1
Turnquist, Tyler, Ast.	.982	19	15	40	1	56	4
Van Pareren, Tim, Exp.	.867	8	3	10	2	15	0
Vazquez, Carlos, D.R.	.500	1	0	1	1	2	0
Vega, Jonathan, Ast.	.800	1	2	2	1	5	0
Zamora, Junior, Mets	.857	2	3	3	1	7	0
Zapey, Winton, Mar.	1.000	1	1	1	0	2	0
Zardis, Alex, Mets	.750	9	2	13	5	20	1

SHORTSTOP

Player, Team	Pct.	G	PO	A	E	TC	DP
Acevedo, Luis, Rang.	.700	1	1	6	3	10	2
Alfaro, Jason, Ast.	.921	46	65	109	15	189	24
Alvarez, Antonio, Pir.	.867	5	6	20	4	30	3
Araujo, Victor, Pir.	.815	16	19	47	15	81	9
Betemit, Wilson, Brav.	.908	50	63	135	20	218	22
Calzado, Napolean, Ori.	.915	11	17	26	4	47	5
De Caster, Yurendell, D.R.	.750	1	0	3	1	4	0
De Los Santos, Eddy, Ast.	.906	21	23	54	8	85	3
Dorrmann, Brian, Yan.	.971	17	23	43	2	68	4
Garabito, Vianney, Yan.	1.000	1	1	2	0	3	0
Garcia, Rafael, Roy.	.914	16	16	37	5	58	4
Guerrero, Jason, D.R.	1.000	1	1	3	0	4	0
Guerrero, Julio, R.S.	.886	35	35	82	15	132	11
Gutierrez, Derrick, Ori.	.911	24	27	75	10	112	11
Hoch, Corey, Ori.	.929	6	5	21	2	28	6
Hopper, Norris, Roy.	.787	9	10	27	10	47	3
Hoshina, Koji, Exp.	.963	5	9	17	1	27	3
Jimenez, Carlos, Tig.	.925	46	85	163	20	268	29
Jimenez, Jonathan, Rang.	1.000	2	8	7	0	15	1
Lane, Ryan, Twi.	.958	5	8	15	1	24	1
Lauterhahn, Dan, Tig.	.875	3	4	3	1	8	0
Leon, Alfredo, Ori.	.933	7	16	12	2	30	3
Linares, Rodney, Ast.	1.000	1	1	1	0	2	0
Lugo, Felix, Exp.	1.000	1	1	2	0	3	1
Malinowski, Scott, Mets	1.000	15	20	29	0	49	6
Martin, Brian, D.R.	.667	1	1	1	1	3	1
Martin, Tommy, Ori.	.953	9	12	29	2	43	7
McKinley, Josh, Exp.	.897	50	71	155	26	252	14
Moore, Frank, D.R.	.857	2	2	4	1	7	0
Moore, Griffin, Roy.	.976	34	50	110	4	164	20
Mundo, Alberto, Brav.	.946	12	21	32	3	56	5
Nelson, Reggie, Tig.	.884	12	23	38	8	69	6
Ojeda, Augie, Ori.	1.000	4	9	16	0	25	4
Paulino, David, Mar.	1.000	10	7	29	0	36	1
Pelfrey, Brice, Pir.	.828	40	71	98	35	204	18
Perea, Carlos, Roy.	.875	7	7	14	3	24	3
Proctor, Mark, Mets	.844	8	11	16	5	32	2
Quinones, Marcus, Rang.	.926	57	85	164	20	269	22
Reding, Josh, Exp.	.938	2	2	13	1	16	1
Reyes, Dadny, Mar.	1.000	2	0	3	0	3	0
Rodriguez, Junior, Yan.	.939	48	74	157	15	246	19
Rodriguez, Luis, Twi.	.917	17	17	49	6	72	11
Rodriguez, Ronny, R.S.	.878	18	20	66	12	98	9
Santos, Angel, R.S.	.818	12	10	26	8	44	5
Seale, Marvin, Mets	1.000	2	3	5	0	8	0
Shuck, Jason, Mets	.929	7	8	18	2	28	1
SOLER, Ramon, D.R.	.944	57	75	209	17	301	36
Stevens, Tony, Twi.	.913	30	31	95	12	138	12
Ugueto, Luis, Mar.	.925	49	58	128	15	201	14
Van Pareren, Tim, Exp.	1.000	3	2	4	0	6	2
Velazquez, Gil, Mets	.958	32	70	113	8	191	23
Watkins, Thomas, Twi.	.868	22	22	44	10	76	4
Wesolowski, David, Mar.	.000	1	0	0	1	1	0

TRIPLE PLAY: Pelfrey.

OUTFIELDERS

Player, Team	Pct.	G	PO	A	E	TC	DP
Alou, Felipe, Roy.	.986	44	66	5	1	72	0
Altagen, Matthew, Tig.*	.912	23	30	1	3	34	0
Amerson, Gordon, Yan.*	1.000	6	8	1	0	9	0
Baez, Ernies, Rang.	.959	31	44	3	2	49	0
Batista, Angel, D.R.*	.975	57	110	8	3	121	3

Player, Team	Pct.	G	PO	A	E	TC	DP
Borjas, Henry, R.S.	1.000	3	3	0	0	3	0
Bronowicz, Scott, Brav.	1.000	1	1	0	0	1	0
Brown, Andy, Yan.*	.972	30	32	3	1	36	1
Brown, Richard, Yan.*	1.000	1	1	0	0	1	0
Brown, Tonayne, R.S.*	.990	51	92	6	1	99	2
Burton, Willie, Pir.	.978	15	42	2	1	45	0
Bystrowski, Robert, Ast.	1.000	38	52	5	0	57	0
Cabrera, Raymond, Ori.	.972	33	66	4	2	72	0
Carpenter, Bubba, Yan.*	1.000	2	2	0	0	2	0
Chourio, Jorjanis, Pir.	.944	26	33	1	2	36	0
Clark, Tommy, Brav.	.917	26	22	0	2	24	0
Cubillan, Jose, Rang.	.975	44	76	1	2	79	0
Davison, Ashanti, Ori.	1.000	4	7	0	0	7	0
De La Rosa, Frank, Tig.	.974	32	34	3	1	38	1
Derosso, Tony, R.S.	1.000	3	5	0	0	5	0
Dominguez, Luis, Ast.	1.000	1	4	0	0	4	0
Edge, Michael, Exp.	1.000	21	27	0	0	27	0
Elder, Rick, Ori.*	.929	15	26	0	2	28	0
Erwin, Christopher, Rang.	1.000	1	2	0	0	2	0
Espinoza, Andres, Exp.	.974	43	71	3	2	76	0
Ferrand, Francisco, Mar.	.917	35	32	1	3	36	0
Fischer, Mark, R.S.	1.000	2	5	0	0	5	0
Fowler, David, Yan.	.980	36	46	2	1	49	1
Galarraga, Luis, Mar.	.966	34	27	1	1	29	1
Garcia, Alfredo, Mets	.978	51	83	4	2	89	1
Gettis, Byron, Roy.	1.000	24	36	1	0	37	0
Gomez, Richard, Tig.	.959	36	45	2	2	49	0
Gonzalez, Felix, Exp.	.968	24	27	3	1	31	0
Graham, Tarik, Roy.*	.902	25	37	0	4	41	0
Green, Richard, Ori.	1.000	4	10	1	0	11	0
Guerrero, Jason, D.R.	1.000	2	1	0	0	1	0
Harts, Jeremy, Pir.*	.951	24	55	3	3	61	1
Hazelton, Justin, Tig.	1.000	2	4	0	0	4	0
Heffernan, Christian, Brav.	.966	25	27	1	1	29	0
Hughes, Brian, Ori.	.973	18	34	2	1	37	1
Hundley, Todd, Mets	1.000	1	2	0	0	2	0
Isenia, Chairon, D.R.	1.000	4	1	0	0	1	0
Johnson, Eric, Pir.	.950	7	17	2	1	20	0
Johnson, Kareem, Twi.	.909	34	29	1	3	33	0
Jones, Andrew (A.J.), Pir.	.975	30	72	6	2	80	2
Jones, Damien, Brav.	.973	47	69	4	2	75	0
Kawabata, Kenichiro, R.S.*	.960	33	44	4	2	50	0
Koone, Chuck, Ori.	.848	22	27	1	5	33	0
Langerhans, Ryan, Brav.*	.975	42	74	3	2	79	0
Lara, Balmes, Tig.	.957	17	22	0	1	23	0
Mack, Antonio, Ori.	.987	37	70	5	1	76	0
Martin, Brian, D.R.	.931	40	52	2	4	58	0
McCorvey, Kenneth, Twi.	.966	40	55	1	2	58	0
McLaughlin, Erik, Brav.	1.000	8	4	0	0	4	0
Mejia, Renato, Mar.	.964	44	49	5	2	56	2
Mendoza, Carlos, D.R.*	1.000	6	13	0	0	13	0
Meseberg, Michael, D.R.	1.000	5	7	0	0	7	0
Miller, Josh, Pir.	.953	19	41	0	2	43	0
Moore, Frank, D.R.	.870	24	18	2	3	23	1
Nanita, Emmanuel, Twi.	.943	29	33	0	2	35	0
Nowlin, Cody, Rang.	.933	45	40	2	3	45	0
Nunez, Edward, Twi.	1.000	3	1	0	0	1	0
Ortiz, Juan, Exp.	.955	46	81	4	4	89	1
Paulino, Waren, Yan.*	1.000	3	2	0	0	2	0
Pena, Jose, R.S.	.950	44	73	3	4	80	0
Pender, Darrell, Tig.	.984	33	59	2	1	62	0
Perich, Joshua, Mets	.952	24	20	0	1	21	0
Pratt, Todd, Mets	1.000	1	2	0	0	2	0
Prosper, Gerard, Mets*	.833	11	9	1	2	12	1
Raines, Timothy, Ori.	.978	52	125	6	3	134	1
Rains, Nick, Mets	1.000	5	5	0	0	5	0
Ramirez, Charlie, Roy.	.984	50	61	1	1	63	0
Reed, Brian, Mar.	.925	56	73	1	6	80	0
Rivas, Justo, Brav.	.980	32	45	3	1	49	1
Rivera, Juan, Yan.	.979	56	86	8	2	96	4
Rodriguez, Carlos, R.S.	.980	35	48	2	1	51	0
Rodriguez, Steve, Tig.	.973	32	34	2	1	37	0
Rollins, Antwon, Rang.	.940	49	105	4	7	116	1
RUAN, Wilken, Exp.	.991	52	108	4	1	113	1
Ryan, Gregory, Rang.*	1.000	6	10	0	0	10	0
Ryan, Kelvin, D.R.	.971	56	95	4	3	102	3
Saffer, Jon, Exp.	1.000	1	2	0	0	2	0
Sajiun, Joel, Twi.	.939	32	31	0	2	33	0
Sandberg, Eric, Twi.*	1.000	2	2	0	0	2	0
Santana, Pedro, Yan.	1.000	16	25	2	0	27	0
Seale, Marvin, Mets	1.000	35	45	3	0	48	0
Seo, Jae, Mets	.750	3	3	0	1	4	0
Shanks, James, Roy.	.987	40	71	3	1	75	1
Sheffield, Jeff, Yan.	.875	9	7	0	1	8	1
Shuck, Jason, Mets	.958	13	20	3	1	24	0
Shumpert, Derek, Yan.	1.000	5	7	0	0	7	0
Smith, Toebius, Brav.	.909	12	9	1	1	11	0
Sosa, Jovanny, Pir.	.903	31	63	2	7	72	0
Southward, Deshawn, Twi.	.946	54	85	3	5	93	0
Stevens, Tony, Twi.	1.000	17	32	4	0	36	1
Stratton, Robert, Mets	1.000	5	4	0	0	4	0
Taveras, Jose, Roy.	1.000	6	10	0	0	10	0
Tillis, Cameron, Roy.	1.000	3	6	1	0	7	0
Tolli, Barry, Tig.	.921	25	35	0	3	38	0
Tucker, Mamon, Ori.	.500	2	1	0	1	2	0
Turnquist, Tyler, Ast.	1.000	8	18	5	0	23	0
Valdez, Angel, Yan.	.907	30	49	0	5	54	0
Vann, Eric, Roy.	1.000	3	9	0	0	9	0
Vasquez, Alejandro, Ast.*	.961	55	70	3	3	76	0
Vega, Jonathan, Ast.	1.000	38	58	4	0	62	0
Walker, Javon, Mar.	1.000	28	32	2	0	34	1
Warren, Christopher, R.S.	.917	19	21	1	2	24	0
Washington, Mo, Pir.	.917	37	62	4	6	72	0
Wright, Charles, Yan.	1.000	9	12	0	0	12	0
Wright, Corey, Rang.*	1.000	9	15	1	0	16	0
Yancy, Michael, Mets	.979	37	43	3	1	47	0
Zapata, Juan, Ast.	.955	49	102	4	5	111	0
Zardis, Alex, Mets	1.000	4	4	0	0	4	0

TRIPLE PLAY: E. Johnson.

CATCHERS

Player, Team	Pct.	G	PO	A	E	TC	DP	PB
Ackerman, Scott, Exp.	.980	12	90	9	2	101	0	3
Adorno, Wilson, Pir.	1.000	3	8	1	0	9	1	2
Alvarez, Nelson, Mets	.971	11	52	16	2	70	1	1
Ayres, Yancy, Roy.	1.000	19	91	15	0	106	0	3
Benham, David, R.S.	.962	3	22	3	1	26	1	0
Brazell, Craig, Mets	1.000	2	28	1	0	29	0	1
Bronowicz, Scott, Brav.	.971	16	86	15	3	104	1	0
Buck, John, Ast.	.983	26	209	21	4	234	1	8
Burke, Paul, Brav.	.982	29	193	24	4	221	0	7
Cardona, Raynier, Pir.	.979	20	121	20	3	144	2	5
Caridi, Tony, R.S.	.974	12	67	8	2	77	0	2
Carreno, Jose, Exp.	.986	38	255	36	4	295	2	4
Casilla, Luis, Ast.	.977	18	122	8	3	133	0	4
Cleveland, Russell, Tig.	.970	25	175	18	6	199	0	12
Cruz, Rafael, Rang.	.979	34	239	40	6	285	2	11
De Jesus, Wilmer, Exp.	1.000	6	58	5	0	63	0	2
Depastino, Joe, R.S.	1.000	4	16	1	0	17	0	1
Diaz, David, Pir.	.978	10	42	3	1	46	1	4
Dito, Robert, Exp.	1.000	6	30	3	0	33	1	3
Edwards, John, Twi.	.981	8	44	7	1	52	0	2
Erwin, Christopher, Rang.	.947	8	33	3	2	38	0	3
Felix, Hersy, Roy.	.971	45	304	29	10	343	1	8
Frawley, Scott, Brav.	.974	7	36	2	1	39	1	2
Fuentes, Omar, Yan.	.986	33	237	38	4	279	2	7
Garcia, Manuel, R.S.	.992	17	120	9	1	130	1	8
Green, Richard, Ori.	.945	13	44	8	3	55	0	4
Gutierrez, Derrick, Ori.	1.000	1	7	1	0	8	0	0
Gutierrez, Fernando, Ori.	.974	30	170	20	5	195	0	13
Hernandez, Jose, Pir.	.987	13	66	9	1	76	1	4
Isenia, Chairon, D.R.	.983	36	253	37	5	295	1	14
Larned, Andrew, R.S.	.900	2	16	2	2	20	1	1
Lopez, Guillermo, Brav.	.993	22	132	18	1	151	0	3
Lough, Aaron, Twi.	.972	24	121	16	4	141	0	4
Massucco, Scott, Yan.	.975	22	169	27	5	201	0	11
McKeel, Walt, R.S.	1.000	6	35	3	0	38	0	1
Monzon, Francisco, Ori.	.975	29	137	20	4	161	0	3
Ochoa, Javier, Mar.	.979	29	216	21	5	242	0	13
Osborn, Jason, Mets	.993	17	117	17	1	135	0	10
Osorio, Israel, D.R.	.989	12	82	5	1	88	1	7
Parker, Chris, Tig.	.967	23	149	28	6	183	1	3
Pena, Rodolfo, R.S.	.992	19	101	18	1	120	0	6
Pratt, Todd, Mets	1.000	1	5	2	0	7	0	0
Resendez, Carlos, Brav.	.977	5	35	8	1	44	0	2
Rhodes, Nicholas, D.R.	.953	20	127	16	7	150	1	6
Rivas, Julio, Mar.	.989	13	73	18	1	92	1	4
Rodriguez, Felix, Yan.	.982	10	48	7	1	56	0	0
St. Pierre, Maxim, Tig.	.971	25	174	29	6	209	1	11
Santana, Emmanuel, Roy.	.947	7	34	2	2	38	0	2
Shrum, Allen, Twi.	.974	38	232	35	7	274	0	2
SMITH, Ryan, Mets	.991	30	172	53	2	227	2	3
Torres, Frederick, Rang.	.979	25	156	27	4	187	1	5
Torres, Rommel, Pir.	.962	26	138	15	6	159	2	7
Valdez, Darlin, Exp.	.857	3	6	0	1	7	0	0
Venales, Luis, Mar.	.980	27	196	46	5	247	4	16

SUMMER CLASS A Gulf Coast League

Player, Team	Pct.	G	PO	A	E	TC	DP	PB
Wade, Michael, Ori.	1.000	5	14	2	0	16	2	1
Whitby, Corey, R.S.	.990	15	95	6	1	102	2	0
Wilson, Vance, Mets	.957	9	35	9	2	46	0	3
Zapey, Winton, Mar.	.965	36	249	28	10	287	1	10

PITCHERS

Player, Team	Pct.	G	PO	A	E	TC	DP
Acosta, Alberto, Yan.	.833	8	1	4	1	6	0
Affeldt, Jeremy, Roy.*	.923	12	3	9	1	13	0
Aguilar, Edwin, Ast.	.800	14	3	5	2	10	0
Alvarez, Wilson, D.R.*	1.000	1	0	1	0	1	0
Anderson, Antwoine, Mar.*	1.000	15	4	6	0	10	0
ANDERSON, Wes, Mar.	1.000	11	7	14	0	21	2
Andujar, Jesse, Exp.	1.000	18	1	8	0	9	0
Appier, Kevin, Roy.	.000	1	0	0	1	1	0
Aramboles, Ricardo, Yan.	.667	10	1	3	2	6	0
Armstrong, Charles, D.R.*	.857	14	0	6	1	7	0
Aucoin, Derek, Mets	1.000	5	0	1	0	1	0
Baldassano, Joseph, Exp.	1.000	14	1	2	0	3	0
Bechler, Steven, Ori.	.929	9	4	9	1	14	0
Beitey, Jason, Rang.	1.000	5	0	2	0	2	0
Belcher, B.J., Rang.	1.000	3	1	0	0	1	0
Bennett, Jeff, Pir.	1.000	13	5	5	0	10	0
Betti, Rich, R.S.*	1.000	3	0	1	0	1	0
Bevil, Brian, Roy.	.500	3	1	0	1	2	0
Blake, Peter, Twi.*	.857	9	1	5	1	7	0
Bobbitt, Josh, Rang.*	.857	19	0	6	1	7	0
Bong, Jung, Brav.*	.941	11	6	10	1	17	0
Brewer, Dustin, Ori.	1.000	14	1	6	0	7	0
Buckles, Bucky, Rang.	1.000	2	0	1	0	1	0
Bullock, Jeremiah, Rang.*	1.000	11	1	8	0	9	0
Bumatay, Mike, Pir.*	.800	13	0	4	1	5	0
Cadena, Nathan, R.S.	1.000	4	1	0	0	1	0
Calvo, Jose, Ast.	1.000	13	2	3	0	5	0
Campos, David, Mar.*	1.000	9	0	5	0	5	0
Centeno, Juan, Ast.	.750	21	2	7	3	12	0
Cepeda, Victor, Tig.	1.000	18	1	0	0	1	0
Chiasson, Scott, Roy.	1.000	13	4	6	0	10	0
Chiavacci, Ronald, Exp.	.875	13	1	6	1	8	0
Chipperfield, Calvin, Tig.	1.000	12	5	4	0	9	0
Chisnall, Wesley, Exp.	.727	13	2	6	3	11	1
Chivers, Jason, Mets*	1.000	12	2	8	0	10	0
Classen, Ender, Pir.	.833	12	3	12	3	18	0
Cooke, Andrew, Twi.*	1.000	17	1	10	0	11	0
Cornejo, Nate, Tig.	1.000	5	6	6	0	12	0
Craun, Robert, Mar.	1.000	12	1	6	0	7	0
Crawford, Carlos, Pir.	1.000	12	0	2	0	2	0
Curtis, Daniel, Brav.	1.000	14	2	6	0	8	1
Dansby, Justin, Brav.	1.000	15	2	5	0	7	0
Deckard, Edward, D.R.	1.000	4	1	2	0	3	0
De La Cruz, Andres, Yan.	1.000	21	3	10	0	13	1
De La Cruz, Fernando, R.S.	1.000	1	0	2	0	2	0
De La Cruz, Francisco, Yan.	.800	3	1	3	1	5	1
DeLaCruz, Juan, Pir.	.750	11	3	6	3	12	1
Denholm, Richard, Twi.	1.000	13	1	2	0	3	0
Dent, Doug, Brav.	1.000	4	0	1	0	1	0
Diaz, Billy, Rang.	.923	13	4	8	1	13	0
Diaz, Luis, Tig.	1.000	25	3	6	0	9	0
Dickson, Patrick, D.R.*	1.000	14	1	5	0	6	0
Dittfurth, Ryan, Rang.	1.000	8	1	5	0	6	0
Douglass, Ryan, Roy.	1.000	9	2	2	0	4	1
Dukeman, Gregory, Brav.	1.000	18	1	9	0	10	0
Dunn, Keith, Yan.	1.000	21	3	3	0	6	0
Earl, Ryan, Tig.*	1.000	6	2	1	0	3	0
Eavenson, Clay, Yan.	.750	12	2	4	2	8	0
Ennis, John, Brav.	.800	8	2	2	1	5	0
Erickson, John, D.R.	1.000	19	1	2	0	3	0
Escalona, Jesus, Ori.	1.000	3	1	1	0	2	0
Espinal, Jose, Twi.	.800	9	0	4	1	5	0
Fereira, Ramon, Ast.	1.000	16	3	3	0	6	0
Figueroa, Carlos, Rang.*	.941	19	3	13	1	17	0
Fischer, Sean, Ori.*	.889	17	0	8	1	9	0
Flock, Rick, Twi.	1.000	2	1	1	0	2	0
Foote, Joe, Twi.	.909	13	2	8	1	11	1
Frazier, Bradley, Twi.	.857	9	3	3	1	7	0
French, Eric, Roy.	1.000	3	1	0	0	1	0
Frey, Christopher, Rang.	.800	10	0	4	1	5	0
Frierson, Andrew, Exp.*	1.000	15	0	10	0	10	0
Gamble, Jr., Jerome, R.S.	.857	11	2	4	1	7	0
Garces, Rich, R.S.	1.000	7	2	3	0	5	0
Garcia, Rosman, Yan.	.895	12	5	12	2	19	1
Garibaldi, Cecilio, D.R.	.889	22	3	5	1	9	1
George, Chris, Roy.*	.750	5	1	2	1	4	0
Getz, Cody, D.R.*	1.000	16	0	5	0	5	1
Gilfillan, Jason, Roy.	1.000	7	0	4	0	4	0
Glaser, Eric, R.S.	1.000	15	1	4	0	5	0
Go, Ho, Pir.	1.000	13	2	6	0	8	0
Gomez, Rafael, Mets	1.000	13	3	6	0	9	0
Gomez, Ricardo, Pir.	.500	9	0	1	1	2	0
Gonzalez, Giovanni, Pir.	1.000	14	2	1	0	3	1
Good, Eric, Exp.*	1.000	6	0	8	0	8	0
Graham, Frank, Mets	1.000	3	0	4	0	4	0
Guerrero, Jason, D.R.	1.000	6	2	2	0	4	1
Guerrero, Junior, Roy.	.917	13	4	7	1	12	0
Guevara, Daniel, D.R.*	1.000	4	0	1	0	1	0
Hafer, Jeff, Mets	1.000	4	1	1	0	2	0
Haigler, Phil, Twi.	1.000	3	4	2	0	6	0
Hamilton, Charles, Roy.	1.000	15	1	3	0	4	0
Hancock, Joshua, R.S.	1.000	5	1	3	0	4	0
Haney, Chris, Roy.*	.500	1	0	1	1	2	0
Harris, Veon, Pir.	1.000	7	2	4	0	6	1
Hebson, Bryan, Exp.	1.000	4	1	1	0	2	0
Hee, Aaron, Mets*	.750	18	0	6	2	8	0
Hernandez, Luis, D.R.*	.929	10	0	13	1	14	0
Hidalgo, Edgar, Rang.	1.000	10	0	3	0	3	0
Hill, Roy, Roy.	1.000	5	0	1	0	1	0
Hill, T.J., D.R.	1.000	7	1	1	0	2	0
Hostetler, Jim, Tig.	1.000	2	1	0	0	1	0
Houle, Marc, Ori.	.800	9	0	4	1	5	0
Huntsman, Brandon, Ori.	1.000	1	0	1	0	1	0
Hurst, Bill, Tig.	1.000	3	0	1	0	1	0
Johnston, Michael, Pir.*	.667	13	1	3	2	6	0
Johnston, Rikki, Tig.*	.944	11	4	13	1	18	3
Kessel, Kyle, Mets*	1.000	4	0	2	0	2	0
Kim, Jae, R.S.	.800	5	2	2	1	5	0
Klein, Cody, Yan.*	.889	17	2	6	1	9	0
Klepacki, Edward, Exp.	1.000	9	2	1	0	3	0
Knowles, Michael, Yan.	.750	8	1	2	1	4	0
Krystofoski, Jay, Mets	.000	1	0	0	1	1	0
Langston, David, Yan.	1.000	15	0	6	0	6	0
Laroche, Jeff, Mar.*	.667	4	1	1	1	3	0
LaRosa, Tom, Twi.	1.000	4	2	0	0	2	0
Ledden, Ryan, D.R.	.800	14	1	3	1	5	1
Lelless, Alexander, Brav.	1.000	14	0	4	0	4	0
Levesque, Benjamin, Pir.	.000	6	0	0	1	1	0
Lima, Frank, Tig.	.941	12	3	13	1	17	0
Lluberes, Alberto, Ori.	1.000	2	1	0	0	1	0
Lopez, Carlos, Exp.	1.000	14	0	5	0	5	0
Lopez, Gustavo, Mar.	.750	9	2	1	1	4	0
Love, Farley, Ast.	1.000	1	0	1	0	1	0
Mancha, Tony, Roy.	.857	20	3	3	1	7	1
Mangieri, John, Mets	.750	16	0	6	2	8	0
Manning, David, Rang.	.750	3	2	1	1	4	0
Marichal, Rafael, Pir.	.857	18	2	4	1	7	0
Marin, Willy, D.R.	1.000	27	0	6	0	6	0
Maroth, Mike, R.S.*	.833	4	0	5	1	6	1
Marrero, Darwin, Exp.	1.000	14	1	1	0	2	0
Marsonek, Sam, Rang.	.750	2	1	2	1	4	0
Martin, Jeff, Pir.	.000	1	0	0	1	1	0
Martinez, Anastacio, R.S.	1.000	12	2	6	0	8	0
Martinez, Lionel, Brav.	.000	3	0	0	1	1	0
Martinez, Obispo, Mets	1.000	3	0	2	0	2	0
Marx, Tommy, Tig.*	.923	12	2	10	1	13	0
Mathys, Jason, Yan.	.000	12	0	0	1	1	0
Mayi, Leonardo, Brav.*	.846	12	1	10	2	13	0
McCormick, Terry, D.R.*	.625	11	2	3	3	8	0
McGill, Frankie, Rang.	1.000	9	3	3	0	6	1
McGinnis, Johnny, Brav.	.714	13	6	9	6	21	0
McKoin, Heath, D.R.*	1.000	10	1	6	0	7	0
Medrano, Juan, Roy.	.727	12	2	6	3	11	1
Melson, Nate, Twi.	.933	12	5	9	1	15	0
Mendez, David, Brav.*	.917	11	3	8	1	12	0
Mikkola, Shaun, Mets	.824	10	2	12	3	17	1
Miller, Aaron, Twi.*	.000	4	0	0	1	1	0
Miller, Greg, R.S.*	1.000	11	2	3	0	5	0
Minaya, Pedro, Mar.	.889	11	0	8	1	9	0
Moon, Chang, Pir.	.857	13	3	3	1	7	0
Morrobel, Juan, Pir.*	1.000	3	0	1	0	1	0
Moses, Stephen, Mets	1.000	14	1	4	0	5	0
Mott, Tom, Twi.	1.000	5	2	4	0	6	0
Nannini, Mike, Ast.	1.000	8	1	8	0	9	1
Norris, Shon, R.S.	1.000	15	1	6	0	7	1
Norton, Jason, R.S.	1.000	3	0	1	0	1	0
Nowakowski, Brian, Twi.	1.000	13	3	0	0	3	1
Nunez, Jose, Mets*	.955	13	1	20	1	22	1
Oswalt, Roy, Ast.	1.000	4	0	1	0	1	0

Player, Team	Pct.	G	PO	A	E	TC	DP
Otanez, Ender, R.S.	1.000	13	1	4	0	5	0
Padilla, Juan, Twi.	.889	17	3	5	1	9	0
Palacios, Refugio, Mets	.000	5	0	0	1	1	0
Paugh, Rick, Pir.*	1.000	4	0	3	0	3	1
Pearson, Jason, Mar.*	.875	11	0	7	1	8	0
Peguero, Kerbin, R.S.*	1.000	9	2	2	0	4	0
Peguero, Radhame, D.R.	.929	11	4	9	1	14	2
Perez, Elvis, Brav.	1.000	11	7	2	0	9	0
Perez, Randy, Ori.*	1.000	8	0	8	0	8	1
Pichardo, Carlos, Roy.	1.000	14	2	2	0	4	0
Pidgeon, Chip, Mets*	.833	16	1	4	1	6	1
Pineda, Isauro, R.S.	1.000	4	1	2	0	3	0
Pineda, Jairo, Ast.	1.000	12	4	11	0	15	0
Pipes, Joey, Ast.	1.000	4	0	2	0	2	1
Pratt, Andrew, Rang.*	.875	12	5	9	2	16	1
Price, Kevin, D.R.	1.000	16	1	2	0	3	0
Pruitt, Jason, Ori.*	1.000	17	1	9	0	10	0
Quarnstrom, Robert, Rang.*	1.000	23	0	6	0	6	0
Ralston, Kris, Roy.	.500	2	1	0	1	2	0
Ramirez, Jose, Tig.*	1.000	2	0	2	0	2	0
Rangel, Julio, Yan.	1.000	3	0	2	0	2	0
Ratliff, Craig, Ori.	.824	10	3	11	3	17	0
Reisinger, Justin, Yan.	1.000	9	2	0	0	2	0
Ridenour, Jeffrey, Rang.	.875	18	1	6	1	8	0
Ridenour, Ryan, Yan.*	.250	4	0	1	3	4	0
Rivera, Homero, Tig.*	.917	16	7	4	1	12	0
Roberts, Marquis, D.R.*	1.000	3	0	3	0	3	0
Roberts, Mike, Rang.	1.000	3	0	3	0	3	1
Rodriguez, Cristobal, Exp.	1.000	8	3	2	0	5	0
Rodriguez, Jose, D.R.	1.000	12	6	3	0	9	0
Rodriguez, Marino, Mar.*	.923	12	1	11	1	13	0
Rodriguez, Tony, Yan.	1.000	6	0	2	0	2	0
Rojas, Frances, Twi.*	1.000	13	1	1	0	2	0
Roller, Adam, R.S.	.889	15	4	4	1	9	1
Rondon, Gabriel, Mets	1.000	8	1	3	0	4	0
Rosario, Rafael, Tig.	.800	22	2	2	1	5	0
Rosario, Reynaldo, Tig.	.875	10	3	4	1	8	0
Rosario, Rodrigo, Ast.	.955	13	9	12	1	22	3
Russo, Mike, Roy.	.750	18	0	3	1	4	0
Ryan, Jeremy, Ast.	1.000	4	1	4	0	5	0
Saneaux, Francisco, Ori.	1.000	3	0	4	0	4	0
Santana, Alfredo, Tig.	.857	22	2	4	1	7	0
Schmidt, Pat, Brav.*	.000	3	0	0	1	1	0
Schreiner, Jon, Exp.	1.000	13	3	5	0	8	0
Schwager, Matthew, Ori.	1.000	12	0	3	0	3	0
Sents, Marcus, Twi.	1.000	9	2	2	0	4	0
Sexton, Patrick, Mets	1.000	10	1	1	0	2	0
Seybt, Paul, R.S.	1.000	16	4	5	0	9	0
Shepherd, Alvie, Ori.	.667	3	0	2	1	3	0
Shields, Drew, Mar.	1.000	13	2	11	0	13	1
Siciliano, Jess, Pir.	1.000	4	0	1	0	1	0
Silverthorn, Will, R.S.*	1.000	11	2	9	0	11	0
Solano, Alexander, R.S.	.929	12	3	10	1	14	2
Solano, Francisco, Roy.	.929	9	8	5	1	14	0
Sosa, Jorby, Yan.	.857	12	0	6	1	7	0
South, Carl, Pir.	1.000	8	2	1	0	3	0
Spurling, Chris, Yan.	.889	13	9	7	2	18	2
Stanford, Derek, Ast.	.750	12	2	4	2	8	0
Stenger, Pat, Twi.	.750	13	2	1	1	4	0
Strange, Patrick, Mets	1.000	4	1	2	0	3	0
Tapia, Rafael, Ori.	1.000	11	2	2	0	4	0
Targac, Matthew, Brav.*	.941	13	3	13	1	17	1
Terwilliger, Rich, Ast.	.800	12	0	4	1	5	0
Thomas, Gaige, Mar.	.733	15	4	7	4	15	0
Tomaszewski, Eliot, Ori.	.857	16	1	5	1	7	0
Torres, Elvin, Yan.	1.000	2	1	0	0	1	0
Trinidad, Fernando, Ori.	1.000	3	0	2	0	2	0
Tucker, Thomas, Exp.	1.000	7	1	7	0	8	1
Turner, Kyle, Roy.*	.833	12	0	5	1	6	0
Underhill, Ray, Twi.	1.000	14	1	3	0	4	0
Urbina, Ulmer, Exp.	.750	5	3	0	1	4	0
Ushiromatsu, Juei, Mets*	1.000	16	1	1	0	2	0
Valdez, Domingo, Rang.	.800	10	3	5	2	10	0
Vallejo, Etanislao, Pir.	.778	13	3	4	2	9	0
Vargas, Claudio, Mar.	1.000	5	2	4	0	6	0
Veras, Enger, D.R.	.600	5	0	3	2	5	0
Vianna, Marcel, Brav.	.818	12	3	6	2	11	1
Villanueva, Bill, Mar.	.950	11	2	17	1	20	2
Wallace, Steven, Roy.	.750	13	0	6	2	8	0
Walsh, Steven, Roy.	1.000	9	0	3	0	3	0
Wamback, Trevor, Exp.	1.000	12	6	1	0	7	0
Weslowski, Brandon, Mets	.960	11	5	19	1	25	0
Wesolowski, David, Mar.	.909	12	4	6	1	11	0
Wheeler, Mike, Ast.	1.000	4	2	0	0	2	0
White, James, Pir.	1.000	12	6	7	0	13	0
Whitecotton, Billy, Ori.	.929	10	2	11	1	14	1
Whiteman, Mike, Tig.*	1.000	12	2	1	0	3	0
Whitfield, Jacob, Twi.*	1.000	7	2	3	0	5	0
Wiggins, Scott, Yan.*	.500	1	0	1	1	2	0
Wilkerson, Byron, Ast.	.818	18	1	8	2	11	0
Wright, Jason, D.R.	1.000	7	1	3	0	4	1
Yarno, Joshua, Ori.	.571	16	0	4	3	7	0

The following players did not have any fielding statistics at the positions indicated or appeared only as a designated hitter, pinch-hitter or pinch-runner: Adam, p; A. Alvarez, of; Araujo, 3b; Backsmeyer, p; Bailey, dh, ph; Bazan, p; Betancourt, p; Brito, p; Bullinger, p; Checketts, p; Checo, p; Conway, of; Dito, p; Erwin, p; Gaillard, p; Garff, p; Gorecki, p; Grantham, p; Gross, dh; Guzman, dh; Hardebeck, p; G. Hunter, p; Jacobs, of; Janzen, p; D. Jefferson, dh; R. Jefferson, dh; Lampley, p; Lugo, of, p; Liniak, dh; Marciante, 3b; Medrano, ss; Mejia, 3b; Merloni, 2b; Moses, of; Munoz, dh; Murphy, p; Ochoa, of; Paulino, p; Paz, p; Pelliciotta, c; Carlos G. Perez, p; Perich, p; Player, dh; Pridie, p; Proctor, 2b; A. Ramirez, p; E. Ramirez, of; Reyes, c; Rollins, c; Rosado, of; Sein, 3b; Seo, p; Smetek, p; E. Smith, p; L. Sopkin, p; Sturtze, p; Torres, ss; Tsujita, of; Turnquist, p; Vazquez, of; Velazquez, 2b; V. Walker, dh; Walter, p; Wojciechowski, p.

LEAGUE CHAMPIONS

Year	Team	Pct.	Year	Team	Pct.	Year	Team	Pct.
1964—	Sarasota Braves	.610	1981—	Kansas City-Gold	.688	1991—	Orioles	.593
1965—	Bradenton Astros	.632	1982—	New York AL	.667		Expos∞	.533
1966—	New York AL	.667	1983—	Texas	.645	1992—	Royals∞	.695
1967—	Kansas City	.614		Los Angeles†	.617		Expos	.593
1968—	Oakland	.650	1984—	White Sox	.651	1993—	Rangers▲	.667
1969—	Montreal	.585		Rangers†	.571		Astros	.593
1970—	Chicago AL	.600	1985—	Yankees§	.705	1994—	Royals♦	.797
1971—	Kansas City	.755		Rangers	.532		Astros	.695
1972—	Chicago NL*	.651	1986—	Reds	.548	1995—	Royals■	.649
	Kansas City*	.651		Dodgers†	.541		Tigers	.579
1973—	Texas	.732	1987—	Dodgers†	.683	1996—	Yankees♦	.638
1974—	Chicago NL	.702		Royals	.635		Rangers	.617
1975—	Texas	.774	1988—	Yankees†	.714	1997—	Mets▼	.700
1976—	Texas	.704		Royals	.619		Rangers	.567
1977—	Chicago AL	.731	1989—	Yankees‡	.651	1998—	Marlins	.633
1978—	Texas	.600		Dodgers	.635		Rangers♦	.567
1979—	Houston	.635	1990—	Expos	.635			
1980—	Kansas City-Blue	.635		Dodgers‡	.603			

*Declared co-champions; no playoff. †League divided into Northern and Southern divisions; won one-game playoff for league championship. ‡League divided into Northern and Southern divisions; won best-of-three playoff for league championship. §Yankees declared champion based on winning percentage when one-game play-off against Rangers was rained out. ∞League divided into Northern, Southern and Central divisions; won best-of-three playoff for league championship. ▲League divided into Eastern, Central and Western divisions; won three-team playoff. ♦League divided into Eastern, Northern and Western divisions; won three-team playoff. ■League divided into Eastern, Northern, Northwest and Southwest divisions; won four-team playoff. ▼League divided into Eastern, Western and Northwest divisions; won four-club playoff. (Note—Known as Sarasota Rookie League in 1964 and Florida Rookie League in 1965.)

SUMMER CLASS A Gulf Coast League

PIONEER LEAGUE

LEAGUE OFFICE

President
Jim McCurdy

Address
P.O. Box 2564
Spokane, WA 99220

Phone
509-456-7615

Teams (affiliation)
Billings Mustangs (Reds)
Butte Copper Kings (Angels)
Great Falls Dodgers (Dodgers)
Helena Brewers (Brewers)

Idaho Falls Braves (Padres)
Missoula (Name to be announced)
 (Diamondbacks)
Medicine Hat Blue Jays (Blue Jays)
Ogden Raptors (Brewers)

1998 FINAL STANDINGS
FIRST HALF

NORTH DIVISION

Team	W	L	T	Pct.	GB
Great Falls (Dodgers)	24	12	0	.667	....
Medicine Hat (Blue Jays)	21	16	0	.568	3.5
Lethbridge (Diamondbacks)	16	20	0	.444	8.0
Helena (Brewers)	12	25	0	.324	12.5

SOUTH DIVISION

Team	W	L	T	Pct.	GB
Ogden (Brewers)	22	15	0	.611	....
Billings (Reds)	22	15	0	.595	....
Idaho Falls (Padres)	19	18	0	.514	3.0
Butte (Angels)	11	26	0	.297	11.0

SECOND HALF

NORTH DIVISION

Team	W	L	T	Pct.	GB
Lethbridge (Diamondbacks)	27	12	0	.692	....
Medicine Hat (Blue Jays)	25	12	0	.676	1.0
Great Falls (Dodgers)	16	23	0	.410	11.0
Helena (Brewers)	9	30	0	.231	18.0

SOUTH DIVISION

Team	W	L	T	Pct.	GB
Idaho Falls (Padres)	28	11	0	.718	....
Billings (Reds)	18	19	0	.486	9.0
Ogden (Brewers)	16	23	0	.410	12.0
Butte (Angels)	15	24	0	.385	13.0

COMPOSITE

Team	M.H.	I.F.	Leth.	Bil.	G.F.	Ogd.	But.	Hel.	W	L	T	Pct.	GB
Medicine Hat (Blue Jays)	....	5	7	4	7	5	4	14	46	28	0	.622	....
Idaho Falls (Padres)	3	....	5	7	5	12	10	5	47	29	0	.618	....
Lethbridge (Diamondbacks)	7	3	....	4	7	5	5	12	43	32	0	.573	3.5
Billings (Reds)	2	6	4	....	5	6	11	6	40	34	0	.541	6.0
Great Falls (Dodgers)	8	3	7	3	....	4	6	9	40	35	0	.533	6.5
Ogden (Brewers)	3	6	3	7	4	....	10	5	38	38	0	.500	9.0
Butte (Angels)	4	3	3	7	2	3	....	4	26	50	0	.342	21.0
Helena (Brewers)	1	3	3	2	5	3	4	....	21	55	0	.276	26.0

Major league affiliations in parentheses.

PLAYOFFS: Idaho Falls defeated Ogden two games to none; Lethbridge defeated Great Falls two games to one; Idaho Falls defeated Lethbridge two games to one to win league championship.

REGULAR-SEASON ATTENDANCE: Butte, 26,061; Billings, 95,533; Great Falls, 74,369; Helena, 36,516; Idaho Falls, 62,087; Lethbridge, 40,998; Medicine Hat, 34,631; Ogden, 99,443. Total—469,638. Playoffs (8 games)—6,872.

MANAGERS: Billings, Russ Nixon; Butte, Bill Lachemann; Great Falls, Dino Ebel; Helena, Tom Houk; Idaho Falls, Don Werner; Lethbridge, Joe Almaraz; Medicine Hat, Rolando Pino; Ogden, Ed Sedar.

ALL-STAR TEAM: 1B—Clint Vaughn, Billings; 2B—Jimmy Gonzalez, Great Falls; 3B—Alex Pelaez, Idaho Falls; SS—Jorge Nunez, Medicine Hat; OF—Jack Cust, Lethbridge; Elpidio Guzman, Butte; Jorge Piedra, Great Falls; C—John Hernandez, Great Falls; DH—Jay Gibbons, Medicine Hat; RHP—Scott Cassidy, Medicine Hat; LHP—Nial Hughes, Great Falls; RP—Dan Mathews, Ogden; Most Valuable Player—Jay Gibbons, Medicine Hat; Manager of the Year—Rolando Pino, Medicine Hat.

1998 BATTING
TEAM

Team	Avg.	G	TPA	AB	R	H	TB	2B	3B	HR	RBI	SH	SF	HP	BB	IBB	SO	SB	CS	GDP	LOB	ShO	Slg.	OBP
Idaho Falls	.304	76	3156	2653	578	807	1225	178	24	64	512	13	29	59	402	3	640	107	50	54	627	2	.462	.403
Medicine Hat	.286	74	2981	2571	508	735	1075	147	20	51	452	16	27	49	318	2	456	111	31	39	571	3	.418	.372
Ogden	.283	76	3025	2606	494	738	1032	140	14	42	401	39	17	40	323	1	519	102	45	47	575	3	.396	.369
Great Falls	.281	75	2958	2604	437	733	1072	150	27	45	368	32	23	32	267	5	485	88	38	55	558	1	.412	.353
Billings	.279	74	2955	2512	484	701	1108	147	13	78	433	19	25	66	333	3	594	25	24	76	561	2	.441	.375
Lethbridge	.275	75	2948	2505	489	689	1048	124	26	61	409	18	33	8	383	8	540	120	53	57	556	1	.418	.376
Butte	.269	76	3072	2550	480	686	1003	124	29	45	405	21	29	42	430	6	528	87	25	66	635	2	.393	.380
Helena	.260	76	2916	2557	381	664	952	142	7	44	309	15	20	44	280	3	602	93	35	74	547	4	.372	.341

TOP QUALIFIERS FOR BATTING CHAMPIONSHIP

Minimum 205 plate appearances. *Lefthanded batter. †Switch-hitter.

Player, Team	Avg.	G	TPA	AB	R	H	TB	2B	3B	HR	RBI	SH	SF	HP	BB	IBB	SO	SB	CS	GDP	Slg.	OBP
Gibbons, Jay, M.H.*	.397	73	339	290	66	115	203	29	1	19	98	0	9	3	37	1	25	2	1	7	.700	.457
Piedra, Jorge, G.F.*	.383	72	325	282	72	108	150	22	7	2	33	3	0	1	39	3	29	16	7	4	.532	.460
Pickler, Jeff, Og.*	.364	71	327	280	55	102	136	22	0	4	49	4	2	2	39	0	25	20	8	4	.486	.443
Cust, Jack, Leth.*	.345	73	315	223	75	77	134	20	2	11	56	0	2	4	86	3	71	15	8	3	.601	.530
Loggins, Joshua, I.F.	.341	71	339	299	66	102	156	20	5	8	64	1	2	2	35	0	60	8	8	7	.522	.411
Pelaez, Alex, I.F.	.340	63	294	262	52	89	132	17	1	8	51	0	2	1	29	0	32	3	1	10	.504	.405
Guzman, Elpidio, But.*	.331	69	327	299	70	99	152	16	5	9	61	1	1	2	24	2	44	40	9	8	.508	.383
Garcia, Alex, I.F.	.320	50	217	178	49	57	87	16	1	4	32	1	0	0	38	0	43	0	1	5	.489	.440
Nunez, Jorge, M.H.	.319	74	347	317	74	101	150	9	11	6	52	1	0	1	28	0	45	31	2	3	.473	.376
Dunaway, Jason, I.F.	.316	67	327	272	54	86	114	16	3	2	47	1	5	11	38	0	55	20	10	3	.419	.414
Stegall, Randy, Bil.	.316	66	302	269	46	85	121	19	1	5	40	6	2	5	20	0	44	2	1	15	.450	.372
Encarnacion, Bienvenido, But.†	.313	69	325	291	46	91	120	10	2	5	44	2	2	3	27	0	40	13	6	5	.412	.375
Candela, Frank, Og.	.311	67	312	257	72	80	89	9	0	0	20	8	2	6	39	0	23	43	10	3	.346	.411
Martinez, Alejandro, Og.†	.311	60	248	222	35	69	98	12	1	5	43	1	3	0	22	0	47	2	2	8	.441	.368
Singletary, Dan, Leth.*	.310	58	254	213	53	66	111	9	6	8	44	0	1	3	37	2	34	15	4	4	.521	.417

DEPARTMENTAL LEADERS: G—Matan, Nunez, Vaughn, 74 each; AB—Nunez, 317; R—Cust, 75; H—Gibbons, 115; TB—Gibbons, 203; 2B—Gibbons, 29; 3B—Nunez, 11; HR—Gibbons, 19; RBI—Gibbons, 98; SH—Collins, 10; SF—Gibbons, 9; HP—C. Miller, 21; BB—Cust, 86; IBB—Cust, Piedra, 3 each; SO—Peters, 100; SB—Candela, 43; CS—Candela, Dunaway, B. Martinez, 10 each; GIDP—Stegall, 15; Slg.—Gibbons, .700; OBP—Cust, .530.

ALL PLAYERS

*Lefthanded batter. †Switch-hitter.

Player, Team	Avg.	G	TPA	AB	R	H	TB	2B	3B	HR	RBI	SH	SF	HP	BB	IBB	SO	SB	CS	GDP	Slg.	OBP
Aalbers, Brady, Bil.	.235	12	37	34	7	8	8	0	0	0	3	1	0	1	1	0	10	1	1	0	.235	.278
Ahlers, Steve, But.	.205	61	256	215	35	44	51	7	0	0	25	3	2	3	33	0	37	6	1	11	.237	.316
Allen, Shane, G.F.	.260	54	190	154	28	40	49	7	1	0	14	1	0	3	32	0	27	8	5	2	.318	.397
Araujo, Orlany, G.F.	.270	61	249	215	37	58	98	18	2	6	45	1	3	5	25	0	35	8	2	9	.456	.355
Arauz, Leobardo, I.F.†	.286	40	166	126	30	36	63	7	1	6	24	0	2	6	32	1	27	3	4	2	.500	.446
Arballo, Carlos, But.*	.000	5	13	10	1	0	0	0	0	0	0	1	0	1	1	0	7	0	0	0	.000	.167
Ayala, Elio, Og.-Hel.	.277	37	132	112	18	31	33	2	0	0	7	3	1	0	16	0	15	1	2	2	.295	.364
Baez, Juan, Hel.	.195	45	148	128	17	25	37	3	0	3	10	3	0	3	13	0	41	5	1	6	.289	.285
Barrett, Andy, M.H.*	.071	8	18	14	1	1	1	0	0	0	0	0	0	0	4	0	4	0	0	0	.071	.278
Bast, Ryan, But.	.222	15	40	36	9	8	14	2	2	0	1	0	0	0	4	0	12	6	0	0	.389	.300
Baston, Stanley, Bil.	.379	12	42	29	8	11	14	1	1	0	5	1	0	1	11	0	7	1	0	1	.483	.561
Beasley, Justin, Leth.	.260	17	59	50	9	13	18	2	0	1	5	1	0	4	4	0	11	0	1	2	.360	.362
Beattie, Andrew, Bil.†	.250	43	168	128	36	32	56	8	2	4	25	1	2	3	34	0	33	3	0	2	.438	.413
Berryman, Brian, I.F.	.000	15	2	1	1	0	0	0	0	0	0	0	0	0	1	0	1	0	0	0	.000	.500
Bordenick, Ryan, Og.	.281	39	156	128	24	36	56	11	0	3	24	1	3	6	18	0	29	0	2	6	.438	.387
Brito, Obispo, Og.	.333	32	124	120	22	40	62	12	2	2	19	1	0	1	2	0	20	5	0	3	.517	.350
Brooks, Jeff, Leth.	.256	68	274	242	33	62	80	10	1	2	38	0	2	5	25	0	52	0	1	5	.331	.336
Campbell, Sean, I.F.*	.291	44	193	165	29	48	80	12	1	6	37	2	3	4	19	1	43	2	4	4	.485	.372
Campusano, Nicholas, Hel.	.261	35	124	115	11	30	40	7	0	1	11	1	1	0	7	0	26	1	0	1	.348	.301
Candela, Frank, Og.	.311	67	312	257	72	80	89	9	0	0	20	8	2	6	39	0	23	43	10	3	.346	.411
Castellano, John, G.F.	.267	35	120	101	10	27	35	5	0	1	16	1	2	1	15	0	12	2	3	2	.347	.361
Ceriani, Matt, Hel.	.226	45	187	155	24	35	48	7	0	2	24	2	1	3	26	0	26	0	2	8	.310	.346
Cintron, Alex, Leth.†	.264	67	285	258	41	68	96	11	4	3	34	3	2	2	20	0	32	8	4	8	.372	.319
Collins, Michael, Og.*	.308	44	171	143	23	44	60	10	3	0	18	10	2	3	13	0	19	4	2	2	.420	.373
Conyer, Darryl, Leth.*	.273	11	29	22	6	6	11	3	1	0	4	0	0	0	7	0	6	2	0	0	.500	.448
Cook, Jon, I.F.	.462	5	18	13	3	6	7	1	0	0	3	0	1	0	4	0	1	0	1	0	.538	.556
Copley, Travis, But.*	.182	3	13	11	3	2	8	0	0	2	7	0	0	0	2	0	1	0	0	0	.727	.308
Corley, Kenny, But.	.300	63	265	213	40	64	98	17	1	5	47	1	6	5	40	2	36	3	2	9	.460	.413
Covington, Kevin, G.F.	.221	40	140	122	26	27	46	4	0	5	15	2	1	0	15	0	39	5	0	2	.377	.304
Cust, Jack, Leth.*	.345	73	315	223	75	77	134	20	2	11	56	0	2	4	86	3	71	15	8	3	.601	.530
Davies, Justin, M.H.*	.269	54	182	145	36	39	43	4	0	0	10	3	0	0	34	0	18	11	4	4	.297	.408
Davis, Jermaine, M.H.	.276	32	102	87	15	24	37	5	1	2	23	0	3	2	10	0	24	2	0	2	.425	.353
Dean, Aaron, G.F.*	.327	44	171	159	22	52	77	15	2	2	24	0	2	2	8	0	30	3	1	4	.484	.363
De La Cruz, Erickson, Og.	.239	54	212	188	29	45	55	8	1	0	23	2	1	2	19	1	25	2	4	4	.293	.314
Dempsey, Nick, G.F.	.295	40	143	129	20	38	57	7	0	4	15	0	1	5	8	0	32	4	2	3	.442	.357
Detienne, Dave, Leth.*	.221	21	77	68	9	15	18	3	0	0	9	2	1	0	6	0	21	7	1	2	.265	.280
Diaz, Angel, But.	.306	50	194	160	38	49	83	10	3	6	33	0	3	3	28	0	36	0	1	6	.519	.412
DiPrima, Giancarlo, Hel.	.284	50	201	176	24	50	59	9	0	0	13	1	0	0	24	0	12	20	6	2	.335	.370
Doucet, Brandon, Hel.	.275	49	197	178	22	49	64	12	0	1	21	0	1	5	13	0	57	7	1	3	.360	.340
Downing, Brad, But.*	.302	70	289	235	38	71	103	15	1	5	42	0	0	4	50	1	55	1	1	5	.438	.433
Downing, Lance, Leth.*	.234	47	175	145	20	34	48	5	3	1	19	1	2	1	26	0	26	4	4	4	.331	.351
Dunaway, Jason, I.F.	.316	67	327	272	54	86	114	16	3	2	47	1	5	11	38	0	55	20	10	3	.419	.414
Dunham, Tray, I.F.*	.278	49	209	176	34	49	64	15	0	0	40	0	3	4	26	0	49	0	0	6	.364	.378
Dunn, Adam, Bil.*	.288	34	151	125	26	36	53	3	1	4	13	0	1	3	22	1	23	4	2	3	.424	.404
Dusan, Joe, I.F.*	.290	61	265	210	50	61	99	12	1	8	50	1	2	2	50	1	66	1	5	4	.471	.428
Eaton, Bill, Og.	.295	35	145	129	28	38	47	6	0	1	14	2	1	3	10	0	20	3	2	1	.364	.357
Encarnacion, Bienvenido, But.†‡	.313	69	325	291	46	91	120	10	2	5	44	2	2	3	27	0	40	13	6	5	.412	.375
Fernandez, Ramon, Og.	.264	56	217	197	35	52	83	11	1	6	35	1	0	1	18	0	60	8	2	0	.421	.329
Figueroa, Eduardo, Hel.*	.283	41	188	152	27	43	67	13	1	3	24	1	3	3	29	1	35	1	2	7	.441	.401
Fleming, Ryan, M.H.*	.306	70	302	255	64	78	106	20	1	2	41	2	4	4	37	0	29	17	3	0	.416	.397
Fox, Brian, Leth.*	.000	1	2	2	0	0	0	0	0	0	0	0	0	0	0	0	1	0	0	0	.000	.000
Fox, Jason, Hel.†	.302	43	198	179	40	54	84	13	1	5	23	2	1	1	15	1	36	21	4	1	.469	.357
French, Ron, I.F.	.239	19	83	67	14	16	26	4	0	2	10	0	4	2	10	0	13	1	0	1	.388	.386
Garcia, Alex, I.F.	.320	50	217	178	49	57	87	16	1	4	32	1	0	0	38	0	43	0	1	5	.489	.440

SUMMER CLASS A Pioneer League

Player, Team	Avg.	G	TPA	AB	R	H	TB	2B	3B	HR	RBI	SH	SF	HP	BB	IBB	SO	SB	CS	GDP	Slg.	OBP
Gibbons, Jay, M.H.*	.397	73	339	290	66	115	203	29	1	19	98	0	9	3	37	1	25	2	1	7	.700	.457
Godfrey, Tim, Bil.†	.318	30	129	110	18	35	45	4	0	2	21	2	1	2	14	0	11	1	1	1	.409	.402
Gomera, Rafael, G.F.	.333	4	13	12	2	4	5	1	0	0	1	0	0	0	1	0	2	0	0	0	.417	.385
Gonzalez, Jimmy, G.F.	.277	69	296	278	43	77	125	17	2	9	61	0	5	2	11	1	32	2	1	7	.450	.304
Guthrie, Kendall, Hel.	.285	49	202	172	25	49	74	13	0	4	22	0	4	3	23	1	50	1	0	4	.430	.371
Guzman, Alexis, M.H.†	.179	36	94	84	11	15	15	0	0	0	3	3	0	1	6	0	21	1	0	2	.179	.242
Guzman, Antonio, Leth.	.276	35	141	127	25	35	61	6	1	6	26	0	0	1	13	0	24	11	2	5	.480	.348
Guzman, Elpidio, But.*	.331	69	327	299	70	99	152	16	5	9	61	1	1	2	24	2	44	40	9	8	.508	.383
Guzman, Julio, Leth.	.258	36	112	93	16	24	37	4	0	3	17	1	3	0	15	0	35	1	2	2	.398	.351
Hall, William, Hel.	.176	29	96	85	11	15	18	3	0	0	5	1	0	1	9	0	27	5	5	2	.212	.263
Hammock, Robert, Leth.	.286	62	259	227	46	65	113	14	2	10	56	0	2	2	28	1	34	5	4	3	.498	.367
Hammond, Derry, Hel.	.216	62	254	232	31	50	104	13	1	13	45	0	3	7	12	0	98	4	3	5	.448	.272
Hazen, Mike, I.F.	.307	61	254	202	57	62	97	14	3	5	30	1	2	13	36	0	50	8	4	1	.480	.439
Hemmings, Scot, I.F.	.275	49	200	171	28	47	71	13	1	3	35	1	3	2	23	0	66	19	2	1	.415	.362
Hernandez, John, G.F.	.286	40	146	133	21	38	54	7	0	3	15	1	1	5	6	0	23	3	0	1	.406	.338
Hubbel, Travis, M.H.	.297	16	47	37	5	11	14	1	1	0	5	0	0	0	10	0	10	1	0	0	.378	.447
Hudson, Orlando, M.H.†	.293	65	273	242	50	71	115	18	1	8	42	0	2	7	22	0	36	6	5	3	.475	.366
Jaramillo, Lee, Hel.	.269	50	192	167	28	45	69	16	1	2	22	0	2	0	23	0	32	2	1	6	.413	.354
Jaramillo, Milko, G.F.†	.277	63	270	249	30	69	93	10	1	4	29	5	2	0	14	0	44	7	6	4	.373	.313
Jones, Travis, I.F.*	.000	31	1	1	0	0	0	0	0	0	0	0	0	0	0	0	0	0	0	0	.000	.000
Joseph, Adolfo, Leth.	.186	22	76	70	10	13	20	2	1	1	9	0	0	1	5	0	24	1	1	3	.286	.250
Juarez, Jonny, M.H.*	.296	39	150	142	17	42	54	7	1	1	22	0	0	3	5	0	12	6	1	1	.380	.333
Kearns, Austin, Bil.	.315	30	134	108	17	34	46	9	0	1	14	0	2	1	23	0	22	1	1	4	.426	.433
Kluver, Hayden, G.F.*	.250	22	70	64	15	16	17	1	0	0	10	1	0	0	5	0	10	3	1	1	.266	.304
Kremblas, Mike, M.H.	.293	59	236	184	40	54	81	15	0	4	36	1	2	9	40	1	30	5	4	4	.440	.438
Layton, Blane, Bil.*	.294	59	259	221	56	65	114	20	4	7	39	3	1	1	33	0	45	3	3	6	.516	.387
Logan, Matt, M.H.*	.266	47	201	173	29	46	69	12	1	3	30	0	1	4	23	0	41	1	1	5	.399	.363
Loggins, Joshua, I.F.	.341	71	339	299	66	102	156	20	5	8	64	1	2	2	35	0	60	8	8	7	.522	.411
Lombardi, Dominick, But.	.219	43	143	96	19	21	24	0	0	1	10	5	1	4	37	0	18	0	0	3	.250	.449
Mackiewitz, Richard, Og.*	.295	65	289	251	45	74	97	15	1	2	45	2	3	6	27	0	37	3	2	4	.386	.373
Markray, Thad, Bil.	.235	70	291	251	43	59	76	11	0	2	31	0	3	4	33	0	64	1	2	8	.303	.330
Martelli, Tony, M.H.	.192	23	65	52	7	10	11	1	0	0	8	0	1	2	10	0	13	1	3	0	.212	.338
Martinez, Alejandro, Og.†	.311	60	248	222	35	69	98	12	1	5	43	1	3	0	22	0	47	2	2	8	.441	.368
Martinez, Belvani, Leth.	.305	63	277	256	56	78	110	11	3	5	25	2	3	4	12	0	30	30	10	7	.430	.342
Matan, Jim, Bil.	.273	74	340	293	61	80	149	13	1	18	65	0	3	5	39	1	66	0	2	14	.509	.365
McAffee, Josh, Leth.	.179	17	65	56	9	10	17	1	0	2	5	0	0	2	7	0	23	0	0	1	.304	.292
Mendez, Francisco, Leth.*	.233	20	74	60	13	14	25	2	0	3	10	0	0	0	14	1	8	2	1	2	.417	.378
Miller, Corky, Bil.	.271	45	178	129	28	35	58	8	0	5	24	2	2	21	24	0	24	1	4	2	.450	.455
Montenegro, Jose, Og.	.184	48	172	147	22	27	37	7	0	1	14	6	1	1	17	0	36	1	2	4	.252	.271
Moreno, Omar, G.F.†	.218	49	156	119	22	26	31	5	0	0	10	3	1	1	32	0	31	7	2	7	.261	.386
Morrow, Alvin, Og.	.221	52	213	163	35	36	61	8	1	5	26	0	0	0	50	0	65	7	2	3	.374	.404
Neal, Steve, Leth.*	.250	43	178	148	16	37	54	8	0	3	20	0	0	2	28	0	50	5	4	4	.365	.376
Nizov, Alexander, But.	.207	33	100	92	15	19	27	6	1	0	9	1	1	0	6	0	15	5	0	1	.293	.253
Nolasco, Jose, But.	.167	16	42	36	7	6	11	2	0	1	4	1	1	0	4	0	16	0	0	0	.306	.244
Nunez, Jorge, M.H.	.319	74	347	317	74	101	150	9	11	6	52	1	0	1	28	0	45	31	2	3	.473	.376
Owens, Jeremy, I.F.	.278	69	331	284	61	79	127	16	4	8	52	0	3	8	36	0	81	30	7	2	.447	.372
Patten, Chris, Hel.	.282	66	284	241	42	68	80	7	1	1	20	2	0	2	39	0	56	4	3	5	.332	.387
Patterson, Marty, Hel.	.182	11	40	33	5	6	10	1	0	1	4	0	1	1	5	0	15	0	0	0	.303	.300
Peckham, Chris, But.	.229	65	256	205	36	47	82	10	5	5	27	4	2	6	39	0	39	4	1	3	.400	.365
Pelaez, Alex, I.F.	.340	63	294	262	52	89	132	17	1	8	51	0	2	1	29	0	32	3	1	10	.504	.405
Peters, Samone, Bil.	.292	72	297	274	44	80	143	22	1	13	46	0	2	8	13	1	100	0	1	8	.522	.340
Pichardo, Gilbert, But.	.154	24	63	52	9	8	10	2	0	0	8	0	1	3	7	0	21	0	0	1	.192	.286
Pickler, Jeff, Og.*	.364	71	327	280	55	102	136	22	0	4	49	4	2	2	39	0	25	20	8	4	.486	.443
Piedra, Jorge, G.F.*	.383	72	325	282	72	108	150	22	7	2	33	3	0	1	39	3	29	16	7	4	.532	.460
Price, Duane, Bil.	.275	31	120	102	21	28	33	2	0	1	14	3	1	0	14	0	32	2	4	0	.324	.359
Proctor, Jerry, G.F.	.255	30	110	106	12	27	46	0	5	3	19	0	0	2	2	0	31	2	2	0	.434	.282
Riggins, Auntwan, M.H.†	.248	41	170	153	30	38	46	6	1	0	18	3	1	3	10	0	34	16	1	0	.301	.305
Rinne, Jim, Leth.	.221	23	82	68	14	15	18	3	0	0	6	0	0	0	14	1	24	1	2	2	.265	.354
Rivera, Francisco, Bil.*	.375	3	13	8	3	3	3	0	0	0	3	0	0	1	4	0	1	0	0	0	.375	.615
Rodriguez, Miguel, Leth.	.375	5	18	16	3	6	9	0	0	1	2	0	0	0	2	0	4	1	1	0	.563	.444
Rojas, Eliezer, Hel.	.293	38	163	140	22	41	45	4	0	0	8	0	1	11	11	0	22	13	1	7	.321	.387
Ross, Justin, But.*	.309	65	306	220	53	68	92	13	4	1	42	0	4	1	81	1	31	7	2	3	.418	.490
Rowan, Chris, Og.	.221	56	226	195	38	43	94	8	5	11	45	1	0	6	24	0	75	4	1	4	.482	.324
Ruiz, Ramon, G.F.	.200	9	30	25	6	5	5	0	0	0	1	0	1	0	4	0	1	0	1	1	.200	.300
Santonocito, Justin, Leth.*	.231	12	44	39	6	9	15	3	0	1	5	0	1	2	2	0	6	0	0	2	.385	.295
Santos, Jose, But.	.262	37	149	130	26	34	63	9	4	4	21	1	2	1	15	0	41	0	0	2	.485	.338
Santos, Juan, M.H.†	.111	15	37	27	2	3	3	0	0	0	1	1	0	1	8	0	13	0	0	1	.111	.343
Schmidt, Bryan, I.F.	.357	4	17	14	5	5	5	0	0	0	2	0	1	1	1	0	1	4	0	0	.357	.412
Senegal, Terence, Bil.	.308	6	17	13	4	4	4	0	0	0	0	0	0	0	4	0	4	2	0	0	.308	.471
Silletti, Pete, M.H.†	.000	2	1	1	0	0	0	0	0	0	0	0	0	0	0	0	1	0	0	0	.000	.000
Singletary, Dan, Leth.*	.310	58	254	213	53	66	111	9	6	8	44	0	1	3	37	2	34	15	4	4	.521	.417
Smith, Fred, M.H.	.252	66	263	226	44	57	85	11	1	5	36	1	2	8	26	0	62	11	3	2	.376	.347
Soto, Luis, I.F.	.273	6	24	22	4	6	6	0	0	0	2	0	0	0	2	0	6	0	0	3	.273	.333
Stegall, Randy, Bil.	.316	66	302	269	46	85	121	19	1	5	40	6	2	5	20	0	44	2	1	15	.450	.372
Stinson, Kevin, Og.	.264	26	105	91	12	24	31	4	0	1	16	0	0	3	11	0	18	0	4	0	.341	.362
Taylor, Corey, Bil.	.200	3	11	10	2	2	4	2	0	0	1	0	0	1	0	0	1	0	0	0	.400	.273
Tena, Luis, But.	.194	14	45	36	7	7	8	1	0	0	1	0	1	0	8	0	15	0	0	1	.222	.341
Thomas, Charles, G.F.	.200	39	131	110	16	22	36	5	3	1	9	1	0	1	19	0	34	3	2	3	.327	.323
Tomaszewski, Dane, G.F.	.296	43	150	135	23	40	70	13	1	5	24	1	1	1	12	1	34	3	1	1	.519	.356
Toomey, Chris, Bil.	.000	3	7	3	1	0	0	0	0	0	0	0	0	2	2	0	2	0	0	0	.000	.571
Tucent, Francisco, Og.†	.305	50	189	164	30	50	63	6	2	1	23	7	0	3	15	0	30	4	3	1	.384	.374
Vaughn, Clint, Bil.	.266	74	324	289	46	77	135	18	2	12	61	0	3	6	26	0	70	2	1	12	.467	.336

Player, Team	Avg.	G	TPA	AB	R	H	TB	2B	3B	HR	RBI	SH	SF	HP	BB	IBB	SO	SB	CS	GDP	Slg.	OBP
Ventura, Henry, M.H.	.214	33	110	103	13	22	33	8	0	1	18	1	1	0	5	0	30	0	1	4	.320	.248
Verdugo, Orlando, I.F.	.000	19	1	1	0	0	0	0	0	0	0	0	0	0	0	0	0	0	0	0	.000	.000
Wade, Bryn, But.	.202	26	102	89	11	18	25	2	1	1	15	0	2	0	11	0	30	0	1	5	.281	.284
Wallis, Jacob, Bil.	.238	32	122	105	14	25	38	7	0	2	20	0	2	2	13	0	29	1	1	2	.362	.328
Warren, Tom, Hel.†	.300	4	13	10	1	3	3	0	0	0	1	0	0	0	3	0	4	0	0	1	.300	.462
Wayne, Tyrone, Hel.	.303	54	217	208	29	63	96	13	1	6	40	1	1	1	6	0	37	7	4	6	.462	.324
Weeks, Paul, I.F.	.289	33	132	114	22	33	56	9	1	4	20	4	0	1	13	0	30	1	1	2	.491	.367
Weichard, Paul, Leth.†	.293	54	227	188	37	55	69	10	2	0	28	1	0	0	38	0	45	19	4	0	.367	.412
West, George, Hel.	.196	47	171	148	16	29	44	7	1	2	14	1	1	3	18	0	22	1	1	8	.297	.294
Wickersham, Jack, I.F.	.333	19	83	75	19	25	35	6	2	0	13	1	0	0	7	0	16	7	2	3	.467	.390
Wilson, Keith, Leth.	1.000	2	2	2	1	2	2	0	0	0	0	0	0	0	0	0	0	0	0	0	1.000	1.000
Yount, Jason, But.	.237	40	157	135	20	32	40	2	0	2	16	0	1	6	15	0	35	2	1	3	.296	.338
Zeber, Ryan, M.H.	.205	14	44	39	4	8	9	1	0	0	9	0	1	1	3	0	8	0	2	2	.231	.273

GRAND SLAMS: Cust, 3; Vaughn, 2; Beattie, Campbell, L. Downing, Hudson, J. Gonzalez, Mackiewitz, Morrow, Peckham, F. Smith, Weeks, 1 each.
AWARDED FIRST BASE ON CATCHER'S INTERFERENCE: Baez (Dunham).

PLAYERS WITH TWO OR MORE TEAMS

Player, Team	Avg.	G	TPA	AB	R	H	TB	2B	3B	HR	RBI	SH	SF	HP	BB	IBB	SO	SB	CS	GDP	Slg.	OBP
Ayala, Elio, Og.	.297	28	90	74	12	22	23	1	0	0	5	3	1	0	12	0	9	0	1	2	.311	.391
Ayala, Elio, Hel.	.237	9	42	38	6	9	10	1	0	0	2	0	0	0	4	0	6	1	1	0	.263	.310

1998 PITCHING

TEAM

Team	W	L	Pct.	ERA	G	CG	ShO	Sv.	IP	H	TBF	R	ER	HR	SH	SF	HB	BB	IBB	SO	WP	Bk.
Medicine Hat	46	28	.622	4.36	74	3	2	19	642.0	662	2825	407	311	57	13	20	37	236	0	527	53	17
Lethbridge	43	32	.573	4.59	75	2	4	12	639.2	661	2890	421	326	41	24	21	49	305	1	491	60	13
Great Falls	40	35	.533	4.59	75	2	2	11	656.1	647	2957	420	335	43	29	21	44	350	9	574	94	11
Idaho Falls	47	29	.618	4.79	76	3	3	20	659.0	695	3069	457	351	46	27	22	31	389	8	602	90	13
Billings	40	34	.541	4.90	74	1	3	17	639.0	691	2940	429	348	36	26	28	38	352	5	564	58	13
Ogden	38	38	.500	5.36	76	2	2	24	651.2	703	2989	473	388	62	15	23	60	354	3	541	72	17
Helena	21	55	.276	6.51	76	2	2	10	648.1	819	3153	591	469	66	12	25	45	398	3	531	80	15
Butte	26	50	.342	7.55	76	5	0	10	641.0	875	3189	653	538	79	18	28	61	352	2	534	69	6

INDIVIDUAL

TOP QUALIFIERS FOR EARNED-RUN AVERAGE TITLE
Minimum 61 innings. *Lefthanded pitcher.

Pitcher, Team	W	L	Pct.	ERA	G	GS	CG	ShO	GF	Sv.	IP	H	TBF	R	ER	HR	SH	SF	HB	BB	IBB	SO	WP	Bk.
Lynch, Pat, M.H.	7	3	.700	2.32	14	14	3	1	0	0	89.1	71	351	33	23	6	1	2	4	16	0	77	2	2
Cassidy, Scott, M.H.	8	1	.889	2.43	15	14	0	0	0	0	81.1	71	325	31	22	4	2	3	5	14	0	82	2	0
Madritsch, Robert, Bil. *	7	3	.700	2.80	14	13	0	0	0	0	80.1	72	341	30	25	3	3	2	1	35	1	87	2	1
Parker, Beau, G.F.	4	2	.667	3.08	16	11	0	0	4	0	73.0	67	312	35	25	2	6	1	6	32	2	72	11	1
Callier, Jeremy, But.	3	9	.250	3.54	19	11	2	0	1	0	101.2	102	433	51	40	7	1	2	8	26	0	78	3	2
Hughes, Nial, G.F. *	8	1	.889	4.05	16	8	0	0	3	0	66.2	64	293	36	30	4	1	3	2	29	1	44	9	0
Sanchez, Simon, Leth.	5	3	.625	4.11	13	13	0	0	0	0	61.1	72	274	39	28	2	2	1	3	25	0	37	6	0
Bido, Jose, Leth.	4	6	.400	4.14	18	7	1	1	0	0	63.0	64	277	38	29	7	2	1	3	19	0	48	6	4
Bauer, Ryan, I.F.	7	2	.778	4.54	17	12	1	0	0	0	77.1	91	341	43	39	10	5	2	1	20	0	62	5	2
Berryman, Brian, I.F.	4	3	.571	4.61	15	14	0	0	0	0	68.1	78	308	48	35	2	2	1	0	33	0	38	9	1
Miller, Jim, Og.	7	5	.583	4.63	15	15	3	1	0	0	101.0	105	441	57	52	10	1	6	12	32	0	75	6	1
Eye, Jake, Og.	3	4	.429	4.65	15	14	0	0	0	0	79.1	75	351	49	41	7	4	3	5	40	0	64	7	0
Kohl, Doug, Leth.	2	1	.667	4.66	13	13	1	0	0	0	63.2	75	289	42	33	5	3	1	5	27	0	43	3	1
Castillo, Wilson, Og.	3	4	.429	4.76	16	10	0	0	4	1	62.1	57	272	37	33	5	2	1	4	37	0	47	10	0
Johnson, Jim, Og. *	5	6	.455	4.87	13	13	0	0	0	0	68.1	75	305	51	37	10	0	2	0	27	0	77	11	1

DEPARTMENTAL LEADERS: W—Cassidy, Hughes, 8 each; L—Callier, L. Martinez, 9 each; Pct.—Cassidy, Hughes, .889; G—T. Jones, 31; GS—Ozuna, 16; CG—Lynch, J. Miller, Salter, 3 each; ShO—Several players tied at 1; GF—File, 26; Sv.—File, Mathews, 16 each; IP—Callier, 101.2; H—J. Miller, 105; TBF—J. Miller, 441; R—Montero, 81; ER—Montero, 67; HR—Montero, 12; SH—Hebert, 7; SF—Russo, 7; HB—J. Miller, 12; BB—Howard, 87; IBB—Verdugo, 3; SO—Madritsch, 87; WP—Howard, 17; BK—Howard, 6.

ALL PITCHERS
*Lefthanded pitcher.

Pitcher, Team	W	L	Pct.	ERA	G	GS	CG	ShO	GF	Sv.	IP	H	TBF	R	ER	HR	SH	SF	HB	BB	IBB	SO	WP	Bk.
Abeyta, Scott, Leth. *	2	1	.667	4.54	24	0	0	0	20	3	35.2	43	167	24	18	3	0	1	3	15	1	38	4	0
Alejo, Nigel, Og.	3	1	.750	6.00	6	3	0	0	0	0	24.0	32	121	18	16	2	1	1	4	14	0	23	3	1
Anderson, Jason, But.	1	1	.500	7.76	23	0	0	0	7	0	29.0	30	149	27	25	2	3	2	3	27	1	33	8	0
Arcangel, Arsenio, Hel.	1	2	.333	8.84	26	0	0	0	8	0	37.2	53	186	39	37	6	0	1	4	17	0	30	9	0
Aronson, Christopher, But.	2	1	.667	10.80	8	0	0	0	1	0	10.0	18	56	21	12	2	1	0	5	4	0	9	1	0
Arroyo, Joel, Og.	1	2	.333	9.38	13	0	0	0	4	0	24.0	31	126	32	25	3	0	1	7	24	0	9	7	0
Baez, Juan, Hel.	0	1	.000	15.00	4	0	0	0	3	0	3.0	4	19	5	5	0	1	0	1	4	0	1	1	0
Barndollar, Jeff, Leth.	0	0	.000	8.18	6	1	0	0	0	0	11.0	15	63	13	10	0	1	3	1	10	0	4	4	2
Barton, Christopher, Hel.	4	8	.333	6.75	14	14	1	0	0	0	74.2	104	359	64	56	4	0	2	9	33	0	59	11	1
Bauer, Ryan, I.F.	7	2	.778	4.54	17	12	1	0	0	0	77.1	91	341	43	39	10	5	2	1	20	0	62	5	2
Bell, Casey, I.F.	2	3	.400	5.56	7	7	0	0	0	0	34.0	41	174	38	21	2	4	0	3	22	0	25	3	0
Berryman, Brian, I.F.	4	3	.571	4.61	15	14	0	0	0	0	68.1	78	308	48	35	2	2	1	0	33	0	38	9	1
Berryman, Chad, But.	0	4	.000	12.10	10	8	0	0	1	0	38.2	85	217	63	52	7	2	3	3	15	0	24	3	0
Bido, Jose, Leth.	4	6	.400	4.14	18	7	1	1	0	0	63.0	64	277	38	29	7	2	1	3	19	0	48	6	4
Birdsong, Tim, Bil.	4	1	.800	1.18	19	1	0	0	9	3	38.0	39	162	13	5	0	1	1	0	17	1	38	0	1
Brooks, Jacob, But.	2	7	.222	7.08	28	3	0	0	14	4	54.2	64	274	53	43	7	1	1	5	39	0	63	8	0
Brown, Zadrian, Bil.	0	3	.000	6.94	16	0	0	0	8	0	23.1	37	119	18	18	2	0	0	2	12	0	25	1	0

SUMMER CLASS A Pioneer League

Pitcher, Team	W	L	Pct.	ERA	G	GS	CG	ShO	GF	Sv.	IP	H	TBF	R	ER	HR	SH	SF	HB	BB	IBB	SO	WP	Bk.
Burgos, Ricardo, G.F.	4	4	.500	3.38	14	6	1	1	6	1	58.2	65	248	25	22	2	3	1	2	7	0	25	3	1
Caceres, Antonio, M.H.	6	4	.600	3.81	21	4	0	0	6	0	59.0	65	257	37	25	3	1	2	3	19	0	30	1	2
Callier, Jeremy, But.	3	9	.250	3.54	19	11	2	0	1	0	101.2	102	433	51	40	7	1	2	8	26	0	78	3	2
Campusano, Nicholas, Hel.	0	0	.000	18.00	1	0	0	0	1	0	1.0	2	6	2	2	0	0	1	0	1	0	1	0	0
Cassidy, Scott, M.H.	8	1	.889	2.43	15	14	0	0	0	0	81.1	71	325	31	22	4	2	3	5	14	0	82	2	0
Castillo, Wilson, G.F.	3	4	.429	4.76	16	10	0	0	4	1	62.1	57	272	37	33	5	2	1	4	37	0	47	10	0
Cavanagh, Andy, Hel.	3	1	.750	3.63	11	10	0	0	0	0	57.0	64	246	32	23	2	0	1	1	24	0	39	3	1
Childers, Matt, Hel.	1	0	1.000	0.64	2	2	1	1	0	0	14.0	9	53	1	1	0	0	0	0	4	1	4	0	0
Coffey, Todd, Bil.	0	0	.000	3.00	3	2	0	0	1	0	12.0	13	48	4	4	1	2	0	2	1	0	8	0	0
Condrey, Clay, I.F.	2	1	.667	2.55	18	0	0	0	17	5	24.2	31	111	12	7	2	1	1	1	4	0	19	3	0
Connell, Brian, Hel. *	1	1	.500	3.06	11	0	0	0	1	0	17.2	15	82	11	6	0	1	0	1	15	0	14	2	0
Cooper, Eric, Bil.	7	2	.778	4.37	22	3	0	0	14	5	47.1	49	203	30	23	2	0	2	2	20	0	48	7	0
Curtis, Mark, M.H. *	6	6	.500	5.94	15	15	0	0	0	0	72.2	79	335	59	48	7	0	2	4	47	0	49	7	1
Darr, Jerry, I.F.	0	0	.000	21.60	2	2	0	0	0	0	5.0	10	34	12	12	2	1	0	2	9	0	1	0	0
Davis, Phil, Leth.	2	2	.500	6.81	20	0	0	0	7	1	35.2	31	174	31	27	2	4	2	6	31	0	36	5	0
Dehart, Casey, Hel. *	3	1	.750	5.79	15	0	0	0	4	3	23.1	26	117	20	15	0	2	1	1	22	1	18	3	1
Dempsey, Nick, G.F.	0	0	.000	9.00	1	0	0	0	1	0	1.0	2	5	1	1	1	0	0	0	0	0	3	0	0
Diaz, Antonio, I.F.	1	1	.500	2.70	14	0	0	0	11	4	20.0	20	84	7	6	1	0	0	2	4	0	16	3	1
Dobson, Mark, I.F.	5	2	.714	2.72	21	1	0	0	4	2	56.1	42	242	25	17	4	2	2	1	31	0	63	7	1
Dotel, Melido, G.F.	4	2	.667	3.88	23	4	0	0	12	0	51.0	41	240	34	22	1	2	6	40	0	63	11	1
Dowell, Brian, I.F.	0	2	.000	13.81	11	0	0	0	3	0	14.1	25	82	26	22	3	0	1	1	14	1	12	4	0
Easton, Eric, But.	0	0	.000	9.27	14	0	0	0	2	0	22.1	42	127	28	23	2	1	0	2	20	0	16	0	0
Elias, Javier, But.	0	0	.000	18.56	4	0	0	0	0	0	5.1	13	30	11	11	2	0	0	1	0	4	0	0
Espinal, Orlando, M.H.	1	5	.167	8.44	7	6	0	0	1	0	26.2	36	129	28	25	8	1	1	6	9	0	30	5	0
Eye, Jake, Og.	3	4	.429	4.65	15	14	0	0	0	0	79.1	75	351	49	41	7	4	3	5	44	0	64	7	0
Figueroa, Claudio, But.	0	0	.000	9.00	7	0	0	0	5	0	11.0	21	59	13	11	2	0	1	0	5	0	7	1	0
Fikac, Jeremy, I.F.	2	0	1.000	2.25	12	0	0	0	6	1	20.0	11	82	5	5	0	0	1	1	8	1	19	1	0
File, Robert, M.H.	2	1	.667	1.41	28	0	0	0	26	16	32.0	24	124	7	5	1	1	2	2	5	0	28	1	0
Forbes, Keith, I.F.	3	0	1.000	5.02	21	0	0	0	6	1	37.2	33	182	27	21	1	2	0	38	2	40	9	0
Fuller, Jody, Leth.	5	1	.833	3.95	18	7	0	0	5	0	54.2	45	225	26	24	5	2	0	2	24	0	41	3	0
Gaud, Perfecto, M.H. *	0	1	.000	4.91	17	0	0	0	9	0	18.1	19	99	16	10	0	1	1	19	0	15	3	0
Geitz, Scott, Og.	1	2	.333	2.98	20	0	0	0	13	2	45.1	38	192	19	15	3	1	1	7	21	1	33	6	1
Giambalvo, Paul, Leth.	5	1	.833	2.48	22	0	0	0	13	2	36.1	28	151	14	10	2	1	0	1	12	0	41	3	2
Gold, J.M., Og.	1	0	1.000	2.61	5	5	0	0	0	0	20.2	21	91	13	6	1	0	1	1	7	0	15	2	1
Gonzalez, Francisco, I.F.	1	1	.500	2.57	5	1	0	0	1	0	7.0	5	31	7	2	1	0	0	0	4	0	3	2	0
Greeny, Burdette, Hel.	1	2	.333	8.36	24	3	0	0	10	0	37.2	67	195	44	35	6	2	0	1	21	0	22	4	3
Guzman, Antonio, Leth.	0	0	.000	9.00	1	0	0	0	0	0	1.0	1	6	1	1	1	0	0	1	0	0	0	0
Guzman, Jonathan, Hel. *	0	0	.000	0.00	2	0	0	0	1	0	3.0	2	12	0	0	0	0	1	1	0	1	0	0
Guzman, Julio, Leth.	0	0	.000	81.00	1	0	0	0	0	0	0.1	1	4	3	3	0	0	0	2	0	1	0	0
Hall, Josh, Bil.	5	4	.556	5.00	14	14	1	0	0	0	81.0	89	363	53	45	6	2	2	4	33	0	50	14	2
Harraid, Jon, Og.	1	3	.250	7.80	19	0	0	0	9	4	30.0	41	158	30	26	1	1	0	4	23	1	24	3	2
Harris, John, But.	1	0	1.000	8.16	16	0	0	0	8	0	28.2	35	132	27	26	7	1	4	3	9	0	22	1	0
Harris, Julian, But. *	2	7	.222	7.69	16	13	0	0	0	0	62.0	77	314	61	53	6	2	3	57	0	39	11	0
Hart, Damien, Bil. *	1	0	1.000	3.00	1	0	0	0	0	0	3.0	4	13	1	1	0	1	0	1	0	0	4	0	0
Hawkins, Ryan, I.F.	2	0	1.000	6.39	7	6	0	0	0	0	25.1	35	135	23	18	0	2	3	1	20	0	16	5	0
Hebert, Cedric, G.F.	6	1	.857	2.55	11	7	0	0	2	1	53.0	40	217	20	15	2	7	2	2	21	1	51	2	1
Herrera, Misael, I.F.	0	1	.000	8.20	11	2	0	0	0	0	26.1	31	138	28	24	2	1	1	4	23	1	25	3	0
Howard, Ben, I.F.	4	5	.444	6.03	15	15	0	0	0	0	68.2	67	354	61	46	2	4	1	4	87	0	79	17	6
Hughes, Nial, G.F. *	8	1	.889	4.05	16	8	0	0	3	0	66.2	64	293	36	30	4	1	3	2	29	1	44	9	0
Hurtado, Ed, But.	2	3	.400	9.73	27	0	0	0	19	6	28.2	41	157	40	31	3	4	1	4	24	0	24	4	1
Hussman, Darrell, Bil.	0	1	.000	8.36	5	3	0	0	1	1	14.0	12	65	15	13	0	0	2	9	0	17	2	0
Huxhold, Adam, M.H. *	0	0	.000	5.40	3	0	0	0	0	0	5.0	4	24	4	3	2	1	0	0	3	0	3	0	0
Isenia, Derrick, G.F.	2	5	.286	6.24	15	9	0	0	4	0	57.2	64	278	58	40	5	3	1	5	33	1	47	7	2
Iwasaki, Junichi, Bil. *	0	0	.000	6.91	9	0	0	0	2	0	14.1	21	76	11	11	2	0	2	1	13	0	11	0	0
Johnson, Jim, Og. *	5	6	.455	4.87	13	13	0	0	0	0	68.1	75	305	51	37	10	0	2	0	27	0	77	11	1
Jones, Fontella, Hel.	3	0	1.000	4.05	23	0	0	0	13	4	40.0	38	172	20	18	3	1	1	0	17	1	50	2	0
Jones, Travis, I.F. *	3	3	.500	3.99	31	0	0	0	8	2	56.1	52	246	29	25	5	0	3	5	21	0	67	9	1
Joseph, Glen, Bil.	0	1	.000	13.50	2	1	0	0	0	0	4.0	3	23	6	6	2	0	0	1	7	0	3	1	0
Kees, Justin, Leth.	5	3	.625	4.32	17	10	0	0	3	0	50.0	45	239	33	24	3	4	2	8	41	0	46	5	0
Kohl, Doug, Leth.	2	1	.667	4.66	13	13	1	0	0	0	63.2	72	289	42	33	5	3	1	5	27	0	43	3	1
Koplove, Mike, Leth.	1	2	.333	3.54	12	1	0	0	4	2	28.0	23	114	12	11	2	0	1	4	3	0	22	0	0
Koronka, John, Bil. *	3	0	1.000	8.04	12	3	0	0	3	0	31.1	47	177	43	28	2	1	3	26	0	36	4	1
Kramer, Aaron, I.F.	4	0	1.000	2.23	6	6	0	0	0	0	36.1	30	152	14	9	0	1	2	1	10	0	22	1	0
Krawczyk, Jack, Hel.	0	1	.000	4.32	7	0	0	0	7	0	8.1	10	41	7	4	1	0	1	0	3	1	11	0	0
Larman, Jayson, Bil.	0	2	.000	4.85	5	1	0	0	1	0	13.0	18	66	9	7	0	1	1	1	5	0	21	0	0
Lawrence, Brian, I.F.	3	0	1.000	2.45	4	4	1	0	0	0	22.0	22	92	7	6	1	0	1	2	5	0	21	0	0
Lewis, Rickey, Hel.	3	6	.333	6.95	12	12	0	0	0	0	57.0	72	285	54	44	8	0	3	4	42	0	44	6	2
Luque, Roger, I.F. *	1	0	1.000	5.28	6	1	0	0	2	0	15.1	13	68	9	9	2	1	2	1	12	0	19	5	0
Lynch, Pat, M.H.	7	3	.700	2.32	14	14	3	1	0	0	89.1	71	351	33	23	6	1	2	4	16	0	77	2	2
Mackoul, Greg, Og.	0	1	.000	5.00	7	1	0	0	3	0	9.0	10	48	6	5	0	0	0	2	13	1	13	1	0
Madritsch, Robert, Bil. *	7	3	.700	2.80	14	13	0	0	0	0	80.1	72	341	30	25	3	2	1	35	1	87	2	1
Martinez, Luis, Hel. *	0	9	.000	10.13	17	10	0	0	2	0	48.0	64	275	73	54	5	1	2	5	66	0	47	14	4
Mathews, Dan, Og.	2	2	.500	2.54	24	0	0	0	24	16	28.1	22	114	8	8	2	0	0	3	1	0	30	4	3
Maysonet, Roberto, Og.	3	2	.600	5.70	14	6	0	0	5	0	42.2	47	202	35	27	5	2	4	5	30	0	33	4	3
McCall, Travis, Leth. *	0	1	.000	13.50	1	1	0	0	0	0	2.2	5	17	7	4	1	0	0	2	0	3	0	0
McClain, Kevin, But.	0	2	.000	24.00	8	5	0	0	1	0	12.0	23	78	33	32	5	0	2	4	21	0	12	5	0
McConnell, Gary, Hel.	1	1	.500	10.19	17	1	0	0	3	0	32.2	49	188	49	37	7	0	3	1	35	0	35	7	1
McCutcheon, Mike, Leth. *	5	3	.625	5.43	17	10	0	0	0	0	64.2	66	291	45	39	4	2	1	3	34	0	40	6	3
McEvoy, Casey, Bil.	6	4	.600	4.89	14	14	0	0	0	0	81.0	71	360	57	44	4	3	11	44	0	64	7	0
Mendoza, Hatuey, Leth.	0	1	.000	27.00	1	1	0	0	0	0	0.2	2	8	4	2	0	0	0	0	1	0	1	1	0
Miller, Jim, Og.	7	5	.583	4.63	15	15	3	1	0	0	101.0	105	441	57	52	10	1	6	12	32	0	75	6	1
Miniel, Roberto, Og.	3	2	.600	4.39	16	0	0	0	7	2	41.0	39	181	24	20	2	1	0	2	24	0	39	1	0

Pitcher, Team	W	L	Pct.	ERA	G	GS	CG	ShO	GF	Sv.	IP	H	TBF	R	ER	HR	SH	SF	HB	BB	IBB	SO	WP	Bk.
Minor, Blas, Og.	0	0	.000	4.50	2	2	0	0	0	0	4.0	4	18	2	2	0	0	0	1	1	0	6	1	0
Montanez, Johen, M.H. ...	0	0	.000	7.88	6	0	0	0	1	0	8.0	14	41	7	7	2	0	0	1	2	0	10	2	0
Montero, Oscar, Og.	4	7	.364	8.96	14	12	0	0	0	0	67.1	88	337	81	67	12	1	3	3	49	0	46	15	3
Moody, Jason, G.F. *	1	1	.500	4.67	14	2	0	0	8	2	27.0	25	120	16	14	3	0	1	0	14	1	35	4	0
Moon, Jared, G.F.	1	5	.167	10.74	19	1	0	0	10	2	32.2	54	186	44	39	5	1	1	1	32	1	25	9	0
Mowday, Chris, M.H.	1	0	1.000	10.13	10	0	0	0	3	0	10.2	12	64	15	12	0	0	0	4	15	0	8	7	3
Murray, Steve, M.H. *	4	1	.800	5.71	14	10	0	0	1	0	58.1	77	256	46	37	9	0	1	1	11	0	41	5	2
Myers, Aaron, Og.	2	0	1.000	3.46	4	4	0	0	0	0	26.0	32	114	16	10	2	1	1	1	8	0	8	0	1
Myers, Rob, Hel.	1	5	.167	7.79	21	0	0	0	9	0	34.2	54	191	40	30	3	0	4	6	27	0	25	10	0
Niehaus, Troy, Leth. *	1	1	.500	5.63	19	0	0	0	7	1	38.1	52	185	36	24	2	0	6	3	18	0	23	3	1
Norris, Mac, Og.	1	0	1.000	11.00	4	0	0	0	2	0	9.0	15	50	12	11	0	0	0	1	7	0	8	1	1
Orloski, Joe, M.H.	7	1	.875	3.92	14	10	0	0	1	0	59.2	71	267	37	26	5	1	2	2	18	0	42	6	1
Ozuna, Adrian, But.	3	4	.429	9.30	16	16	0	0	0	0	61.0	94	321	75	63	6	0	3	6	41	1	63	9	0
Padilla, Charly, But.	1	6	.143	7.97	19	6	0	0	3	0	49.2	71	255	60	44	9	1	3	6	23	0	46	8	0
Parker, Beau, G.F.	4	2	.667	3.08	16	11	0	0	4	0	73.0	67	312	33	25	2	6	1	6	32	2	72	11	1
Penney, Mike, Hel.	1	5	.167	7.38	10	10	0	0	0	0	46.1	63	217	47	38	8	1	4	2	20	0	36	4	1
Piedra, Alex, G.F.	0	0	.000	27.00	3	0	0	0	0	0	1.2	1	10	5	5	1	0	0	1	4	0	0	1	0
Pine, Christopher, Og.	0	1	.000	11.25	3	1	0	0	1	0	8.0	9	37	10	10	1	1	0	0	4	0	6	1	0
Poe, Ryan, Hel.	3	3	.500	4.66	14	5	0	0	2	1	46.1	52	202	30	24	3	1	1	3	15	0	43	1	1
Prinz, Bret, Leth.	4	2	.667	3.09	11	0	0	0	6	0	46.2	49	204	26	16	2	1	0	3	13	0	30	8	0
Regalado, Maximo, G.F. ...	0	0	.000	0.00	3	0	0	0	2	0	5.2	2	21	0	0	0	0	1	0	1	0	5	0	0
Renwick, Tyler, M.H.	1	1	.500	21.38	9	0	0	0	3	0	8.0	10	57	20	19	2	0	2	2	20	1	7	2	1
Rijo, Fernando, G.F.	3	1	.750	4.32	14	6	0	0	3	0	50.0	44	229	34	24	3	4	3	4	35	1	42	6	0
Runk, Dave, Bil.	0	0	.000	7.50	5	0	0	0	2	0	6.0	5	37	8	5	1	0	0	0	12	0	3	3	0
Russo, Dennis, Bil.	1	4	.200	8.26	17	8	0	0	5	0	56.2	83	277	56	52	7	2	7	2	32	0	20	3	3
Ryan, Robert, Bil. *	1	2	.667	1.93	14	0	0	0	11	4	18.2	15	76	4	4	0	0	0	5	5	0	25	0	3
Salter, Cody, But.	4	2	.667	3.51	9	5	3	0	2	0	48.2	48	209	21	19	3	0	0	1	20	0	31	0	0
Sanchez, Simon, Leth.	5	3	.625	4.11	13	13	0	0	0	0	61.1	72	274	39	28	2	2	1	3	25	0	37	6	0
Sellers, Roger, Bil.	0	1	.000	17.18	3	0	0	0	1	0	3.2	8	23	7	7	1	1	0	1	4	0	5	3	0
Smith, Jesse, Hel.	1	3	.250	5.66	12	6	0	0	1	1	47.2	50	229	38	30	2	1	0	5	30	0	28	3	1
Sokol, Trad, Hel. *	0	4	.000	5.62	24	3	0	0	14	4	41.2	47	195	35	26	8	3	1	1	23	0	41	3	0
Stafford, Mike, M.H. *	1	1	.500	2.89	6	4	0	0	5	0	9.1	13	42	7	3	1	1	0	0	1	0	6	1	1
Stanley, Cody, Bil.	1	1	.500	3.03	20	0	0	0	10	1	29.2	32	142	14	10	0	3	3	1	23	2	19	5	0
Stevens, Josh, M.H.	1	0	1.000	2.98	25	0	0	0	5	0	42.1	37	181	17	14	3	0	2	2	13	0	39	1	2
Suares, Orlando, G.F.	1	4	.200	6.65	21	4	0	0	6	0	46.0	50	214	35	34	5	0	2	6	26	1	38	8	0
Tate, Seth, Leth.	0	4	.000	7.06	9	1	0	0	4	0	21.2	30	107	18	17	0	2	1	3	13	0	18	2	0
Taylor, J.K., G.F.	2	3	.400	3.77	15	4	0	0	7	3	43.0	48	187	26	18	3	0	2	3	14	0	43	5	0
Therneau, Dave, Bil.	3	1	.750	3.88	9	9	0	0	0	0	51.0	52	219	27	22	2	4	0	1	16	0	59	1	1
Verdugo, Orlando, I.F.	3	2	.600	3.86	19	4	0	0	15	5	42.0	48	192	23	18	3	1	1	1	20	3	55	1	1
Verigood, Steve, Leth. * ...	2	0	1.000	1.16	15	0	0	0	9	3	23.1	11	88	5	3	0	1	1	0	12	0	17	1	0
Wakefield, Doug, But. *	1	1	.500	7.42	15	1	0	0	9	3	30.1	47	157	33	25	1	0	2	1	21	0	23	4	1
Watkins, Steve, I.F.	0	1	.000	40.50	2	1	0	0	0	0	2.0	10	21	12	9	3	1	0	0	4	0	0	0	0
Williams, Adam, G.F. *	1	2	.333	5.00	10	3	0	0	2	1	27.0	23	125	16	15	1	0	1	0	23	0	32	7	5
Williams, Kris, But.	4	3	.571	5.51	9	8	0	0	0	0	47.1	64	221	36	29	8	1	1	5	9	0	40	3	2
Wilson, Keith, Leth.	0	0	.000	27.00	1	0	0	0	1	0	1.0	4	7	4	3	0	0	0	0	1	0	0	0	0
Woodards, Orlando, M.H. ...	1	3	.250	3.58	26	1	0	0	8	3	50.1	48	215	27	20	4	3	1	2	11	0	58	5	2
Woodrum, Randy, Bil. *	1	0	1.000	3.68	2	1	0	0	0	0	7.1	5	33	3	3	1	0	0	1	4	0	4	2	0
Wooten, Shane, Og. *	1	0	1.000	3.80	13	0	0	0	5	0	23.2	19	103	10	10	1	1	0	2	15	0	27	0	0

COMBINATION SHUTOUTS: **Billings (3)**—Madritsch-Cooper, Therneau-Ryan, McEvoy-Birdsong. **Butte (0)**—None. **Great Falls (1)**—Hebert-Castillo-Moody. **Helena (1)**—Cavanagh-Poe-Greeny. **Idaho Falls (2)**—Hawkins-Dobson-Verdugo, Howard-Dobson. **Lethbridge (3)**—Kees-Prinz-Tate, Sanchez-Bido-Verigood, Fuller-Verigood-Koplove. **Medicine Hat (1)**—Murray-Woodards. **Ogden (1)**—Eye-Alejo-Geitz.
NO-HIT GAMES: None.

1998 FIELDING

TEAM

Team	Pct.	G	PO	A	E	TC	DP	PB	Team	Pct.	G	PO	A	E	TC	DP	PB
Ogden	.954	76	1955	837	136	2928	93	12	Helena	.946	76	1945	850	158	2953	69	16
Lethbridge	.953	75	1919	860	136	2915	76	18	Medicine Hat	.946	74	1926	796	154	2876	74	6
Great Falls	.953	75	1969	858	139	2966	73	29	Butte	.942	76	1923	804	167	2894	67	15
Idaho Falls	.951	76	1977	848	144	2969	72	31	TRIPLE PLAYS: None.								
Billings	.949	74	1917	818	147	2882	82	15									

INDIVIDUAL

FIRST BASEMEN

NOTE: All caps denotes fielding-percentage leader based on 38 games for catchers, 51 for all other non-pitchers and 76 innings for pitchers. *Throws lefthanded.

Player, Team	Pct.	G	PO	A	E	TC	DP
Araujo, Orlany, G.F.	.979	47	399	20	9	428	31
Corley, Kenny, But.	.976	42	348	19	9	376	39
Cust, Jack, Leth.	1.000	1	4	0	0	4	2
Dean, Aaron, G.F.*	.951	6	53	5	3	61	2
Dempsey, Nick, G.F.	.986	32	255	18	4	277	26
Downing, Lance, Leth.	.942	8	62	3	4	69	9
Dunham, Tray, I.F.	.917	1	9	2	1	12	0
Dusan, Joe, I.F.*	.976	57	530	38	14	582	51
Figueroa, Eduardo, Hel.*	.981	40	339	30	7	376	28
Gibbons, Jay, M.H.*	.983	35	334	15	6	355	36
Guthrie, Kendall, Hel.	.979	20	167	17	4	188	20

Player, Team	Pct.	G	PO	A	E	TC	DP
Guzman, Julio, Leth.	.875	2	7	0	1	8	0
Jaramillo, Lee, Hel.	.968	7	55	5	2	62	3
Logan, Matt, M.H.	.981	39	337	25	7	369	35
Loggins, Joshua, I.F.	.983	18	167	9	3	179	14
MACKIEWITZ, Richard, Og.*	.984	59	523	40	9	572	57
Martinez, Alejandro, Og.	.988	18	157	10	2	169	26
Matan, Jim, Bil.	.955	7	61	3	3	67	9
Mendez, Francisco, Leth.	.994	20	161	14	1	176	16
Neal, Steve, Leth.*	.984	43	393	25	7	425	39
Nolasco, Jose, But.	.929	3	12	1	1	14	0
Patterson, Marty, Hel.	.984	7	55	8	1	64	5
Peters, Samone, Bil.	1.000	2	17	0	0	17	1
Santonocito, Justin, Leth.	1.000	3	22	5	0	27	5
Singletary, Dan, Leth.*	1.000	4	35	3	0	38	2
Tomaszewski, Dane, G.F.	1.000	1	4	0	0	4	1

Player, Team	Pct.	G	PO	A	E	TC	DP
Vaughn, Clint, Bil.	.974	66	601	28	17	646	61
Wayne, Tyrone, Hel.	1.000	1	9	0	0	9	1
West, George, Hel.	1.000	3	21	1	0	22	1
Yount, Jason, But.	.963	34	295	18	12	325	23
Zeber, Ryan, M.H.	1.000	2	17	2	0	19	0

SECOND BASEMEN

Player, Team	Pct.	G	PO	A	E	TC	DP
Aalbers, Brady, Bil.	.750	2	2	1	1	4	1
Ahlers, Steve, But.	.941	37	81	96	11	188	27
Allen, Shane, G.F.	.909	4	2	8	1	11	4
Ayala, Elio, Hel.	.955	5	10	11	1	22	2
Bast, Ryan, But.	.909	6	13	17	3	33	3
Baston, Stanley, Bil.	.944	3	6	11	1	18	1
Beattie, Andrew, Bil.	.923	6	11	13	2	26	3
Cintron, Alex, Leth.	1.000	1	1	4	0	5	1
Collins, Michael, G.F.	.896	13	19	24	5	48	6
DiPrima, Giancarlo, Hel.	1.000	2	1	3	0	4	1
Downing, Lance, Leth.	.944	37	60	75	8	143	25
Encarnacion, Bienvenido, But.	1.000	3	4	5	0	9	2
Garcia, Alex, I.F.	.957	31	49	84	6	139	19
Godfrey, Tim, Bil.	.971	27	52	80	4	136	28
GONZALEZ, Jimmy, G.F.	.961	67	132	236	15	383	37
Hudson, Orlando, M.H.	.959	64	128	177	13	318	40
Loggins, Joshua, I.F.	.867	2	4	9	2	15	2
Martelli, Tony, M.H.	.957	16	22	23	2	47	5
Martinez, Belvani, Leth.	.953	48	91	130	11	232	30
Nizov, Alexander, But.	.917	26	40	59	9	108	7
Nunez, Jorge, M.H.	.875	8	13	8	3	24	3
Patten, Chris, Hel.	.925	43	85	113	16	214	27
Pickler, Jeff, Og.	.957	70	130	207	15	352	59
Rojas, Eliezer, Hel.	.930	31	61	85	11	157	17
Schmidt, Bryan, I.F.	1.000	1	1	3	0	4	0
Stegall, Randy, Bil.	.970	42	90	135	7	232	27
Tena, Luis, But.	.850	5	8	9	3	20	5
Tucent, Francisco, Og.	.981	12	23	28	1	52	12
Wade, Bryn, But.	.951	9	21	18	2	41	5
Weeks, Paul, I.F.	.895	28	34	85	14	133	17
Wickersham, Jack, I.F.	.966	18	22	63	3	88	14

THIRD BASEMEN

Player, Team	Pct.	G	PO	A	E	TC	DP
Ahlers, Steve, But.	.863	19	13	31	7	51	0
Araujo, Orlany, G.F.	.949	15	5	32	2	39	3
Bast, Ryan, But.	1.000	2	1	1	0	2	0
Brooks, Jeff, Leth.	.875	67	58	138	28	224	13
Campusano, Nicholas, Hel.	.864	32	20	56	12	88	5
Collins, Michael, G.F.	.952	29	17	43	3	63	1
Corley, Kenny, But.	.867	16	16	36	8	60	6
Detienne, Dave, G.F.	.900	11	10	26	4	40	5
Garcia, Alex, I.F.	.767	15	5	28	10	43	3
Guzman, Alexis, M.H.	.911	23	10	31	4	45	3
Hubbel, Travis, M.H.	.673	15	10	25	17	52	2
Jaramillo, Lee, Hel.	.941	6	5	11	1	17	3
Kearns, Austin, Bil.	1.000	2	0	2	0	2	0
Markray, Thad, Bil.	.883	69	51	130	24	205	14
Martelli, Tony, M.H.	.879	7	4	25	4	33	2
Martinez, Belvani, Leth.	.875	8	1	13	2	16	1
Montenegro, Jose, Og.	.939	48	32	91	8	131	12
Nizov, Alexander, But.	1.000	1	1	1	0	2	0
Nunez, Jorge, M.H.	1.000	2	1	5	0	6	0
Owens, Jeremy, I.F.	1.000	1	0	4	0	4	0
Peckham, Chris, But.	.859	24	15	52	11	78	6
PELAEZ, Alex, I.F.	.967	60	38	138	6	182	10
Riggins, Auntwan, M.H.	.845	40	35	74	20	129	6
Rowan, Chris, Og.	1.000	2	1	1	0	2	0
Ruiz, Ramon, G.F.	.885	9	7	16	3	26	2
Santanocito, Justin, Leth.	.857	7	4	8	2	14	1
Santos, Jose, But.	.786	5	1	10	3	14	0
Stegall, Randy, Bil.	.882	6	4	11	2	17	1
Tena, Luis, But.	1.000	3	2	4	0	6	0
Thomas, Charles, G.F.	.844	28	16	49	12	77	5
Tucent, Francisco, Og.	.837	34	16	56	14	86	6
Wade, Bryn, But.	.846	14	10	34	8	52	2
Wayne, Tyrone, Hel.	.857	2	2	4	1	7	0
Weeks, Paul, I.F.	.875	3	0	7	1	8	0
West, George, Hel.	.893	43	29	80	13	122	9

SHORTSTOP

Player, Team	Pct.	G	PO	A	E	TC	DP
Aalbers, Brady, Bil.	.902	9	13	24	4	41	6
Ahlers, Steve, But.	.971	8	9	24	1	34	6
Ayala, Elio, Og.-Hel.	.870	29	29	71	15	115	21
Bast, Ryan, But.	.727	2	3	5	3	11	1
Baston, Stanley, Bil.	.905	9	12	26	4	42	3
Beattie, Andrew, Bil.	.915	37	56	126	17	199	29
Cintron, Alex, Leth.	.921	66	107	209	27	343	39
Collins, Michael, G.F.	.944	6	11	23	2	36	4
Detienne, Dave, G.F.	.907	10	12	27	4	43	5
DiPrima, Giancarlo, Hel.	.952	47	81	157	12	250	32
Dunaway, Jason, I.F.	.904	67	93	172	28	293	39
Encarnacion, Bienvenido, But.	.905	65	86	181	28	295	34
Garcia, Alex, I.F.	.926	6	10	15	2	27	4
Godfrey, Tim, Bil.	.778	2	2	5	2	9	0
Guzman, Alexis, M.H.	.846	14	6	27	6	39	4
Hall, William, Hel.	.876	27	35	78	16	129	10
JARAMILLO, Milko, G.F.	.927	62	87	154	19	260	34
Markray, Thad, Bil.	.750	2	0	3	1	4	0
Martinez, Belvani, Leth.	.920	11	12	34	4	50	7
Nunez, Jorge, M.H.	.898	65	105	202	35	342	43
Patten, Chris, Hel.	.667	2	1	5	3	9	0
Rowan, Chris, Og.	.892	54	81	159	29	269	47
Schmidt, Bryan, I.F.	.957	3	8	14	1	23	7
Stegall, Randy, Bil.	.894	19	22	54	9	85	11
Tena, Luis, But.	.818	4	3	6	2	11	3
Tucent, Francisco, Og.	.923	2	4	8	1	13	2
Weeks, Paul, I.F.	1.000	3	3	4	0	7	1
Wickersham, Jack, I.F.	1.000	1	0	2	0	2	0

SHORTSTOPS WITH TWO OR MORE TEAMS

Player, Team	Pct.	G	PO	A	E	TC	DP
Ayala, Elio, Og.	.887	25	26	60	11	97	17
Ayala, Elio, Hel.	.778	4	3	11	4	18	4

OUTFIELDERS

Player, Team	Pct.	G	PO	A	E	TC	DP
Allen, Shane, G.F.	1.000	49	61	4	0	65	2
Arauz, Leobardo, I.F.	.978	29	39	5	1	45	2
Arballo, Carlos, But.	1.000	3	3	0	0	3	0
Baez, Juan, Hel.	.890	41	61	4	8	73	1
Barrett, Andy, M.H.	1.000	4	7	0	0	7	0
Candela, Frank, Og.	.951	66	128	8	7	143	1
Conyer, Darryl, Leth.*	.917	11	10	1	1	12	0
Cook, Jon, I.F.	1.000	5	4	1	0	5	0
Covington, Kevin, G.F.	1.000	39	40	4	0	44	1
CUST, Jack, Leth.	1.000	61	78	2	0	80	0
Davies, Justin, M.H.	.977	47	41	2	1	44	0
Davis, Jermaine, M.H.	.889	16	7	1	1	9	0
De La Cruz, Erickson, Og.	.990	53	89	8	1	98	2
Doucet, Brandon, Hel.	.927	49	73	3	6	82	0
Downing, Brad, But.	.905	30	35	4	4	42	0
Dunn, Adam, Bil.	.860	34	35	2	6	43	0
Dusan, Joe, I.F.*	1.000	1	4	0	0	4	0
Eaton, Bill, Og.	.952	34	37	3	2	42	0
Encarnacion, Bienvenido, But.	1.000	1	1	0	0	1	0
Fernandez, Ramon, Og.	.988	48	74	6	1	81	1
Fleming, Ryan, M.H.*	.984	68	113	7	2	122	0
Fox, Jason, Hel.	.988	43	77	5	1	83	0
Gomera, Rafael, G.F.	1.000	2	5	1	0	6	0
Guzman, Antonio, Leth.	.956	27	39	4	2	45	0
Guzman, Elpidio, But.*	.966	69	136	6	5	147	0
Guzman, Julio, Leth.	.946	28	33	2	2	37	0
Hammond, Derry, Hel.	.905	19	35	3	4	42	0
Hazen, Mike, I.F.*	.957	47	66	1	3	70	0
Hemmings, Scot, I.F.	.965	48	76	6	3	85	1
Jaramillo, Lee, Hel.	1.000	22	24	6	0	30	1
Joseph, Adolfo, Leth.	.909	13	18	2	2	22	0
Juarez, Jonny, M.H.*	.911	31	38	3	4	45	0
Kearns, Austin, Bil.	.905	29	32	6	4	42	1
Kluver, Hayden, G.F.*	1.000	19	13	0	0	13	0
Layton, Blane, Bil.*	.944	56	82	2	5	89	1
Loggins, Joshua, I.F.	.954	41	57	5	3	65	1
Matan, Jim, Bil.	.833	6	5	0	1	6	0
Moreno, Omar, G.F.	.881	43	35	2	5	42	2
Morrow, Alvin, Og.	.895	42	47	4	6	57	1
Nizov, Alexander, But.	.667	2	2	0	1	3	0
Owens, Jeremy, I.F.	.968	65	114	7	4	125	0
Patten, Chris, Hel.	.920	15	21	2	2	25	2
Patterson, Marty, Hel.	.750	2	3	0	1	4	0
Peckham, Chris, But.	.966	41	54	3	2	59	1
Peters, Samone, Bil.	.959	70	103	14	5	122	3
Pichardo, Gilbert, But.	.882	19	15	0	2	17	0
Piedra, Jorge, G.F.*	.949	70	124	7	7	138	2
Price, Duane, Bil.	.960	29	47	1	2	50	0

Player, Team	Pct.	G	PO	A	E	TC	DP
Proctor, Jerry, G.F.	.905	29	36	2	4	42	0
Rinne, Jim, Leth.	1.000	15	20	0	0	20	0
Rodriguez, Miguel, Leth.	1.000	1	2	0	0	2	0
Ross, Justin, But.*	.981	65	100	5	2	107	0
Santos, Jose, But.	.615	10	8	0	5	13	0
Senegal, Terence, Bil.	1.000	4	3	0	0	3	0
Singletary, Dan, Leth.*	.935	39	58	0	4	62	0
Smith, Fred, M.H.	.958	64	109	6	5	120	1
Taylor, Corey, Bil.	.857	3	5	1	1	7	0
Toomey, Chris, Bil.	1.000	2	4	0	0	4	0
Ventura, Henry, M.H.	1.000	26	36	2	0	38	0
Warren, Tom, Hel.	.909	4	9	1	1	11	1
Wayne, Tyrone, Hel.	.930	49	69	11	6	86	3
Weichard, Paul, Leth.*	.942	53	109	5	7	121	0
Yount, Jason, But.	1.000	2	1	0	0	1	0

CATCHERS

Player, Team	Pct.	G	PO	A	E	TC	DP	PB
Beasley, Justin, Leth.	.961	10	44	5	2	51	0	1
Bordenick, Ryan, Og.	.974	34	236	28	7	271	2	3
Brito, Obispo, Og.	.970	22	172	23	6	201	0	5
Campbell, Sean, I.F.	.971	26	184	19	6	209	2	14
Castellano, John, G.F.	.973	27	166	12	5	183	4	7
Ceriani, Matt, Hel.	.987	44	347	39	5	391	2	9
Diaz, Angel, But.	.981	39	240	23	5	268	0	7
Dunham, Tray, I.F.	.965	40	296	32	12	340	1	12
French, Ron, I.F.	.992	17	111	6	1	118	0	5
Guthrie, Kendall, Hel.	.982	19	101	10	2	113	1	4
HAMMOCK, Robert, Leth.	.990	52	346	36	4	386	4	12
Hernandez, John, G.F.	.982	40	297	29	6	332	1	13
Jaramillo, Lee, Hel.	.960	15	90	7	4	101	1	3
Kremblas, Mike, M.H.	.974	59	394	58	12	464	2	4
Lombardi, Dominick, But.	.989	43	238	31	3	272	2	3
McAffee, Josh, Leth.	.984	17	104	18	2	124	1	4
Miller, Corky, Bil.	.963	43	319	48	14	381	6	7
Nolasco, Jose, But.	.957	11	58	9	3	70	0	3
Patterson, Marty, Hel.	1.000	1	7	1	0	8	0	0
Rivera, Francisco, Bil.	.967	3	26	3	1	30	0	0
Santonocito, Justin, Leth.	1.000	1	1	0	0	1	0	1
Santos, Jose, But.	1.000	3	17	1	0	18	0	2
Santos, Juan, M.H.	.971	13	65	2	2	69	0	1
Silletti, Pete, M.H.	1.000	1	1	0	0	1	0	0
Soto, Luis, I.F.	1.000	1	2	0	0	2	0	0
Stinson, Kevin, Og.	.986	22	132	14	2	148	0	4
Tomaszewski, Dane, G.F.	.950	15	121	11	7	139	1	9
Wallis, Jacob, Bil.	.988	32	235	17	3	255	2	8
Wilson, Keith, Leth.	.667	1	2	0	1	3	0	0
Zeber, Ryan, M.H.	.953	11	57	4	3	64	0	1

PITCHERS

Player, Team	Pct.	G	PO	A	E	TC	DP
Abeyta, Scott, Leth.*	.857	24	1	5	1	7	1
Alejo, Nigel, Og.	.900	6	2	7	1	10	0
Anderson, Jason, But.	1.000	23	0	8	0	8	0
Arcangel, Arsenio, Hel.	.833	26	1	4	1	6	0
Aronson, Christopher, But.	.800	8	0	4	1	5	0
Arroyo, Joel, Leth.	.833	13	3	2	1	6	1
Baez, Juan, Hel.	1.000	4	0	2	0	2	0
Barndollar, Jeff, Leth.	1.000	6	1	1	0	2	0
Barton, Christopher, Hel.	.950	14	7	12	1	20	0
Bauer, Ryan, I.F.	.957	17	12	10	1	23	0
Bell, Casey, I.F.	.688	7	2	9	5	16	0
Berryman, Brian, I.F.	1.000	15	6	12	0	18	1
Berryman, Chad, But.	1.000	11	5	5	0	10	0
Bido, Jose, Leth.	.900	18	1	8	1	10	1
Birdsong, Tim, Bil.	.857	19	0	6	1	7	0
Brooks, Jacob, But.	.727	28	3	5	3	11	1
Brown, Zadrian, Bil.	1.000	16	1	4	0	5	0
Burgos, Ricardo, G.F.	1.000	14	4	10	0	14	1
Caceres, Antonio, M.H.	1.000	21	2	7	0	9	0
CALLIER, Jeremy, But.	1.000	19	6	20	0	26	1
Cassidy, Scott, M.H.	1.000	15	2	14	0	16	3
Castillo, Wilson, G.F.	.900	16	7	11	2	20	1
Cavanagh, Andy, Hel.	.944	11	7	10	1	18	1
Childers, Matt, Hel.	.667	2	0	2	1	3	0
Coffey, Todd, Bil.	1.000	3	1	1	0	2	1
Condrey, Clay, I.F.	.750	18	2	4	2	8	0
Connell, Brian, Hel.*	.750	11	1	2	1	4	0
Cooper, Eric, Bil.	1.000	22	3	5	0	8	2
Curtis, Mark, M.H.*	.909	15	2	8	1	11	0
Darr, Jerry, I.F.	1.000	2	0	1	0	1	0
Davis, Phil, Leth.	.909	20	2	8	1	11	0
Dehart, Casey, Bil.*	1.000	15	3	7	0	10	1
Diaz, Antonio, I.F.	1.000	14	1	4	0	5	1
Dobson, Mark, I.F.	.900	21	5	4	1	10	0
Dotel, Melido, G.F.	.750	23	7	8	5	20	0
Dowell, Brian, I.F.	1.000	11	1	0	0	1	0
Easton, Eric, But.	.750	14	1	2	1	4	0
Elias, Javier, But.	1.000	4	1	0	0	1	0
Espinal, Orlando, M.H.	1.000	7	1	1	0	2	0
Eye, Jake, Og.	.941	15	8	8	1	17	0
Fikac, Jeremy, I.F.	.667	12	1	1	1	3	0
File, Robert, M.H.	1.000	28	1	6	0	7	0
Forbes, Keith, I.F.	1.000	21	1	5	0	6	0
Fuller, Jody, Leth.	.929	18	2	11	1	14	1
Gaud, Perfecto, M.H.*	.800	17	1	3	1	5	0
Geitz, Scott, Og.	1.000	20	0	11	0	11	0
Giambalvo, Paul, Leth.	1.000	22	2	4	0	6	0
Gold, J.M., Og.	1.000	5	2	2	0	4	0
Gonzalez, Francisco, I.F.	.400	5	1	1	3	5	0
Greeny, Burdette, Hel.	.900	24	3	6	1	10	0
Hall, Josh, Bil.	.667	14	1	3	2	6	0
Harraid, Jon, Og.	.857	19	2	4	1	7	0
Harris, John, But.	1.000	16	1	4	0	5	1
Harris, Julian, But.*	.867	16	4	9	2	15	0
Hawkins, Ryan, I.F.	.833	7	2	3	1	6	0
Hebert, Cedric, G.F.	.923	11	1	11	1	13	2
Herrera, Misael, I.F.	1.000	11	2	6	0	8	0
Howard, Ben, I.F.	.727	15	3	5	3	11	0
Hughes, Nial, G.F.*	.889	16	4	12	2	18	0
Hurtado, Ed, But.	.667	27	2	2	2	6	0
Isenia, Derrick, G.F.	.786	15	4	7	3	14	0
Iwasaki, Junichi, Bil.*	1.000	9	0	2	0	2	0
Johnson, Jim, Og.*	.900	13	3	6	1	10	0
Jones, Fontella, Hel.	.833	23	1	4	1	6	0
Jones, Travis, I.F.*	.917	31	7	4	1	12	0
Joseph, Glen, Bil.	1.000	2	0	1	0	1	0
Kees, Justin, Leth.	.941	17	8	8	1	17	1
Kohl, Doug, Leth.	.882	13	1	14	2	17	1
Koplove, Mike, Leth.	.800	12	1	3	1	5	0
Koronka, John, Bil.*	1.000	12	0	4	0	4	0
Kramer, Aaron, I.F.	.875	6	1	6	1	8	0
Krawczyk, Jack, Hel.	1.000	7	0	2	0	2	0
Larman, Jayson, Bil.	1.000	5	1	1	0	2	0
Lawrence, Brian, I.F.	.900	4	2	7	1	10	0
Lewis, Rickey, Hel.	.769	12	4	6	3	13	0
Luque, Roger, I.F.*	1.000	6	1	3	0	4	0
Lynch, Pat, M.H.	.857	14	5	7	2	14	1
Mackoul, Greg, Og.	1.000	7	1	0	0	1	0
Madritsch, Robert, Bil.*	1.000	14	4	5	0	9	0
Martinez, Luis, Hel.*	.867	17	1	12	2	15	0
Mathews, Dan, Og.	1.000	24	2	1	0	3	0
Maysonet, Roberto, Og.	.875	14	4	3	1	8	0
McCall, Travis, Leth.*	.667	1	0	2	1	3	1
McClain, Kevin, But.	.667	8	2	0	1	3	1
McConnell, Gary, Hel.	1.000	17	5	2	0	7	0
McCutcheon, Mike, Leth.*	1.000	17	3	18	0	21	2
McEvoy, Casey, Bil.	.882	14	3	12	2	17	0
Mendoza, Hatuey, Leth.	1.000	1	0	1	0	1	0
Miller, Jim, Og.	1.000	15	9	11	0	20	1
Miniel, Roberto, Og.	.750	16	2	4	2	8	0
Montanez, Johen, M.H.	1.000	6	0	1	0	1	0
Montero, Oscar, Og.	.800	14	6	10	4	20	0
Moody, Jason, G.F.*	.875	14	1	6	1	8	0
Moon, Jared, G.F.	1.000	19	1	5	0	6	0
Mowday, Chris, M.H.	1.000	1	0	0	0	0	0
Murray, Steve, M.H.*	1.000	14	2	4	0	6	0
Myers, Aaron, Og.	.857	4	1	5	1	7	0
Myers, Rob, Hel.	1.000	21	1	0	0	1	0
Niehaus, Troy, Leth.*	.857	19	2	10	2	14	1
Norris, Mac, Og.	1.000	4	1	0	0	1	0
Orloski, Joe, M.H.	1.000	14	6	7	0	13	2
Ozuna, Adrian, But.	.833	16	1	9	2	12	0
Padilla, Charly, But.	.909	19	2	8	1	11	0
Parker, Beau, G.F.	.867	14	2	11	2	15	1
Penney, Mike, Hel.	.778	10	3	4	2	9	0
Pine, Christopher, Og.	.750	3	0	3	1	4	0
Poe, Ryan, Hel.	1.000	14	2	4	0	6	0
Prinz, Bret, Leth.	.933	11	5	9	1	15	2
Renwick, Tyler, M.H.	1.000	9	1	1	0	2	0
Rijo, Fernando, G.F.	.867	14	6	7	2	15	0
Russo, Dennis, Bil.	1.000	17	1	8	0	9	1
Ryan, Robert, Bil.*	1.000	14	0	2	0	2	1
St. Amand, Reuben, M.H.	1.000	10	0	1	0	1	0

Player, Team	Pct.	G	PO	A	E	TC	DP
Salter, Cody, But.	1.000	9	4	8	0	12	1
Sanchez, Simon, Leth.	.909	13	6	14	2	22	0
Smith, Jesse, Hel.	1.000	12	5	6	0	11	1
Sokol, Trad, Hel.*	1.000	24	5	4	0	9	1
Stafford, Mike, M.H.*	1.000	6	3	1	0	4	0
Stanley, Cody, Bil.	.750	20	0	3	1	4	0
Stevens, Josh, M.H.	.833	25	6	4	2	12	1
Suares, Orlando, G.F.	1.000	21	4	9	0	13	1
Tate, Seth, Leth.	1.000	9	2	7	0	9	1
Taylor, J.K., G.F.	.857	15	0	6	1	7	0
Therneau, Dave, Bil.	.909	9	3	7	1	11	0
Verdugo, Orlando, I.F.	1.000	19	1	3	0	4	1
Verigood, Steve, Leth.*	1.000	15	0	1	0	1	0
Wakefield, Doug, But.*	1.000	15	1	8	0	9	2
Watkins, Steve, I.F.	1.000	2	0	1	0	1	0
Williams, Adam, G.F.*	1.000	10	1	2	0	3	0
Williams, Kris, But.	.800	9	0	4	1	5	0
Woodards, Orlando, M.H.	.909	26	3	7	1	11	0
Woodrum, Randy, Bil.*	1.000	2	0	1	0	1	0
Wooten, Shane, Og.*	1.000	13	1	6	0	7	0

The following players did not have any fielding statistics at the positions indicated or appeared only as a designated hitter, pinch-hitter or pinch-runner: Ayala, 2b; Campbell, of; Campusano, p; Copley, dh; J. Davis, 1b; Davies, 2b; Dempsey, p; Fernandez, 1b; Figueroa, p; B. Fox dh; Antonio Guzman, p; Jonathan Guzman, p; Julio Guzman, p; Hammock, 3b; Hart, p; Hussman, p; Huxhold, p; Jaramillo, 2b; Minor, p; Piedra, p; Regalado, p; Runk, p; Santonocito, ss; Sellers, p; Silletti, of; Wilson, p.

LEAGUE CHAMPIONS

Year	Team	Pct.
1939—	Twin Falls*	.581
1940—	Salt Lake City	.608
	Ogden (4th)*	.492
1941—	Boise	.623
	Ogden (2nd)*	.598
1942—	Pocatello†	.690
	Boise	.683
1943-44-45—	Did not operate.	
1946—	Twin Falls‡	.585
	Salt Lake City†	.585
1947—	Salt Lake City	.618
	Twin Falls†	.600
1948—	Pocatello	.611
	Twin Falls (2nd)*	.595
1949—	Twin Falls	.624
	Pocatello (3rd)*	.595
1950—	Pocatello	.635
	Billings (3rd)*	.571
1951—	Salt Lake City	.618
	Great Falls (3rd)*	.559
1952—	Pocatello	.595
	Idaho Falls (2nd)*	.573
1953—	Ogden	.679
	Salt Lake City (4th)*	.527
1954—	Salt Lake City	.595
	Great Falls (4th)*	.530
1955—	Boise	.588
	Magic Valley (4th)*	.489
1956—	Boise	.561
1957—	Salt Lake City	.650
	Billings†	.582
1958—	Billings†	.582
	Boise†	.615

Year	Team	Pct.
1959—	Boise	.633
	Billings (2nd)*	.523
1960—	Boise†	.686
	Idaho Falls	.650
1961—	Boise	.638
	Great Falls*	.571
1962—	Boise§	.565
	Billings†	.706
1963—	Idaho Falls	.702
	Magic Valley†	.643
1964—	Treasure Valley	.615
1965—	Treasure Valley	.530
1966—	Ogden	.591
1967—	Ogden	.621
1968—	Ogden	.609
1969—	Ogden	.620
1970—	Idaho Falls	.629
1971—	Great Falls	.643
1972—	Billings	.694
1973—	Billings	.629
1974—	Idaho Falls	.569
1975—	Great Falls	.577
1976—	Great Falls	.577
1977—	Lethbridge	.629
1978—	Billings∞	.735
1979—	Helena	.623
	Lethbridge▲	.559
1980—	Lethbridge▲	.743
	Billings	.629
1981—	Calgary	.657
	Butte▲	.557
1982—	Medicine Hat▲	.629
	Idaho Falls	.600

Year	Team	Pct.
1983—	Billings▲	.614
	Calgary	.600
1984—	Billings	.691
	Helena▲	.647
1985—	Great Falls	.771
	Salt Lake City▲	.657
1986—	Salt Lake City◆	.643
	Great Falls	.571
1987—	Salt Lake City◆	.700
	Helena	.657
1988—	Great Falls◆	.754
	Butte	.629
1989—	Great Falls◆	.791
	Butte	.621
1990—	Great Falls◆	.706
	Salt Lake	.618
1991—	Salt Lake City◆	.700
	Great Falls	.657
1992—	Salt Lake	.697
	Billings◆	.697
1993—	Billings◆	.653
	Helena	.589
1994—	Billings◆	.694
	Helena	.611
1995—	Billings	.710
	Helena■	.690
1996—	Helena■	.597
	Ogden	.583
1997—	Great Falls	.556
	Billings■	.549
1998—	Medicine Hat	.622
	Idaho Falls■	.618

*Won four-club playoff. †Won split-season playoff. ‡Ended first half in tie with Salt Lake City and won one-game playoff. §Ended first half in tie with Billings and Great Falls and won playoff. ∞Billings (first place) defeated Idaho Falls (second place) in first place-second place playoff. ▲League divided into Northern and Southern divisions; won two-club playoff. ◆Won two-club playoff. ■League divided into Northern and Southern divisions; won four-club playoff.

MINOR LEAGUE INDEX

TEAMS AND CITIES

Adelanto, Calif. (see High Desert) 480
Aguascalientes, Mexico. 397
Akron, Ohio 438
Albuquerque, N.M. 414
Altoona, Pa. 438
Appleton (see Wisconsin) 521
Arkansas..467
Asheville, N.C. 559
Auburn, N.Y. 536
Augusta, Ga. 559
Augusta, N.J. (see New Jersey)............536
Bakersfield, Calif. 480
Batavia, N.Y. 536
Battle Creek, Mich. (see Michigan) 521
Beloit, Wis. 521
Billings, Mont. 606
Binghamton, N.Y. 438
Birmingham, Ala. 452
Bluefield, W.Va. 574
Boise, Idaho 550
Bowie, Md. 438
Bradenton, Fla. 592
Brevard County, Fla. 504
Bristol, Va. 574
Buffalo, N.Y. 375
Burlington, Iowa 521
Burlington, N.C. 574
Butte, Mont. 606
Calgary, Alberta......................................414
Campeche, Mexico.................................397
Cancun, Mexico 397
Capital City, S.C. 559
Carolina 452
Cedar Rapids, Iowa 521
Charleston, W.Va. 559
Charlotte, Fla. 504
Charlotte, N.C. 375
Chattanooga, Tenn. 452
Chetumal, Mexico 397
Clearwater, Fla. 504
Clinton, Iowa 521
Colorado Springs, Colo. 414
Columbia, S.C. (see Capital City) 559
Columbus, Ga. 559
Columbus, Ohio 375
Comstock Park, Mich.
   (see West Michigan) 521
Cordoba, Mexico 397
Danville, Va. 574
Davenport, Iowa (see Quad City) 521
Daytona, Fla. 504
Delmarva, Md. 559
Des Moines, Iowa (see Iowa).................414
Dunedin, Fla. (Florida State) 504
Dunedin, Fla. (Gulf Coast).....................592
Durham, N.C. 375
Edmonton, Alberta..................................414
Elizabethton, Tenn. 574
El Paso, Tex. 467
Erie, Pa. 438
Eugene, Ore. 550
Everett, Wash. 550
Fayetteville, N.C. 559
Fishkill, N.Y. (see Hudson Valley)..........536
Fort Myers, Fla. (Florida State) 504
Fort Myers, Fla. (Gulf Coast) 592
Fort Wayne, Ind. 521
Frederick, Md. 493
Fresno, Calif. 414

Geneva, Ill. (see Kane County) 521
Great Falls, Mont. 606
Greensboro, N.C. 559
Greenville, S.C. 452
Hagerstown, Md. 559
Harrisburg, Pa. 438
Helena, Mont. 606
Hickory, N.C. 559
High Desert...480
Hudson Valley 536
Huntsville, Ala. 452
Idaho Falls, Idaho 606
Indianapolis, Ind. 375
Iowa..414
Jackson, Miss. 467
Jackson, Tenn. 452
Jacksonville, Fla. 452
Jamestown, N.Y. 536
Johnson City, Tenn. 574
Jupiter, Fla. 504
Kane County 521
Kingsport, Tenn. 574
Kinston, N.C. 493
Kissimmee, Fla. (Gulf Coast).................592
Kissimmee, Fla. (Florida State).............504
Knoxville, Tenn. 452
Lake Elsinore, Calif. 480
Lakeland, Fla. (Florida State)................504
Lakeland, Fla. (Gulf Coast)....................592
Lancaster, Calif. 480
Lansing, Mich. 521
Las Vegas, Nev. 414
Little Rock, Ark. (see Arkansas) 467
Louisville, Ky. 375
Lowell, Mass. 536
Lynchburg, Va. 493
Macon, Ga. 559
Mahoning Valley, Ohio 536
Martinsville, Va. 574
Medford, Ore. (see Southern Oregon) 550
Medicine Hat, Alberta.............................606
Melbourne, Fla. (Gulf Coast) 592
Memphis, Tenn. 414
Mesa, Ariz. 584
Mexico City, Reds...................................397
Mexico City, Tigers.................................397
Michigan...521
Midland, Tex. 467
Missoula, Mont. 606
Mobile, Ala. 452
Modesto, Calif. 480
Monclova, Mexico 397
Monterrey, Mexico..................................397
Myrtle Beach, S.C. 493
Nashville, Tenn. 414
New Britain, Conn. 438
New Haven, Conn. 438
New Jersey 536
New Orleans 414
Norfolk, Va. 375
Norwich, Ct. 438
Nuevo Laredo, Mexico...........................397
Oaxaca, Mexico......................................397
Ogden, Utah 606
Oklahoma City, Okla. 414
Omaha, Neb. 414
Oneonta, N.Y. 536
Orlando, Fla. (Gulf Coast).......................592
Orlando, Fla. (Southern).........................452

Ottawa, Ont. 375
Pawtucket, R.I. 375
Peoria, Ariz. 584
Peoria, Ill. 521
Phoenix, Ariz. 484
Piedmont, N.C. 559
Pittsfield, Mass. 536
Port Charlotte, Fla. (Gulf Coast) 592
Portland, Me. 438
Portland, Ore. 550
Port St. Lucie, Fla. (Gulf Coast).............592
Prince William, Va. 493
Princeton, W.Va. 574
Pulaski, Va. 574
Quad City 521
Rancho Cucamonga, Calif. 480
Reading, Pa. 438
Reynosa, Mexico....................................397
Richmond, Va. 375
Rochester, N.Y. 375
Rockford, Ill. 521
St. Catharines, Ontario 536
St. Lucie, Fla. 504
St. Petersburg, Fla. (Gulf Coast) 592
St. Petersburg, Fla. (Florida State) 504
Salem, Va. 493
Salem-Keizer, Ore. 550
Saltillo, Mexico.......................................397
Salt Lake, Utah.......................................415
San Antonio, Tex. 467
San Bernardino, Calif. 480
San Jose, Calif. 480
Sarasota, Fla. (Florida State) 504
Sarasota, Fla. (Gulf Coast) 592
Savannah, Ga. 559
Scranton/Wilkes-Barre, Pa. 375
Shreveport, La. 467
South Bend, Ind. 521
Southern Oregon....................................550
Spokane, Wash. 550
Stockton, Calif. 480
Syracuse, N.Y. 376
Tabasco, Mexico.....................................397
Tacoma, Wash. 415
Tampa, Fla. (Florida State).....................504
Tampa, Fla. (Gulf Coast) 592
Toledo, Ohio 376
Torreon, Mexico 397
Trenton, N.J. 438
Tucson, Ariz. 415
Tulsa, Okla. 467
Utica, N.Y. 536
Vancouver, British Columbia 415
Vermont..536
Vero Beach, Fla. 504
Visalia, Calif. 480
Watertown, N.Y. 536
West Michigan 521
West Palm Beach, Fla. 592
West Tenn 452
Wichita, Kan. 467
Williamsport, Pa. 536
Wilmington, N.C. 493
Winooski, Vt. (see Vermont) 536
Winston-Salem, N.C. 493
Wisconsin 521
Yakima, Wash. 550
Yucatan, Mexico.....................................397
Zebulon, N.C. (see Carolina) 452

Baseball's Legendary Players...

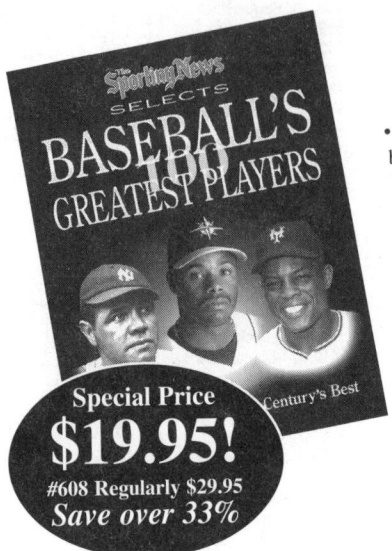

The Sporting News Selects
Baseball's 100 Greatest Players
Foreword by Willie Mays

- A subjective and provocative ranking from 1 to 100 of the best players. Mantle... McGwire... Ruth... Ryan... Feller... Fingers. They're all here, along with 94 others, captured in vintage photographs doing what put them among baseball's greats. Feel the speed of Jackie Robinson, the power of Hank Aaron, the finesse of Ozzie Smith.
  - Large 9" x 11¼" size, hardbound with dust jacket.
  - 224 pages with over 300 beautiful color and historic black and white photos.

Special Price
$19.95!
#608 Regularly $29.95
Save over 33%

" ... guaranteed to help propel the game's great debates in to the next milennium."
—*Newsweek, October 19, 1998*

...And a Legendary Season

Celebrating 70:
Mark McGwire's Historic Season
Foreword by Hall of Fame broadcaster Jack Buck

- Relive, remember and celebrate the power of baseball's new single-season home run king. Accounts of every home run, from No. 1 to No. 70.
- Exclusive arrangement between The Sporting News and the St. Louis Post-Dispatch.
- Large 9" x 11¼" size, hardbound with dust jacket.
- 184 pages with over 200 exclusive color photographs, including game action, home run celebrations and the duel with Sammy Sosa.

Special Price
$21.95!
#621 Regularly $29.95
Save over 25%

For Fastest Service Call Now to Order Toll Free
1-800-825-8508 Dept. GBB9

Or mail to: The Sporting News, Attn: Book Dept. GBB9, P.O. Box 11229, Des Moines, IA 50340.
Please apply sales tax (IL: 6.25%, IA: 5%, MO: 5.975%, NY: 7.2%). **Shipping and handling:** All U.S. and Canadian orders shipped via UPS. No P.O. Boxes please. **Charges:** For U.S. orders, $3.75 for the first book, $1.25 each additional book. For Canadian orders, $6.75 for the first book, $1.25 each additional book. International rates available upon request.

GBB9